THE RISE AND FALL OF THE AMERICAN WHIG PARTY

The Rise and Fall
of the American Whig Party

JACKSONIAN POLITICS
AND THE ONSET OF THE CIVIL WAR

Michael F. Holt

OXFORD
UNIVERSITY PRESS

OXFORD
UNIVERSITY PRESS

Oxford   New York
Auckland   Bangkok   Buenos Aires   Cape Town   Chennai
Dar es Salaam   Delhi   Hong Kong   Istanbul   Karachi   Kolkata
Kuala Lumpur   Madrid   Melbourne   Mexico City   Mumbai
Nairobi   São Paulo   Shanghai   Taipei   Tokyo   Torono

First published by Oxford University Press, Inc., 1999
First issued as an Oxford University Press paperback, 2003
198 Madison Avenue, New York, New York 10016

www.oup.com

Oxford is a registered trademark of Oxford University Press

Library of Congress Cataloging-in-Publication Data
Holt, Michael F. (Michael Fitzgibbon)
The rise and fall of the American Whig party :
Jacksonian politics and the onset of the Civil War/Michael F. Holt.
p. cm.   Includes bibliographical references and index.
ISBN 0-19-505544-6 (cloth) ISBN 0-19-516104-1 (pbk.)
1. Whig Party (U.S.)—History.
I. Title.
JK2331.H63   1999   324.2732'3'09—dc21   98–27020

1 3 5 7 9 8 6 4 2

Printed in the United States of America
on acid-free paper

For my students, 1965–1998

Contents

Illustrations appear after page 552

Preface

THIS IS A HISTORY of a nineteenth-century American political party. It encompasses the careers, aspirations, ideas, and actions of many individual Whig politicians and nameless Whig voters. But it is not primarily a collective biography, a study of political ideology and political culture, or an analysis of the social experience and characteristics of the electorate. Rather, it is the story, told chronologically, of the birth, life, and death of a political organization and of its competitive relationship with other political parties. That life was short—scarcely more than twenty-two years. Yet this history of it, which has taken me almost that many years to write, is a very long book. The reader deserves to know why.

I set five objectives before starting to write. First, I believe that no political party can be fully understood in terms of its own beliefs, actions, and internal quarrels. Its relationships with rival parties must also be incorporated into the analysis. The Whig party operated in a definable two-party system, labeled by historians the Second American Party System, in which its major, but not its only, rival was the Democratic party. A central argument of this study, indeed, is that from the time of the Whig party's birth in the winter of 1833–34 until its death during the 1856 presidential campaign, Democrats played a profound role in shaping its fate. Thus I pay close attention to non-Whig and anti-Whig political actors, not just to the Whigs themselves.

Second, the American federal system, with its jurisdictional division of policy-making responsibilities among national, state, and local governments, had unusual importance for the structure and operations of nineteenth-century political parties. What state governments did often had far more impact on people's lives during that century than did actions taken in Washington. Whigs, therefore, often viewed control of state governments as a vital goal. Like its Democratic foe, moreover, the Whig party was a federation of state and local organizations, each of which had its own experience of internal rivalry and external competition. To write the history of the party as an institution—and not just of a few prominent national leaders—I was therefore compelled to analyze developments in as many states as possible over a period of some twenty years while simultaneously examining Whig attempts to capture the national government and their actions while in it.

I am well aware of the hazards of this approach. Specialists on some states may accuse me of giving their subjects short shrift. I have relied heavily on such specialists' research, but in a project of this scope, my research on individual states could never be as thorough as theirs. More likely, readers may complain that my state-by-state surveys are unnecessary since a few illustrative examples usually would suffice. Occasionally one can generalize about patterns that apply to several states, but conditions in different states often varied sharply. I have sought to get the story straight, and I am convinced that neither the rise nor the fall of the Whig party can be explained without the comprehensive approach I have taken here.

Federalism, of course, implies more than the division of jurisdictional authority among different levels of government. It also connotes interaction among the politicians who acted at each level. Far more than their twentieth-century successors, indeed, nineteenth-century partisan activists cared deeply about the party as a whole, about how it fared at all levels of government, if only because most people voted for or against what parties as institutions seemed to stand for. Since parties could establish their identity before the electorate at all levels of the federal system, and since national leaders were utterly dependent on state and local organizations to obtain or retain national office, connections among local, state, and national politicos were robust. Illustrating the reciprocal connection between politicians in Washington and those who made nominations, conducted electoral campaigns, passed laws, and rewrote constitutions in states thus became a primary objective of this study.

My detailed treatment of states, and occasionally of localities, also stems from a third assumption about nineteenth-century politics. The vitality of the Whig party depended far less on its ability to win the White House than on its strength in Congress, statehouses, and state legislatures. Especially in describing, let alone explaining, the disintegration of the Whig party between the presidential elections of 1852 and 1856, a focus on the state and local arenas that chose subpresidential officeholders is imperative. Thus I have made systematic analyses of Whigs' fortunes in congressional and state elections from the early 1830s until the mid-1850s. Since state legislatures chose United States senators, moreover, to explain the fluctuating strength of the Whigs in the Senate, I have closely studied legislative elections of senators to determine why Whigs were, or were not, elected and why one Whig rather than another got the seat if Whigs prevailed.

Nonpresidential elections had importance far beyond determining who staffed government. Since different states held elections throughout the year almost every year, not uniformly in Novembers of even-numbered years, political leaders read them as their modern counterparts read running public opinion polls. They set strategy and often shifted actions in one place in reaction to earlier outcomes in another. Similarly, internal feuds over nominations and senatorial selections often reverberated long after those choices were made, influencing reactions to policy, patronage, and party strategy. These observations point to a fourth objective that has shaped this study.

Concerned that too much political history written since 1960 sacrificed contingency or change over time in its attempt to explicate underlying structures of collective political behavior, the central tenets of party ideology, or the dominant features of an era's political culture, I have consciously sought to restore a sense of history, of change over time, to my story. Events mattered; they, and not just social structures, economic conditions, fixed political contexts, or ideology, often shaped subsequent behavior. What happened at point A in time influenced what actors did at points B and C. To recapture that constant flux, that importance of contingent decisions and actions, I have tried to write a detailed chronological narrative of developments that occurred simultaneously in numerous different political arenas and that converged to influence subsequent calculations and behavior.

Recapturing those calculations, the various factors that influenced them, and the implications of decisions once made is the fifth goal that I set for myself before starting to write. Hindsight is of great advantage to historians; we know how the story turned out and thus what was pivotal and what was not. By directing our attention to what seems most important to us *now*, however, hindsight can also distort the priorities of historical actors themselves, obscure their sense of possibility and uncertainty, and blind us to their motivations. I have tried to reconstruct those actors' perceptions and expectations, to recapture what they thought they were doing and why, to re-create their world as they experienced it. To do this, I rely extensively on quotations from my sources to allow Whigs themselves, in effect, to narrate their own history in their own words.

This method has other significant implications. Whose words and perceptions matter most, and how representative is the surviving evidence of the viewpoints of the historically inarticulate? To write the story of an institution that eventually encompassed over a million people, one must make choices about perspective or vantage point. For various reasons, I have narrated my story from the perspective of political leaders, officeholders, and political activists, not rank-and-file Whig voters, largely because I believe Whig and non-Whig leaders, not voters, society as a whole, or impersonal forces made the decisions that account for the Whig party's rise and fall. Obviously, developments outside the relatively narrow echelon of political leaders and activists affected the Whig party, and I try to incorporate them in terms of leaders' responses to them. But this is not meant to be a history from the bottom up, a social history of the United States from the 1820s to the 1850s, or even an attempt to mesh social history with political history. It is, instead, an attempt to reintegrate different aspects of a too-often compartmentalized political universe in order to tell the story of a political party.

As a result, some demographic groups are largely missing from its pages. Because African-Americans were disfranchised in all but a few northern states and because the political activists about whom I have evidence were exclusively white, black voices are not heard here. Where possible, I draw heavily on the letters to Whig politicians from their wives, whose partisan zeal I appreciate and whose political acumen I deeply admire, none more so than Emily Baldwin, the wife of Connecticut's Whig Senator Roger Sherman Baldwin, who has recently been rescued from obscurity by the film *Amistad*. But, this is, perforce, a study of white men. I do not call them "elite" white men, for many of the now-forgotten characters who people the follow pages would deserve that appellation only because their words have been preserved on paper.

I knew, as I envisioned the book, that these five goals constituted an ambitious agenda. But once I began to write I also changed the study's chronological scope. When I began my research on the Whigs, I was most interested in answering a single perplexing question: why did the Whig party die as a competitive political organization? My previous studies of the antebellum Republican party and of the Know Nothings convinced me how pivotal the death of the Whigs was to the chain of political developments that triggered southern secession and the subsequent Civil War. For that reason alone, accounting for the party's demise is of vital importance. But profound dissatisfaction with the state of partisan politics in the 1970s, 1980s, and 1990s also increased my desire to find an explanation for the Whigs' death. Anyone who has pondered (and deplored) the longevity and the apparent irreplacebility of the modern Republican and Democratic parties, as I have done, should know that the total disappearance or displacement of a mass major party is an exceedingly rare event in American political history. Why, I asked myself, have the modern Democratic and Republican parties endured for so long, when virtually every index of public opinion, from polling data to low voter turnout, suggests that Americans loathe or ignore them, whereas the Whig party, which helped generate historically high levels of voter turnout, which engendered truly passionate loyalty from voters and leaders alike, and which, I confess, I genuinely admire, ceased to exist? How could such an anomaly—indeed, from my perspective, such an injustice—occur?

Thus, I set out to explain why the Whig party went out of business. My original plan was to write a book that began with Henry Clay's narrow, but traumatic, defeat in the presidential election of 1844 and then traced the party to its grave. During an academic year's leave in 1976–77, I conducted archival research across the country in the expectation of writing such a book. When I set out to write during my next leave in the fall of 1981, however, I found it impossible to compress into a single background chapter the party's history prior to 1844. Thus I decided that I must attempt to tell the whole story.

That decision had profound consequences. I spent the remainder of that academic year bringing the Whigs' story only up to 1844, my anticipated starting point. I made this decision at the Center for Advanced Study in the Behavioral Sciences at Stanford, a glorious environment in which to write but not necessarily the best place to do the research on the party's early years, which I had ignored before arriving there. I relied heavily on secondary works, published collections of politicians' papers, microfilm, and whatever else I could find there, but readers will note a decided difference in the density of archival documentation between the chapters on the years up to 1843 and those covering 1844 and beyond.

My decision that fall also had benefits. Close study of the Whig party's founding and of its early, much-frustrated career increased my faith in the plausibility of the argument I wished to make about the reasons for its death. Just as I intended to argue that the party died primarily because both the reality and the popular perception of Whigs' substantive differences from and conflict with the Democratic party markedly diminished after 1848, I also discovered that the party took root in different states after 1833 only when it managed to carve out distinctive positions on concrete matters of state public policy and to demonstrate the congruence between those positions and the stand Whigs took on national affairs. Such study also led me to recognize two other points that shape the book's argument.

First, for both strategic and principled reasons, the Whig party formed behind an ideological mission. Genuinely appalled by Andrew Jackson's Caesarism, by his apparently flagrant contempt for the separation of powers and the rule of law, a contempt that, early Whigs believed, threatened the people's political freedom, the party's founders tried to rally politicians and voters behind a crusade to save the Revolutionary experiment in republican self-government or, in Henry Clay's words, "to rescue public liberty." Many Whig activists always cherished this mission, and they clung tenaciously to the very name "Whig" because of its association with the Revolutionary founders. Yet that self-conscious devotion to bedrock republican principles clearly had decided limitations in terms of arousing voters' interest or helping Whigs win office. Instead, many voters responded positively to the party only when it developed a distinctive agenda on more concrete matters of public policy. Thus, only after the depression following the Panic of 1837 gave salience to a concomitant republican principle embraced by Whigs— the commonwealth tradition of using the state actively for the benefit of the people—did Whigs succeed in mobilizing enough voter support to become truly competitive with the Democrats.

During the heyday of Whiggery in the 1840s, Whigs' commitment to liberty and republican self-government remained a distinctive but subsidiary weapon in the party's competitive arsenal. Partisan conflict instead revolved primarily around governmental economic policy, territorial expansion, war with Mexico, and slavery expansion into the West. When a number of developments converged to reduce and often end partisan conflict over those matters in the early 1850s, however, ideological concerns about protecting republican self-government and political freedom from liberty-crushing threats again took center stage. This time, however, the menace did not come from executive tyranny. It seemed to come instead from unresponsive politicos, a papal plot, a Slave Power conspiracy, or a heartless northern majority intent upon treating the South as the unequal minority that it in fact was. This reconfiguration of the threat to republicanism and of the ideological crusades necessary to save public liberty helped allow new parties to displace the Whigs as the major anti-Democratic party in American political life.

Second, examination of the party's early years convinced me that serious internal divisions plagued the party throughout its existence, not just in its later years. That recognition, in turn, compelled me to reformulate my central focus on Whigs' competitive relationship with the Democrats as the key to the party's rise and fall. In essence, I now believe, the history of the Whig party can best be understood in terms of a tension or balance between centrifugal forces that always threatened to tear it apart and the centripetal force of conflict with Democrats that held it together. Both the divisive and cohesive forces waxed and waned in response to economic, social, and political events at the state and national levels of the federal system. Neither ceased to have an impact until the party's last days. But over time, the tilt in the balance between them followed a parabolic path, one inverse to that traced by the centrality of ideological concerns about saving republican institutions and principles. During the party's first few years, as during its last six or seven years, divisive forces clearly overpowered the cohesive glue of hostility to Democrats. Yet from approximately the spring of 1837 through the presidential election of 1848, a common determination to defeat Democrats and end Democratic governance held the Whigs together, despite their manifold divisions. Only after the election of the second—and last—Whig presidential administration did the balance between centrifugal and centripetal forces in the party tilt irreversibly and disastrously toward the former.

In the following pages I undertake to describe how and why these transformations occurred. To follow that story, I ask the reader to embark upon a long journey. I hope it is as edifying as it is extended.

Michael F. Holt
Charlottesville, Virginia

Acknowledgments

ONE OF THE PLEASURES of finally finishing a book on which I have worked for so long is the opportunity to thank the many people who helped me along the way. Indeed, precisely because I have been grappling with this study for over two decades, I have been particularly dependent on others for various kinds of support to see it through to completion. One of the costs of taking so long to complete it, however, is the near certainty that I will omit the names of individuals who merit my gratitude, and for those omissions I apologize in advance.

Let me begin with institutions that helped fund my research and writing. During 1976–77 I received a Senior Fellowship from the National Endowment for the Humanities that funded extensive archival research. Aside from my own study at home, the drafting of the manuscript was done at three splendid places: the Center for Advanced Study in the Behavioral Sciences at Stanford in 1981–82; the National Humanities Center in 1987–88; and Downing College, Cambridge, during my year as Pitt Professor of American History and Institutions at the University of Cambridge in 1993–94. I am indebted to the first two institutions for fellowships and also to the University of Virginia for Sesquicentennial Fellowships that allowed me to visit them for a full year. Working on a book was not part of my official job description at Cambridge, but I was given such a humane teaching load that I managed to get a great deal done. Thus I am very grateful to Professor Tony Badger and his colleagues in the History Faculty at Cambridge for inviting me and to the Master and Fellows of Downing College for offering me such warm hospitality during that year. Since 1990, I have been the Langbourne M. Williams Professor of American History at the University of Virginia, and chair leaves associated with that position facilitated my completion of the book.

In 1976–77, I traveled widely in search of material, and I want to thank the following people for finding or providing lodging to me: Claude Barfield; Professor John Milton Cooper; Professor John Hope Franklin; Mr. and Mrs. James W. Henry, Jr.; Mimi Jones; Betsy and Paul Mendelson; Professors Sydney Nathans and Elizabeth Studley; and John Fox Sullivan.

As the list of manuscript collections consulted in the bibliography reveals, I visited a number of archives and libraries, and I want to thank the helpful people at each of them for their aid. The staffs at the Microform and Rare Books Divisions of Alderman Library at the University of Virginia were also a great help. And anyone who has had the privilege of working at the Center for Advanced Study in the Behavioral Sciences and at the National Humanities Center knows how wonderfully supportive and efficient the staffs at those institutions are. I thank them all, and I am delighted that, at long last, I shall have copies of the book on which I labored while benefiting from their help to send them. Before I learned to use a word processor, the secretaries in the Corcoran Department of History at the University of Virginia—Lottie McCauley, Ella Wood, Elizabeth Stovall, and Kathleen Miller—typed seemingly innumerable drafts of seemingly endless chapters, and I am deeply grateful for their help. I also want to thank Diane Cronk for converting the early chapters for which I lacked computer disks into a machine-readable form compatible with the latter chapters.

New and old friends in Stanford, North Carolina, Cambridge, and Charlottesville helped me write the book by diverting my attention to more pleasant activities. Were the book shorter, I'd name them all, but I risk straining the reader's patience already. Thus I shall trust that the individuals whom I mean will know who they are. I cannot thank you all enough.

I am most deeply indebted to fellow scholars who shared material with me, suggested ideas that changed my approach, or carefully read and criticized parts or all of my manuscript. Professors William J. Cooper, Jr., Stephen Cresswell, William W. Freehling, Eugene D. Genovese, and William E. Gienapp kindly sent me materials discovered during their own research. At Stanford, my co-Fellow John Ferejohn, a political scientist of boundless energy and ideas, introduced me to a literature on twentieth-century election analysis that is central to the study. It was also my unique good fortune to be a Fellow at the National Humanities Center when Eugene Genovese was there. To my pleasant surprise, I learned that Gene has a passionate interest in and profound knowledge of antebellum political history. During that year, he read the first ten chapters I had drafted, and they have benefited enormously from his wise suggestions and ruthless editorial pen. He recognizes bloat when he sees it, and he did much to keep this opus from being even longer than it is.

Professor William W. Freehling also read later versions of the first ten chapters, and I am deeply obliged to him for cutting still more fat from my prose and attempting to make it more muscular. Readers familiar with his own books will readily recognize his stylistic input, and my only regret is that a temporarily incapacitating accident and his own busy schedule prevented him from reading more. I know from his pointed letters that he will still find this product too long and too detailed, but I also know that it is a far better book because of the attention he lavished on it.

Over the many years that I was writing this book, I floated ideas before gatherings of my colleagues at the University of Virginia, and their trenchant but sympathetic critiques only confirmed my conviction that I'm privileged to belong to a truly great History Department. In addition, my colleagues Edward Ayers, Charles McCurdy, and Peter Onuf read individual chapters of the manuscript, and they are markedly improved because of their insightful responses. But I am even more indebted for help in bringing this monster to bay to four other people.

My dear friends Professors William J. Cooper, Jr., of Louisiana State University and William E. Gienapp of Harvard University read all but the last two draft chapters and offered numerous keen insights that have reshaped the final version. Loyalty such as theirs defines what is best about the profession we share. My colleague at Virginia Stephen Innes, though a colonialist, insisted upon reading the entire manuscript and constantly prodded me to give him additional chapters. He then gave me a marvelously trenchant, apposite, and helpful critique for revising—and condensing—the manuscript. The labors of these three friends were truly heroic, for the manuscript I sent them and initially submitted to the press was fully twenty percent longer than the final product presented here. Much of the credit for reducing it belongs to my editor at Oxford University Press. That legendary friend of historians at Oxford, Sheldon Meyer, originally arranged a contract for this book after reading the chapters I had drafted in the early 1980s, but when he retired several years ago, he put me in the good hands of Thomas LeBien, who initially, I know, could not believe he was inheriting such a white elephant. In an act of amazing faith and generosity, Thomas went through the entire manuscript suggesting line-by-line and paragraph-by-paragraph deletions while I attempted the same kind of cutting on my own. Together we excised fully 750 manuscript pages from the even more detailed tome that I had originally drafted. That this book has ever reached the printed page—and certainly in a single volume—is largely a product of his help in condensing it and of his confidence in the finished product.

Only a very few of the graduate and undergraduate students I have taught at Yale, Stanford, and the University of Virginia between 1965 and 1998 have read a word of this manuscript. Nonetheless, it is with great pride that I dedicate this book to them. As a glance at my endnotes and bibliography will show, I have heavily relied upon the research papers of those students, the majority of whom were undergraduates when they wrote them. As well, most of the ideas in this book were first tested on undergraduates in my lecture courses on the Coming of the Civil War. But I want to acknowledge something more with this dedication. For almost two decades, many of my students have expressed a seemingly genuine interest in what I was doing and an intention actually to read (and buy!) my book on the Whigs when it finally appeared. Unlike myself and many others, they never seemed to doubt that it actually would appear. I am deeply grateful for this wondrous trust.

My family, who have been forced to endure this long saga with me, have contributed to its completion in a very different way. A superbly efficient manager of our household even while masterfully pursuing a career of her own, my wife Joyce constantly prodded me to finish it. My three children quite literally grew up with this book. When I began research in the fall of 1976, my son Adam was three and my daughter Erin was born. Another daughter, Annie, arrived in the fall of 1981, when I first put word to paper at Stanford. Adam and Erin have now graduated from college, and Annie, who gave me valuable help tracking down illustrations this past summer, is a senior in high school. As they matured, "Dad's Whig book" became a kind of standing family joke, a mirage, a quixotic goal. Though usually offered in the spirit of good-natured joshing, this skepticism was a constant goad, a burr in my saddle, that kept me at it over many long years.

Perhaps the greatest satisfaction I have in finally finishing the book is being able to show them I've done it.

Tradition obliges me to exempt any of those mentioned above from blame for any errors of fact or interpretation that remain in the text. And so they should be, for while I have benefited from advice and different kinds of inspiration, what follows is my own. In a work of this length the laws of probability alone suggest that errors will appear. For those I am solely, if unintentionally, responsible.

M.F.H.

The very life of liberty is maintained only by
the strife of contending parties

American Review, II (July 1848), 69

Chapter 1

"Not Fitted to Make Converts"

"THE WHIGS LOOK FORWARD to the approaching contest with all the confident ardor of men who are conscious of the justness of their cause—and in its righteousness read their claim to certain success."[1] So wrote a Baltimore resident in February 1844 about the impending presidential election to the son of the certain Whig standard bearer, Henry Clay of Kentucky. That winter and spring, through the summer and into the fall, Whigs everywhere forecast triumph. Their own unprecedented harmony, the Democrats' apparent disarray, and faith that they had the superior issues and candidate generated Whig confidence. Their missionary tone, the frequent use of words such as "righteousness" and "redemption," however, derived from another aspect of the race.

Clay's candidacy gave the campaign a special dimension. It vividly reminded Whigs of their ill-starred past even as they contemplated a glorious future. Born in Virginia during the Revolutionary War, Clay had studied law there before moving on to a long and distinguished political career in Kentucky. First a state legislator and interim United States senator, he was elected to the House of Representatives in 1810 and chosen Speaker when he reached Washington. Aside from duty as a peace negotiator at Ghent during the War of 1812, he served as Speaker almost continuously from 1811 to 1825, as secretary of state in John Quincy Adams' administration, and as Kentucky's United States senator for most of the period after 1831. As senator, Clay led the effort to build and define the Whig party. By 1844, most Whigs considered him "the embodyment [sic] and polar star of Whig *principles*."[2]

At the same time, no other Whig leader had suffered so many mortifying setbacks as Clay during, and even before, the Whigs' oft-times losing crusades against Democratic foes. Although the Whigs' chief congressional spokesman, he had been bypassed for their presidential nomination in both 1836 and 1840 on the grounds of "unavailability." When Whigs won power in the latter year and had a splendid chance to enact the sweeping legislative program Clay had done the most to formulate, a cruel twist of fate deprived him of the opportunity. In 1844, therefore, circumstances seemed to offer Henry Clay long overdue personal vindication and his party long overdue dominance. This prospect of atonement generated Whigs' religious language and euphoria.

Clay's long years of frustration began before the creation of the Whig party in 1834. In 1824 and again in 1832 he ran for president, and each time he was soundly thrashed. That record of failure both stigmatized Clay as a loser and, ironically, made the formation of the Whig party both necessary and possible. To understand why and to identify the seeds from which the Whig party grew, a brief review of political developments between 1800 and 1832 is necessary.

I

Like most politically active residents of his native Virginia and of his adopted Kentucky, Henry Clay was an ardent Jeffersonian Republican and a passionate foe of the rival Federalist party during the fitful existence of the so-called first party system. Clay's Jeffersonian pedigree emblemizes a crucial fact. Throughout the Whig party's existence, Democrats repeatedly sneered that Whigs were simply discredited Federalists hiding behind a new name. This superficially cogent accusation proved extraordinarily difficult to overcome. Even historians routinely echoed Democratic propaganda and described Whigs as ex-Federalists.[3] Experts now know better. Massive research in the past forty years has shown that the Whig party evolved not from the Federalists but from divisions within the Jeffersonian Republican party.[4]

After 1800, as the Federalist opposition atrophied, a tension that had always existed among Jeffersonians became more important.[5] On one side moderate nationalists, associated with James Madison, fully accepted the strengthening of the national government inherent in the Constitution. Though appalled by Federalists' excesses and elitism, which seemed to them to endanger republican self-government, they acquiesced in much of the Hamiltonian economic program. Commercial development, they hoped, would provide a constant market for the nation's farmers, and a diversified economy would keep the population industriously employed.[6] Their state governments chartered banks to supply capital for investment and credit to finance the transfer of goods. Frightened by the prolonged diplomatic and military crisis between 1807 and 1815, these development-minded Republicans also sought to strengthen and secure the union. At the end of the War of 1812, therefore, they sponsored congressional legislation to tie together the country's diverse economic regions.

Henry Clay was a leading congressional proponent of this nationalistic Jeffersonian economic agenda. In the following years, his coherent program, known as the American System, included high protective tariffs to nourish American manufacturing and create a home market for American agricultural products, a national bank to provide a sound and uniform currency, and federal subsidization of internal improvement projects to ease the movement of goods. In later years, when federally funded internal improvements became infeasible, Clay instead promoted distribution of federal land revenues to the states for their own improvements.[7]

In 1816, the nationalists pushed through Congress, and President Madison signed, laws effecting two parts of their program: a somewhat protective tariff and a twenty-year charter for the Second Bank of the United States. When the Federalist party disintegrated after 1815, many former Federalists embraced the

Republican party, strengthening this nationalist wing. It would eventually form the initial core of the Whig party.

These developments appalled the other main branch of Jeffersonians, purists known as Old Republicans or Radicals, who feared the degeneration of original Jeffersonian principles.[8] Beginning in 1801 and even more frequently after the nationalistic legislation of 1816, they deplored the dangers of loose construction and consolidation. Republicans' developmental policies, other Radicals feared, threatened the egalitarian and moral basis of republican society and thereby jeopardized the Revolutionary experiment in republican self-government almost all Americans venerated.[9]

Since the Revolution, quarrels over how to achieve and preserve republican institutions had created most political conflict. The British "real Whig" oppositionist tradition, so prominent a part of American Revolutionary rhetoric, had influenced those battles. Revolutionary republicans called on citizens to place the general good ahead of private interests. Officeholders, in turn, must protect citizens' political freedom and legal equality from any concentration of public or private power, and especially from law-granted privileges that gave advantages to some to the disadvantage of others.

While Americans generally agreed on these ends, other aspects of republican theory spawned quarrels over the means of securing them. Disagreements flourished over exactly what the common good entailed and over what government could or should do to promote it without encroaching on popular liberty and equal rights. Contention also developed over which selfish interests, whether political, economic, or religious, sought special privileges that flouted a virtuous commitment to the common good. The defense against these threats lay in citizens' active political participation to oppose those who subverted republican ideals. To Americans of the post-Revolutionary generation, the motto that "The price of liberty is eternal vigilance" was no empty slogan. It was instead the essence of republicanism.

Political leaders had also quarreled about the proper character of a republican society, that is, about what social and economic arrangements would best sustain citizens' virtue, their commitment to the public good or commonweal. A few Radicals groused about the excessive materialism of the market-oriented economy promoted by Clay and other development-minded Republicans. John Taylor of Virginia and Nathaniel Macon of North Carolina, for example, hymned paeans to republican simplicity and to the benefits of a stable agrarian economy that valued hard, honest work. Simultaneously, they preached jeremiads against speculation, arcane financial manipulation, and lust for instant wealth. The egalitarian ethos that had begun to effervesce during the Revolution and spread rapidly thereafter also generated Radicals' laments.[10] According to that ethos, the common good demanded that white men must attain roughly equal condition and, more important, equal rights before the law. Any legal privileges that gave unequal advantages to some seemed to pave a road toward the aristocratic, unrepublican society that all Republicans had accused Federalists of fostering. Radicals like William Duane of Philadelphia and Virginia's Taylor denounced banks and other corporations as bastions of aristocratic privilege inimical to equal rights. They condemned paper banknotes as fraudulent since banks often refused to redeem them for full face value. And they castigated the new monied men as an artificial aristocracy, inherently antagonistic to humble farmers and artisans. To restore social and political equality, they insisted, entrepreneurial policies such as Clay's must be checked.

In the buoyant years immediately following the War of 1812, frightened Old Republicans were a minority in the Jeffersonian party. Outside of a few southeastern states, their cries of alarm resonated faintly. The spirit of nationalism that had helped cause and sustain the war and had then been intensified by Americans' successful escape from that war dulled popular concern about the impending consolidation against which state rights Cassandras wailed. An economic boom blinded most men to the potential pitfalls of a speculative economy. Most important, by 1815, if not long before, most Americans saw no conflict between civic duty (virtue) and economic self-interest. To them, republican citizenship required political participation and vigilance, not economic abnegation. To them, the Declaration of Independence's self-evident truth about the right to pursue happiness freed individuals to seek prosperity. Any other definition of the common good was not merely an abstraction; it was an absurdity.

To most Americans in 1816, Madisonian nationalists like Clay, who had presided over the recent war effort and then passed legislation to rectify national weaknesses, had fulfilled the central duty of elected political leaders. They had preserved the Revolutionary generation's experiment in republican self-government.[11] At the close of Madison's second term in 1817, therefore, nationalists held the upper hand within the Republican party. They would be represented in James Monroe's new Cabinet by John Quincy Adams, the secretary of state and a former Federalist who had joined the Republicans before the War of 1812, and by Secretary of War John C. Calhoun, manager of the Bank charter in the House in 1816 and proponent of federal internal improvements. In Congress, Clay, the long-time Speaker of the House, continued to exert great influence.

The Radical doomsayers, in contrast, were largely ignored. They lacked a sufficient popular following to control the party either in Congress or in most states, and few voters by 1816 seemed interested in these leadership rifts.[12] Nonetheless, Secretary of the Treasury William H. Crawford of Georgia gave the state righters a potential national rallying point, should events create the opportunity for a rally.

The panic of 1819 and the sharp sectional split in Congress between 1819 and 1821 over Missouri's admission as a slave state provided it. Those developments shifted the balance of power toward the Radicals in a number of states and split the Jeffersonian party in the presidential election of 1824. The depression following the panic of 1819 awakened tens of thousands of men to the importance of politics. Farmers who lost their property, artisans who lost their jobs or were paid in worthless paper scrip, and businessmen who faced bankruptcy all turned to government for relief from their economic plight or for retaliation against the forces that they believed had caused it. Thousands voted who had never bothered before or demanded the vote if they did not have it. State politics began to revolve around debtor relief, stay laws, paper money, and banks. Newly politicized citizens seeking positive legislation to promote economic recovery gravitated toward the nationalist or pro-development wing of the party epitomized by Clay. Radicals, however, benefited most from the reaction.

For one thing, thousands of midwestern and southwestern farmers and land speculators, having suffered the foreclosure of mortgages, blamed the Bank of the

United States and the eastern elite for causing the panic. As an attorney for the Bank who oversaw its foreclosures in Kentucky and Ohio, Clay earned resentment for serving the despised Easterners. This inflamed sectional animosity influenced congressional debates over the tariff, internal improvements, and land policy for years thereafter. It also made the juggling of sectional interests part of the task of constructing a national party.

Antibanking sentiment ignited resentment of established elites everywhere. Now farmers and urban working men joined the Radical ideologues in denouncing bankers who seemed both to cause calamitous economic fluctuations and to escape their consequences. When a farmer or artisan could not pay his debts, he usually lost everything he owned and might be thrown into debtors' prison. When banks could not pay their debts, in contrast, they simply suspended specie payments and went about their business. Stockholders in the bank faced no further penalty because of limited individual liability. To many Americans such privileges seemed outrageously unfair, a flagrant violation of the republican principle of equal rights. In state after state, movements emerged to regulate banks, to substitute state-controlled banks for private corporations, or to abolish banks and/or paper money. In sum, the panic created a widespread animosity toward the political and economic establishment that gave the old egalitarian Radicals overwhelming reinforcements.[13]

Simultaneously, Northerners' attempt in Congress to stop the admission of Missouri as a slave state strengthened southern Old Republicans. The problem, according to Old Republicans, was that nationalists' program of aggrandizing national power augured the destruction of slavery. If northern congressmen could demand the abolition of slavery in a new state, they reasoned, they would soon attempt to destroy it in old states. The solution, Old Republicans contended, was to rededicate the party to state rights and strict construction. Newly empowered southern Old Republicans coalesced with key northern politicians, especially Isaac Hill of New Hampshire and Senator Martin Van Buren, leader of the powerful Bucktail faction in New York.[14] Thus did the panic and the Missouri crisis shift the political balance against the nationalist, pro-development wing of the Republicans.

The presidential election of 1824 revealed the degree of the change. Initially five contenders, all of whom called themselves Republicans but who represented different impulses in the party, sought the White House. One, Secretary of War Calhoun, still regarded as a nationalist, eventually dropped out of the race and consoled himself with election to the vice presidency. Of the remaining aspirants, John Quincy Adams and Henry Clay also belonged to the Madisonian nationalist wing, although their images among the electorate differed. Adams of Massachusetts appealed to the regional pride of New England and to Yankees elsewhere who considered slavery immoral, who rankled at the additional political power it gave the South through the Constitution's three-fifths clause, and who blamed the slaveholder Clay for conceding too much to the South by arranging the Missouri Compromise that admitted Missouri as a slave state. Clay, in turn, had greater appeal to those regions and to those voters who sought internal improvements and higher tariffs.

William H. Crawford was the candidate of the state rights Old Republicans. Nominated by a congressional caucus, by now the detested instrument of an insulated Washington establishment, Crawford was stigmatized as the candidate of politicians who violated the first principle of republicanism: government by the people. Instead, those who wanted to smite the political and economic elite turned to the remaining candidate in the field, General Andrew Jackson of Tennessee.[15]

Although Jackson served in the Senate in 1824 and cast votes for a protective tariff and internal improvements, he was still known primarily for his military exploits. The hero of the battle of New Orleans, where in 1815 he had routed the British in the only significant American land victory during the War of 1812, he had also crushed various Indian tribes in the southeastern states and had helped force the Spanish into ceding Florida to the United States in 1819. In a nation where thousands of local militia companies revered military prowess, his achievements guaranteed him wide support.[16] But there was more to Jackson's appeal than martial glory. Though himself a wealthy slaveholding member of Tennessee's plantation gentry, Jackson was a perfect standard bearer for angry voters bent on venting resentments. Westerners and Southerners embraced the Tennessean as a foe of the haughty East. His ownership of slaves and his renown as an Indian fighter only increased his appeal to such men. More important, Jackson was clearly a political newcomer compared to Adams, Clay, and Crawford. All who wanted to throw the establishment out of Washington, or at least out of the White House, could cleave to him.

Jackson and his friends also brilliantly capitalized on spreading popular fears that corruption in government was undermining republicanism. According to the republican ideas with which Americans were indoctrinated, corruption was doubly insidious. It induced officeholders to place their self-interest ahead of the public good and thus reduced their effectiveness as guardians of the people's liberty. At the same time, corruption of private citizens eroded their vigilance and their concern with public life by creating an obsession with materialistic self-advancement. The result would be inevitable. Since neither the people nor their representatives placed a priority on the protection of popular liberty and equality any longer, power would encroach on liberty. Tyranny would prevail, and the people would lose their liberty and equality and be reduced to slavery. Since the mid-eighteenth century, indeed, Americans had believed that slavery was the inevitable result of the loss of republican liberty.

Jackson himself believed that such a process of degeneration had already begun, and in 1824 he and his friend John H. Eaton wrote a campaign document expressing his views that soon became the basis for newspaper editorials endorsing Jackson's election. Known as *The Letters of Wyoming*, the pamphlet labeled the nation's capital a sinkhole of corruption that subverted the very basis of self-government. If virtue continued to be abandoned, it predicted, "freedom of necessity . . . must be laid prostrate." "We are not as we once were," it warned. "The people are slumbering at their posts; virtue is on the wane; and the republican principles with which we set out, are fast declining." But the people could "sustain [their] republican principles . . . by calling to the Presidential Chair . . . ANDREW JACKSON."[17]

Capitalizing on his popularity as a military hero, on regional resentments, on hostility to privileged elites, and on promises to preserve republican liberty, Jackson won a plurality of both the popular and electoral votes. He ran especially well in recently settled states like Illinois, Indiana, Mississippi, Alabama, and Louisiana, in North and South Carolina, and in Pennsylvania and New Jersey. Adams, who placed second in both votes, swept New England and took the bulk of New York's electoral votes. Crawford's strength, aside from Van Burenite support in New York, was confined largely to his native South, especially Virginia and Georgia. Clay, the one avowed champion of a nationalistic economic program, made a dismal showing in this first reach for the presidency, carrying outright only Kentucky, his home state, and neighboring Ohio. Stigmatized in much of the North as a slaveholder, in much of the South as a foe of strict construction, and in much of the recently settled West as an agent of the hated Bank and a critic of Jackson's successful wars against Indians, Clay captured only about 13 percent of the popular vote and came in last in the electoral count.

Nor did his problems in the 1824 election end there. Since no candidate had a majority of the electoral vote, the House of Representatives chose among the top three finishers: Jackson, Adams, and Crawford. Although Clay and Adams did not get along personally, Clay threw his considerable influence among his House colleagues to the New Englander, who then triumphed. When Adams subsequently appointed Clay as his secretary of state and thus his presumable successor in the White House, the embittered Jackson supporters immediately cried that a "Corrupt Bargain" between Clay and Adams had larcenously denied the popular will to keep an encrusted and arrogant elite in power. This charge would haunt Clay for the remainder of his long career.[18]

II

Between 1824 and 1828 a new alignment among politicians and voters began to crystallize. Adams and Clay supporters, divided in 1824, united behind the administration. This Adams party represented that portion of the old Madisonian wing who still believed in positive national legislation to promote economic development. In addition, Daniel Webster of Massachusetts led the remaining Federalists in Congress to support the administration.[19] Federalists not only shared in its patronage but found congenial Adams' bold advocacy of protective tariffs, federal internal improvements, and unprecedented new activities such as the congressional establishment of a national university, a national observatory, and a national naval academy.[20]

The nature and program of the Adams party, in turn, prompted the merger of the followers of Jackson, Calhoun, and Crawford in opposition to the administration and in support of Jackson's candidacy in 1828. The sweeping expansion of national power implicit in Adams' agenda offended state rights men. The apparent hostility of Adams and his attorney general, William Wirt, toward slavery and what slaveholders regarded as their rights alienated Southerners, and their inaction in regard to Indian land titles irritated land-hungry western settlers eager to force Indians off their lands.[21] Furthermore, high protective tariffs were becoming increasingly unpopular in the South, especially in Calhoun's South Carolina, and this sentiment helped drive Calhoun into the Jackson camp. Charges of the Corrupt Bargain, moreover, stigmatized the administration as privileged enemies of the popular will and greatly increased the credibility of the Jacksonian cause.

The Jacksonian opposition to the Adams party quickly developed into a pow-erful combination that won the congressional elections of 1826–27. Nor did shrewd managers of the Jackson coalition rest content with advantages already possessed. Confident that most Southerners would prefer a ticket of Jackson and Calhoun to one headed by Adams, Jacksonian leaders in the Senate such as New York's Van Buren and Levi Woodbury of New Hampshire maneuvered to pass a tariff in 1828 to neutralize whatever appeal Adams had as a proponent of protec-tion in the Midwest and Middle Atlantic states. To get the necessary congressional votes to pass that bill, they willingly made concessions to New England textile interests. Although Southerners shrieked about a "Tariff of Abominations," in the campaign Jackson men took care to pose as champions of protection where they thought they could benefit from such an image.[22] More important than such attempts to manipulate national policy in order to enhance their appeal, the Jack-son men built an organization to exploit the potential of an expanding and pre-viously apathetic electorate.

Appeals for voter support had been relatively less important at the presidential level than for state and local offices. Many states chose to elect presidential electors in state legislatures rather than by popular vote, thus negating the need of or-ganizations to get out the vote. In 1824, one-fourth of the states—Delaware, Georgia, Louisiana, South Carolina, Vermont, and New York—still chose electors in the legislature. Because of the dominance of the Republicans in most parts of the country, moreover, presidential elections since 1800 had generally been less competitive than state and local contests, thereby reducing voter interest in a given state. Some states had also placed property restrictions on the suffrage, reducing the number of eligible voters.

Consequently, prior to 1828, turnout rates in presidential elections were fre-quently lower than in gubernatorial races.[23] In 1824 only slightly more than a fourth of the adult white males voted for president. With voters minimally in-volved, national leaders, to construct winning coalitions, forged alliances with members of local elites in their own states and coalesced with national leaders from other states who had built similar alliances. Politicians, in short, counted on deferential voters to follow where local leaders led. Party building from the cen-ter to the periphery, in sum, had been largely leader oriented rather than voter oriented.[24]

By 1828, however, most states had abolished property qualifications for suf-frage so that virtually all adult white males could vote. By 1828 as well, only South Carolina and Delaware still allowed the legislature to choose presidential electors, and after that date only the Palmetto State clung to that practice. Thus presidential contenders could tap a much larger electorate. As astute Jacksonian managers recognized much more quickly than the Adams party, dealing with a mass electorate required different strategies than could be used with a relatively small one. Voters had to be mobilized directly; alliances of local elites loyal to one political leader or another could no longer win. Issues now had to be framed in terms that were understandable and compelling to relatively less educated and less interested voters. At times this necessity meant presenting specific policies in broad ideological or symbolic terms; at times it meant developing campaign issues that resonated with voters' emotions, values, and prejudices but that had no specific programmatic focus. Strikingly adept at all these tasks, Jacksonians adapted to the new rules of the game much more quickly than the hapless Adams men.[25]

Riding and channeling the waves of resentment mounting against Adams since 1825 and the popular enthusiasm for the hero of New Orleans, the talented Jackson managers organized the Jackson party from the top down. Central committees in Nashville and Washington corresponded voluminously with politicians around the country, who in turn established Jackson clubs and committees at the county and local levels. Sniffing victory that might result in federal patronage or local office, opportunistic politicians in state after state clambered aboard the Jackson bandwagon. They disseminated propaganda that had been mailed from Washington praising Jackson's virtues and dedication to republican principles, reminding voters that he had been the victim of a corrupt and cynical bargain, pillorying the supposed misdeeds of the Adams administration, and lacerating the president himself as an effete intellectual snob who spoke Latin and quoted Voltaire; as a papist or an antipapist, depending upon the audience; and even as a former pimp for the czar of Russia. State and local organizations purchased existing newspapers or established new ones to spread the Jackson gospel. They aroused public interest with mass rallies, parades, barbecues, and pole raisings, all new rituals of American political campaigns. These local organizations, finally, performed the most pragmatic yet important function of political parties in the nineteenth century. They printed and distributed Jackson ballots to voters on election day, for until the end of that century the parties themselves, not government, provided voters with ballots.[26]

The Adams party did not remain inert in the face of these developments. They too gained control of local newspapers, engaged in mudslinging, and developed an organization in various states. Some Adams leaders proved to be effective party managers. For example, Secretary of the Navy Samuel Southard, an old Jeffersonian and son of a former Jeffersonian congressman, created a competitive Adams machine in his native New Jersey. Nonetheless, in most states the Adams organization remained a loose alliance of local elites supplemented by the federal officeholders who remained loyal to Adams. Certainly Adams' campaign apparatus was less extensive and less effective in directly mobilizing voters than the Jackson organization.[27]

The elaboration of an organization gave Jackson a great advantage against Adams in 1828. It was not his only advantage, however. To Southerners and Westerners, Jackson seemed a firmer friend of slavery and foe of Indians than the Yankee president. Moreover, the erudite, Harvard-educated Adams proved a perfect foil for Jackson's campaign to establish himself as the people's champion against a hated northeastern elite. Nor could Adams match Jackson's stirring appeal to fundamental republican values. As a result of this combination a broad, powerful, and heterogeneous movement overwhelmed Adams and swept Jackson into the White House. In 1828, the turnout of eligible voters more than doubled since 1824. Jackson carried 56 percent of the popular vote, and he won in the electoral college by more than a two-to-one margin. Only tiny Delaware, New Jersey, a few congressional districts in Maryland and New York, and Adams' home region of New England resisted the tide.

III

The Adams and Clay forces now found themselves a beleaguered minority. Jacksonians not only captured the White House, but they also controlled both houses of Congress, the House of Representatives by a substantial 138–74 margin. To Clay, Webster, and others fell the classic task of leadership for a minority or "out" party, a task that would preoccupy and define the Whig party for most of its existence—uniting the opponents of the majority and broadening that coalition until it was competitive. Nor did personal ambition alone motivate them. They believed that they had a republican duty to maintain a vigil on the actions of the new government.

Clay, the foremost leader of the opposition, was genuinely appalled by Jackson's election. He feared that Jackson's military background portended a despotism that menaced republican liberty. Clay wrote in the January following the election, for example, that the National Republicans must keep "constantly in view the danger to civil liberty of the predominance of the military spirit" and be prepared to rally the people against it.[28] Rallying the people meant finding attractive issues, picking up converts or defectors from the majority, and winning a decisive share of new voters. Those objectives, in turn, meant waiting for the Jacksonians to alienate former supporters or finding new issues and a new image to win over new supporters.

Surprisingly optimistic about their ability to topple the new regime, National Republicans initially decided to wait quietly for the Jacksonian coalition to disintegrate. Refusing to acknowledge the 1828 election as a repudiation of economic nationalism and of leadership by the traditional political elite they represented, they regarded the outcome instead simply as a triumph by the magnetic Jackson over the aloof and colorless Adams. Hoopla, demagoguery, and Jackson's refusal to take a stand on matters of national policy, they thought, had temporarily dazzled voters, while sheer opportunism had engaged politicians with divergent policy goals in the Jackson cause. Once Jackson clarified his position on matters such as the tariff and internal improvements, they believed, people would regain their senses and desert the Jackson movement as quickly as they had joined it.[29]

In November 1829, for example, Clay wrote to James Barbour of Virginia of his great "hope of a speedy restoration of the reign of reason and common sense." "We must but passively await the inevitable fragmentation of Jackson's alliance," he crowed. "The next session of Congress will . . . greatly add to the dissolvents of that party," Clay again predicted in July 1829. "Whatever the President may say or recommend in his message to Congress, his friends in the body must divide on certain leading measures of policy." Once they did, the dissidents "must, sooner or later, attach themselves to the party which has all along been averse to the General." Hoping for "much" from "discontent and schisms among our opponents," Webster emphatically agreed. "My own firm belief," he wrote to Clay from the Senate in April 1830, "is, that if we were to let the Administration, this session and the next, have their own way, and follow their own principles, they would be so unpopular as that the General could not possibly be re-elected."[30]

In some ways this passive strategy made sense. The members of Jackson's extraordinarily heterogeneous coalition did disagree on policy questions. An alliance of men joined more by ambition for office or common hostility to the

Adams administration than as yet by any positive loyalty to Jackson or his embryonic party, Jacksonian politicians were susceptible to disillusionment. For many voters the attachments and alignments that had developed during the mid-1820s were still new and unfixed. The election of 1828 had mobilized thousands of new voters to throw the "ins" out; a durable realignment of the electorate depended on what Jackson did in office.[31] Thus the possibility of breaking off large chunks of Jackson's coalition theoretically remained open.

But National Republicans badly underestimated the skill with which Jackson solidified his ties to voters. His vigorous advocacy of Indian removal increased his popularity in the South and West. His demand for rotation in office among federal officeholders and his defiant contempt for the snobbish social pretension evident in the so-called Peggy Eaton affair enhanced his image as a foe of privilege and elitism. He cemented his hold on Old Republicans with solicitous respect for state rights, strict construction doctrine. Not only did he echo that doctrine continually in his annual messages and dramatically by his Maysville Veto of May 1830, but he also emphatically supported assertions by southern states of sovereignty over Indians within their borders. At the same time, his willingness to sign other internal improvement legislation and to acquiesce in protective tariffs allowed him to offset the appeal of National Republicans in the West and Mid-Atlantic states on those issues.[32] Thus, in the off-year congressional elections held in 1830 and 1831, the number of National Republican seats in the House fell from 74 to 58, while the Democratic total climbed from 139 to 141. Members with other affiliations occupied the other fourteen seats.

This last figure indicates the second reason why National Republican hopes were dashed. The issues that generated opposition to Jackson did not automatically unite his foes and drive them into the National Republican camp. The case of John C. Calhoun illustrates the point. National Republicans' anticipation of gaining defectors from the Jackson coalition seemed initially to be confirmed when the vice president bolted the Jackson team, taking some southern supporters with him. Personal animosity between the proud South Carolinian and the egotistical president, as well as rivalry between Calhoun and Secretary of State Martin Van Buren to be Jackson's successor, in part caused this rift. Feuding that had divided the administration since 1829 broke into the open in 1831 when Calhoun published a pamphlet detailing his private quarrels with Jackson and when Jackson, at Van Buren's suggestion, reorganized the cabinet to expunge Calhoun allies. Jackson then signaled that Van Buren had replaced Calhoun as his chosen successor by appointing the New Yorker minister to England. In response, National Republicans in the Senate wooed Calhoun by opposing Van Buren's confirmation. When the Senate vote on Van Buren resulted in a tie, the bitter vice president cast the deciding vote against him and thus completed his estrangement from Old Hickory. When Van Buren was named Jackson's running mate by a Democratic national convention in May 1832, National Republican hopes for a more permanent alliance with Calhoun rose even higher.[33]

Yet fundamental disagreements over the tariff issue prevented the absorption of Calhoun and other southern dissidents into the party. By 1828, Calhoun, under pressure from his South Carolina constituents, had shifted from his previous nationalism to a position more in line with southern opponents of protectionism. In that year, he had secretly authored the South Carolina *Exposition and Protest*, which affirmed the right of a state to nullify a tariff law it considered unconstitutional. Jackson's failure to push for tariff revision was one source of Calhoun's alienation from him, and in 1831 Calhoun openly endorsed nullification. Such a stance put him at odds with National Republicans, who iterated their devotion to a protective tariff in a series of addresses and resolutions issued by national conventions in 1831 and 1832 and who agreed with Webster's retort to South Carolina Senator Robert Hayne in 1830 that nullification was treasonous.

Even the passage of a new tariff in July 1832 that lowered rates to the 1824 level could not close the breach between nationalists and nullifiers. In 1832 South Carolina refused to give its electoral vote to National Republican candidate Clay. Instead, in a gesture of protest, the state legislature threw it to John B. Floyd of Virginia. Nor were National Republicans more successful in attracting disillusioned former Jacksonians in other southern states. Dissenters in Alabama, Virginia, Mississippi, Georgia, and North Carolina expressed their anger over developments in Jackson's first term by an abortive effort to substitute P. P. Barbour of Virginia for Van Buren as vice president on Jackson tickets, not by supporting the nationalistic tariff proponent Clay. National Republican expectations of uniting the various opponents of Jackson in the South had aborted.[34]

Nor could they successfully combine all opponents of Jackson in the North. There the problem was not so much that matters of national policy divided the foes of the Jacksonians, most of whom agreed with or at least acquiesced in National Republican positions. Rather, the National Republican leadership's faith in the ability of national issues and a coalition of congressional leaders to rally grassroots voters made them blindly insensitive and, in the end, resistant to important popular currents and political developments at the subnational level that had little to do with national concerns. For most of the nineteenth century, state governments addressed more matters that affected people's everyday lives than did Congress or the president. As a result, many people cared more about controlling state governments than the national regime. Moreover, since an organization could distribute ballots more easily for a single state than for the entire nation, the possibility of starting new parties oriented toward state issues always existed.

National Republicans were especially vulnerable to such a challenge in the late 1820s because permanent voter identifications had not yet been fixed. A new two-party system was still in its incipient stages; it had not yet crystallized. In sum, the same political fluidity that encouraged National Republican leaders to hope for defections from the Jackson movement encouraged other political groups to operate outside the orbit of National Republicans and to challenge their credentials as leaders of the opposition to Jackson. As soon as the presidential election of 1828 was over, National Republican state organizations evaporated in the North, except for a few places like Massachusetts, New Jersey, and Maryland. In this vacuum a new, state-oriented organization called the Antimasonic party displaced the National Republicans as the primary opponent of the Democrats.

Started in 1826 as a protest over the murder of a defecting Freemason in western New York and the apparent effort of Masonic officeholders to cover up the crime, Antimasonry evolved into a defense of republican institutions against the secrecy and power of the Masonic fraternity. Initially its political purpose was to drive all Masons from public office by electing declared Antimasons, but its proclaimed defense of equal rights and civil liberties against the purported Masonic conspiracy quickly developed into a broad condemnation of all privileged corporations and state policies that abetted them. Antimasons vented the anger of farmers who suffered from economic dislocation and who resented the increasing control of urban commercial centers. In addition, they reflected the anxieties of rural evangelical Protestants who were alarmed by what they perceived as an increasing secularization of society and a degeneration, indeed a subversion, of fundamental Christian values. Emphatically embracing the basic republican principle that the people could and must rule themselves, they stressed that simply by voting, the people could install new governors and thereby change government policies. They were happy, declared Antimasons, to represent the "lower classes ... for in this country the lower classes are the head of all. The PEOPLE are SOVEREIGN." By the tens of thousands, disenchanted voters responded to this bracing appeal.[35]

By 1832 the Antimasons had ridden such populistic, antielitist, and moralistic sentiments to a powerful position in several northern states. They controlled the governorship and legislature in Vermont and had come close to winning New York and Pennsylvania. In Massachusetts, Antimasons captured 150 of the 490 seats in the general assembly in 1831, and they were influential in Connecticut and Rhode Island as well. Because Jackson was a Mason and therefore anathema to Antimasons, because the Democratic followers of Jackson in states like New York and Pennsylvania were responsible for the state policies Antimasons abhorred, and because Antimasons properly blamed Democrats in the Senate for frustrating a petition campaign by evangelical Protestants to have Congress stop Sunday mail deliveries and thereby restore the purity of the Sabbath, Antimasons seemed like natural allies for the National Republicans.

Yet a profound difference in style and purpose separated Antimasons from National Republicans. For one thing, many Antimasons distrusted all politicians, not just Democrats, for abetting the Masonic conspiracy. "Antimasonry has no use for any officeseeking, selfish, time-serving politician," they declared. They took "their candidates, not from the exclusive circle of aristocracy, but from the people." With some justice, therefore, Antimasons regarded National Republican patricians as hateful, snobbish, privileged aristocrats. Antagonism toward National Republicans was particularly strong in New England, where National Republicans rather than Democrats controlled state governments. Massachusetts Antimasonic conventions, for example, railed that the state's National Republican party was "completely under the control of the ultra aristocracy, the ultra Federalism, and the ultra Freemasonry of Boston and Worcester." To declare their independence from both major parties, the Antimasons nominated their own presidential candidate, William Wirt, in September 1831.

As early as the fall of 1830, National Republican leaders recognized that "this cursed anti-masonry embarrasses everything, and defeats all attempts at systematic operation against the common enemy." Until their own national convention in December 1831, however, they remained arrogantly confident that they could enlist Antimasonic support against Jackson on their own terms, namely, by stressing national economic policy, not state issues, and by retaining control of the anti-Jackson forces in their own hands. Despite Antimasonry, a New Yorker assured Clay, National Republicans could succeed "under the banner of Clay and the American System." Clay, who was a Mason himself, firmly believed that

Antimasons must join the National Republicans, "for the natural tendency of all divisions of the minority is to cohesion." The National Republicans were stronger than the Antimasons, Clay informed another correspondent, and "upon the laws of gravitation, we ought to draw them to us, instead of being drawn to them." Convinced of the inevitability of such a merger and insisting as well that topics like Masonry, no matter how important they were to voters, should not be discussed by national political leaders, he refused to answer requests from Pennsylvanians and New Yorkers that he denounce Freemasonry or renounce his membership in the order. Antimasons would have to come to Henry Clay. Mohammed would not go the mountain.[36]

Not only did Clay refuse to repudiate Masonry in order to construct a winning anti-Jackson coalition; after Wirt's nomination, he publicly denounced Antimasonry instead. Most other National Republican leaders shared his contempt for the third party, and when the National Republicans' national convention met in December 1831, they nominated Clay unanimously. Despite such obduracy, pragmatic politicians like New York's Thurlow Weed sought to combine the two parties behind common electoral tickets and gubernatorial candidates in Ohio, Pennsylvania, and New York in 1832. In the first two, however, National Republicans simply backed Antimasonic tickets on the understanding that those electors would support Clay in the electoral college if he had a better chance than Wirt to defeat Jackson. More important, New England's Antimasons insisted on running separate tickets for Wirt, and in November he would carry Vermont and drain support from Clay in other states as well.[37]

If most National Republican leaders stubbornly refused to deal with Antimasons as equal partners, they also reacted to "this demon of Antimasonry," as one called it, with fear and revulsion. Antimasonry's insistence that plain people, "the lower classes," should themselves govern challenged deeply held beliefs of National Republican leaders that educated gentlemen such as they, men of demonstrated talent, experience, and breadth of vision, had a right and a duty to rule. They clung to an eighteenth-century version of republicanism that stressed governance by an insulated elite on behalf of the public good rather than other republican values like self-government, equal rights, and liberty. Public issues, they thought, should be decided by reasoned debate among leading public figures, not by referenda at the polls. In their eyes, the egalitarian populism of Antimasonry was just as dangerous as the antiestablishment impulse that had brought Jackson to power. Even though both the Jacksonians and the Antimasons had demonstrated the efficacy of making direct appeals to the electorate and emphasizing basic republican principles, therefore, the National Republicans refused at first to emulate them. They had learned nothing about the changes transforming American politics, or at least they acted that way. This adherence to an outmoded strategy and style constituted the third and overarching reason for the National Republicans' failure to mount an effective opposition to Jackson.[38]

Even though the National Republicans abandoned their initial tactic of passively awaiting events by the middle of Jackson's first term, their underestimation of Jackson's skill, their failure to unite all the foes of Jackson, and their dependence on an old-fashioned leader-oriented strategy continued to plague them. To their credit, National Republicans did recognize by the end of 1830 that they had to attack Jackson openly in order to break up his coalition in Congress and the states.

"The quiescent policy, which it was deemed expedient for us to act upon during the last year, . . . is not fitted to make converts," Alexander Everett of Massachusetts had advised Clay.[39] To most National Republicans in 1831, however, changing tactics simply meant denouncing Jackson's mistakes, proving his unfitness for office to other leaders, and portraying Clay as a politician possessing the traditional qualifications for the presidency.

To be sure, some National Republicans recognized in the fall of 1831 that Clay's long service in the House and Senate, his close identification with the American System, and his purported participation in the Corrupt Bargain made him precisely the wrong candidate to win converts to the National Republican cause. Instead, they predicted accurately, Clay would repel Antimasons and Calhounites and galvanize even disillusioned Democrats behind Jackson. Clay's chances, Oran Follett of Buffalo wrote on the eve of the National Republicans' national convention in December 1831, were as "hopeless as salvation without repentance." The vast majority of National Republican leaders, however, were unwilling to dump Clay in favor of someone more likely to unify the foes of Jackson, such as Supreme Court Justice John McLean, who was popular with the Antimasons. The convention nominated Clay unanimously and then issued a staggeringly long address explaining their action. The address condemned virtually everything Jackson had done since taking office and especially faulted him for "deficiencies" of the "character" and the "dignity, judgment, good temper, discretion, and moderation" necessary for discharging the duties of the presidency. Clay merited support, it contended, because he was "one of the principal founders, and supporters of the American System," because he was a statesman of long and varied experience whose "qualifications and services . . . are too well known to require the aid of our testimony." The very length of this document, the detail in which it reviewed Jackson's record, and its language all indicated that National Republicans were still trying to convert leaders rather than court voters.[40]

IV

By early 1832, even Clay realized that this tack seemed little better than the previous policy of watchful waiting. Dissident Democratic congressmen still clung to Jackson, often professing their personal loyalty to him before voting against his recommended policies. Jackson had neutralized Clay's appeal on internal improvements and the tariff in the North, and those issues in any event were not attracting the support Clay needed in either the North or the South.[41] Thus National Republican leaders recognized that they must find a new issue to wean away Democratic leaders and rouse local elites to action. Eagerly, enthusiastically, and blindly, therefore, they created a new issue, one that hitched the fate of the National Republican party to the Bank of the United States.

Although the charter of the Bank would not expire until 1836, its president, Nicholas Biddle, petitioned Congress for recharter in January 1832. In his annual messages, Jackson had frequently criticized certain provisions of the Bank's operation and called for reform. Biddle knew, however, that Jackson also hoped to roll up a huge popular vote in 1832, and he anticipated that Jackson would not

dare to veto recharter in an election year for fear of reducing his popular major-
ities, especially in Pennsylvania, where the Bank was headquartered. National
Republican leaders like Clay and Webster, in contrast, encouraged and supported
Biddle's recharter effort precisely because they expected Jackson to veto it.

    Such a veto exactly fit their old-fashioned conception of how politics operated.
Correctly, they believed, the Bank was now popular in the South and parts of the
West, which were Jackson strongholds, as well as in the Northeast. A veto, they
calculated, would alienate the businessmen, lawyers, and planters who benefited
from the cheap credit and uniform currency the Bank provided and turn those
community leaders against Jackson. In the Northeast such community leaders
could presumably persuade suspicious Antimasons to support Clay. For two years
Clay had predicted that if he could pry either New York or Pennsylvania from
Jackson he could defeat him, and the veto promised to be just the lever he needed.

    More important, National Republicans calculated that the veto would reduce
Jackson's influence and increase their own strength among congressional leaders.
On the one hand, it could forge a link with Calhoun and South Carolinians. On
the other, it would drive a wedge between Jackson and his remaining congressional supporters, many of whom favored the Bank. A veto, they believed, would
vividly dramatize that Jackson was determined to undermine the position and
authority of traditional political elites. By emphasizing executive usurpation of
congressional prerogatives, they hoped to convince proud Democratic leaders that
Jackson considered his own personal views superior to those of congressional
statesmen. Once Democratic congressmen became convinced of that, National Republican leaders assumed, they would rush to preserve their own status as leaders
by bringing their supposed legions of local supporters into the National Republican camp.[42]

    When rechartering legislation passed Congress with the support of a third of
the Jackson men and when Jackson then vetoed it on July 10, 1832, however,
National Republican hopes were pulverized. Not only did pro-Bank Democrats
fail to bolt once the president declared a party line, but overly eager National
Republicans had forged a mace with which Jackson could bludgeon them, not a
sword for their champion. A masterpiece of political propaganda aimed directly
at voters, Jackson's veto message denounced the Bank as an unconstitutional excess of national authority, as a monstrous concentration of private power that
threatened popular liberty, and as an engine of aristocratic privilege that favored
the rich at the expense of the poor. The message tremendously enhanced Jackson's
credentials as a champion of republicanism and strict construction and as a foe of
the corrupt and entrenched political establishment in Congress. Democratic newspapers and resolutions around the country praised Jackson for saving "the people
from becoming enslaved by the corruptions of a moneyed aristocracy and desperate politicians." The veto marked "the final decision of the President between
the Aristocracy and the People—he stands by the People." "The Jackson cause,"
one paper summarized, "is the cause of democracy and the people, against a
corrupt and abandoned aristocracy."[43]

    Democratic rhetoric proved potent. Americans continued to view powerful,
privileged aristocracy and corruption as the natural enemies of the liberty, equality, and virtue necessary for republics to survive. The similarity of the Democrats'
appeal to the Antimasonic message allowed them in states like New York and

Pennsylvania, where they were on the defensive for supporting state monopolies denounced by the Antimasons, to strike back. As shrewd Antimasonic leaders like Weed instantly recognized in horror, Democrats could now divert attention to the national level and argue that their party opposed the most monstrous threat to republican liberty and equality of all.[44]

All in all, the renewed popularity Jackson and his party won by the crusade against the Monster Bank nullified any advantage Clay may have received from negative reaction to the veto. Having allowed Antimasons to preempt the assault on privilege at the state level, National Republicans could only pose as champions of republicanism by attacking executive tyranny. "THE KING UPON THE THRONE: The People in the Dust!!!" one newspaper thundered. Jackson "has set at utter defiance the will of the people as strongly expressed by their Senators and Representatives . . . he has . . . proved himself to be the most absolute despot now at the head of any representative government on earth." Finally adopting the Antimasonic tactic of calling on the people directly to save republicanism by voting, another National Republican sheet proclaimed, "One more opportunity— *perhaps the last*—is yet afforded us, of strangling the monster of despotism before it shall have attained its full growth, and checking the full tide of corruption before it shall have become too strong to be resisted."[45]

What marked the shift in National Republican tactics even more than their antityrannical rhetoric was their brilliant use of political cartooning to mock Jackson. The most famous and effective of these caricatures was called "King Andrew the First," which portrayed the aged Jackson wearing a crown and regal robes trimmed in ermine, with a scepter in one hand and the veto message in the other, and a copy of the Constitution torn to shreds at his feet. No piece of propaganda summarized so forcefully the National Republicans' conception of how the presidency had been perverted by Jackson, and none symbolized so well their belated turn to the public.

Thus, at the end of 1832, the National Republicans developed the credo upon which the Whig party would be founded and which would remain its central principle. In that year, however, such efforts proved too little and too late. The National Republican organization remained embryonic and truncated compared to the Jackson machine. The party failed even to run electoral tickets in Georgia, Alabama, and Mississippi. Elsewhere Jackson's skill in establishing himself as a paladin of popular liberty and equality blunted the initial attempts to portray him as the subverter rather than the savior of republicanism. Above all, the onus of the Bank of the United States smothered the National Republicans' last-minute attempt to change their own image from a party of the wise and talented to a party of the people. By making Jackson's veto and the Bank central issues in the summer of 1832, the National Republicans had only engaged in self-annihilation.

Jackson registered another smashing triumph in November, and Henry Clay suffered a second humiliating defeat. Although the popular vote was slightly larger than in 1828, Jackson still won 55 percent of it, and he swamped Clay in the electoral college, 219 to 49. Antimasons who refused to back Clay won Vermont and almost a tenth of the popular vote. Clay carried only Kentucky, Delaware, Connecticut, Rhode Island, Massachusetts, and a few congressional districts in Maryland and only about 37 percent of the voters. Clay performed especially dismally in slave states south of Maryland and Kentucky. There, Jackson rolled up an astounding 88 percent of the popular vote.[46]

The election of 1832 clearly stamped the National Republican party as a loser and as the tool of the northeastern elite whom neither Antimasons nor Southerners could support. That stigma was, in the words of Alexander Everett, palpably "not fitted to make converts." Mounting a successful challenge to the dominant Jacksonians required changing that image and developing new strategies, new organizations, and new issues credibly based on republican values. Given the rout of Clay, it also demanded fresh faces to lead the opposition. In sum, competing on even terms with the Jacksonians meant abandoning the National Republican party for a more enticing political vehicle.

Chapter 2

"To Rescue the Government and Public Liberty"

"AS TO POLITICS we have no past, no future," moaned Henry Clay two months after Old Hickory had crushed him. "The will of Andrew Jackson is to govern; and that will fluctuates with the change of every pen which gives expression to it."[1] Although Clay referred to Congress' failure to enact his American System, his words reflected as well National Republicans' gloom. As a tiny minority, they would resist but they could not stop Jackson. The last Congress had frustrated their program, and the next Congress would apparently be even more heavily Jacksonian.

To improve their position, National Republicans had to win over alienated Jacksonians and mobilize new voters. But first, as Clay's lament indicates, Jackson had to do the alienating. Jackson, in short, would largely determine the fate of the anti-Jackson party. The opposition party was locked into a symbiotic relationship with its rival, and he had the initiative.

The recent past had persuaded National Republican leaders that criticism of the Democratic majority alone would not create an effective opposition. They also had to unite those who disliked Democrats. Their failure in 1832 to rally southern dissidents and northern Antimasons demonstrated that unification required compromise. Unless all anti-Jackson men sacrificed some principle, Clay declared, "there can be no union or harmony."[2]

At the same time, National Republican leaders could not conciliate former Democrats at the expense of offending their original supporters. Thus in 1835, when Ohio's Whigs nominated Supreme Court Justice John McLean, a former member of Jackson's cabinet, for president, Clay warned that they "looked too much to support ... from the Jackson ranks, without sufficiently estimating the amount that might be lost in our own."[3]

Because National Republicans disagreed with each other, and with other anti-Jackson men, over which principles should be abandoned, a more effective opposition party proved dauntingly difficult to construct. Over the next eight years, as Jackson's opponents struggled to coalesce and expand the anti-Democratic coalition, the name of the National Republicans, to say nothing of their issues and their nationally oriented strategy, would be jettisoned. Prominent party builders like Clay and Daniel Webster would also learn, to their dismay, that they must temporarily sacrifice their presidential ambitions as well as their principles. Out of this prolonged effort between 1833 and 1840, the Whig party would emerge, larger in numbers, more heterogeneous in composition, and more successful in competing for office than National Republicans had ever been.

I

The national issue that commanded attention after the presidential election of 1832 both divided Jackson's foes and enlarged their ranks. It seemed to point to a complete reshuffling of leadership and voter alignments, not to a more effective anti-Jackson party. In November 1832, immediately after the election, South Carolina nullified the tariffs of 1828 and 1832 and defied the federal government to collect duties after February 1, 1833. Jackson responded with a proclamation on December 10, denouncing nullification as treasonous and warning that he would uphold national laws over spurious pretensions to state sovereignty. In January 1833, he called on Congress to increase his enforcement powers, but to work as well for a lower tariff to defuse the crisis. Congress, in response, passed both the so-called Force Bill, giving Jackson additional powers to collect revenues in South Carolina, and the so-called Compromise Tariff, gradually lowering rates over a ten-year period. After Jackson signed both bills into law, South Carolina nullified the Force Bill but accepted the Compromise Tariff. These actions ended the confrontation, for Jackson now had no need to use the supposedly nullified Force Act.[4]

Yet the Nullification crisis's ramifications extended well beyond its brief duration, especially by increasing southern opposition to Jackson. State righters outside of Calhoun's personal clique detested nullification. But they considered Jackson's willingness to coerce a state and his affirmation of the supremacy of the national government "violent & danger[ou]s in its principles." To them, Jackson's belligerence gave a different meaning to the cry of executive tyranny that National Republicans had raised at the end of the 1832 campaign. Now Jackson was not simply vetoing the people's representatives in Congress; he was threatening to use military power against constituents in the South. Hence, a Georgia newspaper denounced him as "the meanest and most palpable of hypocrites—the most daring, reckless and dangerous of usurpers—and the most self-willed, heartless and bloody of tyrants." Portentously, meetings in South Carolina and a few other states adopted the name Whig in 1833 to signify their resistance to such monarchical despotism. In states such as Virginia, North Carolina, Georgia, Alabama, and Mississippi, moreover, state rights zealots broke with Jackson and often formed independent State Rights factions.[5]

Those defecting politicians constituted only a small minority of southern Jacksonians. The majority of Democratic leaders in Dixie, while dismayed by Jackson's actions, stood by their president. Meanwhile, the vast majority of the Democratic rank and file applauded Jackson's bold Unionism. So great was the continued support for Jackson in the South, indeed, that Senator Willie P. Mangum, who would break with Jackson in 1834 over a different issue, complained at the end of 1833 that Jacksonians slanderously portrayed any Southerner who disagreed with them as a nullifier. "The popularity of Jackson on the one hand and the unpopularity of nullification on the other, give the party in power great advantages in the South."[6]

State rights extremists who bolted in 1833 provided an alternative leadership cadre for any future southern anti-Jackson party. These dissidents differed profoundly from the nationalistic National Republicans who had supported Clay in 1832 and who generally applauded Jackson's stand on nullification. But state rights men such as Senator John Tyler, Benjamin Watkins Leigh, and Littleton W. Tazewell of Virginia; John Branch of North Carolina; John Berrien of Georgia; Senator George Poindexter of Mississippi; and the mammoth 350-pound Dixon H. Lewis of Alabama would play central roles in founding the Whig party in their respective states.[7] When the new Congress would assemble in December 1833, six senators would identify themselves as anti-Jackson State Righters in addition to the two Nullifiers from South Carolina. These eight independent slave state senators would hold the balance of power between the twenty National Republicans and the twenty Jacksonians in that body. As such, their position would have to be considered by any National Republicans who hoped to extend the anti-Jackson party to the South.

In Washington at the start of 1833, however, policy makers only knew that South Carolina had created a crisis, that Jackson had met it, and that some important southern Jacksonians loathed Jackson's stand. National Republican leaders divided sharply over how to respond. Clay, having fared miserably in the South in 1832, privately criticized Jackson's Nullification Proclamation for going too far toward consolidation. Publicly, he ducked the Senate vote on the Force Bill so as not to antagonize southern state righters' sensibilities. Most important, he cooperated with Calhoun, who had resigned the vice presidency and returned to the Senate as a member from South Carolina, to arrange the Compromise Tariff of 1833.

Webster and a number of other northern National Republicans, in contrast, regarded Clay's Compromise Tariff as a surrender of protectionist principles and a sellout of northern interests. Hence, they doggedly opposed it. Moreover, they admired Jackson's strong nationalistic position; many remarked that it echoed Webster's arguments in his debate with Hayne three years earlier. In their eyes, Jackson had erased any reason to fear executive usurpation just at the time southern fears escalated. Now they praised Jackson as the savior of the Union instead of pillorying him as a tyrant. Webster himself lauded Jackson's proclamation in a speech at Boston's Faneuil Hall before resuming his seat in the Senate in December, and once there he managed the passage of the Force Bill, which Southerners considered so offensive. The split between Webster and Clay and the surprising cooperation of the former with Jackson fed speculation that old parties were dead and that a new alignment was forming—nationalists versus state righters, Jackson and Webster versus Clay and Calhoun.[8]

Webster himself fervently prayed for such an alliance. Easily the most imposing figure in American political life, the senator from Massachusetts had celebrated his fifty-first birthday in January during the midst of the crisis. Born in New Hampshire and educated at Dartmouth College, he had moved to Boston in 1816, and for the next thirty-five years he served as attorney and political spokes-

man for its leading bankers, merchants, and manufacturers. A constitutional lawyer of formidable intelligence, learning, and prestige, he had argued many land-
mark cases before the Supreme Court. For all of his intellectual power, however,
Webster's fame and professional success rested on his awesome abilities as an
orator and his commanding physical presence. Five feet ten inches tall, with broad
shoulders and a deep chest, he usually dressed in white trousers, a buff waistcoat,
and a blue coat with brass buttons. But it was his uncommonly large head with
its jet black hair, massive forehead, swarthy complexion, shaggy black brows, and
glowing black eyes that transfixed audiences and caused his admirers to call him
"Godlike Daniel." When he addressed a court, Congress, or a public assemblage,
Webster transported men with the artistically crafted structure, the carefully mod-
ulated tones, the compelling marshaling of facts, and the logical clarity of his
rhetoric. Almost from the day he closed his reply to Robert Hayne in 1830,
schoolboys began to memorize it, and they would continue to do so for much of
the century. Exceptionally few politicians have been so mesmerizing as he.

Despite the fame Webster had earned from his nationalistic oratory and from
his Supreme Court practice, he was not content. His appetites were as large as
his talents. His taste for fine wines, good food, and expensive furnishings caused
him to live beyond the ample income he earned as a lawyer and to borrow heavily
from the Bank of the United States and from wealthy Boston constituents. Similarly, his political ambition caused him to covet the presidency. While he had let
Clay carry the National Republican banner in 1832, he now saw in the Nullification crisis his chance to grasp the only prize he considered worthy of his greatness.[9]

After Congress adjourned in March 1833 with the crisis apparently resolved,
Webster sought an alliance with Jackson. He realized that his own and his constituents' advocacy of a high tariff virtually wiped out any hope of southern
support. Appalled at what he regarded as Clay's apostasy on the tariff, moreover,
he no longer trusted an alliance with Southerners to secure that vital measure.
Instead, he sought to position himself as the preeminent candidate of the North,
and what better way to rally the North, he thought, than to champion the Union
against its southern subverters? Such a stance, he realized, might erase the stigma
he had incurred as a defender of the unpopular Bank of the United States in 1832
and attract previously suspicious Antimasons. The Union issue would allow him
to exploit his reputation as a nationalist while ignoring the nationalistic economic
programs the public regarded as elitist and inequitable. The new tack also accorded
perfectly with his antipathy toward organized parties and his sense that politics
should be conducted instead by high-minded statesmen who were valued for their
dedication to the welfare of the nation, not for their partisan identity. To carry
out this scheme, Webster had to align himself publicly with Jackson, but this
necessity did not deter him. The aged and sickly Jackson seemed unlikely to run
for a third term, and crusading for the Union promised to give Webster an edge
in the North over the general's apparent choice as a successor, Martin Van Buren.

Throughout the spring, summer, and fall of 1833 Webster labored to forge the
new coalition. He arranged for his Massachusetts friends to give a warm reception
to Jackson when the president visited Boston that summer. Newspapers friendly
to him announced that a new era of good feelings existed, in which the old "party
spirit is at rest." Instead, a "new organization" should be founded on "the prin-

ciples of the President's Proclamation." Let us have "no Jacksonians nor National Republicans, as party men—let us have no Free-masons nor anti-masons, no Southrons or Northmen—but let all be for the principles of the Proclamation." While his Massachusetts supporters launched the new party movement, Webster pushed the scheme during a speaking tour of New York, Ohio, and Pennsylvania. Everywhere he warned of "a deep determination among the politicians of the South to produce a separation" and predicted that the "great approaching political division of the whole country is to be between Unionists and anti-Unionists." Everywhere he urged newspapers to stress Unionism.[10]

Had Webster succeeded in 1833, the American Whig party would probably never have been created, certainly not the Whig party that historically existed. But Webster failed. Instead, all he did was to muddle the political situation still further and increase the difficulty of joining the northern and southern opponents of Jackson in a single party. Webster failed because, as Clay had perceived in January, the will of Andrew Jackson and his advisors—and nothing that the opposition itself did—would determine the political future.

II

Webster's attempted rapprochement with Jackson in a new party depended upon a prolongation of the disunionist crisis beyond the winter of 1832–33 and on a lull in Jackson's war against the Bank of the United States. On the banking issue, Jackson and his Democratic supporters stood fundamentally divided from Webster and most northern National Republicans. After his veto of the new charter in July 1832 and his vindication in the November election, Jackson had seemed willing to drop the Bank issue in order to smash the Nullifiers. In the spring of 1833, however, Jackson prepared to take further steps against the Bank. Webster frantically negotiated with the administration to head off any such action. In the spring, Jackson was content to bide his time, humor Webster, and benefit from the famous orator's powerful voice in behalf of his policies. But he was hardly ready to arrange peace terms with Nicholas Biddle's institution. Even as he was being feted by Webster's Boston cronies in June 1833, indeed, Jackson was writing his lieutenants in Washington to make the necessary arrangements to deposit government money in selected state banks rather than in the Bank of the United States.[11]

Jackson's closest advisors, the Kentuckians Amos Kendall and Francis P. Blair, who edited the Washington *Globe*, shared Jackson's hate for the Bank. Like Jackson, moreover, they worried that the disruption of party lines provoked by the Nullification crisis endangered the party's ability to carry out their goals. In March 1833, Kendall advised Jackson that the Democrats required "some decisive act to reunite and inspirit" them. Reopening the war on the Bank by removing the deposits, he counseled, would redivide Democrats from National Republicans. Democrats such as Vice President Van Buren, who questioned the wisdom of removal, also vigorously opposed any alliance with Webster. Van Buren especially had a personal stake in preserving the links with Democratic state righters in the South, a link that could be snapped by coalescing with Webster and other nationalistic National Republicans in the North. Moved by these considerations and even more fundamentally by Jackson's personal hostility to the Bank, his administration announced on September 25, 1833, that beginning October 1, the government would no longer deposit its revenues in Biddle's bank but would instead place them in selected state banks around the country that the opposition soon labeled as "pets."[12]

With this stroke, Jackson reemphasized his command of the political universe and his ability to make parties revolve around his actions, not around the wishes of mere satellites like Webster. As the epicenter of the majority party, he determined what shape the minority party would take. Although it took several months for Webster to admit it, no realignment on the Union issue would occur. Instead, the removal of the deposits inspired the creation of a new anti-Jackson party. With a few exceptions like Webster, National Republicans instantly reopened fire on Jackson as a high-handed tyrant. A writer in the Newark, New Jersey, *Sentinel* epitomized the National Republican reaction. "As Louis of France said, in the plenitude of his despotic glory, 'I am the state,' our Executive Officer openly proclaims, I *am* the Government."[13]

By reinvigorating the issue of executive tyranny, removal of government deposits from the Bank made it more compelling to state rights Southerners who had previously remained loyal to the president. According to the Bank's charter, the deposits could be removed only after congressional committees demonstrated that they were unsafe. Yet recent committee reports had found no evidence that would warrant removal. At the close of the previous Congress in March 1833, indeed, the House had voted by over a two-to-one margin to accept the majority report of its Ways and Means Committee that the deposits were perfectly secure.[14] By executive fiat Jackson had thus ignored Congress' will, removed government funds from an institution where congressional law mandated they be placed, and in the process apparently violated as well the constitutional clause guaranteeing the obligation of contracts. As Senator Mangum of North Carolina put it in a major speech breaking with Jackson the following February, the question was no longer Bank or no Bank, but "law or no law, constitution or no constitution." As Mangum and other Southerners saw it, by placing deposits in state banks chosen for their loyalty to the administration, Jackson had increased his patronage, his power to corrupt politics, and his capacity to yoke politicians to his will. He had wielded the government's sword through the Force Act; now he seized its purse. Finally, Jackson sacked two secretaries of the treasury, who defied his order to remove the deposits, before naming one who would do his bidding. Such behavior menaced the independence of statesmen, as well as the control the Senate supposedly exercised over the cabinet through its power of confirmation, and some senators considered the very dismissal of a cabinet member without Senate permission unconstitutional.[15]

Senate voting patterns show that Southerners considered the removal question one of executive usurpation rather than one involving the economic merits of the Bank. Outside of the border states, only three of sixteen southern senators voted for recharter of the Bank in 1832 and only two supported the resolution to override the veto. But in the spring of 1834, nine Southerners voted for, while seven opposed, Henry Clay's resolution to censure Jackson for removal.[16]

Jackson's foes also charged that the alleged tyrant had caused the severe recession that gripped the nation by the time Congress met in December 1833. In actuality Biddle was the culprit. Even before September, Biddle had responded to the threatened removal of government deposits by curtailing discounts of commercial paper and calling in loans. To create economic discontent that could be mobilized against Jackson, Biddle continued the policy of contraction far longer than economic prudence required. State banks, in response, also retrenched. The resulting sharp reduction in credit and circulating currency forced prices down.

The squeeze was not confined to northern commercial and manufacturing areas. Western farmers, who had borrowed money to buy land, as well as southern bankers, merchants, cotton factors, lawyers, and planters who relied on credit to move their crops, also experienced economic hardship. Many sufferers blamed Jackson for precipitating the crunch. One North Carolinian, for example, told Mangum about a substantial swing of opinion against Jackson in his state: "I admit with you that the question is 'law or no law, constitution or no constitution.' But it is the pecuniary embarrassment, the great and overwhelming distress consequent upon the removal of the deposites [sic], which comes home to the people."[17]

By removing the deposits, Jackson thus greatly expanded the number of his opponents. When Congress assembled in December 1833, however, his foes remained divided. They included nationalistic National Republicans who had previously supported the Bank, Calhoun's Nullifiers who had only recently been sharply at odds with Webster and other Northerners over the tariff, and other state rights men from the South who were alienated from Jackson but despised National Republicans' economic programs. Indeed, most of these men regarded the very name "National Republican" as an insult hurled at them by Jacksonians to cripple their political fortunes in the South. They clung tenaciously to the label "State Rights men" to distinguish themselves from both National Republicans and Nullifiers.[18] Although Webster had not yet given up on an alliance with Jackson, most of the other leaders wanted to unite against Jackson and to prevent the election of Van Buren as his successor in 1836. The problem was how to do it.

III

Clay took the lead in attempting to consolidate the polyglot opposition. At the age of fifty-six, Clay was five years the senior of Webster, his great rival in the anti-Jackson camp. Whereas the granite-like Webster evoked awe and admiration, the irresistibly appealing Kentuckian inspired love, affection, and often rapturous adoration from virtually everyone he met. Where Webster tended to be aloof, somber, and taciturn at private gatherings, Clay was a brilliant conversationalist, sparkling, witty, playful. Tall and thin, with a sandy complexion, a shock of brunette hair that had turned white with age, gray, laughing eyes, and a straight, thin-lipped mouth that broke readily into a smile, the gracious, fun-loving Clay charmed both men and women wherever he went. Neither as profound nor as learned as Webster, he exuded emotion and charisma when he addressed public audiences. The inspirational visions and the warmth of feeling that punctuated his speeches made them almost as effective, at least when heard, as the weighty learning and cold, penetrating reason that made Webster's oratory so compelling.

Both men loved the Union dearly, both could appeal to patriotic sentiment to uphold it, and both longed for the presidency. Although Clay had written a friend in the summer of 1833 that he intended to suspend his quest for that office, he had not relaxed at all his fear and resentment of Jackson. Often imperious and overweening, moreover, he loved to dominate any arena he was in, be it the Senate or simply a dinner party. As Congress convened in December 1833, therefore, he found a situation ready made for his particular talents and personal magnetism, and his natural inclinations moved him to take command of the anti-Jackson forces.[19]

Toward that end, Clay met during the winter of 1833–34 at private dinners with other anti-Jackson leaders to coordinate strategy and to find some common candidate to run against Van Buren. Representing the divergent regional and ideological strains among the anti-Jackson men, the dining partners included the Nullifier Calhoun from South Carolina; the State Rights senator from North Carolina, Mangum, who constantly rejected the notion that he was either a Nullifier or a National Republican; the stalwartly orthodox National Republican from New Jersey, Senator Samuel L. Southard, who had served with Clay in John Quincy Adams' cabinet; and the former president himself, who had returned to Washington as a congressman from Massachusetts. The Antimasonic candidate for governor, Adams might be particularly useful as a bridge to that organization.

Notably absent from these planning sessions was Daniel Webster. Webster continued to hope for a compromise with Jackson, remained independent of the Clay-Calhoun coterie, and even obstructed Clay's initial tactical moves to organize the opposition to Jackson. Only at the end of January 1834, after Jackson had spurned his overtures for some compromise on the Bank with unmistakable finality, and when he was pressed by Biddle, to whom he was financially obligated for loans and a retainer, did Webster openly attack Jackson and thus move reluctantly back into the anti-Jackson camp.[20]

The coadjutors quickly discovered that they could not agree on a common presidential candidate. But they enjoyed more success in deciding upon the forum in which, and the issue with which, they would battle the president. Because Jackson's supporters controlled the House, his foes agreed to concentrate on the Senate, where the combination of State Rights men, South Carolina Nullifiers, and National Republicans outnumbered the Jacksonians 28 to 20. In mid-December, the anti-Jacksonians seized control of the major Senate committees, and the birth of the Whig party can be dated from this parliamentary coup. Neither Clay nor Calhoun took a chairmanship, but Webster, who was still keeping his distance from them, exacted as the price of his future cooperation the chairmanship of the Finance Committee, which would direct the Senate's response to the removal of the deposits. From this power base incipient Whigs launched an all-out war against the administration by refusing to confirm Jackson's appointments of new government directors for the Bank and, in June 1834, of Roger B. Taney, the man Jackson had named secretary of the Treasury the previous September to remove the deposits.[21]

The anti-Jacksonians emphasized removal of the deposits and executive usurpation, rather than a renewed defense of the Bank itself, to galvanize the new coalition and rally popular support. At the end of December, Clay defined the opposition's platform in a ringing three-day speech. "We are in the midst of a revolution, hitherto bloodless, but rapidly tending towards a total change of the pure republican character of the Government, and to the concentration of power in the hands of one man," he warned the Senate. He demanded passage of two resolutions. One rejected Secretary Taney's report to the Senate justifying removal. The other denounced Jackson for trampling on the laws and the Constitution. With these resolutions, the Whig party at its birth focused on its everlasting basic principle: opposition to executive usurpation in general and to Andrew Jackson in particular.[22]

To highlight the removal issue and demonstrate the legitimacy of resistance to Jackson's course, Clay and other Whig leaders encouraged supporters to send petitions to Congress blaming Jackson's high-handed action for causing economic distress and demanding that he restore the deposits. Petitions for relief inundated Congress in February and March. This outpouring, Clay hoped, might turn the House against Jackson, forcing the president to admit his error and restore the deposits. The Bank arranged some of these petitions, seeking to show its indispensability. Anti-Jackson politicians circulated others to manufacture opinion against the president. Most, however, reflected genuine economic suffering.

That suffering, however, also produced disagreement about Whig strategy. Some House and Senate Whigs, hoping to exploit the economic crisis, sought recharter of the Bank rather than redeposit of the federal funds. Webster, ambitious for both objectives, introduced a bill calling for restoration of the deposits *and* an extension of the Bank's charter beyond March 4, 1837.

Those like Webster who wanted recharter, however, formed a minority of the embryonic Whig coalition. The dominant wing, led by Clay, Calhoun, Mangum, and their inner circle, sought only to restore the deposits. They recognized that a defense of the Bank, rather than an assault on Jackson's allegedly despotic action, would revive the elitist image that had wrecked the National Republican party in 1832. Any hint that Whiggery was the discredited National Republican party reborn would especially repel potential southern recruits, who viewed the very name "National Republican" as a political death warrant. Clay warned Biddle in early February against any attempt at recharter. Only executive "usurpation," he maintained, "has convulsed the country. If we put it by and take up the Bank, we may and probably would divide about the terms of the charter, and finally do nothing." Accordingly, Clay forced Webster to table his own bill within a week of offering it, thereby confirming the Kentuckian's leadership. Three days later the chastened Webster helped pass Clay's censure resolutions and echoed Mangum by declaring that the central issue was the "SUPREMACY OF THE LAWS."[23]

In short, the necessity of expanding the National Republican base by incorporating other foes of Jackson dictated Clay's strategy. "I want aid—all the aid that can be given," he pleaded in December. In the winter of 1833–34, Clay sought that aid primarily from the South, where he had run so dismally a year earlier. Rescuing "the Government and public liberty from the impending dangers, which Jacksonism has created," he wrote his Virginia friend Francis Brooke in December, "depends, in my opinion, mainly upon the South." By focusing on executive tyranny rather than on the impending death of the Bank, he told Brooke, he would resume "the campaign of 1777."[24]

By alluding to the Revolutionary struggle for independence against a tyrannical English monarch, Clay encapsulated the main reason the opposition coalition used the name "Whig." That magic label, reverberating with memories of the revered Founding Fathers who had used it during the Revolution, signified that the party's main purpose, at least originally, was resistance to King Andrew Jackson. The name provided an umbrella under which all who opposed Jackson could gather.[25] More important, it struck an ideological chord. By resonating with republican values Americans had cherished since the eighteenth century, it fused National Republicans, Antimasons, and state rights Southerners. Constructing a new party required more than arranging organizational alliances in Washington and the various states. The new party also needed ideological glue, some principle for which it stood.

IV

This last point merits amplification, for the impulse behind the formation of the Whig party has often been misrepresented. Historians have normally portrayed the name "Whig" as a sheer expedient, designed to assemble the widest possible assortment of men who had nothing in common save hatred, fear, resentment, or jealousy of Jackson and his allies. They usually stress the negativism of the Whig party, sneer at its dearth of ideas and ideals, and point to the diversity of its constituent elements as proof of its instability and opportunism. One early student of its formation wrote that "Principles had little part in the origins of the Whig party." Twenty years later, Arthur M. Schlesinger, Jr., called the cry of executive tyranny a façade behind which disgruntled conservatives could hide their greed. "The Whigs," wrote Schlesinger, "in scuttling Federalism, replaced it by a social philosophy founded, not on ideas, but on subterfuges and sentimentalities. As Henry Adams observed, 'Of all the parties that have existed in the United States, the famous Whig party was the most feeble in ideas.' "[26]

As already noted, the men who formed the Whig party in the winter of 1833–34 had often opposed each other over national and state issues during Jackson's first term. Although congressional Whigs in 1834 showed surprising unity in supporting Clay's proposal to distribute federal land revenues to the states and several other measures, original National Republicans and southern state rights men like Mangum remained profoundly at odds over national promotion of economic development.[27] "The principles that you and I hold to be the only conservative principles of our Federative system," Mangum lamented to a North Carolina friend in October 1834, "are scarcely comprehended by the most intelligent of the National Republicans" in "the North & East."[28] Common opposition to Jackson therefore *was*, at least initially, the strongest bond uniting incipient Whigs. Opposition to, and perceived difference from, the Democratic party would, indeed, remain essential to the vitality of the Whig party throughout its lifetime. It was intimately bound to, and decisively shaped by its relationship with, the Democratic majority.[29]

Nonetheless, strictures about the ideological bankruptcy of the early Whig party are wrong-headed. Opposition to executive tyranny was based on principle, a principle with profoundly powerful ideological ramifications. Only a passionate devotion to the Revolutionary experiment in republican government and a common conviction that Jackson threatened it explain how men with such diverse views on other matters formed a united front against him.

From the Whigs' perspective, everything that Jackson had done demonstrated his intention to amass power in his own hands; to upset the constitutionally mandated balance among the branches of the federal government; to subvert or destroy the independence of other political leaders and voters through patronage, the influence of his pet banks, or intimidation; and thereby to crush popular liberty. Convinced that Jackson was following the same classic scenario as King George III in orchestrating a conspiracy against popular liberty, his opponents adopted the name "Whig" to signal their commitment to the independence of the other branches of government and of the people. As Mangum saw it, he and other Whigs were *"The Independents,"* whereas Jacksonians were "the absolute *submissionists,* (I mean submission to the bad influences here in Washington.)" Or, as the Raleigh, North Carolina, *Register* rejoiced in June 1834, "The happy cognomen of Whigs, which all parties opposed to Executive usurpation had adopted," provided "a standard under which . . . men of all parties, could rally in defense of LIBERTY against POWER."[30]

To defend liberty was to give the Whig party at birth a greater ideological legitimacy with the American voting public than the National Republicans had ever enjoyed. By itself the name helped to erase the stigma of antirepublican elitism that had stunted the growth of its predecessor and to supply the credible appeal to republican values necessary for any party that hoped to compete successfully with the Jacksonian Democrats. Through this party, it promised voters, you can perform your duty to preserve the fruits of the Revolution.

Hence the assertion that the adoption of the name "Whig" "fixed attention upon opposition to Jackson rather than upon principles as the reasons for the party's existence" utterly misses the central ideological foundation of the party. Opposition to Jackson was based on principle. Whigs saw themselves acting from the necessity, as Clay had put it, "to rescue the Government and public liberty, from the impending dangers, which Jacksonism has created." "A Whig in its pure signification," pronounced Richmond, Virginia's, *Whig* in April 1834, "means one who prefers liberty to tyranny—who supports privilege against prerogative—the rights and immunities of the people, as ascertained by the equity of nature, the Constitution and the laws of the country, against the predominance of the Crown, or Executive power."[31]

Rank-and-file Whigs repeatedly echoed their leaders' fears about the threat that executive tyranny posed to republican self-government. In 1834, for example, a New Yorker wrote to Clay of his "trembling sense of alarm" about "the measures of the present Executive." Jackson displayed "an unbridled lust of power, that attacked the very foundation of our free institutions." A North Carolinian added that "we are at present under a practical despotism & unless the ballot boxes shall vindicate a violated Constitution, it is fearful to think of our Country's doom."[32]

Previously, northern Antimasons had condemned the power and privilege of the Masonic order and of entrenched officeholders as a threat to republican liberty. By adopting a name and rhetoric signifying opposition to the tyranny of King Andrew, Whigs therefore facilitated the merger between Antimasons in the North and State Rights men in the South. This reaching out to the Antimasons and adoption of the aggressive populistic style that had distinguished them so sharply from the patrician National Republicans was especially apparent in New York rhetoric. Salvation from Jackson's "unlawful" actions rested "IN THE HANDS OF THE PEOPLE," Whig papers proclaimed. The tyrant must be resisted "THROUGH THE MEDIUM OF ELECTIONS." "The time has come," intoned an address of Whig state legislators, "when it must be decided for ourselves and for posterity, whether this government shall be a republic in fact as well as in name, or whether it shall be converted into a monarchy, with the form only of popular power."[33]

Whig denunciations of executive tyranny helped attract Antimasons for another crucial reason. The Antimasonic movement originated in resentment that Masons had literally tried to get away with murder by subverting the legal system. In a fundamental sense, that is, Antimasonry was founded on the proposition that America must have a government of laws and not of men, that no man or group of men, however powerful, was above the law. Thus the Whigs' insistence that their true issue with Jackson was not the Bank, but "law or no law, constitution or no constitution," resonated with Antimasons' deepest values. Antimasons rallied enthusiastically to the new party, one told Seward, because the "common object" of Antimasons and Whigs was "to redeem the Constitution and restore the supremacy of the laws."[34]

By absorbing the great majority of former Antimasons, Whigs accomplished, in ideological terms, a feat of no mean proportion. Perhaps more than any single group in the United States, Antimasons reflected a purist strain of classical eighteenth-century republican ideology that condemned modernization itself—industrialization, commercialization, economic growth and the materialistic values it spawned—as the greatest threat to republican virtue and independence. In contrast, the National Republicans and entrepreneurial Jacksonians who joined them in the Whig party in the North represented par excellence the modernizers in American society, men who lauded economic growth and development, who appealed to materialistic self-interest and considered it desirable, who valued luxury as an incentive to economic effort, not an acid that dissolved pristine virtue. As the historian Daniel W. Howe has argued, when Whigs channeled the republican fears of Antimasons against political degeneration rather than economic change, they "performed the remarkable feat of synthesizing 'virtue' and 'commerce' as political appeals."[35] By merging with populistic Antimasons, in turn, Whigs went even further to shed the elitist image that had wrecked the National Republicans.

V

Other strains of thought besides a common commitment to republicanism facilitated this ideological synthesis. Scottish Common Sense moral philosophy and evangelical Protestantism also contributed to a unique Whig "political culture."[36] All three strains of thought helped produce a critical feature of Whiggery in its formative years. Antipartyism, an aversion to party organization itself, motivated many early Whigs.

Evangelical Protestants insisted on freedom of conscience for an individual. Nothing should interfere with allegiance to Christ; a Christian conscience alone should determine human behavior. Evangelicals had condemned Freemasonry as "an infidel society at war with true Christianity" because it interposed oaths and pagan rituals between a man and his conscience, because its "ceremonies and appendages" struck "at the basis of all morality and religion." This same impulse fueled evangelicals' moral antipathy toward the Roman Catholic church, which, they thought, controlled laymen through the dictates of priests; toward drunkenness and alcoholic consumption, which made men dependent and subverted self-control; and toward Negro slavery, which viciously eradicated all human potential. Such beliefs caused evangelicals to translate their fears of Masonry and the Catholic church into hatred of political parties, especially the Democratic party, which they often associated with both Masonry and Catholics. Because party discipline/ required men to sacrifice their own views for the good of the organization, because it encouraged blind obedience rather than independent action, party organization crushed freedom of conscience and made men moral slaves. In a significant sense the Antimasons had been an antiparty party, and they, as well as many state rights southern men, brought those views with them to the new Whig coalition.[37]

Secular republican ideology reinforced the animus of evangelical religion. Until the 1820s, American political philosophers had damned organized parties, and especially systemic interparty conflict, as destructive of a government devoted to the public interest. This traditional fear of parties, along with a fear that parties inflamed passion at the expense of reason and thereby violated the canons of Common Sense moral philosophy, motivated a number of National Republican patricians. Men like John Quincy Adams and Daniel Webster never fully accepted subordination to the new Whig party. Contemptuous of Democrats' party discipline, Whigs prided themselves on being independents rather than submissionists, on thinking for themselves rather than sheepishly obeying instructions. Whigs, they boasted, "are too independent to wear the collar of party discipline"; they represented the "liberty of Freemen" in contrast to the Democrats' "slavery of party."[38]

By the 1840s Whigs' antiparty sentiment would wane perceptibly, but in the 1830s it strongly fueled their animosity against Democrats in general and Martin Van Buren in particular. To patriarchal Whigs, Van Buren, the architect of the highly centralized Albany Regency machine in New York, which first articulated both the necessity of sacrificing an individual's will to party discipline and the virtue of interparty conflict, epitomized almost everything that was dangerous about the Democratic party. If Van Buren won in 1836, Whigs direly predicted, "the necks of the American people are forever subjected to the yoke of a system of party discipline subversive of personal independence, destructive to freedom of opinion, and fatal to our free institutions."[39]

Jackson, by successfully demanding that the national Democratic convention in May 1835 obediently rubber-stamp Van Buren and Richard M. Johnson of Kentucky as presidential and vice presidential candidates, only increased Whigs' conviction that party dictation meant slavery. An address of Illinois Whigs called "the convention system attempted to be forced upon the American people by the Van Buren party . . . destructive of the freedom of the elective franchise, opposed to republican institutions, and dangerous to the liberties of the people." Anti-Van Buren newspapers in Alabama added "that this odious convention system should be spurned from the embrace of freemen." If conventions continued to usurp the

choice of rulers from the people, "we may linger out a degrading political existence under a caucus despotism—we may wear for a while longer the forms of
freemen; but our spirits will be effectually enslaved."[40]

Antiparty sentiment made Whigs particularly dependent upon issues rather
than party loyalty when conducting campaigns. Antiparty sentiment also may
explain why turnout rates for Whig voters in off-year elections, when no clear
issue seemed to be at stake, were often lower than Democratic turnout rates.
Furthermore, antiparty sentiment may help explain why far more Whigs than
Democrats turned to nonpartisan or apolitical voluntary associations to achieve
certain morally oriented goals: Bible societies, Sunday school unions, temperance
associations, and antislavery or abolitionist organizations. In the 1830s, however,
antiparty sentiment above all else hampered the organization of the Whig party
itself in a number of states like Michigan, Illinois, and Alabama and at the national
level.[41] Revulsion at party dictation was a two-edged sword, at once a weapon
against the Democrats and a bar to fusion within the opposition.

VI

By the time Congress adjourned on June 30, 1834, Whigs had taken significant
steps toward becoming a more competitive anti-Jackson party than the National
Republicans had been. In the Senate the incipient Whig coalition had passed resolutions calling for the government revenues to be replaced in the Bank, censuring
Jackson, and refusing to record Jackson's protest of that censure in its journal. In
the House, however, Democrats had passed resolutions killing recharter, blocking
a return of the revenues to the Bank, and endorsing their deposit in state banks.
Yet even in the House, Whigs smothered an administration-backed bill for the
regulation of the deposits, and in a special election for a new Speaker in early
June they had combined with anti-Van Buren Democrats to elect the pro-Bank
Democrat John Bell of Tennessee over his Tennessee colleague James K. Polk, the
chairman of the Ways and Means Committee and the chief spokesman for Jackson's antibanking policies in the House. More important, with their new name
and with the issues of removal and executive despotism, the Whigs had discovered
a formula with great potential for uniting National Republicans, Antimasons,
Nullifiers, and southern State Righters.

As Whig leaders like Mangum and Clay had recognized as early as the winter
of 1833–34, however, building a congressional coalition could not create a new
party. Whigs now needed to form a more broad-based party in the electorate that
could win state and national elections. The new Whig party had a foundation.
But could it erect a popular edifice?

Chapter 3

"No Opposition Man Can Be Elected President"

"YOU WILL HAVE HEARD the result of our K[entucky] election," an ebullient Henry Clay gushed to Willie P. Mangum in August 1834. "We could not desire that it should have been better—76 out of the 101 members of the [state] H. of R., Letcher's re-election [to Congress in a special election], and 11 of the 12 [state] Senators to be chosen elected on our side." Meanwhile, "Indiana has done nearly as well, and Illinois and Missouri are not much behind her. Ohio will bring up the rear gloriously in the West."[1] Everywhere the new party seemed to be taking hold. Everywhere the various opponents of the Democrats seemed to be rallying behind the Whig banner. Everywhere the Whigs seemed to be riding a wave of resentment against Jackson's actions that would wash Democrats out of office and eventually cleanse the White House itself of the Jacksonian stain.

But Clay, characteristically, was overly sanguine. Convinced of Andrew Jackson's unpopularity in the spring of 1834 and concerned primarily with resisting the tyranny of the national executive, national Whig leaders hoped to transplant their party to the states in 1834 and 1835 and build momentum for the 1836 presidential election by stressing national issues—presidential despotism and Democratic depression. That emphasis, however, proved to be flawed. Economic conditions improved, and disenchantment with the Democratic president dissipated. As a result, Whigs' electoral fortunes fluctuated. Similarly, they sometimes failed to bring all of Jackson's disparate foes into the Whig camp, and they utterly failed to unite behind a single presidential candidate. Thus they could not compete successfully for the office that, according to their ideological standards, especially menaced republicanism if it remained in Democratic hands.

Far more important, contrary to Whigs' initial assumptions, rallying voters against Jackson proved insufficient to launch successful state organizations. Transplanting a nationally oriented party to the states required more than the nutrient of national issues, especially when those issues began to lose their sustaining power. To sink permanent roots in the states, the Whig party had to address matters of state political concern so that citizens would vote Whig in state as well as presidential elections.

Exclusive reliance upon the issue that allowed the creation of the Whig party, in other words, ultimately stunted its growth and hindered its competitiveness at the vital state level. Whigs might initially convert voters with their attacks on Jackson, but to sustain that allegiance they had to demonstrate the congruence between a Whig ideology based on national issues and state affairs. In this task, they also enjoyed only mixed results. Building a victorious Whig party at the local, state, and national levels proved far more difficult than Henry Clay imagined in the bright summer of 1834.

I

During the spring and early summer of 1834, Whigs dramatically extended their new party beyond Washington. Prospects in all-important New York, the nation's largest state, seemed particularly good. In New York City's municipal election in the spring, Whigs triumphed by running against the Democratic recession, and earlier that year, Antimasonic members of New York's legislature called for the dissolution of the Antimasonic party, thus paving the way for a merger of the state's National Republicans and Antimasons in the new organization.

A Democrat facilitated this anti-Democratic merger by allowing incipient Whigs to take a stand on state banking policy that meshed with their attack on Jackson's deposit removal. To save New York's banks from Nicholas Biddle's contraction in the spring of 1834, Democratic Governor William L. Marcy pushed a bill through the state legislature that provided for a potential state bond issue of $6 million. Accordingly, $2 million would be made available to private individuals in upstate New York, and $4 million would go to New York City's banks to cover their deposits and note issues. Led by Thurlow Weed in the editorial columns of his *Albany Evening Journal* and by William Henry Seward in the legislature, Whigs condemned Marcy's plan. Marcy, they charged, tried to rescue Jackson from the disastrous removal of deposits at the expense of the state's taxpayers, who would ultimately have to pay for the bonds issued to privileged individuals. Whigs portrayed an enormous slush fund of state monies with which Marcy could corrupt the polity, just as Jackson had done by depositing federal revenues in his pet banks. Marcy's bullying tactics, continued the Whig indictment, resembled Jackson's executive tyranny.

At the end of his biting address of the Whig minority in the legislature to the people, Seward, who was the Whig gubernatorial candidate in 1834, called on voters to repudiate Jackson, Marcy, and the slavish Democratic legislators and congressmen who had done their bidding and to replace them in November with independent men. The Whigs' fall campaign thus focused on executive usurpation and on *both* national and state banking policy. In New York, the major national Whig themes had been inextricably linked to state politics.[2]

In some other states, Whigs also organized with relative ease in opposition to Jackson, even without distinctive stands on state policy. Ohio's Antimasons and National Republicans also quickly joined the Whig party's campaign in 1834 against removal and party dictation. In Maine, New Hampshire, Massachusetts, New Jersey, Delaware, Maryland, Kentucky, and Louisiana, where the National Republican party had previously taken hold, Whig leaders in Washington could count on the influence of men like Clay, Webster, Southard, and John M. Clayton of Delaware to convert it into the Whig party. In most of those states, former National Republicans contested elections as Whigs in 1834, and an early victory in Louisiana's July gubernatorial contest further fueled Whig hopes of a rising tide against Jackson. In all these states, Whigs could take advantage of preexisting voter cleavages and anti-Jackson organizations to create the new party.[3]

The new Whig party also quickly penetrated slave states where National Republicans had been feeble and Jackson unbeatable. In early 1834 in Virginia, the South's largest state, nationalists from the West, who had backed Clay in 1832, merged in the legislature with the more numerous state rights zealots from the East to condemn Jackson's deposit removal. The new coalition forced the resignation of the pro-Jackson loyalist William C. Rives from the United States Senate by instructing him to vote for restoration of the deposits and elected prominent state righters Littleton W. Tazewell as governor and Benjamin Watkins Leigh as the new senator. In the Senate, Leigh joined his fellow Virginian John Tyler in the Whig camp. Proclaiming that the issue was "a struggle between liberty and power," rather than between Bank or no Bank, and often adopting the name "Whig," this combination then won a convincing victory in the state legislative elections of May 1834.[4]

Meanwhile, in North Carolina, Calhounites led by John Branch, state rights followers of the enormously influential Senator Willie P. Mangum, and a tiny group of National Republicans joined to protest Jackson's removal policy and to contest the August legislative elections. By the summer of 1834, they were often using the name "Whig," although the first statewide Whig convention was not held until December 1835. In Georgia, a pro-Jackson Union party and an anti-Jackson State Rights party, led by John M. Berrien, vigorously fought the congressional elections of 1834 and the gubernatorial contest of 1835. The State Rights party denounced Jackson's action toward the Bank as tyrannical and economically pernicious, but its main platform was support of state rights and hostility to both the Force Bill and Jackson's Nullification Proclamation. In Mississippi, a State Rights Association was formed in the spring of 1834 to protest the Force Bill. By December a Whig convention, denouncing the removal of deposits and Jackson's tyranny, arranged a ticket for the gubernatorial and congressional elections the following November that might gain State Rights support and thus fuse the two major anti-Democratic groups in that state. At the end of 1834, only Alabama, Tennessee, and South Carolina, among southern states, had not yet formed a coherent anti-Democratic party that might align with the Whigs.[5]

Election results during the summer and fall of 1834, however, destroyed Whigs' rosy vision of quickly subduing Jacksonians. Even where the Whigs scored victories, with the exception of Clay's Kentucky, local factors rather than a national trend against Jackson explained the triumphs. The perpetually overoptimistic Clay wrongly interpreted the election of nominal Whigs as governor in Illinois and Indiana in August as referenda against Jackson. Instead, the personal popularity of candidates and the long tradition of chaotic factional rivalries produced the victories; they had nothing to do with national issues.[6]

Success in Louisiana's gubernatorial election in July also stemmed from local factors, not from national anti-Jackson sentiment, even though Whig legislators had denounced removal in the spring. Ethnic rivalries between French Creoles in southern Louisiana and native Americans in the northern part of the state had long shaped state politics. The French had maintained power through suffrage restrictions on potential opponents, gubernatorial patronage, and over-representation in the legislature. When the Democratic candidate for governor in 1834 urged the abolition of suffrage restrictions, reduction of the governor's powers, and legislative reapportionment, the French rallied behind the Whig candidate, a Creole himself, and the Whigs prevailed.[7] These victories in Illinois, Indiana, and Louisiana demonstrated not that Whigs could run successfully against Jackson but that the opposition could, in certain places, exploit state issues and preexisting intrastate rivalries to win irrespective of national issues.

Where the Whig party campaigned almost exclusively against Jackson because it lacked salient state issues, it met defeat. Democrats won the North Carolina legislature in August, and the new legislature immediately tried to force Mangum's resignation. In October, Georgia's pro-Jackson Union party swept the congressional and legislative elections. While the Whigs managed to capture the governorship in Massachusetts, a former National Republican stronghold, Democrats crushed the opposition in Maine and New York and carried New Jersey, Pennsylvania, and Ohio by narrower margins.

Nor did the spring elections in 1835 bring much solace to disheartened Whigs. In New Hampshire, Whigs lost the governorship by almost a two-to-one margin and all five congressional seats. In Connecticut, a state Clay had carried comfortably in 1832, Whigs lost the governorship, both houses of the legislature, and all six U.S. congressional seats. Similarly, Democrats captured both of Rhode Island's congressional seats. Worst of all, the promising start in Virginia proved ephemeral. In May, Democrats elected sixteen of twenty-five congressmen, recaptured the legislature, and quickly passed resolutions of instruction that compelled both Tyler and Leigh to resign from the Senate.[8]

The spring setbacks filled New York's perspicacious Whig leaders with foreboding. "Politically, I am sick at heart," Weed informed Seward after seeing the Connecticut results. "All looks fearfully, hopelessly black." "Virginia has blasted every hope," he added a month later. Albert Tracy, another of Seward's correspondents, was even more demoralized. "The Whigs as a party are without plan, purpose or principle," he lamented. "Their unskillfulness and imbecility . . . deters the young and ambitious from joining them."[9]

Returns from the summer and fall of 1835 only aggravated Whigs' miseries. True, they won eight of thirteen congressional seats in Clay's stronghold of Kentucky, but across the Ohio River in Indiana, which the Whigs had nominally carried in 1834, they elected only one of seven congressmen. While Whigs captured the governorship and eight of thirteen congressional seats in Tennessee, they won only six of thirteen in North Carolina, two of five in Alabama, and neither of Missouri's two seats. Results later in the fall were equally depressing. Victory in Mississippi's gubernatorial contest was offset by the loss of both congressional seats and the legislature by more than a two-to-one margin. Although Whigs secured five of Maryland's eight congressmen, Democrats elected the governor and four congressmen in Georgia, the governor and the lone congressman in Michigan, and a two-to-one majority in both the New Jersey and Ohio legislatures. Whereas the Whigs won 58 percent of the congressional seats filled before

September 1834, they captured only 42 percent in the remainder of that year and a dismal 33 percent in 1835.

II

The causes of the reversal were readily evident. Improving economic conditions in 1834 dissolved discontent and blunted Whig assaults on Jackson as author of the recession. By July, Biddle began to relax his restraints on credit, and this turnabout added credibility to Democratic charges that Biddle had artificially contracted the Bank's operations in order to stir up anti-Jackson sentiment and that he, not Old Hickory, was responsible for economic hardship in the spring. Actually, neither Biddle nor Jackson deserved credit or blame. A marked injection of specie into the economy in 1834 through foreign investment and a favorable balance of trade increased bank reserves and, therefore, loans. As a result, cash in circulation, which had increased by a modest 3 percent between 1833 and 1834, grew by 15 percent between 1834 and 1835 and jumped 38 percent between 1835 and 1836. Expanding money supplies fueled a booming economy between the fall of 1834 and the spring of 1837 that extirpated economic resentment against Democratic policies and Whigs' remaining loyalty to Biddle's bank.[10]

The boom also prevented Whigs from exploiting Jackson's new antibanking initiatives during the remainder of his term. In 1835 and 1836, Jackson aggressively pushed a hard-money policy. His goal was to undermine the circulability of private banknotes by eliminating the government market for them. He urged Congress to bar deposit banks from issuing or receiving notes of small denominations. He ordered his secretary of the Treasury to effect this change through executive circulars to the deposit banks. And in July 1836 he issued a Specie Circular prohibiting the purchase of public lands with paper money. These measures alienated Democratic businessmen, and they would eventually provide ammunition for Whig campaigners. The three-year boom starting in 1834, however, nullified their immediate use as Whig issues.

In several states, Whigs also stood on the losing side of religious and ethnic disputes that weakened their competitiveness in congressional and state legislative elections between 1834 and 1836. In New Jersey, they, like their National Republican predecessors, were morbidly distrusted by dissident Hicksite Quakers, who blamed them for siding with the Hicksites' Orthodox Quaker rivals in legal disputes over Quaker school funds. That distrust kept western New Jersey, and with it the entire state government, in Democratic hands through the elections of 1836, even though virtually all Quakers disliked Jackson himself.[11] In Michigan, virulently anti-Catholic Presbyterians dominated the Whig party and committed it to oppose a provision to allow alien suffrage in the new state's constitution. Presbyterian intolerance alienated virtually all other demographic groups in the state, allowing Democrats to crush Whigs in 1835 and again in 1836.[12]

Even more debilitating to Whig hopes of rallying all anti-Jackson men behind their party, Antimasons persistently retained a separate organization in Massachusetts, Connecticut, Rhode Island, Vermont, and Pennsylvania, despite the Whigs' adoption of a similar ideological position. In Massachusetts, where Antimasons regarded Whigs simply as the same old aristocrats who had dominated the National Republicans, they cooperated with Democrats to come within a single vote of defeating the Whig nominee for United States senator in the 1835 legislature. In Connecticut and Rhode Island, enough Antimasons supported Democrats in 1834 and 1835 to deny Whig control of two states Clay had carried in 1832. In Vermont, Antimasons easily carried every gubernatorial election over both Democrats and Whigs between 1831 and 1836, and when the Whigs and Antimasons finally merged, former Antimasons dominated the party's leadership. In Pennsylvania, normally a Democratic state, Antimasons clearly outnumbered Whigs in the opposition ranks, especially outside of Pittsburgh and Philadelphia. Of forty-six opposition members elected to the state legislature in 1834, for example, thirty-three were Antimasons and only thirteen Whigs.[13]

Where state issues divided Whigs from Antimasons, Whig strategists realized, they must divert Antimasons' attention to national concerns. The removal issue had obviously failed to bring the two groups together by the end of 1834. Whigs therefore increasingly focused their hopes on a common presidential candidate in 1836. That strategy gave the Antimasons, a tiny proportion of the anti-Jackson men nationally, a decisive and disproportionate influence over the selection of the nominee.

To protect liberty from executive tyranny, that nominee would have to defeat Jackson's chosen successor, Martin Van Buren, who seemed eminently more beatable than the charismatic military hero. Virtually salivating at the prospect of campaigning against him, Whigs scourged Van Buren from the moment of his nomination in May 1835 as a corrupt political manipulator and dangerous intriguer. By taking that tack, they could shift the executive usurpation issue from the removal of the deposits, which had failed to move sufficient voters, to Jackson's supposedly dictatorial attempt to impose his successor on his party and on the American people. To anti-elitist Antimasons, they could invoke the horrors of the Albany Regency. To Southerners, they could point out that a slaveholding planter was about to be replaced by a Yankee. With genuine zeal and unbounded relief, Whigs launched a crusade against Van Buren that they hoped would prove more successful than had their forays against Jackson's evisceration of the Bank.

III

Once Whigs shifted their attention to Van Buren's liabilities, however, they confronted the age-old impossibility of beating somebody with nobody. As an impatient North Carolinian warned Mangum in November 1834, "We can never . . . commence operations—with success—without a candidate in the field for the Presidency."[14]

But what candidate could unite nationalistic National Republicans, who distrusted State Rights men and Nullifiers and were distrusted by them, or National Republican patricians and Antimasons, who regarded each other jealously? Every conceivable candidate seemed to have a political past that made him unpalatable to one element or another in the new party, yet, as Whigs recognized, only a single standard bearer who could keep Whigs "together" could "defeat Van Buren and Jacksonianism." "We must run but one candidate lest we break up and divide," protested Kentucky's John J. Crittenden in frustration. Yet the fact remained that while incipient Whigs could unite in opposition to Jackson, Van Buren, executive tyranny, and Democratic economic policies, they could not agree upon a single presidential candidate for 1836.[15]

John C. Calhoun, for one, insisted on going his own way. He acted with the Whig alliance until 1837, but he and his loyal South Carolina supporters were never really of it. The Whig party, indeed, never took hold in Calhoun's fiefdom. "We are aware of the danger . . . of our merging into one or both of the great parties now contending for the Presidency," Calhoun wrote in January 1834. "We are determined to preserve our separate existence on our basis. If there is to be Union against the administration, it must be Union on our own ground."[16]

That ground remained Nullification. But precisely Calhoun's insistence on the constitutionality of state interposition set him apart from National Republican and State Rights Whigs who hoped to bury the divisive issue. When Calhounite editor Duff Green announced in his *United States Telegraph* that the Calhoun men would support no candidate for president who repudiated the right of Nullification, they were furious. I am "shocked with the impudence of D. Green," Clay exploded to Mangum. "Now it is clear that if each element of the opposition . . . will support no Candidate who does not entertain its principles, there can be no union or harmony."[17]

Calhoun's stubborn insistence on sticking to his guns epitomized the disharmony that Clay lamented. By the end of 1834 most Whigs forlornly admitted that they could not hold a national convention without its blowing apart. The antiparty animosity of some early adherents and the desire to condemn the Democratic national convention itself as a menace to self-government further militated against even attempting such an assemblage.

More fundamentally, Whigs' inability to arrange a national convention or agree on a single presidential candidate revealed that the party was still inchoate. To call all who opposed the Jackson administration before 1836 "Whigs" or to speak of a "Whig party" in the mid-1830s is more a literary convenience than an accurate description of fact. Although the opponents of Jackson could cooperate in Congress and although they cheered on each other's efforts in different states, they had developed no central organization. More important, they had not yet formed any institutional loyalties to the new Whig party. Indeed, many foes of Jackson and Van Buren who would later adopt the name "Whig," like the Antimasons in Vermont and Pennsylvania or State Rights men in certain southern states, still eschewed that label in the mid-1830s. It is little wonder that so polyglot and embryonic a coalition failed to hold a national convention in 1835 or 1836.[18]

Instead, Whigs relied by default on newspapers and caucuses of state legislators in different parts of the country to make nominations. At first they hoped that one state's favorite would catch fire elsewhere and that anti-Jacksonians throughout the country would then concentrate behind him. But by the summer of 1835, the party's newspaper in Washington, the *National Intelligencer*, succinctly confessed, "We desire a candidate who will concentrate all our suffrage and we desire what is impossible." With one candidate an impossibility, some Whigs hoped that multiple candidates might deprive Van Buren of the required majority of electoral votes. Then, one of the Whig candidates might prevail in the House of Representatives. Few if any Whigs publicly or privately articulated that hope, however, and there is no evidence of concerted planning among Whigs to bring it about. Indeed, the stigma of the corrupt bargain of 1825 required Whig newspapers to deny any intention of thrusting the election into the House. More pragmatically, some Whigs favored different regional candidates to maximize their advantages in state politics, where they might win control of state governments even if they did not stop Van Buren. As Virginia's James Barbour wrote Clay in the summer of 1835, "By running two popular men," we can secure "the State Government, an object of great importance, and almost a compensation for the loss of our Presidential candidate."[19]

With this priority on winning state elections in mind, Whigs especially rejected as candidates the nationally prominent leaders who had created the Whig party in Congress. Winning required converting former Democrats and Antimasons, and National Republicans, discredited by their association with the Bank of the United States, were deemed exactly the wrong kind of candidates for the chore. Just as Jackson had defined the original shape and thrust of the Whig party, he served as a model of the kind of candidate that Whigs without National Republican antecedents sought. "With Clay, Webster or Calhoun, or indeed any man identified with the war against Jackson and in favor of the Bank or the Bank's Shadow," New York's Thurlow Weed warned, "the game is up." In December 1834, Mangum wrote from Washington that most opposition politicians shared Weed's gloomy prognosis. "Mark it. *No opposition man can be elected President. They may mar, but they can't make,*" he told William A. Graham. "Clay is off— Calhoun is off—& Webster, though anxious for a nomination, must soon find that overwhelming defeat is inevitable."[20]

Ohio's Whigs demonstrated the expedient considerations that motivated the party when, in December 1834, they nominated a native son, Supreme Court Justice John McLean. A supporter of Jackson in 1828, McLean was praised for his potential to attract Democrats in a state Democrats had just carried. He was also presumed to be attractive to Antimasons who had courted him as their own candidate in 1831. Southern Nullifiers and state rights men immediately rejected McLean for lacking any principles, and National Republicans in New England and the border states refused to back an erstwhile Jacksonian.[21] Once his weakness was clear, Ohioans quickly abandoned him for a different candidate who offered a better chance to capture the state.

Ohio's actions particularly offended Clay, who still thirsted for the presidency and counted on Ohio's support. Indignant that the McLean boomlet doomed his chances, he bitterly complained that he, like many Whigs, "could not see the policy or propriety of selecting, as a candidate, a gentleman who was an original friend of Jackson, in preference to all who had been in uniform opposition to him." Clay's fury was understandable, but as usual, he exaggerated his prospects. By the end of 1834, neither Southerners nor New Englanders would support his pretensions.[22]

Nor were Webster's chances much brighter. The collapse of the Union party movement in 1833 had done nothing to quell his lust for the office, and he arranged for Massachusetts Whigs to nominate him in January 1835 in order to head off McLean. Webster succeeded in stopping McLean, who eventually withdrew, but in little else. Even Webster realized that he could get no support from the South. Southern Whigs were not Webster's main obstacle, however; they were willing to let him be the Whig candidate in the North, so long as they could run somebody else in the South.[23]

But too many northern Whigs regarded Webster as a liability. Outside of New England, Antimasons like New York's Weed and Seward considered Webster's Federalist background, his connections with the Boston Brahmins, and his well-known links to Biddle's Bank as dead weight they could not carry. "It is the height of madness to run Webster as a candidate," Seward warned Weed. "To vote for Webster is indirectly to elect Van Buren—and to fix upon the Whigs the perpetual stigma of federalism."[24] Similarly, Whigs in the Middle West, where, outside of Ohio, National Republicanism had been almost nonexistent, were left cold by Webster's political background and regional identity. They wanted a man of their own, just as Southerners did.

In the spring of 1835, both Midwesterners and Antimasons from the Middle Atlantic states began to float the name of a man they considered perfect—General William Henry Harrison. Hero of the battle of Tippecanoe in 1811, a former governor of the Indiana Territory and United States senator from Ohio, an Indian fighter with plain airs, and a long-time resident of the West, even though he had been born in Virginia, Harrison was a marvelously attractive newcomer. True, he had never been a National Republican, but Jackson had sacked him from a minor diplomatic post. He was, in sum, an anti-Jackson man.

Harrison's potential appeal caused Webster's supporters in and outside Massachusetts to complain loud and long of the danger of man worship and military candidates. Harrison, they protested, had insufficient experience, no record on recent issues, no qualifications as a statesman, nothing but fame for a few skirmishes fought in the distant past. To such strictures Harrison's supporters like the Cincinnati *Gazette* tellingly responded, "Harrison takes with the people. . . . Mr. Webster cannot be elected President—General Harrison may be elected. South, West, North, East, all can support General Harrison." If, in the eyes of Webster men, Harrison was just as bad as Andrew Jackson, the general's similarity to the Jackson of 1824 and 1828 made him particularly appealing to Westerners and Antimasons. "If it was right to elect General Jackson because he was a favorite citizen, and not the candidate of officeholders, it is right to elect General Harrison on the same principle," declared the *Ohio State Journal* in 1836.[25]

Harrison adroitly took steps to reassure Whigs that he shared the principles that mattered most. In a public letter he strongly denounced Jackson's executive usurpations and condemned the dictatorial spirit of party. He advocated federal subsidization of internal improvements and endorsed Clay's scheme for distributing federal land revenues to the states for that purpose. He even said he would back a new national bank if events demonstrated its necessity. By such statements, he won the grudging support of former National Republicans like Clay and Clayton of Delaware, although Webster loyalists refused to be budged.[26]

The choice between Webster or Harrison as the preeminent northern Whig candidate remained unclear until the end of 1835. For several reasons, Whigs' decision between the two hinged on Pennsylvania's preference. Having lost New York decisively in 1834 and having virtually conceded it to the Democrats in 1835, Whigs realized they had no possibility of snatching it from the New Yorker Van Buren in 1836. Hence they needed the nation's second largest state to have a chance. In addition, a rift within the Pennsylvania Democratic party assured an opposition victory in the state's gubernatorial election in October 1835 and portended triumph in the Keystone State a year later. Finally, Pennsylvania's primary opposition party remained the Antimasons, not the Whigs, and for the Whigs to have any chance of garnering Antimasonic support throughout the North, they had to accept the favorite of Pennsylvania's Antimasonic party. Waiting until after their victory in October, the Antimasons met in convention at Harrisburg in December 1835. Webster had carefully cultivated support among Pennsylvania's Antimasons—but not enough. The convention, and with it the Whig party of the North, gave its nod to Harrison.[27]

Webster would remain in the race through the November 1836 election. But he was reduced to being a New England candidate and the chief Whig candidate only in Massachusetts. Elsewhere in the North, as well as in the border states and Virginia, Harrison headed the Whig ticket. The Whigs had found a man of the people, an Indian fighter, a military hero of their own.

Other Southerners had settled on a favorite long before. Like Harrison, he had not been a National Republican or a prominent leader of the original Whig forces in the Senate in 1834. During that session, indeed, Senator Hugh Lawson White of Tennessee had remained a staunch supporter of Jackson, as had most politicians in his state. A close personal friend of the president who had faithfully voted against recharter of the Bank and for the Force Bill in the previous session, White considered himself and was presented to southern voters as a true Jacksonian who agreed with his fellow Tennessean on all issues but one: Jackson's insistence that Martin Van Buren be the next president.

Although White's Democratic pedigree, like McLean's, dismayed former National Republicans, most southern Whigs themselves had initially supported Jackson. They had to compete in states that Jackson had swept overwhelmingly. To win converts they needed a candidate with a Democratic background. More important, White possessed three credentials they deemed crucial. He was a Southerner, he owned slaves, and he wanted to keep Van Buren out of the White House. He had been bruited as a possible candidate in 1833 and 1834, but his formal nomination grew out of the exigencies of politics in Alabama and Tennessee, two of the three southern states in which deposit removal had not provided sufficient impetus to launch a viable Whig party.[28]

Jackson had remained so popular in Tennessee that, unlike elsewhere, an opposition party could not organize on the basis of anti-Jacksonism itself. Still, a number of nominally Jacksonian politicians in the state harbored resentment against Jackson's patronage allotment and his antibanking policies. The skirmishing between the two camps crystallized around the rivalry between Congressmen James K. Polk and John Bell, who opposed each other for Speaker of the House both in June 1834 and in December 1835. Jackson sided with Polk, his antibanking spokesman in the House. In retaliation, Bell, in December 1834, helped arrange a meeting of Tennessee's congressional delegation in Washington, which Polk and other Jackson loyalists refused to attend. That meeting then secured White's permission to run him for president. Tennessee's fanciers of White knew that Jackson required his supporters to back Van Buren for president. They also knew that they might discredit those loyalists by running White as a favorite son and demanding another Tennessean in the White House. On that issue and the advocacy of a state program of internal improvements they would eventually elect Newton D. Cannon governor in 1835 over the pro-Jackson, pro-Van Buren William Carroll, and the Tennessee Whig party would be born.[29]

Before the Tennessee caucus announced White's candidacy, the Alabama legislature had nominated him in January 1835. That decision resulted from a combination of the personal supporters of Governor John Gayle, thitherto a nominal Jacksonian, a faction of extreme state righters, and a tiny coterie of National Republicans behind White's candidacy. Calling themselves the White party, this motley proto-Whig coalition contested the Alabama gubernatorial election of 1835 against the Jacksonians on the issues of Van Buren's unfitness for the presidency and the illegitimacy of party conventions.[30]

In sum, White was first nominated because dissident politicians in Tennessee and Alabama wanted to exploit Van Buren's unpopularity in state elections during 1835. To their surprise and northern National Republicans' dismay, fever for the Tennessean then spread across Dixie in 1835 with the speed of an epidemic. White was portrayed not only as the people's candidate against the Democratic convention's dictated choice, but also as slaveholders' defender against northern aggression. "I think our interests imperatively require a Slave holding President," Louisiana's Whig Senator Alexander Porter declared, and he and other southern Whigs constantly pointed to the rising abolitionist movement in the North as the reason that no Northerner, especially the crafty Van Buren, could be trusted in the White House. For it was precisely in 1835 that northern abolitionists began their great campaign to flood the South with antislavery literature and to petition Congress to abolish slavery in the District of Columbia. No Northerner could be relied on to resist that pressure, southern Whigs cried, especially the chameleon-like Van Buren, who had proved he was no friend of the South by supporting the Tariff or Abominations in 1828. If placed in the White House, Van Buren might open up southern mails to abolitionist propaganda. "Vote for a Northern President from a free state," summed up a Virginia Whig paper, "and when the test comes, he will support the abolitionists."[31]

Southern Whigs vilified not only Van Buren but also Democratic vice presidential nominee Richard M. Johnson of Kentucky, who lived openly with his mulatto mistress and their two children. Such a public crossing of the color line shocked southern sensibilities. Even one of Jackson's Tennessee loyalists told him that Johnson was "not only positively unpopular but affirmatively odious" because he flouted social propriety. "In every slaveholding country, this must be so and ought to be so."[32]

Pillorying the obnoxious Democratic nominees, inciting and exploiting visceral fears among white Southerners at the very prospect of abolition or slave insurrection or race mixing that might be caused by abolitionist literature, Whigs across Dixie rallied to the cry: "The cause of Judge White is the cause of the South." In state after state, fearful Democrats howled that the Whigs' "great effort is to excite Southern prejudice" and that "the effort to make a southern sectional party out of the abolition question has been most eagerly pressed by the enemies of the administration." Grudgingly, they confessed the efficacy of that strategy. "Judge White is cutting into our ranks," moaned Virginia's Thomas Ritchie.[33]

Southern Democrats fought back against the Whig onslaught as best they could. They denounced White as an apostate who was now allied with Federalists, minions of Biddle's Bank, and Nullifiers. They charged that White had no chance to be elected, that he was simply a stalking horse for Whigs who would turn to Clay, Webster, or Harrison if the election went to the House. They proclaimed the necessity of party loyalty to protect the gains Jackson had won on behalf of the people against moneyed aristocrats, and they insisted that party principles were more important than men. Over and over they pronounced that Van Buren was "emphatically a FIRM FRIEND OF THE SOUTH." Finally, to stanch the hemorrhaging of their southern support, southern Democratic leaders pressured the Jackson administration and Van Buren to assure southern voters that the Democratic party was safe on the slavery issue.[34]

Democratic leaders in Washington responded with alacrity. Jackson ordered his postmaster general to direct southern postmasters to destroy abolitionist literature and asked Congress for a law banning it from the mails. In addition, he appointed three Southerners to the Supreme Court in 1835 and 1836, including P. P. Barbour of Virginia, the man southern dissidents had run for vice president against Van Buren in 1832, and the new chief justice, Maryland's Roger B. Taney. In May 1836, Van Buren himself helped arrange the gag rule in the House of Representatives under which debate on abolitionist petitions was quashed, and in March 1836 he came out publicly against abolition in the District of Columbia. Privately, he urged northern allies like New York's Governor Marcy and Senator Silas Wright to denounce abolitionist activities in order to prove his reliability to Southerners. His friends circulated a pamphlet that rehearsed his faithfulness to the South. All in all, the frenetic Democratic response to the southern Whig offensive offers telling testimony to its power.[35]

Many northern Whigs blanched at southern Whigs' tactics, for they hoped to enlist antislavery sentiment in the North against the Democrats. From the very inception of the Whig party, its northern and southern wings divided over the slavery issue. In roll-call votes concerning slavery in the House of Representatives in 1836 northern and southern Whigs were sharply polarized, in contrast to their cohesion on economic policies. Southern Whigs took a more proslavery position than southern Democrats, while northern Whigs took a decidedly more antislavery stance than northern Democrats. Much more frequently than northern Democrats, northern Whigs like John Quincy Adams and Joshua Giddings of Ohio introduced the antislavery petitions that so infuriated Southerners, and in 1836 and thereafter, northern Whigs were consistently more unified against the gag rule than were Democrats.[36] In short, spreading the Whig party to the South had a price. It incorporated into the party at its birth a pronounced sectional split over matters relating to slavery, a chasm that yawned so wide that Whigs could accommodate it throughout most of the party's history only by agreeing to disagree, only by allowing northern and southern Whigs to take opposing stands on the issue in their respective sections.

Though sharply divided over slavery, northern and southern Whigs still shared a common cause: defeating Van Buren and Jacksonianism. In Congress, Whigs united behind Clay's land bill, on opposition to the deposit banks, and against Democratic efforts during 1836 to expunge the censure of Jackson from the Senate's journal. Despite regional variations in appeals, moreover, Whigs everywhere lambasted Jackson's dictatorial attempt to impose his successor on the nation and warned that Van Buren would continue King Andrew's pernicious perversions of the republican order.[37]

The "Address to the People" issued by the New York State Whig convention in February 1836 perfectly epitomized the dominant Whig refrain: voters must rescue public liberty in order to save the Revolutionary experiment in republican self-government. Jackson's palpable tyranny and corruption, it averred, called "on all to awake who wish to preserve for themselves something more than the form of a republic." Cataloguing the supposed horrors committed by Jackson and his slavish "minions," it queried, "Could those patriots of former days, who so zealously guarded the security of personal independence and the freedom of individual opinion against the arbitrary exercise of executive power . . . now revisit us, would they be able to recognize the outlines of that system they toiled and bled to establish?" Condemning Jackson's "high-handed attempt to control the free choice of the people in the election of their rulers, and to force upon them a Chief Magistrate" as his most egregious usurpation, it shrilly predicted that if Jackson succeeded, "the form of our government is changed—our constitution subverted, our liberties extinct." Echoing Whig hostility to party proscription and discipline, finally, the address vituperated Van Buren as the architect of "a conspiracy, which seeks to promote the interests of the few at the expense of the many" and subverts "personal independence, . . . freedom of opinion, and . . . free institutions."[38]

Unable to pose as prophets of prosperity or effectively to criticize Jacksonian economic policies during the existing boom and bereft of any national achievements of their own to point to, the Whigs thus resorted to mounting a crusade for political freedom. At stake in the election, they iterated and reiterated, was the very salvation of republicanism.

IV

In 1836 that tocsin was not enough. Despite their impassioned pleas to stop Van Buren and despite the advantages they gained from a three-pronged offensive, they narrowly failed to arouse enough new voters or convert enough old ones to win. The proportion of eligible males who voted increased only from 55.4 percent in 1832 to 57.8 percent in 1836, and since the Whigs captured the bulk of new voters, their inability to evoke an even greater increase in turnout with an essentially ideological appeal proved fatal. Van Buren prevailed by an electoral vote margin of 170 to 124 over his combined opponents. Both in its size and in its geographical distribution, however, the popular vote revealed considerable Whig gains over previous National Republican showings. Nationally, Van Buren eked out a 50.9 percent majority, 764,198 to 736,147. Webster carried Massachusetts, as had Adams and Clay. White won both Tennessee and Georgia, which Jackson had swept almost unanimously in 1832. And Harrison captured Delaware, Maryland, and Kentucky, as had Clay, along with Vermont, New Jersey, Indiana, and Ohio, but he lost Connecticut and Rhode Island, which Clay had won. Obeying Calhoun, South Carolina's legislature refused to vote for White because he had supported the Force Bill in 1833 and instead cast the state's eleven electoral votes for Mangum, the Whig senator from North Carolina. Put another way, where Jackson had lost only eight states in 1832, Van Buren lost eleven.

The results clearly demonstrate the disruptive impact that Jackson's second term and the formation of the Whig party had on voting alignments.[39] Whigs scored their most dramatic gains over previous anti-Jackson showings in southern and western states, where Adams and then Clay had been weakest. Even in states they did not carry—Pennsylvania, Illinois, Missouri, Louisiana, Mississippi, Alabama, North Carolina, and Virginia—Whigs were significantly more competitive than the National Republicans. Van Buren narrowly squeaked by in North Carolina in November, for example, but the Whigs had triumphed in the first popular election for governor there the previous August. In contrast, Whigs were notably weaker in New England than the National Republicans had been. Democrats actually captured a majority of the region's popular vote and four of its six states.

The Whigs clearly attracted a large majority of new voters who had joined the electorate since 1832. As Table 2 indicates, with a few notable exceptions in New England, the anti-Democratic share of the vote grew most markedly in precisely those states where the size of the popular vote increased the most. At the same time, the Whig proportion of the vote was uniformly smaller than the National Republicans' had been in those states where the turnout was lower in 1836 than in 1832.[40] Of the states in which the Whigs scored gains, moreover, only Virginia, Louisiana, and Tennessee showed Democratic losses, but they were never large enough to account for more than a fraction of the Whig growth. In short, Van Buren's candidacy undoubtedly hurt the Democrats in the South, but new voters must have disproportionately supported the Whig party.

These data support Horace Greeley's assertion in 1838 that the Whig party formed as an amalgam of former National Republicans dedicated to the American System, state rights Southerners and Nullifiers, the bulk of Antimasons, dissident Democrats angered by Jackson's "high-handed conduct," and "numbers who had not before taken any part in politics; but who were awakened from their apathy by the palpable usurpations of the Executive."[41] More likely, however, the regional popularity or unpopularity of the candidates, as well as the competitiveness of parties in different states, shaped both the dimension and direction of voter participation. Surely, the presence of White explains a great deal of the Whig surge in the South, as does Harrison's in the Midwest and Pennsylvania, where most Antimasons embraced him.

The substitution of a race between Harrison and Van Buren for one between Clay and Jackson also accounts for the smaller turnout and weakened Whig position in Kentucky. Neither Democrats nor Whigs could be as enthusiastic about their candidates as they were in 1832. Similarly, the shared conviction that Van Buren would win New York depressed both the Democratic and Whig votes, the latter obviously to a greater extent. At the same time, Van Buren's identification as a Northerner helped him run better in New England than the slaveholder Jackson ever had, although infusions of Antimasons also aided the Democrats in Connecticut, Rhode Island, and Massachusetts. Finally, the dominance that Democrats had demonstrated in gubernatorial elections in Maine and New Hampshire in 1835 and especially in 1836 made the outcome of the presidential poll so certain that neither Democrats nor their foes turned out in the same numbers they had in 1832.[42]

By 1836, in sum, a national pattern of two-party conflict had replaced the largely regional one of 1832 in the presidential vote. The Whigs had extended their voting base to the South and West, while competition between the two parties was also generally closer in the Middle Atlantic and New England states than it had been four years earlier. That the opposition's share of the popular

Table 1

Changes in the Opposition's Percentage of the Vote, 1832–1836[a]

	National Republican and Antimason, 1832	Whig 1836	Net Change
New England	60.2%	48.6%	−11.6%
Connecticut	61.2	49.3	−11.9
Maine	45	39.8	− 5.2
Massachusetts	69.4	55.2	−14.2
New Hampshire	42.7	25	−17.7
Rhode Island	56.9	47.8	− 9.1
Vermont	75.5	60	−15.5
Middle Atlantic	45.6	47	+ 1.4
New Jersey	49.5	50.5	+ 1.0
New York	47.9	45.4	− 2.5
Pennsylvania	38.4	48.8	+10.4
Border Slave States	50.1	54	+ 3.9
Delaware	51	53.2	+ 2.2
Kentucky	54.5	53.05	− 1.5
Maryland	50	53.7	+ 3.7
Missouri	0	39.4	+39.4
South Atlantic	16.8	47.3	+30.5
Georgia	0	51.8	+51.8
North Carolina	14.5	46.9	+32.4
Virginia	25.4	43.5	+18.1
Southwest	37.1	50.8	+13.7
Alabama	0	44.8	+44.8
Arkansas	No vote in 1832	36	
Louisiana	38.4	48.2	+ 9.8
Mississippi	0	49	+49
Tennessee	4.7	58	+53.3
Total Slave South	32.8	50	+17.8
Old Northwest	44.5	51.4	+ 6.9
Illinois	27.7	45.2	+17.5
Indiana	32.9	55.9	+23
Michigan[b]	No vote in 1832	45.6	
Ohio	48.5	52.1	+ 3.6

[a]This table is based on the election returns listed in Burnham, *Presidential Ballots 1836–1892*, pp. 3, 5, and 246–54, and Robert V. Remini, "The Election of 1832," I. The regional totals, however, are taken from the table in Silbey, "The Election of 1836," p. 597. I have tried to list the individual states according to Silbey's regional categories, rather than Burnham's, although it is not clear from his table which states were included in each region.

[b]Arkansas and Michigan were admitted as states between the elections of 1832 and 1836, and their votes were not counted until the latter election. Again, it is not clear whether Silbey included them in his regional totals.

Table 2

Relationship Between the Change in the Size of the Total Vote and the Whigs' Share of the Popular Vote, 1832–1836[a]

States	Change in Turnout by Percent	Change in Anti-Democratic Percentage
Alabama[b]	Not contested in 1832	+44.8
Missouri	+250.5	+39.4
Mississippi	+248.4	+49
Georgia	+127.7	+51.8
Tennessee	+106	+53.3
Vermont	+ 83.5	−15.5
Illinois	+ 72.1	+17.5
North Carolina	+ 71.4	+32.4
Indiana	+ 56.7	+23
Massachusetts	+ 38.7	−14.2
Connecticut	+ 30.8	−11.9
Ohio	+ 29	+ 3.6
Maryland	+ 25.5	+ 3.7
Pennsylvania	+ 20.9	+14.4
Virginia	+ 18.7	+18.1
Rhode Island	+ 17	− 9.1
Louisiana	+ 12.9	+ 9.8
New Jersey	+ 9.5	+ 1.0
Delaware	+ 6.1	+ 2.2
New York	− 5.5	− 2.5
Kentucky	− 13	− 1.5
Maine	− 36.6	− 5.2
New Hampshire	− 44.3	−17.7

[a]This table is based on the same voting returns listed in Table 1. The change in turnout is measured not in terms of the proportion of eligible males voting but in terms of the actual vote cast in the two elections. The Spearman rank-order coefficient of correlation between the two variables is +.658.
[b]Ranking Alabama, which had no opposition to Jackson in 1832 and no recorded vote, first may be arbitrary, but surely it was in the top five in terms of growth in turnout, and that ranking does not distort the overall pattern.

vote had increased from 45 to nearly 50 percent of the national total, and that it approached that average in every region of the country, testified to how far the Whigs had traveled in three short years.

Yet those same results also showed that the Whigs still had far to go to fulfill their mission of rescuing the government and public liberty from Jacksonism. As Mangum had predicted at the end of 1834, they might mar but they could not make. Even as a lame duck, Jackson had thwarted them. They could not stop his drive toward hard money, overcome his vetoes, or derail his legatee. Despite Whigs' widespread and multifaceted antipathy toward Van Buren, they could not unite behind a single challenger even though they knew that Van Buren would otherwise win. While they improved their performance in the congressional elections of 1836, they still claimed only 40 percent of the members chosen that year, a slightly smaller proportion than they had won in 1834.[43] Control of any branch of the national government still seemed far beyond their grasp.

Nor did Whigs' record in state elections provide much encouragement. Whigs like James Barbour of Virginia had reconciled themselves to the necessity of running more than one presidential candidate with the hope that the local popularity of different regional candidates could help the party win control of state governments, even if it lost the White House. There is, however, little evidence of such a coattails' effect. Rather, the Whigs won legislative or gubernatorial elections only in those states where the party inherited a National Republican majority or where they carved out a distinctive and advantageous position on salient state issues—that is, where they demonstrated that Whig ideas were relevant to the needs of a state's voters. Where Whigs relied solely on the presidential question in campaigns for state offices or took unpopular stands on state issues, they made their poorest showings, no matter how well their presidential candidates ran.

V

The original objective of the Whig party, a party founded in Congress, was to save public liberty, first by using Congress to check executive tyranny and then by keeping Jackson's hand-picked successor out of the White House. Whigs, of course, had begun to build state organizations, but primarily because state legislatures chose United States senators and because each state's citizens picked a slate of presidential electors. Since Whigs' top priority was to control the national government, moreover, they had relied primarily on charges of Jackson's tyranny and the presidential campaign of 1835–36 to plant and nurture successful state Whig parties.

By the end of 1836, they had failed to achieve their main goal. They had no chance to capture Congress until the next set of elections in 1838–39 or the presidency itself until 1840. Somewhat ironically, therefore, the party's survival in the near-term future, like its durability over the long haul, depended on the viability and vitality of over twenty state Whig organizations, each of which operated in a unique political environment. At the end of 1836 Whig state parties could carry that burden with only varying reliability. During the extended presidential campaign of 1835–36, some were far more successful than others in sinking permanent roots and contesting elections for state offices. Contrary to Whigs' initial expectations, moreover, almost invariably the key to Whigs' success at the state level lay in their ability to go beyond questions stemming from national politics. Success instead depended on Whigs taking appealing stances that differed from those of Democrats on concrete matters stemming from the agendas of state politics and governance that, in the American federal system, were often distinct from those of the national government.

Since at least the spring of 1835, many Whigs had counted on the presidential question to complete the job of building state Whig organizations begun with attacks on Jackson's deposit removal in 1834. Especially in southern and western states, where the National Republicans had been a negligible force, and in northeastern states, where Antimasons still clung to independent existence, they expected to strengthen embryonic state parties by pillorying Van Buren's purported evils and touting their own candidates' supposed strengths, whether it was White's safety on the slavery issue in the South or, in the North, Harrison's popularity among Antimasons, his western residence, and his glamor as an Indian fighter. With the possible exceptions of Indiana, Ohio, Georgia, and Alabama, however, Whig presidential candidates provided very little help to anti-Democratic candidates for state office. In many states, the incipient opposition parties did far better in 1834, when Jackson's tyranny and alleged responsibility for the recession were the issues, than in 1835 or 1836, when the focus was on the impending presidential election. In the West and South, where state Whig candidates depended most heavily on presidential coattails in 1835 and 1836, Whig organizations often remained inchoate or nonexistent. To flourish at the state level, Whigs had to make themselves relevant to state affairs.

Table 3 provides an overview of the presidential campaign's impact on state races. It compares the proportion of the presidential vote won by anti-Democratic candidates in 1832 and 1836 with two measures of Whig (or opposition) performance in state elections between 1834 and 1836: the share of the popular vote won by anti-Jacksonian gubernatorial candidates and, where available, the proportion of seats won by Whigs or their fellow travelers in the lower houses of state legislatures.

Aside from the notable discrepancy between the vote for Whig state and presidential candidates in at least ten states, these figures show that Maine, New Hampshire, Illinois, Missouri, and Mississippi had become so heavily Democratic by 1832 or 1834 that Whig presidential candidates, no matter what their own popularity, could not help state Whig candidates win. When Arkansas became a state in 1836, it joined that category.[44] In Missouri and Mississippi, reliance on presidential coattails not only failed to help Whig state candidates, it helped to retard any self-conscious identification as Whigs by voters and leaders alike until the late 1830s. Missouri's Whigs were so feeble that they preferred to act as a pressure group and throw their support to dissident Democrats who resented Jackson's hard-money economic policies and their prominent Missouri champion, Senator Thomas Hart Benton. In the gubernatorial election of August 1836, for example, Whigs backed a probanking Democrat named William Ashley, who drew 47.7 percent of the vote. But in the same election, Whigs won less than three-tenths of the legislature, and in a markedly smaller turnout in November the Whig electoral ticket drew less than 40 percent. With disputants over state economic policy represented by rival Democratic factions, there seemed little room— or need—for the Whig party.[45]

Partisan identities remained so inchoate and partisan positions on state issues so incoherent in Mississippi that it is an act of generosity even to speak of a state Whig party existing there. The Whigs had held a state convention at the end of 1834 to nominate a gubernatorial candidate for 1835 and to cooperate with the State Rights Association, but by 1835 Whigs there, as in many other southern states, relied primarily on Hugh White's popularity, Van Buren's unpopularity, and the purported abolitionist menace to slavery. As a result, the relevance of the new party to state politics remained unclear, and little consciousness of being Whigs emerged among Mississippi's voters or politicians. In November 1835, when the Whig gubernatorial candidate prevailed with 51.1 percent of the vote, for example, Democrats simultaneously swept both congressional seats in the at-large election with 55.7 percent and captured 69 percent of the seats in the lower house of the legislature. Whigs improved their showing slightly in November

Table 3

Proportion of Popular Vote and Legislative Seats Won by National Republicans, Antimasons, and Whigs, 1832–1836[a]

State	1832P	1834	1835	1836	1836P
N. Hamp. (March)	42.7%	28%L	34%L	23%L	25%
Conn. (April)	61.2%	71%L	39%L	35%L	49.3%
		53%G	47.3%G	45.8%G	
Rhode Is. (April)	56.9%	54%L	49%L	44%L	47.8%
		48.9%G	49/	41.7%G	
			3%G		
Vermont (Sept.)	75.5%	71%L	59%L	73%L	60%
		72.5%G	62%G	55.8%G	
Maine (Sept.)	45%	42%L	38%L	35%L	39.8%
Mass. (Nov.)	69.4%	77%L	55%L	69%L	55.2%
		58.1%G	57.9%G	53.8%G	
New Jersey (Oct.)	49.5%	42%L	32%L	38%L	50.5%
Penna. (Oct.)	38.4%	38%L	68%L	28%L	48.8%
			46.9%G		
New York (Nov.)	47.9%	27%L	22%L	26%L	45.4%
		48.2%G		45.1%G	
Illinois (Aug.)	27.7%	38%L		38%L	45.2%
		52.4%G			
Indiana (Aug.)	32.9%	57.4%G		56%L	51.4%
Ohio (October)	48.5%	62%L	33%L	49%L	52.1%
				51.8%G	
Kentucky (Aug.)	54.5%	74%L	59%L	59%L	53%
				55.8%G	
Missouri (Aug.)	0	32%L		29%L	39.4%
Maryland (Oct.)	50%	76%L	69%L	76%L	53.7%
Delaware (Nov.)	51%	67%L		67%L	53.2%
Virginia (May)	25.4%	59%L	42%L	43%L	43.5%
N. Carolina (Aug.)	14.5%	24%L	44%L	49%L	46.9%
				53.6%G	
Georgia (Oct.)	0		40%L	44%L	51.8%
			47.7%G		
Louisiana (July)	38.4%	57.6%G			48.2%
Arkansas (Aug.)	NV			25%L	36%
				39%G	
Alabama (Aug.)	0		49%L	51%L	44.8%
			35%G		
Mississippi (Nov.)	0		31%L	38%L	48.2%
			51.1%G		

[a]With a few exceptions, the figures on share of state legislative seats (L) are taken from data compiled by Walter Dean Burnham for the Inter-University Consortium on Political Research at the University of Michigan. Gubernatorial returns (G) are taken from the Congressional Quarterly's *Guide to U.S. Elections*. Figures for Connecticut, Vermont, and Pennsylvania combine the Antimasonic and Whig shares, as do the figures for the 1832 presidential vote for those states where there were Wirt and Clay tickets. Months listed in parentheses next to states refer to the time when state elections were held.

1836 by winning 37.5 percent of the legislative seats, but at the same time, White drew 49 percent of the presidential poll. Clearly, many voters made no connection whatsoever between White and other Whig candidates for different offices.[46]

Nor did Mississippi's nominally Whig officeholders develop a much firmer identity with the party. Aside from the nationally oriented election for United States senator in 1836, there was little partisan influence or organization among state legislators even during the election of officers and committee assignments, let alone in voting on matters of substantive state policy, until the late 1830s. In Mississippi, anti-Jackson politicians placed all their hopes on national issues, and by the end of 1836 the state party lacked stability, a coherent identity, and power.

Conversely, inherited National Republican strength, whatever its source, rather than presidential candidates' coattails, clearly accounts for Whig success at the state level in 1835 and 1836 in Delaware, Maryland, Kentucky, and Louisiana. In New England's former National Republican strongholds after 1834, meanwhile, neither Harrison's purported attractiveness to Antimasons nor Webster's favorite-son status in Massachusetts stopped hostile Antimasons, who had long resented National Republican/Whig control of state governments, from helping Democrats to win state elections in Connecticut and Rhode Island and sharply to reduce Whig majorities in Massachusetts from their 1834 high. To recover in state elections, New England's Whigs clearly needed something more tangible than presidential coattails.

Even in Vermont, where Antimasons, not National Republicans or Whigs, dominated the anti-Democratic majority between 1831 and 1836 and where most Antimasons did finally join the Whigs, Harrison had little impact in facilitating that merger or increasing the Whig vote. Fusion first occurred in the gubernatorial campaign of September 1836, when Whigs backed the Antimasonic candidate. That joint candidate won, but with a smaller proportion of the vote than the combined share garnered previously by the two separate parties, just as Harrison's percentage was smaller than the combined share won by Wirt and Clay in 1832. In short, the elimination of the Antimasonic party in New England generally left the Democrats stronger and the anti-Democrats weaker than they had been earlier.

The other northern states where National Republicans had been competitive— New York, New Jersey, and Ohio—underline the central point: in state politics, presidential coattails were no substitute for popular and partisanly distinctive stands on state issues. Whereas New York's Whigs in 1834 had mounted a full-fledged gubernatorial campaign on state as well as national issues for Seward, their well-known state legislative leader, in 1836 they put all their emphasis on the presidential race and gave only tepid editorial and organizational support to Jesse Buel, their superannuated and nondescript gubernatorial candidate.[47] In 1834, Seward garnered 48.2 percent of the vote; in 1836 Buel received only 45.1 percent. In New York's state races, clearly, Whigs were more competitive when they took concrete stands on state issues, when they demonstrated the congruence between national party ideology and matters of state concern.

Ohio and New Jersey suggest that however much concrete and distinctive stands on state issues helped state Whig parties sink permanent roots, they were not enough to carry state elections. For Whigs to win, their distinctive stance also had to have popular appeal. Harrison carried both states in November by comparable majorities, yet Whigs' state candidates in the two met dramatically different fates a month earlier. In Ohio, Whigs won the gubernatorial election and sharply increased their strength in the state legislature over the previous year. In New Jersey, where the legislature still elected the governor, Whig legislative candidates fared almost as badly in 1836 as in 1835, despite Whig triumphs in all six congressional races on the same day and Harrison's victory a month later. Nor does a Democratic gerrymander of the legislature explain New Jersey's result, for a year later, under the same apportionment, Whigs would win 68 percent of the seats. As a native son, Harrison *did* undoubtedly have longer coattails in Ohio than in New Jersey, but the main reason for the different state results is that Ohio's Whigs took the popular, and New Jersey's Whigs the unpopular, side on specific state economic issues.

Between 1834 and 1836 in both Ohio and New Jersey the two parties developed sharply different positions on state economic policies. As in New Jersey, Ohio's Democratic governor recommended legislation to ban bank notes of small denomination in 1835 and 1836, and sharp partisan conflict developed in the legislature over it, as well as over bills to charter banks and other companies.[48] Whig control of the legislature during early 1835 blocked this hard-money initiative, but after Democrats won the 1835 legislative elections, they passed it in 1836. Basing their 1836 state campaign on denunciation of Democrats' antibanking legislation, Whigs recaptured the legislature in October and elected Joseph Vance governor with 51.6 percent of the vote, slightly less than Harrison's proportion a month later.

Because Ohio's Whig party successfully differentiated itself from Democrats on specific state policies, it had, by the end of 1836, developed much greater stability and a clearer partisan identity than its counterparts in Indiana, Illinois, Missouri, and Mississippi. Of all the nation's states, however, by 1836 the emerging two-party system of Whigs and Democrats had developed most completely in New Jersey. Both parties coordinated state and congressional campaigns with central organizations in Trenton composed of legislative caucuses and prominent editors. Candidates for all offices had clear party identities, legislators were organized and disciplined by party caucuses, and elections for legislative offices and state patronage positions, as well as committee assignments, were dominated by the majority party. After 1834, moreover, Whigs and Democrats became sharply polarized against each other in legislative roll-call votes and election campaigns over state policy toward corporations, banks, and paper money.

What differentiated New Jersey from Ohio, where Whigs rebounded on a probanking platform in 1836, was the salience of another state issue: the so-called Joint Companies, the combination of the Camden and Amboy Railroad and the Delaware and Raritan Canal. Jacksonians had arranged that combination, and Whigs attacked it as a privileged Democratic monopoly because it controlled all transportation routes in the state. In 1835 and 1836, Whigs introduced a number of bills to break the Joint Companies' domination by chartering rival transportation concerns, and Democrats fought those bills just as fiercely as Whigs battled the Democrats' hard-money, anticorporation measures.[49]

Given the ethos of the Jacksonian era, New Jersey Whigs' antimonopoly platform intuitively strikes the modern reader as a wonderfully potent weapon, a can't-miss anti-Democratic missile. In fact, their attack on the Joint Companies, a far more powerful monopoly than the banks that Democrats ritualistically flayed, offended far more voters than it pleased. Since the Camden and Amboy Railroad ran through the same West Jersey counties where Whigs suffered from Hicksite Quaker defections, the assault further cemented those counties in the Democratic column. More important, in compensation for its monopoly, the Joint Companies made an annual payment to the state that effectively negated any need for state real estate taxes, but that payment would stop as soon as a single state-chartered competitor entered the transportation field. To break up the monopoly as Whigs demanded, in short, would almost inevitably impose a new tax burden on every landowner in the state. Unquestionably, New Jersey's Whigs *had* a distinctive platform on the state policies salient in state elections, but it was hardly a platform that enthralled most voters. As a result, despite Whigs' success in contests for *national* offices, they could not break the Democrats' lock on the state legislature, which until 1844 elected all of New Jersey's executive officers. In New Jersey, as in New York and New England, Whig state parties badly needed fresh ammunition.[50]

An unpopular stand on a specific state economic policy also put Pennsylvania's Whigs at a fatal disadvantage in the October 1836 state elections. Ironically, however, it also proved far more crucial in facilitating the merger between Antimasons and Whigs than Harrison's presidential candidacy, even though northern Whigs ran him primarily in order to secure Pennsylvania's Antimasonic votes. Almost from the moment of the decisive Pennsylvania Antimasonic state convention in December 1835, that tactic had in fact backfired. An exclusivist or purist faction of Antimasons led by Gettysburg's Thaddeus Stevens bitterly protested the convention's choice of Harrison as a sellout to the Whigs. Stevens instead called for a national Antimasonic convention to meet in Philadelphia in May 1836 to make a separate nomination. It was, nonetheless, Stevens who forged a merger between the state parties in the legislative session of 1835–36.

Because of Democratic rifts, the Antimason Joseph Ritner won the governorship in 1835, and a coalition of Whigs and Antimasons simultaneously captured overwhelming control of the legislature. In exchange for Whig support for authorization to conduct a legislative investigation of the Masonic Order, which later turned into a fiasco, Stevens obtained Antimasonic support for Whig legislation. The two groups coalesced against the Democrats to pass resolutions that instructed the state's Democratic United States senators to vote against resolutions to expunge the Senate's censure of Jackson and for Clay's bill to distribute federal land revenues to the states.

The Whigs and Antimasons also created a distinctive record on state issues. The coalition reapportioned the state senate in a blatantly partisan manner. More significantly, on a party line vote it passed an omnibus bill that gave a state charter to Biddle's Bank of the United States, whose congressional charter expired in March, in return for a large cash bonus to be used to cut taxes and invest in the state's canal system. In addition, Biddle was required to invest additional Bank funds in various transportation projects around the state. Whig papers proudly boasted of this bill as a magnificent achievement that would aid development in the state and eliminate taxes for years, and they confidently made it the centerpiece of their campaign in 1836. This legislative maneuvering, not Harrison's presidential candidacy, which Stevens so bitterly opposed, was chiefly responsible for bringing Antimasons and Whigs together in a single state party behind a distinctively Whiggish program, a party that, after 1836, Whigs, not Antimasons, dominated.

That accomplishment came at a terrible price, for the coalition's legislative record inextricably linked the state's Whig party to Biddle's monster. Able once again to flog the Bank, the previously disrupted Democrats reunited and trounced the Whigs in the state elections of October 1836. Whereas Whigs and Antimasons together had won 38 of 100 seats in the state assembly in 1834 and 68 in 1835, they captured a pathetic 28 in 1836. One month later, Harrison rolled up almost 49 percent of Pennsylvania's vote, but his luster clearly had not rubbed off on state Whig candidates tarred with rescuing the Bank of the United States.[51]

VI

The contrasting fortunes of Whig state parties in slave states where White headed the Whig ticket in 1836 demonstrate even more starkly how important taking distinctive stands on state issues was to the development of competitive and coherent state Whig organizations. In all those states Whigs trumpeted White's southern identity, Van Buren's untrustworthiness on the slavery issue, the northern abolitionist menace, and antipartyism in the presidential race.

As in Mississippi, those were virtually the only issues used in 1835 and 1836 by Alabama's White party and Georgia's State Rights party, neither of which would adopt the Whig label until the late 1830s. White carried Georgia with 52 percent of the vote and lost Alabama with 45 percent, results that accurately prefigured the later strength of the Whig party in the neighboring states. Yet in state elections, or at least state legislative elections in 1835 and 1836, Alabama's proto-Whig party experienced greater success than its Georgia counterpart, even though Georgia's Whig affiliate, the State Rights party, succeeded better than its counterparts in Alabama and Mississippi in building an extensive chain of local, county, and state organizations. Its platform, however, focused exclusively on federal relations between the state and national governments, not on intrastate affairs.[52] In contrast, while Alabama's heterogeneous White party also lacked a distinctive program for state economic policy by 1836, since its inception in early 1835 it had coupled attacks on Van Buren with attacks on the venality of Democratic conventions and the inherent incompatibility between party dictation and republican self-government. The Democrats' *state* convention of December 1835 gave an explicit state dimension to their antiparty crusade in 1836, allowing Alabama's proto-Whigs to run better in the state legislative elections of August than White himself did in November.[53]

Virginia, however, provides the clearest example of the failure of presidential coattails to succor Whigs in southern states. Until 1851, state politics focused on the annual legislative races in May since the legislature, not the electorate, chose the governor. Virginia's incipient Whig party had scored a stunning victory in 1834 when it captured 59 percent of the seats in the lower house of the legislature by campaigning against Jackson's tyranny and blaming him for the depression that still wracked the nation. By the time of the next two elections, the business cycle was on the upswing, as was popular opinion of Jackson. Nor could Whigs fashion a distinctive party platform on state economic affairs, largely because regional conflicts and identities more than partisan affiliation shaped positions on internal improvement projects such as the James and Kanawha Canal. Thus, the Whigs insisted that the preferability of White to Van Buren formed the central issue in both the 1835 and 1836 elections. Yet in 1835, the Whig share of legislative seats fell to 42 percent, and it rose only slightly, to 43 percent, in 1836. Numerous factors undoubtedly contributed to this decline, but neither the popularity of presidential candidates nor a nationally oriented campaign based on the northern menace to slavery could retain the state party in power *within* Virginia.[54]

In contrast, Whigs carried state elections in Tennessee and North Carolina in 1835 and 1836 because they took distinctive party stands on state issues in addition to pushing White for president. The Tennessee Whig party was launched in 1835 solely on the issue of White's presidential candidacy, and White would rack up a larger share of the vote in his home state than anywhere else. As elsewhere, Tennessee's Whig politicians attempted to make the gubernatorial, congressional, and legislative elections of August 1835 referenda on White and Van Buren. Most Democratic candidates, including three-term incumbent Governor William Carroll, tried to deflect this thrust by remaining mum about the unpopular Van Buren until after the state election was over. Nonetheless, the state election of 1835 did not revolve exclusively around presidential candidates or sectional issues. As Whigs recognized, their candidate, Newton D. Cannon, won the gubernatorial election not because he favored White, but because he rolled up huge margins in East Tennessee by advocating an expansive program of state-financed internal improvements and because some voters regarded Carroll's attempt at an unprecedented fourth consecutive term as illegal and arrogant.[55]

The magnitude of Cannon's triumph compared quite favorably with that of White a year later. The gubernatorial election of 1835 brought more men to the polls than had ever voted in Tennessee—27,000 more—indeed, than voted in the subsequent presidential contest. Whereas 55.2 percent of the eligible electorate voted in 1836, between 78 and 80 percent did in 1835. Hence, neither the regional appeal of White nor the southern Whig tactic of agitating the slavery issue can be credited for the great jump in turnout. Cannon attracted 8,000 more votes in 1835 than White won in 1836, and if one counts the votes of a dissident Whig gubernatorial candidate who siphoned off a tenth of the 1835 turnout, Whig candidates in 1835 ran 17,000 votes ahead of White. Because their candidate had the imagination to take a distinctive stand on state issues instead of relying on White's coattails, Tennessee's Whigs scored a most impressive victory in the gubernatorial election of 1835, where they faced a far tougher opponent than Van Buren. That race, not the presidential campaign, put the Tennessee Whig party on a firm foundation.[56]

In no slave state outside Kentucky and Maryland, however, did the Whigs secure so solid a base by the end of 1836 as in North Carolina. As elsewhere, the Whig party formed in North Carolina in 1834 as a disparate coalition opposed to executive tyranny and the economic consequences of deposit removal. By the time of the legislative elections in August of that year, the economy had improved and discontent with Jackson had subsided. As a result, the sweeping Democratic victory caused some Whigs to despair that they could not compete in the state unless they had a popular presidential candidate in the field. Certainly North Carolina Whigs bounded onto the White bandwagon in 1835, and by February 1836 the party's first gubernatorial candidate was proclaiming that "Mr. Van Buren is not one of us. He is a Northern man . . . in soul, in principle, and in action."[57]

But the party quickly moved beyond playing on southern fears of Yankees in 1835 by exploiting regional grievances and aspirations within the state, and it artfully linked its position on those state issues to Whig programs in Congress. Inadequate transportation facilities had aborted economic development in the state's western mountain and piedmont regions, as well as in the northeastern corner near Albemarle Sound. Residents there pleaded for the state to finance internal improvements, but they were rebuffed by the relatively prosperous and predominantly Democratic planters from the coastal plain region who enjoyed the natural benefits of navigable rivers. Even though the merchants of eastern towns also clamored for state aid to transportation, the planters, who feared higher taxes, were able to block action since the old constitution of 1776 gave them grossly unfair overrepresentation in the legislature.

To rally this potential coalition of the frustrated, Whigs took the lead in 1835 in voicing the demand for a new constitution to give the western area a more equitable share of legislative seats and for state aid to internal improvements. Whigs alone were not responsible for the revision of the constitution that occurred in 1835, but once it was ratified, they did carve a distinctive position by pushing for state aid to transportation and education in 1836. They also trumpeted Clay's bill for distribution of federal land revenues to the states, which North Carolina's Democrats opposed, as the way the state could pay for the programs Whigs demanded without burdening the state's taxpayers.

As even Democrats admitted, the internal improvements issue helped the Whig candidate, Edward Dudley, defeat the incumbent Democratic Governor Richard D. Spaight in August 1836 with 53.6 percent of the vote. "The impression has been studiously created that Gov. Spaight is the implacable opponent of Internal Improvement in every shape," lamented the New Bern *Sentinel* after the election. "On the other hand, General Dudley has been held up as a sort of patron of the Internal Improvement policy. . . . This very ground has assisted to elect him as much as any other." In addition, Whigs carried the state senate by a majority of two and came within two seats of capturing the house. The party ran especially well in the western piedmont and mountain areas and in eastern towns, all places that wanted improvements. Once the legislature met in the fall of 1836, moreover, Whig legislators almost invariably voted in larger proportions for state aid to transportation projects than did Democrats, regardless of what region they represented, although on some bills regional conflict was sharper than party conflict.[58]

The importance of this stand on internal improvements to Whig fortunes in North Carolina became clear three months later in the presidential election. Between August and November the Whig press dropped that issue and promoted White almost exclusively on the sectional grounds of protecting slavery from the abolitionist menace. Whereas the August gubernatorial election drew out 67 percent of potential voters, only 53 percent turned out in November. Whereas Dudley secured 53.6 percent of the vote, White garnered only 49 percent. The lesson was evident. The bigger the turnout in North Carolina, the better the Whigs' chances. They could draw out a much larger vote with a program aimed at the specific needs of the state's voters than with a sectional appeal for the defense of slavery.

Throughout Dixie the returns from state elections in 1835 and 1836 exposed the limits of what William J. Cooper, Jr., has termed "the politics of slavery." Cooper marshals massive evidence to demonstrate that Whigs emphasized the abolitionist threat to slavery and the probable unreliability of Van Buren in the campaign for White. Throughout the life of the second party system in the South, he shows further, Whigs and Democrats jockeyed with each other in elections for national office to prove their own party a better defender of the South's peculiar institution than the opponent.[59] Yet in 1835 and 1836 this strategy by itself neither caused the great increase in southern voter turnout since 1832 nor brought the Whigs victory in state elections. Because of a widespread consensus among white Southerners, slaveholders and nonslaveholders alike, that slavery must be protected and sudden abolition prevented, this particular tack simply had little relevance to elections for internal state offices. To win them, Whigs could not depend on presidential coattails or regional patriotism alone. They had to find advantageous positions on relevant state issues.

Although the trend in the South was less ambiguous than that in the North, the races for state office in 1835 and 1836 indicated that Whigs could not win control of state governments by pointing to popular presidential candidates alone. Rather, they did best where they found a clear and advantageous Whig position on state concerns, where they demonstrated that the Whig party was relevant to the needs and grievances of voters at the state level. Since Whigs had failed to do this in most places, their condition in the states by the end of 1836 was just as precarious as it was nationally. To the extent that they had relied on the presidential campaign to breathe life into their party, they now faced four lean years without that sustenance. Yet since they had failed to capture control of either Congress or the presidency, securing a competitive position in state elections became all the more vital to the future health of the party.

VII

At the close of 1836, Whigs must have reviewed the events of the past four years with mixed emotions. They had taken significant steps toward establishing a new and much more competitive party in presidential elections than its predecessor. Still, the Democrats had installed Andrew Jackson's personal choice in the White House, and to add salt to that terrible wound, in January 1837 they would finally expunge the Whigs' censure of Jackson from the Senate journal. Understandably, therefore, Whigs could look forward to their triumphant tormentor's departure from the presidency on March 4, 1837.

Yet once Jackson retired, the party would lose the impetus that had launched it and the cement that had held it together since 1834. Even with Jackson in office, the crusade against executive tyranny had not been enough to bring the Whigs to power in the nation or the states, and his impending departure from the scene almost ensured that they would have to look elsewhere to buttress their appeal. All Whigs shared antipathy to Martin Van Buren, but it was not certain that Van Buren's actual course in office would galvanize the Whigs to action the way fearful anticipations of that course had. Nor was it clear that new voters attracted to the Whig party by the regional appeal of White and Harrison would remain in it if the Whigs ever did unite on a single candidate. The embryonic Whig party was still so new that many voters, especially those who had not been National Republicans and those who despised the notion of party itself, had not yet developed any institutional loyalty to it. Even if the Whigs could rally those voters again in the next presidential campaign, finally, they could not rely on that hope to help them in state and congressional elections prior to 1840.

Despite the giant strides forward, in sum, the Whigs continued to face the same task that had confronted National Republican leaders in 1833. They had to find some formula that would simultaneously hold the coalition together, reinforce the commitment of recent converts, and broaden it still further. Recent experience demonstrated that they could best accomplish this task by taking clear and advantageous stands on concrete issues. At the end of 1836, however, it was impossible to tell what those issues might be.

Chapter 4

"We Have Many Recruits in Our Ranks from the Pressure of the Times"

CAN I OFFER "any consolation to you for the future, as to public affairs?" Henry Clay glumly wrote a friend three days after Martin Van Buren's inauguration. "I lament to say not much." To Clay the new Whig party seemed as ineffectual and divided as the various anti-Jackson elements had been at the beginning of 1833. Unlike some Whigs in Washington, he could entertain no hope of capturing a majority in the next House of Representatives, for Whigs lacked "union as to the ultimate object."[1]

Clay and other Whigs had good reason to despair. They had won only two-fifths of the House seats filled in 1836, and the defeat or forced resignation of party founders like John Tyler and Willie P. Mangum had depleted their Senate strength. Meanwhile, the party had barely begun to organize in the West and Southwest, and in many eastern states it had been thrust into the minority.

Worse, no improvement seemed likely, for no issue appeared ripe for exploitation. Resistance to executive tyranny had given the new party an identity but not a victory. Pennsylvania Whigs' connection with Biddle's Bank had proved to be political poison. The recent attempt in the winter of 1837 to make an issue of Jackson's Specie Circular had floundered when Jackson vetoed a Whig bill altering the system. Now Whigs could do nothing until Congress met again in December. Worst of all, congressional Democrats had defeated Clay's promising proposal to distribute federal land revenues to the states. Instead, in June 1836 bipartisan majorities had passed a Deposit Act that contained a different form of distribution.

Aimed primarily at regulating Jackson's deposit banking system, the Deposit Act also provided that surplus government funds in excess of $5 million should be deposited with state governments, rather than private banks, in proportion to the states' population. These deposits, one-year interest-free loans rather than permanent grants of aid, were to be made in four equal installments at three-month intervals, beginning January 1, 1837. Clay, in contrast, had called for continuing annual grants of land revenues to the states, not a one-year loan. The Deposit Act not only buried Clay's proposal for the immediate future, but also stripped Whigs of their claim to be the sole champions of federal aid to the states, for Democrats seized equal credit for the law.[2]

With old issues gone, Whigs would have to sustain their new party as an anti-Van Buren venture. But the new president's intentions were unclear. He promised in his inaugural address to continue his predecessor's policies, and Whig politicos had sadly learned that most voters tolerated those policies more easily than they did. While the president's course "will not be such as you & I are likely to approve," Webster guessed, the "Country" might find it "acceptable."[3]

Within nine weeks of Van Buren's accession to power, however, an economic collapse swept away the fog that had shrouded the Whigs' political future. On May 10, 1837, banks in New York City suspended specie payments. Financial panic immediately seized the country as banks elsewhere followed suit, credit disappeared, loans were called, and prices plummeted. That panic began a cycle of recession, recovery, and depression that became the dominant force shaping American politics between 1837 and 1844. Those economic fluctuations spawned a political agenda for Whigs and Democrats to battle over in national and state arenas. They allowed Whigs to add support for programs to spur growth and economic recovery to their attacks on antirepublican tyranny. Since governments' response to economic hardship heightened people's political interest, Whigs' chances for broadening their electoral base brightened.

More important, the economic tailspin that began in 1837 ensured that the Whig party would endure. It was not foreordained in 1834 that the Whig party would for twenty years remain the primary political vehicle for almost all the Democrats' foes. Since it was founded primarily to rescue the government from Democratic presidents, it might well have disintegrated after it failed to accomplish that task in 1836, to be replaced by a new party based on different principles. That was exactly what Clay feared, in view of the party's divided and aimless condition at the beginning of 1837.

Had events focused attention on slavery and abolitionism, for example, the party's 1836 problems might have become insurmountable. Abolitionists' continued petitions to Congress, calling for an end to slavery in the District of Columbia, and the proslavery Republic of Texas' appeal for admission to the United States portended sectionally divisive issues that could fundamentally alter political alignments.

The economic crisis in the spring of 1837 channeled political development in a different direction. However shaky its condition, the Whig party was in place to benefit from discontent with the "in" Democratic regime engendered by depression. The slump allowed Whigs to fashion a distinctive national and state program of governmental economic policy, a program that united its northern and southern wings, reinforced the partisan identity of Whig voters, and massively extended that partisan allegiance to new voters. Once created, that partisan identity became a prism through which Whig voters viewed sectional issues themselves. All in all, the economic disaster that followed Jackson's departure from office was the pivotal episode in the growth of the Whig party.[4]

I

The financial panic that began in May 1837 stunningly terminated a seemingly endless and dizzying upward economic spiral. Between the summer of 1834 and the end of 1836, high foreign demand for key export crops like cotton, ample foreign credit for American merchants, and significant infusions of foreign gold and silver doubled the nation's money supply and propelled prices to unprecedented levels, thus ensuring profits to the vast majority of Americans who produced goods for sale.[5] Easy credit and burgeoning money supplies spawned a boom mentality. Private investors started new businesses. State governments frantically launched internal improvement projects such as canals and railroads that they hoped would match the spectacular success of New York's Erie Canal.

The most apparent aspect of the frenzy, however, was massive purchasing of western land. Government land sales exploded from $6 million in 1834 to $16 million in 1835 and $25 million in 1836. As crop prices rose, farmers and planters sought more land so that they could plant more acres to cash in on the bonanza, and they recklessly took out readily available bank loans to do it. But most of those government sales reflected sheer speculation by people who hoped to resell land at a profit to the settlers who were swarming into the North and Southwest in the 1830s.[6]

Dazzled by present prosperity and the prospects for even more in the future, most Americans had ignored warning cries about the vulnerabilities of this economic structure. Both Whig and Democratic spokesmen had long predicted some kind of collapse, and both had ready explanations when it came. Jackson and his antibank advisors, for example, had cringed at the expansion of paper money and banking that followed the removal of deposits. As a result, they had moved toward a hard-money standard in order to restrain the economy and to develop a new Democratic issue to substitute for their victorious war against the Bank. The famous Specie Circular of July 1836 specifically aimed at slowing the land boom and "the ruinous extension of bank issues and credits." And in April 1837, Van Buren defended that Circular as "the only measure that could save the country."[7]

When the panic broke, Democrats quickly condemned bankers for inciting a corrupting speculative spirit that was bound to produce a crash. Private economic actors, not Democratic policies, they insisted, were responsible. Jackson and other Democrats, these spokesmen asserted, had sought to mitigate the damage by returning the country to a hard-money standard. Now, only that standard could cure the disastrous consequences of excessive credit, speculation, overtrading, and paper money.

Whigs, in contrast, blamed Jackson and Van Buren for causing the panic. Since the inception of their party, Whigs had warned that by destroying the Bank of the United States, Jackson had jettisoned the American financial system's stabilizing anchor. Without Biddle's institution to restrain other banks, they charged, currency would lose its uniform value, bank notes would no longer be accepted at face value, and chaos would ensue. Furthermore, Jackson, by placing federal deposits in state banks, first encouraged the overextension of the banking system and then compounded the problem by undermining public faith in the value of bank notes with executive orders banning government use of small notes and the Specie Circular. The Specie Circular further aggravated that pressure by forcing the movement of specie from eastern banks to the West, where the land markets were located. Jackson, in sum, had spurred the expansion of notes beyond the system's capacity to redeem them, and then he had sabotaged confidence in those notes so that people would try to redeem them. To account for the panic and the subsequent economic hardship, Whigs jeered, one need look no further than Democratic incompetence.

Both Whig and Democratic explanations contained elements of truth. Yet external pressure on the economy, not the domestic activities partisans pointed to, mainly caused the collapse. In the summer and fall of 1836, the Bank of England, fearing a drain of its own specie reserves, raised its interest rates and curtailed credit to British firms dealing in the American trade. English merchants, in turn, cut off credit to the United States and began to demand payment of outstanding accounts in bills drawn on England or in specie. That contraction put pressure on American commercial centers, where interest rates on loans rose to prohibitive levels.

Simultaneously, restricted credit in England caused the price of American cotton to plummet in early 1837, for English dealers could no longer get the money to pay high prices for it. Falling cotton prices meant that American merchants who anticipated selling cotton at higher levels faced disastrous losses. Consequently, the value of bills of exchange based on cotton in the United States dropped precipitously. That decline was catastrophic, for the entire American commercial network was largely based on commercial paper secured by cotton exports. Mercantile houses holding those bills as assets found themselves with uncollectible debts and went bankrupt. Even before May 1837, a number of prominent merchants, cotton factors, and brokers with assets totaling $60 million went under. Other merchants who had anticipated paying off outstanding debts to English creditors with the proceeds of cotton sales now needed specie to meet their obligations.[8]

Distress among merchants prior to May menaced bank solvency in two ways. Banks that had made loans to failed firms lost potential assets they needed to cover their own liabilities—their bank notes and customer deposits. Demand from merchants for specie to ship abroad further threatened their specie reserves. To forestall that drain, New York's banks suspended specie payments on May 10, and they were closely followed by banks in New Orleans and other commercial centers. The banks, that is, announced that they would no longer redeem their notes or their deposits at par in specie.

The panic therefore represented a defensive gesture by banks in anticipation of runs on their specie deposits; it did not result from the actual depletion of specie resources. The amount of specie in the country actually increased by 20 percent during 1837. But the banks' action helped decrease the total money supply of bank notes and specie by 16 percent. Once banks suspended specie payments, people no longer would accept bank notes or checks as payment for goods, services, or debts.[9] Bank notes and checks were not legal tender. They were promises to pay the bearer legal tender, that is, specie, promises on which the banks had now reneged. Since banks refused to release specie, the amount of usable currency shrank, and prices sank accordingly.

The ensuing financial panic had important ramifications far beyond banking. Manufacturers unable to sell goods profitably or to secure loans to make up for losses had to close their doors, thus shutting out their workers. Farmers, if they could find credit to move goods to market, had to sell their crops at sharply lower prices than they had anticipated. Often the price received could not cover bank loans they had previously contracted to tide them over until the crop came in or to finance additional land purchases. Nor could they sell land to meet their debts, for if the Specie Circular had slowed land sales, bank suspension slammed them to a halt.[10]

The bank suspension of May 1837 began a bewildering chain of economic fluctuations. By the end of that month, wholesale prices had plunged 22 percent from their high in February, and they remained low for over a year. In May 1838, however, New York's banks resumed specie payments, largely because they received new specie from the Bank of England. Coordinated by Nicholas Biddle, whose Bank of the United States of Pennsylvania still had huge assets, bankers from a number of other states agreed to resume specie payments simultaneously on August 13, 1838. By September 1838 most places were well on the way to recovery, and prices remained at relatively high levels for a year. In October 1839, however, another English contraction of credit forced another American suspension of specie payments and another drop in prices. This time, no rapid recovery followed. Prices continued to fall throughout 1840, 1841, 1842, 1843, and 1844. In July 1840, for example, the general wholesale price level was fully 38 percent below its flush time peak in February 1837, and four years later it was 45 percent below that level. Meanwhile, the nation's money supply shrank from a peak of $276 million in 1836 to $215 million in 1839, $186 million in 1840, and $158 million in 1842.[11]

II

The economic roller coaster had profound political ramifications. Whigs gleefully pronounced the plunge a vindication of their previous warnings, declared Jackson's policies culpable, and began agitating even in 1837 for a new national bank that could bring stability and recovery. Complaining that Whigs were trying "to make the distress of the country subservient to party politics," Democrats stridently denied Democratic responsibility and attributed the collapse instead to over-banking and overspeculation that had fed on an excess of paper money and banking credit. Echoing the hard-money line that Jackson had tried to make official Democratic policy during his last years in office, Democratic newspapers began to insist in the spring of 1837 that to right the economy, the government must outlaw rag currency. Honest citizens would never be safe from wrenching economic oscillations until the bankers' control of currency was ended by prohibiting or restricting the privilege of note issue.[12]

In 1837 Whigs clearly had the better political argument. As the "out" party nationally and in most states, they benefited from voters' inclination to throw the "ins" out during hard times. Both disillusioned Democrats and first-time voters seeking economic recovery flocked to the Whig camp. Starting in the August 1837 state elections and continuing into the fall of 1837 and the spring of 1838, Whigs made dramatic gains almost everywhere. As William Henry Harrison would observe in early 1840, "We have many recruits in our ranks from the pressure of the times."[13]

Of far more long-lasting importance in shaping voter behavior than the panic itself, however, were the sharply contrasting policies Democrats and Whigs advocated to deal with it. In 1837, for the first time, the two parties articulated clear, coherent, and conflicting philosophies about the proper role of *both* state and national governments in the economy and framed concrete legislative programs reflecting those philosophies. While stalemate between the parties from 1837 to

1840 prevented Congress from enacting much legislation that incorporated these divergent orientations, state governments enacted both Whig and Democratic laws dealing with the economy, allowing voters to judge not just what parties said, but what they did.

President Martin Van Buren took the lead in defining the Democrats' response to the panic. According to the Deposit Act of 1836, no bank that suspended specie payments could retain government funds; yet eighty-two of the eighty-eight deposit banks defaulted during the crisis. Van Buren had to determine what to do with new government revenues and how to withdraw existing deposits from state banks without aggravating the crisis. In addition, a dramatic decline in tariff collections caused by sharply reduced imports and the cessation of land sales reduced government revenue to a fraction of its former level. The government's problem abruptly changed from disposing of a surplus to operating with a deficit. To meet these and other demands, Van Buren at the end of May called for a special session of Congress to assemble in September.[14]

During the summer, Van Buren agonized about what to do. On the one hand, he knew that the drive toward hard money had antagonized probanking elements in the party, including some of his closest Albany associates. These powerful Democrats wanted ample credit for economic growth. On the other hand, he recognized that the panic, by rekindling hostility toward paper money and privilege, had greatly strengthened the party's antibanking wing.

Throwing his support to the larger of the party's rival factions, Van Buren took a moderate antibanking position in his message to the special session in September. Events then rapidly forced him even further toward the hard-money camp. He called on Congress first to allow merchants to defer tariff payments, to give deposit banks time to return government funds, to postpone the government's payment on the fourth installment of the rapidly dwindling surplus, and to authorize an issue of Treasury notes to meet government expenses. The Democratic majority in both houses quickly passed those measures over Whig resistance.

Van Buren's subsequent plan for handling government funds stirred intense controversy. He called for the permanent divorce of federal monies from private banks by depositing them instead in a network of government vaults or subtreasuries around the country to be called the Independent Treasury system. He recommended (but did not require) that the federal government refuse to accept notes from banks that had suspended specie payments. He wanted the government to deal in hard money as much as possible. As soon as Congress began debate on the proposal, Calhoun successfully amended the bill in the Senate to require the government to deal exclusively in specie. From that point in the fall of 1837 until the Independent Treasury bill passed in the summer of 1840, hard money was an integral part of the measure.

Van Buren's message emphasized his swing to an antibanking position. Denouncing "corporate immunities," he urged state governments to restrict the privileges of banks they chartered. Thus, he provided a concrete agenda for Democrats in state legislatures as well as in Congress. Throwing the gauntlet down to the Whigs, he explicitly rejected their plea for a new national bank since voters had spurned it as "a concentration of power dangerous to their liberties." Such an institution, he went on, represented "the constant desire among some of our citizens to enlarge the powers of the Government and extend its control to subjects with which it should not interfere."

Repeatedly in the message, Van Buren stressed the doctrine of a negative state that became Democratic dogma for the remainder of the nineteenth century. "The less government interferes with private pursuits the better for the general prosperity." Government intervention into the economy, whether by Congress or state legislatures, inevitably produced justified "complaints of neglect, partiality, injustice, and oppression." Any positive government action created privilege. Government could best preserve equal rights by doing nothing. Ignoring his own call for relief to importers and deposit bankers, Van Buren ringingly proclaimed that government "was not intended to confer special privileges on individuals or any classes of them, to create systems of agriculture, manufactures, or trade, or engage in them either separately or in connection with individual citizens." Demands for relief to help people ruined by the depression should be rejected, for it was not government's "legitimate object to make men rich or to repair by direct grants of public money or legislation in favor of particular pursuits losses not incurred in the public service." Van Buren, in sum, did not simply call for a divorce of government funds from private banks. He called on government to stop aid to economic growth altogether.[15]

Van Buren's message set the tone for Democrats across the nation, and as successive waves of bank suspensions swept the country again in 1839 and 1841, the Democrats' commitment to hard money, antibanking, anticorporation, and negative government doctrines intensified. From Maine to Mississippi and Missouri, Democrats, apparently untroubled by the blatant inconsistency with their own demands for minimal government interference "with private pursuits," advocated and in legislatures voted for policies to force banks to resume specie payments or forfeit their charters, to increase specie ratios or ban paper bank notes altogether, to strip corporate stockholders of their privilege of limited liability, to block the chartering of new corporations, and to end state subsidies for canals, turnpikes, and railroads. When the renewal of hard times in late 1839 threatened the ability of a number of states to meet annual interest payments on bonds they had issued to create state-run banks or to fund internal improvements, most Democrats demanded the repudiation of those bonds rather than tax increases to fund them. In Congress, meanwhile, Democrats pushed for enactment of the Independent Treasury, denounced Whig proposals to raise the tariff as an attempt to aid manufacturing monopolists, and adamantly opposed federal subsidies to state governments or internal improvements.

Everywhere Democrats defended this antibusiness stance in language similar to Van Buren's. Paper money, they fulminated, not only produced speculation and instability; it was the currency of parasitic and aristocratic bankers who used it to cheat honest farmers and mechanics out of their hard-won earnings by refusing to redeem their notes. Bankers must be stripped of their control over the money supply by substituting the people's money—government-minted coins— for the bankers' rags. This "Money Power" flagrantly menaced republicanism. Its gross privileges violated equal rights, and its offer of credit in the form of loans only caused men to surrender their freedom and become slaves by going into debt.[16] Peter D. Vroom aptly summarized this part of the Democratic credo in a speech to the New Jersey constitutional convention in 1844. "If there is any danger to be feared in a republican government, it is the danger of associated wealth, with special privileges, and without personal liability. It is the aristocracy of wealth we have to fear, and that is the only aristocracy from which danger is to be apprehended."[17]

Since government created these privileges through its positive actions, government should do as little as possible. If government acted at all, Democrats asserted, it should be the government closest to the people—the states before the nation, localities before the states—and the purpose of such action should simply be to guarantee equal rights and individual freedom. As the *Democratic Review* put it in 1838, "The democratic creed may be summed up in this brief formula. As little government as possible; that little emanating from, and controlled by, the people; and uniform in its application to all." Only by attacking privilege and protecting equal rights could government advance the general welfare. "By *general good*," declared a Vermont Democrat in 1839, "I do not mean the promotion of riches, splendor, and power in the nation, but the equal protection of every citizen in his rights."[18]

Whigs, in diametric contrast, believed government must promote prosperity. Especially in hard times, government must take positive action to stimulate economic recovery. The electorate, Whigs also believed, would respond positively to such a message. Attacking first Van Buren's proposals to Congress as hard-hearted, they broadened that appeal into a full-fledged defense of positive government. Seizing on the commonwealth tradition of eighteenth-century republicanism, they argued that government as the agent of the people had an obligation to help them.

The proposed Independent Treasury provided Whigs with a concrete target to run against in congressional elections from 1837 to 1840; after the bill passed in July 1840, Whigs immediately campaigned for its repeal. By denouncing Van Buren's efforts to ram his proposal through Congress as executive tyranny, they reinforced the party's original role as a champion of liberty against despotism. They stressed even more the plan's pernicious economic consequences. Removing government money from private banks, they charged, would shrink the reserves on which notes and loans were based, further depress the money supply, and thereby aggravate price deflation. Prices needed to be lifted, not driven down still further, argued Whigs. To promote recovery, the country needed an ample and sound currency, one that would expand rather than diminish credit and confidence. The Democrats' prescription of hard money and restrictions on banks was exactly the wrong medicine. The private banking system must be nourished, not starved, to restore economic health.

Like Democrats, Whigs backed up their rhetoric with action. With remarkable cohesion during the special session of 1837 and regular sessions of Congress thereafter, they voted against every Van Buren recommendation that entailed a retreat by government from its role as partner to, and abettor of, private economic interests. They opposed the Independent Treasury; they voted against postponement of the final deposit payment to the states; they railed against authorization of Treasury notes.[19] Instead of printing its own money as an alternative to bank notes, Whigs cried, the government should remain intimately involved with banks.

This desire was shared by a number of Democrats who called themselves Conservatives, who were appalled by the administration's willingness to shirk responsibility for the economy, and who were infuriated by Van Buren's attempt to dictate party policy. In the summer of 1837, before the special session met, the Conservatives established their own newspaper in Washington called the *Madisonian*. While their foremost spokesmen were Senators Nathaniel P. Tallmadge of New York and William C. Rives of Virginia, Conservative Democrats actually proved more decisive in the House, where party strength was more closely balanced. Together with the Whigs, the Conservatives blocked passage of the Independent Treasury bill for three years.

Van Buren's Independent Treasury proposal thus provoked a realignment at the leadership level. Calhoun and his most devoted acolytes in southern states now rejoined the Democratic party to help the administration secure its passage. The more numerous Conservatives, who were especially strong in New York and Virginia, became potential recruits for the Whigs. Although Conservatives and Whigs disagreed about the desirability of a new national bank, their attitudes toward executive tyranny, the demerits of the Independent Treasury, and the necessity of substantial banking credit were congruent. From 1837 to 1840, Whig leaders would woo Conservatives, and by the time of the presidential election most Conservatives had shifted permanently to the Whig camp.[20]

While the Democratic push for the Independent Treasury dominated the special session, by 1838 and 1839 the parties were battling over other issues as well. Whigs revived and Democrats opposed plans to redistribute federal land revenues to the states. Some Whigs also resurrected the tariff issue, which had been dormant since passage of the Compromise Act in 1833. That act's provisions scheduled the most substantial cuts in duties for 1841 and 1842. Whigs contended that manufacturing and government deficits required an increase in rates rather than the impending reductions. Democrats opposed this proposal, just as they did Whig attempts to relieve ruined businessmen through a national bankruptcy law.

While action stalled in Congress, partisan battles shifted to state legislatures, which traditionally had intervened more actively in the private economic sector than had Congress. Almost all states required banks that suspended specie payments to forfeit their charters. While probanking Democrats initially blocked the implementation of those laws, particularly in New York, Virginia, Pennsylvania, and Ohio, the increasingly disciplined and cohesive parties fought over the forfeitures of charters, over the date by which banks would be forced to resume specie payments to avoid forfeiture, over new charters for banks and other corporations, over stockholder liability, over how much specie banks would have to keep in reserve, and over bans on bank notes. Consistently Whigs took the pro-corporation, probanking, and pro-paper-money side both in their votes and in their rhetoric, while over time more and more Democrats clustered on the opposite side.

These contrasting partisan perspectives on governmental activism also engendered conflicts over social legislation. To a far greater degree than Democrats, Whigs backed state intervention to regulate social behavior: temperance legislation, Sunday blue laws, and the creation of state-run public school systems. Democrats denounced such legislation as intolerable infringements on individual freedom, and although they did not oppose education, they feared that state-supported schools would compel increased state taxation and threaten local supervision of schools.[21] Increasingly, Democrats portrayed Whigs as bigoted and self-righteous religious fanatics intent on imposing their ethical values on others. Whigs retorted that Democrats were immoral deadbeats or dangerous radicals bent on destroying the very fabric of society—property, morality, education, and the rule of law. "Elements of that party," the *American Review* said of Democrats in 1844, support every "dangerously radical opinion, [every] specious, delusive theory, on social, political, or moral points."[22]

Primarily, however, Whig rhetoric focused on the economy and the need for government to get the country moving again. Whig politicians, editors, and pamphleteers articulated a coherent and sophisticated philosophy of the positive state that underlay the position they took in battles over specific policies in Congress and state legislatures. They derided Democratic do-nothingism as niggardly, selfish, and utterly inadequate in a depression. According to Whigs, Van Buren and his cold-hearted Democratic cronies were calling for the government to save itself while abandoning the rest of the population to rot in the decay of depression. As Calvin Colton argued in his 1840 campaign pamphlet *The Crisis of the Country*, "The maxim of Mr. Van Buren, 'Let the people take care of themselves, and the Government take care of themselves,' is as destructive as it is fallacious. . . . The appropriate function of Government is a parental care of the people."[23]

Ringing changes on the principle of beneficent government to which Whigs remained committed for the remainder of their party's existence, Whigs contended that the public welfare or commonweal included far more than equal rights. Government, particularly during a depression, had an obligation to promote economic recovery. Even in good times, argued Whigs, private capital was too small and fragmented to finance economic development. As the agent of the people, the national government therefore should supply that capital, either directly or indirectly. It should subsidize expensive transportation projects or transfer its funds to the states so that they could do it. It should deposit government funds in banks, preferably a new national bank, so that banks could expand money and credit. It should provide tariff protection for American manufacturers to increase their attractiveness to private investors. Meanwhile state governments should provide liberal terms to corporations—especially limited liability for stockholders—to lure capital to them.

According to the Whig analysis, in short, the economy could not grow if it remained atomized and fragmented. Prosperity required economic institutions like banks, manufacturing firms, or railroad corporations that could pool capital and thus accomplish tasks beyond the capacity of individual actors. Government's role was to facilitate the creation of such institutions.

This program, Whigs repeatedly retorted to Democrats, hardly violated equal rights by bestowing privileges on the rich, as Democrats charged. Everyone suffered during hard times, and government as the agent of the people must help them. Their measures would democratize wealth and equalize opportunity. Tariff protection for manufacturers would mean jobs for the unemployed at higher wages than were possible if manufacturers had to compete with cheap goods turned out by the pauper labor of Europe. Limited stockholder liability ensured that less wealthy individuals, no less than the rich, could own businesses. Banking credit, far from enslaving men to debt, as Democrats charged, would open opportunity to all. The economic growth and diversification that would result from Whig programs, they promised, would enhance what the young Illinois Whig Abraham Lincoln called the "right to rise" by increasing individuals' opportunities for upward economic mobility from a dependent to an independent economic status.[24]

"The Whig party is devoted to progress, but it does not seek to destroy," summarized the New York Whigs' legislative address in 1844. "It seeks to establish perfect equality of political rights; but it levels upward, not downwards, by education and benignant legislation, not by subverting established laws and institutions. It is the party of law, of order, of enterprise, of improvement, of beneficence, of hope, and of humanity." "The Whig party have [sic] always been distinguished from their [sic] opponents, by the attribution of a beneficent and protective power to government," echoed the *American Review* at the end of the 1840s. Precisely because Whigs still adhered to that commonwealth tradition of beneficial government, "they assert for themselves the name of 'republicans.' "[25]

No single document captures the ideological chasm that opened between the rival parties after 1837 so perceptively as Horace Greeley's best 1845 editorial. "The Whig party is the champion of general CONCORD or united interests, and thrives upon these," Greeley contended. The Democratic ("Loco Foco") party "is the party of DISCORD, or divided, repugnant, hostile interests and is prospered by whatever makes the separation of interests and classes more broad and palpable." So too, " 'THE COMMONWEALTH' is the term best expressing the Whig idea of a State or Nation, and our philosophy regards a Government with hope and confidence, as an agency of the community through which vast and beneficent ends may be accomplished." In contrast, "Loco Focoism regards Government (not its offices) with distrust and aversion, as an agency mainly of corruption, oppression, and robbery."[26]

In sum, even when Whigs added positive promotion of economic growth to their negative opposition to executive tyranny, they continued to present themselves as paladins of republicanism, just as did the Democrats by fighting for equal rights and freedom. The depression-induced economic agenda vastly broadened the debate between the parties after 1837, but it did not replace the core of that debate. The central argument remained which party could better preserve, protect, and perpetuate republican liberty, equality, and self-government.

Had the Panic of 1837 done no more than clarify the differences in the parties' economic programs and orientation toward government, it would have benefited the Whigs. Hard times gave credibility and urgency to the case Whigs made. But Whigs—and Democrats—did more than talk and write. They voted in Congress and state legislatures in accordance with their divergent views and thus established records for voters to judge. Internal party cohesion and interparty conflict, which had been high in Congress during 1836, rose even higher in the next two Congresses,[27] but the change in roll-call votes in state legislatures was especially dramatic. In virtually every state of the nation, partisan conflict became sharper after the Panic of 1837 than it had been before. In some states, partisan fighting increased immediately in the first session that met after the panic broke out; in others, there was a delay until the second stage of the depression hit in 1839. But almost everywhere Whigs and Democrats took distinctly different stands on state policy that were congruent with their positions on national legislation. Since Democratic state legislators prior to 1836 had often flouted the antibanking, anticorporation, antidevelopment line Democrats took in Congress, this change meant that there was a marked increase in the intensity and clarity of interparty conflict on roll-call votes after the panic (Table 4).

III

The economic oscillations between 1837 and 1840 and the political developments they provoked—the articulation of rival programs, the intensification of partisan combat over concrete policy options in Congress and state legislatures, and the realignment of Calhounites and Conservatives—all had a profound impact on Whig fortunes in the state and congressional elections of 1837, 1838, 1839, and 1840. In these so-called off-year elections—and most of the state and congressional elections even in 1840 were held months before the presidential poll in November—Whigs developed the momentum to win the presidency for the first time.

Although no election is ever a referendum on a single issue, to a remarkable extent Whigs' electoral fortunes followed the fluctuations of the economy. When prices were falling and the economy was depressed, Whigs fared better than they did during the brief recovery from September 1838 to October 1839. Not only their proportion of the popular vote but also the share of seats they won in state legislatures and the House of Representatives, as well as that of governorships, dramatically increased during hard times and fell during the recovery (Tables 5 and 6).[28]

The condition of the national economy alone, however, did not determine Whig fortunes. There are too many exceptions to the general pattern. In some states, especially in the South, Whigs did better during the recovery of 1838–39 than they did during the panic itself. In others, notably Massachusetts and Mississippi, they lost in November 1839 after the second wave of bank suspensions had started. Elsewhere, they retained much of their popular vote and many of the offices they had won even after the recovery began. Their fortunes, in short, rarely fell as fast or as far during the recovery as they had risen during the initial postpanic slump.

Regional variations from the national economic pattern help account for some of these anomalies. The idiosyncratic movement of cotton prices that were based largely on the size of the crop and on foreign demand, for example, clearly affected southern elections. Although the price of cotton fell sharply in early 1837, by autumn it had not dropped as far as the general wholesale price index. Thus Southerners who sold cotton had higher real incomes in the fall of 1837 than did other Americans. In 1838, however, cotton prices continued to drop throughout the year when other prices were rebounding, thereby cutting the real income of cotton growers. Then cotton prices jumped in 1839 while most other prices peaked in July and were dropping rapidly by the fall, especially after the second wave of bank suspensions in October.[29] Accordingly, Whigs did better in Arkansas, Georgia, Mississippi, and North Carolina in 1838 than in 1837 but suffered badly in 1839. In Mississippi, for example, the party's vote and share of offices increased sharply in November 1837, at the depth of the general panic; it improved its position in the legislative races of 1838; and then it lost its legislative majority, the governorship, and both congressional seats in November 1839.[30]

Even the erratic pattern of cotton prices cannot explain all the variation in southern Whigs' fortunes. The realignment of Calhounites and Conservative Democrats provoked by Van Buren's Independent Treasury plan also played a role. The key in Alabama—and to a lesser extent in Mississippi, Tennessee, and Virginia—was the return of Calhounites to the Democratic party. Calhoun's

Table 4

Indexes of Interparty Disagreement on Roll-Call Votes on Economic Issues in Selected State Legislatures, 1835–1844

State	1835	1836	1837	1838	1839	1840	1841	1842	1843	1844
BANKING										
Alabama					43	47	65			
Missouri	16	6.5					80			
Mississippi	0	34.5	33.6	31.1	31.8	55.6	65.5	64.3	61	67.8
New Hampshire	8				77		67			
New Jersey all[a]	83.3	54.3	40.5	72.1	73.1	38.7	65.3	62.9	23.8	NV
special	69	42	35	68	69	16	67	57	NV	NV
North Carolina	NV	NV	NV	NV	NV	69.7	NV	69.4	NV	NV
Ohio	34.5	49	64.5	97	40.5			92	37	
Pennsylvania	8	32	45	79				100	47	
Virginia	37	29	48	62	45	70		66		
CURRENCY AND PAPER MONEY										
Missouri					83.5		71			
Mississippi			41.4	61	50	67.9				33.2
New Hampshire			80	99			90	82		
Ohio		86	74	97	94					
Pennsylvania	11.5			35	16			89	91	
Virginia			70	16				100	62.5	
CORPORATE CHARTERS AND CORPORATE RIGHTS										
Missouri					3	83		35		
Mississippi		12.2	15.5	51.2		14.1	36.4		90	
New Hampshire			41	88	83	75.5		100		
New Jersey (manufacturing)	45	45	16	81	74	15	74	50	53	34
North Carolina				59.5		60.4				95.6
Ohio	47	37	70	74						
Pennsylvania		11		34	35			73.5	74	
Virginia					68					
AID TO INTERNAL IMPROVEMENTS										
Alabama					29	46				
Missouri		68		30.5			71			
Mississippi		27.5	48.9	19.2	12.2	19.4	13	51.3		30.6
New Hampshire					50					
North Carolina										
Subsidies		30.2		29.8		59.8		51.5		64.6
Railroad relief						63.5		55.3		94.6
Ohio		63.5		12.5	14					
Pennsylvania	6		10	53	38			49		
Virginia	14	11	3	9	17					
CHARTERS FOR INTERNAL IMPROVEMENT CORPORATIONS										
Missouri					35					
Mississippi		23.8	15.2	36.5	44.6	20.7		65.5		
New Hampshire					77	77				
New Jersey										
General		30	22	78			67	10		
Joint companies		64								
Ohio		46			10					
Pennsylvania		41	24.5						47	48
Virginia	39									

Table 4 *(continued)*

[a]This table is based on a number of different sources. The figures for Missouri, New Hampshire, Ohio, Pennsylvania, and Virginia are drawn from the tables in Shade and Ershkowitz, "Consensus or Conflict? Political Behavioral in the State Legislatures during the Jacksonian Era." Those figures are sample votes drawn from different years, so blanks indicate that these authors provided no figures, not necessarily that no votes on these issues were held that year. In addition, I have supplemented the votes on banking in Virginia for 1838, 1839, and 1842 with figures from Sharp's chapter on Virginia in *The Jacksonians versus the Banks*. The figures for Alabama are drawn from the tables for votes in 1839, 1840, and 1841 in Thornton, *Politics and Power in a Slave Society*, pp. 463–64. The figures for New Jersey are not the same as those listed in the Shade and Ershkowitz article; rather, they are taken from Levine, *The Behavior of State Legislative Parties in the Jacksonian Era: New Jersey, 1829–1844*, and represent all the votes on those topics, not just samples. Similarly, the figures for Mississippi represent all the votes. They are taken from Table VII in Lucas, "The Period of Political Alchemy: Party in the Mississippi Legislature, 1835–1846," pp. 162–63. The figures for North Carolina are taken from three sources: the samples of five internal improvement votes for 1836 and 1838 in Table 3 of Jeffrey, "Internal Improvements and Political Parties in Antebellum North Carolina, 1836–1860," p. 155; three votes on stockholder liability for 1838 and 1840 in id., "Party Alignment and Realignment in North Carolina, 1836–1860," (paper presented at the Southern Historical Association's annual meeting, 1979), Table 1; and the figures in Table 8 in Kruman's *Parties and Politics in North Carolina, 1836–1865*, p. 57. Kruman's tables begin in 1840, so blanks after that date indicate that no votes on a particular subject were taken. The figures that are underlined indicate the first session held following the outbreak of the panic in 1837.

It should be noted that these figures differ somewhat from those presented in Table 1 of my previous book, *The Political Crisis of the 1850s*, pp. 26–27. There are two reasons for this difference. The sources for New Jersey and Mississippi are different from the ones I relied on there. In addition, I have tried to list the votes under the year in which they occurred, not the year in which the legislative session began. Hence, whenever a legislative session started in December and carried over into the winter of the following year, I have listed the votes in the latter year. I did this because I was especially interested in isolating the votes that occurred before and after the outbreak of the panic and because I wanted to list votes in the year in which they might affect the subsequent elections of that year if the session met before the election.

devoted lieutenant, the mammoth Dixon H. Lewis, and his followers defected from the Alabama Whig party in the summer of 1838 and joined the Democrats. Since the extreme state rights wing of the Whig party was especially strong in the black-belt plantation regions that Whigs had hitherto carried, that shift threw the state into Democratic hands in the state elections of August 1838 and 1839. It also gave the Democrats a sufficient cushion in the legislature to withstand a Whig surge in August 1840, when cotton prices again slumped. The loss of the extreme state rights men left the leadership of the Alabama Whig party in the hands of politicians who stressed positive economic programs rather than state rights and who by 1839 were even trumpeting the merits of a new national bank. That loss, however, also left Alabama's Whigs in a minority.[31]

In Virginia, Conservative Democrats far outnumbered Calhounites, and they helped Whigs' improvement in 1838 and 1839. Determined to keep hard-money Democrats in the legislature from ousting Conservatives' preeminent national leader, William C. Rives, from the Senate, Conservatives ran their own legislative candidates in 1838 and 1839, thereby splitting the Democratic vote and allowing Whig gains in those years. Similarly, Conservatives' refusal to support hard-money Democrats for Congress allowed the Whigs to gain three additional seats in 1839 over their total in 1837 and to increase their share of the popular vote from 43.6 percent in 1836 to 48.2 percent in 1839.[32]

Table 5

Proportion of Congressional and Gubernatorial Seats Won by Whigs in Different Economic Circumstances, 1836–1840[a]

Date of Election and Economic Condition	Congressional Seats	Governorships
January 1836–May 1837 (BOOM)	37.3% ($N = 185$)	37.5% ($N = 16$)
June 1837–August 1838 (PANIC)	65.2% ($N = 69$)	66.7% ($N = 15$)
September 1838–October 1839 (RECOVERY)	49.3% ($N = 223$)	28.6% ($N = 14$)
November 1839–December 1840 (DEPRESSION)	62.3% ($N = 138$)	76.4% ($N = 17$)

[a]This table is based on the results of the congressional elections listed in Congressional Quarterly's *Guide to U.S. Elections*, pp. 568–73, and Kallenbach and Kallenbach (eds.), *American State Governors, 1776–1976: Volume I*, which lists both the results of gubernatorial elections and the date on which state elections were held.

New York's Conservative leaders like Senator Tallmadge and Congressman John C. Clark also called on their followers to support Whig tickets in 1837 and 1838. Clark won reelection as a Whig the latter year, and Tallmadge, who faced reelection by the legislature chosen that year, swapped an endorsement of the Whig gubernatorial candidate, William H. Seward, for Thurlow Weed's promise to persuade new Whig legislators to support Tallmadge. In 1837 the Democratic vote fell by 26,000 and the Whig vote grew by 17,000 since 1836, so Conservative conversions and abstentions contributed to Whigs' astonishing legislative gains. In 1838, however, 1837's Conservative nonvoters apparently returned to the Democratic column. Whigs added 37,000 more votes to their 1837 total, but Democratic turnout increased by 42,000. Still, the combined Whig increment of 54,000 since 1836 more than tripled Democrats' net gain of 16,000, and Whigs prevailed in New York in 1838 despite the economic recovery.[33]

New York's results point to the most arresting feature of the elections held between 1837 and the end of 1840: the extraordinary mobilization of new voters by both Whigs and Democrats. Turnout for both parties usually increased from one election to the next in a leapfrogging pattern of voter recruitment. During the postpanic slump, Whigs outgained Democrats among new voters. They usually retained almost all of those new converts during the recovery and occasionally even increased their totals. That is why Whigs did so much better in congressional, gubernatorial, and legislative elections during the recovery of 1838–39 than during the prepanic boom. Nonetheless, during the brief recovery, Democrats mobilized even more additional supporters to produce their comeback. When prices plunged again after 1839, however, Whigs once again far outpaced Democrats among first-time voters. That surge of additional voters in the spring, summer, and fall of 1840 explains why Whigs won such sweeping victories in the legislative, gubernatorial, and congressional, as well as presidential, elections that year.[34]

Table 6

Whig Share of the Seats Won in the Lower House of the Legislature in All States but South Carolina, 1836–1843[a]

State and Month of Election	1836	1837	1838	1839	1840	1841	1842	1843
New Hamp. (March)	23%	N.A.	**46%**	37%	**38%**	35%	**27%**	**36%**
Connecticut (April)	35%	35%	**73%**	59%	**66%**	**67%**	**32%**	**41%**
Rhode Island (April)	44%	42%	**60%**	44%	**67%**	**76%**	N.A.	**73%**
Virginia (May)	43%	35%	**54%**	52%	**55%**	51%	**37%**	**43%**
Louisiana (July)	N.A.	**N.A.**	35%		46%		57%	
Alabama (August)	51%	**51%**	**41%**	33%	**49%**	**45%**	**33%**	**38%**
Illinois (August)	31%	**52%**		45%		31%		
Indiana (August)	56%	**68%**	**62%**	39%	**78%**	**47%**	**45%**	**45%**
Kentucky (August)	59%	**71%**	**68%**	58%	**77%**	**77%**	**57%**	**62%**
Missouri (August)	29%	**40%**		45%		26%		
N. Carolina (August)	49%	**55%**		61%		44%		
Tennessee (August)		**64%**		44%		52%		**53%**
Maine (September)	35%	**50.5%**	39%	39%	54%	**30%**	**22%**	**34%**
Vermont (September)	73%[b]	**57%**	68%	N.A.	75%	**58%**	**56%**	**51.5%**
Arkansas (October)	25%	**44%**		34%		30%		
Georgia (October)	44%	**N.A.**	50%	43%	57%	**42.5%**	**44%**	61%
Maryland (October)	76%	**60%**	53%	41%	76%	**47%**	**43%**	58%
New Jersey (October)	38%	**68%**	62%	62%	77%	**60%**	**55%**	40%
Ohio (October)	49%	**56%**	47%	32%	71%	**49%**	**42%**	54%
Penna. (October)	28%	**44%**	44%	32%	52%	**36%**	**40%**	42%
Delaware (November)	67%	67%		**100%**		**67%**		
Mass. (November)	69%	**87%**	70%	**52%**	70%	**62%**	**50%**	58%
Michigan (November)		**44%**	40%	**71%**	61%	**11%**	**11%**	11%
Mississippi (November)	37.5%	**50%**	52%	**40%**	54%	**39%**	**33%**	33%
New York (November)	26%	**78%**	64%	**55%**	52%	**26%**	**27%**	29%

[a]With the exception of Alabama and Mississippi, these data on the partisan division of state legislatures were made available by the Inter-University Consortium for Political and Social Research. They were originally collected by Walter Dean Burnham. Neither the original source or collectors of the data nor the Consortium bear any responsibility for the analyses or interpretations presented here. For Alabama, I supplemented Burnham's data with information from *Niles Register*, Volume 51, p. 19, and Thornton, *Politics and Power in a Slave Society*, pp. 34–36. For Mississippi, I utilized what I consider the more reliable data in Table III of Lucas, "The Period of Political Alchemy: Party in the Mississippi Legislature, 1835–1846." N.A. indicates that Burnham found no data available. Results from periods of economic decline are printed in boldface.

[b]In 1836, the Antimasonic and Whig parties in Vermont still ran separate candidates. Thus the figure given represents the combined total of Antimasonic and Whig seats and helps explain the curious fact that the Whig share of seats in Vermont appears to have declined after the outbreak of the panic.

That mobilization of voters in off-year elections has never been equaled in the subsequent history of American politics. Its extent can be measured against the presidential turnout. Nationally, the proportion of eligible males who cast presidential votes jumped from 57.2 percent in 1836 to 80.2 percent in 1840, and the rate was even higher than the national average in fifteen states.[35] That record turnout is normally attributed to the popular enthusiasm roused by the carnival-like Whig presidential campaign that year or to the maturation of partisan organizations that were closely competitive in most states and that turned out every possible voter because every voter was needed.[36]

Most of the increased turnout between November 1836 and November 1840, however, had already been achieved in state and congressional elections prior to the latter presidential poll, including earlier elections in 1840 itself. In some states, turnout in subpresidential races even exceeded the total recorded in the 1840 presidential election, and where the Whigs' presidential candidate secured a larger share of the vote than did Whig candidates early in the year, a decline in the Democratic vote by November almost always explained the difference.[37] Voters responded to what the Whig party stood for as an institution, not simply to an attractive presidential ticket.

Quite unlike the state and congressional elections prior to the presidential election of 1836, moreover, the off-year contests between 1836 and 1840 forged lasting partisan allegiances. Voters did not move massively back and forth between Whigs and Democrats from one election to the next as economic conditions changed. The state and congressional elections of 1837, 1838, 1839, and 1840, not the hoopla of the Whigs' 1840 presidential campaign, converted hundreds of thousands of previous nonvoters into Whigs and transformed a losing party into a winner.[38]

IV

The critical question is why the electorate responded to those elections in the fashion it did. The leapfrogging pattern of voter mobilization suggests that Whigs and Democrats attracted voters from different social and economic milieus and that different economic conditions triggered different Whig and Democratic turnouts. Both parties focused their state and congressional campaigns between 1837 and 1840 largely on the alternative programs advocated in Congress and state legislatures. Promising that their policies would produce recovery, Whigs attracted most new voters during hard times, but they also retained those gains when Whig voters credited the postrecession recovery in part to programs Whig state legislators enacted. Democrats, in contrast, brought out new voters during the recovery by railing against Whig programs as violations of equal rights. Voters, in sum, responded to what government did, not simply to economic conditions.[39]

Demonstrating that connection between policy and popular voting behavior requires one to follow the chronological rhythm of specific policy battles, how parties tried to educate voters about policy alternatives that legislatures had fought over, and the subsequent response of voters in individual states. Since limitations of space (to say nothing of readers' patience) preclude a comprehensive state-by-state survey, a few representative examples must suffice.

New York's Whigs blamed the depression on the Democrats during the 1837 campaign, but they also argued that revival of the economy required more banking credit and expansion of the state's canal system. Even before the outbreak of the panic in May 1837, New York's talented Whig leaders had realized that the Democrats' refusal to allow bank notes of small denomination and to expand the banking system would doom them at the polls. As the state legislative session of 1837 drew to a close in May, Weed exulted to his protegé, Seward, "The whole

People are demanding small notes, and they must know *who* refused them and *how* it was done. . . . We have the Regency on the hip and must keep them there." Weed's only regret as the November 1837 election approached was that the subtreasury bill had not passed Congress. Then Democrats would have had to suffer the consequences of their national, as well as their state, actions.[40] Weed clearly believed that voters responded to governance, not just to economic conditions.

He was right. Whigs scored a stunning triumph in the legislative elections, increasing their proportion of seats in the lower house from slightly more than one-fourth to slightly less than four-fifths. Because Democrats retained control of the state senate, the stage was set for an even sharper polarization over state economic policy when the legislature met in 1838. The Whig house pressed for small notes. The Democratic senate rejected the pressure. By the fall, Whigs were confident that they could pillory the intransigent Democratic resistance to small notes once again.[41] Whigs enjoyed more success in expanding the canal and banking systems, as they had promised in the campaign of 1837. Their programs passed the senate with the aid of Conservatives and other probusiness Democrats appalled by the swing of their party's majority to negative state doctrines. The Whigs authorized a new bond issue to finance canal expansion. More important, they passed and Democratic Governor William L. Marcy, who sided with his party's probusiness minority, signed a free banking act in 1838 that encapsulated the Whig philosophy of the positive state.

That law stated that the system of special bank charters, long attacked by Whigs and Antimasons as a Democratic monopoly, should be ended. Instead, individuals wishing to secure bank charters should receive them automatically if they met certain requirements for capitalization. The capital was to consist of federal and state bonds deposited with a comptroller in Albany rather than specie, and the banks were required to have a specie ratio of only 1 to 8 for their note issue. While some Democrats applauded the antimonopoly aspects of this law, they pushed unsuccessfully for higher specie requirements and individual stockholder liability. Even though Governor Marcy and a few Democrats accepted the measure, it was distinctly a Whig bill. Both it and the canal appropriation were defended as Whig achievements by party newspapers and by the address Whig legislators issued at the end of the session. Whigs campaigned on a record, not just on economic conditions.

Whigs considered the contrast between their desire to expand banks and credit and the deflationary potential of the Democrats' Independent Treasury plan, which Van Buren reendorsed in December 1837, an enormous advantage. "We cannot fail to carry the next election," Weed boasted that month. The restoration of prosperity by the summer of 1838 temporarily dissipated that confidence, for economic recovery, some Whig leaders worried, would "lull" their new supporters "to inaction, and endanger us by default." To counteract such apathy, Whig leaders astutely defined the policy alternatives between the parties as sharply as possible. From around the state, requests cascaded on Weed in Albany and on Seward, the Whigs' gubernatorial candidate, to circulate copies of the as-yet unpassed Independent Treasury bill so that voters could actually read its hard-money provisions. "Our new converts *'wish to see the bill,'*" one wrote Seward. "Speeches and Reports should be printed to show up the Loco Foco party. . . . Our opponents are trying to whip back the Conservatives by telling them *they are the 'friends of the Banks & we are not.'* Let them be exposed on this tack." From Buffalo, the Whig congressional candidate Millard Fillmore asked Seward, "Have you got anything at Auburn showing up the Sub-Treasury in its most odious form that would make a good hand bill? . . . Do send us anything you have on the Sub-Treasury or Small Bills."[42]

Improved economic conditions alone, therefore, did not determine the outcome of New York's 1838 election. With concerted effort, Whigs spelled out the precise alternatives on state and national policy options, on what they had already accomplished, on what they still hoped to do in the future, and on what the rival Democrats had done or hoped to do. As a result, turnout soared, with Whigs gaining 37,000 and Democrats 42,000 additional votes since 1837. Two contradictory impulses explain the Democratic gains. Advocacy of the Independent Treasury and attacks on the Whigs' free banking act and canal bill aroused the party's antibanking majority who had been disappointed in 1837 that Marcy had prevented Democrats from punishing banks for suspending. At the same time, Marcy's signature on the canal and free banking bills appeased Conservatives and other probusiness Democrats who otherwise might have continued to abstain. In any event, Whigs' cumulative increases since 1836 allowed them to retain two-thirds of the assembly seats, cut Democrats' senate majority in half, elect twenty-one of forty congressmen compared to only ten in 1836, and install Seward in the governor's chair.

The new governor quickly moved to add planks to the successful Whig platform. He called on the Whig legislature in 1839 to issue $4 million worth of bonds a year for the next ten years in order to expand the state's canal system, bonds that he claimed could be paid off from canal tolls. Stunned by the extravagance of Seward's grandiose program of canal enlargement, the Democratic senate refused to enact it, which allowed Whigs to make Democratic control of the senate their chief target in the 1839 campaign. The legislature did repeal the small note ban and thus allowed Whigs to take credit for expanding the currency supply during 1839. On those issues, Whigs captured the state senate for the first time in 1839 and thus gained complete control of the state government.

Total control was a mixed blessing. The minimal specie-reserve requirements of the new free banking act, as well as the strength of the old safety-fund banks, allowed New York's banks to resist the wave of suspensions that swept the rest of the nation in October 1839, and state banking was thus effectively removed from the political agenda. But New York hardly escaped the depression that encompassed the nation in 1840. Despite that slump, Seward pressed ahead with his schemes for state aid for internal improvements. Over sharp Democratic resistance, Whigs authorized bond issues worth almost $6.5 million for canal construction and aid to railroad corporations. Thus, Democrats could savage them for recklessly increasing the state's debt.[43] Worse still, nativistic elements in the party persuaded the legislative majority, over Seward's protests, to pass a voter registration law to restrict immigrant voting in New York City. This law had the predictable result of arousing that metropolis's immigrant community against the Whigs. With a controversial Whig record to run against; with Van Buren, who signed the Independent Treasury bill in July, on the ticket as presidential candidate; and with a new gubernatorial candidate to replace Marcy, Democrats made their strongest showing since 1836. Seward narrowly squeaked by in the gubernatorial election, Whigs' majorities in the legislature were reduced, and Whigs lost the congressional seats in New York City they had won two years earlier.

Banking, canal funding, and state fiscal policy also sparked partisan battles in Pennsylvania between 1837 and 1840. Pennsylvania's probanking Democrats were particularly numerous since the state government relied on loans and stock dividends from banks, rather than on taxes, to fund its expenditures. Because they granted a state charter to Biddle's Bank of the United States, the Whig-Antimasonic coalition had been routed in the legislative elections of 1836, but by blaming the panic on Jacksonian policies, they increased their minority in the house in 1837 and exploited their earlier gerrymander to retain control of the state senate.

In the 1838 legislative session, the Democratic house passed and the Whig senate defeated antibanking measures on party-line voting. Together with conservative Democrats, the Whig-Antimasonic coalition also authorized expansive expenditures for the Main Line canal. During the summer, moreover, Antimasonic Governor Joseph Ritner's administration won popularity by securing funds from Biddle's Bank for immediate repairs on a section of the canal damaged by floods. Biddle, moreover, assured Ritner well in advance that he intended to resume specie payments in August, and to gain partisan credit for what Biddle intended to do anyway, Ritner issued a proclamation in July ordering the state's banks to resume on August 13.

That ploy paid dividends in the October 1838 elections when turnout surpassed that of the 1836 presidential election by 40 percent. Ritner lost his bid for reelection, but he garnered 49 percent of the vote in 1838, whereas he had won in 1835 with 47 percent only because of Democratic divisions. Whigs also picked up an additional congressional seat; together with Antimasons, they retained control of the senate; and that coalition came within a whisker of capturing the lower house.[44] The record Whigs established in the legislature and the executive branch, in short, allowed them to benefit from the recovery, while the banks' resumption and the nomination of a probanking conservative named David R. Porter for governor defused the Democrats' antibanking appeal.

Divided control of the legislature blocked passage of controversial bills in 1839, and Porter continued Ritner's policy of funding state expenditures by selling bonds to Philadelphia banks. That dependency on banks left Whigs more vulnerable to economic fluctuations than Democrats. When the Bank of the United States of Pennsylvania led Philadelphia's banks in suspending again, a few days before the October election, Democrats gleefully revived the crippling charge that the coalition had given Biddle his state charter in 1836. The banks' action thus reinforced antibanking sentiment among Democratic voters, but the price slump was not yet severe enough to help Whigs when Pennsylvanians voted. As a result, Democrats increased their majority in the assembly and finally captured the senate.

Complete control of the state government during 1840, when the depression deepened, proved an albatross for Pennsylvania's Democrats. Democratic majorities in each house passed punitive, but differently worded, antibanking bills, but because of this disagreement and Porter's intervention, neither became law. Instead, Whigs combined with probanking Democrats to give banks more than a year to resume specie payments. At the close of the session, a Democratic address blasted this measure as "passed by the Whigs and antimasons, together with a few apostate democrats" and as meriting "the eternal and everlasting execration of every genuine democrat in the commonwealth." Meanwhile, Porter was forced to borrow more money to meet the state's interest payments on previously issued bonds and to continue work on the canal. Admitting that the state could no longer rely exclusively on bank loans, he asked the legislature to levy taxes on real and personal property for the first time since 1836 in order to pay the interest on the new bond issues.

During the 1840 campaign, therefore, the Whigs enjoyed the best of both worlds. They accused Porter of increasing the state debt by $6 million during his two years in office, a debt that required Democrats to reimpose taxes Whigs had abolished in 1836. At the same time, they cited the Democrats' aborted anti-banking bills as examples of radicalism. The Democrats, Whig legislators declared in their address at the close of the session, were "breathing nothing but destruc-tion to the banking and credit systems of the Commonwealth." Posing as pro-tectors of those systems from the "bearded enthusiasts" of the Democratic party, Whigs in October 1840 recaptured both houses of the legislature and gained two additional seats in Congress for a total of thirteen out of twenty-eight. Attacks on the recently passed Independent Treasury Act and the presidential campaign helped this resurgence, but Whigs had also carved a winning platform on state issues.[45]

In New Jersey, Ohio, Connecticut, New Hampshire, Alabama, Louisiana, Vir-ginia, and Mississippi, the same chronological rhythm between legislative action and subsequent elections appeared. Democrats passed or attempted to enact anti-banking and hard-money legislation. Whigs campaigned against those laws, won legislative majorities, and then repealed the laws and often expanded banking credit instead. Democrats, denouncing Whig actions and posing as bank reformers, then often won again in 1838 or 1839. The battle between Mississippi's hard-money Democratic Governor Alexander G. McNutt and Whig legislators was especially ferocious, but virtually everywhere, Democrats' antibanking initiatives in 1839 or early 1840 cost them dearly in the state elections of 1840 when the economy once again turned sour.[46]

Antipodal positions on banking did not develop so quickly in Georgia and Tennessee or in Indiana, Illinois, and Michigan, largely because the Democrats had been deeply involved in creating the dominant banking systems there. Whigs campaigned against the Independent Treasury system in state elections through-out the late 1830s in the first two states,[47] however, and by 1840 sharper party lines had emerged over banking and other economic matters in the three mid-western legislatures. In Michigan, the collapse of a bank prominently affiliated with Democrats during the suspension of October 1839 contributed to Whigs' victory the following month. In Indiana and Illinois, the parties fought over Whig-sponsored canal projects as soon as the panic broke in 1837. Whigs had claimed credit for launching lavish improvement schemes in both states in 1836, and in each, Democrats were quick to assault the projects as extravagantly ex-pensive, ill-conceived, incompetently managed, and boons only to the New York and foreign purchasers of the state bonds with which they were financed. Whigs, in turn, condemned the Democrats for opposing improvements necessary for eco-nomic development. By defending the canals, accusing the Democrats of causing the depression, and charging them with currying the favor of Irish immigrants working on the canal itself, Whigs carried both houses of the Illinois legislature in August 1838. They swept to victory a year earlier in Indiana when they could still focus attention on Democrats' purported responsibility for the panic, and they maintained control in 1838.

The following year, the worm turned. Indiana was the first state to suffer from the contraction of the British market for American bonds in the spring of 1839. Unable to sell new bonds, the state suspended work on the canals in August and confronted the weight of interest payments on the previously sold bonds. Then the Democrats had the best of both worlds. They could both blame the state's Whigs for financial bungling and point to the general prosperity that summer as proving the wisdom of Van Buren's economic policies. For even though the Independent Treasury Law would not be passed until the following summer, Van Buren had refused to restore the deposit banking system fully following the resumption of specie payments. Democrats cited the recovery of 1838–39 as proof that an Independent Treasury system and hard-money currency would work. In August 1839 that appeal succeeded, and Indiana's Whigs were swamped. They fell from a three-fifths majority to a two-fifths minority in the state legislature, and they won only two of seven congressional seats, whereas in 1837 they had captured six. A year later, when plummeting prices gave new salience to Whigs' calls for government-aided economic development, Whigs would capture three-fourths of the legislature.[48]

Aid to state transportation projects and banking also spawned the sharpest partisan battles in Whigs' two main southern strongholds, Kentucky and North Carolina. While Kentucky's parties had been sharply divided over national issues prior to 1837, they, like those in many other states, had cooperated in enacting measures to spur state economic development. In 1832 and 1833 they had joined to charter the Bank of Kentucky and the Bank of Northern Kentucky. Later, they jointly committed the state to fund a massive program of slack-water navigation projects on its rivers to improve transportation. After the panic, however, Democrats attacked the state's Whig-run banks for causing the panic and cheating noteholders by suspension. In response, Whigs defended them as necessary engines of credit. In 1838 and particularly during the recovery of 1839, Democrats had the better of this debate and scored gains in the legislature. In 1839 and 1840, Democrats also vilified the Whig management of the navigation projects as wasteful and demanded an end to further expenditures. Whigs praised those projects as necessary to improve communication within the state, and in 1840 they even advocated an increase in taxes to pay for their completion. Voters were apparently persuaded, for in August they elected a Whig governor and gave the party an even bigger majority in the legislature than it had won in 1837.[49]

The North Carolina Whig party had won the governorship in 1836 largely because of its advocacy of internal improvements, and in the legislative session that year it had given more consistent support to such projects than Democrats. Again, after its victory in 1838, the party proved much friendlier to transportation firms than did Democrats, even though regional rivalries clearly played a role in the roll-call voting. On a bill to provide state aid to the strapped Raleigh and Gaston Railroad, for example, 70 percent of the Whigs but only 30 percent of the Democrats in the house supported the relief bill. Similarly, 74 percent of the

Whigs supported and 69 percent of Democrats opposed state subscription of stock in the Fayetteville and Western Railroad. By 1838, North Carolina's state parties were also sharply at odds over the issue of stockholder liability for corporations, and by the early 1840s they would clash over banking and currency as well. Party platforms in North Carolina tended to focus more on national than state issues, and even in the legislature, resolutions concerning the Independent Treasury or distribution of federal land revenues polarized the parties more sharply than did substantive state legislation. Nonetheless, the rival parties had established distinguishable records on state matters. North Carolina voters knew which party favored internal improvements, banks, and corporate rights and which did not.[50]

Massachusetts, finally, provides an important variation on this central theme by showing that noneconomic state issues could also move voters in the late 1830s. The 1837 economic collapse sharply reversed the surge toward Democrats in 1835 and 1836, even as it clarified differences between the parties on economic policy. Blaming the panic on Democratic hard-money policies and calling for a new national bank, Whigs in 1837 crushed the Bay State Democrats, who loyally, if foolishly, defended Van Buren's Independent Treasury proposal. In 1838, the differences between the parties sharpened. The antibanking wing took firmer control of the Democrats when George Bancroft replaced the conservative businessman David Henshaw as customs collector in Boston. Meanwhile, the Whig legislature delayed the resumption of specie payments and successfully floated a bond issue in England to finance railroad projects in the state. Whigs could thus claim credit for the return of prosperity, which came earlier to Massachusetts than to most other states because its Whig financial community resumed specie payments early in the year. With such a record the Whigs again won the election of 1838.

In that election, however, the Democrats clearly outgained Whigs among new voters and narrowed the gap between the parties. In part, the clearer antibanking, anticorporate privilege stance of the party led to this gain, but the major cause was probably the negative reaction to an antiliquor law that Whigs passed in the spring of 1838 in response to pressure from temperance elements in the party. Aimed primarily at closing down groggeries, that statute banned the sale of liquor in quantities smaller than fifteen gallons. In 1839, Democrats made the fifteen-gallon law the focal point of their campaign. Incumbent Whig Governor Edward Everett praised the law as enlightened social policy. Attacking it for blatantly discriminating against the poor and for puritanically imposing restrictions on individual freedom, Democrats promised to repeal it. Riding this issue, the perennially defeated Democratic gubernatorial candidate, Marcus Morton, scored a stunning upset in 1839. The Democratic vote increased by 24 percent, while the Whig total declined slightly.

Then, in his message to the legislature in early 1840, Morton outlined a sweeping plan to impose restrictions on banks, corporate rights, and state subsidies to railroads. Whigs in the legislature countered with reports and speeches blasting every aspect of this program as inimical to the commonwealth's economic welfare. With the depression of 1840 refocusing attention on economic concerns, and with the contrasting positions of the two parties on the government's economic role clearer than they had ever been, the Whigs demolished the Democrats in the state elections of November 1840. Both parties increased their vote, but Whig gains outpaced the Democrats' by more than four to one.[51]

V

As this survey makes clear, the Whig and Democratic parties advocated specific policies in order to gain office. They attempted to enact those policies once elected. And they expended enormous effort to educate voters about what officeholders had done. Voters knew what the parties stood for in terms of both specific legislation and general goals. They could judge the expected results of those programs because of recent experience with both. And they responded in rational ways to the contrasting programs and party images presented to them.

Repelled by strident Democratic rhetoric about class conflict, appalled by the consequences of the negative state, and attracted by what they perceived as the economic benefits of the Whig program, the vast majority of wealthy businessmen, professionals, and planters supported the Whig party. So did most people in those areas most deeply involved in the commercial economy—farmers who grew cash crops, miners, manufacturers and their workers, artisans, merchants, and tradesmen. In such areas, the Whig promise to promote economic development and restore prosperity through the expansion of banking credit, government subsidies, and economic diversification drew the majority of voters.

In contrast, Democrats received support from the groups most impervious to such promises and most likely to think that Whig programs would create a privileged aristocracy, with enough economic and political power to reduce men to slavery. Throughout the nation, Democratic voting strength was concentrated among subsistence farmers in the most remote and economically underdeveloped regions of states—among voters, that is, who feared becoming ensnared in precisely the kind of commercial-monetary network Whigs wanted to foster. In addition, Democrats drew votes heavily from immigrants, Catholics, and others who resented the self-righteous moral imperialism of the dominant Protestant groups they associated with the Whigs. Ethnic and religious tensions, indeed, sometimes offset the general economic pattern of partisan support. Not just poor Irish newcomers but also long-settled and relatively prosperous Dutch and German farmers in New York and Pennsylvania responded to Democratic charges that Whigs would arrogantly crush freedom in order to impose the religious and social values of dominant ethnic and religious groups on cultural minorities.[52]

There were other exceptions to this demarcation of partisan constituencies. Some voters in market-oriented areas, for example, had clearly been victimized by commercialization, and they retaliated against harmful economic changes by voting Democratic. Nonetheless, each party recruited primarily from pools of potential voters that had different degrees of involvement in and different attitudes toward the market economy, toward the cultural values of the emerging Protestant middle class the market economy spawned, and especially toward promotion of that economy by active governmental intervention. That distinction unravels the complicated relationship among changing economic conditions, the parties' contrasting responses to those conditions, and the variation in election results. The alternating pattern of voter mobilization caused the variation over time in the parties' fortunes because new voters turned out from Whig and Democratic constituencies at different rates during different economic conditions.

Financial turmoil, not low productivity, caused the depressions of the late 1830s. The credit crunch and plunging prices more clearly menaced Whig market-oriented areas than the economically peripheral areas of subsistence farming where Democrats were strongest. Whigs triumphed in the panic period of 1837–38 because they won so many new votes in the areas most crippled by bank suspensions and reduced government expenditures. During the recovery of 1838–39, in turn, Whigs retained the voters they had gained because those voters were pleased with Whig efforts to expand currency and promote growth.

Nonetheless, Whigs won fewer offices during the recovery for two reasons. First, other potential supporters from market-oriented areas saw no need to vote, for the Whig program seemed less necessary during good times than during hard times. Second, Democrats mobilized tens of thousands of new voters from economically underdeveloped regions where men were less concerned about the possible economic consequences of Democratic policies than they were attracted by the Democrats' crusade against debt, high taxes, privilege, and the Money Power.[53] Put differently, potential Democrats did not turn out in unusually large numbers during the panic because they were largely unaffected by it. Nor did economic recovery itself bring them out; the recovery coincided with, but did not cause, the growth of the Democratic vote. New Democratic voters responded instead to the programs Whigs had tried to enact in state legislatures in 1838. For the first time in many states, that is, Whigs' actions provided concrete evidence for Democratic charges against them, just as Pennsylvania Whigs' charter for the Bank of the United States had rejuvenated Democrats there in 1836.

The second wave of bank suspensions and price declines at the end of 1839, in turn, caused another surge of new voters toward the Whigs in market-oriented areas that outpaced the gains Democrats had made elsewhere. Hard times gave new salience to the Whig program. They also intensified popular opposition in market-oriented areas to laws Democrats had enacted. Both state legislation threatening banks and the Independent Treasury Act that Democrats passed in July 1840 were deemed more likely to harm than to help the economy.

This argument that different kinds of new voters responded to party records at different rates under different economic conditions fully accords with the results of longitudinal time-series analyses of contemporary voting behavior by political scientists.[54] It is further supported by additional literary and quantitative evidence from the 1830s. Developments in Tennessee provide a good example. In 1837, the Whigs won the gubernatorial election with an even larger percentage of the vote than favorite son Hugh Lawson White had rolled up in the presidential election of 1836. Both parties gained votes over 1836, but the Whigs gained more: 19,000 compared to 10,000 by the Democrats. Then, in 1839, in an election with an unprecedented turnout, Democrat James K. Polk, after stumping the state denouncing the Whigs as aristocrats and praising hard money, captured the governorship. The Whigs lost about 4,000 votes between 1837 and 1839, but their 1839 total was still considerably larger than in 1836. Polk won because he polled 18,000 more votes than had the Democratic candidate in 1837, not because the Whigs lost votes. To explain where the additional Democratic vote came from, a Whig paper in Memphis argued, "They are the men from the deep gorges of the hills and mountains, and by the sides of the creeks, in the far-off corners of the counties—who take no newspapers and come not into the towns." The closest student of that election agrees with this analysis. Democratic strength in 1839 was concentrated in the least prosperous, most remote regions of the state, whereas Whigs were strongest in the most prosperous counties, areas within the commercial orbit of the state's major trading centers like Knoxville, Nashville, and Memphis.[55]

Extant quantitative data point to the same conclusion. The lack of annual county-level economic data and the spottiness of election returns by county for state and congressional elections prevent a year-by-year analysis of voter mobilization by type of constituency for the late 1830s. But Professor James Roger Sharp has computed indexes of the relative economic status of counties in 1840 for three states—Mississippi, Ohio, and Virginia—and the presidential returns for those counties are readily available.[56] Comparison of the relative gains made by Whigs and Democrats between the presidential elections of 1836 and 1840 in rich and poor counties produces intriguing results.

Perhaps no state had such a sharp class basis in its voting alignment as Mississippi. In 1836 the Democrats carried 70 percent of the vote in the state's fifteen poorest counties, whereas the Whigs carried 60 percent of the vote in its fifteen most prosperous counties. More to the point, between 1836 and 1840 the Democrats outgained the Whigs by a margin of 2,344 to 1,907 in the fifteen poorest counties, while the Whigs outgained the Democrats 2,774 to 989 in the fifteen wealthiest counties. Put another way, in the poorest counties Democrats won 55.1 percent of the new voters, while in the richest counties Whigs secured 74 percent of them. The pattern in Ohio was less clear-cut. There, too, the Whigs outgained the Democrats 8,414 (71 percent) to 3,474 (29 percent) in the fifteen wealthiest counties, but in the poorest fifteen counties they almost matched the Democratic gain, 6,283 to 6,325.

Virginia is the most ambiguous case, largely because many wealthy planting counties in the tidewater and piedmont areas were Democratic, while Whigs gained support in poor western counties that wanted internal improvements. Again, Whigs outpaced Democrats among new voters in the fifteen wealthiest counties 1,296 (56 percent) to 1,023 (44 percent), but the Whigs also outgained the Democrats in the fifteen poorest counties, nine of which were in the present state of West Virginia. Far more new voters, indeed, came out in the poorest counties than in the wealthiest. Whigs captured 4,428 (57 percent) of those new voters compared to 3,352 (43 percent) for the Democrats.

If one divides all the counties in each state into three groups ranked according to wealth in 1840 and assumes that wealth indicates the degree of involvement in the market economy, it is possible to determine what proportion of the total statewide increase in the two parties' votes between 1836 and 1840 came from different kinds of constituencies (Table 7). The absolute figures show that, except for Mississippi's poorest counties, Whigs outgained Democrats in every kind of constituency, in part, no doubt, because of Whigs' theatrical 1840 presidential campaign. Nevertheless, Whigs drew proportionately more of their new vote from wealthy counties and Democrats more from the poorest counties in Ohio and Mississippi. In Virginia the distribution of each party's gain among different economic constituencies was almost exactly the same.

At first glance, the Virginia results confound any theory that Whigs drew additional voters disproportionately from wealthy constituencies, whereas

Table 7

Share of New Voters, 1836–1840, Drawn from Counties
of Varying Economic Status in Mississippi, Ohio,
and Virginia[a]

	Democratic Gain	Whig Gain
	Mississippi (N = 53)	
Wealthiest third	1,424 (21.2%)	3,363 (34.9%)
Middle third	2,385 (35.5%)	3,529 (36.4%)
Poorest third	2,907 (43.3%)	2,803 (28.7%)
	Ohio (N = 71)	
Wealthiest third	5,789 (21.6%)	12,611 (29.8%)
Middle third	10,548 (39.3%)	18,342 (43.4%)
Poorest third	10,485 (39.1%)	11,281 (26.7%)
	Virginia (N = 110)	
Wealthiest third	3,291 (24.4%)	4,703 (24.4%)
Middle third	4,375 (32.4%)	6,597 (34.2%)
Poorest third	5,828 (43.2%)	7,976 (41.4%)

[a]The counties are grouped according to their economic ranking in Appendix A of Sharp, *The Jacksonians versus the Banks: Politics in the States after the Panic of 1837*, pp. 334–42. The increase in vote is measured from the returns in the presidential elections of 1836 and 1840 in Burnham, *Presidential Ballots, 1836–1892*.

Democrats added voters primarily in the poorest regions. Clearly, the Whig campaign in 1840 was efficacious throughout the Old Dominion in attracting recruits. Yet, closer inspection reveals that the Whig party was measurably more successful in relatively prosperous, commercially oriented counties than in isolated, poorer ones even if the data do not permit one to locate different economic regions or constituencies within individual counties.

Seventeen of the thirty-six counties included in the poorest third of Virginia's counties were located in the present state of West Virginia, while only one of the most prosperous thirty-six was found there. West Virginia counties were almost uniformly poor compared with the rest of the state, but if they are ranked only with each other, a predictable pattern appears. In the eight wealthiest among that group of seventeen, Whigs outpaced Democrats among new voters by a 2 to 1 margin, 1,860 to 924. In the remaining nine, the Whigs drew only 51 percent of the new voters, 2,816 to 2,704.

Whigs enjoyed their greatest success among new voters in the western Virginia counties bordering the Ohio River or in the Kanawha River Valley, areas that wanted to develop commercially and that were attracted to the Whig economic program. In Ohio County, which included Wheeling, for example, the Whigs gained 386 new votes between 1836 and 1840, while the Democrats gained only 48. In Kanawha County, Whigs increased their vote by 330, the Democrats by only 96. In Cabell County, located on the Ohio River in the state's extreme western corner and the only western Virginia county among the wealthiest thirty-six, the Whigs outpaced the Democrats 289 to 230 among new voters. That county, like Kanawha and some others, moreover, was large enough geographically to indicate that Whigs gained in the areas along the river, while Democrats attracted votes in remote areas outside the commercial economy. Even in Virginia, therefore, as in Mississippi, Ohio, Tennessee, and other states, the rival parties tended to draw their new voters from different economic constituencies.[57]

In sum, the contrasting party platforms not only attracted different kinds of people, but they also had more salience for new voters under different economic conditions. During periods of economic decline, the Whigs won because they drew out additional supporters in commercial areas most affected by the depression, and they tended to hold them during recovery. They did not increase their vote at the same rate during recovery, however, for new voters in those areas were more likely to respond to hard times than to prosperity. Instead, during periods of prosperity, Democrats usually won, not because Whigs lost votes in commercial areas, but because Democrats mobilized new voters in their strongholds by condemning the newly articulated and often newly enacted Whig programs as a menace to equal rights. Where Whigs continued to win during the recovery, as in New York in 1838 or in Virginia in 1839, it may have been because the prominence of conservative probusiness Democrats in those states' parties prevented them from maximizing their appeal to Democratic constituencies. In New York, Democratic Governor Marcy had signed into law the canal bond issue and the Free Banking Act on which Whigs campaigned, and prominent Conservative Democratic leaders were urging Democrats to support Whigs. In any event, once Democrats acted upon their antibanking, antibusiness animus in those states that they captured during the recovery, those programs turned still more new voters in commercial areas against them when the economy slumped again in 1840. For voters intimately connected with the commercial economy, Whigs rather than Democrats had the proper prescription to bring about economic recovery.

VI

The surge of new voters to the Whigs generated by the divergent party responses to economic conditions in the late 1830s brought them to power in a number of states, greatly increased their strength in Congress, and ensured that the Whig party would survive. Just as the Whig party had planted its strongest roots between the spring of 1834 and the spring of 1837 in states where it took distinct positions on concrete policies, its strength soared after the Panic of 1837 precisely because economic conditions forced the rival parties to take divergent policy positions almost everywhere and made those positions extraordinarily salient to voters who looked to government to advance or retard the growth of the market economy. A sharp contrast with Democrats on measures, not just men, was the nutrient that brought the Whig party to maturity.

The trends established in state and congressional elections between 1837 and 1840 almost ensured the Whigs' triumph in the presidential election of 1840. The party had gained enormous strength during the economic slump of 1837–38 and retained most of it during the recovery of 1838–39. The second wave of bank suspensions and falling prices that began at the end of 1839 obviously spurred another dramatic upswing in Whig fortunes in the spring and summer of 1840 that augured victory in November of that year (see Tables 5 and 6).[58] Equally important, on votes in state legislatures and Congress and in the campaigns that sought consciously to educate voters about the policy differences separating the parties, Whigs and Democrats established records that indelibly etched their contrasting approaches to the economy. Voters had to know generally what policies to expect should one party or the other win the presidential election. Hard times and the Whigs' prescription for ending them, not hard cider, would put a Whig in the White House.

Whig politicians who considered the party's prospects for that presidential race did not enjoy the advantage of such hindsight. Appalled by Van Buren's policies and disgusted with the prolonged Democratic control of the national government, they were determined to win the presidency at all costs in 1840. They could see that the Conservative Democratic revolt against Van Buren and the defection of Calhoun and his most ardent southern followers to the Democrats created both exciting opportunities and difficult challenges. They could also see, from the results during the recovery, that they could lose office just as rapidly as they gained it. To the Whig politicians who gathered in Harrisburg, Pennsylvania, to nominate a presidential candidate in December 1839, in short, the future seemed at once hopeful and uncertain. In addition to other reasons, that uncertainty would frustrate once again the ambitions of the party's foremost national leader, Henry Clay. Instead, the party selected a different standard bearer whose nomination almost inadvertently launched the party into a different kind of campaign than they would have or could have run for the Kentuckian.

The decision to bypass Clay proved one of the most fateful in this nation's history. Had Whig leaders known in December 1839 what would happen to the economy and Whig electoral fortunes during the spring and summer of 1840, or had the Whigs postponed their convention until the following May when the Democrats met, Clay would have undoubtedly been nominated. Had Clay been nominated, he most certainly would have been elected, for 1840 was the Whigs' year. Sadly for Henry Clay, for the Whig party, and especially for the American people, who would soon be launched on the road to Civil War, it was not to be.

Chapter 5

"Harrison and Prosperity or Van Buren and Ruin"

AFTER THE WHIGS' first national convention in December 1839, Henry Clay reportedly exclaimed, "I am the most unfortunate man in the history of parties: always run by my friends when sure to be defeated, and now betrayed for a nomination when I, or any one, would be sure of an election." This lament is probably as apocryphal as Clay's supposed assertion that "I had rather be right than be President," although it surely reflects his sentiments more accurately.[1] Historians often cite them to illustrate Clay's undeniable and understandable personal frustration and Americans' failure between the administrations of Jackson and Abraham Lincoln to elevate great statesmen like Clay, Webster, or Calhoun to the presidency. Instead the parties nominated "available" men—politicians and especially nonpoliticians without stature, experience, or past records and the enemies such records produced.

The Whigs' choice of General William Henry Harrison instead of Clay at Harrisburg has made them seem particularly opportunistic. Whigs, indeed, nominated military heroes rather than civilian leaders in four of the five presidential campaigns they contested, including the only two times they won. That record has led to the illusion that the Whig party was a natural loser, triumphing only when it evaded issues and clung to the coattails of figurehead leaders who had popularity beyond the boundaries of the Whigs' normal voting constituency.

The Whig victory in 1840 is, accordingly, usually attributed to the legendary "Log Cabin–Hard Cider" campaign the party ran in Harrison's behalf. According to this view, hungry Whig politicos nominated the ostensibly apolitical general rather than the prominent Senate leader because they believed that only Harrison could triumph. Then, carefully avoiding issues, they lubricated voters with hard cider and other strong drink; stirred them with ingenious slogans, songs, and symbols rather than hard analysis of programmatic alternatives; and roused them to a frenzy through the brilliant imitation of Jacksonian techniques like parades, mass rallies, and log cabin raisings. Excited, dazzled, and a bit befuddled, voters then poured out in record numbers to sweep Harrison into office. As one historian summarized this interpretation, "Issues counted for little in the 1840 campaign."[2]

Whigs did demonstrate real genius in generating enthusiasm for Harrison, but they deployed far more than hoopla. The overemphasis on ballyhoo during the presidential race ignores the party's equally impressive performance in the state and congressional elections of 1840 that often preceded the presidential poll and that cannot be explained by a coattails' effect. The exclusive focus on parades and carping that Whigs eschewed a national platform in 1840 also belittles the importance of issues in the election, both what was said during the campaign and, more important, the concrete records and programmatic alternatives the parties had created in state legislatures and Congress since 1837. Whigs, in fact, more often avoided specific issues and relied on the popularity of their presidential candidate in the election of 1836, which they lost, than in the election of 1840, which they won.

Worst of all, the traditional interpretation of the 1840 election ignores the political patterns in state and congressional elections since 1836. Those fights over contrasting party responses to economic conditions had brought out many of the new voters who contributed to the record turnout of 1840, and they clearly pointed to a Whig victory in the presidential election once the economy plunged again at the end of 1839. Despite his congenital overoptimism about his own prospects, Clay's prescient assertion in December 1839 that he or anyone else could be elected by the Whigs was, for once, emphatically right.

What is most extraordinary about Clay's statement is not its accuracy but its timing. In December 1839, most Whigs could not foresee what would happen to the economy and to Whig fortunes in 1840. For a variety of reasons, the men who made the decision at Harrisburg, or at least the majority of them, did not believe Clay could win, and they turned opportunistically to a more available candidate. Yet Harrison's purported assets as a standard bearer do not explain his November victory. The inverse relation between economic conditions and the Whigs' political fortunes played the major role in both Harrison's nomination and his subsequent election.

I

The long and bitter scramble for the Whig presidential nomination began almost as soon as the canvass of 1836 ended, and it intensified as the fortunes of potential nominees rose and fell with the fluctuating results of off-year elections. The scent of victory exacerbated rivalries among the aspirants that would have important ramifications for the victorious party. Yet conflicting personal ambitions alone did not shape the race for the nomination. Sectional rivalries growing out of the abolitionist and Texas issues, the machinations of influential state leaders, and especially the decision to hold the national convention in December 1839 also shaped the outcome. Had the convention assembled at an earlier or a later date, its results might have been very different.

From the start, Whigs' central choice lay between nominating a prominent Whig congressional leader, who could rally the party's stalwarts, or a standard bearer not identified with Whig programs, who had appeal to Democrats and new voters. Those of the latter disposition initially leaned almost unanimously toward

Harrison, the party's leading vote getter in 1836, while those who preferred the former divided their support between the Senate giants Webster and Clay.

To many Whigs at the beginning of 1837, running Harrison again seemed the necessary route to success. The shrewd upstate leaders of New York's Whig party, William Henry Seward and Thurlow Weed, believed that Harrison might have won even in 1836 had the party exerted more effort. Two weeks after the polls closed, Seward advised Weed that New York's Whigs must manifest "new zeal for the Hero of Tippecanoe as a candidate by continuation." Weed emphatically agreed that it was "utter folly" for Webster to run and that Harrison "is our man—our only man." Harrison also remained popular among Pennsylvania's Antimasonic Whigs and in Ohio and Indiana. Ohio's Whigs, indeed, formally nominated him for president at their state convention in July 1837, and they repeated that endorsement in May 1838.[3]

Harrison himself continued his quest for the presidency. However ambiguous his stand on issues, he was hardly apolitical. Aided by an able lieutenant in Colonel Charles Todd, Harrison assiduously sought support among other veterans of the Indian wars in which he had won fame, as well as among the numerous militia companies scattered around the country, just as Jackson had done in the 1820s. Pointing to that popularity, Harrison and Todd then corresponded widely with politicos to advertise the general's availability.

Just as in 1835, however, Whig regulars resisted Harrison's pretensions. The upturn in the party's electoral fortunes in the summer and fall of 1837, they believed, demonstrated that the depression was making all the converts Whigs needed and that the party could win in 1840 behind one of its two orthodox statesmen, Clay or Webster.

Even before the outbreak of the panic in May 1837, Webster, who had so stridently protested the party's recourse to irregulars like Harrison and White in 1836 and who had forlornly remained in the race until its bitter end, laid plans for seizing the plum in 1840. Recognizing his palpable weakness in the South and his subordinate position to Clay in the Senate, he utilized his connections with wealthy businessmen in Boston and New York City and his oratorical skills to challenge Harrison in the North. His strategy was three-pronged. He would engineer a nomination by the Whigs in New York City, where his wealthy friends controlled newspapers and the local organization. Then he would use that endorsement to create a bandwagon effect in the rest of the state. Simultaneously, he would make a speaking tour of Harrison's stronghold, the Midwest, in order to demonstrate his popularity outside the Northeast.

Just as he had attempted to use the Nullification crisis in 1833 to rally the North in his behalf, Webster intended to arouse northern sentiments against the South in order to wrest the nomination from Harrison in 1840. The Republic of Texas' pending application for annexation provided his new vehicle. Annexation, which Texans had requested almost as soon as they established the Republic in 1836, could plunge the United States into a war with Mexico, which refused to recognize Texas' independence. Annexation would also mean the acquisition of additional slave territory, for slavery was legal in Texas. In March 1837, Webster powerfully addressed 6,000 cheering partisans in New York City, pledging eternal resistance to "anything that shall extend the slavery of the African race on this continent." The following October he repeated his staunch opposition in a major Senate speech. Webster's implication was clear: northern Whigs could trust no Southerner like Clay or the Virginia-born Harrison, who was mum on the issues. Northern Whigs needed a presidential candidate who forthrightly championed northern interests and values.[4]

Webster probably planned to repeat this theme during his speaking tour of the Midwest, which began in May, but his journey coincided with the arrival of the panic. Hence, Webster changed tack. To enthusiastic throngs in city after city he lambasted the Democratic hard-money policies that, he asserted, had destroyed the credit system on which the prosperity of ordinary Americans depended.

Despite his rhetorical success in the West, Webster failed to make early headway toward the nomination. Harrison's advocates remained unmoved. Ohio's nomination of Harrison in July 1837 symbolized Webster's inability to penetrate Old Tip's fortress, and even before that the movement of his friends in New York had fizzled. That failure stemmed, in part, from the hostility of upstate leaders like Seward and Weed, who continued to consider Webster's Federalist background and his intimacy with Nicholas Biddle's Bank of the United States as fatal liabilities. Within New York City itself, Webster's friends were checked by the partisans of Clay, whose star ascended rapidly once the panic broke. By threatening to repudiate the action of a public meeting called by Webster's friends in June, they forced them to settle for a recommendation, rather than a formal nomination, of Webster and to issue a call to other Whigs to agree that the party's nominee should be chosen by a national convention.[5]

For a number of reasons in the summer of 1837, many Whigs concluded that a national nominating convention should name the party's candidate. The Ohio convention that nominated Harrison in July urged that a national gathering be held in Pittsburgh in May 1838 to select the ticket. Clay endorsed the idea of a convention in a public letter to his New York City supporters in August. Various Whig leaders, however, quickly decided that May 1838 was far too early for a convention. Friends of each aspirant, fearing that the other might get an early advantage, wanted to forestall the decision. Perceptive Whig leaders also wanted to prevent the emerging asperities from dividing the party and damaging it in the important off-year elections of 1837, 1838, and 1839. If one candidate or another clinched the nomination early, the dejected supporters of the others might not work hard enough in state and congressional campaigns. State leaders like Weed did not want to carry the burden of unpopular national leaders during state elections when Whig prospects seemed so bright.

Despite disagreements over the best date, most Whigs deemed a convention imperative. A national convention seemed the best way to concentrate the party behind a single candidate rather than to repeat the multiple-candidate debacle of 1836. Still, not all Whigs embraced the idea with equal enthusiasm. Clay dutifully recommended it to his New York followers in August 1837, but he had little choice since they had used the demand for a convention to block Webster's early efforts. Aware that many Whigs, especially in the South, had vehemently denounced conventions as instruments of party dictation in 1836, Clay worried, with good reason as it turned out, that his full strength might not be represented at a convention because southern Whigs might not send delegates. Harrison, for his part, feared that Clay, the archetypal party insider, could use his Whig congressional supporters to stack the convention. Clay's only "chance of success," he protested in the summer of 1838, was "a packed convention[,] one which will represent the politicians—not the people."[6]

By the time Harrison wrote that letter, however, a convention had already been decided upon. In December 1837, a caucus of congressional Whigs agreed to pressure their state parties to accept a call. Clay hoped for an early gathering, and in mid-April 1838 he confidently wrote his friend Francis Brooke that the convention would be called for some time in the first half of 1839. Later that month, however, the congressional Whigs decided instead on December 1839.[7] As Clay correctly understood, leaders in New York, Vermont, Pennsylvania, and Ohio wanted to postpone the nomination until after the state elections of 1839 so that they could continue to run on efficacious state issues without the burden of defending a presidential candidate.

But Webster also helped delay the convention. His chances had begun to fade almost as soon as the boomlet in New York City collapsed in June 1837. By the end of that year, Weed bluntly told Webster that Harrison was the strongest candidate for 1840. Webster informed at least one friend in February 1838 that he believed Harrison would get the nomination, but as in 1835 and 1836, he stubbornly refused to withdraw until the summer of 1839. Pride and the hope of some last-minute swing in his direction influenced Webster's course, but a jealous determination to stop Clay also motivated him. He had never forgiven Clay for supporting Harrison rather than himself in 1836. By staying in the race, he intended to prevent Clay from locking up the party regulars. For the same reason, Webster told his Massachusetts and New York followers to acquiesce in a convention only if it were held late in 1839. The later the convention, Webster believed, the more time he had to derail Clay.[8]

II

By the spring of 1838, Clay had clearly become the front-runner. In August 1837, he had reported disingenuously to a Louisville editor that "whatever may be my own inclinations or disposition, I shall again be forced into the Presidential arena." In October, his close colleague from Kentucky, Senator John J. Crittenden, wrote that "a vigorous & united effort for one more year must make us triumphant." A month later, Clay himself bragged, "I receive almost daily gratifying proofs of attachment and confidence from all quarters." Because of Whigs' spectacular victories in New York in 1837, "I now hope that I shall live to see the Goths expelled from the Capitol and competent men once more in the Administration of the Government."[9]

In April 1838, Clay gushed that "everything is going on as well as my most zealous friends could desire. Public opinion everywhere, even in Indiana and Ohio, is rapidly concentrating." An attempt to get Pennsylvania Whigs to endorse Harrison had fizzled, and even Ohio's Whigs, though still booming the general, agreed to abide by a convention decision. At the end of May, therefore, Clay cheered that "our Cause everywhere is making sure and certain progress; and that my *particular cause* could hardly be improved."[10]

The grounds for Clay's bravado in the spring of 1838, while seemingly firm enough, turned out to be very slippery. So long as the economy slumped and Whig fortunes rose, the stronger Clay looked, since his spirited Senate resistance to Van Buren's Independent Treasury scheme caused his stock to soar in commercial communities. The obverse of this formula was equally true, however. When the economy and the Democrats rebounded in 1838–39, Clay ceased to look like a winner.

Whatever the economic conditions, Clay retained an asset that could not be matched by either Harrison or Webster—southern support. As in 1836, southern Whigs wanted one of their own in the White House. Since Tennessee Senator Hugh Lawson White showed no inclination to run again, the slaveholder Clay appeared the potential heir. Webster's strident opposition to the acquisition of Texas accelerated southern Whigs' movement in Clay's direction. A Whig editor in North Carolina exclaimed that "Mr. Clay is the only one under [the] circumstances that the Whigs can expect to run with success. . . . Mr. Webster can never get the full Whig vote of the South. His late declarations concerning Texas (right enough perhaps in the abstract) will of themselves like Banquos [sic] ghost stare him in the face and shake their gory or rather *sable* locks at him throughout the contest."[11]

Yet even Clay's popularity in the South proved a two-edged sword, for his southern support was rather shaky and, in attempting to shore it up, he ran the risk of alienating northern Whigs. Alone among the candidates he had to balance the conflicting interests of northern and southern Whigs. Because of his prominence as Senate Whig leader, he could not easily dodge issues that threatened to exacerbate that conflict, especially issues involving slavery.

As early as October 1837, South Carolina's Whig Senator William C. Preston, who refused to follow Calhoun into the Democratic ranks, warned that while Clay remained the only man whom Whigs could elect president, serious obstacles blocked his path to the nomination. Not only were Harrison and Webster in the way, but "there is already a battery opened against him in the South."[12] Although Clay's ownership of slaves made him seem the natural legatee of White's southern support, southern Whigs with state rights views had long mistrusted his nationalism; Clay's American System violated their sense of constitutional propriety and sectional interest.

Satisfying Southerners without alienating northern Whigs in regard to economic policy proved relatively easy. Like Northerners, southern Whigs enthusiastically followed Clay's lead in denouncing and voting against the Independent Treasury bill and Democratic hard-money proposals in order to protect the banking and credit systems. Many southern and some northern Whigs, however, wanted no part of a new national bank, which Clay considered a necessity. Still, in a Senate speech in May 1838, Clay noted that chartering a bank would be inexpedient until public opinion demanded it; and in the fall of that year, he privately conceded that no demand existed. In 1839, in a letter to the state rights ideologue Beverley Tucker, Clay virtually abandoned the rest of his American System. The tariff of 1833, despite its impending reductions, finally settled that issue, he averred, and he no longer saw a need for federal internal improvements. The distribution of federal land revenues sufficed, for the states had made great strides.[13]

The explosive slavery issue posed more problems, for John C. Calhoun and his followers sought an explicit proslavery, prosouthern resolution of that issue from Congress. If Clay condoned any such solution, he realized, he would alienate abolitionists in key northern states like Ohio, New York, and Massachusetts. Worse, he might antagonize the far more numerous northern Whigs who deplored the abolitionists as dangerous agitators but who would brook no political concessions to the South on the issues involving slavery. Yet Clay also knew that he could not desert his southern base on this issue since, as Preston had warned in October 1837, Calhoun and his friends would discredit his credentials as faithful tribune of the South.

Calhoun rejoined the Democratic party in the fall of 1837 in part because he believed that both Harrison and Webster were antislavery. Furthermore, he fumed, "abolitionists, consolidationists, [and] colonizationists" would control the Whig national convention. By "colonizationists," Calhoun meant members of the American Colonization Society like Henry Clay, who would send free blacks to Africa to induce Southerners to manumit their slaves. The soundest friends of slavery, Calhoun believed, were in the Democratic party, and therefore he returned to it with the hope of controlling it.[14]

Yet Calhoun gave the Democratic party little more fealty than he had given the Whigs. In his attitude toward political parties and toward the slavery issue, the South Carolinian was a political wild card who did not match the dominant suit in either party's hand. Most southern politicians believed that the South could best protect slavery through the party system itself. They sought to mute the issue, to convince northern party allies that party unity necessitated removing slavery from the national political arena. They willingly jousted with each other at home as to which party better defended Southern Rights, but in Congress they wanted to bury all discussion of slavery. On both counts Calhoun vehemently disagreed. He did not think that political parties could protect the South or slavery. The clash of the two parties, he thought, only divided the South. Furthermore, instead of avoiding the slavery issue in Congress, Calhoun insisted that the South must confront the North with demands and force Yankee concessions. Precisely that strategy posed Clay's problem.[15]

Determined to "carry the war into the non-slave holding states," Calhoun on December 27, 1837, introduced six resolutions broadly defending Southern Rights and pressed for their passage. The first two restated Calhoun's familiar argument that the nation was a compact of states and that states had jurisdiction over their own domestic institutions—that is, slavery. Both quickly passed. But the other resolutions insisted that the national government must give "increased stability and security to the domestic institutions of the states," that any interference with slavery in the District of Columbia or in federal territories was "a direct and dangerous attack on the institutions of all the slaveholding States," and that any refusal to annex new slave territory discriminated unconstitutionally against the South.[16]

In response, Clay charged that Calhoun's inflammatory resolutions, especially the demand for Texas' annexation, would only strengthen the abolitionist movement and thereby endanger the Union. His counterresolutions concurred that Congress had no jurisdiction over slavery within the states, that Congress should immediately reject any petitions calling for its abolition there, that abolitionist activities endangered the Union, and that no attempt should be made to abolish slavery in the District or in federal territories like Florida. At the same time, however, Clay firmly upheld the right to petition Congress for abolition in areas over which Congress had jurisdiction. He also asserted that Congress had no power to interfere with the interstate slave trade. Most important, his resolutions said nothing about annexing Texas or any other slave territory.

Although Clay failed to substitute all of his resolutions for Calhoun's, he managed, with support from northern Democrats like James Buchanan, to modify Calhoun's most inflammatory statements. The Senate ultimately resolved that Congress should not interfere with, rather than work to increase, the stability and security of the states' domestic institutions; denounced abolitionist activities as a threat to the Union, not as an attack on the South; and eliminated any mention of Texas' annexation. To separate himself still further from Calhoun, Clay stridently denounced him as a Nullifier during a major speech in February 1838.[17]

By the spring of 1838 Clay believed that he had neutralized the slavery issue. He regarded Calhoun's resolutions as a trap to discredit him in either the North or the South, and he rejoiced that he had escaped it. By defending the right of petition and burying the obnoxious Texas resolution, he thought he could appease most northern Whigs. Yet by denouncing the abolitionists, he appealed to the South. And by attacking Calhoun as a Nullifier, he ingratiated himself with southern state rights Whigs like Mangum who had long considered Nullification folly and Calhoun a traitor for his defection to the Democrats.[18]

Hence, even during the debates on Calhoun's resolutions in January 1838, Clay privately exulted that he was losing "nothing neither at the South nor at the North."[19] Later, after Van Buren spurned the overtures from Texas for annexation in order to preserve the intersectional harmony of his own party, Clay rejoiced "that the ridiculous charge against me of being an Abolitionist propagated by the Calhoun school, can deceive nobody."[20] The Kentuckian had in fact managed to satisfy most southern Whigs about his proslavery pedigree by the summer of 1838. Despite the sniping from Calhoun and other Democrats, southern members of his party still favored him.

III

Nonetheless, Clay correctly realized that he was a long way from securing the nomination. Newspaper endorsements meant little. He needed delegate commitments. The South was for him, but he constantly worried that southern states might not attend the convention and he constantly urged his friends to ensure that they did.[21] The real problem, however, lay in the North. Without some northern support at the convention, he could not obtain a majority.

As early as August 1837 Clay had informed his New York supporters that they should promptly press for commitments to him, but by the summer of 1838 the results had been disappointing. Whigs in the Kentucky legislature had formally nominated him in January, and Rhode Island and Maryland had soon followed suit. There things had stalled. Clay had support in Illinois, Indiana, and Ohio, but only the last had made any official nomination and it had gone to

Harrison. Philadelphia's Whigs boomed him, but the more numerous Antimasonic branch of the Pennsylvania Whig party, led by Thaddeus Stevens and Governor Joseph Ritner, won an overwhelming endorsement for Harrison from the state convention that renominated Ritner for governor in March 1838. Prospects in New York seemed just as uncertain. Clay had friends throughout the state, but Webster's allies checked him in New York City and Seward and Weed stalled upstate, fearing that neither Antimasons nor abolitionists would support him. In most of New England, Webster's partisans blocked the Kentuckian.[22]

Clay moved on several fronts in the spring and summer of 1838 to enhance his northern prospects. In the Senate, he sought to take advantage of resentment toward the British along the Canadian border. Rebellion had broken out in Upper Canada against British authorities in late 1837, and Americans along the frontier generally sympathized with the rebels. After being easily routed by British authorities, many rebels fled to the United States, where they tried to raise men and arms to continue the revolt. In response, on December 29, 1837, a British raiding party seized the *Caroline*, an American ship that had been used to run arms to the rebels, on the New York side of the Niagara River. They killed an American on board, set the ship afire, and sent it over the falls. Headstrong Americans in the area demanded revenge, and President Van Buren dispatched General Winfield Scott to keep the peace. Throughout much of 1838, Scott toured the border regions trying to calm Americans down and preserve neutrality. At the same time, his majestic uniformed presence reassured them that the national government would protect them from further assaults. While these commotions stirred the border west of Vermont, Canadian authorities from New Brunswick clashed with the Maine militia over possession of the Aroostook River Valley in the northern part of that state, and eventually Scott was again dispatched to settle the matter peacefully.[23]

Clay saw no serious possibility of war with England, but he saw a chance to score points in the upper North. He made several bellicose Senate speeches defending Maine's right to all the territory it claimed and announcing that if war should occur with England, "it would be a just war, and he would be ready to meet it." As Clay would eventually learn to his dismay, however, the general on the scene, Scott, and not the defiant Senate orator would earn the most political credit from these clashes along the Canadian border.[24]

Clay's covert efforts to advance his cause proved equally futile. Recognizing that New York was crucial, he urged his friends in New York City to arrange a public meeting to endorse him in May 1838. Because of the antagonism of Weed and Seward upstate and Webster's supporters in the city, however, this effort proved stillborn. In June, Clay approached Webster personally and vainly urged him to withdraw. Next, Clay turned to his primary Massachusetts backers like Harrison Gray Otis, Boston's former mayor, and Abbott Lawrence, the wealthy textile manufacturer, urging them to persuade Webster to bow out. They also failed. Spitefully, Webster remained in the race to squelch Clay.[25]

By the end of the summer, Clay's stalled drive for the nomination began to unravel. In September the Boston *Atlas*, thitherto a major Webster paper, withdrew Webster's name from its masthead. Instead of swinging to Clay, however, it charged that Clay was the "darling of aristocratic Whigs, *not the choice* of the democracy of the Whig party." Massachusetts must support Harrison, the *Atlas* insisted. If she could not have her favorite son, she should aid a candidate who was "in truth available."[26] By the end of the year, Otis informed Clay that he could only hope to be named the Bay State's second choice when the Whig legislative caucus endorsed a candidate the following February. Webster, he admitted, remained the state's first choice.[27]

The *Atlas*'s switch to Harrison especially stung because, by the fall of 1838, Whigs elsewhere were also pressing for a more "available" candidate. With the economy recovering between August and the end of the year, Whigs lost control of governorships, state legislatures, and congressional delegations they had won during previous elections in Alabama, Illinois, Maine, Maryland, New Jersey, Ohio, Pennsylvania, and Delaware. True, they captured the governorship of New York and retained offices in North Carolina, Mississippi, and Massachusetts, but their losses raised considerable doubt that a Whig like Clay, the party's preeminent congressional leader, could win.

Once again, the party seemed to need a candidate who could attract Democratic converts. Instead, Clay seemed more likely to deter defections and rally Democrats behind Van Buren. As one Harrison supporter in Pennsylvania told Nicholas Biddle in February 1839, Clay's "long and brilliant career in public life while it furnishes much to admire is fruitful of topics upon which he is vulnerable to the prejudices of the masses."[28]

Almost simultaneously, Harrison's attractiveness to non-Whigs seemed to be reaffirmed when a purported national Antimasonic convention nominated Harrison for president and Webster for vice president on a separate ticket in November 1838. The numbers at that gathering in Philadelphia were small, but its impact on the Keystone State was great. Ritner's defeat for governor in 1838 convinced the Antimasonic members of Pennsylvania's Whig coalition that Harrison offered the only hope of recapturing the state.[29]

Identified far more closely than Harrison with the fortunes of the Whig party as a whole, Clay himself regarded his prospects as desperate by November 1838. The recent elections, he glumly confessed, had been "very unfavorable" to his cause. Deeply discouraged, Clay even contemplated withdrawing his hat from the ring.[30] Grasping at any straw, Clay hoped that recent Whig victories in New York and Virginia might still salvage his nomination if their legislatures endorsed him. Those two large states might convince delegates to the national convention that Clay could win in 1840. Clay viewed the two states as inextricably connected; a nomination from Virginia would, he believed, influence New York. In both states, moreover, an alliance with Conservative Democratic factions, led by his Senate friends Nathaniel P. Tallmadge and William C. Rives, could bolster pro-Clay Whigs. In the winter of 1838–39, therefore, Clay pressed for mergers with the Conservatives and legislative endorsements in both states.[31]

Clay's supporters in New York had begun the maneuver even before the state election in November. Aware that Weed's reservations about Clay's electability posed the biggest obstacle, they had aided the Albany editor's effort to secure the 1838 gubernatorial nomination for Seward instead of the Antimasonic favorite, and likely Harrison supporter, Francis Granger. The Clay men also joined Weed in pushing for an alliance with Tallmadge's Conservative Democrats and backing Tallmadge's reelection to the Senate after the election. Weed welcomed such support, but it hardly improved his opinion of Clay's chances in New York. Indeed, by alienating former Antimasonic Whig leaders from western New York like Granger and Millard Fillmore, who wanted the senatorial nomination for himself, Clay had only increased the enmity of Antimasons. By the end of 1838 Fillmore warned Weed that Seward must not become *"stuck in Clay."* In February 1839, he advised another supporter that the legislature must not nominate Clay, for only Harrison could win. Clay's attempt to capture New York from within had been blocked.[32]

Stymied in the Empire State, Clay pressed all the more feverishly in Virginia. If the Whigs in the Virginia legislature would nominate him, he wrote in December 1838, that "movement would probably be followed and seconded at Albany; and in that case, I think the question would be settled." Clay especially wished a Virginia endorsement to come from a combination of Whigs and Conservative Democrats. Such a merger would not only enhance the Whigs' chances in Virginia; it would also allow Clay's supporters in New York, like Tallmadge himself, to argue that Whigs must choose the candidate who commanded Conservative rather than Antimasonic backing.[33]

Clay worked frantically to facilitate a merger with Conservatives in Virginia by persuading the Virginia Whigs to support William C. Rives' reelection to the Senate in the winter of 1839. "Co-operation between the Whigs and Conservatives will secure a majority against the Administration," he wrote, and "without it the majority may be the other way." Rives held the key to that new majority. "It is manifest that, if we repel the advances of all the former members of the Jackson party to unite with us, under whatever name they may adopt, we must remain in a perpetual and hopeless minority."[34]

Clay's logic was unassailable, even if it flatly contradicted his response to the proposed candidacies of John McLean, Harrison, and Hugh Lawson White in 1835. But he and his friends could not sway die-hard state rights men, who hated Rives for supporting the Force Bill in 1833 and insisted on replacing him with John Tyler. As a result of Tyler's friends' intransigence, the deadlocked Virginia senatorial election had to be postponed to the following year, preventing the legislative endorsement for which Clay yearned.[35]

Clay then adopted a different and very dangerous tack to sway the Virginia legislature before it, and the New York assembly, adjourned. In February 1839, he delivered a blistering speech in the Senate in which he denounced the abolitionists as dangerous disunionists, defended slavery as a necessity, and denied federal power over slavery in the states, the territories, or the District of Columbia. Abolition, he warned, would destroy the nation, "and beneath the ruins of the Union would be buried, sooner or later, the liberty of both races." If Clay could not move Virginia's Whigs by cementing the merger with the Conservatives, he might by reemphasizing his proslavery pedigree.[36]

Clay's bold declarations virtually ensured the South's support for his candidacy, but they failed to secure Virginia soon enough. A state Whig convention would endorse him overwhelmingly in September and Virginians would support him resolutely at Harrisburg in December, but that was far too late to help him in New York. Its legislature, like Virginia's, adjourned without taking any action on the nomination.

As a last resort, Clay toured New York in the summer of 1839 while ostensibly on his way to vacation at the fashionable summer resort of Saratoga. Everywhere the crowds were large and friendly. Even a few abolitionists offered their support. His rearoused hopes were dashed, however, when he reached Saratoga in August. There Weed personally urged him to drop out of the race, for his former connections with the Bank of the United States, his alienation of the Antimasons, and the antagonism of most abolitionists caused by his speech in February all made him too heavy a load for New York Whigs to carry. New York's hard-headed politicos also saw Whig defeats in Indiana, Tennessee, and North Carolina in August 1839 as evidence that Clay was now unelectable. As one Whig who dined with Clay in Albany put it, "The honest truth is, that the recent elections show us that Mr. Clay" can rely on only two states, "Louisiana and Kentucky. . . . Between us, Mr. Clay is *dished* and in my opinion, he thinks so himself."[37]

But Clay, however "disappointed and depressed" by August's "calamitous" results, refused to withdraw from the race. He thought that the people of New York were for him, even if its Whig bosses were not, and that his withdrawal would damage the party irreparably in the South. He therefore determined to await the outcome of the Harrisburg convention.[38]

IV

Because of the reversal of Whig electoral fortunes that began in the fall of 1838 and continued throughout most of 1839, many Whigs looked to Harrison as the most available candidate. But to Weed and other New York leaders, those results had damaged Old Tip's credibility as much as Clay's. After all, Ohio's Whigs, having unanimously endorsed Harrison in both 1837 and 1838, lost state elections in both 1838 and 1839. Pennsylvania's Whig-Antimasonic convention had boomed him in March 1838, but the party had lost in the fall. And in Indiana, where Harrison was supposedly enormously popular, the Whigs suffered a devastating defeat in the congressional and legislative elections of August 1839.

Harrison, recognizing the potential damage of these defeats, moved astutely to separate himself from the party's losses and to reemphasize his popularity among non-Whig voters. His message was clear. The Whig party could no longer win on its issues, but Harrison could still win on personal charisma. In December, Harrison boasted of his support among military veterans, who had formerly enlisted behind Jackson, to Ohio Whig Congressman Joshua R. Giddings. Realizing that New York held the key to the nomination, his campaign manager, Charles Todd, told Governor Seward in February 1839 that Whigs must not "disregard the most available candidate," since "it is our common purpose to effect a redress of grievances by a change of rulers."[39]

This case for Harrison remained compelling to many northern Whigs when the party staggered from defeat to defeat in 1839. Indiana and Ohio stayed safely in his camp, and outside of Connecticut and Rhode Island, which leaned toward Clay, New England also seemed safe for Harrison, especially once Webster issued a public letter of withdrawal during the summer. Most important, though some Pennsylvania Whigs in June chose pro-Clay delegates to the national convention, Pennsylvania seemed secure because Antimasons headed by Charles B. Penrose, one of Thaddeus Stevens' lieutenants and the speaker of the state senate, arranged a September state convention that chose pro-Harrison delegates and declared that

Clay's nomination would fatally offend Antimasons and abolitionists. "No one but Harrison," it proclaimed, "could unite all elements of the party."[40]

New York's upstate leaders remained unconvinced. By the spring of 1839 they were turning to another general, Winfield Scott, who had won enormous popularity in the western part of the state for the way he had handled the border disputes with Canada. Constantly garbed in magnificent full-dress uniforms, laden with medals and trimmed with gold epaulets, the 6-foot 5-inch, 300-pound soldier had cut an imposing, if not quite dashing, figure as he proceeded along the border from Vermont to Michigan arguing that the neutrality laws must be observed. Already renowned in western New York as the Hero of Bridgewater for his exploits at the Battle of Lundy's Lane near the New York border during the War of 1812, Scott appeared to many New Yorkers a more certain winner than the Hero of Tippecanoe.

As one western New Yorker put the case, "Scott's name will bring out the hurra boys. The Whig party were broken down by the popularity and noncommittal character of old Jackson, and it is but fair to turn upon, and prostrate our opponents, with the weapons . . . with which they beat us." To win, "the General's lips must be hermetically sealed, and our shouts and hurras long and loud."[41]

Weed raised Scott's banner with alacrity, and from the summer of 1839 until December he worked to lock up convention support for Scott in New York and other northern states. Weed managed to secure thirty of New York's forty-two delegates for Scott; ten were for Clay and two for Harrison.[42] New Jersey, where Scott, a native of Virginia, now resided, took him as a favorite son; Michigan seemed disposed toward him; and Vermont too swung to the general who had calmed the strife on its borders. Weed also hoped to persuade Pennsylvania's warring factions to agree upon Scott as a compromise candidate, for both the Clay and Harrison conventions were sending rival delegations to the national conclave.

V

When the Whig party's first national convention opened in Harrisburg on December 4, 1839, in sum, what had begun as a three-way race between two regulars—Clay and Webster—and one outsider, Harrison, had become a three-way race between two "non-committal" generals and the party's leading congressional spokesman. By then, Clay's best hope seemed to be that Scott and Harrison might deadlock and that the party might turn to him as a compromise choice. He had solid support from the South, but portentously, all four states unrepresented at the convention were southern—Arkansas, Georgia, South Carolina, and Tennessee. Much of that support was discounted by the politicos at Harrisburg anyway, for in 1839 Whigs had lost elections in which Democrats had made Clay's potential candidacy an issue in Tennessee, North Carolina, Alabama, Georgia, and Mississippi. And the proslavery speeches Clay had made to win southern backing further alienated northern managers like Weed and Stevens.

Clay still had significant support in the North and had a plurality of the entire convention behind him. The delegations from Connecticut, Rhode Island, and Illinois as well as the border slave states of Delaware, Maryland, Kentucky, and

Missouri solidly favored the Kentuckian, and he had minority support in Ohio, New York, and Pennsylvania. With 128 of the 254 delegates necessary to win, Clay might still seize the prize if he could register the votes of his minorities in northern delegations.

But Whig losses in 1838 and 1839 and the subsequent conviction that victory required recruits from Democratic ranks made ambitious leaders like Weed and Stevens determined to stop Clay by neutralizing his plurality. To win in 1840, these leaders spurned a champion of Whig programs and sought instead a military hero with no preexisting political enemies who could broaden the base of the Whig electorate. Weed and Stevens cleared their first hurdle when the dispute between the rival Pennsylvania delegations was settled by deciding to have both represent the state. Since Stevens' pro-Harrison men outnumbered the pro-Clay delegates, the Harrison forces would control Pennsylvania. Then a Harrison delegate from Massachusetts, aided at a critical juncture by Stevens' Pennsylvania henchman, Charles Penrose, persuaded the convention to count the votes in a way that negated Clay's strength by concealing it. Instead of an open vote on the floor by the entire convention, balloting would be done in secret by a committee composed of three-man delegations from each state. Those men were instructed to poll their states and to report the preference of the majority as the vote of the entire delegation. Clay's minorities in the North would not be counted. Belatedly, Clay's floor managers recognized the danger, but after repeated efforts, they failed to reverse Penrose's insidious unit rule. The Southerners had been outmaneuvered by the savvy politicos from New York and Pennsylvania, an egregious lapse that later caused Clay to proclaim, "My friends are not worth the powder and shot it would take to kill them!"[43]

On the first ballot, Clay still led with 103 votes. All the Southerners, all the border states, and Illinois, Connecticut, and Rhode Island supported him. Harrison followed closely with ninety-one votes from Maine, New Hampshire, Massachusetts, Pennsylvania, Ohio, and Indiana. Scott trailed with fifty-seven: forty-two from New York, seven from Vermont, and eight from New Jersey. Michigan's two delegates on the scene were divided between Scott and Clay, and they awaited the arrival of the state's third delegate to break the deadlock.

Frantic secret negotiations ensued. Weed, who had honed his formidable persuasive skills in the lobby of the New York legislature, was a master at such bargaining. After several ballots he had convinced Connecticut to shift to Scott and picked up Michigan's three votes after the arrival of the tardy delegate. Then the count read Scott, sixty-eight; Clay, ninety-six; and Harrison, ninety-one. At this juncture the tall, affable editor with his abundant supply of cigars prepared to approach the delegates from the South, especially North Carolina and Virginia, where he knew of some Scott sentiment.

Thaddeus Stevens beat him to the punch. Wandering among the Virginia delegation in the convention hall, he ostentatiously dropped a letter on the floor that Scott had written to Francis Granger of New York. How Stevens obtained this letter is unknown, but it was dynamite. Scott's letter was a clumsy attempt to win antislavery support in New York, and it immediately had the effect Stevens hoped for. The Virginians stopped all talk of switching to Scott and made it clear that if they deserted Clay, they would swing to Harrison.

As soon as Weed realized that he could get no southern support for Scott, he swung the votes he commanded into the Harrison column to finish off Clay. On the final ballot, New York, Michigan, and Vermont deserted Scott for Harrison, and Illinois abandoned Clay for the same bandwagon. Harrison won the nomination with 148 votes; Clay had 90; and Scott was reduced to 16 from New Jersey and Connecticut. Later, after Leslie Combs of Kentucky read a letter that Clay had written before the convention met pledging his cordial support for the choice of the convention, another one of Clay's friends moved that the nomination be made unanimous.

A combination of poor timing, poor management, and poor attendance had foiled Clay. Clearly, the most important cause of his defeat was the date of the convention itself, for the gathering followed a string of Whig defeats not only in the South but also in Indiana, Maine, Ohio, Pennsylvania, and even Massachusetts. Whigs in those states, as well as in New York, were in no mood to take a chance with the well-known senator, especially since the real impact of the price slump that began late in 1839 had yet to be felt. Had the Whigs chosen to convene in May 1840 when the Democrats renominated Van Buren, for example, prices would have been 16 percent lower than they were in December and the Whigs would have had a string of victories in Connecticut, Rhode Island, and Virginia behind them—a trend that pointed in a very different direction than the results in the summer and fall of 1839.[44]

By itself, the timing of the convention had not been decisive. Clay's friends at Harrisburg had obviously been outmaneuvered by the Scott and Harrison managers like Weed, Stevens, and Charles Penrose. Had state delegations been allowed to split their votes, his support in Ohio, New York, and Pennsylvania might have pushed him so close to the necessary 128 votes on the first ballot that he would have been impossible to stop.

Less obviously but just as significantly, Clay also suffered from the failure of all the southern states to attend the convention. He received every southern vote on every ballot, and he paid a penalty for that firm southern support since it convinced Northerners that he had become too proslavery in order to get it. Yet Clay did not enjoy the full benefits of his popularity in the South because Arkansas, Georgia, South Carolina, and Tennessee were not represented at the convention. While Whigs had no chance of carrying Arkansas, its delegate would have cast the state's three votes for Clay had he arrived in Harrisburg in time for the convention. Nor did the Whigs have a realistic chance of carrying Calhoun's bailiwick; but had Clay supporters such as Senator William C. Preston bothered to come to Harrisburg, they could have added eleven more votes to Clay's column.

Support from Georgia would have been more problematic. Georgia's State Rights party did not send a delegation to Harrisburg because it still considered itself a separate organization and would not endorse Harrison until the spring of 1840.[45] But given the solid southern support for Clay and northern resistance to him at Harrisburg, Georgians, had they attended the convention, would likely have joined the Clay camp, if only to help it overturn the unit rule.

Tennessee's absence from the convention was perhaps more crucial. Neither distance nor distaste deprived Clay of its support. Tennessee's Whig leaders like

John Bell and Hugh Lawson White heartily favored Clay, as did other Whigs among Tennessee's congressional delegation. These men could easily have traveled from Washington to nearby Harrisburg to support him. But a foolish insistence on consistency stopped them. In 1835 and 1836 they had campaigned for Hugh White against Van Buren on the grounds that Van Buren's nomination by a convention denied the people a choice of their rulers, so Tennessee's Whigs had agreed from the moment the national convention was called in April 1838 that they could not possibly attend. Anticonvention sentiment thus cost Clay fifteen sure votes.[46]

Had all four of these missing states attended the convention and supported Clay, the total number of votes would have been 294 and the majority necessary to win the nomination 148. Clay would have received 143 votes on the first ballot exclusive of his support in New York, Ohio, and Pennsylvania, and even the skillful maneuvering of Weed and Stevens would probably have been unable to prevent his picking up the additional five votes, say, in New Jersey, where ailing Whig Senator Samuel Southard favored Clay's nomination.[47] Alternatively, the Clay forces almost surely could have overturned the unit rule on a floor vote, thereby releasing his supporters in New York, Ohio, and Pennsylvania and guaranteeing his success.

Had Clay triumphed, the Whigs necessarily would have nominated a Northerner like New York's Tallmadge for vice president. Harrison's nomination instead ensured that the party would turn to a Southerner to balance the ticket and appease the disappointed Clay men. The names of John M. Clayton of Delaware, Benjamin Watkins Leigh of Virginia, Preston of South Carolina, and Willie Mangum of North Carolina were floated but with no result. The angry Clay supporter Reverdy Johnson of Maryland, who said that Clayton would never consent to benefit from the defeat of Clay, withdrew his name. Leigh, who was at the convention, refused to run. When none of the Southerners most closely associated with Clay would take the second place, the convention by default turned to former Senator John Tyler of Virginia.

The choice of Tyler would later prove to be disastrous. A state rights Democrat who had broken with Jackson over his Nullification Proclamation, he shared none of the views of the nationalistic wing of the party. A bitter personal foe of Conservative Senator William C. Rives, he and a few friends had blocked Clay's attempt to arrange a Whig-Conservative coalition behind Rives' reelection the previous spring. Nonetheless, Tyler had faithfully supported Clay for the nomination and had worked for him at the Harrisburg convention itself. Thus he seemed (quite wrongly) a prototypical southern Clay loyalist. No one else who fit that description would accept the nomination. Tyler, who was on the scene, eagerly agreed to run. Later, the patrician Whig diarist Philip Hone would wittily remark that "there was rhyme but no reason in it." But there was, of course, a reason—to rally the disgruntled southern Whigs behind Harrison. It was simply luck that the Whig ticket also inspired the most famous alliterative campaign slogan in American history—"Tippecanoe and Tyler, Too."[48]

The Whigs left Harrisburg with more than a snappy slogan. Despite their failure to adopt a national platform or issue a formal address to the voters, they defined the central themes of their ensuing campaign. Long before the convention, the strategists who defeated Clay for a more available candidate determined to prevent any formal programmatic commitments that might diminish his availability. One Whig had written to Weed in 1839, for example, "To correct the abuses of the Administration is sufficient motive to vigorous and efficient effort, and in politics, as well as in Philosophy—it is unwise to give more reasons than are necessary." Historians have long fastened on this and similar evidence to show that the Whigs were intent on avoiding issues. But to the Whigs, correcting "the abuses of the Administration" was itself a matter of deep principle. When one of the speechmakers on the convention's last day portrayed that mission in a particularly compelling way, therefore, the party published and widely broadcast his remarks. The Whig campaign, Judge Jacob Burnet of Cincinnati intoned, was a crusade "to save the liberty, the morals, and the happiness of the people, and to rescue the Constitution from the hands of profligate men, under whose management it is sinking into decay."[49]

Although the Whigs had made it abundantly clear since 1837 that they meant economic prosperity when they referred to the happiness of the people, Burnet's delineation of the party's purpose was essentially the same credo that Henry Clay had advanced when he helped found the Whig party in the winter of 1833–34. The party had thrust its founder aside for a more available standard bearer, but the standard itself maintained first principles. As the Whig party launched its presidential campaign of 1840, therefore, it possessed more than a catchy motto. It also had a compelling cause—the restoration of prosperity and the salvation of republicanism itself.

VI

At a testimonial dinner arranged in Clay's behalf by his disappointed southern backers after the convention adjourned, Clay did much to ensure southern support for the ticket by calling for party unity. "We have not been contending for Henry Clay, for Daniel Webster, or for Winfield Scott," he declared. "No! We have been contending for principles. Not men, but principles, are our rules of action." Yet the marvelously imaginative presidential campaign the Whigs waged in 1840 is far better remembered for its slogans, its symbols, and its songs than for its principles. As soon as the convention had adjourned, Democratic newspapers accused the Whigs of fearing "to meet the issue upon all the momentous topics which . . . divide the American people," and many historians have agreed. To them the Whigs seemed to follow the scenario a New Yorker had outlined for Scott in 1839: "The General's lips must be hermetically sealed, and our shouts and hurras must be long and loud." The Whigs themselves appeared to admit that this was their strategy in one of the songs that made the campaign so notorious.[50]

> Mum is the word boys,
> Brag is the game;
> Cooney is the emblem
> of Old Tip's flame.

Without doubt, the Whigs employed flummery, mummery, and hoopla with astonishing ingenuity in order to arouse enthusiasm for Harrison and the Whig party. They rolled giant leather balls across the countryside to attract attention to the anti-Democratic slogans inscribed on them. They held countless parades and processions featuring transparencies and mobile floats. Tippecanoe clubs that proliferated across the country organized and provided supplies for huge rallies that drew tens of thousands of men—sometimes up to 100,000, according to Whig estimates—in Baltimore, in Nashville, in Springfield, Illinois, in Dayton, Ohio, at the Bunker Hill monument, at the Tippecanoe battleground itself, and elsewhere. Undeniably, as well, the Whigs raised sloganeering and political song making to a fine art. Chants such as "Tippecanoe and Tyler, Too," "Van, Van, Van—Van's a Used Up Man," and "Down with Martin Van Ruin!" were not only memorable, they were marvelously effective in bolstering Whig morale. So were the songs Whigs chorused at virtually every party gathering such as

> Farewell, dear Van
> You're not our man;
> To guide the ship
> We'll try old Tip.[51]

Democrats might protest that all the rigmarole that accompanied the Whig campaign was superficial nonsense designed to disguise a senile, unqualified candidate and to evade issues, but they had only themselves to blame for handing the Whigs the central emblems that made that campaign so famous. Shortly after the nomination was announced, Democratic newspapers widely reprinted a story that had first appeared in a Democratic sheet in Baltimore in order to ridicule Harrison's pretensions to the presidency. Taunting an unhappy Clay supporter when news of the decision at Harrisburg became public, the Washington correspondent of the Baltimore *Republican* proudly reported this put-down of Harrison: "Give him a barrel of hard cider, and settle a pension of two thousand a year on him, and my word for it, he will sit the remainder of his days in his log cabin. . . ."[52] The sixty-seven-year-old ex-soldier, Democrats everywhere jeered, was ready for retirement. Nothing in his undistinguished career qualified him for high office.

William Henry Harrison was neither poor nor the resident of a log cabin. While he currently held only the lowly post of a clerk of court, he had been not only a general, but also a territorial governor, a congressman, and a United States senator. Still, shrewd Whigs gleefully seized on this Democratic canard to prove that their candidate was a common man who would represent the poor. "Log-Cabin Candidate," the New York *Daily Whig* indignantly trumpeted, "is the term of reproach given . . . to General Harrison . . . by pampered office-holders . . . who sneer at the idea of making a *poor man* President of the United States." "Gen. Harrison is sneered at by the Eastern office-holders' pimps, as the 'Log-Cabin Candidate,' " echoed a professedly outraged Whig editor from Illinois.[53]

Thus log cabins, hard cider, and the accompanying coonskins that attested to the candidate's frontier background became the dominant symbols of a symbol-laden campaign. Transparencies featuring log cabins were hoisted during parades, log cabins were raised at Whig gatherings, and hard cider was freely dispensed. A weekly campaign sheet, ably edited by the brilliant young Horace Greeley and called the *Log Cabin*, became the Whigs' major newspaper during the race, with a national circulation reaching 80,000 copies a week. One item of the paraphernalia used to publicize this pervasive theme made a permanent contribution to the American vernacular. To quench the thirst of ardent Whigs, a Philadelphia distiller bottled Log-Cabin Whiskey in small bottles shaped like cabins. The liquor became so famous that the name of its distiller, E. G. Booz, soon became a synonym for whiskey itself.

The slogans, symbols, songs, and speeches that glorified log cabins, hard cider, and coonskins had a more serious purpose than providing simple amusement, however. They were meant to draw a sharp contrast between Harrison and Van Buren and to remind voters that Van Buren and the Democrats both were responsible for the depression and refused to help the common man out of it. Whigs eagerly if falsely proclaimed Harrison a poor man because they tried to paint Van Buren as a pampered, aristocratic dandy—much as the Jacksonians had unfairly vilified John Quincy Adams in 1828.

The central weapon in this smear campaign was a scandalously demagogic speech delivered by an obscure Whig congressman from Pennsylvania named Charles Ogle. Entitling his diatribe "The Regal Splendor of the Presidential Palace," the ostensibly horrified Pennsylvanian took three days in April to recount the unrepublican luxury in which Van Buren wallowed. Bewailing the poverty of his unemployed constituents, the congressman contrasted it to the opulence of the White House. Room by room he described its thick "Royal Wilton" carpets, its silk draperies, and its huge gold-framed mirrors. While the poor had to eat hominy and hog meat, he claimed, Van Buren had hired French chefs to prepare gourmet meals served on gold plates with sterling silver service. While they made do with hard cider, Van Buren guzzled champagne. Worst of all, while they were lucky to make 25 cents a day, Van Buren earned $2.81 an hour while living like a king.[54]

This outrageous philippic was widely circulated by the Whigs' central campaign committee in Washington, and throughout the campaign the army of Whig orators who crisscrossed the country rang variations on the same theme. The Whigs were the party of the poor and the Democrats were the party of uncaring officeholders, corrupted by the wealth of office. "The Log Cabin is a symbol of nothing that Van Burenism knows, feels or can appreciate," argued Thurlow Weed in his *Albany Evening Journal*. "It tells of the hopes of the humble—of the privations of the poor— . . . it is the emblem of rights that the vain and insolent aristocracy of federal office-holders have . . . trampled upon."[55]

Whigs did more than simply agitate class antagonisms against the Democrats. They constantly reminded voters that there was a depression, that the Democrats had caused it, that Van Buren argued that government should do nothing about it, and that a Whig triumph was necessary to end it. The theme of one document broadcast by the central committee of Whig congressmen in Washington was encapsulated in its title: "Harrison and Prosperity or Van Buren and Ruin." Campaigning in New Jersey, South Carolina Senator William C. Preston carefully reminded his audience that no previous presidential campaign had ever found prices as low as "wheat at fifty cents a bushel and cotton at six cents." Then, ravaging the Democratic response to such hardship, he proclaimed, "Well indeed may the President, in his marble palace, amid luxurious appliances, with well-paid salary, exclaim 'The people expect too much from Government.' " Ohio's

Whig gubernatorial candidate, Tom Corwin, stressed the same theme when he promised that wheat would be a dollar a bushel under Harrison and forty cents a bushel under Van Buren.[56]

Many Whig speakers and much Whig propaganda simply denounced the Democrats for causing the depression and promised prosperity with a change of regime without delineating Whig measures to effect economic recovery. Furthermore, Whigs in some states, especially in the South, specifically denied that the party favored higher tariffs or a new national bank. But others campaigned differently. In 1840, the Whigs' most important presidential elector in Illinois, Abraham Lincoln, based his campaign for Harrison on the need for a new national bank to supply credit for the common man. Similarly, the brilliant Mississippi orator S. S. Prentiss, while touring the North, openly defended the Bank of the United States with the epigrammatic motto "Credit is the poor man's capital." In New Jersey, Prentiss also stressed the need for a protective tariff, and Pennsylvania's Whigs marched under banners proclaiming "Tip, Tyler, and the Tariff." Stumping for Harrison in North Carolina, Whig George Badger charged that the deflationary impact of the Independent Treasury Act's specie provisions would fall most harshly "upon the poor, and those who are in moderate circumstances and owe money." Furthermore, he pledged that Harrison favored repeal of that act and distribution of federal land revenues to the states. While Harrison personally opposed a new national bank, he added, if a Whig Congress chartered a new one, Harrison would sign rather than veto the legislation.[57]

The disappointed Senate duo of Clay and Webster also injected issues into the campaign on occasion, although God-like Daniel shamelessly posed as a common man and at one point even threatened to use fisticuffs if any Democrat dared call him an aristocrat. In a few speeches, however, Webster specifically lashed out at Democratic deflationary policies as disastrous to the poor and said that government had a duty to provide a sound and ample currency through a new national bank or some other means. Henry Clay, during an address near his birthplace in Hanover County, Virginia, called for the deposit of federal funds in state banks or a new national bank, whichever voters deemed more expedient, and advocated once again his scheme to distribute land revenues to the states. In the same speech, however, Clay also renounced any plans to raise the tariff and said that the compromise schedules of 1833 should remain intact.[58]

More important, voters did not require concrete proposals from campaign orators to know where Whigs stood on the issues. Since 1837 in both Congress and the states, they had outlined their economic program and sharply contrasted it with Democratic alternatives. In 1840, it should be recalled, Massachusetts Whig legislators published a point-by-point rebuttal to Democratic Governor Marcus Morton's anticorporation agenda. Kentucky's Whigs boldly proposed to raise taxes in order to complete the state's river improvements. Pennsylvania Whigs condemned Democrats as "bearded enthusiasts" whose ignorant and visionary schemes would prostrate the state's banking and credit systems. New York's Whig Governor Seward continued to call for lavish expenditures on the canal system; Ohio's Whig newspapers attacked the antibanking policies of the state's Democrats for destroying the credit poor men so badly needed; Virginia, Alabama, and Mississippi Whigs made much of trying to defend state banks from Democratic assaults on them; and Whigs and Democrats in the North Carolina legislature were at well-publicized loggerheads over banking, corporate rights, and subsidies for internal improvements. The epithet "Loco Foco" that Whigs everywhere used to describe Democrats was meant to underline their dangerous economic radicalism. It hardly took campaign speeches to remind the electorate that the two parties were fundamentally at odds over general economic philosophy and specific economic programs.[59]

If the motto "Down with Martin Van Ruin!" encapsulates the central thrust of the Whig campaign, Whigs also used other issues to discredit Democrats and justify reform. Judge Jacob Burnet's widely circulated speech had promised a crusade to save not only the prosperity but also the liberty and morals of the people, and the Whigs addressed those themes as well. To appeal to the sober, churchgoing middle class they portrayed Democrats as an irreligious, immoral rabble who threatened the very foundations of social order. In September, Horace Greeley sounded the tocsin in the *Log Cabin*. "Wherever you find a bitter, blasphemous Atheist and an enemy of Marriage, Morality, and Social Order, there you may be certain of one vote for Van Buren."[60] Such a charge coming from a party that was simultaneously drenching the electorate in booze may seem palpably hypocritical, but it was effective. So was one of the Whigs' biggest campaign innovations that year. In sharp contrast to Democrats, whose demonstrations remained exclusively male and often rowdy affairs, Whigs ostentatiously invited their wives, sisters, and daughters to rallies to testify to the party's family-oriented respectability.[61]

Yet the salvation of liberty and republican self-government constituted the Whigs' second most important theme. Their portrayals of Van Buren as a dissipated, effete monarch reminded voters that Democrats represented executive despotism. To save freedom and republicanism, Whigs iterated and reiterated, the people had to oust their oppressors. The title of Calvin Colton's campaign tract, *The Crisis of the Country*, conveyed the Whigs' sense that republicanism was in danger. Abruptly abandoning Whigs' antipartyism of the mid-1830s, Colton called two-party competition necessary to preserve republicanism by allowing the people to change their rulers. "The two great parties of this country will always remain nearly equal to watch each other, and every few years there must be a change," he asserted. "This is essential to the preservation of our liberties. If power stays always in the hands of one party, the leaders would ruin us."[62]

Other Whigs emphasized the same theme in even more apocalyptic language. "Your Federal Government, which was established with limitations, checks and balances, to preserve the principles of civil liberty, is undergoing a change fatal to its republican character," declared the address of the New York Whig state convention. Like the Revolution, Clay proclaimed in his speech at Hanover County, Virginia, "this contest . . . is to preserve the liberties of the country." The election, declared the Whig Raleigh *Register* in North Carolina, "must determine the great question [of] whether we are to live as SLAVES or FREEDMEN."[63]

As members of a slaveholding society, southern Whigs had an acute sense of the difference between slavery and freedom and a particularly strong fear of enslavement. As they had in 1836, and as they would continue to do in presidential campaigns as long as the Whig party existed, they gave a peculiar sectional cast to this central Whig theme. Like southern Democrats, southern Whigs included the freedom to own black slaves in the concept of liberty for white men, and they attacked Van Buren once again as a menace to that right. In contrast, they portrayed Harrison, a native of Virginia, as perfectly safe on the slavery issue and proudly printed in their newspapers statements that Harrison had made averse to the abolitionists. "The entire portion of that speech relating to abolition," declared the Richmond *Whig* in a fashion typical of Whig papers throughout Dixie, "breathes the most ardent and devoted attachment to the rights and institutions of the South."[64]

Southern Whigs also iterated the standard line that Van Buren tyrannically menaced liberty in general. Even more than their northern compatriots, they focused on a proposal by Van Buren's secretary of war, Joel Poinsett, himself a South Carolinian, to reform the militia system. Poinsett's well-publicized proposal in effect called for mandatory service by all young men in the militia and national supervision of its training. Whigs everywhere, but especially in the South, jumped on this scheme as an attempt to create a standing army, enslave young men, enlarge the patronage at the disposal of the executive, and centralize more power in his hands—power, they implied, that might some day be used against slavery itself. "ONE STEP TOWARD FURTHER MONARCHY," thundered the New Orleans *Bee*. "Strike off these manacles of a cold-blooded party despot, and restore your sons to freedom," urged the Richmond *Whig*. "Expel from the Capitol the man who would subjugate them and you."[65]

Even Harrison himself raised the call to save republican liberty. According to custom in the nineteenth century, presidential candidates did not take to the stump themselves. They left that chore to congressmen, presidential electors, and other politicos. But the old soldier, goaded by Democratic taunts that he was "General Mum" kept in an iron cage by his advisors so that his views would not be publicized, decided to break the tradition. He accepted an invitation to attend an anniversary celebration of the battle of Fort Meigs in June and then toured Ohio, giving some twenty-three speeches to cheering throngs. Harrison stressed the traditional Whig fear of a strong executive. He pledged that he would serve only one term, denounced excessive use of the veto power, and said that he would abide by congressional decisions on most policies. With such declarations, he assured regular Whigs that he adhered to their most important principle—resistance to executive tyranny.

Harrison's stand on specific issues like a new national bank and abolitionism was artfully ambiguous in these speeches, and he personally repeated the nonsense about his residence in a log cabin. Clearly and emphatically, he nevertheless established his credentials as a champion and exponent of republican values. "The old-fashioned Republican rule is to watch the Government," he lectured the sun-scorched multitude at Fort Meigs. "See that the Government does not acquire too much power. Keep check upon your rulers. Do this, and liberty is safe." As a simple republican, he proclaimed to an even larger crowd at Dayton, he was appalled that "the *Government is now a practical monarchy*." If elected, he would reduce "the power and influence of the National Executive"; he would not run for reelection; and he would not attempt to name his successor. Instead he would return "that high trust . . . to the people."[66]

Democrats tried to resist the Whig juggernaut as best they could. They attacked "old Granny" Harrison as a phony hero and claimed that mantle for their own vice presidential candidate, Richard M. Johnson, the purported slayer of Tecumseh. They denounced the Whig campaign as a carnival that insulted the intelligence of the people. Through "banners of Cider Barrels, log cabins, coonskins, gourds, and a hundred other such fooleries," an Alabama Democrat protested, the Whigs were "practicing the most corrupt and unprincipled acts that ever men did, by misleading the ignorant portion of the people." At the same time, Democrats tried to match the Whigs by inventing symbols, songs, and slogans of their own. And they too bequeathed a phrase to the American lexicon when they attempted to coin a nickname for their own candidate to show his common origins. Jackson had been Old Hickory and Harrison was Old Tip. Now Van Buren became Old Kinderhook, which was rapidly reduced in Democratic slogans to O.K., as in "Down with the Whigs, boys, O.K." To counteract the Whig posture as the party of the respectable classes, Democrats both denounced their copious use of spirits to benumb voters and parodied it in ditties such as:

> Hush-a-by-baby;
> Daddy's a Whig,
> Before he comes home
> Hard Cider he'll swig;
>
> Then he'll be Tipsy
> And over he'll fall;
> Down will come Daddy,
> Tip, Tyler and all.[67]

More seriously, Democrats mobilized their control of local postmasterships to distribute copies of the official campaign paper, the *Extra Globe*. Southern Democrats labeled Harrison himself an abolitionist, stressed that abolitionists dominated the Whig party's northern wing, and warned that if Harrison truly did accede to the will of Congress, disaster threatened the South. "PEOPLE OF THE SOUTH," screamed Thomas Ritchie's Richmond *Enquirer*, "You will find out (will it be too late?) that Whiggery and Abolition are BOTH ONE throughout the Northern, middle, and Northwestern States." Whiggery was "Federalism and Abolition United" echoed the *Globe*. In the South as elsewhere, Democrats repeatedly attacked as blatant hypocrisy the Whigs' attempt to pose as the party of the poor. Whatever Whigs said, they insisted, the Whigs were the party of wealthy Federalist aristocrats and bankers. The central Democratic slogan was "SHALL THE BANKS OR THE PEOPLE RULE?" Only the Democratic party, they proclaimed in countless ways, could protect the equal rights and freedom of the people from the privilege and despotism of the corrupt Whig Money Power. Just as the Whigs continued to portray themselves as champions of republican liberty and equality, in short, so did the Democrats. Both parties insisted that the salvation of republicanism was at stake.[68]

VII

For all of the charges and countercharges, for all of the demonstrations and counterdemonstrations, for all of the bandying back and forth of catchy slogans, one fact above all determined the outcome of the election. The depression deepened as the year progressed. The Democratic response of removing federal money from private circulation, restricting the note issues of private banks, and curtailing credit had clearly failed to produce a recovery. The Democratic message that people should not look to their government for aid seemed heartless. In contrast, the Whig call for positive governmental intervention to restore prosperity appeared both promising and necessary.

Despite the circus-like campaign and the tomfoolery, the voters knew what policies they could expect should either party win. They had not only past policies but also the outcomes of these policies to go by.[69] In consequence, the hard-pressed residents of commercially oriented regions turned to the Whigs in even greater numbers than they had in 1837 and early 1838. While the Whigs gained fresh support from all kinds of voters, their appeal to both new and old voters was especially strong among residents of the wealthiest communities whose farmers, planters, and businessmen were most heavily involved in the production and exchange of goods for cash. In the areas most concerned with economic recovery and the promotion of growth, in short, not only the wealthy and the middle class but also many workers who depended on prosperity for jobs surged toward the Whig party.

From March until October 1840, the Whigs rolled up a stunning string of victories in state and congressional elections in which the programmatic differences between the parties had been sharply etched. The voter turnout in those elections often matched and sometimes surpassed the outpouring in the presidential election itself.[70] Only setbacks in heavily Democratic New Hampshire, Arkansas, Illinois, and Missouri and a narrow loss in Maine bucked the Whig trend. Contrary to the calculations of Whig managers at Harrisburg, triumphs in the subnational elections of 1840 demonstrate that the Whigs hardly needed a military hero or campaign hoopla to win the White House. The depression and the perceived party responses to it largely determined the outcome.

In November, Harrison carried nineteen of twenty-six states to crush Van Buren in the electoral vote by a margin of 234 to 60. Old Kinderhook won only Arkansas, Missouri, and Illinois in the West; Alabama, South Carolina, and Virginia in the South; and New Hampshire in the Northeast. The popular vote was closer than the electoral rout indicated. Harrison captured about 53 percent compared to Van Buren's 47 percent, with the newly formed abolitionist Liberty party draining off less than 0.3 percent. Harrison's margins in Maine, New York, and Pennsylvania were perilously thin, but he lost Illinois and Virginia almost as narrowly.

The contest drew a larger proportion of the eligible electorate to the polls than any previous presidential election. The share of adult male voters jumped from 57.8 percent in 1836 to 80.2 percent in 1840, and the rate of participation was even higher than that in fifteen of the twenty-five states that had a popular vote.[71] In absolute numbers the total vote grew by over 900,000 between the two elections, a jump of some 60 percent over 1836. Those new voters constituted 37.5 percent of the total vote in 1840, and the Whigs captured almost three-fifths of them. Surely, the excitement generated by the log-cabin campaign and the furious reaction of Democrats to Whig boasting helped account for this record participation. Surely, the new voters who were brought out primarily by hoopla and free cider helped Old Tip to triumph. Harrison, indeed, ran ahead of gubernatorial and congressional Whig tickets in every state of the nation, and by significant margins in some, like Kentucky, New Hampshire, and Pennsylvania.[72] To that extent, one might credit mummery and meaningless hurrahs for the individual success of Tippecanoe and Tyler too. But Harrison outpaced state and congressional Whig candidates in 1840 largely because Democrats, demoralized by defeats earlier in the year, cast fewer votes for the unpopular Van Buren than they had for state and congressional candidates (Table 8).

By the same token, most of the increment in the Whig popular vote in 1840 occurred in the state and congressional elections that preceded the November balloting, not in the presidential election itself. Such was the case in eleven of the fourteen states that held elections prior to November for which returns are available.[73] The Whig party as an institution, and not simply the popular military hero, enjoyed an immense accession of new voter support in 1840.

VIII

The Whig party did more than win control of the White House, Congress, and many state governments in the elections of 1840. It also established the basic organizational structure, the basic electoral strategy, and the basic voter coalition that would characterize the party until its disintegration in the 1850s. To be sure, the party would be required to address new issues in the future, but always it would pose as the champion of liberty, morals, and prosperity. As they had in 1840, moreover, Whigs would always attempt to demonstrate that their response to an issue differed from that of Democrats. The size of the Whig voter coalition would grow in the future, but never as rapidly or as decisively as it had since 1837. Never again, indeed, would the total vote increase between presidential elections at the same rate it had between 1836 and 1840. It would expand by only 330,000 between 1840 and 1844, by 178,000 between 1844 and 1848, and by 280,000 between 1848 and 1852. Equally important, the size of the vote would never again grow continuously in off-year elections, as it had between 1836 and 1840. Instead, the familiar modern pattern of a drop-off rather than an increase in turnout became more and more frequent in those contests.

Although new voters helped decide some future elections, never again would they weigh as heavily in the total vote or in the calculations of political leaders. After 1840, both Whig and Democratic leaders concentrated primarily on reinforcing the allegiance of previously committed voters to rouse the faithful rather than on making converts. Both parties would continue to use techniques they had adopted in 1840. They developed elaborate organizations coordinated during presidential campaigns by central committees in Washington and extending to states, congressional districts, counties, towns, precincts, and wards that identified voters who favored their party and tried to get them to the polls. Both depended heavily on skillful newspaper editors, who were supported when possible by government printing contracts or other party funds, to denounce the enemy in hyperbolic terms as some dreadful monster intent on destroying republicanism. Both parties utilized hurrah techniques and liberal quantities of liquor to mobilize their constituents and draw the uninitiated into their ranks.

Table 8

Change in the Whig and Democratic Absolute Vote in the Elections of 1840 Measured from the Immediately Preceding Election[a]

		Congressional or Gubernatorial	Presidential
New Hampshire	Whig	− 3,225	+ 5,597
	Democratic	− 997	+ 3,332
Connecticut	Whig	− 334	− 1,238
	Democratic	− 1,863	− 499
Rhode Island	Whig	+ 747	+ 416
	Democratic	− 242	− 155
Virginia	Whig		+11,992
	Democratic		−10,952
Louisiana	Whig	+ 1,561	+ 2,147
	Democratic	+ 267	+ 573
Alabama	Whig		+15,677
	Democratic		+20,950
Illinois	Whig		+15,854
	Democratic		+16,775
Indiana	Whig	+13,334	+ 2,337
	Democratic	+ 3,246	− 6,567
Kentucky	Whig	+ 9,945	− 3,705
	Democratic	+13,808	− 6,567
Missouri	Whig	+ 5,014	+ 671
	Democratic	+ 6,246	+ 373
North Carolina	Whig	+17,800	+ 1,191
	Democratic	+ 4,477	− 2,647
Tennessee	Whig		+ 8,570
	Democratic		− 5,768
Maine	Whig	+10,848	+ 1,015
	Democratic	+ 4,819	+ 615
Vermont	Whig	+ 9,032	− 1,208
	Democratic	+ 744	− 4,991
Arkansas	Whig	+ 1,460	− 628
	Democratic	+ 1,105	− 1,220
Georgia	Whig	+ 6,584	+ 1,045
	Democratic	+ 1,291	− 3,996
Maryland	Whig		+ 8,803
	Democratic		+ 2,802
New Jersey	Whig	+ 4,916	+ 9
	Democratic	+ 2,646	− 97
Ohio	Whig	+43,298	+ 2,599
	Democratic	+21,428	− 5,368
Pennsylvania	Whig		+21,702
	Democratic		+15,848
Delaware	Whig	+ 1,446	+ 1,568
	Democratic	+ 633	+ 421

Table 8 (*continued*)

		Congressional or Gubernatorial	Presidential
Massachusetts	Whig	+20,159	+22,149
	Democratic	+ 4,135	+ 920
Michigan	Whig	+ 3,772	+ 3,864
	Democratic	+ 3,754	+ 3,386
Mississippi	Whig		+ 3,629
	Democratic		− 1,870
New York	Whig	+29,129	+33,131
	Democratic	+34,265	+30,275

ᵃThis table is based on the raw vote totals for congressional and gubernatorial elections listed in Congressional Quarterly's *Guide to U.S. Elections* and the sums for the presidential vote in 1840 listed in Burnham, *Presidential Ballots, 1836–1892*. Changes in the vote are calculated from the immediately preceding election. For every state in which congressional or gubernatorial elections were held in 1840 prior to November, the change registered in the "Congressional or Gubernatorial" column is measured from equivalent elections in 1838 or 1839, whereas the change registered in the "Presidential" column is measured from that previous 1840 election. For the November states of Delaware, Massachusetts, Michigan, Mississippi, and New York, both columns reflect changes from the results of the most proximate election in 1838 or 1839.

Nonetheless, just as in the issue-oriented contests from 1837 to 1840, after Harrison's victory both Whigs and Democrats sought to mobilize voters primarily by defining their differences as sharply as possible. Political leaders palpably believed that voters responded to conflict between the parties. The chief function of party-controlled newspapers was to educate voters about those contrasts. In addition, both parties spent enormous amounts of time and money printing and circulating speeches, pamphlets, and addresses defining where the parties stood on issues and the probable outcomes of their respective policies.

Like the Democrats, the Whigs not only emphasized that they advocated distinctive programs, they also stressed that they represented the values, interests, and needs of the particular groups in society who formed their voting base. Each party drew some support from virtually every element in the social spectrum, whether that element was defined by occupation, class, religion, ethnicity, or regional identity. Nonetheless, Whigs and Democrats attracted distinguishably different constituencies. The new recruits added to each coalition after 1837 reinforced earlier tendencies. The central fault line or cleavage in the electorate separated men with different degrees of experience in and different attitudes toward the market economy and the cultural values it spawned. Broadly put, Democrats were a coalition of those still outside the market economy who feared its spread and those who had experienced and been victimized by market mechanisms. Whigs, in contrast, attracted those who wanted to expand the market sector because they had already enjoyed its benefits or hoped to do so in the future. But that was not the only cleavage in the electorate. The Whig constituency requires closer examination, for it simultaneously contributed to the party's image, placed constraints on leadership strategy because Whig politicians could not flout it, helped engender the factional rivalry that mushroomed in many states and within the national party as a whole, and helped determine how the party would later break up.

Whigs ran well among almost all social classes in cities and trading centers, but they were especially attractive to the economic and social elite of those communities. Of men worth more than $100,000 in New York, for example, 85 percent were Whig; in Boston, 89 percent of a similar category adhered to Whiggery; and in the relatively poorer city of Pittsburgh, three-fourths of the men worth more than $25,000 were Whigs. Not only fear of Democratic radicalism and attraction to the Whig economic platform explain this behavior. For such patricians, belonging to the Whig party was the equivalent of belonging to an exclusive gentlemen's club of social peers.[74]

The economic demarcation between the parties' constituencies was especially clear in a number of southern states because soil types varied from region to region and wealthy and poor counties were separated geographically. Intrastate regional antagonisms therefore often reinforced the different economic needs and values of Democratic and Whig voters. Whigs were strongest in the black-belt plantation regions, where the proportions of both slaves and slaveholders were high: central Georgia, central and southern Alabama, the western delta counties of Mississippi along the river, western Tennessee, the southern sugar-growing parishes of Louisiana, and the bluegrass, hemp-producing center of Kentucky. Louisiana's sugar planters, like Kentucky's hemp producers, not only favored a protective tariff, in contrast to cotton planters, but the majority of the population in those southern parishes was French Creole. In contrast, Democrats dominated the less prosperous areas of northwestern Louisiana, the piney woods regions of eastern Mississippi, the hill country of northern Alabama between the Tennessee River and the black belt, the hilly Cherokee district of northwest Georgia, and the mountainous regions of eastern Kentucky and southwestern Virginia. Not only was the soil of those areas less valuable and less productive, but most of the Democratic voters were nonslaveholders.

There were, of course, variations from this central pattern in every state. In Louisiana, for example, while the French sugar-planting parishes in the southern portion of the state were Whig strongholds, cotton-growing native American planters along the Mississippi River north of New Orleans tended to vote Democratic, as did the poorer farmers in the northwestern sector of the state. Within New Orleans, the South's largest metropolis, in contrast, the ethnic pattern was reversed. There native-born Protestants in general, and the commercial community in particular, tended to vote Whig, whereas recently arrived German and Irish immigrants, most of whom were Catholic, voted Democratic.[75]

In Kentucky, class rather than ethnic lines shuffled with location. In the central, commercially oriented and Whig-dominated bluegrass regions, slaveholders normally voted Whig and nonslaveholders Democratic. Yet in the peripheral areas of the state controlled by Democrats—poor farming communities along the Ohio River to the north, eastern mountainous counties, less developed counties along the southern border with Tennessee, and the Jackson Purchase in the extreme west—wealthy slaveholders voted Democratic, while Whigs drew support from the economic and social outs.[76]

Aside from idiosyncratic South Carolina, Virginia and North Carolina provided the greatest exceptions to the usual electoral cleavage in slave states. In both, most slaveholders voted Democratic, whereas nonslaveholders who lived outside the slaveholding cotton- and tobacco-producing regions voted Whig. In those states remote regions wanted Whig internal improvements, while planters feared the taxes necessary to pay for them. Regardless of region, towns that wanted commercial development like Raleigh, Fayetteville, Newburn, Wilmington, and Ashville in North Carolina and Norfolk, Richmond, Petersburg, Danville, and Staunton in Virginia supported the Whig party much more strongly than did the rural areas of the counties in which they were located. Tennessee offered its own variation on this pattern. Many slaveholders in the wealthiest counties of middle and western Tennessee voted Whig, but so did many nonslaveholders in mountainous eastern Tennessee.[77]

The division of the electorate in many northern states was even more complex because the population was much more diverse. There rival cultural groups were much more frequently in contact, and they often chose one party simply because the hostile group supported the other. These groups might be religious. Everywhere, for example, Catholics voted overwhelmingly for the Democrats, while the Protestants who disliked them the most—Presbyterians, Congregationalists, and Baptists—voted Whig when they lived near them. But Protestants were hardly unified behind the Whig party. Often long-standing rivalries among more or less established denominations determined how men chose political sides. In New England, for example, Congregationalists tended to be Whig, whereas Baptists, Methodists, and in some states even Episcopalians tended to vote Democratic because of residual animosities from earlier battles to disestablish the Congregational church.[78]

At the same time, northern Protestant denominations tended to divide on moral reform. Evangelical men and women stirred by the revivals of the 1820s and 1830s, who saw no separation between religious and secular realms and thought that Christians must ensure that society adhered to God's standards of behavior as revealed in the Bible, tended to support the Whigs. These included New School Presbyterians, Congregationalists, Free Will Baptists, and some Methodists. On the other hand, denominations that believed religious and secular spheres should be kept separate, that frowned on intrusive and especially state-imposed do-goodism, like Catholics, Lutherans, German Reformed churches, and southern Anti-Mission Baptists, tended to vote Democratic. The following statement by Virginia's Anti-Mission Baptists well reflects the resentment that Democratic voters felt toward what they regarded as the moral imperialism of Whig voters. "We have no Christian fellowship for those who advocate the Missionary, Bible, Tract, or Temperance societies, Sunday School Union, anxious seats or anything of that kind as a religious institution or means of grace; nor with any person who communes with a church which advocates any of these institutions." Yet the Whigs attracted precisely those people most likely to belong to such religious organizations, people who wanted to impose moral standards on others through legislation like Sunday blue laws or prohibition, people who favored a culturally homogeneous society and who felt threatened by alien cultural values.[79]

Ethnocultural divisions also fragmented the northern electorate. In most cities, recent immigrants from Germany and Ireland tended to support the Democrats, while recent British immigrants—the Scots, Scotch-Irish Protestants, English, and Welsh, who despised their Catholic countrymen and yearned for assimilation into the community—voted Whig since the Whigs were the party of the upper and middle classes in most communities. Those native-born American Protestants who felt threatened by immigrants also voted Whig, but clearly there was no nation-wide polarization of natives against immigrants. Even so, Whigs who lived in cities near immigrants were much more prone to nativism and openly anti-immigrant political positions than were Whig leaders from rural areas where few if any immigrants or Catholics resided. By the same token, Whigs who lived in those areas of the North that had more than negligible black populations—and those areas were usually cities—were generally more biased against black rights than were Whigs from white rural areas. The seeds of Whig factionalism over the proper party strategy with regard to nativism, prohibition, black rights, and slavery, that is, often lay in the social composition of different communities.

Northern voting alignments also reflected distinctive regional outlooks. While voters within New England divided along religious and economic lines, for ex-ample, Yankee migrants to western New York, northern Pennsylvania, and the northern portions of Ohio, Indiana, and Illinois voted more solidly Whig than did their relatives back in New England. Once they left New England, Yankees came into contact with Democratic demographic groups with conflicting values. In the Midwest, the rival group was primarily Southerners who had settled in southern portions of Ohio, Indiana, and Illinois years before the Yankees arrived in northern portions of those states. In part, this clash reflected different economic orientations as well. Yankees advocated more economic diversification and com-mercial development than did Southerners. Hence, they leaned toward Whiggery. But again, no group unanimously supported one party or the other.[80]

One social distinction was more important than all others. The majority of the middle and upper classes in rural areas, small towns, and large cities supported the Whigs—especially in relatively prosperous areas involved in the production and exchange of goods for cash. The party's economic platform constituted one reason for this support, but not the only one. Whigs portrayed themselves as the party of probity, respectability, morality, and reason—as "the party of law, of order, of enterprise, of improvement, of beneficence, of hope, and of humanity," New York's Whigs put in 1844. By improvement and order, Whigs meant more than physical improvement of the community or social order. They meant self-improvement and self-discipline. They believed that men must be educated, that individuals must control carnal appetites and other dangerous passions with their reason, and that they must develop habits of sobriety, thrift, industry, and self-control. In contrast, the Whigs painted the Democrats as wild-eyed radicals, agrar-ian levelers, "bearded enthusiasts," lawless and lazy drunkards, a contemptible and dangerous rabble. In many communities, those who considered themselves church-going, God-fearing, law-abiding, sober, educated, and respectable probably voted Whig. In turn, they probably associated any manifestation of social disor-der—be it prostitution, public drunkenness, Sabbath breaking, or rowdyism—and any opposition to social improvement—such as resistance to school taxes—with Democrats. In addition to evangelical desire for moralistic legislation, in short, a cultural tone of patrician respectability attracted many Whig adherents. Not only middle-class shopkeepers and artisans but also native-born workers and English,

Scottish, and Scotch-Irish immigrants who yearned for respectability leaned toward the Whigs because of that tone or image.[81]

Precisely Whigs' smug, holier-than-thou attitude, precisely their attempt to distance themselves (psychologically, rhetorically, and often physically) from supposedly uncouth inferiors allowed Democrats to pillory them as silk-stocking snobs. Democrats thus not only capitalized on resentment toward and fear of the Whigs' economic and social programs. They also exploited popular antagonism against Whigs' very tone and image.

Different economic circumstances, different values, different needs, and different sides on a host of ethnic, religious, regional, and cultural rivalries thus all helped to determine why an individual joined the Whigs or the Democrats. Once men attached themselves to a party, moreover, they rarely changed that affiliation, even though they might not participate in every election. Once formed, indeed, party identity caused partisans to vote as much because of what their party had stood for in the past as because of how it stood on current issues. Intense emotions and rational calculations of future benefits had caused hundreds of thousands of voters to affiliate with the Whig or Democratic party between 1837 and 1840. Then party identity itself often shaped behavior. Party adherents would vote as much out of loyalty to their own organization or a negative reaction against the other as because of immediate issues.

After 1840 political leaders could predict how most men would vote. The question was whether they voted at all. To mobilize the troops, Whig politicians developed an organization, used hurrah techniques, and stressed that the parties were in conflict. By demonstrating that interparty conflict existed, they reinforced party identity and capitalized on the animosity between Whig and Democratic voters. They could usually count on their former supporters voting Whig, if only to inflict a defeat on, or to avert the mortification of a victory by, the despised foe. "As a general rule," wrote a Mississippian, "about one half of those who vote look upon the privilege as worthless unless they can use it to gratify a personal hostility or religious antipathies, or to inflict injury on what they hate."[82] Party leaders sought to instigate men "to inflict injury on what they hate" rather than to stay home on election day.

Not all voters, in short, shared leaders' awareness of, or interest in, every issue contested in distant state capitals and Washington. For them nineteenth-century partisan combat resembled the competitive mechanism between fans of opposing twentieth-century college football teams. At most times their support for the team is latent, but the big game with the traditional rival fills the stadium with screaming partisans. Aroused spectators may have little interest in the game's intricacies or even in bettering the team's overall record, but they thirst for triumph over the long-time foe, if only to avoid his taunts. In 1846, for example, a Massachusetts Democrat gloried in a rare triumph over the party's "common and uncompromising enemies; for I deeply feel the truth of the fact that they are our bitterest foes! And a small victory, like this gained over them, gives me more pleasure than I can express in words." Sometimes, more than pride or boasting rights was involved in this yen for victory. Just as with many athletic contests today, Whig and Democratic partisans bet heavily with each other on the outcome of elections. Thus they had a financial as well as an emotional stake in which party won.[83]

Just as it took the event of the game itself to covert latent into active support in the case of football fans, it took conflict to get Whig and Democratic voters to the polls. Hence, Whig newspapers defined how the parties differed on specific issues, and Whig committees distributed pamphlets highlighting the contrast between the parties. Hence, Whigs and Democrats alike welcomed joint debates on the stump, not only to educate voters on where the respective parties stood but also because the spectacle of Whig and Democratic spokesmen actually clashing on the hustings galvanized a party's voters the way a big game excited a team's fans. Thus, in 1851 when a Tennessee Whig deplored "some lukewarmness, not to say defection, among some Whigs," he thought "they need warming up. If we could have a collision on the stump here, it would help us much."[84] The sheer fact of conflict caused adrenalin to flow.

For similar reasons, politicians welcomed attacks from the opposing party because nothing better stirred up the fighting spirit in their own ranks. In 1844, for example, Georgia's Alexander H. Stephens rejoiced that "the Locos seem determined to do what they can by gasconnading, and the only effect of it is I think to arouse the Whigs and make them energetic, and that is all we want." Five years later, a Chicago Whig echoed Stephens: "Whenever a locofoco abuses, or attempts to abuse a Whig—the more I like that Whig—and the more opprobrium a Locofoco Press, attempts to hurl upon him, the closer I cling to him."[85]

Yet interparty conflict involved far more than competition for the sake of competition. Party battles often directly channeled regional, social, economic, religious, and cultural conflict of the deepest sort. If the political parties did not stand for something different from each other, antagonistic social groups would not bother to support one party rather than the other, for they could not score a victory over the other through the political process. That triumph might result in a concrete policy advocated by a social group's party and opposed by its rivals— say, a Sunday blue law, a bank charter, or an internal improvement bill. It might be simply vicarious for some ethnic, religious, or regional groups—the thrill that our party won while theirs lost. But for rival social groups to retain faith in the efficacy of the Whig and Democratic parties as channels for their social conflict, they had to believe that the parties were in political conflict over the various issues with which they dealt, whether or not those particular issues directly touched the interests of the social group.

Casting a ballot also served a political purpose broader than enactment of legislation or humiliation of a traditional foe. Many Americans had come to believe by 1840 that, as Calvin Colton had written in *The Crisis of the Country*, two-party competition was necessary to protect republican liberty from the reckless power of rulers. By voting one party out and the other in, people could change the regime and install new governors more closely in touch with their will. True self-government, in short, necessitated conflict between parties that provided alternative stands on issues so that governmental policy could be changed by changing the party that controlled the government. As a Whig journalist put it in 1848, "The very life of liberty is maintained only by the strife of contending parties." "To carry out in practice the theory of our Republican Government," former Democrat Preston King echoed in 1855, we must "openly and clearly . . . declare principles and measures," and parties must "divide upon them as they are for and against them." Choice was critical to self-government. "Our whole theory of

Government stands upon the idea that the electors of the whole country can and will understand and choose the right." As King implied, in sum, if the electors saw no clear choice between the parties, they would consider republican government in jeopardy.[86]

Ultimately, the very legitimacy of the Whig and Democratic parties and of the two-party system depended upon this belief that party competition provided the best way to perpetuate and preserve republicanism. For that legitimacy to survive, the public had to believe that a change would result when they replaced one set of rulers with another. The parties therefore had to stand for different things, and they had to enact different policies. Just as the Whig party had attracted enough new voters to win the elections of 1840 by advocating policies different from those of the Democrats, they would have to implement different policies in order to retain that voting support.

Certainly, most Whigs expected that revolution in governmental policy after the elections of 1840. After twelve years of seemingly fruitless opposition to the Jacksonians, they finally controlled a popular majority, the White House, both houses of Congress, and most state governments. As the year 1840 closed, Whigs throughout the land rejoiced at their long-delayed chance "to save the liberty, the morals, and the happiness of the people, and to rescue the Constitution."

Chapter 6

"The Whig Party Seems Now Totally Broken Up and Dismembered"

"I NOW REJOICE in the almost certain prospect of the restoration of our common Country to its original prosperity and greatness," an Alabama Whig wrote a month before the installation of the new administration.[1] With control of the presidency, a 29–22 majority in the new Senate, a 133–102 margin in the new House of Representatives, and possession of a majority of state governments, the Whig party stood poised to reform government and to promote economic recovery.[2] The nation's desperate economic condition and the financial disarray of state and national governments required new policies. Their promised alternatives, they believed, would provide the necessary remedy. More than that, they now had the opportunity to restore what they considered the proper balance between the legislative and executive branches of the national government and thus end supposed executive despotism. Harrison had repeatedly pledged to defer to the will of Congress, and Whigs intended to prove that congressional initiative could work. Additionally, the party had its first opportunity to fill the 18,000 offices subject to federal appointment and thus to replace Democrats, whom they scorned as corrupt, incompetent spoilsmen, with public servants of talent and ability.[3] Best of all, from the perspective of Whig politicians, by demonstrating the efficacy of their principles and programs and by using federal patronage to bolster local organizations, the Whig party had a chance to cement the loyalty of those hundreds of thousands of voters who had rallied to the party since 1837 in order to achieve change. They had the opportunity, in short, to effect a durable voter realignment and become a permanent majority party if they could redress the grievances and address the needs that had turned an electoral majority against the Democrats.[4]

Whig leaders in 1841 thought they must act immediately, lest their grand opportunity slip away. As Henry Clay's fellow Kentuckian, Senator John J. Crittenden, put it, Harrison and the Whigs "*must act*. The people expect it, and are entitled to expect it. . . . The real danger is in inaction, and falling behind, and disappointing the high hopes and feelings of the people."[5] This pressure to enact their program decisively shaped Whigs' behavior during the next two years.

As Crittenden's letter reveals, Whigs realized that opportunity entails risk. The chance to succeed implies the chance to fail. And fail they did. Almost every one of their bright expectations went aglimmering. Instead of harmony between the executive and the legislature, they suffered rancorous division. Instead of using appointments to demonstrate the high caliber of Whig officeholders and thus consolidating the party, federal patronage first caused internal party strife and popular disillusionment and then became a weapon utilized against them. Instead of quickly legislating a cogent program for economic recovery, they suffered internal bickering, paralysis, and frustration. Instead of restoring prosperity, they witnessed continuing stagnation and depression. As a result, instead of confirming the allegiance of voters and their control of state and national governments, they suffered some of the most severe reversals in off-year congressional and gubernatorial elections in American history. Table 9 reveals these setbacks, and in the state legislative elections of 1841, 1842, and 1843 Whigs suffered still worse losses. In sum, Whigs' "almost certain prospect" for success turned instead, as John C. Calhoun had presciently forecast within weeks of Harrison's triumph, into a "speedy and utter overthrow."[6]

The story of the first Whig presidential administration is therefore the story of opportunity lost. Although it is a tale often told, most accounts have been biographical and have focused largely on personal rivalries among Whig leaders in Washington. Historians have carefully delineated the early maneuvering by Henry Clay and Daniel Webster for the presidential nomination in 1844 and the subsequent conflict between Clay and John Tyler, who succeeded Harrison as president. Personal rivalry and the clash between the president and the congressional wing of the party have thus been seen as the dominant themes of that administration and as the major causes of the Whigs' downfall.[7]

Table 9

Whig Proportion of Congressional and
Gubernatorial Seats Won Between 1840 and 1844[a]

	Congressional	Gubernatorial
1840	63.2% ($N = 136$)	85.7% ($N = 14$)
1841	60.2% ($N = 103$)	38.5% ($N = 13$)
1842	29.2% ($N = 65$)	27.2% ($N = 11$)
1843	37.5% ($N = 160$)	41.7% ($N = 12$)
1844	37.9% ($N = 145$)	58.8% ($N = 17$)

[a]This table is based on the Congressional Quarterly's *Guide to U.S. Elections.* I have included all the congressional elections in each year, including special elections to fill vacancies, so that the total number of seats contested often exceeds the total number of seats in a given Congress. The number of contested seats in 1842 was unusually low, for the requirement of reapportionment after the census of 1840 and the need of some states to abandon at-large congressional tickets for the district system in compliance with an 1842 federal statute caused a number of states that would normally have held elections in 1842 to postpone them until 1843.

Factionalism did play an important role in the Whig debacle, but it must be understood in a broader context. Rivalry between Webster and Clay, after all, as well as other factional fault lines, had fissured the Whig party since its inception. Such rivalries, endemic to political parties,[8] had not prevented the sweeping Whig electoral success between 1837 and 1840. The problem is why internal division demolished the party's electoral fortunes at some times but not at others. What defined the Whigs' debacle was the party's crushing defeats in state and congressional elections in the early 1840s, exploding all hopes of their quickly becoming a new majority party. How persisting factionalism related to success in the late 1830s but failure in the early 1840s is what must be explained.

Similarly, tension and conflict between the president and the congressional wing of his party are endemic to the American political system. Yet rarely in American history has that tension produced electoral disasters as extensive as those the Whigs suffered in the off-year elections between 1840 and 1844. During the Civil War, for example, Abraham Lincoln and congressional Republicans differed over how to conduct the war. Despite that disagreement, the Republicans remained the majority party. A more apt analogy would be the conflict between Lincoln's successor, Andrew Johnson, and the congressional Republicans. However stunning the similarities between that strife and the battle between John Tyler and congressional Whigs, the two collisions yielded different results. Despite Johnson's use of patronage and his open campaigning against the Republicans, despite his attempt to form a new party, just as Tyler eventually would, the Republicans expanded their congressional majorities in the elections of 1866 by running against the president. The difference between 1866 and 1842–43 was that the Republicans' program was passed over Johnson's objections, thus reinforcing the loyalty and fervor of their voters. Stymied by Tyler, Whigs could pass no such program. Hence, not just personal rivalry for the presidency or factional battles over patronage or disagreements between the president and Congress upended the Whig party during its first presidential administration. The paralyzing effect of those divisions on the attempt to legislate policies did the most damage.

I

Rifts within the Whig leadership at Washington appeared even before Harrison's inauguration. Whigs expected to win the next presidential sweepstakes in 1844, and Harrison's pledge not to seek a second term meant that a new man would reap that reward. Both Clay and Webster, who had been thrust aside for Harrison in 1839, determined as soon as the polls closed in 1840 to be that lucky man. Expecting to manipulate the supposedly malleable figurehead in the White House, they both therefore sought to influence the makeup of the cabinet and the allocation of patronage.

As the party's most prominent congressional leader, Clay expected an offer of the State Department in Harrison's cabinet, but he declined the post even before it was tendered because he preferred to remain in the Senate. With his blessing, Webster received that important slot instead. But Clay hoped to staff the remainder of the cabinet with his friends. He succeeded to the extent that he blocked the rumored appointment of Charles Wickliffe, a Kentucky rival, and secured instead the attorney generalship for his faithful lieutenant Crittenden. John Bell of Tennessee, the secretary of war, and Thomas Ewing, the secretary of the Treasury, could also be considered Clay allies.

Clay was especially anxious for the appointment of John M. Clayton of Delaware. Initially, Clay had suggested Clayton for the Treasury and Ewing for the postmaster general's office. But Webster had prevailed on Harrison to appoint New York's Francis Granger as postmaster general instead and to switch Ewing to the Treasury Department. Frantic to get Clayton into the cabinet, Clay then held a stormy personal interview with Harrison, demanding Clayton's appointment as navy secretary, the remaining cabinet post. Proud and vain, Harrison was determined not to appear subservient to the party's senior statesman and reportedly reminded Clay that he, rather than Clay, had been elected president. Instead, Harrison chose to let Whig congressmen from the South Atlantic states fill the last spot, and they decided on George Badger of North Carolina, who was also friendly to Clay. Thus, despite Clay's failure to win a place for Clayton, his heated argument with Harrison, and Webster's appointment to the most important post, Clay had done well. The other cabinet members were either his outright supporters or at least personally cordial to him.

Stung by the old general's response to his efforts for Clayton, Clay decided not to interfere with lesser patronage appointments, lest he appear too dictatorial. There was, however, one significant exception to this rule. The most important patronage position in the United States, both symbolically and in terms of substantive political influence, was the collectorship of the New York Custom House. The collector could fill some 600 subordinate positions in that office, as well as influence other federal appointments in New York City and Brooklyn. Thus, the post provided a base of power in New York State. The Seward-Weed wing of the New York Whig party, which had opposed Clay's nomination, favored Edward Curtis, a Webster lieutenant, for the job. Clay vehemently opposed Curtis' appointment, but to no avail. When the cabinet chose Curtis, Clay's enemies in New York had seemed to prevail, and Clay had succeeded only in infuriating Harrison still more. Citing Clay's humiliation, the sympathetic Willie P. Mangum predicted a "widening of the breach between Clay and Webster."[9]

Clay still retained one powerful weapon with which to win the presidential nomination he craved—his leadership of the Whigs in the Senate. Indeed, the most significant aspect of the jockeying between Webster and Clay in January, February, and March 1841 was that the two had chosen alternate routes to their common goal. Webster decided to work from inside the administration, while Clay remained outside it.

Necessity as well as personal inclination dictated the choice of these divergent courses. The dynamics of personal or factional rivalry within one party were the same as the dynamics of conflict between the parties. Rivals had to distinguish themselves from each other in order to woo different elements in the same party. They might, for example, adopt different stands on issues or argue for different priorities. Webster and Clay had followed this course in 1833 when Webster took an aggressively northern stand on the Nullification and tariff issues, while Clay tried to appease the South and defuse the crisis in South Carolina with the Compromise Tariff. Again, in 1837, Webster had tried to establish himself as a northern candidate by opposing the annexation of Texas on antislavery grounds, while Clay strove to bury the divisive sectional issue. Now their shared ambition led them once again down different paths.

Aware that he was doomed to play second fiddle to Clay in the Senate, Webster saw the State Department as a distinctive niche for himself. Negotiations with England over the disputed Maine boundary were pending, and skillful management of foreign policy would enhance his reputation as a statesman. Because the Whigs believed that the cabinet was coequal with the president in the executive branch, Webster as its "premier" had a chance not only to shape administration policy but to gain credit for it. Finally, by operating in continuous contact with the president, even during the long spells when Congress was in recess, Webster might win the president's blessing as his successor. At the very least, he could have more direct influence on patronage dispensation than Clay—as his apparent success in the Curtis affair demonstrated.[10]

Clay's reasons for wanting to remain in the Senate were equally compelling. All Whigs expected Congress to formulate Whig policies, and as the party's legislative leader, Clay expected to get the main credit for the program that was passed. Beyond that, he sincerely believed that a comprehensive program of economic legislation was desperately needed to succor the economy and pull the federal government out of debt. He was further convinced that unless the Whig party enacted that program quickly, it would be repudiated at the polls. By uniting his party behind legislative proposals, therefore, Clay could win the gratitude of Whig politicians as well as Whig voters. Such a combination would guarantee his nomination in 1844.

In that belief, Clay and his friends in the Senate like Crittenden used the second session of the Twenty-Sixth Congress, from December 1840 to March 1841, to formulate the Whig program. Mercilessly and obnoxiously taunting the Democrats about the impending overthrow of their measures, Whigs called for repeal of the subtreasury system, incorporation of a new national bank, distribution of land revenues to the states, a new loan to tide the government over until its revenues could be increased, a national bankruptcy law to relieve debtors, and an upward revision of the tariff. To forward that goal, a Whig caucus urged Harrison to call a special session of Congress because of the economic emergency and laid out an agenda for it. They did so, again, primarily because they felt pressure to fulfill the hopes they had raised in the electorate. Hence Crittenden, in the letter quoted earlier, called such a special session *"absolutely necessary."* "The real danger is in inaction, and . . . disappointing the high hopes and feelings of the people."[11]

Not all Whigs were so sanguine about a special session. Some feared that the party was still so divided that a rush to precipitate action could prove calamitous. Far better, they thought, to await the normal session of the new Congress scheduled to meet in December 1841 in order to give the Whigs time to negotiate a program upon which all could agree. New York Congressman Millard Fillmore, for example, wrote to Thurlow Weed in February that "the course of events had unfortunately precipitated upon us the discussion of the proposed measures of the incoming administration." Democrats would benefit if those measures proved "odious," but, given Whigs' promises to restore prosperity, an extra session was now "indispensable or at least politic."[12]

Significantly, one of the Whigs who continued to oppose a special session was Webster. He realized that he could benefit from Clay's prolonged absence from Washington, and he worried about the disruptive potential of hasty action.[13] Clay, in contrast, passionately supported a special session. When he learned that Harrison, with Webster's concurrence, had tentatively decided against it, he sent Harrison a letter virtually instructing him to call the session and writing out a draft for the presidential proclamation.

For Harrison, this insulting "lecture" was the last straw. In reply, he chastised Clay for being too "impetuous" and ordered the mortified Kentuckian to communicate with him in the future only by writing rather than through personal visits to the White House. Clay's imperious letter undoubtedly confirmed the president in his intention not to call a special session. When Ewing reported that the government was in debt and faced an additional deficit of more than $11 million unless additional revenue was quickly raised, however, Harrison reluctantly consented. On March 17 he summoned an emergency session of Congress to meet on May 31, 1841, to address the economic crisis.[14]

Within two weeks of Harrison's inauguration, Clay had fallen out with the new president, and Webster seemed to have won an initial advantage. Both sought to benefit the Whig party as a whole, for only if the party retained its popularity would the nomination in 1844 be valuable. Yet each clearly had a different understanding of what was best for the party and for his own personal ambition. How this conflict might have been resolved had Harrison served out his term can only be speculated. Old Tippecanoe turned sixty-eight just days before his inauguration and was in frail health. Enervated by the hordes of ravenous office seekers who descended on the White House like a swarm of locusts, he contracted pneumonia and died on April 4, one month to the day after his inauguration. Harrison's death immediately changed all calculations, for it brought to the presidency a man of decidedly different values, a man who had not pledged to defer to the legislative will of Congress, and a man who had not foresworn a second term.

II

The accession of John Tyler at first betokened an improvement in Clay's fortunes. Tyler considered himself and was considered by others a Clay man, and he immediately filled some patronage posts with Clay's friends as a gesture of friendship. Tyler was not only the first vice president to serve out another president's term, but at the age of fifty-one he was the youngest man yet to hold that office. Harrison's death, that is, seemed to restore Clay's stature as the undisputed leader of his party, for Whigs could not believe that Tyler, given his relative youth and accidental incumbency, would have the temerity to oppose him. Tyler's pleasant personality further aroused expectations of harmony between the two. The model of a gentleman planter, the Virginian was unfailingly polite, amiable, and apparently eager to please. Members of the cabinet, which he retained, soon wrote Clay that he could count on Tyler's cooperation. By mid-April, Clay himself was informing friends that he expected to pass the entire agenda the Whigs had laid out for the special session.[15]

Whigs in the cabinet and Congress soon discovered that they had mistaken Tyler's courtesy for diffidence, his affability for malleability. Ascetically thin, with a long, angular face, sunken cheeks, and a long, pointed nose, Tyler's very physique betokened rigidity. A former state legislator, governor, congressman, and United States senator, Tyler possessed strong principles and the self-confidence to stand by them. He wanted to work with the congressional Whigs, but the former Democrat belonged to the dwindling state rights faction of the party and had long opposed a national bank, a protective tariff, and federal internal improvements as unconstitutional. His adherence to these beliefs was fortified by the counsel of unofficial advisors from Virginia who were even more ideologically rigid in their affirmation of state rights and strict construction than the president. This group, whom regular Whigs soon castigated as "Impracticables" or the "Virginia Cabal," included Judge Abel P. Upshur, Judge Nathaniel Beverly Tucker, and Thomas R. Dew, president of the College of William and Mary, all of whom resided in Williamsburg, as well as Littleton W. Tazewell and the Virginia Whig congressman Henry Wise. The ideological objections that these men, as well as other Virginia Whig congressmen like Robert M. T. Hunter, Thomas R. Gilmer, and Francis Mallory, raised against the proposed Whig program were contemptuously dismissed by the vast majority of Whigs as "Virginia abstractions."[16]

Even before the special session of Congress assembled at the end of May, Tyler privately informed Clay and other Whigs that he opposed a national bank. In his message to that session, he publicly spelled out which parts of the anticipated Whig program he could accept. He endorsed repeal of the subtreasury, the distribution of land revenues, and new revenue measures including an additional bond issue because the government faced a severe deficit. He indicated, however, that he would reject both new revenue measures and distribution if they required an increase in tariff rates above the 20 percent *ad valorem* duties due to be reached on July 1, 1842, under the Compromise Tariff of 1833. He warned that he would also reject any new bank or fiscal agent for government funds if he thought it unconstitutional. Both duty and honor, he specifically cautioned, would force him to resort to a veto in such a case.[17]

The Whigs thus confronted an immediate challenge to their fundamental principle of congressional supremacy. Tyler clearly intended to shape the Whig program to comply with his wishes. By controlling patronage, he could reward or punish members of Congress, for each had scores of friends at home hungering for some federal plum or other. By using the hated veto, he could block their program and thus jeopardize their future success at the polls. Whigs therefore faced a choice. They could abide by the president's wishes, in order to get part of their program passed and preserve harmony between the executive and legislature, or they could risk Tyler's wrath and party disruption by attempting to pass their entire program. How different Whigs made this choice depended not only on their personal ambition and how they judged the president's firmness, but also on honest disagreements about what was best for the nation and for the Whig party.

Despite Tyler's warnings, Clay and the great majority of congressional Whigs massed behind the whole Whig program. Clay and his supporters quickly seized control of the relevant House and Senate committees when the special session opened. To reduce Democratic obstructionism, the Senate, on Clay's suggestion, resolved to confine its business to the economic measures necessary to relieve the crisis. Later the Whigs unsuccessfully tried to amend Senate rules to limit debate. The all-important Whig caucus, which Willie P. Mangum of North Carolina chaired, agreed to vote down any Democratic amendments. And the Whig leadership kept the House and Senate sitting for seven or eight hours a day, six days a week, despite the suffocating summer heat and humidity.[18]

On June 7, Clay spelled out the agenda. In order to save time and avert duplication of effort, he proposed, the House should immediately begin writing bills for a new loan and an increase in tariff duties while the Senate prepared bills to repeal the Independent Treasury Act, create a new national bank, and distribute land revenues. Undeterred by Tyler's message, he explicitly said he intended a national bank, and on June 10 he introduced a distribution bill that contained no proviso limiting tariff duties to 20 percent, as Tyler wished.[19]

To this agenda Whigs soon added a uniform national bankruptcy act. This legislation consumed both houses of Congress during the special session that dragged on from May 31 to September 13, 1841. Although the measures became inextricably entangled, for purposes of clarity it is useful to separate the banking issue and the Whig response to it. The question of a new national bank first provoked the clash between Tyler and congressional Whigs. That issue preoccupied Washington politicians and their correspondents during the summer. On that rock the Whig program would founder and the Whig party splinter.

On June 7, Clay asked Treasury Secretary Ewing to send Congress a proposal for a new bank that met Tyler's constitutional reservations. Five days later Ewing submitted a bill that had the cabinet's reluctant endorsement. Ewing's bill called for Congress, in its capacity as Washington's municipal legislature, to charter a bank in the District of Columbia. That bank could establish state branches only with the explicit consent of state legislatures. The federal government would subscribe to one-fifth of the bank's $30 million stock. As the fiscal agent of the government, the bank would receive governmental deposits. But it could also engage in normal private banking practices.[20]

Whigs in and outside Congress greeted the administration's proposal with howls of dismay, derision, and anger. For one thing, it struck many as being unconstitutional. By requiring state approval of branches, it seemed to subvert the supremacy of the national government. By restricting the bank's freedom to establish branches and by offering no guarantee against state taxation, Congress would ensure that no private investors would buy stock. "What a bank would be that!" sneered Clay to Kentucky Governor Robert P. Letcher. Not one New York Whig in a hundred approved the Ewing bill, a Whig editor informed Mangum.[21]

Appalled at the inadequacy of Tyler's measure, the Whig majority referred Ewing's bill to a select committee on the currency that Clay chaired. But that committee did not write a new banking measure. Instead, the Senate Whig caucus, meeting in three-hour sessions for four or five consecutive nights, designed a substitute.[22] On June 23, Clay reported the product of the party's labors to the full Senate. It differed from Ewing's plan in two significant respects. It implied that Congress was acting as the national legislature, not as a municipal government, and thereby signaled that Congress was establishing a true national bank.

The bill also authorized the bank to establish branches without prior consent of states. Senate Whigs thus boldly flouted Tyler's will.

The urgency, discipline, and defiance that characterized the Whig majority during June and the remainder of the special session require explanation. Given the risk to the party inherent in angering the president, why did they do it? Many Democrats at the time accused Clay of imperiously lashing his colleagues into line in order to further his own ambition and to demonstrate that he rather than Tyler led the Whig party. Many historians agree. According to this interpretation, Clay acted for personal reasons, not out of concern for the party or its program. He explicitly tried to provoke Tyler into a veto and thereby to eradicate Tyler as the Whig nominee in 1844.[23]

Without question, Clay was jealous of Tyler, and he was determined to demonstrate his undisputed party leadership by pushing his program through. Yet he also sincerely believed that the good of the country and of the Whig party required the passage of the whole program. Whatever Clay's personal motives, moreover, other Whig senators, let alone members of the House, hardly deferred to Clay's will simply to satisfy his personal desires. After the Whig caucus framed the bank bill, Mangum reported that the Whigs had been concerned with putting "the Vessel of State on the right tack," not with the presidential succession. He indicated as well that in the crucial caucus sessions that framed the bill, Clay had remained virtually silent for fear of lending credence to Democratic charges that he was a dictator.[24] Alternately magnetic, imperious, and impatient, Clay led the Whig forces in the Senate. But his colleagues did not slavishly do his bidding.

Nor can institutional considerations fully account for the performance of the congressional Whigs. Granted, many regarded Tyler's stipulations about what he could or could not accept from Congress as a form of executive tyranny, and over time this resentment increased. But above all else, Clay led so effectively because most Whigs agreed with his legislative goals. They too believed that they had to pass their entire program, regardless of Tyler's strict constructionist, state rights scruples.

Congressional Whigs were alarmed about economic conditions and about the political necessity to improve them. Prices had remained low throughout 1840 and the first months of 1841. Commerce had stagnated, and in many places credit had disappeared. Bankers, merchants, planters, and farmers clamored for a national bankruptcy law to relieve their burden of debt. Many state governments that had recently come under Whig control faced insolvency and could not pay the interest, let alone the principal, on their bonds. Without federal aid, in sum, Whig governors and legislatures would have to impose unpopular new taxes. Having already been forced to sell Treasury notes to make up for its revenue shortfall, the federal government expected an additional deficit of $11 million in 1841. Tariff rates were due to drop sharply in 1842 when the major reductions under the tariff of 1833 would take effect. These cuts would deprive the government of $5 million.[25] To most political leaders in the nineteenth century, deficit financing was a calamity. As the majority party, Whigs felt a heavy responsibility to resuscitate both the private and public economic sectors.

As Congressman Christopher Morgan of New York proclaimed in June, "We came here to relieve the country. The eyes of the nation are bent upon us with an intensity which has never before been experienced. The people demand justice at our hands. They demand that we should work and not talk." Calhoun also recognized the Whigs' desperation to deliver on their promises to the electorate. The Whigs feared "the shame and certain overthrow, if a session call[ed] for the purpose of passing their batch of measures, should terminate without doing anything," he reported in July. "This and this alone holds them together, and this and this alone will carry their measures, if they should be carried at all."[26]

Precisely that fear of failure convinced most Whigs that they must pass their entire "batch of measures," no matter what Tyler wanted. His insistence on no tariff duties above 20 percent would cripple any attempt to balance the federal budget. Distribution without substantial increases in tariff revenue would only deplete the federal treasury still further since, aside from borrowing, duties and land sales provided virtually all its revenue. Yet Whigs dared not renege on distribution, for Whig governors and Whig newspapers in the West and South were demanding it to spare those states the unpalatable choice between repudiation of their bonds and new taxes. Simultaneously, New York's Whig Governor William H. Seward was justifying his call for a huge new state bond issue in 1841 with assurances that no new state property taxes would be required since the money from federal distribution could pay off the debt.[27]

Nor were most Whigs willing to sacrifice a new national bank. Only a bank with the power to establish branches where it pleased and to make direct local loans, they believed, could possibly attract private investors and provide the uniform currency and credit necessary to fuel an economic recovery. Only such a bank, moreover, could prevent disaster at the polls because the Whig rank and file demanded it. They believed, in short, that unless they chartered a real national bank, their newly won supporters would abandon them and they would be overwhelmed. "We have deliberately made up our minds to go to the Country & take all the consequences," Mangum explained, "rather than to be forced to do what will be an entire failure, involving loss of personal character & public interest, to say nothing of the dissolution of the party."[28]

The Whig program, even if passed in its entirety, would probably not have spurred an economic revival. But most Whigs were convinced that the whole program was vital. Unless they passed their complete package, they feared, it would not satisfy public demands. Conciliating the president would decimate the party. Half a loaf was not enough.

Fear about "the magnitude of the consequences of failure" caused congressional Whigs to accuse Tyler of placing the party itself in jeopardy by his rigid intransigence. "We are in a crisis as a party," Clay lamented in June, and on July 4 he warned a friend that "Mr. Tyler's opinions about a Bank are giving us great trouble. Indeed, they not only threaten a defeat on that measure, but endanger the permanency, and the ascendancy of the Whig cause." "The Whig party is in a most woeful plight," echoed Mangum, "and there is ground for apprehension that the Session will prove abortive—the consequences of disgrace, disaster & final discomfiture are palpable & appalling."[29]

Far from attempting to provoke Tyler into a veto, in short, the congressional Whig leadership originally feared its consequences. By demonstrating Whig sentiment in the country and in Congress, they hoped to convert the president. Why, rank and file Whigs wondered, did the administration prefer Ewing's bill, "with its Democratic features of establishing branches whereby the constitutional board is virtually surrendered," to a true Whig bill? No real Whig could oppose "*Whig measures*" like Clay's bank bill, a North Carolinian informed Senator William A. Graham. Hence, "the absorbing subject throughout the land is . . . whether since the death of Gen. Harrison, the country is to be considered under a Whig Administration, or not."[30]

Whereas congressional Whigs thought the party would be wrecked unless it met Whig voters' demand for an unadulterated Whig program, cabinet members feared the party would be wrecked if Tyler aborted the whole program through his vetoes. They therefore deemed half a loaf considerably better than nothing at all.[31] Predictably, Webster led the cabinet campaign to arrange a compromise. Since the Massachusetts banking system was sound, he saw no need for Clay's national bank to spur economic recovery. Ewing's alternative, he believed, was perfectly feasible; given Tyler's stubbornness, moreover, it was the only bank Whigs could get. As mediator between Congress and the president, Webster also hoped to advance his presidential candidacy. If Clay provoked a rupture between the president and Congress, Webster could assume the role of party harmonizer and savior.[32]

Through private conversations with Whig congressmen and newspaper articles in the *National Intelligencer*, therefore, Webster worked frantically to win over congressional Whigs to the Ewing bill. The main point, he insisted, was to get "*something . . . done.*" The choice was between "getting no Bank" and "breaking up the Administration" or enacting the "*practicable* and *attainable*" Ewing plan. The "one remedy for the urgent necessities of the country" and "the salvation of the Whig party," Webster wrote in July, "is *union*, immediate UNION. Let us try such a bank as we can agree upon and establish."[33]

These pleas and the lure of patronage weaned enough defectors away from the Whig leadership to produce a stalemate in the Senate. Of the Southerners, William C. Rives and William S. Archer of Virginia, William C. Preston of South Carolina, and John Henderson of Mississippi shared Tyler's state rights scruples to varying degrees. William D. Merrick of Maryland and Alexander Barrow of Louisiana, seeking patronage favors from Tyler, were amenable to the Ewing bill. In addition, Webster's argument that only Ewing's bill could preserve party harmony had great weight with the two senators from Massachusetts, Rufus Choate and Isaac Bates, as well as with Maine's George Evans. Those three, as well as John M. Berrien of Georgia, argued both in the Whig caucus and on the Senate floor that Clay's measure was suicidal, for Tyler would veto it. Some kind of bank was better than no bank, they contended.[34]

By early July, Whig leaders saw that Clay's bill could not pass. While the Kentuckian insisted that "the question is a National Bank or no National Bank," the caucus grudgingly accepted the need to conciliate the administration. Nonetheless, Rives' amendment, restoring Ewing's provision that states must consent to branches, received only eight Whig votes. It was overwhelmed by the main body of Whigs and Democrats, who sought a bill that was so offensive that Tyler must veto it. Indeed, throughout the session the minority Democrats played a brilliant hand, offering little opposition to those measures Tyler agreed with but strenuously objecting to the measures that offended the president's constitutional sensibilities. By ensuring a breach between Tyler and the Whigs, Democrats thought they would guarantee a Democratic victory at the next election.[35]

Late in July the Whig caucus finally agreed upon a concession that might carry enough Whig votes to pass the bill on the Senate floor. On July 23, Clay offered an amendment that states could accept or reject branches. If any state did not act at the first session of its legislature after passage of the law, however, its consent to branches would be assumed. Furthermore, the amendment provided that Congress could subsequently establish a branch after a state rejected one if Congress deemed such a branch vital to the national interest. This transparently cosmetic straddle satisfied no one. Still, the compromise amendment passed (barely), 25 to 24. Rives and Archer joined the Democrats in opposition, while the furious Henderson absented himself from the vote so that it could carry. On July 25, the amended bill passed by a 26–23 margin, with the Virginia Whigs again supporting the Democratic minority.[36]

Compared to the prolonged struggle in the Senate, the House acted with relative dispatch, passing the amended bill after only five days of debate, 128 to 98. Democrats opposed the bill unanimously, while 95 percent of the Whigs favored it. After two months of wrangling and frustration, the Whig majority had finally chartered a new bank, the linchpin of their economic program.[37]

But could the amended bill survive John Tyler's scrutiny? Since early July, Whigs and Democrats alike had predicted that Tyler would veto it, and the president had told several congressmen that he considered Clay's supposedly conciliatory amendment a contemptible hoax. Nor could the cabinet dissuade the president. During July and August their influence upon the president had diminished as he moved closer to the Virginia cabal. Tyler informed the cabinet on August 11 that he intended a veto, but only at the last moment, when it was too late for changes, did he reveal to them the contents of the veto message itself. On August 16, nine days after the bank bill reached his desk, Tyler sent the veto message to the Senate. He castigated the branching provision as an unconstitutional sham. He also denounced the bank's power to discount local promissory notes as both economically pernicious and grotesquely beyond Congress' constitutional authority to regulate the currency.[38]

The night before the veto message officially arrived at the Senate, the Whig caucus tentatively agreed upon a response. They would table the veto message and immediately pass Ewing's original bill. If Tyler dared veto that, the cabinet would resign and the Whigs would read Tyler out of the party. If he signed it, as most Whigs expected he would, then experience with its inadequacies would soon force Tyler himself to request amendments in line with Clay's bill. Either way, Tyler would look like a fool, and congressional Whigs' program would be vindicated.

Attorney General John J. Crittenden discerned a better alternative. Since Tyler really objected not to branches per se but to branches with power to make local loans or discounts on promissory notes without state assent, he excitedly wrote Clay on the morning of August 16, why not confine the branches' power to discounting bills of exchange? As Crittenden and the congressional Whigs perfectly understood, but Tyler apparently did not, such a change would not hamper the power of the bank to boost the economy. Unlike promissory notes, which were in effect loans to individuals, widely used and readily available bills of exchange were commercial notes secured by physical goods in transit that promised payment at a future date when those goods reached their ultimate destination.

To get a loan, a planter or businessman need only obtain a bill of exchange and sell it to the bank at a discount. The bank branch could thus pump money into a local economy simply by financing an interstate or international transaction.[39]

After Crittenden informed his cabinet colleagues of his discovery, Webster and Ewing apparently won Tyler's assent to the change. If the power to discount promissory notes were prohibited, the jubilant cabinet members told congressional leaders, the president would even agree to allow such a bank or Fiscal Agent, as he wanted it called, to establish branches without state consent.

Within two days of the veto message, therefore, the Whigs had miraculously discovered a formula for party harmony and a workable bank. Far more eager to charter a bank than to break with the president, the congressional Whig caucus immediately agreed to pass such a measure under the impression that Tyler was committed to it. Tyler in fact had warned his cabinet members not to make any such intimation to the congressional Whigs, but they, as well as the Whig congressmen who talked to Tyler on August 17 and 18, distinctly gave Congress the impression that Tyler had pledged to sign the bill.[40]

Once again, the Whigs had misjudged the proud Virginian in the White House. On August 19, the very day that the new bill was introduced into the House, his vanity was stung by the Whig reaction to his veto of the first bill. In the Senate, Clay railed that Tyler's kitchen cabinet of Virginians was trying to break up the Whig party in order to form a third party behind their peculiar doctrines. The same day a letter that the Richmond, Virginia, Whig Congressman John Minor Botts had written on August 16 was published. Botts denounced the president's veto but promised that the Whigs would "head" him by passing the Ewing bill, which he was committed to sign, and when that bank failed to attract any investors, Tyler's ignorance about banking would be revealed to the world.[41] Refusing to be intimidated, Tyler resolved not to sign the new bill. He immediately told every congressman he could contact that he would veto the bill, and newspaper correspondents in Washington began to predict it while the new banking measure was still working its way through Congress.

Although Tyler had run out of patience with both the congressional Whigs and his cabinet, he still wished to avert an open rupture. In order to avoid a veto, therefore, he hoped Congress would postpone the whole banking matter until the next regular session convened in December. This time, however, the cabinet's entreaties to congressmen were to no avail. The Whig caucus pressed the matter to a conclusion. Most preferred Tyler to sign the new law. If so, they would have a workable bank and could claim party credit for it. If they could not get the bank, their constituents told them, it was preferable that Tyler veto the bill than that they back down in order to preserve party harmony. For if Tyler vetoed the measure, they could read him out of the party, blame him for sabotaging Whig banking policy, and deny that the Whig party itself was responsible for that failure. If they conciliated the president by delay, they feared that the Whig party itself would be blamed for failing to fulfill its promises.[42]

In short, by August the Whigs had decided that they had more to gain from an open rupture with Tyler than by inaction. If they lost the bank, at least they could argue that it was because Tyler was a traitor to the party and not a real Whig. Clay had laid the groundwork for that claim with his charge that Tyler was trying to start a new party and disrupt the Whigs, an accusation that Whig newspapers had broadcast all summer. With this tack Whigs might lose a bank but regain the unifying issue of executive tyranny. "The Whigs are more firmly united now than before," Letcher told Crittenden on September 3. *"The vetoes are a good cement to hold them together."*[43]

So convinced, Whigs rammed the new bank bill through both houses of Congress on party-line votes within two weeks. Six days later, on September 9, Tyler vetoed it. Whigs might console themselves that their constituents would applaud their faithful adherence to their program and respond to the renewed issue of executive despotism. But they had been forced to sacrifice the keystone of their legislative agenda. As a New York editor warned presciently in July, "If no compromise takes place and the extra session terminates without adopting all or nearly all the measures of reform we cannot go to the people of this State at the next election with any hope or prospect of success."[44]

Despite their disarray on the banking issue, the disciplined Whig majority wielded their control of committees and skillfully employed the caucus to push their other measures through on largely party-line votes, and they received Tyler's signature. But the legislation proved so incomplete, defective, or palpably stopgap in nature that Whigs could not effectively run on that record.

While they successfully repealed the Independent Treasury, for example, they replaced it with nothing, thus leaving unclear what would become of government deposits or how the funds could be used to pump credit into the economy. Whigs also enacted a uniform bankruptcy measure that allowed debtors, rather than creditors, to initiate legal proceedings to scale down debts. But this act seemed to allow the rich to escape the consequences of poor business decisions. Before the law took effect in February 1842, therefore, many of the Whigs' own constituents agitated against it, and within a year, Whig congressmen joined Democrats to repeal it. Such an unpopular measure hardly made an attractive campaign issue.[45]

Nor could the Whig-enacted new loan of $12 million, to cover the federal government's expected deficit, provide a captivating issue. Democrats during the Van Buren administration, after all, had sold bonds and Treasury notes to fund the government; borrowing money was hardly a partisan program, even though votes on the measures were partisan. Worse still, because the government was bankrupt, few subscribers could be found for the Whigs' new bonds, and the loan failed.

Equally a failure from Whig purists' perspective was the new tariff law written by Millard Fillmore, chairman of the House Ways and Means Committee. It only raised duties on goods previously taxed below Tyler's mandated 20 percent level to that scarcely protective rate. Fillmore insisted that Congress must readdress the whole tariff issue at the next session a few months later, but with the stopgap tariff of 1841, Whigs could hardly claim to have restored the government's fiscal stability.[46]

The most important measure passed at the special session, the land bill, was a far cry from Whigs' ideal distribution measure. For years, Westerners generally had wanted a reduction of land prices and the cession of federal lands to the states. In contrast, the Northeast had tried to keep land prices high and prevent cession. Meanwhile, congressmen from the South Atlantic states worried primarily about the impact of land prices on tariff levels since land sales and tariff duties provided virtually all federal revenue. Like Tyler, they therefore opposed the reduction of land prices or loss of land revenue if such measures might produce an increase in tariff duties.

Despite these conflicting sectional positions, the Democrats and Whigs had developed distinctive, opposing partisan stands on land policy. Since 1833, Whigs had favored distribution of land revenues to all the states rather than a reduction of prices or cession of lands to the states. Following the lead of Missouri's Senator Thomas Hart Benton, Democrats pushed for price reductions. Democrats had also sought and Whigs opposed the principle of preemption: squatters who settled on government land before it was sold would have the preemptive right to buy it at the lowest starting price, not bid for it against others at the customary land-office auctions.[47]

A distinctive Whig land law, therefore, would have provided for distribution of revenues among all the states with no provision for preemption, let alone a proviso requiring the suspension of distribution if tariff rates were raised. That was the kind of bill Clay introduced on June 10 in the Senate and the kind of bill that Whigs reported out of the House Committee on Public Lands on June 22. Yet the Whigs were immediately forced to retreat before pressure from their own western wing and from Democrats. The result was a final bill that reflected a compromise among the interests of Whigs and Democrats and of the respective sections.

Fearful of retaliation at home, western Whig congressmen had never hewed to the party line on land policy. Instead, many had voted with Democrats for preemption.[48] Thus, when the Whig measures were introduced in 1841, they were quickly revised in the House and Senate to reflect western demands. Future preemption rights for permanent settlers to 160 acres at the minimum price were guaranteed. Reflecting the Democratic demand for lower prices, the final bill also stipulated that if the minimum price for government land were ever raised, distribution would stop. Democrats and Westerners also extorted two other concessions that reduced the revenues available for distribution to the East: a reservation of 10 percent of the proceeds from sales to the states in which the federal lands were located, before the remainder was distributed among all states, and an outright grant of 500,000 federal acres to each of nine western states, as well as federal subsidies to Alabama and Mississippi for internal improvement projects.[49]

To get a bill out of the House, in sum, the Whig leadership had to make a number of compromises—including the adoption of the hated Democratic preemption formula—that seriously reduced potential distributions to the states. Then in the Senate, the Democrats, acting in conjunction with Whigs from the South Atlantic states, insisted on an amendment that distribution must cease whenever tariff rates exceeded 20 percent. That built-in self-stultification, if Congress raised the tariff at an ensuing session, hardly made the compromised distribution act an attractive Whig achievement. Indeed, although Democrats opposed final passage, they seemed the only winners, for preemption had finally been made permanent.

III

Whigs thus emerged from the special session in September with a truncated legislative record rather than the attractive platform they had expected to take to the voters. They had failed to restore prosperity or the financial stability of state and national governments—and they knew it. All they retained was the fatuous hope that voters would blame John Tyler and not the whole Whig party for the fiasco.

To absolve the party, Whigs tried to isolate Tyler, using the second bank veto message as the pretext. On September 11, two days after Congress received that message, all cabinet members except Webster resigned. Two days later, Whig congressmen adopted a manifesto written by John Pendleton Kennedy, the novelist and Baltimore Whig congressman. Gathering in the public gardens outside the Capitol, they literally read Tyler out of the party. They accused him of betraying and abandoning the Whig party to launch a new organization of Democrats and southern state rights ideologues. The Whig party, they proclaimed, loathed his actions, especially his reviving Jackson's executive tyranny.[50] Most Whig organizations around the country praised this excommunication. Whig newspapers savaged Tyler as the "Executive Ass," "His Accidency," and "a man *destitute of intellect and integrity, whose name is the synonym of nihil*," while public meetings burned the apostate in effigy.[51]

But Tyler, having frustrated the party's program, now frustrated this new strategy. Conciliatory, almost apologetic in tone, his second veto message stressed his support for the great bulk of the Whig program and his desire to work with his congressional Whig partners at the next session for a satisfactory bank.[52] His new cabinet appointments further indicated his desire to remain within and to dominate the Whig family. Ignoring his Virginia advisors' pleas to sack the entire cabinet and to cut his ties entirely with nationalist Whigs, Tyler aimed instead to rally anti-Clay Whigs throughout the nation, regardless of their views on state rights. Two members of the new group, Virginia's Abel P. Upshur, the secretary of the navy, and Attorney General Hugh S. Legaré, a South Carolinian, shared the state rights faith. The other cabinet members, however, were explicitly selected because they belonged to preexisting state Whig factions that favored the congressional Whig program but were known to be hostile to Henry Clay and his presidential ambitions. Walter Forward of Pittsburgh became the new secretary of the Treasury, and John C. Spencer of New York, an ally of Seward and Weed, the new secretary of war. Most blatantly, for the patronage-laden postmaster generalship he chose Clay's most bitter personal enemy in the Kentucky Whig party, Charles Wickliffe.[53]

Above all else, Tyler's retention of Webster, despite his Virginia friends' strident protests, signaled his intention to thwart Clay. Clay's most prestigious and powerful rival within the national Whig party, Webster could deliver to the administration strong support from Massachusetts, other New England states, and New York. When Webster agreed to stay in the State Department, Tyler reportedly exclaimed, "*Give me your hand on that, and now I will say to you that Henry Clay is a doomed man.*"[54]

Jealousy of Clay played a major role in Webster's risky decision to stick with Tyler. He wanted to complete negotiations with England over the troublesome Maine boundary—negotiations that would result in the Webster-Ashburton Treaty of 1842. And he carefully cleared his decision with the Massachusetts Whig congressional delegation so as not to commit political suicide at home. But Webster also regarded the congressional pressure on the cabinet to resign as the work of the imperious Clay, and his prodigious pride prohibited his submission to such dictation. His lust for the presidency also militated against it. If he resigned along with the other cabinet members, he feared, the country would regard this as acquiescence in Clay's claim on the next presidential nomination. By his deluded reasoning, remaining in the cabinet seemed to offer the only chance of securing that prize himself. He recognized that Tyler aspired to the nomination, but he knew that the vetoes had destroyed Tyler's prospects. He, however, might escape their stigma since the Whig press had accused Tyler of overriding the cabinet when he made them. By mediating between the congressional Whig party and the discredited president, he might gain credit for preventing a fatal disruption. By remaining in the cabinet, he also retained access to federal patronage in the fight to wrest the nomination from Clay. Although the congressional Whigs' break with Tyler had greatly increased the consequences of failure, Webster imprudently remained in the new administration for many of the same reasons that he had joined Harrison's old one.[55]

Tyler, Webster, and the other cabinet members immediately demanded that federal officeholders side with the administration against Clay, "There was war," Webster told one late in September. "Mr. Tyler must know his friends." The administration also appointed Clay's enemies in various states to still unfilled offices. Tyler especially courted Thurlow Weed and his powerful organization in New York. Unlike other Whig editors, Weed had not condemned his first veto but had instead urged compromise, as had Weed's extraordinarily able editorial ally, Horace Greeley, in the new but already influential New York Tribune. While the public outcry against the second veto and the cabinet disruption briefly forced Weed and Greeley to denounce Tyler, the president rewarded Weed's friends with postmasterships in the state, while customs collector Curtis directed other plums in their direction in New York City. By October, Weed and Greeley were once again calling for a cessation of warfare and a restoration of harmony between the president and the party, exactly as Tyler and Webster wished.[56]

So too in Massachusetts, New Jersey, Pennsylvania, Virginia, Kentucky, Indiana, Ohio, Michigan, and Maryland, when one wing of a state's Whig party sided with Clay and the congressional Whig majority in 1841, the administration could use patronage to lure their intraparty opponents. While in every state except perhaps Massachusetts the majority of Whig politicians joined congressional Whigs in denouncing Tyler, the proadministration minority, with its control of federal jobs and key newspapers, could sabotage the majority's strategy of rallying the party once again on the issue of executive despotism.[57]

Thus instead of an open battle between a unified Whig party on the one hand and an alliance of Tyler, state rights ideologues, and the Democrats on the other, Tyler's activities split the Whig leadership. Worse, divided leaders, especially pro-Tyler jobholders who refused to mobilize for pro-Clay Whig candidates, had an impact on Whig voters. Fully aware that their legislative failures would disenchant those voters who had rallied to the party since 1837 in order to obtain economic recovery, the Clay leaders now hoped to rouse them instead against Tyler, the traitorous Democrat and executive despot. Such a campaign, however, could not work when local Whig officeholders and influential Whig papers like the Albany Evening Journal, the New York Tribune, and Webster's sheets in Boston defended Tyler as a good Whig, denied that he had wrecked the Whig program, and urged congressional Whigs to work with him in the future. Such conflicting signals to the electorate obfuscated what the Whig party stood for.

Nor, in 1841, did state issues provide Whigs with an effective weapon. With banks closing their doors or suspending specie payments, with state governments on the verge of bankruptcy, and with farmers unable to get loans to move their crops, Whig efforts to aid banks and continue canal construction only stirred the hostility of Democratic constituents without satisfying their own. In Georgia, Mississippi, Pennsylvania, New York, Ohio, and Michigan, Democrats flayed Whig legislatures for economic mismanagement, favoritism toward privileged institutions, and failure to provide any economic relief.[58]

As a result of internal leadership divisions, popular disappointment with Whig achievements at the national and state levels, and confusion among Whig voters, the party suffered disastrous defeats in the fall elections of 1841. Whigs did as well in the congressional elections of 1841 as in those of 1840, since all those contests were rescheduled prior to the meeting of the special session on May 31 and Whig candidates could still run on the promise of future action to promote economic recovery. Similarly, Whigs performed strongly in gubernatorial and state legislative elections held before Tyler's first bank veto on August 16. They won three of five gubernatorial races contested before September and held or increased their previous gains in all state legislatures except Indiana's and, to a lesser extent, Alabama's. In contrast, from September to November, when Whigs' programmatic failure and internal disarray were evident, Democrats vigorously assaulted Whig incumbents and former Whig voters abstained in droves.

Of eight gubernatorial elections held after August, for example, Whigs lost six—in Maine, Georgia, Maryland, Pennsylvania, Michigan, and Mississippi. Whigs were particularly decimated in state legislative races that fall. In the eight states that held legislative elections between March and mid-August, prior to Tyler's first veto, Whigs lost an average of only 3.7 percent of their previous seats. Yet in eleven states holding legislative elections after mid-August, Whig losses averaged 21.7 percent. Maryland vividly illustrates the tidal swing against the Whigs. In its rescheduled congressional elections in the spring, Whigs won six of eight House seats with 57 percent of the total popular vote. But in October, Whigs lost the gubernatorial race with only 49.4 percent of the vote, while their representation in the lower house of the legislature plunged from 76 percent of the seats to 47 percent. Altogether, whereas Whigs controlled both houses of state legislatures in fifteen states in 1840, by the end of 1841 they retained total command in only six states, the same number as Democrats controlled. This shift was portentous since congressional districts were due to be reapportioned in 1842, and now Democratic legislatures would often dominate that vital process (see Tables 6 and 9).

Unpopular positions on state issues undoubtedly contributed to the rout in the fall, but the Whigs' major problem was clearly their failure in Washington to deliver on their promise to enact programs for economic recovery. Tennessee's Democratic Governor James K. Polk, who had narrowly lost his bid for reelection in August 1841 before Tyler's first veto, emphasized the importance of changed circumstances in a postmortem he wrote in early 1842. He had been defeated in August, he complained, because the "obnoxious" Whig measures of the new tariff, the distribution act, the bond issue, and the bankruptcy act "had not been sufficiently developed to be known, and the people acted in view of the liberal promises of *relief and reform* which had been made to them." Now, he added, "they are disappointed and dissatisfied. They now find that they have been deceived."[59]

However obnoxious the Whig measures may have been to partisan Democrats like Polk, the dissatisfaction, disappointment, and consequent refusal to vote of Whig supporters played a larger role in the turnaround. Democrats did not beat Whigs by outgaining them among new voters. Instead, Whigs' disillusioned supporters simply did not vote (Tables 10 and 11). A New York Whig howled about the party's "split into cliques and factions" and about "apathy on the part of the people unexampled, arising solely from disgust at the doings of the Capitol." Predictably, Clay cast the blame for Whigs' demoralization on Tyler. "An army which believes itself betrayed by its commander-in-chief, will never fight well under him," he pouted. "Our defeats have not been produced by any accession of strength to our adversaries, but simply because our friends would not go to the polls."[60]

Many observers now predicted the impending demise of the party. "I now regard the Whigs as destroyed," Calhoun wrote in December. "They can never again rise under their present name, nor on their present issues." "The Whig party now seems totally broken up and dismembered," shrieked an anguished Washington officeholder in October upon seeing the results from Maryland, Georgia, and Pennsylvania. "Some decisive step must be taken soon or unquestionably the Whig party is at an end," the New Yorker Willis Hall warned Mangum the following January. "A rally must be made soon or there will be no party to rally."[61]

Most Whigs believed that the rally depended upon reemphasizing Whig measures and Whig identity. And the best way to reassert Whiggery, they believed, was to commit the party in 1842 to Henry Clay's presidential nomination. Then John Tyler would clearly no longer lead the Whig party. Immediately booming Clay for the presidency, argued Hall, was "the only course which can possibly save the party from destruction." Worries that pushing Clay so soon would widen party divisions were misplaced. "We are at present in greater danger of death from torpidity and mortification than from fear [of Tyler's retaliation]. A fight, even among ourselves, is better than the indifference and disgust that proved so fatal to us last Fall."[62]

IV

Sharply divergent motives thus impelled proadministration and congressional Whigs when Congress reconvened in December 1841, yet in hindsight it is clear that politically both groups engaged in fantasy. Tyler was willing and Webster frantic to restore harmony between the administration and the congressional wing of the party. Clay's congressional followers, in contrast, carried on war to the knife. In the Senate, Whigs rejected Tyler's recent appointments, while in both houses they contemptuously dismissed his legislative proposals.[63] From the start, they sought to prove once and for all that Whigs had read the administration out of their coalition.

Table 10

Party Percentage of the Vote in Congressional and Gubernatorial Elections, 1840–1844[a]

	1840P	1841	1842	1843	1844
New Hampshire					
Whig	44.5%	41.4%G	25.7%G	28.2%G	30.3%G
Dem.	55.5%	56.7%	55.8%	51.6%	53.5%
Liberty	0	2.4%	5.7%	7.7%	11.7%
Ind. Dem.			12.7%	12.3%	4.0%
Connecticut					
Whig	55.5%	56.0%G	46.2%G	46.4%G	49.4%G
Dem.	44.4%	44.0%	49.8%	50.1%	47.3%
Liberty	0.1%		2.5%	3.4%	3.3%
Whig		55.8%C		48.1%C	
Dem.		44.2%		50.9%	
Liberty				1.0%	
Rhode Island					
Whig	61.3%	97.6%G	67.9%G	55.2%G	96.4%G
Dem.	38.3%	0	32.0%	44.6%	0
Liberty	0.4%				
Whig				61.3%C	
Dem.				38.7%	
Virginia					
Whig	49.4%			45.7%C[b]	
Dem.	50.6%			54.3%	
Louisiana					
Whig	59.7%		45.7%G		N.R. Congress
Dem.	40.3%		54.3%		
			N.R. Congress		
Alabama					
Whig	45.6%	43.7%		42.9%C[b]	
Dem.	54.4%	56.3%		57.1%	
		43.3%C			
		58.3%			
Illinois					
Whig	48.9%	49.7%C	45.1%	45.5%	
Dem.	50.9%	50.3%	53.8%	53.2%	
Liberty	0.2%		1.0%	1.3%	
Indiana					
Whig	55.8%	55.5%C		48.4%G	
Dem.	44.2%	44.2%		50.2%	
Liberty				1.4%	
				48.2%C	
				51.1%	
				0.7%	
Kentucky					
Whig	64.3%	Incomplete		56.1%C	52.0%G
Dem.	35.7%	returns Cong.		43.9%	48.0%

Table 10 (continued)

	1840P	1841	1842	1843	1844
Missouri					
Whig	43.2%	N.R. Congress			44.8%C
Dem.	56.8%				55.2%
North Carolina					
Whig	57.5%	52.1%C[b]	53.1%	51.0%	51.9%G
Dem.	42.5%	47.9%	46.9%	42.0%	48.1%
Tennessee					
Whig	55.7%	51.5%G		51.2%G	
Dem.	44.3%	48.5%		48.8%	
		53.3%C		53.1%C	
		46.7%		46.0%	
Maine					
Whig	50.1%	42.7%G	37.3%G	34.6%G	42.0%G
Dem.	49.9%	55.0%	57.0%	55.4%	51.0%
Liberty		1.9%	5.7%	10.0%	7.0%
Vermont					
Whig	63.9%	48.5%G	50.8%G	48.7%G	51.5%G
Dem.	35.5%	44.6%	45.2%	43.7%	38.1%
Liberty	0.6%	6.3%	3.0%	7.5%	10.2%
				50.6%C	52.6%C
				44.0%	37.5%
				5.4%	9.9%
Arkansas					
Whig	43.7%		32.4%C	38.9%G	
Dem.	56.3%		57.4%	47.6%	
Ind. Dem.			10.3%	13.5%	
Georgia					
Whig	55.8%	47.3%G	48.5%C	52.3%G	48.5%C
Dem.	44.2%	53.7%	51.5%	47.7%	51.5%
Maryland					
Whig	53.8%	49.4%G		54.8%C	50.4%G
Dem.	46.2%	50.6%		45.2%	49.6%
		56.9%C			
		43.1%			
New Jersey					
Whig	51.8%		59.3%	(49.1%)C[c]	50.9%
Dem.	48.2%		40.7%	(50.9%)	49.1%
Ohio					
Whig	54.2%		48.5%G	47.7%C	48.7%G
Dem.	45.4%		49.3%	50.0%	48.3%
Liberty	0.4%		2.1%	1.1%	2.9%
Pennsylvania					
Whig	50.1%	45.2%G		44.9%C	48.9%G
Dem.	49.9%	54.4%		53.5%	50.2%
Liberty		0.3%		0.3%	0.9%

Table 10 (continued)

	1840P	1841	1842	1843	1844
Delaware					
Whig	31.2%		50.0%C		50.7%C
Dem.	48.7%		50.0%		49.3%
Massachusetts					
Whig	57.6%	50.4%G	46.6%G	47.7%G	51.8%G
Dem.	41.1%	46.2%	47.9%	44.7%	40.7%
Liberty	1.3%	3.1%	5.4%	7.3%	7.2%
			49.8%C		
			45.5%		
			4.7%		
Michigan					
Whig	52.1%	41.1%G		38.3%C	45.0%G
Dem.	47.9%	55.8%		54.6%	51.0%
Liberty		3.1%		7.0%	4.0%
					37.9%C
					54.8%
					7.3%
Mississippi					
Whig	53.4%	46.8%G		43.7%G	
Dem.	46.6%	53.2%		52.9%	
			Anti-R.D.		
			Pro-R.D.	3.4%	
New York					
Whig	51.2%		46.4%G		47.4%G
Dem.	48.2%		51.8%		49.5%
Liberty	0.6%		1.8%		3.1%
			48.5%C		42.2%C
			50.9%		49.0%
			0.6%		1.8%
				Native Am.	7.0%

[a]This table is based on the same sources for gubernatorial (G) and congressional (C) election returns used in earlier tables. States are again listed in the chronological order in which elections were held. The first column on the left lists the party percentage of the vote in the presidential election of 1840.

[b]These proportions of the congressional vote are based on partial returns: fourteen of fifteen districts in Virginia in 1843, six of seven districts in Alabama in 1843, nine of thirteen districts in North Carolina in 1841. Because returns for only seven of Kentucky's thirteen districts were listed by the Congressional Quarterly's *Guide* for 1841, I did not give those figures.

[c]The New Jersey congressional elections for 1843 provide an especially difficult case to interpret. Popular vote totals for only four of five districts are given, and in one of those, two Whigs opposed each other without a Democratic challenger. In the fifth district the Democrat won with 100 percent of the vote, but no popular total was given. Hence, I have calculated the party percentage of the total vote two different ways. The first figures are based on the absolute votes for the four districts. The figures in parentheses represent an average of the party percentages in all five. They probably reflect the true distribution of party strength better than the first figures.

Table 11

Change in the Whig and Democratic Vote, 1840–1844, Measured from the 1840 Presidential Election[a]

	1841	1842	1843	1844
Alabama				
Whig	− 5,738 (20.1%)		− 8,956 (31.4%)C	
Democratic	− 2,188 (6.4%)		− 8,059 (23.7%)	
Arkansas				
Whig		+ 155 (3%)C		+ 2,416 (46.8%)C
Democratic		+ 2,757 (41.4%)		+ 4,456 (66.9%)
Connecticut				
Whig	− 5,520 (17.5%)C	− 7,898 (25%)G	− 6,197 (19.6%)G	− 1,505 (4.8%)G
Democratic	− 4,875 (19%)	+ 281 (1.1%)	+ 2,133 (8.4%)	+ 3,563 (14.1%)
Delaware				
Whig		− 500 (8.4%)		+ 254 (4.2%)C
Democratic		+ 584 (12%)		+ 1,171 (24%)
Georgia				
Whig	− 5,822 (14.4%)G	− 6,833 (16.9%)C	− 1,633 (4%)G	− 2,233 (55%)C
Democratic	+ 6,531 (20.4%)	+ 3,468 (10.8%)	+ 3,290 (10.3%)	+ 8,394 (26.2%)
Illinois				
Whig	−11,416 (25%)C	− 6,546 (14.4%)G	− 3,288 (7.2%)C	
Democratic	−12,886 (27.2%)	− 941 (2%)	+ 2,039 (4.3%)	
Indiana				
Whig	−15,991 (24.5%)C		− 6,498 (9.9%)G	
Democratic	−12,832 (24.8%)		+ 9,141 (17.5%)	
Kentucky				
Whig			− 1,010 (1.7%)C	+ 1,195 (2%)G
Democratic			+12,368 (27.9%)	+22,496 (69%)
Louisiana				
Whig		− 3,092 (27.4%)G		
Democratic		+ 2,147 (28.2%)		
Maine				
Whig	− 9,832 (21.1%)G	−19,867 (42.6%)G	−29,368 (63%)G	−13,270 (28.5%)
Democratic	+ 1,153 (2.5%)	− 5,346 (11.6%)	−18,570 (40.2%)	− 5,661 (12.2%)
Maryland				
Whig	− 5,213 (15.5%)G		− 6,873 (20.5%)	+ 1,507 (4.5%)G
Democratic	+ 200 (0.7%)		− 6,740 (23.4%)	+ 5,736 (19.9%)
Massachusetts				
Whig	−16,900 (23.2%)G	−17,935 (24.6%)G	−14,975 (20.5%)G	− 3,304 (4.5%)G
Democratic	− 587 (1.1%)	+ 4,537 (8.7%)	+ 2,288 (4.4%)	+ 2,760 (5.3%)
Michigan				
Whig	− 7,484 (32.6%)G		− 7,909 (34.5%)G	+ 1,678 (7.3%)C
Democratic	− 95 (0.4%)		+ 298 (1.4%)	+ 6,802 (32.2%)

Table 11 (*continued*)

	1841	1842	1843	1844
Mississippi				
Whig	− 7,484 (32.6%)G		− 2,073 (10.6%)G	
Democratic	+ 2,049 (12%)		+ 4,105 (24.1%)	
New Hampshire				
Whig	− 5,119 (19.4%)G	−13,933 (53%)G	−13,736 (52.2%)G	−11,794 (43.7%)G
Democratic	− 3,348 (12%)	− 5,971 (18.2%)	− 9,747 (29.7%)	− 6,646 (20.3%)
New Jersey				
Whig			− 4,947 (14.8%)C[b]	+ 4,598 (13.8%)G
Democratic			−11,593 (37.3%)	+ 5,550 (17.9%)
New York				
Whig		−39,924 (17.7%)G		+ 4,598 (13.8%)G
Democratic		− 4,674 (2.2%)		+28,351 (13.3%)
North Carolina				
Whig	−25,493 (55.8%)C[b]	− 6,109 (13.4%)G	−12,213 (26.7%)C	− 3,119 (6.8%)G
Democratic	−15,227 (45.1%)	+ 1,243 (3.7%)	− 9,593 (28.4%)	+ 5,652 (16.7%)
Ohio				
Whig		−30,988 (20.8%)G	−46,641 (31.3%)C	+12,017 (8.3%)G
Democratic		− 4,042 (3.3%)	−16,695 (13.5%)	+21,118 (17%)
Pennsylvania				
Whig	−30,570 (21.2%)G		−52,509 (36.5%)C	+12,017 (8.3%)G
Democratic	− 7,169 (5%)		−34,653 (24.1%)	+16,649 (11.6%)
Rhode Island				
Whig		− 347 (6.6%)G	+ 3,927 (75.3%)G	+ 347 (6.6%)G
Democratic		− 972 (29.8%)G	+ 4,130 (126.6%)	− 3,263 (100%)
Tennessee				
Whig	− 6,370 (10.6%)G		− 4,926 (8.2%)C	
Democratic	+ 2,759 (5.7%)		+ 937 (1.9%)	
Vermont				
Whig	− 8,863 (27.3%)G	− 5,278 (16.3%)G	− 7,980 (24.6%)G	− 4,180 (12.9%)G
Democratic	+ 3,684 (20.4%)	+ 6,121 (34%)	+ 3,973 (22.1%)	+ 2,921 (16.2%)
Virginia				
Whig			−20,863 (48.9%)C[b]	
Democratic			−17,927 (41%)	

[a]This table is based on the same data as Table 10. The changes in each column are measured from the total in the presidential election of 1840. I have excluded heavily Democratic Missouri because of insufficient data.

[b]These figures again are based on only partial returns for the congressional elections and therefore inflate the dropoff suffered by the parties. This inflation is particularly misleading for the Democratic vote in New Jersey for 1843 because the Democrats won 100 percent of the vote in the district for which no returns are listed in the Congressional Quarterly's *Guide*.

In his annual message in December and in a series of special messages to Congress during the spring, Tyler pressed two main legislative priorities. He presented his long promised plan for a fiscal agent known as the exchequer. Designed to combine Whig and Democratic ideas about how to handle governmental monies, as well as meet Tyler's constitutional hostility to a nationally chartered bank, it dissatisfied both Whigs and Democrats. Buried by the Whigs in committee, it never came to a vote until the winter of 1843.[64]

Tyler also stressed that Congress must remedy the federal government's deplorable financial situation. The government, still running at a deficit, had to sell new bonds in order pay off old ones. Yet investors, doubting the government's ability to repay its debts, had purchased only $5 million of the $12 million bond issue authorized at the special session. Revenues from tariff duties were also due to plunge. According to the terms of the Compromise Tariff Act of 1833, rates would drop sharply on January 1, 1842, and then again on July 1, 1842, when they were finally to reach the 20 percent level. Beyond preventing further deficits and restoring faith in public credit, Tyler argued, Congress must make new appropriations for the national defense.[65]

In December 1841, Tyler expressed hope that increased revenues could be found without raising the tariff above 20 percent, but he insisted that distribution must be suspended if rates exceeded that level. By the following spring, as the revenue shortfall became increasingly serious, the Virginian admitted that the tariff had to be raised above the 20 percent level, but he also demanded that distribution cease. In March, he urged Congress to stop distribution even before it passed a new tariff and to allocate land revenues to pay off the debt. Only then, he argued, could the government sell its bonds.[66]

The Whig majority seized on the interrelated deficit, tariff, and distribution questions to finalize their divorce from Tyler. Whereas the president pleaded with Congress for rapid action to restore the government's credit, the Whigs deliberately stalled in order to embarrass him. Furthermore, they insisted on both a higher tariff and continued distribution. Henry Clay, who would resign his Senate seat at the end of March under the disingenuous pretext of attempting to create greater harmony between Congress and the president, took the lead in outlining the alternative Whig program. His series of resolutions committed the Whig party to both a higher tariff and distribution. Spurning Tyler's plea that land revenues should be reserved for reducing the national debt, he insisted instead that they be distributed to the states, which desperately needed them to pay their own debts. From Kentucky, Clay also showered Whigs with advice that the nation's and party's welfare required adherence to distribution, passage of a higher tariff, and the scuttling of Tyler's defense expenditures.[67]

Clay's program, by clearly distinguishing the Whig party from Tyler and from the Democrats, might help win the important congressional elections of 1842 and 1843. Yet this strategy entailed the same risk as the insistence on a national bank in 1841. As the majority party, the Whigs bore the responsibility for enacting legislation. Nonetheless, they pushed a program the president seemed almost certain to veto. To minimize the risk of such frustration, the Whigs delayed action as long as possible in the hope that the worse the government's financial condition became, the greater the pressure on Tyler to eat crow and sign the Whig measures in order to get some revenue. If Tyler still vetoed their measures, the party could blame him for sacrificing the country's welfare because of his hostility to Henry Clay and the Whig party.[68]

Only in June, six months after the session began, did Millard Fillmore, chairman of the House Ways and Means Committee, report tariff legislation to the full House. He proposed first an explicit stopgap measure called the "little tariff" designed to tide the government over until a permanent law could be written. This bill merely postponed the final cuts due under the 1833 tariff from July 1 until August 1. Concomitantly, it postponed the distribution of land revenue scheduled for July 1 for a month as well. The bill passed both houses on decided party-line votes, and on June 29 Tyler vetoed it for illegally continuing distribution while tariff rates remained above the 20 percent level.

The veto infuriated the Whigs and reinforced their animosity toward Tyler. The normally mild-mannered Crittenden wrote Letcher, "My wish is to see the Whig party rid of him—rid of the nuisance." Whigs should "strip him of all disguise" and expose "his true character of enmity and hostility." At the same time, Crittenden told Clay that Whigs' anger at Tyler ensured Clay's election in 1844. "Tyler is one of your *best friends*. His last Veto has served us all well." Clay agreed. Since Democrats would vote to uphold Tyler's veto, he exulted, "*that* will identify them still further with him, and . . . they will have to share with him the odium of its defeat." "The more Veto's [sic] now of right measures the better," Clay iterated in July. Should Tyler cast the expected veto of the Whigs' second tariff bill, House Whigs should initiate impeachment proceedings against him. Democrats would "rally around the President," and "the more complete the evidence shall be of their thorough identification with him the better for us."[69]

To expose Tyler as a Democrat, to clarify Whig differences from Democrats and to rally Whig troops, congressional Whigs wrote a permanent tariff bill they knew Tyler would veto. It coupled an increase in rates far above the 20 percent level with an explicit provision for the continuation of distribution. The bill reached Tyler on August 5. Four days later he vetoed it.

If the Whigs had succeeded in demonstrating that Tyler was no Whig, he forced them to choose between their cherished goals of distribution and a higher tariff. Many southern and western Whigs had gone along with higher tariff rates only because they were combined with distribution, and now the party quarreled over which to keep. "The Whigs are now divided into two parties," Calhoun wrote on August 22, "one preferring the Distribution to the Tariff, and the other the Tariff to the Distribution; and neither willing to join in a bill simply for revenue with us." Disgusted southern Whigs wanted to adjourn without raising any new funds for the administration. As Crittenden told Clay, however, "Our friends of the North seem to be very seriously and sincerely apprehensive that their constituents will be discontented to such an extent as to be fatal to their coming elections if we should adjourn without doing or attempting something more." Southern Whig leaders like Mangum also recognized that as the majority party, the Whigs simply could not shirk their responsibility for providing the government with revenue. In the end, the Whigs chose to pass a tariff and a distribution bill separately. In both houses, southern Whigs deserted the party on the separate tariff act. It passed only because of solid support from Pennsylvania Democrats, and Tyler reluctantly signed it into law because he was desperate for additional revenue. The Whigs reunited on the new distribution act, but Tyler pocket-vetoed it.[70]

Whig efforts to enact a distinctive legislative program in the regular session of the Twenty-Seventh Congress therefore proved as abortive as in the special session. True, they obtained a higher tariff that was popular among manufacturing elements in the North. It levied high specific duties on some items, raised *ad valorem* rates to the levels of 1832, and required that importers pay all duties immediately rather than delaying for up to a year. Thus it provided much more protection for depressed manufacturing areas than had the 1833 tariff and promised as well to raise badly needed additional revenue for the government.[71] But everyone realized that its restorative effects would be slow in coming. And in areas such as Pennsylvania where it was most popular, Democrats could claim equal credit for its passage.

In order to obtain the tariff, Whigs had been forced to sacrifice distribution, thereby alienating some of their southern and western supporters and leaving state administrations that faced crushing debts in the lurch. They had also done little to restore government credit. Bond sales still lagged, and to finance the government in the short term, the Whigs had been forced to issue Treasury notes. Even though these notes bore interest, with their issue the government in effect had printed more money to pay its debts rather than borrowing it, a practice the Whigs had deplored and voted against when the Democrats employed it during Van Buren's administration. Palpably, they had failed to demonstrate the superiority of Whig management.

Even worse, the Whigs paid a high price for their strategy of delaying action until the summer in order to coerce Tyler. The tariff of 1842, their lone positive achievement, passed on August 30, but before that date congressional, gubernatorial, and legislative elections had been held in New Hampshire, Connecticut, Rhode Island, Virginia, Louisiana, Alabama, Illinois, Kentucky, Missouri, and North Carolina. In all except Rhode Island and Kentucky, the Whigs lost, and even in Kentucky they lost seats in the legislature. In March, Thurlow Weed, who still urged reconciliation with the administration, warned presciently in his *Albany Evening Journal*:

> The Whig members of Congress, instead of taking the President "for better or for worse," as wives take their husbands, array themselves against his Administration. This is a source of interminable mischiefs and evils. And what is worse, it's a warfare that will not only bring defeat and disgrace to both parties but is proving destructive to public interests.[72]

Weed shrewdly recognized that voters cared little about who was at fault—Tyler or Congress. All they could see was politicians who were carrying on personal warfare at the expense of the economic recovery the Whig party had promised, and they were not about to spare the party from blame.

The case of North Carolina, which held gubernatorial and legislative elections in August, illustrates the fate of Whigs elsewhere. In March, one resident warned that the Democrats were making hay in the state because the voters saw only "a Whig Congress cut up by Faction, doing nothing scarcely but *idle debate* upon *abstractions*; and a Whig President doing all that can be done to break down that party by whose acts he came into *power*—the country suffering, in the meantime, and becoming *worse* and *worse every day*; and such a state of affairs produced by those who promised better things, and were confided in almost by the acclamations of the people." Two months later, another resident predicted to Senator William A. Graham that the Democrats would carry the crucial legislative elections that would decide the fate of Graham's seat and determine which party could reapportion the state's congressional districts in accordance with the new census, with the cry "of *the promise of better times* not being redeemed."[73] Although the Whigs managed to salvage the North Carolina gubernatorial election, they suffered far more drop-off than the Democrats, and they lost control of the legislature for the first time since 1834. Upon seeing those results, as well as Whig defeats elsewhere, Mangum despairingly protested, "The traitor has destroyed the party, & I fear, we have not time to recover."[74]

To salvage what they could from the legislative debacle, congressional Whigs dramatically reaffirmed their excommunication of the president and exposed Democrats as his primary defenders. House Whigs referred Tyler's veto message of August 9 to a select committee chaired by former President John Quincy Adams and a week later adopted its vindictively partisan report. Inspired especially by Tyler's venomous Virginia enemy, John Minor Botts of Richmond, the committee report castigated everything that Tyler had done since taking office, called his behavior worthy of impeachment, and recommended against formal proceedings only because Democrats could block it. When Tyler sent the House an indignant protest, the Whig majority, on a party-line vote, refused to include it in the House *Journal*, just as the Senate Whigs had done to Jackson in 1834.[75]

Meanwhile, state and local Whig organizations moved to eradicate any hint that the administration or its supporters could be considered Whigs. In the summer and fall of 1842 state conventions in Maine, Kentucky, Georgia, North Carolina, Louisiana, Indiana, Vermont, New York, New Jersey, and even Massachusetts formally endorsed Clay for the presidency. Stalwart Whig papers like the *Albany Evening Journal* and the *New York Tribune* that had formerly urged reconciliation between Congress and Tyler now vilified him. The small band of Whigs in the House who had supported the president—Caleb Cushing of Massachusetts, George Proffit of Indiana, and Wise, Mallory, and Gilmer of Virginia—were purged and denied renomination as Whigs. In succeeding sessions of Congress, the Senate rejected even more of Tyler's nominees.[76]

Yet neither denunciation of Tyler nor unification behind Clay solved the party's problems in 1842 and 1843. For one thing, so long as Webster remained in the cabinet, internal party divisions persisted, especially in Massachusetts. In the Bay State, Webster's personal rival for control of the state party, the affluent and influential textile manufacturer Abbott Lawrence, attempted to exploit the disrepute of the Tyler administration to take revenge on Webster. Lawrence had favored Clay for the nomination in 1839, but Webster's influence had thrown the state to Harrison. When Webster joined the cabinet, Lawrence had sought his seat in the Senate, but Webster secured it instead for his friend Choate. Now Lawrence attempted to banish Webster from the Massachusetts Whig party. In September 1842 he gained control of the state convention, which proceeded to denounce Tyler and his entire administration and to nominate Clay. On September 30, however, Webster delivered a ringing speech in Boston's Faneuil Hall repudiating the convention's actions, defending Tyler, and proclaiming that he was and always would be a good Whig. Given Webster's immense prestige and wide personal following in Massachusetts, the state's voters remained confused about who spoke for the Whig party.[77]

Elsewhere Whigs paid a price for their new unity against the administration in terms of lost federal patronage. Dismayed by the deliberate procrastination of the congressional Whigs during the spring and outraged by suggestions of impeachment in the summer, Tyler abandoned any hope of reconciliation with moderate Whigs. In the spring and summer of 1842 he began to remove Whigs and increasingly to appoint Democrats in their place in an attempt to build up a third party composed of state rights Whigs and Democrats from the South and anti-Van Buren Democrats in the North. The first notable purge occurred in the Philadelphia custom house; Tyler ordered the collector, Jonathan Roberts, to replace some thirty Clay men with Tyler loyalists. When Roberts protested, he himself was sacked. Whereas prior to June 1842 Tyler had appointed primarily Whigs to the federal judiciary upon the advice of Webster, after that date all of his nominees were Democrats. As further evidence of his shift, Tyler directed the administration's newspaper in New York City to support the Democratic gubernatorial candidate in the fall of 1842.

Tyler's courtship of the Democrats accelerated after 1842. Because of deaths, resignations, and Senate rejections, he had to reshuffle his cabinet considerably in 1843 and 1844, and with the exception of the turncoats Cushing and Gilmer, every new appointee was a Democrat: David Henshaw of Massachusetts; John Nelson of Maryland; William Wilkins and James Porter of Pennsylvania, the latter being the brother of Pennsylvania's Democratic Governor David Porter; John Y. Mason of Virginia; and eventually, and most important, John C. Calhoun. But Tyler reached far below the cabinet level to build up a personal organization hostile to the Whigs in Boston, New York, Philadelphia, Cincinnati, St. Louis, and elsewhere. Late in the spring of 1843 and again in 1844, he conducted what was called "the reign of terror" against Whig officeholders and replaced them with Democrats. Symbolic of his strategy, he made great efforts to form an alliance with Tammany Hall, the notorious Democratic organization in New York City.[78] Reviewing Tyler's manipulation of patronage in the fall of 1843, John Davis of Massachusetts complained to Clay, "Corruption and Tyler, and Tyler and Corruption, will stick together as long as Cataline and treason. The name of Tyler will stink in the nostrils of the people; for the history of our Government affords no such palpable example of the prostitution of the executive patronage to the wicked purpose of bribery."[79]

All of these developments had the effect of distilling Tyler elements out of the Whig party. But they also stripped Whigs of federal offices. The loss of local appointive offices, as well as the frustration of the Whig program in Congress, sapped the enthusiasm of state and local Whig organizations as they entered the campaigns of 1842 and 1843. There was little use electing new Whigs or reelecting old ones to Congress, many despaired, since Tyler would only stifle them with the veto. Much better, some openly argued, to let those elections go by default so that the Democratic party would have control of the legislative as well as the executive branch, and thus the Whig party would no longer bear the responsibility for the government's fortunes.[80]

V

Despite the party's rally around Henry Clay during 1842, therefore, it entered the congressional and state elections of 1842 and 1843 divided in some states, demoralized in others, and discredited everywhere for its apparent failure to fulfill its promises. In the fall of 1842 Whigs lost gubernatorial, state legislative, or congressional elections in Maine, Massachusetts, New York, Pennsylvania, Ohio, Arkansas, and Georgia. In 1843 they were defeated in New Hampshire, Connecticut, and Virginia in the spring; Alabama, Illinois, and Indiana in the summer; and Maine, New Jersey, Pennsylvania, Ohio, Michigan, and Mississippi in the fall. In addition, they lost congressional seats in Kentucky, North Carolina, and Tennessee in August, even though they still carried a majority of the vote in those states.

Altogether, the Whigs suffered one of the most staggering reversals in off-year congressional elections ever witnessed in American history. Of the fifty-one Congresses that met between 1835 and 1936, only eight saw as many as 20 percent of the total seats in the House of Representatives shift from one party to another, and the House elected in 1842 and 1843 was one of those.[81] In the Twenty-Seventh Congress, Whigs held a majority of 29–22 in the Senate and 133–102 in the House, with six members listed as Independents. In the next Congress, their margin in the Senate was reduced to 28–25 because of defeats in state legislative elections, while in the House they were in a minority of 79 to 142. As the data in Table 12 indicate, Whig losses were especially heavy in Connecticut, Virginia, Louisiana, Illinois, Indiana, Kentucky, Maine, Georgia, New Jersey, Ohio, and New York, although they also suffered declines in North Carolina, Tennessee, and Michigan.

Paralleling and in part contributing to the thrashing Whigs received in congressional elections was the devastation they suffered in state legislative elections during 1842. Although the Whigs had lost one house of the legislature in a number of states in 1841, their ability to retain control of the other had provided them with a way to check Democratic programs. In 1842, however, they lost control of both houses in a number of states, so that by the end of the year, Democrats completely controlled the legislature in almost as many states as the Whigs had won in 1840 (Table 13). As a result, in 1842 and 1843, Whigs had no way to block Democratic reapportionment schemes or to stop Democratic legislation.

Inevitably, the major leaders of different Whig factions read into these returns what they wanted. Tyler, who was moving irreversibly back toward the Democratic party, later crowed that the Democratic sweep was "the greatest political victory ever won within my recollection . . . achieved entirely upon the vetoes of the Bank bills presented to me at the special session." Webster, who clung to the administration until May 1843 but still hoped to remain a Whig, peevishly interpreted the Whig setbacks as a repudiation of his rival, Clay, and of Clay's strategy of warfare upon the administration. "Blight and mildew afford the same auspices for good crops, as Mr. Clay's name does for political success," Webster wrote Edward Everett, the minister to England, in November 1842. The Whig party could be regarded "as now broken up." "The name may remain, but without entirely new leaders, the members of the party can never again be rallied."[82]

Table 12
Whig Proportion of Popular Vote and Seats Won in
Congressional Elections of 1840–41 and 1842–43[a]

	1840–41	1842–43
New Hampshire		
Seats	0% (N = 4) A.L.	0% (N = 4)
Votes	41.4%	28.2%
Connecticut		
Seats	100% (N = 6)	0% (N = 4)
Votes	55.8%	48.1%
Rhode Island		
Seats	100% (N = 2)	100% (N = 2)
Votes	N.R.	61.3%
Virginia		
Seats	47.6% (N = 21)	20% (N = 15)
Votes	N.R.	45.7%
Louisiana		
Seats	66.7% (N = 3)	0% (N = 4)
Votes	56.5%	45.7%
Alabama		
Seats	0% (N = 5) A.L.	14.3% (N = 7)
Votes	43.3%	42.9%
Illinois		
Seats	66.7% (N = 3)	14.3% (N = 7)
Votes	43.3%	45.5%
Indiana		
Seats	85.7% (N = 7)	20% (N = 10)
Votes	55.8%	48.2%
Kentucky		
Seats	84.6% (N = 13)	50% (N = 10) A.L.
Votes	N.R.	56.1%
Missouri		
Seats	0% (N = 2) A.L.	0% (N = 5) A.L.
Votes	42.8%	N.R.
North Carolina		
Seats	53.8% (N = 13)	44.4% (N = 9)
Votes	52.1%	58%
Tennessee		
Seats	61.5% (N = 13)	45.4% (N = 11)
Votes	53.3%	53.1%
Maine		
Seats	50% (N = 8)	28.6% (N = 7)
Votes	51.1%	34.6%
Vermont		
Seats	100% (N = 5)	75% (N = 4)
Votes	59.6%	50.6%

Table 12 (*continued*)

	1840–41	1842–43
Arkansas		
Seats	0% (*N* = 1)	0% (*N* = 1)
Votes	42.4%	32.4%
Georgia		
Seats	100% (*N* = 9) A.L.	0% (*N* = 8) A.L.
Votes	52.2%	48.5%
Maryland		
Seats	75% (*N* = 8)	100% (*N* = 6)
Votes	56.9%	54.8%
New Jersey		
Seats	100% (*N* = 6) A.L.	20% (*N* = 5)
Votes	51.7%	59.3% (49.1%)[b]
Ohio		
Seats	63% (*N* = 19)	42.8% (*N* = 21)
Votes	53.1%	47.7%
Pennsylvania		
Seats	46.4% (*N* = 28)	54.1% (*N* = 24)
Votes	46%[c]	44.9%
Delaware		
Seats	100% (*N* = 1)	100% (*N* = 1)
Votes	54.2%	50%
Massachusetts		
Seats	91.6% (*N* = 12)	80% (*N* = 10)
Votes	58.1%	49.8%
Michigan		
Seats	100% (*N* = 1)	0% (*N* = 3)
Votes	51.2%	38.3%
Mississippi		
Seats	0% (*N* = 2) A.L.	0% (*N* = 4) A.L.
Votes	46.6%	43.8%
New York		
Seats	47.5% (*N* = 40)	29.4% (*N* = 34)
Votes	51%	48.5%

[a]Where possible, I have used the percentage of the popular vote won in the congressional election, but where those data were unavailable, I have substituted the Whig percentage of the vote in the gubernatorial election held on the same day as the congressional election. "A.L." refers to at-large elections. Here as elsewhere, "N.R." indicates that no returns were available.

[b]Again for the New Jersey elections in 1843, I have calculated the statewide Whig percentage of the vote in two different ways. The first figure is based on the absolute returns for four of the five districts. The second figure, in parentheses, is the mean of the Whig percentage in all five districts.

[c]The Whig proportion of the popular vote in the 1840 congressional elections is based on returns from only twenty-one of twenty-five districts.

Table 13

Partisan Division of State Legislatures, 1840–1844, Arranged by Number of States[a]

	1840	1841	1842	1843	1844
Whigs control both houses	15	6	5	7	8
Houses divided between parties	4	6	3	1	5
Democrats control both houses	5	6	14	11	9

[a]This table is also based on data on the partisan division of state governments made available by the Inter-University Consortium for Political and Social Research.

Clay, alarmed that the party would indeed seek new leaders and desert his presidential candidacy again, minimized the defeats in 1842 and once again blamed "disgust and dissatisfaction" with Tyler's perfidy. The following December he reported buoyantly from New Orleans, "Every where I find great confidence prevailing among the Whigs of their success in 1844," for they knew that "all of the elections of the past fall which have been lost by them" were "lost not by the increased strength of their opponents, but by voters remaining absent from feelings of mortification and disgust, created by the acting President."[83]

None of these self-serving explanations was entirely correct, but Clay was more accurate than either Webster or Tyler. As in 1841, the Whigs lost primarily because of a systemic drop-off in turnout rates among their own disillusioned supporters, not because of increases in the Democratic vote. Of all the states where Whigs lost control of state governments, congressional seats, or both, Democratic gains contributed to the results more heavily than Whig abstentions only in Arkansas, Connecticut, Indiana, Kentucky, and Mississippi. Elsewhere, the failure of Whigs to retain the vote they had achieved in the state and presidential elections of 1840 proved far more important (see Tables 10 and 11).

Historians have long noted this failure of Whigs after 1840 to turn out in nonpresidential elections at the same rate as did Democrats. Some have attributed that abstention to the residual influence of antiparty sentiment among Whig supporters.[84] According to this theory, Whig voters could be brought out only when the stakes were high and the issues clear. Party loyalty alone could never be used to mobilize Whig voters because they never developed intense party loyalty. This analysis minimizes the extent to which Tyler's manipulation of patronage had deprived local Whig organizations of the mechanisms to mobilize voters. More important, it ignores the evidence that the Whig vote soared in the off-year elections of the late 1830s, when the residual influence of antiparty sentiment should have been stronger than in the 1840s.

The crucial difference between the late 1830s and the early 1840s was not the degree of antiparty sentiment but the public perception of what Whig party leaders stood for and would accomplish. Whig voters did indeed respond to issues and programs, but those platforms had to be clear and promising. Instead, in the early 1840s, what the Whig party stood for and how it differed from the Democrats often remained murky. And when its record became clear, it was hardly compelling. Between 1837 and 1840, the Whigs had attracted hundreds of thousands of new recruits by articulating a distinctive and promising program. By failing to fulfill that promise after 1840, the Whigs could not retain the full support they had won earlier.

State issues often depressed Whig turnout further and provided weapons with which the Democrats could mobilize their own constituencies in gubernatorial and state legislative elections. In New York the Whigs suffered, as they had in 1841, from two of Governor Seward's favorite programs. His attempt to secure public funding for Catholic parochial schools in New York City alienated nativistic elements in the party there and contributed to the decline in Whig turnout in 1841 and 1842. At the same time, Democrats pilloried the Whigs' continuing issue of bonds to expand the canal system as ruining the state's credit, and they successfully advocated instead a stop-and-tax policy whereby construction would be halted unless funds were raised immediately by taxes to pay for the canals. In North Carolina, Democrats attacked the Whigs in 1842 and 1843 for their efforts to provide relief to failing railroads. Mississippi's Democrats exploited hostility to banks by demanding the repudiation of state bonds that had been issued to certain banks to raise capital, and the Whigs' resistance to such laws only reinforced the conviction of Democratic voters that the Whigs favored rich and privileged institutions.

Almost everywhere, so long as the economy remained depressed and banks suspended specie payments, the antibanking platform of the Democrats proved far more appealing to Democratic voters than did the efforts of Whigs to aid banks. Put another way, Whigs in a number of states had been given a fair chance to produce economic recovery with their probusiness programs. The enactment of those programs incited Democratic voters against them, as it had in 1838 and 1839. Their failure to produce the promised recovery simultaneously deterred disappointed Whig supporters from voting at all. Developments at the state level, in short, generally reinforced the differential pattern in Whig and Democratic turnout created by events in Washington.[85]

The systemic abstention by Whig voters also left the party vulnerable in several northern states to new challengers for the anti-Democratic vote. Of these, the most important was the recently formed Liberty party, the political arm of the abolitionist movement, which sought to mobilize voters in almost every northern state. During the mid-1830s, most abolitionists had spurned a separate party for fear that the corruption and expediency they associated with parties would dilute the zeal for real reform. Instead they had relied on moral suasion to convince Americans of the sinfulness of slaveholding in the South and of racism in the North, on petitions to Congress calling for eradication of slavery in the District of Columbia, and on interrogation of regular party candidates to determine which ones were more favorable to their goals.

By the late 1830s, a number of abolitionists had grown disenchanted with these tactics. Aside from a few northern Whig congressmen, the petition campaign seemed to fall on deaf ears. From 1836 until 1844, Congress stifled open discussion of antislavery petitions through a formal gag rule in the House and an informal one in the Senate. Interrogating candidates proved less and less useful since abolitionists had no effective sanction against those major party candidates who simply ignored them or who, upon winning office, reneged on promises to back antislavery action. Hence a number of abolitionists became convinced that they could be a more effective pressure group if they established their own party. By aggregating a readily identifiable bloc of voters, they might force regular party politicians to bid for their support. A separate party would also ensure that zealous antislavery men would have genuine abolitionist candidates to vote for and would no longer need to waste their votes on untrustworthy regular party candidates.[86]

The Liberty party's initial plunge into the electoral arena during the presidential contest of 1840 had been far from auspicious. The party received less than three-tenths of 1 percent of the total vote, and only in Massachusetts did its proportion exceed 1 percent. In 1840, partisan attachments were too strong and economic issues too vital to wean any but the most dedicated antislavery men from the regular parties. The opposition of northern Whig congressmen to the gag rule, moreover, provided evidence enough that those who opposed slavery could safely express that antagonism by voting Whig.

Disillusionment with the Whig party after 1840 abetted the growth of the tiny Liberty party. Antislavery men who had clung to Whiggery in order to achieve economic reform saw little reason to remain in the party once it failed to enact that reform. In the Twenty-Seventh Congress, moreover, the Whig majority had proved no more tolerant of abolitionist petitions than had Democratic majorities previously. Eager to push through their economic program without delay, a few Whig congressmen even moved to censure such antislavery Whig stalwarts as John Quincy Adams and Joshua R. Giddings. Although the vast majority of northern Whig congressmen voted against such resolutions, just as they did against the gag rule, the defection of a few Northerners and the solid hostility of southern Whigs on these matters put the Whig party in bad odor among the most committed antislavery men.[87] Tyler's accession to the presidency and his reliance on proslavery Virginia advisors further alienated them from the party. Nor did the Whigs' rally behind Clay's candidacy reassure them, for they had opposed Clay in 1839 precisely because of his antiabolitionist statements.

Abolitionists appealed to and shared the same moralistic fervor for reform that characterized the evangelical Protestant groups who normally supported the Whigs. The Liberty party consequently cut into the ranks of Whiggery. It grew most rapidly in rural strongholds of Whiggery and revivalistic sentiment like northern New England, upstate New York, western Massachusetts, the Western Reserve in northeastern Ohio, and Michigan.[88]

The authenticity of moral antagonism toward slavery among Liberty party voters cannot be questioned, and to an extent, that impassioned antislavery sentiment accounts for the growth of the Liberty party after 1840. The decisive political position it achieved in certain states by 1842 and 1843 nonetheless depended far more on the evaporation of Whig voting support. The data in Table 14 indicate that the Whigs lost far more voters from abstention than from defections to the Liberty party. The ratio of Whig losses to Liberty gains ranged from 2 to 1 in Massachusetts and Vermont, to 4 to 1 in Michigan and Indiana, 7 to 1 in Ohio, 9 to 1 in New York, and 30 to 1 in Pennsylvania. Whatever the Liberty party's success in mobilizing voters, in short, its proportion of the total vote would never have been so large had other Whig supporters continued to turn out.

The Liberty party achieved its greatest proportionate strength in states such as New Hampshire, Maine, and Michigan, where the Whigs declined into a hopeless minority position after 1840. The futility of the Whig cause there freed antislavery voters to support the Liberty party without the fear that their defection might cause the Whigs to lose to the Democrats. In short, the weakening of Whiggery through erosion of its voting base after 1840 did far more to cause the growth of the Liberty party than the growth of the Liberty party did to weaken the Whig party.

Whatever the reasons, the Liberty party achieved a crucial balance of power between the major parties in certain states. In the Connecticut, Massachusetts, and Ohio gubernatorial elections of 1842 and 1843, the small proportion of the vote attracted by the third party could have tipped the elections to the Whigs had it gone to Whig candidates. In Massachusetts, Liberty incursions into the Whig vote, especially in legislative elections, helped the Democrats elect Marcus Morton governor in 1842 when the contest went to the legislature after no candidate received a majority of the popular vote.[89] Even in those states, however, the overall drop-off in the Whigs' vote contributed far more to their defeat than did defections to the Liberty party, and elsewhere Democrats won with absolute majorities. In congressional elections as well, although the Liberty party ran candidates in a number of northern districts, they rarely affected the outcome. Third-party candidates, however, cost the Whigs a seat in Ohio in 1843 and may have contributed to their defeat in three Connecticut districts.[90]

These exceptions aside, the emergence of the Liberty party caused fewer Whig losses in congressional elections than did congressional redistricting. The Constitution required reapportionment of congressional districts according to the census of 1840. In addition, Congress enacted a law in 1842 requiring all states to establish individual congressional districts and to abandon statewide or citywide at-large districts that a number of states had employed until that time. That law, moreover, reduced the number of total seats in the House by increasing the ratio of constituents to representatives and thus forced a reallocation of seats among the states. All this meant that virtually every state in the nation had to redraw its districts in 1842. The political battle waged over reapportionment was so fierce that several states like Ohio, Pennsylvania, New Jersey, Maine, and Vermont, which would have held elections in 1842, were forced to postpone them until 1843.[91]

Where Democrats controlled legislatures, the Whigs were the losers from the reapportionment process. Table 12 lists the proportion of congressional seats and the proportion of the popular vote won by the Whigs before and after redistricting. Those data reveal the disadvantage Whigs endured in a number of states. Abolition of New Jersey's at-large system reduced Whig representation despite an increase in Whigs' popular vote. In North Carolina the Whig vote increased from 52 to 58 percent between 1841 and 1843. But because Democrats had designed the districts, the Whig share of seats fell from seven of thirteen to four of nine. In Tennessee, where the Whigs' proportion of the total vote remained the same in 1841 and 1843, their share of seats fell from eight of thirteen to five of eleven. Elsewhere, relatively small declines in the Whig share of the total popular vote in Illinois, Ohio, Virginia, and New York produced disproportionately large declines in their share of seats.

Very small increases in the Democratic share of the popular vote also produced very large increases in Democratic seats. In 1842–43, the Democratic popular vote

Table 14

Comparison of the Impact of Abstention and the Liberty Party on Whig Fortunes: Changes in the Absolute Party Vote of Northern States in Successive Elections, 1840–44[a]

State	1840P	1841	1842	1843	1844
Maine					
Whig	46,612	− 9,832	−10,035	− 9,501	+16,098
Democratic	46,201	+ 1,153	− 6,499	−13,224	+12,909
Liberty	0	+ 1,662	+ 2,418	+ 882	+ 565
New Hampshire					
Whig	26,297	− 5,119	− 8,814	+ 197	+ 2,233
Democratic	32,801	− 3,348	− 2,623	− 3,778	+ 3,103
Liberty	0	+ 1,273	+ 1,483	+ 660	− 1,459
Vermont					
Whig	32,445	− 8,863	+ 3,585	− 2,702	+ 3,800
Democratic	18,009	− 3,684	+ 2,437	− 2,148	− 1,052
Liberty	319	+ 2,772	− 998	+ 1,673	+ 1,852
Massachusetts					
Whig	72,874	−16,900	− 1,035	+ 2,960	+11,671
Democratic	51,954	− 587	+ 5,124	− 2,249	+ 472
Liberty	1,618	+ 1,870	+ 2,894	+ 2,521	+ 831
Connecticut					
Whig	31,598	− 5,520	− 2,378	+ 1,701	+ 4,692
Democratic	25,283	− 4,825	+ 5,106	+ 1,852	+ 1,430
Liberty	57	− 57	+ 1,319	+ 553	+ 118
New York					
Whig	226,013		−39,924		+44,971
Democratic	212,736		− 4,674		+33,025
Liberty	2,943		+ 4,321		+ 7,873
Pennsylvania					
Whig	144,023	−30,570	−21,939		+64,526
Democratic	143,673	− 7,169	−27,484C		+51,302
Liberty	0	+ 763	− 82		+ 1,885
Ohio					
Whig	148,890		−30,988	−15,570	+44,001
Democratic	123,944		− 4,042	−12,653C	+37,813
Liberty	903		+ 4,231	− 2,701	+ 6,375
Indiana					
Whig	65,307	−15,991		+ 9,493	
Democratic	51,789	−12,832C		+21,973	
Liberty	0	0		+ 1,683	
Illinois					
Whig	45,576	−11,416	+ 4,870	+ 3,258	
Democratic	47,443	−12,886C	+11,945	+ 2,980C	
Liberty	159	− 159	+ 906	+ 261	

Table 14 (*continued*)

State	1840P	1841	1842	1843	1844
Michigan					
Whig	22,993	− 7,484		− 405	+ 9,587
Democratic	21,096	− 95		+ 393	+ 6,504C
Liberty	0	+ 1,167		+ 1,569	− 562

[a]Except where otherwise indicated, these figures are taken from gubernatorial elections. The first column on the left lists the total vote in the presidential election of 1840, but the other columns are not all measured from that total. Instead, they list the changes in the party vote from the immediately preceding election listed in the table. For example, the change in Maine in 1842 is measured from 1841, while the change in New York that year is measured from 1840.

nationwide increased by only about 2 percent. The Democrats' share of House seats, in contrast, increased from 42 to 64 percent. Since the impact of the Liberty party was so slight, the redrawing of congressional districts primarily accounts for this discrepancy.[92]

Comparison of the results for the lower house of the state legislature listed in Table 6 with those for congressional elections listed in Table 12 further highlights the effectiveness of the Democratic reapportionment, since elections for both offices were held simultaneously. In Connecticut, Whigs won 41 percent of the legislative seats in 1843 but none of the congressional seats. In Louisiana in 1842, they won 57 percent of the legislative seats but none of the congressional ones; in Virginia in 1843, 43 percent of the state seats but only 20 percent of the congressional ones; in Indiana, 45 percent of the legislative seats but only 20 percent of the congressional ones; in New Jersey, 40 percent of the legislative seats but only 20 percent of the congressional ones; and in Ohio in 1843, 54 percent of the legislative seats but only 43 percent of the congressional ones. To be sure, the previous success of Whigs in designing favorable assembly districts, differences in the popularity of local and congressional candidates, and differences in the salience of state issues in state and congressional races partially account for the disparity of these results. But Democratic control of both houses of the legislatures that drew the new districts in all of these states except Indiana and New Jersey surely contributed to it.

The Whigs did not suffer everywhere from the redrawing of districts. Although their share of the popular vote in Pennsylvania dropped from its 1840 level, they won a higher proportion of seats in 1843. Even though their electoral performance was woeful in Alabama in both 1841 and 1843, the abandonment of the at-large system allowed them to pick up at least one seat in that Democratic stronghold. The same was true of Georgia. In 1842 the Democratic legislature retained the at-large system in defiance of the new congressional statute. As a result, the Whigs lost all eight seats despite winning 48.5 percent of the vote. But when the Whigs won the gubernatorial and legislative elections of 1843, they designed congressional districts that would benefit their party.[93] Hence in 1844 they carried four of eight seats with precisely the same percentage of the statewide vote. These were exceptions, however. All in all, the ability of Democratic legislatures to shape new congressional districts in most states allowed them to turn small gains in the popular vote into enormous increases in their congressional representation.

VI

The dramatic shift of House seats to the Democrats exaggerated the competitive weakness of the Whigs and disguised the beginnings of a Whig comeback in 1843. Despite the erosion of voting support in some states and the more insistent challenge of the Liberty party for anti-Democratic voters, the Whig party still obtained approximately 48 percent of the popular vote in the congressional elections of 1842–43 compared with approximately 51.5 percent in 1840–41. Even more encouraging, except for Pennsylvania, Ohio, Maine, North Carolina, and Virginia, the erosion of Whig support slowed perceptibly, and in all of those states the Democrats also suffered serious drop-off in 1843. Whigs lost both Connecticut and Indiana that year, but former Whig supporters there rallied to the party once again, although not in the proportions that had melted away in 1841 and 1842. In addition, Whigs increased their share of legislative seats in twelve of the seventeen states that held elections in both 1842 and 1843 while losing ground only in Vermont. Best of all, the Whigs won statewide majorities or pluralities of the vote in Kentucky, Tennessee, and North Carolina in August; in Vermont in September; in Maryland and Georgia in October; and in Massachusetts in November. Equally significant, they recaptured control of the lower house of the Ohio legislature for the first time in three years.

Many circumstances contributed to this minor comeback. Signs of economic recovery appeared by the summer of 1843. Astute local leadership also played a role. In Georgia the brilliant young Alexander H. Stephens, who was destined to become a major figure in the Whig party, stumped across the state in a special congressional campaign and helped himself and the rest of the Whig ticket win. In Tennessee, Ephraim H. Foster rallied the Whigs behind James Jones' campaign for reelection as governor. In Massachusetts, Webster, who was frantic to reinstate himself in the good graces of a party that had come close to ostracizing him, endorsed the Whig ticket, whereas the previous year he had denounced it.

By 1843, Whigs were also able to capitalize on state issues in those states where they returned to power. In Ohio, where Whigs pointed to signs of economic recovery as the product of the Whig tariff of 1842, they also attacked antibanking legislation Democrats had passed in 1842 and 1843 for threatening to abort that recovery by extirpating credit and currency just when they were most needed. Similarly, in Massachusetts, while the Whigs benefited from renewed unity and growing Democratic disarray caused by Tyler's appointment of conservative Democrats to federal offices in the state, they also attacked every part of Democratic Governor Marcus Morton's proposed program to reform taxes, banks, legislative apportionment, and state loans to railroads, just as they had done in 1840. In Georgia, where the cotton economy remained depressed in 1843, Whigs attacked Democrats for mismanagement of the state's finances and for failure to produce relief when they controlled the government. Tennessee's election focused primarily on national economic issues, but Whigs also blasted the Democratic majority of the state senate that had blocked the election of United States senators in 1841 and 1842 and thus deprived the state of representation in the Senate during the second and third sessions of the Twenty-Seventh Congress.[94]

Renewed unity within the party and a clear reaffirmation of its economic principles were most responsible for the improved Whig showing. By 1843 Tyler's courtship of the Democratic party through patronage appointments in Philadelphia, Boston, New York, Tennessee, and elsewhere had become undeniable. No longer were local Whig activists paralyzed by indecision toward the administration. Even though many had been purged from patronage jobs, they now at least agreed that the administration was as much an enemy as the Democrats. In most states, Whigs also came out forthrightly for Henry Clay and the economic principles he had long championed—the high Tariff of 1842, the need for distribution of land revenues, opposition to state repudiation of debts, and, especially in the South, the need for a new national bank. Reflexively the Democrats had run against those traditional Whig programs. Unlike Pennsylvania, where both parties ran as champions of the tariff and both suffered declines in turnout, in the states the Whigs carried, they had once again carved out a clear and distinctive platform. As the Nashville *Banner* boasted of the result in Tennessee, it showed that Andrew Jackson's home was now "A WHIG STATE—A NATIONAL BANK STATE—A TARIFF STATE—A CLAY STATE."[95]

Contrary to Webster's prediction about the need for new Whig leadership after the rout in 1842, many Whigs interpreted the results of 1843 as a vindication of the Kentuckian.[96] Just as Clay had argued, previous defeats could be attributed to the electorate's disgust with Tyler and the apathy it produced. Now that the warfare between Tyler and the Whigs was undeniable, now that Tyler had revealed his true Democratic colors, and now that the party had rallied behind Clay and his principles, it seemed once again on the road to recovery.

Henry Clay's New York friend Peter B. Porter exuberantly wrote to him in October, "On the whole our political prospects are uncommonly bright and promising. The cheering and unexpected result of the elections in Maryland and Georgia, seems to have inspired our friends with new ardor and energy; and we anticipate with a confidence, that we have never before felt, on your triumphant election a year from this time." John Davis of Massachusetts also exulted that the results in Tennessee, Georgia, and North Carolina proved that the country was once again committed to Clay's economic doctrines and his presidential candidacy. "There seems here, in the real Whig party, to be but one sentiment on that head, and it looks to your name as the rallying word."[97]

Despite the setbacks the Whig party had suffered in the elections of 1841, 1842, and 1843, in sum, Whigs showed no inclination to pursue the route they had taken in 1839. This time they would not jettison their foremost leader for an available man. This time they were determined to mount a presidential campaign behind Henry Clay and the programs he had long championed. They were convinced that by running "the embodiment of Whig principles" and drawing the sharpest possible contrast between the Whig and Democratic parties, they would emerge triumphant. To many, the tortuous odyssey of the Whig party and the long frustration of Henry Clay both appeared to be nearing an end. As the year 1843 closed, victory in the next seemed certain.

Chapter 7

"The Whigs Are in High Spirits"

GEORGIA'S WHIGS WERE "active & buoyant, full of hope and energy," exulted Robert Toombs, chairman of the Whig State Central Committee, in January 1844. "I doubt not we shall achieve a brilliant victory in November for Mr. Clay." "The enthusiasm of 1840 is returning," a Baltimore Whig added in February. "The Whigs look forward to the approaching contest," rejoicing in "the justness of their cause—and in its righteousness read their claim to certain success." The following month a Virginian concurred: Nothing "can prevent the election of Mr. Clay, but his death." That spring northern Whigs as diverse as Indiana editor Schuyler Colfax, Ohio's antislavery zealot, Congressman Joshua R. Giddings, and Boston's patrician Robert C. Winthrop also boasted that the Whig "party will succeed by an overwhelming majority at the coming election."[1]

Even though the issues and contestants changed during the 1844 campaign, most Whigs voiced continual certitude about their triumph. "Everywhere the Whigs are confident," Gustavus Henry, a Whig presidential elector in Tennessee, cheered while stumping the state in July. In October one New Yorker felt "just as sure that this state will vote right as I am of anything not yet positively proven," while another bragged that "the state is safe." Only two days before the presidential balloting a Philadelphian gushed, "The Whigs are in high spirits and fully expect to get the state of Pennsylvania, and to elect H. Clay." All these Whigs rejoiced that fate had now given them another opportunity to vindicate "the justness of their cause" and the charismatic leader who best personified the party's principles and the frustrating struggle to establish them. If superior men and superior policies were ever going to prevail, if right and justice were ever to triumph, Whigs believed, 1844 had to be the year. Defeat was, quite literally, unthinkable.[2]

I

Whigs' ebullience in early 1844 now seems unwarranted, indeed incomprehensible. Although they had carried nine states in 1843 and tiny Rhode Island in April 1844, those states could not deliver the electoral vote necessary to win the presidency even if Whigs could carry them again in November. The congressional results of 1843 hardly provided grounds for optimism, and Whigs found themselves in a House minority of 79 to 142 when the new Congress convened in December 1843. Democratic gerrymandering of congressional districts undoubtedly contributed to the lopsided results of 1842 and 1843, but Whigs would have to overcome that same obstacle to capture Congress in 1844. At the same time, the reapportionment following the census of 1840 had reduced the representation of states Whigs might carry, like Vermont, Connecticut, New York, Ohio, Maryland, Kentucky, Tennessee, and North Carolina, and had increased the congressional weight and thus the electoral vote of overwhelmingly Democratic states like Illinois, Michigan, Missouri, Alabama, and Mississippi. By the end of 1843, moreover, President Tyler was actively replacing Whigs with Democrats in local patronage posts, stripping Whigs of their financial and organizational services in the impending campaign.

Despite these cold facts, Clay and other Whigs attributed the party's defeats after 1840 to the disillusionment of Whig voters with Tyler's treachery and to disappointment with the Whigs' failure to enact their program. Whigs had lost, they argued, not because Democrats gained supporters but because Whigs failed to vote. "With the old issues we are safe," declared an Ohioan. "All we want is to bring the voters out." We will win, wrote the chairman of the Whigs' national committee in June, if we "bring the whole Whig force into action." And to bring the Whig majority of 1840 back to the polls, Henry Clay, the "embodiment of the Whig party," was the ideal candidate.[3]

By the beginning of 1844, Clay's nomination seemed virtually certain. In 1841, 1842, and 1843, anti-Clay groups had floated trial balloons for Winfield Scott, Justice John McLean, and even Daniel Webster. The challengers had pressured the congressional Whig caucus in February 1843 to call a national convention for the following year, a convention that the front-runner had initially opposed. But by the beginning of 1844 virtually all Whigs realized that the May gathering would crown Clay.[4]

Whigs' enthusiastic unity behind their most prominent national leader contrasted wonderfully with Democratic disarray. Even when despairing of Whig fortunes during the dark days of July 1843, Maryland's Whig Senator John L. Kerr pointed to "the divisions of the Locos or the Democrats" as a source of Whig hope for 1844. In May 1844, the Bostonian Winthrop predicted the certainty of Clay's election because "the enemy are utterly confounded & distracted," while an Indiana Whig jeered that "any reconciliation" of "the jarring factions of Locofocoism will be superficial & they will enter upon the contests dispirited & with forebodings of defeat."[5]

Whigs were not whistling in the dark. The Democrats began 1844 seriously divided along ideological, sectional, and personal lines. Two weeks before the Democratic national convention, Virginia's powerful Democratic leader, Thomas Ritchie, privately complained that "never have I seen the . . . party in so much danger," for "we are divided by miserable contests and contemptible jealousies." In part, policy disagreements rent the Democrats. Democrats from Pennsylvania and other mid-Atlantic states, for example, staunchly supported a protective tariff, while the great majority of their party loathed the idea. In most states, a minority of the party continued to resist the majority's hard-money, antibanking, anticorporation policies. In Ohio, for example, Democrats feared in 1844 that "the Whig policy is clearly to drag us into Local [banking] matters upon which we are divided," while in New York probusiness, pro-canal-expansion Democrats aligned with Governor William C. Bouck established their own paper in Albany, the *Argus*, to battle the Albany *Atlas*, which represented the party's antibanking, anticanal wing.[6]

These divisions both exacerbated and complicated personal rivalries for the Democratic presidential nomination in 1844. The favorite of the antibanking wing of the party, ex-President Martin Van Buren, led the chase. Infuriated at the willingness of some Democrats to coddle corporations and banks, Van Buren's ardent supporters attributed his defeat in 1840 to the treachery of soft-money elements, and with his renomination and reelection they meant to purge the polluters from the party. Meanwhile, conservative Democrats blamed Van Buren's ideological rigidity and personal unpopularity for the ignominious defeat in 1840, and they intended to deprive the New Yorker of the prize.

South Carolina's John C. Calhoun also vehemently opposed Van Buren's nomination. By December 1843, he had abandoned his quixotic hope for his own nomination, but he still adamantly resisted Van Buren's claims because some of Van Buren's northern supporters had deserted the South on the tariff and on maintenance of the gag rule in the House of Representatives. To protect southern interests, Calhoun and his supporters in Virginia, Georgia, and Alabama increasingly insisted that the Democratic nominee in 1844 must be a slaveholding Southerner.

Tyler's courtship of anti-Van Buren Democrats further fragmented the party. Once Tyler completely abandoned attempts at a rapprochement with the Whig majority and began to fill patronage posts with conservative Democrats, he became as disruptive to the Democrats as he had been to the Whigs, for crucially placed federal officeholders could influence the choice of delegates to the national Democratic convention.

Tyler was clearly trying to build a third party consisting of anti-Van Buren Democrats and southern state rights Whigs, but historians disagree about his motives. Some insist that he sought primarily to advance his policy initiatives, if only by forcing the Democrats to endorse them. Others believe that he was pursuing reelection by running on a third-party ticket or, more likely, by securing the Democratic nomination for himself. Toward that latter end, Tyler's band of officeholding adherents called for a Tyler convention to be held in Baltimore at the end of May, just when the Democratic convention was scheduled to meet in the Monument City. Democrats worried about Tyler's ambitions and his divisive impact on their own ranks, and Whigs agreed that he could only weaken their foes. "Capt. Tyler is going boldly for the nomination against Van Buren," Crittenden gloated to Ohio's Thomas Ewing in March. "This is well."[7]

Though the Democratic party fissured over its impending nomination, most Whigs, like most Democrats, expected Van Buren to emerge as the standard bearer. And Van Buren, Whigs believed, would be the easiest Democrat to defeat. "Van Buren is surely to be the Loco Candidate," Crittenden informed Robert P. Letcher in January, and "that is the *sealed doom* of the party." Similarly, Georgia's Whig Governor George W. Crawford assured Congressman Alexander H.

Stephens that "should Mr. Van Buren be the nominee," we shall hand "Georgia to Mr. Clay by a majority between 5 and 10,000 votes." "Every intelligent Whig" in Washington wants "the contest to be with *him*," North Carolina's Willie P. Mangum summed up. "If we cannot beat Mr. Van Buren, we can beat no one."[8]

As 1844 began, Whigs joyously anticipated rehashing the same diatribes they had hurled against the Little Magician four years earlier. "Against him all the documents are prepared and ready," Clay wrote in December 1843, "and we have nothing to do but publish another edition of them, without revisal or correction, organize, and go ahead." Indiana's voters, Schuyler Colfax concurred, will prove "that they were neither 'drunk' nor 'mad' in 1840." They will show Van Buren "that they cast him out because they were opposed to his Sub-Treasury—his profligate expenditures—his disregard of the petitions of the People—and his retention in office of pampered defaulters."[9]

Above all else, Whigs confidently believed that a race between Clay and Van Buren would dramatically highlight the two parties' contrasting national economic policies, and they were utterly convinced that they had the better side of those issues, just as they did in 1840. Although signs of recovery from the long economic slump were beginning to appear at the end of 1843, Whigs still considered their programs far better calculated to produce prosperity than those of the Democrats. John Tyler's perfidy had blocked those programs, but with Henry Clay as president and a new Whig Congress, the party would at last enact them. "We have always insisted," Horace Greeley declared in the *New York Tribune*, "that the Whig party has only to place its great distinctive principles fairly and fully before the People, advocate them fearlessly and frankly, and *stick to them*, to secure their hearty and early adoption by the great mass of the People."[10]

Greeley and other Whig leaders confidently believed that an issue-oriented campaign would produce triumph in 1844 because it would reinforce the partisan identity and revive the partisan zeal of the men who had voted Whig in 1840 but abstained thereafter. Such a strategy aimed not to convert Democrats but to mobilize Whigs. Hence, the chairman of the Whig Congressional Executive Committee argued that Whigs should circulate documents that contrasted in detail the Whig position on issues from that of the Democrats. Hence, Whigs freely admitted that party rallies and Whig speechifying sought not to change the minds of Democratic voters but to "rouse the luke warm" among their own, "and cause their attendance at the polls."[11]

Precisely because a race between Clay and Van Buren would dramatize longstanding party differences on policy and thereby mobilize the mutually antagonistic Whig and Democratic legions, Whigs salivated at the prospect. Such a race would draw out the maximum vote of both. And, the Whigs firmly believed, the election of 1840, unlike the atypical off-year contests of 1841, 1842, and 1843, demonstrated that when both parties brought out their full vote, Whigs would win.

Contemporaneous developments both in Washington and in a host of state capitals reinforced Whigs' optimism that their issues gave them the advantage. Although 1844 was a presidential election year, the Whigs were just as interested in winning congressional, gubernatorial, and state legislative elections. To do so, they relied on the continuing battles in state legislatures over banking, corporate privileges, subsidies for internal improvements, the repudiation of state bonds, and other state policies to sharpen the differences between the parties and to increase the Whig party's appeal to its constituents.

Georgia's Whigs crowed in early 1844 about the record of the recent Whig-controlled legislature that arranged for payment of the state's debt, put the currency of the state-operated Central Bank on a sound basis, and blocked Democratic efforts to sell off the state-owned and as-yet uncompleted Western and Atlantic Railroad. Largely because of that record on state issues, state chairman Toombs rejoiced, "I have not seen our prospects at any time so bright."[12] Because Ohio's Democrats suicidally nominated a hard-money gubernatorial candidate on an extreme antibanking platform, one Whig informed Clay, "Our friends in Ohio are in high spirits and our enemies depressed in a corresponding degree."[13]

Similarly, in New York, Greeley welcomed an open battle with the Democrats on the canal expansion issue because he believed that a report by a Whig legislator irrefutably demonstrated that the Erie Canal earned enough revenue to pay off the state debt. New bond issues for immediate construction were therefore preferable to the Democrats' stop-and-tax policy. Emphasizing the canal issue, Whig editors like Greeley and Thurlow Weed also knew, would focus the campaign on the state policy that most divided Democrats.[14]

The two parties were also sharply at odds over state economic policy in North Carolina, New Jersey, Pennsylvania, Maryland, Mississippi, and elsewhere in late 1843 and early 1844, and Whigs counted on those conflicts to galvanize their voters. Nonetheless, Whigs looked primarily to national issues in 1844. Tyler's vetoes had revived the Whigs' founding principle of opposition to executive usurpation, and Democrats' applause for those vetoes, including one of a rivers and harbors bill in June 1844, dramatically demonstrated Democratic antipathy to governmentally sponsored economic development. Other congressional actions during the spring of 1844 also reinforced party differences on the land and subtreasury issues. Democrats unanimously supported and Whigs unanimously opposed reinstitution of the subtreasury system, while Whigs supported and Democrats opposed resumption of land revenue distribution, thus providing Whigs with fresh ammunition for their subsequent campaign.[15]

Whigs articulated no clear substitute for the defunct Democratic monetary system. Mindful of past experience and apparently hopeful that voters would forget their congressional agenda of 1841, northeastern Whigs often denied that the party wanted a new national bank and insisted only on a sound, uniform paper currency. Southern and western Whigs, in contrast, boldly proclaimed that a Whig victory would produce a new national bank to provide much needed credit. Still, Whigs unitedly opposed the Independent Treasury and an exclusive specie currency—the fruits, they warned, of a Democratic victory.[16]

The Tariff of 1842 seemed Whigs' most promising issue. Its passage had been their most significant achievement during the Twenty-Seventh Congress. They had predicted that higher duties would increase government revenues and reduce the debt, revive industry and expand employment, reverse the imbalance between imports and exports, cause gold to flow into rather than out of the country, and thereby increase the total money supply enough to fuel a general economic recovery. Many of these predictions had come true by the spring of 1844. The sharp increase in government revenue between June 1843 and June 1844 wiped out the deficit. The balance of trade shifted in favor of the United States, and a surplus of foreign specie came into the country. As a result, the total money stock in the country burgeoned by almost 14 percent between 1843 and 1844. By the last quarter of 1843, the long slump in economic activity ended, and indexes of agricultural and industrial production as well as new construction turned up. That ascent accelerated in 1844.[17]

Whigs proudly asserted that the Tariff of 1842 had reinvigorated the economy. Horace Greeley trumpeted the tariff's virtues almost daily in his influential *New York Tribune*. But Greeley was hardly alone in believing that the tariff provided the Whigs with an invincible issue. In January 1844, Georgia's Toombs jeered that the Democrats no longer dared talk about repealing it. Thus, he looked forward to "the sport I shall have out of them next summer on the stump about their unredeemed pledges to repeal that 'odious Whig Tariff.' " Clay, who made a tour from New Orleans through Alabama, Georgia, and North Carolina in the winter and early spring of 1844, rejoiced that southern Whigs everywhere finally seemed united behind the protective tariff principle.[18]

Nor did Clay exaggerate. Higher cotton prices, chortled North Carolina's David F. Caldwell, proved that a protective tariff for American industry "is decidedly beneficial to the Southern States, & that the clamor of the subject is all humbug." The Virginia state Whig convention in 1844 pledged to campaign in defense of the Tariff of 1842 "in principle and in detail." Southern Whig senators like Georgia's John M. Berrien, Mangum, and Virginia's Rives all gave major speeches in support of the tariff of 1842, while southern Whigs in the House of Representative joined their northern colleagues to form a united front against tariff revision.[19]

Contrary to Toombs' prediction in January, Democrats in the House did try to lower the tariff in the spring of 1844. When the House finally tabled the Democratic McKay tariff bill by a vote of 105 to 99 in May, Greeley proudly reported that only one Whig, the state rights Georgian Absalom Chapel, had joined the Democratic majority in attempting to keep the bill alive, while 77 Whigs and 28 Democrats had voted to table it. The result, he proclaimed, was "the most decisive Whig victory gained in Congress, since the Sub-Treasury was laid on the table [in 1837]."[20]

As the tariff result demonstrated, the Whig party proved far more united, and the Democrats far more divided, during the Twenty-Eighth Congress' first session than previously, especially on the great symbolic issues that could be used to rally the troops—the tariff, revenue distribution, the Independent Treasury, and support for federally funded internal improvements.[21] The vote on the McKay bill also pleased Greeley because Whig congressmen chosen in special elections after Congress convened in December, from districts formerly represented by Democrats, provided the crucial Whig margin. Greeley and other Whigs did not merely hypothesize about the expected appeal of the tariff issue in November. They closely followed election results in the winter and spring of 1844, and they interpreted Whig victories as popular mandates for Whig policies—especially the tariff. After Whigs won Connecticut's April gubernatorial and legislative elections, for example, Greeley crowed: "The *Moral* effect upon the Public sentiment of the Union cannot be overestimated. The struggle has been for great National objects." Later that month, Pennsylvania Whigs interpreted their victory in a special congressional election as a triumph of a protariff Whig over an antitariff Democrat, while New Jersey's Whigs proclaimed their sweep of local township elections a victory for "Clay and Protection."[22]

That these and other local contests turned solely on national issues, let alone the tariff by itself, is doubtful. Nonetheless, Whigs saw those results, just like the early elections of 1840, as establishing an irreversible momentum that would carry the party to victory in the fall. "The result in Connecticut insures, if there was any doubt before, that our success in Novr. is certain," Reverdy Johnson wrote Mangum from Baltimore. "If Connecticut has gone for the Whigs," echoed a North Carolinian, "it almost puts the election of Mr. Clay beyond praying for."[23]

No wonder, then, that Whigs exuded confidence in the spring of 1844. Unprecedented unity behind their presidential candidate and their program, bitter Democratic divisions over men and measures, the expectation that the Democratic presidential nominee would be particularly vulnerable, and the belief that the sharp issue differences between the Whigs and Democrats could once again bring Whigs to the polls all produced a conviction that triumph in November was inevitable. If any additional evidence were needed, the spring's results provided it.

II

Just as Whigs' confidence soared in the spring of 1844, a new issue forced them to revise their calculations about the men and measures upon which the campaign would focus. The transforming issue, Texas annexation, involved the sectionally divisive question of slavery expansion, a dispute with ominous potential to divide both the Whig and Democratic parties along sectional lines. After Texas declared its independence in 1836, virtually all agitation for annexation had emanated from the South, while the most vociferous and vehement opposition had come from the North. When Texans sought admission to the United States, a deluge of hostile petitions, state legislative resolutions, and speeches from northern Democrats, northern Whigs, and northern abolitionists quickly persuaded first Andrew Jackson and then Martin Van Buren to shun the project like a leprous pariah. When calls for annexation reemerged in 1842 and 1843, again they came from southern sources—southern Democratic newspapers; John Tyler's Virginia cronies like Abel P. Upshur, Thomas R. Gilmer, and Henry A. Wise; and a few Democratic politicos like Tennessee Congressman Aaron V. Brown, Mississippi Senator Robert J. Walker, and the Maryland editor Duff Green. But propagandists constituted only a tiny fraction of southern politicians. Most southern Whigs and Democrats remained apathetic or at least silent about Texas because they recognized how dangerously divisive it was. Still, the new clamor for Texas came from the South, and in reply, a storm of protest again poured from the North.

Nor is there any doubt that the legality of slavery in Texas chiefly caused sectional disagreement over annexation. While the assertion by the *Ohio State Journal* in November 1842 that "as a party, in the free states, the Whigs are opposed to the acquisition of Texas" was entirely accurate, the party's most adamant antislavery men led northern Whigs' anti-Texas assault. Veterans of the fight against the gag rule like John Quincy Adams, Joshua R. Giddings, Seth M.

Gates of New York, and William Slade of Vermont published addresses, made speeches, and mobilized grass-roots opposition to annexation. Acquisition of Texas meant slavery expansion, they screamed. The vast, rich Texas soil would guarantee slavery's future economic viability. Slavery extension would thus prolong an immoral and barbaric institution and spawn more slave states, more southern political power in Washington, and more frustration of northern policies like protective tariffs and internal improvements. Indeed, fumed Adams, Giddings, and others, the whole Texas revolution and subsequent pro-Texas agitation proved that a Slave Power conspiracy meant to spread and perpetuate slavery and to increase the South's political power at the North's expense.[24]

Texas annexation, wrote Giddings in April 1844, involved "the great question of *slavery* or *liberty*. Will we extend slavery or will we promote Liberty & Freedom? To give the south the preponderance of political power would be itself a surrender of our Tariff, our internal improvements, our distribution of the proceeds of the public lands," he railed. "In short it would be a transfer of our political power to the slaveholders. And a base and degrading surrender of ourselves to the power & protection of slavery. It is the most abominable proposition with which a free people were ever insulted."[25]

Those Southerners who promoted annexation wanted it for precisely the same reasons Northerners objected to it. True, in propaganda aimed at the North they often denied that the South would benefit from incorporating Texas into the Union. Instead they stressed gains for the North—more land for farmers to buy, increased markets for northern manufactured and agricultural products, and national glory. But such protestations aside, southern enthusiasts for Texas hoped to gain more land, more political power, and more security for the South in general and for slaveholders in particular.

This pro-Texas junto by 1843 harbored the belief—for which some, though not conclusive, evidence existed—that the British sought to make Texas a virtual satellite and would use both political and financial inducements to inveigle Texas authorities into abolishing slavery. Should that happen, proannexation men feared, Texas would become a beachhead for abolitionist activity on the southwestern border of the United States, and the dread disease would inevitably spread to the southern states. To stop this abolitionist plot, proslavery ideologues insisted, Texas had to be saved from perfidious British influence. Annexation must proceed immediately; delay would endanger the entire South.[26]

Both proponents and opponents perceived Texas annexation as a proslavery measure, and neither Whig nor Democratic party leaders wanted to touch it in a presidential election year when support from both sections of the country was considered vital. When Clay first learned that Congress might consider annexation, he warned Crittenden that the Whig majority in the Senate must quash it because such "an exciting topic" could only produce "dissension, discord, and distraction." Van Buren's closest advisers were equally appalled at the prospect. Benjamin F. Butler bluntly warned him that Texas could "prostrate, at the North, every man . . . connected with it," while New York's Democratic Senator Silas Wright predicted that any scheme of annexation that recognized slavery in Texas "is sure to destroy any man from a free State who will go for it."[27] Endorsing annexation, in sum, might cause northern voters to abstain or defect to the growing Liberty party. Openly opposing it on antislavery grounds could alienate southern voters. Far better, most Whig and Democratic strategists believed, to bury the question, just as it had been smothered in the 1830s.

Both Whig and Democratic leaders, however, underestimated the ability of the Virginian in the White House to force the issue upon them. John Tyler made annexation a concrete issue the parties could not avoid, thereby frustrating Whig plans, just as he had done in the past. As president, Tyler could negotiate a treaty of annexation with the Texans and present it to the Senate for ratification. Tyler had been enthusiastic about Texas since the fall of 1841, but Webster's presence in the State Department had deterred him. Once Webster resigned in May 1843, however, Tyler and his friend Upshur, who replaced Webster, made secret and frantic efforts to entice the reluctant Texans into signing such a treaty. The submission of that treaty to the Senate in April 1844 placed annexation and the concomitant problem of slavery extension on the national political agenda.

Tyler lusted after Texas for several reasons. As a Southerner he shared the proslavery leanings, although not the investments in Texas lands and Texas bonds, of some of his Virginia advisors. He also shared their fear of a British conspiracy to force abolition on Texas. Distrusting the minister to England, Edward Everett of Massachusetts, as an antislavery sympathizer, Tyler sent Duff Green to England as a special envoy, and in the summer of 1843 Green wrote Upshur that he had hard evidence that the British government was prepared to make a loan to the Texas authorities so that they could pay slaveholders to emancipate their slaves. This charge ultimately proved to be exaggerated, but Tyler and Upshur believed it and thus frantically courted the Texans.[28]

Personal and political motives also turned Tyler toward Texas. The acquisition of such a vast area, he believed, would bring historical glory to his hitherto inglorious administration. If he could achieve reelection in 1844, he could inflict a stinging rebuke on tormentors in both parties. As a president without a party other than the band of rapacious office seekers he had gathered through his manipulation of patronage, Tyler knew he needed an issue that could generate popular enthusiasm. The major parties already monopolized all salient economic issues. But annexation, he believed, could arouse much support from Southerners in both parties. Then, too, land hunger and Anglophobia could attract northern Democrats. By securing a treaty and demonstrating its popularity, he could thus create a viable third party to reelect him or snatch the Democratic nomination from Van Buren.[29]

For all these reasons, Tyler yearned to present a treaty to Congress before the 1844 campaign began. Even though negotiations did not start in earnest until February 1844, Tyler's annual message in December urged Congress not to be deterred from considering annexation by Mexican threats to declare war should the United States attempt it. By the end of February, Upshur had almost completed a treaty, but on February 28 he suffered a ghastly death when a cannon accidentally exploded on a warship that he and other cabinet members were inspecting. Then Tyler made a fateful decision that ensured that annexation would be presented to the nation in the most explosive way possible. He appointed Calhoun as Upshur's successor.

Calhoun remained a wild card in southern politics. Unlike other southern politicians, he did not believe in political parties or in the wisdom of burying divisive questions for the sake of national party unity. Rather, he sought to unite Southerners of both parties into a solid sectional bloc by confronting the North with sectional ultimatums. Since 1838 Calhoun had promoted Texas annexation to strengthen the South, and Upshur and Duff Green apprised him of the Tyler administration's Texas negotiations. In the Texas project, Calhoun hoped to attain his most cherished political goals. By presenting Texas annexation explicitly as a prosouthern measure and provoking northern resistance to it, he might forge that southern party, across Whig/Democratic lines, he had long dreamed of. Such a tactic might threaten Tyler's attempt to arouse national support for annexation, but Calhoun had no stake in Tyler's career. Although he had publicly withdrawn from the race for the Democratic nomination that February, moreover, he still hungered for Van Buren's defeat. By inciting northern assaults on annexation as a proslavery measure, he believed, he could turn southern Democrats against the New Yorker and thus deny him the nomination. This was the man to whom Tyler entrusted the completion of the Texas treaty.[30]

Calhoun arrived in Washington at the end of March and by April 12 had a signed treaty in his hands. Before Tyler sent it to the Senate, Calhoun wrote a letter to British Minister Richard Pakenham, which he included in the documents accompanying the treaty. The famous Pakenham Letter dragged up again the charge that the British were endeavoring to persuade the Texans to abolish slavery and justified annexation as a defensive move by the United States to save southern slavery from the abolitionist threat. Contrary to the long propaganda campaign designed to convince the North that annexation would not benefit the South or slavery, Calhoun explicitly presented annexation as a proslavery measure. Southern voters, he hoped, would repudiate any party or any politician who dared oppose it. On April 22, Tyler sent the treaty, along with this letter and other documents, to the Senate and requested it to consider them in absolute secrecy. On April 27, a furious antislavery Democrat from Ohio, Senator Benjamin Tappan, released them to the press. By that date, the Texas question was before Congress and the nation in the most divisive form conceivable.[31]

III

Almost all Whigs remained confident even after they learned of Tyler's treaty in April. Until the end of May, they believed that they could still smother the issue. Because the Whigs controlled the Senate, they could easily prevent the two-thirds majority vote necessary for ratification. From December 1843 until April 1844, Clay urged southern Whigs in the Senate to reject any treaty, and by the end of March, Whigs in Washington assured fearful Northerners that all congressional Whigs would unite against it. To strengthen the resolve of Southerners, Clay decided in mid-April to release a public letter opposing immediate annexation.[32]

Nor did Whigs expect Democrats to attempt to resurrect the issue once the treaty was rejected, for Van Buren, who appeared certain to win the Democratic nomination, had as much interest in burying it as Clay. As early as 1838, Calhoun had written contemptuously yet prophetically that "the two prominent candidates Mr. Van Buren and Mr. Clay naturally come together on all questions on which the North and South come into conflict. . . . They of course dread all conflicting questions between the two sections, and do their best to prevent them from coming up, and when up to evade them." Certainly Clay expected Van Buren to assume "common ground" with him against the treaty; indeed, he insisted on publishing a letter against annexation even before the Senate acted or either party's convention met partly because he feared Van Buren would beat him to the punch and gain an advantage in the North.[33]

With both major candidates committed to oppose the treaty, Whig strategists believed, neither party's convention would endorse it. Then the issue would remain the exclusive property of those isolated political mavericks Tyler and Calhoun. They might make a treaty, Whigs believed, but they could not make a president with their third-party movement because of party loyalty among Whig and Democratic voters, an allegiance that would be reinforced by the salience of traditional partisan issues in the campaign. As Clay put it on April 21 while explaining to Crittenden his reasons for writing his Raleigh Letter against annexation, "The public mind is too fixed on the Presidential question, the current is running too strong . . . as to now be affected by Texas." Similarly, when Georgia Whig Congressman Stephens was warned in May that Calhounites in Georgia were demanding ratification of the treaty, he dismissed "the whole annexation project" as "a miserable political humbug got up [by Tyler and Calhoun] as a ruse to divide and distract the Whig party at the South." "But it will avail them nothing," he assured a correspondent on May 17.[34]

At first, it seemed as though Whig expectations would be fulfilled. On April 27, the very day that Tyler's treaty and the Pakenham Letter appeared in the New York press, the major Whig and Democratic papers in Washington published letters from Clay and Van Buren, respectively, opposing immediate annexation and the treaty. Although Calhoun had probably hoped to provoke such letters from the candidates when he wrote the Pakenham Letter, it is unlikely that either of them saw it before putting pen to paper. Clay had forwarded his famous Raleigh Letter to Washington on April 17, the day before Calhoun wrote Pakenham, and he constantly badgered Crittenden after that date to get it into print. Van Buren's letter was dated April 20, before Tyler sent the treaty to the Senate. Four days after the publication of the two letters, the Whig convention unanimously nominated Clay. The short Whig platform endorsed the party's now-familiar economic programs, castigated executive usurpation, and never mentioned Texas. Clearly, the Whigs still hoped to focus the upcoming campaign on traditional issues.

In that hope they would be disappointed. The various elements within the Democratic party who opposed Van Buren's nomination pounced on his public stand against immediate annexation as an excuse for dumping him. Many southern Democrats, while nominally pledged to Van Buren, wanted Texas and believed that annexation could provide them with a much more effective southern issue than hard money. Democratic politicians like Brown, Walker, and Calhoun, while cooperating with Tyler's Virginia friends, were more interested in using Tyler to force the annexation issue on the Democratic party than in using Texas to reelect Tyler. Others, like Lewis Cass' soft-money supporters, however, had far more interest in stopping Van Buren than in acquiring Texas. Fomenting a storm of demands that the party must take up Texas and jettison Van Buren before the Democratic convention met on May 27, they succeeded in derailing the front-runner. Van Buren was thrust aside after a bitter convention fight, and instead the Democrats nominated James K. Polk of Tennessee and George M. Dallas of

Pennsylvania on a platform pledging the Democratic party to "the reoccupation of Oregon and the reannexation of Texas, at the earliest practicable period." Thus, the Democrats had deprived the Whigs of the candidate whom they thirsted to run against and forced them to confront an issue they especially wanted to avoid.[35]

Nevertheless, the unexpected developments at the Democratic convention initially inflated Whigs' optimism since they seemed to perpetuate, indeed to increase, Whigs' advantages. While Whigs had considered Van Buren to be a vulnerable foe, most at first believed that Polk would be even easier to beat. They reacted with the joyous surprise of children opening Christmas presents when they learned what the Democrats had done. After "such a farce as these Baltimore nominations," exclaimed New York's Francis Granger, "we must beat them out of sight," unless, he warned, the very weakness of the Democratic ticket created Whig overconfidence. "It is a *literal disbanding of the party* for this Campaign," a delighted Mangum proclaimed. "We will literally crush the ticket." "We consider it here as giving up the game," professed an astonished Georgia Whig. Clay could scarcely believe his good fortune. "Are our Democratic friends serious in the nominations which they have made at Baltimore of candidates for President and Vice President?" he sarcastically asked Mangum. "We must beat them with ease if we do one half of our duty."[36]

Whigs jeered at the nation's first dark-horse candidate because of his supposed obscurity and lack of qualifications. "What possible chance can such a man stand of being elected President of the U.S. whose qualifications & Claims are so small if not contemptible?" exclaimed a Virginian. Polk "is too small, too feeble," sneered a Tennessee Whig. Despite Polk's previous service as speaker of the House of Representatives and governor of Tennessee, Whigs mockingly and repeatedly chanted "Who is James K. Polk?" After all, he had lost his own state's gubernatorial election in both 1841 and 1843. The American people could not possibly prefer such a political pygmy to the great Whig statesman.[37]

Whigs rejoiced not only at Polk's personal weakness but also at the Democrats' deleterious divisions. Van Burenites were furious that their favorite had been dropped and that Texas had been taken up. When Tyler's treaty came to a vote in the Senate on June 8, eight Van Buren Democrats joined twenty-seven Whigs in rejecting it by a vote of 16 to 35. Similarly, on roll-call votes in the House concerning slavery and Texas, rebellious northern Democrats bolted the party, while the Whigs, in sharp contrast, were far more united in opposition to annexation than they had ever been on any previous votes involving slavery. If the Democrats attempted to make expansionism a central issue of the campaign, it seemed unlikely that they could ever pull the party together. Equally promising from the Whig perspective, the Tyler convention in Baltimore had nominated the president on a Texas platform even after the Democrats had selected Polk. His candidacy would divide annexationists and drain votes from the Democrats, while all the opponents of annexation might rally behind Clay.[38]

IV

By the end of the summer, however, the Whigs' confidence in these supposed advantages had evaporated. Polk ran far better in the South than Van Buren could have, and he also proved more attractive to anti-Van Buren elements among northern Democrats than the New Yorker. Nor could Polk be arraigned as an aristocratic dandy who had cold-heartedly luxuriated in the splendor of the White House while common folk were ground down by the depression.[39]

Similarly, the Democratic wounds healed more quickly than Whigs anticipated. Polk's nomination dumbfounded many Democrats and embittered Van Buren's most loyal followers. Within weeks, however, Democratic politicos realized that a dark-horse candidate and the new issue of territorial expansion would allow them to patch up the damaging divisions that had rent the party before the convention. Polk himself shrewdly promoted party unity by promising not to seek a second term if elected and by assuring Van Buren and his closest lieutenants of his friendship and fidelity to their cherished economic dogmas. At the other end of the Democratic spectrum, Calhoun was so delighted by the derailing of Van Buren and the adoption of the Texas platform that he threw his influence behind the ticket. In South Carolina he quelled a movement to call a southern convention at Nashville that might demand secession were Texas not annexed. In other southern states his allies rejoiced over having a slaveholding advocate of annexation as their candidate.[40]

To guarantee a full Democratic vote, moreover, the Democrats nominated gubernatorial candidates of exceptional popularity. David Tod in Ohio represented the hard-money wing that contained the vast majority of Democratic voters and was the wing most disappointed by Van Buren's defeat. Tod's candidacy ensured that Van Buren's friends in Ohio would exert themselves for the party cause. Similarly, George Bancroft seemed sure to strengthen whatever chances the Democrats had in the Whig bastion of Massachusetts, while even Whigs admitted that Democratic candidates like William O. Butler in Kentucky, Michael Hoke in North Carolina, and Henry Muhlenberg in Pennsylvania would arouse enormous enthusiasm among Democrats, no matter what they thought of the national ticket.[41]

In terms of directly increasing Polk's chances of carrying a state, however, the most significant Democratic gubernatorial nomination was that of Van Buren's friend Silas Wright in New York. Because Wright was the most popular Democrat in the state, New York's Whigs warned, "He is the hardest man for us to beat. He gives them that which before they lacked—strength and union. With *any other* nomination our success was assured," but "now the field is studded with their seried legions—and their consuls and proconsuls and *all* their subordinate officers are at their head, disciplining & marshalling the banded forces."[42]

Like the Whigs, the Democrats were convinced that if they could get out their full vote, they would win. While the Whigs viewed 1840 as the true measure of the two parties' relative strength and the subsequent congressional and gubernatorial elections as flukes, Democrats saw Harrison's triumph as the aberration and Democratic dominance of the midterm elections as proof that they were still the majority party. As Pennsylvania's James Buchanan wrote the Kentucky Whig Robert Letcher in July, "Pennsylvania is a Democratic state by a majority of at least 20,000 and there is no population more steady on the face of the earth. Under all the excitement of 1840 & Mr. Van Buren's want of popularity, we were beaten but 343, and ever since, we have carried our state by large majorities."[43]

Democrats ensured their largest possible turnout by maneuvering Tyler out of the race. Tyler's terms for such a sacrifice were easy to meet. He wanted the virulent personal assaults upon him in the Democratic Washington *Globe* to cease; he wanted assurance that the Democrats who held office under him would not be disqualified in a Polk administration; and he demanded that Democrats ignore the anti-Texas Van Burenites and push for the immediate acquisition of Texas. As Robert Rantoul, the Democrat whom Tyler had appointed customs collector of Boston, wrote to another Massachusetts Democrat, "The Pres. is ready to go for Polk tooth & nail" if "Texas should be backed up *strongly*. This is *true policy & no time is to be lost*."[44]

Anxious to secure the financial and organizational resources available to the federal officeholders Tyler had appointed, Democrats moved adroitly to satisfy Tyler's demands. Polk muzzled the *Globe's* editor, and other Democratic newspapers welcomed Tyler with open arms. Former President Jackson wrote letters implying that Tyler men would be considered as equals in any new dispensation of patronage. Northern Democrats began to boom immediate annexation, although their public enthusiasm for the project varied. Democratic orators and newspapers were most forthright in their advocacy of annexation in states Democrats had little chance of carrying, like Massachusetts and Connecticut; in states they appeared to have little chance of losing, like Illinois, Maine, and New Hampshire; and in states like Indiana, where the combination of Oregon with Texas in the Democratic platform made western expansion in general a viable issue. In states that appeared to be close or where the antislavery vote was strong, like Ohio, New York, Pennsylvania, and New Jersey, in contrast, advocacy of annexation was as muted as it was infrequent.[45]

Still, the Democratic courtship of Tyler proved successful. On August 20 he withdrew from the race and urged all annexationists to unite behind Polk. Tyler himself would later contend that this endorsement and the aid provided by his thousands of followers produced Polk's victory in November. While Tyler probably exaggerated his own impact, the alliance between the Democratic organization and federal patronage holders played an important role in Pennsylvania and New York, changing Whig calculations of what it would take to carry those states. Since Tyler's appointees had especially wooed immigrants to his now-defunct third party, that alliance also ensured Democratic control of the growing immigrant vote in northeastern cities, forcing a decisive revision of Whig strategy.

By themselves, however, these developments during the summer of 1844 did not undermine the chief source of Whigs' confidence growing out of Polk's nomination—their conviction that they would win because of the sharp differences between the parties on concrete issues. Polk had come out vehemently against the Whig tariff of 1842 and the distribution of land proceeds and for the Independent Treasury, with its hard-money, antibanking implications, during his unsuccessful gubernatorial campaigns of 1841 and 1843. To a party that hoped to etch the sharpest possible line separating Whigs from Democrats on these economic issues, Polk initially appeared to be an ideal opponent. The best strategy for the Whigs in Pennsylvania, Clay advised John M. Clayton, was to contrast Clay's well-known support for the protective tariff and distribution with Polk's equally well-known hostility to those measures. "If by such an exhibition of our respective views Pennsylvania remains unmoved, I know not what would operate upon her." Similarly, Greeley boasted in the *Tribune* that Whig victory was certain precisely because the issue differences between the parties were so clear.[46]

Not just Polk's position on economic issues but also his enthusiasm for annexation engendered Whig optimism. Whigs reckoned that they could hold their own on annexation in the South because of the salience of economic issues and

use it to pummel the slaveholding Polk in the North. The clear differences between Clay and Polk on annexation would bring out northern Whigs who had
abstained since 1840 and win back antislavery Whigs who had deserted to the
Liberty party. Against Polk and the Democratic platform Whigs could make the
case that the best way—indeed, the only way—to stop slavery expansion was to
elect Henry Clay. With roll-call voting records in Congress and state legislatures
to supplement Clay's Raleigh Letter as evidence of the party's anti-Texas credentials, Whigs exuberantly embraced hostility to immediate annexation as a partisan
issue in the campaign.[47]

Like the other advantages that seemed so apparent at the end of May, however,
Whig hopes of winning because of the clear party differences on Texas and other
issues diminished during the summer. Concurrent though somewhat different
developments in the North and the South eroded their hopes so that, by the fall,
Whigs would resort to a desperate tactical gamble in order to salvage the election.
It was a gamble they would lose.

V

Like their northern colleagues, most southern Whigs believed that Polk's nomination in May ensured Clay's triumph in November, but their optimism is much
more difficult to understand. To be sure, they too ridiculed Polk's pretensions to
the presidency and praised the potency of Whig economic issues. Nevertheless,
the Democrats had adopted a candidate and a platform committed to annexation,
which had, since 1836, been interpreted as a distinctly prosouthern measure. Their
own candidate, in contrast, was committed against immediate annexation, and
therefore seemed to stand against the interests and needs of slavery. Northern
Whigs might happily denounce annexation on antislavery grounds, but such a
position meant political suicide in the South. How, then, could southern Whigs
have been so sanguine?

Southern Whigs exuded confidence primarily because they found the case that
Clay and other Whig politicians made against immediate annexation compelling.
For one thing, they anticipated that loyal Whigs would automatically oppose anything Tyler or the Democrats wanted. Moreover, Whigs had long opposed territorial expansion on principle because it would make the country ungovernable
and divert energy from necessary internal development.[48] Dismissing Democratic
cries about a British abolitionist plot in Texas, Whigs contended instead that
annexation would threaten the honor, safety, fiscal stability, and very existence
of the nation. Because Texas claimed large areas that clearly belonged to Mexico,
Whigs castigated acquisition as an immoral and perfidious rape of Mexican soil
to satisfy the greed of land-hungry Americans in general and of speculators in
Texas lands and Texas bonds in particular. Tyler was mistaken, Alexander Stephens informed his Georgia constituents in May, in believing "that the people of
this country are as much lost to all sense of national honor as he is of personal."[49]

Worse still, Mexico had never recognized the independence of Texas and had
threatened to declare war on the United States should it attempt annexation.
"Annexation and war with Mexico are identical," proclaimed Clay in his Raleigh
Letter, and such a war would be neither painless nor honorable, especially since

European powers like England might come to Mexico's aid. Throughout the presidential campaign, Whig speakers warned mothers that within months of a Polk victory, their sons would be fighting and dying in some godforsaken part of Texas or Mexico. To enlist the sympathies of women who could influence how their husbands, brothers, and fathers voted, indeed, Whigs enthusiastically welcomed them at partisan rallies during 1844, just as they had in 1840.[50]

Nor, Whig orators proclaimed, would the fruits of such a war be worth the human and financial cost. The United States, still unable to pay off its own debt, would have to assume a Texas debt of $13 million, according to the terms of Tyler's treaty. Worse, annexation would, in Clay's words, "menace the existence, if not certainly sow the seeds of dissolution of the Union." Clay summarized the Whig indictment of immediate annexation in a single sentence at the end of his Raleigh Letter. "I consider the annexation of Texas, at this time, without the assent of Mexico, as a measure compromising the national character, involving us certainly in war with Mexico, probably with foreign powers, dangerous to the integrity of the Union, inexpedient in the present financial condition of the country, and not called for by any general expression of public opinion."

Clay initially exuded confidence that he could oppose immediate annexation even in the South. During his triumphant tour from New Orleans through Alabama, Georgia, South Carolina, North Carolina, and Virginia in March and April, he assured nervous Whig senators, he had found "a degree of indifference or opposition to the measure of annexation that quite surprised me." Urging Crittenden to arrange for the publication of his Raleigh Letter on April 19, he announced, "I entertain no fears from the promulgation of my opinion. Public sentiment is every where sounder than at Washington." Again, on May 6, he boasted to New York's Thurlow Weed, "I am firmly convinced that my opinion on the Texas question will do me no prejudice at the South."[51]

At least until Polk's nomination and even after it, many, if not most, southern Whigs agreed with Clay's assessment. When Democrats in the Mississippi legislature pressed resolutions endorsing annexation in February 1844, Whig papers scorned the project as "supremely ridiculous," and almost two-thirds of the Whig legislators voted against those resolutions. In March 1844 the New Orleans Bee, the most influential Whig paper in the Southwest, admitted that annexation would benefit the nation but rejected it as dangerous and unconstitutional. After the Raleigh Letter's publication, so savvy a political operator as Alexander Stephens pronounced annexation "a humbug" that could have no effect in Georgia, while a North Carolinian assured his congressman that "No. Ca. will not be affected by that measure. . . . Mr. Clay has not nor will he lose a friend on account of his Texas opinion."[52]

Not all southern Whigs, to be sure, were so sanguine even before Polk's nomination. In April, Tennessee's Whig Senator Ephraim H. Foster warned that the Democratic clamor for Texas could hurt in the South and West, and others admitted that "nothing can defeat us but the Texas question."[53] Despite such qualms, when southern Whigs like Foster met the Democrats on the issue, they almost uniformly adopted Clay's position of opposition to immediate annexation. Across the South the Whig press praised the Raleigh Letter as "bold and statesmanlike," southern Whig delegates to the national convention enthusiastically nominated Clay after he had come out against annexation, Southerners made every Whig speech against Tyler's treaty in the Senate, all southern Whig senators except Henderson of Mississippi voted to reject that treaty *after* the Democrats had endorsed immediate annexation, and southern Whigs in the House joined their northern colleagues in voting against it. Henry Clay, in sum, was far from being the only southern Whig politician who confidently believed the Whigs could carry southern states even though they opposed a measure that Democrats and subsequent historians labeled prosouthern.[54]

Resolutely opposing annexation in Congress was one thing for southern Whigs; defending that position on the hustings was another. The Whigs' initial optimism began to melt before the fierce heat of the pro-Texas campaign Democrats mounted in the summer. Southern Democrats, an Alabama Whig lamented, rode the Texas issue "with both whip and spur." Equating opposition to immediate annexation with abolitionism, Democrats castigated Clay and the Whig party as traitors to the South. Democratic papers screamed that the antislavery attack on annexation by northern Whigs exposed "THE COALITION BETWEEN THE CLAY PARTY, AND THE ABOLITIONISTS OF THE NORTH AND THE NORTHWEST." Belittling the threat of war and the dangers to the Union that might result from acquisition, they stressed instead the menace to slavery and the permanent loss of limitless acres of cheap land if Texas were not annexed without delay.[55]

Thrown unexpectedly on the defensive, southern Whigs scrambled to blunt the ferocious Democratic attack. Some tried unsuccessfully to divert debate from Texas to economic issues. A mass Whig rally held in Memphis in June ignored Texas in its resolutions. A meeting in Lexington, Kentucky, in early July complained plaintively that designing politicians used annexation to shift public attention from "far more important questions which should alone decide" the presidential contest. Others endeavored to cast off the fatal stigma of abolitionism and to prove the Whigs' fidelity to the South. The slaveholder Clay, they protested, had always denounced abolitionists and would never betray his homeland. Hostility to slavery had nothing whatsoever to do with their antagonism toward annexation. Some Whigs went so far as to argue, indeed, that annexation would weaken rather than strengthen slavery. Slaves and slaveholders would be attracted to Texas, thereby causing land prices in older regions to plummet as the population declined while simultaneously exposing older areas to ruinous competition from the huge crops that could be grown on its rich soils. That competition would force other slaveholders to migrate themselves or to sell their slaves to Texans. Either way, slavery would be jeopardized.[56]

Such arguments exposed the greatest threat that the Texas annexation issue posed for southern Whigs. It was not so much the hypothetical abolitionist conspiracy against slavery that made Texas a compelling issue in the South. It was the prospect of abundant, cheap, and fertile land, especially to nonslaveholders. In his journey during March and April from New Orleans to Mobile, Montgomery, Savannah, Charleston, Raleigh, and the Virginia tidewater, Clay had met the wrong Southerners. He visited some of the wealthiest areas of the South, where Whig planters and merchants had long deplored the penchant for migration to new lands that characterized their fellow Southerners. Many Whigs in such areas considered it perfectly feasible to oppose annexation, for they had no interest themselves in moving to Texas and were far more interested in the programs of national economic development propounded by Whigs. The same apathy prevailed in certain border areas whose economic activities resembled those in the North more than those in the South. In September, for example, a Whig in Wheeling, Virginia, declared confidently, "We go against Texas, now, always, and in any way."[57]

Such implacable resistance to annexation seemed suicidal to other southern Whigs. The vast majority of the southern white population and much of the Whig constituency consisted of small slaveholders and nonslaveholders who aspired to slaveholding status. Unlike the large planters who resided in the most demographically stable areas of the South, those groups had long identified upward economic mobility with their freedom to move west and buy fresh lands. They could indeed be excited by Democratic warnings that it was now or never for Texas and that on the issue of annexation, the future of the South was at stake. The last thing Whig campaigners among those groups wanted was to have their party labeled the enemy of such southern expansion. Hence, when Tennessee Whig Senator Spencer Jarnagin proposed at the end of the congressional session in June to publish his blistering speech against Tyler's treaty as a campaign document, "the Whig members from Tennessee in a body" threatened that if he did so, they would "denounce him from one end of the State to the other." Similarly, a Virginian worried in July "that heedless & rash men of our party, because the democrats go for *immediate annexation* will run to the opposite extreme, & go *against it at all times*. . . . And when the Whigs occupy that ground in Va., the scepter will depart from Judea."[58]

Within weeks, if not days, of Polk's nomination, therefore, many southern Whigs retreated from the adamant hostility to annexation that southern Democrats and northern Whigs read into Clay's Raleigh Letter and resorted to a more defensible position. Nowhere in that letter, they pointed out, had Clay taken an irreversible stand against annexation. Rather, he stressed only that it was dishonorable and inexpedient "at this time" because the prior consent of Mexico had not been secured and because northern opinion was so strongly against it. Once Mexican assent had been negotiated and sectional harmony restored by a Whig administration, they hinted, Texas could and would be safely acquired. The only difference between Democrats and Whigs, therefore, was that Democrats insisted on annexation immediately, when it was dangerous, while Whigs would achieve it in the near future, when it was safe. As a Georgian advised Senator Berrien on June 3, the Democratic demand for immediate annexation, regardless of the consequences, has "failed here of its objects. Direct opposition to ultimate annexation would perhaps be as unwise as at present unnecessary. Taking as the party ground the position in favor of that measure when the country requires it, and when it can properly be effected, we have thought the safest ground, on which to meet the usual feeling of our people for the acquisition of lands." The Georgia Whig platform endorsed that position in June, Virginia's Rives echoed it in a Senate speech in June that was widely circulated and praised in the South, and southern Whig papers increasingly employed the argument as the campaign progressed.[59]

By seeking to put a southern spin on Clay's Raleigh Letter, southern Whigs followed their traditional strategy. Northern and southern Whigs had long taken a two-faced approach to questions involving slavery. That tactic, espousing one position in the North and another in the South, was possible only if the campaign waged by Whigs in one section did not embarrass Whigs in the other. Had the shift of southern Whigs been confined to newspapers and local Whig campaigners, it might have worked in 1844, as it had in 1836 and 1840. Clay himself, however, apparently felt compelled to shift his position in line with that taken by other southern Whigs. Saving his prospects in the South may have compelled that shift, but he thereby jeopardized the ability of northern and southern Whigs to interpret his position differently.

On July 1, Clay wrote a letter to the obscure Tuscaloosa, Alabama, *Independent Monitor* in which he insisted that his objection to immediate annexation was hardly meant to please northern abolitionists, whom he had long denounced. Instead, he stressed, he was primarily concerned with preserving the Union. While it angered a few abolitionists, this first Alabama letter by itself would probably have done little harm to the northern Whig campaign. Potentially much more damaging was a second letter Clay wrote on July 27 to another Alabama newspaper. This time he asserted that he had no personal objection to annexation and that the existence of slavery in Texas had nothing to do with its propriety. Should the danger of sectional disruption and war he had alluded to in his Raleigh Letter be removed, he indicated, he might consider annexation himself if elected president. At the same time that northern Whigs insisted that annexation must be stopped precisely because of the legality of slavery in Texas, in other words, Clay deliberately minimized the importance of slavery to the matter and promised, as did other southern Whigs, that he himself would "be glad to see it, without dishonor, without war, and with the common consent of the Union, and upon fair and just terms."[60]

Clay's decision to publish the Alabama letters ranks among the biggest mistakes of his long political career. Eventually they would help force a ruinous shift in Whig strategy in the North while they little helped the Whig cause in the South, where Democrats jeered at his vacillation. Precisely why he chose to write them in July—especially the critical second letter—is unclear. Later, Clay would say that he had to write the letters in order to hold southern states in the Whig column, and some historians, blessed with the hindsight knowledge of the closeness of the results, agree that without the letters Clay would have lost additional southern states.[61]

To many Whigs, however, the situation in June and July did not appear so dire as to require the letters. One able student of the election has suggested that Clay wrote them because he was worried about the enthusiasm for Texas in Kentucky, but Crittenden, Clay's closest lieutenant in the state, wrote privately on July 1 that Texas "has passed away as a humbug" in Kentucky. Clay did receive in late June a letter dated June 20 from Stephen Miller, the Alabama editor to whom he had sent the first letter, warning him that Alabama Democrats were pushing Texas "with great assiduity," but on June 24 Clay assured a northern correspondent that signs were good everywhere and that he expected to poll a larger vote than Harrison had in 1840. In the first Alabama letter, in fact, Clay himself expressed the conviction that the Texas question could not hurt the Whigs in Kentucky or Alabama and that it "was a bubble blown up by Mr. Tyler in the most exceptional manner, for sinister purposes, and its bursting has injured no body but Mr. Van Buren."[62]

More to the point, in July before the second letter was written and in early August before it could have been circulated, Whigs across the South expressed confidence that they had blunted the Democratic drive on Texas simply with their own reinterpretation of the Raleigh Letter. There is, in short, abundant evidence, to which Clay must have been privy, that southern Whigs did not believe they needed another statement from Clay himself in late July. Only July 10, for example, Virginia's former governor, David Campbell, assured Rives, "The democratic party will not be able to make anything out of the Texas question." Rives wrote Clay on July 15 that while the majority of Virginia Whigs favored eventual annexation, they were willing to wait until it could be safely accomplished by a Whig administration. Similarly, Whig campaigners in Tennessee boasted in late July and early August that because Texas had failed to dent their ranks, "surely we cannot lose this state." An Alabama Whig reported on August 5 (without mentioning either Clay letter) that while many Whigs in his state wanted annexation, they would never accept it "on the principle of the late shameful treaty." "Some of our Whigs were alarmed when Texas first became the rallying cry of the democratic party," he reported, "but the thing is dead." Even from the remote Democratic stronghold of Arkansas, Whigs crowed that the "Texas humbug" had proved "abortive."[63]

Southern Whigs pounced on the results of elections held during July and August as evidence that they could withstand the Democratic challenge on Texas. On the first Monday in July, Louisiana's Whigs captured the state legislature and one of the two congressional seats they contested. Whigs everywhere were ecstatic because no state in the nation was thought to be more avid for Texas than Louisiana. "If the Texas question has failed in Louisiana where will it not fail?" queried a joyful Georgia Whig, while another reported to the *New York Tribune* that "the news of the Election in Louisiana operates like a dose of jalap upon the poor Locos, whose disappointment and chagrin are pitiable in the extreme." Whigs also pointed to their victory in North Carolina's gubernatorial and legislative elections in the first week of August, after Clay had written the second letter but before it could have been circulated outside of Alabama, as evidence of certain Whig success in November because, they claimed, Democrats had tried to make Texas the central issue in the campaign. Others interpreted the impressive Whig gains in the Missouri and Kentucky legislative elections in early August as signs of an upward Whig trend reminiscent of the one in the summer of 1840 that had culminated in Harrison's triumph. Clay himself reported on August 7, before his second letter could possibly have had any widespread impact, that the Texas issue would do the Whig cause "no prejudice" in the South, where he still expected to carry two-thirds of the states.[64]

In contrast, by the fall, when Whigs and Democrats were for the first time debating the Alabama letters, Whig confidence was clearly eroding. Alabama and Arkansas Whigs might prate about neutralizing the Texas issue, but no one expected Clay to carry those Democratic fiefdoms any more than he could South Carolina or Mississippi. Even so sanguine a forecaster as Horace Greeley, moreover, refused to place Missouri in the Clay column for November because he properly recognized that Whig gains there were attributable to cooperation with dissident Democrats who wanted to prevent the reelection of Thomas Hart Benton to the Senate. Clay could never get such Democratic support.[65]

Even the elections Whigs had won in the summer bore portents of a Democratic surge that might doom them in November, portents that the veteran Clay probably saw. The Whigs dramatically increased their representation in the

Kentucky and North Carolina legislatures, but in each state the Democrats had garnered unprecedentedly large proportions of the gubernatorial vote. With some justice Whigs attributed those gains to local questions and to the undeniable popularity of the Democratic candidates, but there was no gainsaying cold facts: since the presidential election of 1840, the Democrats had increased their popular vote by 17 percent in North Carolina and by an astounding 69 percent in Kentucky, while the Whig vote had remained virtually stagnant.[66]

If the Democrats could gain voters at anything like those rates in Louisiana, Virginia, Tennessee, and Georgia, where the parties were much more closely balanced than in Kentucky or North Carolina and where the Democrats were moving heaven and earth on the Texas issue, Whigs realized, they were in deep trouble. Although many Whigs had initially exulted about the Louisiana results, the hard truth was that their margin in the legislature had declined from what it had been in 1842, while they captured only one of four congressional seats. A low turnout in July made realistic predictions about what would happen in November impossible, but perceptive Whigs knew that Louisiana was too close to call.[67]

Nor, by the fall, did prospects seem more auspicious elsewhere in the South. Virginia's Whigs, for example, continued to predict Clay's victory nationally, but more and more often they despaired of carrying the Old Dominion and its seventeen electoral votes for him. The Whigs' loss of confidence in Tennessee is well reflected in the letters that passed between the Whig elector Gustavus A. Henry and his wife, who, like so many women with Whig husbands, was ferociously partisan. While the sanguine Gustavus boasted in July that the state was safe, his wife was frantic about the real possibility of defeat by September. Urging her peripatetic husband to "work harder than you have ever done," she cried in alarm, "It makes my blood boil to think of James K. Polk being president. Surely the people of these United States have not lost all sense of honour." Though less worried about the outcome, a prominent Maryland Whig was equally perplexed by the apparent surge in Democratic strength. "Who would have thought," John Pendleton Kennedy asked in October, "that this miserable nomination of Polk & Dallas was to give us such trouble?"[68]

Even Clay began to despair by the fall. In September he worriedly wrote Mangum that the close result in North Carolina in August boded ill. "Our opponents are manifestly making great exertions everywhere, and affect if they do not feel great confidence." Although his Alabama letters had neither caused the earlier Whig optimism nor stemmed the apparent Democratic surge by the fall, he feared the appearance of any new charge that could tip the South against him. "Their whole system now seems to be directed to the propagation of the most detestable libels and lies," he warned Mangum. Thus, when his distant cousin, the Kentucky abolitionist Cassius M. Clay, circulated a letter in the North calling on antislavery men to vote for Clay because he sympathized with the abolitionist movement, the beleaguered Whig candidate felt compelled to refute the allegation. On September 2 he published a letter in the Lexington, Kentucky, *Observer* adamantly denying the antislavery sentiments attributed to him and condemning as unconstitutional any congressional interference with slavery in both the states and the District of Columbia. He realized that such a letter would antagonize northern abolitionists, he later admitted to the angry Giddings, but he had been forced to issue it. Efforts to appease the Liberty party in the North were "vain and fruitless," while failure to repudiate his cousin's claims could have cost him as many as four slave states. Just as he had done in July, that is, Clay quite consciously risked offending potential supporters in the North in order to salvage the Whig campaign in the South.[69]

VI

Word of Clay's efforts to propitiate Southerners reached the North at the beginning of September. The nationally circulated *Niles' Register* reprinted the second Alabama letter on August 31. Soon thereafter Clay's September 2 letter, disavowing antislavery sentiments, appeared. The news could not have come at a worse time for northern Whigs. Since May the foundations of their confidence had crumbled one by one. To appreciate the full impact of Clay's letters on northern Whigs, therefore, one must understand what had already happened to them over the summer.

Initially northern Whigs had rejoiced after the Democratic national convention. Instead of running Clay, the Kentucky slaveholder, against Van Buren, the New York nonslaveholder, with all its disadvantages, they now ran against a Tennessee slaveholder who espoused a prosouthern annexation program. The Democratic strategy, fulminated Greeley in the *Tribune*, aimed to satisfy "the ultra Slavery prejudices of the South—the new fanatics enlisted by Calhoun & Co. for a crusade to extend and consolidate Human Bondage." The Philadelphia *North American* proclaimed that the choice for voters was now "Texas and No Tariff, or Tariff and No Texas." In a widely circulated pamphlet, Ohio's Whig state committee called the central question "Polk, Texas, and Slavery; or Clay, the Union, and Liberty." Michigan's Whig state convention added that Polk's agenda had the "avowed purpose of extending and perpetuating the institution of slavery." Because of Polk's commitment to Texas, exulted an Indiana Whig in June, "locofocoism is doomed to bite the dust in November."[70]

Northern Whigs also believed that they had a decisive edge over the Democrats on traditional issues like the tariff, distribution, and the Independent Treasury and with the superior qualifications of their candidate. Seward wrote Weed on June 20 that because of the tariff and Texas issues "we are safe and right," and as late as September 11, he iterated to another correspondent that "the election is to be won or lost on the grounds exclusively" of "Tariff and No Texas." Similarly, Justin Morrill, the chairman of a Whig county committee in Vermont, taunted his Democratic counterpart in August for fearing to debate on "Texas, Public Lands, Tariff, and the Men." On these issues, he insisted, the " 'Democratic' and Whig parties are most emphatically at variance," and "we cannot smother these great National Topics, if we would."[71]

The Democrats, however, proved to be remarkably successful in obfuscating the issue differences that Whigs hoped to clarify. Their ability to neutralize what Whigs saw as their advantage on economic issues frustrated and enraged the Whigs. On no issue, indeed, did the Democrats prove more evasive than on the one on which Whigs had placed their hopes in the spring—the tariff. Almost as soon as Polk received the Democratic nomination, Pennsylvania Democrats pleaded with him to modify his opposition to a protective tariff. For two years they had trumpeted their important role in securing the Tariff of 1842, and in the spring of 1844 the Democratically controlled Pennsylvania legislature unanimously protested any attempts to lower the tariff rates. Polk, realizing that his past opposition to protective tariffs could doom Democrats in the Northeast, penned a letter to a Philadelphia Democrat named John K. Kane in which he artfully shrouded his tariff stance in ambiguity. Admitting that he had always opposed tariffs aimed explicitly to protect manufactured products rather than raise revenue, he said that he favored revenue tariffs with moderate discriminating duties that "afford reasonable incidental protection to our home industry."[72] Meanwhile, the duplicitous Polk privately assured Southerners that one of the first acts of his administration would be to lower duties to the 20 percent *ad valorem* level designated in the tariff of 1833. Had Polk honestly wrote *that* to northern Democrats, the outcome of the election and the subsequent course of American history might have been very different.[73]

Certainly the use to which Democrats put the Kane Letter was anything but forthright. While southern Democrats candidly contrasted Polk's hostility to the protective tariff of 1842 with Clay's defense of it, in Pennsylvania and other northern states Democrats boldly declared that Polk was a firmer friend of that tariff then Clay. "POLK, DALLAS, SHUNK and the DEMOCRATIC TARIFF OF 1842" proclaimed Democratic banners throughout Pennsylvania. "WE DARE THE WHIGS TO REPEAL IT."

Furious, frustrated, and alarmed, Whigs protested the effrontery of these Democratic tactics. From June until the end of the campaign, Greeley's *Tribune* raged against Democrats' fraudulence on the tariff and pleaded with the voters of Pennsylvania, New Jersey, New York, and other northern states not to be bamboozled by it. "In Pennsylvania our opponents have" outdone themselves "in the art of lying and meanness," complained a Whig reporter in August. Aware that Democrats in the South were promoting Polk as a free trader, a Philadelphia Whig sputtered indignantly, "They go for Free Trade where it is popular, and the Tariff where it is popular, . . . solely to deceive the People." Desperately northern Whigs begged evidence from Tennessee with which to expose this hoax, but by the fall they knew that their biggest gun in Pennsylvania had been spiked.[74]

Elsewhere the Democrats were not so brazen. In certain northern states like Maine and New Hampshire, as in the South, they minced no words in their condemnation of all parts of the Whig economic program because they were as confident as the Whigs that they could benefit from such contrasts. While they defended the standard Democratic opposition to the tariff, paper currency, and distribution in Illinois and Michigan, however, they flagrantly insisted that Democrats and Polk wanted federal rivers and harbors improvements just as fervently as Clay and the Whigs did. So too in New Jersey, where the tariff of 1842 was as popular as it was in Pennsylvania, they argued that because Clay and Polk both favored the tariff, a new national bank was the central economic question.[75]

Still, the major Democratic tactic to neutralize any Whig advantage on economic issues, in most of the Midwest as in the South, was to emphasize western expansion in general and Texas annexation in particular. In Michigan, Illinois, and Indiana, Democrats trumpeted the glory of additional land, urged Americans to take possession of Oregon as well as Texas, and stressed the anti-British implications of both Oregon and Texas, thus playing upon the Anglophobia of their constituents, especially Irish and Canadian immigrants.

This tack started an electoral steamroller. In Illinois' August state legislative elections Democrats crushed the Whigs, and Whig strategists knew they had no hope of gaining the state's nine electoral votes in November. That same month, Whigs recaptured control of the lower house of the Indiana legislature and drew even in the state senate, but the Democrats seemed to have the edge in the popular vote. Opposition to Texas annexation had not given Indiana's Whigs the advantage they had counted on. Nor had it persuaded Liberty party voters to return to Whig ranks. Few Whigs, moreover, expected to win Michigan, for the Democrats had carried it decisively since 1840. If Polk captured all three together with New Hampshire, whose loyalty to the Democratic party seemed unshakable, his electoral vote would more than match what the Whigs could count on from their four New England strongholds.[76]

That likelihood left Maine, New Jersey, New York, Pennsylvania, and Ohio as the decisive states in the North, but by September the Whigs had begun to doubt the potency of their No Texas platform in any of them. In both New Jersey and Pennsylvania, where economic issues remained most salient, Democrats were neutralizing the Whigs' protariff platform. Whig strength had declined so much in Maine since 1840 that it seemed unlikely that even the addition of the Liberty vote could put it in the Whig column.

Finally, the Whigs' effort to lure Liberty voters by opposing Texas' annexation in both Ohio and New York seemed stalemated. Democrats muddied the difference between the parties on that issue as well. In Ohio, Democrats ducked the Texas question whenever possible, and if they discussed it at all, they clung to Van Buren's ambiguous position, not to Polk's forthright advocacy of immediate annexation. In New York, Democratic dissembling on Texas frustrated Whig hopes of drawing clear party lines on Texas or No Texas. The long state Democrat address that happily announced the clarity of differences between the parties remained absolutely silent on the Texas issue, as did many campaigners, while a leading Democratic newspaper, the *New York Evening Post*, continued to denounce annexation throughout the campaign. Whigs' difficulty in pinning down where the Democrats stood on annexation was compounded by the Democratic nomination of Silas Wright for governor in early September, for Wright had been a leading figure among the Van Buren Democrats who had fought Tyler's treaty in the Senate. After his nomination, instead of presenting a ringing demand for immediate annexation regardless of the consequences, Wright spoke only vaguely of the peaceful and honorable acquisition of Texas and Oregon within a few years, a position paralleling that taken by southern Whigs.[77]

While Democrats fudged on Texas in New York and Ohio, they brilliantly campaigned to alienate the most advanced antislavery men from Henry Clay and to keep them firmly in the Liberty party. Just as Whigs sought to unite all opponents of Texas annexation behind Clay, Democrats aspired to keep antiannexationists divided. Aware of the moralistic attitudes of the deeply religious evangelical Protestants who supported the Liberty party, Democrats dragged up every charge they could to smear Clay's personal reputation. With telling effect, they lacerated the Kentuckian as a blasphemer, duelist, gambler, profligate, drunkard, and philanderer. As one prominent abolitionist wrote Giddings long after the election, abolitionists never considered "for a moment" voting for Clay. "Why did not the Whigs set up a man of good character? As it was, if Mr. Clay's character had been as good as Mr. Polk's, he would have been elected."[78]

Primarily, however, Democrats attacked the untrustworthiness of the slave-holding Clay on the annexation issue in order to discredit him with the abolitionists. Hence, when Clay's letters on Texas and abolitionism were published in the North in September, both Whig and Democratic politicos immediately recognized their import. Whigs mourned. Democrats celebrated. "Mr. Clay's letter has caused much discussion & some consternation among his friends, & great exultation among his enemies," Webster wrote from New York on September 1 after conferring with Weed and Greeley. "Mr. Weed is quite despairing." Weed indeed was despairing. "Things look blue!" he moaned to Francis Granger on September 3. "Ugly letter, that to Alabama. Can't stand many such." From western New York Seward warned on September 2 that the Alabama letter "jeopard[ize]s, perhaps loses this State."[79]

The results of the Vermont and Maine elections increased Whigs' fears that Clay's vacillation would alienate Liberty party voters and, indeed, drive still more antislavery Whigs to the Liberty camp. The Whigs carried the gubernatorial election in Vermont on September 3 with their largest percentage of the vote since 1840, but, ominously, the Liberty party attracted more voters and a larger proportion of the vote than ever before. The Whig gubernatorial candidate, former Congressman William Slade, a renowned foe of the gag rule and Texas annexation, had been placed on the ticket explicitly to win back antislavery voters. If Slade could not reverse the growth of the Liberty party, how could Clay? The results in Maine on September 9 were even worse. While the Whigs almost doubled their vote since 1843, they still garnered only 42 percent of the total, while the Liberty party siphoned off 7 percent. Realistic Whigs correctly concluded that Maine's nine electoral votes were lost.[80]

The results in Vermont and Maine intensified Whig anxiety about additional defections of antislavery Whigs to the Liberty party in other, more closely balanced states where Whigs might need every vote to win. Clay "is as rotten as a stagnant fish pond, on the subject of Slavery & always has been," ex-Congressman Seth Gates of New York cursed as he deserted the Whigs. Clay's last letter "has produced a bad effect upon . . . the Abolitionists," moaned one New York Whig in early October, and "the Abolition vote will decide the election."[81]

Clay tried to stem further such defections by publishing a final public letter on the Texas question, dated September 23, in the Washington *National Intelligencer*. In it he insisted that all his letters over the summer were perfectly consistent with the original Raleigh Letter and that he had not retreated an inch from his firm opposition to immediate annexation. "Nothing was further from my purpose than to intimate any change of opinion as long as any considerable portion of the confederacy [i.e., the North] should continue to stand out in opposition to the annexation of Texas." That letter apparently allayed antislavery Whigs' suspicions of Clay. On October 5, the very day Clay's final letter was reprinted in *Niles' Register*, Washington Hunt assured Millard Fillmore, the Whig gubernatorial candidate in New York, that the state was safe for the Whigs. "I rejoice to know that at last, we have Mr. Clay's *last letter*. It will do good & we can now stand on solid ground."[82]

Even more important in stanching the flow of northern Whig voters to the Liberty party, their suspicions of James G. Birney, antislavery men's presidential nominee, increased just when their suspicions about Clay began to decline. Word reached the East in October that Birney had denounced Whig economic programs, that he preferred the election of Polk to that of Clay, and that he had accepted a Democratic nomination for the Michigan legislature. To embellish these damaging revelations, Ohio's Whigs circulated a fictitious statement, falsely attributed to Birney, that he had always been a Democrat and that he believed that he was doing the Democratic cause more good by running as an abolitionist than he could by openly supporting Polk. Largely because of these sensational charges, the same New York Whig who predicted on October 2 that the Birney vote could throw New York to Polk wrote on October 30 that two-thirds of the Liberty men would vote for Clay and thus that he would carry the state. Even more reassuring than such predictions, the Whigs eked out a narrow victory in the Ohio gubernatorial election in October despite a significant jump in the Liberty vote, a victory that, according to Ohio's Whigs, guaranteed the Buckeye State for Clay.[83]

By the end of October, in sum, many Whigs had regained confidence that they could hold their own voters in the North, and some still hoped to woo back Liberty men. In September, however, New York and Pennsylvania still seemed in particular jeopardy. Not only had the tariff issue had been neutralized in Pennsylvania, but on September 2 Pennsylvania's Democrats nominated the popular Francis Shunk for governor to replace their previous candidate, Henry Muhlenberg, who had died, and worried Whigs admitted that Shunk seemed unbeatable. On September 8, New York's Democrats nominated Silas Wright for governor, thus ensuring a full Democratic turnout in the nation's largest state, while simultaneously many former Conservative Democrats, who had supported Harrison in 1840, were threatening to sit out the race because Nathaniel Tallmadge had been denied the Whigs' vice presidential nomination.[84]

Worse, in both Pennsylvania and New York, the Polk/Tyler merger might assure the Democrats of a large immigrant vote. That surge of immigrants toward the Democrats had to be offset. Otherwise, the Whigs would lose Pennsylvania and New York and with them the presidency. In September and October, therefore, the Whigs reached out in desperation to the most determined enemies of the rapidly growing immigrant population—nativists and rabidly anti-Catholic Protestants.

VII

In some ways this shift in strategy seems natural, if not inevitable. Ethnic and religious rivalries had influenced American politics since the colonial period, and they had helped to shape the allegiances of some Whig and Democratic voters since the birth of the second party system. The Whigs not only won the support of many native-born evangelical Protestants who often despised Catholics and immigrants; they also consciously portrayed themselves as the party of moral probity, as an organization of church-going, sober, and respectable citizens, while contemptuously stigmatizing the Democrats as godless and immoral. Reinforcing that purported difference was one reason Whig strategists welcomed the attendance of women at their rallies in 1840 and 1844. That Whig image, in turn, caused many immigrants, especially Catholic foreigners, as well as nonevangelical Protestants and the unchurched, who resented the moral imperialism of Whigs, to support the Democrats.

Such ethnocultural tensions had unusual salience in 1844. Democratic demands for Texas and Oregon were presented in ways that stoked the Anglophobia of Irish and Canadian immigrants. At the same time, local federal officeholders in cities were mobilizing immigrants, first for Tyler and then for Polk.[85] Far more critical in alienating potential immigrant and especially Catholic voters from the Whigs, however, was the identity of the man whom the Whigs had chosen as Clay's running mate in May—Theodore Frelinghuysen, a former United States senator from New Jersey and the current chancellor of New York University. If Henry Clay was widely viewed as the embodiment of Whig principles, Frelinghuysen personified the reform impulse of American Protestantism. The son of a famous Presbyterian minister, he was renowned for his prominent participation in the American Tract Society, the American Sunday School Union, the American Board of Commissioners for Foreign Missions, and the American Temperance Union. The organizations with which Frelinghuysen was associated, moreover, attracted not only zealous Protestant do-gooders, but also fanatical anti-Catholic bigots. At a meeting of the American Missionary Society in 1844, for example, two Protestant clergymen denounced the Roman Catholic Church as "the Whore of Babylon" and "the Lady in Scarlet." Frelinghuysen thus suffered guilt by association with men far more prejudiced than he. Several years after the election, indeed, at least one Whig charged that Bishop John Hughes of New York ordered Catholics to vote against the Whig ticket because Frelinghuysen had refused to admonish the offensive ministers publicly.[86]

Perhaps more than any other politician of the day, in short, Frelinghuysen could arouse suspicions among Catholics and immigrants about what the Whig party stood for. Consequently, Democrats were quick to sound the alarm. A Democratic paper in New Orleans, for example, savaged Frelinghuysen as a self-righteous bigot "who boldly attacks religious liberty, demands the unhallowed union of church and state, and contends that the government should legally recognize the religion of the majority."[87]

Precisely why the Whigs nominated Frelinghuysen for vice president is a mystery. Later, some insiders claimed that the convention hoped to facilitate a merger between the Whigs and independent nativist political parties. But in the spring of 1844, the Whigs in general and certainly Clay in particular had no intention of courting the nativists by openly attacking Catholics and immigrants. They had far too much confidence in their traditional issues.

A more plausible guess is that Whigs chose Frelinghuysen to offset Clay's supposed weakness on the "character" issue. Even before the Whig convention assembled, Democrats were flaying Clay as a drunkard, gambler, profligate, and blasphemer. As one Ohio Democrat asserted, "Clay's *duelling* is a bitter pill and many of the moral and reflecting portion of the Whig party refuse to support him." Certainly the Whigs trumpeted Frelinghuysen in a way to assuage those suspicions of Clay among "the moral and reflecting portion" of their party. The national platform of 1844 praised him for giving "his head, his hand, and his heart . . . without stint to the cause of morals, education, philanthropy, and religion," while a Whig magazine identified him as "the *Christian statesman*" who sought to defend the Indians and the sanctity of the Sabbath during his service in the Senate. Later, in fact, Democrats jokingly referred to the supposedly incongruous pair on the Whig ticket as "The Bane and the Antidote."[88]

Yet even this theory implies more premeditation than the existing record sustains. Although the Whigs had every reason to choose their nominee carefully in light of Tyler's betrayal, few Whig leaders seriously considered the matter prior to the convention. Clay shortsightedly left the selection to the delegates and later expressed astonishment at Frelinghuysen's nomination. Southern Whigs favored Delaware's Clayton, but they knew that a free-state man must balance Clay. New Jersey's Whigs nominated Frelinghuysen, but his name rarely figured in preconvention speculation. Instead, men from states with more electoral votes than tiny New Jersey were most frequently mentioned: Maine's Senator George Evans; former Governor John Davis of Massachusetts, who had powerful backing from Webster's rival, Abbott Lawrence; the wealthy Lawrence himself, whom the influential Mangum favored; ex-Congressman Millard Fillmore of New York; Senator Nathaniel Tallmadge, the darling of New York's Conservative Democrats; Supreme Court Justice John McLean of Ohio; and a bevy of Pennsylvania congressmen and ex-congressmen, most prominently Philadelphia's John Sergeant.[89]

Yet each of the most frequently mentioned possible candidates had drawbacks that prevented any preconvention consensus from emerging. Regarded as Webster's man, Evans was tarred by Webster's stubborn loyalty to Tyler. Lawrence and Davis faced opposition from Webster, and resolutions from the Massachusetts legislature in early 1844 calling for elimination of the Constitution's three-fifths clause discredited any Bay State man among Southerners. Southern Whigs also distrusted McLean, whom many Ohio Whig leaders also opposed. None of the Pennsylvanians was deemed popular enough to swing the Keystone State to Clay or capable enough to assume the presidency, an eventuality snake-bitten Whigs had to consider. Regular Whigs both in and outside New York rejected the convert Tallmadge because of their experience with Tyler. Fillmore, who badly wanted the nomination, had the state party's official support. Yet Southerners feared that his popularity among New York abolitionists would sink the ticket in the South. Equally important, Weed, hoping to run Fillmore for governor, privately ordered delegates to knife him.[90]

On the eve of the Whig national convention, in short, "the Vice Presidency" was, in Winthrop's words, "still a very vexed question."[91] That uncertainty appeared when delegates finally filled the second slot. Frelinghuysen led on the first ballot with 101 votes, compared to 83 for Davis, 53 for Fillmore, and 36 for Sergeant. Aside from New Jersey's seven votes, significantly, Frelinghuysen received only three northern votes. Nine-tenths of his support came from the South. Again, on the second ballot, only 16 of his 118 votes came from nonslave states. On the third ballot Frelinghuysen prevailed with 155 votes compared to 79 for Davis and 40 for Fillmore. Northerners gave him fifty-one votes, 30 percent of their total, but 91 percent of Southerners supported him.[92]

Southerners, in short, were primarily responsible for Frelinghuysen's nomination. Possibly they wanted him to balance Clay on the "character issue." More likely, Southerners gravitated to Frelinghuysen because he originally came from New Jersey, a state that bordered on Clayton's Delaware and that in 1844 still possessed a few slaves, and because he seemed less dangerous to Southerners on the slavery issue, despite his long career in humanitarian crusades, than did either Davis or Fillmore. Willing to follow Clay despite his opposition to immediate annexation, they apparently refused to add a potentially unpopular vice presidential candidate to their burden in the South. Such reasoning is understandable, but by placing Frelinghuysen on the Whig ticket with Clay, southern Whigs damaged Whig prospects in crucial northern states even more than Clay's apparent retreat on the Texas annexation issue itself.

By underlining the image of the Whig party as an association of narrow-minded, silk-stocking patricians bent on telling other people how to behave, Frelinghuysen's nomination by itself impaired Whigs' ability to win over Catholics, immigrants, and the unchurched. Certainly it gave a different tone to the Whig campaign than the rough-and-tumble log-cabin, hard-cider theatrics of 1840. What ultimately made the nomination so dangerous, however, was that almost simultaneously with the Whig convention, events in New York City and Philadelphia enhanced the chances that the Democrats could mobilize a wave of new immigrant voters against Clay if the Whig party could be portrayed as anti-Catholic and anti-immigrant.

Private nativist societies had long existed in the United States, inspired by sheer bigotry, superpatriotic fears that the American republic was being undermined by corrupt foreign elements, and sustained Protestant propaganda that the pope was plotting to take over the United States through the emigration of his slavish European minions. Until the early 1840s, however, those societies had been small and relatively apolitical. Then a confluence of developments increased antiforeign and anti-Catholic fears and provided nativists with concrete political issues they could use to establish a party separate from both the Whig and Democratic organizations. Economic competition between native-born artisans and immigrant workingmen increased as jobs disappeared during the prolonged depression. In New York City, a widespread desire for reform of the municipal government, frustrated by both Whig and Democratic politicians, provided a perfect opening for a new party. Equally important, immigration increased in the early 1840s, and so did Americans' repugnance of the social evils they attributed to it: pauperism, crime, public drunkenness, and disorder. Most important, many Americans increasingly feared the political influence of foreigners, especially Catholics. Those anxieties were fed by what seemed to be successful efforts by the Catholic clergy to weaken the control that Protestants exercised over public schools in New York City and Philadelphia and to prohibit the use of the Protestant King James version of the Bible in those schools. Immigrants and Catholics, that is, could be credibly if incorrectly charged with corrupting the political process and subverting the republic by undermining its moral foundations.

The American Republican party emerged as a response to those developments in a number of cities where immigrants were concentrated. It pledged to restore the purity of the political process and to deter further immigration by lengthening the period of naturalization for aliens from five to twenty-one years, by limiting officeholding to native-born citizens, and by protecting the public schools and other social institutions from supposed Catholic assaults upon them. In elections held for state assemblymen in New York City in November 1843, the American Republicans astonished observers by capturing 8,600 votes compared to 14,410 for the Democrats and 14,000 for the Whigs. Even more impressive, the American Republican mayoral candidate, James Harper, triumphed there in April 1844 with 24,570 votes compared to 20,538 for the Democrats and 5,297 for the Whigs. A month earlier, American Republican candidates had swept local township elections in Philadelphia County, Pennsylvania, normally a Democratic bastion.[93]

This performance indicated that the American Republicans could mobilize thousands of new voters, as well as convert both Whigs and Democrats to their cause. In New York, for example, the best estimates are that two-thirds of the nativists' vote in the fall and two-fifths of it in the spring came from normal Democrats. Similarly, they could have carried Philadelphia County only with the help of Democratic voters. For Whigs anxious to carry the critical states of New York and Pennsylvania, therefore, the American Republicans presented a very tempting bloc of voters indeed. If the more than 10,000 former Democrats who supported the American Republicans in New York City in April could be lured to the Whig party, for example, they would almost offset the 16,000 men who voted for the Liberty party in New York State in 1843.[94]

In the spring and summer of 1844, however, most Whigs disdained an alliance with nativists. American Republicans usually reciprocated those feelings.[95] Then an outbreak of rioting between Catholic and immigrant workingmen in the Philadelphia suburb of Kennsington in May, a week after the Whig convention met in Baltimore, reinforced Whig disdain. Those riots and subsequent violence in Southwark in July saw scores of men killed or wounded and at least two Catholic churches, as well as numerous Irish homes, burned to the ground. The Philadelphia riots not only intensified fears and animosities across ethnic and religious lines; they unfairly stigmatized the American Republican party as a band of lawless, church-burning incendiaries who threatened social tranquility. In Philadelphia, even as the Whig *Northern American* praised the goals of the American Republicans and called for revision of the naturalization laws, the Whiggish middle class denounced the violence they blamed on working-class rabble. Elsewhere Whigs recognized that any open association with the American Republicans or their principles would not only infuriate immigrants and Catholics but might also alienate the respectable middle class, whose allegiance Frelinghuysen's nomination was in part meant to secure.[96]

Clay perfectly understood the hazards of nativism. In June, Peter Sken Smith, a leading American Republican from Philadelphia, sent him reports of a mass rally urging a change in the naturalization laws and denouncing the House Judiciary Committee for bottling up nativist petitions on the matter. Clay replied that the spirit behind the American Republican movement was "right" and capable of producing good results "if conducted with discretion and prudence," but he then asked pointedly "whether it be expedient to throw any new issues into the Presidential canvass." Furthermore, Clay denied that he had ever proposed an amendment of the naturalization laws while serving in Congress. In August he told Clayton, an early proponent of cooperation with the nativists, that Pennsylvania Whigs ought to emphasize the tariff and distribution; he said nothing about an alliance with the American Republicans. Similarly, in an August letter to New York City Whigs, urging them to find some way to cooperate with the

American Republicans in the fall elections, Clay again never mentioned the naturalization question. Clay, in short, hoped for American Republican support, but he and most other Whigs carefully eschewed any public antiforeign or anti-Catholic appeals to get it.[97]

Until the deluge of bad news in September, in other words, the Whigs had no intention of openly appealing to or bargaining with the nativists. Yet the withdrawal of Tyler in August and the neutralization of the tariff issue made the situation in Pennsylvania seem desperate. The Alabama letters and Democrats' nomination of Silas Wright clearly imperiled New York. Everywhere, in any case, Democrats were successfully arousing apprehensive immigrants against the Whigs by attacking Frelinghuysen as a fanatic and by charging that the Whigs were bargaining with the nativists. Greeley, for example, protested that Maryland's October state election was in danger because Democrats sought to convert "thousands of Catholic Whigs" with "the base falsehood . . . that the 'Native' movement of Philadelphia and New York was a Whig device, and that *The Whigs raised the riots and destroyed the Catholic Churches in Philadelphia.*" In this situation, many Whigs believed, they might as well openly bid for the nativist vote. Thus Webster, who had called a strategy session in Boston after the Vermont and Maine elections, began in October to urge New York's Whigs to bargain with the American Republicans, while Massachusetts Whig papers began to demand a reform of the naturalization laws.[98]

Chances for a deal with the nativists seemed particularly bright in New York and Pennsylvania. Because American Republicans' strength was largely confined to New York City and Philadelphia County, the nativists there presented separate tickets only for city and county officers, the state legislature, and congressmen, not for governor or president. Whigs might therefore swap support for local nativist candidates in return for American Republican votes for Whig gubernatorial candidates and presidential electors.

Although Pennsylvania Democrats at the time and historians thereafter asserted that such a deal was struck in Philadelphia, the evidence for it is slim. It is clear, however, that the substitution of Shunk for Henry Muhlenberg as the Democratic gubernatorial candidate in early September encouraged Pennsylvania's Whigs blatantly to seek the anti-Catholic vote. Shortly after Shunk's nomination, Whig papers across the state charged that he had participated in laying the cornerstone for a Catholic church in Pittsburgh and, worse still, that he had pledged to help Catholics ban the Bible from public schools. Shunk was a Catholic and an agent of the Catholic conspiracy against the school system, Whig papers falsely shrieked, while Democrats retorted in kind that Whigs believed "there can be no peace until the Catholics are exterminated from this country."[99]

Such rhetoric, as well as reverberations from the bloody riots in May and July, aroused passions on both sides and increased the turnout in Philadelphia County, which cast about 13 percent of the statewide vote, to unprecedented levels in the October elections. Contrary to charges of a bargain, Whigs ran candidates for all local offices and carried the city of Philadelphia itself. But in the county the American Republicans, with the help of some Whig defectors, elected all county officers, the eight-man delegation to the state assembly, and two of four congressmen. Moreover, Whig appeals to the nativists clearly helped the Whig gubernatorial candidate, Joseph Markle, carry Philadelphia County, a traditional Democratic stronghold, by 4,000 votes. Nonetheless, the combined margin of Whigs and American Republicans over Democrats in the election for county commissioners was almost 12,000 votes. Some American Republicans had voted for the Whig state ticket, but not all. If the Whigs had made a bargain, it was a bad one.[100]

The results of Pennsylvania's October election were two-edged. On the one hand, Democrats seized on them as hard evidence that Whigs had indeed trafficked with church burners and broadcast that warning to immigrants throughout the nation. On the other hand, Whigs both inside and outside the state were enormously encouraged by what the result implied for November. The Democrats won the gubernatorial election by only 6,000 votes. The Whigs had increased their vote by 43,000 since 1841 compared to a Democratic gain of 24,000, and Markle's vote actually exceeded Harrison's total in 1840. Because Whig tacticians believed that Polk could never get as many votes as Shunk and that the American Republicans would hold firm in the Whig column, they hoped again for a Whig victory in November. To them wooing nativists appeared to have paid off, and thus the Pennsylvania result hastened the completion of a bargain between the two camps in New York, where cautious Whigs had waited to see what happened in Philadelphia before committing themselves.[101]

As early as August, New York City's American Republicans had approached Whigs about a bargain on the local ticket in November, whereby they would give Whigs two of their congressional nominations and half of the seats on their state assembly ticket if Whigs supported other American Republican candidates. In August, however, the Whigs still hesitated to make any such deal. For one thing, the American Republicans insisted on running a new Whig against an incumbent Whig congressman in one district. For another, Horace Greeley in the *Tribune*, as well as the followers of Seward and Weed, vehemently opposed the bargain because it would weaken the party's integrity and alienate immigrants.[102]

The revelation of the Alabama letters in early September and especially Wright's nomination, however, changed many minds. A New York Whig, who was himself a Catholic, wrote Mangum on September 8, for example, that while American Republicans repulsed him, he now thought that only such an alliance could save the state for Clay. "With this Union we sweep everything—*without* it we may go out of New York in an overwhelming minority—say 10,000," and "we will be whipped 'horse-foot & dragoon.'" Although Whigs outside the state encouraged the alliance, some New Yorkers still demurred. Besides awaiting results from Philadelphia to test American Republicans' trustworthiness, they demanded guarantees of American Republican support for Clay and Fillmore as "a sine qua non." The nativists in turn wanted Fillmore's pledge to work for maintenance of Bible reading in the schools and repeal of the 1842 school law that had stripped control of the city's schools from the Protestant New York Public School Society. Fillmore refused to commit himself on the school law, but he did write the nativists that he favored Bible reading in schools, although not as a legal requirement. That letter, however, was never delivered for Fillmore by Greeley, who had so stubbornly resisted any approach to the nativists. While neither side got the pledges it wanted, by the end of October the Whigs and American

Republicans arranged a common ticket for local offices. Whatever the facts were, moreover, Whigs believed that the American Republicans would deliver their supporters to Fillmore and Clay.[103]

By the end of October, therefore, Whig spirits, which had sagged in September and early October, soared once again. Nativist support seemed to ensure victory in New York and Pennsylvania. Hemorrhaging to the Liberty party had stopped. October triumphs in Ohio, Maryland, and New Jersey augured victory there. Newfound enthusiasm swept over Georgia, despite a narrow defeat in its October congressional elections, as well as North Carolina, Virginia, and Tennessee. Even the recently worried Seward cautiously wrote Clay on October 25 that "the present setting of the current is clearly and strongly . . . flowing rapidly enough to give us success." "Judging from the strong assurances which are given me," Clay added on October 26, "the Whigs will carry all the four great States of New York, Pennsylvania, Virginia, and Ohio," giving me "a larger electoral vote than was given to Gen. Harrison in 1840."[104]

VIII

This preelection optimism left Whigs completely unprepared for the results of the presidential balloting. Of the "four great States" Clay captured only Ohio. Polk carried fifteen states to Clay's eleven and the electoral vote by 170 to 105. The electoral margin was deceptive, however, for Clay came heartbreakingly close to victory. Polk defeated him by only 38,000 votes out of 2,700,000 cast, and the Democrat lacked a popular majority because the Liberty party's vote had burgeoned from 6,200 in 1840 to 62,000 in 1844. Although Clay barely retained Ohio, New Jersey, and Tennessee, he lost eight other states that Harrison had carried in 1840, six of them by exceedingly narrow margins. Relatively minuscule changes in those six states would have thrown the race to him. Had he carried New York, for example, he would have won, yet he lost it by only 5,100 votes (1.05 percent) out of 486,000 cast. Even without New York, he would have triumphed by taking Pennsylvania and Indiana, yet Polk's margin in the former was 7,000 votes, 1.9 percent of the total, whereas Clay lost Indiana by only 2,300 votes, 1.7 percent of the total. Perhaps even more remarkable, the Whigs could have lost both New York and Pennsylvania and still have won with a total of 8,600 additional votes—2,300 in Indiana, 2,000 in Georgia, 700 in Louisiana, and 3,600 in Michigan.

The closeness of the contest proved little consolation. "So unexpected and so calamitous" was this "astounding" result that the Whigs were filled with "gloom and consternation." "The people have been appealed to & have elected a mere *Tom Tit* over the Old Eagle," protested Leslie Combs from Kentucky. Clay's defeat at the hands of such an opponent, indeed, temporarily shattered their faith in the wisdom and viability of popular self-government. "The malcontents of these United States have given the greatest blow to elective government that was ever given," a North Carolinian complained to Clay. "That such a cause, under such a leader, should have been lost, is a reproach to the general intelligence, on which the safety of a Republic rests," added a New Yorker. "Nothing has happened to shake my confidence in our ability to sustain a free government so much as this," a dejected Millard Fillmore, who lost his own gubernatorial bid in New York, reported to Clay. "May God save the country, for it is evident the people will not." More pungent was a furious Virginian who punned, "With a most emphatic by God, I do say it is a disgrace, a lasting disgrace to our God Almighty-God d—n-raggedy-arse-hyena-made Republic to have elected over H. Clay that infernal poke of all pokes James K. Polk of Tenn."[105]

So superior had Whigs' candidates and their position on the issues seemed that many believed that if they could not win in 1844, they could never win. The passage of time would reveal, indeed, that the election of 1844 constituted a fundamental watershed in the history of the Whig party. The unexpected defeat forced disillusioned Whigs to reassess the purpose, the principles, and the viability of their party. Recalculations began almost immediately as dismayed Whigs attempted to identify what had gone wrong. Their list of explanations for Clay's defeat was long and varied, although partisan bias warped some judgments. Still, the heart of the matter was whether Clay and the Whigs had been beaten fairly on the issues. How Whigs answered that question, in turn, largely determined whether they wanted to stick with traditional strategies and leaders or to jettison them for new issues, new men, and perhaps even a new party.

The crux of the debate was encapsulated in the apparently divergent responses of Whig editors Thurlow Weed of the *Albany Evening Journal* and Horace Greeley of the *New York Tribune*. Three months after the election, the shrewd Weed privately wrote Francis Granger that "the Tariff and Texas were distinctly in issue and . . . the people have declared *against* the Tariff and *for* Texas." Yet Greeley in editorial postmortems emphatically declared, "We are beaten not because we were in favor of Protection and opposed to Annexation, but because our opponents concealed or mystified these vital issues throughout two-thirds of the Union, and adroitly but dishonestly made the Election turn on irrelevant and unimportant matters."[106]

Historians have largely repeated this Whig debate. Most have argued that issues, especially the question of annexation, decided the contest. According to this interpretation, Clay's equivocations on Texas drove proslavery voters to the Democrats in the South and antislavery voters to the Liberty party in the North, thereby destroying his chances in both sections. Others, impressed by ample evidence of voter constancy from election to election, have minimized the role of Texas or any other campaign issue and have argued forcefully that party allegiances formed prior to the election, not issues in it, motivated most voters. As Charles G. Sellers puts it, "Probably more voters favored annexation because they were Democrats than voted Democratic because they favored annexation." Yet even Sellers adds, "While candidates and issues would determine only a small percentage of the vote, this marginal effect could be decisive of the outcome."[107]

Foreshadowing later historians, some Whigs did angrily attribute Clay's defeat to the "asinine fatuity of the abolition party." Indeed, if Clay had captured only a third of Birney's 15,800 votes in New York, he would have won the election. Similarly, Clay lost Indiana by 2,300 votes, while Birney attracted 2,100 there. The Liberty party's 3,600 votes in Michigan, added to his own total, would have given Clay that state too.[108]

Although the importance of the enlarged Liberty vote seemed obvious, Whigs disagreed about why antislavery men refused to support Clay. While a few blamed

Clay's waffling on Texas annexation, others discounted the impact of the Alabama letters. Instead they cited the stubborn refusal of abolitionists to vote for Clay because of the "character issue" or because he owned slaves, no matter what he said about annexation or abolitionism, and at least one argued that abolitionists vengefully sought to punish the Whigs for forging a letter supposedly written by Birney.[109]

Some Whigs railed at the obstinacy of the abolitionists, most of them had been well aware of how much the Liberty party had grown since 1840, and their campaign strategy had been aimed as much at containing that growth as at reversing it. But what disturbed the Whigs far more and what they recognized (far better than many historians) as the chief cause of their defeat was the disproportionate and unexpected growth of the Democratic vote since 1840.

The Whigs had gone into the campaign assuming they would win if they could reassemble the forces that had elected Harrison in 1840. If each party achieved a full turnout, they had calculated, Clay would prevail. Hence, the whole point of emphasizing the differences between Democrats and Whigs on Texas annexation and other issues had been to maximize the turnout of previous Whig voters, not to convert Democrats. In many places and on most issues the Democrats had pursued the same strategy. As a result, each party succeeded in bringing out the bulk of its previous supporters. Recent statistical analysis, for example, suggests that Whigs retained at least 87 percent of their 1840 vote in 1844, and fully 95 percent of those who voted Democratic in 1840 also voted for Polk four years later.[110]

Whatever caused the apparent loss of an eighth of Harrison's supporters, those losses did not cause the Whig defeat. Of the seven states in which the Whig vote declined since 1840—Alabama, Maine, New Hampshire, Massachusetts, North Carolina, Tennessee, and Vermont—the Whigs still won the last four, and only in Maine did the diminished Whig turnout provide the Democrats' margin of victory. Elsewhere Whigs gained votes since 1840; Clay's national total surpassed Harrison's by 25,473 votes.[111]

What the Whigs had not anticipated at the beginning of 1844 was the jump of 210,683 votes in the Democratic total since 1840. Some of these recruits may have voted for Harrison in 1840, but the great majority represented new voters. Of the total increase in the presidential vote between 1840 and 1844, indeed, the Whigs captured a minuscule 8.7 percent, the Liberty party garnered 19.1 percent, and the Democrats won a whopping 72.2 percent. Even had all the additional Liberty voters backed Clay in 1844—and many of them probably had defected from the Whigs since 1840—the Democrats would still have outpaced Whigs among new voters by almost three to one.[112]

Inspection of state returns indicates, moreover, that this surge of new voters to the Democrats in 1844, rather than abstention by former Whigs or their defection to the Liberty party, accounted both for the closeness of the result and for Polk's victory. In every northern state that the Democrats narrowly carried—New York, Pennsylvania, Indiana, and Michigan—the difference between the Democratic and Whig gains since 1840 exceeded both the Liberty party's vote in 1844 and the margin by which the Democrats won (Table 15). In Michigan, for example, the number of new Democratic voters since 1840 was almost twice as large as their winning margin, in Pennsylvania it was three times as large, in

New York almost five times as large, and in Indiana eight times as large. In Illinois the Democratic gain far surpassed that of the Whigs, as well as the Liberty party vote, and accounted for nine-tenths of the Democratic margin. New Democratic voters, not new Liberty voters, in short, provided the critical Democratic edge in most northern states. Conversely, in Maine, New Hampshire, Vermont, and Massachusetts, the drop in the Whig vote far exceeded Democratic losses. Whig losses were also larger than the 1844 Liberty vote in all those states except Massachusetts. The ability of Democrats to attract new voters outside of New England and the inability of Whigs to retain their vote in upper New England states thus contributed far more to the result than did the votes siphoned off by the abolitionist candidate.

In the South as well, the decisive Democratic proclivity of new voters accounted for the narrowing of Whig margins in states Whigs retained like Delaware,

Table 15

Changes in the Major Party Vote, 1840–1844, Compared to the Liberty Vote and the Winning Margin in 1844[a]

	Whig Change Since 1840	Democratic Change Since 1840	Liberty Vote, 1844	Winning Margin, 1844
Maine	−12,270	− 479	4,839	11,380D
N. Hampshire	− 8,431	− 5,641	4,161	9,294D
Vermont	− 5,675	− 15	3,894	8,776W
Massachusetts	− 5,353	− 192	10,815	15,375W
Rhode Island	+ 2,109	+ 1,604	5	2,455W
Connecticut	+ 1,234	+ 4,558	1,943	2,991W
New York	+ 6,469	+24,852	15,814	5,106D
New Jersey	+ 4,967	+ 6,454	131	823W
Pennsylvania	+16,361	+23,721	3,152	7,010D
Ohio	+ 6,201	+25,183	8,082	5,964W
Indiana	+ 2,559	+18,394	2,108	2,317D
Illinois	+ 355	+11,539	3,433	13,051D
Michigan	+ 1,252	+ 6,635	3,638	3,546D
Delaware	+ 304	+ 1,098		301W
Maryland	+ 2,461	+ 2,974		3,261W
Virginia	+ 2,223	+ 6,922		5,819D
N. Carolina	− 2,450	+ 5,113		4,361W
Georgia	+ 1,809	+12,133		1,963D
Alabama	− 2,513	+ 3,405		11,399D
Mississippi	+ 361	+ 8,882		6,016D
Louisiana	+ 1,787	+ 6,166		699D
Arkansas	+ 444	+ 2,890		3,942D
Missouri	+ 8,330	+11,293		10,166D
Kentucky	+ 2,154	+19,158		9,000W
Tennessee	− 25	+11,956		267W

[a]This table is based on election returns reported in Burnham, *Presidential Ballots 1836–1892*. The letters D for Democratic and W for Whig in the "Winning Margin" column indicate which party carried the state.

Maryland, Kentucky, Tennessee, and North Carolina; for the expansion of Democratic margins in Alabama, Missouri, and Virginia since 1840; and for Democratic victories in key southern states Harrison had carried in 1840—Georgia, Mississippi, and Louisiana. In Georgia, for example, the Democratic vote grew by six times the Whig gain between 1840 and 1844, and the differential in the parties' number of new voters was five times as large as the Democrats' margin of victory.

Since Democrats hardly organized more thoroughly or campaigned more ardently than Whigs, these figures, at first glance, imply that the Whigs had badly overestimated the ability of their issues and their candidates to stir the electorate. Conversely, they seem to show that the Democratic platform of territorial acquisition and hostility to Whig economic programs had far more appeal to both new voters and traditional Democratic supporters than did Whig policies.

Yet Whigs disputed the causes of the increased Democratic vote even when they agreed upon its importance. Some, for example, blamed Clay's personal unpopularity. "Any other respectable Whig candidate would have received a large majority," the petulant Webster smugly announced. Yet a Virginian who was no friend of Webster similarly interpreted the loss as a "personal" rebuke of Clay. "I believe we have a majority of the people with us upon our principles & measures. With a popular man we could have carried the election easily." The election demonstrated "that our national republican friends must be content to play second fiddle in these national contests, and take pay accordingly."[113] In contrast, many Whigs believed Clay's candidacy had brought great strength to the Whig cause. "The Whig party regard you as the only man upon whom we can rally with one heart and one mind," a Pittsburgher wrote Clay. An Ohioan concurred. "One thing that added greatly to the enthusiasm of the Whigs in the last political contest was a warm personal affectionate attachment to their leader. That personal attachment still continues," he assured the crestfallen candidate.[114]

Those Whigs who remained convinced of the superiority of their candidate and their issues could only attribute the Democratic surge to "the utter mendacity frauds & villainies of Locofocoism." The Democrats, Whigs repeatedly inveighed, relied on "appeals to every bad passion, the hostile instinct of the poor against the rich, lies and calumnies etc etc" to "bamboozle" the masses. Worse still, Whigs charged, Democrats illegally naturalized immigrants and marched them to the polls, openly bought votes or paid the taxes of those who could not meet taxpaying requirements to vote, employed double and triple voting, and stuffed ballot boxes to steal the election from the Whigs in Louisiana, Georgia, New York, Pennsylvania, and elsewhere. "You have lost this state by the most unprecedented frauds and rascality," a New Orleans Whig consoled Clay. "Parishes giving more votes or as many as there are white inhabitants of all sexes & ages being in them. Steamboats chartered to convey voters in the same day at different Polls, and every other species of fraud that could be imagined."[115]

Accusations of corruption accompanied virtually every election in the nineteenth century and are difficult to assess. In this case, however, the charges represented more than sour grapes. Historians agree that the Democrats carried Louisiana, at least, only by padding the vote of Plaquemines Parish, a veritable Democratic rotten borough.[116] The Democratic vote in that parish jumped from 250 in 1840 to 1,007 in 1844, even though only 538 white males over twenty and only 577 over fifteen resided there in 1840, according to the census.

To many Whigs, in short, the apparent Democratic gains consisted largely of illegal or fictitious voters. At the very least, they represented "a most 'unholy alliance' of the most discordant materials"—the ignorant and the ill-informed, the envious and unqualified poor, and the superstitious and malicious foreign-born who had been whipped into an overwhelming horde by "infamous frauds, ... irrelevant issues, ... [and] unblushing misrepresentations." The election had not turned on the parties' respective platforms. Instead, Democrats had employed demagoguery and deceit to assemble an unthinking rabble against an outnumbered coalition of the intelligent, the industrious, and the virtuous. "I never knew a case before where the good and intelligent ranged themselves on one side and the worthless on the other so completely as in the late contest," a New York Whig complained. As a Charlottesville, Virginia, editor put it, "We have seen the will of a large majority of the qualified voters of the country—of the native sons of the soil (as I firmly believe)—contained and set aside by a combination of foreign force & domestic fraud and ignorance against which the intelligence and virtue of the country have, alas! been arrayed in vain."[117]

The disappointing results drove the normally liberal-minded and warm-hearted Greeley to one of his sporadic fits of mean-spirited contempt for Democratic voters. "Is there not illumination, revelry and extra blue rum at the Five Points and in nine-tenths of the three thousand drunkard manufactories of our city?" he sarcastically queried. "Does Not Ignorance and Vice exult; if only to see Intelligence and Virtue perplexed and afflicted? Let universal Rowdyism strain its throat on one more execration of Clay, and three cheers for Polk and Dallas."[118]

Yet even some of the Whigs who denounced Democratic frauds could not deny that Whigs had suffered from certain issues. Southern Whigs in particular blamed their disadvantageous stand on the tariff and especially on Texas annexation. While castigating "fraud the most unparalleled and falsehood the most barefaced," for example, a Georgian concluded that "the preposterous humbug of *Texas* ... ruined us in Georgia." "The Texas question did more to beat us than any other thing," echoed an Alabama Whig. Clay's Kentucky friend Leslie Combs agreed. "I assure you that the Texas question was the *only one* made & openly advocated every where by the Locofocos, & upon it all our losses in the South & West occurred." Another southern Whig summed up the sentiment of many of his colleagues, and of many historians as well, when he flatly asserted, "For anyone now to say that the Texas question had no influence on the Presidential election only makes a fool or an ass of himself."[119]

This insistence that the Texas issue crippled southern Whigs rings true. Even if, as some historians contend, previously formed party loyalty determined the behavior of most voters, Democrats, like Whigs, recognized that interparty conflict over issues was necessary to reinforce that loyalty and get those voters to the polls. Thus southern Democrats had gleefully stressed the parties' differences on immediate annexation, and virtually all southern Democrats who had voted for Van Buren in 1840 also voted for Polk. Furthermore, one *would* be a fool to gainsay the fact that the Democrats captured an awesome 86.1 percent of southern voters who joined the electorate between 1840 and 1844.

Since Whigs had suffered serious erosion of their voting support in the off-year elections of 1841, 1842, and 1843, while the Democrats had already increased their vote in some states before Texas became a partisan issue, a comparison of

Whig and Democratic gains between the last election prior to May 1844 with the presidential results affords a more precise estimate of its impact. By this measure Democrats still garnered 57.6 percent of the total increment in the South, but Texas' impact varied from state to state (Table 16). Whigs actually outgained Democrats in Delaware, Arkansas, and Louisiana after the emergence of the Texas issue. Moreover, Democrats did not need the Texas issue to carry Mississippi and Arkansas; they had already achieved a decisive margin in previous battles over economic issues. The same is probably true of Missouri, Alabama, and Virginia, where most of the gain by both parties after 1843 represented a return to the polls of previously committed voters. Only in Georgia, and to a lesser extent Louisiana, did Democratic gains among new voters after the emergence of the Texas issue prove critical to the result, although such gains also clearly helped Democrats narrow the gap in the slave states that Clay carried.

If annexation sentiment did cause the Democratic surge, hunger for cheap land among nonslaveholders rather than fears of an abolitionist plot among slaveholders apparently constituted the chief appeal of Texas. Throughout the campaign Whigs warned of the lust for land among poor whites, and after the election several complained that the prospect of cheap land in Texas was what made annexation such a compelling issue "among the lower order of people." Whigs, in fact, singled out Georgia as the state where Texas fever was most decisive, and there, they lamented, it reached its height in the hilly northwestern Cherokee District, a fast-growing region populated primarily by nonslaveholders.[120]

Between 1840 and 1844, Georgia's Democrats outgained Whigs in counties where slaves constituted less than 30 percent of the population by 7,080 to 1,772. Both the number of new Democratic voters and the rate of growth in the Democratic vote since 1840 were higher in low slaveholding than in high slaveholding counties (Table 17). Hence, Democrats achieved 58 percent of their total statewide gain in the 43 percent of Georgia's counties with the fewest slaves.

Democrats also recruited new supporters more heavily in the poorest counties with the fewest slaves in Virginia and Tennessee. But in Mississippi, their rate of gain in counties with the heaviest concentrations of slaves almost equaled their gain in counties with the lowest concentration, and in Alabama, Democrats' recruits came primarily from counties where slaves constituted between 30 and 50 percent of the population. In Louisiana, finally, while Democrats gained the most votes in low slaveholding counties, proximity to Texas was more important. The closer a Louisiana parish was to the Texas border, the more its Democratic vote grew after 1840.[121]

More than likely, then, the Texas issue contributed heavily to the Democratic surge in Dixie, and it may have been the decisive issue in the crucial state of Georgia. Nevertheless, it would be, in the words of Virginia's former governor, David Campbell, "mistaken" to argue "that the Texas question decided the Presidential election." The Whigs lost the election in the North, not in the South. If Clay had been able to carry New York and Pennsylvania, he could have lost Tennessee and North Carolina in addition to other southern states and still have won the election. "Had Mr. Clay come out in favor of annexation, he would still have been defeated," Campbell astutely insisted. "The election was decided . . . by the people of New York & Pennsylvania, Michigan & Maine, on considerations and feelings, unconnected with any great national principles or interests."[122]

Table 16

Change in the Parties' Votes Between the Most Recent Election Prior to May 1844 and the Residential Returns[a]

State	Date of Previous Election	Whig Change	Democratic Change	Liberty Change	Margin in 1844
Maine	Sept. 1843	+17,098	+18,091	− 123	11,380D
New Hampshire	Mar. 1844	+ 3,072	− 952	−1,576	9,294D
Vermont	Sept. 1843	+ 2,306	− 3,988	+ 128	8,776W
Massachusetts	Nov. 1843	+ 9,622	− 2,096	+1,912	15,375W
Rhode Island	Apr. 1843[b]	− 1,818	− 2,526	+ 1	2,445W
Connecticut	Apr. 1844	+ 2,739	+ 995	− 47	2,991W
New York	Nov. 1843	+61,313	+44,853	+ 245	5,106D
New Jersey	Oct. 1843[c]	+15,227	+13,479	+ 131	823W
Pennsylvania	Oct. 1843	+68,870	+58,374	+2,471	7,010D
Ohio	Oct. 1843	+52,759	+41,878	+5,649	5,964W
Indiana	Aug. 1843	+ 9,057	+ 9,253	+ 425	2,317D
Illinois	Aug. 1843	+ 3,643	+ 9,500	+2,266	13,051D
Michigan	Nov. 1843	+ 9,161	+ 6,337	+ 902	3,546D
Delaware	Nov. 1842	+ 804	+ 512		301W
Maryland	Oct. 1843	+ 9,334	+10,715		3,261W
Virginia	May 1843	+23,086	+24,849		5,819D
N. Carolina	Aug. 1843	+ 9,760	+14,706		4,361W
Georgia	Oct. 1843	+ 3,442	+ 8,843		1,963D
Alabama	Aug. 1843	+ 6,443	+11,464		11,399D
Mississippi	Nov. 1843	+ 2,435	+ 3,425		6,016D
Louisiana	July 1842	+ 4,879	+ 4,019		699D
Arkansas	Oct. 1842	+ 289	− 1,553		3,942D
Missouri	No returns				
Kentucky	Aug. 1843	+ 3,164	+ 6,790		9,000W
Tennessee	Aug. 1843	+ 1,862	+ 5,428		267W

[a]This table is based on the same sources as earlier tables, although I have supplemented returns for congressional and gubernatorial elections with returns from the *Tribune Almanac*.
[b]I have used the 1843 gubernatorial returns in Rhode Island because the April 1844 election was uncontested by the Democrats. If one uses those later figures, however, the respective changes are Whigs, +1,762; Democrats, +4,659; and Liberty, +5.
[c]The returns for New Jersey in 1843 are incomplete congressional results.

Closer examination of northern voting returns, indeed, suggests that the Texas issue, if anything, helped the Whigs far more than it did either the Democrats or the Liberty party in the North. Whigs' faith in their platform and in the appeal of Clay, that is, was well placed. Whigs substantially outgained the Democrats after the nominations of Clay and Polk and the emergence of the Texas issue in every northern state except Maine, Indiana, and Illinois (Tables 15 and 16). The boost that the issues of 1844 gave Whigs, compared to their relative stagnation between 1840 and 1844, was especially impressive in Maine, Massachusetts, New York, Pennsylvania, Ohio, Indiana, and Michigan. Obviously, much of the increase in the Whig vote between 1843 and 1844 represented a return of former supporters to the polls rather than the recruitment of new voters. Even so, in

Table 17

Growth of the Democratic Vote in Selected Southern States Between 1840 sand 1844 as Distributed among Counties Ranked by the Proportion of Slaves in the 1840 Population[a]

	Absolute Democratic Gain, 1840–44	Rate of Democratic Gain, 1840–44	Proportion of Total Statewide Gain in Each Type of County
Georgia			
0–30% slave (N = 40)	7,080	46.3%	58%
Over 30% slave (N = 53)	5,053	30.2%	42%
Virginia			
Lowest third	2,836	16.1%	40.9%
Middle third	3,207	20.6%	46.3%
Highest third	879	8.3%	12.7%
Alabama			
0–30% slave (N = 18)	687	5.4%	20.1%
30–50% slave (N = 16)	1,689	14.6%	49.6%
Over 50% slave (N = 14)	1,029	10.4%	30.2%
Tennessee			
0–10% slave (N = 34)	5,231	31.1%	38.6%
10–20% slave (N = 12)	3,703	43.7%	27.3%
20–30% slave (N = 12)	1,746	21.4%	12.9%
Over 30% slave (N = 13)	2,612	20.8%	21.2%
Mississippi			
Lowest third	3,001	61.7%	33.5%
Middle third	3,042	41.5%	34.3%
Highest third	2,839	59.1%	32%

[a]I calculated the proportion of slaves in each county's population from the figures listed in the census of 1840. Because the concentration of slaves varied considerably from state to state, I thought it wiser to divide the states differently rather than to use a standard formula. Thus, in Virginia and Mississippi, I have ranked the counties from the lowest third according to the proportion of slaves to the highest third, whereas elsewhere I have grouped counties according to specific proportions of slaves.

every northern state in which Whigs gained votes between 1840 and 1844 except Rhode Island, they achieved that increase after the introduction of the Texas issue.

Equally stunning, comparison of the 1843 and 1844 returns demonstrates that the Whigs mobilized far more additional voters than the Liberty party after the emergence of the Texas issue. In three New England states, the Liberty party's vote actually dropped from what it had been in the preceding election. In Vermont and Massachusetts, moreover, its gains after 1843 may have been drained from the Democrats rather than the Whigs. In New York the Liberty party gained a paltry 245 votes after 1843; the Whigs added 61,000. Indiana's Liberty party increased its vote by 425, but the Whig vote grew by 9,000. In Michigan the jump in the Whig vote after November 1843 was ten times the size of the abolitionists' gain.[123]

In sharp contrast to the case of the South, in short, northern voting returns strongly suggest that the issue differences of 1844 and Clay's candidacy benefited the Whigs far more than the Democrats or the Liberty party—a fact that did not escape the attention of northern Whig politicians. Summary comparisons make the point even more emphatically. Between 1840 and 1844 the increment in the total northern vote was apportioned among the parties as follows: Whigs, 9,778 (4.3 percent); Democrats, 116,997 (63.9 percent); and the Liberty party, 56,301 (30.8 percent). Conversely, the total northern gains between 1843 or the spring of 1844 and the presidential vote were thusly divided: Whigs, 256,629 (54.7 percent); Democrats, 200,383 (42.7 percent); and the Liberty party, 12,389 (2.6 percent). With good reason, then, many northern Whigs had a very different view than southern Whigs about the desirability of perpetuating the issues and strategies on which they had campaigned in 1844.

Or at least some of the issues. Even if Whigs were dramatically more successful than the other parties in bringing additional voters to the polls after 1843, they still recognized that the gains Democrats did make after 1843 were crucial to their victories in northern states. While a few admitted that the promise of immediate territorial expansion in Texas and Oregon engendered some of these accessions in the Midwestern states, most refused to credit the Democratic position on either Texas or economic issues for Democratic gains in New England and the Middle Atlantic states. In New York, for example, Greeley and others pointed to the undeniable impact of Silas Wright on the presidential race. The widely popular Democratic gubernatorial candidate ran ahead of Polk, thus pulling out votes for the presidential ticket that might not otherwise have been there. Moreover, his well-known opposition to Tyler's Texas treaty had helped Democrats obfuscate party differences on annexation.[124]

Primarily, however, Greeley, Weed, and scores of other Whigs around the country pointed quite correctly to a more important cause of the Democratic gains that defeated Clay, a complex of issues and events that most Whigs had considered peripheral to the campaign—the increase in ethnic and religious animosities that had turned the vast majority of foreign-born and Catholic voters against their party. Not only did the fraction of immigrants who had previously voted for Harrison and other Whigs desert the party, Whigs complained, but the Democrats had been terrifyingly successful in mobilizing massive numbers of new immigrant voters behind Polk and their other candidates.

Throughout the North, Whigs howled that they had been inundated by a tidal wave of newly and often illegally naturalized immigrants. "The foreign vote also destroyed your election," Ambrose Spencer informed Clay from Albany, New York, while Fillmore in Buffalo estimated that a unanimous immigrant vote allowed the Democrats to cut the Whig majority in Erie County by 1,000 votes. Whigs in New York City emphatically agreed. "We feel here that the whole result has been changed by the Foreign Votes in this city, and unless some change is made in our Naturalization Laws, that it will soon be too late to prevent an entire foreign control of our government," one wrote his father. "Foreigners who have 'no lot of inheritance' in the matter have robbed us of our birth-right, the 'scepter has departed from Israel,' " chimed the disgusted patrician Philip Hone. "Ireland has reconquered what England lost." "It comes to this," cried an indignant Massachusetts Whig, "that Americans cannot enjoy their birthright—that the destinies of our country are controlled by foreigners—that we are not our own master."[125]

From Cincinnati, Pittsburgh, New York, Baltimore, New Orleans, and virtually every place with significant concentrations of immigrants poured horror stories of thousands of immigrants being naturalized in the last weeks prior to the election, immigrants who gave the Democrats their decisive edge. Weed and Greeley, both exceptionally careful students of election returns, even pointed to examples of small groups of Irish and Germans in upstate counties in New York who joined the Democrats. In the northern tier of counties along Lake Ontario, Greeley added, the Democrats had gained almost 7,000 votes since 1840. Some of these came from Irish workers employed on Canada's public works who came across the border and illegally voted for Polk to protect "Foreigners' Rights," he asserted, but many of the others represented Canadian refugees who had voted for Harrison in 1840. Even from Maine, where the Democratic vote declined slightly between 1840 and 1844 an hysterical Whig wailed that "an army of [20,000] *Irish* paupers, set on and marshaled by their infernal priests," had "prostrated" the Whigs "in the dust." "Something *must* be done," he warned. "The naturalization law must be modified somehow, or we must sink under the weight of the worst of all European influences." The Whigs, Greeley exaggerated at one point, had been crushed by 200,000 foreign votes.[126]

Democrats characterized immigrant voters quite differently than the Whigs did, but they agreed that the foreign vote did the Whigs in. Hence, a delighted supporter wrote Polk that "the true-hearted Adopted Citizens abandoned the Whig party almost *en masse* and supported you with the same zeal and devotedness they did General Jackson. It was an avalanche they could not resist."[127]

Many Whigs could not admit that this avalanche had natural causes. Instead they blamed Democratic fraud and Democratic demagoguery for setting it off. To many Whigs, indeed, the very openness of the Democratic appeals to the ethnic and religious prejudices of immigrants and Catholics during the 1844 campaign was unethical—indeed un-American. "We deplore the want of true American patriotism which our opponents have exhibited throughout this contest, in their appeals to foreigners and religious sects," protested a Whig meeting in New Haven, Connecticut. Similarly the Cincinnati *Gazette* excoriated "the rousing up of the prejudices of foreign Catholics, inducing them to vote against the Whigs because one of our candidates was a Presbyterian, thereby introducing a *religious test* into a political contest." "The Naturalized Citizens have all been carried for Polk by appeals to their Religious and old-world feelings and prejudices," fumed Greeley. Although these complaints conveniently ignored the Whigs' own appeals to antiforeign and anti-Catholic prejudices, the very frequency and indignation with which Whigs alluded to such Democratic propaganda suggests that ethnocultural and religious issues had far more salience in the election of 1844 than in any previous election.[128]

Still more Whigs pointed simply to massive and illegal naturalization of ineligible immigrants who had not yet met the five-year residency requirement for citizenship as the source of the Democratic gain. Democrats could not have won without "the spurious and illegal foreign vote," such Whigs ranted. "It is this that defeated us." In the weeks prior to the election, scores of Whigs protested, judges and, even worse, the clerks of state and municipal courts that Democrats controlled had issued thousands of naturalization papers to undeserving foreigners, some of whom had been on American soil less than thirty days. Explicitly blaming the loss of New York and Pennsylvania on "false and fraudulent votes" rather than on the unpopularity of Whig stands against annexation and for a protective tariff, Webster, for example, asserted in a blistering speech at Boston's Faneuil hall, "There is not the slightest doubt, that in numerous cases different persons vote on the strength of the same set of naturalization papers; there is little doubt, that immense numbers of such papers are attained by direct perjury."[129]

Whatever the extent of illegal naturalization, tens of thousands of immigrants naturalized in the fall of 1844 cast their first presidential vote for Polk. Yet, as some Whigs realized, the ability to vote or even the Democratic agency in securing that ability did not ensure that immigrants would vote Democratic. Thus, while many Whigs blamed Democratic dishonesty for the surge of the foreign vote against them, others, including Greeley himself, thought that the Whigs had primarily themselves to blame. To such men the behavior of immigrants was understandable, if tragic in its consequences. Whigs' flirtation with nativism and alliances with the American Republican party in New York and Philadelphia drove immigrants and Catholics to the Democrats in self-defense. Whig papers and campaigners had embraced the nativists' demand for an extension of the naturalization period to twenty-one years. Whigs had boasted of the American Republican support for their gubernatorial candidate in Pennsylvania, cried Weed. "Can we blame Adopted Citizens, under such circumstance, for leaving us?"[130]

Not only had the embrace of nativism alienated immigrants, Whigs complained, but the American Republicans had betrayed them. While the Whigs had faithfully supported local American Republican candidates as the quid pro quo that these informal bargains demanded, they charged with some justice that former Democrats among the nativists had backed Polk instead of Clay. As a result, Clay's vote in New York City and Philadelphia was lower than it should have been. "Their perfidy has lost us the present election beyond doubt," an angry Whig congressman from Indiana exaggerated. To these Whigs, in short, the attempt to truck with nativists had backfired.[131]

Other Whigs, however, believed that the party had estranged immigrants and Catholics long before Tyler's withdrawal, the revelation of the Alabama letters, and the Democratic nominations of Shunk and Wright in September forced them to turn to the American Republicans for aid. They cited the party's unthinking nomination of Theodore Frelinghuysen, instead of the courting of nativists, as the fatal mistake of the campaign. "Our opponents by pointing to the native Americans and to Mr. Frelinghuysen, drove the foreign Catholics from us and defeated us in this state," Fillmore told Clay. New York's Catholics had voted solidly Democratic, not so much to defeat Clay as to defeat Frelinghuysen, echoed a Long Island Whig. "Mr. F's nomination made the Catholic opposition intense," Leslie Combs informed Delaware's Clayton. Had Clayton been chosen for the second spot, he added, Clay would have won. Clay himself was persuaded of that fact. On December 2, he wrote Clayton that had he been nominated for vice president, "the Catholics would not have been so united against us."[132]

Former Treasury Secretary Thomas Ewing, whose wife was a devout Catholic, also blamed the Whigs' defeat on their haphazard decision at Baltimore. "I felt during the whole canvass that we were suffering greatly by the connexion [sic] of Mr. Frelinghuysen with out ticket. We could have got over the Philadelphia riots, but we could not at all obviate the objections to Frelinghuysen on the part of the Catholics." Whigs, he went on, must learn a lesson from this mistake. "Twice we have been destroyed by an injudicious choice of candidate for the Vice Presidency & in both instances Men were taken up, who had not before been spoken of, or their Merits & popularity weighed." In the future, Whig conventions must adjourn before the vice presidential balloting so that delegates could assess "the merits and demerits" of new men suggested for the office. "You and I could have told this convention at once that Frelinghuysen would destroy us, & we might thus, if one day had been given us, have avoided the Mischief." The Whigs would never make such mistakes with their presidential nominee, Ewing forecast, but they "may again & again with the Vice President unless we take proper measures to avoid it." Little could Ewing have known in January 1845 how accurate this prophecy would prove to be.[133]

IX

Various elements thus produced the traumatic Whig defeat of 1844. The stubborn refusal of deeply religious antislavery men to support a Kentucky slaveholder whom they considered immoral helped keep New York, Michigan, and Indiana out of the Whig column. The lure of cheap lands in Texas and Oregon helped swell the Democratic vote in the South and the West. Democratic fraud cost the Whigs Louisiana and perhaps padded Democratic totals elsewhere. The popularity of Van Buren's close friend Wright helped carry the nation's largest state for Polk, whose nomination Wright had bitterly protested. Most important, the unanticipated salience of ethnic and religious tensions, along with readily exploitable Whig blunders, allowed the Democrats to mobilize an unprecedented number of foreign-born and Catholic voters against the Whigs.

Together these elements prevented the Whigs from finally achieving the vindication they had sought through the nomination of their most revered and renowned champion. Clay's defeat alone, however, was not what made the results of 1844 so disheartening. While the Whigs captured almost three-fifths of the gubernatorial races that year, they won fewer than two-fifths of the seats in the House of Representatives filled in 1844, and their narrow margin in the Senate stood in jeopardy because of losses in key state legislatures.[134] Whigs' high hopes of recapturing control of the government had been almost completely dashed. As a result, the hated Democrats now had the power to enact policies Whigs genuinely dreaded as inimical to the prosperity, the honor, and the security of the republic.

Internal disagreements about why the party had lost, moreover, would prove as crucial as the fact of defeat itself. What, if anything, Whigs wondered, could the party do about the nettlesome Liberty party that threatened their northern base? How should they respond to the new and potent force of Catholics and immigrants that the Democrats had mustered? Should they join with the nativists in an attempt to ban immigrant voting, as those who believed that fraudulent naturalization had doomed the party in 1844 advocated? Or should they shun any further association with nativists and anti-Catholics that might antagonize still more immigrants, as those who insisted that the stigma of Frelinghuysen and American Republicanism had caused the defeat argued?

As most Whigs only dimly perceived at the time, what made this dilemma so perplexing was that they could probably never satisfy the nativists, for the most virulent nativists found the Whigs' anti-Catholic and antiforeign credentials too suspect. Despite the Whigs' bargaining, despite the Whig editorials demanding an extension of naturalization laws, Clay himself had refused to endorse American Republican demands when given an opportunity. In New York, moreover, Fillmore's letter to the New York City nativist B. F. Whitney had never been delivered by Greeley. Theodore Frelinghuysen might frighten Catholics, but he personally did not denounce them in the vitriolic language of some Protestants. In sum, the most extreme antagonists of immigrants and Catholics may not have considered the Whigs sufficiently committed to their cause to merit support. If so, the Whigs in 1844 confronted for the first time a problem that would plague them until the party's demise a dozen years later. To immigrants and Catholics the Whig party seemed impossibly bigoted and hostile. To the most fervent haters of Catholics and immigrants, however, Whigs appeared too moderate, too restrained, too maddeningly neutral in what seemed to them a life-and-death struggle for the soul of the republic. As ethnic and religious antagonisms intensified, as they surely did in 1844, the Whigs had much more to lose than to gain.

At the end of 1844 other choices facing the Whigs were even more basic and more divisive. Whereas some demanded that the party abandon the issues that had failed in 1844 when they seemed invincible, others asserted just as strongly that Whigs could win in the future only by maintaining those policies and clarifying how they differed from Democrats on them. Whereas some believed that only Clay or someone like him could lead the party to future victory, others insisted that the election had demonstrated that no well-known proponent of Whig measures could win and that the party must return to the victorious strategy of 1840. Within weeks of the election, indeed, some were already booming military heroes like Winfield Scott for the nomination in 1848. Most fundamentally of all, Whigs disagreed about what should become of the Whig party itself. Some insisted that "we ought to fight under no other name than that of Whigs." Others argued that they should "form a party under the name of the 'American Republican' and drop that of *Whig*, which appears to be so objectionable to some." While most agreed with Clay that the Whig "minority constitutes a vast power, which, acting in concert, and with prudence and wisdom, may yet save the country," others had been persuaded by the events of 1844 that "the Whigs proper (so called) never *can* rule this nation" and that a reconstitution of parties was necessary, if not imminent.[135]

By the end of 1844, therefore, the high spirits, unanimity, and certitude that had inspired the Whigs during most of the year had given way to demoralization, disillusionment, and divisive uncertainty. The issue, as George H. Colton, editor of the *American Whig Review*, put it only days after the election, was "what the Whig party will do." Together with the results of the Polk administration, which Whigs forecast so accurately, divisions over how to answer that question would largely determine the fate of the Whig party, not only during the next four years but for the remainder of its existence.[136]

Chapter 8

"The Present Administration Are Your Best Recruiting Officers"

"The Whig party seems to be doomed to misfortune—if not to dissolution," one Massachusetts Whig lamented after Clay's shocking defeat. His despair about the party's continued viability was widely shared.[1] Many historians have accepted these Whig obituary notices as correct, if slightly premature. They have interpreted the reasons for Clay's loss as auguries of the Whig party's eventual death and as the beginning of that end. Supposedly, President James K. Polk's policies would greatly inflame tensions over slavery expansion and thus split the Whigs along sectional lines. Allegedly, Clay's defeat had also shown that the Whigs' economic platform was not popular enough either to bring them victory at the polls or to divert public attention from the fatal sectional issues. The appeal of Whig economic issues purportedly continued to deteriorate after 1844, thereby exposing the feebleness of Whig ideas and destroying the fealty voters paid the two-party system.[2]

According to these historians, the inflamation of sectional tensions and the obsolescence of economic issues would lead Whigs in 1848, as in 1840, to eschew a national platform, shun well-known proponents of Whig principles, and nominate another politically inexperienced military hero as their presidential candidate. In the words of one sympathetic historian, "The Whigs had failed to get their message across," and "their policies were not viable enough to be carried to victory by party regulars."[3]

Like traditional interpretations of the 1840 election, however, this pessimistic analysis focuses exclusively on the presidential election year rather than including off-year elections. A broader perspective suggests that the party was robust and its issues vital during the years of Polk's presidency. The Whigs remained internally cohesive in Congress and in many state legislatures between 1844 and 1848. Their record in those legislative bodies remained attractive to the electorate, for they recaptured the House of Representatives and a number of state governments in the midterm elections of 1846–47. In congressional and gubernatorial contests during 1848 itself, Whig candidates who identified with traditional Whig programs ran better than any Whig candidates since 1840. Thus, in 1848, as eight

Table 18
Proportion of Congressional and Gubernatorial
Elections Won by Whigs, 1840–1848[a]

Year	Congress	Governorships
1840	62.2% ($N = 136$)	85.7% ($N = 14$)
1841	60.2% ($N = 103$)	38.5% ($N = 13$)
1842	29.2% ($N = 65$)	27.2% ($N = 11$)
1843	36.8% ($N = 163$)	45.4% ($N = 11$)
1844	37.9% ($N = 145$)	58.5% ($N = 17$)
1845	32.9% ($N = 82$)	36.4% ($N = 11$)[b]
1846	53.6% ($N = 138$)	38.5% ($N = 13$)[b]
1847	45% ($N = 98$)	42.8% ($N = 14$)
1848	57.3% ($N = 143$)	71.4% ($N = 14$)

[a]This table is based on the same sources for returns on congressional and gubernatorial elections as previous tables. I have included both special congressional elections to fill vacancies and regular elections, so the total number of elections may exceed the number of seats in the House of Representatives.
[b]I have excluded from these totals the gubernatorial elections in Rhode Island that were contested between unique, state-oriented parties rather than between Whigs and Democrats. Indeed, the rival candidates in both years were Whigs.

years earlier, the Whig party as a whole, and not just an attractive presidential candidate, scored a convincing victory (Tables 18 and 19). This strong performance raises two questions. Given the widespread Whig despair after Clay's defeat, what accounts for the party's comeback during the Polk years? And since the party recovered in those midterm state and congressional elections, why in 1848 did Whigs select a military hero whose very nomination signaled an abdication of Whig principles?

The reasons Whigs would look to military chieftains for a presidential candidate in 1848 hardly reflected some universal recognition that their issues were dead and that their party was "doomed to misfortune" unless they resorted to a popular hero. For Whigs the months and years following Clay's defeat constituted a period of reassessment, divisive internal debate, and experimentation with strategies that varied from state to state and from year to year. Only by examining closely the changing fortunes of Whigs in congressional and state elections held between 1844 and 1848 can one properly assess the viability of Whig issues and the reasons they ultimately turned to a military hero.

This is not meant to deny that the Whig defeat in 1844 marked a fundamental turning point. Although some historians tend to inter the party prematurely and to oversimplify the reasons for its demise, they are correct about the direction in which it was moving after the traumatic events of that year. They simply have not gauged correctly the speed at which it descended toward its grave.

One can conceive of the history of the Whig party as a fluctuating tension between a centripetal force holding it together and centrifugal forces blowing it apart. Both before and after 1844, the principal cohesive pressure was the party's

Table 19

Proportion of Seats in the Lower Houses of State Legislatures Won by Whigs, 1844–1848[a]

State	1844	1845	1846	1847	1848
New Hampshire	34%	31%	41%	48%	43%
Connecticut	56.5%	59%	48%	59%	55%
Rhode Island	81%	64%	63%	77%	62%
Virginia	56%	41%	45%	54%	48%
Louisiana[b]	52%		44%	52%	
Alabama[c]	33%	38%		38%	
Illinois	34%		33%		31%
Indiana	55%	45%	53%	53%	39%
Kentucky	76%	62%	63%	59%	64%
Missouri	45%		18%		27%
North Carolina	58%		54%		50%
Tennessee	53% (1843)	48%		45%	
Maine	35%	39%	49%	32%	35%
Vermont	64%	58%	59%	51%	N.A.
Arkansas	15%		26%	27%	25%
Georgia	61% (1843)	56%		51.5%	
Maryland	52%	52%	65%	71%	70%
New Jersey	69%	53%	79%	67%	57%
Ohio	57%	61%	54%	54%	53%
Pennsylvania	41%	32%	59%	37%	45%
Delaware	67%		52%		67%
Massachusetts	77%	76%	83%	66%	72%
Michigan	17%	24%	23%	23%	18%
Mississippi	33% (1843)	30%		25%	
New York	36%	42%	71%	73%	84%
Florida		27%	44%		60%
Iowa			30%		28%

[a]This table is based on the data on the partisan division of state legislatures supplied by the Inter-University Consortium for Political and Social Research. They were originally collected by Walter Dean Burnham. Neither Professor Burnham nor the Consortium bears any responsibility for the analyses of these data presented here. The underlined figures indicate the first election held after the first session of the Twenty-Ninth Congress adjourned in August 1846.

[b]Louisiana revised its state constitution in 1845 and changed the date of its elections from July. A special state election for governor and the legislature was held in January 1846. After that, state elections were held in November of odd-numbered years.

[c]Alabama changed from annual to biennial state legislative elections starting in August 1845.

conflict with the Democratic party. As long as voters perceived sharp program-matic and ideological differences between Whigs and Democrats, and as long as the Whig party had a better chance of defeating the Democrats than other anti-Democratic parties, the Whig party would survive. What made the loss in 1844 so important was that at no other time in the party's history did the balance between centripetal and centrifugal forces so favor the former. Never again were Whigs so united. Never again were their differences from the Democrats so clear. And still the Whigs lost. From that point on, the divisive forces within the Whig party would grow stronger and the unifying force of interparty conflict would gradually wane.

Clay's loss accelerated that shift by exacerbating the divisions within the party. After 1844 Whigs split over the best way to seek recovery. Sectional antagonisms over slavery and slavery expansion also increased after 1844, for some Whigs in both the North and the South blamed the attempt to take a nationwide party stand against Texas' annexation for the defeat. They often wished to exploit sectional animosities in order to safeguard the party's base in their own section, regardless of the consequences for the party in the other section. The loss of federal patronage for at least four years ensured that rival factions within different state parties would battle all the more fiercely for control of state organizations and the state offices such control might bring. Pressure to win state elections, in turn, aggravated disagreements about how the party should respond to the abolitionist and nativist challengers who had appeared in 1844. In addition to these problems, emerging regional conflicts over economic development and state constitutional revision, as well as intraparty divisions over newly salient issues such as prohibition, would rend the fabric of state Whig organizations still further. Over and above all these sources of internal strife, and interlocking with many of them, would be the battle for the party's presidential nomination in 1848 itself.

Ironically, Clay's loss, which divided the Whig party in so many ways, also engendered a new passion for unity. James K. Polk's domestic and foreign policies violated virtually every Whig tenet of good government. Whig resistance to that program revived the competitive spirit of Whig voters throughout the nation and revitalized their conviction that the Whig party, and only the Whig party, could best serve the nation's interests and save Revolutionary ideals. Only after a new Whig president replaced Polk in 1849 would the disuniting forces within the party overwhelm the cohesive force of interparty conflict with Democrats.

I

The first decision that confronted Whigs after Clay's defeat was fundamental—whether or not to perpetuate their party itself. So devastating were the November results that some believed that the Whigs, like their National Republican predecessors after Clay's defeat in 1832, must abandon their standard for a new organization with a different name that might attract broader voter support. Fury at the immigrant surge toward Polk caused vengeful Whigs to advocate "the amalgamation of the Whig party with the Native Americans." As a Virginian declared, "We intend to rally again and form a party under the name '*American Republican*' and drop that of *Whig*, which appears to be so objectionable to some."[4]

Proponents of such party suicide were a distinct minority. Most Whig politicians clearly preferred to continue to battle the Democracy as Whigs, and within days of Clay's defeat they sought to rally their discouraged troops. Some, like Webster in a speech to a Whig rally in Boston's Faneuil Hall, stressed that only preserving the Whig party would yield control of state governments. Those governments, insisted Webster, touch "closely all our concerns, all our relations of social life, and all our enjoyments of the fruits of a wise and parental government." In the American federal system states had more direct influence on people's lives than did Washington, and as long as Whigs could capture them, it made no sense to sacrifice the party.[5]

Others attempted to persuade disconsolate Whigs that the party's future was bright. "We assure our brother Whigs throughout the country," vowed a meeting of Connecticut Whigs, "that though defeated, and anticipating the enactment of laws unfavorable to the prosperity of the country, our hearts are still buoyant with hope—and we feel that if our opponents venture to carry out their true principles, they will, in the next contest, give us the victory, with but little effort on our part to obtain it." Similarly, Horace Greeley in virtually every issue of the *New York Tribune* in the two months following the election predicted that once Democrats took power and revealed where they actually stood on the Texas and tariff issues, voters would repudiate them. "The nominal victory of our opponents, won by false pretenses and fraudulent voting, will yet prove their ruin," promised Greeley. Since the Whigs were a large minority that "constitutes a vast power which . . . may yet save the country," Clay himself argued, he did "not see the wisdom of assuming a new name, and giving up our separate organization."[6]

Clay particularly warned against the "great tendency amongst the Whigs to unfurl the banner of the *native* American party." Such a merger, he told Kentucky's John J. Crittenden, would only allow the Democrats to mobilize more immigrant voters. "I am disposed to think it best for each party, the Whigs and the Natives, to retain their respective organizations distinct from each other, and to cultivate friendly relations together." Prominent Whig editors like Greeley, Thurlow Weed, and John H. Pleasants of the Richmond *Whig* rejected a merger with the American Republicans even more emphatically and denied that nativism by itself could be the basis "for a great political party."[7]

Other Whigs emphasized their patriotic duty to preserve the party. At Clay's urging, Whig senators gathered in Washington on March 15, 1845, after the second session of the Twenty-Eighth Congress adjourned, to discuss the party's future. The resulting manifesto ringingly reaffirmed Whigs' original mission: "That the Constitution of the United States, the honor and security of the Country, and all its interests, can only be preserved by maintaining the leading principles, and supporting the leading measures of Policy, of the Whig Party."[8]

An even more remarkable brief for the continuation of the party appeared in the February 1845 issue of the new Whig periodical *The American Review*. No document, indeed, better reflects how the two-party system had matured and how thinking about the role of political parties had changed since the birth of the Whig party in the winter of 1833–34 than this article, which was probably written by the Baltimore Whig congressman and novelist John Pendleton Kennedy. Whereas some early Whigs had been hostile to the very idea of political parties, the author began by asserting the necessity of interparty conflict to the preservation of republicanism itself. "We regard the presence, activity, and vigilance of great political *parties*, in this country, as alike essential to the permanence of liberty and the best security for the virtual and beneficent dominion of constitutional government." So let us "abide by our organization, our principles, our leaders and our name." Since the very "name of WHIG" forcefully indicated "the party of liberty and patriotism and loyalty to *constitutional* government," "Let us cherish the conviction that whatever good can be hoped for the country, must be accomplished through the agency of the Whig party, in *its present form and constitution.*"[9]

By March 1845, if not earlier, therefore, the vast majority of Whigs had determined to persevere as a separate organization. Yet that decision hardly solved all their problems. What could Whigs do in states where Whig principles were not enough to secure control of state governments? How could they contend with the single-idea American Republican and Liberty parties, whose supporters had spurned Whig appeals in 1844 and might continue to do so in future elections? Without those key anti-Democratic voters, how could they possibly overcome the triumphant Democrats, who had gained so many new supporters since 1840? By what routes, in short, could Whigs make a political comeback and recapture the White House?

II

To convince discouraged followers and skeptical new voters that "the Whig party, in *its present form and constitution,*" remained the most effective vehicle for opponents of the Democrats, Whigs had to carry the state and congressional elections in 1845–47. Yet Whigs' ability to achieve these necessary triumphs varied enormously from place to place. Since 1840 the Whigs had apparently fallen into permanent minority status in a number of states. Table 20, which ranks the states according to Clay's share of the popular vote in 1844, lists various indices of Whigs' competitive position vis-à-vis the Democrats and divides the states into three categories: (I) those states Clay carried in 1844 and Whigs normally controlled; (II) states the Whigs lost narrowly in 1844 and were clearly within reach of retaking; and (III) states where Clay lost decisively in 1844, where the margin of the popular vote between Democrats and Whigs had generally exceeded 10 percent since 1840, and where Whig delegations in state legislatures consistently languished in a powerless minority.

Whig prospects of electing governors, congressmen, and United States senators in Alabama, Arkansas, Illinois, Maine, Mississippi, Missouri, and New Hampshire were virtually nil. Texas would join this group of Democratic bastions when it was admitted to statehood in December 1845, for there Whigs bore the crippling stigma of opposing Texas' admission to the Union in the first place. Realistically, Michigan belonged in this category as well. True, Harrison and other Whig candidates had carried it in 1840. Yet, in no state of the Union had the Whigs experienced such catastrophic defeats in state elections after 1840 as in Michigan.[10] And the decreasing share of the popular vote they garnered in the congressional and gubernatorial races of the 1840s effectively precluded a comeback in Michigan unless the party could capture all of the abolitionist vote and win some Democratic converts.

Whigs won only nine of sixty-eight congressional seats filled from this group of states in 1845, 1846, and 1847.[11] Moreover, they refused to contest fourteen of those races, letting the Democrats win by default. Despite small gains in Arkansas, New Hampshire, and Maine in 1846 and 1847, Whigs' record in elections for state legislatures remained equally pathetic. Finally, of fourteen gubernatorial

Table 20

The Competitive Strength of the Whig Party in Different States

	Percentage of the 1844 Presidential Vote			Major Party Margin in 1844[a]	Average Major Party Margin, 1841–44[a]	Average Whig Percentage of Seats in State Legislatures, 1841–44[b]
	Whig	Democratic	Liberty			
Group I						
Rhode Island	60.0	39.9	0.0	+20.1	+50.8	77
Vermont	55.0	37.0	8.0	+18.0	+ 9.7	57
Kentucky	53.9	46.1	0.0	+ 7.8	+ 8.0	68
North Carolina	52.7	47.3	0.0	+ 5.3	+ 4.2	51
Maryland	52.4	47.6	0.0	+ 4.8	+ 3.6	50
Massachusetts	51.7	40.0	8.3	+11.7	+ 5.7	62
Delaware	51.2	48.8	0.0	+ 2.4	+ 1.2	67
Connecticut	50.8	46.2	3.0	+ 4.6	+ 2.3	49
New Jersey	50.4	49.3	0.2	+ 1.1	+ 0.3	56
Tennessee	50.1	49.9	0.0	+ 0.2	+ 1.8	52.5
Ohio	49.6	47.7	2.6	+ 1.9	+ 0.1	50.5
Group II						
Georgia	48.8	51.2	0.0	− 2.4	− 1.8	49
Louisiana	48.7	51.3	0.0	− 2.6	− 5.0	54.5
Pennsylvania	48.5	50.6	0.9	− 2.1	− 5.3	40
Indiana	48.4	50.1	1.5	− 1.7	+ 2.7	48
New York	47.8	48.9	3.3	− 1.1	− 2.9	29.5
Virginia	47.0	53.0	0.0	− 6.0	− 7.4	47
Group III						
Michigan	43.5	49.9	6.5	− 6.4	−10.8	12.5
Mississippi	43.4	56.6	0.0	−13.2	−10.8	35
Missouri	43.0	57.0	0.0	−14.0	−12.2	35.5
Illinois	42.4	54.4	3.2	−12.0	− 7.2	32.5
Alabama	41.0	59.0	0.0	−18.0	−15.0	37
Maine	40.4	53.8	5.7	−13.4	−14.7	30
Arkansas	37.0	63.0	0.0	−26.0	−27.8	22.5
New Hampshire	36.3	55.2	8.5	−18.9	−22.2	32.4

[a]A plus sign indicates that Whigs carried the state; a minus sign indicates that Democrats carried the state.
[b]These are the proportions of Whig seats in the lower house of the state legislature.

elections held in those states in 1845, 1846, and 1847, the Whigs won just one while failing to run any candidate in two.

Whigs and Democrats alike commented on the bleak Whig position in these states. In 1845, a Mississippi Whig moaned in despair, "We have no hope as a party in this state—you know we are in the Egyptian darkness of Locofocoism," while another complained that the Whigs "are disheartened here and will let everything go by default."[12] Arkansas' tiny Whig minority openly admitted that their only hope lay in a possible division among the dominant Democrats.[13] In Illinois a prominent Whig legislator lamented in early 1845, "I have hardly the faintest hope of this State ever being Whig." By the end of that year he had decided to leave politics for private business since "there is precious little use for any Whig in Illinois to be wasting his time and efforts. The state cannot be redeemed. I should as leave think of seeing one rise from the dead." He was right. The Whigs, who had won a dismal 42 percent of the vote in 1844, did even worse in the congressional and gubernatorial elections of 1846.[14] In virtually all the states in this group, many Whigs did not consider it worth their time and effort even to go to the polls in off-year elections because prospects of victory were so slim. In fifteen such races in Michigan, Alabama, Mississippi, Maine, Illinois, and New Hampshire between 1844 and 1848, Whig turnout on average was 19.4 percent lower than it had been in 1844, while the Democratic vote was only 11.3 percent lower than Polk's total, which, of course, had been considerably higher than Clay's in all those states. A furious Greeley complained of the Whig performance in Maine in 1847, "The indifference of the Whigs has left a full victory to our opponents."[15]

Because of their weakness in state and congressional elections, in short, the only plausible road to recovery for such Whigs was to nominate a military hero for president and hope that his appeal across party lines might extend to other Whig candidates. Thus Whigs from these states would overwhelmingly favor the nomination of General Zachary Taylor or General Winfield Scott in 1848. Even those who, like an Arkansas Whig, "would rather go to Clay than for any man," realized that "with him the chances here would be desperate."[16]

Perhaps the most famous example of a devotee of Clay who quickly jumped on board the Taylor bandwagon is Abraham Lincoln, the only Whig sent to Congress from Illinois in the disastrous election of 1846. Lincoln became an ardent Taylor booster in 1847, as did other Illinois Whigs who publicly endorsed Rough and Ready in the summer of that year. He was well aware that he was the lone Whig congressman from Illinois and that the Whigs had to reach far beyond the ranks of their own voters to have a chance of carrying the state. Only Taylor might win the presidency for the Whigs, Lincoln insisted over and over, and equally important, only Taylor could help other Whig candidates in Illinois. "In Illinois, his being our candidate, would *certainly* give us an additional member of Congress, if not more, and *probably* would give us the electoral vote of the state."[17]

In the balloting for presidential nominees at the Whig national convention in June 1848, indeed, delegates from this third group of states would give Taylor and Scott markedly greater support than would Whigs from the first two categories, particularly on the first ballot (Table 22). Where the Whigs were weakest, they did need a popular general to have a fighting chance. Whig leaders, however, never expected to win off-year elections in heavily Democratic states. They looked instead to the states where they were competitive, the states Clay had carried in 1844 and especially the states he had lost narrowly: New York, Pennsylvania, Georgia, Indiana, Louisiana, and Virginia. Those two groups of states, after all, supplied almost four-fifths of the House of Representatives and the Electoral College and three-fifths of the United States Senate. The vast majority of Whigs resided in those states. Here Whigs would make a comeback in off-year elections and score victories in the congressional, gubernatorial, and presidential elections of 1848. Zachary Taylor would not receive a single electoral vote from the non-Whig states in Group III, whose Whigs supported his nomination so enthusias-

Table 21
Fluctuations in the Parties' Proportions of the Vote, 1844–48

	1844P			1845			1846			1847			1848			1848P		
	Whig	Dem.	Lib.	Whig	Dem.	Lib.	Whig	Dem.	Lib.	Whig	Dem.	Lib.	Whig	Dem.	F.S.	Whig	Dem.	F.S.
Group I																		
Rhode Is.	60	99.9		49.1	50.4[a]		49.8	49.2[a]		54.7 49.5	36.3 42.3	6.3 8.2C	60	38.8	1.2	60.8	32.7	6.5
Vermont	55	37	8	47.9	39.1	13	49.1 47	36.5 32.4	14.3 20.6C	48.7	36.7	14.6	43.7	26.6	29.7	47.7	22.6	29.7
Mass.	51.7	40	8.3	48.8	35.3	7.9[b]	53.9	32.7	9.8[b]	50.8	37.5	8.7[b]	49.7[b]	20.4	29	45.4	26.2	28.4
Kentucky	53.9	46.1		51.6	48.4C					53.1	44.3C[b]		53.4	46.6		57.7	42.3	
N.C.	52.7	47.3		42.9	51.1C		54	46		52.4	46		50.5	49.5		55.2	44.8	
Maryland	52.4	47.6		43.3	54.6C[b]					49.5	50.5					52.2	47.7	0.1
Conn.	50.8	46.2	3	51	45.3	3.7	48.6	47.9	3.9	50.5	45.9	3.6	50.3	46.8	2.8	48.6	43.4	8
Delaware	51.2	48.7					49.4 50.6	50.6 49.4C					51.4	48.6C		51.8	47.5	0.7
Ohio	49.6	47.7	2.6				48.3	47.3	4.3				50	49.9		42.1	47	10.9
N. Jersey	50.4	49.3	0.3				51.4	46.C[b]		48.1	51.9		49.7	49.3C[b]		51.4	47.4	1.2
Tennessee	50.1	49.9		49.4	50.6					50.4	49.6					52.4	47.6	
Group II																		
New York	47.8	48.9	3.3				51.5	48.5		53.6	41.7	2.6C	47.9	25.1	27	47.9	25.1	27
Indiana	48.4	50.1	1.5	46.8	51.8	1.4C	48.3	51.7		50.1	49.9C					46	48.8	5.2

Penna.	48.5	50.6	0.9	38.1	51.1[d]		51.3 47.9	48.7C 43.5[d]		44.6	50.8	0.6[b]	50	50		50.2	46.7	3.1
Georgia	48.8	51.2		51.1	48.9		46.9	53.1C		49.1	50.9		49.8	50.2C		51.5	48.5	
Louisiana	48.7	51.3					44.1	53.2[b]		47.2	52.8C					54.6	45.4	
Virginia	47	53		N.A						48.8	51.2C					49.2	50.8	
Iowa							48.9	51.1		48	52.C		48.4	51.6C		44.6	50.5	4.9
Florida				49.6	51.1C		50.8	49.2C					53.3	46.7		57.5	42.5	
Group III																		
Michigan	43.5	49.9	6.5	41.2	50.8	8	43.8	50.1	6.1C	41	53.1	5.9	45.6	47.4	7C	36.8	47.2	16
Mississippi	43.4	56.6		35.2	64.8		33.6	64.7		33.6	64.7					49.3	50.7	
Missouri	43	57					39.4	60.1C					41	59		45	55	
Illinois	42.4	54.4	3.2				36.7	58.2	5.1				33.3	62.5	4.2C	42.4	44.8	12.8
Alabama	41	59		Two dems					55.3		44.7					49.4	50.6	
Maine	40.4	53.8	5.7	40.2	50.7	9.1	40.1	46.9	13	37.2	51.3	11.5	37.8	47	15.2	40.3	45.1	14.6
Arkansas	37	63			No contest			No contest						No contest		44.9	55.1	
New Hamp.	36.3	55.2	8.5	34	51.2	14.8	31.8	48.7	19.5	34.9	51	14.1	46.9	53.1		29.5	55.4	15.1

[a] I have listed the Law and Order percentage under the Whigs and the Liberation party under the Democrats.

[b] In all of these races the balance of the votes went to nativist candidates.

[c] The returns in New York in 1847 are for comptroller. All other returns, except where designated, are for governor, except those marked C, which were for Congress.

[d] These Pennsylvania returns were for canal commissioner, and nativist candidates got the balance of the vote in each case.

Table 22

Proportions of Votes Cast for Military Candidates by
Group at the Whig National Convention, 1848[a]

Percentage for Taylor	First Ballot	Final Ballot
Group I	29.5	56
Group II	38	57
Group III	63	81
Percentage for Taylor and Scott Combined	First Ballot	Final Ballot
Group I	48.5	81
Group II	55	83.5
Group III	68.5	92

[a]Groups are those defined in Table 20. Group II includes Iowa and Florida,
as based on margins in 1846. Group III includes Texas.

tically. It is the Whig comeback in competitive states, therefore, that merits investigation.

III

The top priority for southern Whigs in 1845, a year in which many faced important gubernatorial and congressional elections, was to bury the national issues they believed had hurt them so badly in 1844: the tariff and especially Texas annexation. To do so, they looked to the second session of the Twenty-Eighth Congress, scheduled to meet from December 3, 1844, to March 3, 1845, before Polk was inaugurated. They had known since the previous summer that lame-duck President John Tyler, who had failed to secure Senate ratification for his Texas treaty in June, now intended to seek annexation through a joint resolution of Congress that required only a simple majority in both houses. Tyler's new tack appeared more likely to succeed than his previous one. It provided a chance to settle the Texas question once and for all.

Almost as soon as the polls closed in 1844, therefore, southern Whigs frantically urged their congressmen to support annexation in order to kill the Texas issue before the 1845 campaigns began. "The question was in our way last year, it is in our way now, and will be a thorn in our side until it is . . . put to rest in some way," an alarmed Georgian told Senator John M. Berrien. "The Texas question ought to be put out of the way *immediately*," Leslie Combs warned Delaware's Clayton from Kentucky. "*We cannot now sustain ourselves in opposition to it.*" "If Whigs could be blamed for delaying annexation," a Virginian warned Senator William C. Rives, it "will . . . injure the party in the spring elections." "The Texas question did more to beat us than any other thing," chorused an Alabama Whig to Georgia Representative Alexander H. Stephens. "I think you the Whig leader in Congress had as well dispose of this question at once and Let the Southern Whigs go for annexation immediately if not sooner for we can never come into power until that question is settled."[18]

These frantic entreaties created a dilemma for southern Whigs in Congress. On the one hand, they recognized that the Texas issue had increased the Democratic vote in the South in 1844, and it might damage southern Whigs again if it was not neutralized. Representatives seeking reelection themselves in the congressional elections of 1845 in Kentucky, Virginia, North Carolina, Tennessee, and Alabama, as well as senators whose seats were to be filled by state legislatures chosen that year, had a direct personal stake in eliminating the issue. Beyond considerations of partisan expediency, many of these southern Whigs sincerely believed annexation necessary to protect slavery and the South from the increasingly vehement antislavery and antisouthern attacks emanating from the North. By admitting Texas, argued Tennessee's Whig Congressman Joseph H. Peyton, "The South would acquire a wonderful increase in political power. . . . Can anything be better calculated to check that infernal spirit of abolitionism which is increasing with such fearful rapidity at the North?"[19]

Yet other factors militated against acquiescing to annexation in that session. For one thing, northern Whigs continued to oppose annexation and wanted to delay it as long as possible. Texas' admission was certain once Polk took office and Democrats assumed complete control of Congress in December 1845, they assured the Southerners. But they wanted to prevent admission until that date in order to place total responsibility for annexation upon the Democratic party, to prove to Liberty men that the Whig party, including its southern wing, was reliable, and, most important, to keep the Texas issue alive in the northern state and congressional elections scheduled for 1845. Northern Whigs, that is, knew that they, unlike southern Whigs, had benefited enormously from the emergence of the Texas annexation issue in 1844. It had helped bring former Whig voters back to the polls and stunt the growth of the Liberty party. Thus, they tried to exploit it again in the 1845 elections by passing anti-Texas resolutions in northern state legislatures in order to neutralize the appeal of the Liberty party and woo back antislavery voters. As a New Yorker wrote Virginia's Rives, "All we ask is that our Southern Whig Senators will stand firm upon this question till, our opponents having the power, must take the responsibility, of carrying through the measures."[20]

In addition to a desire to cooperate with northern colleagues, most southern Whig congressmen still hated the very thought of supporting any proposal from the apostate Tyler, especially one that perpetuated the reasons why Tyler's treaty had been repugnant. According to Whigs, that treaty, by calling for the United States to assume the Texas debt, would create an enormous windfall for corrupt speculators in Texas bonds and plunge the nation into war with Mexico. Still more important, many southern Whigs, especially those in the Senate, were convinced that the only way the Constitution permitted the acquisition of foreign territory was through a treaty duly ratified by at least two-thirds of the Senate. In their minds, Whigs who tolerated the attempt to bypass that requirement would abet the subversion of constitutional government, to which the Whig party and they personally were committed. As a perceptive Indiana Whig congressman reported home at the beginning of the session, "The Southern Whigs are in a peculiarly unpleasant situation. They follow the feelings of their people [on Texas annexation] but are not satisfied with the means of doing the thing."[21]

Whipsawed by conflicting pressures of party loyalty, political expediency, regional identity, and principle, southern Whigs in Congress fragmented. Certain that it was impossible to stop passage of annexation in the heavily Democratic House and reluctant to let Democrats get sole credit for it, a group of southern Whigs led by Milton H. Brown of Tennessee moved to present an alternative Whig plan for annexation that would be even more appealing to southern voters than the Tyler measure that Democrats endorsed. In the candid words of one of its backers, Brown's plan was "well calculated to trip the heels of Locofocoism in Tennessee, to prevent them from making capital out of a question that should never have been made a party question." Brown's proposal called for the admission of the entire Republic of Texas as a single slave state rather than as a territory, stipulated that the United States would take responsibility for settling the disputed boundary with Mexico, and provided that Texas would retain both its public lands and the obligation to pay off its debt. More important, it stated that in the future, as many as four additional states could be carved from Texas and that all of those states south of 36°30', the Missouri Compromise line, could enter the Union as slave states if their residents so desired. It was this possibility of gaining as many as ten additional slave state senators from Texas that caused Tennessee's Joseph Peyton to trumpet the Brown plan as a boon to southern political power. With this bold stroke, he exulted, southern Whigs could eclipse the Democrats' claim of being the better proslavery party. Nor, Peyton made it clear, did he care what passage of the Brown proposal might do to northern Whigs. Each sectional wing of the party would have to look out for itself.[22]

Here the potential that the Texas question had always possessed for dividing the Whig party into hostile northern and southern wings appeared to be reaching fruition. Southern Whigs "can never unite with the northern Whigs and do any good," Arthur Campbell exclaimed to his brother. "The northern Whigs are the most cold-hearted—bigoted—selfish & incorrigible people upon earth. . . . They are the abolition party of the U. States. They have no common feelings with us whatever." Similarly, Robert Toombs warned Berrien in February 1845 that southern Whigs would be forced to vote for annexation because "our Northern Whig friends" are "wickedly narrowing it down to a simple question of pro & anti slavery." Once Texas became "purely a sectional question," he feared, its opponents in the South "must need be swept from the political boards."[23]

Still, in the House of Representatives, only 8 southern Whigs joined with 112 Democrats to pass the Brown plan over the opposition of 72 Whigs and 26 Democrats. Four of the five Whigs from Tennessee, where Clay had edged Polk by a mere 267 votes, led this pro-Texas band. Joining the Tennesseans were Willoughby Newton, the only one of four Virginia Whig congressmen seeking reelection in 1845; James Dellet, the lone Whig congressman from Alabama; and both Whig representatives from Georgia, Stephens and Duncan L. Clinch. On the other hand, seventeen southern Whigs voted against annexation, including the entire Whig delegations from Delaware, Kentucky, Maryland, and North Carolina. Altogether 90 percent of the Whigs opposed 81 percent of the Democrats.

The fight over Texas was still predominantly a partisan battle despite its sectional ramifications.[24]

Partisan lines held even more firmly in the Senate. Pressure on southern Whigs became enormous once the Brown plan reached that chamber, for the Whigs still had a slight majority. It could pass, in other words, only with Whig support or acquiescence in the form of abstention. Senator Ephraim Foster of Tennessee, whose term was due to expire in March and who was angling for that year's Whig gubernatorial nomination instead, begged his Whig colleagues to back the Brown proposal. Whigs in the Virginia legislature framed and heavily supported resolutions urging the state's two Whig senators, Rives and William S. Archer, to pass the measure. Berrien's correspondents from Georgia assured him that they agreed with his constitutional objections to annexation by joint resolution, but they also warned that "nothing can save the unity perhaps the existence of the Whig party but the passage of the resolutions by the Senate." Nevertheless, Rives, Archer, Berrien, and the vast majority of southern Whigs refused to budge.[25]

As the session neared adjournment, indeed, it became clear that the Brown plan could not pass the Senate. Not only did all but three or four Whigs oppose it, so did Thomas Hart Benton of Missouri and several Van Buren Democrats from northern states who had voted against Tyler's treaty in June. They wanted the president to negotiate a new treaty with Texas that would admit only the settled area of the huge republic as a slave state and thus open the possibility that some of Texas might be free soil. In the end, only a Democratic amendment giving the president the option of offering Texas admission under the terms of the Brown plan or of negotiating a new treaty brought the dissident Democrats, who clearly expected Polk to exercise the second option, on board. In this new form, the joint resolution passed by the narrow margin of 27–25. Three southern Whigs—John Henderson of Mississippi, who had supported Tyler's treaty in June, Henry Johnson of Louisiana, and William D. Merrick of Maryland—joined twenty-four Democrats in the majority. All of the negative votes came from Whigs, including four-fifths of the Southerners. Even Foster, who had argued so strenuously for the unamended Brown plan, voted nay. Southern Whig votes had provided the margin of victory, but party lines were still sharp. And when the Senate version went back to the House, only one of the eight Whigs who had supported the Brown plan, Dellet of Alabama, voted for it. Six others joined the Whig minority in the negative, and Stephens did not vote. Equally important, all of the Democrats who had opposed the Brown plan now voted for the joint resolution in its new form. Texas' annexation thus passed the House on virtually a strict party-line vote.[26]

The congressional Whig party thus emerged from the Twenty-Eighth Congress with its unity largely intact and the Texas horror settled. But the action of Congress did not resolve the dilemma of Whigs as they turned their attention to the campaigns of 1845. Northern Whigs had clearly failed to stop annexation, and the crucial vote of a few southern Whigs for it promised to exacerbate northern Whigs' problems with the Liberty party in impending elections. Technically, of course, annexation might still have been delayed if Polk had initiated new negotiations with Texas, as many northern Democrats expected. On his last day in office, however, Tyler offered Texas admission under the terms of the Brown plan, and Polk renewed that offer when he assumed power. By July 1845, Texas formally approved those terms.

Many southern Whigs were delighted by the final resolution of the Texas question, but the form of its enactment denied them the political benefits they had anticipated. Southern Whigs were clearly more divided over annexation than southern Democrats, and the majority of the party had continued to vote against it. To the extent that Texas remained a salient issue in southern elections in 1845, therefore, Whigs were still bound to suffer from it. If they somehow avoided the Texas question, moreover, it was not clear to Whigs in most southern states what other issues they could use in 1845 to effect recovery.

IV

Like most off-year state and congressional elections, those of 1845 have received little, if any, serious attention from historians. More congressional seats were at stake in the South than in the North that year, but the contests in both sections merit intensive examination because of the very real problems faced by the Whig party that they reveal. Much more than the narrow defeat in 1844, indeed, the disarray of, and the truly dismal performance by, Whigs in 1845 make their comeback in 1846 and 1847 seem all the more remarkable.

Of the Whigs in all the slave states, those in Georgia suffered the most serious divisions over the Texas question during 1845, yet they also possessed the best chance of diverting attention from them. Georgia, indeed, provides a textbook example of how the American federal system strengthened political parties in the nineteenth century by allowing them to substitute advantageous state issues for unattractive national issues.

Both of Georgia's Whig congressmen had voted for the Brown plan in the House of Representatives, but Berrien, the only Georgia Whig in the Senate, had steadfastly opposed it. This split reflected genuine disagreement about annexation and a growing generational division among Georgia's Whigs. Ambitious younger men like Stephens, Clinch, and Robert Toombs increasingly resented Berrien, whose prestige and determination to remain in the Senate blocked their own aspirations. From 1845 until the final demise of the Whig party in the 1850s, they would use differences from Berrien on slavery matters to end Berrien's control of the Georgia Whig party. Berrien's friends, in turn, regarded the pro-Texas votes of Stephens and Clinch as demagogical attempts to discredit them for being insufficiently proslavery. Principled differences surely counted, but Texas had become a political football for rival Whig factions, just as it had been for rival Democratic factions in 1844.[27]

Whigs from both the pro-Berrien and anti-Berrien camps in 1845 particularly worried that Berrien sought reelection to the Senate from the legislature to be chosen in October, along with a new governor. The longer the intraparty feud over Texas lasted and the longer Whig disputes publicized Berrien's record, the greater the chances that the state election would hinge on precisely the national issues most Whigs hoped to bury. As Toombs, the party's state chairman, told Berrien in February, since "Texas was too strong for us when we were united, how hopeless is the contest when we are divided." Even Berrien's most loyal lieutenants recognized that his support for the Tariff of 1842 and his opposition to annexation in 1844 and 1845 could be a severe liability. They hoped "that no allusion will be made in any way to national politics" because they believed "it would be worse than madness even to allude to them." The Whig campaign should "confine itself exclusively to state issues."[28]

To gloss over intraparty divisions on Texas, Georgia's Whigs ran incumbent Governor George W. Crawford for reelection and concentrated their campaign rhetoric exclusively on his popular record on state economic policy. To Berrien's dismay, they also remained absolutely mum about the impending election for senator. In contrast, Democrats tried to make Berrien and national issues, rather than Crawford and state issues, their focal point. Here was a classic example of how rival parties in the nineteenth century jockeyed to center elections on distinctively different issue agendas generated by the division between national and state jurisdictions.[29]

Perhaps because only state-level offices were directly at stake in Georgia in 1845, the Whig effort at diversion succeeded. Crawford won reelection with 51 percent of the vote, and even though the Whigs lost the state senate, they retained a large enough margin in the lower house to have a majority on the joint ballot. By stressing state issues and ignoring national concerns, the Whigs redeemed a crucial slave state Clay had lost the previous year. Seeing "a Southern state emerging from the abyss of locofocoism," rejoiced one northern Whig, "really galvanized my Whig torpor."[30]

Georgia, however, was the only slave state to ascend from the Loco Foco abyss in 1845. Elsewhere in Dixie the elections that year proved calamitous because the Whigs could not shift attention to state issues. States that Clay had carried toppled into the Democratic deep, and those he had lost sunk even lower into it. In Virginia, for example, where internal regional rivalries prevented a coherent party stand on any state issues, the Whigs unexpectedly lost the state legislative elections in May and, with them, Rives' Senate seat. Equally revealing, they elected just one of Virginia's fifteen congressmen, a net loss of three seats, with even Newton going down to defeat.[31]

Tennessee's Whigs, whose congressional delegation had supported Texas' annexation in 1845 more avidly than that from any other state, fared almost as badly. To capitalize on that pro-Texas record, the Whigs ran Ephraim Foster for governor and made annexation the central issue of the gubernatorial campaign. Democrats correctly chided Foster for talking in favor of annexation but voting against it, while his Democratic opponent, Congressman Aaron V. Brown, had consistently voted for it. Foster lost narrowly, and the Whigs also lost control of the state legislature. Although they retained five of Tennessee's eleven seats in the House of Representatives, moreover, their share of the popular vote in the congressional elections dropped from 53 percent in 1843 to 46.2 percent in 1845.[32]

The trend in other slave states was just as dismal because Whigs lacked issues to mobilize discouraged supporters. North Carolina's Whigs captured only three of nine House seats, and two of those were not contested by the Democrats. Moreover, in the districts that Democrats did contest, the Whig share of the vote dropped from 46.3 percent in 1844 to 42.9 percent in 1845. Kentucky's Whigs gained an additional congressional seat, but their proportion of the statewide vote declined since 1844, a decline reflected by a reduction of their majority in the state legislature. The Whigs' performance in the Alabama and Mississippi elections of 1845 proved to be as pathetic as they expected. Whigs also lost the governorship and control of the state legislature in Louisiana in a special election required by the new state constitution in January 1846, when they garnered a smaller share of the vote than Clay had attracted in 1844. Worst of all was the Whig experience in Maryland, which Clay had carried handily. Controlling all six of the state's congressional seats going into the October election, Whigs lost four of them and saw their share of the vote plummet from 52.4 to 43.3 percent. Despair, apathy, and a lack of viable issues, among other factors, obviously contributed to these reverses. In every southern state except Georgia, the Whig drop-off in voter turnout since 1844 was significantly greater than the Democratic drop-off (Table 23). By early 1846 southern Whigs were clearly in trouble.

V

Greater difficulties plagued northern Whigs in 1845 and early 1846. In contrast to their southern colleagues, they were convinced that they had profited from the tariff and Texas issues in 1844 and could do so again. Greeley asserted in a typical postelection editorial that "We are beaten not because we were in favor of Protection and opposed to Annexation, but because our opponents concealed or mystified these vital issues throughout two-thirds of the Union." The road to Whig victory, Greeley and others concluded, lay in sharply clarifying the differences between the two parties.[33] Such a tactic could revitalize downcast Whigs and might also convert those hoodwinked by Democratic evasions in 1844. Equally important, opposition to annexation might win back antislavery voters who had defected to the Liberty party.

Because the Twenty-Eighth Congress had not altered the Tariff of 1842, defending it remained a secondary weapon in the Whig arsenal in 1845. Texas was a different matter since northern Whigs and Democrats had established such clearly contrasting records on annexation and since virtually all northern Whigs were genuinely appalled by the prospect of another slave state. Even after Tyler and Polk offered Texas annexation in early March, therefore, northern Whigs kept up a steady drumfire against Texas in editorials, party platforms, and legislative resolutions.

Texas had not yet accepted the offer, they argued, and even if it did, Congress could still block its admission as a state if northern opinion were sufficiently aroused. Webster instructed Massachusetts Whigs "to show the People that the question is not yet settled." To foment a public outcry, the Whig-dominated Massachusetts legislature on March 31 published resolutions denying that the joint resolution authorizing Texas' admission was "a legal act" and pledging the commonwealth to use "her utmost exertions in cooperation with other states . . . to annul its conditions, and defeat its accomplishment." In June a corresponding committee of young Whigs circulated a call to Whig and Liberty party leaders throughout the North, urging them to organize nonpartisan public meetings against statehood for Texas. Well into the summer of 1845, Whig candidates and editors in New York, Ohio, and Indiana expressed hope that they could win over Liberty voters and defeat Democrats by highlighting the differences between the

Table 23
Major Party Drop-off Rates in Selected States, 1845–1847[a]

State	1845		1846		1847	
	Whig	Democrat	Whig	Democrat	Whig	Democrat
New Hamp.	13.4	0.8	0.1	−18.1	−13.4	
Rhode Island	−5.1	−62.3	−2.1	−51.8	6.3	10.7
Connecticut	10.1	12	15.2	8.8	8.2	8.2
Virginia	No returns				17.1	24.4
Louisiana			15.1	2.9	0.4	1.8
Alabama	70.9	33.8			−7.9	7.4
Illinois			19.6	0.7		
Indiana	13.3	7.1	15.2	12.4	0.5	4.2
Kentucky	7.7	−14.3			−6.2	−3.8
Missouri			19.2	2.4		
N. Carolina	17	4.7	7.2	12.2	22.6	21.9
Tennessee	5.6	2.7			−2.1	−0.9
Maine	27.5	31.4	15.6	25.8	29.2	26.8
Vermont	22.6	5.8	14.5	5.4	10.6	−0.4
Georgia	13.7	21.4	34.5	29.4	0.4	1.8
Maryland	33.8	8.3			6.4	−5
New Jersey			25.1	31.5	15.8	7.2
Ohio			24.6	23.2		
Pennsylvania	44.4	28.6	39	46.8	20.1	12.7
Mass.	23.5	28.2	18.8	36.3	20.4	23.9
Michigan	32.5	27.4	13.6	13.8	21.5	11.1
Mississippi	24.3	−6.8			29.6	−4.2
New York			14.4	21.1	24.8	42.7

[a]This table is based on the same returns as Table 21. When congressional and statewide elections were held in the same year, I used the statewide returns to calculate drop-off. On Rhode Island, I again put the Law and Order party in the Whig column and the Liberation party in the Democratic column. A negative drop-off indicates that a party drew more votes in that election than it had in the presidential election of 1844.

parties on annexation. As late as September, two months after Texas formally accepted annexation, Michigan's Whigs denounced it as an "outrage" and an "act of National sin and dishonor." They also condemned "the political ascendancy and rule of the Slave Power" and the "arrogant demands of the Slave States ... [whose] power is so often put forth in remorseless sectional hostility to our free institutions."[34]

So long as the issue remained salient and the hope of stopping statehood seemed plausible, the Whigs clearly benefited. In April, Connecticut's Whigs swept to victory on a protariff, anti-Texas platform, winning the governorship, increasing their majority in the state legislature, and replacing the entire congressional delegation of Democrats, who had supported the joint resolution of annexation, with Whigs.[35] After July, however, the prospect of preventing final admission of Texas, given the heavily Democratic Twenty-Ninth Congress, seemed increasingly remote. Continuing a crusade to exclude Texas, therefore, lost its power to rejuvenate discouraged Whig voters, who correctly saw defeat on that issue as virtually certain.

By the summer, further agitation of the issue in states Democrats had carried in 1844 also appeared counterproductive as a means of converting supposedly mystified Democratic voters. From Ohio, New Hampshire, Connecticut, Pennsylvania, and elsewhere in the North the responses to the circular of the Massachusetts anti-Texas committee were uniform on that point. Attempts to organize nonpartisan anti-Texas rallies were doomed, for annexation had become a party question and northern Democratic voters were now determined to achieve statehood for Texas, if only because Whigs continued to oppose it. As an astute Pennsylvanian put it, further opposition to Texas by Whigs and the Liberty party would only increase the pro-Texas fervor of Democrats. "The whole movement would necessarily assume a *party* aspect, and that alone would ensure its defeat. For if the old parties have one principle of action, more influential than another in deciding their conduct, it is *opposition* to *each* other, right or wrong." That shrewd observation testified eloquently to the strength of party loyalty in the North and the inability of even a slavery-related matter like Texas' annexation to disrupt party lines, although it distorts the reasons why many northern Democrats wanted annexation. Most of them desired Texas to expand the realm of America's republican liberty. The observation also underlined the dilemma of Whigs who sought a comeback in states Polk had carried. Prolonged resistance to Texas seemed just as likely to bring angry, proexpansion Democrats to the polls as Whigs.[36]

Worse, continued agitation of the Texas question threatened to aggravate internal divisions within the Whig party. This was especially the case in Massachusetts, the center of the anti-Texas movement. Massachusetts Whig leaders had long been divided between the followers of Daniel Webster and those of his rivals, like the extraordinarily wealthy textile manufacturer Abbott Lawrence and former Governor John Davis of Worcester. In the early 1840s, just when Lawrence was attempting to crucify Webster for remaining in Tyler's cabinet rather than rallying behind Clay, a third distinctive group of Whigs entered the fray for control of the state party. These were the so-called Young Whigs like Charles Francis Adams, John Gorham Palfrey, Charles Allen, and Stephen C. Phillips. Often scions of old, socially prominent families that had been eclipsed economically and politically by the rising industrial magnates, they resented the monopolization of state and national offices exercised by the older men who led both the Webster and Lawrence factions. Frustrated ambition, however, was hardly Young Whigs' only motivation. They despised slavery as immoral and furiously condemned its westward expansion.

Almost as soon as it emerged, the Texas annexation issue had provided grist for this intraparty feud. In 1844, all Massachusetts Whigs had opposed Texas. But the Lawrence faction had stressed nonsectional reasons for doing so, while the Young Whigs had emphasized the sinfulness of slavery and their abhorrence of its possible extension. They had therefore challenged the leadership credentials of Lawrence and his friends because of their attempt to gloss over the moral aspects of the question. As in Georgia, impatiently ambitious younger Whig politicians emphasized their deeply principled, yet sectionally more extreme convictions about the slavery issue to gain an intraparty advantage. This stress on the immorality of slavery and slaveowning would later earn for the Young Whigs the sobriquet of "Conscience Whigs." In late 1843 and throughout 1844, Webster had taken the lead in the anti-Texas movement in order to win their support in his rivalry with Lawrence, and to Lawrence's dismay, that strategy paid off in January 1845, when the Whig-dominated legislature again elected Webster to the Senate.

Later that month, Lawrence, Davis, and others boycotted an anti-Texas meeting in Boston, largely because Webster had organized it. After March, they grew increasingly annoyed at the efforts of Adams, Allen, and Phillips to perpetuate the anti-Texas movement and openly to cooperate in it with both members of the Liberty party and apolitical abolitionists like the notorious William Lloyd Garrison. Textile manufacturers like Lawrence and Nathan Appleton had willingly fought annexation as long as there was a chance to stop it, but by the summer of 1845 they deemed "farther action upon the subject . . . useless." For one thing, they worried that continued agitation of the issue would only alienate southern Whigs, whose help they would need to defeat Democratic efforts to lower the tariff at the impending session of Congress. To these conservative or "Cotton Whigs," preserving the unity of the national Whig party was more significant than wasting "our energies in hopeless efforts upon the impossible." For another, since they stood at the top of the Whig heap in Massachusetts, they feared attempts to change its composition by adding extreme antislavery men to it. To them the existing Whig party and their own governance of the state through it were just fine. Massachusetts Whigs, they correctly believed, did not need potentially disruptive converts from the Liberty party to carry the state, and their opposition negated Young Whigs' efforts to attract extreme antislavery men. In 1845, the Liberty party garnered just as large a share of the Massachusetts vote as it had in 1844.[37]

Elsewhere in the North, attempts to lure Liberty voters into the Whig column proved just as divisive and just as futile. In New York, for example, the state's two most prominent Whig editors, Weed and Greeley, promoted revision of the state constitution to abolish the property requirements for black suffrage. Since New York blacks voted overwhelmingly for the Whigs, the party would gain from enfranchising 10,000 additional black voters, but they also saw suffrage reform as a way to court the political abolitionists. As ex-Governor William Henry Seward candidly explained to Gerrit Smith when soliciting the Liberty party's aid, "In this state the obvious interests of the Whig party (to do no violence to their sympathies) lead to efforts for a convention to extend the Right of Suffrage." With equal bluntness, Weed in the *Albany Evening Journal* warned "the Political Abolitionists, who profess to be the exclusive friends of the people of color," to watch Democrats' certain efforts to block black suffrage. The conservative wing of the Whig party, spearheaded by Greeley's great editorial rival, James Watson Webb of the New York *Courier and Enquirer*, however, stridently opposed any attempt to revise the constitution or to portray the Whig party as a friend of black suffrage. This public brawling destroyed the attempt to forge a distinctive Whig position on the question, as well as any appeal the Whig party might have for Liberty voters.[38]

In New York as elsewhere in the North, in sum, efforts to broaden the Whig constituency in 1845 by courting the Liberty party had clearly failed. Indeed, that year the Liberty party's share of the vote increased, largely at Whig expense, in Vermont, New Hampshire, Maine, and Michigan. Whigs' antislavery efforts had only fragmented the party in key states. Whigs would have to look elsewhere for the road to recovery.

Throughout 1845, in fact, many northern Whigs insisted that nativists would be more valuable recruits than abolitionists or blacks. The Whigs' decision in the spring of 1845 to avoid a formal merger with the American Republican or Native American party, as it was called in different places, failed to quell their enthusiasm for the use of nativism as a Whig issue, especially since nativists might continue to siphon off Whig voters if the party did nothing to neutralize their appeal. That threat became apparent shortly after the presidential election. In December 1844, an independent nativist candidate attracted so many votes in Boston's mayoral election that no one received the majority necessary to carry that normally Whig bastion. Nativist parties also wooed Whig defectors in Philadelphia, Baltimore, Pittsburgh, and Cincinnati, and in April 1845, the bulk of New York City's Whigs continued to support the American Republican rather than the Whig mayoral candidate. The menace grew even graver in the summer of 1845, when nativists nominated separate tickets for governor in Massachusetts and Louisiana, for canal commissioner in Pennsylvania, and for the state legislature in New York.[39]

In the face of this challenge, many Whigs, who themselves considered immigrant voting a threat to republican institutions, contended that the party had to establish its own antiforeign and anti-Catholic credentials. If Whigs could persuade die-hard nativists to support Whig candidates, the party could retake Pennsylvania and New York and widen its margin in other northern and border states. Accordingly, the Whig governors of Maryland and Kentucky asked their legislatures in January 1845 to pass voter registration laws to combat illegal immigrant voting. Webster was convinced that nativism could prove as potent a weapon for Massachusetts Whigs as anti-Texas sentiment, and during the winter of 1844–45 he and other Whigs repeatedly urged Congress to revise the naturalization laws.[40]

This pressure forced the Whig-controlled Senate to make a futile gesture toward nativism during the second session of the Twenty-Eighth Congress, when Texas annexation occupied most attention. Aside from William S. Archer of Virginia, Whig senators had much less enthusiasm for naturalization reform than their angry constituents, if only because they knew they had no chance of getting such a bill past the Democratic House of Representatives. Yet they also recognized the need to appease their supporters' nativist fury, if only symbolically. Thus the Senate Judiciary Committee appointed commissioners to investigate naturalization frauds during the recent presidential election in New York City, Philadelphia, Baltimore, and New Orleans. As if to emphasize the partisan purpose of this inquisition, moreover, they hired a prominent American Republican as one of the investigators in New York. But even before those commissioners reported their findings, the committee's chairman, John M. Berrien, introduced a naturalization reform bill in January 1845.

In essence this would have established an elaborate structure of paperwork, requiring immigrants to report to federal officials and receive certification at frequent intervals from the time they first landed on American shores until the moment they applied for naturalization papers five years later. In short, the purpose of the bill was to make the process of naturalization more difficult and to monitor the movements of immigrant aliens more closely. Significantly, however, it did not require a lengthening of the naturalization period itself, as the nativist parties demanded. No vote was ever taken on Berrien's bill. The best the Whigs could do was, after a strict party-line vote, to secure the publication of 5,000 copies of the final committee report presenting verbatim all the testimony taken in the four port cities that supposedly had documented naturalization fraud.[41]

These feeble efforts hardly persuaded nativists to abandon separate political action. They regarded Berrien's bill as woefully inadequate. More important, although some Whigs tried to demonstrate their anti-immigrant pedigree to mollify the nativists, others tried just as hard to prove to immigrants that the party was untainted by nativism. They condemned antiforeign and anti-Catholic bigotry as morally intolerable and politically unwise. Internal strife over nativism, in sum, proved just as bitter as divisions over the proper response to the Liberty party, and, as in the case of the political abolitionists, the rancorous public quarreling destroyed whatever chances the Whigs might have had of absorbing the nativists. For example, while a Whig rally in New Haven, Connecticut, condemned "the illegal foreign votes that are thrown against us," Whig Governor William Ellsworth urged a Whig meeting in Hartford to spurn nativism. While the Whig Boston *Courier* insisted that the Whig gubernatorial candidate, George N. Briggs, "was heart and soul a Native American" who favored the "entire exclusion from the ballot box . . . of all foreigners," especially Catholics, other Whig newspapermen in Boston insisted that Briggs had "not adopted a single idea of the Natives," that he did not favor extension of the naturalization period to twenty-one years or oppose popery. In New York, the self-described "conservative" Whigs, who opposed constitutional revision and black suffrage, openly sought nativist support by demanding revision of the naturalization laws and condemned Seward, Weed, and Greeley for pampering foreigners and Catholics by opposing Bible reading in public schools. In reply, the "progressive" Weed-Seward-Greeley wing of the party pilloried American Republicans' religious bigotry, blasted naturalization reform as unfair, and declared that New York's Whigs "have definitely taken ground in hostility to the Native movement."[42]

As a result of these internal divisions, the flight of Whig voters to nativist ranks continued in the fall of 1845. Separate nativist and temperance tickets cost the Whigs John P. Kennedy's congressional seat in Baltimore in October 1845, even though Kennedy himself called for reform of the naturalization laws. The results from Pennsylvania that month were even more calamitous. The Native American candidate for canal commissioner drew 9.6 percent of the vote, the Whigs' share of the statewide total plummeted from 48.5 percent in 1844 to 38.1 percent, and they won less than a third of the seats in the state legislature, their worst showing since 1839. A month later, the nativist gubernatorial candidate in Massachusetts garnered 8 percent of the vote, as large a share as the Liberty candidate, and the Whigs lost their statewide majority. In New York, Whigs gained nothing even as the American Republican vote declined. Chastened by their futility, Whigs in early 1846 renounced any plans to merge with nativists or change the naturalization laws.[43]

Unable to exploit a compelling national issue by the summer of 1845 and divided over the wisdom of appealing to nativists and political abolitionists, most northern Whigs fell back on state issues. In most places, however, those concerns only fragmented the party still further in 1845 and early 1846. Ohio was an exception. There the party united against Democrats over state banking policies, and Whigs scored impressive gains in the October 1845 legislative elections by defending their recently passed probanking measures. Pennsylvania was more typical. Whigs from the eastern and western ends of the state, like Democrats, were dividing over the rival claims of the Baltimore & Ohio and Pennsylvania railroads for chartered routes to Pittsburgh. This battle would completely disrupt Whig cohesion in the legislative session that began in January 1846. Similarly, Indiana's Whigs split along regional lines over issues like slavery, state internal improvements, and the repudiation of state bonds issued for construction of the Wabash and Erie Canal, and those divisions apparently contributed to the party's defeat in the congressional and legislative elections of August 1845. Indiana's Whigs held such conflicting views on these matters, contended Godlove Orth, that "no one universal policy should be adopted by our party in the next campaign." Instead, "every district, county, & township must carry on the battle without reference to any other portion of the State." In Connecticut, where Whigs had scored sweeping victories in April 1845 on a protariff and anti-Texas platform, they lost the entire state government in 1846 because of internal divisions between "dries" and "wets" over toughened antiliquor laws and between Hartford and New Haven Whigs over a proposed railroad bridge across the Connecticut River at Middletown. So prolonged were those bitter regional divisions over bridging the Connecticut, indeed, that a year later the politically astute wife of New Haven's most prominent Whig moaned, "Sectional feelings overcome party lines."[44]

Rhode Island provides yet another example of Whig vulnerability to divisive state issues following the settlement of the Texas question. In 1844, the Whigs had rolled up a higher percentage of the vote in Rhode Island than in any other state, but in the April gubernatorial elections of 1845 and 1846 the Whig coalition virtually disintegrated. Legacies of the Dorr Rebellion, those campaigns were conducted by state-oriented parties called the Law and Order party and the Liberation party, which divided over the question of releasing Thomas Dorr from prison and each of which ran a Whig as its candidate for governor. Whigs fractured so badly that in March 1846 one berated the folly of his party's newspapers for making so much of the law-and-order issue when Whigs needed to unite to reelect Senator James F. Simmons to fight Democratic attempts to lower the tariff. Only by focusing attention on national issues, in short, could the Rhode Island Whig party be saved from its suicidal internal bloodletting.[45]

Another New England election in the spring of 1846 surprisingly provided the only other exception, along with Ohio, to the discouraging Whig performance in northern states in 1845 and early 1846. It was, however, an exception that proved the rule, for Whig success depended on a situation that was unique and so temporary that it did not seem to provide a formula for Whig success elsewhere—at least initially. In 1845 and again in 1846, the New Hampshire Democratic party ruptured over the slavery issue when the party's state chairman, future President Franklin Pierce, tried to purge antislavery Democratic Congressman John P. Hale from the party because he had voted against the joint resolution for Texas annexation. Out-of-state Whig leaders like Webster encouraged Granite State Whigs to exploit this rift by forging a coalition with the Liberty party and dissident Hale

Democrats in the legislative elections of March 1846. That coalition, known as the New Hampshire Alliance, carried the legislature and quickly seized the opportunity to bargain for other offices as well.

Like most New England states, New Hampshire required an absolute majority rather than a plurality to secure election. Because none of the three gubernatorial candidates had received the necessary majority, the Alliance in the legislature had the chance to select the winner and to dispose of a United States Senate seat as well. In return for sending Hale to the Senate, it picked Anthony Colby, the Whig candidate, as governor, the first and only Whig governor ever to serve in that Democratic stronghold. Whigs everywhere rejoiced at this unanticipated triumph, but the real strength of the Whig party in New Hampshire was reflected in the 32 percent of the popular vote Colby had won in March. In 1847, when turnout was substantially higher than in 1846 or even in the presidential election of 1844 because of determined Democratic efforts to retake the state, the Whigs received only 35 percent of the statewide vote. As Greeley glumly concluded, the result demonstrated that New Hampshire was solidly Democratic. The apparent Whig success in 1846 had been a fluke.[46]

By the spring of 1846, in sum, northern Whigs, like their southern colleagues, had made a series of false starts. Routes that seemed like shortcuts to power turned out to be blind alleys. In the few states they had carried, they had either exploited ephemeral issues or suffered serious erosion of their voting support. They had failed to come back in the key states of New York, Pennsylvania, and Indiana and seemed in danger in former strongholds like Rhode Island, Connecticut, Vermont, Massachusetts, and Maryland. To pull back apathetic and defecting voters and to overcome the growing Democratic lead, Whigs clearly had to look elsewhere for gripping issues. An indication of where most would look came from a discouraged Indiana Whig in January 1846. Pessimistic about winning the state's impending gubernatorial campaign on state issues that divided the party internally, he wistfully yet accurately predicted, "Congress may kick up some deviltry out of which we can make something to put in our pipes."[47]

VI

Since the Whig party's birth in the winter of 1833–34, its vitality had never depended exclusively on Whigs' initiative or actions or even on economic conditions. Instead, its fate had always been determined primarily by its relationship with its Democratic opponent. The most effective force to counteract the disruptive impulses that had emerged in 1845, therefore, had always been interparty conflict with the Democrats. That conflict could be provoked by Democrats just as easily as by Whigs. Modern research indicates that negative voting against an incumbent party is a more powerful and pervasive political phenomenon than positive voting by those who approve its record, and Whigs, too, had usually benefited more from opposing Democratic policies than from defending their own proposals.[48] Largely unable to define viable issues on their own in 1845, Whigs were rescued by the vigorous determination of Democrats in Washington to enact their own program. The actions of the Polk administration and the Democratic majority in Congress during 1846 and 1847 would reverse the slide that Whigs had experienced in 1845, revitalize the Whig electorate, and spark a dramatic recovery in the midterm congressional and state elections.

Months before the Twenty-Ninth Congress assembled in December 1845, Whigs knew that Democrats would have the power to pass any legislation they wanted, and they regularly predicted the dire consequences of the Democratic program. Whig spokesmen genuinely believed that Democratic policies would bring ruin to the country, yet they also realized that the worst policies for the nation could provide the best Whig platform against Democrats. As the Whig minority in Congress saw it, then, they had a choice between what was best for their country and what was best for their party, a choice of attempting to modify Democratic legislation as much as possible to mitigate its negative results or of letting the Democrats have their way and suffer certain repudiation at the polls. The question, as Whigs most frequently put it, was whether to save the Democrats from their own folly. The Whigs' response to different Democratic policies varied between these alternatives, but consistently throughout the two terms of the Twenty-Ninth Congress, they attempted to highlight the differences between the parties and to stake out a position that would afford them maximum political advantage.

Whigs displayed the most caution on foreign policy. Even though the admission of Texas was assured by December 1845, Polk and most congressional Democrats wanted to keep alive the issue of territorial expansion, from which they believed they had benefited in 1844. Hence, in his inaugural address of March 1845 and again in his annual message to Congress in December 1845, Polk called on the United States to take title to the entire Oregon country north to 54°40', the southern boundary of Alaska, by giving England formal notice that the joint occupation of Oregon by both nations that had existed since 1818 would be terminated. Between those messages, in August 1845, John L. O'Sullivan, editor of the *Democratic Review*, permanently grafted expansionism to the Democratic platform by coining the phrase "Manifest Destiny" to justify the nation's territorial designs.

Polk's proposal initially divided congressional Whigs. Opposed in principle to territorial expansion and adverse to any initiative of the Democratic president, some Whigs refused to vote for the joint resolution notifying England that joint occupation would be ended. Other Whigs regarded such adamant opposition as suicidal. Fearing that the party would be saddled with the stigma of appearing pro-British and unpatriotic, and that Polk was only posturing in order to keep the Oregon question alive until the 1848 presidential election, they wanted to resolve it as quickly as possible. Thus, when the House of Representatives passed the notice to England in January 1846, the Whig delegation was almost evenly divided pro and con.

What allowed Whigs finally to assume a coherent partisan stance on Oregon was the action of Senate Democrats. When bellicose midwestern Democrats in that body raised the cry of "Fifty-four-Forty or Fight" and demanded military preparations to take all of Oregon from Great Britain by force, Senate Whigs urged negotiation or arbitration of the dispute instead, and Whigs across the country railed against Democrats' belligerent recklessness and the dangers of war for Oregon. On Oregon, that is, Whigs posed as propeace rather than antiexpansion. When Polk negotiated and secured ratification in June 1846 of a treaty establishing the northern boundary of Oregon at the forty-ninth parallel, as he had apparently planned all along, relieved midwestern Whigs shifted position and charged Polk with betrayal.[49]

Polk also coveted California, and his efforts to acquire it one way or another from Mexico eventually prompted the outbreak of war with that nation in May 1846, a war Whigs had warned would inevitably follow the annexation of Texas and a war that grew increasingly unpopular as it dragged on until the spring of 1848. Whigs in Congress and throughout the nation castigated Polk's original dispatch of troops under the command of Zachary Taylor to the Rio Grande River as an unwarranted provocation that started the conflict and an unconstitutional usurpation of Congress' power to declare war. When the Democrats in both houses of Congress attached a preamble declaring that Mexico started the war to the initial bills to raise troops and supplies, however, Whigs confronted a dilemma. Knowing the fate of the Federalists for opposing the War of 1812, most were convinced that they had to provide the men and materiel to pursue the war to a successful conclusion. Yet they considered the Democratic assertion of Mexican responsibility for the war a flagrantly spurious attempt to exonerate Polk of culpability. In the end, only fourteen of seventy-seven Whigs in the House and two of twenty-four in the Senate voted against the initial appropriations, which in effect constituted Congress' declaration, or at least recognition, of war with Mexico. This division had a lingering disruptive impact on the party, especially in Massachusetts, where Conscience Whigs exploited Boston Representative Robert C. Winthrop's affirmative vote to attack the Cotton Whigs.[50]

Despite these internal divisions, and despite the willingness of most Whig congressmen to join the Democrats in voting for men and supplies for the army, the Whigs had no difficulty establishing a coherent and distinctive party position on the war. On most roll-call votes in Congress and in state legislatures regarding the war, the rival parties were sharply polarized against each other. For two years, Whigs inside and outside of Congress condemned the war as an immoral aggression to steal territory from a weaker neighbor. They vilified Polk's management of it as grossly partisan and corrupt, especially his treatment of the Whig Generals Taylor and Scott and his attempt to supersede them with Democratic commanders, and they denounced the prospect of a territorial indemnity from it as dangerous to North and South alike. The longer the war lasted, the more vehemently Whigs lambasted the Democrats' insistence on the rape of Mexican territory as the chief obstacle to peace. It was perfectly clear who the prowar and antiwar parties were, and agitation of antiwar sentiment became an increasingly powerful weapon in the Whig arsenal.[51]

While Whig denunciations of the Mexican War became more strident the longer hostilities continued, in 1846 Whigs focused their fire primarily on Democrats' domestic legislation. Here their choice between what they regarded as the best interests of the country versus those of the party was more clear-cut and their decision more cynical. At Polk's command, the Democratic Congress enacted three important economic measures in the summer of 1846 that together marked a frontal assault on the Whig economic program: the Independent Treasury Act, which removed government revenues from private banks and required the government to deal exclusively in specie; the Walker Tariff, which lowered rates on most manufactured goods, raised rates on a number of raw materials imported by American manufacturers, and substituted *ad valorem* for specific duties; and the Public Warehouse Act, which in effect gave government credit to importers and foreign manufacturers by allowing them to deposit imports in government warehouses for up to a year before paying customs duties rather than paying the tariff immediately upon the arrival of the goods. To compound matters, midwestern Democrats defied Polk's wishes and combined with the Whig minority to pass a massive rivers and harbors improvement bill, which Polk vetoed. The veto offended the intended recipients of government aid in New York, Ohio, Michigan, Illinois, Georgia, and along both banks of the Ohio River.[52]

All of these actions presented the Whigs with something they could put in their war pipes. For one thing, Polk's active intervention in the legislative process, like his policies toward Oregon and Mexico, revived the Whigs' cardinal principle of opposition to executive tyranny. More important, they seemed to confirm the prediction that Greeley and others had been making since the election of 1844: that Democratic ascendancy meant economic disaster for the country. Clay himself had confidently forecast at the end of 1844 that "errors" by the Polk administration would generate "abundant cause of public dissatisfaction." Yet, like Clay, most Whigs were prepared to let the Democrats have their way with the tariff and subtreasury because the inevitable depression would spark a Whig comeback. With regard to the Democrats' economic policy, that is, the Whigs attempted to kill not the legislation itself, but rather any attempts to dilute, soften, or delay its impact on the country at large. By their own admission, they chose what was good for the party over what they regarded as good for the country. Only painful experience with Democratic measures, they contended, would turn the electorate permanently against the Democratic party.[53]

Whigs had long maintained that the Independent Treasury system would irreparably harm the economy by draining the banks' specie reserves, undermining public faith in bank notes, and choking commercial credit. In April 1846, after the bill had passed the House, they gleefully pointed to the tightening of credit by bankers as the inevitably disastrous response. Yet when Senate Democrats seemed ready to delay implementation of the bill to ease credit, Whig writers urged congressional Whigs not to let Democrats off the hook. As one Whig urged in the May 1846 issue of *The American Review*, "Let the specie exaction take full effect at once, and the country will not endorse it beyond the term of the present Congress. Will it be wise in the Whigs of the Senate to aid in giving it a shape calculated to purchase a little present relaxation in the money market?" Similarly, in August, when the Democratic leadership in the House made a last-ditch attempt to amend the bill to delay the implementation of its specie clause from January 1 until April 1, 1847, Whigs voted almost unanimously to help kill the amendment, and Greeley in the *Tribune* fulsomely praised them for their action.[54] Clearly, Whigs were more concerned with the political than the economic results of Democratic legislation.

Whig opportunism was even more blatant regarding the tariff. Many Whigs, especially manufacturers, genuinely feared the economic consequences of tariff reduction, which would increase competition from foreign goods and, by increasing gold shipments abroad to pay for them, aggravate the pressure on the currency and the credit supply. Consequently, they wanted congressional Whigs to fight to the last to preserve the Tariff of 1842, which virtually all Whigs credited with ending the prolonged depression between 1839 and 1843. The desire to win southern Whig support for that law, for example, was a chief reason why Abbott Lawrence and Nathan Appleton had opposed the anti-Texas movement of the Young Whigs in Massachusetts in the fall of 1845 and why Lawrence distributed protariff arguments to Whig congressmen early in 1846.[55]

Other Whigs, however, preferred to let the Democrats suffer the voters' reaction against the anticipated depression that tariff reduction supposedly would induce. Such men urged congressional Whigs not to stop Democratic efforts; let them "take the responsibility and the consequences." It is also revealing that many Whig attacks on the impending Democratic measure concerned its hypocrisy, as well as its potential for economic harm. Secretary of the Treasury Robert J. Walker's voluminous report to Congress in December 1845 defending tariff reduction, they pointed out, was based forthrightly on free trade principles, but his proposed bill provided some protection for politically sensitive items like iron, while the McKay bill reported by the House Ways and Means Committee called for even higher levels of protection. Democrats, Whigs jeered, lacked the courage of their own stated convictions.[56]

Although these Whigs would have preferred an even lower tariff to pillory, they regarded the Walker-McKay bill or "The Tariff Reduction and Labor Destruction Bill," as Greeley called it, as sufficiently horrendous to provide Whigs excellent ammunition for the impending congressional and state campaigns in 1846. By June, as the Walker bill progressed through the House, Georgia's Whigs anticipated the final law "with the eagerness of hyenas and jackals waiting only for the final onslaught to be over to rush on to the work of mutilation," while Pennsylvania and New York Whigs salivated at a measure that would doom Democrats in the ensuing elections.[57]

Lest they lose such a potent issue at the last moment, Whigs resisted attempts to alter the bill in the Senate, which was more closely divided than the House and contained a number of protariff Democrats. Businessmen beseeched Whig senators to modify the McKay bill to offer them more protection. Webster, after extensive consultation with northeastern manufacturers and mine owners, prepared a compromise amendment to the Democratic bill, one that would lower rates more gradually and preserve the specific duties businessmen cherished. He was confident that he could garner the votes to adopt the substitute in the Senate and kill the whole bill when it returned to the House. Webster, however, had not reckoned on the determination of Whig politicians to construct a winning platform even at the expense of their constituents' economic interests. When Greeley and his Washington correspondent, "Richelieu," learned of Webster's proposal, for example, they urged Senate Whigs to spurn it: "Stand strongly for the Right. Let them work their will on the Country. . . . Let Polk & Co. break down the Tariff if they can, and let us go to the People once upon a distinct issue of Protection against Free Trade."[58]

In the end, Webster never introduced his amendment because other Whigs would not go along. They wanted the Walker tariff passed, regardless of businessmen's pleas. The worst tariff possible would make the best platform possible. The Whigs, Webster lamented, "wished the administration to make its own Bill and to make it as bad as it pleased." Similarly, a bitter manufacturer concluded with perfect accuracy that Whig politicians were "striving to make political capital to overthrow the present administration at whatever cost to the country."[59]

Once the Democratic program passed Congress, Whigs, exulting that "it is an ill wind that blows no one any good," predicted that they would sweep the 1846 congressional elections and win the White House in 1848 by attacking Democrats' economic package. As William Bebb, Ohio's Whig gubernatorial candidate for 1846, rejoiced, "If the repeal of the Tariff, the passage of the Sub Treasury, the veto of the river and harbor bill and other measures of this administration added to our *state issues* fail to 'stir up the very stones to meeting' we may as well hang our harps on the willows." "If we have not misread the signs of the times," summarized a jubilant Whig in the September issue of *The American Review*, "the tariff of 1846 will precipitate the ruin of its contrivers and hasten the day of our National redemption."[60]

To take maximum advantage of the issues that Democrats had handed them, Whigs made an unprecedented effort in 1846 to provide centralized direction and assistance to the midterm congressional campaigns. Like its Democratic counterpart, the Whig party was a decentralized organization, with no permanent national committee or clear lines of authority from the center to the periphery. Rather, it was essentially a federation or alliance of largely autonomous state organizations that were, in turn, alliances of largely autonomous county and local organizations. Common commitment to the party's principles and common devotion to its victory, rather than a hierarchical model of command and obedience, characterized its operations. Every four years in presidential elections, a semblance of national coordination appeared as Whigs came together in a national convention to nominate the presidential ticket and as a national committee, appointed temporarily for that campaign, dispatched information, money, and speakers to different states and localities to rally support for the standard bearer. Customarily, however, local candidates and organizations were left to their own devices in terms of raising money and defining issues in gubernatorial and congressional campaigns, although out-of-state speakers had occasionally been imported to help gubernatorial and congressional candidates.[61]

In 1846, Whigs considered this normal practice inadequate. They regarded the Democratic measures passed in 1846 as so heinous that national Whig leaders had to orchestrate the various local congressional campaigns in order to take control of Congress from the Democrats. As one furious Whig wrote Webster after the Walker Tariff passed, "I trust you will not leave Washington without *a general concert among all the opponents of such destructive measures, in a plan of action for the next election of Representatives.*" The man who led the effort to coordinate Whig campaigns in 1846, however, was not Webster, but Connecticut's Truman Smith, then serving his third term in the House. Smith lacked the commanding physical presence and oratorical skills of Webster and the legislative talents of Winthrop, Alexander Stephens, Clay, or Crittenden. Yet along with Seward and Weed of New York, Smith was perhaps the party's shrewdest political strategist and manager. He was, moreover, absolutely without peer in terms of looking beyond the parochial concerns of his own district and state to the needs of Whigs as a national organization. Truman Smith, in short, was and would remain until he retired in 1854 the Whigs' closest equivalent to a modern national party chairman.[62]

As soon as Congress adjourned on August 8, 1846, Smith traveled to Boston and then back to Washington again via New York, Philadelphia, and Baltimore in order to raise money for the Whig campaign from outraged manufacturers and businessmen. From Washington and then from his home in the beautiful town of Litchfield, Connecticut, he corresponded with other members of the campaign committee such as Thomas Butler King of Savannah, Georgia, and Senator John Davis of Worcester, Massachusetts, keeping them abreast of developments. Smith hoped to raise $7,500, a not inconsiderable sum for that day, but fell short of his goal. He spent the funds at his command, apparently some $5,500, in two ways.

First, as he had intended since April, he had thousands of copies of Whig speeches against the Democratic measures printed in Washington at a cost of $2,300. Smith had hoped to send these around the country free of charge using the franking privilege of Whig congressmen, but upon arriving back in Washington on September 15, he learned to his dismay that federal law prohibited any congressman from franking documents more than thirty days after the expiration of a congressional session. Thus, only 50,000 documents were distributed in this fashion under the frank of Congressman Alexander Ramsey of Pennsylvania, a member of Smith's campaign committee, who had remained in Washington since August 8, monotonously franking documents. Smith had to box and mail, at the committee's expense, an additional 120,000 documents to other districts.

This stupendous, unprecedented effort to distribute campaign literature in an off-year election demonstrated the conviction of Whig leaders that voters paid close attention to concrete issues. The speeches of congressional Whigs against the new tariff, the Independent Treasury, and the Public Warehouse Act were almost uniformly lengthy, intricately argued, minutely detailed, and teeming with facts, figures, and arcane data on federal revenues, price levels, specie flows into and out of the country, and wage levels in different industries. They were, in sum, difficult and often tediously dull. In 1846, clearly, Whigs believed they could win with closely reasoned arguments addressed to specific issues and that they needed neither slogans, nor songs, nor the glamour of military heroes as their candidates.

Over half of the money Smith raised was devoted to party-building activities in new states, an effort that reflected Smith's solicitude for the good of the national Whig party, especially the congressional Whig party, as a whole. Whigs were outraged that the two new Democratic senators from Texas had provided the narrow margin for victory when the Walker Tariff passed the Senate in late July. Smith therefore sought to offset that additional Democratic strength by building up Whig organizations in federal territories that appeared on the brink of applying for statehood so that the new congressmen they sent to Washington would be Whigs. In 1846, Smith sent some funds to the incipient Whig party in Wisconsin Territory, but his priority that year was Iowa, which had been authorized by Congress to choose a new state government and congressmen in elections scheduled for late October. In September, Smith dispatched J. H. Clay Mudd from Washington to Iowa and gave him $3,000 of the $3,100 then in his possession to buy newspapers, print ballots and campaign literature, and finance

Whig speakers in the Iowa campaign. His goal was to capture the new state legislature and thus send to Congress in December two Whig senators from the nation's newest state.[63]

Despite Mudd's optimistic reports to Smith, the Whigs failed to carry the Iowa elections, but elsewhere in 1846 they scored truly sweeping gains. They picked up fourteen additional House seats in New York, one in New Jersey, five in Pennsylvania, three in Ohio, and one in Georgia, and they held all their seats in other northern states, including the entire Massachusetts delegation. Altogether Whigs won 53.6 percent of the congressional seats contested that year, a dramatic improvement over their performance in 1844 and 1845. They also won gubernatorial races in New York, Ohio, North Carolina, and Massachusetts, where they did much better than in 1845. Although they narrowly lost the election for governor in Indiana in August, they won control of the state legislature. In contrast to the elections held earlier in the year before Democrats in Congress had acted, indeed, the Whigs ran impressively in most state legislative contests after August, especially in Maine, Maryland, New Jersey, Pennsylvania, Massachusetts, and New York. More important for the future, Whigs won a larger proportion of the vote in the fall elections of 1846 than they had in the presidential election of 1844 in every state except Delaware, Georgia, and Ohio and Vermont, two states where the Liberty party still cut into their ranks. Although voter turnout in no state was as large as it had been in 1844, it was uniformly larger than in 1845, and the Whigs had obviously won the lion's share of those returning voters. Reaction against the Democratic program had brought previously demoralized Whigs back to the polls.[64]

VII

Perceptive Whigs, nonetheless, might have found cause for concern even in the midst of this genuinely impressive performance. Attacks on the Polk record did not give the Whigs firm control of the crucial states they would need to carry the presidency in 1848, that is, those states they had lost narrowly in 1844. In Georgia, for example, reapportionment of the congressional districts by the Whig legislature was probably more responsible for the Whigs' success in carrying four of eight seats than the Walker Tariff. The Whigs won only 47 percent of the popular vote in contrast to Crawford's 51 percent the previous year.[65] Pennsylvania's Whigs won the statewide election for canal commissioner in 1846, but with less than a majority of the vote. The Native American candidate still drew 7.5 percent, and Democrats, who had pledged their party in 1844 to a defense of the Tariff of 1842, suffered a significantly larger drop-off than the Whigs as betrayed Democratic voters stayed home on election day. Manifestly, Pennsylvania's Whigs were still vulnerable to a full Democratic turnout if Democratic leaders could induce it. Even in New York, where Whigs scored their biggest gains, they depended in 1846 on more than their opposition to the Democratic record in Congress.

During the off-year elections of 1845, 1846, and 1847, every state in the nation had special peculiarities that influenced the precise shape of political developments within it. In no state, however, were conditions as complex as in New York.

Though unusual in that respect, New York still provides a marvelous microcosm of the trial-and-error method by which Whigs in all states searched for a winning strategy between 1844 and 1848. Whig efforts there in 1846, therefore, merit detailed examination.

Divided into self-styled "progressive" and "conservative" wings, New York's Whig leaders quarreled vehemently about the proper course for recapturing the state. In 1845, the majority who followed Weed, Seward, and Greeley wanted to spurn nativism in order to attract immigrants. They also courted Liberty men and blacks by pushing for a broadening of black suffrage and opposing Texas' annexation on antislavery grounds. The smaller conservative wing, located primarily in the lower Hudson Valley and New York City and represented by papers like the *Express* and the *Courier & Enquirer*, denounced the majority's South-bashing tactics and argued that the party instead should embrace nativism.[66]

But for most of 1846 and especially prior to the passage of the Democratic economic legislation in July and August, which all Whigs opposed, strategic maneuvering for new voters and intraparty strife focused on two state issues. The first concerned revision of the state constitution, which New York's electorate endorsed overwhelmingly in a referendum that scheduled the election of delegates to a state constitutional convention in late April. The convention itself was slated to begin meeting in June.

Conservative Whigs like James Watson Webb and James and Erastus Brooks openly opposed constitutional revision in their newspapers on the grounds that any change was inimical to conservatism, although they also castigated specific revisions pushed by reformers. Among the most enthusiastic of those constitutional reformers were Weed, Greeley, and Seward and their followers in the party's majority wing, who saw a number of advantages in promoting revision.

First, some of the specific changes they advocated, like stripping the governor of most of his patronage powers, substituting single-member assembly districts for countywide general tickets, and replacing the eight huge state senate districts with thirty-two single-member districts, stood to benefit the Whig party. They would reduce the appointments available to the incumbent Democratic administration and increase Whig representation in the state legislature by giving a voice to Whig enclaves trapped in Democratic strongholds.

Second, in early 1846, constitutional revision seemed the best way to add antislavery, black, and immigrant voters to Whig ranks. Both Greeley and Weed pressed for a provision in the new constitution removing the freehold property requirement from black voters, as did a few upstate Whig county conventions controlled by the Sewardites. Weed went even further than Greeley. In the columns of his *Albany Evening Journal*, he advocated suffrage rights for immigrant aliens before they became naturalized citizens, a measure he publicly defended as the best way to stop illegal naturalization but that he also obviously intended as an effort to outbid Democrats for the immigrant vote.

Third, the dominant Whig faction considered reform good politics since it could erase the conservative image so assiduously cultivated by their intraparty rivals and challenge the Democrats' reputation as the party of the people. Indeed, because Van Burenite or Barnburner Democrats supported and Hunker Democrats opposed constitutional revision, Whig leaders saw agitation of constitutional reform as a way further to divide and thus weaken their Democratic foe.[67]

By the early summer of 1846, before Congress had passed Democratic economic legislation, the dominant Whig leadership realized they must change tack. Democrats, most of whom were Barnburners, won control of the constitutional convention, and while some Whig reforms, like reduction of gubernatorial patronage, would probably pass, the new constitution would be no Whig document. Democratic control also doomed expanded black suffrage and alien suffrage, nullifying Whigs' bid to the beneficiaries of those reforms. Weed and Seward, with Greeley's reluctant acquiescence, therefore, jettisoned the strategy aimed at antislavery, black, and immigrant voters for a new one.[68]

Sewardite Whigs now sought to exploit Democratic divisions. They recognized that the Hunkers and Barnburners were deeply split over provisions of the new constitution and over control of the state Democratic machine. They had previously cooperated with the Barnburners to call the constitutional convention in the first place, but once the convention met, they turned to the Hunkers for aid. Barnburners wanted to insert into the state's fundamental charter economic provisions prohibiting state aid to internal improvements, blocking completion of the state's canal system, inhibiting the incorporation of businesses, and imposing unlimited individual liability on stockholders. The Hunkers, in contrast, like the Whigs, had always been more favorable to business interests and especially completion of the canal system than the Barnburners.

Before the convention met in June, the Albany *Argus*, the chief Hunker organ in the state, announced a series of revisions Hunkers could support that were roughly congruent with Whig proposals. More important, on roll-call votes in the convention itself, Hunkers often aligned with the Whigs to moderate the Burnburners' economic proposals and bring them more in line with Whig thinking. Until the convention closed, therefore, it made eminent sense for the Whigs to cooperate with the Hunkers.[69]

More important for the impending gubernatorial election, during the summer the Hunkers privately informed Sewardite Whig leaders that if Whigs chose an acceptable gubernatorial candidate, Hunkers would sit out the fall election and allow the Whigs to win. With Barnburners out of power and stripped of state patronage, Hunkers believed, their chances of controlling the state party machinery would be enhanced. Here was an offer Whigs could not refuse.[70]

Exploiting Democratic divisions thus seemed the clearest road to recovery to Sewardite Whig leaders. Even after the Walker Tariff passed Congress, for example, Seward wrote one of his lieutenants that New York's Whigs could not count on the tariff issue for victory in 1846 because they could never mobilize the full Whig vote in nonpresidential elections. The Whigs' chief hope, he asserted, "arises out of the feud in our enemy's ranks."[71] New York's Whigs, like Whigs elsewhere, were dependent upon their relationship with the Democrats, in other words, but in the Empire State the Democrats' national policies seemed less vulnerable than their internal divisions.

Simultaneously, the prospect of running against Barnburner Silas Wright's record as governor opened up the possibility of securing a bloc of new voters other than blacks, Liberty party members, or immigrants. Wright was anathema to the Anti-Rent movement, the second purely state issue upon which political attention and intraparty squabbling had focused in the first half of 1846. Spread across some fifteen upstate counties but centered in Rensselaer, Albany, Columbia,

Scholarie, and Delaware Counties, the turbulent Anti-Rent movement erupted from the grievances of farmers living on lands once belonging to the colonial manors or patroonships in that area. In some counties, these farmers had long-term leases running for two or three generations of the renter's family, after which the land had to be returned to the proprietor. In others, in return for fee-simple titles to farms, these families or their ancestors had contracted to pay in perpetuity to owners of the estates and their descendants annual payments that the farmers called "rents" but that in reality were lifelong mortgage interest payments on the purchase price of the land, the principal of which was never collected. Technically, the farmers were not tenants or renters since they, and not the original proprietors of the estates, owned the land and paid taxes on it. What the proprietors owned were legally guaranteed contracts obliging the farmers to pay them an annual sum and granting them other privileges, such as the right to sell the farmer's personal property without court trial if the farmer failed to pay rent and to collect one-fourth of the selling price if the farmer sold the property to another man.

Denouncing the system as feudal and unrepublican, increasing numbers of these farmers, beginning in 1839, refused to pay their rents, and they used armed force to prevent public officials from collecting them. In the summer of 1845, a deputy sheriff was killed by a mob of armed farmers in Delaware County, causing Democratic Governor Wright to declare the entire county in a state of insurrection, to have scores of Anti-Renters arrested and imprisoned, to refuse to grant clemency to the men convicted of the official's murder, and to tell the legislature to provide no redress for the Anti-Renters' grievances until farmers everywhere laid down their weapons. In response, the Anti-Renters organized successful state legislative tickets in several counties in the fall of 1845, and in 1846 Anti-Renters across the state flooded the legislature with demands to free the prisoners and to abolish the inequities of the system. Those demands became the hottest issue of the legislative session.[72]

Even more than black suffrage, nativism, and constitutional reform, the Anti-Rent issue divided progressive and conservative Whigs. To the latter the issue was one of law and order, the obligation of contracts, and the rights of property. Accession to Anti-Renter demands, one warned, would lead "to the utter over-throw of all social order, and the ruin of the whole social fabric." In contrast, the Seward-Weed-Greeley wing of the party regarded the rent arrangements as blatantly oppressive and unrepublican restrictions on economic freedom. But they were also mesmerized by the potential voting strength of the Anti-Renters, many of whom had customarily supported Democrats, especially since that vote could so easily be turned against Wright and the Democrats. Over the howls of his conservative editorial rivals, therefore, Greeley ardently championed the cause of the Anti-Renters in the columns of the *Tribune*, which circulated widely in upstate counties and had more influence on Whigs there than in New York City itself. He lavishly praised Whig legislators like Ira Harris of Albany and John Young of Livingston County for leading the fight on behalf of the Anti-Renters' agenda, studiously ignored votes by conservative Whig legislators against that agenda, and falsely blamed Democrats for killing those measures.[73]

By the fall, the factional dispute boiled down to the identity of the Whig gubernatorial nominee to be chosen by a September state convention. Led by

Webb, conservatives threatened to bolt the party if the nominee advocated Anti-Rentism, and they strenuously sought the nomination of Millard Fillmore, the unsuccessful Whig candidate in 1844, who had no ties to the Anti-Rent movement. As author of the Tariff of 1842, Fillmore, conservatives insisted, would be a perfect candidate in a campaign in which the tariff would be a major issue. Sewardite Whigs, on the other hand, wanted to exploit Anti-Renters' anger before it subsided, and they knew that Fillmore could never draw their support. Nor was Fillmore the kind of candidate Hunker Democrats could tolerate; instead, Hunkers would be determined to defeat such a prominent Whig partisan. Because Sewardites wanted to lure Anti-Renters and keep Hunkers at home, they wanted a more palatable candidate.

Instead of throwing their support to Ira Harris, the favorite of the avowed Anti-Renters at the state convention, they backed John Young, who won the nomination. Young was not a member of the tightly knit Seward-Weed clique within the Whig party, and they would eventually rue his selection. But in 1846, Young had the credentials they were looking for. Anti-Renters applauded his votes in the 1846 legislative session, and Hunkers accepted him. To soothe infuriated conservative Whigs and balance the ticket, they then nominated Hamilton Fish, a patrician from Manhattan who was regarded as a foe of Anti-Rentism, for lieutenant governor. Referring to the necessity of juggling the demands of Whigs, Hunkers, and Anti-Renters, Seward concluded, "Our ticket is formed so as neither to offend nor cement any one of three interests, either of which fully secured would give us success."[74]

Although New York Whigs' strategy for defeating the Democrats in 1846 concentrated on internal state affairs, they hardly neglected the national issues that were so prominent in Whig campaigns elsewhere. In addition to lambasting the state's Democrats for stopping canal construction, the address of the Whig state convention and resolutions of different Whig county conventions mainly flayed the Walker Tariff, the Independent Treasury Act, and the Mexican War. Yet the dominant Sewardite Whig leaders obviously regarded divisions within the state Democratic party and the unique Anti-Rent movement as the key to the campaign. Despite the Whig gains in congressional races, indeed, Young was the only candidate on the Whig state ticket to win because only he benefited from Hunker Democratic abstentions and additional Anti-Rent votes. Publicly in the columns of the *Tribune* Greeley trumpeted the results in New York and elsewhere as an outright repudiation of Polk and of the legislation recently passed by the Democratic Congress. Privately, however, he informed Henry Clay that Whigs had elected Young and as many as five congressmen only by capturing the Anti-Rent vote and capitalizing on the growing division between Hunker and Barnburner Democrats. Whether or not such favorable circumstances would ever exist again was unclear.[75]

Though extraordinarily convoluted, Whigs' 1846 campaign in New York was not atypical. In virtually every state, Whigs experienced the same interaction among factional jockeying for power, state issues, and the new national issues generated by Democrats in Washington. State issues and unique state conditions, for example, clearly influenced the outcome in Ohio, North Carolina, and Pennsylvania, as well as in New York. Factional rifts in the party also continued to widen in Massachusetts, Georgia, and elsewhere despite Whigs' success. Nowhere was the Whig party as united and secure as the 1846 results seemed to portend. The record of the Polk administration had indeed provided Whigs with remarkably potent ammunition. By itself, however, it did not guarantee future success, as perceptive Whigs should have known.

VIII

Instead, most Whigs interpreted the 1846 results as a repudiation of Polk's record and dreamed of riding continued attacks upon it into the White House in 1848. "Whiggism ascends," proclaimed one enthusiast. "The present administration are your best recruiting officers, tho' rather expensive." Marveling at the apparent Whig capture of the House of Representatives, a Georgian gushed to Thomas Butler King, "Did you ever see such a rapid and tremendous revolution?" Ohio's Whigs explicitly interpreted their victory as a repudiation of Polk's policies and predicted triumph in 1848 on those issues. The tariff, asserted Massachusetts Senator John Davis, explained the Whig sweep. "We have at last reached an open palpable issue which all can understand, the policy of the administration is enough to excite alarm without coonskins, hard cider, or even a song or a hurrah." Rather than diverting attention to potential Whig presidential nominees for 1848, Henry Clay concluded, "the public mind, I think, had better be left to the fully undisturbed, and undivided consideration of the disastrous measures of the last session of Congress."[76]

Utterly convinced that they could continue to win on economic issues, Whigs worried only that Webster might foolishly reintroduce his compromise tariff proposal when Congress met in December 1846 and thereby "produce the overthrow of that ascendancy which we are now gaining with the country and ought to preserve in 1848." Aware that Pennsylvania's Whigs believed they had "secured positive superiority . . . through the influence of the Tariff issue," Senator Davis assured Clay that he and other Massachusetts Whigs would not support Webster if he resubmitted the bill. Even Massachusetts manufacturers, who liked Webster's plan, would back a Whig platform demanding a complete return to the tariff of 1842. "If this is the best issue to keep before the public and the great end we have in view can be obtained by it then it is our best policy to adhere to it and I have no doubt Mass. will acquiesce in that policy." By the end of November, Whigs rejoiced that Webster had abandoned his scheme.[77]

Buoyed by the results of the 1846 elections and the apparent power of their new issues, Whigs who faced campaigns in 1847 were convinced that they could maintain the party's momentum into the presidential campaign itself. Virginia Congressman John Pendleton exulted, "For my part, I have never doubted since the new Tariff and the war, that the Whigs must carry the election the next time." Whoever the presidential candidate might be in 1848, he predicted, "we shall beat them and beat them badly." As early as August 1846, an excited Tennessee Whig had predicted that "from the signs of the times . . . the canvass next year will be the easiest one for the Whigs since 1840. We have them on the defensive now." By the end of the year, other Tennessee Whigs confidently anticipated victory in 1847 and 1848 because of disgust with Polk. So, too, did North Carolina's Whigs. Although their victory in the North Carolina gubernatorial election in August 1846 had resulted primarily from the unpopularity of the Democratic gubernatorial nominee and his vulnerability on the issue of state aid to railroads, the Whigs had also stressed the tariff in the campaign. In July of that year, moreover, one Tarheel Whig argued that "the war question properly managed may be made to break the Democrats." By January 1847, Whig Congressman Alfred Dockery was even more certain that anger at the war, hostility to territorial acquisition from Mexico, and the virtual certainty that the new tariff and subtreasury measures would bankrupt the government ensured Whig victories in that state's impending congressional elections. Convinced by defeats in 1845 and 1846 "that the majority of Ind. voters are against us" and that "we must avoid as much as possible all merely national politics," Indiana's Whigs also changed their tune dramatically as the August 1847 congressional elections approached. "Attack the Administration at every vulnerable point—upon the Oregon question—the veto of the River and Harbor bill—the subtreasury with a raking fire at the Mexican war," congressional candidate Richard W. Thompson was urged in July 1847. Thompson agreed: "If we can't sustain the issues on which we now stand—we are gone."[78]

Whigs' momentum did appear to continue into the spring and summer of 1847. In March, they almost captured the New Hampshire legislature, even while losing the governorship decisively. In April, they rebounded strongly in Connecticut, where once again they swept the state and congressional elections on the tariff and antiwar issues.[79] In Rhode Island, where the new national issues allowed them to campaign for governor as Whigs for the first time in three years, they amassed 57 percent of the vote and scored striking gains in the legislature, just as they did in Connecticut. Whig candidates also picked up five additional congressional seats in Virginia and made significant gains in the legislature for their strongest showing in the Old Dominion in years. In August they captured two new House seats in Indiana while winning a statewide majority of the vote, added three new congressmen in North Carolina, and recaptured the governorship of Tennessee.

Yet the ability of national issues to sustain the Whig comeback was apparently weakening even in these early elections, especially in the South. However impressive the Whig performance was in Virginia, for example, it still left them with only six of fifteen congressmen and less than a majority of the statewide popular vote in an election in which the Democrats had suffered far heavier drop-off than they did. Virginia Whigs, in short, had good reason to doubt their ability to carry the state on those issues in a presidential campaign. Kentucky's Whigs had increased their share of the vote statewide since 1845, but they lost two congressional seats and saw their majority in the legislature decline. Whigs probably gained congressional seats in North Carolina in 1847, moreover, just as they had in Georgia in 1846, as much because of a Whig-engineered reapportionment of the districts as because of the issues they raised.[80]

The results in Tennessee were equally ambiguous so far as the efficacy of the new national issues Whigs had been so confident of early in the year. Most Whig congressional candidates ran openly against the war and Polk's economic legislation, but the balance of Tennessee's congressional delegation remained exactly what it had been in 1845, six Democrats and five Whigs. Whig gubernatorial candidate Neill S. Brown eked out a narrow victory, but he shunned economic issues, refused to denounce the war, and instead lauded the war hero Zachary

Taylor, whom, he insisted, Whigs should nominate for president in 1848. His tactics, the stalemate in congressional races, and legislative losses by Whigs, like those in Kentucky, suggested that the crusade against Polk's record was losing steam.[81]

If the Whig tide crested in August, it ebbed markedly in the fall of 1847. In September, the Whigs' share of both the popular vote and legislative seats plummeted in Maine and declined in Vermont. Although Whigs carried Ohio and Massachusetts, both their vote and their share of legislative seats sank. They elected the state officers in New York and retained their large majority in the legislature, but only because of massive Democratic abstentions stemming from the Hunker-Barnburner feud. As the Whigs in New York well knew, their future there depended upon preventing the Democrats from reuniting.[82] Elsewhere the news was even grimmer. Georgia's Whigs continued to stumble in 1847. Their margin in the legislature declined, and they lost the governorship because they could not match the growing Democratic vote among nonslaveholders in north Georgia. Worst of all were the results from the Middle Atlantic states, where the Whigs continued to campaign hard on the tariff. Although they picked up two congressional seats and increased their legislative margin in Maryland, they lost the governorship, thus raising doubts about their ability to carry a statewide election. More telling, they lost the governorship and a significant number of legislative seats in both New Jersey and Pennsylvania, where the Native American party still siphoned off vital voters from them. In the fall of 1847, in sum, Whigs' prospects sagged most dramatically in precisely those states where one year earlier they had boasted that economic issues and hostility to the war could carry them to the White House.

Some historians have attributed this turnabout in Whig fortunes between 1846 and 1847 to a change in sentiment regarding the war. According to this interpretation, Whigs won in 1846 because of widespread hostility to the war, but in 1847, as Winfield Scott's army marched victoriously from Vera Cruz to Mexico City, prowar sentiment supposedly increased. Consequently, Whigs fell victim to Democratic charges that their antiwar fulminations were treasonous and were largely responsible for the unwillingness of Mexicans to surrender. Yet there is little evidence that prowar sentiment was greater in 1847 than in 1846 among Whig voters. Certainly, as will be further developed below, Whig politicians retained confidence that an antiwar stance could bring political victory. The reversal in Whig fortunes stemmed instead primarily from the temporarily reduced effectiveness of the Whig assault on the Democrats' economic program.[83]

IX

In November 1846, even as he exuberantly cheered the "tremendous revolution" in Whig fortunes, a Georgia Whig had worried that "the only fear is that the revolution has come too early, its effects may wear out before the next Presidential election."[84] Unfortunately for the Whigs, he was right. Whig campaigns in 1846 and the spring of 1847, when they made their biggest gains, had been based on predictions of what would happen under the Democratic economic program, not on its actual impact. Most of their triumphs and most of their boasting about the power of economic issues occurred before the economic legislation even went into effect. The Walker Tariff did not begin operation until December 1, 1846, and the Independent Treasury Act until January 1, 1847. Indeed, the requirement of the latter law that the government pay out only specie or Treasury notes was not implemented until April 1, 1847. What happened, simply, was that most Whig predictions turned out to be wrong. Despite the conviction of Whig politicians and businessmen alike that the economy would be plunged into disaster—and the private correspondence of Whigs establishes beyond cavil the sincerity of that belief—the nation instead prospered in 1847 and the Democrats reaped the benefit. They could and did say "I told you so," and thus they burst the Whig balloon.

Whigs' case against the Democratic economic program was internally coherent and powerful. By increasing imports, Whigs charged, the low Walker Tariff would propel gold out of the country to pay for them, a net drain on the economy that receipts from exports could never balance. Simultaneously, the Independent Treasury would remove government deposits from banks, reducing their gold reserves still further and quarantining huge sums of money from general economic activity. The inevitable result would be to dry up credit, which Whigs had always considered the vital lubricant that oiled the engine of economic growth. All would suffer, but manufacturers and their workers would be particularly damaged by the low *ad valorem* tariff duties and the public warehousing act that would allow foreign competitors to accumulate inventories on American shores and sell them only when profitable. Worse still, they charged, provisions of the Walker Tariff raising duties on raw materials used by American manufacturers would raise their production costs and render them even less competitive with foreign goods. In addition, Whigs predicted, the federal government itself would go bankrupt. Tariff revenues would decline just when the war required huge new expenditures. Nor could the government finance the war by bond sales since the hard-money clauses of the Independent Treasury Act required their purchase exclusively in gold, which bankers would no longer have in sufficient quantity. Workers, farmers, merchants, manufacturers, and the government itself would be prostrated.[85]

In 1847, however, almost every one of Whigs' predictions proved fallacious. Because of the Irish potato famine and crop failures in Europe at the end of 1846, foreign demand for American grain soared. As a result, the nation enjoyed its most favorable balance of trade in years. Gold and silver flowed into the economy from abroad in record amounts, eastern cities were awash in specie, and farmers earned unprecedented profits. Rather than hoarding its revenues in federal vaults, as Whigs had forecast, the government spent its money on war contracts, thus stimulating industries and recirculating revenues. Commerce, agriculture, and industry all flourished.

The forecast of government bankruptcy also went awry. Government revenues did decline, just as Whigs said they would, and so did the circulation of state bank notes. But the government ingeniously financed the war by selling short-term Treasury notes in small denominations, which could be used as currency. Because Treasury notes earned interest and could be used to pay tariff duties, businessmen demanded them. Bankers, profiting from the sale of Treasury notes, scrambled to handle the loans for which Walker allowed installment payments. The government, in short, pumped much more money into the economy than it took out. Instead of the shrunken money supply and sudden deflation Whigs had dreaded, the amount of circulating currency jumped sharply in 1847, wholesale prices rose, and prosperity prevailed.[86]

As the year 1847 progressed, Whig hopes of exploiting economic issues dimmed perceptibly. Because of increased grain exports, warned a Tennessee Whig congressman in February, "money will be plenty—the Banks easy—Treasury notes in demand and the people prosperous." Since Democrats would get the credit for good times, he glumly concluded, "the Whigs will have heavy work in Tennessee next summer." In the May issue of the *American Review*, a rueful Whig admitted that "all was prosperity, where, according to the apprehensions and predictions of the Whig party, all was to be untoward and disastrous." Galled beyond measure that Treasury notes had averted the currency contraction that implementation of the Independent Treasury Act should have produced, a frustrated Greeley howled that the " 'Independent Treasury' ragmill is at this moment aiding sensibly the general inflation of the currency" because it "vomits forth its promises to pay, of all shapes and sizes." In July a worried New Yorker on a business trip to Pennsylvania aptly summarized the party's dilemma:

> The famine in Europe has produced such an enormous rise in all grains and specie has flowed in on us to such an extent that they have drowned the effects of the Tariff of 46 and somewhat neutralized the effects of the Sub-Try. Besides the mania for Railways in Europe and this country has kept up the price of iron; and the war has called for such enormous supplies, of all its materials, and such immense expenditure of money, that almost every branch of business has been greatly stimulated. Thus, to the great mass, the country appears to be eminently prosperous.[87]

In April 1848, Congressman Meredith Gentry of Tennessee flatly told Webster that it would be a mistake for the Whigs to attempt to repeal the Walker Tariff. "A combination of circumstances at home and abroad has made it eminently successful as a revenue measure and less destructive to our home manufacturers than was anticipated." Because Democrats now had the advantage on economic issues, Gentry concluded, the Whigs' only chance of carrying the presidency in 1848 was to run Zachary Taylor.[88]

The changed perspective on which party benefited from economic issues is plainly revealed in the shifting emphases of the platforms on which they went to the voters. North Carolina's Whigs, for example, made the Walker Tariff and the Independent Treasury centerpieces of their attack during the gubernatorial election of 1846. In 1847, however, Whig congressional candidates campaigned primarily against the Mexican War and territorial acquisition, and the Whig state platform adopted in February 1848 explicitly tried to shift the focus from economic issues to the war. New York's Whigs abandoned economic issues entirely in their official address to voters in 1847, while Democrats continued to boast of the tariff and subtreasury. In 1846, 42 percent of the Whig address had been devoted to economic issues, but in 1847 it focused entirely on the war and slavery extension issues. Even in Pennsylvania, where Whigs continued to attack the Walker Tariff in their platforms of 1847 and 1848, Democrats, who had been grievously embarrassed by the issue in 1846, were defending it in 1847 and 1848 in both state platforms and local resolutions as "the most judicious and equitable that has ever been established."[89]

X

By the summer and fall of 1847, many Whig strategists had shifted their focus to Polk's conduct of the Mexican War and to opposing any territorial acquisition from it. At first blush, that issue too looked unpromising. Considerable evidence, ranging from high rates of volunteer enlistment to popular literature to the cult of hero worship that quickly exalted the names of courageous officers and enlisted men, all suggests that a majority of Americans enthusiastically approved of the nation's first war on foreign soil. Why, then, did Whigs deem opposition to the war a viable platform, especially when the Democrats, led by President Polk himself, continually excoriated them for giving aid and comfort to the enemy by their criticism?[90]

In brief, Whigs correctly recognized that what enthralled the general public about the war was neither its causes nor its possible consequences but the fighting itself and the feats of derring-do in the face of the enemy. Imbued with a romantic fascination with chivalry, martial skills, and foreign places, Americans in the 1840s hungered for military glory and military heroes to reassure them that they still possessed Revolutionary virtues.[91] Therefore, Whigs attempted to distinguish between Polk's culpability for causing the war, his mismanagement of it, and the unworthiness of his purposes, on the one hand, and the stirring activities of American armies on the battlefield, on the other. They focused their attack on incompetent and selfishly envious Democratic civilians in Washington, not on courageous soldiers at the front.

Throughout the war Whigs vilified Polk's ineptitude for prolonging the war and endangering American lives, and they lacerated as mean-spirited his efforts to monopolize credit for winning the war by advancing Democratic generals at the expense of Whigs. Throughout the war they warned of its mounting costs that burdened future generations with a huge debt, and in both December 1846 and December 1847 they hooted that Walker's request for a tax on coffee and tea revealed the bankruptcy of Democratic fiscal policies. Throughout the war they denounced Polk's executive tyranny, first for unconstitutionally provoking the war, then for establishing a tariff in occupied Mexican ports without consulting Congress, and then for ordering American military commanders to claim American jurisdiction in the Mexican provinces of New Mexico and California without congressional authorization. Yet at the same time that congressional Whigs, like the Whig press, vituperated virtually every aspect of Polk's conduct of the war, most continued to vote for the supplies, funds, and troops he needed to prosecute it and to boast that they were doing all they could to ensure the success of American armies.[92]

More important, almost from the moment the shooting started, Whigs attempted to appropriate the lion's share of the military glory that so dazzled the public. Although Zachary Taylor had never even voted, let alone attended a Whig gathering, the Whig press praised "the bravery of that old Whig General Taylor" and "the brilliant Whig achievements of Taylor" when word of his surprising victories at Palo Alto and Resaca de la Palma first reached the United States in late May 1846. Similarly, Whigs promptly labeled the war's first popular martyr, Major Samuel Ringgold, who was killed while directing artillery fire at Palo Alto, a "gallant Whig." Later in the war, when Taylor was publicly quarreling with the Polk administration, even Webster, who already worried about Taylor as a competitor for the presidency in 1848, insisted that the Whigs must take advantage of his popularity by placing "him in opposition to the Administration, not only as a *Whig*, but as a Whig attempted to be injured & kept down by Mr. Polk & Co."

With more justice, Whigs claimed the commanding general of the army, Winfield Scott, who had been mentioned as a Whig presidential possibility for 1848 since Clay's defeat, as an exemplary Whig patriot. They condemned Polk's efforts to keep him from command of the armies in Mexico and to replace him with Democrats like Thomas Hart Benton. And they later basked in the glory of his triumphant campaign from Vera Cruz to Mexico City. As early as June 2, 1846, finally, William E. Robinson or "Richelieu," the Washington correspondent of Greeley's stridently antiwar *New York Tribune*, sounded a refrain that Whigs would echo throughout the war. Only Whig blood and "Whig courage," he asserted, "could rescue the country from Loco-Foco mismanagement." The duplicitous and imbecile Polk administration had plunged Americans into a war it was unprepared to fight, "but they left it to the Whigs to get us out of it."[93]

Not all Whigs condoned this two-faced approach to the conflict. Led by Ohio's Joshua Giddings, the old champion of antislavery petitions, who in 1846 began to cooperate closely with the fervently antislavery Young Whigs of Massachusetts, a few northern Whig congressmen denounced the war from the outset as a southern conspiracy to spread the realm of slavery, flayed the hypocrisy of their Whig colleagues for speaking against the war while voting to support it, and steadfastly refused to vote for men and materiel. The fastest way to end an immoral war of aggression, they logically insisted, was to cut off the lifeblood of the invading armies so that they would be forced to withdraw from Mexico and disband. Even more notorious was the sensational antiwar speech of Ohio's Whig Senator Thomas Corwin, who was not a member of Giddings' clique of antislavery zealots. In February 1847, Corwin boldly proclaimed to a stunned Senate chamber, "If I were a Mexican, I would tell you, 'Have you not room in your own country to bury your dead men? If you come into mine we will greet you with bloody hands, and welcome you to hospitable graves!' "[94]

This dogmatic opposition to the war and the refusal to support American troops divided the Whigs in Congress and frayed tempers on both sides of the issue. It also divided Whig organizations in several northern states, especially Massachusetts. Young Whigs there pounced on the prowar votes of Boston Whig Congressman Robert C. Winthrop to skewer the regulars or Cotton Whigs who controlled the state party for supporting an immoral war to spread slavery and thus flouting the sentiments of Bay State Whigs.[95] Such extremism, however, remained a minor strain in the Whig chorus. On the whole, Whigs avoided being trapped in the unpatriotic posture of criticizing or undermining American armies in the field. In a war in which the two greatest commanders quarreled publicly with the Democratic administration and were extolled as Whigs, in a war in which sons of both Henry Clay and Daniel Webster died in uniform, the Whigs could successfully argue that they were doing more than their share to attain military victory while simultaneously reviling the war's origins and potential outcome.

For the first few months of the war, Whigs concentrated their fire on its unseemly origins. By the fall of 1846 and thereafter, however, they focused on its likely consequences. By then it was clear that Polk intended to seize New Mexico,

California, and possibly additional Mexican territory as an "indemnity" for American expenses in the war. Even in 1844 Whigs had outlined arguments against the dangers of territorial expansion, but they regarded acquisition by military conquest as particularly intolerable. America's mission, they iterated and reiterated, was to spread republican institutions by example, not by coercion. Forceful incorporation of territory into the United States against the will of its inhabitants violated the basic tenet of the Revolutionary experiment in self-government, government by consent of the governed. As Virginia's former Governor David Campbell fulminated to his nephew, "The administration's views on the subject of conquests & occupancy of the country are so wild and despotic and destructive of everything like republican government, that opposition must necessarily be provoked against every movement they make."[96] Just as Whigs insisted that opposition to territorial acquisition was necessary to save the republican principles of the Revolutionary Fathers, however, Democrats extolled it as spreading republican liberty to additional areas of the continent. Thus the battle over expansion became another chapter in the debate over which party better defended republicanism.

The Whigs also employed less exalted themes. Although prominent Whig editors and congressmen had renounced nativism and the drive to revise naturalization laws in early 1846, many Whigs played on Anglo-Saxon and Protestant biases to deter expansion. Reflecting an ethnocentric arrogance shared by most Americans, Whig papers and orators warned that annexing Mexican territory would add to the body politic an ignorant, slavish, superstitious, and mongrel race of Mexicans totally unfit for republican citizenship. As the staid *National Intelligencer* at the capital put it, "The weightier objection . . . is the annexation of a [morally degraded] people who are . . . unfit . . . to sustain a free government."[97]

More important, the coalescing of Whigs around the demand that no territory be taken as a consequence of the war represented a classic case of finding a position on an issue that simultaneously could preserve internal party unity and distinguish Whigs from Democrats. Since most Whigs were determined to share the credit for the military prosecution of the war, opposing acquisition became the simplest way for Whigs to differentiate themselves from Democrats once Polk made it clear that he would not stop the war without a territorial indemnity from the defeated foe. When Polk first made his territorial ambitions clear in August 1846, however, it initially appeared that the expansion issue would divide Whigs internally rather than unite them against the Democrats. The question of territorial acquisition immediately became entangled with the issue of slavery expansion into those territories, and even more than Texas annexation had in 1845, that issue ruptured the party along sectional lines.

XI

As soon as the war began, many northern Whigs and other antislavery groups in the North charged that Polk was acting on behalf of a southern or Slave Power conspiracy to gain additional territory for slavery. When Polk asked Congress for a $2 million appropriation to conduct negotiations with the Mexicans in August 1846, that charge gained credibility, for his intention to force Mexico to sell the

United States territory as the price of peace became clear. Northern Democrats feared that Polk's move would allow their Whig rivals to accuse them of supporting a southern-sponsored war for slavery extension. Those fears crystallized when Hugh White, a New York Whig congressman, demanded that Polk's appropriation bill "be so amended as to forever preclude the possibility of extending the limits of slavery." To prevent Whigs from preempting opposition to slavery expansion, to neutralize the expected Whig charge that they condoned it, and to vent anger at Polk and southern Democrats for their actions on Oregon, the tariff, the Rivers and Harbors veto, and patronage distribution, northern Democrats almost to a man voted for an amendment to the appropriation bill introduced by a thitherto obscure first-term Democratic congressman from Pennsylvania named David Wilmot. Thereafter renowned as the Wilmot Proviso, that amendment barred slavery from any territory to be acquired from Mexico as a result of the war.[98]

The amendment was adopted, and the bill then passed the House on virtually a strict sectional vote. Northern Democrats and all northern Whigs voted for it. Though the amended bill died in the Senate when the first session of the Twenty-Ninth Congress expired, the Wilmot Proviso would be reintroduced in subsequent sessions of Congress, and each time it came to a vote the same sectionally polarized pattern appeared. The Proviso undeniably split both parties along sectional lines.

Antislavery Whigs both in and outside Congress rejoiced at the introduction of Wilmot's Proviso and at the evidence of solid northern support for it. Greeley, for example, immediately endorsed it as *"a solemn declaration of the United North against the further extension of Slavery under the protection of our Flag,"* as did the leading Whig papers in Ohio, Indiana, Illinois, and other northern states. Polk, northern Whigs believed, had resurrected the slavery extension issue that had proved so beneficial to them in 1844 and 1845. Wilmot's Proviso had opened the eyes of Northerners, exulted Ohio's Columbus Delano, one of "the immortal fourteen" who had voted against the original troop authorizations. "The free states ought in my opinion now to take this position openly & avowedly 'Unyielding opposition to the acquisition of any territory by any means unless freedom is guaranteed & slavery prohibited; and like opposition to the admission of any further *slave state.*'"[99]

Despite the subsequent sectional rancor provoked by Wilmot's Proviso, there is little evidence that support for it played a significant role in northern Whig victories in the 1846 elections. Those contests revolved primarily around national economic issues and local concerns. In the fall of 1846 the Proviso still seemed a hypothetical issue. The outcome of the war, let alone the prospect of territorial acquisition from it, was still very much in doubt.

Equally important, perceptive northern Whigs immediately saw what few historians seem to have understood about the Proviso issue in 1846. Since both northern Democrats and northern Whigs had supported it, the Proviso did not offer a distinctive party stance on the war. It differentiated northern Whigs from Southerners of both parties, but not from their northern Democratic rivals. Where they did differ from northern Democrats was on the question of territorial expansion, not slavery extension, for northern Democrats pledged to support territorial acquisition from Mexico if slavery were prohibited from it, while northern

Whigs, as even men like Delano and Giddings admitted, were just as opposed.to territorial conquest as to slavery extension. To highlight that difference seemed to require shifting the issue from the Proviso to territorial acquisition itself.[100]

Developing a distinctive party stance and record on the war also required continued cooperation with southern Whigs, which could never be achieved on the Wilmot Proviso. To the dismay of extreme antislavery Whigs like Giddings and the Young Whigs of Massachusetts, most northern Whigs, like their southern colleagues, were primarily concerned in 1846 and 1847 with returning to power, not with venting sectional grievances. Although Whigs had made great gains in the congressional elections of 1846, control of the House depended upon the ninety seats to be contested in 1847, and most of those seats were in the South. Beyond that, of course, party unity would be necessary to carry the presidential election of 1848. The problem was not simply that the Proviso divided southern Whigs against northern Whigs. It was that opposition to the Proviso in the South, like support for it in the North, could not provide southern Whigs with a distinctive party position to run on in 1847 and 1848 because of the bipartisan sectional consensus against it. To compound the problem, southern Whigs were even more eager than their northern colleagues to demonstrate that they matched Democratic support for American armies in the field because enthusiasm about their exploits in battle was especially avid in the South. Just like northern Whigs, however, southern Whigs quickly realized that opposition to all territorial acquisition offered them a viable and distinct platform.[101]

To fathom southern Whig confidence in the issue, one must understand the reasons for southern opposition to the Proviso. Contrary to the accusations of northern antislavery men, there was no widespread southern conspiracy to spread slavery by attacking Mexico. Most southern Whigs and many southern Democrats, including John C. Calhoun, who joined Whigs in opposing a war of conquest against Mexico, believed and openly argued that slavery could not possibly exist in any territory to be acquired from it. Whatever the accuracy of that analysis—and it was undoubtedly wrong about California—for most Southerners the significance of the Proviso was symbolic, not substantive. They regarded it as a humiliating insult by the northern majority, a denial of the equal rights of white Southerners even when they had no intention of exercising those rights, and an attempt to subjugate Southerners to northern dictation, that is, as an attempt symbolically to reduce white Southerners to the status of slaves. Southerners who were particularly sensitive about defending their individual and collective honor and particularly fearful of enslavement to someone else's power refused to tolerate it. Some Southerners did indeed expect to carry slaves to acquisitions wrested from Mexico. But to most—and especially to most Whigs—Southern Rights, the defense of republican liberty and equality, were at stake, not the extension of slavery.[102]

Since more Southerners were interested in defeating the Proviso than in taking slaves into former Mexican territory, southern Whigs saw No Territory as a perfectly viable stance that distinguished them from southern Democrats, most of whom quickly embraced Polk's territorial ambitions. Thus, when the second session of the Twenty-Ninth Congress convened in December 1846, two Georgia Whigs, Berrien in the Senate and Alexander Stephens in the House, introduced amendments to appropriation bills stipulating that there should be no territorial acquisitions or cessions as a consequence of the war. Southern Whigs argued that since slavery could never be profitably implanted in any cession from Mexico, acquisition would eventually result in adding more free states to the Union even if the Proviso were not attached to it. Forcing a territorial cession from Mexico, indeed, would only ensure a northern effort to impose the galling Proviso on the South and thus provoke dangerous sectional antagonism. If no new territory were acquired, there would be no need for Northerners to inflict the hateful Proviso on the South.[103]

According to southern Whigs, No Territory offered the best hope of simultaneously stopping an immoral war of aggression by making its prolongation pointless, preserving sectional harmony in their party and nation, and protecting Southern Rights from attack. "Can a contest be imagined more frightful and furious than that which this very acquisition of Mexican Territory will excite between the North and South?" a Georgia Whig newspaper queried prophetically in the spring of 1847. "Nothing appears plainer to us than that the North is united on the Wilmot Proviso. The South is united against it. Hence rises a question of lurid and fearful portent." As Tennessee's William B. Campbell, himself a hero of the war, put it at the end of 1847, "The North have the power in Congress and if Mr. Polk gets territory by treaty, will it not be far worse for the South, and better that no territory had been acquired than that it should be admitted as free states. The South will be enclosed by a cordon of free states, which will diminish the value of slave property wherever it may be adjacent to free territory."[104]

At first, the North's most vehement antislavery Whigs viewed the No Territory resolutions offered by their southern colleagues in Congress simply as evidence of Southerners' fear that a united North could indeed impose the Proviso on them. Already convinced "that there can be no permanent *union* as a party between us & the slaveholders," Whigs like Giddings and his Massachusetts Young Whig allies protested "the great efforts . . . to change the issue from the Willmont Proviso [sic] to that of opposing the acquisition of territory." Scorning the conversion of northern Whigs to the No Territory position as "the truckling of doughfaces," Giddings fumed that "it is an insult to common sense to talk of opposing the acquisition of territory and at the same time continue the war."[105]

By the summer of 1847, the vast majority of northern and southern Whigs had nonetheless adopted that incongruous combination. Most northern Whigs joined their southern colleagues in unsuccessfully attempting to attach No Territory riders to appropriation bills in the winter of 1846–47. Once Congress adjourned, most northern Whig papers, even those that had previously endorsed the Proviso, took up the demand for No Territory. "We want no more territory, NEITHER WITH NOR WITHOUT THE WILMOT PROVISO," vowed the *Ohio State Journal* in April 1847, even though it had praised the Proviso the previous August. In a public letter to the voters of his southern Indiana congressional district in June 1847, Whig candidate Richard W. Thompson pledged that he would vote for the Proviso whenever it came before the House, but he insisted that rather than agitating for the Proviso, the Whigs should devote their energies to ending the war and stopping territorial expansion.

I think the Wilmot Proviso . . . was prematurely introduced—not because it asserts any principle which I do not approve, but because it agitates the country with a question not now legitimately before it. It assumes that a portion of Mexican Territory may be acquired by conquest. This admission I am not willing to make. That the present administration desires and designs to acquire territory by the war, I do not doubt, but I have yet seen nothing to satisfy me that the *people* of this Country will approve conduct so at war with the genius and spirit of our institutions. The elections which have taken place since the war began have proven the reverse.

Similarly, Corwin privately advised Thomas B. Stevenson, the editor of the *Cincinnati Atlas*, that insisting upon the Proviso was unnecessary. No Territory was the surest way to stop the spread of slavery, and he and other northern Whigs could always use the Wilmot Proviso as a fallback position if the calamity of territorial acquisition actually occurred. Until that time, opposition to any territorial indemnity from Mexico offered the best hope of gaining the necessary cooperation from southern Whigs and of contrasting the Whig position with that of the Democrats in both sections of the country.[106]

Northern Whigs continued to declare their steadfast opposition to slavery expansion, but they did not insist upon the Proviso as the only or even the most desirable method to stop it. The 1847 state platform of Pennsylvania's Whigs, for example, asserted that "if an addition to our territory be desirable, it should not be . . . attended with an extension of slavery." But it further asserted that "we believe that the interests of North and South, the welfare of the race, and the honor of the nation demand that territory should not be acquired for the purpose of an extension of slavery." Similarly, the state convention of New York's Whigs in October 1847 declared "their uncompromising hostility to the extension of Slavery into any territory now Free which may be hereafter acquired by the action of the Government of our Union." Ohio Whigs stated the party position most forthrightly in the state platform of January 1848: "We deprecate a war of conquest, and strenuously oppose the forcible acquisition of Mexican Territory; but, if additional territory be forced upon us, or acquired by the nation, we shall demand that there shall neither be slavery nor involuntary servitude therein, otherwise than for the punishment of a crime."[107]

Even Massachusetts Whigs seemed to swing into line behind the new position, if only grudgingly. Animosities between the Young Whigs and the party regulars or Cotton Whigs had steadily intensified since 1845. Originating in the division over the Young Whigs' diehard agitation of the anti-Texas issue in 1845, that conflict had focused on Winthrop's votes for war supplies in 1846. In 1847, the dispute shifted to the question of whether the party should make No Territory or the Proviso the centerpiece of its state platform. The state convention in September did iterate the party's customary firm hostility to slavery expansion, but it also endorsed Daniel Webster for president. Webster had been a proponent of No Territory since the winter of 1847, and in a speech to the Whig convention itself he openly defended No Territory as preferable to the Proviso as a means of stopping the spread of slavery.[108]

Perhaps even more important than official platforms in shifting the Whig appeal to No Territory were the editorial columns of Greeley's widely read *Tribune*.

In the fall of 1846, Greeley had called on a united North to rally behind the Proviso to demonstrate to the South its determination that slavery would never spread. By December 1847, however, Greeley candidly admitted that "thousands at the South resist and execrate the Wilmot Proviso . . . not because they really desire the Extension of Slavery, but because they view the proposition as need-lessly offensive and invidious toward the Slave States—as intended to fix a brand upon them." Since Southerners had no intention of spreading slavery, the North no longer needed to push the insulting Proviso. " 'No More Territory' we still think the simplest and safest solution of the impending difficulty; if the South will unite on that the whole danger will be averted."[109]

Obviously, one reason northern Whigs were promoting No Territory rather than the Proviso by the end of 1847 was concern about holding the party together for the impending presidential campaign. As Corwin wrote Kentucky's Crittenden in September, the Whigs would lose that contest if slavery extension rather than territorial expansion became the central issue.

> The Whigs of the South will not sustain any man, in favor of the Proviso, & the Whigs of the North will not vote for *any* man who is opposed to it. . . . Hence arises the great *necessity* of taking early and strong ground against any further acquisition, settle on *that*, & the Wilmot Proviso dies. . . . Whilst this would do *justice* to Mexico, it would restore comparative tranquility to us. It would preserve in its entire strength the Whig party.

Corwin and other leaders who sought party unity, in fact, were enormously pleased that, when the first session of the Thirtieth Congress opened in December 1847, northern and southern Whigs alike appeared determined to rally to the No Territory standard. Rather than driving southern Whigs away from their northern colleagues, the northern Whig platforms that threatened to impose the Proviso if territory were annexed had only increased the commitment of southern Whigs to the No Territory position. As Winthrop, who was elected Speaker of the House by the Whig majority, rejoiced in January 1848, "My view of the Wilmot Proviso has always been that its chief value was in creating an interest North and South against extending our Territory. If the North can be prevented from uniting in such extension for fear the new Territory should be slave & the South for fear it should be Free, we can put an end to all these projects of aggrandisement."[110]

XII

By the end of 1847, in fact, stopping Democratic "projects of aggrandisement" not only seemed more necessary than ever to most Whigs. No Territory also seemed to provide the best issue on which Whigs could win the elections of 1848. Winfield Scott's invading army captured Mexico City in September 1847, and the military phase of the war, the chief source of its popularity, was for all intents and purposes at an end. Americans, observers in both parties believed, now yearned for peace, but the stubborn, if vanquished, Mexicans refused to negotiate an end to hostilities. And they refused to make peace, Whigs repeatedly charged, only because they knew that Polk insisted on dismemberment of their nation.

"This question of Territorial Acquisition is that on which hinges the issue of Peace of War," intoned Greeley in November. "We should have had peace in September but for the inexorable determination of the Executive to acquire a large slice of Mexico by conquest." Until Polk was convinced to renounce his territorial ambitions by continued Whig success at the polls, Whigs asserted, the war would drag on with its staggering expense, its mountainous debt, and its appalling mortality rates as American soldiers continued to die from diseases contracted in their unsanitary encampments scattered across Mexico. Worse still, Whigs warned, the obsessive Polk and his Democratic toadies in Congress now meant to annex all of Mexico to bring the war to a close. That charge received apparent confirmation when Polk, in his annual message to Congress, asked for additional loans and ten more regiments of regular troops to continue the war and insisted that a territorial indemnity from Mexico was an indispensable condition for peace.[111]

Genuinely fearful that Polk intended to conquer all of Mexico and that the war would go on and on, Whigs also recognized that he had helped define the choice before voters exactly as they wanted it, just as he had done with his economic program in 1846. The question was not the Wilmot Proviso, which divided North from South. Rather, the issue was continued war and territorial acquisition versus peace and No Territory, an issue that clearly and sharply divided Whigs from Democrats. Because of war weariness and what seemed to them the palpable immorality and danger of the All Mexico movement, moreover, Whigs believed it was an issue on which they could win in 1848. Expressing "disgust and astonishment" at Polk's annual message, a Rome, Georgia, Whig informed Berrien in December, for example, "I do feel confident that any reasonable method which can be devised to put a stop to this game of blood and disgrace will be sustained by the people." Nor, he averred, was the prospect of territorial cession any more palatable to Georgians than a prolongation of the war. "The great majority of Whigs are opposed to the acquisition of territory in this section of Georgia. And the democracy have seen so little benefit accrue from the annexation of Texas that they are quite indifferent to the matter. I mean the masses." If Georgia, where Democrats had benefited more from the Texas annexation issue than in any other state in the Union, could be carried on a peace and No Territory platform, the future indeed seemed bright.[112]

Even before Polk's message to Congress, Greeley had evinced similar confidence that northern states could be carried on that platform in an extraordinary editorial assessing the contrasting results of the Ohio and Pennsylvania elections in 1847. The Whigs had won in Ohio and lost in Pennsylvania, he asserted, because they had forthrightly opposed the war and territorial conquest in the former while downplaying the war issue in favor of the tariff in the latter. Assailing the war had brought Whig voters to the polls in Ohio; failing to assail it vigorously enough had kept potential Whig voters away from the polls in Pennsylvania. What made this editorial extraordinary was not the accuracy of this contention, although Greeley undoubtedly believed it, but his explicit articulation of the values of the Whig electorate and of the need for concrete issue contrasts to mobilize them to vote.

"The simple truth," Greeley maintained, "is that the strength of the Whig party is its hold on the understandings of the intelligent, the sympathies of the humane, the consciences of the religious among our people. When this fails we are weak as water. We have not a blind, headlong, fiery mass who believe a thing right merely because we affirm it, or who vote and electioneer for whatever is put forth as the 'Regular Whig Ticket.' Unless there are in the issues presented or the contrasted character of the candidates strong moral reasons for preferring the success of our nominations," a very large portion of Whig supporters "will not come out to vote." It was up to Pennsylvania Whigs to mobilize those voters by opposing territorial conquest. Thousands of Pennsylvanians "will not only vote but work for the Whig candidates on the understanding that they thus vote for calling home our troops from Mexico and stopping the butchery going on there, who would not vote at all if they understood the Whigs to favor 'a more vigorous prosecution of the War,' until Mexico shall be thoroughly humbled." Pennsylvania, like the rest of the North, could thus be carried by a strong antiwar and antiexpansion stand.[113]

XIII

Despite the slowing of the Whigs' comeback effort in the fall elections of 1847 and the emergence of the sectionally divisive slavery extension issue, therefore, most Whigs remained optimistic about the party's prospects as the year 1848 began. Although the economic issues that had helped generate the triumphs of 1846 had lost salience, the Whigs had still recaptured control of the House of Representatives. More important, they had found a distinctive issue that could unite all Whigs, bridge the sectional chasm over the Wilmot Proviso by entirely avoiding that issue, mobilize Whig voters, and place the Democrats on the defensive. Whig politicians recognized and openly admitted in the winter of 1847–48 that the party was no more united than it had ever been on the question of voting against supplies to force an immediate cessation of the war and that most Whigs would probably continue to go along grudgingly with Polk's request.[114] Even that disarray did not dismay them, however, for it placed responsibility for ending the war on the Democratic commander-in-chief.

Given Polk's apparent determination to seize all of Mexico and the stubborn refusal of Mexicans to surrender on Polk's terms, the war could last another year. Whigs could thus make the presidential election itself a referendum on the issues of war or peace, All Mexico or No Territory. "The issue in the next campaign, presidential I mean, will be whether we shall annex the whole of Mexico or not," North Carolina Congressman David Outlaw wrote his wife in late January 1848. On February 9, Virginia's Alexander H. H. Stuart echoed that belief. The war would not be terminated, he predicted, "until the issue of 'Conquest' or 'no conquest' is fairly made and tried at the polls in the next presidential election."[115]

As in the off-year elections of 1846 and 1847, that is, Whigs at the beginning of 1848 expected to base the presidential election on a concrete issue over which the parties, rather than the sections, were divided. Once again they would ask voters to judge the record of Polk and his Democratic allies, who had proven to be such effective "recruiting officers" for the Whigs in 1846 and early 1847. In Whigs' minds, in short, the question was not whether they could win the presidency on issues or what those issues would be. Of that they were certain. Rather, the question in most Whigs' minds at the outset of the presidential year was something else, a question phrased succinctly by Connecticut's canny Truman Smith in a letter to William C. Rives in the fall of 1847. The Whig party, Smith insisted, had to find a way to "close this war without any considerable acquisition of territory." That could "only be done through the medium of the next Presidential election. The Whigs must succeed or all the evils of this war will be brought on the country. To do so we must have a proper candidate. Who shall he be?"[116]

Chapter 9

"The Contest for President Should Be Regarded as a Contest of Principles"

"THE WHIGS ADMIT that" the 1844 election "proved" that they could never "succeed of their own unassisted strength" and must "come into power, if at all," only "with the aid of Democratic votes as in 1840," jeered the notorious Rhode Island Democrat Thomas Dorr in January 1848. "Hence," Whigs sought "a *taking* candidate. A brave old soldier they think is the man for them." Many historians have echoed Dorr's charge that the Whigs' nomination of Zachary Taylor in 1848 was an act of desperation, a confession that they could not win on issues.[1]

Dorr's gibe, and the interpretation it prefigured, were in fact only partially accurate. By January 1848, Whig leaders, having squabbled about their nominee for three years, remained far from a consensus. By then most southern Whigs, like northern Whigs from strongly Democratic states, enthusiastically backed Taylor. Despising the war in which he gained fame, many Whigs, however, vehemently opposed him. Others adamantly rejected Taylor because they demanded a committed advocate of Whig programs. They objected to a candidate who, in Dorr's words, "has not made up his mind on any of the great questions of principle & policy that have so long divided the country." Only days after Dorr wrote, indeed, Rhode Island's Whigs officially endorsed Henry Clay for the nomination explicitly because he embodied Whig principles.[2]

Whigs, in short, did not rush en masse to seize Zachary Taylor as their savior. The shifting fortunes of Whig candidates in off-year elections, the aggravation of sectional animosity over slavery extension, state factional rivalries, and, above all else, the oscillating salience of issues all influenced the contest for the nomination. By June 1848, a majority of delegates at the Whig national convention believed that the party did need a "brave old soldier" to win. For a variety of reasons, Taylor was their preferred chieftain. But the choice followed a long and divisive struggle, the wounds of which festered long after the convention and the ensuing election. Opposition to Polk's administration united and strengthened the Whigs in 1846 and 1847. Conflict with the Democrats always did. The simultaneous struggle to choose a Whig candidate to replace Polk, in contrast, dangerously rent them. Since both a diminution of interparty conflict and the deepening of intraparty divisions would ultimately doom the Whig party, the preliminary skirmishing for the 1848 nomination therefore requires explication.

I

Jockeying for the 1848 presidential nomination began as soon as the polls closed in 1844. In the nineteenth century, seekers of the White House did not publicly announce their candidacy, as they do today. Openly to pursue a party's nomination for office, especially the presidency, was bad form. Instead, one supposedly waited for a call to serve from one's party. To make sure that call went to the right man, an aspirant and his friends worked to create support among party leaders, the press, and the rank and file that could produce a majority of delegates at the national convention. Although much of this maneuvering occurred behind the scenes, candidates' major instrument for influencing local leaders and voters was their public posture on contemporary issues.

Competition for the nomination therefore engendered divergent responses among Whig hopefuls and their backers to the issues that emerged between 1844 and 1848. Just as the Whig and Democratic parties took contrasting positions on issues to mobilize their respective electorates, contenders for the nomination had to differentiate themselves to court distinctive elements within the Whig coalition. For the same reasons, existing state factions backed rival candidates to best their intraparty foes for control of state organizations. From the beginning to the end of the long contest, the fundamental division was over what kind of candidate the Whigs needed to win: an orthodox regular like Clay, who championed Whig programs and who could rally the Whig faithful, or a new face, who might bring non-Whigs to the party column by soft-pedaling traditional Whig programs.

Even Clay's warmest admirers initially blanched at the thought of subjecting their beloved leader to the agony of another campaign. Clay, sixty-seven when 1844 ended, himself seemed finally ready to give up the chase. He never definitively refused to run again. But his remarks to Kentucky's Whig electors in December 1844 sounded like a valediction; he privately informed Crittenden that "my anxious desire is to remain during the remnant of my days in peace and retirement"; and his refusal to permit Kentucky's legislature to return him to the Senate reinforced that impression.[3]

Of other Whig regulars, Delaware's John M. Clayton, North Carolina's Willie P. Mangum, and Crittenden himself all drew early mention as possibilities. But the regular who first chased the prize was Clay's long-time rival, Daniel Webster. Himself sixty-two in 1844, Webster had never lost his hunger for the presidency and feared that 1848 might be his last opportunity. "Any other respectable Whig candidate would have recd. a large majority," he churlishly wrote shortly after Clay's defeat. "The Whig party is strong, but it wants good direction." Webster meant to provide that leadership himself. By orchestrating the Massachusetts anti-Texas movement and the drive for naturalization reform in the winter of 1844–45, he clearly sought to woo antislavery and nativist elements within the party.[4]

When economic issues became prominent in the summer of 1846, Webster tried to carve a distinctive stance with his abortive compromise tariff proposal. When his fellow Whigs insisted on a clear choice between the tariffs of 1842 and

1846—and once he was informed he might win the presidency by attacking the Walker Tariff—Webster abandoned his compromise in the next congressional session. Instead, to distinguish himself from other Whig protectionists, Webster began stressing internal improvements to exploit the angry reaction against Polk's veto of the 1846 Rivers and Harbors bill.[5]

Webster's response to the Mexican War also sought to maximize his Whig support. By a stroke of good fortune, he was attending the installation of his friend Everett as president of Harvard College when the Senate voted on the initial war appropriations bills in May 1846. Thus he escaped the wrath that militant antiwar Whigs, including Massachusetts' Young Whigs, heaped on his ally Winthrop for condoning the war. At first, Webster was content to join other Whigs in castigating Polk for unconstitutionally instigating an immoral act of aggression. Antislavery Whigs' enthusiastic response to the introduction of the Wilmot Proviso changed his calculations. Well aware that he needed southern as well as northern support to capture the nomination and win election, Webster from the beginning of 1847 advocated southern Whigs' No Territory position as an alternative to the Proviso while continuing to vote for troops and supplies.[6]

None of Webster's twistings and turnings advanced his candidacy very far. He had never developed a network of friends outside of New England, New York City, and Philadelphia who could organize a viable nationwide campaign.[7] In the fall of 1847, the Massachusetts Whig convention endorsed him, and Webster also locked up the delegates from his native New Hampshire. Elsewhere, Whig politicos resisted his charms. Since 1844, other names had evoked far more enthusiasm among party professionals.

Prior to the summer of 1846, the two front-runners for the nomination pursued decidedly different strategies than Webster. They contended that the party needed a fresh face and must spurn candidates who, like Webster and Clay, carried the baggage of National Republicanism. They and their boosters touted their appeal across party lines and their ability to bring non-Whigs to the party fold.

One was a man whose passion for the presidency had burned almost as long and torridly as Webster's: Associate Supreme Court Justice John McLean of Ohio. Postmaster general in the Monroe and Adams administrations, McLean had supported Jackson for president in 1828, and Jackson had appointed him to the Court in 1829. McLean had flirted with an Antimasonic candidacy in 1832 and was an early aspirant for the Whig nomination in 1836. Following McLean's cue, his supporters in New York, Pennsylvania, Ohio, and Indiana began to boom him in early 1845 as the champion of former Democrats in the Whig coalition.[8]

Sidelined from partisan politics since 1829 by his judgeship, McLean scorned a campaign based on specific Whig programs like Webster's. Instead, he appealed to residual antiparty sentiment among Whigs and especially to jealousy of National Republicans. McLean trumpeted himself as a foe of the corrupt spoilsmen and demagogues who controlled both major parties. As a reformer, he would restore the moral, "pure and elevated" nonpartisan statesmanship of Monroe's administration, when "the glory of our republic was at its height." McLean also boasted that his noninvolvement with traditional Whig issues would allow him to bring tens of thousands of moderate Democrats, Native Americans, Liberty men, and independents to his support. Posing as an outsider, a man above party and narrow partisan considerations who could restore a disinterested republican commitment to the common good, McLean hoped to avoid a national Whig convention and an exclusive Whig nomination. He relied instead on state and local endorsements to force regular Whig leaders to acquiesce in his candidacy.[9]

With his early support concentrated in the North, McLean needed southern followers to secure the nomination. His lieutenants like John B. Mower of New York City and the well-connected and seemingly ubiquitous Washington newspaper correspondent James E. Harvey therefore courted the influential Mangum by promising him the vice presidential candidacy on the McLean ticket. Some Tennessee Whigs like Milton Brown also leaned toward him because he had not opposed Texas' annexation. Meanwhile, McLean and his men targeted the group in the South most likely to respond to his antiparty appeal: the Virginia followers of William C. Rives, Conservative Democrats who had joined the Whig party only in 1840 and who saw themselves as the true guardians of the Jeffersonian Republican heritage of impartial government. Rives' closest supporters had bitterly complained after 1844 that "the Old Adams men," "the ultras who have blundered us into this miserable defeat will utterly ruin the party if the lead is not taken from them." Seeking to capitalize on this resentment, McLean wrote Rives in early 1846, lashing at "the hotheads and iron wills" who have "led the Whigs to defeat for many years past" and pontificating that "a victory on ultra ground can lead to no reform."[10]

McLean's effort suffered from fatal liabilities. He was a prominent Methodist layman, and his "Methodistical cant" caused Whigs, still spooked by memories of Frelinghuysen, to shun another "Psalm-singing Candidate."[11] Legions of Ohio Whigs reviled him, thus jeopardizing his command of his home state. His entire strategy was predicated on the obsolescence of traditional partisan issues and partisan asperities, a strategy that the issue-oriented state and congressional campaigns of 1846–47 negated. McLean admitted as much. While other Whigs credited their triumphs in 1846 to specific attacks on Polk's economic policies, McLean sourly continued to insist "that we should make as few issues as possible and that they should be general."[12] Most important, other possible candidates aroused more enthusiasm among Whig leaders.

At the beginning of 1846, McLean's chief rival was General Winfield Scott, whose battlefield heroics during the War of 1812 seemed more likely to broaden the Whig base than calls for nonpartisan government from the colorless jurist. Scott's name had been raised to the masthead of a few Ohio Whig papers even before 1844 ended. A November 1844 meeting of Philadelphia's Native Americans that boomed a Scott-McLean ticket for 1848 demonstrated the two men's relative appeal to nativists. "We go for success," Savannah's Thomas Butler King candidly told Scott in February 1845. "The people have shown, in all cases, their partiality for military men whenever they have been placed before them. All the civil merits of waggon bills and mill boys cannot give the eclat of a single victory on the battlefield." In March 1845, Ohio Senator Tom Corwin enthusiastically reported from Washington that Scott looked "ten feet high."[13]

The Whigs' dismal electoral performance in 1845 apparently convinced other Whig leaders that a military hero offered the only chance of success. Numerous observers reported in January 1846 that Senators Crittenden, Clayton, and Mangum, all mentioned themselves as potential nominees, had dined with Scott and pledged him their support, although the reports differed as to whether they favored Corwin or Crittenden for the vice presidency. Crittenden denied these rumors, but he admitted that Scott expected the nomination and that he fit the requirements Crittenden thought the Whigs needed, a candidate who would not reunite the feuding Democrats against him. "We all think that if we can be *wise* we can succeed in the next Presidential election." By common consent, Scott was the front-runner in the spring of 1846.[14]

II

The outbreak of war with Mexico in May, passage of Democrats' economic program in midsummer, and the introduction of the Wilmot Proviso in August 1846 rearranged the race. Scott's stock plummeted. In correspondence with Secretary of War William L. Marcy, explaining why he remained in Washington making necessary preparations rather than moving at once to the front to command American forces, Scott complained that he feared "a fire upon my rear, from Washington." In another communication he blurted that a note from Marcy had interrupted him just as he was taking "a hasty plate of soup." To embarrass the Whigs' front-runner, the Democratic administration released these letters to the press. Gleeful Democrats across the country pounced on Scott's unfortunate phraseology to mock him as the "soup candidate" and to joke about the mammoth 350-pounder's ample posterior. Overnight he became a national laughingstock. Perceptive Whigs quickly pronounced him "used up for the Presidentsy [sic]." "Gen. S. has made a fudy of himself," concluded a Massachusetts Whig. "I always thought him an ass, and am more & more convinced of it every day." Scott had "committed suicide on the point of a goose quill," summed up the *Boston Courier*.[15]

McLean initially benefited from Scott's blunders. His lieutenant John Teesdale edited the influential *Ohio State Journal* at Columbus, which began to promote him publicly in March 1846. During the summer his backers reported growing support in Pennsylvania, New York, New Jersey, and various New England states. A mass meeting in Pittsburgh formally launched his candidacy in January 1847, and many Whig congressmen formerly linked to Scott, like Mangum and Maryland's Reverdy Johnson, now scurried into McLean's camp. In late February, Seward informed Weed of the changing scene in Washington. McLean "is quite happy," Seward wrote. "Last Winter he was *alone*. Now he is manifestly the head of a party, and is visited, consulted and flattered as such."[16]

Even as McLean's optimism soared, however, events catapulted other contenders ahead of him. Taylor's initial victories at Palo Alto and Resaca de la Palma and again at Monterrey in September 1846 propeled him into the race as a popular hero who might replace the discredited Scott. Only after Taylor's apparently miraculous victory against overwhelming odds at Buena Vista in February 1847, however, did the Taylor boom achieve real power. Initially, other developments in the summer and fall of 1846 posed a greater challenge to McLean's hopes.

The Whig showing in the congressional and state elections of 1846 and early 1847 convinced many Whigs that the party could win the presidency in 1848 by denouncing the Walker Tariff, the Independent Treasury, Polk's veto of the Rivers and Harbors bill, and the war. Hence, an orthodox regular who championed Whig programs rather than an outsider like McLean or a military chieftain like Scott or Taylor seemed perfectly capable of leading the Whigs to the White House. Faith in the power of Whig issues caused some Whigs in the winter of 1846–47 to caution against the rush to McLean or any hasty nomination. Whigs should postpone all talk about their presidential candidate, urged Crittenden, and focus public attention instead upon "the conduct & measures of the present Administration which is now bringing down daily condemnation upon it, & the party that sustains it."[17]

Indiana's Whigs, upon whose support McLean counted, illustrate the thinking that stymied him. Throughout 1845 and most of 1846, Godlove Orth had bemoaned the disadvantages Hoosier Whigs suffered on both national and state issues. At one point he had insisted that "we must 'stoop to conquer' " and jettison "high-strung Whig doctrine." By February 1847, however, he argued that "upon a calm survey of the issues that must necessarily enter largely—yes almost exclusively into [the 1848 presidential] campaign," he concluded "that the result will be crowned with victory to the Whigs." Insisting that Whig principles were "well known and settled and defined," Orth stated his criteria for the Whig nominee three months later. "I want a man whom I know to be a Whig, who by a long life has shown his devotion to . . . our principles. The contest for President should be regarded as a contest of principles." "If you can't make prosolytes [sic]" by rehearsing Whig principles, another Indianan advised a Whig congressional candidate that year, "you can at least stimulate the Whig party and bring them out at the election." There it was! A campaign based on standard Whig issues aimed at drawing out the Whig faithful rather than making converts would doom the chances of men like McLean, Scott, and Taylor. It was a campaign designed for a regular candidate long identified with Whig programs.[18]

Such sentiments certainly quickened the pulses of those "who by a long life" had demonstrated their devotion to Whig principles. The Whig comeback in 1846, ostensibly on omnipotent economic issues, raised Webster's hopes.[19] It also recharged the ambition of Kentucky's great man, thereby thrilling his legion of loyalists around the country.

In the winter of 1846–47 Clay would not allow his friends to boom him as a candidate, but he carefully hinted at his possible availability. For the moment, Clay was content to await events and to disparage potential rivals in letters that poured forth from Ashland. To check McLean's issueless campaign, Clay insisted that it was far too soon for Whigs to be considering the presidency and that they should concentrate instead on the issues generated by the Democrats. To stifle Webster's budding candidacy, Clay cleverly concentrated on Webster's proposed compromise tariff in the summer of 1846. "As to the Tariff of 1846," Clay advised Pennsylvania's Whigs, who complained that the party's commitment to the Tariff of 1842 had been insufficiently explicit in 1844, "I think our true policy is to go for its repeal, and the restoration of the Tariff of 1842, and nothing else than the repeal of the one and the restoration of the other."[20]

Clay also adroitly played Taylor and Scott off against each other. In April 1847 he told Clayton, who had promoted Scott in early 1846, that he "decidedly prefer[red] Taylor to Scott." Yet a month later, after the news of Buena Vista had created a frenzy in Whig ranks, he informed his zealous backer Daniel Ullmann that attempts to bring Taylor out as a Whig candidate were premature. "There is much reason to hope that the Whig party may be able to elect any fair and honorable man they may choose to nominate." Lest this self-serving suggestion prove too subtle, Clay added, "Up to the battle of Buena Vista, I had reason to believe that there existed a fixed determination with the mass of the Whig party, throughout the United States, to bring me forward again." Besides, Clay predicted, Scott's military successes would undoubtedly cause some Whigs to prefer him to Taylor. "In the collisions which may arise," Clay cooed, "the Whig public may deem it wise and expedient finally to put aside both Generals, and select some civilian." Ullmann got the point. Clay should pretend not to be a candidate until Taylor and Scott killed each other off. *"Then go it with a vengeance."*[21]

The renewed salience of specific issues by the fall of 1846 also allowed McLean's Ohio foes to promote Tom Corwin, the state's junior United States senator, to block McLean's bid. Corwin possessed a number of assets. Although he had long been prominent in the state party, serving as governor from 1840 to 1842, he was new to the national scene and could thus be presented as a fresh face to those Whigs who considered Clay and Webster too old and too vulnerable. In contrast to McLean, Corwin had participated in the fight against the Polk administration. Although the freshman had remained largely silent during the busy 1846 Senate session, he was on record as joining his fellow Whigs to vote against Democratic measures and for the Rivers and Harbors bill. He had announced at the end of that session that the combination of those issues should provide midwestern Whigs with an invincible platform, and that fall he had campaigned across Ohio, flaying the Democrats on behalf of Whig congressional and legislative candidates. A vigorous and spellbinding orator at the age of fifty-two, Corwin was far more popular among Ohio's Whigs than the aloof and antiseptic McLean, who turned sixty-one in 1846.[22]

McLean's friends railed at Corwin's selfish ambition, but the Corwin boom seems to have originated not with Corwin personally, but with Ohio Whigs who despised McLean and feared that if he won the nomination, the national Whig party would not turn to another Ohioan as its nominee for a generation. Dayton's Congressman Robert C. Schenck spearheaded this effort. After Ohio Whigs' triumphs in 1846, Schenck wrote Thomas Butler King, a member of Truman Smith's national campaign committee, that the Whigs could easily win the presidency in 1848 on the same issues they had exploited that year. "Give us Corwin to fight for in 1848, & we'll tell the old story of 1840." Upon returning to Congress in December 1846, Schenck spread the word that McLean could never carry Ohio, while Corwin would sweep it.[23]

Corwin fanned this boomlet in February 1847 with his electrifying speech against the Mexican War and his vote against military supplies. Many Ohio Whigs in the House, including Schenck, had been among the "immortal fourteen" who had refused to vote for men and materiel in May 1846, and most Whigs in the state abhorred the conflict. By assuming national leadership of the antiwar movement, Corwin enormously increased his attractiveness to such men. By the end of February, Ohio's entire Whig congressional delegation boomed him, and the *Ohio State Journal*, no longer edited by McLean's friend Teesdale, declared that Corwin's speech would be "more read and more admired than any other made in Congress for twenty years past." Corwin's sudden fame won him backing outside of Ohio as well. The influential Greeley told several Whigs in the winter and spring of 1847 that he now favored Corwin for the nomination.[24]

Corwin's injection into the race infuriated McLean. What most galled McLean was that Corwin's emergence as the leading antiwar Whig forced him to abandon his calculated reticence on current affairs. Prior to Corwin's speech, McLean himself had privately counseled Whig congressmen to vote against all appropriations for the war.[25] After Corwin preempted the antiwar ground with his February speech, however, McLean wrote an editorial for the *Cincinnati Gazette* that bluntly questioned the patriotism of those who refused to vote for supplies, insisted that Congress had to support the army while the war lasted, and argued that Whigs must concentrate instead on preventing any territorial acquisition from Mexico. This stance offended Ohio's extreme antiwar Whigs but, as McLean informed Teesdale and Rives, it was the best way to win over Pennsylvania and southern Whigs who were adopting exactly that position in the winter of 1846–47. McLean, who had once trumpeted his ability to win over Liberty men, was thus forced to forsake the party's extreme antiwar and antislavery wing and to look for a different constituency.[26]

Antislavery Whigs' growing intransigence also affected calculations about the Whig nominee. Even in 1844 a few had vowed never again to vote for Clay or any other slaveholder. Their conviction that the Mexican War reflected a Slave Power plot to spread slavery, their disgust at Whigs who condoned sending supplies for a proslavery war, and their disdain for the attempt to substitute No Territory for the Wilmot Proviso only increased their demand for an openly antislavery Northerner as a presidential candidate in 1848. Neither Clay, Crittenden, Clayton, Mangum, Webster, nor McLean suited them. By the end of 1846 Massachusetts' Charles Sumner and his fellow Young Whig, Henry Wilson, predicted that they would have to combine with antislavery Democrats and Liberty men "who join in warfare with slavery & the 'Slave Power'" to run a separate northern candidate. "The free state Whigs must dictate the policy of the Party or the Party had better be defeated and broken up," insisted Wilson. The Whig candidate must be explicitly committed against slavery extension. "I for one had rather see the Party defeated than that we should succeed with any slaveholder or any Northern man with Southern principles."[27]

After Corwin delivered his thunderous antiwar speech, antislavery Whigs greeted him as a messiah. Here was the antiwar, antislavery, northern candidate they had prayed for! From the spring until the fall of 1847, antislavery Whigs in Ohio, Massachusetts, and elsewhere became the driving force behind the Corwin movement. What had begun as a stop-McLean tactic became a vehicle for northern resentment against slavery and slaveholders. To the dismay of older, more conservative Ohio Whigs, who insisted that the state party must await and abide by the decision of a national convention, local groups of younger Whigs in the Western Reserve, motivated by "hatred to the War," began booming Corwin for president in April 1847. The Corwin boom, Giddings explained, would increase "opposition to the war and slavery." Since Ohio's Whigs would never vote for a "slaveholder or supporter of the war," he added, "Corwin's early nomination may save us from defeat by preventing the nomination of a man on whom we cannot unite."[28]

New England's Young Whigs were said to be enraptured with Corwin's speech. "I hear it said all around that we must have him for our candidate," reported Wilson. Yet even as they rejoiced that Providence had given them Corwin as a leader, antislavery Whigs voiced doubts. For one thing, Corwin displayed no ambition to be president or to lead an antislavery phalanx. "You know, as I do, in spite of what the public supposes, Corwin is a *timid* man," Greeley advised Giddings. "I don't know anybody more afraid of getting his feet wet." More important, although Corwin had discharged a withering fusillade against the iniquity of the war and the rape of Mexican territory, he had said nothing about the Wilmot Proviso or slavery. "Tell him to come out strong in favor of the Wilmot Proviso," Wilson urged Giddings. "We can give him every state in New England if he will take the right ground against slavery." To these entreaties Giddings could only reply that he was sure Corwin would take "a correct position . . . in regard to slavery" at the next session of Congress in December.[29]

Corwin, in fact, was cut from far more conservative cloth than the antislavery Whigs who so exuberantly embraced him. He passionately opposed the war because he loved the Union, not because he hated slavery or because he yearned for the presidency. Just as Clay had warned in his Raleigh Letter of 1844 about Texas' annexation, Corwin wanted to end the war to avoid sectional conflict over slavery extension, not, as antislavery Whigs wished, to "make a direct issue with the South." Corwin made his position clear in a widely publicized speech at Carthage, Ohio, in September 1847. Criticizing abolitionists as provocateurs of sectional discord, Corwin condemned the Wilmot Proviso as a "dangerous question" and advocated instead that Congress pledge to take no territory from Mexico to prevent disruption of the Union. A few days later, in a letter meant for publication in the *Cincinnati Atlas*, Corwin complained that his speech had been misunderstood and that the Proviso must be adopted if new territory were acquired. Still, he averred, opposition to territorial acquisition was the best way to stop slavery expansion and preserve sectional harmony in the Whig party and the Union.[30]

Deeply disillusioned, antislavery Whigs in Massachusetts and Ohio abruptly jettisoned Corwin. By the end of 1847 they were talking more and more seriously about cutting loose from southern Whigs and launching a new, explicitly antislavery, northern party. The Corwin boom of 1847, nonetheless, had decisively altered the presidential race. His popularity in Ohio gravely challenged McLean's claims to be the state's favorite son. By smoking McLean out on the war, Corwin had also damaged the judge's prospects among antislavery Whigs in other northern states.[31]

Nor did McLean's attempt to offset the loss of antislavery men by courting southern Whigs bear fruit. While the Wilmot Proviso strengthened some Northerners' insistence that the candidate must not be a slaveholder, it also convinced many southern Whigs that he must be one. In the fall of 1846 Southerners largely ignored the Proviso, and the prominence of southern Whigs like Mangum and Reverdy Johnson in the McLean camp in early February 1847 reflected their belief, among other things, that the Whigs' next candidate should come from the North.[32] Yet the acerbic debates that followed the reintroduction of the Proviso in the second session of the Twenty-Ninth Congress changed many Southerners' minds. The turning point came on February 19, 1847, eight days after Corwin's oration against the war.

On that date Calhoun introduced into the Senate a series of resolutions denouncing any congressional legislation to bar slavery from the territories as an unconstitutional deprivation of Southerners' property rights and a humiliating violation of southern equality. Southerners' submission to Wilmot's Proviso, raged Calhoun, would acknowledge their inferiority to Northerners. "I would rather meet any extremity upon earth than to give up an inch of our equality," he thundered. "The surrender of life is nothing to sinking down into acknowledged inferiority." Georgia's Whig Governor George W. Crawford immediately recognized Calhoun's purpose. For twenty years, he correctly noted, Calhoun had been trying to break down party lines in the South in order to form a separate southern party to confront the North. His resolutions marked a renewal of that effort. Immediately after Congress adjourned, Calhoun, in an address at Charleston, openly called on Southerners to abandon the Whig and Democratic parties, shun their national conventions, and combine in a united front behind a proslavery presidential candidate to protect slavery and Southern Rights from northern aggression.[33]

Few southern Whigs believed that Calhoun could create a separate southern party, especially when the economic and war issues of 1846–47 had revived interparty animosities. Both Democratic and Whig papers, indeed, quickly denounced the notion as a product of Calhoun's unslaked ambition for the presidency. A few Whigs did fear that an independent Calhoun candidacy might cut into their southern electorate. What worried them far more, however, was that Calhoun had permanently changed the equation of presidential politics by focusing attention on the danger that the Proviso posed to slavery and Southern Rights. This fear was confirmed as early as May, when Democratic state conventions in Alabama and Georgia and prominent Democratic politicians and newspapers in Virginia, Mississippi, and Florida insisted that their party have a candidate who opposed the Proviso and who would protect Southern Rights. As in 1844, southern Whigs again faced the risk of being one-upped on the slavery issue.[34]

Even before southern Democrats threw down that gauntlet, William Ballard Preston, a Virginia Whig congressional candidate, warned Rives that Southerners would now demand a proslavery candidate who could avert "the impending danger" of sectional dissolution. "General Taylor beyond doubt is the man for the crisis. *He is sound on the slave question. He is not embarrassed by it.*" Taylor could prevent a sectional collision because "his claims address themselves to the patriotism, love, pride, gratitude of the land." Thus, "the South finds him the only man at their command whose position enables us to offer a candidate to the nation with the least hope of success."[35]

Sixteen months before the Whig national convention, Preston outlined southern Whigs' case for Taylor's nomination. As a planter who owned over 100 slaves in Louisiana and Mississippi, he was manifestly safe for the South; as a patriot and war hero, he was acceptable to the North. Taylor, in short, was advanced by Southerners not simply as a proslavery candidate but as the personification of nationalism, who—somehow—would heal the sectional rift unleashed by the Proviso.

Southern Whigs' insistence, as the *Florida Sentinel* put it, that "just as long as the Wilmot Proviso is an open question, WE ARE FOR A SOUTHERN MAN AND A SLAVEHOLDER FOR THE PRESIDENCY," obviously menaced the bid of the Ohioan McLean. Just as Corwin was outflanking McLean among northern antiwar, antislavery Whigs, Taylor seemed capable of outflanking him among proslavery Whigs in the South. And McLean knew it. By the end of April 1847 the frustrated judge complained that Taylor "is rallied upon by a set of politicians determined to give ascendancy to the South, and to advance themselves. They expect to control the administration."[36]

III

Doubt that the Whigs could win the presidency with a regular advocate of Whig economic policies played just as great a role in turning Whigs toward Rough and Ready as southern fears about the Proviso in the spring of 1847. Since Democrats would get credit for the prosperity produced by the unexpected grain sales abroad and by Walker's financing of the war, Tennessee Whig Congressman Meredith P. Gentry predicted in February 1847, Whigs must run Taylor in 1848. The general, he declared, could easily secure the Whig nomination "but for his negroes and cotton bales." Here then was a southern Whig who recognized that Taylor's slaveholding was as great a liability as an asset. He and other Whigs wanted Taylor because changed economic conditions had undermined an issue-oriented campaign.[37]

The most important convert was Crittenden, who began to act as Taylor's unofficial campaign manager. Long an acolyte of Clay, Crittenden took seriously Clay's intention to retire from political life after 1844. Dismayed by the dismal Whig performance in 1845, Crittenden had joined other congressional Whigs in promoting Scott, but unlike them, he had studiously kept his distance from the McLean boomlet in the winter of 1846–47 in the temporary hope that the party could exploit the issues generated by the Democrats. By the spring of 1847 he had abandoned that hope and turned instead to Taylor.[38]

In part, personal considerations shaped Crittenden's shift of allegiance. Though born in Virginia, Taylor was raised in Kentucky, where Crittenden befriended him. Crittenden's first wife was Taylor's cousin, and his son served on Taylor's staff in Mexico. Crittenden corresponded regularly with the general during the war, and it was apparently he who finally persuaded Taylor to toss his hat into the ring.

In letters to Crittenden and others throughout 1846 Taylor adamantly refused to be a candidate, despite the popularity his early victories had won him. Citing his total lack of experience in civil affairs and partisan politics, he insisted that "under no circumstances have I any aspirations for the office" and hoped Clay or Crittenden would be the nominee. During the winter of 1846–47, however, Taylor grew increasingly embittered at the Polk administration and at Scott, and the thought that some Democrat or Scott himself might win the presidency in 1848 because the Whigs proved unable to unite behind a viable candidate enraged him. Thus, when Crittenden obliquely suggested in March 1847 that Taylor could vindicate his reputation in the political arena, Taylor responded in May that while he still preferred "some able & tried Whig, . . . if my friends deem it for the good of the country that I be a candidate . . . be it so."[39]

Beyond personal intimacy, Crittenden turned to Taylor rather than McLean in the spring of 1847 because Taylor possessed what the Ohioan only aspired to— demonstrable appeal across party lines because of his military exploits. Taylor won his greatest victory at precisely the same time that Calhoun sought to unite Southerners in defense of Southern Rights, and martial glory was obviously the chief source of Taylor's appeal. On February 23, 1847, four days after Calhoun introduced his anti-Proviso resolutions in the Senate, Taylor gained a stunning triumph against a much larger Mexican force at Buena Vista. Even though the skill and vigor of Taylor's subordinates, rather than Taylor's generalship, produced the victory, Taylor got the credit.[40] As word of the triumph spread from the Mississippi Valley to the Atlantic Coast in late March and early April, a volcano of enthusiasm erupted for its supposed author. Scores of mass meetings quickly proclaimed Taylor as the people's choice for president, and newspapers of every partisan description began to boom him.

Taylor's meteoric ascent astounded Whig and Democratic politicians alike. Worried friends of other aspirants like McLean and Webster described it as a fever or contagion that must be allowed to run its course. Less biased observers saw an irresistible tide carrying the general toward an inevitable electoral triumph. Two days after reading about the battle, the shrewd Weed wrote, "If Gen. Taylor's life should be spared, he will be our next President. Circumstances over which no man, or class of men, have control, will produce this result."[41]

To a great extent, the Taylor boom of 1847 was spontaneous and nonpartisan. To be sure, some Whigs immediately grabbed for the hero's coattails to exploit his popularity for their party's advantage. Yet for most of 1847 they had no monopoly on his name and prestige. Democrats across the country also rushed to take up the Hero of Buena Vista despite warnings from the Democratic press that nothing was known about his principles. Editors of the Washington Union, the administration organ at the capital, spoke in May of nominating Taylor before the Whigs did because they feared that "nothing but death can prevent Taylor from being our next President." Calhoun's closest followers among southern Democrats, despairing of a separate southern party, urged Calhoun instead to organize "a new National Republican party" behind Taylor's candidacy. If the slaveholding statesman had made too many enemies among both Whigs and Democrats to unite Southerners across party lines, they reasoned, the slaveholding general without political baggage might banish "Whiggery and democracy both . . . from the South." Nativists also claimed Taylor as one of their own, and in September 1847 the national convention of the Pennsylvania-based Native American party recommended him as the "People's Candidate for President." Similarly, many of the mass meetings that mushroomed in the spring and summer of 1847 promoted Taylor as a "People's" or "No Party" candidate rather than as a Whig, Democrat, or Native American.[42]

The attempt to portray Taylor as a nonpartisan, even antiparty, people's candidate ultimately proved to be his campaign's most important aspect. Different men with different motives arrived at that strategy simultaneously. In part, the "No Party" label reflected the determination of genuinely nonpartisan mass meetings to prevent the major parties, which had thitherto controlled the presidency, from denying Taylor the office. To some extent as well, it represented a device by dissident Democrats and Whigs to outflank their intraparty rivals who controlled the regular party machinery and to use Taylor's popularity to capture control of state organizations. In Kentucky, for example, at the same time that Crittenden's lieutenants tried to mobilize Whigs for Taylor, long-time Whig foes of both Clay and Crittenden like Thomas F. Marshall, Robert and Charles Wick-liffe, Ben Hardin, and John Helm organized No Party Taylor meetings to neutralize the regular Whig apparatus that their foes dominated. More important, men who stood outside both major parties seized on the enthusiasm for Taylor as a weapon to smash the monopolistic grip they held on the political life of the nation. The public was disgusted with both the Whigs and the Democrats, declared the *Cincinnati Signal* in an open letter to Taylor in May. It was time for someone to "take independent ground and become president of the people!"[43]

Disparate groups could seize upon Taylor as a potential candidate because he utterly lacked political experience. He had never voted, let alone participated in the activities of any party. Before the Mexican War elevated him to prominence, even his military career had been obscure. In short, he seemed eminently malleable. What people learned of Taylor from newspaper accounts made him appear a perfect choice. He was unpretentious, plainspoken, and plain-dressed—in contrast to the pompous Scott—courageous, and unflappable in the face of the enemy. Taylor thus seemed to embody the virtue and genius of the mythical republican citizen who in time of crisis heroically sprang to the defense of his country.[44] That the Buena Vista battle began on February 22 had extraordinary symbolic significance. Here was a new Cincinnatus, a man who, like the revered Washington, stood above party, a man without personal ambition dedicated to the common good, a man who indeed might be able to restore the glories of the early republic.

Conceiving of himself as nonpartisan, Taylor personally fomented the People's or No Party campaign. Various contemporaries and a number of subsequent historians considered Taylor a babe in the political woods, a hopelessly ignorant and unskilled amateur. Yet the tactics he pursued in 1847 and 1848 and the views he expressed in his private correspondence reveal instead a shrewd political observer with a keen understanding of how he could win the election.[45] Taylor's ideas and strategy were strikingly similar to those of McLean, and they strikingly foreshadowed his postelection agenda.

Throughout 1847 Taylor carefully fostered his image as a No Party man, as a true republican who put the public interest ahead of party goals. He cheerfully accepted nominations from any group that tendered them—Whigs, Democrats, nativists, Calhounites, and independents—"as long," he wrote, "as they continue[d] to use [his name] independent of party distinctions." Both in his private correspondence and in letters published in newspapers across the country, Taylor repeatedly and emphatically insisted that "in no case can I permit myself to be a candidate of any party, or yield myself to any party schemes." Just as McLean had earlier, he declared that while he would accept spontaneous support from the people, he could never acquiesce in his selection by a formal national party convention. It would be an enormous mistake for the Whigs even to hold a national convention, Taylor warned Crittenden and others. As an independent "People's" candidate, he could garner the support of a "strong party of Whigs, Democrats, & Natives." By arousing the mutual animosity between Whigs and Democrats, a convention nomination would also destroy Taylor's "hope of allaying party asperity which has been carried much to [sic] far, for the interest of the country, & the well being of society."[46]

Taylor's attitude toward the presidency and traditional partisan issues also paralleled McLean's. "Although a Whig I do not wish or intend to be a party president in the strict sense of the term if elected," he promised Crittenden in December 1847. "Our affairs ought & must be so managed that the honor & offices of the country could be equally distributed according to numbers among the Whigs, Democrats, & natives." Taylor was equally indifferent to programs Whigs had long considered vital. Publicly, he was artfully ambiguous, refusing to answer queries about his views on banking, the tariff, and internal improvements. Privately, he was more forthright. The idea of a national bank "is dead, & will not be revived in my time." In the future the tariff "will be increased only for revenue"; in other words, Whig hopes of restoring the protective tariff of 1842 were vain. There would never again be surplus federal funds from public land sales to distribute to the states, and internal improvements "will go on in spite of presidential vetoes." In a few words, that is, Taylor pronounced an epitaph for the entire Whig economic program. Such issues, "which have divided the two great parties, Whigs and Democrats," he maintained, should "for the most part be considered as settled at any rate for many years to come, if not by the act of limitation at least by common consent." Thus he scorned the "rabid politicians on both sides [who] hold on to the whole of them with greatest tenacity, and enter their discussion when generally acknowledged to be dead, with the same warmth and zeal, as if the existence of the union depended on their doing so."[47]

Taylor's repeated rejection of party ties, his palpable appeal across party lines, and the possibility that he might indeed win the presidency without the official blessing of either major party account for his attraction to many of the elements that initially boomed him. Patently, the tiny Native American party had no chance of electing a president unless it could break the major parties' lock on most voters. Similarly, Calhounites who saw "Party Organizations" as "the curse of the Union" believed that "Genl. Taylor is the best man to break up those long standing corrupt organizations, which have exercised more despotism over the citizen than ever existed under any other constitutional Government."[48] For the same reasons, Conservative Democratic followers of New York's Nathaniel P. Tallmadge and Virginia's Rives also quickly embraced Taylor as a true people's candidate, as "a Democratic-Republican of our school," as another George Washington who stood above the corrupt strife of parties.[49] The Conservative Democratic wing of the Virginia Whig party, urged William Ballard Preston, must ignore Clay's friends and organize the state for Taylor in order to "be in the van of this great popular, republican and virtuous movement which is to emancipate all from the excesses of party and relieve all from the fearful consequences which successful combinations for vicious party ends have brought upon the land."[50]

To less discontented Whigs, Taylor's nonpartisan appeal posed a dilemma. His obvious attractiveness to non-Whigs thrilled those who, by the spring of 1847, despaired of winning on economic issues or without the help of defecting Democrats. Such men eagerly promoted him as the Whig nominee. In addition to Crittenden's activities in Kentucky, for example, John Pendleton Kennedy worked to have Maryland's state central committee and state convention endorse Taylor in July 1847. Enthusiasm for Taylor "springs from *spontaneous combustion*, and will sweep all before it," Kennedy explained. "We are anxious therefore to place the General in the Whig ranks, and to show that with whatever evil designs Locofocoism *invented* this war, the Whigs have *executed* it with imperishable honor to themselves." Georgia's Alexander H. Stephens arranged for Georgia's state Whig convention in June to nominate Taylor. Like other southern Whigs, he wanted a slaveholding candidate, but he also sought to exploit Taylor's martial luster to cut into the growing Democratic vote among nonslaveholders in north-western Georgia. Yet Stephens also hoped to upstage his intraparty rival Berrien, who continued to favor Clay and deplored "the rage" for "military candidates." Neill S. Brown, the Whig gubernatorial candidate in Tennessee, also promoted Taylor for president in the summer of 1847 to attach military glamor to the Whig cause. For the same reason, the entire Whig delegation to the Illinois state con-stitutional convention that summer endorsed the hero, as had a mass meeting of Iowa Whigs. Undeterred by Taylor's unconventional views, such men wanted a winner regardless of the potential consequences for the Whig party.[51]

Taylor's refusal to commit himself exclusively to a Whig nomination, his ap-parent ignorance of Whig principles, and his preference for a nonpartisan admin-istration of government, however, aroused visceral suspicions among many Whigs. Still haunted by memories of Tyler, they feared they might be buying a pig in a poke. As more and more letters from Taylor appeared during the summer of 1847, more and more Whigs declared their unwillingness to sacrifice everything the Whig party stood for merely to achieve victory behind an announced No Party man. The party, they insisted, must nominate a certifiable Whig.

Rival candidates and their partisans agitated much of this backlash to slow Taylor's accelerating bandwagon. "We want no 'no party' candidate," declared the pro-Scott Harrisburg *Pennsylvania Telegraph*. Clay loyalists, who viewed sup-port for the Kentuckian "to be a duty growing out of *fidelity* to Whig principles," especially fumed at the Taylor boom. Whigs needed a candidate "thoroughly and publicly committed to Whig principles and Whig policy," insisted Virginia's John Minor Botts. Taylor's refusal to accept a convention nomination was outrageous. "If we were to vote for Genl. Taylor on the terms he proposes we could only do so by a disorganization of the Whig party." North Carolina's pro-Clay Whig Congressman David Outlaw chorused the same refrain: "The Whig party cannot without disgrace or dishonor" run any candidate other than an "avowed Whig."[52]

Distrust of Taylor's no-convention, no-party, no-issue posture extended be-yond jealous rivals. Still uncommitted Whigs, especially in the North, voiced similar reservations. To gain northern Whig support, Tennessee's Senator John Bell admitted in December 1847, Taylor must declare unequivocally that he was a Whig and would accept the nomination from a Whig convention. Even that would not be enough for most northern Whigs. "*I go for no man blind*," declared Indiana's Godlove Orth. Taylor must openly endorse Whig principles. Three-fourths of northern Whig congressmen, Indiana Congressman Caleb Smith re-ported from Washington in early 1848, believed "that Genl. Taylor cannot be run with the least prospect of success in the North, if he shall adhere to his present position of declining to give his opinions. The idea of running him as a 'No Party candidate' is out of the question." Taylor's "nomination and election," unaccom-panied by his "unqualified" commitment to Whigs' "known & universally ac-knowledged principles," echoed Buffalo Congressman Nathan K. Hall, "would end in the annihilation of the Whig party." Infuriated by Taylor's acceptance of the Native American nomination in early 1848, Cincinnati editor Thomas B. Steven-son, who ten months earlier had endorsed the general, was even more emphatic. "If we don't get a true blue nominated by the N[ational] Conv[ention]," he exclaimed, "I am for making organizations all over the north, to beat Taylor, believing that next to the success of our principles, that is the best thing we can do."[53]

Northern Whigs opposed Taylor's nomination for three reasons. Even more than their southern colleagues, they were firmly committed to Whig economic programs and sincerely believed that the primary justification for the party's existence was to promote them. Throughout most of 1847 they were convinced that the Whigs could carry northern states with those issues, as they had in 1846. Willingly to abandon those principles for a noncommittal candidate thus struck them as outrageous and suicidal.

Outrage at the Mexican War as an immoral aggression was also especially widespread among northern Whig voters. Northern Whig politicians believed their antiwar constituents simply would not tolerate a candidate whose fame rested on his participation in that heinous invasion. Southern Whigs and prowar northern Whigs who gloried in the military heroics of the war were behind the Taylor candidacy, warned Ohio's Columbus Delano, and if he is run, "distraction, and in the free states, defeat awaits us." "The excitement for Taylor is all over, and I do not know a *single Whig* in this part of the state in his favor," echoed a western New York Whig in January 1848. As the odious war dragged on and as the prospect loomed that Democrats would demand all of Mexico, Taylor's refusal openly to espouse Whig principles appeared especially unconscionable to men from antiwar constituencies. Unless Taylor took "the 'No Territory' ground," unless he "avow his hostility to the prosecution of the Mexican War for the purposes of conquest," northern Whig after northern Whig affirmed, his nomination "would use us up in the northern states."[54]

Northern Whigs' deep hostility to slavery expansion also powered their insistence that Taylor openly renounce territorial acquisition. That some southern Whigs explicitly promoted Taylor because he was a large slaveholder virtually disqualified him for some. Personal hostility to slavery extension, resentment at an apparent southern attempt to dictate the nominee, and a conviction that their northern constituents would never abide a Whig candidate who favored slavery extension all turned them against him. Fervent antislavery Whigs like Henry Wilson and Charles Sumner of Massachusetts denounced Taylor's candidacy from the start and demanded that free state Whigs select their own candidate if Taylor secured the regular Whig nomination. Condemning "the *slave influence*" as unyielding, Charles Hudson of Massachusetts, who was not a Young Whig, snarled that "the southern Whigs want to go for Taylor on the ground of slavery, even if they knew it would break up the Whig party." Repeating Thomas Stevenson's May warning to Crittenden, Corwin iterated in September that Ohio Whigs would support no candidate who was not explicitly pledged against slavery in new territories. Taylor must publicly endorse the Wilmot Proviso to carry New York and other northern states, Greeley editorialized in his influential *New York Tribune*. By the fall of 1847, numerous observers reported that "antislavery sentiment is stronger than the appetite for warriors" among Whig voters in New England, New York, New Jersey, Pennsylvania, and Ohio.[55]

Had northern Whigs known what Taylor was privately writing to southern friends about the proper settlement of the war and slavery extension issues, their objections to his candidacy may have been mitigated. Taylor considered the sectional dispute over slavery the most dangerous issue that had ever threatened the Union, yet he also believed that the Wilmot Proviso was a gratuitous insult invented by agitators to array North against South. It was, concluded this veteran planter and slaveholder, wholly unnecessary. The parts of northern Mexico American armies had occupied were so barren that "no one will, while in his senses, carry his slaves there." Since Mexican law prohibited slavery in that territory and since Northerners in Congress would never tolerate the establishment of slavery there, the best settlement of the war would be to fix the Rio Grande River as the border of Texas and take no additional territory south of 36° 30'. In short, Taylor privately endorsed the southern Whig position of No Territory, which, by the end of 1847, many northern Whigs also embraced as the best way to stop slavery expansion and preserve sectional harmony.[56]

But these views had not been publicized, and northern enthusiasm for Taylor had palpably waned by the fall of 1847. "The Taylor stock is quite flat in this region," mourned a New York Taylor man in October. Taylor's decline raised the hope of other contenders like McLean, Corwin, and Webster. By the end of 1847, however, many northern Whigs were turning to yet another name to stop Taylor and capture the Whig nomination. Previously convinced of the inevitability of Taylor's nomination, New York's sagacious Seward and Weed now believed that Whigs would choose a man for whom they had never evinced much enthusiasm, a man whose closest New York supporters had long fought their control of the state Whig organization. The Whig ticket, Weed told Seward over dinner in October, would be Henry Clay for president and Seward himself for vice president.[57]

IV

Until midsummer of 1847, Clay kept a low political profile. Privately knifing other potential candidates and insisting that the party nominate "an unmistakeable [sic] Whig," he was genuinely reluctant to hazard another campaign.[58] Since 1845, he had repeatedly asserted that only a unanimous demand by the Whig party and a certain prospect of victory could induce him to run again. He well understood why his record as a three-time loser diminished confidence among Whigs that he could lead them to victory. Whig triumphs in the issue-oriented campaigns of 1846 and early 1847 dissipated much of his pessimism, but the apparent ebbing of the Whig tide in the summer of 1847 gave him pause. Furthermore, a prolonged period of mourning occasioned by the death of his son and namesake at the battle of Buena Vista precluded public speeches on current affairs that might signal his reentry into active political life.

Even during this period of quiescence, however, Clay positioned himself for another race by rectifying the weaknesses that were blamed for his downfall in 1844. Some of the reasons Whigs cited for that defeat, such as Democratic fraud, were beyond his personal power to remedy. Others, specifically the antagonism of immigrants and Catholics who believed that he had bargained with nativists, the "character issue" that had caused deeply religious Northerners to reject him as immoral, and his alienation of antislavery Whigs in the North by the Alabama letters, were attributable to the candidate himself. Clay clearly determined not to repeat those mistakes should he run again. Clay's whole effort for the Whig nomination in 1848, therefore, reversed his strategy of 1844. Where he had been portrayed as an ally of nativists, he would now pose as immigrants' friend. Where he had been smeared as a godless profligate, he would embrace organized Christianity. Where he had seemed to bend to the pressure of proslavery Southerners, he would now bid emphatically to antislavery Northerners. Only through such a dramatic reversal of tactics, in fact, could he hope to attract those elements of the Whig party most offended by the Taylor movement.

In the fall of 1844 Clay had welcomed, even if he had not blatantly courted, the support of American Republicans in the crucial states of New York and Pennsylvania. Immediately after that election, however, he had warned Whigs against merging with the nativist party, lest they mobilize still more immigrants against them. By 1847 he was ready publicly to erase any stigma of nativism still attached to him. In January, prior to his son's death, he made a speech at New Orleans calling on Americans to send relief to famine-plagued Ireland. In April, he firmly rejected an inquiry from Peter Sken Smith, Philadelphia's Native American leader, as to whether he would accept the organization's presidential nomination. Greeley later published that reply in the *Tribune* to contrast Clay's rebuff to the nativists with Taylor's willingness to accept their support.

After a Native American national convention recommended Taylor for the presidency in September, Clay intensified his bid to the nativists' targets. He privately asked Smith to return all letters he had written him in 1844 so that they could not be circulated against him in 1848. Then, in a public address in Lexington, Kentucky, in November primarily devoted to the Mexican War, Clay went out of his way to woo Catholics and immigrants. Comparing Mexico to "poor, gallant, generous, and oppressed Ireland," he called for harmony between Protestants and Catholics and boldly asserted that "no potentate in Europe, whatever his religion may be, [is] more enlightened or at this moment so interesting as the liberal head of the Papal See." The contrast with Taylor could not have been clearer.[59]

Even as Clay distanced himself from the most bigoted anti-Catholics, he reassured Protestants on the character issue that had haunted him throughout his public career. Personal tragedy, not cynical calculation, inspired his religious conversion. Forced to ponder the meaning of death by the loss of his son in Mexico, the grief-stricken seventy-year-old statesman was baptized into the Episcopal Church during a private ceremony at his Ashland estate in June 1847. Friendly Whig newspapers broadcast these tidings to the nation, and grateful Protestant clergymen congratulated him for finally becoming "a member of the visible Church of Christ."[60]

Clay's age itself, of course, had also seemed an obstacle precluding another race after his dispiriting defeat in 1844, but by the fall of 1847 he had dissipated some of the qualms it caused. In trips to New Orleans, Baton Rouge, and Mobile in the winter of the year, his excellent health and youthful appearance drew widespread comment. By the summer he himself was surprised at how good he felt, and on a widely reported trip to White Sulphur Springs and then via Baltimore and Philadelphia to Cape May, New Jersey, in July and August he dazzled onlookers with his vigor and stamina, animatedly greeting throngs of admirers for hour after hour at every stop and even frolicking with young women in the surf at the Jersey shore. Newspapers described him as looking forty-five or fifty, not a superannuated relic of the past. Even though he said absolutely nothing about public events on the trip, Clay's energy, elan, and palpable popularity convinced both his admirers and his rivals that he was still a viable candidate.[61]

As Clay made his way homeward in September, a number of Whig presses and public meetings in Ohio, Pennsylvania, and New York boomed him for the Whig nomination and demanded, contrary to the wishes of the Taylorites, that the Whigs hold a national convention to select their nominee. The most important convert to Clay's banner was Greeley, who for most of 1847 had favored Corwin for the nomination and who as late as April 24 had pronounced Clay "out of the question." "What man lives except Henry Clay whom any great proportion of the People really desire to see President?" Greeley asked in the *Tribune* on September 3. Later that fall, as enthusiasm for Corwin among northern antislavery Whigs waned, Greeley, who despised the thought of Taylor's nomination, embraced Clay as the best stop-Taylor candidate even more emphatically. Greeley's conversion, in turn, suggested that "Seward, Weed, Greeley & Co" were now willing to take up the Kentuckian.[62]

By the time Clay reached home on September 19, 1847, he was ready to run again, although he still refused to commit himself irrevocably to the race. The growing resistance to Taylor's nomination among northern Whigs, the widely expressed demand for a candidate committed to Whig principles, the warm reception he had received in the East, and the evidence of support elsewhere in the North revived his optimism that another effort could succeed. A letter to Ashland from Joseph L. White, a New York loyalist, complaining that press accounts indicated that Kentucky's Whigs preferred Taylor to Clay, spurred him to vindicate his status as chief of the state and national party. Above all, he considered Taylor unfit for the office. Like the supporters who beseeched him to run to reaffirm Whig principles, he feared that Taylor's nomination meant abdication of the policies and dissolution of the party he had worked so long to establish. He simply could not tolerate the idea that either he or his creation should be abandoned.[63]

Beginning in late September, Clay rapidly made preparations for his candidacy. After recalling his letters of 1844 from Peter Sken Smith, he attempted to neutralize the impression that Kentucky's Whigs were committed to Taylor. He wrote Crittenden that the organizers of Kentucky's Taylor meetings were his "personal enemies." He had still not decided whether to consent to the use of his name, he informed Crittenden, but he would "regret extremely any collision" between Taylor's friends and his own. The implication was clear: Clay expected Kentucky's Whigs, including Crittenden, to rally behind him should he enter the race. Then, in October, Judge George Robertson and other Clay men in Lexington sent a confidential printed circular to various Whig leaders around the country. Contending that the Taylor meetings in Kentucky had not been as numerous or as well attended as newspaper accounts indicated, it insisted that most Kentucky Whigs still preferred Clay. No direct evidence exists that Clay arranged this circular, but since it met so directly White's concern that Whigs elsewhere believed Kentucky had deserted him, it is difficult to believe he did not. "If the Whig party cannot elect him," Robertson later wrote Georgia's Berrien, "it can elect no one, *as a Whig.*"[64]

Even as he moved to hold Whigs in and outside of Kentucky behind him, Clay wrote to Taylor directly in late September, apparently to persuade the general not to stand in his way should he run again. "I fully agree with you in the necessity for more deliberation in the selection of a candidate for the presidency," Taylor replied on November 4. He added that he had written Crittenden "that I was ready to stand aside, if you or any other Whig were the choice of the party and that I sincerely hoped such might be their decision." He fully understood the importance of harmony within the party, "and whatever may be the decision of the party, I shall be studiously guarded in this particular, and strive to lend my best endeavor to the preservation of unity."[65]

Before Clay received this apparent pledge to step aside, which Taylor would subsequently renege on, he decided to make a public speech to reassert his leadership of the party. Although he continued to view Democrats' economic record as vulnerable, he understood that the prosperity of 1847 had temporarily neutralized attacks upon it.[66] Thus he chose to focus on the issues that most Whigs still believed could carry their party to the White House in 1848—opposition to the war and to territorial acquisition.

Clay, in fact, had to address those matters. Because many southern Whigs were already committed to Taylor, he could win the nomination only with solid support from northern Whigs, many of whom objected to Taylor precisely because he was Southerners' favorite. Clay knew that he was subject to many of the same reservations. The most fervent antislavery Whigs in the North adamantly vowed never to support a slaveholder again, yet Clay, like Taylor, owned slaves. More important, he knew that the vast majority of northern Whigs were committed against slavery expansion, that they insisted that no territory be acquired from Mexico, and that they demanded imposition of the Wilmot Proviso should a territorial cession materialize. Some of these Whigs could accept Taylor's ownership of slaves, but they could not condone his refusal publicly to endorse their No Territory platform. Clay had remained equally silent on the issue, and his commitment against slavery expansion was suspect because of his waffling on Texas' annexation in 1844. To capture the support he needed, Clay had to reassure northern Whigs that he stood with them.

If Clay had any doubts about the necessity of such a public declaration, an editorial in the militantly antislavery *Cleveland True Democrat*, that Clay must have read, given the tone of his subsequent address, dispelled them. Rejecting Greeley's September brief for Clay's candidacy, the *True Democrat* angrily insisted that Clay deserved defeat in 1844 because he had alienated antislavery Whigs with his Alabama letters. Those Whigs had no reason to trust Clay in 1848, it huffed. What had Clay done to secure emancipation in Kentucky? the paper demanded. "What has been his influence in respect to the Mexican War? The day is gone by when Mr. Clay can again receive the votes of Anti-Slavery men in the Whig party, unless he identifies himself, openly and boldly, with the cause of Liberty."[67]

Greeley, who had previously declared in the *Tribune* that Taylor must publicly endorse the Wilmot Proviso before northern Whigs could safely back him, was hard put to respond to this sally, but he tried in an editorial on October 11. Admitting that no candidate could succeed in the North unless he favored the Proviso, he weakly contended that any fair reading of Clay's Raleigh Letter showed that Clay opposed the extension of slavery to any territory thereafter acquired by the United States. The Raleigh Letter of April 1844, muddled as it was by the subsequent Alabama letters, however, hardly met the demands of antislavery Whigs in 1847. Greeley and Clay realized that more had to be done.[68]

Thus it was arranged that Clay would give an address on the war and slavery extension issues. The site was Lexington, Kentucky, but the intended audience was the northern Whig party. When Clay spoke in Lexington on November 13, Greeley had a reporter on hand who was instructed to ride eighty miles to Cincinnati immediately after the speech ended. From there, reports of it would be telegraphed via Pittsburgh and Philadelphia to New York City so that it, or at least the resolutions Clay had carefully written out for distribution, could be printed in the New York papers within twenty-four hours. Then Clay's New York friends would hold a mass rally, using his Lexington remarks as the platform on which to launch his candidacy.[69]

Clay aimed primarily at Northerners, yet he dared not embrace the Proviso itself, lest he completely alienate southern Whigs. Hence, he focused on the No Territory position around which Whigs from both sections had coalesced during 1847. But he took advanced antiwar, antislavery grounds that might appeal to frustrated northern Whigs. Rehearsing the traditional Whig charge that the war was caused by Texas' annexation and presidential aggression, he pointedly asserted that he (like the "immortal fourteen") would never have voted for the original appropriation, polluted as it was by Polk's fraudulent preamble that Mexico had initiated the conflict. He demanded that the House Whig majority in the impending Congress define the war's objectives precisely and stop it immediately if Polk continued to prosecute it for purposes beyond those objectives. Pointing to the dangers entailed in the acquisition of any or all of Mexico, he introduced resolutions declaring that we "are utterly opposed to any purpose like the annexation of Mexico to the United States" and that "we have no desire for the dismemberment of the Republic of Mexico, but wish only a just and proper fixation of the limits of Texas." After announcing that "I have ever regarded Slavery as a great evil" and reminding his audience that he had worked for gradual emancipation, in Kentucky and through the American Colonization Society, he came out squarely against war-induced slavery extension. In language that echoed virtually every 1847 northern Whig platform, his seventh resolution pledged:

> That we do positively and emphatically disclaim and disavow any wish or desire on our part, to acquire any foreign territory whatever, for the purpose of propagating Slavery, or of introducing slaves from the United States into such foreign territory.[70]

V

Determined that "the Whig party ought to take the ground he had assumed at Lexington," Clay intended his resolutions to provide the party platform on the war and territorial acquisition for 1848, just as he had intended the Raleigh Letter to provide the platform on Texas annexation in 1844. Whigs who had already taken that position were happy to chorus his strictures. Whig newspapers praised them; Whig state conventions in Indiana, Ohio, and North Carolina adopted strong antiwar, antiexpansion platforms in early 1848; and Georgia's Whig state legislators introduced resolutions on the war and territorial indemnity in December 1847 that, in the words of a Democrat, "occup[ied] pretty much the position of Mr. Clay in his late speech."[71]

Nonetheless, Clay's attempt to reassert his erstwhile command of the Whig party with the Lexington Address fell short. McLean men bitterly complained that Clay had stigmatized all Whigs who voted supplies and that his "anti-American" speech was "aiding and abeting [sic]" the Mexican enemy. In addition, key New York Whigs like Governor John Young and editor James Watson Webb accused Clay of aiding the enemy and blamed Mexico for starting the war.[72] More important, no consensus developed behind Clay's specific proposal that the new Whig House of Representatives pass a resolution or law to define the objectives of the war and to stop it immediately if Polk refused to abide by their actions. When the Thirtieth Congress assembled in December 1847, the Whig majority was at sea about the proper policy. Some wanted to press for immediate withdrawal of all troops from Mexico. Some opposed new appropriations but would remain silent about troop deployment. Others favored continued supplies for the armies already in Mexico, accompanied by a stipulation that Polk could not order conquest of additional territory. And still others, realistically recognizing that the Democratic Senate would kill any effort to force Polk's hand, admitted that the Whigs had no choice but to do what they had previously done—support the appropriations he requested but oppose the territorial indemnity he demanded. The selection by the Whig caucus and subsequent election of Robert C. Winthrop as Speaker of the House epitomized this last course and signaled that the Whig House would not attempt on its own to halt the war. Only the presidential election, most Whigs admitted, could settle the quesions of war or peace, All Mexico or No Territory.[73]

While many Whigs interpreted Clay's address as an announcement of his candidacy, it also failed to engender the unanimous support he had long stipulated as a precondition for another race. Instead, it established Clay as a leading alternative to Taylor, especially among regular Whigs. This development aggravated personal animosities between the backers of the two rivals and dramatically reinforced the sectional overtones of the struggle. By the end of 1847, what seemed to be at stake was not simply who the nominee would be but whether northern or southern Whigs would control the party.

By insisting in his Lexington Address that "every state has the supreme, uncontrolled and exclusive power to decide for itself whether slavery shall cease or continue within its limits, without any exterior intervention from any quarter" and by shunning the insulting Wilmot Proviso, Clay obviously hoped to retain the support of slave-state Whigs, especially the thousands of old-line Whigs who deeply distrusted Taylor's refusal to embrace the party or its principles. And he enjoyed some limited success. The *Louisville Journal*, Kentucky's chief Taylor newspaper, now conceded that a national convention must choose the Whig nominee; the *Vicksburg Whig* and *Mobile Advertiser* urged Clay's nomination. The intensely partisan wife of Gustavus Henry, a frequent Tennessee Whig presidential elector, pleaded with her husband to work for Clay against Taylor, railing that "Southern Whigs do not deserve the name if they desert him." Just as frequently, however, avowals of admiration for Clay's speech and preference for his candidacy were accompanied by admissions that he could not possibly win and that the party must thus turn elsewhere.[74]

Rather than reviving enthusiasm for Clay, the Lexington Address convinced many southern Whigs that Taylor was their only remaining hope. Clay's naked hunger for the presidency, his willingness, in the words of a scornful Alabama Democrat, to do *"anything* and *everything* that, by any manner of means, may lift him into the presidential saddle" had caused him "to conciliate the Wilmot Proviso men" of the North, thereby "driving off all the South." Southern Whigs not only concluded that Clay had "done himself great injury in his late speech," but they also feared that he had inflicted "much hurt" on all southern Whigs by discrediting their commitment to Southern Rights just when they were facing increasing pressure from southern Democrats and the independent Calhoun movement. "The Whigs will not rally on Mr. Clay, or *any* Whig who swears by his Lexington resolutions," reported an Alabama Democrat, an assessment that could have been extended across the South. "Depend upon it," the Georgian Charles Jenkins reported to John M. Berrien, an ardent Clay man, "unless the Whig party will take ground against the Wilmot Proviso, or present us a candidate above suspicion at the South, Georgia's Whigs will take this matter into their own hands" and select independent electors pledged to Taylor. Clay's "cause is hopeless at the South," he reported three months later. "His candidacy would crush the party in Georgia." "With Mr. Clay we should be in danger of losing all, with Taylor assured of gaining all," echoed North Carolina editor E. J. Hale.[75]

Northern Whigs' reaction, in contrast, was almost all Clay could have wished. As planned, Greeley immediately pronounced Clay the strongest potential candidate northern Whigs could back because his resolutions demonstrated "that the better portion of the South do not desire or expect an extension of our Slave Territory—that far from regarding Slavery as good . . . they profoundly realize that it is a formidable evil to be deplored, limited, and as soon as may be, exterminated." Other northern Whig papers rang changes on the same theme. Weed's *Albany Evening Journal* announced that the speech "settles the Presidential question," while New Jersey's Trenton *State Gazette* insisted that Clay must be "the standard bearer of the great Whig army in the coming battle." Mass meetings called by Clay-dominated Whig committees boomed Clay for president in New York City, Philadelphia, and elsewhere; Rhode Island's state convention formally instructed its delegates to the expected national convention to support him; and observers reported that the great majority of Whigs in Iowa, Indiana, and Connecticut preferred Clay's nomination.[76]

Not all northern Whigs, however, clambered aboard the Clay bandwagon. Supporters of Webster and Taylor remained firm. McLean's livid backers denounced "the 'glory' Whigs—the men 'who would sooner be defeated with Mr. Clay than succeed with anyone else' " and lambasted "the aristocratic, browbeating, dogmatical, selfish, dictatorial simpletons, called Clay Whigs, spread all over the United States." The rancor of McLean men plainly reflected their exasperation that the sudden rush to Clay, the ultimate party insider, seemed within a few weeks to demolish their three-year effort to persuade the party that it needed an outsider like the Ohioan. Yet it also sprang from a more general belief that "defeat will be the result of his [Clay's] nomination." The Kentuckian's age, his record as a loser—especially in 1844, when circumstances had seemed so advantageous— his lack of support in the South, and the near certainty that his nomination could reunite the feuding Democrats against him all convinced a number of Whigs across the North and border slave states that running Clay would be "folly and madness." "I am quite satisfied that Clay stands no chance of success," Buffalo Congressman Nathan K. Hall, like many others, concluded.[77]

Ominously, northern Whigs' biggest objection remained that Clay, like Taylor, was a slaveholder. If they were aware that Clay had infuriated southern Whigs with his remarks at Lexington, zealous antislavery men in Whig ranks were unimpressed. Nor did they buy editorial assertions that Clay had assumed satisfactory antislavery ground. To them, Clay's refusal explicitly to embrace Wilmot's Proviso meant that he could not be trusted as a northern champion against the southern drive for Taylor. "Mr. Clay's notices of slavery and the extension of slavery will not satisfy the North," Seward observed to his wife. More fervent antislavery Whigs like Charles Francis Adams and Giddings, convinced that either Clay or Taylor would get the nomination, now insisted upon preparing "the way for a separation from the Whig party" and for the organization of a new party that could unite all the North's principled antislavery men. Unhappiness with Clay convinced other northern Whigs "that we must have a Northern candidate as the South are bent upon rushing Taylor into the field."[78]

So grave did Clay's liabilities seem that some Whigs correctly suspected that Greeley and other northern Whigs were simply using him as a stalking horse to blunt the Taylor movement. Once Taylor was stopped, they predicted, Clay would be dropped, and some northern Whig like Corwin or McLean or even Scott taken up. Disappointed by his failure to evoke the unanimous support he had previously called a prerequisite, Clay, indeed, drew back from another campaign. Nor was Greeley fully committed to Clay's nomination. Both publicly and privately he admitted that his first objective was to stop Taylor. Clay was his first choice, he announced in the *Tribune*, but after Clay, he would take any civilian in preference to Taylor. Privately, Greeley told Clay himself two weeks after the Lexington Address that should Clay decline to run, he would throw his support to Corwin, and he repeated that determination to others. At the same time, he managed to convince some of McLean's friends in New York that he would back McLean, rather than Corwin, should Clay step down. Ultimately, McLean's New York friends concluded, the influential Weed and Greeley were playing a game to stop all the front-runners and arrange, somehow, for Seward to get the nomination.[79]

VI

By the end of 1847, when Truman Smith asked William C. Rives who would be the best Whig candidate to drive the Democrats from the White House, therefore, no agreement within the party had been reached.[80] Corwin, McLean, Webster, Clay, and Taylor all had proponents. Even the discredited Winfield Scott retained some backing, particularly in Pennsylvania. Yet each possible candidate had grave liabilities so far as many Whigs were concerned. Equally important, by the end of that year, no candidate had created an organization to secure the nomination. Throughout 1847 much speculation about the party's nominee had been voiced, and preferences had been advanced, often vociferously, for and against different men in both private correspondence and public print. Newspapers and letters could reflect and even shape public opinion, but efforts to do so, with a few exceptions like the arrangements for Clay's Lexington Address, had been largely diffuse and uncoordinated.

Public opinion, moreover, was a nebulous and volatile phenomenon that alone could bring about no specific results, despite the naive hopes of some that spontaneous public demands would determine the next president. Picking a presidential nominee required concrete action by specific political leaders. It required bringing public opinion to bear on the political elite who could effect a decision. It required organization of and action by those leaders, not just propaganda. At the end of 1847, little of this concrete work had been done, if only because the presidential election had seemed so distant and the political leaders who could make the choice had been preoccupied with trying to defeat Democrats in state and local races. Actions and events during 1848 would determine who won the Whig nomination.

If the identity of the eventual Whig nominee remained far from clear at the end of 1847, the basis on which all Whigs, including Southerners, intended to run their man was not. They still envisioned the presidential contest as a contest of principles. Specifically, they anticipated that the campaign against the Democrats would focus on the twin questions of war or peace, territorial acquisition or No Territory. They expected to best the Democrats by promising peace without the dismemberment of Mexico and a dangerous increase in American territory. Corwin, Webster, and Clay had all come out forthrightly against the war and a territorial indemnity. McLean would take a similar public stand in early 1848, as would Whig state conventions that met early in the year. Only Taylor's views on the proper resolution of the war were unknown, and his silence constituted one of his gravest liabilities. Many Whigs so hated the war that they rejected Taylor precisely because of his famous role in fighting it. Thomas Dorr's sneer in January 1848 that the Whigs opportunistically sought a "brave old solder" who was noncommittal on issues to attract Democrats grossly misrepresented the vast majority of Whigs at that time. Three weeks after Dorr penned his caustic analysis, indeed, Seward wrote Weed from his home what could have served as Whigs' retort to Dorr: "The war is so odious that no one in this region is thinking about Genl. Taylor as an available candidate."[81]

Chapter 10

"We Must Have the Aid of Gunpowder"

"PRESIDENT MAKING has commenced," Joshua R. Giddings reported from Washington in December 1847.[1] His verb was apt. Although much maneuvering and speculation about the Whig candidate had occurred since 1844, systematic efforts to secure the party's presidential nomination began only with the opening of the Thirtieth Congress.

Almost every event during 1847 that influenced opinion about the nomination—the news of Buena Vista and the subsequent Taylor frenzy, Scott's capture of Mexico City, the convergence of the Whig press and state platforms on the No Territory position, the up-and-down cycle of Whig fortunes in congressional and state elections, Clay's trip east in the summer and his Lexington Address in November—had occurred outside of Washington when Congress was not in session and Whig leaders were widely scattered around the country. Congress not only assembled when many Whig politicians first began seriously to focus on the presidential question, therefore. Its convening also provided the first chance since March 1847 for leading Whigs from different states and regions to meet face-to-face, compare notes, refine calculations, and directly confront opposing points of view.

The congregating of so many officeholders from different states also offered the first opportunity for congressional backers of rival candidates to organize cooperation across state lines and so convert opinion in the periphery. Washington thus became a magnet that attracted elected Whig officeholders, politically influential lawyers with Supreme Court cases like Clay and Seward, and the different aspirants' strategists. Clay men like Greeley and Daniel Ullmann, McLean's lieutenants James E. Harvey and Thomas Dowling, and even Zachary Taylor's brother Colonel Joseph Taylor converged on Washington to make the case for their favorites to the gathered Whig leadership. The ensuing dynamic of group interaction, with its incidents of harmony and friction, agreement and disagreement, fundamentally altered the struggle for the nomination.[2]

Ultimately, decisions at the periphery of the American political system, in states and localities that chose delegates to the Whigs' national convention, determined the outcome of the race. During the first three months of 1848, however, decisions made in Washington had the greatest impact. One of those decisions decisively changed Whig opinion and thus Whig behavior at the periphery; more than anything else, it brought about the nomination of Zachary Taylor. But as much as that outcome itself, the abrasive process by which it was reached opened wounds that debilitated the Whig party during its remaining lifetime.

I

Within two months of Congress' opening, the contest for the nomination had essentially narrowed to a two-man race. Whatever the doubts about Henry Clay's intentions and availability, and whatever solace those doubts gave other hopefuls, events in Washington during December and January convinced most Whigs that only Clay could stop Taylor and become the Whig nominee. After talking to a number of Whig congressmen while in Washington on legal business, Seward grudgingly admitted to his wife in late January that "the presidential canvass . . . seems now to be confined to Clay and Taylor."[3]

Only in December did most southern and northern Whig congressmen fully realize the depth, breadth, and intensity of Southerners' demand for Taylor and rejection of Clay as an apostate who had sacrificed slaveholders' interests and Southern Rights in his Lexington Address. To be sure, a few Southerners—Richmond Congressman John Minor Botts, Georgia's Berrien, Mangum, and several representatives from North Carolina—bravely professed their preference for Clay. Yet majority sentiment in every slave-state Whig delegation except North Carolina's favored Taylor. However strenuously Clay's southern supporters argued, they were effectively spiked among Southerners by the presence of Kentucky's Senator Crittenden and the majority of its Whig representatives. Despite their devotion to Clay, Robertson's secret circular of October, and Clay's warm reception in Lexington, they insisted, Taylor was the stronger even in Kentucky.[4]

Sentiment for Taylor did not spread solely over boarding-house dinner tables and in congressional lobbies. Early in December, seven particularly determined Whig members of the House set about in coordinated fashion to proselytize for Taylor and to commit Whigs from their home states to his nomination. Known as the Young Indians, this small group, which gradually expanded, cooperated with two other blocs of pro-Taylor leaders. The first was Crittenden and his Kentucky lieutenants Brown and Letcher, who had been organizing Kentucky for months, for Kentucky Whigs' preference had enormous influence among those elsewhere. The second was a small group of former Kentuckians living in New Orleans, headed by Albert T. Burnley, a wealthy businessman, and Alexander C. Bullitt, co-editor of the influential Whig *New Orleans Picayune*. In December, when Taylor triumphantly returned to Louisiana, they began in earnest to enlist southwestern Whigs behind his nomination. In Washington, nonetheless, the Young Indians constituted the most active Taylor force.[5]

Unlike the two groups of Kentuckians, the seven Young Indians had no personal ties to, or even a personal acquaintance with, Taylor. Nor did the reinforcing mechanisms of long friendship and common residence, except in Washington itself, bring them together, as it did the other groups. They came from four different states, North and South, and four of them were first-termers.

Five were Southerners—Georgia's congressional veterans Alexander Stephens and Robert Toombs, and three freshmen from Virginia, William Ballard Preston, John C. Pendleton, and Thomas Flournoy. Like most southern Whigs, all five deemed Clay an impossible burden for the party to carry in the South after his speech at Lexington, and they shared the faith that Taylor's credentials as a slaveholder could help protect the party from any imputation that it was unsafe on sectional issues. By itself, however, the slavery issue explains neither their opposition to Clay nor, more intriguingly, the unusual initiative that they, in contrast to other southern Whigs with similar attitudes, displayed in organizing Taylor's support. Like most southern (and northern) Whigs in December 1847, indeed, they still believed that they could use No Territory to avert the insulting Wilmot Proviso, that the war could continue indefinitely, and that the contrast between All Mexico and No Territory would be the central issue of the presidential contest. In sum, in December they, like most southern Whigs, still relied primarily on their platform, not their candidate's regional affiliation, to deal with the slavery extension issue. It cannot explain why they—and not other southern Whigs—became Young Indians.

All five, in fact, had committed against Clay and for Taylor months before Clay spoke at Lexington, when, if anything, Taylor's reliability seemed even more questionable than Clay's. In a widely recirculated letter to the *Cincinnati Signal* in June 1847, Taylor had carelessly given his "decided approval" to its earlier editorial that boomed him as a People's candidate for president while also insisting that Congress apply the Wilmot Proviso to any territory taken from Mexico and that the next president not veto such legislation. Many Whigs interpreted Taylor's letter as a flat endorsement of the Proviso.[6] What mattered most to the five southern Young Indians was the contrast between Clay's fame as "the embodiment of Whig principles" and Taylor's image as a nonpartisan military hero. Behind their choice lay calculations of intraparty factional advantage and interparty competitive needs that would eventually influence most delegates to the Whig national convention.

Toombs and Stephens, for example, were motivated in part by the resentment that they and other ambitious younger Georgia Whigs like William C. Dawson harbored against Berrien, whose insistance upon retaining his Senate seat blocked their own advancement. In 1845 they had forced the postponement of Berrien's reelection by stigmatizing him as unsafe on slavery by contrasting their support for Milton Brown's Texas annexation bill with his adamant opposition to it.[7] But their common support for No Territory in 1847 deprived them of issues to wield against Berrien's reelection in the November legislative session.

The party's presidential nomination was another matter. Berrien was a committed nationalist. His preference for Clay was well known, and, like Clay and Webster, he passionately opposed running soldiers as Whig candidates because it smacked of opportunistic Jacksonism. Since martial ardor and pride in the victorious American campaigns in Mexico were intense in Georgia, Stephens saw Berrien's stand as a potentially fatal blunder. To Berrien's dismay, Stephens skillfully arranged for the Whig state convention in June 1847 to recommend Taylor for president and to nominate Duncan Clinch, a foe of Berrien and a West Point graduate, who rose to the rank of brigadier general commanding troops against the Seminole Indians in the 1830s, for governor. By demonstrating that Berrien was out of step with Whig sentiment in Georgia, they hoped that Whig legislators elected on the same ticket as Clinch in October 1847 might refuse to reelect the obstinately old-fashioned senator. Had news of Clay's Lexington Address reached Milledgeville a few days earlier than it did, this tack may have succeeded, but Berrien was elected before the Whig legislators learned of it. Nonetheless, the same legislature endorsed Taylor for president, and the subsequent eruption of anger at Clay across Georgia caused Berrien's closest allies to warn him frantically to renounce the Kentuckian or suffer grievous consequences. To highlight their differences from Berrien, therefore, Stephens and Toombs became Young Indians when Congress met.[8]

As even Berrien recognized, however, Stephens and Toombs insisted on nominating military men in 1847 and 1848 primarily because they feared that the party could never carry the state legislature or governorship again without attracting Democratic support. Even in the congressional elections of 1846, when Whigs had joyously pilloried the record of Polk and the Democratic Congress, they had won less than 47 percent of the statewide vote. And the chief source of their weakness was clear to all—the seemingly unshakable grip Democrats had on the growing nonslaveholder vote in the Cherokee District of northwestern Georgia. Running military heroes appeared the easiest way to cut into that vote, and hence Whigs from northwestern Georgia clamored more vociferously than anyone else for Clinch's nomination in 1847. After his narrow defeat in October 1847, those same Whigs insisted that Taylor be the Whig nominee. Taylor was a more famous military hero than Clinch. His image as a No Party or People's candidate who repeatedly spurned a regular Whig nomination made him potentially far more attractive to Democrats than Clinch, who had served in Congress as a Whig. "Very many Whigs from the counties North & West say that we are down unless we hoist the Taylor flag," wrote one Georgia Whig. "Nothing can . . . save us but Genl. Taylor—nothing can destroy the Democracy but Genl. Taylor." Gaining control of a party that could not control the Georgia state government had little appeal for Stephens and Toombs. Thus they insisted on, and energetically worked for, Taylor's nomination in December 1847, not only to isolate Berrien but also to win crucial Democratic votes.[9]

Virginia's three Young Indians dearly hoped that Taylor would renounce Whig programs and run a nonpartisan administration, but the same combination of factional rivalry and Whigs' electoral weakness also turned them to Taylor. Whigs had never carried Virginia in a presidential election, and in May 1847 they elected only six of fifteen congressmen while failing to secure a majority of the statewide popular vote when Democratic abstentions were unusually numerous. To win, Virginia's Whigs needed to attract Democratic voters, and this consideration seems particularly to have influenced Thomas Flournoy, who won his congressional seat by a single vote, 650–649.[10]

The other two Virginians, Preston and Pendleton, more secure in their own districts, were Rives men who had long denounced the folly and arrogance of regular, or "ultra," Whigs like Botts, who insisted on emphasizing Whig economic programs and imposing old National Republicans like Clay on the party as its nominee. Unlike the Georgians, indeed, the Rives Whigs did not want to use Taylor's candidacy simply to best their intraparty rivals for control of the state Whig organization. They sought to replace the Whig party with a new organization dedicated to the nonpartisan, republican principles they associated with Jefferson, Madison, and Monroe. The Rives Whigs thus wanted to bypass a regular Whig national convention and to have the state Whig convention, scheduled for February 1848, "nominate Genl. Taylor, as the candidate of the true *Republican* party of the country, saying nothing of Whig economics." Pleading with Rives to write the convention's address, a Richmond editor urged him not to "make the favorite point of the ultras about the origin of the war . . . [and not to] put Genl. Taylor's nomination too exclusively upon the ground that he is *committed* to Whig doctrines," lest it "drive off the locos without some of whom we will probably fail." The Virginia Young Indians, in short, demanded Taylor's nomination to jettison Whig issues and transform the Whig party into something far more palatable.[11]

Antipathy to the Whig party and its programs decidedly did not motivate the two northern Young Indians. One was an obscure freshman congressman from Illinois, the legendary future president, Abraham Lincoln. In both 1840 and 1844 Lincoln had served as an at-large presidential elector for the Whigs, and he had crisscrossed the state ardently and eloquently defending specific Whig economic programs like a national bank, a protective tariff, and distribution of federal land revenues to the states. Few people in the party were so committed to its economic agenda as Lincoln, and Henry Clay had long been his model statesman. Nor, obviously, did Lincoln embrace Taylor because he was a large slaveholder who could protect southern Whigs on the slavery issue. Rather, Lincoln, the lone Whig representative from a heavily Democratic state, believed that only an apparently nonpartisan hero like Taylor could help Illinois Whigs attract the Democratic votes they needed to win additional congressional seats in August and perhaps even carry the state in the presidential contest itself.[12]

Sharing Lincoln's ardor for Whig programs, Connecticut's Truman Smith, the other northern Young Indian, exerted vastly more influence among congressional Whigs than the newcomer Lincoln. The unofficial national party chairman who had coordinated the successful congressional campaigns of 1846–47 and who would perform that same role in 1848, Smith initiated organization of the Young Indians. Unlike Lincoln and the five Southerners, Smith came from a safe Whig state that could be carried by a party regular on orthodox Whig issues. Connecticut had gone for Clay in 1844, the Whigs had won it handily in 1847, and they would do so again in April 1848 by running against the war, territorial annexation, and Democratic economic programs. Unlike the other Young Indians, who risked little at home by supporting Taylor, moreover, Smith defied the wishes of Connecticut Whigs, who decidedly preferred Clay. When Smith published an open letter in the *National Intelligencer* in support of Taylor's nomination, it met a stony reception in the land of steady habits. What moved Smith was his ability to look beyond the needs of Connecticut Whigs to the welfare of the national party as a whole. Certain that the Whigs must win the presidency to avert the pernicious consequences of the Mexican War and aware of the strong sentiment for Taylor in the South, he believed that the Whigs could not prevail with "any man from the free states." Both Clay and Taylor were Southerners, but the dismal performance of regular Whig candidates in Pennsylvania, New Jersey, and Maryland in the fall of 1847 convinced him that the former would not do. Explaining his preference for Taylor, Smith later wrote, "We are a minority party and cannot succeed unless we have a candidate who can command more votes than the party can give him."[13]

Most Whigs in Washington at the end of 1847 were less concerned with the Young Indians' motives than with their activity and effectiveness. "General Taylor seems as formidable now as Napoleon was when expected from Egypt," Seward reported to Weed on January 20. After being lobbied by the Young Indians, Buffalo Congressman Nathan K. Hall also surmised that "Genl. Taylor's chances of success are superior to those of any other candidate." Similarly, North Carolina's David Outlaw, a devoted Clay man, concluded after conversations with his colleagues that "Gen. Taylor is sweeping everything at the South & West, and I go for anybody rather than the present corrupt and unprincipled dynasty."[14]

Because of this aura of invincibility, when the Young Indians tried to enlist at least one Whig representative from every state, some Whigs eagerly boarded the Taylor bandwagon in order, as Hall put it, "to be known as one of his *early friends*." Most of these recruits were Southerners: Tennessee's Meredith P. Gentry, North Carolina's Daniel M. Barringer, Henry Hilliard and John Gayle of Alabama, Florida's E. Carrington Cabell, and others. A few Northerners also joined the Taylor congressional committee, notably Andrew Stewart of Pennsylvania, a renowned advocate of protective tariffs who sought the vice presidency on the Taylor ticket, and Indiana's George Dunn, who, like the Virginians, hoped to bypass a formal Whig nomination and to run Taylor as an independent People's candidate. Altogether, according to Lincoln, between forty and forty-five Whig representatives, including fifteen Northerners, were committed to Taylor by the end of February.[15]

The great majority of the numerically preponderant northern Whigs, nonetheless, regarded the Taylor committee as a southern effort to dictate the party's nominee, and they were infuriated by the tactics of the Taylor zealots. The original intention of the Taylor men—or at least some of them—was to stampede the congressional Whig party into endorsing Taylor on his chosen ground, as a No Party or People's candidate without a national convention or formal party nomination. This most Whigs refused to do. As a result, the Taylor men suffered a series of stunning setbacks in December and January. In late December, the Young Indians tried to arrange an open meeting of Whigs in Washington committed to Taylor's nomination as an independent. It failed completely because so many congressmen refused to attend and because those who did blocked its organization. This presumptuous effort convinced most Whigs that a national convention must choose the nominee and that they must stop Taylor unless he announced himself to be a Whig, openly committed himself to the Whig position against the war and territorial acquisition, and agreed to abide by the decision of the national convention, conditions that more moderate Taylor men like Truman Smith, Barringer, and Tennessee's John Bell had all along recognized must be met.[16]

This determination became clear when Taylor's supporters again tried to commit congressional Whigs to his candidacy without a formal convention nomination. At a Whig congressional caucus held on the night of January 27, fanatical Taylorites from Virginia and Tennessee, caustically dismissed as a "corporal's guard" by Outlaw, attempted to browbeat their colleagues by threatening that no Whig but Taylor could carry Alabama, Virginia, and Tennessee, that Whigs therefore must not risk the chance that a national convention might choose someone else, that southern Whigs would continue to back Taylor "on the noncommittal basis" even if a convention nominated someone else, and "that the Whigs of the North must consent to go for Taylor or be beaten." Outraged rather than intimidated by such blatant extortion, the Whigs voted by a four-to-one margin, with virtually all Northerners and half of the Southerners in the majority, to hold a national convention. A few days later, the caucus called it to meet in Philadelphia on June 7.[17]

II

Both inside and outside Washington, Whigs and Democrats alike interpreted the caucus' insistence upon a convention as a stinging rebuke to, and perhaps a decisive defeat for, Taylor's candidacy. Insiders chosen by regular Whig conventions, not outsiders, mass meetings, or newspaper editors, would select the Whig nominee. Party regulars might now pick one of their own. The northern Whig majority refused to be steamrolled by the party's southern minority. To the delight of suspicious Whigs and anxious Democrats, who "apprehended the greatest danger" from a No Party Taylor campaign, and to the dismay of original Taylor men, Whigs' decision indicated that Taylor would have to jettison his nonpartisan, noncommittal stance to obtain the nomination and thereby probably alienate those Democrats he had attracted with it. As the hostile Indianan Godlove Orth rejoiced, "I am truly glad to learn that the Whigs of the North take the noble stand of requiring Taylor to pass the ordeal of a National Convention & *to require an expression of his political opinions*. Those opinions must accord with the well known principles of the party."[18]

Fury at southern Taylorites' overbearing tactics increased most Whigs' antipathy toward a No Party Taylor candidacy. It also further convinced many Northerners that the party must nominate a committed Whig partisan. Anger at southern intimidation now caused some Northerners to insist that the nominee come from the North. Ironically, however, firsthand experience with southern vituperation of Clay as a traitor and toady to the North erased others' doubts that Clay had taken an adequate antislavery stance in his Lexington Address. Though a slaveholder himself, Clay now seemed perfectly acceptable to many Northerners.

Clay arrived in Washington to argue some Supreme Court cases on January 10, just when angry anti-Taylor Whigs were looking for an alternative. As he had during his trip east in the summer of 1847, Clay mesmerized the throngs who crowded around him with his physical vigor, his mental alertness, and his sparkling conversation. A disgusted Seward reported the fawning of sycophants who begged Clay to enter the race and the excitement he stirred among women in Washington's fashionable society: "That gentleman is bland and persuasive as ever, and one set of admirers only give place to another. Matrons save the gloves he has pressed for relics, and young ladies insist on kissing him in public assemblies." Yet as Seward also noted with alarm, something more occurred than an outpouring of adoration by the faithful. "The influences around him are irresistible and what is more his presence and conversation here are turning the tide of this place in his favor." What transpired, in other words, was a process of reciprocal conversion. Clay's warmest admirers convinced him that he had a chance finally to win the presidency and therefore must enter the race—or at least not publicly withdraw from it. They particularly stressed that northern Whigs would be ruined if Taylor were nominated and that only Clay's candidacy could save them. At the same time, Clay persuaded skeptics among the anti-Taylor men that he was physically and mentally sound enough to serve as president and that his opposition to slavery extension was firm.[19]

More than Clay's presence in the right place at the right time, his personal charm and the backlash against Taylor account for the gravitation of most congressional Whigs toward him. Almost all Whigs, including the Taylor men, still expected the impending presidential campaign to focus on the issues of the Mexican War and territorial acquisition from it. If they had any doubts, Polk's insistence upon a territorial indemnity in his annual message and his request for ten new regiments of regular army troops dispelled them. Most Whigs remained confident that they could win the election by adamantly opposing both. The centrality of the related war and expansion issues is why uncommitted Whigs insisted that Taylor take a stand on them. Anti-Taylor Whigs found Clay so appealing, moreover, because he had articulated the Whig position more forcefully than any other viable candidate. True, Corwin had denounced the war in even more sensational terms, but Corwin's early endorsement by extreme antislavery Whigs rendered him unacceptable to the South.

Clay's northern supporters never envisioned him as an exclusively sectional candidate. They recognized that they needed both southern and northern electoral votes to elect a Whig president, and neither Taylor nor Corwin, they feared, could attract both. Despite the heated rhetoric of southern Taylorites, they believed Clay could carry traditionial southern Whig strongholds on an antiwar, antiacquisition platform because virtually all southern Whigs had pledged themselves to that position. As long as the war continued, and as long as Whigs retained a hope of blocking a territorial cession and thereby avoiding the explosive Wilmot Proviso, Clay struck many Whigs as their strongest man.

Clay thus emerged as the chief stop-Taylor candidate by the end of January 1848, but his status rested largely on the continued salience of the war and expansion issues. Those issues formed Clay's greatest asset and Taylor's greatest weakness—at least from the standpoint of anti-Taylor Whigs. Even though the contest for the nomination had seemingly narrowed to a two-man race, therefore, it remained contingent upon events. As Godlove Orth accurately predicted even as he rejoiced that Taylor had apparently been stopped, "This Mexican War and its probable termination—and the consequences of such termination will all have an important bearing upon our candidate."[20]

III

Whigs' decision to hold a national convention and the concomitant emergence of Clay fundamentally changed the contest for the nomination. Although Taylor had been endorsed by numerous newspapers, mass meetings, Democratic and

Native American gatherings, state legislative resolutions, and even Whig state conventions, few delegates had been named or committed to him because the heterogeneous Taylor movement had sought his nomination by public acclamation. Now the specific politicos who went to Philadelphia, not puffery or even popularity, would determine the nominee. Even states that had previously nominated Taylor, like Maryland, Tennessee, and Georgia, were thus opened to competition, for different men than those who had earlier named Rough and Ready might choose the Whig delegates. The problem for the candidates and their friends now was to secure enough reliable delegates to control the June convention. Now, even though events in Washington would continue to exert a decisive influence on the race, the battleground shifted back to thirty states and the innumerable localities within them that could affect their ultimate decisions.

Developments in Maryland quickly demonstrated how the convention call changed the race for the nomination. Maryland's Whigs had nominated Taylor at their state convention in July 1847, and by the end of that year Maryland seemed as solidly in the Taylor column as the Deep South was. Senator Reverdy Johnson's faction of the Maryland party, known as the "Courthouse clique," led the Taylor Whigs in Maryland, and like some other Southerners, Johnson was intent upon running Taylor as an independent without a formal Whig nomination. Several days after the caucus on January 27, therefore, Johnson called in a Senate speech for Maryland's Whig state legislators to carry out their plans for selecting independent Taylor electors and to refuse to send delegates to the Whig national convention. Johnson's chief rival in the state Whig party, Maryland's other United States senator, James Pearce, responded by insisting that Maryland's Whigs adhere to regular party procedure. As a result of Pearce's speech and the pressure of his followers on the legislature, Whigs in Annapolis dropped plans for a Whig-sponsored independent nomination of Taylor and instead, on February 6, called for state and district Whig conventions to select delegates to the June convention. Eventually, indeed, those conventions would pledge their delegates to go for Clay as long as he had a chance to win the nomination.[21]

By early February, therefore, it was evident that Whig insiders would determine the nominee, that Taylor's momentum could be stopped, and that the race for delegates was wide open. The choice and behavior of delegates to the Philadelphia convention, in turn, resulted from the interaction of a number of variables: the nature of the delegate selection process in each state; the exertions of different candidates and their supporters; conflicting assessments by state and local Whig politicians as to which standard bearer could most help Whig candidates in local, state, and congressional races in 1848; intraparty factional rivalries like those that had brought about the Maryland reversal; and, above all else, events that changed the issues to be confronted in the election and thus impressions of the electability of different men.

Ironically, the process of delegate selection gave Taylor's supporters several advantages. Since each state had as many votes in a Whig national convention as it did electoral votes, the Constitution's three-fifths clause gave slave states more votes than their white population alone justified. Nor did Taylorites' edge end there. Most states sent a number of delegates equal to their assigned voting strength, but there was no requirement that they do so. Sometimes fewer delegates attended and cast a state's entire vote, whether or not they fully reflected

Whig sentiment in the state. Sometimes, as was the case with Louisiana and Indiana in 1848, more than the allotted number attended, and the delegates themselves determined who among them cast the state's votes. In those situations, a majority of delegates for one candidate could deny a state's delegates who favored someone else any vote at all on the convention floor. At Philadelphia, Taylor's friends would ruthlessly exploit both of those openings.

The use of the electoral-vote formula implied that each state would choose two delegates in some statewide body, who would be the equivalent of electors-at-large or senatorial delegates, and that the others would be chosen by separate congressional district conventions. But there was no requirement that state parties do so. As a result, practices varied from state to state. Many states, especially in the North, did hold separate state and district conventions, usually in that order, to pick delegates. Accustomed to holding their state conventions in September, New York's Whigs followed a variation on this practice, choosing the two statewide delegates at a Whig legislative caucus in Albany and leaving the choice of other delegates to district conventions to be held later. In contrast, many southern states and a few northern ones like Indiana, Iowa, and Rhode Island appointed all the delegates at a single state convention. Even then practices differed. Some state parties chose all delegates by a majority vote of the whole convention. Others chose the two senatorial delegates that way and then broke up into separate caucuses of members of the state convention from the individual congressional districts, who then chose the delegates from their own districts.

The differences in procedure were important. The more centralized the decision-making process, the easier it was for a single candidate to garner all the delegates; the more decentralized the process, the more difficult it was. Obviously, the dynamic of a state convention, where all delegates were chosen in a single place on a single day, differed considerably from that of picking the bulk of delegates at widely scattered district conventions held at different times. District conventions were less susceptible to majority sentiment statewide and more reflective of local preferences. District conventions held seriatim also rendered the choice of delegates more responsive to the shifting course of events. These customs were not written rules. They could be changed. Friends of a particular candidate who had a majority at a state convention could insist that it choose all the delegates and dispense with district conventions. That possibility ensured rancorous conflict at many state conventions. And since more southern than northern states picked all delegates at the state convention, the ability of Southerners to concentrate behind a single candidate was considerably greater than that of northern Whigs.[22]

Even the few state Whig conventions held in January prior to the call for a national convention illustrated the intense factional rivalries and the pattern of sectional polarization that would characterize the contest until June. In late January, for example, Rhode Island's state convention picked all four of the state's delegates and pledged them to Clay. A state convention in Iowa, on the other hand, appointed delegates who were instructed for Taylor, though Iowa's Clay Whigs complained that the convention was self-appointed and unrepresentative of Whig opinion. On January 27, the very day of the congressional caucus, Whig members of the Tennessee legislature, together with various Whig editors in Nashville, pronounced themselves the Whig state convention, nominated Taylor, and chose two at-large delegates pledged to him. They also called for district meetings to be held in May to select the state's other delegates, thus allowing Clay men in the state to battle for them. Intraparty factionalism shaped alignments on the nomination in Tennessee, as it did elsewhere, and Clay's supporters included John Bell's most prominent intraparty rivals: ex-Governor James C. Jones, ex-Senator Ephraim Foster, and Gustavus Henry. The influential Knoxville editor William G. "Parson" Brownlow, a partisan of Bell, also continued to support Clay. By the time district conventions met in May, however, issues had changed so substantially that the delegates chosen, like those in most other southern states, unanimously favored Taylor.[23]

Two large northern states also held conventions in January. At Indianapolis on January 12, some Indiana Whigs, led by John Defrees, editor of the influential Indianapolis *Indiana State Journal*, pressed the convention to choose delegates instructed for Taylor. But the majority, most of whom apparently favored Clay, defeated that effort. The convention thus chose uninstructed delegates to the anticipated national convention. Thus they remained vulnerable to changing events and to the lobbying of different candidates. No one could tell how Indiana delegates might vote at the convention.[24]

Neighboring Ohio sent the pivotal delegation to the Whig national convention, and, compared to Indiana, the struggle in the nation's third largest state assumed titanic proportions. Despite intense antislavery sentiment in northern Ohio, Taylor had some support, chiefly among conservative Whig followers of former United States Senator and Treasury Secretary Thomas Ewing. Clay had even more strength at the state convention. In the winter of 1847–48, however, the two largest factions within the Ohio Whig party backed the rival Ohioans Corwin and McLean. Although Corwin himself admitted by the end of 1847 that his chances for the nomination approached nil and was prepared to withdraw, his Ohio friends determined to commit the state Whig party officially to him. McLean and his associates realized that any such action would be fatal to the justice's own chances, and they strove to secure an endorsement for McLean instead or to prevent the meeting from nominating anyone.[25]

The bitter animosity between the Corwin and McLean men spilled over into a battle over the state platform. Since May 1846, Ohio's Whigs had divided deeply over the question of supplying American armies in Mexico. On one side, the most vehement antiwar Whigs—members of the "immortal fourteen" like Joseph Root, Robert Schenck, Columbus Delano, and Joshua Giddings—had embraced Corwin after his famous antiwar speech in February 1847. On the other, McLean, as party insiders knew, had denounced opposition to supplies as unpatriotic in an unsigned editorial printed in the pro-McLean *Cincinnati Gazette*, and conservative opponents of a radical antiwar stance had gravitated to his column or to Taylor's. If the platform embraced the extreme antiwar position of the Corwin men, it would be widely interpreted as a repudiation of both McLean and Taylor. The struggle over the platform gained focus because the party had to nominate a gubernatorial candidate for 1848, and each of the major factions had its favorite. Corwin's backers promoted Delano; McLean's friends pushed Colonel James Collier, who had fought in the hated war and, on several occasions in 1846, stoutly defended the Democratic version of its origins. Attitudes toward the rival candidates for the gubernatorial nomination were inextricably intertwined with the contest for the presidential nomination.

With rival Whig editors hurling vitriol at each other and at the potential gubernatorial and presidential candidates, many Whigs wanted to postpone the state convention from its customary January date until May 1848. But the Corwin men forced the issue. In mid-December 1847, the Corwin-dominated Whig state central committee, at the urging of the pro-Corwin incumbent Whig Governor William Bebb, but over the objections of virtually all Whig state legislators, called a convention in Columbus on January 19. The committee specified that this should be a mass meeting, where everyone who attended had an equal vote, rather than the normal delegate convention, where equal numbers of delegates were allotted to each congressional district and where voting at the convention on both the resolutions committee and for candidates was conducted by district. As the alarmed McLean men suspected, the Corwinites intended to pack this assemblage with their friends around Columbus and from the Miami Valley, who were known as the "Miami boys" or "Xenia clique," to stampede the meeting into nominating Corwin and Delano, and then to select and instruct all the state's delegates to the national convention, which Ohio's Whigs would insist upon holding in a direct slap at McLean and Taylor.

Caught off guard by this coup, McLean's Ohio lieutenants like John Teesdale and Samuel Galloway in Columbus and J. C. Wright, editor of the *Cincinnati Gazette*, frantically tried to expose the custom-breaking scheme of the Corwin-Delano faction and to persuade McLean adherents and friends of other candidates to make the trip to Columbus in the dead of winter. Again, because a mass meeting was planned, it would not do simply to mobilize the relatively small number of professional politicos who might normally attend a state convention. They had to arouse the rank and file.

In this attempt they immediately confronted two obstacles. First, although McLean and his friends had been maneuvering for the presidency since 1845, they had not organized Ohio's Whigs for him since they presented McLean as a nonpartisan reform candidate, not a regular Whig. As a result, they lacked an apparatus even to identify reliable McLean men in different parts of the state. Thus, they had to rely primarily on agitating antagonism to Corwin or Delano, not on mobilizing pro-McLean sentiment, to persuade Ohio's Whigs to attend the meeting in sufficient numbers to stifle the Corwin effort. Second, many rank-and-file Whigs in Ohio distrusted McLean for the same reason they distrusted Taylor. They did not consider him a Whig and doubted his commitment to Whig principles, since McLean, like Taylor, had carefully refused to endorse Whig programs publicly. Therefore Wright, Teesdale, Galloway, and other McLean men in Ohio pleaded with the judge to publish a statement or write a letter they could circulate at the Columbus meeting setting forth his views on Whig economic policies, the war and territorial acquisition, and slavery extension. Without such a statement, they warned, McLean could never get an endorsement from Ohio's Whigs.[26]

McLean therefore published in the Washington *National Intelligencer* a letter dated January 7, stating his position on the war, one that was strikingly similar to those previously taken by Corwin and Clay and strikingly different from the stance he had taken in the anonymously published letter a year earlier. Denouncing the war as "unnecessarily and unconstitutionally commenced," he called on Congress to end it by framing a peace treaty and forcing Polk to effect it through its control of military appropriations. He also urged the Whig House to stop the issuance of any more Treasury notes and to force the administration instead to sell bonds or levy taxes, thus bringing home the cost of the war to the public. Notably, McLean said nothing specific about territorial acquisition or the Wilmot Proviso, and despite the further pleas of his Ohio managers that he do so, he refused. There matters stood when several thousand Whigs assembled in Columbus on January 19 for what one of them later called "the most noisy and uproarious assemblage of the kind ever held in Ohio."[27]

Neither the Corwin-Delano nor the McLean-Collier forces gained clear control of the meeting, despite the strenuous efforts of Governor Bebb on Corwin's behalf. Friends of Clay and Taylor and uncommitted Whigs held the balance of power. Over the vociferous protests of Corwin men, non-Corwinites on the arrangements committee successfully neutralized the chief threat of the mass meeting by insisting that all convention business follow the normal procedure of allotting seats on the platform committee and votes on the floor by congressional district. In other words, no matter how many men the Corwin forces mustered from a particular congressional district, it would have only one seat on the resolutions committee and the same number of votes on the floor as less well represented districts. The Corwin men, in contrast, seemingly won the battle over the platform, which not only insisted on a national convention and strenuously denounced the war, territorial acquisition, and slavery expansion, but specifically praised Corwin's opposition to the war in the Senate.[28] This victory was deceptive. The plank lauding Corwin passed the resolutions committee by a razor-thin 12–11 margin, and a plank endorsing Corwin for president was handily defeated. Given McLean's recent statement on the war, his friends could easily accept the platform, as could Clay men, for some of the planks, like one comparing the dismemberment of Mexico to the notorious partition of Poland, echoed Clay's remarks at Lexington. Although Corwin papers later asserted that the platform implicitly endorsed their man, events quickly revealed that it did not.

When the platform was presented on the convention floor, Lewis D. Campbell of Butler County, the chief spokesman for Bebb and the Corwin managers, passionately insisted that the convention must add the plank the committee had rejected, nominate Corwin, and select delegates pledged to him. Failure to do so, he stated, would deprive Ohio of any influence on the deliberations of Whigs elsewhere. His motion met decisive defeat. Instead, the convention refused to announce a preference for any candidate, although its vow to support "any true Whig" chosen by the national convention reflected the widespread hostility to Taylor in Ohio, as well as lingering suspicion of McLean's Whig credentials. The convention did choose two senatorial delegates to the national convention, but they were uninstructed and, at the time, both leaned toward Clay. Ewing's friends, Clay men, and uncommitted Whigs infuriated by the bulldozing tactics of Governor Bebb and the Xenia clique had combined with McLean's supporters to frustrate Corwin and rebuke the governor.

The same coalition prevailed on the gubernatorial nomination. The Ewing men at Columbus included Ohio's most conservative Whigs, men who were terrified that an *"ultra anti-war* candidate" like Delano on the ticket would prostrate the Ohio Whig party.[29] Nor did they favor Collier. Instead, they rallied on Seabury Ford, the favorite of Western Reserve Whigs. Once the McLean men realized they lacked the votes to nominate Collier, they dropped him and combined with the Ewing faction and the Reserve Whigs to select Ford.

McLean and his friends immediately rejoiced over their triumph at Columbus, but it was a partial victory at best. Corwin and Delano had been stopped, but largely by the Ewing men, who preferred Taylor, and by others hostile to the permanently discredited Bebb. "Bebb and the Miami boys have been completely routed—and the conservatives of our party have gained a great victory," exulted one of Ewing's followers. "The Gov. electioneered for days for Delano & Corwin. . . . And it was the disgust created by his effrontery and impertinence that helped ensure our success." Despite surprising strength at the convention, McLean's friends had failed to secure his own nomination or Collier's. Those failures and the obvious division in the Ohio party scarcely constituted a strong recommendation that Whigs in other states look to Ohio for the party's nominee. McLean still had time to repair the damage if he could capture the district delegates to be chosen in the spring. But that task meant lining up Whig politicos for McLean in twenty-one individual congressional districts, and over sixty-five counties would select the delegates to the district conventions. Winning the district delegates, in short, required the creation of a statewide organization that McLean's managers, by their own admission, had not even begun to build. In the end, McLean would be forced to rely upon an exhausting but fruitless odyssey around the state by his faithful friend, the unemployed former editor Teesdale, to secure the Ohio delegates he needed to be a credible candidate.[30]

Still, Corwin suffered a severe blow. Although he refused to issue a public statement of withdrawal, and although he continued to be named as a second choice by Greeley and other northern Whigs, his Ohio friends' confidence had been shattered. Rather than try to secure the remaining Ohio delegates for Corwin, they took up other candidates to stop the despised McLean. This shift away from Corwin was vastly significant, for Ohio's would be the pivotal delegation at the June national convention.

Many Corwin men, especially from southern Ohio, gravitated to Clay, but others from northern Ohio and the Corwin leaders from the Miami Valley, like Schenck and Campbell, now promoted as the strongest Whig nominee the Hero of Lundy's Lane and Chapultepec, General Winfield Scott. The humiliated Governor Bebb vacillated between the two. In February he told Teesdale that he favored Scott as an alternative to Corwin because "Clay cannot receive assurances of success that will or ought to induce him to run." Yet in early April, Bebb begged Clay to stay in the race, predicted that he could carry Ohio and New York, as well as other states he had won in 1844, promised that Corwin men at the national convention would consider him interchangeable with Corwin, and warned that the northern Whigs would "suffer utter dissolution" if Taylor got the nomination. Overly sanguine as always, Clay placed great stock in Bebb's apparent promise of Ohio support at the convention, an egregious mistake since Bebb, whatever his true intentions, no longer had the ability to deliver Ohio's vote. At the end of January these developments lay in the future. All that was clear was that Ohio's delegates were not committed to a favorite son. They remained to be won.[31]

IV

In February, when the race had seemingly narrowed to a two-man contest between Clay and Taylor, attention shifted to the conventions in Kentucky, North Carolina, and Virginia, all scheduled for February 22, Washington's Birthday and, not coincidentally, the anniversary of Buena Vista. Since each convention would choose all the state's delegates to Philadelphia, forty delegates, and the momentum elsewhere they could generate, were at stake on a single day. But national attention also focused on those three states because the Clay and Taylor forces were far more evenly balanced there than in the Deep South. To make a credible case that Clay could retain crucial slave states for the Whigs, his friends had to stop the election of Taylor delegates, especially in the traditional Whig bastions of Kentucky and North Carolina. Conversely, to demonstrate that Taylor was the choice of Whigs in southern states that the party had a realistic chance of carrying, and not simply of the hopeless Whig minorities in Democratic states like Alabama and Mississippi, Taylor's proponents wanted the endorsement of all three. Given the apparent turnabout in Maryland, if Taylor failed to secure their support, his aura of invincibility would dim and thus his ability to enlist reluctant northern Whigs would diminish.

Just as both camps recognized the potential impact these conventions could have on northern Whigs' choice, they believed that northern Whigs' preference might sway the conventions' decisions. Hence, during February, the rival camps not only marshaled their forces in the three southern states; they also strove to demonstrate their strength in the North.

Still not committed to another race in January and February, Clay was less interested in securing committed delegates than in preventing Taylor from doing so—something he knew Taylorites in Kentucky and Virginia were straining to achieve. Clay and his friends believed that if uncommitted Whigs were sent to the national convention from the three states and learned there that Clay was the favorite of northern delegates, they would swing to the "Embodiment" out of loyalty to the national party. For the same reason, Clay sought an early demonstration from the North that he was the strongest potential candidate in that section. Such evidence, he hoped, would convince Upper South Whigs that they must not nominate Taylor if they genuinely hoped to win the presidency. The northern state to which Clay and his backers looked for such evidence, just as in 1839 when he had tried to influence Virginia's selection of delegates, was New York.[32]

Clay turned to New York for several reasons. Greeley, its leading Whig editor, was already promoting him. Its thirty-six delegates were the biggest prize at the national convention. Most important, since many Whigs thought Clay had lost the 1844 election because New York's antislavery Whigs defected, Clay wanted public assurances from its leading Whigs that he could carry the state in 1848. Before he left Kentucky for Washington in December 1847, Clay urged Greeley to arrange a demonstration on his behalf by Whigs in the New York legislature.

Later his friends begged state comptroller Millard Fillmore to have Weed and other prominent New York Whigs send assurances to Leslie Combs that Clay could win New York so that Combs could circulate them at the impending Kentucky state convention.[33]

Taylor, Clay, Webster, McLean, Scott, and Corwin all had supporters in New York, but Clay's loyalists were the most numerous, the most ardent, and the best organized. Nor, as even the hostile Seward admitted, was there any doubt that Clay could carry New York in 1848. The rancorous Democratic divisions that had handed it to the Whigs in 1846 and 1847 still festered and in fact would worsen in 1848. Any Whig presidential candidate seemed likely to carry New York. To the clamorous Clay men who hungered to atone for the robbery of 1844, that fact, as well as justice to the Kentuckian and to Whig principles, made New York's support for Clay's nomination imperative. As in so many states, however, the presidential question became entangled in intraparty rivalries that in New York were especially visceral. Any attempt to commit New York to Clay was bound to aggravate factional wounds.[34]

Since 1844, New York's self-consciously "progressive" Whigs led by Weed and Seward had clashed with their self-styled "conservative" rivals over nativism, state constitutional revision, Anti-Rentism, black suffrage, and what seemed to conservatives the increasingly radical antislavery stance of the Weed-Seward wing. Yet neither faction was monolithic, and the contest for the presidential nomination jumbled alignments still further. Although Seward and Weed had allies in New York City's wealthy mercantile, banking, and legal community like Simeon Draper and Moses Grinnell, that community, along with wealthy businessmen and lawyers in Brooklyn and in towns along the Hudson River, provided the heaviest concentration of conservative opposition to them. Many of these Whigs had been National Republicans in the early 1830s, rather than Antimasons, and many of their fathers had been Federalists. Millard Fillmore and his Buffalo associates Nathan Kelsey Hall, Solomon G. Haven, and the editor Thomas Foote cooperated with these eastern conservatives but were distinct from them. Like Seward and Weed, Fillmore began his political career as an Antimason, but over the years he and his friends had grown increasingly disillusioned with Weed's control over Whig nominations, state patronage, and canal contracts. The two conservative groups, therefore, were united by common antagonism to Seward and Weed, not by common economic or policy interests or common presidential preferences.[35]

Some of the wealthy Manhattan conservatives, like Hiram Ketchum and Edward Curtis, sought Webster's nomination, but the great majority favored Clay. Repeatedly denounced by McLean's adherents as impractical aristocrats, Clay men dominated the Whig city committee as well as the Young Men's Whig Committee. While most conservative Whigs in the Hudson Valley and western (or upstate) counties also wanted Clay, Fillmore and his closest Buffalo associates did not. In early 1848 Congressman Hall, among others, preferred Taylor to Clay.[36]

To complicate matters, conservative Whigs' leading editorial exponent, James Watson Webb of the New York Courier and Enquirer, came out for Taylor in April 1847 and steadfastly held to him. He was joined in the Taylor camp in early 1848 by Governor John Young, whose nomination in 1846 had been arranged by Weed over Webb's vociferous protests. Webb's commitment to Taylor became a major but not the only reason why Greeley, his editorial rival in New York City, opposed Taylor's nomination and ardently pushed Clay's candidacy beginning in the fall of 1847.

Greeley had long been an ally of Seward and Weed—they were usually considered a triumvirate—yet Seward and Weed did not share Greeley's apparent enthusiasm for Clay. By early 1848 neither doubted Clay's ability to carry New York. They worried instead about his ability to carry the nation. In addition, they feared that if the New York Whig party committed itself to Clay, their downstate conservative foes, the Clay loyalists, would get the credit and would thus enhance their ability to challenge Weed for control of the state organization.[37]

Seward and Weed were also unenthusiastic about Taylor. Weed's *Albany Evening Journal* had boomed Taylor for president in the summer of 1847, but in September, citing Taylor's refusal to endorse Whig principles or to accept a regular Whig nomination, Weed had withdrawn his support. More than Taylor's unorthodoxy compelled this decision. The Seward-Weed faction's strength lay in upstate and western counties, whose fervently antiwar, antislavery Whigs wanted no part of Taylor. As Weed well knew, many of those Whigs preferred Clay's nomination after his Lexington Address. If Taylor won the nomination and the subsequent election, moreover, Webb and Young would have a much stronger claim than Weed to serve as dispensers of federal patronage in New York. Weed and Seward thus feared the nomination of either Taylor or Clay.

They hoped instead that some alternative candidate might emerge if they could keep the state's Whigs from prematurely committing themselves. As George W. Patterson of Chautauqua County wrote Weed in late January, after pronouncing both Taylor and Clay impossibilities, "The true course is to take a *known Whig* of the north, one who has not been mixed up with the war question, and his election would be quite sure." Patterson specifically named Seward himself as the best choice, but Weed was perfectly willing to consider other men, including Corwin, Greeley's second choice.[38]

Weed's desire to stall for time and prevent the New York Whig party from pledging itself to either Clay or Taylor explains his vacillation in the winter and spring of 1848, an oscillation that puzzled contemporaries and has puzzled historians ever since.[39] Weed had a much stronger sense about whom he did not want nominated than whom he did. Given the sentiment among New York's Whigs, preventing an official endorsement of Clay was his biggest problem. Thus Weed secretly helped organize demonstrations for Taylor in order to stop Clay's momentum. Thus he floated trial balloons for Corwin, Webster, Scott, and even John M. Clayton in the columns of the *Albany Evening Journal*. Thus, beginning in February, he insisted that New York's Whigs send unpledged delegates to the national convention, not delegates instructed for Clay, as the Clay men demanded. From Clay's point of view, what made Weed's opposition ominous was less his editorial influence—Greeley's *Tribune* was more than a match for that—than his legendary influence among Whig state legislators from whom Clay sought a public endorsement that might turn the tide in the Kentucky, Virginia, and North Carolina state conventions.[40]

New York City's Whigs responded to Clay's entreaties for aid with alacrity. Greeley and the two Whig city committees arranged mass meetings in December and again in January that demanded Clay's nomination. Well aware that an early commitment by New York to Clay could be decisive, supporters of Webster and McLean helped Webb and the Taylor men in the city schedule a counter-demonstration for Taylor on February 15. Attended by about 500 people, this anti-Clay meeting promoted Taylor's nomination on antiparty grounds that constituted a thinly concealed attack on the party insiders fervently working for Clay. "We need what we have now [behind Taylor]—A PARTY OF THE PEOPLE," declared the meeting's chairman. Without specifically naming Clay, another speaker asserted that it was time for Whigs to jettison "old party shackles" and take up new men. To neutralize the effect of this Taylor meeting and achieve maximum impact on the impending southern state conventions, Greeley and the city's Whig committees then arranged a mammoth Clay demonstration at Castle Garden on February 17, five days before those conventions were to meet. Attended by a crowd variously estimated at between 10,000 and 12,000 people, it left no doubt where New York City's Whigs stood.[41]

Closely coordinated with Greeley's effort in the city, a caucus of Whig legislators met in Albany on the night of February 16 to issue a statement on the presidential race that could be printed in New York Whig papers the next day and then telegraphed to the rest of the nation. Like the majority of the state's rank-and-file Whigs, most Whig legislators wanted Clay's nomination. Even the persuasive Weed, therefore, could not stop them from making some public statement, as Clay requested. But Weed did prevent an explicit endorsement. The caucus adopted two resolutions. One simply praised congressional Whigs for calling a national convention. The other announced that the New York Whig party "expect[ed]" the party's presidential nominee to be "a thorough and blameless Whig of known and well-tried principles and opinions; a statesman of known capacity and qualifications for the highest civil employment, and one who shall fully represent and maintain ... the distinctive doctrines and character of the Whig party of the State." Because Clay seemed to meet these criteria, many Whigs took this as a pro-Clay recommendation. Shrewder observers realized that it was not. Instead, as almost everyone recognized, it expressed New York Whigs' emphatic opposition to Zachary Taylor. Whether this would sway Whigs' decision in Kentucky, Virginia, and North Carolina remained to be seen.[42]

To offset New York's anticipated endorsement of Clay, the Taylor congressional committee laid plans for a demonstration of the general's own popularity among northern Whigs at Philadelphia, the nation's second largest city and commercial entrepot of its second largest state. Organized by Philadelphia members of the congressional Taylor club and their local allies, the Buena Vista Celebration was scheduled for February 22, the same day as the three southern conventions. Since Clay had carried six northern states in 1844 and had narrowly failed to carry New York, Pennsylvania, and Indiana, Taylor's managers sought plausible evidence that Whigs from critical northern states other than New York preferred Taylor to Clay. Otherwise, they feared, Taylor's prospects in the impending Whig conventions in Kentucky, Virginia, and North Carolina might unravel just as quickly as they appeared to be coming apart in Maryland. Each member of the Taylor congressional committee, as well as other prominent Whigs who favored Taylor, like Virginia's Rives and Maryland's John Pendleton Kennedy, was invited to attend the Philadelphia meeting or to prepare letters of support that could be read there. One by one, Truman Smith and Lincoln, Kennedy, Barringer of North

Carolina, Rives, and the others sent off letters that rehearsed their loyalty to the Whig party and its principles, their love of Clay, and their conviction that Taylor alone could lead the Whig party back to the White House. One by one they warned that defeating the Democrats to end the war was too important to risk Clay's nomination.[43]

Aside from the need to exhibit Taylor's purported popularity in a major northern city, his congressional managers chose Philadelphia primarily to shore up Taylor's fading strength in Pennsylvania and New Jersey. Some Whig congressmen from both states were committed to Taylor, and since early 1847 Philadelphia's three-term Congressman Joseph Ingersoll had lauded Taylor both privately and in House speeches as "a Whig—not indeed an ultra-partisan Whig, but a Whig in principle."[44] By the end of 1847, however, enthusiasm for Taylor elsewhere in Pennsylvania and in northern New Jersey had dwindled perceptibly, and support for Clay had risen accordingly. To Taylor's avid Whig supporters in Philadelphia and contiguous areas of southern New Jersey, this trend had to be reversed, for the results of the 1847 gubernatorial elections in the two states had convinced them that Clay could carry neither.

Buoyed by their victories in the 1846 congressional elections, which they attributed primarily to attacks on the Walker Tariff, both Pennsylvania and New Jersey Whigs had made tariff protection the centerpiece of their 1847 campaigns, despite the unexpected prosperity in each state that year. When Clay aroused so much enthusiasm in Philadelphia and at the Jersey shore during the summer of 1847, moreover, his devotees in both states sought to make the anticipated Whig gubernatorial victories a referendum on Clay's personal popularity and his viability as a presidential candidate. Instead, both Whig candidates lost, and in Pennsylvania Whigs were reduced to a meager 37 seats in the 100-member state assembly. As a Philadelphian wrote Rives after that debacle, "Since the election of Pennsylvania, the Whigs here seem disposed to fall back again on Genl. Taylor. Had the result of the election been in their favor, they would certainly have nominated Mr. Clay." "This defeat is considered decisive of Mr. Clay's future prospects," gloated a McLean man from Philadelphia. His friends "did all in their power to make the success of the governor's ticket a Clay triumph and of course would have reasoned themselves into the belief that he would be the strongest man to press for the Presidential nomination." Instead, the loss proved that Clay "has no popularity in this state."[45]

What especially turned Philadelphia's anti-Clay Whigs toward Taylor, however, was the continued strength of the Native American party in Pennsylvania, a party whose voting support was concentrated almost exclusively in the city and county of Philadelphia. Since 1844, Philadelphia Whig associates of Delaware's Clayton, like Morton McMichael, an editor of the Philadelphia *North American*, and Edward Joy Morris, had argued that Whigs could never carry Pennsylvania's statewide elections without nativist support. That judgment seemed to be supported by the results in 1844, 1845, 1846, and 1847. Since Clay had publicly spurned a Native American presidential nomination, his candidacy could not possibly effect the merger they sought. Taylor, in contrast, had been nominated by the Native Americans in September 1847, and he appeared receptive to them. With Taylor as their candidate, Whigs might therefore attract nativist support without resorting to counterproductive immigrant-bashing. "Taylor is the only Whig who can carry Pennsylvania," Morris, who headed the local arrangements committee for the Buena Vista Celebration, later explained. "With Gen. Taylor as the Whig candidate we gain the 15,000 Native American votes without being connected with Nativism politically." With that help Whigs could win the October state legislative elections and put a Whig in the Senate. If the Whig national convention rejected Taylor, however, "the Whig party of this State will be broken up into hopeless confusion."[46]

Despite its elaborate preparations and extensive publicity, the Buena Vista Festival scarcely affected the hunt for delegates in Pennsylvania, New Jersey, or the rest of the North. To mitigate its influence, Clay's numerous Philadelphia friends arranged a public dinner on the following day, where the Kentuckian, who came up from Washington, was lionized. Thus outsiders could not tell whom Philadelphia Whigs preferred. Back in Washington, for example, Outlaw believed that "the reception of Mr. Clay in Phila. will knock the Taylor concern into a cocked hat," while an Illinois Whig who saw both celebrations wrote his wife that the Taylor men had prevailed in this public relations contest. An independent convention composed of Democrats and Native Americans chose a separate Taylor electoral ticket in Harrisburg on February 22, thus undercutting the attempt to present him as a good Whig. Within a week of the Philadelphia extravaganza, moreover, Whigs from the Pittsburgh and Erie congressional districts chose Clay delegates to the national convention, and other districts would subsequently follow suit. When the Pennsylvania state Whig convention met in March, Scott, not Taylor, had the most support. The senatorial delegates it chose were officially uncommitted, but one of them, William F. Johnston, who would unexpectedly become the Whigs' gubernatorial candidate in 1848, was an unabashed Scott man. In addition, that convention insisted "that the Whig candidate for the Presidency, to be worthy of the support of the Whig party, must be known to be devoted to its principles, willing to become their exponent and champion, and prepared to carry them faithfully out in the execution of his official duties." Obviously the Philadelphia celebration had not resolved all doubts about Taylor's Whiggery in the Keystone State.[47]

New Jersey's Whigs seemed equally unimpressed, at least according to one Clay man. Several days after the Philadelphia demonstration, he wrote Greeley's *Tribune* that all the Whigs in the New Jersey legislature, except four or five "croakers," wanted to come out for Clay immediately. "The honest yeomanry of New Jersey are not willing to abandon the glorious old Whig cause for a no party candidate," he vowed. "No! They are for a party candidate." Nineteen-twentieths of the Whigs in New Jersey preferred Clay, he boasted inaccurately. "Yes, gentlemen, your *Native American Managers from Philadelphia* can make no headway among the Jersey Blues." The selection of delegates later in the spring would prove him wrong. Four would back Clay, three Taylor, but the reasons for Taylor's strength, as elsewhere in the North, stemmed from later developments, not the Buena Vista Celebration.[48]

V

Nor did the Clay and Taylor demonstrations in the North discernibly affect the crucial state conventions in Kentucky, North Carolina, and Virginia. Intraparty factional wrangling dominated their proceedings and determined their outcomes.

Because those struggles, which often involved matters other than the presidential nomination, were so intense, finding a formula to hold the party together became a higher priority for many of their participants than resolving the presidential question. As a result, a clear winner emerged in only one of the three.

In Kentucky, where a decision for Taylor could finish Clay's chances, Taylor and Clay leaders sought to avert a blow-up by arranging a truce in November 1847 and publishing it in George Prentice's pro-Taylor *Louisville Journal*. This document insisted that the Whig party must hold a national convention, called on the impending state convention to express no preference on the presidency, and urged it to choose uninstructed delegates. Confident that Clay would not run and reluctant to embarrass their old friend, Letcher, Orlando Brown, Prentice, and Crittenden had been happy to enter this accord. Pleased with the concession on the national convention, unsure of Clay's intentions, and anxious to spare him personal humiliation, Clay's friends like George Robertson and Leslie Combs were too.[49]

As the February convention approached, however, avid Taylorites rejected this bargain and insisted on nominating Taylor and selecting committed Taylor delegates at the state convention. Some of these were Clay's lifelong enemies, but younger zealots particularly exploded when the secret Lexington circular disparaging the Taylor movement was exposed. Reports from Washington about Taylor's setbacks and Clay's reception only increased their determination. To pressure the state convention, they called a separate Taylor meeting in Frankfort on the same day as the official Whig conclave there. "Things are in a most terrible confusion" and the party "in the greatest peril," warned Crittenden's alarmed lieutenants. Convinced that Clay intended to withdraw, Letcher moaned, "But great G-d, if he could have seen the predicament in which he has placed his friends and his party . . . he could not have hesitated a moment about declining." To placate the angry Taylor men and keep the November agreement, therefore, Letcher solicited letters from both Senators Crittenden and James Morehead, as well as from Whig congressmen from other states, promising that Clay would soon announce his refusal to run and urging Kentucky's Whigs not to insult him by nominating Taylor. Robertson obtained a similar letter from Georgia's Berrien.[50]

A fight for the gubernatorial nomination between Archibald Dixon and William J. Graves aggravated the party's problems. Both contenders preferred Taylor for president, but the friends of each threatened to bolt the party should the other get the nomination, thereby jeopardizing the party's ability to capture the state government in the August election. That prospect particularly unnerved Whig leaders, for, as elsewhere, they considered control of the state government as important as control of the White House.

Preserving party harmony thus became the leaders' top priority when the Kentucky state convention opened in the Frankfort Presbyterian Church on February 22. Delegates turned first to the gubernatorial question. Before anyone mentioned Dixon or Graves, a delegate from Logan County proposed Crittenden for governor. Enthusiasm erupted, and protests from Crittenden's friends that he did not want the post were shouted down. Dixon, Graves, and other candidates withdrew, and Crittenden was nominated by acclamation. The state party had escaped a rupture over the governorship, but at a significant long-term cost. Like most southern governors, Kentucky's exerted little influence over legislative policy since a simple majority could override his vetoes, and a new state constitution in 1850 would eradicate the governor's formerly substantial patronage power. As elsewhere in Dixie, the chief function of Kentucky's gubernatorial nominee seems to have been to pull out a large vote of the party faithful in order to elect as many of the legislative candidates on the same ticket as possible.[51] Crittenden, whose rigid sense of personal honor and party loyalty obligated him to accept a nomination he did not want, easily led the Whig ticket to victory in August 1848. But then he languished in Frankfort when he would have been of far more service to the Whig party in Washington.

Over zealous Taylorites' protests, the convention adhered to the November bargain on the presidency. It recommended both Taylor and Clay to the national convention as worthy candidates, promised to support the Philadelphia nominee, and, without instructions, chose all twelve Kentucky delegates. Although some observers mistakenly concluded that eleven were Taylor men, Clay's friends considered this outcome a great victory, especially the commitment that Kentucky's Whigs would support the winner at Philadelphia. Some participants concluded that the result hinged on the reading of the letters from Washington promising that Clay was about to withdraw. Others attributed it to the strength of Clay sentiment at the convention, which supposedly cowed the Taylorites. "The *true* Whigs overwhelmed the available men, & we adjourned perfectly confident of success in August & *hot* for the *nominee* of the Whig convention," crowed Leslie Combs. "Clay 1st of all the world—Taylor next."[52]

Incensed at this rebuff, the separate Taylor meeting in Frankfort, after being reinforced by disappointed Taylorites from the Whig convention, then declared Taylor the clear favorite of Kentucky's Whigs. Telegraphic reports of the two gatherings left Frankfort simultaneously on February 23. Some Whigs elsewhere, confusing the Taylor meeting's action with that of the formal party convention, concluded that Kentucky's Whigs had nominated Taylor. Virginia's Taylor men exploited that distorted impression to score a decisive victory.

The scene of "a very animated and exciting debate in which hard blows were dealt and received," Virginia's Whig convention extended over three days. The congressional champions of the rival candidates—Botts for Clay and Preston and Flournoy for Taylor—traveled from Washington to Richmond to lead their respective forces. Botts first attempted a procedural coup. Each county and city was to have as many votes in the convention as it had in the state legislature. Because the Whig vote was heavily concentrated in a few counties and cities, this arrangement meant that delegates from normally Democratic jurisdictions, whose Whigs favored Taylor far more decisively than those from Whig strongholds, had a majority. Botts therefore proposed that voting in the convention be proportional to the popular vote Clay had received in 1844. If not, he complained accurately, the 170 Whig voters in Shendandoah County would have more votes on the convention floor than the 1200 Whig voters in the city of Richmond. Well aware that a proportional vote would result in a Clay victory, the Taylorite majority killed Botts' proposal. Unable to secure committed Clay delegates, Botts then pushed for an uncommitted delegation and no nomination. Convinced that "with Gen. Taylor as our candidate we must succeed" and that "with Mr. Clay defeat is inevitable," the Taylor forces demanded that the convention nominate Taylor.

For over twelve hours the two sides argued. Then, as Botts appeared close to winning a floor vote on his motion to send unpledged delegates, Preston suddenly announced that he had received telegrams indicating that both the Kentucky and North Carolina conventions had gone for Taylor. Stunned by this false report, the convention crushed Botts' motion 81 to 27 and then adopted a resolution nominating Taylor by an 86–17 vote. It did not explicitly instruct the state's delegates to Philadelphia, but the preference of the state party was clear. Only two of the seventeen delegates selected—one from Botts' own congressional district and the other from a neighboring Whig stronghold—would go for Clay at the convention. The remaining fifteen were staunch Taylor men.[53]

Contrary to Preston's assertion at Richmond, the Raleigh convention of North Carolina's Whigs made no presidential nomination and sent unpledged delegates to Philadelphia. Support for Clay was broader and that for Taylor correspondingly narrower in North Carolina than in any other slave state, with the exception of Maryland. Most of its Whigs, who had lost the state only once since 1838, remained confident of carrying it in the presidential election by opposing the war and territorial acquisition, a confidence reflected in the state platform they adopted. The state's Whig leadership, nonetheless, divided over the presidency, the party's gubernatorial nominee, and the proper strategy for the impending state election in August. Consequently, their state convention also witnessed heated conflict.

Doubtful of Clay's electability outside of North Carolina, two of the state's Whig congressmen, Augustine Shepperd and Daniel M. Barringer, urged the convention to nominate Taylor. Barringer and his constituent E. J. Hale, editor of the influential *Fayetteville Observer*, also feared that the Whigs might lose the August state election unless they endorsed Taylor in February and kept his name atop the Whig ticket from that point on. They anticipated, correctly as it turned out, that the Democrats planned to run a populistic campaign in 1848, pillorying the Whigs as an aristocratic and unresponsive establishment party, and they hoped to use Taylor's image as a nonpartisan People's candidate to parry that expected thrust.[54]

Taylor's most prominent North Carolina backer, however, was United States Senator George E. Badger, whose ambition and arrogance generated the state party's major divisions. A constitutional lawyer of prodigious talent but great conceit, secretary of the navy in the doomed Harrison administration, and highly respected Senate debater, Badger lacked tact and a common touch. He offended many other Whig leaders in the state, including his Senate colleague, the increasingly alcoholic Willie P. Mangum, whom Badger considered his intellectual inferior. Sent to the Senate by a Whig legislature in 1846 to complete the final two years of a resigning Democrat's term, Badger faced reelection by the legislature to be chosen in August 1848. Arguing that "the renomination of Mr. C[lay] would be the signal for the *dissolution*, not the *dismemberment* of *the Whig party*," he pressured the state convention to nominate Taylor to ensure Whig victory in those legislative elections. Secure in statewide elections for governor and president, North Carolina's Whigs over the past decade had been most vulnerable to Democratic challenges in legislative and congressional elections decided in local districts, so Badger's concern was understandable. In addition, Badger maneuvered to secure the 1848 gubernatorial nomination for his eastern North

Carolina kinsman Edward Stanly, who, Badger openly boasted in Washington, would serve two terms and then replace Mangum as United States senator in 1852.

The many intraparty foes of Badger and Stanly exploded at the temerity of Badger's scheme to monopolize the state's highest offices for his own family. Mangum, the state's other four Whig congressmen, and other Whig leaders lined up against both Taylor and Stanly. Because of the angry reaction, Charles Manley, rather than Stanly, won the gubernatorial nomination, and no preference for president was expressed. The majority of Whigs at Raleigh favored Clay, but like Whigs elsewhere they waited to see what he would do rather than commit delegates to him.[55]

VI

At exactly the same time that rival demonstrations in the North and state conventions in the South produced a stalemate, two developments elsewhere fundamentally altered the race. Together they constituted the decisive turning point in the four-year search for a candidate. One should have been predicted but was not. The other upset the predictions of virtually everyone in the Whig party about the focus of the impending presidential election. The first gravely damaged Taylor's chances; the second ultimately killed those of Henry Clay.

A major objective of Taylor's advocates in Washington since the decision of the Whig caucus was to reassure suspicious Whigs about Taylor's Whig credentials. Beginning on February 23, however, New York City newspapers and then the press elsewhere in the nation printed letters that Taylor had written to Peter Sken Smith to accept the Native American party's nomination, to Colonel A. M. Mitchell of Cincinnati, and to independent groups in Harrisburg, Pennsylvania, and Montgomery, Alabama, who had previously nominated Taylor as a People's candidate. In each he emphatically iterated his refusal to be considered the special candidate of any party or "the exponent of their party doctrines." He would accept nominations from Whigs, Democrats, and Native Americans alike, he told Smith, but only if they were made "entirely independent of party considerations." "If the Whig party desire . . . to cast their votes for me," Taylor declared to Mitchell, "they must do it on their own responsibility without any pledges from me."[56]

These letters stunned Taylor's supporters and infuriated party regulars. New York Congressman Washington Hunt, who was helping Weed organize Taylor demonstrations in New York to counteract the rival Clay Whigs, immediately pronounced Taylor's chances hopeless. Evincing "indifference or contempt" toward the Whig party, Taylor's letters, sputtered Hunt, proved that he was not a Whig "unless indeed we have reached a political millennium & the Whig party is to be disbanded." Taylor's letter to Smith "ought to put an end to all idea of his nomination by the Whigs," groaned Thomas Ewing's son. " 'A Northern man with southern principles' was bad enough, but a Southern man with *no principles* may be worse." Kentucky Whigs also "declare[d] they will not support any man who declines being considered the 'exponent' of Whig principles." Taylor's letter to Montgomery "has given a death blow to the hope of his friends & with them, I fear, to the hopes of a Whig triumph," moaned North Carolina's E. J. Hale.

Whigs could not "run anyone but a man who will accept a Whig Convention nomination." No one, however, better expressed the indignation of anti-Taylor Whigs than Indiana's Orth. If the Whigs nominated Taylor after seeing his recent letters, he raged, they would "stultify themselves, discard all their cherished principles—and foresake [sic] the faith of their fathers."[57]

All too aware of this outrage, the Young Indians and other Taylor managers frantically solicited new testimony from the seemingly uncontrollable general that he was indeed a Whig who endorsed Whig programs and positions. Even before this latest batch of letters appeared, Truman Smith had written Taylor in order to "bring out a cautious, judicious exposition of his views on two or three leading points." Similarly, Crittenden, who futilely urged Taylor to be careful in his letters, warned Orlando Brown in late March not to publish a letter in which Taylor was expected to demand a territorial indemnity from Mexico. In March as well, Lincoln prepared a letter that could be issued over Taylor's signature, promising that as president he would not veto a national bank or protective tariff or allow any territorial acquisition from Mexico into which slavery could expand. The Tennesseans Bell and Gentry also begged the hero publicly to embrace Whig principles.[58]

Such pleas accomplished little. Replying to Smith on March 4, Taylor refused to take a public position on Whig domestic policies. Still worse, in early April, a Taylor letter to a Kentucky Democrat indicated his willingness to accept either the Democrats' or Whigs' nomination, and he was rumored among Whig congressmen to have written still other letters lauding the Independent Treasury system and the Walker Tariff. "The man is certainly demented," concluded Indiana's Whig Congressman Caleb Smith. "His friends will now make an effort to get him to come out & take more decided ground in favour of Whig principles. To do this now will only render him more ridiculous." "Taylor cannot get a Whig nomination unless [he] promises to be a Whig president," the shrewd Weed concurred, "and it seems too late for that." Indiana editor John Defrees, who had earlier boomed Taylor in his *Indiana State Journal*, dumped him as too great a liability. "There are thousands of old partizan Whigs who will not vote for a man who says he will not carry out the measures of the party, and I do not very well see how a National Convention, having regard for principle, can nominate him," he told George Dunn, one of the Indiana members on the Taylor congressional committee. Thousands of other Whigs rejected Taylor because he owned slaves and had taken a leading role in the heinous Mexican War, Defrees added. "All this, however, might have been overcome had the 'Old Hero' said 'I am a Whig and should regard it my duty, if elected, to carry out Whig measures.' But he persists in the position that he will not do it, and, I fear, he has 'sinned his day of grace away.' "[59]

Alarmed by Taylor's plummeting prospects, Truman Smith, Crittenden, and southern Taylorites in Washington prepared yet another letter endorsing Whig principles for Taylor to publish. They dispatched it to Baton Rouge on April 11 with Major William Bliss, Taylor's chief aide during the Mexican War. By the time Bliss reached Taylor's home, he discovered that the New Orleans Taylor men had anticipated him. They, in turn, had been stirred to action both by their concern at Taylor's fading chances and by their anger at Clay's dramatic public entrance into the race.[60]

Clay had benefited from the deepening Whig dissatisfaction with Taylor's No Partyism. By the time he left Washington on February 23, his friends had convinced him that he could win the election, and any remaining doubts were dissolved by the tumultuous public reception he received in Philadelphia, New York, and other cities on the way home, as well as by letters he found there from both northern and southern Whigs pleading with him to remain in the race. By April 1, reports that he could carry Tennessee and Louisiana especially encouraged him. "I am persuaded that everywhere, in the Whig states, the Whig masses are for me," he wrote James Harvey, and several days later he explained to another friend that he expected to carry all the states he had won in 1844 plus New York and Louisiana, with the possibility of Indiana and Florida as well. The arrival of letters from Ohio's Governor Bebb and Thomas Stevenson, urging him not to withdraw, and news that on April 6, New York's Whig legislators had named him their favorite, announced he could win the state's thirty-six electoral votes, and chosen two at-large delegates devoted to him clinched his decision. To bury the widespread rumor that he would withdraw from the race at any moment, Clay then released a statement to the press in which he announced his intention to go before the national convention as a candidate. Written on April 10, it appeared in Lexington papers on April 12, eastern papers the following day, and throughout the nation within a week.[61]

Both the fact and the content of Clay's announcement were remarkable. Never before in American history had a candidate shed the fiction of passively waiting to be anointed by his party. The apparent arrogance and naked ambition revealed in Clay's "ukase" shocked and alienated many Whigs. Clay attributed his decision to the warnings "that the withdrawal of my name would be fatal to the success, and perhaps lead to the dissolution of the party with which I have been associated, especially in the free states" and to the assurances "that at no former period did there ever exist so great a probability of my election . . . that New York would more certainly bestow her suffrage upon me than any other candidate and that Ohio would give her vote to no candidate residing in the Slave States but me."[62]

One of the people most incensed by Clay's presumptuous manifesto was the other slave state candidate, the Hero of Buena Vista himself. The previous November, Taylor had promised Clay that he would withdraw from the race if Clay were the Whig candidate, but by April he viewed Clay's announcement as a last-minute attempt to steal a prize he now considered rightfully his. Thus, on April 20, Taylor angrily wrote the editor of the *Richmond Republican* that he intended to remain in the presidential contest as an independent even if the Whig convention nominated Clay or anyone else. Taylor, indeed, flatly and falsely denied that he had ever told anyone he would withdraw from the race if Clay were nominated.[63]

Clay's announcement also infuriated the anxious Taylor clique in New Orleans, but they realized that Taylor now could win the presidency only as the Whig nominee. Hence, he must issue a public declaration of his Whig principles similar to the one the Young Indians had sent from Washington with Bliss. Logan Hunton, Balie Peyton, James Love, and Alexander Bullitt thus drew up such a letter, and on April 21 the first three presented it to Taylor at his Baton Rouge home. Rewritten that evening on the candidate's veranda to his specifications and edited by the New Orleans committee, this letter was addressed to John

S. Allison, a Kentucky tobacco factor, who happened to be visiting Taylor at the time. Dated April 22, the famous Allison Letter first appeared in the *New Orleans Picayune* on April 25 and then was telegraphed to be reprinted throughout the nation.[64]

In this statement Taylor identified himself as "a Whig but not an ultra Whig," stubbornly reiterated his intention "to act independent of party domination" if elected president, condemned aggressive wars of conquest, and called for magnanimity toward the defeated Mexicans. More important, he embraced the fundamental Whig principle of a weak executive by declaring that Congress should set policy regarding the tariff, currency, and internal improvements and that the president should exercise the veto power only when proposed legislation was clearly unconstitutional. Although the Allison Letter was not the forthright endorsement of Whig programs many had demanded, several historians cite it as the decisive event in securing Taylor's nomination because it finally convinced suspicious Whig regulars that Taylor was one of their own. The appearance of the letter did in fact reassure Taylorite Whigs who had worried about his previous statements, but since its impact was offset by the simultaneous publication of Taylor's defiant and duplicitous letter to the *Richmond Republican*, the great majority of Whig regulars continued to oppose him.[65]

VII

An event that occurred two months before the release of the Allison Letter played a far greater role in determining the ultimate outcome at Philadelphia. It vastly expanded Taylor sentiment in the party by tremendously increasing the desperate sense that the party needed a war hero to win the election. Equally important, it prevented the party's anti-Taylor majority from uniting behind Clay. Had all of Taylor's Whig foes in fact rallied behind Clay, Taylor would never have won the nomination.

On February 23, 1848, the same day that Whig state conventions were squabbling in Kentucky and Virginia, the same day that Clay was feted in Philadelphia, and the same day that Taylor's Peter Sken Smith letter appeared in the New York press, President Polk sent the Senate the Treaty of Guadalupe Hidalgo, which would end the war with Mexico. Negotiated by Nicholas Trist in violation of his instructions from Polk, the treaty had arrived by courier from Mexico only four days earlier. It called for the cession to the United States of the former Mexican states of Upper California and New Mexico, as well as the remaining Mexican territory south of the 42nd parallel, some 500,000 square miles in all. In exchange for this immense acquisition, the United States was to pay Mexico $15 million, as well as all claims against the government of Mexico by private American citizens. Polk's submission of this treaty suddenly, unexpectedly, and forcefully reaffirmed that Democrats largely determined the fate of the Whig party.[66]

The treaty created an anguishing problem for Whig leaders. It promised the peace for which they and their constituents had long clamored, yet it also entailed the territorial acquisition they deeply abhorred. Whig senators would be forced to sacrifice a cherished principle whether they voted for or against ratification. Nor could they remain true to both by voting no and leaving it to the Democrats to ratify the treaty. Whigs held twenty-one Senate seats, and it would take only nineteen votes to prevent the two-thirds majority necessary for ratification. The fate of the treaty rested in Whigs' hands, and they faced a stark choice between peace and expansion or continued war and the probability that Polk's administration would seize still more Mexican territory. As a Georgian wrote Berrien, who voted against ratification, "The Southern Whigs are decidedly opposed to the large acquisition of Territory, reported to have been made, but looked also with great apprehension to the continuance of the war, much to be deprecated under any circumstances, but especially so under the auspices of a Democratic administration."[67]

To be sure, a few Democratic observers and northern Whig senators who voted against the treaty, like Daniel Webster and Connecticut's Roger Sherman Baldwin, denied that rejection of the treaty implied rejection of peace. They believed instead that it would cause the Whig-controlled House immediately to halt the war—and without a territorial indemnity—by cutting off funds to American armies in Mexico. Whigs like Congressman David Outlaw, who understood the disarray of House Whigs on the issue of military appropriations, knew that could not happen and feared that rejection would only give Polk an excuse to conquer all of Mexico. "Though I am now, as I have been heretofore, utterly opposed to the acquisition of territory," Outlaw wrote his wife in a judgment shared by many Whigs, "yet were I a Senator, I should vote for ratification of the treaty upon the ground that it is less evil, to have a part, and that a most sparsely settled part of Mexico, than the whole with its mixed breed of Spaniards, Indians, and negroes."[68]

As Whigs immediately recognized, their quandary over the proper policy had significant ramifications for the impending elections. If they rejected the noxious treaty, they would betray their antiwar professions and their antiwar constituents and thus risk punishment at the polls. If they helped secure ratification, they would surrender the last concrete issue they had to use against the Democrats and the issue on which they expected to win the presidency—opposition to both the war and territorial annexation. "In truth we have the wolf by the ears and it is doubtful which is most dangerous, to hold or let go," moaned Buffalo's Nathan Hall on the day the treaty went to the Senate. Hall's New York Whig colleague William Duer was equally alarmed. "If this treaty is rejected [by Whig votes], good bye to the Whig party."[69]

Given their unhappy choice, Senate Whigs were understandably divided. But so too were the Democrats, many of whom angrily denounced the treaty for not securing enough Mexican soil. As a result, both parties fragmented. Nor was there a clear sectional alignment. A Democratic attempt to amend the treaty by increasing the size of the territorial cession failed, as did George Badger's effort to delete the territorial cession from it entirely. Baldwin's motion to incorporate the Wilmot Proviso into the treaty was laid on the table by the votes of all but two Democrats and the southern Whigs. Finally, on March 10, the treaty was approved by a 38–14 vote. Only seven of the twenty-one Whigs joined the opposition on the final roll call.[70]

Slightly less than three months before their national convention, therefore, Whigs lost the central issue they had counted on to carry the presidential election. Mexico's congress did not ratify the treaty until May 30, and Connecticut's Whigs won their April gubernatorial election by campaigning against the war and annexation.[71] Most Whigs, however, recognized that, since the Democrats had achieved both peace and territorial expansion with the aid of two-thirds of the Senate Whigs, they could no longer rail against the war or demand No Territory. Because the country remained prosperous in the spring of 1848, Whigs also lacked salient economic issues. Able to tout a record of peace, prosperity, and the acquisition of Oregon and the Mexican Cession, Democrats, in contrast, appeared almost certain winners. "It is doubtful whether we can beat the scoundrels next Pres. Election," moaned John Defrees. "The war will have been ended—and an immense acquisition of Land will be pointed to as the result of Democracy—the Land stealing, even among our best *Christians*, is popular!"[72]

Worse still, the sole issue left at Whigs' disposal was one they least wanted to face—the Wilmot Proviso. The actual acquisition of Mexican territory made concrete what had hitherto been only a theoretical problem, the question of slavery expansion into that territory, while simultaneously vaporizing the No Territory formula Whigs had used to paper over their sectional divisions on it. As early as September 1847, Tom Corwin had warned Crittenden, "If the President should get a treaty ceding to us any territory *not* a part of Texas (which is already *in* the Union) & the Wilmot Proviso should be a question *pending* at the next Presidential election, I feel confident we shall fail in electing *any* Whig." Southerners would reject any candidate who endorsed the Proviso, and northern Whigs "will not vote for *any* man who is opposed to it."[73]

Both peace and the sudden unavoidability of the slavery extension issue fatally undermined Clay's candidacy, even as he confidently announced his availability to the nation. As the "embodiment of Whig principles," Clay needed an issue-oriented campaign and thought his Lexington Address had outlined a winning platform. Even Whigs who opposed his nomination thought Clay could be elected if the war were still going on in November 1848.[74] The Senate's action on March 10 thus shattered Clay's hopes. All he had left to recommend him to a party that was looking for a winner was the fealty of thousands of Whig loyalists, his reputation as the foremost champion of Whiggery—and his record as a three-time loser.

In the spring of 1848, when every extant issue seemed either to favor the Democrats or to endanger the Whigs, that was no recommendation at all. Across the North, but especially in midwestern states, whose delegates were considered crucial by all contenders, Whig after Whig insisted that Clay would not do. Thus it was only after the loss of the antiwar, No Territory issue in March that large numbers of Whigs resorted to the opportunistic strategy Thomas Dorr had mocked in January. Without any concrete issues to mobilize the Whig electorate, many argued, "what is wanted & what we must have is a candidate that will receive other than strictly Whig votes." Yet they also recognized that "the Locos never can be brought into the support of Mr. Clay" since "opposition to Clay is part of their nature." To win, Indiana's Orth concluded, Whigs must abandon Clay, shun the untrustworthy Taylor, and find "a firm, decided, *available* Whig." "If Mr. Clay is the nominee," echoed scores of other midwestern Whigs, "the Whig party" would again be "doomed to inevitable defeat" and Clay would "be the most beaten man that ever ran the race."[75]

The end of the war with a territorial cession posed the greatest danger to Clay's prospects, but the reigniting of the divisive slavery expansion issue also sharply reversed the considerable momentum Clay had developed in the South since December. Shorn of the No Territory formula's protective shield, southern Whigs became, for the first time, solely dependent on the identity of the party's presidential nominee to meet the Democratic and Calhounite challenge on the slavery issue. To most Southerners, Clay was a hopeless paladin in such a contest, for as soon as the Senate ratified the treaty, thereby obviating No Territory, northern Whigs in the House tried to impose the hated Proviso on the Mexican Cession. And Clay, in his April 10 announcement, smugly portrayed himself as the savior of those very same northern Whigs.

John Berrien's Georgia friend Iverson L. Harris described the dilemma and mindset of southern Whigs precisely. "It has ever seemed to me that the acquisition of territory would necessarily dissolve the Whig party," he mourned, "if the anti-slavery men madly make the exclusion of slavery a sine qua non in their support of a Presidential candidate." Northerners, he grumped, would support Clay because of his antislavery Lexington Address. "Had no territory been acquired [Clay's] opinions (abstractions) would have been a matter of indifference." But now "the very countenance of an anti-slavery man will do the Whig party more prejudice at the South than all other matters combined; there is more involved than even our great interests—they become questions of feeling—passion—and reason is powerless to subdue or even allay them." Now only Taylor's nomination could save southern Whigs from electoral disaster. Without it, the Whig party in the South "will be prostrate for years." Should northern Whigs reject Taylor for an antislavery nominee, indeed, southern Whigs could have "no further fraternity" with them. At stake in Taylor's nomination, in sum, was the continued existence of the national Whig party itself.[76]

Tennessee's Meredith P. Gentry reached the same conclusion. Northern Whigs who wanted to run Clay on antislavery grounds, he explained, had been brought "to the verge of abolitionism." For years they had agitated against slavery and denounced northern Democrats for their "subserviency to the Slave power of the South" in order to win over northern voters. "They commenced this game for political effect," but "those who commenced it as a mere political game, have in many instances worked themselves into the madness of fanaticism. Compel them to take Taylor as a Candidate, and the necessity of their position compels them to breast the storm they themselves have conjured up." In contrast, should Clay or anyone else but Taylor get the Whig nomination, northern Whigs would become "a contemptible abolition faction, the South will be necessarily confined to the dominion of Locofocoism, and the Whig party will be annihilated."[77]

After March 10, in sum, Clay's defeat and Taylor's nomination appeared to be absolutely essential to the political safety, indeed, to the continued existence of the southern Whig party. Clay's April 10 announcement deepened that conviction. Clay "is determined to rule or ruin the party," erupted Robert Toombs after seeing Clay's "Ashland ukase." "He has sold himself body and soul to the Northern Anti-Slavery Whigs." Thus his election posed "the greatest possible danger to the South, and I shall never do any act to aid it." Clay "turned his back upon the South in his Lexington speech and cast his hopes upon the north," chorused Gentry. He was supported in the North only because "of his opposition to Slavery" and therefore, if he won the Whig nomination, "he will be supported at the north upon such grounds as will make it improper & impossible for southern men to sustain him."[78]

Terrified of Clay's nomination, southern Taylor Whigs redoubled their efforts between March 10 and June 7 to send safe Taylor delegates to the Philadelphia convention. On the same day that Taylor penned the Allison Letter, Orlando Brown issued a circular to the Taylor Whigs of Kentucky arguing that the state convention in February had recommended both Clay and Taylor and had selected unpledged delegates only because of assurances from Washington that Clay would withdraw. Taylor was the clear favorite of Kentucky's Whigs, the circular declared, and therefore the state's delegates must vote for Rough and Ready. Tennessee's Whig congressmen bombarded leading Whigs in their state with demands to make sure that Taylor delegates were chosen at the May district meetings. Every vote would count, they warned; an independent Taylor nomination was now impractical. Similarly, Georgia's Whigs, who had initially refused to hold a convention to choose delegates, changed course and called a state convention for May. Despite eloquent pleas from Berrien that the Georgia party stand by Clay, the great majority of the delegates it chose were avid Taylor men, although the device of allowing district caucuses to choose each congressional district's delegate resulted in the selection of a few of Clay's friends like Lucius Gartell. The realization that Taylor might lose the party's nomination and his status as the last hope of proving that southern Whigs were safe on the slavery issue nonetheless drove the vast majority of southern Whig delegates into the Taylor column.[79]

Clay's northern support also eroded. Extreme antislavery Whigs had always rejected him, but most northern Whigs considered the Lexington resolutions a viable platform so long as slavery extension could be stopped by preventing territorial expansion. The cession of Mexican lands and northern Whigs' renewed demands for the Wilmot Proviso thus made Clay's refusal to embrace it a grave liability. On April 6, Corwin warned Clay's friend, the Cincinnati editor Thomas B. Stevenson, that Clay could never win the nomination because "he is not anti-Territory or anti-Slavery enough to meet the inflammatory feeling of the North." Two days later, Stevenson informed Clay that his Ohio supporters "confidently" expected him to "publicly declare against the extension of slavery in the new territories." Significantly, Stevenson also told Clay that he need not endorse the Proviso and thereby destroy his chances in the South. Instead, he implored Clay to insist that the laws regarding slavery that existed in a foreign territory prior to its acquisition remained in force after its acquisition. Thus, just as Florida and Louisiana had automatically become slave territories because Spanish and French law had allowed slavery, the Mexican Cession was free soil because Mexican law prohibited slaveholding. Demanding that this traditional precedent be followed with the Mexican Cession could not offend the South, Stevenson assured Clay, and it would satisfy antislavery Whigs in Ohio, but only if Clay avowed it publicly. That Mexican law prohibited slavery from the Mexican Cession even without the Wilmot Proviso was, indeed, widely believed by Northerners and Southerners, Whigs and Democrats, alike. Thus Stevenson planted the seed from which would grow Clay's famous, but misunderstood, compromise proposals of 1850.[80]

In 1848, however, Clay refused to make any further statements on the slavery extension issue. On May 3, Corwin, who in February had urged Clay to remain in the race, flatly told him that his speech at Lexington no longer satisfied "that portion of the Whigs in the free states, who are violently opposed to the further extension of Slavery," that slavery extension would be the central issue of the presidential election in the North, and that Clay could not now carry Ohio or other northern states if the Democrats chose a nonslaveholding candidate, as was expected. Again, on May 18, the faithful Stevenson warned Clay that large numbers of Ohio Whigs would bolt the party and join a new antislavery organization should either Clay or Taylor get the Whig nomination. Only by issuing the statement against slavery expansion he had earlier advised, Stevenson insisted, could Clay carry Ohio or, of more immediate significance, secure Ohio's votes at the Whig national convention. But Clay would not budge. He had done enough, he told Stevenson. He would leave his fate to the Whig delegates at Philadelphia.[81]

Many northern Whigs had long looked for a northern alternative to Clay and Taylor. Even before ratification of the treaty, some apprehensive Whig congressmen concluded that the struggle between the two rivals' adherents was becoming so rancorous that "it would be better for the Whig party if Clay & Taylor both could be satisfactorily disposed of and some new man less prominent than Mr. Clay yet a decided Whig, placed in nomination." After March 10, far more northern Whigs hoped "that some third man will be taken." The reality that slavery might expand into the Mexican Cession unless the Proviso were adopted convinced a growing number of northern Whigs that "we must have a Northern man for our candidate."[82]

Cries for a northern candidate created no consensus on an alternative to Clay and Taylor, but they resurrected hopes of other aspirants who had largely been forgotten since December. They jump-started Webster's long-stalled candidacy, for example, if only briefly. Shortly after the Senate ratified the treaty with Mexico, Webster delivered a thundering speech denouncing the territorial cession, which his friends then eagerly trumpeted as a "creed for Northern Whigs . . . to rally under." With the aid of Edward Everett and direct encouragement from Webster himself, New York City's Hiram Ketchum published a series of letters in the New York *Commercial Advertiser*, later circulated as a pamphlet entitled "A Whig from the Start," that rehearsed Webster's long support for Whig programs to promote economic growth, his dedication to the supremacy of law and the Constitution, and the necessity of nominating a Northerner. Privately, in letters to Millard Fillmore and Maine's William Pitt Fessenden, Ketchum trumpeted Webster's opposition to slavery expansion, insisted that northern delegates to the Whig convention must resist "all these concessions and compromises which end in making a slaveholder a candidate," and vowed that his cause was "Webster and the free states. Webster & the North."[83]

Webster, Ketchum implausibly contended, could mobilize the Whig vote and garner non-Whig support better than anyone else. Webster was undeniably a Northerner, in contrast to Clay and Taylor, and, unlike Taylor, a committed proponent of Whig programs. Still, Democrats had no more incentive to vote for Webster than for Clay. Nor did members of the Liberty party and other extreme antislavery men, for Webster had dodged endorsing the Proviso just as assiduously as had Clay. Even so orthodox a Whig as Fillmore doubted Webster's availability.[84]

Northern Whigs' aversion to any slaveholding candidate also rejuvenated the hopes of McLean's friends. During April and May, McLean's deluded supporters grew increasingly confident that Greeley and the New York Whigs would dump Clay and turn to the judge rather than Corwin. And McLean picked up significant new support in Indiana from Congressmen Caleb B. Smith, Elisha Embree, and Richard W. Thompson, as well as from Indianapolis editor John Defrees.[85] Moreover, to advance McLean's appeal as a party-healing compromise candidate, his managers sought to worsen relations between the Taylor and Clay camps. Newspaper correspondent James E. Harvey, the most astute and best-informed political operative in McLean's camp, published a story about Taylor's November 1847 letter to Clay promising to withdraw if Clay were nominated, a promise Taylor wantonly broke in his *Richmond Republican* letter. Since Clay's friends would be incensed by the story and Taylor's friends would blame Clay for leaking it, he chortled, "A fierce personal war is to occur between these two divisions, headed by their respective leaders, which of course must result to the advantage of a third candidate."[86]

But even McLean's most optimistic advocates knew that shrewd tactics alone would not snatch the nomination from a deadlocked convention. To do that, three formidable obstacles had to be overcome. First, whatever else McLean was, he was not "A Whig from the Start," and he remained just as vulnerable as Taylor to the determination among northern Whigs that the alternative to Taylor and Clay be a "firm, reliable . . . Whig."[87] Second, McLean had no chance at the convention unless he won solid support from the Ohio delegation. In Ohio, however, McLean lacked a reliable organization and faced bitter opposition from the Corwin men, who, since February, had swung to Clay or Winfield Scott in order to stop him. By early May the most influential Corwin men—Schenck, Lewis Campbell, and Governor Bebb—were all raising Scott's banner. Ohio's delegation to the Philadelphia convention would in fact be surprisingly united, not behind McLean or Clay, as Bebb had predicted, but behind the other great hero of the hated Mexican War.[88]

Here was the third and insurmountable obstacle to McLean's chances in Ohio and at Philadelphia. Just as in 1845, Winfield Scott, "Old Fuss and Feathers," the "hasty plate of soup candidate," once again blocked his bid to become the alternative to regular Whigs like Clay and Webster and to another outsider like Taylor. During April and May, Scott aroused far more enthusiasm among northern Whigs than anyone else. Several reasons explain his phoenix-like rise from the humiliation and ridicule of 1846. Unlike McLean and Taylor, he was deemed a good Whig. Unlike Clay and Taylor, he was a nonslaveholder and yet Virginia born. Most important, unlike Clay, Webster, and McLean, and more justifiably than Taylor, he possessed the sheen of military heroism.

VIII

Between March 10 and June 7, the unexpected obliteration of the Whigs' major issue, Democrats' ability to campaign on peace, prosperity, and territorial expansion, and the suddenly perceived need to attract non-Whig voters led many Whigs from competitive states to the same conclusion reached much earlier by fellow Whigs in Democratic strongholds. Not simply Clay, but no civilian could lead the Whigs to victory in 1848. The candidate, one wrote, must be able to "unite whatever there is left amongst the people of the popularity of the Mexican war and also the opposition to the mode of prosecuting it by the present administration." Running a general "gives us an answer in a word to all the clamor & humbug about the war," urged New York Congressman Washington Hunt while advocating Scott's nomination. "After all, the locofocos rely mainly on the war. . . . With a victorious general we could readily turn the popular current to our side."[89]

During these months some Whigs in Democratic states like Maine and safe Democratic counties in New Jersey selected Taylor delegates to the national convention. Taylor also generated considerable enthusiasm in parts of Indiana. Far more Whigs in Indiana, Ohio, Pennsylvania, and New York, however, now boomed Scott, whose popularity and delegate count in these states ascended like a rocket. "The Whigs have to run either Scott or Taylor or be defeated so badly that you will hardly know we run a candidate," declared Indiana's ex-Congressman Edward McGaughey five days after the treaty was ratified. "To talk of Clay or McLean is worse than madness." Within weeks of McLean's nomination, "the Whig party would be so dead" that "a galvanic battery could not move a muscle in the whole body." No civilian would do! "We must have the aid of gunpowder—the fortress of Locofocoism can not be taken without it." No one expressed so pungently the panicky sense of desperation that drove thousands of Whigs across the North toward military heroes after—*and only after*—the end of the Mexican War.[90]

Battlefield glory was Scott's greatest, but not his only, asset. A few Whigs saw his candidacy as the best solution to the party's bitter divisions over the Wilmot Proviso. So unbridgeable did that chasm appear after March 10, indeed, that some Whigs and Democrats predicted that "Southern and Northern Whigs [could] never agree on the same candidate," and that the party instead would run Taylor in the South and somebody else in the North. As late as May 30, only eight days before the Whigs' national convention met, Illinois' Democratic Congressman John McClernand warned, "It is to be feared that the Whigs will present two candidates, one upon the Northern platform of slavery or rather antislavery, and another upon the Southern pro-slavery platform."[91]

Scott, several astute Whigs realized, offered a way to achieve the same goal—conducting a Janus-faced campaign by running against the Proviso in the South and for it in the North—behind a single candidate. "The Wilmot Proviso brings some perplexity," Hunt informed Weed nine days after the Senate approved the treaty. "Our Southern brethren are restive and fractious, and they sometimes threaten to draw Mason & Dixon's line between us. I tell them they may have their way south of it, & we must manage things for ourselves on the north side." He had conferred with Corwin and Clayton, he went on, and they all agreed that the way to do this was to drop both Taylor and Clay and nominate Scott. As a slaveholder, Taylor would lose the North unless he openly endorsed the Proviso, something he could not do without alienating his southern supporters. Clay was bound to lose the South since Southerners believed he favored the Proviso. Only by publicly denouncing it could he win the South, but then he would lose the North. Scott was "the only man who can run without declaring himself on the Wilmot Proviso." As Godlove Orth, who swung to Scott, put it, "He is a northern man, without being in the least identified with the anti-slavery movement so as to make him obnoxious to the South."[92]

But Scott also carried serious liabilities that advocates of other aspirants were quick to expose. He offended the many Whigs who considered the nomination of any soldier a betrayal of fundamental party principle. Elevating a leading participant in a despised war also risked alienating Whigs who had opposed it on moral grounds, particularly Quakers, who were deemed vital to Whig success in Indiana and Ohio. Taylor's personal animosity toward Scott was widely known among Whig leaders, and many dismissed as fantasy the assumption that Scott would inherit Taylor's support. No nomination, they argued accurately, was more likely to spur a vengeful Taylor into an independent candidacy than that of Scott, and if Taylor remained in the race, realistic Whigs understood, the Whigs could not win. Scott also remained vulnerable to the mockery of Democrats, who could and assuredly would endlessly reprint the foolish letters he had sent Marcy at the beginning of the war.[93]

To many strategists, however, Scott's gravest liability was a different letter he had written before the war started. In December 1844, in a clumsy bid for nativist support, Scott had published a letter over the name "Americus" in the National Intelligencer. The Americus letter denounced the growing political influence of ignorant foreigners and argued that naturalized immigrants should serve for two years in the United States Army before being allowed to vote. Since December 1844, intervening events had monopolized public attention, and most political observers had long forgotten, if they had ever seen, this letter. During one of Greeley's trips to Washington in the spring of 1848, however, McLean's lieutenants, who were eager to quash the incipient Scott boom, showed it to him in old newspaper files. Greeley then flayed the letter and its author in the Tribune. The Whigs, he proclaimed, dared not run anyone who offended immigrants. On this point, at least, Seward and Weed and other like-minded Whigs agreed. Aware that the stigma of nativism had mobilized tens of thousands of immigrants against them in 1844 and had, more than anything else, defeated Clay in key northern states, they had no desire to repeat that mistake.[94]

If Scott had liabilities as a candidate, northern Whigs' frantic hunt for a non-slaveholding military hero caused many to dismiss them. Scott simply excited more enthusiasm among rank-and-file northern Whigs than any other alternative to Clay and Taylor. Unlike the pipe-dreaming McLean men, Clay's friends recognized that fact and the likelihood that Scott could siphon off vital delegates from Clay in Indiana, Ohio, Pennsylvania, and New York.

Their response, with the significant exception of Greeley's exposé of the Americus letter, was not to publicize Scott's weaknesses but to capitalize on his strengths by combining him on the ticket with Clay as the vice presidential candidate. Clay denied any personal responsibility for this initiative, but a Whig paper in Lexington, Kentucky, as well as Clay's champion Botts, in a speech at Philadelphia, broached the idea. Rumors circulated that another Clay lieutenant, Leslie Combs, had gone to New Orleans to meet Scott when he returned to the United States to persuade him to accept the second slot. And when Scott landed in New York City in mid-May, Clay's friends there urged him to take it. Scott, surprisingly, agreed, and he apparently told a Whig member of Congress, whom he took to be a friend of Clay, to inform the convention that he would run for vice president on a Clay ticket. The unidentified individual never delivered the message to the convention. Nor did Scott, driven to bed for weeks with a severe case of diarrhea contracted in Mexico, make any further contact with the convention. Thus was aborted what may have been Clay's last hope.[95]

As Whig delegates converged on Philadelphia in early June, therefore, northern Whigs remained as fragmented as ever over their preferred candidate. Taylor had garnered delegates in Illinois, Maine, and New Jersey, and he had popular support in Indiana, although no one knew what its delegates might do. With the end of the war and continuing absence of salient economic issues, some Pennsylvania Whigs, especially those around Philadelphia who sought Native American help, also frantically promoted Taylor's nomination. Yet the vast majority of northern Whigs still believed that his candidacy would destroy them by keeping orthodox regulars at home on election day and driving antislavery Whigs to the Liberty party or to a new and broader antislavery organization, a threat openly and repeatedly voiced by extreme antislavery Whigs like Giddings and Henry Wilson.[96]

When the Democratic national convention in late May, over the vehement protests of New York's Barnburners, nominated Michigan's Lewis Cass, northern Whigs' alarm that it would be suicidal to run a southern slaveholder increased.[97] Paradoxically, however, Cass' nomination simultaneously presented northern Whigs with a splendid opportunity that also seemed to require nominating a Northerner. Cass was a leading proponent of "popular sovereignty," the formula Democrats had devised to preserve sectional harmony on the divisive slavery expansion question when the Whigs had turned to No Territory. Unlike No Territory, popular sovereignty continued to be viable after the fact of territorial acquisition, for it called on Congress to leave to the residents of the territories themselves the decision regarding slavery.

On the one hand, because Cass had publicly denounced the Wilmot Proviso as unconstitutional and pledged to veto it, his nomination left the Democrats in the North vulnerable to a Whig campaign that advocated the Wilmot Proviso as a surer way than popular sovereignty to keep slavery out of the territories. Roll-call votes in Congress in the spring of 1848 demonstrated that northern Whigs supported the Proviso much more firmly than northern Democrats, but such a campaign would lack credibility if the Whigs nominated a slaveholder who seemed likely to veto the Proviso.

On the other hand, Van Burenite Democrats, committed to the Proviso by the end of 1847, absolutely abhorred Cass. Astute Whigs thus recognized that Cass' nomination greatly increased the chances that Van Burenite Democrats across the North might join the new antislavery party that was apparently forming in the North. With the considerable strength the Van Burenites could bring to such an organization, it might be an even more attractive alternative to dissident antislavery Whigs should the party fail to nominate a nonslaveholder.[98]

Keenly aware of the consequences of not stopping Taylor, northern anti-Taylor Whigs still could not unite on a candidate. Webster controlled the delegates from Massachusetts and New Hampshire, and he still hoped to pick up additional New England delegates while preparing last-minute arguments to sway Southerners.

Clay retained considerable support in New York, Vermont, Connecticut, and Rhode Island, as well as in the new state of Wisconsin, whose delegates were primarily concerned with obtaining federal subsidies for internal improvements. But in Pennsylvania and most of the Midwest, enthusiasm for Clay had cooled considerably. Support for McLean had also eroded in those states, and by the end of May an Indianan who had lobbied his state's delegates for the judge admitted that McLean "cannot be nominated." All the northern delegates must rally on Scott, a Michigan delegate warned on June 2, or "the Whig party is disorganized & disbanded forever."[99]

So fragmented did the northern delegates who arrived at Philadelphia appear that Thurlow Weed, who came as an observer rather than a delegate, sought to unite them at the last moment behind Delaware's John M. Clayton, a short, corpulent, heavy-drinking Yale graduate, who was the only Whig senator from a slave state who had ever voted for the Wilmot Proviso. According to cynics and Weed's enemies within the New York Whig party, Weed pushed Clayton for another reason. Only the nomination of a Southerner would allow the selection of a Northerner to balance the ticket as the vice presidential candidate, and Weed wanted that slot for his friend Seward.[100]

In contrast to the disarray of northern delegates, southern Whigs almost unanimously insisted upon Taylor's nomination because they now considered an independent Taylor campaign impractical. Southerners still regarded Clay as Taylor's chief rival, and the few Clay men who had been chosen as delegates in the Deep South like Georgia's Lucius Gartell, Louisiana's William Brashear, and Alabama's C. C. Langdon received terrific pressure from the Taylorite majorities within their state delegations to go for Rough and Ready. Adding to that pressure, the pro-Taylor members of Congress, now labeled the Palo Alto Club, met every train that came to Washington carrying delegates from the South and West on their way to Philadelphia and frantically browbeat them with the message that only Taylor could lead Whigs to victory. So successful were these lobbying efforts that Clay's managers Greeley and James Harlan conceded defeat before the convention even met. The loss of three delegates in New Jersey and the frenzied pro-Taylor atmosphere in Washington, Greeley warned Clay on May 29, meant that "we are doomed to be beaten and that the men who control the counsels of the Whig party, through the machinery at Washington have resolved to throw overboard a good part of our principles so as to make a surer rush for the spoils."[101]

IX

By June 7, not just delegates and alternates but literally thousands of Whigs had jammed into Philadelphia, straining the capacity of hotels, boarding houses, and private homes to accommodate them. Over 10,000 Whigs were reported to have descended from New York alone, as advocates of different men hoped to stampede the proceedings by packing the galleries of the Chinese Museum, the convention site, and by staging street demonstrations outside. According to some observers, the local Taylor organization, particularly Native Americans dedicated to him, exerted the greatest external pressure on the delegates. Editors, wire workers, and political managers who enjoyed more direct access to delegates on the convention floor and in hotel rooms were also abundant. Three of the Young Indians, Smith, Flournoy, and Preston, were official delegates, as were Gentry and Bell of Tennessee, but Lincoln, Crittenden, Webb, and Taylor's brother also attended the convention to marshall his forces. Meeting nightly at the mayor's office, Greeley, Botts, Leslie Combs, and James Harlan, a Kentucky delegate, captained Clay's troops. James Harvey, Thomas Dowling, and Caleb Smith represented McLean's interests; Hiram Ketchum, Theodore Lyman, and Fletcher Webster, those of Webster. Clayton, Weed's compromise choice, was also there, as was Weed himself, looking for the best way to serve Seward.[102]

Surveys of delegates' opinions on the night of June 6 indicated that the chances of uniting the anti-Taylor forces were dim. Pledged to Webster on the first ballot, the Massachusetts delegation contained three distinct groups, all determined to stop Clay: die-hard Webster loyalists who had always been jealous of him; antislavery Young Whigs like Charles Allen and Henry Wilson, who would stick with Webster but who now welcomed the prospect of Taylor's nomination as an excuse to break up the Whig party and form a new antislavery organization in the North; and the friends of Webster's in-state rival Abbott Lawrence, who were cooperating with Southerners to achieve Taylor's nomination in return for Lawrence's elevation to the vice presidency. Though they dared not vote directly for Taylor, they would help by preventing Massachusetts delegates from defecting to Clay.[103]

Ohio's caucus that night dealt a shattering blow to Clay's bid. Many Ohio delegates had been elected by district conventions favorable to Clay, but ex-Governor Joseph Vance, a delegate-at-large, persuaded twenty of the twenty-three men to go as a unit for Scott and to stick with him throughout the balloting. Vance apparently made the case that only Scott now provided northern Whigs a viable candidate and that the convention would eventually come to him if Ohio held its ground. How sincerely Vance sought Scott's nomination is questionable. Friends of other candidates would later charge that he fronted for Corwin and Bebb, who were determined to stop McLean, or, alternatively, that he was in league with Taylor's Washington managers and acted solely to keep Ohio's votes from Clay. But only the surging sentiment for Scott in the Midwest during the two months prior to the convention can explain why the great majority of Ohio delegates, who viscerally opposed Taylor, agreed to go along with Vance. Whatever the Ohioans' motives, their decision, along with the resolve of the Massachusetts men, doomed Clay's candidacy.[104]

The chances that anti-Taylor Whigs would unite on Scott or some other name were equally remote. The few Clay delegates from the South and border states preferred Taylor, not Scott or Clayton, as their second choice, so northern Clay men had little incentive to rally behind Scott to unite the party. The ubiquitous Weed persistently lobbied against Scott among the delegates, yet Weed proved powerless to swing even the New York delegation to Clayton as a compromise candidate. According to a delegate poll taken on the night of June 6, twenty-nine New Yorkers intended to go for Clay on the first ballot, five for Scott, one for Webster, and only Weed's faithful Chautauqua ally George W. Patterson for Clayton. Admitting defeat, Weed abandoned Clayton and, by the morning of

June 7, was openly working for Taylor, whose New York supporters he considered less dangerous than Clay's. His enemies, at least, charged that he did so because he had worked out a deal with the proponents of a Taylor-Lawrence ticket that Seward would become secretary of state in the new administration.[105]

The convention's organization also advanced Taylor's cause. Clay men served as temporary and permanent officers, but the credentials and rules committee gave Taylor's forces a more concrete edge. Composed of one delegate from each state and chaired by Georgia's Thomas Butler King, a Taylor man, it allowed Arkansas' single delegate, a Taylorite, to cast all three of the state's allotted votes. It called on the oversized Louisiana delegation, most of whom favored Taylor, to pick four men from their ranks to vote for Texas, which had sent no delegates of its own. And it provided that the six Louisiana votes at the convention should be divided among its ten delegates in proportion to the preferences of the eighteen delegates originally appointed by a state convention in Louisiana.[106] Since they had been split between fifteen Taylor men and three Clay men, this decision meant that Louisiana would give Taylor five votes and Clay only one on the first ballot. The Taylorites in the Louisiana delegation, led by Samuel Peters, Cuthbert Bullitt, and Lafayette Saunders, refused to allow William Brashear, Clay's firmest friend in the delegation, to be a voting delegate for either Louisiana or Texas. Instead, Bullitt voted as both a Texas and a Louisiana delegate, and Garnett Duncan, a Taylor man, cast the Louisiana vote for Clay on the first ballot—and only on the first ballot. Finally, to ensure that Taylor garnered all of his scattered support in the free states, the committee rejected the unit rule and called for each delegate to vote individually and publicly as the roll was called, a procedure that rendered delegates vulnerable to pressure from pro-Taylor spectators.

Speech-making prior to the actual balloting further helped Taylor. Duncan announced that he had seen a letter from Taylor to Balie Peyton of New Orleans that took "a decided stand in favor of Whig principles." Later, Lafayette Saunders, attempting to mitigate the damage caused by Taylor's *Richmond Republican* letter, declared that Taylor had assured him that he would abide by the decision of the convention and that his friends would withdraw him should it nominate someone else. Between the statements by the two Louisianans, Ohio's Lew Campbell offered an anti-Taylor resolution, declaring that the convention would consider for nomination only men who had publicly pledged to support the convention's nominee and to promote Whig measures, something Taylor had steadfastly refused to do. When the chair ruled this motion out of order and the convention then tabled Campbell's protest of the ruling, delegates' readiness to capitulate to Taylor was etched too clearly for Clay regulars to miss. "The treatment of such a resolution, in the manner it was disposed of by the Convention," scribbled an angry Clay delegate from the convention floor, "is a virtual dissolution of the Whig party of the Union, by their chosen representatives, and absolves every honest man from being fettered by their decisions."[107]

In the early evening of Thursday, June 8, six names were formally placed in nomination: Taylor, Clay, Webster, Scott, McLean, and Clayton. Before the balloting began, Samuel Galloway, a McLean loyalist at the January Ohio state convention, withdrew McLean's name to spare him the humiliation of a meager vote.[108] His action had important implications for pro-McLean delegates from Indiana.

The voting began shortly thereafter. Because the convention, in sharp contrast to the arrangement for Arkansas and Texas, refused to allow the votes of unrepresented congressional districts from South Carolina and Alabama to be cast or counted, there was a total of 279 votes, with 140 required to win. Slave states, including Delaware, had 111 votes; the free states, 168. Even with the rules rigged to favor Taylor, he could not win without northern support. The first ballot revealed the South's unity behind him, the fragmentation of the North's anti-Taylor forces, and the erosion of Clay's expected strength. McLean got two votes, Clayton four, Webster twenty-two, and Scott forty-three. As had long been expected, Taylor and Clay were the frontrunners, but their order stunned many in attendance. Taylor led Clay 111 to 97, when as late as the previous night, most observers had credited Clay with at least 115 first-ballot votes.[109]

That Clay garnered only one Ohio vote and only five of Kentucky's twelve convinced most attendees that he was finished. As delegates worriedly reported, however, the balloting's clearest pattern was the stark clash between Northerners and Southerners.[110] Of the 111 southern delegates, 85 backed Taylor; three-fourths of Taylor's initial vote thus came from slave states. Aside from Delaware, which clung to Clayton, the twenty-three remaining Southerners went for Clay—all eight of Maryland's delegates, five from both Kentucky and North Carolina, two from Virginia, and one each from Louisiana, Alabama, and South Carolina, which had two self-appointed delegates at the convention. Excepting Delaware, Maryland, and South Carolina, in short, Taylor had majorities in every slave state, narrow in Whiggish Kentucky and North Carolina, heavy in Virginia, Louisiana, and Alabama. Georgia, Tennessee, Mississippi, Texas, Florida, Arkansas, and Missouri went for him unanimously. In contrast to Taylor's 76 percent of the southern vote, 85 percent of northern delegates voted against him.

What devastated Clay was the division in the free states, where he got two-thirds of his total. Taylor won only twenty-six northern votes compared to Clay's sixty-four, yet those sixty-four votes represented only 38 percent of northern delegates. Almost half of the Northerners divided their votes among Webster, Scott, Clayton, and McLean, but it was the crucial defection of forty votes to Scott in Indiana, Ohio, Pennsylvania, and New York—the big northern states on which Clay had counted—that ruined him. Had Clay attracted Scott's forty-three votes, he would have won the nomination on the first ballot despite the stubbornness of the Webster men. Little wonder that Clay and his friends considered the suppression of Scott's willingness to run for vice president on Clay's ticket the key to his defeat.[111]

Equally revealing, just as Clay and even McLean had complained, Taylor did far better among the delegates from Democratic states the party had little chance to carry, as well as among the delegates from Democratic congressional districts in Whig and competitive states, than he did elsewhere. Taylor received thirty-five votes, or a third of his total, from Democratic strongholds like Maine, Illinois, Missouri, Arkansas, Alabama, Mississippi, Texas and South Carolina. Altogether he captured 69 percent of the votes of irredeemably Democratic states; in contrast, Clay received just six votes, or 12 percent of their total. Clay outpaced Taylor in Whig and competitive states, but, again because of the fragmentation of the anti-Taylor vote, his edge was not nearly as decisive as Taylor's margin in Democratic states.[112]

On the second ballot that evening, Taylor gained seven votes while Clay lost eleven. Five first-ballot Clay voters—four Northerners and Duncan—shifted to Taylor, but the other Clay defectors, all Northerners, went to Scott. Clay's southern supporters remained steadfast despite the immense pressure on them. Webster's and Clayton's delegates also stood pat. Thus at the end of the roll call the totals stood: Taylor, 118; Clay, 86; Scott, 49; Webster, 22; and Clayton, 4.

At this point, Clay's adherents pressed successfully for a recess until the following morning in order to shore up Clay's fading support. Rather than make a positive case for Clay or bargain for votes with promises of office, Clay's friends apparently devoted the rest of the night to damning the Scott and Webster men for betraying Whig principles by refusing to rally behind the Kentuckian, a tack that made more enemies than it gained friends. Meanwhile, Weed and other Taylor operators used the recess to play on the ambition of younger men and small-fry politicos among the delegates. Clay was an old man with lifelong friends in every state, they pointed out. If he were elected, he would obviously reward his aged, blue-stocking loyalists with federal jobs. Only a new man would give younger Whigs a crack at the spoils. Simultaneously, southern Taylorites pointed to the sectional pattern of the two votes and increased pressure on southern Clay men to go for Taylor out of regional loyalty. Reverdy Johnson lobbied the Maryland delegation, which had gone solidly for Clay on both ballots. They had been instructed to stick with Clay as long as he had a chance to win, but Clay's decline between the first and second ballots provided the excuse for three Taylor men in the delegation to break ranks.[113]

Taylor's managers were nonetheless badly shaken. Taylor's failure to gain significantly between the first and second ballots, the evidence that Northerners seemed more inclined to shift to Scott than to Taylor, and the undeniable sectional polarization over his candidacy jolted those men who envisioned Taylor as the savior of the national Whig party rather than as a paladin of Southern Rights. Most upset was Truman Smith, the party's unofficial national chairman, who, with the possible exception of Crittenden, had done more than anyone to promote Taylor. That night the unnerved Smith vigorously entreated his colleagues to adjourn the convention without making a nomination.[114]

Widely known for his role as the manager of Whig congressional campaigns, a role he was expected to fill again in the fall, Truman Smith was the convention's most influential and fascinating figure. His mysterious course has long baffled historians. Chairman of the Connecticut delegation, he had joined his colleagues to vote unanimously for Clay on both ballots, despite having publicly defied the pro-Clay Whig sentiment in Connecticut since the previous December. Palpably, he hoped that Taylor would win without his personally having to vote for him, and the question is why. Why would Smith now seek to adjourn the convention rather than be forced to vote for Taylor himself, thereby flouting sentiment he had already flouted for seven months?[115] The intense sectional animosity on the convention floor possibly so frightened this guardian of the national party organization that he wanted to adjourn to avert disruption. More likely, he desperately sought to avoid voting for Taylor, whom he ardently supported, because of the concurrent struggle in the Connecticut legislature over the state's two Senate seats. After a bitter internal brawl among Whigs, Smith and New Haven's Roger Sherman Baldwin had been very narrowly elected senator on May 31, one week before the convention opened. The legislature was still in session, and Whigs could rescind Smith's election if he did anything to anger them.[116]

Hence Smith's reluctance to abandon Clay at Philadelphia. He dared not vote for Taylor and risk alienating any more Whigs in the Connecticut legislature. Other Taylor leaders at Philadelphia, however, would not hear of adjourning the convention without a nomination. Since every vote now seemed necessary to put Taylor over the top, Smith reluctantly decided to vote for Taylor and to use his considerable influence among the rest of the Connecticut delegation and other New England Whigs. That Connecticut came third in the alphabetical roll call of states and that Smith, as chairman of the delegation, would vote first ensured that his vote would have enormous impact in swaying the convention.

The combination of developments on Thursday night clinched Taylor's victory. On Friday morning, even before the balloting began, a New York Clay delegate glumly informed Fillmore that the general would win, and he warned prophetically that the nomination would ignite an uproar from angry Northerners. No changes occurred as Alabama and Arkansas led off the voting on the third ballot. C. C. Langdon, Alabama's lone Clay man, heroically held firm. Then Smith and two other Connecticut delegates announced their switch to Taylor, setting off wild cheering from the pro-Taylor galleries and loud groans from the Clay supporters on the floor. The dike had broken. By the end of the ballot Taylor's total had climbed to 133, just seven short of a majority, Clay's had fallen to 74, Webster's to 17, and Clayton's to a single vote. Scott gained five more votes for a total of fifty-four. In addition to the six votes from Connecticut and Maryland, five other Clay men, only one a Southerner, switched to Taylor. Of Taylor's remaining recruits, Massachusetts' George Lunt was symbolically most important since he broke away from Webster. On this decisive ballot, the slaveholder Taylor gained only five more southern votes compared to ten from the North. Scott gained the other defectors from Clay, Webster, and Clayton.[117]

With Taylor so close to victory, an avalanche of delegates tumbled toward the obvious winner on the fourth ballot. Taylor soared to 171 votes, Scott climbed to 63, Clayton was eliminated, and Clay and Webster, the two greatest statesmen the Whig party boasted, were reduced to the humiliating totals of 35 and 13 votes, respectively. Again, Taylor's gains from the North outpaced those from the South, twenty-three to fifteen. He won majorities from the Maine, New Jersey, and Indiana delegations, while Iowa, Wisconsin, Illinois, and, astonishingly, Rhode Island, which had been Clay's banner state in 1844, now supported Taylor unanimously. The shift of Southerners toward Taylor was much more significant than on the previous two ballots. The inevitability of Taylor's victory, not alarm about slavery or Southern Rights, produced this last-minute movement, but the defections from Clay reduced his count in the slave states to five.[118]

Altogether, between the first and fourth ballots fifty Northerners and twenty-one Southerners had switched to the Taylor column. He could not have won without that northern support, and his gain among Northerners blurred the sharp sectional dimension that had characterized the first ballot. Nevertheless, the polarization between North and South remained stark to everyone in the convention hall. Since a Missouri delegate voted for the first time on the final ballot, slave states had a total of 112 votes, and Taylor received 106 of them. Southern votes now constituted 62 percent of his total rather than the 76 percent on the first ballot, so that Northerners now made up almost two-fifths rather than one-fourth of his vote. But those Northerners constituted only 39 percent of free-state delegates. Although this figure marked a great improvement over his 15 percent on the first ballot, three-fifths of the party's northern wing continued to oppose 95 percent of the Southerners. More important, with the exception of Democratic Illinois and Maine and the swing state of Indiana, Taylor did least well among delegates from the biggest northern states. Pennsylvania gave him twelve of its twenty-six votes; New York, six of thirty-six; Massachusetts, one of twelve; and Ohio, one of twenty-three.

The final ballot also culminated another important trend that had been apparent from the outset. Even on the first ballot Scott and Taylor together had received a majority of the convention's votes, and on each subsequent ballot the military heroes had gained at the expense of civilian candidates. On the ultimate vote, fully 84 percent of the delegates, three-fourths of the Northerners and virtually all of the Southerners, supported the victorious generals. Together, Clay and Webster, the issue-oriented champions of specific Whig measures, had been reduced to a fourth of the Northern votes and a meager 16 percent of the entire convention. Little wonder that Greeley labeled the Philadelphia conclave "a slaughterhouse of Whig principles."[119] As the delegates had conferred with one another both before and during the convention, their sense of desperation as they confronted a campaign with no effective issues had quite obviously spread. With each ballot, more delegates concluded that the Whig party did indeed require the aid of gunpowder to capture the fortress of Loco Focoism.

Both the palpable abandonment of any pretense to an issue-oriented campaign and the Southerners' predominance in Taylor's victorious coalition provoked immediate and angry comment from delegates and observers at the convention. Clay's friends repeatedly accused "the mis-representatives of the Whig party" of committing parricide. "They would not take a true *ultra* Whig & a constitutional conservative slaveholder," fumed Leslie Combs, "and they have gotten an *ultra* slaveholder & no particular Whig." The fury of northern antislavery men at the triumph of the Louisiana slaveholder and at the gloating jubilation of his "hot-headed" Southern supporters, however, had the most immediate impact on the remaining proceedings. Amid the tumult that broke out after the reading of the final tally, John Collier of New York announced that while he had opposed Taylor, he would support the nomination. He then warned, in a thinly veiled reference to the visible and audible anger of northern anti-Taylor men, that the convention could still result in disaster. To preserve harmony it should immediately proceed to the vice presidential nomination, and he wanted Millard Fillmore for that post. Collier's implication was clear. Nominating Fillmore rather than Abbott Lawrence, southern Taylorites' favorite, alone could restore harmony.[120]

Charles B. Allen, a Conscience Whig from Massachusetts, was more intransigent. New York might be satisfied with the nomination, he snarled, but the Bay State was not. "We have a man who will continue the rule of slavery for another four years." Massachusetts "rejected the nominee of the Convention, and . . . Massachusetts would spurn the bribe that was to be offered to her [of a candidate for vice president]." Because not a single southern vote had been cast for a northern Whig, exclaimed Allen, "the Whig Party of the United States is . . . dissolved."[121]

Four Ohioans, whose large delegation had given Taylor but a single vote, next spoke: John Bingham, Samuel Galloway, Daniel R. Tilden, and Lewis Campbell. Even before the third ballot started on Friday morning, the Ohioans had planned to insist that the party adopt the Wilmot Proviso as its platform should Taylor win, and one of the four, variously identified as Bingham, Galloway, or Campbell in the conflicting newspaper reports of the proceedings, introduced a resolution stating that the Whig party would endorse the nomination of Taylor only "on condition that he will . . . adhere to [the party's] great fundamental principles, no extension of slave territory, no acquisition of foreign territory by conquest, protection of American industry, and opposition to Executive patronage." Whoever introduced this resolution—and even its wording differs in the various accounts— all four Ohioans unequivocally declared that their constituents intensely opposed the extension of slavery and would never support Taylor unless he publicly committed himself against it.[122]

Amid yells of approval and disapproval, the chair ruled the resolution out of order and tried to press ahead with nominations for vice president. Before he could restore order, Henry Wilson of Massachusetts shouted a speech above the din. He came to the convention as a Whig prepared to support the nomination of a Whig, he declared disingenuously. But "we have nominated a gentleman . . . who is anything but a Whig, and, sir, I will go home, and so help me God, I will do all I can to defeat the election of that candidate."

It is extraordinarily significant that Wilson, who for over a year had privately objected to Taylor because of his slaveholding and was eagerly planning to build a new antislavery party, publicly justified his bolt from the party by citing Taylor's dubious Whiggery. All of the Ohioans also emphasized and condemned Taylor's lack of party regularity. While antislavery sentiment was a powerful cause of northern Whig opposition to Taylor, in short, they well knew that Taylor's No Partyism generated even deeper discontent among their Whig constituents.

Ohio's Vance and George Ashmun of Massachusetts attempted to restore a modicum of comity to the proceedings by insisting that the men who had spoken did not represent Whig opinion in their states. Ohio and Massachusetts would support the nominee, they declared. The fervent hostility of the Northerners nonetheless left some Southerners "thunderstruck and alarmed" that defeat could be snatched from the jaws of victory. The party seemed to stand on the edge of a schism that would deny Taylor the northern votes he needed for election. It could topple over that precipice if southern hotheads in their moment of exultation tried to press their advantage too far. As sensible Southerners knew, the preservation of party harmony now depended on the vice presidential candidate.[123]

Fourteen names were placed in nomination, including that of New York boss Weed, who had always shunned elective office, but only four Northerners were serious contenders since even extreme proslavery Southerners realized the ticket had to be balanced. Southerners decidedly preferred Lawrence, the millionaire textile manufacturer, for his friends had been cooperating with them for months to achieve Taylor's nomination. Wealthy New York merchants also favored Lawrence, as did many New Englanders out of regional pride. Rumor suggested that Lawrence would supply $100,000 to the party's war chest if he were on the ticket, and that prospect lured additional support. Allen's speech, however, harmed

Lawrence's chances, and Fletcher Webster informed the delegates of his father's decided hostility to Lawrence.[124]

The second prominent candidate was Ohio's Thomas Ewing, a major figure in both his state's and the national Whig party. Since January he had privately lobbied Ohio delegates for Taylor. Immediately prior to the convention he pressed John Sherman, whose brother William Tecumseh Sherman had been raised in the Ewing home, to go for Taylor rather than Scott on the ground that it was more important to have a Northerner as vice president than president since he could break a Senate tie on the Wilmot Proviso. Because most Ohio Whigs knew nothing of Ewing's activity for Taylor, his nomination might provide a way to save that state. Before the voting began, however, Lew Campbell, citing authorization from Ewing and the rest of the Ohio delegation, withdrew Ewing's name from consideration. Neither the other Ohio delegates nor Ewing had given such authorization, and twenty years later, Ewing was still fuming that Campbell had sabotaged his chance to become president. Thus did Campbell gain revenge in June for his defeat in January at the hands of the McLean and Ewing forces.[125]

The New York rivals Seward and Fillmore completed the list. In the spring Seward had asked Weed to withdraw his name in the *Albany Evening Journal*. A man of superb intellect and restless energy, Seward had no interest in the post and was ill-suited for it. By late May, he had changed his mind. Aware that his foes in the New York party were plumping Fillmore for the nomination, he feared the threat that Fillmore, if successful, could pose to the ascendancy of the Weed-Seward faction. Weed came to Philadelphia in early June hoping to secure the nomination for Seward, and that desire was one reason he pushed Clayton and opposed Scott, since Scott's nomination would have mandated a southern vice presidential candidate. Weed also promoted Seward, as did Greeley, as the best candidate to attract Catholic immigrants and help the party carry New York, Pennsylvania, Ohio, and Indiana. Scott, he argued, would alienate those same voters. Precisely because of Seward's pro-Catholic reputation, the numerous Native Americans at the convention warned delegates that Seward's nomination would doom the ticket in Pennsylvania even with Taylor at its head. In fact, once Weed cast his lot with Taylor, he gave up hope for the vice presidency since the deal between Lawrence and the Taylor men seemed too fixed. One of Weed's henchmen in the New York delegation, therefore, withdrew Seward's name before the balloting began. Weed, however, apparently obtained a promise of the State Department for Seward from Colonel Joseph Taylor, whose accommodations in Philadelphia he had arranged.[126]

As early as 1846, New York's conservative Whigs believed that Weed was plotting to make Seward vice president or secretary of state in order to groom him for a presidential run in 1852. If Seward obtained a voice in the distribution of federal patronage in New York, let alone the presidency, they feared, their faction could be crushed. To keep Seward out of the next administration, they came to Philadelphia intent upon securing the vice presidential nomination for Fillmore. As a fallback position, they were prepared to sacrifice Clay and switch to Scott to keep Seward out of the vice presidency.[127]

Once Taylor was nominated, anti-Weed Whigs redoubled their efforts for Fillmore, since they reckoned that if he won, another New Yorker could never be named secretary of state. Seizing on northern Whigs' anger at Taylor's triumph and the damage it did Lawrence, Collier, an anti-Weed man, thus immediately suggested Fillmore's nomination to pacify northern anti-Taylor Whigs. Even as Collier spoke, Harry Bradley, a prominent Vermont Whig, Clay loyalist, and close friend of Fillmore, delivered the same message to Southerners. Seated near the Kentucky, Tennessee, and Louisiana delegations when Taylor's victory was announced and the cries of outrage arose from northern Whigs, he instantly warned them that the party faced ruin if they rubbed salt in northern wounds by pressing ahead with Lawrence and that only Fillmore's nomination could salvage party unity. He then ran over to Solomon Foot, the chairman of the Vermont delegation, who planned to vote for Lawrence because of his New England residence, and urged him to vote for Fillmore instead. Foot and southern Taylor leaders were convinced. Meredith Gentry told the Tennesseans "that the Whig party must be saved" and Lawrence abandoned, Bradley later reported, and the Kentuckians agreed. With the Louisianans, however, "the Lawrence bargain was too strong and I could not detach them."[128]

Bradley's efforts for Fillmore paid off when the voting began. Fifty ballots were scattered among various favorite sons, but Fillmore and Lawrence ran way ahead with 115 and 109 votes, respectively. Lawrence amassed fifty-seven southern and fifty-two northern votes, twenty-six of which were from New England. Fillmore received only twelve New England votes, three of which came from Vermont, and only twenty-three from the South. Tennessee and Kentucky, however, cast thirteen votes for him and thus provided his margin over Lawrence, a lead that probably ensured his triumph on the next ballot. Bradley was immensely proud of his handiwork. "Weed was never more surprised," he later chortled. "He was sure of Taylor & Lawrence & Seward for Secretary of State. He was foiled."[129]

Before the next roll call began, William Tyson, another of Fillmore's friends in the New York delegation, threatened Alabama's Henry Hilliard that unless Fillmore were placed on the ticket, the New York State Whig convention would "make an electoral ticket favorable to Henry Clay and Millard Fillmore." Neither Hilliard nor other southern Taylorites took that threat lightly. Between the two ballots fourteen Southerners shifted from Lawrence to Fillmore.[130] Fillmore easily won on the next ballot with 173 votes compared to 83 for Lawrence.

In the excitement that followed the completion of the ticket, delegate after delegate stood up and pledged his state's support for Taylor and Fillmore. Eager to get to a prearranged mass ratification meeting at Independence Square, no one, save Ohio's Daniel Tilden, even mentioned that the party had not adopted a platform. Tilden again moved that the party pledge itself against the extension of slavery into free territory, but his resolution was promptly tabled. The convention's desire to shun the explosive Proviso is understandable, but given the ticket, a platform that rehearsed the Whig position on economic measures or any other issue also seemed superfluous to most delegates. As a Pennsylvanian boasted in the convention's final moments, Taylor gave the Whigs the only ammunition they needed. From that moment until November, he predicted, Pennsylvania's Whigs would campaign with the cry, "*A little more grape, Captain Bragg.*"[131]

X

Thus ended the long and divisive struggle for the Whig presidential nomination in 1848. One could point to any number of things to account for the result: the divergent procedures in the North and South for selecting delegates; the impatience of younger Whigs with the seemingly inexhaustible ambition of Clay and Webster; personal and factional rivalries; the superior organization and energy of the Taylor managers in Washington; the Allison Letter; the suppression of Scott's willingness to run with Clay; the important decisions on the nights of June 6 and June 8; the selection of Philadelphia, with its concentration of nativists, as the locale for the convention; and the expedient desire to find a winner at all costs. With justice, all of these factors and more were pointed to by contemporaries who sought to explain the outcome.

William Ballard Preston, the Young Indian from Virginia, however, captured the essence most succinctly in a jubilant note to Rives. "The large states of N.Y. Ohio & Pennsylvania in their attempt to exercise a commanding influence in the nomination have in truth exercised but little," he wrote. "The result belongs to those who had but one purpose one choice and one object." Southerners had been extraordinarily united behind Taylor from the beginning to the end. The northern states on which Clay had depended, in contrast, had failed to unite on him, Webster, or anyone else. Factional and personal rivalries in part caused the northern divisions. The main reason why northern Whigs fragmented, however, and why Southerners rallied so cohesively behind Taylor, was the end of the war and the acquisition of the Mexican Cession. Ratification of the peace treaty seemingly destroyed Whigs' last viable issue and left them defenseless to confront the divisive Wilmot Proviso. From March 10 on, growing numbers of northern Whigs reached the conclusion Thomas Dorr had jeeringly attributed to them in January. Forced to find a candidate who could hold southern votes, they lacked concrete issues to mobilize the normal Whig electorate in the North. Thus they believed they required Democratic defectors to win, and to attract them they would need "a brave old soldier" who might prove to be "a *taking* candidate."[132]

Nominating Taylor, however, was a far cry from electing him. Despite the lovefest that ensued at the end of the convention and the confident boasts of triumph, the convention had produced profound bitterness and fractious division. Despite their postconvention euphoria that they had averted a rupture, departing Whigs had good reason to heed the warnings of a Michigan delegate. "Fatal consequences . . . must ensue" from "the flagrant contempt for the wishes & will of the north," J. R. Williams wrote Fillmore. Fillmore should therefore spurn his nomination. The imposition of Taylor upon the Whigs "must lead to an utter dissolution & defeat of the Whig party, to an array of a greater northern against a southern party—the calamities of which no man can foresee."[133]

Chapter 11

"Stimulate Every Whig to Turn Out"

"THE POLITICAL ADVANTAGES which have been secured by Taylor's nomination," southern Whigs cheered after the Philadelphia convention, are "impossible to overestimate." If the Whigs had not chosen a victorious Mexican War general, Meredith Gentry explained, Democrats would have crucified them for treason throughout the campaign "and our overthrow would have been complete." Even more important, Taylor's victory demonstrated that all future aspirants for the presidency must "keep themselves clear upon the negro question." The selection of the Louisiana slaveholder "has scotched if it has not killed abolition. It is literally expurgating the Whig party. For example, Giddings, Root, & Co. will leave now."[1]

That prospective defection of militant antislavery men terrified most northern Whigs. From New England, the Middle Atlantic states, and the Midwest came immediate predictions of a bolt by furious opponents of slavery expansion, not just a few well-known leaders, but tens of thousands of Whig voters. "What in God's name shall be done?" queried a worried New Yorker. "The masses are in rebellion. The rank and file are swearing they'll wheel out by Regiments. Taylor's nomination is regarded as infamous."[2]

These contrasting reactions support traditional interpretations of the 1848 election. According to many historians, sectional disputes over slavery extension and the resulting shift of northern Whigs and Democrats to a new Free Soil party constituted its central story. By this analysis, even though Taylor won, Free Soilers' deep incursions into the Whigs' northern constituency gravely weakened the party's competitiveness and heralded its subsequent disruption.[3] This chapter reassesses how much the sectional split over slavery expansion actually debilitated Whigs in 1848. Northern and southern Whigs had long disagreed about matters involving slavery, yet the cohesive force of interparty conflict had held them together and retained the allegiance of Whig voters despite those divergent sectional views. The question is how successfully that same centripetal pressure operated during the 1848 campaign once the contest was against the Democratic enemy rather than among fellow Whigs.

Whatever historians' preoccupations with the slavery issue, following Taylor's nomination Whigs feared abstentions by Whig regulars disgusted at Taylor's No

Partyism as much as defections by angry antislavery men. "We feel as if we were stripped of every great and strong issue with which to go to the people," the same worried New Yorker complained. "What is there (Taylor being our exponent) left on which to stand?" An embittered Henry Clay chorused that refrain to justify his refusal to endorse Taylor or participate in the campaign. "If it was between Locofoco principles and Whig principles, I would engage in it with all the ardor of which I am capable," he contended. "But alas! I fear that the Whig party is dissolved and that no longer are there Whig principles to excite zeal and stimulate exertion."[4]

This perception that Whigs lacked issues to mobilize their voters better prophesied the election's outcome and significance than did warnings about bolts to a new antislavery party. Since Whigs won the presidency in 1840 and 1848 while running military heroes without platforms, historians normally pair those two elections to demonstrate the Whigs' unprincipled expediency, their policies' unattractiveness, and their electoral weakness. In one important respect this bracketing is valid. Just as in 1840, in 1848 the conditions that caused Whigs to resort to a renowned warrior changed dramatically after the national convention adjourned. Just like Harrison, Taylor would win in 1848 less because of the smell of gunpowder than for other reasons.

Nonetheless, equating the two elections is misleading. The 1840 election was fought over contrasting Whig and Democratic programmatic responses to economic depression, and it culminated a three-year process in which unprecedented numbers of new voters were mobilized. The 1844 presidential election also revolved around concrete issue contrasts, and it induced a turnout rate nearly equal to that of 1840. In the context of previous presidential campaigns, the 1848 election most resembled that of 1836, despite their divergent outcomes. Just as in 1836, when the Whigs ran different regional candidates, in 1848 they would run different campaigns for Taylor in the North and South. In both, Whigs depended heavily on contrasting the images of the parties' respective presidential and vice presidential candidates rather than providing clear alternatives on public policy to attract voters. Consequently, the 1848 election evoked the lowest voter turnout in any presidential election since 1836. The estimated nationwide voting rates of adult white males were 57.8 percent in 1836, 80.2 percent in 1840, 78.9 percent in 1844, and 72.7 percent in 1848. Although Zachary Taylor won in 1848, whereas Henry Clay lost in 1844, Taylor in fact received a smaller share of the actual vote and even less of the potential vote than had Clay in the issue-oriented campaign of 1844.[5]

Aside from the incursion of a separate antislavery party into Whig ranks, therefore, the election of 1848 portended the Whig party's ultimate collapse by demonstrating its inability to retain old voters or to mobilize new ones without demonstrating clear differences from Democrats on concrete issues. That fact creates a paradox. To understand how Taylor won the election, we must understand how the Whigs were able to retain as much of their vote as they did—how they were able to minimize both defections and abstentions. To understand how the election augured the party's demise, we must understand why the Whigs lost the support they did.

I

Whig leaders had good reason to fear that northern antislavery Whigs would defect. Outrage at Taylor's nomination and at Southerners' apparent control of the convention was intense. Discontent erupted immediately in Maine, Vermont, New York, Indiana, Michigan, and elsewhere, but it centered in Ohio and Massachusetts, largely because certain Whig editors and officeholders fomented and organized it. "Stunned Stupefied outraged abased Mortified and enraged to the last degree of endurance" by Taylor's nomination, Albert G. Riddle, a Whig state legislator from Ohio's Western Reserve, for example, was "prepared to pronounce a valedictory to the dead and rotten carcass of the National Whig party." Cincinnati editor Thomas B. Stevenson predicted that over 20,000 Ohio Whigs would defect to a new antislavery party. The Philadelphia convention was the last straw, a young Massachusetts Whig explained. Southerners "have trampled on the rights and just claims of the North sufficiently long and have fairly shit upon all our Northern statesmen and are now trying to rub it in." Northerners must "take a stand" and bring "the South to their proper level."[6]

Plans for a broader antislavery party had been laid in Massachusetts, Ohio, and New York even before the Whig national convention assembled. On May 27, seven Massachusetts Young Whigs (now called Conscience Whigs) gathered in the editorial offices of Charles Francis Adams' Boston *Whig*, the Conscience Whig organ. Including Adams, Charles Sumner, Stephen Phillips, E. Rockwood Hoar, and Henry Wilson, a delegate to the Philadelphia convention, the conferees agreed to convene dissidents should Taylor win the Whig nomination. "I do not know that we ought to regret the result," Adams wrote John Gorham Palfrey, the Conscience Whigs' representative in Congress. "The issue must be made at some time or other, and there is no fairer time than this." Accordingly, on June 10, the day after Taylor's nomination, the group called for a mass protest meeting at Worcester on June 28. Pronouncing Taylor "a candidate whom no Northern Whig is bound to support," they invited all who opposed both Taylor and Cass to meet and to take the steps necessary to unite all northern opponents of slavery extension in a new party.[7]

In Ohio, Salmon P. Chase and the Liberty party launched the new organization. A resident of Cincinnati, a renowned lawyer for free blacks and fugitive slaves, and a one-time Whig, Chase joined the Liberty party in the early 1840s and immediately sought to combine it with antislavery Whigs and Democrats. During 1847, Chase corresponded frequently with Conscience Whigs in Massachusetts, with Joshua R. Giddings in Ohio, and with New York's Barnburner Democrats, who were committed to the Wilmot Proviso. Although he failed to stop the Liberty party from nominating New Hampshire's John P. Hale as its own presidential candidate in October 1847, he continued to favor disbanding the party for a wider coalition. Sensing uneasiness among both Whigs and Democrats in Ohio about their approaching national conventions, Chase on May 17 issued a call, signed by 3,000 antislavery men of all parties, for a "Free Territory Convention" to meet in Columbus on June 21.[8]

Angry Van Burenite Democrats led in New York. At their separate state convention to protest Hunker control of the party in the fall of 1847, the Barnburners adopted the slogan that would identify the new party: "Free Trade, Free Labor,

Free Soil, Free Speech, and Free Men." When Barnburners and Hunkers chose separate delegations to the Democratic national convention in 1848, the Barnburners determined to revolt if the convention did not recognize them alone as New York's official delegates. Infuriated by their treatment in Baltimore and by Cass' nomination, they stormed home. Even as Whig delegates passed through New York City on their way to Philadelphia, the Barnburners held a massive protest rally there and issued a call for a Democratic convention to meet in Utica on June 22 to choose their own "democratic presidential candidate," one who was not the product of "abject subserviency to the slave power."[9]

When most Whig delegates adjourned on June 9 to hasten to Independence Square to celebrate Taylor's nomination, therefore, fifteen angry antislavery men remained behind in the Chinese Museum to precipitate the long-awaited bolt. Including delegates and alternates from Maine, Massachusetts, New York, New Jersey, and Ohio, they commissioned the Ohioans to ask the impending Free Territory Convention on June 21 to call a national Free Soil meeting at Buffalo in early August. From there events proceeded rapidly. Repudiating Cass and Taylor as slaveholders' candidates who refused to oppose slavery extension, the Columbus gathering, which attracted nearly 1,000 Ohioans from all three parties, announced its readiness "to cooperate with any party thoroughly resolved and inflexibly determined to permit no further extension of slavery." It summoned "Freemen of every State and Every Party" to meet in Buffalo on August 9 to select "candidates of Freemen, determined to remain Free." The following day in Utica, Barnburners nominated a presidential ticket of Martin Van Buren and Wisconsin's Henry Dodge, denounced slavery as "a great moral, social, and political evil," proclaimed it both the right and duty of Congress to prohibit slavery in the territories, and appointed the same Barnburner delegates who had gone to Baltimore to attend the Buffalo convention called by the Ohioans. On June 28, some 5,000 Conscience Whigs and a few Democrats met in Worcester and called on "the lovers of Freedom from both parties" in Massachusetts to attend the Buffalo gathering. To facilitate coalition among different antislavery groups, it divided a state committee equally among Whigs, Democrats, and Liberty men.[10]

Prior to the June meetings, a few northern conservatives had greeted the prospective bolt by antislavery zealots with equanimity. Tired of the endless wrangling with the impatient antislavery leaders and confident that the defection could be confined to a few dissidents, they welcomed it, in the words of a Massachusetts Whig, as "a sort of sluice way through which, the Whig party could run off some cumbersome material." The size of the three gatherings and Northerners' enthusiastic response to their actions made it clear, however, that leaders might carry a substantial chunk of the Whig rank and file with them into the new party. Preventing a massive hemorrhage of their northern electorate thus became a top priority for most northern Whig leaders in July.[11]

That goal obviously affected the behavior of congressional Whigs when they addressed the problem of slavery expansion during the summer prior to the Buffalo Free Soil meeting. Even before ratification of the Treaty of Guadalupe Hidalgo, northern House Whigs had unanimously but unsuccessfully attempted to impose the Wilmot Proviso on the Mexican Cession. For the remainder of the session, attention focused on Oregon, where no one expected slavery to be established but that might set a precedent for other territories. After ratification of Polk's Oregon Treaty in 1846, American residents in Oregon, without congressional authorization, formed a provisional government that prohibited slavery in the territory. But many congressmen refused to recognize that government's legitimacy, and some Southerners particularly objected to its ban on slavery. When Congress attempted to create a territorial government of its own, however, it stalemated over the slavery issue. In 1847, the House, on a sectionally polarized vote, passed a bill organizing the Oregon Territory and barring slavery from it. Southerners of both parties vehemently denounced congressional prohibition of slavery, and they killed the House bill in the Senate with the aid of northern Democrats, who favored popular sovereignty. In the spring of 1848, the House's northern majority prepared a similar bill. As a Senate alternative, Jesse Bright, an Indiana Democrat, moved to amend the Oregon bill by specifying that slavery was excluded from Oregon because the Territory was north of the 36° 30' line, which at the time barred slavery in the northern portion of the Louisiana Purchase but not west of the Rocky Mountains. This formula offended most Northerners because it implied that slavery would be permitted south of the Missouri Compromise line, that is, in most of the Mexican Cession.[12]

Before the Senate voted on Bright's amendment, Delaware's Clayton moved simultaneously to break the logjam over Oregon, to find a position on the slavery extension issue that could hold the Whig party together, and to quash the threatened northern Whig revolt by resolving the entire territorial issue before the Free Soil convention met on August 9. By settling the slavery extension question in a way satisfactory to both sections, he could render the divisive Wilmot Proviso irrelevant, just as the Whigs' now-obsolete No Territory platform had once done, thereby demolishing the rationale for a new Free Soil party. On July 12, Clayton moved that the Senate form a select committee to consider the related problems of Oregon and the Mexican Cession; as author of the motion, he automatically became its chairman. Carefully balanced to reflect conflicting partisan and sectional views, the committee's leading figures, aside from Clayton, were three Democrats: Bright, who sought to attach the 36° 30' clause to the Senate's Oregon bill; Daniel S. Dickinson, chief of New York's Hunker Democrats and a leading exponent of popular sovereignty, which would allow residents of territories to make the decision on slavery; and Calhoun, who since early 1847 had repeatedly insisted that the Constitution guaranteed the right to own slaves on every foot of United States territory and that neither Congress nor a territorial government could prohibit it.[13]

After heated discussion, the committee reported a bill on July 18. Immediately dubbed the Clayton Compromise, it created a territorial government for Oregon, specifically allowing the unofficial provisional government's antislavery ban to continue in effect until the new territorial legislature ruled for or against slavery. It also established territorial governments for California and New Mexico, but it explicitly barred those governments from taking any action either establishing or prohibiting slavery.[14] Instead, it left the decision on slavery there to the federal judiciary. Specifically, it authorized any slave brought into those territories to sue in the federal territorial courts to see if slavery legally existed there and provided that the decision of the territorial court could then be directly appealed to the Supreme Court.[15]

Clayton defended his measure as eminently fair to North and South alike. Congress would neither establish nor prohibit slavery in any western territory. The House's ban on slavery in Oregon would be dropped, but the same result would be achieved by adhering to the provisional government's prohibition until the new territorial legislature acted. New Mexico and California, on the other hand, were too underpopulated to allow the same kind of sovereignty to their governments. The conflicting claims of the South and the North about the status of slavery there would be settled by the courts, "by the silent operation of the Constitution itself."[16]

Ignoring Clayton's arguments, Northerners and Southerners of both parties attacked the bill for giving an advantage to the other section. Southerners who had never subscribed to Calhoun's theory protested that the courts would rule that the Mexican prohibition of slavery still applied to the Cession because Congress had not explicitly replaced it. Thus slavery would be effectively barred and the South denied its equal rights. One of the northern Whigs on the select committee, Samuel Phelps of Vermont, in fact defended the bill on precisely those grounds. A few northern Democrats and the vast majority of northern Whigs both inside and outside Congress, however, vehemently assaulted Clayton's bill as a proslavery measure. They objected that it prevented residents of California and New Mexico from prohibiting slavery if they so desired. They complained that men could legally own slaves in the two territories until a definitive court ruling occurred and that therefore slavery would be covertly extended to territory they regarded as free. Nor, they groused, would the judicial system reach a fair decision. The proslavery Polk would appoint the territorial judges, who were bound to rule initially against the slaves and would not issue the writs of habeas corpus seemingly necessary to carry the case on appeal to the Supreme Court. Even if they did, the Court might rule for slavery's legality, refuse to hear the case, or stall for so long that slavery would become firmly established and proslavery state constitutions written.[17]

Behind these objections lay northern Whig fears about the immediate political consequences of the bill. Aware of the impending Free Soil convention at Buffalo, Whigs reasoned that if they surrendered the sure-fire prohibition of the Proviso and allowed slavery even temporarily into free territory by supporting Clayton's measure, they might drive hundreds of thousands of northern voters to the new antislavery party. Opposition to slavery extension among New York's Whigs was vehement, one told Fillmore. "On the local tickets, a man cannot get elected *pathmaster* who is not a most decided 'Free Soil Man.' The feeling is almost as strong as in the times of Antimasonry." Because passage of Clayton's bill would increase the new party's support, it would doom Taylor in New York and New England, Weed warned Seward. Such tocsins were perspicacious. Insisting that "there must be no more compromises with Slavery," the platform of the new Free Soil party would proclaim the Clayton Compromise "an absolute surrender of the rights of the non-slaveholders of all the States."[18]

Over northern Whig opposition, Clayton's bill passed the Senate in the early morning of July 27 by a vote of 33 to 22. Nineteen southern and seven northern Democrats favored the proposal, as did Phelps and six southern Whigs. Ten northern Democrats, eight northern Whigs, and four southern Whigs opposed it. In sum, Whigs split seven to twelve against Clayton's bill, and Democrats divided twenty-six to ten in favor. Northerners opposed the measure by an eighteen to eight margin; Southerners supported it twenty-five to four.[19]

Even as the Senate debated Clayton's plan, observers predicted that Northerners would kill it in the House, yet the fatal stab came from Georgia's Alexander Stephens. As soon as the House took up the Senate bill on July 28, Stephens moved to table it without debate, and his motion passed 112 to 97. Seven Whigs from the Upper South joined Stephens to combine with all seventy-three northern Whigs and thirty-one northern Democrats to bury Clayton's handiwork. Twenty-seven southern Whigs, forty-nine southern Democrats, and twenty-one northern Democrats were in the minority. Again, support for the compromise came primarily from the South and from Democrats, opposition primarily from the North and from Whigs. Still, just as in the Senate, the vote provided a blurred record to take to the electorate. Southern Democrats unanimously supported the measure in both houses, but so did a majority of southern Whigs. Conversely, in both houses, majorities of Northerners from both parties, equally desperate to stem defections to the new Free Soil party, opposed it.[20]

Had Stephens and the seven other southern Whigs voted like most Southerners, the Clayton Compromise would have survived 105–104 and possibly passed. Stephens' motives therefore provoked considerable speculation. In a cogent speech to the House on August 7 and in a public letter to the Milledgeville *Federal Union* at the end of that month, Stephens defended his course by condemning the supposed compromise as a capitulation of Southern Rights that no true Southerner could support. Flatly rejecting Calhounite doctrine, he denied that the Constitution automatically established slavery; rather, it only protected the institution where state or municipal laws had already established it. Because the bill prohibited the passage of proslavery legislation in California and New Mexico, the only law the courts could rely on when deciding the legality of slavery in these territories was the Mexican law abolishing slavery. Hence acquiescence in the bill meant an intolerable surrender of the South's equal rights. Better, he declared, to return the territories to Mexico than to accept such a settlement.[21]

Stephens never abandoned this insistence that only positive territorial or congressional statutes, rather than the aegis of the Constitution itself, could legally establish slavery in federal territories. His conviction was firm, but political factors were also at work. Having cooperated with northern Whig congressmen in the Taylor movement since December, he possibly hoped to extend an olive branch to Whigs still smarting over Taylor's nomination. More likely, he was targeting opponents in the South. Stephens and his Georgia Whig allies repeatedly condemned southern backers of Clayton's Compromise for selling out "our Southern position & Southern Rights." These included every southern Democrat but also his Georgia Whig rival Berrien. Such attacks on disloyalty, Berrien's allies protested, "are shafts sped at you." Toombs, Stephens, and others were "all banded together to advance themselves" by directing "the action of the Whig party."[22]

With the interment of Clayton's Compromise, the House and Senate again stalemated. The House immediately took up its own bill, organizing the Oregon Territory with slavery barred. Southerners and a few northern Democrats tried to remove that stipulation, but most northern Democrats and all the northern Whigs defeated their amendment. The prohibition of slavery from Oregon "practically . . . is of no consequence because no man supposes, that Slavery will ever exist [there], or would if there were no prohibition," admitted North Carolina's Outlaw. "But it is important as manifesting the determination of the Northern States, to appropriate the whole of our late acquisitions to themselves." With the measure viewed as a precedent for the Mexican Cession, the final vote on the House's Oregon bill produced the same sectional polarization between North and South that had appeared in early votes on the Wilmot Proviso.[23]

Once the House bill reached the Senate, Southerners and a few northern Democrats, over the objections of all ten northern Whigs and most northern Democrats, attached Bright's amendment to it and returned the amended bill to the House. The House refused to concur in the Senate amendment on virtually a strict sectional vote. Finally, on August 13, after another all-night session, the Senate receded from its amendment and accepted the House bill, 29 to 25. Despite vociferous southern protests, three Southerners, the Delaware Whig Presley Spruance and Democrats Thomas Hart Benton and Sam Houston, joined Northerners in the majority. In response, Polk noted when he signed the bill that he accepted it only because Oregon was north of the 36° 30' line.[24]

Congress' record on Oregon starkly illuminated the naked sectional polarization that kept the explosive question of slavery's possible extension into the Mexican Cession alive during the 1848 campaign. Yet that record left quite unclear which major party would suffer most from a new antislavery organization in the North or even why such a new party was necessary. Northern spokesmen of both parties could cite their congressmen's votes against slavery extension to deny the need for any new antislavery party. Southerners had clearly fought congressional prohibition, and, just as clearly, a slaveholder headed the Whig presidential ticket. As a counterbalance to this apparent Whig disadvantage, however, northern Whigs brazenly trumpeted the crucial southern Whig votes against Clayton's Compromise as evidence that southern Whigs, like their northern colleagues, were committed to free territory.[25] Democrats had warts of their own. Aside from the northern Democratic Senators who aided Southerners in attempting to extend the 36° 30' line to the Pacific coast and to defeat the House's Oregon bill, Lewis Cass vigorously advocated popular sovereignty, which Clayton had included in his Oregon bill and which the northern majority in the House had rejected in favor of congressional prohibition. Which party could pose as more trustworthy on slavery extension in response to a Free Soil challenge, in sum, remained uncertain.

That challenge crystallized even before the Senate finally passed the Oregon bill. Whatever the hopes of northern Whigs and Democrats, their congressional votes did nothing to slow the momentum that had been growing since June. Over 20,000 elected and self-appointed delegates poured into Buffalo for the August convention. Uniformly zealous, they were a heterogeneous lot: midwestern Democratic proponents of rivers and harbors improvements, which neither party had officially endorsed and Polk had vetoed; labor reformers interested in free homesteads in the West; and even vengeful Clay loyalists from New York City. But most were primarily determined to stop slavery's spread, and they included three main groups: antislavery Whigs from New England and the Midwest; antislavery Democrats, including New York's Barnburners; and Liberty men. Such an assemblage was obviously too huge to be manageable, and from the start the convention operated on a dual track. Most delegates attended what was in effect a mass meeting, where they listened to a succession of speakers who denounced both

Taylor and Cass as lackeys of the Slave Power and called on free men in the North to unite to defend freedom. A separate group consisting of six at-large delegates from each state in attendance and three from each congressional district was responsible for picking a presidential ticket and composing a platform, both of which would then be submitted to the mass meeting for ratification.[26]

Representatives of each of the three preexisting parties had a favorite for the presidential nomination. Most Liberty men pushed their existing nominee, Hale, who made known his willingness to step aside should the convention choose another man. Whigs from Ohio and New England, as well as Salmon Chase, promoted John McLean, the disappointed aspirant for the Whig nomination, but McLean refused to submit his name to the convention. Democrats decisively favored Van Buren, and largely to hold the rebellious Barnburners and attract Democrats elsewhere, Van Buren got the nod.[27] For vice president the convention chose Charles Francis Adams.

The lengthy platform reflected the disparate interests of the incipient Free Soil party's polyglot constituency. One plank called on Congress to subsidize rivers and harbors improvements. Another demanded free homesteads for settlers in the West. The tariff plank, which was written by Joseph L. White, perhaps Clay's staunchest New York friend, called for duties sufficiently high to defray the government's expenses and pay off the debt accumulated in the Mexican War—a plank White insisted was necessary to attract Whig support.[28] Other planks advocated cheap postage, retrenchment of government expenditures, and the election, rather than appointment, of civil servants. Predictably, most of the platform addressed the slavery question. Although it pledged noninterference with slavery in the states where it existed, it incorporated Chase's demand that the federal government divorce itself from slavery wherever it had the constitutional authority, that is, in the District of Columbia, federal military installations, and the territories. Denouncing "the aggressions of the Slave Power," it insisted that Congress bar slavery from all free territory and that there be "no more slave states and no more slave territory." The platform closed with the resounding pledge "that we inscribe on our banner 'Free Soil, Free Speech, Free Labor, and Free Men,' and under it will fight on and fight ever, until a triumphant victory shall reward our exertions."

All of the proceedings on August 9 and 10 evoked an enthusiasm that reminded observers more of a religious revival than a political convention. So fervent, determined, and surprisingly unified was the Buffalo assemblage that the Free Soil party seemed, at least to some, capable of wreaking havoc in the North. Now the Whig party had to confront what many of its most thoughtful members had long dreaded: a new party seemingly capable of mobilizing northern antislavery men of all partisan hues.

II

Two weeks after the Buffalo convention, George Patterson warned Weed that New York's Whig leaders would have "to *work* in order to save our troops from going to Van Buren."[29] Leadership, in fact, largely determined how many Whigs were saved and how many lost. Virtually all northern Whigs—and most northern

Democrats—opposed slavery expansion, but the great majority remained loyal to the major parties. By itself, in sum, antislavery sentiment does not explain who became Free Soilers and who did not. The Free Soil party's ability to siphon off Whig troops varied sharply from state to state, and the disposition of Whig leadership toward the new party largely accounted for the differential. No matter how angry antislavery Whig voters were at the selection of Taylor, most followed the lead of Whig officeholders, editors, and party officials whom they had come to trust and respect. Where significant numbers of prominent Whig opinion makers joined and promoted the Free Soil party, it cut into the Whig rank and file. In contrast, where respected Whig leaders, often renowned antislavery men, spurned the new party and left it dependent on ex-Democrats and Liberty men as spokesmen, the Free Soil party posed a much greater threat to the Whigs' Democratic rivals than to the Whigs themselves.

Influential Whigs played a larger role in Ohio's Free Soil organization than in that of any other northern state. Leaders of the Corwin faction like Columbus Delano and Lew Campbell initially encouraged a bolt after their disappointment at the national convention, as did McLean's lieutenant Samuel Galloway. The Free Soilers' nomination of Van Buren, as well as Corwin's and McLean's adherence to the regular organization, however, brought these men back to the Whig fold. The popular antislavery Whig congressmen from the Western Reserve, Joseph Root and Joshua R. Giddings, in contrast, defected permanently, as did most local Whig politicos and newspaper editors in northern Ohio. "All over the Reserve men who have acted as leaders among the Whigs have abandoned the party for this new platform," complained a loyalist in September. Because of those leaders and "the strong antislavery sentiment here, the defection is alarming." So great was the influence of these men, especially Giddings, in the former Whig stronghold on the Reserve that Whig loyalists—be they state leaders like Corwin and Thomas Ewing, antislavery Whigs from the Reserve itself like future United States Senator Benjamin F. Wade, or outsiders like the New Yorkers Francis Granger and Seward, who were desperately summoned to help save Ohio—could only slow the flight of Whig troops into the Free Soil column, not reverse it. "This Free Soil movement . . . will sweep over the Reserve as Antimasonry did in Western New York," Seward reported.[30]

In sharp contrast, Pennsylvania's Whigs believed their own party could keep slavery out of the West, and their leaders shunned the third party. In Pittsburgh, Whig Congressman Moses Hampton won renomination after pledging his commitment to the Proviso. Running Thaddeus Stevens for Congress, Lancaster's Whigs adopted "free soilism" as their platform and "support[ed] Genl. Taylor on those grounds." In the seventeenth congressional district, Rush Petrikin declined a Free Soil congressional nomination because Samuel Calvin, the Whig candidate, was as good a free-soil man as the district needed. Deprived of influential Whig leaders, the Free Soil party in Pennsylvania depended largely on Democrats like David Wilmot to recruit voting support. As a result, a Philadelphia Whig boasted as early as August that "Free Soil can do no injury to the Whigs in Penna." but might draw as many as 10,000 votes from Cass.[31]

Whig politicos also spurned the new Free Soil party in New Jersey and, more important, in New York. For several months after Taylor's nomination, Horace Greeley petulantly refused to endorse the Whig ticket in his influential *New York*

Tribune, thereby causing Fillmore's friends to accuse him of sabotage. During June and July, indeed, Greeley blessed the preparations for an antislavery revolt. But Greeley never joined the Free Soil party himself, and in September he grudgingly endorsed the Whig ticket as the only one that could defeat the Democrats. Most other New York Whig leaders did not even flirt with the Free Soilers. Citing Van Buren's nomination and the prominence of Barnburners in the state Free Soil organization, they stressed the necessity of remaining faithful to Whiggery. During the campaign, for example, Seward gained notoriety as the most militant antislavery man in the Whig party by declaring in Massachusetts, New York, and Ohio that "slavery can and must be abolished, and you and I can and must do it." But, he declared, "All that is ever to be done for Freedom must originate with the Whig party, and in point of practicability, must be accomplished by it."[32]

In Massachusetts, Conscience Whigs had orchestrated the antislavery revolt. Adams was on the Free Soilers' national ticket, and Stephen C. Phillips became the new party's gubernatorial nominee. Such men, however, represented at best the second echelon of the state's Whig leadership. John Gorham Palfrey did serve in Congress, but he was a relatively obscure first-termer, unlike the well-known Giddings and Root of Ohio, and he was the only Whig in the Massachusetts congressional delegation to embrace the third party. Conscience Whigs hoped that Palfrey's new House colleague Horace Mann, who had been elected in April 1848 to replace the deceased John Quincy Adams, would also endorse it. Mann refused, fearing that he would lose his position as secretary of the state board of education. Realizing their limited influence, the founders of the state's Free Soil party sought to recruit more prominent Whigs to it. Adams and Wilson, though not Palfrey, initially hoped that Webster would lend his enormous prestige to the new organization. Although angered and embarrassed by his inconsequential support at the Whig national convention, Webster nonetheless wanted no part of the Free Soil movement. He admitted as early as June that he would have to swallow his pride and publicly support Taylor, even though he delayed that distasteful obligation until September..With equal futility the Free Soilers solicited support from the orator Edward Everett. By the fall, the front-line leadership of the state Whig party—Senators Webster and John Davis, Governor George Briggs, Abbott Lawrence and Nathan Appleton, Rufus Choate and Everett—and the entire congressional delegation other than Palfrey were campaigning for the Whig ticket.[33]

Elsewhere in New England, even fewer Whig politicians and editors cast their lot with the new party. In Maine, Whig leaders like William Pitt Fessenden and most of the Whig hierarchy remained loyal, thereby reducing Whig defections to the new party. Similarly, an advocate of the Free Soil party in Vermont complained that "a palsy has struck the editors of Whig newspapers . . . all over the State." Because of disputes between the Vermont equivalents of Hunkers and Barnburners, he accurately predicted, most Free Soil support in Vermont would come from the Democrats and the Liberty party, not the Whigs.[34]

With the single exception of lame-duck Democratic Senator John M. Niles, former Liberty party activists provided leadership for Connecticut's embryonic Free Soil party. In contrast, Connecticut's Whig officeholders and editors campaigned actively and ardently against the Free Soil party and on behalf of the Whig nominees. The most important figure in this effort was Senator Roger Sherman Baldwin, whose antislavery credentials were impeccable. With Connecticut's other most prominent Whig, Truman Smith, in Washington superintending the national committee's distribution of documents, the burden of saving Connecticut fell on Baldwin, who crisscrossed the state passionately and cogently explaining to its Whig voters why they must shun the siren call of Free Soilers and stand loyally by the Whig party.[35]

Because the likelihood that Whig voters would defect to the third party depended upon a combination of its attractiveness to them and their alienation from the Whig party, steadfast Whig leaders took two related tacks to deflect the Free Soil challenge. They argued that the Whig party, even with Zachary Taylor as its presidential candidate, deserved voters' continued fealty, and the impressive number of faithful Whig editors, orators, and officeholders enhanced their arguments. They also attempted to discredit the need, the motives, the personnel, and the likely consequences of the Free Soil party. Here the predominantly Democratic tilt of Free Soil leadership in most states, and especially Van Buren's nomination, proved a decisive advantage. Conflict with the Democrats had always been the chief source of Whigs' strength, and it would serve them well again in 1848, when they faced not one opponent but two.

Long before the Buffalo convention, Whigs sympathetic to the Free Soil movement warned that Van Buren's nomination could quash the rebellion stirring in Whig ranks. Inventor and devious manipulator of machine politics, proponent of the negative state, and repeated conciliator of slaveholders, Van Buren epitomized what northern Whigs hated most about Democrats. To place him at the head of an antislavery party struck them as hypocritical, if not ludicrous. Even abolitionists such as Joshua Leavitt suspected that Barnburners had nominated Van Buren at Utica more "to avenge his old quarrel with the Hunkers than for his sympathy with the cause."[36] "Give us good Free Soil nominations & we will leave old parties & unite with you," numerous Whigs told Free Soil organizers before the August convention, "but you need not talk to us about going to Van Buren & the Barnburners." Van Buren, they repeatedly protested, represented "everything we have opposed through life" and was motivated simply by "a desire to injure the politicians who have injured him," not by "a spirit of pure devotion to Freedom."[37]

After the Buffalo convention, relieved Whig regulars voiced almost identical opinions. Because Whigs had opposed Van Buren since the 1830s, few "Whigs— even those strongly tinctured with abolition"—would "vote for him," the North Carolinian Outlaw confidently predicted. From across New York poured assurances that Van Buren's nomination would quell the incipient mutiny in Whig ranks since antislavery Whigs regarded the Free Soil party merely as the product of "a Democratic party quarrel" whose purpose was not "to elect Mr. Van Buren" but "to defeat Gen. Cass." In Massachusetts, Van Buren's selection proved as chilling to potential Whig defectors as apprehensive Conscience Whigs had imagined. By September, members of the Whig state committee pronounced the state safe for Taylor, and in October Phillips, the Free Soil gubernatorial candidate, complained that aversion to Van Buren had deterred at least 25,000 potential Whig recruits from joining the new party.[38]

Nonetheless, it soon became apparent that Van Buren's name alone could not stem Whig rebellion in Ohio, Indiana, Wisconsin, Michigan, and Illinois.[39] Hence Whig speakers and editors redoubled their efforts to discredit the third party. Its domination by Democrats, their dubious motives, and their untrustworthiness on the slavery issue remained constant targets of Whig invective throughout the campaign. Editorials in Pittsburgh's leading Whig paper, which were widely reprinted in midwestern Whig sheets, charged that Van Buren and his fellow Democratic bolters were the same men who "brought about the annexation of Texas, the extension of slavery, the disgraceful Mexican War, the prostration of the Protective Tariff, and numerous other evils which have affected the country." Repeatedly the paper vilified Van Buren as an unconverted Jacksonian and an insincere opponent of slavery. Constantly it denounced as traitors Whigs who would support such a man. Nor were Van Buren's personal intentions alone impugned. Pointing to the New York Barnburners' well-known hopes of regaining control of the state's Democratic organization and to the Conscience Whigs' unsuccessful struggle for power in the Massachusetts Whig party, Whigs savaged the entire Free Soil leadership as ambitious politicos whose lust for office had been frustrated in the major parties. Castigating the selfish purposes of Free Soil leaders, Whigs also condemned the consequences of supporting them. Voting for the Free Soilers would divide the opposition to the hated Democrats and elect Cass. Not only would a Democratic victory place a seal of approval on Polk's obnoxious record, but Cass' jingoistic expansionism ensured further aggressive wars of territorial conquest. Rehearsing the standard Whig refrain that the misguided souls who voted for Birney in 1844 had allowed the election of Polk and with it the annexation of Texas and the Mexican War, northern Whig after northern Whig warned that if additional Whigs now abandoned their party for the Free Soilers, "the consequence is inevitable, more slave territory," just the result honest antislavery men most wanted to avoid.[40]

Antislavery Whigs had no need to betray their objective by voting for Free Soilers, protested Whig leaders. Throughout the North, they accurately insisted, Whigs were pledged to the Wilmot Proviso, and northern Whig congressmen's recent votes demonstrated beyond cavil their determination to stop the spread of slavery. As Baldwin insisted in the speech he made across Connecticut, "The question of free soil . . . is for Congress to decide." Since southern Whigs had helped defeat Clayton's Compromise, spuriously contended one Indiana Whig, "The passage of the Oregon Bill, with a provision similar to the Ordinance of '87, is strong evidence that when the remaining Territories come to be provided with Territorial govts. a like prohibition will be submitted to even by the South." Southern Whig help in defeating Clayton's bill, echoed New York's *Poughkeepsie Eagle*, showed that "while we have a Whig Congress the free labor and free soil doctrine will be triumphant."[41]

Most northern Whigs were not so brazen as to ascribe free soil sympathies to their southern colleagues. Instead they exploited the flexibility the American federal system had long provided both national parties. In the spring of 1848, New York Whig Congressman Washington Hunt noted that southern Whigs threatened to draw the Mason-Dixon line on the Wilmot Proviso issue and that he had told them that "they may have their way south of it, & we must manage things for ourselves on the north side." After June, Whigs conducted the two-faced campaign Hunt envisioned. Whatever appeals the southern Whigs made on Taylor's behalf, northern Whigs presented themselves as the North's preeminent free soil party. In September, Pennsylvania's Whig state convention pledged itself against the extension of "perpetuated bondage . . . which would degrade the nation and bring reproach upon republican principles." Adamant resistance to slavery expansion was the theme of Thaddeus Stevens and other Pennsylvania Whigs; of Seward in his speeches in Massachusetts, New York, and Ohio; of Baldwin in Connecticut; and of northern Whigs everywhere. "The Whigs of the North, and especially the Whigs of Massachusetts," declared the Massachusetts Whig state platform, "may rightfully claim the appellation of the *free soil party*."[42]

The utter superfluousness of a new northern party, Whigs chorused, proved the selfish ambition of Free Soil leaders. What could be accomplished, they asked with much justice, by replacing such staunch Whig friends of freedom with Free Soilers who would vote exactly the same way as northern Whigs did on the territorial issue and who, because of their Democratic background, would vote against Whig interests on other matters? Since everyone in New England opposed slavery expansion, asserted the Boston *Advertiser*, the Free Soilers' platform "can afford no good reason for abandoning other principles of political association, and erecting the standard of a new party."[43] Free Soilers retorted that principles on old issues were irrelevant, for only slavery extension now mattered. Whatever Van Buren's past record, he was a Northerner who was now publicly pledged to the Free Soil platform to impose the Wilmot Proviso on all territories and to sign into law a bill to abolish slavery in the District of Columbia. And certainly no antislavery man could expect the Louisiana slaveholder who headed the Whig ticket to sign a territorial bill that incorporated the Proviso or a ban on slavery in the District.

Citing Taylor's antiveto pledge in the Allison Letter of April, northern Whigs responded that Taylor would not veto the Wilmot Proviso. To stop the spread of slavery, therefore, Northerners need only elect a Whig Congress along with Taylor. It would pass the Proviso, and the faithful Whig Taylor would sign it into law. "The question of free soil as I have before remarked, is for Congress to decide, and we already have a candidate who will not seek to control their action," repeated Baldwin as he stumped across Connecticut. Not only did Whigs have a presidential candidate who would accept the Proviso, in contrast to Cass, bragged Thomas Ewing in a widely distributed public letter, their ticket held the key to its passage: a northern man as vice president who could break a Senate tie between Northerners and Southerners. In Millard Fillmore the Whigs had such a man; with the Kentuckian William O. Butler as their vice presidential candidate, the Democrats patently did not. The best way to achieve free territory was to ignore the hopeless Free Soilers, shun the proslavery Democrats, and vote Whig. Across the North, Whigs promised that Taylor would not veto congressional legislation prohibiting slavery from the territories. That was what allowed northern Whigs, in the words of Connecticut's frustrated Free Soiler John Niles, to take "the position of . . . Taylor and free soil."[44]

With apparent candor, some Whigs like Baldwin and Abraham Lincoln admitted they lacked positive proof that Taylor would not veto the Proviso. They simply inferred it from the Allison Letter, which they trusted since Taylor was an honorable man. Actually, the Whig high command did have more evidence. Prior to the national convention, John Wilson, a proslavery Missouri Whig, interviewed Taylor in New Orleans. On May 10, Wilson reported to Truman Smith that "on the subject of the principle of the Wilmot Proviso (for I put the question direct) he answered *instantly*, that the ordinance of 1787 had been passed by

Congress, approved by Washington and upheld by the Judiciary, and he saw no power left for the President to veto it on constitutional objections." Taylor would sign the Proviso if Congress passed it, and he "would not intrigue or in any way meddle to defeat it in its passage" by Congress. Smith had undoubtedly shown this letter to northern Whigs in Washington like Baldwin and Lincoln, and in late June he sent these quoted excerpts and others to Ewing for private circulation among Ohio Whigs. But Smith insisted that Ewing must not publish them, and he did so for the same reasons Baldwin and Lincoln refused to reveal their sources—to protect southern Whigs. Whig strategists were determined to let Whigs south of the Mason-Dixon line have their own way on the Proviso question, and that way most assuredly was not to admit that Zachary Taylor would sign the insulting Wilmot Proviso into law.[45]

Perhaps because of this reluctance to buttress promises about Taylor's future course with more evidence, many antislavery Whigs discounted them. Despite the barrage northern Whigs leveled at the Free Soilers and Van Buren, despite their repeated trumpetings of their own free-soil record, the slaveholder at the head of the Whig ticket remained northern Whigs' biggest problem. Taylor's position must be convincingly explained to the Whig rank and file, warned the brother of Indiana Whig Congressman George Dunn, an early Taylor supporter. "I wouldn't vote for him myself if I did not regard him as committed substantially to the Wilmot Proviso. . . . There is a deep and growing hostility in the West against the ever encroaching and exacting demands of the South." Michigan's Whigs are *"immovably* opposed to the further extension of slavery & consequent increase of slave representation in Congress & in the Presidential electoral college & *therefore* they look with some fearfullness [sic] upon the coming of Gen. Taylor," wrote one of their number in September. "The great difficulty with us in our efforts with Anti Slavery men is to convince them, that Taylor is right on the Proviso question," confessed a western Pennsylvania Whig as late as October. "The Allison letter, Mr. Mann's letter, & others are insufficient."[46]

Not only uncompromising antislavery Whigs needed reassuring. Ultimately, faith in Taylor's willingness to accept the Proviso rested on faith in his commitment to Whiggery and Whig principles. That was the rub. Far more Whigs than those likely to bolt to the Free Soil party doubted that commitment because of Taylor's No Party campaign before the national convention and his behavior after it. The immediate and widespread stress on Taylor's pledge in the Allison Letter not to use the veto, in fact, was aimed as much at disgusted Whig regulars who had no intention of joining the antislavery revolt as at angry antislavery Whigs who might.

III

Even as nervous Whig leaders watched the gathering free-soil revolt in the summer, they feared that disillusioned regulars might not vote at all. "Where apathy and indifference do not prevail, the most indignant spirit pervades the Whig ranks," an Ohioan reported in July. His juxtaposition and ordering of apathy and anger spoke volumes. Every disillusioned Whig who refused to vote because he considered Taylor's nomination an "abandonment . . . of those principles which have heretofore graced our banner" compounded the damage done by a Whig who defected to the Free Soilers.[47] The very threat of losses to the Free Soilers, in short, increased the necessity of bringing Whigs not attracted by them to the polls. The Whig leadership quickly recognized that winning in 1848 required them not only to minimize bolts to the Free Soilers but also to maximize their residual support.

To be sure, some Whigs believed that Taylor's posture of nonpartisan independence and reputation for battlefield heroics would excite both Whigs and new voters and attract more than enough Democrats to offset any Whig losses from abstention or defection. Now "there was hope for the Whig party," rejoiced Indiana's Whigs upon learning of the decision at Philadelphia. Taylor's "nomination gives the Whigs here, in Illinois, and Mo. new life." Even New England regulars like Winthrop and Vermont's Justin Morrill proclaimed that "Old Taylor is bound to run like prairie fire" among potential Democratic converts. In Pennsylvania, too, the Whigs carefully kept the organization for Taylor's presidential campaign, known there and elsewhere as "Rough and Ready Clubs," separate from the regular Whig apparatus and founded a new newspaper in Philadelphia in order "to work on the Democrats."[48]

Southern Whigs were particularly eager to mine the Democratic vote. Taylor's nomination, Gentry excitedly wrote Whigs in Tennessee after the convention, afforded an opportunity "to Revolutionize the strong Democratic Districts" in the state. Whig speakers should therefore "measure their denunciations of Democracy and infuse a larger quantity of persuasion and conciliation into their speeches than heretofore." In Georgia, where the Democratic vote was mushrooming among nonslaveholders, Whigs speakers also stumped "the Cherokee Counties— the missionary ground of the State."[49]

Wooing Democrats entailed a risk, but one seemingly worth taking. Vigorously assailing the Democrats had been the traditional means for arousing the Whig electorate, galvanizing competitive energies and the will to win. Only confidence that Taylor's status as a slaveholder and fame as a military hero would mobilize Whigs anyway encouraged the leadership to forsake their customary strategy. As they further admitted, winning over Democrats also required Whig speakers to jettison traditional Whig issues that might alienate them and to rely instead on Taylor's military renown to do it. And that is precisely what many southern Whigs initially attempted to do. "Old party issues are worn out and have nearly disappeared," declared the *New Orleans Bee*, a Taylor sheet. "All the old issues are obsolete," chorused a Taylor supporter from Alabama. Taylor deserved election, declared a Rough and Ready Club in Hinds County, Mississippi, because "according to his own declaration, [he] has 'no private purposes to accomplish, no party projects to build up, no enemies to punish, nothing to serve.' " In Louisiana, chortled a New Orleans Whig, the party campaigned for Taylor and Fillmore solely by sending into the parishes groups of young men who with "songs, shouts, music, and banners" foiled the hapless Democrats. Furious at Whigs' reliance on hoopla, a frustrated Georgia Democrat complained that the standard Whig speech consisted of "miscellaneous abuse of Cass and the Democrats, comments on the danger to slavery, and the impossibility of trusting any Northern man . . . and lastly a glorification of Old Taylor's battles."[50]

Some Whigs viewed this outreach to Democrats as more than an opportunistic attempt to increase the party's vote. Sharing Taylor's belief that superheated partisan strife threatened the consensus necessary for republican self-government, they sincerely, if naively, welcomed the chance to restore the supposed golden age of American politics before the advent of Andrew Jackson and mass parties. Taylor would win because he had "plain republican virtues which distinguished 'the better days of the republic,'" gushed Indiana Congressman Richard W. Thompson to his constituents. "He owes no allegiance to any party. . . . He looks to the *people* as the only true source of political power, and will never consent that *politicians*—for the mere purposes of *party*—shall endanger or diminish this power for their own selfish ends and aggrandizement." Taylor's repeated vows not to be a mere party president, chimed another Indianan, ensured "an era of good feeling—good men & good measures all over the land & a mighty abatement of the bitterness of party."[51]

No one was happier about Taylor's nomination than William C. Rives and his Virginia Whig followers. "Your insistence that Whigs are the exponents of the doctrines of the old Jeffersonian Republican party," Rives fawningly wrote Taylor in July, ensured "permanent success" for the Whig party since "the great body of the people in the Country are thoroughly Republican in their sentiments." Because the Rives men controlled Virginia's Taylor campaign, the state platform adopted at a convention in Lexington in September said nothing about specific Whig issues. Instead it extolled Taylor's character and his commitment against executive power as guarantees that basic republican principles would be restored. "The Whigs of Virginia recognize a recurrence to the original and better days of the Republic," they boasted. Taylor's belief in "the legitimate supremacy of the popular will, . . . his lofty personal character, his well known patriotism . . . afford the highest guaranty for an administration of the Government, in his hands, conforming to those republican landmarks."[52]

All Whigs opposed executive usurpation and supported the preservation of republican self-government. Yet those Whigs who believed that Taylor's subscription to these values proved he was a good Whig and that rehearsing his fidelity to them would win the election were a distinct minority—at least among those whose private correspondence is still extant. Far more typical was outrage at the abandonment of traditional Whig policies such men advocated in order to attract Democrats and pessimism that paeans to Taylor's nonpartisan independence could mobilize the Whig electorate. Such a strategy, most Whigs insisted, merely reinforced doubts that Zachary Taylor was a legitimate Whig who merited support from principled Whig regulars.

Predictably, Clay and his many devotees immediately repudiated the ticket. Bitterly and repeatedly he wrote his friends that he would not lift a finger to help Taylor because "the Whig party has been overthrown by a mere personal party," just like the Jackson party. "The Philadelphia convention humiliated itself, and as far as it could, placed the Whig party in a degraded condition" by nominating a man who refused to "pledge himself" to Whig measures and who "is presented as a no-party candidate." Clay's friends were equally indignant. "Thousands" would vote for Cass "to annihilate politically your base and cowardly assassins," snarled a furious Philadelphian. "The last Whig convention committed the double *crime* of *suicide* & paricide [sic]," echoed a New Yorker. "The Whig party as such is dead. The very name will be abandoned, should Taylor be elected, for 'the Taylor party.' "[53]

A few Clay men intended to vote for Cass or Van Buren to punish those who had nominated Taylor, but far more commonly they refused to help Taylor with their money, their time and effort, or their votes. Whig turnout would be so low in New York, they chortled, that only "the dissensions of our opponents," and "not Whig votes," could "save" Taylor. Because of regular Whigs' disgust, ratification meetings in New York City and upstate towns had to be postponed or canceled altogether. Midwestern Whigs also reported "apathy and indifference" and warned that Whig voters would never support Taylor unless Clay publicly endorsed him.[54]

Visceral discontent extended to the South. Clay loyalists in Georgia, Tennessee, and North Carolina also denounced the ticket. "I have no hopes for the Whigs in the next presidential election" and "no interest in the election except for the State elections," declared a North Carolinian who refused to vote for Taylor. "We have had one John Tyler and I don't want another." In Virginia, Richmond Congressman John Minor Botts condemned the ticket as unworthy of support, causing Taylorites to condemn him as "an inexpressible ass" even as they worried "that the discord he has produced may have so disabled us as to lose the state."[55]

Dissatisfaction was hardly limited to Clay's closest friends. Since Taylor's nomination abdicated traditional Whig issues, a New Yorker warned Fillmore, "here our ears are saluted with 'The Kangaroo Ticket' 'The Kangaroo Ticket' 'I would vote it if I thought Taylor would die.' " The inability to hold ratification meetings also terrified Weed's New York lieutenants who sought to mobilize the traditional Whig vote. "If we succeed, it will not be a *Whig triumph*, based upon Whig principles, but a triumph obtained by the aid of disaffected Democrats," complained Indiana's Orth. The nomination alienated "the *very best portion of the party*, who disgusted at our inconsistency will never return." According to another disenchanted Indianan:

> The pageant is old Zack and a new order of things, without principle, object, or aim, torn loose from the landmarks of the past, burying in oblivion the venerated objects of former devotion, sailing with singular sang froid [sic] on the turbid ocean of availability. . . . Now the Whigs openly disclaim any *party issues with the Democrats*. And declare their party is virtually dissolved, dead, and buried![56]

IV

Initially, Whigs attempted to assuage the discontented and arouse the apathetic in their ranks in three interrelated ways. First, they proclaimed it a duty to party and country to vote. To abstain was to betray both. Progressive Whigs like Weed in his *Albany Evening Journal* and conservatives like Massachusetts Congressman George Ashmun and the Albany patrician Daniel D. Barnard in public letters argued that the convention had followed regular procedures and Taylor had won on a fair vote. Therefore, both the delegates who attended it and the constituents they represented had an obligation to support its nominee. "Party conventions are not under the laws of the land; they are therefore governed by the code of honor," maintained a writer in *The American Review*. "The integrity and success of a party depend on its rigid adherence to this code. Whatever be our chagrin or disappointment, the debt of honor must be paid, or we lose all consideration, and therefore all force."[57] Most likely, only a small minority of educated and affluent Whigs ever read the unusually articulate, learned, and well-crafted essays in *The American Review*. Such men, however, formed an influential segment of the Clay loyalists and other regulars who most vociferously protested the nomination. Therefore, its articles, however atypical their rhetorical refinement, illuminate the appeals directed at the disenchanted.

By far the most striking version of this theme of duty appeared in an anonymous essay revealingly entitled "Necessity of Party." No document better shows how Whig thinking about political parties had evolved since the 1830s. In contrast to early Whigs, who denounced parties as inimical to republican self-government and popular liberty, this writer maintained that the preservation of republicanism *required* interparty competition. His theme was the fundamental American axiom that the price of liberty is eternal vigilance. Newspapers could play a vital role in monitoring government and alerting citizens to threats to their liberty, he admitted, but newspapers could also be corrupted by governmental patronage. The more reliable shield of freedom was the ability to vote an incumbent party out of office. Elections, therefore, were the most important struggles "men can engage in," for "the very life of liberty is maintained only by the strife of contending parties." Casting a vote, in other words, was how a citizen performed his historic duty to protect the Revolutionary experiment in republican self-government. "When the Constitution confers the power of suffrage upon a citizen, it imposes a duty. . . . How unworthy, then, of this high privilege are those inert or supercilious citizens, who affect to disregard the elections, or who speak of them as a vain and interested contest of office-seekers. . . . Whoever feels within himself the least spark of that generosity of soul which makes men republicans, is, so far, a POLITICIAN." A true republican, in short, was defined by his active participation in the political arena. The eighteenth-century concept of virtue, the willingness to sacrifice self-interest, including material self-interest, for the common good, had been transformed into a narrower but still vital obligation: the willingness to vote. "Politics, the judging and acting for the honor and prosperity of the nation, is properly an art to which all of *us* are born. *We*, the citizens, who think we have no masters but the laws, cannot be too careful or too vigilant in the power of election, in which we perform the initiative art of government."

Second, in addition to shaming abstainers, Whig leaders insisted that the election could determine vital matters of public policy. Besides those who considered Taylor's nomination a disgraceful abandonment of principle, some Whigs, like New York's James Ogden, believed that the end of the war, the achievement of territorial expansion, however regrettable, and the prosperity attained under the Walker Tariff and the subtreasury system meant that "the question, as to the success of either of the two Presidential candidates, becomes, perhaps, of less consequence than at any previous period of our history."[58] To arouse the indifferent to action, most Whigs therefore strove "to mark the contrast" between the parties, "to set [Whig principles] forth in bold contrast to those of the enemy."

"To present a firm and unbroken front to the enemy," Whig propagandists repeatedly contended, they must "press home upon the public mind the great principles by and for which we exist as a party." Whigs "constantly endeavor to identify the interests of the people with those of the government"; Democrats, in contrast, "opposed every national measure which should call the creative and protective functions of government into action." Admitting that famine in Europe had temporarily produced a favorable balance of trade and prosperity, Whigs nonetheless asserted that the tariff had to be raised and specific duties reimposed to protect American manufacturers and workers from European competition, "to save the industrious Germans in the iron factories of Pennsylvania from ruin." The Subtreasury must be abolished to ensure an ample circulating currency and adequate credit. Congress had not only a right but a duty to fund necessary rivers and harbors improvements. Yet while Democrats were willing to spend millions on unconstitutional and unnecessary wars to conquer new territory, they "declare against all projects of internal improvement." "With EXTERNAL IMPROVE-MENTS they are greatly in love, with *internal* not at all."

Whig spokesmen particularly targeted Polk's record, which, they maintained, accurately forecast what Cass would do in office, since that record "necessarily involved the pretensions of the party that supports him to have its dominion perpetuated." To frighten lethargic Whigs to vote against Cass, therefore, Whigs castigated Democratic enormities under Polk: his unconstitutional, unrepublican, and tyrannical commencement and conduct of the Mexican War; his ballooning the national debt by over $100 million; his economic legislation that would inevitably bankrupt the government and devastate the national economy; and his disdain for domestic improvement.

A dishonorable and antirepublican lust for empire achieved through "rapacity and conquest," war, and crippling debt were the legacies of the Polk administration, and, if possible, the record under Lewis Cass would be even worse. Cass had demanded war with England to get all of Oregon. He supported "our Executive war of conquest and spoilation" against Mexico. "He would not hesitate to make war on his own responsibility, as Mr. Polk has done, with his full sanction and support" to seize Canada, Cuba, or the Yucatan. Cass "seems to look upon the United States as if the country were some monster reptile, that must subsist and swell its huge, unsightly bulk, by gorging itself with every living thing, small and great, that comes in its way." The contrast between Cass and Taylor was clear, declared the Washington *National Intelligencer.* "In Gen. Taylor is presented to us the representative of a constitutional, conservative, and beneficial policy at home, and a peaceful, just, non-intervention policy in regard to foreign Powers." Cass was "the representative of Dorrism and Locofocism, of the Veto upon liberal legislation at home, and of intervention, war, conquest, and annexation with almost every accessible part of the foreign world."[59]

Trumpeting the Whig party's superior principles, of course, meant nothing if men doubted Taylor's commitment to those principles. Therefore the third, and most emphasized component of Whigs' message, rehearsed Taylor's fealty to "the great doctrine which gave us our party designation," "the very foundation . . . the very essence of Whig faith," "opposition to executive usurpation." Over and over, Whig after Whig insisted that Taylor's pledge not to use the veto or to interfere with Congress proved his Whiggery. "He who adopts and maintains this great and distinctive principle is a Whig," declared one writer, "and all Whigs will welcome him to their fellowship." Taylor's Allison Letter clearly embraced Whigs' desire "to see the congress restored to its original powers under the Constitution and the President confined to the proper executive duties of his station." As a lifelong Democrat, in contrast, Cass would not "hesitate, when once in office, to exercise the Executive prerogative with the same arbitrary will that led Louis XIV to proclaim 'I am the State.' " Instead, rhapsodized the *National Intelligencer*, Taylor would "restore the republic to its original purity as administered by the earlier Presidents, before kingly vetoes had *practically* converted the Government into an *Elective Despotism*."[60]

During the summer, however, Seward, Weed, and other perceptive leaders realized that Taylor's Allison Letter did not suffice to reassure skeptical Whigs, if only because Taylor had written so many other letters refusing to be the exponent of any party's principles. Why then, Whig voters asked, should they believe his professed commitment to the fundamental Whig tenet? Additional evidence of the hero's Whiggery was urgently required, and the first place nervous Whig leaders looked for it was in Taylor's official acceptance of the Whig convention's nomination, a reply that seemed agonizingly slow in coming. Unless Taylor accepted the nomination "as a Whig," Weed moaned five weeks after the convention adjourned, he would lose New York and six other northern states critical to Whig success. Weed had Seward prepare a draft letter of acceptance Taylor could use, and the Albany editor had sent it to Taylor's Louisiana cronies with whom he had worked at the convention. To his dismay, however, Rough and Ready rejected Seward's draft. Lamenting Taylor's decision as a "blunder," Weed warned Seward that "the General's letter should be a very good one, or we shall be in a bad box."[61]

Even as Weed wrote, Taylor's letter of acceptance, dated July 15, was on its way to the northern press, and it proved disappointing indeed. Taylor simply and briefly accepted the nomination and promised to carry out his duties faithfully if elected. He did not reaffirm his own Whiggery or his opposition to the veto. He did not even pledge that the Whig nomination was the only one he would accept. William L. Hodge of New Orleans candidly explained to Fillmore the thinking of the Louisiana Whigs who advised Taylor on the letter. "Any promises to carry out Whig measures or that his administration would be predicated upon Whig principles could only drive back into the bosom of the Loco party, thousands and tens of thousands who are desirous of voting for him." Those Louisianans still expected Taylor to carry Democratic bastions like Arkansas, Alabama, and Mississippi, and to do so they needed Democratic votes. "If any of our northern ultra friends think his letter is not strong enough," Hodge added disdainfully, "you and your press also must tell them it is."[62]

Taylor's bland letter of acceptance was bad enough, but he then quickly compounded the damage with other letters penned that summer. Prior to the Whig convention, Taylor had jeopardized efforts to present him as a good Whig with careless epistles like that to Peter Sken Smith. Now, after it, he seemed almost willfully to sabotage Whigs' attempts to reassure and arouse the faithful. Shortly after his tepid acceptance letter appeared, papers published his letter of July 24 to a Philadelphian named George Lippard in which Taylor reasserted his independence: "I am not a party candidate, and if elected cannot be President of a party, but the President of the whole people." The Lippard letter shocked northern Whigs and fanned their fears of massive abstentions and defections to the Free Soilers. "I hope Genl. Taylor has got done writing letters," moaned a member of Weed's organization. "It requires considerable labor to satisfy our friends *he is the* candidate of our party and after his acceptance it is insufferable that he should qualify his position by letters to others. . . . Is there no way to gag him?" Friends of Weed's rival, Fillmore, were also appalled. "The late Lippard letter has produced a most chilling influence," wrote one from Rochester. "We are losing quite a large number of those who have always been true or faithful to our party in consequence of distrust over Gen. T.'s opinions."[63]

Watching in horror as the flames of Whig anger incinerated his chances for the vice presidency, Fillmore frantically wrote Taylor on August 19 that he must counteract the Lippard letter. The northern Whig rank and file demanded absolute proof of Taylor's Whiggery, he warned, because they were still haunted by memories of Tyler's betrayal. Worse still, Free Soil papers charged that southern Whigs, the authors of Taylor's nonpartisan strategy, planned to cut Fillmore and vote instead for William O. Butler, the Democratic vice presidential candidate and, like Taylor, a southern slaveholder.[64] Almost as if on cue, Taylor then provided evidence for Free Soilers' wild charges. Because of his apparent soundness on the slavery issue, Taylor aroused considerable enthusiasm in South Carolina, even though it lacked an organized Whig party and popular voting for presidential electors. On July 20, a meeting in Charleston nominated an independent ticket of Taylor for president and Butler for vice president. In August, Taylor gratefully accepted the Charleston nomination. In another letter to the *Charleston News* he explained that he had accepted the Whig nomination on his own terms and would have just as readily received that of the Democrats had it been offered. He must run, he declared, "without pledges or being trammeled in any way."[65]

If the Lippard letter scandalized northern Whigs, Taylor's South Carolina letters almost precipitated a revolt that would have ended any chance he had of winning the presidency. Word of the letters reached Albany, New York, by telegraphic despatch in the early afternoon of Saturday, August 26. The usually unflappable Weed exploded in rage and had handbills posted calling a protest meeting that night at the state capitol, where he planned to introduce resolutions repudiating Taylor's nomination and launching a new ticket headed by Clay. Fillmore and his friends initially suspected that Weed acted to sabotage Fillmore, either by driving a wedge between Taylor and Fillmore or by bringing about the ticket's defeat. But Weed believed that Taylor's candidacy was doomed in the North and that only a new ticket could salvage Whig congressional candidates. To save his chances for the vice presidency, Fillmore intervened with Weed in the late afternoon as he was preparing his rebellious resolutions in the editorial offices of the *Albany Evening Journal* and persuaded him not to present them. Fillmore and other Whig leaders then tried to calm the crowd of angry Whigs that night by protesting that the South Carolina reports must be false or, if true, that South Carolina's Democrats had dropped Cass for Taylor, not Fillmore for Butler. By Monday morning, August 28, Weed editorially repledged his support to the ticket on the grounds that only Taylor could defeat Cass, and another mass meeting that night also endorsed it.[66]

Nonetheless, the South Carolina letters undid northern Whigs' campaign to rally their troops. "The most sanguine and earnest Taylor men are perfectly dumbfounded and are ready to give up in despair," reported a western New York Whig. "It will be utterly impossible to make the rank & file in this region swallow Taylor now. The universal feeling here is that a new candidate must be started or we lose the state."[67] The shocking letters also gave disgruntled conservative Whigs in New York City an excuse to launch an independent Clay candidacy and thus avenge the Kentuckian's defeat at Philadelphia. "We are at the very brink of a party explosion here," wrote one of Clay's correspondents in early September. "The People will not go *Taylor*—they insist upon having a Whig, a whole Whig, and nothing but a Whig, and are rallying with an enthusiasm, that nothing can stay, or repress, upon your name." On September 7, a mass meeting of furious regulars at Vauxhall Garden named a slate of electors for a new ticket of Clay and Fillmore. Clay's friend Daniel Ullmann begged him not to discourage this revolt. The telegraph had so facilitated communication, he argued, that electoral tickets could be arranged for Clay and Fillmore across the North even at the last moment. Besides, Clay owed it to true Whigs to "let us have a nucleus around which a Whig party may be re-organized after we shall have emerged from the smoke of the present contest. It is the only door open for us, through which we may retreat with a conservative band, which may finally rescue our beloved country from the horrors of military rule or corrupt charlatanism."[68]

The New York City insurgency eerily prefigured future conservative bolts, but how much harm it could have inflicted upon the official Whig ticket is unclear. Calling the Clay men "crack-brained," one New Yorker assured Crittenden that "the move of the aristocratic, crazy Clay idolaters in this city will not change the vote, enough, to be put on paper." Less potentially dangerous than a Clay ticket that bore the imprimatur of Weed and the state Whig leadership at Albany, it nonetheless frightened numerous Whigs. Fillmore denounced the new ticket in a public letter in the *Albany Evening Journal* and refused to serve on it. Men in New York, Pennsylvania, and Washington called on Clay both publicly and privately to renounce it to save Whigs' chance to capture the White House.[69]

Mortified by his rebuff at Philadelphia, Clay had no stomach for an independent candidacy. Unlike his old rival Van Buren, he refused, as early as July 5, to lead an insurgency against his party. Warned in advance about the Vauxhall Garden meeting, he wrote James Brooks that "I am utterly opposed to the use of my name as a candidate for the Presidency," a refusal Brooks published in his *New York Express* the day after that gathering. To extinguish any lingering doubts, Clay then formally wrote the officers of the meeting declining their nomination, and the Whig press widely publicized his declination.[70]

Though stillborn, the September New York Clay insurgency vividly increased the evidence of regular Whigs' deep discontent with Taylor. And if those men could not vote for Clay, they could still abstain. In the longest part of his letter of September 20 refusing the New York nomination, a part he insisted not be published, indeed, Clay provided an extensive list of reasons why good Whigs should *not* support Taylor. By early September, in short, Whig leaders knew that their first attempts to reassure the alienated and arouse the apathetic had failed. It still remained "essential to do something to keep as many of our forces as possible."[71]

V

During August and early September, it also became abundantly clear that blurring partisan differences, eschewing Whig issues, and instead boasting of Taylor's non-partisan independence, republican virtue, and glorious military exploits was failing abysmally to win Democratic converts or energize new voters. By early September, in short, the Whig campaign was in deep trouble, not only in northern Whig strongholds, but in the West and South as well. Something more desperately needed to be done to get Whig troops to the polls in November.

First, the August and September state elections dispelled optimism that Taylor's coattails could help other Whig candidates. Crittenden easily won Kentucky's governorship despite Democratic efforts to turn Clay men against him. Nonetheless, Crittenden's constant defense of Taylor and of Whigs' refusal to adopt a national platform yielded only a few more votes than Whig congressional candidates had amassed in 1847, while his Democratic opponent, Lazarus Powell, an unexpectedly able campaigner, garnered the largest vote yet obtained by a Democrat in Kentucky. If Whigs expected Democratic converts, they did not get them.[72]

North Carolina's Whigs squeaked by with an 854-vote margin out of some 84,000 votes cast in the gubernatorial contest, lost their majority in the state senate, and had it sharply reduced to one seat in the house. As the Whigs had feared, the Democratic gubernatorial candidate, David Reid, found an unusually popular issue in his call for the elimination of the property qualification for voters in state senate elections, an issue Whigs had trouble contending with. Whig candidate Charles Manly's immediate opposition to Reid's proposal offended many Whig voters. Then Whigs charged the Democrats with humbugging the voters and trying to evade their participation in, and approval of, the obnoxious Democratic record in Washington. Finally, Whigs tried to shift the issue away from equal suffrage to equal apportionment of the legislature—"equal power," as they called it—but that proposal divided them along regional lines. Western Whigs ardently favored reapportionment based on the white population rather than the federal ratio, which counted slaves, but eastern Whigs just as adamantly opposed it, a rift that portended difficult times ahead for the North Carolina Whig party. Thus the state issues at stake confounded the Whigs and excited the Democrats. Turnout was unusually large, higher in absolute terms than in the presidential election of 1844, and all of the increased vote went to the Democrats. Reid's vote exceeded Polk's by 2,800, the 1846 Democratic gubernatorial candidate's by 7,000, and the total amassed by Democratic congressional candidates in 1847 by 11,000. With some justice, Whigs claimed they would do better in November. Still, Taylor's name at the top of their ticket had obviously failed to forestall a Democratic surge.[73]

Returns from normally Democratic states dealt the severest blow to Whig hopes. In Missouri, whose delegates had gone unanimously for Taylor at Philadelphia, the Democratic vote soared 20 percent above its levels in 1844 and 1846, leaving the Whig candidate with only two-fifths of the total and Taylor doomed in November. Taylor also lacked coattails in Illinois. The demoralized Whigs did not even contest the gubernatorial election against the Democratic incumbent, but they did run state legislative and congressional candidates. The Whig share of seats in the state house of representatives sank from a dismal 33 percent to 31 percent, and it hovered at 28 percent in the state senate. Again, the Whigs won only one of the state's congressional seats, and they polled only a third of the popular vote, running some 30,000 votes behind the Democrats, another margin that Taylor seemed unlikely to overcome.[74] Finally, in Indiana, where some Whigs had boasted of the converting power of gunpowder and nonpartisanship, Whigs lost control of the lower house of the state legislature, declining from 53 percent of the seats in 1847 to 39 percent in 1848. As realistic Indiana Whigs admitted, Taylor's military reputation backfired against them since his public criticism of two Indiana regiments that deserted at Buena Vista infuriated some Hoosier voters, while Quakers, an important segment of Indiana's electorate, who disliked Taylor's military background altogether, threatened to abstain in November or vote for Van Buren. Gunpowder was proving to be no aid at all in capturing Indiana's sector of the Loco Foco fortress.[75]

Surveying the August results, the vindictive Clay pronounced Taylor a sure loser. To the shaken Whig loyalists conducting the campaign, the results indicated that winning the White House would depend on mobilizing Whig voters in traditionally Whig and closely contested states, not on large-scale Democratic defections or a surge of new voters. The Vermont and Maine results in September reinforced that assessment. Whigs carried the gubernatorial election in Vermont and three of the four congressional seats, as they had in 1846. Yet their absolute and proportionate votes were down since 1847; indeed, they drew less than 44 percent of the total. In contrast, Free Soilers' absolute vote and share of the total doubled what the Liberty party had won in 1847. Even though Democratic losses meant that Taylor would probably carry the state, Whig erosion boded ill for more closely contested states. Maine was a disaster. The Whigs picked up an additional congressional seat, raising their total to two of seven, and their gubernatorial candidate drew substantially more votes than had his three predecessors. Still, he won only 37 percent of the total vote, and Whigs captured only 35 percent of the seats in the lower house of the state legislature. Some observers in Maine blamed the September results on lame effort and poor organization and still predicted Democratic votes for Taylor in November. More realistic Whig politicos knew better.[76]

Reports from the southern states without summer elections also demonstrated that the initial no-issue, no-party, military glory campaign waged for Taylor neither attracted Democrats nor aroused Whigs. Taylor's very nomination by the Whigs' national convention, warned one Georgian, killed any chances of winning Democratic converts in his state. Missionary efforts among Democratic nonslaveholders in North Alabama also quickly foundered. Democrats there reported either a total lack of "enthusiasm" among voters of both parties or that the Whigs' "claptrap about military glory and no-partyism cannot shake the mountain democracy." Meanwhile, in Whig areas of the black belt, abandonment of traditional tactics produced a stultifying indifference. When Whig Congressman Henry Hilliard made a speech for Taylor in Montgomery in late September, his audience was small and unresponsive. "Politics is quiet," concluded a Democratic state official in the capital. "There is no excitement on either side."[77]

Missionary efforts also failed to catch fire among Democrats or ignite Whigs in Tennessee, a state Whigs almost had to carry. In early August, William B. Campbell, a prominent Whig leader from middle Tennessee, complained that "I have not witnessed so much quietness in any general election in fifteen years." By the fall Tennessee Whig leaders were frantic. "The Democrats are making the most desperate effort to carry the State"; they were winning back "the Taylor Democrats" and would "bring their full force to the polls," Governor Neil Brown warned Campbell. Yet Whigs complacently "slumber[ed]." Whig leaders like Campbell must forget about the Democrats and work to "get out [the Whig] vote on election day." Whigs must jettison their wrong-headed and futile focus on Democratic districts and concentrate on strong Whig counties, insisted another of Campbell's correspondents. "Stimulate every Whig to turn out and work on that day. For our opponents are at work." Success, in short, hinged on mobilizing Whigs. Democratic votes must not be expected.[78]

VI

By September, if not earlier, therefore, Whig leaders in both sections had abandoned their reliance on Taylor's nonpartisan heroism and reverted to the traditional tactic of emphasizing differences between the parties and condemning rather than courting Democrats. But southern and northern Whigs went about it in distinctive ways. Southern Whig politicians possessed far fewer options for reinvigorating their rank and file than those available in the North. Unlike the North, where several key states held state and congressional elections in October and November, most slave states did not. In most of the South, Whigs could not expect attractive local candidates to heal intraparty wounds, remind Whig voters of Whig principles, help boost the Whig vote, or create a bandwagon effect. Nor could southern Whigs hope to win many votes by condemning Cass as a warmonger. After all, the Mexican War had been popular in the South, and they boomed Taylor's military exploits to neutralize Democrats' advantage on the issue. They thus doubted the utility of stressing Cass' supposed bellicosity, and to do so in light of the campaign they were making for Taylor would simply expose them as hypocrites.

In sharp contrast to northern Whigs, southern Whigs also did not renew their assaults of 1846 on Democrats' economic record. At first glance, this failure is puzzling. As with northern grain products, the prices of southern export staples, especially cotton, soared in 1847, but they plummeted even further than the prices of northern commodities in 1848, whether measured by the differences with 1847 prices or the differences from the beginning to the end of the year 1848 itself (Tables 24 and 25). At the same time, however, the volume of southern exports swelled in 1848, and the income the region earned from them consequently billowed. The total value of cotton exports, for example, jumped from $43 million to $53 million between 1846 and 1847, but it climbed to $62 million in 1848 for a healthy gain of 17 percent. Similarly, tobacco sales, which had been worse in 1847 than in 1846 increased by 14.3 percent in 1848. In contrast, the total value of wheat exports plunged by 50 percent between 1847 and 1848.[79] In short, Southerners enjoyed relative prosperity during 1848, thus neutralizing any Whig attempt to exploit economic issues.

In the fall, therefore, southern Whigs increasingly emphasized one of their old themes—that Taylor's ownership of slaves meant that Whigs provided greater security to slavery and Southern Rights than did Democrats. Reflecting Whigs'

Table 24

Percentage Drop in Wholesale Prices Between 1847 and 1848 in Five Cities[a]

	June	July	August	September	October	November
New York	17%	15.3%	12%	11.7%	6%	9.6%
Philadelphia	13.5%	10%	9%	6.7%	9%	11%
Cincinnati	33%	33.3%	22.2%	17%	17.7%	12.2%
Charleston	47.4%	44.2%	48%	50%	40%	41%
New Orleans	40.6%	42%	44.5%	47%	42.4%	12.8%

[a]This table is based on Tables 46, 53, 77, 90, and 101 in the appendix of Arthur H. Cole, *Wholesale Commodity Prices in the United States, 1700–1861* (Cambridge: Harvard University Press, 1938). Although each is weighted by different commodities, they measure different things. The table for New York City is the least helpful because it reflects wholesale prices for all commodities, including imported goods. The table for Philadelphia is limited to the prices of domestic commodities and that for Cincinnati to the prices of northern agricultural commodities. Those for Charleston and New Orleans are based on export staples from South Carolina and Louisiana, respectively, and in each, cotton was weighted far more heavily than other products, 85 compared to 15 for rice in South Carolina and 39 compared to 9 for sugar in Louisiana. I have taken cotton prices in these two ports to represent cotton prices across the South.

I constructed the table by calculating the percentage differences in the specified months in the two years, for example, between July 1847 and July 1848.

calculated two-faced strategy on the slavery issue, Truman Smith sent documents to the South, pledging Taylor's and Fillmore's fidelity to southern interests, while simultaneously sending different documents to the North, promising that Taylor opposed slavery expansion and would sign the Proviso. Southern Whigs happily played this cynical game, for they believed they held a winning hand. Whatever northern Whigs claimed about Taylor, they were convinced he would never betray his section. If northern Whigs wanted to hoodwink their electorate, let them.[80]

Significantly, southern Whigs did *not* stress concrete past actions regarding slavery to distinguish themselves from Democrats since their voting records in the recent Congress on Oregon and the Clayton Compromise had been so similar. Instead, Whigs and Democrats alike emphasized what their respective presidential and vice presidential candidates might do in the future. Praising Cass's manly pledge to veto the Wilmot Proviso in his Nicholson Letter of December 1847, Democrats belittled Taylor's cowardly silence. Despite owning some 100 slaves, they insisted, Taylor could not be trusted without a public pledge to veto the Proviso—a pledge he refused to make. Every northern Whig congressman had supported the Proviso, and Whigs across the North promised that Taylor would never veto that odious implement of Yankee tyranny. Thus, Democratic papers in the South vilified the "Two Faces" of the Whig campaign. "The Northern and Southern sections of the Whig party are playing off the boldest attempt at *fraud* ever made upon the American people," declared a Democratic sheet in Florida. "LET THE SLAVEHOLDERS OF NORTH CAROLINA BEWARE! THEY ARE ABOUT TO BE BETRAYED," warned the Democratic organ in Raleigh.[81]

In many slave states, however, Fillmore bore the brunt of Democratic invective. As soon as Whigs chose their ticket, southern Democrats eagerly scanned the ex-congressman's record for incriminating evidence. They discovered that Fillmore,

Table 25

Change in Average Wholesale Prices During 1848 in Five Cities[a]

	Average Price January–March	Average Price September–November	Percentage Change
New York	79	76	− 3.8%
Philadelphia	87.3	82.6	− 5.4%
Cincinnati	72	73.3	+ 1.8%
Charleston	77	60	−20.8%
New Orleans	74.7	62	−17%

[a]This table is based on the same tables from Cole's study of wholesale prices as Table 24.

like most northern Whigs, had consistently voted against the gag rule. Far more damaging, they found and widely printed an 1838 Fillmore letter to abolitionists endorsing congressional abolition of both slavery in the District of Columbia and the interstate slave trade. That letter, chorused the southern Democratic press, irrefutably proved Fillmore's "unsoundness on the question of Southern rights." Did Southerners dare put an avowed abolitionist within a heartbeat of the presidency? "Let every southern man before he goes to the polls put this solemn question to himself."[82]

Southern Whigs could not pooh-pooh so embarrassing a record. When they first learned of Fillmore's nomination, they were as apprehensive as Democrats were hopeful that he had antislavery skeletons in his closet. Southern Whigs thus bombarded Fillmore with questions after the convention about whether he had ever publicly endorsed the Proviso, and they expressed enormous relief when he replied he had not. Citing Democratic attacks on Fillmore's votes against the gag rule, still more demanded a public avowal that he was no abolitionist. But Democrats' unearthing of Fillmore's 1838 letter in early September particularly unnerved them. Virginia's Rives and New York editor James Brooks insisted that Fillmore must issue a public statement to defuse that explosive document. From Georgia, Robert Toombs wailed that the Democrats' exposure of it "has fallen upon us like a wet blanket, & has much injured us in the State."[83]

Fillmore desperately sent southern Whigs ammunition to repel the Democratic assault. In a letter to Alabama's John Gayle, which Whig papers broadcast across the South, Fillmore pledged that he was no abolitionist and would never "assail Southern institutions." On September 13, he sent Brooks a missive intended for southern dissemination dealing with his incendiary remarks about outlawing the interstate slave trade. Apparently referring to the Supreme Court's *Groves v. Slaughter* decision, in which three justices had stated or implied that Congress could not interfere with the interstate slave trade, Fillmore argued that the Court's 1841 decision rendered his 1838 statement moot. He concurred with the decision and would abide by it. Thus he would not abide, he implied, any congressional attempt to end that trade. By late September and early October, at least a few Southerners assured the beleaguered candidate that he had done enough. No more letters were needed.[84]

The major emphasis of the Whig campaign in the fall, however, lay less in defending Fillmore than in attacking Cass. Whatever Cass had written about vetoing the Proviso, Whigs charged, he was manifestly a Northerner and therefore less trustworthy than a native Southerner who owned 100 slaves. And if voters needed evidence of Cass' potential for perfidy, Whigs gleefully proclaimed, they need only look at Martin Van Buren, the original northern man with southern principles and now the candidate of the Free Soil party, that organized embodiment of discrimination against the South.

In trumpeting Taylor's virtues, southern Whigs rarely pledged explicitly that he would facilitate slavery expansion into the Mexican Cession or even veto the Proviso. Rather, southern Whigs promised that Taylor's popularity as a national hero in both sections would enable him somehow to restore sectional comity, stop northern aggressions on southern liberty and equality, and thereby save Southerners from enslavement to a despotic northern majority. Simultaneously, they cited Taylor's identity as a Southerner and slaveholder as sufficient proof, even without any positive pledges, that he would never sacrifice southern interests. Taylor, declared an Alabama ratification meeting, possessed "the same feelings" and had "the same interest in regard to slavery as ourselves." "Will the people of Georgia vote for a Southern president or a Northern one?" asked the Milledgeville *Southern Recorder* in October. "Can Gen. Taylor, a Southerner . . . prove recreant to the institutions of those among whom he has lived, sacrifice his own and your interests?" queried North Carolina's major Whig paper. "Or is it safer to trust Gen. Cass—who is a northern man, with Northern ideas about the matter—who is proclaimed by his neighbors the uncompromising advocate of free soil—who once expressed a desire to VOTE for the *Wilmot Proviso?*" For southern Whigs, those questions could have only one answer.[85]

By its final months, in sum, the presidential campaign in the South had essentially become a shouting match about which party's candidates would better protect the region against the Wilmot Proviso and northern aggression. Democrats pointed to their man's pledge to veto the Proviso; Whigs cited Taylor's Louisiana residence. Yet this difference rested on conflicting promises and threats about what might happen in the future, not on demonstrable differences over concrete policies. Instead, the record of congressional votes on specific legislation demonstrated that southern Whigs and Democrats consistently united in rigid opposition to a statutory ban on slavery extension.

In 1844, in contrast, the two presidential candidates had taken sharply opposed stands on the policy of immediate Texas annexation. More important, in both the House and Senate during 1844, southern Whigs and Democrats had polarized against each other in votes on Texas and, of course, on economic legislation as well. Even in some slave state legislatures, Whig majorities had opposed the Democratic demand for immediate annexation. In 1844, that is, a concrete record established partisan differences over the policy itself. In 1848 there were no differences on the policy, only over which of the two presidential candidates might block the policy everyone in the South opposed.[86]

Only time would tell whether a campaign based on windy rhetoric and Cassandra-like cries of danger could stimulate enough Whigs to carry necessary slave states for Taylor. Evidence from two of them in October, however, should have given Whigs pause about the mobilizing power of their campaign. From North Carolina, whose policy-oriented August gubernatorial election had generated such a high turnout, a Whig warned that there was "very little excitement or feeling manifested by either party. I think Old Zack will carry the State, but not by such a majority as many anticipate." Meanwhile, Georgia's Whigs carried four of eight congressional districts, as they had in 1846. While their statewide vote considerably exceeded their total in that midterm contest, it lagged 3,300 votes behind the turnout for their losing gubernatorial candidate in 1847, and Democratic candidates still garnered a majority of the state's popular vote. At least one Georgia Whig attributed this disappointing performance to over-confidence that kept some Whigs home on election day. But there are other ways to interpret it. In October 1844, when the parties in Georgia and other slave states stood on a concrete record of voting against each other on slavery expansion and other issues, the turnout rate in Georgia's congressional race was 92.2 percent of the eligible voters, and Whig candidates had attracted 40.7 percent of the potential electorate. In 1848, only 72.3 percent of eligible voters participated in the con-gressional races, and Whig candidates garnered only 36 percent of the potential electorate. Like the observation from North Carolina, those figures suggest that a campaign in which the two southern parties agreed upon the fundamental issue and ran only on unsubstantiated promises and charges about their candidates' future course regarding it, rather than on a concrete record of substantive dis-agreement in the immediate past, evoked little voter interest. They suggest, fur-thermore, that if Zachary Taylor carried southern states, it would be in low-turnout elections in which the Democrats did an even poorer job than the Whigs of getting their voters to the polls. Here, then, is a central reason why turnout plunged in 1848.[87]

VII

Northern Whigs, unlike Southerners, did not rely exclusively on the sectionally divisive slavery extension question to arouse their alienated and apathetic troops. Most certainly, they continued to trumpet their free-soil credentials, their com-mitment to the Wilmot Proviso, and their promise that Zachary Taylor would not veto it, in contrast to Cass, who had pledged to do so. Yet northern Democrats replied that popular sovereignty would prevent slavery expansion just as reliably as the Proviso, since nonslaveholders could move into the territories more easily and more quickly than slaveholders. Besides, they bragged, their candidate was manifestly a Northerner, unlike the slaveholder heading the Whig ticket. Just as both parties in the South promised to block enactment of the Proviso, in sum, all three parties in the North pledged opposition to slavery extension. As in Dixie, the dispute concerned means, not ends, unlike 1844, when the parties fundamen-tally disagreed over the policy of territorial expansion itself. According to some Free Soilers like John Van Buren, "The free soil movement . . . compelled all to do homage to its spirit." Others, like Connecticut's John Niles, concluded that Whigs' and Democrats' adamant resistance to slavery expansion neutralized the third party's appeal. Niles perceived the essential point. If all three parties in the North opposed slavery expansion, why should a northern voter prefer one to the other two? Why, indeed, should that individual bother to vote at all?[88]

To mobilize angry and apathetic Whig voters, therefore, northern Whig leaders insisted that other issues were at stake, that the salvation of Whig principles depended upon Whig voters coming to the polls and helping Taylor defeat Cass. In August, Taylor's Lippard and South Carolina letters had undermined this case by deepening suspicion that he had no commitment to the Whig party or its principles. Therefore, Whig politicos demanded additional evidence of Rough and Ready's Whiggery. That was the major purpose of Fillmore's frantic letters to Taylor in July and August.

This time Taylor, at long last, responded to their pleas for help. On September 6, Taylor wrote Fillmore that he regretted "the use that has been made of isolated letters and parts of letters addressed by me to individuals under the seal of *private* correspondence . . . against me and against the Whig party." Thus the press in New Orleans was publishing that very day another letter he had written to John Allison "calculated to correct the misrepresentation in regard to my position before the country as a Presidential candidate." "I trust," he concluded, "it will meet your approbation and that of our friends at the North."[89]

Although it said nothing about specific Whig programs, Taylor's second Allison Letter was a masterstroke. He denounced those who accused him of occupying "an equivocal attitude towards . . . the Whig party." While commander of an army in Mexico that contained brave men from both parties, he explained, he could take no open partisan stance, but "all knew I was a Whig in principle." He had always pronounced himself a Whig when the occasion warranted it, and he proudly accepted Whigs' nomination because "the Convention adopted me as it found me—a Whig—decided but not ultra in my opinions." True, he said that he would have accepted the Democratic nomination, but it could have been offered only on the understanding that he was a Whig. True, he said that he would not be a party president. But he meant that "I am not engaged to lay violent hands indiscriminately upon public officers, good or bad, who may differ in my opinion with me. I am not expected to force Congress, by the coercion of the veto, to pass laws to suit me, or pass none. This is what I mean by not being a party candidate. And I understand this is good Whig doctrine." At last, Taylor had buttressed the keystone of Whigs' case for him. He was a good Whig because he would defer, rather than dictate, to Congress.[90]

The appearance of Taylor's second Allison Letter in mid-September delighted northern Whig leaders as much as his earlier letters had enraged them. Taylor's "frank, manly, independent" statement, editorialized Weed, should cause "thousands of alienated Whigs" to "warm back to General Taylor." The letter "is precisely what we wanted," gushed Fillmore. "It will be immediately published through all our papers, and must give general satisfaction to every true Whig in the state." Along with Clay's refusal to accept the independent nomination from New York City, reported other New York Whigs, Taylor's renewed vows of Whiggery had extinguished the revolt by Clay Whigs and strengthened the party. Taylor's letter was shoring up support among Whigs in Massachusetts and other New England states, echoed House Speaker Winthrop in mid-September.[91]

Important as the second Allison Letter and the free-soil arguments were to northern Whigs' mobilizing efforts, two other developments had equal, and possibly greater, significance. First, Whigs shrewdly selected attractive gubernatorial candidates who helped offset disaffection from Taylor. Four large northern states held gubernatorial elections in the late fall: Ohio and Pennsylvania in October, Massachusetts and New York in November. Massachusetts Whigs ran popular

five-term incumbent George N. Briggs, thus signaling their reaffirmation of traditional principles. Briggs' campaign was inextricably entwined with the campaign
for Taylor, but the other three merit closer attention.

Writing off Taylor's chances in Ohio from the moment of his nomination, its
Whig leaders desperately wanted to win the October state elections. If we cannot
"carry Taylor," worried Corwin, "how are we to carry the October election?"
Ohio's Whigs craved control of the state government because it significantly
shaped economic, social, and political life. The legislature to be chosen in October,
for example, would select two state supreme court judges and a new United States
senator, allot the usual number of less prestigious but still coveted state jobs, and
set state policy for banking and currency, business incorporations, subsidization
of transportation enterprises, and other economic matters that remained objects
of intense partisan competition. The Democratic state platform in 1848, for example, demanded imposition of a tax on banks in the state and hard money,
measures Whigs opposed. During the 1848 legislative session, partisan conflict
had extended to social measures like temperance and state aid to education, but
it had been especially apparent on two issues that would have great impact on
Ohio's future politics and were certain to emerge again in the next legislature.
Democrats backed and most Whigs vehemently opposed revision of the state constitution. In turn, the Whig majority, over bitter Democratic protests, had pushed
through a reapportionment of the state legislature that promised to perpetuate
their control, a law Democrats had challenged as unconstitutional and pledged to
repeal in the next session.[92]

Whig voters' deep interest in their party's agenda for the state government,
in fact, helped answer Corwin's question. "Of one thing there can be no doubt,"
a Whig declared to Thomas Ewing in August. "The *whole* of the Whig party here
are *firm* on the *State issues*." No matter what propensity antislavery Whig voters
displayed toward bolting to the Free Soil ticket in November, Whigs might hold
them in October by focusing on state issues, especially since Free Soilers ran no
gubernatorial nominee. Thus, Ewing was urged to try to rally traditionally Whig
Quaker voters, who despised Taylor's participation in the Mexican War as well
as his slaveholding, by stressing *"state matters."*[93]

The contrast between the Democratic and Whig gubernatorial candidates provided Whigs with their second weapon in the state race. Democrat John Weller
had fought in the Mexican War, which was hated by most Ohio Whigs, and he
emphatically endorsed the Democrats' state and national platforms. Seabury Ford,
Whigs' compromise choice in January and an avowed opponent of slavery expansion, was especially popular on the Western Reserve, where Whig bolts to Van
Buren were most likely. Thus he was precisely the best candidate to hold those
Whigs in October.

Ford, nonetheless, came under enormous and conflicting pressure after Taylor's
nomination to repudiate or endorse him. Chase directly threatened him with a
separate Free Soil candidacy unless he rebuked the Whig nominee, and antislavery
Whigs refused to support him unless he did so. Loyalist Whigs, especially those
from southern Ohio, demanded that he endorse Taylor, both to help hold rebellious Reserve Whigs in the presidential election and to guarantee their own votes
on election day in October. Convinced that either course would alienate more
men than it appeased and that the welfare of Ohio depended on the defeat of

Weller and Democratic legislative candidates, Ford steadfastly refused to announce his presidential preference. By the fall, Free Soil papers were urging antislavery men to support him, and on the Reserve, Free Soilers and Whigs coalesced on state legislative tickets to unite all "that hate Democracy." Dissatisfaction and suspicion persisted in both wings of the party, however, and there is little doubt that because of it, some Whigs in both regions of the state refused to vote in October.[94]

Ford squeaked by with a 314-vote margin out of some 298,000 cast, whereas the Whig pluralities in the three-way races of 1844 and 1846 ranged between 1,300 and 2,300 votes. The turnout rate of 68 percent understandably exceeded the 60 percent rate in the mid-term election of 1846, but it lagged appreciably behind the 78.2 percent rate in October 1844. Results from the congressional and state legislative elections, where Free Soilers ran their own candidates, were even less favorable to the Whigs. In 1846 Whigs had captured eleven of Ohio's twenty-one House seats; in 1848 they won only eight, although both of the victorious Free Soilers, Joseph Root and Joshua Giddings, had Whig lineage. In the state legislative races the Whigs suffered a crippling blow. After the 1847 elections, the state senate had been evenly divided between the parties, and the Whigs had controlled the state house forty to thirty-two. In 1848, the major parties retained an equal number of seats in the senate, but Free Soilers won the balance of power. Because of two contested seats from Hamilton County, the ultimate complexion of the house remained uncertain. But eight victorious Free Soilers had reduced the Whigs to a maximum of thirty-two seats, and those eight men could determine what the legislature did.[95]

New York's Whigs did not nominate their state ticket or pick their slate of symbolically significant presidential electors until the state convention in September. Just as New York's Democrats had brilliantly used the nomination of Silas Wright in 1844 to reunify their party and neutralize dissatisfaction with Polk, New York's Whigs hoped to pick a state and electoral ticket that could heal intraparty wounds and stimulate support for Taylor. At the state convention, conservatives' arch-foe Weed performed one of his most dazzling displays of political wizardry. The electoral ticket was carefully larded with Clay's friends. Weed also blocked the bid of the unpopular Governor John Young for renomination and secured the top spot for Hamilton Fish, a conservative from New York City, with Weed's friend George W. Patterson as his running mate. Some of Weed's allies expressed dismay at his blatant concessions. Yet most Whigs, and particularly the conservatives who had been most likely to abstain, were vastly pleased. Fish's nomination for governor, one rejoiced to Crittenden, would reunite the party in New York. Most New York Whigs would now back Taylor, groaned Free Soil gubernatorial candidate John Dix in October.[96]

The state platform and address to the electorate praised Taylor's opposition to executive despotism, pilloried Cass' warmongering and Van Buren's proslavery record, and reiterated the party's commitment to the Wilmot Proviso. Significantly, they also renewed the assault on the Democratic economic legislation of 1846, which had virtually disappeared from the New York Whig platform in 1847. Attacking Cass' opposition to internal improvements and support for the sub-treasury system, Whigs demanded both the repeal of the Independent Treasury Act to ensure an ample and sound circulating currency and an upward revision of the tariff. Those economic planks represented more than a bid to conservative Whig businessmen. They signaled a conviction that economic issues, which had been so ineffective during the prosperity of 1847, had regained their salience with the Whig electorate. Whigs, in sum, used both an attractive ticket and specific issues to mobilize their latent support.[97]

With New York apparently secure by mid-September and Ohio extremely doubtful, Pennsylvania truly became the keystone to Whig victory in November. With chances of carrying any traditionally Democratic state remote, Whigs knew they had to capture at least two of the nation's three largest states. Hence the wealthy businessmen in New York City and Boston who bankrolled the party were tapped for funds to send to Pennsylvania. When Whig leaders turned their attention to Pennsylvania, they saw a race that was almost impossible to handicap. Both Whigs and Democrats from outside the state, in fact, considered its politics hopelessly corrupt and uniquely byzantine.[98]

Certainly it differed from other northern states Whigs hoped to carry. Unlike Whigs in Ohio, Massachusetts, and New York, those in Pennsylvania had never feared significant defections to the Free Soilers. Unlike Whigs in those states, many Pennsylvania Whigs had vigorously promoted Taylor's nomination as the best way to rescue the party from desperate straits. In 1847, the popular Democratic incumbent Governor Francis Shunk had easily won reelection to another three-year term; his hapless Whig opponent had received less than 45 percent of the vote, in part because the nettlesome Native Americans had siphoned off 4 percent. Worse still, Whig representation in the lower house of the state legislature had plunged from fifty-nine to thirty-seven seats. Then sheer serendipity in 1848 gave the Whigs a vigorous and extraordinarily effective stump speaker as a gubernatorial candidate who could arouse the rank and file. Francis Shunk, who was scheduled to govern until 1851, fell mortally ill, and on July 9, 1848, he resigned the governorship. Pennsylvania had no lieutenant governor, so the speaker of the state senate, the Whig William F. Johnston, became acting governor. Within a few weeks Johnston called for a new gubernatorial election in October.

Although Johnston received the Whig nomination unanimously at a hastily gathered state convention on August 31, he was not a conservative Clay Whig like Fish in New York. In the spring, Johnston had ardently pushed Scott's nomination. Hailing from Armstrong County near Pittsburgh in western Pennsylvania, Johnston had served as a Democrat in the state legislature for ten years. Even then, he had consistently voted with the Whigs in favor of banks, against hard money, and for protective tariffs. At the end of 1846 Johnston converted to Whiggery because of his outrage at the Walker Tariff, which he damned as a betrayal of Polk's promises in 1844. Delighted by the accession of so talented a politician, Whigs had sent him to the state senate in 1847, and in 1848 they made him speaker in the expectation that he would replace the dying Shunk. Perhaps because of his recent conversion to the party, Johnston decided to break precedent and personally stump the state for himself and the rest of the Whig ticket during September and early October. Whigs rejoiced at this decision, for Johnston's formidable oratorical skills might arouse the hitherto alienated and apathetic Clay Whigs.[99]

Johnston's well-publicized break with the Democrats over the tariff issue also made him the perfect exponent for what became Pennsylvania Whigs' central theme that fall. Prior to September, Whigs there had concentrated on reaching out to potential converts by stressing Taylor's nonpartisanship. Conducting the canvass through Rough and Ready Clubs rather than regular Whig committees, they had appealed to Democrats and bargained with nativists. In return for Native American support for Taylor and other Whig candidates in populous Philadelphia County, for example, Whigs promised to back the nativist Lewis C. Levin for Congress and five Native Americans for the state legislature. In addition, Whigs in central and western Pennsylvania stressed their commitment to the Wilmot Proviso and the promise that Taylor would not veto it. With Johnston's nomination, however, the thrust of the Whig campaign shifted markedly to economic questions. Over a third of their new state platform was devoted to the Independent Treasury and tariff issues, and in Johnston's rousing speeches across the state he focused most heavily on the need to repeal the Walker Tariff and restore the Whig tariff of 1842. The Walker Tariff, he repeatedly declared, "had brought or was bringing ruin, stagnation, and business revulsion." By the fall, in short, Whigs were attempting to stimulate their apathetic troops with precisely the same economic issues they themselves admitted had proved so unproductive a year earlier. Like the resurrection of economic planks in the New York Whig platform of September, the Pennsylvania campaign signaled a renewed confidence that the Democratic economic legislation of 1846 was again vulnerable.[100]

Without question, the revived salience of economic issues was the most important development between the Whigs' June convention and the November election because it gave northern Whigs their most effective instrument for mobilizing Whig voters. Clay was defeated at Philadelphia primarily because of northern Whigs' pell-mell rush toward military candidates in the spring, and they had deemed gunpowder candidates necessary then because an issue-oriented campaign appeared hopeless. Aside from the loss of their antiwar and No Territory appeals, the prosperity engendered by Walker's financing of the war and unprecedented grain sales abroad had apparently made their economic programs superfluous. Yet the end of the war stopped the war contracts, government purchases, and injection of Treasury notes into the money supply that had done so much to create prosperity in 1847 and early 1848. Similarly, good harvests in Europe spelled the end of grain exports that had pumped huge quantities of foreign specie into the American economy.

By the fall of 1848, the economy was heading toward recession. By some indices, indeed, the downturn became particularly sharp in July, the month after the Whig convention, and with each successive month as the presidential election approached the deterioration of economic conditions worsened. By September and October, that is, almost all of the ominous predictions Whigs had made in 1846 about the pernicious impact of Democratic economic policies—the drainage of specie reserves, shrinkage of circulating currency, and desiccation of credit, a deleterious imbalance between imports and exports, falling prices, reduced wages and increased unemployment in manufacturing, and shortfalls in government revenue—appeared, finally, to be coming true. Tables 24 and 25 reveal the slump in wholesale commodity prices in five cities. Nationally, wholesale prices of all commodities sank 9 percent but consumer prices only 7 percent in that period. Grain exports in 1848 were half their 1847 level, and domestic prices of foodstuffs also tumbled. The favorable balance of trade was sharply reversed despite the jump in cotton and tobacco exports. In 1847, the country had been a net importer of $24 million worth of gold and silver, largely because of the payments for grain exports. In 1848, a net of $10 million in specie flowed out of the nation's bank reserves to pay for purchases from abroad. This palpable economic slide revivified Whig attacks on the Democrats' Independent Treasury system, Public Warehouse Act, and Walker Tariff.[101]

Recession struck New England as early as the spring, largely because the out-flow of specie had drained the bank reserves used to make business loans. Credit was extraordinarily tight and expensive in Boston and other cities throughout the year. "I never knew it [money available for loans] to remain so scarce for so long a time," complained a Boston businessman in September. Denied access to the short-term loans necessary to meet operating expenses, textile manufacturers were forced to slash wages and lay off workers. Even the immensely wealthy Abbott Lawrence, whose textile enterprise was far less dependent on banks for operating capital than were those of most manufacturers, saw economic ruin ahead.[102] By July, New England Whigs were already blaming the Walker Tariff and the Independent Treasury for causing economic distress, and during the fall they increased their emphasis on economic themes. More than the revived rele-vance of Whig programs explains this tack. Stressing economic issues reminded Whig voters how the parties differed and why Whig victory was essential. All three parties in New England and the rest of the North might denounce slavery extension, but only the Whigs demanded positive government action to aid the economy. Thus, Lawrence told a Vermont ratification meeting that repeal of the subtreasury system and restoration of the tariff of 1842 formed the election's central objectives. Thus, Whig papers in Boston and elsewhere blamed Democratic legislation for ruining the balance of trade, "exhaust[ing] the specie of the coun-try, and bringing the business of the country very nearly to a dead stand." "The only remedy," cried Whigs, "is some change in that system of legislation." Thus the state platform adopted by Massachusetts Whigs in September not only de-fended Whigs as the preeminent free-soil party in the state; it also insisted that it was the *duty* of government to promote prosperity and "to regulate wisely the currency and commerce of the country, to protect the labor and encourage the industry of the people," and to carry out internal improvements. Thus Daniel Webster, in the speeches he made on Taylor's behalf starting in September, fo-cused primarily on economic issues, not slavery extension, not Taylor's character, and not executive despotism.[103]

Friend and foe alike testified to such appeals' impact. Webster's speeches, Mas-sachusetts Whigs told Fillmore, cemented the state for Taylor. "The last card is to be played by Webster's appeal to the pocket-issue!" exclaimed the pessimistic Free Soiler Phillips in mid-October. "This appeal will have great weight under the circumstances, and will effect much more than any of the other pretexts, upon which Genl. Taylor is sustained."[104] Similarly, Connecticut Free Soiler John M. Niles admitted after the election that the tariff issue had been crucial to the Whigs' ability to hold their vote. Throughout the campaign, he had constantly changed his mind about whether the Free Soilers were making greater inroads into the

Whig or Democratic vote, and then his only worry had been that the universal claim by all parties that they opposed slavery expansion might blunt the Free Soilers' appeal. After the election he confessed that the recession, by affecting the many metal shops and small manufacturers in the state, had given the tariff issue unexpected salience. Many manufacturers and their employees had thus voted for Taylor "in hopes of a modification of the act of '46. They expected nothing from Taylor but did from the Whig party." As a result of this Whig success in retaining support, the Free Soil party "got more democratic than Whig votes."[105]

Falling prices gave particular salience to Whig attacks on the Walker Tariff in New Jersey and Pennsylvania. Coal and iron prices plunged in 1848. At the same time, imports of cheap British iron increased 39 percent over their levels of the previous year. Mines, foundries, and rolling mills laid off workers or suspended operations entirely. As a result, Whigs triumphed in both states' October elections. New Jersey had no statewide race, but Whigs, benefiting from a surge in voter turnout, captured four of five congressional seats, retained control of the legislature, and reversed the popular majority Democrats had gained in the gubernatorial election of 1847.[106] The Whigs' real prize was Pennsylvania. Turnout for both parties soared from the previous year, when the Democrats had enjoyed an 18,000-vote margin over the Whigs. In 1848, Johnston won the governorship by 300 votes out of some 337,000 votes cast. Johnston, in fact, polled the largest vote ever attained by any Whig candidate in Pennsylvania until that time, including Harrison in 1840. He attracted 40,000 more votes than the Whig candidate in 1847 and 8,000 more than Clay in 1844. Whigs also won fourteen of twenty-four congressional seats, although that represented a loss of two seats from their remarkable performance in 1846. Furthermore they won forty-five seats in the lower house of the state legislature, and the five Native Americans they backed in normally Democratic Philadelphia County also won.[107]

Almost all Pennsylvania Whigs credited their October victory to Johnston's ability to bring out the entire Whig vote and to the tariff issue. Webster encountered several Philadelphia Whigs in New York City who "all ascribe the change in Pa. to the *Tariffs*, & they wish to make new and stronger efforts on that point" in the three weeks remaining before the presidential election. While Whigs expected that Taylor would get more Democratic votes than the turncoat Johnston, they feared he would not retain all the antislavery voters Johnston had won. Thus Whigs redoubled their efforts to carry the state. Not only did they pour more money into it, they reemphasized the demand for the restoration of the Tariff of 1842, which had apparently been so successful in mobilizing Whigs in October. Throughout Pennsylvania's anthracite coal region, a Whig speaker reported, the Whig slogan was "Taylor, Fillmore, and the Tariff of 1842." Large banners with the same message hung from business establishments in Philadelphia and Pittsburgh.[108]

After the presidential election, Whigs and Democrats alike attributed Pennsylvania's result primarily to the tariff issue. "Thousands voted with us on the tariff question alone," Moses Hampton declared from Pittsburgh. Pointing to Schuylkill County, where the Whigs gained 2,300 votes and the Democrats only 86 between 1844 and 1848, a Philadelphian cited the tariff as the key for Whigs in coal-mining districts. Democrats agreed. "The Whigs as a party would go *down down if it was not* [for] *the tariff principle which keeps them up*," a frustrated

Pittsburgh Democrat sputtered to James Buchanan. Another contended that Democratic losses in the coal regions resulted from "gun powder and the Tariff! which of these had the greatest influence—it will be hard to ascertain." Faced with tumbling wages and the specter of unemployment, Democratic miners could not be kept in the party traces. "They said it was bread and they would not stand to principle." The reports from Pennsylvania, Massachusetts, Connecticut, and elsewhere demonstrate that contentions that the 1848 presidential election revolved around slavery extension alone are nonsense.[109]

VIII

On November 7, for the first time in American history, voters from all the states trooped to the polls on the same day to select a president. Zachary Taylor emerged victorious, with 1,360,967 votes compared to 1,222,342 for Cass and 291,804 for Van Buren, a gain of almost 229,000 votes over the Liberty party's total in 1844. Although Van Buren ran ahead of Cass in New York and Vermont and almost even with him in Massachusetts, he did not win a single electoral vote. Taylor and Cass each carried fifteen states, but Taylor prevailed in the electoral college 163 to 127. Aside from the three states already mentioned, Taylor won Pennsylvania, New Jersey, Connecticut, and Rhode Island in the North. Maine and New Hampshire remained Democratic bastions in Whiggish New England, and the Michigan resident Cass carried every midwestern state, including, most importantly, Ohio and Indiana. In the South, Taylor took Delaware, Maryland, Kentucky, Tennessee, North Carolina, Georgia, Louisiana, and Florida. Between 1844 and 1848, in sum, Taylor's home state, Georgia, New York, and Pennsylvania shifted from the Democratic to the Whig column, while Ohio moved in the opposite direction. As most Whigs had correctly recognized since 1844, the traditional Whig states Clay had carried that year and those he had come close to winning provided the keys to Whig victory. Heavily Democratic states whose Whigs had ardently supported Taylor's nomination contributed nothing to this triumph despite his gains over Clay in some of them.

Unlike Harrison's surging triumph in 1840, widespread voter enthusiasm did not account for Taylor's success. Neither the presence of a popular military hero on the Whig ticket nor the attention devoted by all parties in both sections to the Wilmot Proviso, slavery extension, and sectional rights stimulated a large turnout. Nationwide it declined from about 79 percent of adult white males in 1844 to about 73 percent in 1848. Only in Massachusetts and Louisiana did the rate of voter participation exceed that of 1844. Remarkably, indeed, despite four years of population growth, the actual vote in 1848 was lower than that of 1844 in three New England states, New York, Virginia, North Carolina, and Alabama. As the figures in Table 26 indicate, while Taylor drew a larger share of the actual vote than Clay in a number of states, including eleven of twelve slave states, his share of the potential vote surpassed Clay's only in Pennsylvania, Arkansas, Alabama, Mississippi, and Louisiana.

These results raise important questions. Why did turnout decline, and did the drop-off benefit one party more than another? How did Whigs manage to mo-

Table 26

Proportion of Actual and Potential Votes Won by Clay and Taylor[a]

	Clay			Taylor		
	Actual Vote	Potential Vote	Total Turnout	Actual Vote	Potential Vote	Total Turnout
Maine	41.6%	28.3%	68.1%	40.3%	25.9%	64.4%
N. Hampshire	36.3	24.1	66.4	29.5	18.5	62.9
Vermont	55	37.1	67.4	47.9	30.2	63.1
Mass.	51.7	35.8	69.2	45.4	33	72.6
Rhode Island	60.2	33.4	55.5	60.7	26.3	43.4
Connecticut	50.8	43.8	86.3	48.5	40.6	83.7
New York	47.8	44.6	92.1	47.9	37.9	79.1
New Jersey	50.4	42.3	83.9	51.4	39.5	76.9
Pennsylvania	48.4	37.8	78.2	50.2	38.9	77.5
Ohio	49.6	46.6	94	42.1	38.4	91.3
Indiana	48.4	41.4	85.6	45.9	36.6	79.7
Illinois	42.4	32.8	77.5	42.4	30.6	72.1
Michigan	43.5	34.5	79.4	36.7	27.1	73.8
Delaware	51.2	43.9	85.8	52.6	42.3	80.4
Maryland	52.3	42.6	81.4	52.1	39.6	76
Virginia	46.9	25.4	54.2	49.1	23.2	47.3
N. Carolina	52.6	48.4	92.1	55.1	43.9	79.6
Georgia	48.6	45	92.6	51.5	44.3	86
Kentucky	53.9	43.5	80.7	57.5	42.6	73.9
Tennessee	50.1	45	89.8	52.4	43.7	83.4
Alabama	40.9	32.8	80.3	49.4	34.4	69.7
Mississippi	43.4	37.4	86.1	49.3	39.8	80.7
Missouri	43	33.4	77.8	45	28.1	62.5
Arkansas	36.9	23.4	63.5	44.9	25.1	55.9
Louisiana	48.7	22.9	47.1	54.5	27.8	51.1

[a]The figures for the turnout rates in northern states in this table are taken from Table 1 in Gienapp, " 'Politics Seem to Enter into Everything,' " pp. 18–19. Those for the South are taken from the estimates in *Historical Statistics*, p. 1072. Property qualifications on the right of suffrage in Rhode Island, Virginia, and Louisiana help account for the unusually low turnout rates in those states.

bilize the votes they did, given the overall trend, and to what extent did Taylor's purported appeal to Democrats, nativists, and new voters help them? And what impact did the new Free Soil party have on the outcome in the North? Did it in fact damage the Whigs as gravely as some historians contend?

Democrats suffered and Whigs therefore benefited disproportionately from the slump in turnout. Democratic losses between 1844 and 1848 exceeded, and Democratic gains lagged behind, those of Whigs in every region of the country except the Midwest.[110] The significant decline in the Democratic vote indicates that Lewis Cass' unpopularity may have been as important in explaining the Whig victory as any unique attractiveness of Zachary Taylor. A large number of northern Democrats faithfully followed Van Buren into the Free Soil movement, and the split in the northern Democratic party may have caused other Democrats to stay home on election day either as a response to conflicting loyalties or from a conviction that the divided Democrats could not win.

Not only did the unpopular Cass net some 15,000 fewer votes than Polk in slave states, but he ran significantly behind 1847 or 1848 Democratic gubernatorial candidates in Kentucky, North Carolina, Missouri, Florida, Arkansas, Alabama, and Tennessee. Nonetheless, Democratic declines did not affect the outcome in any slave state except perhaps Florida. It narrowed the margin between the parties in securely Democratic states like Alabama, Mississippi, Arkansas, and Virginia or increased the Whig majority in usually reliable North Carolina, Maryland, Kentucky, and Tennessee. Taylor could have carried all of those states simply by replicating Clay's vote in 1844. In contrast, Georgia and Louisiana shifted to the Whig column because of Whig gains, not Democratic losses (Table 27).

Excluding the new states of Texas and Florida, Democrats lost 17,000 southern votes between 1844 and 1848, while Whigs' total increased by 39,000. On their face, these figures suggest that Whigs succeeded in attracting Democrats, but contemporaries disagreed on whether the missing Democrats abstained or defected to Taylor.[111] Existing statistical studies that measure voter movement between elections in the South suggest greater abstention than defection among previous Democratic voters in 1848. An analysis of voter movements between the congressional elections of 1846 and 1848 in Florida, for example, indicates that almost twice as many previous Democrats sat out as voted Whig. Still, almost a fifth of the 1846 Democrats voted Whig in 1848, and new voters preferred the Whigs by a margin of three to two.[112] A study of the switches between the presidential elections of 1844 and 1848 in Alabama, Mississippi, and Louisiana suggests that about 10 percent of the Polk voters supported Taylor, while another 25 percent abstained.[113] Still another analysis, based on all southern counties, suggests that the Democrats retained 87 percent of Polk's vote in the lower South and 93 percent in the upper South, or 91 percent in the region as a whole, and that the missing Polk voters defected to Taylor. The comparable retention rates for the Whigs were 97, 96, and 97 percent.[114]

Whatever the sources of new southern Whig voters, Whig gains in Dixie were geographically skewed, even though Whigs everywhere presented Taylor as the quintessential Southerner and a hero. Significant Whig gains were disproportionately concentrated in Georgia, Alabama, Mississippi, and Louisiana. His average increase over Clay in those four states was 25.3 percent, compared to 5.5 percent in the four border slave states and 11.2 percent in Virginia, North Carolina, Tennessee, and Arkansas. Taylor ran ahead of North Carolina's Whig gubernatorial candidate, but his gain over Clay among Tarheels was a negligible 804 votes. Given the enthusiasm of Virginia's Rives Whigs about Taylor's supposed attractiveness, his paltry gain in the Old Dominion of 405 votes over Clay speaks volumes about the supposed ability of the slaveholding hero and the slavery issue to stimulate southern voters. Aggregate regionwide figures point to a similar conclusion. The unweighted average total turnout in twelve slave states sank from 79.4 percent in 1844 to 70.5 percent four years later. The average decline in the rate of voter participation of the eight states from the upper South almost doubled the rate of decline in the four Deep South states voting in both years.[115] Equally

Table 27
Differences Between the Major Parties' Share of the Actual Vote in 1844 and 1848[a]

	1844			1848		
	Whig	Democratic	Difference	Whig	Democratic	Difference
Maine	40.4%	53.8%	−13.4	40.3%	45.1%	− 4.8
N. Hampshire	36.3	55.2	−18.9	29.5	55.4	−25.9
Vermont	55	37	+18	47.7	22.6	+25.1
Massachusetts	51.7	40	+11.7	45.4	26.2	+19.2
Connecticut	50.8	46.2	+ 4.6	48.6	43.4	+ 5.2
Rhode Island	60.2	39.9	+20.3	60.8	32.7	+28.1
New York	47.8	48.9	− 1.1	47.9	25.1	+22.8
New Jersey	50.4	49.9	+ 0.5	51.4	47.4	+ 4.0
Pennsylvania	48.5	50.6	− 2.1	50.2	46.7	+ 3.5
Ohio	49.6	47.7	+ 1.9	42.1	47	− 4.1
Indiana	48.4	50.1	− 1.7	46	48.8	− 2.8
Illinois	42.4	54.4	−12.0	42.4	44.8	− 2.4
Michigan	43.5	49.9	− 6.4	36.8	47.2	−10.4
Wisconsin				35.1	38.2	− 3.1
Iowa				44.6	50.5	− 5.9
Delaware	51.2	48.7	+ 2.5	51.8	47.5	+ 4.3
Maryland	52.4	47.6	+ 4.8	52.2	47.7	+ 4.5
Virginia	47	53	− 6.0	49.2	50.8	− 1.6
N. Carolina	52.7	47.3	+ 5.4	55.2	44.8	+10.4
Kentucky	53.9	46.1	+ 7.8	57.7	42.3	+15.4
Tennessee	50.1	49.9	+ 0.2	52.4	47.6	+ 4.8
Missouri	43.0	57.0	−14.0	45.0	55.0	−10.0
Arkansas	37.0	63.0	−15.0	44.9	55.1	−10.2
Georgia	48.8	51.2	− 2.4	51.5	48.5	+ 3.0
Alabama	41.0	59.0	−18.0	49.4	50.6	− 1.2
Mississippi	43.4	56.6	−13.2	49.3	50.7	− 1.4
Louisiana	48.7	51.3	− 2.6	54.6	45.4	+ 9.2
Florida				57.5	42.5	+15.0
Texas				31.0	68.9	−37.8

[a]In the free states and in Delaware and Texas, the share of the vote unaccounted for by these figures went to the Liberty party in 1844 and the Free Soilers in 1848. The percentages are taken from Rayback, *Free Soil,* p. 286.

important, turnout in Kentucky, North Carolina, and Missouri sank markedly between gubernatorial elections in August and the presidential contest in November, while presidential turnout in Alabama lagged behind that in a gubernatorial election the previous year. Granted that southern Democrats deemed their candidate particularly unpalatable, disgruntled Democrats as well as previous nonvoters could vote for a southern slaveholder who was presented as the embodiment of republican nonpartisanship, as another George Washington. Why, then, was voter turnout in the South comparatively so low when both parties insisted that the sole issue in the campaign was the defense of slavery and of Southern

Rights from northern aggression? Why, moreover, was the additional vote Taylor attracted so geographically skewed within the South?

Deep South voters possibly cared more about the slavery extension issue than other Southerners because of the unusually heavy concentrations of slaves and slaveholders in the Deep South. Yet Taylor lived in Louisiana, owned plantations in Mississippi, and was run as a favorite son in both, and that identity probably explains some of the additional Whig vote in those states. More important, non-slaveholders as well as slaveholders had a stake in the defense of Southern Rights and the preservation of slavery, and it would be foolhardy to infer that a lack of interest in those issues caused the lower turnout in 1848 in the upper South or the region as a whole.[116]

Rather, it seems more proper to attribute the apathy reported so extensively in letters and demonstrated by the low turnout to the form the slavery extension issue took in 1848. In 1844, the southern wings of the Whig and Democratic parties had established concrete records of partisan disagreement on Texas' annexation, records that were reinforced by the voting behavior of each party's northern wing. Although those records worked to the disadvantage of the Whigs, they spurred a relatively high turnout for both parties. In 1848, no concrete differences distinguished the parties on the Wilmot Proviso, only conflicting claims as to which presidential candidate offered the South greater security against it. Obviously the Whigs enjoyed the advantage this time, but predictions about an uncertain future lacked the power of concrete differences established in the immediate past to stimulate the electorate to vote.

Northern turnout rates also sagged in 1848, but unlike the South, both major parties suffered a net decline in their absolute votes between 1844 and 1848. Unlike southern Whigs, who proudly displayed their candidate as the party's trump card, in most northern states, and especially traditionally Whig states, Whigs regarded the slaveholding general as a liability, not an asset. Thus, aside from praising Taylor's opposition to the veto and executive usurpation, they had concentrated on attacking Polk's record, denouncing the consequences of a Cass victory, proclaiming the necessity of overturning Democratic economic policies, and rehearsing their commitment to free soil in order to mobilize former supporters and recruit new ones. Such appeals failed to appease all of the distrustful or angry rank and file or to attract enough new voters to replace all those who abstained or defected. The absolute Whig vote declined from 1844 in both New England and the Midwestern states that had participated in the earlier election.[117] It grew by almost 13,000 (3 percent) in the Middle Atlantic states, but that increase lagged behind the gain of 27,800 (6.9 percent) between 1840 and 1844.

Democratic losses were even more severe. The Democratic decline in New England was more than double that of the Whigs, and the heavy drop in New York through defection to Van Buren and abstention also gave the Democrats a huge net loss in the Mid-Atlantic region. The Democrats did gain votes in Cass' home turf in the Midwest, but their increase was quite small compared to the surge they had enjoyed there between 1840 and 1844. To view these net shifts another way, Professor Thomas B. Alexander has estimated that in the North as a whole, Democrats retained 89 percent of Polk's vote in 1844, while the Whigs retained 90 percent of Clay's vote.[118]

Figures for the section as a whole or for even regions within it disguise significant variations among the states. Still, Taylor's vote exceeded Clay's in only two of the northern states he carried, New Jersey and Pennsylvania. As in 1846 and 1847, Whig victory in New York depended upon Democratic divisions, which engendered both defections to Van Buren and Democratic abstentions. Together, Van Buren and Cass outpolled Taylor in the Empire State and three of the New England states Rough and Ready won.

Taylor's success in attracting new voters to the Whig column also varied in Democratic states. Already a hopeless minority, the New Hampshire Whig party lost almost a fifth of its small vote. As had been predicted for months, Taylor's candidacy devastated the party in Ohio. Whigs suffered a net decline of a tenth of their voting strength, and their actual losses may have been substantially larger. One statistical estimate of voter movement between the October gubernatorial election and the November presidential election, for example, suggests that one-fourth of the men who voted Democratic for governor supported Taylor in November. At the same time, over a third of those who had voted for Ford went to Van Buren, while another tenth of Ford's voters abstained.[119] Taylor was also exceedingly unpopular among Whigs in Michigan, many of whom bolted to Van Buren or stayed home on election day.[120] Not only did he draw fewer votes than Clay, but he also ran 7,700 votes (8.8 percent) behind Whig congressional candidates on the same ticket with him. Similarly in Iowa, Taylor received a smaller vote than two Whig congressional candidates had garnered in October, and his proportion of the vote was lower than any received by a Whig since Iowa had become a state. Finally, in Wisconsin, Taylor got only 35 percent of the vote, yet because of substantial Democratic defections to Van Buren since the spring elections, he trailed Cass by only 3 percent.[121]

In Maine, Indiana, and particularly Illinois, however, Taylor increased the Whig vote over Clay's 1844 totals, although the gains obviously did not suffice to carry those states. Taylor added only 783 votes to the Whig column in Democratic Maine, not nearly enough to close the gap between the major parties, even combined with Democrats' heavy net loss of 5,900 votes (13 percent). Regression analysis of the movement of Maine's voters between the two presidential elections suggests that Taylor attracted far more previous nonvoters than that small net gain and that the increment barely offset the desertion of Clay supporters to the Free Soilers and the ranks of nonvoters (see Table 28). The 2,400 votes Whigs gained in Indiana were also neutralized by an even larger Democratic increase. Again, the net change in the Whig vote probably conceals much greater movement of individual voters to and from the party. After the election, Indiana Whigs complained that at least 5,000 Whigs had bolted to Van Buren, while an equal number had abstained rather than vote for Taylor. If so, some 12,500 men, almost a fifth of Taylor's total, voted for Rough and Ready who had not voted for Clay.[122]

Returns from the seemingly impregnable Loco Foco fortress of Illinois shocked Whigs and Democrats alike. Taylor garnered 7,000 more votes there than had Clay and 18,500 more than the Whig congressional ticket in August. At the same time, Cass ran 3,000 votes behind Polk and 9,500 behind Democratic congressional candidates. Taylor's performance was the strongest by a Whig in Illinois since 1840. Although Taylor won the same share of the total vote as had Clay, the margin between the major parties was sharply reduced because of Democrats' marked decline (see Table 27).

Since the Democrats now seemed to be within striking distance and since they suffered significant partisan disadvantages from the adoption of a new state constitution in 1848, Illinois Whigs expressed more optimism than they had voiced in a decade. "Everybody was astonished at the vote," David Davis reported after the election. "The Democracy were terribly scared, the new constitution cutting them off from the [state] patronage and the General Govt. being out of the hands of their friends." Once determined to abandon politics because of Whigs' futility, Davis now envisioned a bright future for Illinois Whiggery, largely because the new constitution had made judgeships, like the one he had just won, and other state offices elective rather than appointive. "The patronage of the Legislature being withdrawn has broken up the Democratic party in this horribly governed state."[123]

Martin Van Buren's Free Soil candidacy obviously contributed to Democratic disarray in both the North and the South. Surprisingly, however, the Free Soil party had only minimal impact on the outcome. In the South, Democrats' reduced vote did not account for Taylor's carrying a single state, although the possible impact of Van Buren's betrayal in deterring a normal increase in the southern Democratic vote cannot be measured. Despite losses to the Free Soilers, the Whigs still managed to carry the four traditionally Whig states in New England. Without question, the havoc wreaked by the Free Soil party on New York's Democrats gave the Whigs its thirty-six electoral votes. Just as clearly, defections to the Free Soilers cost the Whigs Ohio's twenty-three electoral votes. "We are beaten by our friends and not by our old enemies," moaned a Cleveland Whig.[124] In any event, had there been no Free Soil ticket in 1848, and had New York gone Democratic and Ohio Whig, as it had in 1844, 1846, and October 1848, Taylor would still have won the electoral vote, 150–140. Given Cass' sweep of the Midwest, that left New Jersey and especially Pennsylvania, with thirty-three electoral votes between them, as the keys to Taylor's triumph. Taylor won both by a clear, if narrow, majority, and in each the Free Soil party was a negligible presence.[125]

Those two states were the only two free states Whigs carried in which Taylor's vote exceeded Clay's, and one wonders why. Free Soilers' relative weakness in both suggests that fewer Whig voters defected to the third party in Pennsylvania and New Jersey than elsewhere, but their Whigs were still vulnerable to abstention by disgusted regulars that obviously reduced the Whig vote in other northern states. What explains Whigs' unusual success in Pennsylvania and New Jersey in getting out the vote?

During most of the 1840s Whigs had carried New Jersey, and Taylor's gain over Clay there was a modest 1,700 votes. Thus the result might be attributed simply to party loyalty and fixed voting habits. Yet ingrained habit had not stopped Whigs from losing the 1847 gubernatorial election, and Taylor ran almost 8,000 votes (25 percent) ahead of their unsuccessful aspirant that year as well as 3,500 votes ahead of the Whig congressional slate in October. Regression analysis of voter movement between 1844 and 1848, indeed, suggests that Democrats actually retained more of their 1844 vote than did the Whigs. About 3 percent of former Clay voters switched to Cass, and 14 percent abstained. Those losses were more than replaced by former Democrats and previous nonvoters. Over a fifth of Taylor's vote apparently came from men who had not supported Clay.[126] There were some Native Americans in New Jersey, and some of Taylor's new vote could have come from them. But the stagnation in the state's iron and manufacturing industries, which gave renewed salience to the tariff issue, probably accounts for most of it, just as it had sparked the Whig comeback in the congressional elections.

Pennsylvania provided the keystone to Taylor's victory in 1848. Taylor could have lost both Georgia and Louisiana and still have won with Pennsylvania in his column. Without it, he would have lost even though he captured New York. With Pennsylvania, Whigs prevailed despite the loss of every free state to its west. The Whig showing there was simply remarkable. Though closely contested, it was normally a Democratic state. Harrison had won there in 1840 by fewer than 400 votes, Polk had carried it handily in 1844, and Whigs had been crushed in 1845 and 1847. Whigs' smashing triumph in the 1846 congressional elections had broken a skein of Democratic victories, but that year, Democrats disillusioned by passage of the Walker Tariff abstained in droves, an advantage the Whigs did not enjoy in 1848. Precisely because of the difficulty and importance of carrying Pennsylvania, Whigs had poured both speakers and money into it before and after the October state election. Even they, however, could not have anticipated that Taylor would run 25,000 votes ahead of Clay or outpace the 1847 gubernatorial candidate by 57,000 votes and Johnston's October total by 17,000.

This outpouring undoubtedly had multiple sources. Pennsylvania's Whigs had long recognized their need to absorb the separate Native American vote, some of them had explicitly promoted Taylor's nomination in order to attract it, and they had worked assiduously after the Whig convention to ensure it. Nativists provided some of the additional Whig vote, although their party had never polled more than 15,000 votes and many of them had also voted for Johnston.

Certainly nativists claimed after the election that they had provided Taylor's winning edge, as did former Democrats, in order to claim a share of the federal patronage to be dispensed by the new Taylor administration. The Whigs brought out their entire vote for Taylor, argued one Democrat, but "Gen. Taylor's declaration of entire independence of party, and freedom from ultraism of all kinds," not a "conviction among the people of the soundness of Whig measures," attracted the Democrats who provided his winning margin. Loyal Democrats also admitted that they lost votes to Taylor, but their explanation rings truer than such self-congratulatory letters, for it was echoed by virtually every Whig commentator in the state. Whigs, Democrats, nativists, and previous nonvoters surged toward the Whig ticket in 1848 because Whigs promised to restore the Tariff of 1842, a tariff that Pennsylvania's Democrats themselves had pledged to retain in 1844. Zachary Taylor, of course, never promised to restore the tariff. He vowed only to leave domestic legislation to Congress. Unlike the self-promoting politicos who bid for patronage, that is, voters in Pennsylvania and New Jersey who experienced or feared slashed wages, unemployment, and business stagnation, just like those in Connecticut, "expected nothing from Taylor but did from the Whig party."[127]

How Whigs managed to mobilize the northern vote they did is central to any explanation of Taylor's triumph in 1848. Historians obsessed by the slavery extension issue and the emergence of the Free Soil party, however, have paid more attention to Whig losses in the North than to the votes they retained. In net terms, the Whig vote did fall from its 1844 level in the other five northern states Taylor carried, yet the Whigs attracted enough men to equal 94 percent of their 1844 total in New York, 92.6 percent in Rhode Island, 92.4 percent in Connecticut, 90.5 percent in Massachusetts, and 86.4 percent in Vermont. Those figures—like the regionwide estimate that Whigs retained 90 percent of Clay's votes—are surely as impressive as the much smaller numbers lost through defection, disgust, or indifference, and the reasons for them merit scrutiny.

A combination of factors produced the respectable Whig turnout in these and other northern states. Attractive gubernatorial candidates like Briggs, Fish, and Johnston helped. The steadfast refusal of most antislavery Whig leaders to join the Free Soil party and the case northern Whigs made for their own commitment to the Wilmot Proviso undoubtedly contributed. Yet the clearest difference among the three contending parties in the North was not how they stood on slavery expansion. All three declared determined opposition to it. Rather, the parties differed most sharply on their reaction to the Polk administration's record, on executive power, on further territorial expansion, and, above all, on economic policy. Thus Whig attacks on Democratic economic programs also helped the party draw out a large enough vote to carry New York, Connecticut, Rhode Island, Massachusetts, and Vermont, despite the undoubted losses they experienced.

Northern Whigs did suffer losses, and the damage Free Soilers inflicted on them can best be measured in three ways. One is to consider the Free Soilers' impact on the Whigs' competitive relationship with the Democrats since Whigs worried far more about a Democratic than a Free Soil victory in 1848. As New York made abundantly clear, Free Soilers could hurt Democrats far more than Whigs, and the figures on the differential between the major parties' share of the vote in Table 27 indicate that, of the fifteen free states listed, Whigs ran further behind the Democrats than they had in 1844 only in New Hampshire, Michigan, Ohio, and Indiana. Elsewhere, their margin of victory was larger or that of defeat far smaller. In the two new states of Iowa and Wisconsin, the Free Soilers produced divergent results. The Democratic margin in Iowa was larger than it had been in previous state and congressional contests, suggesting disproportionate Free Soil recruitment of Whigs. In contrast, only substantial movement by Wisconsin's Democrats into the Free Soil camp reduced the margin between the major parties to so competitive a level.[128]

More directly, one can attempt statistically to measure the extent of Free Soil incursions into Whig and Democratic voting support and to compare the proportions of Whig converts with those who abstained or crossed over to the Democrats. The Free Soil vote in New Jersey was so tiny that statistical analysis would be fruitless. Van Buren also received an inconsequential vote in Pennsylvania. While a few Whigs may have bolted to him in western counties near Ohio, his support was concentrated in a tier of heavily Democratic northern counties along the New York border in David Wilmot's congressional district. Most Free Soil voters in Pennsylvania, that is, were former Democrats and Liberty men, and attempting through statistical manipulation to measure the size of the Whig defection is hazardous. Estimates for the movement of voters between 1844 and 1848 in the other northern states are more helpful, and they are aggregated in Table 28.[129]

Table 28

Movement of Voters Between the 1844 and 1848 Presidential Elections
Measured by the Percentage of the 1844 Vote[a]

1844		Whig	Democratic	Free Soil	Abstained
				1848	
Maine	Whig	68%	0%	8%	24%
	Democratic	0	69	3	28
	Liberty	0	0	100	0
	Abstained	20	15	2	63
New Hampshire	Whig	75	0	1	24
	Democratic	0	93	5	2
	Liberty	0	0	90	10
	Abstained	10	12	11	67
Vermont	Whig	85	0	9	6
	Democratic	0	61	22	17
	Liberty	0	0	100	0
	Abstained	0	0	10.5	89.5
Massachusetts[b]	Whig	80	0	19	1
	Democratic	0	83	17	0
	Liberty	2	0	98	0
	Nat. American	90	0	0	10
	Abstained	22	4	18	56
Connecticut	Whig	85.5	6	1	7.5
	Democratic	0	80	2	18
	Liberty	0	0	100	0
	Abstained	15	7	4.5	74.5
Rhode Island	Whig	75	0	2	24
	Democratic	0	56	6	38
	Abstained	6	6	1	87
New York	Whig	90	10	0	0
	Democratic	0	31	44	25
	Liberty	0	0	100	0
	Abstained	6	6	0	88
New York[c]	Whig	80	10	10	0
	Democratic	0	29	43	28
	Abstained	28	22	0	50
Ohio	Whig			15	
	Democratic			3	
Indiana	Whig			15	
	Democratic			10	
Illinois	Whig			7	
	Democratic			18	
Michigan	Whig			18	
	Democratic			6	

Table 28 (*continued*)

[a]This table is based on the following sources: The regression estimates for all the New England states except Massachusetts were calculated by my former student Lex Renda; Table 1 in Baum and Knobel, "Anatomy of a Realignment," p. 65; Table VII in Kirn, "Third Party System," p. 37; Sweeney, "Rum, Romanism, Representation, and Reform," p. 118. The estimates for the major party losses to the Free Soilers in the Midwest are taken from Alexander, "Harbinger of the Collapse of the Second Party System: The Free Soil Party of 1848" (a manuscript version of the essay cited in note 136, read at the Conference on Nineteenth Century Political History, University of Nebraska, May, 1987), cited with permission of the author. Scatterplots in Alexander's paper suggest that virtually all Liberty party men in the Midwest voted Free Soil, as did Liberty men in the Northeast.

The category labeled "Abstained" in 1844 includes both men who were legally eligible to vote then but did not and those who became legally eligible between 1844 and 1848.

[b]The regression estimates for Massachusetts measure movement between the gubernatorial election of 1847 and the presidential election of 1848 rather than between the two presidential elections.

[c]These are regressions of the voter movement in New York between the gubernatorial elections of 1844 and 1848.

These estimates indicate that the Free Soil party cut far more deeply into the Whig vote in the Midwest than in the Mid-Atlantic and New England states. Only in Massachusetts did the level of Whig support for Van Buren approach that in the midwestern states. No appreciable number of Whigs backed him in New York, Pennsylvania, New Jersey, New Hampshire, Rhode Island, and Connecticut. Fewer than a tenth of previous Whig voters did in Vermont and Maine. In most of New England, in fact, Whig abstention was a much more severe problem than Whig defection, a point of some importance since men who stayed home because of dissatisfaction with Taylor might be mobilized behind a more appealing candidate in the future. Abstention may also have been a problem for the Whigs in the Midwest in addition to their losses to the Free Soilers. At least one analysis based on all northern counties suggests that while Whigs retained about 90 percent of their vote in the North as a whole, they held only about three-fourths of it in the Midwest.[130] Because none of the available estimates for the Midwest indicate such heavy losses to the Free Soilers, some of the former Clay voters undoubtedly abstained, as midwestern Whigs reported. Proportionately, Democrats suffered equal or greater incursions into their vote from the Free Soilers in New Hampshire, Vermont, Massachusetts, Connecticut, Rhode Island, New York, Pennsylvania, and Illinois. Equally revealing, where we have figures on the behavior of previous nonvoters, they show that such men were far more likely to support one of the major party candidates, and particularly Taylor, than the Free Soilers in all states except Vermont and Massachusetts. A third party widely regarded as a single-issue antislavery party had a markedly limited ability to bring first-time voters or previous nonvoters to the polls.

Finally, one can move beyond the presidential returns to measure Free Soilers' impact on Whig fortunes in state and congressional elections. Ohio has already been discussed. There the Free Soilers cost the Whigs at least two congressional seats and jeopardized Whig control of the state legislature. There Whigs admitted that the results "had prostrated the Whig party" and that "without conciliation [of the Free Soilers] the Whig party of Ohio is doomed to become a small party."[131] In contrast, little evidence exists that Free Soilers contributed to the Whig defeats in the August state and congressional elections in Illinois and Indiana. The new party did run a separate congressional candidate in one of Illinois' seven congressional districts, but Democratic incumbent John Wentworth won with a majority anyway, while the Whig candidate ran far better than his counterpart in 1846 had. And if Indiana's Whigs worried about the defections they had suffered in November,[132] their Whig neighbors in Illinois were too busy rejoicing over the devastating impact the Van Buren candidacy had on the Democrats and the increase in their own vote to be concerned about any threat the Free Soilers might pose.

The situation was more complex in Michigan and Wisconsin. In two of Michigan's three congressional districts all three parties ran candidates, and the Democrats won both with less than a majority of the vote. Had all the men who supported the Free Soilers gone Whig, that is, Whigs would have carried both districts. In the third district, however, the Whigs chose to bargain rather than fight, and together with the Free Soilers they elected William A. Sprague, whom they described as a firm "Taylor Whig." Attempts at fusion with the Free Soilers in other areas did not prevent the Whigs from being routed in the state legislative elections.[133] In Wisconsin, all three congressional districts saw three-way races and each party emerged triumphant in one of them. By draining votes from the Democrats, the separate Free Soil candidate in the second district may have helped the Whig Orasmus Cole win, for he garnered less than a majority of the vote. Democrats won majorities in both houses of the Wisconsin legislature, with the Whigs holding less than a fourth of the seats in each and the Free Soilers the balance. Such figures, like the three-way split in the popular vote, suggested the wisdom, indeed the necessity, of working for a Whig-Free Soil coalition in the future.

Of the Mid-Atlantic states, the Free Soilers had no impact on the state and congressional races in New Jersey or the state contests in Pennsylvania. Two Pennsylvania congressmen elected in October were claimed as Free Soilers. David Wilmot most assuredly was a Free Soil leader, and he would have been reelected as a Democrat had he chosen to run as one. Wilmot's candidacy, in other words, did not deny the Whigs a seat they might have won. In the Twenty-Second District, which the Whigs had carried in 1846, John W. Howe won with the combined backing of Whigs and Free Soilers. Antislavery sentiment was strong in the counties composing the district, and although Whigs outnumbered Free Soilers, as measured by the presidential vote, Free Soil support was vital to Howe's victory. Elsewhere in the state, Free Soilers had no decisive impact on the outcome of congressional races.[134]

The disruptive impact of the Free Soilers on New York's Democratic party was even clearer in state and congressional races than in the presidential contest. Even though more former Whigs apparently voted for John A. Dix, the Free Soil gubernatorial candidate, than for Van Buren, Hamilton Fish won easily because of the divided Democratic vote. More spectacularly, Whigs won thirty-one of New York's thirty-four congressional seats, three-fourths of its state senate seats, and an astonishing 84 percent of the members in the legislature's lower house. If the negative impact of the Free Soilers on the Whigs was clear in Ohio and ambiguous elsewhere, palpably its presence helped the Whigs in New York. Accordingly, they had an incentive to do anything they could to keep the Democrats from reuniting.

Free Soilers' threat to New England's Whigs is more difficult to assess, if only because three of the region's six states would not hold state and congressional elections until the spring of 1849. In the three that voted in the fall of 1848, moreover, results were mixed. As they had in 1846, Whigs won three of Vermont's four congressional seats in September, and they retained control of the state legislature. Such control proved vital to the Vermont Whig party, for the Free Soil gubernatorial candidate got almost three-tenths of the vote, while the Whig Carlos Coolidge received less than 44 percent. Coolidge, that is, would have to look to the legislature for election. Although the Free Soil party in Vermont clearly sapped more votes from Democrats than from Whigs, it still hurt the Whigs and left them vulnerable to a challenge from a Democratic-Free Soil coalition.

In Maine, the dynamic was reversed. There the Democrats lost their secure majority in the gubernatorial election and had it sharply reduced in the state legislature.[135] Maine's Whig minority had an incentive to bargain with the antislavery men in the future, just as their neighbors in New Hampshire had done in the past. Two Whigs won congressional seats in Maine, moreover, only because Free Soil candidates siphoned off votes from their Democratic opponents. In Maine, in sum, Whigs gained rather than lost from the presence of the Free Soilers.

Finally, Massachusetts Whigs palpably suffered from the new party's emergence. Not only did they lose a greater percentage of their former supporters to it than did Whigs anywhere else in the Northeast, but George Briggs polled less than a majority for the first time since 1845, largely because Stephen Phillips attracted 29 percent of the vote. Thus, the gubernatorial election was thrown into the legislature. There Whig control of the forty-member state senate was secure, and proportionately Whigs did even better in the house races than they had done in 1847 (see Table 19). That increase, however, disguised a significant deterioration of Whig strength. Not all towns in Massachusetts could send members to the legislature every year, and in many towns the presence of Free Soil candidates prevented anyone from winning the absolute majority necessary for victory. Because of those stalemates and the state's apportionment law, a number of towns went unrepresented, and the legislature elected in 1848 was significantly smaller than that selected in 1847. The number of seats won outright by Whigs dropped from 196 to 174. Conversely, where the Liberty party had won twelve seats in 1847, Free Soilers captured forty-nine, or a fifth of the total, in 1848, and their potential strength was even greater because they were strongest in many of the towns that went unrepresented that year. As time would soon show, the Massachusetts Whigs were extraordinarily vulnerable to any future alliance of Democrats and Free Soilers that might challenge their control of the commonwealth's government.[136]

The Free Soilers also deprived Massachusetts Whigs of two congressional seats they had captured in 1846. In one district, Charles Allen won outright over Whig and Democratic challengers. In another, John Gorham Palfrey, whom the Whigs had officially read out of the party, siphoned off enough votes in repeated elections to prevent anyone from winning the seat with the necessary majority. That district would go unrepresented during the entire Thirty-First Congress. Some conservative Whigs in Massachusetts might prate that it was "a real blessing to the Whig party . . . to have an occasional sifting such as the Free Soil agitation has given it" and that "we are really all the stronger for the secession of calculating, self-seeking men like Sumner, Adams, Palfrey, *et id genus omne*." More discerning men knew otherwise.[137]

The immediate harm inflicted by the Free Soilers on the northern wing of the Whig party thus varied sharply from state to state. Yet, its real menace to the Whigs would only be determined in the future. If it continued to grow as rapidly as it had during 1848 or if it combined with Democrats against the Whigs in New England, New York, and the Midwest, its potential threat was immense. What happened in the future, in turn, would be determined by the exigencies of political conflict in individual states and by what the new Taylor administration and Congress did about the problem of slavery expansion into western territories.

IX

At the end of 1848, with the significant exception of some Ohioans, most Whigs ignored this cloud on the horizon. Neither the relative decline in their vote, nor the low turnout, nor the sectional division in the party demonstrated by its divergent campaigns in the North and South worried many Whigs. Nor did Whigs' ambiguous message in some places and the accession of Native Americans and Democrats to the Whig column trouble many about precisely who or what was responsible for Taylor's victory. Instead, they were too busy celebrating the overthrow of the Democrats and "the evidence that this result gives of the truly national character of the Whig party, and the soundness of the nation's heart." "Never did true Whigs glory as they do now," Ohio's Benjamin Wade exulted, and he did not gloat alone.[138]

Ominously, however, not all Whigs agreed about what they were celebrating. A Tennessean, for example, proclaimed Taylor's election a "glorious *triumph* of Whig principles," and others interpreted it as ensuring the enactment of specific Whig measures: an increase in tariff rates, repeal of the Independent Treasury, and restoration of federal subsidies for internal improvements. To Kentucky's Leslie Combs, Clay's great friend, the victory meant "the restoration of the *great principles of self government* and the protection of *Human Labour* in practical legislation—1st *majorities* & not *vetoes* are hereafter to govern the country. 2nd Citizens & not foreigners beyond the sea are to be protected in their honest earnings by the sweat of the fires." Other Whigs saw the victory in quite another light. Regular Whigs, warned Georgia's Alexander Stephens, had no sympathy for the Taylor movement or "even now understand it." "The Real Taylor men . . . look upon the late most glorious achievement as a public deliverance and not a *party victory*." They looked "to a *Reform* in the Government and not bounties and rewards for partizan services." Similarly, a New Yorker declared that "public opinion is very decided against some old issues, of the Whig party, and old worn out, political Hacks like Mr. Clay and Webster." Still another New Yorker attributed the triumph not to Whig principles, but to what he called "the Taylor

Republican Party." "The recent revolution, effected by the election of General Taylor upon the principles laid down in the 'Allison Letter,' " he declared in a New York City newspaper, "has completely removed all the old and obsolete platforms of the *Whigs* and *Democrats* and re-established the popular and *Republican* doctrines of *Jefferson, Madison,* and *Monroe.* . . . Old party issues have been totally swept away and a new order of things established under the influence and name of General Taylor whose virtues and patriotism will adorn the brightest page in history."[139]

Aside from the future challenge posed by the Free Soil party—and more broadly the free-soil movement—and the need to resolve the slavery extension issue, therefore, Whigs confronted another problem. Their presidential candidate and most of their gubernatorial and congressional candidates had triumphed in 1848. Exactly what that victory entailed for the administration of government and the course of the Whig party itself, however, evoked sharp disagreement. Conflicts among Whigs about what kind of campaign to run for Taylor were carrying over into disputes about how to proceed after he won. Such uncertainty portended serious trouble ahead.

Chapter 12

"Many Discordant Political Interests to Reconcile"

"THE WHIG PARTY has safely passed through . . . a transition state and will be as enduring as the union itself," one Whig rejoiced after Taylor's election. "Its perpetuity as a great national party, is placed beyond doubt." Optimism abounded among Whigs in the weeks following Rough and Ready's victory. They appeared to be ascending because of their presidential, congressional, and gubernatorial triumphs in 1848, while Democrats plummeted in the opposite direction. "We have precisely changed ground with the locofocos," boasted a New York Whig. "We stand new, fresh, hopeful before the country—full of promise and glittering with the *prestige* of success. They have drooped beneath the weight of odious men, of *names* that stink in the public nose, & of recent measures." Democrats "are regarded as hopeless," while "we have the destiny of the party, in its *new* form, in our hands." "With the right policy by the *incoming* Administration," chorused a Vermont leader, "the locofoco party will never see daylight again."[1]

The modern observer can savor the irony of such predictions. Within a year of Taylor's victory, hopes raised by Whigs' performance in 1848 would be dashed. Within four years, they would be routed by their supposedly discredited foe in the next presidential election. Within eight, the Whig party would totally disappear as a functioning political organization. Four years after that, the perpetuity of the Union itself would be in grave jeopardy, in no small part because of Whigs' disintegration as "a great national party."

Whatever their unintended irony, such predictions provide important clues to what brought the Whig party acropper within a year of Taylor's election. Numerous Whigs rejoiced that Northerners and Southerners had stood behind the ticket despite the corrosive sectional animosity evident at the national convention, profound sectional disagreement over the Wilmot Proviso, and the new Free Soil party's threat in the North. Yet Whigs had maintained unity largely by taking very different tacks on the slavery extension issue in the North and South, and Taylor's triumph had not resolved the divisive issue itself. It could still disrupt the party along sectional lines, a potential enhanced by the Democrats, whose resilience and ability to reshape the immediate political agenda some Whigs so badly underestimated.

After 1848, Whigs' destiny lay exclusively in their own hands no more than it ever had. Interaction with Democrats had always shaped their party's history. As the "out" party after 1848, Democrats could now move to more extreme sectional stances on slavery questions to outflank Whigs in both sections. Cass' defeat, reduced Democratic support everywhere, and northern Democratic defections to the Free Soilers almost ensured that Democrats would adopt new positions that would force Whigs in both sections to respond. That necessity, in turn, enormously increased northern and southern Whigs' difficulty in finding a mutually acceptable policy on slavery extension.

To some extent, however, Whigs could determine their own fate. Here is where allusions to "a transition state" and "the party, in its *new* form" are instructive. Not all Whigs employed such terminology after the election, and some who did probably meant by it only that new men had finally replaced an older generation of Whig leaders symbolized by Clay and Webster. Others, however, insisted that the party's personnel and principles had been fundamentally transformed by the Taylor campaign, that the Whig party itself had been displaced by a new "Taylor party" or "Taylor Republican party." The supreme irony of statements that Taylor's victory ensured the perpetuity of the Whig party was that Taylor and most of the men he gathered around him at the highest echelons of his administration were bent on replacing the Whig party with a new and broader organization based on the coalition that they believed had brought Taylor to power.

That intention guaranteed an internal struggle for the soul of the Whig party. Countless thousands of men who loved it would not brook abandonment of its name or its principles. Some dismissed Taylor's purposes as bizarre; others condemned them as perverse. The internal conflict over the party's future direction decisively shaped disagreements over the administration's policy initiatives, including its policy on slavery extension. More immediately, it influenced the incoming administration's dispensation of patronage. The unseemly scramble for the victor's spoils that immediately developed among hungry Whig office seekers engendered bitter internal divisions within the party in almost every state. Some of those battles reflected and intensified long-established factional rivalries. More generally, they represented conflicts between self-styled original Taylor men, including Democrats, nativists, and political newcomers, bent on changing the Whig party, and orthodox regulars, who had often preferred other candidates for the nomination and who were determined to resist such change and to retain control of the organization. At the same time that Whigs confronted aggressive new challenges from the Democrats and Free Soilers on the slavery extension issue, that is, they suffered debilitating internal fragmentation. The result, by the time Zachary Taylor sent his first annual message to Congress in December 1849, was the loss of much of the promise that had inspired rhapsodic predictions after the victories of 1848.

The combination of external challenge and internal division that would wrack the Whig party appeared even before Taylor's inauguration on March 5, 1849. Developments during the second session of the Thirtieth Congress from December 1848 to March 1849 and within a large number of states exposed the shoals that lay ahead by intensifying intraparty sectional and state factional divisions that ultimately helped destroy the American Whig party. Simultaneously, the maneuvering to determine the composition of Taylor's cabinet not only confirmed the judgment of a Bostonian that the Whig party could be rent "by the jealousies, plans, & counterplots of our great politicians to thwart each other." It also revealed deep disagreement over the kind of administration different Whigs envisioned.[2]

I

If any Whigs harbored illusions that they controlled their own destiny or that common support for the Taylor-Fillmore ticket might end sectional conflict over slavery expansion, the second session of the Thirtieth Congress quickly dispelled them. Sobered by Free Soil incursions into their respective ranks, northern Whig and Democratic congressmen returned to Washington determined to demonstrate their commitment to the Wilmot Proviso or to settle the territorial issue in a way that undermined the third party's rationale. Early in the session, for example, Senator Stephen Douglas, head of the Illinois Democratic party, which had been so jolted by large defections to the Van Buren ticket, introduced a bill that would immediately admit the entire Mexican Cession as a single state of California and thereby skip the territorial stage to which Congress might apply the Proviso. Meanwhile, northern Whigs, who scorned Douglas' plan as a pusillanimous dodge, called on their representatives in the House to push legislation organizing territorial governments with the Wilmot Proviso attached to solve the issue and undercut the Free Soilers.[3]

Free Soilers, in turn, intended to maintain pressure on their major party rivals. Both John Gorham Palfrey and Joshua Giddings unsuccessfully attempted to introduce bills to abolish slavery in the District of Columbia. To deflect that threat, the Whig-dominated northern majority passed a resolution instructing the committee on territories to report bills for California and New Mexico with the Wilmot Proviso attached. Then, on December 21, a New York Whig named Daniel Gott, who had won reelection in 1848 with less than 43 percent of the vote over a strong Free Soil challenger, moved a resolution instructing the House committee on the District of Columbia to report legislation abolishing the slave trade there. Passage of the Gott resolution ignited southern protests, which quickly evolved into an effort by southern Democrats to embarrass southern Whigs.[4]

The political situation in most southern states changed immediately after the presidential election. Blaming their defeat on Whigs' artful ambiguity on the Proviso and on the inadequacy of Lewis Cass' popular sovereignty formula, southern Democrats determined to gain explicit guarantees of southern equality in the territories and to expose the readiness of Whigs to betray Southern Rights. Across the South, Democratic newspapers increased their warnings that Taylor and his Whig supporters would accept the Proviso. Democrats in Florida, Virginia, and elsewhere pushed resolutions through state legislatures demanding formal resistance should the Proviso pass Congress, thus raising the specter of secession. Simultaneously, southern Democrats abandoned popular sovereignty, and more and more of them demanded the extension of the Missouri Compromise line to the Pacific Coast as the only equitable solution for the Mexican Cession, a demand President Polk endorsed in his final message to Congress that December.[5]

Southern Democratic congressmen continued this offensive when they returned to Washington. Virginia Democratic Senator James M. Mason privately told Vice President George M. Dallas that he would work for Virginia's secession if territorial legislation barring slavery were passed. Southern Democrats also rejected Douglas' statehood proposal as merely a disguised attempt to achieve the same end—barring slavery from the Mexican Cession. As a Georgian wrote Democratic Representative Howell Cobb, slaveholders were "wrought up, by the late movements in Congress, into a greater jealousy of their rights." They spurned immediate statehood for the Cession even if it avoided the Proviso, because "the whole population that is to decide the question [of slavery in California] is north of 36 ½ degrees, and the North gets the whole territory as a matter of course." Southerners therefore banded together to defeat those Northerners present in the Senate and to consign Douglas' bill to the southern-dominated judiciary committee, which everyone knew would bury it without floor action.[6]

Incensed by northern proposals for the Mexican Cession in both the House and Senate, southern Democrats were further infuriated by northern support for Gott's resolution on December 21. John C. Calhoun seized on this anger to renew his effort to break up both major parties in the South and to unite Southerners in a separate party. With the aid of Mississippi's Henry Foote, he called a caucus of all Southerners in the House and Senate for the night of December 22 to formulate a southern ultimatum that denounced northern aggression. Calhoun's initiative created a quandary for southern Whigs, who found Gott's resolution as reprehensible as did southern Democrats. Would they remain loyal to their fellow Whigs, who were Northerners, or to their fellow Southerners, who were Democrats?[7]

From the start, as Calhoun himself admitted, the vast majority of southern Whigs wanted no part of the caucus. They regarded it as a preemptive strike to disrupt the Whig party and wreck Taylor's administration before he was inaugurated. "Their real object," complained Calhoun, "is to keep the two wings of their party, North & South, together." Most southern Whigs wanted to postpone any action on slavery until after Taylor took office. "We feel *secure* under General Taylor," Georgia's Alexander Stephens wrote Crittenden. "We are determined to insist upon his controlling the Question." The southern Democrats who embraced Calhoun's movement, echoed Robert Toombs, acted "not on the conviction that Genl. T. can *not* settle our sectional difficulties, but that he *can* do it. They do not wish it settled."[8]

Although southern and northern Whigs alike considered Calhoun's caucus movement "shaped for mere party effect," they disagreed about the proper response to it. Some, like North Carolina's David Outlaw, who was "opposed to geographical parties, or anything which tends to form them," and his fellow North Carolinian Senator George Badger, who considered Calhoun "absolutely deranged" on any matter "concerning *niggery*" and who denounced the meeting as "insane & dangerous," refused to attend. Others, including the Georgians Stephens, Toombs, and Berrien, Clayton of Delaware, and the Kentuckians Thomas Metcalfe and Joseph R. Underwood, went to prevent or dilute any action.[9]

All told, 69 of 124 southern congressmen attended the initial meeting on December 22, which decided that a committee chaired by Calhoun would prepare an address to the Southerners' constituents. When Calhoun's address was reported to a second meeting of the caucus on January 15, Whigs and moderate Democrats condemned it as too radical and sent it back to committee for revision. There, Berrien wrote what Toombs carped was "a weak milk & water address to the whole Union," but Calhoun and his more extreme Democratic adherents rejected the substitute statement as too conciliatory and insisted on issuing Calhoun's original Address to the People of the Southern States.[10]

Ultimately, southern unity broke down completely, and three separate statements were issued to the public. The most important, Calhoun's Southern Address, rehearsed a long series of supposed northern aggressions against Southern Rights and slavery and warned that the Union's preservation depended upon their cessation. It demanded that slaveholders have equal access to the Mexican Cession. "What then we do insist on," Calhoun declared, "is, not to extend slavery," but that slaveholders not be prohibited merely because they owned slaves. Such a denial of equal rights would sink Southerners "from being equals, into a subordinate and dependent condition." More significant than the specifics of the Address was its overall tone. Northern aggressions, warned Calhoun, were leading inevitably to the horrors of abolition and racial equality. Southerners must unite to prevent that cataclysm, and they were justified in using any method of resistance, regardless of the consequences, because their "property, prosperity, equality, liberty, and safety" were at stake. The Address implied, in short, that any Southerner who did not unite in defense of slavery was a traitor to his section and that secession itself might be required to protect the South.[11]

If Calhoun intended his address as a challenge to the honor of southern Whigs, they refused to accept it. So did many southern Democrats. Only 48 of 124 southern congressmen signed the Southern Address, which appeared on February 4, and that total included only two of forty-eight southern Whigs. Some Whigs endorsed Berrien's statement, which was published later, while four Democrats also issued a circular defending those Democrats who refused to sign the Address. Many of these Democrats, significantly, represented districts where nonslaveholders were in a preponderant majority, and they complained that raising the specter of disunion would smash the Democratic party in those regions.[12]

"We have completely foiled Calhoun in his miserable attempt to form a Southern party," gloated Toombs. What the Whig refusal to sign the Southern Address did instead, as observers both inside and outside Washington immediately noted, was to hand southern Democrats a weapon with which to bludgeon southern Whigs. From Virginia to Georgia, from Florida to Louisiana, Democratic papers attacked the Whigs for betraying Southern Rights and declared support of the Address a test to obtain Democratic nomination for office. That theme of treachery remained central to Democratic campaigns throughout 1849.[13]

Southern Whigs had to respond to those assaults or risk defeat in the congressional and gubernatorial elections impending in virtually every slave state in the summer or fall of 1849. Although Whigs had captured the majority of House seats filled in 1848, their continued control of the House depended on the results in 1849, and most of the congressional elections were scheduled for the South. Southern Whigs faced almost certain defeat unless they demonstrated their own loyalty to Southern Rights or found a way to eliminate the immediate issues that gave weight to Democratic criticism. The northern threat to the slave trade in the District of Columbia was defused when enough Northerners in the House retreated and voted to reconsider the Gott resolution, thereby consigning it, in the words of Nathan K. Hall, "to the tomb of the Catapults."[14] But the explosive slavery extension question remained, and southern Democrats immediately charged that Whigs' refusal to sign the Southern Address proved they would betray the South on the territorial issue. Most southern Whigs had returned to Congress prepared to postpone any action on the Mexican Cession until after Taylor took office. But because of their jeopardy in the impending elections of 1849 and the increasing threat that this "dangerous subject" posed "to our beloved country," they could no longer wait for him to formulate a policy.[15]

Northerners' determination to pass the Wilmot Proviso to neutralize Free Soilers' challenge also raised the frightening possibility that they might succeed in the next Congress and confront Taylor with the choice of signing or vetoing a bill that barred slavery from the territories. In early 1849, most southern Whigs still believed that Taylor would veto the Proviso, but if he did, they now realized, he could cripple their northern allies by increasing defections to the Free Soilers. As their refusal to sign the Southern Address indicated, they wanted to hold the national party together, but that effort would be meaningless if northern Whigs were decimated in future elections. At the same time, a small but growing number of southern Whigs that winter began to suspect that Taylor might do the unthinkable and sign the Proviso into law. Everyone realized that enactment of the Proviso with Taylor's blessing would "place the Southern Whigs in a hopeless minority." Any response Taylor made to a congressional ban on slavery in the territories, in sum, would ruin the party in one section or the other. His administration's success and the preservation of the Whigs as a national organization thus required protecting Taylor from the necessity of making a response. And the best way to do that was to settle the territorial question before he took office.[16]

The solution to which southern Whigs resorted was Douglas' California proposal, which had been bottled up in the Senate since early December. Some of them, like Clayton and his frequent correspondent, Kentucky Governor Crittenden, had favored that plan from the time Douglas introduced it, but only after the majority of southern Democrats signed the Southern Address did most southern Whigs turn to it. Skipping the territorial phase and admitting the Mexican Cession at once as a single state struck Whigs as a suitable solution for a variety of reasons, even though everyone expected that California would be a free state. First, given northern Whigs' insistence on enacting the Proviso, they knew they needed Democratic support to pass the measure. Such support seemed probable, not only from northern Democrats like Douglas, who wanted to resolve the territorial issue permanently in order to undermine the Free Soil party, but also from the many southern Democrats who rejected the Southern Address as bad politics and a threat to the Union. Furthermore, the prospect of blocking slavery extension and gaining a new free state might even win over support from northern Whigs like Nathan Hall, who feared the disruptive impact of the territorial issue as much as southern Whigs.

Second, virtually all southern Whigs, convinced "that no sensible man would carry his slaves there if he could," had always regarded the question of slavery extension into the Mexican Cession as symbolic rather than substantive. As Toombs told Crittenden when he described the bill southern Whigs planned to introduce, "It cannot be a slave country; we have only the point of honor to save; this will save it, and rescue the country from all danger of agitation."[17]

Third, if they passed their proposal, they might be able to claim concrete as well as symbolic gains for the South—not just an end to northern aggressions but the actual expansion of the area in which slavery was legal. That paradox is explained by the ambiguity of what men meant by the "territory" in the Mexican Cession that was to be included in the state of California. Texas, a slave state, claimed all the land east of the Rio Grande River as its own, an area that encompassed about a fourth of the former Mexican province of New Mexico and half of the present state of New Mexico, including Santa Fe. At the beginning of the congressional session, residents of New Mexico petitioned for the establishment of civil government in the former Mexican province and asked Congress to protect them from the introduction of slavery into it. Since the petitioners explicitly denied that any of New Mexico belonged to Texas, outraged Southerners in Congress vowed never to tolerate the surrender of lands legally owned by Texas. From the point of view of Southerners, in short, not all of the land acquired in the Mexican Cession had been ceded to the United States government. A healthy chunk of it belonged to the slave state of Texas and hence would never be included in the new free state of California.[18]

The bill southern Whigs eventually introduced blandly—and imprecisely— spoke of erecting a new state "out of and including all that territory ceded to the United States by the recent treaty of peace." Toombs, a major proponent and engineer of the southern Whig plan, explicitly denied that "that territory" included the areas claimed by Texas. He wrote Crittenden on January 22 that the state of California to be proposed in the bill would encompass only the area west of the Sierra Madre Mountains. "This will leave out a very narrow strip, not averaging more than 15 or 20 miles, between this California line and the Rio Grande line of Texas. This Texas line the Democrats are committed to, and some of our very worst Northern Whigs (Corwin, etc.) say, if that line is established they will vote this slip with it to Texas." When southern Whigs proposed to admit the Mexican Cession immediately as a single free state, that is, they by no means envisioned barring slavery from all of the land won from Mexico. They would also be enlarging Texas.[19]

Because Douglas' bill was irretrievably mired in the Senate and because southern Whigs wanted the credit for solving the issue for themselves, they moved in the House, which Whigs controlled. On February 7, three days after publication of the Southern Address, Representative William Ballard Preston of Virginia, one of the original Young Indians and soon to be secretary of the Navy in Taylor's administration, introduced the Whigs' measure and defended it as the "only door" through which the rival sections could reach a mutually acceptable solution on the divisive territorial issue. Despite Preston's passionate entreaties to Northerners to give up the unnecessary Proviso, despite southern Whigs' optimism about the effect of Preston's speech, and despite backing for some sort of statehood bill from President Polk, important Democratic newspapers, and many Democrats in Congress, Preston's bill failed because of northern Whigs' implacable opposition. Whether they recognized its implications for enlarging Texas or feared that any conciliatory step might leave them vulnerable to the Free Soilers, they insisted that the Proviso be applied to the Cession. When Preston's bill came up for a vote on February 27, only five days before Congress adjourned, northern Whigs successfully amended it by barring slavery from the proposed state. The motion to pass the statehood plan in that amended form did not receive a single favorable vote. The Preston bill was dead—and with it the hopes of southern Whigs for settling the territorial issue before Taylor's inauguration and the 1849 elections.[20]

Last-minute attempts to find an alternative solution proved futile. Thus the second session of the Thirtieth Congress adjourned in the early morning of March 4, 1849, without providing for the government of the Mexican Cession or re-solving slavery's status there. Despite the recognition by both southern and northern Whigs that the slavery issue was tearing their party apart, they had been unable to reach an accord. So frayed were the tempers of congressmen after three months of fruitless wrangling that fistfights broke out between Northerners and Southerners in both chambers on the session's final night. "It all grew out of the Slavery question," lamented an Alabamian in Washington. "The whole matter . . . was disgraceful to the Congress of the United States."[21] By the time Zachary Taylor was inaugurated, the façade of national party unity behind his candidacy had cracked, and the sectional fault lines dividing the party were re-exposed. Taylor's administration and the next Congress would have to seek a solution to the territorial issue. And because it remained unresolved, Whigs seek-ing office in the elections of 1849 would have to meet the challenges from Dem-ocrats and Free Soilers on it.

II

Historians have long argued that the widening sectional rift over slavery among Whigs contributed to—and, for some, primarily caused—the Whig party's ulti-mate demise. Yet the sectional fault line was hardly the only intraparty split that weakened the Whigs or that intensified during the months between Taylor's elec-tion and inauguration. Even as congressional Whigs maneuvered futilely for a mutually acceptable resolution of the territorial issue, in the winter of 1848–49 state legislative sessions created or exacerbated rifts within state Whig organiza-tions, laid the foundations for future clashes between Taylor men and orthodox Whig regulars over policy formation and patronage distribution, and demon-strated how Democratic-Free Soil alliances could jeopardize the ability of northern Whigs to control state governments. The unusual volatility and significance of state legislative sessions that winter stemmed primarily, but not exclusively, from the necessity of electing United States senators to the Thirty-First Congress in time for the special Senate session in March to confirm Taylor's cabinet selections. Those decisions had a profound impact on the Whig party.

Of the senatorial elections with relevance for the Whigs, the least significant occurred in Vermont and Florida. Even those, however, illustrated the factional or personal infighting that proved so pernicious to state Whig organizations everywhere and the subsequent consequences such choices could have. Despite the emergence of the Free Soil party and the reduction of the Whigs' share of the popular vote, Whigs dominated both houses of Vermont's legislature after the 1848 elections. Such control virtually ensured the election of a Whig senator, and that certainty fueled the ambitions of rival aspirants. Three-term Congressman Jacob Collamer, who had not been renominated in 1848, angled for the seat of incumbent Whig Senator William Upham, much to the latter's annoyance. Upham fended off that challenge and won reelection, but the result left the disappointed Collamer, a power in the Vermont Whig party, unemployed. By a process of elimination, the starchy and conceited Collamer would emerge as the lone New Englander in Taylor's cabinet. As postmaster general, Collamer would have control over more federal jobs than anyone else in the administration. It was a position that required tact and a touch the Vermonter lacked.[22]

With a margin of thirty-six to twenty-three on a joint ballot over the Democrats, Florida's Whigs had their first opportunity in December 1848 to send a Whig to the Senate. Whig legislators, however, fragmented over regional and personal rivalries. Such divisions might have been overcome had the state's most popular Whig, Representative E. Carrington Cabell, theretofore a moderate on the sectional issue and an ardent Taylor man, consented to move up to the Senate. His unwillingness to do so prevented the squabbling Whigs from uniting behind a single choice and allowed the Democratic minority to dictate the winner. The first attempt at an election ended in a deadlock among four Whig contenders. The second saw twenty-two Democrats combine with eight Whigs to elect Jackson Morton over George T. Ward, the choice of the Whig majority and a much firmer proponent of Whig principles than Morton. Indebted for his election primarily to Democrats, Morton would vote like most southern Democrats rather than like most southern Whigs on the slavery issue during the momentous Thirty-First Congress.[23]

North Carolina's Whigs almost suffered a similar fiasco. Like Vermont, North Carolina had been one of the Whigs' most reliable strongholds during the 1840s, yet there too personal animosities and increasingly virulent regional tensions rent the party. As in Florida, Whigs from the eastern and western portions of the state resented the control that Whigs from its central counties exercised over the state party. To many eastern and western Whigs a conspiracy of the "Raleigh Clique" to monopolize all the state's important offices was evidenced in 1848 by the interim appointment of William M. Battle to the state supreme court and by Charles Manly's gubernatorial nomination—both from Orange and Wake counties near Raleigh.[24]

But more than thirst for office fueled these regional tensions. Mountainous western North Carolina had consistently been the state's Whig stronghold, in large part because Whigs promised to subsidize transportation development.[25] Whig legislators had faithfully voted expenditures for railroad and turnpike construction, but by the end of 1848 the western region had been grossly short-changed in the allocation of funds. The emergence of the free suffrage issue, which almost cost Manly's election in 1848, also increased regional tension. Western Whigs not only protested Manly's initial opposition to free suffrage; they introduced the demand for a reapportionment of the legislature based on the white population instead of the federal ratio, which counted three-fifths of the slaves, a demand opposed by Whigs in the Piedmont and eastern coastal plain alike. After Manly's narrow escape in the August election, Whig Congressman Thomas Clingman of Asheville, a self-proclaimed champion of western interests against central domination, instructed his paper to keep up the cry for reapportionment on the white basis. "Should the clique at Raleigh throw themselves in opposition to the movement," he warned Senator Willie P. Mangum, "it will damage them."[26]

By the time the North Carolina legislature assembled in December 1848 to elect a senator and a permanent supreme court justice, its Whig members were "in a state of shameful disorganization." Yet the Whigs required the strictest cohesion to control events, for the senate was evenly divided 25–25, while the Whigs possessed only a one-vote majority in the house, 60–59. Intraparty dissensions quickly took their toll. Most Whigs favored the election of Judge Richmond Pearson, a westerner, to the supreme court over Graham's appointee, Battle, but some clung to Battle even after the embarrassed judge withdrew from the contest. Finally, Pearson was elected with the aid of a few Democratic votes. Enraged by the stubborn opposition of Battle's friends to Pearson, a few Whigs then aided the Democrats to elect their own John Ellis over Battle to Pearson's now-vacant seat on the superior court.[27]

The debacle in the selection of judges caused Whigs grave anxiety about the senatorial election. The candidate of the Whig caucus was incumbent Senator George E. Badger, but Whig observers in Raleigh predicted his defeat since numerous Whigs opposed him. Many still fumed over his domineering effort to steamroll the state convention in February 1848 into nominating his kinsman, Edward Stanly, for governor and endorsing Taylor over Clay for president. Some complained about his public admission that the Wilmot Proviso was constitutional and about his vote against the Clayton Compromise in the summer, both of which seemed betrayals of Southern Rights. Primarily, Whigs disliked Badger because he "is at the head of this central influence," which "many Whigs are now *execrating*."[28]

When the balloting for senator commenced, two or three Whigs refused to support him, thus denying him the necessary majority. Perhaps because Democrats feared unifying the Whigs behind Badger, they did not nominate a candidate of their own. Instead, they fomented Whig disarray by backing other Whigs against him. That strategy opened up an opportunity for the ambitious Clingman, who rushed back to Raleigh from Washington to engineer a coalition between Democrats and western Whigs behind his own elevation to the Senate. Defending his bid as an act of justice to western Whigs, Clingman bargained blatantly with the Democrats, and he willingly provided written answers to their questions about his positions on economic issues and the territorial question. Evasively ambiguous on the tariff and subtreasury, Clingman was forthright in his denunciation of the Wilmot Proviso as an unconstitutional and tyrannical attempt to enslave white Southerners to northern domination. Its passage, he declared, would necessitate the most extreme southern resistance. Clingman had assumed this defiant stance a year earlier in a congressional speech, but because it was more congruent with the position southern Democrats were then taking on the territorial issue than that of any other North Carolina Whigs, increasing numbers of Democratic legislators began to vote for Clingman on subsequent ballots for senator. Never enough Democrats, however, to bring Clingman victory. Finally Clingman admitted defeat, withdrew from the race, and urged one of his western Whig supporters to go for Badger. Together with a few Democratic abstentions, that was enough to elect Badger on the fifth and final ballot.[29]

Even though most Whigs had stood loyally by Badger and condemned Clingman for his opportunistic trafficking with Democrats, the damage to Whig unity continued after Badger's election. Clingman published an address to his western constituents that justified his course, damned the Raleigh Clique's monopolistic power, and urged western Whigs to send men to the legislature who would resist its attempts to enslave them. Estranged from the power structure of the state Whig party, Clingman thereafter declared himself an independent, and in the mid-1850s he joined the Democrats. A spellbinding orator who brilliantly posed as the defender of his constituents' liberty and equality from the menace of enslavement, whether it came from the North or central North Carolina, Clingman easily withstood repeated Whig attempts to unseat him. Finally, in the late 1850s, the Democrats elevated him to the Senate seat he had long coveted. Far more disastrous to Whig fortunes in the short term than Clingman's defection, the regional animosities that had boiled over in the 1848–49 legislative session caused eastern and western Whigs in 1850 to force a restructuring of the state central committee that demolished the influence of Raleigh Whigs and gutted the committee's ability to raise funds or coordinate statewide campaigns. In a state as closely competitive as North Carolina, this suicidal emasculation of the party's organizational apparatus virtually ensured electoral defeat.[30]

The contest for senator in Pennsylvania reflected personal jealousies rather than regional rivalries, but its outcome engendered a factional struggle that wracked the state Whig party for the next four years. To an extent this battle pitted younger men and newcomers, who had joined or aligned with the Whig party during the 1848 campaign, against older Whig regulars who had often worked for the party since the 1830s, veterans whom the younger men disparaged as "Hunkers." Little separated these groups in terms of state or national policy at the end of 1848, when all Pennsylvania Whigs desperately sought restoration of the Tariff of 1842 and economic recovery. They contended instead for control of the elective and appointive offices at the party's disposal. The leader and hero of ambitious younger Whigs was newly elected Governor William F. Johnston, the recent convert from the Democrats, whom they credited with redeeming the state from Democratic rule and for being "an independent man" rather than "an ultra and violent Whig." The man who became champion of the Whig regulars was the Whig Pennsylvania elected to the Senate in January 1849, James Cooper, a thirty-eight-year-old attorney from Pottsville and a former congressman and state legislator.[31]

By Cooper's own account, he had been the unanimous favorite of the state's Whigs to run for governor in 1848 when Francis Shunk resigned, but he had declined to seek the nomination because he wanted to go to the Senate instead. To help unify the Whig party behind the ex-Democrat Johnston, whom Cooper said most Whigs distrusted as a dishonest and self-serving opportunist, he had accepted Johnston's appointment as state attorney general and urged Whigs to give Johnston the gubernatorial nomination. Then, for reasons Cooper found unfathomable, Johnston had turned against him during the senatorial election and lobbied Whig legislators to vote instead for Johnston's cronies like Thaddeus

Stevens of Lancaster, the old Antimasonic fanatic, or William M. Meredith, president of the Philadelphia City Council. Despite the governor's opposition, which earned Cooper's abiding enmity, Cooper prevailed on the third ballot with all but six of the seventy Whig votes cast.[32]

Johnston's opposition may have baffled Cooper, but his motives are clear. The former Democrat meant to consolidate his personal control of the state Whig party despite the apparent suspicion of many Whig state legislators. To do so, he wielded the state patronage at his command to form alliances with men outside the circle of established Whig leaders, men like Meredith, Stevens, and Cornelius Darragh, head of the young Whig faction in Pittsburgh, whom Johnston appointed state attorney general to replace Cooper. Johnston's primary goal after Taylor's election, however, was to monopolize the federal patronage allotted to Pennsylvania, including an expected cabinet post. He alone could save the Pennsylvania Whig party "from positive and absolute destruction," the ambitious governor immodestly informed Crittenden in January. Pennsylvania's man in the cabinet must not come "from among those personally hostile to me." Johnston thus wanted no Whig as United States senator from Pennsylvania who might challenge his control of federal patronage in the state. As a two-term congressman and four-term state legislator, Cooper had a wide network of friends and an independent power base in the Whig party that placed him securely beyond the governor's control. Hence, Johnston unsuccessfully tried to block Cooper's elevation to the Senate.[33]

Cooper's victory set the stage for a titanic battle between Pennsylvania's Whig governor and Whig senator for the federal offices that Taylor's administration dispensed to the state. Long-time tillers in the Pennsylvania Whig vineyard resented the effort of the newcomer Johnston to build a personal machine, but they could do little to thwart his appointive powers as governor. Therefore, they had to look to federal offices to offset his command of the state spoils. To do that, they necessarily embraced Cooper as their point man in Washington. During Taylor's presidency, Johnston would handily prevail in this struggle, but such a divisive contest between the state's two most prominent Whig politicians boded ill for the party's ability to retain control of a normally Democratic state. The fight over patronage eventually engendered divisions among Pennsylvania's Whigs over the proper resolution of the territorial issue in 1850 and subsequently over the party's presidential nominee in 1852. What began as a battle over patronage became an even more destructive battle over policy and the party's future.

The struggle between Johnston and Cooper in Pennsylvania paled in ferocity to the prolonged and open factional warfare among New York's Whigs over their new senator. For two months, friends of Vice President-elect Fillmore and their conservative allies among Clay Whigs in New York City and the Hudson Valley battled the rival Seward-Weed wing to a standstill. Appalled by "the bitterness of this strife at Albany," unaligned New York Whigs declared that unless the dispute was resolved, "the Whig party will be severed."[34]

Both sides considered the stakes enormous. Seward and Weed dreaded Fillmore's impending accession to the vice presidency because they feared that "the ascendancy of factious councils" in the new administration would wreck their own wing of the New York party through the allotment of federal appointments in the state. Their fear was justified. A month after Taylor's triumph, he promised to consult Fillmore on patronage for the state and to allow him to attend cabinet meetings at which the spoils would be distributed. To check Fillmore's influence in Washington, Weed wanted Seward in the Senate. Rejoicing that Fillmore's election finally provided a chance to smash Weed's machine, Fillmore's friends, in turn, warned him that as a senator Seward "would use his influence and abilities to build up and sustain a party opposed to your interest and the welfare of your friends in this State." Factional rivalry in New York had always involved disagreement over policy as well as competition for office, and the radicalism of Seward's antislavery statements during the 1848 campaign increased conservatives' opposition to his election. Seward had become an abolitionist, they complained. His "ultraism" would shatter Whig unity in Washington and thus destroy any prospect for a successful Taylor presidency. "Seward will be an active 'Architect of ruin' if he comes to the Senate in the present condition of things," warned Congressman Nathan K. Hall from Washington. "Seward will come here to demagogue. He will distract & divide the party and next to Clay is the worst man we or any other people can send to the Senate."[35]

Before the legislature convened, Fillmore papers like the Buffalo *Commercial Advertiser* and Rochester *American* came out publicly against Seward's election. Instead, they and most Fillmorites promoted John A. Collier of Binghamton, a former congressman and state comptroller, who had nominated Fillmore for the vice presidency at the national convention to foil Weed's plans and then served as a presidential elector on the ticket Weed had constructed as a sop to conservatives. Although Fillmore, who remained at Albany until late February to complete important duties as state comptroller, wanted to avoid the appearance of publicly interfering in the contest, he too preferred Collier and was determined at the very least to find some office for his loyal friend. The Sewardites, in turn, regarded Collier with loathing and contempt as an intellectually unqualified, dishonest, and undignified "libertine," "a low buffoon," whose "morals are notoriously profligate to the lowest degree."[36]

Because Whigs held overwhelming majorities in both houses of the new legislature, the struggle for the nomination focused on Whigs' legislative caucus. Weed's organization had skillfully packed Whig assembly tickets the previous fall with firm Seward men, and the Albany editor was confident of ultimate victory. Conservative Whigs dominated the Whig delegation in the state senate, however, and they refused to go into caucus with their house colleagues in order to prevent Seward's inevitable nomination. This fractious and widely publicized deadlock embarrassed unaligned New York Whigs who were concerned primarily with preserving party unity, and they pleaded with the politicians in Albany to find some other man. But Weed, who managed the effort for Seward at Albany, stood resolutely by his man.[37]

Neither Weed nor Fillmore wanted to push the issue to a head. Both hoped to prevent an open rupture because they feared that it could destroy any influence New York's Whigs might have with the new administration. Scornful of Collier, Weed had no wish to humiliate Fillmore. The incoming vice president's ability to exact revenge once the new administration assembled in Washington remained an ominous threat. Besides, he had to work with Fillmore as long as he remained comptroller, for the comptroller headed the canal board that dispensed contracts for canal repairs that winter. Those contracts were among the juiciest patronage plums available to the state Whig party. Finally, the legislature would elect not only a senator but also a new comptroller to replace Fillmore, and in terms of control over state patronage, the comptrollership was the most powerful office in the state. Weed feared that if the Sewardites rode roughshod over Fillmore's friends in the Senate election, they would retaliate on the comptrollership, where Weed hoped to place the self-proclaimed neutral Washington Hunt.[38]

Fillmore's situation was more awkward, and his motives are more difficult to infer. Millard Fillmore was a man of considerable intelligence but weak will. His report as comptroller that winter, for example, contained a brilliantly lucid analysis of the state's safety fund and free banking systems that could have provided a blueprint for the later National Banking System. As a politician, however, the unaggressive Fillmore was no match for the shrewd Weed. Later, even his disgruntled friends would accuse him of timidity and naiveté, and it is difficult to decide which defect was more grave. After the presidential election, for example, Fillmore wrote Taylor praising the mortal enemies Weed and Collier as the two men most responsible for his victory in New York. That winter his friends urged him to threaten Whig legislators with future patronage retaliation unless they supported Collier, but early on he recognized that Collier could not win and refused. Instead, to avert an open defeat at the hands of the Sewardites that might discredit him with Taylor, Fillmore sought a face-saving compromise. He asked Weed to support Collier or his law partner Nathan Hall, who had not sought reelection to Congress in 1848, for the comptrollership, but Weed refused to allow an open Fillmore ally in that important post. Then Fillmore sought pledges of Weed's help in securing a federal job, the lucrative post of naval officer at New York City, for Collier and pledges of Seward's cooperation at Washington.[39]

Finally, under the auspices of Governor Hamilton Fish, a deal was worked out that allowed Seward's election. The patrician Fish did not belong to the Seward-Weed circle, and like Fillmore and his friends he was worried about the "ultraism" of Seward's antislavery statements during the campaign. But Fish could count votes, and he knew Seward had them. To end the unseemly and dangerous infighting, he called Weed, Fillmore, and the leaders of their respective factions in the legislature to a meeting at his home to hammer out a compromise. In return for a cessation of the conservative resistance to Seward and Hunt, it was arranged that Seward would write a letter to Albany pledging not to agitate for abolition in the Senate and to support the Taylor administration in which, of course, Fillmore was to be a major figure. Fish and Fillmore would then circulate the letter to mollify Seward's conservative opponents. In addition, it was agreed that Collier could have the Naval Office at New York City. Significantly, the details of this last understanding were murky. Fillmore left the meeting before they were worked out, but his friends there later recalled that Weed had pledged that Seward would help Fillmore get the appointment for Collier. Weed, in turn, asserted that he had promised only that Seward would not block it; Fillmore himself must secure the post for Collier if he could. Later, after Seward's election, he and Fillmore met at Weed's house and agreed to consult with each other on New York appointments when they got to Washington. Carrying away decidedly different interpretations of what this agreement implied, the two rivals set off for Washington.[40]

III

Whatever the implications of the senatorial decisions in Vermont, Florida, North Carolina, Pennsylvania, and New York for the Whigs' future, that winter Whigs around the country most closely watched the elections in Kentucky and Ohio. Although only the Ohio River separated the two states geographically, their respective selections evoked interest for quite different reasons. Whigs looked to Ohio for clues to how northern Whigs and Free Soilers might interact now that the 1848 elections were over. To many, Kentucky's choice would determine the success of Taylor's administration and the subsequent direction of the national Whig party.

Within weeks of the presidential election, it became clear that Henry Clay, who had not held public office since 1843, desired to return to the Senate in the seat Crittenden had vacated to become governor. Whigs dominated both houses of Kentucky's legislature, and Clay's numerous friends, fully aware of his mortification at Taylor's nomination, were determined to bestow that honor upon him. With Taylor safely elected, even his Kentucky Whig supporters were willing to give Clay one last opportunity to serve. Thus no serious opposition organized within the state to stop Clay, and his election was more coronation than contest.[41]

Outside Kentucky, Clay's prospective return to the Senate struck Whigs with alarm and dread. Recalling Clay's domineering attitude toward Harrison in the winter of 1840–41 and his belligerence toward the apostate Tyler that helped turn the Whigs' first occupation of the White House into a nightmare, they foresaw disaster. More than that, the presence of Webster and Clay together again in the Senate betokened a resurrection of an older generation of National Republican leaders who might resist what many younger Whigs considered salutary changes in men and measures promised by Taylor's election. If "*ultra Whigs*, of the Clay and Webster school of politics" should "give direction to the 'Taylor Republican Party,'" one New Yorker warned Fillmore, "its fate can easily be foretold."[42]

Southerners who had originally boomed Taylor's nomination over Clay rang most of these alarms: Clayton of Delaware, Reverdy Johnson of Maryland, John Pendleton of Virginia, William B. Campbell of Tennessee, Toombs and Stephens of Georgia, Balie Peyton and Albert T. Burnley of Louisiana. While some warned that Clay would complicate settlement of the territorial issue by siding with northern Whigs, the dominant concern was the inevitable friction that would emerge between Taylor and Clay. Clay, they shrieked, was "vindictive & peevish." He would go "into the Senate with unkind & revengeful feelings towards Genl. Taylor" and "throw as many difficulties in Taylor's path" as possible. "He will try to rule or ruin & his rule will be ruin." According to Pendleton, every Whig in Washington for the short congressional session wanted to keep Clay shelved on his Ashland estate. Many northern Whigs, including Fillmore's law partner Nathan Hall, condemned the notion of Clay's election as vehemently as did Southerners. If Clay insisted upon returning to the Senate, moaned New Jersey Senator William L. Dayton, "it would seem as if he had almost been born for the destruction of his friends & is resolved not to disappoint his destiny."[43]

These apocalyptic predictions had some basis in fact. Though deeply humiliated by Taylor's nomination, Clay was willing to support the new administration, particularly since he sought a diplomatic post for his son James, but he and his friends intended to cooperate only so long as Taylor faithfully ran what they considered a Whig administration. That meant adherence to traditional Whig programs and a willingness to share federal offices with all Whigs, not just original Taylor men. What they would not tolerate was an effort to proscribe old-line Whig loyalists to favor the newcomers who had boarded the Taylor bandwagon in 1847 and 1848 or especially to transform the Whig party into a personality cult built around Taylor or to foster an amorphous entity known as Taylor Republicanism that Pendleton and other Taylor men envisioned. Disgust at the attempt "to create a mere *personal* party" behind Taylor had fueled Clay's refusal to help in the 1848 campaign, and his closest friends also regarded it as anathema. "If the accession of Taylor, if Taylorism, should prove Jacksonism Nos. 2—fore God we will fight," proclaimed a New York Clay man shortly after Taylor's triumph. "The reappearance of Mr. Clay in the Senate," exulted Kentucky's Leslie Combs, "will be as terrific to official imbeciles and guerrilla-Whig office-seekers as would the sudden entrance of an old tom cat into a room of cheese-stealing mice & rats." To friend and foe alike, in sum, Clay's restoration to the Senate portended a clash between old-line Whig regulars, "the *old politicians*," and younger Whigs, along with those who had entered the party under the auspices of Taylor's No Party campaign, between those who wanted to preserve the Whig party as it had existed for over a decade and those who wanted to change and broaden it.[44]

In contrast, Ohio's prolonged struggle to name a successor for Democratic Senator William Allen widened the divisions among national Whig leaders over the territorial question by stiffening northern Whigs' insistence that slavery be barred from the entire Mexican Cession. It increased northern Whig adamance because it vividly demonstrated the party's vulnerability in northern states to Free Soil-Democratic coalitions and the consequent necessity of depriving the Free Soil party of its rationale. In all likelihood, the developments in Ohio, along with evidence that similar coalitions were forming in Vermont, Connecticut, and Indiana, directly influenced northern Whig behavior in Congress that winter, particularly the scuttling of Preston's statehood bill with a Proviso amendment.

Historians have long pointed to Ohio's election of the Free Soiler Salmon P. Chase to the Senate as evidence of the growing strength of northern antislavery sentiment and its ability to prostrate northern Whiggery. A recent student of Ohio politics, for example, cites Chase's election as the final nail in the coffin of the state's Whig party, the point at which the slavery issue ended Whigs' competitiveness in the state. The circumstances surrounding Chase's election, however, illuminate a different fact of great importance to a proper understanding of antebellum politics. He owed his success less to his advanced antislavery views than to the exigencies of state politics. Contrary to the assertions of some historians that Americans during the fifteen years before the Civil War were obsessed with the debate in Congress over slavery expansion, the majority of actors in the drama that unfolded at Columbus were not. Their gaze was fixed firmly on control of the state legislature, the state jobs at its disposal, and the policies it might enact for Ohio concerning banks, corporations, taxes, constitutional revision, and other subjects, not on what the state's new senator might do about the slavery issue in Washington. To a large extent, they viewed the Senate seat as a bargaining chip that might gain them advantage on what really mattered.[45]

Ohio's legislative session that winter was the most tumultuous in the nation. It took over a month to select officers and appoint committees to conduct business, two months officially to validate the election of Seabury Ford as governor the previous October, and three months to name a senator. That chaos stemmed largely from an uncompromising battle between Whigs and Democrats for dominance of the state government.[46]

The stage for this fierce struggle was set in February 1848 when Whigs reapportioned the legislature's house and senate districts in order to perpetuate their control. Decisively breaking from traditional gerrymanders that combined counties in legislative districts to increase a party's representation, Whigs also divided Hamilton County, which encompassed populous Cincinnati, into two districts in order to secure for the Whigs two of its five-man house delegation that had been solidly Democratic under the customary system of running at-large countywide tickets. Denouncing the tactic as tyrannical, unconstitutional, and invalid, Democrats demanded its repeal, urged Hamilton Democrats to ignore it during the 1848 legislative elections, and lambasted Whigs as revolutionary anarchists for their flagrant violation of sanctioned practice. Citing Democrats' threats to disrupt the state government and disobey the law, Whigs returned the charge, and the inflammatory rhetoric of both parties made the apportionment act the central issue in the state election that October.[47]

Predictably, the election yielded disputed results. Democrats claimed all five members of Hamilton's house delegation on the basis of the countrywide vote; Whigs demanded the two from the new Cincinnati district they had created. Control of the house, and ultimately of the legislature, hinged on the resolution of this dispute, and both sides vowed to prevent its organization and the appointment of the necessary committees rather than allow the other's attempt at usurpation to succeed. Exclusive of the two contested seats, Democrats had, at most, a margin of two over the Whigs in the house and only one in the senate. Even then, eight Free Soilers in the house and three in the senate held the balance of power between the two rivals. Their leverage, ironically, derived in large part from the Whigs' own gerrymander, for the Whigs had purposely increased the representation of normally secure Whig counties in the Western Reserve, which subsequently elected Free Soil legislators.[48]

All three groups quickly understood that some kind of bargaining, if not an outright coalition, between two of them was necessary. The questions were whether Whigs or Democrats would win Free Soil aid and at what price. The different priorities of the three parties and their internal divisions determined the answers to those questions. Free Soilers were indeed primarily concerned with slavery: they sought the Senate seat and repeal of the state's discriminatory black laws, which restricted various rights of Ohio's free blacks. Although all Free Soilers recognized that the three-way split of the legislature enhanced their chance of success, they disagreed about their senatorial candidate and how to achieve his election.

A few of them favored Chase's election and wanted to deal with the Democrats to secure it. Chase himself visited Columbus frequently that winter and actively promoted this strategy. The majority of Free Soilers, including six of the eight in the house, however, were former Whigs. They pushed Joshua R. Giddings for the senatorship and secured his nomination from the Free Soil caucus. The Whig-Free Soilers also wanted to preserve the new party's independence and to remain neutral in the dispute between the two major parties. They wished to nominate their own candidates for speaker of the two chambers, stand by them, and wait for one of the major parties to come to their men, a plan that resulted immediately in the election of a Free Soil speaker in the senate. Above all, they wanted no trafficking with the Democrats on state economic policy or on the disputed house seats from Cincinnati. Democrats' attempt to steal those seats, fumed a Western Reserve Free Soiler, was "the grossest corruption."[49]

The Free Soil delegation's Whiggish hue initially fostered Whig hopes of cooperation between the two parties. At the very least, Whigs expected the Free Soilers to "act like *Whigs* at the organization" of the legislature. The two groups agreed on much. Aside from abolitionist and Liberty party lobbying efforts, what support there had been for repeal of the black laws during the previous ten years had come from Whigs, and during the 1848 campaign itself Whig candidates, including Ford, had advocated repeal. Like the Free Soilers, Ohio Whigs demanded congressional prohibition of slavery in the territories. Of critical importance, the Whigs did not insist on placing one of their own men in the United States Senate, and they could live with a Free Soiler who pushed enactment of the Wilmot Proviso. Friends of both Thomas Ewing and Justice John McLean would have liked to put their favorites in Allen's seat, but early on they admitted that the complexion of the legislature rendered that goal unobtainable. Whigs, therefore, were willing to concede the Senate seat to the Free Soilers in return for Free Soil help in securing what Whigs considered a far higher priority—control of the legislature. They were determined to implement their new apportionment law by seating the two Whigs from Cincinnati, to stop Democrats from repealing it, and to squelch the expected Democratic efforts to revise the state constitution and overturn Whig economic policies. As one Whig wrote Ewing, the Whigs had to compromise with the Free Soilers to save our "unequaled Banking system—an equitable and fair law of taxation—and an economical administration of state affairs" from "the wild fury of Locofocoism."[50]

Together, Whigs and ex-Whig Free Soilers could have easily dominated the legislature. But the proposed alliance foundered on a large rock. Although Whig-Free Soilers were willing to help Whigs seat their two men from Cincinnati in the house, they insisted on the election of Giddings to the Senate. Aside from the ambitious Chase, whom Whigs reviled, Giddings was the one Free Soiler whom they considered absolutely "out of the question" for the post. As Giddings himself realized, Whigs blamed him for wrecking their party by leading Reserve Whigs into the Free Soil camp. On his election, one Whig legislator snarled, "there can be no compromise."[51]

To the dismay of Democratic friends of incumbent William Allen, most Democrats were also ready to sacrifice his Senate seat to the Free Soilers in return for help in securing the legislature. Aware that their traditional support for the state's black laws and their opposition to the Wilmot Proviso during the 1848 campaign posed obstacles to any bargain, they shamelessly flip-flopped. As soon as the presidential election was over, Democratic papers around the state repudiated popular sovereignty, embraced the Proviso, and endorsed repeal of the black laws. Desperation impelled their about-face. Having lost the governorship for the third consecutive time and confronting the loss of federal patronage once Taylor replaced Polk, they coveted the jobs at the disposal of the legislature—clerkships, judgeships, and state printing contracts—the last of special concern to the primary Democratic deal maker, Samuel Medary, editor of *The Ohio Statesman* at Columbus. To win those jobs, they needed Free Soil help in organizing the house and seating the two Democrats from Cincinnati. Allen's Senate seat seemed a small price to pay for such cooperation, especially since their somersault on the slavery issue indicated it meant little to them. More than sheer opportunism motivated the Democrats, however. Although they were prepared to "abandon the South [and] join the free soilers" on the slavery question, the year-long warfare over the recent apportionment act had invested state issues with great emotional intensity. In addition to winning jobs, therefore, they were determined to repeal it, rewrite the state constitution, and roll back Whig economic legislation.[52]

Prepared though they were to support a Free Soiler for the Senate, the Democrats could not stomach Giddings. Giddings' ardent hatred of slavery and the Slave Power obviously was not at issue. Rather, it was his previous prominence as a Whig and a powerful exponent of Whig economic policy. Salmon Chase was another matter because Chase avidly sought a coalition between Democrats and Free Soilers to promote his own chances of election. He called a state Free Soil convention to meet at Columbus during December while the legislature was in session and wrote its platform to curry favor with the Democrats. To the disgust of former Whigs in the new party, that platform took the Democratic position on everything most dear to Ohio Democrats. It demanded a new constitutional convention, a new tax law, and a ten-hour act for workers; it denounced aid to corporations and the Whigs' recent bank law. Chase also persuaded the two non-Whigs among the Free Soilers' house delegation to oppose the apportionment act and to help the Democrats organize the house. With Chase closely monitoring the negotiations, those two Free Soilers then worked out a bargain with the Democrats that caused both Whig-Free Soilers and Whigs to sputter in rage. In return for Democratic help in electing Chase to the Senate and repealing the black laws, the two renegade Free Soilers, Norton Townshend and John Morse—and only those two of the eight Free Soilers—helped the Democrats elect a Democratic speaker of the house, seat the two Democratic representatives from Cincinnati, place two Democrats on the state supreme court, award a number of district judgeships to Democrats, and make Medary the senate's printer.[53]

Ohio Whigs regarded the consummation of this bargain and the election of Chase, whom they despised, as significant defeats. Although they could have stopped it by agreeing to support Giddings, they blamed Democratic opportunism and Chase's self-serving ambition instead. They vilified the Free Soil-Democratic coalition as "the vilest combination of cutthroat demagogues that ever disgraced or ruled any land." Most important, their defeat convinced them that they must destroy the Free Soil party and win back Whig defectors to have any chance in Ohio. "Unless something is done speedily and efficiently, we are badly whipped in Ohio for some year or two to come," Oran Follett frantically warned Ewing. What had to be done, they repeatedly told members of the Taylor administration, was to cut the ground from under the Free Soilers on the slavery issue. Taylor had to sign the Wilmot Proviso into law when the new Congress met or, preferably, devise a plan that barred slavery from the entire Mexican Cession even before it met.[54]

Yet other aspects of the Ohio story merit emphasis. Although its Whigs considered action by national Whig officeholders necessary to break up the Free Soil party, what most infuriated them was not the loss of the Senate seat to Chase, but the Democrats' success in trading national offices to the Free Soilers in return for control of the state legislature. The Free Soilers promised to give "the Democrats all the offices & [to] carry out all their abominable measures provided they will elect him," moaned one Whig before the consummation of the deal. "Chase's election in itself is not so much to be deprecated although it is bad enough—but the idea of throwing the State into the hands of the locos as a consequence of it is perfectly outrageous." The Democratic-Free Soil coalition in Ohio set a pattern for similar alliances in Indiana, Massachusetts, Connecticut, Vermont, and other northern states. Free Soilers who were primarily concerned with slavery expansion, against which only the national government could act effectively, wanted national offices, whether in the House or the Senate. Northern Democrats, who had little concern with the slavery issue, always demanded state offices in return, for control of state government and the policies it promulgated was their chief goal. Certainly, the main fear of Ohio's Whigs was the Democratic threat to their programs within the state.[55]

That fact, in turn, argues against an interpretation that events of the 1848–49 legislative session destroyed the Whigs as a serious competitive force in Ohio politics. The acid test of the Whigs' influence was not who won appointive or elective offices, but who controlled public policy. Ex-Whigs constituted the majority of Free Soilers, and they agreed with their former colleagues about most aspects of state policy. Together the two groups had a majority in both houses, even with the seating of the two Democratic members from Cincinnati. Together they voted time and again to defeat the Democrats on the repeal of the apportionment act, on banking and currency legislation, on incorporations, on stockholder liability, and on subsidies for internal improvements.[56] The major exception to this record of effective cooperation concerned the calling of a convention to revise the state's constitution, which Whigs had long opposed. There the Free Soilers combined with Democrats to defeat the Whigs, a defeat Whigs properly regarded with alarm.[57] On the whole, however, Whigs enjoyed success on what had always mattered most to them. While a serious problem, the appearance of Free Soilers in the Ohio legislature did not eliminate Whigs' power within Ohio politics—certainly not when public policy is placed where it should be, at the center of political analysis.

IV

However portentous the actions of Congress and of various state legislatures during the winter of 1848–49, many Whigs believed that the party's success hinged on a different set of decisions to be made in the same period—the selection of Zachary Taylor's cabinet. Now that Taylor had served as the Whigs' standard bearer, even fervent proponents of his nomination—Crittenden, Truman Smith, John Pendleton, Alexander Stephens, and Alexander C. Bullitt, among others—admitted that his political inexperience required the appointment of seasoned advisors. Nor did most Whigs trust a novice like Taylor to pick his official team by himself. They bombarded Crittenden, Fillmore, and Smith with conflicting suggestions and importuned them to convince Taylor to wait until he came to Washington and conferred with Whig politicos before making any final decisions. Initially, the apparently unassuming Taylor seemed willing to follow that course. He informed Fillmore and Smith that, with the exception of one man, he would postpone construction of the cabinet until he arrived in the capital in late February. That delay allowed time for rival Whigs to jockey for position. Not just the outcome but also the process of selecting the cabinet had serious consequences for the party.[58]

Agreeing upon the necessity of surrounding Taylor with knowledgeable political hands, Whigs differed sharply about the cabinet's optimal composition. In part their bickering reflected difficult problems that confront any incoming presidential administration. To which states and regions should the six cabinet posts be distributed? Was it better to use them to reward Whigs in party strongholds like Massachusetts and North Carolina for faithful service, to acknowledge the role of key swing states like Georgia and Pennsylvania in putting Taylor over the top, or to boost Whigs in Democratic states like Maine or Virginia by giving them a prestigious cabinet appointment? Whigs from each type of state vigorously advanced their respective claims. Those from the rapidly growing and Democratic midwestern states of Indiana, Illinois, Michigan, Wisconsin, and Iowa were especially vociferous in their clamor for an authentic Westerner in the cabinet. Without one, they contended, the party would never have a chance in a region whose representation in the House and thus in the Electoral College was certain to increase after the impending 1850 census. All of the competing claims could not be satisfied; Taylor and his advisors were bound to offend some Whigs.

Other customary tensions complicated the proper geographical allocation of posts. Within individual states, personal jealousies and factional rivalries ensured strife over every potential appointee. Many Whigs also questioned the wisdom of taking talented men from Congress to serve in the administration if doing so risked losing their seats to Democrats. Beyond those concerns lay a more fundamental and rancorous conflict. Early supporters of Taylor's nomination insisted that the cabinet must be confined to original Taylor men. Backers of defeated contenders like Clay, Webster, and McLean protested just as ardently that internal party harmony could be restored only if they were also represented in the cabinet. This conflict, which would later extend to the distribution of jobs below the cabinet level, involved more than mere contention for spoils. It reflected fundamentally different strategies about how Whigs should compete with the Democrats in the future. Together these cross pressures and contentious disagreements narrowed the choices available to Taylor and almost ensured that he would not pick the best men the party had to offer.

Taylor quickly ruled out making any appointments from Louisiana or New York since he and Fillmore represented those states. But he wanted a man from the Deep South in the cabinet, and he was known to be considering three Whig congressmen from Georgia: Stephens, Toombs, and Thomas Butler King. All three had fervently supported Taylor's nomination, but King, who chaired the House Committee on Naval Affairs in the Thirtieth Congress, appeared to be the front-runner as a possible naval secretary. King, however, was not close personally to Stephens and Toombs and did not belong to their wing of the state party. Distrusting King, Stephens advised Crittenden, whom most Whigs expected to have the greatest influence on Taylor's choices, that ex-Governor George W. Crawford would be the best selection from Georgia. Largely because of Stephens' intervention, Taylor would appoint a man who later caused his administration enormous trouble.[59]

Backbiting over an appointee from New England was particularly vicious. To the dismay of original Taylor men who believed the public opposed "some old issues of the Whig party, and old worn out, political Hacks like Mr. Clay and Webster,"[60] some of Daniel Webster's fervent supporters boldly and unrealistically promoted him for secretary of state. Webster himself had no illusions that Taylor might appoint him. His top priority, other than obtaining a good government job for his son Fletcher, was to keep his Massachusetts rival, Abbott Lawrence, out of the cabinet. Lawrence had the advantage of being an early Taylor man, and he had been the southern Taylorites' favorite for the vice presidential nomination. Many Massachusetts and other New England Whigs thus pushed the enormously successful businessman for secretary of the Treasury. Taylorites outside of New England thought it insane to put a Massachusetts millionaire in that post. The appointment, they warned, would "revive the cry of ancient Federalism [and] Essex Juntoism." Webster, a former Federalist himself, was hardly in a position to make that case against Lawrence. Instead, he and his friends cleverly spread the word that making the wealthy textile manufacturer Treasury secretary would create an unseemly conflict of interest for the new administration, for Whigs expected the new Treasury secretary to draft a new tariff bill with higher rates for presentation to Congress in December 1849. Maine's George Evans, whom Maine Whigs were ardently promoting for a cabinet slot, would make a far better Treasury secretary, the Webster men argued. Lawrence's many advocates responded by smearing Evans as a National Republican, a Webster lackey, and a drunkard who would embarrass the administration.[61]

Such subversion and countersubversion turned Taylor against both Lawrence and Evans and toward Robert C. Winthrop. Yet Winthrop's appointment raised a different problem. He had served admirably as Speaker of the House during the Thirtieth Congress, and most congressional Whigs wanted to keep him in that post if the Whigs retained control of the House. Winthrop was simply too valuable to be removed from Congress.[62]

A similar consideration limited the chances of another contender from New England. Outside of New England itself, many Whigs preferred Connecticut's Senator-elect Truman Smith, the de facto national party chairman, whom one Whig hailed as "the Murat of the [1848] campaign" because of his brilliant leadership of the party's national committee. Whigs in and outside Congress deemed Smith the best-informed and wisest politician in the party. Even those shrewd tacticians Seward and Weed came away from conversations with Smith after the election impressed, indeed almost awed, by his sagacity and keen judgment of the party's personnel. They, the astute Georgian Stephens, and others wanted to place

Smith in the cabinet, preferably as postmaster general. That was a perfect post for the only man in the party who had corresponded with leading Whigs from every congressional district in the country when he distributed documents during the 1846 and 1848 campaigns. Local postmasters could be vital cogs in the Whig organization because they relayed political information between its center and periphery, and no one knew better than Smith which men to place in those sensitive posts.[63]

Seward, Weed, and others wanted Smith in the cabinet for an even more important reason. With the possible exception of Crittenden, whom most Whigs recognized as Taylor's closest advisor and expected to go into the cabinet, no one in the party had done more to secure the nomination and election of Taylor than Truman Smith. No one could question his commitment to the administration's success or detect in him the jealous envy of Taylor they suspected in Webster and Clay. Unlike Crittenden and other original Taylor men, however, Smith vehemently opposed proscribing non-Taylorites from the cabinet and other federal jobs. Concerned as always with the good of the national party, he recognized the need to conciliate, rather than to exclude, other elements of the party, and to build it up in the West and in Democratic states of the South. Thus it was to Smith that Clay men, Websterites, friends of McLean, and those like Seward and Weed, who had backed no particular candidate, looked for influence with the new administration. Without question, Truman Smith's selection was the most valuable one that could have been made for the good of the Whig party.[64]

Yet some Whigs feared removing Smith from the Senate, even though he was a far better party manager and strategist than floor debater or parliamentary tactician. Since Connecticut held legislative elections in April 1849, if the Democrats won control, as appeared likely that winter, they could replace Smith with a Democrat for the full six-year term. Better, those Whigs argued, to keep Smith in the Senate and look elsewhere for a postmaster general. Smith would remain in contention for a post until the very end, but the need to keep his Senate seat in Whig hands, as well as a surge of southern Whig opposition because of his votes for the Wilmot Proviso during the second session of the Thirtieth Congress, forced Taylor to look elsewhere for a New Englander.[65]

Midwestern Whigs also laid claim to the postmaster generalship, and in that region, too, personal, factional, and state rivalries fueled infighting over the proper man. Some Ohio Whigs proposed Thomas Ewing on the grounds of his support for Taylor before and after the national convention and the unlikelihood that Whigs would be able to elect Ohio's new senator in the forthcoming legislature. Thus, they argued, Ewing would be a far better appointment than Tom Corwin, who was already secure in the Senate. Other Ohio Whigs, like Cincinnati's Thomas B. Stevenson, feared the damage that the conservative Ewing might inflict on other elements in the state party, particularly supporters of Corwin and McLean. He argued that if Taylor wanted to honor Ohio symbolically with a cabinet post, he should name Corwin, not Ewing. Corwin would decline in order to keep his Senate seat in Whig hands, and then Taylor, having honored Ohio, could turn to a different state for the Midwest's representative. Stevenson had a specific alternative in mind. He and most Whigs from the other midwestern states strenuously pushed Caleb B. Smith, a three-term Indiana congressman, for postmaster general. They complained that Ewing, who came from eastern Ohio, had no understanding of the needs or personnel of Whig parties elsewhere in the Midwest and demanded that a genuine Westerner be appointed.[66]

Ewing's friends, led by Joseph Vance, who had kept Ohio's delegates from going to Clay at the convention and who spoke with Taylor when he was on his way to Washington, retaliated by attacking Smith's support for McLean's nomination in 1848. As postmaster general, Smith would build up an organization that could secure McLean Whigs' 1852 nomination. Only true Taylor men like Ewing, they contended, deserved cabinet appointments. "There is great effort making by the original Taylor men to prejudice his mind against the appointment of any man who opposed the nomination," fumed the Indianapolis editor John Defrees and other Smith backers. "Should he be so weak as to pursue such a course the Party will be blown to the devil in three weeks."[67]

What was at stake in the construction of the cabinet, Defrees and others worried, was not just that original Taylor men would monopolize its positions. They feared that the Taylorites intended to abandon the Whig party in order to build a new party with a new name. Conciliation and conversion of Democrats, not implementation of Whig policies by Whig personnel, appeared to be Taylorites' goal. Rumors that Taylor was being strongly advised to retain Democrats in federal jobs in order to woo their support appalled them, for a course so reminiscent of Tyler's would outrage "honest Whigs." Some Whig leaders, Cincinnati's Stevenson protested to Caleb Smith, "desire a reconstruction of parties." And the evil genius behind this mad scheme was Taylor's most trusted advisor, Crittenden.[68]

That suspicion was only partially accurate. The impulse to change the name and the policies of the Whig party, to eradicate every trace of what was scorned as the "ultra Whiggery" of "the Clay and Webster school of politics," in order permanently to convert the nativists, Democrats, and new voters who had supported Taylor sprang from numerous men after the election, including Taylor. Everywhere these newcomers identified what they called the "Taylor party" or the "Taylor Republican party" as an entity distinct from the old Whig organization. Everywhere they urged that policies be formulated and appointments made that would keep the new party intact. To attract Democrats, an Illinois resident advised Crittenden, "a new party designation should be adopted in place of Whig." Similarly, a Rough and Ready Club in Natchez, Mississippi, praised Taylor's election as a victory "of the Taylor Republican Party."[69]

That Taylor's Louisiana advisors meant to foster a new party and to jettison old Whig staples along with the Whig name became clear shortly after the election. As early as January 12, 1849, Albert T. Burnley informed Crittenden that Taylor meant to replace the staid Whig *National Intelligencer* in Washington as the administration organ because the *Intelligencer* was too "committed to ultra measures." Taylor wanted Alexander C. Bullitt of New Orleans to edit the new sheet, which, significantly, would be called the *Republic*. Burnley, who would publish the new paper, wrote Crittenden in the summer of 1849 that the Whigs must discard "the old Hunker Whig politicians & the stale, chronic & unpopular doctrines of *ultra* whiggery." By attracting "tens of thousands" of Democrats who "repudiate & despise Locofocism," Taylor could "reconstruct the true old

Republican party." Since "the elements of this Republican party elected Genl. Taylor—they will sustain him if he acts wisely."[70]

While others also wanted to transform the Whig party after Taylor's election, Crittenden wholeheartedly endorsed the project, and he had enormous influence on Taylor. Crittenden was Taylor's first choice for the cabinet, no matter what the post, and he intended to appoint him before consulting Whigs in Washington. But by late November, rumors were circulating that Crittenden hesitated to leave Kentucky; he felt obligated to serve out his gubernatorial term, and he and other Kentucky Whigs distrusted the lieutenant governor who would succeed him.[71]

Though unwilling to leave Kentucky, Crittenden continued to have great influence on the shaping of the cabinet, and he rejoiced that Taylor did not intend "to administer the government as a partisan, or for a party." To advance that goal, Crittenden sought to control events in Washington by securing the appointment of an alter ego as secretary of state, Clayton of Delaware. By early December it was evident to knowledgeable Whigs that Clayton would be Crittenden's man in the cabinet, and the prospect of the Delaware senator as secretary of state appalled Webster, Seward, and, most significantly, Truman Smith. They worried about his heavy drinking, his lack of candor and penchant for backbiting, and his infirm will. Most of all, they questioned Clayton's judgment and also Crittenden's, for whom they knew he would be a catspaw. "I think I see many breakers ahead," moaned the horrified Smith. "I doubt whether the measure of wisdom with which we are likely to be blessed or the temper of the People will allow the admn. to continue over four years."[72]

Clayton was not up to the job of secretary of state, and he knew it. He took it largely because he could not withstand Crittenden's pressure to take it, and throughout his term he leaned shamelessly on the Kentucky governor, nervously soliciting his advice on every move and pathetically begging him to come to Washington to take his place.[73] Yet Crittenden saw great advantages in Clayton's appointment beyond the latter's utter deference to him. First, Clayton had great influence with Whigs in Delaware and, more important, in nearby Philadelphia. Second, the two agreed wholeheartedly that the best solution for the divisive slavery extension question was immediately to form states out of the Mexican Cession and bypass the territorial stage to which Congress might apply the Wilmot Proviso.[74] Most important, they both wanted to replace the Whig party with a new organization based on Taylor's personal prestige and popularity, not on sharply defined doctrine or old Whig policies. "Old Zach is the Rock politically, on which you ought to build," Crittenden wrote Clayton. "There is . . . the source of strength and popularity . . . for the Administration." They would make loyalty or opposition to Taylor himself the main issue, just as Jackson had done twenty years earlier.[75]

Convinced that "we won our victory as *Taylor* men—not merely as Whigs," and determined "to sink the name of the Whig party in that of the Tarylor Republican Party after the election,"[76] Clayton agreed to take the state department in part because of his influence in Pennsylvania, where he first promoted the new party scheme. Immediately after the election, Clayton and his Philadelphia allies like Morton McMichael, Edward Joy Morris, William D. Lewis, and Robert M. Bird, editor of the influential Philadelphia *North American*, organized Taylor

Republican Associations to give permanent institutional form to the campaign alliance between Native Americans and Whigs. Regular Whigs in the area, especially Clay men, fought the proposal tooth and nail. "The Old Fogies in Philadelphia kick angrily against the *Taylor Republican* movement, upon the ground that it must break up the dear Whig party," Bird reported. Clayton himself complained bitterly to Crittenden that "the ultra Whigs in Philadelphia—headed by Josiah Randall—Charles Gilpin & one or two others" labeled Taylor's triumph "an exclusive *Whig* victory," refused "to call themselves 'Taylor men' & insist[ed] on retaining the old name of Whigs," and defiantly reorganized Whig committees as alternatives to the new Taylor Republican Associations. Their myopic stubbornness, he fumed, was driving the nativists away from the new organization. Pennsylvania, in short, provided vivid evidence that any attempt to replace the Whig party would not go uncontested.[77]

Even Crittenden thought Clayton had gone too far in offending old-line Whigs by his rash scheme. Seward and Truman Smith considered it insane. The battle lines that formed over the Taylor Republican movement also fueled an extraordinarily rancorous fight over a cabinet appointment from Pennsylvania. As a vehicle for newcomers to the party, the Taylor Republican movement was an obvious ally for Governor William F. Johnston, the ex-Democrat, who sought to seize control of the state Whig organization from orthodox party regulars. Thus Johnston opposed any cabinet appointment from that wing of the party. Yet it was widely understood that Taylor was interested in one of three elderly and prominent Philadelphia lawyers to serve as attorney general or Treasury secretary—John Sergeant, Horace Binney, and Josiah Randall. The possible choice of one of these patrician old-line Clay Whigs infuriated the younger Taylorites in Philadelphia since they wanted to eradicate the last vestiges of National Republican influence in the party in order to cement their alliance with working-class Native Americans. Johnston immediately informed one of Clayton's lieutenants that it was better that Pennsylvania have no appointment than that one of these three get it. Since "we have many discordant political elements to reconcile," another Clayton correspondent explained, any cabinet appointment from the state would split Taylor's triumphant—and heterogeneous—coalition. The mass of "the Taylor party of Pennsylvania" cared far more about the new administration's policies than about a cabinet appointment.[78]

Yet Clayton wanted a Pennsylvanian in the cabinet to foster his Taylor Republican movement. Because none of the prominent contenders fit his needs, he ordered his Pennsylvania followers to find a suitable man for the Treasury Department. Such an appointment could also keep the old-line Whig Abbott Lawrence out of that important post. For several weeks the search proved fruitless. Then, in early January, two of Clayton's Philadelphia lieutenants recommended the little-known William M. Meredith. An accomplished lawyer who served on the Philadelphia City Council, Meredith had never held national or state office. Nor was he closely identified with the state's manufacturing or financial community. But he had other credentials that mattered far more to Clayton. He had enthusiastically endorsed the formation of the Taylor Republican Association in a speech at its inaugural meeting. Meredith had an "early connection with *the movement*," wrote one of Clayton's allies, and he "would add especial strength to *our* views." Furthermore, Meredith was Johnston's friend, and Johnston, who sought to control all federal appointments in Pennsylvaia, was delighted with the idea of Meredith in the cabinet. Predictably, Whig regulars, including Senator-elect James Cooper, vehemently protested that "Mr. Meredith's appointment will be productive of great pain to many." They wanted a different man to avoid "discord and an open quarrel" in Pennsylvania and to assure regulars of the administration's "entire fidelity to our principles."[79]

Serenely unaware of this feuding in Pennsylvania, Taylor departed Baton Rouge for Washington in early February with only the vaguest ideas about the cabinet's composition. He still hoped to induce Crittenden to join that body when he stopped in Frankfort for consultation with his friend. Despite early rumors that he might give a place to his former son-in-law, the Mississippi Democrat Jefferson Davis, he intended to confine his selections to full-blooded Whigs. He wanted representatives from Georgia and Pennsylvania, was leaning toward Clayton, and preferred Winthrop as the New Englander for the cabinet. Beyond that, he had not considered specific men for specific jobs.[80]

Taylor was stunned and deeply disappointed when, even in person, he could not persuade Crittenden to leave Kentucky, and he spurned Crittenden's plea that he appoint Robert Letcher postmaster general instead. Crittenden's influence on Taylor nonetheless remained substantial. Those who interviewed him after he spoke with Crittenden reported that he had decided on four men, three of whom Crittenden recommended: Clayton as secretary of state, Horace Binney for the Treasury, George W. Crawford for the War Department, and Abbott Lawrence as navy secretary. Unlike his friend Clayton, Crittenden wanted to conciliate Clay regulars in Pennsylvania; hence his acquiescence in Binney, who was to be replaced by John Sergeant if he declined. Crittenden had also always wanted Lawrence in the cabinet, and the conflict-of-interest charge could be avoided by giving him the Navy Department, which carried less prestige than the Treasury. Although no one had been decided upon for attorney general or postmaster general, Taylor also made it clear that he had no intention of naming Caleb or Truman Smith. To obviate the concern that Delaware's Democratic governor might appoint Clayton's successor, Taylor telegraphed Clayton with the offer before he reached Washington. Clayton accepted and immediately resigned from the Senate so that the Whig-dominated Delaware legislature, which was still in session, could elect his successor.[81]

After Taylor reached Washington on the evening of Friday, February 23, ten days before his scheduled inauguration, the Whig hierarchy finally had a chance to press their conflicting advice on him directly. As a result, Taylor reshuffled his plans. Clayton persuaded him to appoint Meredith rather than Binney or Sergeant to the Treasury Department. Taylor offered the postmaster generalship to Tennessee's Meredith Gentry. When he refused to leave the House, Ohio's Ewing was slated for that post instead. Then Taylor learned that the proud Lawrence would not take the navy secretaryship. He had been considering Virginia's William Ballard Preston for attorney general, a post for which Preston lacked adequate legal talent, and when Lawrence declined, he shifted Preston to the naval post. For the attorney generalship he then named Reverdy Johnson, who had eagerly sought it and had resigned his Senate seat in December so that Maryland's Whig governor might appoint his replacement. By the final weekend before his inauguration, therefore, Taylor had performed a minor miracle. By picking four

Southerners and only two Northerners, he had failed to balance the six cabinets posts evenly between the two sections, and his cabinet would have no representative from New England, the staunchest Whig region in the country.[82]

Seasoned party professionals attributed this fiasco to Taylor's naiveté, his susceptibility to the malign machinations of Crittenden and Clayton, and pressure from the South. Virtually no Whig politician in Washington had ever laid eyes on the new president, and they were understandably as curious about the man himself as about his cabinet selections. Almost uniformly they came away with impressions of a guileless political infant. "Genl. Taylor means well, but he knows little of public affairs & less of public men," reported Webster. Seward described Taylor as "the most gentle-looking and amiable of men," but he and Fillmore were both furious that Taylor had committed himself on the cabinet before they reached Washington. "Of course Mr. Crittenden advised all this," ranted Seward, "and of course his advice was at once honest, misconceived, and erroneous. General Taylor relied on it implicitly." On March 1, Seward sent his wife an even more revealing evaluation of Taylor: "He is a sensible and sagacious man, but *uninformed about men*, and will fail to obtain a Cabinet politically strong. It remains to be seen how far honesty and the very purest and exalted patriotism will cover the defect of political sagacity."[83]

Even as Seward penned that letter, the opportunity emerged to repair some of Taylor's damage by assuaging New Englanders' outrage. At the end of the session, Congress created a new Home Department (later renamed the Department of the Interior), so Taylor had a seventh post to fill. New Englanders assumed it would be theirs, and Webster immediately pressed for the appointment of his Maine friend Evans, whom he vigorously defended from the charges of habitual drunkenness. Seward and Fillmore, with the concurrence of Weed, urged Taylor instead to name Truman Smith. They knew that Smith would decline in order to protect his Senate seat, but New England's honor would be mollified. Seward would have preferred that the post then be given to Caleb Smith, but because he knew that Southerners opposed Smith, he hoped that Truman Smith could select a New Englander for the post. Even this opportunity went awry. Taylor did offer Truman Smith the position, but when he declined, Taylor shifted Ewing from the postmaster generalship to the Home Department. As New England's representative, he then appointed Vermont's Jacob Collamer postmaster general. Whether Truman Smith recommended Collamer is unclear, but within days of his appointment the acerbic Vermonter had already offended dozens of office seekers. As a consolation prize for Evans and Caleb Smith, Taylor then appointed both to the new Mexican Claims Commission that would pay off claims by private American citizens against the Mexican government.[84]

V

"The cloud is already rising," an alarmed Tennessean reported home as early as March 12. "I find many are not pleased with Taylor's Cabinet." Dissatisfaction was in fact widespread. North Carolina's Whigs were "indignant" that Democratic Virginia had "a place in the Cabinet to the exclusion of North Carolina." Indianans and other midwestern Whigs angrily protested Ewing's appointment over

Caleb Smith, and the South Bend editor Schuyler Colfax ridiculed the other Northerners, Meredith and Collamer, as weak nonentities. Miffed that his friend Evans had been denied a post, Webster groused that the "construction [of the cabinet] has been botched." Ominously, Clay also complained that all the appointments had gone to "the Taylor men to the exclusion of friends of other candidates." Even Georgia's Whigs, who had twice elected George Crawford governor, worried that his scandalous private life might embarrass the administration. As one later scolded, "The appointment by Mr. Crawford of that man Anderson as his Chief Clerk has met with almost universal reprobation and has subjected Mr. Crawford's private life to scrutiny which cannot but be unpleasant to a gentleman so *extremely sensitive* as he is & has given birth to the foulest conjectures." Horace Greeley, who in early 1849 happily "concede[d] all the places to the originals," rendered a crushing verdict on the whole administration a year later.

> Old Zack is a good old soul, but don't know himself from a side of sole-leather in the way of statesmanship; while his whole cabinet is a horrid mixture, just such as a blind man (or one blind folded) would probably have picked up, if turned in among three or four hundred would be magnates of the Whig party and ordered to touch and take. Clayton is a drunkard, Preston a weak country lawyer, Meredith a good commercial lawyer, but no politician at all, Reverdy Johnson a good lawyer and a bad politician (which is better than none at all)[,] Jake Collamer an upright, attentive, faithful man of business, but a little too conceited to be popular; Ewing an able man and well informed politician, but overbearing and selfish. Such is the Cabinet.[85]

Even though the last-minute changes in personnel appeared slapdash, and even though criticism of the cabinet increased steadily during 1849, Greeley's sour verdict was unfair. The cabinet possessed men of talent, and Taylor, despite his palpable political inexperience, had pursued definite goals in constructing it. Even Ewing's detractors admitted that he was a forceful and seasoned politician, and Truman Smith, among others, expected him to lead the cabinet. One of the few people in Washington acquainted with the obscure Meredith, Webster praised him as "a man of first-rate talent, tho' little experience in politics," and the Pennsylvanian quickly emerged as one of the administration's pillars. Similarly, Seward, an able lawyer himself, applauded the appointment of Johnson because of his immense legal ability. Despite his character flaws and self-doubts, Clayton would labor steadfastly to forward the president's agenda. And even though Crawford had no military background, he had displayed considerable administrative ability as Georgia's governor.[86]

Fair-minded Whigs should also have noted that Taylor acted carefully not to weaken the ranks of elected Whig officeholders, and that constraint limited his choices. Ewing, Crawford, and Meredith held no state or national office in 1849. Collamer had not run for reelection in 1848, and his Vermont constituents had already replaced him with another Whig for the Thirty-First Congress. His selection did far less damage to the party's congressional wing than Winthrop's or Truman Smith's would have done. Both Clayton and Johnson had time remaining in their Senate terms, but both resigned early to allow Whigs in Delaware and

Maryland to elect or appoint Whig replacements. Only with the choice of Virginia's Preston did Taylor risk the loss of a Whig congressional seat, but the party had won 57 percent of the House seats filled in 1848, and its chances of retaining control seemed good even with the probable loss of Preston's seat in 1849.[87] When Taylor later picked sitting congressmen to serve in the executive branch, moreover, he chose men like Indiana's Caleb Smith, North Carolina's Daniel M. Barringer, and Georgia's Thomas Butler King, who appeared to represent secure Whig districts that the party might carry even without those individuals. In many respects, Taylor was in over his head, but far from acting blindly, he showed a solicitous concern for the welfare of the party's congressional wing.

More important, Taylor carefully selected men who might help him settle the divisive territorial question without having to confront the Wilmot Proviso. Aware that the accelerating gold rush to California in early 1849 made the establishment of civil authority there imperative, Taylor scorned Southerners' insistence that slavery be allowed in part or all of the Mexican Cession as an economically unrealistic demand that would block creation of territorial governments. During the week before his inauguration, Taylor also directed Clayton, Ewing, and Senator-elect Seward to lobby congressmen to kill the Democratic effort to abrogate the Mexican prohibition of slavery in the Cession. Its repeal, he realized, would only increase northern opposition to any organization of government without a congressional ban on slavery. As his course in office quickly revealed, Taylor favored immediate statehood for California and New Mexico as the best way to secure civilian government, bypass the territorial stage, and thus avert the possibility that Congress might bar slavery from the area. If Mexican law continued in force until state constitutions were written, he understood, those new states would probably be free, but he counted on that likelihood to induce Northerners to drop their demand for congressional prohibition. That slavery would not be allowed to expand bothered him not at all. As a cotton planter himself, he may have recognized that plenty of land remained within the existing slave states to sustain the southern economy. Certainly, he shared the belief of most southern Whigs and many southern Democrats that slavery could not flourish in the Cession and that therefore only symbolic rights were at stake. Immediate statehood would spare the South the insult of congressional prohibition while giving the North what it wanted—the prevention of slavery's expansion.[88]

Clayton and Preston obviously agreed with this plan; Johnson, from the border state of Maryland, might be expected to go along with it; and Crawford had been recommended by Stephens and Toombs, who had enthusiastically endorsed the Preston bill. The Northerners in the cabinet were less committed to enactment of the Wilmot Proviso than the men from that section whom Taylor rejected. Ewing and Meredith, obviously, had never cast votes in Congress in its favor. Collamer had, but Taylor agreed to appoint him only at the last moment in an attempt to assuage angry New England Whigs.[89] With the exception of Collamer, in short, Taylor tried to pick moderates from both sections, men whom he expected to support a compromise solution to the sectional question that might bar slavery from the Mexican Cession but without the insulting Wilmot Proviso.

Nonetheless, if Taylor's choices showed him to be canny and broad-minded in some ways, they also revealed that he was peevishly narrow-minded in others. Taylor's biggest mistake was ruthlessly excluding friends of Clay, Webster, and

McLean in favor of men who might support his intention of running a No Party administration that could reach out to nativists and Democrats.[90] As non-Taylorites had feared, the cabinet was largely confined to original Taylor men. North Carolina's Whigs might protest the injustice of appointing a Virginian rather than someone from that loyal Whig bastion, but Taylor vindictively never considered choosing a North Carolinian since the state's Whig convention in February 1848 had refused to endorse his nomination. Virginia's state convention, in contrast, had nominated Taylor, and Preston was one of the original Young Indians who wanted to resurrect the old Jeffersonian Republican party. Georgia's Whigs, too, had nominated Taylor, and Crawford, one of Taylor's biggest blunders, was the choice of Stephens and Toombs. Johnson had worked both before and during the national convention to commit Maryland's Whigs to Taylor, and he was the known foe of that state's Clay Whigs, who were led by James Pearce. Ewing had endeavored to line up Ohio for Taylor, while Meredith was advanced by the same men who had arranged the Buena Vista celebration in Philadelphia, men who shared Taylor's goal of merging Native Americans with Whigs in a new party. With the exception of Horace Binney, even the men whom Taylor approached but who subsequently declined appointments—Crittenden, Lawrence, Truman Smith, and Meredith Gentry—had been enthusiastic proponents of Taylor's nomination. Clayton had been a contender himself at the convention, but more as Delaware's favorite son than as a serious rival. Besides, he was Crittenden's man, and manifestly Clayton wanted to replace the Whigs with a new party. Only Collamer was not known as a Taylor man or a new party proponent, but he had the negative virtue of not being Webster's choice as the cabinet's New Englander.

Regular Whigs who had opposed Taylor's nomination as an abandonment of Whig principles could and did complain about the selfish narrowness of Taylor's criteria for selecting his cabinet. The point is that he had criteria. He had not acted blindly. Greeley's savage indictment of Taylor and his cabinet should be seen for what it was—a reflection of the anger he and other regular Whigs felt about the agenda Taylor brought with him to the White House.

From the moment Taylor had first been mentioned as a possible Whig nominee, he had insisted that traditional Whig policies must be shelved and that he would run a nonpartisan, rather than an exclusively Whig, administration in order to build a party of Whigs, Natives, and Democrats. His carefully crafted cabinet demonstrated that he intended to do just that. And just as savvy Whig politicos like Seward and Truman Smith predicted, this delusionary scheme and the cabinet Taylor chose to implement it would have calamitous consequences for the Whig party.

Chapter 13

"Patronage Is a Dangerous Element of Power"

"IF WE CANNOT RALLY a new party—composed of the elements which brought Taylor into power," John M. Clayton warned John J. Crittenden six weeks before Zachary Taylor's inauguration, "we shall be beaten under the old name of Whig this year." To avert that calamity, Taylor must reaffirm his intention to run an all-parties or No Party, rather than exclusively Whig, administration in his inaugural address. If he did, "thousands will join in who never voted with us before." All the Whigs whom Clayton spoke with in Washington concurred in his plan for "some demonstration on the Republican basis."[1]

Here Clayton, one of its chief architects, outlined the central agenda of Taylor's presidency, a term that can best be understood in two phases. During the nine months between his inauguration and the meeting of Congress in December 1849, the sixty-four-year-old president and his men attempted to transform the Whig party into a broader and more inclusive organization. Based on loyalty to Taylor himself, patriotism inspired by Taylor's heroics in Mexico, and a self-conscious dedication to republican principles, this new organization was to be called the Taylor Republican or Republican party. It would abandon what Taylorites deprecated as ultra Whiggery, seek middle ground on issues that had traditionally divided Whigs from Democrats and North from South, and carefully distribute government jobs to non-Whigs, not just Whig regulars.

From its inception, this foolish and utopian initiative provoked angry resistance from most Whigs. The administration's inept patronage policies bitterly divided Whigs against each other and contributed to a truly dismal performance in the crucial state and congressional elections of 1849, thereby neutralizing the solid successes of 1848. By the time Congress assembled in December, the new party initiative had utterly failed, thereby jeopardizing the administration's far more sensible policy proposals. For the remainder of his presidency, therefore, Taylor and the Whig party suffered the consequences of this abortive, fractious, and misguided foray into party building. Since it both exacerbated intraparty divisions and propelled the diminution of interparty differences, the party itself never fully recovered from Zachary Taylor's first nine months in the White House.

I

Only the most perceptive political observer could have discerned Taylor's intentions from the exceptionally brief and bafflingly vague inaugural address he mumbled to the throng gathered before the Capitol on March 5, 1849. Without mentioning Whiggery, he reiterated the Allison Letter's Whiggish principles—his commitment to a nonbelligerent, noninterventionist foreign policy and his willingness to let Congress formulate domestic economic policy. Significantly, in light of Congress' previous inability to settle the divisive slavery extension question, he also asserted Congress' responsibility "to adopt such measures of conciliation as may harmonize conflicting interests and tend to perpetuate [the] Union." Taylor, in short, implied that he had no plans of his own for the Mexican Cession, leaving Northerners and Southerners to speculate how he might react to passage of the Wilmot Proviso.

Contrary to Clayton's hopes, Taylor did not explicitly promise not to be a party president in order to gather his diverse supporters into a new coalition. He suggested his hostility to partisan strife, however, by pledging to emulate George Washington, the original national hero who stood above party, and to base his actions on "those great republican doctrines which constitute the strength of our national existence." Much more clearly than such platitudes, the administration's actions during its first months in office demonstrated how Taylor's aims threatened the very existence of the Whig party.[2]

By the end of March, Taylor moved to replace the staid and orthodox Washington *National Intelligencer*, the major Whig paper in the capital since the founding of the party and a frequent mouthpiece for Clay and Webster, with a new sheet to serve as "the *organ*" of the administration. When cabinet members protested the establishment of this rival influence with the president, Taylor insisted in "very decided . . . language" that it be done. Owned by Albert T. Burnley and co-edited by Alexander C. Bullitt, formerly an editor of the New Orleans *Picayune*, and John O. Sargent, who had written for James Watson Webb's pro-Taylor New York *Courier and Enquirer*, the Washington *Republic* began publication on June 1. Describing the paper's editorial thrust to Crittenden in July, Burnley disdained the economic issues that other Whigs believed had secured key northern states for Taylor in 1848. The administration's success, he argued, depended upon "discarding the old Hunker Whig politicians & the stale, chronic, & unpopular doctrines of *ultra* Whiggery." It would be insane to contend for a new national bank, "for a high protective tariff—for a splendid system of internal improvements—for a distribution of the proceeds of the public lands, etc., etc., etc." Instead, the new Taylor party should seek to *"improve"* but *"not repeal,* the Subtreasury, *improve* [but] not repeal the Tariff of 1846," recommend minimal internal improvements, and use revenue from land sales to pay off the national debt. Such a course, he dreamed, would *"popularize* conservative Whig doctrines" and reaggregate the old Republican party behind Taylor.[3]

Whatever Burnley's and Taylor's policy preferences were, until Congress met in December they drew far less public attention and provoked far less controversy among Whigs than did the distribution of patronage, a task that preoccupied Taylor and his advisors from the moment they took office. Dividing the spoils has been a headache for virtually every incoming presidential administration in

American history, if only because many more people sought offices than there were offices to give. Under Taylor, however, the process proved exceptionally painful and pernicious.

One can easily get the impression from surviving letters that patronage was the only thing politicians, be they small-fry politicos on the periphery or eminent leaders at the center of public affairs, cared about and that the life and death of political parties depended on how offices were allocated. That obsession seems puzzling since only a tiny fraction of the Whig, let alone the national, adult male electorate could hold or would even seek the approximately 18,000 jobs available from the national government. One might well ask, therefore, why both the seekers and dispensers of patronage considered it so important.

One reason is that government jobs paid very well compared to other occupations available in the American economy, particularly an economy still in recession at the end of 1848. At a time when laborers made a dollar a day on the days they could find work and when most skilled artisans' annual income averaged less than $600, government salaries seemed generous indeed.[4] The consulship at Glasgow was said to be worth $7,000 to $8,000 yearly and that at Liverpool even more. Customs collectors in large ports could earn even more, and the naval officer in Philadelphia, New York, or Boston was paid $5,000 annually. Through the assessment of fees and fines, United States marshals could earn $10,000 to $15,000 a year. Government clerks in Washington earned $1,000 or $2,000 annually. Postmasterships in large cities paid $3,000, and even third- and fourth-class postmasters in small towns earned $1,000 a year. Those positions were worth far more to newspaper editors who particularly clamored for them than the salary alone, however. Postmasters had a franking privilege that allowed editors to mail their papers to subscribers free of charge. Moreover, they could charge the government to print contract lettings for mail carriers or lists of letters received since any newspaperman who served as postmaster would give printing contracts to himself. The prospect of high pay, in sum, largely accounts for the rush of office seekers.[5]

Several sitting Whig congressmen coveted foreign missions or lucrative consulships, but most elected Whig officeholders sought federal jobs for their relatives and political friends, not for themselves. They valued patronage for the edge it gave them over intraparty rivals, not for the high salaries. Success in winning positions for friends could enhance leaders' prestige among local party activists and wean the allegiance of job seekers away from factional foes. Failure to land jobs for supporters could drive them into the arms of a rival. Seward, for example, warned Weed that their wing of the New York party would suffer if he could not secure appointments for the hundreds of men who looked to him for influence with the administration. Conversely, friends of Fillmore despaired that Seward's apparent ability to "dictate" New York appointments allowed Sewardites to boast "that their chief is in the ascendant." Pennsylvania's Governor William F. Johnston also recognized that he could raid the Cooper camp by brokering the state's federal patronage. Thus he urged Treasury Secretary Meredith to find jobs for two prominent Cooper supporters in order to "secure the *active* friendship of these gentlemen, both worth detaching from their present alliances."[6]

To politicians who held or aspired to elective office, "*active* friendship" meant help in securing or retaining it. Patronage was the currency politicians dealt in, and the more one amassed, the better one's chances of controlling the party's organizational apparatus that nominated candidates for elective offices. Men who owed government jobs and contracts to a particular patron were expected to repay him with undeviating loyalty, friendly newspaper editorials, campaign contributions, and especially faithful support at local, district, and state conventions. Every federal appointee could render such service, but those who hired subordinates like customs collectors or the superintendents of navy yards were deemed particularly valuable. Voting the right way at, and bringing friends who would vote the right way to, nominating conventions was a condition of employment in these subordinate posts. The more hired hands a politician had in his pocket, the easier it was to pack conventions.

Important as naval officers, postmasters, and customs collectors were to an efficient machine, however, in 1849 Whigs knew that a different federal post had even greater organizational potential since its incumbent could influence a wider geographical area than a single city or congressional district. This was the position of United States marshal, for in 1850 a new federal census was to be taken. That year each marshal would appoint a deputy for every county in his district, and those deputies would hire assistants who would presumably visit—and could proselytize—every voter in the county. At government expense, through the marshals and their deputies, a politician could build a grass-roots organization unrivaled by anything an opponent could contrive. Thus one of Johnston's lieutenants frantically opposed naming a Cooper ally marshal for the Eastern District of Pennsylvania: "The appointment of Deputies to take the Census, will give him the opportunity to raise a party, which will be deeply injurious to the Whig party of this State." Thus Fillmore's friends warned that if Sewardite Palmer V. Kellogg was named marshal for New York's Northern District, "every county in the district will have a deputy to take the canvass thoroughly committed to do Seward's bidding." Kellogg had announced, shrieked another Fillmorite, that he would hire as deputies only men pledged to wage "war to *the knife against you and all your friends*."[7]

The palpable advantages of government jobs to office seekers and Whig politicos, however, hardly explain the widely reported interest that rank-and-file Whigs, who neither sought nor expected jobs themselves, took in their allocation. Popular fascination can be understood in two ways. Men voted Whig in 1848 to change the direction of the national government, and their faith in the responsiveness of the political system, in the efficacy of self-government, required concrete evidence that changes would be made. For most of 1849, however, Taylor's administration concealed its policies for the Mexican Cession and tariff revision from the public. Until December, therefore, changing the personnel of government constituted the only tangible proof that Whigs had accomplished anything by defeating the Democrats.

For most Americans, who never traveled to Washington, local federal officeholders personified the national government. Thus it mattered greatly to Whigs that Democrats be turned out of local post offices and customs houses and good Whigs put in their place. To Whigs at the grass-roots level, only such changes proved the power of the popular will. If ex-Governor James Jones "were appointed to office," one Tennessean reported, "the people would feel more like it was given to them than the appointment of any other man in our State." Whigs had not voted in November simply "to elect a Whig President," argued astute Whigs from Connecticut and New York. "They desired that result, certainly, but chiefly as a means to a greater end"—"to remove [Democrats] & place a better class in their stead." "The people here desire and expect a change," a Pennsylvania Whig congressman complained a month after Taylor's inauguration, "and a refusal to make a change would reduce the Whig party here to a corporal's guard."[8]

More powered such demands than simply a desire to throw the rascals out or to reaffirm republican self-government. Since at least 1840, the dynamic of interparty combat itself, just as much as the programmatic substance of that combat, had activated the competitive instincts of Whigs and Democrats alike. Prior to December 1849, when patronage distribution served as a surrogate for interparty conflict over issues in Washington, Whig voters insisted that Democratic heads roll in order to keep up their élan, to allow them to boast and brag over their fallen foe. They took the same vicarious satisfaction in the decapitation of some hapless Democratic officeholder as they did in watching a Whig spokesman best a Democratic orator during a joint debate on the stump. What mattered to committed partisans was victory over the archrival, no matter what the context of that triumph, and for most of 1849 filling government jobs was the context that attracted attention. The administration must move on appointments with more "*rapidity* or *resolution*," Crittenden chided Clayton in July. Even a wise decision, if slowly made, would produce "no *impression* or *excitement*" among the rank and file. Any sign that Taylor's administration hesitated or refused to remove Democrats, therefore, demoralized the Whig faithful. Consequently, as the perception of such timidity and apparent treachery spread during 1849, increasingly strident alarms about apathy, disillusionment, and anger among Whig troops sounded. "Many—very many, of our hardest working rank & file Whigs feel discouraged," moaned a Michigan Whig on the eve of the state election. "They say it is no use to succeed for if we do Locofocos will be retained in office."[9]

Patronage allocation, in short, profoundly affected the morale and performance of local activists and Whig voters in elections, especially those occurring before the administration provided a policy platform on which Whigs could campaign. Recognizing that fact and the certainty that patronage could tilt intraparty factional balances, Whig after Whig chorused the warning of Indianapolis editor John Defrees that a "proper distribution of offices" was crucial to "the future prospects of the Whig party." For many Whigs, however, distribution by the Taylor administration proved to be anything but proper. Both the process by which it allotted spoils and the selections it made produced consternation and outrage. By November 1849 most Whigs would agree with the caustic assessment Balie Peyton made of the administration's record. "Patronage is a dangerous element of power," he mourned, "a two-edged sword which cuts both ways."[10]

II

Specific appointments inevitably produced discontent and factional squabbling, but the administration's procedures for handling requests also appalled eager Whigs. One problem was Taylor's perceived noninvolvement in the selection process. Within five days of his inauguration, Seward informed Weed that Taylor cast "all responsibility on the Cabinet," and in the succeeding months the impression spread that Taylor was a mere figurehead who absented himself from personnel decisions Whigs deemed vital. That complaint was inaccurate. Taylor attended many of the cabinet meetings where appointments were discussed, and he demanded the best jobs in Louisiana for his friends Samuel J. Peters and Logan Hunton. Taylor also directed plums to his Kentucky relatives. He gave personal attention to major diplomatic appointments, often overriding Clayton, and to the important federal posts in New York City. In addition, Taylor personally dealt with the requests of his defeated rivals Clay and Webster when they sought jobs for their sons, and he secured the appointment of James B. Clay as chargé d'affairs to Portugal when some cabinet members preferred to let Clay grovel interminably. Most significantly, no evidence exists that the cabinet appointed anyone against Taylor's wishes. As Crittenden correctly inferred from Kentucky, "nothing is done but by his dictation or approbation."[11]

Nonetheless, for good reasons, Taylor delegated unprecedented authority to the cabinet on most appointments. Although fewer than 950 of the approximately 18,000 civilian government jobs were direct presidential appointments, sifting through the thousands of applications for them would have been a physically exhausting task. Moreover, Taylor had successfully delegated authority to subordinate commanders in Mexico, and he was most comfortable with that administrative style. He may also have realized that he could use the cabinet as a buffer against complaints from disappointed applicants by shifting responsibility to them.[12]

Yet while the cabinet bore the brunt of popular criticism, Taylor's hands-off style also drew considerable fire. Office seekers and would-be office brokers who swarmed over Washington protested that since they had elected Taylor, not his cabinet, Taylor personally should judge their claims. His apparent abdication of power, in short, betrayed his campaign vows to represent the people as president. Democratic and even some Whig newspapers charged him with weakness, incompetence, and torpor. Rather than the bold tribune Whigs had promised in 1848, he was stigmatized as an insignificant cipher whom selfish Whig politicos manipulated for ends of their own.[13]

By July 1849, tocsins of alarm that Taylor's apparent remoteness and lassitude "will damn us all inevitably" filled Whigs' correspondence. Taylor, Whigs complained, "has yielded too much power to his cabinet." People considered him "a mere man of straw" who "shrinks from responsibility." Because of "the impression that Taylor is removed behind the curtain so that he can neither be seen or approached," sputtered an aghast Indianan, "surely the Whig party is a doomed party." All complaints would stop if people knew that Taylor himself directed appointments, concluded Orlando Brown, Crittenden's Kentucky lieutenant, who had gone to Washington officially as commissioner of Indian affairs but unofficially to advise Taylor and the cabinet about Crittenden's views on policy and patronage. "Yet if the current is not changed and that speedily—if the President does not come to be considered as an acting principal in politics and not merely as a consenting instrument for others, it will be impossible for us to hold our own." "Old Zack is the Rock on which, politically, you ought to build," Crittenden impatiently instructed Clayton. He must be seen as "the active[,] moving[,] energetic cause of all things."[14]

Criticism of Taylor's passivity reflected dissatisfaction with the cabinet's own procedures. Cabinet members appeared purposely to wall themselves off from the public and other Whig politicians, dictating appointments as a closed corporation. They demanded that all applications go to individual department heads, refused to see applicants outside of official office hours, and insisted on interviewing men in groups of two or three rather than individually. They demanded that each applicant or aspiring patron submit letters of recommendation and then refused to read them. Worst of all, although they insisted that each secretary was responsible for the appointments under his department, they considered all major decisions "as a board" and required unanimous consent of the full cabinet before taking any action. Denouncing these "ridiculous formalities," Brown lamented the popular "dissatisfaction" with "the infernal ceremonious checks & balances in official intercourse with the citizens—with the neglect of letters of recommendation—the disinclination to talk to anybody but each other about measures or appointments." An administration that came to office promising to restore republican self-government, sighed Brown, had done nothing to reassure the public "that the Government is in the hands of its citizens."[15]

Closed-door procedures created frustration, but the cabinet's dispensation of jobs provoked widespread outrage among both disappointed job seekers and those who sought no position. Whigs across the country squawked that the cabinet unfairly favored sitting Whig officeholders and their relatives over "working Whigs," the activists who had put those men in elective office. "Activity, labor, zeal, & association with the masses," Whigs griped, had been subordinated to "elevated standing & family influence." These charges had a solid foundation. Lame-duck and newly elected Whig congressmen who sought and often won jobs from the administration included Illinois' Edward D. Baker and Abraham Lincoln, Indiana's Caleb Smith and Richard W. Thompson, Alabama's John Gayle and Henry Hilliard, Pennsylvania's Moses Hampton, North Carolina's Daniel M. Barringer, and Virginia's John Pendleton.[16]

Flagrant nepotism also characterized the cabinet's allotment of jobs. Thomas Ewing appointed his son, in-laws, and cousins to offices at his disposal. At the request of Clayton, Senators Truman Smith and James Cooper, along with Tom Corwin and Caleb Smith, drew up a slate of territorial officers for Minnesota, and Truman Smith and Cooper padded it with relatives. Thomas C. Perkins, the nominee for United States attorney in Connecticut, was related to the state's other senator, Roger Sherman Baldwin, as was Charles W. Rockwell, designated commissioner of customs in the Treasury Department, to Connecticut Congressman John A. Rockwell. James Johnston, brother of Pennsylvania's ambitious governor, was nominated for the lucrative consulship to Glasgow, and Crittenden's son got the even more valuable post at Liverpool.[17]

Even more than the rank favoritism in some appointments, "the delay, hesitation, & indecision exhibited at Washington" ignited a firestorm of protest against the administration. When the dilatory removal of Democrats did not strike Whigs as inexcusable, it produced suspicion of a malign, counterproductive scheme to "conciliate" Democrats at the expense of Whigs. "Loud, very loud complaints are made of the indisposition to act, & of the perfect noncommittalism of Mr. Meredith," Nathan Sargent reported to Crittenden from Washington. "Nothing, they say, is done, or if anything is done, it is delayed and procrastinated so long, that patience is exhausted and gives place to the most bitter complaints." The "temporizing policies" of the cabinet, warned a New Orleans Whig, have produced "a great deal of dissatisfaction here." Alarmed by the cabinet's snail's pace, Crittenden urged Clayton to "execute with *audacity* even, than with any appearance of hesitation or *slowness*."[18]

Whigs who denounced the cabinet's dallying as early as March or April surely overestimated the speed at which it could act. Still, it did procrastinate in making appointments. Aside from an understandable caution in negotiating the minefield of conflicting claims from hungry Whigs, its very procedures forced delay. By demanding letters of recommendation from most applicants and requiring unanimous consent from the full cabinet, it guaranteed postponement of decisions. In addition, when Senate Democrats in March defeated Taylor's nomination of former Indiana Congressman Edward McGaughey as governor of Minnesota Territory and Indiana Whigs then blamed Taylor for blundering, the chastened Taylor and his men abandoned all thought of fast action and waited to make recess appointments.[19]

The cabinet's exasperating indecision and delay, however, primarily reflected deep internal disagreements and conflicting external advice about how fast Democrats should be axed and what purpose patronage allocation should serve. Interior Secretary Thomas Ewing, the veteran politico whom Whig regulars regarded as the most savvy and sympathetic cabinet member, favored swift and extensive decapitations of Democrats. He appointed Whigs as marshals, U.S. attorneys, Indian agents, and land office personnel far more quickly than William B. Preston, George W. Crawford, Jacob Collamer, William M. Meredith, and Clayton acted on positions at their disposal. Postmaster General Collamer inclined toward a similar policy, but Collamer refused to appoint any postmasters in congressional districts represented by Whigs until the appropriate congressman submitted written recommendations for office seekers. Navy Secretary Preston, in contrast, urged caution in sacking Democrats, as did Secretary of War Crawford, who heeded the advice of his patron, Alexander Stephens, that Democrats from Georgia and other slave states be retained in office at least until after the 1849 state and congressional elections.[20]

The close partners Clayton and Meredith, who owed his post at the Treasury to Clayton, pursued Taylor's new party agenda and were thus at odds with Ewing and Collamer. Nominally responsible for all subordinate Treasury officers in Washington and all customs collectors and subtreasurers across the country, Meredith knew virtually nothing about any Whigs outside Philadelphia. Aside from the Pennsylvania appointments, on which he acted as Governor Johnston's pawn, therefore, Meredith insisted on gathering information on the candidates for those coveted positions before acting. His caution was understandable, admitted Nathan Sargent, but "it has been unfortunate for us." By making business capacity and integrity, rather than partisan Whig activity, his chief criteria for customs collectors, moreover, Meredith repeatedly flouted the recommendations of Whig congressmen, notably Florida's E. C. Cabell, North Carolina's Edward Stanly, and Georgia's Senator William C. Dawson. Yet Meredith's hesitation to appoint Whigs also reflected his alliance with Secretary of State Clayton. As Whigs who knew him repeatedly reported, Clayton wanted to use federal jobs "to build up a Taylor party, distinct from, independent of, and superior to the Whig party."[21]

To achieve that goal, Clayton insisted upon honoring job requests from Native Americans, Democrats, and nonpartisan independents who claimed to have supported Taylor, at the expense of Whig contenders for those positions. He also urged retention of all Democratic appointees whose commissions had not yet expired. Clayton's designs infuriated orthodox Whigs who had fought Taylor's nomination as a No Party man and who demanded instant execution of Democrats. "Every day's delay in [removing Democrats] is disastrous," protested one. "A *no party* 'conciliating' course toward the locos will sour our friends and gain strength no where," echoed another. "Any attempt to propitiate Locofocoism proper," the shrewd newspaper reporter James Harvey told Clayton, "will be attended with just as much success as an attempt to propitiate a hungry anaconda." Only massive decapitation of remaining Democrats could save the party. "Any other policy would be suicidal."[22]

A significant minority of party leaders, however, urged the opposite course. For some, retaining Democrats in office fulfilled "those admirable principles of moderation" and nonpartisanship on which, they believed, Taylor had been elected. Most, however, were motivated by less altruistic calculations of partisan advantage. Crittenden, who urged the retention of the Democratic marshal and U.S. attorney in Kentucky, and Stephens, who ordered Crawford to have Collamer retain all Democratic postmasters in Georgia, genuinely believed that such restraint would keep Taylor Democrats in the Whig column for the important congressional and state elections of 1849. Thomas B. Stevenson, the Cincinnati Whig editor, scorned Crittenden's policy of "*Conciliating the Democrats,*" but he understood its rationale. "He thinks patronage will gain accessions to the party."[23]

Most Whig advocates of leniency, who included many 1849 congressional candidates, however, sought temporarily to anesthetize Democratic voters, not win them over permanently to a new Taylor party. They recognized that Democrats, like Whigs, watched patronage decisions closely and that removals could incite vengeful Democrats to come to the polls to retaliate against Whig candidates. Whig politicos from safe party strongholds might demand Democratic blood with impunity, but those from Democratic areas depended less on mobilizing Whigs to win elections than on low Democratic turnout. Warning that anything that aroused the Democratic majority to vote would doom Whig chances in 1849, an Indiana Whig therefore advised a passive course by which "the State will be kept still. That is what we want—until the new administration can organize and show off." Since Taylor's administration could show nothing but its appointments until December, Whigs from Georgia, Mississippi, Indiana, Alabama, Tennessee, Virginia, and North Carolina urged against removals until after their 1849 elections were over.[24]

For every letter to the administration prophesying Whig defeat unless Democrats were purged, in sum, another contended that hasty, wholesale removals guaranteed Democratic victory. To the cabinet, however, one Whig's opinion outweighed all others in setting their patronage policies. And Zachary Taylor fully intended to carry out his preelection promise to reward Whigs, Democrats, and Natives equally. In a silly attempt to court Democrats, for example, Taylor made no effort in March to reverse several of Polk's last-minute Democratic diplomatic appointments, including several Virginians and the notoriously partisan Indiana Senator Edward Hannegan. Democrats dominated both states, and both had pending congressional elections in 1849. Still, regular Whigs from both vehemently protested against this self-defeating appeasement.[25]

More dramatically, the few nominations for domestic posts sent to the Senate in March indicated that the partisan complexion of states would often determine the party identity of their appointees. In an exception to the cabinet's sluggish pace, it quickly nominated customs collectors, customs surveyors, postmasters, naval officers, and U.S. attorneys for the six New England states, but especially the three with spring elections—New Hampshire, Connecticut, and Rhode Island—as well as Virginia, another state that voted in the spring. Probably because of the Vermonter Collamer's influence, the New England posts, even in Democratic Maine and New Hampshire, went without exception to orthodox Whig regulars in an attempt to arouse the Whig faithful. In New Haven, Connecticut, for example, a Whig was appointed customs collector despite petitions from that city's merchants to retain the honest and efficient Democratic incumbent.[26]

In sharp contrast to the New England pattern, the cabinet blatantly courted Virginia's Democrats. Aside from retaining Democratic Virginians in the foreign service, it boldly reappointed four Democrats in the Old Dominion itself to new terms, including Richmond's postmaster and the naval agent at the large Norfolk navy yard. No other Virginia appointments were announced in March, but for the remainder of 1849 Virginia's Democratic postmasters, customs collectors, both U.S. marshals and both U.S. attorneys, and over sixty clerks in Washington retained their jobs. The purpose of what was immediately dubbed the "Virginia policy" was clear to all. Taylor hoped to win Democratic support for Whig candidates or at least to keep Democratic voters away from the polls at the May state and congressional elections.[27]

Sweeping Democratic victories in Virginia convinced most Whigs that the administration's "patent medicine" of appeasement had "been spurned alike by friend and foe." Nonetheless, for the remainder of the year the cabinet retained Democratic postmasters, marshals, attorneys, and customs collectors in North Carolina, Georgia, Alabama, Mississippi, Tennessee, and Kentucky in the foolish hope of helping Whig candidates. "Unless the policy of the Administration is changed & speedily & a new spirit infused into the party," James Harvey bluntly warned Ewing in May after traveling from Virginia to Georgia, "our fate in the Old Dominion will extend over the eight [other] Southern States" in the 1849 elections, and "we shall be a minority in the House." "Working & energetic" Whigs, furious that they had "been discarded" to conciliate "the common enemy," others echoed, were paralyzed by unprecedented "apathy," while "the Locos are in high spirits believing they are safe." Democratic officeholders were indeed smugly complacent. "I have not the most distant idea, that I would be removed," the Democratic U.S. attorney in Alabama informed the Whig lawyer who sought his place. Whigs demoralized by such arrogance, Whig congressmen repeatedly told cabinet members, would not lift a finger in the 1849 contests. Castigating the Virginia policy as "weak & deeply pernicious," Willie P. Mangum instructed Meredith "that you *must* act in *advance* of the elections or lose much."[28]

Much more than disgruntlement over job allocation produced the predicted Whig defeats across the South in the August, October, and November elections. Nonetheless, many furious Whigs attributed their rout to the cabinet's imbecilic patronage policy. From Tennessee, Kentucky, North Carolina, and other slave states came howls that the coddling of Democrats "has almost broken us down." And even where some Democrats were removed, Whigs complained that the administration had "done enough to exasperate our enemies, but not enough to satisfy our friends."[29]

III

In addition to sapping local Whig activists' zest for electoral combat against Democrats, the administration's bungling dispensation of jobs bitterly pitted Whig against Whig. Most of the squawking about retention of Democrats came from orthodox Whigs who had opposed Taylor's nomination, and they found the Whigs who did win positions no more palatable. From the start it was clear that original Taylorites would be favored at their expense. Yet even Taylorites exploded at some of the cabinet's missteps. Crittenden disliked the Kentucky appointments, and by the fall Truman Smith had labeled the cabinet "*incompetent . . . in a political point of view.*" Clayton's diplomatic appointments particularly infuriated southern Taylorites, and his wavering, duplicitous course made him one of the administration's two most loathed figures. Even Bullitt openly vilified him in the Washington *Republic*.[30]

Clayton and Taylor quickly decided to give the French mission to Virginia, and Clayton promised it to Congressman John S. Pendleton, one of the original Young Indians. Then Clayton changed his mind and offered the post instead to William C. Rives. Having already served as minister to France under Jackson, Rives had excellent credentials for the post. But the betrayed Pendleton blamed this humiliating insult for his defeat in the 1849 congressional election.[31]

North Carolina's Whigs, in turn, fumed that Virginia received both a cabinet seat and a foreign mission before they got anything. To appease them, Clayton allotted the Spanish mission to that state. Eager contenders mushroomed among North Carolina's Taylorites: Congressman Daniel M. Barringer, who had promoted himself for months; Senator George Badger's kinsman Edward Stanly; and B. M. Edney, Congressman Thomas Clingman's favorite. Meanwhile, Senator Willie P. Mangum, a strong proponent of Clay's nomination in 1848, pushed Hugh Waddell. Fearful of alienating any of these applicants or their powerful sponsors, the hapless Clayton offered the mission to ex-Governor William A. Graham, a Clay Whig who had not sought it. Yet Graham also personified the Raleigh Clique, whereas Clingman had specifically warned Clayton not to appoint anyone from Orange or Wake counties. Only after furious Whigs from eastern and western North Carolina forced Graham to decline did Clayton give the mission to Barringer, but by then he had earned the enmity of Clingman, Edney, Stanly, Mangum, and Badger.[32]

Clayton also rebuffed other southern Whigs. Alabama Congressman Henry Hilliard never got the foreign mission he coveted. Regional and factional jealousies frustrated the bid of Tennessee's Gustavus A. Henry for a consulship. By July both Clay Whigs and Taylorites in the South execrated Clayton.[33]

Whatever Clayton's blunders—and he insisted that Taylor personally chose every diplomat—every important foreign post, with the exception of Hannegan's retention as minister to Prussia, went to an original Taylor man. Abbott Lawrence got the prestigious mission to England, Rives to France, Barringer to Spain, Robert Letcher to Mexico, and Balie Peyton to Chili. Edward Kent, the Maine Whig who first nominated Taylor at the 1848 convention, won the attractive consulship to Rio de Janeiro. James Watson Webb, who had boomed Taylor in his editorial columns since 1847, was eventually dispatched to Austria, and Crittenden's son went to Liverpool as consul. A few friends of Clay, Webster, Fillmore, and other regulars did secure foreign assignments, but they were a distinct minority. The choicest plums went to Taylor men.[34]

The allotment of domestic jobs tilted still more steeply in favor of Taylorites and against regulars, thereby aggravating intraparty factionalism in many states and infuriating still more Whig congressmen who would ultimately be asked to enact Taylor's policy recommendations. No Whigs were more prominent or more alienated from the administration than those symbols of orthodox or ultra Whiggery, Clay and Webster, both of whom angrily protested their victimization at its hands. "The public patronage has been too exclusively confined to the original supporters of Genl. Taylor," Clay repeatedly complained. So blatant was the discrimination that Crittenden urged Clayton to appoint some recognized Clay men to counteract the "impression" that "all who were friendly to Mr. Clay are proscribed by the Administration." Only after that imprecation and after pressure from Taylor himself did Clayton send James B. Clay to Lisbon.[35]

Webster suffered even more galling treatment. He managed to secure a naval agency in New York City for his wife's brother, but every major appointment in Massachusetts, except that of his friend Franklin Haven as subtreasurer in Boston, went to an ally of Lawrence, the new minister to England: Charles Hudson as naval officer in Boston; Philip Greely, Jr., as its customs collector; William Hayden as postmaster there; and Frederick Coffin as postmaster in Newburyport. Modern observers bored by, and modern academics contemptuous of, petty squabbles among white male politicians might well ask what difference such choices made. The answer is that these men, all Webster's enemies, later bore responsibility for enforcement of the Fugitive Slave Act in Boston and the rest of Massachusetts.

That obligation was emphatically true of the office that mattered most to Webster in 1849, the U.S. attorneyship. Hoping to secure that post for his financially strapped thirty-six-year-old son Fletcher, Webster quickly discovered that the administration had another man in mind. At the 1848 national convention, Tennessee's Meredith Gentry had promised it to the Massachusetts delegate George Lunt, another Lawrence minion, as a payoff for Lunt's switch from Webster to Taylor on the third ballot. Taylor was determined to honor that bargain. Contemptuous of Lunt's scant legal ability and outraged that Gentry could dictate a Massachusetts appointment, Webster exhausted every avenue to block Lunt. Swallowing his immense pride, he trekked repeatedly to the White House to present Fletcher's case to Taylor. He begged help from Ewing and Clayton. He had Fletcher gather recommendations from the Massachusetts bar. He even persuaded Rufus Choate, perhaps the nation's most prominent attorney, to offer to take the position if Fletcher could not get it.[36]

For his ignominious groveling Webster reaped only humiliation. "This business of Fletcher, I confess, has wounded me," he moaned to Edward Curtis, who in turn beseeched Ewing to spare Webster "from the chagrin & mortification of the entire failure of Fletcher's expectations." Taylor and the cabinet refused to budge. Not only did Lunt become U.S. attorney, but Ewing's promise to give Fletcher the U.S. marshalship in Massachusetts as a consolation prize went unfulfilled. Finally, the administration offered Fletcher the much less prestigious customs surveyorship in Boston, and his pathetically eager snapping at that insignificant bone only punctuated his father's impotence with the administration.[37]

Clay and Webster were the most conspicuous losers in the patronage sweepstakes, but they were hardly the only aggrieved Whigs. In almost every state the appointments engendered discontent and bitter intraparty feuds, thereby eroding party unity. Missouri's Clay Whigs protested that its marshalship went to a Taylorite with no prior connection to the Whig party. Proscription of everyone who had opposed Taylor's nomination by Assistant Postmaster General Fitz Henry Warren, the arbiter of all Iowa jobs, its Whigs fumed, produced "more distraction in the Whig ranks in Iowa" than "*all* other causes." In Illinois, a regional battle raged over the appointment of Chicago's Justin Butterfield, a Clay Whig, or ex-Congressman and Taylorite Abraham Lincoln of downstate Springfield as commissioner of the land office. When Butterfield prevailed, Lincoln's ally Congressman Edwin D. Baker spat that "the administration is gone to the devil."[38]

The primary struggle in the Midwest, however, pitted Whigs west of Ohio against Ewing, the Ohioan who dictated virtually all the region's appointments because it lacked enough Whig senators and representatives to challenge him. Michigan, Wisconsin, Iowa, Illinois, and Indiana Whigs furiously complained about Ewing's blatant nepotism and especially his preference for Ohioans at their own states' expense. Ewing, such Whigs railed with considerable accuracy, made willingness to support his own bid for the party's 1852 presidential nomination his sole criterion for appointment. The Indianans who had hoped to place Caleb Smith in the cabinet were especially livid about their abuse at Ewing's hands. "The people want servants, not masters, at the capital," they raged. I warned that Ewing "would be the curse of the administration" when he was appointed, carped Indianapolis editor John Defrees, "and the sequel goes far to prove that I was right."[39] Chafed beyond endurance, Indiana's Whigs, led by Smith, Defrees, and South Bend editor Schuyler Colfax, enlisted other Whig editors like Chicago's Lisle Smith, Milwaukee's Rufus King, and Cincinnati's Thomas Stevenson in a newspaper campaign to oust Clayton, Ewing, and other targets of Whig anger from the cabinet. Across the Midwest, Whigs demanded a cabinet reshuffle.[40]

IV

While midwestern Whigs united in protest against Ewing, patronage distribution elsewhere exacerbated factional divisions in state Whig parties that had often originated in or antedated fights over the 1848 presidential nomination. In Tennessee, for example, "two irreconcilable parties"—pro-Taylor Whigs, led by Congressman Meredith Gentry and Senator John Bell, and their "bitter enemies," anti-Bell Clay Whigs led by ex-Senator Ephraim H. Foster, ex-Governor James Jones, and incumbent Nashville Congressman Washington Barrow—jousted for the spoils. The Taylorites claimed the juiciest plums, but disaffection on both sides over the allotment of jobs was so great that neutral Whigs blamed the party's losses in the August state and congressional elections on "Faction," which "was our powerful enemy," and on the "indolence, inactivity, and entire indifference" produced by "the disaffection of E. H. Foster & a few others."[41]

Maryland, Pennsylvania, and New York, however, best illuminate the pernicious impact of the divisive battles over patronage. In 1848 Maryland's Clay forces, led by Senator James Pearce, had triumphed over the pro-Taylor "Courthouse Clique" of Senator Reverdy Johnson in picking delegates to the national convention. Johnson's subsequent appointment to the cabinet, therefore, appalled Pearce and his allies, for they correctly foresaw that he would become "the sole dictator of Maryland matters." Using the "board" meetings of the cabinet, Johnson systematically blocked all recommendations by Pearce and directed Maryland's jobs to his own friends, even in Pearce's Eastern Shore bailiwick. "Humiliat[ed] and mortif[ied]," Pearce's "very indignant" allies wailed that he "has been utterly repudiated, if not absolutely insulted by the Cabinet." Because Johnson is "the grand almoner for Maryland" and because "every appointment which I have pressed has been denied," the incensed Pearce himself exploded, "my personal resentment will scarcely allow me to maintain terms of civility with the new cabinet." "The selfishness and incapacity of those who should have been the able and disinterested advisors of the honest old soldier," Pearce warned Crittenden, had rendered the victory in 1848 "worse than barren."[42]

Such anguished howls were common, but the Maryland protests were especially ominous for two reasons. First, just as furious Indiana Whigs solicited allies from other midwestern and eastern states in their campaign to change the cabinet, Maryland's aggrieved Whigs communicated with their counterparts in Kentucky, North Carolina, and Georgia to marshal a larger force against the administration. Second, and more important, Pearce's allies bluntly announced their intention to oppose the administration not just on its appointments but also on its policy recommendations when Congress finally met in December. Because the administration "refuse me any share of their confidence," threatened Pearce, "I am not likely to give [it] any support; except as a sense of duty to the country may compel me to sustain the measures which I approve." Blindly or willfully, that is, the administration had stupidly alienated congressional Whigs upon whose support enactment of its policies depended.[43]

Pennsylvania's main antagonists over the spoils were Governor William F. Johnston and Senator James Cooper, but to many Whigs the continued existence of the Whig party itself, not just the personal triumph of either man, seemed at stake. Johnston had demonstrated his determination to crush old-line Whigs in his draconian allotment of state jobs, especially his appointment of Cornelius Darragh, head of Pittsburgh's Young Whig faction, as state attorney general, since Darragh could appoint an assistant in every county of the state. To prevail in a "fierce & animated competition" between older regulars and ambitious upstarts, Johnston allied himself with Clayton and his Philadelphia lieutenants Edward Joy Morris, Morton McMichael, and William D. Lewis, who sought to cement an alliance with Native Americans in order to build a new Taylor party. To facilitate that goal, Johnston removed Isaac R. Davis, a respected and factionally neutral regular, from the chairmanship of the Whig state central committee and replaced him with McMichael, an ardent advocate of Taylor Republicanism. Insisting that "the great mass of the party will never agree to surrender the name Whig," one regular accurately protested that Johnston, McMichael, and their Washington allies intended "to break down the Whig organization by prostrating the prominent men of the party" and "to raise a new party upon its ruins to be called the *Taylor Republican Party*."[44]

That effort's fate hinged on the allotment of the state's federal jobs, and in the struggle for them Cooper, the champion of the regulars, possessed certain resources. The majority of Pennsylvania's Whig voters and "nearly all the active working Whigs" opposed to the new party scheme backed the senator. Cooper also had powerful friends in Washington, notably Truman Smith. Aware of the escalating feud between Johnston and Cooper and utterly contemptuous of Clayton's plan for a Taylor Republican party, Smith urged Ewing to make sure that Pennsylvania's appointments were divided evenly between the two rival factions. Meredith must not be allowed to decide Pennsylvania's appointments himself, Smith warned. Meredith owed his cabinet seat to Johnston's influence, and the administration required "a much more *impartial judge* of Pennsylvania questions."[45]

Meredith was indeed Johnston's man in Washington, and the governor wasted little time in sending him marching orders. "The appointments" for Pennsylvania "should be so arranged as to counteract the schemes of our personal enemies," he commanded two days after Meredith moved into his Treasury Department office. Cowed by Johnston, Meredith quickly exerted complete control over Pennsylvania's jobs, in part because Ewing, to Truman Smith's and Cooper's dismay, came down decisively on Johnston's side, as did Clayton. Following a policy that the cabinet pursued with equally great consequences in other states, Ewing insisted that the success of the Whig party in Pennsylvania hinged on the success of its gubernatorial administration. Johnston must get everything and Cooper nothing.[46]

Against the combination of Johnston, Meredith, Clayton, and Ewing, Cooper and the regulars he represented had no chance. To review Pennsylvania's appointments is to witness the utterly ruthless exercise of political muscle. In March, Meredith named Charles B. Penrose, a Johnston crony, first assistant secretary of the Treasury, while the cabinet ostentatiously signaled its outreach to nativists by appointing William B. Norris, another Johnston favorite, customs surveyor in Philadelphia. When regular or "Old Hunker" Whigs in Pittsburgh recommended Walter Forward, a former United States senator and cabinet member, for postmaster there, Darragh warned Meredith that "Forward is not and has not been an ardent friend of Governor Johnston, and his appointment would not be gratifying to the Governor's friends here." Their choice was Samuel Roseburg. Roseburg got the job.[47]

So it went until Johnston had swept the board. He ordered Meredith to bury Cooper's choice for marshal in the Eastern District, and Meredith did so. Anthony Roberts, a Johnston ally, got that post, and another Johnston man, Alexander Irwin, became marshal in the Western District. Over the livid protests of the Philadelphia bar, John Ashmead, a Native American whom they regarded as hopelessly unqualified, was named U.S. attorney there. Likewise, that city's postmaster and naval officer were Johnston's friends with strong ties to the nativists. Arrogantly and successfully, Johnston ordered Meredith to get his brother the consulship to Glasgow and E. Joy Morris a post in Sicily.[48]

The most powerful patronage post in Pennsylvania, however, was the Philadelphia customs house since the collector could appoint scores of subordinates. After some delay and in order to consolidate "our strength in the City & County" by cementing the friendship of Native Americans, Meredith appointed William D. Lewis to that coveted position. A Clayton lieutenant who had tried to establish Taylor Republican Associations the previous winter, Lewis promised to satisfy "the various political interests here by the union of which the present Administration was brought into power." Lewis therefore immediately appointed James Wallace, editor of the Philadelphia *Sun*, the city's chief nativist newspaper, as one of his chief subordinates. While on the government payroll, Wallace carried on an editorial war with the Philadelphia *Daily News*, the organ of Charles Gilpin, leader of Philadelphia's regular Whigs, who had stubbornly refused to abandon their existing organization for the new Taylor Republican Association. Gilpin was also the regular Whigs' candidate for mayor of Philadelphia in 1849, and when he lost that election, Gilpin blamed Wallace, Lewis, and the Taylor administration.[49]

It is difficult to imagine and certainly to convey how so few people in so short a time could have so wantonly and unnecessarily antagonized so many. Across the state in 1849 anguished and apoplectic recriminations poured from Whig regulars. Pittsburgh's Whigs, who had no love for Cooper, termed the interference of Cornelius Darragh and Johnston against Walter Forward "a monstrous wrong" and an "insult." Declaring Norris' success in Philadelphia a repudiation of the "measures that we have for the last twenty years been contending," a Mifflin County Whig insisted that "this usurper must be removed or the Whig party is utterly ruined in Penna." Because "the veterans of the Whig party" were uniformly proscribed, complained a Chambersburg Whig, the party was "doomed to a most overwhelming defeat" in October. Unless the administration used its patronage exclusively to sustain the Whig party, deposed state chairman Isaac Davis sputtered, "parties are useless and our efforts farcical, and the Whigs had as well disband and surrender the country at once" to "the locofocos." For the Whig party, *this*, the grudging resignation to give up the ghost, was the true fire bell in the night.[50]

In 1849, however, nothing infuriated Pennsylvania's Whigs so much as the appointment of Lewis as Philadelphia's customs collector. Lewis, they cried, "has never been known until recently as Whig." His preference for Native Americans and "Young Taylor Republican men" over Whigs in Philadelphia "together with the effort to cast away or change the name of *Whig* in this section of Pennsylvania," orthodox Whigs exploded, had produced "a feeling of burning indignation & disgust" that "will prove disastrous and disorganizing for a long period." Whig defeat in October, when Lewis' henchman Wallace opposed the Whig ticket, proved the last straw for old-line Whigs. The Whig vote had plummeted since 1848, they charged, only because Whig activists stood "aloof" once they saw Taylor appointing "a class of politicians who are selfish, insidious, and sinister." The Whig party would never carry Pennsylvania again, snarled Charles Gilpin, until the state leadership abandoned the fruitless courtship of Native Americans, jettisoned the divisive Taylor Republican apparatus, and cooperated with orthodox Whigs.[51]

Shorn of the organizational resources accruing to state and federal patronage, vengeful regulars could still pursue two courses to regain command of the state party from Johnston. First, they could try to control local and state nominating conventions by rallying Whigs against the policies of Johnston and his allies in the Taylor administration. That avenue would not be open, however, until after Taylor or Johnston advanced policies that significant numbers of rank-and-file Whigs disliked. In 1850, 1851, and 1852 they would travel it, but in 1849 an alternative route seemed more direct—carrying the battle over federal appointments to a different arena. Regulars were powerless to stop Taylor's cabinet from making recess appointments, but once Congress met in December, Johnston's henchmen would have to be confirmed by the Senate. "I hope our national Senators will discover the true cause of the contemplated Whig downfall, and at once hurl from their places the agents of treachery and sedition," a defiant regular threatened Ewing in August. Like Maryland's Pearce, James Cooper intended to do exactly that. In the fall he publicly vowed to go to Washington and defeat the confirmation of Lewis, Norris, Irwin, and the rest of Johnston's minions.[52]

V

The widely anticipated struggle between Seward and Fillmore for New York's spoils in 1849 spawned divisive distrust and bitterness that infected the New York Whig party for the remainder of its existence. Whatever promises of cooperation the two men had made at Albany, agreement collapsed as soon as they reached Washington. They bickered over the district attorneys, marshals, subordinate officers in Washington departments, and especially the naval office at New York City, which Fillmore demanded for John Collier, whom Seward despised. Each accused the other of bad faith but, given the pressure on both from their respective allies, a break was inevitable. For New York's rival Whig factions, the symbolism, or "moral effect," of controlling appointments mattered as much as the substantive political power it brought. "Each section of the Whig party is watching with the most intense anxiety for the announcement of the first important nomination," warned one Fillmorite, "as that will be taken as indicating which actor is now the controlling voice in the administration."[53]

If many observers saw the contest as a personal duel between Fillmore and Seward for Taylor's favor, each had help from New York allies. Fillmore primarily sought jobs for a small circle of personal friends: Collier; Jerome Fuller, his chief spokesman in the state legislature; his law partner Solomon G. Haven, whom he promoted for a U.S. attorneyship; Buffalo's ex-Congressman Nathan K. Hall, who sought the Minnesota governorship; and Thomas Foote, editor of his organ, the *Buffalo Commercial Advertiser*, who wanted the mission to Constantinople. Nonetheless, since Clay Whigs outside Fillmore's personal circle shared his jealousy of the Seward and Weed "Regency at Albany," important conservative Whig congressmen like David A. Bokee of Brooklyn, James Brooks and J. Phillips Phoenix of New York, Robert Rose of Ontario County, and Abraham Schermerhorn of Rochester joined Fillmore in lobbying against Seward. Most important, Fillmore allied himself with devious ex-Governor John Young, who had broken with Weed after being denied renomination in 1848, who lusted for the customs collectorship in New York City, and who joined his fellow Binghamton resident

Collier to press their cases in Washington during the first months of the administration. To keep the job-rich posts in New York City out of Seward's hands, they relentlessly portrayed him as an abolitionist fanatic to southern Whig congressmen, southern cabinet members, and Taylor's Louisiana friends like Balie Peyton.[54]

As co-leader with Weed of the state party's majority wing, Seward brought even more powerful influences to bear from New York. "Seward's friends are the strongest and deserve the most favors, but the Vice President should have some," the self-professed neutral Washington Hunt informed Clayton. Most of New York's huge Whig congressional delegation also sided with Seward. It included freshmen who counted on Seward to get the right men appointed in their districts, but also three tough, seasoned veterans who came to Washington frequently that spring and who were ruthlessly determined to crush the Fillmore and Clay conservatives. Of these the most important was Albany's John L. Schoolcraft, a wealthy businessman and Weed's handpicked manager of the machine's patronage interests. Another, Orsamus B. Matteson of Utica, who engineered the Sewardites' first coup by duping Clayton, was particularly contemptuous of Fillmore. Allow him nothing, Matteson urged Seward. "The more you whip him, the better he will like you." The third, Elbridge G. Spaulding, the new Whig congressman from Buffalo, proved pivotal in humiliating Fillmore in his own home town.[55]

Seward also received considerable aid from the conservative bastion of New York City itself. The merchants Simeon Draper, Jr., and Moses Grinnell came to Washington frequently to promote Seward's and Weed's choices for the city's federal jobs. More important, James Watson Webb, one-time editorial champion of the conservatives against the Seward-Weed wing and an original Taylor man, defected to the Sewardite camp because he hungered for a foreign mission and mistakenly believed that "Fillmore has *cheated* me, and is playing for the *succession*." Almost deranged by anger and vindictiveness, Webb constantly derided Fillmore to cabinet members as "weak & false—habitually regardless of the truth," a man who "imagines himself cunning, without the capacity for even that low vice." Therefore Fillmore must be kept "weak in this State," and the cabinet should instead "cultivate Seward."[56]

Above all, Seward had the aid of Weed, the legendary mastermind of the state Whig organization, whom even the blundering Fillmore commended to Taylor for special treatment. In the spring Weed traveled repeatedly to Washington, where he beguiled Taylor and the cabinet with the persuasive skills he had honed in Albany for twenty years. Through Weed, Seward obtained a letter in late March anointing him as spokesman for the state's Whig officers and signed by Governor Hamilton Fish, Lieutenant Governor George W. Patterson, and Comptroller Washington Hunt. "All trouble is at an end," Seward exulted after the letter was read to the cabinet, which was determined to favor incumbent Whig state administrations with the spoils. "This seasonable step has removed all difficulties." Even the seemingly obtuse Fillmore recognized that the letter had sealed his doom.[57]

The divergent personalities and political skills of the two main protagonists, in fact, also shaped the outcome of their joust. Physically, the forty-nine-year-old Fillmore was far more prepossessing than Seward, a year his junior. A handsome figure, with a robust physique, blue eyes, and silver hair, Fillmore looked more dignified than the often disheveled Seward, a short, slight man with reddish hair, shaggy eyebrows, a macaw-like nose, and oversized ears. Fillmore not only looked like a statue, he acted like one. Friend and foe alike regarded him as "bland," stolid, passive, phlegmatic, even cold. He dealt with Taylor and the cabinet in formally polite but inconclusive interviews. In contrast to the stiff Fillmore, Seward, though possessing genuine and wide-ranging intellectual interests, had the instincts of a clubhouse pol. Urbane, witty, energetic, and enthusiastic, fond of brandy and cigars, he exuded warmth and charm. He quickly disarmed critics who were suspicious of his antislavery zeal and befriended all the cabinet members except the pompous and hostile Collamer, whom Seward and Weed partially outflanked by establishing close ties to his assistant, Warren. Seward, who had long been friendly with Colonel Joseph Taylor, also quickly formed a close personal relationship with his brother, the president. Before March ended, it was Seward who attended cabinet meetings rather than Fillmore, and Seward, not Fillmore, who defended the administration in newspaper articles.[58]

Personally and politically, in sum, the balance of power tilted overwhelmingly against Fillmore and his conservative allies, and initially Seward and Weed appeared capable of achieving as thorough a rout as Maryland's Johnson or Pennsylvania's Johnston. Matteson struck the first blow by convincing Clayton to appoint a rabid Sewardite, Palmer V. Kellogg, marshal of the state's Northern District, on the false grounds that he was acceptable to both Fillmore and Seward. Shocked and appalled, Fillmore's Buffalo friends then increased pressure on their hesitant champion to secure the few appointments he had made a priority. "It needs but two or three more appts. like that of Kellogg to shake my faith in your ability to secure what is right," Hall bluntly warned. One by one, nonetheless, Fillmore's favorites were slaughtered. Philip Hone, Weed's candidate, won the New York naval office rather than Collier, who also lost the Treasury Department's solicitorship to Weed's man, John C. Clark. Fitz Henry Warren got the post Fillmore wanted for Jerome Fuller. Sewardite James Lawrence became U.S. attorney for the Northern District instead of Haven. Hall was ruled disqualified for the Minnesota governorship. Foote got a chargeship in New Granada, but not Constantinople, and he had been forced to seek Seward's aid to get even that. Most galling of all, Spaulding, with Seward's aid, won the three main jobs in Buffalo—keeper of the lighthouse, postmaster, and customs collector—for Sewardites, and Fillmore's friends especially regarded the selection of Levi Allen over William Ketchum for the last position as a mortifying defeat.[59]

Other jobs in the state also flowed to Seward and Weed. Both the marshal and the U.S. attorney for the Southern District were their lieutenants. Their allies also won key postmasterships in New York, Albany, Troy, Utica, and Syracuse. Yet Seward never enjoyed the unalloyed success and Fillmore never suffered the unmitigated defeat some historians have attributed to them. Weed's allies, in fact, vociferously protested that too many jobs went to Clay conservatives, if not Fillmore's personal friends, especially in congressional districts represented by conservative Whigs. Darrius Perrin, Rochester's postmaster, was a Fillmorite, and Isaac Platt won Poughkeepsie's postmastership over Weed's opposition. Despite Seward's protests, Fillmore and Bokee secured C. B. Stuart's appointment as engineer of the dry dock at Brooklyn's navy yard, and Stuart could hire scores of subordinates. Most important, Weed and Seward lost all the job-rich posts in New York City except postmaster, which went to William Brady. Hone, the naval officer, was a wealthy patrician, not a partisan activist, and William LeRoy, the naval agent, was Webster's brother-in-law, not Weed's subaltern. Seward and Weed did keep the dangerous Young out of the customs house, but Taylor appointed him subtreasurer in New York and named Hugh Maxwell customs collector. Nominally unaligned with either Weed or Fillmore, Maxwell quickly became Young's virtual puppet. The two would throw the considerable forces they could hire behind Fillmore and the Clay conservatives in a prolonged and increasingly bitter battle with Weed for control of the Whig state organization itself.[60]

Outraged by Seward's interference in the Buffalo appointments, mortified that "my recommendations in my own State and even my own city have been disregarded," stung by the growing criticism of friends, and humiliated that the administration had not sought his advice "as to the policy to be pursued," the normally torpid Fillmore finally stirred himself to wage open warfare against his tormentors. Like Maryland's Pearce and Pennsylvania's Cooper, he and his allies determined to seek rejection of Taylor's nominations by the Senate, a tack that, significantly, required them to seek help from Democratic Senator Daniel S. Dickinson. Once aroused, however, Fillmore refused to wait until Congress met. He and his allies determined to effect "a radical change of state officers" in 1849 by capturing the Whigs' state organization from Weed and the "Regency influences at Albany."[61]

Conservatives launched a two-pronged assault on Weed. A consortium including Fillmore, Fuller, Alex Mann, editor of the Rochester American, Young, John Bush, and James Kidd, a wealthy Albany businessman who bankrolled the operation, tried to buy out Weed's interest in the Albany Evening Journal and convert it into a conservative Whig organ. Failing that, they intended to supplant Weed's paper by starting a rival conservative Whig sheet at Albany. During the summer, Weed offered to sell his paper to Fillmore, Bush, and Kidd. But he was only stalling to delay establishment of the new paper, and negotiations broke down. Weed achieved his immediate tactical goal, however; the conservatives' Albany New York State Register did not begin publication until March 1850, too late to help them in 1849.[62]

That delay mattered, for Fillmore's second line of assault in 1849 was to create, for the first time, a statewide conservative Whig organization that could compete with the Weed-dominated Whig state central committee and "counteract the central dictation at Albany." This new organization was to gain control of the county conventions that chose delegates to the state convention, which, in turn, would select the Whigs' state ticket for 1849. That year every important state office except governor and lieutenant governor was up for election: comptroller, treasurer, auditor, secretary of state, state engineer, attorney general, and a canal commissioner—in short, a majority of the canal board. For conservatives shut out of state and federal patronage jobs, capture of the state convention and control of the party's nominations for elected offices appeared to be their last hope to topple Weed's "regency," and they were determined that "no stone" be "left unturned" to bring about that defeat. If Weed retained control of the party's nominations, conservatives were prepared to resort to one last desperate measure to defeat him. They would cooperate with Hunker Democrats, who seemed likely again to nominate a separate ticket, to defeat Weed's Whig candidates and thereby deprive Weed of the state offices.[63]

Building a rival Whig organization from scratch was easier said than done. Young and Maxwell packed the New York City Whig convention with federal employees hostile to Weed, but the real problem was the rest of the state. The state committee's list of local activists was unavailable to Fillmore and was composed primarily of Weed's henchmen in any event. Fillmore therefore had to identify and facilitate coordination among reliable conservatives in scores of counties across the state who could seize command of local and county conventions. To do so secretly, so that Weed could not infiltrate his organization, was impossible in an age without telephones. In May, Jerome Fuller sent out a circular asking for the names of reliable men "opposed to certain Regency influences at Albany." Clumsily, in July and again in September, Fillmore mailed copies of similar circulars over his own signature from Buffalo, thus opening himself up to the charge, which Seward quickly lodged with the cabinet, that the vice president was trying to split the state party. Frustrated conservatives were nonetheless overjoyed at the chance finally to dethrone Weed. "The organization suggested by you is much needed," approved Kidd from Albany. "I long to see the great Whig party of New York the party of the People and not the instrument of intriguants and Demagogues," chimed a recipient from the Hudson Valley.[64]

Inevitably, Weed's men learned of Fillmore's effort, and Whigs from other states who visited New York that fall were astonished by the openness and ferocity of the factional warfare. Seward carped to Meredith that his subtreasurer, Young, was helping Fillmore "to divide and distract" the state party and sent some of the names Fillmore had gathered as men the cabinet should proscribe from federal jobs. Weed redoubled his exertions to control the state convention. He had Horace Greeley and Seward draw up its platform and address in advance. Convinced that the spread of antislavery sentiment in Whig ranks could "defeat the factionalists of our own party," Seward devoted the bulk of the address to denunciations of slavery and slavery expansion, precisely the emphasis that galled conservatives. While Young and Maxwell commanded their employees to oppose the incumbent state administration, and while Bokee circulated a letter he had pried from Navy Secretary Preston asserting that Taylor's administration wanted the present state officeholders dumped, Weed retaliated by ordering the U.S. marshals and their deputies under his command to bring loyal Sewardite delegates to the Syracuse state convention.[65]

Fillmore's counteroffensive of 1849 was therefore crushed. Weed's forces dominated the convention by a two-to-one margin. It nominated his handpicked ticket for state officers and adopted Seward's antislavery address that conservatives found so offensive. Fillmorites left the convention "disgusted & indignant, whispering threats of disunion," but by September their last-ditch ploy of fusing with Hunker Democrats was no longer available. By finessing their differences over the Wilmot Proviso, the Hunkers and Barnburners managed an uneasy union behind a common ticket for the first time in three years. From Buffalo, Spaulding gloated that Fillmore was now ready "to exhibit *the white flag*," but Weed and Seward knew the party's condition was precarious. Democratic reunification ended divisions they had counted on for victory since 1846. Conservative Whigs could still express dissatisfaction by staying home on election day, and reliable rumors circulated that Young and Maxwell were ordering their minions to sabotage the Whig ticket in New York City. The approaching 1849 state election had the earmarks of a calamity.[66]

VI

From its inception, the Taylor administration had shaped its patronage decisions with an eye toward the 1849 state and congressional elections. That year's election cycle also profoundly influenced the policies that the administration prepared to recommend to the new Congress in December. Patronage allocation constituted only one part of the attempt to transform the Whigs into a broader Taylor Republican party. Building a national consensus on issues that had long divided Whigs from Democrats and Northerners from Southerners was its complementary strategy. By any objective standard, the administration's distribution of jobs was an unmitigated disaster for the Whig party. By the same standard, in contrast, the policies it sought to implement were wise, politically shrewd, and potentially of great benefit to the nation. Unfortunately for Taylor and the Whig party, however, those policies became victims of the rancor provoked by the patronage component of the new party initiative.

By far the most pressing and seemingly most intractable problem confronting the new administration was the sectionally divisive territorial question that Congress had failed to resolve prior to Taylor's inauguration. The wave of fortune hunters flooding California's gold fields rendered establishment of civil government in the Mexican Cession imperative. The readiness of northern and southern Democrats to outflank Whigs on the slavery extension issue in the 1849 elections simultaneously increased the difficulty of doing so in a way that was mutually acceptable to Northerners and Southerners and increased the political costs of not doing so. So long as the territorial question remained unresolved, that is, Whig candidates in both sections remained vulnerable to Democratic taunts that Taylor's administration planned to sell out their particular section's rights.

The Democratic-Free Soil coalition's success in the Ohio legislature at the start of 1849 alerted northern Whigs to the danger they faced from similar alliances forming in Indiana, Vermont, Massachusetts, and Connecticut. That threat had already caused them to kill the Preston Bill by adamantly insisting on adding the Wilmot Proviso to it, and in light of the apparent readiness of northern Democrats in 1849 to jettison popular sovereignty and reembrace the Proviso, they saw only political catastrophe in any retreat from it. Ohio Whigs, for example, repeatedly warned Ewing that their only hope lay in cutting "the throat of the Free Soil party" by winning back Whig defectors. To achieve that, Congress must pass and Taylor must sign the Proviso, which "has now become a *sine qua non* with us." Should Taylor instead veto it, "the Whig party is ruined forever."[67]

As the administration well knew, however, southern Whigs facing gubernatorial and congressional campaigns in 1849 could never accept enactment of the Proviso, even if they believed the Cession unfit for slavery. From Virginia to Louisiana, Democrats flayed Whig congressmen for refusing to sign Calhoun's Southern Address and predicted that they would betray the South on the Proviso too. Returning to Georgia from Congress, where he had championed Preston's plan to admit California as a free state, Robert Toombs discovered that "public feeling in the South is much stronger than many of us supposed." Passage "of the Wilmot Proviso would lead to civil war," he warned Preston in May, and even California's admission as a free state would create "bitterness of feeling." "Proslavery feeling is growing stronger and more bitter," echoed Kentucky Congressman C. S. Morehead. Kentucky's Whigs could not bear any additional antislavery weight, Morehead told Clayton. "The Wilmot Proviso must never come before Genl. Taylor for his approval or rejection, if we intend to maintain our party ascendancy."[68]

The spring elections provided ample evidence of how easily Whigs could be whipsawed by antislavery Democratic campaigns in the North and proslavery Democratic campaigns in the South and why it was therefore necessary to resolve the territorial question. The New Hampshire and Rhode Island elections reaffirmed New England Whigs' commitment to the Proviso. Whigs retained control of the state government and both congressional seats in the latter, and by combining with Free Soilers behind a pro-Proviso platform they managed to reelect Congressmen Amos Tuck and James Wilson in the former. Connecticut's results in early April, however, shocked Whigs across the country.

In both 1847 and 1848 Whigs had carried the Nutmeg State handily. As they confidently approached the 1849 elections, they controlled all four House seats, both U.S. Senate seats, the governorship, and both houses of the state legislature. Adamantly opposed to slavery extension, Connecticut's Whig leaders had stressed their commitment to the Proviso to hold the state for Taylor in November 1848, and in 1849 they anticipated a reprise of the three-way presidential race. The state's leading antislavery Democrat, lame-duck Senator John M. Niles, had joined the Free Soilers and would be their gubernatorial candidate. His defection and Gideon Welles' absence in Washington left Connecticut's Democrats under the leadership of a conservative triumvirate—Isaac Toucey, attorney general during the Polk administration's final year; Alfred E. Burr, editor of the Hartford *Times*; and Thomas Seymour, the Democrats' gubernatorial candidate. All three proudly clung to popular sovereignty and openly denounced the Wilmot Proviso as the radical doctrine of traitors to the Democrats.

With Democrats divided and their candidates taking a discredited position on the territorial issue, another Whig triumph seemed assured. Over the angry protests of Toucey, Burr, and Seymour, however, Democrats combined with Free Soilers in three congressional districts and carried all three, even though Whig candidates trumpeted their own antislavery credentials. Because of Free Soil gains in the legislature, moreover, Whigs lost their majority in the house and had it reduced in the senate. Whig legislators still managed to elect Joseph Trumbull governor. Trumbull, however, lacked an outright majority because his vote dropped by 10 percent from Whig turnout in the two previous gubernatorial elections, while Niles, with only 6 percent of the total, had achieved the magical balance of power between the major parties.[69]

Various observers cited anger at the slow removal of Democrats, Trumbull's alienation of Protestants by wooing Catholic voters, and the unpopularity of two of the defeated Whig congressional candidates, Hartford's Charles Chaplin and New Haven's James F. Babcock, for the Whigs' poor showing. But the explanation that carried weight was Niles' boast that "this is altogether a free soil triumph."

Though small, Connecticut's Free Soil party could defeat Whigs by combining with Democrats. Democrats certainly recognized that fact. In the ensuing session, again over the protests of Toucey, Burr, and Seymour, Democratic legislators caucused with Free Soilers and supported Free Soil resolutions instructing the state's two Whig United States senators to vote against confirmation of any federal officeholder who owned slaves and against the admission of any more slave states. As long as the territorial issue gave life to the Free Soil party, in short, Connecticut's Whigs remained vulnerable.[70]

Three weeks after Connecticut's shock, the other blade of the sectional shears closed on Whigs in Virginia. Having won half of the popular vote and six of fifteen congressional seats in 1847, they saw Democrats sweep fourteen districts and their popular vote dip to 45.6 percent in 1849. This wipeout, many southern Whigs complained, exposed the fatuity of not sacking Democratic patronage holders, yet Democrats' exploitation of the slavery issue chiefly accounted for the result. Democrats touted the Southern Address, and Jeremiah Morton, the lone Whig congressional winner, attracted Democratic support and defeated the district's Whig incumbent, John Pendleton, by pillorying him for failing to sign Calhoun's manifesto.[71] In contrast, the state legislative races, in which slavery was not a salient issue, saw Whigs' share of house seats slip only from 48 to 46 percent. Virginia's voters, in sum, singled out Whig congressional candidates, who might betray the South on the territorial issue, for repudiation.

During April, between the Connecticut and Virginia elections, Taylor's administration, following advice from Crittenden and Illinois' Congressman-elect Edward Baker, devised a policy for the Mexican Cession that, it hoped, could satisfy both northern and southern Whigs. "The slavery question is the only really formidable obstacle in the way of the Administration," argued Crittenden, and it could "only be effectively removed by the admission of California into the Union as a State." Like Crittenden, Baker urged Clayton to send agents to California to foster its application for statehood before Congress met in December. "The permanency of Whig ascendancy may depend upon it," since Whigs would get credit for "the settlement of a very dangerous question" and probably two additional Whig United States senators from California to boot.[72]

Having been repeatedly warned that enactment of the Proviso would destroy the Whig party, the administration sought to avoid a formal territorial stage to which the Proviso could be applied by resurrecting the defeated Preston plan through executive, not congressional, initiative. But they were determined to do their petitioners one better. By itself, California statehood would not finesse the territorial question, for it would leave the remainder of the huge Mexican Cession as a focus of agitation over the divisive Proviso. To avert that threat completely, the entire Mexican Cession would have to be admitted as states so that no area remained to require territorial organization by Congress.

That was the administration's bold solution. Savannah Whig Congressman Thomas Butler King was despatched by sea to California to urge its residents to form a civil government, although Clayton explicitly instructed him to say nothing about whether Californians should write a proslavery or antislavery state constitution. Simultaneously, James S. Calhoun, whom Taylor sent as Indian agent to Santa Fe, was to encourage New Mexicans to write a constitution and apply for statehood. Less well known to historians, Utah, then called Deseret, was also encompassed by Taylor's visionary plan. To ensure that the flourishing settlement of Mormons near Salt Lake was included in the statehood scheme, Taylor appointed the Missourian John Wilson as Indian agent to it and instructed him to persuade the Mormons to join the Union as part of the new state of California. If that state proved too large to manage, as it undoubtedly would have, Taylor suggested, it could later be divided.

While Wilson would travel overland and King by sea, Taylor expected the two men to act in tandem. If Wilson obtained Mormons' consent to this stunning proposal, he was to proceed west with Mormon representatives to rendezvous with King in San Francisco, so that the Mormons could attend the California constitutional convention King had arranged and sprawling Utah could be included within the boundaries of the new state of California. King, meanwhile, was to delay proceedings in California until he heard from Wilson and then persuade Californians to include Deseret in their new state. On April 18, Clayton confidently informed Crittenden, "As to California and New Mexico, I have been *wide awake*. The plan I proposed to you last winter will be carried out. The States will be admitted—free and Whig."[73]

Breathtaking in scope and ingenious in conception, Taylor's policy, if successfully implemented, had brilliant political potential. Unlike the aborted Preston Bill, it eliminated the entire territorial question, for the status of slavery in other federal territories was already determined. It could thereby render the Proviso obsolete and eradicate the Free Soil party's rationale. While violating Whigs' preference for a passive executive and an active legislature, the plan's shrewdest feature circumvented Congress by having state governments formed in advance of congressional enabling legislation, thereby depriving northern Whigs of the opportunity and incentive to repeat the torpedoing of the Preston Bill by imposing the insulting Wilmot Proviso. His plan gave them the substance of free soil and two new free states without having to enact it. Nor would they have to stomach the surrender of additional land to the slave state of Texas, for Taylor's plan made no concession to Texas' claim to the entire area east of the Rio Grande. He intended to admit the entire former Mexican province of New Mexico, which stretched almost to San Antonio, as a state.[74] At the same time, northern Democrats who had abandoned popular sovereignty in 1849 and those who had supported Taylor as a national hero in 1848 might be expected to go along.

Southern Whigs who embraced the Preston Bill in February also could be expected to concur. Taylor's plan averted what they most dreaded—enactment by a northern congressional majority of legislation barring slaveholders from the territories and the possibility of a presidential signature on such legislation. Taylor's plan saved southern honor and allowed southern Whigs to assert that, just as they had promised, Taylor had stopped northern aggressions on Southern Rights by resolving the issue that prompted those aggressions.

During the summer and fall, however, far from Washington and the eastern states holding elections, Taylor's plan unraveled. Incredibly, Wilson persuaded the Mormons to become part of California, and several of them, expecting to serve as delegates to the California constitutional convention, accompanied him on the arduous trek across the Sierra Nevada for his planned rendezvous with King. By the time Wilson and the Mormons reached San Francisco, however, it was too late. King reached that city on June 4, only to find that on the previous day, at Monterey, Brevet Major General Bennet Riley, the military governor of California, had issued a proclamation calling a constitutional convention to meet there on September 1. Ignoring his instructions to await word from Wilson about the Mormons' intentions, King plunged into the business of touring California with Riley and General P. F. Smith to sell its residents on applying immediately for statehood rather than awaiting congressional authorization. In September the convention wrote and forwarded to Washington a constitution that prohibited slavery from the new state and claimed its modern-day boundaries. King later unblushingly denied that his mission and Wilson's were related. The furious Wilson, in turn, charged that King had violated his instructions because of his eagerness to secure one of California's Senate seats. Whoever was at fault, an extraordinary opportunity had been lost.[75]

As the administration hoped, California applied for admission as a free state to the Thirty-First Congress, but it did not encompass Utah in its boundaries. Deseret and the Mormons remained in limbo. The vexatious territorial question remained alive no matter what happened to California. The administration's plans for New Mexico also went awry. At the urging of James Calhoun and federal military officers, its residents held a convention in September. Rather than drafting a constitution and applying for statehood, however, they only requested Congress to grant them formal territorial status, a request that left the worsening boundary dispute with Texas unsettled and virtually guaranteed a renewal of the divisive feud over the Proviso. Even before receiving this bleak news, Taylor had despatched a new military commander to New Mexico with orders to advance statehood "if the people of New Mexico desired" it, but the chance to preempt Congress before it met was lost.[76]

VII

Before news of these developments in the West reached Washington, the 1849 elections had been held. And while Taylor's policy for the Mexican Cession was largely intended to shelter northern and southern Whigs from Democratic shafts on the slavery extension issue, he and his advisors wanted to conceal their plans during the 1849 campaigns themselves. As both Crittenden and Morehead anxiously warned Clayton in April, formation of states in the Cession was imperative to avoid enactment of the Proviso, but it was equally imperative, given the sensitivity of Southerners about equal treatment and the demands from Free Soilers for imposing the Proviso on formally organized territorial governments, to avoid any public indication that administration agents had pressured Californians and New Mexicans to apply for statehood and especially that they sought antislavery state constitutions. Morehead was particularly emphatic that "everything connected with it should be kept a most profound secret," even from other members of the cabinet. "The two extremes of North and South are already at work to prevent such a consummation, and if you do not act with circumspection and at the same time with energy, you will find yourself defeated before you know it."[77]

While exposure of the project during the 1849 campaign season carried potential risks, however, the administration's resolute silence left Whig candidates vulnerable to the same Democratic and Free Soil charges that had proved so lethal in Connecticut and Virginia. Southern Democrats endlessly predicted that Taylor would betray the South by signing the Proviso; northern Democrats and Free Soilers chorused that he would veto it. For the welfare of Whig candidates, even North Carolina's former Democratic Senator William H. Haywood admitted, Taylor's "equivocal attitude in this Proviso question" was "the very weakest position he could assume."[78]

Regardless of its impact on Whig candidates, the administration doggedly maintained that position as long as possible. A Cincinnati Whig, for example, frantically warned Ewing in July that the October state elections would "turn mainly or entirely upon the Slavery proviso." Hence, Ohio Whigs "are in embarrassing suspense for want of some revelation of the policy to be expected on that head from the Administration." Yet Ewing refused to divulge that Taylor meant to avert the occasion for enacting the Proviso. Admitting in a letter intended for publication in Cincinnati that Westerners understandably took "the most interest [in] the course of the President on the question of Slavery in the Territories," Ewing affirmed his *belief* that Taylor would sign the Proviso should Congress pass it. But, he added, Taylor "does not say, & he ought not to say anything on the subject in advance of their action." By the end of August many anxious northern Whigs were still in the dark about Taylor's intentions. "The sails of many of the Whig journals seemed to be shivering in the wind, as if uncertain which tack to take," a New Yorker complained. "The administration takes no line of policy and marks out no course of action." As late as November 29, on the very eve of the new Congress, New York's Governor Hamilton Fish begged information from Seward on what Taylor's policy on slavery extension would be so that he would not contradict it in his annual message to the state legislature.[79]

For most of 1849, therefore, Whig candidates were deprived of vital ammunition and left to fend for themselves against taunts about Taylor's probable reaction to the Proviso. Southern election returns in August suggested the wisdom of the administration's calculated silence—but also the foolishness of trying to conciliate Democrats on patronage. In Kentucky, Alabama, and North Carolina, Whigs elected the same number of congressmen as in 1847. Nonetheless, they failed to contest Alabama's governorship and lost seats in both houses of Kentucky's legislature. More ominously, Democrats gained control of Kentucky's impending constitutional convention by charging that Whigs were unreliable on the slavery issue, and everyone expected them to write a constitution that dramatically reversed the partisan balance in the state. In Tennessee, where Democrats flogged Whigs on the slavery issue, the Whig vote declined and the Democratic vote increased by 6 percent. Incumbent Whig Governor Neil Brown was defeated, Whigs lost one congressional seat, and they remained a minority in the lower house of the state legislature. Public knowledge of Taylor's plan, in sum, very likely would have increased Whig losses in those states.[80]

If concealment helped limit southern Whigs' losses in August, however, it proved calamitous for Indiana's Whigs that month. In the doldrums for most of the 1840s, they had won a majority of the legislature and four of ten congressional seats in 1847. In 1848, however, Democrats took the August and November elections handily, and by the start of 1849 some Whigs thought they should avoid running a gubernatorial candidate so as not to incite an overpowering Democratic backlash in August. Others, however, wanted to use that race to win back the approximately 5,000 Whig defectors to Van Buren and an additional 5,000 Whig voters who had abstained rather than support Taylor, but they split over how to do it. Some, described as "ultra," "over-zealous free-soil Whigs," demanded an open merger with Free Soilers behind a common gubernatorial candidate like Joseph Cravens or John H. Bradley, former Whigs who had decamped to the Free Soilers. Insisting that that tack would inevitably alienate conservative Indiana Whigs of southern origin, some, like influential editor John Defrees, argued that the party instead must nominate "some good old-fashioned Whig." Whipsawed by conflicting advice, Whigs straddled. The January state convention adopted a stridently antislavery platform and nominated incumbent Whig Congressman Elisha Embree, one of Taylor's early congressional backers, for governor.[81]

This two-faced strategy instantly collapsed. Pointing out that two Indiana Whig congressmen, George Dunn and Richard W. Thompson, had voted against Gott's resolution to ban the District of Columbia's slave trade, while Caleb Smith had ducked that vote, Free Soilers mocked Whigs' supposed antislavery commitment as sheer hypocrisy. Embree, who had voted for Gott's resolution, declined the gubernatorial nomination, forcing Whigs to undertake an embarrassingly prolonged search for a successor. One Whig after another refused to run, causing Defrees to moan about the party's "*bad fix* about a candidate for Governor" and Democrats to scorn Whigs' feebleness. Finally, in May, a vociferous critic of the Free Soilers, Joel A. Matson, consented to run, thereby ending any chance of recapturing Whig Free Soilers. "The bumbling empyrics who manage" the Whigs, Bradley exploded to Ewing, had handed both the state and congressional elections to the Democrats by alienating Free Soil voters.[82]

Once Whigs muffed their own bid for Free Soil support, Democrats co-opted it. They jettisoned popular sovereignty in 1849 and reembraced the Proviso. They ran fusion legislative tickets with Free Soilers in northern Indiana. Most significantly, in Caleb Smith's congressional district, where Samuel W. Parker ran as the Whig candidate, Democrats backed Free Soiler George W. Julian for Congress in return for Free Soil support for Democratic legislative tickets. An erstwhile Whig like his father-in-law, Joshua Giddings, Julian savaged Whigs' promise to keep slavery out of the Mexican Cession as hollow. Under the slaveholder Taylor, he fulminated, the national administration remained mum about "the alarming encroachments of the Slave Power" and sought to divert public attention by engaging "in a hopeless attempt to drag certain defunct measures of [economic] policy from the grave into which they were sinking and re-animate them with life." The refusal of Taylor's administration to publicize its plans for the Mexican Cession, in sum, only supplied Whigs' Indiana foes with evidence of their purported indifference to the slavery issue.[83]

The August elections, in the words of one stunned Indiana Whig, "proved truly disastrous." Since 1840, Whigs had never trailed Democrats by more than 4,000 votes in a statewide race, but in 1849 the margin was almost 10,000. In contrast to the four Whigs elected to Congress in 1847, only Edward McGaughey won in 1849, along with Julian and eight Democrats. Reduced to only 45.6 percent of the popular vote, Whigs also suffered significant losses in legislative races, trailing Democrats in the next legislature by eighteen seats in the house and eight in the senate, which they still controlled after the 1848 state elections. As a final blow, the Democratic majority approved a call for a constitutional convention that most Indiana Whigs, like those in Kentucky and Ohio, deeply—and properly—dreaded. "We are beat terribly and I fear, finally, in Indiana," exclaimed one disconsolate Whig, and another lamented that "our state is beyond redemption."[84]

Members of Taylor's administration viewed the August returns from the South, where Whig losses were minimal and confined primarily to Tennessee, with equanimity, but they could not shrug off Indiana's results. By the end of August, Whigs had lost a net of twelve congressional seats, and recouping those losses in Maryland, Mississippi, Louisiana, and Texas later that year seemed virtually impossible. Mississippi, Louisiana, and Georgia also had impending gubernatorial elections, but after August the bulk of the remaining elections for state officers and legislators were scheduled for the North—Vermont and Maine in September; Ohio, Pennsylvania, and New Jersey in October; and Wisconsin, Michigan, New York, and Massachusetts in November. The Free Soil party was strong in all those states except Pennsylvania and New Jersey, and the Connecticut and Indiana elections dramatically demonstrated that so long as the administration concealed its policy for the Mexican Cession, Whig candidates could be crucified by Free Soil-Democratic alliances that impugned Taylor's still unknown intentions and took advanced antislavery ground. In Vermont, for example, a Democratic-Free Soil coalition adopted a platform in June that flatly condemned "American slavery [as] a great evil and wrong, which ought to be repented of and abandoned" and that instructed Congress to exclude slavery from the territories, abolish the slave trade in the District of Columbia, and prohibit the admission of any more slave states. Protecting northern Whigs from what a Vermonter called this "most odious and corrupt coalition" required the administration to supply the necessary ammunition for self-defense.[85]

Quite unlike twentieth-century presidents and their cabinet members, who usually feel or feign almost total indifference to off-year state elections that do not directly affect the balance of partisan power in Washington, Taylor and especially his cabinet members cared deeply about the outcome of these impending northern contests. In the nineteenth century, of course, state legislatures elected United States senators, but no Senate seats Whigs currently held or had a chance of taking were affected by the remaining state legislative races in the North. Rather, relations between state and national politicians were far closer than in this century because the sense of common party identity was stronger and because politicians in Washington depended on state and local organizations to mobilize voters for them. Off-year elections were studied for signs of the party's popularity as a whole, not just of an isolated and insignificant segment of it, particularly when state governments had jurisdiction over matters Whigs and Democrats alike deemed vital. State elections, in sum, were the equivalent of modern public opinion polls. That is why Taylor's men were intent upon building up state Whig administrations with federal patronage, and that effort would fail if Whigs lost state elections. Defeat in Pennsylvania would also doom the attempt of Taylor and Clayton to sell northern Whigs on the desirability of creating a new Taylor Republican party. Beyond these considerations, Ewing, Meredith, and Collamer had a personal stake in the welfare of state Whig parties in Ohio, Pennsylvania, and Vermont, and Clayton's interest in Pennsylvania matched Meredith's.

By August all cabinet members were receiving cries of alarm from northern Whigs still facing elections, but Ewing came under the most pressure from his home state. Stung by the success of the Democratic-Free Soil coalition in the winter legislative session, Ohio's Whigs most feared the Democratic threat to their state economic programs, especially since the electorate in October would decide whether to call a constitutional convention as well as pick a new legislature. Unless Whigs won back defectors to the Free Soilers, Columbus Delano warned Ewing, "radical locofocism & radical abolitionism" would control the constitutional convention. To lure back wayward Whigs, counseled another correspondent, "Our contest in 1849 should be on State questions. Our currency and revenue policy, and with them state credit and prosperity are the great questions." Whigs must therefore cultivate Whig-Free Soilers "who have desired and still desire harmony on our currency and revenue policy."[86]

Former Whigs in Free Soil ranks did indeed still cherish the Whig economic program. But they feared that by returning to the Whig party, they would surrender Free Soil machinery to Chase and his friends, who sought a fusion with Democrats "for the sole purpose of putting down our excellent system of Whig state policy." The only way Whigs could safely reunite to save their state economic program, a Whig-Free Soiler told Ewing, was to break down the Free Soilers by guaranteeing free soil in the Mexican Cession, for it was the Proviso issue and only the Proviso issue that Free Soilers were using to fuse with Democrats behind common legislative candidates. "Something must be speedily done to change matters on the Reserve" to avert "the most calamitous consequences," Ewing was warned in May. Whatever Whigs' priorities, in short, they had to neutralize Free Soilers on the slavery extension issue—something they could never do, Ewing was repeatedly told, unless Taylor, not Ewing, made Taylor's intentions for the Mexican Cession public.[87]

After Indiana's August 6 election, therefore, Ewing and other cabinet members knew that they must reassure northern voters that Taylor intended to keep slavery out of the Mexican Cession in order to salvage Ohio and other northern states. Publicizing that intention might hazard Whig prospects in Georgia, Mississippi, Louisiana, and perhaps even Maryland. But nine northern states had yet to vote, five of which Taylor had carried, and in six of them, including the nation's three largest states, Whig governors whom the administration was determined to bolster still reigned.

By early August, in fact, the administration's shroud of secrecy had already been partially lifted. Newspaper stories circulated in Georgia and other Deep South states about Thomas Butler King's journey to California and his speeches urging Californians to apply for statehood. Details of Taylor's three-pronged strategy remained unknown and conventions in California and New Mexico had yet to assemble, but even these stories provoked the hostile reaction among Southerners that Crittenden and Morehead had predicted in April. King's mission "appears to me to betray weakness—and an apprehension in reference to the Slavery question which should have been veiled from the public eye," a nervous Georgia Whig wrote Senator John M. Berrien. Every sensible man in the South knew that free states would eventually be carved from the Mexican Cession, "but why should the President despatch a messenger to hasten an event which will certainly happen?"[88]

By mid-August, in sum, the political cost of reassuring northern Whigs had declined even as the necessity of doing so had increased. The cat was already out of the bag in the South. Southern Whigs would reap the consequences of its escape no matter what the administration told the North. Nonetheless, the administration could not completely reveal its plan, for in August it was still not certain that California and New Mexico would apply for admission as free states. Rather, it could only indicate its opposition to slavery extension in a way that did not commit it to the Wilmot Proviso.

How to get this message out proved as delicate a problem as what to say. The Whigs' biggest difficulty in the North remained distrust of the slaveholder Taylor himself. To allay that suspicion word must come directly from him, not his newspaper or a cabinet member. During the nineteenth century, however, presidents did not hold press conferences. There was no radio or television on which to address the nation, even if there had been a pretext for doing so. Taylor could not issue a proclamation about a policy that had not been fully implemented, nor could he send a message to a Congress that was not in session. Fortunately for the Whigs, however, Taylor had long planned a trip through Pennsylvania and New York to enhance his personal popularity, the rock upon which, Clayton and Crittenden insisted, a new party could be built.

Taylor left Washington by train for Pennsylvania on August 9, three days after Indianans voted and while the new telegraph reported how they had done so. As he traveled west across southern Pennsylvania from Lancaster, York, and Harrisburg to Pittsburgh, he studiously ignored the slavery question and stressed the tariff issue in speeches to crowds along the way. The preferred site for the announcement on slavery had been carefully selected. His target was Ohio's Western Reserve. On August 23 at Mercer, a town south of Erie in northwestern Pennsylvania and, more significantly, close to Ohio and the eastern edge of the Reserve, Taylor made his antislavery declaration. Although the issuance of some free-soil statement cannot be questioned, exactly what Taylor declared is unclear, for newspapers either ignored or disagreed about precisely what he said. According to his most assiduous biographer, he announced, "The people of the North need have no apprehension of the further extension of slavery. . . . The necessity of a third party would soon be obviated."[89]

Taylor said nothing specific at Mercer or anywhere else on his trip about how slavery extension would be stopped. That very night, indeed, he became so sick that he made no more speeches, and newspapers reported on his current health, not his past remarks. Some northern Whigs, therefore, remained mystified about his territorial policy until he sent his message to Congress in December. Others took his opposition to slavery extension as a promise to sign the Proviso. Campaigning against the Free Soil-Democratic coalition on Ohio's Western Reserve, Benjamin Wade rejoiced that "things look bright here" when he read reports of Taylor's remarks. "The Whigs were never in better spirits," and "Old Zack's declaration in favor of free territory altogether make it rather hard sledding" for the enemy.[90]

With considerably less enthusiasm, southern Whigs more accurately grasped the meaning of Taylor's announcement. It explained the purpose of King's mission to California and placed the man whom they had promised would never betray his fellow slaveholders squarely against slavery expansion. However much the Mercer speech may have aided its intended northern beneficiaries, when word of it filtered south in September and October, it crippled Whigs in Georgia, Mississippi, and Louisiana as much as if Taylor had openly endorsed the hated Proviso itself. The prediction of an Alabama Whig the previous December that "the whole South in two years will come out and repudiate Gen. Taylor on account of his slavery notions" was coming true ahead of schedule.[91]

VIII

That most of Taylor's Pennsylvania speeches focused on the tariff reflected an important fact. Slavery extension might be the key issue in Ohio's Western Reserve and in parts of New York and New England, but it was not in Pennsylvania and New Jersey. There the continuing depression in the coal and iron industries generated cries for increased tariff rates, not restriction of slavery. When Pennsylvania's 1849 Democratic state convention again defended the Walker Tariff, therefore, Pennsylvania's Whigs, who believed attacks on that law had won over Democratic voters in manufacturing and mining districts in 1848, happily made demands for more protection the centerpiece of their own platform. "This is the one question upon which the Whigs have always carried Pennsylvania, and it is the only one upon which it can be carried," ex-Congressman Andrew Stewart wrote Meredith in July, advice he repeated to Taylor himself.[92]

Even Taylor's tour, however, did not sufficiently reassure Pennsylvania's nervous and divided Whigs, who feared a catastrophe in the October elections. On August 18, in the midst of Taylor's visit, Morton McMichael, the new chairman of the Whig state committee, urged Meredith, whom everyone expected to formulate the administration's economic policy, to tour the state's coal and iron regions himself in order to inspire confidence that the administration would seek higher duties. "Gen. T's visit has thus far undoubtedly been of service, but in the particular quarters indicated a visit from you I feel confident would be of far more." Five days later, McMichael again begged Meredith personally to reassure the state's depressed mill and mine owners that the administration would "save them from ruin" and to convince "the farmers, mechanics, and laborers—especially those who delve in coal fields & sweat over forges & ply the shuttle"—that it would fulfill the promises Pennsylvania's Whigs had made during the 1848 campaign.[93]

Such pressure meant that the administration had to do more in 1849 than devise a solution for the Mexican Cession. It had to address the economic concerns of crucial constituents. By August, in fact, Meredith was already concocting recommendations for tariff revision to submit to Congress in December. Yet the pleas he received exposed two problems about that effort. First, as with the administration's territorial policies, no one knew precisely what Meredith would recommend. Alerted by the reporter James Harvey, who had seen preliminary drafts of the report, that *it*, not the plan for the Mexican Cession, would be the most important document issued by the administration, the cautious Meredith refused to discuss or release any parts of the report until it was completed. Thus, he spurned McMichael's requests to visit the state.[94]

Second, perfectionism was not the only reason Meredith hesitated to reassure Pennsylvanians that the promises its Whigs had made in 1848 would be honored. Pennsylvania's Whigs had not simply promised a higher tariff, but also repeal of the Walker Tariff and restoration of the highly protective Whig tariff of 1842, just as New England's Whigs had flatly demanded repeal of the Independent Treasury Act to ease the credit crunch that palsied their economy. As Meredith well knew, restoring the tariff of 1842 and abolishing the subtreasury system smacked of ultra Whiggery and thus violated the wishes of Taylor and his closest advisors like Crittenden, Clayton, Bullitt, and Burnley to jettison the stigma of ultra Whiggery and, in Fillmore's words, instead to take "a middle course" on "old party issues." Fulfilling Whig promises, in short, would revive the partisan strife Taylor was determined to abate. Even the sycophantic Andrew Stewart, who had been denied renomination for Congress in 1848, who had unsuccessfully sought a cabinet post, and who still hoped for an appointment from the administration, advised Taylor that in his speeches to Pennsylvanians he must shun ultra Whiggery, lest he alienate Democrats who had supported him. Thus he must say nothing about repealing the subtreasury system or funding internal improvements. Nor, Stewart cooed, need Taylor promise to restore the tariff of 1842, no matter what Pennsylvania Whigs had said in 1848. He should simply tout the advantages of specific rates over *ad valorem* duties, which is precisely what Taylor did.[95]

Meredith had already decided on such a policy, and during the summer and fall he prepared his Treasury report with exceptional thoroughness. Despite pressure from Pennsylvania, he opted to replace *ad valorem* duties with the lowest specific rates that would offer adequate protection, not to return to the high rates of 1842. To ascertain what those rates might be, the former corporation lawyer endeavored to educate himself on the intricacies of the tariff and other federal economic policies. He sent circulars to customs collectors, subtreasurers, and naval officers around the country seeking information on how the public warehouse system, the subtreasury system, and the Walker Tariff were working. In particular, he wanted factual evidence of fraud and gross undervaluation of imported goods under the Democrats' *ad valorem* rates in order to justify replacing them. In July, Meredith also enlisted Isaac R. Davis, Pennsylvania's deposed Whig state chairman, to coordinate an effort to write to Louisiana sugar planters, hemp growers in Kentucky and Missouri, coal mine operators and ironmakers in Pennsylvania and New Jersey, and textile manufacturers in New England to suggest the lowest specific rates that would provide sufficient protection for their enterprises. With the help of Massachusetts Whigs, Davis wrote a new tariff bill, which he forwarded to Meredith in late September, listing precise rates on various products and estimating the differences in revenue it would earn compared to the Walker Tariff. All this information and analysis helped shape the report Meredith prepared for Congress.[96]

Almost totally ignored by later historians obsessed with the sectional crisis but of intense interest to contemporary Whigs, the massive and remarkable report Meredith sent Congress in December encapsulated the Taylor administration's economic policy.[97] Obviously meant to complement Taylor's effort to satisfy both Northerners and Southerners on the territorial question, it reflected his desire to trod "a middle course" on "old party issues" in order to build a new Taylor party.[98] Eschewing traditional Whig charges that the subtreasury system caused depressions by sucking specie from the private economic sector, undermining bank note circulation, and strangling credit, Meredith simply said that Congress should determine the "expediency" of continuing it. He added, however, that the system was understaffed and required changes to facilitate the movement of government specie from points of accumulation to points of expenditure. Similarly, he did not call for repeal of the public warehousing system. Instead, he pointed out that it cost more to administer than it earned, strained the personnel resources of the customs service, and marked a "return to the system of credit upon duties, under a new name and form." A far cry from the angry Whig rhetoric of 1846, these words nonetheless represented a distinctively Whiggish critique.

The bulk of the report, apart from its staggeringly long appendixes, dealt with the tariff, and there Meredith took even more markedly Whig ground. He did not ask for reenactment of the 1842 tariff or present Davis' detailed bill, although he told Congress he could present a bill if requested to do so. Rather, he stressed two reasons for tariff revision that Whigs could—and emphatically did—applaud. Without saying that Whigs had predicted as much for two years, he declared that interest payments on debts incurred to fund the Mexican War ensured government deficits for the foreseeable future unless additional revenues were found, and they could only come from tariff duties. More important, in rhetoric reminiscent of Clay's stirring defenses of the American System, Meredith argued that the government had an obligation to encourage and protect manufacturing because the nation's economic future depended upon expansion of its industrial base.

"All history shows that where are the workshops of the world, there must be the marts of the world, and the heart of wealth, commerce, and power," Meredith asserted. "It is as vain to make these marts by providing warehouses," he skillfully skewered Democrats, "as it would be to make a crop by building a barn." Nor would fostering manufacturing harm agriculture and commerce, for, as Whigs had always maintained, all economic interests were interconnected. The more prosperous manufacturers and their workers became, the more they would consume from farmers and planters and the more they would produce to fuel commerce. The future of American merchants, Meredith contended, lay in shipping manufacturing products, not raw materials. With encouragement, he rhapsodized in a flight of rhetorical fancy, American textile manufacturers could process the South's entire cotton crop, not just the fraction they currently purchased.

To clinch his brilliant argument, Meredith provided a succinct and stunning contrast between the rationales for Democrats' doctrine of the negative state and Whig advocacy of the positive, activist state. "All legislation designed to favor a particular class to the prejudice of others, or to injure a particular class for the benefit of others, is manifestly unwise and unjust," he admitted in a tip of his hat to Democrats. "Nothing can be more destructive of the true interests of the country than such legislation, except the refusal of really salutary legislation under the erroneous impression that it might favor one class to the prejudice of others, while in fact the denial of it injures all classes, and benefits nobody." On the fundamental ideological issue regarding government's economic role, in short, Whigs were right!

Under the Walker Tariff, Meredith maintained, manufacturing interests that should be pulling the economy into a prosperous future lay stagnant and underdeveloped. Because of this, capitalists refused to invest in the necessary plants and machinery to launch an industrial takeoff. At Walker's instruction, goods were evaluated on the basis of foreign production costs, not American market prices, and with pauper labor, foreigners undersold American competitors and threatened

448 THE RISE AND FALL OF THE AMERICAN WHIG PARTY

to drive them entirely out of business. Because *ad valorem* tariff duties were based on a percentage of the foreign price and because that price fluctuated wildly, moreover, the instability and unpredictability of prices for manufactured goods in American markets prevented potential investors from making the necessary calculations of profit margins that would justify their sinking capital into manufacturing. Only permanent price levels that allowed reasonable predictability would foster capitalization of manufacturing, and only specific rather than *ad valorem* duties could produce price stability. Finally, he charged, *ad valorem* duties encouraged fraud and deliberate undervaluation that would drive honest importing merchants, as well as manufacturers, to the wall.

To remedy these evils and thereby catalyze manufacturing development, Meredith recommended four revisions of the Walker Tariff. Rates on foreign products that competed with American goods should be raised, although he listed no precise levels. On certain enumerated staples—coal, pig iron, finished iron products, wool and woolens, cotton textiles, sugar, hemp, and the like—specific duties, a fixed price per ton, yard, bushel, and so on should be substituted for *ad valorem* rates. On those goods on which it was impossible to levy specific duties, moreover, evaluations should be based on the American market price, not the foreign cost of production, so that foreign goods would always be priced higher than the American products with which they competed. Finally, to redress a loud complaint raised against the Walker Tariff, Congress must make sure that the rates on imported raw materials used by American manufacturers were lower than the rates on the finished products they made with those materials.

Here, then, was the blueprint for an economic policy on which Taylor hoped to build a new party that combined Whigs, Democrats, and Native Americans. Meredith had brilliantly tried to find a middle ground between traditional Whig and Democratic positions on economic issues, but the overall tilt suggested that the administration had finally understood the need to pacify Whigs outraged by its disastrous patronage policies. True, the report totally omitted traditional Whig demands for distributing federal land revenues to the states. But it projected those revenues as being inconsequential because so many land warrants had been issued to contractors and soldiers during the war—Mr. Polk's war, Whigs hardly needed to be reminded. The report was equally silent about subsidies for internal improvements, aside from funds for lighthouses, customs houses, and marine hospitals already under construction. Its pointed estimates of government deficits for the future sought to prevent the nettlesome subject of internal improvements from ever coming up for debate, even as they reminded people of the reason for those deficits—a war that Whigs abhorred. While it largely ignored Democrats' public warehousing and subtreasury systems, its gentle jabs at their inefficiency were meant to warm Whigs' hearts. Meredith did not insult Democrats by demanding a return to the Whig Tariff of 1842, and his arguments for protecting American miners and manufacturers and their employees undoubtedly aimed at cementing the allegiance of working-class Democrats and Native Americans who had supported Taylor in Pennsylvania, New Jersey, Connecticut, and other manufacturing states. Nonetheless, his stunning case for governmental promotion of economic development was decidedly a Whig brief. By December 1849, when Meredith presented his report, in sum, the administration appeared to be signaling a retreat from the most destructive aspects of its new party initiative. By December, however, it was too late.

IX

The fall returns shattered whatever possibility had ever existed that Taylor could actually replace the Whig party with a new organization, and they also had enormous impact on Whigs' behavior in the impending congressional session. Without firm evidence of his administration's plans for the Cession and recommendations for economic reform to tout as a platform, Whig candidates fell in droves. What *was* known about King's mission to California and Taylor's free-soil remarks in Pennsylvania proved especially damaging in the South. In Louisiana, a state Taylor had carried, for example, the Whig vote dropped by 6 percent and the Democratic turnout jumped by 20 percent since the previous November. Accordingly, Whigs' share of the total fell from Taylor's 54.6 percent to 48.5 percent in the gubernatorial race. Whigs retained one of Louisiana's four House seats and increased their majority in the lower house of the legislature, but that was small consolation for men who had expected to perpetuate the Taylor coalition in the race. "Well, Campbell, the sun of Buena Vista does not shine on the Whig party of late," moaned Balie Peyton from New Orleans. "Even this city has gone horse, foot, & dragoons for the democrats."[99]

In Mississippi, where ostensibly bipartisan Rough and Ready clubs had been kept intact to manage the campaign, Whigs were thrashed. The state's leading Democrats, Congressman Albert Gallatin Brown, Senator Jefferson Davis, and gubernatorial candidate John A. Quitman, aggressively defended Southern Rights, and by the fall they flatly opposed statehood for California because it would cheat Southerners of their rights in the Mexican Cession. Some Democrats already called California statehood, like passage of the Proviso, grounds for secession. Thrown on the defensive, Mississippi's Whigs joined the state's Democrats in a Calhoun-inspired scheme to call a southern convention at Nashville in June 1850 to prepare a united sectional response to purported northern aggressions. That move, however, failed to save Whig candidates. Democrats swept all four congressional seats, both legislative chambers, and the governorship. In 1848, Taylor trailed Cass in Mississippi by only 729 votes. A year later in the gubernatorial race Democrats won by a margin exceeding 10,000 votes, and Whigs' share of the total plummeted to a pitiful 41 percent. The surge toward Taylor in 1848 had been a one-time blip on the electoral chart; Mississippi remained a Democratic bastion.[100]

Only state offices were at stake in Georgia, and its Democratic leaders were less uniformly militant on the slavery question than Mississippi's. Only one had signed the Southern Address, while Congressmen Howell Cobb and John H. Lumpkin, who represented nonslaveholding districts, had led those southern Democrats who denounced the Address as dangerously disunionist. Cobb and Lumpkin were attacked during 1849 by fellow Democrats for their timidity, however, and in the gubernatorial campaign the state's Democrats stressed Governor George Towns' promise to call a state convention immediately to resist any violation of the South's equal rights—a promise that betokened secession should the Proviso become law.[101]

This Democratic challenge significantly exacerbated tensions between the rival Stephens-Toombs and Berrien factions of the Georgia Whig party. Toombs and Stephens had led the attempt to sabotage Calhoun's southern caucus, ostentatiously walking out before the vote on the Southern Address. They had also enthusiastically endorsed the Preston Bill, even if it admitted another free state. Surprised by the vehemence of anti-Proviso sentiment and the opposition to California statehood when they returned to Georgia, they nonetheless cautioned Whigs to continue to rely on Taylor and to avoid extreme anti-Proviso rhetoric that smacked of secessionism. Such a position was understandable. Their man Crawford was in the cabinet, they controlled the state's federal patronage, and they did not want to appear to abandon Taylor, especially before his intentions for the territories became known. Able to control most Whig papers in the state with the leverage of federal printing contracts, the Stephens-Toombs forces also dominated the party's June state convention. Gubernatorial nominee Benjamin Hill was not their preferred candidate, but the state platform reflected their position on the territorial question. Denouncing the Proviso as "violative of all the Compromises of the Constitution, and making an unjust discrimination against the people of the South," it also expressed full confidence that Taylor would protect Southern Rights. At the insistence of Stephens and Toombs, in sum, Georgia's Whigs, still unaware of King's mission to California, attempted to repeddle the message of 1848.[102]

That message's moderation, in contrast to Democrats' strident rhetoric, opened an opportunity for Berrien and his followers. Ruthlessly excluded from federal jobs because they had preferred Clay for the 1848 nomination, they knew that the ambitious Stephens and Toombs sought to knock Berrien "unceremoniously out of their way." Since "Mr. Toombs would like to be in the Senate & that you should be *out of it*," one wrote Berrien, the pair had used "the antagonism of yr. respective positions on the Slavery question in all its breadth" to "destroy yr. political power for they are perhaps sensible that if they do not destroy you, you will destroy them." Since 1844, indeed, Stephens and Toombs had consistently outflanked Berrien by taking a more extreme proslavery position than he, but their actions in the winter of 1848–49 and their recommendations for Georgia Whigs' 1849 campaign at last offered Berrien a chance to turn the tables and "destroy them." In the Senate that winter Berrien had voted against the California statehood plan, whereas Toombs and Stephens had supported it in the House. Berrien had remained in the southern caucus after they abandoned it, and even though his own address was more moderate than Calhoun's, he had flatly denounced the Proviso as unconstitutional, not just insulting. Now, in sum, he could pose as a more vigilant sentinel of Southern Rights than his nemeses. Hence his Georgia allies in 1849 openly denounced their plea to rely upon Taylor as inadequate and instead promised firm resistance to any proposal that denied southern slaveholders equal access to *all* of the Mexican Cession.[103]

Pregnant with implications for the future, the rival factions' different positions on the territorial question had little impact on the 1849 gubernatorial election itself. While the Democrat Towns breathed fire in defense of Southern Rights, the Whig Hill steadfastly refused to discuss the Proviso and what he might do should it pass or to wrap himself in the protective armor of Taylor's supposed fealty to the South. Hill's attempt to avoid national issues altogether so disgusted Stephens and Toombs that they refused to stump for him. For a while, however, Hill's tack appeared to work. Reporting "no excitement [in middle Georgia] upon the slavery question," Berrien's kinsman Charles Jenkins thought that "our people generally have a strong reliance upon the old General in the last resort." For most of the summer, in fact, the race's outcome appeared to hinge on which candidate won the backing of the state's growing temperance movement, although, as one wag cracked, "It is not a pretty issue to be determined—which drinks the most liquor, Hill or Towns?"[104]

Word of King's mission to California and Taylor's speech at Mercer decisively changed the race. In Georgia, Taylor was reported as calling slavery "a great moral and political evil" and insisting that Congress could bar it from the territories. That news gave Democrats deadly ammunition and made Hill's adamant silence about the Proviso suicidal. Hill ran 4,000 votes behind Taylor and Towns 2,000 ahead of Cass, transmuting Taylor's 3,000-vote margin into a Democratic majority of the same size. Whigs also lost control of the entire legislature, which in the next session would reapportion the state's legislative districts.[105]

Defeat only widened the breach among Georgia's Whigs. Stephens and Toombs blamed Hill for not defending Taylor as safe on the Proviso. Though shaken, they clung to the president and waited to see his still-unknown plans for the Cession. Berrien's friends scorned that analysis. Had Hill simply clung to Taylor, "the Whig party as such would have ceased to exist or been doomed to a hopeless minority for years." His rivals' stubborn and impolitic loyalty to Taylor, one told Berrien, provided the chance to end their "unhealthy and selfish domination." Repeating earlier advice, he urged Berrien to make "a personal address to the Whig party of Georgia" on the slavery issue in the next Congress that outlined "yr. efforts to enforce [i.e., strengthen] their oft repeated declarations & resolutions upon this subject." Berrien refused to waste this opportunity to take a tougher proslavery stance than his rivals. That determination guaranteed his opposition to Taylor's statehood plans for California and New Mexico.[106]

To the north, Whig hopes climbed in September, only to be dashed in October and November. Vermont's Whigs reelected Governor Carlos Coolidge by retaining control of the legislature. The Democratic-Free Soil coalition appeared to backfire by causing conservative Democrats to back their own candidate and driving some Whig-Free Soilers back to their former party. Even without a popular majority, Coolidge ran 3,000 votes ahead of Taylor and his own 1848 total, while the coalition candidate polled 5,000 fewer votes than the combined Free Soil and Democratic totals a year earlier. Vermont's Whigs crowed that they had crushed the odious coalition, and Whigs elsewhere took heart.[107]

With no expectations of carrying Democratic Maine, in contrast, few Whigs were disappointed when the additional voters Taylor had attracted disappeared and the Whig state ticket slumped to its traditional 37–38 percent of the gubernatorial vote. Even in Maine, moreover, two contradictory trends looked promising. The Free Soil vote dropped by a third since the presidential contest, suggesting that the third party might be running out of steam. Because of Free Soil and Whig gains in legislative races, Democrats lost their majority in the state senate and had it reduced to a single seat in the house. Besting Democrats in

Maine's legislature, however, would require Maine's Whigs to cooperate with Free Soilers, a necessity that precluded any relaxation of their adamant opposition to slavery in the Mexican Cession.[108]

Returns from the Midwest helped shatter September's optimism and re-affirmed Whigs' weakness in that burgeoning region, which was certain to gain additional congressional seats and electoral votes after the 1850 census. Illinois had no 1849 elections, but in Wisconsin's legislative elections, Democrats, not Whigs, benefited from a marked decline in Free Soil strength. Michigan's Whigs, in contrast, attempted to forge a coalition with Free Soilers against the dominant Democrats in state races. Although the coalition's gubernatorial candidate drew 45.5 percent of the total compared to Taylor's 36.7 percent, he still ran some 19,000 votes behind the combined total for Taylor and Van Buren, a decline that indicated considerable Whig and Free Soil dissatisfaction with the bargain. Winning less than a third of the house and a fourth of the senate seats, moreover, Whigs' position in the legislature remained hopeless.[109]

Because of its size and Ewing's presence in the cabinet, Ohio was the most important midwestern state to the administration. Taylor had delivered his Mercer speech to help Whigs on the Western Reserve, and because of it, Democratic dissent outside the Reserve about coalition with Free Soilers in it, and faith that Whigs would rally to defend their state economic programs, some Whigs by September rejoiced that "our Locofoco adversaries are manifestly in trouble in almost every part of the state." Despite small Whig gains and Democratic losses, however, Free Soilers elected with Democratic support continued to hold the balance of power in both houses of the legislature. Worse still, Ohioans approved the referendum calling for a state constitutional convention in 1850. Whigs blamed the result on apathy, poor organization, and lack of a coordinated newspaper response to the Free Soil challenge since some Whig papers wooed and others denounced Whig defectors to the third party. Whatever the cause, so long as Free Soilers threatened Whigs' chances, they would insist that slavery not expand into the Mexican Cession.[110]

Since Whigs had lost all midwestern states in 1848, defeats there did not jolt them nearly so much as returns from the New England and Middle Atlantic states Taylor had carried. Combinations between Democrats and Free Soilers stung Whigs in Massachusetts and New York, although the combinations took very different forms in the two states. To the dismay of ex-Whigs like Charles Francis Adams, the Bay State's Free Soilers openly courted Democrats by endorsing Democratic positions on state issues, especially electoral reforms to undermine the influence of Whiggish Boston in the state legislature. Simultaneously, Democrats tried to attract Free Soilers by jettisoning popular sovereignty and declaring in their state platform: "We are opposed to slavery in every form and color, and in favor of freedom and Free Soil wherever man lives throughout God's heritage." This was not the forthright commitment to the Proviso that Free Soilers demanded, and the two parties ran separate gubernatorial candidates, allowing Whig nominee George Briggs once again to get a plurality of the popular vote and win election in the state legislature.[111]

Nonetheless, Whigs' control of that body was much more precarious than it had been after the 1848 elections. Unlike the gubernatorial contest, Democrats and Free Soilers fused behind common legislative candidates and scored dramatic gains at Whigs' expense. The Whig margin plunged from seventeen to eight seats in the senate and from ninety-three to thirty-five seats in the house. What made those results especially ominous was that, because of the peculiarities of the Massachusetts apportionment system, a large number of small towns, where antislavery sentiment was intense, were not entitled to representation in 1849 but would be the following year. If the Free Soil party remained in existence, Whigs' control of the state government stood in grave jeopardy. Like their Ohio brethren, in short, Massachusetts Whigs required a quick resolution of the territorial question that guaranteed free soil.

In contrast to Massachusetts, New York's Free Soil party effectively collapsed when Barnburners returned to the Democratic fold. Democrats had to dodge any statement about the Proviso to achieve their tenuous unity, but they were nonetheless more unified going into the 1849 campaign than they had been in four years. Of the eight officials chosen by a statewide vote, Whigs and Democrats each elected four, with Whigs retaining the four most influential posts—comptroller, treasurer, secretary of state, and state engineer. Even so, it was a close call. Washington Hunt, Whigs' front-runner, won the comptrollership by only 5,900 votes out of over 400,000 cast, largely because Democratic drop-off from the combined Cass and Van Buren totals in 1848 almost tripled Whig drop-off from that year. Statistical analysis, in fact, suggests that over one-fifth of 1848 Whig voters defected to Hunt's Democratic opponent and that only abstentions by 1848 Free Soil and Democratic voters disgusted by the Barnburner-Hunker rapprochement allowed Hunt to win. Hunt had angered some Whigs with his dispensation of canal contracts, but most Whig defectors were probably conservatives who had lost their fight to control the state convention. The willingness of aggrieved Whigs to vote for the enemy in order to punish Weed's organization rather than simply abstain boded serious trouble in the future.[112]

The outcome of the legislative races proved of more immediate concern to Weed and Seward. In 1848, Whigs had compiled huge margins in both chambers because of the Democrats' rupture, and in the house, at least, most Whigs were Sewardites. In 1849, more Whig winners were conservatives, and the reunited Democrats made stunning gains. The phenomenal eighty-six-seat edge in the house that Whigs enjoyed over Democrats and Free Soilers combined after 1848 changed to a two-seat Democratic majority after 1849. Whigs' comfortable sixteen-vote margin in the senate was slashed to a precarious majority of two.

The extraordinary Democratic resurgence in New York would shape the response of Weed and Seward to the great debate over the territories in 1850. The reunified Democrats seriously jeopardized Whig control of New York's state government, the linchpin of Weed's power. Seward and Weed knew that Democrats had reunited only by avoiding an open party stand on the Wilmot Proviso and that the easiest way to redivide them was to compel Democrats in the legislature to vote on the Proviso. Forcing a legislative vote on the slavery extension issue could also reassert the ascendancy of Sewardites over their conservative Whig rivals and perhaps recruit remaining Free Soilers, furious about Barnburners' return to the Democrats, into Whig ranks, thereby reinforcing Sewardites against conservatives. Taking defiant antisouthern ground, in short, seemed to Seward and Weed the best, if not the only, escape from the quandary in which the 1849 elections had left them. Their implementation of the strategy in 1850, and Fillmorites' response to it, would have enormous implications for events that year.[113]

The results from Maryland, Pennsylvania, and New Jersey in 1849 were equally shocking to Whigs, although in none of them did the slavery issue play as significant a role as it did elsewhere. In Maryland, where a Democratic governor would hold office until 1850, Democrats narrowly captured a western congressional seat Whigs had won in 1847 and retained the two seats from Baltimore. They also scored impressive gains in the legislature despite a healthy Whig majority in the statewide popular vote.[114] Whig legislative majorities in New Jersey plummeted from twenty to eight seats in the house and from five to a single seat in the senate. But it was Pennsylvania, the scene of Whigs' most remarkable gains in 1848 and the keystone of the administration's attempt to build a new Taylor Republican party, that dealt Whigs and the administration's hopes their severest blow.

For months, disgruntled Whig regulars in Pennsylvania had warned that apathy and disaffection guaranteed a catastrophe in the October elections, and their prophecies proved self-fulfilling. Dissident Native Americans, who had not shared the jobs allocated by federal patronage holders, combined with Democrats to sweep the local offices and state legislative seats in the city and county of Philadelphia. The spurned nativist faction also ran its own candidate for canal commissioner, the sole statewide office at stake, and he drained 5,400 votes from the Whig ticket, which was reduced to 46.5 percent of the vote. Abstention of 1848 Whig voters was a far graver problem. Statewide in 1849 the party drew 35,000 (21 percent) fewer votes than Johnston had won the previous October and 52,000 (28 percent) fewer than Taylor. In contrast, Democrats' vote dropped by only 20,000 (12 percent) since the previous October and 25,000 (14.5 percent) since November. Democrats won the seat on the patronage-rich canal commission, and in the legislature Whigs were reduced to a two-fifths minority in the house and had their previously secure majority in the senate reversed. Democrats controlled both houses of the legislature for the first time since 1845. The attempt to consolidate a broader Taylor Republican party had manifestly failed.

Angry regulars blamed the attempt by Johnston and state chairman McMichael to supplant Whigs with a Taylor Republican party for the debacle. The state committee "never deign[ed] to consult any of us," fumed one, hence "the great falling off" of the Whig vote since 1848. "They have irretrievably thrown the State into the hands of the Locofocos, for under their lead each succeeding election will be as disastrous as the last one." Johnston and McMichael could "never obtain the confidence of the Whig party," for "the great mass of the party will never surrender the name of Whig."[115]

The similarity of the trend in Pennsylvania, New Jersey, and Maryland also suggests a broader cause of the crippling drop-off in the Whig vote. During 1849 the party had failed to establish a concrete record of achievement that could retain its earlier support. Taylor's administration had issued no clear signal about its intention on the tariff and other national economic policies, and in none of the three states had Whig parties filled that void. Little partisan conflict occurred during the 1848–49 session of Maryland's legislature, perhaps because the Democratic governor could veto any distinctively Whig program. Divided control of Pennsylvania's legislature blocked enactment of Whig policies that could have provided a platform for Whig legislative candidates, even though partisan conflict on roll calls in the Democratic house remained fairly high.[116]

The situation in New Jersey, where Whigs controlled the governorship and both legislative chambers, was more complex. The salient issue during its 1849 legislative session was an outbreak of popular resentment against the Camden and Amboy Railroad's monopoly of transportation in the state. Although Whigs had traditionally opposed the notorious Joint Companies (the Camden and Amboy and the Delaware and Raritan Canal), in 1849 they waffled because state revenue from the railroad, which legally depended upon retention of its monopoly, paid for 90 percent of state expenditures. Chartering new railroads to compete with the Camden and Amboy, in short, would force Whigs into the political suicide of levying property taxes to compensate for the lost annual payments from it. In the legislature, therefore, Whigs joined Democrats in killing proposals for competing lines. During the subsequent election campaign Whig candidates divided along geographical lines, condemning the monopoly in some counties and supporting it in others. This shilly-shallying course infuriated previous Whig voters who hated the Joint Companies. In some counties, independent antimonopoly legislative tickets reaped the votes of angry Whigs. In others, Whigs repudiated the state party for its inaction and ambivalence by voting for Democratic antimonopoly candidates. In still others, Whigs protested by abstaining. As a result, between the legislative elections of 1848 and 1849, the Whig vote declined by an average of 14 percent per county, twice the Democratic rate of decline. Bereft of national or coherent state policies to trumpet, Whigs could neither retain nor mobilize their previous electorate.[117]

X

Election results from individual states dismayed Whigs, but the cumulative totals from 1849 were especially demoralizing. In 1847, they had won 45 percent of the congressional seats and in 1848, 57 percent. In the ninety contests held in 1849, their share plummeted to 30 percent. They had won over two-fifths of the governorships up for election in 1847 and, in 1848, an impressive ten of fourteen (71.4 percent). In 1849, however, they could claim only four of the fifteen elected (26.6 percent), and those were all in New England. In the states that chose legislators in 1849, Whigs controlled both legislative houses in nine states before the elections but only six afterward. States where the two parties split legislatures increased from five to seven, and those with complete Democratic control rose from seven to eight. Even these figures disguise the extent of the Whigs' reversal. In ten states in which Whigs held a majority of the lower legislative chamber going into the elections, the average size of their margin over Democrats was 33.7 seats. Coming out of those contests, their average margin had been reduced to 8.7 seats, and in New York and Georgia, previous Whig majorities had been converted to Democratic majorities. Whigs performed slightly better in states where Democrats controlled the lower house going into the elections. Still, their average deficit in eleven such states dropped only from 22.2 to 19.6 seats, and that small average gain conceals a marked increase in the Democratic margin from 5 to 20 seats in Pennsylvania.

Some Whigs took what solace they could from these dismal results. Clay men and other regulars rejoiced that the elections had extinguished Taylor's misguided attempt to build a new party. After surveying the Ohio and Pennsylvania returns, Kentucky's Leslie Combs, for example, gloated, "The 'Great Taylor Republican Party' which was to overshadow Whig & Democrat & everything is in rather a Blue way—for my friend Clayton. The Govt. at Washington have failed in their *philosophical* experiment." It could not "sit on two stools at once. When the sympathies of the Whigs is second & *last* & the contempt of the Locos obtained— things are in a bad way."[118]

More commonly, Whigs reacted with gloom and despair. "The elections every- where indicate a great cooling in the enthusiasm which brought 'Old Zack' into power," moaned Balie Peyton. "It does seem to me that the Whigs are incapable of maintaining power." And these defeats occurred, he added significantly, "before any measure of the Administration has been presented to the nation." The Whig party had sunk "into a miserable and hopeless minority . . . before a single *mea- sure* has been tried or tested," echoed Elihu B. Washburne from Illinois because "Genl. Taylor permitted himself to go into the hands of a set of mercenary and unprincipled political scape-goats who foisted upon him a cabinet with no hold upon the popular feeling of the country and whose selection was an unpardonable outrage upon the Whig sentiment of the nation."[119]

Precisely because Whigs could not attribute their rout to public repudiation of policies the administration had not yet announced, they usually blamed the dis- aster on the "ignorance, imbecility & ingratitude combined" of the cabinet. Whig after Whig denounced its appointments—its calculated appeasement of Demo- crats, its preferential treatment of newcomers and nativists, and its cold-blooded exclusion of old-line Whig regulars—as "fatuity and madness." As early as July, a New Yorker complained to Weed that "General Taylor's Administration is, or will be crushed—wasted and the interest of the Country, as advocated by the Whig party mined, by the unstatesmanlike conduct of the Cabinet." It "must be dissolved." Otherwise, Taylor's administration "will chain the Whig party to the wheels of the car of Locofocoism for a quarter of a century." After the August and fall returns came in, murmurs of protest escalated to a roar. Alexander Bullitt in the columns of the Washington *Republic*, Schuyler Colfax and his coterie of midwestern editors, Caleb Smith, Truman Smith, Leslie Combs, Tom Corwin, Thurlow Weed, and others all demanded a change in cabinet personnel. "Upon such change depends the very existence of the Whig party," declared the furious Washburne in November.[120]

By November 1849, in sum, incensed Whig politicians blamed the cabinet, not Taylor himself, for the calamitous attempt to build a new party with patronage. Taylor was faulted for his passivity and failure to ride herd on the scoundrels in his cabinet, but not for masterminding a strategy most Whigs repudiated. Yet Taylor's personal insulation from criticism could easily be stripped away, for as insiders like Truman Smith and Orlando Brown well knew, Taylor liked his cab- inet and would resist pressure to change it.[121]

That determination boded ill for relations between Taylor and congressional Whigs who would assemble in December. For months Whig regulars had threatened to put the cabinet upstarts in their proper place once Congress met. The number of angry Whig senators who might challenge the confirmation of Taylor's recess appointees was impressively long: Berrien and Dawson, Badger and Mangum, Pearce, Cooper, Webster, Clay, and perhaps others who would be lobbied by an even longer list of rebellious Whigs in the House.

A potential blowup over the cabinet and patronage was not the biggest problem the party faced. Whigs knew they had run at a disadvantage in 1849 because the administration had not yet presented, let alone enacted, any measure of public policy. This knowledge implied that, to reverse their electoral slide, Whigs would have to pass an attractive program that could remobilize the voters who had brought Taylor to power. Only wise policies now seemed capable of overcoming the damage wrought by foolish appointments.

In three ways, however, Whigs' defeats in 1849 and their angry reaction to those losses jeopardized their ability to agree upon and pass an attractive program. First, their woeful performance in 1849 meant that Whigs would lack a majority in both the House and the Senate. Enactment of legislation would require cooperation with Democrats, Free Soilers, or both. Second, the success of northern and southern Democrats in outflanking Whigs on the slavery extension question reduced the likelihood that northern and southern Whigs could agree upon a policy for the Mexican Cession. Third, congressional Whigs angry at the patronage dimension of the administration's attempt to "rally a new party" might reject its policy dimensions as well. The administration's territorial and tariff reform program was far wiser than its blundering allotment of government jobs. Yet men who castigated Clayton, Ewing, Meredith, and the others for wrecking the party with stupid appointments might also spurn their policy recommendations, as Maryland's James Pearce had already announced.

A different border state Whig, however, emerged as the key player in the first session of the Thirty-First Congress. When news had spread the previous winter that Kentucky's legislature might return Henry Clay to the Senate, Whig after Whig had warned that Clay would come to Washington only to make trouble for Taylor and his administration, only to avenge his loss of the 1848 nomination, only to reassert his command of the Whig party, as he had done with John Tyler. After Taylor's inauguration, in contrast, few Whigs mentioned Clay, or any threat he might pose, in their correspondence. Their attention was diverted in part by their own anger at the cabinet's folly and their preoccupation with the 1849 elections. But Clay also carefully refrained from saying or doing anything that could fuel suspicions that he intended to challenge Taylor. To be sure, astute observers like Ohio's ex-Whig Free Soiler Joseph Root predicted that the growing disenchantment of Whig politicos with the administration would inevitably tempt Clay to rally anti-Taylor Whigs behind him once Congress met. For most Whigs, however, Clay seemed a forgotten man.[122]

Forgotten was the last thing Henry Clay wanted to be. He still seethed at his rude overthrow by his party and at its elevation of an unqualified neophyte like Taylor. Repeatedly, in private, he complained that his friends had been shortchanged by the administration, but just as repeatedly he told his loyalists that they must not complain publicly about the appointments. Unlike Pearce and Cooper, Clay did not seek a showdown over patronage in the Senate. Personal considerations partially account for his reluctance. Clay cared deeply about the success of his son James, whom the administration, after what seemed to Clay an agonizing delay, had appointed to Portugal in August. He would seem like a hypocrite if he then assaulted the cabinet for poor appointments. Any such attack might also cause Taylor or Clayton to withhold the nomination when the Senate met and name another man for Lisbon. Well into 1850, Clay's desire to protect his son from the wrath of the administration and have him succeed in delicate negotiations in Portugal tempered his actions and delayed an open, public break with Taylor. More fundamentally, Clay considered an open fight against Taylor's appointees counterproductive since it would only paint him and his friends as sore losers in a selfish race for spoils.[123]

Unwillingness to battle the administration over patronage did not mean that Clay was prepared to obey the party's new commander-in-chief or to surrender his conviction that he, not Taylor, was its rightful leader. Unfair job distribution was one thing, he wrote in June; the administration's failure "to support and recommend the great measures of the Whig party" would be quite another. Fully aware that large numbers of Whig congressmen who fumed over patronage gave him a potential constituency, he would fight the administration over policy, not patronage, if he chose to fight at all.[124]

When Clay wrote in June, Taylor's new organ, the Washington *Republic*, was already calling for the abandonment of ultra Whig economic measures long identified with him. At that time, therefore, he may have anticipated a battle with the administration over economic policy. While vacationing at Newport in August, however, Clay learned from the reporter James Harvey what the gist of Meredith's proposals would be, and he gave them his hearty approbation. Whether Clay knew more than any other Whigs about Taylor's plans for the Mexican Cession that summer is unknown. But he knew that the disposition of slavery in that area was the most divisive and pressing question facing the nation. If, as many Whigs believed that summer, the sphinx-like Taylor had no plan for the Cession, this might be a question on which Clay himself could devise a policy to reassert his leadership of congressional Whigs.[125]

Slavery was also a pressing issue in Kentucky during the summer of 1849. A small group of emancipationists, led by Clay's cousin Cassius M. Clay, were running a ticket of delegates for the state constitutional convention pledged to a program of state-sponsored gradual emancipation. Ridding Kentucky of slavery had long been a favorite cause of the aged statesman. He had been president of the American Colonization Society for years, and in February 1849, shortly after his election to the Senate, he published a letter in the Lexington press endorsing gradual emancipation. Then, shortly before the August elections and his departure for Newport, Clay circulated "a free soil letter" in the fourth congressional district defending the propriety of Whig candidate Aylett Butler's vote in the previous Congress to apply the Wilmot Proviso to the Mexican Cession. Putting this letter together with Clay's impending return to the Senate, a horrified Taylor Whig from Kentucky asked Clayton with astonishing perspicacity, "Can it be . . . that free soilism may be used by him Clay to overslaugh Taylor & again take the head of the *Whigs himself* hoping still to be made president before he dies?"[126]

Chapter 14

"The Slavery Excitement Seems Likely to Obliterate Party Lines"

"THERE IS A GREAT AND BITTER COMPLAINT against the Administration from all the Whigs, or nearly all," Henry Clay reported upon his return to Washington for the first session of the Thirty-First Congress. Because "the Whigs are so divided & the administration so feeble," even a job hunter recognized that "our party will have an uphill business in sustaining the Appointments of the President." Since Senate Democrats, who outnumbered Whigs thirty-three to twenty-five, with the Free Soilers Salmon Chase and John Hale holding the other two seats, had rejected some of Taylor's first nominations in March on party-line votes, Whigs, Democrats, and Free Soilers all predicted "a great deal of 'cutting and slashing work' " when "the new appointments" came up for confirmation.[1]

Whig anger and Democratic vindictiveness also clouded prospects for congressional enactment of the administration's policy recommendations. But the intensification of sectional squabbling over slavery extension proved an even more formidable obstacle to Taylor's hope of winning immediate statehood for California and New Mexico and thereby finessing the explosive Wilmot Proviso. "Sectional feeling is stronger than I ever saw it before," Georgia's Stephens warned Crittenden in mid-December. "The excitement in the South upon the Slave question is much greater . . . than those who are at the head of affairs here have any idea of." At the same time, he found northern Whigs "insolent and unyielding," totally unwilling "to calm and quiet" the South's "feelings." Sobered by the power of Democratic-Free Soil coalitions in 1849, northern Whigs, indeed, came to Washington convinced that "a compromise by which slavery would be extended would be death to the Whig party." Therefore they vowed "to stand firm on the rights of California and New Mexico to be free." Shocked by the rancorous sectional chasm in both major parties, an Illinois Democrat forecast that "the slavery excitement seems likely nearly to obliterate party lines temporarily."[2]

This situation—a crippled president, a fractious and angry congressional party, a grave sectional crisis over the territories—thus presented an opportunity for Henry Clay to pursue a course that many had predicted from the day of his election to the Senate. "Mr. Clay," chorused forecasters, "will probably put himself at the head of such of the Whigs as distrust Taylor," try "to effect a second compromise," and "lead off so many Whigs that the administration cannot be sustained."[3] In hindsight these prophecies appear astonishingly accurate. Accordingly, historians have often described the prolonged struggle that ultimately produced the Compromise of 1850 as a personal clash between Taylor and Clay and their sharply different policies for the Mexican Cession and other slavery issues. To be sure, historians have properly highlighted the roles of prominent supporting players in this drama, and many have given Democrats their just due for helping to frame and pass the compromise measures. Nonetheless, from the Whig party's perspective, the battle during 1850 has usually been portrayed in bipolar terms—Taylor and his congressional supporters versus Clay and his allies, anticompromisers versus procompromisers.[4]

Though admirably coherent, this scenario distorts the impact of the unprecedentedly long congressional session on the Whig party. Whigs did not divide neatly into pro-Taylor and pro-Clay, anticompromise and procompromise camps. For one thing, some Whigs did not see much difference between Clay's original proposals and those of Taylor, both of which they correctly recognized as compromises. More important, many Whigs did not follow the lead of either Taylor or Clay but instead pursued independent courses. During the heated congressional debates and numerous roll-call votes of 1850, the Whig party splintered into numerous fragments that changed shape over time and assumed the coherence of a bipolar division only toward the session's end.

Bitter feuds over Senate confirmation of Taylor's appointees, personal convictions, factional rifts within state Whig delegations, disagreements about the seriousness of disunionist threats, and calculations about how stands taken in Congress would affect the fortunes of one's faction or party at home all helped fragment the Whig party in 1850. The shaping of the Compromise of 1850 vividly illustrates the intimate connection between state and national politics in the nineteenth century. State legislatures and state nominating conventions met while congressional Whigs struggled with the territorial problem. What happened in those legislatures and conventions decisively influenced Whigs' behavior in Congress, just as developments in Washington shaped how rival Whig factions opposed each other within the states.

As intraparty rivalries intensified, moreover, interparty conflict with Democrats, which had always counteracted those centrifugal forces in the past, weakened perceptibly. Whigs of all varieties—Northerners and Southerners, pro- and antiadministration men, compromisers and anticompromisers—found themselves compelled to cooperate with Democrats of some kind. Sectional divisions over slavery helped blur party differences. Whigs and Democrats from the North or South often acted together rather than concede to demands of fellow party members from the other section. As Seward accurately predicted at the start of the session, would-be compromisers "of both parties" also cooperated with each other to effect a settlement they considered necessary to save the Union. Wherever Whigs stood on the territorial issue, in short, they were driven into the arms of Democrats.[5]

The concomitant feud over patronage also dissolved partisan distinctions. Since Democrats controlled the Senate committees that judged Taylor's nominees, Whigs who sought their confirmation or rejection needed Democratic help to achieve it. That necessity ultimately proved pivotal to passing the Compromise of 1850. Northern Democratic senators with the greatest influence over patronage were deeply committed to a congressional compromise that differed from Zachary Taylor's plan. As the price for their help on appointments, they pressured northern Whigs to support the Democratic alternative. By cooperating with Democrats on both policy and patronage, Whig congressmen helped mute the partisan differences and interparty combat that, along with Whigs' economic policies and commitment to activist government, had sustained the loyalty of Whig voters since the 1830s. Not simply internal divisions, in sum, but also their deadly combination with diminished interparty differences made 1850 a portentous year for Whigs.

I

When congressmen streamed into Washington in late November 1849 for the new session, only a few insiders like Seward had learned of Taylor's intentions. Most people knew that Californians had written a free constitution and would apply for statehood, but because Congress had not authorized their convention and might ignore their application, speculation still centered primarily on whether Taylor would sign the Wilmot Proviso. Many northern Whigs remained doubtful, while some southern Whigs like Georgia's Robert Toombs now feared that Taylor would indeed do so. In their minds, the Svengali-like Seward had bamboozled the cabinet into building up the northern party's antislavery wing with patronage, and they now intended to help it outbid Democrats for Free Soil support by passing the Proviso and securing Taylor's signature to it.[6]

Taylor, of course, meant to evade the Proviso by urging immediate statehood for California and New Mexico. That plan, he hoped, could hold his party together and attract sufficient Democratic support to pass by promising the North the substance of free soil in the Cession while sparing the South the indignity of congressional prohibition. Some able historians argue that Taylor's plan was doomed to defeat because it was "unrealistic" or an inadequate solution for an increasingly grave sectional crisis.[7] Yet Taylor had reason to be hopeful. Southern Democrats would certainly oppose it, but given the ground many northern Democrats had taken against slavery extension in 1849, they seemed unlikely to balk at the immediate admission of two free states. More important, the common rout that northern and southern Whigs had suffered at Democratic hands in 1849 made his plan potentially appealing to both sectional wings of the party.

Shaken by Democratic-Free Soil gains in 1849, personally hostile to slavery expansion, deluged by demands from constituents "that the proviso shall be incorporated in any Territorial Government created by Congress,"[8] and well aware that those constituents would judge their actions at the impending 1850 congressional elections, northern Whig congressmen could never allow the creation of formal territorial governments in the Mexican Cession without an explicit prohibition of slavery. In 1849, moreover, the Sewardite majority in New York's legislature had instructed the state's congressional delegation to fix Texas' western boundary at the Nueces River, and Sewardites would push similar resolutions in early 1850. Thus New York's huge Whig congressional delegation and many other northern Whigs regarded any proposal to legitimate Texas' grandiose claim to all the land east of the Rio Grande River as the kind of compromise to extend slavery that "would be death to the Whig party."[9]

Taylor's plan might appeal to such determined northern Whigs. Free Soilers and their northern Democratic allies seemed committed to the organization of territorial governments with the Proviso. Taylor's proposal to bypass the territorial stage and admit two free states immediately gave Whigs an attractive alternative to run on in 1850, especially as residents of New Mexico would never recognize Texas' boundary claims in any state constitution it drafted when applying for admission. By the end of 1849, in fact, growing numbers of northern Whigs were prepared to adopt alternative methods of stopping slavery expansion. After the Connecticut and Indiana congressional elections, some believed that northern Whig congressional candidates could never trump Free Soilers on the Proviso issue. Conservatives like New York's Daniel D. Barnard, who had long complained that the "Radical" antislavery line taken by Seward and Weed to attract Liberty and Free Soil voters would "denationalize our party and convert it, in this state, into an abolition party merely," worried that continued adherence to the Proviso would permanently alienate southern Whigs.[10] Massachusetts, Michigan, Pennsylvania, New Jersey, Ohio, Indiana, and other northern states also contained conservative Whig factions who chafed at the attempt to outbid Free Soilers for the antislavery vote, and their readiness for a new position offered the administration a potential base of support.

Primarily, however, many northern Whigs no longer deemed the Proviso necessary to stop slavery expansion. Upon learning in November about California's impending application for statehood, for example, Indiana editor John Defrees rejoiced that "the settlement of the slavery question by the California convention will do much to do away excitement on that subject. Let New Mexico do the same—and then let the Gen. Government cede to Maryland the District" to deprive Congress of jurisdiction over slavery and the slave trade there. Then "the infernal nigger business will not injure the Whig party as it has done last year." Northern Whigs like Defrees would readily back Taylor's plan since it would undermine much of the justification for a Free Soil party.[11]

Equally important, the earlier debates on the Clayton Compromise and the Walker amendment[12] convinced most northern Whigs that slavery could legally exist only where positive local law recognized it; that the local laws relevant to slavery in the Cession were the Mexican laws abolishing the institution; and that until Congress, territorial legislatures, or state constitutional conventions explicitly replaced Mexican laws with proslavery legislation, those laws would bar slavery from the Cession. Hence the positive congressional legislation against slavery that Free Soilers demanded was superfluous. The Wilmot Proviso was nothing "but an abstraction, a bugbear, a nonentity," counseled the conservative Nathan Appleton, since "there is no law [in the Cession] by which the master can hold his slave." A Fillmore ally also contended that "we need no laws for the Mexican territories as the laws of Mexico govern (which are opposed to slavery) until we shall pass laws for their future government. Hence, none but slaveholders want affirmative action to protect themselves." Seward's upstate New York constituents also wanted to admit California and leave the rest of the Cession unorganized because it was "under the Mexican law." A surprising consensus had emerged between antislavery Whigs and their conservative rivals in the North. Congress must "not ... pass any territorial bill without the *proviso*," but congressional "noninterference" that left the unorganized Cession under Mexican law was just as acceptable.[13]

When the Thirty-First Congress assembled, in sum, northern Whigs insisted that slavery be barred from the Mexican Cession by one of three methods: inaction that would continue Mexican laws in force, imposition of the Proviso on any formally organized territories, or the immediate admission of free states. Because Taylor's plan incorporated two of these alternatives, it had the potential of drawing strong northern Whig support.

Southern Whig congressional survivors of the Democratic pummeling in 1849 might also find Taylor's plan attractive, if only because Democrats' very militance during 1849 made it promising both as a face-saving alternative to Democratic demands and as a Union-saving measure with which to counter southern Democrats' Union-threatening extremism. During 1849 southern Democrats had not simply pilloried Whigs as potential traitors to Southern Rights; they had demanded guarantees that slavery would expand into the Mexican Cession. Some iterated Calhoun's contention that the Constitution automatically legalized slavery in all federal territories. Others demanded that Congress organize territorial governments that recognized slavery or extend the 36° 30' line to the Pacific coast and protect the right to own slaves south of it by federal law.

Not coincidentally, this latter stance challenged the claim Californians made in their new constitution to all of the Pacific coast from the 42nd parallel to the Mexican border. Democrats across Dixie vehemently objected to immediate statehood for California. Some protested that its proposed boundaries would deny slaveholders a port on the Pacific from which to export crops. Others cited the lack of congressional authorization. More complained that another free state would upset the balance between fifteen free and fifteen slave states in the Senate. Primarily, however, southern Democrats fumed that, by bypassing a formal territorial stage, California had denied slaveholders their equal rights in territories won by southern blood. Immediate statehood for California was just as intolerable as the Proviso.[14]

Most ominously, some southern Democrats in 1849 threatened disunion in response to purported northern aggressions. Democrats initiated Mississippi's call for a regionwide convention to meet in Nashville in June 1850 to hammer out a common strategy of resistance, and that call had cited any congressional attempt to bar slavery from the territories, to abolish it in the District of Columbia, or to interfere with the interstate slave trade as grounds for action. Only the need to retain Whig support for the call, moreover, had caused Mississippi's Democrats to drop California statehood from the list of contingencies justifying secession. Even as Congress assembled, however, Democrats rammed resolutions through the Georgia legislature demanding "that in the event of the passage of the Wilmot Proviso by Congress, the abolition of slavery in the District of Columbia, the admission of California as a state, in its pretended organization, or the continued refusal of non-slaveholding states to deliver up fugitive slaves as provided for in the Constitution, it will become the immediate and imperative duty of the People of this State to meet in Convention to take into consideration the mode and measure of redress."[15]

Most southern Democrats, in sum, would obviously oppose California state-hood, let alone New Mexico's, and a few southern Whig congressmen, who evinced comparable extremism by the fall of 1849, also seemed unlikely to support Taylor's plan. Appalled by Taylor's *"indifference* to the extension of slavery to the territories," Georgia's Berrien returned to the Senate determined to prevent California's admission and to vindicate slavery's legality throughout the Mexican Cession. In November, rumors also circulated that Senator Willie P. Mangum and Representative Thomas Clingman of North Carolina intended to instigate their southern Whig colleagues to issue their own "Address to the people on the subject of Slavery in California" that would "embarrass the Administration and cause a fearful rupture in our ranks." As an alarmed northern Whig warned Fillmore, "Look out for breakers ahead," since Mangum and Clingman now asserted "that neither Congress nor the people of California have any right to prohibit the introduction of slavery into that territory."[16]

Southern Whigs who were determined to stop California statehood at all costs, nonetheless, were atypical. The manifesto against California planned by Clingman and Mangum died stillborn because their fellow North Carolina Whigs ferociously opposed it. By early January, the moderate David Outlaw was predicting that both men would join the Democrats, Mangum because "he has lost influence with his own party" and Clingman because he "has an insane wish to be in the Senate, and thinks there is little hope of reaching that position by Whig votes."[17] All southern Whigs regarded congressional prohibition of slavery from the territories as intolerable, but many were untroubled by the prospect of immediate statehood for California and even for New Mexico. They believed that the whole quarrel over the Cession was about "moonshine" since "no matter what you may do or omit to do at Washington, there will never be slavery in any new territory." "The whole question is an abstract one without any practical bearing," wrote New Orleans editor William L. Hodge, "as there is not nor ever was any prospect for slavery in those territories." Tennessee's William B. Campbell agreed that if California and New Mexico applied for statehood and "exclude slavery in their constitutions, no one will pretend to require that they should be slave states." Georgia's Charles Jenkins concurred. Southerners in Congress must prevent en-actment of the Proviso, he wrote Berrien in December, but he personally could accept any other arrangement that "involved the exclusion of slavery," including immediate statehood, because slaveholders had "no practical interest in the ques-tion." Georgia Democrats' legislative resolutions were thus sheer bluster. The people of Georgia would never secede over the admission of California or even the enactment of the Proviso.[18]

Most southern Whigs, indeed, regarded Democrats' threats of disunion as in-sane, stressed their own devotion to the Union, and openly fought Democratic demands that delegates be sent to the impending Nashville Convention. Most, unlike Clingman and Berrien, flatly rejected the Calhounite doctrine that the Constitution automatically legalized slavery in the Cession and instead contended that only positive local or congressional laws could establish it there.[19] Most re-garded the whole sectional dispute over slavery extension as far more symbolic than substantive. To them, protecting southern equality and "Southern honor" by escaping the stigma of enslavement to northern dictation that congressional prohibition of slavery entailed, rather than actually extending the institution of slavery westward, was the heart of the territorial issue. Even Berrien, who argued that slavery could flourish in California, saw the territorial dispute primarily in symbolic terms. He admitted to his kinsman Jenkins that Northerners in Congress had no intention of abolishing slavery and that slavery could prosper into the unforeseeable future even if its extension were prohibited. Nonetheless, he protested, if the Northern majority could exclude slavery from the Cession, they would gain complete control of the national government. "Slavery will then exist in a double aspect. The African, and his owner, will both be slaves. The former, will as now, be the slave of his owner—but that owner, in all matters within the sphere of federal jurisdiction, will be the doomed thrall of those, with whom he associated on the basis of equal rights." For Berrien, other southern Whigs, and many southern Democrats, in sum, what was at stake in the territorial question was neither the end nor the weakening of African-American slavery. Rather, it was that dictatorial Northerners intended to treat white Southerners themselves as slaves.[20]

That southern Whigs regarded the slavery extension issue primarily as a matter of fending off white slavery rather than spreading black slavery, and that many would accept free states from the Mexican Cession, boded well for their reaction to Taylor's plan. Since Taylor's plan gave southern Whigs a platform that might settle the territorial crisis, evade the stigma of congressional prohibition, and thereby allow them to pose as defenders of the Union against dangerous Democratic hotheads, while simultaneously giving Northerners the substance of free soil, in short, it had more merit and greater potential for passing Congress than some historians have admitted.

Its chances of adoption, however, depended less on its merits than on contingencies over which Taylor had little control. Necessary support from northern Democrats required their willingness to sacrifice narrow partisan advantage. Northern Democratic support also depended on the maintenance of the advanced free-soil, antisouthern ground northern Democratic parties had assumed in 1849. If northern Democratic leaders decided instead that their fire-eating southern colleagues must be appeased, then the chances that they would acquiesce in the administration proposal would plummet.

Unified Whig support was equally problematic. Whigs angry with the allotment of patronage would have to forgive and forget or, at the least, divorce their patronage concerns from matters of policy. Likewise, rival factions within state parties and congressional delegations, whose enmity had been increased by patronage battles, must resist the temptation to strike out on separate paths, as Mangum, Clingman, and Berrien seemed prepared to do. Cooperation across the Mason-Dixon line required the preservation of comity that could be eroded by the abrasive interaction of northern and southern Whigs once Congress opened. Specifically, just as the willingness of southern Whigs to support Taylor's plan depended upon northern Whigs' abandoning the Proviso, northern Whigs' willingness to do that had a price. Because of Free Soil pressure, most of them would resist attempts by southern Whigs to extort concessions weakening the seemingly airtight defenses against slavery expansion contained in the other two alternatives—retention of Mexican law and statehood without a formal territorial stage. To many northern Whigs, indeed, the very word "compromise" connoted morally reprehensible and politically disastrous appeasement. "What do we gain by

Compromise?" Indiana editor Schuyler Colfax asked in February. "We weaken our ranks in the North. We drive from us the Free Soil Whigs whom we won back to our standard last year with our pledges. And we gain nothing in the South."[21] To forego demands for such concessions, southern Whigs, in turn, must heed convictions regarding the impossibility of slavery extension rather than succumb to the taunts and barbs from their Democratic competitors.

Above all, the success of Taylor's plan required speed, for delay would only increase the chances that one or more of the other contingencies could turn against the administration. As Congress prepared to open, in sum, substantial potential support for Taylor's policy existed both in Congress and in the country. But its adoption depended on an extraordinarily large number of cards falling into place. Almost none of them did. The course of events, not the substance of Taylor's plan or the transformation of the "crisis" into one that required a "broad sectional adjustment," doomed the administration to defeat.[22]

II

The odds against preserving Whig unity and passing Taylor's plan lengthened even before he presented it to Congress. Submission of his annual message had to await organization of the House of Representatives. As early as the summer of 1849, the Massachusetts Free Soiler Charles Sumner had predicted that both the Whig and Democratic parties would shatter along sectional lines when the House attempted to select a speaker.[23] Because the speaker appointed all committees, his party would control that chamber. Electing the speaker, in turn, required an absolute majority of those voting, and, in contrast to the Senate, where Democratic dominance was assured, when Congress opened no one could tell which party might marshal the necessary majority.

Nominally, Democrats had the advantage. At full strength they held about 114 safe seats compared to 106 or so for the Whigs. But this edge did not guarantee success. Not all members had reached Washington when voting for speaker began. Even when all were in attendance, Free Soilers held the balance of power, yet few knew the exact size of that critical minority or how it might act in the speakership contest. Newspaper estimates of Free Soil strength ranged from eight to seventeen. The list included former Democrats like Preston King and David Wilmot, as well as men elected by Free Soil-Democratic coalitions like Connecticut's three representatives. Most, however, were former Whigs or men who had run on joint Whig-Free Soil tickets. If all of these men backed their own candidate for speaker, they could prevent either major party from electing its man and perhaps force concessions from one or the other, as Ohio's Free Soilers had in the state legislature. Conversely, if the Free Soilers failed to hang together or nominate their own candidate, their votes might be up for grabs.[24]

If so, Whigs might have an advantage and not simply because most Free Soilers had Whig backgrounds. The sectional balance within the party delegations and the aggressive antislavery stance northern Democrats had adopted in 1849 also seemed to favor them. Exclusive of Democratic-Free Soilers, Southerners outnumbered Northerners sixty-one to fifty among House Democrats. The dominant Southerners could insist upon a southern candidate for speaker whom northern

Democrats and Free Soilers might not support, especially if he had signed Calhoun's Southern Address. Among Whigs, in contrast, the sectional imbalance tilted steeply northward. Unlike the Senate, where the thirteen northern and twelve southern Whigs were almost evenly matched, in the House the thirty southern Whigs could be overwhelmed by seventy-six northern colleagues. Of the thirty Southerners, moreover, only seven came from the Deep South—one from Florida, three from Georgia, two from Alabama, and one from Louisiana—while ten hailed from the hitherto moderate border slave states of Delaware, Maryland, and Kentucky.[25]

The implications of this arithmetic were clear. Any Democratic proposals for the territories would be oriented toward the party's southern majority. Conversely, any Whig proposals, including those of *both* Taylor and Clay, had to satisfy the party's northern majority. Because of their heavy numerical preponderance, northern Whigs expected to choose the Whig candidate for speaker and to chart the party's course. With Whigs running a Northerner and Democrats a Southerner, who would probably own slaves, Whigs' chances of electing the speaker and controlling the House seemed decent. If they could hold Northerners and Southerners together behind their candidate, they might pick up enough votes from disaffected northern Democrats and erstwhile Whigs among the Free Soilers to elect their man.

Encouraged by such calculations, House Whigs caucused on the night of Saturday, December 1, to select their candidate. The overwhelming favorite was the scholarly, bespectacled Boston patrician Robert C. Winthrop, who had performed ably as speaker during the previous Congress. A special target for abuse from ex-Whig Free Soilers like Root, Giddings, and Allen, Winthrop was unlikely to get their votes, but their intransigent hostility might not extend to other former Whigs in Free Soil ranks. Their antagonism, along with Winthrop's moderate record, moreover, made him perfectly acceptable to most southern Whigs.

Most, but not all, Southerners. Before the Whigs could vote on Winthrop, Stephens and Toombs sought to extort a pledge from the northern majority that they would not try to impose the Proviso on the Mexican Cession or to abolish slavery in the District during the ensuing session. Just as two years earlier, when the northern-dominated Whig caucus had called a national convention over the protests of southern Taylorites, the northern majority refused to be bullied and unceremoniously shelved Toombs' motion. In response, Stephens, Toombs, their Georgia colleague Allen Owen, Florida's Edward Carrington Cabell, Alabama's Henry Hilliard, and Virginia's Jeremiah Morton ostentatiously marched out of the caucus, which then nominated Winthrop for speaker.[26]

Two weeks later on the House floor, Toombs justified his bolt. Blasting Northerners' intransigent commitment to the Proviso, he belched defiance. "If by your legislation you seek to drive us from the territories of California and New Mexico . . . and to abolish slavery in this District, thereby attempting to fix a national degradation upon the States of this Confederacy," he exclaimed, "*I am for disunion* and . . . I will devote all I am and all I have on earth to its consummation." When Illinois Whig Edward Baker retorted that disunion was impossible, Stephens sprang to his friend's aid. "I tell this House that every word uttered by my colleague meets my hearty response. . . . I would rather that the southern country should perish . . . than submit for one instant to degradation." Thus did the two Georgians, who had helped sabotage Calhoun's southern caucus explicitly to preserve the Whig party and who had happily promoted California's admission as a free state ten months earlier, emphatically—or so it seemed—mouth the rhetoric of radical proslavery Democrats. It appeared indeed as though "the slavery excitement" would "obliterate party lines."[27]

Long before these speeches, indignant Whigs across the country had denounced the Southerners' bolt and wondered what had provoked it. They recognized that it probably doomed Winthrop's chances of election because some of the six seceders had angrily pledged to oppose him. That all of the bolters except the freshmen Owen and Morton had helped secure Taylor's nomination and that Stephens and Toombs had helped select Taylor's now-reviled cabinet especially enraged Whigs. "Toombs," complained the mild-mannered Winthrop, "is a spoiled child— jealous, impatient, & perverse. He had his own way in respect to the Cabinet, & now he must rule or ruin in the House." Toombs' personality may have explained his action to Winthrop, but other Whigs wondered what "madness" caused it.[28]

Angry about a ruling Winthrop had made during the last Congress, Toombs made no secret of his "personal hostility" toward Winthrop, but his personal peeves do not explain his extreme language on the House floor, the specific content of his resolutions, or the actions of the other bolters. Stephens and Toombs later told an appalled Crittenden that loyalty to the South had motivated them. Apprehensive that Taylor, the cabinet, and the northern Whig majority in Congress had fallen under Seward's influence and meant "to form a coalition with the Free Soilers" by enacting and securing Taylor's signature to the Wilmot Proviso, they had moved resolutely to deter northern Whigs. "My course became instantly fixed," explained Toombs. "I would not hesitate to oppose the proviso, even to a dissolution of the Union." Hence he determined "to prevent the organization of the House going into the hands of the Northern Whig party."[29]

Ultimately, however, these explanations seem self-serving and unsatisfactory. Since all southern Whigs feared enactment of the Proviso, why did Toombs and Stephens, rather than other Southerners, introduce the resolutions, and why did only six of thirty Southerners bolt the Whig caucus when it rejected them? Taylor's refusal to divulge his plan to Toombs at a White House interview prior to the Whig caucus, Toombs told Crittenden, convinced him that Taylor now intended to sign the Proviso. Yet in early December, both Stephens and Georgia Senator William C. Dawson wrote home that they had learned of Taylor's plan, and both pronounced it perfectly acceptable. If they knew of Taylor's plan, how could Toombs not know? And why make such a fuss about the Proviso if they knew Taylor intended to sidestep it? Most important, why go out of their way to threaten secession on the House floor if slavery were kept out of California? Their speeches implied that both the enactment of the Proviso and the admission of California as a free state would be grounds for dissolving the Union since either action constituted legislation barring slavery from it.[30]

Seward came closer to the mark when he explained the bolt as a defensive gesture against taunts by southern Democrats that the Whig party, led by Taylor, meant to sack the South. Alabama's Henry Hilliard, who liked Winthrop and was deeply embarrassed by his action, sheepishly explained that the caucus' rejection of Toombs' resolutions "leaves those of us who come from heavy slaveholding Districts under the necessity of maintaining just now an independent course—

lest we should seem to sanction the course of the caucus on that dangerous question.'' That five of the seven Whigs from the Deep South, where the party had been thrashed in 1849 and where Democrats now threatened secession should Congress admit California or pass the Proviso, joined the bolters suggests that fear of disunion and of Democratic demagoguery on the issue influenced them. Jeremiah Morton did not come from a heavy slaveholding district, even in terms of Virginia, but Morton had won with Democratic support over the regular Whig candidate, John Pendleton, whom he attacked for failing to sign the Southern Address. He, too, felt pressure to veer to the Democratic position.[31]

Toombs, Stephens, and Owens were undoubtedly worried by the Democratic trend in Georgia, especially since Democrats had also won a special congressional election to fill Thomas Butler King's Savannah seat in November, just when Democratic state legislators were pushing their defiant resolutions. Hence they may have sought to neutralize any Democratic advantage by forcefully espousing the Democratic position. Two facts, however, argue against the sufficiency of this explanation. Stephens contemptuously dismissed those ''fighting resolves'' as mere ''braggadocio.''[32] By mid-February, moreover, he and Toombs were working for a compromise that included California statehood, exactly what Democrats and they themselves in December called grounds for disunion.

That about-face suggests that more than an attempt to blunt Democratic criticism spurred Stephens and Toombs. The key to their action lay in their rivalry with Berrien, who returned to the Senate in December determined to expose his Georgia Whig nemeses' supposedly weak commitment to Southern Rights. Unlike Berrien, Stephens and Toombs had bolted Calhoun's southern caucus the previous winter, endorsed immediate statehood for California, and publicly challenged Calhoun's doctrine by admitting the constitutionality, even as they denounced the unfairness, of congressional prohibition and by insisting that only local laws could protect slavery and that Mexico's antislavery laws retained force in the Cession until Congress replaced them. All of these heresies, Berrien and his Georgia lieutenants concluded, left them vulnerable to political destruction.

Berrien's intended weapon was the resolutions on federal relations that the Georgia legislature was formulating as Congress met. Although the Democratic majority had railroaded extreme resolutions through the lower house in November, Whig state representative Charles J. Jenkins, Berrien's closest Georgia ally, successfully moved that the house and senate create a joint committee to draft new resolutions, which everyone expected Jenkins to write. Thus Berrien bombarded Jenkins from Washington with word-by-word instructions for the new resolutions that he thought would annihilate Stephens and Toombs politically. Georgia must condemn California statehood, he ordered. Jenkins must expose, as well, ''the fallacy of the position that *slavery exists only by statute and cannot exist beyond the limit of the state enacting it.*'' He must also attack ''the perversion, or entire misconception that the laws of the conquered country continue in force until repealed by Congress.'' Instead, he should ''show that the laws of Mexico have ceased to exist in California and New Mexico and that a Southern slaveholder has a right to carry his slave there since there is no existing law to forbid it.'' Nor could Congress prohibit slavery there, for the Northwest Ordinance formed no precedent for the Wilmot Proviso. Here, Berrien commanded, Jenkins should stop. The legislature must not threaten secession or give ''even an indication of what in any given circumstances she w[oul]d do." Berrien, in sum, wanted the Georgia legislature to repudiate virtually everything Stephens and Toombs had said since 1847.[33]

Stephens and Toombs had to have known that Berrien hoped to outflank them on the slavery issue, and their strident rhetoric and disruptive behavior in December, especially their willingness to threaten secession when Berrien would not, were meant to foil him by reestablishing their own credentials as champions of Southern Rights. Berrien's Georgia friends certainly interpreted the duo's action as a response to their own more militant position. Their movement, crowed one, "is a tacit admission I take it that they have waited too long in taking decisive ground on the Slavery question."[34]

Equally significant, Berrien's friends warned him, most Georgia Whigs applauded Toombs' and Stephens' bold stand. Thus Berrien found himself once again in danger of being outmaneuvered by his wily antagonists, especially as his attempt to dictate Georgia's legislative resolutions to rebuke their earlier stands was frustrated.[35] Refusing to surrender the advanced proslavery ground to them once again, Berrien later announced his hostility to both the Taylor and Clay plans because both called for California statehood. Only after Berrien had publicly committed himself to this position did Stephens and Toombs begin to work for a compromise that included California's admission. Their defiant behavior in December, in sum, was a preemptive strike to forestall criticism from Democrats and Whigs in Georgia, one that goaded Berrien out onto an extremist limb on the California issue. And as soon as he had crawled out on it, they began to saw it off with consummate skill. Thus did factional rivalry shape the bewildering behavior of Georgia Whigs in the Thirty-First Congress. Thus did selfish and myopic tactical decisions help inflame sectional antagonisms and reduce the chances that Taylor's plan could succeed.[36]

Whatever motivated the six Southerners' bolt, it decisively influenced attempts to organize the House. On Monday, December 3, the House began a three-week marathon that took sixty-three ballots to choose a presiding officer. Democrats ran Georgia's Howell Cobb, and despite his well-publicized opposition to Calhoun's Southern Address, some northern Democrats refused to support him. Nor would all Whigs unite behind Winthrop. The first ballot set a pattern for subsequent roll calls. Cobb received 103 votes, Winthrop won 96, and the remaining members scattered their votes, thus denying either one the necessary majority. Eight or nine Free Soilers consistently voted for David Wilmot or some other member of their group. The six southern Whig bolters cast their votes for Meredith Gentry, who had not yet arrived in Washington to protest their action. After a few ballots Hilliard swung behind Winthrop, but the other five remained in stubborn opposition. A few northern Whigs and Democrats who had won with Free Soil backing also deserted the two caucus candidates and wasted their votes on still other men.[37]

So it went for vote after vote, day after day. Resentments intensified. Tempers frayed. On one occasion, fists flew. This long agony clearly aggravated sectional animosities within both major parties and reduced the likelihood that northern and southern Whigs might combine behind Taylor's plan. Night after night Whigs caucused to reconsider their commitment to Winthrop, and night after night the northern majority, pressured by northern senators and their constituents, pledged to stick by Winthrop rather than succumb to the extortion of Toombs and his fellow bolters, who vowed, in turn, that no northern Whig would be speaker. For northern Whigs, Winthrop's candidacy became a test of sectional will and honor, a test they refused to fail.[38]

Democrats, in fact, splintered long before the Whigs, but sectional jealousies still kept anyone from prevailing. From the first ballot on December 3 through the thirty-ninth ballot on December 11, between 96 and 102 Whigs (including the Philadelphia Native American Lewis C. Levin) steadfastly adhered to Winthrop, but five southern bolters and the Free Soilers resolutely opposed him. Meanwhile, Cobb's support eroded and Democrats fragmented as early as the thirteenth ballot. By the end of the session's first week, between sixteen and twenty men were receiving votes on each ballot. Gradually, however, the Democrats began to coalesce behind Indiana's William J. Brown. By the final ballot on Tuesday, December 11, with 114 votes necessary for election, the tally stood 109 for Brown, 101 for Winthrop, 7 for Wilmot, 5 for the Kentucky Whig Charles S. Morehead, to whom the Stephens-Toombs bolters had suddenly switched that day, and five other votes scattered. Then came an indelible demonstration of the sectional rancor that paralyzed the House.

At their caucus the previous night, Whigs agreed to stick with Winthrop one more day and then, on December 12, to concentrate behind Morehead, who, it was hoped, could hold all of Winthrop's supporters and pick up enough southern Democrats to triumph. Before balloting began on the 11th, Whigs made their intentions known, and by the end of the day, according to Morehead, as many as twenty southern Democrats had promised him support. The switch of Toombs and company from Gentry to Morehead on the 11th, however, irreparably stigmatized him among northern Whigs, who, by this point, would never support anyone Toombs and Stephens favored. At the caucus on the night of the 11th, northern Whigs complained that Morehead's election "would ruin the Whig party in the North," particularly if southern Democrats also supported him. The disappointed Morehead graciously withdrew as the nominee, and the caucus voted to back North Carolina's Edward Stanly instead. But Stanly, a firm Taylor man, had the same drawback as Morehead. Because he represented a slave state, northern Whigs refused to support him.[39]

On December 12 eleven different Whigs—four Southerners and seven Northerners—received votes for speaker, with William Duer of New York leading the pack with a mere twenty-six votes and Stanly garnering only eighteen. The Democrat Brown meanwhile climbed to 112, and his triumph on the next ballot seemed assured. Now Democrats foundered on the rock of sectional distrust. Brown's total included five Free Soilers, who had threatened to help elect him unless Whigs abandoned Winthrop. Shocked southern Democrats immediately demanded to know why Brown, who had "professed great friendship for the South" in the Democratic caucus, got Free Soil votes. Before the day ended, it was proved that Brown had secretly promised Wilmot that, if elected, Brown would allow Free Soilers to name the three committees that dealt with slavery and also support abolition in the District. As Outlaw succinctly wrote his wife, "This exposure has overwhelmed him." Brown never got another vote.[40]

The following day, on the forty-first ballot, a staggering total of thirty different men received votes for speaker. Winthrop and Cobb reemerged as their parties' front-runners, but with only fifty-nine and forty votes, respectively. The stalemate continued until Saturday, December 22, when, after the fifty-ninth fruitless ballot, a Democrat moved that the House vote three more times and, if no one secured a majority on those roll calls, determine the winner by a plurality on the sixty-third ballot. This procedural motion carried 113 to 106, with most Whigs in the majority. Voting against it were the Free Soilers and the five southern Whig bolters, who preferred a stalemate to an enemy's triumph. On the sixty-third and final ballot Cobb edged out Winthrop 102 to 99, an outcome most northern Whigs viewed as a southern as much as a Democratic victory. Southern Democrats were not content with their success in the contest for speaker, however. When the Democratic caucus nominated Pennsylvania's John Forney for the influential clerkship of the House, southern Democrats rebelled and helped elect the Whig candidate, Thomas J. Campbell of Tennessee.[41]

Thus did the southern minority overcome a substantial northern preponderance within the chamber and within the Whig party to organize the House. That victory and the sectional ill-feeling it both reflected and exacerbated decisively influenced the attempt to resolve the territorial crisis. Although Cobb was no fire-eater, one consequence of his election as speaker and of Democratic control of both the House and Senate committees was abundantly clear. The chance that Congress might heed Taylor's policy recommendations measurably declined.

III

Cobb's election finally allowed Taylor to send his annual message, along with the reports of his department heads, to Congress on Christmas Eve. During the three-week delay, speculation about Taylor's intentions had intensified. "Thunderstruck" after seeing Taylor, Indiana Free Soiler George W. Julian sneered that he was "an old, outrageously ugly, uncultivated, uninformed man" who "can't converse in decent language" and who "*cannot* be otherwise than a perfect *tool* in the hands of Clayton & Co."[42] Contrary to this biased assessment, Taylor was infuriated rather than intimidated by southern threats to secede and refused to abandon what he regarded as the best compromise solution to the squabble over the Cession. Taylor, Seward assured Weed, was "as willing to try conclusions with [southern malcontents] as General Jackson was with the Nullifiers." He would make his determination to crush any attempt at disunion unmistakably clear in his message to Congress.[43]

The message, drafted primarily by Clayton, emphasized foreign relations since Taylor's inauguration. It also echoed the recommendations for tariff revision and a congressional reconsideration of the subtreasury system in Meredith's accompanying report, but unlike Meredith, Taylor, in good Whig fashion, called on Congress to fund rivers and harbors improvements. Sandwiched between these sections was a single paragraph dealing with the Mexican Cession. Californians had written a constitution and would apply for statehood, Taylor blandly reported, and he recommended "their application to the favorable consideration of Congress." The people of New Mexico would follow suit "at no very distant period," and "by awaiting their action all causes of uneasiness may be avoided and confidence and kind feeling preserved." Obviously referring to the Free Soilers, he pointedly repeated Washington's warning against political parties characterized by "geographical discriminations" and urged that "we should abstain from the introduction of those exciting topics of a sectional character which have hitherto produced painful apprehensions in the public mind."[44]

Two other passages merit attention. "The Executive has authority to recommend (not to dictate) measures to Congress," Taylor asserted. He would not interfere with Congress' deliberations until it sent bills to him, and he would use the veto "only in extraordinary cases." Members of Congress, when writing legislation, owed "no responsibility to any human power but their constituents." Some southern congressmen took this passage as confirmation of their worst fears—that Taylor would indeed sign the Proviso if Congress enacted it. Instead, he was reassuring Whigs that he would heed Congress' will. Whig congressmen, therefore, could understandably interpret Taylor's recommendations for the Cession not as non-negotiable demands, but as mere suggestions that Taylor would readily abandon if they devised an alternative policy.

Taylor was much clearer about threats to the Union. "In my judgment its dissolution would be the greatest of calamities, and to avert that should be the study of every American," he declared. "Whatever dangers may threaten it, I shall stand by it and maintain it in its integrity to the full extent of the obligations imposed and the power conferred upon me by the Constitution." Time would soon show that this pledge was not mere rhetoric.

Reaction to the message predictably followed party lines. Democrats ridiculed a careless malapropism about foreign relations. Whigs generally praised the tone and substance of the document. The few Whigs who alluded to Taylor's brief remarks about California and New Mexico, including Southerners, applauded them. "We think 'the world' of the Message," summarized one of Seward's New York allies.[45]

Completely neglected by historians, Meredith's Treasury report excited Whigs far more than Taylor's message. "I have read the message with great pleasure," gushed John Pendleton Kennedy. "But above all papers I have ever read of the kind I have never seen anything better than Meredith's. That report alone ought to be a bulwark to Taylor's administration which nothing could shake." Manufacturers in Boston, New York, and Philadelphia were said to be delighted. Even a few Democrats lauded Meredith's recommendations for tariff revision and the subtreasury system. Whatever happened to the territorial issue, it appeared when Congress opened that the administration's economic program stood a chance of winning the bipartisan backing Taylor and Meredith envisioned.[46]

One significant group of businessmen, however, did not join the chorus praising Meredith's report. Importing merchants in Boston and New York City who benefited from the public warehousing system were frightened by Meredith's critique of it as a drain on public revenues. Fear in the mercantile community became outright alienation when, in late January, Meredith laid off New York's superintendent of public warehouses and all of his subordinates on the grounds that the customs service could not afford their salaries. To angry merchants this action seemed abolition of the public warehousing system by administrative fiat. That importing merchants in Boston, New York, and Philadelphia would take the lead in organizing and financing opposition to Taylor's proposal for the Mexican Cession was no coincidence. Resentment of Meredith's economic program prepared the way.[47]

Whatever Whigs' reactions, Democrats in Congress quickly flouted Taylor's recommendations, thereby jeopardizing their adoption. Three days after Taylor's message arrived, Senator Henry Foote of Mississippi moved that Congress' "duty" was "to establish suitable territorial governments for California, for Deseret [Utah], and for New Mexico." Organizing territorial governments that provoked fights over the Proviso was, of course, precisely what Taylor hoped to avert. In early January, Senator James M. Mason of Virginia introduced a harsh fugitive slave bill. At the same time, southern Democrats in both the House and Senate demanded that Taylor send Congress all the administration's correspondence with its agents in California and New Mexico in order to expose Taylor as the instigator of western movements for statehood with free constitutions. During January, Foote and Missouri's Thomas Hart Benton also sparred over a crucial topic that Taylor had ignored in his annual message—the location of the boundary between Texas and New Mexico. Foote insisted that Texas retain all the land it claimed east of the Rio Grande River, while Benton granted New Mexico everything north of the Red River and west of the 102nd meridian, hundreds of miles east of the Rio Grande, in return for a payment of $15 million from the federal government. Democrats emphatically signaled, in short, that Whigs alone would not determine congressional policy.[48]

Taylor clarified his own proposal in special messages to the House and Senate on January 21 and 23 responding to Democrats' demands for information about the administration's activities in California and New Mexico. Protesting that he had instructed his emissaries not to interfere when local residents drafted state constitutions, he freely admitted that he had urged them to write such documents and apply for statehood in order "to put it in the power of Congress, by the admission of California and New Mexico as States, to remove all occasion for the unnecessary agitation of the public mind." Without immediate statehood sectional conflict over slavery extension was inevitable, for "under the Constitution Congress has power to make all needful rules and regulations respecting the Territories of the United States." Hence every acquisition of territory had provoked conflict over whether slavery "should or should not be prohibited in that territory." For the first time, in short, Taylor publicly asserted that Congress had the constitutional right to ban slavery from territories and thus hinted that should Congress pass the Proviso, he would not veto it.[49]

But his proposal would avert the Proviso. Californians had written a constitution and would apply for statehood, and "I earnestly recommend that it may receive the sanction of Congress." In a clear allusion to the northern Whigs' earlier burial of Preston's California statehood bill through a Proviso amendment, Taylor then warned Congress not to "annex a condition" regarding slavery to California's "admission as a State." Such a stipulation would be meaningless since, once admitted, California could change its constitution. Moreover, such congressional dictation denied a state's right to determine its "domestic institutions" for itself, a right, Taylor did not have to add, that Southerners stridently defended. Furthermore, "it is to be expected that in the residue of the territory ceded to us by Mexico the people residing there will at the time of their incorporation into the Union settle all questions of domestic policy to suit themselves."

As for New Mexico, its residents would also seek statehood "at no very distant period." Until they did so, Taylor declared, it would be inexpedient for Congress "to establish a Territorial government . . . especially as the people of this Territory still enjoy the benefit and protection of their municipal laws originally derived from Mexico and have a military force there to protect them from the Indians." Quick statehood for New Mexico would also allow the Supreme Court to resolve its boundary dispute with Texas. If New Mexico instead remained a territory, Congress itself would have to find an adjustment, a task that was impossible without sacrificing the claims of Texas or New Mexico. Because "the question which now excites such painful sensations in the country will in the end certainly be settled by the silent effect of causes independent of the action of Congress," Taylor concluded, "I again submit to your wisdom the policy . . . of awaiting the salutary operation of those causes." Nonaction by Congress, other than the admission of states, would "avoid the creation of geographical parties and secure the harmony of feeling so necessary to the beneficial action of our political system."

Taylor thus brilliantly charted a middle path between sectional extremes defined by the Free Soilers and Calhounites, a path that nonetheless clove to the northern side of the sectional divide in terms of substantive benefits. Taylor could count. Northern Whigs dominated the congressional party. He would save southern honor by averting the "degradation" of congressional prohibition, but he would guarantee the North free soil, under Mexican law prior to statehood and under antislavery constitutions after statehood.

Immediate reaction to Taylor's plan divided along partisan and sectional lines. Free Soilers like Ohio's Edward Wade contemptuously dismissed it as a sellout to the South. Not only did Taylor flatly denounce sectional parties like theirs, but he opposed congressional prohibition of slavery from the territories and seemed to deny Congress' right to deny admission to new slave states. Northern Democratic papers, in contrast, endorsed immediate statehood for California, but they accused Taylor of shamelessly pirating Lewis Cass' popular sovereignty doctrine, which northern Whigs had scorned in 1848, and sneered that his "nonaction plan" for the remainder of the Cession was hopelessly inadequate.[50]

Everything about the plan—the recommendation of immediate statehood, the admission that congressional prohibition was constitutional, the proposal that Mexican law operate until statehood, the apparent animus against Texas—infuriated southern Democrats. Editors and congressmen blasted it as their long-forecasted betrayal of the South by Taylor, as a thinly veiled attempt to keep slavery out of the Mexican Cession that was more loathsome than even the Wilmot Proviso because Taylor tried to accomplish by deceit what Northerners had attempted in the open. Taylor's action in California and New Mexico, thundered Virginia's Congressman James A. Seddon, was "insidious and fatal to the rights and interests of my section." The administration had thrown its "whole weight against the . . . slaveholder."[51]

In the North and border states, Whig papers and politicos fulsomely praised the special message. "The ground taken is just right," proclaimed an enthusiastic

Bostonian, a judgment widely shared by his fellow northern Whigs.[52] Most southern Whigs, in contrast, reacted frostily. While a few Whig papers publicly praised Taylor's plan and while many southern Whigs privately contended that the whole question of slavery extension was a nettlesome abstraction, only one southern Whig congressman responded immediately to Taylor's special message. North Carolina's Clingman denounced it as vehemently as did southern Democrats. The "impudent" plan would leave the South "degraded and enslaved." "Give us . . . fair settlement," thundered Clingman, but do not "cheat us by a mere empty form." If California were admitted, slavery must be guaranteed in the remainder of the Cession. If Northerners would not make such a concession, he would welcome secession, and to stop Taylor's unjust scheme he was prepared to lead filibusters against all appropriation bills. Thus did Clingman, who was obviously courting North Carolina's Democrats to gain a Senate seat, mount the barricades of revolt thrown up earlier by Toombs and Stephens.[53]

Other southern Whig congressmen remained silent, but most were cool to Taylor's proposal. It was not long, however, before they articulated their own proposal as the price of California's admission. Because almost all congressmen agreed that Mexican law barred slavery from the Cession until Congress replaced it, Massachusetts' Julius Rockwell explained to a friend, "it becomes the policy of the South to have territorial govts. established" without the Proviso and to extend the boundary of Texas to the Rio Grande. As to which southern Whig was expected to challenge Taylor by advancing such a scheme, there was little doubt. On the day that Taylor sent his annual message to Congress, Iverson Harris wrote Berrien, "In Georgia the hope is extensively diffused that Mr. Clay means to crown his illustrious life with the adjustment of all of these questions."[54]

IV

Almost seventy-three when he reached Washington in December, Henry Clay suffered from a protracted and enervating cold. Nonetheless, when Clay ventured out for social occasions, he still exhibited the sparkling wit and personal magnetism that had dazzled Washington society for four decades. Even the caustic Free Soiler Julian begrudgingly admitted that Clay exerted "a peculiar power in his presence," and at the traditional White House New Year's levee Clay was "an object of as much attraction as the President himself." "From everybody, of both parties," Clay wrote his wife, "I receive friendly attentions and kind consideration."[55]

For months politicians had speculated about Clay's relationship with the new administration, and the president and his cabinet officers showed Clay every social courtesy, calling at his lodgings and showering him with more dinner invitations than his poor health allowed him to accept. Social politeness did not translate into political intimacy, however. Clayton was an exception. To Clay's delight, Clayton kept him posted on the activities of his son James' efforts in Lisbon to settle a long-disputed American claim against Portugal. With the others, Clay's relations were "civil . . . but nothing more."[56]

Clay's dealings with Taylor himself were also superficially polite, but he still disdained and resented the former general. In January he bluntly told the Free

Soilers Julian and Giddings that the nomination of Taylor "had been & would be the ruin of the Whigs."[57] Clay shared congressional Whigs' anger at Taylor's appointments, but he faulted Taylor primarily for failing to outline a policy during 1849 on which Whigs could successfully campaign. "The elections of this year," he groused to James in early December, "have gone very unfavorably to the Whigs, and without some favorable turn in public affairs in their favor they must lose the ascendancy."[58] Supplying a program that could put the Whigs back on a winning track thus appealed to Clay as a fitting way to turn the tables on the political novice in the White House and the ingrates who had nominated him. Clay could reestablish his own stature as the party's preeminent statesman by doing what the military hero had manifestly failed to do.

The sectional rift within the Whig party and the nation also genuinely alarmed him. The secessionist rhetoric of "Hotspurs" like Stephens and Toombs and the menacing legislative resolutions adopted in the Deep South persuaded him that "disunionist sentiment" had spread further than he had thought. By mid-January he was clearly worried that the Union stood in jeopardy and that Taylor's elliptical December message would not satisfy either section. Nor did Taylor's annual message address what Clay astutely saw was the crux of the problem. As early as the previous June, Clay had written his friend Thomas Stevenson "that more difficulty will be encountered in fixing the boundaries of Texas than in deciding the question of the introduction of Slavery in the new territories." Taylor was also mum about other southern grievances growing out of "the vexed subject of Slavery"—fear of abolition in the District and the emerging demand for a new fugitive slave law. Here then was an opportunity to give a "favorable turn" to "public affairs" that might help the Whigs. By January 2, three weeks before Taylor sent his special message to Congress, Clay had already decided to proffer "some comprehensive scheme of settling amicably the whole question, in all its bearings."[59]

Patriotism, paternal concern for his beloved and endangered Whig party, and jealousy of Taylor, in sum, all motivated Clay. In January, he had no desire to split the Whig party or to lead Whigs into a bipartisan coalition with Democrats. Clay's model was the Tyler administration when congressional Whigs as a body had isolated the president, ignored his recommendations, and rallied behind Clay's leadership to formulate their own program. If Taylor betrayed his pledge to allow Congress to make policy without any interference from the executive and dared to oppose the congressional plan, he might share Tyler's fate. If instead he accepted Clay's formula, then, as one Whig had predicted a year earlier, "all that is done will be attributed to Clay & Taylor will be regarded as a mere tool in his hands." Either way, Clay's revenge would be sweet.[60]

During the first three weeks of January, Clay worked out the details of his plan at night in the seclusion of his hotel rooms, and whom, if anyone, he consulted in that period is unknown. Then, on the night of January 21, after Taylor's special message had been read to the House, the sick Kentuckian braved a cold rainstorm to make an unannounced visit to the house of Daniel Webster. Although Clay had barely spoken to his ancient rival during the previous eight years, he now informed his surprised host of the gist of his scheme, argued that it would satisfy some Democrats and all southern Whigs except the Georgians, and asked Webster's help in saving the Union. Refusing to commit himself to the specifics of the plan, Webster approved its principle and praised Clay's patriotism.

Thus did the two symbols of ultra Whiggery, both of whom resented their displacement by the neophyte Taylor, appear to join forces.[61]

On January 29, before packed galleries, Clay presented to the Senate eight resolutions that together comprised his alternative to the president's plan. Ten months later, after Congress had adjourned, he would assert that his "whole system of measures, as originally proposed, finally prevailed in both houses of congress" to become the famous Compromise of 1850. Throughout his illustrious career Henry Clay had a truly magnificent capacity for self-deception, but some historians have accepted the essential accuracy of this self-serving statement. To appreciate how preposterous it was, in exactly what ways Clay's original proposals differed from Taylor's, and why Whigs reacted to the different plans as they did, one must examine Clay's propositions closely and especially distinguish their content from the rhetorical gloss in which he encased them.[62]

Clay did characterize his resolutions as a Union-saving compromise. "Taken together in combination," he began, they proposed "an amicable arrangement of all questions of controversy between the free and the slave states, growing out of the subject of slavery." They represented "a great national scheme of compromise and harmony" that was imperative, for the Union was in danger. Southerners might secede rather than submit to northern aggressions against slavery. Hence he was asking the North to make a "more liberal and extensive concession" than the South. The North could afford such magnanimity because it was "numerically more powerful than the slave States" and because northern hostility to slavery was but a mere "sentiment without sacrifice, a sentiment without danger, a sentiment without hazard, without peril, without loss." At stake for the South, in contrast, was not only the potential loss of an incalculable amount of property but also insurrection, arson, pillage, murder, and rape—in short, obliteration of "the social fabric, life, and all that makes life desirable and happy." Justice and the Union's preservation required Northerners to make the greater sacrifice.[63]

In modern political jargon, Clay's assessment of his proposals would be called "spin control." It bore little relationship to their substance. Clay hoped to rally all congressional Whigs behind his plan, and, like Taylor, he could count. He offered southern Whigs reassuring words, but his actual recommendations were slanted to appeal to the northern Whig majority.

Clay's plan was more comprehensive and, superficially, more prosouthern than Taylor's. His last four resolutions dealt with subjects Taylor had ignored. One called on Congress to abolish the notorious slave market in the District of Columbia, a demand long pressed by northern Whigs. The other three addressed southern fears and grievances. Congress should declare that it had no power to prohibit the interstate slave trade and that it was "inexpedient" to abolish slavery itself in the District of Columbia without the approval of Maryland, the consent of the District's residents, and "just compensation to the owners of slaves within the District." Finally, Clay asked Congress to enact a "more effectual" fugitive slave law.

Clay obviously intended the three prosouthern resolutions to reassure Southerners that secession was unnecessary, but they bear closer examination. Two of the three entailed no concrete legislation that benefited Southerners. Rather, Clay merely called on Congress to declare that it would not take action against the interstate slave trade or slavery in the District. By asserting that abolition in the

District was "inexpedient," moreover, Clay implied that Congress had the right to do it, a right that southern Democrats and many southern Whigs furiously denied. Finally, while Clay did call for a new fugitive slave law, the law Congress eventually passed omitted provisions Clay included in his own version to provide minimal procedural protection to alleged fugitives, provisions Clay clearly hoped would make the bill palatable to northern Whigs. Even Clay's most overt concession to the South, in short, was framed to garner support from the northern Whig majority.[64]

Clay's first four resolutions, which addressed the Mexican Cession and which formed the heart of his compromise proposal, were decisively pronorthern. The first resolution averred that California "with suitable boundaries" ought to be admitted to statehood immediately upon its application "without the imposition by Congress of any restriction in respect to the exclusion or introduction of slavery within those boundaries." Zachary Taylor had recommended exactly the same thing. From there Clay appeared to diverge from the president. He pointedly explained that he could not agree with Taylor's request that Congress do nothing about the remainder of the Cession until its residents also applied for statehood. Congress had a duty "to legislate for their government if they can, and at all events to legislate for them, and to give them the benefit of law, and order, and security." Thus Clay's second resolution called for Congress to organize the entire remainder of the Cession into an unspecified number of territorial governments, exactly what Taylor had warned Congress not to attempt.

Taylor hoped to dodge conflict over the Proviso, and so did Clay. Yet the wording of his resolution on the territories was even more explicitly antislavery in its implications than Taylor's proposal. "That as slavery does not exist by law, and is unlikely to be introduced into any of the territory acquired by the United States from the Republic of Mexico," the resolution contended, "it is inexpedient for Congress to provide by law for its introduction into or exclusion from any part of the said territory." Thus Congress should establish territorial governments "without the adoption of any restriction or condition on the subject of slavery." In his brief speech on January 29 and in a fuller two-day address in early February, Clay elaborated at length on the meaning of this resolution. Climate and the poor quality of the soil in the remainder of the Cession outside of California guaranteed that slavery could never be profitably established there, and therefore the North should not insult the South unnecessarily by demanding congressional prohibition. More than that, the existing laws in the Cession, the Mexican laws, prohibited slavery in the Cession, and Congress must do nothing to replace those laws when it organized territorial governments. In sum, Clay implied that those laws would continue in force even after Congress created territorial governments unless residents in their territorial legislatures decided to change them, and New Mexico's residents had already shown that they had no intention of doing so.[65]

This analysis significantly reduces the supposed differences between the Taylor and Clay plans. By again using the word "inexpedient," Clay, like Taylor, recognized Congress' right to bar slavery from the territories, but both men argued that the Proviso was unnecessary. Taylor would avoid it by having Congress do nothing until residents in the remainder of the Cession applied for statehood and by allowing Mexican law to operate in the interim. Clay would have Congress organize territorial governments but would bar it from replacing the Mexican antislavery laws. Unlike Taylor, who referred only in general to the laws of Mexico, Clay explicitly and repeatedly emphasized Mexican antislavery statutes in particular as a reason why the Proviso was unnecessary. Thus he went further than Taylor had both in attempting to convince northern Whigs to drop the Proviso and in reassuring them that slavery would never spread into the Cession.

But it was in his third and fourth resolutions dealing with Texas that Clay made his most astonishing bid for northern support. Unlike Taylor, who urged Congress to leave the boundary dispute to the courts after New Mexico became a state, Clay wanted Congress to fix Texas' boundary. And what a boundary he had in mind! Responding to southern demands, he would make the Rio Grande Texas' western boundary, but to appease the North he would lop off the northern half of the area Texas claimed by continuing the southern border of New Mexico from El Paso on the Rio Grande River straight eastward across Texas until it reached the Sabine River between Texas and Louisiana. The area south of that line between the Rio Grande and the Gulf of Mexico would become the new state of Texas. The area north of that line, which included the towns of Dallas and Fort Worth and some 20,000 slaves in 1850, would not become a new state. Rather, it would become part of the Mexican Cession, where, Clay had stressed, Mexican law prohibited slavery. What Clay was proposing, unless the owners of slaves north of his line moved, was outright abolition. Whether Clay realized what he was proposing, it may have been the most startling antislavery measure introduced in Congress before the Civil War. That Clay could later declare in a public speech, and some historians contend, that this measure "as originally proposed" became part of the Compromise of 1850 defies belief![66]

Carefully omitting any reference to compensating Texas for the loss of more than half of the area it claimed in 1850, Clay's fourth resolution proposed that the United States government assume the Texas debt, that is, that Congress fund the bonds that the Republic of Texas had issued between 1836 and 1845 and for which it had pledged customs revenues it lost upon joining the Union. Clay left the precise dollar amount of this funding unspecified, but he insisted that such payment would not be made until the Texas legislature or a state convention passed an "authentic act" that relinquished "to the United States any claim which it has to any part of New Mexico," that is, to all the land north of the boundary line Clay proposed to draw. By this scheme, in short, the state of Texas itself would not receive a nickel. The holders of Texas bonds, most of whom were not Texans or residents of other slave states but northern businessmen, would receive the monetary compensation for slicing in half the nation's largest slave state.[67]

Method rather than malice impelled this proposal. Clay had been thinking about a settlement of the Texas–New Mexico boundary dispute for months. He knew that many Northerners, and especially northern Whigs, totally rejected Texas' claims and would strenuously object to paying it for land it did not own. He must have known as well that Texans themselves would resist any redrawing of their borders. He may also have been informed that holders of Texas bonds did not believe that the Texas state government would pay them off if the United States paid Texas directly.[68] By advocating that the federal government assume that debt, he thus created an incentive for bondholders across the country to lobby Congress on behalf of a boundary settlement Texans themselves would oppose.

He would counter the expected opposition of Texans and other Southerners in Congress, that is, by bringing a new player into the game.

Even as Clay concluded his fervent call for a compromise to save the Union by waving a fragment from George Washington's coffin, southern senators sprang to their feet in angry protest. Unlike some historians, they instantly recognized Clay's sweet talk about the North making greater concessions for the sugar coating it was. Seven Democrats—Thomas Rusk of Texas, Foote and Jefferson Davis of Mississippi, Solomon Downs of Louisiana, James M. Mason of Virginia, William R. King of Alabama, and Andrew Pickens Butler of South Carolina—and the Georgia Whig Berrien denounced the scheme as a flagrant violation of Southern Rights. They had to speak immediately, one after another insisted, lest their silence mistakenly indicate that their states would submit to such an outrage. They pilloried the rape of Texas soil without any compensation, Clay's admission that Congress could abolish slavery in the District, his insistence that Mexican law outlawed slavery in the Cession and should not be replaced, and his willingness to admit California without giving slaveholders a chance to carry their property there. Clay's supposed compromise conceded "the whole question, at once, that our people shall not go into the new Territories and take their property with them," declared Mason. "Is a measure in which we of the minority are to receive nothing, a measure of compromise?" sputtered Davis. "I consider this compromise as no compromise at all," echoed Downs.[69]

While southern Democrats blasted the scheme in toto, they honed in on what Clay maintained about Mexican law, thus again revealing a more acute understanding of Clay's proposals than some historians have subsequently displayed. They recognized that Clay's emphasis on Mexican law, *not* his willingness to organize territories without the Proviso, was the linchpin of his plan. "What matters it whether it be under cover of the acts of the Mexican Government or by the operation of Congressional law, that slavery is excluded?" Davis protested. "What is there in the nature of a compromise here?" queried Butler since Clay insisted "that, by the existing laws in the Territories," slaveholders cannot "go there with their property." Clay cannot "palm off this proposition as a compromise," summarized the Virginian Thomas Ritchie, editor of the Democratic Washington *Daily Union*, since he "asserts that the Mexican edict abolishing slavery is tantamount to the Wilmot Proviso." Therefore "we must now look to clearer, and more generous and more intrepid spirits to save the Union."[70]

Ritchie obviously had Democrats in mind, and ultimately, Democrats who controlled both houses of Congress reshaped the plan Clay intended to unite congressional Whigs into an essentially Democratic compromise. Because Southerners dominated the Democrats in Congress, moreover, the final Compromise made far more concessions to the South than Clay had intended. As the shrewd Truman Smith accurately predicted six weeks after Clay first spoke, "Our northern democracy will *cave in* as usual & the South will do as it pleases except in the matter of California."[71]

Hence the final Compromise differed substantially from the "whole system of measures, as originally proposed" by Clay on January 29. California was admitted as a free state and the slave trade in the District was outlawed. But the borders of Texas were far more generous than Clay and northern Whigs wanted, and

Texas received direct compensation for its surrendered claims, a stipulation Clay had tried to avoid precisely because northern Whigs found it so offensive. The Fugitive Slave Act was easier on purported owners and harsher on alleged fugitives than Clay wanted. Most important, territorial governments were organized without the Proviso but also without the explicit continuation of Mexican law. States carved out of those territories, moreover, were explicitly guaranteed admission by Congress "with or without slavery, as their constitution may prescribe at the time of their admission," and territorial legislatures were granted the power to pass pro- or antislavery laws during the territorial stage. In short, the final Compromise created more potential opportunity for slavery's spread into the Mexican Cession than either the Taylor or Clay plans.[72]

Democrats were primarily responsible for these changes and for the defeat of both the Taylor and Clay plans. But they were not solely responsible. The divergent reactions of Whig congressmen to those and other plans also played a crucial role. Some Whigs like Clay, who invested an emotional stake in the idea of compromise, had little choice but to cooperate with Democrats once they assumed command of the legislative agenda. The motives for the behavior of other Whigs were shaped by events in Washington, in their respective states, and in Texas, and by the simultaneous battle that was raging among Whigs over Senate confirmation of Taylor's appointees.

V

Clay's effort to rally Whigs in and outside Congress behind his plan proved stillborn. The similarity of Clay's proposals to those offered by Taylor a week earlier also stunted support. Both Whig papers in Washington—the *Republic* and the *National Intelligencer*—as well as a few Whig papers elsewhere, with good reason, minimized the differences between the two plans. Clay's plan was more comprehensive than Taylor's and called for congressional action to create territorial governments and to set Texas' boundaries that Taylor opposed. But on the admission of California and the extension of slavery to the remainder of the Mexican Cession the plans were quite similar, as southern Democrats instantly recognized.[73] Most southern Whigs therefore found no more sectional justice or hope of political salvation in Clay's plan than in Taylor's. The savagely accurate attack by southern Democrats on January 29 permanently discredited Clay's propositions. For southern Whigs, to endorse the plan as he presented it would betray the South and sign their political death warrants. Unlike the majority of southern Democrats, most, though not all, southern Whigs were willing to admit California, but they demanded as the price of admission far more concessions on other questions than Clay offered. John Bell, one of the few southern Whig senators besides Clay to speak between early February and mid-March, for example, proposed to offset California's admission by carving two new slave states out of Texas.[74]

Southern Whigs in the House did not immediately offer alternative plans of their own, but men like David Outlaw and Alexander Stephens rejected Clay's plan precisely because they also believed that only positive local law could sustain slavery and that Mexican law continued in force in the Cession until it was replaced. They preferred Clay's idea of forming territorial governments without the Proviso to Taylor's nonaction formula, but they sought territorial governments that could write proslavery territorial legislation if the residents so wished. Furthermore, they insisted that California's admission be contingent upon the organization of such territorial governments. In sum, like Bell, they rejected both the Taylor and Clay plans.[75]

In addition, neither the administration nor most northern Whigs would support Clay's scheme. For one thing, to the extent that Northerners saw it as similar to Taylor's, they had little incentive to back it, especially if they wished to remain in Taylor's good graces on patronage matters. More important, many northern Whigs rejected the very idea of compromise as a pusillanimous surrender to phony threats of secession. "I do not myself propose to enter into any scheme of compromise whatever," Connecticut's Senator Roger Sherman Baldwin informed his wife. "As to the threats of disunion, they do not frighten anybody here." "California will be admitted . . . by decided majorities," predicted one of Seward's Buffalo lieutenants in early March. "Meanwhile the gas will escape, the courage of the turbulent will ooze out. The South will take up its hat and walk out of the house, probably get drunk and swear oaths in barrooms and eating houses, a night's rest and soda water will bring it round and the South will again take its seat."[76]

But the substance of Clay's plan was as objectionable as the idea of compromise itself. Unlike Taylor's plan, Clay's proposal to organize territorial governments without the Proviso opened them to Free Soilers' charges that they had betrayed explicit pledges to prohibit slavery in all formally organized territories.[77] Contemptuous of both the Taylor and Clay plans, Free Soilers intensified the pressure on northern Whigs when, on February 4, Joseph Root forced a vote on a resolution instructing the House Committee on Territories to present bills organizing territorial governments in the Mexican Cession outside of California with slavery explicitly prohibited. This resolution confronted northern Whigs with a Hobson's choice. Supporting the measure meant flouting Taylor's wish that territorial governments not be established; opposing it implied retreat from the Proviso.

Eighteen northern Democrats and fourteen northern Whigs joined a solid southern phalanx to defeat Root's motion 105 to 78. But the deep embarrassment it caused northern Whigs, like southern attacks on Clay's proposals, convinced them, in the words of Truman Smith, that "Genl. Taylor's platform is the best— the only safe one for all parties." "The true way is to admit California & let the Territories alone," echoed Winthrop, who opposed Root's motion. "Any other course will kill Whiggery at one end of the Union." Across the North, Whigs who cared far more about the Free Soil threat in their own section than the welfare of southern Whigs reached the same conclusion about Clay's scheme. "Clay's resolutions on the Slavery question" knock "our position in regard to it, all to the winds," complained a Michigan Whig because they would abort efforts to attract Free Soilers. "Henry Clay's Compromise Bill will not satisfy Whigs in this region," chorused a New Yorker. "The territories had better be left to form states according to President Taylor's plan."[78]

Yet northern Whigs, even with the help of Free Soilers, lacked the political power to enact it. On February 13, Taylor finally sent California's free constitution to Congress. Five days later, Wisconsin's Democratic-Free Soil Congressman

James Doty demanded the previous question on a resolution instructing the House Committee on Territories immediately to prepare a bill admitting California under that constitution. Northerners had a heavy majority in the House; they had the votes to pass the resolution. If the House immediately admitted California, the Senate would probably follow suit. Southern Whig demands for concessions as the price of California's admission would have been rebuffed. Yet the southern minority in the House held a trump card. One of their own was speaker. Stephens and Clingman frantically arranged a filibuster with southern Democrats to frustrate the northern majority. To stop a vote on Doty's motion, Southerners continually moved to adjourn and demanded roll call votes on the motions. Northerners had the votes to defeat adjournment, but the roll calls took precious time. And because Speaker Cobb recognized only Southerners, that minority tied up the House with roll call after roll call until midnight, when Doty's motion ceased to be the order of the day. To the dismay of northern Whigs, who recognized that "our rules present no means of success to the majority," the southern Whig minority had staved off California's immediate admission, but they had done so only by cooperating with southern Democrats who, through Cobb, could control the House agenda. On the question of California statehood, by itself, sectional lines had almost completely replaced party lines.[79]

Stephens desperately organized a filibuster on February 18 because he believed some kind of compromise was necessary to defuse the growing threat of Deep South secession. Southern and northern Whigs did not just jockey for political advantage at home during 1850. They shared a deep commitment to the Union, even if they disagreed profoundly about the seriousness of the threat to it. Unlike Clay and Taylor, Stephens believed that secession could be averted only by making the prior organization of territories into which slavery might expand the price of California's admission. In mid-April, Stephens, Toombs, and possibly Clingman visited Taylor to plead the necessity of their own version of compromise. Unless Taylor pledged to veto the Proviso and supported the organization of such territorial governments before California was admitted, they warned, secession might be unstoppable. Mistakenly interpreting this warning as a threat by the southern Whig congressmen that they themselves would go for secession unless he capitulated, the old soldier furiously declared that he personally would lead troops into the field to put down secession and apparently denounced the three men as traitors who deserved to be hanged to visitors who saw him immediately after the close of the stormy interview. Whatever actually happened, one thing was clear. Southern Whigs who wanted some kind of quid pro quo for California's admission could expect little help from the administration.[80]

Confronted by the insistence of northern Whigs, Taylor, and even Clay that California be admitted with no strings attached, southern Whigs who wanted greater concessions had to look to Democrats for help. Some southern Democrats, of course, adamantly opposed California statehood under any circumstances, and on March 4, John C. Calhoun, whose health was rapidly failing and who would die by the end of the month, voiced the demands of such diehards in a speech that Mason read for him to the Senate. The equilibrium between North and South upon which the security of slavery and Southern Rights depended had been incessantly eroded by northern aggressions, Calhoun protested. Now the willingness of the North to forego California statehood formed the acid test of continued

Union. If California were admitted, the South must secede.[81] Democratic fire-brands like this offered potential southern Whig compromisers no room for ma-neuver, but other southern Democrats and influential northern Democratic leaders moved to frame a compromise southern Whigs could support since it salvaged Southern Rights and might save the Union.

Between December and February, in fact, northern Democrats changed tack on the slavery issue and thereby further dimmed the chances that Taylor's plan could attract enough votes to pass. Key northern Democratic senators like Lewis Cass, the party's standard bearer in 1848, Daniel S. Dickinson of New York, Stephen A. Douglas of Illinois, Jesse Bright of Indiana, and Daniel Sturgeon of Pennsyl-vania feared for the integrity of the national Democratic party and for the Union itself. But they also deeply resented the trafficking with Free Soilers, in which northern Democratic state parties had engaged during 1849, as well as the blithe jettisoning of popular sovereignty, to which they were intellectually and emo-tionally committed. After Congress opened, therefore, they set out to force Dem-ocratic state parties in the North to reverse course once again, shun the Free Soilers, readopt popular sovereignty as the optimal solution to the territorial prob-lem, and support the kind of compromise with the South that southern Whigs sought and that northern Whigs considered anathema.

They achieved considerable success. Cass pressured the Democratic majority in the Michigan legislature to rescind its instructions for him to support the Proviso, and in January 1850 he urged Samuel Medary, the leading Democratic editor in Ohio, to follow a similar course. "The union is in the most eminent danger," he warned, and "nothing can save us but a spirit of moderation from the North and West." Even before Medary received that epistle, Ohio's Democratic state con-vention repudiated its previous coalition with the Free Soilers by defeating res-olutions asserting the right and duty of Congress to prohibit slavery in the ter-ritories. Although Dickinson, leader of New York's Hunker Democrats and an ardent proponent of popular sovereignty, lacked the clout in the New York leg-islature to have his own instructions on the Proviso rescinded, he proudly ignored them and set out to reimpose support for popular sovereignty as a test of party orthodoxy in order to humiliate the Barnburners, whose readmission to the Dem-ocratic party in 1849 he bitterly opposed.[82]

Douglas had proposed immediate statehood for the Mexican Cession in the Thirtieth Congress, but he championed popular sovereignty as the best solution for the territories and the best platform for the Democratic party. Legislative instructions from Illinois to support the Wilmot Proviso infuriated him since they had been adopted in 1849 by a coalition of Free Soil Democrats and Whigs ex-plicitly to force his resignation from the Senate. His allies at home therefore worked to recommit Democrats to popular sovereignty, and by April he was assured that "Wilmot provisoism is dead among the Democrats of Illinois." Penn-sylvania's Democrats also renounced any alliance with the Free Soilers, and by February they were insisting instead on compromise with the South. "This new *test* of democracy" was being enforced at Democratic meetings to select delegates to the party's state convention, reported a Whig. "Prominent men at Washington originated this reorganization, which seems to be general, and no doubt extends to other states." Their rallying cry will be *"the preservation & perpetuity of the Union."*[83]

Northern Democrats of this ilk offered southern Whigs seeking a more palatable compromise the help they needed. During the fierce struggle over Doty's
resolution on February 18, for example, John McClernand, an Illinois Democrat
acting at the behest of Douglas, chairman of the Senate Committee on Territories,
approached Stephens and asked if there was a way out of the crisis. Stephens
apparently set down his terms in writing. California could be admitted only after
territories were organized in the remainder of the Cession without the Proviso,
territories that were "distinctly empowered" to write proslavery laws in the territorial stage and proslavery constitutions when applying for statehood. The following night Stephens and Toombs attended a meeting at the house of their old
Georgia enemy Cobb, along with Democrats Linn Boyd of Kentucky, chairman
of the House Committee on Territories, McClernand and William A. Richardson,
another Douglas lieutenant from Illinois, and John Miller of Ohio. Together they
prepared a compromise plan that Democrats would introduce into the House and
Senate, one that admitted California, reduced Texas' western boundaries in return
for monetary compensation, and organized territorial governments in the rest of
the Cession with the Democratic formula of popular sovereignty. The foundation
was laid for the bipartisan coalition of southern Whigs, moderate southern and
border state Democrats, and northern Democrats that would eventually pass their
own version of compromise, not the plan Clay had proposed.[84]

Thus potential compromisers among southern Whigs were forced to ally themselves with Democrats—sometimes, as was the case of Stephens, Toombs, and
Cobb, with Democrats from their own state. They had little choice, however, if
they hoped to resolve the crisis in a way that did not entail political disaster, let
alone threaten the Union. Besides, whatever the predisposition of a few southern
Democrats like Cobb and Boyd toward compromise, it was primarily northern,
not southern, Democrats who were prepared to bargain. Democratic parties in the
South, in contrast, had moved to the extreme by threatening secession and endorsing the Nashville Convention. By backing compromise, southern Whigs could
still distinguish themselves from the great majority of Democrats in their home
states. Compromise could save their political careers at the same time that it saved
the Union.

Henry Clay was also forced to seek Democratic cooperation in the Senate.
During the first month after Clay introduced his proposal, aside from Badger and
Bell, who did *not* back Clay's plan itself, only Democrats in the Senate had promoted the idea of admitting California in return for other concessions to the
South. Those Democrats, however, had made it clear that they could not accept
Clay's solution to the Texas-New Mexico boundary dispute or his insistence on
the perpetuity of Mexican law. One of the chief Democratic critics of these aspects
of Clay's plan was the Democratic editor Thomas Ritchie, and through the me-
diation of a reporter named James Simonton and Virginia's Democratic congressman Thomas Bayly, chairman of the powerful House Ways and Means Committee, Clay met privately with Ritchie on February 10. In return for editorial
support from the *Union*, Clay apparently agreed to drop his stress on Mexican
law and to accept Democrats' popular sovereignty formula.[85]

Ritchie also pressed Clay to accept Foote's procedural strategy of turning over
to a select Senate committee, rather than to Douglas' existing Committee on
Territories, all the proposals regarding slavery that had been introduced and in-

structing that committee "to procure a compromise embracing all the questions now arising out of the institution of slavery." Everyone recognized that this procedure would inevitably result in combining California's admission with territorial legislation and resolution of the Texas boundary in a single bill. It would create a formal quid pro quo for the admission of California that Taylor, almost all northern Whigs, and Clay himself abhorred. To write what Clay first derisively called—and thereby permanently labeled—an "omnibus" bill, the Kentuckian knew, would be to ensure the opposition of northern Whigs whom he had courted so ardently with his own propositions. Eventually, however, Clay capitulated to that demand as well. That reversal marked his recognition that only help from Democrats and southern Whigs like Badger, who liked the idea better than Clay's own proposal, offered any hope of passing some kind of compromise. Clay reluctantly reached that conclusion, in turn, because of northern Whigs' reaction to developments in March.[86]

VI

While Clay and other southern Whigs solicited Democratic aid to resolve the territorial issue on terms acceptable to the South, the administration and its supporters around the country fumed about the lack of vocal congressional support for Taylor's plan. During February, Southerners who blasted both the Taylor and Clay proposals dominated the debate. Only a few northern Whigs in the House and Jacob Miller in the Senate defended the administration. While Miller's speech was able, friends of the administration grew increasingly disappointed that Clay and Webster had not entered the fray to shield Taylor from Democratic barbs. "Those gentlemen must be sensible that their silence & neglect will have the *effect of opposition,*" carped Crittenden from Kentucky. The administration, he warned Clayton, must have a powerful spokesman in the Senate. Truman Smith, despite his skills as a party manager, would not do, for Smith was an "unadroit, I might almost say *fatal* defender."[87]

With Clay promoting a broader settlement than Taylor, and with other southern Whigs disenchanted with the president's scheme, Daniel Webster, who at the age of sixty-seven was still "the most intellectual looking man" George Julian had ever seen, became the chief hope of administration supporters. Unaware of Webster's meeting with Clay, northern Whigs almost unanimously expected him to back Taylor's plan. During February, in fact, Webster said nothing on the Senate floor as he agonized over what to do. Clay had called for compromise to save the Union, but Webster, whose views oscillated, did not share Clay's sense of crisis. He frequently wrote friends that "the Union is not in danger." "There will be no disunion or disruption. Things will cool off. California will come in. New Mexico will be postponed. No bones will be broken." When Webster announced that he would speak on March 6 or 7, Winthrop, for one, was positive he would endorse Taylor's plan. Yet by late February, Webster was also writing his son Fletcher about the need "to beat down the Northern and the Southern follies, now raging in equal extremes," and by March 1, significantly the very day on which the Senate confirmed Fletcher's appointment as customs surveyor of Boston, he had determined "to make a *Union* speech, and discharge a clear conscience." Until a coterie of close advisors met with Webster on the night of March 6 and read his speech for the first time, no one except Webster himself knew what he intended to say, and both Taylor and Clay eagerly looked forward to the speech.[88]

Both were disappointed. In his controversial Seventh of March speech, Webster neither endorsed nor attacked the Taylor plan, but he also did not embrace Clay's plan. Aware of Southerners' intense hostility to it, Webster went much further than Clay had to appease them, causing Calhoun to applaud Webster's speech where he had condemned Clay's. The speech was less a detailed legislative agenda for compromise than a passionate paean to the Union and a call to reconcile sectional differences over slavery, a reconciliation that Webster insisted was primarily a matter of emotion, not concrete legislation.[89]

Most of Webster's speech reviewed the history of sectional conflict over slavery.[90] He had always abhorred slavery and still did, but the constitutional compact required Northerners to allow Southerners to live in peace with their chattels. Abolitionists, however well intentioned, had done more harm than good and should cease agitation. He had also always opposed slavery extension and still did. He had fought Texas' annexation as long as possible, but Texas had been admitted and slavery was legal on every foot of its soil. Moreover, Webster emphasized, the terms of annexation explicitly allowed as many as four more states to be carved from Texas, and the law required Northerners to admit all of them as slave states if they so desired. Beyond Texas, however, slavery could not and would not go. Very briefly alluding to the desirability of admitting California with its free constitution, he stressed that climate, the law of nature—but, pointedly, not Mexican law, which Clay had emphasized and Webster entirely ignored—barred slavery from the remainder of the Mexican Cession.[91] For Northerners to insist on the Wilmot Proviso if—and Webster himself, quite unlike Clay, did not advocate it—Congress organized territorial governments was therefore superfluous and insulting. Finally, with regard to the Cession, Webster briefly applauded the idea of giving Texas monetary compensation for surrendering its claims to New Mexico, a formula that Bell and others, but not Clay, had broached, but he made no specific boundary proposal himself. Webster also stressed the need for a new fugitive slave law. The Constitution clearly obliged Northerners to return fugitives, and it was unjust for individuals or state legislatures to impede their capture. Therefore, "with some amendments," he would support the bill that Mason had already introduced "with all its provisions to the fullest extent."[92]

Rather than rallying Whigs behind Clay's compromise scheme, Webster further compounded the confusion in Whig ranks. He clearly favored compromise, but many conservative Whigs in the North regarded Webster's compromise as entirely distinct from Clay's. For example, Daniel D. Barnard of Albany urged Fillmore to embrace Clay's scheme as a way to differentiate Fillmore Whigs from Sewardites, whereas ex-Governor and New York City Subtreasurer John Young preferred Webster's to achieve the same goal.[93] More important, Webster immediately followed an erratic course that seemed to contradict what he had said. On the day following the speech, he told Winthrop that he would support "General Taylor's plan, unless he himself should . . . recommend . . . a Territorial Government for New Mexico." Indeed, since Webster had *not* advocated the creation of territorial governments, many thought his speech endorsed Taylor's nonaction scheme, not Clay's compromise. On March 13, Webster enhanced that impression by urging the Senate to admit California immediately and ignore the other questions since no legislation on them could possibly pass. So convinced, he opposed a select committee that would combine all legislation for the Cession in a single bill. If some Whigs saw Webster as the author of an alternative compromise proposal, in sum, his "flitting about like a weathercock" caused others to doubt that he favored any compromise on what northern Whigs deemed the central question—untrammeled admission of California.[94]

Even before Webster performed this volte-face, the *Republic* and the *National Intelligencer* praised his speech just as they had Clay's, implying that Webster represented Taylor. "Let it not . . . be understood that Mr. Webster speaks for the Administration," Weed frantically warned Meredith on March 10. "Gen. Taylor has found a way *round* the 'Proviso' [while] Mr. Webster dashes his brains out against it. In a word, we can sustain ourselves and the Administration only by standing firmly up to Gen. Taylor's plan for California and New Mexico."[95]

As Weed well knew, Webster's speech flabbergasted most northern Whigs. Among commercial circles in northeastern cities and in the South, it drew extravagant praise. By the end of March he had already franked 120,000 copies and was predicting that he would mail out 200,000 by May 1. Most northern Whigs, however, condemned the speech as an unconscionable betrayal, an act of prostitution to win southern support for another presidential bid in 1852. Across the North, Whig papers and speakers denounced Webster as another Benedict Arnold or Judas. "It is not a compromise," sputtered Fitz Henry Warren when urging a Boston Whig editor to denounce Webster. "It is a virtual surrender of everything without even the reservation of marching out with the honors of war." Webster "has ruined himself politically," summarized an upstate New Yorker in an assessment chorused from Maine to the Midwest. "He is dead as a herring & it will be hard work to galvanize him to life."[96]

In the immediate aftermath of Webster's disappointing speech, however, the administration's biggest concern was that it still lacked a powerful champion in the Senate. Taylor himself was reported to be "aggrieved at the course Mr. Clay has taken and at that of Mr. Webster," while Truman Smith sarcastically scorned the failure of "the so-called great men of the Whig party" to support Taylor.[97] By default, therefore, that role fell to the New Yorker Seward, who spoke four days after Webster. Compared to Godlike Daniel, Seward was a poor public speaker. His voice was hoarse and raspy, and he read his speech verbatim in a dull monotone. Nonetheless, no man in the Senate was closer to Taylor's administration, and it had every right to expect him powerfully to advocate its position. On March 11, however, Seward disappointed Taylor almost as deeply as Webster had on the 7th.

Like Webster, Seward had been relatively quiet since Congress opened. In late January, even before Clay spoke, however, he began working on a set speech in which he intended to demonstrate "the certain deliverance of the continent from slavery to be inevitable, and the dissolution of the Union to be impossible." Whatever the context of debate and whatever the administration's needs, in short, Seward determined to deliver an antislavery harangue that might make him the preeminent leader of the North's antislavery Whigs. As he wrote Weed on the morning before he addressed the Senate, "The unlooked for course of Mr. Webster has prepared the way for me in the North, but has rendered of little value the little moderation I can practice in regard to the other portion of the Union." Although Clayton, who had seen his notes for the speech, deplored its extreme "Northern sentiment," Seward added, to suppress that sentiment would conflict "with my view of [political] safety."[98]

Seward's speech emphasized the insidiousness of compromise itself. Legislative compromises were "radically wrong and essentially vicious." He demanded California's immediate admission "directly, without conditions, without qualifications, and without compromise." He would oppose slavery's extension into any of the Mexican Cession and a new fugitive slave law, and he favored the abolition of slavery itself in the District as soon as possible. The idea that compromise was necessary to save the Union was rubbish, since the Union could not split and the South had ample security for slavery in its control of the national government and support from the northern Democratic party.[99]

Lest anyone miss the point, Seward went on to rebut individual advocates of sectional compromise. Calhoun's demand for a formal equilibrium between the fast-growing North and the sluggish South subverted the principle of majority rule. Webster's willingness to admit four more slave states from Texas flouted northern sentiment. Clay's flawed resolutions rested on two false assumptions. They presumed that slavery was a permanent institution in the South that required acknowledgement and protection, when in truth slavery was transient and freedom permanent. Moreover, Clay, like Webster, assumed that slave states had an equal claim to common territories with free states when the Constitution devoted the national domain "to union, to justice, to defence, to welfare, and to liberty." Indeed, there was "a higher law than the Constitution, which regulates our authority over the domain, and devotes it to the same noble purposes." The Mexican Cession was part of God's creation for the good of all mankind. "We are his stewards, and must so discharge our trust as to secure, in the highest attainable degree, their happiness." Slavery must be kept out of the Cession, for it was incompatible with "the security of natural rights, the diffusion of knowledge, and the freedom of industry."

Seward's reference to "a higher law than the Constitution" immediately stoked controversy, but in its context Seward was not calling on men to put conscience ahead of constitutional obligations. Rather, he meant that God had a purpose for the Mexican Cession, and both Webster and Clay had implied much the same thing when they stressed that nature would prevent slavery expansion beyond Texas. Far more important, Seward explicitly rejected their corollary conclusion that, since aridity and parched soil barred slavery extension, Congress need not do so. Slavery might expand despite the climate, Seward warned, and since all human laws were reenactments of God's law, men, as His "stewards," should reaffirm His design with the sanction of civil legislation. Indirectly, that is, Seward demanded imposition of the Wilmot Proviso on the remainder of the Mexican Cession.

As notable as what Seward said was what he did not say. He nowhere mentioned, let alone endorsed, Taylor's plan. That omission appalled Weed, who immediately demanded an explanation for what he considered an inconceivable and perhaps a fatal blunder. Seward lamely and disingenuously replied that praising Taylor's patriotic proposal would have destroyed his speech's symmetry and lengthened an already overlong effort, despite his readiness to work in detailed criticisms of Clay, Webster, and Calhoun.[100] More accurately, Seward also maintained that praising Taylor amounted to hypocrisy in light of what he said. Rather than simply ignoring Taylor, indeed, Seward implicitly repudiated the entire thrust of his recommendations. Taylor presented his plan as a compromise to restore sectional comity; Seward attacked the very idea of compromise as "vicious." Taylor urged congressmen to avoid agitating subjects; Seward purposely introduced one after another, thereby infuriating southern Whigs and Democrats alike and confirming his reputation as a dangerous fanatic. Most important, Taylor called on Congress to admit California and New Mexico as states and to leave the rest of the Cession alone. Seward endorsed California statehood, but he seemed to call on Congress to prohibit slavery in all the remaining Cession in order to give civil sanction to God's will.

Furious that Seward had so heedlessly antagonized southern Whigs like Mangum, Taylor commanded Alexander C. Bullitt to lacerate him in the columns of the *Republic*. Within days of the speech the administration organ, which had praised Clay, Bell, and Webster, accused Seward of repudiating the Constitution and self-righteously posing as God's legislative agent. Everywhere men proclaimed an irreparable breech between the administration and the New York senator, a perception that clearly unnerved Weed.[101]

Why Seward risked the administration's wrath, instead of becoming its chief legislative spokesman, is a vital question. In letters to Weed, Seward sanctimoniously protested that a statesman's reputation depended upon his sincerity, and he therefore had to speak his conscience. He also asserted that northern Whigs in the House would *"cave in"* and submit to compromises unless their antislavery constituencies were aroused to put pressure on them. Hence he called on Weed to have northern newspapers print his speech, and like Webster, he immediately began franking tens of thousands of copies of it for distribution across the North.[102] All of this may have been true, but political needs in New York motivated Seward's speech as much as the compulsion of conscience.

Two crucial developments in 1849 set the stage for New York politics in 1850. First, conservative Whigs of all kinds—Clay men, Websterites, patricians, friends of ex-Governor John Young—had rallied behind the leadership of Millard Fillmore and his western New York allies openly to combat Seward and Weed for control of the state Whig organization. Weed and Seward beat back this challenge, and both because they believed their control of the state party depended on arousing antislavery Whigs and because they wanted to humiliate their foes, they devoted the state Whig platform and address to a denunciation of slavery and its spread. That platform, in turn, convinced apoplectic conservatives like Daniel Barnard, John Spencer, and John L. Dox that their foes meant to abolitionize the Whig party.[103] Second, Democrats made a sweeping comeback in the November elections, capturing four of eight statewide offices, sharply reducing the Whig majority in the state senate, and winning a narrow majority in the house. The Democrats achieved this feat, in turn, only because the Barnburners and Hunkers, who had split in 1846, 1847, and 1848, papered over their differences on the Wilmot Proviso.

To preserve Whig control of the state government and his own faction's control of the state Whig party, Seward wanted his lieutenants to maintain advanced antislavery ground and to portray both Democrats and his intraparty foes as prosouthern doughfaces. To differentiate his followers from their conservative Whig critics and to throw Democrats off balance, therefore, he had an ally named George Geddes introduce a series of antislavery resolutions into the state senate on January 1, 1850, the first day of the legislative session. The Sewardites clearly hoped these measures would disrupt the Democrats, when they were forced to vote on them, and embarrass their conservative Whig foes, who could oppose them only at the risk of alienating their constituents.

Similar to the resolutions the Sewardite majority had rammed through in 1849, Geddes instructed the state's United States senators and requested its United States representatives to abolish the slave trade in the District, to oppose any compromise extending slavery to any part of the Mexican Cession, to prohibit Texas from controlling the area between the Rio Grande and Nueces rivers, and to admit California as rapidly as possible. Unlike the 1849 resolutions, these did not explicitly demand congressional prohibition of slavery in the Cession, but the imprecation that New York's congressional delegation use "all Constitutional means" to resist the spread of slavery implied imposition of the Proviso if necessary. During the six-week legislative debate on the resolutions, indeed, Sewardite Whigs insisted that they had instructed the New York delegation to organize new territorial governments with the Proviso attached.[104]

The Geddes resolutions easily passed the Whig-controlled senate, and Seward's allies in Albany openly hoped that Hunkers and Barnburners would rupture over them in the house, where anguished Democrats frantically tried to delay a vote. Yet conservative Whigs also abhorred them as a transparent bid by "the left wing of our party" for Free Soil support, an attempt that would needlessly alienate southern Whigs and discredit New York's Whigs with Taylor's administration. When Taylor sent his more detailed California message to Congress on January 21, therefore, the Fillmorites seized the opportunity to embarrass the Sewardites by substituting resolutions praising the Taylor plan for the Geddes resolutions. Determined to maintain a different and more blatantly antisouthern position than their intraparty rivals, Sewardites continued to call for imposition of the Proviso, abolition of the District slave trade, and fixing of the Texas boundary at the Nueces—all of which violated the spirit and letter of the president's plan.[105]

Thus an extraordinarily tangled situation emerged in Albany and the rest of New York. Once Taylor fully articulated his plan, Weed and other Sewardite editors like Henry J. Raymond, simultaneously the acting editor of the New York *Courier and Enquirer* and floor manager for the Geddes resolutions in the state house of representatives, had no choice but to endorse it in their editorial columns. Similarly, on the day before Seward spoke in the Senate, Weed pointedly wrote Meredith to assure him of his support for Taylor's plan. At the same time, however, Sewardite legislators strove mightily to defeat the Fillmorite resolutions endorsing the president's policy and to pass instead the inflammatory Geddes resolutions.[106]

On February 15, the Sewardites prevailed in the assembly. Having unceremoniously crushed the pro-Taylor resolutions introduced by John L. Dox, they passed the Geddes resolutions of instruction with the aid of Barnburner Democrats over the opposition of Hunker Democrats. Conservative Whigs felt compelled to go along with the Sewardites even though they found "the antislavery resolutions forced through our legislature . . . hateful." Victory in the legislature, however, left New York's Sewardites hanging in an extraordinarily exposed position. Anti-Weed papers across the state blasted their hypocritical newspaper support for Taylor's plan and proclaimed Fillmore and his allies its only trustworthy champions in the state. The new Albany *State Register*, which began publication in March 1850 and which was edited by Fillmore's friend Jerome Fuller, who constantly sought editorial cues from Fillmore and Nathan Hall, led this assault. The point cannot be made strongly enough. Within New York, Seward's allies demanded imposition of the Proviso on the Cession and other antislavery measures, while his Fillmorite enemies backed the president's plan.[107]

Here, then, is the key to Seward's speech on March 11 and to Weed's panicky response to it. Seward could not endorse the president's plan without betraying his Albany allies, whom he had instigated to take advanced antislavery ground, and without surrendering the initiative to his conservative enemies. Yet by failing to endorse the president's plan, indeed by implicitly opposing it in the substance of his speech, he undermined the spurious contention of Weed and other Sewardite editors that there was no conflict between Taylor's proposal and the pro-Proviso legislative resolutions. More than that, he allowed the Fillmorites to pose as the administration's staunchest New York defenders, and both crestfallen Weed men and exultant Fillmorites knew what that might mean—a complete revolution in who got the state's federal jobs. Across New York, Fillmore's vindictive friends rejoiced that "Seward's speech is fatal to him with the president, cabinet, and Senate and that his ambition has overleaped itself." Even better, the speech "may ensure the rejection of [the] favorite nominees for office" of "this sorrel-topped embodiment of radicalism, demogoguism & abolitionism." Best of all, Seward had handed the Fillmorites the weapon with which to accomplish what they had attempted in 1849—capturing the state Whig organization from Weed. The way to dethrone King Thurlow was obvious, crowed Gideon Hard. "We should organize everywhere on the Taylor platform. Call meetings & strip the mask from these men & let the General Government see them in their true light."[108]

Over time, the unity of the anti-Weed coalition would disintegrate as conservatives increasingly demanded support for Clay's compromise measures. Nonetheless, Millard Fillmore personally and his Buffalo allies like Nathan K. Hall and Solomon G. Haven resolutely stood by "the Taylor platform" until July 2, 1850, when Seward finally announced to the Senate his firm support for Taylor's plan. Once Seward did so, backing it lost its utility for the Fillmorites—its distinctiveness vis-à-vis the hated Sewardites in New York, who, whatever Weed's own reservations, had wildly applauded the senator's morally inspired antislavery stand. Then, and only then, when the sectional crisis had also escalated to a far more dangerous level, did Fillmore and his closest advisors consider supporting a congressional compromise.[109]

VII

In March these developments lay in the unknown future. From Clay's perspective, that month's events had been disastrous. Instead of helping to rally northern Whigs behind Clay's compromise, Webster had ignited a firestorm of protest before which he himself immediately quailed. Seward seemed capable of mobilizing moralistic antislavery northern Whigs against any compromise at all, at least if the demand for franked copies of his speech indicated their attitude. Worst of all was the reaction of New York's conservative Whigs, to whom Clay had always looked first for northern help. Despite their bitterness over patronage, his New York friends cast their lot with Fillmore, and the Fillmorites were proudly trumpeting their allegiance to Taylor's proposal precisely because Seward seemed to oppose it.

In contrast to Whigs, northern Democrats sought a compromise, but one different from Clay's proposal. Procompromise sentiment in New York centered in the Hunker Democratic allies of Dickinson, a longtime champion of popular sovereignty who abhorred the Geddes resolutions of instruction, and in ostensibly nonpartisan Union meetings of merchants in New York City that Democrats helped organize. By March, Democrats in Pennsylvania, Ohio, and elsewhere were also calling for concessions to save the Union and were pushing for a compromise on the basis of popular sovereignty, which Douglas called "that great Democratic principle, that it is wiser and better to leave each community to regulate its own local and domestic affairs in its own way." On March 25, Douglas reported separate bills from the Senate's territorial committee that admitted California as a state and created territorial governments for Utah and New Mexico with "legislative power" over "all rightful subjects of legislation." Shortly thereafter McClernand introduced an identical package of bills in the House.[110]

Southern Whigs like Stephens and Toombs backed this Democratic initiative because it allowed the writing of proslavery local laws in the territorial stage, unlike Clay's original insistence on the perpetuity of Mexico's antislavery statutes. But March's events now reconciled Clay to that Democratic approach. To garner southern support in the Senate, Clay also submitted to Foote's demand that all slavery-related matters be sent to a select committee that everyone expected to write an "omnibus bill" that inextricably tied California's admission to a favorable resolution of the Texas-New Mexico boundary dispute and to organization of territorial governments without the Proviso. Clay, like Douglas, Webster, and northern opponents of any compromise, had previously denounced this procedure, but in early April he came out strongly behind it, a reversal of course that infuriated Zachary Taylor.[111]

Between late March and April 18, when the motion to create a select committee of thirteen finally passed, the Senate engaged in a lengthy and revealing series of votes on Foote's motion. Most of the roll calls concerned amendments that tried to instruct the committee on where to fix the Texas border or whether or not California should be attached to other legislation, votes on which Northerners and Southerners were often sharply polarized against each other. Precisely because of that basic sectional alignment, the roll calls revealed who favored and who opposed compromise.

Consistently supporting Clay were the Whig senators from Maryland, North Carolina, Georgia, Florida, and Tennessee, as well as all southern Democratic senators except Benton, who spearheaded the opposition to an omnibus bill and to any recognition of Texas' claim to New Mexico east of the Rio Grande. That Berrien and southern Democrats, who opposed California's admission on any terms, voted with Southerners, who were willing to accept it in return for other concessions to the South, is explicable. They saw creation of an omnibus bill, which anticompromise Northerners could be expected to oppose, as the best way to stop California's admission. Clay's Kentucky Whig colleague Joseph Underwood, who was a Taylor Whig rather than a Clay loyalist, voted against Clay as frequently as he supported him. Only two northern Whigs ever voted with this southern bloc—James Cooper of Pennsylvania and, less consistently, Webster. Five procompromise northern Democrats gave it steadfast support—Dickinson, Sturgeon, Cass, and Jesse Bright and James Whitcomb of Indiana. Four other midwestern Democrats also frequently joined them—George Jones and A. C. Dodge of Iowa, James Shields of Illinois, and Douglas—although Shields often voted with the anticompromise bloc and Douglas purposely abstained on many embarrassing votes.[112]

Benton forcefully led the opposition to this predominantly southern bloc. He was consistently supported by the two Free Soilers, the six remaining northern Democrats, and all of the northern Whigs except Cooper and Webster. Of great significance, the two Whig senators from the border slave state of Delaware, Presley Spruance and John Wales, also adamantly opposed creation of the committee, proslavery concessions on Texas, and attempts to connect California's admission with anything else.

Two aspects of this voting pattern stand out. Southern Whigs could never have forced concessions as the price of California's admission without Democratic aid, especially the five Northerners who always voted with them. Attitudes toward Taylor's administration also clearly influenced the Whig alignment. With the exception of John Bell, Maryland's Thomas Pratt, and Underwood, who fluctuated, every Whig who voted with the procompromise bloc harbored grievances against the cabinet and Taylor about patronage. This was undeniably true of Clay, Webster, Cooper, Dawson, Berrien, Mangum, and Badger, but the stark contrast between the two Delaware senators and the neighboring Maryland Whigs best makes the case. Both Spruance and Wales were close lieutenants of Clayton, and their faithful opposition to compromise at his bidding defied Whig sentiment in their state. James Pearce of Maryland, in contrast, hated Attorney General Reverdy Johnson, Maryland's cabinet member, and he had previously threatened to oppose administration policies. Pratt, Johnson's ally, could not ignore the procompromise sentiment orchestrated among Maryland's Whigs by such influential figures as John Pendleton Kennedy.[113]

On April 18, the motion creating the committee of thirteen finally carried, 30–22. As expected, Clay became chairman, and he presided over a committee carefully preselected to achieve compromise. Douglas refused to serve on it, and the reluctant Webster attended only its first meeting. The other northern Whigs were Cooper and Samuel Phelps; Berrien, Mangum, and Bell represented southern Whiggery. All three northern Democrats—Cass, Dickinson, and Bright—were ardent compromisers, as was one of the southern Democrats, William R. King, who was joined by Mason and Downs. Of this group only Phelps, Berrien, Downs, and Mason seemed certain to oppose compromise, although Mangum's earlier stance also stamped him as potentially hostile. After a few meetings, which never attracted the full membership, Clay wrote the committee report, which he presented to the Senate on May 8.[114]

Two matters concerning the creation of this committee require emphasis. First, it was charged with addressing all aspects of the slavery question, not just those relevant to the Mexican Cession. Mason, who stridently opposed California's statehood, was included because he had introduced a new fugitive slave bill in early January that the friendly Judiciary Committee had reported out on January 16. After that date, however, diverse proposals for the Cession monopolized attention. Superficially, the fugitive question related only tangentially to slavery extension, and when contemporaries spoke of compromise, they almost always referred only to proposed bargains on the territorial question. Nonetheless, the fugitive issue was integral to the tactics Southerners used to secure concessions on the territorial bills that formed the heart of the Compromise of 1850.[115]

Two months after the Judiciary Committee reported out the fugitive slave measure, when Foote's motion for a select committee was stalled, Cass urged the Senate to take up Mason's bill, but nothing happened. In August, when the fugitive slave bill finally was debated, Cass blamed this delay on Southerners. As he then explained, in March he had asked Foote to urge the bill's southern managers to bring it to a vote because, Cass believed, he had sufficient votes *at that time* (March) to pass it. Foote did so and "reported" to Cass "that they would not; for what cause I shall not undertake to say." Foote, too, attributed the delay to Southerners, but he offered more of a clue about their reasoning than did Cass. Mason and Butler, the chairman of the Judiciary Committee, he explained in August, refused to bring the bill to a vote in March because "it was the opinion of various southern Senators that it was inexpedient to settle that particular point; that the South had other great contests; and that it was better to have a broad than a narrow ground of action." Southerners, in short, saw a connection between the fugitive slave bill and legislation for the Cession, and they purposely stalled its passage so that it could be sent to a select committee along with other bills.[116]

Foote revealed why in a candid speech to the Senate in December 1851. The Fugitive Slave Act, he asserted, "would have been passed by the two houses of Congress at a much earlier period of the session . . . but for the fact that it was not deemed politic by several Southern Senators, who had special charge of the subject," to report the bill "until it should be ascertained that all the other questions connected with the subject of domestic slavery were likely to be satisfactorily disposed of in Congress." Mason and Butler had refused to allow a vote on the bill in March on the grounds that "if the question involved therein should be satisfactorily adjusted at that time, it might prove impossible thereafter to rouse the border states to energetic action in cooperation with the other Southern States, for the vindication of their essential rights." In short, southern Democrats would use the promise of a fugitive slave bill as a carrot to entice help from border state senators, whose constituents had the greatest stake in a new law, on matters of far more importance to them—California, Texas, and New Mexico. As Mason himself confessed during the same debate in 1851, southern Democratic senators in early 1850 freely admitted "that it would be impolitic in Southern Senators [to pass the bill] lest, among other reasons, they weaken their position upon other vital questions affecting the institution of slavery, then before the Senate."[117]

One need only recall the situation in March 1850 to appreciate the logic of this hard-nosed strategy. Six of the eight border state senators were Whigs, and the Whig administration, to whom Delaware's two senators, at least, were devoutly loyal, had recommended admitting California and New Mexico as free states and doing nothing else. The four Whigs from Maryland and Kentucky were not administration loyalists, but the only one of them who had taken a position was Clay, who had recommended the untrammeled admission of California, the retention of Mexico's antislavery laws in the remainder of the Cession, the reduction of Texas to half its size, and the abolition of the District slave trade. Finally, one of Missouri's two Democrats was Benton, who also wanted to shrink Texas, stop slavery expansion, and bring in California alone. Why not then threaten to shelve the fugitive slave bill permanently, which Mason and Butler certainly could do, unless these border men went along with southern Democrats? And if they failed to cooperate on California, Texas, and the rest of the Cession and to oppose abolition of the District slave trade, let them face the wrath of the citizens of Delaware, Maryland, Kentucky, and Missouri, who would be denied a new fugitive slave act. In terms of procedural strategy, in short, the fugitive slave bill was integral, not peripheral, to the Compromise of 1850.

Second, from the moment in late March when Foote's motion to form a select committee became the focus of debate and roll-call voting in the Senate, Whig advocates of the Taylor plan lost, and Democratic advocates of compromise seized, control of the congressional agenda. Taylor's program, which called for nonaction except on California until New Mexico applied for statehood, was moribund, and it could be resurrected only if his congressional supporters could first kill whatever plan the select committee came up with. Friends of the president would now be defined by negative opposition to the compromisers, not positive advocacy of a plan that might realistically be enacted. That some Whigs abetted this Democratic coup galled Taylor and his cabinet. "Old Zack . . . hates Clay," reported a northern newspaperman who saw him in April. "Old Zack is quarreling at Clay openly," repeated another insider. "He evidently don't like the idea of being overlooked in Congress."[118]

Developments outside of Congress also imperiled Taylor's plan. During February and March, anger at Meredith's apparent attempt to undermine the public warehousing system welled up among merchants in Boston, New York, and Philadelphia, and those merchants took the lead in organizing procompromise Union meetings in their cities.[119] Then, in late March, a financial scandal involving Meredith, Reverdy Johnson, and Secretary of War George W. Crawford broke into the open, a scandal that immediately escalated calls from already angry and now embarrassed Whigs for a complete cabinet shake-up.

The details of the Galphin Claim, whose final payment in early 1850 rocked the Taylor administration and instantly made the term "Galphinism" the newest synonym for governmental sleaze, were complex. But the salient points can be quickly summarized.[120] Before the Revolutionary War, a Georgia Indian trader named George Galphin lodged a claim against the British government, and for six decades after the winning of independence, he and then his heirs petitioned both the state of Georgia and Congress to pay it off. The Galphin heirs may have been Whigs; certainly they were well connected to the Georgia Whig party. Since 1832 their attorney had been George Crawford, who during his two terms as governor in the mid-1840s pressed Berrien, Stephens, Toombs, and other Georgia Whig congressmen to push a bill through Congress paying the Galphins. In 1848 they succeeded, and Congress ordered Treasury Secretary Robert J. Walker to pay the Galphin heirs the principal of the claim, about $43,500, or over $760,000 in current dollars. Congress, however, left it to the Treasury secretary's discretion whether sixty years' worth of accumulated interest on the claim, an amount over four times as large as the principal, should also be paid, and Walker deferred a decision on that question.

In 1849 the decision on the interest fell to the new Taylor administration. Preoccupied with preparing his report on the tariff, Meredith referred the claim to the comptroller, who ruled against payment. Then, at Berrien's urging, Meredith sought an opinion from Attorney General Johnson, who ruled in early 1850 that the interest must be paid. Accordingly, Meredith ordered interest amounting to over $191,000 paid to the Galphin heirs, bringing the total settlement to about $235,000 (or $4.1 million in modern dollars).[121]

The size of the payment alone, when the government was already running a deficit, provoked cries of a Treasury raid. Much more embarrassing, Crawford profited immensely from the settlement. No longer the Galphins' attorney of record, he had worked since 1832 on a contingency basis and was due to receive half of any interest payment. Thus, as a direct result of a decision by Johnson and Meredith, Crawford received a windfall of $95,000 (or $1.66 million in modern currency), an enormous sum of money. Neither Meredith nor Johnson knew that Crawford had ever been a lawyer for the Galphins, let alone that he stood to profit from their decision. Crawford had told Taylor about his previous legal work but not about his personal financial stake in the claim.

When news of the payments broke in late March, the decision looked like an act of collusion among the three cabinet members to plunder the public purse for their own advantage and that of other Whigs. Democratic newspapers shrieked for blood. Whig papers, led by the *Republic*, condemned the cabinet for not holding meetings on so huge a claim in order to avoid both the fact and the appearance of impropriety. Public outrage was so intense that, on April 2, Crawford asked the House to investigate his role in the matter. Thus, just when senators were battling over a select committee, House Democrats were gleefully accusing the administration of corruption. Talk of impeachment filled the air, and the three cabinet members were not the only targets mentioned.[122]

The scandal mortified Taylor and embarrassed other Whigs. Since the 1830s, Whigs had always promised to provide more honest and capable government than Democrats, and now a Whig administration, through incompetence or worse, had betrayed the public trust. The administration, intoned Alabama Democrat King, "is destined to go out of office, execrated and despised by every upright and honorable man in the nation." Whigs feared exactly that result. The claim "is enough to finish what little there is left of the present Cabinet," moaned Winthrop. "The Galphin affair," Weed predicted, "will weaken us badly anyhow, and ruin all, I fear, if some do not resign." Seward, Schuyler Colfax, and others concurred. "The dissatisfaction with the Cabinet increases, and their resignation is desired by a very large majority of the Whigs in Congress," summarized David Outlaw on May 12.[123]

When Henry Clay presented his committee report on May 8, therefore, the tarnished Taylor administration could not reclaim the initiative from congressional compromisers. That the cabinet opposed any compromise that entangled California's admission with other matters only further infuriated procompromise Whigs and incapacitated Taylor supporters. Worst of all, complained congressional Whigs, the stubborn Taylor refused to replace his discredited advisors. "The truth is," Weed bluntly warned Meredith, "Mr. Crawford and his friends are costing the Whig party, the Administration, and the country too much. We really cannot afford such expensive luxuries." Because of this obtuse loyalty, a contemptuous Webster predicted, "I fear the Administration is doomed, & the Whig Party doomed with it." Taylor "is an obstinate man," agreed Outlaw. "He did not have when he came here sufficient political information, or experience to qualify him for the office."[124]

With criticism of Taylor and his cabinet growing, on May 8 Clay presented a revised compromise plan consisting of three bills and a twelve-page report explaining their rationale. One bill contained two amendments to Mason's fugitive slave bill, and another abolished the slave market in the District. The third, a huge omnibus bill, that by itself contemporaries identified as "the compromise bill" or "Clay's compromise," linked together all the legislation for the Mexican Cession. On May 8 and again on May 13 Clay urged the Senate to enact the bills. To a degree, he was more conciliatory than in January. Southern Whigs particularly applauded Clay's pointed rejection of Taylor's approach in the committee report. Congress must create territorial governments in the remainder of the Cession because "they are not now, and for a long time to come may not be, prepared for State government." Immediate statehood for New Mexico, in short, was out of the question. Southern Whigs also liked the report's recommendation that Congress refrain from imposing any legislation about slavery on territorial governments and that the people of each territory, when they applied for statehood, "decide for themselves the question of the allowance or prohibition of domestic slavery."[125] Nonetheless, close scrutiny of the report, the bills, and Clay's speeches shows that he had bent to Democratic and southern pressure but not broken completely before it. He still sought primarily to rally northern Whigs behind him.

With one significant exception, the omnibus bill adopted verbatim the bills Douglas had prepared admitting California and creating territorial governments for New Mexico and Utah. Rather than granting their legislatures authority over "all rightful subjects of legislation"—that is, slavery—as Douglas had, they were instead specifically prohibited from passing any law "in respect to African slavery."[126] This was a far cry from popular sovereignty as Douglas and many other Democrats defined it. It meant that a territorial legislature could not prohibit slavery during the territorial stage, but it also meant that a legislature could not pass proslavery laws to replace the existing Mexican laws, thereby neutralizing, if not rendering completely meaningless, the right of residents to write proslavery constitutions at the time of statehood. Southern Whigs who did not believe that slaveholders would ever go into the Cession could live with this phrasing, although they considered impolitic, if not fatal, Clay's insistence in the report that California's example proved that slavery would never spread to any part of the Mexican Cession even if Congress eschewed the Proviso. Most southern Democrats and a few southern Whigs, however, found Clay's new formulation totally unacceptable. Nor did Clay's omnibus bill contain Calhounite language extending the Constitution, with its supposed guarantee of the right to own slaves, over the territories or language guaranteeing congressional admission of states carved from the territories with or without slavery as their constitutions prescribed. Only at the insistence of Southerners would such amendments be added to what later became the final laws. Clay himself was offering the South only the creation of territorial governments without the Proviso as compensation for California's admission.

Clay's continuing attempt to mollify northern Whigs also appeared in the omnibus bill's provisions for the Texas-New Mexico boundary. Clay relented on the draconian border he had first proposed for Texas, but not by much. Now he would set the northern and western borders of Texas along a diagonal line that ran northeastward from a point on the Rio Grande River twenty miles north of El Paso to the intersection of the Red River at the 100th meridian. This proposal would restore to Texas the area between the 32nd parallel and the Red River, which encompassed Dallas, Fort Worth, and some 20,000 slaves, and to that extent Clay retreated before southern pressure. But it would leave Texas smaller than its eventual size and considerably smaller than the area Texas claimed in 1850.[127]

Clay's omnibus bill would also directly compensate Texas for surrendering its claims to part of New Mexico with United States bonds worth a still-unspecified amount. But the bill stipulated that before the government of Texas could spend that money on anything else, it must settle its debt with the holders of Texas bonds. Finally, the bill was silent on the matter of admitting new slave states from Texas to balance California, just as Clay had been in his January resolutions. The committee agreed, Clay explained in his report, that any initiative for carving new states out of Texas must come from the people of Texas themselves, not from Congress.

That Clay still hoped to rally northern Whigs behind this revised compromise became clear when he defended it on May 13. Declaring that he still believed that Mexico's antislavery statutes held force in the Cession, he argued explicitly that because the new territorial governments would be prohibited from passing laws regarding slavery, those Mexican laws barring slavery would remain in force until the population of the territories was numerous enough to write constitutions and apply for statehood. Recognizing that most northern Whigs preferred Taylor's plan, Clay now invited Taylor himself to join the procompromise coalition. When the president had presented his plan in January, Clay admitted, it made sense. But conditions had changed. If Taylor were now to submit a proposition, Clay was sure that "he would not limit himself to a recommendation merely for the admission of California, leaving the territories to shift for themselves." It would instead be "much more comprehensive, and much more general and healing in its character."[128]

Clay admitted in his report that not all members of the committee agreed with the recommendations, and this last-ditch attempt to find a formula to hold the Whig party together, like his first, failed miserably. If most southern Whigs now embraced Clay's omnibus bill as a reasonable compromise, Berrien immediately denounced it, even though his closest advisors had informed him that Georgia's Whigs could accept the admission of California if it were tied to the creation of territorial governments without the Proviso and even though, or perhaps because, Stephens and Toombs now supported such a compromise. If California were admitted at all, Berrien declared as soon as Clay finished reading his report, its southern boundary must be fixed at 35° 30'. Slaveholders must not be excluded from the entire Pacific coast. Mangum, who also served on the committee, and his sidekick Clingman had apparently savaged the proposal even before Clay read it to the Senate, causing the procompromise Outlaw to fume, "The fact is, I do not consider Mangum or Clingman as Whigs." Southern Democrats blasted the insufficient safeguards for slavery in Clay's territorial propositions and the stinginess of Clay's new Texas boundary, which would still substantially reduce the area in which slavery was unequivocally legal. Primarily, however, they personally and their state parties remained hostile to California statehood under any circumstances. They demanded instead the extension of the 36° 30' line to the Pacific, a demand the Nashville Convention would endorse in June.[129]

In part because most northern Democrats lavishly praised Clay's omnibus bill, most northern Whigs, who also thought it gave the South far too much, still spurned Clay's overtures. They found the omnibus bill repugnant because it created a quid pro quo for California's admission and because it organized territorial governments without the Proviso. Although southern amendments would later make the bill even worse from their point of view, Clay's version was bad enough. They could never support it, as Phelps of Vermont, another dissenting committee member, immediately announced on the Senate floor. "I shall vote against any bundling in the matter," Winthrop had vowed in early April. "I certainly will take no bad measures in company with the admission of California. Taylor's plan is still the best." A month later a New Yorker told Thomas Ewing, "The great body of the Whig party are with the administration on the California question. They are against the selfish and suicidal course in the Senate pursued by Clay and Webster. They are as decidedly opposed to *any* compromise, as that necessarily involves an extension of slave territory."[130]

Taylor also refused to alter course. "He is true as steel," wrote an admiring northern reporter on May 3. "He sticks strongly to his plan," echoed another correspondent, who had talked to Taylor three times. "He said if Congress had adopted his recommendations, the whole thing would have been settled three months ago." Though administration insiders knew of Taylor's determination to fight Clay's compromise, it became public knowledge only when Taylor finally replaced Alexander Bullitt and John Sargent as editors of the *Republic*.[131]

Taylor's growing exasperation with Bullitt's unceasing criticism of his cabinet precipitated this editorial reshuffling. The change, which occurred on May 14, "was done by Old Zack," reported a Whig from Washington. "He is determined to throw overboard everybody opposed to the Cabinet, & there seems no alternative but to support the Administration, or go to pot."[132]

Taylor's indignation that Bullitt lavished praise on Clay and Webster and failed to support his own plan adequately, however, lay behind the move. As early as April 19, Taylor privately told Orlando Brown, Crittenden's friend, that he no longer considered the *Republic* the administration's organ, and Bullitt's editorials in May proved the last straw. "We do not see any such discrepancy between the *principle* of [Taylor's] platform and" Clay's committee report, Bullitt editorialized. "We see no necessary enmity to the PRESIDENT in the resolutions of Mr. CLAY and Mr. BELL, [or] the speeches of Mr. WEBSTER, Mr. BERRIEN, Mr. BADGER, and other distinguished Whigs," since "the *settlement* was more important than the *plan* of settlement."[133]

Bullitt and his publisher, Albert Burnley, may have believed this, but Zachary Taylor emphatically did not. Hence, he forced Burnley to sack Bullitt. Pro-Taylor northern Whigs unsuccessfully asked Horace Greeley to succeed Bullitt, and Taylor consulted with Weed about other northern possibilities. In the end, however, they chose another Southerner, Allen A. Hall, an assistant Treasury secretary, former editor of a Whig paper in Nashville, and henchman of John Bell. On May 20, Hall announced in the *Republic* what insiders already knew. Taylor had never wavered from his belief that his January proposal for California's admission as an "independent measure" was "the best practicable."[134]

That shaft forced Clay the following day to do what he had carefully refrained from doing since December—break irrevocably with the administration. "Here are five wounds . . . bleeding and threatening the well being, if not the existence of the body politic," Clay proclaimed to the Senate. Taylor's plan would heal only one, leaving "the other four to bleed more profusely." The committee's bills would salve all five. "I have seen with profound regret" Taylor's "persistence . . . in his own peculiar plan," Clay continued. And then came the ultimate Whig riposte. Given what Taylor had repeatedly said about deferring to the will of Congress, he "ought . . . to permit us to consider what is best for our common country" rather than obstruct the efforts of the people's chosen representatives.[135]

Clay's "arrogant" and "dictatorial" speech appalled pro-Taylor Whigs. "True to his hates he has flung down the defiance to the friends of General Taylor," the outraged Orlando Brown wrote Crittenden. "I am glad myself that he has at last stepped out with his armor on—an avowed enemy though formidable can be met." Clay's unforgivable break with the president, moaned Fillmore's friend Nathan Hall, "will probably end in the dissolution if not the destruction of the Whig party," exactly what Clay sincerely wanted to avoid. Yet, Clay wrote his son, he had no choice. "I had to attack the plan of the Administration for compromising our Slavery difficulties," he explained. "Its course left me with no other alternative."[136]

While the *Republic*'s May 20 editorial ended Clay's hopes of weaning northern Whigs away from the president's plan and left him almost exclusively dependent on Democratic support from the North, other developments also explain the timing of his break. On May 17, a House committee exonerated Crawford, Johnson, and Meredith of collusion on the Galphin claim, even while condemning the payment of interest as unwarranted. That finding, along with the firing of Bullitt, temporarily doomed chances of a cabinet shake-up, which Clay hoped might purge anticompromise elements from Taylor's circle of advisors. Equally important, the mission of Clay's son James to Lisbon, about which he had been so solicitous, appeared a failure by mid-May. Indeed, in the letter of May 27 in which Clay informed James of his attack on Taylor, he also assumed "that your public duties in the port of Lisbon are brought to an unsuccessful close." So convinced, Clay no longer feared administration retaliation against him.[137]

Whatever Clay's motives, the *Republic*'s new editor signaled that the administration would pick up his gauntlet. On May 27, Hall emphatically declared that Taylor still considered his original proposal superior to Clay's, that immediate statehood for New Mexico was the best way to resolve the Texas boundary dispute, and that Taylor steadfastly opposed the "establishment of territorial governments" because he wanted to end "all agitation" on slavery and no territorial bill "could pass Congress without bringing up the . . . proviso." Clay, continued Hall, came to Washington determined to appropriate "to himself the glory of a third compromise." "He came to lead, not to follow. . . . He came to originate measures of compromise, and pacification, not to adopt such as others might recommend."[138]

VIII

Presentation of the omnibus bill and the public rupture between Clay and Taylor helped clarify the confused situation that had existed in Whig ranks since December. No longer could Whigs preserve the fiction that they were not divided. Now Whig politicians and Whig newspapers would have to choose sides for or against the administration. Moreover, Whigs like Bell and Webster, who had preferred a compromise plan different from either Taylor's or Clay's, now had to rally behind Clay's omnibus since it had first place on the Senate agenda. This fact became indisputable when the Senate defeated Douglas' motion to substitute his bill admitting California alone for the omnibus bill. After that defeat, Webster threw his support behind the omnibus, even though he considered it a tactical mistake. By early June, in sum, the divisions within the Whig party were assuming a bipolar form, although some men, like Berrien, continued to denounce both the omnibus and the Taylor plan.[139]

As Whig divisions became clearer, they also grew more rancorous. With Webster and Clay leading the Whig compromisers and anticompromisers rallying behind the administration, the battle seemed to pit ultra Whig regulars against Taylor men, just as did the simultaneous struggle raging over patronage. The split occurred primarily, but not exclusively, along sectional lines, causing Seward to comment caustically that "the North and South, after studying Mr. Clay's juggle for three months, are falling back upon their first positions." Whigs seemed no more capable of bridging their sectional chasm than they had been in December.[140]

The great majority of southern Whigs, including the Stephens-Toombs bolters of December, now rallied behind the omnibus bill, which they saw as the only alternative to the naked admission of California and the secession it might provoke. There were a few exceptions to this rule. Representatives Meredith Gentry of Tennessee and Edward Stanly of North Carolina remained loyal to the Taylor plan, as did Delaware's Whigs. John Bell also voiced a preference for it, but Bell wavered so much that no one could tell how he might eventually vote. Other Taylor men, both in and outside Washington, abandoned the president. Crittenden, for example, reversed course even before Clay presented his report. By early June he was warning Orlando Brown, in words echoing Bullitt's editorials, that "the public is *anxious* for a *settlement*, & comparatively indifferent as to the exact terms, provided that they embrace anything like a *compromise*." Therefore, Taylor must avoid "the responsibility of *defeating* the Bill of the Committee of thirteen, or any other measure of *compromise*." A Mississippian denounced "Old Hal" as "a complete marplot [who] must be first or nothing" for opposing Taylor's plan, which "avoided the only really alarming aggression of the North, 'the Wilmot' and it avoided it on principles entirely just to all parties." Yet he concluded that Clay's opposition doomed any chance that Congress would follow Taylor and that therefore southern Whigs must back the omnibus.[141]

A few southern Whigs—Clingman, Berrien, and Florida Senator Jackson Morton—joined Democrats from their region in opposing any plan that admitted California. Worried that Berrien was assuming a politically untenable position, his closest Georgia friends found his case against California's admission, with its claimed boundaries, powerful but pointless. "California must one day be admitted, and if Slavery cannot be profitable there, it is far better for us that she should not be divided," advised Francis S. Bartow, a Savannah Whig editor. More important, they warned, because there now seemed to be only two Whig positions and because Georgia's Whigs favored Clay's new plan, Berrien's opposition to Clay made him seem an ally of Taylor, whom Georgians now reviled. In short, the rupture between Clay and Taylor made any independent Whig stance impossible unless one was ready to defect to the Democrats, and, unlike Berrien and Clingman, most southern Whigs, including North Carolina's Mangum, who had previously breathed fire and who hated the idea of marching in step with the procompromise Badger, now fell in line behind the omnibus.[142]

In contrast, most northern Whigs still believed that any concessions to southern demands would doom the administration and their own careers, and that sticking to Taylor's plan provided the only feasible way to satisfy their constituents.[143] Dissenters from the prevalent northern Whig position, however, far outnumbered their southern Whig counterparts. In the Senate, both Webster and Cooper came out for the omnibus by early June. Webster and Clay, moreover, had close personal ties to a small number of northern Whigs in the House, a fact of considerable importance since even people who expected the omnibus to pass the Senate knew that the real battle would be in the House, where the huge northern Whig delegation together with the Free Soilers could block it. James Brooks and three other Whig representatives from New York City, as well as Joseph Casey of Pennsylvania, would heed Clay's bidding. George Ashmun of Massachusetts, James Wilson of New Hampshire, David Bokee of Brooklyn, and George G. King of Rhode Island were all deemed Webster's lackeys. Although their impassioned speeches had failed to move most northern Whigs, Clay and Webster could split a few away from their colleagues.[144]

Parallel divisions over the compromise among Whigs mushroomed in most northern states. Procompromise Whigs may have been more fearful about the danger to the Union than anticompromise Whigs. But Webster's private correspondence and public utterances alone raise doubts that fear of secession drove northern Whigs to support concessions to the South. Pocketbook concerns motivated some northern Whig compromisers. Whig merchants in northeastern cities, just like their Democratic counterparts, feared the loss of valuable southern customers if the crisis was not settled on acceptable terms, demanded enactment of the omnibus, and organized Union meetings to support it. Whig manufacturers from Pennsylvania, Rhode Island, and Massachusetts wanted tariff revision, and the longer Congress was tied up by the seemingly interminable debate over slavery, the more impatiently they sought its settlement. When Webster and others warned that southern Whigs would never consider tariff legislation until the compromise passed, therefore, some Whigs in manufacturing and mining areas also backed the omnibus. Seward, for one, feared that this pressure on northern Whig congressmen for a new tariff posed the biggest threat to killing the omnibus.[145]

Constituents' economic demands swayed some northern Whig politicos, but personal and factional political affiliations had a more direct and powerful impact. Webster had a personal following in Massachusetts and other New England states that he could rally. Clay could mobilize more numerous and even more fanatical loyalists in Pennsylvania, New Jersey, New York, and some midwestern states, men who remained as ready to march to his drumbeat as they had ever been. A Whig from Lancaster, Pennsylvania, warned Seward that procompromise sentiment flourished there because "Mr. Clay's name is a tower of strength in our County," and Clay's devotees in Philadelphia, the regulars or ultras who had fought the Taylor Republican movement, organized procompromise rallies. Zealous Clay Whigs in New York's legislature tried to pass resolutions endorsing Clay's January proposal, and after the open break between Clay and Taylor in May, both angry Clay men and Websterites in New York City pressed Jerome Fuller of the Albany *State Register* to endorse the omnibus and renounce Taylor and the *Republic*. Despite repeated pleas from Fillmore and Nathan Hall that Fuller stick to Taylor's plan, the harried editor buckled under that pressure almost immediately. "Henry Clay has hosts of friends in and out of that city upon whom we must retain our hold" and "the Webster men are in favor of territorial governments," Fuller plaintively explained to Fillmore. Moreover, southern Whigs endorsed Clay's omnibus, "and it is important for us to maintain a good standing with them. It is an advantage over Seward and Weed which we must make the most of." From Fuller's vantage point in Albany, the only way to preserve the alliance of anti-Weed Whigs Fillmore had begun to construct in 1849 was to side with Clay and Webster. "To let Clay and Webster fall is to let Weed and Seward walk over the course."[146]

Fuller's candid letters graphically illustrate how preexisting factional rivalries and jealousies spawned by the distribution of federal jobs largely determined which northern Whigs backed the Taylor plan and which swung behind the Compromise. Fuller considered southern Whigs' support crucial for New York's anti-Weed Whigs because he hoped southern Whig senators might vote to reject, rather than confirm, Sewardite appointees. This change of tack at Albany embarrassed Fillmore's western New York supporters, who still favored Taylor's plan, for it allowed Whig papers affiliated with Seward and Weed, which attacked the omnibus, to stigmatize them with guilt by association with pro-Clay doughfaces. Support for Taylor's plan in New York had become so exclusively identified with Fillmore's Sewardite enemies, complained one Fillmorite in early July, that it was "regarded as almost a fixed fact that, one who is not a Sewardite, is, of course, in favor of the omnibus bill, [and] hence our friends in this region labor under a great disadvantage." Blaming this impression on the editorials of the *State Register*, the Rochester *American*, and other pro-Fillmore papers, he warned that unless "that rickety concern of the Omnibus bill" was "abandoned" and the conservative Whig press backed the president's plan, "we must submit to the will of that demagogue Bill Seward."[147]

Such complaints struck Fuller and other Fillmore allies as nonsense. They could never outflank Seward and Weed by taking a harder line against compromise with slaveholders or courting Taylor's favor. Their best policy was to resolve all slavery issues permanently so that Seward and Weed could no longer exploit antislavery sentiment against them and use it to convert the Whig party into "a sectional party." Thus, "we must stay the progress of abolitionism, or we are gone." After a quick trip to Washington to consult with Fillmore, Fuller concluded that "Genl. Taylor's administration is used up. . . . Is it wise to align ourselves too closely with the fortunes of a sinking ship? He may defeat Clay, but in doing so he will use up himself, has done it already." Fillmore's closest confidant, Nathan Hall, who had steadfastly instructed Fillmore to stick with Taylor's plan since January, approached the same conclusion by July. "The President I suppose must desire as you and I do the admission of California & New Mexico as States," he wrote Fillmore, "but with you I fear that this cannot be done. In that event I prefer the Compromise Bill to inaction."[148]

Within New York, in sum, no perfect correlation existed between preexisting factional lines and attitudes toward the compromise. The Weed-Seward Whigs and one wing of their Fillmorite rivals backed the Taylor plan, while eastern anti-Weed Whigs, hard-core conservatives more loyal to Clay and Webster than to Fillmore, swung behind the omnibus. In other northern states, the relationship was much more direct. The Whig faction that controlled federal patronage advocated the president's platform and vilified proponents of compromise, especially Clay and Webster, as traitorous doughfaces who sought to destroy the Whig party. Losers in the patronage sweepstakes promoted compromise and lauded Clay and Webster as pillars of Whig nationalism. In Detroit, Pittsburgh, Philadelphia, and Boston, Whig newspapers with federal printing contracts attacked the compromise, while rival Whig papers, which had been denied that coveted largesse, supported it. Thus did northern Whigs divide against each other.[149]

Two states suffice to illustrate this pattern. In Massachusetts, Abbott Lawrence's wing of the party controlled the state Whig organization and most federal jobs. During the mid-1840s, that notorious Cotton Whig faction had taken a distinctively conservative stance on slavery extension, in contrast to their Conscience Whig and Websterite rivals, but by 1850 positions had changed. With Lawrence absent in London and Nathan Appleton, his fellow textile tycoon, largely retired from politics, leadership of the anti-Webster Whigs had fallen to men who shared the state's prevailing sentiment against any compromise with the South—elected politicians like "Honest" John Davis, Webster's colleague in the Senate; Representatives Winthrop, Julius Rockwell, and Joseph Grinnell; Philo Shelton, a state committeeman; and patronage recipients like William Schouler, editor of the Boston *Atlas*, Boston's customs collector, Philip Greely, Jr., Charles Hudson, the naval officer there, and George Lunt, the United States attorney. Among this group, Shelton, Greely, and Schouler remained in close touch with Seward and Weed, just as did officeholding Whigs in Michigan.[150]

Since Webster's Massachusetts Whig enemies had the inside track with Taylor's administration, he had little to lose, once his son Fletcher won Senate confirmation, and much to gain by opposing it. By working for compromise with southern Whig senators and northern Democrats like Cass, Dickinson, Sturgeon, and Bright, he might influence enough votes to defeat Senate confirmation of Lawrence's minions, who held the Bay State's federal jobs.[151] Once Webster and his Massachusetts organization came out for compromise, the Lawrence men used their papers in Boston, and especially in central and western Massachusetts, to marshal Whig opinion against him. As in New York, the intraparty conflict quickly extended to the state legislature, where, after the Seventh of March speech, anti-Webster Whigs and Free Soilers steamrollered resolutions through the lower house instructing Webster and Davis to insert the Proviso into any territorial bills Congress considered. Because of the gross overrepresentation of Boston in the state senate, Websterites there tabled the resolutions 15–11, but the stalemate bitterly divided the state's Whigs throughout the summer.[152]

Similarly, the strife between Pennsylvania Whig supporters of Governor Johnston and Senator Cooper quickly spawned disagreement over the Taylor and Clay plans. Prior to 1850, little separated the personal views of the two protagonists on the slavery issue. The former Democrat, Johnston, had delighted Pennsylvania's Whigs with his blistering speeches against slavery expansion during the 1848 campaign. Cooper also had a long antislavery record, and his elevation to the Senate in 1849 had been applauded by Quakers and other antislavery Whigs as "a 'free soil' triumph." When Cooper broke with most northern Whigs to vote for the committee of thirteen and publicly announced his support for the omnibus in early June, therefore, Pennsylvania's antislavery Whigs howled that he had betrayed them and wondered "what has brought his present deplorable insanity upon poor Cooper?"[153]

The possibility that Cooper genuinely feared disunion cannot be discounted, but he also wanted to cement the support of the zealous Clay Whigs in Philadelphia and the rest of Pennsylvania, who undoubtedly wanted the sectional controversy resolved. The Whigs' state convention was scheduled to meet on June 19 in Philadelphia, a hotbed of Clay sentiment, and Cooper was determined to seize control of that convention to oust Johnston's allies from state office and the state committee. To gain a majority of the delegates chosen at local and county conventions, Cooper required a weapon to counteract the organizational leverage Johnston gained from his command of the state and federal appointed officials, who could pack conventions with their employees. Lacking organizational resources himself, Cooper had no option but to use an issue to arouse rank-and-file Whigs to attend local conventions and to make the choice of delegates to the state gathering issue-oriented contests. Since the newspapers and politicos loyal to Johnston were firmly committed to Taylor's plan, Cooper tried to mobilize support from Whig regulars by pledging to write a state platform that committed Pennsylvania's Whig party to Clay's compromise as the best and quickest solution to the sectional crisis, as the only plan that could possibly pass Congress and allow it to address other business, which to depression-wracked Pennsylvania Whigs meant action on the tariff.

As soon as Clay presented the omnibus bill on May 8, Cooper's allies in Pennsylvania began offering resolutions at county conventions praising Cooper and Clay for their procompromise stance in order "to create an issue between the Admn. and Mr. Clay" and thus arouse Clay loyalists against Johnston and his allies. As Johnston himself reported to Meredith, "All the Clay & Cooper influence was excited to smuggle into [the state convention] reliable delegates and among [them] our *secret* and worst enemies." With the aid of Clay's Philadelphia friends, the Cooper forces easily won command of the delegations from the city and county of Philadelphia. In a pattern quite similar to those of New York and Massachusetts, however, procompromise Whigs could not make much headway beyond their eastern, urban beachhead. Johnston's forces firmly controlled the state convention. The platform committee defeated pro-Cooper, pro-Clay, and procompromise resolutions, although the votes indicated indisputably that Henry Clay remained more popular among Pennsylvania Whigs than Cooper, their own senator. The platform instead committed the state Whig party to Taylor's plan— statehood for California and New Mexico and no territorial governments. "It is a great triumph for *you*," crowed one of Meredith's friends, "to wheel Penna, moderate, compromising, Clay and Cooper Penna into the line of direct, manly and decided support for the Administration and all its measures."[154]

Cooper and Clay Whigs may have lost the battle, but they refused to suspend the war. By mid-June they were too committed to the omnibus to reverse course, and after the state convention they organized mass meetings in Philadelphia repudiating the Whig platform and endorsing compromise.[155] In Pennsylvania as in other states, intraparty strife over the territorial crisis showed no signs of abating.

In sum, the open breach between Clay and Taylor deepened the chasm separating most northern and southern Whigs from each other, and it unquestionably widened rifts in northern state parties by injecting emotion-laden issues into battles that had previously been confined to scrambles for spoils. These internal divisions prevented Whigs from defining a clear party position on the sectional crisis that differentiated them from Democrats and that might bring Whig voters to the polls at the impending 1850 elections. Who could say what the Whig position was when Whig newspapers in the same city took diametrically opposed stances, when Whig mass meetings repudiated Whig state platforms, and when the Whig governor and Whig senator from the same state, as in Pennsylvania, or two Whig senators, as in Massachusetts, were publicly crucifying each other? Such visceral and vitriolic intraparty feuding could only confuse and paralyze, rather than arouse, the Whig electorate when it was time for Whigs to confront Democrats on the hustings.

The Whigs' difficulty in defining a cogent party position on the sectional issue was aggravated when congressional Whigs on both sides of it openly cooperated with Democrats against Whigs on the other side, thereby muddying the differences between the two parties even further. Once most southern Democrats turned against the omnibus, for example, anticompromise northern Whigs like Seward immediately solicited their aid, along with that of antiomnibus northern Democrats like Douglas and Shields, in order to kill it. In early June, one of Seward's Whig allies, Senator John Clarke of Rhode Island, predicted that twelve Southerners and nineteen Northerners would combine to defeat the bill. His list included eleven southern and five northern Democrats, along with the two Free Soilers, one southern Whig, and twelve northern Whigs. It was an odd combination to be sure, for southern Democrats and northern Whigs disliked the omnibus for opposite reasons. It was a combination nonetheless, and that bipartisan, cross-sectional alliance held together as long as there was a chance that the omnibus might pass. However strange these bedfellows were, moreover, the existence of this coalition was important. If pro-Taylor Whigs could accuse procompromise Whigs of subverting the Whig party by opposing the administration, pro-Taylor Whigs could be accused of betraying it by working arm in arm with Democrats who execrated everything about the Whig party.[156]

In contrast to the procompromise forces, the anticompromise coalition engendered very little cooperation between Whigs and Democrats in the same region, let alone the same state. Both senators from Florida, the Whig Jackson Morton and the Democrat David Yulee, fought the omnibus, and at some local meetings in Georgia, Whigs and Democrats joined together to denounce it, causing one of Berrien's euphoric correspondents to rejoice that "the distinction of democrat & whig is generally passing away." For the most part, however, in the slave states below the border states combat over the compromise was fought on traditional party lines. Similarly, only in a very few northern states like Maine and Wisconsin, which Democrats controlled and where the Free Soil party was a threat to both major parties, did bipartisan cooperation against the compromise emerge. After the introduction of the omnibus bill, for example, Whigs and Democrats in the Maine legislature joined to pass resolutions instructing the state's two Democratic senators to vote against it.[157]

In most northern states, instead, Taylor's adamant hostility to creating territorial governments increased Democrats' support for compromise because they were confident that they could eviscerate pro-Taylor northern Whigs for recklessly endangering the Union. As an Illinois Democratic congressman gloated in June, "This gives opportunity to push the issue of disunion directly at them."[158] Antislavery, anticompromise northern Whigs like Seward would have been delighted to meet that issue head on and to make compromise with the South the focus of interparty, partisan combat in the impending northern elections. But procompromise Whigs from northern and border states rendered it impossible to draw clear lines between the parties.

The *Republic*'s assault on Clay and his omnibus on May 27 forced procompromise Whigs to work closely and publicly with procompromise northern Democrats like Bright, Cass, Dickinson, Douglas, and Sturgeon. "The Democrats are seeking to save their party by the passage of the Compromise Bill," Seward complained to his wife in mid-June. "The principles maintained by us are, therefore, in great jeopardy when all our ancient leaders cooperate with our adversaries." Seward's correspondents denounced Cooper, Clay, and Webster in the same breath with Dickinson, Cass, and Sturgeon as traitors to the North, but their obvious anger did nothing to dissipate the confusion caused by the cooperation between the Whigs' traditional leaders and the Democratic enemy. The "trouble" with the omnibus, wrote one frustrated Whig, was that "it is proved to be the identical 'hobby horse' of which certain men of each party claim paternity." The whole purpose of the omnibus bill, huffed another, was to make Cass "the next Democratic nominee," yet Whigs supported it. Such behavior by the congressional Whig party could never repair the damage done to the rank and file's morale by Taylor's No Party dispensation of patronage in 1849.[159]

Even worse for Whig politicians seeking to arouse an apathetic and disillusioned electorate, the bipartisan procompromise alliance extended to many states. Georgians knew that Cobb, Stephens, and Toombs were cooperating with each other, but the collapse of party lines was especially prominent in the border states and the North. Procompromise meetings in Delaware, a Democrat proudly wrote Clay, were uncontaminated by any "thought or feeling connected with party. . . . Our Senators will find that on questions involving hazard to the Union, the people of Delaware know nothing of parties." He could have written the same thing about Maryland and Kentucky, where Democrats and Whigs, like their representatives in Congress, banded together to support the omnibus. From Philadelphia, New York, and Boston to Detroit, Indiana, and Illinois, Whigs joined their traditional political enemies in meetings demanding a settlement. In Massachusetts, for example, the Democrat Caleb Cushing was urged to run for Congress as the candidate of "Independent Whig & Democratic voters . . . standing upon the Webster . . . platform." Not only was the Whig party divided, but distinctions between Democrats and at least some Whigs appeared to be disappearing. The split between

Taylor and Clay seemed capable of generating a complete realignment or reorganization of parties, one far different from that which the president and Clayton had envisioned for the now-aborted Taylor Republican movement.[160]

Only a minority of Whigs in any northern state supported compromise or aligned themselves with Democrats. Their behavior again raises the question of motivation. Heightened anxiety about disunion, pressure from economic interest groups, loyalty to Clay or Webster, the instinctive impulse of rival factions to oppose each other on issues—all these undoubtedly played a role. But behind certain Whig politicos' and editors' open embrace of Democrats and of what was primarily a Democratic position in the North lay a stark fact. Democrats controlled the Senate, and the Senate disposed of federal appointees.

IX

Democrats and Whigs alike understood that the Senate's Democratic majority would determine the fate of patronage recipients, but that hard fact suggested different possibilities to the two parties when the session opened. Professing shock that Taylor had broken his vow of nonpartisanship by removing Democrats from government jobs, Democrats plotted revenge. Astute Whigs across the country, in contrast, "expected Whigs will defeat Whigs, by soliciting the aid of opposition, locofoco, Senators." In that need for Democratic help on patronage lay the nub of Whig cooperation with Democrats on policy.[161]

Not all Democratic senators returned to Washington in December intent upon purging the bureaucracy, but enough did to cause both Democrats and Whigs to predict massive Senate rejections. Cass, Dickinson, Bright, and Downs of Louisiana were believed to be particularly vindictive. After Cass and his Michigan colleague Alpheus Felch stopped in Buffalo on their way to Washington, for example, Nathan Hall warned Fillmore that Cass "is inclined to make a fight on the nominations as well as the measures of the administration & the warfare will be bitter. It will be indiscriminate."[162]

Senate Democrats flexed their muscle quickly. In January, Dickinson demanded that Postmaster General Collamer justify the removal of Democratic postmasters in New York. Later that month, Maine's James W. Bradbury introduced another resolution requesting the administration to lay "before the Senate" the "charges ... preferred ... against individuals ... removed from office." By insisting that Taylor demonstrate incompetence or malfeasance on the part of decapitated Democrats, Bradbury intended, as Webster recognized, to delay Senate action on appointments "until the President's answer shall come." The Democrats meant to embarrass the administration and let nervous Whig officeholders agonize in uncertainty. Virtually all patronage holders had been appointed after the Senate adjourned in March 1849, and no interim federal appointee could retain his job unless confirmed by the Senate before this session of Congress adjourned.[163]

The Senate never passed Bradbury's resolution, but throughout the spring and into the summer, the Democratic caucus repeatedly voted to delay action on most nominees until the resolution passed and Taylor replied to it. That calculated obstructionism delayed Senate action on the vast majority of Whig appointees until August and September, when the Senate and House were voting on the compromise measures. Thus Democratic senators maximized their leverage to pressure Whigs into voting the way Democrats wished on the compromise itself.[164]

In late January, Webster informed a friend that "any leading Whig Senator, who should be so inclined, might produce rejections, in plenty," by cooperating with Democrats. Yet not all Democrats were equal in the eyes of Whigs who sought a favorable or adverse decision on particular appointments. Committee chairmen who could bottle up nominations or submit hostile reports obviously had clout, but the Democrats mentioned most frequently in Whig correspondence as the arbiters of patronage were William R. King of Alabama, Downs of Louisiana, Douglas, Bright, Cass, and Dickinson. No man in the Senate, indeed, was believed to have more influence over patronage than Dickinson, New York's senior senator, leader of his party's Hunker faction, and chairman of the Finance Committee. That all of these Democrats except Downs became staunch supporters of the Compromise was a fact of incalculable importance. That most Whig senators unhappy with Taylor's appointments eventually joined them was no coincidence.[165]

How Whigs who sought the confirmation or rejection of individual appointees worked with Democratic senators depended primarily on the composition of the Senate delegations from their own states. If both senators from a state were Whigs, their constituents relied on them to cut deals with the Democrats, and Webster, for one, lost no time in seeking the cooperation of Bradbury, Dickinson, and other Democrats.[166] Conversely, Whigs represented by two Democratic senators, as was the case in Virginia, Maine, and all the southwestern and midwestern states except Ohio, pursued one of two courses. They asked a Whig from a different state to run interference for them in the Senate or they worked directly with their own Democratic senators.

Since most complaints about southern appointments involved the retention in office of Democrats who had already been confirmed, disgruntled southern Whigs had little recourse in the Senate. Maine and the midwestern states were another matter. There Whigs had been appointed, men whose proponents and opponents actively lobbied the Senate. Of these heavily Democratic states, Michigan illustrates the tactics used by rival Whigs and how the struggle over patronage affected the battle over compromise measures.

Michigan's antislavery Whigs closely affiliated with Seward won the juiciest patronage plums: Josiah Snow, editor of the Detroit *Tribune*, who had the state's federal printing contracts; Alpheus S. Williams, Detroit's postmaster; Oliver M. Hyde, its customs collector; and Charles Babcock, Indian agent in the state. Aware that their Whig rivals, represented by the Detroit *Advertiser*, had sent a delegation to Washington to defeat Senate confirmation of Hyde and Babcock, Snow begged Seward's help in the Senate on the grounds that Hyde and Babcock "belong to *our* school in views of public policy in relation to slavery, tariffs, etc. The opposition is wholly from the other side on the slavery question." Precisely that conservative effort to defeat Hyde and Babcock caused another of Seward's Michigan allies to warn "that it is expected Whigs will defeat Whigs, by soliciting the aid of opposition, locofoco, Senators." Whether the conservative Whig delegation conferred with Cass, the final arbiter of Michigan nominees, is unknown, but as soon as Cass announced his support for Clay's compromise, the Detroit *Advertiser* began promoting it and denouncing Taylor's obstinate hostility to a general set-tlement. Similarly, Whigs unhappy with the appointments from Indiana and Il-linois began working with Democrats for compromise once it became clear that the Democratic senators from those states wanted it.[167]

States with split Senate delegations created a different dynamic. Ohio's was divided between the Whig Corwin and the Free Soiler Chase, and most Ohio Whigs unhappy with Ewing's distribution of jobs were content to work through Corwin, who adamantly opposed Clay's omnibus, to kill appointments. In con-trast, some of Ewing's favorites, notably Aaron Perry, the Columbus postmaster and editor of the Whigs' state organ there, actively sought Democratic aid in securing their confirmation. Yet Perry and other officeholders could hardly oppose the policy favored by Taylor and Ewing for the Cession. Hence, far fewer Whigs supported compromise in Ohio than in other northern states.[168]

In 1850, four states' Senate delegations were divided between a Whig and a Democrat, and in all four the Democrat was the senior senator, who had the final say on his state's jobs. Hopkins L. Turney of Tennessee had two years' seniority over his Whig colleague Bell, but since Bell had been a cabinet member and speaker of the House, people expected Turney to defer to Bell rather than vice versa.[169] Bell had managed the appointments in Tennessee, and he wanted his friends confirmed, not rejected. He was also considered one of the few southern Whigs who remained loyal to Taylor's administration. Nonetheless, his wavering course on compromise in May, June, and July and his ultimate support of it in August may have been a bid for the necessary Democratic votes on patronage.

All three Whigs from the other states were freshmen who knew they had to work with their Democratic colleagues to sway the Democratic majority. Florida's Jackson Morton, who had been elected by Democratic votes over the choice of the Florida Whig party, could be expected on that account alone to curry favor with the Democrat Yulee. On most roll-call votes concerning both patronage and policy throughout the session, Morton in fact voted the same way as Yulee—that is, like a southern Democrat rather than a southern Whig. Hence, he was one of the very few southern Whigs consistently to oppose compromise.[170] The other two states with split Senate delegations—Pennsylvania and New York—witnessed the most convoluted struggles over Senate confirmation of any states, and none il-lustrate better the intimate connection between Senate action on appointees and battles over the Compromise.

By the time Congress met in December 1849, the rancorous conflict over fed-eral patronage in Pennsylvania between old-line Whig regulars and Johnston's state administration was widely known. Both sides barraged Whig senators from other states with warnings that the confirmation or rejection of Johnston's friends would wreck Pennsylvania's Whig party. Johnston and his job-holding lieutenants knew that freshman Senator Cooper would lead the fight against their confir-mation, and they, as well as Cooper's Democratic predecessor, Simon Cameron, predicted that he would be forced to seek Democratic help to do it. The Democrat whose cooperation Cooper most needed was Daniel Sturgeon, the state's senior senator. As soon as Congress opened, Cooper sought Sturgeon's aid against the federal appointees in Philadelphia, and by mid-January, Sturgeon as well as Dick-inson joined Cooper in presenting remonstrances from Pennsylvania against William D. Lewis, the Philadelphia customs collector, and other Taylor appointees in the state.[171]

Given Democrats' control of the Senate and the probability that Sturgeon's voice would decide Pennsylvania affairs, Johnston, Lewis, and other Whig office-holders realized that lining up support from other Whig senators to offset Cooper would not suffice. They had to compete with Cooper for Sturgeon's favor. Hence Lewis and William I. B. White, Philadelphia's postmaster, hired scores of Democrats to demonstrate to Sturgeon and other Democratic senators that they deserved confirmation. The longer the Senate delayed action on Pennsylvania appointments, the more Democrats nervous Whig officeholders employed. That frantic defensive effort, in turn, further incensed regulars who had been denied jobs. Both rival wings of the Pennsylvania Whig party thus wooed Democrats in a bidding war that simultaneously widened the division between them and blurred the difference between Whigs and Democrats, at least on the allocation of government jobs.[172]

Unlike Johnston's friends, Cooper and his Pennsylvania allies could not offer jobs to Democrats to sway Sturgeon. Nor would they have; their whole point was that government largesse should go to reliable Whigs, not Democrats, Native Americans, or opportunistic newcomers who wanted to junk the Whig party. But they could and did cooperate with Sturgeon and the Pennsylvania Democratic party on policy. Daniel Sturgeon was not as influential a proponent of either popular sovereignty or the Compromise of 1850 as more famous northern Democrats like Cass, Dickinson, and Douglas. But throughout the session he voted with the procompromise, anti-Taylor camp as consistently as anyone in the Senate, and on virtually every roll call Cooper voted right along with him. Back in Pennsylvania, Cooper's friends repudiated the Whig state platform and worked arm in arm with Democrats for a compromise that the state's Democratic party had made a test of Democratic orthodoxy. There were two reasons, then, for Cooper's course that so enraged antislavery Whigs in Pennsylvania. He wanted the help of Clay's friends in his battle against Johnston within the state party, and he wanted to guarantee Sturgeon's help in the Senate in his battle against Johnston over patronage.

No state's Whigs were more obsessed by patronage than New York's, and because of its unique cast of characters, New York surpassed all other states in the byzantine complexity with which Whigs maneuvered to influence Senate decisions on appointees. New York had three, not two, voices in the Senate. Vice President Fillmore could vote only to break ties, but as the chamber's presiding officer, he was expected by his New York allies to exert substantial influence on senators. His rival Seward, though only a freshman, was the ablest, most strident, and, after his Higher Law speech, most famous anticompromise Whig in the Senate. Seward's senior colleague Dickinson was, unquestionably, the Senate's most powerful Democrat. A fervent proponent of popular sovereignty and Clay's omnibus bill, Dickinson was also more interested in playing the role of patronage broker than any other Democrat. The tricornered relationship among these men ensured a drama with a tangled plot.

Both the Seward-Weed Whigs, who had won the bulk of federal jobs in the Empire State, and Fillmore and his conservative Whig allies approached the Senate session with specific agendas. Seward and Weed hoped to win confirmation for their friends and to defeat the few conservatives who had won places, particularly John Young and Hugh Maxwell, the subtreasurer and customs collector, respectively, in New York City. "If it be possible we must get rid of Young," Weed instructed Seward. "The Whig party is not safe with such a traitor in a position of power." So desperate were Weed's and Seward's lieutenants in the city to depose Maxwell, and especially Young, that they initially tried to persuade Taylor to give one or both of them a foreign assignment to get them out of the country.[173]

Fillmorites returned to Washington in December with a much longer hit list. Fillmore and his Buffalo advisors gave priority to ousting Levi Allen and Isaac Harrington from the customs house and post office in that city, but other conservatives were equally determined to axe Weed minions such as Lewis Benedict and Thomas Clowes, postmaster-designates in Albany and Troy, and James R. Lawrence, the United States attorney for the Northern District of New York. At first, Fillmore and his friends hoped to persuade Taylor not even to nominate Allen and Harrington, but by mid-December they decided that it would be easier and politically wiser to defeat their confirmation in the Senate. "If you can't defeat Allen in the Senate," Nathan Hall bluntly warned Fillmore, "you may as well come home, for I should hate to preside over a body which did not take my words for as much as this."[174]

Seward had to contend with Fillmore's influence in the Senate, as well as with lobbying efforts from hostile members of New York's huge Whig delegation in the House, at least half of whom, according to Weed, were Seward's enemies.[175] Yet every interested Whig understood that Dickinson would decide New York's appointments. That fact, in turn, caused Sewardite Whigs grave concern and enormously encouraged Fillmore's conservative Whig allies.

Dickinson hailed from Binghamton, New York. So did the two Fillmore men Sewardites most despised, John Collier and John Young, both of whom were on friendly terms with Dickinson. The duplicitous and ambitious Young, who still hungered for the lucrative customs collectorship in New York City even after he had been named subtreasurer there, huddled with Dickinson at the start of the session and promised to work among conservative Whigs in the New York legislature to secure the Democrat's reelection to the Senate in 1851 if Dickinson, in turn, would exert his influence in the Senate to force Taylor to make Young customs collector. And as dangerous as Young seemed to Sewardites as subtreasurer, they dreaded what he might do to their wing of the party if he gained direct control of the customs house and its hundreds of jobs. Indeed, his indirect control of customs house employees through Maxwell was the main reason Sewardites wanted to get Young out of office. As the Senate term progressed, Young proved far readier than Fillmore to go down the line with the procompromise Dickinson on policy. He urged New York's Whig congressmen to frank copies of Webster's Seventh of March speech to the state to counteract the impact of Seward's Higher Law address. After Clay presented his omnibus bill, this former nemesis of conservative Clay Whigs in New York joined them in pressuring Fuller to abandon the president and back the compromise. He ordered his own and Maxwell's employees to help organize bipartisan procompromise rallies. Young, in short, pulled out all stops to win Dickinson's backing against Seward when the Senate voted on his appointment and Maxwell's.[176]

Collier, who was far more loyal to Fillmore than the self-serving Young, spoke to Dickinson before he left Binghamton for the Senate session and, as he informed Fillmore, urged him "to cultivate friendly relations with you and assured him it would be fully reciprocated by you." Dickinson knew that Seward and Weed had mauled Fillmore on patronage, Collier added. "You may I think talk *fully* and *freely* with him, and he can do a great deal—and I think feels disposed to act favorably in what concerns us both in relation to the action of the Senate upon the appointments in this State." Thus, even before Congress opened, the foundation for a Fillmore-Dickinson alliance against Seward was laid.[177]

At the end of this revealing letter, Collier alluded to the other reason Sewardites feared Dickinson. As the junior senator, Seward would also have to seek Dickinson's aid, Collier accurately predicted, but since the two senators disagreed so deeply on the slavery issue, "they will be naturally and almost necessarily thrown into a rival and hostile attitude." When Collier wrote of Fillmore's reciprocating Dickinson's kindness, he obviously envisioned a quid pro quo. If Fillmore cooperated with Dickinson on policy toward slavery, Dickinson would help him to reject appointments. Precisely the same expectation caused dissident Whigs in Michigan, Illinois, and Pennsylvania to adopt a procompromise position in the spring, but the action of Sewardite state legislators and Seward's March speech rejecting Taylor's approach caused Fillmore Whigs to cling to it.

Nonetheless, anti-Weed Whigs throughout New York unabashedly sought Dickinson's aid, thereby jumbling the lines that had previously separated Whig from Democrat. Dickinson's hostility to patronage-holding Sewardites seemed so certain, because of Seward's previous antislavery record, that panicked Whig postmasters across the state warned Seward that their conservative Whig enemies were working with Dickinson to defeat them. Poughkeepsie's Isaac Platt, who claimed neutrality in the factional rivalry between Weed and Fillmore, protested to Fillmore himself that Whig members of the House "were striving through an arrangement with *Dickinson* to bring about the rejection of all incumbents." Conservative Whigs meanwhile optimistically counted on the "Hunker Senators . . . to go for rejecting all the obnoxious." Nathan Hall and Solomon G. Haven, Fillmore's closest Buffalo allies, were especially confident of Dickinson's help on the Buffalo appointees. "It strikes me you will have no difficulty in the Senate & certainly none if Dickinson will go agt. Harrington & Allen," Hall predicted in January.[178]

Dickinson's bias and his decisive influence on New York appointments appeared so predictable that some of Fillmore's friends urged him to stay out of the Senate fray and let Dickinson do his dirty work for him. The phlegmatic Fillmore himself decidedly preferred such a passive stance so as "not to impair my influence with the administration." Other conservatives, however, insisted that Fillmore actively seek Democratic aid. "Do not hinder their action, but promote it by all means," wrote a Troy Whig seeking the rejection of Thomas Clowes. "It is our political salvation." "You had better see Dickinson & have a confidential talk with him," pressed Hall, who persistently pushed his lethargic friend to take decisive action. Well into the spring and summer, Hall prepared batches of letters for Fillmore to show to Dickinson, Cass, and other Democrats to secure the defeat of Harrington and Allen. In mid-April he listed six senators who would determine the fate of New York's nominees and urged Fillmore to lobby them all: three southern Whigs—Dawson, Bell, and Pearce—and three northern Democrats—Dickinson, Cass, and Douglas. That all of these men later supported the Compromise of 1850, as would Fillmore himself, speaks volumes.[179]

By mid-February, Weed and Seward, like their frantic lieutenants, were convinced that Fillmore "was uniting with ex-Gov. Young and Senator Dickinson to have several N.Y. appointments rejected." They complained to the cabinet that Young and Fillmore had betrayed the party by working with Dickinson, but they knew they had to find a way to counteract that alliance and outbid their rivals for Dickinson's help. Recognizing that Seward could never gain Dickinson's personal confidence the way Young, Collier, and even Fillmore might, they and their friends turned for help to Democrats within New York itself, men who might be more amenable to a bargain and who then might lobby Dickinson on the Sewardites' behalf. Their approach to Dickinson would be indirect, but it had the same result as Young and Fillmore's direct approach—a total collapse of party lines as Whigs cooperated with Democrats.[180]

In Buffalo, for example, Allen and Harrington cut a deal with the local Democratic organization. In the spring mayoral election, they refused to allow their employees to work for the Whig candidate and instead ordered them to cast Democratic tickets. As a result, the Democrats captured that normally Whig stronghold. In return for this help, Buffalo's Democrats then commended them to Dickinson for confirmation.[181]

Weed's approach to Dickinson was even more ingenious. Neither he nor Seward could abandon their rigid antislavery stance to curry Dickinson's favor; to support compromise would surrender their constituents to the Fillmorites. Instead, Weed tried to reach Dickinson through his Democratic counterpart in Albany, Edwin Crosswell, editor of the Albany *Argus*, the major Hunker newspaper in the state. Despite deep partisan differences, Weed and Crosswell had cooperated over the years in several business ventures. One of them was the Canal Bank of Albany, in which Crosswell had invested heavily and the management of which he helped control. In 1849, the Canal Bank shut its doors because of a dearth of funds and suspected fraud. Cries arose for a legislative investigation of the bank that might cost Crosswell a good deal of money and, even worse, result in a criminal indictment and a jail sentence. In return for blocking an investigation into Crosswell's involvement in the bank by the Whig state senate, Weed secured Crosswell's promise to get Dickinson to confirm Weed's friends. As one of Fillmore's outraged correspondents reported from Albany in early January, "The terms of the treaty is Weed is to keep the Whigs right in the Legislature & Crosswell to manage the United States Senate on the confirmation of the Presidential nominations, confirming Weed's friends and rejecting yours." "Crosswell has been very active with his Democratic friends to secure this result," another conservative complained to Webster in April. "He owes his being outside the penitentiary to Weed's exertions."[182]

The longer the Senate delayed action on New York appointments, the more heated became the bidding war between the state's rival Whig factions for Dickinson's help. With both sides wooing him, neither could rest assured that it had consummated a deal until the Senate actually voted. Formerly confident Fillmorites began to panic. "Is it possible that Dickinson and the Democratic Senators are deceiving you?" a worried Buffalo supporter asked Fillmore in March. "You ought to see Gov. Dickinson and Gov. Cass for they say here that they are both to go for Allen," Hall commanded in April. Dickinson had become the absolute broker of New York's patronage, and, as one Whig lamented, "Dickinson understands very well how to beef up a division of Whigs in this state." The problem, however, was not simply that Dickinson and other Democrats used their leverage over appointments to exacerbate Whig factionalism. The longer rival Whigs courted Democrats, the more blurred the lines separating Whigs from Democrats became, and, as elsewhere, this dangerous tendency eventually extended to the slavery issue.[183]

X

At the end of June, a month after the dramatic break between Clay and the Taylor administration, the fate of both patronage nominees and Clay's omnibus bill remained cloudy. The Senate's Democratic caucus still stubbornly refused to take action on appointments. Pro- and anticompromise forces in Congress remained deadlocked as senators fought over a seemingly endless series of amendments that drove an increasingly desperate Clay to the kind of "irritable, impatient, and occasionally overbearing" behavior that alienated even his allies. Partisan lines seemed as chaotic as they had been in December, "in consequence," Outlaw wrote his wife, "of the sectional issues which have arisen."[184]

If anything, developments during June caused friends and enemies of the omnibus to entrench more deeply in their hostile positions. To the dismay of Clay, Berrien and two southern Democrats, Pierre Soulé of Louisiana and Florida's Yulee, successfully tacked amendments onto the bill's territorial provisions enhancing the likelihood that slavery could legally exist in New Mexico and Utah and that they could enter the Union as slave states if they desired. Southerners also rejected Clay's revised Texas border and pressed northern compromisers to grant Texas more land. Meanwhile, lobbyists for Texas bondholders wined and dined congressmen in order to get a better deal for their clients than the omnibus entailed. As Clay realized, all of these changes made the omnibus even more hateful to its northern enemies.[185]

During June, the long-feared Nashville Convention also met. The movement for compromise in Congress sapped the secessionist drive that had once seemed unstoppable, and the gathering proved a fiasco. Some slave states refused to send any delegates at all, while previously chosen Whig delegates from others declined to attend. The unrepresentative rump at Nashville could do little more than endorse the southern Democratic formula of extending the Missouri Compromise line to the Pacific and call for a second meeting after Congress adjourned. This pathetic anticlimax reaffirmed most northern Whigs' conviction that no broad sectional compromise was necessary. At the same time, the convention's recommendation increased most southern Democrats' determination not to allow California's admission. Their adamant hostility to the omnibus, in turn, made them seem even more politically vulnerable to its southern Whig proponents, especially since the June amendments made it more favorable to the South.[186]

The most important developments during June, however, occurred neither in Washington nor in Nashville but on the arid plains of west Texas and in moun-

tainous Santa Fe. While congressmen in Washington debated and debated and
debated, the residents of Texas and New Mexico acted in ways that intensified
the sectional crisis. Furious that federal troops were stationed in Santa Fe and that
Taylor, Clay, Benton, and other Washington politicians refused to recognize the
legitimacy of Texas' grandiose claims to all the land between the Rio Grande and
the Louisiana Territory, the governor of Texas in the spring had asked his legislature for authority to send Texas militia to seize the disputed territory by force.
When it rebuffed him, he instead named Robert S. Neighbors as Texas' "Commissioner" and ordered him to organize new Texas counties in the disputed area.
Starting in El Paso and working his way north toward Santa Fe, Neighbors established several counties whose residents pledged fealty to Texas. When Neighbors reached Santa Fe in May, however, the United States army officers there
refused to allow him to proselytize for Texas. Instead, they persuaded the town's
residents to call a convention and apply for statehood, a goal Taylor had sought
since the previous year. The New Mexican convention in May wrote an antislavery constitution that was overwhelmingly ratified in June and sent on its way to
Washington.[187]

Weeks before it reached Washington, tensions in the Southwest had escalated
to the point of war. When Neighbors returned to Austin in May with the news
of what had transpired at Santa Fe, Texas Governor P. H. Bell immediately called
for a special session of the legislature to meet in August, a session everyone knew
would indeed dispatch Texas troops to occupy Santa Fe.[188] Armed conflict between
the United States army there and the Texas militia impended. Nor would the
anticipated confrontation be confined to those antagonists, for governors and mass
meetings across the Deep South promised Texas military support should confrontation ensue. Unlike South Carolina during its showdown with Jackson over
nullification, Texas would not be isolated. If the failure of the Nashville Convention seemed to scotch the threat of secession, the likelihood of a shooting civil
war between Southerners and the national government seemed to soar at exactly
the same time.

Since January, both proponents and opponents of the Taylor plan had regarded
his suggestion that Congress do nothing about the Texas-New Mexico boundary
dispute and allow the Supreme Court to settle it after New Mexico became a state
as its weakest feature. Yet they disliked it for vastly different reasons. Nonaction
struck proponents of a congressional compromise as a reckless, indeed unconscionable, abdication of responsibility. If nothing was done to resolve the dispute, they
predicted, an armed confrontation between Texans and New Mexicans, with the
United States army caught in the middle, was inevitable, and by June those predictions seemed borne out. When word reached Washington that army officers
in Santa Fe had sent Neighbors packing and that Bell had called a special session
of the Texas legislature, procompromise men became even more convinced that
Congress must enact the omnibus and give Texas a more generous border than
Clay had drawn.

Of much more immediate concern, however, was the past and future behavior
of the federal troops in Santa Fe, for the rebuff of Neighbors appeared to indicate
that Taylor had ordered them to resist Texans with force, an order that guaranteed
a bloodbath in the fall. Livid Southerners pushed a resolution through the Senate
demanding to know if Taylor had commanded those officers "to hold" Santa Fe

against Texas or to "prevent the exercise of her jurisdiction." Taylor replied honestly on June 17 that no such orders had ever been given and that the army had been instructed to observe strict neutrality in the dispute. Referring specifically to Neighbors' effort to organize Texas counties, he then added that he regarded the disputed area to have been "acquired by the United States" from Mexico and that it should "remain" the property of the United States until the boundary dispute was resolved "by some competent authority." Whatever his orders to the army in Santa Fe, in sum, Taylor had no intention of allowing Texas to seize half of New Mexico.[189]

Since Taylor had repeatedly identified the Supreme Court as the only authority competent to settle the boundary dispute, southern Whigs saw the message as an announcement that even the threat of civil war could not force the stubborn old soldier to retreat from his original position. After talking with Taylor in the White House on June 21, Outlaw glumly reported, "The old man . . . did not hesitate to advocate his own plan and condemn Mr. Clay's. . . . It is evident his mind has been poisoned against Mr. C." Such intransigence struck southern Whig compromisers like Outlaw as insane, and when rumors circulated that Taylor, over the protests of the embattled Crawford, was preparing new orders sending more troops to New Mexico and commanding them to resist Texans with armed force, it proved the last straw.[190]

In late June, southern Whigs held a caucus to pick a committee to see Taylor and "inform him, what will probably be the result of a defeat by his Admn. of the Compromise bill, of the disastrous effect of such a policy to our party in the South." One by one in early July the caucus' chosen emissaries, Charles Conrad of Louisiana, Humphrey Marshall of Kentucky, and Toombs, entreated the president to change his mind. Stephens, who purposely had not been selected, also spoke alone with Taylor. Exactly what transpired during these interviews may never be known. But Taylor clearly refused to change his New Mexico policy and may have threatened to send more troops to Santa Fe, a threat that, by some accounts, caused Stephens to tell Secretary of the Navy Preston that he himself would lead a movement in the House to impeach Taylor.[191]

By early July, Taylor and the vast majority of southern Whigs had reached a final parting. In reply to an editorial in the *National Intelligencer* calling on federal troops in Santa Fe to resist Texans, Stephens declared in its columns on July 4 that "the first Federal gun that shall be fired against the people of Texas, without the authority of law, will be the signal for the freemen from Delaware to the Rio Grande to rally to the rescue." Two days later, on July 6, Stephens, Toombs, Owen, Cabell, and Morton, the bolters of December, joined Democrats in the House to pass a resolution censuring Taylor for the Galphin affair.[192]

If Taylor's inflexible course infuriated and alarmed southern Whigs, it endeared him all the more to northern Whig opponents of compromise. From their perspective, what had always been wrong with Taylor's "nonaction" proposal for the Texas-New Mexico boundary was precisely the possibility that Texas might seize the disputed area and thereby "spread" slavery before New Mexico ever became a state. News that Neighbors had successfully established Texas counties around El Paso consternated them, for it seemed to indicate that federal troops would tamely allow Texas imperialism. "If that county of El Paso is lost to New Mexico and given up to Slavery, ever more, I'll blister all those who ought to have prevented it and did not," Greeley fumed to Seward. "This Congress must not adjourn without organizing New Mexico and shutting out Texas somehow, and I shall go hard for Clay's log-roll if something better is not put ahead of it."[193]

The possibility that developments in the west could cause northern Whigs to abandon Taylor and submit to the omnibus to *stop* slavery expansion unnerved Weed. The army's neutrality "hurt the administration," he protested to Meredith. Northern Whigs could not support Taylor's plan if the army stood meekly by and allowed Texas to steal the eastern half of New Mexico for slavery. "The danger is that those movements [to organize Texas counties] made with the approbation of the U.S. officers there, will compel the North to fall back on the Proviso" and thereby desert Taylor.[194]

Accordingly, when Weed learned that troops in Santa Fe had checked Neighbors, that the New Mexicans were finally applying for statehood with a free constitution, and that Taylor would stand firmly by his plan, he was overjoyed. "The New Mexico Constitutional movement 'sets us up.' It is glorious, for that was the only weak point in our 'case.' " Once it was clear that Taylor would never allow Texas to expand, indeed, Weed was certain of success. "The administration stands upon a rock; its opponents have built upon sand."[195]

The administration may not have stood upon a rock, but it certainly stood rock-like. And as long as Taylor adhered to his policy, there was no chance that the omnibus bill could pass Congress because northern Whigs clung to the president. Indeed, the possibility that Taylor could send New Mexico's constitution to Congress provided hope that they could regain the initiative from Clay, Webster, the other procompromise Whigs, and their Democratic allies. Even if they could not, a prolonged stalemate seemed assured.

Thus a dejected Webster wrote on July 4, the very day that Stephens' defiant manifesto appeared in the *Intelligencer*, that prospects for compromise were bleak. "Many, many members do not wish to vote against the President's plan. He seems to have more feeling on the subject than I can well account for, & I believe some members of his Administration take a good deal of pains to defeat the compromise." Webster's pessimism was well founded. As long as Taylor and his cabinet remained in office, no compromise could pass.[196]

That very night, word came from the White House that the president had fallen ill. Independence Day had been sultry in Washington, and after exposing himself to the sun for several hours during a ceremony at the Washington Monument, Taylor had gulped down huge quantities of fresh fruits and vegetables and iced milk. By nightfall he suffered acute stomach pains. That night, at least, the news of his distress seemed regrettable but of little consequence.[197]

Chapter 15

"The Long Agony Is Over"

"THE SUDDEN, & until yesterday, the unexpected death of the President shocks beyond anything I have witnessed," a shaken Senator Willie P. Mangum wrote his wife on July 10. The diarrhea and painful indigestion that afflicted Zachary Taylor on the night of July 4 had been diagnosed by his doctors as "cholera morbus," and they had prescribed doses of quinine and calomel, a compound of mercury and chloride. Taylor probably suffered instead from acute gastroenteritis, an infection of the stomach wall and intestines, and the primitive treatment did him more harm than good. The sixty-five-year-old president managed to conduct business for two days and then began to decline rapidly. By the afternoon of July 9, word spread around Washington that his end was near. At 10:35 that night the "Hero of Buena Vista" died.[1]

As soon as the doleful news spread, stunned Whigs began to speculate about "the effect of Gen. Taylor's death upon the Country" and upon their party. Millard Fillmore's unanticipated ascension to power suddenly created the possibility of change in men and measures. Whigs unhappy with Taylor's cabinet, his as yet unconfirmed appointees, and his territorial policy took heart at this prospect. Among administration supporters, it spawned dread. Thus anguished uncertainty mingled with the gloom that immediately shrouded Whig ranks.[2]

Whig divisions over current affairs alone sufficed to create anxious foreboding about Fillmore's course. But behind Whigs' apprehension lay the traumatic specter of John Tyler, whose accidental presidency had so devastated the party. Inevitably, therefore, almost the first thought that crossed the minds of shocked Whigs, including Fillmore's, was the necessity of preventing a recurrence of that previous nightmare. They sharply disagreed, however, about how best to avert it.

As a Northerner and an orthodox Whig regular, Millard Fillmore was no John Tyler, but ultimately his presidency had almost as deleterious consequences for the Whig party as did the proslavery Virginian's. Whipsawed by conflicting advice, he would shift the stance of the White House toward policy and personnel, and, as most historians have long agreed, that shift facilitated passage of the Compromise of 1850.[3] However beneficial to the nation, that achievement failed to reverse the downward course of the Whig party since 1848. Where Tyler had united Whigs against him, Fillmore's actions deepened Whig divisions and ignited a ferocious and prolonged struggle for the party's 1852 presidential nomination. Where Tyler's obstruction of Whig economic legislation contributed to Whig defeat in state and congressional elections, the divisions caused by Fillmore's actions helped produce the same result in 1850 and 1851. Where Tyler, like Taylor, had unsuccessfully attempted to start a new party, the bipartisan alignments over the Compromise and the electoral defeats many Whigs blamed on Fillmore created the possibility of a partisan reorganization in which other, new parties might supplant the Whigs. Unlike John Tyler, Millard Fillmore cherished the Whig party, but by joining Democrats to settle the controversy over slavery expansion that Tyler helped spawn, he, like Tyler, jeopardized its very existence.

I

Aside from the still fresh memories of Tyler, Whigs' pervasive alarm after Taylor died stemmed from two sources. First, by July 1850 they were so sharply divided over patronage and policy that no one could imagine a middle course by which Fillmore might reunite the party. For Whigs, politics had become a zero-sum game. If some benefited from Fillmore's presidency, their intraparty rivals had to lose. Either Fillmore would retain Taylor's appointees, including the stigmatized cabinet, and adhere to Taylor's plan for the Mexican Cession, or else he would choose new advisors, throw the spoils to the regulars whom Taylor had short-changed, and back the omnibus bill. About the only thing that potential winners and losers in this struggle could agree on was that Fillmore's decision to retain or replace the cabinet would determine his course. As one of Seward's panicked supporters wrote from New York, all would be well if Fillmore followed Taylor's plan, "but if a new shuffle is to be made, and new counsels invoked, I fear the consequences."[4]

Second, no one had a clue what Fillmore might do, and that uncertainty fueled Whigs' anxiety. Like most vice presidents in American history, he had been largely ignored while Taylor was alive, and he seemed a blank sheet on which rival Whigs projected their hopes and fears. Thus, even as preparations for Taylor's funeral proceeded, both friends and foes of the cabinet and of the congressional compromise bravely predicted that Fillmore would align with them while they simultaneously pressed their conflicting claims upon him. Fillmore's endemic caution, his phlegmatic temperament, and his unfailingly courteous response to advice from every quarter only heightened nervousness about his intentions. Contemptuously sneering to his wife that "Providence has at last led the man of hesitation and double opinions, to the crisis, where decision and singleness are indispensable," Seward reported to Weed on July 12, "All men of all parties have called on the P., and all come away without knowing or being able to conjecture anything." Robert C. Winthrop and Thomas Ewing, indeed, were convinced that Fillmore would adhere to Taylor's plan, while Daniel Webster, who saw Fillmore almost daily after July 10, predicted that he would back the omnibus.[5]

The new president was in fact genuinely unsure what to do. Almost two years later, Fillmore told a New York ally that on July 1, 1850, he had informed Taylor that if the Senate deadlocked on the omnibus bill he might cast his tie-breaking vote to pass it. Most historians have accordingly inferred that Fillmore's course was set from the moment he took office. Such a conclusion is logical if only because Seward, Fillmore's chief New York Whig rival, led Senate Whig opposition to the omnibus and because many of Fillmore's New York Whig allies had been pressing him for months to throw in with Webster and Clay behind the Compromise. Nonetheless, even if Fillmore's recollection was accurate, his willingness to back the omnibus on July 1 clearly was contingent on its content, which was then changing almost daily because of Senate amendments. More significantly, whatever Fillmore's resentment of Seward, he knew that all but two northern Whig senators and the vast majority of northern Whig representatives also rejected the omnibus. Most important, he knew that his closest supporters in western New York, like Nathan K. Hall, far preferred Taylor's plan to Clay's. At the time of Taylor's death, in short, Fillmore had not yet committed himself to the omnibus.[6]

The conflicting advice that deluged Fillmore from inside and outside Washington only increased his initial hesitation. Those letters reveal not only how stark the choices confronting Fillmore appeared to most Whigs, but also how closely Whigs identified policy options with specific individuals and therefore how critical they deemed Fillmore's decision about the cabinet. Whigs everywhere greeted the potential changes created by Taylor's death with a mixture of hope and fear, but understandably, emotions ran deepest among New York's warring Whigs because Fillmore was personally involved in their battles. He now had the opportunity not just to adopt a different policy for the Cession but also to reallocate New York's federal jobs. Consequently, both Sewardites and conservatives bombarded the harried president with unsolicited and conflicting advice.

Swallowing his pride, Seward spoke with Fillmore three times on July 10 and urged him to retain all of the cabinet except Crawford and to stick with Taylor's plan. Expecting the worst from his rival, Seward came away from those meetings convinced that Fillmore would back the omnibus and conduct his administration "in the spirit of war and proscription against me, and all with whom I act." Vowing never to crawl to Fillmore again, Seward frantically telegraphed Weed to come to Washington and use his persuasive charm on the president. Too proud to supplicate Fillmore, Weed refused to leave Albany and instead sent Comptroller Washington Hunt, the self-proclaimed neutral in New York's factional war. Hunt was instructed by Weed and Governor Hamilton Fish to tell Fillmore to retain in office all of Taylor's New York appointees, and to insist on statehood for California and New Mexico, while opposing the organization of any territorial governments.[7]

Weed published the gist of his instructions in an imperious editorial in the *Albany Evening Journal* on July 10. Fillmore had two examples to "guide and instruct him": the "inflexible firmness" of Taylor and "the perfidious course and ignominious fate" of John Tyler. If Fillmore "will resist the extension of Slavery and uphold the banner of Freedom," if he "adopts" the measures and "vindicates" the "Policy" of Taylor, Fillmore would have Weed's "hearty support." But "we shall stop short if there be, in the President, any wavers of Principle or any compromises of Freedom."[8]

Even some Sewardites considered this insulting manifesto "extremely dictatorial[,] uncourteous[,] and impolitic," while Fillmore's most conservative allies exploded in rage. Nonetheless, many of Fillmore's New York friends agreed with

Weed's message, if not its tone. Winning Seward's support was more important than propitiating Clay, one wrote from Buffalo. Therefore Fillmore must spurn compromise and adhere to Taylor's plan. "We must give up Clay & Webster both and take care of ourselves as a party," echoed another correspondent. The patrician Governor Hamilton Fish, who commanded Fillmore's respect, also warned Fillmore that a large majority of New York Whigs opposed Clay's compromise and that the state party could not "sustain itself upon its principles."[9]

Other conservatives from eastern New York sent Fillmore the opposite message. The cabinet must be changed, implored Daniel D. Barnard. "The Whigs in Congress must be conciliated. Mr. Clay and his mighty army of friends throughout the Republic must be conciliated." Above all, Barnard insisted, Webster must be appointed to the new cabinet in order "to form a national administration . . . to give you the full confidence and support of both the North and South." Weed and Seward must be shunned, for adoption of "their peculiar & ultra notions" would convert the Whig party, "a national party," into "an Abolition, a free soil, or sectional party." Fuller agreed: "Conciliate Mr. Clay and obtain his support. Act for the good of the whole country & not a section."[10]

Southern Whigs, who had reached the breaking point with Taylor by early July and who feared an eruption of fighting with Texas, also pressured Fillmore to abandon Taylor's cabinet and policies. "For God's sake, save the country," pleaded Kentucky's Leslie Combs. "Save us from civil war & bloodshed. . . . It can be prevented & it ought to be—by a general settlement of the Slavery question." Fillmore must back Clay's compromise to avert bloodletting over the Texas boundary dispute, concurred Louisiana's Whigs. Spurn Seward and form a new cabinet, commanded Alabama's Henry Hilliard.[11] Yet northern Whigs other than New Yorkers bluntly and repeatedly warned Fillmore that aligning with Clay and Webster or appeasing southern Whigs by endorsing the congressional compromise would devastate Whig fortunes from Maine to the Midwest. In New England, Maine's William Pitt Fessenden frantically warned Fillmore, Clay and Webster "have been most decidedly reprobated by a vast majority of Whigs." "The salvation of the Whig party in Ohio depends upon the successful repudiation of *Webster & Clay*," echoed Whigs from the Buckeye State. From neighboring Pennsylvania, the refrain was the same. Passage of the compromise bill "would greatly weaken the Whig party in Penna."[12]

Fully aware that he had to traverse a minefield, Fillmore thus appeared "exceedingly cautious" in charting a course during the first weeks after Taylor's death.[13] But he was not paralyzed by indecision. A loyal Whig since 1834, he hoped to reunite his dangerously divided party. Despite the babel of conflicting advice inflicted upon him and the widespread belief that no middle ground was available, he initially believed it possible to bring Whigs together behind his administration. Postponing decisions on policy, he focused first on matters of personnel, which he considered the key to restoring party harmony.

He began by assembling a new cabinet. On July 10 Taylor's department heads submitted their resignations as a formal courtesy, and by the next day Fillmore decided to accept them.[14] Choosing a new circle of advisors would declare his independence and promised to be widely popular among Whigs. Criticism of Taylor's cabinet had risen for over a year, even among supporters of his territorial policy, and the Galphin scandal pushed it to a fever pitch among congressional

Whigs. Nothing could so effectively signal Fillmore's desire to improve relations between the White House and Capitol Hill as replacing Taylor's official family.

The question, of course, was, with whom? Aware that many Whigs considered Taylor's estrangement from Clay and Webster a blunder, Fillmore consulted them and other procompromise Whigs like James Pearce of Maryland. But he also solicited advice from staunch proponents of Taylor's plan like Winthrop and Truman Smith. This broad survey revealed Fillmore's desire to balance the cabinet not only between Northerners and Southerners, as was customary, but also between Taylor Whigs and the so-called ultras and between friends and foes of Taylor's territorial policy. Both the search process and the final selections also reflected his intention to repair as far as possible Taylor's mistakes in constructing his own cabinet.[15]

Aside from failing to consult congressional Whigs before picking his team, Taylor had been faulted for failing to bring Crittenden into the cabinet, and, with Webster's enthusiastic concurrence, Fillmore immediately recruited Crittenden as his new attorney general. Midwestern Whigs had complained bitterly that Ohio's Ewing did not represent them, and Fillmore, again at Webster's urging, sought someone more to their liking. Friends of Indiana's Caleb B. Smith, whom many Midwesterners had preferred to Ewing, instantly lobbied for his appointment, but as a replacement for Crawford in the War Department, Fillmore first turned to Edward Bates of Missouri, whom Webster specifically recommended as "a *North Western* appointment" who is "well known, not only to the people of Missouri, but also to those of Illinois, Wisconsin, & Iowa & I believe highly respected by the Whigs of those States." Finally, North Carolina's loyal Whigs had stridently protested Taylor's selection of William Ballard Preston from Democratic Virginia over one of their own, and Fillmore sought to heal that wound by appointing William A. Graham as secretary of the navy.[16]

As usual when blueprints for new cabinets were outlined, however, most speculation centered on the so-called premier, the secretary of State. Webster's detailed list of recommendations to Fillmore left that slot blank because his own name had immediately surfaced as a favorite candidate. Certainly, he was the favorite of procompromise Whigs and the bête noire of anticompromise Whigs in the North. Hence, Fillmore's ultimate selection of Webster is usually cited as evidence that he intended from the start to back the Compromise.

Even this appointment, however, suggests Fillmore's initial ambivalence toward the omnibus. Fillmore leaned heavily on Webster for advice following Taylor's death, but he first inclined toward appointing Winthrop to the State Department. And Winthrop adamantly opposed the omnibus bill and any organization of territorial governments. Why pick an acknowledged opponent of the Compromise as his most influential cabinet minister if he had already decided to back it? On July 19, Fillmore offered the post to Winthrop, who flatly declined it and urged Webster's appointment instead on the egregiously mistaken grounds, as he wrote Edward Everett, that Webster favored "*the admission of New Mexico as a State*, in case the Compromise fails, as it will fail. This was Taylor's plan, & it will be Fillmore's plan." Contrary to Winthrop's pipe dream, in fact, Webster passionately urged the Senate to pass the omnibus two days before Winthrop's July 19 interview with Fillmore. Fillmore knew that Webster and Winthrop fundamentally disagreed about the omnibus, yet he preferred Winthrop.[17]

That preference suggests that Fillmore's litmus test for northern members of his cabinet was not whether they favored Taylor's plan or the omnibus, but whether they opposed imposition of the Wilmot Proviso on the Mexican Cession. Since January, opposition to the Proviso, rather than a preference for Taylor's plan or Clay's compromise, had been the issue that separated *all* of Fillmore's New York supporters from their Sewardite rivals. In Seward's Senate speech of July 2, moreover, he had not just finally endorsed Taylor's plan for California and New Mexico statehood. He had also explicitly, rather than implicitly, demanded that Congress bar slavery from any territorial governments it organized.[18]

Every Northerner Fillmore considered for his cabinet had taken an anti-Sewardite or anti-Proviso position, even though all of them but Webster fiercely opposed the omnibus bill. Webster repeatedly called the Proviso unnecessary and insulting, and Francis Granger, one of Fillmore's staunchest New York allies, urged Webster's appointment precisely because New Mexico's recently written state constitution proved Webster right in declaring that slavery extension could be stopped without the Proviso. Placing Webster in the cabinet, wrote Granger, would be a splendid putdown of New York's Sewardites, who were still carping at him "for not deeming the proviso *necessary.*"[19] Winthrop, too, had always opposed the Proviso. That's why Free Soilers scourged him. He had refused to support Joseph Root's February resolution demanding the creation of territorial governments with slavery prohibited, and he favored Taylor's plan because he thought it the best way to avert a divisive up-or-down vote on the Proviso.[20] Congressman Samuel F. Vinton of Ohio, who was briefly considered for a cabinet post, had voted to table Root's motion in February. Senator Tom Corwin, the Ohioan eventually appointed to the cabinet and, like Vinton, a firm proponent of Taylor's plan, had earlier publicly, and at some political cost, denounced the Proviso as unnecessary and divisive. The New Yorker Fillmore selected as postmaster general also agreed with him that it must be avoided to conciliate southern Whigs and to differentiate Fillmorites from Sewardites. Disregarding their stance on the Taylor plan versus the omnibus, Fillmore sought to restore party harmony by appointing Northerners who did not antagonize southern Whigs because of their aggressive antislavery record.

Fillmore's determination to reunite the party before he decided upon a territorial policy explains his initial preference for Winthrop over Webster. The prolonged speakership struggle in December revealed that, with a very few exceptions, Winthrop commanded the respect of all House Whigs, Northerners and Southerners, Taylorites and regulars, pro- and anticompromise men. His appointment would have been a long step toward reconciliation with the entire congressional wing of the party, which had become so alienated from Taylor's advisors. Webster, in contrast, was far more controversial. Northern antislavery Whigs considered him a Judas. In some circles, moreover, Webster had a reputation for, if not outright corruption, being in the pocket of wealthy men who purchased his talents, and it did not help matters that Webster balked at joining the cabinet until monied men in Boston guaranteed to raise a fund to supplement his official salary. As an anonymous correspondent in Washington pungently warned Fillmore on July 16, virtually every Whig paper in the North and all but a dozen northern Whigs in Congress distrusted Webster. "He is a prostitute in morals and something worse in politics. . . . Loose in money matters, tainted with fraud, fixed in profligacy, he is a living ulcer and infection."[21] When Winthrop refused to serve, therefore, Fillmore still hesitated to appoint Webster. Since his selection could build a bridge to party regulars slighted by Taylor and add an experienced statesman with a formidable intellect to the cabinet, however, Fillmore, on July 21, sent Webster's name to the Senate.[22]

By that date Fillmore had settled on four other men. Crittenden accepted the attorney generalship and Graham the Navy Department, although neither had yet reached Washington. They were to be balanced by two Northerners. Corwin's appointment as Treasury secretary was expected to mitigate whatever furor Webster's raised among northern Whigs since he adamantly opposed any concessions to the South in the Cession other than eschewing the Proviso. Corwin, like Webster, had the additional advantage, moreover, of representing a state with a Whig governor who could appoint his replacement in the Senate, and Governor Seabury Ford immediately named Ewing to Corwin's seat to demonstrate Ohio Whigs' continuing commitment to Taylor's policy. In contrast, Governor George Briggs of Massachusetts appointed Winthrop to Webster's seat, thereby shifting its probable vote in an anticompromise direction.[23]

By July 21 Fillmore had also appointed a new postmaster general, his Buffalo law partner and closest political confidant, Nathan K. Hall. Next to Webster, Hall was the most controversial member of Fillmore's team. His views on the territorial issue were unknown to the public, but since January he had ardently preferred Taylor's plan to Clay's, although, as he wrote Fillmore on July 9, if statehood for both New Mexico and California proved unachievable, he would reluctantly back the omnibus.[24] What made Hall a lightning rod was his character. Where Fillmore was mocked by even his supporters as passive, indecisive, and timid, Hall was renowned as a ruthless partisan who wanted all-out war against the Seward-Weed Whigs. In his own words, he had "savagely and angrily" told Washington Hunt in April 1850 that he could no longer sit on the fence, that neutrality was impossible in the struggle between Fillmorites and Weed men. Weed and other Seward allies bravely chortled that Fillmore had committed a blunder because other cabinet members would regard Hall as "a Spy" for the president. But they knew they now faced an enemy with an iron will in the position where he could hurt them the most, head of the most patronage-rich department of the national government. "N. K. Hall is President of the U.S.," moaned a Sewardite from Buffalo. "It will be he who after the Cabinet meeting will go to the private chamber of Mr. F. and revise the decisions."[25]

Fillmore's prolonged effort to fill the other two cabinet seats proved embarrassing. For secretary of war he sought Bates, and for the Home Department, Maryland's James Pearce, his closest friend in the Senate. Had both accepted, significantly, the cabinet would have lacked a representative from the Deep South. This omission was no oversight. Since it had been primarily Deep South Whigs, notably the Georgians Berrien, Toombs, Stephens, and Crawford, who had most infuriated their northern Whig colleagues, the absence of anyone from that region was yet another indication that Fillmore's top priority was to heal the party's wounds.

Nothing was heard from Bates until August 1, when he telegraphed his declination. Next, using Bates as an intermediary, Fillmore turned to another Missouri Whig, Henry Geyer, but on August 6, Geyer also refused to serve. This rebuff ended Fillmore's attempt to find a Missourian who might satisfy mid-western Whigs, and only then did he look to the Deep South. On that ground he rejected Truman Smith's recommendation of Tennessee's Meredith Gentry, a Taylor loyalist, but he also refused to consider a number of names suggested by Smith, Mangum, Berrien, and others: Luke Lea, a former Whig gubernatorial candidate in Mississippi; Judge William Sharkey of that state; Georgia's Toombs; and an Alabama judge. Fillmore clearly sought a Deep South Whig who would not offend Northerners, just as he wanted Northerners acceptable to the southern wing of the party. He wanted no part of Toombs, whom most northern Whig congressmen loathed, or of Sharkey, who had chaired the recent Nashville Convention, or anyone from Alabama, which sent Whig delegates to it. Any hint of proslavery extremism from a state's Whigs disqualified them.[26]

Finally, after six fruitless weeks, Fillmore named Congressman Charles Conrad of New Orleans, who resigned his House seat on August 17 to take the post. Conrad epitomized Fillmore's hope of reuniting the party. He came from the most moderate state in the Deep South, one that had refused to send any delegates to the Nashville conclave. He had been an early and energetic supporter of Taylor in Louisiana and thus a rival of Clay Whigs there, but he was also one of the three men sent by the caucus of House Whigs in early July to persuade Taylor to desist from his defiant stance on the Texas boundary dispute and to support Clay's compromise. Conrad, like Crittenden, in sum, could be a bridge both to the Taylor Whigs, who feared displacement, and to procompromise Whigs.

The secretaryship of the new Interior Department proved the most difficult slot of all to fill. Pearce, Fillmore's first choice, declined because Maryland's Democratic governor would appoint a Democrat to replace him in the Senate. Fillmore next considered Pearce's Maryland ally John Pendleton Kennedy, but because of ferocious opposition to Kennedy from Reverdy Johnson's wing of the party, he decided instead to give the post to Pennsylvania. In many ways his choice from that state, ex-Congressman Thomas McKennan, was inspired. Even in 1849 Pennsylvanians had told Fillmore that McKennan would have been a better cabinet selection than Meredith, and by the summer of 1850 they considered him the only Whig in the state who could patch up the debilitating quarrel between Johnston and Cooper. As a private citizen, moreover, McKennan had taken no public stand for or against the compromise and thus would offend neither side. Yet McKennan hesitated to take on the backbreaking work of the Interior Department because of poor health. He accepted the post on August 9 and then resigned from it on August 26 without ever coming to Washington.[27]

McKennan's almost instantaneous resignation set off another frantic scramble. Pearce again pressed Kennedy's name, but Kennedy preferred the Navy to the Interior Department, which would require persuading Graham to switch hats. Meanwhile Webster and Berrien convinced Fillmore to offer the job to Berrien's Georgia ally Charles Jenkins, but Jenkins refused the offer. Again, Kennedy's name emerged, but because Graham balked at shifting departments unless it was absolutely necessary, Fillmore made one last attempt to find someone else. Finally, in mid-September, two full months after Fillmore was sworn in, Alexander H. H. Stuart of Staunton, Virginia, took the post. At last, the embarrassing ordeal was over.[28]

II

Despite taking longer to assemble than Fillmore had hoped, his official family went far toward meeting his goal of reuniting the party. Most northern Whig congressmen applauded his choices, except for Webster, and Webster's inclusion made them even more appealing to Southerners.[29] His decisions on policy, however, neutralized this gain, for long before Fillmore filled his cabinet, he decided to throw his weight behind the omnibus bill. That decision undoubtedly influenced his ultimate choice of Webster and of a cabinet member from the Deep South. Grousing that Clay had dictated the cabinet's roster, Seward complained to his wife as early as July 24 that administration influence was converting both houses of Congress "to favor the Compromise" and that formerly firm opponents of Clay's bill were now "giving way" before administration pressure. Because of "the tergiversations of the Whig Administration," both Seward and procompromise Whigs now predicted that it would soon pass the Senate and then sail through the House.[30]

Pinpointing what brought Fillmore off the fence within two weeks of Taylor's death is impossible. The reflexive inclination to take a different stance than Seward—who, to the jubilation of his New York backers, came out for Taylor's plan on July 2—pressure from eastern New York conservatives, pleas from southern Whigs, and the influence of Clay and Webster all played a role. Most likely, however, the escalating crisis over the Texas–New Mexico boundary dispute most swayed Fillmore, just as it did Webster. Pressure for a fast resolution of that crisis was enormous, for the Texas legislature was due to meet in special session on August 12. Unless a settlement was found, it would likely send Texas troops against United States forces in Santa Fe, and a bloodbath could ensue. Because the omnibus bill contained a redrawn border between Texas and New Mexico, its rapid passage seemed to provide the quickest solution to the problem.[31]

Fillmore became aware of the urgency of the situation in Texas on July 12 when a letter Texas Governor Peter H. Bell had addressed to Taylor on June 14 finally arrived in Washington. Bell demanded to know if Taylor had ordered or condoned the action of his military commander in Santa Fe, Colonel John Munroe, in calling a convention to establish a new state government "within the rightful limits of the State of Texas." As early as July 13, Texas Congressman Volney Howard pressed Fillmore to respond to Bell's letter; on July 27 the Texas congressional delegation demanded answers during a meeting with Fillmore at the White House; and on August 1 Howard bluntly warned Fillmore that he must disavow and reprimand Munroe before the special legislative session in Texas met. Nor, threatened Howard, should Fillmore attempt to resist Texas' claim to Santa Fe, as Taylor had done. "The state ought not again to be trifled with."[32]

Fillmore thus knew that fast action on the Texas boundary question was imperative. Only two alternatives seemed available—the congressional omnibus bill or immediate statehood. Although official notice of ratification of New Mexico's proposed state constitution had not yet reached Washington by mid-July and could not before August 12, several copies of that document had arrived by July 7. It claimed the boundaries of the old Mexican Department of New Mexico, which would push back the western border of Texas almost to San Antonio in the center of the modern state. That outrageous claim, Congressman Howard fumed to Fillmore, consigned to New Mexico territory that was "within the undisputed limits of Texas!" Thus Fillmore never considered immediate statehood under New Mexico's constitution. Only rapid passage of the omnibus bill appeared to offer a timely escape from the crisis.[33]

To avert a clash between the United States troops at Santa Fe and the Texans, Webster desperately lobbied his recent Senate colleagues during the last week of July to pass the omnibus, and he was thought to speak for Fillmore. "It is quite well, universally understood here that the President desires the passing of the Compromise Bill and his influence is rapidly demoralizing us," Seward lamented to his wife on the morning of July 31. Yet Webster was equally pessimistic. He knew of at least seven northern Whig senators who now wanted the omnibus to pass, he informed a friend. Because they had previously committed themselves to Taylor's plan and refused to appear inconsistent, however, they were *ready to do anything but vote for it."* Both men, paradoxically, proved to be accurate prophets.[34]

III

During the last two weeks of July, the Senate made frantic and extraordinarily confusing efforts to amend the omnibus to break the two-month deadlock over it. One of the most significant of these, because of what its defeat implied, was a motion by Jefferson Davis explicitly to repeal, or declare null, the Mexican statutes abolishing slavery throughout the Mexican Cession. Davis' motion indicated that many men, despite the other changes in the bill's territorial provisions, still believed that those laws would prohibit slavery after the territories were organized. It was defeated 33 to 22. Every northern senator who answered the roll call voted against it, as did four southern Whigs—the two Delawareans, Clay, and North Carolina's George Badger. The stalwart Missouri Democrat Benton and Mississippi's Foote, Davis' archrival, also joined the northern phalanx. Exactly what slavery's status in the territories would be remained murky, but its illegality, as Clay insisted, remained a real possibility.[35]

The haggling, however, focused primarily on the disputed Texas-New Mexico boundary, which had not been changed since Clay reported the omnibus bill on May 8. Benton tried to reduce the area the select committee granted to Texas; Thomas Rusk of Texas demanded everything east of the Rio Grande. Both proposals were summarily rejected. On July 24, Maine Democrat James Bradbury sought to break this logjam by proposing that, rather than attempting to fix the boundary itself, Congress should create a commission composed of representatives from Texas and the United States government to draw the boundary. By that amendment, the rest of the omnibus could become law, including organization of the New Mexico Territory, but the border between Texas and New Mexico would not be determined until later.

Bradbury's motion ignited a flurry of unsuccessful attempts to amend his amendment. But a crucial proviso from the Georgia Whig William Dawson narrowly won adoption. It stipulated that the territorial government of New Mexico, created by the omnibus bill, would have no authority over any of the area east of the Rio Grande until Bradbury's commission reported its boundary. Although it appeared to prejudge the issue by favoring Texas's claims, both it and Bradbury's motion as amended by it passed, despite opposition from every northern Whig except Cooper.[36]

So stood the omnibus bill on July 31, when Fillmore's Maryland friend Pearce objected to Dawson's proviso as patently unfair to New Mexico's claims and moved to remove everything related to New Mexico from the omnibus bill in order to delete it. Pearce, who had steadfastly supported Clay's bill since May, promised to try to restore the New Mexico section, once Dawson's clause was stricken, with a fairer amendment of his own. Nonetheless, Clay was appalled. He recognized, better than the well-meaning Pearce, that removing any one of the building blocks from the omnibus would open Pandora's box. Delighted by this unexpected opportunity, opponents of the omnibus scented blood.[37]

Pearce's motion carried 33–22 and began the complete unraveling of the omnibus bill, for his attempt to restore the section unencumbered by Dawson's proviso failed. With the prospect of endangering a pro-Texas boundary settlement, the Florida Democrat David Yulee then moved to strike everything relating to Texas from the bill. Yulee's motion carried 29–28. Since the organization of the New Mexico Territory without the Wilmot Proviso and a potentially favorable settlement of the Texas boundary had been included in the omnibus to sugarcoat the admission of California for Southerners, their deletion caused Missouri's David Atchison to move successfully to strike California in the hope that all Southerners, regardless of party, might now oppose it. "The omnibus is overturned, and all the passengers spilled out but one," crowed Benton. Its overjoyed opponents danced jigs in the aisles.[38]

The issues and thus the perceived sectional advantage involved in the three roll calls on July 31 differed. Hence each evoked slightly different voting coalitions. Even most of the southern Whigs who favored compromise, for example, joined the majority of southern Democrats who opposed it to support California's deletion once the Texas and New Mexico provisions, whose retention procompromise Whigs supported, had been stripped from the bill. Nonetheless, aggregating the three votes dramatically reveals the extent of sectional division in both parties, as well as the continuing partisan polarization in each section's delegation, a pattern that would reappear in the House. Southern Democrats and especially northern Whigs strongly opposed the omnibus and voted to break it up. Southern Whigs and especially northern Democrats tried to defend it from destruction by opposing all three motions to delete.

Northern Whig opponents of the omnibus exulted over their good fortune, especially Seward, who had despaired of preventing its passage that very morning. One of Seward's allies, Congressman Orsamus B. Matteson of Utica, encountered Fillmore after the Senate votes and relayed the news of the afternoon session to him. According to the contemptuous Matteson, who had once urged Seward to "whip" Fillmore during the patronage struggles of 1849, the president looked "blank enough" and exclaimed, "What a pity!" Fillmore, Matteson gloated to Weed when recounting this episode, "must now 'face the music' and that is not his policy."[39]

Table 29

Percentage of Whig and Democratic Senate Votes Favoring and
Opposing the Retention of the Omnibus Bill Intact[a]

	Against the Omnibus	For the Omnibus
Northern Whigs	87%	8%
Northern Democrats	18%	75%
Southern Whigs	39%	58%
Southern Democrats	68.5%	26%

[a]This table is based on the roll-call votes listed in Hamilton, *Prologue to Conflict*, Appendix B, pp. 193–94. The percentages are calculated on the basis of the total votes the sectional wings of each party could cast when the three roll calls on July 31 are combined. For example, the thirteen northern Whigs had a total of thirty-nine votes, and thirty-four (87.2 percent) of them were cast to break up the omnibus. The difference between the sum of the two columns and 100 percent for each group is the share formed by abstentions. To use the example of northern Whigs again, the missing 5 percent represents abstentions by James Cooper, the lone pro-omnibus northern Whig, on the Pearce and Yulee motions, which seemed so favorable to the North that even Cooper dared not vote against them.

Yet Sewardites and other northern Whigs celebrated too soon. The very night of July 31, after several exhausted senators had gone to a favorite watering hole or home to bed, the Senate passed the remaining section of the overturned omnibus, the Utah Territory bill, by a vote of 32–18. Despite eleven negative votes from all the northern Whigs present on the floor, as well as two more from the Free Soilers, northern Whigs' determination never to allow organization of a territorial government without the Proviso had been foiled. The vote meant, as procompromise men realized and as Sewardites should have, that the Compromise might pass the Senate as individual measures more easily than combined in a single bill, just what Henry Clay had originally proposed and what Webster and Stephen Douglas had argued all along.[40]

IV

The wreck of the omnibus changed the tactics and leadership of the contending sides but not their goals. The session had dragged on for eight months and would soon surpass the record for the longest session of Congress yet held. Temperatures in muggy Washington hovered above 90°, and members' health began to fail. Utterly exhausted and heartbroken, the aged Clay, after petulantly blasting Pearce for destroying his handiwork, departed the capital for Newport, Rhode Island, to recuperate. His starring role in the great drama had ended, and the Democrat Douglas replaced him as manager of the now-separated compromise measures. In August the tiny, wan, and emaciated Alexander Stephens, who had never enjoyed robust health, returned to Georgia to recover. Seward, Senate leader of the Whig anticompromise forces, was also worn out, and his wife begged him to come home to the cooler climate of Auburn, New York, to rest. Duty and political necessity required him to remain in Washington, the New Yorker explained to his alarmed wife. He could not desert the Senate without voting for California and against the other bills. Fillmore wanted the two territorial bills and the Texas boundary proposition to pass both houses separately, he told Weed. "These bills cannot pass the House without disgracing the New York delegation, and perhaps ruining the hopes of the State."[41]

Seward understood the new tactical situation and the ramifications of defeat precisely. Now that the omnibus was shattered, northern Whigs in the Senate were determined to admit California and, if possible, to block all other legislation for the Cession since immediate statehood for New Mexico now seemed impossible. Hence they wanted to place the California bill first on the Senate agenda. Conversely, proponents of compromise hoped to place the New Mexico and Texas bills ahead of California to extort the same price for California's admission that the omnibus would have involved. Their success, as Seward shrewdly grasped, would spell political calamity for northern Whigs. "If the Compromise Bill should pass now and obtain the signature of the President," he wrote Weed on July 28, "what will be the issue on which we go to the Polls?" Seward intuitively knew, in short, that Whig voters could be mobilized only if they perceived conflict between their party and the Democrats. The Senate votes of July 31 displayed dramatic differences between northern Whigs and Democrats, but if Fillmore, the new Whig president, backed the compromise, he could negate that record, align Whigs with the Democratic position, and strip northern Whigs of their best issue. By opening the door to slavery expansion in violation of northern Whigs' pledges, that course, Seward fully realized, entailed electoral disaster for Whigs in New York and other northern states in the impending 1850 elections.[42]

Fillmore, however, was now adamant about passing not only the territorial and Texas bills but also the District of Columbia's slave trade and fugitive slave measures that had always been separate from the omnibus. After the breakup of the omnibus, he intensified his intervention in Congress's proceedings, thus violating the Whig party's founding principle. While word had gone out privately in late July that Fillmore wanted the omnibus passed, by early August the administration had still not taken a public stand. Volney Howard's note of August 1 demanding a response to Texas Governor Bell's letter offered the opportunity to do so, just as it made resolution of the Texas boundary dispute Fillmore's top priority. Fillmore therefore acted to alter the Senate's legislative agenda, for Douglas, supremely confident that all the bills could pass separately, was content to take up California before addressing the Texas boundary and New Mexico bills, just what Fillmore's Sewardite enemies wanted.[43]

The urgency of the Texas boundary dispute and the need to answer Bell's letter also provided Fillmore with a slim chance of finding a middle ground on which the party could reunite. Southern Whigs repeatedly warned Fillmore that he must prevent fighting around Santa Fe. At the same time, northern Whigs emphatically threatened that if he yielded to the "unwarrantable" claims of Texas to everything east of the Rio Grande, "the Whig party is ruined."[44] Thus Fillmore might satisfy Northerners by taking a tough public stand against the saber-rattling Texans and working with congressional Whigs for a Texas boundary to the east of the Rio Grande and Santa Fe. That meant junking Bradbury's commission plan, but it also provided a chance to give Texas more land than Clay's omnibus bill provided. If Texans accepted the new bill, Fillmore could avert civil war and win the plaudits of southern Whigs. It would require close coordination with procompromise Whig congressmen to find a fair boundary, but it just might work.

Beginning August 1, the day after the omnibus overturned, Webster and Fillmore, occasionally consulting with Hall and Corwin, the only other cabinet members yet in Washington, began to draft two messages. One was the administration's answer to Governor Bell, which would go out over Webster's signature. It, in turn, formed the pretext for a message from Fillmore to Congress emphasizing the gravity of the situation and the imperative necessity for a quick solution.[45]

Meanwhile, Fillmore urged his friend Pearce, who had been so instrumental in breaking up the omnibus, to draw up a new boundary between Texas and New Mexico, and Pearce worked closely on one with Douglas. On August 5, in the midst of debate on the California statehood bill, Pearce introduced a new bill for Texas—not New Mexico, to which the Bradbury and Dawson amendments had been attached. This set the western boundary of Texas at its modern location. New Mexico would keep Santa Fe and much, but not all, of the area east of the Rio Grande it claimed. At the same time, Texas was given much more land than the original omnibus granted by carving out the panhandle section of the state. Altogether, angry antislavery Whigs estimated, Texas got 70,000 square miles more than it deserved. Pearce's new bill also included new terms of compensation for Texas that, in effect, paid the state of Texas $5 million for releasing its claims and reserved an additional $5 million to pay people holding Texas bonds. After hearing the bill read on August 5, the Senate went back to debating on California.[46]

That Pearce introduced this bill in the midst of debate over California at the administration's behest, as Webster later explained, became clear the following day. On August 6 Fillmore sent Congress his special message on Texas, along with Governor Bell's letter and Webster's response to it. By coordinating the delivery of this message with the presentation of Pearce's bill, Fillmore intended to shift the Senate agenda from California to Texas, from a northern to a southern priority.[47]

The message that Fillmore and Webster concocted was a political masterstroke. Echoing the stern language of Taylor's June 17 message, Fillmore declared that the boundary dispute was not between residents of New Mexico and Texas but between the United States government and the state of Texas. By the terms of the treaty of 1848 the area claimed by Texas belonged to the United States, and Fillmore was sworn to protect it by his oath of office. If Texas militia invaded United States territory by marching on Santa Fe, they would "become at that moment trespassers, they are no longer under the protection of any lawful authority, and are to be regarded merely as intruders." In such an event, Fillmore would have no choice but to use his ample constitutional and statutory authority to call up the militia and the regular army to repel Texas' aggression.

At the same time, Fillmore continued, Congress had the power to make "an immediate decision or arrangement or settlement" of the "boundary between Texas and the Territory of New Mexico." "All considerations of justice, general expediency, and domestic tranquility" required Congress, not some other body, to fix the border. It was "the first question, or one of the first," growing out of the Mexican Cession, "now requiring decision." Neither the Supreme Court nor a boundary commission could act quickly enough. The United States should indemnify Texas for its concessions, but Congress must act immediately. Nor was that all. "The settlement of other questions connected with the same subject" before Congress adjourned "is greatly to be desired, but the adjustment of this appears to me in the highest degree important."[48]

Together, Fillmore and Webster accomplished the seemingly impossible. Just as northern Whigs demanded, they followed Taylor by defying the Texans, thereby disarming potential northern critics who looked for any signs of betrayal. "It seems that the policy of Mr. F. on the boundary question is one we cannot quarrel with about," admitted one of Seward's dismayed allies. Yet, simultaneously, Fillmore publicly urged the kind of broad settlement involving organization of territorial governments and fixing of the Texas boundary that Taylor had always opposed. Southern Whigs like Mangum purred their approval, and procompromise Democrats like Foote were delighted.[49]

Equally important, the message helped shift the Senate's agenda from California, the only measure on which antislavery Whigs wanted action, to the Texas boundary. On August 7, Pearce moved that his Texas bill take priority over California. The following day the Senate defeated Ewing's motion to pass the California bill first, and on August 9, to the outrage of Seward and other antislavery Whigs, the Texas bill passed easily, 30–20. "One-third of New Mexico was surrendered to Texas, with a purse of ten millions of dollars, to make peace," grumped Seward. "Seventy thousand square miles of free territory made slave, & a gratuity of $10,000,000," fumed John Otis, Maine's lone Whig congressman. "This done by northern Whig votes, who could have defeated it, if they had voted the other way."[50]

The Senate vote on Texas was, in fact, extraordinary. Once the omnibus was broken up, it must be reemphasized, only the Texas bill required concessions from both sections. The other bills clearly favored one section or the other. California statehood, for example, was universally viewed as a pronorthern measure, just as territorial governments for Utah and New Mexico without the Proviso represented concessions to the South. In contrast, northern antislavery men thought Pearce's bill gave Texas too much land, while proslavery Southerners thought it granted Texas far too little. Both Northerners and Southerners who supported it would assuredly be accused of sacrificing sectional interests and could expect potential retaliation from their constituents. Hence its enactment became the key to the passage of all the other compromise measures.

On July 31, with the exception of James Cooper, northern Whigs had united to smash the omnibus because it exacted concessions as the price of California's admission. On August 9, not just Cooper but also six New England Whigs joined six southern Whigs, eleven northern Democrats, and six southern Democrats, including both Texans, in the majority. Furthermore, both New Jersey Whigs were missing or purposely ducked the vote rather than record their opposition. All eight of these northern Whigs had voted against the Utah bill as well as the omnibus, but now the six from New England—Samuel Phelps of Vermont, Truman Smith of Connecticut, John Clarke and Albert Greene of Rhode Island, and both Winthrop and "Honest" John Davis of Massachusetts—helped pass the Texas bill. Had they voted the other way, as Otis noted, Pearce's measure would have lost 24–26. Altogether, indeed, northern Whigs who had fought any west-ward extension of Texas' border beyond the Nueces River for months *supported* the Texas bill, 7–4. Only Ewing, Baldwin of Connecticut, and William Upham of Vermont joined the bitter Seward in the minority, as did two southern Whigs— Underwood of Kentucky, whose motives invite speculation, and Morton of Flor-ida, who, as always, voted with the majority of southern Democrats against what they considered a betrayal of the South. For northern Whigs, it was a stunning reversal. Raising a question that could have been directed at all six New Englan-ders, Maine's aghast Otis asked, "How could John Davis vote for that bill?"[51]

The need to settle the boundary question before the Texas legislature met and thereby avert civil war obviously contributed to the conversion. Winthrop des-perately explained to friends that he and Davis had voted to keep the peace. "The Bill involved no principle—it was a mere question of acres & dollars. But it was the one thing needful for the public peace." Moreover, he pointed out, their vote on Texas did not mean that they now favored all the compromise measures. "If we can now admit California, we shall have nothing to regret. It is not a farthing matter about the Territories. They can get along under their own provisional governments until they are ready to come in as states. I shall stand upon old Zack's system & this Boundary Bill (if it passes the House) will remove any obstacle to its adoption."[52]

Winthrop's exculpatory gloss puts the votes of the New England Whigs in a different light. They may have believed that the Texas bill was necessary to avert civil war, but it also had to be passed before the Senate could take up California. And regardless of what the Senate did with the New Mexico bill, which Winthrop, Davis, Phelps, and every other northern Whig who voted on Texas except Cooper would later oppose, they counted on the huge northern Whig delegation in the House to prevent the organization of territorial governments. In that expectation, they were hardly alone. Illinois Democratic Congressman Thomas Harris reported on August 23 that northern Whigs in the House "now want simply to pass the California bill & the boundary bill to relieve the administration from all its trou-bles & let the territorial bills go." In short, the escalating crisis over the Texas boundary may have persuaded northern Whig proponents of Taylor's plan that opposition to a congressional boundary settlement was now unrealistic, but they were determined to salvage as much of Taylor's original policy as possible by stopping the organization of territorial governments in the House. As they had recognized throughout the long congressional session, the House, not the Senate, posed the crucial barrier to compromise, and for that reason, as soon as the Texas bill passed the Senate, Webster turned all of his lobbying efforts toward the lower chamber.[53]

Yet hope of resolving the boundary dispute while still blocking territorial bills in the House cannot explain why the only northern Whigs who abandoned their previous position came from New England, although the two New Jerseyans who abstained may have been responding to similar pressures.[54] Put simply, the sig-nificant fact was that Zachary Taylor was no longer president. Fillmore was, and Webster was now New England's representative in the cabinet. Webster came to the heart of the matter when he wrote confidently on the morning of August 9, "The R. I. Senators, at last, have waked up." What the Rhode Islanders and other New England Whigs woke up to was not just the impending bloodbath at Santa Fe, but the cold fact that Webster now seemed to command New England's patronage, and he insisted that all the compromise measures pass. For whatever reason, Taylor's cabinet had not sent formal nominations to the Senate for a huge number of interim federal appointees in New England. Unless those men were nominated and confirmed by the Senate before it adjourned, they would, by law, be forced to vacate their offices. And Webster had the power to withhold their names or substitute new ones. On August 11, moreover, Webster moved to take federal printing contracts away from the Boston *Atlas* and give them instead to the Boston *Courier*, a threat that undoubtedly contributed to the shift in Schouler's editorial policies. Nor is it coincidence that Fillmore waited until September 19, after all of the compromise bills had safely passed both houses of Congress, to send to the Senate the names of seventy-four customs collectors, naval officers, and other federal appointees in New England. With the patronage axe poised, New England Whigs who had formerly gone down the line with Taylor caved in.[55]

The six New Englanders' defection on August 9 meant that for one of the few times in the session thus far, majorities of northern Whigs and northern Democrats voted the same way on what, in tactical terms, had become the most important piece of the compromise package. Among Southerners, it is true, Whig and Democratic majorities opposed each other on Texas, but they had already voted together in lockstep for the Utah bill. Seward's nightmare was coming true. Partisan distinctions in both sections' Senate delegations were disintegrating, and the question of what issue Whigs could use against the Democrats in the impending 1850 elections was becoming all the more pressing.

Debate in the Senate remained abrasive, but passage of the Texas bill allowed easy enactment of the other compromise measures. On August 13, California statehood prevailed 34–18. Not a single northern vote was cast against it. John Bell and the two Delaware Whigs joined the majority, as did the Democrats Benton and Houston of Texas. Pearce and both North Carolina Whigs abstained rather than vote against this pronorthern measure. For the most part, however, sectional lines replaced party lines on California.

New Mexico passed on August 15, 27–10. Twenty-three senators, over a third of the membership, missed the vote. Some were out of town and others may have been paired, but many ducked the vote to allow passage of a measure the administration wanted but their constituents opposed. In addition to the discouraged Seward, who went home to Auburn on August 14, five northern Whigs—Baldwin and Smith of Connecticut, Dayton of New Jersey, Clarke of Rhode Island, and Ewing of Ohio—went unrecorded, as did Delaware's Spruance, who had previously voted with the Northerners. Only six of thirteen northern Whigs voted against the organization of New Mexico without the Proviso, and Cooper voted for it. That record distinguished them from northern Democrats, who supported the New Mexico bill 10–3, but the absence of so many northern Whigs precluded any thought of blaming the bill's passage on northern Democrats. Since every southern Whig and Democrat who cast a vote favored the bill, moreover, partisan distinctions evaporated in that section too.

Only after the individual bills that had once constituted the omnibus went to the House did the Senate take up the fugitive slave and district slave trade measures. The former passed 27–12 on August 23. Again, what stood out were the twenty-one abstainers, including five northern Whigs and eight of fifteen northern Democrats, who failed to record a vote against this proslavery legislation. Otherwise, with the exception of the northern Democrats Sturgeon and George Jones of Iowa, who supported the bill, voting went strictly along sectional lines. The public, who would take far more interest in this measure than their congressmen had, found little in the voting records to distinguish between the parties.

The pattern reversed on September 16, when the Senate finally passed the bill abolishing the slave market in the District of Columbia by a 33–19 vote, with 10 abstentions. Now Northerners could safely vote for legislation that their section clearly desired, while Southerners could indicate their support for compromise either by a positive vote or by abstention. Every northern senator who voted, including the two new members from California and the procompromise Cooper, supported the bill, as did six Southerners—Clay, who had finally returned from Newport, his Kentucky colleague Underwood, the two Delaware Whigs, and two defiant Democrats, Benton and Sam Houston. In addition, Pearce and four southern Democrats, at least one of whom was clearly out of town, did not vote. Absent Democrats may have been paired with Whigs because four northern Whigs— Miller, Phelps, Smith, and Upham—also failed to record a vote for the measure. As in most of the preceding roll calls, in sum, the bipartisan sectional solidarity of those who did vote offered little grounds for partisan exploitation at the impending elections.

V

The House delayed action regarding the Mexican Cession until it received all four Senate bills. The central question in the lower chamber was whether its large northern majority would allow anything but California's admission to become law. For months Southerners and procompromise northern Democrats, aided by rulings from Speaker Cobb and Democratic control of crucial committees, had blocked a separate vote on California in order to give the Senate time to pass the omnibus. Once the omnibus was shattered, they sought the same objective by putting the territorial and Texas bills on the House agenda before the California bill, which would certainly pass if it ever came to a vote. The continuing need to prevent the Texas legislature from launching an attack against Santa Fe, moreover, made passage of the Senate's Texas bill compromisers' top priority.[56]

Stopping the northern majority from admitting California through procedural manipulations was one thing. Passing the Texas and territorial bills was another, for that required winning support from hostile Northerners. The Free Soilers and many northern Whigs adamantly objected to the Utah and New Mexico bills because of the absence of the Proviso, but, as in the Senate, the real sticking point was Texas. Since many southern Democrats could be expected to oppose Pearce's bill as a rape of slave territory, northern votes were absolutely essential to get it through. A few northern Whigs were willing to pass it in order to spare the Fillmore administration an armed confrontation with Texas, but most abhorred it as a sellout of free soil. More important, numerous northern Democrats, unlike their counterparts in the Senate, initially vowed to defeat the Texas bill. Ideologically imbued with a hatred of the money power and anything that smacked of privilege, they detested the payoff to speculators in Texas bonds and the shamelessly blatant lobbying by agents of the Texas bondholders on the floor of the House itself.[57]

With some southern Democratic opposition assured and northern Democratic support doubtful, the backing of northern Whigs became essential, and Fillmore's administration strove to secure it. Personally directing that campaign, Webster met almost daily in strategy sessions with procompromise Whigs, the most important of whom were Congressmen William Duer, a Fillmorite from New York, and George Ashmun, Webster's chief lieutenant in the Massachusetts delegation. Truman Smith, who as national campaign chairman in 1848 had provided funds and documents to many of the targeted Whig congressmen, also frequented the House floor to press for settlement. Elbridge G. Spaulding, the Sewardite Whig from Buffalo, attested to the effectiveness of this onslaught. Denouncing Pearce's Texas bill as an outrageous concession to the South, he bitterly complained, "We are very much cut and divided up without concert of action and consequently not *effective* in anything we undertake. ... The Administration hits back upon the *progressive* Whigs in New York through its papers and *patronage* and I come in for my full share of it."[58]

While the administration pressured northern Whigs to support the Texas and territorial measures, the House's Democratic leadership hit upon an extraordinarily astute strategy to enhance the chances of their passage. Recognizing that numerous northern Whigs wanted the Texas boundary question settled but opposed the organization of territorial governments, while northern and southern Democrats wanted the territorial bills but opposed Pearce's Texas trade-off, Linn Boyd, chairman of the Committee on Territories, abetted by John McClernand, Douglas' Illinois ally, and Speaker Cobb, moved to combine the Texas and New Mexico bills into a single measure that was immediately dubbed the "little omnibus."[59] The label was appropriate, for if Boyd was successful, the new bill would create the same tensions inherent in its Senate namesake. Since Democrats controlled the House and insisted that it dispose of Boyd's motion before it considered California statehood or anything else, they could force the hand of those who recoiled from the trap Boyd had laid. In a single brilliant stroke the Kentuckian upset the calculations of northern Whigs like Winthrop and Davis, who expected the House to admit California and settle the Texas boundary while blocking territorial bills, thereby presumably leaving Mexico's antislavery statutes in the rest of the Cession intact.

Boyd's artful motion ignited nine days of emotional debate, dramatically close roll-call votes, and frantic maneuvering for advantage. On September 2, Boyd managed to make his motion the continuing order of the day, but two days later the House moved to bury it by sending the proposal to the Committee of the Whole on a razor-thin vote of 101–100. This tense roll call provided a vivid index of pro- and anticompromise sentiment. Northern Democrats opposed referral in order to save Boyd's little omnibus by a vote of 14–27, as did southern Whigs unanimously, 0–27. In contrast, southern Democrats split evenly, 28–27. Free Soilers unanimously favored referral to kill the compromise, while northern Whigs divided 49–19 in favor. One-fourth of the seventy-six northern Whigs in the House, in short, were prepared to support Boyd's bill and compromise. This group included ten New Yorkers, two Massachusetts men, and four Pennsylvanians, precisely the delegations on whom Fillmore and Webster had exerted the most pressure.[60]

Compromisers then snatched victory from the jaws of defeat by immediately passing a motion to reconsider referral, 104–103, with Speaker Cobb himself casting the tie-breaking vote, and on the second roll call referral itself was defeated by a single vote. Five men switched their votes to carry the motion to reconsider: two of Cobb's fellow Georgia Democrats, New York's lone Democratic representative, another Whig from that state, and an Ohio Whig. The arm-twisting by the administration, now working with the House's Democratic leadership, was being felt.

With Boyd's initiative revived but not yet adopted, crucial efforts were made to amend it. Inexplicably ignored by most previous historians, the most crucial was an amendment offered by a Whig, the Georgian Toombs.[61] Toombs' proposed amendment would have fundamentally altered the legal status of slavery in New Mexico, and it marked a final effort to upstage his Georgia rival Berrien. Throughout the session, Berrien had argued the Calhounite position that the Constitution established the right to own slaves in all federal territories and that no local or federal statutes were necessary to secure that right. Thus he had voted for both the Utah and New Mexico bills in the Senate, even though both in their final form had been stripped of his amendment barring territorial legislatures from establishing or prohibiting slavery and instead once again gave those bodies authority over "all rightful subjects of legislation." More important, Berrien had supported the territorial bills even though Jefferson Davis' move explicitly to repeal Mexico's antislavery statutes throughout the Cession had been defeated. Those votes, Toombs reckoned, left Berrien vulnerable to a proslavery flanking maneuver.

Earlier in the session, both Toombs and Stephens had attempted to expose Berrien's position as inadequately proslavery by demanding a federal slave code in New Mexico and Utah, a demand that had no chance whatsoever of passing. Now, in September, Toombs turned to an even more ingenious alternative. In its entirety his amendment to Boyd's proposed Texas-New Mexico bill read:

That no citizen of the United States shall be deprived of his life, liberty, or property in said Territory [New Mexico], except by the judgement of his peers and the laws of the land; and that the constitution of the United States, and such statutes thereof as may not be locally inapplicable, and the common law, as it existed in the British colonies of North America until the 4th day of July, 1776, shall be the exclusive laws of said Territory upon the subject of African slavery, until altered by the proper authority.[62]

The potential significance of this amendment cannot be exaggerated. The Senate bills for New Mexico and Utah already extended the Constitution and applicable United States statutes to them, as well as granting their territorial legislatures authority over "all rightful subjects of legislation." The key to Toombs' amendment was the application of common law as it stood prior to the Declaration of Independence, for, according to common law, slavery had been legal in all of the American colonies prior to that date. It was a brilliantly imaginative stroke. Where Jefferson Davis had failed to nullify Mexico's antislavery statutes in the Senate, Toombs moved explicitly to replace them with proslavery common law rulings that would have "exclusive" jurisdiction over slavery in the territory. Thus he would legalize slavery in New Mexico, which Northerners and the residents of New Mexico itself considered free soil. By insisting that only some "proper authority," rather than the territorial legislature, could alter that proslavery law, moreover, Toombs seemed to narrow the grant of authority to those legislatures in the Senate bill, at least as that grant pertained to slavery. In short, his amendment would not only legalize slavery; it would inhibit popular sovereignty by barring elected territorial legislators from acting against slavery.

Northerners in the House immediately recognized the proslavery consequences of Toombs' amendment, and their response was just as ingenious as his motion. One moved successfully to divide the proposed amendment at the semicolon after "land" and to vote on the two parts separately. The second or common law clause was summarily crushed by a vote of 134–64. Every northern representative except one Democrat voted to defeat it. Nine Southerners, seven Democrats and two Whigs, joined the majority, but every other Southerner who cast a vote supported the second clause. The muscle of the North in the House of Representatives had at last been flexed.

Equally important, by a voice vote, the House then adopted the first clause of Toombs' amendment, and it was part of the Texas-New Mexico statute the House passed on September 6, although similar wording was never added to the Utah bill. Without the second clause, Toombs' amendment had decisively *antislavery* implications. It stated flatly that any Southerner who dared settle in New Mexico could be deprived of his slave property by the "laws of the land." To many men, including Southerners like Jefferson Davis and Toombs who had tried unsuccessfully to repeal or explicitly replace them, those laws could be Mexico's abolition statutes. Just as important, the wording strongly implied that the territorial legislature of New Mexico could abolish or prohibit slavery by law. However vague the popular sovereignty provisions of the Compromise of 1850 may seem to some historians, very few of whom have even noted Section 19 of the Texas-New Mexico statute, most congressmen had to have believed that New Mexico's territorial legislature was empowered to bar slavery.[63]

Although the first part of Toombs' amendment was adopted, Boyd's proposal to combine New Mexico and Texas itself still faced tough sledding. It was passed on September 5, 107–99, defeated on the third reading the same day, 99–107, resurrected the following morning, and finally passed on September 6, 107–99. On all of these votes every southern Whig except Clingman, who had cast his lot with anticompromise southern Democrats, supported Boyd's measure. On each vote, northern Whigs opposed it by a two-to-one margin, but between twenty and twenty-six northern Whigs voted to keep it alive. On the final vote of passage, twenty-two northern Whigs supported the bill, forty-five opposed, and seven abstained. As in the Senate, northern Whigs who could have killed the bill with negative votes instead supplied the critical margin to pass it.[64]

Analysis of this final vote reveals where the administration's pressure took its greatest toll, for there is no doubt that northern Whigs who supported Boyd's measure betrayed their colleagues and their previous pledges never to allow territorial governments without the Proviso. As a furious Pennsylvania Whig wrote Seward on September 1, "If the territorial bills pass without the proviso, the Whig party is ruined—free soil will then be the cry from one end to the other."[65] New

York's thirty-two Whigs split thirteen to sixteen against the measure with three abstentions, including the harried Sewardite Spaulding. All five Whig congressmen from New York City and Brooklyn backed the measure, as did upstate Fillmorites like Duer, Robert Rose, and Hugh White. Perhaps the most surprising positive vote was that of Abraham Schermerhorn of Rochester, who had previously operated with Seward's faction. That Schermerhorn buckled under pressure is clear, for he was facing a strong challenge from the Fillmorite organization in Rochester to his renomination at precisely the time the House voted, and only after he voted with the compromisers did the Fillmore men allow his renomination.[66] Four Pennsylvania Whigs and an Ohioan, who were Clay men, and four New England supporters of Webster—Samuel Eliot and James Duncan of Massachusetts, James Wilson of New Hampshire, and George King of Rhode Island—supplied the remaining northern Whig support for the bill.

Because of these northern Whig defections and surprisingly heavy southern Democratic support for Boyd's bill, partisan lines were scrambled in both sections. Northern Whigs opposed the little omnibus 22–45, while northern Democrats backed it 32–13. Southern Whigs approved it by a whopping 26–1 margin, while Democrats from Dixie narrowly opposed it, 26–30.[67] In proportionate terms, as in the Senate, northern Democrats and southern Whigs provided the heaviest support for the compromise, but in each section enough Democrats and Whigs voted the same way to blur party lines.

Passage of the Texas-New Mexico bill (which easily cleared the Senate, 31–10, on September 9) facilitated quick action on the other compromise measures by the House.[68] On September 7, California statehood passed 150–56. Every northern representative who voted supported it, as did twenty-seven Southerners, sixteen of whom were Whigs. Thus a majority of southern Whigs openly voted for the admission of California, although no Whig from the Deep South did.[69] The Utah bill passed much more narrowly that same day, 97–85, with thirty-nine men failing to vote, at least twenty-six of whom had voted on the California bill only hours earlier. Only forty-one Northerners supported this prosouthern measure, ten of whom, including five Fillmorites from New York, were Whigs, while forty-seven northern Whigs voted against the bill. At the same time, however, the key to passage were the seventeen northern Whig abstainers, who, if they had cast negative votes, could have defeated it. Nine of those skulkers also hailed from New York, including the desperate Schermerhorn. Massachusetts and Pennsylvania supplied most of the rest, just as they did the other positive northern Whig votes for Utah. Again, the pressure from Fillmore and Webster had succeeded.

A week later the House took up the final two bills. Given its northern majority, it passed the Fugitive Slave Act by the surprisingly large margin of 109–76. Even the thirty-six abstainers probably could not have reversed this outcome had they all voted, for their numbers included Southerners who would have undoubtedly supported the legislation. Nonetheless, the pattern on this roll call again illustrates the heavy pressure brought to bear on northern Whigs to support, or passively allow passage of, the compromise measures. Only thirty-one Northerners supported what was clearly the most proslavery piece of the compromise package. Only two of those thirty-one were Whigs—Samuel Eliot, a Webster loyalist who had replaced Winthrop in Boston's seat, and John L. Taylor, a native of Virginia, who represented a district in southern Ohio—while forty-nine northern Whigs (97 percent of those who voted) opposed the bill. Hence outright northern backing for the Fugitive Slave Law came overwhelmingly from Democrats, not Whigs. Nonetheless, twenty northern Whigs, including eleven New Yorkers, three Pennsylvanians, and three Massachusetts men, did not vote, while New Hampshire's Wilson, Webster's puppet, resigned his seat three days prior to the vote. A few of these men were probably away from Washington—the session, after all, had dragged on to an unprecedented length—but the others, notably Fillmorites like Bokee, Duer, Rose, Brooks, White, and Underhill, simply ducked the vote. They would not or dared not oppose a measure the administration wanted passed, and after the vote, Thaddeus Stevens sarcastically sneered that a page be sent to tell these cowards that they could return to the House floor.[70]

Enactment of the law abolishing the District of Columbia's slave market by a 124–59 margin on September 17 was an anticlimax. Every Northerner who voted predictably supported the bill, and thus every negative vote came from the South. Only four Southerners—two Democrats and two Whigs, the more notable of whom was Tennessee's Gentry—dared to vote for this antislavery measure. Sectional solidarity was virtually complete; partisan differences within the two sections' delegations were nonexistent.

As well he might, Millard Fillmore exulted over the final passage of the compromise bills, which he quickly signed. "The long agony is over," he crowed to Hamilton Fish on September 9. "Though these several acts are not in all respects what I could have desired, yet I am rejoiced at their passage." He was especially pleased that "their success is not owing to any party or section, but portions from both parties & all parts of the Union, have united in their passage." Clay and Webster also exalted the bipartisan support for the compromise measures. Clay repeatedly contended that he had found Democrats like Cass more reliable than Whigs, and at the end of September, Webster congratulated Dickinson, the New York Democrat who had unwaveringly supported the Compromise. Waxing nostalgic about "our companionship in the Senate," Webster gushed, "The more I have known of you, the greater has been my esteem for your character & respect for your talents. But it is your noble, able, manly & patriotic conduct, in support of the great measures of this session, which has entirely won my heart, & secured my highest regard."[71]

The delight of Fillmore, Clay, and Webster that Democrats had joined Whigs in support of the Compromise was genuine and generous. But it had ominous implications for the Whig party. It suggested a propensity to embrace pro-Compromise Democrats at the expense of anti-Compromise Whigs. It betokened an acquiescence in, indeed a desire for, a cessation of partisan conflict that could—and would—ultimately undermine the appeal of the Whig party to the electorate. Interparty combat had always been the nutrient that nourished the Whig party. Programmatic conflict with the Democrats had allowed it to mobilize and retain voting support. Cessation of partisan conflict, therefore, would first enervate and then kill the party.

VI

Cooperation between Fillmore's administration and Democratic senators like Dickinson and Cass extended beyond common support for the compromise measures. The administration also sought help from Democratic senators to resolve intraparty patronage disputes. Though the administration clearly threatened some Whig congressmen directly about patronage decisions, it ultimately expected Democratic senators, not Whig cabinet members, to serve as the administration's hatchet men.

Of all the decisions that confronted Millard Fillmore upon becoming president, none had greater potential for irreparably splitting the Whig party and none seemed less susceptible to a compromise solution than what he did regarding subcabinet-level appointments. Legions of Whigs had been offended by Taylor's choices, and Fillmore, Hall, and Webster had been personally humiliated in their home states. Fillmore had full constitutional authority to sack jobholders who had already been confirmed by the Senate, but those still unconfirmed presented an even more tempting target. By mid-July, the Senate had not yet acted on hundreds of nominations Taylor had made months earlier. For a variety of reasons, ranging from sloth to incompetence to calculated pressure on nominees' congressional sponsors, moreover, the names of hundreds of additional interim appointees had not yet been submitted to that body. Fillmore could reverse Taylor's choices, appease the vengeful, and shift the balance of factional power within the party simply by withdrawing the former, withholding the latter, and replacing both groups with his own favorites.

Little wonder that Whigs of every variety anticipated a reign of terror as soon as Fillmore and his new cabinet turned their attention to patronage. As Thomas Ewing's son delicately phrased it, "The ascension of Mr. Fillmore will to a great extent give prominence to a class of men different from the materiel of the present [Taylor] administration." Winners under Taylor like Weed and Seward feared an all-out war of proscription against their friends. Former losers demanded a "clean sweep" of federal offices, instant decapitation of the remaining Democratic jobholders, and the replacement of Taylor's choices with different Whigs. Reverdy Johnson's enemies in Maryland, for example, clamored for a purge of the Baltimore customs house once Johnson left the cabinet. Similarly, with Clayton and Meredith, who had championed Governor Johnston's favorites for federal sinecures in Pennsylvania, forced into retirement, Johnston's Whig enemies from that state, including Senator Cooper, implored Fillmore to withdraw the nominations of Johnston's most obnoxious lackeys, particularly James Johnston, the governor's brother, to whom Clayton had given the lucrative consulship at Glasgow, and William D. Lewis, Philadelphia's customs collector, whose preference for nativists and newcomers at the expense of veteran Whigs when hiring subordinates was described as "Paradise for Natives, purgatory for Whigs, and hell for an Irish Catholick [sic]." From Michigan to Massachusetts and Maine rose the same refrain: the heads of Taylor's choices must roll and different, presumably better, Whigs must replace them.[72]

Understandably, New York's anti-Weed Whigs clamored most loudly for Fillmore to axe their rivals, and, just as understandably, Fillmore dearly wanted to make amends for his failure to secure positions for friends like John Collier or to stop Spaulding from naming Buffalo's customs collector and postmaster. Placing Hall in his cabinet began to balance the books, but his vindictive allies regarded that appointment as only a down payment. As elsewhere, state and district nominating conventions were impending in New York, and Weed's enemies saw federal patronage as the key to controlling the party organization. Hence they demanded further retribution. One, citing "the *vital importance* of securing this most favorable occasion to so fortify yourself in this great State" against the "corrupt and tyrannical regency" of Weed and Seward, urged Fillmore to purge as many Sewardites as possible. Others singled out U.S. Marshal Kellogg and individual postmasters for eradication. Of particular concern to Fillmore personally were Isaac Harrington, the postmaster, and Levi Allen, the customs collector, in Buffalo. Not only had their nominations mortified him, but his law partner, Solomon G. Haven, whom Fillmore was desperately trying to recruit to run against Spaulding for the Whig congressional nomination in 1850, refused to make that race unless Fillmore personally and instantly removed Harrington and Allen.[73]

Aside from avenging insults and gaining offices for themselves, New York's conservatives wanted Fillmore to exert forceful leadership to dispel his embarrassing, namby-pamby image of "timidity." "The withdrawal of one or two appointments in this State," they urged, "would strike terror in the whole corps of officials holding of the general Government and bring them to the support of the administration." Solomon G. Haven, for example, emphatically advised with regard to axing Harrington and Allen: "*Do not get rid of these men by the action or aid of the Senate. Of all things avoid that.*" Fillmore, in short, could not pass the buck. To gain credit as leader of the anti-Weed Whigs, he would have to do his own dirty work.[74]

Yet Fillmore refused to be a mere factional leader or tool for soreheads bent on revenge. He sincerely—and, some of his allies would say, naively—hoped to reunite, not further divide, the party in New York and in the nation. He realized that any spree of retaliation would so divide the party that it would lose the fall elections, and he would then be blamed for the defeats. Front men for Weed and Seward like Governor Hamilton Fish and Comptroller Washington Hunt warned him not to touch Taylor's appointees in New York, and even some of his own friends agreed. Alex Mann, editor of the pro-Fillmore Rochester *American*, advised "the utmost forbearance and conciliation" because "we shall need all our strength" in the fall. Similarly, in contrast to Solomon Haven's demand that Fillmore himself replace Allen and Harrington, another Buffalo Fillmorite counseled that "the Senate will gratify your desires & cut off both these men. But if not, will not more be perilled by seeming too bloody than gained by exercising this high prerogative in both cases?"[75]

Equally important, Fillmore believed that a middle course that could restore party harmony and still pressure Whig congressmen into supporting the Compromise was possible. To salve his pride and indicate his willingness to decapitate foes if necessary, he would make a very few symbolic removals of Taylor's appointees. To avoid alienating the majority of those men and their champions, however, he would do nothing about their nominations himself and instead would rely on Senate Democrats to reject them. To find jobs immediately for the regulars who had been shortchanged by Taylor, he would do two things. First, he would put the nominations of Whigs that had been held up by Taylor's cabinet, especially the favorites of pro-Compromise Whigs, on a fast track for Senate confirmation. Second, he would sack not the Whigs appointed by Taylor, but the Democrats whom Taylor had stupidly and stubbornly allowed to retain office, and he would replace them almost exclusively with regular Whigs who endorsed the administration's support for the Compromise. By firing Democrats, he could win popularity among Whigs of every variety. As Washington Hunt wrote him, Sewardites could hardly complain if their factional rivals got the bulk of new appointments so long as Fillmore allowed them to retain the jobs Taylor had allocated.[76]

During a two-week period beginning on July 31, Fillmore demonstrated the potential of this plausible strategy. In his first message to the Senate regarding patronage, he withdrew Taylor's appointee as customs collector for the Miami District of Ohio and nominated his own man, undoubtedly a friend of new Treasury Secretary Corwin, who meant to demonstrate that he, not Ewing, was now in charge of Ohio's jobs. More important, he recalled Levi Allen's nomination for customs collector in Buffalo and replaced him with his friend William Ketchum. That single action had almost as great an impact as Fillmore could have hoped. The previously hostile and supercilious Spaulding retreated, lest Fillmore also execute Harrington, whose backing Spaulding needed in his struggle with Haven for the congressional nomination. Hence, when the House voted on the compromise measures in September, Spaulding prudently abstained rather than join other Sewardite Whigs in opposition. Upon learning of Allen's decapitation, another panic-stricken Sewardite from Buffalo gasped, "Much has been said of the timid and noncommittal character of Mr. F. It will be found in one season that he will be neither timid nor noncommittal in the matter of pursuing his own fortunes."[77]

A week later, Fillmore, with Webster's concurrence, nominated Daniel D. Barnard, a prominent procompromise Albany conservative and an opponent of Weed, to the most prestigious foreign post still to be filled, the mission to Prussia, which Taylor, to the widespread indignation of Whigs, had allowed Democratic ex-Senator Edward Hannegan of Indiana to retain. The symbolism of rewarding Weed's enemies in eastern as well as western New York was clear to all. Fillmore, indeed, relied heavily on foreign appointments to make amends to Whigs who had been shunned by Taylor. Later in August, for example, he offered his friend Collier the consulship to Equador, and when the gratified Collier turned it down, Fillmore tendered the post to an Indianan named Cushing specifically to soothe a state that felt shortchanged by Taylor.[78]

Most of Fillmore's new nominations between the end of July and the adjournment of Congress on September 30 went to southern Whigs. Because most southern Whig congressmen backed the compromise, replacing Democrats in the South with their friends rewarded them. Patronage could also swing recalcitrant southern Whigs in a procompromise direction. One reason the formerly anticompromise Berrien voted for the procompromise position on most of the individual measures in August was probably his hope that Fillmore would appoint Charles Jenkins to his cabinet. Florida's Whig Congressman Edward Carrington Cabell, one of the six bolters from the Whig caucus, to give another example, repeatedly clashed with Taylor's cabinet over Florida's appointments, and in part because of Fillmore's new appointments for Florida, in early September, during the procedural votes to merge Texas and New Mexico into the little omnibus and on passage of that measure itself, Cabell voted down the line for the compromise.[79]

Fillmore also greased the skids for quick Senate approval of procompromise Whigs whose nominations had been held up by Taylor's cabinet or the Senate's Democratic majority. The only Taylor appointee in Massachusetts allied with

Daniel Webster, aside from his son Fletcher, was Franklin Haven, the designated subtreasurer in Boston. To punish Webster for his procompromise course, Taylor's cabinet refused to submit Haven's name to the Senate, and Haven had become frantic by the time of Taylor's death. On August 14, after the Senate passed the Texas and California bills, Fillmore sent in Haven's name. The following day, after passage of the New Mexico bill, Haven was confirmed, on the motion of Dickinson, chairman of the finance committee and Webster's procompromise ally, whereas hundreds of other nominees whose names had been submitted the previous winter still awaited action. As soon as Haven was approved, moreover, Dickinson moved and won confirmation of John Young, the subtreasurer in New York City, Fillmore's ally against Weed and Seward and Dickinson's neighbor from Binghamton, New York. The quid pro quo between the Fillmore administration and Dickinson—and the lesson to Whigs in the House who still had to vote on the compromise measures—could not have been clearer.[80]

Finally, the administration possessed one other bargaining chip with which to reward pro-Compromise Whigs. Patronage decisions involving personnel—at least for the jobs with the best salaries and most political clout—required Senate approval. Federal printing contracts that could provide vital financial sustenance to Whig newspapers did not, and pro-Compromise editorials from a Whig congressman's home paper could make a procompromise vote seem much safer. By mid-August, Webster was pressuring his cabinet colleagues to switch contracts for printing departmental notices from William Schouler's anticompromise Boston *Atlas* to procompromise Whig papers in Boston—the *Courier*, the *Bee*, and the *Advertiser*. He was hardly alone in spotting the opportunity. Almost as soon as Fillmore took office, his conservative allies in New York sought federal printing business for the Albany *State Register*, which had been denied it under Taylor. In September the federal officers in Detroit switched their printing from the anti-Compromise Detroit *Tribune* to the pro-Compromise Detroit *Advertiser*, and a similar scenario among Whig papers unfolded in Pittsburgh, where the procompromise *Daily Commercial Journal* replaced the anti-Compromise *Gazette* as the recipient of federal largesse.[81]

On the whole, however, while Congress remained in session, Fillmore bent over backward not to punish anti-Compromise Whigs himself in order to preserve party harmony. Most printing contracts were switched from anti- to pro-Compromise Whig newspapers only after Congress adjourned, and the salient fact about the situation in New York is that conservatives had to beg the administration to give printing business to the *State Register* rather than getting it automatically. Between July 31 and September 30, the final day of the session, when Fillmore made another dramatic move in New York, no other nominations were withdrawn to coerce Whig votes in the House and Senate.

In northern states other than New York, Fillmore's actions were especially erratic and counterproductive. Although he eschewed removals for political reasons, his administration was ruthless in dispatching Whigs whom it suspected of fraud or malfeasance in office. For example, Alex Irvin, the U.S. marshal in western Pennsylvania and a crony of the anti-Compromise Governor Johnston, was fired because of illegal activities. Rather than allowing Senator James Cooper's pro-Compromise allies to name the replacement or even soliciting the opinion of western Pennsylvania Whigs, however, Fillmore, incredibly, replaced Irvin with his own brother William, who spelled his last name Irwin. Even Pennsylvania Whigs who shared Johnston's dislike of the Compromise criticized the move as a transparent attempt to cover up a scandal, a blunder that would doom the prospects of Whig congressional candidates throughout western Pennsylvania by handing Democrats the corruption issue on a golden platter. Richard Wilson, Taylor's nominee for postmaster in Chicago, was also removed for peculation, even though editor Lisle Smith, a friend of both Webster and Clay, protested that the move would devastate friends of the administration in northern Illinois. In contrast, when Oliver Hyde, the Sewardite nominee for customs collector in Detroit and a known leader of the antislavery, anti-Compromise Whigs in Michigan, also had charges of impropriety lodged against him, Corwin refused to sack him to make way for a pro-Compromise Whig. "I thought it best to let him *take his trial in the Senate*," Corwin explained to Fillmore. "I took it for granted you did not wish to withdraw a nomination of yr. predecessor unless *cogent* reasons impelled such a step. I feel quite sure the Senate will reject him."[82]

Here was the key to the administration's calculated leniency toward intraparty foes and anti-Compromise Whigs. The best way to preserve party harmony, Fillmore believed, was *not* to fire Taylor's appointees but instead to allow the Democratically controlled Senate to dismiss all those Whigs whom he and his allies found objectionable. As early as July 15, Fillmore wrote to a friend that he had determined to wait for the Senate to reject, rather than personally to remove, Taylor's nominees for New York and elsewhere.[83] If he had indeed made up his mind by then, it is signficant, for by July 15, Fillmore had not yet picked a cabinet or decided to support the congressional compromise. In other words, Fillmore's decision to duck the responsibility of leadership and rely on Senate Democrats may have been one of the factors that brought him to support the compromise since the Democrats he depended upon, like Dickinson and Cass, were its ardent proponents.

Fillmore's reliance on Senate Democrats to punish his intraparty enemies produced some curious circumstances. The ruthless Hall fired postmasters at will on the suspicion of malfeasance, but he could not touch a hair on the heads of Sewardite postmasters he hated—Isaac Harrington in Buffalo, William Jackson in Syracuse, Thomas Clowes in Troy, or Lewis Benedict in Albany. Instead, just as when Taylor was alive and Fillmore had no influence on appointments, all Hall could do was to cajole Fillmore to make sure that Dickinson stayed in line. Thus on September 2, he frantically telegraphed Fillmore from Buffalo: "I think that you had better see Senator Dickinson personally in reference to Benedict & Harrington. They must not be confirmed if it is possible to prevent it." The situation was not just bizarre; it was surreal. The postmaster general of the United States was telling the president of the United States to crawl to a senator from the opposing party to stop the confirmation of postmasters they had every right to replace themselves.[84]

Similarly, Webster loathed most of Taylor's appointees in Massachusetts, especially Charles Hudson, the naval officer at Boston; Philip Greely, Jr., the customs collector there; and George Lunt, the legal lightweight who had been appointed U.S. attorney instead of his son Fletcher. His friends expected the administration to withdraw those nominations, and Webster repeatedly warned Fillmore that they were antislavery Whigs who sided with Weed and Seward. But he was powerless to axe them. Greely's "nomination will not be recalled, and how it will fare in the Senate, I know not," he sighed to a friend on September 15.[85]

As Webster indicated, the administration had no guarantees that procompromise Democratic senators would or could marshal Senate majorities to reject the men pro-Compromise Whigs found most obnoxious. As it turned out, in fact, the great majority of Seward's allies in New York and of anti-Compromise Whigs in Pennsylvania, Massachusetts, and other northern states were confirmed rather than rejected when the Senate finally voted on them. Those eventually approved included Hudson, Greely, and Lunt from Massachusetts; Oliver Hyde and Charles Babcock from Michigan; Harrington, Clark, Kellogg, Clowes, and Jackson from New York; and Governor Johnston's subalterns in Pennsylvania, including Philadelphia Customs Collector William D. Lewis, whom Senator James Cooper had devoted the entire congressional session to defeating by voting in lapdog fashion with Democrat Daniel Sturgeon.[86] By relying on Senate Democrats, rather than acting directly by withholding or withdrawing nominations, in sum, the administration muffed an opportunity to intimidate anti-Compromise Whigs and bolster its supporters.

In addition, Senate Democrats' postponement of action on the most controversial appointments until the last two weeks of September deprived the administration's supporters in crucial states like Massachusetts and New York of a vital resource in the intraparty battle for control of nominating conventions. Without removals or rejections, pro-Compromise Whigs could neither get control of federal offices themselves in time to influence the selection of delegates nor intimidate the Taylorite incumbents into acquiescing to their wishes regarding nominees and platforms. Worse still from the administration's perspective, some of the nominees held up by the Democrats were its own supporters who refused to participate in the struggle to pack conventions for fear that their Whig enemies would then engineer their rejection by the Senate.

One reason Webster rued his inability to get Hudson and Greely removed before the Senate acted on them in late September, for example, was that the Massachusetts Whig state convention was scheduled for October 1. Convinced, with reason, that at least half of the state committee opposed him and the Compromise, he feared that without action from Washington to chasten the state's antislavery Whigs, the influence of Schouler's *Atlas* and the federal officeholders would be used to secure a platform that endorsed "the insane conduct of Northern men in Congress" and drove "the Whig party of Massachusetts to the very brink of utter separation from all other Whigs." When the Senate confirmed rather than rejected Greely on September 24, therefore, all the desperate Webster could do was to beg his friend Edward Everett to go to the convention in Worcester and "make a speech & *nationalize* the Whig party."[87]

Similarly, district conventions to nominate congressional candidates were scheduled to meet in New York during the middle two weeks of September, and the state convention was slated for Syracuse at the end of the month. Both Fillmore's conservative Whig allies and the Seward-Weed Whigs who competed to control those gatherings knew that patronage holders could order their employees to attend and promise future employment to sway other delegates. The intimidation produced by Fillmore's axing of Levi Allen and appointment of Daniel

Barnard was enough to give the conservatives leverage in some districts. As even Solomon Haven admitted, the penurious Isaac Harrington, fearful that he too would be sacked, remained neutral in the race between Haven and Spaulding for the Buffalo nomination, while Ketchum, Fillmore's replacement for Levi Allen, used promises of customs house jobs to fill the local convention with Haven's friends. Deprived of the necessary support of federal officeholders, Spaulding announced his withdrawal from the race even before the convention met. Fillmorites had enough clout in the Rochester district to force Congressman Abraham Schermerhorn to cast pro-Compromise votes as the price of renomination, and they gave Weed's friends concern in other districts as well.[88]

Fillmore's conservative allies, however, remained at a distinct disadvantage in the struggle to control the state convention. For one thing, Hugh Maxwell, the customs collector in New York City, who had enormous potential influence over delegates because of his ability to hire subordinates in that metropolis, Brooklyn, and the Hudson Valley as far north as Albany, refused to use that influence until he won Senate confirmation, for he feared that Seward would secure his rejection if he did. Lacking the personal and political ties to Dickinson of his assertive ally, Young, to obtain fast action, Maxwell was not confirmed until September 26, the very day the state convention opened.[89]

With Maxwell neutralized during most of September and Young himself in direct control of only a few subordinates, conservative Whigs had few weapons with which to counteract Sewardite control of postmasterships, U.S. attorneyships, and the marshals' offices, to say nothing of state jobs. Thus, the closer the convention approached, the louder conservatives screamed for Fillmore to sack Lewis Benedict in order to send a signal to the delegates. "Nobody will take pains to be on the side of the Administration, if those opposed to it are as safe and as well off as its friends," wrote the frantic Jerome Fuller. Fillmore's attempt to preserve party harmony by relying on the Senate was only encouraging "*Albany Slanderers*" like Weed and Benedict to "*boast* that the *administration dare not re-move*" Benedict, "a Seward abolitionist Whig, and as such not only opposed to you personally but to your administration."[90]

Despite this rising crescendo, Fillmore steadfastly refused to decapitate Benedict or anyone else prior to the meeting of the Whig state convention. Genuinely committed to preserving party harmony and reassured by Washington Hunt, Fish, and others that Weed too wanted unity, Fillmore would do nothing to threaten it. Only when the Whig convention openly ruptured and when the Sewardite majority adopted a platform that intentionally insulted him did Fillmore retaliate. On September 30, two days after the state convention adjourned and the final day of the congressional session, Fillmore withdrew the nomination of the still unconfirmed Benedict and replaced him with James Kidd, the wealthy Albany conservative who had helped fund the Albany *State Register*. Kidd, in turn, was immediately confirmed.[91]

The dramatic last-minute decapitation of Lewis Benedict reflected Fillmore's recognition that his alliance with Democrats had limits on patronage matters, that his conciliatory efforts to restore intraparty harmony had failed, and that he had to harm opponents in order to help his friends. Equally important, Benedict's removal was not intended to secure congressional votes for the compromise measures, as earlier patronage actions had been. All of those bills had already been signed into law. Rather, as with subsequent firings, it was explicitly meant to punish intraparty enemies who would not cease their opposition to the Compromise even after it became the law of the land.

That New York's Whig state convention ruptured over the platform, not the ticket, and that Benedict became the target of Fillmore's wrath because he and his Sewardite allies refused to acquiesce in, let alone openly endorse, the administration's position on the Compromise signaled that factional warfare had entered a new and more deadly phase. Now conflict did not simply revolve around offices or pelf. Rather, supporters and opponents of the administration fought for the power to determine where the party stood on policy and whether it accepted the Compromise of 1850 as a final settlement of sectional strife over slavery. Benedict's sacking, like the concomitant switching of printing contracts in Detroit, Pittsburgh, and other cities, signaled that this was a battle the administration was determined not to lose.

VII

Millard Fillmore's accession to the presidency measurably contributed to the passage of the Compromise of 1850, but it failed to reunite the Whig party, as he had so dearly hoped in mid-July. In Congress and in many states Whigs remained deeply divided over the wisdom, fairness, and necessity of the Compromise, and those disagreements added a volatile policy dimension to long-standing intraparty factional rivalries. Fillmore knew perfectly well why most northern Whig congressmen felt compelled to vote against parts of the compromise package. To preserve as much party unity as possible, he forced his cabinet to eschew a jihad against them on patronage matters. As a payback for that restraint, they expected foes of the Compromise to exhibit similar solicitude for party unity once they had failed to prevent its enactment and to close ranks behind the administration that had treated them so benignly. From the administration's viewpoint, acceptance of the Compromise as a settlement of the four-year-old quarrel over the territories was necessary for the good of the nation and the survival of the Whig party's southern wing.

Across the North, however, most Whigs viewed endorsement of the Compromise as a betrayal of principles and a prescription for electoral disaster. It flouted commitments they had made to northern voters, and, they believed, it nullified their significant advantage over northern Democrats by aping the Democrats' pro-Compromise posture. To mobilize Whig voters and thus maintain the party's competitiveness in the North, such Whigs believed, they must denounce the Compromise as a Democratic sellout to the South even if that required repudiating the Whig administration, which rejoiced in its alliance with Democrats. Continued northern Whig resistance to the Compromise even after it became the law of the land, in turn, was something the Fillmore administration would not tolerate because it alienated southern Whigs, threatened intersectional comity within the Whig party, and, most important, endangered the Union.

Both sides, in sum, considered open warfare for control of the party necessary to save it from extinction. Lewis Benedict was only the first of many casualties in that war, a conflict that raged until the national convention in the summer of

1852, and one that grew so bitter that increasing numbers of Whigs prepared to abandon the Whig party altogether rather than accept their rivals' victory. To counteract such divisive pressures from within, Whigs had always relied on external conflict with Democrats. For the first nine months of 1850, however, Whigs of every variety had openly joined with like-minded Democrats on both patronage and policy matters. Whether Whigs could still mobilize enough voters to carry elections with conflict between the parties apparently attenuated would be determined only by the elections themselves. When Congress finally adjourned on September 30, 1850, weary congressmen could, at long last, go home. For the Whig party, however, the "long agony" was far from over.

Chapter 16

"God Save Us from Whig Vice Presidents"

"IF THE COMPROMISE BILL SHOULD pass now and obtain the [President's] signature," Seward worried in late July 1850, "what will be the issue on which we go to the polls?"[1] The shrewd New Yorker pinpointed northern Whigs' problem throughout Millard Fillmore's presidency. They could mobilize their voters only by differentiating themselves from Democrats. Fillmore's promotion of a measure backed overwhelmingly by northern Democrats could cripple them at the polls. When Fillmore signed the Compromise measures in September and the New York Democratic state platform endorsed them, therefore, Seward's New York allies instructed Weed that the Whigs' state platform must demand revision or repeal of every prosouthern concession Congress had made. Fillmore's pro-Compromise stance, like John Tyler's vetoes nine years earlier, must be publicly repudiated. "We must make war on this administration to save the Whig party from contempt and scorn."[2]

Five days after New York's Whigs met, Daniel Webster penned the administration's response to this declaration of war. "If any considerable body of the Whigs in the North shall act in the spirit of the recent convention in New York," he told a friend, "a new arrangement of Parties is unavoidable." He understood why many northern Whigs opposed the compromise measures in Congress. Now that those bills had become laws, however, loyal Whigs should "resist all attempts at further agitation and disturbance, and make no efforts for another change." Any northern Whigs who "continue to talk about the Wilmot Proviso, and to resist, or seek to repeal the Fugitive Slave Bill, or use any other means to disturb the quiet of the Country" deserved excommunication. "The present administration will not recognize one set of Whig Principles for the North, and another for the South," Webster insisted. "That can be regarded as no Whig Party, in New York, or Mass., which espouses doctrines, and utters sentiments, hostile to the just, and Constitutional rights of the South, and therefore such as Southern Whigs cannot agree to."[3]

Defining precisely the horns of the dilemma that confronted the Whig party, these salvos opened a battle between Fillmore's administration and its northern

Whig critics that lasted from the fall of 1850 to the Whigs' national convention in June 1852. Longtime personal animosities and conflicting political ambitions helped fuel that clash. Fundamentally, however, it revolved around a dispute over how to carry elections, about whether the campaign needs of local Whigs should be placed ahead of intersectional comity within the nation and the national party and of support for the national administration.

I

Simply ignoring the Compromise and using other campaign issues against the Democrats in 1850 and 1851 was not a realistic option for northern Whigs. Still discounting southern threats of disunion, most of them personally detested its prosouthern concessions as an unnecessary surrender to Slave Power intimidation, and they knew that Free Soilers would court anti-Compromise voters if they themselves did not. Because northern Democrats endorsed the Compromise as a fair settlement, therefore, most northern Whigs wanted to trumpet their votes against it in Congress and to promise to gut its most obnoxious provisions as soon as possible. The new Fugitive Slave Act particularly repelled many Northerners. Aside from denying basic rights to blacks, many of whom had resided in the North as free men and women for years and still might be claimed as fugitives, the provisions of the act criminalizing aid to fugitives and fining anyone who refused to join in pursuing them struck Northerners as a Slave Power violation of their own rights. Blaming Democrats for that odious measure, these northern Whigs believed, would make an invincible platform.[4]

Conversely, southern Whigs, who recognized the seriousness of secessionism in a few slave states, sought to celebrate the Compromise for redressing southern grievances. They believed that their Democratic foes, by promoting the Nashville Convention and opposing the Compromise, had aligned themselves with disunionists. That Clay first proposed a comprehensive sectional compromise and that Fillmore's administration decisively embraced it enhanced Whig claims of paternity for the settlement and reinforced southern Whigs' conviction that they could win on a pro-Compromise platform. To ensure those expected triumphs and to undermine residual pockets of secessionist sentiment, however, Fillmore's administration would have to enforce the statutes that northern Whigs found most hateful.

Differing northern and southern Whig priorities whipsawed Fillmore's administration in 1850 and 1851. But he was equally concerned by another threat to his beloved Whig party. Responding to the confusion of party lines in Congress, some Whigs contemplated abandoning the party altogether and allying instead with like-minded Democrats in new coalitions for or against the Compromise. By the summer, talk of partisan realignment and reorganization because "the distinction between whig & democrat is rapidly passing away" and "the old party lines . . . could not be revived" was rampant in both the North and the South. Even Webster, who had always deplored the fierce partisanship of the past fifteen years and who lauded "the softening of political animosities" between pro-Compromise Whigs and Democrats in Congress, contemplated the creation of a new bipartisan Union organization should northern Whig state parties continue to oppose the Compromise.[5]

During Fillmore's presidency, therefore, Whigs had to do more than reconcile profound sectional differences over how best to compete against Democrats. Their party's very survival seemed at stake. To ward off the challenge of potential new parties, Whig politicians and voters alike had to be persuaded not to join them. That task required restoring sufficient internal unity and winning enough elections to maintain the Whig party as a credible competitive force. Again, the problem could be reduced to an essential core. How could fractious Whigs frame platforms on which they agreed that simultaneously distinguished them sufficiently from Democrats to mobilize Whig voters? On what issues would the Whigs go to the polls?

The administration's formula for preserving the national Whig party was crystal clear. It would no longer tolerate the previous unstated agreement between northern and southern Whigs to disagree about matters involving slavery, an implicit truce that had allowed the party to withstand sectional divisions since the 1830s. It would obviate the need for a new pro-Compromise Union party by proving that the national Whig party was pro-Union and pro-Compromise. Condemning attacks on the Compromise that most northern Whigs considered necessary to carry elections, it sought to keep anti-Compromise Whigs from writing party platforms, monopolizing party nominations, and controlling state party organizations. In doing so, it forced most northern Whigs to "make war on this administration to save the Whig party."

Whigs' common conviction that they must win the elections of 1850 and 1851 to preserve their party intact, therefore, fueled an increasingly brutal struggle between Fillmore's administration and its northern Whig opponents. Beginning in March and ending in November, the elections of 1850 had a cumulative and synergetic impact on the internal struggle for control of the Whig party. Whatever factors actually determined those contests, politicians interpreted them as running public opinion polls about developments in Washington. Losses early in 1850, therefore, made Whig leaders in other states all the more desperate to carry elections later in the year; all the more determined to write the platforms upon which, they believed, success depended; and, if they lost those platform battles, all the more willing to repudiate the product of the victors and to sabotage their chances of election. Both by reducing potential Whig turnout and by muddying exactly what Whigs, as a party, stood for and therefore how they differed from Democrats, such actions jeopardized Whig chances of mobilizing enough voters to win.

Further defeats in the fall of 1850, in turn, led to angry finger pointing, produced even more divisive struggles to control subsequent state conventions and legislative elections for United States senators, reinforced northern and southern Whigs' belief that they must put their own electoral success at home ahead of the needs of Whigs elsewhere, and provoked Fillmore's administration to wield its patronage powers against anti-Compromise elements in the party. This assault forced targeted Whigs to rally behind their own presidential candidate for 1852 to block Fillmore and Webster from the nomination. The battle among Whigs was so stark and its deleterious impact on Whig electoral fortunes between 1850 and 1852 so clear that one might easily overlook a crucial fact: Whigs alone had never determined their party's fate. Democratic actions had always decisively shaped it, and they did so again between 1850 and 1852.

II

Whigs carried only four of the eleven states to vote before Congress adjourned on September 30, 1850. A fluke upset gave them one Democratic stronghold, but they lost two reliable, if closely contested, Whig states. Unique elements influenced the outcome in each of the eleven states, but their collective results shaped the behavior of Whig congressmen in Washington and increased the pressure Whigs felt to carry the October and November contests. They also widened the disagreement between northern and southern Whigs about how to do so.

Three New England states, where Whigs confronted Free Soilers as well as Democrats, and Virginia voted in the spring while Taylor was still alive and before Clay submitted his omnibus bill to the Senate. As usual, Whigs swept the legislative and gubernatorial contests in tiny Rhode Island, where the party staunchly backed Taylor's plan, Free Soilers were weak, and Democrats did not contest the reelection of incumbent Whig Governor Henry Anthony. This easy triumph reinforced the commitment of the state's Whig Senators Albert Greene and John H. Clarke to Taylor's plan. Conversely, Free Soilers' negligible strength and Whigs' apparently safe majority over Democrats also help explain why they felt free to abandon it after his death and to support the Texas boundary bill.[6]

Just as predictably, Whigs lost the Democratic Gibraltar of New Hampshire, but the dimension of their defeat and the tactics Democrats used to inflict it etched an indelible lesson for other northern Whigs. Incensed that Whig-Free Soil coalitions elected Amos Tuck, a Free Soiler, and James Wilson, a Whig, to the House of Representatives in 1849, New Hampshire Democrats determined in 1850 to outbid Whigs for Free Soil support. The Concord *Patriot*, Democrats' leading newspaper, endorsed Free Soiler Joseph Root's February resolution demanding immediate congressional organization of territorial governments with slavery explicitly prohibited and condemned Wilson and Robert C. Winthrop, the Whigs' recent speakership candidate, for allowing Root's motion to be tabled out of slavish loyalty to the slaveholder Taylor. Northern Democrats, it baldly lied, opposed slavery expansion more firmly than northern Whigs. With voters apparently content with Democratic state economic policies that year, Whigs were crushed. Their hapless gubernatorial candidate garnered only a third of the popular vote, and they lost nineteen seats in the state house of representatives, reducing their share to a pathetic 31 percent. New Hampshire's results, in short, suggested that a bare hint of appeasing the South could be political suicide in New England.[7]

Connecticut's April state election taught the same lesson, although there the muddying of the Whigs' message as much as Democratic brazenness produced the result. Unlike Rhode Island and New Hampshire, Connecticut was closely competitive, and Whigs had lost three of the state's four House seats in 1849. In 1850, however, Whigs considered it safe. Repudiating the previous year's alliance with Free Soilers, the Democratic state convention nominated doughface Thomas Seymour, a vociferous enemy of the Wilmot Proviso and antislavery men, for

King Andrew the First. LIBRARY OF CONGRESS, LC-USZ62.1562.

William Henry Harrison.
DICTIONARY OF AMERICAN
PORTRAITS, P. 279.

John Tyler. DICTIONARY
OF AMERICAN PORTRAITS,
P. 630.

The Whig Ticket of 1844

Henry Clay, 1852
Daguerreotype by
Frederick Debourg
Richards. NATIONAL
PORTRAIT GALLERY,
NPG.90.24.

Theodore Frelinghuysen.
The American Review, 2 (1845).
COURTESY OF SPECIAL
COLLECTIONS DEPARTMENT,
UNIVERSITY OF VIRGINIA LIBRARY.

Grand National Whig Banner, by Currier. NATIONAL PORTRAIT GALLERY, NPG.82.10.

Treeing Coons. 1844
Democratic Campaign Cartoon.
LIBRARY OF CONGRESS.
LC-USZ62.51254.

Senator Willie P. Mangum of
North Carolina. American
Review (March 1846). COURTESY
OF SPECIAL COLLECTIONS DEPART-
MENT, UNIVERSITY OF VIRGINIA
LIBRARY.

Congressman Meredith P.
Gentry of Tennessee.
American Review (August
1852). COURTESY OF SPECIAL
COLLECTIONS DEPARTMENT,
UNIVERSITY OF VIRGINIA
LIBRARY.

Important Southern Whigs

Senator John Bell of Tennessee. American Review (October 1852). COURTESY OF SPECIAL COLLECTIONS DEPART- MENT, UNIVERSITY OF VIRGINIA LIBRARY.

Congressman Henry W. Hilliard of Alabama. American Review (December 1849). COURTESY OF SPECIAL COLLECTIONS DEPARTMENT, UNIVERSITY OF VIRGINIA LIBRARY.

Important Southern Whigs

Congressman Thomas Butler King of Georgia. American Review (November 1848). COURTESY OF SPECIAL COLLECTIONS DEPARTMENT, UNIVERSITY OF VIRGINIA LIBRARY.

Congressman William Ballard Preston of Virginia. American Review (September 1849). COURTESY OF SPECIAL COLLECTIONS DEPARTMENT, UNIVERSITY OF VIRGINIA LIBRARY.

The Whig Ticket of 1848

Zachary Taylor. DICTIONARY OF AMERICAN PORTRAITS, P. 612.

Millard Fillmore. Photograph by J. H. Whitehurst, ca. 1850. CHICAGO HISTORICAL SOCIETY. ICHI-10287.

THE JUGGLER IN TROUBLE.

GENERAL TAYLOR (as a Chinese Juggler.) I BERRY MUCH 'FRAID DAT SOME OF DESE D——N KIVES TUMBLE DOWN AN CUT MY FINGER. I CAN'T KEEP UM UP MUCH LONGER.

The Chinese Juggler. Anti-Taylor Cartoon in *The John Donkey* (1848). COURTESY OF SPECIAL COLLECTIONS DEPARTMENT, UNIVERSITY OF VIRGINIA LIBRARY.

AN AVAILABLE CANDIDATE.
THE ONE QUALIFICATION FOR A WHIG PRESIDENT.

An Available Whig Candidate. Anti-Taylor Cartoon. LIBRARY OF CONGRESS. LC-USZ62.5220.

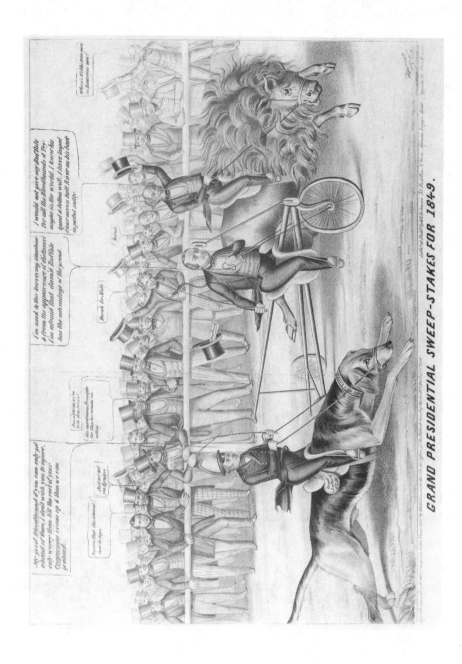

Grand Presidential Sweepstakes for 1849.

President Taylor and his Cabinet. *From left to right,* Reverdy Johnson; William M. Meredith; William Ballard Preston; Taylor; George W. Crawford; Jacob Collamer; Thomas Ewing, and John M. Clayton. Lithograph by Francis D'Avignon after a daguerrotype by Matthew Brady. NATIONAL PORTRAIT GALLERY. NPG.76.53.

Taylor's Two Most Unpopular Cabinet Members and One of Their Victims

Secretary of State John M. Clayton.
DICTIONARY OF AMERICAN PORTRAITS,
P. 119.

Secretary of the Interior Thomas
Ewing. American Review (January
1850). COURTESY OF SPECIAL COLLEC-
TIONS DEPARTMENT, UNIVERSITY OF
VIRGINIA LIBRARY.

Senator James Cooper of
Pennsylvania. American Review
(June 1852). COURTESY OF SPECIAL
COLLECTIONS DEPARTMENT, UNIVER-
SITY OF VIRGINIA LIBRARY.

John MacPherson Berrien.
American Review (May 1847).
COURTESY OF SPECIAL COLLECTIONS
DEPARTMENT, UNIVERSITY OF VIR-
GINIA LIBRARY.

Robert Toombs. American Review
(March 1850). COURTESY OF SPE-
CIAL COLLECTIONS DEPARTMENT,
UNIVERSITY OF VIRGINIA LIBRARY.

Alexander H. Stephens. DICTIONARY
OF AMERICAN PORTRAITS, P. 586.

THE UNITED STATES SENATE. A.D. 1850.

Clay Addresses the Senate. Robert Whitechurch, after Peter Frederick Rothermel, after daguerrotypes. NATIONAL PORTRAIT GALLERY. NPG.77.11.

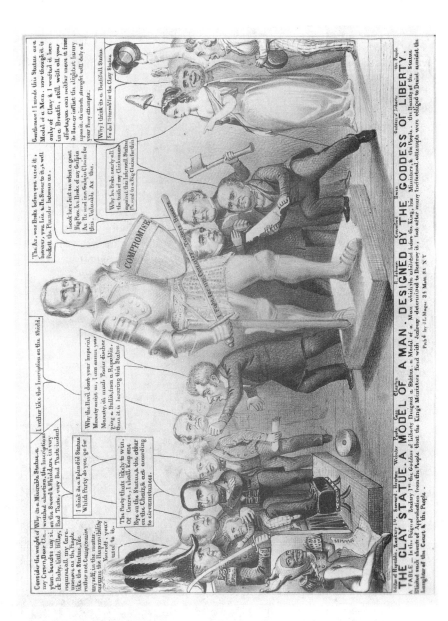

The Clay Statue. LIBRARY OF CONGRESS. LC-USZ62-1424.

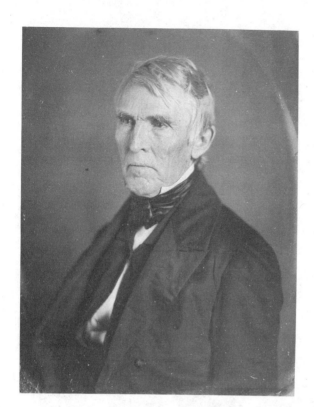

Fillmore's Cabinet

John Jordan
Crittenden, ca. 1855,
Photographer
Unknown. CHICAGO
HISTORICAL SOCIETY.
ICHI-09918.

Daniel Webster. DICTIO-
NARY OF AMERICAN POR-
TRAITS, P. 659.

Fillmore's Cabinet

Alexander H. H. Stuart.
American Review (April
1851). COURTESY OF SPECIAL
COLLECTIONS DEPARTMENT,
UNIVERSITY OF VIRGINIA
LIBRARY.

John P. Kennedy. *American
Review* (December 1846). COUR-
TESY OF SPECIAL COLLECTIONS
DEPARTMENT, UNIVERSITY OF VIR-
GINIA LIBRARY.

Thomas Corwin. American Review (September 1847). COURTESY OF THE SPECIAL COLLECTIONS DEPARTMENT, UNIVERSITY OF VIRGINIA LIBRARY.

Nathan K. Hall. American Review (1852). COURTESY OF SPECIAL COLLECTIONS DEPARTMENT, UNIVERSITY OF VIRGINIA LIBRARY.

Louis Kossuth, Reshuffler of the 1852 Campaign. American Review (December 1851). COURTESY OF SPECIAL COLLECTIONS DEPARTMENT, UNIVERSITY OF VIRGINIA LIBRARY.

The Whig Ticket
of 1852

Winfield Scott. DICTIONARY
OF AMERICAN PORTRAITS,
P. 552.

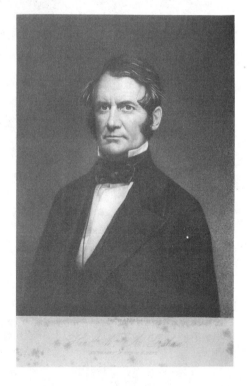

William A. Graham. American
Review (March 1852). COURTESY
OF THE SPECIAL COLLECTIONS
DEPARTMENT, UNIVERSITY OF VIR-
GINIA LIBRARY.

Important
New England Whigs

Truman Smith, Congressman
and Senator from Connecticut.
American Review (November
1852). COURTESY OF THE SPE-
CIAL COLLECTIONS DEPARTMENT,
UNIVERSITY OF VIRGINIA
LIBRARY.

Senator Roger Sherman Baldwin
of Connecticut. American
Review (October 1849). COUR-
TESY OF THE SPECIAL COLLECTIONS
DEPARTMENT, UNIVERSITY OF VIR-
GINIA LIBRARY.

Important New England Whigs

Congressman Robert C. Winthrop of Massachusetts. American Review (March 1848). COURTESY OF THE SPECIAL COLLECTIONS DEPARTMENT, UNIVERSITY OF VIRGINIA LIBRARY.

Congressman George Ashmun of Massachusetts. American Review (September 1852). COURTESY OF THE SPECIAL COLLECTIONS DIVISION, UNIVERSITY OF VIRGINIA LIBRARY.

Important
New England Whigs

Abbott Lawrence of
Massachusetts. American
Review (April 1849). COURTESY
OF THE SPECIAL COLLECTIONS
DEPARTMENT, UNIVERSITY OF
VIRGINIA LIBRARY.

HON. GEO. EVANS,

Senator George Evans of Maine.
American Review (July 1847).
COURTESY OF THE SPECIAL COL-
LECTIONS DEPARTMENT, UNIVER-
SITY OF VIRGINIA LIBRARY.

Daniel Dewey Barnard, conservative spokesman. American Review (May 1848). COURTESY OF THE SPECIAL COLLECTIONS DEPARTMENT, UNIVERSITY OF VIRGINIA LIBRARY.

Thurlow Weed. Matthew Brady Studio. NATIONAL PORTRAIT GALLERY. NPG.81.M203.

Governor and Senator Hamilton
Fish. American Review (December
1848). COURTESY OF THE SPECIAL
COLLECTIONS DEPARTMENT, UNIVER-
SITY OF VIRGINIA LIBRARY. .

Congressman and Governor
Washington Hunt. American
Review (March 1849). COURTESY
OF THE SPECIAL COLLECTIONS
DEPARTMENT, UNIVERSITY OF VIR-
GINIA LIBRARY.

Governor and Senator William Henry Seward. NATIONAL ARCHIVES PHOTO NO. 111-B-5751.

governor, while the state's most prominent Democratic editor, Alfred Burr of the Hartford *Times*, demanded prosouthern concessions in the Mexican Cession. With the state's Whig platform, its Whig press, and Whig Senators Roger Sherman Baldwin and Truman Smith firmly committed against any compromise that allowed slavery expansion west of Texas, Whigs held the high antislavery ground, just as they had in 1844, 1845, 1847, and 1848, when they won sweeping victories.

For various reasons, however, Whigs suffered a narrow but nonetheless shocking defeat. Regional jealousies continued to plague the party, reducing support for gubernatorial candidate Lafayette Foster outside of his own New London County. And as they had so successfully in 1846, Democrats also played the temperance issue like a drum. Roger Baldwin's wife, Emily, whose political zeal and acumen equaled those of any male in the Whig party, astutely, if biasedly, appraised the effectiveness of their two-faced strategy after the returns were in. "The democratic party had worked under all colors and been literally without principles in carrying the election," she reported. "Whatever was most popular in a town, that they seized. Temperance in some, all antitemperance in others. Allied with free soil in many places and in others joined against it and electing . . . out and out . . . proslavery [men]."[8]

Most Whigs in Connecticut and beyond its borders attributed the defeat to the loss of Whigs' advantage on the slavery issue. And Whigs themselves, they admitted, helped blunt that edge. Connecticut's polls were open on April 1 and 2. By those dates, only one New England Whig had spoken in the Senate on the sectional controversy in time to have his speech printed in Connecticut's newspapers—Daniel Webster on March 7. Everyone in Washington knew that Baldwin and Truman Smith favored Taylor's plan, but Smith, an inept orator, shunned the Senate floor, and the frustrated Baldwin could not get it to make a speech until the end of March, when no time remained to circulate it before Connecticut's voters cast their ballots. Thus, even though Whig papers like the Hartford *Courant* flatly asserted that Webster's "ground is not that of the Whigs of Connecticut," Whig leaders blamed their senators' silence in March for allowing Democrats cynically to charge that Webster represented them and gleefully to contrast the votes cast for Root's resolution by Connecticut's three Democratic/Free Soil representatives with the refusal of Winthrop and other northern Whigs to support it.[9] Democrats had gained only about 4,000 votes since 1849, but that was enough to give them a plurality of the popular vote and complete control of the legislature. It elected Seymour and blocked Baldwin's reelection to the Senate, forcing a postponement of that decision to 1851.[10] As in New Hampshire, in sum, Connecticut's Democrats outflanked the Whigs on the slavery issue, and, more than anything else, the loss of Connecticut convinced northern Whigs that identification with Webster's pro-Compromise position was political poison.

Whigs fared no better in the only slave state to vote that spring. While Virginia's Democrats won two-thirds majorities in the state senate, as they had in 1848 and 1849, their margin over Whigs in the house increased from six seats in 1848, when Whigs clutched Taylor's coattails, to eleven seats in 1849, shortly after Taylor was inaugurated and southern Whigs had refused to sign the Southern Address, to thirty seats in 1850, after Taylor had announced his plan for the territories and Virginia Democrats in both houses of Congress had taken a leading role in denouncing both it and Clay's initial proposals.

This trend certainly deterred most Virginia Whigs from embracing Taylor's policy, but they did not interpret the results as public endorsement of the extremist proslavery, anticompromise position assumed by some Virginia Democrats like James M. Mason. For one thing, other Virginia Democrats followed the lead of Thomas Ritchie in Washington and were promoting compromise before the election. For another, Webster's Seventh of March speech, unlike Clay's original proposals, was widely popular among Whigs and Democrats in Virginia. Thus, when Clay presented his more palatable omnibus bill, Virginia's Whigs enthusiastically backed it.

Nor did the elections turn primarily on what was transpiring in Congress. In the spring of 1850, apathy and anger about the continued retention of Democrats in the state's federal patronage posts drove down Whig turnout. More important, the state legislature had scheduled a public referendum during the legislative elections to decide whether a convention to revise the state constitution should be held later that year. Although Virginia's Whigs at the last minute had shifted their stance and now endorsed a convention, since the mid-1840s the party had opposed, while Democrats had advocated, constitutional revision. Thus the convention issue undoubtedly helped Democratic legislative candidates by bringing out proconvention Democratic voters. Whatever the exact causes of the Whigs' defeat, Virginia seemed to be slipping further and further beyond their reach.[11]

III

By the time seven more states voted in August and September, conditions had changed. Taylor was dead; immediate statehood for New Mexico was a dead letter; Whigs and Democrats in the Senate had taken pro- and anticompromise positions on roll-call votes; and Fillmore, despite pleas from Whigs across the North to shun Clay, Webster, and compromise, was doing just the opposite. Five of these contests went according to form, but even they reinforced the divergent convictions of northern and southern Whigs about what was necessary to carry elections.

By the summer both parties in Kentucky, as in its sister border state of Maryland, were booming compromise. Because Kentucky had long been a Whig fiefdom, that consensus helped Whigs win the August legislative elections. Yet all was not well for Kentucky's Whigs. Ratified in May 1850 and due to take effect in 1851, a new state constitution gravely threatened Whigs' monopolistic grip on Kentucky. It stripped the governor of vast amounts of local patronage; required new elections in August 1851 for every office in the state, including the previously appointive judiciary, thus jeopardizing their Whig incumbents; and reapportioned the legislature in ways that decisively benefited Democrats. The 1850 election was the last cakewalk for Kentucky's Whigs.[12]

Safely Democratic Iowa's August election was a mirror image of Kentucky's. Its totally Democratic congressional delegation in Congress firmly supported the Compromise, and by the end of July, so did Iowa Whigs. Lacking a distinctive position to mobilize voters against the incumbent majority party, the Whigs were trounced. Democrats won the governorship, both congressional seats, and virtually the entire legislature. Despite the important offices at stake, indeed, the "me-too" campaign of 1850 generated the lowest turnout rate in Iowa since it became a state. Seriously to challenge, let alone topple, the dominant Democrats, Iowa's Whigs needed to bring new voters to the polls. Manifestly, aping the Democrats' pro-Compromise stance could not do it.[13]

In Indiana, where only legislative seats and local offices were contested in August and where Whigs had stumbled since the 1847 congressional elections, Fillmore's support for the Compromise ruined Whigs' chances for a comeback. As in most northern states, Indiana's Democratic newspapers fervently urged conciliation of the South, and its Democratic congressmen, especially Senators Jesse Bright and James Whitcomb, supported compromise on almost every roll-call vote taken during the session. By attacking that record, Whigs like Theodore Barnett and Schuyler Colfax, who blamed the failure to win back antislavery defectors for Whigs' defeat in 1849, hoped to fuse with Free Soilers on legislative tickets in 1850. Such a coalition, if successful, could replace Bright in the Senate with an antislavery Whig.

To Colfax's great dismay, however, some Whig papers in southern Indiana subverted the chance of coalitions with Free Soilers by praising Clay's omnibus bill in June, and Fillmore's swing behind the Compromise in late July doomed it. "Just as certainly as the Administration links its fortunes to the Omnibus, just so certainly are all our hopes of resurrection lost," Colfax groaned. "We're killed now after what Clay & Webster & [George W.] Crawford have done for us this season." The August elections, which increased Free Soil representation while reducing the Whigs' proportionate strength in both houses to its lowest level since the party's birth, only deepened Colfax's pessimism.[14]

Indiana's returns taught northern Whigs the same lesson as New England's spring results. Where the Free Soil party posed a serious threat, Whigs had to repudiate Fillmore's pro-Compromise position to stem further defections to the Free Soilers and to get their voters to the polls. To win they had to take a tougher stand against the South than their Democratic rivals. September elections in reliably Whig Vermont and stubbornly Democratic Maine reinforced that conviction.

Despite the presence of a vigorous Free Soil party, Vermont was the safest Whig state in the nation. In 1850, its voters would choose congressmen, a governor, and a state legislature, which in turn would elect a successor to incumbent Whig Senator Samuel Phelps. As in 1849, Whigs faced a Free Soil/Democratic coalition, but by September 1850 that alliance was unraveling because northern Democrats' pro-Compromise stance inside and outside Congress decisively refuted Democrats' antislavery pledges. In contrast, Whigs' state platform and leading papers, especially the Burlington *Free Press*, were staunchly antislavery and anti-Compromise. True, by the time Vermonters voted in September, Phelps had wavered by supporting Pearce's Texas boundary bill on August 9, but Vermont's other Whig congressmen defied the administration and voted solidly against the prosouthern parts of the Compromise. Unlike Indiana's Whigs, that is, Vermont's Whigs boasted a congressional record to offset Fillmore's pro-Compromise stance.[15]

Retaining their advantage on the slavery issue, Vermont's Whigs scored an impressive triumph. They won the governorship with an outright popular-vote majority for the first time since 1844, carried three of four congressional districts, as in 1848, and retained comfortable majorities in both houses of the legislature. Nor would Vermont's Whigs sacrifice their antislavery credentials after the election to mollify the Fillmore administration. Over the howls of conservative Democrats and proadministration Whigs, who complained that "our" legislators "always have and always will pass Abolition Resolutions" to satisfy "the strong Abolition feeling in our State," Whig legislators rammed through a personal liberty law that defied the new Fugitive Slave Act, legislation that permanently drove a wedge between grateful Free Soilers and scandalized Democrats. To solidify their antislavery credentials Whig legislators also ousted Samuel Phelps from the Senate and replaced him with Solomon Foot, although Phelps' "sour, saucy, and doggedly aristocratic" personality caused his displacement as much as his Texas boundary vote.[16]

By successfully distancing themselves from Fillmore's pro-Compromise record, Vermont's Whigs appeared more secure than ever. Maine's Whigs, with no members of the Senate and only a single man in the House to establish an antiadministration voting record, could not achieve a similar distance. "Our reliance for success is upon a pretty serious quarrel among the Democrats," moaned Whig congressional candidate William Pitt Fessenden in late August. "If they unite *well*, I shall be defeated."[17]

Totally dominant in the state since 1840, Maine's Democrats were deeply divided. Led by incumbent Governor John Hubbard and Senator Hannibal Hamlin, an original backer of Wilmot's Proviso in the House, who delivered a powerful speech in March supporting Taylor's plan, the free-soil Democratic majority opposed the Compromise. The doughface minority, nicknamed Wildcats, favored compromise with the South and was nominally led by Hamlin's Democratic Senate colleague James W. Bradbury, who voted for all the Compromise measures except the Fugitive Slave Act. Between early May and late July 1850, these contending Democrats fought a bruising battle in Maine's legislature over Hamlin's reelection. Hamlin finally prevailed, but only with the help of Free Soilers and a few antislavery Whigs.[18]

Democrats' rift offered Whigs hope, but it was dashed. Hamlin's stand in Congress prevented Whigs from painting the Democrats as proslavery and also deterred Democratic defections to the Free Soil party that some Whigs tried to instigate. To boot, Maine's Whigs themselves split over the Compromise. Webster's allies captured the Whig senatorial nomination during the summer legislative contest for Webster's close friend George Evans. Trumpeting the Fillmore administration's support for compromise, this faction further hampered Whigs' attempts to exploit antisouthern sentiment even though several Whig congressional candidates were stalwart antislavery men.[19]

Hubbard easily won reelection, and Democrats also increased their margins in both legislative chambers. While Whigs again carried only two of seven congressional districts, however, their anti-Compromise stance made them markedly more competitive in these national contests than earlier. Robert Goodenow won in the third district, which John Otis had carried in 1848. In the sixth, Israel Washburn, Jr., launched his family's remarkable career in national politics when regular and Wildcat Democrats split the opposition vote, allowing Washburn to win with a plurality. Fessenden lost by only 40 votes out of almost 12,000 cast in his district, and James S. Pike trailed the victorious Democrat in his by only some 200 votes.[20]

Despite the dismayingly familiar futility of Maine's Whigs, therefore, they remained competitive enough to exploit any further breach in Democratic ranks. Obviously, however, they had to rely on Democratic dissensions to make further gains, and they had done as well as they had only by flouting Fillmore's support for the Compromise and running staunch antislavery Whigs like Pike, Fessenden, Washburn, and Goodenow. Those men, moreover, deeply offended Webster's loyalists in the state, and even as the campaign wound down, Evans went to Washington to secure Senate rejection of patronage appointees allied with the party's antislavery faction. All of this pointed to trouble ahead.

With the exception of Connecticut, past patterns made the election results from the nine states discussed so far predictable. Such was decidedly not the case, however, with the August contests in Missouri and North Carolina.

Missouri, like its neighbors Arkansas, Illinois, and Iowa, was a Democratic fiefdom. Whigs had never come close to carrying a statewide race for president or governor, and they had languished as a pathetic minority in the state legislature. Since 1834, moreover, only one Whig had served among the twenty-three men Missouri sent to the House of Representatives. So weak were Missouri's Whigs that their closest historian labels them a pressure group, not a party. Yet in August 1850 Whigs carried three of Missouri's five congressional districts, 41 percent of the state house of representatives, and 36 percent of the state senators. Those Whig legislators subsequently achieved a still more astounding feat: the election of Whig Henry S. Geyer to the United States Senate.[21]

The reason for this startling reversal of Whig fortunes can be reduced to three words—Thomas Hart Benton. For years, Benton, a leading opponent of slavery expansion and a champion of Taylor's plan in the Senate, and his rabidly loyal followers had been the target of other Democrats, who shared militantly proslavery Southerners' antipathy toward both the Taylor plan and Clay's compromise. That split allowed Missouri's Whigs, who had no representation in Congress, to join other border state Whigs in promoting Clay's omnibus bill as the fairest compromise between the extreme northern and southern positions.[22]

The Democratic split dominated the 1850 elections because the legislature chosen that year would fill Benton's Senate seat. Benton and anti-Benton Democrats ran separate slates of candidates for the legislature and in four of the state's five congressional districts. In two of those four Whigs triumphed, with popular pluralities of 39.6 and 42.3 percent. In the fifth district, the Bentonians threw their support to the Whig to keep their Democratic rivals from winning. That was the only district Whigs carried with an outright majority. The plurality of seats won by Whigs in the legislature also gave them the balance of power between Benton and anti-Benton Democrats in both chambers. Because Benton's supporters stubbornly insisted on his reelection, while anti-Benton men lacked the votes to choose his successor, the anti-Benton Democrats ultimately supported the Whig Geyer for the Senate in order to purge Benton from it. Thus did Democratic divisions inject new life into the moribund Missouri Whig party just when Democratic actions elsewhere were helping to sap the life from Whig parties.[23]

North Carolina's Whigs would have loved to make their August gubernatorial and state legislative elections a referendum on the Compromise. By July, North Carolina's entire Whig congressional delegation, except Thomas Clingman, was strongly supporting the compromise measures. In contrast, the state's three Democratic congressmen fiercely opposed the package as a sellout of Southern Rights.[24]

Within North Carolina itself, moreover, the parties' platforms and press, led by the Whig Raleigh *Register* and the Democratic Raleigh *Standard*, mirrored the stance of their respective congressional delegations. Partisan differences were crystal clear, and Whigs were confident that they held the edge, especially since they could cite Democratic enthusiasm for the Nashville Convention as evidence that their opponents were disunionists. Had the state election focused on events in Washington, therefore, the Whigs, as usual, would probably have prevailed.[25]

North Carolina's Democrats, however, refused to oblige. On August 1, North Carolinians would elect only a governor and members of the state legislature. Since those new legislators had no Senate seat to fill, no national offices were at stake, and Democrats plausibly argued that state issues should determine those races. On state issues, Whigs suffered several disadvantages. Whig divisions over men and measures and Democrats' demand for equal suffrage (elimination of property qualifications to vote for state senators) threatened to reverse the tiny 854-vote margin by which Charles Manly had defeated Democrat David Reid in 1848.

The disadvantages tipped the balance against them. Considered the creature of the hated Raleigh Clique, Manly was distrusted by both eastern and western Whigs. Although he won renomination at the Whig state convention in June, angry eastern and western Whigs abolished the existing state central committee, which Raleigh Whigs dominated, and replaced it with a totally ineffectual executive committee designed to minimize Raleigh influence. Manly had also proved himself an inept campaigner in 1848 and an unpopular governor after his election, and by sticking with him in 1850, Whigs committed a serious blunder.[26] Furthermore, in 1848 Manly had clearly benefited in western North Carolina because he favored, while Reid opposed, state subsidization of turnpike and railroad construction. After that election, however, William W. Holden, the state's leading Democratic editor, persuaded the state's Democrats to renounce their traditional opposition to internal improvements and support state aid to railroads, thus neutralizing Whigs' best issue.[27]

As if these hurdles were not enough for the Whigs to clear, Manly then committed a fatal mistake during the campaign by charging that if Democrats really favored political reform they would back the white basis for apportioning legislative seats, not just equal suffrage criteria in state senate and house elections. He meant to ridicule both reforms, but the Democratic press leaped on his gaffe to charge that he favored the white basis, a charge that proved lethal among slaveholders in eastern and central North Carolina. Between 1848 and 1850 Manly suffered a net loss of only some 200 votes, although his loss in Rutherford County was heavier than that, and Reid gained 3,400. That small swing was enough to convert Manly's small majority in 1848 to a small majority for Reid in 1850 and to give the Democrats decisive margins in both legislative chambers.[28]

Although Democrats jubilantly boasted that they had won complete control of the state government for the first time since the emergence of the Whig party, North Carolina's Whigs remained a very competitive force. Neither they nor Whigs in other slave states interpreted the defeat as a repudiation of Whig support for the Compromise. The election occurred before Fillmore publicly endorsed a broad congressional settlement and before anti-Compromise votes by North Carolina Democrats in the House established a record they could not fudge. Instead,

Whigs properly attributed the loss to state issues, and they remained confident that they could prevail if elections were focused on what had transpired in Congress during 1850. That confidence was reinforced when they carried six of nine congressional races in 1851.[29]

IV

When Congress adjourned on September 30, 1850, in sum, Whigs had lost three of five gubernatorial elections; retained control of state legislatures in only three of eleven states, not counting their decisive plurality in Missouri; and won only six of eighteen congressional seats. Only in congressional races—and then only because of Missouri—did they run ahead of their 1848 pace. To match their earlier performance, therefore, Whigs had to do exceptionally well in the October and November elections, when most congressmen would be selected that year.

Of the remaining contests for state and congressional offices, only four were scheduled in slave states. Unshakably Democratic Arkansas held legislative elections in October, and although the Whigs gained seven seats in the house, they were still outnumbered two-to-one in that chamber and five-to-one in the state senate. Maryland, where pro-Compromise sentiment was bipartisan and universal, held a gubernatorial election in October, but the normal legislative elections that would have accompanied it were suspended to allow elections of delegates to a state constitutional convention instead. Without partisan disagreement over the Compromise, constitutional revision, which would reapportion the legislature to increase the representation of Baltimore City and County and western counties, became the central issue of the race. As elsewhere, Whigs were at a decided disadvantage on that question. For years Democrats had promoted reform, while overrepresented Whigs in southern Maryland had spearheaded opposition to it. During the fall gubernatorial campaign, Democrats tarred the Whig candidate with his party's opposition to the convention, and the Democrats won with a slightly larger majority (51 percent) than they had polled in 1847.[30] Although the impending constitutional convention posed a potential danger to the party, most Maryland Whigs took their narrow defeat in stride. Some, in fact, positively rejoiced over the outcome. Despite their common support for the Compromise, Maryland's Whigs were deeply divided into hostile factions. Senator James Pearce and his friends, like John Pendleton Kennedy, bitterly opposed former Attorney General Reverdy Johnson and his allies, like Senator Thomas Pratt and the Baltimore customs collector George P. Kane, whom they labeled "a Court House clique, composed of a set of very unprincipled men, selfish, immoral & tyrannical," and whose gambling and "hard drink[ing]" scandalized them.[31] Though Johnson was forced to leave the cabinet after Taylor's death, Fillmore's hands-off policy on appointments left Johnson's friends in control of Maryland's federal jobs. They had used that power to capture the Whigs' gubernatorial nomination in 1850 for William B. Clarke. Johnson's Whig enemies, therefore, uniformly exulted in Clarke's defeat, attributed it to mass abstention among the disgusted rank and file, and smugly interpreted it as a salutary "defeat of the Court House faction" that would revive "the hopes of the orthodox portion of the Whig party."[32]

Whatever role rebellious abstention by angry Whigs played in Maryland's election, their loss of the governorship and of control of the constitutional convention boded ominously for the future. Johnson's friends could retaliate in like manner against friends of Kennedy and Pearce in impending elections, and willingness to accept a Democratic victory in order to punish an intraparty foe bespoke a weakening commitment to Whiggery itself. Maryland Whigs' complacency after their 1850 defeat was unjustified.

Florida, whose tiny population had developed only a fraction of its vast reaches, also voted in October. Whigs had carried its governorship, legislature, and lone House seat in 1848, and Taylor won easily in November of that year. Florida's congressional delegation, with the exception of Whig Senator Jackson Morton, who owed his election to Democrats, had divided along the prevailing partisan lines over the Compromise measures. Meanwhile Whig Governor Thomas Brown vigorously opposed the Nashville Convention as a disunionist conclave; Whig papers praised his stand and endorsed compromise. Democratic papers blasted the governor as a betrayer of Southern Rights and hurled vitriol at the Compromise as a contemptible surrender to northern pressure. Whigs' renomination of Congressman Edward Carrington Cabell, who supported the Texas-New Mexico boundary bill and sent letters to Florida's newspapers lavishly praising Clay, Webster, and their compromise measures, made the Compromise the central issue in the fall elections, for his Democratic opponent demanded resistance to it to the "last extremity." Confident that they held the edge in the congressional campaign, even though Cabell remained in Washington throughout its duration, Whigs hoped it would set the tone for the simultaneous legislative elections, for the new legislature could replace Democrat David Yulee in the Senate with a Whig.[33]

That hope was dashed. Cabell won reelection, but his share of the vote dropped slightly since 1848. Both parties enjoyed small net gains of fewer than 200 voters between the two elections, but it seems likely that there was considerable switching of voters between the two parties. Some men who voted for Cabell also backed Democrats or abstained in legislative races, for Democrats overturned Whig majorities in both chambers and won by razor-thin margins. The Democratic triumph in the legislative races doomed Whig hopes of electing a United States senator. Later, however, a few dissident Democratic legislators who disliked Yulee joined Whigs to replace him with the Democrat Stephen Mallory. Just as the Democratic minority had helped dissident Whigs elect Jackson Morton over the preferred Whig candidate in the legislature of 1848–49, the Whig minority in the 1850–51 session joined dissident Democrats to defeat the preferred candidate of the Democratic majority.[34]

Delaware was the final state below the Mason-Dixon line to elect congressmen and state officials in the fall of 1850. Delaware's tiny population qualified it for only a single seat in the House of Representatives, but Whigs counted on solid Whig congressional delegations from small eastern states like Delaware and Rhode Island to offset the solidly Democratic congressional delegations from geographically large but thinly populated western states like Arkansas and Texas. In particular, Whigs stood no chance of controlling the Senate unless small eastern states like Delaware sent Whigs to that body.

Throughout the 1840s, Delaware had played that strategic role for the Whigs almost as reliably as Rhode Island. Though Whigs had narrowly lost the previous gubernatorial election in 1846, going into the 1850 contests they held majorities in both houses of the legislature, the House seat, and both Senate seats, one of which would be refilled by the legislature chosen in 1850. With regard to the internal politics of the Whig party, Delaware also had special significance, for it was the home base—some would say the political fiefdom—of John M. Clayton, Taylor's controversial secretary of state.

Clayton played a role in Delaware's politics strikingly similar to that of the Democrat Benton in Missouri. Not only did Clayton, like Benton, personally dominate his state's majority party, but, like Benton, he had the iconoclastic reputation of being a free soiler from a slave state. Prior to his inclusion in Taylor's cabinet, Clayton had been the only southern Whig senator ever to cast a vote for the Wilmot Proviso. He had helped formulate Taylor's plan to admit California and New Mexico as free states, and even after Taylor's death he had stubbornly denounced the congressional compromise as a betrayal of Taylor's policy and an unnecessary concession to southern pressure.

By 1850 slaves and slaveholders constituted such a small proportion of Delaware's population that it was even less southern than Missouri, which was itself considered by many contemporaries as more of a western free state than a southern slave state.[35] Hence, nothing like the extreme proslavery, anti-Compromise stance of Benton's Missouri Democratic enemies emerged in Delaware. Instead, Delaware shared the bipartisan enthusiasm for the Compromise evident in Maryland and Kentucky, and Clayton, like Benton, seemed to side with its northern, free-soil opponents. That heresy portended trouble for Delaware's Whig candidates in November 1850. As long as Taylor remained alive, Senators Presley Spruance and John Wales, Clayton's close allies, rigidly adhered to Taylor's plan and fought the omnibus bill. On July 1, Clayton's foremost Democratic rival in Delaware, James A. Bayard, wrote Clay that pro-Compromise sentiment was universal in Delaware, that Clayton's commitment to Taylor's plan embarrassed Delaware's Whigs, and that the two senators were "the mere tools of the Secretary of State," who would be punished when Delaware's electorate went to the polls. In particular, Wales, whose seat was due to be filled, stood in jeopardy. Even though both senators, like Whig Representative John Houston, another Clayton lieutenant, retreated after Taylor's death and voted for the individual Compromise measures, they could not shed the stigma of earlier helping northern, anti-Compromise Whigs.[36]

Clayton's prominence as Delaware's foremost Whig aggravated the party's problems there in two additional ways. First, because of his adamant refusal to abandon Taylor's plan after he left the cabinet and because of the considerable ill will he had earned as a dispenser of patronage while in it, pro-Compromise Whigs allied with Fillmore's administration determined to make him an example by undermining his political base. In particular, they wanted to prevent Delaware from returning him to the Senate to replace Wales, just as Democrats in Missouri determined to dump Benton for his apostasy. Clayton's grip on the Whig party machinery in Delaware seemed so unshakable that they had no chance of dislodging him from within the state party itself by challenging his control of Whig nominations. Thus, they did not, as Clayton feared they would, immediately remove Clayton's lieutenants from federal patronage posts in Delaware.

Instead, they moved to build up Clayton's pro-Compromise Democratic enemies in Delaware, regardless of the consequences that tilt might have for Whigs' electoral fortunes. Clay, who proudly boasted of his alliance with Democrats in the Senate, urged Fillmore to appoint James Bayard to the Interior Department when he had so much difficulty filling that post. Fillmore, who had no intention of breaking openly with the Whig party, wisely ignored that recommendation. In October, however, Fillmore and Webster achieved the same effect by offering a chargéship in Belgium to Bayard's older brother, Richard. Richard Bayard had served as a Whig in the Senate in the early 1840s, but by 1850 Delaware's Whigs considered him an "avowed enemy" of Clayton and much closer to the Democratic party of his brother than to the Whigs. Although this nomination would not be sent to the Senate until December, its announcement prior to the election sent an unmistakable signal to Delaware's Whigs. The administration wanted Clayton and his allies defeated even if that meant sacrificing Delaware to the Democrats. Three-term Congressman John Houston, for one, got the message; he prudently refused to seek renomination.[37]

Second, Clayton was also notorious among Whigs in Washington and Delaware as a heavy drinker, and that reputation alienated temperance elements in the state from the Whig party, which Clayton personified. Whether or not temperance men intended to punish Clayton personally, they ran separate candidates in 1850 for governor and congressman. In a state with so small an electorate as Delaware's, that insurgency was enough to tip the balance. The antiliquor aspirants drew only about 450 votes, but they cut disproportionately into the ranks of anti-Clayton Whigs and allowed the Democrats to win the governorship by 23 votes and the congressional seat by 129 votes out of some 12,000 cast.

Worse still from the Whigs' perspective, Whigs in New Castle County abstained or voted Democratic in the legislative race, thus allowing Democrats to carry that normally Whig bastion. Because each of Delaware's three counties had seven seats in the state house and three in the senate, this revolt was enough to give Democrats majorities in both houses of Delaware's legislature, and they replaced Wales in the Senate with none other than James A. Bayard. Thus did a minuscule number of votes cost the national Whig party a vital Senate seat, as well as a traditionally safe seat in the House. The loss of a Whig United States senator from Delaware, as well as the failure to gain one in Florida, therefore, negated Henry Geyer's surprising election in Missouri.

V

Congressional results from Illinois, Wisconsin, and Michigan in November committed most of their Whigs against the Compromise and Fillmore's position on it. In all three states, moreover, the hope or necessity of winning Free Soil votes explains their adamant stance. Two House races in Illinois served as Whigs' litmus test. When Chicago Democrats, now lashed by Stephen Douglas into unconditional support for all the Compromise measures, dumped incumbent anti-Compromise Democratic Congressman John Wentworth from their ticket, the city's Free Soilers threw their support to the Whig, who came within three percentage points of winning, whereas Wentworth's Whig foe in 1848 trailed him by fifteen points.[38] In the seventh district surrounding Springfield, Whig candidate Richard T. Yates defeated incumbent pro-Compromise Democratic Congressman Thomas L. Harris by lambasting his voting record and demanding repeal of the Fugitive Slave Law and abolition of slavery itself in the District of Columbia.

Initially confident that he could "push the proviso disunion issue on Yates" and thereby secure the votes of pro-Compromise Whigs, Harris howled in November that his defeat "is virtually a condemnation of the compromise by the people of this district." "If this [slavery] issue continues," he fumed, "Illinois will give her vote for any northern Sewardite Whig in 1852." Harris exaggerated, but the results suggested that Illinois Whigs had every reason to support such a presidential candidate in 1852. They had every incentive, in short, to break with Fillmore's administration.[39]

Whig newspapers in Wisconsin also blasted the Compromise and demanded repeal of the Fugitive Slave Act, but so did the state's Free Soil and Democratic sheets. Wisconsin's entire congressional delegation, including two Democratic senators and Democratic Congressman James Doty, indeed, voted against every prosouthern concession in 1850. In Wisconsin, only Fillmore's support for the Compromise distinguished Whigs' position from their opponents', and that distinction was lethal.[40] Whigs dared not even challenge the reelection of Doty or of Free Soil Congressman Charles Durkee, since their anti-Compromise votes were so popular. Whig Orasmus Cole sought reelection, but Democrats and Free Soilers reunited to defeat him despite his voting record. Simultaneously, Whig legislative candidates were reduced to 17 percent of the house and 16 percent of the senate as Democrats captured districts that both Whigs and Free Soilers had carried in 1849. By November 1850, in sum, Wisconsin's Whigs had reached rock bottom, largely because its Democrats retrieved Free Soilers by denouncing the Compromise. Whigs could not convert old voters or mobilize new ones without a distinctive platform, but the 1850 results made it absolutely clear that at least one distinctive platform—identification with Fillmore's pro-Compromise stance—meant self-immolation, a fact that Nathaniel Tallmadge, now a Wisconsin resident, made abundantly clear to Fillmore a month after the election.[41]

Events in 1851 further hardened Wisconsin's Whigs against Fillmore's position. That year its Democrats foolishly pronounced the slavery issue dead and declared they would ignore it in favor of old issues. This incredible misstep threw the state's Free Soilers into the Whigs' arms. In outright defiance of Fillmore's administration, they merged with Free Soilers to elect as governor the Whig Leonard Farwell, who had issued a letter demanding repeal of the Fugitive Slave Act, and, even more astonishing, to win a majority in the state house of representatives.[42]

Pro-Compromise votes by Michigan's Democratic senators and congressmen in 1850, in contrast, infuriated the state's Free Soilers and spurred Michigan's Sewardite Whigs to seek an alliance with them, as they had in 1848 when the two parties combined to elect William Sprague to the House. But the anti-Compromise Whigs, who were led by Taylor's appointees still in office and the editors of the Detroit *Tribune*, faced stiff opposition to this tactic from pro-Compromise Whigs, including Fillmore's brother, whose organ was the Detroit *Advertiser*, to which the administration shifted federal printing contracts that fall. Thus a ferocious internecine brawl ensued to control the state and district conventions that would choose Whig candidates and determine their platform statements on the Compromise.[43]

This struggle resulted in a draw. Fillmorites won narrow control of the state convention, where, by threatening removal of postmasters who resisted them, they adopted a state platform endorsing the Compromise, even though all but

one of the Whigs nominated for statewide office opposed it. In contrast, the Sewardite Whigs won control of the *district* conventions that chose Whigs' congressional and legislative candidates. In all three congressional districts, anti-
Compromise Whigs prevailed over administration men for the nomination;
similarly, most of the Whigs' legislative candidates were antislavery men, chosen
explicitly to attract Free Soil support. As editor Josiah Snow proudly told Seward
later, "Every Whig elected is a free soil Seward doctrine man."[44]

The results of the elections against the Democrats were as mixed as the results
of the Whigs' internal struggle. In 1850, only minor statewide offices were at
stake, and, saddled with a pro-Compromise platform, Whig candidates lost them
all. Together Whig and Free Soil candidates captured a few legislative seats Democrats had won the previous year, but the Democrats' margin was so huge that
these losses meant little. Whig congressional candidates, who ignored the state
platform and blasted the Compromise, however, carried two of three districts and
lost the third by only 400 votes. The losing Whig candidate in that district in fact
garnered about 2,000 fewer votes than the popular Sprague, who refused to seek
reelection, and Snow blamed the defeat on abstention and defection by proadministration Whigs. What most satisfied Michigan's Whigs was their defeat of
Alexander Buel, the Democratic incumbent from the Detroit district, who had
voted for every prosouthern Compromise measure, including the Fugitive Slave
Act. Whigs' share of the total vote rose from slightly less than 46 percent in 1848
and 1849 to 51.3 percent in 1850. For the first time in over a decade, that is,
Whigs won a majority of Michigan's vote, and they did so by openly flouting the
Fillmore administration, defeating its preferred candidates for Whig nominations,
and condemning the Compromise of 1850. That they would sacrifice this beneficial
platform in order to accommodate the administration in the future seemed unlikely.[45]

VI

Prior to Congress' reapportionment after the 1850 census, Iowa, Wisconsin, Michigan, Illinois, and Indiana had a combined total of twenty-five House seats. With
twenty-one seats by itself, Ohio had always been the most important midwestern
state in Whig calculations and, traditionally, the midwestern state where Whigs
were most successful. Though Ohio had also been the northern state where Free
Soilers posed the biggest challenge to Whigs since 1848, prior to Taylor's death
Ohio's Whigs exuded confidence that they could negate the Free Soil threat and
crush the Democrats in the 1850 elections for Congress, governor, and a new
legislature that would fill Thomas Ewing's Senate seat. By the beginning of 1850,
the nettlesome Free Soil/Democratic alliance was falling apart over state policy
toward currency, banks, and other corporations, matters that remained of central
concern in Ohio. Free Soilers of Whiggish antecedents continued to agree with—
and in the legislature to vote with—Whigs on state economic policy. That proclivity embittered their relationships with Free Soilers of Democratic and Liberty
party background, who were Salmon Chase's closest allies, and caused them to
reconsider the wisdom of remaining in the third party.

Fearful of driving away former Whigs by tilting toward the Democrats, Free
Soilers in the 1849–50 legislature refused to help Democrats organize the two

houses, as they had the previous winter. In retaliation, indignant Democrats co-operated with Whig legislators to divide the state jobs between the two major parties and completely shut out the Free Soilers. In addition, the Democratic state convention on January 8, 1850, adopted a platform with hard-money, antibanking planks that infuriated Whiggish Free Soilers and increased their inclination to return to their old party to protect Whig economic programs. As Chase's chief lieutenant in the legislature nervously wrote him in March, "There is a strong disposition now among the Whig Free Soilers in the North part of the State, to unite with the Whigs in local and state politics."[46]

More important, the Democratic state convention emphatically renounced coalition with the Free Soilers by defeating a resolution stating that Congress had authority to bar slavery from territories (thus implicitly repudiating the Wilmot Proviso and the fundamental platform of the Free Soilers) and by adopting another resolution that deplored the absence of Democrat William Allen from the United States Senate (thus implicitly repudiating their complicity in the election of Chase, who replaced Allen). Jettisoning their 1849 commitment to the Proviso in their platform, the Democrats expounded on the virtues of popular sovereignty, and during 1850 Ohio's Democratic papers praised the Compromise that incorporated it. To Free Soilers, Democratic betrayal necessitated running their own gubernatorial candidate to defeat Democratic nominee Reuben Wood. To Whigs, the Democrats' action signaled that Free Soil votes were theirs for the taking.[47]

During the first few months of 1850, Whigs believed that winning back Whig Free Soilers on the Western Reserve required Whig insistence that the Proviso be imposed on the Mexican Cession, but their May state platform praised Taylor, demanded immediate statehood for California and New Mexico without offsetting concessions to the South, and insisted that if Congress instead organized territorial governments in the Cession, it must explicitly bar slavery from that area. Chase's Free Soil friends sneered at this Whig retreat toward "Taylorism in its worst shape," but Ohio's Whigs believed otherwise. By trumpeting "Old Zac's plan," Whig gubernatorial candidate William Johnson wrote Treasury Secretary Corwin in late July, he had been "amazingly successful" in wooing back to the Whig party "the narrow-minded, one ideal descendants of the Roundheads on the Reserve." By adhering to that platform, a Cleveland editor told Seward on July 14, the Whigs could disrupt the Free Soilers' August state convention, retrieve all Whig defectors on the Reserve, and rout the Democrats in October. Since February, indeed, Ohio's Whigs had attempted to outdo each other in execrating Clay, Webster, and Democrats who would appease the Slave Power. Little wonder that Whig after Whig from Ohio warned Fillmore to shun the Compromise and its famous Whig proponents.[48]

With so much riding on continued fidelity to Taylor's plan, Ohio's Whigs were understandably crushed when Fillmore embraced the Compromise instead, especially the Fugitive Slave Law, which provoked paroxysms of rage on the Reserve when it was finally printed in Ohio's newspapers in September.[49] Unlike other northern states, in Ohio Fillmore's course did not seriously divide Whigs against each other. They remained almost unanimously hostile to the Compromise's pro-southern laws. During August and September, however, they could not broadcast their disagreement with an administration that included so prominent an Ohio Whig as Tom Corwin, who, in fact, soon regretted his decision to join the cabinet.

Fillmore's policy, rather, stopped all talk among Whig Free Soilers about returning to their old party and ensured that Free Soilers would run their own candidate for governor against Reuben Wood and Johnson. Whig warnings that Free Soil/Democratic legislative tickets would give hard-money Democrats control of the legislature proved unavailing, for by the fall, the effective arena for settling economic questions in Ohio had shifted from electoral politics to a state constitutional convention, whose delegates were elected in April 1850 and who wrangled endlessly over economic policy. Once Fillmore signed the Compromise measures into law, finally, Democratic newspapers hypocritically accused Ohio's Whigs of betraying their pledge never to allow the organization of territorial governments without the Proviso.[50]

Elsewhere in the North, Whigs had contrasted Whig and Democratic votes on the Compromise in Congress to counteract the embarrassment caused by Fillmore's course. The votes of the Ohio delegation, however, left little room for drawing favorable contrasts. For one thing, Ohio had Free Soilers in both the Senate and the House, and any deviation by Whig congressmen from the Free Soil voting line might be held against them. In the Senate, for example, Ewing joined Chase in voting against Pearce's Texas boundary bill, against Utah, and for California and abolition of the District of Columbia's slave market. For whatever reason, however, Ewing recorded no votes on the New Mexico and fugitive slave bills, both of which Chase opposed, thereby suggesting that Whigs were a less reliable antislavery party than the Free Soilers.

In the House, with the glaring exception of southern Ohio's John Taylor, who voted for the Texas-New Mexico and fugitive slave bills, all of Ohio's Whigs voted in almost identical fashion with the Free Soilers Joshua Giddings and Joseph Root—for California, for abolition of the District slave trade, and against everything else. The problem was that four of Ohio's eleven Democrats in the House voted exactly the same way, thus negating any advantage Whigs might have among antislavery voters in their districts and paving the way instead for Free Soil/Democratic coalitions on legislative and congressional tickets. Only three of the eleven Democrats, moreover, voted in an indisputably pro-Compromise fashion, including two who cast votes for the Fugitive Slave Act. The differences were insufficient to neutralize Democratic taunts that a Whig president had signed the Texas-New Mexico, Utah, and fugitive slave laws.[51]

The cumulative effect of Fillmore's actions, the voting records in Congress, and the campaign conducted by Whigs, Democrats, and Free Soilers in Ohio was to blur the distinctions among the parties, although Free Soilers could still lay claim to being the state's most forthright antislavery party. As a result, voter turnout dropped to its lowest level in over a decade, even though the state's House delegation, a Senate seat, and the governorship were at stake and even though many people were furious about the Fugitive Slave Act. The turnout rate in 1850 trailed that in the off-year election of 1842 by ten percentage points, and it lagged three points behind that of 1846, when partisan differences on the Democrats' economic policies in Congress were drawn so sharply. Undoubtedly, the widespread perception in Ohio that the already elected constitutional convention would settle many of the economic questions that had obsessed Ohioans for over fifteen years contributed to the decline. But the conflicting signals sent by both Whigs and Democrats about where their parties stood on the Compromise and the absence of any differences between them in many congressional districts did so as well. Confused or disgusted voters simply stayed home on election day.[52]

In the gubernatorial race Whigs clearly lost most from the electorate's alienation. In 1848, they had eked out a victory when many anti-Taylor Whigs and Liberty party men supported Seabury Ford. Virtually none of those Free Soil Whigs voted for Johnson in 1850, and about three-fifths of them voted for the Free Soil candidate. The others abstained, as did many other antislavery Whigs who had refused to support either Taylor or Van Buren in 1848 and who were alienated once again by Fillmore's pro-Compromise stance in 1850. Johnson lost to Reuben Wood by 12,000 votes, while the Free Soil candidate garnered 14,000, or 5.1 percent of the total.[53]

Obviously, had everyone who voted Free Soil instead supported Johnson, Whigs could have retained the governorship, and at least one historian has argued that Free Soilers were the biggest winners in 1850 because they helped defeat the Whigs.[54] There is no reason, however, to believe that former Democrats and Liberty men in the Free Soil column would have voted for Johnson had there been no Free Soil candidate in the race. In 1846, for example, the Liberty party had garnered almost 11,000 votes in the gubernatorial election, and if all of those men voted Free Soil in 1850, more recent Whig losses to the third party were small indeed. Equally important, Free Soilers ran a separate candidate explicitly to defeat the Democrat Reuben Wood, not the Whig William Johnson. Genuinely antislavery men, a furious Free Soiler wrote Chase after the Democratic state convention, insisted that "the Hunker Democrats must be beaten out next Oct" since Wood's victory would be "disastrous."[55] If defeating Democrats was the Free Soilers' chief goal, they had stultified themselves.

There are other reasons to question the extent of the Free Soil triumph and the Whig defeat. If one compares the 1850 returns with the November vote for president in 1848, rather than the October gubernatorial returns, the picture is different. The Free Soil vote dropped from 35,523, 10.7 percent of the 1848 total, to 13,747, 5.1 percent of the 1850 total. In short, Free Soil turnout had plummeted by over 57 percent. Similarly, Wood ran 21,000 votes behind Cass, a drop of almost 15 percent. Johnson had only 17,000 fewer votes than Taylor, a drop of about 13 percent, and he won a larger share of the total vote than Taylor had. Since November 1848, in sum, Whigs had lost fewer votes than either of their opponents in both absolute and percentage terms.[56]

Most important, one has to look beyond the gubernatorial race to assess who "won" and who "lost" the 1850 elections. Free Soilers did retain their balance of power in the legislature, but in 1850, unlike 1849, they fused as often with Whigs as with Democrats on legislative tickets, a fact that would prove of enormous importance during the subsequent election for United States senator. Even so, Whigs gained three seats in the state house and one in the senate. In the congressional races, moreover, Whigs won ten seats, compared to eight in 1848, while the Democratic total dropped from eleven to nine. Among the Democratic losers was incumbent Moses Hoagland, who voted for every Compromise measure, and among the Whig winners were incumbents Lew Campbell, whom Free Soilers had supported in 1848 but were now determined "to crush . . . for being a *Whig*,"[57] and John Taylor, the defiant Whig who supported the Compromise, even though a Free Soiler siphoned off a few of the votes he had attracted in 1848. In state legislative and congressional races, in sum, Whigs rather than Free Soilers or Democrats benefited most from the Compromise issue.[58]

Finally, one might look at the two outright Free Soilers elected in 1850. One was Giddings, whom the district's Whigs, to the chagrin of some, did not even bother to oppose and who crushed a Democratic opponent with 78 percent of the vote.[59] The other was Norton Townshend, the Free Soiler of Democratic antecedents who had done so much in the 1848–49 legislature to engineer Chase's election to the Senate. In 1850, Townshend again sought an alliance with Democrats, and he won the Free Soil congressional nomination only over the howling protests of Joseph Root's Whig/Free Soil supporters. So furious were those former Whigs that they ran Root as an independent Free Soil candidate against both Townshend and the regular Whig candidate. Whereas Root had not been opposed by a Whig in 1848 and defeated his Democratic challenger with 57.8 percent of the vote, Townshend won with only 47.6 percent, the Whig garnered 44.4 percent, and Root polled 8 percent.

Unquestionably, the Free Soilers won and the Whigs lost this district, but even this cloud was lined with silver. Townshend's nomination clearly alienated Whiggish Free Soilers and weakened the Free Soil party. Moreover, absolutely no one had been a greater thorn in the side of northern Whigs in the Thirty-First Congress—and for years before—than Joseph Root. It had been Root's resolution about creating territorial governments with the Proviso that so embarrassed northern Whigs in the spring. It had been Root who heaped scorn and contempt on the beleaguered Robert Winthrop. To see Root's defeat by the opportunistic Townshend as a victory for antislavery sentiment and a Whig defeat is to ignore its effect on the remaining northern Whigs in Congress. No matter who won the district, that is, ousting Joseph Root from Congress was a boon for the Whig party.[60]

Nonetheless, Ohio's Whigs themselves saw the 1850 elections as a defeat and sought scapegoats to blame. "With Webster, Clay, & others entertaining their views, for leaders of the Whig party, we are to be overthrown, crushed—annihilated," groaned one. "Those at the North who sustain the fugitive Bill & kindred measures, are *doomed*." To have any Whig support beyond patronage holders, "President Fillmore & his administration" must not "sustain these measures" or "strive to put down those of the party who oppose them." Signing the Fugitive Slave Law "will put Fillmore in as indefensible a plight as that of John Tyler," Ben Wade exploded after stumping the Reserve. "By this measure, the Administration has driven their friends to repudiate them to save the party from utter annihilation," he concluded. "God save us from Whig Vice Presidents."[61]

VII

The four remaining northern states with fall elections—Pennsylvania, New Jersey, New York, and Massachusetts—constituted the heartland of northern Whiggery. Taylor had carried all four, and New York and Pennsylvania provided his electoral vote margin. All but New Jersey had elected Whig governors in 1848. More important, the four together sent six Whigs to the Senate and fifty-eight Whigs to the House of Representatives. Altogether in 1848, Whigs won an astounding 79 percent of the House seats contested in the four states, and those representatives formed 55 percent of the entire House Whig delegation and 76 percent of its Northerners. For Whigs to have any chance of regaining control of Congress and maintaining their credibility as a competitive force, they had to run well in those states.

In no other northern states outside of Michigan, however, were Whigs' state organizations so bitterly riven by the Compromise and by administration pressure to adhere to it. The rivalry between Pennsylvania's Governor William F. Johnston and pro-Compromise elements in the state led by Senator James Cooper has already been discussed. With a Democratic governor, New Jersey's Whigs suffered no such split, but the state's Whig congressional delegation found themselves disowned by the state party. Daniel Webster's immense residual influence among Massachusetts' Whigs, now buttressed by his potential command of federal jobs there, guaranteed a donnybrook in the Bay State. Finally, the escalating feud between Weed, Seward, and their allies, on the one hand, and Fillmore, Nathan Hall, and conservative Whigs from the Hudson Valley, on the other, ensured a ferocious struggle over the platform and nominations in New York. In precisely those northern states where Whigs most needed to mobilize their full strength, in sum, the prospect of doing so seemed most remote.

New Jersey, the smallest and least studied of the four, had always been crucial to Whig power in Congress. Both of its senators and four of its five representatives in the Thirty-First Congress were Whigs. At stake in October 1850 were the governorship, the House seats, and the legislature, which would not only choose a successor to Senator William L. Dayton but also reapportion legislators' districts.[62]

Though spared a potent Free Soil threat, New Jersey's Whig congressmen opposed the Compromise's prosouthern components as staunchly as any northern Whigs. In most free states such antislavery firmness would have won these Whig champions kudos from their constituents. In New Jersey, however, concern for the Union's safety vastly outweighed antisouthern sentiment. By the early summer, New Jersey's Democratic papers were lacerating the Whigs for opposing the Compromise, and, one after another, Whig papers ceased to defend their congressmen's actions and instead welcomed peaceful resolution of the sectional crisis.[63] Having gone far beyond what New Jersey's Whigs would tolerate, all four incumbent Whig congressmen issued public letters at the close of the session, declining renomination to avert certain defeat at district conventions. The Whig state platform said nothing about the Compromise or the behavior of the sitting Whig congressmen. Until election day Democrats painted Whigs as wild-eyed disunionists; Whigs responded with embarrassed silence. In New Jersey, the Compromise was an issue on which Whigs dared not go to the polls. To the extent that any differences separated the parties on the salient national issues of 1850, therefore, Democrats had an edge.

Their advantage on matters of state policy at stake that year proved far more decisive. By exploiting state issues, Democrats had won the governorship in 1847. In 1849, internal divisions among Whigs over antimonopoly protests against the notorious Joint Companies (the Camden and Amboy Railroad and the Delaware and Raritan Canal) had reduced Whig majorities in both legislative chambers.[64] During the subsequent legislative session, Whigs divided over railroad bills designed to challenge the Camden and Amboy's monopoly of rail traffic between Philadelphia and New York City, thereby allowing the Democratic minority instead to fashion a general railroad incorporation bill that carefully protected the privileges of the Joint Companies. Whig legislators' ineffectual performance discredited the party and infuriated opponents of the monopoly, who had supported Whigs in 1849 to break it.

Much more closely affiliated with the Joint Companies than the Whigs who had sided with them, Democrats had no intention of focusing their 1850 campaign on state transportation policy. Their state platform emphasized other reforms that had traditionally united Democrats and divided Whigs: substitution of general for special incorporation laws and the imposition of unlimited liability on stockholders and directors; abolition of property-holding requirements for local officeholders; taxation of the face value of stocks and bonds at rates equal to the assessed value of real estate; increased debtor exemptions; and improved common schools.

That this agenda, on which Whigs remained resolutely mum, gave Democrats the initiative during 1850 became clear in the contrasting gubernatorial campaigns waged by the two parties. Democratic papers praised their candidate, George Fort, for consistently championing every plank in the Democratic platform during his recent service in the state senate. In contrast, Whigs lauded their candidate, John Runk, for his votes in *Congress* against the Democratic measures of *1846*. The sole state matter Whigs mentioned was the last Whig governor's success in retiring the state debt between 1844 and 1847. Self-consciously and suicidally, Whigs portrayed themselves as the party of the past; eagerly, Democrats crusaded as the party interested in New Jersey's future.

The upshot was a smashing Whig defeat. Fort, with almost 54 percent of the vote, rolled up the largest statewide majority in New Jersey's history against Runk. Whereas Whigs had won four of the five House seats in 1848, Democrats won four of the five in 1850 while running 6,000 votes ahead of Whigs in the popular vote. In the legislative races, Democrats drew even with Whigs in the senate and converted a six-seat Whig majority into a four-vote Democratic majority in the house. Then, as if to scourge Whigs for their inept handling of the antimonopoly issue, Democrats used their majority on the joint ballot in the 1851 legislative session to replace Dayton in the Senate with Democrat Robert F. Stockton, president of the infamous Joint Companies.[65]

To some extent Democrats' pro-Compromise stance contributed to this rout, as the reelection of incumbent Democratic Representative Isaac Wildreck with 67 percent of the vote indicated. But the election had been less a referendum on the Compromise than on the future of state policy. Whigs themselves admitted that their ostrich-like refusal to address current state issues cost them the governorship, the legislature, three seats in the House of Representatives, and one in the Senate, losses the congressional Whig party could ill afford. As the Whig Newark *Mercury* bluntly confessed: "The Whigs passed mealy-mouthed resolutions squinting everyway and meaning nothing. Democrats went before the people with reforms, cheerfully and confidently." Then, with extraordinary prescience, the same editor continued: "It is frequently said that . . . the Whig party is a National party, founded upon great principles and not to be disturbed by all the local questions of policy that may arise." Such a stance was a profound mistake. To succeed, Whigs must "plant" themselves "upon those questions of State reform which are justly assuming such prominence in the minds of the people." In the 1830s, in fact, the Whig party had established itself only where it took concrete and distinctive stands on *state* as well as national issues. The failure to do so in the 1850s was suicidal.[66]

Only minor statewide offices were contested in Pennsylvania that October, but the stakes for Whigs were far higher than in New Jersey. Pennsylvania had twenty-four congressmen compared to New Jersey's five, and in 1848 Whigs had carried fourteen districts to the Democrats' eight. Because Lewis C. Levin, the Native American from Philadelphia County, usually cooperated with House Whigs, while the Free Soiler David Wilmot was sharply at odds with his Democratic colleagues, Whigs effectively held three-fifths of Pennsylvania's seats heading into the 1850 elections. Retaining that margin constituted their primary challenge. In addition, should Whigs recapture the legislature in October, they could fill Daniel Sturgeon's Senate seat.[67]

Outside of Wilmot's fiefdom along the New York border and in one or two other districts, the Free Soil party did not seriously threaten Pennsylvania's Whigs. Indeed, Wilmot's refusal to seek reelection in 1850 effectively disbanded the Free Soil organization, although it hardly diminished antislavery sentiment in northern and western areas of the state. In Pennsylvania the biggest menace to Whigs' chances lay in Democratic resurgence and in their own divisions between Governor Johnston and Senator Cooper, and between supporters of Clayton's proposal for a new Taylor Republican party and its orthodox Whig opponents. To reunite their party and defeat the Democrats, Whigs hoped to focus the 1850 campaign on the Democratic Walker Tariff, which, they iterated and reiterated in platforms and private correspondence, had prostrated the state's mining and manufacturing interests and destroyed jobs.[68] In 1850, however, the tariff lost its edge as a Whig weapon. Aside from other problems, such as Democratic attempts to ignore the issue and evidence that workingmen in some industrial areas no longer believed Whigs' claim that higher duties meant higher wages and more jobs, Congress did nothing about tariff rates that year. Southerners, including prominent Whigs, insisted that all slavery questions be resolved before Congress considered anything else, and the session ended with no action. Infuriated by the logjam in Washington, Whig Representative Moses Hampton of Pittsburgh announced at the end of May that he would resign because Southerners, obsessed by their own monetary losses in the form of fugitive slaves, refused to help solve the problems causing far greater financial losses in Pennsylvania's industries. Anger among Pennsylvania Whigs at southern intransigence was intense, but they could hardly blame Pennsylvania Democrats for a blockade their fellow party members helped construct.[69]

Thus the sectional issues and compromise proposals that consumed the entire congressional session became the only available platform for Pennsylvania Whigs, yet on those issues they were divided. Johnston, his allies, and the Clayton Whigs from Philadelphia supported the Taylor plan and opposed further concessions to Southerners. Cooper's allies and the disgruntled regulars who idolized Clay promoted compromise proposals from early on, even to the extent of joining Democrats in mass Union meetings. Whig congressmen elected in 1848 before Johnston took office did not necessarily belong to either faction. Pennsylvania Whigs who voted for prosouthern bills in the House were friendly to Cooper and Clay, but all of those who voted against them were not Cooper's enemies or Johnston's allies. Rather, they voted their consciences or on what they believed was Whig sentiment in their districts.

Whig foes of compromise heavily outnumbered its Whig proponents in Pennsylvania. At the June state convention, prior to Taylor's death, Johnston's forces crushed the attempt by Cooper/Clay Whigs to endorse Clay's omnibus in the state platform. Instead, they demanded California's untrammeled admission as a free state. Even Fillmore's elevation to the presidency and his tilt toward compromise failed appreciably to reverse the imbalance of forces. In July and August, observers reported that outside of Philadelphia, at least three-fourths of the state's Whigs continued to favor Taylor's plan and to execrate compromise; even a few Philadelphia Whigs vilified Cooper for "prostrating himself to the dark spirit of slavery."[70]

The adamant hostility to compromise expressed by the Pennsylvania Whigs' state platform, their press, and most of their congressmen who voted contrasted dramatically with the Democrats' record. With the possible exception of Iowa, no free state's Democrats advocated appeasement of southern demands so unabashedly as Pennsylvania's. The Democrats' state platform in June explicitly demanded "compromise of the existing controversy" and the establishment of formal territorial governments in Utah and New Mexico on the basis of popular sovereignty. Daniel Sturgeon worked unceasingly for compromise in the Senate, and the eight Pennsylvania Democrats in the House voted for compromise as consistently as humanly possible. Six of the eight, indeed, cast affirmative votes for the Fugitive Slave Law. During the spring, moreover, Democratic state legislators pushed for repeal of an 1847 state law that forbade incarceration of suspected fugitive slaves in the state's jails, and only Whig control of the senate stopped them.[71]

On the record, in sum, the differences between Pennsylvania's Whigs and Democrats over conciliating the South were crystal clear. Thus its October elections offered a far better chance for a partisan referendum on that issue than did those in Iowa, Ohio, or Connecticut. That promise, however, was not realized. The refusal of the Cooper/Clay Whigs to adhere to the state platform and the defection of some Whig papers from the anti-Compromise camp presented Whig voters with a discordant cacophony, not a clear call to action. Whatever the partisan polarization in the legislature and Congress, moreover, the passage of the Compromise by mid-September rendered Whigs' state platform obsolete. Concessions had been made to the South in the Mexican Cession and on fugitive slaves; the new Whig national administration and the most prominent Pennsylvania Whig in Washington endorsed them. Even denunciations of Cooper could not reverse those cold facts.

Opposition to pending measures in Congress was one thing; a refusal to recognize the legitimacy of laws on the statute books was another. Although public opinion is impossible to gauge at this distance, most Pennsylvanians, including many Whigs, apparently regarded the settlement of the seemingly interminable sectional debate, no matter what its concessions to the South, with relief and were prepared to acquiesce in it.[72] The Whig state committee's September address to the electorate outlining the issues in the impending elections, in sharp contrast to June's platform, said nothing whatsoever about the Mexican Cession or the Compromise. In effect, that silence invited Whigs in individual congressional districts to take whatever stand they wished on the Compromise. Clearly, however, many Whig leaders believed that taking any position at all would be beating a dead horse.[73]

Even without detailed analysis of the Compromise's impact on Whig contests for nomination and the subsequent elections in all twenty-four congressional districts, certain generalizations are possible. First, Fillmore's administration rarely, if ever, intervened to help pro-Compromise Whigs or to defeat their rivals. Just as it provided no aid to Cooper by removing Taylor's appointees, it did not shift printing contracts to pro-Compromise Whig papers until after the elections were over. Six of the eight anti-Compromise Whig congressmen won renomination, and the other two did not seek it. Second, as Cooper bitterly complained, in contrast to Fillmore's hands-off approach, Johnston apparently tried to punish pro-Compromise Whigs. None of the three pro-Compromise Whig congressmen was renominated, but Chester Butler, who died five days after the congressional session closed, was replaced as the Whig nominee by Henry Fuller, Cooper's closest ally in the state.[74] Third, Whig congressional candidates' ability to take any position they wished on the Compromise did not guarantee that they could draw an advantageous contrast with Democrats. In Pittsburgh and surrounding Allegheny County, for example, where antislavery sentiment was strong and outrage at the Fugitive Slave Act universal, both Whig and Democratic candidates pledged to work for its immediate repeal if elected. Conversely, even where Whigs ran anti-Compromise incumbents, it is not clear that those men emphasized their opposition or criticized Democratic support for the measures during the campaign. Some, like Thaddeus Stevens of Lancaster County, surely did, but others, like Andrew Jackson Ogle, just as certainly did not.[75]

In many districts, in short, differences between the parties became blurred, and Whigs had to rely on the residual loyalty of their voters or the popularity of individual candidates. In most places, that was not enough. As in other northern states, Pennsylvania's turnout rate plummeted in 1850, even below that in the off-year state elections of 1849.[76] Whigs suffered disproportionately from this voter apathy. The total statewide Whig vote dropped by 26,700 (17.1 percent) between the congressional elections of 1848 and 1850 compared to a Democratic decline of 14,320 (9 percent), and Whigs carried only nine districts compared to fourteen in 1848. Whigs, in fact, lost six districts they had won in 1848, and three losers were anti-Compromise incumbents, while they carried one Democratic district only because multiple Democratic candidacies allowed a Whig to win with 42 percent and a considerably smaller absolute vote than his defeated predecessor had amassed in 1848. The inability of Whigs to mobilize their supporters also left the legislature securely in Democratic hands, and in 1851 it replaced Sturgeon with another Democrat, Richard Brodhead.

Many former Whig voters evidently refused to support Whig candidates whose stand on the Compromise they disliked. In the Lancaster County district, where observers reported a significant Clay following during the congressional session, for example, the vote for the vehemently antislavery, anti-Compromise Whig incumbent, Thaddeus Stevens, fell by 3,864 (40.4 percent) between 1848 and 1850, even though Stevens still won. Similarly, the Whig candidate substituted for Charles Pitman in Cooper's home district garnered over 3,000 (30.9 percent) fewer votes than the popular Pitman had in 1848. Two of the defeated anti-Compromise

Whig incumbents, John Freedley and Jesse Dickey, represented districts near Philadelphia where pro-Compromise sentiment was strong. Both suffered declines of over 20 percent in their vote between 1848 and 1850, again suggesting that pro-Compromise Whigs refused to reelect opponents of the settlement.

The failure of more incumbents either to seek or to win renomination probably hurt Whigs even more. With two marked exceptions, the incumbent Stevens and Henry Fuller, Chester Butler's successor, incumbent candidates generally retained a larger proportion of the previous Whig vote than did new men who replaced the victorious Whig candidates of 1848.[77] This pattern suggests that Whigs depended heavily on the skill and popularity of individual candidates to bring out voters and that in some districts the pool of talented leaders was dangerously shallow. In Pittsburgh, which had experienced numerous strikes by disgruntled workers, for example, Whigs foolishly replaced the disgusted Moses Hampton with Thomas M. Howe, a wealthy banker and Episcopalian vestryman, who perfectly fit the silk-stocking, smugly self-righteous image that Democrats loved to paint of Whigs. Howe's vote was almost 30 percent smaller than Hampton's in the entire county and a stunning 45 percent lower in Pittsburgh, where he was best known.[78]

No case better illustrates the dependence of Whigs on capable leadership, however, than what happened in Samuel Calvin's district, which also illuminates how the jealousies endemic to the typical multicounty rural districts of the nineteenth century produced shortsighted decisions. Running west of the Susquehanna River opposite Harrisburg in central Pennsylvania, the district consisted of five counties. Blair and Huntington, the two most populous ones, normally returned Whig majorities; Democrats usually carried Centre, Mifflin, and Juniata by equally steady but smaller margins. The result was a closely balanced congressional district where Whigs needed to mobilize their full vote to win.[79]

A resident of Hollidaysburg in Blair County, Calvin had carried the district in 1846 and again in 1848. He was lionized by his Whig constituents because of his eloquent protariff speeches on the House floor and his implacable opposition to prosouthern concessions in 1850. Thus they were stunned when Calvin announced in late July that he would not run again. Calvin's decision is understandable. He disagreed with the new Fillmore administration on the Compromise. He had been able to accomplish nothing for his constituents on the tariff. And he was suffering through the longest congressional session in history in the suffocating heat and humidity of Washington. News that a few disgruntled Whigs outside Blair County were grumping that Calvin should step aside for a new man was the final straw. Nonetheless, most Whigs in the district begged Calvin to reconsider. They knew that the party needed an experienced champion to win and that Calvin's withdrawal ensured a debilitating scramble for the nomination as each county in the district plumped a favorite son.[80]

When Calvin refused to reconsider his decision, Whigs from Huntington County insisted that they deserved the nomination, especially since a Blair Whig was the nominee for state senator. Calvin's correspondents argued that, aside from Calvin himself, the strongest Whig contender would have been Andrew Curtin, later Republican governor during the Civil War. But Curtin had a fatal flaw. He was ruled out—indeed, he ruled himself out—because he lived in Centre, a Democratic county. According to questionable Whig logic, the congressional nominee had to come only from one of the two Whig counties. Blair had had its chance with Calvin; now it was Huntington's turn.[81]

Thus a Huntington Whig named McCulloch received the Whig nomination for Congress, even though Whigs outside that county considered Curtin "a far abler man." McCulloch was not disliked by Whigs elsewhere in the district. He simply failed to rouse enthusiasm, and that failure proved fatal when apathy among Whigs had been noted even before Calvin withdrew. In October, McCulloch polled almost 2,000 fewer votes than Calvin had in 1848, a drop of 21 percent. Democrats carried the district, and Whigs lost another vote in the House.[82]

Many elements undoubtedly contributed to Whigs' defeat in 1850, but to the extent that Pennsylvania's congressional elections constituted a referendum on the Compromise of 1850, they indicated that most Pennsylvanians, certainly the majority of those who bothered to vote, accepted it. Only one pro-Compromise incumbent, the Native American Lewis Levin, lost, but his defeat was hardly a punishment for his voting record. Instead, rival nativists who had been excluded from federal jobs because of Levin's alliance with Customs Collector Lewis united with anti-Johnston, pro-Compromise Cooper and Clay Whigs to run a separate Whig candidate who siphoned votes from Levin. Other nativists apparently voted Democratic to bring down the domineering Levin.[83] All five Democratic incumbents easily won reelection, and Democrats retained two districts where incumbents declined to run. In contrast, three anti-Compromise Whig incumbents were defeated, and victorious incumbents saw their vote drop.

Whig defeat only exacerbated factional warfare within the party. Governor Johnston, the chief instigator of internal bloodletting, sought reelection in 1851, and his lieutenants retained federal and state jobs. After October, pro-Johnston Whig editors continued to pummel Cooper, the Compromise, Fillmore's administration for attempting to enforce it, and Whigs who joined Democrats in Union rallies. The administration could hardly suffer such impudence in silence, as it had between July and October. Thus it shifted printing contracts to pro-Compromise Whig papers.[84]

Pennsylvania's very location forced the administration to reverse its hands-off stance. Pennsylvania was the likeliest destination of fugitive slaves from Maryland and Virginia, and enforcement of the Fugitive Slave Act immediately became the acid test for southern Whigs of the administration's commitment to southern rights. Johnston's well-publicized record of hindering the pursuit of fugitives and his determination to run an antislavery campaign for reelection in 1851 infuriated Southerners and deeply embarrassed Fillmore. In 1851, unlike 1850, the administration would have to confront Pennsylvania's ambitious Whig governor.[85]

Unlike the situation in most northern states, the Democratic/Free Soil alliance continued to flourish in Massachusetts. The two partners usually ran separate candidates for Congress and governor against the Whigs, but three-way races could deny Whigs the absolute majorities necessary for election. Whigs had been deprived of two House seats in 1848 by Free Soil candidates, and outrage at the Fugitive Slave Act that Webster championed and Fillmore signed guaranteed that Free Soilers would run congressional and gubernatorial candidates to punish the Whigs in 1850.[86] If no gubernatorial candidate won a majority, the election would be thrown into the legislature, where incumbent Whig Governor George N.

Briggs had triumphed in the two previous years. For Whigs, the legislative elections of 1850 were the rub, for Democrats and Free Soilers backed common, not separate, candidates in those races. This Coalition, as it was dubbed, had made considerable gains in 1849 even before Webster's pro-Compromise course handed it a golden issue. Because of the state's peculiar system of representation, moreover, small towns that had been prohibited from sending men to the legislature in 1848 and 1849 could do so in 1850. Antislavery sentiment as well as hostility to Whiggish Boston smouldered in such towns; hence, the chances were good that the Coalition would capture control of the legislature. If so, Whigs knew well before the election, they would give the governorship to a Democrat and Webster's Senate seat, to which Winthrop had been temporarily appointed, to a Free Soiler.[87]

Anti-Compromise Whigs, a heavy majority of the party outside of Boston, wanted to meet this threat by denouncing the fugitive slave law and demanding its repeal. At most, to conciliate Webster's friends, they would ignore the Compromise and Webster's record altogether and plant themselves "upon the old Whig platform and stand as we have stood perfectly erect."[88] Webster and his vengeful Boston allies spurned that strategy, for the "old Whig platform" was openly antislavery. Webster considered the state party "sorely afflicted" with abolitionists and quasi-abolitionists, who were "*afraid* to act a manly part, lest they should lose the State Govt." and who courted antislavery voters through "wicked & abominable" attacks on the Fugitive Slave Act. Infuriated by Whig criticism of his course, solicitous of the southern Whigs' sensibilities, and indignant at the threats from Massachusetts Whigs to resist enforcement of the Fugitive Slave Law, Webster sought vindication. Although Fillmore refused to strip federal patronage from Webster's antislavery Whig foes like William Schouler, Charles Hudson, and Philip Greely, Jr., Webster and his agents nonetheless made it clear that the administration would wage war against any Whigs who continued to flay the Compromise. Webster's opponents, in turn, believed that such an about-face meant "the destruction of the Whig party."[89]

Inevitably, therefore, the two sides collided over Whigs' platform and over congressional and state legislative candidates. Both camps agreed that Briggs, who had won annually since 1843, should run again, but the platform and the address to be issued by the state convention on October 1 were another matter. When Webster urged his friend Edward Everett to go to the Worcester convention and "*nationalize* the Whig party," he wanted more than an endorsement of the national administration and acquiescence in the Compromise. He wanted an acknowledgment that the South deserved the concessions given it and that the Compromise was too essential to saving the Union to be tampered with. He wanted any hint of antisouthern or antislavery language expunged. His intemperate friends wanted still more—an expression of praise for Webster himself.[90]

Everett had no chance of winning such concessions, for Webster's foes controlled the state committee, which wrote the platform and address, and the convention itself. Everett later reported that, to preserve harmony, the documents stressed what Whigs agreed on—the need for a higher tariff and the danger of Coalition control of the state—and kept divisive matters "in the shade." Nonetheless, they hardly fulfilled Webster's hopes, and the resolutions issued later by the district conventions were even worse.[91]

Rather than portraying the laws for the Mexican Cession as a fair intersectional accord, the state platform and address presented them as northern victories over the South. California had been admitted despite the "unwarrantable resistance by a portion of the South." The Texas boundary settlement had kept New Mexico free, and Whig congressmen would make sure that "the present free territories of New Mexico and Utah" were quickly admitted as free states like California. Because of these triumphs, they gloated, "The protracted contest for an obnoxious 'equilibrium' has terminated, and the preponderance is on the side of freedom." The Slave Power that had controlled the nation's policies for so long "has now surrendered its sceptre to the advancing destinies of free States."[92]

Even the few words of praise for southern Whigs offended Webster. To balance a brief expression of confidence in Fillmore and "his distinguished cabinet" in the platform, the address lavishly praised Taylor's attempt to keep slavery out of the Cession as evidence that at least some slaveholders could be trusted by northern Whigs, an encomium that galled Webster. While the state platform closed by calling the Whig party "a National and not a local party" and praising southern Whigs "who have stood by its fortunes with as much firmness and devotion as Whigs of the North," a district convention lauded "those National Whigs of the South" who regarded slavery as "a curse."[93]

On the matter that most concerned Webster and over which Whigs were most divided, the new fugitive slave law and its enforcement, the state platform was utterly silent, while the address criticized the absence of jury trials. District conventions were less reticent. They blasted the act as "arbitrary, unjust, and cruel"; they demanded its immediate amendment or repeal; the Essex County convention even called on the state government to appoint agents to protect Massachusetts citizens against its enforcement.[94]

Grumping to Everett that "the proceedings at Worcester could have been worse," Webster was, in fact, furious. The state's Whigs, he raged to Fillmore, "act a most mean part in the courtship of abolitionism." To bring the state party in line with the administration, Webster's faction now set out to secure Whig congressional nominations for pro-Compromise men—or National Whigs, as they called themselves. In August, during special elections to fill three vacant House seats, Webster dictated his strategy for congressional races: "I much prefer to see a responsible Democrat elected to Congress than a professed Whig, tainted with any degree of Free Soil doctrines or abolitionism."[95]

The August races previewed the later struggles for the fall Whig nominations. For Winthrop's old Boston seat, Webster's friends prevailed twice by nominating pro-Compromise conservatives whom all Whigs in Boston then elected over Democratic and Free Soil opposition: first, Samuel Eliot in August, who arrived in Congress in time to vote for all the measures, including the Fugitive Slave Act, and then William Appleton, a member of the famously rich textile clan, who pledged support for the Compromise and the administration. Conversely, in both August and November, Websterites refused to vote for the Whig nominee in the Essex County district, Charles Upham, whom Webster considered an abolitionist. "If all those, who disapproved of Mr. Webster's 7th of March speech, are to be sacrificed," complained Upham after Websterite abstentions denied him the necessary majority in August, "where will the administration find support in Massachusetts?"[96]

In addition to Appleton, Webster was initially satisfied with only two other Whig nominees for the fall: George Davis, who replaced George Ashmun, Webster's chief congressional lieutenant during the 1850 session, in the sixth district, and the third district's incumbent, James Duncan, whom Webster had pressured to support at least the Texas-New Mexico bill. Almost everywhere else the Websterites were routed. Upham was nominated again for the full term in the second district. Orin Fowler, who had received both the Free Soil and Whig nominations in 1848, accepted both again in 1850. The replacements for incumbents Julius Rockwell and Joseph Grinnell, John Z. Goodrich and Zeno Scudder, were staunch antislavery, anti-Compromise men. And no Whig, regardless of his opinions, stood a chance against incumbent Free Soiler Charles Allen in the Worcester district. Webster considered all these men wild-eyed fanatics.[97]

The most closely watched and most symbolically freighted nomination fight, however, occurred in the eighth district. Its enormously popular Whig incumbent, Horace Mann, who had won over 80 percent of the vote in 1848, had not just voted against every concession to the South. He had infuriated Southerners by his repeated tirades against slavery and slaveholding as sinful. Applauding this record, the district's Free Soilers nominated Mann as their own candidate in 1850. The question was whether its Whigs would also renominate him. To do so would signal their contempt for Webster, the Fillmore administration, the South, and the Compromise.

Anti-Webster Whigs on the state committee and in Boston urged Whigs to choose Mann to keep the seat in Whig hands. The district's Websterites, insisting on a pro-Compromise administration loyalist, surprisingly secured the nomination of Samuel Walley instead. But even they justified that choice on the grounds that Walley had a better chance than Mann of securing southern Whig consent to amending the "arbitrary, unjust, and cruel" Fugitive Slave Act. And even on that platform Walley had no chance of defeating Mann, a certainty that may explain why anti-Webster Whigs allowed his nomination as a gesture toward party harmony.

Websterites enjoyed greater success in naming Whig candidates for the legislature in and outside Boston. That success spelled trouble for Winthrop, as he well knew. Though Winthrop, like his Senate colleague John Davis, supported the Texas boundary bill, he angered Webster by voting against the territorial bills and the fugitive bill. "I am literally between two fires," Winthrop explained to his Baltimore friend John Pendleton Kennedy. Although he got along with Webster himself, Webster's "peculiar friends have a basilisk eye for all who did not follow the track of his 7th of March Speech. On the other hand, the Free Soilers do not forget my old opposition to them, nor forgive my vote for the Boundary bill." Whoever won control of the legislature, in short, Winthrop knew his days in the Senate were numbered. Whigs were in such disarray because of divisions over the Fugitive Slave Act, indeed, that Winthrop doubted that "Massachusetts Whiggery will survive the shock which this and other things have given it."[98]

Winthrop's pessimism proved well founded. In the three-way gubernatorial contest, Briggs' plurality of the vote slipped below 47 percent, the worst Whig showing since 1842. Despite impressive gains, Democrats still won less than three-tenths of the total. Because Coalition candidates won decisive majorities in both legislative houses, however, the election of Democrat George S. Boutwell was assured. Culminating a surge that had been building for two years, the Coalition converted an eight-seat senate minority into a ten-seat majority and a thirty-five-seat deficit in the house into a forty-eight-seat advantage. Winthrop's fate seemed sealed.[99]

The outcome of the congressional elections was almost as bad. After 1848, Whigs held eight seats to the Free Soilers' one; the fourth district was never represented because stubborn Free Soil support for John Gorham Palfrey in repeated runoffs denied Whigs the necessary majority. In November 1850, only five Whigs triumphed—Appleton, Davis, Duncan, Fowler, and Scudder. Mann crushed Walley, who garnered less than a third of the vote, while the hapless Whig Ira Barton ran even more poorly against the victorious Free Soiler Allen. Three races yielded no winner in November, but in special runoff elections the following May those districts chose representatives. Democrat Robert Rantoul, Jr., defeated Upham in the second district, in part because Webster Whigs abstained. In the seventh district, Goodrich, who openly scorned Webster, prevailed, and in the long-unrepresented fourth district the Whig Benjamin Thompson, whom Websterites considered tolerable if undistinguished, finally secured the necessary majority to defeat the persistent Palfrey. When the smoke had settled, in sum, Whigs held seven of ten, not eight of nine, seats, their House delegation would be sharply split between Webster and anti-Webster men, and the majority of the entire Massachusetts delegation execrated the Fugitive Slave Act.[100]

Bay State Whigs did not wait until May to blame each other for their losses. Upham castigated Webster for exercising "a fatal influence" in New England because he whored after southern support for the presidency, while Schouler's Boston *Atlas* faulted Whigs for alienating antislavery voters by failing to attack the Compromise and Fillmore's administration vigorously enough. In contrast, pro-Webster sheets like the Boston *Advertiser* attributed the setback to Whigs' refusal to embrace the Compromise and the administration more enthusiastically. Snorting that the election was "all bad," Webster himself ascribed the result to Whig opposition "to the peace measures of the last session." Again he called on fellow cabinet members like Corwin to strip the *Atlas* of federal printing contracts, and again he urged Fillmore to sack Greely and Hudson. Equally significant, the furious Webster, who had returned to Massachusetts, vowed personally to oversee enforcement of the Fugitive Slave Act to prove to the South that northern members of the administration would do their duty. As elsewhere, in sum, electoral defeat only exacerbated intraparty animosity. In terms of rancor, depth of penetration into the cadre of local party leaders, and damage inflicted on Whigs' electoral fortunes, however, divisions among Massachusetts' Whigs paled next to those in New York.[101]

VIII

At 5:18 P.M. on September 27, a Fillmorite frantically telegraphed the president from Syracuse, site of New York's Whig state convention: "Affairs at a crisis. Convention split open. Granger and your friends gone to another house."[102] This unprecedented rupture destroyed efforts to hold New York's Whigs together that had begun as soon as Taylor died. Negotiated by intermediaries between Thurlow

Weed and Fillmore like Comptroller Washington Hunt and Governor Hamilton Fish, that truce rested on a mutually agreed-upon formula to deal with political reality.[103]

Level-headed leaders from both Whig factions recognized how much rode on the 1850 elections. They also saw clearly that, in the words of one Fillmore advisor, "we shall need all our strength" to have a chance in November because Barnburner and Hunker Democrats had reunited behind a pro-Compromise platform and gubernatorial candidate Horatio Seymour.[104] The importance of the 1850 elections for New York's Whigs cannot be exaggerated. Barnburner defections to Free Soil candidates in 1848 had allowed Whigs to win an astounding thirty-two of New York's thirty-four House seats, and retaining as many of them as possible was a top priority. The legislature to be elected in 1850 could also replace Daniel S. Dickinson in the Senate; to do so, Whigs had to reverse the slide they had suffered in 1849. Important state administrative positions were also at stake. Although Democrats had captured four statewide offices a year earlier, Whigs still controlled the three most powerful ones—governor, lieutenant governor, and comptroller. The first two of these, as well as a seat on the canal commission would be filled in 1850, and if Whigs were defeated, they would lose control of the all-important canal board that annually distributed contracts for repairs that lubricated the Whig machine along the entire length of the Erie Canal.

With so much at risk, Weed, Fillmore, and their saner allies implicitly agreed to mobilize full party strength. Having insulted Fillmore in July, Weed quickly abandoned any thought of packing the state ticket with Sewardites, causing the Albany patrician Daniel D. Barnard to crow a week before the convention that "the [Albany *Evening*] Journal of last evening shows signs of cowering." Fillmore, for his part, followed Alex Mann's advice to conciliate anti-Compromise Whigs in order to win the elections. After replacing Levi Allen with William Kethcum in the Buffalo customs house, he steadfastly resisted demands to decapitate additional Sewardites like Palmer V. Kellogg, Thomas Clowes, and Lewis Benedict.[105]

The linchpin of this tenuous rapprochement was agreement that Washington Hunt should run for governor. Having worked with Hunt in Albany, Weed believed he held him in his pocket. Conservatives were equally confident that he was a loyal Fillmore man. *"He is your friend,* no matter what may be said to the contrary,"* wrote one from New York City. Fillmore congratulated Hunt on his impending nomination weeks before the convention met, and he carefully heeded Hunt's warning not to sack any more Sewardites.[106]

Aside from his understandable determination to secure Buffalo's congressional nomination for his law partner Solomon G. Haven, Fillmore's commitment to party unity behind the state ticket was sincere. Four days prior to the state convention he informed Daniel Ullmann, a New York City delegate and an ardent Clay man, that Ullmann must not offend anti-Compromise Whigs at Syracuse. "They are good men and we want them all."[107] Yet Fillmore's willingness to make peace with Sewardites had limits. He would brook no attack on the Compromise or on his congressional Whig allies who had supported it. Samuel P. Lyman explained this quid pro quo to Weed after a conversation with an administration insider. To preserve party unity, Fillmore was willing to let "by gones . . . be by gones" with respect to patronage, but he would not tolerate a platform that offended southern Whigs. Fillmore condemned "any [such] measure" as indicating a "willingness to sacrifice the Whig party of the Union for the sake of a temporary triumph in the State of New York."[108]

Fillmore's conservative Whig allies from the Hudson Valley were even more adamant about the platform. Since 1847 they had complained that Seward's speeches, the state platforms Weed had dictated, the legislative resolutions of 1849, and the galling Geddes resolutions of 1850 all proved that Weed and Seward were intent on "abolitionizing" the Whig party to court first Liberty and then Free Soil voters. Convinced that this Sewardite tack would have disastrous consequences for the national Whig party and the Union itself, conservatives saw Fillmore's pro-Compromise stance as both correct in principle and splendidly useful for dethroning Weed and capturing control of the state organization. They could now make the case to rank-and-file Whigs that the Union's safety required repudiation of Seward's "Higher Law" stance and endorsement of the Compromise. Conservative Whigs across the state, Barnard told Fillmore, were determined "that the Convention *shall do right.*"[109]

A pro-Compromise platform was precisely what Weed and his subalterns across New York would not accept, for they genuinely hated slavery and the possibility that it might spread westward. In part, nonetheless, this refusal *did* reflect expedient calculations about what was necessary to win. To them victory in New York *was* more important than the feelings of southern Whigs or of the administration. Both before and after the state convention, correspondents urgently warned Weed that Whigs could mobilize their supporters only by renouncing the Compromise and vigorously attacking the Fugitive Slave Law. Moreover, they *did* hope to attract the remaining Free Soilers, whom Barnburners had abandoned to return to the Democrats. As one of these indignant survivors wrote Weed six days before the convention, "Can't you give us a plank from the Buffalo [Free Soil] platform in your resolutions at Syracuse on the 26th, & put one of the old Whig Liberty men on for one of the minor offices?" If Whigs did so, "we will float 15,000 strong to the Whig ship . . . & you know very well to which wing of the Whig party the new accession would be attached." Weed could hardly ignore so tempting a prospect.[110]

Deep-seated principle, however, primarily motivated Sewardite foot soldiers who attended local meetings and went to Syracuse as delegates. Such men, Hunt admitted to Fillmore, "consider the gratification of their particular views more important than the success of the party and the administration which embodies its principles." Hunt was only half right. To such men, Fillmore's administration emphatically did not represent the principles of New York's Whig party. Those principles had repeatedly been spelled out since 1846 in local resolutions and state platforms, in speeches on the hustings, and in legislative resolutions of instruction to the state's congressional delegation—adamant opposition to slavery and its spread west of the Nueces River. Far from embodying those principles, Fillmore and House Whigs who had supported or abstained on the Texas-New Mexico bill, the Utah bill, and the Fugitive Slave Act had betrayed them. Traitors deserved repudiation, not endorsement.[111]

This principled dispute between conservatives and Sewardites over the Compromise's propriety, as well as the sheer number of offices at stake, guaranteed ferocious factional struggles over legislative and congressional nominations, no matter what agreements had been reached on the state ticket. New York's Whig congressmen had divided almost down the middle on the crucial resolution of the Texas boundary dispute. Seward had opposed the Texas bill in the Senate; on the House's Texas-New Mexico bill, New York's huge Whig delegation had divided thirteen for and sixteen against, with three abstentions. Scorning support of this bill as a betrayal of Whig principles, Sewardites sought to block renomination of Fillmorites like David A. Bokee, James Brooks, J. Phillips Phoenix, Walter Underhill, Robert Rose, and William Duer, the last of whom announced his refusal to seek renomination even before the congressional session closed. Simultaneously, Fillmorites forced Spaulding out of the race for the Buffalo nomination; pressured Abraham Schermerhorn of Rochester to support the Texas-New Mexico bill to secure renomination, a capitulation that infuriated Sewardites in Monroe County; and vigorously challenged Orsamus B. Matteson and other anti-Compromise incumbents. Meanwhile, the two New York City freebooters—Subtreasurer John Young and his toady, Customs Collector Hugh Maxwell, over whom Fillmore exercised no control—sought to nominate conservatives for the legislature in New York and to commit the Syracuse platform to the Compromise.[112]

Struggles over congressional and legislative nominations did not necessarily ensure a breakup at the state convention. Combatants on both sides, in fact, expected that successful nominees, no matter what their faction, would get the support of all rank-and-file Whigs if the party could maintain a semblance of unity. They wanted to control, not disrupt, local organizations. The threat to harmony at Syracuse came from elsewhere. Local politicos in Weed's faction planned to endorse Seward's course in the Senate as faithfully expressing New York Whigs' principles. By implication, such a move would condemn Fillmore and pro-Compromise Whig congressmen. Neither Weed nor Seward orchestrated this spontaneous effort, but both realized that it could disrupt the convention.[113]

Informed of the plan by Ullmann, Fillmore responded, "I should regret to see any controversy in the convention about the relative merits of our Whig Senator and myself." Because he considered himself "at the end of my political race," he cared nothing about a personal endorsement in the platform. "But not so, with those gallant men who have stood by me, and by the country in the darkest hour of its peril. . . . Pray do not let them be sacrificed." To avert the implied condemnation of his friends, Fillmore sent William Duer to Syracuse as a delegate from Oswego County, even though Congress had not yet adjourned. With him Duer carried the platform Fillmore wanted, a platform Hunt assented to before the convention opened.[114]

Leaders from both factions descended on Syracuse to marshal their respective delegates. Weed set up shop in a hotel room. He was aided by federal officeholders like Kellogg, Clowes, Benedict, and Syracuse's own postmaster. Horace Greeley, who had once favored the Compromise but now deprecated its abandonment of free-soil principles, roamed the convention floor. To aid Duer, Young and Maxwell came up from New York City; they were joined by other Fillmorites: Alex Mann of Rochester, James Kidd and Jerome Fuller of Albany, and A. K. Hadley of Troy. All had previously determined that if Sewardites made "mischief," they "shall be defied, & the proper remedy resorted to."[115]

On September 26 the hopelessness of preserving harmony immediately became apparent.[116] The two sides squabbled over the preliminary organization and even over the hour to start the convention. Though Weed's forces had a clear majority, they acquiesced in Francis Granger's selection as permanent chairman, just as Fillmore's friends hoped. After deploring the party's divisions and begging for reconciliation, Granger appointed an evenly balanced platform committee that included Duer and John T. Bush from the Fillmore camp and Andrew Bray Dickson from Weed's. After deadlocking for hours over Duer's demand to present the platform he had brought with him, one Sewardite relented, and Duer read it to the delegates that night. The convention then recessed until the following morning without taking any action on the platform or nominations.

The salient planks of Duer's platform, which he insisted was dictated by Fillmore, praised Fillmore's virtues and declared that New York's Whigs had "the utmost confidence in his administration of the government and his maintenance of the well-known principles of the Whig party." They iterated New York Whigs' adamant opposition to slavery extension and their belief that Congress had a right to prohibit it. Nonetheless, they "acquiesce[d]" in the Texas-New Mexico boundary bill and the creation of territorial governments for New Mexico and Utah "in the confident belief that those acts of conciliation will result in the exclusion of slavery" and "restore cordial sentiments and fraternal ties" between the sections. Finally, they admitted that the state's "Whig Senator and Representatives" had adopted "differing and antagonistic views" on the Compromise measures, but praised "the honest purposes and patriotic motives" of both sides and their toleration for each other. About the explosive Fugitive Slave Law, the platform was silent.

In sum, Fillmore's support for compromise was said to represent Whig principles, Seward was not named, prosouthern concessions were accepted without protest, and votes for and against them deserved equal respect. Sewardites could not stomach that litany. With undoubted input from Weed and Greeley, during the night's recess they drafted alternative resolutions and plotted procedural strategy.

At the start of the next morning's session William Cornwell, a Sewardite from Cayuga County, immediately moved to nominate the ticket before debating the platform. Despite vigorous objections from Duer and Bush, the motion carried by a voice vote. Duer, Bush, and nineteen other Fillmore men then announced that they refused to participate in nominating candidates because the platform had not yet been debated, let alone adopted. The majority brushed aside their complaints and proceeded to select the ticket. Hunt easily won the gubernatorial slot with eighty-seven of eighty-nine votes cast. For lieutenant governor the convention chose the eminently conservative George J. Cornell of New York City rather than Fillmorites' favorite, Hadley of Troy. Not closely affiliated with Webster or Clay Whigs in New York City, Cornell, like his good friend Hamilton Fish, stood independent of all factions. Ebeneazer Beach, another neutral, was nominated for canal commissioner.[117]

As soon as the ticket was completed, again before a single word had been uttered in defense of Duer's platform, Cornwell proposed a substitute set of resolutions. He accepted six of Duer's planks word for word and other language that was noncontroversial, but he zeroed in on the points of disagreement. Cornwell's revisions contained a resolution dealing exclusively with the state's House delegation. It expressed confidence in their motives but omitted any reference to their disagreements or their mutual tolerance of them. Like Duer, he praised the admission of California, but he intransigently rejected acquiescence in the territorial bills. Pointedly emphasizing the omission of the Wilmot Proviso from them "on the assumption that Slavery is excluded by other causes," Cornwell's plank proclaimed "the solemn duty of Congress" to impose the Proviso on those territories at "the first indication" that slavery would be introduced into them. (Like Duer, significantly, Cornwell omitted any reference to the new Fugitive Slave Law.) Whereas Duer offered separate resolutions praising the deceased Taylor and lauding Fillmore, Cornwell combined references to the two men in a single plank. By citing the "clear judgment and Roman firmness" Taylor had displayed "at a crisis in our country's history," Cornwell, in contrast to Duer, alluded to Taylor's opposition to Congress's compromise. The remainder heralded Fillmore's "experience, fidelity, and enlightened statesmanship." The omission from this plank leaped out at the delegates. Praise for Fillmore's "maintenance" of Whig principles had been jettisoned.

The bombshell came with the plank that immediately followed the reference to Fillmore. In an obvious attempt to highlight the contrast, it read:

> Our thanks are especially due to the Hon. William H. Seward for the signal ability with which he has sustained in the United States Senate, those beloved principles of public policy so long cherished by the Whigs of the Empire State, expressed in State and County conventions, as well as on the votes and instructions in our State Legislature. . . .

This was not exactly an endorsement of the "Higher Law" speech, but the message was loud and clear. Seward in opposing concessions to the South, not Fillmore and his congressional Whig allies who supported them, represented New York's Whigs.

Pandemonium erupted once Cornwell finished reading his resolutions. Their adoption, warned Duer, meant disruption of the Whig party. At Duer's request, Cornwell's substitute platform was returned to the platform committee, which was doubled in size to include Cornwell as well as staunch Fillmore men like Ullmann and James R. Thompson of Rochester. Attempts at compromise failed. The committee deadlocked 8–8 over the rival platforms, and the decision went to the convention floor. Duer demanded an up-or-down vote on Cornwell's substitute, again warning that adoption would rupture the party. Unfazed, Weed's forces carried it, 75–42. Duer then demanded separate roll calls on the individual planks. When the resolution praising Seward passed 76–40, Duer and his thirty-nine supporters began to march ostentatiously out of the hall. Granger, who remained in the chair and who had presided with scrupulous fairness, then gave a short speech calling this the saddest day of his political career, relinquished his gavel, and followed Duer and his colleagues out the door. Granger, in short, did not lead the exodus, but forever afterward the bolters and other Fillmore men would be called Silver Grays in reference to Granger's hair. The remaining delegates, some stunned, others taunting the defeated minority, then named a new state committee dominated by Weed's cronies and adjourned. They did not even bother to name a committee to officially extend nominations to the party's ticket.

The bolters reassembled in another building that night and named Granger as their chairman. The following morning they called for a new state convention to be held at Utica on October 17 and issued an address defending their action. The Whig party in the nation's largest state lay in shambles.

Recriminations flew immediately. The bolters' address laid down a line that would be echoed privately and publicly by Silver Grays up to and beyond the November election. Sewardites had caused the split because they wantonly insisted upon a plank that they knew was offensive to Fillmore and would cause a rupture. Weed's minions wanted "to convert the Whig party of this State into an abolition party, or rather to destroy the Whig party, and build up an abolition party on its ruin." Sewardites intended to reagitate the slavery question by renewing efforts to impose the Proviso on the territories. Silver Grays stood by the Compromise and rejected "all attempts to disturb it."[118]

To the contrary, retorted Weed, Silver Grays were engaged in an "insane and incendiary attempt to distract and divide the Whig Party of the Empire State." Hypocritically ignoring the presence of Sewardite patronage holders from across the state at Syracuse, he criticized Young, Maxwell, and Duer for abandoning their official duties in New York and Washington to come to Syracuse to orchestrate a rupture they had planned in advance. "We stand firmly on the Whig platform of 1848," he intoned. Fillmore and Duer had once pledged themselves to uphold its principles. "The Whig party must stand where it stood in past conflicts and triumphs. Any departure, by the Convention, from cardinal principles—any faltering in the path of duty—any Compromise of the cause of Freedom, would have left the Whig party defenceless and naked." Thus Duer, who acted as Fillmore's agent, caused the split. Fillmore ruptured the party because he jealously would not tolerate approval of Seward's course against him. "The Whig party [was] broken and shivered by one whom it has elevated to the highest office in the Republic!"[119]

Pragmatic leaders from both camps understood that restoring party unity before November was essential, but they disagreed about how to repair the breach. Weed, underestimating the anger of many Silver Grays, expected the bolt to fizzle for lack of popular support, forcing the bolters to back the ticket. Neither he nor his allies, therefore, saw any need for concessions. Some Sewardites, in fact, worried mainly that, to appease conservatives, the convention had foolishly omitted any condemnation of the Fugitive Slave Act and that some Fillmorites' support for Hunt's nomination would arouse suspicion of him among antislavery Whigs. To mobilize those voters, they warned, Hunt must publicly denounce the fugitive law, an action that would only further antagonize Silver Grays.[120]

Conservatives' reactions varied. Those with Whig nominations like Solomon Haven sought reconciliation in order to bring out a full Whig vote. Washington Hunt and George Cornell were especially frantic. Both, Cornell wrote Fillmore, liked Duer's platform and were prepared to acquiesce in any resolutions adopted at Utica, but they were terrified that Silver Grays would press them to renounce the Syracuse platform publicly. Such a repudiation would turn Sewardites against them and Silver Gray congressional candidates, thus dooming them all to defeat. Hence, continued Cornell, the two had agreed that Hunt should simply announce his acceptance of the nomination, which appeared in Weed's paper on October 2, without any reference to the platform.[121]

Fillmore sympathized with the bolters, and on September 30 he withdrew Lewis Benedict's nomination as Albany's postmaster to indicate his displeasure with Weed. But, Fillmore told Ullmann, he would remove no one else until he saw what Weed did. "I am very anxious to save the Whig party of N.Y. entire if I can." Other conservatives, in contrast, were ready to sacrifice the party to ruin Sewardites. Nathan Hall suggested that Silver Grays simply sit out the state election, throw the state administration to Democrats, and thereby strip Weed of state patronage. "A masterly inactivity will I think be the most wise when we get to the polls." Hotheads like Young, Maxwell, and C. B. Stuart wanted all-out war. Such men not only demanded that Fillmore sweep all Sewardites, not just Benedict, out of federal offices. They wanted a new ticket nominated at Utica to "draw out a *full* vote of the *National* Whigs." It was "better to have a *minority* standing upon the *National* Platform *which is right* than a *majority* vote for the *Ticket* with a Platform that is *undefined* or *totally wrong.*"[122]

This suicidal strategy appalled the vote-seeking Haven. The Utica convention should never have been called; the bolters should simply have protested against the platform and endorsed the ticket. It was foolish to make war on the Weed wing "when they control the power & patronage of this State, controlled its stocks, its banks, & its immense Canal revenues—had all the party organization of the State, and the active politicians in it." Had Fillmore replaced federal appointees with his own men earlier, they would have had the resources to battle for the party's machinery. As it was, "It is impossible for the staid sober men of the State, who attend to their own business, to prevent such active[,] wellfed[,] and reckless *'sons of bitches'* from controlling to some extent our nominating conventions."[123]

Fillmore agreed with Haven. "I think it madness at this late hour to nominate another ticket," he told Granger. "We have no time—no organization." The Utica convention should therefore readopt Duer's platform and endorse the Syracuse ticket. Hunt and Cornell should not be required publicly to accept that platform, reject the Syracuse platform, or even acknowledge the Utica nomination. "In this way the ticket may be elected, or at all events, we shall save many members of Congress, sheriffs, clerks, assemblymen, etc. etc. which we cannot afford to lose."[124]

Conservatives in New York City, particularly wealthy merchants on whom Whigs depended for campaign contributions, however, flatly refused to tolerate a "stealth candidate." They would not support Hunt without knowing where he stood on the Compromise. Private assurances were not enough. Hunt would have to endorse the Duer platform publicly, they threatened, or they would vote Democratic. To appease these intransigents, it was arranged that Hunt would write a public letter to Granger approving the Duer platform in advance of the Utica convention. The convention then would readopt that platform, reiterate the Silver Grays' reasons for bolting the Syracuse convention, and endorse the Syracuse ticket. Diehards who wanted a new ticket insisted on one additional condition— the appointment at Utica of a rival state Whig committee "composed exclusively of Union Whigs!" They would grudgingly support Hunt, but they were determined to demonstrate publicly their continued independence of Weed.[125]

This carefully planned scenario was followed to the letter, although Fillmore was so nervous that hotheads still might go too far at Utica that he sent his personal secretary, Robert Campbell, from Washington to oversee the meeting. Dated October 11 and printed in Whig papers, Hunt's letter to Granger admitted that he had approved of Duer's platform before the Syracuse convention, deplored the party's divisions, and lauded both anti- and pro-Compromise Whig congressmen for their rectitude and patriotism. Even though he personally disliked the Texas boundary agreement and the territorial bills, Hunt said, "we must acquiesce in the constitutional action of Congress." Hunt did not fully support the Compromise, however. Obviously informed by Weed about the restlessness of rank-and-file Sewardites, he also declared, "I deplore the passage of the Fugitive Slave Law, in its present form. . . . It could not have been well considered and needs essential modifications."[126]

Delighted by the success of their plans for Utica, Fillmore's closest Silver Gray allies accepted this statement. Even Weed's taunts that Silver Grays were "Leaders without Followers—Officers without Troops" did not dint their confidence that the party had reunited sufficiently to carry the elections and that Silver Grays had remained faithful to conservative principles by issuing their own platform and creating their own state committee. From their point of view, indeed, it was the Sewardites who were crawling in repentance, not National Whigs.[127]

Unity, however, remained elusive. Rumors abounded that Sewardites planned to knife Silver Gray congressional nominees in some districts, while Silver Grays would cut Sewardites in others. Lewis Benedict, the Weed man sacked from the Albany postmastership, traveled to Rochester and Buffalo and openly opposed the election of Schermerhorn and Haven. In the latter district a local Sewardite named Seth Hawley repeatedly challenged Haven at his speaking engagements, charging that Haven and Fillmore had betrayed Whig principles by endorsing the Compromise. So rancorous and vindictive was the feuding that Hamilton Fish wrote Seward in disgust two weeks before the election, "I fear that some of our professing Whig friends are becoming tired of belonging to a party in power. Intolerance seems, in some quarters, to have destroyed reason, & personal hatred, to have become superior to party attachment." After the election, Fish admitted to Fillmore that both sides cut rivals from the tickets they cast.[128]

The multiplicity of tickets made available to the electorate, some of which were clearly intended to sabotage certain men, was an even greater problem. While George Cornell was not Silver Grays' first choice for lieutenant governor, for example, he was much friendlier with Manhattan's Silver Grays than with Weed and the Sewardite faction. Prior to the election he complained to Fish that Weed was distributing Whig tickets along the Erie Canal that excluded his name altogether. Cornell was also omitted from a separate ticket distributed by what was left of the Anti-Rent party, a ticket that included Hunt for governor and Barnburners on the Democratic ticket for other offices.[129]

The Anti-Rent ticket, as well as Hunt's denunciation of the Fugitive Slave Act, engendered a last-minute development pregnant with present and future danger to the Whigs. New York City merchants, pressured by southern customers to demonstrate their fealty to the entire Compromise, refused to support Hunt, despite his endorsement by Silver Grays at Utica, and called for a Union Safety meeting to be held at Castle Garden at the end of October. Thousands of normally Whig merchants signed the petition calling this assemblage, but its orchestrators were a small group of men who plotted to break up both parties and to form a bipartisan Union party consisting of pro-Compromise Whigs and Democrats. "They are playing the very Devil here with the Whig ticket & getting up a Union party," wrote one of Fish's correspondents. The plotters included Robert West, the editor of the ostensibly nonpartisan New York *Journal of Commerce*, who in advance of the meeting prepared a Union ticket consisting of the Democrat Horatio Seymour for governor, Cornell for lieutenant governor, and pro-Compromise Whig and Democratic congressional candidates from New York City and Brooklyn. Among his coadjutors were Democrats, who hoped to line up Whig support for Seymour in November and Dickinson in the impending senatorial election, and the schemers Young and Maxwell, who hoped a bipartisan Union coalition would increase their own chances of winning the Senate seat. Most significant, however, was Daniel Webster, who sent a letter to be read at the Castle Garden meeting praising its organizers as "abject slaves to no party" and pledging that he himself would support that party "whose principles and practice are most calculated to uphold the Constitution and to perpetuate the glorious Union."[130]

Attended by thousands, the Castle Garden meeting adopted resolutions approving the Compromise as a "fair" settlement, expressing determination to enforce the Fugitive Slave Act, renouncing allegiance to old parties, and pledging to support no candidate "at the ensuing, or any other election," for state office, the legislature, or Congress "who is known or believed to be hostile to the peace measures recently adopted by Congress, or any of them, or in favor of re-opening the questions involved in them for renewed amendment." This clause targeted Hunt, who had called for amendment of the Fugitive Slave Act, but also Fish, Weed's preferred Whig candidate for Dickinson's Senate seat, who had also denounced the fugitive measure. Upon adjournment, a Union Safety Committee appointed by the meeting then endorsed the *Journal of Commerce*'s Union ticket as the "Anti-Disunion, Anti-Abolition, Anti-Seward, Anti-Demagoguism Ticket." Fully aware of the gullibility of the Whig merchants who had attended the meeting and of the harm it could do Hunt and his own prospects for the Senate, the patrician Fish exploded: "The Castle Garden meeting was the design of knavery. It was the adulterous offspring of political trickery, perpetrating violence upon political ignorance and stupidity. The trickster of the Journal of Commerce determined to set a trap for the benefit of Dickinson and Seymour; so he baited it with the word 'Union'' & drove the game toward it."[131]

Though dismal, the election's results were not so bad as many Whigs had feared. Hunt squeaked by Seymour in the gubernatorial election with a plurality of fewer than 300 votes out of over 229,000 cast. Only Hunt's presence on the Anti-Rent ticket produced this small margin, for conservatives in several upstate districts cut him and in New York City he ran 3,500 votes behind Cornell, who was on the Union ticket. Hunt drew about 3,500 fewer votes than Fish had won in 1848 and almost 17,000 fewer than Fillmore had garnered in his losing run for governor in 1844. If some conservatives refused to support Hunt, so did the remaining Free Soilers. Because Hunt had endorsed the Duer platform, they scattered their votes or stayed home. Altogether, the gubernatorial turnout dropped 23,672 votes between 1848 and 1850, while the proportion of potential voters who came to the polls was the lowest of any gubernatorial election since the 1830s. Hunt's undistinguished performance was, nevertheless, the best by any statewide Whig candidate. Cornell and Beach were abandoned by upstate Sewardites; Democrats captured both the lieutenant governorship and the canal commission post. Only Hunt's narrow victory denied them control of the canal board.[132]

The backstabbing of Whig candidates on the state ticket was so selective from county to county that Whigs managed to regain control of the state legislature. They retained their two-seat margin in the senate and converted a two-seat Democratic majority in the assembly into a thirty-eight-seat Whig margin. Dickinson's days in the Senate were apparently numbered, but who the Whigs might put in his place remained in doubt, especially as the senate, which voted in separate session for United States senators, was so closely divided and would be the center of Silver Gray strength in Albany.

In contrast, the congressional races were a flat-out disaster. Whigs lost fifteen seats to Democrats, so that the delegation was evenly divided seventeen to seventeen, not tilted thirty-two to two in the Whigs' favor. Democratic reunification was the primary cause of this reversal. Whigs had carried eleven of the fifteen lost districts in 1848 only by pluralities that were often quite small. Once Hunkers and Barnburners supported common candidates in 1850, therefore, Whigs suffered defeat even though they often garnered a much higher proportion of the vote than in 1848. Charles F. Clarke, a staunch Sewardite, for example, won with 39.7 percent in 1848 but lost with 48 percent in 1850; Orsamus B. Matteson, that inveterate Fillmore hater, won with 42.4 percent in 1848 and lost with 49.6 percent in 1850; John Thurman won in 1848 with 42.6 percent, while his successor as Whig nominee lost with 49.2 percent. Viewed differently, Whigs retained nine of thirteen majority Whig districts but only eight of the nineteen they had won with pluralities.

Only eleven incumbent Whig congressmen won renomination in 1850, including four of fourteen pro-Compromise incumbents and seven of eighteen anti-Compromise men. Of the former, three won reelection—James Brooks and George Briggs in New York City and Abraham Schermerhorn, who had been pressured by Rochester's Silver Grays to defect to the Fillmore camp. Other pro-Compromise men were forced off the ticket, although it is unclear how many were replaced by Sewardites. Brooklyn's David Bokee was denied renomination because Staten Island demanded his district's nomination under rotation, and the Whig who replaced him, and won, was probably pro-Compromise, as was Walter Underhill's victorious successor in New York City. While some upstate Fillmorites like Elijah Risley from Chatauqua County and Hugh White were replaced by Silver Grays, it is likely that anti-Compromise Sewardites replaced Duer, John Thurman, and George Andrews on the Whig ticket.[133]

The case of J. Phillips Phoenix, a pro-Compromise Whig incumbent whose district encompassed northern New York City and Westchester County, and one of the few Whigs to prevail with an absolute majority in 1848, illustrates both the complexity of the nomination fights and the jealous backstabbing that hindered Whig efforts. Seward's allies opposed Phoenix's renomination because of his pro-Compromise votes, but conservatives also opposed him because he was a corrupt ingrate who had won in 1848 by buying illegal votes and then refused to contribute any of his salary to the party's coffers for the 1850 campaign. When Phoenix loyalists and anti-Phoenix conservatives split at the convention, Sewardites surprisingly captured the nomination for James Bowen of Dobbs Ferry. The furious Phoenix then persuaded another Whig named Rodman to enter the race against Bowen, and Maxwell and Young exerted all their efforts to distribute Rodman rather than Bowen tickets at the polls. Bowen ran last, the total Whig vote was much smaller than in 1848, and a Democrat carried the district with a plurality in the three-way race.[134]

Only four of the seven anti-Compromise incumbents won reelection: John L. Schoolcraft, Weed's Albany lieutenant, Henry Bennett; William A. Sackett; and Lorenzo Burrows, who was rumored by Weed's agents in Washington to have sold out to Fillmore after Congress adjourned but who would have been known to his constituents by his solid record of anti-Compromise votes. The others fell victim to reconstituted Democratic majorities and sabotage from Silver Grays. Matteson, who lost by 117 votes out of 15,500 cast even though his own vote increased by 1,617 (26.5 percent) between 1848 and 1850, is a classic case. Despite his antisouthern votes, he fumed after the election, Barnburners and other Free Soilers supported his Democratic opponent. Even worse was the treachery of the Silver Grays, who cast 300 votes for the Democrat, thus costing Matteson a net 600 votes, and who, led by young Roscoe Conkling and the Utica *Gazette*, openly boasted that they had caused Matteson's defeat.[135]

Some Sewardites who replaced anti-Compromise incumbents as Whig nominees also suffered defections by disgruntled Silver Grays, but most benefited from the anti-Compromise records of their predecessors.[136] As Whig turnout rates demonstrated, indeed, how New York's Whig congressmen voted on the Compromise in September influenced the November results in their districts, whether or not the incumbents themselves ran. Opposition to the Compromise expanded the Whig vote, whereas support for it usually contracted that vote. In the fourteen districts whose Whig congressmen voted for or abstained on prosouthern concessions, Whigs lost an aggregate of 8,663 votes (9.1 percent) between 1848 and 1850, and the four pro-Compromise incumbents who ran again suffered an even larger aggregate decline of 11.9 percent. Altogether, Whigs lost votes in eleven of those fourteen districts, and of the three where they gained votes, the biggest increase came in a district where a Sewardite replaced the Silver Gray John Thurman. Conversely, Whigs gained votes in eleven of the eighteen districts represented by congressmen who opposed prosouthern concessions, and while their aggregate gain in all eighteen was only 3,050 votes (2.7 percent), in those eleven districts it was 6,223 (9.2 percent). In five of the seven anti-Compromise districts where the Whig vote fell, including two carried by incumbents John L. Schoolcraft and Henry Alexander, vengeful Silver Gray abstentions caused the decline, but the biggest losses came in districts where Sewardites refused to support Silver Grays who defeated Sewardites for Whig nominations. John A. King's successor on Long Island ran 736 votes (16.7 percent) behind King's 1848 total and lost. Haven, Fillmore's law partner, who pledged to resist any amendments to the Fugitive Slave Law, carried the Erie County district, but he ran 1,009 votes (13.2 percent) behind Spaulding's poll in 1848 and apparently carried the normally Whig district only with the aid of pro-Compromise Hunker Democrats.[137]

The experience of the Sewardite Whig who replaced William Duer in the Oswego district vividly illustrates what an incubus a predecessor's pro-Compromise record could be. Even a fresh candidate, complained one Weed man, could not overcome Duer's disgrace. At every Whig rally Democratic hecklers raised the cry that Whigs could not be trusted by antislavery voters because Duer had voted for Texas-New Mexico and Utah, because Duer had ducked the vote on the fugitive slave bill, because Fillmore had signed that hated law and demanded obedience to it, and because Duer had introduced the pro-Compromise, pro-Fillmore platform at Syracuse. Nor would antislavery Whigs support the party's legislative ticket, for Democrats charged that it was pledged to support Duer for the Senate seat. The upshot of these deadly tactics was that Free Soilers supported the Democrat, while Sewardites stayed home. "Our people were afraid that they should again be deceived," sighed one correspondent. "I found many such on election day & after pressing them to vote, they would say who can we trust, since Duer has turned traitor." Whereas Duer had won with 8,107 votes (48.2 percent), his tarnished Whig successor lost with 7,136 (45.9 percent).[138]

The disparate success rates of pro- and anti-Compromise candidates, and the evidence that both Silver Grays and Sewardites had sabotaged factional rivals, perpetuated the debilitating internal divisions that, almost everyone admitted, had nearly wrecked the party. "Our movements were impeded at every step by internal jealousies and strife," Hunt wrote Fillmore ten days after the election. "The great question for you and me and all of us is to determine whether the Whig party can be preserved." Both Hunt and Fillmore wanted to hold it together, but scores of local politicos did not. With the election's conclusion removing the need for an uneasy marriage of convenience, they preferred divorce.[139]

Convinced that Weed and Seward would never jettison their antislavery stance and that conservatives would always writhe under their tyranny inside the party, furious Silver Grays called for a parting of the ways. "The Silver Greys are boisterous—boast that the Whig party is broken up, etc.," an upstate Whig reported to Weed. Many conservatives insisted that Fillmore purge more Sewardites from federal offices, and a few were sacked by the end of the month. Without administration approval, Maxwell fired the few remaining Seward men in the customs house, and the Silver Gray congressman Brooks urged Fillmore to uphold him. "We must either break down the negro party in this city, or all be painted black—and to keep ourselves white, Maxwell must be sustained in all his removals."[140]

More ominous still, as Hamilton Fish warned Fillmore, Silver Grays were "openly advocating the Union of a portion of the Whig party with the Hunker portion of the Democratic party" in the legislature to put Duer or Dickinson in the Senate. Even before the election, Ullmann had warned Fillmore "that there can be no permanent union between the two sections [of the state Whig party]. I am also pretty certain that the Hunker and Barnburner sections of the Locofocos in this State will ultimately assimilate with their respective sections in our ranks." Any such reorganization would doom all hopes of preserving the Whig party, yet by mid-November at least some Silver Grays wanted to push it to fruition.[141]

After the election, angry Sewardites were equally prepared to let the Silver Grays go—if not go in peace. Silver Grays, they fumed, were an albatross, not an asset, during the campaign. They sabotaged Whig candidates, and their demand that Hunt embrace the Duer platform further reduced the Whig vote. "If the Silver Grays had not endorsed our Ticket, we should have done better," declared one. "Men believed that we were sold to the South, if not to be their slaves, to be their doughfaces which was worse." The Duer platform had ruined Whigs' chances, echoed another. Only continued attacks on the Fugitive Slave Act and slavery extension could save the party. As James Bowen, himself a victim of Silver Grays' treachery, assured Seward, "Without them, we shall move on a harmonious party, & gather strength in every campaign. My only fear is that timid friends will endeavor to make a hollow peace to be broken at a more critical juncture." Alvah Hunt, the new governor's brother, was blunter in a note to Weed: "Give the Traitors Hell hereafter."[142]

IX

By the end of November, in sum, Whigs were more deeply divided than at any other time in their history. The pressure to carry elections had widened, not healed, rifts over the Compromise and patronage. And the elections' results inflicted a grievous, if not yet mortal, wound on the party. Granted, aside from setbacks in Iowa and Indiana, Whigs did surprisingly well in the region where the party had always been weakest—the West. The upsets in Missouri, the comeback in Ohio's congressional elections, the creditable performance in Illinois, and the upsurge in Michigan pointed to a brighter future, and Whigs also stood on the verge of an astounding triumph in Wisconsin. Setbacks in the East and South, however, more than balanced these gains. They lost chances to replace Democratic senators in Pennsylvania and Florida. They had lost a governor and possibly a senator in Connecticut, as well as the governorship of North Carolina and Maryland. New Jersey's Democrats routed them and Delaware's gained complete control of the government, thus costing Whigs two Senate seats. Even in Kentucky and Maryland, where they retained control of state legislatures, they encountered trouble from new state constitutions, as they also would in Ohio and Indiana. Worst of all, Whigs experienced grievous congressional losses in their core New England and Middle Atlantic bastions.

Summary comparisons best reveal the damage. In 1848, Whigs won ten (71.4 percent) of the fourteen governorships contested; in 1850, they captured only three (23 percent) of thirteen. In 1848, Whigs carried eighty two (57.3 percent) of the 143 House races; in 1850, they elected only 57 (42.2 percent) of 135 congressmen chosen.[143] Theoretically, Whigs still had a chance to control the House during the Thirty-Second Congress. To do so, they would have to dominate the congressional contests scheduled for 1851. Since Whigs had won only 30 percent of the House elections in 1849, however, that possibility seemed remote.

More than past history dimmed prospects of a comeback in 1851. Most elections that year would be held in the South, and during 1850 northern Whig candidates almost everywhere denounced the Fugitive Slave Act and the territorial bills, just those features of the Compromise southern Whigs hoped to trumpet as southern victories delivered by the Whig party. Convinced that Fillmore's "Administration has driven their friends to repudiate them to save the party from utter annihilation," most northern Whigs, indeed, contemptuously scorned Fillmore's and Webster's solicitude for southern Whigs' electoral needs. By choosing instead to "make war on this administration to save the Whig party from contempt and scorn," they heedlessly threatened to make the Whig party an object of "contempt and scorn" in South.[144]

While southern Whigs enthusiastically praised the attempts of Webster and Fillmore to secure their region's rights, moreover, northern Whigs openly execrated Webster and called on "God [to] save us from Whig Vice Presidents." As the extent of northern Whigs' autumn debacle became clearer, indeed, they no longer waited for Providence to deal with Fillmore. A public dinner for Clayton in Wilmington, Delaware, a Whig meeting in Bangor, Maine, and a Sewardite editorial in a New York paper all arrived at a similar solution. They boomed General Winfield Scott for the Whigs' 1852 presidential nomination to stop Webster or Fillmore from winning the presidency in his own right. By the fall of 1850, therefore, the intraparty struggle over patronage and the Compromise became inextricably entangled with the next presidential race, still two full years away.[145]

The administration's Whig opponents had thrown down a gauntlet. Now Fillmore, Webster, and other administration supporters had to meet that challenge. In doing so, they had not only to weigh the strength of contending factions in different northern states and to balance the conflicting needs of northern and southern Whigs. They also had to respond to developments in the South and North that seemed to threaten the existence not just of the Whig party but of the nation itself.

Chapter 17

"Fillmore . . . Is Precisely the Man for the Occasion"

"MY ONLY OBJECT IS TO save the country [and] to save the Whig party, if possible," Millard Fillmore assured Hamilton Fish on November 21, 1850. Fillmore wanted no quarrel with angry northern Whigs who vilified him. He shared their hatred of slavery. He understood their outrage at the Fugitive Slave Act, but, he explained, Whig principles regarding the veto required him to sign that deeply flawed law. Most important, because he owed his present position to his beloved Whig party and had no interest in its 1852 nomination, "I should regard any attempt on my part to divide the Whig party as suicidal."[1]

Yet Fillmore's commitment to party reunification clearly had limits. Saving the country, not the Whigs, was his top priority. Northern Whigs, he believed, focused too selfishly on their own resentments and electoral fortunes. They did "not fully appreciate the dangers to which we are exposed from the South, and the infinite importance of setting an example of maintaining the Constitution in all its parts." The fugitive slave law "must be executed" and "sustained against attempts at repeal." Henceforth, he would therefore regard as good Whigs all who "sustain me in sustaining the laws." Whigs who opposed that effort were enemies of the Whig party "and would be treated accordingly."[2]

By dangers from the South, Fillmore meant more than southern Whigs' electoral welfare, about which he was genuinely solicitous. As soon as Congress admitted California, hotheads in several southern states initiated formal steps toward secession. To blunt that threat, Fillmore was prepared "to bring the whole force of the government" to sustain the fugitive slave law in the North. Its determined implementation might do more than undermine popular support for secession. As Fillmore told Fish, enforcement would set an example; it would show Southerners that, if necessary, he would use force to stop secession in order to save the country.[3]

This course only earned Fillmore execration from many northern Whigs, who pooh-poohed talk of secession and blamed Fillmore's needless capitulation to southern pressure for their rout at the polls in 1850. Tens of thousands of other Whigs, however, recognized that Fillmore was pro-Union, not a prosouthern doughface, and they esteemed him precisely because they took disunionism seriously. Some were northern conservatives who increasingly called themselves National Whigs to indicate their devotion to the country, not just to northern Whigs' electoral success. Most resided in the South and the border states. "You know Fillmore, and therefore know how safe a man he is for us at this time," Baltimore's John P. Kennedy gushed to Richard Pakenham, the former British minister. "Plain, direct, honest, and manly, with a sound judgment and great discretion, he is precisely the man for the occasion."[4]

Even some of Fillmore's greatest admirers, however, no longer believed that his twin goals of saving the country and the Whig party were compatible. To secure the former, they advocated abandoning the latter for a bipartisan Union party of pro-Compromise Whigs and Democrats. Infuriated by defiant Whig state conventions in New York and Massachusetts, Webster thundered that "a new arrangement of Parties is unavoidable" and that "there must be a Union party." Kennedy argued that bipartisan congressional support for compromise pointed to "the creation of a great National Union Party which will . . . obliterate the present divisions." The main impetus for a new party, however, came from the South, where, many contended, only it could stop secession.[5]

Developing tremendous momentum during the winter of 1850–51, the Union party movement challenged Fillmore's hope of saving the Whig party as much as did the defiance he encountered from northern anti-Compromise Whigs. If southern Whigs fused with like-minded Democrats in a new party, he knew, pro-Compromise northern Whigs would probably follow suit. Their defection would abdicate control of northern Whig organizations to anti-Compromise men and possibly drive them into an explicitly antisouthern alliance with Free Soilers that could provoke the disunion he sought to avert. To Fillmore, therefore, the dangers from the South included both the secession movement and the Union party movement formed to prevent it. To demonstrate that neither secession nor a new party was necessary, he set out to prove that the Whig party was reliably pro-Union and could win elections on those grounds. This course enormously enhanced Fillmore's popularity among southern Whigs, who by 1852 clearly wanted him as the party's presidential nominee. Simultaneously, however, that course convinced more and more northern Whigs that Millard Fillmore was anything but "the man for the occasion."

I

As the next Whig in the White House would later say about a far graver crisis, the occasion that confronted Fillmore's administration in the late fall of 1850 was piled high with difficulty.[6] Its most vindictive northern allies bellowed for massive decapitations of holdover Taylor appointees, a move that could destroy state organizations. It also had to address unavoidable problems of governance that inevitably had implications for voters' attitudes toward the Whig party. It faced an embarrassing diplomatic flap with important domestic political ramifications. Enforcement of the unpopular fugitive slave law placed an unprecedented administrative burden on the executive branch. Most important, it had to defuse, rather than inflame, secessionist movements in the South while simultaneously demonstrating its even-handedness and firmness to Whig critics in the North. This combination of problems required all the sound judgment and discretion Fillmore and his advisors possessed.

The administration met these challenges with considerable skill. Fillmore subordinated the demands of bloodthirsty allies to the good of the party. To hold Whigs together for impending senatorial elections in the Rhode Island, New York, Massachusetts, and Ohio legislatures, as well as for spring elections in Connecticut and Rhode Island, with six representatives and another Senate seat at stake, he eschewed a divisive purge of patronage holders. Daniel Webster and Nathan Hall favored much more aggressive action against anti-Compromise Whigs than did Fillmore himself. After the Massachusetts elections, Webster again demanded that his cabinet colleagues strip William Schouler's Boston *Atlas* of federal printing contracts and that they be awarded to pro-Compromise Whig sheets. In New York, by mutual agreement, Webster assigned contracts for printing federal laws to the Albany *State Register* and the Rochester *American*, while Hall gave the lucrative post office printing in New York City to the *Commercial Journal*, organ of the Union Safety Committee.[7]

Prior to the spring of 1851, this cabinet-led retaliation was confined almost exclusively to a few newspapers, not personnel. Fillmore steadfastly prevented his advisors from axing jobholders for whose heads pro-Compromise Whigs clamored: William D. Lewis and John Ashmead in Pennsylvania; Palmer V. Kellogg and Thomas Clowes in New York; and Charles Hudson and Philip Greely, Jr., in Massachusetts. He repeatedly pleaded with his allies instead to patch up their differences with intraparty enemies. As late as February 23, 1851, he could honestly tell Washington Hunt that he personally had ordered the removal of only two Sewardites in New York—Levi Allen and Lewis Benedict. Only later would the administration take its gloves off on patronage.[8]

Webster, in consultation with Fillmore, Edward Everett, and a state department clerk named William Hunter, handled the diplomatic spat with Austria even more adroitly. Inherited from Taylor's administration, this dispute involved American reaction to the unsuccessful Hungarian rebellion against the Hapsburg Empire during 1848 and 1849. Scrupulously observing neutrality, Taylor had nonetheless sent A. Dudley Mann to Hungary to report on developments in case success might warrant American recognition of Hungarian independence. Austrian spies intercepted Mann's instructions, and when the Austrian chargé to Washington, Chevalier J. G. Hülsemann, complained to the administration about improper American interference in Austrian affairs, Rough and Ready was furious. To tweak the Austrians for violating the confidentiality of diplomatic papers, he sent the administration's instructions to Mann to Congress along with a message trumpeting his determination to recognize Hungarian independence had the revolt succeeded.[9]

Both Hülsemann and Austrian authorities in Vienna were livid about this calculated swipe, but the brunt of their anger fell on the new administration. In a note to Webster, Hülsemann accused the United States of insulting the Austrian Empire and desiring its overthrow. Webster brilliantly seized on this opening to score political points. Few Hungarian refugees lived in the United States in 1850, but German and Irish immigrants cheered any attempts by subordinate nationality groups to gain political independence from authoritarian regimes like Austria's. Thus Webster could gain credit for Whigs among burgeoning and traditionally Democratic immigrant groups. Primarily, however, the occasion offered

Webster a chance to sing paeans to American nationalism that would, he hoped, "touch the national pride and make a man feel sheepish and look *silly* who should speak of disunion."

Webster's long public reply to Hülsemann was a political masterpiece. Reaffirming American commitment to neutrality in foreign conflicts, it rehearsed America's historic mission to advance freedom everywhere through its own republican example. Americans, hymned Webster, always wished success to peoples contending for self-determination and political independence. If Austria contemplated any retaliation for this stance, he boasted in full knowledge that Austria lacked the fleet to damage the United States, the American people were "quite willing to take their chances and abide their destiny." Indeed, Austria should remember that compared to the vast United States, "The possessions of the House of Hapsburg are but a patch on the earth's surface."[10]

Most Americans lustily cheered this bombast. In 1851, therefore, Congress demanded that Lajos Kossuth, leader of the Hungarian revolt, be released from his Turkish detention, and it invited him to visit the United States. For the moment, however, Webster had triumphantly resolved the diplomatic squabble. In the winter of 1850–51 the administration could turn its attention to a far graver matter—quelling disunion.

The threat of southern secession required far more than bravado or carefully crafted hymns to nationalism. Yet it also demanded more than wholesale capitulation to southern pressure, and Fillmore and Webster were in fact resolutely determined to resist secession. Their problem was to demonstrate their firmness to Northerners without pushing southern extremists over the edge.

The secessionist menace came from several sources. One was the radical fringe who had attended the Nashville Convention in June 1850 and deplored its failure to precipitate disunion. After denouncing the admission of California, the reduction of Texas, and abolition of the District of Columbia's slave trade as blatant violations of Southern Rights, the Nashville Convention called for another regionwide convention to meet in November to assess Congress' achievements, and some delegates, especially those from South Carolina, went home demanding secession. Radicals, in sum, regarded the Compromise as grounds for disunion, although the Nashville Convention's second session ultimately proved to be even more of a dud than its first.[11]

The more concrete threat came from governors in Deep South states who could act on their own. On September 23, after receiving official notification of California's admission, Georgia's Democratic Governor George Towns, citing the legislature's January resolutions, called for a state convention to meet on December 10 to consider secession, and he set a date in late November to select the delegates. On September 26, Mississippi's Democratic Governor John A. Quitman ordered a special state legislative session to meet on November 18 and announced that he would urge it to call a secession convention. Popular agitation for special legislative sessions in South Carolina and Alabama portended the same result. Governor Whitemarsh Seabrook of South Carolina was an especially avid secessionist, but he realized that South Carolina's reputation for radicalism could stigmatize disunionist movements elsewhere. Thus he, as well as Alabama's governor, a moderate who opposed secession, refused to summon their legislatures and instead awaited the outcome of developments in Georgia and Mississippi.[12]

Even before Congress adjourned, in sum, Fillmore and his advisors knew of the southern danger. Ironically, it provided the same opening for mending political fences with dissident northern Whigs that Fillmore and Webster had astutely exploited in their August replies to Texas Governor P. H. Bell's threats to march Texas militia against Santa Fe. Virtually all southern politicians who sought secession were Democrats. Since southern Whigs were appalled by secessionism, the administration would not offend them by taking a firm stance against Democratic disunionists that simultaneously pleased northern Whigs.

Webster salivated at this opportunity to earn approval from northern Whigs. When federal district attorneys in Georgia, Mississippi, Alabama, and South Carolina telegraphed warnings about the depth of secessionist sentiment and the determination of Democratic governors to exploit it, Webster instantly proposed that he or Fillmore telegraph a circular to every United States attorney in the country setting forth "fully and explicitly, the duty of the Executive Government of the United States . . . in case of a collision between the authority of a State and that of the United States." Such a tough-minded proclamation, argued Webster, would be "quite applicable to the present state of things, and be a good *Union* paper, to send to Congress with your annual message." Webster, in sum, meant not only to cow secessionists; he intended to show Northerners that the administration played no favorites when it insisted on obedience to the laws.[13]

Without awaiting approval from Fillmore, Webster, who was in New England at the time, drafted such a circular, which reminded potential secessionists of the fate of South Carolina's Nullifiers, against whom Congress had authorized the use of military force if necessary. Webster mailed this draft to Fillmore, who then circulated it among other cabinet members for advice. Both Interior Secretary Alexander H. H. Stuart, a Virginian, whose department had formal authority over United States marshals, and Hall vigorously objected that Webster's bellicose language and especially his caustic references to South Carolina's retreat over Nullification would inflame, not intimidate, secessionists. Consequently, Webster's proposed circular was never sent. The administration decided instead to watch developments in the South carefully while using its enforcement of the fugitive slave law in the North to indicate its refusal to tolerate lawbreakers.[14]

Although the administration eschewed saber rattling to frighten potential secessionists, it did not rely solely on northern law enforcement to dissuade southern extremists. It was sworn to uphold neutrality laws that forbade American citizens from interfering with or attacking foreign countries. Between 1850 and 1853 the most daring American violators of the neutrality laws, the so-called filibusterers, were Southerners whose chief target was the Spanish possession of Cuba. By fomenting and joining a revolution of resident sugar planters against Spanish authorities, these southern crackpots believed, they could ultimately secure Cuba's annexation to the United States and thus enlarge the realm of slavery. By cracking down on southern filibusterers, who usually set sail for Cuba from ports on the Gulf coast, Fillmore's administration, in turn, could balance its enforcement of the fugitive slave law in the North.

By a fortuitous coincidence, the most prominent southern filibusterer when Fillmore took office was Mississippi's secessionist Governor Quitman. A hero of the Mexican war who found the lure of combat almost irresistible, Quitman became involved during the spring of 1850 with Narciso López, a Venezuelan expatriate, who had once lived in Cuba and who had already attempted unsuccessfully to invade it in 1849. Quitman hosted López and other filibusterers at the governor's mansion in Jackson. He traveled to New Orleans in April to arrange supplies for the expedition and to grease the skids for it to avoid naval patrols when it left New Orleans. Rumor circulated that he even accepted military command of the reinforcements that would back up López's May assault on Cuba. That assault was aborted and López was chased by the Spanish navy back to the United States, where he immediately began planning another sortie.

In June 1850, López was arrested in New Orleans. To appease or perhaps overawe the authorities, he implicated various Americans who had helped him, like John L. O'Sullivan, the famous Democratic proponent of Manifest Destiny; John Henderson, Mississippi's former Whig senator, who was practicing law in New Orleans; and Quitman. They and others were indicted by a federal grand jury for violating the neutrality laws in late June and were ordered to appear in federal district court in New Orleans in December. All of this occurred under Taylor's administration, but Fillmore's team inherited the task of overseeing the prosecution by United States Attorney Logan Hunton in December. Despite the delicacy of the federal government's prosecuting a sitting governor and despite delays secured by defense attorneys, the administration refused to drop the proceedings. Ultimately Quitman, who succeeded in getting Mississippi's special legislative session in November to call a secession convention to meet in the fall of 1851, resigned the governorship on February 3, 1851, and went in the custody of a United States marshal to New Orleans for his trial. When the cases against two of Quitman's co-defendants ended in hung juries, however, Hunton dropped the charges against them, Quitman, and all the others on March 3, 1851.[15]

Now Quitman gained the status of martyr as well as military hero and avid secessionist, but Fillmore's administration had demonstrated its willingness to prosecute Southerners as well as Northerners who broke the law. For the remainder of his term, indeed, Fillmore vigilantly tried to rein in the filibusterers, and in April and October 1851, he issued proclamations threatening to arrest and fine anyone who joined their illegal expeditions. Not coincidentally, these proclamations coincided with the use of federal force to implement the fugitive slave law in the North. What is more, Fillmore used precisely the same language against southern as against northern lawbreakers. He called "upon every officer of this Government, civil or military, to use all efforts in his power to arrest for trial and punishment every such offender against the laws of the country."[16] Fillmore's purpose of playing no favorites between North and South was clear. Without question, however, northern enforcement of the fugitive slave law constituted the administration's central strategy for curbing secession.

II

Technically, implementation of that law was a judicial, not an executive, responsibility. The new United States commissioners designated to hear cases brought by slaveholders or their agents had judicial status; the marshals and deputies whom commissioners could order to apprehend fugitives were considered officers of federal courts. Nonetheless, the administration appointed the commissioners, it had responsibility for United States marshals and attorneys, and it was deter-mined that the law be enforced and alleged fugitives returned to the South re-gardless of the costs to the government in money and manpower. On this point, Fillmore, Webster, Stuart, and Attorney General John J. Crittenden were in full agreement. "There must be no flinching, nor doubt, nor hesitation," insisted Webster.[17]

Despite public protest meetings and scathing editorials threatening forcible re-sistance to the Fugitive Slave Act, its initial implementation during the fall of 1850 went smoothly. Northern blacks, who had always regarded slave hunters as kidnappers and occasionally armed themselves to ward them off, increased their vigilance, and many blacks fled immediately to Canada to escape the law's oper-ation.[18] The great majority of whites, however, obeyed the law. Alleged runaways were captured and returned to the South without incident in New York, Penn-sylvania, Indiana, Illinois, and Massachusetts by the end of the year. In early November even Webster, who had been apoplectic about threatened defiance dur-ing October, assured Fillmore from Boston that "the excitement caused by the Fugitive Slave Bill is fast subsiding, & it is thought there is now no probability of any resistance, if a fugitive should be arrested." Ten days later he crowed, "We can kill off Free Soilism, in the whole of New England, in twelve months by energy and decision."[19]

Fillmore exhibited both. On October 8, a mob of armed and angry blacks in Detroit threatened to rescue a fugitive in federal custody, forcing the marshal to call out troops. When two Democratic federal judges in Pennsylvania requested Fillmore two weeks later to issue a general order allowing federal judges to deploy federal troops to enforce the law, therefore, he ordered the commander of the United States Marines in Philadelphia to make his troops available if U.S. mar-shals called for them or if federal judges certified that they were necessary. A few days later, Fillmore dispatched additional troops to Boston to aid federal author-ities there. "I have therefore commenced mildly—authorizing this force only at the last resort but if necessary," he told the absent Webster. "I shall not hesitate to give greater power, and finally to bring the whole force of the government to sustain the law."[20]

In his December annual message to Congress, Fillmore declared "that to the utmost of my ability and to the extent of the power vested in me I shall at all times and in all places take care that the laws be faithfully executed." Signifi-cantly, he coupled that pledge with a warning that Americans "instigate no rev-olutions, nor suffer any hostile military expeditions to be fitted out in the United States to invade the territory or provinces of a friendly nation." The laws, in sum, would be enforced in *both* the North and the South.[21]

Although fugitives continued to be remanded to their owners without resis-tance in most places throughout 1851 and 1852, three incidents in 1851 tested the administration's determination. The most important in terms of the admin-istration's response occurred in Boston on February 15 when a mob of blacks assaulted the federal marshal and his deputies, forcibly seized a fugitive named Shadrack from a federal courtroom, and spirited him to Canada. On September 11, a crowd of armed blacks in Christiana, Pennsylvania, shot and killed a Mary-land slaveholder and wounded his son to prevent their capturing two fugitives, who also escaped to Canada along with their defenders. The following month, blacks and white abolitionists snatched a slave named Jerry from authorities in Syracuse.[22]

The Shadrack rescue deeply embarrassed the administration. On February 18, Fillmore issued a proclamation calling on citizens to obey the laws and commanding "all officers, civil and military, and all other persons, civil or military" in the vicinity to aid by all means in their power "in quelling this and other such combinations." He also directed the federal attorney to prosecute everyone who had participated in the rescue. In a message to the Senate the following day, Fillmore asked Congress to facilitate enforcement by changing the law to allow him to call state militia into national service without first issuing a proclamation calling on lawbreakers to desist and disperse and by clarifying the president's authority to use the regular army and navy to implement laws.[23]

Especially mortified by the events in Boston, Webster took personal charge of the arrest and prosecution of Shadrack's rescuers. His need to work through local federal officials was a problem. He trusted U.S. Marshal Charles Devens and the federal commissioners, but he regarded Customs Collector Greely and Naval Officer Charles Hudson as untrustworthy anti-Compromise men. The key federal official was U.S. Attorney George Lunt, the man who had beaten his son for the office, the Whig who had abandoned Webster and supported Taylor at the 1848 Whig national convention, and an incompetent lawyer whom Webster deemed a dolt.[24]

Because Webster and Fillmore considered conviction of the rescuers vital as a signal to Southerners, Webster, on February 25, 1851, ordered Lunt to hire Charles Loring and Rufus Choate, the state's preeminent lawyer, to help him prosecute the government's case. Lunt, however, proved obdurate and held out for a junior subordinate. Nothing helped. The trials against four blacks and four white abolitionists in late May and June ended in hung juries and dropped charges.[25]

This failure to secure convictions, which would later be repeated in Pennsylvania, was offset by another fugitive case in Boston while Webster was on the scene. On April 3 city officials arrested a fugitive slave named Thomas Sims for theft. Abolitionists tried to secure his release, but they were rebuffed first by federal authorities and then by state courts that refused to issue a writ of habeas corpus for a federal prisoner. When abolitionists urged blacks to arm themselves and take Sims by force, the Whig mayor called out two companies of state militia. On April 11, Sims, guarded by 300 armed men, was loaded onto a navy brig and sent to Savannah. Two days later Webster rejoiced at the government's success and particularly the decisions by both state and federal courts upholding the constitutionality of the Fugitive Slave Act. "I cannot but think that these judgments will settle the question, with all sane men in Mass."[26]

III

To conservative Whigs, indeed, Sims' successful rendition and judges' refusal to countenance opposition to the fugitive slave law more than balanced the Shadrack rescue. By the spring of 1851 they loudly applauded the administration's success in overcoming various challenges. "How thickly the testimonies in favor of the administration crowd us from all quarters," Baltimore's Kennedy cheered to Interior Secretary Stuart. History would record "as the chief glory of the present administration that they have identified themselves with a new era of peace and prosperity." From Kennedy's perspective, moreover, those achievements had immense political implications. "I regard every man who now places the Compromise in the front of his creed a good and true Whig—and every convert to the administration on that ground a new recruit to the standard of Whig principles."[27]

Kennedy's readiness to consider any pro-Compromise man, regardless of formal partisan identification, as an adherent of Fillmore and a recruit to Whig principles is significant. Kennedy ardently wanted to create a new bipartisan Union party, and he envisioned Fillmore's administration and pro-Compromise Whigs as its rallying point. Some members of Fillmore's cabinet—especially Webster, who saw a Union party as a vehicle for his presidential ambitions—welcomed this prospect. Millard Fillmore himself emphatically did not. Possessing the prize Webster still hungered for and uninterested in another term himself, he viewed the Union party movement that mushroomed in the winter of 1850–51 as at best a useful though temporary check on secessionism and at worst as a Democratic ruse to seduce gullible Whigs that must be undermined in order to achieve his second goal—saving the Whig party.

Even before Taylor's death, Whig and Democratic cooperation on opposite sides of the compromise struggle in Congress had spawned predictions of an imminent realignment. As soon as Fillmore replaced Taylor, interest in fusing the "patriotic hearts and minds" from "all parties" in a new "Union party" quickened.[28] By October, as bipartisan Union meetings proliferated in northern cities, excitement about a new party spread. Baltimore's Kennedy fanned it, and the Silver Gray bolt in New York spurred widespread predictions that Silver Grays and Hunker Democrats would ultimately combine against Barnburners and Sewardite Whigs to form the nucleus of a new national party.

Webster's letter to New York's Castle Garden meeting in October raised this excitement to a fever pitch. Praising the Union Safety Committee that was circulating a separate, predominantly Democratic Union ticket as "abject slaves to no party," Webster pledged, "With you, I declare that I 'range myself under the banners of that party whose principles and practice are most calculated to uphold the Constitution and to perpetuate our glorious Union.' " While Winthrop, who had taken Webster's Senate seat, huffed that Webster's letter disgraced a Whig administration and dismissed "all this fuss about the Union" as "nonsense," Kennedy, who attended the Castle Garden meeting, was jubilant. Webster's letter, he told his wife, announced "the beginning of a great Conservative National party which will overwhelm the old divisions of Whig and democrat and make a new order of politics." Anxious to perpetuate that momentum, Webster arranged for a mass Union meeting in Boston in November, and he gave his blessing to a bipartisan Union meeting in Philadelphia arranged by conservative Whig Josiah Randall.[29]

Henry Clay also endorsed the new party. At a barbecue at Lexington, Kentucky, in October, Clay praised the bipartisan cooperation behind the Compromise in what, his antislavery cousin Cassius M. Clay snarled, was a transparent attempt "to bring over a number of the democrats to form a 'Union' party—which means a *slavery party*, strong enough to carry him or his 'Executor' and friends into power." Then, in a November speech to a special joint session of the Kentucky legislature, Clay announced that continued resistance to the fugitive slave law in the North "will lead to the formation of two new parties, one for the union and the other against the union." Devoted as he was to Whig principles, if northern Whigs grafted abolitionism onto the Whig creed by continued opposition to the Compromise, "from that moment I renounce the party and cease to be a Whig." If a new Union party were necessary, "I announce myself, in this place, a member of that union party, whatever may be its component elements."[30]

The primary drive for a Union party, however, came from the South. Talk of merging pro-Compromise Whigs and Democrats occasionally emerged in North Carolina, Tennessee, and other southern states during the fall of 1850,[31] but the Union party took concrete form only in Mississippi, Alabama, and Georgia, the last by far the most important of the three. Georgia's election on November 25 for delegates to the convention that Governor Towns had called was not simply the most direct referendum on the Compromise held in the country that year. Secessionists in South Carolina and Alabama awaited events in Georgia and Mississippi before acting. The special session of the Mississippi legislature summoned by Quitman met on November 18, one week before Georgia's elections, but since opponents of secession managed to postpone the state convention there until November 1851, events in Georgia would effectively determine secession's fate across the South. Those events, therefore, played a vital role in Fillmore's attempt to save the country.

The most populous state in the Deep South and the only one, aside from Louisiana and sparsely settled Florida, where Whigs were competitive, Georgia was also crucial to Fillmore's hope of saving the Whig party. Whigs had carried Georgia for Taylor and Fillmore in 1848 and elected four of eight congressmen. In 1850 both United States senators were Whigs. Any threat to the Georgia Whig party therefore directly impinged on Whigs' congressional strength. On that score, developments in Georgia seemed particularly ominous. Georgia would help save the country from secession, but in doing so it presaged the demolition of the Whig party.

During the campaign for delegates to the December state convention, as Alexander Stephens informed Crittenden, "old party lines [were] obliterated and forgotten." The battle was fought between embryonic Union and Southern Rights coalitions that drew support from both major parties. The division was hardly equal. The vast majority of Whigs and almost half of the Democrats joined the Union coalition. The remaining Democrats were joined by a small Whig rump in the Southern Rights camp. For Democrats, this realignment during 1850 and 1851 proved only temporary; many Georgia Whigs, in contrast, would never return to their old party. Since similar patterns ensued in Mississippi and Alabama, developments in Georgia merit close examination.[32]

At first blush, the gravity of the secessionist threat in Georgia by itself appears to explain the emergence of Union and Southern Rights parties. Georgia harbored rabid secessionists with whom Governor Towns sided. After the Nashville Convention, they successfully urged formation of Southern Rights Associations in most of the state's counties, and on August 22, a statewide Southern Rights rally at Macon actually called for immediate secession. Most county Southern Rights Associations, however, fervently renounced disunionist intentions and instead contented themselves with denouncing the proposed compromise as an insult to Southerners and demanding the extension of the Missouri Compromise line to the Pacific coast. In short, the great majority of the Southern Rights men sought to exploit anti-Compromise sentiment to secure political power within the state, not to remove it from the Union. Even avid secessionists admitted that publicizing their aim would prove suicidal in any popular election. For exactly that reason, the Unionist foes of Southern Rights men grossly exaggerated the threat of secession in order to maximize their vote. Authentic secessionists, in sum, were far too weak to provoke the political realignment that occurred.[33]

Union and Southern Rights men crystallized into political parties, as distinguished from ad hoc blocs, indeed, only after the threat of secession had already been crushed. Unionists' confident prediction that if Towns called a convention the "traitors who seek dissolution will not muster a corporal's guard" proved accurate. In November, Southern Rights candidates carried only ten of Georgia's ninety-three counties, and Unionists outpolled them approximately 46,000 to 24,000. In the convention itself, delegates favoring the Compromise and cessation of agitation outnumbered their foes 240 to 23. That crushing triumph effectively ended the threat of secession throughout the South for ten years. Yet it was only at the convention, after the victory had been won, that the Union coalition gelled into a party that sought to perpetuate its existence, a move that forced Southern Rights men to follow suit. Obviously something more than the menace of disunion itself spawned partisan reoganization.[34]

The formation of new parties in Georgia—and later in Alabama and Mississippi—stemmed from changes in the competitive relationship between Whigs and Democrats, from rancorous feuds within both parties, and especially from ambitious politicians' attempts to exploit the sectional controversy to score a knockout blow against factional rivals or to save threatened political careers. Three aspects of interparty conflict facilitated realignment. First, the legislature rescheduled Georgia's congressional elections from even-numbered years, as had been the case throughout the 1840s, to odd-numbered years beginning in October 1851. Had those contests been slated for October 1850 rather than October 1851, the pyramid of conventions necessary to nominate candidates and the subsequent campaigns, which would have been underway long before Towns called the state convention, would most likely have reinforced partisan identities among politicians, the press, and the electorate and thereby inhibited the abandonment of old parties. Conversely, the absence of such elections allowed the campaign for convention delegates to focus exclusively on the question of accepting or resisting the Compromise, an issue that fostered cooperation between Whigs and Democrats on both sides.

Second, by 1850 Whigs and Democrats in Georgia, as was also true in Mississippi and Alabama, had ceased to battle over state economic issues. However radical Towns was on sectional issues, he was a conservative with Whiggish views on state financial policy, and Whigs praised the part of his legislative message in November 1849 dealing with it. This agreement was important, for almost everywhere in Georgia, as elsewhere in the nation, proponents of a Union party pointed to the abatement of partisan conflict over economic issues as justification for replacing the Whig and Democratic parties with new coalitions formed around current sectional questions.[35]

Third, Whigs' competitiveness vis-à-vis Democrats in Georgia had deteriorated markedly by 1850, and Whigs' chances of winning elections in Alabama and Mississippi were even more remote. Whether or not new parties were necessary to stop secession, they seemed necessary to put Whigs in office. In part, this perception reflected what historians have called "the politics of slavery" or "loyalty politics."[36] By this analysis, since northern Whigs proved far less willing than northern Democrats to appease Southerners during the recent congressional session, continued affiliation with the national Whig party meant political annihilation in Dixie. Specifically, some historians have attributed Toombs' and Stephens' readiness to desert the Whig party to their fury at antislavery Whigs. Similarly, Berrien's Whig allies, who rejoiced during the summer that "the old party lines are broken down" and that "there will never be another election between the old parties," wanted to deal no longer with Northerners as mere "parcels of the great National parties."[37]

Equally if not more important, by 1850 Whigs' prospects for controlling the state government were declining dramatically. As a result, state leaders within Georgia whose focus was the legislature and the governorship, not national officeholders issuing directives from Washington, launched the reorganization of 1850. After dominating the state government from 1843 to 1847, Whigs lost the governorship in 1847 and again by a larger margin in 1849, when Democrats also won small majorities in both houses of the legislature. Even in 1848, Whig congressional candidates garnered only 47 percent of the statewide popular vote, while Taylor benefited from the refusal of Democrats to support Cass. Especially worrisome were Democratic incursions into Whig support in the rice plantation belt along the coast that appeared in 1849 and even more emphatically in a special congressional election to replace Thomas Butler King, who resigned to remain in California. In 1848 the popular King crushed Democrat James Jackson by 57 to 43 percent, but in February 1850, Jackson, who would join the majority of southern Democrats in adamantly opposing the Compromise, defeated his Whig opponent.[38]

Democrats' tack of courting normally Whiggish slaveholders with the aggressive proslavery, Southern Rights platform they adopted in 1849 and continued to push in 1850, in sum, appeared capable of building a permanent statewide majority that could doom Whig gubernatorial aspirants. But that was not all. In February 1850 the new Democratic majorities in the legislature tried to ram through bills to reapportion both congressional and state senate districts so as to force Toombs and Stephens into the same district and to cement control of the senate. So outrageous did Whigs find these gerrymanders that all but one Whig bolted the house for four days to deny the Democrats a quorum. Eventually Whigs, with the aid of a few Democrats from the upcountry Cherokee district, who saw the measure as a power grab by black belt Democrats, blocked the congressional redistricting. But the senate reapportionment passed, thus jeopardizing Whig hopes of ever again controlling that chamber. The handwriting was on the wall. Unless Whigs could recapture the vote of slaveholders or cut into the Democratic vote elsewhere, they seemed doomed to minority status.[39]

Most Whig leaders eventually decided on the latter course, but at first they tried to stanch the hemorrhaging of slaveholders toward the enemy by matching Democrats' proslavery zeal. Almost all Whig legislators voted for the militant

Georgia resolutions threatening secession should California be admitted, as well as for appropriations to hold elections to send delegates to Nashville. Indeed, the original house resolutions in November were introduced by a Whig who sought, in the words of the Savannah *Republican*, "to set the Whig party right before the public on slavery." Yet those same votes reinforced a fissure within the Democratic party that Whigs had long recognized but that they could only now exploit.[40]

For years Georgia Democrats had divided along lines of geography and principle. One wing of the party was composed overwhelmingly of nonslaveholders from the mountainous upcountry regions like Cherokee. Fervent disciples of the Jacksonian faith, these men were staunch nationalists who had opposed Nullification, and they remained suspicious of the commercial mentality and proslavery zealotry of the black belt. Their preeminent leader was Howell Cobb, speaker of the House. Indeed, these nonslaveholding constituencies usually sent more Democrats to Congress than did their intraparty rivals because they were the safest Democratic districts in the state. The other wing of the Democrats was concentrated in the slaveholding areas that Whigs usually controlled. Known as the Chivalry, this wing contained many Calhounites who shared their hero's desire to destroy both major parties and combine all Southerners into a single organization. This wing, to which Towns belonged, seized control of the party machinery in 1849, and they were the ones pushing the extreme proslavery, Southern Rights agenda reflected in the Georgia resolutions. They hated Cobb because of his public repudiation of Calhoun's Southern Address in 1849 and his support of the Compromise in 1850.[41]

For different reasons, various groups within the Chivalry saw advantages in converting the Democratic party into a Southern Rights organization in 1850. Some sought to consolidate their control of the state party and increase the number of converts from Whiggish slaveholders. Reapportioning congressional districts was a complementary effort to increase their representation in the House. Others saw a Southern Rights organization as the fruition of Calhoun's long-sought southern party. A minority including Towns hoped to effect secession. All of these variants left Cobb and his followers, who heartily reciprocated the Chivalry's hatred, in the cold and up for grabs.

Understandably, therefore, the idea of forming a Union party was first broached publicly by the house Whigs during their February bolt to prevent a quorum. By building a new coalition devoted to stopping secessionists, they might pick up support from Cobb's followers, who distrusted proslavery extremists even more than Whigs did. This call in February produced no results, but when Union rallies were held during the summer to counteract the formation of Southern Rights Associations, nonslaveholding Democrats flocked to them. Fear of losing control of the state government permanently, in sum, caused Georgia's desperate Whigs to hatch the Union party idea, but its success depended on divisions within the Democratic party. As had been the case since the birth of the Whig party, its fate was inextricably linked to what Democrats did.

Whig politicians too were divided, although more by generational rivalries for office than by ideology or geography. The exception to this pattern was a tiny bloc of proslavery extremists. A few Whig newspapers, notably the Augusta *Republic*, edited by James M. Smythe, represented this small faction, and they had a few representatives in the legislature, though none in Congress. Despite the support most Whig legislators gave the Georgia resolutions, this extremist fringe recognized their lack of influence on the party's mainstream. Hence, they avidly embraced the new Southern Rights organization, in which they might have more clout.

Many supporters of Berrien also gravitated to the Southern Rights cause, as would Berrien himself. Neither he nor almost all of them were secessionists. A firm nationalist, Berrien was a close friend of Webster, and in 1848 he supported Clay rather than Taylor for the Whig nomination. That record allowed his younger rivals in the party, Toombs and Stephens, who hungered for Berrien's Senate seat, to try to undermine Berrien by taking more advanced proslavery ground than he on every sectional issue that emerged between 1844 and 1848. Berrien then sought to turn the tables on his tormentors after the 1849 election. In the Senate during 1850 he lacerated Stephens for his earlier position that Mexican law barred slavery in the Cession, and he stridently opposed California's admission as a free state to establish his prosouthern credentials. Berrien's intransigent hostility to both the Taylor and Clay plans and his own proposal for dividing California at the 35° 30' line put him closer than any other Georgian in Congress to the position taken by the Nashville Convention. Since the Nashville platform was the platform of the emerging Southern Rights Associations, proslavery zealots among the Whigs like Smythe, who had long disdained Berrien, and anticompromise Democrats began to sing the senator's praises during the summer.[42]

These developments convinced most of Berrien's followers that the way to advance their own careers in Georgia and to perpetuate Berrien's career in the Senate was to embrace the Southern Rights cause. They knew that the followers of Stephens and Toombs, aided by the federal patronage Taylor had given them, now dominated the state Whig party and would give short shrift to either Berrien or his followers when it was time to make nominations. They, too, recognized that the Whigs seemed to be sinking inexorably into a statewide minority and that if something was not done, Democrats would control the legislature elected in 1851 that chose Berrien's successor. By siding with Southern Rights Democrats, who had already ridden to power in the state by pushing an aggressive proslavery platform and who were now praising Berrien to the skies, they could do three things. They could gain the necessary allies to defeat Toombs and Stephens, whom the Georgia press had identified since the spring as pro-Compromise men, and perhaps put Berrien men in their places. They could construct a coalition in the legislature that might return Berrien to the Senate as a reward for his manly stand in 1850. And, if the Southern Rights movement swept the entire South, as they expected it would, they could make Berrien its presidential candidate in 1852.[43]

Not all of Berrien's followers accepted this rosy scenario. Democrats, some accurately warned him, dominated the Southern Rights movement, and they would never reelect Berrien to the Senate. By joining the Southern Rights camp, Berrien men simply would become the tail wagged by a Democratic dog. Others recognized the Southern Rights cause as a sure loser because of the stigma of secessionism and doubted the wisdom of joining it. "There are many genuine Southerners," wrote one, "who will not go for disunion upon the California question." Still others, including Berrien's kinsman and closest lieutenant, Charles Jenkins, were put off by the secessionists in the Southern Rights camp and joined the Union coalition to put them down. For months, in fact, Jenkins and others warned Berrien that he would only isolate himself by opposing the Compromise since most Georgians cared far more about ending agitation than extending slavery.[44]

Unwisely, Berrien ignored these warnings. Convinced that the Compromise represented an ignominious defeat for the South that must be resisted and desperate to win reelection, he threw his support to Southern Rights candidates when he returned to Georgia in October. Before leaving Washington, however, Berrien tried to carve out a position of resistance that distinguished him both from the secessionists, whom he abhorred, and from Democrats in the Southern Rights organization. This was a totally impractical and unconstitutional proposal for economic nonintercourse with the North in which the Georgia legislature would impose a confiscatory tax on all northern goods that entered the state in order to keep them out.[45]

That Berrien committed the political suicide against which his saner friends had warned was evidenced by two facts. Southern Rights candidates in only one of Georgia's ninety-three counties, Burke, endorsed his platform of economic nonintercourse. In addition, when Berrien sought election to the convention himself as a Southern Rights delegate from Savannah, he suffered humiliation. Southern Rights Democrats in Savannah, led by Congressman James Jackson, wanted to monopolize the Southern Rights movement for themselves. Thus they refused to cooperate when Berrien's Whig friends suggested a joint ticket that included Berrien. Those Whigs then refused to nominate Berrien on the grounds that it was undignified for a four-term United States senator to grovel for votes in a local election against Democrats who ostensibly shared his anti-Compromise views. To demonstrate indelibly who controlled the Southern Rights organization, Savannah's Democrats then nominated Berrien as one of *their* candidates, an insulting gesture that Berrien's proud Whig friends refused to let him accept. Berrien would be back in Washington when the Georgia convention met in December. That physical distance from the center of action perfectly symbolized how out of touch with Georgia this immensely learned Whig stalwart had become. He would linger on in the Senate until the spring of 1852, but his career as the leading force in Georgia politics was effectively finished.[46]

Conversely, the Union party movement finally allowed Stephens and Toombs to displace Berrien, a goal they had sought since 1844. Throughout 1850, their oscillations in Congress between concerted efforts to secure passage of the compromise package and hair-raising speeches threatening secession and demanding federal protection for slavery in the territories baffled many Georgia Whigs. But on the central matter at issue—whether California's admission justified resistance—the differences separating Berrien from Toombs and Stephens were crystal clear. As early as March 11, Toombs published a letter to Governor Towns in Georgia's newspapers declaring that a compromise package that included California offered no justification for calling a state convention or seeking secession. Although Toombs, like most Southerners, voted against the California bill when it came before the House in September, he then announced, "I do not consider the admission of California an aggression upon the South." Stephens, who returned to Georgia for a month in mid-August and thereby missed key congressional votes on the Compromise, made a number of speeches defending it as an end to northern aggression against the South. The continued resistance that Berrien demanded, he insisted, was unnecessary.[47]

Since Toombs and Stephens had been cooperating for months with Cobb and other pro-Compromise Democrats in Washington, the shift of Cobb's followers in Georgia to the Union coalition opened the way for the duo to follow their Whig supporters back home into a new alliance that could finish Berrien and advance their own careers. When Congress adjourned, Toombs, Stephens, Allen Owen, and Whig Senator William C. Dawson campaigned in Georgia for Union candidates among Whig constituencies, just as Cobb and other pro-Compromise Democratic congressmen canvassed for Union tickets in Democratic strongholds. Leadership of the Southern Rights cause was left to Berrien, the state's two anti-Compromise Democratic congressmen, and various state politicians.

That Stephens and Toombs sought to purge Berrien and not just to stop secession became clear at the Milledgeville convention in December. During a recess, Toombs, who by mutual agreement between the two was slated for Berrien's Senate seat, insisted that the Union forces organize a Union party across the state to contest the 1851 state and congressional elections. Cobb's Democratic followers in the Union coalition, sensing the chance to drive Southern Rights Democrats from power within the state by running Cobb for governor, readily agreed. Southern Rights men rightly protested that this conversion of an ad hoc Union coalition into an office-seeking party was totally unnecessary and a transparent grab for office. The November election, they insisted, had emphatically determined that Georgia would accept the Compromise and not secede. Like Stephens and Toombs, they recognized that a Union party campaigning demagogically against the phantom of secession would sweep the 1851 elections. Haplessly watching events from Washington, Berrien understood instantly that formation of a Union party meant the end of his Senate career. Only his belief that Stephens, not Toombs, would displace him was mistaken.[48]

Toombs and Stephens sought more than victory in Georgia's 1851 elections and the destruction of Berrien. They hoped to build a permanent national Union party that would replace the Whigs and run its own presidential candidate in 1852 and thereafter. Thus they encouraged incipient Union party movements in other southern states, and they returned to Washington in the winter of 1850–51 seeking northern recruits from among pro-Compromise Democrats and Whigs. Meanwhile, their Georgia allies seconded the call from New York City's Union Safety Committee for a national Union party convention to meet in Washington on February 22, 1851, the highly symbolic birthday of that city's namesake.

The Milledgeville convention not only launched the Union party, its resolutions, drafted by Charles Jenkins, also provided that party's platform in Georgia, Alabama, and Mississippi. Intended to refute the charge that pro-Compromise men were cowardly submissionists, the famous Georgia Platform provided southern Unionists with impenetrable armor by making it absolutely clear that Georgia's acceptance of the Compromise was not absolute. Its acquiescence depended upon full compliance by Northerners in whose hands lay "the destiny of the Union."[49]

Sharply noting that parts of the Compromise were unjust to the South, the Georgia Platform nonetheless declared that the package as a whole negated the need for immediate secession. It pledged that Georgia "would abide by it as a permanent adjustment of this sectional controversy." Permanence was the key, and Georgians would make no more concessions to northern demands. They would resist "to a disruption of every tie that binds her to the Union" any congressional action that touched slavery in the District of Columbia, that refused the admission of new slave states, that tried to bar slavery from Utah and New Mexico, or that modified or repealed the new fugitive slave law. In a clear warning to Fillmore's administration, the final resolution declared, "That it is the deliberate opinion of this Convention that upon a faithful execution of the *Fugitive Slave Law* by the proper authorities depends the preservation of our much beloved Union." In sum, secession had been temporarily shelved, not permanently renounced. Any of the actions still loudly being demanded by many northern Whigs would provoke it.

Most Southern Rights men in Georgia applauded this belligerent manifesto as representing their own position. Only diehard secessionists and Berrien, miffed that his nonintercourse idea had been completely ignored, continued to grouse. Yet their agreement with the Union party's platform did nothing to deter the organization of that party, which justified its existence by the recalcitrance of the secessionist fringe. Southern Rights men had little choice but to convert the local Democratic organizations they still controlled into a Southern Rights party to save their own careers from the Unionist onslaught. Whigs who had cooperated with them in 1850, similarly, had no choice but to support Southern Rights candidates for state and federal offices, for their former Whig allies in the Union organization totally shunned them, refusing even to print Berrien's speeches in the papers they controlled. With Berrien cornered, they showed no mercy.[50]

One of Berrien's Whig followers, a Southern Rights legislative candidate in 1851, shrewdly intuited what was going on in Georgia. Furious about being forced to cooperate with Democrats because Union party leaders were flogging the dead horse of secession to secure selfish ends, he exploded, "I am unable to see any good reason, why this slavery agitation should break up old parties in Georgia, when no such consequence has followed in other states." Since secession was now a chimera, the "rank & file" were ready "to return to old party lines." Only "some of the leaders" who desired "to control the affairs of Georgia" were determined on "breaking up old & forming new parties." With astonishing prescience, he then predicted the rapid demise of the Union party. "This Constitutional Union party may subserve the purposes of its founders for the present," but "it cannot endure" since "the South has acquiesced in the *adjustment*" and "Parties cannot be maintained on past questions." This small-fry politico from Athens, Georgia, could not know it, but he had written an apt epitaph not only for Georgia's Union party, but also for the national Whig party.[51]

For the present, however, the Union party most certainly did subserve the purposes of its office-hungry founders. Continuing to praise the Compromise a year after it passed, Cobb ran for governor against Charles J. McDonald, a Southern Rights Democrat, who defended the right while denying the necessity of secession, continued to pillory the Compromise, and blasted the Union party as Whiggery in disguise. This tack won back many Democrats who had sat out the 1850 convention elections but pried few, if any, Democrats from the Union party. Cobb breezed into office with three-fifths of the popular vote, a landslide by Georgia standards, and Union candidates—Stephens, Toombs, and four Democrats—carried six of the eight congressional districts.[52]

The outcome of the legislative elections, which mattered most to Toombs and Berrien, was even more one-sided. Union men outnumbered their Southern Rights foes 104–29 in the house and 39–8 in the senate. Long certain of defeat, Berrien particularly abhorred the prospect that Toombs would get his seat. To avert that mortification, he announced that he would not seek reelection in the hope that this sacrifice might sway the legislature's Union majority to support his kinsman Jenkins rather than the hated Toombs. The Stephens-Toombs juggernaut was not to be denied, however; they elected Toombs to the Senate on the session's very first day. Thus Stephens and Toombs won their long war with Berrien. In the process, they willfully helped destroy the most important state Whig organization in the Deep South.[53]

IV

Developments in Mississippi and Alabama can be quickly sketched. Despite impressive performances in the presidential elections of 1840 and 1848, between 1839 and 1849 Mississippi's Whigs had never won the governorship, elected only two of the twenty-two men Mississippi sent to the House of Representatives, and averaged less than a third of the seats in the legislature. Even more than Georgia's Whigs, in short, they badly needed a transfusion of Democratic blood to restore their competitive vigor.

There, too, Democratic divisions over the Compromise and the potential isolation of a prominent Democrat who needed Whig help to save his career offered them a chance. The Democrat was Senator Henry S. Foote, who had strongly supported the omnibus measure and later the Compromise, and who was censured by Democrats during the special November legislative session for his apostasy from Mississippi Democratic orthodoxy.[54]

Foote, whose Senate seat would be filled by the legislature elected in 1851, in sum, burned his bridges to the state's Democratic leadership. He now needed new allies to prolong his career, just as Whigs had long needed reinforcements to launch theirs. It seemed like a marriage made in heaven, and Quitman's push for secession provided the opportunity to hold a ceremony. After Quitman's call for a special legislative session, pro-Compromise Whigs agreed with Foote to hold a meeting in Jackson to organize a bipartisan Union party on November 18, 1850, the same day the special session met. Pressure from it and Democratic legislators from strongly unionist nonslaveholding districts forced postponement of the state's secession convention until the following November.[55]

Mississippi's Union party thus faced two elections in 1851, one in September for delegates to the state convention and the regularly scheduled November election for congressmen, governor, and state legislators. As in Georgia, Whigs constituted the great majority of Union party supporters, and they hoped that since "the issue now with us is union or disunion," Whigs might actually "carry the State next year." Since they were even more dependent than their Georgia counterparts on securing Democratic aid, however, they gave all four congressional nominations to Democrats, while Foote himself ran as the Union candidate for governor. Just as in Georgia, moreover, Whigs ran on the Union ticket for the legislature and convention in traditionally Whiggish plantation regions, while Democrats received Union nominations in nonslaveholder strongholds.[56]

As in Georgia, finally, Democrats who demanded repudiation of the Compromise or secession formed a Democratic State Rights party, which in June 1851 nominated Quitman, the state's most renowned secessionist, for governor. Even though their platform admitted that immediate secession was inexpedient, Quitman's well-known radicalism sank the State Rights cause.[57] In the September election for delegates, Unionists prevailed by a margin of 28,277 to 21,421, and in November the convention by an overwhelming vote of 72–17 adopted a resolution condemning secession as "utterly unsanctioned by the Federal Constitution." The size of September's popular vote, which reversed the 10,000-vote majority Quitman had won in 1849, sealed his fate, and four days after the September elections he withdrew as a gubernatorial candidate. Jefferson Davis, who had adamantly opposed the Compromise in the Senate but who was no secessionist, replaced Quitman, and he ran much closer to Foote than Quitman could have. Nonetheless, Foote won, as did three of four Union party congressional candidates, and, as in Georgia, the Union party piled up heavy majorities in the state legislature.[58]

Alabama followed a different pattern than either Mississippi or Georgia, but there too black belt Whigs combined with hill-country Democratic nonslaveholders in a Union coalition that swept to a massive victory in the August 1851 state legislative and congressional elections. Democratic Senator Jeremiah Clemens, who owed his election primarily to Whig legislators and who took a pro-Compromise stance in 1850, became the leading Democratic proponent of a Union coalition just as Cobb and Foote did in Georgia and Mississippi.[59] Its main proponents, however, were Whigs who swung to a pro-Compromise position in 1850 and who, by the fall of that year, were clearly winning support from thousands of north Alabama Democrats because of that stance. Unlike Mississippi, Whigs received at least three of the seven Union party congressional nominations for 1851, and two of those Whigs as well as three Union Democrats won in August. The results of the legislative races were even more decisive. Altogether, Union tickets carried about two-thirds of Alabama's counties.[60]

That Whig politicians in Alabama, like those in Georgia and Mississippi, seized on the Union party as a way to advance their careers is illustrated by the case of Henry Hilliard, the state's most prominent Whig, who represented the Montgomery district in the Thirty-First Congress. Hilliard had been one of the bolters from the Whig caucus in December 1849, but like his fellow Alabama Whig John Allston, he supported the Compromise to secure sectional peace. Ambitious for higher office, Hilliard refused to run for the House again in 1851. He unsuccefully sought a diplomatic post from Fillmore's administration, but he immediately sensed that the Union party movement offered an alternative route for advancement. Thus Hilliard supported efforts to construct a national Union party in Congress during the winter of 1850–51, he campaigned hard for his Whig/Union successor as congressman from the Montgomery district, and he could barely contain his glee when the Union party swept the legislature. Because he and other Whigs had joined the Union party, he exulted, "For the first time I am in a majority in my State & now believe that I shall reach the Senate."[61]

V

These developments had only begun when Millard Fillmore sent his annual message to Congress in December 1850. He could not know that Georgia's November election would effectively stymie secessionism everywhere in Dixie. Nor did he know that the pro-Compromise Union movement would transform itself into a political party. Instead, it seemed to offer the best hope of checking secession and saving the country. He therefore paid Georgia's Unionists heed as he drafted sections of the message pertaining to the Compromise, for Stephens bluntly warned the administration that Fillmore must insist that Northerners had an obligation to uphold the Union by obeying the Fugitive Slave Act. Even before he submitted his message, indeed, Fillmore had a letter published in the Washington *Republic* assuring Georgians of his complete compliance with that law.[62]

Fillmore declared to Congress that the Compromise measures were "a settlement in principle and substance—a final settlement of the dangerous and exciting subjects which they embraced." Since Congress could not now change the laws regarding California, the Texas boundary settlement, Utah, and New Mexico, they were "final and irrevocable." As for the others, Congress should adhere "to the adjustment established by those measures until time and experience shall demonstrate the necessity of further legislation to guard against evasion or abuse."[63]

Fillmore later told New York's Governor Washington Hunt that these controversial statements were necessary to deter secession. Fillmore's rival, Seward, understandably viewed things differently. "It is quite evident, from the message," he griped to Weed, "that the Whig party is required to occupy the Castle Garden platform." Both Fillmore's attempt to reassure New York's new governor and Seward's allusion to a New York City meeting point to a crucial fact. Fillmore was as concerned about the Whig party in New York as about events in the South. As Seward apparently intuited, Fillmore echoed the stance of the Castle Garden meeting, not to foment the surging Union party movement in New York or elsewhere, but to check its growth by coopting its platform for the Whig party.[64]

By December 1850, that growth seemed formidable. Northern bipartisan Union rallies were spreading from coastal cities into the interior as far west as Ohio, Michigan, and Iowa. Within New York, many of Fillmore's Silver Gray allies loudly demanded fusion with pro-Compromise Hunker Democrats. Louisiana's Democratic Senator Solomon Downs publicly endorsed a new party at a November rally in New Orleans. Thus Washington was abuzz with rumors in December, especially after Toombs and Stephens arrived from Georgia and, along with Speaker Cobb, began to proselytize for the new party. Whig Senator John Bell was so unnerved by Stephens' approach that he apprehensively wrote lieutenants in Tennessee to ascertain Whig attitudes toward a Union party there.[65] By the end of December the Ohio Free Soiler Joshua R. Giddings, hardly a potential recruit, predicted that a Union coalition of Whigs and Democrats would elect Ohio's new United States senator during the winter legislative session and that a national Union party would soon bury both major parties. The Whig party, he jeered, would "never again rally under that name with its present leaders or policy." Both Whigs and Democrats "will soon be swallowed up by the Unionists."[66]

Giddings welcomed this development, for it opened the way for merging Free Soilers with anti-Compromise Whigs and Democrats into a broad, exclusively northern antislavery party. That prospective realignment appalled Fillmore, who hoped to save the Whig party by rallying all its elements behind his administration. If pro-Compromise Whigs abandoned the party for a coalition with Democrats, Fillmore recognized, they would abdicate control of state Whig organizations to anti-Compromise men, who would then seek reinforcements from Free Soilers. Fillmore wanted pro-Compromise Whigs to stay and fight rather than switch.

Enthusiasm for a merger with Hunker Democrats among Fillmore's Silver Gray allies in New York who sought to put down "Seward, Weed *et id omne genus*" and to escape "the despotism of Weed" especially alarmed him.[67] His most immediate concern was a proposal that John Young and Hugh Maxwell openly advocated in New York City: that Hunkers and Silver Grays unite in the new legislature to reelect Democrat Daniel S. Dickinson to the Senate rather than the consensus Whig choice, Hamilton Fish. Fish himself, who had regarded the Union party movement from its inception as a Democratic trick to dupe gullible Whigs, warned Fillmore on November 18 that the proposed merger aimed at Dickinson's election and that Fillmore must therefore publicly denounce the creation of a Union party to prevent a permanent rupture of New York's Whigs.[68] These warnings prompted Fillmore's assurance to Fish that he hoped to save the Whig party and would do nothing to divide it. Eschewing the public pronouncement Fish demanded, Fillmore instead privately wrote allies like Solomon Haven and Jerome Fuller denouncing any alliance with Hunkers.[69]

To a far greater extent than events in Georgia or pleas from New York Whigs associated with the Castle Garden Union movement, the advice Fillmore received from Fish and Washington Hunt, the departing and incoming Whig governors of New York, shaped his annual message and the course he pursued during the winter of 1850–51. Within two days of each other during the third week of November, both men implored Fillmore to help reunite and thus preserve New York's Whig party.[70] The simultaneity and similarity of these letters suggest a concerted effort to double-team the president.

Both Fish and Hunt argued, as they had prior to the election, that saving the New York party required Fillmore to forgo a pogrom against Sewardites still holding federal jobs. Weed and other Sewardites, they vowed, would zealously cooperate with the administration if Fillmore left patronage holders untouched. A purge, in contrast, would permanently alienate them from Fillmore and his Silver Gray allies. Whig divisions, they chorused, were confined for the moment to leaders. The rank and file had not yet split, and Fillmore could prevent them from doing so. Whig voters, according to Hunt, "are for Whig principles and will not consent to be divided up into personal factions." Whig voters would remain united unless Silver Grays allied with Hunkers in the legislature, echoed Fish, who obviously had a personal stake in preserving party cohesion in that body.

Other than patronage, the two continued, the major source of intraparty division that fall had been over the Compromise's territorial and Texas boundary provisions. Those wounds were bound to heal, for the new laws forever settled those questions. "These questions therefore no longer remain to divide us," declared Fish. "The sectional agitations which have ... shattered the Whig party must gradually subside," chimed Hunt. "The territories being disposed of, the great cause of sectional conflict is removed." When Fillmore declared the territorial aspects of the Compromise irrevocable, in sum, he heeded not just the demands of Georgia Unionists but also the advice of New York Whigs that the sooner the sectional question was buried and forgotten, the faster the state party would reunite.

The Fugitive Slave Law was another matter. Both Fish and Hunt condemned its retroactive implications that threatened blacks long resident in the North and its lack of jury trials. Both pointed to the legitimacy of northern Whig outrage. Both urged Fillmore to tolerate dissent against the law, though not resistance to its enforcement, and to remain open to possible revisions. Demands for changes, insisted Fish, "may be entertained without being cause for separation between Whigs." Avoid declaring the fugitive law "unalterable," urged Hunt. "That would make it a 'higher law' than the Constitution." Fillmore's insistence on the finality of the Compromise seemed to ignore these pleas, yet he in fact went as far toward meeting them as southern pressure would allow by alluding to possible future revisions to remedy abuses and evasions revealed by experience.

Fillmore also heeded their advice on matters other than patronage and the Compromise. Both asserted that rank-and-file Whigs were eager to support a reunited Whig party and Fillmore's administration, but Fish emphasized the continuing threat that a Union party posed to Whig reunification, while Hunt stressed positive ways Fillmore could rally Whigs. Whig voters could be reinvigorated, reunited, and remobilized, insisted Hunt, by an emphasis "on the original measures and principles of the Whig party."

Fillmore clearly took this advice to heart. The dominant theme of his annual message with regard to government *policy* was not the finality of the Compromise or his determination to enforce the fugitive slave and neutrality laws. Its longest sections instead resurrected the traditional Whig case for an activist state in general and for a higher tariff and federal subsidization of internal improvements, including a Pacific railroad, in particular. To an astonishing degree, Fillmore iterated in detail almost every charge Whigs had made against the Walker Tariff in 1846. He called for abandonment of its *ad valorem* duties, which cut government revenue, provided insufficient protection to manufacturers, and encouraged fraud as shippers and importing merchants undervalued goods on bills of lading to secure lower duties. He urged Congress to substitute specific for the variable *ad valorem* rates and to end the heinous provision that placed higher rates on the raw materials used by American manufacturers than on the finished goods they made with them.[71]

By rehashing Whig themes from 1846, Fillmore thus attempted to leap back to the last election prior to the sectional controversy over the Mexican Cession, to an election that focused on economic issues, to a campaign during which Whigs throughout the country had rallied behind a distinctive Whig economic platform and had apparently ridden that platform to victory. The longest part of his message, in sum, attempted to ignore the sectional conflict, to advocate "the original measures and principles of the Whig party," and to shift the agenda from what divided Whigs to what united them and distinguished them from Democrats.

Fillmore thus moved indirectly rather than overtly to undermine a bipartisan Union party. By proclaiming the benefits of an activist state, decrying the invidiousness of *ad valorem* tariff duties, and explicitly defending the constitutionality of federal internal improvements, Fillmore moved explicitly to differentiate Whigs from Democrats. By coopting the Union party's position on the Compromise and reaffirming traditional Whig economic principles, he sought to negate the need for, and scuttle the possibility of, bipartisan cooperation. He sought to demonstrate that he was a Whig, not a Union party man.

VI

By itself, Fillmore's annual message did little to reunify the Whig party or to derail the Union party movement. Yet by the end of March 1851, developments in both Washington and the states suggested that the Union movement might be confined to its Deep South base. It stalled because the conditions that fostered it in Georgia, Alabama, and Mississippi did not exist elsewhere. To flourish, the Union party required at least three things: a rationale in the form of a disunionist threat or a credible opposition party that refused to accept the Compromise; the willingness of *both* Whig *and* Democratic politicians to abandon old organizations for new ones; and the abatement or cessation of partisan conflict on issues other than the Compromise. The absence of one or more of these elements stifled the proposed realignment.

Though no test votes on slavery or the Compromise occurred during the short congressional session to promote a possible Union coalition, the Georgians maneuvered to convert their state Union organization into a permanent national party. Stephens drafted a Union pledge and circulated it for signatures first among all the southern Whigs in the House and Senate and then, with the aid of Speaker Cobb, among southern and northern Democrats. Simultaneously, Silver Grays like William Duer solicited signatures from pro-Compromise northern Whigs. Dubbed the Round Robin by its critics, this document pledged that its signers, in order to protect the Union, would maintain the compromise "settlement inviolate" and "resist all attempts to repeal or alter the acts aforesaid." Nor would they support for state or federal elective office "any man, of whatever party, who is not known to be opposed to the disturbance of the SETTLEMENT aforesaid, and to the renewal, in any form, of agitation upon the subject of slavery." Signed by forty-four men, the Round Robin was printed in the New York *Express*, the paper of Silver Gray Congressman James Brooks, who signed it, as well as in the Democratic Washington *Union*, which did not endorse it.[72]

Stephens and others saw this document as a blueprint for a national Union party.[73] Along with the failure of the proposed Union party's national convention for February 22 to materialize, however, the paucity of support for the Round Robin instead demonstrated the difficulty of building such an organization. The Round Robin's forty-four signers represented approximately one-third of the representatives and senators who had voted for compromise measures that required some sacrifice of sectional interests. Thirty-nine of the forty-four were Whigs, but only ten of those were Northerners: Cooper of Pennsylvania, Boston's lameduck Congressman Samuel Eliot, who opposed creation of a Union party, and eight of New York's thirteen Silver Grays.[74] Representation from southern Whigs was far more respectable. Henry Clay and all six of Kentucky's Whig representatives signed. So did Senator Thomas Pratt and the entire Maryland Whig delegation in the House; Senator Willie P. Mangum and four of six North Carolina Whig representatives; four of Tennessee's five Whig representatives; the lone Whig representatives from Florida and Louisiana; Henry Hilliard of Alabama; both of Virginia's Whig representatives; and all the Georgia Whigs who had joined the Union party—Toombs, Stephens, Allen Owen, and Senator William C. Dawson.

Yet there were notable absences from the ranks of pro-Compromise southern Whigs: Senator George Badger and Congressman Edward Stanly from North Carolina; John Bell and a Whig representative from Tennessee; Delaware's three Whigs; Joseph Underwood, Clay's Senate colleague from Kentucky; and James Pearce of Maryland, Fillmore's closest Senate friend.[75] Nor is it clear how many of the southern Whigs who signed, aside from Hilliard, the Georgians and Kentuckians, and perhaps the Louisianan Henry Bullard, were prepared to join Democrats in a Union party.[76] Nonetheless, the most glaring aspect of the Round Robin is that only five Democrats signed it. They included four Southerners: Senator Thomas Rusk of Texas and Foote, Cobb, and Clemens, each of whom was committed to a Union party in his home state. But no other Democrats from those states, let alone from Maryland, Kentucky, or Louisiana, signed. Especially revealing was the total absence of northern Democrats other than California's Senator William Gwin, a beneficiary rather than an architect of the Compromise, for no bloc had backed compromise more solidly in 1850 than they. Why they refused to sign is clear. They saw no reason to join a new party and share credit with Whigs for saving the Union. They believed they could win as Democrats on a pro-Compromise platform in the North by tarring anti-Compromise northern Whigs with the stigma of disunionism. As Stephen Douglas, who indignantly refused to sign the Round Robin, declared in a Senate speech, "The Democratic party is as good a Union party as I want, and I wish to preserve its principles and its organization and to triumph upon its old issues."[77]

Pro-Compromise Democrats, in sum, undermined the Union party movement. By mid-March, moreover, many Whigs had evinced equal disdain for combining with Democrats, no matter what their stand on the Compromise. When Bell sounded out his Tennessee lieutenants about a Union party, he received a crescendo of catcalls. "You speak of the desire to form a Union party," Thomas A. R. Nelson wrote. "I have no objection to the Whigs becoming the chosen champions of the Union," but "I am opposed to changing our name or abandoning the old standards." Both parties in Tennessee were equally devoted to the Union, another declared, but "on most other important questions, on which there can be a difference of opinion, they differ now as they have always done. A union of heterogeneous bodies! It is absurd." "The great mass" of northern Whigs "cannot & will not affiliate" with a Union party, echoed Detroit's Whig editor Henry Barns, for they regarded it "as a Webster plot." Thomas Ewing, who faced reelection by the Ohio legislature that winter and who, like Giddings, feared the creation of a Union coalition during that contest, received similar tidings when he tested opinion at home. True Whigs, he was told, saw the Union movement as a "humbug"; they would not swerve from the previous state platform that endorsed the Taylor plan against compromise. "No *coalition* with *Locofocos* even under the plausible title of *Union party* can succeed."[78]

VII

If the Union party movement stalled during the spring of 1851, it was far from dead. Its strength in Alabama and Mississippi and its continuing potency in Georgia were yet to be demonstrated in elections between August and November. In addition, pro-Compromise Democrats and Whigs in certain northern states, notably those where Democrats had formed coalitions with Free Soilers and where anti-Compromise Whigs controlled state Whig organizations, like Massachusetts, New York, Connecticut, and Rhode Island, still saw mutual advantages in such a merger if it progressed elsewhere. Ultimately, therefore, the fate of the Union party movement in 1851 hinged on the electoral fortunes of southern Whigs outside of Georgia, Alabama, and Mississippi. For if southern Whigs could not win state and congressional elections on their own with a pro-Compromise platform, they might follow the example of their counterparts in the Union party's three Deep South strongholds and abandon the Whig party for the new organization. And if Whigs across the South did so, then the likelihood that Northerners would follow suit would increase exponentially. As Jerome Fuller, the Albany editor and Union party proponent, told Fillmore in January, "A mere bargain between Nationals and Hunkers in the North to unite and form a Union party would not be worth a straw. The current events at the South must determine whether a union party can be formed, and bring its members together."[79]

Aside from Georgia, Alabama, and Mississippi, eight other slave states held congressional and/or gubernatorial elections in 1851. As usual, Whigs were routed in the Democratic bastions of Texas and Arkansas. Since the mid-1840s Virginia had become almost as predictably, if less lopsidedly, Democratic. In 1849 Whigs had carried only one of the state's fifteen congressional districts, although they had added another in a subsequent special election.

For various reasons, however, they expected to do much better in 1851. First, Virginia's Whigs, like their two representatives in the Thirty-First Congress who signed the Round Robin, were ardently pro-Compromise. In contrast, while half of the Virginia Democrats in the House supported the Compromise, the other half, both Democratic senators, and much of the Democratic press vigorously opposed it both before and after its passage.[80] Thus Whigs hoped to label the enemy as secessionist fire-eaters and pose as the Union's only reliable defenders.[81] Second, Virginia's Whigs recruited the most able and renowned men in the party to run as congressional candidates. Ex-Congressmen Thomas Flournoy, William Goggin, and John Minor Botts all accepted nominations. In the Ninth and Tenth Districts, James F. Strother and Charles J. Faulkner were men of considerable talent. Third, Virginia's Whigs, quite unlike those in other states, expected to benefit from the new state constitution that was completed in May 1851. Indeed, the congressional elections, which were normally held in May, were postponed to October on the same day as the referendum on the constitution. If it were adopted, legislative contests and the state's first popular gubernatorial election would be held in December.

Although Whigs were a decided minority at the constitutional convention, they gave far more proportionate support to its final adoption than Democrats, and they expected to reap benefits from its more popular features. The constitution not only made the governorship elective rather than appointive, it also broadened the suffrage by removing property-holding requirements. That provision, Whigs believed, would benefit them in cities like Richmond, Norfolk, Petersburg, and Lynchburg, where they had traditionally been strong. Both chambers of the legislature were enlarged, and the districts were reapportioned to give western Virginia, where nonslaveholders constituted the vast bulk of the population, a majority of house seats, whereas eastern Virginia retained a majority in the senate. This change too would benefit the party, Whigs trumpeted, for western areas were far more appreciative of Whig support for internal improvements than was the East. To exploit that presumed popularity, they not only ran a Westerner named George Summers for governor, they also boasted of Whigs' strong support at the convention for measures that would ease state funding of internal improvements. All in all, Whigs believed, their backing for the constitution and the provisions they had helped write into it would rejuvenate the party.[82]

This optimism proved unfounded. Even though many Democrats continued to denounce the Compromise for sacrificing Southern Rights, they neutralized the Whig advantage by supporting legislative resolutions in the spring that acquiesced in the finality of the measures, the same formula pushed by Fillmore. By the time of the October congressional elections, disagreement about the Compromise was a dead issue. One reflection of this consensus was that, even though Whigs had recruited an all-star team to run in some congressional districts, they offered no challenger to Democrats in six of fifteen districts. This abdication not only portended party collapse, it nullified any advantage Whigs might gain from turnout in the constitutional referendum. Although the constitution, which Whigs backed more avidly than Democrats, carried by a seven-to-one margin, Whigs again carried only two districts, the Ninth and Tenth, and Democrats, regardless of how they had voted on the Compromise, usually won by far bigger margins than they had two years earlier. Because of the pro-Compromise consensus and the absence of Whig candidates, moreover, total turnout in the congressional contests was a pathetic 44,000 compared to over 80,000 in the simultaneous constitutional referendum and 126,000 in the subsequent gubernatorial election.[83]

Nor did expansion of suffrage and legislative reapportionment help Whigs markedly in December. Summers lost the gubernatorial contest with 47 percent of the votes, 59,476 to 67,074, the customary proportion Whigs had drawn before the abolition of property requirements. Whigs' share of seats in the legislature's lower chamber increased from only 39 to 43 percent. In the senate, it declined from 34 to 32 percent. Virginia's Whigs, in sum, remained a respectable but maddeningly persistent minority.

The Compromise had even less influence on Maryland's congressional elections. The three Whigs and three Democrats in its House delegation had voted similarly on the measures, and popular sentiment in the state almost unanimously favored them. Personalities and local factional squabbles thus dominated the campaigns, and in October, Whigs actually gained a seat in Baltimore formerly held by a Democrat. Yet this nominal success failed to conceal the problems that afflicted the state party and that stemmed from discontent over revision of the state constitution.

Despite Whig opposition in the legislature and in popular referenda, Maryland's citizens authorized a constitutional convention that met from November

1850 to May 1851, the product of which was popularly ratified in June 1851. Among other changes, the new constitution made a host of previously appointive state and local offices, including judges and justices of the peace, elective, created new state offices that would be filled in the 1851 election, and reapportioned the legislature to the Whigs' disadvantage. Whig strength in Maryland had always centered in the oldest, slaveholding, tobacco-growing counties of southern Maryland and the Eastern Shore, which under the old constitution had grossly disproportionate representation in the legislature, thereby almost guaranteeing Whig control. Democrats, in turn, were strongest in heavily populated Baltimore and Baltimore County, as well as western Maryland, the areas most enthusiastic about constitutional revision. The new constitution changed the method of electing senators and thereby opened that chamber to Democratic penetration. It also reduced the size of the house, stripped the usually Whiggish counties of at least ten seats, increased the Baltimore County delegation by one seat, and doubled Baltimore City's representation from five to ten.[84]

Other aspects of the movement for constitutional revision also damaged Whigs. Because opposition was identified with their party, Whigs in Baltimore and western Maryland who wanted revision abandoned the organization for fusion "union" or "reform" organizations during the election of delegates and the voting on ratification. The convention's proceedings, which dragged on far longer than anyone believed necessary, only increased the impatience with and antipathy toward established politicians in both parties. As a result, during the 1851 elections in the fall, when Maryland's voters had the opportunity to elect more officeholders than they ever had before, a host of independent candidates – some representing self-proclaimed antiparty, reform organizations, others self-nominated – contested regular party candidates for local offices, judgeships, the legislature, and Congress. No disagreements on specific issues spurred these insurgent candidacies; indeed, precisely the absence of policy disputes encouraged them because both major parties now seemed interested only in the spoils of office. Independents' agenda was simply to destroy the monopoly that regular parties exercised over public office, to restore power to the people.[85]

Thus, even though Whigs won four of six congressional seats, their local organizations were in disarray. In the solidly Whig First District north of Washington, incumbent Whig Congressman Richard J. Bowie of Montgomery County, who had run unopposed in 1849 and staunchly supported the compromise measures, received a serious challenge, not from a Democrat but from an "Independent" Whig in neighboring Prince Georges County, who was also named Bowie. In the Sixth District on the Eastern Shore, which had been represented by Whig John Kerr in 1850, the regular Whig nominee was defeated by "Independent" Whig Joseph S. Cottman. Independent candidacies together with the legislative reapportionment took an even heavier toll on Whigs in the state and legislative races. Democrats, already holding the governorship, in 1851 swept the new state offices and most of the elective judgeships. Independents, whose qualifications were dubious, took the others. Democrats evenly divided the new senate with Whigs, who had consistently dominated that body since the early 1830s. In the newly apportioned house, where Whigs had held a majority of 57 percent in 1850, they fell to a minority of 42 percent.

Despite Whigs' gain of one congressional seat, therefore, Whigs both inside and outside Maryland regarded the results as a defeat. Significantly, indeed, few commentators even mentioned the congressional returns and concentrated instead on Whigs' loss of the legislature, Democrats' sweep of state offices, the infusion of unqualified men into the judiciary, and the palpable erosion of their voter support as former Whig voters defected to "reform" tickets. "Our judges are below medicocrity, and lower in inverse ratio, according to the squares of the distances of the elevation of the Court—the Court of Appeals being the worst—inferior to the run of our students' mock court," lamented the intellectual Kennedy. "The other officers—I mean, not judicial—are shocking to behold. Ours is a horrible Q.E.D. against reform." The populistic upsurge boiling up in Ohio, Kentucky, Indiana, and other states as well as Maryland, it would seem, had a high price—at least if one were a Whig.[86]

In other southern states, however, Whigs successfully tarred Democrats with the stigma of secessionist radicalism and thus exploited the unionist sentiment embodied by the Union party elsewhere. Louisiana, a strongly competitive state, offers a good example. The four House seats as well as the legislature were at stake in 1851, and the new legislature would fill Solomon Downs' Senate seat. Despite talk of starting a Louisiana Union party in 1850, none materialized. Instead Democrats split along the lines they had taken on the Compromise. Two of the state's three Democratic representatives, as well as Pierre Soulé, cast solidly anti-Compromise votes, and once back in Louisiana they defended that record. Although they shunned secessionism, Southern Rights Associations formed to defend them as champions of the proslavery cause. This move left the pro-Compromise Downs isolated from the majority of his party; nonetheless, Downs stumped the state in defense of the settlement in 1851, occasionally accompanied by Whig congressional candidates. Charles Conrad's move to the War Department in 1850 prevented any Louisiana Whig from voting on the Compromise, but his successor, Henry Bullard, signed the Round Robin, while the Whig press like the New Orleans *Picayune*, once again edited by Alexander Bullitt, former editor of the Washington *Republic*, wholeheartedly defended the settlement and castigated Democrats as disunionist "extremists."[87]

Defense of the Compromise and the Union was not Whigs' only weapon. They also urged that the next legislature call a new constitutional convention that could reapportion the legislature, exempt homesteads from debt, provide for an elective judiciary, and, above all, eliminate the restrictions on banking and other corporations contained in the 1845 constitution. Democrats were not adverse to all these revisions, but they wanted them made by legislative amendment, not a new constitutional convention, which, they charged, was certain to increase New Orleans' representation in the legislature. This stance gave Whigs the advantage, especially in the South's largest city.[88]

This combination of issues powered impressive Whig gains. While they carried only two of the four congressional districts, they thereby doubled their representation in the House. More important, Whigs gained complete control of the legislature, and in January 1852 the Whig majority selected Judah P. Benjamin to replace Downs in the Senate. Thus Louisiana was one of the very few states where Whigs took a Senate seat from Democrats, although Benjamin would not serve until the Thirty-Third, not the Thirty-Second, Congress. In addition, over concerted Democratic opposition, Whig legislators also pushed through a bill providing for an April referendum on the question of calling a constitutional convention, and when it passed, Lousiana's Whigs appeared to be on a roll.[89]

North Carolina's Whigs also managed to make the August congressional elections a referendum on disunionism. Without state offices at stake, they could evade the divisive free suffrage and reapportionment questions that had so hurt them in 1850. With the marked exception of Thomas Clingman, the renegade Whig from Asheville, who had joined Democrats in opposing the Compromise in 1850, the lines between the parties were crystal clear. Both Whig senators and the other five Whig representatives supported compromise, and all three Democratic representatives opposed it, a division mirrored in the party press.

Even though all three Democrats and four of the six Whig incumbents ran again in 1851, however, the race focused less on the merits of the Compromise, which even Democrats grudgingly accepted by the summer of 1851, than on the related question of secession. In the state legislature and on the hustings, Democrats defended the right, if not the expediency, of secession to defend Southern Rights from northern aggression. Whigs not only denied the right of secession, they approved the use of federal force against South Carolina should it attempt secession that year. As one Whig reported, the congressional race in his district "has been conducted in reference chiefly to the issue of Secession, and acquiescence in the measures of the compromise, and the course of the administration." The last reference was important, for North Carolina's Whigs, like those elsewhere in the South, publicly and privately trumpeted their approval of Fillmore and pointed to his administration's fairness toward the South as a reason to elect Whigs and reject any hint of secession.[90]

Many North Carolina Democrats, however, staunchly upheld the Union and rankled at their party's extremism in 1851. For a while, therefore, Whigs hoped to pick up their votes. But either because of the unpopularity and ineptitude of certain Whig candidates such as Burgess Gaither, who opposed the apostate Clingman, and Calvin Graves, who contested Democratic incumbent Abraham Venable, or because of partisan animosities that kept Democrats from backing rabid Whigs like Edward Stanly, few conversions occurred.[91] As a result, all three Democratic incumbents prevailed, while Whigs carried the same six districts they had in 1849, although the victorious Clingman, who still claimed to be a Whig, should probably be counted as a Democrat since all Democrats in his district supported him.

Three aspects of this Whig triumph stand out. First, while North Carolina as a whole was an intensely competitive state, most congressional districts were extremely uncompetitive, in part because of the Whigs' gerrymander in the 1840s. Of nine districts, only in Stanly's did fewer than five percentage points separate the winner from the loser, and in no other district was the margin less than ten. In most districts, indeed, it surpassed twenty or thirty percentage points, whether carried by Whigs or Democrats, and incumbents Whig Joseph Caldwell and Democrat William Ashe ran unopposed. Compared to 1849, when only two districts produced such lopsided results and voter turnout was significantly higher, these results suggest that the partisan polarization over the Compromise and secession questions effectively cemented the majority party's control of each district by depressing the vote of its opponent.

Second, Democrats immediately recognized their disadvantage on sectional questions. How many votes Ashe may have drawn in a contested race is unclear, but the total Democratic vote dropped from 38,606 in 1849 to 17,857 in 1851. Even if Ashe's district is excluded from the 1849 total, Democrats drew 30,666 elsewhere that year, and in 1850 David Reid attracted over 45,000 votes for governor. Clearly, many Democratic voters rejected the party's extremist stance, and the party quickly abandoned it. The Democrats' leading editor, William W. Holden of the Raleigh *Standard*, informed the fire-eating Venable that Democrats must now silence their guns and accept the finality of the Compromise measures. Whigs, in turn, recognized that Democratic capitulation stripped them of their best issue. "As to Politicks [sic], the secession feeling is dead in N.C.," one sighed. "I only fear it is too dead for the good of the Whig party." With the secession issue still alive, he thought, Whigs could carry the 1852 state election "by 5000 or 10,000 majority." As it was, he lamented, "they are now *backing out* from secession & will press State & constitutional questions, on all which they outmanage the Whigs."[92]

Yet in the same letter, this despairing Whig pointed to the third important impact of the 1851 elections. "Nothing will gain us" victory in the next state elections, he predicted, "except the popularity of the present Whig administration, which is, I assure you, very real in this state. We can point to it with pride & as fair illustration of Whig policy." Even before the congressional elections in August, indeed, North Carolina's Whigs concluded "that the Whigs of the South cannot rally for the next Presidency on any other person so readily as on Mr. Fillmore." Nothing better illustrates the chasm that continued to separate northern from southern Whigs.[93]

In no slave state in 1851 were the political stakes so high and in none did the Whigs score so impressive a victory as in Tennessee. Not only were the eleven-man congressional delegation, the legislature, and the governor to be elected in August. The new legislature could also replace Democrat Hopkins L. Turney in the Senate. Even more important to Tennessee's Whigs, the new legislature would reapportion not just the state's congressional districts but also the legislature itself, and the new districts could not be altered for a decade. As the Whigs' gubernatorial candidate put it, whichever party won control of the legislature "may without seriously outraging the other, so arrange the Legislature that the political complexion of the State will be permanent for the next 10 years." As a result, "the victory of a Whig governor would be valueless without the Legislature."[94]

Clearly recognizing the consequences of the August elections, Whigs in early 1851 despaired of carrying them. They had no worries about the pro-Compromise positions taken by Bell and Whig congressmen, all of whom had voted even for California's admission. They saw that stance as a source of strength, especially since Turney opposed the Compromise in the Senate and the Democrats' gubernatorial candidate, incumbent William Trousdale, repeatedly called it outrageous. Elected in 1849 on a platform pledging defense of Southern Rights "to the last extremity," Trousdale was Tennessee's equivalent of Georgia's George Towns. Although he did did not call for secession, he had as governor endorsed the Nashville Convention and its anticompromise resolutions. The Democrats' 1851 platform acquiesced in the finality of the Compromise, but it made that acceptance conditional on complete northern compliance with the laws. Throughout the 1851 campaign, moreover, Trousdale repeatedly attacked each of the individual measures as southern defeats, a stance that Whigs believed exposed the hypocrisy of the Democratic platform. Because Trousdale as governor also opposed any increase in the state debt to fund railroad construction, a stance that angered residents of East Tennessee, he seemed especially vulnerable.[95]

The Whigs' problem at the beginning of the year was finding a gubernatorial candidate behind whom they could rally. Tennessee's Whigs were bitterly divided by factional rivalries and personal enmities that had little to do with issues, although they frequently led to differences over potential presidential candidates. In part, divisions reflected age-old jealousies among the state's three well-defined and self-conscious geographical regions—East, Middle, and West Tennessee— jealousies that mandated the balancing or rotation of the party's candidates for the governorship and Senate. Whigs from mountainous East Tennessee in particular felt shortchanged. Distribution of federal patronage in Tennessee also engendered immense anger, for under both Taylor and Fillmore, Senator John Bell and his allies like ex-Governor Neill Brown, Congressman Meredith Gentry, Nashville editor Allen Hall, and East Tennessee's Thomas A. R. Nelson monopolized the jobs and newspaper printing contracts. Bell was Tennessee's most eminent Whig, but many in his party despised him as a "cold hearted, selfish, and artful scoundrel." So deep was the anger at Bell that many of his rivals, especially ex-Governor James "Lean Jimmy" Jones, wanted the new legislature, if Whigs won control, to forsake the tradition of electing senators late and fill Bell's seat as well as Turney's. "Bell's day is *over*," growled Felix Zollicoffer, editor of the Nashville *Republican Banner*. "He must *not* be re-elected."[96]

Tennessee's governorship was a largely honorific post since the governor lacked the veto power and the legislature distributed most state patronage, but a strong gubernatorial candidate was deemed essential to carrying the legislature, since he had to stump the entire state defending the Whig cause. That grueling and expensive responsibility deterred some potential candidates, and the expectation that the legislature might fill both Senate seats deterred others who wanted to remain available for the federal office. At the same time, candidates for the Senate like Jones and Bell wanted to derail potential opponents by inducing them to run for governor. The man whom both Bell and his opponents hit on to fill that bill was William B. Campbell, a circuit court judge and Mexican War hero from Carthage in Middle Tennessee. Both Bell and Gentry pleaded with Campbell to run, as did their factional rival, Nashville editor Zollicoffer. Campbell's refusal to run, argued Zollicoffer, would "strike upon the Whig party *as a death-knell.* . . . We are *lost*, if you do not stand by us, *now, and of consequence, forever.*" On Campbell's candidacy, declared another Whig, rested "the destiny of the Whig party, not only in Tennessee, but all over the Union."[97]

But Campbell, miffed that he had never been offered a federal job by Taylor or Fillmore and fearful that he would lose money by running for and serving as governor, balked. Finally, promises that the party would raise the money for him and immense pressure from across the state persuaded the reluctant Campbell to become the standard bearer. Whigs' platform praised the Compromise as a final settlement of sectional controversy, and throughout the campaign, Campbell and other Whig speakers lauded its wisdom and patriotism and heaped encomiums on Fillmore for supporting and enforcing it. Campbell, moreover, repeatedly insisted that he preferred Fillmore as the Whigs' presidential candidate, while Democrats, unbelievably in light of developments since July 1850, dredged up the charge that Fillmore was an abolitionist. Helped in East Tennessee by his support for aid to railroad construction and by the withering speeches of Nelson, who filled in for him in joint debates with Trousdale when he fell ill, Campbell garnered about 3,000 more votes than his unsuccessful predecessor and edged out Trousdale 63,423 (50.7 percent) to 61,648 (49.3 percent). Whigs agreed that Campbell's victory marked "a triumph of the *Compromise* and the *Union* over an anti-Compromise *factionalist.*"[98]

Because only 22 percent of Tennessee's white families owned slaves in 1850 and because even most slaveholders were staunch unionists, the only surprising thing about this victory over Trousdale was how close it had been. Trousdale's total, indeed, declined by fewer than 100 votes from 1849 to 1851, a fact that indicates that even yeoman Democrats who disliked his reputation as an extremist loyally stood by their party. That steadfastness combined with other factors to prevent Whigs from using their pro-Compromise position to similar advantage in the concurrent congressional elections.

As in most other slave states, Tennessee's congressional districts were flagrantly gerrymandered. Whigs ran no candidates in three of the districts Democrats controlled, just as Democrats mounted no challenge to Whig incumbents Meredith Gentry and Christopher Williams. Nor were most Democratic incumbents as vulnerable to attacks of extremism as Trousdale. Although Hopkins Turney had opposed compromise in the Senate, all seven Democratic members of the House gave it varying degrees of support. Three supported all the measures except the District slave trade ban; the other four also opposed California, but all supported the crucial Texas-New Mexico bill.[99] Consequently, Whigs failed to make any gains in the congressional races; just as in 1849, they won only four of the eleven House seats, although they came within 16 votes of 13,000 cast of carrying a fifth district.[100]

Whigs scored their greatest triumph in the legislative races, the focal point of their campaign. They converted a three-seat deficit in the house into a three-seat majority and increased their margin in the senate from three to seven seats. Whig control immediately set off a scramble for the open Senate seat when the legislature met in October. Favorites from each of the state's three regions demanded the prize: Thomas A. R. Nelson, who had filled in so ably for Campbell, from East Tennessee; Gustavus A. Henry, a frequent presidential elector, who claimed a payback for his efforts in repeatedly canvassing the state, from Middle Tennessee; and Bell's enemy James Jones, who now lived outside of Memphis in West Tennessee, the area of the state where slaveholding and cotton growing were most prevalent. Each man had such strong claims that for weeks the Whig caucus could not make a choice. Finally, after the angry Henry withdrew, Jones prevailed over Nelson, who was furious that Campbell did not back him, and Jones easily defeated Trousdale, the Democrats' candidate. The party was so divided that it abandoned all thought of trying to replace Bell.[101]

Despite the embarrassing squabble over United States senators, the legislature's Whig majority, at Campbell's urging, passed a bill providing for the loan of state credit to railroads that could connect East Tennessee with Virginia and Georgia and thereby redeemed the party's campaign pledge. Whigs also reformed the state's legal system and passed a free banking act. Most important, the defeated senatorial aspirant Gustavus Henry wrote and Whigs passed an ingeniously partisan redistricting bill for the state's congressional and legislative districts.

Notorious thereafter as the Henrymander, the districting act, as Governor Campbell jubilantly reported, would secure "to the Whigs a majority in both branches of the Legislature & 7 out of the 10 members of Congress."[102]

Tennessee's elections of 1851 had three results of enormous importance for the state and national Whig parties. First, by ensuring the Whigs a powerful base in the legislature and a more competitive chance in congressional elections, the Henrymander enhanced the Whig party's longevity in Tennessee and guaranteed that even its successors would offer far stronger opposition to Democrats than was true in most southern states. The Henrymander did not work perfectly. By adding the two most heavily Whig counties in the state to the hitherto securely Democratic first congressional district, for example, Whigs achieved their goal of forcing Democrat Andrew Johnson out of Congress, but Johnson then won the governorship in 1853. Nonetheless, more successfully than Whigs in any other state, North or South, Tennessee's tilted the political playing field in their direction and guaranteed that so long as the national Whig party endured, opponents of Democrats in Tennessee would adhere to it.

Second, Campbell's vigorous defense of the Compromise and of the Fillmore administration convinced the vast majority of Tennessee Whigs that running Fillmore on a pro-Compromise platform in 1852 offered the party its best chance in the presidential election. "Tennessee may be put down as sound on the Union question, for the Compromise & for Mr. Fillmore or a sound Union man for the next Presidency," Campbell assured his uncle after his victory.[103]

Third, not all Tennessee Whigs shared that conviction, for in James Jones the state elevated to the Senate a man with even higher aspirations. Jones dreamed of the vice presidency or the White House itself, and since his intraparty rivals like Bell and Gentry were wholeheartedly in the Fillmore camp, hitching his star to the incumbent did not stike Jones as the best way to realize those dreams. He would look elsewhere, just as he had backed Clay in 1848, when Bell and Gentry promoted Taylor. Because of Jones' naked ambition, Tennessee's Whigs became more deeply involved in and more divided by the maneuvering for the Whigs' presidential nomination in 1852 than those from any other slave state.

If Tennessee produced the Whigs' most significant southern victory in 1851, neighboring Kentucky, the home of Clay and the cradle of Whiggery, inflicted their most stinging defeat. For only the second time since the formation of the Whig party in the winter of 1833–34, Democrats won half of the state's House delegation by gaining one seat from the Whigs. With the addition of only 120 votes in another district, Democrats would have completely reversed the six-to-four margin Whigs had won in 1847 and 1849.[104] Even more embarrassing, for the first time ever, Whigs lost the governorship when Democrat Lazarus Powell, who had lost to Crittenden in 1848 by over 8,000 votes, edged out Whig Archibald Dixon by fewer than 1,000. Whigs were hardly crushed, but a former bastion was now closely competitive.[105]

This setback stemmed primarily from the popularity of a rising Democratic star who stole a traditionally Whig congressional seat and from the palpable unpopularity of Dixon.[106] Democrats' new star was John C. Breckinridge, who defeated Clay's old friend Leslie Combs in the eighth congressional district that encompassed Clay's Ashland farm, as well as Lexington and Frankfort. Breckinridge clearly cut into the Whig vote and mobilized previously despondent Democrats. Democrats had not even contested the district in 1849 against Whig Charles Morehead, although a separate nativist candidate had. But Breckinridge ran 1,100 votes ahead of Powell's vote in the district during the 1848 gubernatorial race and 600 votes ahead of Powell in 1851. Breckinridge's coattails, indeed, made the eighth district the only one in the state where Powell gained votes since 1848.[107]

The victorious Powell actually attracted over 2500 fewer votes in 1851 than he had three years earlier; he won because Dixon ran almost 11,000 votes behind Crittenden. The new constitution in part accounted for this drop-off, for it reduced the number of days on which Kentuckians could vote from three to one. Nonetheless, Dixon clearly alienated many Whigs. Abrasive and ambitious, he selfishly demanded the gubernatorial nomination because he had stepped aside for Crittenden in 1848. This, of course, was a self-serving version of history, for the reluctant Crittenden, who had to sacrifice a Senate seat to run for governor, had been selected in desperation to end a standoff between Dixon and another man. To prevent another contentious convention in 1851 Whigs gave the nomination to Dixon, but many obviously rankled at his browbeating tactics.

Equally important, the 1850 constitutional convention increased Dixon's unpopularity with a small but significant constituency. Because of agitation by Cassius M. Clay's Emancipationist party for a provision mandating gradual emancipation in the new constitution, Dixon fought on the convention floor to bolster the state's commitment to slavery. This stand infuriated antislavery men, who ran Cassius Clay as an Emancipationist gubernatorial candidate against him. While Clay garnered only about 3,600 votes, many were Whig defectors and others were previous nonvoters who obviously disliked Dixon. As some Whigs argued prior to their state convention, the Whigs would probably have been better off had they run little-known John B. Thompson, the party's successful candidate for lieutenant governor.[108]

The new constitution also reapportioned the state's legislative districts, and Whigs had to struggle to retain control of that body. They did so, but their majority in the house was reduced from fourteen seats to ten, and, in the senate, from twelve to two. This victory meant that the new Whig legislature could fill the Senate seat of Joseph R. Underwood, Henry Clay's stubbornly independent Whig colleague. Yet when the legislature met in November 1851, the party again faced problems with the grasping Dixon.

Underwood's term actually did not end until March 1853, but the openly antislavery stance he had taken during Kentucky's constitutional elections in 1849 and his siding with northern antislavery Whigs in the Senate during so many roll-call votes in 1850 made him an albatross to the party. Dixon now demanded this Senate seat as a reward for making the gubernatorial run. The immensely popular Attorney General Crittenden also wanted it, for the beginning of the term would coincide with the end of Fillmore's administration. Congressman Charles Morehead, who did not seek reelection in 1851, Judge George Robertson, and Congressman Humphrey Marshall, who won reelection in 1851, also threw their hats into the ring.[109]

The result was paralysis and a divisive struggle that dashed Whigs' hope that the legislative majority might reorganize and reenergize the party. Crittenden's entry into the race caused the friends of Henry Clay, who still simmered over

Crittenden's support for Taylor in 1848, to back Robertson. Dixon's friends refused to withdraw him on the grounds that he had stepped aside for Crittenden in the 1848 governor's race; Crittenden's allies retorted that precisely Crittenden's willingness to make that race justified his return to the Senate. To the dismay and growing anger of Whig newspapers, the Whig caucus could agree on no one, and vote after vote on the floor of the legislature produced no winner since Whigs divided among the rivals. Finally, after a month of fruitless balloting, both Crittenden and Dixon agreed to withdraw. Fifteen men now presented their claims. From this melee Whigs chose the man with the fewest enemies, a man whom no one could possibly imagine in the United States Senate, and the man whom the legislature ultimately sent there—newly elected Lieutenant Governor John B. Thompson, whom Democrats greeted with the derisive jeers that Whigs had heaped on James K. Polk in 1844.[110]

Within days of Thompson's election, while the legislature remained in session, Henry Clay announced from Washington that he would resign his seat effective September 1852. Thus the legislature could elect someone to the remainder of his term, which ran until March 1855. Crittenden immediately refused to allow consideration of his name, but the unmitigatedly selfish Dixon again grabbed for the ring. After another unseemly quarrel among Whigs, who divided their votes on six roll calls among Dixon and other contenders, Dixon finally prevailed on December 30. Thus in the Thirty-Third Congress, Kentucky, represented for so many years in the Senate by the irrepressible and enormously gifted Clay and the brilliant if more taciturn Crittenden, would send Thompson, whom many considered a nonentity, and Dixon, the only Kentucky Whig ever to lose a statewide election to the Democrats and a man who was now thoroughly hated by a substantial minority of the party.

VIII

Despite setbacks in Kentucky and the Maryland state elections, southern Whigs' performance at the polls in 1851 checked the spread of the Union party across Dixie and thereby boosted Fillmore's effort to save both the country and the Whig party. By ardently embracing the Compromise and Fillmore himself, they demonstrated that Whigs could win on the terms Fillmore laid down and did not need a Union party. Although Whigs lost a congressional seat and the governorship in Kentucky, they still retained control of the legislature and both Senate seats, and they obviously had a chance to carry the state again if they mobilized the Whig voters alienated by Dixon. In Tennessee they took the governorship and a Senate seat from the Democrats, and while they elected only four men to the House, the Henrymander promised much greater success in the future and control of the legislature for a decade. In Maryland, where they lost the state government, they picked up an additional congressman and retained both United States senators. In Louisiana, they also added a House seat, captured the legislature, and replaced a Democratic United States senator with a Whig. In North Carolina, where both United States senators were still Whigs, they kept a majority of the House seats, and a two-thirds majority if Clingman is considered a Whig. Only in Texas,

Arkansas, and Virginia did they continue to languish in a minority, and in the last they suffered no net loss in Congress.

Altogether, exclusive of Alabama, Georgia, and Mississippi, of the fifty-eight House seats filled from the South in 1851 Whigs won twenty-three (39.6 percent), or twenty-four (41.3 percent) if Clingman is considered a Whig, a respectable improvement over their 31.6 percent success rate in 1849. If one were to add Whigs elected to Congress under the Union or Southern Rights label in those three states, the total would be thirty-one of seventy-seven seats or 40.3 percent, and, in addition, Georgia's Union party elected Toombs to the Senate for the Thirty-Third Congress. Union Whigs, of course, had abandoned the party, but Fillmore could hope that if the party nominated a pro-Compromise man for president in 1852, they might return to the fold. Whatever Whigs who had joined Union parties might do in the future, indeed, the sweeping success of Union parties in Mississippi, Alabama, and Georgia, as well as Whig triumphs elsewhere in the South, pointed to an undeniable fact. No presidential candidate could carry the South in 1852 without an unshakable commitment to enforcement and preservation, without alteration, of the Compromise measures. That fact, Fillmore hoped, might bring northern Whigs to their senses.

Yet during 1851 most northern Whigs showed little evidence of ackowledging it. And, as Fillmore well knew, however crucial southern Whigs were in checking the growth of the Union party, they alone could never save the Whig party. Their unanimity behind the Compromise and their enthusiasm for Fillmore himself starkly contrasted to the response in the North, where Whigs were divided and often deeply hostile to the president. The North, not the South, in short, posed the real challenge to saving the Whig party on Fillmore's terms. Not only was it far more difficult to persuade northern Whigs that they could win by rallying behind the finality of the Compromise. Northern Whigs' very divisions made Fillmore's control of patronage potentially a far more important weapon in influencing the outcome of intraparty battles over it. Given the position of southern Whigs, Fillmore had no need or inclination to wield the patronage axe in the South to force compliance with the administration. The North was another matter, and despite his reluctance to make removals in the winter of 1850–51, pressure to do so increased inexorably during 1851, as did the potential damage of doing so to Whigs' electoral fortunes.

Only five northern states held congressional elections in 1851, but there were a number of important state elections. In addition, at least four incumbent northern Whig senators faced stiff but potentially winnable reelection challenges in state legislatures, and Fillmore's own New York Whigs had a chance to displace Daniel S. Dickinson if they made peace with each other. The political situation confronting Fillmore in the North, in sum, was far trickier than that in the South. Putting Whigs in office, and especially in the Senate, required reunifying a fractiously divided party that could be further rent by clumsy attempts from Washington to dictate platforms or threaten jobholders.

In the North, in sum, Fillmore's twin goals of saving the country by quelling agitation against the Compromise and saving the Whig party by not dividing it further were often conflicting, not complementary, as they were in the South. There he had to balance his desire to commit the party to the finality of the

Compromise against its potential risks to Whig electoral fortunes. And there, quite unlike the South, he faced an additional aggravating complication that ultimately subverted his efforts to reunify and reinvigorate the party. This did not come from his overt intraparty enemies, the anti-Compromise Whigs, who continued to vilify him and boom Winfield Scott for the next presidency. It came instead from the unslaked ambition of his nominal ally, the secretary of state.

Chapter 18

"Webster Is Now Engaged in Strenuous Efforts to Secure the Succession"

"WHILE YOU AND I ARE TOGETHER . . . in the administration of the Government," Daniel Webster assured Millard Fillmore in October 1851, "that Administration will not be bi-faced, but will be one in principle and purpose." On most challenges confronting Fillmore's administration, the two men in fact saw eye to eye. They cooperated brilliantly to extinguish the fire over the Texas-New Mexico boundary and to secure passage of the Compromise. They shared a commitment to its finality. They completely agreed on Webster's nationalistic manifesto to Hülsemann and on the need for vigorous enforcement of both the Fugitive Slave Act and the neutrality laws.[1]

On two matters of critical political importance, however, Webster and Fillmore parted company, so much so that Webster's portrait of unanimity was disingenuous, if not wantonly hypocritical. The first concerned the administration's response to intraparty strife among northern Whigs. While Fillmore insisted that all the Compromise measures must be enforced and should be acknowledged as a permanent settlement, he sincerely hoped to reunite feuding Whigs and promote the party's success at the polls. He opposed massive, regionwide purges of anti-Compromise Whigs from federal jobs as suicidally destructive. To facilitate reunification, he tolerated intentionally vague platform statements about the Compromise so long as they did not explicitly repudiate it. To allies who threatened to sabotage factional rivals, he counseled forbearance and stressed the imperative of party loyalty. The passage of time, he appeared to believe, would heal all wounds, especially if Whigs could bury the hatchet and coalesce around a new agenda.

This patient, tolerant stance sorely exasperated Webster. Rather than conciliating anti-Compromise Whigs, he advocated total war against them. Where Fillmore hoped to bury disagreements over the Compromise and stress different issues on which all Whigs could agree, Webster demanded that northern Whig platforms explicitly endorse the Compromise for what he believed it was—a crowning achievement of statesmanship, including his own, that was justified by the legitimate demands of the South and the need to preserve the Union from reckless fanatics. Unlike Fillmore, who admitted the justice of northern Whig complaints about slavery and the fugitive slave law even as he ignored them, Webster intended to expunge every hint of antisouthern sentiment from the northern Whig party. Similarly, from the moment he joined Fillmore's cabinet, Webster sought to axe anti-Compromise Whigs from appointive office in order to punish enemies and crush dissent. As for those holding elective office, Webster intervened repeatedly in different northern states to block their renomination or reelection. Unlike Fillmore, Webster much preferred the triumph of a Democrat to that of a Whig if he was not emphatically pro-Compromise. Personal vindication, not party success, was Webster's goal.

These different attitudes toward the electoral fortunes and future of the Whig party both contributed to and resulted from the two men's disparate responses to the Union party movement. Fillmore feared and tried to subvert it; Webster embraced and fomented it. To him, combination with like-minded Democrats in a new party seemed far preferable to continued affiliation with a Whig party dominated in the North, as he saw it, by small-minded politicos who always put victory at the state level ahead of the good of the country as a whole.[2]

Different temperaments and the different political situations Fillmore and Webster confronted in their home states of New York and Massachusetts in part account for their contrasting reactions to anti-Compromise Whigs and the Union party. Primarily, however, they derived from a single difference of circumstance. Fillmore occupied the White House and had little interest in seeking it again in 1852; in contrast, Webster lusted for the presidency.

That gnawing ambition shaped everything Webster did in 1851, but he remained undecided about the best way to fulfill it. At times he looked to a possible Whig nomination, and he sought to crush anti-Compromise Whigs to strip power from men who opposed his selection and to win southern Whigs' support. At other times, he despaired of obtaining that nomination, in large part because he eventually came to believe that Fillmore, despite professions to the contrary, sought reelection and would have an inside track with northern patronage holders and southern Whigs. At these times, Webster pointed to the strength of the Union party in Georgia, Alabama, and Mississippi to justify building it in the North as the vehicle to carry him to the White House.[3]

Webster's ruthless self-interest in reaching that destination was clear to everyone by the end of 1850. To succeed, Winthrop predicted in December, Webster "must be less repulsive to his old friends." As the months passed during 1851, Webster's hostility toward Whig enemies and disregard for Whig welfare as he pursued the presidency became even more evident. "Webster is now engaged in strenuous & incessant efforts to secure the succession," wrote the disgusted Truman Smith in August. "If he expects me to enter the field [on his behalf], he will be greatly disappointed."[4]

Webster, with his single-minded pursuit of the presidency during 1851, inflicted as much damage on the northern Whig party, especially in New England, as any one individual possibly could. He negated Fillmore's efforts to reunite rival factions and inflamed bitterness instead by refusing to let bygones be bygones with regard to the Compromise. Internal divisions and disadvantages on state policies were severe enough by themselves to jeopardize Whig success in many states, but Webster instigated one Whig defeat after another, not only at the polls but also in senatorial elections. As a result, northern Whigs enjoyed markedly less success than their southern counterparts in 1851. Those losses reinforced the conviction of most northern Whigs that they needed a candidate other than Webster or Fillmore in 1852. But they had even greater significance for the party's future. However much intraparty strife weakened the Whig party and contributed to defeat, the cumulative decline of Whig strength in the Senate, the House, and state governments threatened the very existence of the Whig party. Hence the combination of circumstances that produced defeat in state after state must be recounted.

I

When Fillmore assembled his new cabinet in 1850, he announced only one fixed rule regarding federal patronage. He would not tolerate its manipulation to advance the prospects of a cabinet member or anyone else for the party's 1852 presidential nomination.[5] Not interested in the nomination himself, Fillmore did not view his own dispensing of patronage to friends as a double standard. Instead, the ban stopped Webster from sacking enemies who held federal jobs in Massachusetts and elsewhere.

In frustration, Webster therefore flirted with the Union party movement almost from its inception. He sent his approving letter to New York City's Castle Garden Union meeting in the fall of 1850, urged his followers in Boston to organize a Union meeting there, and by letter endorsed a similar effort in Philadelphia. But to keep alive his chances for a Whig nomination, Webster also sought to defeat the renomination or reelection of elected Whig officeholders who had not supported all the Compromise measures, especially the Fugitive Slave Act. By purging such leaders, he could increase his chances of winning support from their state organizations. Alternatively, driving anti-Compromise men from office might ingratiate him with Democrats and allow pro-Compromise Whigs to control local and state Whig committees, which could then provide an organizational infrastructure for a bipartisan Union party.

Webster focused first on the New England states, where he had the greatest following. He paid little attention to Vermont and Maine in 1851, for their congressional delegations, including the disposition of Senate seats, had been determined in 1850. Instead, Webster concentrated on the four remaining New England states, three of which had congressional and gubernatorial elections scheduled for the spring of 1851 and three of which also considered the reelection of incumbent Whig United States senators whom Webster regarded as unsound. Webster saw those elections as the launching pad for a Union party, but ultimately they, as well as senatorial elections in Ohio and New York, finished any chance that party had in the North. By revealing the disastrous consequences for Whigs of flirting with Democrats, those elections discredited the very idea of coalition politics. They also demonstrated how continuing Whig divisions over the Compromise could decimate Whig strength in Congress, and in New England, Webster and his vindictive allies served as the firing squad.

Like Delaware and New Jersey, tiny Rhode Island was crucial to Whigs' chances of controlling Congress. That January the Whig-dominated legislature chosen in 1850 was to replace Albert Greene, who declined to seek another Senate term, perhaps because of vocal opposition from a small group of Websterites headed by John O. Charles and W. G. Gibbs.[6] Webster aggressively lobbied Rhode Island's Whigs to back a conservative named Whipple for the Senate, but instead the Whig legislative caucus nominated former Senator James F. Simmons, politically inactive since 1847 and therefore lacking any public record on the Compromise. Repudiating the caucus, Webster's friends clung to Whipple. This split opened an opportunity for ex-Governor William Sprague, who for his own reasons set out to stop Simmons. Unable to sway the anti-Webster Whig majority, Sprague backed a protariff Democrat named Charles James and persuaded thirteen Whigs to join all of the Democrats in electing him over the indignant opposition of the remaining Whig majority.[7]

This outcome not only cost Whigs another valuable Senate seat. It also put bipartisan cooperation in an exceedingly bad light, since James was exposed as making flatly contradictory promises to Whig and Democratic legislators to secure their votes. The fiasco in the legislature completely shattered the Whig party for the April elections, as pro- and anti-Webster men refused to cooperate. When the anti-Compromise Whig majority nominated Josiah Chapin, a favorite of the state's tiny Free Soil party, for governor, some Websterites threw their support to the Democrat Philip Allen, a pro-Compromise man, while others abstained.[8] As a result, Whigs lost the governorship for the first time since the early 1830s, Democrats captured the state senate, and the Whig majority in the house sank from seventeen to four seats. In the popular vote, Whig majorities of 59 percent in 1849 and 80 percent in 1850 were reduced to a 46 percent minority because of Websterite defections and Democratic gains.

The results of the congressional elections were almost as bleak. Anti-Compromise Whig incumbent Nathan Dixon did not run, but his successor, Charles Jackson, was no more popular among Websterites. Jackson drew only 38 percent of the vote against the same Democrat Dixon had defeated in 1849 with 56 percent. In the other district, in contrast, anti-Compromise Whigs loyally backed Webster's ally George King, who squeaked by with only 51 percent of the vote, a sharp drop from his two-thirds majority in 1849. In his district, Democrats inspired by the chance finally to win the governorship turned out in unusually high numbers.[9] Another Whig stronghold had been penetrated, largely because Webster's friends preferred Whig defeat to the victory of Whig rivals.

In neighboring Connecticut the Senate seat at stake belonged to Roger Sherman Baldwin, an ardent antislavery Whig who had failed to win reelection in 1850 and who, along with Senator Robert C. Winthrop of Massachusetts and Pennsylvania's Governor William F. Johnston, was one of Webster's three main targets in 1851. Baldwin's fate hinged on the outcome of the April legislative elections, which coincided with contests for governor and Congress. Although a Free Soil-Democratic coalition won three of four congressional seats in 1849, and although Democrats captured the governorship and the legislature in April 1850, Connecticut's Whigs exuded optimism about the 1851 elections after they swept the local elections in the fall of 1850. Intraparty divisions over the Compromise and Democratic attempts to lure pro-Compromise Whigs into a Union party in the New Haven congressional district, however, confounded those hopes.[10]

Since Connecticut was a relatively small and closely balanced state, defections to Democrats in even a single congressional district could cost Whigs heavily.

Terrified that New Haven's carriage manufacturers, whose southern trade left them anxious to register support for the Compromise, would force their employees to vote Democratic and withhold the money that customarily bankrolled their own party, Whigs therefore tried to run in 1851 as a pro-Union party that tepidly acquiesced in the Compromise as a finality. But they could hardly outflank Democrats with such a tack. With doughface incumbent Governor Thomas Seymour again heading their ticket, Democrats advanced a platform that wholeheartedly embraced all Compromise measures, including the fugitive slave law. Repudiating their former coalitions with Free Soilers in congressional races, they ran ardent pro-Compromise men in all four districts.[11]

The tilt of pro-Compromise Whigs toward Democrats in the New Haven district decisively influenced the statewide result. Democrats again won the congressional seat there and in two other districts. Only in the Hartford district, where Charles Chapman nosed out the Democratic incumbent by fewer than fifty votes, did Whigs prevail. Seymour again defeated Lafayette Foster for governor with a slightly larger plurality than in 1850. The all-important legislative races would again determine the governorship as well as the Senate seat.[12]

In contrast to their disappointing performance in the gubernatorial and congressional contests, Whigs made marked gains in the legislative races. They won a three-seat majority in the senate and reduced the Democratic margin in the house to four. Since the Democratic delegation remained divided between doughfaces and Free Soilers who could agree on Seymour's reelection as governor but not on Isaac Toucey's elevation to the Senate, the chances that Whigs could reelect Baldwin, who easily secured the nomination from the Whig caucus, seemed good. Yet three to five "Union-safety Whigs" consistently refused to support Baldwin because he was an anti-Compromise man. Rumors circulated in Connecticut that Webster had orchestrated this obstinate minority, and Baldwin complained of that fact to Winthrop. Though unprovable, Webster's complicity seems almost certain.[13] In any event, the Whig dissidents and Democratic divisions once again prevented any election. Baldwin's career was finished. The stubborn vindictiveness of a few Websterite Whigs had cost the party another United States senator.[14]

The Democratic stronghold of New Hampshire had no senatorial election in 1851, but its congressional and gubernatorial elections that year deeply interested its most famous native son. Webster saw New Hampshire as potentially fertile ground for a Union party, but only if New Hampshire's Whigs spurned the alliances with Free Soilers they had formed in 1849 and earlier. During his trip to New England in the fall of 1850, therefore, Webster exerted pressure on New Hampshire's Whigs to recant their antislavery agitation and coalition. He achieved some success, but far from enough to justify his exultant boasts to Fillmore that Free Soilism would be wiped out within a year. Webster secured a Whig congressional nomination for his old friend, ex-Governor Anthony Colby. He also approved the Whigs' gubernatorial candidate, and he condoned the Whig platform as the best he could get given prevailing Whig sentiment. That evasive document said not a word about the Compromise or the fugitive slave law, but it did call for obedience to all laws and condemn nullification, provisions that could be interpreted as repudiating resistance to the fugitive slave law.[15]

Webster may have hoped that on this platform Whigs could either outflank New Hampshire's Democrats, who in 1850 had shamelessly and successfully attacked Whigs as prosouthern appeasers, or lure pro-Compromise Democrats into a Union coalition. In 1851, however, Democrats flipflopped once again and defended the Compromise far more explicitly and enthusiastically than the Whigs. Democrats ran their two incumbent congressmen, Harry Hibbard and Charles Peaslee, who had both voted for all the Compromise measures, and they dumped their first gubernatorial nominee when he criticized the Fugitive Slave Act and replaced him with a staunch pro-Compromise man. Far from succumbing to the siren call of a Union party, in sum, New Hampshire's pro-Compromise Democrats drove anti-Compromise elements from their own party and told voters that Democrats were safer unionists than Whigs.[16]

Democratic Congressmen Hibbard and Peaselee easily won reelection, but Amos Tuck and Jared Perkins, behind whom Whigs and Free Soilers combined in defiance of Webster's pressure, also triumphed. In the gubernatorial election, Democratic incumbent Samuel Dinsmoor was reduced from a majority to a plurality as almost one-sixth of the 1850 Democratic voters decamped to the Free Soilers, whose vote soared from 12 to 21 percent of the total cast. Democratic divisions allowed marked Whig gains in the state legislature, but not enough to overcome the huge Democratic cushion. Thomas E. Sawyer, the Websterite Whig who ran for governor, garnered a whopping 32 percent of the total, while Colby won an even smaller proportion of his district's vote. Democratic tribulations, in sum, did not translate automatically into Whig gains. The results underlined emphatically that only alliance with Free Soilers offered Whigs hope in the Granite State. Webster's political embrace seemed a kiss of death, but, amazingly, his New Hampshire loyalists ignored that lesson. In 1852 they would send Webster delegates to the Whig national convention.[17]

II

Quite naturally, Massachusetts commanded Webster's greatest attention during 1851. There his allies' vindictiveness peaked, and there Webster's selfish penchant for putting personal advancement ahead of Whig welfare became most clear. Webster counted on Massachusetts to launch his presidential campaign and was thus determined to wipe out anything about the Massachusetts Whig party that offended Southerners. That agenda guaranteed intraparty bloodletting, for in 1851 Bay State Whigs faced a powerful Democratic/Free Soil Coalition that had won control of the state legislature in November 1850. Any shift by Massachusetts Whigs toward Webster's position on national affairs, therefore, would only enhance their enemies' power within the state.

In early 1851 the legislature would choose the governor and was scheduled to fill Webster's old Senate seat, now held by Winthrop, who had outraged Webster by refusing to vote for the fugitive slave bill. Months before the November 1850 election, Whig papers warned that Coalition control of the next legislature would produce a Democratic governor and a Free Soil senator, most likely the pedantic, unctuous, and radically antislavery Charles Sumner. As soon as the Coalition-dominated legislature opened on January 1, 1851, things went as badly as Whigs predicted. Democrat George S. Boutwell was immediately installed as governor, and as if to accentuate the opportunistic nature of the alliance between Democrats and Free Soilers, a Democrat became speaker of the house and a Free Soiler president of the senate.[18]

Initially, disposition of the Senate seat also proceeded with clock-like efficiency. To humiliate Winthrop, in late January Coalition legislators selected Democrat Robert Rantoul, Jr., for the remaining few weeks of his term. But Free Soilers insisted that one of their own get the new, full six-year term. The self-righteous Sumner, Winthrop's chief Massachusetts tormentor since 1846, had positioned himself to be the Coalition's Senate candidate for over a year. While he never retreated from his extreme antislavery ground, he made sure that Free Soil platforms incorporated Democratic positions on state economic policy. His ascent to the Senate seemed assured when both Free Soil and Democratic caucuses in January overwhelmingly nominated him and when the senate, which in Massachusetts voted separately from the house for United States senators, elected him two weeks later. In the house, however, the Coalition locomotive derailed.[19]

Although some Free Soilers opposed alliance with Democrats or Sumner's election or both, the real problem came from a bloc of pro-Compromise Democrats, who began to protest immediately after the November election that they had cooperated with Free Soilers solely to wrest the state government from the hated Whigs. Helping the Coalition put an antislavery fanatic in the Senate, these dissident "regular" Democrats raged, was "a gross outrage on our principles."[20] Their leader in the house was the chairman of the Democratic State Executive Committee, Caleb Cushing. An immensely learned scholar and eminent jurist, Cushing was a Tyler Whig turned Democrat. In the summer of 1850 Webster's friends approached Cushing about running as a bipartisan, pro-Compromise, pro-Webster Union candidate for Congress, but instead he campaigned as a Democrat for the legislature and was elected with the help of Webster's friends in his Newburyport district. Supported by twenty-five to thirty like-minded Democrats, Cushing bolted the Democratic caucus as soon as it endorsed Sumner and vowed never to support him. Without this crucial bloc of votes, the Coalition in the house failed to muster the necessary majority for Sumner on roll call after roll call.[21]

This wrench in the Coalition's plans unexpectedly offered the Whig minority a possibility of snatching victory from the jaws of defeat. Cushing was prepared to support a conservative pro-Compromise Whig like Webster's ally Edward Everett. More important, although Whigs were badly outnumbered in the house, what counted was not the total membership but how many legislators were present and voting on roll calls for senator. Because the session dragged on for five months, legislators frequently quit Boston to return home. Each party therefore faced the problem of getting members back to Boston in time for votes, and in this regard Whigs had a decisive advantage. Spearheaded by Amos A. Lawrence, a member of the fabulously wealthy textile clan, Whigs raised a fund to pay for train fares to bring legislators back for key roll calls. If Whigs could not pull a coup when Coalition absentees were numerous, moreover, so long as Cushing and his dissident Democrats refused to support Sumner, Whigs had the votes to prevent any election at all if no one broke ranks.[22]

Unity was the rub, for the prolonged stalemate over the senatorial election aggravated Whig divisions evident during the 1850 campaign. Even though Winthrop was the Whig caucus' overwhelming choice for the full term, Webster and his legislative lieutenants insisted upon making an example of Winthrop to demonstrate the political oblivion that awaited Whigs who refused to support all the Compromise measures. This vindictiveness baffled and deeply hurt the mild-mannered and deeply conservative Winthrop, who had once read law with Webster.[23] But Webster saw the Senate election as a chance to advance the Union party movement in Massachusetts already launched by the bipartisan Union rally in Boston arranged by his friends. The unusual political situation in Massachusetts, with both parties sharply split over the Compromise, indeed, undoubtedly helps explain Webster's enthusiasm for the new party, since the pro-Compromise Democratic minority whom his old friend Cushing led seemed very likely recruits for a new Union party. Thus, while his preferred candidate for the Senate was the ultraconservative Whig Samuel Eliot, he and his friends were fully prepared to back a Union Democrat instead. In January, Webster ordered his allies to assist the birth of the new organization. It was "the duty of the Whigs in the Massachusetts Legislature to join with honest conservative Democrats, & elect any good man of either party," he commanded. He personally would "not hesitate" to vote for "a sound, sensible, Union man of the Democratic party, if I could not elect a decided Union Whig" since now was the time "for friends of the Union to *unite*, & rally in its support."[24]

Webster and his fawning Whig acolytes "are really *green enough* to believe that they can detach democrats from their party to help them make a 'Union party'!" sneered the contemptuous Charles Upham, "and all for the sake of the Presidency." Verdant they were. Moses Stuart, head of the Andover Theological Seminary and a Webster disciple, revealed his naiveté when he wrote Webster in April that he preferred Sumner to Winthrop "on the desperate ground of, *the worse the better*" in terms of driving pro-Compromise Whigs and Democrats together. "I think a *Union party*, taking the Corps *d'elites* of the two *quondam* parties bids fair to become the order of the day, in the North & the South." If it did, "I expect, if I & you live, to see you in the *White House*."[25]

Stuart's fantasy recognized at least one reality. Long before April, it had become evident that the only choice was between Winthrop and Sumner. Webster's Whig followers and Cushing's Democrats, combined with disciplined support for Winthrop by other Whigs, blocked Sumner's election throughout January, February, March, and most of April.[26] As the end of the legislative session approached, however, a few antislavery Whigs and a handful of Cushing's Democrats decided to support Sumner rather than postpone the election to the next legislature. On April 24, on the twenty-sixth ballot, Sumner finally prevailed by a majority of exactly one vote.[27]

Websterite and anti-Webster Whigs alike regarded Sumner's victory as a grievous defeat and the Coalition as an abomination. Not only did the Coalition send Sumner to the Senate and blatantly trade for office; it proposed election reforms to replace the state's traditional majority requirement with a plurality decision, advocated a state constitutional convention to effect them, and passed economic legislation all Whigs reviled.[28] Whigs' common antagonism toward the Coalition, in short, opened an obvious way to reunite the party for the November elections, but the prolonged struggle over the senatorship eliminated that possibility. Furious that Websterites were prepared to sacrifice Winthrop for a pro-Compromise Democrat, the majority of Whigs determined to nominate Winthrop for governor later that year. Nonetheless, they made a peace offering to Webster's faction to restore party harmony. Conceived by Samuel Hooper, a Whig state legislator, and aired in William Schouler's Boston *Atlas*, this treaty had two parts.

Since Webster regarded the Whig state committee, chaired by George Morey, as uniformly hostile to him, it would be enlarged to include more Webster men, though not enough to give them a majority. With regard to the state platform, Whigs would agree to disagree, as they had done during the legislative session. They would insist on obedience to all laws, including the fugitive slave law, but they would tolerate criticism of that statute and demands for its revision to protect blacks' rights.[29]

Webster and his allies angrily spurned the offer. Miffed that the Whig majority had refused to support Eliot or a Democrat for the Senate, furious that Webster had been denied the use of Boston's Faneuil Hall for a pro-Union rally on the pretext that it might provoke a riot by foes of the fugitive slave law, and incensed that the Whig majority refused to accept the Compromise's finality, they insisted on battling for outright control of the party and were prepared to abandon it if they lost.[30] As soon as Schouler printed his peace offering, Whig papers affiliated with Webster like the *Bee* and the *Courier* denounced it. Webster told friends that he would have nothing to do with the Whig state committee, even if a few of his allies were added to it, because it was so intent on carrying the state elections that it would whore after antislavery votes and thereby discredit the Massachusetts Whig party with southern Whigs and Union men. Both Whig and Democratic leaders were "*National,* and justly appreciate[d] great national objects," Webster wrote Democrat David Henshaw. "But there are thousands in each party, who are more concerned for state, than for national politics, whose objects are all small." Webster also flatly repudiated the live-and-let-live platform proposed by Schouler as an "utter absurdity." "I, for one, shall have nothing to do with the Whig party, if a part of their 'platform' be . . . to 'agitate' for the modification of the Fugitive Slave Law." Any attempt to revise or repeal that law would "break up, forever, the Whig party of the Union."[31]

As Webster saw it, Winthrop's candidacy for governor would ensure the same disruption. Webster wanted a formal presidential nomination from Massachusetts in 1851 that would increase his appeal to southern Whigs or proponents of the Union party, and he and his allies were convinced that running Winthrop as the Whig candidate for governor would undercut that appeal. Within a month of the legislature's adjournment, therefore, pro-Webster newspapers were questioning Winthrop's fitness and electability. Simultaneously, Webster's lieutenants tried unsuccessfully to marshal support for alternative Whig nominees more satisfactory to Webster, like Samuel Walley or Rufus Choate.[32]

When his initial efforts to derail Winthrop failed, Webster prepared openly during May, June, and July 1851 to abandon the Whigs and cast his lot with the Union party. By then, he was convinced that "Mr. Fillmore shall try his chances" for the Whig nomination. By then, as well, he was thoroughly disgusted with the Massachusetts Whig party and persuaded that since the Union party would sweep the South, "the present organization of the Whig party cannot be continued throughout the United States." Apparently never considering that strife over the Compromise, the only rationale for a Union party, could prove ephemeral, he urged his Massachusetts allies "to call a meeting of the Union men of all parties," for if the new party took root there, "New Hampshire is not unlikely to follow the example." That meeting or a petition campaign organized by his friend Franklin Haven would boom Webster as the Union party's presidential candidate.[33]

Both the proposed bipartisan Union convention in June and the petition campaign, however, fizzled. In desperation, therefore, Webster and his friends jumped back from the Union to the Whig horse and again sought an endorsement from the September Whig state convention on grounds that could attract both southern Unionists and pro-Compromise Democrats like Cushing's supporters. As Webster and his acolytes saw it, Winthrop's nomination for governor by that body would totally negate the effect of any endorsement of Webster's presidential candidacy by alienating the conservatives Webster hoped to woo. Once it became clear that the boomlets for Walley and Choate had failed, therefore, Webster, through an intermediary, tried to persuade Winthrop to postpone his candidacy until 1853 on the grounds, as Winthrop sputtered, that his nomination in 1851 "would not be *satisfactory in Georgia!*" When Winthrop indignantly refused to withdraw, Webster commanded his friends to boycott the state convention: "A convention which shall nominate me, for one high office, & Mr. Winthrop for another, would be an inconsistency."[34]

The state convention's nomination of Winthrop on a platform that added calls for revising the Fugitive Slave Act to planks denouncing the Coalition's actions reinforced Webster's alienation from his state's Whig party. Nonetheless, in November the Whig total increased by almost 8,000 votes over the Whig vote in 1850 despite approximately 1,100 defectors to the Democratic column. Websterite Whigs almost surely accounted for those bolters, but even those votes, if added to Winthrop's total and subtracted from the Democrats, would not have given Winthrop the necessary majority. The election again went to the legislature, and since the Coalition, despite the defection of Cushing's Hunkers, narrowly retained control of that body, Governor Boutwell's reelection was assured. Still, the willingness of Websterite Whigs to support a Democrat and their overt joy at Winthrop's defeat, just like their attempt to stop his nomination, underlined their willingness to wage open war on anti-Compromise Whigs.[35]

III

During the winter and spring of 1851, while Webster concentrated on developments in New England, Millard Fillmore responded in a markedly different fashion to the concurrent senatorial election in New York. Where Webster sought to defeat Whigs who were not totally pure on the Compromise, Fillmore vigorously worked for the election of a Whig who criticized the fugitive slave law. Where Webster urged cooperation with Democrats, Fillmore actively discouraged it. Where Webster spurned ambiguous platforms, Fillmore was prepared to forgo a statement on principles to secure Whig success. Nonetheless, New York's election also deepened factional animosities among Whigs and damaged their chances at the polls. It also pushed Fillmore into using patronage against his New York rivals in ways he would not permit Webster to adopt in other states. And it was Fillmore's wielding of the axe in New York and the gratitude it earned him from his Silver Gray allies that, more than anything else, convinced the ambitious Webster that the president himself was his chief rival for the Whig nomination.

New York provided Whigs with a splendid chance to gain a new senator who could partially offset losses elsewhere in 1851. Despite Democratic gains in 1850's congressional races, continued bickering between Hunker and Barnburner Dem ocrats over legislative candidates allowed Whigs to secure a thirty-six-seat majority in the house and a two-seat edge in the senate.[36] Hamilton Fish was the consensus Whig choice to replace the Democrat Daniel S. Dickinson. Although some Sewardites and Silver Grays preferred a different man more closely identified with their respective factions, Weed, Seward, and Fillmore acknowledged that the party could unite only on Fish, and Fillmore himself enthusiastically supported him. Nonetheless, Fish's election inevitably became entangled with and embittered the rift between Sewardites and Silver Grays.[37]

With the exception of sacking Lewis Benedict, Fillmore had worked hard since the Silver Gray bolt of September 1850 to restrain his allies and restore party harmony, and by December those peace efforts appeared to be bearing fruit. Seward, back in Washington for the congressional session, told Fillmore at the White House that he wanted reconciliation, and from early December 1850 to early March 1851, Seward remained resolutely mum on the slavery issue, to the great dismay of supporters who feared a retreat from "higher law" ground. If anything, Weed seemed even more eager to please. Alerted by Corwin that Fillmore would be gratified by an editorial endorsement of his annual message, Weed, to Fillmore's delight, warmly praised it in the Albany *Evening Journal*, although he studiously omitted any reference to the Compromise's finality. Weed also talked seriously of retiring from the fray, of going on an extended trip to Europe, and even of selling his paper, the state's flagship Whig journal, to the Silver Grays. With both Seward and Weed silenced, the chances of rallying the state party behind the administration and its measures brightened.[38]

Even during the fall of 1850, however, Fillmore recognized that the state legislative session starting in January 1851 posed the biggest obstacle to his hope of saving the New York Whig party from irreparable disruption. Still mutually hostile, many Sewardites and Silver Grays distrusted the thaw in relationships at the top of the party hierarchy. Seward's friends repeatedly warned that the duplicitous and vengeful Fillmore intended to axe jobholders no matter what he promised. Especially his acquiescence in the bloodletting by John Young and Hugh Maxwell in New York City, they warned cabinet members, would provoke "the cry of Tylerism" since "these reptiles sting the bosoms in which they are warmest." By January 1851, Seward, Weed, and their followers insisted that Fillmore could "unite and consolidate" the New York party only by decapitating Young, "the Knave," and Maxwell, his "Dupe." And in retrospect, it is clear, Fillmore should have done so.[39]

Silver Grays were even less happy about the unsigned truce during November and December, especially when Seward and Weed made support for the administration contingent upon retaining patronage posts. "Any trust or confidence bestowed on any of that crew, will be misplaced, and surely be abused & betrayed," insisted Jerome Fuller. "They will stab you, they will stab every National Whig at the first opportunity." Their "uncompromising hatred" and selfishness, warned Silver Grays, would be revealed when Weed bulldozed the Whig members of the new canal board to deny National Whigs lucrative contracts for repairs. If Fillmore's friends did not get at least half of that state boodle, they cried, more removals from federal jobs must be made.[40]

The likelihood that men so suspicious and resentful of each other could keep the peace when they came together seemed remote. Yet the meeting of the legislature created additional problems. However much Weed and Fillmore—to say nothing of the desperate Hunt and Fish—might want to hold the party together, they lacked total control over their respective troops. Even Weed, whose influence over legislators was legendary, could not prevent every single Sewardite from making a speech or presenting a resolution that might precipitate a blowup. Fillmore, who had to direct his forces from Washington rather than Albany, was at an even greater disadvantage. He had some trustworthy lieutenants in the legislature, but he had little influence on conservatives from New York City. In outright defiance of his wishes, Young and Maxwell continued to urge the legislature's Whig delegation to reelect Dickinson and construct a Union party rather than reunite the Whig party behind Fish. Even worse from Fillmore's perspective, the Silver Gray press was utterly reckless. To Fillmore's dismay, those papers continued to pillory Weed throughout December despite his endorsement of the president's annual message, and during the legislative session they embarrassed Fillmore by refusing to endorse Fish and praising Whig legislators who opposed him, by making demands upon Sewardites far beyond those that Fillmore himself asked, and, most explosively, by falsely insisting that Fillmore sought the 1852 nomination.[41]

Equally problematic was the fundamental matter of the basis on which Whigs could reunite other than common support for Fish. In November the factional rivals supported Washington Hunt on vastly different grounds, and distrust of Hunt by both sides caused considerable abstention. The party's tenuous unity, in sum, encompassed flatly contradictory stances on the slavery issue. As even Joseph Varnum, Jr., the Silver Grays' leader in the state house of representatives, admitted about the impending legislative session, "We shall certainly divide if any slavery resolutions are introduced."[42]

The problem was not simply the near inevitability that some legislator, possibly a Democrat bent on mischief, might introduce resolutions for or against the Compromise that could ignite an explosion. Fillmore himself, in his public and private letters, his orders to troops and marshals, and his annual message, had altered the equation by demanding acquiescence in the finality of the Compromise, total compliance with the fugitive slave law, and, most important, postponement of any attempts to revise that statute. Fillmore wanted loyal followers who sustained his administration's measures, not equal partners with their own agenda. He made that clear to Fish in November, and on the back of a letter he received in January 1851 warning against any alliance with Weed's faction, he jotted, "No alliance proposed. I am anxious for union & harmony but it must be their supporting the administration."[43]

If Fillmore's Silver Gray allies carped at his leniency toward Sewardites on patronage, his firm stand on finality delighted them. Coupled with the secessionist threat in the South, it allowed them to portray any Whigs who refused to accept finality as dangerous disunionists whom, they believed, Whig voters would repudiate. More than this, they yearned to avenge the slur in the Syracuse platform that Seward, not Fillmore, represented the ideals of New York's Whigs. As the legislative session approached, therefore, they demanded a public demonstration of adherence to Fillmore from the Sewardites as a precondition for their backing Fish. That some Silver Grays wanted simply to humiliate the Sewardites became clear when Fuller in the *State Register* insisted that Sewardites "accept" the merits of the Compromise rather than merely "acquiesce" in its finality, an escalation of terms that incensed Fillmore.[44]

Sewardites found the demand for prior concessions as a precondition for allowing Fish's election unconscionable. Endorsing Fillmore's position and abandoning criticism of the Compromise and especially of the hated fugitive slave law, they complained, would destroy the Whig party's credibility. Besides, they railed, it was degrading for the majority of the party to submit to extortion by the minority. In the legislature, where Sewardites outnumbered Silver Grays by fifty-nine to twenty-three in the house and by fourteen to three in the senate, indeed, the Sewardite majority was even larger than it had been at Syracuse; nonetheless, in each chamber, Silver Grays had enough votes, when combined with Democrats, to block Fish's election. Although Weed and others hinted that they might publicly endorse the administration in some way after Fish's election, to make that endorsement a precondition for support was intolerable. Even the willingness to make a postelection acknowledgment of loyalty evaporated, moreover, when Thomas Foote printed rash editorials in the Buffalo *Commercial Advertiser* asserting that Fillmore intended to run again in 1852. Those statements implied that an endorsement of the administration was an endorsement of Fillmore's nomination for a new term, something Weed's men, who were already booming Winfield Scott, would never do.[45]

These festering tensions made almost everything that happened in Albany during January a test of wills, a matter of saving or losing face, that widened rather than bridged the chasm between rival factions. On every occasion when Silver Grays expected a concession, they met what they perceived as insulting defiance. First came the delivery of Washington Hunt's inaugural address to the legislature and the announcement of his initial appointees. Neither side fully trusted Hunt's self-proclaimed neutrality, and Silver Grays especially looked for evidence that he would give their faction a fair shake. Instead, they regarded his appointees as Sewardites "of the rankest kind." Since lame-duck Governor Fish had already appointed a man they distrusted as an interim replacement for Hunt in the all-important position of comptroller, the head of the canal board, they immediately concluded that Weed intended to keep his monopoly over state jobs.[46]

Nor were they happy with Hunt's inaugural message. They expected Hunt to toe the line Fillmore had laid down in his own annual message. Sewardites, in contrast, wanted Hunt to repeat his campaign demand for immediate revision of the fugitive slave law.[47] Hunt responded characteristically to these cross pressures by straddling, and to most Silver Grays, although apparently not to Fillmore himself, a straddle did not suffice. Just as he had urged Fillmore in respect to Fillmore's annual message, Hunt devoted most of his own message to traditional Whig economic arguments. He promoted protective tariffs, internal improvements, and an amendment of the 1846 state constitution to facilitate enlargement of the Erie Canal system. But he also sought to reassure Anti-Renters in ways that nettled conservatives. Fuller considered his eulogies to Zachary Taylor too fulsome and his praise of Fillmore too faint, a complaint other Silver Grays echoed. On the all-important litmus test, Hunt continued to call for minor revisions in the fugitive slave law, and, in sharp contrast to the Round Robin then circulating in Congress, he insisted that men have the freedom to discuss and criticize it.[48]

The organization of the legislature itself increased the rancor between the two sides. During the preceding weeks, Silver Grays repeatedly cited the election of the house's speaker as the key test of Whigs' fealty to Fillmore. In particular, they demanded the defeat of Henry J. Raymond, a newspaperman and prominent Sewardite from New York City. Their logic was clear, if reductionist. Raymond's election as speaker would identify Fish as a Seward man unless counteracting resolutions were passed by the Whig caucus endorsing the Compromise. Raymond's defeat, however, would mark a repudiation of Sewardism, obviate the need to press a vote on divisive resolutions, and magically transform Fish into a Fillmore man in the eyes of Whigs elsewhere in the nation. Symbolism, in short, was everything.[49]

Yet symbolism also reduced the leverage available to the outnumbered Silver Grays. Unwilling to boycott the Whig caucus, which would have reinforced their reputation as bolting soreheads who put personal resentment ahead of party loyalty, they had no choice but to attend the caucus, futilely run Varnum as their candidate against Raymond, and sit by mutely when Raymond won an easy victory. Once the caucus had decided, moreover, similar demands of party loyalty and legitimacy required them to support him on the house floor, where he won the post.[50]

Then Raymond, who later in 1851 would start the *New York Times* as a pro-Seward, pro-Scott organ, added insult to the Silver Grays' injury. By party tradition, the speaker automatically named the runner-up for the caucus speakership nomination, in this case Varnum, as chairman of the ways and means committee. Raymond, however, refused to appoint Varnum unless he pledged that he and all other Silver Grays would refrain from introducing resolutions accepting the Compromise or endorsing Fillmore and his annual message. The livid Varnum refused. From that point on Silver Grays boycotted Whig caucuses, and Raymond packed the committee chairmanships with Sewardites. Rupture appeared more and more likely.[51]

Varnum, in fact, had no intention of introducing pro-Compromise resolutions, for he, like Fillmore, knew that an up-or-down vote on them would destroy the party. Thus, when a Democrat and a Silver Gray later introduced such resolutions and a Sewardite Whig countered with one calling for repeal of the fugitive slave law, Varnum and most Sewardites cooperated to bury the inflammatory measures in Whig-controlled committees. Yet Varnum possessed resolutions that were drafted in Washington by Congressman James Brooks, Postmaster General Nathan Hall, and Webster. These praised the administration and endorsed Fillmore's call for acquiescence in the finality of the Compromise. Fillmore himself urged Silver Gray legislators to force a vote on these resolutions to test the Weed faction's allegiance to the administration.[52] When Varnum introduced them, however, they too were buried in the judiciary committee, which Sewardites controlled. Thus the issue boiled down to a simple choice. Would the house judiciary committee release the Varnum resolutions and would the Sewardites support them prior to the house vote for senator, thus placing Fish on a pro-Fillmore platform, or would the Sewardites press for a vote on Fish before allowing a vote on Varnum's proposals? On that procedural question the fate of the New York Whig party appeared to hang.[53]

Conflicting external pressure on legislators was immense. From Washington, William Duer, Brooks, Webster, and the hard-nosed Hall, who orchestrated the false reports that Fillmore wanted the 1852 nomination, all sent unauthorized messages professing that Fillmore wanted Silver Gray legislators to throw away their votes to deny Fish the election unless Varnum's resolutions were adopted.[54] Young came up from New York City and demanded that Fish be stopped. Simultaneously, Weed, aided by Sewardites from western New York, urged that the resolutions be stymied and threatened that if any resolutions were passed, they would be those denouncing the fugitive slave law. Varnum took this threat so seriously that he abandoned efforts to pry his own resolutions out of committee. Meanwhile, Samuel Lyman, who knew Fillmore's wishes, reported to him that his so-called friends were misrepresenting him as implacably opposed to Fish's election.[55]

During the week before February 4, the scheduled date of the senatorial vote, frantic efforts were made to break the logjam. Varnum, despairing of any actions on his resolutions, went to New York City to extract a pledge from Fish that he supported Fillmore's position on finality. Specifically, he asked Fish to respond in writing to a letter from the three Silver Gray state senators asking him to endorse Fillmore's annual message and thereby renounce any attempt to change the fugitive slave law if elected. Far more fair-minded than his allies, Fillmore himself later admitted that Fish could make no such pledge "without degrading himself," and Fish, who abhorred the fugitive slave law, adamantly refused. Instead, he showed Varnum his correspondence with Fillmore and a speech he intended to give at a public dinner, which, unsurprisingly, was almost identical to Hunt's inaugural address. To die-hard Silver Grays that was not nearly enough. Meanwhile Fillmore finally recognized that both his cabinet and the Silver Grays in Albany were out of control. Fearful of being blamed for Fish's defeat, he forced Hall and Webster to telegraph the legislators and countermand their earlier orders to oppose Fish. Those pro-Fish messages, however, were partially offset when, during this same crucial week, the canal board announced its new dispensation of jobs and contracts, from which Silver Grays were totally excluded, as they had long angrily predicted.[56]

As a result, Fish initially failed to win election. Only a few Silver Grays in the house threw away their votes, and Fish easily prevailed. The senate, where only two votes separated the parties, was another matter. Fifteen Democrats lined up behind their man, and fifteen Whigs, including Fillmore's lieutenant, George Babcock, voted for Fish. One Whig missed the vote, however, and James Beekman, a Silver Gray from New York City, ostentatiously wasted his vote on Francis Granger to deny Fish the necessary majority. Beekman, moreover, announced that for personal reasons, as well as Fish's refusal to send a written pledge endorsing Fillmore's message, he would never vote for Fish, no matter how many votes were held or how many telegrams arrived from Washington. Worse still from Fillmore's perspective, Fuller in the *State Register* lauded Beekman for saving the administration from disgrace and rebuking Weed, while the renegades Young and Maxwell, together with the Union Safety Committee, had cannon fired in New York City to celebrate Fish's defeat. To aggravate the situation, Henry Clay, who still hoped to force Silver Grays to cooperate with Dickinson's Hunkers in a Union party, wrote Maxwell a letter praising Beekman's stand and Maxwell's support of him, a letter Maxwell happily showed to everyone he encountered. Weed, in response, editorially savaged the administration for blocking Fish. New York's Whigs stood on the brink of the rupture that Fillmore desperately hoped to avert.[57]

Immediate attempts at damage control proved futile, in large part because animosity between the two camps had become so great. Talk of finding some other candidate was quickly dismissed. Fillmore blasted Fuller for misrepresenting him, and he forced Fuller to admit in his paper for the first time that Fillmore wanted Fish elected. The obstreperous Beekman held the key, however, and Fillmore's efforts to sway him directly or through friends failed. So did efforts to persuade Beekman to allow the election to go to a special joint session of the house and senate, where the large Sewardite majority in the house could overcome his obstructionism. Proposals to resurrect Varnum's resolutions or to change them so that Sewardites could support them to convert Beekman also came to naught. Weed made it unmistakably clear that his troops would block any vote on those resolutions unless Fillmore first removed Young and Maxwell, and the furious president, who believed that he had made every concession that honor allowed, flatly rejected that extortionate demand. "If harmony can be restored on no other grounds" than the "sacrifice of a friend," Fillmore huffed to the frantic Hunt, then "this discord must reign."[58]

Finally, at 1 A.M. on March 19, after another futile ballot earlier that month, the logjam on the senatorship broke. Beekman never relented, but senate Democrats, anxious to remove the Senate seat as an issue from the impending fall elections because it had so divided Barnburners and Hunkers in the legislative races of 1850, allowed the vote to proceed even though two of their members were absent. That allowed Whigs to elect Fish 16–13 despite Beekman's stubborn ballot for Granger.[59]

IV

Fish's election failed to restore party unity. By the third week of February, Millard Fillmore had clearly been pushed beyond the limits of even his monumental patience. The ruthless exclusion of Silver Gray friends from state patronage by the canal board, Weed's refusal to allow a vote on the Varnum resolutions, and particularly Weed's arrogant demands for the heads of Young and Maxwell finally convinced Fillmore to launch retaliatory strikes against Sewardites. During the last week of February and the first three weeks of March, Fillmore's New York friends prepared a list of victims for the chopping block: Thomas Clowes, postmaster of Troy, as well as postmasters in Auburn, Oswego, and elsewhere; Elias Pond, customs collector in Rochester; and, most important, Marshal Palmer V. Kellogg and his deputies. The removal of Kellogg, warned the faithful Babcock, meant "open war in the party in this state," but "this is infinitely preferable to the present state of things."[60]

Fillmore waited for over a month after mid-February to launch his purge. He could make interim appointments without the need of Senate confirmation only after Congress adjourned in early March. Nor did he want to turn Sewardite legislators against Fish, whom he had publicly endorsed, as long as it was possible that he could still win the senatorship. On March 27, eight days after Fish's election, the guillotine dropped. John Bush replaced Kellogg as marshal for the northern district. James R. Thompson, a Silver Gray from Rochester, who had been fired from his state job by the canal board, took Pond's place as customs collector there. Silver Grays took the jobs of Clowes and other Sewardite post-masters. The joy of Fillmore's friends knew no bounds. "It is an emphatic proof that the Administration not only in words but in deeds makes adherence to the settlement a test question," cheered Duer.[61]

Nor did Fillmore stop there. He gave the lame-duck Duer a foreign post, but focused primarily on finding an appropriate place for his Binghamton friend John A. Collier. Fillmore's loyalty to Collier anguished respectable allies, for Collier was a notorious womanizer with a fondness for young girls and other men's wives. He had also been fined for exposing himself to women on the sidewalk through the ground-floor front window of an Albany hotel. Fillmore was none-theless determined to find something for him. In December 1850, he contemplated replacing the Sewardite John C. Clark with Collier as solicitor for the treasury, but the intervention of scandalized friends, who hinted that they would inform Mrs. Fillmore of Collier's sordid reputation, deterred him.[62]

Then, in early May 1851, the Manhattan patrician Philip Hone, naval officer in New York harbor, suddenly died, and Fillmore placed the Albany flasher at the top of his list of possible replacements. Again consternated Silver Grays from Albany to Washington pleaded with the president not to tarnish his administration by appointing so disreputable a rake. Fillmore finally relented and instead named David A. Bokee, the former Silver Gray congressman from Brooklyn, to the influential post. Bokee's appointment in July reinforced the lessons of March, for Bokee was an avowed foe of Weed and a personal enemy of Fish, who begged Fillmore not to appoint him. The message was loud and clear. At least in New York the administration would play the patronage card to force compliance with its wishes.[63]

Weed responded to Fillmore's patronage offensive by excoriating the administration in the *Evening Journal*. All talk of resurrecting the Varnum resolutions stopped. Instead, Weed was rumored to be pressing for the passage of resolutions that openly condemned the Compromise or approved Seward. If those failed, Weed was expected to get every Sewardite legislator to sign a vehemently anti-Compromise address at the end of the session. Meanwhile, Silver Grays circulated their own address among legislators that endorsed Fillmore's annual message. Despite Fillmore's cooperation with Weed in securing Fish's election, in sum, the Whig party remained bitterly divided over patronage and principles.[64]

Then, suddenly in April, the storm clouds dissipated, and intraparty harmony suddenly emerged for the first time since 1844. The reason for this miraculous reunion was not, as some contemporaries and later historians suggested, that Weed wilted before administration pressure in order to protect the federal jobs his men still occupied.[65] Rather, in April, Whigs stumbled across a new issue that united their party and redivided the Democrats. It bore no relation whatsoever to Fillmore, the Compromise, or slavery. It illustrated a fundamental fact about the federal structure of American government in the nineteenth century: state policies often mattered more to politicians and the public than the actions of Congress or presidents. The issue that saved the New York Whig party from almost certain disaster was enlargement of the state's Erie Canal system.

To unify fractious Whigs, Washington Hunt had tried to soft-pedal the sectionally and factionally divisive slavery issue in his inaugural message and to return instead to the party's traditional economic themes. As part of this strategy, he called on legislators to amend the state constitution to facilitate enlargement of the Erie Canal by improving the main east-west channel and completing construction of north-south feeder canals. Since the 1830s Whigs had advocated funding enlargement through bond issues that would eventually be repaid with revenues from tolls. Deficit financing divided Hunker Democrats, who favored it, against Van Burenites, who opposed it. In 1842 the dominant Van Burenites slowed construction with their stop-and-tax law, and in 1846 they wrote that approach into the new state constitution. One of its pertinent provisions allocated annual revenues from canal tolls to sinking funds to defray general expenses and pay off the existing debt before any annual surpluses over those amounts ($1.85 million) could be spent on repairs and new construction. Another prohibited new bond issues for canal construction worth more than $1 million unless the legislature first won approval of the new debt in a popular referendum and accompanied it with real estate taxes that could pay off the bonds' interest and principal. Hunt sought to lift those restrictions.[66]

Hunt contemplated beginning the lengthy process of constitutional revision, but Whig legislators seized on an alternative he had mentioned in his message but rejected as a violation of the constitution's spirit and letter—as indeed it was. By this device the state would sell "revenue certificates," not bonds to which the future credit of the state was pledged, to fund enlargement. The annual surplus revenue from canal tolls allotted by the constitution for repairs and construction— that is, the surplus after the yearly payments to the sinking funds—but no other state funds, particularly those that depended on land taxes, would be pledged to pay the holders of these certificates for a number of years. They would be a form of debt that would be extraordinarily attractive to investors because of the huge surpluses earned from tolls on the mainline Erie Canal. But they would not be, or so their advocates maintained, bonded indebtedness as defined by the constitution, since their holders could not seek any payment by the state other than canal revenues. In short, with revenue certificates the legislature could finesse the requirement to secure permission in a popular referendum and to levy land taxes to pay off the bonds. Ingenious Whigs had raised smoke and mirrors to an art form.[67]

On March 13, in the midst of the stalemate over Fish's election and Varnum's resolutions, a Sewardite assemblyman from Buffalo named Orlando Allen, responding to a letter from Seward urging Whig legislators to expand the canal system, introduced a bill calling for the issue of $9 million in revenue certificates to fund immediate completion of all canals. Some Silver Grays carped that the Nine Million Loan, as it was quickly dubbed, would only give more leverage to the Weed-controlled canal board, but others recognized that the potential boodle was so large that there would be plenty of room for Silver Grays and Sewardites alike to feed at the government trough. Thus, when Whigs sought legal opinions to justify the constitutionality of this quintessential pork barrel scheme, they went to administration supporters, not Sewardites, in order to eliminate any suspicion that it was a factional rather than a party measure. Not only did John C. Spencer, one of the state's most eminent jurists and the Silver Gray most responsible for dissuading Fillmore from appointing John Collier, write a brief. Daniel Webster himself also delivered an opinion assuring New Yorkers that the proposed revenue certificates were not bonds subject to the constitutional limitations.[68]

The political benefits of the Nine Million Loan went far beyond increasing the pelf available to Whig contractors and investors. Whig voters across New York, who had no possibility of sharing the boodle themselves, shouted enthusiastically for the proposal. Simultaneously, the scheme initially split the Democrats, while the certain opposition of Barnburners could make it a defining issue in the 1851 election. When the bill steamrolled through the house on April 4 by a vote of 75–27, for example, all of the negative votes came from Democrats, while only four supported it. Fourteen Democrats, all from districts along proposed canal routes, abstained rather than vote against a Whig measure of such direct benefit to their constituents. The senate provided Whigs with even better campaign fodder. Twelve Barnburner senators announced their immediate resignations, and another absented himself to deny the quorum necessary to vote on the measure. Unable to act, the senate adjourned *sine die.* On April 19 Hunt then issued a proclamation denouncing Democrats for their outrageous obstructionism, ordering special elections in May to replace the twelve senators who had resigned, and calling a special session of the senate to meet in June. In May, Whigs carried seven of the twelve special elections, and in late June, on a straight party-line vote, senate Whigs passed the Nine Million Loan.

Long before this triumphant outcome, Whigs realized that they had discovered a truly golden issue, and they refused to jeopardize it by continuing quarrels over Fillmore, the Compromise, slavery, or even patronage. Babcock, the Silver Gray senator from Buffalo, urged Fillmore to make no further removals in order to nurture the party's newfound unity, a request with which the delighted president happily complied. Weed "and his friends now talk of harmony, and say the Canal Bill will unite us," the recently appointed U.S. Marshal Bush told Fillmore in April, while Thomas Foote, long a visceral foe of Weed, announced in early May that "the break-up at Albany [i.e., the adjournment of the senate because of Democratic resignations] will do good by uniting the Whigs and by substituting a new issue of agitation for that of slavery."[69]

Seward and Weed, not Fillmore, in sum, discovered a way to reunify the New York Whig party without Sewardites endorsing the administration's position on the Compromise. Instead, their formula depended on ignoring slavery altogether and focusing on something else. United by the new and apparently invincible canal expansion issue and the momentum from the May results, New York's Whigs seemingly faced only one final hurdle on the road back from disruption— reuniting the rival regular and Silver Gray state committees.[70]

Whigs were anxious "to rally together on their common and undisputed principles and forget or lay aside the topics on which they differ, or to unite on them as far as possible," Spencer reported to Fish in June. Even Fuller was now prepared "to go for harmony in the party." Negotiations involving Hunt, Spencer, Foote, Varnum, Babcock, and Weed, among others, began in July to find a formula to ensure a harmonious state convention that fall. Attempts to draft an address dealing with the Compromise that all Whig legislators could sign at the end of the special summer session aborted, however, for Sewardites rejected the Silver Gray demand that it condemn agitation for repeal of the fugitive slave law as unpatriotic and unwise. Nonetheless, the common commitment to canal expansion allowed Whigs to overcome even this obstacle. They agreed to divide the fall state ticket evenly between Silver Grays and Sewardites, and a committee was appointed to bring the two state committees together so that they could jointly issue the call for the state convention. That summit occurred in Albany in early August when both state committees called the convention and issued the so-called Albany Platform, which had been drafted by Spencer. It insisted upon obedience to all constitutional laws while admitting the right of men to criticize and seek revision of statutes they found offensive. However unsatisfactory some administration supporters found this compromise manifesto, most Whigs had long since turned their attention to the canal issue. Fillmore himself was overjoyed. "I congratulate you and the country upon the *union* of the Whig party in N. York," he exulted to Webster.[71]

V

That Fillmore boasted to Webster of Whig reunion in New York testifies to his blindness toward the widening chasm between the two men. Webster contemptuously scorned the Albany Platform as precisely the kind of live-and-let-live platform he rejected in Massachusetts. Refusing even to allow his friends to attend a state convention where Winthrop would be nominated, he spurned as a sellout the deal to split the New York ticket evenly between Sewardites and Silver Grays. He deplored the reunification of the party in New York because it increased the difficulty of building a Union party there. More important, Fillmore's willingness to sack Sewardites and appoint his own friends convinced him that Fillmore had decided—or would be forced by his New York allies like Hall who wanted to retain patronage—to seek the party's nomination in 1852. And he was especially angry that his patronage-holding enemies in Massachusetts like Philip Greely, Jr., and Charles Hudson justified their opposition to Webster's own nomination on the spurious grounds of supporting Fillmore for the prize. That promise, Webster jealously concluded, explained Fillmore's refusal to axe them.[72]

Webster misjudged Fillmore's intentions in 1851; he had not decided to seek the nomination. Although he and especially his Silver Gray allies concluded that his dramatic removals forced Weed to seek a rapprochement in New York, moreover, he also recognized that hope of winning in the fall on the canal expansion issue did most to reunite the New York party.[73] Fillmore comprehended, in short, that the best way to save the Whig party was to prove that it could still win. Unlike Webster, therefore, from the summer of 1851 on, he refused to do anything that could jeopardize Whig victory in New York or elsewhere. No more removals occurred in New York, and Fillmore used patronage only sparingly elsewhere. Yet his restraint in the name of party unity did not guarantee victory in New York's fall elections, for he had no control over the New Yorkers who were most enthusiastic about Webster's Union party scheme: the New York City Union Safety Committee.

The tenuous Whig alliance behind the Albany platform held through the September state convention. The state platform expressed confidence in Fillmore's administration, called for obedience to the Compromise measures, and admitted the right of individuals "in a constitutional manner" to seek modification of any of the "Peace Measures." As arranged previously, the convention also carefully divided the state ticket among Sewardites, Silver Grays, and neutrals with no ostensible factional affiliation. George Patterson of Chautauqua County, a close Weed ally and the nominee for comptroller, was the most prominent Sewardite on the eight-man state ticket, and Daniel Ullmann, the candidate for attorney general, was the leading Silver Gray.[74]

At stake in the 1851 election, aside from the legislature, were six of the nine positions on the all-important canal board. Although Whigs had distributed $3 million worth of revenue certificates immediately after passage of the Nine Million Loan bill in June, the new board would allot the balance. Since the three holdovers on the board, two canal commissioners and the lieutenant governor, were all Democrats, Whigs needed a near sweep to retain control. Since most Whigs wanted to focus the fall campaign on the benefits of canal expansion, the issue that had brought such spectacular success during the special May senatorial elections, such a sweep seemed feasible.

Almost from the moment the state convention adjourned, however, Whig strategists encountered unforeseen setbacks. They counted on the canal issue not only to unite and mobilize their own voters but also to divide Hunker and Barnburner Democrats. They expected to pick up procanal Hunker votes in areas benefited directly by the proposed enlargement. Yet Democrats proved far more united and energetic than Whigs anticipated. Hunkers found the prospect of a Whig canal board distributing the boodle just as appalling as Barnburners found the distribution itself. Thus, for quite different reasons, both factions were determined to capture the canal board.[75]

The struggle for control of the canal board also generated controversy over Ullmann's nomination. The attorney general not only sat on it, but he also had to defend the constitutionality of the Nine Million Loan in court from legal challenges Barnburners immediately brought against it. The attorney general also had to deal with the claims of Anti-Renters, who sought state intervention to end the quit-rent system. Like other Silver Grays, Ullmann rabidly opposed Anti-Renters, whereas his Democratic opponent, Levi Chatfield, vocally championed their cause. From the start, therefore, Whigs had to write off the small but potentially crucial Anti-Rent vote. They hoped instead to pick up enough offsetting votes from procanal Democrats and Whigs, for Chatfield had published a pamphlet denouncing the loan as illegal. Chatfield's stance seemed to give Ullmann an advantage among upstate proponents of canal expansion; the problem was that the views of the Manhattan lawyer on the canal issue were utterly unknown in the areas where it mattered most. Throughout the two-month campaign, therefore, suspicious upstate Whigs pressed Ullmann to write public letters endorsing expansion (which he did) and to speak in its defense along the canal itself (which he did not). Whether letter writing alone was sufficient to mobilize enough votes to offset the loss of Anti-Renters was the problem.[76]

That problem, in turn, was complicated by an unavoidable fact. Most, though hardly all, upstate Whigs interested in canal expansion were Sewardites who hated the Compromise and scorned New York City merchants who clamored for appeasement of the South. Ullmann, in contrast, was renowned as a Silver Gray bolter in 1850 and a fervent champion of finality. That is why Silver Grays demanded his inclusion on the ticket. Despite the accord reached by factional leaders on the Albany Platform, in sum, animosities between rank-and-file Sewardites and Silver Grays remained intense.

They were fanned by New York City's Union Safety Committee, which had not participated in the love fest at Albany. In September it demanded that both Whig and Democrat platforms explicitly renounce agitation against or alteration of any of the Compromise measures. Neither party complied with this ultimatum, but the Union Safety Committee found the Whigs' platform especially offensive. Therefore it sought signed pledges from businessmen in New York City and upstate towns that they would not vote for anyone who did not unequivocally oppose revisions of the fugitive slave law. By election day, according to one estimate, at least 20,000 merchants in New York City alone had signed the pledge, which precluded them from voting for Sewardites on the Whig ticket. Worse still from the Whigs' perspective, the Union Safety Committee then circulated its own state ticket, consisting of three men from the Democrats' slate and four from the Whigs', including Ullmann.[77] After his nomination Ullmann was warned, even by Fillmore's allies like George Babcock, that any hint of association with the Castle Garden crowd would be the kiss of death among upstate Whigs, who already distrusted his commitment to canal expansion. As soon as the Union Safety Committee placed Ullmann on its ticket, therefore, rumors spread that upstate Sewardites would knife him. Silver Grays, in turn, vowed retaliatory strikes against Patterson and other Sewardites.[78]

Merchants not only refused to vote for many Whig candidates, but they also withheld contributions to the Whigs' war chest. So, significantly, did patronage-holding Whig allies of the Union Safety Committee—Young, Maxwell, and the new naval officer, David Bokee, a well-known friend of Webster. While privately assuring Fillmore that they supported the whole Whig ticket, they openly endorsed pro-Compromise Democrats over Whig candidates, not only on the state ticket but for the assembly and state senate as well. The chagrined Fillmore knew of their apostasy, but he refused to condemn it publicly, thus implicating himself as their accomplice.[79]

The result was a Whig disaster. Only two of eight candidates on the Whig state ticket won, and both were on the Union Safety ticket. Ullmann lost, however, for he was cut by upstate Sewardites and opposed by Anti-Renters who supported Chatfield. Democrats thus gained control of the new canal board. Silver Gray and Sewardite legislative candidates, knifed by factional foes, went down in droves. The huge advantage Whigs had won in May's special senate elections vanished; the thirty-two seats were now evenly divided, giving the Democratic lieutenant governor the deciding vote.[80] Whigs' thirty-eight-seat cushion in the house shrank to two. Silver Grays crowed that Weed and Seward were now "flat on their backs." In contrast, Weed moaned that "a gallant, glorious party has been used up." Sewardites blamed the treachery of Silver Grays, the cupidity of Whig merchants, and the timidity of Fillmore, who refused to crack down on Maxwell, Young, and Bokee. Most of all, however, anti-Compromise Whigs blamed the blind presidential ambition of Daniel Webster, who had publicly sanctioned the Castle Garden meeting, who still saw the Union Safety Committee as a nucleus for a Union party, and who, they sputtered, sought Whig defeat as a way to discredit Winfield Scott's presidential candidacy. "Webster has succeeded better under Fillmore than he did under Tyler, in breaking up the Whig organization and forming a third party," fumed Fish.[81]

VI

By November 1851, most other northern states had already voted. Whether or not Fillmore's administration or Webster on his own tried to bolster their pro-Compromise forces, moreover, almost everywhere Whig candidates were crushed. Ohio, the other northern state with a crucial senatorial election in early 1851, provides a good example.

Throughout 1851 both Fillmore and Webster refrained from intervening in the Buckeye State, in part because they could not identify any reliable pro-Compromise Whig politicos who might benefit from federal aid. With striking unanimity, Ohio's Whigs hated the Fugitive Slave Act, deplored Fillmore's insistence upon implementing it, and complained that "Webster and Clay have contributed more to the annihilation of the Whig party in Ohio than any other causes combined." In sharp contrast to this overwhelming sentiment, moreover, by early 1851 virtually every Whig paper in the state was pledging fealty to the administration and tempering attacks on the Fugitive Slave Act in order to keep federal printing contracts, so nothing could be gained by switching them to other editors.[82]

Primarily, however, Fillmore and Webster hesitated to intervene in Ohio because, next to Massachusetts, the Free Soil party retained its greatest disruptive potential there. Both men wanted to avert the election of another Free Soil United States senator from Ohio in the winter of 1851 and Free Soil gains in the fall elections. They realized that their insistence on finality was burden enough for Ohio's Whigs to carry, and they refrained from any pogrom against jobholders that might drive still more angry Whigs to the Free Soil camp.

The Senate seat at stake in the winter of 1850–51 was Corwin's, to which Ewing was appointed by Seabury Ford in July 1850.[83] As in Massachusetts, the legislature could confirm or replace Ewing for the remaining three months of that term, as well as fill the new full-term seat. Both Ewing and the Free Soiler Joshua R. Giddings sought that prize. Although each sounded alarms about a Union party possibly coalescing during the legislative session to defeat them, Whigs' anti-Compromise sentiment rendered such a possibility remote. In addition, Ohio's Whigs and Democrats remained sharply at odds over state economic policy, not only in the legislature but even more so at the state constitutional convention sitting in Cincinnati while the legislature met at Columbus.[84]

Some interparty bargaining in the legislature was inevitable, however. Free Soilers still retained the balance of power in both chambers.[85] Ewing and Giddings feared a Union party in the election for senator, indeed, because Whigs and Democrats had bargained in the 1849–50 session to divide the state patronage between themselves in order to exclude Free Soilers totally. Many predicted the reemergence of this so-called People's Line coalition to give one party the state jobs and contracts and the other the Senate seat. Common contempt for Free Soilers, if not mutual support for the Compromise, might cause Whigs and Democrats to cut a deal.

Considerable sentiment existed among Whig and Democratic legislators for renewal of the People's Line in 1850–51, but significant elements in both parties wanted instead to forge a coalition with Free Soilers by giving them the Senate seat in return for control of the legislature and its spoils. Exploiting Fillmore's vow to enforce the hated fugitive slave law, newly elected Democratic Governor Reuben Wood, whose nomination and campaign during 1850 had infuriated Free Soilers, denounced the fugitive law in his December inaugural address and demanded the complete abolition of slavery in the District of Columbia. Wood's nakedly opportunistic somersault so enraptured Free Soilers, from Salmon P. Chase and Giddings on down to local politicos, that the chances of consummating another Democratic-Free Soil bargain surged. But conservative Democrats, Ohio's equivalent of New York's Hunkers and Cushing's Democratic bloc in Massachusetts, were appalled at the thought of supporting Giddings, the Free Soilers' favorite, for the Senate. Nor would they support the nominee of the Democratic caucus, Henry Payne of Cleveland. Without complete Democratic support, the putative Democratic/Free Soil alliance lacked the votes to elect the senator or to distribute the remaining spoils. Whigs now had their chance.

Whigs, however, were even more badly fragmented than the Democrats. Some believed that Ohio Whigs had been so thoroughly indoctrinated with antislavery views by Whig "stumpers" for six years and were so repelled by the prosouthern course of Fillmore, Clay, and Webster that the party's only future lay in repudiating the Compromise and reaffirming antislavery orthodoxy, whatever the risk of alienating the administration.[86] Like northern anti-Compromise Whigs elsewhere, they were already booming Winfield Scott for the next presidential nomination, and they also advocated cooperation with Free Soilers in the legislature. No Whigs could tolerate elevating the traitor Giddings to the Senate, but they argued that a staunch Whig foe of the Fugitive Slave Act could attract enough Free Soil votes to win.

Others preferred the opposite tack. They were so incensed at Free Soilers' "corruption & selfishness" in pursuit of office since 1848 that their top priority was "to put them down." These Whigs favored the People's Line bargain with Democrats on patronage, and they would accept a stalemate that postponed the senatorial election until the next legislature or even support a Democrat to keep a Free Soiler out of that office. The Free Soilers' "*object* is *office* & their motto 'office by bargain or any other means,'" snarled one such Whig. "Quit buying meat at their stalls & they will soon be out of the market."[87]

Between these poles stood straight-out Whigs composed primarily of Ewing's followers. They shunned bargains with either Free Soilers or Democrats on both patronage and the Senate seat. Such men came as close as any Ohio Whigs could to Millard Fillmore's model of good Whigs. They refused to endorse the Compromise openly, but since they had received most of Ohio's federal jobs when Ewing was in the cabinet, they considered it impolitic to flout Fillmore and embarrass Corwin by running a known opponent of the fugitive slave law for the Senate. They would grudgingly acquiesce in finality, and, as would occur in New York, they wanted to rally the party on different issues, such as opposition to the new state constitution then being drafted in Cincinnati. Their preferred candidate for the Senate was the incumbent Ewing, although some favored other conservatives like Samuel Vinton or Henry Stanbery.[88]

Pulled in three directions, the Whig caucus in January rejected Ewing, Vinton, and Stanbery and nominated a nonentity named Hiram Griswold on the pretext that he could gain Free Soil backing. Calling this claim spurious, Ewing's friends attacked Griswold as a stalking horse for proponents of the People's Line who were prepared to let the Democrats have the Senate seat in return for control of state patronage. On that ground they refused to support him.

Neither all the Whigs nor all the Democrats, in sum, united behind their caucus candidates for the Senate. Nor would they vote for Giddings or any other Free Soiler. Stalemate ensued, just as in New York, Massachusetts, Connecticut, and Rhode Island. It was not until February 16, 1851, two and a half months after the session began, that state jobs were finally distributed, and here the People's Line finally prevailed to shut out the Free Soilers. No agreement was reached on the senator, however, and most legislators assumed that the decision would pass to the next legislature.

Then, in mid-March, the situation suddenly changed. The constitutional convention in Cincinnati finally completed its business and scheduled a popular referendum on its handiwork for June. The new constitution was not as bad as many Whigs had feared, for Whig delegates had combined with conservative Democrats to defeat the most radical economic proposals such as a clause authorizing the state legislature to repeal every bank charter in the state. But the Democratic majority in that body reapportioned the legislature in a way that, as Whigs complained, would "render it utterly impossible for the Whigs to obtain a majority in the next Legislature." Alarmed that this would be their last chance for at least a decade to elect a United States senator, the Whig caucus frantically reassembled and replaced the unpopular Griswold with Benjamin Franklin Wade. A resident of the Western Reserve, the hotbed of antislavery sentiment and Free Soil strength in Ohio, Wade had remained loyal to the Whig party. Since October 1850, however, he had given hair-raising speeches against enforcement of the fugitive slave law even though he himself was a judge. With the aid of Free Soil votes and the abstention of disgruntled Democrats who still refused to support Payne, the Whigs then elected Wade to the Senate.[89]

Wade's election was a Whig triumph, but it resembled a pyrrhic victory. The selection of so extreme an antislavery man could hardly please Southerners or Fillmore even though federal officeholders in Ohio tried to reassure him that Ohio's Whigs would confine their antislavery sentiment "within legitimate bounds." Wade's election, in sum, aggravated rather than reduced the difficulty of reuniting the national party. Within Ohio itself, the blatant bargaining over the Senate seat and the flagrant pursuit of lucrative state jobs at the disposal of the legislature by Whig legislators themselves convinced many Whig voters that "the present Ohio Legislature is the most infamously corrupt that ever assembled."[90]

This burgeoning disgust with legislators who arrogantly assumed "that they embodied all the wisdom and ability of the State," and with a political system that had become unspeakably polluted, pointed to immediate trouble for Ohio's Whigs in the impending June referendum on the new constitution. Although Whigs stifled what they considered the most obnoxious proposals from the Democratic majority at the constitutional convention, they still regarded the new charter with horror. It reapportioned the legislature to deprive Whigs of a majority, and it menaced an activist, prodevelopment state by restricting appropriations, limiting the ability to fund internal improvements through bond issues, prohibiting county governments from buying stock in railroads, and increasing taxation on, and stockholder liability in, banks. It mandated new elections for every state office in October 1851. Furthermore, in what Whigs regarded as an invitation to demagoguery and incompetence, it made elective all the posts legislators had previously appointed—state executive offices below the governorship, the Board of Public Works, and all state judgeships.

Yet Whig voters lauded precisely this attempt to strip the legislature of patronage. As elsewhere, a disgust with politics and politicians that had nothing to do with the slavery issue was boiling up, and it would cost Whigs heavily. Although some Whig delegates refused to sign the new constitution in protest against the offensive clauses, and although almost every Whig editor and politician in the state went "against it tooth and toe nail," in June at least half of the normal Whig voters either supported the document or abstained, allowing it to pass narrowly. Such voters, in sum, disregarded the harm the new constitution did to their party's competitiveness and program. They did so, as one Whig explained, "to give the people directly, as far as they will, the appointing power."[91]

"Election all wrong," the young Cincinnati Whig Rutherford B. Hayes tersely jotted in his diary after the votes were counted in October. "Democrats take all and would have taken more if there had been more to take." Democrats, indeed, swept all the previously appointive state offices, rolled up huge majorities in both houses of the legislature, and trounced the Whigs by an unprecedented margin in the gubernatorial contest. Whig candidate and Ewing ally Samuel Vinton was reduced to 42.4 percent of the vote.[92] Surly Whigs attributed their rout to anger at Fillmore and Webster and looked desperately for an attractive presidential candidate to spark a comeback in 1852. "Here in Ohio we are a little devoured," one confessed, "but Scot [sic] is a talisman with us."[93]

VII

In some other northern states the administration played the patronage card against anti-Compromise Whigs, but removals were erratic and often hardened animosity toward Fillmore and his cabinet. Even where administration intervention did not cause Whig defeats, moreover, the outcome of the 1851 races reinforced the conclusion drawn by many northern Whigs at the end of 1850: only repudiation of Fillmore and Webster offered them a scintilla of hope for the future.

Dispensation of federal jobs in the nation's newest state was calamitous. Because California's entire congressional delegation was Democratic, the administration had no firsthand knowledge of the situation on the West Coast. It treated federal jobs there as sinecures for friendly eastern Whigs, much to the annoyance of men already in California. Thomas Butler King's appointment as customs collector in San Francisco fanned pique into outrage. How much this discontent affected the outcome of California's 1851 elections is unclear, but Democrats elected both congressmen. In the gubernatorial race John Bigler, brother of Pennsylvania's Democratic gubernatorial candidate, nosed out his Whig competitor by about 440 votes.[94]

To the extent that midwestern results outside of Ohio secured support for the administration, Fillmore, not Webster, won credit. Whether it was his original determination not to allow cabinet members to advance their own presidential prospects with patronage or confidence gained from the apparently salutary moves in New York in March is unclear. But Fillmore took charge of midwestern appointments himself. When he won personal credit from grateful Whigs, therefore, Webster's jealousy only increased.

Iowa, for example, had no major elections scheduled for 1851, and its Whigs had already thrown their support to the Compromise the previous year. Nonetheless, Iowa's Whigs had long complained that the cabinet, out of deference to the state's two pro-Compromise Democratic senators, allowed Democrats to control the government's land office there. As soon as the Senate adjourned in March, therefore, Fillmore named a Whig as surveyor general. By itself, this appointment could not improve the electoral prospects of Iowa's outnumbered Whigs, but it did, Fillmore learned, cement Iowa's support for his renomination in 1852 if he wanted it.[95]

In Wisconsin, Fillmore used patronage in a more heavy-handed fashion to redress the party's factional balance. James D. Merrill was named postmaster of Milwaukee after Congress adjourned in March, largely because he pledged to start a proadministration newspaper to rival the Sewardite sheet of Rufus King, who had previously secured the post office for a friend from Taylor. Merrill's appointment, however, failed to deter Wisconsin's Whigs from coalescing with Free Soilers in the gubernatorial and legislative elections of 1851 when they won their unprecedented victory. The triumph argued that defiance of, rather than compliance with, the administration's pro-Compromise stance still provided the route to success in the North.[96]

Michigan posed a delicate problem for Fillmore, for he knew that only Free Soil support had allowed Whigs to capture two of its three congressional seats in 1850. He therefore attempted a complicated straddle on patronage. To woo antislavery Whigs and Free Soilers, the administration appointed former Whig/Free Soil Congressman William Sprague as Indian agent there. This move won widespread applause from antislavery Whigs in Michigan, disconcerted Fillmore's Silver Gray allies in New York, and would have been inconceivable on the part of Webster. Simultaneously, however, Fillmore, whose brother led Michigan's pro-Compromise Whigs, attempted to silence the state party's dominant Sewardite wing that was already booming Scott for the 1852 nomination. Apprised of the administration's get-tough policy, Detroit's federal officeholders—Alpheus Williams, Charles Babcock, and Oliver M. Hyde—abandoned assaults on the administration and the Compromise in order to keep their jobs. Meanwhile the pro-Fillmore Detroit *Advertiser*, fattened by revenues from government printing contracts, made concerted efforts to buy out the Detroit *Tribune*, a pro-Seward, pro-Scott sheet. Despite pledges of loyalty from cowed officeholders in Michigan and gratitude among anti-Compromise Whigs for Sprague's appointment, the Whig majority in the state legislature endorsed Winfield Scott for president in late March. Sewardite Whigs also dominated the Whig state convention in September. They not only nominated an antislavery man who won Free Soil backing for governor, but they also selected four Scott men and only two administration supporters as delegates to the anticipated Whig national convention in 1852. In response, Fillmore's supporters sat out the election in an effort to depress the Whig vote and thereby discredit Scott. Consequently, the Whig/Free Soil vote dropped from 23,561 (45.7 percent) in 1849 to 16,901 (41.3 percent) in 1851. Such sabotage hardly won friends for the administration from the party's dominant wing.[97]

In contrast, Fillmore won acquiescence in finality from Illinois Whigs, who like their counterparts in Iowa faced no elections in 1851. During the summer and fall of 1850, many Illinois Whigs endorsed the Compromise, and strategic removals by the administration in late 1850 increased Whigs' flight toward its position. In January 1851 Democratic resolutions praising the Compromise for resolving the sectional conflict received almost unanimous support from Whig state legislators, and by the end of 1851 Whig papers openly condemned continued opposition to the Fugitive Slave Act. Nonetheless, as events would soon show, near-unanimous acquiescence in finality did not translate into support from Illinois Whigs for either Fillmore's or Webster's nomination.[98]

Outside of Ohio, the midwestern state of greatest concern to the administration was Indiana, which held congressional elections in August. Like their Illinois neighbors, many Indiana Whigs embraced Clay's compromise in 1850, and the party's crushing defeat in that year's legislative elections clearly sapped the will of Whigs still inclined to oppose the administration's position. At the constitutional convention during the winter of 1850–51, Whigs joined Democrats in passing pro-Compromise resolutions by a vote of 90–25. Opposition came almost entirely from delegates representing Quaker and Free Soil strongholds in the Whitewater River Valley in southeastern Indiana. By the spring the state's leading Whig paper, John Defrees' *Indiana State Journal*, argued that agitation against the fugitive slave law should cease until it had a fair trial. Most indicative of Whigs' shift, however, was the retreat of South Bend editor Schuyler Colfax. For two years Colfax had argued that Whigs must seek Free Soil votes with a hard-line antislavery stance, and he had bitterly vilified the pro-Compromise tilt of Clay, Webster, and Fillmore for ruining Whigs' hopes in the 1850 elections. In 1851 Colfax accepted the finality of the Compromise, and that summer he was nominated as a Whig congressional candidate on a platform that echoed verbatim the language of Fillmore's annual message regarding the Compromise and the fugitive slave law. Fillmore, in sum, had no need to use patronage to whip Indiana's Whigs into line behind finality.[99]

As in Illinois, however, acquiescence in finality did not equal support for Webster's presidential pretensions. By the spring of 1851 Defrees and Colfax, as well as other Whig editors, were booming Scott for the 1852 nomination.[100] Individual Whig congressional candidates, moreover, took divergent stances on the Compromise. Whig incumbent Edward McGaughey, who had voted against the Texas-New Mexico bill, abstained on Utah and, incredibly, *supported* the Fugitive Slave Act, insisted during his campaign against pro-Compromise Democrat John G. Davis that he still wanted to impose the Wilmot Proviso on Utah and New Mexico in a vain—and, from this distance, ridiculous—attempt to win Free Soil support. Samuel Brenton, the Whigs' candidate in the Tenth District, also openly solicited Free Soil backing. In sharp contrast, Samuel W. Parker, who had been defeated by Free Soiler George W. Julian in 1849 and again challenged him in 1851, recognized that Democratic support for the Compromise dissolved the basis for the Democratic/Free Soil coalition of 1849. Thus he posed as a pro-Compromise Fillmore loyalist in hopes of winning over or keeping home Democrats, who had no candidate of their own in 1851. A third variant was represented by Colfax, who challenged Democratic incumbent Graham Fitch. Elected with Free Soil support in 1849, Fitch in 1850 had voted against the fugitive slave and Utah bills but for the crucial Texas-New Mexico bill. Hampered by a platform that embraced finality, Colfax could not stop Free Soilers from reendorsing Fitch. In most other districts, little separated Whigs from Democrats on the Compromise.[101]

Whatever advantage or disadvantage Whig congressional candidates had on the slavery issue, their prospects were threatened by another factor that had nothing to do with it. The August elections coincided with a popular referendum on the new state constitution hammered out between October 1850 and February 1851. For years in the state legislature Whigs had opposed calling a convention and thereby earned a reputation for obstructionism. The vote for delegates in 1850 had occurred on the same day as the legislative elections when Democrats won such a resounding victory, and although party lines apparently did not hold in contests for delegates, Democrats still won a lopsided majority.[102] Although Whigs applauded many of the new constitution's provisions, the Democratic majority added some that Whigs found repellent. As elsewhere, restrictions were placed on state debt and on the ability of local governments to buy stock in railroads. Of greater political significance, the new constitution allowed immigrant aliens to vote in all elections after one year's residence in the state, four years before they were eligible for naturalization, a provision that was calculated to inflate the Democratic vote. Finally, a separate clause prohibited free blacks from settling in the state. Most Whigs did not oppose this measure, but the resistance to it in the convention had come from Whigs and Free Soilers. Given the pervasive racist sentiment in Indiana, Whigs knew that the popularity of this discriminatory measure would provoke a high turnout of voters who would most likely go Democratic in races for elective offices.[103]

It could have been worse. With the aid of some Democrats, Whigs blocked the most radical antibanking measures at the convention. Unlike the Ohio and Kentucky constitutions, moreover, Indiana's did not require new elections for all state officials. Thus Whigs in 1851 escaped the impossible task of running against the immensely popular Democratic incumbent, Governor Joe Wright, whose name at the top of the ticket would certainly have increased the Democratic vote. Nonetheless, the constitution seemed so popular, especially its provisions reflecting the rising tide of antipolitician, antiofficeholder sentiment in Indiana and elsewhere, that Whig papers tried to deflect its consequences by endorsing ratification. That proved to be no contest. In August the new constitution passed by an enormous majority, 113,230 to 27,638, and the prohibition of black settlement won by an even wider margin, 113,828 to 21,873.[104]

Given this landslide and another rout by Democrats in the legislative elections, Whig candidates for Congress ran surprisingly well.[105] The incumbent McGaughey lost to Davis, but Whigs won two of ten seats compared to one in 1849. Parker defeated Julian, undoubtedly to the administration's delight, and Brenton, who had Free Soil backing, edged out his Democratic opponent in the Tenth District. Colfax lost by fewer than 250 votes out of over 18,000 cast, and he blamed his defeat on ballots illegally deposited by railroad workers.[106] In three other districts, including McGaughey's, the margins against Whigs were just as slim. Still, the total Whig vote of 68,493 was about 2,000 less than the party had polled in 1849, while the Democratic vote grew by 5,000. With fewer than a third of the seats in the legislature, only a fifth of the new House delegation, and a declining proportion of the statewide popular vote, Indiana's Whigs remained in dire shape. With the Democratic vote bound to grow because of the enfranchisement of alien immigrants and the invincible Wright heading the Democrats' state ticket in 1852, Indiana's Whigs might well conclude that they needed the aid of gunpowder in the 1852 presidential election, just as they had in 1848.

Of the six midwestern states, in sum, Whigs openly defied the administration by seeking Free Soil support only in Michigan and Wisconsin. In the other four, Whig papers silenced their criticism of the Compromise and embraced finality, whether expediently or enthusiastically. Yet Wisconsin provided the Whigs' only statewide triumph after Ohio elected Wade to the Senate, and both of those victories, like one of the two congressional successes in Indiana, were attributable to Free Soil support. Of the four states that acquiesced in finality, moreover, only Iowa's Whigs were enthusiastic about Fillmore's nomination for 1852. Nowhere in the Midwest, significantly, was there any hint of support for Webster.

VIII

The two remaining northern states, New Jersey and Pennsylvania, therefore provided Webster's only hope of building northern support for his presidential aspirations outside of New England to counteract the possibility that New York might support Fillmore's nomination. Whatever New Jersey's Whigs thought about Webster or the Union party, the administration made no attempt to reallocate federal jobs there in 1851. Nor could Webster punish any Whig candidates that year. The state's new congressional delegation had been chosen in 1850, and even before Congress adjourned that year, the state Whig party had fled from the anti-Compromise stance of its Whig congressmen. All four Whig incumbents retired without seeking renomination, and one of the offending Whig senators was already bound to be purged by the new Democratic legislature elected that year. Hence little could be gained by removing Whigs who already swore fealty to the administration and finality, and Fillmore forbade patronage manipulation simply to advance someone's presidential prospects.

Neither adherence to the Compromise nor control of federal jobs, however, prevented New Jersey's Whigs from suffering the worst defeat in the party's history in the October 1851 legislative elections. As in 1850, those elections revolved around discontent with the Whig stand on state issues like railroads, taxes, and reform, not slavery or the Compromise. In the house, Whigs plummeted from 48 to 25 percent of the seats; in the senate, they dropped from 50 to 35 percent. Ineptitude on state, not national, policy had been responsible, but to aghast Whigs another former bastion now resembled New Hampshire.[107]

Neighboring Pennsylvania, the nation's second largest and politically most important state, in contrast, seemed tailor-made for a patronage offensive that might shift the balance of factional power and force compliance with finality. The identity of whom to punish and whom to reward in Pennsylvania was crystal clear. Incumbent Governor Johnston and his allies, who included most state and federal patronage holders as well as the state's leading Whig papers, opposed adoption of the Compromise in 1850, and after its passage they remained vociferous critics of the fugitive slave law. Johnston's rivals, regular Whigs who idolized Henry Clay or Daniel Webster and Senator James M. Cooper's friends in central Pennsylvania, had supported the Compromise and joined Democrats in Union rallies to praise it. Nonetheless, no state so clearly illustrated the contrasting responses of Webster and Fillmore to anti-Compromise Whigs.

By the beginning of 1851, the Johnston and anti-Johnston Whigs were bitterly split over the question of repealing the state's 1847 antikidnapping statute that forbade the retention of captured fugitives in the state's jails. That question gave a concrete state policy dimension to Fillmore's demand that agitation against the fugitive slave law cease forthwith. Not only did Democrats make repeal of that law their top priority for the 1851 state legislative session; so did Cooper's allies on the grounds that only repeal could quash secessionism in the South. Philadelphia's bipartisan Union meeting of November 1850, which had been organized by Webster's allies Josiah Randall and John Riddle, demanded repeal, and after that meeting Joseph P. Sanderson's Philadelphia *Daily News*, Cooper's major newspaper, ran editorials with headlines like "The Policy of the [Fillmore] Administration Re-endorsed. . . . The Act of 1847 Condemned. Its Repeal Demanded." Johnston, his newspapers, and his lieutenants in federal jobs, in contrast, adamantly opposed repeal on the grounds that it would doom Johnston's reelection, and they openly repudiated Fillmore's formula of finality. Johnston sent special messages to the legislature to rally Whigs against repeal, and he openly denounced Southerners who demanded it for interfering in Pennsylvania's internal affairs.

With Fillmore's blessing, therefore, Webster personally intervened in Pennsylvania to champion the administration's cause (and to build up support for his own nomination). Wangling an invitation to address the legislature in Harrisburg in order to secure Whig support for repeal, he called on it in early April to reassure the South of the state's devotion to the Union by complying fully with the Compromise measures. Undaunted, Johnston immediately followed him to the dais and proclaimed that nothing Pennsylvania did or did not do would threaten the Union, a reply that Webster correctly took as a personal rebuff. When the Democratic majority finally pushed repeal through the legislature over the opposition of all Whigs except Cooper's few allies at the end of the session, Johnston defiantly killed the measure with a pocket veto.[108]

Nor was this the only evidence of Johnston's contempt for the administration. Through Philadelphia Customs Collector William D. Lewis and Morton McMichael, editor of the pro-Johnston, anti-Compromise Philadelphia *North American*, Johnston had allied himself with former Secretary of State Clayton, who had launched the presidential boom for Winfield Scott the previous fall. In 1851 the pro-Johnston press eagerly raised Scott's banner, and from the moment the legislature assembled in Harrisburg, Johnston pressed the Whig caucus formally to nominate Scott. Opposition from Cooper's few legislative allies frustrated Johnston in February, but in March the majority of the inexperienced Whig legislators succumbed to Johnston's whip, to his free whiskey, and to the wheedling of McMichael, who traveled to Harrisburg for the occasion. After a night of revelry and arm twisting at Johnston's quarters, forty of the fifty-four Whig assemblymen and senators signed a card calling for Scott's nomination in 1852. Terrified that this endorsement might be repeated at the June state convention, anti-Johnston Whigs hastily organized a mass pro-Fillmore rally in Philadelphia and circulated the state with calls for nominating Fillmore, not Scott.[109]

At precisely the time that Fillmore dropped the guillotine on Sewardite, anti-Compromise officeholders in New York, in sum, Johnston and his Pennsylvania subalterns had made themselves obvious targets for similar sanctions. Conversely, outside of New York and Massachusetts, no Whig in the North appeared so natural an ally for Fillmore and Webster to succor than James Cooper. To boot, Fillmore had the perfect opportunity to act. From the moment Fillmore assumed the presidency, Cooper and other anti-Johnston Whigs pressed him to sack the entire crew of federal jobholders in Philadelphia, but their chief target had always been Customs Collector Lewis. In late 1850 Cooper's allies had published charges that Lewis had forged most of the letters recommending his appointment and confirmation. The Treasury undertook a closely watched four-month investigation of these accusations, and Cooper, Josiah Randall, Charles Gibbons, and other anti-Johnston Whig regulars clamored for the administration to smite Johnston and build up the pro-Compromise, proadministration wing of the party by replacing Lewis.[110]

Webster itched to launch a pogrom. He knew that Southerners considered Pennsylvania's compliance with the fugitive slave law of crucial importance. He also knew that no northern Whig, with the exception of Seward, was so hated by Southerners as Johnston, who went out of his way to snub southern governors. Pennsylvania was also central to his presidential aspirations. Aside from New England and New York City, Philadelphia housed the only Whigs openly promoting his nomination, and throughout 1851 he repeatedly visited Philadelphia to coordinate their activities. Livid at Johnston's insulting behavior when he visited Harrisburg and convinced that Johnston's defiant antislavery stance must not be tolerated, he urged Fillmore in March to initiate a purge. In April, Webster shifted public printing in Philadelphia from the *North American* to the *Inquirer*, a sheet promoting his candidacy, and to Cooper's *Daily News*. "I have no confidence whatever, in Gov. Johnson [sic], or his professions, & not much in Mr. W. D. Lewis," he bluntly warned Fillmore in May.[111]

Incredibly, however, Fillmore refused to punish Johnston or his cohorts. On April 16, at Fillmore's direct command, Corwin issued a letter to the Philadelphia press dropping all charges of forgery against Lewis as groundless and giving him what amounted to a slap on the wrist. The pro-Johnston press, particularly Johnston's new personal mouthpiece, the Harrisburg *Daily American*, edited by young Edward McPherson, crowed that Lewis' retention demonstrated that Fillmore sided with the governor rather than the malcontents who opposed him.[112]

Johnston's Whig foes found Fillmore's decision as incomprehensible as it was indefensible. In an interview with Fillmore, the hapless Cooper exploded in rage and threatened that he would now support Scott for president, an outburst for which he and his friends quickly apologized. "We could not under any circumstances go over to Genl. Scott and his friend Gov. Johnston without an entire abandonment of principle," declared Randall. But they could and would ground their arms, cease to compete for control of the state organization, and sit out the state election, he warned. How, they bitterly asked, could Fillmore and Corwin muff the best chance they had of gaining sufficient leverage to stop the nomination of Johnston and Scott at the state convention? "It is a striking fact," complained Charles Gibbons, "that while Gov. Johnston is making war upon everybody who sustains the policy of the National Administration, he is able by some power which nobody here understands, to use its patronage in promoting his own schemes."[113]

The historian is equally bewildered. Why did Fillmore repeatedly give the cold shoulder to Cooper, who seemed so natural an ally? Why did he refuse to axe Johnston's allies when he decapitated Sewardites in New York, Michigan, and Wisconsin? Why retain so sleazy and perfidious an operator as Lewis in office? Why not lower the boom on a crowd that so richly deserved it? Absolutely nothing else about Millard Fillmore's entire presidency remains so puzzling or seems so dumbfoundingly stupid as his response to Pennsylvania's Whigs. Was this simply another example of Fillmore's congenital indecisiveness or could there possibly have been method behind his madness?

Answers to such questions can only be inferred. It is tempting to suggest, for example, that Fillmore's response to Pennsylvania proves beyond cavil his disinterest in seeking the presidency again. Unlike Webster, he was not bothered by Johnston's support for Scott, since, like most Washington insiders, he knew that Scott warmly supported the Compromise and consequently did not fear his possible nomination. Scott aside, however, the open opposition of Johnston and his men to the Fugitive Slave Act argued for action. Instead of Fillmore's disinterest in the presidency, therefore, the key to his behavior probably lies in the inherent tension between his twin goals of saving the country and saving the Whig party.

No state posed so stark and agonizing a choice between those goals as did Pennsylvania. Johnston was no moderate, like Washington Hunt or Hamilton Fish or Robert Winthrop or Samuel Vinton. Through his well-publicized clashes with the governors of Maryland, Virginia, and Georgia over Pennsylvania's lax enforcement of fugitive slave laws, he had become anathema to the South. Fillmore had as much reason to defeat his renomination as did Webster, who openly denounced Johnston on his many trips to Philadelphia and urged his friends to vote Democratic should Johnston be the Whig nominee.[114] Simultaneously, however, Johnston and his lieutenants like Lewis and John Ashmead, the U.S. attorney in Philadelphia, seemed indispensable to keep Pennsylvania in Whig hands, and in 1851 no state in the nation seemed more important to the party's future than Pennsylvania. After the losses of Connecticut and Rhode Island in the spring, when Fillmore had no way of anticipating the Whig upset in Wisconsin the following November, only three northern states still had Whig governors—Vermont, New York, and Pennsylvania. Losing Pennsylvania's statehouse would have a profoundly demoralizing effect on Whigs elsewhere, yet everyone knew that retaining it in the face of Pennsylvania's normal Democratic majority required a candidate who might cut into the Democratic vote like the ex-Democrat Johnston. More important, winning required maintaining the coalition between Whigs and Native Americans that had carried Pennsylvania for Johnston and Taylor in 1848.

Solicitude about that tenuous alliance best explains Fillmore's otherwise unfathomable decisions regarding Ashmead, Lewis, and the other federal officials in Philadelphia. U.S. Attorney Ashmead, for example, was a Native American himself, as he repeatedly reminded Fillmore.[115] But Lewis was the linchpin to the alliance between Natives and Whigs. Cooper, Gibbons, Randall, and other regular

Whigs objected to Lewis precisely because he appointed so many Natives and Taylor Democrats as subordinates. In their minds only true blue Whigs deserved federal jobs, and they wanted one of their own ilk to replace him. They were not the only group lusting after Lewis' influential post, however. Lewis won appointment largely through the efforts of former Native American Congressman Lewis C. Levin, who had promised Clayton and McMichael his support for a Taylor Republican party if Lewis got the job. Yet Levin and his henchman, Lewis, were opposed by a rival Native American faction who wanted the collector's job for Peter Sken Smith.[116]

Replacing Lewis, in short, could have been even more divisive than retaining him. If Fillmore gave the job to Smith, he would infuriate Cooper and the regular Whigs as well as Levin's faction of nativists. Appointing a regular rather than Smith might drive both wings of the Native American party to run their own gubernatorial candidate, who would undoubtedly siphon off enough votes to throw the election to the Democrat William Bigler. Far better, it seemed, to keep the support of at least Levin's faction of nativists by retaining Lewis.

The key to keeping the state administration in Whig hands, however, was Johnston himself, not Lewis. That, at least, is what Fillmore and Corwin were told by Whigs whom they trusted—William Reed, the elected district attorney of Philadelphia, and James E. Harvey, an influential newspaperman currently on the staff of McMichael's *North American*. Fillmore's obvious confidence in these two was misplaced, for they fronted for Johnston. The hook they dangled before the president was the argument that only Johnston could possibly get the necessary Democratic and Native votes to carry Pennsylvania for the Whigs. Yet, they warned, this indispensable man would refuse to run unless Lewis was retained, and, if Johnston withdrew, Democrats would rack up huge majorities. To reinforce this threat, Johnston coyly refused to announce his intention to seek renomination until after Corwin issued his letter of April 16.[117]

If the imperative necessity of Johnston's candidacy was the hook dangled by Harvey and Reed, the bait was the promise that if Fillmore eschewed a patronage assault against Johnston's friends, Johnston would make sure that the Whig state convention adopted a pro-Compromise, proadministration platform and refrained from making any presidential nomination. Conversely, any mistake in Washington with regard to patronage would only ensure an endorsement of Scott and deter Johnston from running. Whether out of desperation or gullibility, Fillmore swallowed this baloney, and once he was hooked, Harvey and Reed played the line like championship fishermen. When the directorship of the Philadelphia mint opened up in May and Cooper pleaded for the appointment of a friend, Harvey warned of the implications: "We have a sensitive & nervous candidate & a delicate campaign to manage and therefore it is desirable if possible to avoid new troubles." If Cooper got a single crumb, in short, Johnston would refuse to run. The promise of a proadministration platform was also abandoned in May. The only way to hold the party together, cooed Harvey, was to make no references at all to Fillmore or the Compromise.[118]

Their vow that no presidential endorsement would be made also had to be broken. Here Harvey and Reed brilliantly exploited Webster's strenuous efforts to line up Pennsylvania for his own nomination to play on Fillmore's commitment to Whigs' electoral success and antipathy toward a Union party. Webster and his

Pennsylvania friends were openly pushing for an endorsement from the Whig state convention, they argued, and Johnston would therefore be powerless to stop the delegates from nominating Scott in order to block the nakedly ambitious Webster. Cooper, Gibbons, Randall, and the whole anti-Johnston crew were already vowing to support Bigler rather than Johnston, complained Harvey and Reed, and Webster repeatedly boasted in Philadelphia that Bigler's victory over Johnston would be a triumph for the Union party. Narrow-minded and selfish Websterites, not the heroic Johnston, caused all the party's problems.[119]

Johnston's betrayal of Fillmore climaxed in June at the Lancaster state convention, where Johnston's forces outnumbered Cooper's 92–27. Those delegates who bothered to vote nominated Johnston unanimously on the first ballot. Efforts by Cooper's friends to obtain an outright endorsement of the fugitive slave law's finality were crushed. Instead the platform, most of which dealt with traditional Whig economic themes like the tariff, vaguely asserted that the adjustment measures "shall be faithfully observed and respected" by Pennsylvania's Whigs, a sharp contrast to the Democrats' explicit pledge to "observe and execute" the Fugitive Slave Act. The platform did rehearse the willingness of Pennsylvania's Whigs to carry out all provisions of the Constitution, if not the specific fugitive law that had been passed to do so, but it coupled that pledge with a needlessly belligerent declaration that southern complaints to the contrary were "a libel upon the fair fame of the citizens of the Commonwealth." Expressing "unbounded confidence" in Fillmore's administration because of its fidelity to Whig economic measures in one plank, it urged Scott's nomination for the presidency in another. As if this platform were not sufficient to enrage conservatives, Johnston then broke precedent by coming personally to Lancaster to accept the nomination. Arguing that all existing laws deserved respect and obedience, he pointedly insisted that had he been in Congress in 1850, he would have voted against the Texas boundary and fugitive slave bills and that both required immediate revision.[120]

Johnston's spokesmen, Reed and Harvey, unblushingly blamed the convention's outcome on Cooper's friends, who, they asserted, had forced the nomination of Scott to stop that of Webster and scuttled a plank promising the rendition of fugitive slaves that Johnston had personally written because it did not unwaveringly oppose revision of the Fugitive Slave Act. Conservative Whigs, in contrast, were furious, especially at Johnston's acceptance speech, and none more so than the frustrated Webster. "I am quite prepared to see the defeat of Gov. Johnson [sic], & its necessary consequences upon the fortunes of Genl. Scott," Webster huffed. From that point on, in fact, Cooper and his friends, as well as Webster's Philadelphia lieutenants, announced their intention to support Bigler in order to defeat Johnston and discredit Scott. Once again, where Fillmore sought Whig success, Webster sought revenge.[121]

In several campaign speeches Johnston continued to criticize the Fugitive Slave Act, and Whig papers and local platforms, especially in western Pennsylvania, also stressed the party's antislavery, antisouthern credentials. Nonetheless, Whigs tried to focus the race on economic issues, particularly on the need for tariff revision and on Johnston's success in reducing the state debt. Democrats in rebuttal largely ignored economic matters and stressed the sectional consequences of the campaign. Because of Johnston's open contempt for the fugitive law, they harped, his reelection could precipitate southern secession. The Union's safety, they cried, depended upon Bigler's victory.[122]

Democratic scaremongering benefited enormously from the so-called Christiana Riot in Lancaster County in September during the last weeks of the campaign. Even though blacks perpetrated the murder of a Maryland slaveholder and the wounding of his son, Democrats held Johnston and the Whig party responsible for inciting their violence through the example they set in defying the fugitive law. They further pilloried Johnston, quite unfairly, for failing to pursue the "rioters" vigorously enough, and even the farfetched attempt by U.S. Attorney Ashmead, a Johnston ally, to charge some white bystanders at the affray with treason against the United States failed to blunt that charge. Together with the determination of Cooper's friends and Websterites to defeat Johnston, the riot ensured Bigler's election.[123]

Johnston polled almost 10,000 more votes than he had in 1848, and Whigs actually gained four seats in the assembly and recaptured the state senate. Nonetheless, Bigler defeated Johnston by almost 9,000 ballots. About 1,900 Native Americans abandoned Johnston for a separate nativist candidate, and others, according to the vindictive Peter Sken Smith, voted directly for Bigler. Still, defections to Bigler by Cooper's central Pennsylvania friends and Webster's Philadelphia minions palpably contributed to the defeat. Despite the statewide gain by Whigs, there was a swing of about 1,400 votes against Johnston in Cooper's Schuylkill County, between the two elections, and in Philadelphia City and County Johnston's vote dropped by about 2,200. "We have been defeated by Whig treachery," groused Edward McPherson. "Gibbons of Phila voted an open ticket for Bigler & that whole faction did the same." Other Whigs as well as Democratic friends of Bigler agreed; Webster, Cooper, and their vindictive friends had defeated Johnston. "Governor Johnston has been sacrificed—not destroyed," thundered the Berks County *Intelligencer*, "to gratify the vengeful spirit of a disappointed domestic rival [Cooper]—to remove a supposed obstacle to the ambitious schemes of a Presidential aspirant [Webster]—and to minister to the cupidity of a misguided and mistaken commercial interest [Philadelphia merchants who feared the loss of southern business if Johnston won]."[124]

Other aspects of the election had equally critical implications. In 1850 Pennsylvanians ratified a constitutional amendment requiring popular election of state supreme court judges, and in 1851 both Whigs and Democrats ran full slates of five judges. In selecting their ticket, Democrats rejected the bid of Philadelphia judge William D. Kelley and instead nominated his Irish Catholic colleague on the county bench, James Campbell. Both decisions had profound consequences. The furious Kelley, theretofore a stalwart and immensely popular Democrat, bolted the party and accepted the Whig and Native American nominations for county judge in Philadelphia. By bringing Democrats to the Whig ticket, he helped Whigs retain a 2,600-vote majority in the city and county in 1851 and thereby elect the state senators necessary to give Whigs a majority. Kelley would also go on to win fame as a Whig and even more so as a Republican. Foolishly, Democrats had handed their enemies a most powerful champion in "Pig Iron" Kelley.[125]

Campbell's impact on the race was far more important and problematic, for everyone considered his nomination a blatant payoff to Irish Catholics and a palpable symbol of their growing influence in the Democratic party. Some Whigs attributed the vast bulk of the 18,000-vote increase in the Democratic total be-tween 1848 and 1851 to a surge of immigrant Catholics attracted by Campbell's name on the ticket. But Campbell's nomination also infuriated Protestants and anti-Catholic bigots in Democratic ranks, and for months before the election Dem-ocratic leaders feared that Catholic haters would bolt to the Whigs. Not many did in the gubernatorial election, at least outside Philadelphia, but Campbell was the only Democrat on the state ticket to lose. The refusal of so many Protestant Democrats to support him, in turn, enraged Catholics. ''The Catholicks [sic] of this place are up in arms at the defeat of Judge Campbell and have declared themselves Whigs hereafter,'' warned one frantic Democrat from central Penn-sylvania. By appealing to those resentful Catholics, Harvey promised Fillmore, ''Pennsylvania will be recaptured next fall by 10,000 easily.'' Thus was planted the poisonous seed that would ultimately prove fatal to the Whig party.[126]

For the national administration, therefore, the loss of Pennsylvania had a silver lining. The rancorous Democratic divisions caused by Campbell's nomination and defeat and the prospect of picking up alienated Irishmen raised hopes of salvaging the state in 1852. At the same time, Bigler's victory ensured repeal of the state's antikidnapping law in 1852 and underlined the political futility of continued op-position to the Compromise. Johnston's defeat removed from office a major ob-stacle to Fillmore's goal of reuniting southern and northern Whigs. It also ap-peared to chasten Johnston's supporters. Criticism of the Fugitive Slave Act and of the administration by Whigs lowered to a whisper almost everywhere in the state. The Harrisburg *Daily American* instantly blamed Fillmore as well as Web-ster for the defeat, but it ceased publication within two weeks of Bigler's victory. Lewis and Harvey hastened to ingratiate themselves with Fillmore and other members of the administration in order to avert a postelection purge. Johnston's defeat, along with that of Samuel Vinton in Ohio and of Michigan's Whigs, moreover, temporarily deflated Winfield Scott's presidential balloon. Scott could not get the vote of a single Democrat, Quaker, or Union Whig in Pennsylvania, wrote one of Fillmore's supporters, and even Scott's proponents seemed to agree. Daniel Webster could barely contain his glee. ''As to the 'North American', it is clear that Mr. Clayton & Mr. Harvey are a little in doubt, which way to steer, since the Penna election,'' he chortled.[127]

Webster was the last person to have celebrated Pennsylvania's results. His presidential prospects there were now dead, for his name was mud among the vast majority of Pennsylvania Whigs. Fillmore, Corwin, and Crittenden, but no-tably not Webster, received vows of loyalty from Johnston's friends after the election. Scott supporters pledged allegiance to Fillmore, moreover, precisely be-cause they believed he would not run in 1852. At the same time, the man anti-Johnston Whigs and Native Americans now urged to carry the pro-Compromise, pro-Union banner in 1852 was not Webster. Rather, it was Fillmore himself.

IX

Whatever the reasons, northern Whigs suffered far more heavily at the polls during 1851 than did their southern colleagues. Where southern Whigs captured two-fifths of the House seats contested that year, northern Whigs won only 23 percent. Where southern Whigs gained a governorship from the Democrats in Tennessee and additional United States senators there and in Louisiana and Missouri, northern Whigs prevailed in only two of ten gubernatorial races in 1851, and they lost previously held Senate seats in Massachusetts, Connecticut, Rhode Island, and New Jersey. Altogether the cumulative impact of the 1850 and 1851 elections on the Whig party had been decimating. When the new Thirty-Second Congress opened in December 1851, Democrats outnumbered Whigs by 140 to 88 in the House and 35 to 24 in the Senate.[128] If Free Soilers are added to the total, Whigs held approximately 39 percent of the seats in each chamber. Even worse was the condition of Whigs in the states. At the end of 1851 Whig governors served in only five of the thirty-one states—Vermont, New York, Wisconsin, Florida, and Tennessee—and Whigs had lost New York's most recent statewide race. Similarly, Whigs controlled both houses of the legislature in only four states—Vermont, Kentucky, Tennessee, and Louisiana—whereas Democrats could boast of that honor in fully sixteen states, including the former Whig bastion of New Jersey. Union parties with substantial Democratic minorities controlled legislatures in that party's three strongholds, while in six states power was divided.[129]

Understandably, therefore, many Whigs believed that the party's future as a competitive organization depended upon victory in the 1852 presidential election. At the end of 1851, however, who their candidate might be remained a mystery. Everywhere in the North where anti-Compromise Whigs had openly boomed Winfield Scott—in Michigan, Indiana, Ohio, Pennsylvania, New York, and Maine—they had lost. Those losses did not necessary dim enthusiasm for Scott, as Webster and some Fillmore men mistakenly believed, but they along with other northern results convinced even Scott's supporters that opposition to the Compromise must be jettisoned. In contrast, southern Whigs who heaped praise on Millard Fillmore had usually won, but Fillmore had as yet shown no inclination to run. Nor could southern votes alone ever elect a Whig president. Webster avidly sought the Whig nomination, but he was anathema to most northern Whigs and not considered seriously by Southerners. And Henry Clay, finally, had admitted the realities of age and the near certainty that 1852 would be a Democratic year by refusing to allow his name to be considered.[130]

"Can nothing be done to prevent our going into a hopeless minority?" asked an anxious Pennsylvania Whig after the fall's defeats. The party in Pennsylvania and elsewhere remained angrily divided, he warned. "Should we go into the Presidential contest next Fall, situated as we are at present, we shall be beaten beyond peradventure, no matter who may be our candidate." Scott's friends had been silenced, for he now had no chance for the nomination. The main problem, therefore, was uncertainty among pro-Compromise Whigs as to "the views of the Administration in reference to the Presidency. Who is to be our candidate? Are President Fillmore and Mr. Webster rivals? Without knowing who [sic] to centre on, how can we act effectively?"[131]

Chapter 19

"Scott & Scott Alone Is the Man for the Emergency"

"THE SESSION WILL BE SPENT more in President making than anything," Ohio's freshman Senator Ben Wade wrote home in January 1852. "Soon everything will give way to this one idea." Newspapers also reported "positively no transaction of Congressional business" because of the obsession with "who shall be President in 1853." As in 1840, 1844, and 1848, the gravitational forces of the political universe in 1852 pulled every public event, every policy controversy, and every personality dispute into the orbit of the impending presidential election.[1]

If 1852 inevitably resembled other presidential years, Truman Smith concluded that Whigs confronted "exactly the same situation" as they had in 1848. Once again, Whigs required a military hero to win. "We are a minority party and can not succeed unless we have a candidate who can command more votes than the party can give him," he counseled a North Carolinian on May 1, 1852. "Every consideration which justified us in going for Taylor in /48 requires that we should go for Scott now."[2]

Although a Whig now occupied the White House, Whigs' "situation" *was* strikingly akin to that four years earlier. Once again the convening of a new Congress crystallized the scramble for their nomination. Just as prosperity engendered by wartime financing and grain exports had temporarily neutralized traditional Whig economic appeals in early 1848, so a boom spawned by California gold strikes, surging foreign investment, and frenetic railroad construction appeared to eliminate economic issues in 1852. Just as sectional divisions over possible enactment of the Wilmot Proviso influenced northern and southern Whigs' respective preferences for the nominee and dictated their subsequent Janus-faced campaign in 1848, so poisonous sectional strife over the Compromise threatened to contaminate the 1852 nomination contest and to cripple Whig efforts during the following campaign. And just as defeats in the state and congressional elections of late 1847 combined with loss of the antiwar issue in March 1848 had convinced many Whigs that they needed gunpowder to capture the fortress of Loco Focoism, so northern Whigs' losses in the off-year elections of 1850 and 1851 persuaded many that they needed a famous general to maximize their vote in 1852.

Conditions in 1852, however, formed a mirror image rather than an exact replica of those in 1848. In 1848, Taylor's appeal to the vital Native American vote in Pennsylvania helped him secure nomination and election; in 1852, nativists there and elsewhere vehemently opposed Winfield Scott. In 1848, most southern Whigs zealously sought, and most northern Whigs vigorously opposed, Taylor's nomination; in 1852, northern Whigs led the drive for Scott, whereas almost all Southerners tried to derail him. Suspicious of Taylor's No Party tactics, northern Whigs in 1848 demanded concrete evidence of his fidelity to Whig principles; his southern backers would dispense with pledges, platforms, and even a formal convention nomination. In 1852, in contrast, Southerners insisted upon irrefutable proof from Scott that he deemed the Compromise measures a final settlement of the slavery controversy.

Social, economic, and political developments between 1848 and 1852 produced these reversals. Quarrels over slavery-related issues exacerbated suspicion of individual Whig leaders, eroded intersectional comity within the party, and complicated the task of selecting a presidential nominee behind whom all Whigs would rally. In addition, Whig control of federal patronage had aggravated factional rivalries within state parties and personal animosities among leaders since 1849. Job allocation under Taylor and Fillmore vividly reminded small-fry politicos that it mattered greatly not just whether a Whig, but also which Whig, occupied the White House. Most important, however, were changes Whigs could not control. Sectional, factional, and personal disagreements had wracked the Whig party since its formation, yet the powerful glue of conflict with the Democrats had always contained those divisive forces. Competitive zeal, in turn, had always depended on the clarity of differences with Democrats over specific policy options and general principles of governance. By 1852 the deepening of sectional, factional, and personal divisions among Whigs coincided with a diminution of differences from, and a waning of policy conflict with, the Democrats. By decreasing opportunities to deflect attention to issues that united Whigs against Democrats, these developments focused Whig leaders all the more narrowly on what divided them—sectional quarrels, the identity of the nominee, and calculations about patronage. Simultaneously, the disappearance of party differences made voter apathy as formidable an obstacle as sectional anger to mobilizing voters, thereby increasing the pressure to find a candidate who might rouse enough voters to win. Apathy, moreover, easily shaded over into alienation from the major parties and their leaders precisely because those politicians seemed concerned only with the spoils of office, not with providing alternative solutions to the electorate's grievances and problems. Hence, far more Whigs than in 1848 questioned the value of maintaining allegiance to an organization they now deemed purposeless. For such skeptics, the ability to win the presidency again in 1852 became a crucial test of whether the Whig party could, would, or should survive as a political organization.

I

Together three developments—the 1850–51 defeats of northern Whigs, the corresponding success of southern Whigs who defended the Compromise of 1850, and the emerging power of new Union parties in the Deep South—profoundly influenced the scramble for the Whig presidential nomination in 1852. Each different electoral trend particularly affected the prospects and calculations of one of the three chief contenders for that prize—Fillmore, Webster, and Scott.

Webster fixated on the Union party's apparent rejuvenation. Its Deep South victories combined with palpable northern Whig and Democratic divisions over the Compromise resurrected attempts in the late fall of 1851 to cobble together a national Union party for the presidential election. Anti-Compromise or Sewardite Whigs were so dominant in most northern states, argued Union party proponents like John O. Sargent, editor of the Washington *Republic*, and John P. Kennedy, that the National Whig minority must combine with northern pro-Compromise Democrats and then align with the southern Union parties. "Neither Whig nor Democratic conventions can make a President on old party grounds," Kennedy wrote Winthrop in December. "Nothing can succeed with the people but a strongly compacted conservative party."[3] Prospects for a new party seemed so bright that several of Millard Fillmore's most ardent supporters envisioned Fillmore himself heading the Union ticket. "New organizations are forming in spite of leading minds of the old line," Oran Follett told the president in late November 1851 while arguing that now was the time to build a Union party around Fillmore. "You have only to cut loose from the anti-Compromise Whigs to rally to your support Union men enough to elect you as the honored head of a great Union party," echoed Daniel Lee, a Georgia newspaperman then working for the Patent Office in Washington.[4]

Nonetheless, Fillmore still spurned a new Union party. In sharp contrast, Webster, having orchestrated attempts to launch his presidential bid for a year, eagerly sought to bring it to fruition. Whig divisions and Whig defeats across the North convinced him by November 1851 that "there can be no *entire Whig Ticket* nominated for President & Vice President." He therefore instructed the Boston organizers of a November mass meeting to nominate him that "the *Union* idea should be kept up, & strongly put forth," and he was enormously pleased when its resolutions did so. Simultaneously, Benjamin Balche of Newburyport, Massachusetts, the self-appointed chairman of the imposingly titled but thinly manned National Union Party Organizing Committee, now broadcast Union presidential tickets pairing Webster with Georgia's Howell Cobb.[5]

Webster, the earliest, most avid, and most hopeless aspirant for the Whigs' 1852 nomination, turned to the Union party again in the winter of 1851–52 from a mixture of realism and desperation. The seventy-two-year-old statesman knew 1852 would be his last chance to grasp the maddeningly elusive prize and that his chances for the Whig nomination ranged from unpromising to improbable. He retained enough prestige in Massachusetts and New Hampshire to capture their delegates, but his prospects among Whigs elsewhere in the North seemed remote. He had allies but also many enemies in Rhode Island, Connecticut, and Maine. He might pick up a few delegates in New York City by cooperating with Sewardites against Fillmore men, but he had no strength whatsoever upstate.[6] In Pennsylvania, on which he had lavished so much personal attention during 1851, his name was mud, and even James Cooper's friends, furious at the administration's cold shoulder on patronage, had abandoned him.[7] Across the Midwest most Whigs execrated him. And in the South, Webster knew only too well, Whigs who had not joined the Union party palpably preferred Fillmore to himself.

Capturing an exclusive Whig nomination seemed a very long shot indeed, and given Whig losses in 1851, winning with it seemed doubtful.

In contrast, building a bipartisan Union party offered numerous possibilities. Since the powerful Union parties in Alabama, Georgia, and Mississippi were widely expected to preserve their independence from both major parties, they could form a separate power base from which Webster could rival Fillmore's popularity in the South, especially since the two men's sharply contrasting attitudes toward a Union party were well known. To increase support among southern Union men, Webster promised Alabama's Henry Hilliard a juicy diplomatic post if he would support his nomination, and in the winter of 1851–52 he ostentatiously befriended Mississippi's Henry S. Foote, who had already been elected the Union governor of Mississippi, whom Kennedy considered the perfect running mate for Webster on a Union ticket, and who returned to the Senate for six weeks that winter before his January inauguration.[8]

Not only might the three (four if South Carolina went along) Deep South state Union parties give Webster a beachhead in Dixie, but the apparent trend of events suggested that they could provide the nucleus for a national organization. Once other southern Whigs and pro-Union Democrats understood that Union men from Georgia, Alabama, and Mississippi would boycott the major parties' national conventions, he calculated, they too might defect to a Union party and drag along with them pro-Compromise Northerners from both parties who found fellow party members still too anxious to propitiate antislavery elements. Webster was told in November that Missouri's new Whig Senator Henry Geyer expected the formation of a Union party in that state before the presidential election, and he knew of Kennedy's efforts to organize the party in Maryland. On the eve of the congressional session, moreover, pro-Compromise Democrats from both sections angrily stormed out of the House Democratic caucus when it tabled resolutions committing the party to the Compromise's finality, and in the Senate during December and January, Southern Rights Democrats blocked any action on Foote's finality resolutions. Frustrated and rebuffed, pro-Compromise Democrats, too, might find a Union party alluring. Then, in a widely discussed speech to the House on February 3, Florida's Whig Congressman Edward Carrington Cabell raised the possibility of a massive defection of southern Whigs to the new party. If northern Whigs continued to press for Scott's nomination, warned Cabell, he and other southern Whigs were prepared to abandon the Whig party in order to "act in harmony with the Union Constitutional party." Immensely heartened by all of these omens, Webster in speeches in New York City in late February continued to speak of "the formation of a Union party, of which he would be the head."[9]

By mid-March, however, even Webster admitted that the Union party had again aborted.[10] By then, both pillars supporting his renewed hopes of a Union nomination had crumbled. First, like many others in Washington in the winter of 1851–52, Webster believed that Fillmore would stand aside, publicly announce his refusal to accept a presidential nomination, and thus leave "the coast . . . clear" for Webster to monopolize the pro-Compromise elements in the Whig party and drag them with him into the Union party.[11] But Fillmore, after a period of waffling and mixed signals, had a change of heart. On January 22, 1852, the Washington *Republic*, the administration's organ, denied that Fillmore would withdraw. In the context of Whig politics that winter, not withdrawing was equivalent to tossing

Fillmore's hat into the ring. Webster's friends were furious, and Webster himself was crestfallen, for they all recognized the consequences of Fillmore's decision. As the Washington correspondent of the Philadelphia *Public Ledger* put it, Fillmore and Webster both "run on the same combination and merely weaken each other, while Gen. Scott comes in under a combination entirely different, being thus able to beat up Union Whigs in detail." With Fillmore still a possibility, in short, Webster could never monopolize the backing of pro-Compromise Whigs or line up the crucial support of federal patronage holders, who now would not dare to cross the president in backing delegates to the Whig convention or, more significantly, by following Webster into a Union party that Fillmore disdained. And without solid backing from pro-Compromise Whigs, Webster's chances of persuading Union Democrats to make him the Union presidential candidate plummeted.[12]

At exactly the same time that Fillmore toppled one prop buttressing Webster's Union party strategy, moreover, the other—the belief that the Union parties from Alabama, Georgia, and Mississippi could serve as the nucleus for a broader Union party—was also rapidly collapsing. Like many other people, Webster reckoned between November 1851 and February 1852 that the Whigs and Democrats already in those state Union parties would never return to their old parties. That was indeed the intention of Union men when the new Congress opened in December. Both former Whigs and former Democrats in Georgia's Union delegation, for example, refused to attend the major party caucuses. Contending that "the *mission* of the Constitutional Union party is not fulfilled yet," Alexander Stephens contemptuously dismissed the Whig party as "dead" and condemned the Democratic caucus for embracing former Free Soilers and Southern Rights men. Stephens, indeed, worked with southern Democratic congressmen friendly toward Howell Cobb, Georgia's Union governor, to introduce finality resolutions into the Democratic caucus in order to precipitate a bolt of pro-Compromise Democrats should the caucus defeat them.[13] Simultaneously, Robert Toombs urged southern Whigs to introduce finality resolutions in the Whig caucus, and Toombs fully expected that northern Whigs' refusal to pass them would provoke a bolt by Southerners and "cutt [sic] them all off from their national organization and therefore shut them out of the Whig national convention." Mississippi's Foote returned to the Senate with precisely the same goal in mind—to force a vote on finality that could shift pro-Compromise men away from anti-Compromise colleagues in both old parties. And his successor, Walter Brooke, a one-time Whig elected by the Union majority in the Mississippi legislature, pledged that he would never support "the nominees of the next *Whig Convention*, because I fear the Convention will not be sound on the compromise."[14]

Yet events in Washington and in the three states themselves stymied these plans and undermined the new party movement. In Washington, new congressional recruits for a Union party once again failed to materialize. Southern Whigs, though undeniably suspicious of their northern colleagues and frightened by the possibility of Scott's nomination, refused that winter to abandon their party, a fact made abundantly clear by none other than Florida's Cabell on the opening day of the House session. Foote failed to force a Senate vote on his finality resolutions, and Democrats maintained an uneasy unity. Pro-Compromise Democrats in the House were angry about their caucus' tabling of finality resolutions, but the selection of Linn Boyd, a staunch Compromise man, as speaker appeased most of them. Most important, Democrats deemed it folly to abandon a party on the verge of winning the presidency.[15]

Southern Rights Democrats in Georgia, Alabama, and Mississippi shrewdly seized on this likelihood to shatter the bipartisan Union coalitions in those states. They demanded the immediate reorganization of the Democratic party, and by the time Congress opened, they had already called state conventions to select delegates to the Democratic national convention and invited their former colleagues in Union parties to attend them.[16] Union Democrats found this pressure to return to the Democratic party nearly irresistible, for if they allowed Southern Rights men alone to reclaim the mantle of Democracy and send delegates to the party's national convention, they faced the risk of losing any claim on federal patronage should Democrats win the presidency. Thus, in January, Union Democrats in the Georgia legislature tried to commit the Union party to send its own delegation to the Democratic national convention, while in Alabama and Mississippi more and more Democrats drifted back to the old party.[17]

Democrats bent on redrawing old party lines also brilliantly exploited state legislative sessions that winter to disrupt Union coalitions. In Alabama, Democrats used the legislature's allotment of patronage to drive a wedge between Whigs and Democrats in the Union coalition. By January 1852, when a state convention reorganized the Democratic party, only a dozen of over thirty Union Democratic legislators continued to cooperate with Union Whigs. When Mississippi's legislature convened in January 1852, Democrats repeatedly forced roll calls on old economic questions such as banking, the disposal of state lands, and payment of the long-repudiated Planters' Bank bonds. These votes utterly fragmented the Union coalition and repolarized Whigs and Democrats against each other.[18]

Having previously pledged that they would never return to the Whig organization, Union Whigs in all three states frantically tried to preserve the Union coalition and to stem Democrats' defection.[19] Nonetheless, their inability to retain Democrats in Deep South Union state organizations virtually doomed prospects for a Union party in 1852. Conservative Whigs' disinterest outside those states also helped abort it. Before Congress opened, for example, Samuel Eliot, the ultraconservative Websterite Whig from Boston, scoffed at attempts by John O. Sargent to recruit him. The whole idea of a Union party was ludicrous, he laughed, for by the end of 1851 no one anywhere opposed the Union. "How can a party exist without an opposition?" he pointedly asked Sargent. "And what party is going to stand permanently in opposition to the Constitution?" A Union party "cannot live alone, & it cannot find a vis-a-vis."[20]

Aside from his astute understanding of what was necessary for a political party to exist—namely, conflict with a rival party—Eliot grasped a point of central importance. By the end of 1851, northern Whigs who had railed against the Compromise for eighteen months were ready to foreswear continued attacks in 1852. They signaled that resignation during the organization of the House and during the Senate debates on Foote's resolution, from which they assiduously abstained in order to avoid saying anything whatsoever about slavery or the Compromise. Again, southern Whigs never fully trusted this abjural of antislavery agitation by northern Whigs, but it robbed both them and pro-Compromise northern Whigs of any pretext for bolting the party and encouraged them instead to battle for control of its nominee and platform. With pro-Compromise Whigs and Democrats apparently comfortable in their old parties and the existing Union parties disintegrating with each passing day, hopes for a national Union party in 1852 expired. As Webster's long-time nemesis, Boston Customs Collector Philip Greely, Jr., jeered in reference to Webster's boasts of forming a Union party with himself at its head, "Uncle Dan is a dead man, & upon a dead horse."[21]

II

Southern Whig congressmen did not abandon the Whig party in December 1851 because of the contrast between House Whigs' initial caucus on the morning of Monday, December 1, and its Democratic counterpart the preceding Saturday night. Spurred on by Toombs, southern Whigs planned to introduce finality resolutions at the caucus and to bolt when the northern Whig majority rejected them. Webster knew and approved of this scheme, as did Silver Grays like New York's James Brooks, since they fully expected the breakup to drive pro-Compromise Whigs into the Union party.[22] The surprising result of the Democratic caucus, however, abruptly altered southern Whigs' plans.

To lure Southern Rights and Free Soil Democrats back into the party fold for the presidential campaign, Democrats tabled finality resolutions sought by pro-Compromise men, arguing that the Democratic national convention, not a House caucus, should enunciate party principles. Whatever the excuse, Democrats' action suddenly raised for southern Whigs the irresistible prospect of making the 1852 presidential campaign in Dixie a replay of the 1850 and 1851 congressional races when they donned the pro-Compromise, pro-Union mantle and pilloried Democrats as soreheaded agitators and outright secessionists. To make this case, of course, southern Whigs first required the adoption of their own finality resolution by the Whig caucus, and to the astonishment of politicians in and outside Washington, the Whig caucus passed it on a voice vote with barely a murmur of dissent. Only hours later, both Brooks and Cabell taunted Democrats on the House floor that Whigs, including the majority of *northern* Whigs, now were clearly a safer pro-Compromise party than the Democrats.[23]

Exactly what occurred at the Whig caucus may never be known. Reporters were barred and no attendance was recorded, nor were votes or speeches. The best source, the angry debate on the House floor that same day, is filled with conflicting claims about its size, composition, and significance. Union and Southern Rights Whigs from Georgia and Alabama boycotted the meeting, and only a fraction of the remaining eighty-six Whigs showed up.[24] How big that fraction was and how many Northerners it contained are unclear. The safest conclusion is that the caucus attracted about half of the Whig members, that few Northerners dissented openly on the voice vote, and that those who disliked the finality resolution silently allowed it to pass in order to preserve *Whig* unity for the impending election.[25]

Whatever their satisfaction with the caucus vote, southern Whigs knew that it alone could not undergird another pro-Compromise campaign in 1852. They demanded a presidential candidate openly committed to finality. "We are willing to take a northern man," wrote Tennessee's Whig Governor William B. Campbell, but only one "who is undoubted on the compromise." Throughout 1851, indeed, their newspapers had repeatedly vowed that southern Whigs could support no one for president in 1852 except a forthright Union man who, according to the New Orleans *Bulletin*, "must avow himself boldly and openly, as have FILL-MORE and WEBSTER, the friend and staunch advocate of the compromise as a final settlement of all the questions connected with slavery." "This," echoed the Memphis *Eagle*, "is a *sine qua non* with every man in the South."[26]

By the end of 1851, Fillmore and Webster were virtually the only possibilities considered by most southern Whigs. Unlike 1848, 1844, 1839, or 1836, they lacked a slaveholding favorite son. Taught by Taylor in any event that even a slaveholder could take antisouthern stances, southern Whigs insisted on platform commitments in 1852. They gravitated to Fillmore and Webster because both personified the platform they wanted—an irrefutable commitment to enforcement of the fugitive slave law and to finality. What Southerners meant by finality was quite specific: no renewed efforts to have Congress bar slavery from any territories, prevent the admission of new slave states carved out of them, or change one word of the Fugitive Slave Act, and an insistence that further agitation of the slavery question by anyone, North or South, would not be tolerated. Almost all southern Whigs, moreover, considered Fillmore a far more reliable exemplar of these tenets than Webster.

Southern Whigs admired Webster's role in passing the Compromise in 1850 and in defending it and the Union in speech after speech thereafter. They never doubted his unshakable commitment to retention and enforcement of the Fugitive Slave Act. They cheered his defiance of northern antislavery elements in the party. Nonetheless, southern Whigs never completely trusted Webster. Some recalled his flirtation with Massachusetts' Conscience Whigs in the mid-1840s, when he strongly opposed Texas' annexation and slavery extension. Others remembered his Federalist background and his lifelong devotion to Massachusetts' manufacturing and mercantile interests. Most important, Southerners cited Webster's speech in Buffalo in the summer of 1851, when he was trying to court the Sewardites and Weed men. The territorial provisions of the Compromise together with climate, he assured his Buffalo audience, guaranteed that no additional slave states would *ever* be added to the Union. To southern Whigs this remark rendered Webster not only unelectable but undeserving of election.[27]

Fillmore, in contrast, was regarded as sound. He had committed himself to finality in his annual message of December 1850 and again in December 1851. Ignoring Hamilton Fish's pleas to recommend revision of the Fugitive Slave Act, in that latter message he ringingly reaffirmed his determination to enforce it and castigated its opponents as enemies of the Constitution itself. What a North Carolinian said of Whigs in his state, therefore, applied to the entire South: "all are for Fillmore." During the spring of 1852 Whig state conventions in Maryland, Kentucky, Missouri, Virginia, Tennessee, North Carolina, Florida, and Louisiana endorsed him, as did less official Whig assemblages in the Union states of Georgia, Alabama, and Mississippi. And in March, Henry Clay, now mortally ill, took one final stab at his old rival Webster and urged Whigs to nominate Fillmore in a public letter to a New York newspaper.[28]

If southern Whigs overwhelmingly preferred Fillmore's nomination by the end of 1851, neither then nor later did Fillmore actively seek it. Since entering the presidency in 1850, he had refused even to discuss the 1852 race other than to forbid the allotment of patronage to benefit any aspirant for the party's nomination, a policy Webster found maddeningly restrictive. When the Boston mass meeting nominated Webster in November 1851, Fillmore told Everett he did not care a whit who the Whig candidate was so long as he was devoted to the Union, and Fillmore clearly considered all the most often mentioned possibilities—Webster, Crittenden, and Scott—to be in that category. Thus he concluded that he could bow out. In November and December, Fillmore told both his cabinet and Buffalo editor Thomas Foote that he would publicly announce his withdrawal. Only pleas from Alexander H. H. Stuart that an announcement could hurt Whig chances in Virginia's December gubernatorial election prevented Fillmore from saying so in his annual message. As insiders and reporters correctly stated, he postponed his withdrawal until January.[29]

Meanwhile, pro-Compromise Whigs from both sections pleaded with Fillmore to remain in the race. Consciously or unwittingly, they played on Fillmore's love of the Whig party and his determination to commit it to finality. Only Fillmore could possibly carry Iowa and Indiana for the Whigs, argued correspondents from each. John Ashmead, the U.S. attorney in Philadelphia and a Native American, swore that Fillmore was the only Whig whom that third party would back and thus the only Whig who could win Pennsylvania. "The idea of Genl Scott carrying the state of Pennsylvania is preposterous," declared Ashmead. "He cannot receive one Native American vote."[30]

Putting the Whig party on proper ground, declared his petitioners, necessitated Fillmore's candidacy. If Fillmore withdrew, Alabama's Hilliard warned, the Union party would make a separate nomination that could end any hope of reunifying the party or winning the election. More than that, as Fillmore well knew, independent action by the Union party would keep Whigs from Georgia, Alabama, Mississippi, and possibly other southern states from attending the Whigs' national convention. Without full southern participation, the chances of adopting a pro-Compromise platform were remote.[31]

His closest allies from New York echoed that message. Seward and the other managers of Winfield Scott's candidacy, they charged, wanted to impose an anti-Compromise platform on the party that would drive Southerners from it. According to Fillmore's friends, antislavery Whigs had given up on 1852, but they hoped to blame the defeat on southern Whigs' refusal to support the party's candidate in order to gull angry northern Whigs into joining a new, exclusively northern, antislavery party by 1856, when Seward himself expected to run. The only way to foil this scheme, Fillmore was told, was to get enough pro-Compromise delegates at the convention to adopt the right kind of platform. Yet pro-Compromise Whigs would never battle to control the district conventions that selected delegates if Fillmore withdrew, for his withdrawal would guarantee Scott's nomination and pro-Compromise Whigs' exclusion from federal jobs if he won. Only the promise of patronage down the road from a new Fillmore administration could guarantee the grass-roots effort necessary to succeed. Only a majority of delegates, in sum, could produce the kind of platform Fillmore wanted, and only the hope of making Fillmore the nominee could bring enough right-minded delegates from the North and South to secure it.[32]

These pleas did the job. Convinced, as he later wrote, that his withdrawal "would not only endanger the perpetuity of those measures, which I deemed so essential to the peace and welfare of the country, but would sacrifice many friends who had stood by my Administration," Fillmore had the *Republic* refute the rumors that he intended to withdraw. He would "sacrifice" his own wishes for the "cause" of committing the party to the end of sectional agitation.[33] Yet behind this decision lay a more pragmatic consideration. Fillmore's correspondents flatly and repeatedly told him that Webster by himself could never stop Winfield Scott from winning the nomination. If Scott ran without a pro-Compromise platform, it would forever shatter the Whig party, since Scott, as Fillmore knew, was anathema to southern Whigs.[34]

Many southern Whigs revered Scott's achievements as a soldier. He was, after all, a legitimate hero of two wars, and while his partisan opponents tagged him with the sarcastic sobriquet of "Old Fuss and Feathers," his admirers alternated between "Old Chippewa" in reference to the War of 1812 and "Old Chapultepec" in reference to his capture of Mexico City.[35] It was not Scott himself, but his northern advocates, notorious opponents of the Compromise and the fugitive slave law like Seward, Johnston, and Ben Wade, whom southern Whigs feared and detested. From their point of view, Seward, author of the hateful "higher law" doctrine, had bewitched Zachary Taylor into betraying the South, and Scott, no matter how imposing physically and professionally, would simply be putty in Seward's demonic hands. "Not one Southern state would cast its vote for him," warned the Savannah *Republican.* "The fact that he comes forward under the auspices of Mr. Seward of New York and Gov. Johnston of Pennsylvania . . . is enough to damn him to utter defeat in this section of the Confederacy." As Tennessee's Whig Congressman Christopher H. Williams warned in January, moreover, "If Genl Scott should be the Whig nominee . . . the Whig party as a national party will be forever disbanded." Scott's nomination, in short, might not only ensure Whig defeat, but it would also convert the party into an exclusively northern, antislavery party, exactly what Fillmore and his conservative New York allies had long dreaded. The need to avert that disaster and keep Southerners in the party is what ultimately persuaded Fillmore to "sacrifice" his inclinations for the good of the "cause."[36]

III

If southern Whigs gravitated to Fillmore in order to perpetuate the platform they had ridden to victories in 1850 and 1851, most northern Whigs seized on Winfield Scott to rectify the problems that had caused their own defeats in those years. Even Whigs like Horace Greeley, who considered Scott a pompous fool, had concluded by February 1851 that "we must run Scott for President, and I hate it" because only Scott seemed capable of diverting attention from embarrassments that plagued northern Whigs in 1850 and 1851 and of bypassing still other obstacles that loomed ahead in 1852. Democrats who understood that pro-Scott Whigs wanted "to reduce the [presidential] contest to a personal struggle" between Scott and his Democratic opponent were right. Scott's proponents expected a campaign based on men, not measures, and they were convinced that "Scott & *Scott alone* is the man for the emergency."[37]

Scott had no connection to the quarrels over patronage and the Compromise that produced earlier defeats. In addition, his presumed popularity as a military hero could counteract the defeatism and demoralization that threatened Whig success. Reuniting the party by ignoring previous quarrels, reviving Whig spirits, energizing the rank and file, and mobilizing non-Whigs, especially in the North, were the central concerns of Scott's proponents. Only making a fresh start with a fresh face like Scott seemed to offer an antidote to past ills.

Truman Smith, for example, repeatedly faulted "the utter want of tact & skill displayed by our Whig statesmen when in power" for producing Whig electoral defeats, but he also cited the stigma of corruption tainting Taylor's administration. And to Whigs' horror, even Fillmore's official family became mired in muck when the details of the spurious Gardiner claim and Treasury Secretary Corwin's involvement in securing its payment were exposed in 1851.[38] Given the odium of both previous Whig administrations, Smith and others believed that the party must find a presidential candidate with no official connection to either of them. Hence Smith believed that uniting behind Scott offered Whigs their only chance of victory. Scott had served as interim secretary of war under Fillmore during July and August 1850 when Fillmore could find no civilian to take that post. Unlike Webster and other cabinet members, or Fillmore himself, however, he distributed no jobs and was untarnished by scandal. His reputation rested on his triumphant military career; he was Mr. Clean.

Scott's status as outsider also might heal intraparty quarrels over the Compromise. Just as Whigs in 1848 sought a candidate with no record on the Wilmot Proviso to hold both northern and southern Whigs behind him, Scott's supporters wanted a nominee who had taken no public stance on the Compromise. Yet beyond this negative asset—no record that offended either pro-Compromise or anti-Compromise Whigs—Scott's supporters counted heavily on his personal popularity to mobilize the largest vote possible. When they declared "that the only platform we can fight upon in the North is *Scott*, Scott alone," northern Whigs meant more than a rejection of southern Whigs' demand for an explicit platform commitment to finality, although they indeed meant that too. They recognized that no platform could help Whigs, for old issues seemed obsolete and emerging matters of popular concern too divisive to rouse Whig voters from their defeatism and lethargy. Had Whigs believed that they could mobilize the electorate with an issue-oriented campaign, Scott's nomination would not have seemed so vital. Only the conviction that northern Whigs lacked a decisive edge on *any* issue made Scott's nomination seem indispensable.[39]

Scott's proponents believed that the North held the key to victory in 1852. Certain southern states—Texas, Arkansas, Mississippi, Alabama, and South Carolina—seemed untakable by Whigs, they themselves hailed primarily from free states, and the North had 176 electoral votes to the South's 120. As would happen eight years later, a party could amass an electoral vote majority without a single southern elector, and some of Scott's proponents, like Boston editor William Schouler, spoke in 1851 of electing him exclusively with northern votes so that he "owed nothing to the South." Saner advocates like Smith admitted the need for some southern support. Nonetheless, he believed that Scott, if nominated, could get 133 of the 149 electoral votes necessary to win from Vermont, Massachusetts, Rhode Island, Connecticut, New York, New Jersey, Pennsylvania, Ohio, and Indiana and that he also had a good shot at carrying normally Democratic Maine, Iowa, Wisconsin, and Michigan. In contrast, Smith argued, neither

Fillmore nor Webster, who had been millstones dragging down the northern Whig party in 1850 and 1851, could garner more than seventy-five electoral votes.[40]

Scott's supporters thus pinned their hopes on the region where Whigs had done worst in 1850 and 1851. Since 1848, Taylor's margins of victory in Rhode Island, Connecticut, New York, New Jersey, and Pennsylvania had been wiped out by Whig losses and Democratic gains, and Whigs had fallen even further behind the Democrats in Maine, Ohio, Indiana, Illinois, and Iowa. To sweep most of the North, as Scott's supporters asserted that he and he alone could do, Whigs counted on remobilizing Whig voters who for one reason or another had abstained since 1848 and on adding to them to counteract Democratic gains during that interval.

To do so, most Whigs knew they could not count on the elements that had brought northern successes in 1848. In many states that year, most significantly New York, they had benefited from Free Soil incursions into the Democratic vote. By 1852, however, many of those Democratic bolters had already returned to the party fold, and Democratic leaders were frantically rounding up the remaining strays. Fillmore's friends George Babcock and Thomas Foote, for example, believed that no Whig could carry New York in 1852 because the Barnburners and Hunkers had reunited.[41] In 1848 Native American voters had provided Whigs' edge in Pennsylvania, and while many of Scott's advocates did not yet believe nativists' angry vows never to support him, they knew that openly courting them in 1852, as they had in 1848, would alienate two vital constituencies. One was the regular Whigs who had rallied behind Senator James Cooper, who fumed over the patronage given nativists, and who abstained or defected in 1851 in order to defeat Johnston's reelection bid. The other was the burgeoning immigrant vote, which everyone knew would be a central factor in 1852.

Most important, Whigs realized that their northern victories in 1848 had stemmed from their ability to mobilize Whig voters disenchanted with Taylor's nomination by promising that they would pass and Taylor would sign the Wilmot Proviso and by resurrecting attacks on Democratic economic policies when the economy slumped during the fall of 1848. In 1852, however, neither of those issues was available. Imposition of the Wilmot Proviso on territories seemed a dead letter to all but fanatical antislavery men, and, for reasons to be explained below, most—though hardly all—of Scott's northern backers thought it counterproductive to agitate against the Compromise and the Fugitive Slave Act that year. As New York Governor Washington Hunt, admittedly a moderate but nonetheless a strong proponent of Scott's nomination, put it, "For one I am ready to proclaim that our action as a party has no more to do with Southern *niggers* than it had fifteen years ago."[42] Of greater moment here, with each passing month in 1852, more and more Whigs recognized that they could not use economic issues that year or perhaps ever again.

IV

By 1852, diverse developments had rendered much of the Whigs' traditional economic program obsolete and blurred the distinction between them and Democrats on the few remaining economic questions requiring governmental action. Whigs always contended that economic growth and prosperity demanded the positive governmental intervention that they alone advocated. By their logic, the atomized American economy lacked the concentration of private capital necessary to diversify and expand. Thus government must supply investment capital directly through subsidies to large projects like canal and railroad construction or else facilitate its accumulation in private hands by chartering banks and other corporations, by limiting stockholder liability to increase people's willingness to buy stock, and by encouraging investment in manufacturing and mining with protective tariffs.

To Whigs, banks and tariffs were integrally linked as the keys to prosperity, for the oil that lubricated the engine of economic growth was credit. Individuals' ability to borrow beyond their existing resources and to use those loans to transport products, start businesses, pay workers' weekly wages, buy land to farm, and earn the profits from which to repay loans generated expansion and opened opportunity for upward mobility. Banks and businesses provided the necessary credit, and since the specie resources of the United States were limited, it came primarily in the form of paper bank notes, bills of exchange secured by goods in transit, and promissory notes.

The credibility of those paper devices ultimately depended on assurance that they could, if necessary, be redeemed in specie. Thus the supply of credit and interest rates for it ultimately depended on the nation's specie reserves. That is why Whigs regarded the tariff as so crucial. To them the biggest threat to the nation's specie reserves and thus to the availability of credit was an unfavorable balance of foreign trade. If the value of imports exceeded the value of exports, Whigs believed, specie would be drained abroad, and credit, the economy's lubricant, would dry up. Hence protective tariffs did more than shelter American manufacturers, mine operators, and workers from foreign competition. By limiting imports, they also slowed the exodus of specie and preserved the credit supply that freed men to pursue their economic ambitions beyond the limits of their restricted individual financial capacities.

Most Democrats, of course, had always castigated this program as baneful and unnecessary. They viewed credit from its dark flip side, as debt, as a trap rather than a release. They denounced its public form—bonds—as a burden on taxpayers and its private forms as threats to individual autonomy, as insidious inducements to self-enslavement. They attacked banks and other corporations as privileged monsters that violated the principle of equal rights before the law. They vilified paper money as a cheat and a fraud. They dismissed protective tariffs as pandering to manufacturers, who would inevitably raise prices to unjust and unjustifiable levels if shielded from foreign competition. What is more, they denied that active government intervention into the private economic sector was necessary to achieve growth or enhance the public welfare. "There is, perhaps, no more dangerous heresy taught in our land than that the prosperity of the country is to be created by its legislation," intoned Pennsylvania's Democratic Governor William Bigler in his inaugural message of 1852. "The people should rely on their own individual efforts, rather than the mere measures of government for success."[43]

To Whigs' chagrin, by 1852 Bigler's analysis seemed correct. Since 1849 the economy had been soaring even without Whigs' governmental programs, primarily because of a huge increase in the specie supply fueled by the California gold strikes and by truly unprecedented British investment in the American economy. Thus, while the value of imports continued to exceed that of exports, as Fillmore noted in his December 1851 annual message, the total international flow of funds favored the Americans.[44] Much of the British investment, in turn, went into railroad stocks and bonds, funding a spectacular construction boom that tripled the amount of track in operation from 6,000 to 18,000 miles between 1849 and 1854. Railroad construction itself had important stimulative multiplier effects. It provided markets for and thereby revived the previously prostrate iron and coal industries. It gave jobs to at least some among the swelling tide of European immigrants. It allowed cheaper and faster movement of agricultural goods and thus increased the productive acreage and profits of farmers.

Together these and other developments undercut the rationale for Whigs' program and eliminated many of the specific issues Democrats and Whigs had fought over since 1837. The huge new supplies of specie, for example, ended all talk about the pernicious impact of the Independent Treasury system. Simultaneously, they rendered moot many of the old quarrels over banking and paper bank notes, for now there was ample specie to back notes. As a result, Democrats' traditional aversion to banking and credit softened, a fact evidenced by substantial Democratic support for free banking acts in midwestern legislatures and increased demands from Democrats for the chartering of more banks in states like Pennsylvania. To be sure, many Democratic editors and politicians such as Pennsylvania's Governor Bigler clung to the old Jacksonian faith and continued to denounce banks, paper money, and special privilege. Nonetheless, in state after state, partisan combat over old banking questions waned perceptibly, and even Whigs pooh-poohed the idea of a new national bank.[45]

Similarly, the railroad boom reduced old partisan disputes over the funding of internal improvements. While some of the earlier roads had been built at state expense, almost all railroads since the mid-1840s were private corporations, not public enterprises built with state funds, as canals had been. The necessity of securing charters, rights of way, and other privileges from state legislatures put railroads on the policy agendas of officeholders, but almost everywhere the competition for state favors pitted locality against locality or company against company, not party against party. Similarly, the lack of state funding did not mean that railroads relied entirely on private financing. Public support, however, usually took the form of investment by local rather than state governments, and those local bond issues or bond endorsements usually had bipartisan backing. In Congress, state legislatures, and city councils, Democrats proved just as enthusiastic about railroads as Whigs.

Prosperity also nullified Whig attacks on the low Walker Tariff. The unprecedented supplies of gold destroyed the argument that protection was necessary to secure credit supplies. Railroad construction and other business activity provided ample markets for iron manufacturers and coal miners; indeed, since the American iron industry did not yet have the rolling mill capacity to meet the demand for rails, anyone with a stake in the rapid construction of roads—and such people, ranging from stockholders to potential customers, numbered in the hundreds of thousands—had a stake in keeping the duties on foreign rails low. By the early 1850s, large textile firms also considered high duties unnecessary and counterproductive in that they only encouraged smaller, less efficient competitors to enter the business. All in all, the Whig demand for higher tariffs had also become moot.[46]

In the late 1840s and early 1850s, new state constitutions further eroded partisan conflict over economic questions by restricting state indebtedness and aid to internal improvements, mandating general incorporation acts that ended conflict over special charters, encouraging legislatures to pass free banking acts that had the same effect, and substituting biannual for annual legislative sessions, thereby halving the opportunity for partisan confrontation. As a result, partisan combat over most economic questions in both Congress and state legislatures declined appreciably from the starkly polarized levels of the 1840s. This trend appeared in the Thirty-First Congress and would be even clearer in the Thirty-Second. Some economic questions in certain states, like New York's Nine Million Loan, continued to engender sharp interparty conflict, and the rate at which levels of partisan disagreement sank between 1848 and 1854 varied from state to state. Nonetheless, from Louisiana to Wisconsin, from North Carolina to Connecticut and New Hampshire, party differences on economic policies diminished.[47]

By early 1852 Whigs admitted that prosperity had apparently blunted the need for their programs, thereby spiking a once powerful gun for that year's presidential campaign. Even Whigs' public statements implied surrender. In his December 1851 message, Fillmore again alluded—briefly and perfunctorily—to the need for tariff revision and to the constitutionality of federal internal improvements. But he conceded that people had been blinded to the need for these policies by the plenitude of gold pouring out of California. Kentucky's Whig state platform in February, written by Henry Clay's old friend Leslie Combs, chorused Whigs' traditional refrain about protecting American labor but entirely omitted the words "tariff" and "duties." Virginia's state Whig platform in April flatly opposed protective tariffs and condemned lavish federal internal improvements. And in June, Whigs' national platform said absolutely nothing about banking and currency, defended the constitutionality but made no case for the urgency of congressional aid to rivers and harbors improvements, and adopted a milk-and-water tariff plank that Democrats accurately hooted was now identical to their own. Absent from it was any reference to the special needs of northern manufacturers, the threat of foreign pauper labor, the desirability of specific rather than *ad valorem* duties, or the need to reduce imports to protect credit.[48]

In November 1851, Wisconsin's Nathaniel P. Tallmadge privately outlined the obviation of Whigs' economic issues with stunning acuity. Pointing, as Fillmore would, to the huge excess of imports over exports as a reason why a protective tariff would at some point again be necessary to fend off "disastrous results," he admitted, "The famine in Ireland by reason of the demand for our breadstuffs, mitigated the evils of the tariff of 1846, and when that ceased the evil day was put off by the discovery of California gold. This, with our Government stocks, state stocks, railroad stock etc. etc. etc. which are sent abroad, may put it off still farther." The United States had to have a much higher tariff, echoed Ohio's Ben Wade to his wife. "But this will never be done until a fatal breakdown brings men to their senses. And this would have happened long ago, except for the enormous quantities of gold from California." Whigs and Democrats now stood so close together on the issues of tariffs and internal improvements, a New Orleans Whig told Fillmore in February 1852, that in the approaching campaign "many of the issues that have heretofore been made will scarcely be mooted at all."[49]

Other Whigs believed that prosperity permanently rendered Whigs' whole approach to governance obsolete and wiped out forever disputes that had justified the Whig and Democratic parties' existence. "The real grounds of difference upon important political questions no longer correspond with party lines," the young Cincinnati Whig Rutherford B. Hayes wrote in his diary in September 1852. "Politics is no longer *the topic* of this country. . . . Government no longer has its ancient importance. . . . The people's progress, progress of every sort, no longer depends on government." Daniel Barringer's brother, a resident of Baltimore, sounded the same note in early 1853. Bankers who were investing in railroads, he reported, "say that never before has the world been so largely and regularly supplied with gold." Therefore, "the great dividing lines between the two old parties are fast melting away" and "issues formerly momentous are now of comparatively trifling importance."[50]

Democrats also noted "the rapid approximation of Whig doctrines" to their own on economic questions. "There is now nothing but the *name* left to distinguish Democrats from Whigs," New York Barnburner Jabez Hammond informed Seward in November 1851. John Van Buren, the former president's son, also predicted that the impending presidential campaign would be issueless, a "dreary waste of petty plans, personal schemes, and small dodges," not "great questions" on which rival "parties took sides," as in earlier elections.[51]

Soaring prosperity thus spiked the heaviest artillery of northern Whigs, who felt enormous pressure to bring their voters back to the polls and to mobilize new recruits to offset Democratic gains since 1848. To many, therefore, only a presidential candidate who could arouse voters on his own, without an economic platform, seemed to offer hope. New Jersey's Whigs, for example, wanted a candidate who diverted voters' attention from their bumbling inability to handle emerging state issues dealing with economic reform in 1850 and 1851. They therefore sent a solid Scott delegation to the Whigs' national convention.[52]

Indiana also illustrates the desperation that turned northern Whigs to Scott. In October 1852 (the date of state elections had been changed from August by the new state constitution) Indiana's Whigs had to run against popular incumbent Democratic Governor Joe Wright. Without any issues to ride, Whigs considered Wright invincible, and thus their first choice for gubernatorial candidate, Henry S. Lane, flatly spurned pleas from the state convention and the Whig legislative caucus that he run. Without issues, he repeated, the race was hopeless. Similarly, the party's preferred candidate for the state supreme court refused on the grounds that it would be "ruinous" even to enter a state ticket against a Wright-led Democratic slate. "Think of the excitement that will exist next Oct.," he complained. "The Presidential election approaching—every bog-trolling Irishman in the land voting—the Whigs in the minority by more than 10,000. The Democrats straining every nerve to carry the State elections in order to come, like so many victorious troops, to the battle for President. . . . What can any Whig hope under the circumstances?" Unsurprisingly, therefore, Indiana's Whig state convention in February 1852 chose national convention delegates and a slate of presidential electors pledged to Scott, even though almost all delegates to that convention were pro-Compromise and wanted "to quiet agitation" by "saying nothing about slavery" in their state platform.[53]

V

If proponents of Scott's nomination hoped to substitute his personal popularity for now defunct economic issues, they also sought to divert attention from troubling new social issues percolating into the public arena in the early 1850s. By far the most important was the escalating crusade against liquor. For decades temperance associations had sought to reduce the consumption of alcoholic beverages, but they had relied primarily on moral suasion to convince tipplers to renounce strong drink. When they resorted to state authority, it usually took the form of local option licensing laws to regulate the number of taverns, inns, and "groceries" that sold liquor by the drink. By taxing those who sold booze, they sought to reduce consumption by raising its cost. The passage of the famous Maine Law in 1851, however, drastically ratcheted up the use of state police power, for that statute mandated a statewide ban on the manufacture, sale, and consumption of alcoholic beverages. Maine's example inspired temperance forces elsewhere to seek similar legislation.

Agitation for state-imposed prohibition laws swept across the North by the end of 1851 and appeared in some slave states as well. Reformers flooded legislatures with demands to emulate Maine's model, interrogated candidates from all parties as to how they stood on the issue, and, ominously, vowed to vote for no one, regardless of party affiliation, who opposed passage of the law. Boasting that a petition signed by 130,000 people was forcing Indiana's legislature to consider a Maine Law, one Whig declared, "Why, many of us no more think of voting for any man, unless he be right on this question, than we would vote for a free negro." Prohibition "bids fair to eradicate for a time all party lines," echoed a frantic Whig from Geneva, New York, in March 1852. "The Temperance question is far more important to the people of this State than any other that agitates the public mind," chorused another New York Whig in August. Whigs and Democrats alike would vote "for temperance men only," regardless of "the consequences" to "the two political parties."[54]

Temperance had, in fact, never been a strictly partisan issue. Both Whig and Democratic parties encompassed its proponents and opponents, and votes concerning strong drink in state legislatures prior to the 1850s were usually nonpartisan.[55] Party leaders usually avoided official party stances on the divisive liquor question, and the fissures in Maine's Democratic party over that state's liquor law amply confirmed the wisdom of this hands-off posture. By 1851, however, zealous prohibitionists would no longer tolerate neutrality; they demanded open commitments from the parties and threatened to run their own independent candidates if they did not get them. Northern Whigs proved especially vulnerable to such pressure because their core electorate, the self-defined "respectable" middle classes who prided themselves on their sobriety, their female-centered home life, and their regular attendance at Protestant churches, enthusiastically took up the cry for prohibition.

The Whig constituency, however, included a number of groups who opposed prohibition—merchants, innkeepers, and liquor dealers; farmers who sold products to breweries and distilleries or simply converted apple crops into hard cider; men from all socioeconomic classes who enjoyed a drink; and independent thinkers who believed state governments had no business telling people what they could and could not consume. If prohibition became an issue in the 1852 elections, as seemed likely at the start of the year, and if Whigs endorsed it in platforms or established a partisan record on it with their votes in legislatures, they could alienate crucial supporters from the party.[56]

Connecticut's spring election dramatically illustrated prohibition's perils for Whigs. Sobered by the Democratic success in blaming Whigs for enforcing unpopular local license laws in 1850, Whigs, like Democrats, tried to duck prohibition in 1851 by ignoring calls from temperance organizations to take an official stance on the liquor question. Silence did not avert another Whig defeat that year, and in 1852 Whigs decided to reverse course again. By then, Connecticut's Whigs had renounced any thought of running against the Compromise, and state economic issues were quiescent. At the close of the 1851 legislative session, however, Democratic Governor Thomas Seymour pocket-vetoed a measure to call a referendum on prohibition. With Seymour heading the Democratic ticket again in 1852 and Democrats still refusing to answer inquiries from Maine law proponents, Whigs decided openly to court dries.[57]

Although the Whigs' platform said nothing about the Maine Law, their gubernatorial candidate, Green Kendrick, was an ardent prohibitionist, and Whig legislators had strongly supported the referendum bill in 1851. When Whig legislative candidates in 1852 pledged to support the Maine Law, therefore, temperance groups publicly endorsed them; in response, the Democratic press came out vigorously against state-imposed prohibition. Former Senator Roger Sherman Baldwin, among other Whigs, questioned the wisdom of their party's new tack. While the influence of the new issue "baffles calculations on both sides," he warned, "past experience has generally shown that the Whigs are the greatest losers when any new issue of this sort is brought into the election."[58]

April's election results further convinced Baldwin that "the Maine law issue operated as such collateral issues generally do, very much against the Whigs." For the first time since 1843, Democrats won the governorship with an absolute majority of the vote. Seymour's total increased by 1,600 votes (5.3 percent) between 1851 and 1852, while the Whig total dropped by 515. These shifts widened the margin Democrats had already gained over Whigs from 1,300 to 3,400 in a state Taylor had carried. Statistical analysis suggests that almost one-sixth of the 1851 Whig voters either defected to the Democrats or refused to vote when the party embraced prohibitionism. Whigs partially compensated for these losses because they outrecruited Democrats among previous nonvoters by a four-to-one margin. Nonetheless, the losses were substantial, and according to Baldwin they came not in cities, where he expected them, but from farmers who sold hard cider. That fact was reflected in the legislative races, where Democrats captured the senate and widened their house majority from four to twenty-eight seats. Whatever the sources of the shifting voters, Whigs knew that prohibitionism had been political poison. "We have been defeated" more thoroughly than "for many years," moaned the Hartford *Courant*, because of "the introduction into the canvass of a *side issue*—of a question that was merely moral in its bearing."[59]

In early 1852, few people expected prohibition to be directly at stake in the impending presidential campaign. Regulating alcoholic consumption fell squarely within the jurisdiction of state and local governments, not national authorities. Nonetheless, voters wishing to reward or punish parties for their stands on it at the state level could influence the presidential turnout in November. Whigs' experience in Connecticut (and in New Hampshire, where Whigs also suffered losses that spring after embracing prohibition) signaled that courting dries had significant costs and that they needed a presidential candidate who could reawaken the enthusiasm of Whig voters alienated by that tactic. To many Connecticut Whigs, Scott appeared to be that man.[60]

Rewinning the allegiance of Whig wets offended by a pro-Maine Law stance, however, constituted far less than half of the problem posed by prohibitionism. The much graver danger, as most Whigs knew, was the political awakening of Irish and German immigrants. They might troop to the polls in unprecedented numbers in 1852 and vote Democratic in order to punish Whigs for what they regarded as intolerant and unconscionable attacks on cherished mores, as bigoted infringements on the individual liberties they had fled the Old World to secure.[61]

An anticipated surge in the immigrant vote loomed over all political calculations in 1852. Since 1846 almost half a million Europeans a year had entered the United States. Most were Irish or German, most were Catholic, and almost all settled in the North and border states. By 1852, those who had arrived in 1846 and 1847 could meet the five-year requirement for naturalization, and in any event, Whigs believed with some foundation, Democrats had long employed fraudulent naturalization to inflate their vote. In addition, several midwestern states like Indiana, Iowa, and Wisconsin allowed unnaturalized aliens to vote. For decades, most immigrants, except for British and Scots-Irish Protestants, traditionally voted Democratic when they bothered to vote at all. Despite Whig complaints during the 1840s, however, the majority of recent immigrants, whether from disinterest or ineligibility, had not participated in American elections. They were a sleeping giant waiting to be aroused.[62]

As astute Whigs realized, anger at holier-than-thou do-gooders trying to cut off immigrants' supplies of whisky and beer might be the prod that did so. In that event, as the results in New Hampshire and Connecticut indicated, Whigs would be the losers. Whereas opponents of prohibition abandoned the Whigs when they embraced it, dries among Democrats had shown little inclination to defect to the Whigs. That was why Baldwin warned that Whigs were always "the greatest losers" when such issues emerged. In sum, Whigs could never hope to mobilize a unified force of Maine Law advocates to counteract a surge of new immigrant voters toward the Democrats if prohibition remained an issue by the fall campaign. Far better, it seemed, to drop that hot potato and rely on their candidate's popularity.

Even if Whigs managed to shun the prohibitionist cause, however, they correctly expected an outpouring of new immigrant voters in 1852, and they knew that unless they cut into that vote, they were goners. In December 1851, indeed, something other than prohibition also aroused immigrants' political zeal, an event that momentarily overshadowed the impending presidential campaign, only to be quickly sucked into its vortex. It altered the calculations of every Whig and Democratic presidential aspirant, illustrated the difficulty of formulating a programmatic appeal to potential new foreign-born voters without also alienating members of one's own party, aggravated sectional and factional divisions among Whigs, and ultimately forced them to seek different ways to woo newly politicized immigrants. The explosion that set off these shock waves was detonated on Saturday, December 6, when the Hungarian exile Louis (Lajos) Kossuth arrived in New York City.

VI

Kossuth had led an attempt to win Hungarian independence from the Hapsburg Empire in Austria. When Russian troops intervened to help the Austrians crush the rebellion, Kossuth ignominiously fled to Turkey, leaving thousands of his followers to be mowed down by Austrian firing squads. In Turkey the sultan placed Kossuth's entourage under house arrest until they were "rescued" by an American naval vessel sent by order of Congress and carried to the United States. Despite Kossuth's unseemly abandonment of his troops, Americans considered him a hero, a freedom fighter, a Magyar George Washington.

Dapper and dashing, a splendid orator who dazzled crowds with his fluent English, the diminutive Kossuth ignited almost unprecedented excitement and adulation from celebrity-worshipping Americans. A Kossuth mania swept the East Coast even before he landed. Hundreds of thousands of people turned out to gawk at him in New York and other cities he visited, and they roared enthusiasm at his every word. Yet Americans expected that the grateful Kossuth, after accepting the applause of admiring crowds, would simply settle somewhere in the United States and enjoy the benefits of American liberty, as had so many other refugees from the revolutions of 1848. Kossuth instead turned out to be the most disruptive and politically embarrassing foreigner to set foot on American shores since Citizen Genet.[63]

Kossuth announced in his very first speeches in New York that he wanted Americans to contribute funds to reenergize the failed Hungarian revolt. More important, he demanded that the United States government recognize Hungarian independence; that it officially warn Russia not to intervene on the side of Austria when the fighting renewed or face American military intervention on the side of the Hungarians if it did; and that it send an American fleet to the eastern Mediterranean to give teeth to that ultimatum. As he had in England on the way to the United States, furthermore, Kossuth also suggested the formation of an Anglo-American alliance to help Hungary against Austria and Russia. In sum, Kossuth insisted that Americans renounce the traditions of neutrality and nonintervention in European affairs that had been the cornerstones of American foreign policy since Washington's administration, a policy that Fillmore and Webster had enforced so vigorously. What is more, by the hundreds of thousands, adoring crowds screamed their approval of everything he said.[64]

Even before Kossuth's arrival, Webster and other Whigs expected that Democrats would use him to revive their jingoistic program of spread-eagle expansionism and to expose Whigs' supposed "timidity" in enforcing neutrality laws against filibusterers. In particular, they feared that Democrats' cries for intervention to help Europeans struggling for liberty against autocratic regimes would galvanize support from Irish and German immigrants. To counteract this potential Democratic appeal, Webster ordered his friends to have copies of his Hülsemann letter and a dinner speech he had given in Buffalo printed in German and distributed in the South and West. "They would suit the foreign population, I think, better than anything else," he hoped. Yet even the bombastic Hülsemann letter paled next to the calls for direct intervention in Europe that Democratic presidential aspirants like Senators Lewis Cass and Stephen A. Douglas immediately raised after Kossuth spoke in New York. Thus the wildly enthusiastic reception Kossuth received seemed to give Democrats yet another advantage. As the pessimistic Winthrop put it, Kossuth's "advent" would "conspire with other circumstances in giving the Democracy an easy return to power."[65]

Almost overnight, Kossuth threatened to inject a foreign policy question—intervention or nonintervention—into the center of the impending presidential race. According to Tennessee Whig Congressman William Cullom, a rare Southerner who advocated Scott's nomination, "This Compromise question will be a secondary element in the presidential canvass. . . . Other new and more immediate issues will enter the canvass such as intervention." Kossuth seemed so popular, indeed, that Whigs could neither ignore him nor allow Democrats alone to side with him. As the Philadelphia *Public Ledger* put it, "Each party, each clique of each party, would appropriate the great Magyar as an electioneering machine for the next Presidency." Kossuth, in short, did not displace the anticipated issues of the impending presidential campaign. He provided an issue; he filled a vacuum.[66]

Various contenders for the Whigs' nomination scrambled to align themselves with Kossuth so that Democrats alone did not bask in his reflected glory. Fillmore's supporters urged him to invite Kossuth to the White House even before the Hungarian landed in New York, and he later reluctantly did so. Webster's friends, too, wanted him to "take a strong hold of this Kossuth movement," and Webster arranged for Foote to introduce a Senate resolution on December 7 that officially welcomed Kossuth to the United States and invited him to visit Washington.[67]

Webster quickly learned that Kossuth must be handled as gingerly as nitroglycerin. As secretary of state, Webster dared not endorse Kossuth's demands that Americans abandon neutrality and nonintervention. Equally important, the Senate debate provoked by Foote's resolution of welcome and roll-call votes on inviting Kossuth to address Congress starkly exposed Southerners' nearly unanimous hostility to the Magyar and his cause. Rhetorical endorsement of rebellions for liberty frightened Southerners, who worried about setting a precedent for government intervention on behalf of abolition or slave rebellion in the South. When Congress eventually arranged a public dinner for Kossuth, therefore, Southerners, led by Georgia's Stephens, engineered a counter dinner to reaffirm their commitment to Washington's doctrine of nonintervention in European affairs. Consequently, as soon as Southerners protested Foote's original motion, Webster, fearful of further alienating Southerners, had Foote withdraw it.[68]

Webster's temporary retreat allowed Scott's managers to cash in on the Kossuth mania. As the army's highest-ranking officer, Scott himself dared not make any public pronouncements about American foreign policy, especially since his commander-in-chief adamantly clung to neutrality and nonintervention. Indeed, Scott's supporters wanted him to make no public statements whatsoever. His propensity for malapropisms such as "fire in my rear" and "a hasty plate of soup" was notorious. Scott's managers rather than Scott himself, in sum, had to make the case for Scott's nomination. Of these, none was so important as Seward, with whom Scott was inextricably identified.[69]

Seward seized Kossuth's cause with gusto. His lieutenants in New York City, Henry J. Raymond and Simeon Draper, immediately took Kossuth under their wing when he arrived there, and other followers urged him to exploit Kossuth's popularity. Always a fervent champion of human freedom who had long sought to lure immigrants to the Whig column, Seward introduced his own joint resolution welcoming Kossuth to the United States. This quickly passed both houses of Congress before Kossuth aired his demands for a change in American foreign policy, but knowledge of Kossuth's agenda failed to deter Seward. Southerners might scream and Silver Grays like James Brooks might denounce Kossuth on the House floor, but Seward saw political points to be won, both for himself in the long run and for Scott in the near term.[70] To embarrass conservative intra-party rivals, moreover, in December 1851 and again in January 1852, Seward delivered powerful speeches denouncing Russia's suppression of Hungarian independence as a blow to human freedom, but he carefully refrained from threatening that the United States would use force to stop such intervention in the future. Seward's friends were delighted by these orations, and Seward immediately arranged with New York printers to publish a million copies of them for distribution in the North and West, where immigrants were concentrated.[71]

By the time Kossuth reached Washington in late December after another tumultuous reception in Philadelphia, Whig leaders were divided over him, and everyone recognized the implications for the impending presidential campaign. Seeing a chance to win votes in the North, especially among immigrants, northern Scott men lavishly praised Kossuth's attempt to win political freedom. Fillmore, in contrast, was incensed that Kossuth publicly challenged his administration's foreign policy, acutely solicitous about not offending Austrian or Russian ministers any further, and embarrassed that he had invited Kossuth to the White House. When Webster finally brought Kossuth to meet him on the afternoon of December 31, therefore, Fillmore bluntly declared that the United States would never abandon neutrality and nonintervention so long as he was president. Angered by this rebuff, which Fillmore made sure the press printed, Kossuth addressed the House of Representatives a week later, urging it to ignore the president and to adopt the agenda he had set forth in New York. Southerners and Silver Grays had failed to stop the invitation to Kossuth to speak on January 7 and a congressional dinner in his honor that evening. But their warnings had effect. Kossuth's speech evoked only stony silence; any prospect that Congress would recognize Hungary, threaten Russia, or officially condemn Russia's actions in 1849 was dead.[72]

Webster, still hoping to benefit from Kossuth's popularity, sought a position between Seward's warm embrace and Fillmore's cold shoulder. Aware that he could not renounce nonintervention but also that the pro-Hungarian speeches of Seward and of Democrats had eclipsed his earlier Hülsemann letter, Webster sought to refurbish his reputation as a champion of republican liberty. Telling Fillmore that he must attend the congressional dinner for Kossuth to defuse Democratic charges about the administration's insulting response to the Magyar, he joined Seward and Democrats like Cass and Douglas at the gathering and toasted the prospect of Hungarian independence without committing the United States to do anything that helped achieve it. Both Whig and Democratic politicos, sneered Baltimore's indignant Kennedy after the dinner, were engaged "in a ludicrous and disgusting competition for whatever amount of popularity they may be able to get out of the great Hungarian Pretender," who refused to accept the refusal of Congress and the president to change America's foreign policy.[73]

Kossuth, indeed, would not take no for an answer. If the country's political leaders rejected his demands, he would go over their heads to the people. Five days after the congressional dinner, Kossuth left Washington to make a speaking tour of the West, where he hoped not only to raise money but also to arouse so much enthusiasm for intervention that the government would be forced to change course. Such a speaking tour could benefit only Democrats politically. Conservative and southern Whigs so heartily approved of Fillmore's rebuff to Kossuth that wooing foreign voters by praising him, as even Seward and Webster now recognized, would only further divide the party for the presidential campaign. Without official responsibility for foreign policy, Democrats, in contrast, could court foreign votes by promising to change it if they won the White House.[74]

VII

One response to Kossuth, however, offered Whigs a different way to seek immigrant voters. Kossuth aroused immigrants even more than native-born Americans, but he also divided foreigners against each other. Recently arrived Germans saw in Kossuth a kindred spirit, but many Irishmen were infuriated by his proposed Anglo-American alliance. More important, before Kossuth left New York City for Washington but after Seward's speech praising him, Archbishop John Hughes, the nation's leading Roman Catholic prelate, denounced him. Seward's friends at first dismissed this criticism, but they soon realized that Kossuth outraged other Catholic clergymen as well as lay Catholics. As a Maryland Whig informed Fillmore, Kossuth's "appeal is to the Protestantism of the country to interfere by arms, if necessary, for the religious as well as the civil liberty of Hungary, against the Pope and the Jesuits." Catholics, in short, viewed Kossuth's proposed war against the Hapsburg Empire as a war against their church.[75]

For every German who cheered Kossuth, therefore, a Catholic Irishman booed him. "Kossuth is taking the *people* by storm, and no mistake," wrote one Philadelphia Democrat. "Our German people are crazy, and Bishop Hughes' *denunciation of him* is widening the break between the Irish & Germans." From St. Louis to Chicago, Cincinnati, Cleveland, Pittsburgh, Philadelphia, New York City, Brooklyn, and Boston, the refrain was the same. Germans loved Kossuth, but "the Catholics here are *Anti-Kossuth*, to a man."[76]

A personal friend of Hughes who had long championed Catholics' rights, Seward was embarrassed by Hughes' condemnation of Kossuth. Seward therefore immediately sought to right himself with those whom a Brooklyn ally called "the bigoted Catholics, who did not approve of your advocacy of the noble and generous Magyar" by broadening his appeal to all immigrants. He supported resolutions of sympathy for Irish exiles who had been the target of British persecution and introduced a Senate bill to force merchant ship owners to improve the sanitary conditions of immigrant passengers.[77]

Other Whigs, however, decided that the best tack was to forget the Germans, whom Kossuth was turning against the Whigs by denouncing Fillmore's nonintervention policy, and to concentrate on the Irish, who hated Kossuth. Lew Campbell, a Whig congressman from Dayton, Ohio, and a major player in the Scott organization, for example, chided Boston editor Schouler for his overenthusiastic praise of Kossuth. Schouler must keep his eye on the ball, Campbell warned. Their top priority was to elect Scott. To win Ohio's Catholics for Scott, Campbell announced proudly, he had voted against the House resolution welcoming Kossuth, and that vote "shall *tell* in the fight for Old Lundy's Lane."[78]

More than Irish Catholics' anger at Kossuth made Whigs believe their votes were takable in 1852. In Massachusetts, Boston's large Irish community, a mainstay of the Democratic coalition, chafed against Democrats' alliance with Free Soilers from western Massachusetts, who were notoriously anti-Irish, strongly pushed enactment of a Maine Law, and wanted to reduce Boston's representation in the legislature. Schouler, the target of Campbell's rebuke, relished the prospect of converting them to Whiggery in order to break up the Coalition. By backing a bill in the legislature to give alien immigrants equal rights with citizens to own real estate, Whigs "are fast becoming the Liberal party," Schouler boasted to Seward. "The Irish in & about Boston all swear by me, and I like them."[79]

Prohibition was the key issue to Boston's Irish, however. In 1851, Free Soil legislative candidates had campaigned for a Maine Law, and in the 1852 legislative session they, along with most Whigs and those Democrats who sought to preserve the Coalition, passed one, to the fury of the Irish, who now seemed even more likely to defect from the Democratic column. In hopes of holding both dries and the Irish in the subsequent gubernatorial campaign, Democrats nominated a Maine Law proponent for governor and a wet for lieutenant governor. In response, Whigs ran an opponent of the Maine law for governor and a temperance man for lieutenant governor. And if that did not suffice to bring Irish into the Whig column, Boston's Whigs circulated a separate ticket devoted to repeal of the recently passed Maine Law featuring the Whigs' gubernatorial candidate and the Democrats' nominee for lieutenant governor. Proponents of the new Maine Law countered with a separate prohibition ticket headed by Horace Mann, Free Soilers' gubernatorial candidate and an ardent prohibitionist, and the Whigs' candidate for lieutenant governor.[80]

The relevance of this tangled maneuvering over prohibition to the presidential campaign was that Schouler and other Massachusetts proponents of Scott's nomination believed that Scott could attract the alienated Irish without taking a stand one way or the other on liquor. Scott, after all, had commanded American troops in a war against England, Irishmen's archenemy. More important, Scott was believed to have particular appeal to Catholics.

Scott's supporters among Pennsylvania Whigs certainly counted on that appeal. Catholics among Pennsylvania's Democrats were furious with their traditional party because James Campbell, the Irish Catholic from Philadelphia, was the only Democrat on the statewide ticket who lost in 1851. Even before the Kossuth mania further outraged Catholics, in short, Pennsylvania's Irish Catholic votes appeared to be up for grabs, and as a Webster supporter from Philadelphia wrote in March, "The Scott men here count on the Roman Catholic vote." Precisely the vows of Pennsylvania's Irish Catholics that "they will never vote the Democratic party again," indeed, made Scott's Pennsylvania supporters so heedless of Native Americans' threats never to support Scott, for Catholic voters far outnumbered Native Americans.[81]

Irish Catholics' anger at the Democratic party in Massachusetts, Pennsylvania, and other states like Illinois, of course, did not ensure that they would vote Whig in 1852.[82] That is why most northern Whigs considered the nomination of "Scott & *Scott alone*" absolutely critical. An Episcopalian himself, Scott educated his two daughters in convents, and one converted to the Catholic faith and joined a nunnery. Scott also took particular care during his march across Mexico to prevent his troops from desecrating Catholic churches. To be sure, this record offended anti-Catholic bigots among Whigs, one of whom fulminated against "our *military, sapheaded, Roman Catholic Scott,*" who had "compelled the American Armies to prostrate themselves in the mud whenever a *crucifix*, or an idolatrous *Doll Baby* passed along," and who would therefore "get every roman catholic vote in the United States." Yet this presumed appeal to Catholics is precisely why his advocates wanted him nominated. Aware in the winter and spring of 1852 that the immigrant vote was bound to be larger in crucial northern states, fearful that Kossuth was arousing Germans against the Whigs in every city he visited, and certain that Whigs would be crushed if all immigrants went Democratic, they saw Scott's supposed popularity among Catholic immigrants as yet another reason why he offered Whigs their only hope.[83]

VIII

Convinced that with Scott "we can be successful" and that "without him we *will be* defeated," and dismissing Fillmore and Webster as "dead dogs" who had dragged northern Whigs down to defeat in 1850 and 1851 and would do so again in 1852 unless displaced, Scott's supporters arrived in Washington in December 1851 supremely confident that he would win the nomination. They quickly organized a Scott club under the day-to-day management of Assistant Postmaster General Fitz Henry Warren and James Pike, the Maine newspaperman once again reporting for the New York *Tribune*. They began to proselytize among Whig congressmen. And they had Pike prepare a campaign biography. They of course knew of southern Whigs' antipathy toward Scott, but for a variety of reasons they tended to discount it—at least initially.[84]

For one thing, in December and January they believed that, if necessary, they could bulldoze Scott's nomination through over southern opposition. Like others, they did not expect any delegates from South Carolina, Georgia, Alabama, and Mississippi at the Whig convention. Their absence would reduce the vote against Scott and, more important, the number of votes Scott needed for a majority. In addition, while Sewardites from New York never believed that Fillmore would not run, other Scott supporters accepted the accuracy of the rumors about his intentions. Fillmore's withdrawal would leave the South without its preferred candidate and reduce the race for northern delegates to Scott and Webster, and as they counted noses among Whig congressmen, they concluded that *"no body"* favored Webster. If Fillmore threw in the towel, in short, Scott would win in a walk.[85]

Most Scott men, however, wanted Southerners to support, or at least acquiesce in, Scott's nomination. Even after they learned that Fillmore was not withdrawing, they evinced confidence that they could get that backing by arguing that only Scott could win enough electoral votes, especially in the North, to bring victory. As Philip Greely of Boston put it in March, "I trust that our Southern friends will soon begin to see 'that success is worth more than pride.' We *can* succeed if they will come in cordially to support the only man who can be nominated." Even Webster feared that southern Whigs would succumb to the argument of Scott's *"availability,"* and in December and January, Seward and others cheered that "the South breaks."[86]

Southern Whigs insisted on more than a case of electability. They demanded that the nominee explicitly pledge himself to the Compromise's finality, and as the year opened, Scott had not done so. Seward initially hoped that Southerners would support Scott "without his giving a disclaimer that would ruin him in N.Y. & Pennsylvania." Yet even the few southern Whigs who favored Scott, like Tennessee Senator James Jones, who angled for the vice presidential nomination on a Scott ticket, his Tennessee lieutenant Congressman William Cullom, and North Carolina's Edward Stanly insisted that Scott could never be run in the South without declaring that not a single word of the Compromise measures should be altered. Other Southerners like Humphrey Marshall of Kentucky, Florida's Cabell, John Moore of Louisiana, and Tennessee's Christopher Williams and Meredith Gentry insisted even more adamantly that Scott must make a pledge before he could be considered. Scott's northern supporters found this demand both puzzling and annoying. They knew, and they knew that southern Whig congressmen admitted, that Scott was pro-Compromise, that while serving as interim secretary of war in 1850, Scott had done everything he could to persuade congressmen to pass the Compromise measures. "Genl. Scott is as open for the Compromise as any man in Tennessee," Cullom wrote his governor in January, and later Willie P. Mangum and Stanly publicly asserted the same to justify their support. Leading southern Whigs' personal knowledge of Scott's fidelity to the Compromise, Scott's northern managers believed, should suffice. "There must be no pledges, no resolutions, no compromise issue," and they hoped that "the South will come to that ground."[87]

But Southerners in and outside the Scott camp would not relent. Lew Campbell attributed their obstinacy to their sense of honor. Southerners, he explained, felt bound by the vows they had made when they foolishly signed the Round Robin the previous winter never to support anyone for office who was not explicitly pledged to finality. Pike came nearer the mark when he stressed that southern Whigs wanted to preserve the pro-Compromise platform on which they had won in 1850 and 1851. Ultimately, he believed, they would back Scott even without a pledge.[88]

Pike may have gauged pro-Scott Southerners like Jones and Mangum, who also had vice presidential ambitions, but he fundamentally misread Gentry, Cabell, and others who hoped for a Fillmore candidacy. Rather than "let byegones be byegones," as Pike predicted, such men were determined to compel a surrender from northern Whigs, and they threatened on the House floor to bolt the party if Scott were nominated without a finality pledge. Northern Scott men opposed a pledge, Gentry railed, because, just as in 1848, they wanted to foment "the prejudices of the North against the South." They intended to run Scott "upon such ground that hostility to the fugitive slave law and the compromise generally, with strong denunciations of the same, and furious appeals to the prejudices against Slavery and the Slave States, can be indulged in by his Northern supporters." Scott's northern managers, he carped, whored after "that Abolition element at the North" that "has hung like a millstone about the necks of those in the South who have for years struggled for the ascendancy of the Whig party." Tennessee Governor William B. Campbell, the recipient of Gentry's warnings, concurred that Scott was "out of the question" because of his "equivocal position on the compromise & the warm support of such men as Seward & Greeley." For years southern Whigs had been "growing weaker, in consequence alone of our affiliation with such men as Seward"; it was "now good time to cut loose from them."[89]

However understandable their suspicions, Southerners like Gentry and Campbell misread Scott's managers' intentions, and their accusations have misled subsequent historians. In 1852 most of Scott's northern backers had no intention of continuing to agitate against slavery or the Fugitive Slave Act in order to appeal to Free Soilers and abolitionists. Southern Whigs, not Scott's northern supporters, wanted to keep the Compromise issue alive.[90]

Scott's strategists, in contrast, hoped to attract antislavery voters simply by avoiding a pro-Compromise pledge from Scott and a pro-Compromise platform. Much as Democrats benefited from silence on the prohibition issue when Whigs embraced it, Whigs, who correctly believed that Democrats would adopt a pro-Compromise platform, expected to pick up anti-Compromise voters by taking no position at all. They did not want to seek their vote openly by running against the Fugitive Slave Act or the Slave Power. The risks of an antislavery campaign aimed at wooing Free Soilers far exceeded its benefits. Reassuring conservative National Whigs, who had produced northern Whig losses in 1850 and 1851 by bolting or abstaining, was the central task.[91]

Ample evidence indicates that most of Scott's supporters had renounced all thought of campaigning against slavery, the South, or the Compromise in 1852. First, northern Whigs allowed a finality resolution to pass at the poorly attended House caucus on December 1, and during the vote for speaker of the House, when Whigs scattered their votes among twelve different men, the only clear anti-Compromise Whig in contention, Thaddeus Stevens, drew a grand total of sixteen votes.[92] Second, not all of those who wanted Scott's nomination were anti-Compromise Whigs, at least not by the beginning of 1852. Delaware's John M. Clayton had initiated the Scott boom, more out of anger at his treatment by Fillmore's administration than resentment of the Compromise, and the legislative caucus of Delaware Whigs that endorsed Scott's nomination hardly wanted to denounce the Fugitive Slave Act. Rather, they believed that with Scott "we have the cards in our hands to win the game, and if we play them right Delaware will be redeemed." The majority of the Indiana Whig state convention that sent a solid delegation of Scott delegates to the national convention were pro-Compromise, and Indiana Whig leaders like John D. Defrees and Schuyler Colfax were anxious to appease southern Whigs as well as National Whigs in the North. Convinced that Scott was staunchly pro-Compromise, Illinois' Whigs also picked a Scott delegation. Connecticut and New Hampshire Whigs abjured antislavery agitation, as had New Jersey's by 1850.[93]

Individual northern Whigs tried to reassure Southerners and northern National Whigs of this fact. Explaining to William Schouler, the anti-Compromise and pro-Scott editor, why he had given a conciliatory speech in the Senate, Massachusetts' John Davis argued, "We need as a party some common & satisfactory ground to rally upon." Therefore congressional Whigs should "rock the subject to sleep without giving or exacting pledges." "There is not an agitator in the whole Whig party here, at the moment," echoed Robert Winthrop from Boston, "nor one who cares to disturb anything that has been done." Connecticut's Truman Smith repeatedly wrote Southerners that he did not want to overturn Fillmore's pro-Compromise position; he favored Scott because only Scott could win. "The North have acquiesced & will acquiesce in these measures," he assured Southerners. Northern and southern Whigs differed on only one thing: "we of the North wish to let the whole subject drop and to sink quietly & forever into oblivion whereas some of our Southern friends (mistakenly I think) wish us to be all the while affirming & affirming that the thing is dead & shall never be revived."[94]

Needlessly alienating Silver Grays or abandoning the Whig party for a new antislavery coalition with Free Soilers is precisely what Seward and other Scott managers did not want to do in 1852. To them, fabricating antislavery bona fides for Scott in order to appease fanatics seemed suicidal. The beauty of Scott was precisely that his views were unknown, that he could be all things to all people, that he had publicly said nothing that would antagonize either pro-Compromise or anti-Compromise men. And it was exactly on this point—the determination to keep Scott from publicizing his views in order to reunite Whigs *in the North*—that Scott's managers ran afoul of southern Whigs' demand for a written commitment to finality.

By publicizing his enthusiasm for the Compromise or vowing to oppose changes in the fugitive slave law, as Southerners demanded, Scott would mimic the detested Fillmore and Webster and thereby lose his chief appeal to the vast majority of northern Whigs—namely, that he was *not* Fillmore or Webster. The goal of Seward and other Scott men was to hold pro- and anti-Compromise Whigs together *without* siding with either bloc. That is why they insisted that "Scott, & Scott alone" was "the only platform we can fight upon in the North."

To help ensure a platform-free campaign, Seward and other Scott managers purposely smothered all talk of slavery and the Compromise. They accepted the Whig caucus' action on December 1 and abstained from the Senate's debates on Foote's finality resolution because they believed that "silence is our true policy." Although Seward made countless Senate speeches in 1852—on Kossuth and Russian aggression, on British persecution of Irish exiles, on the unsanitary conditions for immigrants on ships, on rivers and harbors improvements, on disputes over Canadian fisheries—he said nothing whatsoever about slavery or the Compromise. By June, Free Soilers like Joshua Giddings, supposedly the targeted recruits of Scott's managers, were denouncing Seward for betraying his antislavery principles to propitiate Southerners. Similarly, for the first time in years, Sewardites in the New York legislature introduced no inflammatory antisouthern resolutions, and Fillmore's secretary, Robert Campbell, happily announced that Woollies and Silver Grays could therefore unite for the impending campaign.[95]

The wisdom of Sewardites' refusal to attack the Compromise or slavery in 1852 became clear during New York's spring contests to select district delegates to the Whig national convention. From Rochester, customs collector and Fillmore ally James R. Thompson complained that he could not mobilize rank-and-file Silver Grays against Scott's forces, who had muted the issue that might arouse them. "We want some issue of Compromise & antiCompromise. We cant [sic] attach Sewardism to Scott & the odds is greatly against us here." He then added what the consequences of Scott's nomination and election would be: "a Seward triumph that grinds us to powder." Thompson palpably referred to the *patronage*, not the *policy*, consequences of Scott's victory, a consideration that motivated many in the Scott camp. Indiana's Schuyler Colfax, for example, told Seward that he supported Scott because Scott was pro-Compromise, an utter necessity in Indiana, and because Scott, unlike Fillmore and Webster, would not proscribe from office Whigs who had formerly opposed the Compromise.[96]

Northern Whigs, in sum, supported Scott's nomination and opposed that of Fillmore or Webster because they hungered after victory and its spoils, not because they wanted to renew assaults on slavery, the Compromise, or the South. Free Soilers scented their retreat toward expediency even in the fall of 1851. "The Whig party is hopelessly given over to Slavery," groused Vermont's Edward A. Stansbury. "It will, more and more, grapple the Slave Power to itself, and slough off all but the despots and the partizans [sic] of despotism."[97]

IX

Most Scott men wanted no party statement whatsoever about slavery or the Compromise in 1852, but a few recommended acceding to southern Whigs' demand that Scott issue a pledge to support finality. This split largely reflected the prospect of winning back Free Soil Whigs and the degree to which quarrels over the Compromise had divided state Whig parties. The stronger National Whigs were in a state party, and the more adamantly they had insisted earlier on explicit acceptance of finality, the more implacably anti-Compromise Whigs in those states opposed any statement by Scott. Thus Sewardites from New York, Webster's enemies like Greely and Schouler in Massachusetts, Israel Washburn of Maine, and the Ohioans Wade and Lew Campbell pleaded, exhorted, and demanded that Scott say nothing. They did count on blocking a separate Free Soil nomination so that antislavery men would have no alternative to the Whigs once Democrats endorsed finality. Everywhere their message was the same. Scott "should write no letters"; "keep pens away from him," make "no pledges," and the result would be certain Whig success.[98] On the other side and much to Seward's dismay, both John Defrees and Schuyler Colfax of Indiana prepared letters for Scott to issue; Truman Smith favored some kind of new Allison Letter from Scott; and Clayton, working through James E. Harvey, the Washington correspondent for the Philadelphia *North American*, pressed for one in order to win southern support for Scott's nomination, as did other Southerners in Scott's camp.[99]

During the first four months of 1852, therefore, two tests of will took place in Washington over Scott's issuing a letter: between northern and southern Whigs and between members of the Scott camp itself. On February 8, Ben Wade boasted to his wife that at that evening's meeting of the Scott club he had browbeaten potential appeasers into "a final & irrevocable decision" that Scott must say nothing. Within a week, however, Harvey assured Clayton that northern and southern Whigs were about to agree on a letter Scott could issue. On February 26, Cullom promised that a letter from Scott was imminent; eight days later, Lew Campbell asserted that Scott "remains *firm*" and that his northern supporters remained adamant that no statement be issued. Almost weekly, rumors floated that a letter from Scott was in press, and that possibility repeatedly forced Seward and other hard-liners to scramble to stop it. Those like Colfax, who were not privy to the arguments in Washington, argued that an ambiguous letter could forestall a platform commitment, which would be far more harmful to northern Whigs. Some Southerners, however, played a deeper game.[100]

Tennessee's breathtakingly ambitious James Jones, who was serving his first months in national office, whom several northern Whig newspapers mentioned as Scott's running mate, and who wangled a vice presidential endorsement from the same Tennessee Whig state convention that demanded Fillmore's presidential nomination, spotted an opportunity to leapfrog to the head of the political pecking order. As the naive Cullom wrote various Whigs in Tennessee, if Jones could entice a finality pledge from Scott, it would ruin Scott among anti-Fillmore Whigs in the North. They would then turn in gratitude to Jones, who had braved other southern Whigs' anger to support Scott, as the best man to keep Fillmore and Webster from gaining the nomination. Lean Jimmy Jones, of all people, might head the Whig ticket! Jones' game, however, was too clever by half. Once others learned of his scheming, his unpopularity among most Tennessee Whigs, and his rashness when he finally spoke in the Senate, Scott's northern managers dropped him from their list of possible running mates.[101]

Throughout January, February, and March the tug of war over a letter continued. Hard-liners in Scott's camp like Lew Campbell frequently voiced the hope that "the pressure of our Southern Whig friends is abating somewhat" and that "they will *cave* if we but hold out," but the pressure from Southerners, especially men like Gentry, Williams, and Cabell, proved relentless.[102] Tension escalated when Whigs from outside Washington pressed for a congressional Whig caucus to issue the call for the national convention. Its meeting had been delayed for months because Southerners refused to attend unless Scott first committed himself. Attendance at a caucus that called a national convention, just like attendance at the convention itself, was, by long tradition, equated with a commitment to back whomever the convention nominated, and in March, Scott still seemed the front-runner. If a caucus were called, therefore, southern Whigs might introduce a finality resolution that could provoke an explosion. Unlike the poorly attended House caucus on December 1, by the spring so much publicity had been given to Southerners' demand for a pledge from Scott that his managers believed passage of another finality resolution would doom his chances. At the same time, by

March, Southerners, who still feared they could not stop Scott at a national convention because Alabama, Georgia, Mississippi, and South Carolina would send no delegates desperately sought a pro-Compromise commitment from Scott's northern supporters if they could not get it from Scott himself.[103]

Fully aware of the risk, congressional Whigs finally agreed to caucus on April 9, and Scott's camp exerted every effort to avoid an embarrassing confrontation. On April 6, North Carolina's Edward Stanly sent a public letter to the Washington *Republic* admitting that most southern Whigs favored Fillmore but also blasting Gentry, Williams, Cabell, and others for vowing never to support Scott unless he publicly pledged himself. Stanly knew that Scott "was as earnest, ardent, and zealous a friend of the Compromise measures as there was in the United States." North Carolina, Stanly averred, wanted a man like Scott whose patriotism was clear, not "a man who writes letters and makes pledges just before an election." Democrats intent on mischief, however, neutralized whatever soothing impact Stanly's letter had, for on the very day it appeared in the *Republic*, two Georgia Democrats forced the House to vote on a formal finality resolution. This roll call starkly revealed how deceptive the outcome of the two caucuses at the start of the session had been. Now two-thirds of the northern Democrats supported and 70 percent of the northern Whigs opposed the resolution.[104]

That vote confirmed southern Whigs' worst fears. An angry Virginian immediately informed Webster that southern and northern Whigs must split and make separate nominations. "That vote left to me, and to other Whigs from the slaveholding states," Kentucky's Humphrey Marshall later protested to the House, "no evidence whatever that a faithful adherence to the compromise" or a determination to "proclaim" it "as a final settlement . . . would henceforth be considered as part 'of the Whig creed.' "[105]

The likelihood of a rupture was so obvious when the caucus was gaveled to order by North Carolina's Mangum on the evening of Friday, April 9, that his Senate colleague George Badger immediately pressed for adjournment. Truman Smith, in response, insisted that the gathering proceed with its purported agenda: naming the site and date of the national convention. Kentucky's Marshall then tried to force a vote on the same finality resolution the Whig caucus had passed on December 1, and Gentry, David Outlaw of North Carolina, and Thomas Walsh of Maryland vowed that southern Whigs could never cooperate with Northerners who refused to swear to the permanence of the Fugitive Slave Act. Thaddeus Stevens, Truman Smith, Lew Campbell, and Samuel Parker of Indiana angrily opposed the motion. To avert further strife, a motion to adjourn and reconvene on Tuesday, April 20, was adopted. Before the attendees departed, Mangum, who automatically chaired joint caucuses because of his seniority as the Whig with the longest continuing congressional service, announced that next time he would rule Marshall's divisive motion out of order since the caucus should only call a national convention, not write the party's platform.[106]

Tension between northern and southern Whigs soared during the eleven-day interval. On Saturday, April 10, the New York *Tribune* printed a blistering report from James Pike that accused southern Whigs and Fillmore's administration of breaking the unstated but vital agreement between northern and southern Whigs to disagree on matters involving slavery, "upon which, in the very nature of things, they could in fact do no otherwise than differ." "It is in a word," he steamed, "a very plain attempt to make Northern Whigs take Southern ground on the subject of Slavery. It is an attempt to destroy the old divisions, by making one side surrender to the other." Northern Whigs, vowed Pike, would never capitulate to the extortion of "Mr. 'KIT' WILLIAMS, and Mr. HUMPHREY MARSHALL, and Mr. E. CARRINGTON CABELL, *et id genus omnes*."[107]

On Wednesday, April 14, the Democratic Washington *Union* ran an editorial on Pike's letter entitled "The Ultimatum of the Northern Whigs" that attempted to incite southern Whigs to open revolt. Pike's main point, insisted the *Union*, was that there "never can be any agreement or community of opinion between Whigs of the North and Whigs of the South in relation to sectional questions." Pike, the paper gibed, had let the cat out of the bag. Northern Whigs regarded the passage of the Compromise as an "odious" betrayal and would never submit to its finality. They intended to run Scott without any pledges in order to woo "the antislavery elements of their own section," and even if Scott now released a letter, Pike had made it clear that it could not be trusted.[108]

Southern threats and Pike's reckless report further divided the Scott forces. Fulminating that a few southern "ultraists" were trying to extort "humiliating concessions" from Northerners, Henry J. Raymond's *New York Times* assured Southerners of northern Whigs' "acquiescence" in the "existing laws" and of their "aversion to any further agitation of Slavery and the incidental issues to which it has given rise." On April 16, Mangum came out openly in the Senate for Scott on the grounds that he was perfectly safe on the Compromise, as had William Ward, a Kentucky Whig, earlier in the House.[109] Complaining that the party was being "buffeted about by extreme men" in both sections, Truman Smith warned that unless Southerners were reconciled to Scott's candidacy, Whigs faced "overwhelming defeat" in the fall. Meanwhile the intransigent Philip Greely urged Seward from Boston not to yield an inch at the next caucus and to let Cabell, Marshall, and other southern soreheads walk out if they wished.[110]

The Whig caucus on April 20 thus met in an atmosphere of extraordinary tension. With Mangum publicly in Scott's camp and prepared to disallow a finality resolution, several Southerners refused to attend: Dawson and Berrien of Georgia, as well, of course, as Toombs and Stephens; John Bell of Tennessee; North Carolina's Badger; all the Maryland Whigs from the House and Senate; Alabama's two Union Whigs; and all but one Missouri Whig. Some Northerners, too, absented themselves, and Seward, the lightning rod for Southerners, remained conspicuously outside the meeting, although he was close by in an anteroom to lend direction to Scott's forces. Altogether, only 70 to 75 of the 116 congressional Whigs were present.[111]

When Humphrey Marshall again pressed his finality resolution at the start of the meeting, Mangum ruled it out of order. Marshall demanded a vote on the chair's ruling, and when it was upheld 46–21, Marshall angrily stalked out. Gentry then tried to amend the motion to call the national convention with a proviso that no Whigs who participated in the call would be bound to support its nominee unless the convention adopted a finality platform. When this amendment, after an angry debate, was also defeated, Gentry and Christopher Williams of Tennessee, North Carolina's Outlaw and Clingman, Florida's Cabell and Senator Jackson Morton, John Strother of Virginia, Louisiana's two Whig congressman, and Senator Walter Brooke, the Unionist from Mississippi, also departed. When the smoke cleared, only Stanly, Alfred Dockery, James Morehead, and Mangum of North Carolina, Cullom and Jones of Tennessee, a few Kentuckians, and the lone Missouri representative remained from the slave states.

Crowing that the caucus marked "the entire disorganization of the Whig party, as a national party," the Washington *Union* quoted extensively from the testy debate. The moderate Outlaw announced that to carry any slave state Southerners must have an explicit, public pledge from Scott himself, rather than private assurances from his surrogates, that "*each and all*" of the compromise measures was "a final adjustment of the slavery question," a warning echoed by even the North Carolinians who remained in the caucus. To this tocsin Maine's Israel Washburn defiantly retorted that northern Scott men would "never consent that the finality of the compromise measures shall be made a part of the Whig creed; and any candidate, whether he be General Scott or any other man, who insists upon that, or who is nominated by a convention which affirms or requires it, cannot . . . obtain the vote of a single northern State—not one." This blast, asserted the *Union*, showed that Southerners could never again trust the Whig party and that Democrats alone adhered to the Compromise.[112]

As if to ratify the *Union*'s analysis, the southern bolters published a manifesto refusing to cooperate with the Whig party unless it formally embraced finality, and numerous southern Whig papers insisted that the national convention, scheduled for Baltimore on June 16, must adopt a pro-Compromise platform or Southerners would abandon its nominee. These actions panicked some of Fillmore's northern supporters. Since they were competing with Sewardites to elect delegates and could afford nothing that offended rank-and-file northern Whigs, they bitterly complained that Southerners' attempt to dictate a platform in caucus, when only the national convention could frame it, would drive infuriated Northerners toward Scott. If Southerners boycotted the convention, as the bolters threatened, moreover, they would deprive Silver Grays of necessary southern allies and thereby ensure that Seward, Johnston, and other northern Scott men wrote the platform. Fillmore himself, in contrast, viewed the bolt as a wake-up call to spur southern Whigs to attend the convention in order to obtain an appropriate platform, and he hoped "almost against hope, that in some way or other its action may be made to harmonize and give satisfaction both to the North and the South." Aware that Scott's New York supporters were driven primarily by animosity toward him, he offered once again to withdraw his name from consideration immediately to produce a harmonious convention.[113]

The southern bolt also further divided Scott's backers. All along, those recommending a conciliatory letter from Scott had argued that a pro-Compromise platform, especially one adopted at the South's insistence, would do far greater harm in the North than any personal statement from Scott, for a platform would implicate as accessories northern Whig convention delegates. Simultaneously, pro-Scott southern Whigs like Stanly, who had defied their section's clear sentiment, became all the more importunate in demanding a statement from Scott that justified their action. Pressure thus increased to get Scott to say something in advance of the convention to forestall a platform. Former hard-liners like Massachusetts' Charles Hudson and Philip Greely, Jr., aware that their state's pro-Webster delegates would support a finality platform, now prepared letters that Scott could issue. So did Horace Greeley, although he and others hoped to delay publication until after the convention so that Scott would not be seen as appeasing Southerners in order to win the nomination. Schouler and Truman Smith meanwhile escalated their private attempts to assure Southerners that Scott was a sound pro-Compromise man in order to blunt the demand for a pro-Compromise platform.[114]

These efforts had only minimal results. In what Greeley considered a "first-rate" public letter, Virginia's John Minor Botts asserted that he had talked to Scott and found him perfectly sound on the Compromise. Only the impropriety of appearing to seek the nomination, cooed Botts, prevented Scott from making that commitment public. Botts also promised Schouler privately that he would fight any attempt by Southerners at the national convention to force a finality platform on the party. Yet even Botts, like Stanly, expressed annoyance that the pro-Scott northern press refused to print publicly what northern Scott men freely admitted privately—that Scott was ardently pro-Compromise and wanted no change in the Fugitive Slave Act. Without a public pledge, warned Stanly, southern convention delegates would demand a pro-Compromise platform, and if Northerners refused to give them one, they would bolt the convention and the Whig party would be destroyed.[115]

Intransigents among Scott's supporters, in contrast, insisted that allowing Scott to make a pledge after Southerners had bolted would constitute craven capitulation to southern intimidation and ruin all chances of holding northern antislavery voters. "If we yield to the South we are gone irrevocably!" cried one. Even having Scott issue a letter after the convention, in lieu of a platform, struck Seward and some of his New York allies as humiliating. " 'Finality' must be avoided by hook or crook," insisted one Sewardite. "The fate of the party now & for years depends upon avoiding that obnoxious issue." As an alternative way to avert a pro-Compromise platform and still mollify Southerners, some suggested saving Southerners' face at the convention by having Scott delegates scatter their votes for a few ballots rather than ramming through his nomination immediately. Implacable Israel Washburn was far more realistic when he admitted that nothing could now stop a platform fight. "The battle is to be lost or won at Baltimore on the question of the finality resolutions." If all northern delegates "will only stand like a rock there will be no trouble." By late April, however, even Scott's most sanguine supporters knew that the real question now was whether the Scott forces would have enough rock-like delegates, not just to defeat a pro-Compromise platform but to win the nomination itself.[116]

X

Despite their bravado at the beginning of the congressional session, Scott's backers knew by spring that they faced a dogfight for control of the national convention. "The greatest danger is that the South in convention will to a man go for Fillmore and that he will get scattering votes North enough to nominate," an alarmed Lew Campbell warned in March. "We must be particular about that. We must not lose a single delegate where we can help it." The delegate selection process had in fact been proceeding for months before the Whig caucus called a national convention, and, despite the few pro-Scott Southerners, Fillmore seemed assured of virtually unanimous support from the southern delegates who attended except those from Delaware. To make certain that there was no wavering from Fillmore, moreover, Virginia, Kentucky, and Louisiana sent two or more delegates to represent each congressional district and insisted that those delegates, or a majority of them, concur before the district cast its vote.[117]

By April, when Southerners bolted the Whig caucus, the question was not whether southern delegates at Baltimore would back Fillmore. It was whether all slave states would be represented. By then the four states with Union parties—Alabama, Georgia, Mississippi, and South Carolina—still had made no arrangements to pick delegates, and Whigs affiliated with those Union parties, like William C. Dawson of Georgia and Arthur F. Hopkins of Alabama, had told Fillmore that they had no intention of doing so.[118] In addition, by April, North Carolina's Whigs, who faced a crucial gubernatorial election in August, still had held no state convention that could choose its delegates. They had not dared to call one because of continued antipathy toward the central clique and virulent regional disagreement over committing the state party to the legislature's reapportionment on the white basis as a response to incumbent Democratic Governor David Reid's anticipated use of the "free suffrage" issue.[119]

Alerted by April's two fractious caucuses, Fillmore and Southerners in his cabinet—Crittenden, Stuart, Charles Conrad, and William A. Graham—pressed for a full southern attendance. Even Webster, who by April knew that his only chance at the convention was to block a quick Scott victory and emerge as a compromise choice if Fillmore and Scott deadlocked, worked through Tennessee's John Bell to persuade Georgians to attend. And he personally pleaded with conservatives in South Carolina to send delegates. Working through Arthur Hopkins, Joseph Baldwin, and Henry Hilliard in Alabama, the administration succeeded in arranging a May state Whig convention to pick delegates that only Whigs who had never joined the Union party would attend, and their Alabama contacts assured them that Mississippi Whigs also would pick delegates. Graham contacted friends in North Carolina to make sure his state sent men, and they in turn also tried to induce the few Whigs in South Carolina to select a delegation. Aside from North Carolina, the machinery that picked these delegates was jerry-rigged, but by early June it was clear that the entire South would be represented at Baltimore.[120]

The South's full attendance and its near unanimity for Fillmore meant that Scott's forces would have to marshal 149 of the North's delegates, or 146 if they could count on Delaware's 3 votes, to obtain a convention majority.[121] Despite their earlier bluster, it was unlikely that they could ram Scott's nomination through with northern votes alone. Fillmore seemed assured of Iowa's delegates, probably some of Michigan's and Wisconsin's, and undoubtedly a minority of New York's. In New England, Webster posed the biggest threat to Scott's friends. Although they were certain Scott could carry Massachusetts, they knew that the majority, if not all, of its thirteen delegates would go for Webster, as would New Hampshire's.[122]

Rhode Island and Connecticut picked delegates at early spring state conventions to nominate gubernatorial candidates for the April elections. Because their Whigs feared that a presidential endorsement might offend supporters of nonendorsed candidates and thus reduce the party's gubernatorial vote, both states chose unpledged delegations, leaving both open to imprecations from Fillmore's and Webster's influential friends.[123] California, which would be represented by Whigs already in the East, was also subjected to intense lobbying. The northern states where Scott's managers were determined not to "lose a single delegate where we can help it," therefore, were Maine, Vermont, New York, New Jersey, Pennsylvania, Ohio, Indiana, Illinois, and Michigan, although they, too, battled for every delegate they could get from other New England states, California, and Wisconsin.

In 1848, northern Whigs hoping to block Taylor's nomination had suffered because Southerners chose delegates at state conventions, thereby increasing the likelihood of unanimous delegations, whereas most northern states selected most delegates one by one at individual congressional district conventions, thereby increasing the likelihood of divided delegations. In 1852, therefore, Scott's forces in several states sought to discard the traditional district system and pick all the delegates at state conventions they controlled.[124]

Michigan's Sewardite Whigs led the way at the party's state convention in September 1851, where they chose four Scott and two Fillmore men as delegates to the national convention. Whether anger at the refusal of proadministration Whigs to support the state ticket that year or a response to pleas from Scott's managers in Washington not to lose a single vote caused the change is unclear, but when Michigan's delegation reached Baltimore it was unanimously for Scott.[125]

Vermont's antiadministration Whigs attempted to follow suit in October 1851. Whig members of the state legislature and other Whigs who happened to be in Montpelier pronounced themselves a state convention and picked the two at-large delegates, as well as all of the delegates representing the state's four congressional districts. "We beat the Websterites, *with* their allies, horse, foot, and dragoons," one Scott man later boasted. Yet this preemptive strike was neither so draconian nor so effective as it at first seemed. Though the "convention" endorsed Scott rather than Webster, it did not pledge the delegates to Scott. Its two senatorial delegates were Justin Morrill, whom even Fillmore's friends described as a moderate, and the newspaper editor Harry Bradley, Fillmore's long-time friend, who sought a patronage post and whose "vote in Convention may be considered in the market." Of the four delegates chosen for congressional districts, moreover, only one was a staunch Scott man; the other three were described as "out & out Compromise, Fillmore or Webster men." The so-called state convention, moreover, blundered by naming four congressional delegates since Vermont had four seats in the Thirty-Second Congress. According to the new reapportionment that took effect in the 1852 elections and determined the number of delegates each state would have in the national convention, however, Vermont was eligible for only three district delegates. Furthermore, three of the four men chosen in October resided in the same one of the new congressional districts, while the newly drawn third district had no delegate at all. Thus the Vermont delegation could be challenged on the ground that the state "convention" was unrepresentative, that it violated party tradition by not allowing individual congressional districts to select their own delegates, and that the delegation it picked did not represent all of the new congressional districts. The attempt of Scott's friends to jump the gun had backfired.[126]

Elsewhere Scott's forces were equally ruthless but more effective. Regularly elected state conventions in Indiana enthusiastically, and in Illinois, after astute tactical sleight of hand by Sewardites who boasted that "we managed it well & trapped the Silver Grays," endorsed Scott, chose all the delegates, and imposed a unit rule on each delegation so that their pro-Scott majorities could cast all the votes. Ohio picked delegates by the traditional district system, but the Scott forces there, at Lew Campbell's urging, also imposed a unit rule. In New Jersey, Senator Jacob Miller, ex-Senator William L. Dayton, and former Congressman James King, all of whom had voted against the Compromise in 1850 and were implicitly repudiated by the state party thereafter, dominated the state Whig convention, demanded that it pick all the state's delegates, and committed them to Scott. Although the New Jersey state platform made no specific mention of the Compromise measures, it pledged the state's Whigs to oppose "all discussion on the subject of slavery or the agitation of any measures having reference thereto." As elsewhere, in short, pro-Scott did not automatically mean antislavery.[127]

Scott's supporters flexed their muscle most nakedly in Pennsylvania. Several district conventions in the Philadelphia area had already picked convention delegates, at least half of whom favored Fillmore, when the Whig state convention met in Harrisburg in March. Dominated by allies of ex-Governor William Johnston, this gathering, like the 1851 state convention, endorsed Scott. It then flouted what one Webster man called "time-sanctioned custom" by naming the state's entire delegation to the national convention and replacing all but one of the Fillmore men already chosen from Philadelphia with Scott supporters. Johnston himself was named an at-large delegate. In line with the Scott camp's strategy of burying sectional issues in 1852, the state platform said nothing about the Compromise or slavery, reassured southern Whigs that Pennsylvanians had "none but the kindest feelings for their Whig brethren of the whole country," and "earnestly appeal[ed] to them to forget past differences, forgive past grievances, and move in a solid column" against the common Democratic foe. The true temper of Pennsylvania's Scott men reappeared, however, in their defiant response to the manifesto of the eleven southern bolters from the April 20 Whig caucus. "We can elect Scott without the aid of the South," declared a Pittsburgh paper, "and there never will be harmony and repose, in the relations of the two wings of the party until we show these disorganizers not only that we *can* do without them, but that we mean to carry our man in spite of them."[128]

New York required finesse rather than brute force. Disagreement about a potential gubernatorial nominee was so divisive that Whigs wanted to put off their state convention until long after the June national convention met. Sewardites, in any event, sought reconciliation with Silver Grays, and strong-arm tactics like those of Johnston's allies in Pennsylvania would have been self-defeating. Thus supporters of the different contenders faced a district-by-district battle, and since both Fillmore and Webster had considerable support in the New York City area, Scott could never capture all the delegates. Some upstate districts quickly selected Scott men. Where Silver Grays held the patronage posts, as in Buffalo, Rochester, Oswego, Albany, and Troy, however, Fillmorites prevailed or else fractiously divided district conventions sent rival Scott and Fillmore delegates to Baltimore.[129]

In New York City and Brooklyn, which together picked seven delegates, the federal patronage holders, particularly Customs Collector Hugh Maxwell and Naval Officer David A. Bokee, proved far friendlier to Webster than to Fillmore. By early March, when the delegate elections were at hand, indeed, even Fillmore's closest allies like Daniel Ullmann pleaded with him, as Weed and Seward had done for a year and a half, to sack Maxwell. Since Whig merchants who had contributed to the Union Safety Committee also preferred Webster to Fillmore, and since James Watson Webb's New York *Courier and Enquirer* openly endorsed Webster and savagely attacked Fillmore, Webster had significant strength in the metropolis. Recognizing that Fillmore posed a far greater threat than Webster to Scott and that they lacked the strength in "this sink of Silver Greyism" to pick straight-out Scott delegates on their own, Sewardites joined forces with the Webster men against Fillmore. The upshot was that Moses Grinnell, a Webster man, defeated a Fillmorite in one district, and Scott men carried four of the other six, although often by dubious practices that prompted challenges at the national convention.[130]

During late March and April, attention in New York and especially in Washington focused on the meeting of the Whig legislative caucus in Albany that traditionally chose the two at-large delegates and announced the state's Whigs' presidential preference. Silver Grays were badly outnumbered by pro-Scott men in both chambers, and in April the caucus endorsed Scott by a 50–15 vote. Nonetheless, to propitiate Silver Grays, the Sewardite majority agreed to postpone the selection of at-large delegates until a more representative body of state Whigs met. Since the regular Whig state convention would not meet until September, the decision fell to an assemblage of the previously chosen district delegates in New York City on June 11, when they were on their way to Baltimore. Dominated by Scott men, it chose J. L. Talcott, a staunch Scott man, and Simeon Draper, a Sewardite merchant who, like his close friend Grinnell, now leaned toward Webster.[131]

Despite nominally controlling thirty of thirty-five New York votes for Scott on the eve of the convention, Scott's friends knew that at least seven of their men would be challenged. Hence, it was far from clear that Scott had enough delegates to win the nomination, let alone block a pro-Compromise platform. As Horace Greeley alarmedly but accurately predicted in April, "Everybody in the Free States is going pell mell for Scott, and so any number of the most inveterate Hunkers are slipping into the National Convention as Scott men, to help endorse the Fugitive Slave Law and thus saddle us with a load that (with St. Paul) 'neither we nor our fathers were able to bear.' " Greeley probably had in mind delegates from Illinois, Indiana, and New Jersey, but Maine's George Evans best exemplified such fifth columnists. Pro-Scott Whigs in no northern state went as far as those in Maine to conciliate pro-Compromise Whigs. Prior to the state convention in early June, five congressional districts chose ardent Scott men, including the abrasive James Pike, whose April 10 column had so infuriated Southerners. The state convention, where Scott's backers had a decisive majority, chose the other two district delegates as well as the at-large delegates. For those latter two slots it coupled the anti-Compromise William Pitt Fessenden with Evans. Evans swore that he would honor the state party's endorsement of Scott, but for decades no man in New England had been more loyal to Webster than he. Prior to Maine's convention, moreover, Evans had stated unequivocally that he favored a platform commitment to finality. With nominal Scott delegates like Evans and moderates from other states who favored concessions to the South, Scott's managers had every reason to doubt that they could meet Israel Washburn's test—that northern Scott delegates "stand like a rock" against a pro-Compromise platform.[132]

XI

By early June no one knew who would control the convention, and supporters of all three contenders made desperate last-minute attempts to sway delegates. Long before June, Webster and his agents planned to lobby unpledged delegates from New England as well as some of the Midwesterners. In addition, Webster invited as many southern delegates as possible, especially those from South Carolina, to confer with him on their way to Baltimore. Their argument was that only Webster could carry the vital state of New York since Sewardites, who cooperated with him, would never vote for Fillmore and immigrants would never support Scott because of his previous nativist letters. Webster delegates at the convention, no matter how small their number, should therefore stick to Webster for as many ballots as it took for the Fillmore delegates to give up the ghost and throw their support to him. That strategy assumed a deadlocked convention, but it also counted on Fillmore delegates' willingness to take Webster, not Scott, as a second choice.[133]

Southerners seeking Fillmore's nomination and a pro-Compromise platform were equally active. By June, they had lost hope of securing any letter from Scott prior to the convention and dismissed any letter after the convention as certain to ''be a shilly, shally affair.'' Thus Williams and Gentry of Tennessee, Marshall, and others pressed southern delegates to hold out for an acceptable platform. The day before the convention, Florida's Cabell and Tennessee's Gentry declared once again in the House that the convention must write a pro-Compromise platform and pick a candidate who would sustain it. Pointedly attacking Scott and praising Fillmore, Cabell warned, ''If Northern Whigs . . . are resolved to go on with the slavery agitation, and to repeal the fugitive slave law, the party ought not to be preserved.''[134] Aside from publicly intimidating Scott's supporters, southern Whigs met privately in Washington and again in Baltimore on the night of June 15 and the following morning to plot strategy. They wrote a platform and apparently agreed to insist upon its adoption before any nominations were made as the price of their continued participation in the convention. Significantly, the southern Fillmore men won concurrence in this strategy from Webster's New England delegates on the night before the convention began.[135]

Unknown to these Southerners, on June 10 Fillmore drafted a letter of withdrawal that he entrusted to George Babcock, his floor manager at the convention. This letter, which Babcock was to give to the president of the convention, who would then read it to the delegates, rehearsed Fillmore's decision not to seek reelection upon ascending to the presidency in July 1850 and the reasons he had delayed making that announcement the previous winter. He specifically instructed Babcock to decide for himself precisely when, during the convention, the letter should be revealed, but Fillmore insisted that ''you will not suffer my name to be dragged into a contest for a nomination, which I have never sought, [and] do not now seek.''[136]

Fillmore's withdrawal, in sum, depended upon the proceedings of the convention itself, and in delegating responsibility for announcing it to his supporters, he guaranteed that he would indeed be dragged into a contest for the nomination. By June 10, Fillmore's closest advisors were certain that together Fillmore and Webster would have a majority of delegates and that Fillmore could win. On

June 11, Nathan Hall wrote from Buffalo that Fillmore must hang on because victory was within reach. The following day, another Silver Gray brought the Iowa delegates to the White House for personal lobbying by the president. And still another supporter, John Barney, promised to attend the convention to bring Webster's delegates into Fillmore's column.[137]

In the final week before the convention Scott's managers were frantic. Meeting almost nightly at Seward's house or the Scott club, they argued furiously over what could be done to head off a pro-Compromise platform and secure the necessary votes to select Scott. Over Seward's protests, Pike and others promised Southerners that Scott would release a letter on the Compromise after he got the nomination if Southerners would relent on their demand for a platform. Clayton of Delaware tried a different tack by floating a Scott-Crittenden ticket in hopes of at least winning more southern votes for Scott, if not blocking a platform. Fearing "a 'Silver Gray' explosion of the Whig Convention," Seward knew that the once overconfident Scott forces faced the battle of their lives.[138]

Democratic actions raised the stakes for all contenders and thereby demonstrated once again the inextricable relationship between the Whig and Democratic parties. On June 5, the Democratic national convention nominated Franklin Pierce of New Hampshire for president and William R. King of Alabama for vice president on a pro-Compromise platform. Though eschewing the code word "finality," it pledged that Democrats would "abide by and adhere to a faithful execution of . . . the compromise measures, settled by the Congress of 1850: 'the act for reclaiming fugitives from service or labor,' included." Democrats would oppose any effort to change or repeal the Fugitive Slave Act as a violation of "an express provision of the Constitution." And they would "resist all attempts at renewing, in Congress or out of it, the agitation of the slavery question under whatever shape or color the attempt may be made." Democrats, in sum, made it emphatically clear that they sought the pro-Compromise vote. Whigs now had to decide if they would also compete for it or seek a different constituency.[139]

XII

Slightly before noon on Wednesday, June 16, the longest, most rancorous, and most debilitating Whig national convention ever to meet commenced in the grand hall of Baltimore's Maryland Institute. Presidential nominating conventions were the apogee of the party apparatus. Like meetings of Congress, only on a much larger scale, they brought together men from different regions of the country who had often never laid eyes on anyone outside their own state. They invited fractious confrontation and placed a premium on skillful management to avoid it. Averting an explosion and preserving party unity were consequently top priorities of the men who made local arrangements for the Baltimore convention.

Decorated with red, white, and blue bunting and with portraits of Washington and of the dying Henry Clay, the hall featured two huge banners on opposite walls. One quoted Webster's famous reply to Hayne: "Liberty and Union, Now and Forever, One and Inseparable"; the other echoed across the hall: "The Union of the Whigs for the Sake of the Union." Such platitudes and equally gaseous rhetoric about common commitments to unity, comity, and fair play for the good of the party, however, were quickly and repeatedly punctured by the strife between anti- and pro-Scott forces over the convention officers, the composition of committees, procedural rules, delegates' credentials, and even the veracity of newspaper reports about the proceedings. With tempers shortened by Baltimore's suffocating June heat and humidity, enmities could not be concealed. Speeches were greeted with boastful cheers or derisive jeers, hisses, and angry catcalls, depending upon the identity of the speaker and auditors. So antagonistic and confused were the preliminary jousts that balloting for president did not begin until the evening of the third day's session. The convention, indeed, took an unprecedented six days to complete its work.[140]

Aside from naked animosity and distrust, from the din inside a hall packed by over 3,000 people, and from exhaustion attributable to the extraordinary heat, what caused and conditioned the prolonged struggle were the following facts. Scott's backers, who hoped to secure his nomination without any platform, let alone a pro-Compromise document, had failed to secure the majority they needed. Together, Webster's and Fillmore's delegates could control the convention—if and when they worked as a team. Equally important, Scott men dominated only nine state delegations—those of Maine, New York, New Jersey, Delaware, Pennsylvania, Ohio, Indiana, Illinois, and Michigan. In addition, California was divided, but leaned toward Scott. With Iowa and fourteen slave states, Fillmore's forces controlled fifteen. Websterites dominated Massachusetts and New Hampshire, and together Fillmore and Webster men controlled Rhode Island, Connecticut, and Vermont. This imbalance was a crippling handicap to Scott men, for although they dominated the northern states with the largest delegations, committees traditionally consisted of one member from each state. Procedurally, that is, the number of states mattered more than the number of delegates. For example, the three pro-Scott committee members from Ohio, Pennsylvania, and New York, who collectively represented eighty-five votes, could be outvoted by four Webster and Fillmore members from New Hampshire, Texas, Arkansas, and Florida, who collectively represented only sixteen. With Scott men outnumbered on every committee by a two-to-one margin, in sum, they were bound to lose every important committee fight—on permanent officers, on credentials, and on the platform.

The first day's session on June 16 did little more than name committees on permanent officers and credentials and in the evening session, over some Northerners' protests, install Maryland's John G. Chapman as the convention's permanent president. Opposed by outnumbered Scott men in committee, that choice was portentous, for Chapman chaired the southern caucus on June 15 and 16 that prepared a pro-Compromise platform. Particularly annoying to northern Scott delegates was the inflated size of southern delegations that had sent two or more men for each vote they had, a practice that bolstered the presence of Southerners on the convention floor and gave them an enormous advantage on voice, as opposed to roll-call, votes.[141] The debate on this matter quickly revealed the reciprocal suspicions among delegates and featured at least one classic exchange. Ohio's John Sherman moved unsuccessfully to table the report recommending Chapman until the credentials committee made clear who among southern delegations had authority to vote. A Maryland delegate then objected with a point of order that

Sherman had no right to speak after a motion to table. When he insisted that "I stick to my point of order," Sherman shot back: "Stick to your seat."

During the evening recess, as supporters of all three contenders paraded through Baltimore's streets, serious work was done in private. Webster's delegates caucused and vowed to stick by him until Webster withdrew his name; some of Fillmore's supporters, probably led by John Barney, meanwhile spread the word that Fillmore wanted his delegates to back Webster should Fillmore withdraw. Pennsylvania's Johnston, meanwhile, huddled with John Minor Botts in an attempt to break into the Virginia delegation, and other Scott men floated rumors that Scott would send a letter on finality to the convention to reassure Southerners. Botts and Johnston both told reporters that Scott would win on the third or fourth ballot.

Ill temper increased during the second day's session. The credentials committee again failed to report, so the convention continued to quarrel over precisely who could speak or vote. After the adoption of procedural rules that allotted each state the equivalent of its electoral votes, T. B. Duncan of Louisiana introduced resolutions calling for the immediate appointment of a platform committee consisting of one man from each state, allowing each state's delegation to designate its representative, and requiring the convention to vote on the platform it reported before taking up the presidential nomination. As Duncan proudly declared, his purpose was "to know if our [Southerners'] principles are your [Northerners'] principles" and to ascertain "whether we are all of one party or not." Recognizing this strike for what it was—an attempt to force the decision on a platform before the nomination and to ram the Southerners' prewritten platform through a committee Scott's foes would dominate—northern Scott men sought to table Duncan's resolutions or adjourn to delay a vote. Nonetheless, the first resolution passed comfortably, 199 to 97, over the opposition of Scott delegations from New York, New Jersey, Indiana, Ohio, and Michigan, as well as Wisconsin. The rules for this vote required each state's entire total to be recorded as its majority wished, and, ominously for Scott hard-liners who opposed any platform whatsoever, ten of the twenty-three Ohio delegates favored the resolution, while Pennsylvania and Illinois voted in favor with the Fillmore and Webster delegations.[142]

The convention's first roll-call vote, therefore, demonstrated that Scott men were bound to lose on the issue of whether or not to adopt any platform. To give Scott's forces a better chance than they otherwise would have to influence that platform, therefore, a Pennsylvanian named Jessup immediately introduced an explosive amendment to Duncan's second resolution, which called for each state delegation to appoint one man to the platform committee. Charging that the one-state, one-vote rule on committees was patently unfair to large states with the most delegates and electoral votes, Jessup moved to weight representation on the platform committee by allowing each member to cast his state's entire vote during committee roll calls. That way, for example, New York's member would have thirty-five votes and Florida's only three rather than being treated as equals. That way the nine members from Scott states could outvote the entire South, as outraged Southerners were quick to protest.

Not quickly enough, however, for Jessup's stunning initiative caught Fillmore and Webster men flatfooted. Demanding the previous question before Southerners mounted a counterattack, Scott's backers forced a vote on the Jessup amendment and scored their only victory on a procedural vote during the entire convention, 149–144. On this roll call, states were not required to vote as a unit, and the results thus suggested the balance of forces within individual delegations. Every slave state except Delaware and, surprisingly, Missouri, which divided 6–2 in favor with one abstention, cast unanimous votes against Jessup's motion.[143] The pattern of the free states was far more complicated.[144] Vermont's delegation was in turmoil and did not vote. Maine was solidly in favor, but the other New England states, where Webster men dominated, voted against: New Hampshire 0–4; Massachusetts 3–10, Connecticut 2–4, and Rhode Island 0–4. California split 2–2, Wisconsin 1–3 against, and New York 31–4 in favor. All of the other northern states, including Iowa, voted unanimously in favor. The four Fillmore men from New York immediately protested that six Scott delegates whose credentials were being contested had voted with their state's majority and should not be counted. Despite those protests, furious complaints from Southerners that Jessup's amendment violated the equal rights of states and substituted majority tyranny for traditional Whig conservatism, and attempts to replace Duncan's motion as amended by Jessup with a less controversial substitute, Jessup's amendment stood when the convention angrily adjourned for the night, although the convention had not yet adopted the resolution to which it was attached.

As everyone was aware, the total vote for Jessup's amendment equaled the precise number of votes necessary for nomination. Victory though the vote was for Scott men, however, the total exaggerated Scott's strength. Aside from the disputed seats from New York, Missouri was instructed for Fillmore, and he seemed assured of Iowa's votes. Nonetheless, the vote on Jessup's amendment spawned frantic maneuvering during the second night's recess, especially among the Webster and Fillmore men. To the consternation of Fillmore's lieutenants, Webster's forces again vowed to stand by him rather than switch to Fillmore. This was outrageous, Barney reported to Fillmore from Baltimore. By his count, Scott would get 137 votes on the first ballot, Webster 40, and Fillmore 119. Since it took 149 to win, it would be far easier to transfer 30 of Webster's delegates to Fillmore than all but 10 of Fillmore's to Webster, especially as he knew of at least 12 votes from Kentucky, Virginia, and North Carolina that would go for Scott rather than Webster if Fillmore withdrew. "Prudence requires Mr. Webster's phalanx to join your Legion," Barney told the president.[145]

During the same night, the cantankerous Jessup, as well as other Scott men anxious to conciliate Southerners, had second thoughts about his inflammatory amendment. The vote to adopt Duncan's first resolution revealed that a substantial number of Scott delegates would accept a platform. No matter how gratifying the vote on Jessup's amendment was to Scott men, anyone who could count realized that even under Jessup's formula Webster and Fillmore men could outvote Scott's representatives on the platform committee, for in divided states like Wisconsin, Connecticut, and Massachusetts, to say nothing of Missouri and Iowa, anti-Scott men would pick the committee members. Infuriating Southerners for what could only be a pyrrhic victory did not seem worth the cost.

A third crucial development also occurred that night. The credentials committee, heavily dominated by anti-Scott men, met until 1 A.M. Obviously swayed by the vote for Jessup's amendment, they contrived to strip Scott of at least seven votes from Vermont and New York. Their report sparked a ferocious dispute the following morning.[146]

Friday, June 18, the convention's third and most pivotal day, proved one of the most important in the party's entire history. At the outset, Jessup moved to withdraw his controversial amendment, and, significantly, the majority that adopted it acquiesced.[147] This action allowed the immediate appointment of a platform committee, each of whose members would have only one vote. It included a distinguished and diverse group: William Pitt Fessenden of Maine; Vermont's ex-Governor Carlos Coolidge; George Ashmun, Webster's loyal ally from Massachusetts; New York Sewardite A. B. Dickinson; ex-Governor Johnston from Pennsylvania; Clayton of Delaware; Louisiana's determined Duncan; Crittenden's friend Orlando Brown from Kentucky; Felix Zollicoffer of Tennessee; and Georgia's Senator William C. Dawson. As soon as the committee was named, the platform already drafted by the southern caucus was submitted to it, as were other resolutions.

The platform committee's diverse membership ensured some lively debates during its meetings, but the one-state, one-vote rule guaranteed defeat of the Scott men, at least in committee. That fact became clear when the credentials committee finally reported. Aside from admitting a nonvoting, though pro-Scott, delegation from the District of Columbia, it effectively stripped Scott of at least six and perhaps seven votes, one from Vermont and the remainder from New York. In Vermont it denied Porteas Baxter, a pro-Scott man chosen at a June district convention from the new third congressional district, which had been left unrepresented by the October state convention. Instead it admitted all six delegates chosen the previous October and left it up to them how to cast the state's five votes. Since at least four of those six were pro-Compromise, anti-Scott men, this decision left the Vermont delegation in the hands of Scott's enemies.[148]

Seven districts required action in New York. In one, the committee seated Grinnell, the Websterite, instead of his Fillmorite opponent. In four, it named Fillmorites rather than the Scott men who had already voted for Jessup's amendment. Its decision on the remaining two district disputes was more insidious, for it seated both the Silver Gray and his pro-Scott opponent in each and stipulated that the vote of the districts could not be cast on any roll call unless the rival delegates concurred. Since everyone at the convention realized that such agreement would never be reached, this decision effectively deprived New York of two votes while simultaneously counting those two votes in the total from which a majority had to be constructed. More precisely, Scott still needed 149, not 148 votes, and he was robbed of 6 votes from New York and 1 from Vermont that his floor managers had counted on. New Yorkers—Silver Grays and Sewardites alike—screamed in protest at this emasculation, while Southerners hooted in derision for them to shut up, especially since one of the delegates rendered a eunuch was the despised Sewardite Henry J. Raymond, editor of the *New York Times*.[149]

While New Yorkers fumed, Florida's Cabell pressed for the previous question on adoption of the committee report. This motion produced the third critical roll call at the convention and, according to Solomon G. Haven, revealed that together the Fillmore and Webster forces had a majority of forty-seven votes. While the report was adopted 164 to 117, Haven's estimate was overly optimistic. Altogether thirteen pro-Scott delegates from Indiana, Illinois, New Jersey, Pennsylvania, and Michigan broke ranks and supported adoption. No votes were cast from the disputed districts in New York, which split 4–24 against, however, and only 5 of Missouri's 9 votes were cast. Scott's opponents would pick up additional votes from those states. Predictably, every southern vote cast and twenty-nine of the thirty-three New England votes outside of Maine favored adoption.

Appointment of a platform committee without Jessup's amendment and adoption of the credentials committee's report marked stinging defeats for the Scott forces. When Southerners moved to adjourn for a few hours until the platform committee reported, therefore, Ohioans attempted to salvage the chief objective of Scott men—nomination without a platform—by moving that the convention proceed immediately to presidential balloting without waiting for the platform. Surprisingly, Southerners' attempt to stop this effort by moving adjournment was initially defeated by twenty-five votes. At that point, Maine's George Evans, the Websterite in Scott clothing, declared that it was obvious that the convention would never allow a nomination until a platform was adopted, and, with the aid of a favorable ruling from Chapman on a loudly disputed voice vote, Evans won adjournment. Chapman's selection as permanent president and Maine's inclusion of Evans to appease Websterites had together produced the convention's decisive turning point. Now a pro-Compromise platform was inevitable.

George Ashmun reported the platform to the evening session. With only slight modifications, it was the same platform drafted by the southern caucus on June 15 and 16. The critical eighth plank announced that the Whig party "received and acquiesced in" the Compromise measures, "the Act known as the Fugitive Slave law, included . . . as a settlement in principle and substance" of the matters they addressed. It pledged Whigs to "maintain them and insist upon their strict enforcement." If "time and experience" showed the need for further legislation to guard against abuse or evasion, moreover, that new legislation must not "impair their present efficiency." Like the Democrats, finally, the plank said that Whigs "deprecate all further agitation of the question thus settled, as dangerous to our peace; and will discountenance all efforts to continue or renew such agitation whenever, wherever, or however the attempt may be made." Like the Democratic platform, in short, the Whigs' meant finality without using the word.[150]

The Compromise plank drew most of participants' attention at the convention and virtually all the attention of later historians, but two other planks proved critically important during the subsequent campaign. The third resolution endorsed the stance of Fillmore's administration and of Southern Whigs against any intervention in European affairs and thus effectively put the party on record against Kossuth. It thus lengthened the odds against cutting into the expected new German vote. As a member of Kossuth's entourage wrote Seward immediately after he read it, "What a pity that the Whig platform could not be more favorable or at least less hostile! You could have had the german vote of all the western States, which could have secured the election."[151]

The fifth plank adopted word for word the Southerners' tariff resolution, which called for a revenue tariff with "a just discrimination, whereby suitable encouragement may be afforded to American industry, equally to all classes, and to all portions of the country." This was the plank that Democrats mocked as a total surrender of Whigs' protectionist pretensions, the plank that appeared in both Whig and Democratic newspaper versions of the Whig platform, and the plank that appears in supposedly authoritative collections of national party platforms.[152] Astonishingly, however, it was not the tariff plank written by the platform committee.

The following day William F. Johnston, Pennsylvania's member on the committee, angrily protested that the plank reported in newspaper accounts was not what the committee had adopted. He had successfully amended the Southerners' plank in committee, he insisted, by inserting a vital demand for specific rather than *ad valorem* duties. The plank should read, he declared and the committee chairman Ashmun concurred: "and in laying such duties sound policy requires a just discrimination and protection from fraud by specific duties whereby suitable encouragement may be afforded to American industry. . . ." The importance of specific duties to Whigs who wanted a protective, not just a revenue, tariff cannot be exaggerated. Nor can it be doubted that the platform committee inserted that phrase, for northern and border state Webster and Fillmore men were just as committed to specific rates as northern Scott men.[153] Yet for whatever reason, while the journal of the convention recorded the plank as Johnston wrote it, the versions of the platform that went out to the public and that have come down to posterity never included the critical words about specific duties. Whatever opportunities booming economic conditions still allowed Whigs to make a case for protectionism had been closed by their own inadvertence, indifference, or sheer incompetence.

On Friday night, however, delegates focused on the controversial Compromise plank, not the truncated tariff resolution. In the hubbub that ensued after Ashmun read the platform, Webster's eminent Massachusetts ally Rufus Choate got the floor first. Intentionally and gratuitously insulting Scott's backers, he exultantly declared that the platform "affirmed the finality of the Compromise," argued that the Democrats' platform had left the Whigs with no alternative but to do so, and praised the prescience of Webster's notorious Seventh of March speech. Then, in a direct stab at Scott's delegates, he insisted that honor required Whigs to go forth to the country with an explicit platform and a candidate committed to it rather than an uncommitted and two-faced candidate who told northern audiences "No platform—agitation forever" and southern audiences "No platform—but a letter in every man's breeches pocket."

This shaft was aimed at southern Scott backers like Botts and Jones who circulated among the delegates swearing they had letters to prove that Scott was pro-Compromise. After an Ohioan angrily urged Scott to spurn the obnoxious platform should he win the nomination, Botts tried to respond. Protesting Choate's acerbic language, he denied that Scott had written any letters to influence delegates at the convention. Then, as if not recognizing the contradiction, he pulled out of his own pocket and read a letter that Scott had written ex-Senator William Archer of Virginia on the day before the convention began. In that letter Scott said that he had decided not to write anyone at the convention itself before the nomination, but that, should he receive it, he would send a letter of acceptance that affirmed his strong approbation of the Compromise measures. Botts, in short, quoted a letter from Scott announcing to the convention that Scott was pro-Compromise in order to demonstrate that Scott had written no letters to influence the convention. To refute Choate's charge, he had seemingly proved it, thus bringing waves of derisive laughter down on his head. Yet Botts was hardly the bumbler he seemed. He had cleverly seized an opportunity to make public for the first time a letter from Scott himself approving the Compromise and promising to make that approval much more explicit if he won the nomination.[154]

After this exchange the convention proceeded to vote on the platform. Since its adoption was certain, Scott's floor managers spread the word that Scott men were free to vote for it to conciliate the South. As Pike wrote Seward, arms had to be twisted to get certain men to do so, and he had promised them that a paragraph of Scott's acceptance letter would explicitly repudiate "the doctrine of making the compromise a party test."[155] Voluntarily or grudgingly, at least half of the Scott delegates supported the platform, and it carried easily 226–66. Every Southerner, including Delaware's three Scott delegates, was in the majority, and all the negative votes came from Scott men. Yet the roll call revealed where hard-liners and moderates in the Scott camp were concentrated, if not precisely who they were. Michigan was the only free state unanimously opposed. Iowa, California, New Hampshire, Vermont, Massachusetts, and Rhode Island were unanimously in favor, but so was New Jersey, a Scott state. Wisconsin split 4–1 in favor, as did Connecticut, where one delegate abstained. Maine divided 4–4, Indiana, 7–6, Illinois, 6–5, and Pennsylvania, whose heavily pro-Scott delegation was headed by William F. Johnston, gave the platform 25 of its 27 votes. Even in Ohio, eight of twenty-three delegates voted in favor. Only New York joined Michigan as a bastion of opposition. There only three delegates, who probably included the Webster-leaning Grinnell and Draper, joined the eight Fillmore men in favor, while the remaining twenty-two delegates who could vote opposed it.[156]

If Scott's strategists bowed to the inevitable by releasing delegates to support the platform, hard-liners still considered its adoption a decisive defeat. "The wretched platform, contrived to defeat General Scott in the nomination, or sink him in the canvass, comes to him like the order of a superior power," Seward carped to his wife, "and he is incapable of understanding that it is not obligatory on him to execute it." The North "as usual," he lamented, had divided in the face of "intimidation" from a united South, "and so the platform adopted is one that deprives Scott of the vantage position he enjoyed."[157]

Muzzled and voteless, Henry J. Raymond tried to salvage some benefit from this disaster. On Friday night he telegraphed a dispatch to the *New York Times* that appeared in the Saturday issue and that caused the convention's biggest blowup. He reported that the New York delegation was outraged by the credentials committee's action and would refuse to support the convention's nominee if it cost Scott the nomination. But he also predicted that Scott would win on the third or fourth ballot on Saturday because "Kentucky, Tennessee, Virginia, and one or two others will give Scott the nomination. . . . The Northern Whigs gave way on the Platform, with this understanding. If Scott is not nominated, they will charge breach of faith on the South."

Raymond's allusion to a quid pro quo swapping northern votes for the platform in exchange for southern votes for Scott accurately reflected the hopes of Scott's managers, but it represented wishful thinking, not hard evidence. The balloting for president began on Friday night, after the platform was adopted, but before it did, southern Scott men made one more attempt to provoke the break in anti-

Scott southern ranks that Raymond predicted. Tennessee's Lean Jimmy Jones declared that he knew from personal conversations with Scott that he would accept and endorse the pro-Compromise platform just adopted because Scott "was an ardent supporter and friend of the Compromise measures from the day they were first presented to Congress by Henry Clay and that he was opposed to touching them in any manner, shape, or form."[158]

Botts and Jones barely dented southern opposition to Scott, however. On the first ballot and on five additional votes cast on Friday night, Scott's support from the South ranged between four and six votes, three from Delaware and between one and three from Virginia. Jones of Tennessee, who angrily denied that he intended to betray his state's wishes, apparently abstained rather than support Scott, for Tennessee cast only twelve of its thirteen votes. More significant was the general stability of the vote and the deadlock it signified. Nomination required 149 votes. On the first ballot that night Fillmore had 133, Scott, 131, and Webster 29. On the remaining five ballots Scott's vote fluctuated between 130 and 134, Fillmore's between 130 and 133, and Webster's surpassed 29 only once when it reached 30. Indeed, during forty ballots on Saturday, the convention's fourth long and contentious day, Scott never went lower than 131 or higher than 136, Fillmore fluctuated between 133 and 126, and Webster ranged between an irreducible 28 and his high of 32. Of the few switches that occurred, moreover, one fact was clear. Delegates swung back and forth between Scott and Webster and between Scott and Fillmore, but there was virtually no traffic in either direction between the Fillmore and Webster columns. By the end of Saturday's extraordinarily long and turbulent day of voting, the pattern stood pretty much where it had started on Friday night: Scott 134, Fillmore 127, Webster 31.

The breakdown of support can be discerned from the first ballot for which we have state-by-state data. Maine, New Jersey, Delaware, Indiana, Illinois, and Michigan were unanimous for Scott. He also garnered twenty-two of Ohio's twenty-three votes, twenty-six of Pennsylvania's twenty-seven, and twenty-four of New York's thirty-three. Two men in the Connecticut, Massachusetts, and California delegations backed him, as did one from Virginia, New Hampshire, Vermont, Rhode Island, and Wisconsin. Aside from a surprising three of Wisconsin's five delegates, two from New York, and one from California, Webster's strength came exclusively from New Hampshire, Massachusetts, Vermont, Connecticut, and Rhode Island. Fillmore took 115 of the 119 votes cast by Southerners, along with 7 from New York, all 4 from Iowa, and a scattering of 1 each from Vermont, Rhode Island, Connecticut, Pennsylvania, Ohio, Wisconsin, and California.

The lesson of these ballots was crystal clear. Both Scott and Fillmore were within striking distance of the nomination, and the irreducible Webster bloc of twenty-eight votes stood in each man's way. Aside from a few individuals in New Hampshire, New York, and Wisconsin who switched back and forth between Webster and Scott, Scott's managers had little hope of cutting into Webster's vote; they concentrated on prying Southerners away from Fillmore. Fillmore's managers, in turn, engaged in desperate negotiations during recesses on the 18th and 19th to bring Webster men into the Fillmore column.

The stubbornness of Webster's New England base infuriated Fillmore's Baltimore floor managers. From the moment the convention opened, operatives like Barney, Haven, and B. M. Edney, a North Carolinian employed in the Interior

Department, huddled with Massachusetts Webster delegates like Choate and William Hayden and pleaded with them to abandon Webster and support Fillmore. If Fillmore instead withdrew, they pointed out, they could not deliver all of his votes to Webster. Enough Southerners would then break to Scott to nominate him, they warned, but Webster's delegates refused to believe it. "No men ever were more mistaken," the disgusted Haven wrote Fillmore on Friday. At daybreak that morning, Barney had traveled to Washington to plead with Webster himself to turn his delegates over to Fillmore, but Webster was as unmovable as his delegates. Aware that he had sacrificed his popularity in the North to aid the South in 1850, he believed southern Fillmore men owed him their support. "My friends will stand firm," he telegraphed a Maryland delegate on Saturday morning. "Let the South answer for the consequences. Remember the 7th of March."[159]

During the prolonged balloting on Saturday, June 19, which caused Elihu Washburne, an Illinois Scott delegate, to say "that the Whig party is about to pass through the dark valley of the shadow of death," Fillmore's operatives grew angrier at Websterites' stubbornness as they saw Fillmore's total decline negligibly but perceptibly. After the convention adjourned Saturday night until Monday morning, Fillmore's friends doubled their efforts during the recess. At a meeting on Saturday night, they proposed that if Webster could bring forty votes from the North, Fillmore's men would break to him, but if he could not, then Webster's delegates should support Fillmore. Webster's friends shunned the deal. On Sunday morning, Edney offered a different bargain. On Monday, he proposed, 4 Webster delegates should shift to Fillmore on each ballot until he reached 145, 4 short of the necessary 149. This movement should frighten the Scott men into switching to Webster to stop Fillmore, and if Webster could get seventy-five northern votes in this fashion, Edney would deliver seventy-five southern Fillmore men to Webster. Alternatively, if Webster could not get seventy-five northern votes, then his supporters should go to Fillmore. This proposal, too, was rejected. Meanwhile, Barney and Brooklyn's David A. Bokee arranged a delegation from Baltimore to speak with Webster in Washington on Sunday. As of Sunday night, however, Webster would not budge. If he withdrew in favor of Fillmore, Webster contended, enough of his New England delegates would go to Scott to nominate him.[160]

The inability of the Webster and Fillmore delegations in Baltimore to unite their combined majority is puzzling, but the behavior of the principals back in Washington strikes the modern observer as positively surreal. During the entire convention week, the two men who had worked so closely together for two years never saw or spoke to each other. True, Fillmore and Webster had occasionally been at odds, especially over Fillmore's willingness to take patronage from his New York enemies while refusing to allow Webster to do the same in Massachusetts, Pennsylvania, and elsewhere. Nonetheless, they agreed with each other about so much that was at stake in Baltimore that one wonders why they simply did not meet themselves for an hour or two and resolve the deadlock. Concern about the impropriety of openly maneuvering for the presidency is an obvious answer, but newspapers were already reporting that their men in Baltimore met at every opportunity to arrange a deal.

Mutual pride and Webster's resentment may offer a better explanation. Fillmore was certainly prepared to turn his delegates over to Webster, but he had promised his friend Babcock that Babcock alone should make that decision.

Besides, as Fillmore was head of the administration, making the first overture to a subordinate would be unseemly. Webster's pride was monumental; since January, moreover, his anger that Fillmore had refused to withdraw had festered and the proceedings in Baltimore had brought it to a flash point. Webster spent most of Sunday afternoon, indeed, cursing Fillmore and his southern supporters as duplicitous ingrates. Whatever the reasons why the two men failed to communicate directly with each other, rather than through their Baltimore emissaries, that lapse almost produced a fiasco of legendary proportions.[161]

On Monday morning, Webster conceded the hopelessness of his situation. Early that morning he sent a note to Fillmore saying that he had informed his friends in Baltimore to throw their support to the president and that Fillmore should be nominated by one o'clock that afternoon. But Fillmore had also had enough. As he replied to Webster, he too had sent a messenger to Baltimore that morning urging his friends to withdraw his name and cast their support to Webster, "which I presume will be done unless the knowledge of your communication shall prevent it." The possibility existed that both men's names would be withdrawn, leaving Scott alone in the field.[162]

That ludicrous denouement was averted. Neither the Webster nor the Fillmore men at Baltimore would obey instructions. As Francis Granger later wrote Fillmore, Babcock had acted superbly. "There was never a moment when your withdrawal would have secured Mr. Webster's nomination. There were never more than 94 of the 116 Southern votes which sustained you that could have been given to him." By keeping Fillmore in the race, moreover, the Southerners who planned to switch to Scott if he dropped out would have to desert openly to do so and thus earn the execration they deserved. As for Webster's friends, chided Granger, "Some of them, as you know, were Scott men at heart. The rest, Choate included, seemed to me to act like a parcel of school boys, waiting for the sky to fall that they might catch larks. Such another collection of respectable out of place gentlemen was never seen."[163]

Another factor stopping a simultaneous withdrawal, however, was that the convention did not immediately recommence balloting when it reconvened on Monday morning. It spent several hours instead debating a motion from a Georgian to expel Henry J. Raymond. That angry debate, during which Raymond implied that Cabell was a liar and Cabell threatened to challenge Raymond to a duel, provided sufficient time for the Fillmore and Webster managers to compare notes, decide that it would be pointless for both men to withdraw, and determine to keep both in the race on the grounds that the instructions canceled each other out.[164]

On the first two votes after balloting resumed, Scott gained 3 votes from Missouri to bring his total to 137. On the next, the forty-ninth, ballot, Cranston of Rhode Island abandoned Webster and joined Scott's column, a shift that caused enormous excitement in the spectator galleries.[165] By the fifty-second ballot Scott's total stood at 148, 1 vote shy of nomination, Fillmore had declined to 119, and Webster was down to 26. In a normal convention there would have been a landslide in Scott's direction as everyone tried to side with the winner, but the long and acrimonious struggle had cemented most delegates to the man with whom they started. On the fifty-third and final ballot, Scott edged over the top with 157 votes, Fillmore got 114, and Webster retained only 21—4 of Wisconsin's

5 votes, 1 from California, 1 from New York's faithful Grinnell, and the remainder from New England, including the 11 diehards in Massachusetts who refused to back Fillmore.[166]

Between the first and last ballots the following shifts had occurred: Scott picked up two Fillmore and six Webster votes from New England, including those of all four New Hampshire Webster men. Very early in the balloting, New York's Simeon Draper had also moved from the Webster to the Scott column.[167] Otherwise, his gains came at the expense of Fillmore: one in California, one in Pennsylvania, one in Ohio, one in Iowa, three in Missouri, three in Tennessee, and seven in Virginia.[168] Although Kentucky and North Carolina had been repeatedly rumored to harbor Scott supporters, they remained solidly opposed to Scott, as did the other slave states. Still, the thirteen southern votes made the difference. Scott could have won without the eight votes he gained in New England. The thirteen southern votes, in contrast, were indispensable, and they equaled all of the gains Scott had made elsewhere.

Many of these Southerners obviously decided over the Sunday recess to switch to Scott to break the stalemate, and as if to justify the vote he had finally dared to cast, Tennessee's Jones immediately stood and read a letter from Scott, dated Sunday, June 20. One sentence long, it said: "Having the honor to be a candidate of the Whig Convention, I will accept the nomination, with the platform of principles the Convention has laid down." Whether Jones actually had a letter from Scott of that date—he had promised on Friday that Scott would accept the platform—will never be known, but hard-liners among Scott men considered any acknowledgment of the platform by Scott a blunder. "In God's name have no slip here," Pike had written Seward. Scott's letter of acceptance must explicitly repudiate "making the compromise a party test." Most important, "The letter of Gen. S. should be sent *by the committee*." If Scott wrote what Jones read, in sum, he proved to be the loose cannon his managers had always feared.[169]

While Scott's northern managers would later try to repair the damage caused by Scott's convention letter in his official letter of acceptance, Jones' speech allowed southern delegates to follow customary ritual and accede to the nomination. With varying degrees of enthusiasm, speakers from Georgia, Alabama, Mississippi, and even South Carolina announced their support for the nominee, as did a Massachusetts delegate. However sincere or hollow these pledges, everyone knew that a Southerner had to be placed on the ticket to balance Scott, and thus the convention moved to select the vice presidential nominee.

Altogether, nineteen men received votes on the first ballot for vice president, and all but one—New York's hapless Silver Gray Richardson, who got three sympathy votes for being denied a vote during the convention by being paired with Raymond—were Southerners. Three men from Kentucky, four from Tennessee, three from North Carolina, two from Maryland, two from Missouri, and one each from South Carolina, Florida, Virginia, and Alabama got votes. The leader was Missouri's Edward Bates, with ninety-seven votes, followed by William A. Graham of North Carolina with seventy-four. Crittenden of Kentucky got ten and Jones of Tennessee, once the front-runner for the slot, a meager five. Both withdrew their names after that ballot.

Aside from favorite sons like Florida's Governor Thomas Brown, the home states of serious candidates were not accidental. Missouri, Tennessee, and Virginia were the states that had put Scott over the top, and northern Scott men wanted to reward them. The front-runner Bates, for example, got only six southern votes, aside from his own state's nine, although the other contender from Missouri, John W. Crockett, got all twelve of Tennessee's votes, as well as seven from the North. All of Bates' remaining votes came from the North, and he ran especially well among Midwesterners, who considered him one of their own.[170] In contrast, Kentucky, Maryland, and North Carolina, whose various contenders received a total of 143 votes, were traditional Whig states that solidly supported Fillmore and whose votes were considered vital in November. In the end, the necessity of appeasing them rather than rewarding southern bolters to Scott carried the day. Graham won on the second ballot by a vote of 232 to 52 for Bates.

Graham's nomination was perfectly logical. Unlike Mangum and Stanly, other North Carolinians who received votes, Graham had never supported Scott, and he was a member of Fillmore's official family. Unlike Crittenden of Kentucky, who was also in the cabinet, Graham's name was not withdrawn. And unlike Senator James Pearce, the leading vote getter from Maryland, Graham hailed from a state with ten, not just eight, electoral votes. Since Jones had already pledged to work as hard for the ticket as possible in Tennessee, shoring up North Carolina seemed the top priority. As soon as his nomination was announced, indeed, a North Carolina delegate pledged that the Scott-Graham ticket would carry North Carolina by at least 10,000 votes.

XIII

The ticket of Scott and Graham represented a desperate attempt to preserve the party as a bisectional organization. Although one wag immediately predicted that a ticket coupling a North Carolinian with "Old Fuss and Feathers" would be derisively labeled "Tar and Feathers," it linked the clear favorite of most northern Whigs with a slaveholder closely associated with the runner-up and eminently acceptable to Southerners who distrusted Scott.[171] Given Webster's anger that no Southerner cast a single vote for him at the convention, probably no Southerner could appease Webster loyalists, but Scott, not Graham, was expected to carry New England for the Whigs.

Nonetheless, the ticket by itself could not heal the wounds opened up at and before the convention. One reminder of those divisions came in the convention's last minutes when Pennsylvania's irascible Jessup moved that at the next national convention no state be allowed more delegates than it had votes, a slap at the overrepresentation of the South that had so infuriated northern Scott men. More important were the divergent sectional reactions to the outcome. Southern Whigs in and outside the convention cheered the adoption of the platform and Graham's nomination. Their response to Scott, in contrast, was tepid, if not downright chilly, and they always coupled promises to support the ticket with the contingent demand that he embrace the platform. Both Botts and Jones had specifically pledged that Scott's letter of acceptance would explicitly endorse the Compromise, and for Southerners much hinged on what Scott would actually say in that epistle. Many Northerners' reactions were succinctly captured by Charles Dana, the New York newspaperman: "Hurrah for the nomination & damn the platform!"[172] Appalled by the letter Jones read, Scott's managers hoped to repair the damage in the official letter of acceptance. No letter acceptable to them could possibly say everything that Southern Whigs now anticipated.

When the Whig convention finally adjourned, in sum, most northern and southern Whigs still deeply disagreed about what the thrust of the ensuing campaign should be. That chasm could not be papered over by obligatory promises to support the ticket. During the entire six days of the convention, in fact, delegates for different candidates and from different regions enthusiastically united on only two occasions. Both were commemorations of Henry Clay, the party's mortally ill founder, who had championed its cause for so many years. That Whigs were far more united when they looked to the past than when they confronted the future spoke volumes.

What Clay thought of the convention's outcome is unknown. He lay dying during its proceedings. A little after 11 A.M. on June 29, eight days after the convention adjourned, the only man on whom Whigs seemingly still could unite expired. Word of Clay's death, which Whigs had anticipated for months, went out to the nation in the next day's papers. By an eerie and ominous coincidence, the same editions of papers on June 30 that announced the doleful news also carried the acceptance letters of Winfield Scott and William A. Graham that had such grave implications for the future of the party that Clay had personified in the past.

Chapter 20

"Like Pissing Against the Wind"

"THE WHIG CAUSE never was more vulnerable in its platform and in the person of the individual hoisted up on the rickety scaffolding," a Louisiana Democrat jeered on the very day that Henry Clay died. Other Democrats shared this confidence, but they were struck less by the shakiness of the Whigs' platform than by its similarity to their own. Pennsylvania's Governor William Bigler told Franklin Pierce that Whigs had purposely "assimilated" Democratic doctrines "to reduce the contest to a personal struggle between General Scott and yourself, relying as they evidently do on the brilliance of his military career to secure success."[1]

Bigler erred. Whigs did not intentionally mimic Democratic principles in order to contrast the candidates. Most southern Whigs fought Winfield Scott's nomination until the bitter end, while many of Scott's northern supporters regarded the platform as an unconscionable price to pay for his nomination. On the same day that Scott was nominated and Tennessee's James Jones read a letter from him accepting the platform as "laid down by the Convention," for example, Horace Greeley wrote of the platform in his widely read New York *Tribune*: "We defy it, execrate it, spit upon it."[2]

If Bigler mistook Whig intentions, he correctly judged the result of the Whig and Democratic conventions. More than any presidential election since 1836, the 1852 campaign focused on the character and reputation of the opposing presidential candidates rather than on alternative public policies. Southern Democrats' campaign tactics, northern Whigs' disgust with their platform, and the Democrats' selection of Pierce, a man particularly vulnerable to personal attack, all contributed to that focus. Primarily, however, it resulted from the elimination of issue differences between the parties. Their indistinguishable positions on the Compromise and the irrelevance of economic issues because of prosperity forced them to appeal for votes by contrasting their nominees.

The lack of programmatic differences between the two parties, their opportunistic efforts to fill that void with ad hominem attacks, and the resulting disaffection and disinterest among the electorate together produced one of the election's two most important results. Despite the anticipated mobilization of tens of thousands of new immigrant voters, turnout rates in November 1852 fell to the lowest level since 1836, a plunge never equaled again during the nineteenth century. Whigs suffered most from voter apathy, but the election also loosened Democrats' and Free Soilers' grip on the electorate's allegiance. And the weaker voters' partisan loyalties became, the greater grew the opportunities for new parties to steal them away.

Abstention from the polls was not uniform across the nation. Total turnout fell much further and Scott ran far more poorly in the South than in the North. This sectional differential was the election's second most important result. The disgusted response of Florida's truculent Edward Carrington Cabell to the convention's outcome suggest some reasons for it. "We got an antiFreesoil platform, with the candidate of the Freesoilers, nominally on it. I will *not vote for Scott*, though I shall not go for Pierce."[3] Southern Whigs' refusal to support the ticket despite the pro-Compromise platform crippled Scott in Dixie and drove down turnout rates among Democrats, who saw no need to vote once it became clear that Scott's showing, especially in the Deep South, would be pitiful. But the "antiFreesoil platform" Cabell and his co-agitators like Meredith Gentry, Christopher Williams, and Humphrey Marshall had helped force on the party vastly complicated the challenge facing northern Whigs. It guaranteed that Scott would not get Free Soilers' endorsement and forced desperate northern Whigs to seek other ways to arouse support.

Despite the considerable problems Whigs faced, many Whig leaders, especially the party's high command who orchestrated the campaign from Washington, convinced themselves that victory was certain. Although some prescient Whigs had long predicted defeat in 1852, even a few of the previous naysayers converted and remained optimistic until the votes were cast. For the historian blessed (or cursed) with hindsight, explaining that confidence is far more difficult than explaining the outcome itself.

I

Since voters in individual states would decide the presidential election, Whigs depended on state and local leaders to bear the brunt of grass-roots campaigning. Far more than any other presidential election contested by the party, however, in 1852 Whigs tried to coordinate the campaign from Washington. In part, this attempt reflected Winfield Scott's residence in the capital. Preventing Scott from issuing the damaging letters that Clay wrote in 1844 and the all-too-independent Taylor published in 1848 was an even more pressing incentive for the Whigs who had engineered Scott's nomination to surround him with a campaign team in Washington. For the only time in their history, moreover, Whigs commanded the national executive branch during a presidential campaign. With the glaring exception of Daniel Webster, who brooded bitterly about his humiliation at Baltimore, Fillmore, his administration, and the administration's Washington newspaper, John O. Sargent's Washington *Republic*, rallied loyally behind the party's ticket. Not only did cabinet members such as Secretary of War Conrad, Attorney General Crittenden, and Treasury Secretary Corwin relay information between

Washington and their home states of Louisiana, Kentucky, and Ohio, but their cooperation allowed Scott's managers to launch the campaign's most important innovation.

Nominal responsibility for the campaign rested with the national committee. Manned almost exclusively by Scott's original supporters, it raised and allocated funds, recruited and dispatched speakers, and wrote, printed, and distributed campaign literature. Connecticut's Senator Truman Smith once again chaired the operation, with Fitz Henry Warren, the assistant postmaster general, as his vice chairman. The most influential members and committee staff were Congressman Henry D. Moore of Philadelphia, the Maine newspaperman James S. Pike, North Carolina Senator Willie P. Mangum, ex-Congressman John Minor Botts of Richmond, John M. Clayton from nearby Delaware, Senator Ben Wade of Ohio, and Alexander H. Greene of New York, Seward's young secretary and his agent at the Baltimore convention. Within hours of Scott's nomination, the committee arranged for New York publishers to print a million copies of Pike's campaign biography of Scott and hired German printers to translate documents.[4] Campaign strategy, however, was also charted by many of Scott's original backers who remained in Washington until Congress adjourned in early September, such as Seward, John L. Schoolcraft, and Ohio's Lew Campbell. Usually the two groups concurred, but at least once, disagreements led to disarray.

As soon as the Baltimore convention adjourned, Whig leaders in Washington frantically tried to bridge the chasm between anti- and pro-Compromise men. The Washington *Republic* instantly raised the banner of Scott and Graham to signal administration approval. In mid-July, Fillmore himself magnanimously wrote a letter for publication to Philadelphia in which he endorsed Scott as a true Whig who was devoted to the Compromise and deserved all Whigs' support.[5] Scott's managers reciprocated. Comprehending the fear he aroused among southern Whigs and New York's Silver Grays, Seward announced in late June that he would neither seek nor accept a cabinet position should Scott win. Until Congress adjourned, Seward carefully avoided all personal contact with Scott in order "to show that he is not under my dictation."[6]

Given Seward's supposedly malign influence over Taylor as United States senator, these actions failed to mollify suspicious Southerners. Instead, they looked to Scott's official letter of acceptance for fuller evidence of his commitment to finality. "If Scott's avowals shall be satisfactory to run on the compromise, I may give him my vote," wrote Tennessee's previously hostile Whig Governor William B. Campbell on June 26. Yet hard-line northern Scott managers, who hated the platform and were appalled by the note Scott had apparently given Jones to read at the convention, were determined to use that acceptance letter to erase any impression that Scott flatly opposed revision of the fugitive slave law or that he considered commitment to finality a test of party orthodoxy.[7]

Dated June 24, two days after Scott received official notification of his nomination, Scott's reply did not appear in the press until five or six days later when news of Clay's death was announced.[8] Exactly who wrote it is unclear. Scott's biographer asserts that only Scott could have written a statement so transparently devoid of political guile. Yet at the end of June, Wade, an insider in the preconvention Scott club, wrote his wife that two of its members, whom he refused to name, composed it and that they had made as strong a bid for the Free Soil vote "as they dare under the circumstances."[9]

Anything but guileless, Scott's acceptance letter artfully attempted to reunite the party for the forthcoming campaign and to increase its ranks. Unable to reconcile the divergent attitudes toward the platform, Scott (or his ghost writers), in sharp contrast to the promises Botts and Jones had made at the convention to sway southern votes, said nothing directly about slavery, the Compromise, or even the platform; he merely accepted the nomination "with the resolutions annexed." His only other reference to the intraparty gulf was to insist that sectional harmony required him and other Americans to "know no South and no North" and to discountenance "any sedition, disorder, . . . or resistance to the law or the Union . . . in any part of the land." This promise could be interpreted as a pledge to implement the fugitive slave law but also as a vow to crack down on secessionists and filibusterers. As to the all-important veto power—which Southerners wanted used and Northerners wanted renounced in case Congress repealed or revised the fugitive law—Scott straddled by saying it must be "cautiously exercized, and under the strictest restraints and necessities."[10]

A long draft that Horace Greeley sent Pike on May 29 suggests the ideas that influenced, if not exactly who wrote, Scott's letter.[11] Greeley emphatically insisted that Scott reject southern demands for pledges to veto bills that revised or repealed the fugitive law, a rejection implicit in Scott's letter. In addition, Greeley, like other northern Scott managers, stressed that full acceptance of the Compromise must not be made a litmus test, as pro-Compromise Whigs had demanded in the Round Robin of 1851. Scott's letter promised that in order "to cultivate harmony and fraternal sentiments throughout the Whig party" he would appoint or retain in office only qualified Whigs, "without attempting to reduce [the administration's] members, to exact conformity to my views." However tepidly Scott endorsed the platform, in short, he would not require other Whigs to do so. Yet these well-chosen words could also reassure Southerners and northern pro-Compromise men that they too would have a chance for federal jobs. Finally, they signaled that Scott, unlike Zachary Taylor, had no intention of pursuing a No Party or all parties patronage policy.

Other parts of the letter also strongly suggest Greeley's influence on whoever wrote it. Should the convention adopt a pro-Compromise platform, Greeley argued in May and June, Whigs could still bid for Free Soil voters with a plank endorsing homestead legislation. Free soil had always meant more to the third party than slaveless territories; it also meant free government land to encourage rapid settlement of the West. "A Free Land plank," Greeley urged, "would almost act as a chloride to a compromise infection."[12] Since the Whigs' national platform said nothing whatsoever about a homestead bill, Scott's acceptance letter attempted to rectify that omission. Scott could not fully endorse free land; too many northeastern and southeastern Whigs still clung to the vain hope of distributing federal land revenues to the states. The letter recommended instead that Congress change the laws regarding the public domain "so as to secure an early settlement of the same, favorable to actual settlers, but consistent, nevertheless, with a due regard to the equal rights of the whole American people in that vast national inheritance." Along with the studied noncommittalism on finality, this back-handed embrace of cheap land marked the bid to Free Soilers by the letter's authors "as strong as they dare make it under the circumstances."[13]

The second new substantive proposal in the letter reflected the previous decision by Scott's managers to seek Irish Catholic votes and their desire to mollify Germans angered by the platform's endorsement of Fillmore's nonintervention policy that seemed intentionally to insult Kossuth. Whatever Scott's purported appeal to Catholics, Greeley, Seward, and other Scott men were only too well aware of Scott's nativistic letters from the mid-1840s that, during 1852, Democrats dredged up and reprinted to turn immigrants against him. Scott's most notorious—and clumsy—bid for Native American backing, the "Americus" letter of 1844, had demanded that all immigrant men serve two years in the American armed forces after naturalization as a prerequisite to enfranchisement. Now his managers sought to put a favorable spin on that impolitic proposal. The acceptance letter called for admitting to immediate citizenship any immigrant aliens who served in the armed forces during a period of war for only one year and were honorably discharged. In short, military service was now presented as a voluntary way to shorten the naturalization process by four years, not as a mandatory method of prolonging it. This proposal, crowed Raymond's *New York Times*, "refutes the allegations of his political enemies, that he is . . . hostile to the rights and interests of foreigners."[14]

Appearing in the same newspaper editions as Scott's letter, William A. Graham's acceptance of the vice presidential nomination overtly attempted to conciliate Southerners and other pro-Compromise Whigs. He had served for two years in Fillmore's administration, he proudly announced, and the Whig platform fully reflected its policies during that period. Should Scott and Graham win, "so far as I shall be invested with authority, a faithful adherence to these doctrines may be expected."[15]

Additional efforts to sell Scott to southern Whigs began simultaneously with publication of the two acceptance letters and continued nonstop until November. Like so much else about the 1852 Whig campaign, they largely ignored the parties' records and platforms and concentrated instead on reassuring Southerners about Scott's reliability and instigating fear and suspicion of Pierce, who was almost completely unknown to Southerners. Propaganda aimed at southern Whigs was reduced essentially to a simple assertion: our guy is not as bad as their guy.

Ostensibly, Whigs had little room to maneuver. New Hampshire's Democratic party had been fully committed to the Compromise since early 1851; Pierce had personally driven the Free Soiler John Atwood off the Democratic state ticket that year; and Pierce's letter accepting the Democratic nomination was far more forthright in endorsing the Compromise than was Scott's. Pierce, in sum, was the archetypal doughface. Whigs tried to sow doubts about him by reminding Southerners that the notorious Free Soil Senator John P. Hale, who was nominated in August as the Free Soilers' presidential candidate, hailed from New Hampshire and was once a Democrat, just as they had stigmatized Lewis Cass in 1848 by pointing to Martin Van Buren. But Whigs needed more.

They found it when they discovered a skeleton in Pierce's closet. Responding to hecklers during a speech in New Hampshire in January 1852, Pierce incautiously declared that he disliked the fugitive slave law because it was inhumane. Such words were harmless so long as Pierce remained a nonentity outside of New

Hampshire, but when he unexpectedly won the Democratic presidential nomination in June, they became a smoking gun. Before the end of the month Sargent's Washington *Republic*, which had vociferously defended the fugitive law for two years, was daily printing the charge that Pierce opposed and would therefore never enforce the act. Fully aware of the credibility of Fillmore's organ with Southerners, consternated Democrats in Washington screamed for Pierce to rebut this lethal canard.[16]

Southern Whig papers widely reprinted this charge, and later it, along with other assaults on Pierce's character and testimonials to Scott's soundness on everything that mattered to Southerners, was gathered in a series of campaign pamphlets. Compiled by the national committee, these tracts formed the core of Whigs' propaganda campaign in both sections. With titles like "The Contrast," "Pierce and His Allies," and "Franklin Pierce and His Qualifications and Intentions for the Presidency," they reflected Whigs' emphasis on candidates, not programs. Truman Smith not only oversaw the preparation and distribution of these materials, he personally wrote each of them. "I have never exerted myself so much," Smith complained. "I thought I worked as hard as I could in /48, but I worked harder now."[17]

Smith aimed "The Contrast" and "Pierce and His Allies" especially at the South, and he later congratulated himself that they had done the Whig cause much good there. The latter pamphlet stressed Pierce's untrustworthiness on the Compromise by pointing to the Democratic-Free Soil coalition in certain northern states, notably Massachusetts, which, one Masschusetts Whig argued, should "surely" strike "all Southern men as heretical and damnable."[18] In "The Contrast," Smith unfavorably compared Scott's brilliant military career to Pierce's ostensibly cowardly record as a brigadier general in Mexico. Although Pierce had won official commendations from Scott himself for his participation in some very hard fighting, Pierce's experience in Mexico had been luckless indeed. When the horse on which he was mounted to lead his brigade on a charge bucked, Pierce was thrown violently against the pommel of his saddle, fell to the ground, fainted from his painful groin injury, and lay there ignominiously as his brigade marched by and an underling shouted, "Take command of the brigade, General Pierce is a damned coward." At the next encounter, Pierce, this time safely afoot to lead the charge, twisted a knee he had hurt during the previous fall and collapsed to the ground as his troops again marched by and beyond him. Finally, when his brigade participated in the storming of Chapultepec, Pierce again missed the fray, for he lay prostrated behind the lines with diarrhea. Whigs gleefully mocked this ill-starred showing, for Southerners with a fetish for manly honor reviled any hint of cowardice.[19]

Aiming more directly at his southern audience, Smith also gathered in "The Contrast" every testimonial to Scott's nationalism, devotion to the Compromise, and independent character he could find. Most of these came from predictable sources: southern Whig editorials and speeches from southern Whig politicians. But some were unexpected. Mississippi's Union governor and former Democrat Henry S. Foote was quoted as telling a Democratic mass meeting that he personally knew Scott was sound on the Compromise. More surprising, John A. Quitman, Mississippi's secessionist former governor, who had served under Scott in Mexico, provided a ringing endorsement. As a Democrat, Quitman announced, he could not vote for Scott; nonetheless, Scott was the only Whig whom he could ever support for president. Moreover, the charge that Scott would be Seward's puppet was sheer "*stuff!*" No one was more independent or more "true to the South." Thus, Quitman told a Democratic rally, "I have been surprised and astonished that among the Whig party there should be found a single man unwilling to give him a cordial and hearty support."[20]

These, then, constituted the array of Whig appeals that the Whigs' high command in Washington aimed at the South. Southern Whig papers and speakers offered their own variations on them, and they often reminded voters that many of the same Democrats who now embraced Pierce and finality had only recently been promoting secession. But the central question was how well this message played in Dixie. Could the palliatives offered by Whig leaders soothe suspicious southern Whig voters?

II

"The South have been humbugged already by the pledges of Taylor & I trust they will not be simple enough to be humbugged again," a Democrat wrote Pierce from Washington when Scott's acceptance letter first appeared. Most southern Democrats, indeed, reacted with contempt to Scott's letter, and they remained confident that it could not mitigate southern Whigs' deep distrust of him. There was "not the slightest enthusiasm anywhere" for Scott, asserted a Democrat from Raleigh, North Carolina. Whigs were "downcast, dispirited, and distressed," echoed a Mississippian. In late July a Louisianan summed up what Democrats across Dixie saw as southern Whigs' response to Scott: "The Whigs in this state are bolting in all directions—they are cut to pieces." Given Whigs' revulsion toward Scott, Louisiana Democratic leaders advised New Orleans' leading Democratic newspaper editor, Democrats must not reawaken Whigs' party loyalty by traditional partisan assaults, but should instead further undermine Whigs' confidence in their candidate.[21]

Convinced that true Southerners should regard Scott's nomination as insulting evidence that hostile Northerners now controlled the Whig party, southern Democratic papers constantly portrayed the election as a referendum on sectional loyalty. Equally convinced by their own rhetoric that any southern votes for Scott would mark "a degree of degradation which the Southern character has never before reached," Democrats believed that Whig support for Scott was literally inconceivable.[22]

Initially, at least, Southern Democrats' confidence seemed justified. Within a week of Scott's and Graham's letters' publication, nine southern Whig congressmen, led by the six Unionists from Mississippi, Alabama, and Georgia, announced in the Washington *National Intelligencer* that they could not support Scott because he had refused to endorse finality before or after the convention. In July, moreover, Robert Toombs denounced Scott on the House floor as a stalking horse for antislavery men in a speech that Whigs later circulated in the North as one of their own campaign documents. Whig Representative Charles J. Faulkner of Virginia and Tennessee's Williams and Gentry, who had vowed throughout the spring that they would never support Scott unless he committed himself before the convention, also signed the defiant manifesto. Florida's Cabell did not, but as the only Whig congressman from the Deep South who faced a reelection campaign in 1852, he tried to distance himself from Scott by writing Florida's Whig state convention that he could not support him. In addition, North Carolina's renegade Congressman Thomas Clingman completed his four-year march toward the Democrats by openly pledging to support Pierce and King.[23]

Since this opposition was expected, neither it nor Democrats' crowing fazed Scott's managers, who had always written off the Deep South. For over a decade Democrats had dominated Mississippi and, to a lesser extent, Alabama, and once Democrats abandoned their Union coalitions early in 1852, it became clear that Whigs could not prevent Democrats from carrying them any more than they could stop Democratic victories in South Carolina, Arkansas, and Texas.[24] Hopes of carrying Georgia in 1852 had also long since died, but a rout there in November could prove more serious. Georgia had always contributed more to Whig congressional strength than any other Deep South state. If influential Union Whigs like Toombs and Stephens, not content with renouncing Scott, openly defected to the Democratic party and carried their large personal followings with them, Georgia's Whig party might never rebound, despite the efforts of Senator William C. Dawson and John M. Berrien, who resigned his Senate seat in May, to rally the state's Whig politicos and voters behind the Scott ticket. Georgia's Whigs' fate after 1852, in sum, might well be determined by the presidential campaign.[25]

Whigs outside Georgia were therefore heartened when Whig papers in Atlanta, Macon, Savannah, and Columbus ignored Stephens and Toombs and endorsed Scott. More important, although a few Whigs instantly threatened to vote for Pierce, by July Union Whigs loyal to Stephens had joined him in rebuffing pressure from Union Democrats to support Pierce for fear of being absorbed "into all the evils of locofocoism." Instead, they insisted, Georgia's Union party should "reject both the regular nominees & hoist the banner of [a] third candidate." When Georgia's remaining Union Democrats, including Governor Howell Cobb, endorsed a Union electoral ticket pledged to Pierce at the Georgia Constitutional Union party's last state convention in mid-July, therefore, Union Whigs called a new state convention to make an independent nomination. They carefully scheduled it for Macon in August on the day before the pro-Scott Whigs met in state convention there, thereby briefly raising false hopes that the two Whig assemblages might combine behind Scott.[26]

Determined to inflict a humiliating defeat on Scott, averse to a merger with Democrats, and hopeful of "putting an end to these party conventions and irresponsible bodies . . . who now virtually make choice of our chief magistrates," Stephens and his Georgia followers had decided upon the identity of their candidate by early July. As if to prove their spite, or sense of justice, it was the embittered Webster, who was privately telling friends to join him in voting for Pierce. Some Georgians approached Webster directly, and Stephens secured permission to run him from his disappointed Massachusetts loyalists like George R. Curtis, who planned to use the Georgia nomination as an excuse to run a separate Webster ticket there as well. In August, Georgia's Unionist Whigs chose an electoral slate pledged to Webster and their own Charles J. Jenkins for vice president. If Scott ever stood a chance of carrying Georgia, that nomination destroyed it. Stephens, moreover, had clearly burned his bridges to the Whig party. Nonetheless, the Union Whigs' decision to spurn the Democrats encouraged hope that all Whigs might still reunite after the presidential election.[27]

Even more heartening to Whigs, in neighboring Florida, Cabell grudgingly recanted his opposition to Scott.[28] Despite residual anger among longtime residents of Florida at Scott, who had denounced them in an 1836 report as cowards because of their panicked reaction to some Indian raids, Florida's Whig press and the popular incumbent Whig Governor Thomas Brown quickly endorsed the general's nomination. Although Brown would campaign hard for the Whig ticket in the fall, he declined to seek renomination, and the Whig state convention in July chose as his successor George T. Ward, a delegate to the Baltimore convention, who also strongly endorsed Scott. The determination of Florida's Whigs to repudiate Cabell's repudiation of Scott became even clearer when his letter refusing to support Scott was read to that convention. Ward instantly and angrily refused to accept the gubernatorial nomination or run on the same ticket with Cabell unless he retracted it. To preserve the strongest and most harmonious ticket possible, the convention then induced Cabell to write another letter in which he agreed to "acquiesce" in Scott's nomination. Florida's Democratic press jeered that the state Whig party had committed "political suicide" and that "the body will be embalmed and kept over ground till *November*, when it will be laid in the grave." Since voters would not register their opinions until October, however, Whigs elsewhere could hope during the summer that this small, but symbolically important, Whig outpost might be preserved.[29]

Contrary to Democratic jeers, Louisiana Whig leaders, except for newly elected Senator Judah P. Benjamin, also rallied behind the ticket. Even more heartening to the Washington campaign team, most upper South Whigs, who had always formed the backbone of southern Whig support, responded positively to the ticket. In Virginia, which gave Scott eight votes on the final ballot in Baltimore, Congressman James Strother, ex-Senator William Archer, Secretary of the Interior Alexander H. H. Stuart, and ex-Congressman Botts praised the nominee, while the Richmond *Whig*, the state's most influential Whig paper, proclaimed, "Scott's letter is all his *friends* could desire, and a great deal more than his *enemies* can digest." Months before the national convention, Kentucky's longtime Whig state chairman promised Seward that state's support for Scott should he be the nominee, and virtually the entire Whig leadership, from sitting United States senators and incumbent congressmen on down through local politicos and editors in Missouri, Kentucky, Maryland, Delaware, and North Carolina, threw their weight behind the ticket. Particularly noteworthy to Scott's northern managers was the silent acquiescence he received from southern Whig congressmen who had bolted the second Whig caucus in April, like North Carolina's David Outlaw and especially Kentucky's Humphrey Marshall, who even more than Gentry, Williams, and Cabell had brought the party to the brink of sectional disruption.[30]

No state better illustrates the tendency of upper South Whigs, despite a few well-known but atypical dissidents, to rally behind the ticket than Tennessee. After the convention only William G. "Parson" Brownlow's Knoxville *Whig* echoed Gentry and Williams in repudiating Scott, whereas the rest of the Whig press, including the flagship Nashville *Republican Banner*, endorsed the ticket. So did most of the state's Whig leadership. Senator Jones and his lieutenant, Congressman William Cullom, had long since been committed to Scott, and in July other

Whig congressmen, Governor Campbell, and, most important, Senator John Bell, the state's most prominent Whig and Jones' foremost intraparty rival, joined them. Like other Southerners, Bell had favored Fillmore's nomination, and he had privately applauded the heavy-handed efforts by Gentry, Williams, and others to extort a pro-Compromise platform from the Whig convention. Furthermore, Bell had angrily and publicly rejected rumors that he was pro-Scott like Jones. Thus his series of letters to the state's Whigs in July endorsing Scott as someone whose principles were perfectly compatible with Southern Rights had considerable impact.[31]

By the end of July, Gentry and Williams had clearly failed to carry Tennessee Whigs into revolt with them. Whig Governor Campbell and Democratic Congressman Andrew Johnson concurred that "Gentry has most foolishly destroyed himself and is a ruined man among his constituents." Campbell's letters reflect the sea change that occurred among Tennessee's Whigs during the two months following the convention. Although Campbell vowed throughout the spring never to support Scott, on June 26 he expressed a grudging willingness to cast his own vote for him. At that point, however, he refused to campaign personally for the ticket, and he cited as the Whigs' only hope of carrying Tennessee Democratic weaknesses: Pierce was a less distinguished political pygmy than even Polk, and unlike 1844, Democrats had no Texas annexation issue to ride. By late July he reported that Tennessee's Whigs were now zealous for Scott and that he himself could campaign for the ticket "warmly." On August 17 he exulted that "there can be no doubt now but that Scott will run like *wild fire*."[32]

The few August state and congressional elections prolonged Whigs' hopes about the South by indicating that support for Scott was not necessarily fatal. Whereas Whigs won three of five Missouri's House seats in 1850 because of Democratic divisions, in 1852 they retained only two. Nonetheless, this was an outstanding performance in that former Democratic bastion, especially as Whigs lost a seat primarily because Thomas Hart Benton himself ran in the St. Louis district Whigs had carried two years earlier. Nonetheless, Whigs remained a distinct minority among Missouri's voters, winning 43 percent of the total popular vote in the congressional contests and 41 percent in the gubernatorial election, while Whigs' share of seats in the lower legislative house declined from 41 percent to a more normal 31 percent. Scott's nomination, in sum, failed to reduce the previous gains Whigs had made with Missouri's voters, but Pierce was certain to carry it in November.[33]

Nor did North Carolina's August gubernatorial and legislative elections, which Whigs watched closely since Graham was on the national ticket, shake their confidence. Incumbent Democratic Governor David Reid defeated his hapless Whig opponent, John Kerr, with 53 percent of the vote, a landslide by North Carolina standards, while in the legislative races Whigs won a majority of the house for the first time in six years and Democrats increased their margin in the senate. Although almost a tenth of the men who voted Whig for governor in 1850 now abstained, neither Whig nor Democratic leaders in North Carolina attributed these results to either party's presidential candidate. Instead they pointed to Reid's effective exploitation of the free suffrage issue; Kerr's unpopularity among western North Carolina Whigs because he opposed a constitutional convention to reapportion the legislature on the white basis and distribution of the state's public school fund; the intrusion into the state race by the magnetic maverick Clingman, who, from Washington, endorsed Pierce for president and urged his mesmerized constituents to support Reid as well; and, with regard to Democratic losses in the legislature, the selection of incompetent candidates in eastern North Carolina who could not compete with very strong Whig slates. Concerning "the prospect for Whig success in the Presidential election," one Whig reassured Graham in early September, "we have no cause for either despondency or despair." Kerr's defeat was not "evidence of a declension of the Whig cause."[34]

Attributing the North Carolina defeat to local factors, knowledgeable northern Whig leaders also continued to count on North Carolina's electoral votes for Scott. "The aspect of our affairs South is much better than I anticipated they ever would be & our intelligence leads us to believe we shall carry Louisiana, Tennessee, Kentucky, & Maryland," Truman Smith rejoiced in late August to Thurlow Weed, now back from Europe. "We have strong hopes of N. C. notwithstanding the result of the recent election."[35] Exactly what Smith heard from the South is unclear since no collection of his incoming correspondence has ever been found. Yet other southern Whigs besides North Carolinians exuded optimism. In early September, B. H. Sheppard, chairman of Tennessee's Whig state committee, assured Seward that the state was safe for Scott. A week later a Virginian reported that "all the Whigs" believed that Scott's prospects in the Old Dominion were "becoming more bright and favorable every day."[36]

How, one asks, could Whigs and Democrats have read the southern electorate so differently? In part because of Whig attacks, Pierce clearly failed to arouse much enthusiasm among southern Democrats, and Whig observers possibly concentrated on Democratic apathy, just as Democrats counted on Whigs' refusal to turn out for Scott. In addition, the infrequency of southern elections that summer concealed the electorate's mood, causing Whig activists who displayed unity and vigor in nonelectoral arenas to project that enthusiasm onto the silent electorate.

In Louisiana, where Whigs won in 1851 and elected Benjamin to the Senate in early 1852, for example, Whig leaders focused their attention during the spring and summer on a constitutional convention that Whigs had called over the opposition of Democrats and to which Whigs elected a majority of delegates. Those delegates worked cohesively and successfully to achieve Whigs' foremost goal: revision of the 1845 constitution to allow the legislature to charter banks and fund internal improvements for the first time in seven years. Success had followed success, in sum, and Whig leaders may have assumed that this momentum would continue into November, when the referendum on the new constitution would be held simultaneously with the presidential election. Had they examined the workings of the convention more closely, however, they might have been less sanguine. To achieve what Whig delegates wanted on banking and other economic provisions in the new constitution, they made a Faustian bargain with Democrats to change the basis of representation in the legislature in ways that reduced the influence of Whiggish New Orleans and increased the representation of Democratic cotton planters, thereby almost ensuring that Whigs could never control the legislature again. Rather than signaling Whigs' optimism about future political prospects, this was the act of men who, having secured certain specific goals through the partisan political process, were preparing to abandon it.[37]

There is another possible explanation for Whigs' misreading of the South. Although Truman Smith was not the only member of the national committee who counted Louisiana and other slave states as certain for Scott, his optimism is the most puzzling, for Smith was as unsentimental a realist as the Whig party possessed. Prior to the Whig national convention, he himself wrote off all the South but the border states and argued that the election had to be carried in the North. Yet on October 7, less than four weeks from election day, he told a Californian that in addition to seven certain northern states, Scott would carry Delaware, Maryland, North Carolina, Kentucky, Tennessee, and Louisiana. "We expect also Florida & our friends on the other side of the Potomac even talk of carrying Va. & I shall not be astonished if they do." Complaining that he was exhausted since he had to write all the Whig documents himself, Smith significantly added that those pamphlets "have produced a great effect in the South & have contributed to work a great revolution in that section in favor of Scott." One sees here the delusion of authorial pride. Having worked so hard to convince southern Whigs to vote for Scott, he convinced himself that he had done so.[38]

III

Unlike the South, where Scott's chances seemed surprisingly bright, in the North the reaction to Scott initially proved cooler than his managers anticipated. To be sure, northern Whigs who had previously promoted Scott as the party's savior rejoiced that "present appearances indicate a triumphant election," and midwestern Whigs voiced particular confidence.[39] Yet even some of Scott's strongest proponents expressed doubts. To some the platform posed a potentially insuperable hurdle. Ohio's Lew Campbell pronounced it "a dead weight" in his state. In New York, where Greeley ringingly repudiated the platform, upstate Sewardite Whigs were so embarrassed by it that they refused to hold ratification meetings in areas where Silver Grays were numerous, lest they be forced to ratify the platform as well. Seward himself angrily told his wife that if the state Whig convention in September adopted the national platform, he would immediately resign from the Senate. The platform's pro-Compromise planks worried such men, but many also complained that the endorsement of nonintervention that so offended the Germans aroused by Kossuth "gives us no votes in the South & cripples us in the North." With good reason, therefore, northern Whigs ignored, when they did not explicitly renounce, the platform during the remainder of the campaign and instead contrasted their candidate's purported virtues to the weaknesses of his foe.[40]

Yet many anti-Compromise Whigs now questioned Scott's reliability as a standard bearer. They viewed his impetuous letter to Jones at the convention as evidence of his penchant for shooting himself in the foot. "Feathers will be more fussy than ever and I shall be greatly surprised if he does not throw himself into the hands of the enemy immediately," Seward's young secretary wrote the senator's wife. "I am getting a little afraid of Gen. Scott," another New Yorker warned Seward. "I know you made him, & we've got him and it's better Scott than anybody else in the world and all that, but I am a little afraid of his vanity & letter writing."[41]

To most of the Whig high command in Washington and to many northern Whigs, however, Scott remained the party's best, if not its only, card. And they needed that "tower of strength" to overcome the many other problems they faced.

Sudden trepidation among Scott's early supporters was one thing; the distinct lack of enthusiasm among conservatives who had preferred Fillmore or Webster was quite another. Conservative leaders promised support for the ticket, if only because of common antipathy to the Democrats, but often they added that such support was contingent on exactly what Sewardites refused to give—untempered endorsement of the national platform. At the grass-roots level, moreover, both Whigs and Democrats reported unprecedented apathy and indifference, especially among conservatives. "No enthusiasm exists in this region for Scott," a Philadelphia Democrat reported. Neither Native Americans nor the pro-Compromise merchants who had supported Senator James Cooper and Fillmore would vote for him. "Should the state and local conventions create some political action, there may yet be a spirited campaign," the loyal Francis Granger warned Fillmore from western New York, "but at present, there is a want of interest never before witnessed. No enthusiasm for Scott nor anything for Pierce." From southeastern Ohio Whigs portrayed "alarming apathy and indifference," a cry echoed even in distant California.[42]

Conservatives' disaffection and distrust deepened when Sewardite Whigs rejected the platform. Yet the problem of apathy and indifference extended far beyond disgruntled Silver Grays and Websterites. The fundamental reason, as both Whigs and Democrats recognized, was the irrelevance of economic issues that had long fueled partisan conflict. Pennsylvania's Democrats rejoiced that the Tariff issue "has lost much of its potency" for Whigs because the national platform nullified their traditional claim to be "the *exclusive* friends" of protection and because the boom in railroad construction had brought prosperity to ironmakers and anthracite coal miners who had normally gone Whig to secure now unnecessary tariff protection. "I never did see in the whole course of *my* political experience such apathy and want of confidence on the part of the Whigs," reported a gleeful Pennsylvania Democrat. Without the tariff issue, another chortled to Pierce at the end of September, Whigs' "great argument . . . against you here, is the fainting at the Battle in Mexico—it is doing them no good."[43]

Whigs agreed, and some desperately urged leaders in Washington to resurrect traditional economic issues in order to reawaken and reunite the troops. Henry C. Carey, for years the nation's most erudite and famous advocate of tariff protection, complained to John O. Sargent in early July that Whig politicians lacked the courage of their convictions. Citing a temporary credit crunch in Philadelphia as justification, he urged Sargent to get Fillmore immediately to send a special message to Congress demanding a higher tariff. If Congress passed such a bill, "it would be *a Whig measure*, & the Whigs would profit by it." If the Democratic majority defeated such a bill, "the party would go to the country upon the issue— their only one." Then, revealing a spreading disillusionment with Whig leaders, Carey immediately lamented, "It would be a bold measure, & for that reason it will not be adopted. The Whigs have little faith in the truth of their own doctrines, & less in the common sense of the people."[44]

Whigs from New York and Massachusetts also implored Seward to energize Whigs by demanding higher tariffs and rivers and harbors improvements. They are "unquestionably Whig measures," argued Seth Hawley. Seward was sympathetic, but he told the Boston editor William Schouler that he simply had no time to prepare a tariff speech until the next session of Congress, after the election. Attempts to breathe life into the tariff issue thus expired.[45] Nor did anything come of proposals to promote internal improvements, an issue of special importance to midwestern Whigs. A rivers and harbors bill was introduced into Congress in July, but, as one New York Whig congressman warned Weed, since it contained no subsidies for western projects, western Whigs would vote against it, thereby allowing midwestern Democrats to portray Whigs as the enemies of internal improvements. By the end of the session, no legislation had passed for which Whigs could claim credit.[46]

The two parties, however, still differed on foreign policy, an issue of considerable concern to many Whig leaders. Prior to Democrats' national convention, many Whigs feared that they would endorse a policy of spread-eagle expansionism that at best condoned aggressive action to acquire Cuba and at worst sanctioned armed intervention in Europe in a bid for German votes.[47] Democrats did not go that far, but their national platform, by defending the Mexican War as "just and necessary" and celebrating "the results of that war, which have so manifestly justified the policy and conduct of the democratic party," indicated a yen for future aggressive foreign adventures. Belligerent Democratic United States senators reinforced that impression by attacking the administration's response to provocations by the British navy in the Canadian fisheries as proof that Whig foreign policy consisted of cowardly appeasement.[48]

Whig leaders' fear that reckless Democrats might drag the country into war with Spain over Cuba, with Great Britain over the North Atlantic fisheries, or with German states and Austria to appease Kossuth was genuine, and they personally believed that this terrifying prospect necessitated the preservation and triumph of the Whig party. Nonetheless, three things prevented Whigs from using foreign policy to arouse their demonstrably lethargic electorate in 1852. First, no evidence existed that rank-and-file Whig voters appreciated the threat or would have responded to it if they had. Second, emphasizing Whig opposition to foreign adventurism would be counterproductive in some southern states—especially Louisiana—for Whigs there reported that Scott's greatest handicap was not his tepid Compromise stance but his evident intention to crack down on filibusterers. Most important, many alarmed Whigs saw the platform's commitment to neutrality and nonintervention as driving the entire and vastly enlarged German vote into the Democratic column. To emphasize foreign policy, in sum, was to write off Ohio, Indiana, Illinois, Wisconsin, Michigan, and perhaps New York. Like tariff protectionism and rivers and harbors improvements, foreign policy could not be used to combat Whig apathy. Scott's strategists had to look elsewhere.[49]

IV

The first place some looked was to Scott himself. Personal campaigning by major party presidential candidates was simply not done, but Scott's position as commanding general offered opportunities to place him before the public on ostensibly nonpolitical trips that could remind voters of his glorious military achievements. As soon as Scott was nominated, therefore, Whigs in Washington and upstate New York made arrangements for a huge rally in late July at Niagara Falls to celebrate the anniversaries of Scott's triumphs at nearby Chippewa and Lundy's Lane. Veterans of both the War of 1812 and the Mexican War were to be brought in by special trains to cheer their former commander, and Whigs from western New York, northwestern Pennsylvania, and northern Ohio, which had relatively easy access to Buffalo by boat service across Lake Erie, would assemble to kick off the campaign and shake off Whig listlessness.

Although Fillmore's Buffalo allies urged Attorney General Crittenden to keep Scott from personally attending because any hint of electioneering would be fatal, Sewardites considered Scott's presence absolutely essential. He would be carefully scripted by his campaign managers so as to avoid blatantly political remarks and other blunders, but he had to be there to arouse Whig enthusiasm. "Our western friends are very, *very* sanguine that staying away will be awful," warned Simeon Draper from New York City. Lew Campbell proposed that Scott go from Niagara Falls into Ohio to awaken its Whigs as well, and he busily telegraphed Ohio Whig leaders to make local arrangements.[50]

This initial attempt to excite torpid Whigs aborted. George Morey, chairman of the Massachusetts Whig state committee, begged Truman Smith to keep Scott away from the celebration, and, in Campbell's contemptuous words, "Uncle Truman & others *caved.*" Word was sent that Scott had fallen ill and could not attend. The celebration took place, but even Whigs admitted that it fizzled. Democrats jeered about a complete flop. Campbell was livid. "This business will prove disastrous. Don't count on Ohio any longer," he fumed. "We have too many cooks at work, and if the broth is not all spoiled already, it will be, unless we all determine to act in our own latitude—leaving those at a distance from us to operate at the dictates of their own discretion." Why on earth did Morey of Massachusetts interfere in a rally planned for western New York? he angrily asked Boston's Schouler.[51]

Why indeed? What Morey wrote Truman Smith is unknown. Since both the War of 1812 and the Mexican War had been vastly unpopular in Massachusetts, at least among likely Whig voters, he may have feared anything that reminded them of Scott's prominent role in those contests. More than most Whigs, those in Massachusetts, especially Webster and his followers, had also long railed against the dangers of a military man in the White House. Primarily, indeed, Morey probably sought to contain the damage caused by Webster's expected independent presidential candidacy that was bruited by his diehard followers within days of the Whig national convention and actually launched in Massachusetts two weeks after Georgia's Union Whigs nominated him on August 17.[52]

No one in Massachusetts believed that a splinter Webster ticket could prevent Scott from carrying the state, but the revolt betokened sabotage of the Whig state ticket that would once again prevent a Whig majority and allow the hated Democratic/Free Soil Coalition to recapture the legislature, name the new governor, and send a Free Soiler to the Senate.[53] In northern states outside of Massachusetts, an independent Webster ticket could prove far more damaging to Scott's chances. Whigs expected New York's race to be extremely close, and Scott needed every Whig vote to prevail. "The great object now is to elect Scott," argued one Sewardite, "and one flank of the Whig army cannot do it without the aid and cooperation of the other." As early as July 14, however, angry conservatives in New York City approached Webster about running a ticket for him there. Democrats encouraged the effort with funds and press support. And Whigs groaned that if any significant fraction of Silver Grays threw away their vote to Webster, Scott would lose. Even Vermont's Whigs feared that defection of Websterites to a separate ticket might deprive Scott of that bastion.[54]

Separate Webster tickets raised an even more insidious threat. Native American parties and other nativist groups like New York City's Order of United Americans detested Scott's flip-flop on naturalization and his obvious sympathy for Catholics. As Pennsylvania's Native American leader Lewis C. Levin wrote in October, "The feeling among my friends is intense—intense hostility to the Whigs." Because they believed Whigs' charges, aimed at wooing Catholic voters for Scott, that Pierce was an anti-Catholic bigot, most nativists favored Pierce's election to reward his "Anti-Popery." They realized, however, that open support for Pierce might drive immigrants and Catholics toward Scott. To prevent that and to entice nativist Whig voters away from Scott, those nativists, with the full encouragement of Democratic leaders, nominated separate Webster tickets in New York, New Jersey, and Pennsylvania.[55]

If independent Webster tickets threatened to siphon off pro-Compromise Whigs and nativists from Scott, Whig hopes of preventing a separate Free Soil candidacy evaporated when Free Soilers in July called for a national convention at Pittsburgh in August. Democrats like Pennsylvania's Governor Bigler and some Whigs believed that any Free Soil nomination would be "the end of Scott," but Whig strategists like Seward, Weed, and Schuyler Colfax hoped that the damage could be contained if Ohio Senator Salmon P. Chase rather than New Hampshire's Hale was the nominee. Chase was anathema to Whigs and Whig-Free Soilers in Ohio, and his selection might still allow Scott to get most of the antislavery vote. Hale, in contrast, had frequently cooperated with New Hampshire's Whigs and might lure away antislavery Whigs disgusted with their party's platform. Weed urged Schouler, while Colfax implored Seward, to persuade Hale not to accept the nomination if offered. "If you can't influence Hale, I don't know who in our party can," cried Colfax. The selection of Hale and Indiana's George W. Julian as the Free Soil candidates in August and Hale's acceptance of that nomination were therefore severe setbacks.[56]

Virtually all the Free Soil leaders—Chase, Charles Sumner, Henry Wilson, and Hale himself—knew they had no chance of winning the presidency, and they far preferred Scott to Pierce. Hale therefore decided to break precedent and tour Ohio and Michigan in September after Congress adjourned. By blaming Democratic leaders in those states for Texas' annexation and the growth of the Slave Power, he believed, he would turn normal Democrats against Pierce and cut more deeply into the Democratic than the Whig vote. The prospect of this tour at first panicked Ohio Whig leaders, and they begged Seward to come to the state to counteract it. Once Hale reached Ohio, however, Whigs in Washington mistakenly concluded that he hurt Democrats there far more than Whigs. Nonetheless, Hale's candidacy meant that Whigs could count on neither Free Soil nor nativist votes for Scott.[57]

V

By early September Scott's northern campaign was clearly floundering. The Hale and Webster tickets threatened to siphon off votes. Pro-Compromise conservatives remained discontented, and New Yorkers widely predicted sabotage or abstention by Silver Grays.[58] The rank and file exhibited unprecedented indifference. No national issues were available to arouse them, and the first attempts to use Scott himself to do so had been badly bungled.

Whigs responded to their plight in four ways. They stepped up efforts to vilify and denigrate Pierce personally. They mounted an extraordinary campaign to court immigrants and Catholics to reduce the Democratic vote and offset the loss of Free Soilers and nativists. With the crucial help of Secretary of War Conrad and the blessing of Fillmore, they found an excuse to send Scott on a speaking tour of Ohio, Kentucky, Indiana, and New York in order to counter Hale's campaign swing and excite their immobilized troops. Finally, they resorted to state and local candidates and, where possible, to state issues to unify and rouse Whig voters.

From the moment Pierce was nominated, Whigs belittled him as an unknown who patently lacked qualifications for the presidency. The more they learned about Pierce, the easier a target he seemed. His unfortunate military career was widely mocked, and the charge of cowardice was extensively bruited. Whigs reminded antislavery constituencies of his blatant subservience to the South. When Whigs learned that Pierce once had a serious drinking problem, they ignored the evidence that he had since reformed and pilloried him as a hopeless drunkard. Linking Pierce's war record with his purported fondness for liquor, Whigs across the North joked that Pierce was the "Hero of Many a Well Fought Bottle."[59]

Whigs criticized Pierce's drinking through a whispering campaign, not in the party's official documents. Fearful of offending opponents of prohibition, Whig strategists wanted no part of the rum issue. Prohibition's contribution to Whig defeats in New England's spring elections helps explain Whigs' refusal to emphasize Pierce's drinking. More important, criticizing drinking would undermine their effort to align Catholics and immigrants behind Scott. Since Whigs had long been identified with evangelical Protestantism and moral reform and since many conservative, pro-Compromise northern Whigs decidedly disliked immigrants, Catholics, and Seward's sympathy for them, this campaign marked a dramatic and risky shift of tack. Ultimately it, and the concomitant renunciation of prohibitionism, proved to be the Whigs' biggest blunder of 1852. To Scott's strategists, however, it appeared imperative. They expected a hugely expanded foreign-born vote in 1852, and they knew that unless they cut into it, Democratic victory was certain.[60]

The disaffection of Irish Catholics from certain state Democratic parties and their clergy-led opposition to Kossuth had caused Scott's strategists to salivate over the possibilities of a pro-Catholic campaign for six months prior to the Whig convention. Even in Ohio, Indiana, Illinois, Michigan, and Wisconsin, where unnaturalized aliens could often vote and where the enlarged German vote was expected to be crucial, Whigs believed that a pro-Catholic tilt might offset Kossuth's efforts to turn Germans against them. Catholic Germans bitterly disliked the atheistic "Forty-Eighters" who responded most enthusiastically to Kossuth's appeal.[61] The Democrats' nomination of Pierce clinched Whigs' decision to seek Catholic and immigrant voters, for Pierce seemed particularly vulnerable to the charge of anti-Catholic bigotry.

In 1850 New Hampshire, like many other states between 1848 and 1853, revised its state constitution, and Pierce presided over the convention that did so.

At the referendum in 1851, voters rejected the fifteen amendments it had written. At Pierce's urging, three amendments, now unencumbered by those voters had found most objectionable, were resubmitted to the electorate in March 1852. One of them called for a repeal of the old constitution's ban on officeholding by Catholics, and it failed again, primarily because a two-thirds majority was necessary for approval. Although Pierce led the drive to remove the ban, the amendment's defeat could be attributed to New Hampshire's Democrats since they had a heavy majority in the state. As the state's Democratic leader, Pierce was vulnerable to the same charge. Thus, as soon as Pierce was nominated on June 7, Whig papers around the country, under headlines such as "To Your Tents, Catholics!", charged that Pierce had in fact led the drive to defeat the pro-Catholic amendment and was an enemy of the Catholic faith. "Catholicism appears to be the leading question of the day," a stunned Cincinnati Democrat wrote Pierce in late June, and from Whigs and Democrats alike came reports that Catholics would vote for Scott en masse. "I fear there are more probabilities of Scott's success than we democrats are willing to believe," a frantic New York City Democrat wrote a southern friend in mid-July. "I find that he would receive the entire Catholic vote of our Town, if the election took place tomorrow, and they are nearly all *democrats!*"[62]

Whig leaders eagerly fanned this potential revolt. In addition to his acceptance letter proposing a way to shorten the naturalization period, Scott sent the editor of the Catholic Boston *Pilot* another letter that he had written in 1848 "retracting his Native Americanism & ordering 5000 extra copies for distribution among the Irish & German Catholics in Ohio & Pennsylvania." William E. Robinson, an assistant editor of the New York *Tribune*, prepared a pamphlet that rehearsed the charge that Pierce had led New Hampshire's Democrats in retaining the anti-Catholic constitutional provision and listing the many reasons why Catholics could trust Scott. Fearful of the 15,000 new German voters enfranchised by Indiana's revised state constitution, Schuyler Colfax even got Truman Smith to solicit Weed's help in lining up the Catholic hierarchy for Scott. Weed should drop everything and travel to Cincinnati to confer with Bishop John B. Purcell, argued Smith, for Purcell's word was law with midwestern Catholics and his endorsement of Scott could save Indiana, Ohio, and other midwestern states. Whether Weed made this trip is unknown, but at least some Democrats believed that Catholic bishops, if not the humbler priests, solidly supported Scott.[63]

Special appeals to the Irish, such as copies of Seward's speech commiserating with Irish victims of English persecution, and to the Germans were also broadcast. Henry D. Moore of the national committee assumed responsibility for preparing and distributing German-language copies of all Whig documents. In cities without a German-language Whig newspaper, Whigs sought to buy or start them. Wisconsin's Whigs proved especially vigorous in the pursuit of the foreign born. They distributed German-language editions of Scott's biography and other campaign documents, and they also printed 5,000 copies in Norwegian, for they estimated that Wisconsin harbored 6,000 to 8,000 Norwegian voters.[64]

Whigs also used state and local tickets to appeal to immigrants. In Massachusetts, they ran an opponent of prohibition for governor to help pry Boston's Irish away from the Democrats. In Cincinnati, Whigs placed a German on their state legislative ticket specifically to attract German votes, and when they carried the city in October's congressional and legislative elections, Whigs poured into the streets shouting, "Hurrah for the Germans!" "They gave us the victory," reported one Whig. "This victory almost assures the German vote for Scott next month."[65]

Illinois' Whigs also aggressively pursued Catholics. Democratic Senator James Shields urged his Illinois lieutenants to put Gustave Koerner, a Protestant German, on the Democratic state ticket for lieutenant governor to exploit the sudden new political interest of Germans fanned by the Kossuth mania, and they did so. To make sure that they did not offend those Germans angered by Catholic attacks on Kossuth, Democrats also bypassed the front-runner for the gubernatorial nomination because he was Catholic and chose the Protestant Joel A. Matteson instead. This switch infuriated Catholics, and Whigs believed Democrats had committed a major mistake that they could exploit. Lacking a prominent Catholic to run as their own gubernatorial candidate, they nominated for lieutenant governor *"a good & true Whig whose wife & daughters are communicants of the Holy Catholic church, though not one himself."* Illinois Whigs thus regarded the nomination of Scott as perfect for the pro-Catholic campaign they intended to run, and one Chicago Whig leader assured Seward that they would use the anti-Catholic charge against Pierce "to the best advantage."[66]

At least one Illinois Whig congressional candidate also bid strenuously for Catholic support. Elihu B. Washburne worried about both his district's numerous Free Soilers, who could split the anti-Democratic vote, and the large, normally Democratic Irish Catholic vote. To neutralize the first threat, he begged Horace Greeley, whose New York *Tribune* circulated even in northwestern Illinois, to endorse him because Washburne vehemently opposed Whigs' national platform. Now ruing his impetuous response to the platform in June, Greeley refused since such a statement could kill Whig hopes in the South. "You can be elected easily enough, and by help from another quarter," advised Greeley. "The *Catholics* are strong in your district, and they are going to elect Gen. Scott and will take care of his friends." Washburne dealt with the Free Soil threat in another manner. The same printer under contract to prepare the district's Whig tickets also printed its Free Soil tickets. At Whigs' urging, he prepared 3,000 Free Soil tickets with Washburne's name as the Free Soil congressional candidate. "I have not printed the Free Soil candidate's name at all," he chortled to Washburne. But Washburne remained very nervous about the "very large Irish Catholic vote in the district," and to sway it he asked Seward to get him a letter of recommendation from New York's Archbishop John Hughes. Seward replied rather testily that Hughes never wrote such letters, and instead he sent a copy of his speech sympathizing with the Irish. In part because of these efforts, Washburne edged out his Democratic competitor 7,392 to 7,106, while the betrayed Free Soiler polled only 2,200 votes.[67]

The maneuvering for Irish and German voters in Illinois illustrates an obvious but crucial fact. Democrats fought vigorously to retain their Catholic and immigrant supporters and to win over the new voters from those constituencies. They too sought endorsements from Catholic clergymen and the Catholic press such as the Boston *Pilot*. They too chose candidates and campaign speakers because of their appeal to target groups. In Pennsylvania, for example, both George W. Woodward, a Democratic candidate for the state supreme court, and James Campbell, the Irish Catholic whose defeat in 1851 ignited the Catholic rebellion and whom Governor Bigler had appointed state attorney general to pacify the Catholics, crisscrossed the state to hold the Irish in the Democratic column. Democrats too aimed specific appeals at Germans in their own language. They repeatedly reprinted Scott's "Americus" letter, and they broadcast German translations of his acceptance letter in which Scott's suggestion of voluntary military service as a way to abbreviate the naturalization period was transmuted into a mandatory requirement that would lengthen it. Democrats even charged that Scott had ordered the flogging and execution of German volunteers in Mexico out of sheer anti-German prejudice.

This savage counterattack blunted Whigs' offensive in many areas. Whigs' "desperate effort" to "carry off the Irish Catholic vote" would "fail," a prominent Indianapolis Democrat told Pierce. In late July a Brooklyn Democrat echoed, "The Whigs is [sic] sorry they meddled with religion as it has influenced them very much. The respectable Catholics has [sic] all went [sic] to work for you and the Irish in general is [sic] working hard for you." Two months later James Campbell assured Bigler that Philadelphia's "Whigs are playing for the foreign vote here as elsewhere, in which they are going to be most egregiously deceived." By early September, reports that virtually all Irishmen and Germans would go for Pierce far outnumbered predictions of significant Whig inroads into the immigrant vote.[68]

VI

Clearly worried by Democrats' effective counterattack, members of the Whig national committee especially feared the false charges Democrats aimed against Scott in German. Together with continued reports of Whig torpor, especially in Ohio, they turned Whigs to new tactics. The national committee flooded Ohio with thousands of documents, speakers, and money in September. Truman Smith personally wrote at least 200 letters to Whig politicos there urging them to take to the stump. More important, Whigs decided to put Scott on the road to stimulate Whigs and reassure the Irish and Germans.[69]

The excuse for this transparent political junket, Whigs' biggest tactical innovation of the campaign, came from an army appropriations act passed on August 31. It authorized Fillmore to send a group of army officers to examine a site at Blue Lick Springs, Kentucky, for the possible construction of a home for aging army veterans. Secretary of War Conrad ordered Scott to head this team, and rather than proceeding directly to Kentucky, Scott's managers routed him through areas where the immigrant vote was crucial—through Pittsburgh to Cleveland, then down to Columbus, and from there south into Kentucky, across Kentucky to Louisville, then up into Indiana and back to Cincinnati. From there Scott moved north to Sandusky on Lake Erie, by boat to Buffalo, across northern New York to Albany, and then down to New York City. Scott left Washington on September 18; that he was in Ohio at the same time as Hale was hardly coincidental.[70]

Scott did little more in Pittsburgh than show himself to crowds and praise army veterans, but during a downpour in Cleveland he made his first heavy-handed bid for the immigrant vote. "Fellow Citizens of Cleveland!—and when I say *fellow citizens*, I mean all American citizens, both native and adopted citizens," he began. When a member of the drenched audience shouted a response to his remarks, Scott replied as if on cue: "I love to hear the Irish brogue. I have heard it before on many battlefields, and I wish to hear it many times more!" In Columbus, Scott held a carefully arranged interview with some Germans in front of reporters. When the Germans repeated the Democratic charge about his mal-treatment of their countrymen in Mexico, Scott thundered that it was "a false and groundless lie!" In his speech there he again waxed lyrical about "the rich [Irish] brogue" and "the gallant men of Erin who in such great numbers have followed me to victory." Whig newspaper accounts, meanwhile, stressed his easy interaction with the people, his decided lack of "Fuss and Feathers," and his great impact on Whig voters.

Members of the national committee in Washington were overjoyed by the apparent success of Scott's junket. "Since the General's trip to Ohio the skys [sic] seem to smile more brightly there," wrote one in late September. Henry Moore, head of the German subcommittee, declared that Scott's remarks in Columbus had saved the German vote. A Pittsburgh Whig who campaigned in both New York and Ohio after Scott had been there pronounced both states as well as Pennsylvania safe for Scott. Even the hardheaded Weed wrote Seward on Sep-tember 25 that because of Scott's speeches "we shall most likely carry this State [New York], and there is a possibility of General Scott's election."[71]

Not all Whigs applauded Scott's campaign swing, however. "For God's sake, Seward, keep Scott at home. One more Cleveland speech and 'we are ruined,' " sputtered a furious Boston Whig. " 'Oh, that rich brogue! I love to hear it' Just write him some speeches and forward as soon as possible—don't trust him a single minute *alone*—if you do the game is up." Scott's speeches and Whigs' aggressive courtship of Catholics and immigrants in fact thoroughly alienated a crucial bloc in the party's constituency—native-born Protestants who despised Catholics and foreigners. From the start, Democrats, especially in Pennsylvania, predicted that the Whigs' blatantly crude courtship of Catholics would backfire because it was so offensive to Presbyterians, Methodists, and the Protestant Scots-Irish who hated their Catholic countrymen. "Hundreds of protestant Whigs here, could by no possibility be induced to vote for Scott if they believed he was tinctured with Catholicism," wrote one in late July. "Many honest Protestants among the Whigs are disgusted at the course Scott has taken to secure the Catholic vote & will vote against him," echoed another three months later. Perspicacious Democrats were not alone; some Whigs also recognized that alienating Protestants by wooing Catholics was a disastrous, and perhaps irredeemable, mistake.[72]

VII

However severe the revolt of angry Protestant Whigs might be, many Whigs appeared oblivious to the threat. "Pennsylvania is all right," a Philadelphian re-ported on September 20. Scott would win because "the party never was better organized than it is now" and because "the full Whig vote will be out & accom-panied by many that were never given for a Whig candidate before." A Pitts-burgher echoed that confident prediction two weeks later. Pennsylvania's Whigs thus joined those in Massachusetts, Seward, Weed, and other Whigs in New York, some Ohioans after Scott's tour, and the Washington high command in forecast-ing victory.[73] Aside from contempt for Pierce as a political pygmy, the expected inroads into the immigrant vote, and optimistic appraisals of Scott's tour, Whigs' confidence derived from their purported advantages in several key state races to be decided simultaneously with or shortly before the presidential contest.

In 1844, Democrats had helped salvage enough northern states to elect Polk by running exceptionally strong state tickets, and Whigs hoped to turn the tables in 1852. In addition to Illinois, New York and Michigan held gubernatorial and congressional elections on the same day as the presidential contest, while Wisconsin and Delaware had congressional elections scheduled.[74] Iowa, Pennsylvania, and New Jersey would elect congressmen in October, and Indiana had a gubernatorial contest as well. Maine and Vermont elected both congressmen and governors in September.

Though Whigs always considered Vermont safe for Scott, the dimensions of their September triumph caused confidence to surge among Whig leaders elsewhere. Whigs swept all three congressional races, more than doubling their foe's vote in two districts, carried the three-way gubernatorial contest with a plurality, and elected Erastus Fairbanks governor with their dominant majority in the legislature. Vermont, in sum, remained solidly Whig; the national platform had not mobilized antislavery men against them.

In Maine, Whig hopes rested less on the strength of gubernatorial candidate William G. Crosby, who had won only 40 percent of the vote in 1850, than on Democrats' rancorous divisions over prohibition, which resulted in rival Democratic gubernatorial tickets. Thus, even though Crosby's own proportion of the vote declined to 31 percent in 1852, Whigs both in and outside Maine took heart when incumbent pro-Maine Law Democratic Governor John Hubbard's total sank to 44 percent, the worst showing by a regular Democratic candidate since the formation of the Whig party.[75] Not only did Crosby and the renegade wet Democratic candidate Anson Chandler between them have a majority of the vote, but Whigs could hope that Democrats' acrimonious division would reduce Pierce's vote in November. In addition, Hubbard's failure to win a majority threw the gubernatorial election into the state legislature, and because of Democratic divisions, Whigs dramatically increased their share of seats in the house from 34 to 46 percent and in the senate from 19 to 39 percent. If Whigs could strike a bargain with one of the Democratic factions, they might yet elect Crosby governor. Most important, Whig candidates did extraordinarily well in Maine's congressional elections. They carried three of six districts, an event reminiscent of 1840, the only year a Whig presidential candidate had carried Maine.[76]

No state figured more heavily in Whigs' calculations of assembling an electoral vote majority than New York, and surprisingly, Whigs exuded more confidence about it than about any other northern states except Vermont and Massachusetts.[77] Aside from Democratic predictions that Pierce was certain to carry New York, Whig complacency about it is puzzling because Democrats seemingly possessed so many advantages while Whigs confronted so many problems there. Democrats, for example, appeared likely to obtain a huge new foreign-born vote from the burgeoning immigrant populations of New York City, Brooklyn, Buffalo, and Albany and from the construction crews working to complete the New York Central Railroad. Given Greeley's assurance to Elihu Washburne that Catholics were going to put Scott in the White House, Whigs may have considered Catholic support certain, especially since they counted on Seward's reputation as a champion of immigrants and Catholics to neutralize the immigrant threat.[78] Nonetheless, New York Whigs' sangfroid in the face of it is stunning given the anxiety voiced by Whigs elsewhere.

More striking than Whigs' apparent complacency about the foreign vote was their equanimity over the divisive Compromise issue. Recent experience indicated that divisions between Hunker and Barnburner Democrats provided their best hope of carrying New York. The Barnburner bolters of 1848 had returned to the Democratic fold by 1852, however, and Democrats of all kinds embraced Pierce's nomination and the Democrats' pro-Compromise platform with enthusiasm. In contrast to Democratic harmony, Sewardite and Silver Gray Whigs remained deeply divided over their own national platform. They often refused to hold ratification meetings together, a rupture over the platform at the state convention in September appeared inevitable, and predictions of Silver Gray sabotage of Scott in November were rampant. Even the sanguine Greeley admitted, "Our State is certain unless our Silver Grays behave worse than Judas Iscariot and Benedict Arnold ever knew how to." Given Democratic unity and Whig division over the Compromise, how could Whigs be so serenely confident about New York?[79]

The answer is that New York's Whigs expected their congressional candidates and state ticket to reunify their party, while Democrats' divisions over canal expansion would neutralize their agreement on the national platform, depress Democratic turnout in November, and thereby help elect Scott. Just as Massachusetts Whigs bid for conservatives by giving their congressional nomination in the Fourth District to the Websterite Samuel Walley after he grudgingly agreed to endorse Scott, Sewardites allowed Fillmorites to have congressional nominations in Buffalo, Rochester, and New York City in the belief that Silver Gray congressional candidates had a stake in maximizing Whig turnout to achieve their own elections, thereby helping Scott in the process.[80]

However pragmatic the dispensation of Whig congressional nominations was, for many months achieving unity on a state ticket and especially on a state platform appeared far more problematic. In 1850 feuding Whigs had combined uneasily behind Washington Hunt, who had won by the narrowest of margins. Hunt's appointments and annual message in 1851, however, angered conservatives, and then, in his January 1852 message, he infuriated antislavery Whigs by condemning abolitionists and explicitly renouncing his earlier demands for revision of the Fugitive Slave Act. To boot, he then announced that he would not seek renomination. Seward's most fervent antislavery followers therefore demanded that the 1852 gubernatorial nomination go to a flat-out anti-Compromise man. Appreciating the need to harmonize the party, Seward instead promoted the conservative New York City merchant Moses Grinnell for the post. But Grinnell's friend, and Seward's other closest lieutenant in New York City, the merchant-auctioneer Simeon Draper, was also interested in the nomination. So was the Manhattan lawyer Daniel Ullmann, who was anathema to Sewardites but far more palatable to Silver Grays, who demanded "a true[r] friend of Mr. Fillmore for Governor" than either Grinnell or Draper.[81]

More than continuing divisions over the Compromise, however, blocked the nomination of anyone from New York City. As early as March, Seward was warned that "prohibition or not, Maine law or not, will be the issues tried by the people." Seward and Weed desperately wanted to avoid the divisive prohibition issue, for the Whig coalition possessed men who passionately supported opposite sides of it. Since both Grinnell and Draper dealt in liquors and wines, both offended temperance men. Ullmann too was distrusted by prohibitionists, if only because his views on the Maine Law were unknown and because he resided in a city that upstate dries considered Sodom and Gomorrah.[82] This dilemma laid the ground for Washington Hunt's resurrection from his self-consigned political grave, and by mid-August Hunt was the favorite for the nomination.[83]

Hunt was, in fact, the most available of all the potential Whig gubernatorial candidates. He had offended neither dries nor wets. He remained in the middle on the slavery issue when neither Sewardites nor Silver Grays could accept an outright member of the opposing faction. Indeed, to Seward and Weed, who clearly wanted to conciliate Silver Grays in some fashion, he offered hope of finessing a disruptive battle over the state platform. To Silver Grays they could emphasize Hunt's January message and the fury it evoked from antislavery Whigs to prove that they were willing to acquiesce in the Compromise even if the state platform said nothing about it. To their own supporters they could stress their success in nominating Scott and defeating Fillmore, the necessity of mobilizing a full Whig vote, and the undesirable alternatives among Silver Grays like Ullmann if Hunt was not nominated. Most important, Hunt provided the best chance to divert the state election, and with it the presidential election, away from the national issue that divided them and united Democrats to a state issue that united them and bitterly divided their foes. As George Bancroft wrote Franklin Pierce a month after his nomination, "The issue [outcome] here will depend on the Canal issue."[84]

Although the scramble by the Whig rump on the canal board to distribute the remaining revenue certificates and repair contracts in December 1851 discredited New York's Whigs, by the close of the legislative session in the spring of 1852 Whigs believed they held a considerable advantage on the canal expansion question. Democrats on the state's highest court ruled the Nine Million Loan unconstitutional, and the new canal board, headed by Democratic Comptroller George Newell, refused to honor either the revenue certificates or the repair contracts. In the legislature, meanwhile, Democratic majorities readopted the stop-and-tax policy, and by the time the legislature adjourned, no new bonds had been issued or the taxes to pay them passed. Thus Whigs believed that they could pose once again as the state's only champions of immediate expansion, especially after a feared special summer session of the legislature, which might have issued new bonds complying with constitutional requirements and thereby relieved Democrats of the anticanal stigma, never met. Thus Whigs behind Hunt, a fervent proponent of immediate expansion, could pillory Democrats for opposing progress. As Hunt himself wrote, Whigs "in the canal counties" most urgently pressed his renomination. Or, as a Buffalo Silver Gray bluntly put the matter, "The Canal Contractors are determined to nominate Hunt or some other man whom they think they can control."[85]

If the canal issue could rally Silver Gray contractors to the ticket in November, no matter what the state platform said about the Compromise, it could also divide Democrats. By doing nothing about canals in 1852 other than refusing to pay Whig contractors, Democrats preserved their tenuous alliance between Hunkers who wanted to push expansion under Democratic auspices and Barnburners who remained hostile to it. Picking a Democratic state ticket for the fall election, however, could blow the party apart, especially since proexpansion Hunkers hated Horatio Seymour, Democrats' most likely nominee.[86] Democrats tried to bridge this chasm at their state convention. To Barnburners' dismay, their platform entirely ignored the court's decision against the Nine Million Loan, Newell's refusal to pay contractors, and what, if anything, the future policy of Democrats on the canal question might be. Seymour got the gubernatorial nomination, but to balance him, Democrats picked a well-known proponent of expansion for canal commissioner. Signs of mutiny at this straddle appeared immediately. If the Democrats lost, forecast one, "it will be owing" to "the unfortunate position of the canal question," while another warned Pierce that Whigs had a strong state ticket and a much more popular position on canal expansion than the Democrats.[87]

Although Marcy predicted that a Whig rupture over the Compromise would offset Democratic divisions over canal policy, the Whig state convention in late September was the most harmonious in four years. Hunt was renominated for governor by acclamation. The rest of the ticket, apparently constructed at Weed's direction, included men with no known stand on the Compromise whom Silver Grays could not possibly find offensive.[88] The platform, which, according to Raymond, expressed in "unmistakable terms" the measures to which Whigs were pledged and put "a clearer and more exact construction" on some planks of the Baltimore platform, also received unanimous support. The controversial Compromise plank of the national platform received no such clarification; instead, it was fudged. Since Whigs were a national party, the state platform maintained, "an honest acquiescence in the decision and action of the late National Convention of the Whig party upon all subjects legitimately before them, is the duty of every Whig."

This purposely vague plank was then balanced by one that lavishly praised "the President and his Cabinet," especially for "maintaining the honor of the nation untarnished abroad" and "promptly answering every attempt to embroil us in a foreign war." Lest this praise for Webster's Hülsemann letter, Fillmore's rebuff of Kossuth, the crackdown on southern filibusterers, and the administration's stand on the Canadian fisheries compound the alienation of Germans angered by the nonintervention plank of the national platform, a separate resolution denounced violations of the laws of nations "for the furtherance of the interests of despotism"—that is, Russia's intervention against Hungary—and pledged "generous and active sympathy with, and moral support to, all oppressed nations and races struggling to assert their liberties." Other emendations of the national platform called for tariffs with specific duties, a land policy that encouraged both rapid settlement *and* distribution of land revenues to the states, and subsidies for rivers and harbors improvements "as fast as such appropriations can be effectively and economically expended."[89]

The heart of the platform, however, was the plank on the canal issue. The canal system, Whigs thundered, must be vigorously expanded and completed "at the earliest possible day without imposing taxes on those sections least interested in these noble works." The canals would "certainly and promptly" pay for themselves "if speedily completed." Rejection of Democratic obstructionism could not have been clearer.

Although Democratic campaigners tried to defuse the canal issue by promising enlargement under a new constitutional bond issue with the necessary tax support, Whigs remained confident that they held the edge because they were certain that Democratic divisions would defeat not just Seymour but Pierce in November. When Weed told Seward that New York was safe for Scott on September 25, he exulted, "The feud between Barnburners and Hunkers rages bitterly. This will weaken them greatly." Three weeks later, another Whig from western New York added that only hunger for federal spoils was still holding the Democrats together. "The Canal question is bound to be their death in this state certainly."[90]

VIII

"We are getting good tidings from all points," Fitz Henry Warren informed Seward from national committee headquarters on September 28. "Unless we are greatly misled by the statements of our friends the election of Genl. Scott is quite certain." Nine days later Truman Smith predicted that Scott would carry eight slave states, along with Vermont, Massachusetts, Rhode Island, Connecticut, New York, New Jersey, and Pennsylvania in the North, and he also had great hopes for Ohio, Indiana, Illinois, Michigan, and Wisconsin. Two days after that, a Pittsburgh Whig pronounced Ohio, New York, and Pennsylvania safe.[91]

"Scott has not moved the masses as was expected," a Pennsylvania Democrat more accurately concluded, "and the campaign has not been judiciously conducted by our Whig adversaries." Despite numerous Whigs' confident predictions, indeed, others continued to worry about the intractable indifference among their rank and file. "In Illinois there is no political excitement at all," a Whig complained in mid-October. "I would like to see General Scott elected President," young Rutherford B. Hayes wrote in his diary on September 24. "But there is so little interest felt by the great body of thinking men that I shall not be surprised at his defeat." "Genl. Apathy is the strongest candidate out here," reported another Cincinnati Whig, while a Baltimore newspaper announced, "Let either [party] win that may; we have nothing at stake."[92]

State and congressional elections during the second week of October shattered most Whigs' hopes. Arkansas went predictably Democratic, but under the new apportionment Democrats now won two House seats, not one, as well as the governorship and complete control of the legislature. In Iowa, surprisingly, Whigs elected one of two congressmen. That gain was primarily attributable to discontent with the defeated Democrat over a local railroad question, however, and Democrats still maintained a narrow statewide majority in Iowa. No one believed Scott could carry either state.[93]

Results from states Whigs expected Scott to win were more significant. In Florida, George Ward lost the gubernatorial election by 292 votes out of almost 9,000 cast; Cabell succumbed even more narrowly, 4,590 to 4,568. Although the Whig vote was comparable to the totals in 1848 and 1850, over half of the men who supported Thomas Brown for governor in 1848 refused to vote at all in 1852, and a tenth of Brown's voters defected to the Democratic column. Even substantial gains from previous Democrats and nonvoters could not make up for that hemorrhaging. Cabell actually won slightly more votes in 1852 than in 1850; nonetheless, almost a tenth of his previous supporters voted for his opponent, and an equal proportion abstained. Discontented Whig voters' rebellion was felt most heavily in the state legislative elections. The Whigs, who trailed the Democrats by only one vote in each house after 1850, were reduced to one-third of the seats in both. Florida's small but doughty Whig party had been gutted.[94]

Suspicion of Scott clearly contributed to Whig defections in October, and, coupled with discouragement over that month's heartbreaking losses, it produced a rout in November. Total turnout declined by 21 percent since October, but Whigs suffered most from the electorate's disaffection. Scott retained only two-thirds of Ward's support, and Pierce thumped him 4,318 to 2,875. By another measure, only slightly more than a third of the Floridians who voted for Zachary Taylor in 1848 stood by Scott. Over a fifth switched to the Democrats, and almost half abstained.[95]

Although Maryland's Whig Senator James A. Pearce warned in the spring of 1852 that the state's new constitution "must place the Whig party in a minority for years to come," Whigs escaped that ignominy in October since legislative and congressional elections were postponed until the following year. Local elections took place, however, and Baltimore's mayoral contest should have alarmed the Whigs' high command. The Whig candidate lost because a Baptist minister circulated a letter warning that if he won, "the city & the state would be given up to the Pope." If Protestants refused to vote for a Whig mayoral candidate suspected of having pro-Catholic sympathies, Whigs should have wondered, why would they vote for Winfield Scott?[96]

The remaining northern elections pointed to disaster in November. Indiana's Whigs had said that they would have to hold Democrat Joe Wright's majority below 3,000 for Scott to have a chance there. Wright instead romped through by 19,000 votes, and Democrats won two-thirds majorities in both houses of the legislature. New congressional elections were also required since Indiana had gained a new seat under reapportionment. Although Whig candidates in the aggregate ran slightly better than their martyred gubernatorial candidate, they won only one of the eleven seats compared to two of ten the previous year. "Every Irish Catholic I found or heard of, stands faithfully by us," one Democrat crowed, and the new immigrant vote so feared by Whigs appears to have gone by over a three-to-one margin against them. Scott's prospects in Indiana were now hopeless.[97]

On the day before the congressional elections in neighboring Ohio, the state's most important Whig editor exuded optimism. "The State is just as thoroughly stirred up as it can be," he reported to Thomas Ewing. "If the signs do not prove to be mere 'surface indications,' we shall do extremely well." Surface indications they indeed were. Whereas Whigs had won ten of Ohio's twenty-one House seats in 1850, in 1852 they captured only seven of twenty-three. Lew Campbell won reelection and Whigs carried the Cincinnati district, but Free Soilers, whom Whigs hoped would hurt Democrats rather than themselves, carried two districts in the Reserve and deprived Whigs of majorities in at least five other districts, allowing Democrats to win with pluralities. In the only statewide race, Whigs almost halved the Democratic margin in 1851, but they still garnered only 47.4 percent of the total. Reports of apathy may have been exaggerated, for, as in Indiana, three-fourths of the eligible electorate voted in October. Consequently, Whigs could not expect a surge of new voters in November to overcome their shortfall. Despite bright spots like Dayton and Cincinnati, information from elsewhere in the state indicated Scott's defeat.[98]

Once reliably Whig, New Jersey continued its slide into the Democratic column. As in 1850, Whigs won only one of five congressional seats, and their sole victor edged out his opponent by fewer than 200 votes out of over 15,000 cast. Turnout was slightly higher than it had been two years earlier, but the Whigs' share of the vote, 46.3 percent, remained exactly what it had been. Nor did the state legislative races provide solace. Whigs' share of house seats rose only from 25 to 35 percent, the same proportion they held in the senate. In four short years, New Jersey's Whigs had become uncompetitive.[99]

Pennsylvania completed the rout. In 1850, Whigs had carried nine of its twenty-four House seats, and in 1851 Governor William F. Johnston went down to defeat by only 12,000 votes. In 1852, Whigs elected nine of twenty-five congressmen and trailed Democrats in the statewide race for canal commissioner by 20,000 votes. Third parties severely damaged Whigs. A Free Soil congressional candidate who got 9 percent of the vote allowed a Democrat to win with a plurality of 29 votes. In the Philadelphia area three Native American candidates, who together amassed 7,224 votes, allowed Democrats to carry two districts with pluralities of less than 47 percent. Since both nativists and Free Soilers seemed certain not to vote for Scott, even the still-hoped-for Catholic surge toward him in November might not suffice. Statewide turnout had plunged since 1851, and the total Whig vote trailed Johnston's by almost 26,000. Nativists and Free Soilers together accounted for less than half of that deficit. Whigs' widely reported apathy about an issueless race and disgust with their party's pro-Catholic campaign undoubtedly caused the bulk of it. If Catholic immigrants did vote Whig in October, they dramatically failed to offset the defection of men who hated them or who saw no reason to vote at all. As one Philadelphia Democrat assured Governor Bigler after seeing the returns, "We may consider this state as safe for Pierce."[100]

IX

"Notwithstanding the *indigo* twist of Pennsylvania returns, I have full faith in the election of Genl. Scott," Schouler wrote Seward on October 16. "We are by no means discouraged," a Cincinnati Whig echoed to William Pitt Fessenden. "We honestly expect to carry Ohio, & we have good hope of Pennsylvania." Kentucky, Tennessee, and Louisiana, he added, were all "certain." Pennsylvania's unbowed if delusionary Whigs, Lewis Levin scoffed three days before the presidential election, were "making the most stupendous efforts" to secure both the nativist and the Irish Catholic vote for Scott. But others knew that October's elections had broken the party's back. "I don't know how it is but my presentiments all favor our being licked and no cyphering & no argufying can make them any better," New York's Charles A. Dana wrote his fellow newspaperman Pike. The brother of Pennsylvania's ex-governor put it best when he wrote retrospectively in December that "the election last year and the first election this year had entirely prostrated the Whigs." Aptly summarizing the frustration of Whig campaigners unable to mobilize apathetic voters who saw little at stake in a personality contest, he added, "To make a fight in November was something like pissing against the wind, when blowing about sixty miles to the hour."[101]

On November 2 Whigs suffered the most stunning defeat in the party's history. Scott carried only Vermont, Massachusetts, Kentucky, and Tennessee for a total of 42 electoral votes; Pierce won 254 electoral votes from the remaining twenty-seven states. Whig gubernatorial candidates on the same ticket with Scott were mowed down in Illinois, Michigan, and New York, where Hunt lost to Seymour by 23,000 votes despite running 7,000 ahead of Scott. Congressional hopefuls fared almost as badly. Whigs lost Delaware's only seat, both of California's, all three in Wisconsin, and all four in Michigan. In New York, where Whigs had won thirty-two of thirty-four House seats in 1848 and seventeen of thirty-four in 1850, they were reduced to eleven of thirty-three; in addition, their share of seats in the state assembly plummeted from 51 to 33 percent, while the senate, because of holdovers, remained evenly divided. Finally, in Louisiana, where the new constitution won overwhelming ratification, Whigs lost the governorship and both legislative houses in the new elections mandated for December.

Only Illinois and Massachusetts offered a ray of hope. Illinois Whigs garnered less than 42 percent of the statewide vote, but they won four of nine congressional districts, their best showing in the party's history, largely because separate Free Soil candidates allowed them to carry three districts with pluralities. Whigs won five of eleven House races in Massachusetts with outright majorities in November and four more after runoff elections. More important, Whigs finally broke the Democratic/Free Soil Coalition's control of the legislature by gaining a one-seat margin in the senate and a ten-seat house majority over Hunker Democrats and the Coalition combined. Although John Clifford won only a 45 percent plurality, Whig control of the legislature ensured his election, as well as that of a Whig to the Senate.[102]

Even Illinois and Massachusetts, however, could not disguise how disastrous 1852 was for the Whig party. Whigs won only three of twelve gubernatorial elections contested that year. After the legislatures in Maine and Massachusetts resolved undecided elections in early 1853, they controlled governorships in only five of thirty-one states: Wisconsin, where the party was clearly in jeopardy; Maine, where it remained a decided minority and utterly depended upon Democratic divisions; Tennessee, where the popular William B. Campbell itched to retire and enter private business; Vermont; and Massachusetts. Everywhere else, now including all-important New York, along with Pennsylvania and Ohio, Democrats reigned. Whigs' standing in Congress was equally perilous. In 1848, Whigs had won 57 percent of the House seats contested. In 1850, that proportion slumped to 42.2 percent, and in 1852 it plummeted to 29.1 percent. Democratic command of so many state legislatures also threatened Whig strength in the Senate, and between the Thirty-Second and Thirty-Third Congresses, Whigs slipped from twenty-four (39 percent) to twenty-one (33.7 percent) seats.

Democrats gleefully hooted that the Whig party had "suddenly departed this life, on the 2nd inst." and mockingly asked, "Who ever dreamed that Whiggery would squat & shrivel—& collapse and die of overfeeding on its own aliment—humbuggery?"[103] Stunned Whigs meanwhile searched for language adequate to describe "the disastrous result—the complete Waterloo overthrow of the entire

Whig forces." "Waterloo" was in fact a favorite metaphor, and the finality of that legendary defeat spoke volumes. "The Whig party have not only been defeated, but, as a national party annihilated in the late contest," an Ohioan groaned. "What a tremendous general wreck it is," declared an Illinois Whig. "Was there ever such a deluge since Noah's time?" Henry Raymond asked Seward. "I can see no resurrection of the Whig party *as such.*" Seward himself was more restrained, but he too initially believed the party might be finished. "Well!" he despaired to Weed, "the play is played out for this time and played out practically for us perhaps forever." "God help the Whig party," chorused an Alabamian. "I fear it is a mere abstract idea."[104]

Others expressed resignation at the result. It confirmed what he and Fillmore had long believed, Nathan Hall wrote the president: no Whig could win in 1852. "I see that Greeley speaks of disbanding the party, & Weed seems astounded," the defeated William Kent serenely wrote Seward. "After all, was it surprising? We call this election a catastrophe, but was it more than the natural conclusion of a long descending series? Have we carried an election anywhere in the last two years?" The election merely confirmed, wrote another of Seward's correspondents, that the Whigs were "a minority party & can never be otherwise except upon a division of the Democratic party," a view echoed by Fillmorite Whigs. Many Silver Grays, indeed, consoled themselves that the election repudiated Seward's leadership and vindicated Fillmore's. "We are whipped—some say terribly," gloated one. "I say, the more the better. May the lesson not be lost upon our party."[105]

The rout induced a kind of gallows humor in some Whigs. "The number who supported the *late* Winfield Scott is so small that there is no danger of being overlooked in the crowd," Hayes quipped from Cincinnati. "Our Waterloo is so huge that we are not kept several days dangling in suspense between the heaven of success and the pit of despond, but are compelled to make one big plunge." "We are beaten so preposterously," he added, "that we can't lay our defeat to any neglect or blunder on the part of any of Scott's friends" since "no prudence or sagacity, no industry or expense, could have averted the result."[106] Bitterly disappointed, most Whigs, however, demanded to know what had happened, who was to blame for the debacle, and what future, if any, the Whig party had.

"How unavailing have been all our efforts! how overwhelming and disastrous our defeat!! how sad and unexpected our disappointment!!!!" moaned Virginia's John Minor Botts. What, he asked, could explain such a defeat? The primary cause, he answered, was southern Whigs' "senseless and insane apprehension of Sewardism and its influence upon Gen. Scott." Others located the source of the defeat in the North. "The Whig party was practically defeated for the next presidential term when Clay & Webster deserted Genl Taylor & the North and took prominent seats in the proslavery omnibus," complained Schouler. Since 1850, "we have wilted as a party like leaves of the maple in the forest." The splenetic Lew Campbell pointed to "that cursed platform" imposed on Scott at the Whig convention. "It drove from us the Anti-Slavery Whigs & free Soilers, whilst Webster & Fillmore drove their stiletto into us from the rear." "The Slave power obtained its platform" at Baltimore, echoed Massachusetts' John Davis, and thus forced Scott to stand "on the same ground as Pierce with the disadvantage of an apparent abandonment by the Whigs of their former professions."[107]

Yet in the same letter Davis offered other explanations. Scott's supposed "personal popularity" was illusory. "Foreigners were misled & deceived by an issue artfully raised about Nativism & Naturalization and Scott lost the vote of multitudes predisposed in his favor." Others, too, blamed Democrats' huge new vote from immigrants, not a reduced Whig vote, for the slaughter. "The truth is, Judge, we are overwhelmed by the Foreign vote," John Teesdale informed John McLean from Akron. "It has been accumulated with wonderful rapidity for two or three years past; and now the whole flood breaks on us at once." Yet from nearby Cleveland, Whig editor John Barr complained about just the reverse. Scott's foolish pro-Catholic tilt lost the election, he snapped. "Our Whig papers here made so much ado about Catholic Irish, that quite as many American Whigs voted for Pierce as Democratic Irish for Scott." The Pittsburgh *Gazette* also attributed the defeat to the "coldness produced among zealous Protestants from the courting of the Catholic vote."[108]

These conflicting reactions and explanations powerfully influenced what different Whigs did in the future, but they also raise many questions. Had the Whig party in fact been annihilated in November? Was the source of the defeat to be found in the North or the South? If the former, was it attributable to a growth of the Democratic vote, especially from foreigners, or to an unnatural reduction of the Whig vote? If the latter, was low Whig turnout caused by the defection of antislavery Whigs alienated by the platform, conservatives determined to knife Scott and his manager Seward, Protestants and nativists infuriated by the Whigs' pro-Catholic campaign, or, as Davis suggested, by Whigs' overreliance on Scott's personal popularity rather than issue differences to mobilize the Whig vote? The short answers to the first two questions are, respectively, no and both. With respect to the last two, the answer is all of the above, but the weight of the different factors varied from state to state.

Whig candidates were massacred on November 2, but rhetoric about the party's death was overwrought. In amassing almost 1.4 million votes, Winfield Scott drew more popular support than any previous Whig presidential candidate. Nationally, Pierce got 50.9 percent of the popular vote compared to Scott's 44 percent, and the absolute margin between the two was 214,000 votes out of over 3 million cast. Aside from the four states Scott carried, Whigs ran creditably in Louisiana, North Carolina, Connecticut, Delaware, Pennsylvania, New York, Ohio, and Iowa. In the last three, as well as in Indiana, Illinois, Michigan, and Wisconsin, Scott ran well ahead of Taylor and of Whig gubernatorial candidates in elections held prior to 1852. A greater accumulation of new votes by Democrats in those states, as well as in New Jersey, Pennsylvania, and California, not a smaller Whig vote, explains Scott's defeat (see Tables 30, 31, and 32).[109]

The story in the South was far different. In the eleven states that later formed the Confederacy, Scott garnered scarcely four-fifths of Taylor's total in 1848. With only 42.5 percent of the vote cast, his was the worst showing ever recorded by a Whig presidential candidate south of the border states.[110] Yet even that figure disguises significant regional variation. In the six Deep South states that cast popular votes, Scott won only 37.5 percent, and in Texas, Alabama, and Georgia his share was even smaller, in part because Webster, who died one week before the balloting, still won 5,324 votes (9.2 percent) from Georgia's defiant Whig Unionists, while a Southern Rights ticket received 2,205 (5 percent) in Alabama.

Table 30

Popular Votes, Proportions of the Vote, and Turnout Rates in 1852[a]

	Turnout Rate		Democratic	Whig	Free Soil
	1848	1852			
Alabama	69.7%	45.3%	26,881 (60.9%)	15,038 (34.1%)	
Arkansas	55.9%	48.6%	12,173 (62.2%)	7,404 (37.8%)	
California		75.7%	40,626 (53.4%)	35,407 (46.6%)	100
Connecticut	72.3%	72.3%	33,249 (49.8%)	30,359 (45.4%)	3,160
Delaware	80.4%	75%	6,318 (49.9%)	6,293 (49.7%)	62
Florida	64%	56.9%	4,318 (60%)	2,875 (40%)	
Georgia	86%	54.8%	34,705 (61.4%)	16,660 (29.4%)	
Illinois	70.5%	64.7%	80,597 (51.8%)	64,934 (41.8%)	9,966
Indiana	78.5%	80.3%	95,340 (52%)	80,901 (44.2%)	6,929
Iowa	90.7%	80.2%	17,763 (50.4%)	15,856 (45%)	1,604
Kentucky	73.9%	64.2%	53,806 (48.4%)	57,068 (51.3%)	265
Louisiana	51.5%	48.7%	18,647 (51.9%)	17,255 (48.1%)	
Maine	68.4%	61.2%	41,609 (50.6%)	32,543 (39.6%)	8,030
Maryland	76%	72.8%	40,020 (53.1%)	35,066 (46.5%)	281
Mass.	64.6%	57.8%	44,569 (35.6%)	52,683 (42%)	28,023
Michigan	74.5%	71.3%	41,842 (50.4%)	33,859 (40.8%)	7,237
Mississippi	80.7%	61.7%	26,876 (60.5%)	17,548 (39.5%)	
Missouri	62.5%	46.3%	38,353 (56.1%)	29,984 (43.9%)	
New Hamp.	67.4%	65.7%	29,997 (56.8%)	16,147 (30.6%)	6,695
New Jersey	82.7%	79.8%	44,305 (53.2%)	38,556 (46.3%)	350
New York	79.6%	84.7%	262,083 (50.2%)	234,882 (45%)	25,329
N. Carolina	71.4%	65.8%	39,744 (50.4%)	39,058 (49.5%)	59
Ohio	77.5%	80.6%	169,220 (47.9%)	152,526 (43.2%)	31,682
Pennsylvania	76.3%	72.6%	198,568 (51.4%)	179,174 (46.4%)	8,525
Rhode Is.	41.1%	57.8%	8,735 (51.4%)	7,626 (44.8%)	644
Tennessee	83.4%	72.9%	57,018 (49.3%)	58,898 (50.7%)	
Texas	69.6%	42.6%	13,552 (72.9%)	4,995 (27.1%)	
Vermont	70.5%	63.5%	13,044 (29.7%)	22,173 (50.6%)	8,621
Virginia	47.3%	63.3%	73,858 (55.6%)	58,572 (44.1%)	291
Wisconsin	58.3%	59.6%	33,658 (52%)	22,240 (34.4%)	8,814
U.S.	72.7%	69.6%	1,601,474 (50.9%)	1,386,580 (44%)	156,667 (5.1%)

[a]These returns are based on the table in the Nichols' article "The Election of 1852." The totals and percentages differ slightly from those in Gienapp, *Origins of the Republican Party*, p. 28. The figures on turnout are those listed in *Historical Statistics*, p. 1072. These are based on percentages of adult white males (and blacks, where they could vote). Gienapp's figures in " 'Politics Seem to Enter Into Everything,' " pp. 18–19, are based on his estimates of eligible voters in northern states and are therefore slightly higher in most cases.

Only Louisiana, where Scott got 48.1 percent and trailed Pierce by 1,400 votes, bucked this regional trend. In dramatic contrast, Scott took 47.2 percent of the vote in North Carolina, Virginia, Tennessee, and Arkansas. In the four border slave states of Missouri, Kentucky, Maryland, and Delaware, Scott ran more strongly still, with 48 percent. Scott, indeed, ran far better in those eight slave

Table 31

Changes in the Parties Vote for President, 1848–1852

	Democrats	Whigs	Free Soil
Alabama	− 4,292 (13.8%)	−15,444 (50.7%)	
Arkansas	+ 2,872 (30.9%)	− 183 (2.4%)	
Connecticut	+ 6,198 (22.9%)	+ 41 (0.1%)	− 1,845 (36.9%)
Delaware	+ 408 (6.9%)	− 147 (2.2%)	
Florida	+ 1,304 (43.2%)	− 1,206 (29.5%)	
Georgia	− 10,087 (22.5%)	−30,851 (64.9%)	
Illinois	+ 24,682 (44.1%)	+12,081 (22.9%)	− 5,736 (36.5%)
Indiana	+ 20,782 (27.9%)	+10,601 (15.1%)	− 1,104 (13.7%)
Iowa	+ 6,525 (58.1%)	+ 5,926 (59.7%)	+ 501 (45.4%)
Kentucky	+ 5,014 (10.3%)	− 9,505 (14.3%)	
Louisiana	+ 3,268 (21.2%)	− 1,232 (6.7%)	
Maine	+ 1,779 (4.5%)	− 2,582 (7.3%)	− 4,066 (33.6%)
Maryland	+ 5,533 (16%)	− 2,677 (7.1%)	
Massachusetts	+ 9,288 (26.3%)	− 8,387 (13.7%)	−10,035 (26.4%)
Michigan	+ 11,100 (36.1%)	+ 9,912 (41.4%)	− 3,156 (30.3%)
Mississippi	+ 276 (1%)	−14,967 (58%)	
Missouri	− 1,512 (3.7%)	− 2,714 (8.3%)	
New Hampshire	+ 2,234 (8%)	+ 1,366 (9.2%)	− 865 (11.4%)
New Jersey	+ 7,425 (20.1%)	− 1,453 (3.6%)	
New York	+147,763 (129.2%)	+16,279 (7.4%)	−95,181 (79%)
North Carolina	+ 3,934 (11%)	− 5,037 (11.4%)	
Ohio	+ 14,438 (9.3%)	+13,870 (10%)	− 3,841 (10.8%)
Pennsylvania	+ 25,864 (15%)	− 6,249 (3.4%)	− 2,748 (24.4%)
Rhode Island	+ 5,089 (140.4%)	+ 846 (12.5%)	− 85 (11.6%)
Tennessee	− 1,209 (2.1%)	− 5,341 (8.3%)	
Texas	+ 1,908 (16.3%)	− 286 (5.4%)	
Vermont	+ 2,096 (19.1%)	− 949 (4.3%)	− 5,716 (39.9%)
Wisconsin	+ 18,657 (124.4%)	+ 8,493 (61.8%)	− 1,609 (15.4%)

states than in the free states, which cast more than twice as many popular votes as the slave states and where Scott got 43.4 percent compared to 49.9 percent for Pierce and 6.7 percent for Hale.

Whigs' refusal to vote because they distrusted Scott, expected defeat, or were simply indifferent to the outcome of a personality contest with no clear programmatic differences at issue clearly damaged the Whigs in Dixie more than a surge of new Democratic voters after 1848. Only in Virginia, where the 1851 constitution broadened suffrage rights, did Scott outpoll Zachary Taylor, but Democrats' increase since 1848 doubled Whigs' gain. Everywhere else, even in slave states where Whigs remained competitive, the Whigs' vote dropped—dramatically so in Alabama, Georgia, Mississippi, and North Carolina. Few previous southern Whig voters, however, apparently supported Pierce. The Democratic vote also declined between 1848 and 1852 in Alabama, Georgia, Missouri, and Tennessee, though by only a fraction of the Whig slump. Elsewhere Democratic gains over 1848

Table 32

Difference Between Whig and Democratic Presidential Vote in 1852 and the Most Proximate Preceding Gubernatorial Election in Selected States[a]

	Democrats	Whigs	Date of Election
Connecticut	+ 1,625 (5.1%)	+ 2,118 (7.5%)	April 1852
Delaware	+ 317 (5.3%)	+ 315 (5.2%)	November 1850
California	+17,451 (75.3%)	+12,675 (55.7%)	November 1851
Florida	− 310 (6.7%)	− 1,461 (33.7%)	October 1852
Georgia	−11,929 (25.5%)	−26,689 (61.6%)	October 1849
Indiana	+ 2,381 (2.6%)	+ 7,254 (9.8%)	October 1852
Iowa	+ 4,277 (31.7%)	+ 4,453 (39%)	October 1850
Kentucky	− 1,015 (1.8%)	+ 3,045 (5.6%)	August 1851
Louisiana	+ 188 (1%)	− 152 (0.9%)	November 1849
Maine	−21,596 (34.1%)[b]	+ 4,414 (15.7%)	September 1852
Maryland	+ 3,680 (10.1%)	+ 208 (0.6%)	October 1850
Massachusetts	+ 680 (1.5%)	−11,596 (18%)	November 1851
	+ 5,806 (14.9%)	− 9,550 (15.3%)	November 1852
Michigan	+18,015 (75.6%)	+16,958 (100.3%)	November 1851
	− 949 (2.2%)	− 803 (2.3%)	November 1852
Missouri	− 8,141 (17.5%)	− 2,722 (8.3%)	August 1852
Mississippi	− 6,241 (18.8%)	− 5,448 (23.7%)	November 1849
New Hampshire[c]	− 750 (2.4%)	− 2,260 (12.3%)	March 1852
New Jersey	+ 4,582 (11.5%)	+ 4,026 (11.8%)	October 1850
New York	+47,731 (22.2%)	+20,268 (9.4%)	November 1850
North Carolina	− 8,740 (18%)	− 3,935 (9.1%)	August 1852
Ohio	+23,564 (16.2%)	+31,421 (25.9%)	October 1851
Pennsylvania	+12,069 (6.5%)	+ 1,140 (0.6%)	October 1851
Tennessee	− 4,630 (7.5%)	− 4,525 (7.1%)	August 1851
Vermont	− 1,957 (13%)	− 1,622 (6.8%)	September 1852
Virginia	+ 6,784 (10.1%)	− 904 (1.5%)	December 1851

[a]I have used the 1849 gubernatorial elections in Georgia and Mississippi since the vote in 1851 did not reflect regular party strength. Similarly, although a Whig contested Democrat Henry Collier in Alabama in 1851, his total was so low that it would distort results to use it. Nonetheless, it is significant that Pierce's total in Alabama trailed Collier's by almost 12,000.

[b]The Maine figures are calculated on the basis of the combined Democratic vote for Anson Chandler and John Hubbard.

[c]In New Hampshire, John Hale's vote for president lagged behind John Atwood's for governor by 2,788 (29.4 percent). Both presidential candidates from that state, in sum, attracted fewer votes than their parties' candidates in March, extraordinary testimony to the lack of interest the presidential race aroused.

were modest given four years' of population growth and the manifest unpopularity of Lewis Cass in 1848 (see Table 31).

Since Taylor appealed to Southerners as a native son and since Cass failed to evoke their enthusiasm in 1848, indeed, inverse movement in the two parties' votes between the two presidential contests was almost inevitable. A better gauge of the 1852 race's impact on southern voters, therefore, is the differential between its results and those of a gubernatorial election held between the presidential contests (see Table 32). By that measure, Scott still cost Whigs votes in every slave state except Delaware, Maryland, and Kentucky, where he outpolled Archibald Dixon, Whigs' losing gubernatorial candidate in 1851. But the deficit in some states, particularly Louisiana and Mississippi, was notably smaller. What this comparison shows more dramatically, however, is either how unpopular Pierce was in the South or, more likely, how disinterested both southern Democrats and southern Whigs were in the result. The substantial Democratic drop-off in Georgia, Mississippi, and Alabama, where Pierce ran 30 percent behind Henry Collier's 1851 vote, might be attributed to certainty about November's outcome. But neither overconfidence nor defeatism can explain why the decline in Democratic turnout since the gubernatorial elections of 1851 or 1852 exceeded that of Whigs in Kentucky, Missouri, Tennessee, and North Carolina. With both parties' platforms pledged to finality and little else apparently at stake, southern voters, like many Northerners, saw no reason to vote at all.

Louisiana, Tennessee, and North Carolina provide the best evidence of this phenomenon. Louisiana witnessed the lowest turnout decline of any slave state between 1848 and 1852, and aside from Delaware, it was the only slave state to give voters a choice in November on something besides the presidency—ratification of the new state constitution, over which Whigs and Democrats were at odds. Everyone in Tennessee knew that the 1851 state election would determine future state policy toward railroad construction and free banking, as well as congressional and state legislative apportionment. Those matters inspired a higher turnout than 1852's issueless beauty contest. North Carolina's parties fought the August 1852 gubernatorial contest over salient state issues, 79 percent of the potential electorate voted, and David Reid won by a margin of 53 to 47 percent. Three months later, turnout fell to 66 percent, twice as many Democrat as Whig voters dropped out, and the margin between the parties fell below 1 percent.[111]

While voter turnout in the North dipped only from 77.1 to 75.3 percent between 1848 and 1852, compared to an average arithmetic decline of 19.9 percent in the fifteen slave states, that minuscule decrease masks considerable variations from state to state and among the three parties.[112] Increased turnout that primarily benefited Democrats in populous states like New York, Ohio, and Indiana offset decreases elsewhere.[113] In western states with rapidly growing populations, the absolute size of the vote grew substantially in four years; any decline in turnout rates, therefore, merely reflected an increase in the pool of potential voters. In the four New England states of Maine, New Hampshire, Vermont, and Massachusetts, in contrast, calculated abstention and sheer apathy reduced the vote.

Significantly, Free Soilers suffered greater declines in turnout than either Whigs or Democrats in every northern state except New Jersey and Pennsylvania. The Free Soil vote and the proportion of the vote were almost halved in four years. Much of that drop occurred in New York, where Barnburners returned to the Democratic column, but the Free Soil vote sank appreciably in Connecticut, Illinois, Maine, Massachusetts, Michigan, Pennsylvania, and Vermont as well. Some former Free Soilers voted for Scott or Pierce, but many sat out the election, apparently in despair that revising the Compromise was now hopeless.[114]

After the election, Georgia's vindictive Toombs gloated that "it must have satisfied the northern Whigs, that free soil don't pay any better at the North than at the South. If their candidate had no other merit, he was certainly *available*.

What would they have done with an unpopular candidate?" Toombs may have referred to the purported defection of pro-Compromise Whigs, but if he meant that antislavery men refused to support Scott, his reasoning is questionable. True, had Scott received all of Hale's votes, he would have carried Connecticut, Ohio, and, surprisingly, Delaware. But it is doubtful that without Hale in the race, all of those men would have voted, and Whigs' platform, not their candidate, caused Free Soilers to run Hale. Hale and other Free Soil leaders sought to hurt Democrats more than Whigs, and in New York, where over three times as many former Free Soilers voted for Pierce than for Scott, that hope clearly backfired. In Connecticut, Indiana, Massachusetts, and Ohio, however, far more of Martin Van Buren's former backers supported Scott than Pierce, and the same is probably true of Michigan, where Scott doubled the vote of the 1851 fusion Whig/Free Soil gubernatorial candidate. In Ohio, moreover, some of Cass' 1848 voters did desert to Hale. Whigs lost a few voters to the Free Soilers in Illinois, Indiana, and Connecticut, but in none did those defections affect the outcome.[115]

Even in New York, over a third of the increased Democratic vote did not come from former Free Soilers, and in other northern states where Democrats gained the most votes between 1848 and 1852, Free Soilers constituted only a minuscule fraction of the increment. Most of this gain instead most likely came from immigrants, about whom Whigs complained vociferously. Turnout by foreign-born voters jumped substantially in 1852, and the Germans preponderantly and the Irish overwhelmingly favored the Democrats. Whigs' pro-Catholic campaign, in sum, failed dismally. "The Catholic question was brought to bear heavily on us in this State," a Wisconsin Democrat wrote, "but by untiring efforts, and a complete and most effective system of operators, that ridiculous movement was thoroughly *headed off*."[116]

Nonetheless, some Whigs did defect to Pierce. Proportionately most significant in Ohio, Massachusetts, and Connecticut, these turncoats also existed in Indiana, Maine, and New York. Some undoubtedly represented angry Protestants disgusted by Whigs' pro-Catholic campaign for Scott, and the Whig decline in Maryland in part reflected the same impulse. Pierce's election, concluded Hayes in Cincinnati, was "a sort of *anti*-Catholic triumph," while Cleveland's John Barr also bemoaned defection by anti-Catholic Protestants. In Pennsylvania, where Protestant Whigs' disillusionment and nativists' anger were most widely reported, however, very few of Taylor's 1848 voters supported Pierce. There they simply sat out the election, depriving Scott of over 15,000 votes. Abstention also greatly exceeded defection in New Jersey, New York, Maine, and Massachusetts, where almost a third of Taylor's voters stayed home.[117]

Conservatives miffed by Scott's nomination and by many northern Whigs' contempt for the platform also contributed to this outflow. Websterite Whigs had been sufficiently strong in Connecticut to block Baldwin's reelection to the Senate, and they undoubtedly constituted a considerable fraction of 1848 Whig voters who supported Pierce or abstained and whose votes could have given Scott that state. The same was probably true in Vermont, New Hampshire, and Maine, where a fifth of Taylor's voters abandoned Scott. In New York, where Sewardites railed about "the treachery of Silver Grays" and Washington Hunt groaned to Hamilton Fish that "the backbone of the Whig party was broken by those internal divisions which you and I have so long deplored," conservatives' sabotage clearly hurt Scott, although Democrats' huge additional vote would have defeated him even without those abstentions. One index of this sabotage is that Scott ran almost 7,000 votes behind Hunt. Defection by conservatives in New York City, where one Democrat reported that Websterites voted for Pierce and other Whigs who had earlier supported the Castle Garden Union ticket abstained, was especially severe. Even Silver Gray congressional candidates suffered from this calculated abstention. Our "periodic feuds" and "the shameful defection of the disappointed proved stronger than the principles which now divide the two great parties," concluded a demoralized Fish.[118]

In Massachusetts almost half of Taylor's supporters defected to Pierce or abstained, and frustrated Websterites surely contributed to that hemorrhage. John Clifford, a conservative acceptable to them, ran almost 10,000 votes ahead of Scott in the gubernatorial election held a week later. John Davis complained that those Whigs who posed as Union savers by insisting on finality looked "assiduously for favorable opportunities to trample upon all Whigs who differed from them in opinion." Davis had good reason to complain; Websterites elected about thirty members of the state legislature. They held the balance of power, and as the price of supporting Clifford in the legislative election of governor, they insisted that Davis be replaced in the Senate.[119]

Yet the electorate's widely reported apathy also surely contributed to abstention by Democrats as well as by Whigs on November 2, especially in Maine, Vermont, New Hampshire, and Massachusetts, where the absolute vote, not just the turnout rate, declined between 1848 and 1852. Those four, of course, were among the least competitive two-party states in the nation, and a combination of defeatism and overconfidence further depressed turnout by Free Soilers as well as Whigs and Democrats, especially in Vermont. Still, the issueless nature of the presidential contest unquestionably tranquilized the electorate.

In Massachusetts, for example, the state election's central issue was the Maine Law, and that contest evoked a turnout of 73.9 percent compared to 67.8 percent only a week earlier. One reason Clifford ran so far ahead of Scott, indeed, is that he got 8,000 votes on a separate anti-Maine Law ticket, many of which were apparently from Democrats who had supported Pierce, the notorious "drunkard." Similarly, Horace Mann, the Free Soilers' gubernatorial candidate and the most ardent prohibitionist in the race, drew over 8,000 (31.1 percent) more votes than Hale had a week earlier, in part because he was also on a separate pro-Maine Law ticket. The liquor issue obviously mattered more to voters than stale debates about the finality of the Compromise or who was the superior general in the Mexican War. People would vote when public policy was at stake. Maine's September gubernatorial election had also revolved around the liquor issue, and 12,000 more men, almost one-tenth of the potential electorate, voted in it than for president. Whigs had hoped that one of the warring Democratic factions might boycott the presidential election, and many Democrats did. Pierce drew slightly fewer votes than John Hubbard alone had in September, and he trailed the combined vote of Hubbard and Anson Chandler by over 34 percent. Even in New Hampshire, home of two presidential candidates, turnout dropped between March and November, and, incredibly, both Pierce and Hale ran behind their parties' gubernatorial candidates, as did Scott. Men voted when differences over policy were clear; in an issueless personality contest they did not bother.[120]

X

For Whigs in 1852, answering the question of whether the Whig party was now "dead—dead—dead," as Lew Campbell angrily growled two days after the election, involved much more than recapitulating the popular vote or compiling reasons for Scott's defeat. However competitive the party remained at the polls outside the Deep South, Whigs could not gainsay their candidates' massacre that year. Ultimately, therefore, the Whig party's life or death boiled down to a matter of psychology. Did Whigs have the will to carry on despite their rout?[121]

In a defiant letter dictated twelve days before he died in October, Daniel Webster spurned pleas from his closest New York supporters to renounce the independent tickets launched in his name. Defending the motives of soreheads, he explained, "Probably they think they see indications that within a fortnight, the Whig party in the United States will have become merely Historical." After the election, many Democrats and Free Soilers as well as some Whigs agreed. "Is there any Whig party now?" Philadelphia's Customs Collector William D. Lewis asked John Clayton. "Did not 'Godlike' Daniel prophecy truly?" Reminding Clayton of their effort in 1849 to replace the Whig name with the Taylor Republican party, he queried, "Can we get clear of it now in the new organization which our great rout renders inevitable?" From western Pennsylvania James Johnston concluded: "The Whigs are out of heart and I think many will seek new party connections." "As a party organization we are extinct, and are of 'the things that were, but now no more forever,'" despaired an Indiana Whig. Why continue a hopeless struggle? he asked. For twenty-five years the party had been "butchered and slaughtered." Its two great leaders, Clay and Webster, were now dead. Why "keep up an opposition that stimulates our adversaries to excesses and which will constitute their apology for such excesses?"[122]

If some Whigs were prepared to ground arms, others looked to the reorganization of parties to which Lewis alluded. Anti-Compromise Whigs in particular spoke of merging with Free Soilers to oppose expansionistic foreign policies designed to spread slavery that they expected from Pierce, and four days after the election, Charles Sumner tried to tempt Seward into negotiations aimed at launching a new antislavery party. Even without such a merger, many of Seward's New York allies wanted to drive Silver Grays permanently from the party, no matter how small a minority such an ostracism rendered them. Silver Grays retorted by proposing a new and purified Whig party from which all hint of Sewardism and antislavery sentiment was distilled. Referring to one such effort in Rochester, a Sewardite asked sarcastically, "Can you conceive that sane men would believe they could bring Fillmore out in 1856 with a *great* chance for success? and yet these noodles really *do* think so! There is no knowing what effect the 'Rochester Knockers' [spirit rappers] will next produce on men's minds."[123]

Though deeply discouraged, most Whigs vowed to soldier on. "Cast down but not dismayed there are many here eager to reorganize against our opponents," a defeated Whig candidate reported from New York City. "There is a slight pulsation in the region of the heart which shows that life is not wholly extinct, but the doctors differ as to the probability of restoration to his wonted vigor," a successful Whig congressman wrote Israel Washburn about the party in Pittsburgh. "I am willing to stay here and battle for the good cause," Schouler told Seward from Boston. "We cannot disband," William Kent insisted. Seward himself wanted no part of a party reorganization either in New York or the North as a whole. "No new party will arise, nor will any old one fall," he replied to Sumner. Instead, Seward and many other leaders recommended that Whigs remain quiescent until their wounds healed.[124]

Some Whigs based their decision on pragmatic grounds. Virginia's Botts declared that he intended to stand by the Whig organization since it was far easier to disband an old party than to build a new one. Others stressed patriotic duty. From his post as consul to Argentina, Maine's conservative Edward Kent argued plaintively to Israel Washburn, who clearly wanted to merge with Free Soilers, that he had always worried that "the defeat of Scott, especially if he was largely deserted in the Slave States, would [lead to] the abandonment of the national Whig party & the formation out of . . . its northern section, and of other materials, a substantially sectional party." Any such party, he warned, would jeopardize "the Union."[125]

Primarily, however, Whigs determined to hang on because they believed they could win again in two or four years. Separately but almost simultaneously, Whigs across the nation reached the same conclusion. Democrats' sweep was so huge that they were bound to fall apart once they distributed patronage and tried to formulate policy, especially if Whigs indulged in what Simeon Draper called "a good *sound sleep*" and thereby deprived Democrats of the cohesive pressure provided by external competition. "In the very magnitude of the defeat I find omens better for the future," piped an Illinois Whig. "The Democrats go in with such overwhelming power that they must fall to pieces." An Alabamian concurred: "Democracy have the sway, and I say let them have their own way, for the next four years. Give them rope and they will hang themselves." "We say to ourselves, let us see how Mr. Pierce shall administer the government," Hugh Maxwell wrote Fillmore from New York. Some predicted that Democratic economic policies would rouse the electorate against them when depression followed. Others pointed to inevitable attempts to expand slavery "by purchase, stealing, or war" that would bring at least northern voters back to the Whig party. Whatever it was, Whigs agreed, Democrats were bound to do something that alienated their own supporters and allowed Whigs to mount a triumphant counterattack. "To talk of abandoning the Party is to me absurd," William Kent wrote Fish in January. "Everything was against us [in New York], yet our vote was immense. Let General Pierce form his cabinet, &, what is more important, fill his offices, & we shall see, whether we assist it or not, a formidable rising up in this state in opposition."[126]

At the close of the most disastrous election year in the Whig party's history, in sum, most Whigs wanted to battle on. By pursuing a policy of "masterly inactivity," they would await the inevitable Democratic blunders.[127] Whigs had always functioned better as outs than as ins. The party was founded on opposition to Democratic governance, it survived for almost twenty years because of that role, and now Whigs could oppose it again in Washington as well as in twenty-seven states. As one Whig had said of the comeback in 1846–47, Polk's administration had been the Whigs' best recruiting officer. Why could they not expect the same kinds of gifts on a silver platter from Franklin Pierce? Why not indeed?

Chapter 21

"Now Is the Time to Start New; the Old Issues Are Gone"

"The Whigs are sullen of course but more united in Congress by far than at the last session," Tennessee's William Cullom reported from Washington in December 1852. "They seem confident that they are only postponed for a season." Also impressed by congressional Whigs' unity, New York's Seward concurred that they wanted "to be quiet and wait without committing ourselves until a breach shall occur in the ranks of the majority." Outside of Washington, too, Whigs of all varieties agreed that "if we keep still and quiet" "the Democratic party must soon divide itself." "If we will be wise," summarized Virginia's John Minor Botts, "we shall have little to do but hold out our hats to catch the fruit as it falls in 56."[1]

The Whigs' own history after defeats in 1836 and 1844 and the entire course of American political history demonstrate that outs can mount comebacks by exploiting ins' mistakes. Whig predictions, moreover, were largely accurate. During Pierce's administration Democrats divided over patronage and policy, and they committed blunders that produced massive defeat at the polls. Whigs, however, did not reap the fruit of voters' backlash in the congressional elections of 1854–55 or in the 1856 presidential election. After 1852, instead, the Whig party disintegrated and was displaced. Decomposition was marked during 1853. In 1854 and 1855 erosion accelerated so that by 1856 only a shadow of a once formidable party remained.

What requires explanation, therefore, is why Whigs' eminently reasonable assumptions in the winter of 1852–53 proved erroneous. Since Whigs correctly predicted that Democrats would divide and alienate most American voters, why did Whigs fail to benefit from their opponents' woes? Why did the Whig party waste away when the Democrats provided so much nutriment to revive it? Addressing those questions forms the agenda of the remaining chapters.

Although Whigs' reactions to the party's plight after the crushing defeats of 1852 differed, virtually all of them factored Democrats' imminent disruption into their calculations for the future. Thus the Whig party's fate continued to be shaped by its interaction with the Democratic party. What was common to all those calculations and what gave coherence to the kaleidoscopic pattern of events during 1853, in turn, was the need of both Whigs who hoped to preserve the party and those who sought new allegiances to find distinctive identities that could attract voters. The central theme of 1853, in sum, was the search for new issues to fill the void that had emerged in 1852.

I

By itself, Whigs' "Waterloo" defeat in 1852, which caused Horace Greeley to moan in the New York *Tribune* that the party had been "not merely discomfited but annihilated," cannot explain the frustration of Whig expectations.[2] To be sure, the rout in the electoral vote combined with heavy losses in congressional, gubernatorial, and state legislative races made the 1852 debacle unusually severe. Nonetheless, the margin between the Democratic and Whig shares of the nationwide popular vote was hardly insurmountable; nor had many Whig voters, even in the South where the Whig totals declined most sharply, defected to the enemy. Reviving the party, therefore, appeared to be largely a matter of remobilizing temporarily demoralized or alienated supporters and of courting new voters, not of converting lifelong enemies.

Nor was Whig strategy that winter manifestly illogical. What Greeley called the "quiescent policy" offered Whigs several advantages.[3] Temporarily postponing nominating conventions and eschewing efforts to define distinctively Whig, but potentially divisive, positions in speeches and platforms could provide time to heal the party's factional and sectional wounds. Equally important, as outs Whigs could finally escape fractious quarrels over patronage. Similarly, waiting for Democrats to take some unpopular action could allow Whigs to rally against it, just as opposition to Democratic policies had united Whigs during Polk's administration.

Democrats and Whigs alike, moreover, correctly recognized that without the "external pressure" provided by active Whig opposition, Democrats almost certainly would divide over issues and patronage allocation once Pierce was inaugurated. As the astute Truman Smith snapped, "I have got tired of officiating as a sort of hoop to the democratic barrel! keeping the heading & staves in place by outside pressure." Although Democrats united behind Pierce's candidacy in 1852, potential rifts among them were manifold. Distrust between pro-Compromise Democrats and those who had supported coalition with Free Soilers in the North and extremist Southern Rights demands in the South was especially deep-seated. As Nathan K. Hall accurately predicted, Pierce tried to gloss over these differences by constructing a "piebald cabinet," but by the summer of 1853 his attempt to please everyone had instead infuriated numerous Democrats, particularly pro-Compromise men in both sections.[4]

Squabbling among Democratic leaders in Washington and state capitals might produce an image of disarray, incompetence, and selfish preoccupation with spoils that disillusioned previous Democratic voters. Whigs knew that their own rifts in 1841–42 and again in 1850 had paralyzed government and engendered disproportionate Whig drop-off in off-year elections. Democratic divisions might have a similar effect.

The calculated policy of watchful waiting until Democrats ruptured or blundered, however, rested upon a chain of seriously flawed assumptions. Most fundamental was the delusion that time was on Whigs' side, that Whigs could passively wait for Democrats to self-destruct while healing their own factional and sectional rifts. Conflict with Democrats had always been the chief counterweight to Whigs' internal divisions. If they ceased fighting Democrats for some indefinite period, there was no guarantee that they would cease fighting each other. Nor would the passage of time necessarily reverse the apathy and alienation of previous Whig voters that eroded Whig strength. If the opposition party's purpose was to oppose the majority, an abdication of that role, no matter how temporary, could increase, not decrease, popular disenchantment and turn still more former Whig supporters into nonvoters.

Above all else, the strategy of lying low and waiting to reap the fruits of the anti-Democratic harvest in 1854 or 1856 presupposed that primarily Whigs would benefit from a voter backlash against Democrats. In the winter of 1852–53 this assumption too had a patina of plausibility. The tiny Native American party was an annoyance chiefly in Pennsylvania. More important, Free Soilers, not Whigs, clearly lost the most votes between 1848 and 1852. Since the 1852 campaign underlined the national consensus on the Compromise's finality, the antislavery party might shrivel to its abolitionist base. Politics could then revert essentially to a two-party contest between Democrats and Whigs, a zero-sum game in which Democratic losses automatically meant Whig gains. As the Whigs would learn to their dismay, however, new players could enter the game. Those new players could define the issues before the electorate just as readily as Whigs and Democrats, and rather than generating a Whig revival, their new issues could—and would—devastate the Whig party.

II

Aside from passivity's unsuitability for Whigs' immediate needs in 1853 when they had to provide voters some reason to come out and vote for Whig candidates, the strategy of watchful waiting presupposed that all Whig leaders saw it as a means toward the same end. The shared expectation that Democrats would inevitably come acropper, however, did not indicate consensus about how to respond to Democratic divisions, what the future shape of the Whig party would be, who should control the organization, or whether it deserved perpetuation at all. At the start of 1853 most Whig leaders and voters hoped to preserve the party in order to fight again another day. Most loved the party, and most were deeply committed to Whig principles of social order and Union, activist domestic governance to improve people's lives, and a nonaggressive foreign policy. Most sincerely believed Whigs would govern more wisely than Democrats. "It will not do for us to think of joining any other party, whatever some may say to the contrary," declared Ohio's Ben Wade, an original Scott supporter and militant antislavery Whig. "The country cannot survive the destruction of Whig principles." The country would always look to Whigs "to set things right," echoed Fillmorite John P. Kennedy a few months later. Most Whigs, in sum, still saw a vital need for their party.[5] Agreement on preserving it, however, did not indicate complete consensus. If the sobering shock of defeat produced a semblance of harmony among previously divided Whig congressmen during the winter of 1852–53, Whigs outside the capital remained deeply divided along factional and sectional lines. From the moment of Scott's defeat, therefore, jockeying for advantage against intraparty foes commenced.

Seward, for example, was content to remain in the Whig party and temporarily assume a passive stance, not simply because he, like Greeley, expected that divisions among New York's Democrats might hand Whigs victory in the 1853 state elections. He also believed that once Fillmore left the White House and Whigs reassumed the role of an opposition party, Silver Grays would be exposed as the "Croakers, Irregulars, [and] Disorganizers" that they were. Thus his followers would rise to dominance in New York, across the North, and in the nation as a whole.[6]

Many of Seward's northern followers had even less use than he for pro-Compromise Whigs. They spoke angrily of purifying the party in the North by driving conservatives from it. They wanted "the line [to] be squared and distinctly drawn between Anti-Slavery & Pro-Slavery Whigs." Convinced that in the North "the only question available is Freedom against Slavery," they sought reinforcements from the ranks of the apparently collapsing Free Soil party. From their perspective, the chief reason to postpone Whig conventions and the writing of Whig platforms was not to mend fences with conservative rivals and southern Whigs, but to allow time for negotiations that would bring former Free Soilers into the Whig fold. They did not, however, want to jettison the Whig party's southern wing. Like Seward, they sought to retain a national, bisectional organization. But they did insist that northern antislavery Whigs no longer be muzzled, as they were by the 1852 national platform, that northern and southern Whigs again agree to disagree about slavery.[7]

This prescription for the future Whig party appalled southern Whigs and conservative Northerners. "We can never have peace & security with Seward, Greeley & Co. in the ascendant in our national affairs & we had better *purchase them* by the destruction of the Whig party than of the Union," Georgia's defiant Robert Toombs thundered after Scott's defeat. The continued prominence among northern Whigs of antislavery zealots convinced even moderate southern Whigs like North Carolina's Senator George Badger and Tennessee's John Bell that an unbridgeable sectional chasm would continue to divide the party if Seward and his ilk led its northern wing. "The Seward party are an incubus upon us—universally so at the South," William L. Hodge, a Louisianan who had worked for Fillmore's administration, concluded by September 1853.[8]

Precisely because Silver Grays and other northern conservatives believed that the Sewardites' "game undoubtedly is, to monopolize the name of Whig, control the party, and make it abolitionist," they feared that lying low, as Seward and Greeley advised, might allow the suspected Sewardite strategy to succeed. In Ohio and New York, therefore, conservative Whigs moved quickly after Scott's defeat to call local and state party conventions, from which they excluded Sewardites, to define what the Whig party stood for according to their own views and thereby to block any infusions from former Free Soilers.[9]

Ohio conservatives' success in calling and dominating a Whig state convention on February 22, 1853, over Sewardites' protests turned Sewardites themselves against the policy of lying low.[10] As Ohio Sewardites learned, their calculated inactivity merely allowed their conservative intraparty rivals to strike first. Furious that the Whigs who wrote the Ohio state platform in February referred to Whigs as "the *'National Conservative'* party," one Ohio Sewardite sputtered, "I am not a National Conservative Whig in the sense they intend, and am sick of endeavoring to make the most of an equivocal position." Silence was a mistake. We "must be committed to some political position or party ere long." Unless Seward or another trusted national leader spoke up and defined a position around which antislavery Whigs could rally, he warned, "many will be wandering off into other organizations or become permanently disgusted with every attention to public affairs."[11]

Nor were splits over the slavery question the only Whig divisions that the "quiescent policy" could not heal. During the winter of 1852–53 Whigs in Maine and North Carolina squandered an opportunity to elect at least two United States senators because of intraparty sniping. In Massachusetts it forced an uneasy compromise on the party's successful candidate.

In Maine, the problem stemmed from Whigs' need to prolong the division between Wildcat and regular Democrats. To propitiate the Wildcats, who had allowed Whig state senators to elect him, and to prevent the Democratic majority from reuniting, Whig Governor William Crosby appointed many Wildcats to state jobs and thereby outraged Whig regulars who had been out of power for years. The same dynamic shaped the legislature's contest for the Senate seat. The Whig state senators elected with Wildcat complicity were numerous enough to give Whigs a majority on a joint ballot of the two legislative chambers. Thus Whigs had a splendid chance to replace Democratic Senator James Bradbury. Several Whig senators refused to support Whig candidate William Pitt Fessenden, however, because that refusal had been the price of Wildcat acquiescence in their own election. No Democrat took the seat, but selection of the United States senator was postponed until after the 1853 legislative elections, when Whigs might not do as well as they had in 1852.[12]

Old regional jealousies, as well as resentments spawned by the recent presidential campaign, prevented North Carolina's Whigs from filling the Senate seat of Willie P. Mangum, who announced his intention to retire when he endorsed Scott's nomination in April 1852. While Democrats had a fragile two-seat legislative majority on the joint ballot, they would not rally behind James Dobbin, their caucus' choice. Even fewer would support the Democrats' fallback candidate, Whig apostate Thomas Clingman. Democratic fractiousness offered Whigs a realistic chance to seize the senatorship, but between five and eleven Whig legislators refused to support their top contender, Kenneth Rayner. Since Rayner hailed from eastern North Carolina, some western Whigs found him unacceptable. Rayner's main problem, however, was his refusal to endorse the Scott-Graham ticket in 1852, a stance that some Whigs viewed as treason. Whigs took solace in the fact that both Dobbin and especially the turncoat Clingman had been stopped. But the stalemate meant that George Badger alone represented the state in the Senate during the first session of the Thirty-Third Congress and that the legislature elected in August 1854 would fill both Senate seats.[13]

The Massachusetts legislature was to pick a successor to the deceased Webster's longtime antagonist, Whig Senator John Davis. Whigs elsewhere invested great symbolic importance in the Massachusetts decision, for, as Thurlow Weed wrote Springfield editor Samuel Bowles, "It would help the cause in other states to see the Whig Party, amid all its embarrassments, strong enough to elect a Whig Senator." With good reason, however, Weed feared that internal Whig divisions might destroy this chance. A small bloc of Webster's acolytes together with an even smaller group of antiCoalition Democrats held the balance of power between the Whig majority and the Coalition. The Websterites would never condone Davis' reelection, and they vehemently opposed replacing him with Robert C. Winthrop. As a compromise the party settled on the scholarly and extraordinarily cautious Edward Everett, an ally of Webster, but not one who had worked actively in Washington for the Compromise measures. Time would show Whigs that his election was a mistake.[14]

More portentous than continuing intraparty divisions that could neutralize any benefit from anticipated Democratic splits, by 1853 a minority of Whigs wanted to jettison the Whig party altogether. How large that minority was is impossible to estimate, but such men fell into different categories. The most fascinating group—because of what they signified about the party's perceived bankruptcy— were men who had no interest in starting or joining new parties. Instead, because of the prosperity during the early 1850s, Whig and Democratic agreement on remaining economic questions, and the bipartisan commitment to squelch further agitation of the slavery issue, they no longer believed that the Whig party served any useful purpose. They spoke of retiring from political life altogether and devoting their attention to making money or other matters. And they included some extraordinarily important Whig politicians. Historians have long noted that the deaths of Clay and Webster in 1852 deprived Whigs of their two foremost national leaders, but they have not appreciated how many second-tier leaders who might have replaced them also abandoned the party when it most needed them.

Thomas Ewing, the former United States senator and cabinet member from Ohio, represented these refugees from the political arena. After his unsuccessful bid for reelection to the Senate in 1851, he devoted his attention almost entirely to private business activities, not politics.[15] Governor William B. Campbell of Tennessee, the state's most popular Whig, also yearned for private life. Adamantly refusing to seek reelection in 1853, he counted the days until he could escape office, move to New Orleans, and set up as a cotton factor. "Politics is at a low ebb here," he wrote his uncle after his successor had been chosen, "and I daily feel rejoiced that I am done with it."[16] The Boston patrician Winthrop, whose touchy sense of personal dignity bordered on arrogance, also abandoned political life in early 1853. In January, he refused to allow his name to be used as a Senate candidate before the legislature, in part because he feared that the malignant opposition of "Webster toadies" would guarantee yet another humiliating defeat. But he also complained that a return to Washington would force him into "a daily contact with the thing I loathe."[17]

Unlike Ewing, Campbell, and Winthrop, who still sympathized with the Whig cause even if they no longer wanted personally to participate in it, two influential Whigs whose service to the Whig party had been vital now rebuked it. One was Horace Greeley, who had fallen out with his allies Seward and Weed and who was engaged in a ferocious competition for subscribers with other Whig editors in Manhattan like James Watson Webb and especially Henry J. Raymond of the fledgling *New York Times*. Scorning as "blockheads" Whigs who spoke of resurrecting the party in 1853, Greeley saw the quiescent policy that he urged as more than a temporary lull during which Whigs could regroup. Convinced that the Whig party had begun a process of terminal disintegration, he said almost nothing about party politics in the columns of his *Tribune* throughout 1853. When he did, both in his paper and privately, he argued that keeping the Whig party alive foolishly endangered enactment of policies Whigs favored since Whig advocacy only guaranteed Democratic opposition. His advice, therefore, was for Whigs to disband, support a friendly Democrat such as Missouri's Thomas Hart Benton for speaker of the House when Congress met in December, and ally with Democrats who favored Whiggish projects like federal subsidies for a railroad to the Pacific Coast. The goal, he insisted at the end of April, should not be a revival of two-party competition but the "general fusion of all parties."[18]

The politician who greeted Greeley's call for Whigs to abdicate their opposition role most enthusiastically was also the Whig whose loss could do the party more harm than that of Clay, Webster, Ewing, Campbell, Winthrop, and Greeley combined—Truman Smith, the party's de facto national chairman since 1842. Throughout 1853, in letters to newspaperman James Pike, his California friend John Wilson, and Weed, Smith lacerated his party's futility and savaged its leaders with extraordinary scorn and contempt. "Galphinisms & Gardnerisms," "*stealing on a large scale*," and "a remorseless scramble for the Spoils" had disgraced the party under Taylor and Fillmore, he railed to Pike in March. Rather than support another "Old Fogie of the Whig party" for president in 1856, he intended to "encourage the presentation of a *Democratic* candidate who favors tariff revision and Rivers & Harbors improvements but who opposes further territorial annexation & war."[19]

"I have washed my hands now & foorever of all further intermeddling in party politics," Smith told Wilson and Weed the following August. Spurning Weed's plea to help rally Whigs for a comeback attempt, he declared that he would "never again lift a finger to put the Whig party in power" or "step across Pa. Av." to place a Whig in the White House. The only presidency that interested him now was that of two copper mining companies in Michigan to which he had just been appointed. "What do you expect to gain by the resuscitation of the Whig party of your State?" he pointedly asked Weed. Nationally, "the party is not worth preservation." "The Whig party should" instead "be broken down & put out of the way."[20]

Smith's contempt for Whigs and Whiggery is simply extraordinary. No other Whig had been more devoted to the party's welfare as a national institution. No one had paid more attention to the nuts and bolts of running congressional and presidential campaigns on a nationwide scale. No other Whig had been so willing as he to seek the compromises across sectional lines necessary to preserve the party's national competitiveness. That such a dedicated party man was now so disillusioned with it, now so ready "to have Whiggery charred & burned," now so eager to escape political life altogether spoke volumes about the impediments to a Whig comeback.[21]

The belief that Whigs could lie low for some indefinite period and then rally their troops again to the clarion call of battle, in short, was folly. Campbell, Winthrop, and Smith were not the only Whigs who saw no point in continuing the fray. "These party names of Whig and Democrat now mean nothing and point to nothing," a journalist wrote in April. Devoid of "principles and measures," their rivalry was perpetuated solely "as a means of political intrigue and an avenue for the attainment of office." Politics now completely lacked national principles, a New Yorker echoed in September. It had become a mere "scramble for the spoils & a fight about Men rather than measures." As an angry Ohioan warned Seward in February in a somewhat different context, unless Whigs defined what they stood for and thereby justified the party's continued existence, "many will be wandering off into other organizations or become permanently disgusted with every attention to public affairs."[22]

The second half of this prophecy described Whigs who wanted to quit political life completely. The first points to a different group of former Whigs who would no longer support the party. It also highlights the most egregious flaw in the strategy of quiet passivity that many Whig leaders advocated in the winter of 1852–53.

III

"No new party will rise, nor will any old one fall," Seward had retorted to Charles Sumner's postelection proposition that northern antislavery Whigs and Free Soilers merge in "a new organization," a new "party of Freedom."[23] In the narrow sense that no existing party disappeared and no new antislavery party appeared during 1853, Seward's prediction proved accurate. Nonetheless, Whigs' biggest mistake in waiting passively until they reaped the fruit of Democratic dissensions and mistakes in 1854 or 1856 was their assumption that Whigs could monopolize opposition to the Democrats and thereby automatically benefit from popular wrath against them.

During the twentieth century, American electoral politics has always been organized around the same two major parties—Republicans and Democrats—in large part because the adoption of state-printed ballots in the 1890s measurably increased the difficulty of launching a third party to challenge them. Since those major parties had an automatic slot on the ballots governments prepared and since the legal hurdles for other parties to get on those ballots were so high, Republicans and Democrats effectively monopolized voters' choice. During this century, therefore, the Republican party has been the only realistic alternative to the Democrats. Thus it, and not some other party, has usually benefited when voters sought to punish Democrats and to replace them in office.[24]

In the 1850s and for most of the nineteenth century, however, the rules of the political game encouraged rather than inhibited the creation of new parties. Instead of state-printed ballots that gave legally recognized major parties pride of place and disadvantaged other groups who sought to be listed on them, political parties printed and distributed their own ballots. As a result, it was far easier for new parties to challenge the old ones. As Whigs would learn to their dismay, therefore, politics in the 1850s was not a zero-sum game. Animosity toward Democrats did not translate automatically into support for Whigs. Voters had other options, especially in races for state and local offices that often had different, and for voters more salient, policy agendas than did officials in Washington. By siphoning off former Whig voters and eroding their allegiance to the Whig party, those new subnational parties were every bit as damaging as a new antislavery coalition to the survival, let alone the comeback, of the Whig party. Unlike their twentieth-century Republican successors, in sum, Whigs could not monopolize opposition to Democrats, and that simple, if easily overlooked, fact more than anything else explains the death of the Whig party.[25]

Although Seward and most other Whig leaders wanted to perpetuate the Whig party as a national, bisectional organization, in 1853 a minority of militant antislavery Whigs yearned for a merger with Free Soilers and antislavery Democrats into a new antislavery party. Such men were generally small-fry politicos, religiously inspired antislavery zealots, or simply former Whig voters who were fed up. There was a fine line, moreover, between Sewardites who wanted to lure Free Soilers into the northern Whig party in order to strengthen their own faction and to reaffirm the party's antislavery commitment, on the one hand, and antislavery Whigs who had viewed Seward as their spokesman and who now wanted to combine with Free Soilers in a new party, on the other. Their numbers, therefore, are impossible to calculate.

Some were not even Northerners. Kentucky's Cassius M. Clay, for example, had long since abandoned his famous cousin's Whig party to advance the antislavery cause. "The Whig party has had its day," he told Seward. "It had long since lost most of its measures, and its late disgraceful minority proves that its vitality is gone also." What was more, "your usefulness in the Whig ranks is at an end." If Seward stubbornly clung to the Whig party, Clay warned, "you would daily lose your own troops who will join *us!*"[26]

Some of Seward's troops were indeed prepared to defect. "The Whig party sought their own graves, by compromising with slavery at Baltimore," protested an Ohioan in late November 1852. "The time must soon come," he vowed, "when, regardless of consequences, the issue of freedom or slavery will be tried in this country." "The Whig party as such is completely used up and appears to be doomed," a New York Sewardite chorused the following February. "The only hope appears to me to be in the union of all lovers of freedom. The only question available is Freedom against Slavery."[27]

These passionate howls, ironically, help explain why Seward himself had no interest in trying to build a new antislavery party in 1853, why none took shape that year, and why even the remaining Free Soilers looked beyond the slavery question to perpetuate their party. The Free Soil party could not possibly recover its strength or a new antislavery coalition possibly be built until someone made an issue of "Freedom against Slavery." Disgruntled small-fry politicos and impatient abolitionists in Ohio, New York, or Massachusetts could not make slavery a live issue, that is, *do* something that convinced a majority of northern voters, who now seemed prepared to acquiesce in the Compromise's finality, that a new antislavery party was necessary. Only politicians in Washington could do that. Yet both the departing Fillmore administration and the incoming Democrats were pledged to squelch any new agitation of the slavery issue, and for most of 1853 Congress was not in session. Starting an antislavery fire required new fuel that no one of consequence seemly likely to supply.

Nonetheless, some northern Whigs' desire to agitate against slavery in order to build a new party or revive their own convinced a wholly different group of

Whigs that they must abandon the Whig party and seek new alliances. Like other Whigs, these men fully expected that the Democratic party would rupture within months of Pierce's inauguration, but they did not see that impending division as the spark to ignite a Whig revival. Rather, the prospect that pro-Compromise or Union Democrats would be most offended by the new administration caused them to resurrect plans for building a bisectional Union party from conservative Whigs and Democrats.

Within two weeks of Scott's defeat, Daniel Lee, a Georgia newspaperman who had served in Fillmore's administration and who now edited the Silver Gray Rochester *American* in New York, wrote him that "the conservative and filibustering elements" of the Democrats would soon "separate, adding the former to the patriotic Whigs North & South, who sustain your Administration." His friends in the Georgia and Alabama Union parties controlled major newspapers in those states, he added. Thus, "arrangements are in progress for the Union men of the whole country to cooperate in effecting a perfect national organization." Lee's allusion to southern Union parties and especially to his native Georgia was important. Throughout 1853 proponents of a Union party looked to Georgia and New York as the pillars on which to build it. And by the end of that year, many conservative Whigs, especially ex-members of Fillmore's administration and Fillmore himself, embraced the Union party idea.[28]

To summarize briefly, by the start of 1853 the Whig party was already fragmenting into at least five groups of very uneven size: conservative, pro-Compromise northern and southern Whigs who wanted to remain in the party and do battle with antislavery northern Whigs for control of it; Sewardites who were prepared to stay in the party, hoped to dominate it, and looked to former Free Soilers as allies in that struggle; men who yearned to quit politics for private life, some of whom believed the Whig party had outlived its usefulness; antislavery Whigs who wished to combine with Free Soilers in a new organization; and conservatives who thought a battle with Sewardites was hopeless and who looked toward a combination with conservative Democrats in a new Union party. That a party containing men of such different dispositions might hold together and stage a comeback at some future date, as Whig optimists envisioned, was problematic.

Nor was it only Whig politicos who could launch new parties that siphoned off voters whom other Whig politicians expected to mobilize when they sounded the charge. Rank-and-file Whigs' vulnerability to incursions by new parties was forecast in a remarkable letter from a disgruntled New York Whig to Seward in the spring of 1852. Anticipating Truman Smith's vitriolic criticisms, he declared that thousands of citizens held both Whig and Democratic congressmen in "utter contempt" because of "their neglect of the real interests of the nation, their apparent incapacity to discover anything better to occupy" their minds "than the tricks of demagogues to arrange for place and profit." Because their elected leaders were "imbeciles," he warned, "thousands of Whigs, tired of the present condition of things, are debating in their minds the propriety of abandoning their old association in the hopes that by a new crystallization a better development will be realized."[29]

That angry and disillusioned Whigs would eagerly embrace new parties that seemed responsive to popular grievances, even if those parties openly opposed

Whig candidates, became clear in some local and state races in 1852 when the excitement stirred by the presidential campaign held most voters in party traces. The Whigs' triumph in the Massachusetts state election in November had been the party's most satisfying victory that year. In the gubernatorial race, however, there had been five separate tickets, two of which took a more forthright stand for or against prohibition than either the Whigs, the Democrats, or the Free Soilers. Granted, Whigs had operated behind the scenes to launch the ticket opposing prohibition in order to lure alienated Irish voters from the Democrats. The more important fact is that those two tickets captured a tenth of the previous Whig vote and almost a tenth of the cast vote. In the Whig bastion of Pittsburgh in October a bigot named Joe Barker, who had won the mayoralty as a "People's and Anti-Catholic Candidate" in 1850 and who was renowned for his hostility to the enforcement of liquor laws, attracted a fourth of the vote in the race for county sheriff, while his Whig opponent captured little more than a third, a significantly smaller share than other successful Whig candidates on the same ticket.[30]

These elections were ominous for two reasons. First, they illustrated the ease with which splinter tickets could enter state and local races and the vulnerability of Whigs to them. Second, they highlighted the salience of anti-Catholicism and prohibition (or hostility to prohibition) to certain voters, issues that Whigs had purposely spurned in 1852 and that could be injected into the political arena by others when Whigs renounced them. As events soon revealed, indeed, they were the first breezes of an impending hurricane.

IV

Whigs, therefore, could not simply stand pat in 1853. To compete in the elections that year, to stem defections to new parties, and to restore the confidence of those who now deemed the party purposeless and corrupt, they had to justify the Whig party's perpetuation. They could hope that Democrats might eventually contribute to that rationale by angering voters, but they could not wait for Democrats to do so. They had to find an issue or issues that reestablished a distinctive and relevant identity for the party. Among Whigs across the nation, therefore, 1853 was marked by a flailing, often unsuccessful, search for issues that polarized Whigs against Democrats and thereby rejuvenated the party.

Seward, for one, intuitively recognized this need. Prior to the congressional session in December 1852, he pressed his friend Samuel Ruggles for facts and arguments he could use in a speech promoting construction of a railroad to the Pacific coast. "We can't fight Locofocoism with its own fire & I see nothing but this fire to fight them with," Seward succinctly explained.[31] In the same speech he went out of his way to revive the tariff issue for Whigs by arguing that the duties on iron, and particularly iron rails, should be raised rather than lowered, as so many railroad men demanded. In his final annual message to Congress, Fillmore also tried to breathe life into the tariff issue that the Whig platform of 1852 had abdicated. Far more thoroughly than he had in his 1850 message, Fillmore trotted out the entire arsenal of traditional Whig arguments for protection. He pilloried the Walker Tariff's *ad valorem* duties as invidious inducements to fraud, and he denounced that law's differential rates on raw materials and finished goods as pernicious disincentives to manufacturing. Flatly declaring that the United States needed "discriminating protective duties," the code words so conspicuously absent from the 1852 national platform, Fillmore recounted in detail the country's unfavorable balance of trade, the resulting outflow of specie to Europe that siphoned off almost the entire yield from the California gold strikes, the reluctance of capitalists to invest in manufacturing unless they were protected "from ruinous competition from abroad," and the need "to protect and encourage the labor of our own citizens." A protective tariff with specific duties, he hymned in language reminiscent of Henry Clay, "would place the mechanic by the side of the farmer, create a mutual interchange of their respective commodities, and thus stimulate the industry of the whole country." Friends of both Fillmore and Seward praised these efforts to revive the tariff issue, but the reigning prosperity continued to blunt its utility.[32]

Both Fillmore and Seward also addressed foreign policy, a topic many Whigs thought provided the greatest potential for drawing a line between themselves and expansion-minded Democrats. Alluding obliquely to his efforts to squelch filibusterers, Fillmore announced that he had assured both England and France that the United States had no designs on Cuba and that he personally regarded "its incorporation into the Union at the present time as fraught with serious peril." With regard to Democratic enthusiasm for Kossuth's calls for intervention in Europe, Fillmore was more emphatic. Rehearsing his commitment to strict neutrality and nonintervention in foreign wars, he chastised those who "now said . . . that this policy must be changed" and "that we ought to interfere between contending sovereigns and their subjects for the purpose of overthrowing the monarchies of Europe." "This," warned Fillmore, "is a most seductive but dangerous appeal to the generous sympathies of free men."[33]

Franklin Pierce's initial actions as president reinforced the belief that foreign policy might replace economic issues and slavery as the focal point of two-party conflict. In his inaugural address Pierce went out of his way to repudiate Fillmore's cautious approach by brashly proclaiming, "The policy of my Administration will not be controlled by any timid forebodings of evil from expansion." The location of the United States rendered "the acquisition of certain possessions not within our jurisdiction eminently important to our protection." That Pierce had annexation of Spanish Cuba and more of Mexico in mind became clear from his diplomatic appointments. To Spain he dispatched the notoriously reckless Louisiana champion of filibusterism and slavery expansion Pierre Soulé. To Mexico he sent the South Carolina fire-eater James Gadsden.[34]

Along with the selection of Mississippi's Jefferson Davis as secretary of war, these appointments indicated that Pierce would favor Southern Rights Democrats over pro-Compromise Union men, and southern Union Democrats resented them accordingly. But they also betokened a belligerent, expansionist foreign adventurism that genuinely appalled many Whigs, at least some of whom believed that voters could be rallied by opposition to it. Yet opposition to expansionism also failed to develop as a Whig panacea. Only some Democrats, many of whom adopted the label "Young America," promoted that policy. Other Democrats, as both Daniel Lee and Truman Smith had noted, opposed filibusterism, and Lee had cited them as potential recruits for a Union party.

With no new national issues to exploit in 1853, astute Whigs instinctively turned to state issues for desperately needed ammunition. In Ohio, they sought to exploit negative reaction to a new tax Democrats had imposed on banks' assets, a reaction that Cleveland editor John Barr predicted could "give Whigs the ascendancy [next fall], especially in the legislature."[35] In Illinois, some Whigs sought to ban "intoxicating drink" in order to break "the shell of the Democracy."[36] Samuel Bowles of Springfield, Massachusetts, argued that since Whigs had been "beaten out" by the Coalition in elections for delegates to an impending state constitutional convention, "our only hope is in making a State question" out of its actions. Pushing a single-district system of legislative representation, which could split Democrats and Free Soilers, he believed, "affords the best chance for the Whigs to make head against the Opposition." If defeated at the convention, "let us go to the people & fight it out there." Such a stand "is our only present hope of 'saving the state,' i.e. "the Whig party." "Now is the time to start new," he insisted. "The old issues are gone, we can't live under them."[37]

V

By the time of the spring elections in 1853, however, no compelling new Whig platform had yet emerged, and Whigs paid a terrible price for their failure to find one. In 1851, Virginia's Whigs had won two of fifteen House seats, wracked up 47 percent of the vote in the first popular election for governor, and made gains in the lower house of the legislature under the reapportionment dictated by the new state constitution. Because of congressional reapportionment, Virginia had only thirteen House seats to fill in 1853. Whigs failed even to run candidates in six districts, and they lost all seven they contested. Of those seven, the Whigs' share of the vote exceeded 45 percent in only four, and in two it fell below 40 percent. In contrast, a combination of increased representation from the west and multiple Democratic candidates in other districts produced the strongest Whig showing in legislative races since 1848. A net Whig gain of eight seats reduced the Democratic majority in the house from twenty-two to six and increased the Whig share from 43 to 48 percent. Nonetheless, Democrats still controlled the legislature and the governorship, and now there would be no Virginia Whig presence whatsoever in Congress.[38]

Lack of salient national issues also ruined Whig congressional candidates that spring in New England. The size of the Whigs' vote and their share of the total dropped everywhere. In New Hampshire, where they won two of four seats in 1851 through alliances with Free Soilers, they lost all three reapportioned districts. In the former Whig bastion of Rhode Island, George King had resisted the state's swing toward Democrats in 1851 by winning with 51.2 percent in the first district. Even though King's absolute vote grew by over 40 percent between 1851 and 1853, he lost in 1853 with less than 46 percent of the total, while the hapless Whig candidate in Rhode Island's other district attracted fewer than a tenth of its voters. Whigs had carried one of Connecticut's four districts in 1851, and their statewide total of 28,886 votes constituted a respectable 49.1 percent of the total. In 1853 their total vote sank to 24,891 (42.7 percent), and they lost all four seats. As in Virginia, in sum, Whig congressional candidates were completely shut out.

Whereas Whigs had won six of twenty-five congressional seats in the four states with spring elections in 1851, they were zero for twenty-two in 1853.[39]

Unlike Virginia, New England's state elections provided little solace for Whigs. Rhode Island's incumbent Democratic Governor Philip Allen won by his largest majority in three years, while Whigs were reduced to less than a third of the seats in the state house of representatives. In New Hampshire, Whig gubernatorial candidate James Bell won 2,270 (11.4 percent) fewer votes than his humiliated predecessor in 1852, Whigs' share of the total dipped to 31 percent, their proportion of house seats plummeted to 30 percent, and they elected only one of twelve senators. Once again, however, Connecticut best augured future developments.

In 1852, Connecticut's Whigs had tried to exploit prohibitionist sentiment by running Green Kendrick, a well-known dry, for governor and by urging their legislative candidates openly to endorse passage of a Maine Law. That strategy backfired when Kendrick won only 45 percent of the vote, and Whigs lost twenty house seats and six in the state senate. Nonetheless, most political observers in Connecticut expected that prohibition would again be the central issue in the 1853 state election, if only because a coalition of Whigs and Free Soilers in the legislature still sought to pass a Maine Law and because the Democrats' gubernatorial candidate, incumbent Governor Thomas Seymour, adamantly opposed it.

Confident that "the sinking carcass of Maine Lawism" was "a no go," Democrats eagerly wanted to make the election another referendum on prohibition by openly opposing it. As they suspected, however, Whigs changed tactics and tried "hard to effect, this year, by *indirect* means & *side issues* what they failed to accomplish last year by more *open* & *direct* means." Stung by the 1852 results, the 1853 Whig state convention directed candidates on the Whigs' statewide ticket to spurn all inquiries from temperance groups. It also purged prohibitionist sympathizers from the new state ticket. Henry Dutton, Whigs' gubernatorial candidate, particularly offended dries, for as state senator in 1850 he had helped bury a prohibition bill in order to save the Whig governor from having to sign or veto it. In sharp contrast to the studied silence of the state ticket, however, many Whig legislative candidates ran as open proponents of the Maine Law.[40]

With both Whig and Democratic gubernatorial candidates decidedly unsympathetic to prohibition, the question was whether temperance men would run candidates of their own or support the Free Soilers, who had endorsed the Maine Law a year earlier. Arguing that the Free Soil party must not pollute itself by taking a stand on a side issue like prohibition, at least one Free Soiler strenuously urged that the party keep hands off and force temperance men to make their own nominations. Most Free Soilers, however, disliked drinking and drinkers intensely. The party therefore nominated Francis Gillette for governor on a pro-Maine Law platform, and Gillette won the endorsement of temperance groups. In legislative races Free Soilers ran their own candidates in a few districts, but more often they supported Whigs or Democrats committed to a Maine Law.[41]

Free Soilers, in sum, were the only Connecticut party officially committed to prohibition in the gubernatorial race, but in the simultaneous legislative races Whigs and Democrats both ran dries and wets. Already demoralized by Scott's decisive defeat the previous November, Connecticut's Whigs, especially dries among them, were confused and often paralyzed with indecision by this bewildering situation. "The Whigs expect defeat," Emily Baldwin shrewdly wrote her absent son on election day. "They are disheartened & divided by temperance, Maine Law & abolition. While the opposite are in high feather from the Presidential election and all hang together." Democrats concurred. "The Whigs here seem disposed to let the election go pretty much by default," wrote a Democrat from the eastern shoreline town of Lyme. "Upon the whole things look, as if the Democracy would have their own way, without much of a struggle."[42]

Renouncing prohibition proved even more disastrous for Connecticut's Whigs than embracing it had been. Dutton was crushed. Between April 1852 and April 1853 Whigs lost almost 8,000 votes, a fourth of their 1852 total, and their share of the total plunged from 45 to a dismal 34 percent. Almost a tenth of Kendrick's 1852 supporters backed Gillette. Combined with recruits from previous nonvoters, those defectors increased the Free Soilers' vote by 6,000 and their share of the total from 4.6 to 14.8 percent. By stressing prohibition, and *not* the slavery issue, that is, Connecticut's Free Soilers garnered the biggest vote since the party's formation. Even more worrisome for Whigs, wets as well as dries abandoned the Whig party. Twice as many Kendrick voters as those who defected to Gillette decamped to the Democratic column in 1853, and Seymour's 51 percent of the vote represented the largest share won by a Democrat since 1837. Another index underlines Whig dissolution. Winfield Scott had won 2,000 more votes in November than Kendrick had the previous April, yet in April 1853 almost a fifth of Scott's supporters refused to vote at all.[43]

Demoralization and the divisive prohibition question also decimated Whig legislative candidates. As recently as 1851 Whigs had retained control of the senate, and by winning 49 percent of the house seats they had remained within four votes of the Democratic majority. In 1852, Whigs' share of house seats dropped to 40 percent, and the Democrats' majority increased to thirty-eight seats. Simultaneously, Whig strength in the senate was halved, and Democrats took firm control. In 1853, Whigs lost yet another senate seat to the Democrats, and in the house they were almost wiped out. Reduced to three-tenths of the seats, they now trailed the Democrats by seventy-seven votes. By 1853, in sum, Connecticut's Whig party had been torn apart. This collapse surely reinforced Truman Smith's conviction that the party was finished.

Two municipal elections that spring were also ominous harbingers. In Detroit an open assault by the Catholic clergy on the city's public school system and their demand that the public school fund be divided to support Catholic schools infuriated Protestants. Democrats split as Catholic supporters of the bishop "nominated a city ticket pledged to destroy the schools of this city by hook or crook" and Protestant Democrats nominated an Independent ticket against them. Caught flatfooted and now embarrassed by their pro-Catholic campaign in 1852, Whigs made no nomination of their own and supported the anti-Catholic ticket. The anti-Catholic Independent ticket easily prevailed, but Whigs' support of it indicated that others besides Whigs could define the political agenda and that Whig voters, disenchanted by their own party's pro-Catholic tilt in 1852, would readily support an openly anti-Catholic party.[44]

Cincinnati's mayoral election that spring demonstrated even more emphatically former Whig voters' readiness to punish their old party for its flirtation with Catholics. There, too, popular outrage at a perceived Catholic assault on public schools fueled an anti-Catholic backlash that shattered the existing parties. Four parties contested the mayoralty. The regular Democratic candidate tried to avoid the religious issue, but he was generally viewed as the favorite of Bishop John Purcell and the Catholic hierarchy, who petitioned the Ohio legislature in February for a division of the public school fund. The Whig candidate, backed strongly by the city's major Whig paper, dubbed himself an Independent and took a moderate proschool, anti-Catholic stance—far too moderate for most Protestants. Hence a new Free School party nominated a virulently anti-Catholic and anti-immigrant bigot, who was denounced by the regular Whig press as totally unfit for office. His candidacy, in turn, caused anti-Catholic Germans, who feared the nativism of the Free School candidate and who resented native-born Democrats' dominance of that party's local organization, to run a fourth, Anti-Miami ticket.[45]

Because foes of the Democrats split the anti-Catholic vote, Democrats won with 40 percent of the total. Still, three-fifths of Cincinnati's electorate chose anti-Catholic parties, and the Free School party alone took 35 percent of the vote. More important, Whigs, who had carried the city in the congressional election of October 1852, now won less than a fifth of the cast vote. Over three times as many former Whigs supported James Taylor, the Free School candidate whom the Whig press had denounced, as supported the Whig-backed Independent. More worrisome still, Ohio had held a referendum on prohibition in 1851, and almost two-thirds of the Cincinnatians who had then voted against liquor supported Taylor, twice the number retained by Whigs. That fact was ominous, for prohibition would become a central issue in the fall state election. The storm clouds that combined prohibitionism, nativism, anti-Catholicism, and antipartyism into the most powerful political force in the North, a storm that would shatter Whiggery, were gathering visibly on the horizon.[46]

VI

Prohibition played a role—often a decisive role—in almost every northern state election during 1853. Coupled with the propensity of men who now disgustedly rejected both major parties to start or support new parties in order to repudiate the old ones, it usually wreaked havoc on the Whig electorate. In every northern state where Whigs failed to find a defining new issue of their own, indeed, internal division, defection, and abstention mocked their hopes for a comeback.

California was one of very few states where prohibition was not a central issue in 1853, but its gubernatorial and legislative elections directly tested Whigs' hopes of benefiting from Democratic divisions. They also showed how even the vaguest of platforms, if relevant to voters, could keep Whigs competitive. Having come within a whisker of winning the governorship in 1851 and within 5,000 votes of defeating Pierce in the much larger turnout of 1852, California's Whigs remained within reach of the Democrats, and in 1853 their status as outs was a distinct advantage. The same antiparty, antipolitician sentiment mushrooming in the East appeared in California, in part because, as one Whig admitted, "The Whigs and Dems agree on virtually every policy for the state except patronage." By posing as clean government reformers, Whigs might therefore benefit from anti-incumbent animosity, especially as Governor John Bigler, whom Democrats renominated, was especially unpopular.[47]

Whigs, however, split over strategy. Led by John Wilson, Truman Smith's friend, some wanted to forsake Whig nominations altogether, "postpone our party issues if we have any," and instead merge with "the better portion of the Democratic party by means of an *independent movement.*" "Let the leading issue be opposition to the present corrupt set & their measures, & go for competence & honest men of either party," argued one such advocate. Others, including the majority of the Whig state committee, believed that rabidly hostile anti-Bigler Democrats would support a separate Whig nominee who could win by at least 12,000 votes. Especially if Whigs committed themselves to a new constitutional convention that would divide the state in two, argued one advocate of this strategy, Whigs could rout the Democrats "horse, foot, & dragoons."[48]

For various reasons, most Whigs opposed a constitutional convention. As a result, Whigs made their own nominations for governor and the legislature but without a concrete platform other than throwing the rascals out. By itself that was almost enough. Bigler won by a slightly larger margin than in 1851, but his 1,500-vote majority was markedly smaller than Pierce's a year earlier. Some dissident Democrats may have voted for the Whig candidate who ran 2,400 votes ahead of Scott, but defections were not nearly as numerous as optimistic Whigs had predicted. And in the legislative races where dissident Democrats presumably supported their own candidates, Whigs were slaughtered. They fell from a dismal 35 to 15 percent of the house seats, and in the senate their minority shrank to 23 percent. Democrats would subsequently engage in a blood feud over the Senate seat the new legislature was to fill, but the elections had already demonstrated that Democratic rifts did not translate into Whig victories.[49]

Fortunately for Whigs in Iowa, Illinois, and Indiana, they faced neither congressional nor important state elections in 1853. Wisconsin's Whigs were not so lucky. The Whig alliance with Free Soilers that had elected a majority of the state house of representatives and Governor Leonard Farwell in 1851 collapsed in 1852 because of the Whigs' national platform, and Democrats swept the elections that year. Farwell's refusal to run again in 1853 because he wanted to pursue private business affairs shattered attempts to revive the coalition behind a People's ticket that year. Anti-coalition Whigs, Democrats, and Free Soilers, now running as the People's party, each nominated their own gubernatorial candidates. Worse still from Whigs' perspective, only Edward Holton, the People's candidate, pledged to sign a prohibition law should the next legislature pass one. The liquor issue annihilated the Whig party. Holton ran second, with approximately 22,000 votes (39.3 percent); the Whig candidate drew a pathetic 3,300 votes (6 percent). Faced with a choice between a sterile old party and a new one with a decisive stand on a salient new issue, Whig voters abandoned their old party in droves.[50]

Prohibitionism also contributed to Whigs' collapse in Ohio. Although Ohio's Whigs had not won a state election since 1848, the popular vote margin between them and Democrats remained narrow. By cooperating with ex-Whigs among Free Soilers in the legislature on economic policy, moreover, they had managed to stop Democratic measures prior to 1852. That year's legislative reapportionment dictated by the 1851 constitution gave Democrats overwhelming control, and they used it to pass the bank tax many Whigs saw as the party's salvation.[51]

Despite their mutual suspicions, both Sewardite Whigs and the conservatives, who had seized control of the 1853 state convention, reviled the Democrats' bank tax. "If the Whig party will now do its duty, we might succeed," wrote one conservative in January. "The Democrats having made the *Hard money* issue, let us make no other issue & put them on the *defense*. They cannot defend this issue before the people." Since Whiggish Free Soilers, businessmen who were normally apathetic about politics, and probanking Democrats also hated that new law, making opposition to it the focal point of the Whig campaign, as Sewardite Whigs also urged, offered a realistic chance of carrying October's state elections.[52]

For two reasons, these hopes foundered. Whigs could not capture either the governorship or the legislature unless they won support from Free Soilers. Attempts to form fusion Whig-Free Soil legislative tickets in northern Ohio sputtered, however, when Free Soilers demanded as the price of cooperation that Whig legislative candidates commit themselves to Joshua Giddings' "ultra views of Slavery," to Salmon P. Chase's reelection to the Senate, and to the formation of a new antislavery party "for all time to come." Chase remained a pariah even to Western Reserve Whigs, and they refused to commit suicide by dissolving the Whig party in a new coalition. "This is more than we can stand," complained Sewardite John Barr, who sought Free Soil support for Whig candidates "to check the rampant and destructive Locofocoism . . . in this State," not a new party. "I care as little for names as anyone, but I am not to be driven from the support of Whig principles, or from acting with the glorious old party, sink, or swim," echoed Ben Wade.[53]

Simultaneously, "inveterate Silver Grays," who shared Sewardites' horror at the bank tax, opposed any cooperation with Free Soilers. That is why they engineered the gubernatorial nomination of the conservative southern Ohio congressman Nelson Barrere in February. The brief Whig platform, which called Whigs the "National Conservative party" and pledged them to uphold the Union and oppose Democrats' state policies, left Free Soilers cold. They therefore nominated their own gubernatorial candidate and, where Whigs spurned fusion on their terms, their own legislative candidates.[54]

Whigs' hope of focusing the election on the bank tax also foundered. Since 1851, when voters had ratified a clause of the new constitution authorizing the legislature to attack liquor, prohibitionist sentiment had burgeoned in Ohio. Unlike banking policy, which still polarized Whigs and Democrats against each other, temperance divided both parties internally. Hence, neither the Whig nor the Democratic state convention in 1853 said anything about it. Prohibitionism was particularly strong among Free Soilers, and even though some complained that stressing it rather than slavery would be "to throw away the *stack* to clinch at straw," Free Soilers featured it in their campaign. Their gubernatorial candidate, Samuel Lewis, vigorously called for passage of a Maine Law, and the state's leading temperance paper endorsed him. Free Soil legislative candidates also pushed prohibition, and on that issue, rather than banking or slavery, they often fused with Democrats or Whigs. Some Whig legislative candidates, sensing that prohibition was the only issue that aroused popular interest in 1853, also took up the cry. "The Maine Law will enter largely into the contest," Whig Congressman Lew Campbell reported from the Miami Valley. "I am not exactly a Maine Law man, but I say, Heaven send us anything that will help break down Locofoco-ism."[55]

That Whigs were perceived as less committed Maine Law men than Free Soilers was precisely the problem. By the summer Whigs knew they faced another defeat. Reports of apathy among Whig voters abounded, and Whig politicos spoke of going fishing rather than campaigning. The result was even worse than Whigs feared. In a poll that brought out fewer than three-fifths of the eligible voters, Democrats won the governorship easily. The Whig vote plunged by almost 34,000 (28.2 percent) since 1851 and by an even more alarming 66,734 (43.7 percent) since the presidential election in 1852. Accordingly, Whigs' share of the total plummeted from 42 percent in 1851 and 43 percent in 1852 to 30 percent in 1853. Meanwhile, Samuel Lewis, the clearest prohibitionist in the race, tripled the vote of his predecessor in 1851, ran far more strongly than Hale or even Martin Van Buren had, and raised Free Soilers' share of the total to 17.5 percent, its all-time high. Altogether, Whigs retained only two-thirds of their voters from the 1852 state election.[56]

After the election, Ohio's most important Whig paper, the *Ohio State Journal*, attributed the defeat to prohibition, blaming some Whigs for failing to vote, while Whig wets defected to the Democrats in order "to uphold and sustain the free and unrestricted traffic in ardent spirits." Few Whigs apparently supported the Democrats' gubernatorial candidate, but many dries bolted to the Free Soil column. In legislative races, however, wet Whigs who bothered to vote did support Democratic candidates. Whigs who had won only twenty-six house and nine senate seats in 1851 sank to seventeen in the house and seven in the senate. Whigs, in sum, had been routed, and the prohibition issue, combined with apathy, caused their obliteration.[57]

VII

Prohibition also contributed to Whiggery's unraveling in the Middle Atlantic and New England states, but their elections illuminated additional problems that afflicted the party. In 1852 Maine's Whigs exploited Democratic divisions over liquor to elect three of six congressmen, gain control of the legislature, and thereby put William Crosby, who won less than a third of the popular vote, in the governor's office. Democratic dissension over prohibition, and now over allocation of federal jobs, continued into 1853, and Whigs again stood to profit from it. This time the wet Wildcat faction controlled the Democratic state convention, which nominated Albert G. Pillsbury, a moderate opponent of prohibition, as the regular Democratic candidate for governor. Their platform said nothing about the Maine Law. Dry Democrats, who had previously supported Hubbard, bolted and nominated Anson P. Morrill, chairman of a recent state temperance convention, on a platform pledged to retain the Maine Law. Whigs renominated Governor Crosby, and Free Soilers again entered their own candidate, who defended the Maine Law even more strenuously than Morrill.[58]

Democratic division and the four-way race guaranteed that Maine's legislature would again choose the governor, but Whig prospects of success were anything but sure. A Senate seat was at stake in the legislative elections, and Wildcat Democrats who now ran as regulars seemed unlikely to help Whigs control the legislature again. In addition, Crosby alienated a number of Whigs because he had appointed Democrats to office and because his senate supporters had blocked Fessenden's election to the Senate in February. Finally, some Whig dries had voted for Hubbard rather than Crosby in 1852, and with more committed Maine Law men in the race than he, their support in 1853 was doubtful.[59]

The September gubernatorial results underlined how completely the prohibition issue had disrupted Maine's politics. Pillsbury, the Wildcat or regular Democratic candidate, emerged with a plurality of 43 percent. The two dry candidates, Morrill and the Free Soiler, took 24 percent between them, with Morrill running modestly ahead. With almost 33 percent of the reduced vote, Crosby ran only slightly better than he had a year earlier. More important, both the Whig and Democratic coalitions fragmented. While Crosby's net vote declined by only 2,000 between 1852 and 1853, analysis suggests that he retained only about 65 percent of his previous supporters. The balance split evenly between presumably wet defectors to Pillsbury and abstainers. Fragmentation of Hubbard's and Chandler's 1852 supporters was even more severe, as they divided among all the available candidates or joined the ranks of nonvoters. Results in the crucial legislative elections were just as chaotic. But the key fact was that after September, eleven senate seats remained to be filled by the successful senate candidates, and whoever won those senate seats could determine who became governor.[60]

Jockeying for advantage began even before the senate met. Morrill's supporters among Democratic legislators vowed to support no one but him for governor. Nonetheless, Whig divisions were more portentous, for they forecast which Whigs would later abandon the party and which would not. Whigs who had no love for Crosby spoke of uniting all the proponents of the Maine Law, that is, the opponents of the Wildcat Democrats, into a new coalition that would back Morrill for governor, Fessenden for United States senator, and Crosby for state supreme court justice and thereby split the Democratic party forever. "The effect of a coalition will be destructive of the harmony of the Whig party," the panicked Crosby protested to Fessenden. "You & I must stand or fall together." If Fessenden's friends supported Morrill, he warned, "*my friends*, & that includes all the aspirants for state patronage, will feel themselves aggrieved," and their only satisfaction "will be in defeating you."[61]

Fessenden's reply was frosty. Whigs' best strategy, he averred, was to combine all foes of the Wildcats, a goal with which his Whig allies like Israel Washburn, Jr., concurred. "Although I do not see that you and I must 'stand' together since your election by no means involves mine, yet a Whig governor is a good thing *per se*." Hence, he *personally* would not engage in any deals. Instead, he ambiguously wrote, he would work to carry "into effect the decrees of the Whig party to the best of my power."[62]

Despite continuing suspicion between pro-Crosby and pro-Fessenden Whig legislators, by mid-February both men had won election. "We now have what no reasonable Whig could have expected, a Whig Administration & Whig Senator," exulted one of Fessenden's friends. Even he, however, admitted that Whigs' rift pointed to trouble ahead. Crosby and Fessenden were, in fact, supported by very different coalitions. In the senate, which had exclusive authority to pick the governor, Whigs split evenly between Crosby and Morrill, and Crosby won only with the support of Wildcat Democrats determined to defeat Morrill. In the joint-session's election of United States senator, in turn, Crosby's avenging friends, whom one Whig termed "wild cat Whigs" representing "the stationary conservatism of venerable Whig antiquity," refused to support Fessenden. He won only by combining Morrill Democrats and Free Soilers with the majority of Whigs against the Wildcats.[63]

The rift widened in early 1854. Crosby and Fessenden disagreed about the party's future course. Crosby was now determined to give state jobs only to Whigs and only to his loyalists among them. Aware of his dependence on Morrill Democrats and determined to build a broader coalition against the anti-Maine Law Wildcats, Fessenden, in contrast, implored Crosby to appoint at least some Morrill men and above all not to remove Morrill himself from the state job he held. Even in victory, in sum, divisions between Whigs seeking a broader anti-Democratic coalition and those hoping to preserve an exclusive Whig party intensified. And while this contentious debate waxed in the early months of 1854, Congress was debating an even more controversial matter that exacerbated it—the Kansas-Nebraska bill.[64]

If division marred Whigs' victory in Maine, a startling defeat stunned them in Vermont, which by 1852 had become northern Whigs' safest stronghold. There, as elsewhere, trouble erupted over the liquor issue. In late 1852, a coalition of Whig and Free Soil legislators, aided by some Democrats, passed an anti-liquor license law, not a full-fledged prohibition act. But two-fifths of Whig legislators, fearing a wet backlash, opposed the license law, and Whig papers denounced it. Whigs' nervousness increased when a popular referendum on the law passed by only 300 votes out of more than 44,000 cast. When Whigs renominated Governor Erastus Fairbanks in 1853, therefore, they tried to finesse the liquor issue by declaring "that this is not a party question, and never should be." Democrats, in contrast, flatly denounced the new license law as a Whig measure and called for its repeal. As elsewhere, therefore, the Free Soilers, who ran their own gubernatorial and legislative candidates and who had strongly supported the new law in the legislature, were the most clear-cut proponents of prohibition in the race. Furious at the backsliding by their own party, a few dry Whigs, led by prominent editor E. P. Walton, then endorsed the Free Soilers' gubernatorial candidate. Recognizing that their hope of wresting the legislature from the Whigs and thus electing the new United States senator depended upon cooperation with Democrats, however, Free Soilers refused to attack Democrats' antiliquor stance in what Whig Justin Morrill disgustedly called a "chicken-hearted" display.[65]

By August, once-confident Whig leaders were deeply worried. Bulwarked by the funds and organizational resources of federal jobholders, Vermont's Democrats made their most vigorous effort in years. At the same time, overconfident Whigs seemed too complacent and dry Whigs too cross-pressured to vote at all. Even worse, wet Whigs who opposed the license law threatened to scratch Whig legislative candidates or "desert us for Rum openly" by voting Democratic. Efforts to awaken Whigs to the danger proved too little and too late. In September, Fairbanks got 2,600 fewer votes than a year earlier, reducing his share from 49.3 to 44.1 percent. Conversely, Democrats gained 3,000 votes, boosting their share from 31 to 38 percent. The Free Soil gubernatorial candidate lost about 1,000 votes between 1852 and 1853, and his percentage slipped from 19.6 to 17.5. Nonetheless, and more important, pro-Maine Law Free Soilers doubled their representation in the legislature and gained the balance of power between the two major parties. The chance of throwing Whigs out of power for the first time since the party's birth proved too tempting, and Free Soilers joined Democrats to elect Democrat John Robinson governor. Democrats, however, refused to send a Free Soiler to the Senate, and as a result the legislature failed to choose anyone to replace Whig Senator Samuel Phelps.[66]

In Massachusetts, Whigs' other remaining New England bastion, prohibition became inextricably entwined with the Democratic/Free Soil Coalition's attempt to revise the state's constitution in 1853 because support for prohibition had a decidedly regional cast. When the state legislature passed a Maine Law in 1852, it was supported by Whigs and Coalition members from thinly populated western towns that were decidedly hostile to Boston and its growing Irish population. Opposition to the law came primarily from eastern Democrats sensitive to the views of their Irish and working-class constituencies. Whigs exploited Irish Catholics' antipathy toward the Coalition's nativism and the prohibition law to win the 1852 gubernatorial election, but they failed to defeat a referendum to call a constitutional convention long sought by the Coalition.[67]

Whigs' lethargy and internal division over constitutional reform allowed the Coalition in March 1853 to elect the majority of delegates to that convention. They had two priorities: preserving the majority rule in statewide elections so that multiparty races for governor would almost always be thrown into the legislature, where the Coalition could bargain, and increasing the already disproportionate representation of small towns that were the heartland of Free Soil strength. These proposals were included in the constitution submitted to the electorate on the same day as the 1853 state election.

The constitution offended three groups. Irish Catholic Democrats from eastern Massachusetts opposed any increase in the strength of western Democrats and Free Soilers, who had inflicted the hated Maine Law on them and whom they quite properly regarded as bigoted enemies of their faith and mores. Pro-Compromise Democrats disliked anything that prolonged the Coalition, and a few weeks before the November election, Caleb Cushing, whom Pierce had appointed attorney general, tried to rally them against the constition and behind their own dissident ticket of National or Hunker Democratic candidates by issuing a public letter, quickly labeled the "Cushing ukase," which declared that Pierce's administration would no longer tolerate Democrats who cooperated with Free Soilers.[68] Whigs, however, stood to lose most under the new constitution, which by increasing the representation of small towns would guarantee Coalition control of the legislature. Hence Whigs denounced the new constitution "as shameless a party manoevre as was ever concocted" and urged their supporters to defeat it.[69]

Massachusetts Whigs, in sum, found a compelling new state issue around which the party rallied. Because dissident Democrats agreed with them about the constitution, they not only defeated it, they triumphed in the state elections as well. Total turnout dropped by about 14,000, including a 3,000-vote Whig decline, since 1852, but with almost 46 percent, Whig gubernatorial candidate Emory Washburn's plurality was slightly larger than John Clifford's a year earlier. Democrats ran second with 27 percent, and Free Soiler Henry Wilson, who garnered almost 8,000 fewer votes than Horace Mann in 1852, was third with 22.5 percent. The anti-Coalition Hunker candidate attracted less than 5 percent, but his 5,500 votes, drawn almost entirely from wet Democrats who had supported Clifford in 1852 and conservatives, proved crucial.

Had Whigs possessed modern statistical methods, they would have known that they retained more of their 1852 electorate than either Democrats or Free Soilers and that they gained more votes from other parties than those rivals. What Whigs could see was even more important. The presence of dissident Democratic legislative tickets deprived Democrats of some seats by preventing the necessary majorities and threw others to the Whigs. Whigs retained narrow control of the senate, and they increased their margin in the house over Hunker Democrats and Coalition members combined from ten to sixty-four seats. Washburn's elevation to the governorship was thus assured.[70]

Best of all for Whigs, the new constitution lost by about 5,000 votes. Nearly unanimous opposition from the Whigs provided the biggest bloc of negative votes, but the margin of victory came from dissident Democrats and even a few Free Soilers. Seventy percent of the Hunker Democrats, approximately 3,900 men, voted against ratification. In Massachusetts, Democratic divisions, along with Whig unity behind a new state-oriented issue, produced Whigs' victory.[71]

Three other results of the Massachusetts election were portentous. First, Sumner blamed his new Senate colleague, Edward Everett, for leading the Whig charge against the constitution, a view that betokened trouble between the two when they went to Washington. Second, while Sumner called the defeat "a calamity to the Liberal cause," it had far more pragmatic implications for Sumner himself. Along with Cushing's ukase, it effectively finished the Massachusetts Coalition that put Sumner in the Senate. As a disconsolate pro-Coalition Democrat wrote Gideon Welles the follow February, "Cushing's ukase, aided by one or two other circumstances that would have been powerless without it, 'crushed out' the most genuine and hopeful democratic movement that was ever organized here." Sumner, that is, now lacked a secure base in the legislature, which would determine his reelection. He needed to revitalize antislavery sentiment, and as a United States senator he, quite unlike the small-fry politicos who wrote Seward, could make an issue of Freedom against Slavery when Congress met in 1854. Third, within Massachusetts the group credited with or blamed for the constitution's defeat was Irish Catholics in Boston and its environs. Their supposed responsibility, in turn, helped fan the embers of Massachusetts nativism into a conflagration.[72]

New York, where Whigs had been promoting state canal enlargement since 1851, produced northern Whigs' only other triumph in 1853, and as in Maine and Massachusetts, it depended primarily upon Democratic divisions. Though contention over canal expansion contributed to Democratic rifts, feuds between Hardshell Hunkers, led by ex-Senator Daniel S. Dickinson, and Softshells and their new Barnburner allies over the allocation of the party's nominations and appointments primarily caused them. Pierce's distribution of federal patronage pushed these disputes beyond the breaking point, and the two rival factions nominated their own state tickets in 1853.[73] Whigs knew that Pierce's blunders had handed them victory on a silver platter. "We are stronger today than we ever were before," wrote one Whig in June. "The trumps are all in our hands for this year and probably for many years to come." Even better, Whigs could again focus their campaign on canal expansion, which united them and divided Democrats since, in early 1853, Whig and Hard state legislators passed a constitutional amendment allowing the enlargement aimed at by the Nine Million Loan bill in 1851.[74]

Getting "men of the right stamp" on the Whig ticket was the pothole on the comeback trail. Precisely because Democratic divisions meant that Whigs could win with only a fraction of their normal vote and precisely because control of the canal board now seemed more important than ever, the prospect of certain victory aggravated rather than mitigated Whigs' own internal divisions. Distrust between Silver Grays and Sewardites remained rancid after Scott's defeat, and in a few spring muncipal elections Silver Grays supported Democratic candidates to defeat Sewardite foes. As Whigs' October state convention approached, therefore, the rival factions jealously eyed each other. Both knew Whigs would "have control of the Canals," and therefore both wanted "men of the right stamp" on the Whig ticket.[75]

Fearing that Weed intended to exclude them entirely from the state ticket, Silver Grays insisted that some of the slate go to their own men, such as George Babcock for comptroller or Daniel Ullmann for attorney general. If "Weed & Co exhibit their intolerance to the utmost extent" by "forcing obnoxious men on us," they vowed, they would refuse to vote or support the Hards. The prospect that Hards, who shared Silver Grays' antipathy toward antislavery men, would nominate a procanal ticket, indeed, provided defiant Silver Grays with such an attractive fallback position that in some localities they did not even bother to contest the selection of delegates to the Whig state convention. And if the Hard ticket proved unacceptable, some Silver Grays threatened, they would bring out a separate ticket of their own that would get Hard support. "In either way," predicted John C. Spencer before the Democrats formally split, "the nucleus of a new and honest party that can work together, will be formed."[76]

Sewardites welcomed an intraparty brawl. "I would go in with all my soul to put Greyism out of the party," declared one. "A glorious opportunity to vindicate the Whig party & remove from it the crushing weight of the Baltimore platform will be lost unless the plainest & [most] outspoken resolutions be passed," wrote another. "We can do so now with safety—let Silver Grays join the Hunkers—the Whig party will be vastly stronger internally & externally without them." The course to "complete victory" was "plain and simple," urged still another Sewardite. "Make no compromise with slavery beyond the strict letter of the Constitution and eschew all sympathy with the treacherous Silver Grays."[77]

Much to the consternation of Silver Grays, allies of Seward and Weed easily dominated the convention, but neither Weed nor Seward wanted to alienate Silver Grays by reaffirming the party's hostility to the Fugitive Slave Act. Under Weed's guidance, the platform was completely silent on the slavery issue and the divisive prohibition question. It instead emphasized canal enlargement. Weed also adroitly arranged a superficially balanced state ticket, even to the point of angering followers who complained that antislavery Whigs had resurrected, not crushed, Silver Grays with the ticket.[78]

Despite apathy caused by overconfidence, residual Silver Gray disaffection, and confusion caused by the volatile Maine Law question in legislative races, Whigs, as Washington Hunt predicted, elected their "state ticket & Legislature very easy." Democrats lost thirty-eight seats in the house, and their remaining contingent was evenly divided between Hards and Softs. The Whig share of seats soared from 33 to 61 percent, and in the senate it jumped from 50 to 72 percent. The entire Whig state ticket also won, causing one Seward lieutenant to rejoice: "I congratulate you on the result of the Election. Another *1840* seems to be approaching—1837 has already returned."[79]

The scope of Whig gains in the legislature between 1852 and 1853 resembled that between 1836 and 1837, but this glowing comparison was misguided. In 1837 and 1838 Whigs triumphed in New York and elsewhere because new voters surged into their party, not because of Democratic divisions. In contrast, turnout in New York plunged from 84 percent in 1852 to only 59 percent in 1853, and victorious statewide Whig candidates attracted some 81,000 fewer votes (33.5 percent) than the defeated Hunt had a year earlier. Statewide, moreover, Whig candidates won with less than 44 percent of the vote, while Hard and Soft candidates evenly split almost 52 percent between them. Both significant Silver Gray defections to the Hard ticket and heavy abstention by 1852 Whig voters contributed to the depressed Whig total that year.[80]

Democratic divisions and hope of directing canal enlargement, in sum, brought Whigs victory in the nation's largest state. But even their triumph revealed the toll taken by internal division and apathy. Whigs might crow about majorities in the legislature "quite as large as any good Whig could desire" and about the absence of anything "to prevent our holding the State for some time," but Silver Grays' action pointed to a quite different future. Even before the votes were cast, Fillmore, who urged his friends to support the ticket, noted that New York politics were "in a *snarl*" and that only Democratic divisions made Whig victory certain. That triumph, he added, would "disorganize the Whig party as the democrats are now disorganized" since "*Woollies*" would control the state administration and proscribe " '*Silver Grays*' or National Whigs" from all state jobs.[81]

VIII

Quite unlike Whigs in Massachusetts and New York, those in Pennsylvania and New Jersey failed to develop a compelling issue in 1853, and they suffered the consequences. The difference between the fortunes of Pennsylvania's and New York's Whigs is especially puzzling, for not only were Pennsylvania Democrats' divisions potentially as explosive as Democratic rifts in New York, but Pennsylvania's economy also resembled New York's. With its Main Line Canal system, newly completed Pennsylvania Railroad, and numerous other railroads under construction, its commercial center of Philadelphia, its extensive coal mining areas, and its iron foundries, glass factories, and textile mills, Pennsylvania was one of the nation's three most economically complex and advanced states. Both the legislature's agenda and Bigler's correspondence in 1852–53 indicate that concrete economic policies concerning banks, coal-mining companies, and railroads generated intense interest around the state. Yet Whigs' failure to define a distinctive and unifying state economic issue was emphasized by their insipid single-sentence 1853 state platform: "The Whigs of Pennsylvania adhere steadfastly to the cherished and often avowed principles of their party." That meaningless statement, growled Pittsburgh's major Whig paper, "measurably weakened" party ties and produced "indifference and apathy" in "the public mind."[82]

Given the cornucopia of economic issues in the state legislature and the rifts among Democrats, what prevented Pennsylvania's Whigs from mounting a campaign in 1853 as compelling as that of their New York neighbors? One answer is that Pennsylvanians would elect only a canal commissioner and state legislators that year. More important, the complex public policy questions associated with a modern economy defied exploitation by statewide political parties, quite unlike expansion of the Erie Canal system, which was a state, not a private, responsibility. Questions involving railroads and coal companies generated intense interest, but it was highly localized in individual communities. Railroad policy aligned region against region, not party against party.

Banking policy seemed an exception to this pattern, and in 1853 legislative roll-call votes on banking and currency generated levels of partisan conflict reminiscent of those of the 1840s prior to the California gold strikes. But that conflict was misleading. By the early 1850s, Pennsylvania's Democrats sharply divided over banking. New charters passed the legislature with considerable Democratic support, only to be vetoed by Governor Bigler. Attempts to override those vetoes polarized the parties against each other and thus camouflaged the considerable Democratic support for the original bills.[83]

Unable to find a compelling state economic platform in the 1853 legislative session and fully aware of apathy among their supporters, Pennsylvania's Whigs in the summer tried to manufacture a statewide issue by demanding sale of the state's Mainline Canal system to private investors, but Democrats refused to take the bait and oppose such a sale. In this void, Whig legislative candidates in certain localities like Pittsburgh committed themselves to passage of a Maine Law to mobilize votes. Where Whigs did not, independent protemperance tickets challenged them. As elsewhere, prohibition divided both Democrats and Whigs internally, and its injection into the race confounded everyone's calculations.[84]

This crazy-quilt pattern paralyzed some Whig voters and drove others, along with some Democrats, to splinter parties. The issueless statewide contest for canal commissioner brought out barely half of the potential electorate, and Whigs won barely two-fifths of the cast votes, the worst showing in the party's history. Apathy clearly afflicted Whigs more than Democrats. Since the hotly contested and unsuccessful campaign for William F. Johnston's reelection in 1851, the Whig vote had plunged by 60,000 (33.7 percent), while the Democrats had lost only 33,600 (18 percent). Measured against the lower-profile race for canal commissioner in October 1852, Whig turnout declined by 33,664 votes (22.2 percent) compared to a Democratic loss of only 18,684 (10.9 percent). Even worse, over 7,700 Native Americans still backed their own canal candidate rather than the Whig, Native Americans won four of five legislative seats from Philadelphia County, and an Independent pro-Maine Law ticket, whose stated goal was "to break down for once the power of party organization in this city," swept all of eight of Philadelphia City's normally Whig assembly seats. When the smoke had cleared, Whigs were reduced to a pathetic 26 of 100 seats in the house and a four-vote minority in the senate.[85]

As in Pennsylvania, the economic questions pressing upon New Jersey's government were far too complex for partisan exploitation. The cross-cutting impact of railroad legislation, taxes, and other state economic issues had long since split the once-dominant Whigs and toppled them from power.[86] The gubernatorial and legislative elections of 1853 further punctuated their disarray. After the crushing losses of 1852, some Whig papers and politicos in New Jersey concluded that "the Whigs are a used up party," an organization barely "breathing the breath of life."[87] Desperate to revive the vigor of their moribund party, Whigs in 1853 tried to combine prohibitionists, nativists who had bitterly opposed Scott, and remaining Whig voters interested in economic projects blocked by the Camden and Amboy Railroad into a new, potentially broader coalition. They did so, however, in hopelessly inept fashion, for their platform ignored the liquor question completely and instead stressed the antimonopoly issue, on which Joel Haywood, their gubernatorial candidate, a favorite of the state's small Native American party, and a strong prohibitionist, was unfit to run since he had been a consistent supporter of the Joint Companies.[88]

A chaotic race ensued. Democrats pilloried Haywood as a prohibitionist fanatic and an anti-immigrant bigot. Whig legislative candidates stressed different issues in different parts of the state. Democratic legislative candidates endorsed a Maine Law where prohibitionist sentiment was strong. And temperance men, who distrusted Whigs' commitment to prohibition because of their platform's silence, successfully ran independent legislative tickets in some counties. Although Haywood carried lightly populated southern New Jersey, where antimonopoly and prohibitionist sentiment was most intense, he lost northern New Jersey, where immigrants were concentrated and opposition to prohibition was strongest. Statewide he got 47.4 percent of the vote, only a slight improvement over his defeated predecessor in 1850, and Whigs remained a powerless minority in the legislature.[89]

IX

However dismal, northern Whigs' performance in 1853 did not drastically reduce Whig strength in Congress. They lost four House seats in New England, to be sure, and Vermont's surprising defeat temporarily cost them another Senate seat. Even in Vermont, however, Free Soilers and Democrats had failed to elect a U.S. senator, and elsewhere, as in Ohio or California, sitting Democratic or Free Soil United States senators, not Whigs, were most affected by the results of legislative elections. Northern Whigs, in sum, could still hope to increase their representation in Washington in 1854, when the great majority of northern states held congressional elections.

The preservation of the Whig party as a competitive national organization depended far more upon the southern than the northern elections of 1853, since many House and important Senate seats were at stake. In addition, a much larger proportion of southern than northern Whigs had refused to vote in 1852. The South's 1853 state and congressional elections thus posed a crucial test of the party's ability to restore their allegiance. Though unquestionably ominous, the wipeout in Virginia's May congressional elections could be attributed to

Democrats' traditional strength there. Virginia had also voted before the expected Democratic dissensions had time to fester or demoralized Whigs had time to regroup. What happened later in Maryland, Kentucky, Tennessee, and North Carolina, where Whigs remained strongly competitive, and in Georgia, where they had once been powerful, would provide a more accurate gauge of the party's future. Without the albatross of Winfield Scott, could southern Whigs rebound?

Although many Southerners favored the Maine Law, prohibitionism and anti-Catholicism played a lesser role in most southern congressional and state elections than in the North. Maryland was the only slave state where the Catholic clergy joined their northern counterparts in attempting to raid public school taxes to fund parochial schools. Outside of Maryland, Kentucky, Missouri, and Louisiana, Catholics and immigrants were not numerous enough to arouse much concern— at least in 1853. In most southern states, therefore, feuds among Democrats had the greatest influence on the 1853 elections. Unfortunately for Whigs, they usually were not enough to help them win.

Missouri was a marked exception to this rule. Under the congressional reapportionment that took effect in 1852, Missouri was entitled to seven federal representatives. Since the legislature had not yet drawn up new districts by the time of the August elections that year, Missouri elected only five congressmen, two of whom were Whigs and another, Thomas Hart Benton. In August 1853, therefore, Missouri had two additional House seats to fill. Benton's impending return to Congress shattered the majority Democrats once again along pro- and anti-Benton lines, and Whigs consequently won both seats. Thus, when the Thirty-Third Congress met in December, Whigs controlled four of seven House seats and a senatorship from one of the most solidly Democratic states in the nation.

Democratic divisions over congressional candidates also portended Whig gains in Maryland, where discipline among both parties began to break down in 1851 after ratification of the state's new constitution. "I was mortified to find so much disorganization in Maryland . . . owing entirely to domestic contestions," one appalled Democratic observer reported to Washington in October 1853. But Whig organization proved little better, and failing to exploit a glorious opportunity, they elected only two of six congressmen in 1853 compared to four of six in 1851.[90] Maryland's gubernatorial election in 1853 featured a straight-out race between Democrat Thomas Ligon and the recently retired Whig Congressman Richard Bowie. Both Democrats and Whigs predicted their man would win, but Democratic unity carried the day. Exploiting Democratic divisions over prohibition, however, Whigs won both houses of the legislature for the first time since 1849 and all the offices on the state ticket other than governor.[91]

Prohibition's impact on Maryland's elections bears emphasis. In the fourth congressional district, "a Maine Liquor Law organization" threw its support to Thomas Walsh, the only incumbent Whig from the Thirty-Second Congress to seek reelection in 1853. Yet that support did not spare Walsh from defeat and may have contributed to it by causing a few hundred Whig wets to shift to his rival, who claimed to be an Independent Democrat, not a regular Democrat.[92] More likely, the temperance endorsement meant little to dries, since Congress had no jurisdiction over liquor. By running separate tickets in heavily Democratic Baltimore and fusing with Whigs elsewhere, however, prohibitionists helped Whigs win state offices. At the same time, third-party legislative tickets, like the proliferation of independent congressional candidates, demonstrated how extensively anti-incumbent, antiparty sentiment pervaded Maryland. "The result of the elections," the *Baltimore American* accurately observed, "shows with great significance the abatement of party feeling, and the difficulty of organization under party banners."[93]

Although some Kentucky Whigs were ready to abandon their party by the summer of 1853, others, buoyed by Scott's victory in the state and their success in a special 1852 congressional election to replace Humphrey Marshall, looked forward confidently to August's congressional and legislative elections. Unlike Maryland, where only one of four Whig incumbents sought reelection to Congress in 1853, for example, three of Kentucky's five incumbents ran. In addition, Clement S. Hill, who had lost the fifth district in 1851, reentered the fray. Most important, in the eighth district, former congressman and governor Robert P. Letcher, now back from a stint as minister to Mexico, contested Democratic upstart John C. Breckinridge, who had usurped that former banner Whig district in 1851. However demoralized Whigs elsewhere seemed, in short, Kentucky's displayed the old fighting spirit.

Spirit without compelling issues, however, was not enough.[94] As they had since 1834, Whigs carried both chambers of the legislature. Yet they won only fifty-five house seats, exactly the same as their 1851 total and the smallest number controlled by Whigs since the party's formation in 1834. They did pick up two additional senate seats, yet, with the exception of 1851, their share of senators was the lowest since 1838. Despite the strong slate of congressional candidates, moreover, Whigs again won only five of ten House seats. Though Letcher attracted almost 1,000 more votes than Leslie Combs in 1851, he also lost to Breckinridge, the Democrats' new star. Elsewhere too, Democrats seemed on the rise. While the statewide Whig total increased by almost 5,000 votes (9.8 percent) between 1851 and 1853, the Democratic total grew by 12,000 (24 percent), and in 1853 Democrats ran almost 7,000 votes ahead of Whigs in the state as a whole. Tradition, in sum, kept Whigs securely in power, but they failed to roll back the gains Democrats had been making since 1848.[95]

Tennessee was the other slave state carried by Scott, but as 1853 opened, its Whigs were far less sanguine than Kentucky's about August's gubernatorial, congressional, and legislative elections. On the one hand, their 1852 reapportionment of the congressional and state legislative districts seemed to give them a clear edge over the Democrats, and the program of railroad aid and a free banking law they had enacted were popular, especially in East Tennessee. On the other hand, those achievements exhausted the party's state agenda, and they lacked compelling state issues for 1853.[96]

Ironically, moreover, the reapportionment that Whigs expected to help them control the state for a decade also fomented Whig rifts. Many legislative districts were now so securely Whig that several Whig aspirants ran, thereby threatening to allow Democrats to win with pluralities. More important, to drive Democrat Andrew Johnson from Congress, the Henrymander added the heaviest Whig counties from the old second district to Johnson's first district. Whig Congressmen Albert G. Watkins, who represented the second district in the Thirty-Second Congress, lived in one of the transferred counties, and he refused to stand down in favor of the Whig candidate preferred by the old first district's Whigs. Consequently, two Whig candidates ran in the new first district in 1853, and by dividing the heavy Whig majority, they allowed a Democrat to win with only 37 percent of the vote. The reapportionment did succeed in forcing Johnson not to seek reelection, but that freed him to become the Democrats' gubernatorial candidate instead.[97]

Leadership feuds also split the Whigs. Endemic jealousies among prominent Whigs from the state's three main geographical regions—West, Middle, and East Tennessee—seemed sure to flare again over the choice of a gubernatorial nominee and when the legislature elected in August tried to fill John Bell's Senate seat. The refusal of Congressmen Meredith Gentry and Christopher Williams to endorse the national ticket in 1852 was a new source of intraparty rancor. To the dismay of their supporters, neither won renomination in 1853, and Gentry, for one, blamed Bell for stirring up opinion against him, thereby jeopardizing Bell's reelection to the Senate. What made these resentments all the more threatening is that the only prominent Whig whom all factions trusted, Governor William B. Campbell, refused to run again.[98] Without an obvious gubernatorial candidate, Whigs first approached Gustavus A. Henry of Middle Tennessee, the party's most effective stump speaker, but he initially refused on the grounds that he had already exhausted himself crisscrossing the state as a presidential elector in 1852.[99] Late in the spring, however, Henry relented and agreed to run, believing that his Democratic opponent Johnson, known for his rough-hewn mannerisms and lack of formal education, was vulnerable on a number of fronts. *"I will ruin him,"* boasted Henry.[100]

Although Whigs regarded Johnson as an "arch demagogue" who lacked the education to be governor, Johnson in fact possessed superb political instincts. Even the overconfident Henry eventually admitted that Johnson was "as smart a fellow as I have met in many a day." As early as December 1852 Johnson sensed the antiparty, antipolitician mood emerging across the nation, and to capitalize on it he had preferred to be run for governor as a People's candidate without a formal convention nomination. His demand for reapportioning the legislature exclusively on the basis of the white population appealed to the nonslaveholder majorities in East Tennessee. In 1852, moreover, the legislature passed a state constitutional amendment providing for the popular election of all judges in Tennessee, and the referendum on that amendment coincided with the gubernatorial poll in August. Johnson vigorously endorsed the amendment for "bringing the government nearer to the people, as originally designed by our republican ancestors." Like so many politicians since the days of Andrew Jackson, in sum, Johnson posed as the paladin of republicanism, the champion of popular self-government. He, not Henry, defined the winning issue.[101]

The gubernatorial contest was close. Henry ran some 2,300 votes behind Campbell in 1851 and lost to Johnson by the same margin. Defections in East Tennessee proved crucial. Campbell attributed them to the popularity of the white basis among nonslaveholders. Henry blamed vote swapping by friends of Whig legislative candidates and, in the first congressional district, of the rival Whig congressional candidates. Whigs, he fumed, agreed to vote for Johnson in return for Democratic votes for the Whig legislative and congressional candidates they preferred. "I was regarded as a sort of merchandise on the market & vended to the highest bidder," howled Henry. However accurate Henry's analysis, Whigs did retain control of the legislature, although even the Henrymander did not prevent their losing the senate by one seat.[102]

When the Henrymander became law in 1852, Governor Campbell rejoiced that it ensured Whigs seven of the state's ten congressional districts. In 1853, however, Whigs won only five, a net gain of one over 1851. In the "safe" first district, where rival Whig candidates squandered the chance to take Johnson's old seat, moreover, the death of the successful Democrat allowed Whigs to carry it in a special election early in 1854. And in the new tenth district, they came within 6 votes, out of over 10,000 cast, of unseating incumbent Democrat Frederick Stanton. Of the Whig victors, the most important were the incumbent William Cullom, Emerson Etheridge, who ran unopposed in the new ninth district, Nashville editor Felix K. Zollicoffer, and Charles Ready.

No sooner had the polls closed than Whigs divided over the impending selection of United States senator. Like Kentucky's Archibald Dixon after his defeat in 1851, Henry demanded the Senate seat as reward for his sacrifice of time and health during the grueling gubernatorial campaign. Henry's ambition frightened the incumbent Bell. Both came from Middle Tennessee, and Henry's challenge, along with Meredith Gentry's bitter opposition, could divide Bell's support there, opening the way for a claimant from East Tennessee like Thomas A. R. Nelson. Nelson had lost the other Senate seat to Jones in 1851, and he could justly assert that he merited the party's nomination since Middle and West Tennessee had controlled the plums for years and since East Tennessee Whigs needed party recognition to offset Democrats' selection of Johnson for governor.[103]

An exhausting marathon ensued. Whigs would not unite behind a single candidate, and forty-nine ballots were required before Bell was reelected. Even then, he owed his success to Democratic supporters of A. O. P. Nicholson, who sought to stop the Democrat Aaron V. Brown from exploiting the Whig rift to seize the seat.[104] Bell's reelection meant that Tennessee's Whigs would have both senators and five representatives when Congress opened in December. Its size, but especially its behavior, made Tennessee's the most exceptional southern Whig delegation in that body.

Elsewhere in Dixie, Whigs' fortunes were dismal. An attempt by North Carolina's Whig congressional candidates to resurrect the call for distribution of federal land revenues to the states to fund expansion of North Carolina's railroad network did little good. Whigs elected only three of eight congressman in 1853 compared to six of nine in 1851. Veteran Whig Congressman David Outlaw went down to defeat, and other experienced Whig incumbents like Edward Stanly, Joseph Caldwell, and Alfred Dockery refused even to seek reelection. Altogether, Whig candidates attracted only 32,000 votes, less than two-fifths of the total and far less than they had won in either August or November 1852. Coupled with a loss of a United States Senate seat because of the legislative stalemate, Whigs' dominance of the state's congressional delegation had ended.[105] The Whigs' slump extended to Louisiana, where Theodore G. Hunt was the only victor among four Whig congressional candidates, whose proportion of the popular vote was smaller than that won by Winfield Scott, and where Whig representation in the state legislature slumped from 58 to 38 percent in the house and from 53 to 37 percent in the senate. And in Mississippi, Alabama, and Georgia, the question was not whether the Whigs would decline, but whether the Whig party could be revived after the successful bipartisan Union coalitions of 1851 dissolved in 1852.

The history of Alabama's Whigs can be briefly told. The old two-party lines did not reemerge in 1853; instead, fragmentation that weaned former Whigs away from their old allegiance continued. Whig voters placed a priority on defeating the more obnoxious Democrat in multicandidate congressional and legislative races, not on electing Whigs. The strength of the Whig party itself was best illustrated in the gubernatorial election. There a Whig named Earnest opposed the new champion of the Jacksonian faith, John A. Winston, as well as a dissident Union Democrat. Winston won with 65 percent of the vote. Polling fewer than 10,000 votes, Earnest ran second with 20 percent. The Alabama Whig party had effectively evaporated.[106]

In contrast to Alabama, Mississippi's Whigs initially made a vigorous effort to revive the party in 1853. Never had Mississippi so "required a thorough organization of the friends of law, order, and good government," the party's organ intoned from Jackson in January. "By the united action of the good old Whig party, the State may yet" be redeemed. In calling for a state Whig convention in June, the Whig executive committee stressed traditional Whig issues like state funding for internal improvements and repayment of the long-repudiated Planters' Bank bonds. Even earlier, two self-nominated Whigs entered the race for state judge against Charles D. Fontaine, the Democratic candidate, and other Whigs presented themselves for the governorship, the congressional seats, and the legislature.[107]

Then, as had so often been the case during the history of the Whig party, Democratic decisions reshaped Whig actions. Democrats split at their May state convention. Eager to reclaim his old Senate seat, which became vacant in March 1853, Union Governor Henry S. Foote insisted as the price of his reentry into the Democratic fold that the party commit itself to his election and split the state ticket evenly between Union and Southern Rights Democrats. When the convention refused to submit to such extortion, Foote stormed out and vowed to back legislative candidates who were former Unionists, whether Whigs or Democrats, and who might support his Senate candidacy. While Democrats nominated a Southern Rights man for governor, they nonetheless named Union men for state treasurer, secretary of state, and an at-large congressional seat.[108]

Furious at this leniency toward Union men, Southern Rights Democrats denied renomination to all three Union Democrats who had won congressional seats in 1851. Meanwhile Congressman Albert Gallatin Brown, the lone Southern Rights Democrat to resist the Unionist tide in 1851, declined renomination, secured the candidacy for his friend Wiley P. Harris, announced that he sought the Senate seat coveted by Foote, and pledged to campaign across the state to see that anti-Foote Democrats got into the legislature.[109] Nominally, in sum, the governorship, five House seats, and the legislature were at stake in Mississippi's election, but popular attention focused on the race between Brown and Foote for the Senate seat the new legislature would fill.

With the Democrats resplitting along Union/Southern Rights lines, Mississippi's Whigs abandoned their attempt to resurrect the state party on economic issues and opportunistically seized the chance to reforge the triumphant bipartisan

Union coalition of 1851. The Whig state convention in June eschewed separate nominations and merely recommended Whigs who had already nominated themselves. Whig papers denounced "the *spirit of party*," called for the election of "pure patriots, without regard to old party distinctions," and endorsed Foote for the Senate. In two congressional districts, Whig conventions nominated the incumbent Union Democrats, whom their party had spurned, as *Whig* candidates, and even one of Charles Fontaine's Whig opponents appealed for Democrats' votes on the "no party . . . ground of long acquaintance and superior qualification."[110]

Whigs' tack toward nonpartisanship almost succeeded. With 46 percent of the vote, their gubernatorial candidate ran better than any Whig since 1841. Nevertheless, his total fell about 2,000 votes short of Foote's in 1851, while the Democrat John McRae ran 4,000 votes ahead of Jefferson Davis that year. Some, but not all, Union Democrats, in short, supported the Whigs. Similarly, the two Union Democrats whom Whigs had adopted as their own congressional candidates came achingly close to winning, and Whig candidates also ran respectably in a third district and in the statewide, at-large race. The fact remains, however, that Whigs lost all five House seats and the governorship, and in the legislative races, the key elections in 1853, Whigs slipped back to their traditional minority status. The new Democratic majority would send Brown to the Senate in January 1854. What proved to be Mississippi's Whigs' last gasp came up short even when they shed their Whig clothes for the garb of Unionism.[111]

Georgia's Whigs fared no better, but their most influential leaders renounced any connection to the old Whig party even more emphatically. "If the Whig party is incapable of rising to the same standard of notoriety as the motley *crew, which offers* peace under the name of the Democracy," growled the intransigent Toombs in December 1852, "it is entitled to no resurrection [and] it will have none!" Toombs' ally Alexander Stephens was equally determined to smother the rebirth of Georgia's Whig party. Undeterred by Howell Cobb's warning that "a reorganization of the Union party" was "impracticable," Stephens sought exactly that. Thus the Georgia papers loyal to Stephens and Toombs pressed for a reunion between Whig regulars, who had grudgingly supported Scott, and the anti-Scott Whigs on a Union party, not a Whig party, basis.[112]

Not all Whigs who had rallied behind the national ticket in 1852 accepted this arrangement, especially allies of ex-Senator John M. Berrien. They implored Berrien in the spring to run for governor in 1853 so that the *Whig* party, not a Union party, could be reorganized behind his candidacy. Their rationale for calling on the aged statesman, aside from hatred of Stephens and Toombs, was the implausible argument that Berrien, a Savannah resident who had not contested a popular election for thirty years, could get more votes than any other Whig in the upcountry, traditionally Democratic Cherokee district. Berrien, who possibly saw through this nonsense or knew that Stephens and Toombs were grooming his kinsman and closest political ally, Charles Jenkins, for the Union gubernatorial nomination, refused to tilt at windmills. Efforts to resurrect a Whig party thus failed.[113]

Most delegates at the Whig state convention in June opposed any reunification with the national Whig party. Stephens wrote its address to the electorate, and the splenetic Toombs composed the platform. Among other things, they denounced both the Whig and Democratic parties as faithless to their pledges on the economy and public lands and insisted that the maintenance of the Georgia platform and the promotion of the interests of Georgia's citizens were more important than any national party. The gubernatorial candidate Jenkins had not only written the Georgia Platform and run for vice president on the Webster ticket. During the campaign he repudiated "for himself and party all alliances with national parties." Pierce's appointment of Free Soilers and secessionists, he argued, revealed the Democrats' unreliability on the Compromise's finality, and the continued dominance of Sewardites among northern Whigs tainted that party too. "I maintain that the best hope of the country is the promotion of a new National Conservative party."[114]

Jenkins openly bid for former Union Democrats' support, a strategy ostensibly abetted by the Southern Rights background of his Democratic opponent, Herschel Johnson. Yet Johnson vigorously denied that he sought secession. He denounced the Union party as a Whig wolf in sheep's clothing. He blamed Jenkins for destroying the old Union party, and he accused him of elitist hostility to the political rights of the poor, a charge to which Jenkins was particularly vulnerable. Johnson also shrewdly fanned the hostility of Whig regulars who had supported Scott by emphasizing Jenkins' role on the Webster ticket in 1852. For at least two months after Jenkins' nomination, indeed, Scott Whigs continued to implore Berrien to enter the race as the Whig candidate since Jenkins renounced that affiliation. Only a public letter from Berrien endorsing Jenkins in September stopped those pleas, but even then Whig suspicion of Jenkins as an apostate may have cost him the election.[115]

With over 47,000 votes, almost triple the count for Scott and within 400 of Zachary Taylor's 1848 total, Jenkins drew more support than any Whig in the history of state elections. Still, he ran some 500 votes behind Johnson. Though Jenkins drew more votes than any other Whig ever had in the Cherokee district, statewide he ran some 10,000 votes behind Cobb in 1851, clear evidence that many Union Democrats, like Cobb himself, had returned to the Democratic fold. Jenkins blamed his loss on Johnson's demagogic use of the "Algerine Law" issue, low Whig turnout in southwestern Georgia, where there were few Whig papers to spread his message or print Whig ballots, and the inveterate hostility of Scott Whigs. Estimates of voter movement between the 1852 presidential election and the 1853 election suggest, indeed, that one-fourth of the 16,000 Whigs who cast Scott ballots abstained in 1853. They also indicate that less than a tenth of Pierce's supporters defected to Jenkins.[116]

Jenkins' opposition to prohibition, as Stephens worried, may also have hurt him. Jenkins complained that in many legislative districts with Union majorities, Union Whigs ran rival temperance and antitemperance legislative candidates. With no legislative candidates of their own in those districts, Democrats promised to vote for the Whig legislative candidate their Whig friends backed in return for those Whig votes for Johnson. This tactic may have helped defeat Jenkins, but it also helped Whigs achieve a very respectable performance in the legislative races. Union Whigs won half of the senate and 45 percent of the house.[117]

To dissociate themselves from Whiggery and reforge a bipartisan Union party, Georgia's Whigs also refused to run congressional candidates against two Democratic/Union incumbents who now ran as Democrats. Of the six other Whig Union candidates, only two—Stephens and David Reese—won election, although several other races were exceptionally tight. Still, the effort to resurrect a bipartisan Union party had clearly failed. Union votes had come almost exclusively from former Whigs, and they had not been enough to bring the relabeled party back to power. By the end of 1853 even Stephens, who still wanted no part of Whiggery, conceded the hopelessness of preserving a separate Union party in Georgia.[118]

Like their northern counterparts, in sum, southern Whigs failed to come back in 1853 and instead fell further behind the Democrats. The defeat in Tennessee removed the last southern Whig governor, and with the losses in Wisconsin and Vermont, Whig governors served in only two of thirty-one states—Maine and Massachusetts. After the 1853 elections, Whigs controlled both houses of the legislature in only two of fifteen southern states—Maryland and Kentucky. In contrast, Democrats had complete control in nine. By another index, of the twenty-eight southern state houses and senates for which data from the elections of 1852 and 1853 are available, Whigs constituted less than 40 percent in fifteen.[119]

In 1853, Whigs also lost an aggregate of nine House seats in Virginia, North Carolina, Maryland, Kentucky, Louisiana, and Alabama, almost half the total they had elected from those states in 1851. The net gain of three seats from Missouri and Tennessee could not compensate for those losses. In the Thirty-Third Congress, Whigs would hold only twelve of the thirty Senate seats from the South— thirteen if the fiery Toombs were considered a Whig. Of ninety-one slave-state representatives, only twenty-three (25 percent) were Whigs, and three of those had been elected as Union Whigs.[120] Like northern Whigs, in sum, southern Whigs were in desperate shape at the end of 1853.

X

Thus, Whigs' search for compelling state or national issues in 1853 usually failed. In the Deep South their revival of the Union issue brought Whig voters back to the polls and restored the anti-Democratic opposition to respectability, at least in Mississippi and Georgia. But it did not help most Whig congressional candidates win, and it necessitated renunciation of the Whig name and the existing national Whig party. A quixotic demand for distribution of federal land revenues could not stop Whig defeat in North Carolina or Tennessee. Canal expansion in New York and opposition to the new state constitution in Massachusetts proved successful state issues, but in those states, like Maine, Whigs also depended on Democratic divisions. In Kentucky, Whigs relied on traditional strength and prestigious candidates, not compelling issues, to hold power, but Democrats made the greater gains among the electorate. In California and New Jersey, finally, Whigs exploited popular anger at incumbent Democratic regimes to remain respectably competitive minorities—but minorities nonetheless.

In most states, Whigs either failed to find a distinctive issue and lost votes through abstention or took the unpopular side of issues made by others and suffered defection. Strikingly, only in New Jersey did the head of the Whig state ticket take an uncompromisingly favorable position on the Maine Law. Elsewhere Whigs who gave only tepid endorsement, remained resolutely silent on the liquor question, or actively opposed prohibition paid a terrible price for those stances.

In Wisconsin, Ohio, Vermont, and Connecticut, Free Soilers salvaged their own party and threatened to eclipse the Whigs by seizing the issue. In Tennessee and Georgia, pro-Maine Law Whigs supported Democratic gubernatorial candidates in order to get prohibitionist Whigs into the legislature. In Michigan, Pennsylvania, Maryland, New York, New Jersey, and elsewhere, independent temperance tickets confused state and local elections. In most states, indeed, anger at incumbents was not channeled through the Whig party. Instead, splinter tickets siphoned off Whig voters by demanding clean government, the ouster of spoilsmen, the repudiation of Catholics, and the implementation or evisceration of antiliquor laws.

The seepage of some Whig voters toward new parties and the abstention of many more meant that popular allegiance to the Whig party was far weaker at the end than at the start of 1853. Well might Whig leaders who hoped to preserve the party thus look with relief to the opening of the Thirty-Third Congress in December. With its huge Democratic majorities, that Congress had always been the trump card for Whigs who wanted to stand pat during 1853. They expected those Democratic majorities to divide over confirmation of Pierce's controversial appointees and to do something that offended the electorate and sent them racing back to the Whig party to punish and oust the offenders. They expected the Democrats to create the winning issue they themselves had been unable to find in 1853, an issue against which all Whigs would rally.

Whigs hopeful of reviving the party were not the only political actors who eagerly looked to the new congressional session. So did Democrats, who, despite easy triumphs in most states, fissured along various lines during 1853. Animosity among former Union and Southern Rights Democrats in Mississippi and Alabama was almost as fierce as that between pro- and anti-Benton Democrats in Missouri, Hards and Softs in New York, and Wildcats and Maine Law Democrats in Maine. Protestant and Catholic Democrats warred in Michigan, Ohio, and Pennsylvania. Independent tickets, devoted to breaking the power of party organizations, cut into the Democratic vote in those states and Maryland as well. Everywhere, moreover, anger at Pierce's patronage allocation exacerbated intraparty tensions, and an effort to prevent Senate confirmation of many appointees seemed certain. Many incensed Democrats, indeed, looked to the meeting of Congress primarily as an opportunity to humiliate the administration.

Though Whig feebleness camouflaged Democratic difficulties in most states, the Democratic party too seemed to stand at the brink of disintegration, and Democratic leaders knew it. Like the Whigs, moreover, they instinctively recognized that only a revival of traditional interparty conflict *over concrete policies* could halt intraparty fragmentation. The best way to reunite the fractious party in Pennsylvania, a Pittsburgh Democrat wrote Caleb Cushing in July, was for Pierce to launch a policy initiative "that will raise invective from the other side and compel us to quit our domestic squabbles." The Democratic party would be "shivered to atoms," a St. Louis Democrat warned Illinois Senator Stephen A. Douglas in December, unless Pierce or the Democratic majority in Congress promptly marked "out a line of sound national and Democratic policy." Only the "boldest and most decided action can turn the current." Douglas needed no such warning. A month before receiving this letter, he wrote an Illinois lieutenant that "the party is in a distracted condition & it requires all our wisdom, prudence, &

energy to consolidate its power and perpetuate its principles." He intended to provide that necessary leadership when Congress met in December.[121]

Whig proponents of a new Union party also looked eagerly to the new Congress to hasten the alliance between conservative Whigs and Democrats that had failed to gel during 1853 itself. The Whigs' continued erosion at the polls, indeed, increased such advocates' numbers. Not privy to Democratic plans to heal that party's divisions with partisanly distinctive policy initiatives, such Whigs were fully aware of Democratic divisions themselves. They especially noted the anger of pro-Compromise southern Democrats at Pierce's tilt toward Southern Rights men, the continuing feuds between Union and Southern Rights Democrats in Alabama and Mississippi, and the Hard/Soft rupture in New York. Coupled with the apparent determination of Georgia's Whigs to preserve an independent state Union party and the strife between Silver Grays and Sewardites in New York, Democratic rifts, they believed, provided the materials for a successful Union party.

In September, Fillmore loyalist William L. Hodge pleaded with Fillmore to have New York's Silver Grays and Hunkers merge into a new "Union party," make "it the nucleus of a new party organization," and drop "old party names." Pierce's administration had been "an absolute abortion," he maintained. "The whole Union Democratic party at the South are ready to cut loose from them." Since southern Whigs were solidly unionist, "I have no doubt the Southern Union Democrats would readily unite with them & make one general sweep of every Southern state in the Canvass of 1856." Everything, Hodge insisted, depended upon New York's Silver Grays. "There is no *national success for us unless we can clear our skirts of Sewardism*, which will ruin us in the South." But "if we play our cards right at the North, especially in N. York, the Southern Whig party could attract & swallow up the Union democrats, & whether you still called it the Whig or the Union party it would to all practical purposes be the former."[122]

On October 3, two days before New York's Whig state convention, Fillmore wrote Hodge that a merger between Silver Grays and Hunkers was impossible in 1853. Hungry for control of state canal contracts, too many Silver Grays still hoped for a fair shake from the as yet unnamed Whig ticket that was sure to win. The Democratic split that raised the possibility of a merger, in short, also deterred it—at least in 1853. Whigs would not swap sure victory and a possible share of its spoils for a risky new alliance. When Hards ran dead even with Softs in the November election, moreover, Fillmore concluded that they were far less likely to seek an alliance with Silver Grays than if they had been humiliated, for now they stood within reach of taking over the state Democratic party.[123]

Nonetheless, by the fall of 1853 Fillmore himself finally acknowledged the necessity of forging a new Union party. One reason, unquestionably, was his expectation of becoming the Union party's presidential nominee. To bring the party to fruition, he began to plot with other members of his former administration, especially Kennedy and Stuart. On October 14, prior to the New York election but after he knew that Sewardites would monopolize canal patronage and thereby further alienate his own allies, Fillmore wrote Kennedy one of the most illuminating letters in American political history. Yet neither the writer nor the recipient of this brilliant analysis, which so incisively identified what eroded loyalty to old parties and what was needed to build new national parties, could appreciate its irony. For they did not know what their historian does—what Stephen A. Douglas intended to do in the forthcoming Congress in order to save the Democratic party from being "shivered to atoms."[124]

New York Whigs' inevitable rupture, Fillmore told Kennedy, "will leave the national Whigs and democrats to act unitedly on national affairs if they can agree upon a common platform and name. Probably the sooner this takes place the better." But, he added,

> what new combinations will grow out of this, it is difficult to foresee, as national parties can only be formed by the action of the general government. Parties are broken up by local causes and that centrifugal force which throws individuals and masses beyond the attraction of the central power; but new parties of a national character can only be gathered from these fragmentary *nebula* of dissolving systems by the magnetism of some great national and centripetal force at Washington. Will any question present such a magnet at the ensuing session of Congress? If so, then we may hope to see a national Union party which will cast off the secessionists of the South and the abolition freesoilers of the North and rally around the Constitution and sustain it in its purity.

Kennedy could barely contain his enthusiasm for the idea. "A Union party, against all seceding fragments . . . seems now to be inevitable," he replied. "Neither National Whig nor National Democrat can henceforth hold communion or acknowledge fellowship with the freesoil section of either party." Whigs would numerically dominate the new party, especially in the South, and thus it would represent Whig principles. Hence, "the Whigs may willingly part with their name and external form." Kennedy also agreed with Fillmore that "this winter will bring forth many developments to enable us to compute the probability of the new organization." If Union Democrats were honest in their professions of opposition to Pierce, "we may regard" the Democratic party's "dissolution and the reconstruction [as] certain."[125]

Kennedy moved immediately to proselytize for the new party. "Can *we* now make a perfect Union party which shall consolidate the Whigs of every state into a compact mass so completely national as to make the contest of 1856 an easy victory?" he asked his friend Winthrop in early December. All southern Whigs would eagerly join a new Union party. "How will it be with the Whigs of the North? In other words what is the strength of national Whigs in New England? Can you not throw off all abolitionism from the Whig party by a public renunciation of fellowship with those who entertain it?" To woo converts in the South, Kennedy urged Fillmore to accompany him on an ostensibly nonpolitical tour of southern states in the spring of 1854, a trip the now nakedly ambitious Fillmore was eager to take.[126]

Stuart also agreed with Fillmore "that the sooner the present parties are broken up and new ones formed, adapted to the practical issues of the day, the better." National Whigs and Union Democrats had more in common with each other than either had with rival factions in their old parties. "I should be very willing to drive a trade, & bargain off Seward & his gang for Dickinson & the hards; especially as we should get the whole South to boot!" "The Whig party has fulfilled its appropriate mission," he concluded, "& it may now honorably ground its arms."[127]

Fillmore and others who sought to replace the Whigs with a Union party all looked to the action of the new Congress to advance it. What Stephen Douglas and the Democrats did there, however, was not all that frustrated their vision of a grand conservative party. Other actors had been at work in 1853. To explain the confusing voting patterns in New York City in November 1853, a German Democrat contemptuously cited "the secret working and complotting of the Order of United Americans, lately called the 'Know Nothings,' who for the sake of their paltry designs in their notorious nothingness strived to create some confusion." Still, he admitted, "they have been successful to a certain degree."[128]

Started in 1849 as a superpatriotic secret society called the Order of the Star Spangled Banner, the Know Nothings were taken over by the Order of United Americans in 1852. Confined initially to New York City, they operated outside the orbit of both Whigs and Democrats, and for most of 1853 they were more interested in recruiting members to a social fraternity than in political activity. But the spread of the organization had been fueled by the same nativistic, anti-Catholic hatreds that exploded in several local elections during 1853, and in the fall they used the cohesive power of their oath-bound members to back anti-immigrant and anti-Catholic candidates in certain races. What appeared in New York was hardly the "paltry designs" of a "notorious nothingness." Rather, it was a strike of lightning that heralded an impending tornado.[129]

Chapter 22

"This Nebraska Business Will Entirely Denationalize the Whig Party"

"THERE MUST BE SOME MODIFICATION of party relations before the close of the present session of Congress," Alexander H. H. Stuart excitedly wrote Millard Fillmore in early December 1853. Convinced that the California gold strikes had permanently settled partisan disputes over economic policy and that congressional Democrats' anger at Pierce's administration had inflicted an "irremedial wound" on the Democrats, Stuart, like John P. Kennedy, Solomon G. Haven, and other Fillmore allies, believed that the impending Democratic crackup augured a merger of National Whigs and antiadministration Democrats in a new Union party. When dissident Democratic United States senators cooperated with Whigs in December to defeat Pierce's preferred candidate for Senate printer, Fillmore himself exulted that "a *nucleus* has been formed around which the *Union men* of all parties may rally and form a *Union party*."[1]

Those hoping to revitalize the Whig party also rejoiced at Congress' opening. Although Democrats outnumbered Whigs 159–71 in the House and 37–22 in the Senate, Seward described congressional Whigs as "a happy set of men" since the long-predicted Democratic rupture over Senate confirmation of Pierce's controversial appointees was now imminent. Better still, as one Whig congressman reported, "the administration is without [any] policy" around which feuding Democrats might reunite. With Democratic bloodletting now inevitable, advised Tennessee Senator John Bell, "The Whigs who are prudent will take no active part against the adminn. for the present, but let the elements of distraction accumulate before they make a combined attack."[2]

What happened in Congress during that session would indeed weaken the Democrats and help define the postsession "phase of politics." Those developments, however, prevented the "combined attack" by Whigs that Bell envisioned, and they also frustrated advocates of a new Union party. On December 14, Iowa's Democratic Senator Augustus Dodge introduced a bill to organize the area west of Missouri and Iowa into a Nebraska Territory. The seemingly innocuous bill was immediately sent to the Senate's Committee on Territories, which Stephen A. Douglas chaired. What Douglas and others, including Whigs and Free Soilers, did with that measure helped transform American political life and propel the Whig party to its grave.

Developments elsewhere that December also portended things to come. While Whigs across the nation looked expectantly to Washington for ammunition, two independent, reform-oriented nativistic splinter parties—a Citizen's Union Party and a Young Men's League—outpolled both Whigs and Democrats in Boston's mayoral election.[3] Emblematic of the grass-roots, antiparty revolt that had bubbled up during 1853 in the form of anti-Catholic, antiliquor, and antiwireworker tickets, the Boston insurgents also heralded the emergence of the Know Nothings as a powerful third party that, in 1854 and 1855, sought to punish Whigs and Democrats alike for their pro-Catholic, proimmigrant tilt.

The reaction to the Nebraska bill and the eruption of Know Nothingism together produced smashing Democratic defeats, derailed the Union party movement, and permanently eclipsed the Whig party. Many southern Whigs' support for the Kansas-Nebraska Act in the spring of 1854 reopened and deepened the sectional chasm in the national party. Unlike earlier rifts over the Wilmot Proviso and the Compromise of 1850, this split proved irreparable. Between the act's passage and the presidential election of 1856, new parties emerged in the North that gutted the Whig party by siphoning off its constituency. Despite the desire of many southern Whigs to preserve the national organization by arranging another armistice with Northerners in 1856, as they had in 1848 and 1852, no credible northern wing of the party with which to make terms remained. By 1855, indeed, southern Whigs who wished to continue active opposition to Democrats had to seek new political homes.

Most chose the new Know Nothing or American party. The secret, antiforeign, anti-Catholic Know Nothing organization arose in response to social, political, and economic developments that antedated the introduction of the Kansas-Nebraska Act. Given the outbreak of antipartyism, anti-Catholicism, and prohibitionism in 1852 and 1853, a populistic party that vented those feelings would probably have grown in 1854 and 1855 even without its passage, especially since the last six months of 1854 and first five months of 1855 witnessed a sharp economic recession that aggravated tensions between native-born and foreign workers. Nonetheless, Know Nothingism's most rapid growth coincided with a furious northern backlash against the Nebraska Act that both contributed to that growth and spawned still other new northern coalitions organized explicitly to stop slavery expansion and Slave Power aggressions. Two new parties—the Know Nothings and the Republicans—thus vied with each other and with Whigs to mobilize anti-Democratic voters. By the end of 1855 they had displaced the Whig party as the major opponent of the Democrats and thereby destroyed its utility as a political organization.[4]

The rise of the Republican and Know Nothing parties after 1853 has been thoroughly studied.[5] The intent here is not to retell that story. The remaining chapters focus instead on how Whigs contributed and reacted to events that precipitated and then completed the party's final death throes. This chapter deals with the framing of the Kansas-Nebraska Act and its initial impact on the Whig party prior to the adjournment of Congress in August 1854. The next three assess the varying tribulations of Whigs outside of Washington during the state and congressional elections of 1854 and 1855. And the last describes the stillborn attempt to resurrect the Whig party during the 1856 presidential campaign.

I

From the moment of Winfield Scott's defeat, Whigs in both sections had looked wistfully to the Democratic majorities in Congress to do something against which Whigs could once again rally. No such galvanizing issue emerged from Washington during the winter of 1852–53, but the new Thirty-Third Congress was another matter. For a brief moment at the start of 1854, it looked as though the long-awaited Democratic blunder might indeed provoke a "combined attack" by Whigs that could rejuvenate their party.

When Congress met in December 1853, Senator Stephen A. Douglas had sought official organization of the area west of Missouri and Iowa for almost a decade. Long a champion of building up the West as a balance wheel between Northerners and Southerners, Douglas knew that settlers eager to move there could not gain legal title to land until Congress officially organized a territorial government and the land office surveyed and placed land on sale. For similar reasons, various proposals to build railroads with government land grants across that immense area to the Pacific coast required formal territorial organization. By the end of 1853, finally, Douglas was looking for a concrete Democratic policy to reunify his fragmenting party, "to consolidate its power and perpetuate its principles." To supply it, he envisioned a three-pronged program: organizing the Nebraska territory, allotting federal land grants from it to subsidize construction of a Pacific railroad, and encouraging settlement with a homestead bill.[6]

The hurdle blocking passage of a Nebraska bill was that, according to the Missouri Compromise of 1820, slavery was "forever prohibited" from the contemplated Nebraska Territory. Southern Democrats refused to vote for the bill unless those insulting terms were changed. Anger at what seemed a denial of southern equality primarily caused their intransigence, but some southern Democrats were also determined to buttress slavery in Missouri by ensuring that areas west of it did not become free-soil refuges for fugitive slaves. In addition, key southern Democratic senators, who sympathized with New York's Hardshell Hunkers, sought to redefine Democratic orthodoxy in order to test Softshell and Barnburner appointees when they came before the Senate for confirmation. Since the Democratic platform of 1852 committed the party to the finality of the Compromise of 1850, these Southerners insisted that its territorial provisions should be applied to all federal territories, not just Utah and New Mexico. They would substitute popular sovereignty in the Nebraska territory for the eternal prohibition of slavery north of 36° 30' contained in the Missouri Compromise.[7]

For different reasons, Douglas hit upon the same formula to secure the organization of the Nebraska territory. Douglas believed that all Democrats would rally behind a policy that reaffirmed the party's commitment to local self-determination, the basic republican principle of self-government. Since Whigs had generally opposed western development, moreover, it might provoke Whig opposition, the external pressure necessary to reunite feuding Democrats. The critical point here is that, to the extent that Douglas succeeded in reclarifying the line that differentiated Democrats from Whigs, he might also, willy-nilly, breathe life into the torpid Whig party.[8]

In the initial stages, Democrats monopolized the framing of legislation in the Senate. Only two Whigs—Bell and Edward Everett of Massachusetts—served on Douglas' committee. Bell was not in Washington when it wrote the bill, and Douglas was determined to report out a measure southern Democrats could accept, regardless of any protests from Everett. Douglas, however, desperately wanted to avoid outright repeal of the Missouri Compromise line since he knew that many Northerners regarded that thirty-four-year-old provision as sacrosanct. He wanted Democrats to go before the country behind the positive platform of western development and popular sovereignty, not responsibility for repealing that prohibition against slavery expansion. Through legislative sleight of hand he thus hoped to substitute the principles of the 1850 compromise for those of the 1820 compromise. He dismissed as nonsense the idea that slavery might spread to the area in question.[9]

Ignoring Everett's futile dissent, Douglas reported a bill on January 4, 1854, that organized the entire area between the Missouri Compromise line and the Canadian border into a Nebraska Territory and provided, in the language of the Utah and New Mexico laws, that any states formed out of the immense territory could be admitted with or without slavery, as their constitutions prescribed. The bill further declared that the legislative power of the territorial government would extend to all rightful subjects, including slavery, but Douglas ambiguously implied in his accompanying report that until the territorial legislature acted, the 1820 prohibition against slavery would continue to have legal force. On one point— repeal of the Missouri Compromise line itself—the committee's report was clearer. It did *not* recommend either "affirming or repealing the 8th section of the Missouri act."[10]

Seward immediately wrote his wife that Douglas had gone as far toward repeal as he dared. A few days later, he told Weed that the administration, not Douglas, had designed the measure to conciliate Hardshell Hunkers into accepting confirmation of Softshell and Barnburner appointees, while Democrats more perceptively interpreted it as a test devised by Hards to embarrass Soft appointees and force resignations if they did not go along with it. Whatever its impact on Democrats, Seward and other northern Whigs immediately determined to oppose the "infamous Nebraska Bill." Of greater importance, Seward also voiced hope "that we shall get up a division in the South on the subject" and "draw [John M.] Clayton out to lead an opposition to 'the repeal of the Missouri Compromise.' " "That," he wrote Weed, "is the word." Since Douglas's original bill explicitly did *not* "repeal" the Missouri Compromise line, northern Whigs obviously wanted to portray it that way in order to outrage northern voters, who might then be mobilized against Democrats in the impending 1854 congressional elections. Though unelaborated, Seward's hope that southern Whigs would also oppose "repeal" probably rested on its clear violation of the implicit promise southern Whigs had made when they helped foist the 1852 national platform upon the party—namely, that the Compromise of 1850 was a final settlement and would preclude any further sectional disputes over slavery.[11]

If Seward believed that the first version of Douglas' bill was so "infamous" that the entire Whig party might rally against it, southern Democrats immediately complained that it failed to replace the 1820 ban on slavery extension. As most people interpreted the original draft, a decision regarding slavery would be made only when application for statehood occurred; during the entire territorial stage, that is, the previous ban would apply. Key southern Democratic senators therefore pressed Douglas for modifications, and on January 10, Douglas had newspapers print a twenty-first section of the bill that had supposedly been omitted by clerical error. This made emphatically clear what Douglas had always intended: that the residents of the territory, through the territorial legislature, could make the decision on slavery if they so chose. This change not only made the displacement of the Missouri prohibition more explicit. It also increased the likelihood of southern Whig opposition to the measure, for Southerners condemned a decision on slavery by territorial legislatures before statehood as "squatter sovereignty" that robbed Southerners of equal rights. Had that been the final form of the bill, that is, southern Whigs would have considered its Democratic supporters vulnerable to attack.[12]

These changes, therefore, still failed to satisfy certain Southerners. In addition to disliking Douglas' explicit incorporation of squatter sovereignty, they recognized that the Missouri Compromise ban could possibly still apply until the territorial legislature made a decision. If so, only nonslaveholders would elect that legislature, and its decision would be foreordained. Thus southern Democrats and Whigs contemplated moving for outright repeal of the Missouri ban. Two weeks before Douglas reported out his original bill, indeed, Georgia's Whig Senator William Dawson had predicted that someone in the House would move for explicit repeal. Like many Whigs, he expected the motion to come from Hardshell Democrats or their southern Democratic allies.[13]

Philip Phillips, a Democratic representative from Alabama, did urge outright repeal in early January, but in the Senate, Kentucky Whig Archibald Dixon beat Democrats to the punch. After consulting with Tennessee's James Jones, Dixon announced on January 16 that, when it was in order, he would propose an amendment that neither the Missouri prohibition nor squatter sovereignty should apply to Nebraska or any other territory. As if to emphasize for Southerners the implications of not adopting repeal, the Massachusetts Free Soiler Charles Sumner immediately offered a counteramendment that explicitly reaffirmed the Missouri restriction in Nebraska.[14]

Seward, who from early January on clearly hoped to stigmatize Democrats for attempting to repeal the Missouri restriction, later claimed to have prompted Dixon's amendment as a way of forcing Democrats to make that move and turning northern opinion against them. Since Dixon's threatened amendment was so extreme that it could never pass Congress, posturing as a more ardent proslavery man than southern Democrats in order to goad them into repeal, as Seward hoped, may indeed have been his purpose.[15] Other evidence, however, argues against such a possibility. On January 24, Dixon told the Senate that he had no idea how radical his proposed amendment was. Explicitly citing the gossip that his motion was a Whig attempt to embarrass Democrats, he also denied any partisan motives. "Upon the question of slavery, I know no Whiggery, and I know no Democracy," he declared. He was, instead, "a pro-slavery man" who sought to maintain the "rights" of his "slaveholding constituency."[16]

It is tempting to suggest that just as Milton Brown had added a proslavery amendment to the joint resolution for Texas annexation in December 1844 in order to prove southern Whigs better defenders of Southern Rights than southern Democrats, Dixon and Jones sought to benefit Whigs in Dixie by attacking a restriction many Southerners now regarded as an insulting denial of southern equality. Yet Dixon and Jones, who enthusiastically endorsed Dixon's surprising initiative, each had more selfish motives. Both were men of burning ambition who needed to mend fences with Whigs in their home states by enhancing their leadership credentials. Dixon's reelection to another Senate term, indeed, would be decided by the Whig majority of the Kentucky legislature, which was sitting in Frankfort while Congress met in Washington, within five weeks of the day he threatened to introduce his proslavery amendment. Dixon had always ridden the slavery issue to advance his career within Kentucky. By posing as a nonpartisan champion of slaveholders' rights, he might even pick up votes from Democratic legislators to offset opposition from Whigs who despised his self-centered lust for office. Just as the actions of New York's Whig legislators in early 1850 forced Seward's Higher Law speech, the impending decision by Kentucky's legislature spurred Dixon's move in 1854.[17]

Dixon's threatened amendment in combination with Sumner's embarrassed Douglas and altered the political calculus. Dixon demanded an explicit repeal of the Missouri restriction that could outrage Northerners and thereby inhibit northern Democratic congressmen from supporting the bill. But he also sought to gut the popular sovereignty formula for territorial self-government that Douglas considered the linchpin of his bill, the feature that defined it as a Democratic measure. Dixon's proposed amendment asserted that "citizens of the several States or Territories shall be at liberty to take and hold slaves within any of the Territories of the United States or of the States to be formed therefrom." Dixon's amendment, in sum, implied that neither a territorial legislature nor even a state constitutional convention could bar slavery from the contemplated territory. Taken literally, it would legalize slavery in every new state thereafter admitted to the Union. One of the most extreme proslavery pieces of legislation ever aired in Congress, it could not pass. Nonetheless, Southern Democrats immediately understood its political threat to their own proslavery credentials, especially once Sumner highlighted the implications of not seeking direct repeal. Refusing to be outflanked by southern Whigs, they insisted that Douglas incorporate some form of repeal in the bill.[18]

Dixon's shaft forced a week-long series of frantic negotiations among Democrats, including President Pierce and some of his cabinet, from which Whigs were excluded. The goal was to concoct a recognizably Democratic bill by saving popular sovereignty and to present a more palatable version of repeal. Douglas reported this measure on January 23, and Pierce's administration spread the word that support for it was the new test of party orthodoxy. Douglas' revised bill now created two territories—Kansas, directly west of Missouri, and, to the west of Iowa, Nebraska, whose northern boundary would be the border with Canada. Rather than directly "repealing" the ban of 1820, it declared that the Missouri prohibition had been "superceded [sic] by the principles" of the Compromise of 1850 and was therefore "inoperative and void." And, in sharp contrast to Dixon's amendment, it did not legalize slavery in the territories but left the decision, at least implicitly, to their residents. As revised two weeks later, the bill explicitly asserted that "the true intent and meaning of this act [is] not to legislate slavery into any territory or state nor to exclude it therefrom, but to leave the people thereof perfectly free to form and regulate their domestic institutions in their own way, subject only to the Constitution of the United States." This was not the flat grant of power to the territorial legislature included in earlier versions, but, significantly, it still strongly implied what Southerners abhorred as squatter sovereignty—an early decision on slavery by territorial legislatures.[19]

II

The January 23 version of the bill offered the best chance that a unified Whig party might rally against it. Here was the controversial Democratic legislative initiative that Whigs had yearned to run against for over a year, one that, like the Independent Treasury bill of the late 1830s or the Walker Tariff, the Independent Treasury, and the Mexican War of the late 1840s, might spark a Whig comeback. Douglas' authorship and Pierce's endorsement stamped it indelibly as a Democratic measure. Equally important, the junking of Dixon's inflammatory language excused Whigs from blame for repealing the Missouri restriction on slavery extension, for, whatever its language, the bill did repeal it. As Seward wrote his wife on January 29, without once mentioning Dixon's threatened-but-never-moved amendment, "The 'Hards,' finding fault with Douglas' equivocations in his first bill, insisted on the repeal of the Missouri Compromise." Seward, like most Whigs in Washington, attributed this action to the Hards' "purpose of ruining the 'Softs,'" but the important point was that the spotlight had been taken off Dixon and southern Whigs, even though Dixon himself immediately endorsed Douglas' new bill. Responsibility for framing the legislation could be laid exclusively upon Democrats. Not only might Whigs count on the habitual inclination of Whig politicos and voters to oppose any Democratic measure once the differences between the parties had been made clear. There was also much about the bill that Whigs of all varieties, Northerners and Southerners, antislavery Sewardites and pro-Compromise conservatives, despised.[20]

All northern Whigs, but especially antislavery men who had so bitterly execrated the Compromise of 1850 and the 1852 platform as betrayals of freedom, northern interests, and northern Whigs' long-standing principles, abominated Douglas' measure. Sewardites repeatedly charged, and many of them undoubtedly believed, that, regardless of climate, slaveholders would take their chattels anywhere they legally could and that consequently the bill opened the possibility of slavery extension into a vast area long promised exclusively to nonslaveholders, especially northern nonslaveholders. In addition, they knew that the bill, and most certainly its passage into law, could revive the Free Soil party and with it resurrect the hated Free Soil/Democratic coalitions that had so discomfited Whigs in Ohio, Massachusetts, and elsewhere. The political necessity of averting a Free Soil revival combined with visceral revulsion at the prospect of slavery expansion to mobilize northern antislavery Whigs against the bill.

Until May, therefore, northern Whigs' top priority was to stop enactment of the *bill* into *law*. Instantly in January, Whig newspapers, state legislators, and local politicos affiliated with Seward flayed Douglas' bill. Whigs alone, of course, did not have the votes in Congress to prevent passage if Democrats united behind the bill, and by early February a Senate majority for it seemed certain. Rather, the Whigs' goal was to arouse the northern public in order to intimidate northern Democratic representatives, who faced elections in the fall of 1854, into helping Whigs defeat the odious measure in the House. And from January almost to the last minute, northern Whigs expressed confidence that they would have the necessary votes to do so.[21]

Even if Douglas' measure failed to pass, Seward and his northern Whig allies also expected considerable political dividends from opposing it. For over a decade they had believed that fighting slavery extension and portraying northern Democrats as doughfaced lackeys of an aggressive Slave Power offered northern Whigs their best chance to win elections. During 1853, Seward's most zealous antislavery supporters had unavailingly demanded that he and other northern Whigs make an open issue of Freedom versus Slavery in order to expunge the stigma stenciled upon the party by the 1852 national platform.[22] Now, suddenly in 1854, the Democrats handed them a terrific issue on a silver platter. Northerners regarded the bill "as *base* and *fraudulent*," Connecticut's former Senator Roger Sherman Baldwin excitedly wrote Truman Smith from New Haven. "It will do us good politically at the coming election." So convinced, northern Whig congressmen did everything they could to make Douglas' bill as repulsive as possible to northern voters. As Ohio Congressman Lew Campbell wrote in May, if he and other opponents could not prevent enactment, their "policy" was to "drive" the bill's backers to pass it "by some desperate means—overriding the rules, or disregarding our rights—so that it may go to the country with as much odium as can be heaped upon it."[23]

More than the prospect of pillorying Democrats' responsibility for the bill to defeat them in the 1854 elections caused Sewardite Whigs to salivate. That tack could also trump their conservative intraparty rivals who had long tried to bury the slavery issue precisely to prevent Sewardites from using antislavery rhetoric to control northern Whig organizations. The Kansas-Nebraska bill discredited the promises of pro-Compromise Whigs that pledges to finality in the 1852 Whig and Democratic platforms meant the end of Slave Power aggressions and exposed conservatives' opposition to the Taylor plan and the Wilmot Proviso in 1850 as a fatal mistake. Northern anger at the bill was so intense and so widespread, moreover, that Whig conservatives, who themselves reviled it, had no choice but to follow Sewardites' lead. "If the Missouri Compromise is repealed, then nothing remains but sectional war," declared a pro-Compromise Whig from Maine. "The feeling is intense & bitter & the National Whigs as they are called are beyond all others mortified, enraged, and determined." Democrats' contention that the Nebraska bill was the logical extension of, indeed was inherent in, the Compromise of 1850, in sum, demolished conservatives' case for leading the northern Whig party.[24]

In early 1854, therefore, Sewardite Whigs had no intention of abandoning the national Whig party for a different kind of northern coalition with Free Soilers or of attempting to drive northern conservatives and Southerners from it. The more Whigs who remained in the party, the greater the chances that it could win office, and the greater the benefits control of it might yield to them. Seward, for example, had a personal stake in keeping New York's Silver Grays in the party as long as his followers dominated local Whig organizations and the nominations they made. He was up for reelection in the legislature to be chosen in the fall of 1854. Hence he needed a Whig majority in that body. The angry northern Whig reaction to the Nebraska bill virtually guaranteed that most Whig legislative candidates would be his allies, not Silver Grays, but to ensure their election he wanted to retain as many votes in the Whig column as possible. What Sewardites counted on, in fact, was that all Whigs would unite behind their leadership in opposition to the bill, for the more united Whigs were against it, the better the chance of pinning the blame solely on Democrats and the more credible the case that Whigs should reap the credit for trying to defeat it.

Conservative northern Whigs instantly recognized the untenable position in which Douglas' measure placed them. "If I determine to vote against the bill," Haven moaned to Fillmore in late January, "my greatest regret will be that I shall be thereby compelled to go with the woolly headed crowd from the north." By late January, however, Haven and other northern Whig conservatives had no alternative but to oppose the bill. Even more than other Whigs, they considered the Democrats' pretense that in 1850 Congress had extended popular sovereignty to all territories, not just Utah and New Mexico, sheer demagoguery, a transparent fabrication, an outright lie. "Clay & Webster could have, & would have, blown this Bill to atoms," fumed the outraged Robert C. Winthrop. "Overthrowing the Compromise of 1820," echoed Truman Smith, was "the last thing which either Mr. Clay or Mr. Webster would have assented to."[25]

More important, northern conservatives recognized that the measure, and especially its passage, would "renew the old strife between sections & make it rage more furiously than ever," thereby betraying "the promise of that cessation of agitation which the Compromise of 1850 held out." Winthrop, indeed, could only explain Douglas' measure as a "deliberate design to keep alive an active Free Soil Party at the North" since Democrats wanted to negate "all our late victories over the Coalition." Thoroughly appalled by this threat to the sectional peace they had promised, pro-Compromise or National Whigs knew that consistency alone required them to join Sewardites in opposing the Nebraska bill.[26]

Douglas' bill, therefore, forced together and kept intact the entire northern wing of the Whig party by stopping conservatives aligned with Fillmore from bolting to a new Union party. It was precisely in December 1853 and January 1854, when Sewardite Whigs in Albany ruthlessly excluded Silver Grays from canal contracts and jobs, that Fillmore's closest Whig allies tentatively decided to abandon the Whig party permanently for a new alliance with anti-administration Democrats.[27] Nonetheless, however much Sewardite actions in Albany infuriated Silver Grays, Democratic actions in Washington abruptly stopped talk of such a new party. For one thing, the alignments among Democrats over the bill confounded the calculations of conservative Whigs. Hardshell Hunkers and other antiadministration Democrats, whom they had targeted as potential allies in a Union party, were precisely the Democrats who most aggressively pushed Douglas' measure. "The Hards of the North (together with some Softs) will vote for it," Haven lamented. "So we are isolated from the hards, and made particularly subordinate & secondary amongst the Whigs of the north," since opposition to the bill "gives a decided preponderance to the woolly headed influence of the north."[28]

Silver Gray leaders, however, had no choice but to join Sewardites in opposing the Nebraska bill since their constituents angrily demanded that they do so. As Ogden Hoffman, a Silver Gray, enthused to Seward in early March, "The Nebraska bill has had one good effect, to atone for its many sins. It has united the Whig party, & broken down the foolish partition wall, which separated one portion from another." Or, as a visceral anti-Sewardite conservative despaired later that spring, "The Nebraska Swindle has driven National & Sectional Whigs into the same camp where they must mess together."[29]

Particularly embarrassing to Fillmore's northern allies was the prospect that their joining Sewardites in opposition to the bill would destroy Fillmore's popularity in the South and thereby kill his prospects for the presidency in 1856. On the one hand, they knew they had to oppose the bill in order to retain any credibility with northern Whig voters. On the other, southern Fillmorites like Virginia's Stuart and Daniel Lee, the Georgian now editing the pro-Fillmore Rochester *American*, warned Fillmore that Southerners much preferred Douglas' doctrine of congressional noninterference to the Missouri prohibition and that, consequently, "the National Whigs are about to commit a great blunder on the Nebraska question." I hope, Lee pleaded, that "you will not be found in the same boat."[30] Most conservative northern Whigs, however, saw only one escape from their quandary. They wanted southern Whigs to join them in opposing the bill by portraying it not as a Slave Power aggression against the North to spread slavery, but as a "question of *plighted faith*," that is, a flagrant violation of the party's pledge to finality. "It is upon this point that a chivalrous Southron might make a stand which would cover him with honor," Winthrop advised Kennedy.[31]

As Douglas' bill stood on January 23, there was still a chance that most southern Whigs might oppose it. Southern Whigs in and outside Congress considered the principle of congressional noninterference more palatable than the Missouri restriction, and for this reason alone some undoubtedly found the bill irresistible. Dixon publicly endorsed Douglas' new version on January 24 because it repealed the Missouri restriction, and Tennessee's "Lean Jimmy" Jones quickly concurred with him. In addition, the erstwhile Georgia Whigs Stephens and Toombs, who still exerted great influence among their former Whig colleagues from Dixie, avidly supported the bill because they thought it vindicated the Georgia Platform. Since they had already renounced allegiance to the national Whig party and sought to replace it with a new regionwide organization more faithful to Southern Rights, moreover, they believed that pressuring southern Whigs to support the bill could drive a permanent wedge between them and the northern wing of the party. Their intention is clear, but what such an anti-Democratic, non-Whig, pro-Southern Rights organization might accomplish in national politics is not, at least to this modern observer. Nonetheless, both sought passage of Douglas' Kansas-Nebraska bill. Stephens was indisposed by illness until mid-February, but Toombs, who had now finally replaced Berrien in the Senate, worked actively for passage from January on. Citing Stephens and Toombs by name, John Bell, who ultimately voted against the measure, later complained that from the start its "most zealous" southern Whig backers hoped "that there would no longer be a Whig party" since they sought "to get up a new party."[32]

On January 23, when Douglas presented his revised version of the Kansas-Nebraska bill, however, most southern Whigs still wanted to preserve the Whig party, few of them had as yet committed themselves to the bill, and they had numerous reasons to oppose it. For one, the rejection of Dixon's amendment and inclusion of a provision that seemed to condone squatter sovereignty meant that proslavery southern Whigs could attack the measure in a politically viable way. Hence, virtually every southern Whig newspaper editorial and every southern Whig congressional speech against the bill condemned it for enacting squatter sovereignty. For another, northern Whigs like Ohio's Ben Wade and Connecticut's Truman Smith instantly warned Southerners that their support of the bill meant permanent disruption of the national Whig party. That was a threat most southern Whigs, quite unlike Toombs and Stephens, did not take lightly. In addition, there was virtually no grass-roots pressure on southern Whig congressmen to go along with the bill. To the contrary, many southern Whigs, just like many southern Democrats, believed that nothing would be achieved by changing the law for Nebraska since climate would render plantation slavery unprofitable there.[33]

Thus the South's gain would be purely symbolic rather than substantive. It would be what Tennessee's Bell pronounced an "abortive abstraction." Against that gain Southern Whigs had to weigh the certain renewal of antisouthern agitation in the North, the probable political resurrection of the most fanatical antislavery groups there, the alienation of their northern Whig allies and likely rupture of the national Whig party, and a threat to the survival of the Union itself. To many southern Whigs that price seemed far too high merely to gain repeal of a law they had accepted for nearly thirty-five years. Richmond's John Minor Botts published a public letter against the bill in the Washington *National Intelligencer* in mid-February. Denouncing the measure as "odious in principle, uncalled for by any political exigency," and certain to reopen "the floodgates to future agitation on the slavery question," a public meeting of Whigs in Wilmington, Delaware, chaired by ex-Senator John Wales, "earnestly" petitioned Clayton to oppose it. William A. Graham, the party's vice presidential candidate in 1852, urged North Carolina's Whig congressmen to vote against it, and Kentucky's United States senator-elect Crittenden privately pleaded with his state's Whig congressional delegation, including Dixon himself, to do likewise in order to avert sectional strife and preserve comity between northern and southern Whigs. Initially, the southern Whig press was just as unenthusiastic. The New Orleans *Bee* and New Orleans *Bulletin*, the Louisville *Journal*, the Raleigh *Register*, and the Savannah *Republican*, among other papers, flayed the measure as Democratic demagoguery, warned against igniting an antislavery conflagration in the North that would jeopardize sectional peace, and reminded southern Whigs that their 1852 platform committed them to oppose any revival of the slavery question.[34]

Though most southern Whig protests against Douglas' bill appeared during formal debates on it between February and May, it was on January 23 that the chances of rallying most Whigs against the measure peaked. Just as northern and southern Whigs had united against Texas annexation in 1844 and behind the No

Territory formula in 1847, all Whigs might oppose Douglas' bill and campaign on that opposition in both sections to revive the party. Outrage at the bill by committed nationalists stymied the threat of a bolt by conservatives to a new Union party—and with it the potential loss of vital northern Whig voting support. Southern Whigs seemed to have reason and sufficient political cover to resist the bill. Northern Sewardites eagerly anticipated the prospect of leapfrogging ahead of their conservative rivals, trouncing the Democrats, burying the Free Soil party by rendering it unnecessary, and still retaining an alliance with southern Whigs. A clear-cut, nationwide, two-party partisan battle, not a sectional clash, appeared to be on the horizon. Douglas and the Democrats had seemingly worked a miracle. The chance for a powerful bisectional comeback lay within Whigs' grasp.

III

That chance evaporated within twenty-four hours of Douglas' presentation on January 23. The following day, newspapers published a protest from the few remaining Free Soil officeholders in Washington entitled "The Appeal of the Independent Democrats in Congress." Signed by Senators Salmon P. Chase and Charles Sumner and four House members, including Joshua Giddings and the abolitionist Gerrit Smith, it lacerated Douglas' measure as "a gross violation of a sacred pledge," as "part and parcel of an atrocious plot" to spread slavery and exclude northern whites from the new territories, and as a "bold scheme against American liberty" that would subjugate the entire nation "to the yoke of a slave-holding despotism." If the bill passed and this audacious Slave Power aggression succeeded, they vowed, they—that is, Free Soil politicians—would "go home to our constituents, erect anew the standard of freedom, and call on the people to . . . rescue . . . the country from the dominion of slavery."[35]

The manifesto appeared a week before formal debate on Douglas' proposal even started. Free Soilers, therefore, defined the purpose of Douglas' measure before he himself could do so. More important for the Whigs, they preempted the ground of opposition to it. They thereby cast anyone inclined to oppose the bill for any other reason as a fellow traveler of abolitionist fanatics. "The cry of abolitionism" raised by "that address of Chase, Sumner, Giddings and Company," complained one Ohio Whig editor, who sought to mobilize Whigs against Douglas' measure, "came near swamping us altogether."[36] By exaggerating and impugning southern responsibility for the bill, by portraying it as a southern assault on the liberty and future economic prospects of northern whites, the "Appeal" converted what, only hours earlier, had been shaping up as a partisan struggle between Democrats and Whigs into a sectional brawl. In achieving this transmutation, the tiny group of Free Soil congressmen had a far more devastating impact on the Whig party than even they probably intended.

With their clarion call to arouse the North, Chase, Sumner, and Giddings obviously hoped to revive the flagging fortunes of the Free Soil party by enlisting antislavery Democrats and Whigs behind the Free Soil banner.[37] Most northern Whigs needed no scolding from Free Soilers to oppose the bill, especially after the Pierce administration defined it as the new test of Democratic orthodoxy. Some, like Ohio's Wade, clearly hoped Whigs and Free Soilers would combine behind the Whig banner.[38] Initially, that is, the northern Whigs most likely to bolt to the Free Soilers saw no need to follow their lead since northern Whig editors and legislators were already denouncing the bill for opening up the floodgates to slavery extension. If anything, the prospect that Free Soilers might profit the most politically from passage of the measure by erecting "anew the standard of freedom" in the North only intensified northern Whigs' desire to stop its enactment.

By identifying opposition to the bill with abolitionist extremism, however, the "Appeal" deepened the embarassment of conservative northern Whigs who personally despised the bill and saw no political alternative but to oppose it. They wanted to fight the bill on grounds of its threat to national tranquility and its violation of the concord reached in 1850, in ways, that is, that could persuade pro-Compromise southern Whigs to oppose it and thus preserve harmony between northern and southern Whigs. The Free Soilers' bold strike seemed to eliminate the middle ground on which Whigs with diverse attitudes might cooperate. How could conservatives now try to stop a bill that had been painted as prosouthern without alienating Southerners and driving them into its support?

Writhing in agony at this dilemma, conservatives begged their congressional spokesmen like Haven and Everett to retrieve the initiative and present the case against the Nebraska measure in less inflammatory, nonsectional terms. Informing Everett in early February of his personal hostility to the repeal of the Missouri Compromise, Fillmore fretted, "If our people intend to oppose its repeal," they should move "a proper amendment and not suffer themselves to be placed in the false position of following the lead of known and avowed *abolitionists*." Appalled that that Free Soilers and anti-Compromise Sewardites led the charge against Douglas' bill, thereby winning plaudits from angry northern voters, Winthrop also pleaded from Boston for Everett to make a Senate speech around which conservatives and southern Whigs could rally since, he insisted, it was the friends of finality who would lose the most by the bill's passage. And yet, as he was still protesting over a year later, Free Soilers had driven "off the only persons who could have prevented" its passage. They "usurped a lead which belonged to others, and gave an odor of abolition to the whole movement."[39]

How effectively Free Soilers had staked out the anti-Nebraska ground became clear in February when Everett attempted to articulate the conservative case against the Nebraska bill in the Senate. With his friend Webster now dead, Everett was easily the most renowned and accomplished orator in American public life, and conservatives like Fillmore and Winthrop looked upon him as a natural rallying point. To Winthrop's delight, Everett cited his intimacy with Webster to shred Douglas' rationale that the Compromise of 1850 had already superseded the Compromise of 1820 by extending popular sovereignty to all territories. In order to conciliate southern Whigs and rally them against the measure, Everett also stressed their conviction that climate would prevent slavery from ever taking hold in Kansas and Nebraska. Given that prospect, Everett implored, southern friends of the Compromise and sectional harmony should join him in opposing Douglas' measure.[40]

Whatever conservatives like Winthrop thought of this tack, it infuriated Free Soilers and Sewardite Whigs, who wanted to stress the real threat of slavery expansion in order to increase northern opposition to the bill. Aimed at reassuring

Southerners about the motives for opposition to Douglas' bill, Everett's speech struck Sewardites and even some conservative northern Whigs instead as a "*milk & water* speech" that anesthetized Northerners just when they needed to be aroused into pressuring northern Democratic congressmen to vote against the bill. It smacked too much of Webster's opposition to the Wilmot Proviso in 1850. It was quintessential doughfacism, and when painful kidney stones later forced Everett to miss the Senate vote on adoption of the Kansas-Nebraska bill, he inadvertently undermined conservatives' credibility even further. Everett thus found himself an odd man out, reviled by Whigs in New England and scorned by most northern Whigs in Congress, and he would resign his Senate seat in June before the session ended. Clearly, however, Free Soilers' success in sectionalizing debate over the bill most discomfited him. "Why should I persevere in this contest?" he forlornly asked his niece in May 1854. "I do no good. I gain no credit. I have no future. The Country is given over to ultraism on both sides, and moderate counsels are despised alike at the South and the North."[41]

When Winthrop subsequently complained that Free Soilers had driven "off the only persons" who could have stopped passage of the Nebraska bill, however, he did not refer to northern conservatives like Everett. In neither the Senate nor the House could the few northern Whigs who failed to vote have stopped passage had they been present, and every northern Whig in Congress who cast a vote, whatever his factional affiliation or ideological orientation, voted against passage. Rather, the Whigs most alienated by the Free Soilers' "Appeal" were Southerners, and, at least in the House, their support provided the margin of victory.

With the exception of one-time Whigs who had won as Union candidates in 1853 and openly repudiated Whiggery, the southern Whigs who came to Congress in December 1853 were loyal party men. Most had rallied faithfully behind Scott's candidacy in 1852 and sought the resuscitation of the Whig party. Of those old-line Whigs, moreover, twenty of twenty-one representatives and nine of twelve senators hailed from the border states, North Carolina, or Tennessee, the slave states where the Whig party had always been strongest, most committed to national harmony, and most adverse to reckless proslavery propagandism.[42] The unusual enthusiasm within Missouri for the formal organization of Kansas and Nebraska might make it difficult for Senator Henry Geyer and the four Whigs in the Missouri House delegation to vote overtly against the measure,[43] but northern Whigs had every reason to expect support against it from conservatives such as Clayton of Delaware, James Pearce and Thomas Pratt of Maryland, George Badger of North Carolina, Bell of Tennessee, and John B. Thompson of Kentucky, as well as from Whigs in those states' House delegations.

Free Soilers' insulting manifesto ended that possibility by rendering any opposition to the Nebraska bill for whatever reason betrayal of the South. To most Southerners in Congress, including southern Whigs, its passage now became a matter of southern honor, just as resistance to the Wilmot Proviso had been. As Jewett reported to Fillmore from Washington in mid-February, "It is unfortunate that the free soil Senators have been suffered to lead off the opposition. This fact more than anything else has contributed to unite Southern sentiment on the bill."[44]

Little evidence exists that the Free Soil assault, which northern antislavery Whigs immediately echoed, created much enthusiasm among rank-and-file southern Whigs for a measure they still considered solely symbolic. Rather, by citing northern attacks, southern Democratic newspapers made support of the bill a test of fealty to Southern Rights. Given their unhappy experience since 1844 with Democrats' one-upmanship on the slavery issue, that was a test most southern Whigs refused to flunk. By February and March, southern Whig editors who had previously denounced the bill as a reckless and useless provocation of renewed sectional strife fell silent or changed their tone. Southern Whig congressmen, proclaimed the Richmond *Whig*, must leave no doubt about "the soundness of Southern Whigs upon the questions involving the peculiar institutions of the South."[45]

Perceptive northern Whigs like Truman Smith, and especially conservatives who desperately sought to preserve an alliance with Southerners, began to worry about southern Whigs' seepage from the anti-Nebraska camp within a week of the "Appeal's" publication. "This movement if consummated," the indignant Smith privately protested on the last day of January, "will be a finishing blow to the Whig party. No man has struggled . . . as I have to preserve it as a national party," but "I shall have nothing to do with any Southern Whig who joins Stephen A. Douglas in introducing into Congress & into the country another controversy on the subject of slavery."[46]

During February, southern Whigs not only endorsed Douglas' bill. Key representatives and senators collaborated actively with its Democratic sponsors to revise the bill in order to enhance its chance of passage. North Carolina's Badger and Clayton successfully moved amendments that made the bill more palatable to southern Whigs while simultaneously attempting to make their support for it more palatable to northern Whigs, for, it must be emphasized, southern Whigs by no means intended their support to disrupt the national Whig party. Meanwhile a number of southern Whigs from both the House and Senate participated in bipartisan caucuses that refined the language regarding popular sovereignty and the rationale for replacing the Missouri Compromise's restriction. Presented to the Senate by Douglas on February 7, this new language, while still insisting that the bill intended neither to establish nor prohibit slavery in the two territories, declared the Missouri restriction "inoperative and void" because it was "inconsistent with the principle of congressional nonintervention with slavery in the States and Territories, as recognized" by the "Compromise Measures" of 1850. This apparently minor modification, by stressing the "congressional nonintervention" rather than the local self-determination aspect of popular sovereignty, was far more attractive to Southerners than Douglas' earlier twenty-first section. That section had forthrightly—far too forthrightly for most Southerners—insisted that "all questions pertaining to slavery in the Territories . . . are to be left to the decision of the people residing therein, through their appropriate representatives." With the aid of southern Whigs, that is, the emphasis concerning the decision on slavery extension had been shifted from action by territorial legislatures to nonaction by Congress.[47]

What appeared to many to be the "finishing blow" to the national Whig party, however, occurred in the Senate after these collaborations were completed. On the morning of February 15, the ultraconservative Washington *National Intelligencer*, still regarded by many as the official organ of Whiggery, strongly condemned repeal as dangerous to sectional harmony and implied that almost all Whigs in Congress would consequently vote against it. Most southern Whig senators, who now favored repeal, were embarrassed by that implication since the Senate's upcoming schedule for floor debate would keep them from refuting it publicly. At Clayton's urging, therefore, nine of them—Clayton, Bell, Badger, Dawson, Dixon, Jones, Geyer, Pratt, and Judah P. Benjamin—together, significantly, with the ex-Whig Toombs gathered briefly in a Senate lobby upon adjournment of that afternoon's session to discuss a response to the *Intelligencer's* editorial. Some would later call this meeting a "caucus" whose agenda had been scripted in advance. At least Bell and Benjamin, however, were simply grabbed by friends as they left the Senate chamber and had no foreknowledge of what the impromptu meeting was about, and Bell later vehemently protested that he left after a few minutes before the "caucus" reached any final decisions.[48]

Toombs was selected to preside, and that choice alone says much about the tenor of the gathering. He presented a formal resolution that was adopted with no audible dissent. It declared "that we disapprove of the course of the National Intelligencer upon the Nebraska bill, and that, in our opinion, it does not truly represent the opinions of the Whig party of the South." Clayton, Badger, and Bell were then deputized to take this protest to the *Intelligencer* office, but they never did so. Instead, prior to the dispersal of the brief meeting, it was decided that Badger, who was already scheduled to speak to the Senate the next day, be authorized to announce "that the southern Whigs were a unit in favor of the bill." On February 16, Badger accordingly declared that he had the "authority" of all his southern Whig colleagues to assert that "we all agree as one man—every southern Whig Senator" that the bill must be passed because it repealed the Missouri restriction.[49]

Southern Whig senators proved almost as good as their word. When the Senate, after a marathon sixteen-hour session, voted at 5 A.M. on March 4, nine southern Whigs supported final passage, and they provided almost a fourth of the thirty-seven votes in favor. Only Bell, who first announced his opposition during debate the previous afternoon, joined the six northern Whigs still on the floor among the minority of fourteen. Pearce, Toombs, and Clayton missed the vote, as did three northern Whigs. How Pearce might have voted is unclear, but his absence, like that of Maryland's two Whig representatives from the final House vote ten weeks later, suggests a conscious attempt to avoid offending southern or northern colleagues by not voting at all.[50] Toombs most certainly would have supported it, but Clayton, who had already announced his approval of repeal, later asked to be recorded against the bill on the grounds that it incorporated squatter sovereignty.[51]

Furious northern Whigs later condemned the February 15 meeting of southern Whig senators as "the funeral of the National Whig party—or rather the choking & stabbing—preparatory to the funeral on the last night of the Nebraska bill" and Badger and Clayton as the party's "executioners." Even if all nine southern Whigs who cast votes for the bill, along with the absent Pearce and Clayton, had joined Bell in opposition, however, the bill would still have passed 28–24. Even the addition of the three absent northern Whigs—Everett, Pennsylvania's James Cooper, and Vermont's Samuel Phelps—to this hypothetical Whig phalanx could not have overcome the pro-Nebraska Democratic majority in the Senate. Rather, it was in the House, where southern Whigs were more evenly divided over the measure, that their support would prove crucial.[52]

Heavy northern majorities, the greater susceptibility of northern Democratic representatives than senators to public pressure, and different rules all made the prospect of stopping the Nebraska bill in the House better than in the Senate. An attempt to assign the Senate bill to the Committee on Territories, where it could expect favorable treatment, indeed, was defeated. Instead it was sent to the Committee of the Whole, whose rules and pre-existing agenda seemed, initially at least, to guarantee burial. Thus Connecticut's Truman Smith, who fumed at the betrayal of southern Whigs in the Senate, could crow as late as April 27 that "this vile measure . . . is just as good as dead! dead! It will never see daylight in the House of Rep." In addition to unrelenting administration pressure on wavering northern Democrats, therefore, the bill's Democratic sponsors in the House needed all the help from southern Whigs they could get to excavate the bill from its apparent grave and secure passage.[53]

At least ten of the twenty-four southern Whig congressmen, however, were distinctly unenthusiastic about the measure, and seven of them—Louisiana's only Whig representative, two of North Carolina's three, and four of Tennessee's six Whig congressmen—openly opposed it in debate and later voted against it. Together with all northern Whigs, Free Soilers, and anti-Nebraska northern Democrats, they managed, through constant demands for adjournment that required time-consuming roll-call votes, to stall the efforts by Democrats to pry the bill out of the Committee of the Whole. Other southern Whigs or ex-Whigs, however, provided the margin and the methods by which the bill's managers ultimately did so.

To resurrect the Nebraska bill from the bottom of the Committee of the Whole's agenda, those bills ahead of it had to be set aside on individual votes. Those votes were taken by teller as members filed past, not by roll call, so how individuals voted was not recorded. Nonetheless, the Georgians Stephens and Toombs worked closely with administration managers of the bill to secure southern Whig votes, and it seems clear that southern Whigs helped provide the margins by which bills were set aside. Stephens would also discover or remember an obscure procedural rule by which the Nebraska bill was finally removed from the Committee of the Whole without the possibility of further amendment on the House floor and forced to a vote on final passage. "If I had not been here the Bill would never have been got through," Stephens crowed to a friend. "I took the reins in my own hand and drove with whip & spur until we got the 'wagon' out of the mud."[54]

Two votes best gauge southern Whigs' impact on passage. The first was a roll call on May 15 in the House, not the Committee of the Whole, that required a two-thirds vote to postpone consideration of a Pacific railroad bill from May 16 to May 24 in order to allow continued action on the Nebraska bill in committee. Had that procedural roll call been defeated, it is likely that the Nebraska bill would have been permanently buried, but it passed by a margin of 123–53, 16 more than the necessary two-thirds majority.[55] On this vote, southern Whigs divided fifteen for, two against, and seven not voting. Two of the majority—Sion Rogers and Richard Puryear of North Carolina—and three of the abstainers—Theodore

Hunt of Louisiana and William Cullom and Robert Bugg of Tennessee—would later vote against final passage, along with Nathaniel G. Taylor and Emerson Etheridge of Tennessee, who voted Nay on this procedural roll call. Had those five, plus the four other abstainers—two each from Maryland and Kentucky—voted Nay, the two-thirds majority would have been denied.[56]

On May 22 the Kansas-Nebraska bill finally passed the House by a margin of 113–100. Southern Whigs split thirteen for, seven against, and four not voting. One of the abstainers, Samuel Carruthers of Missouri, missed the vote because he was paired with an absent northern Whig, and he later announced that he would have supported passage, as did the three Missouri Whigs who voted.[57] Had half of those fourteen southern Whigs—say, Felix Zollicoffer and Charles Ready of Tennessee, John Kerr of North Carolina, and the four Kentucky Whigs who voted Yea—instead voted Nay, the bill would have been defeated. Southern Whigs, in sum, provided the critical margin of victory even if 100 of the 113 votes came from Democrats.

Equally noteworthy, however, is how much less lopsided southern Whig support for passage in the House in May was than it had been ten weeks earlier in the Senate. One-third of the southern Whigs whose opinions are known—almost two-fifths if the three Georgia and Alabama Unionists are excluded from the total of House Whigs—joined a unanimous northern Whig delegation in voting against passage. The three other abstainers—the two Maryland Whigs and Kentucky's Presley Ewing, whom Crittenden had urged to vote against the bill—also probably desired its defeat even if they dared not vote openly against it. While Missouri and Kentucky Whigs, like the Whig senators from those states, gave solid backing to the bill, Whig representatives from Louisiana, Tennessee, and North Carolina stood predominantly against it, and Maryland's Whigs had refused to support it.

Southern Whig opponents cited squatter sovereignty, the impossibility of carrying slavery into the new territories, and the necessity of preserving sectional comity to justify their opposition to the bill. But, it seems clear, they were also determined to stand by what Bell called the "patriotic and noble Whigs at the North, who . . . have acquiesced in the compromises of 1850—those who are opposed to the plans of the abolition organization, and entertain no purpose of pressing their antislavery feelings to the point of disunion." What motivated the southern Whig opponents of the Nebraska bill, in short, was a desire to prevent the sectional disruption of the Whig party. As they saw it, "the tendency of this bill is to stimulate the formation of a sectional party organization . . . the last and most fatal evil which can befall this country."[58]

IV

The tocsin John Bell sounded against a sectional reorganization of parties in May was hardly the first mention of that nightmarish specter. Speculation about a political realignment in which parties that exclusively represented the North or the South displaced the nationwide, bisectional competition between Whigs and Democrats began in early February when events seemed to presage such a reshuffling. Caucuses of pro-Nebraska southern Whig and Democratic congressmen in Washington portended a bipartisan fusion in Dixie. Simultaneously, in community after community across the North, meetings that combined Whigs, Democrats, Free Soilers, and the politically unaffiliated gathered to protest the Nebraska bill as an outrageous southern aggression against the rights, interests, expectations, and moral convictions of Northerners. Along with the acrimonious debate in Congress and angry recriminations traded by northern and southern editors, these cross-party sectional gatherings in early 1854 seemed harbingers of intrasectional unity and permanent intersectional conflict. Understandably, if incorrectly, therefore, some historians have dated the death of the Whig party in early 1854 and attributed it to sectional divisions over the Nebraska bill that drove exasperated Whigs to new parties.[59]

Some Whig leaders and editors from both sections did speak angrily in early 1854 about breaking away from former allies in the other section—what Whigs often called the "denationalization" of their party—and it is important to assess how representative and successful they were. It is even more important to emphasize the crucial distinction between, rather than to conflate, the readiness of some northern and southern Whigs to separate from each other and their readiness to abandon existing state and local Whig organizations in the North and South in order to join new sectional parties. Three separate but related steps were necessary for the collapse of national party organizations and the creation of sectional parties in their place. The first was a permanent rift between northern and southern leaders of the Whig party, or at least the majority of those leaders in each section. The second was an abandonment of the resulting sectional wings of the party by both Whig leaders and Whig voters. The third was the combination of those defecting Whigs with Democrats—and, in the North, with Free Soilers and abolitionists, as well—in new sectional phalanxes that were overtly hostile to the rival section.

By May 1854, when the Kansas-Nebraska Act finally passed and was signed by Pierce, a few Whigs in and outside Washington voiced a willingness to take all three steps. Since many northern Democrats opposed the Nebraska bill and half of them in the House voted against final passage, formation of a new sectional party seemed especially likely in the North. Significantly, however, in both North and South, the most ardent advocates of new sectional parties were primarily men who had already abandoned the Whigs and Democrats for third-party action.

Far more Whig leaders, though still probably not a majority of them, demanded or grudgingly accepted the inevitability of at least a temporary separation between the northern and southern wings of the Whig party because of the rancor stirred up by the Nebraska issue. The absolutely crucial point with regard to the dating of, *and the explanation for,* the death of the Whig party is that most of them saw no need to take steps two or three—abandoning their local Whig organizations and combining in new sectional parties with their former political enemies from the same section. They understood what it has been difficult for subsequent historians to comprehend. Aside from sessions of Congress themselves—and in the first session of the Thirty-Third Congress, Whigs and Democrats remained internally cohesive on most measures other than the Kansas-Nebraska Act—northern and southern Whigs did not need to cooperate with each other until it was time to nominate a presidential candidate in 1856.[60] By that time a reconciliation across sectional lines might be possible. In the meantime—

in 1854 and 1855—a sectional split between Whig leaders over national policy need not be fatal to the Whig party itself since Whig organizations could be preserved in both northern and southern states to compete with Democrats. Prior to 1850, after all, northern and southern Whigs had always campaigned in opposite ways on slavery questions. Why, some Whigs implicitly asked, could they not do so again?

Reactions of southern Whigs during the first half of 1854 well illustrate the vast difference among the three steps outlined above. Bitter accusations from northern Whigs about Southerners' betrayal of the Whigs' national platform and of a sacred intersectional compact, and particularly their statement that no Northerner could coexist with slaveholders in the territories, deeply affronted southern Whigs' honor and convinced a number of them that they must deal no longer with their northern Whig tormentors. Thus southern Whig editors rang changes on the same theme: the necessity of seceding from the national Whig party. Northern Whigs' slurs about Southerners, concurred Georgia's Savannah *Republican* and Milledgeville *Southern Recorder* in March, necessitated the termination of a "party association that will not admit and treat us as *equals*." "The Whigs of Florida have already *waived* their party affinaties [sic] and allegiance with northern Whigs until they should give unmistakable evidence of repentence," echoed the Tallahassee *Florida Sentinel* in June. And in May, the Petersburg, Virginia, *Intelligencer* attempted to orchestrate a regionwide bolt by calling for a separate southern Whig convention to decide all southern Whigs' future course. "Such a convention as we propose may be termed *sectional*," its editor defiantly declared. "Well, let it be so. It is *sectional*, and *meant to be so*."[61]

At least some southern Whigs, in sum, *were* prepared to "denationalize" the Whig party. There is very little evidence, however, that many were yet prepared to abandon southern Whig state parties or to combine with Democrats in a new sectional party of the type that Calhoun and his acolytes had long envisioned.[62] Though southern state legislatures, usually with heavy bipartisan majorities, endorsed the Nebraska measure along with newspaper editors from both parties, no mass public meetings in support of the bill, comparable to the North's anti-Nebraska meetings, were held.[63]

Southerners' widely noted public lethargy about the Nebraska bill no doubt helped dull Whig interest in bolting the party. Ignoring that disinterest, the two dispeptic ex-Whigs from Georgia, Toombs and Stephens, hoped to convert the depleted Georgia Union party, to which they still clung, into a bipartisan southern party that could force cooperation and concessions from Northerners still interested in intersectional comity. In 1854, they worked closely with both pro-Nebraska Democratic congressmen and the Pierce administration, and they rejoiced at the wedge the Nebraska controversy drove between northern and southern Whigs. Toombs told Solomon G. Haven in February that he "sought the entire separation of the South as a party from the north." In June, Stephens wrote supporters in Georgia that the country was now in better condition for a *"reorganization"* of parties than it had been in 1852, when he first attempted it. If southern Whigs and Democrats remained aloof from any cooperation with Northerners until they accepted the finality of both the Compromise of 1850 and the Kansas-Nebraska Act, Stephens rosily predicted, southern Whigs could ultimately achieve "a sound national party" upon "broad national, Republican principles." Neither other Whigs nor Georgia Democrats, however, showed much interest in this idea during 1854.[64]

Prior to Congress' adjournment in August 1854, in fact, most southern Whigs had little interest in combining with southern Democrats, abandoning local and state Whig organizations, or, most significantly, separating permanently or even temporarily from their northern Whig counterparts. A number of indices point to this conclusion. Most pro-Nebraska southern Whig congressmen did not intend their support for the bill to indicate a break with northern Whig colleagues or a bolt from the party. Clayton expressly voiced regret that northern Whigs were angered by southern support for the bill, and Badger clearly intended his amendment to alleviate northern concerns that repeal of the Missouri prohibition would automatically reinstate the proslavery French laws in the territory.[65] On matters not related to Nebraska, moreover, southern and northern Whigs continued to cooperate. At the close of the congressional session in August, Bell reported that all southern Whig congressmen, except Stephens and Toombs, had abandoned the attempt "to get up a new party, & are willing to be anointed Whigs, at least until they perceive that the party is more clearly doomed than it seems at present."[66]

Within the South itself, numerous Whigs expressed second thoughts about the wisdom of the Nebraska bill and of splitting from northern Whigs for separate action or new combinations. To the Petersburg Intelligencer's call for a separate southern Whig convention, for example, the Mobile, Alabama, Register retorted in July with a list of fifteen prominent southern Whig papers that opposed the scheme of sectionalizing the party as "impolitic, uncalled for and mischievous." On July 1, the Louisville Journal proclaimed that "if we have at any time expressed fears of the imminent disruption and dissolution of [the Whig party's] present organization, we have never felt the slightest apprehension of its death." Admitting that southern Whig support for the Nebraska bill had been a huge blunder because it so incensed "our Northern allies," George Bryan, the stalwart though isolated Whig from Charleston, South Carolina, worried in August if "the unity, the nationality of the Whig party [were] a possible thing." Others answered emphatically that it was or was at least worth working to restore.[67]

Indeed, some southern Whigs believed they had already found a national champion who would preserve the party and lead it to victory. Despite the qualms of some northern friends and the necessity of postponing his plans to proselytize for a new Union party, Millard Fillmore, accompanied by John P. Kennedy, toured the Mississippi Valley and a few other southern states in the spring of 1854 before Congress finally passed the Nebraska bill. From everywhere he went—indeed, from southern cities he never got near—came stunning reports of extraordinary Whig enthusiasm for Fillmore, of certainty that he could carry the South as a presidential candidate in 1856, and, most important, of renewed commitment among the rank and file to the Whig party itself. So long as a northern Whig like Fillmore appeared capable of winning the Whig presidential nomination in 1856—and to many southern Whigs in 1854 it apparently seemed inconceivable that he would not—most southern Whigs had no intention of breaking away from northern Whigs or abandoning southern Whig organizations. As the jubilant Virginian Stuart concluded at the end of Fillmore's trip in mid-May, "The Nebraska bill, which was intended to demolish the Whig party, seems likely [instead] to perform that kind of office for its inventors." A far more important indication of southern Whigs' determination to adhere to the old organization in 1854 was that in every slave state that held congressional or gubernatorial elections prior to November, the Whigs, rather than some new party, continued to do battle with the Democrats.[68]

Southern Whigs' enthusiasm for Fillmore and the Whig party, however, did not negate the chief threat to national Whig unity: fury among northern Whigs that southern Whig votes for the Nebraska bill constituted an unforgivable betrayal. Some southern Whigs openly condemned that support as a mistake, and others—Kennedy and George Bryan, for example—expressed the hope that northern Whigs' anger would dissipate once it became clear that slavery would not expand to either Kansas or Nebraska. Still others sought to propitiate Northerners in an attempt to save the national party. On July 1, for example, a St. Louis Whig begged Fillmore to indicate what "course the Whigs of the South should pursue to secure the cooperation of their Northern brethren, and to avoid the consequences of the Douglas bombshell."[69]

Though this Whig's willingness to support restoration of the Missouri Compromise's restriction on slavery extension in order to prevent sectional rupture was wildly atypical—even southern Whigs who rued the Nebraska Act considered its repeal politically impossible—his diagnosis of the menace to Whig unity was on the mark. All southern Whigs, except those in Delaware, proved willing to retain the Whig label during the elections of 1854, but ultimately, their continued loyalty to the party, and with it the future of the national Whig party, depended upon northern Whigs' willingness to let bygones be bygones. As John Bell wrote home in August, "The course of the Northern Whigs will decide whether we can unite with them or not."[70]

V

From the moment of Badger's announcement on February 16, the chances that northern Whigs would bolt the party and unite with others in a new northern antislavery party had always been greater than the chances that southern Whigs would defect. With varying degrees of dismayed regret or bitter outrage, northern Whigs declared that, as a bisectional or national coalition, the Whig party was finished. "We no longer have any bond to Southern Whigs," Seward wrote his wife on the very day Badger spoke. "This Nebraska business will entirely denationalize the Whig party," Thurlow Weed concurred. The Nebraska bill has provoked "the ultimate disruption and *denationalization* of the Whig party," chimed the *Ohio State Journal* from Columbus in mid-April. "The Whig party has been killed off effectually by that miserable Nebraska business," echoed the disgusted Truman Smith in May. The "break" was "final," he declared. "We could not heal it if we would & would not if we could." At their mid-February meeting, southern Whigs "had made up their minds to sever forever all further connection with their northern brethren," snarled Ben Wade. "And most effectively have they done it. After this I hope to hear no more of national parties."[71]

Initially, northern conservatives also fumed at southern Whigs' betrayal and seemed just as certain that, as Haven moaned, "it cuts off all communion between us & the Whigs of the South." "What party are we to belong to hereafter?" asked one of Hamilton Fish's correspondents. "Not the Whig party I fear—for it seems to me that it must cease to exist as a national party" because of "the unanimous desertion of us on this question by the southern Whigs." The speeches by Clayton and Badger, groaned Maine's conservative Edward Kent in March, "ring forever the knell of the Whig party as a national party." "Never was a greater mistake made than in passing the Nebraska bill," summarized Winthrop in June. Had southern Whigs only rallied "en masse" against it, "we should have had a party now & a President two years hence. As I see it, nothing ahead but discord & deviltry."[72]

Most Free Soilers did all they could to foment such "discord & deviltry" by pressing northern Whigs to join a new, exclusively northern, antislavery party in protest against the Nebraska Act and slavery extension. Precisely the presence of a preexisting sectional third party in the North, indeed, increased the likelihood of building a broader sectional party there. "Whigs who have any patriotism will not attempt to reorganize their party now," argued Samuel Lewis, Ohio's 1853 Free Soil gubernatorial candidate,[73] and other Free Soilers begged northern Whig leaders to repudiate their southern Whig allies and abandon northern Whig organizations in order to form such a party. "It is *impossible* to unite the north on the old Whig basis," a Maine Free Soiler told Whig Senator William Pitt Fessenden. Northern Whigs must "give up the idea of reconstructing the old Whig party" and instead unite with all other antislavery men "on equal terms." "You must separate from the Southern Whigs or all is lost," declared Massachusetts' Henry Wilson to Maine's Whig Representative Israel Washburn, Jr. "Our friends in this State will make any concessions but we will do all we can to crush the *national* Whig party," he warned. "Decide and we can sweep the free states—continue to act with the Southern Whigs and you will fail and ought to fail. Now is the time for action, bold decisive action." "The Whig party has been a noble party in its day, in many respects," Gamaliel Bailey, editor of the Free Soil Washington *National Era*, wrote James S. Pike, yet another Maine Whig and a Washington reporter for both Greeley's New York *Tribune* and Weed's *Albany Evening Journal*. But "we all know that it was not organized with any view to antislavery issues, that as a *National* party it has never been sufficient to the protection of Freedom, that the great Question now before us must be met by a different kind of organization, by new tactics, by new ideas."[74]

The primary target of Free Soil supplications, however, was Seward, the preeminent leader of the North's antislavery Whigs. Boston's abolitionist minister Theodore Parker urged him to help organize a national, or at least regionwide, convention of northern antislavery men in the summer of 1854 to launch a new party. "The time has come to dissolve the infamous union of Whigs of the North and South," echoed Wilson. Seward was Wilson's preferred presidential candidate for 1856, cooed the Free Soiler, but not if he was the candidate "of the united Whig party. I will never act with or vote for the candidate of the Badgers', Toombs', & Dixons' of the South." Instead Wilson would "do all in my power" to build a new antislavery northern party and "to defeat all efforts to reconstruct and hold up the national Whig party." He hoped Seward, too, "will do all in your power to make a North—to combine in one great party all the friends of freedom."[75]

The very stridency of Free Soilers' language, the very urgency of their pleas that northern Whigs repudiate alliance with Southerners, point to a fact of central importance—and deep embarrassment to those who attribute the Whig party's death to a sectional rupture over the Nebraska Act. By the time Congress adjourned on August 7, 1854, few northern Whigs in Washington or in the states were inclined to break permanently with their southern Whig allies, let alone to abandon northern Whig organizations for new affiliations with Democrats and Free Soilers. To the contrary, many seemed disposed "to reconstruct and hold up the national Whig party."

During the ten-week struggle over the Nebraska bill in the House, for example, there was no coordination among its polyglot Free Soil, Whig, and Democratic opponents. "Party names & prejudices are the cords that bind the Sampson of the North," moaned Bailey, who, along with Preston King, the former Barnburner and Free Soil congressman from New York, sought for weeks to arrange a caucus of anti-Nebraska men to agree upon tactics. They finally succeeded only on the evening of May 21, when final passage on the following day was certain, and even the frantic Bailey admitted at that point that the only hope of launching a new party from Washington was the issuance of an address protesting the act signed by all its opponents "without distinction of party."[76]

As Bailey's list of the men who arranged this last-minute caucus indicated, moreover, even among anti-Nebraska Whig representatives, three separate blocs operated independently of each other. The floor leaders of the most ardent antislavery northern Whigs—the Whigs most likely to bolt the party for an alliance with Free Soilers—were Ohio's Lew Campbell, Maine's Israel Washburn, and his brother, Illinois Congressman Elihu B. Washburne, who had added an "e" to the family name. Three Massachusetts Whig congressmen—Thomas Eliot, Edward Dickinson, and John Z. Goodrich—cooperated closely with this group. Significantly, however, the firmest New York Sewardites in the House—Russell Sage, Orsamus B. Matteson, and Edwin B. Morgan—conspicuously conceded leadership of antislavery Whigs to non-New Yorkers not closely identified with Seward. The harsh antisouthern stance assumed by Campbell and Washburn caused southern Whig opponents of the bill—Hunt of Louisiana, Rogers and Puryear of North Carolina, and Etheridge, Bugg, Cullom, and Taylor of Tennessee—to give them a wide berth and, for the most part, to steer an independent course. When these Southerners cooperated openly with northern Whigs, it was with the third distinctive bloc, northern conservatives like Fillmore's spokesman Haven, the Massachusetts Websterite Samuel Walley, Philadelphia's Joseph Chandler, E. Wilder Farley of Maine, and Ohio's John Taylor. Northern conservative Whigs, in sum, provided the most obvious bridge across the chasm that threatened to separate northern and southern Whigs over the Nebraska bill. They provided the first—but hardly the last—hope of preventing the denationalization of the Whig party.[77]

Conservatives like Haven and Farley had no intention of breaking with southern Whigs or cooperating with Free Soilers because of the Nebraska bill. Despite the discouragement Haven expressed in February about being cut off from southern Whigs after Badger's announcement, he and other conservatives took heart from the greater southern Whig opposition to Nebraska in the House. Even Truman Smith, who had given up on the Whig party before the session opened, who resigned his Senate seat in disgust in late May, and who vowed never to have anything to do with southern Whig supporters of the bill, singled out Hunt, Cullom, and Etheridge for praise. Conservatives deemed their courageous stand against Nebraska, along with Bell's, the reason that the alliance with southern Whigs could and should be preserved. Now that Democratic support for the Nebraska Act had once again derailed the possibility of building a new Union party, moreover, conservatives like Haven rejoiced at Fillmore's enthusiastic reception in the South. Together with the continuing strength of conservatives in Philadelphia and New York City, it resuscitated their hope that conservatives could take control of the national Whig organization and make Fillmore Whigs' presidential nominee in 1856. But that possibility depended upon retaining an alliance with southern Whigs.[78]

If hope of reviving an alliance with southern Whigs that could win the 1856 nomination for Fillmore motivated some northern conservatives, their revulsion at cooperating with antislavery fanatics killed any thought of merging with Free Soilers. Long before the Kansas-Nebraska Act passed Congress, indeed, conservatives had moved to expunge any Free Soil taint from the anti-Nebraska movement. They sought to keep anti-Nebraska protests as moderate as possible, to focus them exclusively on the injustice of overturning the Missouri restriction, and to prevent Free Soilers from so radicalizing anti-Nebraska meetings with demands for abolition in the District of Columbia or repeal of the Fugitive Slave Act that southern Whigs would be permanently alienated.

In Massachusetts, for example, Winthrop addressed a protest meeting at Boston's Faneuil Hall to tone it down, and for the same reason he asked Everett to write noninflammatory anti-Nebraska resolutions for the Massachusetts legislature to pass. These were not the only Whigs worried about the radicalization of the Whig party. "The Southern Senators are not so much to blame as those scoundels from the North," Judge David Davis of Illinois advised Julius Rockwell, the Massachusetts Whig who had been appointed to take Everett's Senate seat, in July. "Try to save the Whig party," he implored. "I don't fancy it being abolitionized—although no one can be more opposed to [the] admission [of] Nebraska than I am." After his resignation from the Senate, Everett worked successfully toward that same goal, and by the end of August he rejoiced in relief that in Massachusetts "there will be no *fusion* of the Whigs and freesoilers."[79]

In Ohio, ex-Senator Thomas Ewing diverted his attention from his salt and coal-mining businesses long enough to send a public letter to a state anti-Nebraska convention at Columbus in March. Alerted by an enthusiastic friend that circumstances might make Ewing himself president in 1856, Ewing clearly hoped to quash Free Soil radicalism and hold open the possibility of southern Whig support. His letter insisted that the meeting's resolutions should, with "calmness, prudence, and consideration," focus exclusively on the threatened repeal of the Missouri restriction, "single and alone." He also flagrantly courted Southerners and thereby infuriated antislavery extremists by proposing that "a due proportion of newly acquired territory should be opened to the unobstructed occupancy of each section of the Union." Since this remarkable statement implied that slaveholders had a legitimate right to take slaves to at least some federal territories, it seemed to endorse the idea that Kansas should be slave and Nebraska free. Ewing's ally Oran Follett, editor of the Columbus *Ohio State Journal*, went even further to appease southern Whigs. In mid-April he bitterly announced that the Nebraska bill had denationalized the Whig party, but only a few days later he attempted to renationalize it. Citing the danger that on "this Missouri question" the entire North could be bulldozed "into freesoil-ism or semi-abolitionism," he argued that Whigs should ignore the repeal of the Missouri Compromise to avoid "the Abolition taint." In late April, therefore, he floated an editorial proposal that would concede to Southerners the right to take slaves to the new territory but abolish the three-fifths rule regarding representation of slaves in Congress for any new states admitted from it. "We would not seek to abolish slavery," he excitedly wrote Ewing. "We would simply sink it to its municipal character, and when it will no longer confer political power, it will soon pass away."[80]

Hostile to Free Soilers and determined to reach out to southern Whigs, northern conservatives also shunned attempts by Free Soilers to orchestrate the formation of a new party from Washington. The principal part of what Seward dismissed as Free Soilers' scheme for "dissolving the Whig party" was to bring as many anti-Nebraska men from all parties together as possible to issue a public protest that could launch the new party.[81] On June 20, Free Soilers succeeded in arranging a gathering of anti-Nebraska congressmen at the National Hotel to write an address. Drafted by a committee of Whigs and Democrats, the meeting's address sought to attract as many signatures as possible. Thus its tone was, in Seward's words, of "utmost moderation," in contrast with the Free Soilers' appeal in January.[82] Though the protest blamed the Nebraska Act on Pierce's administration and "the slaveholding power," though it condemned the law as a violation of both parties' 1852 national platforms, and though it rued the possible spread of slavery, it spoke only of restoring the Missouri Compromise line and recovering "the ground lost to freedom," not the full antislavery agenda pushed by Free Soilers. It also failed to call for creation of a new sectional party. Indeed, it explicitly repudiated sectionalism. "We appeal in no sectional spirit," vowed the authors. "We appeal to the North and to the South, to the free states and to the slaveholding states themselves."

According to Free Soilers and northern Whigs now desirous of a new antislavery coalition with them, the "tame" language and lack of a "trumpet tone" in the address, and the failure to name the men who had signed it, would prevent the consolidation of anti-Nebraska forces in the North. Still, southern anti-Nebraska Whigs considered the address offensive, and precisely because they did so, the small bloc of conservative northern Whig congressmen headed by Haven, Chandler, and Walley refused to sign it. Even though the address had been intentionally watered down to gain support from such conservatives, sneered Israel Washburn in disgust, six or seven "weak-backs" from the North "would have nothing to do with" it. Washburn thought he knew why. The goal of "southern Whigs & Fillmore men" was to make Fillmore president, and that goal required "acquiescence in the Miss. repeal & unquestioning submission to the Slave Power to be secured by continuing the present national organization of the Whig party."[83]

The furious Washburn was one of the few northern Whig congressmen who, by the summer of 1854, were clearly ready to bolt the Whig party for a new antislavery coalition that would wage unrelenting political war against slavery expansion and southern slaveholders. His brother Elihu, the Massachusetts Whigs Thomas Eliot and Edward Dickinson, Ohio's Senator Ben Wade and Congressman

Lew Campbell, and the just-resigned Connecticut Senator Truman Smith also seemed ready to form a broader anti-Nebraska coalition to conduct the 1854 campaigns in the North.[84] Prior to Congress' adjournment in August, however, most northern Whigs evinced little interest in abandoning northern Whig organizations for a new sectional party. Aside from deep-seated distrust of former Free Soil and Democratic enemies, they were convinced that the contrast between Democratic responsibility for, and their own opposition to, the Nebraska Act guaranteed Whig victories in the 1854 elections. If anti-Nebraska Democrats and Free Soilers wanted to support Whig candidates in order to repudiate Pierce, Douglas, and the Democratic party, they were delighted to accept that support. But they saw no need to jettison the Whig party in order to get it, and in many parts of the North they believed they could win without it. In sum, they saw no need for a new antislavery party to win. And they had no desire to share either the glory or the material benefits of those impending triumphs with Democrats and Free Soilers, as formally joining new parties would surely require them to do.[85]

Northern Whigs who spoke of riding the anti-Nebraska wave to power clearly expected Free Soil and even anti-Nebraska Democratic support without the need of formal new parties. By early April, for example, constituents of Illinois Whig Congressman Richard Yates informed him that the universal outrage in his district among all parties made his reelection certain. "The Whig party of the North is, this day, stronger than at any other period" because Democrats could be blamed for the Nebraska bill, a Pittsburgh Whig informed James Pollock, Pennsylvania's Whig gubernatorial candidate, in May. The hope that Whigs could win reinforcements from Free Soilers with a few sops—in sharp contrast to the complete abandonment of the Whig party for a new coalition in which all anti-Nebraska elements were treated "on equal terms," as Free Soilers demanded— was made clear by Russell Errett and D. N. White, editors of the Pittsburgh *Gazette*, one of the most influential Whig papers west of the Alleghenies. In July they proudly called the anti-Nebraska address issued by the Whig state committee a "platform broad enough to secure the cooperation of every Anti-Slavery man in the State." Similarly, on May 26, just at the time Free Soilers in Washington were trying to orchestrate the creation of a new party, Thurlow Weed declared in the Albany *Evening Journal* that only Whigs could win in 1854 and that, "so far, we have not found freedom *practically* advanced one step except by the Whig party." In case anyone missed the point, Weed iterated two months later: "Having found the Whig party of the North, on all occasions, and in every emergency, the most efficient and reliable organization both to resist the aggressions of Slavery and to uphold the cause of Freedom, we concur . . . that it is best, now and ever, 'for the Whig party to stand by its colors.' "[86]

VI

No antislavery Whigs opposed a new antisouthern party so intransigently and thereby did more to frustrate the plans of Free Soilers, in fact, than did Seward, his New York Whig allies in Congress, and their mentor, Weed, in Albany. To Theodore Parker's pleas that Seward help arrange a national convention that could combine all antislavery men, Seward coldly replied, "We are not yet ready for a great National Convention at Buffalo or elsewhere.... The *States* are the places for activity just now. They have elections for Senators & Congressmen coming off in the Autumn." Seward's reference to "Senators" makes it clear how much his own reelection spurred his and Weed's determination to preserve the Whig organization. It also reflects how much his and his allies' confidence that Whigs could defeat Democrats with the anti-Nebraska issue rested on the outcome of state contests earlier that year.[87]

New England's spring elections in 1854 did not constitute a clear referendum on the Nebraska bill. They occurred between Senate and House action on the measure, when many people still expected it to be stopped in the House. In all three states, moreover, Democratic candidates tried to ignore the Nebraska issue or contended that it was irrelevant to gubernatorial and legislative contests, while rival Democratic papers in a particular state often took opposite stands, endorsing or condemning the bill. Nonetheless, Whigs everywhere campaigned against Democratic responsibility for the odious measure, and by mid-April it was clear that anti-Nebraska sentiment helped them, if only by depressing Democratic turnout. New England's results also seemed to show that Free Soilers would cooperate with Whigs against Democrats even without a formal merger. What Seward and other Whigs who believed that what Congress did would spark a Whig comeback apparently ignored about those results, however, is that Whigs alone did not benefit from anti-Nebraska sentiment and that voters had far more on their minds than just Nebraska.

Rhode Island's elections produced the least ambiguous Whig victory, if only because they were two-party contests. Whigs prevailed in the gubernatorial contest primarily because of Democratic abstentions, not Whig gains. The Democratic vote plunged by almost 40 percent from the previous year. With 58.4 percent of the vote compared to his predecessor's 42.9 percent, William W. Hoppin became the first Whig governor in four years.[88]

New Hampshire's March elections were symbolically important because they occurred in Franklin Pierce's home state, but they suggested less cause for Whig confidence than Rhode Island's. To Pierce's chagrin, his state party refused to mention, let alone endorse, the Nebraska bill, and only that silence probably prevented Whigs and Free Soilers from scoring a major upset. Former Congressman Amos Tuck, however, exaggerated when he jubilantly concluded that "the Whigs and free soilers are welded together in this State, and cannot again be separated." The two camps shared an antipathy to the Nebraska bill and to the state's reigning Democratic dynasty, but they ran their own candidates for the legislature and governor.[89]

Free Soilers, indeed, appeared to benefit more from the anti-Nebraska backlash than Whigs. After the 1853 elections, Democrats had enjoyed a fifty-two-seat majority in the state house of representatives over the combined forces of Whigs and Free Soilers, but in 1854 Democrats lost twenty-three seats, Whigs gained eleven, and Free Soilers added seventeen, thereby reducing the Democratic margin to one. Still, holdovers with the power to fill empty seats left the senate securely in Democrats' control, and in the gubernatorial contest their majority slipped only from 54.7 to 51.3 percent between 1853 and 1854. In the latter race, indeed, the Free Soilers, with some success, blatantly attempted to encourage Whig defections by running former Whig Congressman Jared Perkins as their candidate. He ran

3,000 votes ahead of his Free Soil predecessor in 1853 and increased the third party's share of the cast vote from 14 to 19 percent. Meanwhile, James Bell, the Whig candidate in both years, suffered a decline in his absolute and proportionate votes despite the Whig crusade against Nebraska.[90]

Nor did Connecticut's results point unambiguously to the ability of the Nebraska issue to revive Whiggery. In 1853, when prohibition remained the most salient issue, Connecticut's Whigs had suffered a disaster. They had plummeted to a meager 34 percent of the popular vote in the gubernatorial election, 30 percent of the seats in the lower house of the legislature, and less than a fourth of the senate seats. When 1854 opened, many politicians in the state expected that prohibition would again be the central issue. Democratic Governor Thomas Seymour had vetoed a local-option temperance law that the legislature passed in 1853. Even though the most ardent dries opposed the bill as too weak, that veto, together with the Free Soil party's abandonment of its pro-Maine Law candidate, Francis Gillette, and Whigs' determination to stick with the notorious wet Henry Dutton caused prohibitionists to nominate their own legislative and gubernatorial candidates, headed by Hartford Whig Charles Chapman for governor. The Nebraska bill, in sum, was only one of several issues. Nonetheless, outrage against it—even the Democratic Hartford *Times* denounced it—was so widespread that Whigs shunned all other issues and expressed confidence that their anti-Nebraska stance would produce victory, especially since Connecticut's Democratic Senator Isaac Toucey had voted for the bill in March.[91]

At first blush, April's results seemed to prove that confidence well founded. Whigs recaptured control of the state senate and helped reduce the Democrats from a 65 percent majority to a 40 percent minority in the house by adding forty-two new Whig seats. Those gains guaranteed election of a Whig governor by that body, as well as the ability of Whigs to choose a successor to Senator Truman Smith. Thus Whig papers like Greeley's New York *Tribune*, Henry J. Raymond's *New York Times*, and Samuel Bowles's Springfield, Massachusetts, *Republican* hailed the results as a spectacular Whig triumph. "We have had another political revolution in Connecticut growing out of the excitement in relation to the Nebraska Kansas outrage and the Maine law temperance question," Roger Sherman Baldwin wrote his son.[92]

Baldwin's inclusion of prohibition was crucial; Whigs' ability to win with the Nebraska issue was not nearly as clear-cut as it appeared to Seward and other Whigs in Washington. While the Connecticut legislature would elect the Whig Dutton governor, he in fact received a smaller vote and a smaller proportion of the vote than he had in the 1853 debacle. There were four gubernatorial tickets, and anti-Democratic voters refused to combine behind the wet Dutton. Despite the Nebraska issue, Free Soilers' total plunged from 8,926 (14.6 percent) in 1853 to 2,560 (4.2 percent) in 1854. Their decline, in turn, reflected defections to the prohibitionist Chapman, whom angry dries kept in the race after the emergence of the Nebraska issue specifically to prevent opponents of the Democrats from concentrating behind the hated Dutton. Chapman drew over 10,000 votes (17.4 percent) compared to Dutton's 19,465 (31.8 percent). Dry Whigs who bolted the party for the Free Soiler Francis Gillette in 1853 continued to boycott the straight Whig ticket. Even dissident Democrats and previous nonvoters preferred Chapman to Dutton, despite the Nebraska issue.[93]

The rebellious prohibition party also elected seven men to the lower house of the legislature, and Free Soilers also added six seats to bring their total to seventeen. Splinter parties, rather than the Whigs, in sum, gained almost a fourth of the seats lost by Democrats. Many of the new Whig members, moreover, were either outright Free Soilers or abolitionist sympathizers who had been put on Whig tickets to attract antislavery voters who normally refused to support Whigs. "The election is a glorious triumph of F[ree] D[emocratic] principles," gloated one Free Soiler. "The Whigs do not claim it as a Whig victory—it is *ours*." That boast was surely overblown, but Whigs acknowledged their dependence upon an alliance with Free Soilers when the new legislature met in May, a month after the elections. That body had already planned to elect a successor to Truman Smith, whose Senate term ended in March 1855, but Smith's resignation allowed it to name someone to complete his term as well as his successor. Although Whigs constituted the overwhelming majority of the anti-Democratic forces in both legislative chambers, they conceded from the start that a non-Whig, either the prohibitionist Chapman or Francis Gillette, the Free Soilers' pro-Maine Law gubernatorial candidate in 1853, should succeed Smith immediately. Prohibitionists and a number of Whigs tried to hold out for Chapman, but Gillette ultimately got the nod, while Lafayette Foster, the Whigs' unsuccessful gubernatorial candidate in 1850 and 1851, was given the new six-year Senate term that began in March 1855.[94]

Connecticut's Whigs had undeniably rebounded behind the Nebraska issue. But antislavery and antiliquor sentiments had tended to fragment opponents of the Democrats, not unite them behind the Whig party. Whigs' subsequent cooperation with Free Soilers in the legislature, moreover, suggested that many of them might indeed be prepared to abandon the Whig organization to "unite with the Free Democracy on the broad platform of freedom from rum and Slavery."[95]

Seward, Weed, and New York's Whigs, however, most emphatically were not—at least not in 1854. Like Whigs in Pennsylvania, Massachusetts, Vermont, and elsewhere, they believed that they could ride the Nebraska issue to victory in 1854. They therefore spurned formal mergers with Free Soilers in a new party. Yet what most differentiated Sewardites from other northern Whigs who wanted to perpetuate state and local Whig organizations—and what most infuriated Free Soilers about their refusal to jettison the Whig party—was that Sewardites also sought to keep conservative Silver Grays in the New York party, and Silver Grays adamantly opposed any cooperation whatsoever with Free Soilers. Of greater importance still, Seward, Weed, and their closest New York lieutenants were resolutely determined to preserve an alliance with southern Whigs. They insisted on maintaining the Whigs as a national party.

Even in February, when Seward wrote of a split with southern Whigs and Weed warned that Nebraska would "denationalize the Whig party," their tone had been one of regret and sorrow, not bitterness or glee. "I cannot see how or where good can come out of it," Weed had said despairingly to Fish. Once it became clear that Bell in the Senate and even more southern Whigs in the House would oppose the Nebraska bill, therefore, they instantly reached out to the Southerners. With the enthusiastic concurrence of their New York lieutenants in the House like Matteson and Morgan, they lavishly praised Bell, Etheridge, Cullom, Hunt, and the others, as well as northern conservatives like Haven, in their papers, the *Albany Evening Journal* and the *New York Times*. Thus, when Henry J. Raymond, the editor of the *Times*, privately urged Maine's Fessenden to resist "a formal disbandonment of the Whig party" and argued in his editorials against the "disbanding of a strong, disciplined, and well organized [Whig] army," he emphatically meant to include southern Whigs and northern conservatives as soldiers in it.[96]

Seward contemptuously regarded as "absurdities" the "schemes" of Free Soilers for "dissolving the Whig party," and he did all he could personally to keep southern Whigs under the Whig umbrella. On February 17 and again on May 26, Seward delivered Senate speeches against the Nebraska bill, and he previewed the latter in an important speech in New York in early May. He blasted the fraudulence of the Democratic rationale for the bill, condemned the overturning of the Missouri Compromise as unconscionable, iterated the impossibility of slavery and free labor coexisting in the new territories, and described the difference between freedom and slavery as one "between truth and error, between right and wrong." But he did not declare war against Southerners or engage in scaremongering about the threat of slavery expansion, as Wade and some other northern Whigs did. Rather, he spoke calmly, if resolutely, about accepting the South's challenge to compete for control of Kansas and Nebraska and reassuringly about the certainty that Northerners would win such a contest and thereby bring sectional agitation over slavery to a close. The Union would endure, Seward insisted; North and South could not separate. The nation, he hymned in what many correctly interpreted as an effort to get men to look beyond current sectional quarrels, was destined for a glorious future of development and expansion. Since most southern Whigs—even those who had voted for the Kansas-Nebraska Act— agreed with Seward's conclusion that slavery would never be established in the new territories and yearned for the intersectional harmony he promised in the future, Seward's argument, as furious Free Soilers were quick to see, represented a peace offering to them.[97]

"I wish I could take as hopeful a view as you do of the future that awaits us, on this question," gushed the conservative Everett after reading a copy of Seward's May speech. "Your hopeful bearing, & assurances—the future which you see & depict—have done more to encourage me than anything else I have seen or heard," chimed Raymond from New York City. Coupled with Weed's simultaneous editorial in the *Albany Evening Journal* calling for preservation of the Whig party, that same speech caused Gamaliel Bailey to snap, "Seward hangs fire." He and Weed clearly meant to preserve the Whigs as a "*National* party." Referring to Seward's New York preview of that May speech, Henry Wilson protested, "I think I see in it an idea of going on to concentrate the Whig party as a National Party—to keep up the union of the Northern and Southern Whigs." Seward had suddenly become the darling of conservatives and southern Whigs since he sought the preservation of the Whig party, yelped the proponents of a new party from Maine, "and every earnest friend of freedom regrets it."[98]

VII

When Congress adjourned on August 7, 1854, in sum, the sectional disagreement among Whigs over the Kansas-Nebraska Act had not yet completely denationalized the party, let alone destroyed its local and state organizations in the North and South. The future of the Whig party remained unclear. Some men spoke of abandoning the party, and key northern Whig leaders were prepared to combine with Free Soilers and anti-Nebraska Democrats in a new sectional party. But others were not. They wanted to make the northern Whig party the anti-Nebraska party, and Seward and Weed in particular fought to preserve the Whigs as a national party and to sabotage a formal merger with Free Soilers that would require a break with northern conservatives and southern Whigs. By mid-summer they appeared to be so successful that many Whigs dreamed of electing the next president in 1856 and anticipated that the fight for the party's nomination would be between those old New York rivals, Seward and Fillmore. All the signs, Fillmore's Warwick Kennedy assured a friend in early October, pointed to the election of a new Whig president two years hence.[99]

At the same time, precisely the refusal of Sewardites and conservatives to abandon the party and combine with Free Soilers, as well as their efforts to soften the antisouthern tone of anti-Nebraska rhetoric, gave heart to southern Whigs like John Bell. "The course of the Northern Whigs will decide whether we can unite with them or not," he predicted on August 10. "The Whigs of Massts have set the example of declining any party or other annexion with the abolitionists & freesoilers. This is noble conduct, & I hope will have a decided effect in moderating the violence of Whigs in other states."[100]

In June, Seward had also emphasized that "the *States* are the places for activity just now. They have elections for Senators & Congressmen coming off in the Autumn." Ultimately, in fact, the Whig party's fate was determined not in Washington, but in the state and congressional elections of 1854 and 1855. When Whigs prepared to campaign for those elections, however, they confronted a bewildering complexity of problems and difficulties that made sectional resentments within the national party seem simple by contrast. In the North, for example, the willingness of Whigs to preserve the old party or to abandon it for new coalitions varied not only from state to state, but also from congressional district to congressional district within individual states. Once Whigs shifted their attention from Washington to the states, moreover, in both North and South they discovered that voters did not always share the agenda or priorities of Whig congressmen. Instead, they encountered a cluster of issues that had nothing to do with slavery but mattered far more to many Whig and non-Whig voters than the Nebraska bill. Most important, once Whigs focused on developments within the states, rather than those in Washington during the first half of 1854, they collided with a burgeoning Know Nothing movement that abruptly shattered all calculations based on the potential impact of "this Nebraska business" and that threatened, far more seriously than did the entreaties from Free Soilers for a new antislavery organization, to disembowel the Whig party.[101]

Chapter 23

"The Whig Party, as a Party, Are Entirely Disbanded"

"THE WHIG PARTY OF THE NORTH is, this day, stronger than at any former period," Pittsburgh's William Larimer wrote James Pollock in March 1854, several weeks after Pennsylvania's Whig state convention selected Pollock over Larimer as the party's gubernatorial nominee. "Occupying as she now does, the true Republican ground, the policy of the opposition is making her a *unit*, and is doing more to render her *invincible* than all the efforts of her most astute political tacticians could accomplish." Many northern Whigs shared Larimer's confidence that Democratic responsibility for the Nebraska bill guaranteed Whig victories that year. That Larimer was an erstwhile Free Soiler epitomized Whigs' hope that all opponents of Nebraska and other Democratic measures might now rally behind the Whig banner. That he saw opposition to slavery extension and Slave Power aggressions as a reaffirmation of fundamental republican principles illustrates the remarkable persistence of those inherited values. That Larimer, like many others, capitalized "Republican" unintentionally indicated one route by which a different organization would usurp the Whig party's mission to rescue public liberty.[1]

By late March, indeed, when Larimer wrote Pollock, and certainly by May, when newspapers published his letter, other political observers would have disputed his rosy prediction about Whigs' unity and invincibility. Northern Whigs might condemn slavery expansion and Slave Power aggressions to win at home in 1854, but that tack could permanently alienate Southerners from the party. Nor were northern Whigs united about how best to exploit anti-Nebraska sentiment. Some advocated abandoning the party, if only temporarily, for broader anti-Nebraska coalitions to ensure that Democratic candidates were rebuked. Others, hoping to preserve northern Whig organizations intact, often feuded over how far the party should go to reach out to non-Whigs, particularly militantly antislavery Free Soilers. Astute observers, moreover, doubted Whigs' invincibility because they doubted that the upcoming elections would be clear-cut referenda on the Nebraska Act and other actions by Democrats in Washington. Ominous evidence existed during the spring and summer of 1854 that voters insisted instead that politicians confront matters that fell within the jurisdiction of local governments and state legislatures, matters that often divided Whigs against each other.

Yet Whig leaders dared not straddle or evade them, for the groups most intensely interested in those issues threatened to start new parties to address them if the existing parties would not.

Because the vast majority of the elections slated for 1854 and 1855 involved neither governorships nor congressional seats but instead state legislators and local officials chosen from relatively small districts, they would occur in precisely the geographically limited arenas where new parties could easily distribute ballots and mount credible challenges to the major parties. Once insurgent organizations made the decision to print tickets of their own, moreover, they might run their own candidates for Congress and statewide offices as well. All in all, the new concerns transforming the political agenda outside of Washington threatened to rend, not unite, the Whig party and to render it anything but invincible.

Northern Whigs' hopes in particular were jeopardized by the same cluster of issues that had divided and drained the Whig vote in 1853: the cry for reform to cleanse government of arrogantly unresponsive, spoils-oriented politicos associated by the public with both major parties; burgeoning resentment of immigrants; and escalating anger at Catholics. Northern states also suffered from what one Indiana Democrat called the temperance "disease." In New England's spring elections of 1854, when Whigs tried to exploit mushrooming anti-Nebraska sentiment, zealous prohibitionists fragmented the potential Whig vote, and they seemed likely to remain a divisive force in Vermont, Maine, and Massachusetts that fall. From New York, Democratic Governor Horatio Seymour, who had apparently sewed up the wet vote by vetoing an antiliquor bill in 1853, assured Secretary of State William L. Marcy that prohibition would dominate the 1854 race and chortled that Whigs were "at a loss in the Maine Law question" because of their internal divisions over it. Whig friends of Seward agreed that the prohibition issue would be critical in the fall elections and that it would undoubtedly "trouble us" and "play the very 'dickens' with party lines." Nonetheless, dry Whigs bluntly insisted to Seward and his lieutenants that the party could not carry New York in 1854 on the anti-Nebraska issue alone, that "party leaders should understand that the people are in *earnest* in their advocacy of the Maine Law," and "that the *Whigs must sail* in our cold water ship or sink."[2]

Ultimately, however, the biggest threat to the unity, the invincibility, and indeed the very existence of the Whig party came from the rapid growth and increasing political militance of the still-secret, anti-immigrant, anti-Catholic, and antiparty Know Nothing fraternal order. In January, Democrats from New York City, the birthplace of the order, shrieked to Marcy that "Native American sentiment" was "never so strong before." Instead of worrying about the possible spread of slavery to Kansas and Nebraska, a Whig told Hamilton Fish, artisans feared that the "thousand evils . . . to the working classes" caused by "the vast influx of immigrants" might drive "American *mechanics*" from eastern "cities to western wilds." With a barely concealed allusion to the readiness of Know Nothings to run their own candidates if necessary, another nativist prophetically warned Fish that "you may rest assured that it will not be the Nebraska bill that will decide the next State election, but a sterner and more exalted question will determine the result."[3]

Unfortunately for the Whigs, that prediction proved all too accurate. The elections of 1854 and 1855 did not revolve exclusively around the Nebraska and slavery extension issues. Nor did the Whig party remain a unit, mobilize all the various opponents of the Democrats behind the Whig banner, or prove invincible. Instead, those elections witnessed the continued fragmentation of major party lines, the emergence of a bewildering variety of new coalitions that challenged Whigs' credentials as leaders of the anti-Democratic opposition, and an accelerating exodus of once-loyal Whigs to new political homes. Even though Democrats suffered a massive rebuke at the hands of the electorate, as Larimer and others predicted, the Whig party, too, became a casualty of voters' wrath. By December 1855, when the new Thirty-Fourth Congress met, not one but two new parties appeared to have displaced Whigs from their role as the Democrats' chief political opponents. Their ability to hijack what had been the Whigs' primary political function since the early 1830s convinced all but a few diehards that the Whig party had outlived its usefulness and should be given a decent burial.

I

The purpose of this and the following two chapters is to describe the process by which new parties displaced the Whigs as vehicles for anti-Democratic political action during 1854 and 1855, to outline the divergent reactions of Whig voters and politicians to it, and to suggest why it occurred. The congressional, state, and local elections between August 1854 and December 1855 were the most labyrinthine, chaotic, and important off-year contests in all of American political history. To help the reader comprehend what occurred during them, therefore, certain themes and conclusions must be elaborated at the outset.

Three interrelated, but analytically distinguishable, political processes occurred simultaneously over the course of those elections. First, a majority of the American electorate, particularly in the North, turned against the Democratic party. This realignment, which continued into the 1856 presidential election, went both ways. It involved both the movement of first-time voters and former Democratic supporters to anti-Democratic ranks and the mobilization of first- and second-generation immigrants and some Whig defectors behind the Democratic banner.

Second, the Whig party failed to benefit from the realignment against the Democrats. Rather, it disintegrated. This collapse had two separate aspects, and historians' failure to keep both aspects in view largely accounts for their contentious dispute over the past thirty years as to whether sectional conflict over slavery or ethnocultural issues killed the Whig party. On the one hand, the sectional chasm dividing northern from southern Whigs widened. Incensed by the anti-southern posture many northern Whigs assumed to win the elections of 1854, most southern Whigs by the end of that year renounced allegiance to the national Whig party. Within the North, on the other hand, the Whig party suffered crippling internal erosion as former supporters decamped for new political homes rather than using the Whig party itself to punish offending Democrats. What weakened the Whig party in the North was not necessarily the same as what split the national organization, but both toxins had a poisonous effect.

The emergence of an astonishing variety of new political movements in 1854 and 1855 that challenged the Whigs for the anti-Democratic vote constitutes the third process that contributed to the turbulence of those years. These new coalitions not only sought to displace the Whig party in 1854 and 1855. They also attempted to combine and broaden their ranks; to establish their durability; to transform themselves from temporary, often localized protest movements into permanent, national political parties; and to compete with each other, as well as with the Whigs, to become the major opponent of the Democrats by the time of the 1856 presidential election. A process of building new parties, in sum, accompanied and accelerated the processes of voter realignment and Whig disintegration. Whigs' sharply divergent reactions to these new parties had as profound an influence on Whigs' behavior as did their ingrained aversion to Democrats.

Essentially, what happened to the Whig party in 1854 and 1855 is that it bled to death. Or at least it was bled to the point where it no longer possessed the vitality or will to perform its traditional function. It became so depleted of personnel in both the North and South that diehards who remained in it eventually, and almost always regretfully, recognized that it was useless any longer to hold legislative caucuses, call nominating conventions, or run candidates for office on tickets with the Whig—and only the Whig—label. The date at which different Whigs reached that decision varied from state to state and from locality to locality. The central point here is that the demise of the Whig party refers to the cessation of its activities as a political institution. It does not connote the death of individual Whigs, their loss of a sense of identity as Whigs, or their abandonment of Whig principles, for which many expressed admiration long after the party itself ceased to operate.[4]

Although the process of Whig attrition was cumulative, it did not proceed at a constant rate. It oscillated in response to fast-changing developments that affected both the decisions of different Whigs about leaving the party and the destinations they then chose. Those fluctuations and the sense of contingency they inspired had two main sources. One was the sequential nature of the prolonged election cycle between August 1854 and November 1855, during which the new members of the Thirty-Fourth Congress were selected. Conditions and the political calculations based upon them varied not only from state to state, and often from congressional district to congressional district, but also from month to month. New parties did *not* emerge everywhere simultaneously in the summer and fall of 1854 to displace the Whig organization. In a number of places Whigs preserved the party intact and contested the 1854 elections under the Whig banner. Elsewhere, however, the party was severely weakened, if not entirely replaced, by new challengers. The momentum these rivals generated in 1854 convinced even Whig leaders in those states where the party had survived, and often flourished, that year, that future prospects lay elsewhere.

No matter how successful Whigs were in some states in 1854, they closely watched the fate of Whig candidates elsewhere to assess the party's future. They calculated whether there would be enough Whig congressmen to secure a majority in the next House of Representatives, whether Whigs controlled enough state legislatures to replenish the party's dwindling strength in the Senate, and whether Whigs remained sufficiently competitive in enough states that it was arithmetically possible to secure a majority of the nationwide electoral vote in the presidential election of 1856. Once it became clear that Whigs no longer possessed the requisite numbers to achieve those goals, most Whig leaders gave up on the party. Many men elected as Whig governors, Whig state legislators, and Whig congressmen in 1854 themselves abandoned the Whig party within a year, and often within a few months or weeks, of their victories in order to join new organizations that apparently had a better chance of gaining majority control of the new Congress and electing the next president.

If the diverse and changing results of the sequential elections from August 1854 to November 1855 helped to shape the spatial and chronological pattern of Whig disintegration, so did the simultaneous process of transforming the ad hoc coalitions and secret societies that entered the political fray in 1854 into durable political parties. The fast-paced internal changes within these rival organizations affected their attractiveness to different Whigs. In addition, the increasing evidence that they intended to broaden and perpetuate themselves and might have a better chance than the Whig party itself of controlling Congress and the White House in 1856 altered the thinking of Whigs who had seen their support for them in 1854 as a temporary act of expediency or protest, not necessarily as a permanent break from the Whig party. Once Whigs politicos became enmeshed in the process of party building, moreover, they often devoted their attention to ensuring their own control of the new organizations rather than to reviving the Whig party itself. New commitments, in short, diverted the time, energy, and talent necessary to sustain old relationships.

Quite obviously, different Whigs contributed and responded to this process of erosion and displacement in different ways. Some left the party early and eagerly because their alienation from it had passed the point of no return and because they reacted enthusiastically to the appeal of new parties. Others abandoned the party solely to perpetuate careers in new parties that seemed to promise defeat of the hated Democrats. Others left the party only reluctantly and involuntarily, when they had no choice but to support a different party or cease political participation altogether, and a not insignificant number of one-time Whigs did simply toss in the towel. A tiny minority clung bitterly and intransigently to the Whig party. Viscerally disliking the new parties that sought to displace it, they hoped against hope that the disruptive developments of 1854 and 1855 would prove ephemeral and that the Whig party would somehow reclaim its role as the vehicle for the anti-Democratic opposition in 1856 and thereafter.

Aside from the impact of contingent events and short-term chronological changes, two other variables influenced Whig leaders' divergent reactions to the developments of 1854 and 1855.[5] One was the geographical and political context in which they were situated. Outside of the South, much depended on the competitiveness of the Whig party in different states and localities by the end of 1853. Whigs in areas where the party was weakest were the most prone to seek new affiliations or alliances. One can also categorize leaders by the level of the federal system at which they operated. Small-fry local politicos whose aspirations for advancement up the ladder of political offices had been frustrated or members of dissident, minority factions within Whig state parties often jumped immediately at the opportunity provided by new affiliations to win state or local office. In contrast, seasoned, established, and nationally oriented leaders who personally had no interest in any subnational office often awaited the results of the 1854 contests before they determined upon a course of action. Although events between August 1854 and December 1855 repeatedly reshaped the decisions made by Whigs, the watershed event was the elections in October and November of 1854. More than anything else, their results, and especially the stunning strength of Know Nothings they revealed, forced Whigs of all varieties into major recalculations.

The second variable that influenced the divergent responses of Whig leaders and voters was the nature, composition, and agendas of the rival organizations that emerged in 1854 and 1855 to challenge the Whig party's role as the vehicle for anti-Democratic political action. Put briefly, to fully understand the displacement of the Whig party, one must first examine its competitors.

II

That the new organizations were anti-Democratic is of the utmost importance. Both the fusion anti-Nebraska coalitions, which appeared in some northern states in 1854 and which would not be successfully combined into a regionwide Republican party until early 1856, and the still-secret Know Nothing fraternity won support from disillusioned Democrats as well as Whigs.[6] Nonetheless, both sought to oust Democrats from office in order to reverse the direction of Democratic governance. Thus they offered Whigs a chance to continue their long-time opposition to the Democrats. Many Whigs, indeed, initially viewed the new organizations less as competitors to or replacements for the Whig party than as pliable instruments Whigs might manipulate to advance the cause of Whig candidates by bringing non-Whigs to their support.

The ability of Whigs to continue political opposition to Democrats through the new organizations, however, hardly explains why Whigs preferred them to the regular Whig party itself or why they preferred one alternative to the other. The different organizing principles and political agendas of the new movements provide the explanations. They gave priority to different issues; that is, they stressed different actions by Democrats that demanded immediate redress and reversal. But they also made a compelling case that their sense of urgency and their new organizational schemes for rallying political support made them far more likely than the Whig party itself to secure the redress of grievances many Whigs shared with them.

Although northern Whigs courted Free Soil support in some states in 1854, those attempts to broaden the Whig vote must be distinguished from the formal anti-Nebraska coalitions that emerged elsewhere. The former usually entailed attempts to secure outside support for Whig candidates after exclusively *Whig* conventions had met and nominated them as *Whig* candidates. The latter involved open cooperation by Whig leaders with Free Soilers and anti-Nebraska Democrats to arrange statewide conventions or mass meetings that purposely eschewed the Whig label so as not to offend non-Whigs and that carefully constructed state tickets representing all of the participating parties, not just Whigs. In short, they required a conscious decision by Whig leaders to suspend operations as a separate Whig party and instead to enfold themselves and their followers in a broader and different organization. Thus, when Indiana's Whig leaders fused with other groups to present "People's" rather than Whig tickets in 1854, a Democrat could assert with accuracy that "the Whig party, *as a party*, are entirely disbanded. They have not *as a party*, brought out a single candidate."[7]

In Michigan and Wisconsin these new coalitions called themselves the Republican party in 1854, and proponents of forming an exclusively northern Republican party existed elsewhere as well. In most northern states, however, the names adopted by these protest movements—Anti-Nebraska, Anti-Administration, Fusion, Independent, People's Party, and numerous hyphenated permutations that indicated attitudes toward the Maine Law, public schools, and so on—reflected their inchoate, ad hoc nature. Their composition, the degree to which they incorporated anti-Nebraska Democrats, the proportionate strength and influence of Whigs within them, the issues other than condemnation of the Nebraska Act on which they campaigned in 1854, and, of particular interest here, the degree to which these new statewide alliances penetrated individual congressional districts and localities to displace regular Whig organizations and candidates in 1854 varied widely from state to state. Successful arrangement of fusion tickets for governor and other state officials, in other words, did not automatically ensure similar degrees of interparty cooperation, and thus the suspension of independent Whig efforts, in congressional and state legislative races during 1854. Local pockets of straight-out, fusion-resisting Whigs endured far longer in the North than many historians have acknowledged.

By itself, the prospect that anti-Nebraska coalitions were more likely than Whigs alone to defeat Democrats attracted some Whigs to them, but these coalitions also threatened the continued existence of the Whig party in still other ways. First, Whig politicians who helped form them often announced that the Whig party was not adequate to meet the present emergency and must be shelved, if only temporarily. With Whig congressmen still in Washington until mid-August 1854, influential Whig newspaper editors often first made this case. In Ohio, Oran Follett of the Columbus *Ohio State Journal* and William Schouler of the Cincinnati *Gazette* promoted new organizations. In Indiana, both South Bend's Schuyler Colfax and Indianapolis' John D. Defrees, editor of the *Indiana State Journal* and chairman of the Whig state committee, did so. Pro-fusion Whig leaders insisted, as Free Soilers had since 1848, either that the old issues that had once divided Whigs from Democrats were settled and obsolete or that traditional partisan disagreements must be put into abeyance and political efforts directed instead to the resolution of a far more pressing and dangerous crisis. The Whig Chicago *Tribune*, for example, declared itself "sick and tired of party organizations which are dead and lifeless," while Joseph Warren, editor of the Detroit *Tribune*, insisted that, since Michigan's Whigs had "suffered defeat after defeat of the most overwhelming and hopeless character for the last 14 years," they should instead support a movement that "irrespective of old party organizations" would "combine the whole anti-Nebraska, antislavery sentiment of the State, upon one ticket."[8]

The emergency that required the cessation of independent Whig action was, of course, the threat of slavery extension to Kansas and Nebraska. Everywhere anti-Nebraska coalitions insisted that Northerners must forget former party differences and unite to stop slavery's spread by replacing Democrats in Congress with men who would repeal the Nebraska Act, restore the Missouri Compromise line, impose new statutory bans on slavery in the territories, or resist the admission of any more slave states to the Union. The policy demands and degree of antislavery radicalism of these coalitions varied, but they all insisted that Northerners must combine in exclusively northern political organizations that no longer dealt with putative southern allies.

In sum, anti-Nebraska coalitions required a cessation of independent Whig activity, but they also further separated northern from southern Whigs. Whigs elected on anti-Nebraska tickets seemed unlikely to cooperate with former party allies from the South in upcoming sessions of Congress or during the 1856 presidential campaign. Just as Ben Wade and Truman Smith had done before Congress adjourned, many procoalition Whig politicians vowed never again to cooperate with southern Whigs. Since the betrayal by southern Whigs had already destroyed the national Whig party, they declared, now only an exclusively northern party could defend northern liberties and rights from a Slave Power conspiracy to extend slavery. As Oran Follett put it in the *Ohio State Journal*, "There is no longer a National Whig or Democratic party" because southern Whigs and Democrats had "turned their backs on the compromises of 1820 and 1850."[9]

Beyond their obvious expediency to Whigs who had long languished in a political minority, in short, anti-Nebraska coalitions seemed preferable to the Whig party precisely because they were exclusively northern, precisely because they seemed prepared to meet the threat posed by southern slaveholders more directly and adamantly than northern Whig organizations that still preached the necessity of party fellowship with Southerners, and precisely because they called for an end to partisan disputes that seemed outmoded or inconsequential when compared to the sectional threat. Conversely, precisely this sectional cast of the anti-Nebraska coalitions rendered them anathema to southern Whigs and to conservative northern Whigs, at least some of whom had hoped to create a new national Union party even before the introduction of Douglas' Nebraska bill.

The antisouthern thrust of the anti-Nebraska coalitions had two additional implications that help explain the embryonic Republican party's incursions into the ranks of northern Whiggery. First, since they called upon Northerners to mobilize politically to check Slave Power aggressions, any events—whether in Washington, Kansas, or elsewhere—that focused public attention on slavery and that increased northern animosity toward, and fear of, Southerners tended to reinforce their case that Northerners needed an exclusively northern party to defend northern rights and interests. Second, by identifying a compelling cause that required political action and an immediate political target, northern Democrats who subserviently abetted Slave Power aggressions, the anti-Nebraska coalitions simultaneously highlighted the hollowness into which the strife between spoils-oriented Whigs and Democratic parties had apparently degenerated by 1853 and reinvested political participation with important purpose.

This last point merits elaboration. Neither the anti-Nebraska coalitions nor the Know Nothings lured men away from the Whig party simply because they offered them a way to perpetuate opposition to Democrats, because they focused more pointedly on new concerns than the Whig party itself seemed capable of doing, or because they offered a better chance to defeat Democrats than the Whig party. To be sure, all of these considerations mattered. But the new parties also succeeded in usurping Whigs' ideological mission.

Whatever programs and policy positions had been grafted onto the platform of the Whig party since its formation in the early 1830s, it was founded to rescue public liberty, to save the Revolutionary experiment in republican self-government from the threat that King Andrew Jackson and his Democratic minions posed to it. From the 1830s on, Whigs continued to insist that they were dedicated to the defense of republican principles and institutions. And, as the language of Larimer's letter to Pollock indicates, the felt need to protect and perpetuate republicanism still mattered deeply to men in the 1850s.

The new organizations emerging in 1854 and 1855 co-opted Whigs' mission to defend republicanism by portraying themselves as better able to do so. They insisted that powerful new threats to America's experiment in republican self-government had emerged that made executive tyranny and the other antirepublican bogeys against which Whigs had campaigned seem tame by comparison. They explicitly and repeatedly invoked the key code phrases of the familiar republican idiom—power, tyranny, corruption, conspiracy, and enslavement versus liberty, freedom, self-government, majority rule, and republicanism itself. And they summoned voters to join a crusade in defense of republican principles and institutions that, they argued, far exceeded in importance stale partisan quarrels fought between now irrelevant parties. They initially portrayed themselves, in short, not as officeseeking political parties, but as patriotic Minute Men springing to freedom's defense. Anti-Nebraska coalitions and the Know Nothings, however, saw different dangers to republicanism that approached from different directions. In effect, they wanted to wage the battle to rescue public liberty on different fronts.

The anti-Nebraska coalitions insisted that the threat to republican liberty and self-government now came from the South, from a Slave Power conspiracy to spread slavery in defiance of the majority North, and from an attempt by domineering slaveholders to treat northern white men themselves like slaves rather than as free and equal citizens. "The sectionalism of the South," declared the *Ohio State Journal* in July 1854, had delivered "a blow at the Republicanism of our institutions and the free labor of the North." To save them, chimed Gamaliel Bailey in the *National Era*, Northerners must "rally as one man for the reestablishment of liberty and the overthrow of the Slave Power."[10] In June, a month before the Ohio People's party anti-Nebraska convention met in Columbus, Follett predicted in the *Ohio State Journal* that "we shall soon find a common name in the pure Republicanism of our object." The state platform adopted by Michigan's new Republican party in July 1854 identified that label. The Kansas-Nebraska Act, it declared, was intended "to give to the Slave States such a decided preponderance in all measures of government as shall reduce the North . . . to a condition too shameful to be contemplated." To meet this threat of enslavement, a new party was necessary, and its name would signify its mission. "That in view of the necessity of battling for the first principles of republican government, and against the schemes of aristocracy the most revolting and repressive with which the earth was ever cursed, or man debased, we will co-operate and be known as Republicans until the contest be terminated."[11]

In 1854, it must be stressed, their overtly antisouthern thrust and their attempt to combine men from all parties in exclusively northern organizations, not anti-Nebraska sentiment itself, distinguished Whigs who joined anti-Nebraska coalitions from northern Know Nothings, as well as from northern Whigs who spurned coalition. For many northern Whigs, there was no incompatibility between the objectives of the Know Nothings and those of anti-Nebraska men. Both groups offered compelling reasons to smite the Democrats. The difference between Know Nothings and the anti-Nebraska coalitions, rather, stemmed from the mode and geographical scope of their organization, from the grievances against Democrats to which they gave priority, and from the primary threat to Americans' republican self-government they identified. Know Nothings mobilized secretly rather than publicly. Their organization penetrated extensively into the South as well as the North. And they did not see the Slave Power as the chief threat to American freedom.

The menace came not from the South but from Rome. A Catholic conspiracy or papal plot, Know Nothings cried, sought to subvert America's republican institutions and to steal control of government from the hands of native-born Protestants. That plot was powered by the huge waves of European immigrants inundating the United States in the 1840s and 1850s, and it was abetted by corrupt Democratic and Whig politicos who obsequiously whored after immigrant and Catholic support. It had become so dangerous by 1854 that it "was the duty of every American and naturalized protestant citizen throughout the Union," of Southerners as well as Northerners, that is, "to use his utmost exertions to aid the cause by organizing and freeing the country from that monster," which sought "to plant its flag of tyranny, persecution, and oppression among us."[12]

Social and economic grievances spawned by the rapidly growing immigrant population undoubtedly contributed to the growth of Know Nothingism. The new and menacing political influence of Catholics and immigrants by the early 1850s, however, created the Know Nothings' political agenda. Among other things, that influence was manifested by the outpouring of new immigrant voters for Pierce in 1852, by demands of Catholic clergymen for local ordinances or state laws to ban Bible reading from public schools and to divide school funds to provide tax revenues for Catholic schools, and by the blatant awarding of political jobs to Catholics, most notoriously Pierce's appointment of the Philadelphia Catholic James Campbell as his postmaster general. Nativist spokesmen shrieked that Roman Catholicism was inimical to American republicanism because it was a "despotic faith" that was "diametrically opposed to the genius of American Republicanism," because its "crafty priesthood" taught "anti-republican sentiments," and because Catholics' assault on the public school system threatened "the very Citadel of Republican strength." Smashing that threat, cried Know Nothings, was imperative to "guarantee the three vital principles of Republican Government— *Spiritual Freedom, Free Bible,* and *Free Schools.*"[13]

Republican self-government, in sum, stood in jeopardy because Protestant Americans no longer ruled America, because the existing political parties shamelessly and unpatriotically kowtowed to Catholics and foreigners. Thus the political goal of Know Nothings—and only of Know Nothings, they stressed—was to reduce, indeed to obliterate, the political influence of Catholics and foreigners. They and they alone would make sure that only native-born Protestants gained elective and appointive public office. They and they alone would stop immigrants from voting by revising the state constitutions that allowed aliens to vote before naturalization, by enacting requirements that even naturalized immigrants wait years after they technically became citizens before they could vote, and by imposing stiff literacy qualifications on the right to vote that could keep foreigners from the polls. They and they alone sought control of Congress in order to increase the naturalization period from five to twenty-one years and to pass laws that would prevent European nations from dumping criminals and paupers on American shores.

Know Nothings tapped into and articulated a remarkably deep and widespread anxiety about, and antipathy toward, foreigners and Catholics, and those sentiments helped fuel the dazzling growth of the order in 1854. Urban artisans and mechanics, who blamed immigrants for driving down wage scales and driving up the cost of food and rent, may have been particularly susceptible to those sentiments. But the bias and certainly the propensity to join Know Nothing lodges was not confined to a particular class or even to large cities, where concentrations of Catholics and immigrants were most dense. During the first seven months of 1854, prior to Congress' adjournment, anti-Catholic sentiment and Know Nothing lodges appeared in remote country hamlets as well as large cities and in slave states like Virginia, Alabama, Mississippi, and Louisiana as well as in New England, Middle Atlantic, and midwestern states.[14]

The ferocity of nativism and the rapidity of Know Nothingism's spread especially stunned Democrats, not just because they knew they were the order's chief political target but also because they recognized that thousands of Democrats, long galled by the influence of Catholics and immigrants in their party, had become "altogether deranged on Nativism" and were flocking to the order.[15] Many Whigs were equally startled by the intensity of anti-Catholicism and the extensive geographical range of the Know Nothing movement it helped fuel. "How people do hate Catholics," marveled the Whig Rutherford B. Hayes after Know Nothings swept Cincinnati's congressional and state legislative elections in October. But anti-Catholicism also erupted in small towns. "The 'Know Nothings' . . . are a great power even out here in the country," a Whig warned Thurlow Weed from upstate Geneva, New York in June. Calling himself "astonished" that the Know Nothing "mania" was sweeping up even third-generation Germans in Pennsylvania, Fillmore's close advisor, William L. Hodge, declared in July that Know Nothings would not only "govern the fall elections" in New York and Pennsylvania, but they were also already "overwhelmingly powerful" in Virginia and his home state of Louisiana.[16]

Voters who demanded that politicians take steps against Catholics and immigrants, in sum, refused to be denied. Although Democrats were Know Nothings' most obvious targets, that determination menaced the Whig party as well. The momentum generated by Know Nothings might attract Whigs looking for a winner, and Know Nothings' agenda could attract zealous Protestants who had long supported the party primarily because immigrants and Catholics supported the Democrats. But Know Nothings' insistence that they and they alone would do something to counteract the papal plot was especially important.

For one thing, they obviously expressed an urgency about the Catholic threat that many staid and complacent Whig leaders did not share. That Know Nothings had a specific agenda for state and local officials to undertake when northern Whigs were focusing their campaigns on the Nebraska bill in most states was also significant. Know Nothings, that is, often seemed more relevant than Whigs in elections for local offices, and even in the spring of 1854, Know Nothings defeated Whigs in small Pennsylvania towns by electing men whom no one but Know Nothings even knew were candidates.[17]

More important, when Know Nothings clamored that Catholics had become a political threat only with the aid of sycophantic politicians, they included Whigs along with Democrats among the traitors. Granted, Democrats were primarily responsible for the pro-Catholic actions that most infuriated nativists, but Whigs too had eagerly supplicated Catholic and foreign support, most notably in the recent 1852 presidential campaign. Former Whigs who embraced Know Nothingism harshly attacked this betrayal by Whig politicians. "A *secret American movement*" had emerged to combat Catholicism, Judge Ross Wilkins of Detroit wrote Supreme Court Justice John McLean, because "*both* parties had courted what was called the foreign vote" [emphasis mine]. Catholics had achieved power, sneered Tennessee's vitriolic Whig-turned-Know Nothing editor William G. "Parson" Brownlow, only because "the worst class of American politicians, designing demagogues, selfish office-seekers, and bad men, calling themselves Democrats and 'Old-Line Whigs' " had wooed them to secure "the Catholic vote." Chastising Seward, Weed, and Horace Greeley by name, New York's veteran nativist Thomas R. Whitney in his Know Nothing tract, *A Defence of the American Policy*, insisted that venal "political leaders who have yielded to [the] pretensions and demands" of the "Romish Church," "whether Democrat, Whig, or Native American," must "be repudiated from Maine to California."[18]

Know Nothing leaders and propagandists portrayed the order as a refuge for those who believed that all existing parties were controlled by corrupt spoilsmen and wire pullers and that honest, responsive government could be restored only by driving them from office. And without question, at least some people regarded the order as an antiparty, reform organization that would restore republican self-government not just by stifling the Catholic conspiracy, but also by purging self-interested politicos from the political system and returning political power directly to the people. "This new and mysterious party called 'Know Nothings' may, and I think will, do good in ridding the country of the trading and trafficking politicians," argued a Virginia Whig in December 1854. Looking back on the Know Nothing outburst in 1859, Connecticut's Gideon Welles, who despised it, acknowledged that "thousands flocked into the order, not that they approved its principles, but for the purpose of relieving themselves from the obligations and abuses of the old organizations."[19]

Know Nothings themselves waxed euphoric about the order's potential for smashing all the existing parties, driving their corrupt leaders from office, and restoring a more pristine politics that honestly reflected the will of the people. Philadelphia Whig editor Morton McMichael wrote in the *North American* that the mayoral triumph of the Know Nothing Robert T. Conrad, McMichael's co-editor of that Whig sheet, in June 1854 had been the "triumph of popular intelligence and virtue, solicitous for the public welfare, over party organization and objects, as such." A New York Know Nothing bluntly insisted later that year that "*we* are determined to give old party lines and old party hacks a glorious drubbing this fall." Everywhere, in fact, Know Nothings promised to reject professional, office-seeking politicos clad "in the cast off garments of Whiggery or Democracy" and to elevate to office instead new men "fresh from the ranks of the people."[20]

Know Nothings' call for restoring power to the people clearly enhanced their image as champions of republican self-government. Just as clearly, calls for the obliteration of old party lines and the repudiation of candidates associated with

Whiggery menaced the Whig party's very existence. Some Whig politicians, especially those identified with the pro-Catholic campaign for Winfield Scott in 1852, were prominent Know Nothing targets. In New York, the goal of Know Nothingism was "to sweep Sewardism & Political Catholicism off the face of the Earth," and "particularly to defeat Mr. Seward's re-election to the Senate."[21]

Nonetheless, neither the importance of an antiparty impulse to Know Nothings' early success nor the danger that Know Nothingism posed to the Whig party in 1854 should be exaggerated.[22] The Know Nothings undoubtedly attracted sincere antiparty reformers who did indeed want to destroy all the old parties. How influential they were among Know Nothings in 1854 and how many initiates knew of their intentions are unclear, however. One man's hack, after all, is often another man's statesman, and all Know Nothings did not regard all politicians, especially all Whig politicians, with equal contempt. Many of the candidates they backed in 1854, especially candidates for Congress and statewide office, were not amateurs "fresh from the ranks of the people," but instead veteran politicians, the great majority of whom were Whigs.[23]

Just as modern-day calls for imposing term limits on congressmen are often aimed at entrenched and apparently unbeatable officeholders from the other party, vows to drive hack politicians from office may sometimes have been self-interested cant. They often reflected the frustration of soreheads who had long been galled by the dominance of the other party or of rival factions within their own party and who saw Know Nothingism as a way to bring old enemies down. This is not to suggest so much the hypocrisy of Know Nothings as to point to the order's potential malleability and manipulability, its capacity to serve very different ends for different people. It could indeed be a vehicle for bigots, alarmed Protestants, and authentic antiparty reformers; it could serve as a temporary home for anti-Nebraska men until some better antisouthern alternative came along; but it could also serve as a refuge for conservatives who feared the control that antislavery Whigs exerted over the regular Whig party. It could be a weapon wielded by one Whig faction against another, but Whigs could also seize upon it as a powerful ally against dominant Democrats that would bring the Whig party back to power.

What made Know Nothings seem so malleable to so many different groups was the nature of their organization. In 1854, Know Nothings, despite their concrete demands upon government, were not yet a political party that publicly nominated its own exclusive candidates in open conflict with the preexisting parties. Rather, they were a secret society that sought to secure the election of men who agreed with their goals. They did so either by infiltrating existing parties and seeking to control their nominations or by throwing the weight of the organization behind candidates already nominated by existing parties. In short, Know Nothings were a pressure group, rather like the contemporaneous temperance associations, whose influence often seemed up for grabs.

It was, to be sure, a very peculiar pressure group. Its secret grips, signals, passwords, and elaborate superpatriotic initiation rituals struck even veteran Whig politicians who joined the order like Congressman Solomon G. Haven as "puerile," if not downright "foolishness."[24] The pledge to absolute secrecy about belonging imposed on members, moreover, meant that men who joined local lodges in one place did not know whether men who joined lodges elsewhere were also members, and this ignorance often led to some hilariously stilted written correspondence between them as they sought to feel each other out and to indicate that they belonged to the order without openly saying so.[25]

Yet the Know Nothings were a pressure group, nonetheless, and one that had vast potential power because of their secret organization. By the summer of 1854, they had developed a pyramid-like organization ranging from local lodges or councils to countywide to state councils to a grand national council. More important, one of the Know Nothings' membership oaths required members to support candidates endorsed by the order, regardless of those candidates' party affiliation. These endorsements for local and congressional candidates were usually made by majority vote within the local lodges, but statewide candidates in most states were endorsed by state councils, sometimes after polling opinion within local lodges.

These practices meant that Know Nothings could deliver an unusually disciplined and solid vote from their membership. They also meant that those who gained control of the Know Nothing machinery, from local lodges to state councils, could determine who got that vote. Thousands of Democrats joined the order in 1854, and to retain them, Know Nothings did occasionally endorse Democratic candidates for whom Whig members would have to vote. At the same time, however, the Know Nothings' organization meant that Whig candidates could get Democratic votes if Whigs gained control of the machinery. Whigs could join the order, in sum, not to destroy the Whig party but to bring reinforcements to its aid. Allegiance to the one, at least originally in 1854, did not necessary imply a cessation of allegiance to the other.

It is often difficult to tell from this distance, in fact, exactly who was trying to take over whom in 1854. By the fall, Know Nothings were trying to infiltrate Whig meetings and conventions to dictate their nominations, but just as often, Whig politicos signed up with the Know Nothings in order to control the order's endorsements. In New York, for example, where Seward and Weed were indeed the primary targets of many Silver Gray Whigs who joined the order, Sewardites themselves joined lodges to negate their opposition to Seward. Understandably, just as many Democrats regarded the threat by temperance associations to run separate tickets in 1854 as "a hypocritical devise [sic] of the wireworking Whigs" to trick dry Democrats and thereby "elate & resuscitate the almost expiring Whig party," so many Democrats regarded Know Nothingism as "the new invention of the Whigs" that sought to gull resentful Protestant Democrats. Just as often, however, Democrats admitted that Know Nothings were a threat to Whiggery, "demanding the disbanding of the Whig *organization, name*, & everything." Know Nothings had dominated every People's party convention in Indiana by the end of September, reported one Democrat, and "Whigs have had to play second fiddle to them." Similarly if some Whigs considered the order a powerful ally— "Whig thunder" one Nashville Whig called it in December 1854—others moaned that the Know Nothings and the resentments vented by them "have destroyed everything like party discipline, and many staunch old Whigs are floating off they don't know where."[26]

By 1855, the American party that evolved from the secret order would clearly be recognized as a substitute for and therefore a threat to the Whig party, but in 1854 Know Nothingism's import for the Whigs was anything but clear. The order's growth and potential power were apparent, but it often seemed a prize

Whigs could capture and use rather than a menace that might gut the Whig party. The very plasticity and manipulability of the order, in sum, meant that its impact upon the Whig party and upon the fortunes of Whig candidates varied considerably from state to state in the elections that year.

Know Nothingism ultimately proved lethal to Whiggery, paradoxically, because it was not as malleable as it originally seemed. Whatever the original intentions of Whigs who joined the order may have been, once they became enmeshed in its oath-bound machinery, either they were seduced by its potential to become a substitute for the Whig party itself or they discovered, to their chagrin, that they were abetting men who did indeed mean to drive the Whig party out of business. First appearances, in short, proved deceptive. Men could not remain simultaneously loyal to both the Whig party and the Know Nothing organization.

III

In 1854 anti-Nebraska coalitions and the Know Nothings initially had their greatest impact in northern elections. Six slave states, however, also voted that year, and with the exceptions of South Carolina, where no Whig party had ever existed, and Delaware, their contests featured the traditional combat between Whigs and Democrats. By itself, that fact undermines assertions that sectional anger stirred up by the Nebraska debates, and especially southern Whigs' fury at northern Whig assaults on their support for the Nebraska measure, instantly caused southern Whigs to desert the Whig party. Southern Whigs instead gave every indication that they hoped to perpetuate the national Whig organization.

Residents of Missouri and neighboring Arkansas went to the polls in early August, when their incumbent congressmen were still in Washington and could not campaign personally. Whigs had no prayer of carrying Arkansas, a Democratic stronghold since its statehood in 1836, and they again lost both congressional seats.[27] In sum, regardless of what happened to Whig parties elsewhere, Whig prospects in Arkansas were hopeless, and it is little wonder that Whigs, led by the explorer Albert Pike, initiated the formation of Know Nothing lodges in the fall of 1854 and sought to recruit dissident Democrats to them in order to increase their strength. By August 1855 Democratic leader Senator Robert Johnson could, with prefect accuracy, pronounce the Whig party in Arkansas "*notoriously extinct.*"[28]

Missouri's results differed dramatically and bordered, indeed, on the astounding. In what was once one of the nation's most reliable Democratic states, Whigs won six of seven congressional races and increased their strength in both chambers of the state legislature.[29] Missouri's Whigs had already exploited the rift between pro-Benton and anti-Benton Democrats to win four House seats and elect a United States senator. Earlier, however, Whig candidates had been almost solely dependent on those divisions, and they had often won with pluralities in multicandidate races, not by convincing majorities. In 1854, in contrast, four of six won with majorities of greater than 51 percent. Samuel Carruthers, who had attracted less than 40 percent of the vote in 1853, garnered 58 percent a year later.[30] Unlike the situation in Arkansas, Missouri's Whigs appeared to be very much on the rise.

Unlike Arkansas as well, the Nebraska issue was absolutely central to Missouri's elections, and Whigs' success disproves the contention that Nebraska killed southern Whiggery. It did not, however, largely because Missouri's Democrats were more deeply divided by it than were Whigs themselves. Benton represented the St. Louis congressional district during the Thirty-Third Congress, and he, as well as his Democratic allies in Missouri, vehemently opposed repeal of the Missouri Compromise line. In contrast, Senator David R. Atchison, leader of the state's anti-Benton Democrats, was a primary architect of the Nebraska bill, and his Missouri allies demanded its passage. Previously, Whigs had allied with one or the other of the warring Democratic factions, but in 1854 Missouri's Whigs themselves divided over the Nebraska bill. Three Whig congressman whom pro-Benton Democrats had helped elect, along with Carruthers, whom Bentonites had bitterly opposed, and Whig Senator Henry Geyer voted or announced support for the bill. When Whig district conventions renominated all four incumbents and praised their pro-Nebraska position, Benton Democrats now opposed all but one of them. In contrast, both of the new Whigs elected to join the incumbents—Gilchrist Porter and Luther Kennett, who defeated Benton in St. Louis—were known as anti-Nebraska men, and Democrats, at least, reported considerable anti-Nebraska sentiment among Whigs across the state. Whigs could win, in sum, no matter how they stood on Nebraska.[31]

Kennett won without aid from either pro- or anti-Benton Democrats, but he did get vital help from elsewhere. As a rapidly growing city with a huge German population, St. Louis was one of the first places west of the Mississippi where Know Nothings organized. On July 22, three weeks before the election, an anti-Benton Democrat frantically reported that "the new element introduced into our politics, the 'Know Nothings,' disturbs all calculations. All depends upon their course." Between the writing of this dispatch and election day, the Whigs apparently worked out a deal with the Know Nothings. In return for purging several foreign-born candidates from their local ticket and pledging that Kennett would join the order *after* the election, Whigs won Know Nothing support for him.[32]

Kennett did join the Know Nothings after the election, as did reelected Whig Congressman James Lindley sometime before the Thirty-Fourth Congress met. In contrast, Gilchrist Porter adamantly refused to join the order and pronounced himself a Whig during his entire congressional term, while Carruthers and Mordecai Oliver openly denounced the order and would vote with Democrats against American candidates for House speaker when the new Congress met. Unlike Arkansas, where the tiny Whig party appeared to move en masse into Know Nothingism, in short, Missouri's nativist order had a divisive rather than a unifying impact on the Whig party. The St. Louis *Missouri Republican*, the most influential Whig paper in the state, vehemently denounced Know Nothings in 1854, and in April 1855 it backed an anti-Know Nothing Whig for mayor against the Know Nothing candidate. And divisions over Know Nothingism in the new legislature helped stop the Whig minority from picking a new United States senator.

With full attendance in the joint legislative session that in late 1854 would fill the Senate seat for which both Atchison and Benton hungered, there were sixty

Whigs, fifty-seven anti-Benton Democrats, and forty-three Benton Democrats. Since none of the three groups had the majority necessary to prevent a stalemate, ambitious Whigs and Democrats alike looked to Know Nothings for help. At least one contender for the Whigs' caucus nomination, James S. Rollins, joined the order to gain its influence, and so too, astonishingly, did the Democratic incumbent Atchison, apparently in the hope that Whig members of the order might support him and offset the visceral opposition of Bentonites to his reelection. In the end, Know Nothings helped no one. Whigs from western Missouri, who distrusted Know Nothings as anti-Nebraska men, spurned Rollins' bid and instead nominated a vehemently pro-Nebraska, proslavery Whig outsider named Alexander Doniphan, and even Know Nothing Whigs stuck by him in subsequent roll calls. Voting went according to party and factional lines, not according to membership in the order, and the resulting stalemate forced a postponement of the election until the following winter.[33]

Missouri's Whigs, in sum, had done so well on their own in the August 1854 elections that a good many of them actively resisted merging the party with the Know Nothings. Like other southern state organizations, however, they could not ignore what happened to Whig fortunes elsewhere in 1854 and 1855. During the latter year, when the state held no important elections, most Whigs drifted toward the American party that had evolved out of the secret order. Thus, when the still defiant St. Louis *Missouri Republican* in November 1855 called for a Whig state convention to meet to nominate candidates for the 1856 races, the rival *Missouri Democrat* jeered, "An invitation to the ghostly and grinning skeletons of some cypress-decked necropolis to walk forth once more under the joyous sky would not be more absurd and mournfully ludicrous."[34]

No congressmen were due to be elected in North Carolina in 1854, and its August contests for governor and members of the state legislature consequently revolved primarily around states issues, particularly state subsidization of railroad expansion into eastern and western parts of the state and revisions of the state's constitution.[35] Nonetheless, Whig leaders, who had seen the number of Whig congressmen reduced from five to three in the 1853 elections, considered the legislative contests especially crucial, for the new legislature would fill both of the state's United States Senate seats. Thus Whigs mounted an extraordinary effort to capture it, demonstrating beyond cavil that they, too, had no intention of abandoning the Whig party in 1854.

North Carolina's Whigs had long relied on the statewide speaking tours and joint debates of rival gubernatorial candidates, even more than upon state platforms, to define the issues at stake in state contests and to rouse the faithful to vote for Whig legislators as well as governor. As a result, Whig legislative candidates in North Carolina, as in most states, indeed, were often obscure and inexperienced small-fry politicos. For several reasons, however, in 1854 North Carolina's Whigs abandoned this customary strategy.

Whigs' problem in 1854 was not men but measures. Their gubernatorial candidate, ex-Congressman Alfred Dockery, was able and experienced, and he ran against Thomas Bragg, not the popular David Reid, who refused renomination in the hope of securing one of the Senate seats. By 1854, however, little differentiated the two parties on state subsidization for railroad construction. Their state platforms agreed on it, and during the joint debates between Dockery and Bragg, Bragg came out flatly for state subsidies, thereby neutralizing Whigs' advocacy of state railroad promotion. The other salient state issues—free suffrage and legislative reapportionment on the white basis—divided Whigs along regional lines. Since the legislature itself blocked reapportionment, by the 1850s western Whigs demanded a constitutional convention to adopt this and other reforms. Whigs' supporters among slaveholders in central and eastern North Carolina, however, strongly opposed the white basis, whether by statute or constitutional revision. In this situation, the Whig state platform adopted in February straddled by calling for a state constitutional convention but only if it preserved the present apportionment of the legislature.[36] This plank provoked a storm of protest from western Whig meetings and Whig newspapers, but Dockery clung to it because he knew that the Whigs would be pulverized in "the Eastern and Middle counties" if "we go into the campaign with a change of the basis upon our banner."[37] The straddle thus spiked one of Whigs' two biggest guns in the west, just as Bragg's prorailroad stance had spiked the other.

By the spring and early summer, then, Whigs clearly could not rely on Dockery's coattails to retake the legislature. Rather than run the typically obscure men as candidates in 1854, therefore, they ran "our strongest men for the legislature," many of whom had long been retired, few of whom had any interest in spending dreary months in Raleigh, but all of whom recognized that the necessity of controlling the legislature in order to elect the two United States senators required a significant personal sacrifice. Former Governor, Senator, Secretary of the Navy, and Whig vice presidential candidate William A. Graham ran for the state senate. Former Governor John Morehead and former Congressmen David Outlaw and Daniel M. Barringer, as well as prominent Whigs like William Cherry and Samuel F. Patterson, who had once been mentioned as potential gubernatorial nominees, all ran for the legislature in 1854. When Barringer's wife complained that she was "*mortified*" that he would consent to run for so lowly an office after just serving as United States minister to Spain, he explained that he had "good reasons for yielding" to the demands of his constituents "*at the present time. It is a critical period in the affairs of our State. All our best men are being called upon.*"[38]

Whigs' "best men" were not enough. Dockery ran almost 4,000 votes ahead of his predecessor in 1852, and he cut the Democratic margin from 6 to 2.2 percent. Nonetheless, he still lost to Bragg by 2,100 votes. Some of the Whigs' best men won election to the legislature, but they still suffered a net loss of five seats in the house, converting a four-vote majority into a six-vote minority, and in the senate they lost two more seats and fell to two-fifths of the total.[39]

Although the North Carolina Whig party obviously remained quite competitive, the narrow defeat, especially after so much effort, had to have been demoralizing. After the expulsion of Vermont's Samuel Phelps and the resignation of Connecticut's Truman Smith and Massachusetts' Edward Everett from the Senate, Whigs held only nineteen of its sixty-two seats. Thus the North Carolina result severely damaged the hopes of Whigs across the nation of regaining control of Congress' upper chamber. "Our little company of Whigs here are mourning over the great defeat in N. Carolina," George Bryan groaned from Charleston, South

Carolina. If only Fillmore and John P. Kennedy had visited Raleigh on their southern swing in the spring, he pipe-dreamed, "the event might have been different."[40]

Florida's Whigs also were in disarray as they prepared for the state's October congressional and legislative elections. By 1853, only three Whig papers remained in operation, one each in Jacksonville, Tallahassee, and Pensacola. E. C. Cabell, the popular former Whig congressman, had announced his retirement from politics to engage in business. And in 1854 demoralized Whigs could not even agree to hold a statewide convention to nominate their congressional candidate; they relied instead upon county conventions to pick their man.[41]

Ex-Governor Thomas Brown, whose former popularity, it was hoped, would reinvigorate the party, eventually got the nod. But Brown quickly infuriated pro-Nebraska Whigs by announcing that he would have opposed the Nebraska bill had he been in Congress in 1854, since it unnecessarily insulted northern Whigs, and by stating that he would work amicably with northern Whigs in Congress if elected. Pro-Nebraska Whigs openly heckled Brown at rallies and bolted meetings that endorsed him on anti-Nebraska grounds. Brown began the race "with such a prospect of defeat before him as no Whig candidate has had for many a day," taunted one Democratic editor, but, undaunted, Brown and his friend Richard K. Call continued to condemn the Nebraska Act as an unnecessary provocation and to stress the vital necessity of preserving the national Whig party and its principles.[42]

Brown's heroic effort rejuvenated Florida Whiggery, but not sufficiently to restore its majority status. Democrats easily retained control of the legislature, which sent David Yulee back to the Senate to replace Jackson Morton, thus reducing the Whig remnant in that body even further. In the congressional contest, Brown amassed only four votes fewer than Cabell had won in 1852, but he still lost by almost 1,100 votes to the same Democrat who had defeated Cabell by only twenty-two votes. Brown's stance clearly alienated large slaveholders. Despite gains elsewhere in the state, he retained less than a fifth of Cabell's 1852 voters in heavy slaveholding counties in central Florida.[43]

Although local Whig candidates did surprisingly well in county elections during 1855, 1854 was the last statewide race run by Florida's Whig party. During 1855 Know Nothing lodges appeared in Florida, and in November a public American state convention met in Tallahassee. Brown, who chaired that American convention, and Richard K. Call, who was prominently mentioned for the American party's vice presidential nomination in 1856, led most of Florida's Whigs into the new organization, but some Whigs, as they would elsewhere in the South, moved instead into the Democratic party.

Florida's October election, in fact, was the last statewide campaign Whigs ever ran in the South. As usual, Whigs ran no candidates in South Carolina's congressional elections, and by November 1854 the American party had replaced the Whigs in Delaware, the final southern state to hold elections that year. Only nominally a slave state, Delaware economically and politically had long resembled its Middle Atlantic neighbor Pennsylvania, where Know Nothings became a powerful political presence in 1854. Know Nothing lodges were organized in Delaware during 1854 as well, but the alliance of Delaware's Whigs with them had less to do with a process of osmosis than it did with the predominance of Senator John M. Clayton within the state's Whig party.

Although Clayton himself apparently never joined the Know Nothing fraternity because he abhorred its secrecy, in October 1854 he issued a public manifesto calling for the creation of an open American party based upon its principles. As soon as the polls closed in 1854, he urged Know Nothing candidates in other states to get their state councils to renounce secrecy, and well into 1855 he complained bitterly about "the silly jealousy between the *outside* & *inside* Americans" that was "eating into the very vitals of the best party the country ever had."[44] Whatever his squeamishness about secrecy, Clayton enthusiastically embraced nativism and anti-Catholicism, but his longtime hope of replacing the Whig party best explains his advocacy of a new American party. Convinced by Whigs' sectional rift during debates over the Nebraska bill in 1854 that "the old parties, as National parties, are broken up & their power gone," he pleaded with other Whigs to help form an American party to replace them.[45]

Clayton's determination that the American party operate publicly also stemmed from his recognition that many Delaware Whigs, including heavyweights such as former Congressman John W. Houston, shared his hostility to the order's secrecy. In 1854, therefore, Delaware's Know Nothings publicly announced their own candidates, who had been secretly nominated in the lodges, in order to preempt the Whigs and prevent them from running their own slates. In this they succeeded, but Clayton's public endorsement of an American party in October may have been crucial in persuading fractious Whig outsiders to swing behind the Know Nothing candidates.[46]

With the backing of most Whigs as well as Democratic defectors to the order, the Know Nothing candidates swept to victory in November. Know Nothings won nineteen of twenty-one seats in the state house of representatives and eight of nine seats in the state senate. Know Nothing congressional candidate Elisha D. Cullen, a lawyer who *was* apparently "fresh from the ranks of the people" and without previous political experience, narrowly defeated Democratic incumbent George Riddle, who himself had narrowly defeated the Whig Houston in 1852.[47] Peter F. Causey, the Know Nothings' gubernatorial candidate and a well-known Whig, won far more impressively than Cullen. Causey had run for governor twice before as the Whig candidate; he lost in 1846, a Whig year otherwise, with 6,012 votes (49.4 percent), and again in 1850 with 5,978 votes (48.1 percent). He won in 1854 as a Know Nothing with 6,941 votes (52.6 percent), a gain of almost 20 percent since his most recent candidacy.

If Delaware was the only slave state in which Know Nothings completely displaced the Whig party by the end of 1854, it was emphatically not the only slave state penetrated by the order that year. As noted, Know Nothings were operating in St. Louis by July and possibly as early as April 1854. Elsewhere in the South, however, the order made its greatest headway in states without 1854 elections like Virginia, Maryland, Georgia, Alabama, Mississippi, Louisiana, Tennessee, and Kentucky, and it probably did so precisely *because* there were no elections in those states. Had Whigs and Democrats been engaged in campaigns against each other that year, politicos from both parties may have viewed the order as a possible threat. Without elections and the partisan fervor whipped up by them, in contrast, men could view the order as a pressure group that they could join without discarding their old party allegiances.

The order sprouted like kudzu across the South during the hot summer of 1854. Kennedy noted its presence in Maryland by early July. In August a New Orleans Whig exultantly told Fillmore that the order already had 10,000 members in that city and a proportionate number elsewhere in Louisiana. If his estimates were anywhere near accurate, his prophecy of certain "triumph" for "the *glorious old Native American party*" in its new "form" in 1855 was realistic, for the entire vote in Louisiana in 1852 had been less than 36,000. That same month another Whig reported that the order was spreading in Georgia, especially around Savannah, and even earlier an Alabama Democrat worried about the growth of "this stupendous and far-spreading leprosy" in his state. By November and December even Mississippi Democrats wondered how to stop "the progress of this extraordinary movement," and by January 1855 Solomon G. Haven, who was in close touch with Know Nothing leaders from Virginia, reported that there were at least 60,000 members out of a voting population of 170,000 in the Old Dominion.[48]

Southern Know Nothingism is usually interpreted by historians as simply a continuation of Whiggery, as a refuge for conservative Union-loving Whigs who were driven to it not by nativism, but by their fear of sectional agitation and the emerging Republican party in the North. Three aspects of the spread of Know Nothings among Southerners in 1854, however, refute that interpretation. First, many southern Whigs did not join the order, and when 1854 ended they still contemplated independent political action as Whigs in 1855.[49] Second, Know Nothingism originally grew in the South for the same reasons it spread in the North—nativism, anti-Catholicism, and animosity toward unresponsive politicos— not because of conservative unionism. In January 1855, for example, ex-Governor William B. Campbell of Tennessee wrote, "I have been astonished at the widespread feeling in favor of their principles—to wit, Native Americanism & anti-Catholicism—it takes everywhere." Later that year, an apprehensive Mississippi Democrat complained that Know Nothingism "has been eagerly embraced" because the order allowed "men of the very meanest capacity . . . to vote now according to birth and religion" and "to inflict injury on what they hate."[50] Third, and most important, southern Democrats joined the order by the thousands in 1854. By November, Virginia's Alexander H. H. Stuart reported that "many of the democrats who are tired of party dictation have joined the order." "I am sorry to see so many of our Democratic friends taking up with the 'Know Nothings,' " complained Mississippi's Democratic Senator Albert Gallatin Brown in December, and three months later he moaned, "*Know Nothingism* like the *measles* is catching."[51]

Most Democratic politicos were terrified by the heavy Democratic defections to the order in the South, and they bent every effort to break up the order and to woo those men back to the Democratic column *before* the 1855 elections. Southern Know Nothings, in turn, fought to retain their Democratic members, and they used nominations to do so. That effort had a vital impact on Whig reactions to the order as the 1855 elections approached. One reason many Virginia Whigs kept their distance from the order in the winter of 1854–55, for example, was a belief that Virginia's Know Nothings would insist upon nominating a Democrat for governor in order to demonstrate their independence from Whig control, as Know Nothings in fact did in Mississippi to prove the order was "no *Whig trick.*" Ultimately, however, former Whigs received the vast majority of southern nominations made by the American party in 1855.[52]

By May 1855, when Virginians voted, many southern Whigs had concluded that their old party had been obliterated. To understand fully why they did so and why many southern Whigs continued to regard the Know Nothings with suspicion, however, one must first examine what happened to the Whig party in the North during the elections of 1854 and how both Whigs and northern Know Nothings behaved in the aftermath of those elections. What happened in the North, rather than the nature of the southern American party itself, primarily shaped the outcome of the South's 1855 elections.

IV

Unlike the South, not a single free state witnessed completely straightforward two-party races between Whigs and Democrats. Know Nothings affected the results in many states, and where they did not, temperance men and Free Soilers did or else anti-Nebraska coalitions replaced the Whigs entirely. The upshot was a paradox. Northern Whig candidates were far more successful than southern Whigs in 1854, but by the end of that year the northern wing of the party had been weakened, or at least altered, far more than its southern counterpart. And where Whig state and local organizations had not eroded internally, they had assumed a corrosive antisouthern stance that dissolved the ties binding northern and southern Whigs together. Northern rather than southern elections inflicted mortal damage on the Whig party in 1854.

In distant California, for many reasons the most idiosyncratic of all free states, Whigs showed every intention of preserving the party intact. As in Missouri, Maine, New York, and, in 1854, Indiana, their potential success hinged on bitter splits within the dominant Democratic party, thus revealing once again how much Democrats determined Whigs' fate. By 1854, the most important of these Democratic divisions pitted Northerners against Southerners and focused on the rivalry between Tennessee-born Democratic Senator William Gwin and David Broderick, a New Yorker, who hungered for Gwin's Senate seat. When California's two incumbent Democratic congressmen sided with Broderick, Gwin's followers ran their own candidates against them, thus opening a golden opportunity for California's Whigs to capture the two seats. For two reasons, however, they again squandered it.

First, northern and southern Whigs also fell victim to sectional jealousies. By the summer, when Whigs held a state convention to nominate congressional candidates, word of the Kansas-Nebraska Act had reached the state. Northerners in the party wanted to take a stand against it or at least run northern-born men for Congress. A few Southerners, led by a militantly proslavery Tennessee Whig named Crabb, in contrast, sought to endorse the act in the state platform.[53] Ultimately the platform, like the subsequent Whig congressional campaign, ignored Nebraska altogether and instead trumpeted the same anticorruption, clean-government reform themes the party had used against the Democrats in 1853.

Southerners at the convention, however, exerted sufficient control to claim both congressional nominations for southern men, G. W. Bowie and Cal Benham. Many northern Whigs, angered by their rebuff at the convention, apparently refused to vote for them.[54]

Second, the Know Nothing order that burgeoned in California that summer in response to incipient anti-Chinese sentiment endorsed the two anti-Broderick Democratic congressional candidates. Given the sectional divisions in both parties and the pervasive hostility to wire-pulling politicos, Know Nothing influence proved decisive. "But for the Know Nothings, the Whigs would have carried the State," one disconsolate Whig wrote Fillmore after the election. Both anti-Broderick Democrats won seats in Congress, whereas in the legislative races, where Know Nothings backed Whigs, Whigs tripled their numbers in the house from twelve to thirty-six and lost one seat in the senate.[55]

After the election, some frustrated northern Whigs spoke of combining with Broderick Democrats in a new party against Southerners from both old parties. But when the badly divided new legislature failed to elect a new United States senator to Gwin's seat, southern Whigs and Democrats, who were determined to topple Democratic incumbent John Bigler in the 1855 gubernatorial race, took the lead by combining anti-Bigler forces in the Know Nothing party. Missouri's John Wilson and Tennessee's Bailie Peyton, who had fought Crabb's pro-Nebraska platform during the 1854 convention, led Whigs en masse into the American party, but the Democrat who did the most to form this coalition was Henry S. Foote, the former Democratic United States senator and Union governor from Mississippi, who palpably hungered after one of the state's two Senate seats. In 1855 Know Nothings ran ex-Whig J. Neely Johnston for governor, and he defeated the despised Bigler by about 4,000 votes. Know Nothings also gained control of the legislature.[56]

The California American or Know Nothing party was an oddity. Although there clearly was nativist sentiment in the state, Know Nothings recruited both Catholics and foreigners. Thus it was primarily the bipartisan anti-Bigler reform organization some Whigs and Democrats had spoken of creating in 1853. Yet it was also very clearly a party dominated by Southerners, and some northern Whigs who had no choice but to support it in 1855 angrily complained that the thrust of that campaign "was not that Americans shall rule" but that the new, antisouthern Republican party must not gain control of the national government. As one disgusted northern Whig put it, "Americanism was a mere pretext behind which to conceal the great question of the day and the prejudice against foreigners in our mining counties was eagerly seized hold of to forward the covert scheme of electing *Foote* and Crabb to succeed Gwin and [John B.] Weller" in the Senate. Such discontent meant that the Republican party had potential recruits in California, but by September 1855 the Whig party itself had been utterly displaced. A month later, one San Franciscan accurately observed, "The Whig party seems to be defunct in this State."[57]

V

That same assessment could have been applied to the Whig party by the end of 1854 in four midwestern states where anti-Nebraska coalitions displaced it—Wisconsin, Michigan, Indiana, and Ohio. The extent of cooperation among anti-Nebraska elements varied in those states, as did the enthusiasm of Whigs about joining new organizations. What the states had in common was more important. By the end of 1853, the Whig party in each was in desperate shape. In the most recent gubernatorial election in each state, the Whig proportion of the vote ranged from 43.3 percent in Indiana and 41.6 percent in Michigan in 1852 to 30.3 percent in Ohio and 6 percent in Wisconsin in 1853. In none of the four states did Whigs hold more than a third of the seats in the popular branch of the state legislature. Only one of the eight United States senators from the four states was a Whig, and in the House of Representatives that sat during 1854, the proportions of Whigs were: Wisconsin, zero of three; Michigan, zero of four; Indiana, one of eleven; and Ohio, seven of twenty-one. So forlorn did Whig prospects appear at the start of 1854 that no arrangements had been made in any of the four states to hold Whig state conventions.

Given their pathetic condition, Whig leaders understandably greeted the uproar caused by the Kansas-Nebraska Act as the chance to get outside aid even if that opportunity required a cessation of independent political action. From early March until late June, for example, New York's Horace Greeley, who advocated the formation of Republican parties across the North, excitedly urged his Indiana protegé Schuyler Colfax to arrange fusion tickets that combined Whigs and Free Soilers throughout the state. "Anti-Nebraska and anti-Rum," he crowed, "ought to unite Whigs and Free Soilers and carry your state this Fall." Any Whigs who refused to support "men on a Free platform . . . ought not to win." In the following months, both Whig Senator Ben Wade and Whig Congressman Lew Campbell of Ohio urged Whig editors in that state to promote anti-Nebraska alliances, and, as already noted, Whig editors in all four states did so.[58]

The intensity of anti-Nebraska sentiment among Whig politicians and voters in those four states—and everywhere in the North, for that matter—cannot be gainsaid. Furious that seven of ten Indiana Democrats in the House voted for the "perfidious" repeal of the Missouri Compromise in May, the determined Colfax vowed, "The North shall remember to expunge the expungers." Whig politicos and editors from all four states publicly fulminated against Slave Power aggressions and southern Whig betrayal.[59] By itself, the intensity of anti-Nebraska outrage predisposed the minority Whigs in all four states toward coalition in order to ensure that Democrats were defeated, but two other factors facilitated the creation of anti-Nebraska coalitions. Democrats in all four states, but especially Indiana, were deeply split over Nebraska, and thus anti-Nebraska Democrats seemed likely recruits. In addition, to varying degrees in all four, prohibitionism, nativism, and Know Nothingism further fragmented the Democratic rank and file and further alienated the electorate from the reigning Democratic state parties. In none of the four states, consequently, was antislavery sentiment the sole issue in the 1854 campaign or the only element in the formation of anti-Nebraska coalitions.

Both Whig needs and existing issues and circumstances, therefore, pointed to the relatively easy formation of anti-Nebraska coalitions in Wisconsin, Michigan, Indiana, and Ohio. July state conventions formalized anti-Nebraska alliances in all four, and they swept to impressive triumphs in the October and November elections. Individual Whig politicians who embraced coalition, moreover, palpably benefited from that decision. In Wisconsin, where there was no statewide race, anti-Nebraska men elected two of three congressmen, including Cadwallader C.

Washburn, the Whig brother of Elihu and Israel Washburn(e), and their majority in the new legislature sent Free Soiler Charles Durkee, whom Whigs had helped reelect to Congress in 1850, to the Senate. In Michigan, the entire coalition state ticket, including the zealous prohibitionist and stridently anti-Catholic Detroit Whig Jacob Howard, who ran for attorney general, triumphed, as did three of the state's four congressional candidates, all of whom were Whigs who had independently been endorsed by Know Nothings. Headed by a one-time Whig, Indiana's anti-Nebraska state ticket won, as did nine anti-Democratic congressional candidates, five of whom were Whigs, compared to one Whig and ten Democrats elected only two years earlier. And in Ohio, where anti-Nebraska candidates swept all twenty-one congressional districts in 1854, fourteen of the new representatives were Whigs.[60]

However inevitable coalition appeared in the spring and however much Whigs apparently benefited from it in the fall, there was nonetheless some Whig resistance to it in all four states, as there would also be in Illinois and Iowa. If only because Democratic disarray and vulnerability created the possibility of Whig victories even without coalition, dissident Whigs held out against the gravitational forces pulling anti-Pierce administration men together. Thus Ohio Free Soilers seeking coalition feared "that the hunker Whigs will *again* seek to make capital from the division of the democratic party" by attempting "to reorganize their party now." Similarly, Indiana's Whig state committee chairman John Defrees, a proponent of coalition, had to fend off the demands of Whigs who wanted to preserve an independent "organization of the Whig party, for the present contest."[61] This resistance was far more significant in Iowa and the lower midwestern states that bordered on the Ohio River than in Wisconsin and Michigan. As a result, the anti-Nebraska coalitions assumed a different form in the former than in the latter, and Whigs in the two blocs of states perceived them as serving different functions. Simply put, far more Wisconsin and Michigan Whigs viewed the coalitions created in 1854 as a final and irrevocable break from the South than was the case in Ohio and Indiana.

The differences stemmed from demography and recent political history. A much greater proportion of the residents in Iowa, Illinois, Indiana, and Ohio than in Michigan and Wisconsin had southern antecedents and kinfolk still living in the South. As a result, Whig leaders who lived among them or personally shared their southern heritage recognized the need to propitiate the sensibilities of their constituents. This attitude by no means precluded opposition to slavery extension and the Nebraska Act. Many of the Southerners in the Midwest had left the South to escape the economic and social dominance of slaveholders, and they abhorred the prospect of its establishment in Kansas and Nebraska. But solicitude for the concerns of southern-descended constituents did foster conservatism and an aversion to anything that might threaten the Union, whether southern aggression against a hitherto sacrosanct sectional compromise or the self-righteous antislavery, South-bashing rhetoric they associated with abolitionists and Free Soilers.

Readiness to cooperate with Free Soilers as equal partners was the second thing that differentiated Michigan and Wisconsin Whigs from those in the lower Midwest. In contrast with Ohio and Indiana Whigs, Michigan and Wisconsin Whigs had joined pragmatically with Free Soilers to back common congressional and gubernatorial candidates as early as 1850, and the platforms adopted by Republican coalitions in those states incorporated much more of the radical Free Soil agenda than those of anti-Nebraska coalitions elsewhere. In Wisconsin, for example, even a tiff between the state's most prominent Whig editor, Rufus King of the Milwaukee *Sentinel*, and his Free Soil counterpart, Sherman Booth, over the latter's supposed responsibility for preventing legislative passage of a prohibition bill in early 1854 failed to stop coalition against the Nebraska Act. When Booth called for a statewide convention to meet in July, Whig papers endorsed the call. Taking the name "Republican," that convention adopted a platform that incorporated the Free Soil agenda. It demanded repeal of the Fugitive Slave Act as well as of the Nebraska law and pledged resistance to slavery extension and to the admission of more slave states. Subsequently, local Whig organizations embraced the Republican label and called on Free Soilers and anti-Nebraska Democrats to combine with them. Few, if any, Whigs, moreover, failed to support Republican candidates who ran on this platform.[62]

Although it took Michigan's 1854 Republican coalition over a full year to develop into a coherent political party, Michigan's Whigs made a more thorough repudiation of national Whiggery and former southern Whig allies in 1854 than those from any other northern state. Paradoxically, however, the party's demolition resulted primarily from the determined resistance of some Whigs to any fusion whatsoever. For years, Michigan's Whigs had been split between an antislavery, antisouthern Sewardite majority associated with Joseph Warren's and Henry Barns' Detroit *Tribune* and pro-Fillmore conservatives aligned behind the Detroit *Advertiser*, which denounced the Nebraska Act as outrageous but also argued that Whigs should exploit anti-Nebraska sentiment by preserving a separate organization for the fall elections and by spurning alliance with other anti-Nebraska men. When Free Soilers precipitously nominated their own state ticket in February 1854 and subsequently refused to abandon it in order to cooperate with Whigs, they provided additional ammunition for the *Advertiser*'s case that Whigs should go it alone.[63] This impasse infuriated Whigs who sought coalition. By June one Whig paper noted despairingly that Free Soil and conservative Whig intransigence guaranteed separate anti-Democratic tickets in the fall, and that possibility prompted Warren's angry insistence that Whigs surrender their "love for an empty name" and his call for an all-parties anti-Nebraska convention on July 6. Finally, in late June, a mass meeting of Free Soilers agreed to drop their ticket and attend the meeting Warren had called. Relieved pro-coalition Whigs then vindictively set out utterly to humiliate the conservatives who had opposed coalition by making it as radically antisouthern as possible.[64]

Not only did the July state convention adopt the name Republican and nominate the Free Soiler Kinsley J. Bingham for governor. Whig attendees agreed to a platform that incorporated Free Soil demands for "abrogation" of the Fugitive Slave Act and abolition of slavery in the District of Columbia as well as repeal of the Nebraska Act, a platform that even the pro-Republican Greeley considered "a little too steep." Furthermore, to neutralize criticism from the *Advertiser* that a handful of self-appointed Whig leaders were trying to sell the Whig party body and soul to Free Soilers and abolitionists, pro-coalition Whigs attempted to legitimize abandonment of separate action with rank-and-file Whigs by holding a series of local and district meetings that ratified the actions taken in July. During

August and September, local or district Whig conventions met on the same day as, or a few days after, Fusion, Independent, or Republican conventions and endorsed their nominees for Congress and the state legislature. Ostensibly as a concession to the *Advertiser*, finally, pro-coalition Whigs agreed to hold a Whig state convention in October, the last ever held in Michigan, where the majority of delegates shouted down demands from conservatives for a separate Whig state ticket and endorsed the Republican candidates on a platform that denounced "the undying efforts of the Slave Power for political supremacy."[65]

Despite the *Advertiser*'s continued grumbling, election returns suggest that most conservative Whigs supported Republican candidates in 1854 rather than abstaining. The reason they did so appears to have been the Know Nothing order that emerged in Michigan by June, which grew independently from, but parallel to, the Republicans that year and which reflected the anti-Catholic animosity that had erupted in local elections in 1853 and 1854. Whatever the *Advertiser* thought of Free Soilers and coalition, it had taken stridently anti-Catholic positions in Detroit politics, and during 1854 it openly justified the growth of Know Nothingism. Many conservatives, therefore, probably joined lodges in 1854, and once those lodges endorsed Republican state and congressional candidates, membership vows required conservatives to support them. Together, that is, Republicanism and Know Nothingism gutted the Michigan Whig party, and the vindictive Warren could barely suppress his glee. "I think we shall not be troubled hereafter with any more attempts to galvanize the Whig party into life," he gloated to Seward after the fall election. "The sooner AntiSlavery Whigs and antislavery democrats combine their strength the better for the cause of freedom."[66]

Warren's determination to bury the Whig party was shared by few procoalition Whigs in Indiana and Ohio, where there was much greater Whig resistance to even a temporary cessation of independent activity. Deep distrust of Free Soilers and the larger numbers of conservative Whigs convinced even Whig proponents of coalition that they must control the anti-Nebraska movements or at least keep Free Soilers from dominating them. In Ohio, for example, Whig editors and officeholders dared not push for coalition until Whig intervention at a mass anti-Nebraska meeting in March excluded Free Soil demands and confined protests to repeal of the Missouri Compromise line. Similarly, nine day's before Indiana's anti-Nebraska convention in July, Whig leader Godlove Orth insisted that *"The Whigs must control that convention—without SEEMING to do so."*[67]

The need to reassure reluctant Whigs had several results. In both Indiana and Ohio the anti-Nebraska coalitions shunned the name Republican because of its radical connotations and instead called themselves "People's" movements. Their state and local platforms eschewed Free Soil planks attacking slavery in the District of Columbia and the Fugitive Slave Act and instead confined themselves to demands to restore the status quo by reimposing the Missouri restriction on Kansas and Nebraska.[68] Unlike Michigan's Whigs, who pledged to enlist in the Republican cause until the struggle against the Slave Power ended, moreover, procoalition Whigs in Ohio and Indiana explicitly emphasized that no permanent alliance with anti-Nebraska Democrats and the hated Free Soilers was contemplated and that cooperation in 1854 was temporary. In Ohio, for example, Whigs at the People's state convention insisted that no state committee be appointed in order to indicate the alliance's evanescent quality. Four days after it met, Schouler, who worked for coalition, cooed in the *Cincinnati Gazette* that "the Whig party and the Union will stand. . . . It makes no difference by what name you call it, its principles are undying." Similarly, Indiana's Defrees denied that the People's state convention was launching "a permanent organization."[69]

Implacable Whig resistance to coalition below the statewide level reveals why Whig editors had to sugar-coat what many Whigs deemed an exceptionally bitter pill even with the watered-down anti-Nebraska platforms. In Ohio, for example, Whig conventions in the eighth, tenth, and fifteenth congressional districts flatly refused to coalesce with other anti-Nebraska men and instead nominated straight Whig tickets for congressmen and state legislators. As if to punctuate Whig antipathy to coalition, Oscar Moore, who replaced four-term incumbent John Taylor as the Whig nominee in the tenth district, repeatedly proclaimed his loyalty to the national Whig party. In the second district defiant Whigs renominated J. Scott Harrison, an archetypal Whig conservative, despite Free Soilers' refusal to endorse him, and in the third district a Whig convention also renominated Lew Campbell without consulting other anti-Nebraska men.[70]

In most Ohio districts, People's, not Whig, conventions nominated the coalition's congressional candidates, and in many places where Whigs failed to control those nominations, their aversion to coalition was especially glaring. When the People's convention in the eleventh district nominated a Democrat, Whigs refused to support him and forced his replacement by Valentine Horton, a Whig who had Know Nothing backing. Whig rebellion against coalition was perhaps sharpest in the two Western Reserve districts represented by incumbent Free Soilers Ned Wade and Joshua Giddings. Although Whigs realized that it was futile to run their own men against them, local Whig organizations loudly refused to endorse their renomination and reelection even though Ned Wade was Ben Wade's brother, and large minorities of Whigs abstained rather than support them on election day. Despite all attempts to assure Whigs that coalition was moderate and temporary, indeed, about one-fourth of the Ohio voters who had supported Whigs in October 1852 sat home on election day in October 1854 rather than vote for the coalition ticket.[71]

Similarly, Horace Greeley's plea that Indiana's Whigs combine with Free Soilers and return George W. Julian to the House fundamentally misread Whig attitudes in that state. Most Indiana Whigs, particularly those in Julian's home district, detested Free Soilers. At the People's state convention in July, delegates shouted down an attempt by Julian to substitute a more radical platform that in effect called on the North to repudiate the Compromise of 1850, and not one of the slots on the People's state ticket or one of the eleven People's congressional nominations went to a Free Soiler.[72] More than perverse jealousy explains why Whigs shut out Free Soilers from People's nominations. Unlike Ohio's, Indiana's Free Soilers were not numerous enough to give Whigs a majority against the dominant Democrats.[73] Only by cutting into Democratic ranks could the People's coalition win, and Whigs therefore targeted dissident Democrats, not Free Soilers, as their preferred allies in 1854. The opportunity came when the Democratic state convention in May, at the instruction of Democratic Senator Jesse Bright, not only committed the party to the Nebraska Act and thereby effectively read anti-Nebraska men out of the party but also opposed passage of a Maine Law and denounced the Methodist clergy who sought it for interfering in political affairs.

When furious anti-Nebraska Democrats called for an anti-Nebraska meeting at Indianapolis in July, Whig state committee chairman Defrees and other Whig editors endorsed the call. In addition, the People's state convention itself not only called for restoration of the Missouri restriction. It also demanded passage of the Maine Law and defended the right of clergymen to participate in politics.[74]

If procoalition Whigs sought help from dissident Democrats in the People's movement, they still intended to control the People's state convention "without SEEMING to do so." Whigs did just that. Whigs claimed three of the five slots on the state ticket nominated at Indianapolis, six of the eleven subsequent People's district conventions nominated Whigs for Congress, and when the People's convention in the third congressional district had the temerity to nominate an anti-Nebraska Democrat named John Hendricks for Congress, furious Whigs nominated veteran Whig leader George Dunn and forced Hendricks to withdraw from the race to avoid splitting the anti-Democratic vote. Altogether, that is, in a state where Whigs had seemed a hopeless minority at the start of 1854, they seized seven of eleven congressional nominations.[75] Whigs dominated the Indiana People's movement because they seized control of the state's Know Nothing order. In no other state in 1854 did Whigs manipulate the secret nativist fraternity so expertly to advance their own partisan purposes. And they could do so, in large part, because of the integral relationship between nativism and prohibitionism in Indiana.

A state temperance convention in January had not nominated its own ticket, as many politicos had feared, but it had urged subsequent meetings of its local and county affiliates to run their own legislative candidates if neither Whig nor Democratic nominees pledged themselves to enact a Maine Law. Those local affiliates began to meet in February, the same month that the first Know Nothing lodge appeared in the state. Since one of the membership vows of Indiana's Know Nothing order pledged members to support passage of a Maine Law, it seems likely that temperance men seized upon the secret society as a device to ensure a consolidated prohibitionist vote in October. Since many of those dries were Democrats who would be bound by Know Nothing vows to support candidates endorsed by the order, astute Whigs like Orth and Colfax instantly recognized its potential for locking up Democratic votes if Whigs could control the order itself.[76]

How Whigs managed to do so is unclear, but that they used the order to serve their own purposes is undeniable. Two days before the People's state convention met in Indianapolis, the first meeting of the Know Nothing state council with representatives from local lodges gathered secretly in the city, chose Whig activist Orth as president of the state council, and nominated a state ticket. The same Know Nothings then attended and controlled the People's convention and selected the identical ticket. A similar scenario unfolded in ten of the state's eleven congressional districts. Know Nothings met prior to district People's conventions, secretly chose a congressional nominee, and then infiltrated the People's convention so thoroughly that the same man was nominated. The exception to this pattern proved the rule. Know Nothings had not met yet to select a candidate when the People's convention in the third district nominated the Democrat John Hendricks. Instead, Know Nothings threw their endorsement to Hendricks' rebellious Whig rival George Dunn, and that endorsement, possibly more than anything else, forced Hendricks out of the race. In sum, every anti-Democratic congressional candidate in Indiana was a Know Nothing or had Know Nothing backing.[77]

The beauties of Know Nothingism for ambitious Whigs went beyond the permeability of the order's secret machinery. In a state long dominated by Democrats, Know Nothings' antiparty, antipolitician rhetoric proved perfect for Whig needs. Thus Defrees happily asserted in the Indianapolis *Journal* that supporters of the People's movement were "unawed by party dictation." Whigs and Democrats alike also recognized what a powerful combination anti-Nebraskaism, prohibitionism, and nativism was. By September Orth predicted "a glorious victory" for "the friends of Freedom Temperance and our *Native Land*," and after the election Defrees, a Know Nothing sympathizer and probably a member, crowed that "American Principles" contributed to the victory and that Know Nothingism was an instrument of "the *people*, to overthrow the corruption that continued [Democratic] party success has spread through all departments of the Government." Long accustomed to easy Democratic triumphs over the hapless Whig foe, the bitter Democrat John Law, in contrast, complained that "the Whig party . . . have *no existence* in Indiana." Instead, Whigs had "united themselves with the abolitionists, the anti-Nebraska men, the Maine Liquor Law men, and the 'Know Nothings' the most dangerous of all."[78]

Finally, as in Michigan and Ohio, Know Nothingism allowed procoalition Whig leaders to persuade many of their party's most conservative elements to cooperate in a movement they otherwise would have spurned. Nonetheless, in Indiana as in Ohio, resentment among conservative Whigs about the apparent abandonment of the party ran deep. Between a tenth and a fifth of Whigs who voted for Winfield Scott in 1852 abstained in 1854 rather than support People's candidates.[79] For whatever reason, Whig abstainers in Ohio and Indiana had not joined Know Nothing lodges by the fall of 1854, but what often linked them with conservatives who joined the coalition via Know Nothingism is what most differentiated them from men like Michigan's Joseph Warren. Many Ohio and Indiana Whigs were not yet prepared to burn all bridges to their erstwhile southern Whig allies. The dilution of anti-Nebraska platforms in the two states and the insistence by editors like Defrees and Schouler that coalition was only temporary were emphatically not simply opportunistic ploys to induce suspicious conservative Whigs to support People's tickets. They were instead conscious efforts to hold the door open for future alliances with southern Whigs who also deplored the reopening of sectional agitation. The outraged Free Soiler Julian recognized that fact when he spat in disgust after his failure to modify the Indiana People's platform that "every Doughface in Indiana can demand the restoration of this compromise."[80]

Equally important, however, by late 1854, Whig leaders who entered People's movements in Ohio and Indiana via Know Nothingism and still sought to perpetuate alliances with southern Whigs believed that it could now be done only through, or in conjunction with, the Know Nothing order. This belief reflected a recognition that Know Nothingism had attracted tens of thousands of ardent nativists and antiparty reformers who would never abide an attempt to resurrect Whiggery, as well as a recognition that Whiggery had been so weakened elsewhere that an open American party of the type advocated by Clayton now represented perhaps the best chance of creating a new bisectional organization to oppose the Democrats.

The point here is that some men who authentically hated the Nebraska Act and slavery extension and who helped engineer the anti-Nebraska coalitions of 1854 still wanted no part of a permanent, exclusively northern antislavery party. It seems likely that such Whig politicos originally embraced Know Nothingism precisely because they saw it as a bridge to potential southern allies who could help them control the Thirty-Fourth Congress and win the presidency in 1856. In Indiana, for example, Orth concluded by 1855 that since "the 'fusion' party had outlived its usefulness and the Whig party cannot be galvanized into existence again," Know Nothings offered the best hope to build a new bisectional organization. "I want to preserve the nationality of our order *if it can be done without a sacrifice of principle.*"[81] Meanwhile, Ohio Congressman Lew Campbell, who pressed for cooperation among all anti-Nebraska men in Washington and promoted fusion within Ohio during the spring of 1854, simultaneously joined a Know Nothing lodge in Washington in order to line up southern Whig/Know Nothing backing for his run for the speakership of the House when Congress met in December 1855 or even the presidency in 1856.[82] Similarly, the ex-Boston editor William Schouler, now in Cincinnati, endorsed Know Nothing candidates in that city during 1854 even as he promoted a fusion anti-Nebraska coalition. Once the 1854 election was over, moreover, Schouler entered into correspondence with other Whig editors from around the country to make arrangements for holding a *Whig* national convention in 1856 that would reunite the northern and southern wings of the party by running an anti-Nebraska southern Whig like Kentucky's Garrett Davis, who was also a Know Nothing, for president.[83]

VI

Outside of Wisconsin, Michigan, Indiana, and Ohio, indeed, Whigs from every northern state were determined to preserve distinctive Whig organizations, if not ties to southern Whig allies, in 1854. Nonetheless, what occurred in them explains why even northern Whigs who hoped to retain an alliance with their southern counterparts doubted by the end of 1854 that they could do so through the Whig party itself. In some states—Iowa, Vermont, Pennsylvania, and a few congressional districts in Illinois, for example—Whigs could not resist reaching out to Free Soilers for help, thereby reducing the likelihood of future cooperation with southern Whigs. In Pennsylvania and other northern states, moreover, ambitious Whig candidates either joined Know Nothing lodges or sought to enlist Know Nothing aid, thereby compromising the likelihood of their future independent action as Whigs. And in the few states like Maine, Massachusetts, and New York where some Whig leaders defiantly refused to combine with any other group, other Whigs successfully orchestrated massive defections by the Whig rank and file to new organizations. Only New Jersey's Whig party escaped the 1854 elections anywhere near intact, and by the time New Jersey's November returns were in, even its Whig leaders realized that the Whig party must ally with Know Nothings to have any chance of remaining a national force.

Iowa and Illinois, which occupied opposite banks of the Mississippi River, illustrate how events forced even grudgingly reluctant midwestern Whigs to abandon the party. In Iowa, which voted in August, a few ambitious and committed leaders dragged the Whig party into an alliance with Free Soilers in 1854 that many rank-and-file Whigs considered both unnecessary and repugnant. Pro-fusion leaders then used their control of elective offices to make the new alliance permanent. Most Illinois Whigs, in contrast, staunchly resisted fusion during the 1854 campaign. Nonetheless, during the winter of 1854–55 they found it neces-sary to sacrifice one of their champions in order to replace the pro-Nebraska Democrat James Shields in the Senate with an anti-Nebraska man. By reducing even further the possibility that the Whig party might ever control the Senate again, that lost opportunity along with events elsewhere in 1855 convinced re-alistic Whigs that continued allegiance to the party was fatuous.

In 1852 Winfield Scott ran only 1,900 votes behind Pierce in Iowa, and the narrowness of this margin made that year's 1,600 Free Soil voters an obvious target as Whigs prepared for the gubernatorial, congressional, and state legislative elections of 1854. For two reasons, however, many Whigs shunned their support. First, Iowa's tiny Free Soil party was led by genuinely egalitarian ideologues, abolitionists who wanted not just to stop slavery's spread, but to eradicate it as well as all antiblack laws within Iowa itself. Many Iowa Whigs, especially those who favored Fillmore's nomination in 1852, considered Free Soilers' abolitionist proclivities and racial egalitarianism simply too extreme, and Free Soilers, who reciprocated that distrust, displayed their own contempt for fusion by nominating their own gubernatorial candidate in January 1854.[84]

Second, by the start of 1854, abstention by disillusioned and disgusted Dem-ocratic voters seemed so likely that Whigs might be able to win even without Free Soil aid. Once again, in sum, the condition of and actions by Democrats vitally shaped what Whigs did. The Democratic party was riven by internal feuds over rival railroad schemes seeking state and congressional subsidies. It opposed prohibition when demand for a Maine Law was burgeoning, and temperance men threatened to run their own tickets. It stubbornly defended the absolute ban on banking in the state's 1846 constitution that even many Democrats themselves considered anachronistic and inimical to economic development. When all three Iowa Democrats in Congress supported the Nebraska bill, finally, they outraged even southern-born conservatives.

When the Iowa state Whig convention met in late February 1854, most Whigs expected to focus at least their state campaign on the prohibition issue and to run independently of the Free Soilers. Free Soilers, including that party's guberna-torial nominee, who attended the Whig convention as a delegate, persuaded them otherwise. If Whigs nominated James W. Grimes on a platform that strongly condemned the Nebraska bill and endorsed prohibition, the Free Soilers promised to withdraw their ticket and support the Whig slate. Grimes was the key to coalition. A young New England-born and-educated lawyer, he had attended the Whig national convention in 1848 and served several terms in the legislature, but he was not known as a Whig activist and he had cast no previous votes for or against antiblack laws that might alienate Free Soilers from him. Confronted with an offer they could not refuse, Whigs nominated Grimes, who then bent every effort to cement a permanent fusion and thus bury the Whig party, to which he had little attachment.[85] Furthermore, during the campaign, he stressed the slavery extension issue and soft-pedaled prohibition in order to attract support from anti-Nebraska Germans. In July, he wrote Illinois Whig Congressman Elihu Washburne to solicit endorsements of his candidacy from Free Soilers Salmon Chase and Joshua Giddings. And he kept his distance from one of the Whig congressional candidates, James Thorington, because Thorington was also a Know Nothing.[86]

Iowa's conservative Whigs were furious. "James W. Grimes has been nominated for Governor in connexion with an out & out abolition ticket," one protested shortly after Grimes' selection. "His own Whiggery has been greatly suspected. I feel no interest in the Canvass—having but little confidence in either party." Whigs therefore insisted upon nominating their own congressional candidates, thereby spurning further coalitions with Free Soilers, but in the second district the opposition united behind Thorington. Grimes and Thorington won in August, and anti-Nebraska men, the majority of whom were Whigs, would also control the state legislature. But some disgusted conservative Whigs refused to vote for Grimes, and over three-fourths of previous Whig voters abstained rather than support the Free Soilers on the rest of the state ticket.[87]

Because Iowa was the first northern state to vote in 1854, eastern Whigs watched its results closely, and Greeley initially pronounced them a victory of a "Whig Anti-Nebraska, Anti-Whiskey ticket." As Greeley's own interest in promoting new Republican parties in New York and elsewhere grew during the fall, however, he changed his tune. In a later editorial, Greeley flatly denied that "the late victory of the Anti-Slavery and Anti-grog-shop ticket in Iowa" was "a victory of the Whigs." "The Whig party, as such, never could have gained that success," he intoned, even though former Whigs constituted almost 70 percent of Grimes' vote. "It was not done by either of the old organizations but by that new party of the People which the Nebraska outrage has brought to life in all Northern States and which, we do not doubt, is destined substantially to triumph everywhere."[88]

Grimes attempted to bring Iowa's "new party" to maturity when the new legislature met. He called on it to pass forthright resolutions condemning repeal of the Missouri Compromise, to enact a strict antiliquor law, and to repeal the ban against banking activity in the state. He also persuaded Whig legislators to put a Free Soiler on the state supreme court. Most important, he intervened in the election of a new United States senator to prevent Whig regulars, who protested the abandonment of the party, from winning that prestigious office. At least a dozen conservative Whigs boycotted a caucus of anti-Nebraska men and refused to support its nominee, former Assistant Postmaster General Fitz Henry Warren. Free Soilers also balked at Warren, and they instead backed young James Harlan, a Whig who had previously cooperated with the third party. As a result, on the first ballot opponents of incumbent pro-Nebraska Democrat Augustus Dodge fragmented among three candidates—Harlan, Warren, and Ed Johnson, the candidate of the "National Whigs." After that ballot Dodge withdrew, and Democrats in desperation agreed to back a different National Whig in the hope of luring dissidents into a coalition. In response, the anti-Nebraska caucus now united on Harlan, but he won only because Grimes twisted the arms of seven Whig conservatives to vote for him.[89]

In the spring of 1855, some Whigs as well as Know Nothings competed in Iowa's local elections. By April and May of that year, however, Grimes was writing Chase that "it seems to me that it is time to thoroughly organize the Republican party," and Grimes probably wrote the call for the first statewide Republican convention in 1856 that did so. Along with his Free Soil allies, who joined him in repudiating "the shibboleths of Whiggery" clung to by "Old Hunkerish" Whigs, Grimes had done more than any single individual to destroy the Iowa Whig party as an independent political force.[90]

Across the Mississippi River from Iowa, Illinois' Free Soilers tried to organize a Republican party at a state convention in Springfield in October 1854, but it proved a complete fizzle. Whigs from the northern half of Illinois had cooperated with Free Soilers in 1852, when Whigs won four of nine House seats, and they were ready to do so again in 1854. Whigs from central and southern Illinois, however, refused to abandon their old party, thereby dooming rapid formation of a statewide Republican organization. When Springfield Whig Abraham Lincoln was named to a Republican state committee by the small October gathering, for example, he declined to serve.[91]

Only a single, relatively minor statewide office was contested in Illinois that year, and Whig newspapers nominated their own man for that office even before the abortive Republican convention met. The congressional races, because of almost solid support from incumbent Democratic congressmen for the Nebraska bill, were considered far more important. In five of the nine House districts Whigs made no pretense of fusion whatsoever and ran straight Whig tickets against Democrats. Two of their candidates, James Knox in the fourth district and Richard Yates in the sixth, were incumbents who simply announced their intention to run again and were accepted without formal convention nominations. In still another district, the eighth, Whigs ran state legislative tickets but nominated no one for Congress. Instead they backed anti-Nebraska Democrat Lyman Trumbull against the regular, pro-Nebraska Democratic nominee.

Only in the three northernmost congressional districts did Whigs fuse with Free Soilers, but even there some Whigs resisted. In the northwestern first district, which bordered on Wisconsin, Galena Whig incumbent Elihu Washburne, who had squeezed by with a 300-vote margin and less than 44 percent of the vote in a three-way race in 1852, avidly sought Free Soil support in 1854. Yet Whigs in the district, "who fear they shall loose [sic] their identity as Whigs" if they cooperated in an anti-Nebraska coalition, insisted that a separate Whig convention nominate Washburne on the same day that a fusion Republican convention also did so. Washburne's fusionist friends were embarrassed by this separate Whig nomination, but he refused to repudiate it, even though it caused anti-Nebraska Democrats to run their own candidate.[92]

In the third or Bloomington district, Free Soilers also held the balance of power in 1852, but because many Whigs opposed coalition with them in a new Republican party, Whig incumbent Jesse Norton, who won with only 46 percent of the total in 1852, originally announced himself as a Whig candidate for reelection who would stand down only if a Whig convention replaced him. No such Whig convention ever met. Norton, meanwhile, joined the Know Nothings to enhance his chances. Nonetheless, a Republican convention also nominated him on a platform that called for repeal of the Fugitive Slave Act and imposition of the Wilmot Proviso on all territories. Fuming at that platform's radicalism, the Joliet *Signal*, the district's leading Democratic paper, in a transparent attempt to drive conservative Whigs away from him, accused Norton of renouncing "his allegiance to the old Whig party," repudiating "the old Whig platform," and trampling "upon the ashes of the immortal Clay." In campaign speeches for Norton, Abraham Lincoln neutralized these wild charges by insisting that the Whig party still existed in the district, despite Republicans' endorsement of Norton. Nor did many, if any, Whigs abandon Norton in November. His vote surpassed the combined total for Whigs and Free Soilers in 1852, and he won with over 62 percent of the total.[93]

The second or Chicago congressional district witnessed the most confusing race and the least successful attempt to combine the anti-Democratic opposition. Unlike most large cities, Chicago housed a powerful Free Soil party that had drawn over 13 percent of the vote in 1852, and its leaders were the state's most zealous advocates of forming a Republican party. Like other northern cities, however, Chicago also saw a burgeoning Know Nothing movement in 1854. Anticipating a race against incumbent anti-Nebraska Democrat "Long John" Wentworth, proponents of fusion were willing to seek Know Nothing support to marshal every vote they could get. Their real problem, however, came from what the Free Soiler Zebina Eastman called "old fogy Whigs," who were appalled at the thought of combining with Free Soilers. Whigs chose delegates to a fusion or Republican nominating convention in September, but even before it met, the pro-fusion Whig editor Richard S. Wilson of the Chicago *Tribune* feared "the difficulty that may grow out of the ultra Whigs insisting upon a nomination of their own."[94]

That fear proved prophetic. The Republican convention attracted Whigs, Free Soilers, and Know Nothings, but its congressional nomination went to the Democratic Mayor James Woodworth, who also had the endorsement of Know Nothings. Conservative Whigs found Woodworth's nomination intolerable. Instigated by the Chicago *Journal*, long a competitor and ideological rival of Wilson's Chicago *Tribune*, they nominated their own man, Robert S. Blackwell, a move that the Democratic *State Register* jeered was "a sickly effort on the part of the Chicago Journal clique to resist the crushing out of the old [Whig] name with the surrender to abolitionism."[95]

The campaign grew even more complicated because the Democrats refused to renominate Wentworth and chose a pro-Nebraska regular in his place. That move caused anti-Nebraska Democrats, who were dissatisfied with both Woodworth and Blackwell, to nominate a fourth candidate. Despite the four-way race, Woodworth, the Know Nothing Republican, still won with a majority. Nonetheless, Blackwell attracted about a fifth of the total vote, and his 2,600 supporters represented almost two-fifths of the Whig vote in 1852. The Chicago Whig organization had not been completely supplanted, but it had been ripped apart.

The bitterest disappointment for Illinois Whigs came in the winter of 1854–55 when the legislature selected a new United States senator. Anti-Nebraska men controlled both chambers, and Whigs far outnumbered Free Soilers and anti-Nebraska Democrats in each. Believing their preponderance in the opposition justified the selection of a Whig to replace James Shields, Whigs rallied behind Lincoln, who resigned the legislative seat he had just won to make himself available for the Senate. Both Know Nothings and Republicans opposed Lincoln, the latter because they doubted his antislavery fervor and because he had spurned the Republicans and instead made "indiscreet professions of Whiggery 'and nothing else' " during the recent campaign. Republicans, as one wrote, "rejoice[d] at the death of Whiggery" and refused to allow the revival of "old Whig doctrines" that Lincoln's election would signal.[96]

Within the legislature itself, a small bloc of anti-Nebraska Democrats who refused to elevate any Whig to the Senate ultimately doomed Lincoln's chances. That intransigence, in turn, caused some Whig legislators to cling to Lincoln in retaliation. When divisions among the anti-Nebraska men threatened to allow a pro-Nebraska Democrat to slip into the Senate seat, Lincoln urged the Whig legislators to swallow their pride and support Lyman Trumbull, the favorite of the anti-Nebraska Democrats, and Trumbull won the senatorship. Lincoln's magnanimous intervention helped inflict a stinging blow on Douglas and the pro-Nebraska Democrats, who despised Trumbull as a turncoat, but it also hastened the dissolution of the Illinois Whig party by promoting the fusion that Lincoln and the great majority of Whigs had rejected in 1854.[97]

VII

Three New England and three Middle Atlantic states also held elections in the fall of 1854. Whigs in all six tried to ride the anti-Nebraska issue to power, but they met only mixed success. What most differentiated these six states from each other, however, was the influence of Know Nothings on the 1854 races. In Vermont, Maine, and, surprisingly, New Jersey, Know Nothings had only a minimal impact during 1854. In Massachusetts, New York, and Pennsylvania, in contrast, they proved so central to the outcome that Know Nothingism doomed all hopes of resurrecting the national Whig party.

Know Nothings had the least impact on Vermont, but Vermont's Whigs courted Free Soilers so aggressively during the 1854 campaign that they helped frighten southern Whigs and northern conservatives out of the Whig organization. Following their upset defeat in 1853 in which prohibitionist Whigs had deserted the party, Whigs at their June 1854 state convention adopted a platform that denounced the repeal of the Missouri Compromise as "palpable perfidy to a solemn pledge of Freedom" and included the Free Soil demand for repeal of the Fugitive Slave Act. In addition, Whigs nominated Free Soiler Oscar Shafter to run for lieutenant governor. For governor, they bypassed former Governor Erastus Fairbanks, whom prohibitionists loathed, and instead chose Judge Stephen Royce, whom the Whig press called a "firm and consistent Whig."[98]

Despite the party's transparent reach for Free Soil support, which caused former Senator Samuel Phelps to complain that "the Whig party of Vermont has become an ultra abolition party," fusion almost failed because of the prohibition issue that prompted prohibitionist defections in 1853.[99] Royce may have been a "firm and consistent Whig," but dries doubted his commitment to the Maine Law. Their suspicions impelled a rebellion. On July 13, three groups gathered simultaneously in Burlington: the Free Soil state convention, the state convention of Vermont's temperance association, and an anti-Nebraska mass meeting that encompassed the other two groups. To the Whigs' dismay, the anti-Nebraska mass meeting refused to endorse Royce and Shafter and instead nominated the prohibitionist E. P. Walton, who had orchestrated the bolt from the Whig ticket in 1853, for governor and a different Free Soiler for lieutenant governor, nominations that the Free Soilers immediately ratified. Walton declined on the spot, reendorsed Royce, and persuaded the Free Soilers and temperance men to do so too, but Whigs were forced to replace Shafter with the Free Soiler named by the anti-Nebraska meeting.

Cooperation was almost as rocky in the congressional races. All three incumbent Vermont congressmen were Whigs who had voted against Nebraska and who had been opposed by Free Soilers as well as Democrats in 1852. Two of them, Alvin Sabin and James Meacham, sought reelection. Meacham was nominated by a straight Whig convention, an action to which Free Soilers acquiesced, and Sabin by a nonpartisan anti-Nebraska mass meeting that the Democratic press labeled Republican. In the second district, Whigs insisted on running their own man, Justin Morrill, whose repeated pledges of exclusive fealty to the Whig party caused the Free Soilers to run Oscar Shafter, who seemed likely to attract Whig votes, against him.[100]

Vermont was a Whig state, and Whigs swept the elections, primarily because of a huge decline in Democratic turnout since 1852. With the support of Free Soilers, Royce ran some 6,700 votes ahead of Fairbanks in 1853 and won with 62 percent compared with Fairbanks' 44 percent. All three Whig congressional candidates won, Meacham and Sabin by huge majorities and Morrill by a safe margin in his three-way race. Shafter, the champion of Free Soilers disgusted by the stubborn independence of Whigs, got about 15 percent of the vote. As a sop to Free Soilers, the new Whig majority in the legislature elected a Free Soiler to the remaining three months of the Upham/Phelps Senate term, but for the full six-year term they chose an orthodox Whig regular, former Postmaster General Jacob Collamer, whom the outnumbered and outraged Free Soilers fruitlessly opposed with their own candidate. That lopsided division of booty, like the Whigs' monopolization of the gubernatorial and congressional nominations, faithfully reflected the balance of power among Vermont's anti-Democratic majority.

By the end of 1854, in sum, Vermont's Whigs had not fused with Free Soilers in a new party; rather, they had attempted to co-opt Free Soil support with a minimum of concessions. Their state platform was militantly antislavery and therefore deeply offensive to southern Whigs. Nonetheless, Morrill's nomination for the open House seat in 1854 and especially the selection of Collamer, who had served in Zachary Taylor's cabinet, for the Senate over the protests of Free Soilers indicated that Vermont's Whigs were not yet ready to give up the ghost. By giving top priority to the success of the party within their state, regardless of its consequences for Whigs elsewhere, however, they helped sever the ties that bound the northern and southern wings of the Whig party together.

Many Maine Whigs also adopted radical antislavery positions that inevitably offended Southerners and conservatives, but unlike Vermont, where the anti-Nebraska uproar helped reunite the state Whig party, in Maine it shattered the Whigs, who had already split over the proper response to Democratic rifts over prohibition. Newly elected Senator William Pitt Fessenden, Congressman Israel Washburn, Jr., and influential newspaper reporter James S. Pike all favored an alliance with the dissident pro-Maine Law Morrill Democrats, who had helped elect Fessenden to the Senate. In contrast, Governor William Crosby, who had been opposed by Morrill Democrats in the legislature, and conservative Whig

Congressman E. Wilder Farley condemned alliance with any Democratic faction. During the spring and summer of 1854 continued Democratic disarray over the governorship, which promised even further defections to the Morrill faction, and passage of the Nebraska Act, which increased some Whigs' desire to combine with them, intensified these Whig divisions.

Anti-Nebraska outrage within Democratic ranks was so widespread that one Democrat called the party "completely *abolitionized.*" Nonetheless, the regular, anti-Morrill faction stubbornly tried to ignore it altogether by nominating the rotund, protemperance Albion K. Parris for governor without any platform. That evasive stance alienated both wet and dry Democrats. The former nominated Shepard Cary for governor on a platform that attacked the Maine Law as unconstitutional but also ignored Nebraska. Dry Democrats once again nominated Anson Morrill on a platform that denounced the Nebraska Act, called for repeal of the Fugitive Slave Act, and enthusiastically praised the Maine Law.[101]

Morrill Democrats' strong antislavery stance caused Free Soilers to forsake a separate gubernatorial candidacy in 1854, endorse Morrill, and call on all anti-Nebraska men to rally behind him. As one Portland Free Soiler wrote Fessenden, "The Whigs of the North" must "give up the idea of reconstructing the old Whig party, and meet all other citizens on equal terms who favor the right," for "it is *impossible* to unite the North strongly on the old Whig basis."[102] Many Maine Whigs agreed. In May the Bangor *Whig and Courier* asserted that the Nebraska outrage was "irresistibly driving together all men, of all parties, who sincerely deprecate human bondage, and who are opposed to the universality of the slave power." Fessenden, Washburn, Pike, and the pro-Compromise conservative Edward Kent, who was appalled by southern Whig support for Nebraska, all urged Whigs to unite behind Morrill's candidacy.[103]

Conservative Whigs, who considered Morrill "highly objectionable to every consistent Whig," nonetheless insisted on holding their own state convention in late June and nominating their own gubernatorial candidate, Isaac Reed, on a platform that condemned repeal of the Missouri Compromise but explicitly refused to cooperate with legislative candidates who refused to support Reed's gubernatorial candidacy. The apoplectic Kent fumed about "tender-toed & impracticable Whigs" who "want everything to be Whig & nothing but old Whigs." As in 1853, the gubernatorial campaign featured a four-way race, and the horrified Fessenden groaned that the anti-Nebraska forces would "be beaten by the utter folly of men calling themselves *Whigs!*" "Nothing but party *depletion* will produce the right state of mind in that class of Whigs," snarled Free Soiler Austin Willey.[104]

Whig stubbornness also prevented cooperation among anti-Nebraska men in several congressional races. In the first, or Portland district, Whigs eschewed a separate nomination. Instead, they joined Morrill Democrats and Free Soilers at an anti-Nebraska meeting to nominate Whig John Wood, a close friend of prohibitionist Neal Dow, on a platform that denounced the Nebraska bill and also called for repeal of the Fugitive Slave Act. Portland's Know Nothing lodge also endorsed both Wood and Morrill, and Wood won easily.[105]

Whig incumbents Samuel Benson and Israel Washburn, Jr., were both assured of renomination, and both sought formation of a broader anti-Nebraska coalition. Even though Benson had won handily in 1852 with Whig votes alone, the straight

Whig convention that renominated him in the fourth district won the support of other anti-Nebraska elements by adopting a platform that condemned the Slave Power conspiracy, called for repeal of the Fugitive Slave Act, and urged abolition in the District of Columbia. Benson, who in 1852 had won by 3,300 votes over his closest competitor in a three-way race, amassed 77 percent of the total in 1854 and crushed his sole Democratic opponent by 8,200 votes.

However much Washburn desired fusion, an exclusively Whig convention renominated him in the fifth district. Nonetheless, Whigs reached out to Morrill Democrats and Free Soilers by proclaiming that repeal of the Missouri Compromise nullified all compromises with the South. Washburn cruised to reelection as a Whig, but he and his constituents were obviously prepared to join an exclusively northern Republican party.

In the other three districts, Whig resistance to abandonment of their party was more substantial. In the second district, after Whigs initially made their own nomination, they and the Free Soilers eventually rallied behind John Perry, the Morrill Democratic candidate and Morrill's closest ally in the state. Although Whig papers outside the district praised its Whigs for "sacrificing old prejudices and party ties," and although C. J. Gilman, the original Whig nominee, unselfishly endorsed Perry, many Whigs from Gilman's home town of Brunswick were so miffed by his forced withdrawal that Perry had to beg Fessenden to try to rally them to his support. Fessenden did so, and Perry easily carried the district.[106]

In the sixth district, Whigs and other anti-Nebraska men utterly failed to cooperate. When an anti-Nebraska meeting listed the names of Whigs it could support for office, indignant Whigs rebuffed those choices and instead nominated Noah Smith, a strong Maine Law proponent, the speaker of the state house of representatives, and the runner-up to Isaac Reed for the straight Whig gubernatorial nomination, for Congress. Another anti-Nebraska convention then rejected Smith and selected a Morrill Democrat.

But the third district, represented by the archetypal antifusion Whig diehard, the conservative E. Wilder Farley, saw the most bitter brawl between regulars and pro-fusion Whigs. Although Farley voted against the Nebraska bill in May, even before Congress adjourned, Ebeneazar Knowlton, a radically antislavery and prohibitionist Baptist minister, announced that he would run as a Free Soiler against him unless Farley pledged himself to seek repeal of the Fugitive Slave Law and abolition in the District, as well as restoration of the Missouri Compromise line. In a public response, Farley defiantly declared repeal of the first and restoration of the last politically impossible, a stance with which virtually all anti-Nebraska southern Whigs agreed. He also refused to have anything to do with a proposed anti-Nebraska nominating convention and announced, "I shall adhere to the Whig party" because it was "sounder than any other" party on slavery and other issues. "I cannot abandon it" since "the best hopes of the country depend upon its continuance as a political organization."[107] When the unfazed anti-Nebraska meeting then nominated Knowlton, a convention of intransigent Whigs nominated Farley, endorsed Isaac Reed for governor, and demanded "the perpetuity of the National Whig organization." Farley had won a four-man race in 1852 with only 36 percent of the vote, so his stubborn independence was suicidal. In September he retained barely three-fifths of his 1852 vote, and he garnered barely a quarter of the total. Knowlton handily won the three-way race.[108]

It requires solomonic wisdom to determine whether the 1854 election inflicted greater damage on the Whig or the Democratic party in Maine. Morrill ran far ahead of his three competitors in the gubernatorial race, and between a fourth and a half of previous Whig voters supported him. The hapless Reed, who retained fewer than half of Crosby's voters from 1852 and 1853, garnered only 15 percent. As in 1852, Whigs won three of the six House seats, but their only victors— Wood, Benson, and Washburn—had fused with or been endorsed by other anti-Nebraska men and run on militantly antislavery platforms that precluded further cooperation with southern Whigs. Where Whigs tried to preserve an independent organization, they were swamped. Farley got only 26 percent of the vote in the third district and Smith only 19 percent in the sixth.[109]

Almost as emphatically as possible, Maine's electorate had repudiated diehard Whigs' call for "the perpetuity of the National Whig organization." The Augusta *Kennebec Journal*, which had explicitly rejected pleas for a new fusion party in 1854, admitted as much. Two months after Maine's polls closed, it pronounced an epitaph for the Whig organization and pledged its allegiance to the new Republican party. The first Republican statewide convention, held on Washington's birthday in 1855, nominated Morrill as the Republican candidate that year. Know Nothings also extended their organization to other parts of Maine in 1855, but they also endorsed Morrill and were absorbed into the emerging Republican party by the time of the September election.[110]

Nonetheless, a few Whig leaders stubbornly refused to give up. In both 1855 and 1856, despite the protests of Kent, Fessenden, and even Noah Smith, "straight out Whigs," who refused to agree with the party's majority "that the old Whig organization is dead & was sundered by Southern Whigs on the Nebraska bill," held rump state conventions and ran separate gubernatorial candidates who, notably, explicitly condemned Know Nothingism and nativism as well as the new Republican party. Whiggery had essentially become a refuge for men who completely rejected the new political order. In 1855 their candidate drew 11,000 votes, 9.6 percent of the total and about two-fifths of the Whigs who had supported Winfield Scott in 1852. By September 1856 this stubborn residue shrank to 6,600 men, or 5.5 percent of the cast vote.[111]

If most Maine Whigs emphatically rejected the plea for "the perpetuity of the National Whig organization," New Jersey's far more moderate Whigs just as emphatically hoped to extend its existence. Free Soilers were a negligible presence in New Jersey, and Whigs could therefore eschew inflammatory antisouthern rhetoric when focusing congressional campaigns against Nebraska.[112] Since pro-Nebraska Democrats represented four of the five House districts contested that year, Whigs blamed the Democratic party, not the South, for wantonly violating intersectional comity. Although prohibitionism and nativism were openly aired issues in the 1853 election, nativists exerted influence in only two of five congressional districts, and there they served as allies rather than competitors to Whig candidates.

Whigs ran their own candidates in four of the five congressional districts and all four won, thereby reversing the Whig/Democratic ratio of the two preceding congressional elections. Two were nominated by straight Whig conventions—the lone Whig incumbent, Alexander C. M. Pennington, in the fifth district and Dr. George Robbins in the second, where the Whig convention declared that they "firmly adhere to the Whig organization" and needed no coalition with other anti-Nebraska men. James Bishop, the Whig victor in the third district, was nominated on the same day by separate Whig and anti-Nebraska conventions, but Know Nothings may have been as instrumental to his triumph as anti-Nebraska Democrats. Only after the votes were in did a Know Nothing newspaper reveal that Bishop was a member of the order. His Democratic opponent, incumbent Samuel Lilly, had depended on immigrant support, it crowed, whereas Bishop "had never occupied any other than the American platform" and therefore received "the whole American vote."[113]

The two other races especially underlined Whigs' commitment to the continuation of the Whig party as a national organization. The only district Whigs did not carry, the heavily Democratic fourth, had been carried in 1852 by pro-Nebraska incumbent George Vail with three-fifths of the vote. There Whigs ran no candidate of their own and instead backed an independent anti-Nebraska Democrat. Yet even there, where Whigs apparently had no chance of winning, that support came only grudgingly. The Whig Newark *Daily Advertiser*, commenting from outside the district, hoped "the Whig party there" would not "compromise its own integrity" by endorsing the anti-Nebraska Democrat. A few days later, a Whig convention at Morristown did so on the grounds that "good men" must "forego their party predilections and make common cause" with others against "those entrusted with power" who, "in an act of reckless legislation," threatened "the Constitution, Justice, Liberty, and Union." The fourth district's Whigs, in sum, did not rail against slavery, southern treachery, or Slave Power aggressions, as did other northern Whigs. Instead, they cited Democratic recklessness to justify their temporary digression from the Whig fold, and to emphasize their antipathy toward a permanent new northern party, they simultaneously vowed their allegiance to the national Whig party.[114]

A Whig carried the first district, which encompassed the state's six southernmost counties, but it witnessed the state's most confused race. As would be the case well into the twentieth century, zealous prohibitionists were proportionately most numerous in these southern counties, and when none of the other parties addressed that issue in the congressional contest, they ran their own man. The district also harbored a small Native American party that, unlike the obsessively secret Know Nothings, operated publicly. Seeking to beat Whigs to the punch in exploiting anti-Nebraska sentiment, it nominated a young Whig named Isaiah Clawson as the Native American candidate for Congress on an anti-Nebraska platform. Clawson would declare himself a Know Nothing by the time the Thirty-Fourth Congress assembled, but whether he was a member in 1854 is unknown.

Native Americans' preemptive strike caught the Whigs, who expected to run their own man, completely off guard. The state's flagship Whig paper, the Trenton *State Gazette*, urged the district's Whigs to rally behind Clawson since he had "always heretofore . . . been a consistent Whig," but local Whig papers complained that "endorsement of the Native candidate would be a suicidal measure, utterly destructive of our party organization." Only after "warm discussion," the reading of numerous testimonials to Clawson's Whig pedigree, and the adoption of a platform that lauded the national Whig party as "the only true conservative party" did a district Whig convention endorse Clawson. Again, what is striking is the total absence of the South-bashing sectional rancor voiced by Whigs farther north and the continued fealty to the national Whig party as a bisectional alliance of Northerners and Southerners.[115]

Know Nothings who attended the Whig convention possibly provided Clawson's winning edge among Whig delegates. Certainly Clawson's Democratic opponent denounced him as a Know Nothing and tried to focus the race on the evils of Know Nothingism to divert attention from Nebraska. Clawson carried the normally Democratic district, but with only a 43 percent plurality since the independent prohibition candidate siphoned off over a fourth of the voters, including a healthy minority of the Whigs. Pro-Nebraska Democrats suffered a dramatic repudiation. They lost almost two-fifths of their 1852 supporters, and their share of the total plummeted to 30 percent.[116]

The electorate's determination to punish Democrats for the Nebraska Act allowed New Jersey's Whigs to stage an impressive comeback in congressional races without repudiating their external ties to southern Whig allies. Nonetheless, the party did not reattain its previous vigor, for it suffered the same internal erosion that occurred elsewhere in the North over nativism and prohibition. Whigs were forced to back the candidate originally chosen by Native Americans in the first district, and even then they lost votes to a separate temperance candidate. Know Nothings and independent prohibitionists particularly damaged the major parties in the legislative races. When the returns were counted, insurgent minor party candidates had elected twenty-two members of the lower house compared to eighteen Whigs and twenty regular Democrats, and at least fifteen of those insurgents had Know Nothing support. Together with Know Nothings' stunning showing in neighboring Pennsylvania and New York, this nativist surge within New Jersey convinced the state's Whig editors who hoped to reunite the national Whig party in 1856 behind a southern anti-Nebraska Whig presidential candidate that their candidate must also be a Know Nothing.[117]

VIII

The 1854 election results from the five southern and ten free states discussed above had ambiguous implications for the Whig party's future. Aside from Arkansas, South Carolina, and Delaware, where Whigs folded themselves into the American party, southern Whigs appeared to be flourishing. Nonetheless, the heartbreaking losses in North Carolina and Florida cost Whigs three Senate seats they could ill afford to lose given the party's weakness in the Senate already. At the same time, Whig candidates for the House of Representatives ran far more successfully than they had in 1852. Whigs had won only twenty-four of seventy-seven House seats from these fifteen states in 1852; in 1854, Whigs captured forty-three of those seats. Of thirty-seven Whig victors from the free states, however, only nine won as straight Whigs, and four of those from Vermont and Maine took such strident antislavery stands that Free Soilers willingly supported them. In contrast, twenty-one of the victors won on Republican, People's, or fusion tickets, and together with Democrats and Free Soilers who triumphed on such tickets, thirty-five congressmen with some kind of anti-Nebraska coalition label had been elected. Based on these results, that is, new party men seemed to have almost as good a chance as Whigs to control the next House, to say nothing of the Senate, where the election of Durkee, Harlan, and Trumbull gave the incipient Republican party momentum.

Based on returns from these fifteen states, Know Nothings posed almost as serious a challenge to Whigs' traditional role as the major anti-Democratic party. Of the northern Whig congressional winners, at least twenty were, or had been endorsed by, Know Nothings, and the addition of Missouri's two Whig Know Nothings brought the total to twenty-two. Counting Democrats with Know Nothing backing as well as Delaware's Elisha Cullen, indeed, the total number of nativist representatives elected by the fourteen of these states that held congressional elections was thirty-one, compared to forty-three Whig winners.[118]

This assessment of the Know Nothing threat to Whiggery, however, is incomplete. It omits the three remaining northern states with 1854 elections—Massachusetts, New York, and Pennsylvania. Altogether the ten free states previously discussed, including Ohio, Indiana, and Illinois, possessed a combined total of sixty-six House seats and seventy-six electoral votes. By themselves, Massachusetts, New York, and Pennsylvania were eligible for sixty-nine seats in the House and would cast seventy-five electoral votes. Thus it was the course of events in these three states that Whigs elsewhere, especially in the South, watched most closely for clues to the Whig party's fate. In August, indeed, Tennessee Senator John Bell explicitly said that the course and fate of Whigs in those three states and Ohio would "decide whether we [southern Whigs] can unite with them or not."[119]

Ohio's Whigs clearly disappointed Bell's hopes by fusing with Free Soilers, and Whigs in Pennsylvania and New York would do so by reaching out for Free Soil support to guarantee Whig victory. Their militantly antislavery and anti-southern stand jeopardized future cooperation with Southerners, but even it failed to prevent fatal internal erosion of Whig strength. Know Nothings, not incipient Republican parties, made lethal incursions into the ranks of Pennsylvania, New York, and Massachusetts Whiggery that dashed Whigs' hopes of riding the anti-Nebraska issue back to power and that doomed the future viability of the Whig party as an independent political force in the North. Results from those three states formed the critical turning point that drove the great majority of Whigs who had hoped to preserve the Whig party into a frantic search for new political homes. Those three states' elections in 1854 effectively demolished the Whig party as a competitive organization.

Chapter 24

"Confusion Worse Confounded"

"THE, SO-CALLED, Whig Convention in this State surrendered at discretion to the abolitionists," Louisiana's Charles M. Conrad, Millard Fillmore's secretary of war, railed to the ex-president after reading newspaper accounts of the proceedings while on a business trip to New York City in September 1854. Whigs' platform amounted "to a declaration of perpetual warfare against the South"; therefore, it was "impossible for Southern Whigs to cooperate with the authors & abetters of these measures." New York's Whigs, like those in Vermont and Massachusetts, Conrad raged, aimed at "a virtual dissolution of the Whig party" that would result in "a new arrangement of parties" and in a new northern "organization based on merely sectional issues." To avert that catastrophe and retain southern Whig support in 1856, Fillmore must repudiate New York Whigs' actions and help "to form a new national party."[1]

Other Southerners also viewed northern Whigs' virulently antisouthern stance in 1854 as lethal to the continued "nationality of the Whig party." "What are we to do with our Northern allies?" George S. Bryan asked Fillmore's close advisor John P. Kennedy in August. Although Bryan recognized that northern Whigs' antislavery bluster was only "political & for local power," he still wondered, "Can we of the South maintain brotherly relations with men whose power is based on sectional association against *our section*?"[2]

Both Conrad and Bryan correctly perceived the fatal impact that northern Whigs' campaigns during 1854 had on southern Whigs' allegiance to their old party. Yet Bryan understood northern Whigs' motives better than did Conrad. Outside of Wisconsin, Michigan, and perhaps Maine and Vermont, most northern Whigs, even in Indiana and Ohio, viewed the campaigns of 1854 as sui generis. They did not seek the creation of a permanent new northern party "based on merely sectional issues"—at least not in 1854. Instead they hoped to resurrect disintegrating northern Whig organizations that year by exploiting anti-Nebraska, anti-slavery-extension sentiment to defeat Democrats. Once they revivified the northern Whig party with those anticipated victories, they expected to rebuild bridges to southern Whig allies so the two sectional wings could rally again for the next presidential election.

Because Bryan, unlike Conrad, appreciated Know Nothings' surging power, he also understood why the 1854 results from Pennsylvania, Massachusetts, and New York, the three northern states that most decisively influenced Whigs' calculations for the future, forever dashed those hopes. Nativism and prohibitionism produced an earthquake that confounded Whig expectations of a comeback on the Nebraska issue, transformed the political landscape, and caused "the dissolution of the Whig party" in all three states. Aftershocks from it in 1855 shaped New England's spring elections, changed northern Whigs' calculations elsewhere, and sent Whigs across the South scurrying to new political homes. Although Conrad was right that northern Whigs' extreme antisouthern rhetoric would permanently alienate southern Whigs, Know Nothings' stunning strength in Massachusetts, New York, and Pennsylvania in 1854, not the emergence of Republican parties that year, propelled "the new arrangement of parties" that Conrad feared.

I

Anti-Catholicism and nativism had been powerful political forces in Pennsylvania long before 1854. The Catholic James Campbell's appointment as postmaster general intensified the growing animosity between Protestant and Catholic Democrats, and in early 1854 Democratic state legislators introduced bills to divide the public school fund with Catholics, thereby fueling Protestant charges of a Democratic-aided papal assault against republican institutions. Meanwhile, thousands of zealous Methodists and Presbyterians in Pennsylvania were alienated by Whigs' courtship of the Catholic vote in 1852. To make amends, Whig papers and politicos in 1854 sharply reversed course to side emphatically with Protestants against Catholics. In Philadelphia, the Whig press cheered the Whig/Know Nothing Robert Conrad's election as mayor in June as an anti-Catholic triumph. Across the state, the Pittsburgh *Gazette*, the most influential Whig sheet in western Pennsylvania, proudly boasted by March and April that "the Whig party always was and is, the standard bearer of Protestantism and Free Soilism," while "the papers and leaders of [the Democratic] party have always been ready to yield to the wishes and demands of Popery." The Whig state platform adopted in March not only included the traditional demand for a protective tariff and condemned the as yet unpassed Nebraska bill as "a deliberate breach of plighted faith" and "a high-handed attempt to force slavery into a territory now free from it by law." It also declared that universal education (i.e., the teaching of Catholics in public, not parochial, schools) and religious liberty should be the goals of all state laws. And later, Whigs explicitly accused Governor William Bigler, whom Democrats renominated, of favoring the division of the public school fund demanded by the Catholic clergy.[3]

Whig strategists, in short, obviously recognized the powerful anti-Catholic currents in the state. Many Whig politicos therefore struck a Faustian bargain with Know Nothings when the order burgeoned across the state during the first half of 1854. Others like Pittsburgh's William Larimer, however, dazzled by the apparent potency of the anti-Nebraska issue, refused to sell their souls to nativism. In retaliation against that defiance, Know Nothings prevented Pennsylvania's Whigs from winning a revitalizing party victory.[4]

The Nebraska bill, which Democratic Senator Richard Brodhead and eleven of Pennsylvania's sixteen House Democrats supported, outraged both Whigs and Free Soilers, who together captured 48.6 percent of Pennsylvania's vote in 1852, *and* many Democrats, especially in northern counties along the New York border. When the March Democratic state convention totally ignored it, indignant anti-Nebraska Democrats vowed that they would never support Bigler or anyone else who did not openly condemn the measure. When Bigler, an archetypal trimmer, said nothing about Nebraska even after the Democratic state committee endorsed the law that summer, defection or abstention by anti-Nebraska Democrats seemed certain.[5]

Bigler's straddle on Nebraska explains why Whigs salivated at the prospect of running anti-Nebraska campaigns against him and other Democratic candidates. Widely reviled by dissident Democrats, Bigler seemed especially vulnerable in 1854, even without the Nebraska issue. He had infuriated Democratic politicos across the state with unpopular local appointments. He alienated antiprohibition Democrats by allowing a referendum on that subject to be placed on the ballot in October, and he then offended dries by refusing to commit himself to sign a Maine Law should the referendum authorize one.[6] He angered Germans by failing to veto a bill that required beer-hall owners to pay the same license fees required of taverns that sold hard liquor. Later, when he reversed himself and denounced that law, he enhanced his reputation for flip-flopping. His frequent vetoes of bank incorporation bills in the spring antagonized residents of communities that sought additional banking facilities. Yet his failure to veto a bill that allowed the sale of the Pennsylvania Mainline Canal to the Pennsylvania Railroad offended residents along the public works. Finally, his appointment of James Campbell as state attorney general in 1852, suspicion that he had helped secure Campbell's place in Pierce's cabinet, and his apparent sympathy for Catholic attempts to divide the public school fund earned him execration from the state's most rabidly anti-Catholic Democrats, to say nothing of Protestant Whigs.[7]

Just as anti-Nebraska Whig congressional candidates differed sharply from Democratic incumbents who had voted for that measure, Whig gubernatorial candidate James Pollock presented a clear contrast to Bigler on all of these matters except sale of the unprofitable Main Line Canal.[8] A Scots-Irish Presbyterian with a puritanical streak, Pollock was far more acceptable to anti-Catholics than Bigler, and during the campaign he vowed to defend the public school fund from Catholic assaults. He won the support of prohibitionists, if not outright endorsement from the state temperance association, by pledging to sign "every measure of moral or political reform" the legislature passed that did not violate the state constitution. His embrace of Whigs' anti-Nebraska platform, finally, highlighted Bigler's waffling on the slavery extension issue.[9]

During the early spring, therefore, Whigs expressed confidence about capturing the rich booty at stake in October: seats on the supreme court and canal commission as well as the governorship; the twenty-five congressional seats; and the new state legislature, which would select a successor to Whig Senator James Cooper. Convinced like his fellow Pittsburgher Larimer that all antislavery men would rally behind Pollock, D. N. White, editor of the Pittsburgh *Gazette*, boasted on March 24 that "the Whig party was never stronger" and predicted that in October it would "give evidence of vitality never possessed by it before." The Harrisburg

Telegraph agreed that Whigs had "a platform broad enough to admit every Whig, every friend of freedom, and every American."[10]

After March, however, Whig confidence was rudely jolted. In part because the Whig platform, passed when most Northerners still expected the House to kill the Nebraska bill, failed to demand its repeal, Free Soilers and anti-Nebraska Democrats spurned Pollock and other Whig candidates. Gamaliel Bailey of the Free Soil Washington *National Era* sneered that "Pennsylvania Whiggery is simply old fogeyism" and tried to get Free Soilers to nominate David Wilmot in order to drive Pollock from the field and create a fusion anti-Nebraska coalition.[11]

Free Soilers' disdain for Pollock and the widely rumored Wilmot candidacy panicked some Whigs, especially the Pittsburgh *Daily Gazette*'s editors, White and Russell Errett, who had counted on rallying Free Soilers behind the Whig ticket. In what proved to be a huge mistake, they therefore sought to head off a Free Soil nomination by dropping all references to anti-Catholicism and prohibitionism from the paper's editorial columns and exclusively stressing Whigs' opposition to slavery and slavery extension. They pleaded with Free Soilers in April not to nominate a separate candidate, especially Wilmot, behind whom Whigs would never unite since Wilmot opposed protective tariffs. "We are not so wedded to the Whig organization or name as to refuse to enter any better organization for the purpose of resisting the encroachments of slavery," the *Gazette* declared. But "the Whig party of Pennsylvania as now organized, is a large, powerful and tolerably well disciplined party." Its March platform had purposely avoided the divisive prohibition and nativist questions to focus on two issues that united Whigs and Free Soilers—sale of the public works and opposition to the Nebraska bill. "What is to be gained, then, by relinquishing this organization, and accepting an independent candidate?"[12]

Wilmot in fact had no interest in breaking from the Democratic party again, but in late May, Free Soilers nominated the little-known David Potts for governor. His selection satisfied neither national Free Soil leaders hoping to build a new anti-Nebraska coalition nor Whigs. Worried that the obscure Potts would split Pennsylvania's anti-Nebraska voters, Bailey reluctantly concluded that Pollock had the best chance of unifying them. Sill angry that the Whigs' March platform was confined to a condemnation of the Nebraska bill, he urged pro-fusion Whig newspaperman James S. Pike to get Pollock to write "a stiff antislavery letter" that repudiated all compromises with slavery, called for repeal of the Fugitive Slave Act, and sought to "denationalize slavery, by excluding it from every inch of soil within Federal jurisdiction."[13]

Whether Pike contacted Pollock is unknown, but Pollock wrote a public letter in July that called for restoration of the Missouri Compromise line and declared that Congress had no authority to establish slavery in any territory. Other Whigs also moved vigorously to appease Free Soilers. Immediately after the Free Soilers' May state convention, Pittsburgh's White asserted that "we are willing to make any reasonable sacrifice of party ties to a great and undying principle." In June, he and Errett helped rig the Allegheny County Whig convention to make that sacrifice. It put a Free Soiler on the state legislative ticket and adopted radical antislavery resolutions.[14]

Condemning the effort to "propagate, confirm, and diffuse the national sin and shame" of slavery, that platform vowed to oppose its further extension, the admission of more slave states, and any further compromises with the South. "For the future the South must take care of itself—take care of its peculiar property; supply its own bloodhounds and doughfaces," Allegheny County's Whigs warned. Lest this defiant language prove insufficient, Whigs added a plank that Gamaliel Bailey himself could have written and that Errett, a confidant of Bailey, probably did write: "That in view of the dangers of the crisis—a crisis overriding all former party distinctions—we hereby pledge ourselves to the camp of Freedom—we inscribe Free Men to Free Labor and Free Lands upon our banner, and enlist for the whole war."[15] This platform and the Whig state committee's July address, which took far more strident antisouthern ground than the March state platform, trumpeted White, were "broad enough to secure the cooperation of every Anti-Slavery man in the State." Coupled with Pollock's letters, they were at least enough to cause a Free Soil meeting in August to withdraw Potts and endorse Pollock.[16]

By essentially placing all their eggs in the antislavery basket, Pennsylvania's Whigs helped alienate Southerners from the party. But they hardly solved all their problems within Pennsylvania. That exclusive emphasis utterly ignored the divisive but increasingly salient prohibition question. That evasive stance, like the waffle of Whigs and Democrats in the 1854 legislative session on the Maine Law, left cold water men icy. Although most dries ultimately backed the moralistic Pollock for governor, prohibitionists ran independent Maine Law legislative tickets against regular Whig candidates in Erie, York, and Philadelphia counties. Elsewhere they backed independent Know Nothing legislative candidates against Whigs.[17]

Independent anti-Whig Know Nothing tickets posed the biggest threat to Whig control of the legislature, and Know Nothings menaced Whig statewide and congressional candidates as well. During the spring, at exactly the time some Whig newspapers ceased to attack Catholics and boasted that the party was eschewing nativistic attacks on immigrants in order to focus on the Nebraska issue, Know Nothing lodges mushroomed across the state. That spring Know Nothings won a number of local elections, often defeating regular Whig candidates, and in June, Know Nothing-backed Whig candidates scored decisive victories in Philadelphia's municipal elections. Reporting to James Buchanan, now minister to England, about the "overwhelming majorities" Know Nothings won in the spring, one Lancaster Democrat whinged, "Politicians are dumbfounded—editors are completely smashed into the middle of chaos, and the people stand amazed." "The Old Whig Party is undoubtedly annihilated," he added. If Bigler were defeated, "it will not be a *Whig* victory."[18]

That prediction proved accurate. As elsewhere, Know Nothings had the potential to help Whig candidates against Democrats in Pennsylvania, and some Whig politicos rushed to join the order after its impressive showing in the spring. In Philadelphia, the Whig Conrad obviously did so before his election as mayor. By early June, Andrew Curtin, the state Whig chairman and a future Republican governor, had also joined, and he immediately contacted other Know Nothings about supporting the entire Whig state ticket. After Conrad's victory, Pollock himself traveled to Philadelphia, where Conrad arranged for his induction into the order. Nothing, however, shows how profoundly Know Nothingism altered the political calculus than the behavior of William Larimer, who in late March wrote Pollock that "the Whig party of the North" had never been stronger since Democratic actions made "her a *unit*" and rendered "her *invincible*." Three months later, in June, Larimer became a Know Nothing.[19]

Some Whig candidates, in short, benefited from the order's support, but Know Nothingism still proved extraordinarily damaging to Pennsylvania's Whig party. For one thing, in Pennsylvania, Know Nothings did not have to pick their candidates from only the Whig and Democratic tickets. The independent Native American party also fielded candidates, and if Know Nothings backed them, Whigs would be denied anti-Democratic votes. For another, while anti-Catholicism primarily motivated Pennsylvania's Know Nothings, the order's nativism prevented it from supporting any foreign-born Whig candidates while alienating Protestant immigrants, who had previously voted Whig, from any Whig candidates suspected of being Know Nothings. Most important, many of the numerous former Antimasons among Pennsylvania's Whigs, men who still despised all secret organizations, furiously opposed the Know Nothings even though they shared their animosity toward Catholics. "The old antimasons are rising strong in opposition to Know Nothingism," reported a Democrat from Somerset, and White of the Pittsburgh *Daily Gazette*, himself an old Antimason, waged open warfare against the secret order as "unwise, dangerous, and Anti-American" from July 1854 on.[20]

Whigs, in sum, divided sharply in their reaction to Know Nothingism. Consequently, Know Nothings rivaled Whigs almost as often as they helped them in races from statewide offices down to county clerkships. In late August local Know Nothing lodges began to choose from among the three parties' candidates for governor, supreme court justice, and canal commissioner. Those selections were confirmed at a meeting of the Know Nothing state council in October. The Whig Pollock, who had joined the order, rather than the Native American Benjamin R. Bradford, got the Know Nothing nod for governor, but in the supreme court race, Know Nothings endorsed the Native American Thomas H. Baird rather than the Whig candidate, thereby virtually ensuring reelection of Democratic incumbent Jeremiah S. Black. For canal commissioner, Know Nothings chose the pro-Nebraska Democrat Henry S. Mott, a member of the order, and rejected Whig George S. Darsie, a Presbyterian lawyer and former state senator from Allegheny County, because Darsie was born in Scotland. Most Pennsylvania Know Nothings undoubtedly opposed the Nebraska Act, as they did elsewhere in the North, but Mott's endorsement emphatically shows that one's stand on Nebraska was largely irrelevant to Know Nothings. It also shows that nativistic suspicion of all foreigners, not simply anti-Catholicism, impelled the order. If a Scottish Presbyterian could be blackballed by the fraternity, no foreigner, no matter how anti-Catholic, was safe.[21]

Pollock was the only triumphant Whig candidate for statewide office. He defeated Bigler by over 35,000 votes, and his 55 percent majority in a three-way race was the best showing by any Whig, including Harrison and Taylor, in the state's history. As promised, Free Soilers, who with very few exceptions shunned the Know Nothings, backed him, but Know Nothings contributed well over half of his total, including virtually all of the previous Democratic voters who supported him. If Pollock won as a Whig, moreover, he was clearly ready to abandon the party. Two weeks after his victory, he wrote Delaware's Clayton and agreed with him about the desirability of launching a new American party. "The old parties, as National parties, are broken up & their power gone," concurred Pollock. "We have the material for a 'liberal, tolerant, highminded, and truly American party' and it will be used."[22]

What Know Nothings gave with one hand they took with the other. In the race for canal commissioner the Democratic Know Nothing Henry Mott defeated the hapless Whig Darsie, 274,074 to 83,331, compared to Pollock's 204,008 to 167,001 victory over Bigler. That approximately 120,000 Know Nothings accounted for the difference became clear in the state supreme court balloting, the one race where Know Nothings backed the Native Americans rather than a major party candidate. Democratic incumbent Black won with 167,010 votes (45.6 percent), virtually the same number as Bigler drew. But the Know Nothing-backed Native American Baird ran second with 120,576 (32.9 percent), while the Whig candidate, now abandoned by Whigs who had joined the order, drew only 78,571 (21.5 percent). In sum, loyal Whigs had been reduced to about 80,000 voters, approximately 23 percent of the active electorate and less than 15 percent of the state's potential electorate. Of Whigs who voted for Winfield Scott in 1852, half remained in the party column, almost a third defected to the Know Nothings, and the remainder did not vote. Because Democratic defectors to the Know Nothing column almost equaled the number of Whigs in the order and because the Know Nothings dramatically outrecruited Whigs among previous nonvoters, the Know Nothings had replaced the Whigs as the major opponent of Pennsylvania's Democrats by October 1854.[23]

Know Nothings also wreaked havoc on Whigs in congressional races. In four of the state's twenty-five House districts—the eighth, fourteenth, fifteenth, and sixteenth—Whigs fielded no candidates against the dominant Democrats. In three of those districts Know Nothings threw their support to Independent Anti-Nebraska Democratic candidates, thereby seizing control of the anti-Democratic opposition, and two of those Democratic Know Nothings, J. J. Pearce and Lemuel Todd, triumphed. Everywhere else Whigs ran candidates, but Know Nothings still caused trouble. In the southeastern sixth district, which Whigs had carried handily since 1846, Know Nothings backed anti-Nebraska Democrat John Hickman against veteran Whig state legislator John Broomall and thus took that seat from the Whigs. In the northwestern and heavily Democratic twenty-fourth district, Know Nothings also backed the regular Democratic nominee, an anti-Nebraska man named David Barclay, against a Whig named Arthurs. Arthurs drew a pitiful 25 percent of the vote compared to 34 percent won by his Whig predecessor in 1852, and he ran an astonishing 5,120 votes behind the Know Nothing-backed Pollock in his district. In the fourth district, one of four in Philadelphia, Know Nothings helped elect Jacob Broom, the Native American candidate who had been that party's 1852 presidential nominee, over the Whig John Lambert and a pro-Nebraska Democrat. Broom opposed the Nebraska Act during his campaign, but unlike virtually every northern Whig congressional candidate in 1854, he flatly announced that if elected he would *not* support its repeal unless Southerners agreed to it, thus illustrating once again that how one stood on the slavery issue was *not* what mattered most to Know Nothings.[24]

In at least three other districts—the second in Philadelphia, the ninth in Lancaster, and the eighteenth, composed of Somerset and three other counties—Know Nothings split the Whig vote by backing one Whig candidate against another.[25]

Elsewhere, at least ten "regular" Whig candidates, including Henry Fuller, James Cooper's close ally, who became the major Know Nothing candidate for speaker of the House when the Thirty-Fourth Congress met, secretly joined the order before nomination, between nomination and the election, or after the election and thus had at best divided loyalties to the Whig party.[26] Altogether, fifteen Whigs were elected to Congress in 1854, compared to nine in 1852, but twelve (80 percent) of those men were or would become Know Nothings. Combined with the victorious Barclay, Hickman, Broom, Pearce, and Todd, members of the order filled seventeen of Pennsylvania's twenty-five seats, all but four of those won by anti-Nebraska men.

Know Nothings' challenge to Whigs was equally extensive in state legislative races, where Whigs already confronted independent temperance tickets. Across the state, Know Nothings ran their own independent tickets against regular Whig slates, chose slates from all of the existing parties that included Democrats and Native Americans rather than Whigs, or usurped Whigs' opposition role altogether. One or more Democrats were always included on these tickets to demonstrate their independence from Whiggery, yet one-time Whig voters supported them in droves. As one astonished Democrat reported to Simon Cameron after the election from northwestern Venango County, "We are whipt in everything, a most unaccountable victory by the 'Know Nothings.' " "Know Nothingism has knocked the spots off us here," echoed another bewildered Democrat from central Huntingdon County. "The Whigs on the day of the election . . . disbanded & went over in a body" to the Know Nothings.[27]

Three localities, each of which had traditionally been a Whig stronghold—Philadelphia, Lancaster, and Pittsburgh—illustrate the devastation Know Nothingism inflicted on Whiggery. One can begin with Lancaster, some sixty miles west of Philadelphia in the southeastern portion of the state. In late spring, Lancaster's county (and district) Whig convention renominated Congressman Isaac Heister as well as a full Whig ticket for the legislature and local offices. Although Heister, like all northern Whig congressmen, voted against the Nebraska bill, he represented the conservative faction of the Lancaster Whig organization, which had secured his nomination in 1852 explicitly to unseat his antislavery Whig predecessor, Thaddeus Stevens. In retaliation, Stevens and many members of his Whig faction joined the Know Nothings in the summer of 1854. The order, probably at Stevens' instigation, ran another Whig, Anthony E. Roberts, a crony of ex-Governor William F. Johnston, who had served as United States marshal in Philadelphia under Taylor and Fillmore, as the Know Nothing candidate against Heister and his Democratic opponent. Nominated first as an Independent Whig by a rump Whig convention of the Stevens wing and then later by a public Know Nothing meeting, Roberts won the three-way race with 6,561 votes, 40.5 percent of the total. Heister trailed with 5,371 (33.2 percent), 3,470 fewer votes than he had received in 1852, when he racked up almost 58 percent of the total.

In Lancaster's state legislative races, Democrats highjacked seats Whigs would have won by joining the Know Nothing order. Led by a dissident Democrat named Reah Frazer, who was publishing articles against Bigler in the local *Know Nothing Register* by July, three Frazer Democrats won slots on an independent Know Nothing ticket along with two Stevens Whigs. That ticket defeated the regular Whig slate in October. Know Nothings' sweep in Lancaster, moaned one Democrat, "can be explained only by the hostility to foreigners and Catholics," but the revived impetus that the Nebraska Act gave Thaddeus Stevens' antislavery wing of the local Whig party surely contributed to it.[28]

Pittsburgh's Know Nothings did not defeat the regular Whig congressional candidate, David Ritchie. They coopted him instead by inducting him into the order after his June nomination by the convention D. N. White had rigged to promote fusion with the Free Soilers, not the Know Nothings. By the fall Ritchie's membership, like Pollock's, was widely known. Know Nothings helped Ritchie cruise to a much more imposing victory in 1854 than he had won in 1852.[29] In other races, however, nativists decimated the Whig party, whose chief editorial spokesman, White, virulently denounced them. Aside from Pollock and Ritchie, there were ten other men on the Whig ticket in Pittsburgh. Of these only two Whig assembly candidates, both of whom were Know Nothings, triumphed.[30] Three Democrats, two of whom were pro-Nebraska, and five Native Americans carried the county, and all of them, like the four victorious Whigs, were Know Nothings.[31]

Because a United States Senate seat was at stake, state legislative races were especially significant and illuminating. Whigs had gone all out to win those races by adopting a radical antisouthern, antislavery platform at their June convention and by placing a Free Soiler on their assembly ticket. He ran dead last among the five Whig assembly candidates. Democratic Know Nothings won the senate seat and one assembly seat. C. S. Eyster and D. L. Smith, the two victorious Native American assembly candidates, were both dissident Whigs who had been denied nomination by the Whig convention in June and who joined the order and the Native American party explicitly to advance their careers and to punish the Whig party.[32]

J. Heron Foster of the Pittsburgh *Dispatch*, the city's leading Know Nothing editor, attributed Know Nothings' sweep to popular anger at the political power of foreigners and Catholics, and Democrats concurred that "the momentary supremacy of bigotry and prejudice" and "the power of political frenzy" had produced the result. D. N. White and those Whigs who sought to use the anti-Nebraska issue first to resurrect Whiggery and then to build a new northern party were furious. Convinced that Know Nothings had diverted and diluted the anti-Nebraska vote and that they could now control any Whig meeting, White called for his old party's utter dissolution. No Whig convention must meet or any Whig nomination be attempted, he declared, until the Know Nothing blight was eradicated. Admitting that this task required cooperation with the Democratic enemy, he and like-minded Whigs then persuaded incumbent Whig Mayor Ferdinand Volz, who had won election rather easily in January 1854, to run as a Whig-Democratic fusion candidate in January 1855 against the Know Nothing candidate, who had the backing of the city's other Whig paper. Volz triumphed, but the Know Nothing vote had increased by 55 percent since October as virtually all native-born Whig voters, except those who had been Antimasons, shifted to the Know Nothing column.[33]

Whig disintegration continued later in 1855. In the fall elections Whigs nominated no local or state candidates of their own. Instead, some Whigs voted Democratic to preserve January's anti-Know Nothing coalition, most voted Know Nothing, and still others, led by White and the county Whig committee, futilely tried to transfer the Whig vote to the new Republican party. Volz ran for mayor again as a Whig in January 1856, but with less than half of his 1854 vote, he lost badly. For all intents and purposes the Pittsburgh Whig organization had been destroyed by January 1855. The bright hopes raised by the Nebraska Act in the spring of 1854 had been dashed.[34]

Philadelphia's population dwarfed both Pittsburgh's and Lancaster's, and the city's Whig organization began to unravel as soon as Robert Conrad won the mayoral election in June 1854. Since Conrad was the regular Whig nominee, Whig politicos who had not joined the Know Nothings were shocked by his proscription of everyone but members of the order from the offices at his command. "The consequence is, *real fright and disgust* on the part of the Whigs," one Democrat reported in mid-July, and he subsequently repeated that "Know Nothingism has broken up the Whig organization," that "the *old Whig* managers are outsiders completely in the new order of things and they will not surrender power quietly," and that "thousands of the *old line* Whigs are in *open rebellion*."[35]

Rivalry between Whigs and Know Nothings wrecked Whigs in Philadelphia's congressional and state legislative races, where Maine Law tickets joined American Union (Know Nothing) tickets in competing with Whig and Democratic slates. As noted above, in Philadelphia's fourth congressional district, Know Nothings helped elect Native American Jacob Broom over the Whig nominee. In the first and third districts, in contrast, Know Nothings backed the regular Whig nominees, Edward Joy Morris and William Millward, against pro-Nebraska Democrats. It was in the second district that bloodletting between Know Nothings and Whigs was most copious.

The second was the only Philadelphia district represented by a Whig during the Thirty-Third Congress, and three-term incumbent Joseph R. Chandler was one of the party's most respected men. A moderate on the slavery issue, he had voted against the Nebraska Act and been a key player, after it passed, in attempting to draft an anti-Nebraska statement that all Whigs could support. Yet Chandler committed an unpardonable sin so far as Know Nothings were concerned; he had recently converted to the Roman Catholic faith. Thus Know Nothings infiltrated the Whigs' district convention and threw its nomination to Job R. Tyson instead of Chandler.[36] Regular Whigs were livid. Declaring that the "present nominees of the Whig party, or so-called Whig party, are very objectionable to a large number of Whigs," a rump convention of outsiders nominated Chandler as an Independent Whig for Congress, as well as their own slate for the legislature. Tyson and the other Know Nothing/Whigs won, but Whiggery was shattered. Chandler had triumphed with approximately 6,600 votes in 1852, 62.4 percent of the total. In 1854, Chandler garnered fewer than 1,200 votes (12 percent), while Tyson got 5,655 (55 percent). Know Nothings had displaced Whigs there, as elsewhere. As one Democrat moaned, "The tornado has been so stunning and overwhelming."[37]

Attempts to elect a new United States senator when the legislature met in January 1855 only punctuated the demise of Pennsylvania Whiggery. There is no need to detail the legislature's tribulations other than to say that when an attempt was made to hold a straight Whig caucus, only eight men appeared, in contrast to the ninety-one who attended a Know Nothing meeting. The primary contenders for the Senate seat, Whig State Chairman Curtin and the notoriously ambitious and corrupt Democrat Simon Cameron, had both joined the Know Nothings by the time of the balloting, and the selection of Cameron was ultimately defeated because the majority of Whig/Know Nothings refused to support him. Viewing the Whig disarray in this contest, reelected State Supreme Court Justice Jeremiah S. Black wrote Buchanan in February, "The Whigs are gone hook & line." Even though a few Whigs stood "obstinately on the old platform" and refused to coalesce with Know Nothings, most Whigs did "not pretend now to have an organized existence."[38]

The previous October a Philadelphia Whig had provided a fuller epitaph for his party. In Ohio and Indiana, he admitted, antislavery sentiment helped produce Democratic defeats. "But here the 'American Union party' 'Know Nothings'" dropped "all other issues as secondary" and fought the battle "against a powerfully organized foreign and Catholic party—a party coquetted with by Buchanan—bought by Pierce and whose 'rich Irish brogue' Scott was so fond of hearing." "We see the work [of the Know Nothings] finished in the North," he continued: "the destruction of the old party organizations between which the administration of the government and the destinies of the country have vibrated for the last quarter of a century." Not only was the Democratic party "gone—disbanded—exterminated." In addition, "the old northern Whig party has ceased to exist—it is swallowed up[,] routed[,] and merged into the great 'American Union party.'" With respect to the entire North in the fall of 1854, this assertion was an exaggeration. But in Pennsylvania, the Whig party was not *"invincible,"* as Pittsburgh's William Larimer had boasted in March. It had instead been "swallowed up" almost whole by a rival new organization.[39]

II

Know Nothings also shattered the Massachusetts Whig party in 1854, but the secret order's composition in the Bay State was unique. As a result, it ruined Whiggery for slightly different reasons than it did in Pennsylvania and New York. Anti-Catholicism, nativism, and prohibitionism powered Know Nothingism in Massachusetts, as elsewhere. The difference between it and other states lay in Free Soilers' response to the nativist party. Only a few current or former Free Soilers joined the order in New York and Pennsylvania in 1854; in contrast, the majority of Massachusetts' proportionately much larger Free Soil party enlisted in the Know Nothing crusade.[40]

Massachusetts had been one of Whigs' few bright spots in 1853. They had discovered a winning issue—opposition to the new state constitution written by the Free Soil/Democratic Coalition—and used it to disrupt the once-dominant Coalition. Mistakenly, Free Soilers blamed the defection of Irish Catholic Democrats from Boston and its environs for the constitution's defeat and the Whigs' victory in the gubernatorial and legislative elections.[41] As a result, nativist and anti-Catholic sentiments among Free Soilers outside of Suffolk County escalated. Democratic responsibility for the Nebraska bill in 1854 cauterized the split between Free Soilers and Democrats and left the former looking for a new path back to power.[42]

Some Free Soilers, led by Henry Wilson, the party's 1853 gubernatorial nominee, pressed northern Whigs to fuse with them in a new antislavery party, a prospect that terrified conservative Whigs.[43] Massachusetts Whigs ultimately spurned fusion with Free Soilers in 1854, but less because of conservative fears than because of residual Whig bitterness against Free Soilers and the universality of antislavery, anti-Nebraska sentiment in the Bay State. Conservative influence in the Whig party was on the wane, and antislavery Whig leaders like Ezra Lincoln saw anti-Nebraskaism as a potentially unifying and winning Whig issue, just as opposition to the 1853 constitution had been.[44]

Thus in June, the Whig state committee issued a tough address rejecting fusion and condemning Free Soilers for their previous participation in the noxious Coalition. The Whig state convention adopted a platform that called for revision or repeal of the Fugitive Slave Act as well as repeal of the Nebraska bill. It also reaffirmed its rejection of fusion with Free Soilers and nominated a full Whig slate, headed by incumbent Governor Emory Washburn. Whigs followed suit in later district conventions by nominating straight Whigs for Congress and rejecting cooperation with Free Soilers.[45]

Whigs' hard-line antislavery stance disconcerted conservatives. Edward Everett had rejoiced in late August that "there will be no *fusion* of the Whigs and free soilers," but by the fall he was grumping about the implications for intersectional comity of the stance the party had taken. "The Whig party is—to use the French expression—completely demoralized; and will have little else to do for some time to come but to follow a 'freesoil' lead," he moaned. "The Southern Whig papers say that the Northern Whigs can no longer be trusted, and that the National Whig party is used up. There is a good deal of truth in the last part of this."[46]

Whereas conservatives rued the antisouthern posture adopted by Massachusetts Whigs, their rejection of fusion infuriated Free Soilers. Rebuffed by the Whig convention, a few Free Soilers, led once again by Wilson, called for a Republican state convention in early September. Although that convention nominated Wilson as the Republican candidate for governor, it attracted so few people, almost all of whom were disgruntled Free Soilers, that erstwhile Young Whig and Free Soil leader Charles Francis Adams scoffed that it was little more than "a drum and fife [corps] without followers."[47]

Henry Wilson was ceaselessly ambitious, but he was no fool. He accepted the Republican nomination because he hoped to get the endorsement of the Know Nothing order, which had been growing like topsy in Massachusetts since early in the year. So numerous had Know Nothings become by the summer that even the Whigs' Ezra Lincoln admitted that "the result of our State election will depend upon the Know Nothings." That was a crucial admission from a leader who sought Whig victory on an anti-Nebraska, antisouthern platform, for incumbent Governor Emory Washburn, the Whig candidate, refused to join the order. In contrast, Wilson and many other Free Soil politicos became members in the spring at the same time as they were loudly demanding the creation of a new northern antislavery party. A desire to punish Irish Catholics, whom they blamed for the defeat of the constitution and the collapse of the Coalition, motivated such men, but it is just as obvious that they saw Know Nothingism as an alternative route to office should their hopes for a fusion antislavery party abort.[48]

Once antislavery Whigs rejected fusion, therefore, Free Soilers streamed into Know Nothing lodges to control their nominations and endorsements. Free Soilers never dominated the order numerically. Tens of thousands of Democrats and Whigs also rushed into it. The Whigs who joined, moreover, were not staunch antislavery men like Lincoln, Julius Rockwell, or John Z. Goodrich, the most likely candidates to join Free Soilers in a new antislavery organization. Rather, they were often Wesbterites unhappy about the thrust of the Whigs' 1854 campaign. Ultimately, indeed, the Know Nothings nominated and then publicly announced as their own gubernatorial candidate not Wilson, but Henry J. Gardner, a politically obscure Boston merchant and former Websterite Whig.[49]

At the leadership level, in sum, Know Nothingism represented an unlikely coalition of the two groups most unhappy about the actions of the Whig state convention: Free Soilers and Websterites. Among the rank and file, it represented not only those who sincerely despised the state's large Irish Catholic population, but also those who yearned for political reform and who were sorely disappointed that the Whig-controlled legislature in 1854 failed to follow through on promises to clean up government. That "debauched" legislature, wrote one disgusted Whig, had reached "the extremity of degradation" and engaged in "the most corrupt log-rolling and pipe-laying that Massachusetts has ever witnessed."[50]

Massachusetts Know Nothingism thus consciously repudiated the Whig party, as well as Catholics and immigrants. Yet it also measurably advanced Free Soilers and their goals. Although Wilson lost the order's gubernatorial endorsement, veteran Free Soil politicos deftly won seven of the eleven Know Nothing congressional nominations. Nor was Wilson permanently blocked. He used his Republican gubernatorial nomination as leverage to gain an even bigger prize. He and Gardner made a secret deal whereby Wilson declined the Republicans' nomination a few days before the election so that Republicans could not name another man; in return, he secured a pledge of Know Nothing support for election by the legislature to the remaining three years of Everett's Senate term.[51] Though Websterite Whigs and thousands of Democrats flocked to the Know Nothing order along with Free Soilers, moreover, Massachusetts Know Nothings were thoroughly antislavery and anti-Nebraska too. Indeed, Gardner, who had served two terms in the legislature without taking a public stand on any controversial issue and thus earned a reputation as a third-rater, was as shrewd and ambitious as Wilson. Suddenly changing spots, he presented himself as the strongest antislavery man in the race and began denouncing the defining article of the Websterite faith, the Fugitive Slave Act. Dismissing his earlier votes against prohibition, he also now demanded a restrictive Maine Law. To call this rank opportunism misses the point. Acutely aware of public opinion, Gardner bent accordingly.[52]

But Massachusetts Know Nothingism also differed from the movement in other states like New York for an additional and quite significant reason. Unlike the politically ambitious and socially suspect Gardner or the most bitter Websterites who saw Know Nothingism as a vehicle for revenge against Whig factional foes, many of the state's wealthiest, most socially prominent, and best-educated conservative Whigs like Winthrop and Everett clung tenaciously to the Whig organization, even though they were asked on numerous occasions to join the secret nativist order. Principled revulsion at Know Nothings' bigotry and proscriptiveness, as well as love of Whiggery, help account for their stubborn adherence to the old party. As early as 1853, for example, Everett refused to speak to the Order of United Americans because he considered nativism pernicious. Nonetheless, sheer social snobbery also explains their aversion to Know Nothingism.[53]

The naked contempt for the Know Nothings expressed by the Harvard-educated bluebloods who had once dominated Massachusetts Whiggery is stunning. "The *personnel* of the Native American party here has been of a very repulsive character," huffed the patrician Winthrop. Henry Gardner, he added tellingly, "is not of the Gardner family to which I belong, either by pedigree or principle." Mocking Gardner as "that rickety vermin," Ezra Lincoln moaned that Know Nothings "have spawned upon us the veriest race of spaniel ministers, lying toothpullers & bargaining priests that were ever showered upon any unoffending people." The order had "made a most preposterous string of nominations. People—most of whom—one has never heard of before," sneered an appalled Everett, "small traders, mechanics, & artisans, wholly unknown to the public." As for Gardner, he was "a man of some cleverness, but no solidity of character & no qualifications for high office."[54]

Nonetheless, Gardner and other Know Nothings won one of the most sweeping victories ever achieved by an American political party. Contemporaries disagreed, as have later historians, about the reasons for the Know Nothing explosion, but its decimation of the once-dominant Massachusetts Whig party was unmistakable. Know Nothings won every seat in the state senate and all but a handful in the huge lower house. In the four-way gubernatorial race, where Wilson still received a few Free Soil votes, Gardner won with an astonishing 63 percent of the total, while the hapless Whig incumbent, Emory Washburn, ran second with 21 percent. Between 1853 and 1854, Washburn's total plummeted by 32,000 votes, 5,000 more than he received in 1854, and more Whigs who had supported Winfield Scott in 1852 backed Gardner than remained in the Whig column. That latter fact is especially telling, since, of course, diehard Webster Whigs refused to vote for Scott in 1852.[55]

Returns from the House races proved especially devastating to the future of Whiggery. All eleven Massachusetts congressmen had voted against the Kansas-Nebraska bill in 1854, and nine of those men were Whigs. Only seven of the nine Whig incumbents ran again, but all of them, as well as the two Whig replacement candidates, were defeated by Know Nothings. The only two incumbents who won reelection had joined the Know Nothings too: the Free Soiler Alexander De Witt and the ambitious Democrat Nathaniel P. Banks. Of the victorious Know Nothings, moreover, only two had formerly been Whigs, and one of them, Linus Comins, who defeated the Websterite Whig incumbent, Samuel Walley, in the fourth district, had fluctuated like a shuttlecock between the Whig and Free Soil parties.

Regular Whig candidates were not simply defeated; they were obliterated. Of the eleven, four amassed between 30 and 32.1 percent of the vote, and they were the front-runners among Whigs! Only two of the others drew more than a fourth of the vote, and three failed even to reach the 20 percent mark. That talented anti-Nebraska Whig incumbents like John Z. Goodrich, William Appleton, Charles Upham, and Thomas D. Eliot, whose defeat even the Free Soiler Charles

Sumner lamented, were cast aside for Know Nothings demonstrates beyond cavil that something in addition to the Nebraska Act was on voters' minds.[56]

Whiggery's demolition by Know Nothings stunned men within and outside the Bay State. How, wondered Illinois Whig David Davis, could Massachusetts voters have defeated so many anti-Nebraska Whig incumbents and thus given solace to the South? "The Know Nothings have smitten Whig and Democrat hip and thigh in Massachusetts," wrote the crusty New York patrician George Templeton Strong in his diary. "If *we* are in a fix, how is it with the *Whigs*," a Massachusetts Democrat rationalized. "If there be anything then in the idea that misery loves company, we surely have company enough in our overthrow." "Poor old Massachusetts!" Winthrop groaned after the election. "Who could have believed the old Whig party would have been so thoroughly demoralized in so short a space of time?"[57]

Weeks before the election, astute Whig conservatives had worried about Free Soil infiltration of the Know Nothings and especially about the rumored bargain between Gardner and Henry Wilson. Wilson's subsequent election to the Senate, therefore, only punctuated the humiliation of Massachusetts Whigs. But it did more than that. Along with senatorial elections during 1855 in New York and New Hampshire, it attached the stigma of antislavery radicalism to northern Know Nothings. And that stigma, far more than the nativist, anti-Catholic tenets of Know Nothingism itself, crippled Know Nothing candidates in most southern states during the elections later that year.

III

Know Nothingism mushroomed in New York as well, but its politics were far more complicated than those in Massachusetts or Pennsylvania. Since New York possessed the nation's largest bloc of House seats and electoral votes and was home to Fillmore and Seward, the two northern Whigs most frequently mentioned as possible Whig presidential candidates in 1856, its politics were also far more consequential.

At first glance, New York's Whigs seemed more successful than their Bay State brethren in 1854. Nonetheless, Know Nothingism and, even more so, prohibitionism so damaged the unity and integrity of New York's Whigs and Democrats that developments there had even more profound consequences for the future of the national Whig party. By demonstrating the impossibility of holding the traditional Whig and Democratic coalitions together, New York augured a fundamental reorganization of American political life rather than the reinvigoration of the second party system that Seward sought in the spring of 1854. Internal divisions smashed Whig hopes of turning the election into a referendum on slavery extension and a demonstration that Whigs could carry the state for a favorite son in 1856. As a result, events in New York altered the calculations of almost every Whig who looked ahead to the presidential contest.

Like other northern Whigs, Seward's New York followers voiced supreme confidence in 1854 that opposition to the Nebraska bill would bring victory in the fall state and congressional elections and provide them the inside track for the national party's 1856 presidential nomination.[58] Silver Grays were every bit as appalled by Douglas' measure as Sewardites, if for somewhat different reasons, and they wanted Whigs' state platform to condemn it vigorously. Only a call for repeal of the Fugitive Slave Act might alienate them, and that was a call Weed and Seward were determined to muzzle. An attack on the Fugitive Slave Act like that made by Whigs in Vermont, Massachusetts, or Pennsylvania could doom their whole effort to keep the party united. If for no other reason than to ensure Whig control of the new legislature so that Seward might be reelected to the Senate in 1855, they bent over backward to preserve Whig cohesion, and throughout the spring, Whig and Democratic commentators alike commented on Whigs' apparent harmony.[59]

Despite their unwonted agreement on the slavery issue, however, at least five different threats menaced and ultimately subverted Whigs' unity. First was the residual jealousy between Silver Grays and Sewardites. Despite their common antipathy to the Nebraska Act, many resentful Silver Grays were determined never again to play second fiddle to Seward and Weed. A donnybrook for control of the Whig organization and its nominations was thus irrepressible. Second was an attempt during the summer to launch a fusion Republican party in New York that could fatally weaken the Whigs by siphoning off their angriest antislavery supporters. The third and fourth threats were the intensification of nativist and prohibitionist sentiments, which, by the summer, displaced Nebraska as the key issues in the fall elections. The fifth, ironically, was the continuing rift among the state's Democrats between Hardshell Hunkers led by ex-Senator Daniel S. Dickinson and the alliance of Softshell Hunkers and Barnburners, led nominally by Secretary of State William L. Marcy and incumbent Governor Horatio Seymour. By the summer, the entanglement of these five elements caused seasoned Whig leaders to moan in bewilderment that "so many strange elements [were] afloat" "that we are to have political chaos—'confusion worse confounded' for a time."[60]

As was the case since the party's founding, Whigs' relationship with the rival Democrats largely determined their fate. Paradoxically, Democratic divisions simultaneously encouraged Whig cohesion and jeopardized it. On the one hand, just as in 1853, when separate Hard and Soft tickets guaranteed Whig victory and thereby deterred bolts by dissident Silver Grays who hoped to share in the spoils of certain Whig triumph, Democratic divisions in 1854 promised Whigs control of the governorship, the legislature, and most congressional seats if they could hold together. That prospect increased the likelihood of an intraparty battle for nominations, but it also seemed to ensure that rival Whigs would remain within the party, at least until nominees were named. On the other hand, the near impossibility that either Democratic faction by itself could defeat a united Whig party gave both a powerful incentive to provoke Whig division.

Internal disagreements within both Democratic factions over the Nebraska bill in 1854 complicated their rivalry. Five Hardshell Democratic congressmen voted against it, but in early July a Hard convention nominated Greene Bronson for governor on a platform that endorsed Nebraska and stridently denounced the alliance between Softs and Barnburners as "unmanly and dishonest." Hards also ran congressional candidates against Softs in at least twenty-four of the state's thirty-three House districts.[61]

Fearful of offending the administration, especially with Marcy in the cabinet, Softs dared not repudiate the Nebraska Act. Nor could they endorse it, for it outraged Barnburners and many Softs themselves, and, given the separate Hard ticket, Soft leaders knew they had no chance whatsoever of carrying the state if they alienated Barnburners by endorsing the Nebraska Act. Softs therefore renominated Seymour in early September on a platform that straddled the Nebraska issue and tried to focus the campaign on other matters. Whigs and Free Soilers alike mocked this "sniveling, twaddling, ropedancer balancing proposition." Both Democratic factions were thus vulnerable if Whigs could remain united and keep their campaign focused against the Nebraska Act and further slavery extension.[62]

Acutely aware of this fact, Hards and Softs each sought to split the Whigs to even the odds in November. Some Hards hoped to break off the Silver Grays, whom they saw as potential allies. Simultaneously, anti-Nebraska Hards, dissatisfied with their faction's July platform, began to cast about for new political moorings. They sought different Whig allies.[63] Hards and some Softs, therefore, encouraged an effort by Free Soilers (or Free Democrats, as they had called themselves since 1852) to create a fusion antislavery coalition in New York that year. Anti-Nebraska Hards did so because they needed a new party; pro-Nebraska Hards, in contrast, simply hoped that if enough antislavery men abandoned the Whig party for a new Republican coalition, the remaining Silver Grays, now less confident of Whig victory, might combine with them.

The occasion for launching an antislavery fusion party was a statewide anti-Nebraska convention scheduled to meet in Saratoga Springs on August 16. The original calls for this convention, issued by mass anti-Nebraska meetings in New York City and Albany, said nothing about nominating a state ticket. Instead, they simply invited New York's voters "to consider" what was necessary "For the protection of the Free States from Southern aggression and Northern treachery; For the recovery of the rights of the Free States . . . and For the rescue of the General Government from the control of the Slave Power."[64]

That language opened the door for proponents of a new party. So did the mechanism for selecting delegates to Saratoga. County mass meetings were to choose five delegates from each of the state's 128 assembly districts, and those county meetings might be steamrolled into demanding a fusion party. Of particular concern to Whig strategists, Horace Greeley enthusiastically pushed the new party bandwagon in his *New York Tribune.* Frustrated by the apparent intention of Seward and Weed to maintain ties to southern Whigs and by the waffling of Whig legislators during the spring on the Maine Law, Greeley hoped to build a Republican party in New York on an anti-Nebraska, prohibitionist platform. That Greeley also hoped the new party would nominate him for governor was widely known.

Hardshell Democrats, either cynically or sincerely, and a few Softs abetted this drive for Republican nominations at Saratoga in order to break up the Whig party. At the Saratoga convention itself, indeed, a Hard introduced the resolution to form a Republican party. A few Silver Grays, who hoped that Republican nominations might lure Sewardites from the Whig party so that their own faction could control it, joined the cry for fusion nominations. Sensing the danger to Whig unity, one appalled Whig complained to Weed that his county's meeting had been "controlled by Abolitionists, Free Democrats & Softs, pushed on by a few inveterate Silver Greys[,] all of whom ardently desire the dismemberment of the Whig party."[65]

Suspicious "that a ticket is to be nominated at Saratoga," major leaders from all Whig factions cooperated to avert this threat. Nothing, indeed, better illustrates their consensus on the Nebraska issue and their desire to preserve party unity in 1854 so that one or both of them might enjoy the fruits of the anticipated Whig victory. Fillmorites like Solomon Haven and James Kidd raged at "the disorganizers seeking to break up the Whig party" by "going over to the Abolitionists."[66] Ex-Governor Washington Hunt worked to ensure that his county's mass meeting sent to Saratoga reliable delegates who would "resist the *fusion* scheme, and . . . secede if a ticket is formed."[67] Weed, who had always questioned what "good" the Saratoga convention "will do," recognized how difficult it was to build the organizational apparatus for a new party. He also understood that the remaining Free Soilers represented only a fraction of the Silver Gray Whigs who would be alienated by an attempted coalition. What was worse, he wrote Hunt, by drawing away antislavery Whigs, a Republican nomination would leave Silver Grays and other anti-Weed men in control of the existing Whig organization. That eventuality would menace what seemed certain Whig victory in the fall and, with it, Seward's reelection to the Senate by the new legislature. Having already publicly spurned Free Soil overtures for a merger, Weed now urged his lieutenants around the state to "have friends in it [the Saratoga convention] to guard against mischief," reliable Whig delegates who were committed to preserving "the integrity of the Whig party."[68]

Weed personally set out to persuade Greeley to abandon the new-party effort during an interview in New York City in late July. Appealing to Greeley's antipathy to the burgeoning Know Nothing movement by warning that Silver Grays and Know Nothings would cooperate to carry the state if the Whig party were split by Republican nominations, thereby stopping Seward's reelection, which was vital to the antislavery cause, Weed prevailed upon Greeley to change his editorial tack in the *Tribune*. On July 26, Greeley disgustedly wrote his Indiana protegé, Schuyler Colfax, "We shall have no nomination at Saratoga, and, alas! no fusion at all, which will do harm in all the 'fusion' states. It will tell heavily against us that we carry all the States Whig that we can, and go 'fusion' where we can do no better."[69]

With Greeley, who chaired the resolutions committee at Saratoga, now on board, enough loyal Whig delegates on the floor, and unexpected help from the Barnburner Preston King, who still hoped the Soft convention in early September would oppose Nebraska, Weed's friends beat back attempts to make separate nominations at Saratoga. Instead, the convention adjourned to meet again at Auburn in late September, after the Whig and Soft conventions, in the hope that the continuing threat of a new ticket would force both to condemn the Nebraska outrage. Since the Whigs were certain to do so, the fusion menace to Whig hopes had seemingly been checked.[70]

The suppression of fusion nominations, however, did not completely disarm Democrats seeking to rend the Whigs. Hostility to slavery extension was hardly the only issue in the impending election, as New York's Whig congressional delegation had been warned repeatedly during the spring. Both nativism and prohibition had the potential to split Whigs, and by the summer these issues seemed to matter far more than Nebraska to vast numbers of them. "Whig or Democrat will have nothing to do with the election this fall," wrote one Whig in early August. "The temperance and Catholic questions" were now the central issues in New York, echoed another upstate Whig later that month. Residents of rural districts harbored "a deep conviction of the necessity of a prohibitory law, & determination to obtain such a law even at the expense of other favorite measures or party ties." Zealous Protestants demanded that "some check should be given to the wily schemes of political demagogues who pander to the prejudices and passions of our foreign population." As a result, "The Nebraska-Kansas bill is obsolete, or in the language of its famous Author 'is superceded & inoperative' in comparison with these immediate & practical questions."[71]

Precisely because these questions transfixed so many Whig voters, Democrats, having failed to divide Whigs with a new antislavery party, seized on them to accomplish that goal. The Softs' renomination of Seymour consciously targeted wet Whigs who adamantly opposed passage of a Maine Law. In March, Seymour vetoed a prohibition law passed by a bipartisan legislative majority.[72] His veto instantly established Seymour as the darling of the "liquor *interest*," drinkers, and those who opposed sumptuary legislation on principle as unconscionable state interference with individual freedom. So popular among liquor dealers and tavern owners was Seymour, indeed, that at least one important Soft tactician feared that he would be identified "as the *rum candidate*," thereby deterring "many sober & temperance democrats from *voting at all*."[73]

Other Soft strategists correctly saw great advantages in running Seymour again. His nomination diverted attention in at least the gubernatorial and legislative campaigns from the nettlesome Nebraska question to liquor. It could negate the rebellious Hards, since, one Soft calculated, at least half of the Hard rank and file would vote for Seymour rather than Bronson if the right to drink were clearly at stake. Best of all, since Seymour had already preempted the anti-Maine Law position, Whigs faced a dilemma. They dared not nominate a wet themselves, lest they thereby provoke outraged temperance men to run a separate Maine Law candidate who might siphon off tens of thousands of Whig voters. Yet if Whigs ran a zealous prohibitionist, or even a passive temperance man who seemed willing to sign prohibitionist legislation, uncounted numbers of anti-prohibition Whigs might defect to Seymour or abstain. Softs could not split the Whigs over the slavery issue, but they might do so with the liquor question.[74]

Though Seymour had staked out the antiprohibition position, Whig leaders wanted to hold their own wet voters if at all possible.[75] Finding a gubernatorial candidate who could appeal to Whigs on both sides of the liquor issue, therefore, proved to be Whigs' thorniest problem prior to the state convention at Syracuse on September 20. Flatly warned by leading prohibitionists "that the *Whigs must sail* in our cold water ship or sink" and aware that dries would run their own candidate unless Whigs "nominate a well known Temperance man for Governor," they also worried that the "avowal" to sign a prohibition measure that antiliquor men now demanded as a sine qua non "will alienate great numbers of the political party to which the candidate may belong."[76]

Conflicting advice deluged Weed, who once again hoped to engineer the Whig nomination. During April, in the weeks immediately following Seymour's veto, when a bolt by appreciative wet Whigs seemed likely, Weed toyed with the idea of running Seward himself for governor. By mid-May, however, Weed admitted that "the Maine Law question would be fatal to Seward as a candidate for Governor" since the most fanatical prohibitionists "would never support him."[77] Greeley, who ached to be governor, was disqualified for the opposite reason. Even before he pushed for nominations at Saratoga, Greeley demanded daily in his *New York Tribune* that the Whigs' gubernatorial candidate must pledge to sign a prohibition law. Since any candidate who publicly sympathized with prohibitionists would instantly be consigned to "his political grave," wrote another Whig, the party's best hope was "to keep Greeley quiet."[78]

Nonetheless, the pressure on Whigs to appease prohibitionists was inexorable. Thus, in late June, when Weed broached George W. Patterson's name to John M. Bradford, Bradford replied that if Patterson "cannot get the whole Maine law vote it would be madness to nominate him." A better choice, Bradford suggested, would be State Senator Myron H. Clark, a loyal Sewardite, who as author of the vetoed prohibition bill would pose the clearest alternative to Seymour on the liquor question. Clark, he argued, would get all the Sewardites, who, by his grossly inflated estimate, constituted nine-tenths of the Whig rank and file, all the Free Soilers, and the whole Maine Law vote. "He would lose all Whigs who love anti-Maine Lawism more than the party," but "so I think would any man we should nominate." Since Seymour had locked up the anti-Maine Law vote, only an ardent dry would do.[79]

Were the divisive prohibition question Weed's only problem, holding the party together would have been difficult enough. But as he and other Whigs well knew, Know Nothings also threatened Whig unity, and particularly Weed's long domination of the party. While Softs used the liquor issue, Hards seized on Know Nothingism to split the Whig party after fusion nominations were blocked at Saratoga. And they did so primarily because Know Nothingism was also the vehicle that some Silver Grays used to capture control of Whig nominations from Weed and Seward.

As elsewhere, Know Nothing lodges spread across New York State during 1854 in response to intense grass-roots anti-immigrant, anti-Catholic, and antiparty resentments. However sincere those resentments were, both Hards and Silver Grays quickly sought to exploit the secret, oath-bound fraternity to advance their factional interests. Silver Grays wanted to use its tightly disciplined machinery to counter Weed's control of regular Whig county organizations in a pitched battle to select delegates to the Whig state convention and to name Whig candidates for the legislature and Congress. Hards looked for a direct alliance with Silver Grays by seeking control of Know Nothing lodges and their candidate endorsements.

A concerted Silver Gray challenge to Weed's control of the Whig party emerged almost simultaneously with, but separately from, Know Nothingism. Significantly, Fillmore himself did not orchestrate either movement. During the spring, Fillmore was repeatedly informed by his closest advisors of the Know Nothings' astonishing power and of their likely support for his presidential candidacy in 1856. He and they, however, saw no need to join the order to get that support, and they awaited the results of the 1854 elections before determining upon a course of action with regard to it. Since Haven planned to run for reelection as a Whig and since Fillmore still hoped that Silver Grays would be treated fairly at the Whig state convention, moreover, during the summer they were far more interested in quashing fusion nominations at Saratoga than in spawning a different independent party.[80]

For similar reasons, Fillmore initially abstained from Silver Grays' challenge for the Whigs' gubernatorial nomination. He certainly knew that many Silver Grays, despite their opposition to the Nebraska bill, still yearned to break "the power and cohesion of the Seward dynasty" and would resist an attempt by Weed to impose a radical antislavery platform on the Whig party since they "will not go Nigger when a White Man is at stake."[81] Nonetheless, Fillmore bided his time as younger men outside his inner circle launched an effort to control the state convention. The instigator was Daniel Ullmann, the New York City lawyer who had helped lead the Silver Gray bolt in 1850, run unsuccessfully for attorney general in 1851, and grudgingly stepped aside for Washington Hunt as the Whig gubernatorial nominee in 1852.

Starting in April, Ullmann began to write to veteran anti-Weed Whigs across New York to ascertain what his prospects for the Whig gubernatorial nomination might be and what the chances were of constructing a statewide organization to rival the regular, Weed-controlled Whig committee structure. He asked Albany's James Kidd, for example, for a copy of the mailing list of reliable conservatives Fillmore had compiled in 1849. Aside from widespread sympathy for a concerted challenge to Weed, Ullmann received three key pieces of information from his numerous correspondents. First, Know Nothingism was spreading like wildfire across the state, and nativists hated Weed, Seward, and Greeley because of their well-known sympathy for Catholics and foreigners. Second, prohibitionism was the dominant sentiment among upstate Whigs. Dries would support no one, regardless of his factional affiliation, who was not committed publicly or privately to signing a Maine Law, and they were congenitally suspicious of anyone from that den of iniquity, New York City. Third, and most important, in most places Silver Grays were heavily outnumbered by Sewardites and could never select pro-Ullmann delegates to the Whig state convention unless they could lure Sewardites to the Ullmann camp.[82]

In July a group calling itself the New York Central Whig Association formed to coordinate Ullmann's drive for the Whig nomination. Second-tier Silver Gray leaders like Benedict Lewis, Robert C. Wetmore, and Stephen Sammons directed the NYCWA, and its corresponding secretary was Marcellus Ells. Significantly, both Ells and Sammons were influential Know Nothings. On August 1, the NY-CWA published a circular making the case for Ullmann's nomination. Touting Ullmann's fidelity to "all our favorite measures," his "earnest" advocacy of canal expansion, and his "determined" opposition to the Nebraska bill, it asserted that no one else could "more readily unite and cement the party."[83]

"The party" in question was the Whigs, and the NYWCA was presented to the public exclusively an as organization of Whigs. Nonetheless, Ells was a leading Know Nothing, and many of the men who wrote to him, other NYCWA leaders, or Ullmann openly identified themselves as Know Nothings or included the tell-tale phrase "I know nothing" in their letters. By August, Ullmann himself had probably joined the order, and he certainly had by September 20, when the Whig state convention met.[84]

Many Silver Grays never became Know Nothings, but cooperation between the two groups was almost inevitable. Genuine nativists despised the pro-Catholic, proimmigrant proclivities of Weed, Seward, and Greeley, and many conservative Whigs shared that animosity. Determined to shove Weed and Seward aside, Silver Grays swarmed into the order, and by early August one Whig reported to the NYWCA that "the Know Nothings are to exert considerable influence in the Whig caucuses this Fall." Accordingly, veteran Silver Grays like John L. Dox boasted openly "that the know nothings and silver grays would carry the state by 30,000 this fall."[85] Precisely because many Silver Grays flocked to Know Nothingism, Hardshell Hunkers followed suit in the admittedly unlikely hope that, should Ullmann fail to get the Whig nomination, Know Nothings instead might endorse Bronson. Regardless, from the perspective of Weed, Seward, and their lieutenants, Hards' movement into Know Nothing lodges only aggravated the threat to their own control of the Whig party and Seward's reelection. "Silver Gray treachery & Know Nothing activity may defeat the Whig ticket," one Sewardite warned Weed. "You should know that secretly the K. N. are pledged against you & Seward & *Abolitionism*."[86]

Sewardites responded to the Know Nothing threat in various ways. Some, like Greeley, openly defied the order and demanded war to the hilt against the nativists.[87] Others, like Weed's favorite, George Patterson, refused to have anything to do with them. Still others, including Weed himself and some of Seward's closest advisors, believed that Sewardites themselves must infiltrate the order to counter Silver Gray influence within it. Sewardites should join the order to disrupt it and thus "get back our true men and disavow the traitors," advised one Syracuse Whig. So many Seward Whigs followed this tack to control Know Nothing lodges that one outraged correspondent of the Senator complained that they had "thrown away 'both their honor and their weapons' " since they would be bound by the order's oaths of allegiance to oppose him.[88]

Once it appeared that Know Nothings might elect a majority of delegates to the Whig convention, moreover, other aspirants for the gubernatorial nomination besides Ullmann joined the order in a bid for their help. Of the Sewardites, Myron H. Clark, the prohibitionist state senator, proved boldest. As the apoplectic Elbridge Spaulding, who sought the gubernatorial nomination himself, raged to Weed, Clark's friends in Canandaigua created a bogus Know Nothing lodge that inducted him so that he could claim to be a Know Nothing when the Whig convention met. Ullmann, too, received angry warnings that Clark would be his main competitor in a planned caucus of Know Nothing delegates to the Whig gathering.[89]

With ample reason, therefore, a perplexed Weed dejectedly confessed to Patterson three days before the state convention that he could no longer control it. Anti-Nebraska sentiment, which he had counted on to hold Whigs together and defeat the Democrats, would not be the campaign's leading issue. Know Nothings and Silver Grays were organized against him. The prohibition issue remained a headache, with prohibitionists planning to hold a convention at Auburn to nominate their own man unless the Whig candidate satisfied them. "I don't see how we are to get through the Convention safely," he moaned. "The breakers ahead cause serious apprehension. Unless we hit right the Auburn Conventions will act." Nor was that all. "The 'Natives' and 'Silvers' " would insist upon the nomination for lieutenant governor if they did not get the governorship itself. "This is the worst aspect of the question."[90]

IV

Thurlow Weed had never suffered many Whigs' penchant for overoptimism, and in 1854 his fears again proved all too accurate. At the convention he discovered that non-Know Nothing, nontemperance delegates were divided between Spaulding and his man Patterson. Maine Law men threatened to form an independent ticket if either were nominated and instead insisted on Levi Harris, who had little support outside their circle. Meanwhile, Know Nothing delegates, who caucused before the convention officially opened, demanded that the nominee be a member, but they were divided among Clark, Ullmann, Joseph Savage, and William Campbell. Incensed that Clark might derail months of effort to nominate Ullmann, Silver Gray Know Nothings passed around a document known as the Canandaigua Circular, signed by James W. Barker, the president of the Know Nothings' state and national councils, and members of the official Ethan Allen Council in that town, asserting that Clark "belongs to a spurious Order here & is not a member of our Order."[91]

In part because of Silver Gray opposition to Clark, but primarily because his nomination would appease zealous temperance men, Weed decided to back him at a conference between the two men on the night before the convention opened.[92] With Weed's support, Clark won the nomination on the third ballot. Henry J. Raymond, the Sewardite editor of the *New York Times* and a prominent foe of the Maine Law, got the nod for lieutenant governor. In an effort not to further alienate Silver Grays, who had been completely excluded from the major slots on the state ticket, the Whigs' platform condemned the Nebraska Act but suggested no remedy for it. On enforcement or revision of the Fugitive Slave Act, it was utterly silent, as it was on both the Maine Law and nativism. Within a week, the adjourned Saratoga convention and the state temperance meeting at Auburn endorsed the ticket.[93]

Given the difficult circumstances Weed faced, his reluctant swing from Patterson to Clark made sense. He knew that Sewardites would never tolerate a Silver Gray nominee, and Clark was even more rabidly antislavery than Seward. As a deputy United States marshal in 1850, indeed, he had vowed never to enforce the Fugitive Slave Act and had helped fund a new Whig paper that denounced the Compromise.[94] His prohibitionist credentials were impeccable, and he might lure Know Nothings to boot. In the short run, moreover, Clark's nomination seemed to pay dividends, as the actions at Auburn implied.

Still, the choice of Clark reflected Weed's desperation. Many Whigs regarded him not simply as a cold-water fanatic, but also as a dimwit who was totally unqualified to be governor. "Mr. Clark is a respectable citizen without a single qualification for Gov.," Francis Granger huffed upon learning of the decision at Syracuse, and later he asserted that "thousands of Seward Whigs . . . will not vote for Clark, from a knowledge of his utter want of fitness." Similarly, Alex Mann, Rochester's Silver Gray editor, reported "wide and deep dissatisfaction with the nomination of Clark among the Whigs of this section, and it is by no means confined to Silver Grays." Incensed by the nominations of a simpleton like Clark and his hated editorial rival Raymond, Greeley bitterly railed against Weed to Seward, and after the election he announced to Seward "the dissolution of the political firm of Seward, Weed, & Greeley by the withdrawal of the junior partner."[95]

Incompetence was hardly Clark's only liability. As Weed had been amply warned, Clark's prohibitionist zeal infuriated wets. Terrified at the prospect of Clark as governor, "the liquor dealers," as even Weed admitted, made "a tremendous effort to elect Seymour." In New York City they printed and distributed 17,000 Seymour tickets at their own expense. "We lose more Whigs than you would anticipate," Washington Hunt bluntly told Weed two weeks before the election. "Many of our best outdoor men are those who keep or resort to places of entertainment," and they "are ready to sacrifice party, country and everything, sooner than be deprived of the 'critter.'"[96] Hunt was as flummoxed as he was discouraged by the chaos that followed Clark's nomination. "There never was a time when party ties seemed of so little account," he groaned. "The new questions have destroyed everything like party discipline, and many staunch old Whigs are floating off they don't know where."[97]

Among the new questions that threatened Whig discipline, Hunt listed an open bolt by Know Nothings and Silver Grays who were even more offended by the actions at Syracuse than were hard-drinking Whigs. The nomination of Clark and Raymond, in fact, detonated an explosion that ended Whig unity based on common anger at the Nebraska Act. The long-simmering resentments of Silver Grays now erupted in an outpouring of anger and spleen that proved irrevocable. Because Silver Grays now had Know Nothings as both an ally against and an organized alternative to the Sewardite-dominated Whig party, their defection was irreversible.

To be more precise, Whig attempts after the convention to cement endorsements of the Syracuse ticket at Auburn mortally wounded the party. In the first few days following the convention, at least some Silver Grays seemed disposed to support the ticket. Since Weed's preference for Patterson or Spaulding as the nominee was well known, some Silver Gray papers, including Fillmore's personal mouthpiece, the Buffalo *Commercial Advertiser*, and the Albany *State Register*, initially crowed that Clark's nomination marked a defeat for Weed. Francis Granger, whose silver locks had given the National Whigs their sobriquet, for one, was not fooled. Demanding to know how the *Commercial Advertiser* could reach such an erroneous conclusion, Granger bluntly told Fillmore that "W. has not a more pliant tool in the State" than Clark, that Weed had marshaled support for him at Syracuse, and that, unless Silver Gray papers repudiated the ticket, "we here [in Canandaigua] must consider it, as a formal disbanding of the Silver Grays."[98]

Within days of this outburst, the actions at Auburn dispelled the illusions of other Silver Grays. Between September 25 and 27, the Free Democrats, the adjourned Saratoga convention, and the state temperance convention met in Seward's home town. Refusing to ratify the Whig ticket, Free Soilers pressed the remnants of the Saratoga convention to nominate a genuine fusion ticket by substituting a Barnburner for Raymond in the second slot. Orchestrated by Weed, Edwin Morgan, and Seward himself, the numerous Whig delegates at the anti-

Nebraska gathering fended off this threat and secured endorsement of the entire Whig ticket. But they also supported resolutions that, quite unlike the Syracuse state platform, repudiated both major parties' 1852 national platforms and their commitment to the finality of the Compromise of 1850, vigorously condemned the Fugitive Slave Act, and called for an exclusively northern convention to nominate a presidential ticket in 1856. What is more, after many Whigs had left to go home, the remaining anti-Nebraska men and Free Soilers agreed to name a Republican state committee, even if there was no Republican state ticket, and the Whigs who were still in town made no protest against it.[99]

Delighted by the endorsement of Clark and Raymond, neither Seward nor Weed apparently recognized what public perception of their complicity with the actions at Auburn meant. Their careless indifference allowed hotheads at Auburn to wreck within a few hours everything they had done over nine months—indeed, during the four years since the Silver Gray bolt in 1850—to hold the New York Whig party together. The attack on the Compromise and the Fugitive Slave Act and the apparent sympathy for an exclusively northern Republican party, not the condemnation of the Nebraska Act at Syracuse, reopened the party's wounds over slavery. Newspaper accounts of the Auburn meetings, not of the official Whig state convention on September 20, caused the furious Charles Conrad to protest to Fillmore that the "so-called Whig convention" had "surrendered at discretion to the abolitionists," that the resolutions accompanying the endorsement of Clark and Raymond "amount to a declaration of perpetual warfare against the South," and that Fillmore and other National Whigs must repudiate the ticket and help form a new *national party* since "it would be impossible for Southern Whigs to cooperate with the authors & abetters of these measures."[100]

Furious Silver Grays instantly recognized the consequences of what had transpired at Auburn. "The Whig candidates have all gone over to a sectional Seward abolition movement and I hold them utterly unworthy of support as Whigs," protested one. Since they were "loaded down with isms," he raged, "it would be a publick [sic] disgrace as well as the ruin of what is left of the Whig party to have them elected."[101]

Some Silver Grays initially spoke of supporting Seymour or Bronson or simply abstaining en masse to bring down Clark and Raymond. Sitting out the election, however, might simply demonstrate the Nationals' weakness and unwillingness to fight, thereby encouraging southern Whigs to leave the party.[102] To persuade Southerners that they continued to have powerful allies in New York and to coordinate strategy for the state election, therefore, leading Silver Grays met in Albany on October 24. Fillmore, who publicly took no part in the 1854 campaign in order to conceal his continuing political ambition, did not attend, but he privately kept abreast of the proceedings.[103] The Albany gathering made two important decisions. First, to reassure southern Whigs that Silver Grays repudiated the actions at Auburn, they issued a circular that was disseminated widely among conservative Whigs in New York, other northern states, and, most significantly, the South. It announced that conservatives planned to issue an address on the day after the election "in which the principles of the National Whig party will be plainly declared" and called for another Whig convention, purified of Sewardite influence, at Albany in January 1855 "to re-instate the old Whig party on its old platform recently discarded at Auburn." It went on to list the principles on which the "National Whig party" would be based: opposition to "the Nebraska bill as a violation of the Missouri Compromise"; continued enforcement of the Fugitive Slave Act; and a firm pledge "to oppose all propositions for the fusion of the Whig party with any other for the purpose of forming a sectional party based upon the agitation of the day." The circular concluded on a ringing and ominous note. "The time for decisive action has arrived, as the coming winter will determine whether a National Whig party will cease to exist."[104]

As late as October 24, 1854, in short, many Silver Grays still hoped to perpetuate the Whig organization and to have it nominate Fillmore for president. Their circular said absolutely nothing about Catholics, foreigners, Know Nothings, or the Maine Law. Nonetheless, their second decision at Albany recognized the necessity to continue their implicit alliance with Know Nothings. Through a private letter-writing campaign they would throw Silver Gray support to Ullmann, whom Know Nothings, acting on their own, had nominated for governor at a convention in New York City on October 4.

Know Nothings' refusal to endorse Clark, Bronson, or Seymour and their nomination of Ullmann signaled their transformation from a secret pressure group into an alternative party. They had good reasons for making the switch. Nativists had a concrete political agenda they wanted enacted, but to force politicians to address it, they needed to demonstrate their strength among the electorate or elect men of their own. James W. Barker, who had taken over the struggling Order of the Star Spangled Banner in 1852 and personally directed its astounding growth since then, hoped to do so at first by infiltrating the Whig convention, but even before it met, he had called a Know Nothing convention for October 4 to make its own nominations should those at Syracuse be unacceptable. Barker and other sincere nativists, moreover, were indignant at Sewardites' cynical attempt to capture local lodges, outraged by the insulting selection of the "bogus" Know Nothing Clark, and miffed that neither the Hards, the Softs, nor the Whigs had said one word against the Catholic and foreign menace. At their insistence, Ullmann was nominated to show the order's electoral power, but since they planned a campaign that would operate primarily through the lodges themselves, they saw no need to publish a platform.[105]

As was the case prior to the Whig convention, Know Nothings and Silver Grays cooperated against Seward and Weed—and now Clark—but they did not merge completely. Many Silver Grays never joined the Know Nothings, others waited to do so until after the election, and a few simply found it inconceivable to vote for anyone without a formal Whig nomination. Fillmore punctuated many Silver Grays' inclination to hold Know Nothings at arm's length. Fillmore deemed Ullmann "a good national Whig and . . . in all respects qualified for the office." But when Stephen Sammons directly asked him to endorse the Know Nothings publicly in order to swing Silver Grays behind Ullmann and thereby build "a united force that could well harmonize in the future," Fillmore answered coldly that he could do "nothing."[106]

Know Nothings wanted Silver Gray help for two reasons. First, despite the order's rapid spread, they recognized that by themselves they lacked a majority of the state's voters. Of particular concern, although they disseminated the Canandaigua Circular among lodges across the state to discredit Clark's phony Know Nothing credentials, they still feared that many lodges might support him rather than Ullmann since Clark's supporters spread the false rumor that Ullmann had been born in Calcutta, India, and was therefore ineligible to be a Know Nothing. So likely did it appear that all Know Nothings would not rally behind Ullmann, indeed, that a few members strenuously opposed his nomination on the grounds that it would only split the anti-Democratic vote and throw the election to Seymour or Bronson. Second, Know Nothings also desperately needed money to pay for the printing and distribution of ballots and campaign posters. They regarded patrician Silver Grays as men with deep enough pockets to provide the necessary cash.[107]

If some Know Nothing leaders unabashedly solicited Silver Gray help, many rank-and-file members detested the need for it. They distrusted Silver Grays as pompous bluebloods or jaded hacks, not new men "fresh from the ranks of the people."[108] Nonetheless, more pulled the two groups together than pushed them apart. Although Ullmann carefully kept his distance from the Albany Silver Gray conclave and although it refused to endorse him publicly, Know Nothings and Silver Grays shared a commitment to "a complete *annihilation* of the Weed and Seward Regency." Your "nomination by the 'Know Nothings,' " Mann told Ullmann, "will give many in this quarter, besides the members of the 'mysterious order' an opportunity to vote for a candidate whom they like and know to be qualified." Fillmore, who publicly took "no part in politics this fall," also hoped for Ullmann's election, and he now privately began to urge his friends to join Know Nothing lodges. Cooperation between Know Nothings and Silver Grays on the state ticket, in short, was nearly complete.[109]

Inevitably it spilled over into local contests to nominate Whig legislative and congressional candidates, and it was in those struggles between September 20 and late October that Know Nothings took their most devastating toll on the Whig organization. Across the state, stunned Weed men reported Know Nothing and Silver Gray takeovers of local conventions. "At our caucus they rushed in from their Council room in a body—controlled it—elected their delegates—& ajd [adjourned] in a few moments," gasped one Sewardite. "They acted like zombies."[110] Here is where the Hards' infiltration of Know Nothing lodges paid dividends. Know Nothing Whigs aided Silver Gray outsiders in pitched battles within Whig meetings against Weed's allies. If they won, Know Nothings endorsed the Silver Gray candidate, and Democratic Know Nothings were under oath to support him too. But where Sewardites won Whig nominations, Know Nothings endorsed Democrats—and usually Hard Democrats—and Silver Grays, whether Know Nothings or "outsiders," followed their lead. Referring to one legislative ticket, for example, a Silver Gray Know Nothing gloated, "The Whig party, as a *party*, are broken up in Troy. . . . The Seward Whigs in Troy are about two-thirds of the party but the Silver Grays will have a man that the Democrats will unite on, or they will have a Democrat that the Whigs will unite on, and *no Seward Whig will go to the legislature from Troy, mark that*." "*We are* determined to give old party lines and old party hacks a glorious drubbing this fall, and learn them *hereafter* a lesson they will not forget during a lifetime," echoed another Know Nothing from western New York.[111]

This determination took its greatest toll on Sewardite Whig candidates in the congressional races. "Chaotic" barely begins to describe the confusion of those contests. When the smoke had settled, only five of the state's thirty-three districts

featured the customary two-candidate races. Whigs nominated one or more candidates in all thirty-three districts; Hards and Softs each nominated men in all
but three, although the Soft or Hard candidate withdrew from two before the
final balloting; and Know Nothings made endorsements in at least twenty-two
races. In addition, four Free Soilers and two independent temperance candidates
entered the lists.

Democratic divisions gave Whigs their anticipated advantage in many congressional races. Whigs carried twenty-seven of the state's thirty-three districts,
compared to only eleven in 1852, and they won nine of those seats with pluralities
smaller than the combined Democratic vote. Nonetheless, Whigs suffered considerable disarray, to which the Know Nothings contributed. At least five races saw
rival Whigs competing against each other, and the total would have been six had
not George W. Patterson, the Sewardites' nominee in the Chautauqua/Cattar-
augus district, withdrawn and endorsed anti-Nebraska Soft incumbent Reuben
Fenton, a future Republican governor, against Francis Edwards, the Silver Gray
and Know Nothing candidate, who defeated Fenton. Disagreements over prohibition produced two Whig candidates in Long Island's first district, which was
carried by a Democratic Know Nothing. In three districts, however, Know Nothings backed Whig challengers against regular Whig nominees, and in one, New
York City's fifth district, Silver Gray and veteran nativist Know Nothing Thomas
R. Whitney won the seat. In the Oneida district, finally, the incumbent Sewardite
Orsamus Matteson faced a challenge from a Silver Gray who tripled the proportion of the vote won by Matteson's Silver Gray opponent in 1852, thereby reducing Matteson's share of the vote from 50 percent in 1852 to 38 percent in
1854.

Know Nothing influence spread far beyond these districts. Altogether, Know
Nothings backed thirteen Whig candidates, eleven of whom were victorious. Incumbent Russell Sage of Troy was a Sewardite, but most of the others appear to
have been Silver Grays, like Buffalo's Haven and Lockport's Thomas Flagler or
prominent nativists who had probably joined the secret order. In addition, nine
Softs and two Hards had Know Nothing backing; four of those Democrats won.
In sum, the fifteen Know Nothing winners, four Democrats and eleven Whigs,
almost matched the sixteen non-Know Nothing Whig victors.

The toll Know Nothings took on Whig voting strength, however, is best illuminated by popular voting percentages. New York's congressional districts can
be divided into three categories: the eleven carried by Whigs whom Know Nothings endorsed and who thus got votes from Democratic members of the order;
the sixteen carried by non-Know Nothing Whigs who were often opposed by
Know Nothing Whig or Democratic rivals; and the six carried by Democrats, four
of whom were themselves Know Nothings backed by Silver Gray insiders and
outsiders. Victorious Whig Know Nothings averaged 58.1 percent of the vote, and
in those districts Whigs' share of the vote on average increased by 12.4 percent
between 1852 and 1854. In stark contrast, the share of the vote amassed by victorious non-Know Nothing Whigs averaged only 45 percent, a *decrease* of 0.1
percent between 1852 and 1854. Worst of all were Whig fortunes in the six
districts carried by Democrats. In those districts, Whigs' mean share of the vote
in 1854 was a pitiful 26 percent, on average an astounding 16 points *lower* than
in 1852. Know Nothings, in short, shattered the normal voter alignment.[112]

Whigs from inside and outside New York, however, focused primarily on the stunning evidence of partisan fragmentation in the four-way gubernatorial race. The bitter election was a cliffhanger, and the final results were not known for several weeks. The prohibitionist Sewardite Whig Clark narrowly edged out the antiprohibitionist Soft Seymour, 156,804 (33.4 percent) to 156,495 (33.3 percent). The Hard Bronson ran last with a dismal 33,850 votes (7.2 percent). The big news was Ullmann's total of 122,282 (26 percent).

For at least three reasons, Ullmann's vote is not an accurate gauge of Know Nothing strength in New York. First, his nomination came so late that ballots for him could not be distributed throughout the state. Second, his correspondence indicates overwhelmingly that nonmembers supported him where Ullmann ballots were available. Third, Ullmann's friends and Sewardites both testified that some Know Nothings—how many is unknown—supported Clark rather than Ullmann because they thought Clark was a member and were suspicious of Ullmann's commitment to a Maine Law and his possible foreign birth. Nonetheless, even a quick glance at New York's 1852 presidential returns, when Winfield Scott got 235,000 votes, indicated both that the state's Whig party had been fractured and that Ullmann attracted considerable support from non-Whigs.

Modern statistical analysis confirms that conclusion. Whig voters from 1852 who turned out in 1854 divided almost evenly between Clark and Ullmann. Wet Whigs offended by Clark did not bolt to Seymour as predicted; instead, they either abstained or supported Ullmann. Whig divisions reflected intriguing splits among different Protestant denominations, but far more significant was the evidence that Know Nothings could attract new voters and Democrats, who constituted a third of Ullmann's vote, in much larger numbers than did Clark. That fact, as much as Silver Gray defection to Ullmann, made the Know Nothings a dangerous threat to the survival of the Whig party.[113]

V

Know Nothings' dramatic success in New York, on top of their victories in Pennsylvania and Massachusetts, shocked observers in and outside the Empire State and instantly altered the calculations of Whigs everywhere. "The large vote for Ullmann reinvigorates the Silver Grey faction," moaned one of Seward's friends. "Who could have believed that K. N. fanaticism was so extensive and so well organized?" Conversely, Silver Grays in New York and their allies outside of it counted on that same discipline to stop Seward's reelection to the Senate when the new legislature met. New York's results indicated that Seward "is about to realize the fruits of his Catholic proclivities," chortled a Rhode Island conservative. "The greatest strength of Seward's influence in the State," chorused Baltimore's John P. Kennedy, "cannot cope with the antagonistic force of the Know Nothings and the National Whigs—which two seem to me to have sufficient affinities to make their combination hereafter inevitable." Even New York's defeated Democrats agreed that Know Nothings had "torn the Whig strength to pieces."[114]

If Know Nothingism seemed to have gutted northern Whiggery, the harsh antislavery, antisouthern rhetoric adopted by many Whigs in Pennsylvania,

Massachusetts, and New York simultaneously seemed to preclude any further cooperation between them and Southerners. "The old parties, as National parties, are broken up, & their power gone," Pennsylvania's victorious James Pollock had concluded even before the Massachusetts and New York results came in. On election day in Massachusetts, one week after New Yorkers voted, Edward Everett, the Bay State's devoted unionist, glumly predicted that northern and southern Whigs could never again cooperate. The platform on which Clark carried New York was "purely sectional," and "the Whig party in the nonslaveholding states is completely abolitionized." Thus, Everett complained to Fillmore, the planned attempt by New York's Silver Grays to resurrect a "National Whig" organization in 1855 would prove stillborn. It was not just that fury against the Nebraska Act in the North "has strengthened the free-soil wing of the Whig party, at the expense of the Conservative wing." In addition, as North Carolina's William A. Graham wrote Fillmore, "Southern Whigs" regarded northern Whigs as "so infest[ed]" by "Abolitionism or Free soilism" that they welcomed their defeat.[115]

Precisely this perception that cooperation between Northerners and Southerners within the Whig party was now impossible prompted Delaware's Clayton, with the blessing of Pennsylvania's Pollock, to promote a public American party to replace the Whigs as the "new national party" Conrad had called on Fillmore to help build in September. Sewardite Whigs from New York regarded Clayton's project as sheer fantasy, for they now believed that Northerners and Southerners who opposed Democrats could never cooperate in any common party. Others beyond Clayton's immediate circle of friends, however, were more sanguine. If Know Nothings would abandon their secrecy and especially if northern Know Nothings "assume a political position in harmony with the conservative National party of the South," that is, with southern Whigs, Kennedy concluded after seeing Know Nothing strength in New York, that party would carry the 1856 presidential election.[116]

Fillmore and his numerous northern and southern Whig backers came to the same conclusion. Only *after* the results of the Pennsylvania, Massachusetts, and New York elections were clear did Fillmore and his conservative Whig allies decide to infiltrate the Know Nothing movement in order to convert it into the Union party they had sought since 1853—in some cases, indeed, since 1850. Fillmore's association with Know Nothingism, whose anti-Catholic and nativist bigotry Sewardites already despised, in turn, ensured that Seward, Weed, and their friends across the North would do all in their power, even to the point of abandoning the Whig party for a new "organization based on merely sectional issues," to defeat it. This titanic struggle lasted until the presidential election in November 1856. Even before 1856 began, however, the Whig party would be shattered into smithereens. Not even all the king's horses and all the king's men, let alone the few diehard Whig fossils who tried to do so, would be able to put it back together again.

Chapter 25

"Let, Then, the Whig Party Pass"

SOUTHERN WHIGS' "only chance" was now "a diversion—a change of names," South Carolina's George S. Bryan concluded two months before the North's crucial October and November elections. Northern Whigs' attacks "against *our section*" destroyed "the nationality of the Whig party" and rendered it impossible for southern Whigs "to maintain brotherly relations" with them. In the future, therefore, southern Whigs must tout "Fillmore & the Know Nothings—or whatever better than can be devised."[1]

On seeing the returns from Pennsylvania, Massachusetts, and New York, John P. Kennedy agreed. Know Nothings could form the core of his long-sought Union party. "National Whigs" and Know Nothings must inevitably combine in New York and other northern states, and "the National Democrats of the North must seek their fellowship hereafter in the same combination." Their interest was to cooperate "with the conservative National party of the South," Kennedy maintained, for in Dixie, Know Nothing "sentiment is thoroughly National and will enlist the support of the whole Whig party and, I doubt not, the National democratic party also." Across the South, he added, those groups "constitute in sentiment and policy one party" that "looks with extraordinary unanimity to Mr. Fillmore" for 1856.[2]

Kennedy's dream appalled most northern Whigs. Furious that Know Nothing strength in the North's fall elections had "demonstrated that, by a majority, Roman Catholicism is feared more than American Slavery," they refused "to have the Whig organization broken up, or merged, into either Temperance or Know Nothing organizations." Nor would they surrender antislavery principles to propitiate southern Whigs. "True friends of Freedom," one snarled, must never again allow political cooperation between Northerners and Southerners.[3] Only by intransigently rejecting cooperation with Southerners and reemphasizing their own antislavery, antisouthern credentials, not propitiating Know Nothings, insisted intransigent Sewardites like Orsamus Matteson, could northern Whigs prevent Free Soilers from seizing control of the fusion Republican movement that many of them now believed to be the North's only hope.[4]

These dramatically divergent reactions to Know Nothings' success in 1854 outline the millstones between which the Whig party was ground to powder. Starting immediately in November and December 1854 and extending throughout 1855, most southern and conservative northern Whigs, led by Fillmore and his acolytes, abandoned the Whig organization and flocked to the Know Nothing order to convert it into a new bisectional Union party that could make Fillmore president. In response, northern Whigs of the Sewardite ilk, who continued to fear that Slave Power aggressions might succeed unless the North was rallied against them, declared "war" against Know Nothingism.[5] Almost inevitably they gravitated toward the emerging Republican party in order to smash the nativists and to prevent Free Soil extremists from dominating it.

The odd men out in this reshuffling were a few die-hard Whig patricians typlifed by Edward Everett and Robert C. Winthrop of Massachusetts; Washington Hunt, Daniel D. Barnard, and Hamilton Fish of New York; Thomas Corwin of Ohio; James Pearce of Maryland; Georgia's Charles Jenkins; Kentucky Congressman William Preston; Virginia's William C. Rives; and William A. Graham and George E. Badger of North Carolina. Repulsed by Know Nothings' principles and personnel, appalled by the Republican party, and sickened as ever by the thought of cooperating with Democrats, these men fumed at their futility. They continued to hope that somehow, some way, the storm would pass and Whiggery could be revived.

I

"I am an individual Whig, but where is my party?" moaned Daniel Barnard, Albany's silk-stocking diehard, in late December 1854. "Where are the Whig elements that are to act in concert, with one leading faith, over the great length and breadth of this great country, to carry a Presidential election?" In New York, the state most pivotal to continued cooperation between northern and southern Whigs, "what calls itself the Whig party now . . . is just no Whig party at all. It has not one element of nationality in its whole composition; and it is the mere broken remnant of a party at that."[6]

New York's November election propelled its long-feuding Silver Gray and Sewardite Whig factions to a permanent parting of the ways. Convinced that the results "have done more to break the back of the Weed & Seward faction than anything that has ever occurred" and opened the way for conservatives "to sweep the Union in '56," Silver Grays wondered only if they should "fight" Sewardites in the future "as 'National Whigs,' or as the 'American Party.' " To bring about a complete merger between Know Nothings and Silver Grays against the Sewardites, John T. Bush, now publisher of the *Albany State Register*, urged Fillmore that Silver Grays should cultivate Know Nothing leaders like Ullmann and James W. Barker, and "our papers should now defend this order and provoke as much denunciation of them, and Silver Gray Whigs jointly, from the Wooly organs, as possible."[7]

Fillmore emphatically agreed with his New York henchmen. Previously dismissing Know Nothings as merely "a disturbing force," he had encouraged Silver Grays' proposed postelection National Whig convention as a device to compete for control of the state Whig organization. November's stunning results changed his mind. Since Sewardites could use state offices to fend off a conservative challenge and since so many Silver Grays had already defected to the Know Nothings in any event, he now viewed Know Nothings as "the best remedy for existing evils."[8] Continued allegiance to the Whig party, in short, now struck Fillmore and his friends as a dead end, not a path to power. In early December, accordingly, Granger and other Silver Grays canceled the planned Albany conclave of conservatives, thereby signaling that National Whigs could no longer survive in the northern Whig party.[9]

Ullmann's strong showing after his last-minute nomination simultaneously convinced Fillmore and his allies that Silver Grays could control the Know Nothing organization, which now offered a better vehicle than Whiggery for a conservative national party. Aware that Massachusetts' Edward Everett was "gloomy" about "the prospect for *conservative* Whigs," Fillmore assured him in mid-December "that *Know Nothingism* or *Americanism* is fast purging a political party from sectionalism and slavery agitation, and may lay the foundation of a party useful to the country and entirely national in its character." The Know Nothing order, he repeated to Virginia's Alexander H. H. Stuart, "presents the only chance of preserving a National party at the North" as well as "the only hope of forming a truly national party, which shall *ignore* the constant and disturbing agitation of slavery." For that reason, "I give it my countenance."[10]

Unmentioned in Fillmore's letters was what others had been saying for months. What one called "the resistless Know Nothing element" could also be "useful" in making Fillmore president once again. That prospect, rather than a sudden conversion to nativism, spurred their sudden appreciation of the secret order. Unlike conservative Whigs from eastern New York, Fillmore had never condemned Catholics or immigrants. As a founder of New York's Antimasonic party, moreover, he abhorred the order's secrecy and agreed with Congressman Solomon G. Haven that its initiation rituals were "puerile."[11] Nonetheless, since Fillmore also agreed with Haven "that the material could be worked (perhaps usefully) into a national fabrick which should be of service," he now discovered virtues even in nativism and secrecy. With Seward's pro-Catholic and proimmigrant proclivities clearly in mind, Fillmore told Stuart that Know Nothingism could "take away the inducement for demagogues, of both parties, to pander to the foreign vote and corruptly chaffer for its purchase at every election." Aware, too, of conservatives' inability to pry New York's Whig organization from Weed's grip, he touted the order's secret selection of candidates in lodges as an antidote to the "*fraud* and *bribery*" and the "disorderly and riotous" behavior that had prevented "respectable gentlemen" from attending Whigs' primary meetings. For all these reasons, Fillmore concluded, "the KNs are the best remedy for existing evils."[12]

Once New York's returns were in, therefore, Fillmore pressed his New York Whig allies to join Know Nothing lodges if they had not already done so. Fillmore and Kennedy also bombarded conservative Whigs elsewhere like Everett, Robert C. Winthrop, and Virginia's Stuart, with imprecations to give up on Whiggery and convert to Know Nothingism.[13] While Fillmore and Kennedy privately lobbied Whigs to switch to Know Nothingism, New York's Silver Grays publicly announced their abandonment of Whiggery. In January 1855, the Albany *State Register*, New York's flagship Silver Gray organ since 1850, asserted that there was no longer a Whig party in either the South or the North. Discounting "men who claim to be Whig leaders and masters of ceremonies [i.e., Sewardites]," it asked, "Whether there is in sober truth any such thing as a Whig party embracing Whig masses? An organization based upon Whig principles, advocating a Whig policy?" Both the Whig and the Democratic parties "have become practically obsolete . . . [and] are broken into irreconcilable fragments." Since New York's Whig organization had become "a mere abolition party, its leaders abolitionists, a mere sectional party," the old Whig party was "dead" and could never "be galvanized into a new existence." "Instead of all this foolish talk about the Whig party and the Locofoco party," concluded editor Samuel H. Hammond, "why not step out independent American men, kicking away these old party fetters that have so long been rusting into the flesh, . . . and gather on a broad American platform?"[14]

II

Whether public or private, these arguments sought to surmount a series of interrelated obstacles that Fillmore and his advisors confronted once they decided to cross the Rubicon and leave the Whig organization. Most basically, by casting his lot with the Know Nothings in anticipation of riding the nativist wave into the White House in 1856, Fillmore instantly acquired a personal stake in making sure that wave did not ebb. To help secure Know Nothings' continued success at the polls, he had to persuade as many Whigs as possible to join him in abandoning ship and supporting Know Nothing, not Whig, candidates in 1855. New England's spring elections would be his first target, but far more important were southern contests later that year since Southerners were critical to his presidential aspirations.

Continued Know Nothing success, however, would not benefit him unless he cleared additional hurdles. For one, whatever Kennedy and other Fillmore lieutenants said about Know Nothings' preference for Fillmore's presidential candidacy in 1856 and about the order's potential to become the long-sought Union party, Know Nothing strength in 1854 primarily reflected intense anti-Catholic, anti-foreign, and antiparty resentments. Populistic nativists would not necessarily look kindly on the intrusion of seasoned pols like Fillmore's friends or on the candidacy of a nonmember like Fillmore, who had never publicly expressed any anti-Catholic or nativist sentiments. Original Know Nothings, in sum, must be reassured that Fillmore shared their agenda.

Fillmore could not do so publicly, however. He knew that hundreds, perhaps thousands, of Whigs like Everett and Winthrop reviled the anti-elitist demagoguery, secrecy, and anti-Catholic bigotry of Know Nothings and were "vehement in [their] denunciation" of the order.[15] An open embrace of Know Nothingism would simply discredit Fillmore with such men, not encourage the conversions he needed. Any public endorsement of Know Nothing principles, moreover, would shatter Fillmore's calculated pose of noninvolvement in political affairs and expose his ambition for the presidency.

Fillmore, therefore, moved privately on two fronts to reassure nativists. In early January 1855 he sent a confidential letter to Isaac Newton, a Philadelphia Know Nothing and former Whig, who had worked for Stuart in the Interior

Department during Fillmore's presidency. Fillmore instructed Newton to circulate it among Pennsylvania's Know Nothings, but he insisted that the letter must not be published. In it he denounced "the corrupting influence which the contest for the foreign vote is exciting upon our elections," deplored the perversion of "the ballot-box—that great paladium of our liberty—into an unmeaning mockery, where the rights of native-born citizens are voted away by those who blindly follow their mercenary and selfish leaders," and protested "the large disproportion of offices which are now held by foreigners at home and abroad." All this, he declared, caused the cheeks of every "true-hearted American" to "tingle with shame and mortification." Thus it was time for "our country to be governed by American-born citizens."[16]

More delicate was the matter of whether Fillmore should personally join the Know Nothing fraternity. Originally, Fillmore and his friends like former Post-master General Nathan K. Hall hoped that he would not have to demean himself by doing so. They relied implicitly, however, on the advice of Haven, who sought opinions from other Know Nothing congressmen in Washington during December and January. Haven initially advised against Fillmore's joining. Know Nothings, he wrote, would make no presidential nomination until mid-1856, and every lodge in the country would know it within ten days if Fillmore did join, thus effectively throwing his hat in the presidential ring. No one in Fillmore's inner circle wanted his name "hawked about" as a presidential contender until 1856, and they encouraged Fillmore to make an extended trip to Europe that would keep him out of the country, and out of the public eye, from May 1855 until June 1856. By mid-January, however, Haven became convinced that Know Nothings would nominate no one but an insider. Thus he arranged for Fillmore's private induction into the order at Fillmore's Buffalo home in late January 1855.[17]

Both Fillmore's letter to Newton and his initiation also addressed two far more serious problems hindering his objectives. And it was these, more than anything else, that caused Fillmore and Kennedy to press conservative Whigs to ignore their disdain for Know Nothings and follow them into the nativists' camp. First, after November 1854, Fillmore was not the only ambitious politico who realized that Know Nothings might elect the next president. Fillmore therefore sought to outmaneuver potential competitors for Know Nothings' nomination.

Fillmore became a Know Nothing and sent his letter to Newton to neutralize those threats. Since New York's Know Nothings insisted upon retaining their secrecy and rejected pleas by John M. Clayton for open action, Fillmore and his managers calculated that insiders who belonged to the order, rather than outsider fellow travelers, would name the nativists' candidate from among their midst. That calculation clearly influenced his letter to Pennsylvania's Newton since he and his managers especially feared the popularity of Delaware's Clayton among nativists. To hedge their bets on the secret order's control of the nomination, however, Kennedy, the co-manager of Fillmore's presidential campaign along with Haven, never joined a Know Nothing lodge so that he could maintain his credibility with men who wanted to jettison the Whig party for a new bisectional nativist party but who vehemently rejected secrecy.[18]

The same tactics could also stymie another outsider who hoped to ride the anti-Catholic, antiparty eruption into the White House—Supreme Court Justice John McLean. Possibly the only man in antebellum America whose thirst for the presidency was as unquenchable as Daniel Webster's, McLean had flirted with the Antimasonic nomination in 1832, bid for the Whig nomination in 1836, and orchestrated a concerted effort for the party's 1848 laurels by presenting himself as a No Party reformer. Now he saw the antiparty, antipolitician, clean-government impulse behind Know Nothingism as the perfect opportunity to achieve his long-sought goal. After the 1854 returns came in, McLean obsequiously showered letters on Know Nothings in New York, Pennsylvania, Ohio, and Michigan, praising their organization as "the party of the people" that could save the government from "cliques," "demagogues," and "political traders and gamesters," and warning them to "suffer not the political hacks of any party to enter into your organization or to control your action." That advice, if heeded, could certainly have checked Fillmore, but by joining the order, when McLean himself did not, Fillmore might trump McLean's bid for the Know Nothings' favor.[19]

Fillmore could outflank outsider Whigs by joining the order but not Democratic hopefuls who also became Know Nothings. By far the most prominent of these in the winter of 1854–55 was Texas' famous Senator Sam Houston. Houston aroused enormous enthusiasm among Democratic Know Nothings, whose support had to be retained if Know Nothings were to elect a president. He was also extraordinarily popular among anti-Nebraska Democrats in the North who were not members, for Houston had opposed the Nebraska Act. Fillmore might compete for Democratic/Know Nothing support by renouncing the Whig party, as he did privately and Hammond did publicly in his *Albany State Register* manifesto, but Fillmore's best hope against Houston—and against New York's George Law, who later emerged as Fillmore's primary Democratic challenger for the Know Nothing nomination—was to make sure that former Whigs outnumbered former Democrats among Know Nothings. That was a major reason why he urged conservative Whigs to join the order after the 1854 elections.[20]

It was not, however, the most important reason. Fillmore sought reelection in 1856 primarily because he sincerely believed that the renewed sectional agitation over the Nebraska Act endangered the Union and that he offered the best hope of rallying a bisectional Union party that could save it. Southern Democrats who pressured Douglas and Pierce into renouncing their party's 1852 platform pledges had to be driven from office, but so too did anti-Nebraska Whigs who courted Free Soil support in 1854 by adopting vehemently antisouthern platforms or, even worse, by joining fusion and Republican coalitions. Only the Know Nothings now seemed capable of defeating all three political groups that menaced the Union, but that was true if—and only if—Know Nothings could be converted into a bisectional Union party that, in both the North and the South, would now "*ignore the constant and distructing agitation of slavery.*" That task, in turn, seemed to require massive reinforcements by conservative Whigs who had thus far remained indifferent or hostile to the Know Nothings' anti-Catholic, anti-immigrant crusade.

Specifically, Fillmore needed additional conservative Whig infusions into Know Nothing ranks to accomplish three critical political goals. First, to defeat southern Democrats and to make sure that southern Know Nothings supported his own nomination for president, Fillmore had to persuade southern Whigs, many of whom despised the secrecy, bigotry, and proscriptiveness of Know Nothings, to abandon the old party and join the nativists. At the same time, he had to bring southern Whigs on board without driving Democratic Know Nothings out of the order, for unionist Whigs and Democrats must combine to carry traditionally Democratic slave states. During December and January, therefore, Fillmore and Haven were already deeply involved in advising Whigs from Virginia, the first slave state to vote in 1855, not to do anything that offended Democrats in the order and thereby jeopardized Know Nothing chances of winning the May gubernatorial and congressional elections.[21]

Fillmore realized, however, that Know Nothing success in the South ultimately depended upon achieving two other goals in the North, both of which required converting more conservative northern Whigs to Know Nothingism. To convince southern Whigs, upon whom his hope for the presidency had always rested, to follow him into the Know Nothing party, Fillmore and his inner circle had, first, to demonstrate that in the North genuine conservatives who would *"ignore"* antislavery agitation, rather than anti-Nebraska zealots, controlled Know Nothing machinery. For this reason, among others, they planned to "exclude the Nebraska bill and the temperance question from discussion in the paper" when the *State Register* was converted to a Know Nothing organ, but they also required help from hostile conservatives outside New York like Everett and Winthrop to displace antislavery men from power in the order. Kennedy told a New York Know Nothing in February 1855, for example, that he must "impress upon the association in New York and all north of it" that to achieve success the order must "declare and show itself to be thoroughly *national*. Its whole virtue as a supreme political agency depends upon its sober—I may say religious—determination to crush all mischievous *sectionalism* which is now struggling for ascendancy in American politics."[22]

Second, Fillmore and his boosters had to show that northern Know Nothings who eschewed attacks on the South could in fact carry elections in 1855 against both northern Democrats, who defended the Nebraska Act, and anti-Nebraska parties, whether Whig or Republican, that engaged in South bashing to win northern votes. Unless they could do both, southern Whigs might shun Fillmore's new vehicle and turn instead to the southern-oriented Democrats themselves as the best way to check South bashers in the North. To win in the North, and thereby help Know Nothings in the South, as many reliable National northern Whigs as possible had to aid the Know Nothing cause.

III

In 1855 these three tasks—attracting more southern Whigs to Know Nothingism without alienating Democratic Know Nothings, ensuring that conservative Whigs controlled northern Know Nothing parties, and winning northern elections without attacking the South—preoccupied Fillmore and, after he departed for Europe, his inner circle of advisors. All ultimately proved beyond their power to accomplish. Know Nothingism could not be harnessed by any single group, and its performance at the polls that year owed little if anything to Fillmore's agenda. At the same time, events continued to inflame sectional antagonism. As a result, northern anti-Nebraska Know Nothings refused to cease antisouthern agitation, while anti-Nebraska Whigs, Democrats, and Free Soilers outside the order strained every nerve to crush it. This ferocious battle between pro-Know Nothing and anti-Know Nothing Whigs nearly obliterated what remained of northern Whiggery.

In the South most, but never all, Whigs backed Know Nothing or American candidates in 1855, yet their conversion owed little to Fillmore's efforts or to his potential presidential candidacy. And it drove most Democrats who had joined the order in 1854, when few elections were held in the slave states, back to their former party. Reduced essentially to a shrunken Whig base, southern Know Nothing parties did not prove nearly as powerful as the effusive Kennedy predicted. Southern Whig conversions to Know Nothingism instead produced two results: the decimation of the southern Whig party and a sectional split among Know Nothings at a national council meeting in June 1855 that eerily resembled the rancorous Whig national convention of June 1852.

Control of Whig state organizations in New York by Sewardites and by even more rabidly antisouthern men in Vermont, Pennsylvania, and the Midwest drove Fillmore and Silver Grays out of the Whig party toward the Know Nothings. Yet they could not escape conflict with antislavery men by fleeing to the nativist order. Though a few conservative Whigs joined the Know Nothings in the Midwest, Fillmore lacked leverage over the ex-Whig leaders who engineered Know Nothing participation in the anti-Nebraska fusion movements in Wisconsin, Michigan, Indiana, Ohio, and several congressional districts in Illinois. Rather than ignoring slavery to facilitate cooperation with Southerners and to convert Know Nothingism into a national Union party, for example, John Defrees, Godlove Orth, and Schuyler Colfax, the Indiana Whigs who skillfully manipulated Know Nothingism to gain control of Indiana's People's party and who hoped to "preserve the nationality of our order," would do so only "if it can be done without a sacrifice of principle." Throughout the spring of 1855 they insisted that both "a strong Anti-Slavery feeling" and "a strong American feeling . . . must be preserved & united if possible, else both go by the board."[23]

Ohio's Whig/Know Nothings even more adamantly resisted renunciation of open opposition to slavery extension. No presidential candidate from a slave state would do, Lew Campbell angrily told Schouler when he boomed Kentucky's Garrett Davis. At the mere hint of that, "the influence of Greeley & [Gamaliel] Bailey & co. will destroy the K. N. element." For Know Nothingism to remain viable in the Midwest, it must remain an avowedly anti-Nebraska, anti-Slave Power party. Men with such beliefs were hardly prepared to abdicate antislavery agitation, as Fillmore wished.[24]

More important, at the start of 1855 the tenor of Know Nothingism in Pennsylvania, Massachusetts, and New York had to give southern Whigs pause. Many of their victorious gubernatorial and congressional candidates who had been identified by newspapers as Know Nothings ran vehemently antisouthern campaigns. The first tests of Fillmore's effort to demonstrate conservatives' control of northern Know Nothingism, therefore, were senatorial elections scheduled for the early months of 1855 in all three of those key states. To entice southern Whigs to combine with Know Nothings, northern Know Nothing state legislators must elect conservatives to the Senate. As Haven told Fillmore in December, the election of "a national man" from Massachusetts like Julius Rockwell, Winthrop, or Rufus Choate, each of whom indignantly refused to have anything to do with Know

Nothingism, but especially Seward's defeat by Know Nothings in New York's legislature, "would open up a nice future for our folks." "The Order would be hailed everywhere as having accomplished a great work," and "the South would no longer be restrained if that were to happen."[25]

It was not to be. Know Nothings dominated the Pennsylvania legislature, yet no acceptable conservative candidate for the Senate emerged there. Conservative Whig incumbent James Cooper was never considered, even though he courted Know Nothing support.[26] Instead, a three-way race split the Know Nothing caucus among two avowedly anti-Nebraska Whigs who would be anathema to Southerners: ex-Governor William F. Johnston and Andrew Curtin, the Whig state chairman who had written the antislavery Whig address in July 1854, and the opportunistic Democrat Simon Cameron, who joined the order after the October elections to advance his senatorial ambitions. Residual jealousies between ex-Whigs and ex-Democrats in Know Nothing ranks and a strenuous lobbying campaign against Cameron by the fervently antislavery Whig-Know Nothing Thaddeus Stevens prevented any selection whatsoever. The only solace Fillmore and his friends could derive from Pennsylvania was that no one offensive to the South had been named.[27]

Results from Massachusetts were far grimmer from Fillmore's perspective. Not only did its Know Nothing legislature pass resolutions demanding repeal of the Nebraska and Fugitive Slave Acts, but, for the remaining three years of Everett's Senate term, it elected Free Soiler Henry Wilson, who had become a Know Nothing only after his efforts to lure Massachusetts Whigs into a new Republican coalition aborted. Everett, who predicted Wilson's election from the moment Know Nothings swept the state, mourned his triumph as an indication that in the North "there is a great increase in antislavery feeling," while "conservative views are paralyzed." Winthrop, who adamantly spurned Kennedy's pleas to cooperate with Know Nothings, saw Wilson's victory as a signal that southern Whigs must *not* abandon the party for Know Nothingism. "I hope our Southern friends understand what Massachusetts *Know Nothingism* is," he growled.[28]

Of far greater consequence to Fillmorites and southern Whigs was the New York contest over Seward's Senate seat. By the end of 1854, Seward was in a curious position. On the one hand, his refusal to abandon the Whig party that year and his insistence on holding out olive branches to southern Whigs earned him contempt from Free Soilers and other Northerners intent upon building a new antislavery fusion organization. On the other, his moderation failed to mitigate the hatred of Silver Grays and the suspicion of southern Whigs, who still regarded him as the North's preeminent antislavery Whig. Consequently, Seward's defeat was considered essential to the success of southern Know Nothingism. "It will hurt us greatly in this part of the country if he should be elected by 'Know Nothing' votes," North Carolina's Whig/Know Nothing Kenneth Rayner warned New York's Ullmann in January. "For God's sake, have him defeated, if possible."[29]

Seward was certainly New York's preeminent Whig politician, and Weed had tried to preserve the Whig organization intact in 1854 primarily to ensure Seward's reelection. On paper that task seemed easy. Along with capturing the governorship and the vast majority of congressional seats in November 1854, New York's Whigs won overwhelming majorities in both houses of the state legislature. The problem, of course, was that some of those successful Whigs were Know Nothings, and both committed nativists among the Know Nothings and Silver Grays who had joined them to vent displeasure with the Whig ticket pledged to stop Seward.[30] So widely known was the intention of Know Nothings and Silver Grays to use "every means their conceivable meanness can invent to defeat" Seward that Democrats crowed about the "division within the Whig ranks," while out-of-state Whigs like Rhode Island's John O. Charles and Pennsylvania's Edward McPherson predicted that Seward's "imprudent" hostility to nativism ensured his defeat.[31] Seward himself was so pessimistic that on Christmas Eve he wrote Weed volunteering to decline reelection to help the Whig cause, an offer Weed emphatically rejected.[32]

Three things, in fact, operated against the Know Nothings and to Seward's advantage in the senatorial contest. First, whereas Silver Grays, Know Nothings, and Democrats could agree on opposing Seward, they could not agree on a common champion, and by late January, Haven had concluded that, without a consensus candidate of their own, the Know Nothings' only hope was to postpone the senatorial election until the next legislature.[33] Second, Seward had support outside of straight Whig ranks. In some districts Sewardite Whigs helped elect Democrats in exchange for their pledges to support Seward's reelection. More important, Know Nothings' ability to stop Seward depended on disciplined cohesion within their ranks. Yet some of the Whig/Know Nothing legislators were Sewardites who intended to vote for the incumbent if they could do so without being expelled from the order.[34] Third, and most important, loyal Weed Whigs controlled both the governorship and the canal board, and thus they had the patronage resources to woo even the most inveterate Silver Gray and Know Nothing legislators into Seward's camp. "Clark, by all consent, is a miserable man," whined Barnard in late January. "The offices are held for sale." Three days before the crucial vote, E. R. Jewett, a prominent Silver Gray leader, dejectedly predicted Seward's election because Clark refused to make any appointments until after the Senate election. "This unites all applicants and their friends in his [Seward's] behalf, who act as if the zeal they manifest is to be the criterion of their claims."[35]

These factors combined to return Seward to the Senate on February 6 with 87 of 160 votes. By one estimate, twenty-nine of thirty-six Whig/Know Nothings voted for Seward, while only seven held out against him. It was a crushing blow to Fillmore's plans and to Know Nothings' hopes. Sewardite Whigs were quick to celebrate Seward's victory—significantly, not as an elixir for the Whig party, but as poison for Know Nothingism. "Hindooism in New York has met with an Artic [sic] calamity—the beak is too far below the water line to have any hope for the craft," crowed one. "Your election yesterday will carry consternation into the camp of 'Sam,'" echoed another, "and from it may be dated his decline."[36] Such exultant gibes were wildly premature. The supposedly obtuse Myron Clark came closer to the mark when he warned Seward that, because "there is still so much of the spirit of vandalism or 'Hindooism', such a fever or rage for some new organization, or a breaking up of the old ones amongst us," even Seward's reelection had failed to insulate the Whig party from danger.[37]

Rather than permanently slowing Know Nothing momentum, Seward's reelection instead had a paradoxical impact on the rival Whig camps that had fought over it. By indicating that Sewardite Whigs could run New York's state government even without the help of Silver Grays, it encouraged Sewardites' hopes that the New York Whig party, and with it the northern Whig party, might continue to be a viable political force. Thus it delayed, if only for a few months, any serious consideration by New York's remaining Whigs about joining the antislavery fusion movement that was mushrooming elsewhere. Yet Seward, Weed, and other leaders of the truncated New York Whig party were as hardheadedly realistic as any leaders the Whig party ever produced. Given the "rage for some new organization, or a breaking up of the old ones amongst us," they knew that the acid test of northern Whiggery's survival was the ability of northern Whigs outside of New York to emulate their performance by defeating Democrats, Know Nothings, *and* Republicans in 1855. Simultaneously, Seward's victory meant that, at least until the next New York election in November 1855, Fillmore and his conservative Whig allies must also look beyond New York for evidence to persuade southern Whigs that northern Know Nothings were controlled by conservatives who, by abjuring agitation of the slavery issue, could defeat both pro-Nebraska Democrats and anti-Nebraska forces, whether Whig, Republican, or Know Nothing. Pro- and anti-Know Nothing New York Whigs, moreover, looked to exactly the same place for the evidence they needed. And both were sorely chagrined by what occurred in New Hampshire, Rhode Island, and Connecticut that spring.

IV

Tiny Rhode Island clearly disappointed those who hoped to preserve the Whig party, but it hardly fulfilled Fillmore's wishes. With the Nebraska question neutralized by Rhode Island Democrats' anti-Nebraska votes in Congress, attention focused on whether its Whigs, who had ended a skein of Democratic victories by electing William Hoppin governor and capturing the legislature in 1854, would merge with Know Nothings in the gubernatorial and congressional races.[38] Deploring the rush of good Whigs into the Know Nothing order, the Providence *Journal* considered even certain defeat on a straight Whig ticket "no sufficient reason why we should abandon our party" and praised those Whigs "who have not been seduced into new combinations, and who are not ashamed of the name, the principles, or the organization of Whigs."[39]

The majority of Rhode Island's Whigs were so seduced, however, and Governor Hoppin, who apparently joined the order before the end of 1854, led them. A Whig convention renominated Hoppin in March, but Know Nothings then immediately named him as their own candidate. Adding over 1,300 votes to his 1854 total, Hoppin crushed his Democratic opponent, a vociferous critic of Know Nothingism, with 81.5 percent of the vote, compared to 58.4 percent in 1854. Know Nothings also overwhelmingly won both House seats, appropriating Whig candidate Nathaniel Durfee in the first district and popular anti-Nebraska Democratic incumbent Benjamin Thurston, whom Whigs dared not oppose, in the second.[40]

Rhode Island, in sum, demonstrated that Whigs could not withstand the surging Know Nothing movement. But it hardly produced a Know Nothing movement purged of anti-Nebraska sentiment. Both congressmen-elect were anti-Nebraska men. Rhode Island's Know Nothings bolted the national council meeting in June

1855 when it failed to condemn the Nebraska measure. And Hoppin won reelection again in April 1856 as a joint American and Republican candidate. By April 1855, however, it *was* clear that the Whig party had effectively ceased operation in another northern state.

New Hampshire and Connecticut also heralded the Whig party's demise, but they gave even less solace to Fillmore than to Seward and Weed. Rather than providing unionist ballast to the soaring Know Nothing movement, as Fillmore hoped, many conservative Whigs in both states, like their counterparts in Maine and Massachusetts, clung to the crumbling Whig party that Fillmore abandoned or sat out the election, thereby forfeiting leadership of Know Nothings to others. Many antislavery Whigs, the men most likely to follow Seward's lead on sectional issues, also refused to abandon Whiggery. Their stubbornness may have temporarily gratified the New Yorkers, but the thrashing that holdout Whigs received at the hands of Know Nothings quickly chastened them.

New Hampshire's politics were complicated because the existing Democratic, Whig, and Free Soil parties, following custom, all nominated gubernatorial candidates in the summer of 1854, months before the March 1855 election and months before the Know Nothing frenzy swept the state. A singular fact nonetheless emphasized Know Nothings' power. Both incumbent Democratic Governor Nathaniel Baker, whom Democrats renominated for 1855, and Whig candidate James Bell, who had lost to Baker in 1854, joined Know Nothing lodges before the end of that year in hopes of their endorsement. Anti-Nebraska Democrats, who wanted to repudiate Pierce's administration, and Free Soilers also rushed into the order. So headlong was politicos' flight into the secret society that the Websterite Whig Boston *Courier* complained that Whigs and Free Soilers "virtually disbanded themselves" to whore after Know Nothing support, while the pro-Pierce Democratic Concord *New Hampshire Patriot* warned that Know Nothings were controlled by the "log-rolling and wire-pulling ambitionists of the whig and freesoil fusion party."[41]

Antislavery men dominated New Hampshire's Know Nothing party, and, ignoring Baker and Bell, they nominated Ralph Metcalf, an anti-Nebraska and anti-Pierce Democrat, for governor because, as the Free Soiler John P. Hale explained, they wanted the help of anti-Nebraska Democrats in electing "two Senators of the right stamp to the next Congress from New Hampshire."[42] In the state's three congressional districts, the various foes of the administration—Whigs, Free Soilers, anti-Nebraska Democrats, and Know Nothings—held separate conventions to choose candidates. Nonetheless, all opposition groups ended up agreeing on common candidates, all three of whom were Know Nothings. All these Know Nothing candidates, as well as Know Nothing legislators, swept to decisive victories, thus ending Democrats' decades-long domination of New Hampshire.

The gubernatorial race best demonstrates how Know Nothings decimated Whiggery and absorbed Free Soilers, precisely the group Fillmore did not want in the new party. Metcalf won with 32,783 votes (50.7 percent), and Baker, whose vote dropped by 2,700 since 1854, polled 27,055 (41.8 percent). Far more striking, the Free Soil vote plummeted by almost 90 percent between 1854 and 1855, and statistical estimates suggest that almost all of the defectors, many of whom were Whigs attracted by Jared Perkins' candidacy in 1854, went Know Nothing in 1855.[43] Just as dramatically, the Whig Bell's total dropped from 17,028 (29.4

percent) in 1854 to 3,436 (5.3 percent) in 1855. Three-fourths of New Hampshire's Whigs had decamped to the Know Nothings, and Bell himself had decamped with them.[44]

Observers outside the state quickly recognized the implications of Free Soilers' and Whigs' absorption into New Hampshire's Know Nothing party. Indiana's Schuyler Colfax, who wanted all anti-Nebraska men to rally behind the Know Nothing, not the Whig or Republican, banner, rejoiced that Know Nothings' sweep meant that New Hampshire would send Hale back to the Senate, as indeed the legislature did in June. That act, along with Wilson's election in Massachusetts, Colfax exulted, "will show Anti-Slavery men that the indiscriminate attacks [on Know Nothingism] of the [National] Era & Tribune are unjust as well as mistaken." New Hampshire's Know Nothing party, in short, represented exactly what neither Fillmore nor Seward wanted.[45] Clearly, New Hampshire Know Nothings were not potential Fillmore men; just as clearly, Seward and Weed knew by June that Whiggery was dead in the Granite State, and that, as elsewhere, its antislavery Whigs now sought to join the new Republican party.[46]

Know Nothings also decimated Whiggery as an independent force in Connecticut. Free Soilers and Maine Law men futilely warned that "the cause of Liberty and Temperance" would be "swallowed up by the 'one idea' that Roman Catholicism is the great bugbear and the only question that interests the freemen of this country." To no avail, staunch old-line antislavery Whigs like ex-Senator Roger Sherman Baldwin and his sons also protested against any Whig fusion with the nativists. Two weeks before the April election, Baldwin's shrewd wife, Emily, ruefully admitted that Know Nothings had infiltrated most Whig meetings and "draw more from the whig ranks than any other." The day after Know Nothings swept the April gubernatorial, legislative, and congressional elections, reducing staunchly anti-Nebraska Whig incumbent Governor Henry Dutton, whom Free Soilers endorsed in 1855, to a mere 14 percent of the vote and putting virtual nonentities rather than veteran Whig politicos in Congress, she reported accurately that "the present result of this new party is to break up the Whig influence and to put forward an entire set of new men." Anti-Nebraska Democrat Gideon Welles, who detested the bigotry and proscriptiveness of Know Nothings, agreed: "Our election has resulted in a rout & break up of the old parties."[47]

V

New England's spring elections and the winter's senatorial selections punctuated two developments begun in the fall of 1854: the fragmentation of the anti-Democratic vote and the Whig party's irreversible dissolution. As shrewd observers recognized, those developments also indicated that pro- and anti-Know Nothing Whigs could largely determine whether, and on what basis, anti-Democratic elements might combine for the 1856 presidential race. By the spring of 1855, indeed, virtually every political leader's calculations explicitly or implicitly revolved around that impending presidential contest. And to shape its outcome, two battles among Whigs raged simultaneously for the remainder of 1855: one between anti- and pro-Know Nothing Whigs over the nature of the new anti-Democratic party; and one between anti-Nebraska Whig/Know Nothings and

Fillmorite conservatives for control of the Know Nothing organization. Tellingly, almost no protagonist in these fights suggested that the Whig party itself should or could survive.

Less obviously but just as significantly, the same developments in the winter and spring of 1855 suggested that southern Whigs might profoundly affect the outcome of both battles. The nature of New England's victorious Know Nothing coalitions set back Fillmore's hope of converting the nativist order into a Union party and decreased the likelihood that other northern conservatives would help displace antislavery men as Know Nothing leaders in the North. Thus Fillmore became all the more dependent on aid from Southerners in national gatherings of Know Nothings to accomplish his goals. Conversely, those who wanted to combine all northern antislavery men in a new Republican party would have welcomed an exodus of anti-Nebraska Whigs from the Know Nothings, but the spring results reduced the likelihood that such men could be pried away—unless Southerners did something that forced them from the order.

Even if northern anti-Nebraska Whig/Know Nothings could be weaned from the order, moreover, the fall and spring elections demonstrated indelibly that anti-Catholicism and nativism could not be ignored—let alone repudiated, as New York's Whig remnant appeared bent on doing—by any non-Know Nothing anti-Democratic coalition. Determined to focus the public's attention on the slavery issue, proponents of a Republican party lamented that nativism's strength in the spring "shows that *we* have lost the precedence, so far as New England is concerned." Many admitted as well "how idle it would be for us to hope to triumph in '56 in direct antagonism to the K[now] N[othings], as we should be with Seward for our leader & the *Tribune* for our oracle!" Midwestern Whigs like Indiana's Schuyler Colfax and Ohio's Lew Campbell, who sought to rally anti-administration men behind the Know Nothings and were convinced that no party that repudiated their anti-Catholic, antiforeign agenda could carry the North in 1856, also castigated New York Whigs' "insane course" that had "butchered up matters so as to have hatred where there should be fusion." Free Soil friends of Salmon Chase, who understood the necessity of including Know Nothings in any antislavery organization, and anti-Nebraska Democrats like Gideon Welles joined the cry and blamed Weed's and Seward's pigheaded decision to cling "to the Whig party too long" and to run a "strict Whig ticket" in New York for the disarray of the North's anti-Nebraska forces. Along with Sewardites' insistence upon running separate Whig tickets against anti-Nebraska Know Nothing coalitions in Connecticut and New Hampshire, fumed Free Soilers, that stubbornness showed "a persistent purpose not to let the old Whig party with all its history of Clay & Webster & Fillmore abominations die out." Only by overcoming "Whig stupidity," therefore, could a "union of all Anti Nebraska parties" be effected.[48]

If almost all politicos recognized that Whiggery was doomed and that nativist sentiment could not be ignored, antislavery Whig/Know Nothings who wanted to perpetuate the nativist party, like Fillmore and his inner circle of Whig advisors, believed that most southern Whigs would join the American party. Throughout 1854 and the first half of 1855, moreover, most of them still expected to cooperate with their southern counterparts behind a common presidential candidate in 1856. Yet they also believed that Fillmore's nomination or the conversion of the nativist movement into a Union party that eschewed an anti-Nebraska platform would destroy Know Nothingism in the North by driving men like themselves from it and guaranteeing the opposition of antislavery outsiders to it. " 'Sam' will be proslavery in all the slave states—but 'woe betide him' if the smell of that fire is on him in a free state," warned Indiana Whig Samuel W. Parker in May 1855. "The old codger's sons North and South will have to 'agree to disagree' on the Slavery question—or else be ground to powder." Since some southern Whigs had condemned the Nebraska Act before its passage and even more did so afterward, Indiana Whig/Know Nothing leaders like Colfax and Godlove Orth expected southern Know Nothings to tolerate a call for its repeal in a national platform. Others, notably Ohio's Campbell, were willing to avoid any antislavery statement in the expected platform from the Philadelphia national council meeting in June, so long as northern Know Nothings were left free to demand that repeal in their own states.[49]

Further to build a bridge to Southerners in 1854–55, but also to stop them from fixing irrevocably on Fillmore as their presidential candidate, midwestern Whig/Know Nothings touted various southern Whig/Know Nothings who might be palatable to Northerners as possible nominees: Garrett Davis, Schouler's favorite; Tennessee's Whig Congressman William Cullom, who had voted against the Nebraska bill; Missouri's Edward Bates; and North Carolina's Kenneth Rayner, a prominent nativist, who had taken no public stand on the Nebraska issue. The important corollary point, however, is that anti-Nebraska Whig/Know Nothings sought utter control of northern Know Nothing organizations so that they could dictate to southern Know Nothings who could—but especially who could not—be the candidate if Southerners expected northern help in electing him. The refusal of Sewardite Whigs in New York and elsewhere to combine with them frustrated that objective by cracking the northern solidarity believed necessary to negotiate with Southerners from a position of strength and instead opened the possibility that some northern Know Nothings would back an unacceptable doughface.[50]

While picking the proper man to win the White House in 1856 was the ultimate objective of both Fillmorite conservatives and anti-Nebraska Whigs, both groups knew that their battle to control the Know Nothing organization could be determined by two interim contests, both of which might turn on what southern Know Nothings did. One was the election of the new speaker of the House when the Thirty-Fourth Congress met in December 1855, for, after the 1854 elections, antiadministration men expected to dominate that body. As early as the fall of 1854, therefore, jockeying began to shape a decision that would be made a full year later.

"The Speaker should be *Whig*," declared Indiana's Parker when endorsing Ohio's Lew Campbell, the favorite of Colfax and other midwestern Whig/Know Nothings who had cooperated with anti-Nebraska fusion movements in 1854. During the winter of 1854–55, Campbell was also mentioned prominently in caucuses of anti-Nebraska congressmen that included anti-Know Nothing Sewardites, but so were Massachusetts' anti-Nebraska Democrat Nathaniel P. Banks, who was reelected as a Know Nothing in 1854, and Maine's Israel Washburn, Jr., the favorite of those promoting the Republicans as an alternative to Know Nothings. Expecting a dogfight, Campbell orchestrated a letter-writing campaign through Ohio's Whig/Know Nothing Congressman-elect Samuel Galloway in the spring of 1855 to line up support. Colfax arranged for the entire Indiana Know Nothing congressional delegation to operate as a unit for Campbell in December, and he promised that Michigan's Know Nothing/Republican congressmen would act with them.[51]

As potential rivals to these northern anti-Nebraska men, Know Nothings occasionally mentioned Southerners, but the man they most feared and the hope of the Fillmorite conservatives was Buffalo's Solomon G. Haven. After New England's spring elections, in fact, electing Haven speaker represented one of the two last chances Fillmorites had of demonstrating to southern Whigs that conservative Unionists, rather than antislavery zealots bent on repealing the Nebraska Act, controlled northern Know Nothing organizations.[52] During the nine months Congress was out of session between March and December 1855, therefore, Haven, too, engaged in a vigorous correspondence campaign to line up support. Campbell and other northern opponents of Haven feverishly predicted that proadministration Democrats would back Haven to defeat more militant anti-Nebraska alternatives, but the conservatives understood from the start that Haven had no chance without considerable southern support.[53]

What Southerners did could also determine the outcome of the Philadelphia national council meeting in June 1855, the second contest that might determine the future direction of Know Nothingism and thus the future course of Whigs inside and outside the order. Even if that meeting retained the order's secrecy, it was expected to issue a public platform spelling out where the order stood on the slavery issue. Thus antislavery Whig-Know Nothings seeking to commit the order to repealing the Nebraska Act and conservatives hoping to quash sectional agitation struggled during the spring to control it. Only if antislavery New England Know Nothings attended the Philadelphia conclave, Indiana's Colfax wrote E. W. Jackson of Massachusetts, would he go, "so that we can make a *demand* that the anti-slavery sentiment of the North shall be respected & consulted in the National nomination."[54] "Our order must & will be nationalized," insisted Kentucky's Garrett Davis in a typical southern reponse to that determination. The national council meeting must stress the order's "all-sacrificing devotion to the union," avoid any public statements on slavery, and thus "prevent the proscription of any man, or set of men, from sectional considerations."[55]

By late May 1855, however, the chief concern of those who wanted to ensure cooperation between northern and southern Know Nothings was not whether the council would openly condemn the Nebraska measure. It was, rather, that southern delegates might insist upon an avowedly proslavery, pro-Nebraska statement. A movement would be made at Philadelphia to give the order a *"Southern"* character, warned North Carolina's Kenneth Rayner, author of the order's third or "union" membership degree.[56] One of Schouler's Massachusetts correspondents agreed in late May that "the great fear now is that, the South will go into the order so generally as to utterly swamp it, with a view to taking care still & forever of their darling institution." "If this is done," he added, "the North must stand up resolutely against such tricks. We shall be better posted up after the Convention in Phila. in June."[57]

Two elections outside of New England in the spring of 1855 heightened apprehensions of a sectional showdown at Philadelphia that might determine which

Whigs entered and which Whigs left the Know Nothing movement. In March, the elections for a territorial legislature in Kansas inflamed the North. So-called border ruffians from Missouri poured into Kansas, stuffed ballot boxes with illegal votes, and secured a vehemently proslavery territorial legislature. This brazen violation of popular sovereignty undercut predictions that southern Whigs had repeated since the spring of 1854 "that slavery will never find its way into Nebraska" and caused Greeley, who was booming an anti-Know Nothing Republican party, to announce ominously in the *Tribune* that "an inevitable collision is before us, between the North and the South, on the question of Slavery Extension." To keep Greeley's Republican party from absorbing all northern antislavery voters, anti-Nebraska Whig/Know Nothings like Indiana's Orth and Colfax therefore redoubled their efforts to secure an explicit condemnation of slavery extension at Philadelphia.[58]

If Kansas' March territorial election increased northern Whig/Know Nothings' insistence upon a repudiation of the Nebraska Act by the national council meeting, the results of Virginia's May gubernatorial and congressional contests ensured that southern Know Nothings would fight tooth and nail against it. Since Virginia was the first slave state to vote in 1855, it also provided the first test of Fillmore's ability to lure southern Whigs into the Know Nothing order. To most observers inside and outside the order, indeed, Virginia's was the pivotal southern election in 1855.

VI

During 1854, long before Fillmore decided that Know Nothingism was "the best remedy for existing evils," Southerners of all partisan varieties rushed into Know Nothing lodges in response to the same anti-Catholic, antiparty, and nativist impulses that fueled their growth in the North. Nonetheless, throughout the spring and summer, most southern Whig officeholders and editors ignored Know Nothingism and instead called for continued cooperation with their northern Whig counterparts. Some condemned the Nebraska Act as a foolish and needless insult to Northerners that "was in reality, what Northern Whigs regarded it, a Democratic trap to catch the South, and destroy the Whig party." Others, lamenting that any southern Whigs had opposed the measure, still argued that southern Whigs had far more in common with northern Whigs, despite their predictable disagreements over slavery, than they did with Democrats and that therefore the Whig organization must be preserved.[59]

By discrediting the Whig name and organization in the eyes of Southerners, northern Whigs' anti-Nebraska campaigns in 1854 compelled most southern Whig leaders to abandon Whiggery and seek refuge in the new nativist movement. Southerners had little interest in the Nebraska measure since slavery could never exist in the two new territories, Charles Conrad told Fillmore in late December, "but the clamor that has been raised against it by the antislavery party" has "awakened a much stronger feeling in its favor and few even of those who were originally opposed to it, would now favor any attempt to repeal it." Thus, "any attempt to revive old party divisions [between Whigs and Democrats] will be abortive." For this reason, Conrad added, in Louisiana as in the rest of the South, "the Whig party has, more or less, merged in the 'Know Nothing' organization."[60]

Not all southern Whigs upset by northern Whigs' antislavery stance saw Know Nothings as their best resort. Some self-proclaimed "old Henry Clay Whigs" gravitated toward the Democrats since northern Democrats, unlike northern Whigs, contained "a reputable number of union men, who will accord to the South their rights."[61] Others preferred futile independence to joining any new party. And still others angrily declared Whiggery's survival as if their mere assertions could keep the party alive. "Is the Whig party to be dissolved or is it to preserve its organization?" asked a Kentucky editor in February 1855. Since "the two great parties, which have so long divided the American people and held sway alternately over the national administration, . . . are mutually dependent, and one cannot exist without the other," the Whig party must endure despite the rise of Know Nothingism. Know Nothings "tell us the Whig party is dead," echoed a Tennessee congressional candidate. "Fellow citizens, I do not believe them. Its winding sheet has been placed upon it by those who have an interest to get it out of the way. No! No! the Whig party is not dead, but only sleepeth, and when it arises from its slumbers and its lion voice is heard to roar through the land, it will frighten away all these little fellows who want to put it aside." More realistic was North Carolina's Whig Congressman John Kerr when he announced his candidacy for reelection in May 1855: "I am aware that the Whig party is now disbanded, but Whig principles and Whig measures are not on that account less dear to me."[62]

By May 1855, indeed, Know Nothings, now calling themselves the American party, had displaced Whiggery as Democrats' major opponent across Dixie. "I think the Whig party of the South is dissolved and the divisions of the parties for the immediate future will be Hindoo and Democrat," a Whig informed Seward from Louisville in late March, and two days later, Kentucky Democratic Congressman John C. Breckinridge concurred that Know Nothings had displaced Kentucky's Whigs and that whatever happened in 1855, "the Whigs will be unable to resume their position in the state, and we shall control it." The American party, glowed Knoxville's former Whig editor Parson Brownlow, an early Know Nothing enthusiast, would "swallow up all other parties" and remain "free from the trading, huckstering spirit of party, which has divided and distracted the Whig party." Since "old party lines of Whig and Democrat" had been "obliterated, and new ones drawn," agreed the Whig Greensboro, North Carolina, *Patriot* in May, Whigs must now rally behind the Know Nothings. "The Whig party has been divided, denationalized, and destroyed beyond all hope of resuscitation and reorganization," summarized Alabama's Democratic Senator Clement C. Clay in July. In most states, "the very name has perished, and not a banner bearing the Whig insignia flutters in the breeze."[63]

As elsewhere in the South, Know Nothing lodges mushroomed in Virginia, the South's largest and still most influential state, during the summer and fall of 1854 for reasons extraneous to the slavery issue or Millard Fillmore's designs. By the end of 1854 Know Nothing membership was estimated at 60,000 out of a total potential electorate of 170,000, and between one-third and two-fifths of those members were thought to be ex-Democrats.[64]

Democratic strength in the order gave Virginia's Whigs pause about joining it, for they feared that Know Nothings would insist upon running ex-Democrats for governor and Congress to demonstrate their independence from Whiggery. The likelihood of this calculated freeze-out increased in December when Democrats nominated as their gubernatorial candidate Henry Wise, the erstwhile pro-Tyler Whig congressman who rejoined the Democracy after Whigs expelled Tyler from their party. A spellbinding speaker and acerbic debater who was chosen because he had written a withering anti-Know Nothing manifesto, the apostate Wise was anathema to many Democrats. Fearing that Know Nothings would run a Democrat for governor to attract anti-Wise Democratic voters, some Whigs vowed to shun the new party.[65]

Even beyond Democratic influence in the organization, other aspects of Know Nothingism provoked mixed reactions from Virginia Whig leaders. Some abandoned Whiggery and joined the order enthusiastically, either because they agreed with its nativist agenda or because they saw in it an opportunity to jump-start long-stalled careers. When New Jersey Whig/Know Nothing editors arranged a public dinner in Newark to boom Richmond's John Minor Botts for president, for example, Botts told it that "if the Whig organization is to be broken up, it leaves no alternative for us but to choose between the two other parties, the Know Nothings on the one hand and the Good-for-Nothings on the other." Thus, he gladly joined the Know Nothing crusade against the Democrats.[66] Yet others were insurmountably repelled by the order's secrecy and proscriptiveness. A widely circulated editorial by Vesparian Ellis in the Washington *American Organ* stating that Virginia's Know Nothings would nominate no one but full members of the order infuriated many Virginia Whigs, who vowed to vote against it solely because it proscribed outsiders.[67]

In the winter of 1854–55, despite the rise of Know Nothingism within the state and the ferociously hostile antisouthern rhetoric of northern Whigs in the 1854 elections, in fact, many Virginia Whigs still hoped to preserve an independent Whig organization that could cooperate with, but resist absorption by, the Know Nothings. Foremost among these was Staunton's Alexander H. H. Stuart, Fillmore's former cabinet member, who expected a formal Whig gubernatorial nomination early in 1855, which, he hoped, Know Nothings would then endorse. Lacking a state committee to call a Whig convention, Whig editors from Richmond, Fredricksburg, Norfolk, Lynchburg, Petersburg, Charlottesville, and Staunton decided instead to boom Stuart as the Whig candidate in their newspapers beginning in February. Whigs, and in particular Fillmore and Solomon Haven, worried, however, that by preempting the Know Nothings they might drive Democrats from the order and that Know Nothings might reject Stuart as an outsider.[68]

The intervention by Fillmore and Haven stopped the separate Whig newspaper nomination of Stuart. It thereby effectively made the death of organized Whiggery in Virginia the price of cooperation with Know Nothings. One index of how much Whigs sacrificed by this bargain came from the concomitant congressional races. In 1853, Democrats carried all thirteen House seats when the demoralized Whigs contested only seven of them. In 1855, Know Nothings ran candidates in ten districts, yet only five of those men were former Whigs. And the two Know Nothing victors were both ex-Democrats.[69] Even Know Nothingism, that is, could not put a Virginia Whig in Congress.

Democrats also got Know Nothings' nominations for lieutenant governor and state attorney general, but their March state convention picked a Whig to run for governor. Unlike Stuart, or even Haven's preferred candidate, James Strother, whose prominence as Whigs may have alienated Democratic/Know Nothings from the ticket, Thomas S. Flournoy had not held public office since his single congressional term ended in March 1849. And that term had been notable for only one thing—Flournoy's membership in the Young Indians, who promoted Zachary Taylor's nomination as a No Party candidate against Henry Clay. Whatever his potential appeal to Democratic/Know Nothings and anti-Wise Democrats, Flournoy proved a poor choice for two reasons. First, after accepting the Know Nothings' nomination in a public letter that scathingly attacked Catholics and demanded their exclusion from office, he adamantly refused to campaign or make public speeches. This abdication left the field clear for Wise, Virginia's most compelling orator, who began to crisscross the state immediately after his December nomination lashing out at Know Nothings' intolerance and subversive secrecy.

Second, and of greater importance in terms of the election's impact beyond Virginia, both Flournoy and his Democratic running mate for lieutenant governor were vulnerable to attack as being hostile to slavery. A major thrust of Wise's campaign and those of many Democratic congressional candidates, indeed, was that northern Know Nothings' support for the election of Seward and Henry Wilson to the Senate proved that Virginia's Know Nothings had leagued themselves with abolitionist foes of the South. Virginia's Democrats, promised Wise, "will defend the state against agrarianism, free-soilism and abolitionism, now threatening to invade the South from Northern and non-slaveholding councils of Know Nothingism."[70]

The belief that antislavery men dominated northern and especially New England Know Nothings also inhibited Virginia Whigs from joining the new party even when they sympathized with its nativist goals. Across the North, Rives warned a friend, a "strong anti-slavery feeling . . . has infused itself among them." Wilson's election in Massachusetts and Know Nothings' gubernatorial campaign in New Hampshire left "no doubt that in . . . all the New England States, it is strongly injected with the spirit of free-soilism & abolition." Hence, there was "very much . . . doubt whether the *order* can ever *nationalize* itself."[71]

Despite such doubts and Flournoy's refusal to campaign, he still ran a respectable race against Wise, who won with 83,224 votes (53.2 percent) to Flournoy's 73,244 (46.8 percent). No previous election in Virginia had ever generated such a large turnout, and Flournoy ran almost 15,000 votes ahead of Scott in 1852 and 14,000 ahead of George Summers, the Whigs' gubernatorial candidate in 1851. While Vesparian Ellis angrily attributed the relatively narrow defeat to "the *foreign vote introduced into Virginia since 1852 & now* employed on the railroads in that State," most Whig/Know Nothings in Virginia and other slave states blamed the antislavery and abolitionist image of northern Know Nothings for undercutting Virginia Know Nothings' attempt to run as "a National Union Party." "The Whigs would not vote with the American party in many of the counties," David Campbell reported to his nephew, then president of Tennessee's Know Nothing state council, in a typical postmortem. "They were not prepared to join a party that was so little to be relied on in the free states." Foreigners had hurt Virginia's Know Nothings, reported Alabama's major Know Nothing newspaper, but they also "had another enemy to fight—Massachusetts."[72]

Virginians voted on May 24, two weeks before the Know Nothings' national council was scheduled to meet in Philadelphia. By the end of May, Virginia's results had been telegraphed to other slave states with elections still to be held in August, October, or November and where Know Nothings fully—and accurately—expected a replay of Wise's attack on the antislavery virus infecting northern Know Nothingism unless something were done at Philadelphia to exterminate or expunge it. Southern delegates thus descended on the Know Nothing conclave determined to stop the kind of anti-Nebraska platform sought by Colfax, Pennsylvania's notorious William F. Johnston, and the Bay State's still more notorious Henry Wilson.

VII

By June 1855, in sum, the Whig party had already disintegrated in most states, but the Philadelphia Know Nothing national council meeting could go far to settle whether former Whigs from the North and South could cooperate with each other in the order and thus, indirectly, what options might be available to non- and anti-Know Nothing/Whigs. Original nativists like James W. Barker, the Know Nothings' national president, and important Whig/Know Nothings—Ohio's Campbell, Massachusetts Governor Henry Gardner, Kentucky's Garrett Davis, and North Carolina's Rayner, to name just four—hoped that the Philadelphia meeting could preserve intersectional comity by avoiding any controversial statement on slavery and focusing instead on the nativist program Know Nothings had in common. The odds, however, were very much against them. Jolted by Wise's victory in Virginia, most southern delegates vowed to demonstrate that New Englanders did not speak for the party on the slavery issue. The elevation of Free Soiler John P. Hale to the Senate by New Hampshire's Know Nothings while the council was meeting only intensified that determination.

Northern anti-Nebraska Whig/Know Nothings also confronted Fillmore's attempt to ignore slavery agitation in order to convert Know Nothingism into a Union party, although little evidence exists that Fillmore's inner circle sought to engineer the outcome at Philadelphia to achieve that goal.[73] The New York delegation, indeed, was led by Barker, who opposed Fillmore's presidential aspirations.[74] Nonetheless, Silver Grays had publicized that project, and in March the New York State Know Nothing council published a platform, written by Baltimore's John P. Kennedy, that portrayed the Americans as a national Union party.[75] Anti-Nebraska Know Nothings, in reply, threatened to have none of it. "The K. N. of the Free States will *Bolt* the Convention at Philadelphia if the[y] undertake to make a National Platform," vowed one of Weed's saboteurs in the order on May 30. "The course of affairs in Kansas will compel [sic] us to go for a restoration of the prohibition of slavery in Kansas and Nebraska," Henry Wilson wrote Schouler in mid-April. If he could not secure even a moderate antislavery platform at Philadelphia, he subsequently promised a friend, he "would blow their party to hell."[76]

Wilson thus became the lightening rod of a rancorous gathering that lasted from June 8 to June 15. Efforts of moderates like Rayner and Kentucky's Albert T. Burnley to keep peace failed totally, and they later railed at the "fools and demagogues" who "were trying to pervert the order into a great antislavery element in one section & a pro-slavery element in another section" for wrecking it.[77] Several nonsectional questions also generated intense controversy. The council denied requests from Southerners and especially Louisianans that native-born Catholics be allowed to join the order, and the eighth section of its platform ringingly reaffirmed its hostility to Catholics. Delegates also debated whether the order should jettison its secrecy and rituals, an abandonment that the council eventually recommended to, but did not require of, "subordinate councils." Nonetheless, the assemblage quickly degenerated into an angry sectional melee.[78]

Southerners immediately denounced the Massachusetts delegation and especially Wilson for their antislavery extremism, and Wilson retorted, "We intend to repeal the Fugitive Slave Act, and we mean that Kansas will never come into the Union as a slave State—no, never." The battle carried over into the platform committee, which delivered both a minority northern report calling for the restoration of the Missouri Compromise prohibition and admission of Kansas and Nebraska as free states and a prosouthern majority report. After the minority report was rejected, the majority's was adopted by a vote of 78–63, when eleven Northerners—four each from New York and California, two from Pennsylvania, and one from New Jersey—joined all the Southerners except those from Delaware to defeat the remaining Northerners.

The defeated Northerners met separately the next morning and adopted a protest. Spurning demands from Wilson that the delegates immediately urge northern Know Nothings to join the Republican party, they instead simply reaffirmed their commitment to restoring the Missouri Compromise and their devotion to other nativist principles. Fifty-three Northerners signed this document, and ten others from Pennsylvania and New Jersey signed a similar protest that Pennsylvania's former governor Johnston drafted. Altogether, that is, sixty-three of seventy-five Northerners in attendance rebuked the majority's platform. The most conspicuous absentees from these protests were the entire delegations from New York and California, as well as a few delegates from Pennsylvania, Illinois, and New Jersey.[79]

What incensed most Northerners was Section Twelve of the majority platform. It blamed "obnoxious acts" and "violated pledges"—that is, the Nebraska's Act's repeal of the Missouri Compromise line—on the Whig and Democratic parties, but it pledged Know Nothings "to abide by and maintain the existing laws upon the subject of slavery, as a final and conclusive settlement of that subject, in spirit and substance." In short, it opposed any attempt to repeal the Nebraska Act and the Fugitive Slave Act. In addition, it announced "the sense of the National Council that Congress ought not to legislate upon the subject of slavery in the territories" or interfere with slavery in the District of Columbia.

If this sounded eerily like the finality pledge that Fillmore had tried to impose on the Whig party since 1850, the platform's Section Three—which was apparently ignored by delegates during the hubbub in Philadelphia and has since been forgotten by most historians—rhetorically achieved virtually all that Fillmore and

Kennedy could have wished in terms of converting the Know Nothings into a Union party. Praising "the maintenance of the union of these United States as the paramount political good," it advocated "uncompromising antagonism to every principle of policy that endangers it" and "the suppression of all tendencies to political division, founded on geographical discrimination, or on the belief that there is a real difference of views between the various sections of the Union."

Four different groups of Whigs came away from Philadelphia with renewed hope, if for vastly different reasons. By spurning the platform, northern Whig/ Know Nothings did not feel bound by it, and by standing up to Southerners, they believed they had reaffirmed their antislavery credentials for northern voters. As yet, that is, they saw no need to abandon Know Nothingism in the North, especially since every northern state council sanctioned their action explicitly or implicitly.[80]

Free Soil/Know Nothings like Wilson and non-Know Nothing northern outsiders, conversely, saw the flare-up as preparing the way for a Republican party since they expected a wholesale exodus of outraged antislavery men from Know Nothing ranks. One of these, Samuel Bowles, editor of the Springfield, Massachusetts, *Republican*, was hired to report on the proceedings by the New York *Tribune*, and he worked closely with Wilson at Philadelphia to foment a northern bolt.[81] Northern delegates, Bowles inaccurately alleged in his final dispatch, agreed to "throw up the American organization as an organization in order to unite the North in an all-powerful and effective party against the aggressiveness of Slavery."[82] New York's increasingly isolated Sewardite Whigs similarly spied new opportunities in the events at Philadelphia. "I congratulate you on the brightening prospects of last week," one told Seward the day after delegates left Philadelphia. "Secrecy is gone; Nativism is gone, and only anti-Catholicism remains, and that is shivering." "The Know-nothings, thank God, are in their graves," echoed Charles A. Dana, who was editing the *Tribune* in Greeley's absence.[83]

Millard Fillmore was already in Europe when the Philadelphia convention met, but his inner circle were just as jubilant about its results. The national council constructed an almost perfect platform for a Fillmore candidacy. It identified the Americans as a national Union party, and Section Twelve exempted, indeed prohibited, Fillmore from making any public statement about the Nebraska Act that could offend Northerners or Southerners. Brushing off the sectional split over it as predictable and temporary, Kennedy insisted to the still skeptical Winthrop that "the platform of the Convention" provided the basis for "a National party" that could bridge "the chasm between the Slave and free states" and oppose "an anti-slavery hating combination" in the North. All that was necessary for its success even in Massachusetts, argued Kennedy, was that "you and Clifford, Everett, Choate, Lawrence, Appleton and the *rest of you*" embrace the "Phila. platform."[84]

Yet it was southern Know Nothings, almost all of whose delegates to Philadelphia were former Whigs, who believed they had won the most. They had not just smothered a demand for repeal of the Nebraska Act. By apparently forcing antislavery Northerners out of the party, they also demonstrated their toughness and fidelity to southern interests. Democrats, they fantasized, could no longer rail against them as allies of abolitionists. A replay of Wise's campaign now seemed impossible. Whatever had happened in Virginia, the way was open to sweep the South's remaining elections—and to sweep the South's remaining Whig holdouts into the new American party.

VIII

Northerners' walkout at Philadelphia, southern Whig/Know Nothings believed, removed the major obstacle stopping other Whigs from joining them. Union-loving southern Whigs no longer had any excuse for not joining the Americans, crowed the New Orleans *Bee*, since "the Whigs can scarcely be said to exist." The Philadelphia convention was the only instance in American political history "where the friends of the Union had the nerve to force its enemies from their own councils into a separate organization," boasted the Charlotte *North Carolina Whig*. Hence, "the South may now stand upon this platform as a unit, if they wish to preserve the Union." "The ejection of these men [the Massachusetts Know Nothings] from the Convention in Philadelphia, is . . . a restoration of confidence in the South," concurred Kennedy. "If the Convention had met before the Virginia election and had done the same thing then, Wise would have been overthrown by an overwhelming vote."[85]

These predictions—both about a headlong rush of holdout Whigs into the new American party and about the insulation of southern Know Nothings from loyalty politics on the slavery issue—proved badly mistaken. Of seven other southern gubernatorial elections in 1855, Know Nothings carried only Kentucky, where former Whig Congressman Charles S. Morehead took the statehouse back from the Democrats. Hopeful that they had defused the slavery issue, Know Nothing gubernatorial and congressional candidates across the South made "the Pope and Catholics" their "great Hobby" during the campaigns.[86] Like Wise, Democrats elsewhere criticized that intolerance, but even after the Philadelphia convention, Democrats repeatedly charged that southern Know Nothingism represented an antislavery fifth column.

No Democratic gubernatorial candidate played the slavery card so relentlessly or effectively as Tennessee's Andrew Johnson against Meredith Gentry. In no southern state had more congressional Whigs opposed the Nebraska Act, and Tennessee's Know Nothings chose Gentry in part because he was not in Congress in 1854 and, indeed, had been denied renomination in 1853 because of his strident opposition to Winfield Scott as a figurehead for northern antislavery Whigs. That record offended pro-Scott and anti-Nebraska Whigs, but it was expected to protect Gentry from the charge of being soft on the slavery issue. By exhuming and repeatedly attacking ostensibly antislavery votes that Gentry had cast during his long and exemplary period of service in Congress, however, Johnson defeated Gentry by the same narrow margin he had gained over Gustavus Henry in 1853.[87]

Anti-Nebraska Whig congressional incumbents who ran as Know Nothings in 1855, like Tennessee's William Cullom and Louisiana's Theodore Hunt, also faced charges of betraying slavery. Both lost, and Cullom attributed his defeat in part to "the cry of Abolitionist."[88] Nonetheless, southern Know Nothings ran far better in later congressional races than they had in Virginia. Whereas they won only two (15.4 percent) of Virginia's House seats, they carried twenty-five (41.7 percent) of sixty congressional elections in Alabama, Georgia, Kentucky, Louisiana, Maryland, Mississippi, North Carolina, Tennessee, and Texas.

Altogether, Know Nothings won twenty-seven of seventy-three House seats in slave states that sent only nineteen Whigs to Congress in 1853. They won one seat each in the traditional Democratic bastions of Mississippi and Texas, and two in Alabama, but most victories occurred in states where Whigs had been competitive or dominant. The relevant questions with respect to southern Whigs, therefore, are to what extent they benefited from their absorption into the new American party and how complete that absorption was.

Of eight southern Know Nothing gubernatorial nominees in 1855, only Flournoy, Gentry, Morehead, and Louisiana's Charles Derbigny were Whigs. Only Morehead won, but Whigs had not elected a governor anywhere in the South since 1851. Former Whigs did even better with regard to Know Nothing congressional nominations outside Virginia, capturing thirty-nine (68.4 percent) of fifty-seven, and they dominated Know Nothing congressional slates in Maryland, Kentucky, Tennessee, North Carolina, Louisiana, and Georgia. Twenty-two of the twenty-seven southern Know Nothings elected to Congress in 1855 were former Whigs, compared to nineteen Whigs who won House seats in 1853. By these measures, Whig leaders marginally benefited from trading the Whig label for the American brand name.

Even so, the transition from Whiggery to Know Nothingism in the South was conflicted, often costly to individual Whig politicos, and far from complete. At least two Whig-Know Nothings got to Congress by defeating loyal and vociferously anti-Know Nothing Whig incumbents. In Kentucky, Humphrey Marshall, a leader of the anti-Scott forces in 1852, routed William Preston, who mourned that "the old Whig party by which I was elected is disbanded," who pronounced himself "an independent candidate" while vilifying Know Nothings' bigotry and secrecy, and who attracted Democratic support in a losing effort.[89] Similarly, North Carolina's pro-Nebraska Whig Congressman John Kerr won a Democratic endorsement, even after announcing "I am *now, as ever,* a Whig," because of his strident denunciations of Know Nothingism. But neither that help nor his proslavery credentials spared him from being crushed by the Know Nothing newcomer Edwin Reade in North Carolina's fifth district.[90]

These were not the only anomalies in the congressional results. At least four Whigs or former Whigs, who attracted Democratic support, defeated Whig/Know Nothing rivals by running as anti-Know Nothing Independents or Whig Independents: Thomas Bowie in Maryland's sixth district along the western shore of Chesapeake Bay; Albert G. Talbott, who carried Kentucky's fourth district by only 16 votes out of over 13,000 cast; Georgia's Alexander H. Stephens, who stridently denounced Know Nothing intolerance even as he publicly refused to endorse Democratic candidates; and Albert Watkins, a former Whig congressman, who defeated sitting anti-Nebraska Whig (and now American) incumbent Nathaniel G. Taylor in East Tennessee's heavily Whig first district. In sum, at least twenty-six Whigs were elected in slave states in 1855, but they were sharply, if unevenly, divided by Know Nothingism itself.[91]

Know Nothingism, in short, did not simply replace (or forcibly displace) the southern Whig party. It also turned former Whigs against each other, provided a new arena in which to renew old factional struggles, and drove some Whigs into an alliance with Democrats to crush a movement they abhorred. Occasionally, as in Tennessee's first congressional district, disagreements about the Nebraska Act or the Know Nothings' purported unreliability on the slavery issue contributed to these divisions, but most often they reflected divergent reactions to Know Nothings' attempt to restrict the political rights of Catholics and foreigners.

There is little evidence of Whig resistance to Know Nothingism in Mississippi or Alabama, where even Henry Hilliard, the state's most eminent Whig, publicly endorsed the new American party and its principles.[92] Most Whig leaders and Whig newspapers in Louisiana also readily embraced it in 1855. But many Creole Catholic Whigs in the sugar plantation parishes refused to support Know Nothing candidates that year, despite the state platform's repudiation of the national council's anti-Catholic Section Eight and the nomination of a Catholic for governor. And the state's leading Whig officeholder, Senator Judah P. Benjamin, a Jew born in the West Indies, issued a public statement in August 1855 blasting the party's bigotry and proscriptiveness as "a wretched fall from the the proud tradition of the gallant Whigs of the older time" and pronouncing himself henceforth a party-less Whig independent.[93]

In North Carolina, too, Whig resistance went beyond Kerr's bold stand. In the sixth congressional district, incumbent anti-Nebraska Whig Congressman Richard Puryear was first renominated by a Whig convention before Know Nothings later endorsed him. In debate, he defended Know Nothing principles but also "denied that he had deserted his Whig friends or foresaken one Whig principle held dear by them." Even more defiant was Whig leader James Caldwell, who announced in the spring that he would run as a Whig against incumbent Democratic Congressman Burton Craige. When Democrats suggested he was a Know Nothing, he issued a public card declaring that "he was not the Know Nothing candidate, but was 'a Whig of the old line, a Henry Clay Whig,' and expected to be supported by that party." When the Know Nothings then nominated a Democrat to face Craige, the bitter Caldwell withdrew and endorsed Craige.[94]

The Know Nothing explosion especially wreaked havoc on the unity of Whig leaders and, to a lesser extent, of Whig voters in Maryland, Kentucky, Tennessee, and Georgia, states that, along with North Carolina, were once the most reliable Whig polities in the South. Two complementary dissolvents appear to have been at work. Whiggery's collapse as an organized, competitive party freed longtime Whig factional rivals to go their separate ways. Simultaneously, the anti-Catholic bigotry and proscriptiveness of Know Nothingism provided a new dividing line between former Whig allies.

In Maryland, for example, previous rivalries between Reverdy Johnson's Court House clique and the Whig faction aligned behind Senator James Pearce and John P. Kennedy only marginally affected divergent reactions to Know Nothingism. The key was the order's anti-Catholicism, resort to violence in Baltimore elections, and insistence on putting no one but full members in public office. Catholic planters whose families had been in Maryland since the seventeenth century crucially contributed to Whig dominance in the Eastern Shore and southern Maryland tobacco-growing counties between the Potomac and the Chesapeake. Significantly, neither John R. Franklin nor August R. Sollers, the Whigs who represented the two districts on the Chesapeake's opposite shores in the Thirty-Third Congress, sought reelection once it became clear that Know Nothings would pick the nominees. The list of eminent Whigs who refused to join the order also included Kennedy; United States Senators Pearce and Thomas G. Pratt, who called the anti-Catholic Eighth Section of the Philadelphia platform "suicidal"; Reverdy Johnson, who, unlike Pearce, issued a forceful public denunciation of Know Nothing intolerance; and Johnson's brother-in-law Thomas Bowie, who won a House seat as an anti-Know Nothing Independent Whig.[95]

Pearce remained publicly silent throughout much of 1855, but in September he sent John M. Clayton a revealing letter that illustrated the isolation he and many Whigs increasingly felt. Complaining that the American party "allow no connection except with duly admitted and sworn members," and that it could never become "a National" party since "the whole North is so inflamed on the Slavery question," he also refused "to be a tail to that [Democratic] kite." Thus "I am quite hopeless of any political changes acceptable to me," especially as "the Whig party if not forever at an end is so broken up that I see no probability of its reunion."[96]

Less eminent Whigs were more willing to cooperate with Democrats against Know Nothings' anti-Catholic bigotry. Meetings of old-line Whigs in St. Mary's County, first settled by Catholics in the 1630s, and Frederick, which encompassed another concentration of Catholics, protested "know nothingism as still more alarming" than "northern abolitionism" and vowed that since "the principal issue before the people is between Know Nothingism and anti-Know Nothingism," they would cooperate with Democrats in the anti-Know Nothing party. Maryland's 1855 elections, which produced four Know Nothing congressmen out of six chosen and a heavily Know Nothing legislature, in fact, also produced the most dramatic voter realignment experienced by any slave state. The old southern and Eastern Shore counties where Whigs had been strongest became Democratic bastions, whereas former Democratic strongholds in northeastern counties and especially Baltimore went Know Nothing.[97]

The urbane Kennedy lived in Baltimore, the site of Maryland's most extraordinary voter realignment and campaign violence. As he repeatedly told confidants, the main reason he did not join the Know Nothings was to conceal his main purpose—converting the order into an electioneering machine for Fillmore. But he hoped that the new Know Nothing legislature would send him to the Senate to replace Pratt, his old Court House clique antagonist. When it instead rejected him because he was not a member and chose his sworn-in brother Anthony, whom he considered "a good fellow whom everybody likes" without a brain in his head, John Kennedy's bitterness knew no bounds. Blasting the "wretched condition of that organization in its personnel," he warned that old-line Whig outsiders like himself would be even less likely to cooperate with it in the future. "The truth is," he railed to his friend Winthrop, "the party is a very mean one in this state.... If it is not reformed and strengthened by an infusion of men of sense, into it, it will go to pieces all over the country."[98]

Hostility to Know Nothings' anti-Catholicism also contributed to Whig resistance in Kentucky. The *Bardstown Herald*, which led the opposition to joining the Americans, was printed in the county with the state's largest concentration of Catholics. Even more important was sheer resentment among Kentucky's Whigs, who prided themselves as being the nation's oldest and most loyal party members, at being shoved aside. As elsewhere, Know Nothingism emerged in

Kentucky's local elections of 1854 as an independent antiparty movement that denounced Whigs and Democrats alike, and most Whig leaders spurned it. "The principles generally imputed to the Know Nothings are not our principles," announced the state's leading Whig newspaper in August 1854.[99]

Hope of preserving a separate Whig organization lasted as late as February and March 1855 even though uncertainty sparked by the North's elections caused Whig leaders to postpone a scheduled Whig state convention from February 22 to April. Before it ever met, however, third parties forced the Whigs' hand. In December 1854 the state's temperance association nominated a gubernatorial candidate, and the Know Nothings, meeting secretly, followed suit in February by nominating a different man, Judge William Loving. By then, a few Whig papers had endorsed Know Nothing principles, but it was not until mid-March that the Danville *Kentucky Tribune* openly attacked Catholics and that Louisville's George D. Prentice, in an article entitled "The Whig Party of Kentucky," called on Whigs to forgo a race in 1855 and back the Americans on the ground that "many of the old measures that once divided the two parties [Whigs and Democrats] were settled by incorporation into the policy of the country."[100]

Belated recognition that developments in the North ended any hope of preserving a national Whig party spurred this change. But Prentice's announcement launched a full-scale attempt by Kentucky's Whig leaders—or most of them—to seize Know Nothing machinery from its original founders and convert the order from a nativist, anti-Catholic, and antiparty populistic protest into a conservative Unionist Whig vehicle. Kentucky's Whigs, in sum, attempted at the state level what Fillmore and his friends sought on the national level.

Relentlessly, old-line Whigs shoved original Know Nothings aside. When Know Nothing gubernatorial candidate Loving withdrew because of ill health, the Whig-dominated state council replaced him with ex-Congressman Morehead, whom most Whigs had expected to nominate as their own gubernatorial candidate in April. In the seventh (Lexington) congressional district, where former Native American congressional candidate Stephean Trabue had announced himself as the Know Nothing candidate, the Whig-controlled district council replaced him, first with Whig James Robertson and then with Alexander Marshall, who had formerly been both a Whig and a Democrat. Most important, in the Louisville district, Whigs secured the American congressional nomination against Whig incumbent William Preston for Humphrey Marshall, even though the Know Nothing *Louisville Courier* had previously denounced him by name as an example of "men who have broken down in the old parties to which they belonged, and who are now seeking to advance themselves by riding into power on the popularity of the new organization."[101]

Prentice, Senator-elect John J. Crittenden, Marshall, Albert T. Burnley, incumbent Congressman Leander Cox, and many other Whig leaders went along with this coup. But many others did not: Preston; Senator Archibald Dixon, who had already been replaced by Crittenden; Senator John B. Thompson, whose seat was safe for four more years; former Senator Joseph R. Underwood; congressional candidate Albert Talbott; and Henry Clay's son James B. Clay, among others. Contempt for Know Nothing principles in part explains their refusal, but the division between Whigs who became Know Nothings and those who clung to Whiggery in 1855 most resembles the split between Whigs who had boomed

Zachary Taylor for the 1848 nomination and Henry Clay loyalists. Prentice, Crittenden, and Burnley were all leaders of the Taylor boom, and Morehead had privately chastised Clay for refusing to endorse Taylor once he had the Whig nomination.[102] James B. Clay's loyalties in that ancient controversy are obvious, but Underwood was a Clay man and Dixon was a foe of Crittenden, if not an outright Clay man. Other than Talbott, the holdouts did not become Democrats in 1855, but their antipathy to Know Nothingism belied assertions that all southern Whigs would back Fillmore if he were the American party's presidential nominee.

More recent feuds help explain Whig divisions over Know Nothingism in Tennessee. The emergence of anti-Scott and pro-Nebraska Whigs like Gentry, Parson Brownlow, and Nashville Congressman Felix Zollicoffer as Know Nothing leaders alienated pro-Scott and anti-Nebraska Tennessee Whigs, who correctly saw it as an attempt by old foes to purge them from power. Because of their popularity in their districts, both Emerson Etheridge and Cullom managed to secure Know Nothing congressional nominations, but Cullom specifically attributed his defeat in part to the unpopularity of Gentry among his constituents.[103] Senator James Jones, whose vigorous support for the Nebraska Act failed to mitigate the enmity he had earned from Gentry and his ilk for Jones' equally vigorous support of Scott in 1852, however, refused to join the new party. He remained a Whig, he announced in a public letter in July, "and so far as the recognition of the correctness of principles go, I expect to live and die one."[104] Nor did John Bell endorse the party until after his enemy, Gentry, lost. Lamenting that there was no more "glorious old Whig party," he announced on October 8, 1855, that he could never join the secret Know Nothing fraternity but would support the public American party because it was a conservative unionist organization.[105]

Whether or not Know Nothingism could serve their personal ambition, however, appears to explain other Tennessee Whigs' divergent reactions to it. Furious that a separate Know Nothing candidate blocked his attempt to run as a Whig for Congress in the tenth district, for example, Walter Coleman insisted that "the Whig party is not dead," and he bitterly, if futilely, complained that "its winding sheet has been placed upon it by those who wish to get it out of the way."[106] Tennessee's first congressional district, redrawn by Whigs between 1851 and 1853, illustrates how Know Nothingism became a new battleground for old Whig antagonists. Since early 1854, when Whig Nathaniel Taylor won a special congressional election against Albert G. Watkins, formerly the Whig congressman from the old second district but now a resident of the first, the furious Watkins had vowed to take the seat from Taylor in 1855. Both men joined the order to seek the Know Nothings' endorsement, and when Taylor got it, the vindictive Watkins shifted course. Castigating local Know Nothings as bitter personal enemies, he secured Democrats' endorsement by running as an Independent. Supported by Democrats and anti-Know Nothing/Whigs, Watkins then narrowly edged out Taylor.[107]

In no state, however, did Know Nothingism wreck what remained of Whiggery so completely as Georgia. By 1855, of course, internal Whig divisions had already thoroughly disrupted the party. The feud pitting Stephens, Toombs, and William Dawson against John Berrien, Charles Jenkins, and others in the 1840s helped shape the Union/Southern Rights realignment of 1850–51. In 1852, when many

Union Whigs, including United States Senator Dawson, loyally rallied behind Scott's presidential candidacy, Stephens and Toombs arranged a separate electoral ticket for Daniel Webster that their most loyal followers backed even after Webster died. Stephens and Toombs then orchestrated a "Conservative" or "Republican" convention in 1853 that explicitly repudiated the national Whig party and nominated Charles Jenkins for governor.[108]

Whatever Toombs and Stephens called themselves, however, they still despised Democrats who had been Southern Rights men, and their constituents, as one told Stephens in 1855, did not consider them any *"less the Whig[s]"* because "the old *landmarks* which divided you and them [Democrats] still exist."[109] In 1853, moreover, both pro- and anti-Scott Whigs, as well as some Union party Democrats, rallied behind Jenkins, Berrien's kinsman and close associate, who came within 500 votes of defeating Democrat Herschel Johnson. Residual antagonisms between Whigs and Democrats, in sum, survived all the shuffling of party labels and lines in Georgia. And in early 1855, many Whigs expected Jenkins once again to carry their banner, whatever it was labeled, in a rematch against the hated Johnson. A few Whig proponents of the so-called Columbus movement in southwest Georgia, however, called on all Georgians to combine behind Johnson to erect a unified phalanx against the North.[110]

The eruption of Know Nothingism shattered any chance that Georgians would unite in a single party or that Whigs would rally again as a unit behind Jenkins. Instead Georgians—Whigs and Democrats alike—divided into Know Nothings and the "Anti-Know Nothing party."[111] Though many Whigs poured into Know Nothing lodges, Stephens and Toombs both issued withering public letters denouncing the order's secrecy and intolerance and damning it as an abolitionist trick. Even earlier, Stephens had protested that "the old Whig party is about to be sold out to the Know Nothings" and insisted that "to *crush* them out I would join with any man." Stephens had intended to retire from Congress, but his abhorrence of the possibility that a Know Nothing might replace him caused him to run as an Independent in the eighth district, as did his brother Linton in the seventh. Democrats endorsed both Stephens brothers even though each publicly denounced Democratic gubernatorial candidate Johnson, and Know Nothings, most of whom were former Whig idolators of Stephens and Toombs, ultimately ran candidates against both brothers.[112]

Unlike Stephens and Toombs, indeed, "nearly all the old Whig leaders" ardently embraced Know Nothingism. These included not just the duo's old Whig foes like Berrien and Savannah editor Francis Bartow, but also former friends like William S. Jones, who edited the Augusta *Chronicle*; Dawson, whose Senate term expired in March; ex-Congressman Eugenius Nisbet; Mayor Thomas Miller of Augusta, whom one Stephens loyalist called "a bonafide traitor"; and even former Governor and Secretary of War George W. Crawford, whom the same Stephens ally said was "galvanized (not Galphinized) into a spasmodic effort" for the Know Nothings.[113]

Democrats also became Know Nothings, and in the vain hope of attracting still more of them, Georgia's American party bypassed the respected Whig Jenkins, who refused to join the secret order, and nominated Democrat Garnett Andrews for governor. An inept campaigner whose Democratic background alienated many Whigs who would have undoubtedly voted for Jenkins, Andrews was a terrible choice. In 1853 Jenkins drew 47,128 votes (49.7 percent) and lost to Johnson by only 510. In 1855, Andrews garnered only 43,358 (41.8 percent) and lost to Johnson by 10,778. Andrews also ran 2,300 votes behind the aggregate total for the eight Know Nothing congressional candidates, five of whom were former Whigs, including the state's two Know Nothing victors.[114]

Whigs who shunned this internecine brawl between pro- and anti-Know Nothing Whigs because they had friends on both sides saw careers come to an abrupt halt. David A. Reese, the Union Whig elected to Congress with Stephens in 1853, for example, refused to seek a nomination from either side. But the greatest casualty was Jenkins. Author of the revered Georgia Platform, Jenkins, because of his close ties to both Union Whigs and the Berrien camp and because of his strong showing in 1853, was the single Georgia Whig with the greatest potential for reuniting Whiggery's long fractured ranks. Refusing to demean himself by joining a Know Nothing lodge, to denounce old friends on either side, or to run as an Independent, he placed himself on the sidelines in a June public letter: "I have concluded, therefore, that being neither a Democrat nor a Know Nothing, there is no place for me in this contest."[115] His abdication was personal, but he had written an appropriate epitaph for the southern Whig party.

IX

Many northern Whigs whose support Fillmorites sought for the American party also remained on the sidelines in 1855 rather than join a new party or cooperate with Democrats against the Know Nothings and Republicans. Winthrop quickly deflated John Kennedy's hope that Know Nothings' June national platform would persuade conservative Whig leaders in Massachusetts to aid them. First, he informed Kennedy, "the bolters [who repudiated that platform as insufficiently antislavery] are a vast majority in this State." Second, "there are no *dramatis personae*" of old conservative Whig leaders to endorse the platform, for age itself had taken its toll on them. Abbott Lawrence was "very ill" and would sail for Europe if he did not die. Nathan Appleton was "about, but quite feeble," and Rufus Choate was hobbled by "water on the knee." And Winthrop himself refused "to be found higgledy-piggledy with Wilson, Gardner & Co."[116]

Edward Everett also expected antislavery men to control Know Nothingism throughout 1855 and then to cooperate with Seward, "notwithstanding his early and persistent denunciations of it." Thus conservative Whigs must continue to oppose Know Nothings. "If the conservative Whigs had an able leader," he wrote his niece, while shunning that role himself, "they could make a very important stand" in Massachusetts in 1855. "But I do not see that they could rescue the state from the freesoil K. N.s—owing to the impossibility of coalescing with the democrats" since Democrats would never demand repeal of the Nebraska Act, a sine qua non for even conservative Massachusetts Whigs.[117]

In New York, Washington Hunt and Hamilton Fish also remained isolated. Complaining to Weed "that the Whig party is to be swallowed up in fusion," Hunt published a letter in the New York *Commercial Advertiser* in August "declaring my purpose to remain a Whig, even after the party has been dispersed." As for the cost of this stance, "I understand perfectly that my views of duty will separate me from all the political movements of the day." Hunt's letter "expresses my sentiments better than any of the Manifestoes of the day," Winthrop rejoiced to Kennedy. "Here in Massachusetts, Fusion is in full progress. I have refused to have any part or lot with it."[118]

The fusion that Winthrop and Hunt resisted was an attempt after the Philadelphia Know Nothing national council meeting to unite antislavery Know Nothings and antislavery outsiders like the Sewardites in the new Republican party. Fusion's success varied widely from state to state. Holdout Whig conservatives resisted it. But so too did many anti-Nebraska Whig/Know Nothings, who repudiated Section Twelve of the Americans' national platform specifically to avert the collapse of independent northern Know Nothing parties. Nonetheless, together with Know Nothingism, fusion helped pulverize what remained of northern Whiggery.

In the three New England states with fall gubernatorial and legislative elections, fusion proved most complete in Vermont, yet even there it met some resistance. By adopting what one appalled conservative Whig called "an ultra abolition" stance in 1854, Vermont's Whigs swept the governorship, the legislature, and the three congressional seats, and in early 1855 the Whig legislature then sent Jacob Collamer back to the Senate. Know Nothing lodges existed in Vermont, but by the summer of 1855, almost all Whig leaders—Governor Stephen Royce, Senators Solomon Foot and Collamer, and the three Whig congressmen elected in 1854—had committed themselves to the Republican movement. Royce won reelection as a Republican with 25,699 votes (59 percent) compared to the 27,811 (62.4 percent) he had amassed as a Whig in 1854. Former supporters who deserted his column may have voted for a separate American candidate, who garnered 3,631 votes (8.3 percent), but Republicans clearly commanded the state. The once-indomitable Vermont Whig party had been extinguished.[119]

Maine's conservative Whigs proved more numerous and stubborn. In 1854, most of Maine's Whig leaders and about half of the party's former voters supported fusion with Free Soilers and anti-Nebraska Democrats behind Anson Morrill's successful gubernatorial candidacy. In February 1855 those elements, as well as virtually all of Maine's Know Nothings, held a Republican convention that renominated Morrill on the most radically antislavery platform adopted anywhere in the North that year. Die-hard Whigs, who secured only 15 percent of the vote for Isaac Reed in 1854, however, defiantly called a Whig convention that renominated Reed on a platform denouncing Know Nothingism, demanding dilution of the prohibition law, which the fusion legislature had just stiffened, and castigating the new Republican party as "the offspring of a corrupt fusion of men of opposite political opinions, and associations aided recently by a secret political organization of the most dangerous character."[120]

Even before the "straight Whig" convention met, pro-fusion Whigs like Edward Kent and Noah Smith protested that "these straight out Whigs are manifestly determined to ruin us all if they can & they will openly or covertly join or aid the Hunkers in smothering northern sentiment." Pro-fusion Whigs, insisted another, must issue an address stating "boldly & with cleanness that the old Whig organization is dead throughout the union & was sundered by the Southern Whigs on the Nebraska bill." These anguished cries proved prophetic. Though three-tenths of Reed's 1854 supporters went Republican in 1855, reducing his vote from 14,000 in 1854 to 10,645 (9.6 percent), Whig holdouts still denied Morrill a majority. And since the conservative Whigs combined with Democrats on legislative candidates, they had enough men to elect the Democrat Samuel Wells governor over Morrill in the legislature's runoff contest.[121]

"A portion of the old Whig party . . . are not yet ready to abandon the name & the organization but cling tenaciously to both," Kent groaned to Seward after the election. A minority of these diehards, "composed" of once "prominent . . . leaders, is determined to join the Democratic party" since they were "hunkers and proslavery at heart." The rest "are with us in feeling" against "the Slave Power & its outrages," but they are "frightened by the cry of sectionalism and disunion."[122]

Old line Whigs and anti-Nebraska Whig/Know Nothings, though still enemies, together stymied the Republican movement in Massachusetts. During the three months after the Philadelphia Know Nothing meeting, Henry Wilson, Know Nothing Governor Henry J. Gardner, and anti-Know Nothing Whig editor Samuel Bowles strove to combine the state's anti-Nebraska elements. "I hope our Whig friends will go promptly with the movement," Wilson told Bowles. But conservatives like Winthrop and Everett instead longed for a coalition of "the great conservative interests" to "crush" Wilson. Thus Whigs held their own state convention and nominated the old Websterite Samuel Walley for governor on a platform denouncing the Republican party, even though the Republican state convention a few days earlier had nominated Whig Julius Rockwell "in the hope," Everett believed, "to catch the Whig votes."[123]

Furious that Republicans had spurned him, Gardner, running again as a Know Nothing, won the four-way race with a plurality of 51,497 (37.7 percent), a dramatic drop from the 81,503 (62.6 percent) he had achieved a year earlier. Rockwell, with 36,714 votes (26.9 percent), ran second, and the Democrat Edward Beach ran third with 34,728. Walley, the champion of intransigent Whigs, garnered only 13,296 votes, a decline of 14,000 from Emory Washburn's total a year earlier. The Whig proportion of the cast vote slumped from a fifth to less than a tenth. More of Washburn's 1854 supporters voted for Rockwell and Beach, indeed, than stuck with Walley, and while a fifth of Gardner's 1854 voters went Republican and another 15 percent reverted to the Democratic column, virtually none came back to the expiring Whig party. Measured differently, Whigs retained only about 7 percent of Winfield Scott's 1852 supporters; two-fifths of those men were now Republicans, a fourth remained Know Nothings, and almost a fifth did not bother to vote.[124]

Attempting to account for Whigs' pitiful vote, Everett explained that "the repeal of the Missouri Compromise shattered us." In 1854 many conservative Whigs went Know Nothing since Gardner was a former Webster Whig. In 1855, some voted Republican, but "a great many conservative Whigs voted for the democratic candidate. Had it not been that the democratic party, as supporters of the Administration, had to endorse the Nebraska concern, the conservative Whigs would have joined them almost *en masse*." Nonetheless, he exulted, "we Whigs are well satisfied with the result, which so completely demolishes the paltry 'fusion' intrigue." Republicans were annoyed by Whig holdouts, but they more accurately blamed the continuing appeal of Know Nothingism. According to Wilson, they had "overestimated the power of the antislavery sentiment and underestimated the power of old organizations." "The people will not confront the issues at present," another griped. "They want a Paddy hunt & on a Paddy hunt they will go." Consequently, "the hope of a united North in 1856 is the merest moonshine."[125]

The results certainly raised doubts that Massachusetts' most conservative men could be rallied behind Fillmore's candidacy on the American ticket in 1856. To fend off the Republican challenge, moreover, Massachusetts Know Nothings had trumpeted their anti-Nebraska and antislavery credentials. Thus they also appeared likely to oppose Fillmore if he ran on the 1855 American platform with its despised Section Twelve.[126]

Most northern Know Nothings who protested Section Twelve of the Philadelphia platform, in fact, wanted no part of fusion. They still believed that they could maintain their organization as both a nativist and an antislavery party in the North, yet still cooperate with southern Americans in the impending presidential campaign. To facilitate that cooperation, the bolters called a meeting of northern Know Nothings in Cincinnati in late November to which they invited E. B. Bartlett of neighboring Covington, Kentucky, the new national president of the order. Massachusetts, Vermont, Rhode Island, and Pennsylvania sent delegates to this gathering, including Pennsylvania's ex-Governor Johnston. But the most important delegations came from the midwestern states of Michigan, Wisconsin, Indiana, Illinois, and especially Ohio.[127]

Rejecting a pro-fusion platform proposed by Thomas Spooner, president of Ohio's state council, which announced that "since the slavery issue is paramount" Know Nothings would "cheerfully unite" with anyone opposed to Slave Power aggressions, the Cincinnati meeting instead adopted a far more moderate platform endorsed by its president, Thomas Ford, also of Ohio. Those resolutions called for another National Council meeting in February at Philadelphia a few days before the Americans' national nominating convention met there, demanded that Section Twelve be replaced with a plank that called for restoration of the Missouri Compromise line, insisted that Congress refuse to admit any slave states formed in Kansas and Nebraska Territories, and firmly repudiated "coalescing with any party which demands the postponement or abandonment of American principles, or the disorganization of the American party."

That plank, warned one Cincinnati Republican, meant "that the Republicans will have to enter upon the Presidential contest without calculating on much aid from those still adhering to the K. N. Organization." According to Schouler's fuller assessment in the Cincinnati *Gazette*, northern Know Nothings clearly spurned fusion with the Republicans and still desired cooperation with southern Americans. Because of the Nebraska outrage, however, "the Northern members of the American party cannot with safety to their party, respect for themselves or regard for principle, wink out of sight this great question. It is one that must be met." Unless Southerners agreed to this change, he warned, Know Nothingism in the North was finished.[128]

This demand severely disappointed Fillmore's friends who had expected "a just and liberal construction of the principles of the Philadelphia resolutions" that reaffirmed Know Nothingism's conversion into a bisectional Union party. Northern and southern Know Nothings in Congress, Haven wrote Fillmore two weeks later when the new Thirty-Fourth Congress commenced, "constantly quarrel about Platforms & to save me from perdition I can contrive no way to prevent it."[129] Yet northern Know Nothings' determination at Cincinnati, both to reject absorption by the Republicans and to insist on stopping slavery expansion in Kansas and Nebraska, was easily comprehensible. The Cincinnati meeting was carefully scheduled to follow all of the North's 1855 elections so that delegates could plot future strategy based on their results. What happened at the polls shaped what they did in the Queen City.

In Pennsylvania, Know Nothings almost totally stifled attempts to launch an independent Republican party or to preserve Whiggery as an independent force. They infiltrated and controlled the initial Republican state committee, insisted on restoration of the Missouri Compromise in their own platform, and ultimately forced anti-Democratic elements to coalesce behind Thomas Nicholson, a Know Nothing, as the opposition's candidate for canal commissioner. In local elections during the winter and spring of 1855, Whigs had divided votes between Know Nothings and anti-Know Nothing Democrats, but the remaining Whigs still held a state convention that nominated a candidate for canal commissioner. According to delegate Alexander K. McClure, it was "an assembly of leaders without rank and file" since Whiggery's remaining adherents were "a few old Scotch-Irish Whigs, most of whom would have been compelled to lie awake at night to decide whether they most hated Know Nothingism or Democracy." McClure himself, like D. N. White and Russell Errett of the Pittsburgh *Gazette*, helped form a Republican party in 1855 that also nominated a candidate for canal commissioner—the controversial Passmore Williamson, who had been arrested for defying the Fugitive Slave Act. Nonetheless, Know Nothings heavily outnumbered other opponents of the Democrats. When their leaders called for a meeting of three members each from the American, Whig, and Republican state committees at Harrisburg on September 27 to agree upon a fusion candidate, McClure represented the Whigs and accepted Nicholson.[130]

A few Whigs, however, insisted on keeping their own candidate in the race. So did two other groups: Republican ideologues, who refused to cooperate with Know Nothings, and the anti-Know Nothing Native American party. The Native American got 4,056 votes (1.2 percent), but that was almost twice as much as the showing of the last statewide Whig candidate to run in Pennsylvania, who attracted only 2,293 votes (0.7 percent). "There are about enough Whigs left to keep us in remembrance that there was once such a party, and no more," joked one Democrat. "The Whig party is defunct," accurately chimed another. Some of the Whigs who had not yet joined the Know Nothings in 1854 went Republican, but Williamson attracted only 7,226 votes (2.2 percent). Over two-fifths of those 1854 Whig holdouts, however, refused to vote in 1855, and the rest went for Nicholson, as did the great majority of 1854 Know Nothings.[131] With 149,745 votes (46 percent), Nicholson was clearly the major opposition candidate, even though he still lost by over 12,000 votes to the victorious Democrat. Little wonder that Pennsylvania's delegates to the Cincinnati conclave had little interest in abandoning the Know Nothing organization for a merger with the Republicans.[132]

Ohioans were the key delegates at Cincinnati, and at first blush, Ohio's state election seemed strikingly different from those in Pennsylvania, Massachusetts, and Maine. Few Ohio Whigs contemplated running their own gubernatorial candidate in 1855. Virtually all non-Democrats hoped to preserve the polyglot anti-Nebraska People's coalition that swept the 1854 congressional races and that planned to nominate a state ticket in July at a Columbus convention. The major question was who would control those nominations: Whig/Know Nothings like Lew Campbell, who wanted to preserve his ties to southern Know Nothings at least until after the speakership election in the impending session of Congress, or non-Know Nothing and often virulently anti-Know Nothing Free Soilers who sought to convert the People's coalition into a Republican party. "We are battling the Know Nothings," declared Joshua R. Giddings. "We refuse to go into Convention with, or to recognize them as allies. We are determined to have a Republican Convention, a Republican *nomination*, and Republican Candidates without surrender, without compromise." Just as adamantly, Campbell insisted that the Know Nothings, whose Ohio membership had swollen to about 130,000 by the spring of 1855, were too "formidable" to be insulted and that while they were "strongly Anti-Slavery," they would "not consent to abandon other reforms ... to remedy other palpable wrongs besides Slavery!"[133]

Each side correctly suspected the other of plotting earlier nominations to preempt the decision at Columbus, and each pushed favorites for the gubernatorial nomination. Know Nothings strongly preferred Jacob Brinkerhoff, a member of the order and a former Free Soil Democrat, whom Campbell had promoted since December 1854. Free Soilers and non-Know Nothing antislavery Whigs like Senator Ben Wade favored Salmon Chase, whose nomination, Campbell warned Schouler, "will ruin us" because he was an outsider and anathema to old-line Whigs.[134] Nonetheless, many Know Nothings were so eager to unite antislavery voters that they would accept Chase, who for months had been trying to get his friends to stop attacking the nativists in order to forge a Republican majority.

The most important pro-Chase Know Nothing was Thomas Spooner, president of the state council. An ex-Free Soiler, rather than a Whig like Campbell, Spooner enthusiastically supported merging the Know Nothings into an exclusively northern Republican party. Using his authority as president, Spooner quashed attempts by Know Nothings to make separate nominations at a June council meeting. The way was thus prepared for Ohio's Whigs, Free Soilers, anti-Nebraska Democrats, and Know Nothings to combine in the Republican party. Yet the mutually suspicious groups still had to construct a mutually acceptable ticket.[135]

Adopting the Republican label, the July convention gave Chase its gubernatorial nomination on a platform that focused almost exclusively on the slavery issue and was utterly silent on nativism. But the eight other slots on the state ticket went to Know Nothings, including Thomas Ford, the candidate for lieutenant governor. Prominent among the northern protesters at Philadelphia, the ex-Whig Ford later opposed Spooner's motion at Cincinnati for a merger between northern Know Nothings and Republicans. One reason for that stance, clearly, was that the Know Nothing preponderance on the July Republican ticket did not assuage dissident Know Nothings and conservative Whigs. They immediately nominated Allen Trimble, a septuagenarian former governor, to oppose Chase.

Chase won, but he polled over 22,000 fewer votes than others on the ticket, while Trimble got over 24,000 (8 percent), almost all of whom were former Whigs. Considerably fewer than half of Ohio's one-time Whigs, indeed, could stomach the hated Chase. Of those who supported Winfield Scott, only a third backed Chase, a fourth went to Trimble, and 44 percent abstained. Yet almost all of Trimble's voters supported anti-Nebraska candidates in 1854, and they also backed Ford and other ex-Whig Know Nothings on the Republican ticket. For that reason, Ford and most Ohio delegates to the Cincinnati Know Nothing meeting broke with Spooner and spurned a merger with Republicans. For the same reason, however, they also insisted on free soil and restoration of the Missouri Compromise line, a position starkly at odds with Fillmore's vision of the American party.[136]

X

Fillmore's confidants like Kennedy and Haven drew far more solace from New York's results since the Know Nothings, whom his Silver Gray allies now almost completely controlled, won the few statewide offices at stake that year. Yet even New York Know Nothings, who refused explicitly to repudiate Section Twelve of the American party platform in order to hold the door open for future cooperation with Southerners and who boycotted the postelection Cincinnati gathering precisely because they expected it to jettison that controversial plank, knew that they could not explicitly endorse it. In August, therefore, a state council meeting at Binghamton condemned the repeal of the Missouri Compromise, insisted that slavery "should derive no extension from such repeal," and asserted that the slavery issue had "no rightful place in the platform of the National American Party."[137]

Because Sewardite Whigs' 1854 victory caused them stubbornly to shun both the Republican and Know Nothing movements, the 1855 New York election is important primarily for completing the northern Whig party's obliteration as an independent political force. Discomfited by their isolation from antislavery men elsewhere and aware after New England's spring elections that even hostility to slavery extension could not preserve northern Whiggery, Seward, Weed, and their various lieutenants began to plot in May and June to merge their forces with New York's Free Soilers and anti-Nebraska Democrats in an anti-Know Nothing Republican party. Seward made no public statement until the fall, but the key decisions came in July. Early that month Seward privately endorsed the formation of a Republican party in Indiana. Three weeks later, Weed wrote Seward that within New York itself "the necessity of getting in line with other states is imperative."[138]

Weed briefly toyed with the idea of calling a People's convention, as had been done in midwestern states a year earlier,[139] but instead he and others hit upon the idea of holding simultaneous Whig and Republican state conventions in Syracuse on September 26 to combine the two organizations. Even before this proposal was published in Whig newspapers, Haven had doubted "that there will be a Whig State Convention" in New York that year. Once the plan was broadcast, Weed's intentions were clear. "The Whig party is dissolved by the formal action of its leaders with a view to its reconstruction," former Democratic Governor Horatio Seymour told Secretary of State Marcy. Fillmore's friends and Washington Hunt concurred that "the Whig party is sick unto death," "moribund," and "foreordained . . . to be swallowed up in fusion" with the Republicans, a merger for which Sewardite Whig newspapers were "straining every nerve."[140]

Many Sewardites optimistically endorsed the plan. The Republican movement was spreading like wildfire and would crush "Hunkerism, Know Nothingism and all its allies," one wrote Governor Myron Clark in early August. "This Republican movement cant be resisted—other states having gone so far with it," chimed another Weed lieutenant. Weed and Seward themselves were far more skeptical of success, at least in 1855. "It is possible that the state may be carried this fall," Weed told Seward to justify his call for simultaneous conventions. "There are elements enough, if combined, to effect it." Seward was even more reluctant to abandon the Whig organization. In September, when he congratulated Edward A. Stansbury upon his election as chairman of Vermont's new Republican state committee, he warned, "The revolution is inaugurated and it will prevail, but not everywhere, all at once. . . . We are by no means at the end but only at the beginning of the end."[141]

Democrats and Silver Gray Know Nothings were certain that fusion would fail abysmally. Assuming like so many others that Weed's stance in the *Albany Evening Journal* represented Seward's thinking, Seymour told Marcy that Seward's objective for the Republican organization was "to get entirely clear from the Silver Grays & induce a portion of the Democratic party to act with him." Yet, Seymour predicted, "he will lose a large number of Whigs," and few Democrats would join the "new organization." Given the "disastrous" handling of canal repairs by the incumbent Whig state administration and the obnoxious new prohibition law that Clark had signed, he added, Democrats should win the election on state issues. Only the effort of Whig papers that embraced the Republican movement "to excite the minds of the northern people against the South" gave him pause.[142]

Convinced that New York's election "must be between the Democracy & the Americans," Haven assured Fillmore that "Fusion is out of the question . . . unless the extreme sectional Whigs fuse by voting the Democratic nomination" rather than running a Republican ticket. Confident about the power of the anti-Catholic issue, other Know Nothings believed that they could easily undercut the Republican movement by demonstrating that "Black republican" leaders "have long slept with [Archbishop John] Hughes" and "that Seward and Pierce have a common interest in crushing out the American sentiment in the country." Mocking Weed's effort to divide what was left of the Whig carcass, Nathan K. Hall rejoiced that Washington Hunt's letter clinging to Whiggery signaled that many Whigs "will not go into the Republican fusion movement."[143]

Hunt, in fact, was not the only old-line Whig appalled by the Republican movement. "Whig young men will not follow the lead of King Weed & Company," crowed one Democrat, who expected Whig reinforcements for his party. "The total abandonment of the Whig party leaves all Whigs to form such political associations as best comports [sic] with their notions and ambition." More important, some conservatives wanted to preserve the Whig organization itself. In New York City, a Silver Gray wrote Fillmore in early October, "a strong organization of the Whigs will still be kept up to resist this [Republican] movement." Citing a meeting of those Manhattan Whigs, Hunt told Hamilton Fish, the state's most prominent Whig holdout, that "thousands of Whigs in the [upstate] counties will not vote the fusion ticket." And a week later, a worried Weed man from Oswego warned that "the Whigs who were once in the habit of contributing funds are now openly opposed to us & openly call a meeting . . . to resuscitate the old Whig party."[144]

Jeering that old-line Whig "opposition to the Republican movement is by no means equal to the Clay opposition to Taylor [in August and September 1848] which flattened out so completely," one Sewardite dismissed the New York City meeting in early October as "a miserable abortion." Nonetheless, he warned that in 1856 Republicans must bring in "the Trimbles of Ohio[,] the Winthrops & Walleys of Mass.[,] and the Bradishes & Fishes of N.Y." since "it seems to be hopeless in 1855." Indeed, a second straight-Whig convention in Manhattan on October 23 attracted delegates from thirty-one counties. They adopted resolutions by Robert A. West, the editor of the *Commercial Advertiser*, who probably arranged the meeting, that condemned the Republican movement and declared that the Whig party still lived. By late October, however, even most of these conservatives admitted that the mass of Whigs who had not joined the Know Nothings accepted the new Republican party, and they therefore resolved not to run their own candidates.[145]

A month earlier, the incorporation of Sewardite Whigs into the new Republican party occurred with barely a hitch at Syracuse. Seward told one Whig delegate that "it didn't make a difference" whether he attended the Whig or the Republican convention. "He said we would go in by two doors, but we would all come out through one." Whigs, in fact, attended both conventions that initially met in separate locations. Committees from each agreed upon a common ticket and platform before formal merger was attempted. Free Soilers Preston King and Abijah Mann got the nominations for secretary of state and attorney general, but Whig James Cook was selected for comptroller to assure Whigs that, along with the executive officers chosen in 1854, Whigs would still control the all-important canal board.[146]

The platform demanded slavery's exclusion from all territories, condemned Missouri's border ruffian outrages in Kansas, and opposed the admission of any new slave states. Significantly, it did *not* call for reimposition of the Missouri Compromise line, perhaps because New York's Know Nothings, like those elsewhere in the North, had in effect done so.[147] As to Know Nothingism itself, the platform was forthright: "We repudiate and condemn the proscriptive and antirepublican doctrines of the order of Know-Nothings, and all their secret constitutions, oaths, rituals, and organizations." The Whig convention approved both the ticket and the platform, as did the Republicans, after some grousing about the platform's complete silence on prohibition.

Once they had ratified the platform and ticket, Whigs adjourned and marched across town to the Republican gathering. Led by Weed himself, they entered to thunderous applause, and the combined membership then reratified the ticket and platform; added a renowned dry as Republican candidate for the state court of appeals, which would decide upon the constitutionality of the 1855 prohibition act; and appointed a Republican state committee. The New York Republican party was launched—after the New York Whig party had willfully committed organizational suicide.

Thunderous applause at Syracuse was not enough to bring Republicans victory. Winning pluralities in the four-way statewide races, Know Nothings captured all three executive posts, as well as control of the legislature and canal board. In the race for secretary of state, for example, Know Nothings won with 148,557 votes (34.1 percent), an increase of 26,000 over Ullmann's poll in 1854 despite an overall decline in turnout of 33,000 since that election. Republicans ran second with 136,698 (31.4 percent), 20,000 fewer than Clark had received a year earlier. The Soft and Hard Democratic candidates trailed with 91,336 (21 percent) and 59,353 (13.6 percent), respectively. "If we fail this fall," Seward's friend George Baker predicted three weeks before the election, "it will be because the people have read more about the Pope and Bishop Hughes than about Slavery and Equal Rights." Anti-Catholicism, indeed, clearly remained a powerful force among New York's voters, a force that the new Republican party, in a display of righteousness some Sewardites considered more foolish than brave, had explicitly repudiated.[148]

Yet Democrats who complained that "this hurricane of Know Nothingism has been contributed to largely by the 'straight out Whigs' who rushed blindly in, to defeat republicanism" were also correct.[149] As historian William E. Gienapp has demonstrated, Know Nothing voter support shifted dramatically from 1854 to 1855; antislavery men now voted Republican, while more conservative Whigs replaced them in American ranks. As one Whig consoled Hamilton Fish, "There is one thing about this contest quite discernible—that where they [Know Nothings] were strong last year they have now lost & where they were weak now they are strong." "To my mind," he wistfully added, "this is an indication that ere long they will die out."[150]

Only three-fifths of Ullmann's 1854 supporters continued to vote Know Nothing; the remainder divided evenly among Republicans, Democrats, and abstainers. Conversely, whereas approximately one-fifth of Myron Clark's supporters went Know Nothing in 1855 and a smaller fraction abstained, the others moved into the Republican column. Indeed, they provided virtually all of the Republican votes. Free Soilers had voted for Clark in 1854, but even when measured against the 1852 presidential vote, Whigs outnumbered Free Soilers among 1855 Republican voters by five to one. Exceptionally few former Democrats supported the new party. The same estimates suggest that three-tenths of Winfield Scott's 1852 supporters abstained in 1855, while the remainder divided almost evenly between Republicans and Know Nothings.[151]

New York's Whig party had been completely shattered. With its demise, all but diehards admitted, Whiggery as an independent political force had evaporated as thoroughly in the North as in the South. Hunt pragmatically attributed the collapse in New York and other free states to the transfer of "nearly all the [party's] machinery," its newspapers and local organizations, to the Republicans or Know Nothings, making it necessary for those who sought to perpetuate Whiggery "to reorganize and wait for better times." Seward, who loved the Whig party as much as Hunt, offered a deeper explanation of what had happened. No party could exist, he wrote organizers of Indiana's Republican party in July, unless it "admits and justifies the claim of every man of whatever race or clime or faith to equal protection with all others in the enjoyment of the inalienable Rights of Life and Civil and Religious Liberty and the pursuit of happiness" guaranteeed by the Constitution and the Declaration of Independence. Though "the Whig party" originally "cloth[ed] itself with the traditional policy of the Revolutionary fathers," it had abandoned its commitment to liberty for men of every race and faith. Seward implied, in sum, that Whigs' mission to save the Revolutionary experiment in republican self-government by rescuing public liberty had run its course. The issue now was the freedom of northern whites of whatever religious or ethnic background and indeed of blacks, and Whigs either ignored that issue or sided with the foes of freedom. New parties were necessary.[152]

Yet it was on October 12, 1855, on the steps of the state capitol in Albany, that Seward delivered his most poignant public valedictory for the Whig party. It was time, he argued, for antislavery men to abandon Whiggery and rally to the new Republican party. Whatever the Whig party's past accomplishments, the past must be left behind; the battle against the Slave Power required a fresh start. "Shall we report ourselves to the Whig party? Where is it? 'Gentle Shepard' tell me where?" he asked. "It was a strong and vigorous party, honorable for energy, noble achievements, and still more noble enterprises." Yet "it was moved by panics and fears to emulate the Democratic party in its practiced subserviency" to the Slave Power. "It yielded in spite of your remonstrances and mine, and now there is neither Whig party, nor Whig, south of the Potomac." Then came the moving peroration. "Let, then, the Whig party pass. It committed a grievous fault, and grievously hath it answered [for] it. Let it march out of the field, therefore, with all the honors."[153]

XI

Millard Fillmore's friends did not mourn the death of the Whig party in New York or anywhere else. By their analysis, New York's results proved that the American party, now purged of antislavery men and firmly in the hands of Unionists, could carry New York and thus deliver it to Fillmore in 1856. Even sweeter, they had "routed the Fusion republicans," stripped them "of power & patronage" in New York, and thereby "destroyed Sewardism." Best of all, Seward's futile efforts to "break down the American party there, by consolidating the whole force of abolitionism, Whig and Democratic, in a republican fusion against it" had succeeded only in driving conservatives in both the South and North into the arms of the American party. Therefore, crowed Kennedy, "the Whigs especially" who had thus far spurned the American movement must now look to it "as the chief repository of that national conservatism which has been the distinctive point of their creed."[154]

Republicanism had hardly been "routed" or Sewardism "destroyed" in New York. Events in the following weeks and months quickly revived both. Even as he "grieve[d] for the disappointment of so many good friends" and hung his "head with shame" at the Know Nothing victory, Seward predicted that no "other termination of the canvass would have been better calculated to promote our ultimate success." Know Nothings' boasts were "just so much gas in any ascending balloon. . . . But the balloon is always sure, not only to come down, but to come down *very quick*." The presidential election of 1856 would determine the rivals' true strength. "The 'Know Nothings' will inevitably disappear in the heat of the great national contest," Seward told his son. "A year is necessary to let the cheat wear off."[155]

Nor were die-hard Whigs yet prepared to give up the ghost by joining either the Know Nothings or the Republicans. "I agree with you fully that we ought to preserve the Whig organization," Hunt wrote Fish on December 20, 1855. Even though almost all Whig newspapers and "active politicians who are looking for patronage advancement" in the North and South had gone over to the Republicans, the Know Nothings, or, in the South, the Democrats, there were still "in every state (or nearly all) a respectable body of men, respectable for numbers and intelligence, who are still Whigs and will not act with any of the other parties except as a choice of evils for the time being." Certain "that neither the K. N. or the Fusion [Republican] combination can be of long duration," Hunt predicted that "one presidential election will finish them both." Whoever won it, "then all or nearly all the honest Whigs who are now acting in either of the factions, will be glad to resume the Whig name and do battle again for national Whig principles." Holdout Whigs like Hunt, Fish, Winthrop, and others must therefore hold "a National Convention" in 1856 "to demonstrate that we are still alive as a national party."[156]

Kennedy, Seward, and Hunt each articulated what had been on the minds of Whig politicians since the party first began to disintegrate after the 1852 election. Anything might happen in off-year state and congressional elections. But the final fate of the Whig party would be determined only by the presidential campaign of 1856.

Chapter 26

"The Whig Party Is Dead and Buried"

"THE WHIG PARTY died of too much respectability and not enough people."[1] That, at least, was the opinion of Edward Stafford, a Republican newspaper editor from Jackson, Mississippi, five years after the Civil War. A review of the reasons for the party's rise and fall demonstrates the manifold inadequacies of Stafford's witty epitaph. As this last chapter also seeks to show, however, Stafford quite accurately described the party's final death throes in 1856.

I

By the end of 1855, so many one-time Whig voters and leaders had deserted their former party for new organizations that it did indeed have far too few people to contest the presidency in 1856. But Stafford's sarcastic gibe fails to explain why the Whigs had been reduced to that condition by the start of 1856. To the extent that he posited a causal connection between his two variables—that the Whig party had too few supporters because its self-righteous aura of respectability and social superiority turned most American voters against it—his analysis is manifestly wrong. Although the majority of the nation's politically active wealthy citizens supported the Whig party, it had never been the exclusive preserve of the rich. Although the often self-consciously respectable, God-fearing, church-going, sober middle classes in towns and cities across the nation also tended to be Whig, moreover, the party could never have dominated almost every city in the country or the small towns and prosperous agricultural regions that constituted the core of its strength if only the social elite and smugly fastidious middle classes composed it.

Nor was a sense of social and moral superiority the main reason even the upper and middling classes gravitated to Whiggery. Whig supporters were attracted by the commonwealth tradition of republican government Whigs espoused and Democrats so vigorously rejected. Inherited by the Whigs from the Madisonian wing of the Republican party to which Henry Clay had belonged, this tradition held that government at all levels of the federal system should be used positively to elevate people economically, socially, and morally through the internal development of the nation's civic institutions and economic infrastructure rather than through foreign expansionism and adventurism, the only positive use of government that Democrats championed and one that appalled most Whigs.

Initially, however, a related, but equally powerful, republican conviction engendered the Whig party. This was the belief that the fundamental purpose of the Revolutionary experiment in republican self-government was to protect personal and popular (or public) liberty from concentrations of arbitrary and tyrannical power that would lead inevitably to the people's figurative "enslavement" unless actively resisted and repudiated. Whigs' commitment to this bedrock tenet never wavered. It explains why so many of them cherished the very name "Whig," with its reverberations of the Revolutionary struggle. Nor did Whigs view it as separate from their concomitant commonwealth belief in an activist state, which Whigs hoped would liberate people from restrictive conditions, debilitating character defects, and unhealthy dependencies. Similarly, Whigs advocated government promotion and subsidization of economic growth and diversification through the expansion of banking credit and currency, the granting of corporate privileges, tariff protection, and internal improvements because they sincerely believed that such diversification enhanced individuals' economic freedom by expanding their opportunities for upward economic mobility.

In the winter of 1833–34, however, economic prosperity obviated the need for and the electoral appeal of such programs. Instead, the Whig party formed around a crusade to save public liberty and republican self-government from Andrew Jackson's supposedly tyrannical executive usurpations that upset the constitutional balance between branches of the national government and that seemed to violate the laws of the land. While these concerns facilitated a coalition of various anti-Jackson leaders, they did not ensure Whig success at the grass-roots level. Indeed, the party flourished at the state level only when it took concrete, partisanly distinctive stands on state public policies and demonstrated the congruence between its founding principles and state affairs. Nor, manifestly, did a crusade against executive tyranny combine the heterogeneous Whig legions behind a single presidential candidate in 1836. Only the Panic of 1837 and Democrats' response to it allowed Whigs to unite behind a positive agenda for government-aided economic recovery and to make a persuasive case to the electorate for the necessity of positive governance, the interrelatedness of what state and national governments did, and the inadequacies of the Democratic alternatives.

From the start, indeed, Whigs were deeply divided between Northerners and Southerners over slavery and other matters; between National Republicans and later converts, whether former Jacksonians, Antimasons, or southern State Rights men; between self-styled progressives and self-conscious conservatives; and among ambitious politicos and their personal devotees, be they Clay, Webster, and others who chafed at those titans' pretensions to the party's presidential nominations or factional rivals in Vermont, Massachusetts, New York, Pennsylvania, Ohio, Maryland, Virginia, North Carolina, Tennessee, Georgia, and so many other states. Those divisions, utterly omitted from Stafford's caustic postmortem, contributed far more than "too much respectability" to the Whig party's death.

From the beginning, these centrifugal forces were counteracted by a powerful centripetal pressure that Stafford also failed to recognize. That cohesive force was deeply principled opposition to Democrats and a common abhorrence of what Democrats stood for, or, at least in Whigs' biased eyes, seemed to stand for—executive suppression of the legislative will; the negative, do-nothing state; war-mongering expansionism; corruption; subservience-to the demands of their Catholic, immigrant, and rum-swilling constituents; and, by the mid-1840s, Union-threatening and liberty-crushing Slave Power aggression. If anything, indeed, Stafford's omission of the synergistic relationship between Democrats and Whigs in the death—and life—of the Whig party is even more glaring than his silence about its internal divisions.

If Stafford's epigrammatic epitaph is manifestly incomplete, why, then, was the Whig party at death's door when 1856 began? Only the cumulative and combined impact of many factors can explain the party's demise. The problem—and the source of disagreement among historians who have seriously considered it—is how to weigh or prioritize those many factors. Focusing on the party's woes during its last six or eight years, some historians attribute the party's demise to increasingly hostile sectional antagonism over slavery and to sectionalism's inseparable concomitant, many northern and southern Whigs' genuine fears about the danger that sectional agitation posed to the Union. Others cite the increasingly fractious infighting among Whig leaders. Still others stress the uniquely subversive impact of new issues like nativism and prohibitionism on the Whig electorate in the 1850s. All of these did indeed contribute to the party's ultimate collapse, but historians too often view those corrosive forces as mutually exclusive. More important, any explanation that focuses only on the party's final years misses the mark. The reasons for the party's death can be found in the same dynamics that first allowed it to rise and flourish.

In essence, the history of the Whig party was encapsulated in the fluctuating balance between the divisive centrifugal forces that threatened to tear it apart and the centripetal pressure of conflict with and difference from the Democrats that held it together. Between 1834 and 1854 that balance followed a parabolic and surprisingly symmetrical trajectory, with its apogee in 1844. Beginning in 1834, only common opposition to Jackson united the new coalition. Divisive forces were clearly stronger, as evidenced by the three-headed presidential campaign in 1836, the holdout of Antimasons in some northern states and State Rights parties in some southern states, and sharp sectional splits between northern and southern Whigs over slavery and the gag rule in Congress.

Even before 1837, however, a few state parties—in Ohio, North Carolina, and New Jersey, for example—managed to rally behind distinctive state programs and against their Democratic opposites. After the Panic, the balance between centrifugal and centripetal forces tilted increasingly toward the latter in response to the dramatic sharpening of programmatic differences between the two parties at both the national and state levels of the federal system. Personal rivalries for the 1840 presidential nomination notwithstanding, hard times and the major parties' divergent remedies for them rallied growing numbers of Whig voters and brought both northern and southern anti-Democratic holdouts into the Whig fold.

Division flickered again in the break with Tyler, and disarray in Washington dearly cost Whigs in the off-year elections between the spring of 1841 and late 1843 as disillusioned and disappointed new supporters stayed home on election days. But that split also solidified the vast majority of Whigs against Tyler and·

behind Henry Clay and his programs. Thus, in the presidential campaign of 1844, Whigs were never more unified and their differences from the Democrats were never sharper. Yet still the Whigs lost a heartbreakingly close election.

After that election, the parabolic trajectory of the balance between cohesive and divisive forces in the party turned downward. Almost immediately internal rifts intensified—over the reasons for Clay's defeat, over the next presidential nominee, over Texas' annexation, over the response to the Native American and Liberty parties, and within certain state parties like those of Massachusetts, New York, and Georgia. Nonetheless, common opposition to the economic policies of James K. Polk and his Democratic congressional allies and to the Mexican War kept the balance tilted toward centripetal pressures, allowed the Whigs to rebound in the 1846–47 state and congressional elections, and helped them win the congressional, gubernatorial, and presidential elections of 1848. Almost from the moment of Zachary Taylor's election in November 1848, however, interparty conflict between Whigs and Democrats diminished and intraparty divisions among Whigs dangerously escalated. By 1854 the balance between centrifugal and centripetal forces had returned approximately to its starting point in 1834, yet with an absolutely crucial difference: the emergence of powerful and attractive new parties that could siphon off the Whigs' leadership cadre and electorate.

II

To a large but not exclusive extent, therefore, explaining the Whig party's expiration requires explaining the shifting relationships after 1844 between the forces of interparty conflict and intraparty division. The diminution of the first and exacerbation of the second together did alienate Whig voters, provoke their defection, and thereby contribute to the problem of "not enough people." The danger for the historian, however, lies in totally conflating the reasons for the two divergent trends.

At times the two processes *did* stem from a common cause, and never more so than with the exacerbation of sectional conflict over slavery extension after 1848. That divided Whigs against each other along North-South lines and within a number of states. Simultaneously, in Congress during 1850 and in a number of states that year and later, it caused some Whigs to side with Democrats of like mind against intraparty foes, thereby diminishing the perception of difference between the parties. Yet, however principled disagreements were between rival Whigs over whether to emphasize preservation of the Union and intersectional comity within the Whig party, on the one hand, or protection of sectional rights and interests, on the other, principle alone did not cause those divisions. In Massachusetts, New York, Pennsylvania, Michigan, North Carolina, Tennessee, and Georgia, those disagreements also reflected the preexistence of rival factions motivated in many cases by different issues or simply by the conflicting ambitions of rival politicos. Those rivalries had been dramatically intensified, indeed, by so nonideological a matter as federal patronage allotment by the Taylor and Fillmore administrations. And even where state organizations did not divide over slavery, as in Maryland, Virginia, and Ohio, rancorous internal feuds weakened the party.

Similarly, the weakening of Whigs' competitive position against, and the diminution of their conflict with, Democrats helped spur internal Whig division over the best strategy for coping with their plight, and those processes coincided in time. But they were distinct and must be analyzed separately. Nor can analysis focus solely on the Whigs and the societal conditions to which they reacted.

From the time of the Whig party's birth, Democrats vitally determined its fortunes and fate. Opposition to the Democrats and Democratic policies was always the strongest glue holding the Whigs together and the strongest incentive for men to go to the polls to vote Whig. Sometimes the biggest Democratic target emerged in Washington, whether it was Jackson's Caesarism, Van Buren's wrongheaded and cold-hearted response to the depression, or Polk's warmongering and seemingly vulnerable economic program. Just as often, however, it appeared in individual states, whether New York Democrats' opposition to canal expansion, Ohio, Louisiana, and New Jersey Democrats' hard-money policies, North Carolina and Tennessee Democrats' opposition to railroad subsidies, or Mississippi Democrats' bond repudiation.

Any shift by Democrats toward Whiggish stands on issues such as Pennsylvania Democrats' embrace of tariff protection in 1844, Midwestern Democrats' endorsement of internal improvements in the 1840s and 1850s, North Carolina Democrats' acquiescence in railroad aid after 1848, or Alabama Democrats' shift to a probanking stance in 1849, therefore, could dull both party differences and men's incentive to vote Whig. Logrolling deals between the two parties in state constitutional conventions in Virginia, Louisiana, and Maryland had the same effect. The burgeoning prosperity after 1848 based on California gold strikes and increased foreign investment, however, did the most to blunt Whigs' economic appeals. Prosperity undermined the justification for Whigs' positive governmental programs; drove far more Democrats in a probanking, probusiness, prodevelopment direction; and, with the boom in railroad construction, divided both parties along regional and interest group lines, thereby further blurring interparty differences.

Democratic decisions after 1848 on the slavery issue also gravely damaged the Whigs. Blaming their defeats that year on the Whigs' artful Janus-faced campaign, the Democrats trumped it with one of their own in 1849. Swinging to a more adamant antislavery stance, often in combination with Free Soilers, in the North and to a more extreme proslavery stance in the South, where some Whigs felt compelled to go along, they outflanked the Whigs in the 1849 elections. Thus they made it impossible for Whigs from the two sections to unite behind Taylor's plan for the Mexican Cession or the congressional Compromise. Then pro-Compromise Democrats helped lure Whigs away from their party in Georgia, Alabama, and Mississippi, and subsequently they left them stranded in non-Whig Union parties in 1852.

Whigs themselves, of course, also contributed to the diminution of interparty differences. Genuine devotion to the Union undoubtedly motivated Millard Fillmore's insistence that all Whigs acquiesce in the finality of the Compromise of 1850, but his administration's stance injured northern Whigs even as it helped their southern counterparts. Egregious Whig blunders that reflected defective political judgment also muddled interparty differences. The abortive attempt to displace the Whig party with a new Taylor Republican party wrought electoral havoc in 1849 and intensified internal Whig divisions. The hope that it could succeed was sheer fantasy, as the Taylor administration itself seemed finally to recognize. Similarly, the hopes of the Georgians Stephens and Toombs and of Daniel Webster that they could replace the Whig party with a permanent Union party incorporating pro-Compromise Democrats were surreal. As events in the Deep South in 1852 demonstrated and as Webster's close Boston friend Samuel Eliot argued, no Union party could exist without a "vis-a-vis," without a coherent anti-Union opponent. By 1852 no such party was to be found.[2] Sewardite Whigs were equally guilty of mistakes that erased interparty differences. However understandable, their desperate decision during the 1852 presidential campaign to compete with Democrats for Catholic and immigrant votes was a colossal blunder. It failed dismally in the short run and permanently alienated an important, rapidly growing sector of the anti-Democratic electorate in the long run. Nor did Whig leaders prove much more skillful in handling the other powerful and divisive new social issue that emerged in the early 1850s—prohibition. By 1853 Free Soilers profited at Whigs' expense from the issue in Connecticut, Ohio, and Wisconsin, while in Maine and Massachusetts, Whigs tried to forge coalitions with dry or wet Democrats that further diminished interparty differences.

Whigs' internal divisions deepened and widened after 1848 even as the reality and perception of conflict with Democrats declined. Without question, the most important and pernicious of those divisions was the split between northern and southern Whigs, and among northern Whigs themselves, over matters related to slavery and slavery expansion that preoccupied the attention of politicians in Washington after Taylor's election. Yet the rifts intensified by the Taylor administration's bungling patronage policies and Fillmore's attempts to rectify them were almost as damaging. They increased the difficulty of rallying the party behind a presidential candidate in 1852 and simultaneously helped convince one-time supporters that spoils, rather than distinctive programs, was all that party leaders cared about.

Equally pernicious and divisive were the selfish ambition and dogmatic intolerance of so many Whig leaders, who often acted with heedless disregard for the party's welfare in order to advance their personal careers or simply to humiliate Whig rivals. Daniel Webster heads this list of self-centered villains. Many Whigs after 1847 also saw Henry Clay acting from spiteful selfishness, although perhaps just as many viewed him as the party's savior, as, of course, did Clay himself. But second-tier politicos who sought personal advancement at the expense of intraparty foes, whatever the cost to internal party harmony, like New York's John Young and Hugh Maxwell, Pennsylvania's William F. Johnston, Maryland's Reverdy Johnson, Kentucky's Archibald Dixon, North Carolina's Thomas Clingman, and Georgia's Robert Toombs, also did the Whigs immense harm. If Democrats always helped determine Whigs' fortunes, in short, many of their wounds were self-inflicted.

All of these things—the loss of distinctive and viable issues, corrosive sectional division and distrust, bitter factional and personal rivalries, ineptitude in handling new issues—weakened the Whig party, alienated many of its former supporters, and left it on the ropes by the end of 1853. By themselves, however, they did not kill it. Shorn of responsibility for national and most states' patronage by the election results of 1852, Whigs escaped a divisive burden and could profit from the toll it took on Democrats. By the time Fillmore left office in March 1853, moreover, sectional tensions had abated and along with them the threat to Whig integrity from a new Union party. True, in most places Whigs failed to develop a compelling platform in 1853 when abstention and defection to minor parties continued to weaken voters' allegiance to the party. Even that year, however, they exploited Democratic divisions in Maine, Massachusetts, New York, Missouri, and California to run creditable campaigns, and they remained quite competitive in Florida, Louisiana, and the upper South. More important, they correctly expected Democrats in the new Thirty-Third Congress to do something against which all Whigs could unite and rally, as they had during the administrations of Polk, Van Buren, and Jackson.

The Democrats' Nebraska Act supplied the anticipated provocation, but for three vitally important reasons Whigs could not mobilize their former legions against it. First, the tiny bloc of Free Soilers in Congress managed to define the Nebraska bill as an aggressive Slave Power attempt to spread slavery against the wishes of the North rather than as a Democratic violation of sectional peace that threatened the Union. This brilliant tactical coup prevented northern and southern Whigs from uniting against it and goaded most southern Whigs in Congress instead to support it. Southern Whigs' defection, in turn, caused outraged northern Whigs either to seek new antislavery allies, as the Free Soilers hoped, or to ignore southern sensibilities during the 1854 elections in the belief that southern Whigs had signaled their willingness once again to let northern and southern Whigs disagree on slavery-related matters. The Nebraska Act thus badly damaged intersectional comity in the party, although some Whigs in both sections continued to hope that it might be restored in time for the 1856 election.

Restoration failed in large part because of the second development that frustrated Whig hopes of a united rally against Democratic actions. Many Whig and Democratic voters in the North, where most of the 1854 elections occurred, proved as, if not more, motivated by prohibitionist zeal and anti-Catholic, anti-immigrant, and antiparty rancor as by anti-Nebraska sentiment. Despite Whig efforts to revive the party on anti-Nebraska platforms, therefore, many one-time Whig voters bolted to the Know Nothing party and to splinter prohibition tickets. In the Midwest, they expressed their multivalent grievances against the Democrats through new fusion parties that displaced the Whigs as the primary vehicle for anti-Democratic political action. Whatever the destination of Whig defectors, by the end of 1854 the northern Whig party itself was so decimated that neither northern conservatives nor Southerners who had hoped to preserve the Whig organization for the 1856 presidential campaign believed it was any longer worth the effort.

These developments point to the third and most important reason why Whig hopes of rallying the party foundered. Politics in the nineteenth century was not a zero-sum game. Voters were not restricted to a choice between two major parties, so that one always gained from the electorate's anger at the other. Since parties printed and distributed their own ballots, it was easy to start new parties that might grow rapidly if they discovered compelling issues, as the Know Nothings and the embryonic Republican party manifestly did. Though easily overlooked, this ability to challenge existing major parties for access to the electorate, more than anything else, explains why the Whig party lacked "enough people" to remain a viable political force by the end of 1855.

Whigs were absolutely correct to expect that Franklin Pierce's administration and the Democratic Congress would alienate the American electorate. Where they erred was in their corollary assumption that they alone would benefit from the voters' disgust and anger. Their poisonous leadership feuds, their unseemly and often corrupt scramble to feed at the public teat, the obsolescence of much of their traditional economic platform, their attempts to maintain bisectional comity in the face of escalating sectional antagonisms, their waffling on the prohibition issue, and their disastrous solicitation of Catholic and immigrant support in 1852 alienated far too many voters for the party ever to regain their trust. For too many people, the Whig party had become part of the problem, not its solution. Thus, when both Know Nothings and Republicans found compelling ways to revive and usurp the party's original ideological mission of saving republican liberty from conspiracies against it, a mission that Whigs had seemingly abandoned, the party's days were numbered.

III

In this broader context, Edward Stafford had a point when he cited "too much respectability" as a cause of the Whigs' demise. Neither the partisan preference of most wealthy families for the Whigs nor the privileged educational background and social eminence of many Whig leaders necessarily drove the "people" away from the Whig party. Rather, the temperament instilled by privileged social backgrounds rendered many Whigs inflexible and inept political leaders. They were frequently too conservative, too cautious, too disdainful of political infighting, too slow to recognize the need to alter course in the face of public pressure for the party's benefit. The adamant, politically costly, and ultimately unsuccessful opposition by Whig leaders to constitutional revision in Maryland, Kentucky, North Carolina, Ohio, and Indiana is one such instance where Whigs undoubtedly suffered from "too much respectability," where innate conservatism put them on the losing side of an issue.

The presidential campaign of 1852 is another. No doubt 1852 was a Democratic year, but arguably the party would have been far wiser to run Fillmore on the platform his friends dictated than Winfield Scott. Sewardite northern Whigs had already decided not to run against the Compromise that year, and they had staked too much on Whig success in state or congressional races in Massachusetts, New York, Pennsylvania, and elsewhere to bolt if Fillmore were the nominee. Fillmore quite possibly could have run as creditably in the North as Scott, and he most certainly would have run better in the South. Even Stephens and Toombs could not have stopped Georgia's Whigs from backing him, his nomination would also have finished the Alabama and Mississippi Union parties, and Whigs in other southern states would have been spared considerable backbiting.

Thus, though defeated, the party would have emerged from the election far stronger and more united than it was, especially, indeed, if Fillmore were defeated. Yet Sewardites did not prevent Fillmore's nomination. Rather, it was the ostrich-like stubbornness of the blue-blooded Websterites in the Massachusetts delegation to the Baltimore national convention. Of them, Francis Granger, Fillmore's friend and as conservative a man as the Whig party possessed, angrily wrote: "The rest, Choate included, seemed to me to act like a parcel of school boys, waiting for the sky to fall that they might catch larks. Such another collection of respectable out of place gentlemen was never seen."[3] Naive and amateurish gentlemen who had long made the Massachusetts Whig party the same kind of private club its National Republican and Federalist predecessors had been simply would not do. At decisive moments like the Baltimore convention, the Whigs too often lacked hard-headed realists.

"Too much respectability" also hurt the Whig party after 1852. For one thing, the self-consciously sober, church-going, respectable Protestant middle classes who formed the party's base across the North *were* far more vulnerable to incursions by new prohibition, nativist, and antislavery parties than were Democratic constituencies. For another, precisely the conservative, cautious, safely respectable aura that so many Whig leaders cultivated made the Whig party seem precisely the wrong vehicle to channel, let alone to lead, crusades against new liberty-threatening conspiracies that voters identified with the Democrats. However much Whig leaders condemned Democrats' assault on a sacrosanct sectional compromise in 1854, they did not seem the men to take on the Slave Power. Moreover, despite the Protestant bona fides of Whig leaders and their unquestionable social revulsion toward immigrants, they could not be trusted to lead a populistic crusade to ensure that Protestant Americans ruled America.

Repelled by the hurly-burly of politics and grass-roots popular enthusiasms, many former Whig leaders simply could not or would not confront or adjust to political convulsions after 1853. Precisely their conservative abhorrence of the Republicans and their snobbish contempt for the populistic Know Nothings caused respectable gentlemen like Robert Winthrop, Edward Everett, Rufus Choate, Hamilton Fish, Daniel D. Barnard, James Pearce, William C. Rives, William A. Graham, and others of their ilk to stand on the sidelines during 1855 and to cling to the shell of the rapidly disintegrating Whig party. It was precisely such out-of-place, respectable gentlemen on whom Washington Hunt counted at the end of 1855 to preserve the Whig party so that it could fight again another day. They, too, would willingly suspend disbelief, blindly ignore disconcerting realities, and await a miracle to save the party.[4]

IV

Announcing in January 1855 that "the Whig party is dead," an Illinois Democratic editor chortled, "In a few years they will be as few and far between as the old Federalists, the National Republicans, the National Bank, or the Tariff party men." Diehards like Hunt hoped to stop such Whig scattering. Hunt admitted that the depleted party could not elect a president on its own in 1856. His goal, rather, was "to preserve the Whig organization" by holding a "National Convention to demonstrate that we are still alive as a national party," a scheme he hawked to other New York conservatives in early 1856. Assuming that neither the Know Nothing nor the Republican party could be "of long duration" and that both would be finished by "one presidential election," he believed that after its conclusion, "all or nearly all the honest Whigs who are now acting in either of the factions, will be glad to resume the Whig name and do battle again for national Whig principles."[5]

This strategy of waiting out events in 1856 and then resurrecting the Whig party was itself hostage to those events. Hunt mistakenly assumed that the surging sectional, ethnic, and religious animosities that fed the rise of the Know Nothing and Republican parties would subside during 1856. He calculated that neither Republicans nor Know Nothings would generate sufficient momentum in 1856 to endure. Yet it was just as likely that at least one of them would do so well that Whigs who had joined it would never consider returning to the Whig fold. And he blithely presumed that conservatives like himself and Fish who still clung to Whiggery would continue to stand apart from all other parties rather than being pressured by the exigencies of the presidential election itself to join one, a decision that could prove permanent, not temporary.

Other conservative Whigs, indeed, believed that it was foolish to preserve the Whig organization and that Whig principles, certainly Whigs' commitment to the Union, could best be perpetuated by aligning with the American party and "National Democrats" behind Fillmore's presidential candidacy. Insisting that Fillmore's chances would be ruined "by a regular, formal, old party nomination," John P. Kennedy, for example, envisioned the creation by newspaper endorsements of a platform-free Union coalition behind Fillmore that would displace the Whig party even as it was "altogether dependent upon the cordial support it may get from" conservative Whigs.[6] Vermont's ex-Congressman Andrew Tracy envisioned a different destination for men like Hunt and Kennedy. Like other Vermont Whigs in December 1855 and January 1856, Tracy urged his successor, Justin Morrill, to help build up the Republican party as a replacement for the Whigs. "As for that hybrid animal, [the] national Whig[s]," he sneered, "the sooner they unite in name, as they already have, in feeling, with the Pierce Democracy, the better for us." Conservative Whigs, in sum, could just as likely join the Democrats as rally behind Fillmore. And whatever they did, northern antislavery Whigs like Tracy hardly seemed ready to reunite with them in the Whig party after 1856.[7]

At the start of 1856, therefore, still uncommitted Whigs might be lured by three different parties. Complete retirement from political activity also powerfully beckoned many of them. Spurning a request to join the Republicans late in the year, George Ashmun, Webster's chief lieutenant in the House during 1850, exclaimed, "I am clear, & intend to keep clear, of all party associations. I have had enough of them, more than enough, & have accomplished an absolute disenthralment from the slavery, worse than African, which they involve."[8] Diehards who hoped to preserve the Whig party, therefore, had to do something to hold the remaining Whigs together and keep them politically engaged. During January they debated their options.

Some, like Hunt and New York City Whig editor Robert A. West, wanted to make immediate preparations for a Whig national convention. They waited, however, for a conclave of Whigs in New York City on January 10 that had been arranged by James A. Hamilton, son of the famous Federalist, to plot the party's future course. Ultimately, only a few patrician Whigs from New York City and Boston attended the gathering, but Hamilton claimed to have letters supporting his plans from Whigs in at least nine states. Insisting that his tiny assemblage therefore represented "the sentiment of the Whig party," this "select number of leading Whigs," as Daniel Barnard called them, "determined that there should be no national Whig convention, and of course no separate Presidential nomination." Rather, after the other parties named their candidates, Hamilton would "summon another meeting by letter, which meeting should decide what course the Whigs should pursue." In the meantime, Hamilton would urge his Whig correspondents to refrain from joining other parties and to remain ready for independent action.[9]

Even this gathering was plagued by "too much respectability." Hypocritically, West warned Fish when reporting on its proceedings that Hamilton was *not the people's man enough* to lead the Whig remnant out of the wilderness. "His tastes and ideas are too much above those of the masses for him to enter into their feelings or make sufficient allowance for their intellectual obtuseness, mental ignorance, or moral obliquity." West, in short, was every bit the snob that Hamilton was. Only such out-of-touch fossils sought to rejuvenate Whiggery.[10]

As had always been the case, keeping the organizational machinery of the party in working order was the job of leaders, not rank-and-file Whig voters, no matter how passionate their loyalty to the Whig name and principles. The problem, therefore, was how many Whig leaders remained to take on this task and whether they had the capacity to accomplish it. That capacity, in turn, involved their own talent, commitment, and sagacity, but it also hinged heavily on the political situation they confronted.

Die-hard Whigs consciously chose to wait out events until the summer before acting, but almost every development between early February and the end of June 1856 damaged prospects of preserving the Whig party either behind Fillmore's candidacy or without him. In retrospect, Kennedy and others who urged remaining Whigs to rally around Fillmore identified the only possibility, however remote, of preserving the Whig party as a functioning political body. While the magnetic forces that pulled remaining Whigs toward the Republican and Democratic parties constituted part of the Whig party's final act in 1856, therefore, Whigs' reaction to Fillmore's campaign gave that denouement its central theme.

If Fillmore won or even if he ran second in the three-candidate presidential race of 1856, his unionist coalition could provide Whigs a vehicle in which to persevere as the nation's primary anti-Democratic party. Achieving either goal, like the resuscitation of the Whig party itself, however, hinged upon a fundamental requirement: limiting the growth of the Republican party. For that reason, the factors that caused Fillmore to run a distant third in 1856 drove the final nails into the Whig party's coffin. Rather than sustaining the possibility of its post-election resurrection, the events of 1856 buried it beyond hope of revival. Since those events have been very ably analyzed elsewhere, and since the main focus here is on the remaining Whigs who watched them as spectators rather than shaping them as active participants, they can be quickly sketched.[11]

V

While conservative elitists from New York dithered during January, the House of Representatives in Washington was locked in a nine-week struggle to elect its speaker that dramatically underscored the improbability of putting the Whig party back together. Democrats were outnumbered in the House by almost two to one, and only about seventy Democrats were Pierce administration loyalists. Excluding anti-Nebraska Democrats, who clung to the Democracy even as they opposed Pierce, straight Whigs, Know Nothing/Whigs, Know Nothing/Democrats, Know Nothings of Free Soil or nonpartisan background, and anti-Nebraska fusionists, many of whom by December 1855 sought an exclusively northern and overtly antisouthern Republican party, constituted the polyglot opposition. Amazingly, the largest single non-Democratic bloc was the 117 one-time Whigs, exactly half of the total House membership, elected in 1854–55 in the best performance by Whig congressional candidates since 1846–47.[12]

These one-time Whigs, however, included Northerners and Southerners, Know Nothings, non-Know Nothings, and overt anti-Know Nothings who had often courted Democratic support, beneficiaries of the northern anti-Nebraska fusion movements, and northern conservatives intransigently opposed to a new anti-slavery northern party. With Whig reunion behind a common candidate for speaker apparently unlikely, the central question when Congress convened, therefore, seemed to be whether northern and southern Know Nothings, approximately 115 of the members, or various northern anti-Nebraska men who numbered a few more, including many Whigs and Whig/Know Nothings, would seize the prize and other posts all parties coveted—the House clerk, sergeant-at-arms, doorkeeper, postmaster, and printer.[13]

Since Northerners constituted the majority of the opposition, anti-Know Nothing Republicans like the editor Gamaliel Bailey and Joshua R. Giddings, who sought the speakership himself, insisted on a Northerner with "back-bone" and no nativist affiliation.[14] But it quickly became clear that only an anti-Nebraska Know Nothing could win. This imperative might allow a coalition between straight Whigs and Know Nothing/Whigs from both sections behind a common candidate. When the initial Democratic caucus issued a statement praising the Nebraska Act and blasting Know Nothings, causing southern Americans and most southern Whigs to vow never to support any Democrat who had participated in it, the chances of such a bisectional Whig coalition seemed to improve.[15]

Whig/Know Nothings had a plausible ticket for such a deal that might help resuscitate the national Whig party. For over a year, Ohio's Lew Campbell had courted southern Whig support for the speakership race. When Tennessee's Whig/Know Nothing William Cullom, whose courageous anti-Nebraska stance in 1854 earned him the admiration of northern Whigs and cost him reelection in 1855, announced his candidacy for the House clerkship, the possibility of reuniting Whigs behind that duo increased.

For various reasons, however, it never materialized. First, southern and northern Know Nothing congressmen immediately quarreled over the platforms adopted at Philadelphia in June and at Cincinnati in November, causing Fillmore's frustrated lieutenant Solomon G. Haven to complain, "To save me from perdition I can contrive no way to prevent it." Second, some Republicans initially backed Campbell as sufficiently "extreme," and their support alienated both conservative northern Whigs and all southern Americans from him. Instead, they supported northern moderates like Pennsylvania's Henry Fuller, James Cooper's Whig friend and a Know Nothing "who has no record on national matters but is a national Whig," or New Jersey's Alexander Pennington, who had voted against the Nebraska bill but won reelection as a straight Whig with no connection to either Republicans or Know Nothings. Third, anti-Nebraska Democrats and Democratic Know Nothings refused to support any ex-Whig for speaker, especially since the Whig Cullom seemed assured of the clerkship. Instead, they, along with most New England members, eventually rallied behind Massachusetts' Nathaniel P. Banks, an anti-Nebraska Democrat and prominent Know Nothing. As a result, Campbell never got more than eighty-one votes, far from the necessary majority. After a few ballots, he grudgingly withdrew his candidacy, and most northern anti-Nebraska men then clung to Banks, whom Republicans, seeking permanently to displace the Whig party, quickly anointed as their standard bearer.[16]

In early February, Banks finally won a plurality vote over the South Carolinian William Aiken, who had replaced the Democrats' original candidate. Not a single Southerner voted for Banks, while all but a handful of one-time northern Whigs in Congress did so. Even though Cullom and several other southern Whig/Know Nothings won the coveted House patronage slots, the opportunity of using the speakership contest to reunite Whigs had been lost.

Since early December, most Northerners had viewed this struggle in nakedly sectional terms, and they urged their congressmen to "stick to Banks at all events" to prove that "there is a North." Vermont, one former Whig wrote Justin Morrill, was pervaded by "but one feeling . . . *fear* that the Slave Power will ultimately triumph." Thus one Pennsylvania Whig convert to Republicanism pronounced Banks' victory "a great triumph for the North." Since Maine's Republicans needed a "demonstration of the fact that we had a party" in Washington, echoed Edward Kent to Congressman Israel Washburn, Jr., "the election of Mr. Banks electrified us all." And Washburn himself crowed, "The importance of this victory cannot well be overestimated." In sum, Banks' triumph, coupled with a Republican organizational meeting in Pittsburgh on February 22 that called for a national nominating convention in June, gave powerful momentum to the new Republican party. Whigs now had two potent rivals for their role as the primary anti-Democratic party.[17]

Know Nothings, in fact, also took some solace from the result. Many nativists considered Banks "a straight out and out K. N.," and over 70 of his 105 winning votes came from Know Nothings. Half of those northern Know Nothings now wanted to leave the nativist fraternity to become Republicans, but the others were still determined to keep northern Know Nothings independent of Republicans and to give anti-Catholicism and antiforeignism equal billing with free-soilism. In addition, as the appalled Republican Bailey grumped, only intervention by pro-southern Washington Know Nothings had put Banks over the top. They persuaded southern Know Nothings and northern conservatives like Jacob Broom, Scott Harrison, and Bayard Clark to scatter their votes or abstain rather than support the Democrat Aiken.[18] In return, Republicans supported Know Nothing candidates for clerk, sergeant-at-arms, doorkeeper, and postmaster. Even Solomon G. Haven, who complained that Know Nothings in the House had been "disunited, broken up, and fragmentary," believed that "all this difficulty & disorganization" ensured that Know Nothings would nominate Fillmore for president as the best way to restore sectional harmony in their party.[19]

The Americans nominated Fillmore at Philadelphia three weeks later, but Haven erred about the restoration of sectional harmony. Republican gloating over Banks' election virtually ensured a sectional donnybrook. Since the summer of

1855, Fillmore's supporters from the border states and New York had feared another "fatal" platform fight in which Northerners sought to replace the pro-slavery Section Twelve of the 1855 platform with an explicit demand for restoration of the Missouri Compromise line. Such a fight might increase northern support for Fillmore's main competitor for the nomination, George Law, a free-spending ex-Democrat from New York. Therefore, they had been trying for months to postpone the scheduled American national convention and its nomination from February to July.[20] Banks' triumph killed any chance of delay.

Furious that some seventy northern Know Nothing congressmen backed Banks, southern Americans now demanded a convention to provide evidence that other northern Know Nothings were not antisouthern. Haven and other Fillmore managers now realized that an immediate platform statement was necessary to appease them. Equally important, the impetus that Banks' triumph and the call for a June Republican convention gave to the Republican party created the specter of wholesale northern Whig/Know Nothing defections to the Republicans unless Fillmore's nomination provided a rallying point to stop them. "We had no alternative between a nomination now or being switched off onto the Republican track before the convention reassembled [in July]," Haven assured Fillmore. That same prospect simultaneously galvanized the determination of antislavery northern Know Nothings intent upon avoiding absorption by Republicans to repudiate Section Twelve, lest its retention force them into Republican ranks.[21]

Sectional wrangling therefore wracked both the preliminary American national council meeting and the subsequent nominating convention in Philadelphia. At the former, Northerners jettisoned the entire 1855 American platform with its odious Section Twelve. With the aid of conservatives from New York, Pennsylvania, and Massachusetts, however, Southerners on the council then adopted a new platform written by the Washington, D.C., lodge. Unlike the 1855 platform, it contained no explicit reference to slavery, let alone declare the finality of existing laws regarding slavery. But it explicitly endorsed the principle of popular sovereignty and called for all laws to be obeyed until repealed. It did not, that is, incorporate Northerners' demand for reimposition of a congressional ban on slavery north of 36° 30'.[22]

Outraged by this setback, many northern delegates to the subsequent convention refused to participate in any presidential nomination unless the convention repudiated the council's handiwork and adopted the platform they wanted. Their abstention increased Fillmore's chances of winning, and his managers at Philadelphia, who included Haven, Kennedy, and Alexander H. H. Stuart, pushed their advantage by insisting on an immediate nomination without a new platform. Delighted with the council's noncommittal platform, which one furious Indianan condemned as "so covered in verbiage that [the Americans] would be able to elect a President before the people discovered what it meant," they saw the chance once again to present Fillmore himself as *"the best platform"* on which to build a "national party."[23]

Fillmore won the nomination, but with meager northern support.[24] The sectional breach in the party had been widened, not bridged, as Fillmore's strategists had hoped. Upon Fillmore's selection, indeed, some seventy northern bolters formally repudiated his nomination because an anti-Nebraska platform had not been adopted, named themselves North Americans, and called for a new North American convention to meet in New York City on June 12, five days before the scheduled Republican convention in Philadelphia. Law's New York delegates issued a protest of their own, and the Albany *State Register*'s editor, Samuel Hammond, now completely in Law's pocket, promised the bolters that Law's friends would help substitute a new candidate for Fillmore in June.[25]

Some of the bolters from Ohio and Iowa wanted to join the Republican party immediately rather than form a separate North American party, and many Republicans, badly underestimating Know Nothings' continued commitment to anti-Catholicism and nativism, believed that the Americans' split guaranteed North Americans' support for the Republican nominee instead of Fillmore. "It is not a dead lion they are attempting to run but a dead ass," hooted Andrew Tracy. "The nomination of Fillmore has ruined the Americans here," echoed a Bostonian. "It falls like a wet blanket."[26]

Conversely, Fillmore's friends initially dismissed the bolt as insignificant. Some of the protesters at Philadelphia, they believed, were Republican saboteurs whose departure marked a good riddance.[27] Their bolt would enhance Fillmore's vote in the South, especially among National Democrats whom Kennedy had targeted as recruits for two years. More important, Fillmore's lieutenants confidently expected to bring the majority of bolters and the rank-and-file northern Know Nothings whom they represented back to Fillmore's camp by stressing Fillmore's commitment to Know Nothings' nativist agenda.

Fillmore's closest advisors all wanted him to delay any official letter of acceptance until he returned to the United States in June, but they urged him in writing it to take explicitly "Protestant" ground and rehearse the cry that "Americans must rule America." In the interim, they published Fillmore's 1855 pro-Know Nothing letter to Pennsylvania's Isaac Newton, and they leaked word that Fillmore had in fact joined the order. In addition, Fillmore's friends relied upon the order's oaths of allegiance to keep members in line. Thus they rejoiced when state councils like New York's immediately endorsed Fillmore's nomination, and they had E. B. Bartlett, the order's national president, replace northern state councils that refused to do so with new state councils that would. They also called yet another national council meeting in New York for June when North Americans convened to further remind members of their organizational obligations, and they strove to make sure that Southerners were fully represented at it to counteract the expected influence of Republicans among the North Americans.[28]

Between Fillmore's nomination in February and his return to New York from Europe on June 22, however, three developments virtually doomed his prospects—and with them Whiggery's only possibility of revival. Once again, Democrats critically influenced the fate of the Whig party. Pro-Compromise National Democrats, who had been infuriated by Franklin Pierce's patronage policies and by his endorsement of Douglas' sectionally inflammatory Nebraska Act, were not just a figment of John P. Kennedy's imagination, and he confidently predicted that "the National Hard Democrats North and South are much too offended with the administration and the Softs" ever to support the Democratic nominee in 1856.[29] In early June, however, Democrats bypassed both the palpably incompetent Pierce and the seemingly reckless Douglas and nominated instead the old Pennsylvania wheelhorse James Buchanan. As the candidate of the anti-Pierce Democrats, he seemed likely to reward National Democrats with federal plums if elected, and they dropped any plans of bolting the party. Freed of any responsibility for the Nebraska Act because he was absent in England, the sixty-five-year-old Buchanan, a former U.S. representative, U.S. senator, and U.S. secretary of state, also seemed to personify conservative experience, in contrast to the callow Pierce. In addition to squelching defections by conservative Democrats, therefore, his nomination made the Democratic ticket far more palatable to Union-loving Whigs still searching for a new political home and increasingly worried by the rise of the Republican party.

The other two developments between February and the end of June drove northern antislavery Whig-Know Nothings toward the Republican column. Fillmore's friends expected to deter that movement by playing on those Know Nothings' loyalty to the order and still-vibrant nativist prejudices. A bigger problem, of course, was what Haven despairingly called "the old eternal question of slavery over again, only very much intensified" by northern anger at border ruffian outrages in Kansas that opened the possibility that slavery might actually be established in that territory. To soothe North Americans' concerns on this front, Fillmore's friends, in his absence, assured them that Fillmore had deplored the passage of the Nebraska Act and now favored statehood for Kansas under any constitution written by "bona fide" residents of the territory, not proslavery Missouri invaders. Primarily, however, they expected to present Fillmore as the only man who could save the Union from sectional agitation.[30]

This holding action depended on the absence of events that increased northern anger at the South, and in May 1856 two new provocations exploded. The so-called sack of Lawrence, an antislavery stronghold in Kansas, by a posse of Missouri border ruffians on May 21 and the brutal caning of Massachusetts Senator Charles Sumner by South Carolina Representative Preston S. Brooks in the Senate chamber itself the following day totally changed the election. "Bleeding Kansas" and "Bleeding Sumner" electrified the North and gave Republicans an almost invincible combination of issues, for both incidents exposed white Southerners, the Slave Power, nakedly treating white Northerners like slaves. Northern fury was intense, widespread, and of immense political significance.[31]

Fillmore's Know Nothing backers, holdout Whigs, and joyful Republicans instantly recognized the political consequences. Republicans would gain—and Fillmore would lose—votes in the North. The likelihood that the impending North American convention would shun Fillmore and merge with the Republicans soared. "The late outrageous proceedings in Kansas & the assault on Mr. Sumner have contributed very much to strengthen the Republican party" and had laid "Conservatism, in all its forms, ... prostrate," Everett moaned to Fillmore in early July. "Brooks has knocked the scales from the eyes of the blind, and now they *see*!" exulted a Vermont Republican. "The color is *red bloody* and their wrath is hot."[32]

Even before shocks from Kansas and Washington changed the race and reduced the possibility that North Americans would ever back Fillmore, Republicans and their Know Nothing allies rigged the North American convention so that it ultimately supported the Republican nominee at Philadelphia, John C. Frémont, without first naming him themselves at New York and thereby driving antislavery Germans from him. To achieve this, they used Banks as a stalking horse for Frémont, even though many of Banks' fervent supporters in New York were clueless about Banks' double-dealing. Banks, not Fillmore, got the North American nomination, and the delegates then were persuaded to remain in New York until Banks replied. By prearrangement, Banks delayed his response until after Republicans nominated Frémont. Then he declined the North Americans' offer and urged them instead to endorse Frémont, which most of them did.[33]

The day after North Americans succumbed to this trick, Fillmore landed in Manhattan. Dated May 21, his letter formally accepting the American nomination had preceded him by several weeks, and it was circulated among North American delegates to hold them in Fillmore's column. After the events of May, however, they found Fillmore's pledge to quiet sectional agitation and scrupulously defend the rights of both sections, as he previously had while president, palpably inadequate; they now wanted an outright champion of the North.[34]

By June 22, in sum, Fillmore's prospects were bleak, and during the next four months they grew steadily bleaker. Nonetheless, Fillmore and his advisors battled to the end. By the fall, they sought to throw the election into the House of Representatives, where, they dreamed, the opponents of the front-runner, whether Buchanan or Frémont, would help elect Fillmore rather than let a hated foe win. That desperate strategy, of course, required carrying enough states for Fillmore to stop either of his foes from amassing a majority of electoral votes. To keep northern Know Nothings out of Frémont's column, they fanned the false rumor that Frémont was Catholic, a charge that more than anything else prevented him from winning the election. To weaken Buchanan in the South, they charged that the Democratic platform on which he ran sanctioned squatter sovereignty in the territories, a doctrine still anathema to most Southerners. To Union-loving conservatives in both sections, they trumpeted Fillmore's rescue of the nation between 1850 and 1853 and argued with increasing stridency, but rapidly decreasing credibility, that Fillmore, not Buchanan, had the best chance of beating Frémont.[35]

With National Democrats apparently mollified by Buchanan's nomination and most antislavery northern Know Nothings moving inexorably to the Republicans, these Unionist appeals were increasingly aimed at die-hard Whigs like Hunt, Fish, and Everett who had yet to make a commitment. Such conservative Whigs were always envisioned by Fillmore's friends as a key building bloc of their long-sought Union coalition. Their wholehearted and unanimous support for the champion of the Compromise of 1850 had never been questioned. By mid-1856, moreover, both Fillmore's managers and die-hard Whigs themselves believed that "Old Guard" Whigs held "the balance of power" in the election. Yet in 1856, when Fillmore desperately needed their help, it proved surprisingly elusive.[36]

VI

The political cross winds buffeting "straight," "Old Line," or "Old Guard" Whigs between January and July drove them in different directions and left many too paralyzed to act. Since Republicans and Democrats considered the Americans' choice of Fillmore essentially a "*Whig* nomination," they worried that "the old Whig party," and especially northern Silver Grays, would "rally in union with the Know Nothings on Fillmore."[37] Most die-hard, non-Know Nothing conservative Whigs *did* regard Fillmore's candidacy as the best hope of keeping their party intact and his election as the nation's best hope of ending sectional strife. Some, like North Carolina's William A. Graham and George Badger, therefore, quickly threw their support to him, as did "the old Whigs of Florida."[38]

New York's diehards also rallied behind Fillmore after his nomination at Philadelphia. James Hamilton immediately pressed Fish to help call a national Whig convention in the summer to endorse Fillmore and thereby "rally multitudes of the solid & conservative men of the country." "If anybody wants to see the true Whig party reconstructed & substantially placed in power again," piped Daniel Barnard in April, he should "take the American party at their offer, & bring in an administration with Mr. Fillmore at its head." National Whigs should hold a convention to preserve "the organization of the Whig party, that it may be prepared to resume its mission when the ephemeral factions of the day have been dissolved—an event which must speedily follow the canvass of 1856," counseled West's New York *Commercial Advertiser*. That convention, however, must not "present a distinct presidential nomination." Whigs must support Fillmore "not because of, but notwithstanding his nomination by the American party." New York's "old line Whigs," Hunt promised Fish, "will hold a convention some time this summer" and "take our position boldly."[39]

The uncertain dates and provenance of these proposed conventions, the vagueness of Hunt's prospectus for them, and especially West's obvious embarrassment at the Know Nothing imprimatur on Fillmore speak volumes. The Americans' nomination of Fillmore and his three-month delay in accepting it left Whigs in a perplexing quandary. Old-line Whig leaders feared that the Whig party would completely disintegrate unless they took some dramatic public action to reinvigorate it, yet they also knew that too quick a public embrace of Fillmore could have a high cost. If Whigs officially endorsed Fillmore *before* he responded to the American convention, they would appear to hijack him as their own man and possibly cause Democratic/Know Nothings and nativist true believers to renounce him.

One such true believer was Know Nothing editor Vesparian Ellis, who wanted Know Nothings to supplant, not provide life support to, the dying Whig party. Whigs who publicly endorsed Fillmore to resurrect Whiggery behind his candidacy would "drive every democrat out of our ranks & make the issue one of whiggery & democracy," he ranted. "Let outside Whigs *keep quiet & vote* as they please when the time comes." Fillmore must be run exclusively as "the *American* Candidate, or he will be defeated."[40] For haughty Whig bluebloods like Everett, Winthrop, and Charleston's George S. Bryan, who condemned Know Nothingism as "about an equal mixture of blind machinery, imbecility, & craft," however, the major problem was precisely that Fillmore *was*, or might consent to be, the Know Nothing, not the Whig, nominee. Such stuffed shirts simply could not stomach an open alliance with a party they despised as the vehicle of bigots, riffraff, and thugs. "Our Whigs are exceedingly exclusive and they parade their Whiggery as a badge of aristocracy, sometimes in a very obnoxious manner," one pro-Fillmore Massachusetts Know Nothing complained during the summer. "They paralyze us here, and also do the cause harm elsewhere." As Edward Stafford would later jeer, in short, the Massachusetts Whig rump harbored "too much respectability."[41]

Old line Whigs balked, in part, at Fillmore's running mate on the American ticket. They considered Tennessee's Andrew Jackson Donelson, nephew of the Democratic demon himself and erstwhile editor of the hated Democratic Washington *Union*, "a bitter pill," far too bitter for many Whigs to swallow. Thus North Carolina's George Badger, though willing to disregard his own abhorrence of nativism to back Fillmore, carped, "The association of Donelson with Fillmore hurt us here with Whigs who had a strong dislike of him, whilst it will not gain a single vote."[42]

Donelson, however, was not the main problem. Anti-Know Nothing southern Whigs in particular raged that Fillmore's acceptance of the American nomination would signal his betrayal and abandonment of the party they loved and wished to preserve. Rather than support such a traitor, they warned, they would bolt Whiggery for the Democrats. That threat also forced Whigs to delay any public endorsement of Fillmore until his intentions were clear. "The nomination of Fillmore is coldly received," rejoiced a New Orleans Democrat in March. "The old line Whigs consider it a political assassination." A month later Charles Conrad, Fillmore's former secretary of war, warned the ex-president that neither he nor other Louisiana Whigs could support him if he ran as the candidate of anti-Catholic bigots. Fillmore "must not permit himself to be *possessed* by the Know Nothings—to be their mere [i.e., exclusive] party exponent," Bryan warned Kennedy. Old line Whigs harbored too "much revulsion at the idea of his having become a member of the order." These alarm bells were more than sound and fury. When Americans lost North Carolina's state elections in August, two months after Fillmore's acceptance of the American nomination, Badger cried, "Our old line Whigs have behaved like apes—have turned democrats—have ruined the State. Heaven help us!"[43]

Southern old line Whigs were at least willing to back Fillmore as an independent Unionist candidate. Such was not the case with Pennsylvania's "large body of old national Whigs, who will not support Fillmore" and would, it was reported, vote Democratic or Republican rather than "strengthen the Know Nothings." Their peculiarly intense obduracy seems inexplicable. But the explanation is obvious once one recalls the history of the Whigs in question. They were the Cooper-Clay Whigs who fought Clayton's attempt in 1849 to combine Whigs with Native Americans in a Taylor Republican party, who bitterly protested Fillmore's refusal to remove William D. Lewis from the Philadelphia custom house in 1850–51 so as not to alienate nativists, and who proudly supported incumbent Whig Congressman Joseph R. Chandler in 1854 after Know Nothings ruthlessly dumped him because Chandler was a Catholic. Old chickens were coming home to roost at Fillmore's expense in Pennsylvania. But so long as there was a chance of holding such "old national Whigs" in the party fold, Whigs there, as in other states, could not endorse Fillmore publicly until they knew his response to the Know Nothings.[44]

If Whig diehards could be damned by embracing Fillmore before his return from Europe, however, they were also damned if they failed to do so. Unless and until some collective, recognized body of Whigs such as a national convention indicated that the party meant to preserve itself as an independent political force, discouraged Whig loyalists around the country would hang suspended in uncertainty or, worse, look elsewhere for a political home. The longer old guard Whig gentlemen waited to act, in short, the fewer they and their followers were and the more vulnerable they became to incursions by Republicans, Democrats, and Know Nothings.

Even before May's pivotal sectional shocks drove many "straight Whigs and conservatives" toward the Republican column, Republicans took aim at uncommitted Whigs. In New York they urged Governor Myron Clark to help "get back a great many Old Whigs, who have not joined any organization" with a careful dispensation of highly visible state jobs. Massachusetts Republicans struck in July by organizing a straight Whig ratification meeting for Frémont. "It has convinced the fossils that they are not paramount, and has divided the [Whig] party," one exulted, a conclusion with which discouraged Whig conservatives agreed. In Indiana, where Whig/Know Nothings played a central role in organizing the party in the spring, they eschewed even the name "Republican" and wrote a moderate state platform in order, as one furious Free Soiler sputtered, to woo "Know-nothings and old fossil Whigs who have just emanated from their old political graves where they have been 'persevering to rot.' "[45]

As Pennsylvania and North Carolina indicated, however, the Democrats were a likelier destination than the Republicans for National Whigs if they were allowed to float free. Common antipathy to Know Nothings' bigotry and to Republicans' apparent sectional extremism drew them together. In late fall 1855, Kentucky's Archibald Dixon, Henry Clay's successor in the Senate, announced his conversion to the party of Jackson. After Banks' election, the trickle of prominent Whigs toward the Democrats became a torrent, for many doubted that Fillmore, especially if he ran as a Know Nothing, could win. In the spring, Georgia's Robert Toombs and Alexander H. Stephens, who had abandoned the Whig party in 1850 but persistently kept their distance from the Democrats, finally joined that party, and Stephens' brother Linton was a Georgia delegate to the Democratic national convention. Appalled by Know Nothingism and Republicans' surging prospects, key local Whig leaders in Michigan and Indiana, along with Maryland's Reverdy Johnson, became Democrats as well. By midsummer the list of Whig leaders who openly endorsed Buchanan as the best hope of defeating Frémont was stunning: Tennessee Senator James Jones; Maryland Senators Thomas Pratt and James Pearce; North Carolina's ex-Congressman Daniel M. Barringer; Georgia's Charles Jenkins, Henry Clay's son James, and Rufus Choate.[46]

Prominent Whig defectors gave Democrats a powerful weapon, especially in the slave states where Whigs had once been most competitive and that Fillmore therefore had to carry to have a chance. Both crestfallen Whig converts to Know Nothingism like Tennessee's William G. Brownlow and anti-Know Nothing Whigs like George Bryan shrieked about the "utterly faithless" Whigs who supported Buchanan, while Democrats rejoiced at their coup. Thanking North Carolina's Barringer for his support, Kentucky's John C. Breckinridge, the Democratic vice presidential candidate, spelled out its consequences for the election and the postelection prospects of the Americans. "The very choicest spirits of the old parties now stand together—and the K. N. party . . . is literally composed of the fag ends of other organizations," he exulted. "It may continue for a little while as a disturbing element in certain localities, but its pretentions as a national party have already fallen into common contempt."[47]

Whig/Know Nothings committed to Fillmore's candidacy tried to combat Republican and Democratic incursions by bidding for old line Whigs themselves.

They did so primarily by contrasting Fillmore's Whig background to the Democratic lineage of his two opponents, by stressing Fillmore's Whiggish conservatism and unionism, and by arguing that Fillmore in fact had a better chance to stop Frémont than did Buchanan. Some even deigned to dirty their hands with the kind of one-on-one personal politicking most Whig gentlemen had long disdained. Calling himself the only prominent Indiana Whig to remain loyal to Fillmore, Richard W. Thompson was one such stalwart. "Thompson is making desperate exertions to carry his points," gasped an astonished Republican in June. "He does what he has seldom done before; he is on the streets, and at the corners in season and out of season trying to inveigh old Whigs to his scheme of resuscitating the Whig party" behind Fillmore.[48]

VII

Well before the summer, therefore, old line Whigs who hoped to revive their party by preserving its independence as an organization knew that there would be little left to preserve unless they counteracted these incursions. Hesitant to endorse Fillmore until they learned his reaction to the American nomination, they had to do something in the interim to show that Whigs were "still alive as a national party."

Those demonstrations varied. Primarily, however, die-hard Whigs relied on proclamations that the party still survived from newspapers still loyal to it, like West's New York *Commercial Advertiser* and especially the Washington *National Intelligencer*, and from a series of county and state Whig conventions that showed the Whig flag even if they usually refused to nominate Whig candidates. During the spring, for example, local Whig meetings were held in Boston, Staunton and Charlottesville, Virginia, and Washington, D.C., while straight Whig state conventions met in Iowa, Kentucky, Maryland, and Rhode Island. In the summer, after Fillmore's return, small Whig state conventions also assembled in Virginia, New York, Maine, and Massachusetts. In northern states like Massachusetts and Rhode Island, where a semblance of Whig organization still existed, the purpose of these avowals was "to keep the Whig party from falling into the Fremont current." In the South, where few Whig candidates had been run in 1855 and conversions to the Democrats were soaring in 1856, Whigs insisted "the Whig party [must] be reorganized" to "preserve unimpaired their distinct political character amid the many conflicting organizations by which they are surrounded and sought to be absorbed."[49]

For admirers of the Whig party, including this historian, these poignant manifestos make for painful reading. They portray the pitiable condition to which the party had been reduced, predict the most pernicious consequences of its demise, and punctuate Whigs' seemingly endless capacity for self-delusion, their pathetic propensity to cling to pie-in-the-sky fantasies in the face of unwelcome realities. One is reminded, indeed, of Granger's cutting remark about the "out of place" Websterites at the 1852 Whig convention who waited "for the sky to fall so that they might catch larks."

Old line Whigs' calls to battle usually admitted that Whigs had "ceased to be an organized and active party in political affairs," that they had been "shorn of [their] former strength" because "many men . . . had attached themselves temporarily to other organizations," and that they were therefore "in a minority compared with the three other great parties into which the country is divided." Yet they then declared that, for three reasons, those prodigal sons could and must be won back. The first was to resolve the sectional crisis other parties had caused. That crisis required Whigs to "keep the good old Whig party alive, distinct, and organized, to serve as a nucleus around which all these dispersed conservative republican elements may rally at the critical juncture to save the Republic." The second was "to prepare the way for a national reorganization of the Whig party when the phrenzy of the hour shall have passed." The third, equally delusionary goal was to keep die-hard Whigs "together" so that they could exert "the balance of power" and "turn the scale of the Presidential election" in 1856 itself.[50]

If the remaining Whigs all recognized the necessity for "a concert of action between the various companies and regiments of the Whig army" so that "the Whig party" could "survive the present changes and disruption of parties" and "control the result of the next Presidential election," however, they deeply disagreed on how this should "be done."[51] New York Whigs like Barnard and West argued that the best course was to eschew any separate Whig nomination and throw Whigs' collective support to Fillmore. Yet Whig meetings and newspapers in Washington, Kentucky, Maryland, Virginia, and North Carolina flatly repudiated an early endorsement of Fillmore and insisted that only a national Whig convention, which Barnard and West dreaded would nominate someone other than Fillmore, could "give due expression to the political opinions they still entertain."[52]

With no representative body of Whigs in Congress to call a national convention, however, it was unclear who could or would do so. Many Whigs looked to the prestigious Washington *National Intelligencer* to call the convention, but it refused to do anything or, ominously, even to mention Fillmore as the likely Whig nominee until Whig meetings gave it some direction. Finally, the Kentucky Whig state convention on April 12, which bitterly attacked Whigs who had jumped ship to the Know Nothings and sought to *stop* Whigs from nominating Fillmore, called for a convention of loyal Whigs from across the country to meet in Louisville in July. But this action was so irregular that some Whig papers in the East announced the date of the proposed Louisville convention as July 4, while others announced it as July 30. Because of this confusion, suspicion that the intention was to blackball Fillmore, and Louisville's distance from the East, this assemblage never met.[53]

VIII

When Fillmore arrived in New York on June 22, therefore, he and his advisors faced a cruel dilemma. Well aware of the anti-Know Nothing Whigs' decided coolness toward Fillmore's candidacy as an American, they still believed such conservatives could be won over by stressing Fillmore's devotion to the Union and attacking the sectional extremism of Republicans and Democrats. In late June, however, their top priority was to repair the damage caused by North Americans' nomination of Frémont the day before Fillmore returned. Stopping the hemorrhage of northern Whig/Know Nothings to the Republicans seemed more pressing than reassuring anti-Know Nothing Whigs. Stressing Fillmore's Unionism was manifestly insufficient to staunch that outflow. In addition to playing the anti-Catholic card against Frémont, therefore, they decided to reemphasize Fillmore's personal allegiance to the American organization and its founding nativist principles. Perhaps more than anything else Fillmore could have done, that tack risked alienating Whig diehards still further.

By long custom, presidential candidates did not make campaign speeches. Since Fillmore had been out of the country for over a year and out of the public limelight for almost four years, however, he attempted to jump-start his campaign by giving a series of public addresses as he moved north from New York City to Albany and then west toward his home in Buffalo. His advisors like Haven and Stuart were so delighted by these speeches that they had them published as a campaign pamphlet entitled *Fillmore at Home*. "The old line Whigs seem to be coming round right," gushed Haven at the end of June after reading accounts of them. Fillmore should say nothing more.[54]

Old line Whigs, in fact, applauded most of what Fillmore said. At Albany, Rochester, and elsewhere he primarily rehearsed his patriotic devotion to the Union. He attacked Democrats for reopening sectional agitation with the Nebraska Act and Republicans for cynically inflaming that agitation to arouse the North. Fearful of offending Southerners, however, Fillmore resolutely refused to publicize his own solution to the Kansas crisis—the repeal of unfair proslavery territorial legislation, the holding of honest elections protected from border ruffian incursions to choose a new legislature and a constitutional convention, and rapid admission to statehood under a constitution written and approved exclusively by legitimate residents of that territory, not interlopers from Missouri.[55] Instead, he warned that either a Democratic or a Republican victory would "break asunder the bonds of our Union and spread anarchy and civil war through the land." Only he stood above the sectional fray. "If there be those at the North who want a President to rule the South—if there be those at the South who want a President to rule the North—I do not want their votes," he declared. "I stand upon the broad platform of the Constitution and the laws."[56]

Two of Fillmore's otherwise unexceptionable speeches, however, deeply incensed anti-Know Nothing Whig holdouts. For six months old guard Whigs had pronounced the Whig party still alive and, if not exactly well, still capable of reorganization and rejuvenation. Yet in a speech to New York City's Whig General Committee on June 23, Fillmore hymned a dirge over the party's "grave." For years, he mourned, the time had been "approaching when that noble Whig party, of which I was ever proud, would be inevitably destroyed." Clay's defeat in 1844 started the process, and "the canker worm that has been gnawing at the very vitals of that party has at last, I fear, destroyed it" and "carried it to the grave." "But, sir," he immediately added, "a phoenix . . . has arisen from its ashes that is yet to save the country." Just as the Compromise acts that had rescued the country in 1850 "were not the measures of one party" but the handiwork of both Whigs and Democrats, that new party must not be exclusively Whig. Rather, it must combine "conservative Whigs—old-line Whigs, true Whigs" with "true-hearted Democrats" in a new organization.[57]

Having urged Whigs to give up the ghost as a separate party, Fillmore, a few days later at the Hudson River town of Newburgh, assured Know Nothings that he was now no longer a Whig but one of their own. He was proud to be the American candidate, "for I am an American and with the Americans." Not opposed to all immigrants, he would still "exclude the pauper and the criminal." Tolerant of all religious creeds, he would "exact from all faithful allegiance to our republican institutions." Thus, "if any sect or denomination, ostensibly organized for religious purposes, should use that organization or suffer it to be used for political objects, I would meet it by political opposition." The safety of the republic required "that, independent of all foreign influence, Americans will and shall rule America." Avowedly no longer a Whig, Fillmore trumpeted his Know Nothingism.[58]

These announcements appalled anti-Know Nothing Whigs who wanted to preserve the party, but then Fillmore further compounded the damage by adamantly refusing to accept "straight" Whig endorsements lest Americans be offended by them. Fillmore's carefully calculated response to the proffered support from Virginia's state Whig convention in mid-July is a case in point. Flatly contradicting Fillmore's speeches in New York, its resolutions credited Whigs alone with resolving previous sectional disputes that Democrats had caused, angrily accused Democrats of stealing "Whig propositions as [their] own, regardless of having denounced them," so as to deny Whigs "credit" for them, and "condemn[ed] the thought of disbanding the Whig party, and of any remission of its untiring exertions." In addition, the platform flatly opposed repeal of the Nebraska Act and, though calling Fillmore the best of the three presidential alternatives available, refused to surrender Whigs' separate identity by merging with the Americans.[59]

Fillmore consulted with Virginia's William C. Rives and John S. Carlisle, as well as with Haven, before replying. "The few who composed this meeting," warned Carlisle in a scathingly accurate assessment of die-hard Whigs' impotence and naiveté, "are men who cannot see what is passing around them and do not know that the idea of reviving *the Whig party by its name is utterly hopeless.*" Stick by what you told the New York Whig committee—that the Whig party had already been "carried to the grave," echoed Haven. "Give no old party a chance to either pamper you or complain of you." Thus, Fillmore frostily wrote Rives, Virginia's Whigs "were indiscreet in laying down a platform on the slavery question & for my acceptance." By adopting a Whig platform, he "would but increase the jealousy of the American Democrats who are constantly told that the American party is the old Whig party in disguise." Nor could he publicly sanction its commitment against repeal of the Nebraska Act. "I cannot be one thing to the North and another to the South," he sputtered, "nor one thing to the American party and another to the Whig party."[60]

Fillmore's frustration is understandable, and some former Whig officeholders who had never joined the Know Nothings and still-loyal Whig editors accepted his proclaimed independence from their old party and pledged their personal support.[61] Nonetheless, his rebuff of die-hard Whig loyalists caused many to respond in kind. Some, like North Carolina's Daniel Barringer, who angrily cited Fillmore's speeches as evidence that "there is no organized Whig party—and no Whig candidate in the field," petulantly defected to the Democratic party in retaliation.[62] Others demanded that Whigs nominate someone else to resurrect the party that Fillmore had so insultingly consigned to oblivion. To Fillmore's great chagrin, the leaders of these recalcitrants were Joseph Gales and William W. Seaton, editors of die-hard Whigs' flagship newspaper, the Washington *National Intelligencer*. Gales and Seaton loathed the Know Nothings and absolutely refused to support Fillmore as a Know Nothing candidate. Until mid-September they repeatedly insisted that their only allegiance was to the Whig party, and they repeatedly complained that "there is no Whig candidate in the field."[63]

Within weeks of Fillmore's return to Buffalo, he and his campaign managers recognized their mistake; old line Whigs would not automatically support him as an American candidate. Daily the Republicans seemed to grow stronger in the North, in part, as Everett told Fillmore, because "events in Kansas & the outrages in Washington have done much to break down the straight Whig organization." As Republicans surged, more and more conservatives, frightened by the threat of disunion should Republicans win, deemed Buchanan, rather than Fillmore, the best hope of stopping Frémont. Whig support therefore seemed more and more necessary, yet still-uncommitted Whigs demanded some "united action" by Whig leaders "to give due expression to the opinions they still entertain" before committing themselves to a candidate. And the only Whig leaders sending signals to rank-and-file Whig diehards about what to do were the growing list of prominent Whigs who announced their support for Buchanan. So massive was the flight by renowned Whigs to the Democrats, indeed, that Ohio's Thomas Ewing had to deny newspaper reports that he, too, had endorsed Buchanan, even though he leaned toward him.[64]

Starting in July, therefore, Fillmore personally or through intermediaries begged still-neutral Whig leaders like Everett, Winthrop, Fish, and Ohio's ex-Senator Tom Corwin to announce their support publicly in order to counteract other Whigs' endorsements of Buchanan. Opinion molders such as he, Fillmore pressed Everett, had no right to abandon politics and remain "inactive or neutral." Democrats were driving the "ship of state . . . directly upon the rocks of perdition, and if she founders, we must go down with her." Both Everett and Winthrop published affirmations of support, but even they doubted their influence on Bay State voters. It was not just that some Websterites like Choate announced for Buchanan, while others like Samuel Walley came out for Frémont. As Everett warned, Fillmore's embrace of Know Nothingism "is what will prevent you, more than anything else, from being more cordially supported by the straight Whigs of this State."[65]

Haven was blunter about the folly of relying on elitist political has-beens, no matter how blue their blood, to carry Massachusetts. "Such men as Choate, Everett, Winthrop etc. are good for their own votes, but they are the fossil remains of too low and ancient a strata to stir up the surface in the least now." Hating Know Nothings as "too contemptible for them to fight," yet "too powerful for them to conquer," bitter Whig diehards would never "give any portion of such a party a hand, even in a good cause."[66]

Haven was right on both counts. As Edward Stafford later contended, respectable gentlemen like Everett and Winthrop no longer molded opinion. Whigs who despised Know Nothings still refused to work for Fillmore's election even after a state Whig convention in September tepidly recommended him. "Our Whigs prefer that the great cause should be entirely ruined rather than [a]bate a hair of their exclusive aristocracy of feeling," fumed one Fillmore American. Winthrop shared his anger at Whigs' stubbornness, this Know Nothing admitted, but

Winthrop "lacked and always will lack that sort of pluck which is now needed to make those fellows do right."[67]

Haven also dismissed an endorsement from the Whig grandee Fish "as not worth enquiring about" since "he cannot control more than his own vote." But virtually every old guard Whig in New York state considered Fish, a sitting United States senator, absolutely the key figure to lead a revival of the National Whig party and swing the remaining Whig holdouts behind Fillmore. Pouting that Weed and Seward had merged the state Whig organization with the Republicans in 1855 without ever consulting him, Fish resolutely remained on the Whig fence during the first half of 1856. Fillmore dearly wanted him to jump off. A New York Whig state convention attended by Fish's old guard acolytes backed Fillmore on August 14, but Fish himself stubbornly remained neutral until mid-September, when, to pro-Fillmore Whigs' consternation, he came out publicly for Frémont because Fillmore had deserted the Whig party.[68]

Corwin, one-time darling of the free-soil Whigs now at work building the Republican party, agreed with Fillmore that "the Whig party *as such* is dead & buried." But he was not a Know Nothing; nor could he ever vote Democratic. Since he had always opposed slavery extension and since the Republicans were the only party openly committed against its spread, he leaned toward Frémont. But he could never campaign publicly for a party led in his state by Free Soilers like Chase and Giddings.[69] Corwin, therefore, considered endorsing Fillmore, but only, he told Fillmore's agents, if the ex-president publicly avowed his private opposition to slavery extension. At this demand, Fillmore balked. He knew from his southern correspondents that publicizing his preferred policy for Kansas would utterly ruin his chances in the South. With negotiations stalemated, Corwin, citing his need to concentrate on his business affairs, broke them off.[70]

By early September, therefore, Fillmore's attempt to shore up conservative Whigs' support had stalled. Fish and Corwin held back, and he knew that in Massachusetts Everett and Winthrop were hardly enough. The prestigious *National Intelligencer* stubbornly denied its support under the pretext of awaiting "some unanimous decision on the part of the 'Old Line Whigs.'" Friends from New Jersey, a northern state absolutely critical to his chances of amassing enough electoral votes to throw the election into the House, warned of Whig losses to the Republicans. And he was certain that Republicans, because of "the outrage upon Mr. Sumner and upon the people of Kansas," would sweep the September state elections in Maine and Vermont. Yet Southerners had been warning him for months that they could never stop Whigs from going to Buchanan without concrete evidence that Americans could carry enough northern states to win themselves or to keep Frémont from winning.[71]

IX

In desperation, therefore, Fillmore and his campaign team resorted to precisely what pro-Fillmore old line Whigs recommended against in January, to what Fillmore and Haven calculatedly spurned in July, and to what Know Nothing true believers always sought to stop—Fillmore's nomination as a Whig by a straight Whig national convention to be held in Baltimore on September 17. The last Whig national convention ever held, this rump meeting had *not* been arranged by Fillmore's friends. To the contrary, it was called by anti-Know Nothing Whigs who sought to ensure their party's independence so that Whigs would rally to it once again after the election was over. It was first suggested, in fact, by the same Virginia Whig state convention on July 16 whose determination to preserve Whiggery's independence Fillmore so contemptuously scorned. Aware by mid-July that the proposed Whig meeting in Louisville would fizzle because of the confusion over its date, the Virginians recommended the September convention as an alternative, and straight Whig papers like the *Intelligencer* enthusiastically embraced it.

Now desperate for a Whig endorsement and fearful that this gathering might back someone else, Fillmore frantically urged his non-Know Nothing old guard Whig friends to attend it to make sure that it indeed nominated Fillmore. Loyally they did so. Among others, the delegates included the following pro-Fillmore Whigs: Benjamin O. Tayloe from the District of Columbia; William L. Hodge from the same city but representing Louisiana; George Lunt of Massachusetts; James M. Townshend of Connecticut; Joseph F. Randolph of New Jersey; James Spruance, son of Delaware's former Whig United States senator; ex-Congressman Richard J. Bowie of Maryland; Edward Bates of Missouri; Senator John Bell of Tennessee; John Janney, William L. Goggin, William C. Rives' son Alex, and Wyndham Robertson, who had sent Fillmore word of the state's July Whig convention nomination, from Virginia; former governors William A. Graham and John M. Morehead of North Carolina; and Granger, Hunt, David A. Bokee, James Kidd, James A. Hamilton, A. K. Hadley, and other Silver Grays from New York.[72] Refusing even to mention the American party or its principles, the convention nominated Fillmore and Donelson, declaring that their election promised the best hope of saving the Union.[73]

What is most noteworthy about this forlorn gathering, however, is that it managed to combine "too much respectability" with "too few people." The air of unreality that had characterized die-hard Whigs throughout 1856 was omnipresent. Altogether only 144 men attended, the smallest national convention held by any political party since Antimasons met in 1831. No delegates whatsoever appeared from Maine, New Hampshire, Vermont, Rhode Island, California, Wisconsin, Michigan, South Carolina, or Texas, and most of the states represented sent only a handful of men. The sixty-nine New Yorkers, indeed, composed almost half of the total count. Most of the delegates, moreover, were political nonentities, despite the presence of a few prominent Whigs.

Politically obscure they may have been, but the aristocratic Hamilton and the Albany banker Kidd must have felt comfortable in this gathering of wealthy, middle-aged amateurs who were no more attuned to the mood of, or capable of mobilizing, average voters than they were. Describing the delegates as "quiet, respectable, black waist coat individuals, whose very air stamps them unmistakably as gentlemen of the old school," a reporter from the Democratic New York *Herald* scoffed, "I could have hardly imagined that so many intelligent men could be got to engage in this resurrectionist business. With all their antiquatedness . . . they are as confident of electing Fillmore as orthodox Christians are of the coming of the millennium."[74]

More sadly still, the veteran newspaperman Hodge, who had worked since 1853 to build a Union party behind Fillmore, made exactly the same point without the saving grace of sarcasm. The convention, he gushed to Fillmore, "was without exception the finest body of men I ever saw assembled on any occasion—staid, sober, solid, respectable—two-thirds of them over fifty years of age." Since the speeches were uniformly "decorous, eloquent, & highly appropriate," he added, the convention would "make its mark." "These proceedings, have aroused the Whigs throughout our widespread land," would "lead to the resuscitation of the Old Whig Party," and would guarantee Fillmore's election, echoed another delusionary delegate.[75]

Such old fogies, such "respectable" gentlemen, could neither elect Fillmore nor resuscitate the Whig party. Indeed, their convention could not even persuade Gales and Seaton, who still insisted there was no genuine Whig in the race, to endorse Fillmore, although they did allow Hodge to write an unsigned editorial for the paper that did so. Nor, after Democrats won the crucial October elections in Pennsylvania and Indiana, thereby indicating beyond cavil that only Buchanan had a prayer of defeating Frémont, could the convention's action stop still more conservative Whigs from fleeing to the Democrats. All the Whig elitists at Baltimore managed to do was infuriate genuine nativists. "Your *pretended* friends have destroyed you!" Pennsylvania's veteran Native American Lewis C. Levin exploded to Fillmore.[76]

X

Levin's outburst was as farfetched as hopes that the Whig convention could save the election for Fillmore. His chances of winning or even running second expired long before September. Fillmore, whatever his other flaws, was often capable of quite perceptive political analysis. He knew when his campaign had been doomed. "If Freemont [sic] is elected," Fillmore wrote William A. Graham on August 9, "he will owe his election entirely to the troubles in Kansas and the martyrdom of Sumner; and the Republicans ought to pension Brooks for life!!"[77]

No pension was offered since Frémont did not win in 1856. Buchanan, although carrying only 45 percent of the popular vote, captured 174 electoral votes, 58.6 percent of the total, and the White House with that majority. Frémont ran second with 33 percent of the popular vote and 115 electoral votes, all from the North, where he carried all but five states. Fillmore finished a distant third. With 871,731 votes (21.6 percent), he ran 500,000 votes behind Winfield Scott in 1852, and he carried only Maryland's eight electoral votes.

The national totals were humiliating enough, but the skewed sectional distribution of the popular and electoral votes finished all hope of preserving a national, bisectional Whig party. Fillmore's own vote itself was divided fairly evenly. His 476,485 votes in the South represented 54.6 percent of his total, and his 43.9 percent of the slave states' vote virtually equaled Scott's 44.2 percent in 1852. Fillmore, in fact, ran almost 110,000 votes ahead of Scott in Dixie, but Buchanan surpassed Pierce's total by over 150,000.

By themselves, these comparisons raise questions about Nathan Sargent's angry complaint that Fillmore was defeated by "the treachery, the faithlessness, & the utter lack of pride & spirit exhibited by . . . a great portion of the Old Whigs—the Henry Clay Whigs" in Kentucky, North Carolina, Tennessee and other slave states who either supported Buchanan or abstained. Prominent Whig leaders in the South—including one of Henry Clay's sons—had indeed endorsed Buchanan, but most rank-and-file Whigs, whatever they thought of Know Nothingism, appear to have voted for Fillmore, if they bothered to vote at all, out of traditional enmity to Democrats. According to one statistical estimate of southern voter movement between presidential elections, indeed, Fillmore retained 86 percent of 1852 Whig voters (91 percent if one excludes Georgia and Texas from the analysis), 84 percent of Zachary Taylor's voters, and 86 percent of 1844 Whig voters. By the same estimates, barely a tenth of one-time Whig voters could have supported Buchanan. Whatever its label, in short, the electoral core of the Whig party in Dixie had held together, and in that section a potential base for a resurrected Whig party existed.[78]

Among them, Kentucky, Tennessee, and North Carolina possessed thirty-four electoral votes. Had they gone to Fillmore rather than Buchanan, the election would have gone to the House. But in none of the three states did Whig conversions to Buchanan explain the result. In both Kentucky and Tennessee the margin between Buchanan and Fillmore barely exceeded 7,000 votes, and in each, Fillmore's gain over Scott since 1852 surpassed that margin. Statistical analysis of voter movement in Kentucky suggests that about one-tenth of previous Whig supporters failed to vote at all, but even had they backed Fillmore, they could not have overcome the new non-Whig voters in the Democratic column. In North Carolina as well, few Whigs apparently defected to Buchanan. But almost one-sixth of Winfield Scott's supporters abstained, and there Fillmore, who trailed Buchanan by 12,000 votes, also ran 3,000 votes behind Scott's 1852 total. Recovering all the former Whig strength in Dixie, in sum, would require jettisoning the American label.[79]

The real problem lay in the North, where most former Whigs joined a different party than their southern counterparts. That trend can be measured in various ways. Fillmore's 395,000 northern votes, though 43.4 percent of his own total, represented a puny 13.4 percent of the northern votes cast. His share exceeded an embarrassingly low one-sixth of the turnout only in Pennsylvania (17.9 percent), New York (20.9 percent), New Jersey (24.1 percent), and California (32.8 percent), the only free state where he ran ahead of Frémont. Scoring what historian William E. Gienapp aptly calls a "victorious defeat," the Republicans not only won the electoral vote in eleven of sixteen free states. They captured 45.2 percent of that section's popular vote, more than three times the proportion won by Fillmore, and, equally important, almost 4 percent more than the Democrats' 41.4 percent. Republicans, indeed, carried eight states with outright majorities in the three-way race. Whatever the situation in the South, in sum, by the end of 1856 Republicans had clearly become the major anti-Democratic party in the North, and their supporters, just as clearly, had no interest in reuniting with Whigs who backed Fillmore in the South, at least in the near future.[80]

Viewed differently, in 1852 the partisan breakdown of the northern popular vote was: Democrats, 49.8 percent; Whigs, 43.6 percent; and Free Soilers, 6.6 percent. In 1856, it was Republicans, 45.2 percent; Democrats, 41.4 percent, and Americans, 13.4 percent. Almost 650,000 more Northerners voted in 1856 than in 1852, so the proportions for each year do not represent the same number of voters. Buchanan, in fact, garnered some 80,000 more votes than had Pierce in free states. Nonetheless, Democrats had clearly suffered devastating proportionate losses over four years, while over twice as many former Whigs appear to have become Republicans than voted for Fillmore. Professor Gienapp's valuable estimates of voter movement between elections allow more precise delineations of how former Whig voters fragmented in 1856. In Connecticut, for example, more Scott voters supported Buchanan than Fillmore, and Frémont outpaced Fillmore among former Whigs by a ratio of five-to-one. In no other state in his sample were Whig defections to the Democrats so large, but the split of former Whigs between Republicans and Americans often was. The Republican/American ratio among 1852 Whig voters in Illinois was almost two-to-one, in Indiana three-to-one, in Maine seven-to-one, in Massachusetts, where more Democrats than Whigs supported Fillmore, eleven-to-one, in New York, three-to-two, and in Ohio, five-to-two. Only in Pennsylvania was the split relatively even. Frémont also far outpaced Fillmore among 1854 Know Nothing voters everywhere but New York and Pennsylvania.[81]

The key assumption for those old line Whigs who hoped that one-time Whig supporters would regain their senses after 1856 and return to a reconstituted Whig party was that both the new American and Republican parties would prove ephemeral. The American party did disintegrate rapidly after 1856, but most ex-Whigs in it showed little interest in resurrecting the Whig party. During the campaign's frantic last month, Fillmore refused pleas to allow Americans in Pennsylvania and New Jersey to form fusion tickets with Republicans to stop Buchanan from carrying them and the election on the grounds that the American party was "a national Union party." And after the election, he and others spoke vainly of reorganizing and strengthening the nativist American party, not of reviving the Whigs.[82]

More important, the majority of northern Whigs who had joined the Republican party had no intention of deserting it. Republicans already controlled most northern states, and if they could attract Fillmore's northern voters, they stood in reach of carrying Pennsylvania, New Jersey, Indiana, Illinois, and California. Why should ex-Whigs in the Republican party, who had long hated Democrats, leave it when it so clearly appeared to be a winner? Why should ex-Whigs who supported Fillmore in the North stick with the American party, rather than join their former colleagues in the Republican party, especially if it could be made more palatable to them? For both groups, there was no reason. By 1860 all but 80,000 of Fillmore's 395,000 northern voters would join the Republicans to help elect ex-Whig Abraham Lincoln president.[83] The Whig party had been displaced—permanently.

What finally buried the Whig party, therefore, was the extraordinary Republican surge in the North. It lodged most northern Whigs in a different party than their southern counterparts, and there was no immediate prospect that they could reunite. Unlike conservative old guard Whigs who abstained or voted Democratic in disgust at Fillmore's embrace of Know Nothingism, moreover, antipathy to anti-Catholicism and nativism did not drive most of them to the Republican column. Many had themselves been Know Nothings, and Republicans, in addition to arranging a common front behind Frémont, used anti-Catholic appeals to attract them.[84] Nonetheless, as Fillmore knew, they went Republican primarily because of their outrage at slavery expansion and Slave Power aggressions against the North—specifically, against Senator Charles Sumner and northern residents of Kansas. Explaining why Republicans would sweep the former Whig bastion of

Vermont, one Fillmore loyalist confessed in early July, "The outrage upon Mr. Sumner and upon the people of Kansas has strengthened them as a party and placed it out of our power to carry this State unless Congress settles the Kansas question soon." In late October, another Vermonter reported that attempts to revive the Whig party there and in the rest of New England by ratifying the action of the Baltimore Whig convention had failed. "The mass of the Whig party in N. Eng." simply refused "to keep their former organization" and went as a "body" to the Republicans because of the "deep & extensive revulsion of feeling at the present state of things."[85]

That is the point. Neither Congress nor the election of 1856 settled the Kansas or broader sectional questions. The new Democratic administration only helped exacerbate "the present state of things," thereby fueling the continued growth of the Republicans and dooming any chance of resurrecting the Whig party. The intensity of northern anger at Slave Power aggressions and the aid it gave Republicans cannot be exaggerated. Northerners felt a profound need for a party that championed the North. They saw themselves being reduced to slavery, the antithesis of the public liberty they cherished, because Democrats allowed Southerners to destroy republican self-government. "What has taken place in Kansas and at Washington within the last few months," screamed one Massachusetts Republican in July 1856, "is a disgrace to the country and a reproach to our republican form of government." "It is high time that the people of the whole country should know and understand, that the degraded negro is not the only class of *slaves* among us; but that the arrogance of the *'Slave Power'* tramples ruthlessly upon *all* who presume to fix the limits of its dominion," echoed an Ohioan. The people "are perfectly furious," concurred a Pennsylvanian, "and nothing but the vent which our election affords, prevents [them] from resorting to arms."[86]

XI

Within four and a half years of the 1856 presidential election, Northerners and Southerners did take up arms to vent their reciprocal fury at each other. From the moment he assumed the presidency in 1850, Millard Fillmore had seen the potential bloodbath coming. If either the Democrats or the Republicans won in 1856, he predicted that year, "Civil War and anarchy stare us in the face."[87]

As argued in the first parts of this chapter, sectional division was *not* the only thing that destroyed the Whig party and drove it to its grave. But the death of the Whig party clearly contributed to the outbreak of war, if only by clearing the way for and, in the form of essential northern Whig converts, aiding the rise of the Republican party as the major opponent of Democrats in American political life. That achievement, largely completed by the end of 1856, allowed Republicans, rather than a differently constituted anti-Democratic party, to capture the votes of Northerners who wanted to punish the Democrats in 1860. And their victory in the presidential election provoked Deep South secession and the subsequent war.

The death of the Whig party thus had consequences, and none graver than the outbreak of the Civil War in April 1861. This is not to say that there never could have been a civil war had a bisectional Whig party survived. If anything, this study should show how rapidly contingent events could change things. But surely the circumstances provoking that war and its chronology would have been different. The historical Civil War, the one that started in April 1861, resulted primarily from the fact that an exclusively northern and overtly antisouthern Republican party, not a bisectional Whig party, benefited most from anger at Democrats in 1856 and defeated Democrats for the presidency in 1860. That southern fire-eaters who had unsuccessfully sought secession for decades could have exploited the election of a Whig president, supported by southern Whigs, to trigger disunion seems doubtful indeed.[88]

To the extent that the Whig blunders, heedlessly selfish decisions, and failed strategies outlined at the start of this chapter contributed to the death of the Whig party, therefore, they also indirectly helped cause the Civil War. The more important question, however, is whether Whigs inflamed the escalating sectional antagonism that helped destroy the party and disrupt the nation, as Fillmore had so presciently forecast. By even raising this question, one risks attack as an unreconstructed revisionist, as a purveyor of the long since discredited argument that a "blundering generation" of narrow-minded or misguided political leaders, not irreconcilable and popularly rooted sectional differences over slavery and slavery extension, "caused" the Civil War.

For over thirty years, the accepted interpretation of the war's coming in the academy has been that it resulted from basic social, economic, and ideological differences between the sections deriving from the presence of African-American slavery in the South and its absence from the North. In its cruder—and more common—formulation, the "forces" that caused the war were self-generating and operated toward their inevitable conclusion almost without the need of human agency. And most certainly, this argument goes, specific political leaders cannot be held accountable for the war since the sectional conflict producing it involved mass public opinion and sensibilities growing out of different economic and social systems, not something so epiphenomenal as politics.

Yet sectional differences over slavery had existed for decades without causing a shooting war, and the Whig party itself survived for two of those decades despite them. As even the most compelling modern critic of the revisionists recognizes, moreover, the Civil War resulted from a specific chain of events. And those events did not just happen; they were not just products of sectional differences. Rather, specific human actors—and, yes, specific political leaders—usually caused them to happen.[89]

The questions, then, are, how many of these actors were Whigs and who were they? Whigs are hardly blameless. Without question, John Tyler and his cabinet, who decided to seek Texas' annexation to secure Tyler's reelection and salvage his historical reputation, are most blameworthy. Had Henry Clay been nominated in December 1839 and elected in 1840, as he surely would have been, he would not have sought Texas' annexation in 1844. Nor would he have provoked the subsequent Mexican War, with its legacy of dispute over slavery extension into the Mexican Cession. But Tyler and his cronies were hardly alone. Stephens, Toombs, Thomas Clingman, and a few other southern Whigs, usually for narrow political gains, helped ratchet up the provocative southern demands that so infuriated the North. Next to Tyler's Texas adventurism, moreover, no Whig action did more to destroy the party and bring on the war than southern Whigs' easily avoidable support for the Nebraska Act in 1854, a mistake that many of them later rued. Similarly, some northern Whigs—John Quincy Adams and his son Charles Francis, Joshua Giddings, Henry Wilson, Weed, Seward, Greeley, Ben Wade, William F. Johnston, Roger Sherman Baldwin, and others—helped whip up northern anger in response to these perceived aggressions.

To the extent that politicians, rather than nonpartisan actors, were responsible for the events that inflamed sectional animosities and helped lead to war, however, Democrats and Free Soilers, by any objective standard, deserve more blame than Whigs. As the historian William W. Freehling demonstrates so persuasively, southern Democrats and the Calhounites who operated as a pressure group upon them launched most of the assaults that outraged the North along the road to disunion. In Dixie, Whigs were far more often conservative unionists victimized politically by Democratic aggression than they were aggressors themselves. And during the secession crisis of 1860–61, Whigs in virtually every state of the South provided the leadership of and most votes for the opposition to immediate secession, whereas Democrats led the rush to leave the Union.[90]

Likewise, it was always northern Democrats, not northern Whigs, who folded before pressure from the South, thereby encouraging still more southern aggressions. Antislavery northern Whigs did take a harder sectional line than northern Democrats, and they did play the antislavery card to win elections in the North. But most of them usually acted on the defensive, only after southern or northern Democrats had created an issue, and many were motivated as much by a recognition of how southern aggressions, if not stopped, would endanger the Union as by antislavery and antisouthern sentiment. Most, emphatically, were not abolitionists who sought to destroy the South's domestic institution or sectional tyrants who sought to dictate to white Southerners.

Seward is a perfect example. After the most extreme antislavery Whigs bolted to the Free Soil party in 1848, no other northern Whig was so frequently condemned as a dangerous fanatic by Southerners and his conservative New York Whig rivals as Seward. Yet when the crunch came in 1854, Seward's true conservatism showed. Supremely confident that Northerners could win any contest with slaveholders for the territories without a new party and certainly without a war, Seward, to the dismay of infuriated Free Soilers and the consternation of some outraged northern Whigs, sought to preserve his ties to southern Whigs and to save the Whig party as a bisectional organization. Again, during the secession crisis, five years after he had become a Republican, Seward and his New York editorial allies like Weed and Henry Raymond responded more positively than any other Republicans to pleas from southern ex-Whigs that secession in the upper South might be stopped if the exclusively northern Republican party dropped its South-bashing, antislavery rhetoric and joined antisecessionist Southerners in a new, bisectional Union party. Millard Fillmore himself could have done no more.[91]

Yet Seward's efforts, like Fillmore's, came to naught. They did so primarily because other Republicans, led by another ex-Whig, President Abraham Lincoln, refused to follow the example of earlier northern Democrats by acceding to southern demands and thereby destroying the new Republican party itself. Lincoln's attitude toward a Union party would change, but his intransigence in the winter of 1860–61 helped provoke the Civil War that many northern and southern

Whigs had long hoped to avert. That Lincoln was the president who made this decision, like the rise and triumph of the Republican party itself, was a direct result of the death of the Whig party to which Lincoln himself had clung until early 1856. There would have been no Civil War without an underlying sectional conflict, but a specific chain of political events and politicians' decisions both aggravated that conflict and explain why that war started in April 1861. And among the most important links in this chain of causation were the decisions and developments that put the Whig party in its grave.

XII

Five years after that unimaginably sanguinary war ended, Edward Stafford offered his epitaph for the Whig party. He did not write in 1870 from sheer whim. Rather, he was responding to widespread talk in the South about reviving Whiggery to replace the Republicans as the Democrats' primary partisan opponent. Such talk had appeared sporadically in the late 1850s. During the secession crisis and the war itself, moreover, proposals for building a Whig-based Union party of the type envisioned by John P. Kennedy had flourished. Because southern Whigs largely opposed secession in 1860–61, moreover, even during the years of the Confederacy, Southerners elected them to express hostility to the Democrats who brought on secession and now led the Confederacy. This habitual Whig opposition to the hated Democrats continued immediately after the war, when former Whigs won most of the appointive and elective offices in the South under the terms of President Andrew Johnson's Reconstruction policies.[92]

Even after passage of Congress' Military Reconstruction Acts in 1867 and 1868 added adult black males to the southern electorate and thereby launched the formation of Republican parties across the South, former Whigs, most of whom had languished out of office during the late 1850s, landed on their feet. In most southern states, they ended up leading both the Republican and Democratic (or Conservative) parties between 1868 and 1872. Often having far more in common with their fellow ex-Whigs in the opposition than they did with the mass base of their newly adopted parties, ex-Whigs in both talked of reviving the Whig party.[93]

Stafford hoped to squelch this talk with his caustic putdown. He need not have bothered. Like the surreal visions of Whig resurrection voiced so poignantly during 1856, prospects of Whig revival after the Civil War were sheer fantasy. Having embedded themselves in power across the North by managing the successful northern war effort, Republicans had no inclination whatsoever to abandon their party for resurrected Whiggery. And without northern allies who shared their hatred of and contempt for Democrats, southern Whigs had no hope of ever reviving the Whig party.

At least one tough-minded North Carolina Whig recognized that fact—and as early as 1865, when prospects that antisecessionist southern Whigs might rise to power again seemed bright. Unlike any other state in the nation, in North Carolina Democrats' opponents reassumed the Whig label and ran Whig candidates in the late 1850s. They almost won the governorship in 1860 and gained additional recruits by opposing immediate secession in early 1861. Thus a formal Whig organization still existed there when the Civil War began. Born in 1830 and therefore far too young to seek office as a Whig during the party's heyday, Zebulon Vance imbibed Whig principles from his family, and he became one of the most energetic and effective Whig leaders during its second coming. In 1862 he was elected governor for the same reason former Whigs in North Carolina and elsewhere were elected to the Confederate Congress in 1863—to express opposition to the administration of ex-Democrat and Confederate President Jefferson Davis. During his tenure in office, indeed, Vance earned fame as an unusually effective and obstreperous critic of the Richmond authorities.[94]

The very opposite of the old fogies who tried to save the Whig party in 1856, Vance, in sum, was exactly the kind of youthful, vigorous, ambitious, and skillful politician to lead a revival of the Whig party. But he was also realistic enough to know the task was impossible. When asked to do so in 1865, therefore, he replied with cold finality: "The [Whig] party is dead and buried and the tombstone placed over it and I don't care to spend the rest of my days mourning at its grave."[95] To this brutally candid and totally accurate extinguisher, there was—and is—only one appropriate response. Amen!

Notes

Chapter 1

1. Beverly C. Sandrin to James B. Clay, Baltimore, February 20, 1844, Thomas J. Clay MSS.

2. J. W. Mighels to Henry Clay, November 11, 1844, Henry Clay MSS (LC).

3. See, for example, Binkley, *American Political Parties*, and Schlesinger, *Age of Jackson*. For one historian who questions the very concept of a first party system by denying that Federalists and Jeffersonians developed the permanent organizations and voter identifications necessary to qualify as genuine parties, see Formisano, "Deferential-Participant Politics," and id., "Federalists and Republicans."

4. This literature is too vast to list here, but for examples see Benson, *Concept*; Livermore, *Twilight of Federalism*; McCormick, *Second American Party System*.

5. The following analysis is largely my extrapolations from the insights in Ellis, *Jeffersonian Crisis*. The links between Jeffersonianism and Whiggery are also suggested by McCoy, *Elusive Republic*, pp. 236–59; Birkner, "Politics, Law and Enterprise"; and especially Howe, *Political Culture*, pp. 49–50, 90–91, 109, and passim.

6. The best study of the economic thought of the Jeffersonians is McCoy, *Elusive Republic*, but see also Appleby, *Capitalism*.

7. The best modern analyses of Clay during the 1820s can be found in Peterson, *Great Triumvirate*, and Remini, *Henry Clay*. For the Republicans' schizophrenia about the constitutionality of federal internal improvements, which would help explain Madison's veto of Calhoun's bonus bill in 1817 and Clay's later shift to a formula of federal revenue sharing, see Larson, "Jefferson's Union."

8. Aside from Ellis, my portrait of the Radicals is drawn from Brown, "The Missouri Crisis"; Phillips, "Democrats of the Old School," and Phillips, "Pennsylvania Origins"; Risjord, *Old Republicans*; Schlesinger, *Age of Jackson*, pp. 18–29; and Sellers, *Market Revolution*, pp. 34–136.

9. The literature on republican ideology and its relationship to older "commonwealth" or "country" political ideas is now so familiar that it seems unnecessary to cite it all again. Much of it is conveniently summarized and cited in the Introduction to Elkins and McKitrick, *Age of Federalism*, pp. 3–29, 757–61. On the inculcation of veneration for the Revolutionary generation's achievements, however, see Welter, *Mind of America*, pp. 3–218 and passim; and Forgie, *Patricide*, pp. 3–53 and passim. For interpretations of how republican ideology was transformed between the Revolution and the Jacksonian period, see Ross, "Transformation of Republican Ideology," and Kruman, "Second American Party System."

10. On the egalitarian thrust of the Revolution that displaced the hierarchical conceptions of classical republicanism, see Wood, *Radicalism*.

11. On James Madison's own postwar popularity, see McCoy, *Last of the Fathers*, pp. 11–20.

12. To the extent that Americans bothered to vote at all between 1808 and 1828, turnout was usually higher in state than in presidential or congressional elections. Prior to 1819, however, it is not clear that, except for a few places, these state elections pitted candidates from the rival Republican wings against each other. Prior to that year, indeed, turnout was usually greatest in elections where Federalists still contested Republicans. See Tables I and II in McCormick, "New Perspectives."

13. The political ramifications of the Panic nationally and in individual states have been described in a number of works, but for able summaries, see Sellers, *Market Revolution*, pp. 103–201; and Remini, *Jackson and the Course of American Freedom*, pp. 39–54.

14. Brown, "Missouri Crisis."

15. On the influences in the 1824 campaign, see McCormick, *Second American Party System*; the two articles by Kim Phillips cited in note 8; Ratcliffe, "Role of Voters"; Marshall, "Genesis"; and Sellers, "Banking and Politics."

16. Remini, *Jackson and the Course of American Freedom*, pp. 75–76.

17. Ibid., pp. 12–38, 74–99; quotations are from pp. 76–77.

18. The best modern treatment of the maneuvering in the House is found in ibid., pp. 85–99, and in Remini, *Henry Clay*, pp. 251–72. See also Carroll, *Origins of the Whig Party*, pp. 6–12; and Poage, *Henry Clay*, pp. 4–5.

19. Nathans, *Webster*, pp. 18–24.

20. For a succinct, exceptionally insightful interpretation of Adams' presidency, see Skowronek, *Politics Presidents Make*, pp. 110–27. It, in turn, draws heavily from the best modern treatment of the Adams administration, Hargreaves, *The Presidency of John Quincy Adams*.

21. Brown, "Missouri Crisis"; Pessen, *Jacksonian America*, pp. 293–99; Howe, *Political Culture*, pp. 40–42; Remini, *Jackson and the Course of American Freedom*, p. 258.

22. For the "Tariff of Abominations," see Niven, *Van Buren*, pp. 194–201.

23. McCormick, "Political Development."

24. Marshall, "Strange Still-Birth."

25. Ibid.; McCormick, *Second American Party System*; Nathans, *Webster*, pp. 1–7, 22–47, and passim; Formisano, "Toward a Reorientation," 61.

26. Robert V. Remini has analyzed the building of the Jackson organization between 1825 and 1828 and the nature of its campaign appeal in a number of works, among which are *Election of Andrew Jackson; Andrew Jackson*; and, most recently, *Jackson and the Course of American Freedom*, pp. 100–42. In the last book, he demonstrates how the Jackson campaign stressed the need for reform to stamp out corruption and thus save republican liberty.

27. Remini, *Henry Clay*, pp. 323–28; Nathans, *Webster*, pp. 26–27; Carroll, *Origins of the Whig Party*, pp. 13–16; Birkner, *Southard*, pp. 75–89.

28. Henry Clay to Francis Brooke, January 10, 1829, in *Works of Henry Clay*, IV, p. 217. The figures on party strength in Congress come from *Historical Statistics*, II, 1083.

29. On May 29, 1830, Webster explicitly wrote Clay that "the Tariff and Internal Improvements" would be "the great ground of difference" between new parties and that Jackson's stand on them must produce "discontent and schisms among our opponents from which much is now to be hoped." *Works of Henry Clay*, IV, pp. 274–76.

30. Clay to Barbour, November 21, 1829, quoted in Carroll, *Origins of the Whig Party*, p. 30; Clay to J. J. Johnston, July 18, 1829, and Webster to Clay, April 18, 1830, May 29, 1830, in *Works of Henry Clay*, IV, pp. 238–40, 260, 274–76. See also Clay to H. Niles, November 25, 1828, J. J. Crittenden to Clay, December 3, 1828, and Clay to Francis Brooke, January 30, 1829, ibid., pp. 213–21; Nathans, *Webster*, pp. 29–31.

31. Richard P. McCormick, in the works cited above, makes the point that it took sixteen years for the second party system to crystallize. Yet in some states the alignments that appeared in 1828 probably already represented previously fixed attachments. See, e.g., Benson et al., "Toward a Theory of Stability"; and Ratcliffe, "Politics in Jacksonian Ohio."

32. Remini, *Andrew Jackson*, pp. 106–32; Remini, *Jackson and the Course of American Freedom*, pp. 257–79: Ellis, *Union at Risk*, pp. 13–73; Carroll, *Origins of the Whig Party*, p. 56.

33. This story is well told in a number of sources: Remini, *Andrew Jackson* and *Andrew Jackson and the Course of American Freedom*, pp. 203–352; Nathans, *Webster*, pp. 31–47; Freehling, *Prelude to Civil War*.

34. The best recent treatment of the Barbour movement is Cooper, *Politics of Slavery*, pp. 11–22.

35. I have interpreted the origins and course of Antimasonry at greater length in Holt, "Antimasonic and Know Nothing Parties," pp. 575–620. All quotations of Antimasonic rhetoric in this and subsequent paragraphs are drawn from that essay. See also Kutolowski, "Antimasonry Reexamined"; Formisano, *Transformation of Political Culture*, 197–221; and Goodman, *Toward a Christian Republic*.

36. Peter B. Porter to Clay, October 6, 1830, Clay to John Bailhache, November 24, 1830, Clay to J. J. Johnston, July 23, 1831, Clay to Francis Brooke, June 23, and October 4, 1831, in *Works of Henry Clay*, IV, pp. 284, 288–91, 300–03, 306–09, 314–17.

37. Carroll, *Origins of the Whig Party*, pp. 48–53; Shade, "Political Pluralism," pp. 80–81.

38. The quotation is from W. B. Lawrence to Clay, November 18, 1830, in Carroll, *Origins of the Whig Party*, p. 49. My portrait of the National Republicans' orientation is based on Marshall, "Strange Still-Birth," and Nathans, *Webster*, pp. 29–49.

39. Alexander H. Everett to Henry Clay, October 29, 1830, quoted in Nathans, *Webster*, p. 36.

40. Oran Follett to Major G. Camp, December 13, 1831, quoted in Carroll, *Origins of the Whig Party*, p. 67; see ibid., pp. 43–68, for evidence of others who doubted Clay's ability to unite the anti-Jackson men. The Address of the National Republican Convention, December 1831, is reprinted in Remini, "The Election of 1832," pp. 553–66.

41. Russo, "Major Political Issues," p. 6 and passim; Carroll, *Origins of the Whig Party*, pp. 55–57.

42. Remini, *Jackson and the Bank War*; Wilburn, *Biddle's Bank*; Carroll, *Origins of the Whig Party*, pp. 57–70; Nathans, *Webster*, pp. 41–47; Marshall, "Strange Still-Birth"; Clay to Francis Brooke, April 19, 1830, and to J. J. Johnston, April 30, 1830, in *Works of Henry Clay*, IV, pp. 260–61, 264–65.

43. Remini, "The Election of 1832," p. 509.

44. For the Democrats' use of the veto to offset liabilities on state issues, see Benson, *Concept of Jacksonian Democracy*, pp. 47–63. On Weed, see Van Deusen, *Weed*, pp. 63–64.

45. Remini, "The Election of 1832," pp. 511–12.

46. Ibid., p. 515; Cooper, *Politics of Slavery*, p. 5. Wirt carried Vermont, and Robert Remini estimates that Wirt got 8 percent of the popular vote compared to Clay's 37 percent. Yet even Remini's estimate of Clay's vote may be too high and, correspondingly, that of Wirt's too low since three separate electoral tickets were in the field in at least eight states. See Shade, "Political Pluralism," pp. 80–81.

CHAPTER 2

1. Henry Clay to Francis Brooke, Washington, January 17, 1833, in *Works of Henry Clay*, V, pp. 347–48.

2. Henry Clay to Willie P. Mangum, August 26, 1834, in *The Mangum Papers*, II, p. 191.

3. Clay to ?, Ashland, July 14, 1835, in *Works of Henry Clay*, V, pp. 392–95.

4. The best account of this episode, which stresses Jackson's desire to avoid the use of force, is Freehling, *Prelude to Civil War*, pp. 260–97. For the congressional enactment of the so-called Compromise of 1833, see Peterson, *Olive Branch*; Peterson, *Great Triumvirate*, pp. 212–33; and Remini, *Henry Clay*, pp. 412–35.

5. Willie P. Mangum to Charity A. Mangum, Washington, December 15, 1833, in *The Mangum Papers*, I, p. 589; Augusta *Courier*, n.d., quoted in Cole, *Whig Party in the South*, p. 17. On the general reaction to the nullification crisis in the South and its role in launching State Rights organizations, see, ibid., pp. 17–24; Cooper, *Politics of Slavery*, pp. 52–57; Murray, *Whig Party in Georgia*, pp. 54–63; Folsom, "Party Formation," 221–23; Thornton, *Politics and Power*, pp. 21–28; McCormick, *Second American Party System*, pp. 192–93, 205–06, 241–42, 197–301.

6. Willie P. Mangum to David L. Swain, Washington, December 22, 1833, in *The Mangum Papers*, II, pp. 51–56. See also Mangum to John Beard, Philadelphia, October 7, 1834, ibid., pp. 212–19.

7. Cole, *Whig Party in the South*, pp. 1–38 and passim; Cooper, *Politics of Slavery*, pp. 43–97; Folsom, "Party Formation"; Williams, "Foundations," 115–29; and Thornton, *Politics and Power*, pp. 20–39.

8. Carroll, *Origins of the Whig Party*, pp. 71–117; Nathans, *Webster*, pp. 48–61.

9. For this portrait of Webster, I have relied on Nathans, *Webster*; Brown, *Webster*; and Dalzell, *Webster*.

10. *Boston Daily Evening Transcript*, June 20, July 29, 1833, and *Boston Courier*, August 8, 1833, quoted in Nathans, *Webster*, pp. 64–66. I have borrowed heavily from Nathans' perceptive analysis of this episode, pp. 61–73, but see also Carroll, *Origins of the Whig Party*, pp. 71–117, and Brown, *Webster*, pp. 15–55.

11. Nathans, *Webster*, pp. 61–66; Carroll, *Origins of the White Party*, pp. 81–83.

12. Amos Kendall to Andrew Jackson, March 20, 1833, quoted in Latner, "A New Look," 956; Curtis, *Fox at Bay*, pp. 39–46. The announcement on September 25 came from interim Treasury Secretary Roger B. Taney, whom Jackson had appointed specifically to make it.

13. *Sentinel*, October 4, 1833, quoted in Birkner, "Politics, Law and Enterprise," p. 328.

14. There had been a series of investigations of the Bank since 1830, most of which were biased for or against it according to the predispositions of various committee members. Sellers, *Polk: Jacksonian*, pp. 178–95.

15. Mangum to Duncan Cameron, Washington, February 7, 1834, in *The Mangum Papers*, II, pp. 72–75. That the pets were selected for their political reliability is demonstrated in Gatell, "Spoils of the Bank War."

16. Cooper, *Politics of Slavery*, pp. 50–52.

17. Samuel Hillman to Mangum, February 16, 1834, in *The Mangum Papers*, II, pp. 81–83. For an analysis of the contraction's impact on Tennessee, see Sellers, *Polk; Jacksonian*, pp. 196–210. A splendid example of a northern Whig's case against Jackson's economic blunders is William Henry Seward's "Six Million Dollar Loan Speech" of April 10, 1834, reprinted in Van Deusen, "The Whig Party," 369–78.

18. Mangum to David L. Swain, Washington, December 22, 1833, loc. cit.

19. For this sketch, I have drawn heavily on the stunning portrait of Clay in Schlesinger, *Age of Jackson*, pp. 82–83, and the admirable analysis of Clay in Howe, *Political Culture*, pp. 123–49. Clay's personal magnetism is also described at length in Remini, *Henry Clay*. For Clay's temporary renunciation of presidential ambition, see Clay to Francis Brooke, May 30, 1833, in *The Works of Henry Clay*, V. pp. 360–63.

20. Van Deusen, "Whig Party," p. 337; Nathans, *Webster*, pp. 66–73, 85–87; Brown, *Webster*, pp. 56–66; Darling, *Political Changes*, pp. 85–129.

21. Ibid.; Carroll, *Origins of the Whig Party*, pp. 101–17. Both Nathans and Brown correct Carroll's erroneous assertion, p. 210, that Clay maneuvered Webster into accepting the chairmanship to force his hand.

22. Birkner, "Politics, Law and Enterprise," pp. 339–40; Clay's speech is quoted in Remini, *Henry Clay*, pp. 447–49.

23. Brown, *Webster*, pp. 64–66, Clay to Biddle, February 2, 1834, quoted p. 65; Nathans, *Webster*, pp. 75–78, Webster quoted p. 77. Clay and Mangum also urged Virginians and North Carolinians to mount opposition to Jackson in their state legislatures on the removal question, not recharter. Clay to Francis Brooke, December 16, 1833, January 14, 1834, in *Works of Henry Clay*, V, pp. 375–77; Mangum to David L. Swain, Washington, December 22, 1833, loc. cit.

24. Clay to Francis Brooke, December 16, 1833, loc. cit.

25. According to Remini, *Henry Clay*, pp. 456–59, a speech that Clay made to the Senate on April 14, 1834, was primarily responsible for affixing the Whig name to the new opposition coalition.

26. Carroll, *Origins of the Whig Party*, pp. 171, 124–27; Schlesinger, *Age of Jackson*, 106–

11, 267–82. The quotation is from p. 279. Howe's *Political Culture*, the fullest exploration of Whig thought, constitutes a retort to this indictment of intellectual sterility.

27. Alexander, *Sectional Stress*, pp. 9–11; McCormick, "Was There a 'Whig Strategy' in 1836?" 50–52.

28. Willie P. Mangum to John Beard, October 7, 1834, in *The Mangum Papers*, II, pp. 212–19.

29. My thinking about the interrelatedness of parties in any party system has been influenced by Sartori, *Parties and Party Systems*, pp. 25–28, 43, and passim.

30. Howe, *Political Culture*, pp. 69–95; Mangum to David L. Swain, December 22, 1833, loc. cit. Raleigh *Register*, June 10, 1834.

31. Carroll, *Origins of the Whig Party*, p. 124; Clay to Francis Brooke, December 16, 1833; Richmond *Whig*, April 8, 1834, quoted in Simms, *Rise of the Whigs*, p. 86. "The name Whig made its appearance in North Carolina," recalled the Raleigh *Register* on January 23, 1846, "when *power* first began to encroach on the rights of the people. . . . The name implies opposition to misused power, and we glory, as does every true Whig, in the name."

32. Alexander Coffin to Henry Clay, May 12, 1834, in *Works of Henry Clay*, II, pp. 383–84; Isaac Croom to Mangum, Lenoir County, N.C., April 13, 1834, in *The Mangum Papers*, II, pp. 143–44.

33. *New York Daily Advertiser*, March 21, 22, 1834, quoted in Nathans, *Webster*, p. 80; Seward's Address of the Whig Minority in the legislature is reproduced in Van Deusen, "The Whig Party," pp. 379–83.

34. James Mowatt to William Henry Seward, N.Y.C., September 20, 1834, Seward MSS (RU).

35. Howe, "Virtue and Commerce," 351; Appleby, "Origins of American Revolutionary Ideology." Kathleen Kutolowski questions the extent of anticommercial sentiment among Antimasons in western New York in "Antimasonry Reexamined."

36. My reference here, of course, is to Howe's superb *Political Culture*, on which I rely heavily for the following discussion.

37. In this and the following paragraphs, I have relied heavily on Howe, *Political Culture*, pp. 23–98 and passim; and Formisano, "Political Character." The quotations came from my essay "The Antimasonic and Know Nothing Parties," p. 587.

38. Hofstadter, *Idea of a Party System*; Howe, *Political Culture*, pp. 28–68; Welter, *Mind of America*, pp. 173–74, 196; Ann Arbor *State Journal*, October 26, 1837, quoted in Formisano, "Political Character," p. 702; and Silbey, "Election of 1836," p. 585.

39. Wallace, "Changing Concepts"; address of the New York Whig State Convention, February 1836, in Van Deusen, "The Whig Party," p. 395; Ann Arbor *Michigan Emigrant*, quoted in Formisano, "Political Character," p. 702.

40. Latner, "A New Look," p. 965; Illinois Whig caucus of 1835 quoted in McCormick, *Second American Party System*, p. 284; Huntsville (Ala.) *Southern Advocate*, May 26, 1835, quoted in Thornton, *Politics and Power*, p. 32.

41. Howe, *Political Culture*, pp. 52–54, 142, 157–59, 280; Formisano, "Political Character"; McCormick, *Second American Party System*, pp. 282–93; Thornton, *Politics and Power*, pp. 32–37.

CHAPTER 3

1. Henry Clay to Willie P. Mangum, Ashland, August 26, 1834, in *The Mangum Papers*, II, p. 191. *Niles Register*, Volume 46, p. 443, lists the Whigs as winning 74 of 100 seats in the lower house of the Kentucky Legislature.

2. Van Deusen, *Weed*, pp. 65–69, 86–89; id., *Seward*, pp. 23–28. Seward's speech against the Six Million Dollar Loan and the Address of the Whig Legislators are reproduced in Van Deusen, "The Whig Party," pp. 369–83. The standard study of the formation of the Whig party at the state level is McCormick, *Second American Party System*. I have utilized it in my discussion of every state, and because it is organized by states, I shall eschew the repeated listing of page citations in these notes.

3. In addition to McCormick, see Ratcliffe, "Politics in Jacksonian Ohio"; Darling, *Political Changes*, pp. 126–27; Birkner, "Politics, Law and Enterprise," pp. 350–67; Kirwan, *Crittenden*, pp. 96–97; Van Deusen, "The Whig Party," pp. 336–38.

4. Simms, *Rise of the Whigs*, pp. 63–86; Washington *National Intelligencer*, April 3, 1834, quoted in ibid., p. 84; Cole, *Whig Party in the South*, pp. 28–38.

5. Williams, "Foundations," pp. 119–24; *The Mangum Papers*, II, p. 216, note; Murray, *Whig Party in Georgia*, pp. 58–65.

6. See the sections on Illinois and Indiana in McCormick, *Second American Party System*.

7. Ibid., p. 28.

8. *The Mangum Papers*, I, p. xxxii; Murray, *Whig Party in Georgia*, p. 61; Carroll, *Origins of the Whig Party*, p. 126; Silbey, "Election of 1836," p. 582; Simms, *Rise of the Whigs*, p. 98. For returns in gubernatorial elections I have used Kallenbach and Kallenbach (eds.), *American State Governors*. Figures on congressional elections come from the Congressional Quarterly's *Guide to U.S. Elections*.

9. Weed to Seward, April 13, May 13, 1835, Albert H. Tracy to Seward, April 14, 1835, Seward MSS (RU).

10. Nathans, *Webster*, pp. 82–83; Sellers, *Polk: Jacksonian*, pp. 221–22; Temin, *Jacksonian Economy*, pp. 61–68; Josiah Randall to Willie P. Mangum, Philadelphia, December 12, 1834, in *The Mangum Papers*, II, p. 236. The percentages are based on the figures for currency in circulation outside the Treasury listed in *Historical Statistics*, p. 993. For estimates that continuing hostility to the Bank of the United States cost the Whigs the New York election in 1834, see William H. Seward to William W. Tredway, November 8, 1834, and Dudley Selden to Seward, November 12, 1834, Seward MSS (RU).

11. For more on this bitter feud among Quakers and how Democrats exploited Hicksite wrath against National Republican Governor Elias P. Seeley and United States Senator Theodore Frelinghuysen, see Birkner, "Politics, Law and Enterprise," pp. 330–36, 364–67, 382–83.

12. Formisano, *Birth of Mass Political Parties*, pp. 81–97.

13. Nathans, *Webster*, pp. 83–89; Holt, "Antimasonic and Know Nothing Parties," pp. 590–92; Snyder, *Jacksonian Heritage*, pp. 49–81. See also the sections on these states in McCormick, *Second American Party System*.

14. R. H. Alexander to Willie P. Mangum, Raleigh, November 29, 1834, in *The Mangum Papers*, II, pp. 224–26.

15. Crittenden quoted in Silbey, "Election of 1836," p. 585.

16. John C. Calhoun to Francis W. Pickens, January 4, 1834, and to Christopher van Deventer, January 25, 1834, in Jameson, "Correspondence of Calhoun," pp. 326–30.

17. John C. Calhoun to Francis Pickens, April 15, 1834, and to Duff Green, September 20, 1834, ibid., pp. 335–36, 341–42; Clay to Mangum, Ashland, August 26, 1834, in *The Mangum Papers*, II, p. 191; see also Matt M. Moore to Mangum, April 17, 1834, and Orlando Brown to Mangum, December 21, 1834, ibid., pp. 147–48, 250–52; Henry Clay to Francis Brooke, April 17, 1834, in *Works of Henry Clay*, V, p. 382.

18. For a forceful argument that no coherent national Whig party existed by 1836 and that incipient Whigs pursued no concerted strategy that year, see McCormick, "Was There a 'Whig Strategy' in 1836?". Additional evidence on the embryonic state of Whig organization and partisan loyalties can be found in Shade, "Political Pluralism." For evidence that Whigs shared enough of a common bond to monitor and participate vicariously in the campaigns of their fellows in different states, see Brantz Mayer to William Henry Seward, Baltimore, September 21, 1834, Joseph M. Root to Seward, Norwalk, Ohio, October 23, 1834, and Thurlow Weed to Seward, Albany, March 8, April 13, October 16, 1834, Seward MSS (RU).

19. *National Intelligencer*, July 1, 1835, quoted in Carroll, *Origins of the Whig Party*, p. 145; Weed to Seward, June 15, 1835, Seward MSS; Clay to ?, July 14, 1835, James Barbour to Clay, August 2, 1835, in *Works of Henry Clay*, II, pp. 392–99; Nathans, *Webster*, pp. 90–91.

20. Thurlow Weed to Francis Granger, November 23, 1834, quoted in Kirwan, *Crittenden*, p. 127; Mangum to Graham, Washington, December 17, 1834, in *The Mangum Papers*, II, pp. 245–47.

21. Nathans, *Webster*, pp. 91–95; Mangum to William A. Graham, December 17, 1834; Or-

lando Brown to Mangum, December 21, 1834, in *The Mangum Papers*, II, pp. 245–47, 250–52; John C. Calhoun to Lewis S. Coryell, Fort Hill, S. C., August 10, 1834, in Jameson, "Correspondence of Calhoun," p. 340.

22. Clay to ?, Ashland, July 14, 1835, in *Works of Henry Clay*, II, pp. 392–95; Willie P. Mangum to John Beard, Philadelphia, October 7, 1834, in *The Mangum Papers*, II, pp. 212–19.

23. Mangum to John Beard, October 7, 1834; James Barbour to Henry Clay, August 2, 1835, loc cit.; Nathans, *Webster*, pp. 90–103.

24. Seward to Weed, February 15, March 15, 1835, quoted in Brown, *Webster*, p. 113; Nathans, *Webster*, p. 95. See also Weed to Seward, March 8, 1835, and Albert H. Tracy to Seward, April 14, 1835, Seward MSS (RU).

25. Cincinnati *Gazette*, September 18, 1835, quoted in Carroll, *Origins of the Whig Party*, p. 141; *Ohio State Journal*, October 15, 1836, quoted in Fox, "The Bank Wars," p. 265; Nathans, *Webster*, pp. 95–103; Brown, *Webster*, pp. 110–23.

26. Silbey, "The Election of 1836," p. 587; Clay to ?, Ashland, July 14, 1835, loc cit.

27. Henry Clay to John Bailhache, Ashland, September 13, 1835, in *Works of Henry Clay*, V, pp. 399–400; Brown, *Webster*, pp. 98–99, 124–48; Nathans, *Webster*, pp. 94–98; Snyder, *Jacksonian Heritage*, pp. 69–71.

28. My account of the southern Whig campaign for White in 1835 and 1836 rests heavily on Cooper, *Politics of Slavery*, pp. 74–97, and Silbey, "Election of 1836."

29. Sellers, *Polk: Jacksonian*, pp. 234–303; McCormick, *Second American Party System*, pp. 227–36.

30. Thornton, *Politics and Power*, pp. 30–35.

31. Alexander Porter to Jesse B. Harrison, January 12, 1836, quoted in Cooper, *Politics of Slavery*, p. 81; Richmond *Whig*, April 7, 1835, quoted in Simms, *Rise of the Whigs*, p. 100. While Harrison would officially head the Whig ticket in Virginia, the electors on it had been chosen originally as White men and Virginia's Whigs ran as supporters of both.

32. Alfred Balch to Andrew Jackson, April 4, 1835, quoted in Latner, "A New Look," p. 964.

33. Raleigh *Register*, December 22, 1835, W. H. Roane to Frank Blair, May 7, 1835, and Thomas Ritchie to Francis Blair, March 27, 1835, quoted in Cooper, *Politics of Slavery*, pp. 81, 83–84; Washington *Globe*, n.d., quoted in Silbey, "Election of 1836," p. 594.

34. The quotation is in Silbey, "Election of 1836," p. 590, and in Cooper, *Politics of Slavery*, p. 91.

35. See Cooper, *Politics of Slavery*; Silbey, "Election of 1836"; and Holt, *Political Crisis*, pp. 28–29.

36. Alexander, *Sectional Stress*, pp. 11–13 and passim; Van Deusen, "The Whig Party," p. 341. Thurlow Weed lamented that the southern campaign for White would only help Van Buren in the North in Weed to Seward, September 30, 1835, Seward MSS (RU).

37. Silbey, "Election of 1836," pp. 592–95; Kirwan, *Crittenden*, p. 128.

38. Van Deusen, "The Whig Party," pp. 390–96.

39. While the statistical state-by-state correlation between the 1828 and 1832 results was +.93, it was only +.22 between 1832 and 1836. Silbey, "The Election of 1836," p. 597. In certain states like Ohio, however, the county-by-county product-moment correlation between the 1836 vote and that of 1832 was exceptionally high. See Ratcliffe, "Politics in Jacksonian Ohio," p. 14.

40. The Spearman rank-order coefficient of correlation between the states, as ranked by growth in turnout and change in the anti-Democratic share of the popular vote, is +.658.

41. *Tribune Almanac for 1838*, quoted in Burnham, *Presidential Ballots*, pp. 1–2.

42. The significance of the regional identification of candidates is a central theme in McCormick, *Second American Party System*; Silbey, "Election of 1836," pp. 595–99.

43. According to results listed in the Congressional Quarterly's *Guide to U.S. Elections*, pp. 562–67, the anti-Jacksonians captured 43 percent of House seats filled in 1834, 32.7 percent in 1835, and 40 percent in 1836. These figures include the South Carolinians identified as State Righters or Nullifiers.

44. Walton, "Second Party System in Arkansas," pp. 127–30.

45. Mering, *Whig Party in Missouri*, pp. 28–40.

46. This and the following paragraph are based largely on Lucas, "Political Alchemy," an

admirable piece of research and analysis that the author generously loaned me. The figures on party strength in the legislature are based on Lucas' estimates listed in Table III, p. 133. William G. Shade provides further statistical evidence that there was no relationship between state and national politics and thus no coherent Whig party in Mississippi or elsewhere before 1836 in "Political Pluralism," pp. 77–112, esp. pp. 90–91.

47. Van Deusen, *Weed*, pp. 86–87, 93.

48. Shade, *Banks or No Banks*, pp. 23–28. For the partisan dimensions of roll-call voting patterns in the Ohio and New Jersey legislatures between 1834 and 1836, on which assertions about the two states in the following paragraphs are based, see Ershkowitz and Shade, "Consensus or Conflict?"; and Levine, *New Jersey*.

49. Levine, *New Jersey*, passim.

50. Ibid., pp. 157–67.

51. The previous three paragraphs are based on Snyder, *Jacksonian Heritage*, pp. 50–85.

52. Murray, *Whig Party in Georgia*, pp. 56–66.

53. Thornton, *Politics and Power*, pp. 29–34.

54. Simms, *Rise of the Whigs*, pp. 94–116, 167–92. For evidence of the lack of a party dimension to voting in the legislature in 1834 and 1835, see the figures for Virginia in the various tables in Ershkowitz and Shade, "Consensus or Conflict?"

One might argue that the joint Harrison-White electoral ticket in Virginia blunted the Whigs' attempts to pose as southern defenders of slavery and to attack Van Buren as untrustworthy on the abolitionist issue, yet the evidence is overwhelming that Virginia Whigs pursued that strategy.

55. Sellers, *Polk: Jacksonian*, pp. 267–92. It is true that advocacy of White rather than the internal improvements issue probably accounts for the overwhelming victory Whigs appeared to win in the legislative elections of 1835. But as Sellers has ably demonstrated, that majority should be regarded as a White rather than a Whig victory. It quickly dissipated when the legislature met in the fall of 1835.

56. Bergeron, *Antebellum Politics in Tennessee*, pp. 35–63, argues that the presidential question was the central issue in the 1835 campaign. But he also sharply disagrees with Cooper that slavery was the central issue in the presidential election in Tennessee. I have used the figures he gives on pp. 45–46 for my calculations.

57. Raleigh *Register*, February 23, 1836, quoted in Cooper, *Politics of Slavery*, p. 82; R. H. Alexander to Willie P. Mangum, Raleigh, November 29, 1834, in *The Mangum Papers*, II, pp. 224–26.

58. Williams, "Foundations," pp. 121–29; Kruman, *Parties and Politics*, pp. 3–28; Watson, *Jacksonian Politics and Community Conflict*, pp. 198–245 and passim; Jeffrey, "Internal Improvements," 111–56. See especially pp. 111–22 and Tables 2 and 3, pp. 152, 155.

59. Cooper, *Politics of Slavery*. Freehling, *Road to Disunion*, pp. 298–99, reaches an identical conclusion about the inapplicability of Cooper's paradigm to internal southern state politics.

CHAPTER 4

1. Clay to Francis Brooke, Washington, March 7, 1837, in *Works of Henry Clay*, V, p. 412.

2. According to Thomas Alexander's figures, 67 percent of the Democrats and 98 percent of the Whigs in the House of Representatives supported the final bill. *Sectional Stress*, p. 131, vote 50.

3. Webster to Hiram Ketchum, January 28, 1837, quoted in Nathans, *Webster*, p. 106.

4. While I stress the formative impact of the panic more than he, William G. Shade's brilliant essay, "Political Pluralism," provides systematic evidence for this point.

5. The analysis in this and the following paragraphs is drawn from: Temin, *Jacksonian Economy*; Shade, *Banks or No Banks*, pp. 40–59; Curtis, *Fox at Bay*, pp. 64–85; Sharp, *Jacksonians versus the Banks*, pp. 3–49; McFaul, *Politics of Jacksonian Finance*; Timberlake, "Specie Circular and Distribution"; and idem., "Specie Circular and Sales."

6. Temin, *Jacksonian Economy*, pp. 88–91, 124.

7. The Specie Circular is quoted in Shade, *Banks or No Banks*, p. 42; Van Buren is quoted in Curtis, *Fox at Bay*, p. 71.

8. Here I rely heavily on the analysis in Temin, *Jacksonian Economy*, pp. 136–47.

9. Ibid., Table 3.3, p. 71.

10. Ibid., Table 4.3, p. 124.

11. Ibid., Tables 3.2, 3.3, and 5.2, pp. 69–71, 159, and pp. 148–71.

12. Martin Van Buren to Andrew Jackson, April 24, 1837, quoted in Curtis, *Fox at Bay*, p. 71; see ibid., pp. 70–85, and Shade, *Banks or No Banks*, pp. 40–59.

13. William Henry Harrison to Nathaniel P. Tallmadge, February 22, 1840, quoted in Gunderson, *Log-Cabin Campaign*, p. 12.

14. Curtis, *Fox at Bay*, pp. 64–85 and passim.

15. *Messages and Papers of the Presidents*, III, pp. 324–46.

16. I am particularly indebted to the analysis in Thornton, *Politics and Power*, pp. 39–58, for this point.

17. Vroom quoted in Welter, *Mind of America*, p. 80.

18. *Democratic Review* (1838) and Edward D. Barber quoted in Welter, *Mind of America*, pp. 90, 185.

19. For partisan conflict on congressional votes from 1837 through most of the 1840s, see Alexander, *Sectional Stress*, and Silbey, *Shrine of Party*. Votes in the House during the special session are recorded in Alexander, pp. 24–30, 137–44.

20. Curtis, *Fox at Bay*, pp. 86–151; Friedman, *Conservative Democrats*; Sharp, *Jacksonians versus the Banks*, pp. 3–24; Cooper, *Politics of Slavery*, pp. 101–19; and Schlesinger, *Age of Jackson*, pp. 227–66.

21. For differences on social legislation and cultural perspective, see especially Ershkowitz and Shade, "Consensus or Conflict?"; Benson, *Concept of Jacksonian Democracy*; and Formisano, *Birth of Mass Political Parties*.

22. *American Review*, quoted in Welter, *Mind of America*, p. 15.

23. Ibid., p. 127.

24. Boritt, *Lincoln*.

25. Whig address and *American Review* quoted in Welter, *Mind of America*, pp. 18, 123.

26. *New York Tribune*, November 29, 1845.

27. Alexander, *Sectional Stress*, pp. 20–21, 24, 32.

28. For an explanation of the data used to construct these tables and for citation of the political science literature relevant to the impact of economic conditions on off-year elections, as well as additional tables, graphs, and analysis that document this fluctuating pattern in Whig fortunes, see my "The Election of 1840, Voter Mobilization, and the Emergence of the Second American Party System" in Holt, *Political Parties*, pp. 151–91.

29. Compare Tables 3.3 and 3.6 in Temin, *Jacksonian Economy*, pp. 71, 103, and see his analysis of cotton prices, pp. 152–54. For example, cotton prices in New Orleans were 12.5 percent lower in the fall of 1837 than they had been in the fall of 1836, but the general wholesale price index was down 18.5 percent.

30. Compare the cotton prices listed in Table 3.6 in Temin's book with the figures in Table 6 and with the figures on the Whigs' share of the popular vote and accompanying graphs in Holt, "The Election of 1840," pp. 172–80.

31. Thornton, *Politics and Power*, pp. 34–39. For the other states, see Cooper, *Politics of Slavery*, pp. 113–15; Cole, *The Whig Party in the South*, pp. 47–52; and Sellers, *Polk: Jacksonian*, p. 376.

32. Friedman, *Conservative Democrats*, pp. 31–39; Sharp, *Jacksonians versus the Banks*, pp. 215–38.

33. Friedman, *Conservative Democrats*, pp. 39–47; Van Deusen, *Weed*, p. 104.

34. See Table 5 in Holt, "The Election of 1840," pp. 182–85.

35. *Historical Statistics*, p. 1072.

36. See, for example, Gunderson, *Log-Cabin Campaign*; Chambers, "Election of 1840"; and McCormick, "New Perspectives." The presidential election of 1840 will be examined in Chapter 5.

37. Table 5 in Holt, "The Election of 1840," pp. 182–85.

38. For a statistical analysis that shows the hardening of partisan allegiance after 1837, see Shade, "Political Pluralism," pp. 88–93.

39. This argument is based on the theory of retrospective voting advanced in Fiorina,

Retrospective Voting, and in complementary work by other political scientists. I discuss that literature and its applicability to nineteenth-century elections in my essay "The Election of 1840."

40. Thurlow Weed to William Henry Seward, Albany, May 16, 1837, Seward MSS (RU). See also Weed to Seward, March 12, 19, 31, April 16, 18, October 19, 25, 1837, Seward MSS (RU). In addition, the account of New York politics in this and the following paragraphs is based on Van Deusen, *Weed,* pp. 93–119; id., *Seward,* pp. 43–76; Sharp, *Jacksonians versus the Banks,* pp. 297–305; Benson, *Concept of Jacksonian Democracy,* pp. 89–109; and Friedman, *Conservative Democrats,* pp. 39–46.

41. Christopher Morgan to Seward, March 1, 1838, Seward to Christopher Morgan, March 5, 1838 (draft), N. P. Tallmadge to Seward, March 4, 1838, Seward to N. P. Tallmadge, March 14, 1838, Thurlow Weed to Christopher Morgan, October 4, 1838, and Millard Fillmore to Seward, October 22, 1838, Seward MSS (RU).

42. Weed to Seward, December 2, 10, 1837, Day Otis Kellogg to Seward, October 8, 1838, Henry Raynor to Seward, October 14, 1838, and Fillmore to Seward, October 22, 1838, Seward MSS (RU).

43. This account of the battles over railroad and canal subsidies is based on my colleague Professor Charles W. McCurdy's brilliant forthcoming study of New York's Anti-Rent controversy.

44. After the October election, Whigs held forty-four seats in the house, Democrats possessed forty-eight, and the eight seats from Philadelphia County were disputed because of the closeness of the returns. An impasse ensued when the new legislature met in December, with each party claiming control of the house. Mobs milled in the streets, and to prevent violence, the governor called out the militia, which was armed with shotguns, earning for this episode the sobriquet of "the Buckshot War." Democrats eventually seated their disputed Philadelphia representatives and controlled the house, but had the Whigs prevailed, they would have had 52, not 44, seats in the 100-member chamber.

45. For Pennsylvania, I have relied on Snyder, *Jacksonian Heritage,* pp. 112–50; Sharp, *Jacksonians versus the Banks,* pp. 289–96 (Democratic legislative address of 1840 quoted on p. 294); and Mueller, *Whig Party in Pennsylvania,* pp. 43–66. The Whig legislative address of 1840 is quoted in Mueller, p. 63.

46. On New Jersey, see Levine, *New Jersey,* pp. 112–42. Sharp, *Jacksonians versus the Banks,* pp. 55–73, 114–16, 123–32, and 239–43, covers the battles in Mississippi, Alabama, Louisiana, Ohio, and Virginia. But for Ohio, see also Shade, *Banks or No Banks,* pp. 79–84, 102–03, and for Mississippi, see Lucas, "Political Alchemy." For Connecticut and New Hampshire I have used Morse, *Neglected Period,* pp. 300–09; McFaul, *Politics of Jacksonian Finance,* pp. 87–90; Niven, *Welles,* pp. 167–87; and Cole, *Jacksonian Democracy in New Hampshire,* pp. 185–96.

47. Murray, *Whig Party in Georgia,* pp. 67–95; Sellers, *Polk: Jacksonian,* pp. 321–77.

48. For Michigan, Indiana, and Illinois, I have relied on Shade, *Banks or No Banks,* pp. 53–54, 60–102; Roll, *Dick Thompson,* pp. 23–35; Goodrich, *Canals and American Economic Development,* p. 197; Boritt, *Lincoln,* pp. 8–62; Johannsen, *Douglas,* pp. 61–70.

49. Volz, "Party, State, and Nation," pp. 22–25. The Whig share of seats went from 59 percent in 1839 to 77 percent in 1840.

50. For the data on legislative voting and sharply different interpretations of the significance of state issues to Whig fortunes in North Carolina, see Jeffrey, "Internal Improvements"; id., "Party Alignment and Realignment"; and Kruman, *Parties and Politics,* pp. 3–28, 55–85, and passim.

51. Darling, *Political Changes,* pp. 202–43.

52. Studies that identify the Whig and Democratic electorates are too numerous to be listed. The books previously cited in this chapter by Sharp, Thornton, Donald Cole, and William G. Shade, as well as Shade's "Political Pluralism," support these generalizations. See also Oakes, *Slavery and Freedom,* pp. 107–13; two studies by Harry L. Watson: *Jacksonian Politics and Community Conflict* and *Liberty and Power;* Johnson, *Shopkeeper's Millennium;* Howe, "Evangelical Movement"; and Sellers, *Market Revolution.* Finally, for a brilliant analysis of how the economic, social, and religious changes transforming the United States between 1815 and 1850 produced cleavages in the electorate that explain the Democratic and Whig voting bases, see Hays, "Politics and Society."

53. The crucial point that Democrats were less interested in the economic consequences of economic policies than in the maintenance of equal rights is made by Welter, *Mind of America*, p. 90.

54. Again, I have discussed the results of that research and its applicability to these elections in my "The Election of 1840." For a challenge to the applicability of this political science research to nineteenth-century elections, see Formisano, "The New Political History." Formisano's article is a forceful critique of my essay, and it requires a thorough response that I shall not attempt here. Unlike Formisano, I remain convinced that the contemporary research I have cited is relevant to the late 1830s.

55. Memphis *Enquirer*, August 23, 1839, quoted in Sellers, *Polk: Jacksonian*, p. 374. See the same page for Sellers' analysis. See also Bergeron, *Antebellum Politics in Tennessee*, pp. 50–52.

56. Sharp, *Jacksonians versus the Banks*, pp. 334–42.

57. Mills Thornton provides evidence for economic differences between Whig and Democratic voters within Alabama's counties in his *Politics and Power*, pp. 41–42. Harry L. Watson's superb study of party formation in Cumberland County, North Carolina, also demonstrates that the Whig and Democratic parties attracted voters with different levels of involvement in, and different attitudes toward, the market economy and that between 1836 and 1840 the Whig vote grew in wealthier, more commercially oriented sections of the county, while the Democrats recruited in the remote areas hostile to the urban commercial sector. Watson, *Jacksonian Politics and Community Conflict*, pp. 246–81 and passim.

58. See also the graphs and tables in Holt, "The Election of 1840," pp. 172–80.

CHAPTER 5

1. The first statement is attributed to Clay by Henry Wise in his memoirs, *Seven Decades of the Union*, and is quoted in Gunderson, *Log-Cabin Campaign*, p. 68. The second was attributed to Clay by South Carolina Senator William C. Preston and is quoted in Van Deusen, *Clay*, p. 318.

2. Murray, *Whig Party in Georgia*, p. 94. See also Gunderson, *Log-Cabin Campaign*, pp. 28, 73–74, 96, 115, and passim, and Schlesinger, *Age of Jackson*, pp. 267–305. Howe, *Political Culture*, pp. 1–22 and passim, persuasively rebuts the canard that Whigs were unprincipled opportunists.

3. Seward to Weed, November 17, 1836, quoted in Gunderson, *Log-Cabin Campaign*, p. 41; Weed to Seward, April 18, 1837, Seward MSS. For able summaries of the struggle for the nomination, see Gunderson, *Log-Cabin Campaign*, pp. 41–66; Nathans, *Webster*, pp. 104–29; Van Deusen, *Clay*, pp. 320–36; id., *Weed*, pp. 109–11.

4. Webster quoted in Nathans, *Webster*, p. 108; *The Mangum Papers*, II, p. 513, note. Nathans, *Webster*, pp. 104–29, presents the most perceptive analysis of Webster's attempt for the nomination.

5. Nathans, *Webster*, pp. 114–18; Gunderson, *Log-Cabin Campaign*, p. 42.

6. Clay to the New York Committee, August 6, 1837, in *Works of Henry Clay*, V, pp. 415–17; William Henry Harrison to William Ayres, August 22, 1838, quoted in Gunderson, *Log-Cabin Campaign*, p. 50. On Clay's fears, see Nathans, *Webster*, pp. 117–18, and Van Deusen, *Clay*, p. 322. For evidence that those fears were well grounded, see Hamilton C. Jones to Willie P. Mangum, December 22, 1837, in *The Mangum Papers*, II, pp. 513–14.

7. Clay to Brooke, April 14, 1838, in *Works of Henry Clay*, V, pp. 426–27.

8. Henry Clay to Willie P. Mangum, Washington, May 31, 1838, in *The Mangum Papers*, II, pp. 525–26; Nathans, *Webster*, pp. 116–24; Harrison Gray Otis to Clay, Boston, January 11, 1839, in *Works of Henry Clay*, V, pp. 437–38. See also Dalzell, *Webster*, pp. 65–69.

9. Clay to George D. Prentice, August 14, 1837, in *Works of Henry Clay*, V, p. 418; Crittenden to Willie P. Mangum, October 11, 1837, and Clay to Mangum, November 17, 1837, in *The Mangum Papers*, II, pp. 511–13.

10. Clay to Brooke, Washington, April 14, 1838, in *Works of Henry Clay*, V, pp. 426–27; Clay to Mangum, May 31, 1838, in *The Mangum Papers*, II, pp. 525–26.

11. Hamilton C. Jones to Mangum, December 22, 1837, in *The Mangum Papers*, II, pp. 513–14. See also William A. Graham to Mangum, October 11, 1839, ibid., III, pp. 18–20; Cole, *Whig Party in the South*, pp. 53–58; and Cooper, *Politics of Slavery*, pp. 119–26.

12. William C. Preston to Willie P. Mangum, October 4, 1837, in *The Mangum Papers*, II, pp. 508–10.

13. Clay to Francis Brooke, October 9, 1838, in *Works of Henry Clay*, V, pp. 428–29; Clay to Beverley Tucker, October 10, 1839, in Tyler, *Letters . . . of the Tylers*, I, pp. 601–02; Curtis, *Fox at Bay*, pp. 130–31; Van Deusen, *Clay*, p. 320. See also the sections of Cole and Cooper cited in note 11.

14. John C. Calhoun to Duff Green, July 27, 1837, to James Edward Calhoun, September 7, 1837, and to Anna Maria Calhoun, September 8, 1837, in Jameson, "Correspondence of Calhoun," pp. 374–79. See also William C. Preston to Willie P. Mangum, October 4, 1837, April 7, 1838, in *The Mangum Papers*, II, pp. 508–10, 519–20. That Calhoun and other South Carolinians, who were committed to the perpetuation of slavery, feared that white Southerners from other states were eager to abandon slavery if the proportions of blacks in their populations could be reduced is a central theme of Freehling, *Road to Disunion*.

15. See the very perceptive analysis of Calhoun in Cooper, *Politics of Slavery*, pp. 103–18.

16. John C. Calhoun to James Edward Calhoun, December 24, 1837, January 8, 1838, and to Anna Maria Calhoun, December 24, 1837, in Jameson, "Correspondence of Calhoun," pp. 386–88; Curtis, *Fox at Bay*, pp. 118–19; Van Deusen, *Clay*, pp. 314–15.

17. Curtis, *Fox at Bay*, pp. 118–24; Van Deusen, *Clay*, pp. 309–19; Cooper, *Politics of Slavery*, pp. 121–24. Able accounts of this debate can also be found in Peterson, *Great Triumvirate*, pp. 274–77, and Remini, *Henry Clay*, pp. 507–15.

18. Clay to Francis Brooke, January 13, 1838, in *Works of Henry Clay*, V, pp. 423–34.

19. Clay to Peter B. Porter, January 10, 26, 1838, quoted in Van Deusen, *Clay*, p. 317.

20. Clay to Mangum, May 31, 1838, loc. cit.; for Van Buren's desire to finesse the sectionally divisive Texas question, see Curtis, *Fox at Bay*, pp. 152–69.

21. Clay to Mangum, May 31, 1838, in *The Mangum Papers*, II, pp. 525–26.

22. Clay to the New York Committee, August 6, 1837, in *Works of Henry Clay*, V, pp. 416–17; Nathans, *Webster*, pp. 118–29; Van Deusen, *Clay*, pp. 320–34; Gunderson, *Log-Cabin Campaign*, pp. 43–47; Van Deusen, *Weed*, pp. 109–10; Snyder, *Jacksonian Heritage*, pp. 141–42.

23. I have relied for the details of this border conflict on Curtis, *Fox at Bay*, pp. 170–88, and Elliott, *Scott*, pp. 332–66.

24. Van Deusen, *Clay*, p. 321; Clay to Francis Brooke, January 13, 1838, in *Works of Henry Clay*, V, pp. 423–24.

25. Nathans, *Webster*, pp. 118–24.

26. Boston *Atlas*, September 14, 15, 1838, quoted in ibid., pp. 123–24.

27. Clay to Francis Brooke, October 9, November 3, 1838, and Harrison Gray Otis to Clay, December 24, 1838, in *Works of Henry Clay*, V, pp. 428–31, 433–34; Nathans, *Webster*, pp. 123–24.

28. Charles B. Penrose to Nicholas Biddle, February 29, March 1?, 1839, quoted in Carroll, *Origins of the Whig Party*, p. 161.

29. Mueller, *Whig Party in Pennsylvania*, pp. 56–58; Snyder, *Jacksonian Heritage*, p. 141.

30. Clay to Francis Brooke, November 3, 1838, in *Works of Henry Clay*, V, pp. 429–31.

31. Clay to Brooke, December 20, 26, 1838, January 7, 18, 28, 1839, ibid., pp. 432–40; Van Deusen, *Clay*, pp. 325–27.

32. Fillmore to Weed, December 26, 1838, quoted in Gunderson, *Log-Cabin Campaign*, p. 44; for the New York maneuvers, see ibid., pp. 44–47; see also Rayback, *Fillmore*, pp. 97–110.

33. Clay to Brooke, December 20, 1838, in *Works of Henry Clay*, V, pp. 432–33.

34. Clay to Brooke, December 26, 1838, ibid., pp. 434–36.

35. Simms, *Rise of the Whigs*, pp. 131–34; Tyler, *Letters of the Tylers*, I, pp. 587–93; Seager, *And Tyler Too*, pp. 127–32.

36. For Clay's speech and the southern reaction, see Van Deusen, *Clay*, pp. 317–19; Cooper, *Politics of Slavery*, pp. 122–25.

37. John C. Spencer to William Henry Seward, Albany, August 18, 1839, Seward MSS (RU). For New York abolitionist opposition to Clay, see Seth M. Gates to Seward, NYC, November 23, 1839, ibid.

38. Weed to Seward, August 16, 1839 (quotations), Seward MSS (RU); Van Deusen, *Clay*, pp. 327–29; Gunderson, *Log-Cabin Campaign*, pp. 46–47.

39. Harrison to Giddings, December 15, 1838, and Charles Todd to Seward, February 8, 1839, quoted in Gunderson, *Log-Cabin Campaign*, pp. 49, 51.

40. Ibid., p. 56; Charles B. Penrose to Seward, November 20, 1839, Seward MSS (RU).

41. M. Bradley to Weed, August 29, 1839, quoted in Gunderson, *Log-Cabin Campaign*, p. 52; for the campaign by Weed on Scott's behalf, see pp. 51–56.

42. Weed to Seward, Harrisburg, December 4, 1839, Seward MSS. Gunderson, citing Weed's autobiography, says that the figures were twenty for Scott, ten for Clay, and two for Harrison. I have assumed that Weed misremembered since he referred to thirty Scott men in the letter cited above and since New York had forty-two delegates at the convention.

43. For the convention itself, I have relied on the following: Gunderson, *Log-Cabin Campaign*, pp. 57–66 (Clay is quoted on p. 68); Van Deusen, *Clay*, pp. 331–33; Seager, *And Tyler Too*, pp. 132–35; Bain and Parrish, *Convention Decisions*, pp. 24–27. The proceedings of the convention are also printed in the appendix of Van Deusen, "The Whig Party," pp. 401–10.

44. See Table 32 in Temin, *Jacksonian Economy*, p. 69.

45. Murray, *Whig Party in Georgia*, pp. 89–91.

46. On Tennessee, see Sellers, *Polk: Jacksonian*, pp. 370–77; Parks, *Bell*, pp. 159–69; and Atkins, " 'A Combat for Liberty,' " pp. 162–63. I am deeply indebted to Professor Atkins for sending me a copy of his dissertation.

47. On Southard's position, see Winfield Scott to Seward, Washington, December 9, 1839, Seward MSS (RU); and Birkner, *Southard*, pp. 182–85.

48. For the vice presidential nomination, see especially Seager, *And Tyler Too*, pp. 134–35. Hone's diary entry for August 17, 1841, is quoted on p. 435.

49. C. Davis to Weed, November 13, 1839, and Burnet's speech, quoted in Gunderson, *Log-Cabin Campaign*, pp. 65–66.

50. Harrisburg *Keystone*, December 11, 1839; M. Bradley to Weed, August 29, 1839; and the Whig ditty, all quoted in ibid., pp. 59–66, 62, and 115.

51. Gunderson, *Log-Cabin Campaign*, provides the fullest description of the campaign, and unless noted otherwise, I have taken my information from him. There seems no point in providing a specific page citation for every slogan and ditty quoted here.

52. Baltimore *Republican*, December 11, 1839, quoted in ibid., p. 74.

53. Washington *National Intelligencer*, January 14, 1840, and *Northwestern Gazette and Galena Advertiser*, January 17, 1840, quoted in ibid., p. 75.

54. Ibid., pp. 101–05.

55. The *Log Cabin* reprinting the *Evening Journal*, May 23, 1840, quoted in ibid., pp. 110–11.

56. Ibid., pp. 149, 194, 211.

57. For Lincoln's campaign themes see Boritt, *Lincoln*, pp. 63–78; Prentiss and the Pennsylvania Whig banner are quoted in Gunderson, *Log-Cabin Campaign*, pp. 189–91. Badger's speech is quoted and described in Thomas E. Jeffrey, "State Parties and National Politics: North Carolina and the Second American Party System, 1815–1861" (draft manuscript), chapter IV, pp. 17, 20, and Chapter V, p. 16.

Throughout his book, Gunderson argues that the major Whig effort was to avoid issues, not to make them, but other historians have recognized more accurately that there were real issues involved in the campaign. See, for example, Howe, *Political Culture*, pp. 7–8, 90, 142, and Brock, *Political Conscience*, pp. 3–70, especially 3–5.

58. For Webster during the campaign, see Nathans, *Webster*, pp. 130–47; Van Deusen, *Clay*, pp. 335–36.

59. See Chapter 4.

60. *Log Cabin*, September 5, 1840, quoted in Gunderson, *Log-Cabin Campaign*, p. 132. On Whig appeal to evangelical Protestants, see especially Carwardine, "Evangelicals." Carwardine argues, p. 49, "that for pious evangelicals the election of 1840 was not a vacuous campaign devoid of issues . . . but rather . . . had a profound religious significance."

61. On the presence of women at Whig rallies, see Varon, "Tippecanoe and the Ladies, Too."

62. *Crisis of the Country*, quoted in Welter, *Mind of America*, p. 192.

63. New York Whig Address for 1840 and Clay, quoted in ibid., pp. 31, 210; Raleigh *Register*, October 9, 1840, quoted in Kruman, *Parties and Politics*, p. 3.

64. Again, the best account of the presidential campaign in the South is Cooper, *Politics of Slavery*, pp. 126–48. The Richmond *Whig*, March 24, 1840, is quoted on p. 137. On the anti-abolitionist tone of both parties' campaigns in 1840, see Volpe, "The Anti-Abolitionist Campaign of 1840."

65. New Orleans *Bee*, June 30, 1840, and Richmond *Whig*, March 6, 1840, quoted in Cooper, *Politics of Slavery*, p. 134. For more on Poinsett's militia scheme and its deleterious impact on the Democratic campaign, see Curtis, *Fox at Bay*, pp. 199–202, and Gunderson, *Log-Cabin Campaign*, pp. 94–95, 228–29.

66. Harrison's speech at Fort Meigs is quoted in Welter, *Mind of America*, p. 195; the speech at Dayton is quoted in Chambers, "Election of 1840," p. 678. Harrison's campaign efforts are fully, if hostilely, described in Gunderson, *Log-Cabin Campaign*, pp. 161–72. Failing to recognize the centrality of republican values, Gunderson unduly minimizes the importance of Harrison's pledges to reduce the power of the presidency and to protect the people's liberty.

67. The Democratic campaign is described in Gunderson, *Log-Cabin Campaign*, pp. 219–47. The Alabama Democrat's remarks are in Samuel Forwood to William S. Forwood, October 5, 1840, quoted in Thornton, *Politics and Power*, p. 48.

68. Richmond *Enquirer*, July 24, 1840, quoted in Cooper, *Politics of Slavery*, p. 140; *Washington Globe*, September 25, 1840, and Democratic slogan quoted in Gunderson, *Log-Cabin Campaign*, pp. 228–29.

69. Modern political scientists have coined the phrase "retrospective voting" to describe how voters incorporate evaluations of past party records in office into the decisions they make at the polls. See Fiorina, *Retrospective Voting*, pp. 83, 197, and passim.

An obvious question raised by my insistence on the centrality of issue-oriented voting is why Whigs continued to run a hoopla campaign after the economy had turned sour. One reason, clearly, is that they were determined to capture the presidency and saw how effective hoopla was in arousing voters. Another may be that they did not know what we now do—that voters' attachment had hardened during the congressional and state elections of the late 1830s and early 1840. What they did know was that in 1836 there had been very little relationship between how people voted for president and how they voted for other offices that year and in 1835. They may have (wrongly) believed, that is, that they still had to run a different kind of campaign for president than for their congressional and gubernatorial candidates.

70. In addition to Tables 5, 6, and 7 in this study, see the additional tables and the graphs in Holt, "The Election of 1840."

71. *Historical Statistics*, p. 1072.

72. See Table 3 in Holt, "The Election of 1840," p. 176.

73. Pennsylvania's October congressional returns are incomplete, and they are not included in this calculation.

74. Gatell, "Money and Party"; Rich, " 'A Wilderness of Whigs' "; Holt, *Forging a Majority*, p. 76; Dalzell, *Webster*, p. 59. This proclivity of the rich to support the Whigs did not hold everywhere, however. See Folsom, "Politics of Elites."

75. Documentation for the general pattern was cited earlier, but for Louisiana see McCrary, *The Louisiana Experiment*, pp. 19–65.

76. Volz, "Party, State, and Nation," pp. 13–17. See especially notes 26, 28, and 29 for the statistical correlations.

77. On North Carolina, see Kruman, *Parties and Politics*, pp. 3–28, and Watson, *Jacksonian Politics and Community Conflict*; on Virginia, see Sharp, *Jacksonians versus the Banks*, pp. 247–73, and Shade, *Democratizing the Old Dominion*; on Tennessee, see Sellers, *Polk: Jacksonian*, pp. 374–75. For the South in general, see the maps in Cole, *Whig Party in the South*.

78. Goodman, *Christian Republic*; Cole, *Jacksonian Democracy in New Hampshire*, pp. 136–59; Benson, *Concept of Jacksonian Democracy*, pp. 278–87.

79. The quotation is taken from Brock, *Political Conscience*, p. 42. The now-notorious "ethnocultural" interpretation of Jacksonian voting behavior is elaborated in Benson, *Concept of Jacksonian Democracy*; Formisano, *Birth of Mass Political Parties*; Kleppner, *Third Electoral*

System, pp. 59–74; and Shade, "Pennsylvania Politics." See also the perceptive discussion of Whigs' evangelical religious orientation in Johnson, *A Shopkeepers' Millennium*. For the southern antagonism to the aggressive efforts of evangelical denominations to proselytize and to Christianize society at large, see Wyatt-Brown, "Antimission Movement." For general discussions of the impact of religious and ethnocultural influences on political behavior, finally, see Kelley, *Cultural Pattern*, and Carwardine, *Evangelicals and Politics*.

80. For the Midwest, see Formisano, *Birth of Mass Political Parties*; Kleppner, *Third Electoral System*, pp. 59–74; Shade, *Banks or No Banks*, pp. 158–67; Fox, "Politicians, Issues and Voter Preference"; and Flinn, "Continuity and Change," 524–27.

81. New York Whig Legislative Address of 1844, quoted in Welter, *Mind of America*, p. 18. This analysis rests heavily on Howe, *Political Culture*, pp. 21–42 and passim. For how this emerging middle-class mentality reflected changing economic and social relations among classes in developing industrial communities, see Johnson, *A Shopkeeper's Millennium*.

82. Wiley P. Harris to John F. H. Claiborne, August 30, 1855, Claiborne MSS (MDAH). I have developed this theory of the dynamics of party loyalty and interparty interaction at greater length in Holt, *Political Crisis*, pp. 1–38 and passim.

83. R. G. Lee to Nathaniel P. Banks, Boston, September 3, 1846, Banks MSS (Ill.SHL). For evidence on betting, see, for example, G. H. Steele to R. W. Thompson, Indianapolis, January 5, 1849, Thompson MSS (Ind.SL).

84. Felix K. Zollicoffer to William B. Campbell, July 14, 1851, CFP.

85. Alexander H. Stephens to James Thomas, July 16, 1844, in Phillips, "Correspondence of Toombs, Stephens, and Cobb," pp. 59–60; L. Lisle Smith to Elihu B. Washburne, Chicago, February 19, 1849, Washburne MSS (LC).

86. "Necessity of Party—the Press—the Locofoco Platform," *American Review*, II (July 1848), 69; Preston King to Francis P. Blair, November 21, 1855, Blair-Lee MSS (Princeton University Library).

CHAPTER 6

1. John Van Hook, Jr., to Willie P. Mangum, February 1, 1841, in *The Mangum Papers*, III, pp. 103–04.

2. The figures on party strength are taken from Silbey, *Shrine of Party*, p. 238, note 3. There were also six Independent Whigs in the House; eventually they supported President John Tyler rather than the Whig majority. There was an odd number of men in the Senate because Tennessee had only one senator in the special session.

3. I take this figure from Brock, *Political Conscience*, p. 76. All of these offices, of course, were not filled directly by the president; many subordinate positions in customs houses, post offices, navy yards, and so on were filled by men whom the president and his cabinet appointed.

4. Whig leaders in 1841 intuitively sensed what modern research on voter realignments has demonstrated. A surge of dissatisfied voters can eject one party from power and give dominant control of government to its opponent. But for the new governing party, in this case the Whigs, to confirm the allegiance of those new supporters and retain power, its officeholders must pass legislation that alleviates the dissatisfactions that turned voters against the old governing party in the first place. Clubb, Flanigan, and Zingale, *Partisan Realignment*, pp. 11–45 and passim.

5. John J. Crittenden to Robert P. Letcher, January 30, 1841, in Coleman, *Crittenden*, I, pp. 140–42.

6. John C. Calhoun to Andrew Pickens Calhoun, November 22, 1840, in Jameson, "Correspondence of Calhoun," p. 467. For the results in state legislative elections, see Table 6.

7. Poage, *Clay*, pp. 1–122; Van Deusen, *Clay*, pp. 336–57; Chitwood, *Tyler*; Seager, *And Tyler Too*, pp. 141–288; Dalzell, *Webster*, pp. 30–58; Nathans, *Webster*, pp. 143–214. These valuable studies are often biographical and it would be unfair to fault them for focusing on personality, but for a welcome corrective that stresses the systemic flaws in the Whig conception of congressional government, rather than personal rivalries, as the reason for party failure, see Brock, *Political Conscience*, pp. 71–113.

8. Sundquist, *Dynamics*, pp. 32, 304.

9. These maneuvers are treated in considerable detail in Poage, *Clay*, pp. 14–32, and

Nathans, *Webster*, pp. 148–60. Mangum to William A. Graham, March 27, 1841, in *The Mangum Papers*, III, pp. 128–29. See also Henry Clay to Francis Brooke, December 8, 1840, January 7, 1841, Peter B. Porter to Clay, January 28, February 20, 1841, and Clay to William Henry Harrison, March 15, 1841, in *The Works of Henry Clay*, V, pp. 446–52. Though Curtis' appointment was a Webster victory, Webster in fact abstained from the cabinet vote on the post.

10. The best discussions of Webster's motives are in Nathans, *Webster*, pp. 149–51, and Dalzell, *Webster*, pp. 30–38.

11. Crittenden to Robert P. Letcher, January 30, 1841, loc. cit. See also Kirwan, *Crittenden*, pp. 147–48; Poage, *Clay*, pp. 21–32; Van Deusen, *Clay*, p. 39; Nathans, *Webster*, pp. 154–58.

12. Fillmore to Weed, February 6, 1841, quoted in Brock, *Political Conscience*, p. 81.

13. Nathans, *Webster*, pp. 154–58.

14. Ibid.; the most detailed account of the exchange between Clay and Harrison is in Poage, *Clay*, pp. 28–32.

15. My account of the growing rift between Tyler and Congress and the course of legislation in 1841 and 1842 is based on the detailed accounts in the works listed in note 7. I shall not burden the reader with continuous citations to specific pages in those books, and hereafter will only document direct quotations and material based on other sources.

16. See, for example, Willie P. Mangum to Duncan Cameron, June 26, 1841, Priestly H. Mangum to William A. Graham, July 7, 1841, and Willie P. Mangum to C. L. Hinton, August 13, 1841, in *The Mangum Papers*, III, pp. 181–87, 191–92, 215–16. In his splendid biography of Henry Wise, Craig Simpson demonstrates that Wise was not as close ideologically or personally to Tyler as were other members of the so-called Virginia Cabal. Personal resentment of Clay apparently explained his support for Tyler as much as his views on policy. Simpson, *A Good Southerner*, pp. 45–60.

17. *Messages and Papers of the Presidents*, IV, pp. 40–51.

18. John C. Calhoun to Thomas G. Clemson, July 11, 1841, in Jameson, "Correspondence of Calhoun," pp. 480–81; Willie P. Mangum to William A. Graham, July 10, 11, 1841, in *The Mangum Papers*, III, pp. 193–95.

19. Stephenson, *History of the Public Lands*, pp. 54–57.

20. Brock, *Political Conscience*, pp. 91–93, disagrees with virtually every other account of the Ewing plan by asserting that it specifically prohibited the Bank from discounting promissory notes. This power would become a major source of contention between Tyler and the congressional Whigs, and they included it in their own bill.

21. Henry Clay to Robert P. Letcher, June 11, 1841, in Coleman, *Crittenden*, I, pp. 156–57; Nathans, *Webster*, p. 166, note 16; Mordecai N. Noah to Mangum, June 13, 1841, in *The Mangum Papers*, III, pp. 166–67.

22. Willie P. Mangum to Duncan Cameron, June 26, 1841, in *The Mangum Papers*, III, pp. 181–87. This remarkably detailed letter provides a full account of Whig consideration of the bank bill in the caucus.

23. John C. Calhoun to Thomas G. Clemson, July 11, 1841, in Jameson, "The Correspondence of Calhoun," pp. 480–81. Chitwood, *Tyler*, pp. 209–51; Seager, *And Tyler Too*, pp. 151–71; Poage, *Clay*, pp. 37–106; Nathans, *Webster*, pp. 162–80.

24. Mangum to Duncan Cameron, June 26, 1841, loc. cit.

25. The Compromise Tariff of 1833 provided that duties in excess of 20 percent should be reduced by one-tenth of that excess annually until January 1, 1840. Then on January 1, 1842, half of the remaining excess would be cut, and on July 1, 1842, the remaining excess would be eliminated. The great bulk of the reduction, in short, was delayed until 1842.

26. *Congressional Globe*, 27th Cong., 1st Sess., p. 53; Calhoun to Thomas G. Clemson, July 11, 1841, loc. cit.

27. Stephenson, *History of the Public Lands*, p. 30. The states that had been forced to suspend payment on their debt and would thus benefit from distribution included Pennsylvania, Maryland, Ohio, Indiana, Illinois, Michigan, Arkansas, and Louisiana. In 1841, Ohio, Indiana, Michigan, and Louisiana had Whig governors who could be helped politically by distribution. Wellington, *Political and Sectional*, p. 75.

28. Mangum to Duncan Cameron, June 26, 1841, loc. cit.

29. Clay to R. P. Letcher, June 11, 1841, in Coleman, *Crittenden*, I, pp. 156–57; Clay to Francis Brooke, July 4, 1841, in *Works of Henry Clay*, V, pp. 454; Mangum to Duncan Cameron, June 26, 1841, loc. cit.

30. All quotations come from Priestley H. Mangum to William A. Graham, July 7, 1841, in *The Mangum Papers*, III, pp. 191–92. For more on fear of a veto, see Willie P. Mangum to C. L. Hinton, August 13, 1841, ibid., pp. 215–16.

31. The best analysis of the cabinet reaction to the conflict over the bank bill is Nathans, *Webster*, pp. 161–80. See also Kirwan, *Crittenden*, pp. 147–55; and Parks, *Bell*, pp. 181–88.

32. Nathans, *Webster*, pp. 161–80; Dalzell, *Webster*, pp. 37–40.

33. Webster to Hiram Ketchum, July 16, 17, 1841, quoted in Nathans, *Webster*, p. 155, and Dalzell, *Webster*, p. 37.

34. Willie P. Mangum to Duncan Cameron, June 26, 1842, and to William A. Graham, July 10, 11, 1841, loc. cit.; John C. Calhoun to Andrew Pickens Calhoun, July 26, 1841, in Jameson, "Correspondence of Calhoun," pp. 482–83; Poage, *Clay*, pp. 49–66.

35. Clay quoted in Poage, *Clay*, p. 52; Mangum to Graham, July 10, 1841, loc. cit.; Brock, *Political Conscience*, pp. 87–97.

36. John C. Calhoun to James H. Hammond, August 1, 1841, in Jameson, "Correspondence of Calhoun," pp. 483–85; Poage, *Clay*, pp. 63–66.

37. Alexander, *Sectional Stress*, p. 157, vote 65.

38. Nathans, *Webster*, pp. 171–73; Poage, *Clay*, pp. 67–78; John C. Calhoun to Thomas G. Clemson, July 23, 1841, and to Andrew Pickens Calhoun, July 26, 1841, in Jameson, "Correspondence of Calhoun," pp. 482–83; Willie P. Mangum to C. L. Hinton, August 13, 1841, in *The Mangum Papers*, III, pp. 215–16.

39. Crittenden to Clay, August 16, 1841, in Coleman, *Crittenden*, I, pp. 159–60.

40. Nathans, *Webster*, pp. 173–77; Poage, *Clay*, pp. 79–91; Chitwood, *Tyler*, pp. 237–51.

41. Botts' "coffee-house letter" is reprinted in Tyler, *Letters . . . of the Tylers*, II, p. 112, note 1.

42. Reverdy Johnson to Willie P. Mangum, August 27 and 29, 1841, James D. Ogden to Henry Clay, August 30, 1841, in *The Mangum Papers*, III, pp. 222–29.

43. R. P. Letcher to Crittenden, September 3, 1841, in Coleman, *Crittenden*, I, pp. 160–62.

44. Mordecai M. Noah to David Lambert, July 18, 1841, in *The Mangum Papers*, III, pp. 200–02. In his letter of August 30 to Clay, James D. Ogden explicitly called the national bank "the keystone of the party's arch."

45. In July 1842, a North Carolina Whig warned both Mangum and Graham that the Bankruptcy Act was so "odious" that "it is doing more to allay the zeal of Whigs than every thing else." J. H. Long to Mangum and Graham, July 7, 1842, in *The Mangum Papers*, III, p. 366; see ibid., p. 266, note 11; and Alexander, *Sectional Stress*, p. 167, vote 14.

46. Rayback, *Fillmore*, pp. 122–25.

47. The history of land policy, as well as detailed accounts of the framing of the Land Act of 1841, can be found in Wellington, *Political and Sectional*, passim, and Stephenson, *History of the Public Lands*, pp. 19–65. See also Robbins, *Our Landed Heritage*, pp. 72–91.

48. In 1838 and 1840, for example, whereas 60 percent of the Whigs in the House had voted against preemption, while about 90 percent of the Democrats had favored it each time, about four-fifths of Whig congressmen from midwestern and southwestern states had voted in favor of it. Alexander, *Sectional Stress*, p. 139, vote 63, and p. 151, vote 37.

49. The Land Act of 1841 can be found in *Statutes at Large*, V, pp. 453–58. The studies by Wellington, Stephenson, and Robbins cited in note 47 make it clear that previous proposals for the actual cession of public land to western states had come from Democrats, especially John C. Calhoun.

50. Poage, *Clay*, pp. 92–106.

51. The quotations are listed in Chitwood, *Tyler*, p. 318; see also ibid., pp. 249–51.

52. *Messages and Papers of the Presidents*, IV, pp. 68–72.

53. Nathans, *Webster*, pp. 181–84; Chitwood, *Tyler*, pp. 269–89.

54. Possibly apocryphal, this quotation is based on a letter written by Tyler's son in 1883. It is quoted, among other places, in Chitwood, *Tyler*, p. 273.

55. In addition to Nathans, Chitwood, and Poage, see Dalzell, *Webster*, pp. 37–55, for an admirable discussion of Webster's motives for remaining in the cabinet and his actions while in it.

56. Manuscript diary of Phillip R. Fendall, September 23, 1841, quoted in Nathans, *Webster*, p. 182; Van Deusen, *Weed*, pp. 118–24; id., *Greeley*, pp. 84–87.

57. For factionalism in Massachusetts, see Dalzell, *Webster*, pp. 61–80; in Pennsylvania, see Mueller, *Whig Party in Pennsylvania*, pp. 66–69, 83–84; Snyder, *Jacksonian Heritage*, pp. 151–52, and Hall, *Politics of Justice*, pp. 48–51. In Virginia the split was between state rights men like Wise, Gilmer, and Upshur and Clay supporters like Congressman John Minor Botts of Richmond; on Michigan, see Streeter, *Political Parties in Michigan*, pp. 37–42; on Indiana, see Hall, *Politics of Justice*, pp. 52–54; on Ohio, see Holt, "Party Politics in Ohio," pp. 54–61; on Maryland, see Willie P. Mangum to Duncan Cameron, June 26, 1841, loc. cit.

58. Murray, *Whig Party in Georgia*, pp. 96–99; Sharp, *Jacksonians versus the Banks*, pp. 73–79; Snyder, *Jacksonian Heritage*, pp. 152–59; Van Deusen, *Weed*, pp. 114–25; Shade, *Banks or No Banks*, pp. 98–100; Holt, "Party Politics in Ohio," pp. 60–61.

59. James K. Polk to John C. Calhoun, February 23, 1842, in Jameson, "The Correspondence of Calhoun," pp. 884–85. The best analysis of the Tennessee campaign is Sellers, *Polk: Jacksonian*, pp. 431–44.

60. Nicholas Carroll to Willie P. Mangum, October 28, 1841, in *The Mangum Papers*, III, pp. 247–50; Clay to Francis Brooke, October 28, 1841, in *Works of Henry Clay*, V, p. 455.

61. Calhoun to Thomas G. Clemson, Washington, December 31, 1841, in Jameson, "Correspondence of Calhoun," pp. 500–01; David Lambert to Willie P. Mangum, October 14, 1841, and Willis Hall to Mangum, January 31, 1842, in *The Mangum Papers*, III, pp. 244–46, 282–83.

62. Hall to Mangum, January 31, 1842; see also Reverdy Johnson to Mangum, August 27, 1841, in *The Mangum Papers*, III, p. 222.

63. Seager asserts that the Senate rejected more of Tyler's appointees than those of any other president in American history. *And Tyler Too*, p. 227.

64. Chitwood, *Tyler*, pp. 291–93; Nathans, *Webster*, pp. 185–89.

65. *Messages and Papers of the Presidents*, IV, pp. 74–89.

66. See messages of March 8 and March 25, 1842, ibid., pp. 102–03, 106–11.

67. Stephenson, *History of the Public Lands*, pp. 55, 73–87; Seager, *And Tyler Too*, pp. 165–68; Henry Clay to John J. Crittenden, Ashland, June 3, July 16, 1842, in Coleman, *Crittenden*, I, pp. 180–81, 188–89.

68. Rayback, *Fillmore*, pp. 127–32.

69. Crittenden to R. P. Letcher, June 23, 1842, Crittenden to Clay, July 2, 1842, and Clay to Crittenden, July 16, 1842, in Coleman, *Life of Crittenden*, I, pp. 183–86, 188–89; Clay to Willie P. Mangum, July 11, 1842, in *The Mangum Papers*, III, pp. 367–68.

70. Calhoun to Thomas G. Clemson, August 22, 1842, in Jameson, "Correspondence of Calhoun," pp. 514–15; Crittenden to Clay, August 12, 1842, in Coleman, *Life of Crittenden*, I, pp. 192–93; and Willie P. Mangum to Henry Clay, June 15, 1842, to Priestley H. Mangum, August 10, 1842, and to Charity A. Mangum, August 14, 1842, in *The Mangum Papers*, III, pp. 358–60, 376–80. See also the perceptive analysis of the shifting voting blocs on the different tariff bills in Brock, *Political Conscience*, pp. 102–06.

71. See the able discussion of the protective features of the 1842 Tariff Act in Rayback, *Fillmore*, pp. 126–36. See also Baack and Ray, "Tariff Policy." This important article points out that the actual tariff rate on textile goods was far higher than the *ad valorem* rate. "While the ad valorem duty was 30% between 1843 and 1846, the actual tariff rate was more on the order of 291.24%" because of minimum evaluations on British goods (p. 107).

72. *Albany Evening Journal* (n.d.), quoted in Brock, *Political Conscience*, p. 106.

73. Jonathan H. Jacobs to Willie P. Mangum, March 4, 1842, John D. Hager to Mangum, July 19, 1842, and Priestley H. Mangum to Graham, May 12, 1842, in *The Mangum Papers*, III, pp. 296–98, 332–35, 371–72.

74. Willie P. Mangum to Priestley H. Mangum, August 10, 1842, ibid., pp. 376–77.

75. Morgan, *Whig Embattled*, pp. 48–54; Chitwood, *Tyler*, pp. 298–302; Alexander, *Sectional Stress*, p. 171, votes 102 and 188. On the first vote 95 percent of the Whigs voted to accept and

100 percent of the Democrats voted to reject the select committee report. On the second vote, 93 percent of the Whigs supported and all Democrats opposed a resolution denying Tyler's right to protest House proceedings.

76. John J. Crittenden to R. P. Letcher, June 23, 1842, and to Henry Clay, July 2, 1842, in Coleman, *Crittenden*, I, pp. 183–86; Poage, *Clay*, p. 107; Seager, *And Tyler Too*, p. 170; Van Deusen, *Greeley*, p. 87. In 1843, Wise and Gilmer were elected to Congress as Democrats.

77. Nathans, *Webster*, pp. 194–200; Dalzell, *Webster*, pp. 61–77.

78. Nathans, *Webster*, 195; Chitwood, *Tyler*, pp. 269–89, 367–85; Seager, *And Tyler Too*, pp. 161–71, 209–42; Hall, *Politics of Justice*, pp. 44–59; Brock, *Political Conscience*, pp. 107–08.

79. Davis to Clay, Worcester, October 14, 1843, in *Works of Henry Clay*, V, pp. 480–81.

80. See, for example, Willie P. Mangum to Priestly H. Mangum, August 10, 1842, and John Leeds Kerr to Willie P. Mangum, July 22, 1843, in *The Mangum Papers*, III, pp. 376–77, 462–64. Kerr served as United States senator from Maryland in the Twenty-Seventh Congress.

81. Campbell, "Party, Policy, and Political Leadership," p. 7.

82. John Tyler to Alexander Gardiner, July 11, 1846, quoted in Seager, *And Tyler Too*, p. 170; Webster to Edward Everett, November 28, 1842, quoted in Nathans, *Webster*, p. 201.

83. Clay to Nicholas O. Britton, September 23, 1842, and Clay to Francis Brooke, December 30, 1842, in *Works of Henry Clay*, V, pp. 470–74.

84. The classic statement of this argument is Formisano, "Political Character." But see also Shade, "Political Pluralism," pp. 77–111, especially pp. 79, 82; and Howe, *Political Culture*, pp. 280, 301–02, and passim.

85. In addition to the sources in note 58 on state politics in these years, see Van Deusen, *Seward*, pp. 55–86; Kruman, *Parties and Politics*, chapters 1–3 and Tables 8 and 9; Cooper, *Politics of Slavery*, pp. 149–66; and Cole, *Whig Party in the South*, pp. 64–103.

86. The literature on the abolitionist movement is too vast to list here, but the best study of the origins of the Liberty Party is Sewell, *Ballots for Freedom*, pp. 3–106.

87. Barnes, *Anti-Slavery Impulse*, pp. 177–90; Stewart, *Giddings*, pp. 71–74. For the voting pattern of congressional Whigs on matters relating to slavery, see Alexander, *Sectional Stress*, pp. 155–76.

88. Stewart, *Holy Warriors*, pp. 77–79; id., "Abolitionists, Insurgents, and Third Parties"; Sewell, *Ballots for Freedom*, passim; Benson, *Concept of Jacksonian Democracy*, pp. 120–21; Howe, *Political Culture*, pp. 150–80 and passim; for an example of a contemporary's recognition of the problem, see John Davis to Henry Clay, October 14, 1843, in *Works of Henry Clay*, V, pp. 480–81.

89. Darling, *Political Changes*, pp. 281–93.

90. The Congressional Quarterly's *Guide to U.S. Elections*, p. 578, shows three of four Democrats winning in Connecticut in 1843 with less than a majority of the popular vote. Although it lists no Liberty candidates in those districts, it may indeed have been Liberty men who siphoned off the balance of the vote. It should be noted, however, that in the one district Democrats carried with a majority, a separate Liberty candidate, who attracted 5.1 percent of the vote, was listed.

91. For some evidence of the partisan disputes over reapportionment in different states, see Holt, "Party Politics in Ohio," pp. 70, 85; Mueller, *Whig Party in Pennsylvania*, pp. 80–81, 87; and Sellers, *Polk: Jacksonian*, p. 471, a discussion of Democratic success in Tennessee.

92. The relationship between the increase in the share of House seats and the nationwide increase in the share of a party's popular vote from one congressional election to the next is technically known as the "swing ratio." For Democratic candidates in all elections between 1836 and 1972, it averaged only 1.8, yet in 1842–43 it was 10. See Clubb, Flanigan, and Zingale, *Partisan Realignment*, pp. 172–84, especially Figure 5.3a. The extent of the Democratic increase in the proportion of the popular vote in 1842–43 can only be approximated because congressional returns are incomplete. I calculated this figure by adding up the total popular vote and deriving the Democratic proportion of it in 1840–41 and 1842–43. Where congressional returns were unavailable but gubernatorial returns from the same day were, I utilized the gubernatorial returns. By this calculation the Democrats won 48.4 percent of the popular vote in the congressional elections of 1840–41 and 50.5 percent in those of 1842–43. In the April 6, 1844, issue of the

New York Tribune, Horace Greeley asserted that Democrats had gerrymandered congressional districts against the Whigs in two-thirds of the states.

93. Georgia's Whigs exulted in the districting scheme as soon as they had completed it. See Robert Toombs to Alexander H. Stephens, January 1, 1844, in Phillips, "Correspondence of Toombs, Stephens, and Cobb," pp. 53–54.

94. Murray, *Whig Party in Georgia,* pp. 104–06, 115–16; Sellers, *Polk: Jacksonian,* pp. 454–57, 469–89; Nathans, *Webster,* pp. 215–18; Dalzell, *Webster,* pp. 77–82; Holt, "Party Politics in Ohio," pp. 71–74; Shade, *Banks or No Banks,* pp. 104–06; Darling, *Political Changes,* pp. 293–311.

95. Nashville *Republican Banner,* August 11, 1843, quoted in Sellers, *Polk: Jacksonian,* p. 489.

96. See especially the discussion of the Tennessee campaign in Sellers, *Polk: Jacksonian,* pp. 469–89; Poage, *Clay,* pp. 107–20; Cooper, *Politics of Slavery,* pp. 153–66.

97. Porter to Clay, October 11, 1843, and Davis to Clay, October 14, 1843, in *Works of Henry Clay,* V, pp. 478–81.

CHAPTER 7

1. Robert Toombs to John M. Berrien, January 28, 1844, Berrien MSS; Beverly C. Sandrin to James B. Clay, February 20, 1844, T. J. Clay MSS; A. Patterson to Samuel F. Patterson, March 23, 1844, Patterson MSS; *New York Tribune,* April 8, 1844; Robert C. Winthrop to Edward Everett, April 26, 1844, Everett MSS; Joshua R. Giddings to Maria Giddings, April 28, 1844 (quotation), Giddings MSS.

2. Gustavus V. Henry to Marion Henry, July 24, 1844, Henry MSS; Charles A. Davis to Henry Clay, October 4, 1844, H. Clay MSS (LC); Washington Hunt to Millard Fillmore, October 5, 1844, MFP-O; Arthur Ritchie to H. B. Murdoch, October 30, 1844, Murdoch-Wright Family Papers.

3. J. C. Wright to Clay, September 5, 1844, H. Clay MSS (LC); Willis Green to William C. Rives, June 19, 1844, Rives MSS.

4. Poage, *Clay,* pp. 107–12.

5. John Leeds Kerr to Willie P. Mangum, July 22, 1843, in *The Mangum Papers,* III, pp. 462–64; Winthrop to Edward Everett, May 11, 1844, Everett MSS; Caleb Smith to Thomas Ewing, May 12, 1844, EFP.

6. Ritchie to Howell Cobb, May 16, 1844, in Phillips, "Correspondence of Toombs, Stephens, and Cobb," p. 56; H. C. Whitman to William Allen, April 27, 1844, Allen MSS. Analyses of the Democratic divisions that influenced the nomination of 1844 can be found in Paul, *Rift;* Sharp, *Jacksonians versus the Banks,* pp. 133–47, 285–305; and especially Sellers, *Polk: Continentialist,* pp. 14–66, 129–30. I have largely relied on Sellers for the following two paragraphs as well.

7. Crittenden to Ewing, March 10, 1844, EFP; Sellers, *Polk: Continentalist,* pp. 20–21; Chitwood, *Tyler,* p. 284; Seager, *And Tyler Too,* pp. 209–42.

8. Crittenden to Letcher, January 28, 1844, Crittenden MSS (Duke); Crawford to Stephens, March 6, 1844, Stephens MSS; George W. Crawford to John M. Berrien, February 13, 1844, Berrien MSS; Mangum to Paul Cameron, February 10, 1844, in *The Mangum Papers,* IV, pp. 41–43.

9. Clay to John Pendleton Kennedy, December 3, 1843, quoted in Kirwan, *Crittenden,* p. 177; *New York Tribune,* April 8, 1844.

10. *New York Tribune,* July 2, 1844.

11. Willis Green to William C. Rives, July 23, 1844, J. S. Shirrer to Rives, July 23, 1844, and James S. Penn to Rives, September 3, 1844, Rives MSS.

12. Toombs to Alexander H. Stephens, January 1, 1844, in Phillips, "Correspondence of Toombs, Stephens, and Cobb," pp. 53–54; Toombs to Berrien, January 28, 1844, Berrien MSS; Murray, *Whig Party in Georgia,* pp. 116–20.

13. Trester, "David Tod," 170; J. Sloane to Clay, May 9, 1844, Henry Clay MSS (LC).

14. *New York Tribune,* May 23, 1844.

15. Ibid., June 15, 1844; Alexander, *Sectional Stress*, pp. 180–85, votes 8, 32, 50, 51, 56, and 57.

16. Robert Winthrop to Edward Everett, August 1, 1844, Everett MSS; *New York Tribune*, June 14, 15, October 7, 1844; Cooper, *Politics of Slavery*, pp. 153–66; Boritt, *Lincoln*, p. 105.

17. *Historical Statistics*, pp. 886, 993, 1104, 1106. I also used the graph on "American Business Activity Since 1790," published by The Cleveland Trust Company in 1966, which used monthly commodity and security prices between 1815 and 1861 to measure deviations from a long-term trend line based on a composite index of commodity outputs. These monthly figures show that the deviation from the long-term trend in April 1843 was −19; in August 1843, −12; in November 1843, −8; in March 1844, −2; and for most of 1844, −1. Prices and productivity, in short, were moving up even though they did not recover completely from the depression until the end of 1845.

18. See, for example, *New York Tribune*, June 14, 27, 1844; Toombs to John M. Berrien, January 28, 1844, and Clay to Berrien, March 23, 1844, Berrien MSS; Clay to John J. Crittenden, March 24, 1844, Crittenden MSS (Duke).

19. D. F. Caldwell to Daniel M. Barringer, April 10, 1844, Barringer MSS; Cole, *Whig Party in the South*, pp. 99–102; Cooper, *Politics of Slavery*, pp. 155–66; *New York Tribune*, April 17, 1844; Henry Clay to Rives, August 19, 1844, Rives MSS; Alexander, *Sectional Stress*, pp. 51–56.

20. *New York Tribune*, May 13, 1844.

21. Alexander, *Sectional Stress*, pp. 20–21, 51–56, 180–85.

22. *New York Tribune*, April 1, 3, 9, 10, 12, 17, 26, 30, May 3, 13, 1844.

23. Johnson to Mangum, April 5, 1844, Mangum MSS; David F. Caldwell to Daniel M. Barringer, April 10, 1844, Barringer MSS.

24. *Ohio State Journal*, November 5, 1842, quoted in Tutorow, "Whigs in the Old Northwest," pp. 69–70. See also Tutorow, *Texas Annexation*, pp. 17–46, and Merk, *Slavery*, pp. 3–11 and passim. On pp. 205–11, Merk reprints an antiannexation address issued by Adams and twelve other northern Whig congressmen on March 3, 1843.

25. J. R. Giddings to J. A. Giddings, April 28, 1844, Giddings MSS.

26. Merk, *Slavery*, pp. 3–32 and passim; Cooper, *Politics of Slavery*, pp. 182–89. The best account of the basis for these fears is now Freehling, *Road to Disunion*, pp. 353–439.

27. Clay to Crittenden, December 5, 1843, in Coleman, *Crittenden*, I, pp. 207–10; Butler to Martin Van Buren, April 6, 1844, Van Buren MSS (LC); Silas Wright to Van Buren, n.d., quoted in Foner, "Wilmot Proviso," 267. For evidence that Massachusetts Whig leaders wanted to smother the Texas issue to protect Clay, see Nathans, *Webster*, pp. 219–20, and Formisano, *Transformation*, p. 326.

28. See the accounts cited in note 26. For Webster's role in delaying Tyler's plans for annexation, see Dalzell, *Webster*, pp. 40–58. England's role in the tangled maneuvers that eventuated in the annexation of Texas was complex. Briefly put, the English government did want to prevent the acquisition of Texas by the United States and was endeavoring to mediate between Mexico and Texas to perpetuate the latter's independence. Moreover, English authorities did favor abolition in Texas and elsewhere and had proposed to the Mexican government that they would try to secure abolition in Texas in return for Mexican recognition of Texan independence. Finally, abolitionists had approached the British government asking for a loan to Texas to start the abolition process, but the British authorities had never promised to grant it. Indeed, exaggerated talk by abolitionists about the probability of such a loan may have been as responsible as letters from Duff Green and Texas agents in England for the rumors of official governmental support for an abolitionist plot in Texas. A careful treatment of this complicated story is Pletcher, *Diplomacy*, pp. 86–88, 113–207, esp. pp. 121–22, but see as well Freehling's splendid account in *Road to Disunion*, pp. 353–439.

29. In addition to the works by Merk, Cooper, Paul, and Pletcher cited above, see Seager, *And Tyler Too*, pp. 209–42.

30. Paul, *Rift*, pp. 38–47, 79–113; Sellers, *Polk: Continentalist*, pp. 40–61; Merk, *Slavery*, pp. 44–82.

31. The Pakenham Letter is reprinted in the appendix to Sellers' essay "The Election of 1844," pp. 818–21.

32. Clay to J. J. Crittenden, March 24, April 17, 19, 21, 1844, Henry Clay MSS (LC); Clay to Mangum, April 14, 1844, Mangum MSS; William Hayden to Mangum, April 5, 1844, in *The Mangum Papers*, IV, pp. 92–93; Crittenden to Thomas Ewing, March 30, 1844, EFP; *New York Tribune*, April 1, 1844; Washington Hunt to Alvah Hunt, April 4, 1844, Knollenberg Collection.

33. John C. Calhoun to Armistead Burt, January 24, 1838, in Jameson, "Correspondence of Calhoun," pp. 388–90; Clay to Crittenden, April 21, 1844, Henry Clay MSS (LC). At least one member of Tyler's Cabinet, Secretary of War John C. Spencer, expected both Clay and Van Buren eventually to support the treaty in order to neutralize the issue. Silas Wright to Martin Van Buren, April 8, 1844, Van Buren MSS.

34. Clay to Crittenden, April 21, 1844, Henry Clay MSS (LC); Alexander H. Stephens to James Thomas, May 17, 1844, in Phillips, "Correspondence of Toombs, Stephens, and Cobb," pp. 57–58.

35. Sellers, *Polk: Continentalist*, pp. 40–107; Paul, *Rift*, pp. 114–68.

36. Francis Granger to Thomas Ewing, June 7, 1844, EFP; Willie P. Mangum to Priestley H. Mangum, May 29, 1844, and Clay to Mangum, June 7, 1844, in *The Mangum Papers*, IV, pp. 127–29, 134; Grieve Edvine to John M. Berrien, June 3, 1844, Berrien MSS.

37. Geo. S. Yerby to Willie P. Mangum, June 29, 1844, in *The Mangum Papers*, IV, pp. 140–42; William B. Campbell to David Campbell, August 14, 1844, CFP; Sellers, *Polk: Continentalist*, pp. 100–01, 139–41.

38. Merk, *Slavery*, p. 81; Alexander, *Sectional Stress*, pp. 51–54; Sellers, *Polk: Continentalist*, p. 133.

39. *New York Tribune*, June 1, 12, 1844; Sellers, *Polk: Continentalist*, p. 101.

40. Sellers, *Polk: Continentalist*, pp. 101–03, 109–16, 123–28; Cooper, *Politics of Slavery*, pp. 205–06.

41. Trester, "David Tod," pp. 162–78; Sharp, *Jacksonians versus the Banks*, pp. 123–59; Maizlish, "Triumph of Sectionalism," pp. 48–58; *New York Tribune*, August 1, 15, 19, 26, 1844; Williams, "Graham and the Election of 1844"; Gibson, "Opinion in North Carolina," 7–10; Snyder, *Jacksonian Heritage*, pp. 179–82; James Buchanan to Robert P. Letcher, July 27, 1844, Crittenden MSS (Duke).

42. Nicholas Carroll to Willie P. Mangum, September 8, 1844, in *The Mangum Papers*, IV, pp. 180–84; Sellers, *Polk: Continentalist*, pp. 129–31.

43. Buchanan to Letcher, July 27, 1844, Crittenden MSS (Duke).

44. Rantoul to Nathaniel P. Banks, August 9, 1844, Banks MSS (Ill.SHL).

45. Sellers, *Polk: Continentalist*, p. 131; Tutorow, *Texas Annexation*, pp. 61–77; Bruser, "Political Antislavery," pp. 80–83; Van Bolt, "Sectional Aspects," 121–28.

46. Clay to Clayton, August 29, 1844, Henry Clay MSS (LC); *New York Tribune*, July 2, 1844.

47. Holt, *Political Crisis*, pp. 42–45.

48. Clay to Crittenden, December 5, 1843 in Coleman, *Crittenden*, I, pp. 207–10; Merk, *Manifest Destiny*, pp. 34–44; Wilson, "Concept of Time."

49. Stephens to James Thomas, May 17, 1844. The Whig case against Texas annexation is well summarized in the two books by Merk, *Slavery* and *Manifest Destiny*. I have also relied on Tutorow, *Texas Annexation*, pp. 1–117; Pletcher, *Diplomacy*, pp. 137–47; Williams, "Graham and the Election of 1844," pp. 38–42; Clay to Crittenden, December 5, 1843, loc. cit.; and Clay's Raleigh Letter of April 17, 1844.

50. See, for example, the letter of Samuel Medary to Polk, November 10, 1844, quoted in Tutorow, *Texas Annexation*, p. 74; Varon, "Tippecanoe and the Ladies, Too."

51. Clay to Willie P. Mangum, April 14, 1844, Mangum MSS; Clay to Crittenden, March 24, April 19, 1844, Henry Clay MSS (LC); Clay to Weed, May 6, 1844, copy, Henry Clay MSS (Duke).

52. *Jacksonian Southron*, February 7, 1844, quoted in Lucas, "Political Alchemy," p. 92; for the vote in the Mississippi legislature, see Lucas, "The Second Party System in Mississippi," pp. 35–36; *New Orleans Bee*, March 28, 30, 1844, cited in Tutorow, *Texas Annexation*, p. 23;

Stephens to James Thomas, May 17, 1844, loc. cit.; David F. Caldwell to Daniel M. Barringer, June 12, 1844, Barringer MSS.

53. William Kinney to Willie P. Mangum, April 29, 1844, in *The Mangum Papers*, IV, pp. 121–22; Ephraim H. Foster to William B. Campbell, April 6, 1844, CFP. I am indebted to Professor William J. Cooper, Jr., for bringing this latter letter to my attention. For additional evidence of early Whig fears of the Texas issue, see George F. Platt to Alexander Stephens, April 30, 1844, Stephens MSS; James Lyons to William C. Rives, June 14, 1844, and S. A. Wales to Rives, June 29, 1844, Rives MSS.

54. Cooper, *Politics of Slavery*, pp. 208–09; Merk, *Slavery*, pp. 78–81.

55. *New York Tribune*, July 3, 1844; Cooper, *Politics of Slavery*, pp. 196–216.

56. For the Memphis meeting, see *New York Tribune*, June 14, 1844; the quotation from the Lexington meeting is taken from Poage, *Clay*, p. 142; Cooper, *Politics of Slavery*, pp. 211–12. A particularly good example of the Whig case against the pernicious economic consequences of annexation is a circular issued to his constituents by the Virginia Whig Congressman William Goggin, on January 1, 1845, in the *Richmond Semi-Weekly Whig*, January 10, 1845. Although it deals with an earlier period, there is an excellent discussion of the economic consequences of western emigration for older southern states and of the Whiggish attempt to promote internal economic development in order to stop it in Watson, *Jacksonian Politics and Community Conflict*, pp. 45–59 and passim.

57. Oakes, *Ruling Race*, pp. 146–47, 192–224; J. S. Shirrer to William C. Rives, September 14, 1844, Rives MSS.

58. Arthur Campbell to David Campbell, September 8, 1844, CFP; Jeremiah Morton to William C. Rives, July 1, 1844, Rives MSS; Oakes, *Ruling Race*, pp. 51–57, 69–91, 147–50.

59. Grieve Edvine to Berrien, June 3, 1844, Berrien MSS; James Lyons to Rives, June 14, 1844, Rives to Clay, July 15, 1844, draft, Morton to Rives, July 16, 1844, Nathaniel Tallmadge to Rives, July 25, 1844, Rives MSS; Cooper, *Politics of Slavery*, pp. 209–10; Poage, *Clay*, pp. 141–45.

60. The most detailed discussion of these letters is in Poage, *Clay*, pp. 143–45. For the letters themselves, see Clay to Stephen F. Miller, July 1, 1844, in *The Works of Henry Clay*, V, pp. 490–91; and Clay to Thomas M. Peters and John M. Jackson, July 27, 1844, in the appendix to Sellers, "The Election of 1844," pp. 855–56.

61. Clay to Joshua R. Giddings, September 21, 1844, Giddings-Julian MSS; Cooper, *Politics of Slavery*, p. 218; Dalzell, *Webster*, p. 91.

62. Poage, *Clay*, pp. 140–43; Crittenden to Waddy Thompson, July 1, 1844, Waddy Thompson MSS; Stephen Miller to Clay, June 20, 1844, quoted in Cooper, *Politics of Slavery*, p. 211; Clay to Nicholas Davis, June 24, 1844, Henry Clay MSS; Clay to Stephen F. Miller, July 1, 1844, loc. cit. I am indebted to Professor William J. Cooper, Jr., for giving me his notes on the letter of Crittenden to Thompson.

63. Campbell to Rives, July 10, 1844 and Rives to Clay, July 15, 1844, draft, Rives MSS; Gustavus A. Henry to Marion Henry, July 24, 28, 1844, Henry MSS; William B. Campbell to David Campbell, August 14, 1844, CFP; A. Brackett to Erastus Fairbanks, August 5, 1844, Fairbanks MSS; L. Evans to Jesse Turner, August 19, 1844, Turner MSS.

64. R. B. Cuyler to Thomas Butler King, July 18, 1844, King MSS; *New York Tribune*, July 12, 15, 24, August 8, 15, 16, 26, 1844; James Harvey to Willie P. Mangum, July 23, 1844, in *The Mangum Papers*, IV, pp. 159–61. Clay to Epes Sargent, August 7, 1844, Boston Public Library. Again, I am greatly indebted to Professor Cooper for sharing his notes on the Clay letter to Sargent with me.

65. Adam Huntsman to James K. Polk, September 20, 1844, Adam Huntsman MSS (Tennessee State Library), and the Milledgeville, Georgia, *Federal Union*, September 17, 1844, show Democratic awareness of the Alabama letters by September. Again, I am indebted to Professor Cooper for these references. *New York Tribune*, August 26, 1844.

66. *New York Tribune*, August 19, 26, 1844. In Kentucky the Whig proportion of seats in the lower house of the legislature increased from 62 percent in 1843 to 76 percent in 1844. In North Carolina, it increased from 44 percent in 1842 to 58 percent in 1844. Changes in the popular vote in the two states between 1840 and 1844 show dramatic Democratic gains.

	Vote for President 1840		Vote for Governor 1844	
	Whig	Democratic	Whig	Democratic
Kentucky	58,597	32,593	59,792	55,089
N. Carolina	45,705	33,781	42,586	39,433

67. *New York Tribune*, August 26, 1844. In 1842 Whigs had captured 57 percent of the seats in the lower house of the legislature; in 1844 they won 52 percent.

68. Wm. L. Savage to Thomas Ewing, July 6, 1844, EFP; William H. McFarland to David Campbell, August 27, 1844, William C. Rives to Campbell, September 24, October 25, 1844, CFP; G. A. Henry to Marion Henry, July 24, 28, 1844, and Marion Henry to G. A. Henry, September 26, 1844, Henry MSS; John Pendleton Kennedy to Philip C. Pendleton, October 17, 1844, copy, Kennedy MSS.

69. Clay to Mangum, September 11, 1844, Henry Clay MSS (LC); Clay to Giddings, September 21, 1844, Giddings-Julian MSS; Sellers, *Polk: Continentalist*, p. 147.

70. *New York Tribune*, June 1, 27, 1844; *North American*, June 3, 1844, quoted in Mueller, *Whig Party in Pennsylvania*, p. 102; Tutorow, *Texas Annexation*, pp. 67–70; Van Bolt, "Sectional Aspects," p. 128.

71. *New York Tribune*, June 27, 1844; Seward to Weed, June 20, 1844, quoted in Sellers, *Polk: Continentalist*, p. 146; Seward to Samuel B. Ruggles, September 11, 1844, Seward MSS (LC); Morrill to J. W. D. Parker, August 2, 1844, Morrill MSS.

72. Sellers, *Polk: Continentalist*, pp. 116–23.

73. Ibid., pp. 120, 126–27. Despite exposing Polk's promises to Southerners, Sellers defends the candor of the Kane letter because Polk seemed to endorse both protection and discrimination in favor of manufactured products. But that is a dubious judgment, for the central issue in 1844, especially in Pennsylvania, was where Polk stood on the Tariff of 1842, not some hypothetical measure. Publicly Polk refused to say anything about that measure even as he privately told Southerners that he wanted to replace it.

74. See, for example, *New York Tribune*, June 27, July 6, October 7, 1844; James E. Harvey to Thomas Butler King, August 7, 1844, King MSS; Reynolds McFarland to James M. Bell, September 10, 1844, James Bell MSS; Truman Smith to William B. Campbell, August 18, 1844, CFP.

75. Sellers, *Polk: Continentalist*, pp. 122–23; Tutorow, *Texas Annexation*, pp. 61–72; *New York Tribune*, June 15, July 6, 1844.

76. *New York Tribune*, August 26, 30, 1844. For evidence that Indiana's Whigs worried about the incursion of the Liberty party into their strength, see Schuyler Colfax to Richard W. Thompson, June 11, 1844, Thompson MSS (Lincoln Life Foundation).

77. On Ohio, see P. B. Ewing to William L. Savage, n.d. (July 1844 folder), EFP; Tutorow, *Texas Annexation*, pp. 66–67; and Maizlish, "Triumph of Sectionalism," pp. 58–60. On New York, see Sellers, *Polk: Continentalist*, pp. 129–31; Benson, *Concept of Jacksonian Democracy;* pp. 230–32; and *New York Tribune*, November 8, 9, 16, 1844.

78. William Lawrence to William Allen, March 29, 1844, and H. C. Whitman to Allen, April 27, 1844, Allen MSS; Sellers, *Polk: Continentalist*, p. 141; *New York Tribune*, November 9, 1844; Lewis Tappan to Joshua R. Giddings, December 19, 1845, Giddings MSS.

79. Daniel Webster to Edward Curtis, September 1, 1844, Webster MSS; Weed to Granger, September 3, 1844, Granger MSS; Seward to Weed, September 2, 1844, quoted in Sellers, *Polk: Continentalist*, p. 147.

80. William Slade to Joshua R. Giddings, June 6, 1844, Giddings MSS; Winthrop to Everett, September 14, 1844, Everett MSS.

81. Seth M. Gates to Giddings, October 2, 1844, quoted in Sellers, *Polk: Continentalist*, p. 147; John Lorimer Graham to William C. Rives, October 2, 1844, Rives MSS.

82. Clay's letter of September 23, 1844, is quoted in Poage, *Clay*, p. 147; Hunt to Fillmore, October 5, 1844, MFP-O.

83. Sellers, *Polk: Continentalist,* pp. 148–49; John Lorimer Graham to William C. Rives, October 30, 1844, Circular from the Whig State Central Committee of Ohio, October 11, 1844, Rives MSS.

84. Snyder, *Jacksonian Heritage,* p. 184; Nathan Sargent to Willie P. Mangum, August 21, 1844, in *The Mangum Papers,* IV, pp. 179–80; *New York Tribune,* October 7, 1844; Edward Jenkins to William C. Rives, June 5, 1844, Rives MSS.

85. *New York Tribune,* April 6, 1844; Seager, *And Tyler Too,* pp. 230–42.

86. Benson, *Concept of Jacksonian Democracy,* pp. 241–42; John S. Wendell to Clay, March 11, 1848, Henry Clay MSS (LC).

87. *Louisiana Courier,* July 19, 1844, quoted in Redard, "Election of 1844 in Louisiana," 426.

88. William Lawrence to William Allen, March 29, 1844, H. C. Whitman to Allen, April 27, 1844, Allen MSS; Whig Platform of 1844 in appendix to Sellers, "Election of 1844," p. 807; *The American Review,* I (January 1845—but issued in the fall of 1844), pp. 99–103; Snyder, *Jacksonian Heritage,* p. 184.

89. Peter B. Porter to Clay, October 13, 1843, in *Works of Henry Clay,* V, p. 479; Clay to Weed, May 6, 1844, Henry Clay MSS (Duke). The generalizations about potential candidates in this and the following paragraphs are based on the following letters: James Watson Webb to W. H. Morrell, January 12, 1844, Willie P. Mangum to John M. Clayton, March 16, 1844, Reverdy Johnson to Mangum, March 23, 1844, Mangum and James T. Morehead to Clayton, March 25, 1844, B. W. Leigh to Mangum, March 28, 1844, Clayton to Mangum, March 30, 1844, Richard H. Atwell to Mangum, April 17, 1844, S. P. Walker to Mangum, April 30, 1844, in *The Mangum Papers,* IV, pp. 13–14, 65–68, 74–76, 79–87, 104–06, 121–22; Robert C. Winthrop to Edward Everett, April 26, May 11, 1844, Everett MSS; Thomas Corwin to Thomas Ewing, April 8, 1844, EFP; William H. Seward to William Woodbridge, April 6, 1844, Seward MSS (RU). Of these letters, only two even mentioned Frelinghuysen before the convention.

90. In addition to the letters listed above, see Dalzell, *Webster,* pp. 89–90, for Webster's hostility to Davis; Van Deusen, *Weed,* pp. 132–33, 362, note 5; Rayback, *Fillmore,* pp. 147–51.

91. Winthrop to Everett, April 26, 1844, Everett MSS. On the night before the convention, a Whig wrote Mangum from Baltimore, "The *East, Ohio & Inda* stand firm for Davis. Fillmore gains, and so does Frelinghuysen. McKennan is brought out today, but nothing is known, more than you can conjecture about the matter of the V. P. at Washington." S. P. Walker to Mangum, April 30, 1844, in *The Mangum Papers,* IV, pp. 121–22.

92. I have used the report on the convention's proceedings in the *New York Tribune,* May 3, 1844.

93. For the background of the American Republican movement I have relied on Billington, *Protestant Crusade,* pp. 1–211; Benson, *Concept of Jacksonian Democracy,* pp. 114–22; Leonard, "American Republican Party"; and Feldberg, *Philadelphia Riots.*

94. Estimates of Democrats voting American Republican are taken from Leonard, "American Republican Party," pp. 164–72, 183; Feldberg, *Philadelphia Riots,* pp. 95–96, 164–67.

95. Leonard, "American Republican Party"; Van Deusen, *Weed,* pp. 131–35.

96. Feldberg, *Philadelphia Riots,* pp. 99–168. Within three days of the Kennsington riot, indeed, Thurlow Weed, who had backed James Harper for mayor of New York City in April, wrote that the Whigs must spurn any connection with "the Philadelphia Native Americans." Weed to Alvah Hunt, May 11, 1844, Knollenberg Collection.

97. Clay to Peter Sken Smith, June 17, 1844, Clay to Clayton, August 29, 1844, Henry Clay MSS (LC); John C. Hamilton to John M. Berrien, August 27, 1844, Berrien MSS.

98. *New York Tribune,* October 3, 1844; John Lorimer Graham to William C. Rives, October 30, 1844, Rives MSS; Nathans, *Webster,* pp. 222–23; Charles A. Davis to Clay, October 4, 1844, Henry Clay MSS (LC).

99. Mueller, *Whig Party in Pennsylvania,* pp. 104–13, quotation on p. 111; Snyder, *Jacksonian Heritage,* p. 185; Feldberg, *Philadelphia Riots,* pp. 165–68, properly expresses skepticism about the existence of such a bargain.

100. Feldberg, *Philadelphia Riots,* pp. 164–68.

101. James E. Harvey to Thomas Butler King, October 22, 1844, King MSS; Nicholas Carroll to Willie P. Mangum, October 15, 1844, in *The Mangum Papers*, IV, pp. 214–16; John C. Hamilton to Millard Fillmore, October 8, 1844, Henry Davies to Fillmore, October 14, 1844, V. M. Smith to Fillmore, October 27, 1844, MFP-O.

102. John C. Hamilton to John M. Berrien, August 27, 1844, Berrien MSS.

103. Nicholas Carroll to Willie P. Mangum, September 8, October 7, 15, 1844, in *The Mangum Papers*, IV, pp. 180–84, 205–07, 214–16; Henry E. Davies to Millard Fillmore, October 1, 1844, John C. Hamilton to Fillmore, October 8, 11, 1844, Solomon G. Haven to Fillmore, October 2, 1844, Fillmore to B. F. Whitney, October 28, 1844, draft, and Horace Greeley to Fillmore, November 8, 1844, MFP-O; Charles A. Davis to Clay, October 4, 1844, Henry Clay MSS (LC); W. Niles to William C. Rives, October 29, 1844, John Lorimer Graham to Rives, October 30, 1844, Rives MSS.

104. For the quotations, see Seward to Clay, October 25, 1844, Henry Clay MSS (LC); Clay to William B. Campbell, October 26, 1844, CFP. Dozens of similar letters could be cited.

105. Thomas Nevitt to Clay, November 24, 1844, E. Pettinger to Clay, January 1, 1845, Henry Clay MSS (LC); Richard W. Thompson to Millard Fillmore, January 8, 1845, MFP-O; Leslie Combs to John M. Clayton, November 20, 1844, Clayton MSS; John L. Lawrence to Clay, November 25, 1844, Fillmore to Clay, November 11, 1844, Henry Clay MSS (LC); William M. Cooke to William C. Rives, December 14, 1844, Rives MSS.

106. Weed to Granger, February 25, 1845, Granger MSS; *New York Tribune*, November 16, 1844. See also the *Tribune* for November 8, 9, 15 and for December 15, 23, 1844. I say "apparently divergent responses" because Weed and Greeley both believed Whigs could win on issues once the electorate had a taste of the Democratic alternatives.

107. For historians who consider the Texas issue decisive, see note 26; Sellers, *Polk: Continentalist*, pp. 108–9, 159. For other historians who minimize the impact of issues, especially the Texas issue, on voting behavior, see Benson, *Concept of Jacksonian Democracy*, pp. 123–40, 254–69, and passim; Alexander, "Voter Partisan Constancy," pp. 78, 92–93, 116, and passim.

108. S. M. Chester to Clay, November 13, 1844, Henry Clay MSS (LC). See also "A Native Whig" to Millard Fillmore, November 9, 1844, MFP-O; Fillmore to Clay, November 11, 1844, Ambrose Spencer to Clay, November 21, 1844, Henry Clay MSS (LC); David Davis to William P. Walker, February 1845, draft, David Davis MSS.

109. Daniel Webster to Edward Everett, December 15, 1844, Webster MSS; *New York Tribune*, November 9, 1844; John Lorimer Graham to William C. Rives, November 19, 1844, Rives MSS.

110. Alexander, "Voter Partisan Constancy," pp. 92–95.

111. Some of the absolute decline in the Whig vote may have reflected defeatism. Different states held the presidential election on different days in 1844, beginning on Friday, November 1, and extending to Thursday, November 14. Because most of the crucial states voted before November 6, Whig voters in many of the states voting later may have known the results and been discouraged. Maine, Massachusetts, and Alabama voted on November 11, Vermont on November 12, and North Carolina on November 14. New Hampshire and Tennessee, however, voted on November 4 and 5, respectively. For election dates, see *Tribune Almanac for 1844*, p. 60.

112. The proportions alluded to in this paragraph are calculated by dividing the total increase in the vote between 1840 and 1844 by the gains of the three parties. Were one to begin with the estimated proportions of the 1840 vote each party retained, the figures would be slightly different. Given the decline in the Democratic vote during 1840 from earlier congressional and gubernatorial contests to the presidential balloting in November, it is likely that some of the increase in the Democratic total of 1844 also came from normal Democratic supporters who had failed to vote for Van Buren in November.

113. Webster to Everett, December 15, 1844, Everett MSS; James F. Strother to William C. Rives, November 17, 1844, Rives MSS. Another correspondent complained to Rives that Virginia could have been carried "if the old Adams men had not been allowed to take the lead and undo all we did in 40 without them." James Lyons to Rives, November 11, 1844, Rives MSS.

114. Thomas Baird to Clay, November 30, 1844, Stephen Russell to Clay, March 4, 1845, Henry Clay MSS (LC).

115. The quotations are from Ambrose Spencer to Clay, November 21, 1844, and William L. Gould to Clay, December 18, 1844, Henry Clay MSS (LC); V. Bouligny to Clay, December 4, 1844, Thomas J. Clay MSS; and Charles Oliver to Clay, November 29, 1844, Henry Clay MSS (Lilly Library, Indiana University). For similar lamentations, see David Campbell to William B. Campbell, December 23, 1844, CFP; and *New York Tribune*, November 9, 1844.

116. Redard, "Election of 1844 in Louisiana," p. 428; Sellers, *Polk: Continentalist*, p. 159; Burnham, *Presidential Ballots*, p. 30.

117. William L. Gould to Clay, December 18, 1844, Henry Clay MSS (LC); George H. Colton to John P. Kennedy, November 13, 1844, Kennedy MSS; Gilbert H. Sayers to Clay, December 21, 1844, Thomas H. Baird to Clay, November 30, 1844, and Allan B. Magruder to Clay, November 21, 1844, Henry Clay MSS (LC).

118. *New York Tribune*, November 13, 1844.

119. William L. Gould to Clay, December 18, 1844, Henry Clay MSS (LC); H. M. Cunningham to Alexander Stephens, December 21, 1844, Stephens MSS; Combs to John M. Clayton, November 20, 1844, Clayton MSS; Arthur Campbell to James Campbell, November 21, 1844, and to David Campbell, November 17, 1844, CFP.

120. Gould to Clay, December 18, 1844, Henry Clay MSS (LC); Cunningham to Stephens, December 21, 1844, Stephens MSS (LC).

121. For Louisiana I have relied on the multiple regression and correlation analyses in Redard, "Election of 1844 in Louisiana," pp. 430–33. Note that the Whigs lost some 2,500 votes in Alabama between 1840 and 1844. Since the party was strongest in the wealthiest counties with the most slaves in that state, Democratic gains in counties more than 30 percent slave could well represent the conversion of former Whig voters. Long ago, indeed, Arthur Cole noted that Whig losses in the South occurred in the black belt plantation areas, while Democratic gains came in the areas with few slaves. Cole, *Whig Party in the South*, pp. 115–16.

122. David Campbell to Arthur Campbell, February 11, 1845, CFP.

123. See also Renda, "Retrospective Voting."

124. *New York Tribune*, November 8, 9, 16, December 23, 1844.

125. Ambrose Spencer to Clay, November 21, 1844, Hone to Clay, November 28, 1844, Henry Clay MSS (LC); Fillmore to Weed, November 6, 1844, Weed MSS (RU); Simeon Baldwin, Jr., to Simeon Baldwin, November 23, 1844, BFP; Amos Abbott to William Schouler, November 16, 1844, Schouler MSS.

126. Charles Henry Hall to John C. Hamilton, January 1, 1845, J. Burnet to John M. Berrien, February 14, 1845, Berrien MSS; J. W. Migels to Clay, November 11, 1844, Thomas H. Baird to Clay, November 30, 1844, C. L. Leary to Clay, November 14, 1844, Theodore Frelinghuysen to Clay, November 9, 1844, Henry Clay MSS (LC); V. Bouligny to Clay, December 4, 1844, T. J. Clay MSS; *New York Tribune*, November 6, 9, 11, 13, 1844, October 10, 1846.

Because the federal census of 1840 did not list information on place of birth and because the immigrant population grew rapidly in any event, it is impossible to analyze statistically the behavior of foreign-born voters. But it is likely that Whigs were generally correct. In Buffalo and Erie County, New York, where the German and Irish populations were growing rapidly, for example, Democrats outgained Whigs between 1840 and 1844 by 1,363 to 118 votes. In New York County, where Whigs made some gains through their cooperation with the American Republicans, the Democrats still attracted 1,000 more new voters than they did. In Pennsylvania, Whigs outpaced Democrats among new voters in populous Philadelphia County because of their alliance with the American Republicans, but the Democratic vote grew dramatically between 1840 and 1844 in areas of German settlement such as Berks, Bucks, Lehigh, and Schuylkill counties, while in Allegheny County, site of Pittsburgh and a traditional Whig bastion, Democrats outgained Whigs by 1,170 to 464 votes. Finally, J. Burnet claimed that Democrats illegally naturalized 1,500 Germans within two weeks of the election in Cincinnati, and the Democrats outdrew Whigs by 3,100 to 1,300 among new voters in Hamilton County, Ohio. For more on the surge of non-British immigrants to the Democrats in New York State, see Benson, *Concept of Jacksonian Democracy*, pp. 138–76.

127. W. E. Cramer to Polk, November 13, 1844, quoted in Sellers, *Polk: Continentalist*, p. 158.

128. The resolutions of the New Haven meeting are enclosed with P. S. Galphin et al. to

Clay, November 16, 1844, Henry Clay MSS (LC); Cincinnati *Gazette* quoted in the *New York Tribune*, November 16, 1844; for Greeley's lament see ibid., November 11, 1844.

129. Thomas Nevitt to Clay, November 24, 1844, Henry Clay MSS (LC); Draft of Webster's Speech at Faneuil Hall, dated November 10, 1844, Webster MSS; and the sources cited in note 128. Whigs also pointed to a surging Democratic immigrant vote in Illinois and Michigan, where, as they lamented, aliens could legally vote prior to naturalization. See, for example, *New York Tribune*, August 26, 1844, and Tutorow, *Texas Annexation*, pp. 76–77.

130. Philo D. Mickles to Millard Fillmore, November 14, 1844, MFP-O; *New York Tribune*, November 9, 11, 1844; *Albany Evening Journal*, quoted in ibid., November 13, 1844. See also the speech of Connecticut Governor William Ellsworth printed in ibid., November 28, 1844; and Seward to Henry Clay, November 7, 1844, copy, Seward MSS (RU).

131. Samuel Sample to Schuyler Colfax, December 1, 1844, Colfax MSS (NIHS); *New York Tribune*, November 6, 12, 1844. Comparison of state and congressional returns with the presidential tally in New York City and Philadelphia suggests that complaints of American Republican betrayal were justified.

132. Fillmore to Clay, November 11, 1844, Gilbert H. Sayers to Clay, December 21, 1844, Henry Clay MSS (LC); Combs to Clayton, November 20, 1844, Clay to Clayton, December 2, 1844, Clayton MSS.

133. Thomas Ewing to Timothy Childs, January 3, 1845, EFP.

134. See Table 9. Three Senate seats held by Whigs were to be filled in 1845 by legislatures that Democrats carried in 1844. The Whig margin in the Senate during the 28th Congress was twenty-eight to twenty-three, with one vacancy.

135. Thomas Butler King to Winfield Scott, February 15, 1845, draft, King MSS; William J. Hough to William Allen, December 9, 1844, Allen MSS; George Tucker to William C. Rives, November 16, 1844, J. J. Fry to Rives, November 13, 1844, Rives MSS; Clay to Crittenden, November 28, 1844, Henry Clay MSS (LC); Arthur Campbell to James Campbell, November 21, 1844, CFP.

136. G. H. Colton to J. P. Kennedy, November 13, 1844, Kennedy MSS.

CHAPTER 8

1. Leverett Saltonstall to Clay, December 10, 1844, Henry Clay MSS (LC). For additional examples of Whig pessimism after Clay's defeat, see Chapter 7.

2. For typical examples of historians who sneer at the bankruptcy and unpopularity of Whig programs by 1848, see Nevins, *Ordeal: Fruits*, p. 194; and Brock, *Political Conscience*, pp. 151–53 and passim. For the argument that sectional issues replaced economic issues after 1844 and thus destroyed the Whig party, see also Maizlish, *Triumph of Sectionalism*.

3. Boritt, *Lincoln*, p. 145; see also Brock, *Political Conscience*, p. 188, and Potter, *Impending Crisis*, p. 81.

4. F. S. Bronson to Henry Clay, November 20, 1844, Henry Clay MSS (LC); J. J. Fry to William C. Rives, November 13, 1844, Rives MSS.

5. Draft of Webster's speech, November 10, 1844, Webster MSS; William L. Gould to Clay, December 18, 1844, Henry Clay MSS (LC).

6. Resolutions of Whig meeting in New Haven, Connecticut, November 14, 1844, with P. S. Galphin et al. to Clay, November 16, 1844, Henry Clay MSS (LC); *New York Tribune*, November 9, 1844; Clay to Crittenden, November 28, 1844, Crittenden MSS (LC); Clay to John M. Clayton, December 2, 1844, Clayton MSS.

7. *New York Tribune*, December 18, 1844; *Albany Evening Journal* quoted in ibid., November 13, 1844; John H. Pleasants to Rives, December 23, 1844, Rives MSS.

8. I have relied on the minutes of this meeting of March 15, 1845, in the Webster MSS. Clay, in the letters to Crittenden and Clayton cited above, urged Whigs in Congress "to have an early consultation and to adopt some system of future action."

9. "The Result of the Election," *The American Review*, I (February, 1845), 113–20. No author was listed for the article, but George H. Colton, owner of *The American Review*, had written Kennedy after the election asking him to contribute an article on the election outlining what the Whigs' future course should be. Colton to Kennedy, November 13, 1844, Kennedy MSS.

10. In legislative races, this weakness was largely attributable to representation based on at-large county tickets, rather than single-member districts, which denied Whigs a share of seats commensurate with their popular vote. For Whig complaints about the apportionment of the legislature, see the Michigan Whig State Platform for 1845, *New York Tribune*, September 27, 1845.

11. This total includes special elections to fill vacancies as well as regularly scheduled elections. My sources for the congressional races are the Congressional Quarterly's *Guide to U.S. Elections* and the *Tribune Almanac*.

12. Duncan McKenzie to Duncan McLaurin, November 2, 1845, McLaurin MSS; P. B. Barringer to Daniel M. Barringer, June 26, 1845, Barringer MSS; B. F. Dill to John A. Quitman, September 7, 1847, Claiborne MSS.

13. C. F. M. Noland to Jesse Turner, October 22, 1845, Turner MSS.

14. David Davis to John Henry, February 11, 1845, Davis to John Rockwell, December 17, 1845, and Davis to William P. Walker, December 6, 1845, David Davis MSS.

15. *New York Tribune*, September 17, 20, 1847.

16. C. F. M. Noland to Jesse Turner, February 23, 1848, Turner MSS.

17. Abraham Lincoln to T. S. Flournoy, February 17, 1848, in *Collected Works of Lincoln*, I, p. 452; see also Lincoln to Taylor Committee, February 9, 1848, Lincoln to Usher F. Linden, February 20, March 22, 1848, and Lincoln to Jesse Lynch, April 10, 1848, ibid., pp. 449, 453, 457–58, 463–64.

18. N. C. Barnett to John M. Berrien, February 18, 1845, Berrien MSS; Leslie Combs to John M. Clayton, November 20, 1844, Clayton MSS; James Lyons to Rives, November 11, 1844, Jeremiah Morton to Rives, December 11, 1844, W. E. Sutton to Rives, January 31, 1845, Rives MSS; H. M. Cunningham to Alexander H. Stephens, December 21, 1844, Stephens MSS (LC).

19. Joseph H. Peyton to William B. Campbell, February 16, 1845, CFP.

20. Holt, *Political Crisis*, pp. 44–45; *New York Tribune*, February 6, 1845; Daniel Webster to Robert C. Winthrop, December 29, 30, 1844, January 10, 1845, Winthrop MSS; Webster to Samuel Hurd Walley, March 8, 1845, Webster MSS; copy of the anti-Texas resolution passed by the Massachusetts legislature, March 31, 1845, in Adams Family Papers; Dalzell, *Webster*, pp. 91–97; A. G. Johnson to Rives, December 2, 1844, Joseph R. Ingersoll to Rives, February 18, 1845, Rives MSS.

21. *Messages and Papers of the Presidents*, IV, pp. 334–56; John P. Kennedy to Elizabeth Kennedy, December 12, 1844, Kennedy MSS; Samuel Sample to Schuyler Colfax, January 15, 1845 (quotation), Colfax MSS (NIHS); Brock, *Political Conscience*, pp. 156–63; Cooper, *Politics of Slavery*, pp. 219–23; Merk, *Slavery*, pp. 140–59.

22. Sample to Colfax, January 15, 1845, Colfax MSS; John P. Kennedy to Elizabeth Kennedy, December 12, 1844, Kennedy MSS; Joseph H. Peyton to William B. Campbell, February 16, 1845, CFP. For details of the Brown plan, see the books by Brock, Cooper, and Merk cited in note 210.

23. Arthur Campbell to James Campbell, November 21, 1844, CFP; Robert Toombs to Berrien, February 13, 1845, Berrien MSS.

24. *Congressional Globe*, 28th Cong., 2nd Sess., p. 194; Silbey, *Shrine of Party*, pp. 60–62.

25. William E. Sutton to Rives, January 31, 1845, James F. Strother to Rives, February 2, 1845, and James Tallmadge to Rives, February 19, 1845, Rives MSS; Toombs to Berrien, February 13, 1845, Charles Jenkins to Berrien, February 15, 1845, N. C. Barnett to Berrien, February 18, 1845, Berrien MSS; Daniel Webster to Franklin Haven, February 2, 1845, and Webster to Edward Everett, February 26, 1845, Webster MSS.

26. *Congressional Globe*, 28th Cong., 2nd Sess., pp. 360, 372; see also the section of the books by Merk, Cooper, and Brock listed in note 21; see also Sellers, *Polk: Continentalist*, pp. 214–23.

27. Allen F. Owen to John M. Berrien, January 2, 1845, Samuel Dickson to Berrien, February 3, 1845, Charles J. Jenkins to Berrien, February 3, 15, April 22, 1845, Berrien MSS; S. T. Chapman to Alexander H. Stephens, February 4, 1845, Stephens to James Thomas, February 11, 1845, Stephens MSS (LC); Toombs to Stephens, February 16, 1845, in Phillips, "Correspondence of Toombs, Stephens, and Cobb," pp. 63–64. For more on the Georgia Whig divisions, see Walton, "Georgia's Biennial Legislatures."

28. Toombs to Berrien, February 13, 1845, and J. R. A. Merriweather to Berrien, April 21,

May 10, 1845, Berrien MSS. See also C. B. Strong to Berrien, April 25, May 9, June 10, 1845, Berrien MSS. By 1845, the Tariff of 1842 was drawing increasing criticism from Georgia's Whigs because its high rates on English iron rails increased the state government's costs for constructing the Western and Atlantic Railroad. Throughout the winter of 1844–45, indeed, Governor Crawford bombarded Berrien and Stephens with pleas to secure a reduction of rates on railroad iron.

29. Toombs to Stephens, January 24, 1845, in Phillips, "Correspondence of Toombs, Stephens, and Cobb," pp. 60–62; S. T. Chapman to Stephens, February 4, 1845, Stephens MSS (LC); Charles J. Jenkins to Berrien, April 22, August 6, 1845, and Francis S. Bartow to Berrien, July 30, August 3, 1845, Berrien MSS.

30. James E. Harvey to Thomas Butler King, October 20, 1845, King MSS.

31. For Whig expectations and disappointment in Virginia, see J. J. Fry to Rives, January 23, 1845, and Jno. Pendleton to Rives, May 1, 1845, Rives MSS. A year later, when the Whigs also lost the legislative elections, the chief Whig paper in the state openly admitted that the party could find no state issues with which to contest the elections. Richmond *Whig*, April 19, 1846.

32. Bergeron, *Antebellum Politics in Tennessee*, pp. 77–80. The percentages are calculated from the figures in Congressional Quarterly's *Guide to U.S. Elections*, pp. 78–80.

33. *New York Tribune*, November 16, 1844.

34. Webster to Samuel Hurd Walley, March 8, 1845, Webster MSS; copy of Massachusetts anti-Texas resolution, March 31, 1845, Adams Family Papers; Dalzell, *Webster*, pp. 102–05; *New York Tribune*, March 13, September 4, 27, 1845; Maizlish, *Triumph of Sectionalism*, pp. 62–64; Samuel Sample to Schuyler Colfax, June 8, 1845, Colfax MSS (NIHS).

35. William Ellsworth to Roger Sherman Baldwin, April 9, 1845, and Roger Sherman Baldwin to S. C. Phillips, Charles Allen, and Charles Francis Adams, July 3, 1845, copy, BFP.

36. Joshua Giddings to S. C. Phillips, Charles Allen, and Charles Francis Adams, July 7, 1845, Salmon P. Chase to S. C. Phillips et al., July 2, 1845, William W. Ellsworth to S. C. Phillips et al., July 2, 1845, and Julius Lemoyne to S. C. Phillips et al., July 22, 1845, Adams Family Papers. The best modern analysis of Whig and Democratic attitudes toward expansion in general and Texas annexation in particular is now Morrison, *Slavery and the American West*. For his discussion of Texas, see pp. 13–38.

37. For these developments, see Brauer, *Cotton versus Conscience*; Dalzell, *Webster*, pp. 91–107; Donald, *Sumner*, pp. 135–41; Charles Francis Adams to Louisa C. Adams, January 24, 1845, and Abbott Lawrence to Charles Francis Adams, November 17, 1845, Adams Family Papers; Abbott Lawrence to William C. Rives, January 17, 1845, Rives MSS; Nathan Appleton to C. F. Adams, John Gorham Palfrey, and Charles Sumner, November 10, 1845, copy, Appleton MSS.

38. Stanley, "Majority Tyranny"; William Henry Seward to Gerrit Smith, January 21, 1845, Seward MSS (RU); *Albany Evening Journal*, quoted in the *New York Tribune*, January 13, 1845. See also the *Tribune*, January 9, March 11, April 20, 24, May 17, 20, June 9, 18, and July 2, 3, 1845.

39. L. Saltonstall to Henry Clay, December 10, 1844, Henry Clay MSS (LC); George Wm. Boyd to John Quincy Adams, April 7, 1845, Adams Family Papers; *New York Tribune*, December 17, 1844, January 17, April 10, 1845; S. M. Troutman to James M. Bell, November 13, 1844, James Bell MSS; Abbott Lawrence to Edward Everett, March 31, 1845, Everett MSS.

40. *New York Tribune*, November 26, 1844, January 7, 9, 1845; draft of Webster's speech, November 10, 1844, Webster to David P. Hall, November 26, 1844, and Webster to Robert C. Winthrop, December 13, 29, 1844, Webster MSS; copy of the Massachusetts legislative resolution, March 31, 1845, in Adams Family Papers; George Tucker to William C. Rives, November 16, 1844, and John H. Pleasants to Rives, December 23, 1844, Rives MSS.

41. Jno. C. Hamilton to John M. Berrien, January 15, 1845, and J. Burnet to Berrien, February 14, 1845, Berrien MSS; Samuel Sample to Schuyler Colfax, December 1, 1844, Colfax MSS (NIHS); *New York Tribune*, March 10, 1845; U.S. Congress, *Senate Documents*, 28th Congress, 2nd Sess., Volume II, Documents 59 and 173; *Congressional Globe*, 28th Cong., 2nd Sess., pp. 389–90, 3030.

42. Resolutions of the New Haven Whig meeting, November 14, 1844, included with P. S. Galphin, et al. to Henry Clay, November 16, 1844, Henry Clay MSS (LC); Ellsworth's speech in the *New York Tribune*, November 28, 1844; Boston *Courier*, quoted in the *Pennsylvania*

Telegraph (Harrisburg), October 29, 1845; "Boston Correspondence," *New York Tribune*, November 7, 1845. For the quarreling in New York, see the *New York Tribune*, December 18, 1844, January 24, February 18, March 12, 20, 21 (quotation), April 5, 7, 10, May 17, 20, June 9, September 4, November 4, 14, 1845.

43. *New York Tribune*, September 26, November 5, December 31, 1845, January 1, 3, 1846; John P. Kennedy to Philip C. Pendleton, October 9, 1845, copy, Kennedy MSS; William Henry Seward to Thurlow Weed, January 1, 1846, and John Tayler Hall to Weed, February 17, 1846, Weed MSS (RU).

44. On Ohio, see Maizlish, "The Triumph of Sectionalism," pp. 74–95; and Sharp, *Jacksonians versus the Banks*, pp. 140–52. On Pennsylvania, see Holt, *Political Crisis*, p. 112; and Mueller, *Whig Party in Pennsylvania*, pp. 131–32. On Indiana, see Samuel Sample to Schuyler Colfax, December 8, 1844, Colfax MSS (NIHS); *New York Tribune*, February 1, 1845; and Godlove Orth to Colfax, August 16, 1845, Orth MSS. On Connecticut, see *New York Tribune*, April 16, 1846; Roger Sherman Baldwin to S. D. Hubbard, March 28, 1846, Emily Baldwin to Edward Baldwin, April 12, 1846, May 12, 1847 (quotation), BFP; A. E. Burr to Gideon Welles, June 17, 1846, Welles MSS (NYPL); Welles to Isaac Toucey, June 23, 1846, Welles MSS (LC). Since the proposed railroad line needing the Middletown bridge would connect New Haven with Boston, New Haven Whigs favored the bridge, while Hartford Whigs, fearing disruption of river traffic, opposed it.

45. *New York Tribune*, November 21, 1845, April 2, 1846; Thomas J. Stead to Samuel F. Man, March 18, 1846, Jenckes MSS.

46. Sewell, *Ballots for Freedom*, pp. 126–30; Daniel Webster to James Wilson, March 16, 1846, and Webster to Anthony Colby, May 20, 1846, Webster MSS; John P. Hale to Joshua R. Giddings, April 5, 1846, Giddings MSS; Franklin Pierce to Edmund Burke, November 18, 1846, March 2, 1847, Burke MSS; *New York Tribune*, March 15, 1847. Both Whig and Democratic turnout in 1847 soared above their respective levels in the presidential election, and it has been estimated that the proportion of eligible males voting in New Hampshire's elections was 66.4 percent in 1844, 71.9 percent in 1846, and 77.2 percent in 1847. See Table 1 in Gienapp, " 'Politics Seems to Enter into Everything,' " pp. 18–19.

47. Godlove Orth to Schuyler Colfax, January 27, 1846, in Schauinger, ed., "Orth Letters," 39, pp. 378–80.

48. Among works by political scientists, I have been primarily influenced by Kernell, "Presidential Popularity"; Fiorina, *Retrospective Voting*; Bloom and Price, "Voter Response"; and Hibbing and Alford, "Electoral Impact."

49. *Messages and Papers of the Presidents*, IV, pp. 373–84, 392–98; Merk, *Manifest Destiny*, pp. 29, 46, 62–64; Sellers, *Polk: Continentalist*, pp. 358–415. In the House vote to give notice, 52 percent of the Whigs voted yea and 48 percent nay. Alexander, *Sectional Stress*, p. 188, vote 11. For evidence of the strategic considerations dividing the Whigs on Oregon, see the Washington correspondence and editorials in the *New York Tribune*, January 8, 17, 20, 31, February 5, 13, March 25, June 20, 1846; "The Whig Party, Its Position, and Duties," *The American Review*, II (December 1845), 554–56; William B. Campbell to David Campbell, December 22, 1845, March 8, 1846, CFP; William Henry Seward to Thurlow Weed, January 3, 6, 22, 1846, Weed MSS (RU); and Truman Smith to William C. Rives, February 24, 1846, Rives MSS.

50. The situation in Massachusetts is detailed in Brauer, *Cotton versus Conscience*; Donald, *Sumner*, pp. 143–49; and Dalzell, *Webster*, pp. 113–22. Winthrop privately justified his vote in the following terms, which reflect the dilemma of many Whigs: "The Mexican War Bill presented the most difficult case for an honest man to give a satisfactory vote upon, which I have ever met with. I could not bear the whole Massts. Delegation should be mixed up with a little knot of ultraists against supplies; and altho' the preamble of the Bill did not tell the whole truth, I thought that the rejection of our Minister by Mexico was, under all circumstances, a pretty serious affront, & one which at least *divided* the responsibility of the war." Winthrop to Edward Everett, June 7, 1846, Everett MSS.

51. For the votes in Congress and state legislatures, see Alexander, *Sectional Stress*, pp. 57–69; Silbey, *Shrine of Party*, pp. 172–88; and Holt, *Political Crisis*, p. 47. The standard account of Whig opposition to the war is Schroeder, *Polk's War*, but see also: Howe, *Political Culture*,

pp. 92–93; Bolchin, "Caleb B. Smith's Opposition"; Boritt, "Lincoln's Opposition"; Gilley, "Polk's War"; id., "Tennessee Whigs"; and Graebner, "Party Politics." Typical examples of Whig denunciations can be found in *The American Review*, IV (December 1846), 545–47; V (May 1847), 433–46; VI (October 1847), 331–46; VI (December 1847), 553–60; and I (January 1848), 1–14.

52. The specific appropriations in the vetoed Rivers and Harbors bill were printed in *The Whig (Tribune) Almanac for 1847*, p. 38.

53. For example, see the *New York Tribune*, December 20, 1844, January 7, 17, 18, 1845; Thurlow Weed to Francis Granger, February 12, 1845, Granger MSS; Henry Clay to John J. Crittenden, November 28, 1844, Henry Clay MSS (LC); and Clay to John M. Clayton, December 2, 1844, Clayton MSS.

54. *New York Tribune*, April 14, 1846; "The Independent Treasury," *The American Review*, III (May 1846), 465–68; "Finance and Commerce," ibid., 556–57; *New York Tribune*, August 8, 1846.

55. Abbott Lawrence to William C. Rives, January 17, 26, 1846, Rives MSS. I provide a much fuller analysis of Whigs' predictions about the baneful economic consequences of tariff reduction, the Independent Treasury system, and the Public Warehouse Act in my "Winding Roads to Recovery: The Whig Party from 1844 to 1848," in Holt, *Political Parties*, pp. 192–236.

56. Abbott Lawrence to William C. Rives, January 17, 26, 1846, Rives MSS; *New York Tribune*, August 14, 1845; "Mr. Walker's Report and Bill," *The American Review*, III (April 1846), 335–48; ibid., III (May 1846), 466; *New York Tribune*, February 27, May 9, June 17, 18, July 6, 15, 1846.

57. *New York Tribune*, July 6, 1846; Truman Smith to Nathan Appleton, April 9, 1846, Appleton MSS; John B. Lamar to Howell Cobb, June 24, 1846, in Phillips, "Correspondence of Toombs, Stephens, and Cobb," pp. 82–84; H. King to Thomas Butler King, June 22, 1846, King MSS; James Bowen to Thurlow Weed, July 21, 1846, Weed MSS (RU). Significantly, Seward doubted that the Whigs could carry New York on the tariff issue in 1846. Seward to James Bowen, September 25, 1846, Seward MSS (RU).

58. Webster's attempt to arrange a compromise tariff can be followed in great detail in the Daniel Webster MSS for July 1846; Dalzell, *Webster*, pp. 109–12; *New York Tribune*, July 23, 24, August 8, 1846.

59. Daniel Webster to James K. Mills, July 21, 24, 1846, Webster to Fletcher Webster, July 27, 29, 1846, and Joseph Balch to Webster, July 25, 1846, Webster MSS.

60. Moses Stuart to Daniel Webster, August 3, 1846, Webster MSS; Thomas Corwin to Thomas Ewing, August 1, 1846, and William Bebb to Ewing, August 10, 1846, EFP; *The American Review*, IV (September 1846), 228. For other examples of Whig confidence that they could win by campaigning against the Democratic economic legislation of 1846, see *New York Tribune*, August 12, September 3, 1846; R. Fisher to Thomas Butler King, August 3, 1846, and S. Jardin to King, August 6, 1846, King MSS.

61. For a superb analysis of the decentralized nature of the Whig organization in a crucial state, see Booraem, *Republican Party in New York*, pp. 79–115 and passim.

62. Moses Stuart to Webster, August 3, 1846, Webster MSS; ZT:SWH, p. 63.

63. For this and the preceding three paragraphs, see Truman Smith to Thomas Butler King, September 16, 17, October 13, 1846, King MSS; Smith to John Davis, September 16, October 26, 1846, John Davis MSS. On Whig fund-raising efforts, see also Leo W. Blunt, July 20, 1846, and James G. King, July 30, 1846, to Thomas Butler King, King MSS; Abbott Lawrence to Nathan Appleton, August 4, 1846, Abbott Lawrence MSS; and Lawrence to Daniel Webster, August 4, 1846, Webster MSS. No central collection of Truman Smith's papers, alas, has survived, a great misfortune for a historian of the Whig party.

To convert the dollar amounts listed here and elsewhere in this study to 1995 dollars, one should multiply by a factor of 17.5. Thus Smith's original target of $7,500 was $131,250 in 1995 dollars. I have taken this conversion ratio from Hummel, *Emancipating Slaves*, p. 39.

64. For figures on turnout I have relied on William Gienapp's table, cited in note 46.

65. On the Whigs' delight with the reapportionment, see Robert Toombs to Alexander H. Stephens, January 1, 1844, in Phillips, "Correspondence of Toombs, Stephens, and Cobb," pp. 52–53.

66. See the sources cited in notes 42, 47, and 48 above. See also the *New York Tribune*, November 17, 20, December 2, 1845, April 1, May 2, 4, 5, August 20, 1846.

67. *New York Tribune*, April 26, May 17, 20, June 18, September 17, 1845, February 23, 28, March 2, 4, April 1, 21, May 2, 4, 5, August 13, 20, 1846; John Bradley to Thurlow Weed, February 1, 1846, Benton Rose to Weed, February 6, 1846, Alvah Hunt to Weed, February 17, 1846, John Tayler Hall to Weed, March 19, 1846, Washington Hunt to Weed, April 4, 1846, and Seward to Weed, April 5, 1846, Weed MSS (RU); Seward to John McLean, March 20, 1846, Seward MSS (LC); John T. Bush to Millard Fillmore, March 11, 1846, MFP-O.

68. Horace Greeley to Schuyler Colfax, April 22, 1846, Greeley-Colfax MSS; *New York Tribune*, April 27, May 2, 4, 5, June 2, July 2, 9, 21, 31, 1846.

69. *New York Tribune*, April 24, 26, May 3, 14, 1845, March 9, July 2, 9, October 12, 1846. For the analysis of Hunker and Barnburner voting in the constitutional convention, I have relied on Merkel, "Party and Constitution Making." Merkel convincingly disproves the existence of a Whig-Democratic consensus on economic issues in the convention, a notion advanced by Meyers, *Jacksonian Persuasion*, pp. 236–37. As Merkel demonstrates, most votes in the convention divided sharply along party lines, and the compromises forced upon the Barnburner majority were the product of Hunker aid to the Whigs, not agreement between most Democrats and most Whigs on economic policy.

70. Bush to Fillmore, March 11, 1846, MFP-O; Greeley to Weed, March 13, 1846, Seward to Weed, August 10, 1846, Philander B. Prindle to Weed, October 15, 1846, Weed MSS (RU); Greeley to Henry Clay, November 15, 1846, Henry Clay MSS (LC). To strip Barnburner Governor Silas Wright, whom Democrats renominated in 1846, of patronage, Hunkers also joined Whigs at the constitutional convention in voting to limit the governor's appointment powers.

71. Seward to James Bowen, September 25, 1846, Seward MSS (RU).

72. The best existing secondary account of the Anti-Rent movement is Ellis, *Landlords*, pp. 225–312. It will be supplanted, however, by a brilliant study of the legal issues involved in this prolonged controversy that my colleague Charles W. McCurdy is writing. I have also utilized David D. Barnard, "The 'Anti-Rent' Movement and Outbreak in New York," *The American Review*, II (December 1845), 587–98, which has a prolandlord bias, and the following issues of the *New York Tribune*: November 10, 11, December 2, 1845, January 9, 12, 17, March 4, 30, April 1, 6, May 5, 6, 15, 1846. Wright did commute the death sentences of the two men convicted of the murder to life imprisonment, but he refused to release other Anti-Renters convicted of lesser charges.

73. Barnard, "The 'Anti-Rent' Movement," loc. cit., p. 596; in addition to the issues of the *Tribune* cited in note 72, see those for July 31 and August 13, 1846; Van Deusen, *Greeley*, pp. 97–115; id., *Weed*, pp. 142–53; Greeley to Weed, May 14, 1846, Weed MSS (RU).

74. For this and the preceding paragraph, see *New York Tribune*, July 31, August 13, 26, 27, September 25, 26, October 7, 8, 14, 15, 29, 1846; Seward to Weed, August 10, 1846, Seth Hawley to Weed, August 21, 1846, Weed MSS (RU); B. F. Hall to Fillmore, August 21, 1846, J. L. White to Fillmore, August 27, 1846, D. O. Kellogg to Fillmore, September 17, 1846, J. L. Kellogg to Fillmore, September 27, 1846, Philip Hone to Fillmore, October 20, 1846, MFP-O; Fillmore to Artemus S. Childs, October 8, 1846, Millard Fillmore MSS (HSP); Greeley to Clay, November 15, 1846, Henry Clay MSS (LC); Seward to James Bowen, September 25, 1846, Seward MSS (RU).

75. *New York Tribune*, September 3, October 14, November 7, 20, 1846; Greeley to Clay, November 15, 1846, Henry Clay MSS (LC). Young, in fact, ran far better and Wright ran far more poorly in Anti-Rent strongholds than in the rest of the state, and regression analysis suggests that within Anti-Rent counties far more former Wright voters defected to Young or abstained than was true elsewhere. As a result, Wright retained only about three-fifths of his 1844 vote in Anti-Rent counties but three-fourths of it elsewhere in the state. Statistical analysis also suggests that Democrats who backed Young would not back Fish. For this analysis I have relied on a superb paper by my doctoral student John R. Kirn. See the tables on the 1846 election in his "Elections, Roll Calls."

76. John Couper to Thomas Butler King, November 17, 1846, R. R. Cuyler to King, November 12, 1846, circular of the Whig State Central Committee of Ohio, October 17, 1846, and Robert C. Schenck to King, October 25, 1846, King MSS; Davis to Clay, November 13, 1846,

Clay to John S. Littell, November 17, 1846, Henry Clay MSS (LC). See also the speeches by Webster and John M. Clayton ascribing the Whig victory to economic issues in the *New York Tribune*, November 10, 11, 1846.

Clay's fellow Kentuckian Crittenden also warned in January 1847 that it was too soon to consider the presidential nomination for 1848 because any Whig candidate would divert attention from "the conduct & measures of the present Administration which is now bringing down daily condemnation upon it, & the party that sustains it." Crittenden to George B. Kinkead, January 10, 1847, Crittenden MSS (Duke).

77. James E. Harvey to William Hayden, November 6, 29, 1846, Schouler MSS; Davis to Clay, November 13, 1846, with Abbott Lawrence to John Davis, November 12, 1846, enclosed, Henry Clay MSS (LC); Walter Forward to Millard Fillmore, October 26, 1846, MFP-O.

78. Jno. C. Pendleton to William C. Rives, November 23, 1846, January 31, 1847, Rives MSS; Sam W. Fite to William B. Campbell, August 13, November 24, 1846, John Bell to William B. Campbell, November 22, 1846, CFP; R. H. Kingsburgh to Nathan Appleton, June 18, 1846, Appleton MSS; Charles L. Hinton to Samuel F. Patterson, July 10, 1846, and Alfred Dockery to Duncan McLaurin, January 9, 1847, McLaurin MSS; Godlove Orth to Schuyler Colfax, January 27, 1846, in Schauinger, "Orth Letters," 39, 378–80; T. H. Nelson to Richard W. Thompson, July 5, 1847, Thompson MSS (Ind.SL); Thompson to H. J. Hilton, July 16, 1847, Thompson MSS (IU).

79. On the impact of the war and tariff issues in Connecticut, see John M. Niles to Gideon Welles, April 11, 1847, and William G. Pomeroy to Welles, May 11, 1847, Welles MSS (NYPL); A. E. Burr to Welles, April 13, 1847, Welles MSS (Conn.HS).

80. For an example of Whig doubts in Virginia, see William Ballard Preston to William C. Rives, February 28, 1847, Rives MSS; on North Carolina's reapportionment, see Walton, "Elections to the Thirtieth Congress," 196, and the *New York Tribune*, January 16, 1847.

81. Bergeron, *Antebellum Politics in Tennessee*, pp. 80–83, and William B. Campbell to David Campbell, January 23, 1848, CFP.

82. Horace Greeley to Schuyler Colfax, September 18, 1847, Greeley-Colfax MSS.

83. Walton, "Elections to the Thirtieth Congress," 186–202, provides a convenient summary of historians who cite changing sentiment on the war. Walton's main thesis is that southern Whigs began to boom Taylor for president in 1847 in order to help them in the congressional elections that year by neutralizing criticism that the Whigs were antiwar. He concludes that there is little evidence that Taylor helped Whig candidates or that their antiwar stance hurt them. In this admirable article, Walton takes no cognizance of the declining efficacy of economic issues from 1846 to 1847, and thus his interpretation differs markedly from my own.

84. R. R. Cuyler to Thomas Butler King, November 12, 1846, King MSS.

85. Again, readers interested in a fuller analysis of Whig assumptions about the baneful economic impact of Democratic policies should consult my "Winding Roads to Recovery." In addition to the sources, I cite there, I rely here on the following articles in the *American Review*: "Mr. Walker's Report and Bill," III (April 1846), 335–48; "The Independent Treasury" and "Finance and Commerce," III (May 1846), 465–68, 556–57; "Finance and Commerce," III (June 1846), 662–63; "Finance and Commerce," IV (July 1846), 95–98; "Finance and Commerce," IV (August 1846), 199–204; "The Tariff of 1846," IV (September 1846), 215–28; "Mr. Secretary Walker's Agricultural Project for the United States," IV (September 1846), 410–15; "The Twenty-Ninth Congress," IV (December 1846), 545–50; and "The Twenty-Ninth Congress," V (May 1847), 433–46.

86. Virtually every economic statistic available bears out this portrait. Exports in merchandise and grain exceeded imports, but imports of gold and silver dramatically exceeded exports in 1847. The value of wheat exports jumped 300 percent in 1847 over 1846. Circulating currency expanded by 15.7 percent in 1847, even though state bank note circulation dropped slightly that year. Government receipts were down and deficits up, but the wholesale price index rose from 83 in 1845 and 1846 to 90 in 1847. For the relevant tables, see *Historical Statistics*, pp. 203, 886, 899, 993, 1104, and 1106. For Walker's financing of the war, see Shenton, *Walker*, pp. 87–98, and Cohen, *Business and Politics*, pp. 40–62.

87. Meredith P. Gentry to William B. Campbell, February 20, 1847, CFP; *American Review,*

V (May 1847), 436; *New York Tribune*, August 23, 1847; Daniel Ullmann to Henry Clay, July 12, 1847, Henry Clay MSS (LC).

88. Meredith P. Gentry to Daniel Webster, April 13, 1848, Webster MSS.

89. For North Carolina, see the sources cited in note 80; the North Carolina Whig platform of 1848 is printed in the *National Intelligencer* (Washington), March 2, 1848. The figures on New York are based on a content analysis of party addresses in Harp, "Character of Party Dialogue," pp. 30–32. Only the Hunker address in 1847 focused on national economic policy; the Barnburner address that year concentrated on slavery expansion and the internal party dispute. My analysis of Pennsylvania rests on my *Forging a Majority*, pp. 49–53. The quotation is from the resolutions of the Allegheny County Convention, *Pittsburgh Morning Post*, January 13, 1848. For more on the Democrats and the tariff issue in Pennsylvania, see Snyder, *Jacksonian Heritage*, pp. 194–202. Despite their defense of the Walker Tariff, Democrats still tried to shift attention to other matters; 51 percent of the space in their 1847 and 1848 platforms was devoted to the Mexican War.

90. The best study of the popular reaction to the war is Johannsen, *To the Halls*. For Polk's denunciation of the Whigs in his annual messages of December 1846 and December 1847, see Schroeder, *Polk's War*, pp. 63–64, 148–49.

91. Johannsen, *To the Halls*, pp. 68–143 and passim.

92. The summary of Whig arguments against the war in this and subsequent paragraphs is based on the sources listed in note 51. For attacks on Walker's requests for duties on tea and coffee, see the *New York Tribune*, December 18, 1846, January 4, 8, March 2, 1847.

93. *New York Tribune*, June 2, 9, 11, 18, 1846, January 12, 25, 1847; Daniel Webster to Fletcher Webster, April 18, 1847, Webster MSS; Winfield Scott to Robert P. Letcher, June 5, 1846, Crittenden MSS (Duke). On Ringgold, see Johannsen, *To the Halls*, pp. 123–27. For fuller accounts of the hostile relations between Generals Taylor and Scott and the Polk administration, see Hamilton, *Zachary Taylor*, pp. 217–230; Elliott, *Scott*, pp. 417–596; and "The Administration: Its Treatment of General Scott," *The American Review*, I (June 1848), 553–72. *The American Review* renumbered its volumes beginning in 1848.

94. Corwin's speech quoted in Graebner, "Corwin and the Election of 1848," 163. The activities of Giddings and other extreme antiwar Whigs are covered extensively in Schroeder, *Polk's War*, pp. 29–32 and passim, and Stewart, *Giddings*, pp. 110–40. For vivid examples of Giddings' scornful attitude toward his fellow Whigs, see Giddings to J. A. Giddings, December 20, 1846, January 4, 1847, Giddings MSS; and Giddings to Horace Greeley, December 27, 1846, Giddings-Julian MSS. Scores of letters in the Giddings MSS and the Adams Family Papers for 1846 and 1847 document this intraparty feud, as well as Giddings' link with the Young Whigs of Massachusetts.

95. Donald, *Sumner*, pp. 140–59; Dalzell, *Webster*, pp. 114–22; Stewart, *Giddings*, pp. 110–40; Schroeder, *Polk's War*, pp. 59–62.

96. David Campbell to William B. Campbell, December 24, 1846, CFP.

97. *National Intelligencer*, February 28, 1848; Schroeder, *Polk's War*, pp. 155–56; Johannsen, *To the Halls*, pp. 164–74.

98. Schroeder, *Polk's War*, p. 46; Foner, "Wilmot Proviso"; Morrison, *Democratic Politics*.

99. *New York Tribune*, August 12, 1846; Schroeder, *Mr. Polk's War*, p. 49; Columbus Delano to Joshua R. Giddings, August 25, 1846, Giddings MSS.

100. See, for example, the reports on Whig and Democratic positions in Congress and the New York legislature in the *New York Tribune*, January 23, 27, 1847; Joshua R. Giddings to Charles Francis Adams, August 12, 1847, Adams Family Papers.

101. Walton, "Elections to the Thirtieth Congress;" Schroeder, *Polk's War*, pp. 82–88; John McLean to John Teesdale, April 6, 1847, McLean MSS (OHS).

102. My views on the southern stake in the Proviso issue are further elaborated in Holt, *Political Crisis*, pp. 52–56. See also Cooper, *Politics of Slavery*, pp. 238–44; Lander, *Reluctant Imperialists*, pp. 63, 71–73, and passim.

103. Cooper, *Politics of Slavery*, p. 228; Schroeder, *Polk's War*, p. 86.

104. *Augusta Daily Chronicle and Sentinel*, May 18, June 17, 1847, quoted in Schroeder, *Polk's War*, p. 124; William B. Campbell to David Campbell, November 20, 1847, CFP. For

additional statements by southern Whigs that acquisition would endanger, not benefit, the South, see Alfred Dockery to Duncan McLaurin, January 9, 1847, McLaurin MSS; William Ballard Preston to William C. Rives, February 28, 1847, Rives MSS; Richmond *Whig*, March 27, 1847; and Rives to David Campbell, September 13, 1847, CFP.

105. Daniel P. King to Charles Francis Adams, January 17, 1847, Giddings to Adams, August 12, 1847, Adams Family Papers; Charles Sumner to Giddings, January 22, 1847, Giddings MSS.

106. *Ohio State Journal*, April 13, 1847, quoted in Schroeder, *Polk's War*, p. 124; see ibid., pp. 86–87, for votes in Congress; Richard W. Thompson to ?, June 8, 1847, draft, Thompson MSS (Ind.SL); Corwin to Thomas B. Stevenson, September 23, 1847, Stevenson MSS. See also John McLean to William C. Rives, February 27, 1847, Rives MSS; and McLean to John Teesdale, April 16, 1847, McLean MSS (OHS).

107. Philadelphia *North American and United States Gazette*, March 12, 1847; *New York Tribune*, October 9, 1847; Washington *National Intelligencer*, January 26, 1848.

108. Dalzell, *Webster*, pp. 122–41.

109. *New York Tribune*, December 4, 1847.

110. Corwin to Crittenden, September 2, 1847, Corwin MSS (OHS); Corwin to Thomas B. Stevenson, December 10, 1847, Stevenson MSS; Andrew S. Fulton to David Campbell, January 1848, CFP; Robert C. Winthrop to John P. Kennedy, January 24, 1848, Winthrop MSS.

111. Schroeder, *Polk's War*, pp. 89, 124–41; Johannsen, *To the Halls*, p. 130; *New York Tribune*, November 16, 1847; "The President's Message—The War," *The American Review*, I (January 1848), 1–14; "The National Finances: The War Debt," *The American Review*, I (February 1848), 170–78.

112. William H. Underwood to John M. Berrien, December 19, 1847, Berrien MSS.

113. *New York Tribune*, October 19, 1847.

114. Truman Smith to William C. Rives, December 17, 1847, Rives to Jno. C. Pendleton, December 28, 1847, Rives MSS; David Outlaw to Emily Outlaw, December 20, 1847, January 7, 1848, Outlaw MSS; Andrew S. Fulton to David Campbell, January 1848, CFP.

115. David Outlaw to Emily Outlaw, January 23, 1848, Outlaw MSS; Alexander H. H. Stuart to Richard W. Thompson, February 9, 1848, Thompson MSS (Lincoln National Life Foundation).

116. Truman Smith to Rives, October 18, 1847, Rives MSS.

CHAPTER 9

1. Thomas Dorr to Edmund Burke, January 13, 1848, Burke MSS; see sources listed in notes 2 and 3, Chapter 8.

2. William H. Seward to Thurlow Weed, February 5, 1848, Weed MSS (RU); Dorr to Burke, January 13, 1848, Burke MSS; *New York Tribune*, January 24, 1848.

3. Poage, *Clay*, p. 152; Clay to John J. Crittenden, November 28, 1844, in Coleman, *Crittenden*, I, pp. 223–25.

4. Daniel Webster to Edward Everett, December 15, 1844, Everett MSS; Rayback, *Free Soil*, p. 95.

5. Moses Stuart to Webster, August 3, 1846, Edward Everett to Webster, December 5, 1846, Webster to James A. Hamilton, June 16, July 1, 1847, and Webster to Thomas Butler King, July 1, 1847, Webster MSS.

6. Dalzell, *Webster*, pp. 114–41.

7. Ibid., pp. 256–57.

8. Rayback, *Free Soil*, pp. 1–10; Maizlish, *Triumph of Sectionalism*, pp. 80–84.

9. Maizlish, *Triumph of Sectionalism*, pp. 80–82; James Harvey to McLean, April 24, 1846 and McLean to Harvey, May 1, 1846, draft, McLean MSS (LC); McLean to John Teesdale, December 11, 1846, McLean MSS (OHS); Elisha Whittlesey to William C. Rives, August 30, 1846, Rives MSS.

10. William Miner to McLean, April 24, 1846, McLean MSS (LC); John B. Mower to Willie P. Mangum, June 8, 1846, James E. Harvey to Mangum, August 25, October 24, 1846, in *The Mangum Papers*, IV, pp. 448–49, 479–81, 500–502, 515–16; Elisha Whittlesey to William C. Rives, August 30, 1846, James Lyon to Rives, November 11, 1844, James F. Strother to Rives, November 17, 1844, and McLean to Rives, February 19, 1846, Rives MSS. Harvey, one of the

most influential behind-the-scenes players in the Whig party, was simultaneously the Washington correspondent for the Philadelphia *North American*, the Boston *Atlas*, the Richmond *Whig*, and a Maryland paper. James E. Harvey to Daniel Webster, June 11, 1846, Webster MSS.

11. A. H. Shepperd to Willie P. Mangum, May 20, 1846, George C. Collins to Mangum, July 14, 1846, *The Mangum Papers*, IV, pp. 438–39, 455–57; Rayback, *Free Soil*, p. 7.

12. Maizlish, *Triumph of Sectionalism*, pp. 84–85; McLean to John Teesdale, October 16, 1846, McLean MSS (OHS).

13. William J. Hough to William Allen, December 9, 1844, Allen MSS (LC); *New York Tribune*, November 8, 1844; T. B. King to Winfield Scott, February 15, 1845, draft, King MSS; Corwin to Oran Follett, March 13, 1845, quoted in Rayback, *Free Soil*, p. 3.

14. William H. Seward to Thurlow Weed, January 6, 1846, Weed MSS (RU); Arthur Campbell to James Campbell, March 8, 1846, CFP; John J. Crittenden to Robert P. Letcher, March 9, 1846, Crittenden MSS (Duke); Rayback, *Free Soil*, pp. 3–4.

15. Elliott, *Scott*, pp. 425–29; William S. Robinson to William Schouler, June 12, 1846, Schouler MSS; Amos Sawyer to Thurlow Weed, June 22, 1846, Weed MSS (RU); *Boston Courier*, June 15, 1846, quoted in Rayback, *Free Soil*, p. 5.

16. Maizlish, *Triumph of Sectionalism*, p. 84; Rayback, *Free Soil*, pp. 9–10; W. Jones to William C. Rives, February 27, 1847, Rives MSS; Seward to Weed, late February 1847, in *Seward at Washington*, pp. 37–38; McLean to Teesdale, December 22, 1846, February 7, 1847, McLean MSS (OHS).

17. John J. Crittenden to George B. Kinkead, January 10, 1847, Crittenden MSS (Duke).

18. Godlove Orth to Schuyler Colfax, August 16, 1845, Orth MSS; Orth to Colfax, February 11, May 9, 1847, in Schauinger, "Orth Letters," 39, 384–89; T. H. Nelson to Richard W. Thompson, July 5, 1847, Thompson MSS (Ind.SL).

19. Everett to Webster, December 5, 1846, Webster MSS; C. F. Adams to Joshua R. Giddings, May 19, 1847, Giddings MSS.

20. Clay to John S. Littell, November 17, 1846, Henry Clay MSS (LC); Clay to John Pendleton Kennedy, December 27, 1846, Kennedy MSS; Clay to John M. Clayton, April 16, 1847, Clayton MSS; Clay to Henry White, November 27, 1846, in *The Works of Henry Clay*, V, pp. 537–38; Walter Forward to Millard Fillmore, October 26, 1846, MFP-O.

21. Clay to Clayton, April 16, 1847, Clayton MSS; Clay to Ullmann, May 12, 1847, Ullmann to Clay, July 12, 1847, Henry Clay MSS (LC).

22. Corwin to Thomas Ewing, August 1, 1846, EFP; Robert Young to McLean, December 25, 1846, McLean MSS (LC).

23. Rayback, *Free Soil*, pp. 9–10; Maizlish, *Triumph of Sectionalism*, pp. 84–88; Wm. Miner to McLean, September 28, 1846, James Harvey to McLean, October 12, 1846, Robt. Young to McLean, December 25, 1846, John Teesdale to McLean, April 28, 1847, McLean MSS (LC); McLean to Teesdale, September 26, December 11, 1846, McLean MSS (OHS); Schenck to T. B. King, October 26, 1846, King MSS. For evidence of Corwin's hesitancy to become a candidate, see Corwin to William Greene, May 30, June 7, July 25, 1847, in Hamlin, "William Greene Papers," 18–23.

24. Seward to Thurlow Weed, late February 1847, in *Seward at Washington*, pp. 37–38; *Ohio State Journal*, February 20, 1847, quoted in Maizlish, *Triumph of Sectionalism*, p. 84; Henry Wilson to Joshua R. Giddings, February 6, 1847, Greeley to Giddings, April 24, 1847, Giddings MSS.

25. McLean to Teesdale, September 26, December 11, 1846, February 7, 1847, McLean MSS (OHS).

26. Maizlish, *Triumph of Sectionalism*, pp. 85–86; McLean to Rives, February 27, 1847, Rives MSS; McLean to Teesdale, April 6, 1847, McLean MSS (OHS); Thomas B. Stevenson to John J. Crittenden, May 1, 1847, Crittenden MSS (LC).

27. Joshua R. Giddings to Joseph A. Giddings, January 31, 1846, William Slade to J. R. Giddings, April 27, 1846, C. F. Adams to J. R. Giddings, December 16, 1846, Charles Sumner to J. R. Giddings, January 7, 21, 22, 1847; and Henry Wilson to Giddings, February 6, April 10, 1847, Giddings MSS; J. R. Giddings to Horace Greeley, December 24, 1846, Giddings-Julian MSS.

28. J. R. Giddings to C. F. Adams, April 16, 1847, Adams Family Papers; Giddings to Horace Greeley, April 16, 1847, Giddings-Julian MSS.

29. Greeley to Giddings, April 24, 1847, Giddings MSS; Henry Wilson to Giddings, April 10, 1847, Giddings to C. F. Adams, March 15, 1847, Adams Family Papers.

30. Graebner, "Corwin and the Election of 1848"; Wilson to Giddings, April 10, 1847, Adams Family Papers; Maizlish, *Triumph of Sectionalism*, pp. 89–90; Rayback, *Free Soil*, p. 94; Corwin to Thomas B. Stevenson, September 23, 1847, Stevenson MSS.

31. Giddings to C. F. Adams, August 12, December 7, 1847, January 10, 1848, C. F. Adams to John G. Palfrey, December 11, 23, 1847, Adams Family Papers.

32. W. Jones to William C. Rives, February 27, 1847, Rives MSS.

33. Calhoun quoted in Rayback, *Free Soil*, p. 28; George W. Crawford to John M. Berrien, February 23, 1847, Berrien MSS.

34. Rayback, *Free Soil*, pp. 30–33; Cooper, *Politics of Slavery*, pp. 234–38.

35. William B. Preston to William C. Rives, February 28, 1847, Rives MSS.

36. *Florida Sentinel* quoted in Rayback, *Free Soil*, p. 42; McLean to Teesdale, April 29, 1847, McLean MSS (OHS). The most forceful case that southern Whig support for Taylor was motivated primarily by the need to neutralize the Proviso issue by running a slaveholding candidate is made in Cooper, *Politics of Slavery*, pp. 244–53.

37. Meredith P. Gentry to William B. Campbell, February 20, 1847, CFP.

38. J. J. Crittenden to G. B. Kinkead, January 10, 1847, in Coleman, *Crittenden*, I, pp. 268–69; ZT:SWH, p. 64.

39. Kirwan, *Crittenden*, pp. 203–5, Taylor to Crittenden, May 15, 1847, quoted p. 205; Taylor to Crittenden, January 26, 1847, in Coleman, *Crittenden*, I, pp. 270–78; Crittenden to Taylor, March 23, 1847, Crittenden MSS (Duke); ZT:SWH, p. 40.

40. For a superb assessment of Taylor's military record in Mexico, see Bauer, *Zachary Taylor*, pp. 166–214. The battle of Buena Vista actually began on February 22, 1847, Washington's Birthday, a fact that would later prove to be of great symbolic significance.

41. Caleb B. Smith to J. R. Giddings, May 21, 1847, Horace Greeley to Giddings, April 24, 1847, Giddings MSS; George Ashmun to Daniel Webster, June 14, 1847, Webster MSS; James E. Harvey to Willie P. Mangum, June 3, 1847, in *The Mangum Papers*, V, pp. 65–68; Seward to his wife, March 31, 1847, in *Seward at Washington*, p. 42; Weed to ?, April 3, 1847, Weed MSS (LC); F. H. Davidge to Mangum, August 1, 1847, Mangum MSS (SHC, UNC).

42. Rayback, *Free Soil*, pp. 41–55; Edward S. Harden to Howell Cobb, May 3, 1847, in Phillips, "Correspondence of Toombs, Stephens, and Cobb," pp. 87–88; James Hamilton to John C. Calhoun, April 24, 1847, in Jameson, "Correspondence of Calhoun," pp. 1117–19; James Edward Henry to Samuel F. Patterson, August 24, 1847, Patterson MSS.

43. Poage, *Clay*, p. 155; Rayback, *Free Soil*, p. 48, quote from *Cincinnati Signal*, p. 49; Clay to Crittenden, September 26, 1847, Henry Clay MSS (LC).

44. ZT:SWH, pp. 21–24; Nevins, *Ordeal: Fruits*, pp. 198–99; Rayback, *Free Soil*, pp. 36–44.

45. Holman Hamilton disagrees with this traditional portrait and presents Taylor as a shrewd political strategist in ZT:SWH, pp. 41–51. In contrast, K. Jack Bauer's more recent biography reasserts the traditional critique of naiveté; Bauer, *Zachary Taylor*, pp. 215–38.

46. Zachary Taylor to Jefferson Davis, August 16, 1847, draft, Taylor to ?, December 16, 1847, draft, Taylor to Joseph Taylor, January 1, 1848, draft, Taylor to William M. Murphy, et al., January 23, 1848, draft, Taylor MSS (LC); Taylor to *Cincinnati Signal*, May 12, 1847, quoted in Rayback, *Free Soil*, p. 50; Taylor to Crittenden, September 15, 1847, March 25, 1848, Crittenden MSS (LC); ZT:SWH, pp. 40–47.

47. Taylor to Crittenden, December 16, 1847, Crittenden MSS (LC); ZT:SWH, p. 43; Taylor to Robert C. Wood, September 27, 1847, in Samson, *Letters of Zachary Taylor*, pp. 131–37; Taylor to Jefferson Davis, August 16, 1847, Taylor MSS. Davis married Taylor's daughter Sarah Knox Taylor in June 1835, but she died within three months of the wedding.

48. Alexander Bowie to John C. Calhoun, April 13, 1847, Duff Green to Calhoun, April 16, 1847, R. K. Crallé to Calhoun, April 18, 1847, and Fitzwilliam Byrdsall to Calhoun, July 19, 1847, in Jameson, "Correspondence of Calhoun," pp. 1107–27.

49. Stoddard Judge to N. P. Tallmadge, March 10, 1847, W. M. Bayard to Tallmadge, July 1847, N. T. Eldridge to Tallmadge, August 12, 1847, Philip Potter to Tallmadge, October 15, 1847, Tallmadge MSS.

50. Preston to Rives, December 18, 1847, Rives MSS.

51. John P. Kennedy to Thomas Turner, May 4, 1847, copy, Kennedy MSS; Iverson S. Harris to John M. Berrien, May 9, 1847, Berrien MSS; Berrien to Webster, June 21, 1847, Webster MSS; Rayback, *Free Soil*, p. 44; Walton, "Elections to the Thirtieth Congress."

52. McLean to John Teesdale, April 29, 1847, McLean MSS (OHS); Daniel Ullmann to Henry Clay, July 12, 1847, Botts to Clay, August 24, 1847, Henry Clay MSS (LC); Joseph L. White to Clay, September 4, 1847, Crittenden MSS (Duke); David Outlaw to Emily Outlaw, February 11, 23, 1848, Outlaw MSS.

53. John Bell to Wm. B. Campbell, December 23, 1847, CFP; Godlove Orth to Schuyler Colfax, May 9, 1847, in Schauinger, "Orth Letters," 39, 386–89; Caleb B. Smith to Allen Hamilton, February 15, 1848, Hamilton MSS; Nathan K. Hall to Millard Fillmore, January 9, 1848, MFP-O; Stevenson to Crittenden, May 1, 1847, Crittenden MSS (LC); Stevenson to Caleb B. Smith, March 6, 1848, Smith MSS.

54. Columbus Delano to Joshua R. Giddings, May 25, 1847, Giddings MSS; George W. Patterson to Thurlow Weed, January 28, 1848, Weed MSS (RU); Caleb B. Smith to Allen Hamilton, February 15, 1848, Hamilton MSS; Hall to Fillmore, January 9, 1848, MFP-O; Thomas B. Stevenson to J. J. Crittenden, September 1, 1847, Crittenden MSS (LC).

55. Wilson to Giddings, April 10, 1847, Giddings MSS; Charles Hudson to William Schouler, June 28, 1847, Schouler MSS; Stevenson to Crittenden, May 1, September 1, 1847, Crittenden MSS (LC); Corwin to Crittenden, September 2, 1847, Corwin MSS (OHS); *New York Tribune*, August 12, October 14, 1847; James Dunlap to John McLean, December 29, 1847, McLean MSS (LC); Godlove Orth to Schuyler Colfax, September 9, 1847, in Schauinger, "Orth Letters," 39, 389–90; William P. Walker to David Davis, September 5, 1847, David Davis MSS; Smith to Allen Hamilton, February 15, 1848, Hamilton MSS.

56. Zachary Taylor to Jefferson Davis, July 27, August 16, September 18, 1847, April 20, 1848, in McIntosh, et al., ed., *Papers of Jefferson Davis*, pp. 198–204, 208–14, 217–23, 304–11; Zachary Taylor to Joseph P. Taylor, January 1, 1848, Taylor MSS.

57. N. T. Eldridge to P. Potter, October 7, 1847, Tallmadge MSS; John McLean to Thomas Ewing, October 6, 1847, EFP; Seward to Home, October 14, 1847, in *Seward at Washington*, p. 55.

58. John Minor Botts to Clay, quoting a letter from Clay, August 24, 1847, Henry Clay MSS (LC).

59. Clay to Epes Sargent, February 15, 1847, quoted in Brock, *Political Conscience*, p. 185; Poage, *Clay*, p. 159; *New York Tribune*, September 11, 1847; Peter Sken Smith to Clay, November 6, 1847, Henry Clay MSS (LC); Clay to Horace Greeley, December 10, 1847, De Coppet Collection; Greeley to William E. Robinson, February 8, 1848, Greeley MSS (NYPL). A copy of Clay's Lexington Address can be found in *The Tribune Almanac for 1848*, pp. 7-16.

60. Poage, *Clay*, p. 160; E. C. Wines to Clay, August 16, 1847, in *The Works of Henry Clay*, V, pp. 547–48.

61. Poage, *Clay*, pp. 159–61; Rayback, *Free Soil*, pp. 125–26; Clay to Daniel Ullmann, August 11, 1847, in *Works of Henry Clay*, V, pp. 543–45; Thomas B. Stevenson to J. J. Crittenden, September 1, 1847, Crittenden MSS (LC).

62. Rayback, *Free Soil*, pp. 125–26; Greeley to Joshua R. Giddings, April 24, 1847, Giddings MSS; *New York Tribune*, September 3, 1847; Poage, *Clay*, p. 162; Van Deusen, *Greeley*, pp. 119–21; Thomas J. Dowling to John McLean, October 30, 1847, McLean MSS (LC); Joseph L. White to Clay, June 28, 1847, Crittenden MSS; White to Clay, September 4, 1847, Crittenden MSS (Duke).

63. White to Clay, September 4, 1847, Crittenden MSS (Duke); Clay to Crittenden, September 21, 26, 1847, Henry Clay MSS (LC).

64. Clay to Crittenden, September 21, 26, 1847, Henry Clay MSS (LC); copy of Robertson's Lexington Circular, October 1847, Clayton MSS; Robertson to Berrien, November 30, 1847, Berrien MSS.

65. Taylor to Clay, November 4, 1847, Henry Clay MSS (LC). The gist of Clay's letter of September 27, 1847, must be inferred from Taylor's reply.

66. Clay to Daniel Ullmann, August 11, 1847, Henry Clay MSS (LC).

67. Cleveland *True Democrat* quoted in the *New York Tribune*, October 11, 1847. Edited by E. S. Hamlin in 1847, the *True Democrat* would subsequently become a leading Free Soil paper in Ohio.

68. *New York Tribune*, October 11, 1847.

69. Kirwan, *Crittenden*, pp. 210–24; "Mr. Clay's Resolutions," *The American Review*, VI (December 1847), 553–60.

70. The Lexington Address is printed in *The Tribune Almanac for 1848*, pp. 7–16.

71. W. H. Seward to Frances Seward, January 19, 1848, in *Seward at Washington*, p. 60; Washington *National Intelligencer*, January 28, March 2, 1848; Luther J. Glenn to Howell Cobb, December 1, 1847, in Phillips, "Correspondence of Toombs, Stephens, and Cobb," p. 89.

72. J. B. Mower to McLean, December 6, 12, 1847, Thomas Dowling to McLean, December 7, 1847, McLean MSS (LC); N. K. Hall to Millard Fillmore, January 9, 1848, MFP-O; *New York Tribune*, November 26, 1847, January 10, 1848; Seward to Frances Seward, January 19, 1848, in *Seward at Washington*, p. 60; Seward to Weed, January 10, 1848, Weed MSS (RU).

73. N. K. Hall to Millard Fillmore, January 9, 1848, MFP-O; Truman Smith to William C. Rives, December 17, 1847, Rives to John C. Pendleton, December 28, 1847, draft, Rives MSS; Andrew S. Fulton to David Campbell, January 1848, CFP; David Outlaw to Emily Outlaw, December 20, 1847, January 7, 23, 1848, Outlaw MSS. Two virulently antiwar Whigs, Joshua R. Giddings of Ohio and John Gorham Palfrey of Massachusetts, as well as Amos Tuck, a product of the coalition among Liberty men, Whigs, and Hale Democrats in New Hampshire, voted against Winthrop, thereby disgusting regular Whigs at the fanaticism of antiwar zealots. See Ezra Lincoln to William Schouler, December 12, 1847, Schouler MSS.

74. Lexington Address in *Tribune Almanac for 1848*, pp. 7–16; Clay to Greeley, December 10, 1847, De Coppet Collection; Rayback, *Free Soil*, p. 148; Cooper, *Politics of Slavery*, p. 252; Marian Henry to Gustavus A. Henry, January 1848, Henry MSS; William P. McConnell to Thomas Butler King, March 6, 1848, King MSS; John P. Kennedy to Richard Pakenham, November 28, 1847, copy, Kennedy MSS; David Outlaw to Emily Outlaw, January 19, 21, 1848, Outlaw MSS.

75. Franklin W. Bowden to William P. Browne, November 24, 1847, Browne MSS; Charles Jenkins to John M. Berrien, December 13, 1847, March 11, 1848, Iverson L. Harris to Berrien, December 15, 1847, Berrien MSS; David Campbell to William B. Campbell, November 24, 1847, CFP; E. J. Hale to Daniel M. Barringer, January 21, 1848, Barringer MSS; William Ballard Preston to Rives, December 18, 1847, Rives MSS; Thomas M. Peters to George S. Houston, March 1, 1848, Houston MSS; Cooper, *Politics of Slavery*, pp. 225–68.

76. *New York Tribune*, November 19, 25, 26, December 21, 1847, January 24, 27, 1848; *Albany Evening Journal* quoted in Poage, *Clay*, pp. 166–67; Trenton *State Gazette* quoted in Rayback, *Free Soil*, p. 128; Samuel Hannah to Caleb B. Smith, January 25, 1848, Smith MSS; Harry Bradley to Millard Fillmore, February 18, 1848, MFP-O; James F. Babcock to Roger Sherman Baldwin, February 12, 1848, BFP; Thomas Dowling to McLean, December 7, 1847, McLean MSS (LC).

77. Thomas Dowling to McLean, December 7, 1847, J. B. Mower to McLean, January 3, 1848, H. Vallette to McLean, January 26, 1848, McLean MSS (LC); N. K. Hall to Fillmore, December 30, 1847, MFP-O; Seward to Weed, January 20, 1848, Weed MSS (RU). See also Samuel Hannah to Caleb B. Smith, January 25, 1848, and William H. Barnett to Smith, February 8, 1848, Smith MSS; and Jno. Ewing to George Dunn, February 9, 1848, Dunn MSS.

78. William Seward to Frances Seward, November 1847, in *Seward at Washington*, pp. 57–58; Charles Francis Adams to John Gorham Palfrey, December 11, 23, 1847, Giddings to C. F. Adams, January 10, 1848, Adams Family Papers; Samuel Galloway to John McLean, January 10, 1848, misdated 1847, McLean MSS (LC).

79. Thomas Dowling to McLean, October 30, December 23, 1847, February 26, 1848, John Teesdale to McLean, February 9, 1848, misdated 1847, J. B. Mower to McLean, February 15, 21,

March 12, April 2, 19, 24, May 15, 1848, McLean MSS (LC); Greeley to Clay, November 30, 1847, Henry Clay to Wife, February 18, 1848, Clay to James B. Clay, February 1, 1848, Henry Clay MSS (LC); *New York Tribune*, January 25, 1848; Cyrus Prentiss to Weed, January 28, 1848, Weed MSS (LC).

80. Truman Smith to Rives, October 18, 1847, Rives MSS.

81. Thomas Dorr to Edmund Burke, January 13, 1848, Burke MSS; Seward to Weed, February 5, 1848, Weed MSS (RU).

CHAPTER 10

1. Joshua R. Giddings to Charles Francis Adams, December 15, 1847, Adams Family Papers.

2. Seward to Frances Seward, January 19, 23, 29, 1848, in *Seward at Washington*, pp. 60–62.

3. Seward to Frances Seward, January 29, 1848, ibid., p. 62.

4. See Seward's letters cited in note 2; David Outlaw to Emily Outlaw, January 21, 1848, Outlaw MSS; John J. Crittenden to Albert T. Burnley, January 8, 1848, Crittenden MSS (Duke); Giddings to Adams, December 15, 1847, Adams Family Papers.

5. *ZT:SWH*, pp. 63–65.

6. Ibid., p. 43; Rayback, *Free Soil*, pp. 49–50. So widespread was this belief that as late as February 1848 New York's free-soil Barnburner Democrats considered making him their own candidate. J. R. Doolittle to Mary Doolittle, February 12, 1848, and Doolittle to Zachary Taylor, February 22, 1848, Doolittle MSS.

7. For the details of Georgia's Senate election, see Walton, "Georgia's Biennial Legislatures," 140–55. Berrien was sixty-six at the start of 1848. Dawson was sixteen years younger, and Stephens and Toombs were thirty-six and thirty-seven, respectively.

8. Berrien to Daniel Webster, June 21, 1847, Webster MSS; Walton, "Georgia's Biennial Legislatures," pp. 145–46. Berrien was elected on November 15. The Milledgeville *Southern Recorder*, the major Whig paper in the state capital, did not carry stories of Clay's speech until November 23, 1847.

9. Berrien to Webster, June 21, 1847, Webster MSS; J. S. Locke to Berrien, July 4, 1847, Iverson L. Harris to Berrien, December 15, 1847, Berrien MSS.

10. See Table 23 for the Democratic drop-off rate in 1847. For the vote in Flournoy's district, see Congressional Quarterly, *Guide to U.S. Elections* (Washington, 1975), p. 586. Because Whigs generally ran better in slaveholding than in nonslaveholding regions of the South and because three-fifths of the slaves counted in the apportionment of congressional districts within slave states, the total number of voters in southern congressional districts carried by Whigs was usually considerably lower than the total turnout in northern congressional districts. Even so, the 1,300 votes cast in Flournoy's district was an unusually small vote.

11. John C. Pendleton to Rives, November 19, 1847, William Ballard Preston to Rives, December 18, 1847, James Lyons to Rives, February 16, 1848, Rives MSS.

12. Boritt, *Lincoln*, pp. 63–147; Abraham Lincoln to T. S. Flournoy, February 17, 1848, to Usher F. Linder, February 20, March 22, 1848, and to Jesse Lynch, April 10, 1848, in *Collected Works of Lincoln*, I, pp. 452–64.

13. Truman Smith to Rives, October 18, 1847, Rives MSS; Truman Smith to Daniel M. Barringer, May 1, 1852, Barringer MSS; James Babcock to Roger Sherman Baldwin, February 12, 1848, Baldwin Family Papers. Hamilton in *ZT:SWH*, p. 63, asserts that Crittenden encouraged Smith to form the Young Indians, but his evidence for that statement is unclear.

14. Seward to Weed, January 20, 1848, Weed MSS (RU); Hall to Fillmore, December 28, 1847, MFP-O; David to Emily Outlaw, January 21, 1848, Outlaw MSS; Giddings to Adams, December 15, 1847, Adams Family Papers.

15. Hall to Fillmore, December 28, 1847, MFP-O; *ZT:SWH*, pp. 63–64; E. J. Hale to Daniel M. Barringer, January 4, 1848, Barringer MSS; John Ewing to George Dunn, February 9, 1848, Dunn MSS; Lincoln to Usher Linder, March 22, 1848, *Collected Works of Lincoln*, I, pp. 457–58. Without naming them, Lincoln asserted that in addition to himself and Smith, there were two Whigs from Indiana, three from Ohio, five from Pennsylvania, and four from New Jersey

in the Taylor group. Dunn was a freshman from a normally Democratic district. Like Flournoy, he had won by a single vote out of a total of 15,000 in 1847, so his preference for a No Party campaign is understandable.

16. John Gayle to William Crawford, December 11, 1847, Sarah Crawford MSS (Duke); Hall to Fillmore, December 28, 30, 1847, January 9, 1848, MFP-O; David Outlaw to Emily Outlaw, January 19, 28, 30, 1848, Outlaw MSS; John Bell to William B. Campbell, December 23, 1847, CFP; E. J. Hale to Daniel M. Barringer, January 4, 1848, Barringer MSS.

17. David Outlaw to Emily Outlaw, January 28, 30, 1848, Outlaw MSS; Hall to Fillmore, January 28, 1848, MFP-O; Washington *National Intelligencer*, February 5, 1848.

18. Fillmore to James Woods, February 5, 1848, De Coppet Collection; Franklin Pierce to Edmund Burke, February 1, 1848, Burke MSS; Godlove Orth to Caleb B. Smith, January 30, 1848, Smith MSS; John McLean to John Teesdale, February 7, 1848, McLean MSS (OHS); John Ewing to George Dunn, February 9, 1848, Dunn MSS.

19. William Rockhill to Allen Hamilton, January 15, 1848, Hamilton MSS; Poage, *Clay*, pp. 168–69; Seward to Frances Seward, January 19, 29, 1848, in *Seward at Washington*, pp. 60–62; Seward to Weed, January 20, 22, 1848, Weed MSS (RU); Henry Clay to James B. Clay, February 1, 1848, Clay to H. L. Duncan, February 15, 1848, Henry Clay MSS (LC).

20. Orth to Caleb Smith, January 30, 1848, Smith MSS.

21. *New York Tribune*, October 9, 1847, February 15, 1848; Washington *National Intelligencer*, February 7, March 25, April 29, 1848; Z. Collins Lee to John McLean, March 24, 1848, McLean MSS (LC).

22. The southern states that chose all delegates at a state convention included Texas, Arkansas, Missouri, Mississippi, Florida, Georgia, Kentucky, North Carolina, and Virginia. Rayback, *Free Soil*, p. 158.

23. *New York Tribune*, January 24, 27, 1848; Bergeron, *Antebellum Politics in Tennessee*, pp. 90, 95.

24. John H. Sanders to McLean, January 12, 1848, McLean MSS (LC); Samuel Hannah to Caleb B. Smith, January 25, 1848, Godlove Orth to Smith, January 30, 1848, and William H. Bennett to Smith, February 8, 1848, Smith MSS.

25. Thomas Corwin to William Greene, December 24, 1847, January 24, 1848, in Hamlin, "William Greene Papers," 25–27; William H. Seward to Frances Seward, January 23, 1848, in *Seward at Washington*, p. 62.

My account of the Ohio Whig convention in this and subsequent paragraphs is based on the following: Rayback, *Free Soil*, pp. 159–62; Maizlish, *Triumph of Sectionalism*, pp. 90–93; letters to John McLean in the McLean MSS (LC) from John Teesdale, December 15, 1847, January 4, 7, 11, 19, 20, February 9, 1848, Samuel Galloway, January 7, 10, 1848, William Miner, December 25, 26, 1847, January 8, 21, 1848, J. C. Wright, January 7, 1848; McLean to John Teesdale, December 25, 1847, McLean MSS (OHS); *National Intelligencer*, January 26, 1848; and Henry Stanbery, January 14, 1848, A. Banning Norton, January 20, 1848, Philemon B. Ewing, January 20, 1848, Dr. Boerstler, January 22, 1848, and N. H. Swayne, January 23, 1848, all to Thomas Ewing, EFP.

26. McLean's paper, the *Cincinnati Gazette*, and McLean in private correspondence had taken a position on territorial acquisition and the Wilmot Proviso, but McLean had made no public statement that rank-and-file Whigs could identify as his. Maizlish, *Triumph of Sectionalism*, p. 90.

27. An undated newspaper fragment of the January 7 letter is in the McLean MSS (LC); A. Banning Norton to Thomas Ewing, January 20, 1848, EFP.

28. Specifically, the territorial plank read: "Resolved, that we deprecate a war of conquest, and strenuously oppose the forceful acquisition of Mexican Territory; but if additional territory be forced upon us, or acquired by the nation, we shall demand that there 'shall be neither slavery nor involuntary servitude therein, otherwise than for punishment of crime.' " The quoted words were taken from the Wilmot Proviso. Washington *National Intelligencer*, January 26, 1848.

29. Henry Stanbery to Thomas Ewing, January 14, 1848, EFP.

30. A. Banning Norton to Thomas Ewing, January 20, 1848, EFP; for the subsequent efforts

of McLean's friends, see J. C. Wright to McLean, February 21, 1848, and the numerous letters from Teesdale to McLean in February, March, and April 1848 McLean MSS (LC).

31. Teesdale to McLean, February 9, 26, 28, March 2, 6, 1848, J. C. Wright to McLean, March 3, 1848, McLean MSS (LC); McLean to Teesdale, March 1, 1848, McLean MSS (OHS); William Bebb to Henry Clay, April 4, 1848, Thomas B. Stevenson MSS.

32. Henry Clay to H. L. Duncan, February 15, 1848, Henry Clay MSS (LC); L. C. Holmes to Millard Fillmore, February 4, 1848, MFP-O.

33. Clay to Greeley, December 10, 1847, De Coppet Collection; L. C. Holmes to Fillmore, February 4, 1848, MFP-O.

34. Seward to Thurlow Weed, February 5, 1848, Weed MSS (RU); Dudley Selden to Weed, February 3, 1848, Weed MSS (LC).

35. For further background on the divisions in New York, see Carman and Luthin, "Seward-Fillmore Feud"; and Rayback, "Silver Grey Revolt."

36. Dalzell, *Webster*, p. 292; Thomas Dowling to McLean, October 30, December 7, 1847, J. B. Mower to McLean, January 3, 1848, McLean MSS (LC); Greeley to Clay, November 30, 1847, Henry Clay MSS (LC); Hall to Fillmore, December 28, 1847, January 9, 1848, MFP-O.

37. Weed and Seward had reason to fear the wrath of New York City conservatives. In 1847, one of them wrote Crittenden that he had only two political objectives: "First the election of Mr. Clay or yourself & secondly the punishment of Seward & Co. for defrauding the country of Mr. Clay in 1840—until these men are destroyed there will be no peace in all Israel and but little of principle." Joseph L. White to Crittenden, June 28, 1847, Crittenden MSS (LC).

38. Seward to Weed, February 5, Mary 27, 1848, George W. Patterson to Weed, January 28, 1848, Minos McGowan to Weed, March 23, 1848, Weed MSS (RU); Rayback, *Free Soil*, p. 162.

39. For different attempts to make sense of the course of Weed, Seward, and Greeley, see Poage, *Clay*, p. 163; *ZT:SWH*, pp. 61–63; and Rayback, *Free Soil*, pp. 162–64.

40. Richard M. Blatchford to Seward, February 15, 1848, Seward MSS; Washington Hunt to Weed, February 15, 21, 25, March 19, 30, 1848, Samuel Partridge to Weed, February 22, March 23, 1848, Weed MSS (RU).

41. *New York Tribune*, February 16, 17, 18, 1848; Boston *Daily Advertiser*, February 18, 1848; David B. Ogden to McLean, January 15, 1848, J. B. Mower to McLean, February 26, 1848, McLean MSS (LC); Nicholas Carroll to Crittenden, February 20, 1848, Crittenden MSS (LC); Poage, *Clay*, p. 170.

42. Hamilton Fish to John M. Berrien, February 22, 1848, Berrien MSS; *New York Tribune*, February 27, 19, 1848; N. K. Hall to Fillmore, February 23, 1848, MFP-O; Hiram Ketchum to William Pitt Fessenden, March 10, 1848, Fessenden MSS (WRHS). There is a newspaper clipping of the resolution, filed for February 15, 1848, in the Thomas J. Clay Papers with the penciled notation, apparently by Clay's son, that the resolution was a nomination of Clay.

43. John P. Kennedy to E. J. Morris et al., February 20, 1848, Kennedy MSS; Edward Joy Morris to Rives, February 15, 1848, Rives MSS; Daniel M. Barringer to Philadelphia Committee, February 16, 1848, draft, Barringer MSS; Lincoln to Taylor Committee, February 9, 1848, *Collected Works of Lincoln*, I, p. 449.

44. Mueller, *Whig Party in Pennsylvania*, p. 145; David Outlaw to Emily Outlaw, February 11, 1848, Outlaw MSS.

45. Mueller, *Whig Party in Pennsylvania*, pp. 146–67; John P. Kennedy to E. Joy Morris, February 20, 1848, Kennedy MSS; George Tucker to William C. Rives, October 26, 1847, Rives MSS; R. J. Arundel to John McLean, October 15, 1847, McLean MSS (LC).

46. Daniel Ullmann to Clay, February 18, 1848, Henry Clay MSS (LC); Mueller, *Whig Party in Pennsylvania*, p. 146; J. B. Mower to McLean, April 19, 1848; Rayback, *Free Soil*, pp. 168–69; Edward Joy Morris to J. P. Kennedy, May 6, 1848 (quotation), Kennedy MSS.

In 1846, 14,000 of the 15,000 Native American votes in the state came from Philadelphia City and County (Mueller, p. 133). In 1847, a Native American gubernatorial candidate attracted 11,247 votes, or about 4 percent of the statewide total.

47. David Outlaw to Emily Outlaw, February 23, 1848, Outlaw MSS; David Davis to Sarah Davis, February 24, 1848, David Davis MSS (CHS); Cornelius Darragh to John McLean, March

2, 1848, McLean MSS (LC); Poage, *Clay*, p. 170; Mueller, *Whig Party in Pennsylvania*, pp. 147–48. The proceedings of the Buena Vista Celebration (or Festival) were later published in pamphlet form.

48. *New York Tribune*, February 28, 1848.

49. Peterson, *Great Triumvirate*, pp. 435–36.

50. My account of events in Kentucky in this and subsequent paragraphs is based on: ibid.; Kirwan, *Crittenden*, pp. 211–14; Poage, *Clay*, pp. 171–73; Volz, "Party, State, and Nation," pp. 38–46; Letcher to Crittenden, January 15, February 16, 21, 1848, John S. Helm to Crittenden, January 11, 1848, P. Swigert to Crittenden, February 24, 1848, John Bibb to Crittenden, December 25, 1847, Addison White to Crittenden, February 5, 1848, Thomas Metcalf to Crittenden, February 8, 1848, Crittenden MSS (LC); George Robertson to John M. Berrien, February 29, 1848, Berrien MSS; John P. Kennedy to Elizabeth Kennedy, April 16, 1848, Kennedy MSS.

51. For the general weakness of governors in the Upper South, see Wooster, *Politicians, Planters, and Plain Folk*, pp. 57–78, especially pp. 58–59. For the reliance on the coattails of the gubernatorial candidate to help elect legislative candidates, see Kruman, *Parties and Politics*, pp. 43–45.

52. Kirwan, *Crittenden*, pp. 211–14; P. Swigert to Crittenden, February 24, 1848, Crittenden MSS (LC); George Robertson to Berrien, February 29, 1848, Berrien MSS; Leslie Combs to Daniel Ullmann, February 24, 1848, Ullmann MSS.

Kirwan's conclusion that the result was a clear defeat for Clay and a victory for Taylor, because Clay did not secure the nomination or committed delegates and because eleven of the twelve chosen favored Taylor, strikes me as untenable. Clay did not seek committed delegates, five of the twelve supported Clay at the convention for three ballots—indeed, Clay was shocked that the others did not—and the pledge to support the nominee of the national convention, given Taylor's position at the time, was a victory for Clay.

53. Richmond *Enquirer*, February 24–29, 1848; Rayback, *Free Soil*, p. 149; Poage, *Clay*, p. 173; James Lyons to William C. Rives, February 16, March 1, 1848, R. E. Scott to Rives, February 21, 26, 1848, Rives MSS.

54. Kruman, *Parties and Politics*, p. 119; Washington *National Intelligencer*, March 2, 1848; E. J. Hale to Daniel M. Barringer, January 4, 21, 1848, Barringer MSS; Augustine Sheppard to Lyndon Swaim, March 21, 1848, Swaim MSS.

Hale feared that a Democrat would run as an independent who attacked convention dictation of nominees, an appeal that would resonate with the many Whigs angered by the tight control over Whig nominations by a central committee drawn from Raleigh and its environs. Instead, the eventual Democratic gubernatorial nominee, David M. Reid, demanded elimination of the property requirement for the right to vote in state senate elections, or equal suffrage, an issue with great appeal to many Whig voters in western North Carolina. Kruman, *Parties and Politics*, pp. 85–90, 145–53; Harris, *Holden*, pp. 28–31.

55. Kruman, *Parties and Politics*, p. 148; London, "Badger"; David Outlaw to Emily Outlaw, January 19, 23, February 10, 22, 23, 24, 29, March 3, 1848, Outlaw MSS; David L. Swain to William H. Battle, April 7, May 3, 1848, Battle Family Papers. On Mangum's fondness for alcohol, see Brock, *Political Conscience*, p. 86. The Democratic senator whom Badger replaced had resigned in 1846 rather than obey instructions from the Whig state legislature to vote against the Walker Tariff.

56. *New York Tribune*, February 24, 1848; Rayback, *Free Soil*, p. 154.

57. Washington Hunt to Thurlow Weed, February 25, April 7, 1848, Weed MSS (RU); Philemon B. Ewing to Thomas Ewing, March 2, 1848, EFP; James Harlan to Caleb B. Smith, March 5, 1848, Thomas B. Stevenson to Smith, March 6, 1848, Smith MSS; E. J. Hale to Daniel M. Barringer, April 7, 1848, Barringer MSS; Orth to Schuyler Colfax, April 29, 1848, in Schauinger, "Orth Letters," 39, 390–93.

58. Washington Hunt to Thurlow Weed, February 15, 1848, Weed MSS (RU); Crittenden to Orlando Brown, March 25, 1848, Crittenden MSS (Duke); "What General Taylor Ought to Say," [March ?] 1848, *Collected Works of Lincoln*, I, p. 454; Kirwan, *Crittenden*, pp. 216–18; *ZT: SWH*, p. 77.

59. Extract of Taylor to Smith, March 4, 1848, in Truman Smith to Thomas Ewing, n.d.

(May 1848 folder), EFP; Caleb Smith to John McLean, April 10, 1848, McLean MSS (LC); Weed to Patterson, April 9, 1848, quoted in *ZT:SWH*, p. 74; John Defrees to George Dunn, April 18, 1848, Dunn MSS.

60. Meredith P. Gentry to William B. Campbell, April 18, 1848, CFP; James Bowen to Thurlow Weed, April 26, 1848, Weed MSS (RU); James E. Harvey to John McLean, April 27, 1848, McLean MSS (LC); *ZT:SWH*, pp. 76–77; William C. C. Claiborne to Henry Clay, April 26, 1848, Henry Clay MSS (LC).

61. Henry Clay to James B. Clay, February 21, 1848, Thomas J. Clay MSS (LC); Clay to James Harvey, April 1, 1848, David Davis MSS; William Bebb to Clay, April 4, 1848, Stevenson MSS; Thomas B. Stevenson to Clay, April 8, 1848, Clay to S. S. Prentiss, April 12, 1848, Clay to James Brooks, April 13, 1848, Henry Clay MSS (LC); Thomas Dowling to John McLean, April 14, 1848, McLean MSS (LC); *New York Tribune*, April 6, 7, 1848; Poage, *Clay*, p. 170.

Although the resolution of the New York Whig legislative caucus declared that New York's Whigs preferred Clay's nomination, it did not instruct the state's delegates to vote for him. The lack of such instructions may have reflected Weed's influence, although most observers saw the resolution as a defeat for Weed and Seward (Greeley to Clay, April 28, 1848, Henry Clay MSS). More likely, Whig legislators believed that they could not bind the thirty-four delegates chosen by district conventions. Even without such instructions, the vast majority of New York delegates would vote for Clay at Philadelphia.

62. Poage, *Clay*, pp. 173–75; printed excerpt of April 10 announcement in Henry Clay MSS (LC); Thomas Dowling to John McLean, April 14, Mary 4, 1848, McLean MSS (LC); Meredith Gentry to William B. Campbell, April 18, 1848, CFP.

63. Taylor's letter is reproduced in Rayback, *Free Soil*, pp. 155–56.

64. *ZT:SWH*, pp. 77–79; William C. C. Claiborne to Clay, April 26, 1848, Henry Clay MSS (LC). As the three New Orleans men were leaving Baton Rouge on the morning of April 22, Bliss arrived on the same steamboat that was to carry them back to New Orleans. They showed Bliss the Allison Letter, and Bliss pronounced it superior to the various drafts he had brought with him from Washington.

65. *ZT:SWH*, pp. 75–81; Kirwan, *Crittenden*, pp. 218–20; Rayback, *Free Soil*, pp. 155–57; Crittenden to Clay, May 4, 1848, Crittenden MSS (Duke); Thomas Dowling to McLean, May 4, 1848, McLean MSS (LC); C. S. Morehead to Clay, May 3, 1848, Henry Clay MSS (LC); Thomas Ewing to Crittenden, May 26, 1848, draft, EFP.

66. David Outlaw to Emily Outlaw, February 23, 1848, Outlaw MSS.

67. Charles Jenkins to John M. Berrien, March 11, 1848, Berrien MSS.

68. William Rockhill to Chester Stocker, March 6, 1848, Rockhill MSS; Roger Sherman Baldwin to Edward L. Baldwin, March 19, 1848, R. S. Baldwin to Simeon Baldwin, March 19, 1848, BFP; David Outlaw to Emily Outlaw, February 23, March 6, 21, 1848, Outlaw MSS.

69. Nathan K. Hall to Millard Fillmore, February 23, 1848, MFP-O; Duer to Weed, March 7, 1848, Weed MSS (RU).

70. Potter, *Impending Crisis*, pp. 5–6; Johannsen, *Douglas*, pp. 216–17; R. S. Baldwin to Edward L. Baldwin, February 26, 1848, BFP.

71. James F. Babcock to R. S. Baldwin, March 22, 1848, BFP; Mark Howard to James M. Barnard, April 5, 1848, Howard MSS.

72. John D. Defrees to Caleb B. Smith, April 4, 1848, Smith MSS; for additional evidence that Whigs thought the Democrats would win an issue-oriented campaign, see Meredith P. Gentry to Daniel Webster, April 13, 1848, Webster MSS.

73. Corwin to Crittenden, September 2, 1847, Corwin MSS (OHS); see also Godlove Orth to Caleb Smith, January 30, 1848, Smith MSS.

74. See, for example, Caleb Smith to Allen Hamilton, February 15, 1848, Hamilton MSS.

75. Samuel Partridge to Thurlow Weed, March 23, 1848, Weed MSS (RU); John Edwards to George Dunn, April 3, 28, 1848, Dunn MSS; Orth to Schuyler Colfax, April 29, 1848, in Schauinger, "Orth Letters," 39, 390–93; A. Babcock to Millard Fillmore, April 7, 1848, MFP-O; David Davis to William P. Walker, May 16, 1848, David Davis MSS; J. M. Huntington to John McLean, March 28, 1848, McLean MSS (LC).

76. Harris to Berrien, March 25, 1848, Berrien MSS.

77. Gentry to William B. Campbell, April 18, 1848, CFP. For a modern analysis of how the attempt to win antislavery voters away from the Liberty party caused northern Whigs to internalize antislavery sentiments, thereby pushing northern Whigs to adopt more extreme antislavery positions, see Stewart, "Abolitionists, Insurgents, and Third Parties."

78. Toombs to James Thomas, April 16, May 1, 1848, in Phillips, "Correspondence of Toombs, Stephens, and Cobb," pp. 103–05; Gentry to William B. Campbell, April 18, 1848, CFP. See also John Bell's letter to Campbell of the same date.

79. *ZT:SWH*, p. 83; Washington Barrow to William B. Campbell, April 1, 1848, David Campbell to W. B. Campbell, March 21, 1848, Gentry and Bell to Campbell, April 18, 1848, CFP; Lucius J. Gartell to Henry Clay, April 15, 1848, Henry Clay MSS (LC); S. S. Locke to Thomas Butler King, May 11, 1848, King MSS; Murray, *Whig Party in Georgia*, pp. 132–33.

80. Corwin to Stevenson, April 6, 1848, Stevenson MSS; Stevenson to Clay, April 8, 1848, Henry Clay MSS (LC). For other references to Mexican law prohibiting slavery in the Cession, see Francis Granger to Thomas Ewing, January 10, 1848, EFP; and Henry L. Benning to Howell Cobb, February 23, 1848, in Phillips, "Correspondence of Toombs, Stephens, and Cobb," pp. 97–103.

81. Corwin to Clay, May 3, 1848, Stevenson to Clay, May 18, 1848, Henry Clay MSS (LC); Clay to Stevenson, May 20, 1848, Stevenson MSS.

82. Nathan K. Hall to Millard Fillmore, February 23, 28, 1848, MFP-O; David Outlaw to Emily Outlaw, February 28, 1848, Outlaw MSS; Caleb Smith to Allen Hamilton, March 26, 1848, Hamilton MSS; Orth to Caleb Smith, January 30, 1848, Smith MSS; Washington Hunt to Thurlow Weed, March 19, 1848, Weed MSS (RU); Thomas Dowling to John McLean, March 24, 1848, McLean MSS (LC).

83. Dalzell, *Webster*, pp. 145–46; Peterson, *Great Triumvirate*, pp. 439–40; Hiram Ketchum to Fessenden, March 10, 24, April 11, May 1, 30, 1848, Fessenden MSS (WRHS); Charles March to Daniel Webster, April 2, 1848, Webster to Edward Everett, May 22, 1848, Webster MSS.

84. Fillmore to Ketchum, May 9, 1848, MFP-O.

85. Thomas Dowling to John McLean, March 24, April 26, 1848, James E. Harvey to McLean, April 12, 1848, John D. Defrees to McLean, April 16, 1848, John B. Mower to McLean, April 20, 24, 1848, Caleb Smith to McLean, March 29, April 22, May 1, 1848, McLean MSS (LC); O. H. Smith to John M. Berrien, May 20, 1848, Berrien MSS.

86. Zachary Taylor to Clay, November 4, 1847, Harvey to Clay, May 3, 1848, Henry Clay MSS (LC); Harvey to McLean, May 16, 1848, McLean MSS (LC). In a private letter to Clay dated April 30, 1848, Taylor tried to explain away the *Richmond Republican* letter by disingenuously dissembling that he was in the hands of others who had nominated him and whom he could not betray. They, not he, insisted upon his avowal to remain in the race no matter what the Whig convention did. Only they could withdraw his name.

87. Godlove Orth to Schuyler Colfax, April 29, 1848, loc. cit.; Lewis D. Campbell to Caleb B. Smith, May 4, 1848, Smith MSS; Harvey to McLean, May 2, 1848, McLean MSS (LC).

88. John Teesdale to John McLean, April 26, 29, 1848, Thomas Dowling to McLean, April 28, May 12, 1848, Caleb Smith to McLean, May 1, 1848, Lewis Benedict to McLean, May 4, 1848, McLean MSS (LC).

89. C. W. Hester to George Dunn, April 24, 1848, Dunn MSS; Washington Hunt to Thurlow Weed, April 17, 1848, Weed MSS (RU).

90. Edward McGaughey to Caleb B. Smith, March 15, 1848, Smith MSS; McGaughey to George Dunn, May 23, 1848, Dunn MSS. For evidence of support for Taylor or Scott in different parts of the North, see Greeley to Clay, April 28, May 29, 1848, Henry Clay MSS (LC); Washington Hunt to Weed, May 19, 1848, Weed MSS (RU); William H. Bogart to Fillmore, May 9, 1848, Jerome Fuller to Fillmore, May 15, 1848, MFP-O; Thomas Ewing to John Sherman, May 26, 1848, EFP; William H. McCrillis to William Pitt Fessenden, May 29, 1848, Fessenden MSS (WRHS); Godlove Orth to Schuyler Colfax, April 29, 1848, loc. cit.

91. Thomas Corwin to Caleb Smith, May 10, 1848, Smith MSS; Corwin to Thomas B. Stevenson, March 3, 1848, Stevenson MSS; William Rockhill to Allen Hamilton, March 16, 1848, Hamilton MSS; McClernand to Charles H. Lanphier, May 30, 1848, Lanphier MSS; Thomas B. Stevenson to Clay, May 22, 1848, Henry Clay MSS (LC).

92. Hunt to Weed, March 19, 1848, Weed MSS (RU); Orth to Colfax, April 29, 1848, loc. cit.

93. Thomas B. Stevenson to Caleb Smith, March 6, 1848, John Defrees to Caleb Smith, April 4, 1848, Smith MSS; James Harvey to John McLean, April 12, 1848, Robert Howard to McLean, April 27, 1848, Thomas Dowling to McLean, May 12, 1848, McLean MSS (LC); Thomas B. Stevenson to Henry Clay, May 18, 1848, Joseph L. White to Clay, May 26, 1848, Henry Clay MSS (LC); Thomas Ewing to John Sherman, May 26, 1848, EFP; Daniel Webster to Hiram Ketchum, May 27, 1848, Webster MSS.

94. Elisha Whittlesey to John McLean, April 12, 1848, J. B. Mower to McLean, April 20, 1848, Thomas Dowling to McLean, April 26, May 1, 1848, James Harvey to McLean, May 1, 1848, McLean MSS (LC); David M. Nagle to Henry Clay, May 1, 1848, Henry Clay MSS (LC).

95. Henry Clay to James Brooks, April 13, 1848, Greeley to Clay, April 28, 1848, Joseph L. White to Clay, May 26, 1848, Winfield Scott to Clay, July 19, 1848, Thomas B. Stevenson to Clay, August 10, 1848, John Minor Botts to Clay, August 23, 1848, Henry Clay MSS (LC); Clay to Thomas B. Stevenson, August 14, 1848, Stevenson MSS; Thomas Dowling to John McLean, May 1, 4, 1848, McLean MSS (LC). Clay believed that Garnett Duncan of Louisiana was the Whig to whom Scott referred. Scott's biographer guesses, plausibly, that it was Washington Hunt. Neither Duncan nor Hunt favored Clay's nomination. Elliott, *Scott*, p. 592.

96. William H. McCrillis to William Pitt Fessenden, May 29, 1848, Fessenden MSS (WRHS); E. Joy Morris to John P. Kennedy, May 6, 1848, Kennedy MSS; Henry Wilson to Daniel Webster, May 31, 1848, Webster MSS; Horace Greeley to Schuyler Colfax, April 3, 1848, Greeley-Colfax MSS; Rayback, *Free Soil*, pp. 171–85.

97. See, for example, Seward to Weed, May 27, 1848, Weed MSS (RU).

98. Henry Wilson to Charles Francis Adams, June 3, 1848, Adams Family Papers.

99. H. E. Eastman to Amos A. Lawrence, April 28, 1848, Amos A. Lawrence MSS; C. S. Morehead to Henry Clay, May 3, 1848, Henry Clay MSS (LC); Daniel Webster to Hiram Ketchum, May 27, 31, 1848, Webster to Edward Everett, May 29, 1848, Webster MSS; John A. Watkins to Leslie Combs, May 15, 1848, Ullmann MSS; E. W. Huntington to George Dunn, May 31, 1848, Dunn MSS; J. R. Williams to Millard Fillmore, June 2, 1848, MFP-O.

100. Jerome Fuller to Millard Fillmore, June 1, 4, 6, 1848, John T. Bush to Fillmore, June 6, 1848, MFP-O; Henry Wilson to Charles Francis Adams, June 3, 1848, Adams Family Papers; Hunt to Weed, June 4, 1848, Weed MSS (RU); James Harvey to John McLean, April 12, 1848, McLean MSS (LC).

101. William Ballard Preston to William C. Rives, May 30, 1848, Rives MSS; Henry S. Levert and C. C. Langdon to Henry Clay, May 29, 1848, Greeley to Clay, May 29, 1848, and James Harlan to Clay, June 2, 1848, Henry Clay MSS (LC).

102. The best secondary account of the convention, on which I have relied heavily in this and the following paragraphs, is *ZT:SWH*, pp. 86–97. See also Rayback, *Free Soil*, pp. 194–200, and Kirwan, *Crittenden*, pp. 220–22. A memoir by an individual who describes himself as the convention's official reporter is Dyer, *Great Senators*, pp. 68–86. On the impact of the Native Americans, see George C. Collins to Henry Clay, June 10, 1848, Henry Clay MSS (LC); and Edwin G. Lindsey to Millard Fillmore, April 7, 1851, MFP-BHS.

103. John T. Bush to Millard Fillmore, June 6, 1848, Jerome Fuller to Fillmore, June 4, 1848, Harry Bradley to Fillmore, June 20, 1848, MFP-O; Henry Wilson to C. F. Adams, June 3, 1848, Adams Family Papers; Amos A. Lawrence to Members of the Philadelphia Convention, June 1, 1848, draft, Amos Lawrence MSS; John O. Sargent to Thomas Butler King, April 22, 1848, King MSS; Dalzell, *Webster*, p. 147; Greeley to Henry Clay, April 22, June 21, 1848, Henry Clay MSS (LC).

104. Leslie Combs to Henry Clay, June 10, 1848, John Sloane to Clay, June 22, 1848, Thomas B. Stevenson to Clay, June 12, 19, July 26, August 10, 1848, John L. Lawrence to Clay, June 23, 1848, P. Van Trump to Clay, July 26, 1848, J. M. Botts to Clay, August 23, 1848, Henry Clay MSS (LC); Clay to T. B. Stevenson, August 14, 1848, Stevenson MSS; William Miner to John McLean, June 13, 1848, James Harvey to McLean, August 30, 1848, McLean MSS (LC).

105. Jerome Fuller to Millard Fillmore, June 6, 7, 1848, John T. Bush to Fillmore, June 6, 1848, Harry Bradley to Fillmore, June 20, 1848, MFP-O.

106. A Louisianan represented Texas on this committee.

107. John L. Lawrence to Clay, June 9, 1848, Henry Clay MSS (LC); *ZT:SWH*, pp. 91–92.

108. Rayback, *Free Soil*, p. 196, note 21.

109. John T. Bush to Millard Fillmore, June 6, 1848, MFP-O. The votes of the individual delegates on all four ballots at the convention can be found in the Washington *National Intelligencer*, June 16, 1848. On the first ballot, Webster had one vote from New York, three from Maine, and all eighteen from Massachusetts and New Hampshire. Scott's total was divided as follows: Ohio, twenty; Indiana, nine; Pennsylvania, six; New York, five; Michigan, two; and Illionis, one.

110. Leslie Combs to Henry Clay, June 10, 1848, James Harlan to Clay, June 15, 1848, John L. Lawrence to Clay, June 23, 1848, Henry Clay MSS (LC); Jerome Fuller to Millard Fillmore, June 9, 1848, MFP-O; Meredith Gentry to William B. Campbell, June 18, 1848, CFP.

111. Henry Clay to Thomas B. Stevenson, August 14, 1848, Stevenson MSS; Stevenson to Clay, August 10, 1848, Henry Clay MSS (LC).

112. John McLean to Caleb Smith, March 23, 1848, Smith MSS; Clay to James Brooks, April 13, 1848, Henry Clay MSS (LC). The combined influence of sectionalism and partisan strength can be seen in the following table, which uses the same categories as Tables 20 and 22, to which the delegates from Wisconsin and South Carolina are added. In every group, ranged from the strongest Whig to the strongest Democratic, Taylor drew a higher proportion of votes in the South than the North. The only northern Whigs for whom Taylor had significant appeal, on the other hand, came from Democratic states. Even in the South, moreover, Taylor was considerably weaker in Whig states (Group I) than in those Clay had lost in 1844. Conversely, with the exception of the southern states Clay had carried in 1844, Clay's strength was concentrated in the northern states he had won or come close to carrying. His relative weakness in the North (38 percent) reflected his negligible vote in Democratic states as well as losses to Scott and Webster. Altogether, Clay won 48 percent of the votes from northern states in Groups I and II.

Percentage of Delegates for Clay and Taylor

	Group I		Group II		Group III		Regional Average	
	Tay.	Clay	Tay.	Clay	Tay.	Clay	Tay.	Clay
North	9%	34%	14%	57%	39%	17%	15%	38%
South	58%	38%	92%	8%	93%	7%	76%	20%
Group average	29.5%	36%	37%	43%	69%	12%		

113. Dyer, *Great Senators*, pp. 68–75; *ZT:SWH*, p. 93; Horace Greeley to Henry Clay, June 21, 1848, J. Morrison Harris to Clay, May 1848, John G. Proud to Clay, June 11, 1848, Henry Clay MSS (LC).

114. James Harvey to John McLean, August 30, 1848, McLean MSS (LC); Kirwan, *Crittenden*, p. 222.

115. Rayback, *Free Soil*, p. 197, note 23; *ZT:SWH*, pp. 93–94; Dyer, *Great Senators*, pp. 72–73; Truman Smith to John Davis, August 8, 1848, John Davis MSS. In this letter, Smith said he lobbied for Taylor immediately before the convention because of his conviction that Taylor was the only man whom Whigs could elect.

116. For more on the fascinating battle among Connecticut's Whigs over both Senate seats during May 1848, a battle that reflected both north/south and east/west regional tensions in the state, see Holt, "Rethinking," 97–111, especially 104; Emily Baldwin to Edward L. Baldwin, May 11, 23, 1848, C. Bissell to Roger Sherman Baldwin, May 12, 1848, Roger Sherman Baldwin to Emily Baldwin, May 17, 24, 1848, Emily Baldwin to R. S. Baldwin, May 19, 24, 27, 1848, James F. Babcock to R. S. Baldwin, May 27, 1848, and Dennis Kimberly to R. S. Baldwin, June 1, 1848, BFP; Alfred E. Burr to Gideon Welles, September 27, 1847, Welles MSS (NYPL); Burr to Welles,

November 5, 1847, William J. Hammersley to Welles, December 27, 1847, April 13, 1848, Welles MSS (LC).

117. Jerome Fuller to Millard Fillmore, June 9, 1848, MFP-O; Dyer, *Great Senators*, p. 76.

118. John G. Proud to Clay, June 11, 1848, Henry Clay MSS. Clay retained one vote each from Virginia, North Carolina, South Carolina, Alabama, and Kentucky.

119. Peterson, *Great Triumvirate*, p. 441.

120. John L. Lawrence to Henry Clay, June 9, 1848, David Graham to Clay, June 9, 1848, Leslie Combs to Clay, June 10, 1848, Henry Clay MSS (LC); Harry Bradley to Millard Fillmore, June 20, 1848, MFP-O; *ZT:SWH*, p. 95. See also the excerpts from the *New York Tribune*'s account of the convention reprinted in the Appendix to Van Deusen, "The Whig Party," pp. 436–44, especially p. 440.

121. Newspaper and hence the secondary accounts of the speeches in the confusion following Taylor's nomination differ. In this and following paragraphs, I have relied primarily on the *National Intelligencer*, June 12, 1848, which includes the bracketed phrase in the quotation in its original report. But I have supplemented the *Intelligencer*'s account with Van Deusen's appendix and the descriptions by Hamilton and Rayback.

122. Jerome Fuller to Fillmore, June 9, 1848, MFP-O.

123. Harry Bradley to Millard Fillmore, June 20, 1848, MFP-O; Dyer, *Great Senators*, pp. 79–80.

124. Bradley to Fillmore, June 20, 1848, MFP-O; John O. Sargent to Thomas Butler King, April 4, 22, 1848, King MSS; John O. Sargent, Hugh Maxwell, M. H. Grinnell, and Simeon Draper to Nathan Appleton, May 16, 1848, Appleton MSS; John Lorimer Graham to William C. Rives, June 15, 1848, Rives MSS; J. R. Williams to Millard Fillmore, June 10, 1848, MFP-O. Webster denied that he personally had interfered to stop Lawrence. Daniel Webster to R. M. Blatchford, June 10, 1848, Nathan Appleton MSS.

125. Thomas Ewing to John Sherman, May 26, 1848, typescript copy of letter from Thomas Ewing, Jr., to the editor of the *Springfield Republican*, October 11, 1933, quoting William Bebb to Crittenden, November 24, 1848, and Thomas Ewing to John Sherman, January 22, 1867, EFP.

126. Seward to Weed, March 29, May 27, 1848, Weed MSS (RU); Jerome Fuller to Millard Fillmore, June 1, 4, 6, 7, 9, 1848; John Bush to Fillmore, June 6, 1848, Harry Bradley to Fillmore, June 20, 1848, MFP-O; Edward G. Lindsey to Fillmore, April 7, 1851, William I. A. Birken to Fillmore, December 25, 1850, MFP-BHS; *ZT:SWH*, p. 88.

127. *Ibid*; Joseph L. White to Millard Fillmore, August 27, 1846, MFP-O; J. L. White to John J. Crittenden, June 28, 1847, Crittenden MSS (LC).

128. Harry Bradley to Fillmore, June 20, 1848.

129. Ibid; for the votes on the vice presidential nomination, I have used the *Tribune* account reprinted in Van Deusen's appendix.

130. William Tyson to Millard Fillmore, March 28, 1849, MFP-O.

131. Van Deusen, "The Whig Party," Appendix, p. 444.

132. William Ballard Preston to William C. Rives, June 9, 1848, Rives MSS; Daniel Webster to Hiram Ketchum, June 11, 1848, Webster MSS: Thomas Dorr to Edmund Burke, January 13, 1848, Burke MSS.

133. J. R. Williams to Fillmore, June 10, 1848, MFP-O.

CHAPTER 11

1. Meredith P. Gentry to William B. Campbell, June 18, 1848, CFP.

2. E. D. Culver to Millard Fillmore, June 11, 1848, MFP-O.

3. Maizlish, *Triumph of Sectionalism*, pp. 73–146; Rayback, *Free Soil*, pp. 303–10 and passim; Nevins, *Ordeal: Fruits*, pp. 211–16; Brock, *Political Conscience*, pp. 184–232; Mayfield, *Rehearsal for Republicanism*, p. 126.

4. E. D. Culver to Fillmore, June 11, 1848, Henry Clay to Committee at Louisville, June 28, 1848, draft, Henry Clay MSS (LC).

5. These estimates of turnout can be found in *Historical Statistics*, 1072. Clay received 48.13 percent of the votes cast in 1844; Taylor gained 47.28 percent of those cast in 1848.

Multiplying those figures by the respective turnout rates in the two years indicates that Clay won 37.9 percent of the potential vote and Taylor only 34.34 percent.

6. Albert G. Riddle to Joshua R. Giddings, June 12, 1848, quoted in Maizlish, *Triumph of Sectionalism*, p. 99; Rayback, *Free Soil*, p. 205; Thomas B. Stevenson to Henry Clay, June 19, 1848, Henry Clay MSS (LC); William H. Howe to Roger Sherman Baldwin, Jr., July 25, 1848, BFP.

7. Frank Otto Gatell, " 'Conscience and Judgment' "; call for Worcester Convention quoted on p. 27; Charles Francis Adams to John Gorham Palfrey, May 26, June 10, 1848, Adams Family Papers.

8. Rayback, *Free Soil*, pp. 99–112, 181–83; Mayfield, *Rehearsal for Republicanism*, pp. 86–91, 101–02.

9. Rayback, *Free Soil*, pp. 60–77, 171–81, 201; Sewell, *Ballots for Freedom*, pp. 145–49.

10. Rayback, *Free Soil*, pp. 205–13; Mayfield, *Rehearsal for Republicanism*, pp. 108–11; Boston *Daily Advertiser*, June 12, 1848. The fifteen Whigs at Philadelphia, not all of whom would leave the party in 1848, were: Lewis O. Cowan and Samuel Bradley of Maine; Charles Allen, Henry Wilson, and Daniel Alvord of Massachusetts; Isaac Platt, John C. Hamilton, and Robert Colby of New York; Horace Conger of New Jersey; and Lewis D. Campbell, Samuel Galloway, John C. Vaughan, Stanley Mathews, John Burgoyne, and H. B. Hurlburt of Ohio (Rayback, *Free Soil*, p. 205, note 20).

11. J. N. B. to William Schouler, May 1848, Schouler MSS; for additional evidence of the enthusiasm for a new free-soil party among Northern Whigs, see J. Sloane to Henry Clay, June 22, 1848, Henry Clay MSS (LC); Thomas Treat to Millard Fillmore, July 4, 1848, D. H. Davis to Fillmore, July 8, 1848, MFP-O; Thurlow Weed to William Henry Seward, July 29, 1848, Seward MSS (RU).

12. Potter, *Impending Crisis*, pp. 63–73; David Outlaw to Emily Outlaw, July——, July 31, August 1, 1848, Outlaw MSS.

13. The other members of the select committee were Missouri Democrat David R. Atchison and Whigs Joseph Underwood of Kentucky, Samuel S. Phelps of Vermont, and John H. Clarke of Rhode Island.

14. Clayton's bill provided for the presidential appointment of executive and judicial officials for California and New Mexico, but it explicitly forbade the creation of a popularly elected territorial legislature, as in Oregon. Instead, the appointed executive and judicial officials together were to exercise legislative authority in the two territories. The bill is printed in *Congressional Globe*, 30th Cong., 1st Sess., 1002–05.

15. The bill allowed a slave, or presumably an attorney for a slave, to seek a writ of habeas corpus from a federal district judge or the territorial supreme court and provided that the Supreme Court would hear an appeal on the decision to award the slave habeas corpus, which would temporarily free the slave.

16. Clayton's speech is quoted in the Washington *National Intelligencer*, July 19, 1848.

17. *Congressional Globe*, 30th Cong., 1st Sess., 953–1002. See also Seward to Weed, July 25, 1848, Weed MSS (RU); David Outlaw to Emily Outlaw, July 23, July——, 1848, Outlaw MSS; Thomas B. Stevenson to Henry Clay, July 26, 1848, Henry Clay MSS (LC); Andrew S. Fulton to David Campbell, July 25, 27, 1848, CFP; Rayback, *Free Soil*, p. 252.

18. T. C. Peters to Fillmore, July 11, 1848, MFP-O; Weed to Seward, July 29, 1848, Seward MSS (RU). The platform of the Free Soil party is printed in the appendix to Kraditor, "Liberty and Free Soil Parties," pp. 876–78.

19. *Congressional Globe*, 30th Cong., 1st Sess., p. 1002; Potter, *Impending Crisis*, p. 74.

20. Seward to Weed, July 25, 1848, Weed MSS (RU); David Outlaw to Emily Outlaw, July 23, 1848, Outlaw MSS; Andrew Fulton to David Campbell, July 25, 27, 1848, CFP; *Congressional Globe*, 30th Cong., 1st Sess., p. 1007; Rayback, *Free Soil*, p. 253. The seven southern Whigs who helped Stephens table the bill included three Kentuckians, two North Carolinians, and one each from Tennessee and Virginia. Significantly, Robert Toombs and the two other Georgia Whigs, as well as prominent southern Taylor men like Gentry, Ballard Preston, and Thomas Flournoy, voted in the minority against Stephens.

21. *Congressional Globe*, Appendix, 30th Cong., 1st Sess., 1103–07; Alexander H. Stephens

to Milledgeville *Federal Union*, August 30, 1848, in Phillips, "Correspondence of Toombs, Stephens, and Cobb," pp. 117–23; A. H. Stephens to Duncan L. Clinch, October 7, 1848, Stephens MSS (LC).

22. Ibid.; Rayback, *Free Soil*, p. 253, note 101; Iverson L. Harris to John M. Berrien, August 23, 1848, Berrien MSS.

23. Washington *National Intelligencer*, August 2, 3, 1848; David Outlaw to Emily Outlaw, August 1, 1848, Outlaw MSS; Alexander, *Sectional Stress*, p. 199, votes 84 and 85.

24. Washington *National Intelligencer*, August 12, 14, 1848; Roger Sherman Baldwin to Emily Baldwin, August 11, 1848, BFP; Daniel Webster to Richard M. Blatchford, August 13, 1848, Webster MSS; Alexander, *Sectional Stress*, p. 200, vote 100; Potter, *Impending Crisis*, pp. 75–76.

25. *Poughkeepsie Eagle*, August 5, 1848, clipping in MFP-O; Boston *Daily Advertiser*, September 14, 1848; A. B. Conditt to George Dunn, September 1, 1848, Dunn MSS.

26. For the creation of the Free Soil party, I have relied on Rayback, *Free Soil*, pp. 201–30; Mayfield, *Rehearsal*, pp. 108–25; Sewell, *Ballots for Freedom*, pp. 152–69; and Blue, *Free Soilers*, pp. 44–80.

27. E. Harrington to Salmon P. Chase, August 5, 1848, Chase MSS (LC).

28. Rayback, *Free Soil*, p. 226, note 105. For additional evidence that vengeful Clay Whigs joined the free-soil movement, see George W. Patterson to Thurlow Weed, August 19, 1848, Weed MSS (RU).

29. Patterson to Weed, August 24, 1848, Weed MSS (RU).

30. Henry Howe to Roger Sherman Baldwin, September 27, 1848, BFP; Seward to Weed, October 27, 29, November 6, 1848, Weed MSS (RU); P. Hitchcock to Thomas Ewing, June 12, 1848, A. Banning Norton to Ewing, August 7, 1848, EFP; Ewing to John J. Crittenden, October 15, 1848, Ewing MSS (OHS); John W. Allen to Crittenden, September 90, 1848, Crittenden MSS (LC); Benjamin F. Wade to Caroline Wade, July 21, October 27, 1848, Wade MSS; John W. Allen to Millard Fillmore, November 2, 1848, MFP-O; Thomas B. Stevenson to Henry Clay, June 19, July 26, August 10, 24, October 2, 1848, Henry Clay MSS (LC); Thomas Corwin to Thomas B. Stevenson, June 13, 1848, Stevenson MSS.

Several of Clay's friends believed that the only possible explanation for the treachery of the Ohio delegation at the national convention was that Corwin wanted to foment an antislavery revolt so that he could lead the new Free Soil party. See John Minor Botts to Clay, August 23, 1848, Henry Clay MSS (LC).

31. S. Todd to John J. Crittenden, September 27, 1848, John M. Clayton to Crittenden, October 12, 1848, Moses Hampton to Crittenden, November 26, 1848, Crittenden MSS (LC); Thaddeus Stevens to Abraham Lincoln, September 7, 1848, David Davis MSS; B. Rush Petrikin to Samuel Calvin, October 2, 1848, with clipping of Petrikin's Address to the Electors of the Seventeenth Congressional District, September 30, 1848, Calvin MSS; E. Joy Morris to Amos A. Lawrence, August 4, 1848, Amos Lawrence MSS; Holt, *Forging a Majority*, p. 56.

32. Horace Greeley to Clay, June 20, 1848, Henry Clay MSS (LC); T. W. Williams to Fillmore, July 28, 1848, MFP-O; Greeley to Schuyler Colfax, September 15, 1848, Greeley-Colfax MSS; Rayback, *Free Soil*, pp. 203, 213; Van Deusen, *Greeley*, pp. 122–25; Blue, *Free Soilers*, p. 112; Seward to Edward J. Fowle, August 26, 1848, Seward MSS (RU); Elisha Whittelsey to Oran Follett, October 11, 1848, in Hamlin, "Follett Papers," 30–31.

33. Charles Francis Adams to J. G. Palfrey, May 26, 1848, Henry Wilson to C. F. Adams, June 3, 1848, Palfrey to Adams, June 7, 1848, Adams Family Papers; Boston *Daily Advertiser*, June 14, 15, 1848; Daniel Webster to Fletcher Webster, June 19, September ?, 1848, Edward Everett to Daniel Webster, August 4, 1848, E. Rockwood Hoar to Webster, August 13, 1848, Webster to E. R. Hoar, August 23, 1848, Webster MSS; Stephen C. Phillips to Salmon P. Chase, October 19, 1848, Chase MSS (LC); Gatell, "Bolt," 38–40.

34. A. Willey to Charles Francis Adams, June 16, 1848, Joseph W. Porter to C. F. Adams, July 3, 1848, Edward A. Stansbury to C. F. Adams, June 26, July 5, 1848, Adams Family Papers; Boston *Daily Advertiser*, September 12, 13, 1848; Blue, *Free Soilers*, p. 117.

35. A. E. Burr to Gideon Welles, June 24, 1848, John M. Niles to Welles, October 8, November 8, 1848, Welles MSS (LC); John M. Niles to Welles, September 17, 1848, Welles MSS

(NYPL); Hugh White to Roger Sherman Baldwin, September 4, 1848, Amasa Mason to Baldwin, September 25, 1848, E. A. Andrews to Baldwin, October 3, 1848, A. Brewster to Baldwin, October 3, 1848, and draft of speech in New Haven by Baldwin, September 8, 1848, BFP.

36. Joshua Leavitt to Joshua R. Giddings, July 6, 1848, quoted in Blue, *Free Soilers*, p. 80; see also A. E. Burr to Gideon Welles, July 24, 1848, Welles MSS (LC).

37. Thomas Mumford to Charles Francis Adams, July 17, 1848, Samuel Lyman to Adams, July 17, 1848, Seth Gates to Adams, July 24, 1848, Seth Webb to Adams, July 27, 1848, and C. F. Adams to J. G. Palfrey, July 30, 1848, Adams Family Papers; Samuel Lyman to J. G. Palfrey, July 30, 1848, quoted in Gatell, "Bolt," 43.

38. David Outlaw to Emily Outlaw, August 10, 1848, Outlaw MSS; Solomon G. Haven to Millard Fillmore, August 14, 1848, H. B. Lathrop to Fillmore, August 28, 1848, George Morey to Fillmore, September 3, 1848, Silas Stillwell to Fillmore, September 19, 1848 (quotation), and Philip Greely to Fillmore, September 26, 1848, MFP-O; *ZT:SWH*, p. 112; Stephen C. Phillips to Salmon P. Chase, October 19, 1848, Chase MSS (LC).

39. Thomas B. Stevenson to Henry Clay, August 29, September 9, October 2, 1848, Henry Clay MSS (LC); Adams Jewett to Salmon P. Chase, September 1, 1848, Chase MSS (LC); John W. Allen to J. J. Crittenden, September 9, 1848, William Woodbridge to Crittenden, September 12, 1848, R. W. Thompson to Crittenden, October 21, 1848, Crittenden MSS (LC); John Defrees to George Dunn, September 5, 1848, Dunn MSS; John Defrees to Thurlow Weed, September 30, 1848, Weed MSS (RU); Schuyler Colfax to Caleb B. Smith, November 16, 1848, Smith MSS.

40. Citations for the Pittsburgh *Gazette* can be found in Holt, *Forging a Majority*, p. 58; Boston *Daily Advertiser*, June 15, August 11, 18, 19, September 11, 1848; Hugh White to Roger Sherman Baldwin, September 4, 1848, draft of Baldwin's speech at New Haven, September 8, 1848, BFP; see also Abraham Lincoln's campaign speeches in Massachusetts and Illinois, *Collected Works of Lincoln*, II, pp. 1–14.

41. Ibid.; A. B. Conditt to George Dunn, September 1, 1848, Dunn MSS; *Poughkeepsie Eagle*, August 4, 1848, clipping in MFP-O; Resolutions of Whig meeting in Roxbury, Massachusetts, Boston *Daily Advertiser*, September 14, 1848.

42. Washington Hunt to Thurlow Weed, March 19, 1848, Weed MSS (RU); Pennsylvania Whig State Platform of 1848, *Pittsburgh Commercial Journal*, September 16, 1848; Boston *Daily Advertiser*, September 14, 15, 1848; Van Deusen, *Seward*, pp. 109–10. See also sources in note 40.

43. Boston *Daily Advertiser*, August 11, October 28, November 4, 1848.

44. Draft of Baldwin's Speech at New Haven, September 8, 1848, BFP; C. B. Stebbins to Fillmore, July 5, 1848, *Poughkeepsie Eagle*, August 5, 1848, clipping, MFP-O; public letter of Thomas Ewing, June 30, 1848, typescript copy, EFP; Stevens to Lincoln, September 7, 1848, David Davis MSS; John M. Niles to Gideon Welles, October 29, 1848, Welles MSS (NYPL).

45. Roger Sherman Baldwin to Thomas Ritchie, August 28, 1848, draft, BFP; Lincoln's speech at Jackson, Illinois, October 21, 1848, in *Collected Works of Lincoln*, II, pp. 11–12; Truman Smith to Thomas Ewing, June 30, 1848, with extracts from John Wilson to Truman Smith, May 10, 1848, EFP. Baldwin specifically denied accusations that Ritchie had printed in the Washington *Union* that Baldwin had letters from Taylor explicitly pledging not to veto the Proviso. Ritchie circulated such reports, Baldwin charged, in order to discredit Taylor in the South.

46. William M. Dunn to George Dunn, June 26, 1848, Dunn MSS; Alexander Kelsey to Millard Fillmore, August 21, 1848, B. B. Chamberlin to Fillmore, October 3, 1848, MFP-O; William Woodbridge to J. J. Crittenden, September 12, 1848, Crittenden MSS (LC).

47. P. Van Trump to Clay, July 26, 1848, Henry Clay MSS; Godlove Orth to Schuyler Colfax, July 11, 1848, in Schauinger, "Orth Letters," 39, 393–94. Democrats also commented on the same combination of apathy and anger among Whigs. See, for example, Edwin Crosswell to Horatio Seymour, July 29, 1848, typescript copy, Fairchild Collection.

48. A. T. Ellis to George Dunn, June 12, 1848, Dunn MSS; Edward McGaughey to Henry S. Lane, June 20, 1848, Henry Lane MSS (IU); Justin Morrill to Thomas Hale, June 19, 1848, Morrill MSS; Robert C. Winthrop to Edward Everett, July 5, 1848, Everett MSS; Report on the

Maine election, Boston *Daily Advertiser*, September 13, 1848; John H. Bryant to Millard Fillmore, August 7, 1848, MFP-O; Mueller, *Whig Party in Pennsylvania*, pp. 148–49.

49. Meredith P. Gentry to William B. Campbell, June 18, 1848, CFP; Charles Jenkins to John M. Berrien, July 15, 1848, Berrien MSS; George W. Crawford to Thomas Butler King, July 30, 1848, King MSS.

50. Charles Jenkins to John M. Berrien, July 15, 1848, Berrien MSS; *New Orleans Bee*, March 23, 1848; John A. Calhoun to Joseph White Lesne, July 10, 1848, quoted in Thornton, *Politics and Power*, p. 175. K. McKenzie to Duncan McLaurin, October 14, 1848, McLaurin MSS; Resolutions of Raymond Rough and Ready Club, enclosed with John B. Peyton to Millard Fillmore, August 9, 1848, William Hodge to Fillmore, October 21, 1848, MFP-O; W. H. Hull to Howell Cobb, July 22, 1848, quoted in Cole, *Whig Party in the South*, p. 132.

51. John P. Kennedy to George Sanburn, October 15, 1848, copy, Kennedy MSS; Richard W. Thompson to Edward Duff et al., June 29, 1848, Thompson MSS (Ind.SL); S. W. Parker to Caleb B. Smith, July 1, 9, 12, 1848, Smith MSS.

52. Rives to Taylor, July 11, 1848, draft, Rives MSS; clipping from *Richmond Times*, October 3, 1848, with Rives to Millard Fillmore, October 28, 1848, MFP-O.

53. Clay to Committee at Louisville, June 28, 1848, draft, Clay to George M. Curtis, July 4, 1848, draft, Clay to James Lynch et al., September 20, 1848, draft, George C. Collins to Clay, June 10, 1848, John G. Proud to Clay, June 11, 1848, Willis Hall to Clay, June 28, 1848, Thomas B. Stevenson to Clay, June 19, 1848, Henry Clay MSS (LC); Thomas B. Stevenson to Caleb Smith, June 12, 1848, Smith MSS.

54. Edwin Bryant to Clay, June 11, 1848, C. S. Morehead to Clay, June 22, 1848, P. Van Trump to Clay, July 26, 1848, Nicholas Dean to Clay, July 27, 1848, Henry Clay MSS (LC); H. B. Eastman to Amos A. Lawrence, June 14, 1848, Amos Lawrence MSS; David S. Crandall to Thurlow Weed, June 19, 1848, Weed MSS (RU); David S. Crandall to Millard Fillmore, June 19, 1848, MFP-O; C. A. Trowbridge to J. J. Crittenden, September 15, 1848, Crittenden MSS (LC).

55. Alexander Fleming to M. B. Fleming, June 22, 1848, Fleming MSS; John Minor Botts to Henry Clay, July 3, 1848, Henry Clay MSS (LC); John Pendleton to J. J. Crittenden, September 14, 1848, Robert Toombs to Crittenden, September 27, 1848, Charles W. Morgan to Crittenden, October 12, 1848, and Balie Peyton to Crittenden, October 21, 1848, Crittenden MSS (LC).

56. E. D. Culver to Fillmore, June 11, 1848, MFP-O; Seward to Weed, June 10, 1848, David S. Crandall to Weed, June 19, 1848, Weed MSS (RU); Godlove Orth to Schuyler Colfax, July 11, 1848, loc cit; Erlem Bratney to George Dunn, August 12, 1848, Dunn MSS.

57. Boston *Daily Advertiser*, June 14, 1848; Daniel D. Barnard's letter and Weed's editorial can be found in "The Nomination—General Taylor," *The American Review*, Vol. II (July 1848), 3–4, 7–8. Unless specified otherwise, all the quotations in this and the following eight paragraphs are taken from various articles in that Whig periodical. It would be tedious and repetitious to list individual page citations for each. The articles I relied on are: "The Future Policy of the Whigs," Vol. I (April 1848), 329–340; "The President's Message," ibid., 384–396; "The President and His Administration," Vol. I (May 1848), 437–452; "The Nomination—General Taylor," Vol. II (July 1848), 1–8; "Necessity of Party—The Press—The Locofoco Platform," ibid., 8–14; "The Whigs and Their Candidate," Vol. II (September 1848), 221–34; and "Party Discontents," Vol. II (October 1848), 331–40.

58. James D. Ogden to Thomas Butler King, June 13, 1848, King MSS.

59. *National Intelligencer*, June 10, 1848; for similar arguments, see Thomas Ewing's public letter of June 30, 1848, EFP; and Boston *Daily Advertiser*, June 14, July 18, 20, 1848.

60. *National Intelligencer*, June 29, 1848.

61. Weed to T. B. King, July 15, 1848, King MSS; T. C. Peters to Weed, July 2, 1848, Weed MSS (RU); Weed to Seward, July 27, 1848, Seward MSS (RU).

62. ZT:SWH, p. 117; William L. Hodge to Fillmore, July 19, 1848, MFP-O.

63. ZT:SWH, p. 120; Patterson to Weed, August 14, 24, 1848, Edward Dodd to Weed, August 18, 1848, Weed MSS (RU); Fillmore to Solomon Haven, August 19, 1848, D. A. Kelsey to Fillmore, August 21, 1848, MFP-O.

64. Fillmore to Taylor, August 19, 1848, Fillmore MSS (original in Zachary Taylor MSS, University of Kentucky).

65. Thomas Y. Simons to Jefferson Franklin Jackson, September 8, 1848, Jackson MSS; Rayback, *Free Soil*, pp. 270–71; Joshua L. Brown to Thurlow Weed, August 29, 1848, Weed MSS (RU).

66. Fillmore to Solomon Haven, August 19, 1848, Fillmore to D. A. Kelsey, August 24, 1848, Fillmore to Zachary Taylor, August 28, 1848, Thomas Foote to Fillmore, August 30, 1848, James O. Putnam to Fillmore, August 30, 1848, Weed to Fillmore, September 26, 1848, A. K. Hadley to Fillmore, February 17, 1855, MFP-O; Fillmore to Erastus Brooks, February 10, 1855, in Severance, "Millard Fillmore Papers," 11, 350–51; Fillmore to Weed, September 27, 1848, Weed MSS (RU).

67. Joshua L. Brown to Weed, August 29, 1848, Weed MSS (RU).

68. Nicholas Dean to Clay, August 5, 1848, Daniel Ullmann to Clay, August 9, 1848, Henry Clay MSS (LC).

69. John B. Mower to J. J. Crittenden, September 11, 1848, Crittenden MSS (LC); Fillmore to Zachary Taylor, September 16, 1848, MFP-O; Morton McMichael to Clay, September 9, 1848, Thomas J. Clay MSS; Washington *National Intelligencer*, September 11, 1848.

70. Clay to George Curtis, July 5, 1848, Clay to N. B. Meade and J. W. King, September 11, 1848, Clay to James Lynch et al., September 20, 1848, Henry Clay MSS (LC); Washington *National Intelligencer*, September 29, 1848; Rayback, *Free Soil*, p. 273.

71. Edward Dodd to Weed, August 3, 1848, Weed MSS (RU).

72. Kirwan, *Crittenden*, pp. 224–31. Powell polled 57,397 votes compared to Polk's 52,000 in 1844 and 55,000 for William O. Butler, the Democrats' gubernatorial candidate, that year.

73. Alex Fleming to M. B. Fleming, June 22, 1848, Fleming MSS; Alfred Dockery to Robert L. Caruthers, July 25, 1848, Caruthers MSS; William L. Battle to Lucy Battle, August 6, 1848, Battle Family Papers; Willie P. Mangum to John S. Pendleton, August 26, 1848, Mangum MSS (Duke); Washington *National Intelligencer*, August 14, 1848; Kruman, *Parties and Politics*, pp. 61, 86–90. Although absolute turnout in August 1848 exceeded that in November 1844, the rate of turnout did not. It was 92.1 percent in 1844 and 84.2 percent in August 1848.

74. The Whig reluctance to run a candidate against the Democratic incumbent, Augustus French, may have reflected French's stand on a new state constitution ratified in the spring, which offended Democrats and ingratiated Whigs. French intervened in the convention to defeat antibanking clauses, and he vigorously endorsed the constitution that forbid alien suffrage, previously allowed in Illinois, thereby potentially reducing the Democratic vote; mandated a new tax specifically to pay off the state debt; stripped the legislature of patronage and made most state and local offices elective; and called for circuit judges to be elected by district, rather than at-large statewide, thereby allowing Whigs to win four of seven circuit judgeships in 1848.

See David T. Gregg to Charles H. Lanphier, February 14, 1848, Thompson Campbell to Lanphier, March 9, 1848, and John Roberts to Lanphier, June 15, 1848, Lanphier MSS; D. H. Whitney to David Davis, March 1, 1848, David Davis to Julius Rockwell, December 7, 1848, David Davis MSS; Letter of J. S. W., April 24, 1848, Washington *National Intelligencer*, April 29, 1848; McCormack, *Koerner Memoirs*, I, p. 524.

75. Thomas Foote to Millard Fillmore, October 1, 1848, MFP-O; Isaac E. Johnson to George Dunn, July 2, 1848, Dunn MSS; John Defrees to Thurlow Weed, September 30, 1848, Weed MSS (RU); R. W. Thompson to J. J. Crittenden, October 21, 1848, Crittenden MSS (LC).

76. Clay to Nicholas Dean, August 24, 1848, Thomas J. Clay MSS; Boston *Daily Advertiser*, September 12, 13, 1848.

77. Iverson Harris to John M. Berrien, July 14, 1848, Berrien MSS; James Meeks to Bolling Hall, August 1, 1848, Hall MSS; F. G. Norman to George Houston, July 27, 1848, A. C. Matthews to Houston, August 7, 1848, Houston MSS; Elmore J. Fitzpatrick to Reuben Chapman, September 23, 1848, Reuben Chapman MSS (Governors' Records, ADAH).

78. William B. Campbell to David Campbell, August 7, 1848, Neil Brown to William B. Campbell, October 1848, S. M. Blythe to William B. Campbell, October 30, 1848, CFP.

79. *Historical Statistics*, p. 899.

80. Truman Smith to Alexander H. Stephens, October 2, 1848, Stephens MSS (LC); John McLean to John Teesdale, December 10, 1848, McLean MSS (OHS).

81. Richmond *Enquirer*, September 15, 1848, Tallahassee *Floridian*, September 16, 1848, Raleigh *Standard*, November 8, 1848, all quoted in Cooper, *Politics of Slavery*, p. 260.

82. Ibid., p. 261. The first quotation apparently comes from the Richmond *Enquirer*; the second is from the Jackson *Mississippian*, September 18, 1848.

83. W. G. Snethen to Fillmore, July 11, 1848, Fillmore to W. G. Snethen, July 14, 1848, copy, E. C. Cabell to Fillmore, July 11, 1848, William L. Hodge to Fillmore, July 13, 1848, William C. Rives to Fillmore, September 6, 1848, James Brooks to Fillmore, September 7, 1848, MFP-O; Toombs to Crittenden, September 27, 1848, Crittenden MSS (LC).

84. Fillmore to John Gayle, July 31, 1848, Fillmore to John B. Peyton, August 20, 1848, in Severance, ed., "Millard Fillmore Papers," 11, pp. 280–81; William L. Hodge to Fillmore, September 7, October 21, 1848, Fillmore to James Brooks, September 13, 1848, William L. Goggin to Fillmore, September 20, 1848, Richmond *Times*, October 3, 1848, clipping with Rives to Fillmore, October 28, 1848, MFP-O; Finkelman, *Imperfect Union*, pp. 266–71.

85. William J. Penniman to John M. Clayton, December 3, 1848, Clayton MSS; Richmond *Times*, October 3, 1848; Thornton, *Politics and Power*, pp. 179–80; clipping of Dallas County, Alabama, Whig ratification meeting in R. H. Chamberlayne to Millard Fillmore, June 24, 1848, MFP-O; Milledgeville *Southern Recorder*, October 3, 1848, quoted in Cooper, *Politics of Slavery*, p. 262 (see pp. 262–63 for quotations in a similar vein); Raleigh *Register*, October 21, 1848, quoted in Kruman, *Parties and Politics*, pp. 120–21.

86. For voting records in the House of Representatives, see Alexander, *Sectional Stress*, pp. 51–54, and particularly the sharp divisions between southern Democrats and Whigs on votes 40, 58, 59, 62, 63, and 65, pp. 181–82. In the Senate, every southern Whig but one had voted against ratifying Tyler's treaty of annexation.

87. Will B. Walton to William B. Campbell, October 3, 1848, CFP; S. S. Locke to Thomas Butler King, October 26, 1848, King MSS. I have interpolated the figures for turnout rates in the Georgia congressional elections of 1844 and 1848 from the figures for presidential turnout rates for those years listed in *Historical Statistics*, p. 1072. The following table gives the total Democratic and Whig votes in the elections referred to.

	Whig	Democratic
1844 Congress	38,111	40,377
1846 Congress	27,563	31,187
1847 Governor	41,941	43,219
1848 Congress	38,651	38,908

88. John Van Buren to Joshua Giddings, December 11, 1848, Giddings-Julian MSS; John M. Niles to Gideon Welles, October 8, 1848, Welles MSS (LC).

89. Taylor to Fillmore, September 6, 1848, MFP-O.

90. The entire text of the second Allison Letter is printed in *ZT:SWH*, pp. 121–24.

91. Weed quoted in ibid., p. 125; Fillmore to Taylor, September 16, 1848, copy, Philip Greely to Fillmore, September 26, 1848, Debs Lake to Fillmore, September 30, 1848, MFP-O; Ogden Hoffman to J. J. Crittenden, September 30, 1848, Crittenden MSS (LC); Robert Winthrop to John P. Kennedy, September 19, 1848, Kennedy MSS.

92. Tom Corwin to Thomas B. Stevenson, June 13, 1848, Stevenson MSS; P. Hitchcock to Thomas Ewing, June 12, 1848, D. C. Pinkerton to Thomas Ewing, July 1, 1848, EFP; Luther Ruien to Caleb Smith, July 1, 1848, Smith MSS; Maizlish, *Triumph of Sectionalism*, p. 78.

My assertions about partisan conflict in the Ohio legislature are based on two unpublished papers by my former students who calculated indexes of party disagreement and internal party cohesion on roll-call votes for 1848 and other sessions: Hampel, "Ohio Whig Party," and Shadle, "Consensus." The following table lists the number of roll calls and average indexes of partisan disagreement for various categories of legislation in 1848.

	Number of Votes	Average Index of Disagreement
Business incorporations and stockholder rights	11	38
Banking and currency	16	71
Internal improvements	27	65
Constitutional revision	3	67
Social reform	3	47

Stephen Maizlish argues, in his admirably detailed study of Ohio, that state economic policy lost salience for voters after 1846, largely because the Democrats decided that their own internal strife over it was destroying their party (*Triumph of Sectionalism*, pp. 40–50). But he ignores continuing Whig interest in state policy and the relatively high levels of partisan legislative conflict over it after that date. The figures listed above were lower than those for 1847; nonetheless, they indicate that on average, between two-thirds and 85 percent of Whigs and Democrats opposed each other when voting on the roll calls included.

93. D. C. Pinkerton to Thomas Ewing, July 1, 1848, Van Brown to Ewing, August 23, 1848, EFP.

94. Maizlish, *Triumph of Sectionalism*, pp. 113–15; P. Hitchcock to Thomas Ewing, June 28, 1848, William L. Perkins to Ewing, July 24, 1848, EFP; Joseph Vance to J. J. Crittenden, October 24, November 13, 1848, Crittenden MSS (LC); E. S. Hamlin to John McLean, September 16, 1848, McLean MSS (LC); Salmon P. Chase to James A. Briggs, September 27, 1848, Chase MSS (LC); James Ferguson to Austin Brown, September 27, 1848, Austin Brown MSS; Thomas Ewing to Crittenden, November 3, 1848, Ewing MSS (OHS).

95. Maizlish, *Triumph of Sectionalism*, Appendix A, Table 2, p. 242; Congressional Quarterly's, *Guide to U.S. Elections*, pp. 584, 588; Hampel, "Ohio Whig Party," Table 4; E. S. Hamlin to McLean, September 16, 1848, McLean MSS (LC); William Bebb to Crittenden, November 24, 1848, Crittenden MSS (LC). Whigs in Root's district ran no candidate against him, but some Whigs in Giddings' district backed his Democratic opponent in a futile attempt to unseat him. The impregnable Giddings still won 62.7 percent of the vote compared to 60.6 percent in 1846, when a separate Liberty party candidate had siphoned off 13 percent of the vote. In short, Liberty men more than compensated for any Whig defections to the Democrat in 1848.

96. T. S. Williams to Fillmore, July 28, 1848, C. B. Stuart to Fillmore, August 31, 1848, Fillmore to Taylor, September 16, 1848, MFP-O; Edward Dodd to Thurlow Weed, August 3, 1848, George W. Patterson to Weed, August 14, 1848, Weed MSS (RU); Nicholas Dean to Clay, September 5, 1848, Henry Clay MSS (LC); Greeley to Schuyler Colfax, September 15, 1848, Greeley-Colfax MSS; Ogden Hoffman to Crittenden, September 30, 1848, Crittenden MSS (LC); John A. Dix to Francis P. Blair, October 18, 1848, Blair-Lee MSS; Van Deusen, *Weed*, pp. 163–64.

97. My analysis of the New York Whig platform is based on an admirable content analysis of party platforms in Harp, "Character."

98. Philip Greely to Fillmore, September 26, October 12, 1848, Weed to Fillmore, October 13, 1848, N. K. Hall to Fillmore, October 23, 1848, James Lynch to Fillmore, October 24, 1848, MFP-O; Daniel Webster to ?, October 16, 1848, Webster MSS; Philip Greely to Weed, October 20, November 6, 1848, Weed MSS (RU); Truman Smith to Daniel M. Barringer, October 20, 1848, Barringer MSS; Daniel S. Dickinson to S. Brewster, October 23, 1848, Fairchild Collection.

99. Snyder, *Jacksonian Heritage*, pp. 215–17; Mueller, *Whig Party in Pennsylvania*, pp. 149–51; John H. Bryant to Fillmore, September 4, 1848, B. B. Chamberlin to Fillmore, October 3, 1848, MFP-O; S. Todd to Crittenden, September 27, 1848, Crittenden MSS (LC).

100. Mueller, *Whig Party in Pennsylvania*, pp. 148–53, Johnston quoted on p. 152; Snyder, *Jacksonian Heritage*, pp. 214–18; Holt, *Forging a Majority*, pp. 48–53, 289, note 47; John Bryant to Fillmore, August 7, September 23, October 5, 1848, MFP-O; Frederick J. Fenn to Samuel Calvin, October 9, 1848, Calvin MSS.

101. *Historical Statistics*, pp. 201, 886, 899, 993, 995, 1104, and 1106. In 1966 the Cleveland Trust Company published a chart of American business activity between 1790 and 1966 that

measured yearly and monthly fluctuations above and below a standardized mean. In short, it measured surges and declines in economic conditions. Constructed from wholesale commodity prices, data on output and consumption in industries like coal, iron, and textiles, and information on railroad construction, that chart best demonstrates the slide in economic activity that began at the end of 1847 and accelerated in July 1848, immediately after the Whig convention. During 1847, economic activity was, on average, 12 points above the standardized mean for the entire period 1790 to 1966. Business activity also hovered above that mean during the first six months of 1848 by an average of +2.6 points. Beginning in July, however, it sank below the mean and continued in the negative category for the remainder of the year. The average index for those last six months was −2.8 points, that is, 2.8 points below the mean or 5.4 points below the average for the first half of the year. For the last three months of 1848, it was −4 points. In short, the closer the presidential election came, the worse the condition of the economy grew.

102. Washington *National Intelligencer*, February 4, 1848; James M. Barnard to Mark Howard, March 20, September 12, 1848, Howard MSS; Abbott Lawrence to Nathan Appleton, August 11, 1848, Abbott Lawrence MSS. Why Lawrence and the other Boston Associates were less dependent on commercial banks than other manufacturers for operating capital is brilliantly explained in Dalzell, *Enterprising Elite*, pp. 79–112 and passim.

103. Boston *Daily Advertiser*, July 4, 18, 20, September 14, October 15, 16, 28, November 2, 4, 1848.

104. George Morey to Fillmore, September 3, 1848, Philip Greely to Fillmore, September 26, 1848, MFP-O; Stephen C. Phillips to Salmon Chase, October 19, 1848, Chase MSS (LC).

105. Niles to Gideon Welles, September 17, October 29, 1848, Welles MSS (NYPL); Niles to Welles, October 8, November 8, 1848, Welles MSS (LC).

106. Eiselen, *Pennsylvania Protectionism*, pp. 212–13. Turnout rates in New Jersey were 58.2 percent in 1846, 68.1 percent in 1847, and 73.7 percent in October 1848. Those figures, however, still lagged behind the 82.3 percent rate in October 1844. Gienapp, " 'Politics Seems to Enter into Everything,' " pp. 18–19.

107. Turnout in Pennsylvania was 41.5 percent in 1846, 61.9 percent in 1847, and 70.6 percent in October 1848. In October 1844 it had been 78.2 percent. Gienapp, " 'Politics Seem to Enter into Everything,' " pp. 18–19.

108. Charles B. Penrose to Crittenden, October 24, 1848, Charles H. Delavan to Crittenden, October 25, 31, 1848, Crittenden MSS (LC); Daniel Webster to ?, October 16, 1848, Webster MSS; Jacob Abell to Fillmore, October 31, 1848, MFP-O.

109. Moses Hampton to Crittenden, November 26, 1848, John Kennedy to Crittenden, November 26, 1848, Crittenden MSS (LC); Robert Orr to James Buchanan, October 4, 1850, Buchanan MSS (HSP); Hendrick B. Wright to James Buchanan, November, 13, 1848, quoted in Mueller, *Whig Party in Pennsylvania*, p. 159.

110. The following table lists changes in the parties' totals in different regions between 1844 and 1848. The four new states of Iowa, Wisconsin, Florida, and Texas are included, and the Free Soil gains are measured against the Liberty party vote in 1844.

	Whig	Democrat	Free Soil
New England	−15,457	−33,211	+ 52,142
	(−8.3%)	(−18.7%)	
Mid-Atlantic	+12,851	−118,483	+116,230
	(+3%)	(−26.8%)	
Midwest	+16,360	+36,207	+ 64,054
	(+5.6%)	(+11.5%)	
South Atlantic	+12,639	−1,677	
	(+7.3%)	(−1%)	
South Central	+21,317	−10,407	
(Ky., Tenn., Ala., Miss.)	(+12.8%)	(−5.9%)	
Southwest	+14,380	+11,539	
(Ark., La., Tex.)	(+28.9%)	(+17.8%)	

111. James F. Cooper to Howell Cobb, November 11, 1848, in Phillips, "Correspondence of Toombs, Stephens, and Cobb," p. 137; William Dickinson to George Houston, December 17, 1848, Houston MSS; Thornton, *Politics and Power*, pp. 179–80.

112. Calabro, "Collapse in Florida," p. 16. Calabro used the congressional election of 1848 rather than the presidential because turnout was substantially higher in October than in November. His regression estimates are contained in the following table.

	1848		
1846	Whig	Democratic	Nonvoters
Whig	88%	6%	6%
Democratic	18%	49%	33%
Nonvoters	18%	12%	70%

113. See Table I in McCrary, Miller, and Baum, "Class and Party." These estimates, it must be noted, cannot logically account for the substantial increase of the Whig vote in all three states, and their reliability has been questioned in Benson, "Mistransference Fallacy," 127.

114. Table 13 in Alexander, "Voter Partisan Constancy," pp. 98–99. Unlike the other two studies cited, Alexander does not consider movements to and from the nonvoting category. Hence his estimates of Democratic losses must appear as Whig gains when many probably did not vote at all. Because the overall participation rates were down, however, more faith can be placed in his estimates of the share of its 1844 vote that each party retained.

115. Again, Professor Alexander's estimates of voter movements between 1844 and 1848, cited in note 114, suggest that almost twice the proportion of Democrats switched to Taylor in the lower South as in the upper South. In the eight upper South states, the unweighted average arithmetic decline in the turnout rate was 8.3, compared to 4.6 in the four lower South states with popular votes in 1844, although the increased turnout in Louisiana offset sharp drop-offs in the other three.

116. That nonslaveholders had a racial, economic, ideological, or symbolic stake in the defense of slavery and Southern Rights seems to me a central point of consensus among scholars who disagree about much else when interpreting the antebellum South. It seems unnecessary to list all the works by William J. Cooper, Mills Thornton, James Oakes, Bertram Wyatt-Brown, George Frederickson, Eugene D. Genovese, and Harry L. Watson, among others, that I have in mind. Watson, "Conflict and Collaboration," synthesizes much of the relevant literature, as does Thornton, "Ethic of Subsistence."

117. When totals from Iowa and Wisconsin are excluded, the Whigs' vote in the Midwest declined by 7,307 (2.5 percent) between 1844 and 1848. Whigs gained votes in Indiana and Illinois but lost them in Michigan and heavily in Ohio, where the Whig total declined by 16,435 (10.6 percent). In the six New England states, the total decline was 15,457 (8.3 percent).

118. Alexander, "Voter Partisan Constancy," pp. 98–99. Even including Iowa and Wisconsin, the Democratic gain in the Midwest between 1844 and 1848 was 36,207 compared to a gain of 61,757 in the four other midwestern states between 1840 and 1844.

119. Joseph Vance to Crittenden, November 13, 1848, William Bebb to Crittenden, November 24, 1848, Crittenden MSS (LC); Table 4, Appendix C, in Maizlish, *Triumph of Sectionalism*, p. 244. In making these calculations, I have converted the negative estimates in the table to zero and reduced the positive estimates proportionally to their size.

120. William Woodbridge to Daniel Webster, November 27, 1848, Webster MSS; Formisano, *Birth of Mass Political Parties*, p. 30.

121. Current, *Wisconsin*, pp. 202–04.

122. John Defrees to Weed, September 30, 1848, Weed MSS (RU); Richard W. Thompson to Crittenden, October 21, 1848, Crittenden MSS (LC); Schuyler Colfax to Caleb B. Smith, November 17, 1848, Thomas Dowling to Smith, January 5, 1849, misdated 1848, Smith MSS.

123. Elihu B. Washburne to Cadwallader C. Washburne, November 12, 1848, Washburne

MSS (Norlands); David Davis to Julius Rockwell, December 7, 1848, David Davis MSS. For the changes in the new state constitution that caused Whig hope and Democratic despair in Illinois, see note 74.

124. John W. Allen to William H. Seward, November 13, 1848, Seward MSS (RU).

125. The Free Soilers' share of the vote was 1.1 percent in New Jersey and 3.0 percent in Pennsylvania.

126. My former doctoral student Lex Renda calculated the following regression estimates for New Jersey voter movement between the presidential elections of 1844 and 1848. The small Liberty and Free Soil totals (131 and 849 votes, respectively) were included in the Nonvoters categories for 1844 and 1848.

	1848			% of 1848
1844	Whig	Democrats	Nonvoters	Electorate
Whig	29	1	5	35
Democratic	2	31	2	35
Nonvoters	6	2	22	30
% of 1848 electorate	37	34	29	100

127. E. G. Lindsey to Millard Fillmore, January 28, 1851, MFP-BHS; Adam Diller et al. to J. J. Crittenden, November 11, 1848, Crittenden MSS (LC); John M. Niles to Gideon Welles, November 8, 1848, Welles MSS (LC).

128. Current, *Wisconsin*, pp. 202–04.

129. Alexander, "Harbinger," pp. 28, 30, also concludes that identifying Whig bolters to the Free Soil party in Pennsylvania is impossible because virtually all of the gain this party enjoyed over the Liberty party in 1844 came from former Democrats. Examination of county-level returns suggests that if Whigs did defect to the new party anywhere in the state, it was most likely in a few western counties near Ohio like Beaver, Mercer, and Crawford.

130. Alexander, "Voter Partisan Constancy," Table 13, pp. 98–99. The large number of estimated abstentions in New England and the net decline in both major parties' votes between 1844 and 1848 may in part reflect the movement of 1844 voters out of the region to other states.

131. McLean to John Teesdale, December 10, 1848, McLean MSS (OHS); Joseph Vance to J. J. Crittenden, November 13, 1848, Crittenden MSS (LC).

132. O. H. Smith to Crittenden, November 16, 1848, Crittenden MSS (LC); Schuyler Colfax to Caleb B. Smith, November, 17, 1848, Smith MSS.

133. A. M. Baker to Fillmore, October 23, 1848, MFP-O; Formisano, *Birth of Mass Political Parties*, p. 30. Whigs won only 18 percent of the seats in each house of the Michigan legislature in 1848.

134. Howe edged out a Democrat by 348 votes. In November, Taylor ran behind Cass by 1,072 votes in the counties composing the district, while Van Buren garnered 1,776 votes, a gain of 968 over Birney's total in 1844.

135. Democrats' share of the Maine gubernatorial vote fell from 51.3 percent in 1847 to 47 percent in 1848. Their membership in the lower house of the state legislature dropped from 78 percent in 1847 to 55 percent in 1848; they remained overwhelmingly dominant in the state senate, however.

136. The best analysis of the peculiar apportionment law in Massachusetts and its relationship to fluctuations in Free Soil and Whig strength in the legislature is Sweeney, "Rum." After the 1847 elections 295 men were sent to the lower house of the state legislature; after the 1848 elections, 243 were sent. As with all figures for the partisan composition in state legislatures, I have used the data from the Inter-University Consortium for Political and Social Research at the University of Michigan. For an analysis of the apportionment system that gave Massachusetts Whigs firm control of the state senate, as well as of the reasons for George Briggs' customary popularity, which made his low vote in 1848 unusual, see Formisano, *Transformation of Political Culture*, pp. 299–301, 329.

137. John H. Clifford to Robert C. Winthrop, November 19, 1848, Winthrop MSS.

138. Thomas Foote to Fillmore, November 9, 1848, MFP-O; Benjamin F. Wade to Caroline Wade, November 21, 1848, Wade MSS.

139. John W. Head to Robert L. Caruthers, December 9, 1848, Caruthers MSS; Fillmore to Zachary Taylor, November 11, 1848, copy, Leslie Combs to Fillmore, November 10, 1848, Harry Bradley to Fillmore, November 28, 1848, John Bowson to Fillmore, with unidentifiable newspaper clipping entitled "The Taylor Republican Party" enclosed, November 23, 1848, MFP-O; John B. Mower to Crittenden, November 12, 1848, Crittenden MSS (LC); Alexander H. Stephens to Crittenden, December 5, 1848, Crittenden MSS (Duke).

CHAPTER 12

1. A. C. Brown to Millard Fillmore, November 21, 1848, Harry Bradley to Fillmore, November 28, 1848, MFP-O; Theodore Barnett to Caleb B. Smith, December 6, 1848, Smith MSS.

2. Philo Shelton to Thurlow Weed, January 22, 1849, Weed MSS (RU). March 4, the normal date for an inauguration, fell on a Sunday, and Taylor waited until Monday, March 5, to be sworn in.

3. A number of secondary accounts provide good analyses of the second session of the Thirtieth Congress. In this and subsequent paragraphs I have relied most heavily upon Johannsen, *Douglas*, pp. 240–51; Potter, *Impending Crisis*, pp. 82–89; Brock, *Political Conscience*, pp. 241–56; and especially Cooper, " 'The Only Door.' "

4. Potter, *Impending Crisis*, p. 84. Palfrey's bill called for congressional abolition in the District; Giddings proposed a plebescite by the residents of the District on the continuation of slavery there. Gott, who had won with 49.2 percent of the vote in 1846, garnered only 42.2 percent in 1848, and his absolute vote was also smaller that year. In 1848, his Free Soil opponent won 38.5 percent and the Democrat 19.5 percent. Congressional Quarterly's *Guide to U.S. Elections*, pp. 583, 588. Apparently Gott's desire to placate his own antislavery constituents, rather than any preconcerted northern Whig plan, motivated his resolution, and even other northern Whigs considered its preamble unnecessarily insulting to the South. See Nathan K. Hall to Fillmore, December 30, 1848, MFP-O.

5. Hopkins Holsey to Howell Cobb, January 29, 1849, in Phillips, "Correspondence of Toombs, Stephens, and Cobb," 142–45; John Beire to Daniel M. Barringer, February 3, 1849, Barringer MSS; Daniel Lee to Fillmore, January 25, 1849, MFP-O; Potter, *Impending Crisis*, p. 88.

6. Brock, *Political Conscience*, pp. 245–46; Thomas B. Stevenson to Caleb B. Smith, December 12, 25, 1848, Smith MSS; N. K. Hall to Fillmore, January 8, 1849, MFP-O; Hopkins Holsey to Howell Cobb, February 13, 1849, in Phillips, "Correspondence of Toombs, Stephens, and Cobb," pp. 148–52.

7. Brock, *Political Conscience*, pp. 243–44; Cooper, *Politics of Slavery*, pp. 269–70.

8. John C. Calhoun to James E. Calhoun, January 17, 1849, Calhoun MSS; Alexander H. Stephens to John J. Crittenden, January 17, 1849, draft, Stephens MSS (Duke); George E. Badger to Crittenden, January 13, 1849, Robert Toombs to Crittenden, January 13, 1849, Crittenden MSS (LC); Robert T. Scott to Reuben Chapman, January 27, 1849, Reuben Chapman MSS (Governors' Records, ADAH).

9. Robert C. Winthrop to Edward Everett, January 31, 1849, Everett MSS; David Outlaw to Emily Outlaw, January 15, 1849, Outlaw MSS; Badger to Crittenden, January 17, 1849, Toombs to Crittenden, January 22, 1849, Crittenden MSS (LC); Stephens to Crittenden, January 17, 1849, draft, Stephens MSS (Duke).

10. Potter, *Impending Crisis*, pp. 84–86; Brock, *Political Conscience*, pp. 246–47; Toombs to Crittenden, January 22, 1849, Crittenden MSS (LC).

11. Holt, *Political Crisis*, p. 69.

12. The two Whigs who signed the Southern Address were John Gayle of Alabama and Patrick W. Tompkins of Mississippi. The four Democrats who denounced it were Howell Cobb and Joseph Lumpkin of Georgia, and Linn Boyd and Beverly Clarke of Kentucky. For evidence that southern Democrats from nonslaveholding hill regions feared and resented the radicalism of the Southern Address, see Robert T. Scott to Reuben Chapman, January 27, 1849, Reuben

Chapman MSS; and Hopkins Holsey to Howell Cobb, January 29, 1849, in Phillips, "Correspondence of Toombs, Stephens, and Cobb," pp. 142–45.

13. Toombs to Crittenden, January 22, 1849, Crittenden MSS (LC); Hopkins Holsey to Howell Cobb, January 29, February 13, 1849, in Phillips, "Correspondence of Toombs, Stephens, and Cobb," 142–45, 148–52; Henry W. Hilliard to John M. Berrien, May 8, 1849, in McCrary, "Hilliard"; P. Fauntleroy to Henry Bedinger, January 17, 1849, Bedinger-Dandridge MSS; John Phillips to James McDowell, February 5, 1849, McDowell MSS; Alexander Stephens to George W. Crawford, March 20, 1849, Stephens MSS (LC); Cole, *Whig Party in the South*, pp. 140–46.

14. N. K. Hall to Fillmore, January 12, 1849, MFP-O; Potter, *Impending Crisis*, p. 88.

15. Dan Coleman to Daniel M. Barringer, January 10, 1849, Barringer MSS.

16. See the letters of Stephens and Toombs to Crittenden cited in note 9; Hopkins Holsey to Howell Cobb, January 29, 1849, loc. cit.; William Penniman to John M. Clayton, December 3, 1848, Clayton MSS; William L. Hodge to Fillmore, November 16, 1848, N. K. Hall to Fillmore, January 8, 1849, and Daniel Lee to Fillmore, January 25, 1849, MFP-O.

17. J. J. Crittenden to John M. Clayton, December 19, 1848, Clayton MSS; Toombs to Crittenden, January 22, 1849, Crittenden MSS (LC); Daniel Lee to Fillmore, January 25, 1849, MFP-O.

18. Brock, *Political Conscience*, pp. 244–45; *ZT:SWH*, p. 181.

19. *Congressional Globe*, 30th Cong., 2nd Sess., p. 477; Toombs to Crittenden, January 22, 1849, Crittenden MSS (LC).

20. Cooper, " 'The Only Door'," loc. cit.

21. Robert T. Scott to Reuben Chapman, March 5, 1849, Reuben Chapman MSS.

22. William Upham to Justin Morrill, September 23, 1848, Morrill MSS; for the characterization of Collamer as conceited, see Horace Greeley to Schuyler Colfax, March 17, 1850, Greeley-Colfax MSS.

23. Doherty, *Whigs of Florida*, pp. 22–23, 31–32.

24. My account of North Carolina in this and subsequent paragraphs relies on Kruman, *Parties and Politics*, pp. 145–59; Walton, "Elections . . . in North Carolina"; Jeffrey, "Clingman"; Kruman, "Clingman"; Inscoe, "Clingman."

25. Table 1 in Jeffrey, "Clingman," 369.

26. Thomas L. Clingman to Willie P. Mangum, September 1, 1848, Mangum MSS (Duke).

27. J. R. Hargrave to Daniel M. Barringer, December 13, 1848, J. M. Long to Barringer, December 15, 1848, Barringer MSS.

28. Long to Barringer, December 15, 1848, Barringer MSS; David L. Swain to William H. Battle, December 16, 1848, Battle Family Papers.

29. B. G. A. Love to Thomas Clingman, December 16, 1848, B. M. Edney to Clingman, December 16, 1848, Clingman-Puryear Family Papers; D. F. Moore to Daniel M. Barringer, December 29, 1848, Barringer MSS.

30. D. F. Moore to Barringer, December 29, 1848, J. R. Hargrave to Barringer, January 18, 1849, Barringer MSS: Kruman, *Parties and Politics*, pp. 149–50.

31. Harry Woods to Samuel Calvin, November 17, 1848, Calvin MSS; Adam Diller to John J. Crittenden, November 11, 1848, Crittenden MSS (LC); B. B. Chamberlain to Millard Fillmore, January 11, 1849, MFP-O; for the factional division in Pittsburgh, see Holt, *Forging a Majority*, pp. 73–74.

32. Mueller, *Whig Party in Pennsylvania*, pp. 160–61; James Cooper to Millard Fillmore, March 13, 1851, MFP-BHS. Cooper told Fillmore that when Johnston was still a Democrat, Whigs had bribed him to whitewash a legislative investigation of the deal in the 1830s by which Thaddeus Stevens obtained a state charter for the Bank of the United States. He also said that in 1848 Johnston became president of the state senate, the post from which he became acting governor upon Shunk's resignation, against the will of senate Whigs, by threatening to help elect a Democrat unless the Whigs supported him.

33. Ibid; William F. Johnston to J. J. Crittenden, January 17, 1849, Crittenden MSS (LC); Townsend Haines to William M. Meredith, March 17, 1849, Meredith MSS.

34. Trumbull Cary to Thurlow Weed, December 15, 1848, Washington Hunt to Weed, January 28, 1849, Weed MSS (RU).

35. Seward to Weed, May 27, 1848, Weed MSS (RU); Zachary Taylor to Fillmore, December 4, 1848, N. K. Hall to Fillmore, December 25, 1848, January 9, 1849, E. T. Osgood to Fillmore, January 19, 1849, David B. Ogden to Fillmore, January 22, 1849, MFP-O; James Watson Webb to Seward, January 28, 1849, Weed to Seward, January 28, 1849, Seward MSS (RU).

36. Benjamin Harwood to Seward, December 10, 1848, Richard M. Blatchford to Seward, December 10, 1848, Seth Hawley to Seward, January 23, 1849, Weed to Seward, March 11, 1849, Seward MSS (RU); Andrew Bray Dickson to Weed, November 24, 1848, George W. Buck to Weed, December 12, 1848, David H. Abell to Weed, December 1848, Seward to Weed, January 4, 1849, Weed MSS (RU); William A. Cornwall to Fillmore, December 17, 1848, N. K. Hall to Fillmore, December 20, 25, 1848, MFP-O; John C. Spencer to C. B. Penrose, April 12, 1849, Meredith MSS.

37. Weed to Seward, December 2, 10, 12, 1848, January 9, 16, 1849, Seward MSS (RU); Washington Hunt to Weed, December 12, 16, 1848, January 22, 28, 29, 1849, Washington Hunt to Alvah Hunt, January 21, 1849, and Washington Hunt to Morgan Johnson, January 19, 1849, Weed MSS (RU); N. K. Hall to Fillmore, December 20, 25, 1848, January 9, 1849, Alfred Babcock to Fillmore, December 30, 1848, MFP-O. There were 107 Whigs in the house and 24 in the senate, and Seward was believed to be assured of 70 to 80 votes if the caucus met.

38. Ibid. Weed to Seward, March 11, 1849, Seward MSS (RU). For a description of the powers of the comptroller, see Gideon Hard to Fillmore, November 20, 1848, and D. O. Kellogg to Fillmore, November 29, 1847, MFP-O. Not only did the comptroller chair the canal board, he also supervised the deposit of state funds in different banks and the regulation of banks and railroads. He had more direct impact on businessmen in the state than any other public official.

39. See Fillmore's Comptroller's Report, December 30, 1848, in Severance, "Millard Fillmore Papers," 10, 275–83, and for contemporary praise of it, see Schuyler Colfax to Fillmore, March 10, 1849, MFP-O; Weed to Seward, December 10, 12, 1848, January 16, 28, March 11, 1849, Seward MSS (RU); Seward to Weed, December 5, 7, 1848, David H. Abell to Weed, December 18, 1848, Weed MSS (RU); Fillmore to Taylor, November 11, 1848, Thomas Foote to Fillmore, November 14, 1848, N. K. Hall to Fillmore, December 20, 26, 1848, January 8, 1849, James Woods to Fillmore, January 9, 1849, E. T. Osgood to Fillmore, January 19, 1849, MFP-O.

40. Weed to Seward, January 28, February 4, March 11, 1849, James Watson Webb to Seward, January 28, 1849, Seward MSS (RU); Seward to James Watson Webb, February 1, 1849, Weed MSS (RU); N. K. Hall to Fillmore, February 11, 1849, Jerome Fuller to Fillmore, March 16, 1849, Gideon Hard to Fillmore, March 18, 1849, MFP-O; Van Deusen, *Seward*, pp. 112–15.

41. Poage, *Clay*, pp. 189–91.

42. Ibid.; John Bowson to Fillmore, November 23, 1848, MFP-O.

43. Clayton to Crittenden, January 23, 1849, Johnson to Crittenden, December 12, 1848, Pendleton to Crittenden, December 22, 1848, Burnley to Crittenden, January 12, 1849, Dayton to Crittenden, December 14, 1848, Crittenden MSS (LC); Stephens to Crittenden, January 17, 1849, draft, Stephens MSS (Duke); William B. Campbell to David Campbell, February 23, 1848, CFP; N. K. Hall to Fillmore, December 26, 30, 1848, January 8, 12, 1849, MFP-O; Philo Shelton to Thurlow Weed, January 22, 1849, Weed MSS (RU); J. G. Marshall to George Dunn, January 28, 1849, Dunn MSS; Poage, *Clay*, p. 190.

44. Henry Clay to Nicholas Dean, August 24, 1848, Thomas J. Clay MSS; Nicholas Carroll to Henry Clay, November 11, 1848, Henry Clay MSS (LC); Leslie Combs to John M. Clayton, January 22, 1849, Clayton MSS; Philo Shelton to Weed, January 22, 1849, Weed MSS (RU); Thomas B. Stevenson to Caleb Smith, December 7, 1848, January 5, 18, 1849, Smith MSS; John A. McClung to Crittenden, January 6, 1849, Crittenden MSS (LC).

45. Maizlish, *Triumph of Sectionalism*, pp. 121–46; Potter, *Impending Crisis*, pp. 49, 73, and passim.

46. In addition to the chapter in Maizlish's book cited above, my account of the Ohio legislative session in this and subsequent paragraphs relies on the following secondary works: Holt, "Party Politics in Ohio," 319–402; Pershing, "General Assembly of Ohio," 222–83, especially 232–42; Erickson, "Repeal of Ohio's Black Laws"; and Blue, "Ohio Free Soilers."

47. To prevent passage of the law, Democrats withdrew from the state senate to deny the quorum necessary to enact legislation, yet senate Whigs found a pretext to pass the law anyway. That action and the Democratic attempt at obstructionism in part generated the charges of revolutionary anarchism. Traditionally, Hamilton County had been awarded five house and two senate seats, although only one of the two senators was elected each year. The Whig apportionment law of 1848 created one district out of the first eight wards of Cincinnati and allocated two house and one senate seat to it. It was the district Whigs expected to carry. The other district, consisting of Cincinnati's remaining wards and the rest of the county, was allotted one senate and three house seats. Democrats were expected to carry it easily. The reason the state senator elected in 1848 did not raise a dispute was that he would represent the safe Democratic district. In 1849, the senate contest in the controversial Cincinnati district would produce the same kind of conflict that the house election did in 1848.

48. John Harris to Fillmore, December 15, 1848, MFP-O; Oran Follett to William H. Seward, November 30, 1848, Seward MSS (RU); James Ferguson to Austin Brown, December 9, 1848, Brown MSS; John L. Miner to John McLean, December 14, 1848, McLean MSS (LC). Authorities disagree about the exact strength of the three parties in the two chambers, and my figures in the text represent an amalgam of their estimates and the data gathered by Walter Dean Burnham for the Inter-University Consortium for Political and Social Research at the University of Michigan. Burnham lists thirty-three Democrats, thirty-one Whigs, and eight Free Soilers in the house, which means that Whigs and Democrats were at even strength before the resolution of the disputed Cincinnati seats.

49. Edward Wade to Albert G. Riddle, December 10, 1848, Riddle MSS; E. S. Hamlin to John McLean, December 9, 1848, John L. Miner to McLean, December 12, 1848, John Teesdale to McLean, January 5, 1849, McLean MSS (LC); Salmon P. Chase to Belle Chase, December 30, 1848, Chase MSS (LC); Samuel Lewis to Joshua R. Giddings, March 20, 1849, Giddings-Julian MSS.

50. Oran Follett to Seward, November 30, 1848, Seward MSS (RU); A. S. Brewer to Thomas Ewing, November 27, 1848, David Peck to Ewing, November 27, 1848, George Riles to Ewing, January 16, 1849, William Bebb to Crittenden, November 24, 1848, EFP; Salmon Chase to Belle Chase, February 15, 1849, Chase MSS (LC); John L. Miner to McLean, December 14, 1848, John Teesdale to McLean, January 5, 1849, McLean MSS (LC).

51. Giddings to Albert G. Riddle, November 25, 1848, Riddle MSS; Miner to McLean, December 14, 1848, McLean MSS (LC); George Riles to Thomas Ewing, January 16, 27, 1849, EFP; Salmon Chase to Belle Chase, February 15, 1849, Chase MSS (LC).

52. H. C. Whitman to William Allen, January 29, 1849, Allen MSS; A. S. Brewer to Thomas Ewing, November 27, 1848, David Peck to Ewing, November 27, 1848, EFP; Alfred Thomas to Salmon Chase, February 1, 1849, Chase MSS (LC); R. G. Corwin to Caleb Smith, February 7, 1849, Smith MSS.

53. Salmon Chase to Belle Chase, December 30, 1848, February 15, 1849, Chase MSS (LC); E. S. Hamlin to Chase, January 19, 27, 1849, Chase MSS (HSP); John Woods to Thomas Ewing, January 24, 1849, George Riles to Ewing, January 23, 27, February 13, 1849, EFP; R. G. Corwin to Caleb Smith, February 7, 1849, Smith MSS.

54. James H. Briggs to Thomas Ewing, March 10, 1849, Oran Follett to Ewing, April 30, 1849, E. N. Sill to Ewing, April 6, 1849, EFP; Oran Follett to Fillmore, March 10, 1849, J. Ridgeway to Fillmore, December 12, 1848, MFP-O. Historians who insist that Chase's election increased the pressure on northern Whigs to oppose concessions to the South on slavery extension, in sum, are absolutely correct.

55. B. S. Cowen to Thomas Ewing, April 9, 1849, EFP; R. G. Corwin to Caleb Smith, February 7, 1849, Smith MSS; John Reaves to John McLean, January 31, 1849, McLean MSS (LC); Alfred Thomas to Chase, February 1, 1849, Chase MSS (LC); Samuel Lewis to Giddings, March 20, 1849, Giddings-Julian MSS.

56. The following table lists the average index of disagreement between Whigs and Democrats, Free Soilers and Democrats, and Free Soilers and Whigs on roll-call votes in the state house of representatives during the 1848–49 session. It indicates that most Free Soilers voted with the Whigs against the Democrats on most matters except constitutional revision.

	No. of Votes	Whig/ Democratic	Free Soil/ Democratic	Free Soil/ Whig
Business incorporation	33	71	71	10
Stockholder liability	19	83	75	10
Banking and currency	8	100	86	13
Internal improvements	26	67	64	8
Slavery and race	9	40	58	15
Constitutional revision	9	84	14	72

Note: These figures are taken from the tables in Shadle, "Consensus."

57. Columbus Delano to Thomas Ewing, April 10, 1849, Oran Follett to Ewing, April 30, 1849, EFP; Boston *Daily Advertiser*, April 3, 1849.

58. Crittenden to Clayton, November 14, 1848, Clayton MSS; Alexander C. Bullitt to Crittenden, December 3, 1848, John Pendleton to Crittenden, December 22, 1848, Crittenden MSS (LC); Alexander Stephens to Crittenden, January 17, 1849, draft, Stephens MSS (Duke); Robert C. Winthrop to John P. Kennedy, November 14, 1848, Kennedy MSS; Seward to Weed, December 10, 11, 1848, Truman Smith to Seward, January 7, 1849, Weed MSS (RU); Zachary Taylor to Fillmore, December 4, 1848, James Watson Webb to Fillmore, December 22, 1848, MFP-O; Washington Barrow to William B. Campbell, January 6, 1849, CFP.

59. William L. Hodge to Fillmore, December 11, 1848, MFP-O; Stephens to Crittenden, January 17, 1849, draft, Stephens MSS (Duke).

60. J. B. Mower to Crittenden, November 12, 19, 1848, Crittenden MSS (LC); for other examples of the determination to purge all vestiges of Clayism, Websterism, and National Republicanism, see S. Pleasonton to John M. Clayton, November 22, 1848, Clayton MSS; John Bowson to Fillmore, November 23, 1848, MFP-O; and E. Joy Morris to Daniel M. Barringer, November 10, 1848, Barringer MSS.

61. Richard M. Blatchford to Crittenden, December 4, 1848, Nathan Appleton to Crittenden, November 20, 1848, John Pendleton to Crittenden, December 22, 1848, John Clayton to Crittenden, December 13, 1848, James S. Pike to Crittenden, January 26, 1849, Joseph Grinnell to Crittenden, January 31, 1849, Crittenden MSS (LC); Daniel Webster to Hiram Ketchum, November 27, 1848, February 9, 1849, Webster MSS; Weed to Seward, December 2, 1848, Seward MSS (RU); Philo Shelton to Weed, November 27, 1848, January 22, 1849, Weed MSS (RU); Elihu B. Washburne to Cadwallader C. Washburn, December 12, 1848, Washburne MSS (Norlands); Harry Bradley to Fillmore, November 28, 1848, William Pitt Fessenden to Fillmore, January 26, 1849, Nathan Appleton to Fillmore, February 6, 1849, MFP; Crittenden to John Davis, January 26, 1849, Philip Greely to John Davis, January 20, 22, February 23, 1849, John Davis MSS; Daniel Ullmann to John M. Clayton, December 5, 1848 (quotation), Clayton MSS.

62. Alexander C. Bullitt to Crittenden, December 3, 1848, Crittenden MSS (LC); Thomas B. Stevenson to Caleb Smith, February 16, 1849, Smith MSS.

63. Thomas Dowling to Caleb B. Smith, February 21, 1849 (quotation), Smith MSS; Weed to Seward, December 2, 10, 12, 1848, March 4, 1849, Seward MSS (RU); Seward to Weed, December 10, 11, 1848, February 27, March 1, 4, 1849, Weed MSS (RU); Stephens to Crittenden, January 17, 1849, Stephens MSS (Duke); Washington Barrow to William B. Campbell, January 6, 1849, CFP.

64. Ibid.; R. G. Corwin to Caleb Smith, January 19, 1849, Schuyler Colfax to Caleb Smith, March 3, 1849, Smith MSS; Caleb Smith to Allen Hamilton, December 20, 1848, Hamilton MSS; Truman Smith to Seward, January 7, 1849, Weed MSS (RU).

65. Washington Barrow to William B. Campbell, January 6, 1849, CFP.

66. William Bebb to Crittenden, November 24, 1848, EFP; Caleb Smith to Allen Hamilton, December 20, 1848, Hamilton MSS; Thomas B. Stevenson to Caleb Smith, December 12, 1848, January 9, 1849, R. G. Corwin to Caleb Smith, January 19, 1849, Schuyler Colfax to Caleb Smith, March 3, April 2, 1849, Elihu B. Washburne to Caleb Smith, May 4, 1849, Smith MSS.

67. Thos. B. Stevenson to Caleb Smith, December 7, 1848, February 16, 1849, John Defrees to Smith, February 18, 1849, Colfax to Smith, March 3, 1849, Smith MSS.

68. Stevenson to Caleb Smith, January 5, 18, 27, 1849, Smith MSS.

69. John Bowson to Fillmore, November 23, 1848 (quotation), A. D. Chaloner to Fillmore, December 4, 1848, Zachary Taylor to Fillmore, December 4, 1848, clipping of the resolutions of the Natchez Rough and Ready Club, January 22, 1849, MFP-O; J. W. White to John M. Clayton (quotation), April 30, 1849, Clayton MSS; Nathaniel Pope to Crittenden, November 19, 1848 (quotation), Crittenden MSS (LC).

70. Albert T. Burnley to Crittenden, January 12, July 22, 1849, Crittenden MSS (LC).

71. Alexander C. Bullitt to Crittenden, December 3, 1848, John Pendleton to Crittenden, December 22, 1848, Crittenden MSS (LC); William L. Hodge to Fillmore, December 11, 1848, MFP-O; Seward to Weed, November 29, 1848, Weed MSS (RU); T. B. Stevenson to Caleb Smith, December 7, 1848, Smith MSS; Stephens to Crittenden, January 17, 1849, Stephens MSS (Duke); Kirwan, *Crittenden*, pp. 235–37.

72. Crittenden to Clayton, November 14, December 19, 1848, Clayton MSS; Clayton to Crittenden, December 13, 1848, Crittenden MSS (LC); Seward to Weed, November 29, December 10, 11, 1848, Truman Smith to Seward, January 7, 1849, Weed MSS (RU); James Watson Webb to Fillmore, December 12, 1848, MFP-O; Daniel Webster to Hiram Ketchum, November 27, 1848, Webster MSS.

73. Poage, *Clay*, pp. 188–89, and the numerous letters between the two in the Crittenden and Clayton Papers.

74. Crittenden to Clayton, December 19, 1848, Clayton MSS.

75. Crittenden to Clayton, November 14, 1848, July 8, 1849, Clayton MSS.

76. Seward to Weed, December 3, 1848, Weed MSS (RU); Clayton to Crittenden, November 8, December 13, 1848, January 23, 1849, Crittenden MSS (LC).

77. E. Joy Morris to Daniel M. Barringer, November 10, 1848, Barringer MSS; A. D. Chaloner to Fillmore, December 4, 1848, MFP-O; Morton McMichael to Clayton, December 3, 1848, Robert M. Bird to Clayton, n.d., Clayton MSS; Clayton to Crittenden, December 13, 1848, Crittenden MSS (LC).

78. Crittenden to Clayton, December 19, 1848, William D. Lewis to Clayton, December 18, 1848, E. C. Reigart to Clayton, February 19, 1849, Clayton MSS; Seward to Weed, December 3, 11, 1848, Weed MSS (RU); Seward to Josiah Randall, November 29, 1848, Seward MSS (RU); William L. Hodge to Fillmore, December 11, 1848, MFP-O; Thomas B. Stevenson to Caleb Smith, February 16, 1849, Smith MSS.

79. William D. Lewis to Clayton, December 18, 1848, M [McMichael?] to Clayton, n.d., Robert M. Bird to Clayton, n.d., Townsend Haines to Clayton, March 1, 1849, Clayton MSS; William B. Reed to Fillmore, March 2, 1849, Gideon Ball to Fillmore, March 2, 1849, Isaac Davis to Fillmore, March 3, 1849, MFP-O.

80. Alexander C. Bullitt to Crittenden, December 3, 1848, Crittenden MSS (LC); William L. Hodge to Fillmore, December 11, 1848, MFP-O; *ZT:SWH*, pp. 137, 151.

81. Thomas B. Stevenson to Caleb Smith, February 16, 1849, Smith MSS; Leslie Combs to Fillmore, February 23, 1849, MFP-O; Memo by Thomas Ewing on Clayton's appointment, May 1849, EFP; Webster to ?, February 22, 1849, Webster to Richard M. Blatchford, February 25, 1849, Webster MSS; Crittenden to Clayton, December 19, 1848, Clayton MSS; Crittenden to John Davis, January 26, 1849, John Davis MSS.

82. *ZT:SWH*, pp. 147–52; Seward to Weed, November 29, 1848, February 27, 1849, Weed MSS (RU); J. J. Burnett to William B. Campbell, March 12, 1849, CFP.

83. Webster to Richard M. Blatchford, February 25, 1849, Webster MSS; Seward to Weed, February 27, March 1, 1849, Weed MSS (RU); Seward to Wife, March 1, 1849, in *Seward at Washington*, p. 101.

84. Seward to Weed, February 27, March 1, 4, 1849, Weed MSS (RU); Webster to Clayton, March 3, 4, 1849, Clayton MSS; J. J. Burnett to William B. Campbell, March 12, 1849, CFP.

85. Burnett to Campbell, March 12, 1849, CFP; E. J. Hale to Daniel M. Barringer, March 12, 1849, Barringer MSS; Schuyler Colfax to Caleb Smith, March 3, April 2, 1849, Smith MSS; Webster to Franklin Haven, March 10, 1849, Webster MSS; Horace Greeley to Thomas B.

Stevenson, February 27, 1849, Henry Clay to Stevenson, April 21, 1849, Stevenson MSS; Iverson L. Harris to John M. Berrien, August 17, 1849, Berrien MSS; Greeley to Schuyler Colfax, March 17, 1850, Greeley-Colfax MSS.

86. Truman Smith to Thomas Ewing, April 6, 1849, EFP; Webster to Franklin Haven, March 10, 1849, Webster MSS; Seward to Weed, March 4, 1849, Weed MSS (RU).

87. In 1847 Preston won by only 325 votes in a district Democrats had carried handily in 1843 and 1845, and some of his constituents considered him the only Whig they could elect in 1849. In any event, the Whigs lost the seat with a different candidate in May. See ? to William Ballard Preston, January 26, 1849, and John B. Floyd to Preston, February 19, 1849, Preston MSS.

88. William L. Hodge to Fillmore, December 11, 1848, MFP-O; *ZT:SWH*, pp. 142–43, 152–53. According to Robert W. Fogel, the most recent estimates of econometricians indicate that in 1850 the entire cotton crop of the South was grown on only 6 percent of the cultivated acreage in the cotton regions of the South and that output could be doubled simply by converting 1/15th of the land planted in other crops to cotton. In essence, that is what happened during the 1850s. See Fogel, *Without Consent*, p. 71.

89. Seward wrote Weed on March 4 that Southerners objected to both Caleb and Truman Smith on the grounds that they were antislavery men, yet Collamer could hardly have been more acceptable to them. Collamer had steadfastly supported the Gott resolution and voted against efforts to reconsider it. Both Caleb Smith and Truman Smith, in contrast, refused to vote on the original motion to pass the Gott resolution, even though both were on the House floor, and both later supported reconsideration. Collamer, in short, was a more hard-line antislavery man than either Smith. *Congressional Globe*, 30th Cong., 2nd Sess., 83–107, 212–16.

90. Taylor did not regard McLean as an ultra Whig like the supporters of Clay and Webster, but he did dislike him as a rival and considered his letters to newspapers on current affairs improper behavior for a Supreme Court justice. Alexander C. Bullitt to Crittenden, December 3, 1848, Crittenden MSS (LC).

CHAPTER 13

1. Clayton to Crittenden, January 23, 1849, Crittenden MSS (LC).

2. *Messages and Papers of the Presidents*, V, pp. 4–6.

3. *ZT:SWH*, pp. 170–71; Walter Taylor to William H. Seward, April 1, 1849, William L. Hodge to Seward, June 2, 1849, Seward MSS (RU); Balie Peyton to William B. Campbell, April 14, 1849, CFP; Albert T. Burnley to Crittenden, January 12, July 22, 1849, Crittenden MSS (LC).

4. For the pay of skilled and unskilled labor, see Holt, *Forging a Majority*, pp. 28–31; and Wilentz, *Chants Democratic*, pp. 117, 405.

5. E. Joy Morris to Daniel M. Barringer, November 10, 1848, Willie P. Mangum to Barringer, May 30, 1849, Barringer MSS; Summers, *Plundering Generation*, pp. 23–40.

6. Seward to Weed, March 6, 1849, Weed MSS (RU); Nathan K. Hall to Millard Fillmore, March 10, 1849, MFP-O; William F. Johnston to William M. Meredith, May 7, 1849, Meredith MSS.

7. John Defrees to Thomas Ewing, March 14, 1849, EFP; Townsend Haines to William M. Meredith, March 17, 1849, Meredith MSS; N. K. Hall to Fillmore, March 10, 1849, Thomas Foote to Fillmore, March 12, 24, 1849, Gideon Hard to Fillmore, March 18, 1849, and Dennis Bowen to Fillmore, March 24, 1849, MFP-O.

8. William B. Campbell to David Campbell, May 14, 1849, CFP; Thomas Foote to Millard Fillmore, April 4, 1849, MFP-O; Samuel D. Hubbard to John M. Clayton, May 22, 1849, Clayton MSS; Samuel Calvin to Fitz Henry Warren, April 5, 1849, Calvin MSS.

9. Crittenden to Clayton, July 20, 1849, Clayton MSS; C. A. Trowbridge to Thomas Ewing, October 15, 1849, EFP.

10. John Defrees to Caleb B. Smith, May 23, 1849, Smith MSS; Balie Peyton to William B. Campbell, November 7, 1849, CFP.

11. *ZT:SWH*, pp. 203–18; Seward to Weed, March 10, 24, 1849, Weed MSS (RU); Zachary Taylor to Henry Clay, May 28, 1849, Henry Clay MSS (LC); Walter Cunningham to William

H. Seward, June 27, 1849, Seward MSS (RU); Crittenden to John M. Clayton, July 10, 1849, Clayton MSS.

12. *ZT:SWH*, p. 204; Bauer, *Zachary Taylor*, pp. 259–60.

13. *ZT:SWH*, pp. 216–17; Millard Fillmore to Edward Everett, July 11, 1849, Everett MSS; Orlando Brown to John J. Crittenden, July 10, 1849, Crittenden MSS (LC); J. G. Marshall to Richard W. Thompson, April 23, 1849, Thompson MSS (Ind.SL).

14. Abraham Lincoln to John M. Clayton, July 28, 1849, Crittenden to Clayton, July 8, 1849, Clayton MSS; Fillmore to Everett, July 11, 1849, Everett MSS; Orlando Brown to Crittenden, July 10, 1849, Nathan Sargent to Crittenden, July 15, 1849, Crittenden MSS (LC); J. G. Marshall to Richard W. Thompson, April 23, 1849, Thompson MSS (Ind.SL).

15. W. W. Carter to William M. Meredith, May 2, 1849, William C. Dawson to Meredith, June 15, 1849, Meredith MSS; Orlando Brown to Crittenden, June 27, July 10, August 29, 1849, Crittenden MSS (LC).

16. C. S. Morehead to John M. Clayton, March 14, 1849, Thompson MSS (Lincoln National Life Foundation); John Pendleton to John J. Crittenden, May 22, 1849, Crittenden MSS (LC); E. D. Baker to John M. Clayton, March 20, 1849, Clayton MSS; Willie P. Mangum to Daniel M. Barringer, May 30, 1849, Barringer MSS; Moses Hampton to Thomas Butler King, April 5, 1849, King MSS; Henry Hillard to Nathan Appleton, May 21, 1849, Appleton MSS; *ZT:SWH*, pp. 209–12; Elihu B. Washburne to Thomas Ewing, May 4, 1849, EFP.

17. *Senate Executive Proceedings*, pp. 83, 84, 88, 106, 110, 145; Clayton to Crittenden, April 18, 1849, Crittenden MSS (LC); Truman Smith to Elihu B. Washburne, March 26, 1849, Washburne MSS (LC); John Defrees to Caleb Smith, October 1, 1849, Smith MSS.

18. Nathan Sargent to Crittenden, July 15, 1849, Crittenden MSS (LC); William L. Hodge to Seward, June 2, 1849, Seward MSS (RU); James E. Harvey to Clayton, May 5, 1849, Crittenden to Clayton, July 20, 1849, Clayton MSS.

19. *ZT:SWH*, p. 206; *Senate Executive Proceedings*, p. 90; Seward to Weed, March 24, 1849, Weed MSS (RU); Weed to Seward, April 1, 1849, Walter Cunningham to Seward, May 4, 1849, Seward MSS (RU); Edward McGaughey to Caleb Smith, April 16, 1849, Smith MSS. The Senate always met in a special March session after a presidential nomination to confirm cabinet members, but Democrats' pretext for rejecting McGaughey was that he was constitutionally ineligible for the post since he had served in the Congress that formally organized the Minnesota Territory.

20. Russell Sage to Seward, May 2, 1849, Walter Cunningham to Seward, May 4, 1849, Seward MSS (RU); Seward to Weed, March 24, 1849, Weed MSS (RU); Alexander H. Stephens to George W. Crawford, March 20, 1849, Stephens MSS (LC); *ZT:SWH*, pp. 203–09.

21. Nathan Sargent to Crittenden, July 15, 1849, Crittenden MSS (LC); E. G. Spaulding to Seward, March 30, 1849, Seward MSS (RU); E. C. Cabell to William M. Meredith, June 3, August 28, 1849, William C. Dawson to Meredith, June 15, 1849, Edward Stanly to Meredith, June 29, 1849, Meredith MSS; Daniel Lord to John M. Clayton, March 30, 1849, J. W. White to Clayton, April 30, 1849, Clayton MSS; Thomas Foote to Millard Fillmore, April 11, 1849 (quotation), MFP-O.

22. Charles D. Drake to Crittenden, April 2, 1849, Crittenden MSS (LC); John Drew to Thomas Ewing, April 9, 1849, James E. Harvey to Ewing, June 7, 1849, EFP; Samuel Kramer to William M. Meredith, March 21, 1849, Harvey to Meredith, May 28, 1849, Meredith MSS; David A. Bokee to Millard Fillmore, May 12, 1849, MFP-O.

23. H. H. Hunter to Thomas Ewing, March 7, 1849, Nicholas Dean to Ewing, April 4, 1849, Crittenden to Ewing, June 4, 1849, EFP; Stephens to George W. Crawford, March 20, 1849, Stephens MSS (LC); Thomas B. Stevenson to Caleb Smith, January 5, June 12, 1849, Smith MSS.

24. D. S. Woods to Caleb Smith, December 15, 1848, David Kilgore to Smith, January 5, 1849, D. McGuire to Smith, April 11, 1849, Smith MSS; John Defrees to Thomas Ewing, April 5, 1849, John Bell to Ewing, April 19, May 1, 1849, Patrick W. Tompkins to Ewing, June 1, 1849, William Alston to Ewing, June 16, 1849, EFP; P. B. Barringer to Daniel M. Barringer, July 17, 1849, Barringer MSS.

25. O. P. Q. to Thomas Ewing, June 7, 1849, EFP; Edward McGaughey to Caleb Smith, April 16, 1849, Smith MSS.

26. *Senate Executive Proceedings*, pp. 73–88; J. W. White to John M. Clayton, April 30, 1849, Clayton MSS; S. D. Pardee to Samuel D. Hubbard, February 27, 1849, James F. Babcock to Roger Sherman Baldwin, March 1, 1849, BFP.

27. *Senate Executive Proceedings*, pp. 73–86; William Peterson to Thomas Ewing, May 31, 1849, O. P. Q. to Ewing, June 7, 1849, Ewing to Joseph Ligon, June 13, 1849, EFP.

28. Harvey to Ewing, May 5, 1849, Patrick W. Tompkins to Ewing, June 1, 1849, O. P. Q. to Ewing, June 7, 1849, EFP; Willie P. Mangum to Meredith, April 2, 1849, William C. Dawson to Meredith, June 15, 1849, Meredith MSS; Joseph A. Acklim to Jefferson Franklin Jackson, June 2, 1849, Jackson MSS.

29. Leslie Combs to Millard Fillmore, October 8, 1849, MFP-O; Nathan Sargent to John J. Crittenden, July 15, 1849, Crittenden MSS (LC).

30. Truman Smith to Caleb Smith, October 28, 1849, Smith MSS; Seward to Weed, March 24, 1849, Weed MSS (RU); Orlando Brown to Crittenden, June 27, July 10, August 29, 1849, A. T. Burnley to Crittenden, July 22, 1849, Crittenden MSS (LC); Crittenden to Orlando Brown, July 26, 1849, Crittenden MSS (Duke); Crittenden to Clayton, July 20, 1849, Clayton MSS.

31. John Pendleton to Crittenden, May 22, 1849, Crittenden MSS (LC).

32. Willie P. Mangum to Daniel M. Barringer, May 30, 1849, Thomas L. Clingman to Barringer, June 21, 1849, Barringer MSS; Clingman to Clayton, July 5, 1849, Clayton MSS; William H. Haywood to Francis P. Blair, July 15, 1849, Blair-Lee MSS; Mangum to William A. Graham, March 1, May 24, 1849, in *The Mangum Papers*, V, pp. 135–26, 149–50.

33. Balie Peyton to Gustavus A. Henry, April 14, 1849, Henry MSS; Walter Cunningham to Seward, June 23, 1849, Seward MSS (RU).

34. Cunningham to Seward, June 27, 1849, Seward MSS (LC); *Senate Executive Proceedings*, pp. 106–16.

35. Henry Clay to Nicholas Dean, June 21, 1849, Henry Clay MSS (LC); Clay to Thomas B. Stevenson, April 21, 1849, Stevenson MSS; Crittenden to Clayton, June 1, 1849, Clayton MSS.

36. Daniel Webster to William B. Preston, March 7, 1849, Webster to Franklin Haven, March 10, 1849, Webster to Fletcher Webster, March 26, 27, 28, April 12, 1849, William LeRoy to Daniel Webster, March 23, 1849, Webster MSS; Webster to Thomas Ewing, May 1, 1849, EFP; Dalzell, *Webster*, pp. 160–61.

37. Webster to Edward Curtis, April 3, 1849, Webster MSS; Curtis to Ewing, May 8, 1849, EFP; Dalzell, *Webster*, p. 161.

38. A. B. Chambers to Thomas Ewing, June 9, 1849, EFP; Elihu B. Washburne to Caleb Smith, May 4, 7, 21, November 17, 1849, Justin Butterfield to Smith, June 5, 1849, Smith MSS; Truman Smith to Elihu B. Washburne, March 26, 1849, Washburne MSS (LC); A. G. Henry to Joseph Gillespie, June 2, 1849, Gillespie MSS; E. D. Baker to David Davis, June 20, 1849, David Davis MSS; *ZT:SWH*, pp. 209–12.

39. William Woodbridge to Thomas Ewing, March 29, 1849, Elihu B. Washburne to Ewing, April 26, 1849, EFP; Washburne to Caleb Smith, May 4, 1849, Thomas Dowling to Smith, July 27, 1849, Hugh O'Neal to Smith, July 30, 1849, John Defrees to Smith, October 1, 1849, Smith MSS.

40. Thomas Corwin to Millard Fillmore, August 7, 1849, Thomas Foote to Fillmore, October 9, 1849, MFP-O; Schuyler Colfax to Caleb Smith, September 27, November 3, 8, 1849, Truman Smith to Caleb Smith, October 28, 1849, Elihu B. Washburne to Caleb Smith, November 15, 1849, Smith MSS.

41. Albert T. Burnley to John J. Crittenden, February 20, 1849, Boyd McNairy to Crittenden, August 6, 1849, Crittenden MSS (LC); Neil J. Brown to John Bell, March 27, 1849, John Bell MSS; Bell to Thomas Ewing, April 9, May 1, 1849, EFP; William B. Campbell to David Campbell, May 14, August 19, 1849, CFP.

42. J. J. Sanford to Daniel M. Barringer, August 9, 1849, Barringer MSS; James Pearce to John M. Berrien, May 21, 1849, T. W. Spencer to Berrien, July 13, 1849, Berrien MSS; Pearce to Crittenden, July 14, 1849, Crittenden MSS (LC); Crittenden to John M. Clayton, July 23, 1849, Clayton MSS.

43. Alexander Evans to William M. Meredith, August 9, 1849, Meredith MSS; Pearce to Berrien, May 21, 1849, Berrien MSS.

44. B. B. Chamberlain to Millard Fillmore, January 11, 1849 (quotation), Isaac R. Davis to Fillmore, March 3, 1849, MFP-O; Townsend Haines to Clayton, March 1, 1849, Clayton MSS; Morton McMichael to William M. Meredith, August 18, 1849, Meredith MSS; J. E. Bradley to Thomas Ewing, October 12, 1849 (quotation), EFP.

45. Truman Smith to Ewing, April 6, 1849, C. F. Hoeckley to Ewing, May 7, 1849, J. E. Bradley to Ewing, August 19, 1849, EFP; George W. South to Zachary Taylor, April 22, 1849, Meredith MSS.

46. Johnston to Meredith, March 7, 1849, H. H. Watts to Meredith, March 9, 1849, Ewing to Meredith, April 25, 1849, Meredith MSS.

47. C. F. Hoeckley to Thomas Ewing, May 7, 1849, EFP; Cornelius Darragh to Meredith, March 8, 1849, Meredith MSS; *Senate Executive Proceedings*, pp. 86, 98.

48. Johnston to Meredith, March 9, July 14, 1849, Townsend Haines to Meredith, March 17, 1849, Sydney G. Fisher to Meredith, March 20, 1849, and Meredith to Johnston, April 23, 1849, Meredith MSS; *Senate Executive Proceedings*, pp. 98, 105, 106, 109, 133.

49. Meredith to Johnston, April 23, 1849, Henry White to John M. Clayton, April 23, 1849, Morton McMichael to Meredith, May 4, 1849, William D. Lewis to Meredith, May 10, June 3, 4, July 15, November 16, 1849, P. C. Ellmaker to Meredith, November 1, 1849, Meredith MSS; James Buchanan to Edmund Burke, June 4, 1849, Burke MSS.

50. Robert M. Riddle to Millard Fillmore, March 21, 1849, MFP-O; H. M. Brackenridge to Meredith, April 4, 1849, Isaac R. Davis to Morton McMichael, May 8, 1849, Meredith MSS; Sherman Zook to Samuel Calvin, May 29, 1849, Calvin MSS; John E. Bradley to Thomas Ewing, August 8, 19, 30, 1849, EFP. Probably because of complaints from the Whig bastion in Pittsburgh, the cabinet eventually appointed Walter Forward chargé to Denmark.

51. F. Fraley to Meredith, May 5, 1849, Charles Gilpin to Meredith, October 17, 1849, William D. Lewis to Meredith, November 15, 1849, Meredith MSS; James Pettus to Thomas Ewing, August 3, 1849, John E. Bradley to Ewing, October 12, 1849, EFP.

52. James Pettus to Ewing, August 3, 1849, EFP; William D. Lewis to Meredith, November 16, 1849, Meredith MSS.

53. Seward to Weed, March 1, 6, 7, 8, 9, 10, 15, 1849, Weed MSS (RU); Weed to Seward, March 11, 17, 1849, Seward MSS (RU); N. K. Hall, March 10, 1849, Thomas Foote, March 12, 1849, Gideon Hard, March 18, 1849, Jerome Fuller, April 24, 1849, all to Fillmore, MFP-O.

54. Seward to Weed, March 8, 22, 25, 1849, Weed MSS (RU); Walter Cunningham to Seward, March 30, April 3, 1849, Seward MSS (RU); letters to Fillmore from C. B. Stuart, March 10, 1849, Robert Rose, March 14, 1849, David A. Bokee, March 17, May 12, 1849, and James Brooks, March 19, 1849, MFP-O.

55. Hunt to Clayton, April 18, 1849, Clayton MSS; Matteson to Seward, March 23, 1849, William T. Jackson to Seward, April 17, 1849, Seward MSS (RU).

56. Robert Rose to Fillmore, March 14, 1849, MFP-O; Henry J. Raymond to James Watson Webb, July 13, 1849, Webb MSS; Webb to Clayton, n.d. (1849 folder), Clayton MSS; Webb to Meredith, May 17, 1849, Meredith MSS.

57. Seward to Weed, March 24, 29, Weed MSS (RU); Seward to George W. Patterson, March 29, 1849, in *Seward at Washington*, p. 108; Fillmore to Francis Granger, April 17, 1849, MFP-O; Van Deusen, *Weed*, pp. 166–69.

58. Seward to Weed, March 1, 4, 10, 24, 29, 1849, Weed MSS (RU); Weed to Seward, April 16, April——, 1849, Russell Sage to Seward, May 2, 1849, Walter Cunningham to Seward, May 4, 1849, Seward MSS (RU); N. K. Hall to Fillmore, March 10, 17, 1849, Millard Fillmore to Abigail Fillmore, March 25, 1849, MFP-O; *ZT:SWH*, pp. 165, 209; Van Deusen, *Seward*, pp. 113–15; Rayback, *Fillmore*, pp. 196–205.

59. Thomas Foote to Fillmore, March 12, 19, May 22, 1849, Robert Rose to Fillmore, March 14, 1849, N. K. Hall to Fillmore, March 17, 22, 26, April 14, 1849, Gideon Hard to Fillmore, July 30, 1849, MFP-O; Seward to Weed, July 13, 1849, Weed MSS (RU); Weed to Fillmore, John T. Bush, and James Kidd, July 20, 1849, Knollenberg Collection.

60. Seward to Weed, March 9, August 13, 1849, Charles Stetson to Weed, July 7, 1849, Weed MSS (RU); Weed to Seward, March 15, 1849, Isaac Platt to Seward, April 17, 1849, Frederick Whittlesey to Seward, April 20, 1849, Seward MSS (RU); Weed to Meredith, June 2, 1849, Meredith MSS; Alex Mann to Fillmore, April 19, 1849, John T. Bush to Fillmore, June 1, 1849, John L. Dox to Fillmore, September 24, 1849, MFP-O.

61. Fillmore to Seward, April 17, 1849, Seward MSS; Fillmore to Francis Granger, April 17, 1849, Jerome Fuller to Fillmore, May 2, 1849, MFP-O; Fillmore to Edward Everett, July 11, 1849, Everett MSS (MHS); Charles E. Clarke to Seward, May 14, 1849, Weed MSS (RU).

62. Jerome Fuller, May 2, September 10, 19, 1849, Alex Mann to Fillmore, July 27, September 18, 1849, MFP-O; Fillmore to William Johnson, July 30, 1849, Fillmore MSS (LC); Seward to Weed, July 13, 1849, Weed MSS (RU); Weed to Fillmore, Bush, and Kidd, July 20, 1849, Knollenberg Collection.

63. Fillmore to William S. Johnson, August 10, 1849, Fillmore MSS (LC); John L. Dox to Fillmore, September 9, 1849, John Young to Fillmore, September 21, 1849, MFP-O; Seward to Meredith, August 3, 1849, Meredith MSS.

64. E. G. Spaulding to Weed, September 3, 1849, Weed MSS (RU); Erasmus Pershine Smith to Weed, August 31, 1849, Weed MSS (LC); N. K. Hall to Fillmore, July 27, 1849, James Kidd to Fillmore, July 28, 1849, E. Crosby to Fillmore, July 30, 1849, C. Swain to Fillmore, August 9, 1849, John Saunders to Fillmore, August 9, 1849, MFP-O. A copy of the July 24 circular signed by Fillmore can be found in MFP-BHS.

65. Congressman William A. Sackett to Weed, August 19, 1849, August 4, 1849, Weed MSS (LC); Seward to Weed, July 14, 1849, Weed MSS (RU); Seward to Meredith, August 3, 1849, Weed to Meredith, October 6, 1849, Meredith MSS; Weed to Seward, September 18, 1849, Seward MSS (RU); John L. Dox to Fillmore, September 18, 1849, MFP-O; Schuyler Colfax to Caleb B. Smith, September 27, 1849, Smith MSS. Seventy percent of the address that Seward wrote dealt with slavery extension.

66. Schuyler Colfax to Caleb Smith, September 27, 1849, Smith MSS; Gideon Hard to Fillmore, September 29, 1849, Daniel D. Barnard to Fillmore, November 9, 1849, MFP-O; E. G. Spaulding to Weed, October 7, 1849, J. H. Lathrop to Weed, October 14, 26, 1849, Seward to Zachary Taylor, October 18, 1849, copy, Weed MSS (RU); Weed to Meredith, October 21, 1849, Meredith MSS. For New York Democrats' tenuous reunion in 1849, see Mayfield, *Rehearsal for Republicanism*, pp. 141–47.

67. C. G. Blake to Ewing, July 10, 1849, Rufus King to Ewing, July 21, 1849, EFP.

68. Toombs to William Ballard Preston, May 18, 1849, Preston MSS; C. S. Morehead to Clayton, April 10, 1849, Clayton MSS; Cole, *Whig Party in the South*, pp. 145–47.

69. James Babcock to Roger Sherman Baldwin, January 24, 26, 1849, BFP; Alfred E. Burr to Gideon Welles, February 15, March 19, 1849, M. A. Osborn to Welles, March 26, April 3, 1849, Welles MSS (LC); John M. Niles to Welles, March 26, April 5, 1849, Burr to Welles, July 12, August 9, 1849, Welles MSS (NYPL).
The total votes for each party were:

	1847 (Governor)	1848 (Governor)	1848 (President)	1849 (Governor)
Whig	30,137	30,717	30,318	27,300
Democrat	27,135	28,525	27,051	25,106
Liberty-Free Soil	2,135	1,728	5,005	3,520

70. Niles to Welles, April 5, 8, 1849, Burr to Welles, July 12, 1849, Welles MSS (NYPL); Niles to Welles, May 13, 1849, Welles to ?, November 3, 1849, draft, Welles MSS (LC); Boston *Daily Advertiser*, April 17, 1849; J. W. White to John M. Clayton, April 30, 1849, Clayton MSS; Thomas Foote to Fillmore, April 4, 1849, MFP-O.

71. P. Fauntleroy to Henry Bedinger, January 17, 1849, Bedinger-Dandridge Family Papers;

John Phillips to James McDowell, February 5, 1849, McDowell MSS; John Pendleton to Crittenden, April 30, 1849, Crittenden MSS (LC).

72. E. D. Baker to Clayton, March 20, 1849, Crittenden to Clayton, April 11, 1849, Clayton MSS.

73. *ZT:SWH*, pp. 176–82; Clayton to Crittenden, April 18, 1849, Clayton MSS. For evidence of the little-known Utah aspect of Taylor's plans, see John Wilson to Zachary Taylor, December 24, 1849, Wilson to Ewing, May 13, 1850, EFP; Wilson to John Davis, April 29, 1850, John Davis MSS; and Truman Smith to John Wilson, February 12, 1850, John Wilson MSS. I am obliged to Professor William E. Gienapp for making available to me photocopies of the important Wilson Papers at Berkeley.

74. *ZT:SWH*, pp. 180–82.

75. See the letters from Wilson cited in note 74.

76. *ZT:SWH*, p. 182.

77. C. S. Morehead to Clayton, April 10, 1849, Crittenden to Clayton, April 11, 1849, Clayton MSS.

78. William H. Haywood to Francis Preston Blair, July 13, 1849, Blair-Lee MSS.

79. Rufus King to Ewing, July 21, 1849, Ewing to J. C. Wright, July 30, 1849, draft, EFP; George H. Andrews to James Watson Webb, August 30, 1849, Webb MSS; Fish to Seward, November 29, 1849, Seward MSS (RU).

80. Washington Barrow to Clayton, August 5, 1849, William T. Ward to Clayton, August 17, 1849, Clayton MSS; Joshua Bell to Crittenden, June 9, 1849, Crittenden MSS (LC); R. H. Stanton to John W. Stevenson, November 27, 1849, Stevenson Family Papers (LC); Washington Barrow to William B. Campbell, August 7, 1849, CFP.

81. D. S. Woods to Caleb Smith, December 15, 1848, S. W. Parker to Smith, December 27, 1848, Thomas Dowling to Smith, January 1, 5, 1849, John Defrees to Smith, April 18, 1849, Smith MSS.

82. Defrees to Caleb Smith, April 18, 1849, S. W. Parker to Smith, July 10, 1849, Smith MSS; John H. Bradley to Thomas Ewing, May 18, 1849, EFP.

83. Schuyler Colfax to Caleb Smith, May 12, 16, June 12, 1849, James H. Hunt to Smith, June 12, 1849, Smith MSS; George W. Julian to G. C. Starbuck, June 1849, draft, Julian MSS.

84. Godlove Orth to Schuyler Colfax, August 18, 1849, in Schauinger, "Orth Letters," 39, 400; Hugh O'Neal to Caleb Smith, August 12, 1849, R. A. Clements to Smith, September 1, 1849, Smith MSS.

85. John M. Clayton to Zachary Taylor, August 13, 1849, Taylor MSS; Boston *Daily Advertiser*, June 6, 1849; D. W. Clarke to Clayton, August 4, 1849, Clayton MSS.

86. Delano to Ewing, April 10, 1849, B. S. Cowen to Ewing, April 9, 1849, EFP.

87. Thomas Bolton to Salmon P. Chase, April 23, July 30, 1849, Chase MSS (HSP); William Dennison to Ewing, May 14, 1849, C. G. Blake to Ewing, July 16, 1849, Rufus King to Ewing, July 21, 1849, EFP.

88. Iverson L. Harris to Berrien, August 17, 1849, Berrien MSS.

89. *ZT:SWH*, p. 225. Like other historians, I have relied on Hamilton's quotation from this speech, for which he provides no citation. A search of two Whig papers from Ohio, two from Pennsylvania, and the *Albany Evening Journal* and the New York *Tribune* yielded no accounts of the speech, even though Greeley's *Tribune* had a reporter traveling with Taylor who described his trip from Pittsburgh north to Erie. Part of the problem was that Taylor immediately became ill after his stop in Mercer. Since there was a cholera epidemic that summer and people feared Taylor may have contracted the disease in Pittsburgh, newspapers started to print telegraphic dispatches about his condition, rather than delayed accounts of his speeches as they had done for his stops in other Pennsylvania towns. Nonetheless, other primary evidence clearly indicates that Taylor said something about opposing slavery extension and the irrelevance of a Free Soil party at Mercer.

90. Ben Wade to Caroline Wade, September 10, 1849, Wade MSS.

91. William Penniman to Clayton, December 3, 1848, Clayton MSS; Cooper, *Politics of Slavery*, pp. 227–28.

92. Stewart to Meredith, July 17, 1849, Meredith MSS; Stewart to Taylor, August 8, 1849, Taylor MSS; Mueller, *Whig Party in Pennsylvania*, pp. 164–65.

93. McMichael to Meredith, August 18, 23, 1849, Meredith MSS.

94. Harvey to Meredith, August 26, 1849, Meredith MSS.

95. Fillmore to Edward Everett, July 11, 1849, Everett MSS; Stewart to Taylor, August 8, 1849, Taylor MSS; *ZT:SWH*, p. 25.

96. Meredith's papers between July and December 1849 are filled with letters related to this effort. Among the most illuminating are those from Robert L. Martin, July 27, Philip Greely, Jr., August 30, Benjamin Bannen, September 11, Isaac R. Davis, September 19, 22, 24, and Charles Hudson, October 6, 1849, Meredith MSS. See also Meredith to Nathan Appleton, November 6, 9, 1849, Appleton MSS.

97. With its lengthy tables and appendices, Meredith's report filled an entire, unusually thick, volume of the House Executive Documents, but the gist of his recommendations, on which these paragraphs are based, came in his twenty-four-page introduction to those data. U.S. Congress, Thirty-First Congress, 1st Sess., *House Executive Documents*, Volume 2, Executive Document 4.

98. In July, while complaining that he had no knowledge of the administration's intentions, Fillmore used these words to predict what it would do. See Millard Fillmore to Edward Everett, July 11, 1849, Everett MSS.

99. Peyton to William B. Campbell, November 7, 1849, CFP.

100. Cole, *Whig Party in the South*, pp. 146–49. Patrick W. Tompkins, the Whig congressman who signed Calhoun's Southern Address, did not seek reelection in 1849.

101. Murray, *Whig Party in Georgia*, pp. 141–42; Schott, *Stephens*, pp. 98–105; William Hope Hull to Howell Cobb, January 26, 1849, Lumpkin to Cobb, March 12, 1849, and John W. Burke to Cobb, March 22, 1849, in Phillips, "Correspondence of Toombs, Stephens, and Cobb," pp. 142, 156–58.

102. Murray, *Whig Party in Georgia*, pp. 141–42; Schott, *Stephens*, pp. 98–105; Iverson L. Harris to John M. Berrien, August 17, 1849, Berrien MSS.

103. Ibid.

104. Murray, *Whig Party in Georgia*, pp. 141–42; Jenkins to Berrien, July 16, 1849, Iverson L. Harris to Berrien, October 6, 1849, Berrien MSS.

105. Schott, *Stephens*, p. 104.

106. Ibid., p. 105; Iverson L. Harris to Berrien, August 17, October 6, 1849, Berrien MSS.

107. Jacob Collamer to Zachary Taylor, September 11, 1849, Taylor MSS; Ben Wade to Caroline Wade, September 10, 1849, Wade MSS.

108. In Maine, Taylor had garnered 35,125 votes (40.3 percent) in November 1848, whereas the Whigs' gubernatorial totals in 1847, 1848, and 1849 were, respectively, 24,308 (37.2 percent), 30,026 (37.8 percent), and 28,260 (38.3 percent). In 1848, Free Soilers had drawn 11,978 votes in September and 12,096 in November, but in 1849 their total was 8,025.

109. The lack of statewide returns for Wisconsin in 1849 prevents comparison with 1848, but in Michigan, where Taylor had garnered 29,947 votes and Van Buren 10,393, in 1848, Flavius Littlejohn, the Whig-Free Soil gubernatorial candidate, got only 23,561 in 1849.

110. Ben Wade to Caroline Wade, September 10, 1849, Caroline Wade to Ben Wade, September 19, 1849, Wade MSS; William Dennison to Thomas Ewing, September 16 (quotation), October 6, 1849, Aaron F. Perry to Ewing, December 16, 1849, EFP; Maizlish, *Triumph of Sectionalism*, pp. 149–53. As for other Ohio elections, different scholars who have examined Ohio's legislative returns give different numbers for Whig gains and Democratic losses in 1849, yet they concur that Free Soilers continued to hold the balance of power in both chambers even though they lost two seats in the house and one in the senate.

111. My chief source for this and the following paragraph is Kevin Sweeney's invaluable "Rum." The Democratic platform is quoted on p. 120. Whigs' gubernatorial vote dropped from 61,640 (49.7 percent) in 1848 to 54,009 (49.4 percent) in 1849; meanwhile, the Democratic vote increased by 5,000 and the Free Soil vote declined by 11,000 between the two years.

112. Democrats were elected as attorney general, canal commissioner, prison inspector, and judge of the state appeals court. In 1848, Taylor won 218,603 votes (47.9 percent); in 1849, Hunt

garnered 205,034 (50.7 percent), a net loss of 13,569. In contrast, with 199,134 votes, Hunt's Democratic opponent ran 35,696 votes behind the combined total for Cass and Van Buren.

The regression estimates for voter movement between the 1848 and 1849 *state* elections are:

		1849			% of 1849 Electorate
		Whig	Democratic	Not Voting	
1848	Whig	30	8	0	38
	Dem.	1	13	6	20
	Free Soil	4	13	4	21
	Not voting	0	0	21	21
	% of 1849 elect.	35	34	31	100

These figures are taken from Kirn, "Third Party System," Table IX, p. 60. By Kirn's estimates, about 46,000 Whig voters went Democratic in 1849, not just the 13,500 indicated by the difference between Taylor's and Hunt's totals. Kirn used the 1848 gubernatorial, not presidential, returns, but Whig Hamilton Fish's 218,280 poll was virtually identical to Taylor's total.

113. I shall document these assertions in the next chapter, but my point is to explain Seward's oft-noted but puzzling refusal to endorse the Taylor plan in his famous "Higher Law" speech against Henry Clay's compromise proposals.

114. In 1847, Whigs won four congressional seats to the Democrats' two, although Democrats led in the gubernatorial vote, 34,368 to 33,730. In 1849, when the parties evenly split the six-man congressional delegation, Whigs won the aggregate popular vote in those contests, 30,699 to 25,974.

115. J. E. Bradley to Thomas Ewing, October 12, 1849, EFP; Charles Gilpin to Meredith, October 17, 1849, Meredith MSS; Mueller, *Whig Party in Pennsylvania*, pp, 162–67.

116. For the voting patterns in the lower houses of the Maryland and Pennsylvania legislatures, see Holt, *Political Crisis*, pp. 115–16, and Mueller, *Whig Party in Pennsylvania*, p. 162.

117. For the tangled and much neglected New Jersey story, I have relied on Lex Renda's excellent "Railroads, Revenue, and Reform," pp. 33–50.

118. Leslie Combs to Millard Fillmore, October 12, 1849, MFP-O.

119. Balie Peyton to William B. Campbell, November 7, 1849, CFP; Washburne to Caleb Smith, November 15, 1849, Smith MSS.

120. Thomas Foote to Millard Fillmore, October 9, 1849, Combs to Fillmore, October 12, 1849, Henry Davis to Fillmore, October 19, 1849, MFP-O; Charles Stetson to Weed, July 7, 1849, Weed MSS (RU); Schuyler Colfax to Caleb Smith, September 27, November 3, 8, 1849, Truman Smith to Caleb Smith, October 28, 1849, Washburne to Smith, November 15, 1849, Smith MSS; Robert Letcher to Crittenden, July 10, 1849, Crittenden MSS (LC).

121. Brown to Crittenden, July 10, 1849, Crittenden MSS (LC); Truman Smith to Caleb Smith, October 28, 1849, Smith MSS.

122. Joseph Root to Joshua R. Giddings, June 12, 1849, Giddings MSS.

123. Henry Clay to Nicholas Dean, June 21, 1849, Henry Clay MSS (LC); James Harvey to Meredith, August 26, 1849, Meredith MSS. The best study of the vital impact that James B. Clay's mission to Portugal had on Henry Clay's behavior in 1850 is Bearss, " 'How All Occasions Do Inform.' "

124. Clay to Nicholas Dean, June 21, 1849, Henry Clay MSS (LC).

125. James Harvey to Meredith, August 26, 1849, Meredith MSS.

126. William T. Ward to Clayton, August 17, 1849, Clayton MSS; Joshua Bell to Crittenden, June 9, 1849, Crittenden MSS (LC); Peterson, *Great Triumvirate*, pp. 378–79; Volz, "Party, State, and Nation," pp. 69–75.

CHAPTER 14

1. Henry Clay to Thomas B. Stevenson, December 21, 1849, Stevenson MSS; David Outlaw to Emily Outlaw, December 2, 6, 17, 1849, Outlaw MSS; C. H. Wiley to David F. Caldwell, January 7, 1850, Caldwell MSS; Simon Cameron to Edmund Burke, June 13, 1849, Thomas Dorr to Burke, October 3, 1849, Burke MSS; Joseph Root to Joshua R. Giddings, June 12, 1849, William L. Hodge to William H. Seward, January 4, 1850, Seward MSS (RU); N. K. Hall to Millard Fillmore, November 20, 1849, N. C. King to Fillmore, November 30, 1849, Francis Granger to Fillmore, December 12, 1849, MFP-BHS.

2. Alexander H. Stephens to John J. Crittenden, December 17, 1849, draft, Stephens MSS (Duke); Oliver Butler to Caleb B. Smith, September 15, 1849, Smith MSS; Seward to Thurlow Weed, November 30, December 3, 1849, Weed MSS (RU); Alexander Stephens to Linton Stephens, December 2, 1849, quoted in Schott, *Stephens,* p. 107; William H. Bissell to William Martin, February 5, 1850, Bissell MSS.

3. James C. Marshall to George Dunn, January 28, 1849, Dunn MSS; Joseph Root to Joshua R. Giddings, June 12, 1849, Seward MSS (RU); see also Seward to Weed, December 3, 1849, Weed MSS (RU).

4. Nevins, *Ordeal: Fruits,* pp. 219–341; Poage, *Clay,* pp. 183–264; *ZT:SWH,* pp. 229–359; Hamilton, *Prologue to Conflict.* In this and following chapters, I shall designate attitudes toward the final Compromise measures that passed in September 1850 as pro- and anti-Compromise. But to refer to vaguer attitudes toward the idea of compromise itself during 1850, before the final package of laws was formulated, I shall use the lowercase "compromise."

5. William H. Bissell to William Martin, February 5, 1850, Bissell MSS; Seward to Weed, December 3, 1849, Weed MSS (RU).

6. Seward to Weed, November 30, 1849, Weed MSS (RU); Weed to Seward, December 7, 1849, Seward MSS (RU); Stephens to Crittenden, December 17, 1849, draft, Stephens MSS (Duke); John M. Berrien to Charles J. Jenkins, December 10, 1849, Berrien MSS; Robert Toombs to John J. Crittenden, April 25, 1850, in Coleman, *Crittenden,* I, pp. 364–66.

7. Nevins, *Ordeal: Fruits,* p. 257; Potter, *Impending Crisis,* pp. 92–94.

8. Anthony C. Brown to Seward, February 2, 1850, Seward MSS (RU); John L. Dox to Fillmore, January 30, February 2, 1850, MFP-BHS.

9. Resolutions of the Legislature of New York, January 17, 1849, U.S. Congress, *House Miscellaneous Documents,* 30th Cong., 2nd Sess., Document 6. I originally wrote this chapter seven years before the publication of Mark J. Stegmaier's immensely detailed and valuable *Texas, New Mexico, and the Compromise of 1850.* Although I am heartened that Stegmaier agrees with me about the centrality of the Texas-New Mexico boundary issue to the Compromise of 1850, his research on this episode is far more thorough than mine, and his book supersedes the sources I have used. His book has forced me to make some revisions in this and the following chapter, but I continue to cite the sources, particularly my students' unpublished seminar papers, that I originally used to draft them.

10. John C. Spencer to John M. Clayton, August 25, 1849, Clayton MSS; Daniel D. Barnard to Millard Fillmore, November 9, 1849, MFP-O; Barnard to Fillmore, December 15, 1849, John T. Bush to Fillmore, January 5, 1850 (quotation), MFP-BHS.

11. John Defrees to Caleb B. Smith, November 16, 1849, Smith MSS.

12. At the very end of the Thirtieth Congress' second session in March 1849, Wisconsin's Democratic Senator Isaac Walker had tried to amend an appropriations bill with a clause that explicitly abrogated all Mexican laws, including the prohibition of slavery, in the Mexican Cession. That amendment passed the Senate, but in the House northern Whigs successfully amended Walker's amendment specifically to retain Mexico's antislavery ban in the Cession. The Senate balked and killed both amendments, but the fierce two-day debate had alerted everyone to the continuing force of Mexico's antislavery laws in the Cession.

13. Nathan Appleton to Henry Hilliard, December 22, 1849, Appleton MSS; John L. Dox to Fillmore, January 30, February 2, 1850, MFP-BHS; Anthony C. Brown to Seward, February 2, 1850, Seward MSS (RU).

14. This summary of the southern Democratic position in 1850 is based on my reading of the congressional debates and numerous secondary sources.

15. Cole, *Whig Party in the South*, p. 149; Johannsen, *Douglas*, p. 263; copy of Georgia legislative resolutions, January 26, 1850, Berrien MSS.

16. Charles Jenkins to Berrien, December 1849, Berrien to Jenkins, December 10, 1849, January 7, 1850, Berrien MSS; John S. Williams to Fillmore, November 17, 1849, MFP-O.

17. David to Emily Outlaw, December 9, 1849, January 10, February 16, 1850, Outlaw MSS; C. H. Wiley to David F. Caldwell, January 7, 1850, Caldwell MSS. Outlaw's Whig colleague Edward Stanly also attributed Clingman's radicalism to his desire to win a Senate seat "on the excitement he is trying to raise." Edward Stanly to David F. Caldwell, March, 1, 1850, Caldwell MSS.

18. William L. Hodge to Seward, January 4, February 20, 1850, Seward MSS; William B. Campbell to David Campbell, January 9, 1850, CFP; Charles Jenkins to Berrien, December 1849, A. J. Miller to Berrien, January 5, 1850, Berrien MSS. Jenkins gauged the Georgia Whig mentality accurately. In January 1850 two-thirds of the Whig legislators, most of whom had earlier acquiesced in the Democrats' bellicose resolutions, signed a manifesto protesting that the admission of California should not be grounds for calling a state convention. Cole, *Whig Party in the South*, p. 158.

19. Cole, *Whig Party in the South*, pp. 146–62. That the antebellum South was not a united phalanx on virtually anything up through the secession crisis of 1860–61 itself is, of course, a central argument of Freehling, *Road to Disunion*.

20. Nathan Appleton to Henry Hilliard, December 22, 1849, Appleton MSS; Berrien to Charles Jenkins, January 7, 1850, Berrien MSS.

21. Schuyler Colfax to Caleb B. Smith, February 16, 1850, Smith MSS.

22. The language is Potter's in *Impending Crisis*, pp. 92–94.

23. Charles Sumner to Joshua R. Giddings, July 3, 1849, Giddings MSS.

24. Joseph Root to Joshua R. Giddings, June 12, 1849, Seward MSS. Because one Massachusetts seat went unfilled for the entire session, the House had a total of 230 members prior to the admission of California. For good reasons, historians have varied in their estimates of party strength. Mine are based on the party identifications in the *Biographical Directory of Congress* and other information. I estimate that of the 230 members there were 114 Democrats, 106 Whigs, 2 Whig-Free Soilers, John Howe and William Sprague, one Native American who was expected to cooperate with the Whigs—Philadelphia's Lewis C. Levin—and 7 Free Soilers.

25. The estimates of the sectional balance within each party are based on the identifications in the *Biographical Directory of Congress* and Robert C. Winthrop to Edward Everett, December 23, 1849, Everett MSS. Altogether there were 91 representatives from the slave states and 139 from the free states.

26. David Outlaw to Emily Outlaw, December 2, 3, 1849, Outlaw MSS; Henry Hilliard to Nathan Appleton, December 4, 1849, Appleton MSS; Robert Toombs to John J. Crittenden, April 25, 1850, in Coleman, *Crittenden*, I, pp. 364–66, and Hamilton, *Prologue to Conflict*, p. 38.

27. Schott, *Stephens*, pp. 108–09; Smith, *Presidencies of Taylor and Fillmore*, p. 107.

28. Howell Cobb to Wife, December 2, 1849, in Phillips, "Correspondence of Toombs, Stephens, and Cobb," p. 117; Robert C. Winthrop to John P. Kennedy, December 4, 1849, John P. Kennedy to Winthrop, December 4, 18, 1849, Kennedy MSS; David Outlaw to Emily Outlaw, December 2, 1849, Outlaw MSS; Robert C. Winthrop to John H. Clifford, December 3, 1849, Winthrop MSS; Seward to Weed, December 4, 1849, Weed MSS (RU); Weed to Seward, December 7, 1849, Seward MSS (RU); Francis Granger to Millard Fillmore, December 12, 1849, MFP-BHS.

29. David Outlaw to Emily Outlaw, December 3, 1849, Outlaw MSS; Robert C. Winthrop to John H. Clifford, December 3, 1849, Winthrop MSS; Winthrop to John P. Kennedy, December 4, 1849, Kennedy MSS; Iverson L. Harris to John M. Berrien, December 17, 1849, Berrien MSS; Toombs to Crittenden, April 25, 1850, loc. cit.; Stephens to Crittenden, December 17, 1849, Stephens MSS (Duke).

30. Schott, *Stephens*, pp. 107–08; Iverson L. Harris to John M. Berrien, December 24, 1849, Berrien MSS.

31. Seward to Weed, December 4, 1849, Weed MSS (RU); Henry Hilliard to Nathan Appleton, December 4, 1849, Appleton MSS: Winthrop to Kennedy, December 4, 1849, Kennedy to Daniel D. Barnard, December 10, 1849, letterbook copy, Kennedy MSS; Cole, *Whig Party in the*

South, p. 146. Morton's district in the northern neck of Virginia had a smaller proportion of slaves in its population in 1850 than any other congressional district east of the Blue Ridge Mountains.

32. Stephens to James Thomas, February 13, 1850, draft, Stephens MSS (Duke).

33. Charles Jenkins to John M. Berrien, December 1849, Iverson Harris to Berrien, December 24, 1849, Berrien to Charles Jenkins, December 10, 1849, January 7, 1850, Berrien MSS.

34. Iverson Harris to Berrien, December 17, 24, 1849, A. J. Miller to Berrien, January 5, 1850, Berrien MSS.

35. Jenkins never received the most detailed suggestions for the Georgia resolutions that Berrien mailed from Washington, and, in any event, the Democratic majority insisted on passing their own resolutions. Jenkins to Berrien, February 26, 1850, Berrien MSS.

36. Berrien delivered his first speech against California statehood on January 29, 1850. Much later in the session, Berrien successfully amended the territorial provisions of the omnibus bill by revising the language regarding the authority of territorial legislatures over slavery. His amendment barred those bodies from establishing or prohibiting slavery but opened the possibility that they could pass laws protecting property rights in slaves. In a tit-for-tat response, both Toombs and Stephens, who had previously said that only local laws could protect slavery, then called in the House for federal slave codes to protect slavery in the territories. I rely here on Morrison, "For Buncombe or Principle," pp. 36–45.

37. This and the following paragraphs are based on an analysis of the roll-call votes for speaker between December 3 and December 22, 1849 in the House Journal, 31st Cong., 1st Sess. There are good secondary accounts of the speakership struggle in ZT:SWH, pp. 243–53, and Smith, Presidencies of Taylor and Fillmore, pp. 106–07.

38. Seward to Weed, November 30, 1849, Weed MSS (RU); Winthrop to John H. Clifford, December 15, 1849, Winthrop MSS; Winthrop to Edward Everett, December 11, 16, 1849, Everett MSS.

39. Winthrop to Clifford, December 15, 1849, Winthrop MSS; Winthrop to John P. Kennedy, December 16, 1849, Kennedy MSS; Charles Morehead to John J. Crittenden, December 25, 1849, Crittenden MSS (LC); Poage, Clay, p. 196.

40. David Outlaw to Emily Outlaw, December 12, 1849, Outlaw MSS.

41. Howell Cobb to Wife, January 11, 1850, in Phillips, "Correspondence of Toombs, Stephens, and Cobb," pp. 181–82; Thomas L. Harris to Charles H. Lanphier, January 12, 1850, Lanphier MSS; Robert C. Winthrop to Edward Everett, December 23, 1849, Everett MSS; Winthrop to John H. Clifford, December 22, 1849, Winthrop MSS.

42. George W. Julian to Isaac Julian, January 25, 1850, Giddings-Julian MSS.

43. Seward to Weed, November 30, 1849, Weed MSS (RU).

44. Messages and Papers of the Presidents, V, pp. 9–24.

45. Seth C. Hawley to Seward, December 25, 1849, Simeon Draper to Seward, December 26, 1849 (quotation), William L. Hodge to Seward, January 4, 1850, Seward MSS (RU); William B. Campbell to David Campbell, January 9, 1850, CFP.

46. Daniel Webster to Peter Harvey, December 30, 1849, Webster MSS; Kennedy to Winthrop, December 25, 1849, letterbook copy, Kennedy MSS; Simeon Draper to Seward, December 26, 1849, Seward MSS (RU); Edwin M. Stanton to William M. Meredith, January 5, 1850, Meredith MSS.

47. Philip Greely, Jr., to James S. Pike, January 15, 1850, Pike MSS; Carlos G. Houston to Seward, January 21, 1850, Simeon Draper to Seward, January 25, 28, February 2, 1850, Seward MSS (RU); Simeon Draper to William M. Meredith, March 28, 1850, Meredith MSS. I am indebted to Professor William E. Gienapp for loaning me a microfiche copy of the Pike MSS.

48. ZT:SWH, pp. 262–63, 273–76; Anderson, "Texas Boundary Dispute," pp. 10–16. The best modern study of the Texas boundary issue is Stegmaier, Texas, New Mexico, and the Compromise of 1850, but I have often used preliminary Senate votes analyzed by Anderson, but not Stegmaier, to identify pro- and anticompromise senators. Maps in Stegmaier, pp. 94 and 96, show the different Benton and Foote proposals for Texas. Each man also wanted to carve new states out of Texas to balance California's admission.

49. Messages and Papers of the Presidents, V, pp. 26–30. Taylor's descriptions of his official

instructions to Thomas Butler King and Colonel George McCall, the agent to New Mexico, were accurate, but Mark Stegmaier has uncovered evidence that, unknown to Secretary of War Crawford, McCall had been instructed orally by Taylor and Colonel William Bliss, Taylor's son-in-law and private secretary, to take an active role in launching New Mexico's statehood movement. Stegmaier, *Texas, New Mexico, and the Compromise of 1850*, pp. 68–78.

50. Edward Wade to Albert G. Riddle, February 3, 1850, Riddle MSS; *ZT:SWH*, pp. 266–68.

51. Seddon and Howard are quoted in *ZT:SWH*, pp. 272–73.

52. Ibid., pp. 268–69; John P. Kennedy to Elizabeth Kennedy, January 22, 1850, Kennedy MSS; Philip Greely, Jr., to James S. Pike, January 25, 1850, Pike MSS. Scores of additional northern letters could be cited.

53. *ZT:SWH*, pp. 270–71.

54. David Outlaw to Emily Outlaw, February 14, 1850, Outlaw MSS; Julius Rockwell to David Davis, January 25, 1850, David Davis MSS; Iverson Harris to John M. Berrien, December 28, 1849, Berrien MSS.

55. George Julian to Isaac Julian, January 25, 1850, Giddings-Julian MSS; Henry Clay to Lucretia Clay, December 28, 1849, January 2, 1850, Thomas J. Clay MSS (LC); Peterson, *Great Triumvirate*, p. 453.

56. Henry Clay to James B. Clay, December 4, 1849, to Susan Clay, December 15, 1849, and to Lucretia Clay, December 28, 1849, Thomas J. Clay MSS. For a discussion of the negotiations with Portugal, see Smith, *Presidencies of Taylor and Fillmore*, pp. 72–73; and *ZT:SWH*, pp. 190–91, 371.

57. George Julian to Isaac Julian, January 25, 1850, Giddings-Julian MSS.

58. Henry Clay to James B. Clay, December 4, 1849, Thomas J. Clay MSS.

59. Henry Clay to Thomas B. Stevenson, June 18, 1849, Stevenson MSS; Henry Clay to Boyd McNairy, January 26, 1850, Henry Clay MSS (LC); Henry Clay to James B. Clay, January 2, 1850, Thomas J. Clay MSS.

60. Henry Clay to James B. Clay, December 29, 1849, Henry Clay MSS (LC); Joseph Root to Joshua R. Giddings, June 12, 1849, Seward MSS (RU); James G. Marshall to George Dunn, January 28, 1849, Dunn MSS.

61. Poage, *Clay*, pp. 199–200; Peterson, *Great Triumvirate*, p. 455.

62. Clay's remark came in a speech to the Kentucky legislature in Frankfort on November 15, 1850. There is a draft of the speech in the Henry Clay MSS (LC).

63. For Clay's speech and resolutions, see *Congressional Globe*, 31st Cong., 1st Sess., pp. 244–46.

64. By the time Clay spoke, Virginia's Senator James M. Mason had already introduced a new fugitive slave bill, and Clay said little about it in either his short speech of January 29 or his two-day address in early February. Yet he privately wrote friends that he was concerned about protecting free blacks who were falsely accused of being fugitive slaves, and in his report from the select committee of thirteen in May he proposed two clauses to be inserted into the law. Those provisions would have allowed alleged fugitives to testify in their own behalf before the commissioners hearing their cases in the North; required the purported owner to obtain a court affidavit from his home state attesting to his ownership of the slave; and, most important, forced the owner to post a bond of $1,000 with federal authorities, which he would forfeit if the alleged fugitive were not given a jury trial in the owner's home state to determine the fugitive's actual status. None of these requirements was included in the final statute (the provision about the court affidavit was made optional rather than mandatory), and testimony by captured fugitives was explicitly banned. See Henry Clay to R. H. Walworth, March 11, 1850, Henry Clay MSS (LC); U.S. Congress, *Senate Committee Reports*, 31st Cong., 1st Sess., Report 123, pp. 24–25; and U.S., *Statutes at Large*, Volume 9, 31st Cong., Chapter 60, pp. 462–65.

65. Recall that the residents of New Mexico had petitioned the Thirtieth Congress to create a territorial government for them and to bar slavery from it.

66. I was first alerted to the antislavery implications of Clay's Texas boundary proposal by the manuscript of Freehling's *Road to Disunion*, pp. 496–97. The estimate of 20,000 slaves is Professor Freehling's. In his recent *Texas, New Mexico, and the Compromise of 1850*, pp. 98–99, and note 27, p. 372, Stegmaier notes that Clay stipulated the continuation of the "southern

line of New Mexico," and that in early 1850 no one knew exactly where that line would be located. He also argues vigorously that Clay could not have knowingly intended to bring about emancipation in Texas north of the 32nd parallel. If Clay realized how many slaveholders lived north of the line he proposed, he undoubtedly expected those men to move to keep their slave property. Nonetheless, I think Clay intentionally proposed stripping so much land from Texas to appeal to northern Whigs, although his stipulation of the Rio Grande, rather than the Nueces, as Texas' southwestern boundary was a bone tossed to Southerners.

67. Clay did say that his third and fourth resolutions were inextricably linked, but rather than admitting that federal assumption of the Texas debt was compensation for the surrender of Texas's claims to New Mexico, he insisted on just the opposite—that is, that Texas should surrender its claim to New Mexico as compensation to the United States government for assuming its debt. Clay clearly believed, that is, that it made a major difference to Northerners whether the United States compensated Texas or Texas compensated the United States. His plan would benefit the holders of Texas bonds, not the State of Texas.

68. On the bondholders' distrust of the Texas state government, see James A. Hamilton to John Bell, May 1, 1850, John Bell MSS.

69. For the initial reactions to Clay's plan on January 29, see *Congressional Globe*, 31st Cong., 1st Sess., pp. 247–52.

70. Ibid.; Washington *Daily Union*, January 7, 1850.

71. Truman Smith to John Wilson, March 14, 1850, Wilson MSS.

72. The final laws that comprised the Compromise of 1850 can be found in United States, *Statutes at Large*, Volume 9, pp. 446–65. To compensate Texas, Congress authorized the issue of $10 million of United States bonds. Half of that amount was to be paid directly to the Texas government without any stipulation as to how it spent the money. The other $5 million was retained in Washington to pay off Texas bondholders. As I will argue in the next chapter, even with the provisions that were incorporated into the territorial laws, many congressmen at the time of their passage *still* believed that Mexico's antislavery statutes would hold force until directly replaced. This was especially true of the Texas-New Mexico statute, which, unlike the Utah law, contained a provision explicitly allowing the expropriation of property by "the law of the land." Exactly what that law was in New Mexico remained a source of dispute.

73. ZT:SWH, p. 298.

74. Ibid.; Parks, "John Bell," 340–42. Stegmaier, *Texas, New Mexico, and the Compromise of 1850*, pp. 105–08, identifies Webster as the original author of Bell's plan. Northern Whigs' anger upon learning of it apparently deterred Webster from offering it himself.

75. David Outlaw to Emily Outlaw, February 14, 1850, Outlaw MSS; Alexander H. Stephens to James Thomas, February 13, 1850, draft, Stephens MSS (Duke); Schott, *Stephens*, p. 113; Julius Rockwell to David Davis, January 26, 1850, David Davis MSS.

76. Lewis Henry Morgan to William H. Seward, February 2, 1850, Anthony C. Brown to Seward, February 2, 1850, Simeon Draper to Seward, February 9, 1850, Seth C. Hawley to Seward, March 3, 1850 (quotation), Seward MSS (RU); John L. Dox to Millard Fillmore, January 30, February 2, 7, 1850, MFP-BHS; Roger S. Baldwin to Emily Baldwin, March 3, 1850, BFP; John Davis to George Briggs, March 3, 1850, Briggs MSS.

77. Ibid.; David Outlaw to Emily Outlaw, February 18, 1850, Outlaw MSS.

78. Hamilton, *Prologue to Conflict*, p. 66; Truman Smith to John Wilson, March 14, 1850, Wilson MSS; Winthrop to William Schouler, February 19, 1850, Schouler MSS; Winthrop to John P. Kennedy, March 1850, Kennedy MSS; Winthrop to Edward Everett, January 30, March 3, 1850, Everett MSS; Josiah Snow to Seward, January 31, 1850, S. C. Hawley to Seward, February 11, 1850, Edwin B. Morgan to Seward, February 12, 1850, Seward MSS (RU); Henry Carter to James S. Pike, April 17, 1850, William Schouler to Pike, April 25, 1850, Pike MSS.

79. Robert C. Winthrop to William Schouler, February 15, 1850, Schouler MSS; David Outlaw to Emily Outlaw, February 18, 1850, Outlaw MSS; Hamilton, *Prologue to Conflict*, p. 67; Schott, *Stephens*, p. 113.

80. Several historians date this stormy interview in February after the marathon session on the 18th, but they disagree about the substance of the meeting and who attended it. See, for example, Poage, *Clay*, pp. 207–08; ZT:SWH, p. 300; Schott, *Stephens*, p. 114. The fullest treat-

ment was Stegmaier, "Taylor versus the South," but in *Texas, New Mexico, and the Compromise of 1850*, pp. 103, 112, Stegmaier recants on his February 20 date for the meeting and now puts it in mid-April. Taylor, however, did meet with an unidentified group of Southerners in mid-February, when he also pledged to lead federal troops personally against any secession movement.

81. *ZT:SWH*, pp. 303–05.

82. Hamilton, *Prologue to Conflict*, p. 92; Josiah Snow to Seward, January 31, 1850, Seward MSS (RU); Lewis Cass to Samuel Medary, January 26, 1850, Medary MSS; Maizlish, *Triumph of Sectionalism*, p. 154.

83. Johannsen, *Douglas*, pp. 251–56, 262–303; S. S. Hayes to Stephen Douglas, April 13, 1850, Douglas MSS; Gideon Ball to William M. Meredith, February 19, 1850, Meredith MSS.

84. Hamilton, *Prologue to Conflict*, p. 88; Poage, *Clay*, pp. 206–07; Schott, *Stephens*, pp. 113–14; Johannsen, *Douglas*, pp. 272–73. I say that Stephens "apparently" wrote down his terms for a compromise because the only evidence for this assertion is Stephens' own post-Civil War history/memoir, *A Constitutional View of the Late War Between the States*. I have found no contemporary evidence that he put his terms for territorial governments in writing, and Johannsen credits Douglas, not Stephens, with the language of the bills the House and Senate territorial committees reported.

85. Hamilton, *Prologue to Conflict*, p. 66; Nevins, *Ordeal: Fruits*, pp. 272–73; James Simonton to Thomas Ritchie, July 10, 1852, included with Thomas Ritchie to Richmond *Enquirer*, December 6, 1852, newspaper extract in Henry Clay MSS (LC).

86. Simonton to Ritchie, July 10, 1852; Hamilton, *Prologue to Conflict*, p. 62; Poage, *Clay*, pp. 211–17; London, "Badger," pp. 103–04.

87. Hamilton, *Prologue to Conflict*, pp. 63–65; John J. Crittenden to John M. Clayton, February 18, 1850, Clayton MSS; T. M. Brewer to William Schouler, March 8, 1850, Schouler MSS.

88. George W. Julian to Isaac Julian, January 25, 1850, Giddings-Julian MSS; Moses McGowen to William H. Seward, March 7, 1850, Seward MSS (RU); T. M. Brewer to William Schouler, March 8, 1850, Schouler MSS; Winthrop to Edward Everett, March 3, 1850, Charlie Everett to Edward Everett, March 5, 1850, Everett MSS; Daniel Webster to Franklin Haven, January 13, 1850, to Peter Harvey, February 13, March 1, 1850, to Edward Everett, February 16, 1850, to Fletcher Webster, February 24, 1850, Webster MSS; Dalzell, *Webster*, pp. 175–77; *ZT:SWH*, p. 313.

89. On Calhoun's reaction, see Hamilton, *Prologue to Conflict*, p. 79. The many historians who call Webster's speech an endorsement of Clay's compromise err because they assume that support for the idea of compromise automatically meant support for Clay's version, ignore the differences between Clay's original resolutions and the compromise he eventually backed, and minimize the difference between what Clay and Webster actually said in January and March since the two men ended up on the same side. To contemporaries like Calhoun those differences were crucial.

90. The best summary and analysis of Webster's speech, upon which I have heavily relied, is Dalzell, *Webster*, pp. 178–95. See also Nevins, *Ordeal: Fruits*, pp. 286–91.

91. Again, contemporaries paid closer attention to the details of the speech than have the historians who call it an endorsement of Clay's plan, and they noted Webster's careful omission of any reference to Mexican law. Reflecting the opinion of most northern Whigs, a dismayed Winthrop wrote, "The argument from *Nature*, too, is, at best, pretty loose, and is much less satisfactory to our friends than that from the Mexican law, to which W. does not allude." Winthrop to Edward Everett, March 17, 1850, Everett MSS.

92. Dalzell, *Webster*, p. 183.

93. Daniel D. Barnard to Millard Fillmore, January 31, 1850, John Young to Fillmore, March 14, 1850, MFP-BHS; Nathan K. Hall to Fillmore, March 11, 1850, MFP-O; Truman Smith to John Wilson, March 14, 1850, Wilson MSS.

94. Dalzell, *Webster*, pp. 197–98; Robert C. Winthrop to Edward Everett, April 7, 1850, Everett MSS; T. M. Brewer to William Schouler, March 14, April 1850, James S. Pike to Schouler, April 21, 1850, Schouler MSS; Daniel Webster to Willie P. Mangum, April 19, 1850, Webster MSS.

95. Seward to Weed, March 22, 1850, Weed MSS (RU); Nathan K. Hall to Fillmore, March 11, 1850, MFP-O; Weed to Meredith, March 10, 1850, Meredith MSS; Hamilton, *Prologue to Conflict*, p. 79.

96. Daniel Webster to Fletcher Webster, March 31, 1850, to Peter Harvey, April 7, 1850, John Pendleton to Webster, March 12, 1850, Webster MSS; Winthrop to John P. Kennedy, March 15, 1850, Kennedy MSS; Roger S. Baldwin to Emily Baldwin, March 8, 1850, Emily Baldwin to Roger S. Baldwin, March 14, 1850, BFP; Fitz Henry Warren to William Schouler, March 9, 1850, Schouler MSS; Lyman A. Spaulding to John L. Schoolcraft, March 28, 1850, Seward MSS (RU).

97. T. M. Brewer to William Schouler, March 8, 1850, Schouler MSS; Truman Smith to John Wilson, March 14, 1850, Wilson MSS.

98. Van Deusen, *Seward*, p. 120; Seward to Weed, January 25, March 11, 1850, in *Seward at Washington*, pp. 121, 124–25.

99. I have relied on the able summaries of the speech in Van Deusen, *Seward*, pp. 122–24, *ZT:SWH*, pp. 316–19; and Nevins, *Ordeal: Fruits*, pp. 299–301.

100. Van Deusen, *Seward*, pp. 125–26, ably summarizes the exchange between Seward and Weed. See also Weed to Seward, March 14, 15, 26, 1850, Seward MSS (RU); and Seward to Weed, March 15, 22, 1850, in *Seward at Washington*, pp. 129–30.

101. Van Deusen, *Seward*, p. 125; *ZT:SWH*, pp. 321–23; Weed to Seward, March 15, 26, 1850, Joshua R. Giddings to Joshua A. Giddings, March 16, 1850, Seward MSS (RU); N. K. Hall to Millard Fillmore, March 17, 1850, MFP-O; Jerome Fuller to Fillmore, March 20, 1850, Alex Mann to Fillmore, March 22, 1850, MFP-BHS.

102. Van Deusen, *Seward*, pp. 125–26; Seward to Weed, March 15, 22, 1850, in *Seward at Washington*, pp. 129–30. Seward cited no evidence that most northern Whig congressmen were prepared to compromise in March, and I have found none.

103. See, for example, Gideon Hard to Millard Fillmore, April 4, 1850, MFP-BHS.

104. *Albany Evening Journal*, January 2, 1850; Daniel D. Barnard to Millard Fillmore, January 31, 1850, John L. Dox to Fillmore, February 2, 1850, Gideon Hard to Fillmore, February 9, 1850, MFP-BHS.

105. John L. Dox to Fillmore, January 30, February 2, 7, 1850, Daniel D. Barnard to Fillmore, January 31, 1850, Gideon Hard to Fillmore, April 4, 1850, MFP-BHS; Henry J. Raymond to Seward, January 19, February 15, 1850, James Bowen to Seward, January 21, 25, February 3, 1850, Robert H. Pruyn to Seward, February 1, 1850, Hamilton Fish to Seward, February 9, 1850, Seth C. Hawley to Seward, February 19, 1850, Seward MSS (RU).

106. Weed to Meredith, March 10, 1850, Meredith MSS; D. D. Barnard to Fillmore, January 11, 1850, John L. Dox to Fillmore, February 2, 7, 18, 1850, MFP-BHS.

107. Henry J. Raymond to Seward, February 15, 1850, Seward MSS (RU); John L. Dox to Fillmore, February 17, 18, 1850, D. D. Barnard to Fillmore, February 25, 1850, Gideon Hard to Fillmore, April 4, 1850, MFP-BHS; Nathan K. Hall to Fillmore, March 11, 17, April 2, 22, May 23, 1850, MFP-O; John C. Spencer to Daniel Webster, April 11, 1850, Webster MSS; Millard Fillmore to Oran Follett, April 30, 1850, Millard Fillmore MSS (Cincinnati Historical Society, in microfilm edition).

108. Weed to Seward, March 26, 1850, Seward MSS (RU); Hall to Fillmore, March 17, April 2, 1850, MFP-O; Jerome Fuller to Fillmore, March 20, 1850, Alex Mann to Fillmore, March 22, 1850, Leonard Rising to Fillmore, March 29, 1850, Gideon Hard to Fillmore, April 4, 1850, MFP-BHS.

109. James Bowen to Seward, February 3, 1850, Weed to John L. Schoolcraft, July 5, 1850, copy, Seward MSS (RU); Jerome Fuller to Fillmore, May 28, June 6, 14, 1850, John H. White to Fillmore, July 3, 1850, MFP-BHS. Readers of my *Political Crisis* will note a shift in my interpretation here, for there I erroneously telescoped developments by listing Fillmore and his Whig followers as supporters of Clay's plan from the start. Clay and Webster Whigs in New York did support a compromise, especially after the presentation of Clay's omnibus bill in May, but Fillmore's closest allies preferred Taylor's plan until July.

110. Johannsen, *Douglas*, p. 279; Hamilton, *Prologue to Conflict*, pp. 89, 203; for the Union Meetings in New York City, see Foner, *Business & Slavery*, pp. 24–31.

111. Hamilton, *Prologue to Conflict*, p. 92; Poage, *Clay*, pp. 210–17; James S. Pike to William Schouler, April 21, 1850, Schouler MSS.

112. This and the following paragraph are based on the analysis of Senate roll calls in Anderson, "Texas Boundary Dispute." Summary figures best reveal the disproportionately southern and Democratic composition of this bloc. Altogether it contained ten southern Whigs, seventeen southern Democrats, two northern Whigs, and nine northern Democrats. Anderson used a different sample of roll calls than does Stegmaier in Appendix B of his *Texas, New Mexico, and the Compromise of 1850*, pp. 325–30, for Stegmaier's sample of twenty-five roll calls includes no votes before June. Though I question the conflation of roll calls before and after Taylor's death to identify compromisers and anticompromisers early in the session, Stegmaier has demonstrated more authoritatively than any previous scholar the extent of cooperation within an anticompromise bloc of northern Whigs, northern Free Soilers, and southern Democrats.

113. James A. Bayard to Henry Clay, July 1, 1850, Henry Clay MSS (LC); Joseph Gales to John P. Kennedy, March 3, 1850, Kennedy to Rufus Griswold, March 9, 1850, letterbook copy, Kennedy MSS.

114. U.S. Congress, *Journal of the Senate*, 31st Cong., 1st Sess., pp. 299–303; Hamilton, *Prologue to Conflict*, pp. 94–95; Stegmaier, *Texas, New Mexico, and the Compromise of 1850*, p. 135.

115. Here I am in utter retreat from my previous argument in *Political Crisis*, p. 82, that the Fugitive Slave Act was "peripheral to the real concerns of the Compromise of 1850." I have been forced to recant by a brilliant seminar paper by a University of Virginia undergraduate, Jane Lemley, "The Passage of the Fugitive Slave Act of 1850" (May 1989), the best study of the framing of the Fugitive Slave Act I have ever seen.

116. *Congressional Globe*, 31st Cong., 1st Sess., pp. 1573 (Foote) and 1588 (Cass).

117. Ibid., 32nd Cong., 1st Sess., pp. 113–14. Mason, in his speech on these pages, quotes Foote's speech a few days earlier.

118. James S. Pike to William Schouler, April 21, 1850, Schouler MSS; Theodore Barnett to Caleb B. Smith, April 24, 1850, Smith MSS. Stegmaier, *Texas, New Mexico, and the Compromise of 1850*, p. 102, argues persuasively that the Taylor plan ceased to be a viable option even earlier in the House, when James Doty's resolution for the untrammeled admission of California was blocked by a southern filibuster on February 18.

119. Simeon Draper to Seward, January 28, February 2, 1850, Seward MSS (LC); Simeon Draper to Meredith, March 28, 1850, Meredith MSS.

120. For more detail, see my discussion of the Galphin Claim in Woodward, ed., *Responses*, pp. 75–78.

121. Allen A. Hall to Meredith, April 11, 1850, Meredith MSS. On March 18, 1850 Berrien wrote John Milledge, one of the Galphin attorneys, asking for $1,899 as a fee for his help in getting Meredith and Johnson to expedite payment of the interest. Berrien MSS.

122. *ZT:SWH*, pp. 345–53.

123. William R. King to N. Blue, April 11, 1850, Blue MSS; Winthrop to John P. Kennedy, March 1850, Kennedy MSS; Seward to Weed, April 1, 1850, Weed MSS (RU); Weed to Seward, April 4, 1850, Seward MSS (RU); Schuyler Colfax to Caleb Smith, April 19, 1850, Theodore Barnett to Smith, April 20, 1850, Smith MSS; David Outlaw to Emily Outlaw, May 12, 1850, Outlaw MSS.

124. Weed to Meredith, May 31, 1850, Meredith MSS; Alexander H. Stephens to John J. Crittenden, May 7, 1850, Stephens MSS (Duke); David Outlaw to Emily Outlaw, May 12, 1850, Outlaw MSS; Daniel Webster to Jonathan Prescott Hall, May 18, 1850, Webster MSS; John J. Crittenden to Albert T. Burnley, April 29, 1850, Crittenden MSS (Duke). I have found no evidence to prove it, but the stigmatization of Reverdy Johnson for his involvement in the Galphin affair may have been one reason that Thomas Pratt kept his distance from the administration and joined Johnson's enemy, James Pearce, in backing a congressional compromise rather than Taylor's plan.

125. U.S. Congress, *Senate Committee Reports*, 31st Cong., 1st Sess., Report No. 123, pp. 4–6. The three bills are printed on pp. 12–26 of the report, and the omnibus bill fills pp. 12–24. For the reactions of southern Whigs to the bills and the report, see Alexander Stephens to

Crittenden, May 7, 1850, Stephens MSS (Duke); David Outlaw to Emily Outlaw, May 13, 16, 1850, Outlaw MSS; Francis S. Bartow to John M. Berrien, May 21, 1850, Charles J. Jenkins to Berrien, May 29, 1850, and Iverson Harris to Berrien, June 1850, Berrien MSS.

126. Hamilton, *Prologue to Conflict*, pp. 95–96; Johannsen, *Douglas*, pp. 285–86.

127. A Mississippi Whig wrote in June that "Clay's [compromise] is hotly opposed by all extreme Southerners—particularly in reference to Texas." Patrick Henry to Gustavus A. Henry, June 20, 1850, Henry MSS.

128. Bearss, " 'How All Occasions Do Inform,' " pp. 69–70. Clay is quoted in Ms. Bearss' excellent thesis.

129. Hamilton, *Prologue to Conflict*, p. 95; J. L. Locke to Berrien, March 23, 1850, Iverson L. Harris to Berrien, April 25, 1850, Charles J. Jenkins to Berrien, May 15, 1850, Volney Howard to Berrien, May 5, 6, 1850, Berrien MSS. Berrien, it should be noted, received conflicting advice from Georgia because Whig foes of Stephens and Toombs had always contained two quite distinct groups: conservative Unionists like Locke, Jenkins, and Francis S. Bartow, and diehard state rights men like Harris and Volney Howard, who should not be confused with the Texas Democratic congressman with the same name. Harris and Howard were prepared to abandon the Whig party for a new Southern Rights coalition, and in the letters cited above, Howard excitedly wrote that party lines were collapsing in the South over California's admission. By offering a bill fixing California's southern boundary at the 36° 30' line as a substitute for the select committee's report, Howard cheered, Berrien could become the leader of a new Southern Rights party in Georgia, win the backing of all Georgia Democrats except the Cobb wing of that party, and leave Stephens and Toombs stranded in a minority. Berrien's entire course until August, I believe, was an attempt to bring that end about. As it turned out, Stephens and Toombs not only neutralized Berrien's efforts to outflank them in Congress, but when such a reorganization of parties did occur in Georgia in 1850–51, Berrien was its victim rather than its beneficiary.

130. Winthrop to Edward Everett, April 7, 1850, Everett MSS; D. H. Abell to Thomas Ewing, May 7, 1850, EFP. Scores, if not hundreds, of other letters from northern Whigs could also be cited to substantiate this point.

131. James S. Pike to William Schouler, May 3, 1850, Charles Russell to Schouler, May 18, 1850, Schouler MSS.

132. Theodore Barnett to Caleb B. Smith, May 14, 1850, Smith MSS; *ZT:SWH*, pp. 324–25, 333–34; Poage, *Clay*, pp. 229–31.

133. Orlando Brown to Crittenden, April 19, 1850, John J. Crittenden MSS (LC); *Republic*, May 6, 9, 1850, quoted in Bearss, " 'How All Occasions Do Inform,' " pp. 71–72.

134. Poage, *Clay*, pp. 230–31; *ZT:SWH*, p. 334; Horace Greeley to James S. Pike, May 16, 1850, Pike MSS; Charles T. Russell to William Schouler, May 18, 1850, Schouler MSS.

135. *ZT:SWH*, pp. 335–36; Nevins, *Ordeal: Fruits*, p. 319.

136. Roger S. Baldwin to Emily Baldwin, May 22, 1850, BFP; Seward to Weed, May 22, 1850, in *Seward at Washington*, p. 134; Orlando Brown to John J. Crittenden, May 23, 1850, Crittenden MSS (LC); Nathan K. Hall to Fillmore, May 23, 1850, MFP-O; Henry Clay to James B. Clay, May 27, 1850, Thomas J. Clay MSS.

137. The fullest account of this aspect of Clay's decision is Bearss, " 'How All Occasions Do Inform,' " pp. 74–89.

138. *ZT:SWH*, pp. 336–37; Poage, *Clay*, p. 233.

139. Johannsen, *Douglas*, p. 287; Webster to Franklin Haven, May 18, 1850, and to Peter Harvey, May 29, 1850, Webster MSS.

140. Seward to Wife, June 3, 1850, in *Seward at Washington*, p. 137.

141. David Outlaw to Emily Outlaw, May 13, 18, 1850, Outlaw MSS; Truman Smith to John Wilson, May 9, 1850, Wilson MSS; Seward to Wife, July 1, 17, 1850, in *Seward at Washington*, pp. 141–43; Crittenden to John M. Clayton, April 6, 1850, Clayton MSS; Crittenden to Orlando Brown, April 30, June 7, 1850, Crittenden MSS (Duke); Patrick Henry to Gustavus A. Henry, June 30, 1850, Henry MSS.

142. C. B. Strong to Berrien, May 19, 1850, Bartow to Berrien, May 21, 1850, Charles Jenkins to Berrien, May 15, 29, 1850, Iverson Harris to Berrien, June 1850, Berrien MSS; for the bad

blood between Mangum and Badger, see David Outlaw to Emily Outlaw, December 9, 1849, Outlaw MSS.

143. Eliza (Mrs. John) Davis to James S. Pike, June 9, 1850, Pike MSS; Horace Mann to Lewis Campbell, July 3, 1850, Campbell MSS (OHS); Lewis Campbell to Seward, July 2, 11, 1850, Schuyler Colfax to Seward, April 27, 1850, Philo Shelton to Seward, May 9, 1850, Seth C. Hawley to Seward, May 14, 1850, William James to Seward, May 20, 1850, Seward MSS (RU).

144. Seward to Wife, June 13, 1850, in *Seward at Washington*, p. 139; T. M. Brewer to William Schouler, April 26, 1850, Schouler MSS; Joseph Root to Joshua R. Giddings, June 12, 1849, Benjamin Mumford to Seward, April 10, 1850, and James Wilson to Seward, May 26, 1850, Seward MSS (RU); Webster to Peter Harvey, April 7, 1850, Webster MSS. For the belief that the House would never allow the organization of territorial governments without the Proviso, see Thomas Corwin to J. A. Briggs, March 20, 1850, Corwin MSS (OHS); Weed to William M. Meredith, March 10, 1850, Meredith MSS; Winthrop to Everett, March 17, 1850, Everett MSS; Alexander H. Stephens to Crittenden, May 7, 1850, Stephens MSS (Duke); Webster to Franklin Haven, May 18, 1850, Webster MSS.

145. Foner, *Business & Slavery*, pp. 21–33; Hamilton Fish to Seward, February 9, 1850, A. Herr Smith to Seward, July 5, 1850, Augustus P. Steele to Seward, August 6, 1850, Seward MSS (RU); Seward to Weed, March 12, 1850, in *Seward at Washington*, p. 129; Roger S. Baldwin to Emily Baldwin, March 5, 1850, BFP; Webster to Peter Harvey, April 15, May 29, June 2, 1850, Webster MSS; J. O. Charles to Fillmore, June 27, 1850, MFP-BHS.

146. D. G. Eshleman to Seward, April 9, 1850, James Bowen to Seward, February 3, 1850, Seward MSS (RU); Jerome Fuller to Fillmore, May 28, June 6, 14, 1850, MFP-BHS.

147. Horace Greeley to James S. Pike, May 16, 1850, Pike MSS; Greeley to Seward, May 17, 1850, Seward MSS (RU); Van Deusen, *Greeley*, pp. 136–39; John H. White to Fillmore, July 3, 1850, MFP-BHS.

148. Nathan G. King to Fillmore, June 11, 1850, Fuller to Fillmore, June 14, July 9, 1850, Nathan K. Hall to Fillmore, July 9, 1850, MFP-BHS.

149. On Detroit and Michigan, see Josiah Snow to Seward, January 16, 31, March 27, September 16, 1850, Seward MSS (RU). On Pittsburgh and Philadelphia, see Holt, *Forging a Majority*, pp. 86–87; James Cooper to Fillmore, March 31, 1851, MFP-BHS; and S. Coryell to Samuel Calvin, June 28, 1850, Calvin MSS. For the split among Illinois Whigs over the omnibus, see Thomas L. Harris to C. H. Lanphier, June 24, August 12, 1850, Lanphier MSS. In Boston the *Courier* and the *Advertiser* remained loyal to Webster and plumped for compromise. The Boston *Atlas*, edited by William Schouler who had federal printing contracts and employed rabidly antislavery correspondents in Washington like T. M. Brewer and James S. Pike, virulently and persistently attacked Webster, Clay, and the very idea of compromise. Numerous letters in the Webster, Schouler, and Pike papers detail this rift.

150. For example, see Philo Shelton to Weed, May 9, 27, 1850, and Philip Greely, Jr., to Weed, September 4, 1850, Weed MSS (RU).

151. Shelton wrote Weed on May 9 that Webster had told southern Whig senators that Greely had written an anticompromise article in the *Atlas* in order to get those Southerners to vote against Greely's confirmation. Greely himself feared to attack Webster publicly, lest Webster block his confirmation. See Shelton to Weed, May 9, 1850, Weed MSS (RU); and Philip Greely, Jr., to John Davis, May 9, 1850, John Davis MSS.

152. Poage, *Clay*, p. 219; Webster to Willie P. Mangum, May 1, 1850, Webster MSS; William Schouler to James S. Pike, April 25, 1850, Pike MSS; Philo Shelton to Seward, May 9, 1850, Seward MSS (RU).

153. Seward to Wife, June 13, 1850, in *Seward at Washington*, p. 139; J. Fulton to Seward, July 28, 1850, Seward MSS (RU); Isaac Fisher to Samuel Calvin, July 22, 1850, Calvin MSS.

154. Morton McMichael to Meredith, May 10, 1850, R. C. Ellmaker to Meredith, June 5, 1850, William D. Lewis to Meredith, June 20, 1850, William F. Johnston to Meredith, June 25, 1850, H. M. Watts to Meredith, June 26, 1850, Isaac R. Davis to Meredith, June 26, 1850, Meredith MSS. Reports on how badly the Cooper and Clay forces were defeated at the state convention varied. Lewis, the Philadelphia customs collector, boasted that the Cooper forces were

outnumbered by a five-to-one margin on the resolutions committee. Probably more reliable is Watts' tally of the actual votes. A resolution lauding Clay failed to pass on a 15–15 tie vote, one to consider the omnibus bill was defeated 20–10, and the resolution praising Cooper's course in the Senate was crushed 23–7.

155. H. M. Watts to Meredith, July 2, 1850, Meredith MSS.

156. Seward to Wife, May 22, 1850, in *Seward at Washington*, p. 134; John H. Clarke to Meredith, June 1, 1850, Meredith MSS. Clarke counted Wales of Delaware as a northern Whig and said that Wales' colleague Spruance was undecided. Again, Stegmaier's *Texas, New Mexico, and the Compromise of 1850* provides definitive evidence of the existence of this anticompromise bloc, and his list of anticompromise senators, pp. 328–29, closely resembles Clarke's.

157. Volney Howard to John M. Berrien, July 18, 1850, Berrien MSS; Daniel Webster to Franklin Haven, July 4, 1850, Webster MSS.

158. Thomas L. Harris to C. H. Lanphier, June 24, 1850, Lanphier MS.

159. Seward to Wife, June 16, 1850, in *Seward at Washington*, p. 140; A. Gould to Seward, May 18, 1850, Worthington G. Snethen to Seward, May 21, 1850, J. Fulton to Seward, July 27, 1850, Seward MSS (RU).

160. James A. Bayard to Clay, July 1, 1850, Henry Clay MSS (LC); H. M. Watts to Meredith, July 2, 1850, Meredith MSS; Foner, *Business & Slavery*, pp. 21–33; Crittenden to Orlando Brown, June 7, 1850, Crittenden MSS (Duke); James Morse to Caleb Cushing, June 27, 1850, Cushing MSS; Johannsen, *Douglas*, pp. 283–84; Alfred Gilmore to J. Alexander Fulton, June 26, 1850, Fulton MSS.

161. Thomas Dorr to Edmund Burke, October 3, 1849, Burke MSS; William R. King to N. Blue, April 11, 1850, Blue MSS; Henry Barns to Seward, January 18, 1850 (quotation), Seward MSS (RU); William H. Bissell to Joseph Gillespie, December 15, 1849, Gillespie MSS.

162. Nathan K. Hall to Fillmore, November 20, 1849, Nathan G. King to Fillmore, November 30, 1849, MFP-BHS; William L. Hodge to Seward, January 4, 1850, Jacob Morris to Seward, January 11, 1850, Seward MSS (RU).

163. Jacob Morris to Seward, January 11, 1850, Seward MSS (RU); *ZT:SWH*, p. 263; Daniel Webster to Franklin Haven, January 24, 1850, Webster to Charles A. Stetson, February 15, 1850, Webster MSS; Philip Greely, Jr., to James S. Pike, January 25, 1850, Pike MSS.

164. Webster to Charles A. Stetson, February 15, 1850, Webster to Edward Curtis, June 7, 1850, Webster MSS; Nathan K. Hall to Fillmore, June 8, 1850, MFP-O.

165. Webster to Franklin Haven, January 24, 1850, Webster MSS; Nathan K. Hall to Fillmore, April 9, 1850, MFP-O; Solomon G. Haven to Fillmore, January 27, 1850, MFP-BHS.

166. Webster to Peter Harvey, January 9, 1850, Webster to Franklin Haven, January 24, 1850, Webster to Edward Curtis, June 7, 1850, Webster MSS.

167. Josiah Snow to Seward, January 16, 31, March 27, 1850, Henry Barns to Seward, January 18, 1850, Seward MSS (RU); Johannsen, *Douglas*, pp. 283–84.

168. Columbus Delano to Thomas Ewing, June 10, 1850, EFP; H. Reed to Seward, May 2, 1850, Seward MSS (RU).

169. John H. Clarke to Meredith, June 1, 1850, Meredith MSS.

170. For the similar voting patterns of Morton and Yulee on the procedural votes breaking up the omnibus and the final compromise measures, see Hamilton, *Prologue to Conflict*, pp. 192–94.

171. William F. Johnston to Fillmore, December 4, 1849, MFP-BHS; James F. Sanderson to Seward, December 21, 1849, Harry Schell, Jr., to Seward, February 23, 1850, Owen Marrin to Seward, July 20, 1850, Seward MSS (LC); William M. Biddle to John M. Berrien, January 2, 1850, Berrien MSS; Daniel Webster to Franklin Haven, January 24, 1850, Webster MSS; William D. Lewis to Thaddeus Stevens, January 21, 1850, Stevens MSS; Cornelius Darragh to Meredith, February 1, 1850, Meredith MSS; Simon Cameron to Edmund Burke, June 15, 1849, Burke MSS; *Senate Executive Proceedings*, pp. 116–19.

172. John H. Bryant to Fillmore, December 4, 28, 1849, G. S. Walker to James Cooper, September 6, 1850, with James Cooper to Fillmore, September 1850, and Miller N. Everly to Fillmore, January 6, 1851, MFP-BHS.

173. Weed to Seward, December 19, 1849, March 2, 1850, James Bowen to Seward, December

18, 1849, Richard M. Blatchford to Seward, December 6, 1849, Simeon Draper to Seward, December 7, 1849, Seward MSS (RU).

174. Fillmore to Nathan K. Hall, December 18, 1849, Hall to Fillmore, December 2, 13, 22, 1849, January 27, 1850, Solomon G. Haven to Fillmore, January 27, 1850, MFP-BHS; Theodore Parmalee to Seward, December 21, 1849, Seward MSS (RU).

175. Weed to Seward, December 2, 1849, Seward MSS (RU).

176. Simeon Draper to Seward, December 7, 1849, Richard M. Blatchford to Seward, December 6, 1849, James Bowen to Seward, December 18, 1849, William H. Scott to Seward, July 3, 1850, Seward MSS (RU); John Young to Fillmore, March 14, 1850, MFP-BHS.

177. John Collier to Fillmore, December 2, 1849, MFP-BHS.

178. Isaac Harrington to Seward, January 8, 1850, Jacob Morris to Seward, January 11, 1850, J. M. Ackley to Seward, March 11, 1850, Seward MSS (RU); Nathaniel G. King to Fillmore, November 30, 1849, Lathrop Cook to Fillmore, January 19, 1850, Isaac Platt to Fillmore, January 26, 1850, W. F. Willard to Fillmore, February 13, 1850, Solomon G. Haven to Fillmore, January 27, 1850, MFP-BHS; N. K. Hall to Fillmore, January 27, 1850, Fillmore MSS (LC).

179. Fillmore to Nathan K. Hall, December 18, 1849, W. F. Willard to Fillmore, January 2, 1850, Russell Sage to Fillmore, February 23, 1850, MFP-BHS; Nathan K. Hall to Fillmore, January 25, 31, April 9, 1850, MFP-O.

180. Weed to Seward, February 19, 1850, Seward MSS (RU); Weed to Meredith, March 2, 1850, Meredith MSS.

181. Nathan K. Hall to Fillmore, January 25, April 10, 1850, MFP-O; Dennis Bowen to Fillmore, March 3, 1850, Nathan K. Hall to Fillmore, May 26, 1850, MFP-BHS; Buffalo *Morning Express*, March 7, 1850, with Elbridge G. Spaulding to Weed, March 11, 1850, Weed MSS (RU).

182. Gideon Hard to Fillmore, January 4, 1850, John C. Spencer to Fillmore, August 7, 1850, MFP-BHS; John C. Spencer to Webster, April 11, 1850, Webster MSS; Summers, *Plundering Generation*, p. 218.

183. Dennis Bowen to Fillmore, March 8, May 21, 1850, MFP-BHS; Nathan K. Hall to Fillmore, February 16, April 2, 9, May 26, June 8, 1850, MFP-O; John C. Spencer to Daniel Webster, April 11, 1850, Webster MSS.

184. John S. Williams to Gideon Welles, June 30, 1850, Welles MSS (LC); Webster to Franklin Haven, July 4, 1850, Webster MSS; David Outlaw to Emily Outlaw, June 25, 1850, Outlaw MSS.

185. Eliza Davis to James S. Pike, June 9, 1850, Pike MSS; John S. Williams to Gideon Welles, June 30, 1850, Welles MSS (LC). Berrien's amendment changed the prohibition on territorial legislatures from passing any laws "in respect to African Slavery" to any laws "establishing or prohibiting African Slavery." This revision allowed laws that recognized a property interest in slaves—for example, laws that made theft of a slave a felony. Yulee's amendment explicitly extended the Constitution and the laws of the United States to Utah and New Mexico. It reflected the disputed Calhounite contention that the Constitution guaranteed the right to hold slaves in all federal territories while also implicitly replacing Mexico's antislavery laws. Soulé's said that Congress had to admit any states formed out of Utah and New Mexico with or without slavery as their constitutions prescribed. Hamilton, *Prologue to Conflict*, pp. 98–99. For the Texas bond lobby, see ibid., pp. 118–32. For the motions to revise the Texas border, I have relied on Anderson, "Texas Boundary Dispute."

186. Cole, *Whig Party in the South*, pp. 168–73.

187. ZT:SWH, pp. 374–78; Stegmaier, *Texas, New Mexico, and the Compromise of 1850*, pp. 115–33.

188. Official notice of Bell's call for the special session apparently did not reach Washington until July 24, 1850, but rumors about it began to circulate in June. Stegmaier, *Texas, New Mexico, and the Compromise of 1850*, p. 182.

189. Ibid.; *Messages and Papers of the Presidents*, V, pp. 47–48. Six hundred additional troops had been dispatched to Sante Fe before Taylor sent his June 17 message to Congress, and in a cabinet meeting on July 2 or 3, Taylor told the cabinet that he was going to change the orders for the troops in New Mexico so that they would resist any armed attempt by Texans to seize Santa Fe. Stegmaier, *Texas, New Mexico, and the Compromise of 1850*, pp. 155–56.

190. David Outlaw to Emily Outlaw, June 21, 1850, Outlaw MSS. On Taylor's actions, see the preceding note.

191. David Outlaw to Emily Outlaw, June 25, 1850, Outlaw MSS (quotation); *ZT:SWH*, pp. 380–82; Poage, *Clay*, pp. 237–39; Stegmaier, "Taylor versus the South"; Stegmaier, *Texas, New Mexico, and the Compromise of 1850*, pp. 158–64.

192. Schott, *Stephens*, p. 120; *ZT:SWH*, p. 391; *Albany Evening Journal*, July 9, 1850.

193. Horace Greeley to Seward, May 27, 1850, Seward MSS (RU).

194. Weed to William M. Meredith, May 31, 1850, Meredith MSS.

195. Weed to Meredith, June 25, 1850, Meredith MSS.

196. Webster to Franklin Haven, July 4, 1850, Webster MSS.

197. *ZT:SWH*, pp. 388–89.

CHAPTER 15

1. Willie P. Mangum to Charity A. Mangum, July 10, 1850, in *The Mangum Papers*, V, pp. 180–82; *ZT:SWH*, pp. 388–93.

2. Willie Mangum to Charity Mangum, July 10, 1850, loc. cit.; John Pendleton Kennedy to Elizabeth Kennedy, July 10, 11, 1850, Kennedy MSS.

3. Smith, *Presidencies of Taylor and Fillmore*, dissents from this traditional view for reasons I do not find fully compelling.

4. Harmon Goodrich to William Henry Seward, July 11, 1850, Seward MSS (RU).

5. John Pendleton Kennedy to Elizabeth Kennedy, July 10, 11, 15, 1850, Kennedy MSS; Seward to Wife, July 12, 1850, Seward to Weed, July 12, 14, 1850, in *Seward at Washington*, pp. 145–46; Thomas Ewing to Philemon Ewing, July 10, 1850, Ewing MSS (OHS); Thomas Ewing to Millard Fillmore, July 18, 1850, Henry Hilliard to Fillmore, July 11, 1850, MFP-BHS; Robert C. Winthrop to Edward Everett, July 16, 1850, Everett MSS; Daniel Webster to Franklin Haven, July 11, 1850, Webster MSS.

6. Millard Fillmore to James Brooks, May 24, 1852, John White to Fillmore, July 3, 1850, Jerome Fuller to Fillmore, July 10, 1850, and N. K. Hall to Fillmore, July 9, 1850, MFP-BHS. My guess is that if Fillmore did have such an interview with Taylor, it was on July 2 or 3, after Seward finally came out for Taylor's plan in the Senate, not on July 1, the day before Seward spoke.

7. Seward to Wife, July 10, 11, 12, 1850, Seward to Weed, July 12, 14, 1850, in *Seward at Washington*, pp. 144–46; Weed to Seward, July 10, 1850, Seward MSS (RU).

8. *Albany Evening Journal*, July 10, 1850.

9. Garet G. Heermance to Seward, July 14, 1850, Seward MSS; Daniel D. Barnard to Fillmore, July 10, 1850, Jerome Fuller to Fillmore, July 10, 1850, Thomas J. Siser to Fillmore, July 10, 1850, James Diefendorf to Fillmore, July 11, 1850, MFP-BHS; Hamilton Fish to Fillmore, July 22, 1850, Fish MSS.

10. Daniel D. Barnard to Fillmore, July 10, 1850, Jerome Fuller to Fillmore, July 10, 1850, MFP-BHS.

11. Leslie Combs to Fillmore, July 10, 1850, D. F. Royrdon to Fillmore, July 22, 1850, Henry Hillard to Fillmore, July 11, 1850, MFP-BHS.

12. William Pitt Fessenden to Fillmore, July 15, 1850, S. Mason to Fillmore, July 17, 1850, John Peterson to Fillmore, August 1, 1850, William Graham to Fillmore, August 3, 1850, MFP-BHS. See also Lindley M. Moore to William H. Seward, July 17, 1850, Seward MSS (RU).

13. Daniel Webster to Franklin Haven, July 21, 1850, Webster MSS.

14. William H. Seward to Wife, July 11, 1850, in *Seward at Washington*, p. 145; Daniel Webster to Franklin Haven, July 11, 1850, Webster MSS.

15. John P. Kennedy to Elizabeth Kennedy, July 12, 1850, Kennedy MSS; Winthrop to Edward Everett, July 16, 1850, Everett MSS; Truman Smith to Fillmore, July 15, 1850, MFP-BHS; Daniel Webster to Fillmore, July 11, 1850, Webster to Franklin Haven, July 11, 1850, Webster MSS; Henry Clay to James B. Clay, July 18, 1850, Thomas J. Clay MSS.

16. Webster to Fillmore, July 11, 1850, Webster MSS; Theodore Barnett to Caleb B. Smith, July 15, 1850, Smith MSS.

17. John P. Kennedy to Elizabeth Kennedy, July 11, 1850, Kennedy MSS; Winthrop to Everett, July 19, 1850, Everett MSS; Dalzell, *Webster*, pp. 205–06.

18. Van Deusen, *Seward*, p. 131.

19. Francis Granger to Fillmore, July 16, 1850, MFP-BHS.

20. In February and March, Winthrop wrote several friends that he had voted to table Root's motion, yet the *House Journal*, unless there is a misprint, indicates that he abstained rather than voted against Root. *House Journal*, 31st Cong., 1st Sess., 452.

21. A True Friend to Fillmore, July 16, 1850, MFP-BHS; Webster to Franklin Haven, July 21, 1850, Webster MSS; Dalzell, *Webster*, p. 205.

22. Seward to Weed, July 16, 1850, in *Seward at Washington*, p. 147; Dalzell, *Webster*, p. 204.

23. Webster to Fillmore, July 11, 19, 1850, Thomas Ewing to Fillmore, July 18, 1850, MFP-BHS; Daniel Webster to Franklin Haven, July 21, 1850, Webster to Fletcher Webster, July 23, 1850, Webster MSS; John Woods to Samuel Galloway, July 23, 1850, Galloway MSS.

24. N. K. Hall to Fillmore, July 9, 1850, MFP-BHS.

25. N. K. Hall to Fillmore, April 3, 1850, MFP-O; Weed to Seward, July 23, 1850, Seth C. Hawley to Seward, July 27, 1850, Seward MSS (RU).

26. Truman Smith to Daniel Webster, August 5, 1850, Webster MSS; Edward Bates to Fillmore, August 1, 1850, Henry Geyer to Fillmore, August 6, 1850, Willie P. Mangum to Fillmore, August 6, 1850, MFP-BHS; Cole, *Whig Party in the South*, pp. 168–71.

27. James Pearce to Fillmore, July 19, 1850, William B. Reed to Fillmore, March 1, 1849, Thomas McKennan to Fillmore, August 26, 1850, MFP-BHS; Daniel Webster to Franklin Haven, July 21, 1850, Webster MSS; David McClure to Samuel Calvin, July 16, 1850, Calvin MSS; John P. Kennedy to Elizabeth Kennedy, August 12, 1850, Edward Stanly to Alex Randall, September 3, 1850, with Alex Randall to John P. Kennedy, September 4, 1850, Kennedy MSS.

28. James Pearce to John P. Kennedy, September 26, 1850, Kennedy to Pearce, September 27, 1850, Edward Stanly to Alex Randall, September 3, 1850, Kennedy to Philip C. Pendleton, September 21, 1850, Robert C. Winthrop to Kennedy, September 29, 1850, Kennedy MSS; Daniel Webster to Fillmore, August 26, 1850, Charles Jenkins to Fillmore, September 8, 1850, MFP-BHS.

29. John Otis to James S. Pike, August 9, 1850, Pike MSS; John Otis to William Schouler, August 10, 1850, Schouler MSS.

30. Seward to Wife, July 24, 25, 1850, in *Seward at Washington*, p. 149; Seward to Thurlow Weed, July 21, 28, 1850, Weed MSS (RU).

31. Thurlow Weed to Mrs. Frances Seward, July 4, 1850, Weed to John L. Schoolcraft, July 5, 1850, Seward MSS (RU); Daniel Webster to Peter Harvey, July 19, 1850, Webster MSS.

32. A copy of Bell's letter is included in *House Executive Documents*, 31st Cong., 1st Sess., Doc. No. 82, 6–7; Volney Howard to Fillmore, August 1, 1850, MFP-BHS; Stegmaier, *Texas, New Mexico, and the Compromise of 1850*, pp. 170, 187.

33. Howard to Fillmore, August 1, 1850, MFP-BHS; Stegmaier, *Texas, New Mexico, and the Compromise of 1850*, p. 164; Potter, *Impending Crisis*, pp. 110–11, n. 33. Stegmaier, p. 164, states that the cabinet, which met without the dying Taylor, decided on the night of July 7 to press for New Mexico statehood with the boundaries claimed by the just-arrived constitution. The boundary between New Mexico and Texas recognized by the government of Mexico can be found in Hammond's *United States History Atlas* (Maplewood, N. J.: Hammond, Inc., 1984), p. U-21.

34. Seward to Wife, July 31, 1850, in *Seward at Washington*, p. 151; Webster to Franklin Haven, July 26, 1850, Webster MSS; Charles Clarke to Thurlow Weed, July 29, 1850, Weed MSS (RU).

35. Anderson, "Texas Boundary Dispute," pp. 40, 55–56.

36. Smith, *Presidencies of Taylor and Fillmore*, pp. 173–75; Anderson, "Texas Boundary Dispute," pp. 41–44. I have relied on Anderson's tables for the Senate votes.

37. Smith, *Presidencies of Taylor and Fillmore*, pp. 177–78.

38. Hamilton, *Prologue to Conflict*, pp. 110–117.

39. Orsamus Matteson to Thurlow Weed, August 1, 1850, quoted in ibid., p. 116.

40. Cooper and Samuel Phelps were the missing or abstaining northern Whigs. Eight southern Whigs, including Berrien and Jackson Morton of Florida, supported the Utah bill, as did most southern Democrats. The weary Clay and Mangum were absent, while John Bell and, surprisingly, Pearce joined northern Whigs in the minority. Southern Democrats who voted supported the bill 12–0, as did northern Democrats 12–3.

41. Robert C. Winthrop to Edward Everett, August 1, 1850, Everett MSS; Seward to Wife, August 2, 1850, Seward to Weed, August 2, 1850, in *Seward at Washington,* p. 151.

42. Seward to Weed, July 28, 1850, Weed MSS (RU); Seward to Wife, August 9, 1850, in *Seward at Washington,* p. 153; Hamilton, *Prologue to Conflict,* pp. 133–37.

43. Hamilton, *Prologue to Conflict,* pp. 135–36.

44. William Graham to Fillmore, August 2, 1850, MFP-BHS.

45. Webster to Fillmore, August 1, 3, 5, 6, 1850, MFP-BHS; Smith, *Presidencies of Taylor and Fillmore,* p. 181; Webster to Franklin Haven, August 9, 1850, Webster MSS.

46. Seward to Wife, August 9, 1850, in *Seward at Washington,* p. 153; John Otis to William Schouler, August 11, 1850, Schouler MSS. Pearce's original bill did not divide the $10 million compensation to Texas; he did so in an amendment to his own bill on August 9, the day the Texas bill passed the Senate.

47. Webster to Franklin Haven, August 9, 1850, Webster MSS; Seward to Wife, August 9, 1850, in *Seward at Washington,* p. 153.

48. *Messages and Papers of the Presidents,* V, pp. 67–73.

49. Seth Hawley to Seward, August 8, 1850, Seward MSS (RU); Mangum to Fillmore, August 6, 1850, MFP-BHS; Webster to Fillmore, August 7, 1850, Webster MSS.

50. Seward to Wife, August 10, 1850, in *Seward at Washington,* p. 153; John Otis to William Schouler, August 11, 1850, Schouler MSS.

51. John Otis to William Schouler, August 11, 1850, Schouler MSS.

52. Robert C. Winthrop to John P. Kennedy, August 10, 1850, Kennedy MSS; Winthrop to John H. Clifford, August 11, 1850, Winthrop MSS.

53. Thomas L. Harris to Charles H. Lanphier, August 23, 1850, Lanphier MSS; James S. Pike to William Schouler, August 25, 1850, Schouler MSS; Daniel Webster to Peter Harvey, August 11, 1850, Webster to Charles H. Thomas, August 12, 1850, Webster MSS.

54. Hamilton, *Prologue to Conflict,* p. 138, suggests that abstaining Whig senators may have been paired with absent Democrats rather than purposefully ducking the vote.

55. Webster to Franklin Haven, August 9, 1850, Webster to Peter Harvey, August 11, 1850, Webster to Thomas Corwin, September 3, 1850, Webster MSS; John Otis to James S. Pike, August 9, 1850, Pike MSS; *Senate Executive Proceedings,* p. 234.

56. Hamilton, *Prologue to Conflict,* pp. 51–55.

57. Ibid., p. 155; Thomas Harris to Charles H. Lanphier, August 22, September 4, 1850, Lanphier MSS; Alphonzo Taft to Daniel Webster, August 23, 1850, Webster MSS; E. G. Spaulding to William Schouler, August 31, 1850, Schouler MSS.

58. Webster to Fillmore, August 23, 1850, MFP-BHS; Webster to Franklin Haven, September 5, 1850, Webster to William Duer, September 6, 1850, Webster MSS; E. G. Spaulding to William Schouler, August 31, 1850, Schouler MSS.

59. Hamilton, *Prologue to Conflict,* pp. 156–57. Boyd's original motion of August 28 included Utah in his proposed bill, but he deleted it the next day. McDonald, "Politics of Compromise," pp. 11–12. I have relied on this exemplary and remarkably thorough undergraduate paper for much of my discussion of proceedings in the House.

60. The other northern Whig "defectors" were James Wilson of New Hampshire, long considered Webster's lackey; James Meacham of Vermont, another New Englander vulnerable to Webster's influence; and Edward McGaughey, the lone Whig in the Indiana delegation. Significantly, Ashmun, who was clearly in Washington, abstained, as he would on all the other crucial roll calls in the House except the vote to pass the District slave-trade bill. Two Pennsylvania and two New York Whigs, including the buffeted Spaulding, also did not vote, thus subtracting their support from the anticompromise ranks. Figures for this and all other House roll calls concerning Boyd's proposal were taken from the tables in McDonald, "Politics of Compromise," Appendixes A and B.

61. Stegmaier's exhaustive *Texas, New Mexico, and the Compromise of 1850*, pp. 289–90, does note Toombs' amendment, but I decidedly disagree with his characterization of the part of the amendment included in the final Texas-New Mexico statute as a "small addition." I think it changed the meaning of the legislation.

62. Toombs' proposed amendment is quoted in McDonald, "Politics of Compromise," p. 15, and it can be found in the *Congressional Globe*, 31st Cong., 1st Sess., 1753.

63. U.S., *Statutes at Large*, Volume IX, p. 452. For the contrasting argument that the legislation left the power of New Mexico's legislature to bar slavery ambiguous by a historian apparently unaware of Section 19, see Potter, *Impending Crisis*, pp. 115–17.

64. The votes here, as throughout this section, are based on tables in McDonald, "Politics of Compromise," and McDonald relied on the appendixes in Hamilton, *Prologue to Conflict*, for the party identity of House members. Like Hamilton, therefore, his number of northern Whigs totals seventy-four, not seventy-six, the total I list above in the text. My total includes Rufus Goodenow of Maine, who is absent from Hamilton's table and who, for whatever reason, must have been absent from Congress during a considerable part of the session, and Daniel King of Massachusetts, who died in July and was not replaced.

65. William Neal to Seward, September 1, 1850, Seward MSS (RU).

66. David Abell to Thurlow Weed, August 5, 1850, Weed MSS (RU). C. B. Stuart wrote Fillmore on September 23, 1850, that he had been in Rochester when the convention renominated Schermerhorn and said, "This was owing to his *last* vote on the Boundary—which has placed him in the right position with the Whigs of Monroe." MFP-BHS.

67. The Pennsylvania Native American Lewis C. Levin provided the other positive vote, and if he is considered a northern Whig, then twenty-three of them backed the Texas-New Mexico bill.

68. Since the combined Texas-New Mexico bill represented a new piece of legislation, it required action by the Senate, which had passed separate bills. The lopsided margin by which it passed reveals how thoroughly opposition to the compromise in the upper chamber had collapsed. Only six northern Whigs voted in the negative, while Truman Smith and the two Delaware Whigs supported the bill. The remaining northern Whigs abstained. U.S. Congress, *Journal of the Senate*, 31st Cong., 1st Sess., pp. 612–13.

69. Border state Whigs voted unanimously for California, and Tennessee's Whigs favored it 4–1. One Virginian and two of six North Carolina Whigs completed the total.

70. Hamilton, *Prologue to Conflict*, p. 182.

71. Fillmore to Hamilton Fish, September 9, 1850, Fish MSS; Webster to Daniel S. Dickinson, September 27, 1850, Webster MSS. For Clay, see Remini, *Henry Clay*, pp. 730–65.

72. Philemon Ewing to Thomas Ewing, July 13, 1850, Ewing MSS (OHS); Alex Mann to Millard Fillmore, July 12, 1850, James Cooper to Fillmore, July 15, 1850, "Anti-Reverdy Johnson" to Fillmore, July 17, 1850, D. O. Kellogg to Fillmore, August 5, 1850, MFP-BHS; William H. Seward to Wife, July 10, 1850, in *Seward at Washington*, p. 144; John Armitage to Samuel Calvin, July 20, 1850, Thomas McNamara to Calvin, July 26, 1850, Calvin MSS; Owen Marrin to Seward, July 20, 1850, Seward MSS (RU). Numerous other examples of letters from Whigs demanding the replacement of Taylor's appointments can be found in the files for July 14 and 15, MFP-BHS.

73. James R. Thompson to Fillmore, July 29, 1850, Aurelius Conkling to Fillmore, August 7, 1850, Daniel D. Barnard to Fillmore, July 12, 1850, Jerome Fuller to Fillmore, July 11, September 10, 12, 1850, John C. Spencer to Fillmore, August 7, 1850, Solomon G. Haven to Fillmore, July 19, 31, 1850, MFP-BHS; James O. Putnam to Fillmore, July 18, 1850, MFP-O.

74. Jerome Fuller to Fillmore, July 11, 1850, Solomon G. Haven to Fillmore, July 31, 1850, MFP-BHS.

75. Hamilton Fish to Millard Fillmore, July 22, 1850, Fish MSS; A. H. Calhoun to Fillmore, July 11, 1850, Alex Mann to Fillmore, July 12, 1850, Washington Hunt to Fillmore, July 25, 1850, MFP-BHS; James O. Putnam to Fillmore, July 18, 1850, MFP-O.

76. John Armitage to Samuel Calvin, July 20, 1850, Calvin MSS; Washington Hunt to Fillmore, July 25, 1850, Joshua Fry to Fillmore, August 12, 1850, MFP-BHS.

77. *Senate Executive Proceedings*, p. 210; Seth C. Hawley to Seward, August 8, 1850, Seward

MSS (RU). All subsequent information about nominations and Senate actions comes from this Senate journal, pp. 210–72. Elbridge Spaulding may also have been trying to save the job of Franklin Spaulding, Taylor's nominee for customs collector in Niagara, New York, who I assume was related to him. If so, his case well illustrates how the alliance between Fillmore and Senate Democrats worked. Fillmore did not remove Franklin Spaulding, but Dickinson, who controlled the calendar since he chaired the Finance Committee, delayed the Senate vote on him until September 26, well after Elbridge Spaulding had abstained on crucial votes in the House rather than oppose compromise measures like the little omnibus. On September 26, Spaulding was defeated by a vote of 17–23, even though northern Whigs including Seward supported him. Only one Democrat, Thomas Hart Benton, voted to confirm, and nineteen of the twenty-three negative votes came from Democrats.

78. Webster to Fillmore, August 7, 1850, Webster MSS; Webster to Fillmore, August 21, 22, 26, September 17, 1850, John A. Collier to Fillmore, August 29, 1850, MFP-BHS. Hannegan, Polk's midnight appointee, resigned as minister to Prussia in January 1850, but no one had been named to replace him until Fillmore nominated Barnard.

79. Hamilton, *Prologue to Conflict*, p. 196.

80. *Senate Executive Proceedings*, pp. 217–19.

81. John C. Spencer to Fillmore, August 7, 1850, MFP-BHS; Webster to Peter Harvey, August 11, 1850, Webster to Thomas Corwin, September 3, 1850, Webster MSS; Josiah Snow to William H. Seward, September 16, 1850, Seward MSS (RU); Holt, *Forging a Majority*, pp. 86–87.

82. *Senate Executive Proceedings*, pp. 219, 236; George Welch to Samuel Calvin, August 27, 1850, William K. Hamilton to Calvin, September 3, 1850, Calvin MSS; Thomas Corwin to Fillmore, August 13, 1850, C. R. Starkweather to Fillmore, August 18, 1850, L. Lisle Smith to Fillmore, August 19, 1850, Nathan K. Hall to Fillmore, August 19, 1850, MFP-BHS.

83. D. O. Kellogg to Fillmore, August 5, 1850, MFP-BHS.

84. N. K. Hall to Fillmore, September 2, 1850, John Young to Fillmore, August 21, 1850, D. D. Barnard to Fillmore, September 17, 1850, MFP-BHS.

85. Webster to ?, September 15, 1850, Samuel Lawrence to Webster, June 19, 1850, Benjamin Curtis to Webster, August 31, 1850, Webster MSS; Webster to Fillmore, September 11, 1850, MFP-BHS.

86. *Senate Executive Proceedings*, p. 233.

87. Webster to Everett, September 26, 1850, Everett MSS; Philo Shelton to Thurlow Weed, May 9, 1850, Philip Greely, Jr., to Weed, September 4, 1850, William Schouler to Weed, September 16, 1850, Weed MSS (RU).

88. David Abell to Thurlow Weed, August 5, 1850, Weed MSS (RU); N. K. Hall to Fillmore, September 7, 1850, Solomon G. Haven to Fillmore, July 31, September 1, 14, 1850, MFP-BHS; Seth C. Hawley to Seward, August 17, September 21, 1850, Seward MSS (RU).

89. John Young to Fillmore, August 21, 1850, Daniel D, Barnard to Fillmore, September 17, 1850, MFP-BHS.

90. Jerome Fuller to Millard Fillmore, September 10, 15, 1850, John Young to Fillmore, August 21, September 12, 1850, Lot Clark to Fillmore, September 6, 1850, C. B. Stuart to Fillmore, September 7, 1850, Daniel D. Barnard to Fillmore, September 17, 1850, MFP-BHS.

91. Washington Hunt to Fillmore, September 18, 1850, Daniel Ullmann to Fillmore, September 21, 1850, Fillmore to Daniel Ullmann, September 22, 1850, D. D. Barnard to Fillmore, September 30, 1850, MFP-BHS; Samuel Lyman to Thurlow Weed, September 23, 1850, Weed MSS (RU); *Senate Executive Proceedings*, p. 272.

CHAPTER 16

1. William Henry Seward to Thurlow Weed, July 28, 1850, Weed MSS (RU).

2. Alex Williams to Thurlow Weed, September 19, 1850, Weed MSS (LC); Seth Hawley to Seward, September 1, 1850 (quotation), Seward MSS (LC).

3. Daniel Webster to Peter Harvey, October 2, 1850, Webster MSS.

4. Holt, *Political Crisis*, p. 88. For the enforcement of the Fugitive Slave Act, see Campbell, *Slave Catchers*.

5. Charles Sumner to George W. Julian, June 6, 1850, Giddings-Julian MSS; Volney Howard to John M. Berrien, July 18, 1850 (quotations), C. B. Strong to Berrien, July 15, 1850, Iverson Harris to Berrien, August 2, 1850, Berrien MSS; Webster to Harvey, October 2, 1850, Webster MSS.

6. Unlike the Democrats, the Free Soilers did run a candidate against Anthony, but Anthony outpolled him by a five-to-one margin in a low-turnout election. Whigs also retained over 60 percent of the seats in each house of the legislature. The results for all elections discussed in this chapter, unless noted otherwise, are taken from Congressional Quarterly's *Guide to U.S. Elections*, and the data on partisan strength in state legislatures were supplied by the Inter-University Consortium for Political and Social Research at the University of Michigan.

7. Renda, "The Polity and Party System," pp. 185–190, 207, 214. Renda's splendid dissertation provides an excellent analysis of Democrats' manipulation of state economic issues in the 1850 campaign. Democrats outnumbered Whigs in New Hampshire's tiny state senate by eleven to one.

8. Emily Baldwin to Roger Sherman Baldwin, April 4, 1850, BFP. This account of Connecticut is also based on the following sources: Renda, "The Polity and the Party System," pp. 173–76, 206, 215; Gideon Welles to Chauncey F. Cleveland, November 3, December 19, 1849, Chauncey F. Cleveland to Welles, January 16, 1850, Welles MSS (LC); Gideon Welles to Chauncey Cleveland, January 21, February 21, 1850, Welles MSS (Connecticut Historical Society); Emily Baldwin to Roger Sherman Baldwin, February 26, March 2, 13, 23, 24, 1850, Samuel Hubbard to R. S. Baldwin, March 14, 1850, Anson Baldwin to R. S. Baldwin, March 27, 1850, Dennis Kimberly to R. S. Baldwin, April 8, 1850, Roger Sherman Baldwin to Emily Baldwin, March 3, 8, 25, April 5, 1850, BFP.

Since 1848, Whigs from eastern Connecticut had complained that both United States senators, Baldwin and Smith, lived west of the Connecticut River. Since Whigs expected to renominate Baldwin as their senatorial candidate when the legislature met after the election, Whigs tried to appease easterners by replacing incumbent Governor Joseph Trumbull of Hartford, who also lived west of the Connecticut, with Foster, a resident of Norwich. But that action offended Trumbull's friends, and Foster ran behind Trumbull's 1849 totals everywhere in the state except New London County.

9. Hartford *Courant*, March 16, 1850, quoted in Renda, "The Polity and the Party System," p. 175.

10. In the legislature, free-soil Democrats helped elect Seymour governor, but they refused to support the Democratic candidate for the Senate, Isaac Toucey, an even more notorious doughface, and instead voted for John M. Niles. That split prevented Democrats from filling the Senate seat, but Democrats also had enough votes to stop Baldwin's reelection.

The changes in the gubernatorial vote and the partisan distribution of seats in the legislature in Connecticut between 1849 and 1850 were as follows.

Popular Vote for Governor

	1849	1850
Whig	27,300 (48.8%)	28,209 (46.9%)
Democratic	25,106 (44.9%)	29,022 (48.3%)
Free Soil	3,520 (6.3%)	2,877 (4.8%)

Share of Legislative Seats

	House	Senate	House	Senate
Whig	111	13	100	6
Democratic	97	8	108	10
Free Soil	14	0	4	5

11. John Pendleton to Daniel Webster, March 12, 1850, Webster MSS; J. W. Spaulding to Thomas Ewing, May 16, 1850, EFP; White, "Virginia Constitutional Convention," pp. 7–18.

12. Volz, "Party, State, and Nation," pp. 59–64, 69–82. The 1850 results left Whigs with fifty-seven seats and Democrats with forty-three seats in the house of representatives; in the senate, Whigs outnumbered Democrats twenty-five to thirteen. In contrast, after the 1848 elections, in which Crittenden was elected governor, the Whigs enjoyed margins of sixty-four to thirty-three in the house and twenty-seven to eleven in the senate.

13. Rosenberg, *Iowa*, pp. 36–54. For the figures on turnout, see Gienapp, " 'Politics Seem to Enter into Everything,' " pp. 18–19. Iowa's turnout rate in August elections was 76 percent in 1846, 78.7 percent in 1847, and 78.4 percent in 1848, falling to 64.8 percent in 1849 and 62.7 percent in 1850.

The changes between 1848 and 1850 in the popular vote for congressmen and partisan representation in the state legislature were as follows:

Statewide Vote for Congressmen

	1848	1850
Whig	11,478 (47.4%)	11,710 (45.9%)
Democratic	12,266 (50.6%)	13,182 (52.2%)
Free Soil	485 (2%)	408 (1.9%)

Seats in the Legislature

	House	Senate	House	Senate
Whig	11	8	4	6
Democratic	28	10	35	13
Free Soil	0	1	0	0

14. Van Bolt, " 'Eternal Agitation,' " 358–63; Schuyler Colfax to William H. Seward, March 26, April 27, 1850, Seward MSS (RU); Theodore Barnett to Caleb B. Smith, May 6, 1850, Schuyler Colfax to Caleb Smith, February 18, March 8, July 20, August 10, August 21, 1850, Smith MSS.

The changes in the partisan share of seats in the Indiana legislature between 1849 and 1850 were as follows:

	1849		1850	
	House	Senate	House	Senate
Whig	40	21	37	17
Democratic	59	29	55	34
Free Soil	1	0	8	0

15. Isaac L. Scribner to William H. Seward, August 31, 1850, Seward MSS (RU); Harry Bradley to Millard Fillmore, October 24, 1850, John H. Peck to Fillmore, November 2, 1850, MFP-BHS; E. A. Stansbury to George W. Julian, October 30, 1850, Giddings-Julian MSS.

16. Harry Bradley to Fillmore, October 24, 1850, Thomas Hale to Fillmore, April 23, 1852, MFP-BHS; E. A. Stansbury to George W. Julian, October 30, 1850, Giddings-Julian MSS; E. D. Barber to Salmon P. Chase, February 24, 1851, Chase MSS (LC); Justin Morrill to Solomon Foot, September 20, 1850, (description of Phelps), Morrill MSS.

17. William Pitt Fessenden to Fillmore, August 24, 1850, MFP-BHS.

18. Hunt, *Hamlin*, pp. 35–69.

19. James S. Pike to William Schouler, August 25, 1850, Schouler MSS. A veteran newspaper reporter and Whig congressional candidate in 1850, Pike tried to instigate Democratic defections to the Free Soil congressional candidate in his district by secretly writing campaign speeches for the Free Soiler.

20. The changes in the vote for governor and for the share of legislative seats between 1849 and 1850 in Maine were as follows:

Popular Vote for Governor

	1849	1850
Whig	28,260 (38.3%)	32,308 (40.0%)
Democratic	37,534 (50.9%)	41,220 (51.0%)
Free Soil	8,025 (10.9%)	7,271 (9.0%)

Seats in the Legislature

	House	Senate	House	Senate
Whig	59	11	58	6
Democratic	76	14	93	25
Free Soil	16	5	18	0

21. Mering, *Whig Party in Missouri*, p. 138.

22. Ibid., pp. 166–80. My discussion in this and the following paragraph relies solely on Mering's pages cited here, and Mering is so interested in splits among Democrats and Whigs that he says nothing about what position Missouri Whig candidates took on the Compromise during the August election. Because the Missouri Whig press later lauded the Compromise, I surmise that Missouri Whig candidates endorsed it as a perfect middle ground between the warring Democratic factions.

23. The representation of Whigs and the two Democratic factions in Missouri's legislature after the 1850 elections was as follows:

	House	Senate
Whigs	53	12
Benton Democrats	48	13
Anti-Benton Democrats	27	8

I have reversed the strength of Benton and Anti-Benton Democrats as listed by Walter Dean Burnham in the data he submitted to the Inter-University Consortium. I have done so because of the relative strength of the two factions described in Francis Preston Blair, Jr., to Francis Preston Blair, Sr., August 17, 1850, Blair-Lee Papers.

24. In a paper written for a seminar on the Compromise of 1850, one of my students, at my suggestion, calculated indices of support for the Compromise for North Carolina's House delegation. Based on fourteen roll-call votes, including the votes and various amendments on Boyd's motion to combine Texas and New Mexico, as well as the votes on the final measures themselves, his tabulation assigned a score of 2 to every positive pro-Compromise vote, 1 to every abstention, and 0 to every anti-Compromise vote cast. Thus, a perfect pro-Compromise score was 28. The scores of the five orthodox Whigs ranged between 26 and 20. Clingman scored 9. The three Democrats scored 7, 7, and 3. This method, which can be applied to any state's delegation, reveals in a different way the dominant pattern of voting I suggested in the previous two chapters, as well as identifying exceptions to the rule, like Clingman. Hunter, "Delegation Divided," Table 3.

25. Cooper, *Politics of Slavery*, pp. 285–95; Kruman, *Parties and Politics*, pp. 124–33; Harris, *Holden*, pp. 37–41.

26. Edward Stanly to David F. Caldwell, March 1, 1850, Caldwell MSS.

27. Kruman, *Parties and Politics*, pp. 65–68, 149–51; Harris, *Holden*, pp. 51–53.

28. Kruman, *Parties and Politics*, pp. 93, 151; Harris, *Holden*, pp. 35–41. The changes in the

popular vote and partisan share of legislative seats between 1848 and 1850 are listed below. I have used Kruman's figures for partisan strength in the legislature rather than those from the Inter-University Consortium.

	Popular Vote for Governor			
	1848		1850	
Whig	42,536 (50.5%)		42,341 (48.5%)	
Democratic	41,682 (49.5%)		45,058 (51.5%)	
	Seats in the Legislature			
	House	Senate	House	Senate
Whig	61	25	55	22
Democratic	59	25	65	28

29. For evidence that Whigs blamed the result on state issues, see the letters from Whigs to William A Graham cited in Harris, *Holden*, p. 40, n. 43. Since Thomas Clingman was one of the victorious Whig candidates in 1851, it may be more accurate to say that Whigs won five of nine districts.

30. Evitts, *Matter of Allegiances*, pp. 16–38; see also Bowers, "Ideology."

31. John P. Kennedy to Robert C. Winthrop, September 9, 1850, copy, Kennedy MSS; Truth to Thomas Corwin, n.d. [October 1850], Corwin MSS (LC).

32. John P. Kennedy to J. D. Whelpley, October 3, 1850, copy, Kennedy to Robert C. Winthrop, October 7, 1850, copy, Kennedy to J. Sherrod Williams, October 22, 1850, copy, Kennedy MSS; James A. Pearce to Thomas Corwin, October 1, 5, 1850, John Pickett to Corwin, October 5, 1850, Corwin MSS (LC).

33. Doherty, *Whigs of Florida*, pp. 35–48. The quotation is from the Jacksonville *Florida Republican*, September 26, 1850, p. 43.

34. Ibid. Doherty provides no popular vote totals for the legislative elections, and I cannot account for the Whigs' defeat in them. Doherty also says that the Democrats had a 31–28 majority on the joint ballot in the legislature, figures that differ slightly from those supplied by the Inter-University Consortium, which I list below. Regression estimates of voter movements between the two elections suggest that about 10 percent (380) of 1848 Democratic voters supported Cabell in 1850, whereas about 9 percent (395) of his 1848 voters defected to the Democrats. The regression estimates are contained in Calabro, "Two-Party System in Florida," pp. 22–23.

The changes in the popular vote for congressmen and representation in the Florida legislature between 1848 and 1850 were as follows:

	Popular Vote for Congress			
	1848		1850	
Whig	4,382 (53.5%)		4,531 (52.8%)	
Democratic	3,805 (46.5%)		4,050 (47.2%)	
	Legislative Seats			
	House	Senate	House	Senate
Whig	24	12	19	9
Democratic	16	7	20	10

35. Recall that Webster wanted Fillmore to appoint a Missourian to his cabinet to represent the Midwest, not the South. See also Freehling, *Road to Disunion*, pp. 32, 538–41. In 1850,

slaves constituted less than 3 percent of Delaware's population and only about 13 percent of Missouri's.

36. James A. Bayard to Henry Clay, July 1, 1850, Henry Clay MSS (LC).

37. John M. Clayton to John J. Crittenden, August 8, 1850, Clayton to Edward Stanly, August 23, 1850, Crittenden MSS (LC); John W. Houston to John M. Clayton, December 23, 1850, Clayton MSS; James Pearce to John P. Kennedy, September 2, 1850, Kennedy MSS; Daniel Webster to Richard H. Bayard, October 6, 1850, Webster to Millard Fillmore, October 19, 1850, Webster MSS.

38. Johannsen, *Douglas*, pp. 283–84; Thomas L. Harris to Charles Lanphier, June 24, 1850, Lanphier MSS.

39. Thomas L. Harris to Charles H. Lanphier, June 24, August 12, October 18, November 6, 1850, Lanphier MSS; John B. Shaw to Richard T. Yates, August 22, 1850, Yates MSS; Johannsen, *Douglas*, pp. 299, 303. In 1848, a Free Soiler had drawn 1.1 percent of the congressional vote in the seventh district, allowing Harris to defeat his Whig rival that year by 49.8 to 49.1 percent.

40. Current, *Wisconsin*, pp. 201–09; Hamilton, *Prologue to Conflict*, pp. 191–200.

41. Nathaniel P. Tallmadge to Millard Fillmore, December 12, 1850, January 6, 1851, MFP-BHS.

42. Current, *Wisconsin*, pp. 209–10; William Duane Wilson to Fillmore, October 24, 1851, Nathaniel P. Tallmadge to Fillmore, November 7, 1851, MFP-BHS. Tallmadge claimed that Whig support for and Democratic opposition to a free banking act in Wisconsin had produced the result, and he insisted that Farwell's hostility to the Fugitive Slave Act drove Whig voters away from him. The extent of the revolution in Wisconsin politics in 1851 can be illustrated by the longitudinal change in party strength in the state legislature.

	House			Senate		
	Whig	Dem.	F.S.	Whig	Dem.	F.S.
1848	16	35	15	4	12	3
1849	17	41	8	4	12	2
1850	11	48	7	3	14	2
1851	35	25	6	6	12	1

43. Josiah Snow to Seward, September 16, November 15, 1850, George E. Pomeroy to Seward, October 28, 1850, Seward MSS (RU).

44. Ibid.

45. Josiah Snow to Seward, November 15, 1850, Seward MSS (RU). The change in the three parties' share of the popular vote in Michigan between 1848 and 1850 was as follows:

	Whigs	Democrats	Free Soilers
1848 (Cong.)	30,108 (45.6%)	31,244 (47.4%)	4,567 (7.0%)
1849 (Gov.)	23,561 (45.7%)	27,845 (54.3%)	
1850 (Cong.)	30,929 (51.3%)	29,260 (48.7%)	

The Whigs' share of seats in the state house of representatives rose from 18.4 percent in 1848 to 29.2 percent in 1849 to 35.3 percent in 1850; in the state senate the change was from 18.1 percent in 1848 to 22.7 percent in 1849 to 27.2 percent in 1850.

46. Salmon Chase to Belle Chase, January 15, 1850, C. R. Miller to Salmon Chase, January 21, 1850, Edward Hamlin to Chase, March 11. 1850, Chase MSS (LC); Aaron F. Perry to Thomas Ewing, December 16, 1849, EFP.

The average indexes of likeness or agreement between Whigs and Free Soilers, on the one hand, and Democrats and Free Soilers, on the other, on roll-call votes concerning economic policy in the Ohio house of representatives during its 1849–50 session were as follows:

Policy Category	No. of Votes	Whig/F.S.	Dem./F.S.
Business incorp.	8	74	50
Altering charters/stockholder liability	8	52	65
Banking and currency	68	83	34
Internal improvements	49	69	65

These figures are drawn from the tables in Shadle, "Consensus."

47. Maizlish, *Triumph of Sectionalism*, pp. 154–55; Salmon P. Chase to Belle Chase, January 15, 1850, Chase to Edward Hamlin, February 2, 1850, Adams Jewett to Chase, February 3, 1850, Chase MSS (LC).

48. Maizlish, *Triumph of Sectionalism*, p. 166; Aaron F. Perry to John McLean, February 14, 1850, McLean MSS (LC); Aaron Perry to Thomas Ewing, May 7, 1850, Van Brown to Thomas Ewing, May 10, 1850, EFP; William Johnson to Thomas Corwin, July 24, 1850, Corwin MSS (LC); John Barr to William H. Seward, July 14, 1850, Seward MSS (RU).

49. John Coon to Thomas Corwin, October 24, 1850, Corwin MSS (LC).

50. Maizlish, *Triumph of Sectionalism*, p. 168; Aaron Perry to Thomas Ewing, September 4, 1850, EFP; John Miller to Samuel Galloway, September 17, 1850, Galloway MSS. On Corwin's regret at joining Fillmore's cabinet, see John L. Schoolcraft to Thurlow Weed, August 12, 1850, Weed MSS (RU). For reports on the wrangling over economic policy at the state constitutional convention, which continued until the spring of 1851, see Van Brown to Thomas Ewing, May 10, September 11, 1850, Jacob Blickensderfer to Ewing, June 15, 1850, EFP.

51. Unlike Chase in the Senate, both Giddings and Root failed to vote on the District slave trade bill. To measure the degree of support members of Ohio's House delegation gave the Compromise as a whole, I used the votes on the five final measures as well as the three procedural roll-call votes on framing the Texas-New Mexico bill, listed in the appendixes of Hamilton's *Prologue to Conflict*, to construct a composite index. I assigned a score of 2 for every positive or pro-Compromise vote, 1 for every abstention, and 0 for every negative vote. Thus a perfect pro-Compromise score was 16 and a perfect anti-Compromise score was 0. Because both the California and District slave trade bills were viewed as antislavery, pronorthern measures, however, the archetypal northern anti-Compromise score was 4. By this index, both Root and Giddings scored 3. Six of eight Whigs scored 4, and another, 5. John Taylor's composite score was 10. Of the Democrats, four scored 4, one, 8, three, 10, one, 12, one, 14, and Moses Hoagland a perfect 16. Whigs opposed the critical Texas-New Mexico bill by a margin of 1–7, while Democrats opposed it more narrowly 4–5, with two abstentions. All eight Whigs including Taylor voted against the Utah bill; Democrats split 3–4, with four abstentions. Six of eight Whigs voted against the Fugitive Slave Act, Taylor supported it, and Robert Schenck recorded no vote. Democrats split 2–6 with three abstentions. In sum, there were differences between the voting records of Whigs and Democrats, but they were not very dramatic.

52. Maizlish, *Triumph of Sectionalism*, pp. 241–42. The turnout rate in 1850 was only 57.3 percent. Not only was this rate lower than that in previous off-year congressional races, but it lagged behind the level in odd-year elections when only legislative seats and minor statewide offices were at stake. See Gienapp, " 'Politics Seems to Enter Into Everything,' " pp. 18–19.

53. See the tables in Maizlish, *Triumph of Sectionalism*, pp. 244–45.

54. Ibid, pp. 156–57.

55. Adams Jewett to Salmon P. Chase, February 3, 1850, Chase MSS.

56. The change in the parties' share of the popular vote from 1848 to 1850 was as follows:

	Whig	Democratic	Free Soil
1848 (Gov.)	148,766 (49.9%)	148,452 (49.8%)	
1848 (Pres.)	138,656 (42.1%)	154,782 (47.0%)	35,523 (10.7%)
1850 (Gov.)	121,105 (45.1%)	133,093 (49.6%)	13,747 (5.1%)

57. J. Dustin Ward to Lewis Campbell, August 28, 1850, Lewis Campbell MSS.

58. The size and share of the three parties' statewide vote in the congressional elections of 1848 and 1850 were as follows:

	Whigs	Democrats	Free Soilers
1848	118,193 (43.2%)	136,217 (49.8%)	18,996 (7.0%)
1850	108,913 (42.9%)	127,843 (50.4%)	16,901 (6.7%)

In constructing this table, I have credited the vote of Free Soilers who ran on joint tickets, like Giddings, to the Free Soil column, but I counted Campbell, John Crowell, and Eb Newton, Crowell's successor in 1850, as Whigs. I have also interpolated the size of the Free Soil vote when it was not listed in the returns given in the Congressional Quarterly's *Guide to U.S. Elections* and the major parties' share did not equal 100 percent.

59. B. White to Thomas Corwin, September 30, 1850, Corwin MSS (LC).

60. After the election, the jubilant Townshend wrote Salmon Chase, "My election was a damper to the Whigs & whig free soilers of this region. . . . Our opponents both of the Root & Worcester [Whig] parties have been very bitter." Norton S. Townshend to Salmon P. Chase, October 10, 1850, Chase MSS (HSP). Townshend's close alliance with Chase has led me to follow Maizlish, *Triumph of Sectionalism*, p. 156, in crediting Townshend's victory to the Free Soil rather than the Democratic column, but the *Guide to U.S. Elections* lists Townshend as a Democrat and Root as the Free Soil candidate in the district, while Blue, *Free Soilers*, p. 183, argues that "Giddings was the lone Free Soiler from Ohio returned to Congress."

61. E. F. Sadler to Thomas Corwin, October 24, 1850, Corwin MSS (LC); Benjamin Wade to Caroline Wade, November 5, 1850, Wade MSS.

62. My account of New Jersey in this and subsequent paragraphs is based almost entirely on Renda, "Railroads, Revenue, and Reform," pp. 38–79. I shall eschew specific page citations except for quotations.

63. For a survey of Whig newspaper sentiment in New Jersey, see ibid., p. 60.

64. Because Democrats had chartered the Joint Companies and were closely associated with them, Whig attacks on those transportation monopolies seemed a natural issue for the party. But for several reasons many Whigs opposed such attacks. Some represented counties that benefited from the railroad or the canal. Others believed the charters represented a contract that could not be constitutionally breached. Most important, about 90 percent of the state's revenue was derived from fees and dividends the Joint Companies paid the state. Anything that lessened those firms' revenue could necessitate real estate tax increases that many Whigs were loath to levy.

65. In 1848, the total Whig popular vote for congressmen was 36,668 (50.2 percent), compared to the Democrats' 36,379 (49.8 percent). In 1850, the comparable figures were: Whigs, 33,299 (45.8 percent) and Democrats, 39,368 (54.2 percent). In 1848, Taylor ran ahead of Cass 40,009 (51.4 percent) to 36,880 (47.3 percent). In 1850, Fort bested Runk 39,723 (53.8 percent) to 34,054 (46.2 percent).

66. Newark *Mercury*, November 6–9, 1850, quoted in Renda, "Railroads, Revenue, and Reform," p. 78 and front quotes.

67. I include in this total of Whigs John W. Howe from a western district north of Pittsburgh. Howe was elected on joint Whig/Free Soil tickets in 1848 and again in 1850. He cooperated with the Free Soilers in the speakership election during December 1849 but with Whigs on other

votes. Congressional Quarterly's *Guide to U.S. Elections* lists his affiliation as Free Soil in 1848 but Whig in 1850.

68. Holt, *Forging a Majority*, pp. 90–91; Mueller, *Whig Party in Pennsylvania*, pp. 167, 172–73; H. M. Watts to William M. Meredith, May 31, 1850, Meredith MSS; J. W. Megary to Samuel Calvin, June 10, 1850, S. Coryell to Calvin, June 28, 1850, James T. Hale to Calvin, July 10, 22, 1850, and Thomas McNamara to Calvin, July 22, 1850, Calvin MSS.

69. Holt, *Forging a Majority*, pp. 87–91; Mueller, *Whig Party in Pennsylvania*, pp. 172–74; see also the letters to Samuel Calvin cited in the previous note. Daniel Webster blamed the refusal of southern Whigs to consider tariff revision during the 1850 session on their anger at the fanatical attacks northern Whig congressmen had made on slavery and the South during the compromise debates. See Webster to Edward Everett, September 26, 1850, Webster to Franklin Haven, September 27, 1850, Webster MSS.

70. Holt, *Forging a Majority*, p. 86; Mueller, *Whig Party in Pennsylvania*, pp. 174–75; S. Coryell to Samuel Calvin, June 28, 1850, Thomas McNamara to Calvin, July 22, 1850, Calvin MSS; William Neal to William H. Seward, September 1, 1850, Seward MSS (RU). For the ferocious opposition of Whig papers affiliated with Johnston to Cooper, see James Cooper to Millard Fillmore, March 13, 1851, MFP-BHS. This long, bitter letter provides a remarkable review of the strife between Johnston and Cooper since 1848.

71. Holt, *Forging a Majority*, p. 85; Mueller, *Whig Party in Pennsylvania*, pp. 170–71. Five of the eight Democrats compiled perfect pro-Compromise scores of 16, and the other three had scores of 15. The average index of partsian disagreement in the state house of representatives on Democrats' attempt to repeal the 1847 antikidnapping law was at least 35 points higher than the disagreement index in any other issue area in 1850. Holt, *Political Crisis*, pp. 115–16.

72. In late October, Cooper wrote Webster that most Pennsylvanians applauded the settlement of the sectional crisis and that a "sound national feeling . . . begins to prevail throughout this State." Cooper, of course, is a biased source. Cooper to Webster, October 21, 1850, Webster MSS.

73. Holt, *Forging a Majority*, pp. 86–87; Mueller, *Whig Party in Pennsylvania*, p. 175.

74. Cooper to Fillmore, March 13, 1851, MFP-BHS.

75. Holt, *Forging a Majority*, p. 87; Mueller, *Whig Party in Pennsylvania*, p. 175. I infer Ogle's acquiescence in the Compromise from a letter Webster wrote Fillmore in June 1851, after Ogle had been defeated for reelection, describing him as the most able man in the Pennsylvania delegation during the Thirty-First Congress and saying that Speaker Howell Cobb believed the same thing. During 1851, indeed, Ogle became a leader of the anti-Johnston Whigs in the state. See Webster to Fillmore, June 6, 1851, MFP-BHS; Mueller, *Whig Party in Pennsylvania*, p. 179.

76. Turnout in 1850 was 55.3 percent, in contrast to 70.6 percent in the October elections of 1848 and 57.4 percent in 1849, when only candidates for canal commissioner and the legislature ran. The mean turnout rate for the period 1840–60 was 65.4 percent, so the 1850 participation rate dipped ten points below that average. See Gienapp, " 'Politics Seem to Enter Into Everything,' " pp. 18–19, 22.

77. Not counting Stevens, the average rate of decline in the Whig vote for the six other incumbent candidates was 16.5 percent. Excluding Fuller, who drew more votes than Butler had in 1848, the average rate of decline in the six districts where new candidates replaced Whig incumbents was 20.4 percent.

78. On Pittsburgh, see Holt, *Forging a Majority*, pp. 84–113, and Tables 16 and 23, pp. 327, 335. In January 1850 an anti-Catholic demagogue named Joe Barker, who pledged to resist enforcement of local antiliquor laws, won Pittsburgh's mayoral election over both Whig and Democratic candidates by running strongly in working-class wards. In October both Native American and Protestant party congressional candidates competed against the Whigs and Democrats.

79. Alexander K. McClure to John Penn Jones, July 26, 1850, Samuel Calvin MSS.

80. J. W. Megary to Calvin, June 10, 1850, Samuel Royer to Calvin, July 20, 1850, James T. Hale to Calvin, July 22, 1850, Thomas McNamara to Calvin, July 22, 1850, John Penn Jones to

Calvin, July 24, 1850, Samuel S. Blair to Calvin, July 25, 1850, Alexander K. McClure to Calvin, July 26, 1850, John Armitage to Calvin, August 7, 1850, and David McClure to Calvin, August 7, 1850, Calvin MSS.

81. Alexander K. McClure to Calvin, July 26, 1850; Andrew G. Curtin to Calvin, August 12, 1850, Joseph A. Kemp to Calvin, August 20, 1850, Calvin MSS.

82. S. Coryell to Calvin, June 28, 1850, James T. Hale to Calvin, July 22, 1850, Joseph A. Kemp to Calvin, August 20, 1850, John Penn Jones to Calvin, September 12, 1850, Calvin MSS.

83. William N. Everly to Millard Fillmore, October 19, 1850, MFP-BHS; Mueller, *Whig Party in Pennsylvania*, p. 176. Levin's vote fell from 4,897 in 1848 to 4,164 in 1850, while that of his Democratic opponent increased from 4,228 to 5,352. The separate Whig candidate in 1850 attracted 609 votes.

84. John H. Bryant to Millard Fillmore, November 11, 1850, James Cooper to Fillmore, March 13, 1851, MFP-BHS.

85. For Johnston's actions and speeches with regard to fugitive slaves and the southern complaints in 1849 and 1850, see Mueller, *Whig Party in Pennsylvania*, pp. 168–74, 181–88; and Slaughter, *Bloody Dawn*, p. 98.

86. On Free Soil opposition to fusion, see Donald, *Sumner*, pp. 185–89; for the opposition of conservative, pro-Compromise Democrats, see Benjamin Barstow to Caleb Cushing, November 5, 1850, Cushing MSS. Cushing led the Democrats opposed to the alliance with Free Soilers. Charles Allen of Worcester was the Free Soiler elected to Congress in 1848; the fourth district went unrepresented during the entire Thirty-First Congress despite twelve runoff elections because ex-Whig Free Soiler John Gorham Palfrey ran so closely to Whig Benjamin Thompson in the three-way races.

87. Whigs explicitly warned voters of this bargain in the address issued by their state convention. Boston *Daily Advertiser*, October 3, 1850. On the representation system, see Sweeney, "Rum, Romanism, Representation, and Reform," 116–37.

88. Charles Hudson to John Davis, September 11, 1850, J. Dexter to Davis, September 17, 1850, John Davis MSS.

89. Ibid.; Philip Greely, Jr., to Thurlow Weed, September 4, 1850, Weed MSS (RU); Webster to Peter Harvey, October 2, 1850, Webster to Fillmore, October 14, 24, 1850, Webster MSS; Dalzell, *Webster*, pp. 214–19.

90. Webster to Edward Everett, September 26, 1850, Webster to Peter Harvey, October 2, 1850, Webster MSS. I infer what Webster meant by "nationalize" from his letter to Harvey.

91. Everett to Webster, October 5, 1850, Webster MSS.

92. The platform and address are printed in the Boston *Daily Advertiser*, October 2, 3, 1850.

93. See the resolutions of the Eighth District convention, Boston *Daily Advertiser*, October 31, 1850.

94. Boston *Daily Advertiser*, October 30, 31, November 5, 1850.

95. Webster to Everett, October 8, 1850, Webster to Fillmore, October 24, 1850, Webster to Harvey, August 11, 1850, Webster MSS.

96. Amos A. Lawrence to William Appleton, October 25, 1850, Amos Lawrence MSS; Samuel Lawrence to Millard Fillmore, October 26, 1850, Webster to Fillmore, October 24, 1850, MFP-BHS; Boston *Daily Advertiser*, October 28, 1850; Charles Upham to Henry L. Dawes, September 14, 1850 (quotation), Dawes MSS; Boston *Daily Advertiser*, August 19, 1850. Daniel King, the Whig elected to Congress from the second district in 1848, died in late July 1850, necessitating the special election. The other August election occurred in the fourth district, where Palfrey's Free Soil candidacy produced continued stalemates.

97. Boston *Daily Advertiser*, October 23, 1850; Humphrey Gould to Henry L. Dawes, November 5, 1850, Dawes MSS; Webster to Fillmore, October 14, 24, 1850, Webster MSS.

98. Winthrop to John Pendleton Kennedy, October 18, 1850, Kennedy MSS.

99. Sweeney, "Rum, Romanism, Representation, and Reform," 121. The change in the gubernatorial vote between 1848 and 1850 was as follows:

	Whigs	Democrats	Free Soilers
1848	61,640 (49.7%)	25,323 (20.4%)	36,011 (29%)
1849	54,009 (49.3%)	30,040 (27.4%)	25,247 (23.1%)
1850	56,778 (46.8%)	36,023 (29.7%)	27,636 (22.8%)

100. Edward Everett to Daniel Webster, May 27, 1851, Webster MSS; John Z. Goodrich to Henry L. Dawes, May 31, 1851, Dawes MSS.

101. Charles Upham to Henry L. Dawes, November 20, 1850, Dawes MSS; Webster to Fillmore, November 13, 15, 1850, MFP-BHS; Webster to Corwin, November 13, 1850, Corwin MSS (LC); Boston *Daily Advertiser*, November 16, 1850.

102. B. F. Hall to Fillmore, September 28, 1850, MFP-BHS. Because the bolt took place on the afternoon of September 27, I have assumed that a telegraph operator in Syracuse or Washington misdated the telegram. The bolters did remain in Syracuse overnight and met on the morning of September 28, but many had returned home by that afternoon. This fact and the breathless urgency of the telegram suggest that it was sent on the 27th.

103. Hamilton Fish to Fillmore, July 22, 1850, copy, Fish MSS; Washington Hunt to Fillmore, July 22, 25, 1850, MFP-BHS.

104. Alex Mann to Fillmore, July 12, 1850, MFP-BHS.

105. Hamilton Fish to Millard Fillmore, July 22, 1850, copy, Fish MSS; Washington Hunt to Fillmore, July 22, 1850, Alex Mann to Fillmore, July 12, 1850, D. O. Kellogg to Fillmore, August 5, 1850, Barnard to Fillmore, September 17, 1850, Jerome Fuller to Fillmore, September 15, 1850, MFP-BHS; Samuel P. Lyman to Weed, September 23, 1850, Weed MSS (RU). For more on Barnard's relations with Weed, see Penny, "Barnard versus Weed."

106. C. B. Stuart to Fillmore, September 7, 1850, John Lorimer Graham to Fillmore, September 9, 1850, Hunt to Fillmore, September 18, 1850, MFP-BHS.

107. Fillmore to Daniel Ullmann, September 22, 1850, Ullmann MSS.

108. Lyman to Weed, September 23, 1850, Weed MSS (RU); Fillmore to Ullmann, September 22, 1850, Ullmann MSS.

109. Barnard to Fillmore, September 17, 1850, Jerome Fuller to Fillmore, September 20, 1850, Hiram Ketchum to Fillmore, September 30, 1850, MFP-BHS.

110. Alexander B. Williams to Weed, September 19, 1850, John C. Underwood to Weed, September 20, 1850 (quotation), Simeon Draper to Weed, October 2, 1850, Edward Dodd to Weed, October 7, 1850, Weed MSS (RU).

111. Washington Hunt to Millard Fillmore, September 18, 1850, MFP-BHS; Minos McGowen to Weed, October 7, 1850, Edward Dodd to Weed, October 7, 1850, Weed MSS (RU); John S. Bowron to Seward, October 5, 1850, Seward MSS (RU).

112. C. B. Stuart to Fillmore, September 7, 23, 1850, Solomon G. Haven to Fillmore, September 14, 1850, Alex Mann to Fillmore, September 16, 1850, Jerome Fuller to Fillmore, September 20, 1850, John Young to Fillmore, September 29, 1850, James R. Thompson to Fillmore, October 2, 1850, James Brooks to Fillmore, October 3, 1850, Joseph Hartwell to Fillmore, October 27, 1850, J. Phillips Phoenix to Fillmore, November 6, 1850, Charles Shepard to Robert Rose, October 8, 1850, MFP-BHS; David Abell to Thurlow Weed, August 5, 1850, Orasmus B. Matteson to Weed, September 13, 1850, Samuel P. Lyman to Weed, December 1, 2, 5, 7, 8, 20, 1850, Weed MSS (RU); Seth Hawley to William Henry Seward, September 21, 1850, Simeon Draper to Seward, September 17, 1850, Seward MSS (RU).

113. Daniel Ullmann to Fillmore, September 21, 1850, MFP-BHS; Seward to Weed, 1850, in *Seward at Washington*, p. 156.

114. Ullmann to Fillmore, September 21, 1850, MFP-BHS; Fillmore to Ullmann, September 22, 1850, Ullmann MSS; *Albany Evening Journal*, October 2, 16, 1850; Rayback, "Silver Grey Revolt," 160.

115. Daniel D. Barnard to Fillmore, September 17, 1850 (quotation), John Young to Fillmore, September 29, 1850, Nathan K. Hall to Fillmore, October 1, 1850, MFP-BHS; Van Deusen, *Greeley*, pp. 140–41.

116. The following account of the convention, which is extensive because of its importance, is based on the following sources: *Albany Evening Journal,* September 27, 28, 1850; Boston *Daily Advertiser,* October 1, 2, 1850; John Young to Fillmore, September 29, 1850, Hiram Ketcham to Fillmore, September 30, 1850, MFP-BHS.

117. A candidate for prison inspector was also chosen.

118. Boston *Daily Advertiser,* October 2, 1850; John Young to Fillmore, September 29, 1850, Hiram Ketcham to Fillmore, September 30, 1850, MFP-BHS.

119. *Albany Evening Journal,* September 28, October 1, 2, 17, 1850.

120. John Young to Fillmore, September 29, 1850, MFP-BHS; Simeon Draper to Thurlow Weed, October 2, 1850, Weed MSS (RU); *Albany Evening Journal,* September 28, 1850.

121. Young to Fillmore, September 29, 1850, Haven to Fillmore, September 29, 1850, Cornell to Fillmore, October 7, 1850, MFP-BHS.

122. Fillmore to Daniel Ullmann, October 3, 1850, Ullmann MSS; Nathan Hall to Fillmore, October 1, 1850, Hugh Maxwell to Fillmore, September 28, 1850, John Young to Fillmore, September 29, October 2, 1850, C. B. Stuart to Fillmore, October 3, 1850, Daniel Ullmann to Fillmore, October 5, 1850, J. R. Mower to Fillmore, October 6, 1850, MFP-BHS.

123. Haven to Fillmore, October 6, 1850, MFP-BHS.

124. Fillmore to Francis Granger, October 9, 1850, Fillmore MSS (Ontario County Historical Society, in microfilm edition); D. O. Kellogg to Fillmore, October 8, 1850, MFP-BHS.

125. Daniel Ullmann to Fillmore, October 11, 1850, John Young to Fillmore, October 12, 1850, Hugh Maxwell to Fillmore, October 12, 1850, Daniel D. Barnard to Fillmore, October 14, 1850, Francis Granger to Fillmore, October 19, 1850, MFP-BHS; Robert G. Campbell to Fillmore, October 17, 1850, MFP-O.

126. *Albany Evening Journal,* October 16, 1850. Upon the advice of Granger, Hiram Ketcham, James Brooks, and other Silver Grays, who apparently wanted to deny Weed any more ammunition about federal officeholders orchestrating New York conventions, Campbell did not go to Utica. Instead he contented himself with coordinating Silver Gray forces in Albany and New York City. Robert G. Campbell to Fillmore, October 17, 1850, MFP-O.

127. *Albany Evening Journal,* October 17, 1850; Francis Granger to Fillmore, October 19, 1850, Charles A. Davis to Fillmore, October 19, 1850, MFP-BHS; Hugh White to Thomas Corwin, October 21, 1850, Corwin MSS (LC); B. Thompson to Hamilton Fish, October 21, 1850, Fish MSS.

128. D. G. Garnsey to Fillmore, October 28, 1850, Alex Mann to Fillmore, November 6, 1850, William Frary to Fillmore, November 6, 1850, Fish to Fillmore, November 18, 1850, MFP-BHS; Moses H. Grinnell to Thomas Corwin, October 30, 1850, Corwin MSS; Hamilton Fish to Alvah Hunt, November 4, 1850, Knollenberg Collection; Henry Montgomery to William H. Seward, October 6, 1850, Hamilton Fish to Seward, October 24, 1850, Seth Hawley to Seward, November 8, 1850, Orsamus B. Matteson to Seward, November 8, 1850, Seward MSS (RU).

129. George J. Cornell to Fillmore, October 7, 1850, MFP-BHS; Cornell to Hamilton Fish, October 23, 1850, Fish MSS; Fish to Alvah Hunt, November 4, 1850, Knollenberg Collection.

130. Foner, *Business & Slavery,* pp. 34–54; Dalzell, *Webster,* p. 219; Washington Hunt to Alvah Hunt, October 31, 1850, Knollenberg Collection; Hamilton Fish to Seward, October 24, 1850, Seward MSS (RU); James P. Thomas to Hamilton Fish, October 23, 1850, George J. Cornell to Fish, October 28, 1850, A. W. Bradford to Fish, November 9, 1850, Fish MSS; Moses H. Grinnell to Thomas Corwin, October 30, 1850, Simeon Draper to Corwin, November 4, 1850, Corwin MSS (LC).

131. Foner, *Business & Slavery,* pp. 48–50; Fish to Alvah Hunt, November 4, 1850, Knollenberg Collection.

132. Foner, *Business & Slavery,* p. 50; Gienapp, " 'Politics Seem to Enter into Everything,' " p. 18; *New York Tribune,* November 7, 19, 1850; Alvah Hunt to Hamilton Fish, November 6, 1850, George Cornell to Fish, November 9, 1850, Fish MSS; Alvah Hunt to Thurlow Weed, November 9, 1850, Starr Clark to Weed, November 13, 1850, Lyman Spalding to Weed, November 18, 1850, Weed MSS (RU); D. O. Kellogg to Millard Fillmore, November 16, 1850, Fish to Fillmore, November 18, 1850, MFP-BHS; Lyman Spalding to William H. Seward, November 18, 1850, Seward MSS (RU). The parties' vote for governor in 1848 and 1850 was as follows:

	Whig	Democratic	Free Soil
1848	218,280 (47.9%)	114,457 (25.1%)	123,360 (27.1%)
1850	214,614 (49.6%)	214,352 (49.6%)	

133. Charles Shepard to Robert Rose, October 8, 1850, C. B. Stuart to Millard Fillmore, October 21, 1850, D. L. Garnsey to Fillmore, October 28, 1850, MFP-BHS; Hugh White to Thomas Corwin, October 21, 1850, Corwin MSS; Starr Clark to Thurlow Weed, November 13, 1850, Weed MSS (RU).

134. Joseph Hartwell to Fillmore, October 27, 1850, J. Phillips Phoenix to Fillmore, November 6, 1850, MFP-BHS; Moses H. Grinnell to Thomas Corwin, October 30, 1850, Simeon Draper to Corwin, November 4, 1850, Corwin MSS (LC); James Bowen to William H. Seward, November 12, 1850, Seward MSS (RU). Phoenix had won with 5,601 votes, 55 percent of the total, in 1848; Bowen and Rodman together mustered only 3,919 votes, (51.6 percent of the total) in 1850. The disparity suggests either that Phoenix did buy a lot of illegal votes in 1848 or that disgusted conservatives who refused to support either Bowen or Rodman sat out the election.

135. Henry Montgomery to William H. Seward, October 6, 1850, Matteson to Seward, November 8, 1850, Seward MSS (RU); William Frary to Fillmore, November 6, 1850, MFP-BHS.

136. One example of an anti-Compromise Whig who replaced an anti-Compromise Whig incumbent and who was then abandoned by Silver Grays was Russell Sage, a close friend of Weed, who lost in the Troy district north of Albany. His predecessor had won with 6,055 votes (53 percent); Sage lost with 5,594 votes (49 percent). Another example was the successor to the eighth district's Ransom Halloway, who lost in 1850 with 5,942 votes (48.9 percent) compared to Halloway's 6,301 votes (51.2 percent) in 1848. Anti-Compromise incumbents John L. Schoolcraft and Henry Alexander also lost a few votes; Schoolcraft won because Whigs had a normal majority in his district, while Alexander, who had won with 47.2 percent in 1848, lost despite increasing his proportion slightly. On the Silver Grays' knifing of Sage and Schoolcraft, see Alvah Hunt to Thurlow Weed, November 9, 1850, Weed MSS (RU); D. O. Kellogg to Millard Fillmore, November 16, 1850, MFP-BHS; Orsamus B. Matteson to Seward, November 8, 1850, Seward MSS (RU).

137. Spaulding had carried the district with 56.9 percent of the votes; Haven won 55.2 percent. On Sewardite abandonment of and Hunker support for Haven, see Seth Hawley to William H. Seward, November 8, 1850, Seward MSS (RU). Whereas the four renominated pro-Compromise incumbents suffered an aggregate decline of 11.9 percent between 1848 and 1850, the seven anti-Compromise incumbents who ran in 1850 enjoyed an aggregate gain of 8.7 percent.

138. Starr Clark to Thurlow Weed, November 13, 1850, Weed MSS (RU).

139. Washington Hunt to Millard Fillmore, November 16, 1850, MFP-BHS; Fillmore to Hamilton Fish, November 21, 1850, Fish MSS.

140. D. E. Sills to Weed, November 15, 1850, Weed MSS; William Frary to Fillmore, November 6, 1850, James Brooks to Fillmore, November 16, 1850, MFP-BHS; Weed to Thomas Corwin, November 12, 1850, Corwin MSS (LC); Henry B. Northrop to William H. Seward, November 27, 1850, William Wasson to Seward, December 5, 1850, Seward MSS (RU). Silver Grays' conviction that antislavery Whigs were problack is the source of their contemptuous epithet for Sewardites, "Woolly Heads" or "Woollies," in reference to blacks' curly hair.

141. Hamilton Fish to Fillmore, November 18, 1850, Daniel Ullmann to Fillmore, October 5, 1850, Joseph B. Varnum to Fillmore, November 22, 1850, MFP-BHS; A. W. Bradford to Hamilton Fish, November 9, 1850, Fish MSS; Weed to Corwin, November 17, 1850, Corwin MSS (LC).

142. Seth Hawley to Seward, November 8, 1850, James Bowen to Seward, November 12, 1850, Seward MSS (RU); Alvah Hunt to Weed, November 9, 1850, Charles Stetson to Weed, November 10, 1850, Starr Clark to Weed, November 13, 1850 (quotation), Lyman Spalding to Weed, November 18, 1850, Weed MSS (RU).

143. These summary figures include the seven seats in South Carolina, which I have excluded

from my analysis throughout this study. Surprisingly, a Whig candidate won one of those seats in 1850. The total number of seats for 1850 is lower than that for 1848 because Georgia, like Arkansas, rescheduled its congressional elections to odd-numbered years.

144. Benjamin Wade to Caroline Wade, November 5, 1850, Wade MSS; Seth Hawley to Seward, September 21, 1850, Seward MSS (RU).

145. Samuel Dinsmore to William H. Seward, September 30, 1850, John Bowron to Seward, November 18, 1850, Seward MSS (RU); *New York Tribune*, November 18, 1850.

CHAPTER 17

1. Washington Hunt to Millard Fillmore, November 16, 1850, Hamilton Fish to Fillmore, November 18, 1850, MFP-BHS; Millard Fillmore to Hamilton Fish, November 21, 1850, Fish MSS; Fillmore to Daniel Webster, October 17, 1850, Millard Fillmore MSS (Ind.HSL, in microfilm edition of Fillmore Papers); Fillmore to Webster, October 23, 1850, Webster MSS.

2. Fillmore to Hamilton Fish, November 21, 1850, Fish MSS; Fillmore to Webster, October 23, 1850, Webster MSS.

3. Fillmore to Webster, October 28, 1850, Webster MSS.

4. Webster to Fillmore, October 14, 1850, Webster MSS; John Pendleton Kennedy to Richard Pakenham, October 13, 1850, letterbook copy, Kennedy MSS.

5. Webster to Peter Harvey, October 2, 1850, Webster MSS; Kennedy to Richard Pakenham, October 13, 1850, Kennedy MSS.

6. The reference here is to David Donald's famous essay "Abraham Lincoln: Whig in the White House," in his *Lincoln Reconsidered*, pp. 187–208.

7. Webster to Members of the Cabinet, November 13, 1850, draft, Webster MSS; N. K. Hall to Fillmore, January 1851, James D. Merrill to Jerome Fuller, January 31, 1851, MFP-BHS.

8. Millard Fillmore to Washington Hunt, February 23, 1851, copy with Henry E. Davies to Fillmore, March 17, 1851, MFP-BHS. Secretary of the Treasury Corwin told Cincinnati Whig editor Thomas Stevenson in mid-October 1850 that he personally had made only twelve removals since taking office and that the cabinet had not yet agreed upon any concerted policy with regard to removals. Corwin to Thomas B. Stevenson, October 14, 15, 1850, Stevenson MSS.

9. Daniel Webster to Fillmore, October 3, 1850, William Hunter to Webster, October 4, 15, 1850, Webster to Edward Everett, October 20, December 21, 1850, Fillmore to Webster, December 20, 1850, Webster MSS; *Messages and Papers of the Presidents*, V, p. 41. For background on this affair, see Rayback, *Fillmore*, pp. 327–29, and Dalzell, *Webster*, pp. 225–27.

10. The preceding two paragraphs are based on Rayback, *Fillmore*, pp. 327–29, and Dalzell, *Webster*, pp. 225–26.

11. Barnwell, *Love of Order*, pp. 105–09.

12. Shryock, *Georgia and the Union*, p. 296; May, *Quitman*, p. 244; Barnwell, *Love of Order*, pp. 123–24.

13. Webster to Fillmore, October 25, 1850, Webster MSS.

14. Alexander H. H. Stuart to Fillmore, November 4, 1850, Nathan K. Hall to Fillmore, November 11, 1850, Webster MSS.

15. These two paragraphs are based on May, *Quitman*, pp. 236–52; for later efforts of the administration to enforce the neutrality laws against López and other filibusterers, see Rayback, *Fillmore*, pp. 321–24. For more on López, see Chaffin, *Fatal Glory*.

16. *Messages and Papers of the Presidents*, V, pp. 111–12.

17. Webster to Fillmore, October 29, 1850 (quotation), Fillmore to Webster, October 23, 1850, Webster MSS; Fillmore to Webster, October 17, 1850, Fillmore MSS (Ind.HSL). The standard account of the operation of the Fugitive Slave Act is Campbell, *Slave Catchers*.

18. Slaughter, *Bloody Dawn*, pp. 43–58 and passim; Nevins, *Ordeal: Fruits*, pp. 380–89.

19. Campbell, *Slave Catchers*, pp. 114–16, 199; Webster to Fillmore, November 5, 15, 1850, MFP-BHS.

20. Campbell, *Slave Catchers*, p. 115; Fillmore to Webster, October 23, 28, 1850, Webster MSS; Webster to Fillmore, October 29, November 5, 1850, MFP-BHS; *Messages and Papers of the Presidents*, V, p. 103. The two Democratic judges were George Kane and Robert Grier.

Fillmore waited for two months after ordering the use of federal troops before he solicited an opinion from Supreme Court Justice John McLean to ascertain if such action was constitutional. Fillmore to John McLean, January 6, 1851, McLean MSS (LC).

21. *Messages and Papers of the Presidents*, V, pp. 78–80.

22. Campbell, *Slave Catchers*, pp. 116, 148–57; the Christiana riot is described in vivid detail in Slaughter, *Bloody Dawn*.

23. *Messages and Papers of the Presidents*, V, pp. 101–06, 109–10.

24. Webster to Fillmore, November 15, 1850, MFP-BHS. The administration would face the same embarrassing situation after the Christiana riot in Lancaster County, Pennsylvania, for the United States attorney for eastern Pennsylvania who had to prosecute the government's case was John Ashmead, a crony of Governor William F. Johnston, who ardently opposed the Fugitive Slave Act. I shall discuss the Christiana riot later in the context of the 1851 Pennsylvania election.

25. George Lunt to Webster, March 31, 1851, Webster to Fillmore, April 4, 13, 1851, Webster to Lunt, April 4, 1851, Webster MSS; Webster to Fillmore, April 5, 1851, Henry Sargent to Fillmore, April 5, 1851, MFP-BHS; Campbell, *Slave Catchers*, pp. 150–51.

26. Campbell, *Slave Catchers*, pp. 117–20; Webster to Fillmore, April 13, 1851, Webster MSS.

27. John P. Kennedy to Alexander H. H. Stuart, April 17, 1851, letterbook copy, Kennedy MSS.

28. J. S. Skinner to Fillmore, July 12, 1850, MFP-BHS; Charles A. Davis to Webster, August 9, 1850, Webster MSS.

29. Daniel Ullmann to Fillmore, October 5, 1850, MFP-BHS; John P. Kennedy to J. D. Whelply, October 12, 1850, Kennedy to Elizabeth Kennedy, October 31, 1850, Kennedy to Robert C. Winthrop, November 10, 1850, Kennedy to John C. Pendleton, November 12, 1850, letterbook copies, Robert C. Winthrop to John P. Kennedy, November 12, 1850, Kennedy MSS; T. L. Walters to Daniel M. Barringer, October 7, 1850, Barringer MSS; Robert C. Winthrop to Edward Everett, December 31, 1850, Everett MSS; E. M. Wright to Henry L. Dawes, November 27, 1850, Dawes MSS; Josiah Randall to Daniel Webster, November 11, 1850, Webster MSS; Boston *Daily Advertiser*, November 26, 1850; Dalzell, *Webster*, p. 219.

30. Cassius M. Clay to William H. Seward, October 24, 1850, Seward MSS (RU); draft of Clay's speech to the Kentucky legislature, November 15, 1850, Henry Clay MSS (LC). By Henry Clay's "Executor," Cassius Clay may have meant Fillmore.

31. M. C. Fulton to Howell Cobb, November 6, 1850, in Phillips, "Correspondence of Toombs, Stephens, and Cobb," pp. 217–18.

32. Alexander Stephens to John J. Crittenden, October 24, 1850, draft, Stephens MSS (Duke).

33. Shryock, *Georgia and the Union*, pp. 275–345; William Law to John M. Berrien, September 11, 1850, James M. Smythe to Berrien, September 12, 1850, Charles Jenkins to Berrien, September 14, 1850, Benjamin Good Stiles to Berrien, September 20, 1850, Berrien MSS; Stephens to Crittenden, October 24, 1850, Stephens MSS (Duke).

34. James Meriweather to Howell Cobb, August 24, 1850, in Phillips, "Correspondence of Toombs, Stephens, and Cobb," pp. 210–12; Stephens to Crittenden, October 24, 1850, Stephens MSS (Duke); S. T. Chapman to Alexander H. Stephens, August 31, 1850, Stephens MSS (LC); Shryock, *Georgia and the Union*, pp. 319–36. Shryock's estimate that almost half of the Democrats voted the Union ticket seems plausible. In the 1849 gubernatorial election, Democrats had outpolled Whigs 46,643 to 43,349, while the vote in 1850 stood 46,616 to 24,499. Without statistical analysis, the partisan distribution of the 19,000 1849 voters who stayed home in 1850 is impossible to determine. Nonetheless, the differential between the 1849 Democratic and 1850 Southern Rights votes suggests that those Democrats who voted in 1850 split their vote evenly between the two camps. According to maps in Shryock, pp. 109, 320, moreover, of forty-two counties carried by Democrats in 1848, only eight elected Southern Rights delegates and five others sent divided delegations; twenty-nine sent Union delegates. Conversely, only two of the fifty-one counties Taylor had carried sent Southern Rights delegates, while forty-six sent solid Union delegations.

35. Shryock, *Georgia and the Union*, p. 218; James A. Meriweather to Howell Cobb, August 24, 1850, M. C. Fulton to Cobb, November 6, 1850, in Phillips, "Correspondence of Toombs,

Stephens, and Cobb," pp. 210–12, 217–18; C. B. Strong to John M. Berrien, July 15, 1850, Charles Jenkins to Berrien, February 5, 1851, Berrien MSS; Holt, *Political Crisis*, pp. 118–19.

36. Cooper, *Politics of Slavery;* Freehling, *Road to Disunion.*

37. C. B. Strong to John M. Berrien, July 15, 1850, Volney Howard to Berrien, July 18, 1850, Iverson Harris to Berrien, August 2, 1850, Berrien MSS; Shryock, *Georgia and the Union,* p. 345; Schott, *Stephens,* pp. 107–08, 118–19.

38. For Democratic gains in the rice belt see Hoisington, "From Whig to Union."

39. Shryock, *Georgia and the Union,* pp. 235–36; Murray, *Whig Party in Georgia,* pp. 145–46; Hoisington, in the M. A. thesis cited above, has discovered that Shryock and Murray err in asserting that the senate redistricting bill was defeated.

40. Savannah *Republican,* November 13, 1849, quoted in Shryock, *Georgia and the Union,* p. 221; for the legislative roll calls, see ibid., pp. 218–36. The eighth resolution listing California's admission and other grounds for calling a state convention passed 92–28, as did the bill requiring it. Twelve of sixty-three Whigs and sixteen of sixty-six Democrats composed the minority.

41. For the Democratic divisions, see Shryock, *Georgia and the Union,* and Montgomery, *Cracker Parties.*

42. C. F. McCoy to Samuel Calvin, July 11, August 13, 1850, Calvin MSS; C. B. Strong to John M. Berrien, July 15, 1850, Volney Howard to Berrien, July 18, 1850, Iverson Harris to Berrien, August 2, 1850, William Law to Berrien, September 11, 1850, James M. Smythe to Berrien, September 12, 1850, Berrien MSS.

43. In addition to the letters to Berrien cited in the previous note, see Benjamin Good Stiles to Berrien, September 20, 1850, and Alfred Iverson to Berrien, October 23, 1850, Berrien MSS. For the newspaper opposition to Stephens and Toombs as compromisers, see Shryock, *Georgia and the Union,* pp. 247, 312–13; Schott, *Stephens,* p. 121.

44. William Law to Berrien, September 11, 1850, Charles Jenkins to Berrien, September 14, 1850, February 5, 1851, Berrien MSS.

45. Shryock, *Georgia and the Union,* pp. 268–69, 315–17; Berrien's correspondence is filled with invitations to speak at Southern Rights rallies, which he did.

46. Shryock, *Georgia and the Union,* p. 317; William Law to Berrien, November 3, 1850, Berrien MSS.

47. Schott, *Stephens,* pp. 108–26; Shryock, *Georgia and the Union,* pp. 247, 266; S. T. Chapman to Alexander H. Stephens, August 31, 1850, Stephens MSS (LC); Toombs' House speech in September is quoted in Leibiger, "Georgia and the Compromise of 1850," p. 28.

48. Shryock, *Georgia and the Union,* pp. 334–45; Charles Jenkins to John M. Berrien, February 5, 1851, Francis S. Bartow to Berrien, February 28, 1851, Iverson L. Harris to Berrien, March 12, 1851, C. Doughtery to Berrien, March 31, 1851, Berrien MSS.

49. Francis S. Bartow to John M. Berrien, December 16, 1850, Charles Jenkins to Berrien, December 19, 1850, Berrien MSS; my summary of, and quotations from, the Georgia platform are based on Shryock, *Georgia and the Union,* pp. 330–32.

50. Shryock, *Georgia and the Union,* pp. 330–32; Francis S. Bartow to Berrien, December 16, 1850, Charles Jenkins to Berrien, December 19, 1850, February 5, March 21, 1851, Iverson L. Harris to Berrien, March 12, 1851, C. Dougherty to Berrien, March 31, 1851, Berrien MSS.

51. C. Dougherty to Berrien, March 31, 1851, Berrien MSS.

52. Cobb defeated McDonald by a margin of 57,414 to 38,824. In contrast, Towns had defeated his Whig rival in 1849, 46,643 to 43,349, while Unionists won in 1850, 46,616 to 24,499. These figures suggest that the 19,000 1849 voters, who abstained in 1850 returned to the polls in 1851 along with 6,000 new voters and that these 25,000 divided 11,000 for Cobb and 14,000 for McDonald. One of my former undergraduate students ran an ecological regression analysis to estimate voter movement between 1849 and 1851. Because he did not weight his county voting data by population, I do not have total faith in his results, but they are plausible. They suggest that of 1849 Whig voters, 82 percent voted for Cobb, 12 percent supported McDonald, and 6 percent abstained. Approximately one-third of 1849 Democrats supported Cobb, while two-thirds went for McDonald; those who abstained in 1849 but voted in 1851 divided evenly between the Union and Southern Rights parties. Bobo, "Revelry, Reorganization, and Ruin," p. 19.

53. Shryock, *Georgia and the Union,* pp. 354–58; Schott, *Stephens,* p. 139; Charles J. Jenkins

to John M. Berrien, July 23, 1851, C. Doughtery to Berrien, August 24, 1851, Iverson L. Harris to Berrien, September 28, 1851, Francis S. Bartow to Berrien, November 5, 1851, Berrien MSS.

54. Cole, *Whig Party in the South*, pp. 148–49, 169–71, 186.

55. Miller, "A New Perspective," pp. 86–90; Cole, *Whig Party in the South*, pp. 185–87; May, *Quitman*, pp. 247–48.

56. P. B. Barringer to Daniel M. Barringer, November 18, 1850 (quotation), Barringer MSS; A. Hutchinson to Charles D. Fontaine, April 5, 1851, Fontaine MSS; the books by Cole and May, as well as the thesis by Miller cited above, all document this pattern.

57. Even ardent supporters of Quitman recognized that his reputation as an immediate secessionist would doom the Southern Rights cause. See George T. Swann to John A. Quitman, July 18, 1851, and Frederick W. Quackenboss to Quitman, July 23, 1851, Claiborne MSS.

58. Miller, "A New Perspective," p. 227, n. 21; May, *Quitman*, pp. 248, 254–64. The resolution adopted by the Mississippi convention is quoted on p. 264. In 1849, Quitman defeated his Whig rival, 33,117 to 22,996; in 1850, Foote nosed out Davis, 27,836 to 26,301. These figures suggest that about 5,000 Democrats supported Union delegates in the convention election, while about 6,500 abstained in September. Some 5,000 of those abstainers returned to support Davis in November, but Foote held almost all of the 28,277 votes Union convention delegates had attracted.

59. Thornton, *Politics and Power*, pp. 180–96, 468–69. In December 1849 Clemens was elected with sixty-seven votes in the legislature, fifty of which came from Whigs, over the choice of the Democratic caucus.

60. Ibid., pp. 182–202.

61. Henry W. Hilliard to Nathaniel Niles, August 13, 1851, Niles MSS.

62. Stephens to Crittenden, October 24, 1850, Stephens MSS (Duke); Shryock, *Georgia and the Union*, pp. 313–15.

63. *Messages and Papers of the Presidents*, V, p. 93.

64. Fillmore to Washington Hunt, February 23, 1851, with Henry E. Davies to Fillmore, March 17, 1851, MFP-BHS; Seward to Thurlow Weed, December 4, 1850, Weed MSS (RU).

65. George Frazier to Millard Fillmore, December 16, 1850, MFP-BHS; Adams, *Whig Party of Louisiana*, pp. 206–07; John P. Kennedy to Elizabeth Kennedy, Decmeber 9, 10, 1850, Kennedy MSS; Charles Ready to John Bell, January 3, 1851, Thomas A. R. Nelson to Bell, January 10, 1851, John Bell MSS.

66. Joshua R. Giddings to Edward Wade, December 28, 1850, Giddings-Julian MSS; Giddings to Milton R. Sutliffe, December 30, 1850, Sutliffe MSS.

67. Hiram Ketcham to Fillmore, December 13, 1850, Jerome Fuller to Fillmore, December 15, 1850, January 4, 1851, MFP-BHS.

68. Fish to Fillmore, November 18, 1850, MFP-BHS; Hamilton Fish to Alvah Hunt, November 4, 1850, Knollenberg Collection; A. W. Bradford to Hamilton Fish, November 9, 1850, Fish MSS; Moses Grinnell to Thomas Corwin, October 30, 1850, Thurlow Weed to Corwin, November 17, 1850, Simeon Draper to Corwin, November 26, 1850, Samuel Lyman to Corwin, December 7, 1850, Corwin MSS (LC); Moses Grinnell to John J. Crittenden, November 18, 1850, Crittenden MSS (LC).

69. Jerome Fuller to Fillmore, December 15, 1850, January 4, 1851, Solomon G. Haven to Fillmore, January 1, 1851, MFP-BHS.

70. Washington Hunt to Fillmore, November 16, 1850, Hamilton Fish to Fillmore, November 18, 1850, MFP-BHS. All quotations in the following four paragraphs are from these two letters, unless noted otherwise.

71. *Messages and Papers of the Presidents*, V, pp. 83–91.

72. Samuel P. Lyman to Simeon Draper, January 20, 1850, Weed MSS (RU). A draft note in John M. Berrien's papers declining to sign the Round Robin is labeled, "Answer to Mr. Stephens." From this fact as well as the fact that Stephens was always listed by contemporaries as one of the people circulating the pledge, I have concluded that Stephens wrote the Round Robin. See, for example, E. G. Spaulding to Weed, January 20, 1851, Weed MSS (RU).

A copy of the Round Robin was printed at the bottom of the second page of the Democratic Washington *Union* on January 22, 1851. Editor Thomas Ritchie did not endorse it, but instead said he printed it to satisfy the curiosity of his readers. A list of those who signed the Round Robin, taken from the New York *Express*, can be found in the *Union*, January 30, 1851.

73. John Bell to William B. Campbell, January 25, 1851, CFP; Charles Ready to John Bell, January 3, 1851, Thomas A. R. Nelson to Bell, January 10, 1851, John Bell MSS; "Answer to Mr. Stephens," January 24, 1851, draft, Berrien MSS.

74. Eliot made his opposition to a Union party clear later. See Eliot to John O. Sargent, November 10, 1851, Sargent MSS.

75. Calling Underwood pro-Compromise may be questionable, for he had often voted against Clay's position on roll calls during the session and opposed the final Texas boundary bill. Yet he voted for all the other Compromise measures, including the pronorthern California and District slave trade bills. Similarly, while Delaware's Whigs opposed compromise as long as Taylor was alive, all three voted for the final measures. The absence of Berrien, who declined Stephens' request to sign, and of the anti-Compromise Whigs Senator Jackson Morton of Florida and Representative Thomas Clingman of North Carolina is more understandable.

76. Bullard had been elected to fill Charles Conrad's seat when Conrad became Secretary of War.

77. Johannsen, *Douglas*, p. 340.

78. Charles Ready to John Bell, January 3, 1851, Thomas A. R. Nelson to Bell, January 10, 1851, John Bell MSS; Henry Barns to Fillmore, February 10, 1850, MFP-BHS; C. Prentiss to Thomas Ewing, February 8, 1851, R. P. S. Baker to Ewing, February 10, 1851, EFP.

79. Jerome Fuller to Fillmore, January 4, 1851, MFP-BHS.

80. Democratic Representative Thomas Bocock, for whatever reason, missed all the votes on the Compromise measures recorded in Hamilton's *Prologue to Conflict*. The other twelve Democrats split 6–6.

81. Cole, *Whig Party in the South*, pp. 191–92.

82. For Whig optimism about the constitution and its impact on their electoral fortunes, see John C. Rutherford to William C. Rives, March 25, 1851, William M. Burwell to Rives, April 1851, Rives MSS; S. R. Mumford to Fillmore, March 25, 1851, MFP-BHS; David Campbell to William B. Campbell, May 19, July 25, 1851, CFP; John Minor Botts to Alexander H. H. Stuart, November 30, 1851, Stuart MSS (University of Virginia).

With good reason, the Virginia constitutional convention of 1850–51 has normally been interpreted in terms of the sectional tension between east (Tidewater and Piedmont) and west (Shenandoah Valley and Trans-Allegheny). Certainly the most crucial issue, reapportionment of the legislature, pitted one region against the other. Yet curiously, historians have overlooked the partisan dimension of many of the votes; Whig and Democratic majorities often voted the same way, but Whigs were usually far more cohesive than the sharply divided Democrats. On the vote on final adoption of the constitution, for example, Whigs divided 32–7 in favor, while Democrats split 43–32. Similarly, while Democrats voted more solidly than Whigs to strike a restriction prohibiting subsidization of internal improvements altogether, on other measures—for example, defeats of efforts to bar loans to railroad corporations or to prohibit bond issues unless taxes to pay them were also imposed—Whigs provided far more support for internal improvements than Democrats. This analysis of votes at the convention relies on White, "Virginia Constitutional Convention," pp. 18, 24.

83. White, "Virginia Constitutional Convention," p. 24. The old suffrage requirements applied during the congressional elections. Nonetheless, turnout was exceedingly low. In only one of the nine contested districts did it surpass 8,000 votes, and in most it was less than 5,000.

84. The account in this and subsequent paragraphs is based on Evitts, *Matter of Allegiances*, pp. 13–42; Bowers, "Ideology"; and Green, "Whig Party in Maryland." Green's analysis of roll-call votes in the Maryland legislature shows that in 1848, on five roll calls concerning the question of calling a constitutional convention, an average of 88 percent of the Whigs opposed while Democrats unanimously favored the call. Similarly, on sixteen roll calls in the 1850 session, an average of 85 percent of the Whigs opposed and 96 percent of the Democrats favored the convention call. In the subsequent referendum deciding whether to call the convention in May 1850, as well as the June 1851 ratifying referendum, opposition was concentrated in traditionally Whiggish counties in southern Maryland and on the Eastern Shore.

85. The growing populistic rebellion against the regular parties and the politicians who led them as corrupt, selfish wire pullers was hardly confined to Maryland. It also helped fuel movements to revise and ratify constitutions in Ohio, Indiana, and Kentucky. For evidence of this boiling antiparty sentiment in Maryland, see the sources listed in the previous note. For the nationwide phenomenon, see my *Political Crisis*, pp. 130–38 and passim; and "Politics of Impatience."

86. John P. Kennedy to Robert C. Winthrop, November 15, 1851, letterbook copy, Kennedy MSS.

87. Alexander C. Bullitt to John O. Sargent, March 6, 1851, Sargent MSS; Solomon Downs to John F. H. Claiborne, September 24, October 8, 1851, Claiborne MSS; Adams, *Whig Party of Louisiana*, pp. 198–213. The third Democrat in Lousiana's House delegation during 1850, John Harmanson, missed all the votes on the Compromise because he was fatally ill, and he died in November. The only Democratic incumbent who ran again in 1851 was Isaac Morse of the fourth district.

88. Adams, *Whig Party of Louisiana*, pp. 211–12, 215–16.

89. Ibid., pp. 215–19, 251. On p. 211, Adams says that the 1851 legislative elections resulted in a Whig majority in the house of 53–44 and an even 16–16 split in the senate. The figures compiled by Walter Dean Burnham for the Inter-University Corsortium at Michigan indicate even larger Whig gains: a 56–41 Whig majority in the house and 17–15 majority in the senate.

90. Kruman, *Parties and Politics*, pp. 125–133; James W. Osborne to William A. Graham, June 13, 1851, August 21, 1851 (quotation), John Kerr to Graham, August 6, 1851, in *Graham Papers*, IV, pp. 120–21, 182–83, 191; Edward Stanly to Millard Fillmore, June 16, 1851, MFP-BHS.

91. James W. Bryan to William A. Graham, July 7, 1851, John Kerr to Graham, August 6, 1851, James Graham to William A. Graham, August 17, 1851, in *Graham Papers*, IV, pp. 142–43, 182–83, 187.

92. Kruman, *Parties and Politics*, pp. 132–33; Rufus Barringer to Daniel M. Barringer, September 7, 1851, Barringer MSS.

93. Rufus Barringer to Daniel M. Barringer, September 7, 1851, Barringer MSS; James W. Osborne to William A. Graham, June 13, 1851, in *Graham Papers*, IV, pp. 120–21.

94. William B. Campbell to David Campbell, April 14, 1851, CFP.

95. Felix Zollicoffer to William B. Campbell, March 22, 1851, Hugh Preston to Campbell, May 1, 1851, CFP. I have used the following secondary accounts for the Tennessee election: Bergeron, *Antebellum Politics in Tennessee*, pp. 119–22; Walton, "A Matter of Timing," 129–48; Walton, "Second Party System in Tennessee"; and Atkins, " 'Combat for Liberty,' " pp. 380–437. I am deeply indebted to Professor Atkins for sending me a copy of his valuable dissertation. The Democrats' 1849 platform, which vowed resistance to the Wilmot Proviso "to the last extremity," is quoted on p. 380.

96. William B. Campbell to David Campbell, February 9, 1851, Felix Zollicoffer to William B. Campbell, February 9, 1851, CFP. On patronage disputes, see also Parks, *Bell*, pp. 233–39, 263–67.

The terms of United States senators ended on March 3 of odd-numbered years; Bell's, for example, was due to expire on March 3, 1853. Tennessee's legislature met in October of odd years after the August elections; therefore, while it could elect a senator for the new Congress that began in December of that year, it elected "late" since the new senatorial term officially began on March 4, after the old one expired. Since the new Senate always met in special session during the March following presidential elections to confirm the cabinet and other appointees of the new president, Whigs had an excuse to replace Bell in the 1851 legislative session. Both Meredith Gentry and gubernatorial nominee William B. Campbell wrote letters saying that both Senate seats were at stake in the 1851 legislative elections. Meredith P. Gentry to William B. Campbell, March 9, 1851, William B. Campbell to David Campbell, April 14, 1851, CFP. On the date of senatorial elections, see Walton, "A Matter of Timing."

97. John Bell to William B. Campbell, January 25, 1851, Felix Zollicoffer to Campbell, February 3, 1851 (quotation), February 9, 1851, A. M. Savney to Campbell, February 18, 1851 (quotation), Meredith Gentry to Campbell, March 9, 1851, CFP.

98. William B. Campbell to David Campbell, February 9, April 14, September 2, 1851, Felix Zollicoffer to Campbell, February 9, 1851, B. H. Shepperd to Campbell, June 6, 1851, Alex Williams to Campbell, June 17, 1851, Thomas A. R. Nelson to Campbell, July 9, 1851, E. Alexander to Campbell, July 15, 1851, William G. Brownlow to Campbell, July 16, 1851, Rolfe S. Sanders to Campbell, August 10, 1851 (quotation), CFP; Bergeron, *Antebellum Politics in Tennessee*, pp. 119–22; Atkins, " 'A Combat for Liberty,' " pp. 422–31.

99. Whigs in Democrat Isham G. Harris's district charged that he had voted against both the California and Texas-New Mexico bills and therefore should be opposed as an anti-Compromise man, but however radical Harris' speeches may have been, he voted for Texas-New Mexico. H. V. Cummins to Gustavus A. Henry, March 15, 1851, Henry MSS.

100. The Congressional Quarterly's *Guide to U.S. Elections* incorrectly lists William H. Polk, who defeated incumbent Democrat James H. Thomas, as a Whig. Polk was instead a unionist Democrat. Because Democrats ran two candidates in two districts where Whigs had no challenger and the Whigs' vote was artificially low in Gentry's district, where he had no opponent, the Democrats far outpolled Whigs in the total congressional vote for the state, 54,158 to 47,957.

101. E. Alexander to William B. Campbell, September 18, 1851, David H. R. Campbell to David Campbell, November 20, 1851, William B. Campbell to David Campbell, November 30, 1851, CFP; Gustavus A. Henry to Marion Henry, November 14, 21, 1851, Henry MSS; Bergeron, *Antebellum Politics in Tennessee*, pp. 111–12.

102. Gustavus A. Henry to Marion Henry, November 21, 1851, Henry MSS; David H. R. Campbell to David Campbell, November 20, 1851, William B. Campbell to David Campbell, November 30, 1851, February 15, 1852 (quotation), CFP. In accordance with the reassignment of House seats after the Census of 1850, Tennessee's delegation was reduced from eleven to ten.

103. William B. Campbell to David Campbell, August 9, 1851, quoted in Atkins, " 'A Combat for Liberty,' " p. 429.

104. Since 1835 Whigs had won sixty-four of the ninety-two elections for the national House of Representatives in Kentucky or 69.5 percent. Only in 1843 had Whigs and Democrats evenly divided the delegation, five to five; Whigs won seven of ten seats in 1845 and six of ten in both 1847 and 1849.

105. The Congressional Quarterly's *Guide to U.S. Elections* lists the returns as Powell, 54,821, and Dixon, 54,023. Yet the closest study of Kentucky, on which I have depended, gives the results as 54,613 to 53,763. Even by the *Guide*'s more generous estimate of Dixon's vote, he ran 10,959 votes behind Crittenden's total in 1848, a drop of almost 17 percent. Cassius M. Clay ran as an independent Emancipationist candidate and attracted 3,621 votes, almost all of which apparently came from Whigs and previous nonvoters. See Volz, "Party, State, and Nation," pp. 96–97.

In the statewide totals for congressmen, Whigs narrowly outpolled Democrats, 50,842 to 50,355. Democrats, in sum, converted the former Whig stronghold into a closely competitive state.

106. Volz, "Party, State, and Nation," pp. 87–102.

107. Ibid., pp. 98–99.

108. J. Speed Smith to John J. Crittenden, January 28, 1851, Crittenden MSS; Volz, "Party, State, and Nation," pp. 99–100; Volz's regression estimates, p. 97, suggest that Dixon retained only about 70% of the Whigs who voted for Crittenden in 1848. A few bolted to the Democratic column, about 7 percent voted for Clay, and almost one-fifth simply abstained.

109. Volz, "Party, State, and Nation," pp. 106–08.

110. Ibid., pp. 108–13.

CHAPTER 18

1. Daniel Webster to Millard Fillmore, October 12, 1851, Webster MSS. For their agreement on strict enforcement of the neutrality laws, see Fillmore to Webster, April 16, 1851, Millard Fillmore MSS (LC); Webster to William S. Derrick, acting secretary of state, April 25, 1851, Webster to Fillmore, April 25, 1851, Webster MSS.

2. See, for example, Webster to Peter Harvey, May 4, 1851, and to David Henshaw, June 11, 1851, Webster MSS.

3. For evidence of these calculations, see Webster to Edward Curtis, May 1851, Webster to Peter Harvey, May 4, 1851, Webster to Franklin Haven, June 11, 1851, Webster MSS.

4. Winthrop to Everett, December 31, 1850, Everett MSS; Truman Smith to John Wilson, August 16, 1851, Wilson MSS.

5. Rayback, *Fillmore*, pp. 333–37; Fillmore to the Whig National Convention, June 10, 1852, draft, MFP-O.

6. Whigs held majorities of forty-two to twenty-five in the house and nineteen to ten in the senate.

7. W. G. Gibbs to Daniel Webster, April 4, 1851, Webster MSS; Thomas Dorr to Edmund Burke, April 9, 1851, Burke MSS. The *Biographical Directory of Congress* identifies James as a protariff Democrat. It is impossible to tell from the letters cited above whether the Whigs who voted for James were Websterites, but Gibbs blamed Whigs' refusal to accept Whipple for the result.

8. Ibid.

9. The Whig vote for Jackson dropped by 700 votes (24 percent) from that won by Dixon two years earlier, while King's raw vote was larger in 1851 than in 1849. His margin narrowed because of a dramatic increase in turnout by the rejuvenated Democrats.

10. Emily Baldwin to Roger Sherman Baldwin, Jr, November 10, 1850, Emily Baldwin to Roger Sherman Baldwin, December 10, 1850, E. A. Andrews to R. S. Baldwin, July 29, 1850, James F. Babcock to Baldwin, December 14, 1850, BFP.

11. James F. Babcock to Roger Sherman Baldwin, February 6, 24, 1851, Roger Sherman Baldwin to Emily Baldwin, February 26, 1851, BFP; Colin M. Ingersoll to Thomas Seymour, February 28, 1851, Thomas Seymour MSS; Renda, "The Polity and the Party System," pp. 177–79.

12. Seymour's vote increased from 29,022 (48.3 percent) in 1850 to 30,077 (49 percent) in 1851; Foster got 28,209 (46.9 percent) in 1850 and 28,756 (46.9 percent) in 1851.

13. I have found no letter that demonstrates beyond cavil that Webster was behind the Whig opposition to Baldwin, but such a letter might exist in some manuscript collection that I did not examine.

14. T. C. Perkins to Roger Sherman Baldwin, June 19, 20, 1851, F. Parsons to Baldwin, July 3, 1851, Roger Sherman Baldwin to Robert C. Winthrop, July 7, 1851, copy, (quotation), BFP; J. D. Baldwin to John M. Niles, September 19, 1851, copy, Welles MSS (LC). Regional jealousies that had long complicated Connecticut's politics also contributed to Baldwin's defeat, for when Baldwin stalled, Lafayette Foster, the defeated gubernatorial candidate from eastern Norwich, tried to marshal support for the Senate seat on the grounds that since Truman Smith had previously taken the East's seat, he deserved Baldwin's. Foster failed because Free Soilers in the house refused to allow any Whig but Baldwin to have the office. See the letter of J. D. Baldwin, who blamed the defeat on "hunker Whigs," to Niles.

15. Webster to Fillmore, November 15, 1850, MFP-BHS; Webster to Peter Harvey, May 4, 1851, Webster MSS; Renda, "The Polity and the Party System," p. 192.

16. Renda, "The Polity and the Party System," pp. 190–91.

17. Ibid., pp. 191, 214. Dinsmoor's percentage dropped from 55 in 1850 to 47 in 1851. Whigs gained nineteen seats in the house and one in the senate, but because Free Soilers opposed Democrats in a number of house districts and prevented anyone from attaining the necessary majority, Democratic losses in the house totaled fifty-two, far more than the Whig gains. Even so, Democrats retained healthy margins of thirty-four in the house and eight in the senate, ensuring Dinsmoor's reelection as governor.

18. Boston *Daily Advertiser*, October 3, 1850; Donald, *Sumner*, pp. 183–204. I have relied heavily on Donald's splendid narrative of the election for my account. Walter Dean Burnham's data on file with the Inter-University Consortium for Political and Social Research suggest that the Coalition's majority was forty-three seats in the house and fourteen in the senate. Sweeney, "Rum, Romanism, Representation, and Reform," 121, gives the majority as forty-eight seats in the house and ten in the senate. Both Burnham and Sweeney list figures only for the Coalition as a whole and do not break it down by Free Soil and Democratic members. Donald, p. 189,

however, states that Free Soilers and Democrats caucused separately and that eighty-five men attended the Free Soil caucus. He does not make it clear whether that caucus included both senators and representatives or only the latter, but either way, Democrats outnumbered Free Soilers by almost two-to-one.

19. Donald, *Sumner*, pp. 182–95.

20. I. W. Beard to Caleb Cushing, November 16, 1850, P. W. Leland to Cushing, January 9, 1851 (quotations), B. H. Cheever to Cushing, November 18, 1850, Thomas J. Whittlemore to Cushing, November 29, 1850, John T. Heard to Cushing, November 29, 1850, H. C. Merriam to Cushing, January 25, 1851, Cushing MSS.

21. James Morss to Cushing, June 27, 1850, J. S. Colley to Cushing, November 11, 1850, Cushing MSS; Donald, *Sumner*, pp. 192–93. For evidence of the continuing close relationship between Webster and Cushing, see Fletcher Webster to Cushing, October 14, 1850, Cushing MSS.

22. Donald, *Sumner*, p. 198; Ezra Lincoln to Amos A. Lawrence, February 10, March 7, April 24, 1851, Amos Lawrence MSS.

23. H. A. Wise to Edward Everett, February 6, 1851, "Charlie" Wise to Everett, February 9, 1851, Everett MSS.

24. B. H. Cheever to Caleb Cushing, November 18, 1850, Cushing MSS; Daniel Webster to T. B. Curtis, January 20, 22, 1851, David Henshaw to Webster, April 21, 1851, Webster MSS; Donald, *Sumner*, p. 191; Dalzell, *Webster*, p. 228.

25. Charles Upham to Henry L. Dawes, November 20, 1850, Dawes MSS; Moses Stuart to Webster, April 18, 1851, Webster MSS.

26. Donald, *Sumner*, p. 191, asserts that "about 165" Whigs consistently voted for Winthrop. Since Burnham and Sweeney put Whig strength in the house between 171 and 174 votes, Donald's figure suggests that a few Whigs, undoubtedly Websterites, scattered their votes, although it is possible that the deficit simply reflects the absence of some Whig legislators.

27. Ibid., pp. 200–02.

28. Sweeney, "Rum, Romanism, Representation, and Reform," 124–25; for Whig disgust with, and confidence that they could successfully run against, the record of the Coalition in the legislature, see Moses Stuart to Webster, April 18, 1851, Webster MSS; James M. Barnard to Mark Howard, June 4, 1851, Howard MSS; George T. Davis to Henry L. Dawes, July 11, 1851, Dawes MSS.

29. Samuel Hooper to William Schouler, April 12, 1851, Schouler MSS; Dalzell, *Webster*, pp. 228–31.

30. While the senatorial election in the legislature was moving toward its climax in April, it should be recalled, Webster was in Boston to oversee the prosecution of Shadrack's rescuers and the extradition of Thomas Sims. Thus, when Webster sought to speak at Faneuil Hall that month, excitement over the fugitive law was at fever pitch.

31. David Henshaw to Webster, April 21, 1851, Fletcher Webster to Daniel Webster, May 2, 1851, Daniel Webster to Fillmore, April 18, 1851, to Franklin Haven, May 9, 1851 (quotation), to Fletcher Webster, May 9, 1851, to Peter Harvey, May 4, June 3, 1851, and to David Henshaw, June 11, 1851, (quotation), Webster MSS; Dalzell, *Webster*, pp. 228–31.

32. Robert C. Winthrop to Edward Everett, July 9, 29, August 6, 1851, Everett MSS; Winthrop to Roger Sherman Baldwin, July 11, 1851, BFP; Winthrop to John Clifford, August 11, 1851, Winthrop MSS; Winthrop to John Davis, September 2, 1851, John Davis MSS; Webster to Peter Harvey, May 4, 1851, Webster MSS; Dalzell, *Webster*, pp. 231–34.

33. Daniel Webster to Edward Curtis, May 1851 (quotation), Webster to Peter Harvey, May 4, 1851 (quotation), Webster to Franklin Haven, June 11, 1851, Webster MSS.

34. Winthrop to John H. Clifford, August 11, 1851 (quotation), Winthrop MSS; Edward Everett to Webster, September 2, 1851, Webster to Everett, September 3, 1851 (quotation), Webster MSS; Aaron Hobart to Caleb Cushing, May 30, 1851, John F. Heard to Cushing, June 4, 1851, Cushing MSS; Dalzell, *Webster*, pp. 232–33.

35. Dalzell, *Webster*, pp. 233–34; Sweeney, "Rum, Romanism, Representation, and Reform," 126–29, especially Table VI. After the 1851 elections, Coalition majorities were reduced from

ten to six seats in the senate and from forty-eight to ten seats in the house. Issues such as constitutional revision, prohibition, and anti-Catholicism also impinged on the 1851 Massachusetts election, and I will examine it again later in a different context.

36. Hunkers wanted to return their leader, Daniel S. Dickinson, to the Senate, while Barnburners wanted to replace him with John Van Buren. Hence members of the rival factions refused to vote for the other's legislative candidates and allowed Whigs to win a majority of seats. Hamilton Fish to Daniel D. Barnard, January 23, 1851, Barnard MSS.

37. Lyman A. Spalding to Thurlow Weed, November 18, 1850, Weed MSS (RU); Thurlow Weed to William H. Seward, January 8, 19, 1851, Christopher Morgan to Seward, January 9, 1851, Seward MSS (RU); Joseph B. Varnum, Jr., to Fillmore, November 22, 1850, Solomon G. Haven to Fillmore, December 21, 1850, January 1, 1851, Jerome Fuller to Fillmore, January 4, 1851, MFP-BHS; Thurlow Weed to Samuel P. Lyman, December 5, 1850, copy, Corwin MSS (LC); Horace Greeley to Schuyler Colfax, December 26, 1850, Greeley-Colfax MSS.

Free Soilers had no representation in the state senate; they held two seats in the house compared to the Democrats' forty-four and the Whigs' eighty-two.

38. Millard Fillmore to Hamilton Fish, November 21, 1850, Fish MSS; John C. Clark to Thurlow Weed, December 2, 1850, Seward to Weed, December 4, 1850, John L. Schoolcraft to Weed, December 5, 1850, Weed MSS (RU); Weed to Seward, November 25, 1850, Schuyler Colfax to Seward, December 20, 1850, John L. Schoolcraft to Seward, December 25, 1850, Harry P. Whitbeck to Seward, January 20, 1851, Seward MSS (RU); Samuel P. Lyman to Fillmore, December 8, 1850, Hugh Maxwell to Fillmore, December 25, 1850, MFP-BHS.

39. Weed to Corwin, November 17, 1850, February 2, 1851, Samuel P. Lyman to Corwin, January 2, 1851, Corwin MSS (LC); Moses Grinnell to John J. Crittenden, November 18, 1850, Crittenden MSS (LC); Samuel P. Lyman to Weed, December 4, 7, 1850, January 2, 3, 4, 1851, John L. Schoolcraft to Weed, December 5, 1850, February 1, 1851, Orsamus B. Matteson to Weed, December 12, 1850, January 23, 1851, William A. Sackett to Weed, January 20, 1851, Elbridge G. Spaulding to Weed, January 20, 21, 29, 1851, Weed MSS (RU).

40. Jerome Fuller to Millard Fillmore, December 7, 15, 1850, January 4, 1851, Hiram Ketchum to Fillmore, December 13, 1850, Solomon G. Haven to Fillmore, December 18, 1850, Daniel Ullmann to Fillmore, December 23, 1850, Hugh Maxwell to Fillmore, December 25, 1850, Alex Mann to Fillmore, January 27, 1851, MFP-BHS.

41. Samuel P. Lyman to Thurlow Weed, January 8, 13, 1851, Weed MSS (RU); Weed to Thomas Corwin, February 2, 1851, Corwin MSS; Samuel P. Lyman to Henry Raymond, January 24, 1851, Raymond MSS; Washington Hunt to Hamilton Fish, February 4, 1851, Fish MSS; Millard Fillmore to Jerome Fuller, February 3, 1851, copy, Fillmore to Washington Hunt, February 23, 1851, copy, Joseph B. Varnum, Jr., to Fillmore, November 22, 1850, Hugh Maxwell to Fillmore, January 13, 1851, Samuel P. Lyman to Fillmore, February 3, 5, 9, 1851, Jerome Fuller to Fillmore, February 7, March 22, 1851, Thomas Foote to Fillmore, February 7, 1851, MFP-BHS.

42. Varnum to Fillmore, November 22, 1850, MFP-BHS.

43. Fillmore to Fish, November 21, 1850, Fish MSS; James Edwards to Fillmore, January 1, 1851 (Fillmore's notation on back), MFP-BHS.

44. Solomon G. Haven to Fillmore, December 18, 1850, Joseph Varnum, Jr., to Hamilton Fish, November 22, 1850, Robert G. Campbell to Fillmore, November 27, 1850, John T. Bush to Fillmore, January 6, 1851, Fillmore to Jerome Fuller, February 23, 1851, copy, MFP-BHS.

45. Joseph B. Varnum, Jr., to Millard Fillmore, January 13, 26, February 9, 1851, Jerome Fuller to Fillmore, March 22, 1851, Samuel P. Lyman to Fillmore, February 3, 4, 5, 9, 1851, MFP-BHS; Alexander Graham to William H. Seward, February 7, 1851, Thomas C. Chittenden to Seward, February 12, 1851, Seward MSS (RU); Hamilton Fish to Daniel D. Barnard, January 23, 1851, Barnard MSS; E. G. Spaulding to Thurlow Weed, January 29, 1851, Weed MSS (RU); Thurlow Weed to Thomas Corwin, February 2, 1851, Corwin MSS (LC).

46. Jerome Fuller to Fillmore, December 15, 1850, January 4, 1851, MFP-BHS.

47. Washington Hunt to Fillmore, November 16, 30, 1850, February 10, 1851, Hamilton Fish to Fillmore, November 18, 27, 1850, Hiram Ketchum to Fillmore, December 13, 1850, Solomon G. Haven to Fillmore, January 1, 1851, Fillmore to Washington Hunt, February 23, 1851, copy,

MFP-BHS; Morton McMichael to Simeon Draper, December 26, 1850, Simeon Draper to Thurlow Weed, December 30, 1850, Weed MSS (RU); Weed to Seward, January 8, 1851, Seward MSS (RU).

48. Jerome Fuller to Fillmore, January 4, 1851, John T. Bush to Fillmore, January 6, 1851, Fillmore to Hunt, February 23, 1851, copy, MFP-BHS; Christopher Morgan to William H. Seward, January 9, 1851, Seward MSS (RU).

49. Joseph B. Varnum, Jr., to Fillmore, November 22, 1850, Robert G. Campbell to Fillmore, November 26, 1850, John T. Bush to Fillmore, January 6, 1851, MFP-BHS.

50. In addition to the letters cited in the preceding note, see Solomon G. Haven to Fillmore, December 18, 1850, and Joseph B. Varnum, Jr., to Fillmore, January 13, 1851, MFP-BHS.

51. John Bush to Fillmore, January 6, 1851, Joseph B. Varnum, Jr., to Fillmore, January 13, 15, 1851, MFP-BHS.

52. Here the distinction between pro-Compromise resolutions that stressed the merits and fairness of the individual measures and acquiescence in the Compromise's finality, which said nothing about the merits of the legislation, must again be stressed. The former praised the substance of the Compromise; the latter simply recognized it as the law of the land without implying approval. Webster would undoubtedly have preferred the former, but given Fillmore's rage at Fuller's demand for positive approval as the price of support for Fish, he dared not go beyond insisting upon acquiescence in finality.

53. Thurlow Weed to Thomas Corwin, February 2, 1851, Corwin MSS (LC); E. G. Spaulding to Weed, January 29, 1851, Weed MSS (RU); Daniel Webster to Hiram Ketchum, February 1, 1851, Webster MSS; Washington Hunt to Hamilton Fish, February 4, 1851, Fish MSS; Joseph B. Varnum, Jr., to Fillmore, January 13, 15, 26, February 9, 1851, Nathan Hall to Fillmore, January 13 and January, 1851, Jerome Fuller to Fillmore, February 7, 1851, Samuel P. Lyman to Fillmore, February 5, 9, 1851, Fillmore to Jerome Fuller, February 23, 1851, copy, Fillmore to Washington Hunt, February 23, 1851, copy, MFP-BHS.

54. Legislative elections of United States senators required an absolute majority, rather than a plurality, of those voting in each chamber. Thus, in the house, the twenty-three Silver Gray votes, if scattered among different Whigs like Francis Granger or William Duer, combined with the votes of forty-four Democrats for their candidate and the two Free Soilers, could prevent the fifty-nine Sewardites from achieving a majority. In the senate, where Whigs outnumbered Democrats only seventeen to fifteen, the three Silver Grays also held the balance of power.

55. In addition to the letters cited in note 53, see Samuel P. Lyman to Fillmore, February 4, 1851, and F. S. Faxton to Fillmore, February 7, 1851, MFP-BHS.

56. Varnum to Fillmore, February 1, 1851, John T. Bush to Fillmore, February 3, 1851, Samuel P. Lyman to Fillmore, February 4, 1851, F. S. Faxton to Fillmore, February 7, 1851, Jerome Fuller to Fillmore, February 7, 1851, Fillmore to Washington Hunt, February 23, 1851, copy, MFP-BHS; Hamilton Fish to Thurlow Weed, February 1, 1851, Weed MSS (RU).

57. Washington Hunt to Hamilton Fish, February 4, 1851, Fish MSS; Samuel P. Lyman to Fillmore, February 1851 (misdated January), Jerome Fuller to Fillmore, January 7, 1851, Joseph B. Varnum, Jr., to Fillmore, February 9, 1851, Hugh Maxwell to Fillmore, February 18, 1851, MFP-BHS; Hamilton Fish to Henry Clay, February 18, 1851, Henry Clay MSS (LC); Fish to Weed, February 20, 1851, Weed MSS (RU).

58. Samuel P. Lyman to Thurlow Weed, February 23, 1851, Weed MSS (RU); Lyman to Fillmore, February 5, 9, 1851, Jerome Fuller to Fillmore, February 7, 1851, Hiram Ketchum to Fillmore, February 10, 1851, Fillmore to Jerome Fuller, February 23, 1851, copy, Fillmore to Washington Hunt, February 23, 1851, copy, MFP-BHS; Henry J. Raymond to William H. Seward, February 6, 1851, Seward MSS (RU).

59. Rayback, *Fillmore*, p. 285; John T. Bush to Fillmore, March 4, 1851, Jerome Fuller to Fillmore, March 19, 1851, MFP-BHS.

60. Fillmore to Washington Hunt, February 23, 1851, copy, Francis Granger to Fillmore, February 20, 1851, John T. Bush to Fillmore, March 4, 1851, A. K. Hadley to Fillmore, March 4, 1851, John C. Spencer to Fillmore, March 5, 1851, James R. Thompson to Fillmore, March 11, 1851, Nathan K. Hall to Fillmore, March 14, 1851, George R. Babcock to Fillmore, March 17, 1851, Jerome Fuller to Fillmore, March 19, 26, 1851, MFP-BHS.

61. William Duer to Fillmore, March 27, 1850, MFP-BHS.

62. John A. Collier to Fillmore, October 4, 9, 1850, John C. Spencer to Fillmore, December 6, 1850, MFP-BHS. Spencer's letter relates the story of Collier's exposing himself to women; Spencer also asked Fillmore to consider what his wife would think of Collier.

63. David A. Bokee to Fillmore, May 5, 1851, Jerome Fuller to Fillmore, May 8, 1851, Nathan Hall to Fillmore, May 23, 1851, Hamilton Fish to Fillmore, June 4, 1851, Thomas Foote to Fillmore, June 8, 1851, William L. Hodge to Fillmore, July 7, 1851, MFP-BHS.

64. Robert G. Campbell to Fillmore, April 9, 1851, Daniel Webster to Fillmore, April 15, 1851, MFP-BHS; Fillmore to Daniel Webster, April 16, 1851, Fillmore MSS (LC); Henry J. Raymond to William H. Seward, February 6, 1851, Seward MSS (RU).

65. Rayback, *Fillmore*, pp. 285–86; John T. Bush to Fillmore, April 20, 1851, MFP-BHS.

66. The standard account of the Erie Canal in New York politics in this period is Shaw, *Erie Water West*. Aside from manuscript sources, however, I have relied primarily on an unusually able undergraduate senior thesis written under my supervision: Reed, "Politics of Internal Improvements."

The Stop-and-Tax Act of 1842 suspended all work on canals, levied a real estate tax to help defray the state's general expenses, and consigned revenue from canal tolls to a sinking fund to pay interest and principal on the existing debt, which in 1842 totaled $26 million.

67. Reed, "Politics of Internal Improvements," p. 63. On the attractiveness of revenue certificates to banks and other potential investors, see William L. Marcy to Andrew Jackson Donelson, May 7, 1851, Donelson MSS. Marcy considered the scheme flatly unconstitutional, but he admitted that the arguments for it were so plausible and the financial incentives so irresistible that the bill was bound to pass.

68. Samuel B. Ruggles to Seward, January 18, 1851, Seward to Samuel B. Ruggles, January 23, 1851, Seward MSS (RU); Jerome Fuller to Fillmore, March 19, 1851, John T. Bush to Fillmore, April 20, 1851, and George R. Babcock to Fillmore, April 21, 1851, MFP-BHS. Spencer's opinion was printed in the *Albany Evening Journal*, March 17, 1851. A draft of Webster's brief, dated April 11, 1851, is in the Webster MSS. Both are cited in Reed, "Politics of Internal Improvements," p. 68. Webster's reaction to events in New York and his possible motive for writing this brief at Weed's behest will be discussed below.

69. Thurlow Weed to Hamilton Fish, April 6, 1851, Fish MSS; John T. Bush to Fillmore, April 20, 1851, George R. Babcock to Fillmore, April 21, 1850, Thomas Foote to Fillmore, May 2, 1851, M. P. Bemus to Fillmore, May 2, 1851, MFP-BHS.

70. For additional evidence of Whig confidence in the issue, see Charles Cooke to Thurlow Weed, May 30, 1851, Seth C. Hawley to Weed, May 30, 1851, and Alvah Hunt to Weed, June 6, 1851, Weed MSS (RU). Democrats were correspondingly pessimistic, believing that the canal issue and the resignation of the Democratic senators would crucify them in the fall. William L. Marcy to Andrew Jackson Donelson, May 7, 1851, Donelson MSS; William C. Bouck to Horatio Seymour, June 4, 1851, Fairchild Collection.

71. John C. Spencer to Hamilton Fish, June 14, 1851, Fish MSS; Jerome Fuller to Fillmore, June 16, 1851, James Brooks to Fillmore, July 1, 1851, N. K. Hall to Fillmore, July 20, 1851, John C. Spencer to Fillmore, July 22, 1851, Thomas Foote to Fillmore, July 24, August 2, 1851, MFP-BHS; John C. Spencer to John O. Sargent, August 18, 1851, Sargent MSS; Fillmore to Webster, August 4, 1851, Webster MSS.

72. Charles W. March to Webster, April 17, 1851, Webster to Edward Curtis, May 1851, Webster to Peter Harvey, May 4, 1851, Hiram Ketchum to Webster, May 10, 1851, Webster to Franklin Haven, June 11, 1851, Edward Everett to Webster, September 2, 1851, Webster to Everett, September 3, 1851, Webster MSS; Philip Greely, Jr. to Fillmore, March 5, June 19, 1851, MFP-BHS.

73. On Fillmore's disinterest in another race for the presidency, see Fillmore to Isaac Newton, July 31, 1851, Millard Fillmore MSS (Yale University, microfilm edition of Fillmore MSS).

74. Foner, *Business & Slavery*, p. 70; N. K. Hall to Fillmore, August 15, 1851, MFP-BHS; Simeon Draper to Thurlow Weed, August 30, 1851, Weed MSS (RU); Oran Follett to Thomas Corwin, September 14, 1851, Corwin MSS (LC).

75. Oran Follett to Thomas Corwin, September 14, 1851, Corwin MSS (LC); Philo C. Fuller

to Millard Fillmore, October 6, 1851, MFP-BHS; George R. Babcock to Daniel Ullmann, October 13, 1851, Ullmann MSS.

76. George R. Babcock to Daniel Ullmann, September 4, 13, October 13, 1851, E. G. Spaulding to Ullmann, September 20, 1851, Ullmann to Spaulding, September 24, 1851, copy, E. Andrews to Ullmann, September 29, 1851, S. C. Hart to Washington Hunt, October 1, 1851, with Washington Hunt to Ullmann, October 5, 1851, S. P. Allen to Ullmann, October 23, 1851, Ullmann MSS; Robert Morriss to Hamilton Fish, October 15, 1851, Fish MSS.

77. Foner, *Business & Slavery*, pp. 69–74.

78. Horace Greeley to Daniel Ullmann, September 14, 1851, George R. Babcock to Ullmann, September 13, 1851, B. Thompson to Ullmann, October 25, 1851, James Henry to Ullmann, October 26, 1851, Ullmann MSS; Winthrop Atwell to Dewitt Clinton Littlejohn, September 20, 1851, John L. Schoolcraft to Thurlow Weed, October 28, 1851, Weed MSS (RU); John M. Bradford to Hamilton Fish, October 15, November 8, 1851, Fish MSS.

79. Thurlow Weed to George W. Patterson, October 30, 1851, Weed MSS (RU); David A. Bokee to Fillmore, October 30, 1851, Hugh Maxwell to Fillmore, October 31, 1851, Hamilton Fish to Fillmore, November 1, 3, 1851, MFP-BHS; Fillmore to Hamilton Fish, November 2, 1851, Fish MSS.

80. After the May 1851 elections, the Whig margin over Democrats in the senate had increased from seventeen to fifteen to twenty-four to eight.

81. Gilbert Davis to Millard Fillmore, November 7, 1851, MFP-BHS; Seward to George W. Patterson, November 13, 1851, Hamilton Fish to Thurlow Weed, November 15, 1851, Weed MSS; Fish to Daniel D. Barnard, November 10, 1851, Barnard MSS; Weed to Fish, November 16, 1851, quoted in Carman and Luthin, "Seward-Fillmore Feud," 343.

82. Maizlish, *Triumph of Sectionalism*, pp. 167–68; Thomas Corwin to J. D. Ward, December 13, 1850, Corwin MSS (OHS); Aaron F. Perry to Millard Fillmore, March 20, 1851, Daniel Webster to Fillmore, August 10, 1851, N. K. Hall to Fillmore, October 6, 1851, Oran Follett to Fillmore, November 19, 1851, MFP-BHS; ? to Thomas Ewing, January 9, 1851 (quotation), EFP. (The page of this critical letter with the signature is missing.)

83. The subsequent account of Ohio's senatorial election is based on the following sources, and I shall eschew further citation except for quotations: Maizlish, *Triumph of Sectionalism*, pp .157–64; Trefousse, *Wade*, pp. 60–69; Aaron F. Perry to Thomas Ewing, October 30, 1850, January 19, 22, 1851, Thomas Ewing to ?, November 13, 1850, draft, John Greiner to Ewing, December 20, 1850, January 10, 15, 18, 23, February 11, 1851, P. B. Ewing to Thomas Ewing, January 11, 1851, A. Banning Norton to Ewing, February 1, March 18, 22, 1851, EFP; Samuel Foner to Thomas Corwin, December 22, 1850, Edwin Corwin to Thomas Corwin, February 6, 1851, Corwin MSS (LC); E. S. Hamlin to Salmon P. Chase, December 23, 1850, George Hoadly to Chase, December 24, 1850, Chase MSS (LC).

84. ? to Thomas Ewing, January 9, 1851, EFP.

85. According to the data Walter Dean Burnham compiled for the Inter-University Consortium for Political and Social Research, there were thirty-four Whigs, thirty-two Democrats, and six Free Soilers in the house and seventeen Whigs, sixteen Democrats, and three Free Soilers in the senate.

86. John Greiner to Thomas Ewing, December 20, 1851, ? to Ewing, January 9, 1851, EFP.

87. L. Atkinson to Thomas Ewing, February 5, 1851, ibid. Atkinson was not a member of the legislature.

88. For evidence of the Whigs' hope of running against the new constitution in the fall elections, see John Greiner to Thomas Ewing, January 18, 1851, Simeon Brush to Ewing, February 4, 1851, EFP. Vinton, it will be recalled, had helped Taylor at the 1848 national convention by persuading Ohio's Whigs to back Scott rather than Clay.

89. A. Banning Norton to Thomas Ewing, March 18, 22, 1851, EFP. For Wade's speeches, see the pages in Trefousse's biography cited in note 83.

90. Aaron F. Perry to Millard Fillmore, March 20, 1851, MFP-BHS; A. Banning Norton to Thomas Ewing, March 22, 1851, EFP.

91. A. Banning Norton to Thomas Ewing, March 22, 1851, Thomas Ewing, Jr., to Hugh B. Ewing, June 8, 1851, EFP; William E. Russell to Thomas Corwin, July 8, December 1, 1851,

Corwin MSS (LC). My description of the new Ohio constitution is drawn from Hampel, "The Ohio Whig Party," pp. 25–31. The constitution passed with 53.5 percent of the vote in June.

92. Williams, *Hayes Diary*, I, p. 399 (entry for October 15, 1851). The change in the popular vote for governor and the parties' share of legislative seats between 1850 and 1851 was as follows:

	Vote for Governor	
	1850	1851
Whig	121,105 (45.2%)	119,550 (42.4%)
Democratic	133,093 (49.7%)	145,656 (51.6%)
Free Soil	13,747 (5.1%)	16,910 (6.0%)

	Seats in Legislature			
	House	Senate	House	Senate
Whig	34	17	26	9
Democratic	32	16	68	25
Free Soil	6	3	2	1

The reapportionment of the legislature by the new constitution, which increased the size of house and reduced the senate, clearly worked to the Whigs' disadvantage, as they had feared.

93. R. W. Clark to John G. Davis, October 20, 1851 (quotation), John G. Davis MSS; E. Connor to Thomas Corwin, October 25, 1851, William E. Russell to Corwin, December 1, 1851, Corwin MSS (LC); William E. Russell to Thomas Ewing, November 2, 1851, EFP; Maizlish, *Triumph of Sectionalism*, pp. 171–72.

94. For complaints by California Whigs about Fillmore's patronage decisions, see Truman Smith to John Wilson, November 29, 1850, January 5, November 3, December 3, 1851, John Wilson MSS; John Wilson to Millard Fillmore, April 28, 1851, J. H. Clay Mudd to Truman Smith, December 4, 1851, MFP-BHS.

95. C. L. Hall to Fillmore, November 19, 1850, George Madeira to Fillmore, March 31, November 18, 1851, MFP-BHS.

96. James D. Merrill to Millard Fillmore, January 31, March 22, 1851, MFP-BHS.

97. Jacob M. Howard to Millard Fillmore, November 12, 1850, Solomon G. Haven to Fillmore, April 3, 1851, A. M. Baker to Fillmore, December 1, 1850, May 4, June 30, 1851, O. M. Hyde to Fillmore, June 21, 1851, MFP-BHS; Josiah Snow to William H. Seward, March 8, 26, 1851, Henry Barns to Seward, April 22, May 19, October 2, December 4, 1851, Jacob Howard to Seward, September 17, 1851, Seward MSS (RU).

98. S. Francis to Millard Fillmore, January 22, 1851, MFP-BHS; John Moses to Richard Yates, November 19, 1851, Yates MSS.

99. Willard Smith, "Colfax," 273, 276–77; Van Bolt, " 'Eternal Agitation,' " 363, 367.

100. Smith, "Colfax," 278; Van Bolt, "Indiana in Political Transition," 151.

101. George W. Julian to Henry Hoover, April 23, 1851, copy, Julian MSS; Joseph O. Jones to John G. Davis, July 27, 1851, John Davis MSS; Schuyler Colfax to John O. Sargent, October 27, 1851, Sargent MSS; Van Bolt, " 'Eternal Agitation,' " 364; Smith, "Colfax," 276–77.

102. This discussion of the background to the convention is based on an analysis of roll-call votes on calling the convention in the Indiana legislature, as well as on a correlation analysis of the votes for delegates in Hampel, "Indiana Constitutional Convention."

103. Hampel, "Constitution-Making"; Smith, "Colfax," 273–76; Van Bolt, "Indiana in Political Transition," 136–41; Samuel Brenton to Allen Hamilton, January 23, 1851, William Holman to Hamilton, April 5, 1851, Hamilton MSS.

104. Ibid.

105. Between the elections of 1850 and 1851, Whig proportions of seats in the legislature dropped from 37 to 36 percent in the house and from 34 to 20 percent in the senate.

106. Schuyler Colfax to John O. Sargent, September 23, October 27, 1851, Sargent MSS.

107. The best analysis of the 1851 elections in New Jersey is found in Renda, "Railroads, Revenue, and Reform."

108. Mueller, *Whig Party in Pennsylvania*, pp. 168–69, 181–86; Josiah Randall et al. to Daniel Webster, November 11, 1850, James Cooper to Webster, April 29, 1851, Webster MSS; Joseph P. Sanderson to Millard Fillmore, March 6, 1851, Webster to Fillmore, April 4, 1851, MFP-BHS. Roll-call votes on repeal of the 1847 law provoked higher levels of interparty conflict in the 1851 legislature than did those on any other issue. See Holt, *Political Crisis*, pp. 115–16.

109. W. J. Sanders to Millard Fillmore, February 18, 1851, Joseph P. Sanderson to Fillmore, March 6, 1851, J. G. Moore to Fillmore, March 8, 14, 1851, MFP-BHS; Josiah Randall to Webster, March 21, 1851, Webster MSS.

110. John H. Bryant to Fillmore, November 11, 1850, James Cooper to Fillmore, December 21, 1850, March 13, 1851, William D. Lewis to Thomas Corwin, March 19, 1851, MFP-BHS; William F. Johnston to Fillmore, April 11, 1851, Corwin MSS (LC); Josiah Randall to Webster, March 21, 1851, John S. Riddle to Webster, April 7, 1851, Charles Gibbons to Webster, April 28, 1851, Webster MSS.

111. Webster to Fillmore, March 17, 1851, Josiah Randall to Webster, March 21, 1851, Webster MSS; Webster to Fillmore, April 4, May 1, 1851, James E. Harvey to Fillmore, June 16, 1851, MFP-BHS; James E. Harvey to Thomas Corwin, April 27, 1851, Corwin MSS (LC). For Johnston's repeated snubs of governors from Maryland, Virginia, and Georgia, see Mueller, *Whig Party in Pennsylvania*, pp. 168–69, 186.

112. Joseph P. Sanderson to Fillmore, March 6, 1851, James E. Harvey to Fillmore, April 20, 1851, William D. Lewis to Fillmore, April 21, 1851, MFP-BHS; James E. Harvey to Thomas Corwin, April 27, 1851, Corwin MSS (LC); Charles Gibbons to Daniel Webster, April 28, 1851, James Cooper to Webster, April 29, 1851, Webster MSS.

113. James Cooper to Fillmore, April 18, 19, 1851, MFP-BHS; Charles Gibbons to Daniel Webster, April 28, 1850, James Cooper to Webster, April 29, 1851, Josiah Randall to Webster, April 30, 1850, Webster MSS.

114. James E. Harvey to Thomas Corwin, April 16, 1851, Corwin MSS (LC); William B. Reed to Fillmore, June 7, 1851, James E. Harvey to Fillmore, July 7, 1851, MFP-BHS.

115. John Ashmead to Millard Fillmore, July 12, 1851, February 27, March 25, 1852, MFP-BHS.

116. E. G. Lindsey to Millard Fillmore, January 28, April 7, 1851, Daniel Webster to Fillmore, March 17, 1851, Peter Sken Smith to Fillmore, March 24, April 7, 1851, MFP-BHS; John S. Riddle to Webster, April 7, 1851, Webster MSS.

117. Mueller, *Whig Party in Pennsylvania*, p. 178; Harvey to Corwin, April 16, 27, 1851, Corwin MSS (LC); William B. Reed to Fillmore, June 7, 1851, MFP-BHS.

118. Cooper to Fillmore, May 2, 1851, James E. Harvey to Fillmore, April 27, May 28, June 16, 1851, William B. Reed to Fillmore, June 7, 1851, MFP-BHS.

119. Ibid.

120. Mueller, *Whig Party in Pennsylvania*, pp. 179–80; Holt, *Forging a Majority*, pp. 95–100; J. R. Flanigen to Fillmore, June 28, 1851, MFP-BHS.

121. James Brooks to Millard Fillmore, June 27, 1851, James E. Harvey to Fillmore, July 7, 1851, MFP-BHS; Daniel Webster to Hiram Ketchum, June 27, 1851, Webster MSS.

122. Holt, *Forging a Majority*, pp. 98–100; Mueller, *Whig Party in Pennsylvania*, pp. 181–82; Edward McPherson to J. B. McPherson, June 17, 1851, McPherson MSS; Solomon Krick to J. Alexander Fulton, August 25, 1851, Fulton MSS.

123. Mueller, *Whig Party in Pennsylvania*, pp. 181–90. The best account of the Christiana Riot and its aftermath is Slaughter, *Bloody Dawn*. Slaughter, however, is obviously unfamiliar with Pennsylvania Whig politics. Thus he fails to realize that one of the reasons Ashmead brought the hopelessly unsustainable charges of treason against bystanders is that he was trying to curry favor with Fillmore and Webster, lest they sack him, as Cooper immediately demanded, because he belonged to Johnston's machine. Nor does he seem to appreciate the delicious irony that Maryland authorities asked none other than Senator Cooper to help Ashmead prosecute the case and that Cooper accepted. Cooper's contempt for Ashmead's incompetence as a lawyer

strikingly resembled Webster's disdain for Lunt in Massachusetts. See Cooper to Webster, October 21, 1851, Webster MSS.

124. Mueller, *Whig Party in Pennsylvania*, pp. 190–91; Edward McPherson to J. B. McPherson, October 16, 1851, McPherson MSS; Peter Sken Smith to Fillmore, October 15, 1851, J. W. S. to Fillmore, October 18, 1851, James E. Harvey to Fillmore, October 19, 23, 25, 1851, clipping of the Berks County *Intelligencer* with letter of October 25, William D. Lewis to Fillmore, October 19, 1851, MFP-BHS; E. H. Penniman to William L. Bigler, October 19, 1851, Bigler MSS; William L. Hirst to J. Alexander Fulton, August 26, 1851, Fulton MSS.

In 1848, when there was no separate Native American candidate for governor, Johnston won by about 300 votes, 168,522 to 168,225. In 1851, Bigler garnered 186,459 votes, Johnston, 178,034, and the Native American, 1850.

125. Mueller, *Whig Party in Pennsylvania*, pp. 176–77, n. 4; Francis Wharton to Jeremiah Sullivan Black, September 18, 1851, Black MSS; E. H. Penniman to William L. Bigler, October 19, 1851, Bigler MSS.

126. G. G. Wescott to William Bigler, January 16, 1851, William F. Small to Bigler, January 20, 1851, Henry M. Phillips to Bigler, January 28, 1851, Benjamin Brewster to Bigler, February 17, 1851, E. H. Penniman to Bigler, October 19, 1851, James Macmanus to Bigler, October 23, 1851 (quotation), Bigler MSS; Joseph Hemphill to James Buchanan, July 16, 1851, J. C. Van Dyke to Buchanan, October 18, 1851, Buchanan MSS (HSP); N. D. Strong to J. Alexander Fulton, July 22, 1851, R. A. Lamberton to Fulton, July 28, 1851, Fulton MSS; James E. Harvey to Fillmore, October 19, 1851, Miller N. Everly to Fillmore, November 15, 1851, MFP-BHS.

127. William D. Lewis to Thomas Corwin, October 16, 1851, Corwin MSS (LC); J. W. S. to Fillmore, October 18, 1851, James E. Harvey to Fillmore, October 19, 23, 1851, William D. Lewis to Fillmore, October 19, 1851, Daniel Webster to Fillmore, November 16, 1851, MFP-BHS; James E. Harvey to John J. Crittenden, November 5, 1851, Crittenden MSS (LC).

128. These figures, taken from *Historical Statistics*, p. 1063, apparently include Whigs and Democrats elected under Union and Southern Rights labels with their respective major parties.

129. In New York and Maryland the senate was evenly divided, and if strength in joint sessions were considered, New York could be added to the Whig list and Maryland to the Democratic one.

130. Henry Clay to Daniel Ullmann, June 14, 1851, Ullmann MSS.

131. Benjamin Matthias to William A. Graham, November 21, 1851, in *Graham Papers*, IV, pp. 216–17.

CHAPTER 19

1. Benjamin F. Wade to Caroline Wade, January 28, 1852, Wade MSS; Philadelphia *Public Ledger*, Washington Correspondence, January 14, 1852.

2. Truman Smith to Daniel M. Barringer, May 1, 1852, Barringer MSS; Truman Smith to William B. Campbell, May 15, 1852, CFP.

3. For Sargent's interest in a Union party, see James D. Ogden to John O. Sargent, September 17, 20, 1851, Samuel Eliot to Sargent, November 10, 1851, Sargent MSS; for Kennedy's continuing advocacy of the idea, see John P. Kennedy to Henry C. Carey, April 30, 1851, Kennedy to Daniel Webster, July 10, 1851, and Kennedy to Robert C. Winthrop, December 20, 1851, copies, Kennedy MSS.

4. Oran Follett to Millard Fillmore, November 19, 1851, Daniel Lee to Fillmore, July 27, December 4, 1851, February 13, 1852, MFP-BHS.

5. Daniel Webster to Franklin Haven, November 21, 28, 30, 1851, National Union Party [Benjamin Balche] to Webster, October 20, 1851, Webster MSS; Henry A. Wise to Edward Everett, November 28, 1851, Everett MSS; Benjamin Balche to Howell Cobb, January 10, 1851, in Phillips, "Correspondence of Toombs, Stephens, and Cobb," pp. 220–21.

6. Aside from having a common desire with Websterites to stop Fillmore from sewing up the city's delegates to the national convention, Seward needed their help to secure the Whig gubernatorial nomination in 1852 for Moses Grinnell, a Manhattan merchant who was close to Webster's friends in the mercantile community and on the Union Safety Committee. Grinnell's nomination, Seward believed, could reunify the state Whig party without giving Silver Grays

the governorship. See Simeon Draper to Daniel Webster, January 1852, James Watson Webb to Webster, February 8, 1852, Webster MSS; Henry J. Raymond to William H. Seward, March 15, 1851, Seward MSS (RU).

7. An Old Fashioned Webster Man to Webster, Philadelphia, October 28, 1851, Webster MSS; John M. Clayton to John J. Crittenden, October 27, 1851, James E. Harvey to Crittenden, October 28, 1851, Crittenden MSS (LC).

8. Philadelphia *Public Ledger*, January 14, 1852; Oran Follett to Millard Fillmore, November 19, 1851, Daniel Lee to Fillmore, December 4, 1851, Webster to Fillmore, December 20, 1851, MFP-BHS; Henry S. Foote to Millard Fillmore, December 22, 1851, MFP-O; John P. Kennedy to Robert C. Winthrop, December 20, 1851, copy, Kennedy MSS; Daniel Webster to Henry Hilliard, April 7, 1851, Edward Everett to Webster, November 22, 1851, Webster MSS; William H. Seward to Thurlow Weed, December 26, 1851, Weed MSS (RU). Foote resigned his Senate seat on January 8, 1852; his successor, Walter Brooke, a Union Whig, was sworn in on March 11, 1852.

9. Charles March to Daniel Webster, November 23, 1851, Webster to Franklin Haven, November 30, 1851, Webster MSS; Seward to Weed, December 26, 1851, Weed MSS (RU); William Schouler to Seward, December 20, 1851, James B. Swain to Seward, February 24, 1852, Seward MSS (RU); Cabell's speech is quoted in Cole, *Whig Party in the South*, pp. 230, 233n. The Democratic caucus, which met on Saturday night, November 29, 1851, will be discussed further below.

10. Webster to Everett, March 13, 1852, Webster MSS.

11. Webster to Franklin Haven, November 14, 28, 1851, Webster MSS. For other reports that Fillmore intended to announce his withdrawal from the race in December or January, see Joseph C. Kennedy to John M. Clayton, December 10, 1851, Clayton MSS; and the Washington Correspondence in the Philadelphia *Public Ledger*, January 23, 1852.

12. Henry A. Wise to Edward Everett, January 24, 1852, Fillmore to Everett, February 16, 1852, Everett MSS; Webster to Franklin Haven, January 22, 1852, Simeon Draper to Webster, January 1852, Webster MSS; Philadelphia *Public Ledger*, January 24, 1852.

13. Alexander Stephens to Linton Stephens, December 10, 1851, and the letters to Howell Cobb from Robert Toombs, December 2, 1851 [misdated January 2, 1851], Alexander Stephens, November 24, 26, December 5, 1851, Thomas D. Harris, November 29, 1851, and George W. Jones, December 7, 1851, all in Phillips, "Correspondence of Toombs, Stephens, and Cobb," pp. 218–20, 264–74.

14. Ibid.; see also Howell Cobb to Alexander H. Stephens, December 3, 22, 1851, Stephens MSS (LC); Daniel Lee to Millard Fillmore, December 4, 1851, MFP-BHS. Brooke is quoted in Cole, *Whig Party in the South*, p. 218.

15. Andrew Jackson Donelson to Howell Cobb, October 22, 1851, George W. Jones to Cobb, December 7, 1851, January 25, 1852, John Slidell to Cobb, January 28, 1852, in Phillips, "Correspondence of Toombs, Stephens, and Cobb," pp. 262–77. The reason southern Whigs expressed continued faith in the party will be examined below, but Cabell's December speech, in which he proclaimed the Whig party now safer on the finality of the Compromise than the Democrats, can be found in U.S. Congress, *Congressional Globe*, 32nd Cong., 1st Sess., pp. 8–9.

16. In addition to the letters to Cobb cited in previous notes, see Herridon L. Henderson to John Bragg, January 15, 1852, A. Lopez to Bragg, January 24, 1852, Bragg MSS; Cole, *Whig Party in the South*, pp. 212–14; Nevins, *Ordeal: Fruits*, pp. 377–79; Thornton, *Politics and Power*, pp. 195–99; and Shryock, *Georgia and the Union*, pp. 356–63.

17. In addition to the sources cited in the previous note, see Howell Cobb to Alexander H. Stephens, December 22, 1851, Stephens MSS (LC); Stephens to Cobb, November 26, 1851, in Phillips, "Correspondence of Toombs, Stephens, and Cobb," pp. 265–67; Edward Everett to Daniel Webster, November 22, 1851, Webster MSS; Arthur F. Hopkins to Millard Fillmore, March 3, 1852, William C. Dawson to Fillmore, March 15, 1852, MFP-BHS; Thomas E. Joby to John Bragg, December 10, 1851, Herridon L. Henderson to Bragg, January 15, 1852, A. Lopez to John Bragg, January 24, 1852, Bragg MSS.

18. For Alabama, see Thornton, *Politics and Power*, pp. 195–97; for Mississippi I have relied primarily on two unpublished papers written by graduate students at the University of Virginia,

copies of which are in my possession: Hoerl, "Land, Rails, and Gresham's Law," and Mittendorf, "Mississippi Politics." Both possess tables showing changes in the Rice Indexes of Cohesion over time on various issues that graphically illustrate the disunity of the Union coalition. In 1848, for example, five votes on banking produced an average Whig cohesion score of 85; on two votes on banking in 1852 the Union average was only 6.5. In 1848, the average Whig cohesion on eleven votes concerning the Planters' Bank bonds was 74.5; in 1852, the Union coalition mustered a cohesion index of only 30.9 on ten such votes. In 1848, on twenty-one votes on land policy, Whigs retained an average cohesion score of 73.6; four votes on land policy produced a Union score of only 34.7. In contrast to these votes on state economic policy, the index of Union cohesion on the vote for United States senator in 1852, when Brooke was elected, was 85.2.

19. Henry Hilliard to Fillmore, January 26, 1852, Arthur F. Hopkins to Fillmore, March 3, April 22, 1852, William C. Dawson to Fillmore, March 15, 1852, MFP-BHS.

20. Samuel Eliot to John O. Sargent, November 10, 1851, Sargent MSS.

21. Philip Greely, Jr., to William H. Seward, March 1, 1852, Seward MSS (RU). These contentions about northern Whigs will be documented more fully below, but see the speeches by Lewis Campbell, James Brooks, and E. C. Cabell, *Congressional Globe*, 32nd Cong., 1st Sess., pp. 5–9; and William H. Seward to Thurlow Weed, December 26, 1851, Weed MSS (RU).

22. Robert Toombs to Howell Cobb, December 2, 1851 [misdated January 2, 1851], in Phillips, "Correspondence of Toombs, Stephens, and Cobb," pp. 218–220; Webster to Franklin Haven, November 30, 1851, Webster MSS; speeches of Brooks and Cabell, December 1, 1851, *Congressional Globe*, 32nd Cong., 1st Sess., pp. 5–9.

23. *Congressional Globe*, 32nd Cong., 1st Sess., pp. 5–9. Brooks read the Whigs' resolution into the *Congressional Record*, p. 6. It said that the "adjustment measures" formed the best "system of compromise" possible "and that therefore they ought to be adhered to and carried into full execution, as a final settlement in principle and substance of the dangerous and exciting subjects which they embrace."

24. Alexander, *Sectional Stress*, p. 18, lists ninety-two Whigs in the House for this session. To get the figure of eighty-six Whigs, I have subtracted the two Union Whigs from Alabama, the two Union Whigs from Georgia, and the two Southern Rights Whigs from Georgia. The Whig caucus in fact never nominated a candidate for speaker, and Whigs scattered their votes among several people on the House vote.

25. *Congressional Globe*, 32nd Cong., 1st Sess., pp. 5–9; George W. Jones to Howell Cobb, December 7, 1851, in Phillips, "Correspondence of Toombs, Stephens, and Cobb," pp. 269–71; John Z. Goodrich to William Schouler, April 26, 1852, Schouler MSS. Goodrich, a Massachusetts Whig at the caucus who dissented from the finality resolution, bitterly complained in this last letter about the false portrait of northern acquiescence in finality that Brooks and Cabell presented on the House floor.

26. William B. Campbell to David Campbell, February 15, 1852, CFP; New Orleans *Bulletin*, July 11, 1851, Memphis *Eagle*, November 11, 1851, both quoted in Cole, *Whig Party in the South*, pp. 227–28. Cole, pp. 223–44, amasses irrefutable evidence that the vast majority of southern Whigs preferred Fillmore or Webster and opposed Scott as untrustworthy. See also Cooper, *Politics of Slavery*, pp. 322–25.

27. Alabama's Joseph G. Baldwin wrote Alexander H. H. Stuart, "Webster won't do. His declaration that there should be no other slave state is *fel de re* here." Howell Cobb, in replying to a proposed Union party ticket of Webster and Cobb, declared that "*no man*—Whig or Democrat, great or small—can or ever will receive the support of the South for the presidency who advocates the doctrines avowed by Mr. Webster in his Buffalo speech." Baldwin to Stuart, April 16, 1852, Stuart MSS (University of Virginia); Cobb to C. W. Denison, February 3, 1852, in Phillips, "Correspondence of Toombs, Stephens, and Cobb," pp. 278–79. See also J. Muir to Thomas Corwin, March 11, 1852, Corwin MSS (LC).

28. Millard Fillmore to Daniel Webster, November 29, 1851, with answers on back from Webster, Crittenden, and William A. Graham urging Fillmore not to change the section of his annual message on the Fugitive Slave Act, as Fish requested, MFP-BHS; *Messages and Papers of the Presidents*, V, pp. 137–39; Dennis Heart to Willie P. Mangum, March 31, 1852, in *The*

Mangum Papers, V, pp. 221–23; Henry A. Wise to Edward Everett, March 20, 1852, Everett MSS.

29. Rayback, *Fillmore*, pp. 333–37; Joseph C. Kennedy to John M. Clayton, December 10, 1851, Clayton MSS; Fillmore to Everett, November 28, 1851, Everett MSS; Fillmore to Whig National Convention, June 10, 1852, draft, MFP-O.

30. George Madeira to Fillmore, November 18, 1851, Richard W. Thompson to Fillmore, January 6, 1852, John Ashmead to Fillmore, July 12, 1851, February 27, March 25, 1852, George W. Knight to Fillmore, April 7, 1852, MFP-BHS.

31. Henry Hilliard to Fillmore, December 9, 1851, MFP-BHS.

32. Oran Follett to Fillmore, November 19, 1851, Henry Hilliard to Fillmore, December 9, 1851, George R. Babcock to Fillmore, March 8, 1852, MFP-BHS.

33. Fillmore to President of the Whig National Convention, June 10, 1852, draft, Fillmore to George R. Babcock, June 12, 1852, MFP-O; Fillmore to Edward Everett, February 16, 1852, Everett MSS.

34. William H. Garland to Fillmore, February 17, 1852, Daniel Lee to Fillmore, March 26, 1852, MFP-BHS.

35. See, for example, Lewis Campbell to William Schouler, January 15, 1852, Schouler MSS.

36. Savannah *Republican*, July 1, 1851, quoted in Cole, *Whig Party in the South*, pp. 225–26; Christopher H. Williams to William B. Campbell, January 26, 1852, CFP.

37. Horace Greeley to Schuyler Colfax, February 12, 1851, quoted in Nevins, *Ordeal: House*, p. 26; William Bigler to Franklin Pierce, June 26, 1852, Pierce MSS; Joseph C. Kennedy to John M. Clayton, December 10, 1851, Clayton MSS.

38. Truman Smith to John Wilson, January 5, August 16, October 14, 1851, Wilson MSS. George C. Gardiner, one-time dentist, land speculator, and spectacularly brazen bunko artist, presented a completely spurious claim to the Mexican Claims Commission created under the terms of the Treaty of Guadelupe Hidalgo to pay off the debts the government of Mexico owed to U.S. citizens. While still in the Senate, Corwin served as Gardiner's lawyer, working on a contingency basis, before the claims commission on which his cousin, Robert C. Corwin, sat. Upon his elevation to the cabinet, Corwin sold his share to another lawyer for $81,000. Thus he netted none of the $484,000 the commission awared Gardiner. Nonetheless, the later revelation that Gardiner's claim was utterly false and the obvious fact that Corwin had been able to sell his share of the claim for so much only because of his presumed influence on his cousin created a scandal. See Summers, *Plundering Generation*, pp. 159–61.

39. James S. Pike to Thurlow Weed, January 30, 1852, Weed MSS (RU).

40. John O. Charles to Millard Fillmore, March 17, 1851, MFP-BHS; Charles A. Dana to James S. Pike, May 1852, Pike MSS; Truman Smith to Daniel M. Barringer, May 1, 1852, Barringer MSS.

41. George R. Babcock to Fillmore, March 8, 1852, Thomas Foote to Fillmore, April 19, 1852, MFP-BHS.

42. Washington Hunt to Hamilton Fish, April 4, 1852, Fish MSS.

43. Philadelphia *Public Ledger*, January 21, 1852. This summary of Whig and Democratic positions on economic policy recapitulates arguments I've already developed in previous chapters, and I see no need for additional documentation here.

44. *Messages and Papers of the Presidents*, V, pp. 123–24. I have documented the argument in this and subsequent paragraphs in Holt, *Political Crisis*, pp. 106–13, 270–71, 297–99.

45. On free banking acts and Democratic support for them in the Midwest, see Shade, *Banks or No Banks*, pp. 145–88; for Democratic demands on Pennsylvania's Bigler to sign bills chartering new banks, see the letters in the Bigler MSS dated April 10, 13, 17, 19, 1852. Letters from other Democrats dated April 20, 21, 23, 1852, however, applaud his vetoes of the same banking bills. For the diminution of legislative conflict over banking and currency, see Table 3 in Holt, *Political Crisis*, p. 175.

46. In July a Pennsylvania Democrat, after making a trip through the state's iron-making and coal-mining districts, reported: ''The tariff people—especially the discontented *coal* and iron people are satisfied[,] for the increased demand for rail way iron has set them to work & we

hear no more complaints." Governor Bigler also told Franklin Pierce that the tariff issue "has lost much of its potency" in Pennsylvania. Benjamin Brewster to Edmund Burke, July 19, 1852, Burke MSS; William Bigler to Pierce, June 26, 1852, Pierce MSS.

For evidence that those involved in railroad construction wanted to keep duties on imported rails low, see Alfred Kelley to Thomas Ewing, February 11, 1851, EFP; and Isaac R. Diller to Stephen A. Douglas, February 2, 1853, Douglas MSS.

47. On Congress, see Alexander, *Sectional Stress*, pp. 77–84; and Silbey, *Shrine of Party*, pp. 121–36. On pp. 115–16 of *Political Crisis* I provide a table showing the decline of indices of disagreement in various state legislatures in the early 1850s. After I wrote that book, Marc Kruman published indices for North Carolina, while my own graduate students generated figures for Louisiana and Wisconsin and a more complete analysis of votes in Kentucky, Connecticut, New Hampshire, and Ohio. The changes in the average indices of disagreement in those states on banking and currency, business incorporations and stockholder privileges, and internal improvements were as follows:

State	1848	1849	1850	1851	1852	1853	1854
			Banking and Currency				
Louisiana	42.5		69.7		48.8	40.3	39.1
Ohio	71	100	74	77	50		51
Kentucky	30	29	26	22		31	
Connecticut	73	67	48	59	69		43
New Hamp.			No Votes during These Years				
N. Carolina					10.1		21.6
Wisconsin	27	40	36	9	36	6	32
		Business Incorporations and Stockholder Liability					
Louisiana	59.1				16.3	26.5	26.5
Ohio	38	76.3	54.5	73.8	44.4		53
Kentucky		19	17	12		42	
Connecticut			No Votes during These Years				
New Hamp.	36	31	38	47	25	37	44
N. Carolina	54.6						
Wisconsin		15	13				
			Internal Improvements				
Louisiana	30.5		18.7		18.4	32	14.5
Ohio	65	67	59	61	30		33
Kentucky	33	9	41	10		43	
Connecticut	31	33				10	67
New Hamp.		55	57	62	13		
N. Carolina	41.8		37.9		10		24
Wisconsin	12	20	31	15	22	18	31

These figures can be found in Kruman, *Parties and Politics*, pp. 57, 72, 82–84; Volz, "Party, State, and Nation," p. 143; Renda, "The Polity and the Party System"; Ames, "Conflict and Consensus"; Shadle, "Consensus"; Pilkington, "Louisiana House of Representatives."

48. *Messages and Papers of the Presidents*, V, pp. 113–39; Kentucky Whig platform, enclosed with Leslie Combs to Millard Fillmore, February 26, 1852, MFP-BHS; Washington *National Intelligencer*, April 17, 1852; the Whig national platform is reprinted in the appendix to Van Deusen, "The Whig Party," pp. 478–79. For Democratic jeers at the Whig retreat on the tariff and confidence that Whigs could no longer use the issue against them, see William V. Pettit to Franklin Pierce, June 5, 1852, William Bigler to Pierce, June 26, 1852, Pierce MSS; Benjamin Brewster to Edmund Burke, July 19, 1852, Burke MSS; and Holt, *Forging a Majority*, pp. 104–05.

49. Nathaniel P. Tallmadge, Jr., to Thomas Corwin, November 7, 1851, Corwin MSS (LC);

Benjamin F. Wade to Caroline Wade, March 15, 1852, Wade MSS; W. H. Garland to Fillmore, February 17, 1852, MFP-BHS.

50. Entry for September 24, 1852, in *Hayes Diary*, pp. 421–22; Charles Barringer to Daniel M. Barringer, February 4, 1853, Barringer MSS.

51. William Bigler to Franklin Pierce, June 26, 1852, Pierce MSS; Jabez D. Hammond to William H. Seward, November 12, 1851, Seward MSS (RU); John Van Buren to Francis P. Blair, February 28, 1852, Blair-Lee MSS.

52. On New Jersey, I have used Renda, "Railroads, Revenue, and Reform," pp. 80–86.

53. David McDonald to Henry S. Lane, January 17, 1852, (quotation), D. P. Holloway to Lane, February 3, 1852, Lane to Holloway, February 4, 1852, J. L. King et al. to Lane, February 10, 1852, Lane to J. L. King et al., February 15, 1852, Henry Lane MSS (IU). For the actions of the Whig state convention, see John D. Defrees to John J. Crittenden, February 28, 1852, Crittenden MSS (LC); and Schuyler Colfax to William H. Seward, March 5, 1852, Seward MSS (RU). The complaint about Irishmen referred to the provision in Indiana's new constitution that unnaturalized immigrant aliens could vote. Other Indiana Whigs, as we shall see, feared a huge new German vote even more. Whigs' eventual nominee for governor ran almost 20,000 votes behind Wright in October, winning only 43.3 percent of the vote, the Whigs' worst showing since the party's founding.

54. John S. Davis to David F. Caldwell, February 19, 1852, Caldwell MSS; John M. Bradford to William H. Seward, March 3, 1852, Seward MSS (RU); Alex Brooks to Benedict Lewis, August 22, 1852, Daniel Ullmann MSS. The best general accounts of the prohibition movement in these years are Tyrell, *Sobering Up*; and Danenbaum, *Drink and Disorder*.

55. See Table 3 of Holt, *Political Crisis*, p. 116.

56. Robert H. Morris to Hamilton Fish, February 10, 1852, Fish MSS; William J. Rogers to William L. Bigler, October 4, 1852, Bigler MSS.

57. The account of Connecticut in this and following paragraphs is based, in part, on Renda, "The Polity and the Party System," pp. 180–84. Roll-call votes involving the slavery issue had produced sharp polarization in the Connecticut legislature in 1850 and would again in 1854, but no votes concerning slavery were held in 1851, 1852, or 1853. Holt, *Political Crisis*, p. 116.

58. Roger Sherman Baldwin to Emily Baldwin, March 13, 1852, Baldwin to Roger Sherman Baldwin, Jr., March 19, 1852, BFP.

59. Roger Sherman Baldwin to Emily Baldwin, April 10, 1852, BFP; Hartford *Courant*, April 10, 1852, quoted in Renda, "The Polity and the Party System," p. 183; see also Renda's regression estimates of voter movement between 1851 and 1852, p. 213.

60. After the Whig national convention, where only two of Connecticut's six delegates consistently backed Scott, Baldwin complained that the other four flouted the wishes of most Connecticut Whigs, who preferred Scott. Roger Sherman Baldwin to Emily Baldwin, June 27, 1852, BFP. For the 1852 spring campaign in New Hampshire, see Renda, "Polity and the Party System," pp. 192–96.

61. The evidence of immigrant opposition to prohibition is overwhelming, but for a recent examination of German attitudes, see Levine, *Spirit of 1848*, pp. 90, 141, 143, 245.

62. This assertion about low turnout rates among immigrants, which cannot be conclusively proved, rests on the following information. According to the census of 1850, which I reaggregated from manuscript schedules, there were 11,557 white males aged twenty-one or more living in Pittsburgh. Of these, only 4,137 (35.8 percent) were native born or the adult sons of native-born men living at home. Almost 65 percent of the adult male population, that is, was first- or second-generation immigrant. In the presidential election of 1848, when the estimated turnout rate for Pennsylvania as a whole was 77.5 percent, only 5,365 (46.4 percent of the 1850 total) Pittsburghers voted, and turnout was especially low in the wards with the heaviest concentrations of immigrants. Similarly, in the gubernatorial election of 1851, when statewide turnout was 70.7 percent, the total vote in Pittsburgh was only 4304 (37.2 percent of the 1850 total). That discrepancy between city and state turnout rates suggests that, for whatever reason, immigrants voted at lower levels than the native-born. The data on which these estimates are based can be found in Tables 4, 16, and 23 of Holt, *Forging a Majority*, pp. 319–34; and Gienapp, " 'Politics Seem to Enter Into Everything,' " pp. 18–19.

Pittsburgh's exceedingly low turnout level is hard to square with estimates by Robert W. Fogel that during the 1840s *already naturalized* immigrants voted at the same rates as the total electorate. Yet Fogel's figures also show that in 1848 little more than half of the male immigrants already in the northern workforce by 1840 had even bothered to take out naturalization papers, a stunning index of immigrants' political disinterest. For the northern turnout figures, see the table in Gienapp, pp. 18–19. For Fogel's estimates, see Tables 2 and 3 in Fogel, "Modeling Complex Dynamic Interactions," 16–17.

63. My account of the excitement Kossuth engendered rests primarily on Spencer, *Kossuth*; for contemporary descriptions of his speaking style and public persona, see John P. Kennedy to Robert C. Winthrop, December 20, 1851, copy, Kennedy MSS; Simeon Draper to William H. Seward, December 19, 1851, Seward MSS (RU).

64. Spencer, *Kossuth*, pp. 53–54.

65. Daniel Webster to Edward Everett, November 21, 1851, Webster to Franklin Haven, November 21, 1851, Webster to Abbott Lawrence, December 29, 1851, Edward Everett to Webster, December 9, 1851, Webster MSS; Robert C. Winthrop to John Davis, December 13, 1851, John Davis MSS; John P. Kennedy to Robert C. Winthrop, January 24, 1852, copy, Kennedy MSS.

66. William Cullom to William B. Campbell, January 17, 1852, CFP; Philadelphia *Public Ledger*, January 8, 1852; Henry A. Wise to Edward Everett, December 12, 1851, Everett MSS.

67. Gilbert Davis to Millard Fillmore, December 3, 1851, MFP-BHS; B. H. Cheever to Caleb Cushing, December 12, 1851, Cushing MSS; William H. Seward to Thurlow Weed, December 26, 1851, Weed MSS (RU).

68. Webster to Franklin Haven, December 23, 1851, Webster MSS; Ben Wade to Caroline Wade, December 10, 1851, Wade MSS; Henry A. Wise to Edward Everett, January 3, 1852, Everett MSS; Alexander Stephens to John J. Crittenden, February 17, 1852, Crittenden MSS (LC); Seward to Weed, December 26, 1851, Weed MSS; Seward to William Schouler, January 12, 1852, Schouler MSS. For southern attitudes toward Kossuth, see Spencer, *Kossuth*, pp. 95–106. Although a joint resolution welcoming Kossuth to the United States easily passed the House by a vote of 181–16, a later motion to allow Kossuth to address the House met stiffer opposition, 111–56, when most Southerners from both parties opposed it. See Alexander, *Sectional Stress*, pp. 217, 220.

69. Ben Wade to Caroline Wade, December 10, 1852, Wade MSS; Edwin B. Morgan to Seward, January 27, 1852, Seward MSS (RU).

70. Walter Cunningham to Seward, December 7, 20, 1851, Henry J. Raymond to Seward, December 8, 1851, William Schouler to Seward, December 20, 1851, Louis Kossuth to Seward, December 21, 1851, Seward MSS (RU); Seward to Weed, December 26, 1851, Weed MSS (RU); Seward to Schouler, January 12, 1852, Schouler MSS; Seward to Home, December 7, 1851, in *Seward at Washington*, p. 175; Henry A. Wise to Edward Everett, December 31, 1851, Everett MSS. Seward actually invited Kossuth to stay with him when Kossuth reached Washington, but Kossuth declined because his entourage was so large.

71. Van Deusen, *Seward*, pp. 139–40; Frederick Seward to Thurlow Weed, January 31, 1851, Weed MSS (RU); Richard M. Blatchford to Seward, December 13, 1851, Thomas Doremus to Seward, December 15, 1851, Simeon Draper to Seward, December 15, 26, 1851, William Schouler to Seward, January 1, 1852, Seward MSS (RU); Seward to Schouler, January 12, 1852, Lewis Campbell to Schouler, January 17, 1852, Schouler MSS.

72. Webster to Fillmore, December 30, 1851, N. K. Hall to Fillmore, January 13, 1852, MFP-BHS; Henry A. Wise to Edward Everett, December 31, 1851, January 2, 3, 1852, Everett MSS; John P. Kennedy to Elizabeth Kennedy, January 7, 1852, Kennedy MSS; Spencer, *Kossuth*, pp. 87–89.

73. Kennedy to Robert C. Winthrop, December 20, 1851, January 24, 1852, copies, Kennedy MSS; Webster to Fillmore, January 7, 1852, MFP-BHS; Robert Bird to John M. Clayton, January 12, 1852, Clayton MSS; Spencer, *Kossuth*, p. 91.

74. Seward to Webster, January 10, 1852, Webster MSS; Robert Bird to John M. Clayton, January 12, 1852, Clayton MSS; Isaac Jones to Fillmore, February 9, 1852, MFP-BHS.

75. Walter Cunningham to Seward, December 20, 1851, Simeon Draper to Seward, December 26, 1851, William Cooney to Seward, February 16, 1852, Seward MSS (RU); Isaac Jones to Millard Fillmore, February 9, 1852 (quotation), MFP-BHS.

76. G. G. Wescott to William Bigler, December 22, 1851 (quotation), James Burnside to Bigler, December 27, 1851, Bigler MSS; E. W. H. Ellis to Joseph Wright, March 19, 1852 (quotation), Wright MSS; William Cooney to Seward, February 16, 1852, Seward MSS (RU); on the division between Germans and Irish Catholics in St. Louis, see Frank Blair, Jr., to Francis P. Blair, January 31, 1852, Blair-Lee MSS; and McCormack, *Koerner Memoirs*, I, p. 582.

77. William Schouler to William H. Seward, February 14, 1852, William Cooney to Seward, February 16, March 8, 11 (quotation), 13, 1852, Charles Lee to Seward March 4, 1852, Peter Walker to Seward, March 4, 1852, Seward MSS (RU); James Shields to Charles H. Lanphier, February 6, 1852, Lanphier MSS. Significantly, Shields told Lanphier that, just like Seward, he intended his pro-Irish speeches to balance his courtship of Germans with pro-Kossuth speeches.

78. Lewis Campbell to Schouler, January 17, 1852, Schouler MSS.

79. Schouler to Seward, February 14, 1852, Seward MSS; On the nativism of Massachusetts Free Soilers, see Sweeney, "Rum, Romanism, Representation, and Reform."

80. Sweeney, "Rum, Romanism, Representation, and Reform," 129–30.

81. Robert L. Martin to James Watson Webb, March 12, 1852 (quotation), Webb MSS; see also George F. Lehman to James Buchanan, October 30, 1851 (quotation), Buchanan MSS (HSP); James E. Harvey to John J. Crittenden, November 5, 1851, Crittenden MSS; and James Burnside to William L. Bigler, December 27, 1851, Bigler MSS.

82. On the potential revolt of Catholics in Illinois, who were offended by the Democrats' gubernatorial nominee in 1852, see S. Francis to Richard Yates, May 10, 1852, Yates MSS.

83. S. C. Stearns to John McLean, April 9, 1852, McLean MSS (LC); for the conversion of Scott's daughter to Catholicism, I have relied on Gienapp, *Origins*, p. 22. Yet I dissent from Gienapp's otherwise superb account of the 1852 election in that book and in his important essay "Nomination of Winfield Scott." Gienapp argues vigorously that Scott's strategists did not consider seeking the Catholic vote until after the Whig national convention in June; prior to the convention, they counted instead on wooing Free Soil voters in the North by preventing Scott from making any public statement on the Compromise and then running an antislavery campaign. I disagree for two reasons. First, every letter I have quoted or cited above indicating that Whigs hoped Scott would attract Irish and Catholic votes preceded the Whig convention in June. Second, as I show below, I think Gienapp exaggerates Whigs' reliance on the Free Soil vote and their anticipation of running an antislavery campaign if Scott remained silent on the Compromise. Scott's managers' top priority was to reunite northern Whigs by winning the allegiance of pro-Compromise Silver Grays, not wooing Free Soilers. Thus, while they did hope Scott could avoid a commitment on the Compromise, they had no intention of running an anti-Compromise, antislavery campaign if he won the nomination.

84. Miller Pennington to Samuel Galloway, January 14, 1851 (quotation), Galloway MSS; Ben Wade to Caroline Wade, February 8, 1852 ("dead dogs"), Wade MSS; Seward to Weed, December 26, 1851, William A. Sackett to Weed, January 30, 1852, James S. Pike to Weed, January 30, 1852, Weed MSS (RU).

85. William A. Sackett to Weed, January 30, 1852, Weed MSS (RU); on the expectation that Deep South states with Union parties would not attend the Whig national convention, see Philadelphia *Public Ledger*, Washington Correspondence, January 14, 1852.

86. Philip Greely, Jr., to Seward, March 19, 1852, Seward MSS (RU); Webster to Franklin Haven, November 28, 1851, Webster MSS; Seward to Weed, December 26, 1851, Sackett to Weed, January 30, 1852, Pike to Weed, January 30, 1852, Weed MSS (RU). For arguments to Southerners that only Scott could garner the necessary electoral votes, see Truman Smith to Daniel M. Barringer, May 1, 1852, Barringer MSS; and Smith to William B. Campbell, May 15, 1852, CFP.

87. Seward to Weed, December 26, 1851, Sackett to Weed, January 30, 1852, Pike to Weed, January 30, 1852, Weed MSS (RU); Cullom to William B. Campbell, December 9, 1851, January 14, 1852 (quotation), Truman Smith to Campbell, May 15, 1852, CFP; T. M. Brewer to William

Schouler, January 11, 1852, Charles Russell to Schouler, April 16, 1852, Schouler MSS; see also Edward Stanly's public letter to the Whigs of North Carolina, Washington *National Intelligencer*, April 8, 1852.

88. Lewis Campbell to William Schouler, January 17, 1852, Schouler MSS; Pike to Weed, January 30, 1852, Weed MSS (RU). T. M. Brewer also reported that southern Whigs only asked for some "assurance" that would do northern Whigs "the least possible harm—the simplest assurance from Scott himself that he will let the compromise remain undisturbed and is opposed to the renewal of agitation." Brewer to Schouler, January 11, 1852, Schouler MSS.

89. Cole, *Whig Party in the South*, pp. 229–34; Meredith P. Gentry to William B. Campbell, December 27, 1851, William B. Campbell to David Campbell, February 15, 1852, CFP.

90. In saying that the protests of southern Whigs like Gentry—and one might add as well the letters of Silver Grays—have led historians astray into thinking that northern Whigs affiliated with Scott hoped to run an antislavery campaign in 1852, I count myself among the primary offenders. See my mistaken interpretation of Gentry's letter in *Political Crisis*, pp. 96–97. But I have plenty of company from other able historians. In his analysis of the strategy of Scott's managers in the works cited above, for example, William E. Gienapp argues that securing Free Soil support for Scott was their primary goal, and he strongly implies that they intended to run an openly anti-Compromise., antislavery campaign to get it. See also Cooper, *Politics of Slavery*, pp. 322–30.

91. Regression analysis of New York's voting patterns suggests, for example, that in 1849 Whigs had already picked up slightly less than a fifth of the 1848 Free Soil vote, or 4 percent of the potential electorate, but that in 1851 the same percentage of 1850 Whig voters bolted to the Democrats and others abstained. Altogether in 1851, Whigs lost one-seventh of their 1850 voters or 5 percent of the potential electorate. Kirn, "Third Party System in New York State," Tables IX, XII, pp. 40, 45.

In Ohio, in contrast, few if any Whigs defected to the Democrats after 1848, but about three-eighths of the Whigs who voted for Van Buren in 1848 were abstaining by 1850 and 1851. See Maizlish, *Triumph of Sectionalism*, Tables 4, 5, 6, pp. 244–46.

After 1848, Massachusetts Whigs had always won a plurality of the popular vote, which would suffice in presidential but not gubernatorial elections. Thus they were confident about carrying the state for Scott if he were the nominee. When Whigs like Philip Greely spoke about attracting Free Soil votes to break up the Coalition, therefore, their eye was on the state election in 1852, not the presidential contest.

92. *Congressional Globe*, 32nd Cong., 1st Sess., p. 9.

93. On Delaware see John Allderdice to John M. Clayton, February 25, 1852 (quotation), Clayton MSS; on Indiana, see Schuyler Colfax to Seward, January 27, March 15, 1852, Seward MSS (RU); John D. Defrees to John J. Crittenden, February 28, 1852, Crittenden MSS (LC). The Illinois Whig convention did not officially endorse Scott, and Fillmore had numerous supporters in it. But it chose a solid pro-Scott delegation and imposed a unit rule on it in part because delegates believed Scott shared their pro-Compromise beliefs. Samuel Lisle Smith to Seward, February 4, 19, 1852, Seward MSS (RU); John Moses to Richard Yates, March 28, 1852, Moses Cassell to Yates, April 24, 1852, J. M. Ruggles to Yates, May 3, 1852, Yates MSS.

At the Whig national convention, John Minor Botts would try to convince southern Whigs that Scott favored finality by pointing to Scott's endorsement of the pro-Compromise New Jersey state platform of 1852.

94. John Davis to William Schouler, February 5, 1852, Schouler MSS; Winthrop to Crittenden, May 13, 1852, Crittenden MSS (LC); Truman Smith to Daniel M. Barringer, May 1, 1852, Barringer MSS; Smith to William B. Campbell, May 15, 1852, CFP. Smith sent the same assurances to John Wilson in California even before Congress assembled: "The idea is now disseminated all over the slave states that Genl. Scott is disposed to sympathize with the abolitionists or at least that he is regarded by them with favor. But this is utterly false—I speak as of my own knowledge." Smith to Wilson, October 14, 1851, Wilson MSS.

95. William Schouler to Seward, December 20, 1851 (quotation), Joshua R. Giddings to Joseph A. Giddings, June 10, 1852, Seward MSS (RU); Seward to Weed, December 26, 1851, Weed MSS (RU); Robert G. Campbell to Fillmore, January 5, 1852, MFP-BHS.

96. Thompson to Fillmore, May 12, 1852, MFP-BHS; Colfax to Seward, March 15, 1852, Seward MSS (RU).

97. E. A. Stansbury to George W. Julian, September 7, 1851, Giddings-Julian MSS.

98. Anthony C. Brown to Seward, February 25, 1852, Philip Greely, Jr., to Seward, March 1, 1852, Alvah Hunt to Seward, March 17, 1852, Seward MSS (RU); Lewis Campbell to William Schouler, January 17, March 5, 1852, Schouler MSS; Ben Wade to Caroline Wade, December 10, 1851, February 8, 1852, Wade MSS.

99. Schuyler Colfax to Seward, January 27, March 15, April 2, 1852, Seward MSS (RU); Seward to William Schouler, January 12, 1852; Schouler MSS; William Cullom to William B. Campbell, December 9, 1851, CFP; James E. Harvey to John M. Clayton, February 15, 1852, Clayton MSS.

100. Ben Wade to Caroline Wade, February 8, 1852, Wade MSS; James E. Harvey to John M. Clayton, February 15, 1852, Clayton MSS; Cullom to William B. Campbell, February 26, 1852, CFP; Lew Campbell to William Schouler, March 5, 1852, Schouler MSS; Colfax to Seward, March 15, April 2, 1852, Seward MSS (RU). The text of Colfax's proposed letter for Scott accompanies his March 15 letter. It was cleverly phrased to leave open the loophole that Congress might revise the fugitive slave law.

101. William B. Campbell to David Campbell, February 15, 1852, Christopher H. Williams to William B. Campbell, February 19, April 27, 1852, William Cullom to Campbell, February 26, 1852, Meredith Gentry to Campbell, March 24, 1852, CFP; William Cullom to Robert L. Caruthers, March 14, 1852, Caruthers MSS; Andrew Johnson to David T. Patterson, April 4, 1852, in *Johnson Papers*, pp. 30–31.

102. Campbell to William Schouler, March 5, 1852, Schouler MSS; E. C. Cabell to Daniel M. Barringer, March 14, 1852, Barringer MSS.

103. Simeon Draper to Seward, March 3, 1852, Philip Greely, Jr., to Seward, March 2, 1852, James Forsyth to Seward, March 4, 1852, Washington Hunt to Seward, April 4, 1852, Seward MSS (RU); Meredith Gentry to William B. Campbell, March 24, 1852, CFP.

104. Washington *National Intelligencer*, April 8, 1852; Cole, *Whig Party in the South*, p. 235; Alexander, *Sectional Stress*, p. 218.

105. G. A. Tavener to Daniel Webster, April 8, 1852, Webster MSS; Marshall quoted in Cole, *Whig Party in the South*, p. 235.

106. *New York Tribune*, April 12, 1850; *New York Times*, April 12, 1852.

107. *New York Tribune*, April 10, 1852.

108. Washington *Union*, April 14, 1852. This issue of the *Union* for Wednesday is misdated April 10. The 10th was a Saturday.

109. *New York Times*, April 14, 20, 1852; Washington *National Intelligencer*, April 17, 1852; Charles Russell to William Schouler, April 16, 1852, Schouler MSS.

110. Greely to Seward, April 14, 1852, Seward MSS (RU); Truman Smith to John Wilson, April 12, 1852, Wilson MSS.

111. My account of the Whig caucus is based on the reports in the Washington *Union*, April 23, 1852, and the *New York Times*, April 22, 1852. The *Union* attributed its account to the report James Harvey had made to the Philadelphia *North American* and to other reports to the Baltimore *Sun*. These accounts, as usual, differed about the total number of men initially in attendance and about how many Southerners, eleven or seventeen, withdrew.

112. Washington *Union*, April 23, 1852.

113. Cole, *Whig Party in the South*, pp. 239–40; Oran Follett to Millard Fillmore, April 27, 1852, MFP-BHS; Fillmore to Oran Follett, May 3, 1852 (microfilm edition of the Fillmore Papers).

114. Philip Greely, Jr., to Seward, May 22, 27, 1852, Seward MSS (RU); Edward Stanly to William Schouler, May 10, 1852, John Minor Botts to Schouler, May 19, 1852, Schouler MSS; Philip Greely, Jr., to James S. Pike, May 15, 27, 1852, Horace Greeley to Pike, May 29, 1852, June 13, 1852, Pike MSS; Truman Smith to Daniel M. Barringer, May 1, 1852, Barringer MSS; Smith to William B. Campbell, May 15, 1852, CFP.

The letter Greeley ultimately prepared was enclosed with his letter to Pike on June 13 and dated June 20, so that Scott could issue it *after* he won the nomination. The letter itself was preposterously verbose and windy, worse than anything the foot-in-mouth Scott could have written.

115. Edward Stanly to William Schouler, May 10, 1852, John Minor Botts to Schouler, May 19, 1852, Schouler MSS; Philip Greely, Jr., to James S. Pike, May 15, 1852, Pike MSS. Botts' public letter was dated May 3, the day he said he spoke with Scott, and appeared in the Richmond *Whig* on May 11. Cole, *Whig Party in the South*, p. 243.

116. Philip Greely, Jr., to James S. Pike, May 3 (quotation), May 15, 1852, Charles A. Dana to Pike, May 15, 1852, Pike MSS; Seth C. Hawley to Seward, June 4, 1852 (quotation), Seward MSS (RU); Israel Washburn, Jr., to William Schouler, May 5, 1852 (quotation), John Minor Botts to Schouler, May 19, 1852, Schouler MSS; William H. Seward to Wife, June 2, 4, 1852, in *Seward at Washington*, pp. 183–84.

117. Campbell to Schouler, March 5, 1852, Schouler MSS. As in 1848, most southern states chose all the district delegates at state conventions. For the multiple representation of southern states, which in effect gave each delegate only a fraction of one vote, see the debates at the convention, *New York Times*, June 17–23, 1852.

118. William C. Dawson to Fillmore, March 15, 1852, Arthur F. Hopkins to Fillmore, March 3, 1852, MFP-BHS; Hopkins to William A. Graham, April 6, 1852, in *Graham Papers*, IV, pp. 283–87.

119. Charles C. Raboteau to David F. Caldwell, March 17, 27, 1852, Caldwell MSS; resolutions of Buncombe and Henderson County meetings, with Marcus Erwin to Thomas Clingman, April 16, 1852, Clingman-Puryear MSS; John H. Bryan to William A. Graham, April 5, 1852, in *Graham Papers*, IV, pp. 280–81.

120. William A. Graham to James W. Bryan, April 17, 1852, James W. Osborne to William A. Graham, May 26, 1852, in *Graham Papers*, IV, pp. 290, 302–04; Webster to ?, April 13, 1852, Webster to James L. Pettigru, June 5, 1852, George Abbot to Webster, May 15, 1852, Webster MSS; Arthur F. Hopkins to Fillmore, April 22, 1852, Henry Hilliard to Fillmore, June 1, 1852, George S. Bryan to Fillmore, June 3, 1852, MFP-BHS; Joseph G. Baldwin to Alexander H. H. Stuart, April 16, 1852, Stuart MSS (LC); Cole, *Whig Party in the South*, p. 241.

121. The District of Columbia was allowed to send a delegation to the convention, but according to newspaper accounts, they did not vote in roll calls on the nominee. The total number of votes at the convention was 296, but since some southern states sent three or more men to represent each congressional district, the total number of accredited delegates was considerably larger.

122. S. Lisle Smith to William H. Seward, February 19, 1852, Philip Greely, Jr., to Seward, March 19, May 22, 27, 1852, D. S. Palmer to Seward, March 31, 1852, Seward MSS (RU); S. Lisle Smith to Elihu B. Washburne, February 20, 1852, Washburne MSS (LC); James Kidd to Millard Fillmore, February 27, 1852, MFP-BHS.

123. Daniel Webster to Franklin Haven, February 6, 1852, Charles J. Lanman to Webster, March 4, 1852, Webster MSS; John O. Charles to Fillmore, May 8, 1852, W. Channing Gibbs to Fillmore, June 4, 1852, MFP-BHS.

124. I have found no explicit complaints about the district system that split northern anti-Taylor Whigs in 1848, but the procedural changes that Scott majorities rammed through in several states certainly suggest that they had learned a lesson in 1848.

125. Jacob Howard to William H. Seward, September 17, 1851, Henry Barns to Seward, October 2, December 4, 1851, Seward MSS (RU).

126. D. W. C. Clarke to William Schouler, December 16, 1851 (quotation), Schouler MSS; Thomas Hale to Millard Fillmore, April 23, 1852 (quotation), MFP-BHS; Harry B. Stacy to Porteas Baxter, June 11, 1852, Justin Morrill MSS.

127. Samuel Lisle Smith to Seward, February 4, 19, 1852, Schuyler Colfax to Seward, March 15, 1852, Seward MSS (RU); John S. Butterfield to Fillmore, June 2, 1852, MFP-BHS; Lew Campbell to William Schouler, March 5, 1852, Schouler MSS; William Pennington to Daniel Webster, June 28, 1852, Webster MSS; New York *Herald*, June 3, 19, 1852.

128. John H. Bryant to Fillmore, March 18, 1852, P. L. Ellmaker to Fillmore, March 26, 1852, George W. Knight to Fillmore, April 7, 1852, MFP-BHS; Charles March to Webster, April 8, 1852, Webster MSS; Mueller, *Whig Party in Pennsylvania*, p. 194, Pittsburgh *Commercial Ad-*

vertiser, May 3, 1852, quoted in Mueller, pp. 195–96; the Whig platform can be found in the Pittsburgh *Gazette*, March 30, 1852.

129. The battles in individual congressional districts can be traced in numerous letters in the Seward and Fillmore Papers. George R. Babcock, Fillmore's ally from Buffalo, who represented the Erie County district at the national convention, promised to attend a meeting of all the state's delegates on June 11, 1852, in New York City, where disputes over seats would be addressed. But he wisely urged Fillmore to let the national convention, where Fillmore's strength would be significantly greater than in this New York meeting, decide these disputes. Babcock to Fillmore, June 3, 1852, MFP-BHS.

130. Daniel Ullmann to N. K. Hall, January 27, 1852, R. C. Wetmore, James Price, and Daniel Ullmann to Fillmore, March 6, 1852, Ullmann MSS; Hugh Maxwell to Fillmore, March 6, 1852, Thomas Foote to Fillmore, March 18, 1852, John O. Charles to Fillmore, May 8, 1852, MFP-BHS; James Watson Webb to Daniel Webster, February 8, 1852, Charles March to Webster, April 12, 1852, Webster MSS; Simeon Draper to Seward, March 9, 1852, James Bowen to Seward, March 11, 1852 (quotation), James Kelly to Seward, April 10, 1852, Horace Greeley to Seward April 20, 1852, C. A. Stetson to Seward, May 13, 1852, Seward MSS (RU). For the credentials fights at the national convention, see *New York Times*, June 19, 1852.

131. For the maneuvering prior to, and the decisions of, the Whig legislative caucus, see James R. Thompson to Millard Fillmore, March 29, 30, 1852, MFP-BHS; Henry J. Raymond to William H. Seward, March 15, 27, 1852, Seward MSS (RU); *New York Times*, April 10, 13, 1852. For reports of the meeting of delegates in New York City stating that "the feeling between the Fillmore and Scott men was very bitter," see the New York *Herald*, June 12, 1852. Despite an anti-Whig bias, issues of the *Herald* for May and June also carry helpful accounts of battles over delegates in individual congressional districts.

132. Horace Greeley to Seward, April 20, 1852, Seward MSS; George Evans to William Pitt Fessenden, May 22, 1852, Fessenden MSS (WRHS); Philip Greely, Jr., to James Pike, June 4, 1852, John Otis to Pike, June 5, 1852, Pike MSS. Maine's Whig state convention met on June 3 and chose Evans and Fessenden as at-large delegates, as well as the delegates from the first and third congressional districts. The other five districts chose delegates on their own earlier; Pike represented the seventh district. New York *Herald*, June 4, 1852. The delegation would unanimously favor Scott, the only New England delegation to do so.

133. Webster to ?, April 13, 1852, Webster to James L. Pettigru, June 5, 1852, Charles Morehead to Webster, June 11, 1852, Webster to Humphrey Marshall, June 15, 1852, Webster to Richard M. Blatchford, June 22, 1852, Webster MSS.

134. Christopher Williams to William B. Campbell, June 3, 1852, CFP; William H. Seward to Wife, June 17, 1852, in *Seward at Washington*, p. 186; Cabell's speech is quoted in Doherty, *Whigs of Florida*, p. 53.

135. Cole, *Whig Party in the South*, p. 245; *New York Times*, June 17, 1852; New York *Herald*, June 17, 1852.

136. Fillmore to President of the Whig National Convention, June 10, 1852, draft, Fillmore to George Babcock, June 12, 1852, copy, MFP-O.

137. John Barney to Fillmore, June 11, 1852, N. K. Hall to Fillmore, June 11, 1852, E. R. Jewett to Fillmore, June 12, 1852, MFP-BHS. Fillmore told Babcock to keep his letter absolutely secret, and he made no reference in the June 10 or June 12 letter to endorsing Webster. Barney, therefore, must have referred to something Fillmore said, not anything he wrote.

138. Barney to Fillmore, June 11, 1852, MFP-BHS; Seward to Wife, June 2, 4, 6, 10, 17, 1852, in *Seward at Washington*, pp. 183–86; Horace Greeley to James S. Pike, June 13, 1852, Pike MSS.

139. Holt, "Democratic Party," p. 559.

140. Unless otherwise noted, all information on the convention proceedings is taken from the *New York Times*, June 17–23, 1852, and the New York *Herald* for the same dates. Most secondary accounts have focused primarily on the balloting for president and to a lesser extent the adoption of a platform, and they have largely ignored the three days of bickering that preceded the presentation of a platform. See, for example, Dalzell, *Webster*, pp. 259–77; Rayback, *Fillmore*, pp. 354–63; and Gienapp, "Nomination of Winfield Scott," 408–09. For the Whig party

as an institution, however, the first three days were as just as important as the ballots on which most historians have focused. Happily, they are treated seriously in Cole, *Whig Party in the South*, pp. 245–49, additional testimony to the enduring value of that now eighty-year-old work. Still, my account must give them proper due, and its length reflects the convention's lasting significance.

141. Virginia, for example, sent forty-five accredited delegates to cast its fifteen votes. The exception to this pattern of overrepresentation was South Carolina, which had no organized Whig party; only four men claimed the right to cast its eight votes.

142. Maine apparently did not vote on this resolution; at least, newspaper accounts did not record a vote by Maine.

143. The report in the *New York Times*, June 18, 1852, listed all eight of Maryland's votes against, while the report of the New York *Herald* for the same day said that all eight Maryland delegates voted in favor. I assume there was an error in transcription at the *Herald* office, for the only way to arrive at the total of 144 negative votes on which both papers agreed was to count Maryland as against.

144. For the North I rely on the fuller vote totals in the *Herald*.

145. John Barney to Fillmore, June 17, 1852, Solomon G. Haven to Fillmore, June 18, 1852, MFP-BHS; see also Raymond's report to the *New York Times*, June 18, 1852. The basis for Barney's calculations is unclear; perhaps he simply subtracted the six Missouri, four Iowa, and two other votes from the total supporting Jessup's amendment to arrive at the Scott vote. But he wrote before the critical credentials committee reported.

146. Despite the questionable proceedings in Pennsylvania, the credentials committee apparently considered nothing other than challenges in New York and Vermont and the propriety of admitting a nonvoting delegation from the District of Columbia.

147. Technically, of course, the mover of an amendment cannot withdraw it, if it has been adopted, without another vote. Jessup did not refer to the amended Duncan resolution, but rather to his motion to attach the same amendment to a substitute resolution offered by a Maryland delegate. Since that motion had not yet been voted on, he could do it alone, and the substitute motion, which provided for the one-state, one-vote formula, was adopted in place of the amended Duncan resolution. The northern majority that had adopted Jessup's amendment acquiesced, therefore, by not attempting to introduce something like Jessup's amendment themselves when he withdrew it, a fact commented on specifically by the *Herald*'s correspondent in his report appearing in the June 19 issue.

148. Aside from the reports in the June 19 issues of the *Herald* and the *Times*, see New York *Herald*, June 4, 1852; Henry B. Stacy to Porteas Baxter, June 11, 1852, Justin Morrill MSS; Solomon G. Haven to Millard Fillmore, June 18, 1852, MFP-BHS.

149. The disputes over these individual districts can be followed in the reports in the New York *Herald* for May and June 1852. But the case involving Raymond, which ignited the convention's most vitriolic debate, requires explanation, for it involved the twenty-second congressional district from the northern part of the state bordering on Lake Ontario, while Raymond lived in New York City. Two men, a Silver Gray named Richardson and a Scott man named Bruce, claimed to represent the district after the two sides tied at the district convention. Both came to Baltimore, but Bruce became sick after the first day (probably because of too much strong drink, if the *Herald*'s reporter can be believed), and he went home. Before he left, Bruce signed a blank proxy and told the chairman of the pro-Scott state delegation to fill in the name that would go before the credentials committee. After two New York Whigs turned down the request to substitute for Bruce, the chairman (probably Simeon Draper, although it is unclear from the reports) approached Raymond, who had come to the convention not as a delegate but to report the proceedings to his newspaper. Raymond agreed to serve, the chairman wrote in Raymond's name, and the proxy was submitted to the credentials committee along with Richardson's claim.

The soap opera did not end there. While its chairman, a Virginian named Watts, was out of the room on Thursday night, the committee agreed to seat both Richardson and Raymond. Watts found this decision so outrageous—he later said Raymond had no more right to represent the twenty-second district than he did to represent California and that neither man had proper credentials—that when he read the committee report on Friday morning, he apparently omitted any reference whatsoever to the disputed twenty-second district, causing both Richardson and Raymond to demand to know who had the right to speak and vote for the district. I say "apparently," for the newspaper reports are unclear as to exactly which portions of the report Watts read, but Richardson's anger was just as evident as Raymond's. See *New York Times*, June 19, 22, and especially 23, 1852. On the deadlock at the convention in the twenty-second district itself, see the New York *Herald*, May 15, 1852.

150. For grammatical reasons, I have changed the participial form "impairing" in the platform to "impair." Aside from minor changes in the prelude to the platform, the one significant change from the southern caucus' platform occurred in the Compromise plank and constituted a small concession to Northerners. The Southerners' platform singled out the Fugitive Slave Act a second time, thereby highlighting its importance. "And so far as the Fugitive Slave Law is concerned," it read, "we will maintain the same, and insist on its strict enforcement." The committee's platform deleted this second specific reference to the fugitive law and referred to all the Compromise measures when it said that "we shall maintain them and insist upon their enforcement." The two documents can be found in *New York Times*, June 17, 19, 1852.

151. Francis Pulszky to Seward, June 20, 1852, Seward MSS (RU). This letter is misdated June 2 by the staff of the Rush Rhees Library, but obviously it could not have been written until after the platform was adopted.

152. See, for example, Johnson, *National Party Platforms*, p. 20.

153. Recall that a major Whig argument against the Walker Tariff in 1846 had been the absence of specific duties; that Webster, as Ashmun well knew, in trying to arrange a compromise to stop passage of the Walker bill in 1846, had sought above all to protect specific duties even if at lower rates; that Treasury Secretary William Meredith had stressed the need for specific rates in his widely admired report in December 1849; and that Fillmore himself had repeated that emphasis in his December 1850 annual message.

154. The account of Botts' speech is much fuller in the *Herald* than in the *Times*, although the *Herald* was especially contemptuous of Botts' supposed blunder.

155. James S. Pike to Seward, June 16, 1852, Seward MSS (RU). Pike referred to the letter that Horace Greeley had written on May 29 for Scott to issue after he got the nomination and that he had mailed to Pike on June 13. It contained such a paragraph, and it can be found in the Pike MSS with Greeley to Pike, June 13, 1852. Despite Pike's letter, the evidence I cited earlier clearly indicates that many Scott delegates were eager to conciliate Southerners.

156. Most secondary accounts list the vote as 227–66 but do not make clear the source of that total. The embarrassed *New York Times*, in an obvious attempt to keep from New York's Whigs the extent of northern capitulation, gave no figures at all in its issue for June 19. The New York *Herald* for that date lists the total as 226–66 and gives the breakdown for each state, but its figures add up only by including California's 4 votes with the majority rather than with the opposition, as the *Herald* lists them.

157. Seward to Wife, June 18, 1852, in *Seward at Washington*, pp. 187–88; Gienapp, "Nomination of Winfield Scott," 408. Seward's belief that northern Scott delegates had collapsed before southern intimidation raises additional questions about Pike's assertion that they had to be forced to support the platform.

158. Jones' speech is quoted in the June 19 issue of the *Herald* and is omitted from the *Times* report that day.

159. John Barney to Millard Fillmore, June 17, 18, 19, 20, 1852, Solomon G. Haven to Fillmore, June 18, 1852, B. M. Edney to Fillmore, June 20, 1852, MFP-BHS; Webster to Daniel Jenifer, June 19, 1852, Webster MSS.

160. Elihu B. Washburne to Algernon Sydney Washburn, June 19, 1852, A. S. Washburn MSS; John Barney to Fillmore, June 20, 1852, B. M. Edney to Fillmore, June 20, 1852, MFP-BHS; Webster to ?, June 20, 1852, Webster MSS; Dalzell, *Webster*, pp. 269–73.

161. On Webster's surly mood, see Dalzell, *Webster*, p. 272.

162. Webster to Fillmore, June 21, 1852, Fillmore to Webster, June 21, 1852, MFP-BHS.

163. Granger to Fillmore, June 30, 1852, MFP-BHS.

164. During Saturday's long session, a clerk from James Watson Webb's New York *Courier*

and Enquirer had telegraphed him and Moses Grinnell that he had seen Raymond's telegraphic dispatch to the *New York Times*, in which Raymond charged that if Southerners did not vote for Scott after Scott men voted for the platform, it would be "a breach of faith." This telegram fell into the hands of Southerners, who interrupted the balloting on Saturday to read it and charge that Raymond had accused Southerners on the platform committee of making a corrupt bargain to support Scott. This outrageously false accusation, charged a Georgian on Monday, justified Raymond's expulsion. Raymond demanded the floor to defend himself, and there then ensued a long but exceedingly informative debate involving Raymond, Georgians, Cabell, Grinnell, Duncan of Louisiana, who read the telegram to the convention on Saturday, the Virginia chairman of the credentials committee, and members of the platform committee that, among other things, contains the fullest account of how Raymond was named a delegate and what the credentials committee did with his case. Raymond acquitted himself well, and the convention ultimately tabled the motion to expel by voice vote. *New York Times*, June 22, 23, 1852.

165. After the convention W. Channing Gibbs wrote Fillmore that Cranston had betrayed Rhode Island's Whigs by the way he voted at Baltimore. Gibbs to Fillmore, June 30, 1852, MFP-BHS.

166. My state-by-state breakdown of the vote and the switches between the first and last ballots is taken from the account in the *New York Times*. It lists Scott's total as 158, but the individual state votes for him add up to 157.

167. Reports of the convention do not identify who cast individual ballots; I have inferred that Grinnell and Draper cast the two Webster votes from New York on the first ballot and that Grinnell stuck by him, as he pledged, at two caucuses of the Webster men.

168. With eight votes in Scott's column on the final ballot, Virginia, Scott's native state, was the only slave state aside from Delaware to give him the majority of its votes.

169. Pike to Seward, June 16, 1852, Seward MSS (RU).

170. Recall that Webster urged Fillmore to appoint Bates as secretary of war in July 1850 because Bates was considered a Westerner, not a Southerner. Bates got every vote from Indiana, Illinois, Iowa, Wisconsin, and Arkansas. Massachusetts also gave all thirteen of its votes to Bates, evidence that may support the case of some contemporaries and historians that Massachusetts men really wanted Scott nominated even if they stuck with Webster. See, for example, Dalzell, *Webster*, pp. 274–77.

171. For the wonderful "Tar and Feathers" label, see John P. Kennedy to John Morris, July 4, 1852, copy, Kennedy MSS.

172. Charles A. Dana to James S. Pike, June 21, 1852, Pike MSS.

CHAPTER 20

1. Charles Gayarre to John F. H. Claiborne, June 29, 1852, William L. Bigler to Franklin Pierce, June 26, 1852, Pierce MSS; Andrew Johnson to Sam Milligan, July 20, 1852, in *Johnson Papers*, pp. 67–70.

2. *New York Tribune*, June 21, 1852.

3. E. C. Cabell to Daniel M. Barringer, July 10, 1852, Barringer MSS.

4. Charles A. Dana to James S. Pike, June 21, 1852, Pike MSS; Benjamin Wade to Caroline Wade, July 2, 1852, Wade MSS. I have pieced together this list from correspondence in various manuscript collections, especially the Seward Papers.

5. Henry C. Carey to John O. Sargent, July 2, 1852, Sargent MSS; W. Channing Gibbs to Millard Fillmore, June 30, 1852, George R. Babcock to Fillmore, July 15, 1852, MFP-BHS; Elliott, *Scott*, p. 631.

6. Elliott, *Scott*, p. 628; William H. Seward to Frances Seward, August 7, 1852, in *Seward at Washington*, p. 191.

7. William B. Campbell to William Cullom, June 26, 1852, copy, CFP. For an example of a hard-liner angered by Jones' action, see Lewis D. Campbell to William Schouler, July 6, 1852, Schouler MSS.

8. Scott's letter, for example, was first printed in the *New York Times* on June 30, 1852.

9. Benjamin F. Wade to Caroline Wade, June 30, 1852, Wade MSS. Elliott, *Scott*, p. 625, asserts that the forthrightness, naiveté, and clumsy prose of the letter indicate that neither Seward nor any other Scott manager wrote it.

10. *New York Times*, June 30, 1852. In a letter Schuyler Colfax prepared months before the Whig convention for Scott to issue to reassure Southerners, he had explicitly left open the possibility that Scott would approve any attempt to revise the fugitive slave law. This insistence was common among Scott's northern supporters. Schuyler Colfax to William H. Seward, March 15, 1852, Seward MSS (RU).

11. Horace Greeley to James S. Pike, May 29, June 13, 1852, Pike MSS. The letter, dated June 20 by Greeley because he thought the convention would be over by then, is filed with his June 13 letter, but Pike dates it May 29 on the back. We may never know who the two authors to whom Wade alluded were, but my guess is James Pike and Lew Campbell.

12. Greeley to Pike, June 13, 1852 (quotation), Pike MSS; Greeley to Seward, June 13, 1852, Seward MSS (RU); Greeley to Schuyler Colfax, June 13, 1852, Greeley-Colfax MSS.

13. In its editorial commentary on Scott's letter in the June 30, 1852, issue, the *New York Times* implicitly noted the omission of a flat call for free land by arguing that the important point was to encourage early settlement favorable to actual settlers. "We hail the introduction of this principle into the creed of the great Whig party as a first step towards a new and beneficent policy in regard to the Public Lands."

14. *New York Times*, June 30, 1852; for Democratic uses of the earlier letters before and immediately after the convention, see Daniel M. Haskell to William H. Seward, June 7, 1852, Seward MSS (RU); and Albany *Argus*, June 25, 1852; for Greeley's admission that the earlier letters were damaging, see Horace Greeley to Schuyler Colfax, July 15, 1852, Greeley-Colfax MSS. For Whigs' recognition that they must conciliate Germans offended by the platform, see Charles A. Dana to James S. Pike, June 21, 1852, Pike MSS; and Seth Hawley to William H. Seward, June 26, 1852, Seward MSS (RU).

One additional phrase in the acceptance letter hints that others besides Scott wrote it and helps resolve disagreements among historians about what occurred at the Whig convention itself. One reason northern Whigs were so appalled by Scott's statement, which James Jones read on June 21, was that they knew that if Scott committed himself to a pro-Compromise platform prior to the nomination itself, he would be seen as capitulating to southern pressure and accordingly weakened in the North. Jones read the letter as being dated Sunday, June 20, and newspaper accounts like that in the *New York Times* on June 22 printed that as the date of Scott's message, which was clearly worded in anticipation of a possible nomination: "I will accept the nomination, if tendered to me, with the Platform laid down by the Convention." Since no one at the convention saw the note in Jones' hands and since he spoke some minutes after the final ballot ended (how long after is impossible to determine from newspaper accounts), Scott's Washington managers saw a chance to rectify even this potential embarrassment by postdating Scott's letter to Monday, June 21, *after* he learned of his nomination. Thus the acceptance letter declared: "Not having written a word to procure this distinction, I lost not a moment after it had been conferred in addressing a letter to one of your members, to signify what would be, at the proper time, the substance of my reply to the Convention." For historians' disagreements about the date of Scott's note to Jones, compare Gienapp, *Origins*, p. 19, with Cole, *Whig Party in the South*, pp. 254–58.

15. *New York Times*, June 30, 1852.

16. Nichols, *Pierce*, p. 206; James Dew to Franklin Pierce, July 14, 1852, Pierce MSS.

17. Truman Smith to John Wilson, October 7, 1852, Wilson MSS.

18. B. F. Johnson to Elihu B. Washburne, September 16, 1852 (quotation), Washburne MSS (LC); Henry Wilson to Seward, July 8, 1852, Seward MSS (RU); George B. Loring to Caleb Cushing, July 19, September 24, 1852, Cushing MSS; Benjamin Bristow to Franklin Pierce, July 28, 1852, Pierce MSS.

19. On Pierce's misfortunes in Mexico, see Nichols, *Pierce*, pp. 161–66; on Southerners' cult of honor, which made any hint of cowardice so damaging, see Wyatt-Brown, *Southern Honor*, and Ayers, *Vengeance and Justice*.

20. Elliott, *Scott*, pp. 629–30, with quotation from "The Crisis" of Quitman's speech; Cole, *Whig Party in the South*, pp. 267–68.

21. B. B. French to Franklin Pierce, June 27, 1852, James G. Fitzgerald to Pierce, July 20, 1852, Pierce MSS; Henry A. Wise to James Buchanan, July 20, 1852, Buchanan MSS (HSP); Thomas Bragg to John Bragg, July 11, 1852, Bragg MSS; B. F. Dill to Charles D. Fontaine, July

6, 1852, Fontaine MSS; A. G. Penn to John F. H. Claiborne, June 25, 1852, John Slidell to Claiborne, July 6, 1852, Claiborne MSS.

22. Richmond *Enquirer*, September 7, 1852, quoted in Cooper, *Politics of Slavery*, pp. 336–37. Cooper's account of the election in the South, pp. 327–41, is most valuable.

23. The card appeared on July 5, 1852. Cole, *Whig Party in the South*, pp. 259–60; Elliott, *Scott*, pp. 627–38; Christopher Williams to William B. Campbell, June 3, 1852, Meredith Gentry to William B. Campbell, July 1852, CFP; Cabell to Daniel M. Barringer, July 10, 1852, Barringer MSS.

24. Cole, *Whig Party in the South*, pp. 261–68; Henry Hilliard to Millard Fillmore, August 3, 11, 1852, MFP-BHS; Daniel Webster to Fillmore, July 25, 1852, Webster MSS; John Clemens to Franklin Pierce, September 24, 1852, Pierce MSS; John Barnes to John Bragg, July 22, 1852, F. S. Lyon to Bragg, July 27, 1852, Bragg MSS.

25. Cole, *Whig Party in the South*, pp. 263–69.

26. Ibid., pp. 263–65. The first quotation is from the Milledgeville *Southern Recorder*, quoted on p. 265; Murray, *Whig Party in Georgia*, pp. 166–67; J. R. Sneed to Alexander H. Stephens, July 13, 1852 (second quotation), Stephens MSS (LC). For some Whigs' intention to vote for Pierce, see W. W. Wigins to A. W. Venable, July 17, 1852, and Herschel V. Johnson to Franklin Pierce, July 21, 1852, Pierce MSS.

27. The quotation, apparently from a public letter by Stephens, is in the Milledegeville *Southern Recorder*, July 13, 1852, quoted in Murray, *Whig Party in Georgia*, p. 166; John L. Stephens to Daniel Webster, August 3, 1852, Webster MSS; George R. Curtis to Alexander H. Stephens, August 13, 1852, Stephens MSS (LC); Robert C. Winthrop to John P. Kennedy, August 23, 1852, copy, Winthrop MSS; William H. Seward to William Schouler, August 22, 1852, Schouler MSS. On Webster's bitterness and determination to vote for Pierce, see Dalzell, *Webster*, pp. 278–304; and George S. Bryan to John Pendleton Kennedy, September 25, 1852, Kennedy MSS. Bryan, a delegate to the Baltimore convention from South Carolina, spoke with Webster in Washington on his way back to Charleston.

28. This paragraph is based on Doherty, *Whigs of Florida*, pp. 51–55, and Cole, *Whig Party in the South*, p. 269.

29. Jacksonville *News*, quoted in Doherty, *Whigs of Florida*, p. 55. Cooper, *Politics of Slavery*, pp. 328–29, points out that virtually all southern Whigs stressed the platform and Scott's commitment to it.

30. Richmond *Whig*, June 30, 1852, quoted in Cole, *Whig Party in the South*, p. 261; Richard Pindell to William H. Seward, April 28, 1852, Seward MSS (RU); Lewis D. Campbell to William Schouler, July 6, 1852, Schouler MSS. In North Carolina, Whig papers affiliated with the dissidents Clingman and Rayner, the Ashville *News* and Wilmington *Commercial*, continued to oppose Scott, but for evidence that the majority of Whigs supported the Scott-Graham ticket, see Kruman, *Parties and Politics*, pp. 133–35. While Humphrey Marshall, unlike some other southern Whigs, did not openly denounce Scott, he was clearly crestfallen at the result. He resigned his House seat on August 4, 1852, before the session ended, and temporarily ceased all political activity.

31. Cole, *Whig Party in the South*, pp. 261–63; John Bell to ?, July 13, 1852, Bell to ?, July 31, 1852, drafts, John Bell MSS; Andrew Johnson to David T. Patterson, July 15, 1852, in *Johnson Papers*, pp. 65–66.

32. Andrew Johnson to Sam Milligan, July 20, 1852, in *Johnson Papers*, pp. 67–70; William B. Campbell to William Cullom, June 26, 1852, and to David Campbell, June 29, July 29, August 17, 1852, CFP.

33. As usual, all data on state and congressional elections are calculated from the returns in the Congressional Quarterly's *Guide to U.S. Elections* and Burnham's figures on the partisan share of state legislative seats supplied by the University of Michigan's Inter-University Consortium for Political and Social Research.

34. David F. Caldwell to John Kerr, June 14, 1852, draft, Seaton Caldwell to David F. Caldwell, Caldwell MSS; Thomas Bragg to John Bragg, July 3, 11, 1852, Bragg MSS; David L. Swain to William A. Graham, July 6, 1852, Samuel F. Patterson to Graham, September 2, 1852 (quotation), in *Graham Papers*, IV, pp. 341–42, 385–88; Thomas L. Clingman to J. F. E. Hardy, July

18, 1852, draft, Clingman-Puryear MSS. For an expert account of the 1852 state election, see Kruman, *Parties and Politics*, pp. 96–100. My assertion that almost one-tenth of previous Whig voters abstained is based on a regression estimate in McFaden, "Sections, Slaveholders, and Safe Concessions," p. 14.

Whigs' share of seats in the lower house of the state legislature changed from 54 percent in 1846 to 50 percent in 1848 to 46 percent in 1850 to 52 percent in 1852. Whereas Democrats controlled the senate twenty-seven to twenty-three after the 1850 elections, their margin increased to twenty-eight to twenty-two in 1852.

35. G. B. McGudry to Samuel F. Patterson, September 20, 1852, Patterson MSS; Truman Smith to Thurlow Weed, August 21, 1852, Weed MSS (RU).

36. B. H. Shepperd to William H. Seward, September 2, 1852, Seward MSS (RU); John Campbell to William B. Campbell, September 10, 1852, CFP.

37. Wyndham Robertson to James Buchanan, November 8, 1852, Buchanan MSS (HSP); Pilkington, "Louisiana House of Representatives," pp. 11–19.

The Louisiana constitution of 1852 changed the basis of legislative apportionment from qualified white voters to total population, white and black. Since the size of the house and senate remained the same, this change forced a reapportionment to increase the representation of plantation areas with heavy slave populations. Whiggish sugar planting regions obviously benefited from this change, as did Democratic cotton regions, but New Orleans would see its legislative delegation reduced in size. In addition, by allowing resident aliens to vote immediately upon naturalization, rather than requiring a two-year delay after naturalization, as did the 1845 constitution, the 1852 document most likely increased the size of the Democratic vote in New Orleans.

38. Truman Smith to John Wilson, October 7, 1852, Wilson MSS; for other overly optimistic reports from the national committee about Whig prospects in the South, see Fitz Henry Warren to William H. Seward, September 28, 1852, Arthur W. Fletcher to Seward, September 28, 1852, Seward MSS (RU).

39. Roger Sherman Baldwin to Roger Sherman Baldwin, Jr., July 19, 1852, BFP; B. Thompson to Daniel Ullmann, June 26, 1852 (quotation), Ullmann MSS; L. S. Geyer to Elihu B. Washburne, July 11, 1852, Washburne Papers (LC); A. P. Stinson to William H. Seward, July 12, 1852, Seward MSS (RU); Joseph K. Smith to Thomas Corwin, June 21, 1852, John G. Love to Corwin, July 28, 1852, Corwin MSS (LC).

40. Lewis D. Campbell to William Schouler, July 6, 1852 (quotation), Schouler MSS; Darrius Perrin to Daniel Ullmann, Rochester, June 30, 1852, Ullmann MSS; William H. Seward to Frances Seward, August 7, 1852, in *Seward at Washington*, p. 191; William Jackson to William H. Seward, June 25, 1852, Seth Hawley to Seward, June 26, 1852, E. Pershine Smith to Seward, July 4, 1852, John Defrees to Seward, July 19, 1852, Schuyler Colfax to Seward, July 24, 1852 (quotation), Seward MSS (RU). Many northern Whigs joined Greeley in openly execrating the platform. The Pittsburgh *Daily Gazette*, the most influential Whig paper in western Pennsylvania, for example, flatly rejected it, as did that city's Whig ratification meeting. As one Democrat said of Pittsburgh's Whigs, "They almost all curse that platform." See Holt, *Forging a Majority*, pp. 105–06.

41. Alexander H. Greene to Frances Seward, July 9, 1852, John M. Radford to William H. Seward, August 5, 1852, Seward MSS (RU).

42. Seth Hawley to William H. Seward, August 11, 1852 (quotation), Seward to John Wilson, August 30, 1852, Seward MSS (RU); Edward Everett to Millard Fillmore, June 30, 1852, Babcock to Fillmore, July 15, 1852, MFP-BHS; Benjamin Thompson to Daniel Ullmann, June 26, 1852, Darius Perrin to Ullmann, June 30, 1852, Ullmann MSS; Washington Hunt to Hamilton Fish, June 25, 1852, Fish MSS; Vincent L. Bradford to J. Alexander Fulton, August 10, 1852 (quotation), P. Frazer Smith to Fulton, August 24, 1852 (quotation), Fulton MSS; Francis Granger to Millard Fillmore, August 25, 1852 (quotation), Granger MSS; Truman Smith to Thomas Ewing, September 22, 1852, EFP; John Gordon to John Wilson, July 5, 1852, John Wilson MSS.

43. William L. Bigler to Franklin Pierce, June 26, 1852 (quotation), A. D. Wilson to Pierce, September 29, 1852 (quotation), Pierce MSS; Charles Bruner to J. Alexander Fulton, July 11, 1852, Ulysses Mercer to Fulton, July 26, 1852, Isaac Hughes to Fulton, August 13, 1852, Fulton

MSS; B. F. Sloan to William L. Bigler, September 11, 1852, Bigler MSS; Benjamin H. Brewster to Edmund Burke, July 19, September 3, 1852 (quotation), Burke MSS.

44. Henry C. Carey to John O. Sargent, July 2, 1852, Sargent MSS. One of Seward's correspondents expressed the growing lack of faith in the Whig party even more vividly the previous April. Warning Seward that citizens held Congress in "contempt" for its "neglect of the real interests of the nation," he added, "Thousands of Whigs, tired of the present condition of things, are debating in their minds the propriety of abandoning their old association in the hopes that by a new crystallization a better development may be realized." Thus the best course for Whigs in 1852 was to allow the Democrats to win the presidency "and wait patiently for the new organization." George Bacon to Seward, April 14, 1852, Seward MSS (RU).

45. E. Pershine Smith to William H. Seward, July 11, 1852 (quotation), Seth Hawley to Seward, August 11, 1852 (quotation), Seward MSS (RU); Seward to William Schouler, August 7, 1852, Schouler MSS.

46. Marius Schoonmaker to Thurlow Weed, July 29, 1852, Weed MSS (RU).

47. See, for example, Isaac Jones to Millard Fillmore, February 9, 1852, MFP-BHS; Truman Smith to William B. Campbell, May 15, 1852, CFP; and especially Edward Everett to H. Jewell, October 20, 1852, Everett MSS. Everett's remarkable letter was an attempt to rouse Whigs from their lethargy by warning of the catastrophic foreign policy consequences should Democrats win.

48. See Daniel Webster to Millard Fillmore, August 4, 1852, Webster MSS; and Frederick Seward's editorial note in *Seward at Washington*, p. 193. When British naval vessels stopped and forced American whaling and fishing boats to leave the contested waters, Fillmore and Webster responded with conciliatory diplomacy rather than the bellicose actions Democrats demanded. The Democratic platform is reprinted in Nichols and Nichols, "Election of 1852," 951–53.

49. On the fear of Louisiana's Whigs regarding Scott's statement on filibusterers, see Fitz Henry Warren to William H. Seward, September 28, 1852, Seward MSS (RU).

50. T. N. Parmalee to John J. Crittenden, July 6, 1852, Crittenden MSS (LC); George Holley to William H. Seward, July 19, 1852, Simeon Draper to Seward, July 20, 1852, Seward MSS (RU); Lew Campbell to William Schouler, July 21, 1852, Schouler MSS; Elliot, *Scott*, pp. 633–34.

51. Campbell to Schouler, July 21, 1852, Schouler MSS; Seth Hawley to William H. Seward, August 11, 1852, Seward MSS (RU); Thomas Foote to Millard Fillmore, August 7, 1852, MFP-BHS; William L. Marcy to Franklin Pierce, July 19, 1852, Pierce MSS; Marcy to Augustus Campbell, July 30, 1852, Marcy MSS (LC).

52. Robert C. Winthrop to John P. Kennedy, August 23, 1852, copy, Winthrop MSS; Daniel Webster to Fletcher Webster, August 26, 1852, Webster MSS; Elliott, *Scott*, p. 628; Dalzell, *Webster*, pp. 274–304.

53. Henry Wilson to William H. Seward, July 8, 1852, Seward MSS (RU); Winthrop to Kennedy, July 29, 1852, Kennedy MSS; Henry Vose to Henry L. Dawes, August 7, 1852, E. H. Kellogg to Dawes, August 28, 1852, Dawes MSS; Philip Greely, Jr., to Thurlow Weed, October 12, 1852, Weed MSS (RU).

54. "Anon" to Daniel Webster, July 14, 1852, Moses Grinnell et al. to Webster, September 24, 1852, Webster MSS; N. S. S. Beman to William H. Seward, July 9, 1852 (quotation), George Foster to Seward, August 9, 1852, Seward MSS (RU); William Kent to Hamilton Fish, July 29, 1852, Fish MSS; George Foster to Thurlow Weed, August 27, 1852, Weed MSS; Carlos Baxter to Justin Morrill, October 6, 1852, Morrill MSS.

55. Lewis C. Levin to William L. Marcy, October 15, 1852, Marcy MSS (LC); John McKeen to Franklin Pierce, September 28, 1852, Pierce MSS; E. A. Penniman to William L. Bigler, October 13, 15, 1852, Bigler MSS; Richard J. Mapes to Daniel Webster, October 10, 1852, Webster MSS. For the characterization of Pierce as an embodiment of "Anti-Popery," see the splenetic anti-Catholic letter of Watson G. Hayes to William H. Seward, August 23, 1852, Seward MSS (RU). Scores of letters from Pennsylvania testify to the hatred of that state's Native Americans toward Scott. Whigs' campaign to woo Catholics and immigrants will be discussed below.

56. William L. Bigler to Franklin Pierce, June 26, 1852, Pierce MSS; J. B. Turner to William H. Seward, July 8, 1852, Henry Wilson to Seward, July 8, 1852, Joseph Garlinghouse to Seward,

July 20, 1852 (quotation), Schuyler Colfax to Seward, August 2, 1852 (quotation), Seward MSS (RU); Thurlow Weed to William Schouler, August 7, 1852, Schouler MSS.

57. Gienapp, *Origins*, pp. 19–20; Salmon P. Chase to E. S. Hamlin, June 28, August 3, 1852, Chase MSS (LC); see also the following letters to Seward, John Barr, September 9, 1852, Aaron F. Perry, September 9, 1852, John Sherman, September 16, 1852, Fisher A. Foster, September 28, 1852, Arthur W. Fletcher, September 28, 1852, Joseph Warren, October 6, 1852, Seward MSS (RU). Fisher Foster told Seward that before Hale left Washington, he told the New Hampshire member of the Whig national committee "that he wished to make a great many Free Soil votes in Ohio, but he hoped to make them all from the Democratic party—and our accounts from there show that he is doing both."

58. On New York, see, for example, Seth Hawley to William H. Seward, August 11, 1852, Seward MSS (RU); and Samuel D. Partridge to George Dennett, June 29, 1852, Pierce MSS.

59. Nichols, *Pierce*, pp. 209–10; Nevins, *Ordeal: House*, p. 41.

60. See my analysis in the previous chapter; Holt, *Political Crisis*, pp. 119–27; and Gienapp, *Origins*, pp. 21–26.

61. For Schuyler Colfax's fear that Germans would decide the Indiana election, see Colfax to Seward, July 24, 1852, Seward MSS (RU); for Colfax's belief that the Catholic clergy could lead Germans into the Whig column, see Truman Smith to Thurlow Weed, September 19, 1852, Weed MSS (RU).

62. Nichols, *Pierce*, pp. 181–86, 209–10; John W. Lawrence to Henry Bedinger, July 13, 1852 (quotation), Bedinger-Dandridge Papers; Andrew A. Eyster to Franklin Pierce, June 29, 1852 (quotation), Pierce MSS. Pierce's incoming correspondence for June, July, and August contains scores of letters detailing Whig use of the anti-Catholic charge. See also the numerous letters in the J. Alexander Fulton MSS. Fulton, a Democratic leader, polled Democrats throughout Pennsylvania to see how grave the threat of Catholic defections was. All reported that Whigs actively sought the Catholic vote, many expected to lose it, and some predicted that Protestant Whigs, angered by the blatant courtship of the Catholics they hated, would abstain or defect to Pierce. For Whig expectations of getting the Catholic vote, see Lew O. Edwards to Thomas Corwin, Cincinnati, June 7, 1852, Corwin MSS (LC); William B. Campbell to David Campbell, Nashville, July 29, 1852, CFP; Richard L. Wilson to William H. Seward, Chicago, June 21, 1852, and John I. Fay to Seward, Detroit, September 1, 1852, Seward MSS (RU).

63. George Emery to Franklin Pierce, Boston, June 26, 1852 (quotation), George M. Dallas to Pierce, July 3, 1852, Paul R. George to Pierce, July 11, 1852, Thomas McGee to Pierce, July 26, 1852, Pierce MSS; Truman Smith to Weed, September 19, 1852, Weed MSS (RU); Gienapp, *Origins*, p. 22. Robinson's pamphlet was entitled *Franklin Pierce and Catholic Persecution in New Hampshire*. Whigs erred about Purcell; he favored Pierce. See J. B. Purcell to William J. Barry, June 25, 1852, enclosed with Barry to Franklin Pierce, July 1, 1852, Pierce MSS.

64. Charles A. Dana to James S. Pike, June 21, 1852, Pike MSS; David Nagle to William H. Seward, July 20, 1852, Seward to Schuyler Colfax, July 31, 1852, Henry Barns to Seward, September 6, 1852, Arthur W. Fletcher to Seward, September 9, 1852, Henry H. Booth to Seward, September 15, 1852, William J. Miller to Seward, September 18, 1852, Champion S. Chase to Seward, October 16, 1852, Seward MSS (RU).

65. Rutherford B. Hayes to Sardis Birchard, October 12, 1852, in *Hayes Diary*, I, p. 424.

66. George H. Rives to William H. Seward, February 10, 1852, Richard L. Wilson to Seward, June 21, 1852 (quotations), Seward MSS (RU); James Shields to Charles H. Lanphier, February 6, 1852, Lanphier MSS; John Moses to Richard Yates, March 28, 1852, Yates MSS; Richard L. Wilson to Elihu B. Washburne, July 20, 1852, Washburne MSS (LC); *Koerner Memoirs*, I, pp. 564, 588, 598–99.

67. Elihu B. Washburne to Seward, September 17, 1852, Seward MSS (RU); Greeley to Washburne, September 15, 1852, Seward to Washburne, September 22, 1852, Nathan C. Greer to Washburne, Waukegan, n.d., Washburne MSS (LC).

68. This and the preceding paragraph are based on Elliott, *Scott*, p. 638; the following letters to Franklin Pierce: George F. Emery, Boston, June 26, 1852, Samuel W. Black, Pittsburgh, July

12, 1852, William J. Brown, Indianapolis, July 14, 1852 (quotation), Edward Lynch, Brooklyn, July 24, 1852 (quotation), Thomas McGee, Buffalo, July 26, 1852, and A. D. Wilson, Williamsport, Pa., September 29, 1852, Pierce MSS; W. W. H. Davis to Caleb Cushing, Philadelphia, September 10, 1852, Cushing MSS; David Nagle to William H. Seward, July 20, August 13, 1852, William J. Miller to Seward, September 18, 1852, Seward MSS (RU); James Campbell to William L. Bigler, September 21, 1852 (quotation), E. A. Penniman to Bigler, October 9, 1852, George W. Woodward to Bigler, October 16, 1852, Bigler MSS. The J. Alexander Fulton Papers also contain many letters on the situation in Pennsylvania.

69. William J. Miller to Seward, September 18, 1852, Fisher A. Foster to Seward, September 28, 1852, Arthur W. Fletcher to Seward, September 28, 1852, Seward MSS (RU).

70. Elliott, *Scott*, pp. 635–41. Scott reached Pittsburgh and Cleveland on September 19 and left New York in mid-October. My subsequent remarks on the content of his speeches are taken from the same pages in Elliott.

71. Ibid., pp. 640–41; Thurlow Weed to Seward, September 25, 1852 (quotation), Arthur W. Fletcher to Seward, September 28, 1852 (quotation), Fisher A. Foster to Seward, September 28, 1852, W. I. Madeira to Seward, October 9, 1852, Seward MSS (RU).

72. P. C. H. Harris to William H. Seward, September 24, 1852 (quotation), Seward MSS (RU); Jesse Young to J. Alexander Fulton, July 28, 1852 (quotation), J. W. Maynard to Fulton, August 3, 1852, P. Frazer Smith to Fulton, August 24, 1852, Fulton MSS; John H. Brinton to Franklin Pierce, October 6, 1852, John H. Davis to Pierce, October 25, 1852 (quotation), Pierce MSS; Alvah Hunt to Hamilton Fish, August 28, 1852, Fish MSS. For additional quotations and citations, see Holt, *Political Crisis*, p. 126; and Gienapp, *Origins*, pp. 25–26. Professor Gienapp and I have examined many of the same manuscript collections, and on this point, as on so many others, we concur.

73. G. B. McGudry to Samuel Patterson, September 20, 1852, Patterson MSS. W. I. Madeira of Pittsburgh and Weed, as well as the confident reports from Massachusetts and Ohio, have already been cited. For Seward's confidence about New York, see Anna Ella Carroll to Seward, September 27, 1852, and Arthur W. Fletcher to Seward, September 28, 1852, Seward MSS (RU); Seward to Elihu B. Washburne, September 22, 1852, Washburne MSS (LC).

74. The Massachusetts elections were also clustered in November, but the crucial state elections were held one week after the presidential and congressional contests on November 2. The referendum on Louisiana's new state constitution was scheduled for November 2 as well, and if it carried, new elections for all statewide officials and state legislators were to be held in December.

75. C. N. Bodfish to Franklin Pierce, June 8, 1852, Pierce MSS; Gienapp, *Origins*, pp. 48–50, 489–90.

76. William G. Crosby to Stephen Stark, December 18, 1852, Fessenden MSS (WRHS); B. F. Johnson to Elihu B. Washburne, September 16, 1852, Washburne MSS (LC). Only the state senate voted for governor if no candidate had a popular-vote majority, and sitting senators also decided state senate contests in which no candidate won a majority. Eight seats remained unfilled after the September elections, and those seats could determine control of the senate. Crosby wanted Whigs already in the senate to bargain with Democrats to choose the Whig candidate, rather than a factional rival, in disputed senate districts and thereby give the Whigs a clear senate majority. This deal worked, and Crosby was elected governor in late December 1852 or January 1853. That, in turn, created friction among Whigs, for Whigs brought into the senate by this deal refused to support William Pitt Fessenden, Whigs' candidate for United States senator. See the next chapter and Israel Washburn, Jr., to Fessenden, February 12, 1853, Fessenden MSS (WRHS).

77. In addition to the letters to Seward and Weed cited above, see Arthur W. Fletcher to Seward, October 12, 1852, Charles W. Beers to Seward, October 17, 1852, and William Schouler to Seward, October 28, 1852, Seward MSS (RU).

78. David Nagle to William H. Seward, July 20, August 11, 1852, William J. Miller to Seward, September 4, 18, 1852, Seward MSS (RU); Alvah Hunt to Hamilton Fish, August 28, 1852, Fish MSS; Horace Greeley to Elihu B. Washburne, September 15, 1852, Washburne MSS (LC).

79. John Roberts to Salmon P. Chase, June 16, 1852, Chase MSS (LC); Greeley to Washburne, September 15, 1852, Washburne MSS (LC).

80. Solomon G. Haven to Millard Fillmore, September 25, 1852, James R. Thompson, Rochester, October 2, 1852, MFP-BHS. Haven noted that he had been renominated unanimously; where Sewardites needed Silver Gray help on the presidential ticket, that is, they made no attempt to deny Silver Grays nomination.

Walley's endorsement of the Scott ticket in Massachusetts was extraordinarily grudging. He began his acceptance speech by proclaiming that the Whig party had done Daniel Webster an "irreparable wrong" and had thereby "brought discredit on themselves." *New York Times*, September 24, 1852.

81. Henry J. Raymond to William H. Seward, March 15, June 4, 1852, Seward MSS (RU); A. H. Savage to Benedict Lewis, Jr., August 12, 1852 (quotation), Ullmann MSS; Hamilton Fish to Thurlow Weed, August 18, 1852, Weed MSS (RU). Letters in the Ullmann Papers for July, August, and September are by far the best source for Silver Gray attitudes toward New York's state election in 1852.

82. John M. Bradford to William H. Seward, March 3, 1852 (quotation), Horace Greeley to Seward, April 20, 1852 (quotation), Seward MSS (RU); Alex Brooks to Benedict Lewis, Jr., August 22, 1852 (quotation), D. R. Barker to Lewis, August 27, 1852, Ullmann MSS. The priority that pro-Compromise Silver Grays as well as antislavery Sewardites put on the Maine Law issue corrects the mistaken tendency of some historians to identify prohibitionism and antislavery as complementary attitudes of the same people. The liquor issue cut across the fault line established by the slavery issue.

83. Greeley to Seward, April 20, 1852, Raymond to Seward, June 4, 1852, Seward MSS (RU); Alex Mann to Benedict Lewis, Jr., August 14, 1852, Ullmann MSS; Washington Hunt to James Watson Webb, July 31, August 22, 1852, Webb MSS.

84. Robert G. Campbell to Millard Fillmore, January 5, 1852, MFP-BHS; George Dawson to Thurlow Weed, January 8, 1852, Weed MSS (RU); Seth Hawley to William H. Seward, January 3, 1852, Alvah Hunt to Seward, January 8, 1852, Henry J. Raymond to Seward, January 11, 1852, Seward MSS (RU); George Bancroft to Franklin Pierce, July 9, 1852, Pierce MSS.

85. James R. Thompson to Millard Fillmore, March 30, 1852, MFP-BHS; C. A. Mann to George Newell, May 20, 1852, Marcy MSS (NYSL); Lewis Morgan to William H. Seward, May 14, 1852, Seth Hawley to Seward, May 21, 1852, Seward MSS (RU); Washington Hunt to Hamilton Fish, June 25, 1852, Fish MSS; Hunt to James Watson Webb, July 31, 1852 (quotation), Webb MSS; B. Thompson to Benedict Lewis, Jr., August 11, 1852 (quotation), Ullmann MSS.

86. J. T. Hatch to William L. Marcy, July 28, 1852, William J. Russell to Marcy, August 2, 1852, Marcy MSS (LC); J. T. Hatch to George Newell, August 9, 1852, Marcy MSS (NYSL). By 1852 the divisions among New York Democrats were more complex than ever. Hunkers divided into Hardshell and Softshell factions over the question of receiving Barnburners back into the party. To win the support of Barnburners, Softshells, headed by William L. Marcy and Seymour, embraced their hard-line opposition to canal expansion.

87. A. C. Flagg to George W. Newell, September 23, 1852, Marcy MSS (NYSL); William L. Marcy to A. Campbell, September 8, 1852, C. Stebbins to Marcy, October 14, 1852 (quotation), Marcy MSS (LC); V. W. Smith to George Dawson, September 3, 1852, Weed MSS (RU); A. Birdsall to Franklin Pierce, September 28, 1852, Augustus Schell to Pierce, September 29, 1852, Pierce MSS.

88. William L. Marcy to A. Campbell, September 8, 1852, Marcy MSS (LC); *New York Times*, September 23, 24, 1852. I have inferred that Weed constructed the ticket because its jewel was William Kent, the widely respected jurist and candidate for lieutenant governor, whom Weed at first approached unsuccessfully about accepting the nomination. Fish wanted Kent to run for Congress to prevent James Brooks' renomination. See William Kent to Weed, August 17, 1852, and Fish to Weed, August 18, 1852, Weed MSS (RU).

89. The platform can be found in the *Times*, September 23, 1852. Raymond's spin on the proceedings appeared the following day.

90. Weed to Seward, September 25, 1852 (quotation), Charles W. Beers to Seward, October 17, 1852 (quotation), Seward MSS (RU); Willis Sumner to George W. Newell, October 31, 1852, Marcy MSS (NYSL).

91. Fitz Henry Warren to Seward, September 28, 1852, W. I. Madeira to Seward, October 9, 1852, Seward MSS (RU); Truman Smith to John Wilson, October 7, 1852, John Wilson MSS.

92. John H. Brinton to Franklin Pierce, October 6, 1852 (quotation), Pierce MSS; David Davis to ?, October 17, 1852 (quotation), David Davis MSS; *Hayes Diary*, I, pp. 421–22; *Baltimore County Advocate*, September 4, 1852, quoted in Evitts, *Matter of Allegiance*, p. 49; James Johnston to Edward McPherson, December 3, 1852, McPherson MSS. The quotation about "Genl. Apathy" is taken from Sewell, *Ballots for Freedom*, p. 249.

93. William P. Hills to William L. Bigler, October 8, 1852, Bigler MSS. Democrats won 51.3 percent of the statewide vote in Iowa; in 1850 their majority had been 53 percent.

94. Doherty, *Whigs of Florida*, p. 56. Ward won 4,336 votes compared to 4,626 for James Broome; in 1848 Thomas Brown's 4,147 votes represented 53.3 percent of the active electorate. My assertions about voter movement between elections are based on interyear regression estimates in Calabro, "Two-Party System in Florida," pp. 27–28. According to Calabro's estimates, almost one-fifth (18 percent) of the 1848 Democratic voters supported Ward in 1850.

95. Calabro, "Two-Party System in Florida," Table 8, p. 27.

96. James A. Pearce to Thomas Corwin, March 1, 1852, Corwin MSS (LC); Arthur W. Fletcher to William H. Seward, October 22, 1852, Seward MSS (RU).

97. W. A. Gorman to Franklin Pierce, October 16, 1852, Pierce MSS. Wright won with 92,959 votes (54.7 percent) to 73,647 (43.3 percent) for Nicholas McCarty, his Whig foe. A Free Soil candidate apparently garnered the balance. In the congressional elections, all of which were two-way races, Democrats won 89,787 votes (53.8 percent) to the Whigs' 76,957 (46.2 percent). For the breakdown of the immigrant vote in Indiana, see Tables 1.9 and 1.10 in Gienapp, *Origins*, p. 486. Gienapp's estimates are for the presidential vote and apply to all immigrant voters, not just new ones enfranchised by the 1851 constitution. Yet Wright's vote was only slightly smaller than Pierce's in November, almost 16,000 votes larger than his own total in 1849, and 18,000 votes more than Democratic congressional candidates had won in 1851, the last election before the new state constitution enfranchised alien immigrants. Since Indiana's native-born voters tilted Democratic far less disproportionately than immigrants, I assume that newly enfranchised immigrants divided the same way as other immigrants.

98. A. F. Perry to Thomas Ewing, October 11, 1852, EFP; Rutherford B. Hayes to Sardis Birchard, October 12, 17, 1852, in *Hayes Diary*, I, pp. 424–26. The totals in the 1852 popular vote for congressmen were: Democrats, 141,411 (48.1 percent); Whigs, 128,468 (43.7 percent); and Free Soil, 24,044 (7.2 percent). The margin for the statewide vote is taken from Gienapp, *Origins*, Table 2.16, p. 496. For estimates on turnout in all northern states between 1840 and 1860, see id., " 'Politics Seem to Enter Into Everything,' " pp. 18–19.

99. The statewide popular vote in the congressional races was: Democrats, 44,393 (53.7 percent) and Whigs 38,270 (46.3 percent). The totals in the 1850 gubernatorial election were: Democrats, 39,723 (53.8 percent) and Whigs 34,054 (46.2 percent).

100. E. A. Penniman to William L. Bigler, October 13, 1852, Bigler MSS. In 1851 the vote for governor was: Democrats, 186,499 (50.9 percent); Whigs, 178,034 (48.6 percent); and Native Americans, 1,850 (0.5 percent). The corresponding totals for canal commissioner in 1852 were: Democrats, 171,551 (51.2 percent); Whigs, 151,601 (45.2 percent); Native Americans, 8,187 (2.4 percent); and Free Soilers, 3,843 (1.2 percent). The turnout rate dropped from 70.7 percent in 1851 to 63.3 percent in 1852.

101. Schouler to Seward, October 16, 28, 1852, Seward MSS (RU); Allison Owen to Fessenden, October 22, 1852, Fessenden MSS (WRHS); Lewis C. Levin to William L. Marcy, October 31, 1852, Marcy MSS (LC); Dana to James Pike, October 1852, Pike MSS; James Johnston to Edward McPherson, December 3, 1852, McPherson MSS.

102. Clifford received only 53,500 votes on the regular Whig ticket, some 11,000 fewer than Winthrop had a year earlier, but he got over 8,000 votes on the anti-Maine Law ticket, raising his total to 9,000 votes more than Scott won a week earlier. That gain indicated how important the prohibition issue was in Massachusetts. See Sweeney, "Rum, Romanism, Representation,

and Reform," Table IX, p. 131. I have also used Sweeney's figures on the number of legislative seats, pp. 121, 133, rather than those provided by the Inter-University Consortium, which vary sharply from them.

103. N. B. Markle to John G. Davis, November 8, 1852, John Davis MSS; Thomas L. Harris to Stephen Douglas, November 22, 1852, Douglas MSS.

104. Edwin R. Campbell to William H. Seward, December 15, 1852, F. J. Stratton to Seward, November 22, 1852, Raymond to Seward, November 6, 1852, Seward MSS (RU); Stephen A. Hurlbut to Elihu B. Washburne, November 8, 1852, Washburne MSS (LC); John Minor Botts to William Schouler, November 12, 1852, Schouler MSS; Seward to Thurlow Weed, November 4, 1852, Weed MSS (RU); L. R. Davis to T. J. McClellan, December 18, 1852, Buchanan-McClellan Papers.

105. N. K. Hall to Millard Fillmore, November 3, 1852, S. J. Wright to Fillmore, November 3, 1852 (quotation), A. S. Linn to Fillmore, December 24, 1852, MFP-BHS; Worthington G. Snethen to William H. Seward, November 4, 1852, William Kent to Seward, November 10, 1852, Seward MSS (RU).

106. Rutherford B. Hayes to Sardis Birchard, November 3, 10, 1852, in *Hayes Diary*, I, pp. 429–32.

107. John Davis to William Schouler, November 4, 1852, Botts to Schouler, November 12, 1852, Schouler MSS; Moses Kimball to Henry L. Dawes, November 3, 1852, Dawes MSS; William Schouler to William H. Seward, November 10, 1852, Seward MSS (RU); Lewis Campbell to Israel Washburn, November 4, 1852, Israel Washburn MSS (LC).

108. Davis to Schouler, November 4, 1852, Schouler MSS; Teesdale to McLean, November 19, 1852, McLean MSS (LC); *Browning Diary*, pp. 79–80; John Barr to William H. Seward, November 8, 1852, Seward MSS (RU); James Johnston to Edward McPherson, December 3, 1852, McPherson MSS; Pittsburgh *Daily Gazette*, November 4, 1852.

109. While Scott improved on Johnston's 1851 gubernatorial vote in Pennsylvania, he ran over 6,000 votes behind Taylor there, and the Democratic vote grew by four times that amount between 1848 and 1852. Scott also ran slightly behind Taylor in New Jersey, but Democratic gains between 1848 and 1850 provided the margin of victory. Nonetheless, a combination of defeatism after the October elections, apathy, and defection by nativists and Protestant Whigs, who may have voted for Webster had he lived, probably accounted for the reduced Whig vote in both states. The Free Soil vote in New Jersey was negligible, and very few, if any, Pennsylvania Whigs defected to the Free Soilers. See Gienapp, *Origins*, p. 29, n. 72, and Table 1.8, p. 485.

110. Cooper, *Politics of Slavery*, p. 340.

111. Kruman, *Parties and Politics*, p. 136.

112. The figures for the North are from Gienapp, *Origins*, p. 28, n. 69. The average for the fifteen slave states is unweighted, but the turnout rates themselves, of course, are based on a ratio of active voters to the total adult white male population.

113. Gienapp's figures on turnout are comparable in the direction, if not the dimension, of change with those I have used in Table 33, with the following exceptions. He finds a slight decrease in Ohio, not an increase, a slight decrease in Connecticut, and a small increase in Michigan between 1848 and 1852.

114. Holt, *Political Crisis*, p. 129; Gienapp, *Origins*, pp. 28, n. 68, and pp. 482–85.

115. Ibid.; Robert Toombs to John J. Crittenden, December 5, 1852, Crittenden MSS (LC). Gienapp's estimates suggest that 1 percent of Taylor's voters went for Hale in Illinois, Indiana, and Connecticut. In the last state that would equal approximately 300 voters, not enough to overcome Pierce's 3,000-vote margin.

116. John A. Bryan and J. A. Noonun to Gideon Welles, November 14, 1852, Welles MSS (LC); Gienapp, *Origins*, pp. 482–86; Gienapp, " 'Politics Seem to Enter Into Everything,' " Table 4, p. 29. Gienapp's estimates of immigrant turnout in this last table apply only to New York, but it probably increased at comparable rates in other states. See also the citations to Professor Robert W. Fogel's research in the preceding chapter, note 71. Gienapp's estimates of voter movement in New York between 1848 and 1852 suggest that over half of the increased Democratic vote came from people other than ex-Free Soilers.

117. *Hayes Diary*, I, p. 430; John Barr to William H. Seward, November 8, 1852, Seward

MSS; Gienapp, *Origins*, p. 30, notes 78 and 80, and pp. 482–85. Although Scott ran only 6,249 votes behind Taylor's total in Pennsylvania, Gienapp's estimates suggest that about 8.7 percent of Taylor's voters, over 15,000 men, abstained.

118. George Bull to William H. Seward, November 6, 1852, William Kent to Seward, November 10, 1852 (quotation), Simeon Draper to Seward, November 12, 1852, Henry Schermerhorn to Seward, January 10, 1853, Seward MSS (RU); Washington Hunt to Hamilton Fish, November 10, 1852 (quotation), Fish MSS; A. C. Flagg to George W. Newell, November 3, 1852, Marcy MSS (NYSL); Hamilton Fish to Daniel D. Barnard, November 24, 1852 (quotation), Barnard MSS; Gienapp, *Origins*, pp. 29–30.

Whig congressional candidates were wiped out in Brooklyn and New York City, both Silver Gray bastions. Even though that urban area gained an additional seat under reapportionment, Whigs' total vote for Congress dropped by 17,040 (34.3 percent) between 1848 and 1852. Rochester's Silver Gray candidate also met defeat, but in Buffalo the victorious Solomon G. Haven increased his 1850 vote by almost 25 percent. Undoubtedly Sewardites also refused to vote for well-known Silver Grays like Joseph Varnum and James Brooks, whom they particularly hated. Brooks, whose district was altered under the new apportionment, received only 3,398 votes in 1852 compared to 8,357 in 1850.

119. John Davis to William Schouler, November 4, 1852, Schouler MSS; Samuel Bowles to Henry L. Dawes, November 13, 1852, Dawes MSS; Thurlow Weed to Samuel Bowles, January 2, 1853, Bowles MSS; Robert C. Winthrop to John P. Kennedy, January 13, 1853, Kennedy MSS.

120. For these states I have used the turnout rates listed by Gienapp in " 'Politics Seem to Enter Into Everything,' " pp. 18–19. For prohibition's salience in the Massachusetts state election, see William Schouler to William H. Seward, November 6, 1852, Seward MSS (RU); and R. T. Paine to Roger Sherman Baldwin, November 17, 1852, BFP. For the breakdown of the multiticket gubernatorial vote in Massachusetts, see Sweeney, "Rum, Romanism, Representation, and Reform," p. 131. Mann got 3,600 votes on a separate Temperance ticket.

121. Campbell to Israel Washburn, November 4, 1852, Israel Washburn MSS (LC).

122. Webster to Moses Grinnell et al., October 12, 1852, quoted in Dalzell, *Webster*, p. 300; Lewis to Clayton, November 13, 1852, Clayton MSS; James Johnston to Edward McPherson, December 3, 1852, McPherson MSS; E. J. Terry to Richard W. Thompson, November 13, 1852, Thompson MSS (Ind.SL); Gienapp, *Origins*, pp. 32–33.

123. Charles Sumner to William H. Seward, November 6, 1852, George Bull to Seward, November 6, 1852 (quotation), John Bradford to Seward, November 8, 9, 1852, F. J. Stratton to Seward, November 22, 1852, Seward MSS (RU); John Davis to William Schouler, November 4, 1852, Schouler MSS; Daniel Lee to Millard Fillmore, November 5, 1852, MFP-BHS.

124. James Bowen to William H. Seward, November 3, 1852 (quotation), Seward to Gerrit Smith, November 10, 1852, William Kent to Seward, November 10, 1852 (quotation), William Schouler to Seward, November 10, 1852 (quotation), Simeon Draper to Seward, November 12, 1852, Seward MSS (RU); Thomas M. Howe to Israel Washburn, November 14, 1852, Israel Washburn MSS (LC); Gienapp, *Origins*, pp. 33–34, Seward to Charles Sumner, November 9, 1852, quoted on p. 34.

125. Botts to Schouler, November 12, 1852, Schouler MSS; Kent to Washburn, December 27, 1852, Israel Washburn MSS (Norlands).

126. Worthington G. Snethen to Seward, November 4, 1852, John M. Bradford to Seward, November 9, 1852 (quotation), Simeon Draper to Seward, November 12, 1852 (quotation), Seward MSS (RU); Stephen A. Hurlbut to Elihu B. Washburne, November 8, 1852 (quotation), Elihu Washburne MSS (LC); L. R. Davis to T. J. McClellan, December 18, 1852, Buchanan-McClellan Papers; Hugh Maxwell to Millard Fillmore, November 10, 1852 (quotation), MFP-BHS; John Davis to William Schouler, November 4, 1852, Schouler MSS; William Cullom to William B. Campbell, December 22, 1852, CFP; William Kent to Hamilton Fish, January 29, 1853 (quotation), Fish MSS. Some Democrats also believed that their party must fragment because its majorities were so large, Whig opposition was too weak to exert the necessary "external pressure to keep it together," and the *"cohesive ties of public plunder"* were inadequate to please the hordes of job seekers. See Andrew Johnson to Sam Milligan, December 28, 1852, in *Johnson Papers*, pp. 100–103.

127. William Schouler to Seward, November 10, 1852, Seward MSS (RU).

CHAPTER 21

1. William Cullom to William B. Campbell, December 22, 1852, CFP; William H. Seward to William Schouler, December 25, 1852, John Minor Botts to Schouler, February 4, 1853, Schouler MSS; John Barr to William H. Seward, January 22, 1853 (quotation), Seward MSS (RU); Daniel Lee to Millard Fillmore, November 15, 1852 (quotation), Nathan K. Hall to Fillmore, February 13, 1853, MFP-BHS.

2. The *Tribune* is quoted in Van Deusen, *Greeley*, p. 172.

3. Horace Greeley to Schuyler Colfax, January 18, 1853, Greeley-Colfax MSS.

4. Andrew Johnson to Sam Milligan, December 28, 1852 (quotation), in *Johnson Papers*, pp. 100–04; Truman Smith to James S. Pike, March 27, 1853, Pike MSS; Nathan K. Hall to Millard Fillmore, February 13, 1853, MFP-BHS; Alexander H. H. Stuart to Fillmore, August 1, 1853, MFP-O. The controversy among Democrats caused by Pierce's patronage allocation is examined in Nichols, "Kansas-Nebraska Act"; and Nichols, *Pierce*, pp. 247–93.

5. Wade to Lew Campbell, June 27, 1853, Lewis Campbell MSS; John P. Kennedy to Joseph G. Kennedy, October 6, 1853, copy, Kennedy MSS.

6. Seward to William Schouler, December 25, 1852, Schouler MSS.

7. George W. Bull to William H. Seward, November 6, 1852, John M. Bradford to Seward, November 8, 1852, John Barr to Seward, January 22, 1853, April 13, 1853, Henry Sill to Seward, February 24, 1853, and George Olmsted to Seward, February 28, 1853, Seward MSS (RU); Schuyler Colfax to William Schouler, February 1, 1853, Schouler MSS.

8. Robert Toombs to John J. Crittenden, December 5, 1852 (quotation), Crittenden MSS (LC); F. J. Stratton to William H. Seward, November 22, 1852 (quotation), Seward MSS (RU); William L. Hodge to Millard Fillmore, September 26, 1853, MFP-O; Cooper, *Politics of Slavery*, pp. 343–44; Cole, *Whig Party in the South*, p. 275.

9. George W. Bull to William H. Seward, November 6, 1852, John Barr to Seward, January 22, 1853, George Olmsted to Seward, February 28, 1853, Seward MSS (RU); John C. Spencer to Millard Fillmore, September 5, 1853 (quotation), MFP-O; P. J. Wagner to Fillmore, January 6, 1853, MFP-BHS.

10. Here as elsewhere in this chapter I use the term "Sewardites" to describe not only Seward's northern Whig correspondents but all northern Whigs who opposed the Compromise in 1850 and 1851, vigorously disputed the presidential nomination of either Fillmore or Webster in 1852, and viewed Whigs' national platform that year as a betrayal of their antislavery principles.

11. John Barr to William H. Seward, January 22, 1853, George Olmsted to Seward, February 28, 1853 (quotation), Seward MSS (RU); Benjamin F. Wade to Milton R. Sutliffe, February 13, 1853, Sutliffe MSS.

12. William G. Crosby to Stephen Stark, December 18, 1852, Israel Washburn, Jr. to William Pitt Fessenden, February 12, 1853, Crosby to Fessenden, May 5, 15, 1853, Fessenden MSS (WRHS).

13. Morrill, "Presidential Election of 1852," 347; Walton, "Elections in North Carolina," 185–87; Kenneth Rayner to David F. Caldwell, April 4, 1853, Caldwell MSS. During the 1852–53 legislative session, Democrats had a six-seat majority in the senate and Whigs held a four-seat edge in the house. On joint ballots, therefore, Democrats had a narrow eighty-six to eighty-four margin if everyone voted. But everyone did not vote, and abstentions and scattered votes produced the deadlock. Rayner's total from Whigs ranged between seventy-nine and seventy-three votes.

14. Thurlow Weed to Samuel Bowles, January 2, 1853, Bowles MSS; Robert C. Winthrop to John P. Kennedy, January 13, 1853, Kennedy MSS; Winthrop to Edward Everett, January 17, 24, 1853, Everett MSS.

15. Ewing's absorption in private affairs after mid-1851 is documented by various letters from 1851, 1852, and 1853 in EFP.

16. William B. Campbell to David Campbell, September 23, 1853, CFP.

17. Robert C. Winthrop to John P. Kennedy, January 13, April 14, 1853, Kennedy MSS; Winthrop to Edward Everett, January 17, 24, 1853, Everett MSS.

18. Horace Greeley to Schuyler Colfax, January 24, 1853, Greeley-Colfax MSS; Greeley to

William H. Seward, February 6, 1853, Seward MSS (RU); Truman Smith to James S. Pike, March 27, 1853, Pike MSS; Van Deusen, *Greeley*, pp. 172–78, New York *Tribune*, April 30, 1853, quoted on p. 178.

19. Truman Smith to James S. Pike, March 27, 1853, Pike MSS.

20. Truman Smith to John Wilson, August 28, 1853, John Wilson MSS; Smith to Thurlow Weed, August 29, 1853, Weed MSS (RU).

21. Smith to Weed, August 29, 1853, Weed MSS.

22. George Olmsted to Seward, February 28, 1853, Seward MSS (RU). The writer in the *North American Review* and the New Yorker J. S. McLaury are quoted in Gienapp, *Origins*, pp. 65.

23. Charles Sumner to William H. Seward, November 6, 1852, Seward MSS (RU); Seward to Sumner, November 9, 1852, quoted in Gienapp, *Origins*, p. 34.

24. For evidence that Democrats and Republicans cooperated in many states to adopt the Australian ballot during the 1890s explicitly to deny third parties access to the electorate, see McCormick, *From Realignment to Reform*, pp. 114–18; Reynolds and McCormick, "Outlawing 'Treachery' "; and Argersinger, "Place on the Ballot."

25. Again, I have explored this contrast between the fate of the Whigs in the 1850s and their twentieth-century Republican successors at greater length in "The Mysterious Disappearance of the American Whig Party," in Holt, *Political Parties*.

26. Cassius M. Clay to Seward, June 9, 1853, Seward MSS (RU).

27. F. J. Stratton to William H. Seward, November 22, 1852, Henry Still to Seward, February 24, 1853, Seward MSS (RU).

28. Daniel Lee to Fillmore, November 15, 1852, MFP-BHS.

29. George Bacon to Seward, April 14, 1852, Seward MSS. For additional evidence of the mushrooming antipolitician, antiparty sentiment expressed by Bacon, see Holt, *Political Crisis*, pp. 132–38.

30. Sweeney, "Rum, Romanism, Representation, and Reform," 31; Holt, *Forging a Majority*, pp. 110–15, 335.

31. William H. Seward to Samuel Ruggles, November 6, 1852, Seward MSS (LC).

32. Van Deusen, *Seward*, p. 147; *Messages and Papers of the Presidents*, V, pp. 169–71; Daniel Lee to Millard Fillmore, November 15, 1852, MFP-BHS; Robert Wickliffe to Seward, June 14, 1853, Seward MSS (RU).

33. *Messages and Papers of the Presidents*, V, pp. 163–82.

34. *Messages and Papers of the Presidents*, V, p. 198.

35. John Barr to Seward, April 13, 1853, Seward MSS (RU).

36. J. A. Chesnut to Richard Yates, June 18, 1853, Yates MSS.

37. Samuel Bowles to Henry L. Dawes, May 13, 1853, Dawes MSS.

38. For evidence of multiple Democratic candidacies, see Thomas H. Averett to Walter Coles, April 13, 1853, Coles MSS. The data from the Inter-University Consortium for Political and Social Research include no results for Virginia's state senate elections in 1853, but Democrats retained control. Because Whigs failed to contest so many congressional districts, I have not calculated their proportion of the total statewide vote.

39. In Rhode Island, Whig candidates had won 45.8 percent of the vote in 1851, and in 1852 Scott had won 44.8 percent. In 1853 the Whigs' share sank to 35.1 percent. New Hampshire's Whig candidates won 22,424 votes (42.4 percent) in 1851; two years later they captured 20,871 votes (42.0 percent).

40. Gienapp, *Origins*, pp. 52–55; Julius Clark to Joseph R. Hawley, January 29, 1853, J. R. Stewart to Hawley, March 6, 1853, Moses Pierce to Hawley, March 15, 1853, Hawley MSS; Charles H. Pond to Thomas Seymour, February 11, 1853, March 8, 1853 (quotation), W. S. Carter to Seymour, March 16, 1853 (quotation), Seymour MSS.

41. J. R. Stewart to Joseph R. Hawley, March 6, 1853, Moses Pierce to Hawley, March 15, 1853, Joel Fox to Hawley, March 21, 1853, John Boyd to Bartlett & Hawley, March 28, 1853, Findley M. Fox to M. H. Bartlett & Co., March 28, 1853, Hawley MSS. Joseph Hawley and M. H. Bartlett co-edited a Free Soil newspaper in Connecticut.

42. Emily Baldwin to Roger Sherman Baldwin, Jr., April 4, 1853, BFP; J. C. Comstock to Thomas Seymour, March 23, 1853, Seymour MSS.

43. For a more extensive analysis of the Connecticut vote and its role in punctuating the long-term disintegration of the Connecticut Whig party, see Gienapp, *Origins*, pp. 52–56, 491–93.

44. Joseph Warren to Seward, March 15, 1853, Seward MSS (RU); Formisano, *Birth of Mass Political Parties*, pp. 215–29.

45. Gienapp, *Origins*, pp. 62–64. Native-born Democrats had formed a secret club known as the Miami Tribe to stop Germans from getting Democratic nominations; hence, angry Germans called themselves the Anti-Miami party. On pp. 61–62, Gienapp also provides an able discussion of the role of the school issue in the rise of anti-Catholicism. I have offered my own analysis of that phenomenon, which would transform northern politics, in my *Political Crisis*, pp. 161–66.

46. Gienapp, *Origins*, pp. 63–64, 495.

47. Roger Sherman Baldwin, Jr., to Emily Baldwin, San Francisco, October 31, 1852, BFP; Henry A. Craft to John Wilson, Stockton, June 3, 1853 (quotation), Madison Whitehall to Wilson, Sacramento, June 13, 1853 (quotation), John Wilson MSS.

48. Henry Craft to John Wilson, June 3, June 12, 1853, Madison Whitehall to Wilson, June 13, 1853, John Wilson MSS.

49. In 1851 Bigler won with 23,175 votes (50.5 percent) to the Whigs' 22,732 (49.5 percent); in 1853 his margin was 38,940 (51 percent) to 37,454 (49 percent). The letters cited above indicate that some Whigs opposed pushing for a new constitutional convention because they feared that former residents of southern states would try to legalize slavery in California. Others opposed dividing the state in two, and still others doubted that Democrats who wanted revision would support it if Whigs alone ran a ticket dedicated to it.

50. This and the previous paragraph are based on Current, *Wisconsin*, pp. 214–17. Neither Current nor Walter Dean Burnham's data for the Inter-University Consortium for Political and Social Research supply returns for Wisconsin's legislative elections, but Democrats presumably retained their majorities. The extent of the defection from the Whigs is suggested by comparing the gubernatorial returns from 1851 and 1853 with the presidential results in 1852. Remember that Farwell won with Free Soil support in 1851 and that Holton ran as a People's, not a Free Soil, candidate even though he had first been nominated by Free Soilers.

	Whig	Democratic	Free Soil
1851	22,319	21,812	
1852	22,210	33,658	8,814
1853	3,304	30,405	21,886

51. Whigs narrowly won the gubernatorial election in October 1848, and Cass' margin over Taylor in November was 4.9 percent. In 1850 the Democratic margin was 4.5 percent, and it increased to 9.3 percent in 1851. The strong Whig effort for Scott in 1852, however, reduced the percentage difference between Democrats and Whigs to 4.7. Similarly, in legislative contests after 1847, Whigs retained a respectable proportion of the house and senate until they were wiped out under the new apportionment of the 1851 constitution.

52. John Barr to William H. Seward, April 13, 1853, Seward MSS (RU); Daniel Peck to Thomas Ewing, January 10, 1853 (quotation), EFP; Gienapp, *Origins*, p. 57.

53. Ben Wade to Milton Sutliffe, February 13, 1853, Sutliffe MSS; John Barr to William H. Seward, July 19, 1853 (quotation), Seward MSS (RU); Wade to Lew Campbell, June 27, 1853 (quotation), Lewis Campbell MSS.

54. John Barr to William H. Seward, April 13, 1853 (quotation), Seward MSS (RU); Wade to Campbell, June 27, 1853, Lewis Campbell MSS.

55. R. W. P. Muse to Salmon P. Chase, July 12, 1853 (quotation), J. M. Tweed to Chase, September 8, 1853, Chase MSS (LC); Lew Campbell to Benjamin F. Wade, August 16, 1853, Wade MSS; Gienapp, *Origins*, pp. 56–59; Maizlish, *Triumph of Sectionalism*, pp. 181–85. According to regression estimates in Gienapp's book, p. 488, during the 1851 referendum on prohibition in Ohio, Whigs split almost two-to-one in favor, Democrats divided one-to-three against, and the Free Soilers who voted were unanimous in support. For evidence that the temperance

question also divided the major parties in the Ohio legislature and thus generated less clear-cut partisan conflict on roll-call votes than banking, see Holt, *Political Crisis*, pp. 115–16.

56. On Whig apathy and resignation to defeat, see Gienapp, *Origins*, pp. 58–59; Maizlish, *Triumph of Sectionalism*, pp. 184–85; and Wade to Campbell, June 27, 1853, Lewis Campbell MSS. The Ohio totals in gubernatorial and presidential elections are conveniently listed in Maizlish, pp. 241–42. I have used the regression estimates of voter movement in Gienapp, p. 494.

57. *Ohio State Journal*, October 14, 1853, quoted in Gienapp, *Origins*, p. 59. In 1853 Free Soilers added seven seats in the house and one in the senate; they, not Democrats, benefited most from the Whigs' loss of seats.

58. M. McDonald to Caleb Cushing, March 11, 1853, Francis O. J. Smith to Cushing, March 14, 1853, E. K. Smart to Cushing, April 14, 1853, Nathan Clifford to Cushing, August 16, 1853, Cushing MSS. Named attorney general by Pierce, Cushing was New England's representative in the cabinet, and the cited letters reveal the linkage between Democratic disputes over patronage and those over prohibition. See also, Gienapp, *Origins*, pp. 50–51.

59. Gienapp, *Origins*, pp. 48–49, 489. On hearing that pro-Crosby Whig senators had refused to support Fessenden for the Senate, Congressman Israel Washburn, Jr., erupted: "Now if this be so (& I can hardly believe it) ought not these gentlemen to understand that if they desire the cordial, earnest, & effective support of the Whig party for Mr. Crosby they must support its nominations fairly & so as to remove all suspicion of a wish on their part, or his, to defeat you?" Washburn to William Pitt Fessenden, February 12, 1853, Fessenden MSS (WRHS).

60. Gienapp, *Origins*, p. 489. Morrill won 11,012 votes (13.2 percent) and the Free Soiler Ezekiel Holmes, 9,039 (10.8 percent). Crosby took 31 percent in 1852. I have taken the gubernatorial results from the Congressional Quarterly's *Guide to U.S. Elections*, p. 410. After September, the seat count in the house stood at sixty-five Whigs (43 percent), seventy-six Democrats (50.7 percent), and nine Free Soilers (6.3 percent). In the senate, it was ten Whigs, eight Democrats, and two Free Soilers, with eleven seats still to be filled because no contenders for them had won the necessary popular-vote majority.

61. William G. Crosby to Fessenden, November 18, 1853, Fessenden MSS (WRHS).

62. Israel Washburn, Jr., to William Pitt Fessenden, January 30, 1854, ibid.; Fessenden to Crosby, November 20, 1853, Lincoln MSS (IU). I have no idea why this letter concerning Maine politics ended up in this small collection of Lincoln's correspondence.

63. Isaac Reed to Israel Washburn, Jr., February 10, 1854 (quotation), Israel Washburn, Jr., MSS (Norlands); William Pitt Fessenden to Governor Crosby, February 11, 1854, copy, S. C. Fessenden to W. P. Fessenden, February 11, 1854, F. H. Morse to W. P. Fessenden, February 12, 1854 (quotation), Fessenden MSS (LC); Gienapp, *Origins*, pp. 129–30.

64. Ibid.

65. Justin Morrill to J. H. Harris, August 19, 1853, draft, Morrill MSS; Montpelier *Vermont Watchman*, April 15, 1853, quoted in Olberg, "Party Formation in Vermont," p. 16. Olberg's roll-call voting analysis indicates that the 1852 license law passed the house by a vote of ninety-one to ninety and that on seven roll-call votes concerning liquor that session, an average of 79 percent of Free Soilers and 59 percent of Whigs took an antiliquor stance, while 64 percent of Democrats took a proliquor position. The referendum, which determined whether the new law should go into effect in March or December—not whether it became law—went in favor of the earlier date by 22,215 to 21,904.

66. The totals in the gubernatorial race were: Whigs, 21,118; Democrats, 18,287; Free Soilers, 8,370. In January 1853 Whig Senator William Upham died, and Whig Governor Fairbanks appointed Whig Samuel Phelps to his seat. The term ran until March 1855, but the U.S. Constitution stipulated that no interim appointee could remain in the Senate beyond the next meeting of the state legislature unless it elected him. Thus it was Phelps' seat at stake. When the legislature failed to replace him, Phelps returned to Washington for the Thirty-Third Congress in December 1853, but in March 1854 the Senate's Democratic majority ejected him on the grounds that constitutionally an appointee could not serve in two different congresses.

67. My account of Massachusetts rests heavily on Sweeney's superb "Rum, Romanism, Representation, and Reform," which is also the source of data on voting patterns.

68. For local Democratic reaction to Cushing's letter, see C. B. H. Fessenden to Caleb Cushing, November 2, 1853, J. Nayson to Cushing, November 3, 1853, and George B. Loring to Cushing, November 11, 1853, Cushing MSS. Since pro-Coalition and antislavery Democrats despised Cushing, his appointment to the cabinet marked another of Pierce's extraordinary blunders.

69. Edward Everett to Mrs. Charles Eames, November 15, 1853 (quotation), copy, Everett MSS; A. M. Ide to Caleb Cushing, November 8, 1853, Cushing MSS.

70. I have taken the count of the legislative seats from Sweeney's article. My assertion that wet Democrats, who had supported the Whig (and anti-Maine Law) candidate Clifford in 1852, swung to the Hunker or National Democratic candidate in 1853 is based on arithmetic manipulations of Sweeney's estimates. They indicate that 8 percent of the 44,000 1851 Democratic voters, or 3,520 men, supported Clifford in 1852 on either the Whig or Repeal tickets. They also show that 5 percent of Clifford's 62,200 voters in 1852, or 3,110 men, backed the Hunker Democrats in 1853.

71. It is unclear who supplied the ballots for and against the new constitution at the November referendum. But parties distributed their own ballots, and Sweeney's estimates suggest that 98 percent of Whig voters opposed, that 71 percent of Hunker Democrats opposed, and that 94 and 93 percent of Democratic and Free Soil voters, respectively, supported, the new constitution. Therefore it seems likely that parties printed Yes or No on the party ballots they distributed or that their poll workers handed out a ballot on the constitution with a Yes or No vote when they gave voters the party ticket. The vast majority of votes on the constitution, in sum, probably reflected what various party leaders had decided, not what individual voters thought about it. If this surmise is accurate, the decision of Cushing's anti-Coalition Democrats to run a separate ticket proved crucial.

72. Sumner to Seward, November 15, 1853, Seward MSS (RU); J. D. Baldwin to Gideon Welles, February 23, 1854 (quotation), Welles MSS (LC); Moses Bates to Caleb Cushing, November 15, 1853, Fisher A. Hildreth to Cushing, November 17, 1853, Cushing MSS; Sweeney, "Rum, Romanism, Representation, and Reform," 136–37. Though the letters to Cushing cited above attributed the defeat to "the foreign vote" and "the Catholics," Sweeney's regression analysis on Boston itself suggests that the Irish abstained rather than voting for or against the constitution.

73. These well-known Democratic feuds in New York require no detailed documentation. But they can be followed in the Cushing MSS, the Tilden MSS, the Fairchild Collection of Horatio Seymour Papers, and the Marcy MSS (LC).

74. Benjamin Thompson to Daniel Ullmann, June 25, 1853 (quotation), Ullmann MSS; Washington Hunt to Thurlow Weed, August 21, 1853, September 18, 1853 (quotation), Weed MSS (RU); Gienapp, *Origins*, p. 41.

75. Hunt used these words in his letter to Weed cited in the preceding note, and so did the Silver Gray Benjamin Thompson in his letter to Daniel Ullmann of June 25, 1853. For the Rochester spring elections, see Henry J. Brent to Caleb Cushing, May 18, June 8, 1853, Cushing MSS.

76. John C. Spencer to Millard Fillmore, September 5, 1853 (quotation), MFP-O; Henry Genet to William H. Seward, September 23, 1853, Seward MSS (RU); Thompson to Ullmann, June 25, 1853, September 20, 1853 (quotation), N. G. King to Ullmann, August 1, 1853, N. W. Davis to Ullmann, August 27, 1853, Thomas H. Bond to Ullmann, September 11, 1853, Darius Perrin to Ullmann, September 21, 1853, William C. Hasbrouck to Ullmann, September 21, 1853, George B. Warren to Ullmann, September 27, 1853, Ullmann MSS.

77. John M. Bradford to William H. Seward, September 10, 1853 (quotation), Lyman A. Spalding to Seward, September 28, 1853 (quotation), Samuel Wilkerson to Seward, October 6, 1853, Seward MSS (RU); John T. Clark to Charles Cook, September 25, 1853 (quotation), Weed MSS (RU).

78. John T. Bush to Millard Fillmore, October 6, 1853, Henry E. Davies to Fillmore, October 7, 1853, MFP-O; Samuel Wilkerson to William H. Seward, October 5, 1853, Seward MSS (RU); Van Deusen, *Seward*, p. 150; Gienapp, *Origins*, p. 41.

79. Washington Hunt to Thurlow Weed, November 3, 1853, Weed MSS (RU); George E. Baker to William H. Seward, November 15, 1853, Seward MSS (RU).

80. Gienapp, *Origins*, pp. 42, 487. Although I have tried to extrapolate from Gienapp's regression estimates in the text, it should be noted that they are based on the difference between the presidential vote in 1852 and the 1853 results, while my assertion of a total Whig loss of 80,000 votes used Washington Hunt's vote, which was 7,000 larger than Scott's.

81. Washington Hunt to Thurlow Weed, November 3, 1853 (quotation), Charles Cooke to Weed, November 15, 1853 (quotation), Weed MSS (RU); Millard Fillmore to John P. Kennedy, October 14, 1853, Kennedy MSS,

82. The Whig state platform can be found in the Pittsburgh *Gazette*, March 28, 1853, and the complaints of political indifference in the issues of May 17, 23, 1853. For the economic questions generating interest in the state, see the files for January to June, 1853, Bigler MSS. Roll-call voting patterns for the Pennsylvania legislature in 1853 can be found in Holt, *Political Crisis*, pp. 115–16.

83. Since Whigs held only 38 percent of the house seats in 1853, considerable numbers of Democrats had to support bank bills for them to pass so that Bigler could veto them. For evidence of Democratic anger at Bigler's bank vetoes in 1853, see Holt, *Forging a Majority*, p. 119. In 1853 the index of partisan disagreement on banking legislation in the Pennsylvania legislature was 70; in contrast, on corporate rights, which involved bills like that for the Pennsylvania Coal Company, it was 46.9 and on railroad bills it was only 38.

84. Mueller, *Whig Party in Pennsylvania*, pp. 203–06; Holt, *Forging a Majority*, pp. 116–21; Thomas Houston to J. Alexander Fulton, January 5, 1853, Fulton MSS; Thomas C. Macdowell to Simon Cameron, September 13, 1853, Cameron MSS; James Reynolds to James Buchanan, September 20, 1853, Buchanan MSS (HSP); Charles A. Black to William Bigler, September 2, 23, 1853, G. G. Wescott to Bigler, October 10, 1853, Bigler MSS. The index of partisan disagreement on legislative votes regarding prohibition was only 16.3 in 1852 and 26 in 1853. Prohibition, that is, evoked far less partisan cohesion than any economic issue.

85. The 1853 Pennsylvania returns for canal commissioner can be found in Mueller, *Whig Party in Pennsylvania*, p. 206; those for 1851 and 1852 are on pp. 190 and 200, respectively. For turnout rates, see Gienapp, " 'Politics Seem to Enter Into Everything,' " pp. 18–19. The turnout rate in 1853 was 51.3 percent; between 1840 and 1860, only the 41.5 percent rate in 1846 was lower. For the description of the Independent legislative slate in Philadelphia, see William Pettit to John M. Niles, December 8, 1853, Welles MSS (LC).

86. Whigs had last carried New Jersey in 1848. New Jersey remains the least studied of all northern states in the antebellum period, and I have relied almost exclusively on Renda, "Railroads, Revenue, and Reform." Renda demonstrates that beginning with the 1849 legislative session, Whigs achieved much less cohesion on roll-call votes concerning economic legislation than Democrats and that not only railroad legislation but also taxes and even public education involved trade-offs between interest groups and localities that utterly fragmented statewide party coalitions. The very complexity of the issues now on the government's agenda, in sum, prevented statewide party organizations from addressing them, lest they lose votes in some communities while attempting to gain them in others.

87. Renda, "Railroads, Revenue, and Reform," pp. 125–36; the *Gloucester Constitution*, November 9, 1852, and *Sussex Register*, November 6, 1852, are quoted on pp. 124–25.

88. Ibid., pp. 137–38; for the background of the temperance issue in New Jersey, see pp. 108–16.

89. In addition to Renda's M. A. thesis, I have used Kierner, " 'The Motley Party.' " The 1853 election is analyzed on pp. 13–21.

90. Robert McLane to Caleb Cushing, October 14, 1853, Cushing MSS; McLane to William L. Marcy, October 21, 1853, Marcy MSS (LC); Evitts, *Matter of Allegiances*, pp. 57–58.

91. McLane to Marcy, October 21, 1853, Marcy MSS; Z. Collins Lee to William H. Seward, October 13, 1853, Seward MSS (RU); John Thompson to James Buchanan, February 20, 1854, Buchanan MSS (HSP). In the 1850 gubernatorial election, the results had been Democrats, 36,349 (51 percent); Whigs, 34,858 (49 percent). In 1853 they were Democrats, 39,087 (52.8 percent); Whigs, 34,939 (47.2 percent). In the legislature, Whigs increased their share of seats in the house from 41 percent in 1851 to 53 percent in 1853; the corresponding change in the senate was from 50 to 64 percent. In heavily Democratic Baltimore, Whigs threw their support to an independent

Maine Law ticket that included five Whigs and five Democrats and that defeated the regular, antiprohibition Democratic legislative ticket. See Evitts, *Matter of Allegiances*, pp. 61–62; and Bowers, "Ideology," 206–07.

92. McLane to Cushing, October 14, 1853, Cushing MSS. In 1851 Walsh won narrowly, 6,683 to 6,453; in 1853, he lost almost as narrowly, 6,440 to 6,792.

93. *Baltimore American*, November 4, 1853, quoted in Bowers, "Ideology," 208–09.

94. Little separated the contending parties in 1853. Democrats asserted that old Whig measures like a national bank and federal internal improvements were now dead letters, and they even praised the deceased Henry Clay to win over former Whig voters. Whigs, in reply, blasted the hypocrisy of the Democrats' crocodile tears for Clay. That the main argument was over a corpse symbolized the bankruptcy of partisan debate. Volz, "Party, State, and Nation," pp. 133–47.

95. I have included in the 1853 Democratic total, and thus in the gains Democrats made between 1851 and 1853, 5,590 votes cast for a dissident Democratic candidate in the first district who ran unsuccessfully against Speaker of the House Linn Boyd. A Whig had garnered 3,400 votes against Boyd in 1851, while another dissident Democrat that year had won 1,460. Thus it is likely that Whigs contributed some of the votes I have counted as Democrats.

96. William B. Campbell to David Campbell, February 15, 1852, CFP; Felix Zollicoffer to William Schouler, April 4, 1853, Schouler MSS.

97. William B. Campbell to David Campbell, July 4, 19, 1853, CFP; Andrew Johnson to David T. Patterson, December 3, 1852, and to Albert G. Graham, December 10, 1852, in *Johnson Papers*, pp. 92–97. Nathaniel Taylor and Watkins split 9,300 votes (63 percent) between them, allowing Democrat Brookins Campbell to win with 37 percent. Campbell, however, died on December 25, 1853, without ever going to Washington. Nathaniel Taylor won a special election in early 1854 and took the seat in March. The furious Watkins would oppose him again in 1855.

98. John Bell to William B. Campbell, January 6, 1853, CFP. For resentment of Bell among Tennessee's Whigs, see above, Chapter 18.

99. Gustavus A. Henry to William B. Campbell, n.d. (1853), CFP.

100. Gustavus A. Henry to J. A. Shackelford, June 3, 1853 (quotation), G. A. Henry to Marion Henry, July 3, 1853, Henry MSS; William B. Campbell to David Campbell, July 4, 1853, CFP.

101. William B. Campbell to David Campbell, August 10, 1853 (quotation), Thomas J. Campbell to William B. Campbell, September 9, 1853, CFP; Gustavus A. Henry to J. O. Shackelford, June 3, 1853, Henry MSS; Andrew Johnson to David T. Patterson, December 3, 1852, to Albert G. Graham, December 10, 1852, to A. O. P. Nicholson, September 8, 1853, and to the Democrats of Maury County, September 18, 1853 (quotation), in *Johnson Papers*, pp. 92–97, 167–71.

102. William B. Campbell to David Campbell, August 10, 15, 1853, Gustavus A. Henry to William B. Campbell, August 26, 1853 (quotation), CFP. The gubernatorial results in 1851 had been: Whigs, 63,423 (50.7 percent); Democrats, 61,648 (49.3 percent). In 1853, they were: Whigs, 61,163 (49.1 percent); Democrats, 63,413 (50.9 percent). The changes in the legislature, the first to be elected under the Henrymander, were:

	House		Senate	
	Whigs	Democrats	Whigs	Democrats
1851	39	36	16	9
1853	44	31	12	13

For figures on the legislature, I have relied on *Johnson Papers*, p. xx; and William B. Campbell to David Campbell, August 15, 1853, CFP.

103. William B. Campbell to David Campbell, August 10, September 23, 1853, John Bell to W. B. Campbell, August 14, 1853, Gustavus A. Henry to W. B. Campbell, August 26, 1853, CFP; G. A. Henry to Marion Henry, October 9, 14, 1853, Henry MSS.

104. Cave Johnson to James Buchanan, November 20, 1853, Buchanan MSS (HSP).

105. Kruman, *Parties and Politics*, pp. 153–54.

106. On Winston, see Thornton, *Power and Politics*, pp. 321–30. The returns from the 1853 legislative elections are apparently missing, but it is clear that while some Whigs were elected, Democrats controlled both chambers. Bolling Hall was elected speaker of the house, and Clement Clay, Jr., expected the race for the Senate seat to be between himself and a Union Democrat like George Houston whom the Whig minority would support. David C. Humphreys to Bolling Hall, September 7, 1853, G. T. Yelverton to Hall, September 9, 1853, Clement C. Clay, Jr., to Hall, September 30, 1853, Hall MSS.

107. Cole, *Whig Party in the South*, pp. 278–80, Jackson, *Flag of the Union*, January 28, 1853, quoted on pp. 278–79; Joshua Whitman to Charles D. Fontaine, January 7, 1853, Fontaine MSS.

108. Under the reapportionment after the census of 1850, Mississippi gained a fifth House seat. Because of a stalemate between the Union-dominated house and the Democratic senate, however, the legislature failed to redraw the districts and the new seat had to be filled in a statewide race in 1853. Mittendorf, "Mississippi Politics," pp. 46–47.

109. Albert G. Brown to John F. H. Claiborne, May 6, October 16, November 15, 1853, Claiborne MSS.

110. Cole, *Whig Party in the South*, p. 280; N. S. Price to Charles D. Fontaine, June 15, 1853, Fontaine MSS.

111. On Fontaine's defeat by a Whig named Scruggs, see the note attached to Joshua Witman to Charles Fontaine, January 7, 1853, Fontaine MSS. The proportions of the vote won by Whig congressional candidates—Union Democrats ran as the Whig candidates in the first and second districts—were as follows: first, 48.4 percent; second, 49.3 percent; third, 44.4 percent; at-large, 45.9 percent. Wiley P. Harris, Democratic candidate in the fourth district, Brown's old bastion and the most heavily Democratic district in the state, ran unopposed.

The shift in legislative seats was as follows:

	1849		1851		1853	
	House	Senate	House	Senate	House	Senate
Whig	36	10			37	10
Democratic	62	20			60	20
Union			63	11		
Southern Rights			35	21		

112. Toombs to John J. Crittenden, December 5, 1852, Crittenden MSS (LC); Howell Cobb to Alexander H. Stephens, February 2, 1853, Stephens MSS (LC); Murray, *Whig Party in Georgia*, pp. 170–71.

113. E. C. Cain to John M. Berrien, April 3, 1853, D. R. Mitchell to Berrien, May 5, 1853, William H. Underwood to Berrien, May 9, 1853, Berrien MSS.

114. Charles J. Jenkins to John M. Berrien, August 17, 1853 (quotations), Berrien MSS; Murray, *Whig Party in Georgia*, pp. 171–74.

115. Charles J. Jenkins to John M. Berrien, August 17, October 7, 22, 1853, William Hunter to Berrien, September 7, 30, 1853, Berrien MSS; Alexander Stephens to John Bird, July 20, 1853, Stephens MSS (LC); Murray, *Whig Party in Georgia*, pp. 173–75. Jenkins' vulnerability to the charge of privileging the rich stemmed from his support for the so-called Algerine Law, a municipal ordinance passed by his home town of Augusta in 1841 that limited the suffrage in city elections to those who owned property worth $1,000 or more.

116. Charles Jenkins to John M. Berrien, October 7, 22, 1853, Berrien MSS; Murray, *Whig Party in Georgia*, p. 174. The regression estimates come from an undergraduate seminar paper, Bobo, "Revelry, Reorganization, and Ruin."

117. Alexander H. Stephens to John Bird, July 20, 1853, Stephens MSS (LC); Jenkins to Berrien, October 22, 1853, Berrien MSS. The changes in the Whig and Union proportions of seats in the state house and senate between 1849 and 1853 were as follows:

	House	Senate
1849	49% Whig	50% Whig
1851	78% Union	83% Union
1853	45% Union Whig	50% Union Whig

118. Murray, *Whig Party in Georgia*, p. 175.

119. No returns for Alabama's 1853 legislative elections are reported in the data from the Inter-University Consortium.

120. The total of twenty-three southern Whigs in the House includes Nathaniel Taylor, who was elected in a special election in Tennessee's First District in early 1854.

121. Charles Shaler to Caleb Cushing, July 21, 1853, Cushing MSS; Samuel Treat to Stephen A. Douglas, December 18, 1853, Douglas MSS; Douglas to Charles H. Lanphier, November 11, 1853, Lanphier MSS.

122. Hodge to Fillmore, September 26 (quotation), 30, 1853, MFP-O.

123. William L. Hodge to Millard Fillmore, October 6, 1853, MFP-O; Fillmore to John P. Kennedy, December 15, 1853, Kennedy MSS.

124. Fillmore to John P. Kennedy, October 14, 1853, Kennedy MSS; Samuel Treat to Stephen A. Douglas, December 18, 1853, Douglas MSS.

125. Kennedy to Fillmore, November 26, 1853, copy, Kennedy MSS.

126. John P. Kennedy to Robert C. Winthrop, December 4, 1853, copy, Millard Fillmore to John P. Kennedy, January 14, 1854, Kennedy MSS.

127. Alexander H. H. Stuart to Millard Fillmore, December 6, 1853, January 3, 1854, MFP-O. The quotations come from both letters, but I have mixed them rather than following Stuart's sequential order.

128. M. Gross to Caleb Cushing, November 14, 1853, Cushing MSS.

129. On the origins of Know Nothingism, see my "The Antimasonic and Know Nothing Parties," pp. 593–94; Gienapp, *Origins*, pp. 92–93; and Anbinder, *Nativism & Slavery*, pp. 20–51.

CHAPTER 22

1. Alexander H. H. Stuart to Millard Fillmore, December 6, 1853 (quotation), January 3, 1854, Solomon G. Haven to Fillmore, December 12, 17, 1853, MFP-O; John P. Kennedy to Robert C. Winthrop, December 4, 1853, copy, Millard Fillmore to Kennedy, December 15, 1853 (quotation), Kennedy MSS.

2. Jeffrey L. Dugger to Richard Yates, January 22, 1854, Yates MSS; William H. Seward to Thurlow Weed, December 12, 1853, Weed MSS (RU); Solomon G. Haven to Millard Fillmore, December 17, 1853 (quotation), MFP-O; John Bell to William B. Campbell, December 13, 1853, quoted in Parks, *Bell*, p. 282.

3. Handlin, *Boston's Immigrants*, p. 355, n. 85.

4. For an alternative interpretation of the growth of northern Know Nothingism that discounts economic factors, acknowledges even while downplaying nativism and anti-Catholicism, and stresses instead anti-Nebraska or antislavery sentiment, see Anbinder, *Nativism & Slavery*. Delineating my disagreements with Anbinder's interpretation would require a separate essay. My own interpretation of Know Nothingism is presented in *Political Crisis*, pp. 154–81, and two essays, "The Antimasonic and Know Nothing Parties" and "The Politics of Impatience." In *Origins*, pp. 69–102 and passim, William E. Gienapp supports my argument that Know Nothingism grew for reasons independent of the Nebraska Act and that it played a central role in gutting northern Whiggery. Like Anbinder, however, he minimizes the role of economic dislocation and

hardship in spawning Know Nothingism. In contrast, Fogel, *Without Consent or Contract*, pp. 354–80, gives the economic immiseration of native-born laborers and their resulting resentment of immigrant competition top billing in his explanation of Know Nothingism.

5. See, for example, the studies cited in the preceding note.

6. Stephen A. Douglas to Charles H. Lanphier, November 11, 1853 (quotation), Lanphier MSS; Holt, *Political Crisis*, pp. 144–48; Johannsen, *Douglas*, pp. 395–434; and Nichols, "Kansas-Nebraska Act."

7. In addition to the sources cited in note 6, see Cooper, *Politics of Slavery*, pp. 346–52; Freehling, *Road to Disunion*, pp. 536–65; and Wolff, "Party and Section."

8. For an explicit statement of Douglas' hope that his bill "will form the test of Parties," see Stephen A. Douglas to Charles H. Lanphier, February 13, 1854, Lanphier MSS. For his confidence that popular sovereignty embodied "the great principle of self government" and that "surely the people of this country are never going to decide that the principle upon which our whole republican system rests is vicious & wrong," see Stephen A. Douglas to Howell Cobb, April 2, 1854, in Phillips, "Correspondence of Toombs, Stephens, and Cobb," p. 343.

9. Parks, *Bell*, pp. 284–85; Johannsen, *Douglas*, pp. 395–434. I have relied heavily on Johannsen's wonderfully detailed analysis of the Senate's action on the Kansas-Nebraska bill in this and succeeding paragraphs. Like Douglas, northern Whig congressmen recognized that popular sovereignty had far more positive appeal than the negative onus of repealing the Missouri restriction. See, for example, Solomon G. Haven to Millard Fillmore, February 18, 1854, MFP-O. That awareness explains why northern Whigs from the start portrayed Douglas' bill as repeal.

10. Johannsen, *Douglas*, p. 406.

11. Ibid., pp. 407–08; Seward to Weed, January 7, 8, 1854, Weed MSS (RU); Jabez Hammond to William H. Seward, February 28, 1854, Seward MSS (RU); for other Democratic reactions to the bill voicing the delight that Hards had established a litmus test for Softs, see Holt, *Political Crisis*, p. 146. My inference about Seward's calculations regarding southern Whig behavior rests on many contemporary statements that repeal violated the spirit and letter of the platform southern Whigs had imposed on the party. See, for example, Truman Smith to John Wilson, May 26, 1854, John Wilson MSS.

Seward's hope of portraying Douglas' bill as "the repeal of the Missouri Compromise" casts light on his subsequent claim that he later instigated Kentucky Whig Senator Archibald Dixon to try to amend Douglas' bill with an open repeal of the Missouri Compromise restriction. Seward's claim has provoked considerable dispute among historians, if only because the sources, mostly consisting of reminiscences written much later, conflict with each other. William J. Cooper and William W. Freehling both argue persuasively that Dixon needed no prodding from Seward to do what the exigencies of southern politics demanded, and they are surely correct that some Southerner, Whig or Democrat, would have moved for outright repeal without northern prompting. But their argument says nothing about Seward's intentions in January 1854. Seward's supposed intervention with Dixon is compatible with the position he had assumed since 1850—namely, that northern and southern Whigs must once again agree to disagree about slavery issues and take opposite positions in each section when seeking votes. Initially in 1854, however, Seward apparently saw explicit repeal as the best way to force southern Whigs to join northern Whigs in opposing Douglas' bill. But if Seward expected Clayton to rally southern Whigs against repeal, that rally would surely have been less likely if a southern Whig, rather than a Democrat, first proposed it. At the very least, that is, if Seward approached Dixon, as he later claimed, he changed his mind after January 8.

12. On southern Whig contempt for squatter sovereignty, see Cole, *Whig Party in the South*, pp. 288–92.

13. William C. Dawson to Linton Stephens, December 21, 1853, Alexander H. Stephens MSS (LC).

14. For Sumner's amendment, see Donald, *Sumner*, p. 250. In January, when both Dixon and Sumner spoke, the Nebraska bill had not yet been formally placed on the Senate agenda for debate and possible amendment. Thus, on January 16, Dixon did not offer an amendment that required a vote to adopt or reject it. Rather, he only announced his intention of offering an

amendment when appropriate. Democrats could thus head off the amendment and a vote on it by changing the bill before it was formally placed on the Senate agenda.

15. As Freehling puts it, in *Road to Disunion*, p. 553, "an exasperated Southern Whig had defied the Democracy to go all the way for the South."

16. *Congressional Globe*, 33rd Cong., 1st Sess., pp. 239–40.

Dixon's very protests that he did not act for the partisan purpose of embarrassing southern Democrats, of course, may be read as evidence that he did.

17. Freehling, *Road to Disunion*, p. 555, stresses the parallel between Dixon's proposed amendment and the one moved by Brown in 1844. The overweening Dixon had infuriated many Kentucky Whigs by demanding the party's 1851 gubernatorial nomination, then losing the race because of abstention by disgusted Whigs, and then demanding one of the Senate seats at the disposal of the Whig legislature as a consolation prize for running the gubernatorial race in the first place. Dixon was serving out the term to which Clay had been elected in early 1849, a term that ended on March 3, 1855. In sum, he badly needed to burnish his reputation with Kentucky Whigs or, alternatively, to woo Democrats in order to offset Whig opposition to him. Since Kentucky's Whigs had always been nationalists rather than proslavery extremists, winning favor with Democrats may have been his primary intention, an interpretation supported by his immediate endorsement of Douglas' revised bill on January 24. In any event, his proposed amendment failed to mitigate Kentucky Whigs' animosity. In early February 1854, the legislature elected Dixon's old nemesis, John J. Crittenden, to replace him for the term that began in March 1855. See Cole, *Whig Party in the South*, p. 299, n. 58, citing a February 24 newspaper account of a public dinner in Kentucky honoring Crittenden's election to the Senate.

Jones had outraged many Tennessee Whigs by his naked ambition for the vice presidential nomination in 1852 and his early support for Scott's candidacy when the vast majority of Tennessee's Whigs preferred Fillmore. Since support for Scott prior to the Whig national convention was interpreted as an antislavery, antisouthern stance, moreover, Jones had even more incentive to reaffirm his proslavery credentials by supporting repeal of the Missouri Compromise line. Regardless of Seward's later claims and the likelihood that some Southerner of either party might move for repeal, that is, there were specific political reasons why these two men seized the initiative.

18. Johannsen, *Douglas*, p. 411.

19. Freehling, *Road to Disunion*, pp. 552–60. The quoted passage reaffirming popular sovereignty was actually presented by Douglas in a later amendment on February 7, not in the January 23 version of the bill. That version dropped the twenty-first section and reverted to the original language of the January 4 bill granting the territorial legislatures authority over "all rightful subjects of legislation." *Congressional Globe*, 33rd Cong., 1st Sess., p. 353; Johannsen, *Douglas*, pp. 405–18.

20. Seward to Wife, January 29, 1854, in *Seward at Washington*, pp. 217–18. Seward and others could legitimately blame repeal on Hard pressure, for two days before Dixon offered his amendment, the Washington *Sentinel*, edited by Beverley Tucker, the man Hards had helped elect Senate printer over the administration's preferred candidate, demanded that Douglas change the bill to include overt, direct repeal. Johannsen, *Douglas*, p. 411.

21. William H. Seward to Wife, January 29, 1854, in *Seward at Washington*, pp. 217–18; Hamilton Fish to Thurlow Weed, January 25, February 3, 1854, Weed MSS (RU); John Minor Botts to William Schouler, March 26, 1854, Lewis Campbell to Schouler, May 22, 1854, Schouler MSS; Truman Smith to John Wilson, April 27, 1854, Wilson MSS; Elihu Washburne to James S. Pike, May 8, 1854, Israel Washburn to Pike, May 13, 1854, Lewis Campbell to Pike, May 14, 24, 1854, Pike MSS.

22. On November 26, 1853, *before* the opening of the congressional session, for example, Ohio's Lew Campbell wrote William Schouler, who had agreed to move from Boston to take over the Cincinnati *Gazette*, "The hour looks dark for Whigs in Ohio, but the *live young fellows* can win. The *Old Silvers* have tried long enough. Let us now go to work and galvanize the concern and put it on the platform it occupied before '48, where it naturally belongs, and will feel easy." Schouler MSS.

23. Roger Sherman Baldwin to Truman Smith, February 18, 1854, BFP; Campbell to James S. Pike, May 22, 1854, Pike MSS; William H. Seward to New York Anti-Nebraska Meeting, January 28, 1854, in *Seward at Washington*, p. 218.

24. Edward Kent to Israel Washburn, March 9, 1854, Israel Washburn MSS (Norlands). That Sewardites intended to heavyhandedly remind northern Whig voters of conservatives' fatal mistake in supporting the Compromise was made clear in Seward's letter of January 28, 1854 to a New York anti-Nebraska meeting, cited in note 23. "It is quite clear," he wrote, "that if we had maintained our ground on the laws of freedom which then protected New Mexico and Utah, we should not have been attacked in our stronghold."

25. Solomon G. Haven to Millard Fillmore, January 29, 1854, MFP-O; Robert C. Winthrop to Edward Everett, February 6, 13, 1854, Millard Fillmore to Everett, February 8, 1854, Everett MSS; Truman Smith to Roger Sherman Baldwin, January 28, 1854, BFP.

26. Solomon G. Haven to Millard Fillmore, January 29, 1854, MFP-O; Robert C. Winthrop to Edward Everett, February 6, 13 (quotation), 1854, Everett MSS; Winthrop to John Pendleton Kennedy, January 31, February 27, 1854 (quotations), Kennedy MSS; Edward Kent to Israel Washburn, March 9, 1854, Washburn MSS (Norlands).

27. John T. Bush to Fillmore, January 19, 1854, MFP-O.

28. Solomon G. Haven to Millard Fillmore, February 12, 1854, MFP-O.

29. Ogden Hoffman to William H. Seward, March 5, 1854, Seward MSS (RU); B. Thompson to Daniel Ullmann, May 16, 1854, Ullmann MSS. Democrats also noted that the Nebraska bill induced the previously divided New York Whigs to reunite. See, for example, T. M. Parmalee to Caleb Cushing, February 15, 1854, Cushing MSS.

30. Winthrop to Kennedy, January 31, February 27, 1854, Kennedy MSS; Daniel Lee to Fillmore, February 9, 1854, Alexander H. H. Stuart to Fillmore, February 16, 1854, MFP-O.

31. Winthrop to Kennedy, February 27, 1854, Kennedy MSS.

32. John Bell to William B. Campbell, August 10, 1854, CFP; D. A. Reese to Linton Stephens, May 20, 1854, Alexander Stephens MSS (LC); Schott, *Stephens*, pp. 163–73. Solomon Haven spoke with Toombs in the Senate chamber on February 17 while Seward was speaking against the Nebraska bill, and he reported to Fillmore that Toombs hoped the bill would produce "the entire separation of the south as a party from the north." Haven to Fillmore, February 18, 1854, MFP-O.

33. John P. Kennedy to Robert C. Winthrop, February 19, 1854 (quotation), copy, Kennedy MSS; Alexander H. H. Stuart to Millard Fillmore, February 16, 1854, MFP-O; Truman Smith to John Wilson, January 31, April 27, 1854, John Wilson MSS; Cole, *Whig Party in the South*, pp. 285–305 (for Wade's warning to southern Whig senators, see p. 304, n. 77). For evidence that some southern Democrats also believed that repeal of the Missouri restriction was of little practical consequence because slavery would never be established in Kansas or Nebraska, see William B. W. Dent to Herschel V. Johnson, June 13, 1854, Johnson MSS; and J. L. M. Curry to Clement Claiborne Clay, July 5, 1854, Clement C. Clay MSS. "So far as the introduction of slavery [into Kansas or Nebraska] is concerned," Curry wrote Clay in explaining southern apathy about the bill, "such a consummation is hardly hoped for."

34. John Bell's long speeches in late May justifying his vote against Nebraska summarize almost all the arguments other southern Whigs made against the bill. They can be found in *Congressional Globe*, 33rd Cong., 1st Sess., *Appendix*, pp. 755–57, 939–48, quotation on p. 945. See also John Minor Botts to William Schouler, March 26, April 9, 1854, Schouler MSS; E. R. Jewett to Millard Fillmore, February 18, 1854, MFP-O; J. Wales et al. to John M. Clayton, February 13, 1854, Clayton MSS; Orsamus B. Matteson to Thurlow Weed, May 22, 1854, Weed MSS (RU); John J. Crittenden to Presley Ewing, March 6, 1854, Crittenden to Archibald Dixon, March 7, 1854, Crittenden MSS (LC); Cole, *Whig Party in the South*, pp. 285–99; Cooper, *Politics of Slavery*, pp. 351–54; and Volz, "Party, State, and Nation," pp. 168–69.

35. The "Appeal" is quoted in Johannsen, *Douglas*, p. 418.

36. Oran Follett to Thomas Ewing, May 1, 1854, EFP.

37. Joshua R. Giddings to Joseph R. Hawley, March 13, 1854, Hawley MSS.

38. Benjamin F. Wade to Milton R. Sutliffe, April 21, 1854, Sutliffe MSS; Ben Wade to Caroline Wade, May 6, 1854, Wade MSS.

39. Fillmore to Everett, February 8, 1854, Winthrop to Everett, February 6, 13, 1854, Everett MSS; Winthrop's public letter of October 15, 1855, is quoted in Gienapp, *Origins*, p. 73.

40. Winthrop to Everett, February 13, 1854, Everett to Mrs. Charles Eames, March 21, 1854, Everett to ?, April 24, 1854, Everett MSS; Edward Kent to Israel Washburn, March 9, 1854, Israel Washburn MSS (Norlands).

41. Edward Kent to Israel Washburn, March 9, 1854 (quotation), Robert C. Winthrop to Edward Everett, February 13, May 12, 1854, Edward Everett to ?, April 21, 1854, Everett to Mrs. Charles Eames, March 21, May 5, 12 (quotation), 1854, Everett MSS; Robert C. Winthrop to John P. Kennedy, February 27, 1854, Kennedy MSS; Donald, *Sumner*, p. 257.

42. The few outright Whigs from the lower South—other than the independent Union Whigs from Alabama and Georgia, James Abercrombie, Alexander Stephens, Robert Toombs, and D. A. Reese—included Representative Theodore G. Hunt of Louisiana and Senators Judah P. Benjamin of that state, William C. Dawson of Georgia, and Jackson Morton of Florida.

43. In July a St. Louis Whig wrote Fillmore that nine-tenths of Missouri's Whigs opposed repeal of the Missouri Compromise line but that because Missourians were so anxious to have Nebraska formally organized, Missouri's Whig congressmen were obligated to support the bill. Henry W. Williams to Millard Fillmore, July 1, 1854, MFP-O.

44. E. R. Jewett to Millard Fillmore, February 18, 1854, MFP-O.

45. Truman Smith to John Wilson, January 31, 1854, Wilson MSS; Cooper, *Politics of Slavery*, pp. 351–54, Richmond *Whig*, quoted on p. 354.

46. Smith to John Wilson, January 31, 1854, John Wilson MSS; Solomon G. Haven to Millard Fillmore, January 29, February 12, 1854, Charles Davies to Fillmore, February 1, 1854, E. R. Jewett to Fillmore, February 18, 1854, MFP-O. Clayton's speech is quoted in Cole, *Whig Party in the South*, p. 293.

47. *Congressional Globe*, 33rd Cong., 1st Sess., pp. 222, 353; Nichols, *Blueprints for Leviathan*, pp. 99–103; Johannsen, *Douglas*, p. 428. Clayton's amendment, reflecting the emerging anti-immigrant feeling among Whigs, restricted the right to vote and hold office in the territories to citizens. Since immigrants were thought to be hostile to slavery extension, barring them from political participation in the territories was considered prosouthern. Simultaneously, Clayton's amendment made the bill more difficult for House Democrats from the North to support, and it would be deleted from the version that the House passed. Badger's amendment had a different purpose. Aware of the sensitivity among southern Whigs to Northerners' charge that repeal of the Missouri prohibition marked an aggressive attempt actually to extend slavery—an extension that southern Whigs continually denied would occur—Badger stated explicitly that repeal of the Missouri ban would *not* automatically reinstate the laws that legalized slavery in the Louisiana Territory prior to the adoption of the 1820 prohibition. Put differently, Badger sought to mollify northern Whigs about the motives of southern Whigs in order to preserve party unity on other issues during the remainder of the congressional session. Unlike Toombs and Stephens, neither he nor other old line southern Whigs saw their support for the Nebraska bill as cause for a permanent sectional rupture of the Whig party. Certainly, they did not *intend* to precipitate a rupture by supporting the bill.

48. James Pearce of Maryland, John Thompson of Kentucky, and Jackson Morton of Florida did not attend. Tennessee's Whig Representative William Cullom later claimed to have been at this impromtu gathering, but he probably confused it with a different, bipartisan caucus a few days earlier that hammered out the final wording of the repeal and popular sovereignty provisions of the Nebraska bill, which the Senate, ironically, adopted on the afternoon of February 15. The caucus, and particularly Bell's role in it, were later angrily debated at great length in both the House and Senate, and those speeches provide the best accounts of it. *Congressional Globe*, 33rd Cong., 1st Sess., *Appendix*, pp. 755–57, 902, 939–48.

49. For the quotations see Toombs' account of the caucus and William Churchwell's citation of Badger's Senate speech, ibid., pp. 756, 902; Cole, *Whig Party in the South*, p. 293; William Henry Seward to Mrs. Seward, February 16, 1854, in *Seward at Washington*, p. 219. Churchwell,

a Democratic congressman from Tennessee, received a report of the caucus from Toombs and later used it on the House floor to accuse Bell of betraying his word as well as the South when he voted against the bill.

50. In May, Pearce supported the revised version of the bill reported back to the Senate from the House, the passage of which was absolutely certain, and in March some newspapers declared that he would have supported the bill had he been present for the vote on March 4. Yet Pearce did not attend the southern Whig meeting on February 15, and on February 17, when Solomon Haven warned him that passage of the bill in its present form would outrage the North and strengthen the antislavery wing of the northern Whig party, Pearce told Haven that he hoped the bill would be modified to mollify northern Whigs prior to its passage. Haven to Millard Fillmore, February 18, 1854, MFP-O.

51. *Congressional Globe*, 33rd Cong., 1st Sess., pp. 532, 550. Everett, James Cooper, and Samuel Phelps of Vermont were the northern Whigs who missed the vote. Joining Bell in opposition were two Free Soilers, four northern Democrats, and only six northern Whigs—Seward and Hamilton Fish of New York, Truman Smith of Connecticut, Solomon Foot of Vermont, William Pitt Fessenden of Maine, and Ben Wade of Ohio. Subsequent attempts by Everett and Clayton to have negative votes recorded were ruled out of order.

Over a month after the Senate vote, John Minor Botts reported that Bell had been so frightened by the anger of other southern Whigs when he spoke against the Nebraska bill in the afternoon of March 3 that he had determined to duck the final vote on it. According to Botts, only pressure from Seward and three Tennessee Whig representatives who were also publicly committed against the bill—William Cullom, Emerson Etheridge, and Robert Bugg—finally persuaded Bell to stand up and cast a negative vote. John Minor Botts to William Schouler, April 9, 1854, Schouler MSS.

52. Edward Kent to Israel Washburn, March 9, 1854, Israel Washburn MSS (Norlands). One might stretch my counterfactual case totally beyond the boundaries of plausibility by adding the vote of Toombs to the negative column. In that case, theoretically, a 24–24 tie would have developed, and with no vice president to break it (William R. King had died in 1853), a tie could have defeated the bill. Yet if one is going to add absent Whigs, one must also add absent Democrats, and three Democratic senators, including Florida's Stephen Mallory, missed the vote. He certainly, and the others probably, would have supported the bill and secured its passage.

Phelps undoubtedly opposed the measure, and he most likely failed to vote because his right to represent Vermont in the Senate was under challenge. He had been appointed in January 1853 to fill the seat upon the death of William Upham, but in the fall of 1853 the Vermont legislature had failed to ratify that gubernatorial appointment by formally electing him. On March 16, 1854, twelve days after the vote on Nebraska, the Senate's Democratic majority expelled Phelps, and the seat would remain empty until the new Vermont legislature, elected in September 1854, chose Lawrence Brainerd, a Free Soiler, to complete Upham's term during the second session of the Thirty-Third Congress.

53. Truman Smith to John Wilson, April 27, 1854, John Wilson MSS. The best account of maneuvering in the House is Nichols, *Blueprints for Leviathan*, pp. 104–21.

54. Nichols, *Blueprints for Leviathan*, pp. 110–20; Schott, *Stephens*, pp. 166–70; D. A. Reese to Linton Stephens, May 20, 1854, Alexander H. Stephens to Thomas W. Thomas, May 23, 1854, Stephens MSS (LC).

55. *Congressional Globe*, 33rd Cong., 1st Sess., p. 1195; Nichols, *Blueprints for Leviathan*, p. 116, cites a different vote of postponement that carried 137–66 and set May 20 as the closing date for debate on the Nebraska bill. What explains the discrepancy between his total and the vote listed on p. 1195 of the *Globe* is unclear.

56. Here and elsewhere, unless noted otherwise, my total of twenty-four southern Whig representatives includes the three Unionists, Stephens and Reese of Georgia and Abercrombie of Alabama.

57. *Congressional Globe*, 33rd Cong., 1st Sess., pp. 1254–55.

58. The quotations come from John Bell's speech of May 25, 1854, which can be found in the *Congressional Globe*, 33rd Cong., 1st Sess., *Appendix*, p. 948.

59. Eric Foner, for example, has written: "We can date almost exactly the final collapse of

the [second-party] system—February 15, 1854—the day a caucus of southern Whig Congressmen and Senators decided to support Douglas' Nebraska bill despite the fact that they could have
united with northern Whigs in opposition both to the repeal of the Missouri Compromise and
to the revival of sectional agitation." Foner, "Politics, Ideology," p. 26. Foner here confuses
earlier bipartisan caucuses attended by Whigs from both houses of Congress with the February
15 meeting of southern Whig senators, but he is absolutely correct that the demise of the Whig
party was central to the collapse of the second party system. Nonetheless, Foner minimizes the
number of Whig leaders who wanted to stop a sectional rupture in the party and thus dates it
prematurely. Although he alludes to erosion from local Whig organizations over temperance and
nativism in a note on the same page, he also seems to equate the rupture of Whigs' national
leadership along sectional lines with the party's death. Yet a sectional rift among Whig politicians
in Washington over the Nebraska issue did not automatically necessitate the abandonment of
local and state Whig parties in the North and South, spell an end to their competitiveness, or
indicate a readiness among Whig voters and politicos to join new sectional parties.

60. The most thorough study of roll-call voting patterns during the first session of the
Thirty-Third Congress, which documents the continued cohesion among Whigs and Democrats
on votes not related to Nebraska, is Wolff, *Kansas-Nebraska Bill.*

61. For the newspaper quotations, see Cole, *Whig Party in the South*, pp. 305–06; Cooper,
Politics of Slavery, pp. 357–58.

62. Cole, *Whig Party in the South*, pp. 306–07.

63. For state legislative resolutions from Tennessee, Louisiana, and Georgia, see Nashville
Republican Banner, March 3, 1854, and Washington *National Intelligencer*, March 8, April 1,
1854.

64. D. A. Reese to Linton Stephens, May 20, 1854, Stephens MSS; William B. W. Dent to
Herschel V. Johnson, June 13, 1854, Johnson MSS; Haven to Millard Fillmore, February 18,
1854, Fillmore MSS (MFP-O); Schott, *Stephens*, pp. 173–74, and Cole, *Whig Party in the South*,
p. 307, for quotations from Stephens in June.

65. Cole, *Whig Party in the South*, p. 293; London, "Badger: His Last Years in the Senate,"
246–47.

66. John Bell to William B. Campbell, August 10, 1854, CFP. Clayton was probably an
exception to Bell's generalization. He had broached the possibility of forming a new party in
1853, and his nativistic amendment to the Nebraska bill, as well as one denying immigrants
eligibility for homesteads under a bill debated in July, were clearly meant to appeal to the
burgeoning Know Nothings, with whom those amendments, and Clayton, were wildly popular.
See D. Rodney King to John M. Clayton, n.d., J. W. Wheelwright to Clayton, July 18, 1854, and
F. A. Pettis to Clayton, July 19, 1854, Clayton MSS.

67. Cole, *Whig Party in the South*, p. 307; Louisville *Journal*, July 1, 1854, quoted in Volz,
"Party, State, and Nation," p. 171; George S. Bryan to John P. Kennedy, August 23, 1854,
Kennedy MSS; Logan Hunter to John J. Crittenden, September 22, 1854, Crittenden MSS (LC).

68. Alexander H. H. Stuart to Millard Fillmore, May 18, 1854, MFP-O. For other reports
about enthusiasm for Fillmore spawned in different parts of the South by his trip, see John P.
Kennedy to Elizabeth Kennedy, Mississippi River, March 23, 1854, George Bryan to John P.
Kennedy, Charleston, April 5, 1854, Kennedy MSS; Joseph G. Baldwin to Alexander H. H. Stuart,
Mobile, April 15, 1854, Stuart MSS; B. Edwards Gray to Fillmore, Washington, May 26, 1854,
MFP-O.

69. Stuart to Millard Fillmore, May 18, 1854 (quotation), John P. Kennedy to Fillmore, May
28, 1854, Henry W. Williams to Fillmore, July 1, 1854 (quotation), MFP-O; George S. Bryan to
John P. Kennedy, August 23, 1854, Kennedy MSS.

70. John Bell to William B. Campbell, August 10, 1854, CFP.

71. William H. Seward to Frances Seward, February 16, 19, 1854, in *Seward at Washington*,
pp. 219, 222; Thurlow Weed to Hamilton Fish, February 19, 1854, Fish MSS; *Ohio State Journal*,
April 19, 1854, quoted in Foner, *Free Soil*, p. 194; Truman Smith to John Wilson, April 27, May
26 (quotation), 1854, John Wilson MSS. Wade's Senate speech is quoted in Cole, *Whig Party
in the South*, pp. 304–05, n. 79.

72. Solomon G. Haven to Millard Fillmore, February 12, 1854, MFP-O; B. D. Silliman to

Hamilton Fish, March 4, 1854, Fish MSS; Edward Kent to Israel Washburn, March 9, 1854, Israel Washburn MSS (Norlands); Robert C. Winthrop to John P. Kennedy, June 1854, Winthrop MSS.

73. Samuel Lewis to Salmon P. Chase, April 17, 1854, Chase MSS (HSP).

74. A. Willey to William Pitt Fessenden, July 12, 1854, Fessenden MSS (WRHS); Henry Wilson to Israel Washburn, May 28, 1854, Washburn MSS (LC); Gamaliel Bailey to James S. Pike, May 30, 1854, Pike MSS.

75. Henry Wilson to William H. Seward, May 28, 1854, Seward to Theodore Parker, June 23, 1854, copy, Seward MSS (RU).

76. Gamaliel Bailey to James S. Pike, May 21, 1854, Pike MSS.

77. George E. Baker to William H. Seward, May 14, 1854, Seward MSS (RU); Haven to Fillmore, July 1, 1854, MFP-O. In his letter to James Pike of May 21, Gamaliel Bailey listed Campbell, Washburn, Walley, and Chandler as the Whig negotiators who arranged the multiparty anti-Nebraska caucus. Democrats were represented in those negotiations by Gilbert Dean of New York, Nathaniel P. Banks of Massachusetts, and Senator Charles James of Rhode Island, who voted against the Nebraska bill in the Senate and who, it will be recalled, had been elected by the Rhode Island legislature in 1851 with the help of thirteen dissident Whigs over the choice of the Whig caucus, James F. Simmons. In his letter of July 1 to Fillmore, Haven asserted that within Congress he was the recognized leader of northern conservative Whigs who "would only go where I would go, & would not go beyond me."

78. On the revival of conservatives' confidence in preserving an alliance with southern Whigs and nominating Fillmore, see Solomon G. Haven to Fillmore, June 29, July 1, 1854, Alexander H. H. Stuart to Fillmore, May 18, 1854, B. Edwards Gray to Fillmore, May 26, 1854, Isaac Hazlehurst to Fillmore, July 7, 1854, William L. Hodge to Fillmore, July 21, 1854, MFP-O. For Truman Smith, see Smith to John Wilson, March 6, April 27, 1854, John Wilson MSS. Smith, who had sneered that the Whig party deserved death throughout 1853, returned to Congress for only one purpose: to work for passage of a federally chartered and subsidized Pacific railroad. In March he concluded that support for the Nebraska bill from California's two senators killed any prospect of passing that legislation, and in April he announced he would resign his seat on May 24.

79. Robert C. Winthrop to Edward Everett, February 6, 1854, Everett to Mrs. Charles Eames, August 31, 1854, Everett MSS; Winthrop to John P. Kennedy, February 27, 1854, Kennedy MSS; David Davis to Julius Rockwell, July 15, 1854, copy, David Davis MSS.

80. J. W. Jones to Thomas Ewing, February 9, 1854, Thomas Ewing to Columbus Anti-Nebraska Convention, March 14, 1854, copy, John Teesdale to Thomas Ewing, April 6, 1854, Oran Follett to Ewing, May 1, 1854, EFP.

81. Seward to Weed, May 29, 1854, Seward to Frances Seward, May 31, 1854, in *Seward at Washington*, p. 231; Gamaliel Bailey to James S. Pike, May 21, 30, 1854, Pike MSS.

82. Gienapp, *Origins*, pp. 89–90; Washington *National Intelligencer*, June 22, 26, 1854. A committee of seven Democrats and six Whigs apparently drafted the address, but newspapers failed to identify who they were. The address was printed in the June 22 issue of the *Intelligencer*, and my quotations in this paragraph come from that report.

83. Gamaliel Bailey to James S. Pike, quoted in Gienapp, *Origins*, p. 90; Edward Kent to Israel Washburn, June 25, 1854, Washburn MSS (Norlands); New York *Courier & Enquirer*, quoted in Washington *National Intelligencer*, June 26, 1854; William H. Seward to Frances Seward, June 22, 1854, in *Seward at Washington*, p. 234; Israel Washburn to James S. Pike, June 24, July 1, 1854 (quotations), Pike MSS.

84. Gienapp, *Origins*, p. 89; Gamaliel Bailey to James S. Pike, May 30, 1854, Pike MSS; Lewis Campbell to William Schouler, May 14, 1854, Salmon P. Chase to Schouler, May 28, 1854, Schouler MSS. For Elihu B. Washburne's eager embrace of Free Soil support for his reelection in 1854, see Solon C. Mimms to E. B. Washburne, August 24, 1854, B. Seeholm to Washburne, September 17, 1854, and Zebina Eastman to Washburne, September 18, 1854, Washburne MSS (LC).

As will be argued below, many anti-Nebraska northern Whig candidates welcomed Free Soil support in 1854, but they often believed they could get it without abandoning the Whig party or even seeking separate Free Soil nominations. By itself, in sum, soliciting Free Soil votes by no means indicated a desire to break up the Whigs and join a new party. Washburne was nominated separately by Whigs and Free Soilers, however, and the obvious confidence that Free Soilers like Seeholm and Eastman placed in his sincerity suggests that he, like his Maine brother, sought a new northern party to replace, not just provide additional support to reinforce, the Whig party.

85. For examples of northern Whigs' confidence and northern Democrats' fears that anti-Nebraska sentiment would make northern Whigs invincible in 1854, see George Patterson to Thurlow Weed, March 16, 1854, Weed MSS (RU); George E. Baker to William H. Seward, May 10, 1854, Seward MSS (RU); Holt, *Political Crisis*, p. 149.

86. J. B. Turner to Richard Yates, April 8, 1854, Paul Selby to Richard Yates, April 8, 1854, Yates MSS; William R. Larimer to James Pollock, quoted in Pittsburgh *Daily Gazette*, May 3, 1854; the Pennsylvania Whig address and the editors' reactions to it can be found in ibid., July 20, 22, 1854; for the attempt of Pittsburgh's Whigs to court Free Soil support without abandoning the Whig organization, see Holt, *Forging a Majority*, pp. 136–38; *Albany Evening Journal*, May 26, July 13, 1854, quoted in Gienapp, *Origins*, p. 83.

87. Seward to Theodore Parker, June 23, 1854, Seward MSS (RU).

88. Data on the returns for Rhode Island's legislative elections for 1854 are missing, so they cannot be compared to the 1853 results. Whigs gained about 900 votes between 1853 and 1854, and some of these may have come from Rhode Island's tiny Free Soil organization, which had no separate candidate in 1854. Disaffection among Democratic voters, however, clearly helped Whigs more than new supporters. Between 1853 and 1854, the Democratic vote fell from 10,371 to 6,484, whereas the Whig vote climbed from 8,228 to 9,112.

89. Amos Tuck to Israel Washburn, March 18, 1854, Washburn MSS; J. H. Wright to Caleb Cushing, March 18, 1854, Cushing MSS; Renda, "The Polity and the Party System," pp. 278–85.

90. Renda's regression estimates in "Polity and the Party System" suggest that 6 percent of Bell's 1853 supporters switched to Perkins in 1854; Bell lost about 500 votes between the elections, while Democratic turnout declined by about 1,200. I have used Renda's figures, p. 376, for changes in the legislature.

91. Renda, "Polity and the Party System," pp. 273–78; for expressions of Whig confidence in the Nebraska issue, see Roger Sherman Baldwin to Truman Smith, February 18, April 4, 1854, Baldwin to Bishop Perkins, March 28, 1854, BFP.

92. Roger Sherman Baldwin to Roger Sherman Baldwin, Jr., May 18, 1854, BFP; for the delight of Whig papers, see Gienapp, *Origins*, p. 85, n. 66.

93. For more on the Connecticut election, see Renda, "Polity and the Party System," pp. 285–88; and Gienapp, *Origins*, p. 85–86. Regression estimates by both Renda and Gienapp suggest that almost half of the 1853 Free Soil voters and one-seventh of the 1853 Democratic voters supported Chapman in 1854 and that he drew far more votes than any other candidate from previous abstainers.

94. M. H. Bartlett to Joseph R. Hawley, March 27, 1854, Moses Pierce to Hawley, March 27, 1854, H. Hammond to Hawley, March 30, 1854, C. M. Steele to Hawley, April 11, 1854 (quotation), Edmund Tuttle to Hawley, April 12, 1854, Julius Pratt to Hawley, April 18, 1854, Hawley MSS; Roger Sherman Baldwin to Roger Sherman Baldwin, Jr., May 18, 1854, BFP. The data from the Inter-University Consortium list no legislative returns for Connecticut, so the exact numbers in the senate are unclear. In the letter cited above, however, Baldwin said that the proportion of Whigs to Free Soilers in the senate was about the same as in the house. And in the house, as Lex Renda shows in "Polity and the Party System," p. 375, there were 110 Whigs, 17 Free Soilers, and 7 prohibitionists in opposition to 89 Democrats. After the 1853 elections, in contrast, there had been 145 Democrats, 68 Whigs, and 11 Free Soilers in the house and 15 Democrats, 5 Whigs, and 1 Free Soiler in the senate.

95. The quotation is from Edmund Tuttle to Joseph R. Hawley, April 12, 1854, Hawley MSS.

96. Weed to Hamilton Fish, February 19, 1854, Fish MSS; Edwin B. Morgan to Thurlow Weed, March 8, 1854, O. B. Matteson to Weed, April 22 (quotation), May 18, 22, 1854, Weed

MSS (RU); Haven to Fillmore, July 1, 1854, MFP-O; Elihu B. Washburne to James S. Pike, May 8, 1854, Israel Washburn to Pike, May 13, 1854, Pike MSS; Raymond's letter to Fessenden and his editorial are quoted in Gienapp, *Origins*, p. 83.

Haven, who hated the necessity of cooperating with Sewardite "Woollies," it should be noted, was unimpressed by the favorable notices he got in the Sewardite press. He told Fillmore in the letter cited above that only his influence with other northern conservatives and southern anti-Nebraska Whigs caused those papers to shift from abusing to praising him. Those papers, he wrote, acted "from compulsion & not from love." Haven may have been correct about the motives of Morgan and Matteson, who arranged the favorable press reports, but his analysis only underscores to what lengths Sewardites would go in order to keep conservatives and Southerners under the Whig umbrella.

97. Seward to Thurlow Weed, May 29, 1854, Weed MSS (RU); for Seward's Senate speeches, I have relied on the descriptions in Van Deusen, *Seward*, pp. 152–54; and Nevins, *Ordeal: House*, pp. 140, 301. Nevins interprets Seward's acceptance of a contest for control of the territories between freedom and slavery as defiant of the South, but what pleased conservatives like Edward Everett, while miffing Free Soilers, was his equanimity and certitude that Northerners would prevail, a certitude that undercut the rationale for forming a new, exclusively northern party.

98. Henry Wilson to William H. Seward, May 28, 1854, Henry J. Raymond to Seward, May 30, 1854, Edward Everett to Seward, June 16, 1854, Seward MSS (RU); Gamaliel Bailey to James S. Pike, May 30, 1854, Pike MSS; Edward Kent to Israel Washburn, June 25, 1854, Washburn MSS (Norlands); A. P. Willey to William Pitt Fessenden, July 12, 1854 (quotation), Fessenden MSS (WRHS).

99. John Pendleton Kennedy to M. F. Tupper, October 7, 1854, copy, Kennedy MSS.

100. John Bell to William B. Campbell, August 10, 1854, CFP.

101. William H. Seward to Theodore Parker, June 23, 1854, Seward MSS (RU); Thurlow Weed to Hamilton Fish, February 19, 1854, Fish MSS.

CHAPTER 23

1. William Larimer to James Pollock, March 28, 1854, in Pittsburgh *Gazette*, May 3, 1854. Larimer lost the nomination to Pollock in part because he had only recently returned to the Whigs from Free Soiler ranks and Whig delegates, now confident of success, insisted that the nomination go to a Whig regular. For more on how the republican idiom suffused and defined resistance to the Nebraska bill, see Holt, *Political Crisis*, pp. 151–54; and Gienapp, *Origins*, pp. 4–5, 72, and passim.

2. On Indiana, see L. G. Matthews to William H. English, December 23, 1853 (quotation), English MSS; William Noel to John G. Davis, January 27, 1854 (quotation); A. D. Billingsley to Davis, May 13, 1854, John G. Davis MSS; and S. J. Ensley to Joseph Wright, February 24, 1854, Wright MSS. On New York, see Horatio Seymour to William L. Marcy, February 21, 1854, Marcy MSS (LC); John Austin to George E. Baker, April 18, 1854, Edward C. Delavan to William H. Seward, May 16, 1854, Seward MSS (RU); and George W. Patterson to Thurlow Weed, May 8, 1854, Weed MSS (RU).

3. L. R. Shepard to William L. Marcy, January 28, 1854, Marcy MSS (LC); George W. Morton to Hamilton Fish, February 27, 1854, Marcellus Ells to Fish, February 14, March 21, 1854, Fish MSS.

4. One index of the longevity of Whig identity and the continued influence of Whig principles on men who had once been affiliated with the party is the frequency with which historians stress the importance of that Whig heritage during the Civil War and Reconstruction. See, for example, David Donald's famous analysis of the Republican Abraham Lincoln's presidency, "Abraham Lincoln: Whig in the White House," in Donald, *Lincoln Reconsidered*; Boritt, *Lincoln*; Alexander, "Persistent Whiggery in the Confederate South"; and Perman, *Road to Redemption*.

5. Former Whig voters, of course, also abandoned the Whig party, often before leaders did, and in the analysis of the 1854 and 1855 elections below, I shall attempt to show when they did so and where they went. I focus on leaders here, however, for two related reasons. It is easier

to ascertain and document the motives and reactions of leaders than of voters. We must infer the motives of the rank and file primarily from the remarks of contemporary observers and from how they voted. As noted above in the text, however, political leaders limited the range of political expression for voters by nominating the candidates and printing the ballots from which they had to choose. If Whig voters backed candidates who ran in open opposition to formally nominated Whig candidates, we can infer that they were prepared to leave or temporarily bolt the Whig party. But if Whig leaders refused to make formal Whig nominations and instead collaborated in the creation of fusion tickets that eschewed the Whig label, it is difficult to know, other than inferring from the abstention rate of previous Whig voters, whether they approved or disapproved of this leadership decision. Similarly, if, as was often the case, Whigs nominated candidates who afterward joined or accepted secret endorsements from the Know Nothings, we cannot know if Whig voters believed they were voting for a Whig or a Know Nothing. Whatever the insurgent inclinations of the Whig electorate, in sum, it was ultimately Whig leaders who decided to abandon the formal, independent operations of the Whig party, and that is the second reason for focusing on them.

6. The tortuously difficult process by which the Republican party was formed from the inchoate anti-Nebraska coalitions and from northern Know Nothings is superbly analyzed in Gienapp, *Origins*.

7. John Law to William L. Marcy, September 25, 1854, Marcy MSS (LC).

8. All the evidence about editors and quotations from Whig papers in this paragraph are taken from Gienapp, *Origins*, pp. 104, 108, 113–14, 122.

9. Columbus *Ohio State Journal*, June 27, July 27, 1854, quoted in Burnet, "Creating the 34th Congress," p. 430. For other examples of such statements by the Ohio Whigs Wade, Follett, and Schouler, see the quotations cited in Maizlish, *Triumph of Sectionalism*, pp. 190, 198.

10. *Ohio State Journal*, July 17, 1854, quoted in Burnet, "Creating the 34th Congress," pp. 430–31; Washington *National Era*, May 22, 1854, quoted in Berger, *Revolution*, p. 36.

11. *Ohio State Journal*, June 5, 1854, quoted in Maizlish, *Triumph of Sectionalism*, p. 199. The Michigan Republican platform is printed in Trefousse, "Republican Party," pp. 1185–88. For additional examples of these changes rung on the republican theme, see Holt, *Political Crisis*, pp. 152–54, 189–91; and Gienapp, *Origins*, pp. 71–77, 353–73, and passim.

12. Charles G. Irish, Jr., to Daniel Ullmann, March 1855, Ullmann MSS. My intention here and in the paragraphs below is not to provide a full-scale analysis of Know Nothingism. I have attempted a more thorough treatment in two articles, "Politics of Impatience" and "The Antimasonic and Know Nothing Parties," and in *Political Crisis*, pp. 156–70. See also Gienapp, *Origins*, and Anbinder, *Nativism & Slavery*.

13. Holt, *Political Crisis*, p. 162.

14. Anbinder, *Nativism & Slavery*, pp. 33–51, vigorously assaults arguments I have previously made that economic dislocation made the Know Nothings particularly attractive to young working-class artisans and lower-middle-class shopkeepers because the membership of four northeastern Know Nothing lodges he examined was not confined to those groups. But Anbinder provides no extended analysis of Know Nothingism in Ohio Valley cities, which unquestionably suffered economic dislocation in 1854, or a statistical analysis of Know Nothing voting support anywhere. Granted, some men who voted for Know Nothing candidates never joined the order, but it seems undeniable that the Know Nothing vote was particularly strong in working-class neighborhoods of Pittsburgh, Cincinnati, Louisville, and St. Louis, just as it was in the industrial towns of Philadelphia County that had recently been merged with Philadelphia City.

Anbinder's contention, p. xii, that "southern Know Nothingism bore little resemblance to its northern counterpart," also strikes me as untenable. Is it credible that Know Nothingism in Baltimore, Wheeling, Louisville, St. Louis, New Orleans, or even Savannah grew for different reasons than it did in Philadelphia, Pittsburgh, Cleveland, Cincinnati, or Chicago? After all, even William B. Campbell, president of the Know Nothings' state council in Tennessee, a state with few large cities, wrote on January 4, 1855, "I have been astonished at the widespread feeling in favor of their principles—to wit, Native Americanism & anti-Catholicism—it takes everywhere." William B. Campbell to David Campbell, January 4, 1855, CFP.

Know Nothingism in the South was not different from Know Nothingism in the North, and it is precisely the simultaneous spread of the order in the South in 1854—before it converted itself publicly to the American party—when it was penetrating the North that raises questions about Anbinder's insistence that antislavery sentiment, not nativism, primarily explains that northern growth after May 1854.

Anbinder further contends, pp. 43–45, that until the end of May 1854 the order remained "a small-scale urban movement" and that it extended beyond large cities to small towns and the countryside starting only in June because of temperance and especially anti-Nebraska sentiment. That assertion, too, strikes me as dubious. His own evidence, p. 53, shows the strength of Know Nothings in small Pennsylvania towns prior to June, as do the examples, which I could easily have multiplied, that I give in the text below. Know Nothingism extended well beyond the boundaries of big cities—and of the North—before June, although his corollary contention that anti-Nebraska outrage often influenced the vote for Know Nothings and against Democrats even in the North's local elections is undoubtedly correct.

15. John Oscar Lorain to William L. Bigler, January 10, 1854 (quotation), E. A. Penniman to Bigler, June 8, 1854, Bigler MSS. The studies of Know Nothingism listed above all cite considerable evidence that Democrats joined the Know Nothings in droves.

16. Rutherford B. Hayes to Sardis Birchard, October 13, 1854, in Williams, ed., *Hayes Diary*, I, p. 470; Charles B. Ewing to Thomas Ewing, Jr., April 5, 1854, EFP; John M. Bradford to Thurlow Weed, June 24, 1854, Weed MSS (RU); William L. Hodge to Millard Fillmore, July 21, 1854, MFP-O.

17. Anbinder, *Nativism & Slavery*, p. 53.

18. Ross Wilkins to John McLean, January 11, 1855, McLean MSS (LC); William G. Brownlow, *Americanism Contrasted with Foreignism, Romanism, and Bogus Democracy*, excerpted in Silbey, *Transformation of American Politics*, pp. 53–57. The quotation from Whitney is taken from the excerpt from his *Defence* included in the appendix of my essay on "The Antimasonic and Know Nothing Parties," pp. 681–82.

19. J. H. Shirrard to William C. Rives, December 21, 1854, Rives MSS; Gideon Welles, draft article, October 1859, Welles MSS (Conn.HS).

20. George W. Mitchell to Alexander H. H. Stuart, June 20, 1854, Alexander H. H. Stuart MSS (LC); J. J. Henry to Daniel Ullmann, October 10, 1854, Ullmann MSS; Moses Kimball to Henry L. Dawes, August 28, 1854, Dawes MSS; Pittsburgh *Gazette*, February 24, 1855; Philadelphia *North American and United States Gazette*, June 8, 1854, quoted in Burnet, "Creating the 34th Congress," p. 538.

21. James R. Thompson to Daniel Ullmann, March 24, 1855, Ullmann MSS; Horace Greeley to Schuyler Colfax, August 24, 1854, Greeley-Colfax MSS.

22. I now believe that I myself am probably guilty of such exaggeration in my previous publications on the Know Nothings.

23. Nonetheless, many men elected as Know Nothings to state legislatures and local offices were relative newcomers who seemed, especially to Whigs, both socially and politically obscure. Hence the patrician Boston Whig Edward Everett complained that one of the Know Nothings elected to Congress in Massachusetts was "some obscure person whose name I do not recollect," and in the legislature, of which Know Nothings won almost total control in November 1854, "the men brought forward & elected to office are for the most part small traders, mechanics & artisans, wholly unknown to the legislature." Similarly, Emily Baldwin, the extraordinarily perceptive wife of Connecticut's former Whig United States senator, observed that Know Nothings in that state intended to "put an entire set of new men in office who are very little known in any way." "Some of them [are] young men only four years from College and others are quite uneducated and as it now appears unfitted for their places." Edward Everett to Mrs. Charles Eames, November 13, 1854, Everett MSS; Everett to Millard Fillmore, December 16, 1854, MFP-O; Emily Baldwin to Roger Sherman Baldwin, Jr., March 17, April 11, 1854, BFP.

24. Haven to Millard Fillmore, December 9, 1854, MFP-O.

25. See, for example, many of the letters in 1854 to Daniel Ullmann and other New York Know Nothing organizers in the Ullmann MSS, as well as the correspondence between Millard Fillmore and Haven, Alexander H. H. Stuart, and John P. Kennedy that year.

26. Vivus W. Smith to William H. Seward, September 4, 1854, Seward MSS (RU); William

Fuller to John G. Davis, February 4, 1854 (quotation), John G. Davis MSS; William S. Hirst to William L. Bigler, June 10, 1854 (quotation), Bigler MSS; A. Bussey to William H. English, July 13, 1854 (quotation), English MSS; J. Glancy Jones to James Buchanan, July 9, 1854 (quotation), Buchanan MSS (HSP); John Law to William L. Marcy, September 25, 1854 (quotation), Marcy MSS; J. J. Billings to John Bell, December 11, 1854 (quotation), Polk-Yeatman Papers; Washington Hunt to Thurlow Weed, October 24, 1854 (quotation), Weed MSS (RU).

27. The data collected by the Inter-University Consortium list no returns for Arkansas' legislative elections in 1854.

28. These two paragraphs on Arkansas are based on the analysis in Burnet, "Creating the 34th Congress," pp. 177–86. The quotation from Johnson appeared in a letter dated August 26, 1855, which Burnet found in the Memphis *Daily Appeal*, October 4, 1855, p. 182.

29. In the state house of representatives, Whigs' numbers grew from thirty-nine (31 percent of the total) to forty-eight (37.5 percent); the increase in the Senate was smaller, from eleven (33 percent) to twelve (36 percent).

30. In the only district Whigs did not carry, they ran no candidate of their own and instead let pro-Benton and anti-Benton candidates fight it out. The absence of a Whig candidate in the sixth district makes attempts to calculate the proportion of the total statewide vote by the two parties misleading. The more important point is that Whigs carried *every* congressional district in which they ran a candidate.

31. Frank Blair, Jr., to Francis P. Blair, Sr., March 19, 1854, Blair-Lee MSS; Henry W. Williams to Millard Fillmore, July 1, 1854, MFP-O. My analysis of the Missouri campaigns is based largely on Burnet, "Creating the 34th Congress," pp. 94–136.

32. Thomas C. Reynolds to Caleb Cushing, July 22, 1854, Cushing MSS; Burnet, "Creating the 34th Congress," pp. 108–111.

33. Frank Blair, Jr., to Francis P. Blair, Sr., January 28, October 23, 1855, Blair-Lee MSS. In the latter letter, the younger Blair presents evidence that Atchison joined the order. My analysis of the legislature's attempt to elect a new United States senator is based upon Burnet's research on Missouri, but the inferences as to why Whigs rejected Know Nothings are mine, not his.

34. St. Louis *Missouri Democrat*, December 3, 1855, quoted in Burnet, "Creating the 34th Congress," p. 144.

35. R. B. Scott to W. L. Scott, July 4, 1854, quoted in Kruman, *Parties and Politics*, p. 78. In the analysis below, I have relied heavily on Kruman's analysis of the 1854 campaign, pp. 75–79, 100–01.

36. The relevant plank is quoted in Kruman, *Parties and Politics*, p. 100.

37. Alfred Dockery to David F. Caldwell, March 10, 1854, Caldwell MSS.

38. Daniel M. Barringer to Elizabeth Barringer, June 23, 1854, Barringer MSS; see also J. R. Stubbs to David F. Caldwell, May 19, 1854, Caldwell MSS; and William W. Holden to Thomas L. Clingman, June 17, 1854, Clingman-Puryear Papers. For Patterson's 1854 race, see Kruman, *Parties and Politics*, p. 156.

39. The totals in the gubernatorial race were: Bragg, 48,705 (51.1 percent); and Dockery, 46,644 (48.9 percent). In contrast, in 1852 Whig candidate John Kerr had lost to Reid with 42,993 votes (47 percent). It is impossible to pinpoint what determined the outcome of individual legislative races, but at least some Whigs blamed their losses on defections to independent temperance tickets distributed by the Sons of Temperance. See Frank Amfield to David F. Caldwell, June 24, 1854, A. F. McDaniel to Caldwell, July 4, 1854, Caldwell MSS; Kruman, *Parties and Politics*, pp. 155–56.

40. George S. Bryan to John P. Kennedy, August 23, 1854, Kennedy MSS.

41. For Florida's 1854 election, I have relied on Doherty, *Whigs of Florida*, pp. 58–61; Calabro, "Collapse of the Two-Party System in Florida"; and Burnet, "Creating the 34th Congress," pp. 306–19.

42. *Floridian and Journal*, July 13, 1854, quoted by Burnet in a draft, not the final version, of "Creating the 34th Congress." My analysis in these paragraphs rests entirely on Burnet's section about Florida and on the pages in Doherty, *Whigs of Florida*, previous cited.

43. These assertions are based upon regression estimates of voter movement in Calabro, "Two-Party System in Florida," pp. 35–39. Calabro ran both statewide estimates based on

county-level returns as well as separate regional estimates for counties in eastern, central, and western Florida. The statewide estimates suggest that Brown attracted only four-fifths of Cabell's 1852 vote and three-fifths of his 1850 vote. Erosion was far heavier in middle Florida, conversely, former Whigs were most loyal in the western counties.

44. Clayton's October manifesto was printed in the New York *Herald*, October 4, 1854, and is quoted in Burnet, "Creating the 34th Congress," p. 755. For his correspondence with Know Nothing politicians, see James Pollock to John M. Clayton, October 30, 1854 (quoting an earlier letter of Clayton to him), P. F. Causey to Clayton, November 23, December 22, 1854, June 6, 1855, Edward Joy Morris to Clayton, February 21, 1855, and Daniel Ullmann to Clayton, July 18, 1855, Clayton MSS; and Clayton to Daniel Ullmann, June 26, 1855 (quotation), Ullmann MSS. In December 1854, Solomon G. Haven, who by then had joined the order, told Fillmore that Clayton was not a member. Haven to Fillmore, December 9, 1854, MFP-O.

45. Pollock to Clayton, October 30, 1854, Clayton MSS.

46. For evidence that a significant fraction of Delaware's Whigs despised the secrecy of the Know Nothings and were not members of the order, see John W. Houston to John M. Clayton, May 1, 1855, P. F. Causey to Clayton, June 6, 1855, and George Pepper Norris to Clayton, December 17, 1855, Clayton MSS.

47. Cullen won with 6820 votes (51.9 percent) to Riddle's 6,334 (48.2 percent); in 1852 Riddle, with 6692 votes (50.2 percent), had defeated Houston, with 6,630 (49.8 percent). Since Riddle's vote declined by 358 votes between the two elections while Cullen ran ahead of Houston by 190 votes, it seems likely that Democratic converts to Know Nothingism made the difference, especially if some Whigs refused to support Cullen *because* he was a Know Nothing.

The Biographical Directory of Congress does not list any previous political affiliation for, or any previous offices held by, Cullen prior to his election, unlike most of its brief biographical summaries. Hence Cullen may well have been a new man, "fresh from the ranks of the people."

48. John P. Kennedy to Millard Fillmore, July 5, 1854, William Christy to Fillmore, August 3, 1854 (quotation), Solomon G. Haven to Fillmore, December 20, 1854, January 10, 1855, MFP-O; George S. Bryan to John P. Kennedy, August 23, 1854, Kennedy MSS; J. L. M. Curry to Clement Claiborne Clay, June 30, 1854 (quotation), C. C. Clay Family Papers; John J. McRae to J. F. H. Claiborne, November 10, 1854, Wiley P. Harris to Claiborne, December 8, 1854 (quotation), Claiborne MSS. For more evidence of the order's spread in Virginia, see Alexander H. H. Stuart to Millard Fillmore, November 11, 1854, MFP-O; and J. H. Shirrard to William C. Rives, December 21, 1854, January 29, 1855, Rives MSS.

49. On Virginia, for example, see Alexander H. H. Stuart to Millard Fillmore, November 11, 1854, January 1, 1855, Solomon G. Haven to Fillmore, December 20, 1854, MFP-O; J. H. Shirrard to William C. Rives, December 21, 1854, January 16, 1855, Rives MSS.

50. William B. Campbell to David Campbell, January 4, 1855, CFP; Wiley P. Harris to J. F. H. Claiborne, August 30, 1855, Claiborne MSS.

51. Alexander H. H. Stuart to Millard Fillmore, November 11, 1854, MFP-O; Albert Gallatin Brown to J. F. H. Claiborne, December 17, 1854, March 29, 1855, Claiborne MSS. For evidence of Democratic support for Know Nothings in Alabama, see George S. Houston to Thomas A. Hendricks, August 19, 1855, John G. Davis MSS; Houston to Thomas J. Key, June 20, 1855, Houston MSS.

52. On Virginia, see Solomon G. Haven to Millard Fillmore, December 20, 1854, MFP-O; Joseph Segar to Daniel Ullmann, December 9, 1854, Ullmann MSS; J. H. Shirrard to William C. Rives, January 16, 1855, Rives MSS. On Mississippi, see E. L. Acee to Charles D. Fontaine, 1855, William L. Sharkey to Fontaine, May 3, 1855, A. L. McWilliams to Fontaine, May 4, 1855, Fontaine MSS. Fontaine, a young Southern Rights Democrat, was the Know Nothing gubernatorial candidate in Mississippi in 1855.

53. William W. Shepard to William H. Seward, September 15, 1854, Seward MSS (LC); Bailie Peyton to John Bell, February 3, 1856, John Bell MSS.

54. William W. Shepard to William H. Seward, September 15, 1854, Seward MSS; for the thrust of the Whig campaign in California, I have relied on Burnet, "Creating the 34th Congress," pp. 197–201.

55. John G. Baldwin to Millard Fillmore, September 30, 1854, MFP-O. The two victorious

Democrats garnered 36,819 and 36,542 votes, respectively, and the two Whigs won 34,741 and 34,411. The 45 percent of the house seats Whigs held was the largest share they ever won in that body.

56. William W. Shepard to William H. Seward, September 15, 1854, September 18, 1855, Cornelius Cole to Seward, September 19, 1855, Seward MSS (RU); Raul G. Ridley to John Wilson, May 29, 1855, Wilson MSS; Bailie Peyton to John Bell, February 3, 1856, John Bell MSS; John Bigler to William L. Bigler, September 12, 15, 1855, Bigler MSS. Know Nothings won 56 percent of the seats in the state house of representatives in 1855, but they divided the senate evenly with Democrats.

57. William W. Shepard to William H. Seward, September 18, 1855, Cornelius Cole to Seward, September 19, 1855 (quotations), and H. S. Love to Seward, October 19, 1855 (quotation), Seward MSS (RU); Samuel F. May to Nathaniel P. Banks, March 4, 1856, Banks MSS (LC).

58. Horace Greeley to Schuyler Colfax, March 12 (quotation), June 5, 20 (quotation), 1854, Greeley-Colfax MSS; Benjamin F. Wade to Milton Sutliffe, April 21, 1854, Sutliffe MSS; and Lew Campbell to William Schouler, May 14, 1854, Schouler MSS.

59. Schuyler Colfax to Kline Shryock, May 23, 1854, Colfax MSS (CHS).

60. For the congressional campaigns and lineage of anti-Nebraska congressional candidates I have relied on Burnet's extensive coverage of each state in his "Creating the 34th Congress." In addition, I have drawn heavily from the following secondary sources which the reader should consult for further detail: Gienapp, *Origins*, pp. 104–21; Anbinder, *Nativism & Slavery*, pp. 68–73; Current, *Wisconsin*, pp. 217–24; Formisano, *Birth of Mass Political Parties*, pp. 234–53; Maizlish, *Triumph of Sectionalism*, pp. 187–224; and, for Indiana, Brand, "Know Nothing Party in Indiana"; and Van Bolt, "Fusion Out of Confusion." Assertions about individual states below are based on these sources, and I shall eschew further citations to them except to cite direct quotations.

61. Samuel Lewis to Salmon P. Chase, April 17, 1854, Chase MSS (HSP); John D. Defrees to Samuel Judah, September 21, 1854, quoted in Van Bolt, "Fusion Out of Confusion," 377.

62. Without regression analysis, it is hazardous to estimate the extent of abstention by Whigs angered at the coalition with Free Soilers in the Republican party, but gross figures suggest very little defection. In 1854 the total vote for the three Republican congressional candidates was 32,321; in 1852 Whig totals ranged from 18,199 votes in the congressional election to 22,240 in the presidential race and the Free Soilers from 9,400 votes in the congressional election to 8,800 in the presidential race. Together, in sum, Whigs and Free Soilers had 31,000 between them in 1852, quite close to the Republican total in 1854. Since the entire Wisconsin congressional delegation, all Democrats, voted against the Nebraska Act in 1854, I assume that Democratic defections to the Republican column that year were minimal, but regression analysis could prove otherwise.

63. Joseph Warren to William H. Seward, November 12, 1854, Seward MSS (RU). For the details on Michigan, I have relied on Formisano, *Birth of Mass Political Parties*, pp. 217–65.

64. Detroit *Tribune*, quoted in Gienapp, *Origins*, p. 104; Formisano, *Birth of Mass Political Parties*, p. 241.

65. Gienapp, *Origins*, pp. 104–05; Horace Greeley to Schuyler Colfax, July 26, 1854, Greeley-Colfax MSS; for the radicalism of the platform and later Whig meetings, see Formisano, *Birth of Mass Political Parties*, pp. 242–43, 244–47.

66. Formisano, *Birth of Mass Political Parties*, pp. 249–53; Gienapp, *Origins*, pp. 105–06, n. 13. Joseph Warren to William H. Seward, November 12, 1854, Seward MSS (RU).

In the gubernatorial poll in 1854, the Republicans won 43,652 votes (53 percent) and the Democrats, 38,676 votes (47 percent). In contrast, in the presidential election of 1852, the totals had been: Democrats, 41,842 (50.4 percent); Whigs, 33,859 (40.8 percent); and Free Soilers, 7,237 (9.8 percent). Since Democrats lost about 3,200 votes between 1852 and 1854, while the sum of the 1852 Whig and Free Soil votes was approximately 41,000, these figures suggest that most Whigs, whatever the strictures of the *Advertiser* against fusion, voted the Republican ticket and that former Whig voters constituted about three-fourths of the Republican coalition.

67. Godlove Orth to Schuyler Colfax, July 4, 1854, in Schauinger, "Orth Letters," 40, 54.

68. Ohio's state People's platform did go slightly further by endorsing the Free Soil demand that no more slave states be admitted to the Union.

69. *Cincinnati Gazette*, July 17, 1854, quoted in Maizlish, *Triumph of Sectionalism*, p. 200; *Indiana State Journal*, July 20, 1854, quoted in Burnet, "Creating the 34th Congress," p. 345.

70. All my evidence on individual congressional districts is taken from Burnet, "Creating the 34th Congress," pp. 432–76. I have not included Harrison and Campbell among the straight Whig nominees because both were Know Nothings who were publicly endorsed by Know Nothing newspapers prior to the election. Campbell, indeed, joined the order before he left Washington in the summer, and in the third district there were initially separate Whig and Know Nothing tickets, each headed by Campbell. The non-Know Nothing Whig candidates for the legislature and local offices on the separate Whig ticket eventually withdrew before the election, lest they divide the anti-Democratic vote.

71. For the statewide voter movement between 1852 and 1854, see Table 4.3 in Gienapp, *Origins*, p. 500. Inspection of the returns from the first and fourth congressional districts from 1852 and 1854 suggest that it was arithmetically impossible for the victorious People's candidates, both of whom were one-time Democrats, to have rolled up such heavy majorities unless virtually all previous Whig voters supported them, as do Gienapp's regression estimates of voter movement in Cincinnati between 1853 and 1854, ibid, p. 501. In contrast, in Edward Wade's district, total turnout declined by 17 percent between 1852 and 1854, and almost all of that decline apparently came from fractious Whigs. Wade attracted about 2,400 more votes in 1854 than in 1852, when both Whig and Democratic candidates had opposed him, and very few of those additional votes could have come from Democrats. But Whigs had garnered over 4,000 votes in 1852, suggesting that some 1,600 Whigs, or 40 percent of the total, abstained rather than support Wade. Similarly, total turnout plunged by 25 percent in Giddings' district between 1852 and 1854, and his total in the latter year was over 2,800 votes (30 percent) smaller than the combined Whig and Free Soil votes in 1852. Indeed, if those 2,800 voters were all recalcitrant Whigs, they represented over two-thirds of the normal Whig vote.

72. For the congressional nominations, Parker's House speech, and events in Parker's and Julian's district, I have relied on Burnet, "Creating the 34th Congress," pp. 332–90. For Julian's humiliation at the People's state convention, see Gienapp, *Origins*, p. 110. For Colfax's concerns, see Schuyler Colfax to Kline Shryock, July 24, 1854, copy, Schuyler Colfax MSS (Ind.SL); and Horace Greeley to Colfax, June 5, 20, 1854, Greeley-Colfax MSS. For identifications of the previous affiliations of the men on the People's state ticket, see John Law to William L. Marcy, September 4, 1854, Marcy MSS (LC).

73. In the presidential election of 1852, for example, when Indiana's voter turnout surpassed 80 percent, the totals for the three presidential candidates were: Pierce, 95,340 (52 percent); Scott, 80,901 (44.2 percent); and Hale, 6,929 (3.8 percent).

74. These events are detailed in Van Bolt, "Fusion Out of Confusion." For evidence of Democratic fears that the party's opposition to prohibition and the alienation of Methodists would produce Democratic defeats, regardless of the Nebraska Act, see, S. J. Ensley to Joseph Wright, February 24, 1854, John Hunt to Wright, July 22, 1854, Wright MSS.

75. Information on congressional nominations is again taken from Burnet, "Creating the 34th Congress." People's conventions nominated candidates in all eleven districts, and in the four where Democrats received them, Whigs had attracted only 47 percent of the vote in 1852 in one and 46 percent in the other three.

76. Anbinder, *Nativism & Slavery*, pp. 71–72.

77. This paragraph is based primarily on Burnet's systematic study of congressional races, but for the events at Indianapolis, see also Gienapp, *Origins*, pp. 109–11.

78. *Indiana State Journal*, August 30, October 12, 14, 1854, quoted in Burnet, "Creating the 34th Congress," pp. 344, 383–84; Godlove Orth to Schuyler Colfax, September 29, 1854, in Schauinger, "Orth Letters," 40, 54–55; John Law to William L. Marcy, September 4, 25, 1854, Marcy MSS (LC).

79. John Law to William L. Marcy, September 4, 1854, Marcy MSS; Gienapp, *Origins*, Table 4.1, p. 498. I waffle in my estimate of how many Whigs abstained because of uncertainty over how to weigh the negative estimate in one of the columns of Gienapp's table.

80. Julian's diary entry for August 5, 1854, quoted in Gienapp, *Origins*, p. 110.

81. Godlove Orth to Schuyler Colfax, February 5 (quotation), June 23, 1855, in Schauinger, "Orth Letters," 40, 62–63, 66; Orth to Will Cumback, April 14, 1855 (quotation), Schuyler Colfax to Cumback, April 16, 1855, Cumback MSS.

When national meetings of the Know Nothings in 1855 and 1856, in order to placate Southerners, refused to call for repeal of the Nebraska Act, Orth, Colfax, and Cumback, like many other northern Know Nothings, would bolt the order and join the new Republican party. Thompson, in contrast, hated the Republicans and was the key leader of the American party's presidential campaign in Indiana.

82. On Campbell's presidential ambitions, see Orsamus B. Matteson to William Schouler, December 14, 1854, Lewis D. Campbell to Schouler, December 26, 1854, January 1, February 15, 1855, Schouler MSS. The three letters from Campbell allude to his aspirations for the speakership as well, but see also Samuel W. Parker to Samuel Galloway, May 10, 1855, and Campbell to Galloway, May 16, 22, 1855, Galloway MSS.

83. Isaac Tucker to William Schouler, November 27, 1854, Orsamus B. Matteson to Schouler, December 14, 1854, Lewis Campbell to Schouler, December 26, 1854, January 1, 1855, Garrett Davis to Schouler, January 3, 19, 1855, Ezra Lincoln to Schouler, February 21, 1855, Schouler MSS.

84. For Iowa's disputes over antiblack legislation, the background of its Free Soilers, and their ultimate merger with Whigs in 1854, see Robert R. Dykstra's brilliant *Bright Radical Star*. For events in Iowa, I have also relied on Burnet, "Creating the 34th Congress," pp. 160–76, and Rosenberg, *Iowa*, pp. 84–144.

Of the obstacles inhibiting cooperation between Whigs and Free Soilers in 1854, Dykstra, p. 116, writes "that only a miracle could have brought Whigs and Free Soilers together, given the record of mutual betrayal that so bitterly divided them."

85. Dykstra, *Bright Radical Star*, pp. 116–17.

86. James W. Grimes to Elihu B. Washburne, July 13, 1854, Washburne MSS; Grimes to James S. Pike, August 14, 1854, Pike MSS; Dykstra, *Bright Radical Star*, pp. 126–27. Burnet identifies Thorington as a Know Nothing.

87. John T. Henry to David Davis, February 27, 1854, David Davis MSS; Gienapp, *Origins*, pp. 121–22, and Table 4.7, p. 502; Dykstra, *Bright Radical Star*, p. 127, and Table B.5, p. 288. Dykstra estimates that almost four-fifths of the Whigs abstained rather than vote for the Free Soilers, who were crushed by their Democratic opponents.

In the state legislative contests, Democrats retained a one-seat margin in the senate, compared to the nine-vote majority they had after 1852, but anti-Nebraska men won a ten-seat margin in the house, and Grimes admitted that there was "a small Whig majority on joint ballot according to old party lines." Grimes to James W. Pike, August 14, 1854, Pike MSS.

88. The first quotation is taken from the *New York Tribune*, August 10, 1854, and is cited by Burnet, "Creating the 34th Congress," 165. The second is quoted in Rosenberg, *Iowa*, p. 106, but he gives no date for the issue of the *Tribune*. For the makeup of Grimes' vote, see Table 4.7 in Gienapp, *Origins*, p. 502.

89. For the senatorial election, I have used Burnet, "Creating the 34th Congress," pp. 166–72; Dykstra, *Bright Radical Star*, p. 127; and Rosenberg, *Iowa*, pp. 111–13. Harlan's election was also achieved only because the Whig minority in the senate defied a vote by its Democratic majority not to go into joint session with the house to hold the election. Democrats thus challenged Harlan's election as invalid, and two years later, in January 1857, after Harlan had sat during the first term of the Thirty-Fourth Congress, the Senate's Democratic majority declared Harlan's election illegal.

90. The quotes from Grimes and an Iowa Free Soil meeting are in Dykstra, *Bright Radical Star*, pp. 129–30. Rosenberg, *Iowa*, pp. 129, suggests that Grimes wrote the initial call for the Republican state convention held on February 22, 1856.

91. On Illinois, I have relied primarily on Gienapp, *Origins*, pp. 122–27, and Burnet, "Creating the 34th Congress," pp. 685–752.

92. Solon C. Minns to Elihu B. Washburne, August 25, 1854, B. Seeholm to Washburne, September 17, 1854 (quotation), Washburne MSS (LC).

93. Joliet *Signal,* quoted in Springfield *Illinois State Register,* October 2, 1854, quoted in Burnet, "Creating the 34th Congress," p. 698. Burnet is also my source for the gist of Lincoln's speeches in the district. The party totals for the 1852 and 1854 elections were as follows:

1852		1854	
Whig	8,268 (46%)	Whig/Republican	10,474 (62.8%)
Dem.	8,092 (45%)	Democrat	6,215 (37.2%)
F.S.	1,603 (9%)		

94. Zebina Eastman to Elihu B. Washburne, September 18, 1854, Richard S. Wilson to Washburne, September 19, 1854, Washburne MSS (LC).

95. Springfield *Illinois State Register,* September 23, 1854, quoted by Burnet, "Creating the 34th Congress," pp. 695–96.

96. Zebina Eastman to Elihu B. Washburne, December 14, 1854, C. H. Ray to Washburne, December 16, 29 (quotation), 1854, Washburne MSS (LC); J. O. Wilkerson to Richard Yates, December 10, 1854, Zebina Eastman to Yates, January 11, 1855 (quotation), Yates MSS.

According to lists of the new legislature's composition that Lincoln himself drew up, there were nine Whigs and five anti-Nebraska Democrats in the senate; in the house, twenty-eight Whigs, fourteen anti-Nebraska Democrats, and one abolitionist constituted the anti-Nebraska forces. *Collected Works of Lincoln,* II, pp. 296–98.

97. Abraham Lincoln to Elihu B. Washburne, February 9, 1855, in *Collected Works of Lincoln,* II, pp. 304–06; Gienapp, *Origins,* pp. 174–75.

98. The Whig state platform can be found in the Burlington *Free Press,* June 8, 1854, and the characterization of Royce can be found in ibid., June 14, 1854. Both are quoted by Burnet, "Creating the 34th Congress," pp. 220–21. Aside from cited correspondence, my account of Vermont is taken wholly from Burnet, pp. 212–35.

99. Nathan K. Hall to Millard Fillmore, December 5, 1854, MFP-O. Phelps, it will be recalled, had attended the first months of the Senate session in 1854, but he had refrained from speaking or voting until the Senate decided on his disputed claim to his seat. The Senate's Democratic majority rejected that dubious claim on March 16, 1854, leaving the vacant seat to be filled by the Vermont legislature elected in September.

100. For an example of Morrill's pledges of loyalty to the Whig party, see Justin Morrill to_____Barrett, October 11, 1854, draft, Morrill MSS.

101. John Abbot to Caleb Cushing, February 24, 1854, Cushing MSS; Israel Washburn, Jr., to James S. Pike, June 24, 1854, Pike MSS; Gienapp, *Origins,* pp. 129–33.

102. A. Willey to William Pitt Fessenden, July 12, 1854, Fessenden MSS (WRHS).

103. Bangor *Whig and Courier,* May 27, 1854, quoted in Burnet, "Creating the 34th Congress," pp. 249–50; Edward Kent to Israel Washburn, Jr., June 21, 25, July 27, 1854, Washburn MSS (Norlands); William Pitt Fessenden to James S. Pike, August 14, 1854, Pike MSS.

104. In order of appearance, the quotations are from George W. Ladel to Israel Washburn, Jr., July 29, 1854, Edward Kent to Washburn, June 25, July 27, 1854, Washburn MSS (Norlands); William Pitt Fessenden to James S. Pike, August 14, 1854, Pike MSS; and Austin Willey to Fessenden, July 12, 1854, Fessenden MSS (WRHS).

105. For Maine's congressional races, I have relied heavily on Burnet, "Creating the 34th Congress," pp. 236–304. On p. 300, n. 32, Burnet cites a September 8, 1854, issue of the Portland *Eastern Argus* as evidence that Know Nothings endorsed Wood and Morrill. Gienapp, *Origins of the Republican Party,* p. 132, also argues that Know Nothings accounted for the support Morrill would receive from previous nonvoters.

106. *Kennebec Journal,* July 14, 1854, quoted by Burnet, "Creating the 34th Congress," p. 264; John Perry to William Pitt Fessenden, August 18, 1854, Fessenden MSS (LC).

107. *Kennebec Journal,* August 9, 1854, quoted in Burnet, "Creating the 34th Congress," pp. 268–69.

108. *Kennebec Journal,* September 8, 1854, quoted in ibid., 269. In 1852, Farley received

5,255 votes (36.4 percent); in 1854, his total sank to 3,587 (26.3 percent). Knowlton won in 1854 with only 5,995 votes, most of which presumably came from non-Whigs.

109. For estimates of voter movement from 1852 and 1853 to 1854, see Tables 5.1 and 5.2 in Gienapp, *Origins*, pp. 503–04.

110. Gienapp, *Origins*, pp. 133, 203–08; Austin Willey to Salmon P. Chase, March 25, 1855, Chase MSS (LC).

111. Gienapp, *Origins*, p. 133, and Table 7.8, p. 512; George R. Ingersoll to William Pitt Fessenden, February 25, 1855, Edward Kent to Fessenden, May 21, June 6, 1855 (quotations), Noah Smith to Fessenden, June 8, 1855, and George R. Ingersoll to Noah Smith, June 12, 1855 (quotation), Fessenden MSS (WRHS).

112. In the 1852 presidential election in New Jersey, Free Soilers cast only 350 of the 83,000 ballots deposited.

113. Newark *Daily Advertiser*, October 6, 1854, and Elizabeth *New Jersey Journal*, November 14, 1854, quoted by Burnet, "Creating the 34th Congress." Aside from Burnet's dissertation, for New Jersey I have relied on Kierner, " 'The Motley Party.' "

Both abstention by anti-Nebraska Democrats and new support from Know Nothings apparently contributed to Bishop's victory in the third district. In 1852, the respective party totals were: Democratic, 10,193 (55.1 percent); and Whig, 8,315 (44.9 percent). In 1854, they were Whig, 9,051 (54.4 percent); and Democratic, 7,603 (45.6 percent). The Democrat Lilly, in sum, lost about 2,500 votes between the two elections, while Whigs gained 700 votes. It seems likely that Democrats accounted for those gains, but it is just as likely that many of those Democratic defectors had joined Know Nothing lodges, as, of course, did many of the Whig repeaters. As pointed out earlier in the text, nativism and anti-Nebraska sentiment were complementary, not conflicting, reasons for supporting northern Know Nothings.

114. Newark *Daily Advertiser*, October 10, 20, 1854, quoted in Burnet, "Creating the 34th Congress," p. 766. With Whig aid, Peter Osborne, the anti-Nebraska Democrat, reduced Vail's majority in the district, but Vail still won. In 1852 the party totals were: Democratic (Vail), 9,247 (59.6 percent); and Whig, 6,247 (40.4 percent). In 1854, they were: Vail, 7,281 (51.7 percent); and Osborne, 6,816 (48.3 percent).

115. Newark *Daily Advertiser*, quoting the Trenton *State Gazette*, August 25, 1854, and reporting on the first district Whig convention, September 15, 1854, cited in Burnet, "Creating the 34th Congress," p. 763.

116. The partisan totals in the two elections were as follows: in 1852, Democrats, 7,185 (51.3 percent), and Whigs, 6816 (48.7 percent). In 1854, Whig/Native American, 6,269 (42.9 percent); Democrats, 4,383 (30 percent); Prohibition, 3,949 (27.1 percent).

117. The count of legislators elected in 1854 is taken from Kierner, " 'The Motley Party,' " pp. 11, 29. For the New Jersey Whig editors' presidential calculations, see Isaac M. Tucker to William Schouler, November 27, 1854, Schouler MSS.

118. I use the term "nativist" to describe congressmen who were endorsed by Know Nothings, were members at the time of their election, or are known to have become members by the time the Thirty-Fourth Congress met in December 1855. My count depends heavily on Burnet's dissertation and other secondary works previously cited. It includes Cullen of Delaware, two Missouri Whigs, the two anti-Broderick Democrats elected in California, three Michigan Republicans, the nine People's victors in Indiana (four Democrats and five Whigs), eight Whigs and Timothy Day in Ohio, a Whig and a Democrat elected on Republican tickets in Illinois, James Thorington, the Know Nothing Whig from Iowa, and two Whig Know Nothings from New Jersey. In discussing Ohio in the text, I stated that straight-out Whig conventions that repudiated coalition nominated three of the victors. That is true, but two of those Whigs were subsequently endorsed by Know Nothings.

119. John Bell to William B. Campbell, August 10, 1854, CFP.

CHAPTER 24

1. Charles M. Conrad to Millard Fillmore, September 28, 1854, MFP-O. Pennsylvania's Whigs were not on Conrad's list of offenders, but they could have been.

2. George S. Bryan to John P. Kennedy, August 23, 1854, Kennedy MSS.

3. Holt, *Forging a Majority*, pp. 131–36, containing the quotations from the *Daily Gazette*. The March Whig platform can be found in the *Daily Gazette*, March 20, 1854, and the July Whig address in the Pittsburgh *Morning Post*, July 21, 1854. Morton McMichael's enthusiasm over Conrad's victory in Philadelphia is described in the preceding chapter.

4. Larimer's March letter to Whig gubernatorial candidate James Pollock is quoted at the beginning of Chapter 23. It is printed in the Pittsburgh *Daily Gazette*, May 3, 1854.

5. For an especially devastating Democratic critique of Bigler's tendency to straddle or evade all tough issues, including Nebraska, see Edward J. Fox to Simon Cameron, July 29, 1854, Cameron MSS. See also the following letters to Bigler for warnings about the defection of anti-Nebraska Democrats: David Wilmot, March 3, 1854, E. B. Chase, May 15, June 14, 1854, Henry M. Phillips, May 28, 1854, R. B. Little, June 12, 1854, William J. Garvin, June 14, 1854, John C. Knox, July 6, 1854, Bigler MSS.

6. As in other states, prohibitionist pressure had been growing in Pennsylvania for several years, but because the issue divided both parties internally, the Democratic-dominated 1854 legislature refused to pass a prohibition law that might be unpopular. Instead, to test the political winds—and absolve parties from responsibility—it authorized a referendum that would in effect be a public opinion poll. Voters would be given a chance to indicate whether they favored or opposed passage of a stringent antiliquor law by the next legislature.

7. Literally scores of letters in the Bigler Papers, the James Buchanan Papers (HSP), and the Simon Cameron Papers (DCHS) could be cited to support these assertions. In addition to my own book on Pittsburgh and Burnet, "Creating the 34th Congress," pp. 525–647, I have used the following secondary sources for Pennsylvania: Gienapp, "Nebraska, Nativism, and Rum"; id., *Origins*, pp. 139–47; Anbinder, *Nativism & Slavery*, pp. 57–68; and Gerrity, "Philadelphia Whigocracy." Unless noted otherwise, evidence for all assertions about the 1854 campaign in Pennsylvania can be found in one or more of these sources.

8. An unwieldy system linking railroad track, canals, and inclined planes over the Allegheny Mountains, Pennsylvania's Main Line Canal lost so much freight traffic to the Pennsylvania and Baltimore and Ohio Railroads after their completion that the revenue generated by tolls could no longer pay for the expensive annual repairs, let alone the still unpaid bonds issued to fund its construction. Hence considerable pressure emerged from taxpayers who did not use the canal to sell it. The problem was that only the Pennsylvania Railroad appeared to have the financial resources and economic incentive to buy it, and many people feared giving that railroad company a monopoly over east-west transportation within the state.

9. For evidence of Pollock's popularity among Protestants, prohibitionists, and anti-Nebraska men, see J. Patrick to William L. Bigler, June, 1854, W. H. Hutter to Bigler, August 11, 1854, R. B. Little to Bigler, June 12, 1854, and James E. McFarland to Bigler, September 12, 1854, Bigler MSS.

10. Pittsburgh *Daily Gazette*, March 24, 1854; Harrisburg *Telegraph*, March 18, 1854, quoted in Burnet, "Creating the 34th Congress," p. 530. That the *Telegraph* specified "every American" may simply have referred to members of the Native American party, whose support had been crucial to every statewide victory Whigs had won since the mid-1840s; more likely, it indicated a hope that Know Nothings too would support Pollock and other Whig candidates.

11. *National Era* quoted in Gienapp, "Nebraska, Nativism, and Rum," 433.

12. Pittsburgh *Daily Gazette*, April 19, 1854, quoted in Burnet, "Creating the 34th Congress," p. 533.

13. Gamaliel Bailey to James S. Pike, June 4, 1854, Pike MSS.

14. Gienapp, "Nebraska, Nativism, and Rum," 434–35; Holt, *Forging a Majority*, pp. 136–38. The following two paragraphs are also based primarily on these pages of my Pittsburgh book. Allegheny County, which encompassed Pittsburgh, sent five representatives and one senator to the state legislature.

15. In his letter to James Pike of June 4, Bailey cited Errett as one of the Pennsylvanians he would write to in order to get Pollock to take a stiffer antislavery stance.

16. Pittsburgh *Daily Gazette*, June 23 (comments on Allegheny County Whig platform), July 20 (address of state Whig committee), and July 22 (comments on that state address), 1854. Gienapp, "Nebraska, Nativism, and Rum," 435, n. 27, cites a letter from Pollock, dated June 19,

endorsing the Whig state committee's address, but it was not published in newspapers until a month later.

17. For reports of the independent prohibition tickets in Erie, York, and Philadelphia, where Maine Law men ran their own candidates against both Whigs and Know Nothings, as well as Democrats, see J. P. Sherwin to Simon Cameron, August 31, 1854, A. Cummings to Cameron, September 13, 1854, D. F. Williams to Cameron, September 25, 1854, and V. S. Eckert to Cameron, October 4, 1854, Cameron MSS; and Henry Welsh to William L. Bigler, October 3, 1854, Bigler MSS. Because Cameron sought Cooper's Senate seat and therefore corresponded with virtually every legislative district in the state, his papers contain a treasure trove of information on the legislative races.

According to D. F. Williams, the Whig county committee in York made a deal with temperance men who distributed their own Temperance assembly ticket. The Whig committee printed Whig tickets with the names of Temperance candidates on it. In retaliation, wet Whigs printed their own tickets under the Whig label, tickets that included the names of a few Democrats. The liquor issue, in sum, utterly shattered York's Whig party.

18. J. Franklin Reigart to James Buchanan, July 28, 1854, Buchanan MSS (HSP); Anbinder, *Nativism & Slavery*, p. 53.

19. William Larimer to James Pollock, March 28, 1854, in Pittsburgh *Daily Gazette*, May 3, 1854; for Larimer's induction into the order in June, see John C. Dunn to Simon Cameron, November 25, 1854, Cameron MSS. For Curtin and Pollock, see Gienapp, *Origins*, p. 144.

20. Isaac Hugus to Simon Cameron, August 18, September 24 (quotation), 1854, Cameron MSS; Holt, *Forging a Majority*, pp. 142–44. Not all former Antimasons proved so fastidious in their opposition to secret societies. Thaddeus Stevens, for example, became a Know Nothing.

21. J. Ellis Bonham to Jeremiah Sullivan Black, August 29, 1854, Black MSS; Anbinder, *Nativism & Slavery*, pp. 58–59; Holt, *Forging a Majority*, p. 73.

22. James Pollock to John M. Clayton, October 30, 1854, Clayton MSS. My assertions about voting support for Pollock and other state candidates are based on the detailed analysis in Gienapp, "Nebraska, Nativism, and Rum." His regression estimates of voter movement between elections indicate, among other things, that almost no Free Soilers voted for the Know Nothing Thomas Baird in the supreme court race, that men who did support Baird against the Whig Smyser in that race constituted 54 percent of Pollock's vote, and that, while previous Whigs divided evenly for and against prohibition in the referendum held on election day, virtually all of the dries voted for Pollock and they outnumbered wets in his column by over five-to-one.

23. Anbinder, *Nativism & Slavery*, p. 62, conveniently lists the totals for all three statewide races. I have used Gienapp's estimates of how 1852 Whig voters behaved in 1854. See especially Table 2 on p. 456 of "Nebraska, Nativism, and Rum."

24. All of the assertions about congressional races in these paragraphs are based on Burnet, "Creating the 34th Congress," which analyzes every House race in Pennsylvania, as it does for every state in 1854 and 1855.

25. The second and ninth districts will be discussed in more detail below. In the eighteenth, John R. Edie of Somerset, who later emerged as perhaps the most prominent Know Nothing in the state, won the regular Whig nomination after considerable dispute. He was opposed by the Whig J. H. Cresswell from a different county in the district. It is impossible to say whether local jealousies within the district, rather than anti-Know Nothing sentiment, inspired Cresswell's candidacy, but residual Antimasonic sentiment and therefore hostility to Know Nothings was strong there. In any event, Cresswell, Edie's only opponent, was crushed. Edie racked up 72 percent of the vote.

26. In addition to Fuller, these Whig congressional candidates included Pittsburgh's David Ritchie; Philadelphia's Edward Joy Morris and William Millward; Samuel Purviance; John C. Kunkel, David F. Robinson; James H. Campbell; John Covode; and John Allison, who was nominated separately by the Free Soilers before Whigs also named him.

27. The quotations are from R. M. De France to Simon Cameron, October 12, 1854, and J. R. Anderson to Cameron, October 12, 1854, Cameron MSS. Letters to Cameron in August, September, and October 1854 from the same collection document the presence of independent Know Nothing tickets in counties across the state.

28. J. Franklin Reigart to James Buchanan, July 28, 1854, George Sanderson to Buchanan, September 14, 1854, James L. Reynolds to Buchanan, October 23, 1854 (quotation), Buchanan MSS (HSP); Reah Frazer to Simon Cameron, September 26, 1854, Cameron MSS.

29. Ritchie's vote increased from 4,939 (52.2 percent) in 1852 to 5,705 (60.6 percent) in 1854. The district encompassed all of Pittsburgh and most of Allegheny County.

30. The remainder of the ticket included candidates for state canal commissioner and state supreme court justice, five assembly seats and one state senate seat, and two county offices.

31. Holt, *Forging a Majority*, p. 145.

32. John C. Dunn to Simon Cameron, June 28, October 15, 1854, Cameron MSS.

33. Holt, *Forging a Majority*, pp. 140–53; Alfred B. McCalmont to William L. Bigler, October 16, 1854 (quotation), Bigler MSS.

34. Holt, *Forging a Majority*, pp. 151–74. Running as a straight Whig, Volz won the mayorality with 57.5 percent of the vote in January 1854. In 1855, as the fusion anti-Know Nothing candidate, he drew 300 more votes for a total of 2,406, but his percentage fell to 55.3. In 1856, Volz got 1,030 votes (26.5 percent). He ran slightly behind the Democratic candidate, and a Know Nothing won with 1,499 votes (38.6 percent).

35. G. G. Wescott to William L. Bigler, July 14, August 25, and September 7, 1854, Bigler MSS; see also Daniel S. Jenks to James Buchanan, September 22, 1854, Buchanan MSS (HSP).

36. Gerrity, "Philadelphia Whigocracy." Chandler had also apparently promised not to seek a fourth term, and some Whigs cited his betrayal of that pledge as justification for dumping him.

37. Daniel S. Jenks to James Buchanan, September 22, October 13 (quotation), 1854, Buchanan MSS (HSP); speeches at the rump Whig convention appeared in the Philadelphia *Public Ledger*, September 8, 1854, quoted in Burnet, "Creating the 34th Congress," p. 543. The congressional returns listed in the Congressional Quarterly's *Guide to U.S. Elections* give no vote for Chandler and portray the contest as a two-way race between Tyson and his Democratic opponent. Therefore, I have relied on the returns listed in Gerrity, "Philadelphia Whigocracy," 189, n. 86. Chandler received 1,196 votes to Tyson's 5,655. Chandler had won 6,594 votes in 1852.

38. Black to Buchanan, February 17, 1855, Buchanan MSS (HSP). Burnet, "Creating the 34th Congress," p. 597, lists the figures attending the Whig and Know Nothing caucuses. Accounts of the Pennsylvania senatorial election can be found in Gienapp, *Origins*, pp. 172–73; and Anbinder, *Nativism & Slavery*, pp. 150–54. On p. 153, n. 67, Anbinder says that twenty-six Whigs voted for Cameron and twenty-seven voted against him. Whether those totals include non-Know Nothing Whigs is unclear.

39. Robert J. Arundel to John McLean, October 14, 1854, McLean MSS (LC).

40. For evidence of this divergent behavior of Free Soilers in the three states and of the proportionately greater strength of Free Soilers in Massachusetts than elsewhere, compare Table 5.3 with Tables 5.4, 5.6, and 5.7 in Gienapp, *Origins*, pp. 504–06; for the influence of anti-Catholicism, nativism, and prohibitionism in Massachusetts politics prior to 1854, see Sweeney, "Rum, Romanism, Representation, and Reform."

41. See my analysis of the 1853 election in Chapter 21.

42. The secondary literature on Massachusetts, which informs my analysis throughout this section, is extensive and of high quality. In addition to Gienapp, *Origins*, pp. 133–39, and Anbinder, *Nativism & Slavery*, pp. 87–94, see Formisano, *Transformation of Political Culture*, pp. 329–35; Baum, *Civil War Party System*, pp. 24–35; and Mulkern, *Know Nothing Party in Massachusetts*. As with other states, for information on congressional races, I have drawn on the section on Massachusetts in Burnet, "Creating the 34th Congress," pp. 839–83.

43. For examples of conservative concern about radicalization of the Whig party and a possible merger with Free Soilers, see Robert C. Winthrop to John P. Kennedy, January 1, February 27, June 1854, Kennedy MSS; Winthrop to Edward Everett, February 6, 13, March 10, 1854, Everett MSS; Winthrop to John H. Clifford, July 25, 1854, copy, Winthrop MSS.

44. Edward Everett to Mrs. Charles Eames, June 7, 1854, Everett MSS; Philo C. Shelton to

Thurlow Weed, June 6, 1854, Weed MSS (RU); Ezra Lincoln to William Schouler, August 14, 1854, Schouler MSS.

45. Gienapp, *Origins*, p. 134; Ezra Lincoln to William Schouler, August 14, 1854, Schouler MSS. At least two of the regular Whig congressional nominees withdrew prior to the election when Know Nothings endorsed their incumbent rivals, the Free Soiler Alexander DeWitt in the nineth district and Democrat Nathaniel Banks in the seventh district. Last-minute Whig replacements in both districts were slaughtered. De Witt and Banks were both members of the order, and they, like the nine Whig congressmen, voted against the Nebraska bill.

46. George B. Loring to Cushing, August 27, 1854, Cushing MSS; Everett to Mrs. Charles Eames, August 31, October 9, 1854, Everett MSS.

47. Gienapp, *Origins*, pp. 134–35.

48. Lincoln to Schouler, August 14, 1854, Schouler MSS.

49. Though largely unknown outside of Boston, Gardner was hardly a political neophyte. He had served on the Boston city council, in the state legislature, and on the Whig state committee.

50. John H. Clifford to Robert C. Winthrop, April 9, 1854, Winthrop MSS.

51. The deal between Gardner and Wilson was known even before the election, and between November and the legislature's election of Wilson to the Senate, Whigs complained about it even more bitterly. See, for example, Robert C. Winthrop to John H. Clifford, November 1, 1854, Winthrop to John P. Kennedy, December 27, 1854, copy, Winthrop MSS; Edward Everett to Mrs. Charles Eames, November 4, 16, 1854, January 13, 1855, Everett MSS.

52. Gienapp, *Origins*, p. 136; Anbinder, *Nativism & Slavery*, pp. 91–92.

53. For the aversion of Everett and Winthrop to nativism and secret societies, see Edward Everett to William B. Weis, February 14, 1853, Everett MSS; and Robert C. Winthrop to John H. Clifford, November 16, 1854, Winthrop to John P. Kennedy, December 27, 1854, copies, Winthrop MSS.

54. Robert C. Winthrop to John P. Kennedy, January 3, 1855, copy, Winthrop MSS; Ezra Lincoln to William Schouler, October 28, 1854, Schouler MSS; Everett to Mrs. Charles Eames, October 9, 1854, Everett MSS; Everett to Millard Fillmore, December 16, 1854, MFP-O.

55. For the estimates of voter movement between 1852 and 1854, see Table 5.3 in Gienapp, *Origins*, p. 504. Gienapp's estimates suggest that when one includes abstentions and a few defections to the Democrats, approximately 36 percent of the 1852 Scott voters supported Washburn. Gienapp, p. 136, n. 29, lists the gubernatorial returns for 1854 as: Whig, 27,279 (21.1 percent); Democratic, 13,742 (10.7 percent); Republican, 6,483 (5 percent); and Know Nothing, 81,503 (63.2 percent). In 1853, Washburn had garnered 59,224 votes (45.9 percent).

56. Sumner's lament is contained in his letter to Julius Rockwell, November 26, 1854, which is quoted in Burnet, "Creating the 34th Congress," p. 851.

57. David Davis to Julius Rockwell, March 4, 1855, David Davis MSS; Nevins and Thomas (eds.), *Diary of George Templeton Strong*, entry for November 15, 1854, II, p. 197; Isaac O. Barnes to Caleb Cushing, November 4, 1854, Cushing MSS; Robert C. Winthrop to John H. Clifford, November 16, 1854, copy, Winthrop MSS.

58. George W. Patterson to Thurlow Weed, March 16, 1854, Weed MSS (RU); see also George E. Baker to William H. Seward, May 10, 1854, Seward MSS (RU).

59. For evidence of these assertions about Weed and Seward's intentions, see Orsamus B. Matteson to Thurlow Weed, April 22, May 18, 22, 1854, Weed MSS (RU); Henry J. Raymond to William H. Seward, May 30, 1854, Seward MSS (RU); and especially the copy of the Circular of the "New York Central Whig Association," August 1, 1854, in the Weed MSS and Solomon Vurmich to New York Whig Central Association, August 6, 1854, Ullmann MSS. For comments on Whig unity, see Ogden Hoffman to Seward, March 5, 1854, E. Pershine Smith to Seward, May 3, 1854, Seward MSS (RU); B. Thompson to Daniel Ullmann, May 16, 1854, Ullmann MSS.

60. The three quoted passages come respectively from B. Thompson to Daniel Ullmann, May 16, 1854, Ullmann MSS; Thurlow Weed to George W. Patterson, July 11, 1854, copy, Weed MSS (RU); and Washington Hunt to Hamilton Fish, August 2, 1854, Fish MSS.

61. Berger, *Revolution*, pp. 29–31. In addition to Berger's book, which, despite its title, focuses almost exclusively on the years between 1854 and 1856, my main secondary sources for

New York are Gienapp, *Origins*, pp. 147–60; Anbinder, *Nativism & Slavery*, pp. 75–86; and, for the congressional elections, Burnet, "Creating the 34th Congress," pp. 778–838.

62. The Softs' platform pronounced the Nebraska Act "inexpedient and unnecessary" but also "opposed . . . any agitation" to restore the Missouri Compromise line or "tending to promote any sectional controversy in relation thereto." The scornful critique of it is from the *New York Tribune*, September 8, 1854. Both are quoted in Berger, *Revolution*, pp. 45–48. For an especially illuminating example of Softs' anguish about how to handle the Nebraska issue, see Herman J. Redfield to Marcy, July 15, 1854, Marcy MSS (LC).

63. Lyman Spalding to Thurlow Weed, August 3, 1854, Orson Nicholson to Weed, August 10, 1854, Weed MSS (RU); Berger, *Revolution*, p. 30.

64. I have used an undated copy of the call in the Hamilton Fish MSS.

65. Orson Nicholson to Thurlow Weed, August 11, 1854, Weed MSS (RU); Berger, *Revolution*, pp. 36–37; Gienapp, *Origins*, pp. 150–51.

66. Washington Hunt to Thurlow Weed, July 30, 1854, Weed MSS (RU); Solomon G. Haven to Millard Fillmore, July 26, 1854, MFP-O; James Kidd to Daniel Ullmann, July 15, 1854, Ullmann MSS.

67. Washington Hunt to Weed, July 30, 1854, Weed MSS (RU); Hunt to Hamilton Fish, August 2, 1854, Fish MSS.

68. Thurlow Weed to George W. Patterson, July 11, 1854, copy, Lyman A. Spalding to Weed, August 3, 1854 [misdated 1853], Orson Nicholson to Weed, August 11, 1854, Weed MSS (RU); Washington Hunt to Hamilton Fish, August 2, 1854, Fish MSS.

69. Horace Greeley to Schuyler Colfax, July 26, 1854, Greeley-Colfax MSS; Gienapp, *Origins*, p. 152.

70. Gienapp, *Origins*, pp. 152–53; Berger, *Revolution*, pp. 39–41.

71. B. H. Davis to New York Central Whig Association, August 4, 1854, Sam J. Mills to New York Central Whig Association, August 12, 1854, Ullmann MSS. As will be explained in the text below, the New York Central Whig Association was an organization put together by Daniel Ullmann and other Silver Grays to secure the Whigs' gubernatorial nomination for Ullmann and thereby deny it to one of Weed's allies. Literally scores of other letters from the Ullmann and Weed Papers attest to the salience of nativism and prohibitionism among Whigs.

72. Though dries were proportionately more numerous among Whigs than among Democrats, New York's parties, like those of other states, had long divided internally in the legislature when forced to vote on concrete policies affecting drinking. On twenty-two roll-call votes concerning liquor regulation in the New York assembly between 1847 and 1853, for example, the average index of partisan disagreement was only 39.7, the average Rice Index of Whig cohesion was 53.7, and the average Rice Index of Democratic cohesion was 31.9. By contrast, on seventeen roll-call votes on the partisanly polarizing canal expansion question in 1851, the average indexes of disagreement, Whig cohesion, and Democratic cohesion were 81.9, 85.1, and 78.8, respectively. I have taken these figures from Tables A9 and A11 in Kirn, "Second Party System in New York State." Kirn, who is my doctoral student, kindly gave me a copy of this stimulating paper.

73. Herman J. Redfield to William L. Marcy, July 15, 1854, Marcy MSS (LC).

74. Henry S. Randall to William L. Marcy, June 20, 1854, Marcy MSS (LC).

75. For Whigs' recognition of Seymour's popularity with wets, see Washington Hunt to Hamilton Fish, April 8, 1854, Fish MSS; John Austin to George E. Baker, April 18, 1854, Seward MSS (RU).

76. Edward C. Delevan to William H. Seward, May 16, 1854, Seward MSS (RU); N. W. Davis to Daniel Ullmann, May 20, 1854, Ullmann MSS, Edwin D. Morgan to Hamilton Fish, May 2, 1854, Fish MSS.

77. Washington Hunt to Hamilton Fish, April 8, 1854, Fish MSS; Eliphalet Nott to Thurlow Weed, April 3, 1854, Weed to George W. Patterson, May 10 (quotation), 29, 1854, copies, Charles Adams to Weed (detailing the publication of Seward's drinking habits), July 14, 1854, Weed MSS (RU).

78. George W. Patterson to Thurlow Weed, May 20, 1854, Weed MSS (RU); Harvey Green to Marcellus Ells, August 7, 1854, Ullmann MSS.

79. John M. Bradford to Weed, June 24, 1854, Weed MSS (RU).

80. Solomon G. Haven to Millard Fillmore, June 29, July 26, 1854, William L. Hodge to Fillmore, July 21, 1854, MFP-O; John P. Kennedy to Fillmore, July 4, 1854, copy, Kennedy MSS.

81. Alex Mann to Daniel Ullmann, June 20, 1854, Solomon Vurmich to New York Whig Central Association, August 6, 1854, Ullmann MSS.

82. See the following letters, all addressed to Daniel Ullmann in the Ullmann MSS: Darius Perrin, April 28, 1854, B. Thompson, May 16, 1854, N. W. Davis, May 20, 1854, Alex Mann, June 20, July 13, 1854, James Kidd, July 15, 1854, A. Wolcott, August 16, 1854. In the same collection, see also A. Perry to Robert C. Wetmore et al., August 2, 1854, R. B. Warren to Marcellus Ells, August 7, 1854, Socretezo Smith to Ells, August 11, 1854, E. E. Pettengill to Ells, August 8, 1854.

83. I have used the copy of the circular in the Weed MSS (RU).

84. E. J. Hoony to Ullmann, June 26, October 17, 1854, H. M. Morgan and G. M. Henry to Ullmann, June 28, 1854, Solomon Vurmich to NYWCA, August 6, 1854, A. Wolcott to Ullmann, August 16, 1854, Ullmann MSS.

85. Horace Greeley to Schuyler Colfax, August 24, 27, September 7, 1854, Greeley-Colfax MSS; Alex Mann to Daniel Ullmann, June 20, July 13, 1854, A. Perry to Robert C. Wetmore et al., August 2, 1854, A. J. Calhoun to Marcellus Ells, August 9, 1854, Ullmann MSS; Elbridge G. Spaulding to Thurlow Weed, August 8, 1854, Weed MSS (RU).

86. Lyman Spalding to Thurlow Weed, August 3, 1854 [misdated 1853], Weed to George W. Patterson, September 17, 1854, copy, Weed MSS (RU); Charles A. Dana to James S. Pike, September 1, 1854, Pike MSS; Washington Hunt to Hamilton Fish, August 2, 1854, Fish MSS.

87. Greeley to Schuyler Colfax, August 27, September 7, 1854, Greeley-Colfax MSS; Charles Dana to James S. Pike, September 1, 1854, Pike MSS; E. G. Spaulding to Thurlow Weed, August 8, 20, 1854, Weed MSS (RU); George E. Baker to William H. Seward, September 5, 1854, Seward MSS (RU).

88. Nathan G. King to Daniel Ullmann, September 8, 1854, Ullmann MSS; Vivus W. Smith to William H. Seward, September 4, 1854, Myron O. Wilder to Seward, November 2, 1854, Seward MSS (RU).

89. Elbridge G. Spaulding to Thurlow Weed, August 20, 1854, Weed MSS; L. L. Parsons to Daniel Ullmann, September 16, 1854, Nathan G. King to Ullmann, September 16, 1854, Ullmann MSS. King called Clark and Flavius Littlejohn, another Whig aspirant, "bogus if members." Other Know Nothing contenders for the Whig nomination included Joseph Savage and Judge William Campbell. Anbinder, *Nativism & Slavery*, p. 77.

90. David H. Abell to Thurlow Weed, September 10, 1854, Weed to George W. Patterson, September 17, 1854, copy, Weed MSS (RU).

91. Thurlow Weed to George W. Patterson, September 23, 1854, copy, Weed MSS (RU); L. L. Parsons to Daniel Ullmann, September 27, 1854, J. P. Faurot to Ullmann, September 27, 1854, Ullmann MSS. Faurot, who was president of Ethan Allen Council No. 113 in Canandaigua, sent Ullmann a copy of the circular from which I have quoted.

92. Myron H. Clark to Thurlow Weed, September 19, 1854, Weed MSS (RU).

93. Gienapp, *Origins*, p. 154; Berger, *Revolution*, pp. 53–54.

94. Francis Granger to Millard Fillmore, September 23, 1854, MFP-O.

95. Gienapp, *Origins*, pp. 153–54; Francis Granger to Millard Fillmore, September 23, 1854, MFP-O; Alex Mann to Daniel Ullmann, October 9, 1854, Granger to Ullmann, October 17, 1854, Ullmann MSS; Horace Greeley to William H. Seward, October 25, November 24, 1854, Seward MSS (RU).

96. Washington Hunt to Thurlow Weed, October 21, 1854, Henry J. Raymond to Weed, October 28, 1854, and Weed to George W. Patterson, October 28, 1854, copy, Weed MSS (RU); Warren T. Worden to William L. Marcy, September 23, 1854, Marcy MSS (LC).

97. Hunt to Weed, October 21, 1854, Weed MSS (RU).

98. Granger to Fillmore, September 23, 1854, MFP-O.

99. Gienapp, *Origins*, p. 154; Berger, *Revolution*, pp. 56–58.

100. Conrad to Fillmore, September 28, 1854, MFP-O.

101. George F. Comstock to Daniel Ullmann, October 6, 1854 (quotation), Ullmann MSS; David O. Kellogg to Millard Fillmore, October 7, 1854, MFP-O.

102. Kellogg to Fillmore, October 7, 1854, MFP-O; S. Potter Bradford to Marcellus Ells, August 24, 1854, O. L. Sheldon to Daniel Ullmann, October 10, 1854, Hiram Kling to Ullmann, October 12, 1854, Ullmann MSS.

103. Francis Granger to Millard Fillmore, October 19, 24, 1854, E. R. Jewett to Fillmore, October 24, 1854, MFP-O; Fillmore to John P. Kennedy, November 1, 1854, Kennedy MSS.

104. Francis Granger to Millard Fillmore, October 24, 1854, E. R. Jewett to Fillmore, October 24, 1854, MFP-O. Granger's letter of October 24 was the conservatives' circular; Jewett's explained what else occurred at Albany. Edward Everett, William A. Graham, and Charles M. Conrad were among the out-of-state Whigs sent copies of this circular.

105. Vivus W. Smith to William H. Seward, September 4, 1854, Seward MSS (RU); Anbinder, *Nativism & Slavery*, pp. 77–79.

106. D. O. Kellogg to Millard Fillmore, October 7, 1854, Stephen Sammons to Fillmore, October 16, 1854, E. R. Jewett to Fillmore, October 24, 1854, MFP-O; Fillmore to John P. Kennedy, November 1, 1854, Kennedy MSS. On the back of Sammons' letter to Fillmore is a notation from Fillmore saying that he answered on October 21 that he could do "nothing."

107. See the following letters to Daniel Ullmann in the Ullmann MSS: Charles S. Olmsted, October 11, 1854, E. M. Holbrook, October 12, 1854, Charles G. Irish, October 14, 1854, J. C. Colver, October 14, 1854, J. M. Coley, October 15, 1854, Lyman Bradley to Ullmann, October 17, 1854, S. H. Hammond, October 17, 1854, Stephen Sammons, October 25, 26 (quotation), 1854, L. L. Parsons, November 11, 1854.

The rumor that Ullmann, who was born in Wilmington, Delaware, had been born in Calcutta apparently originated with a man who claimed to have been Ullmann's classmate at Yale College. Although Know Nothings did all they could to refute the charge, it is the reason Know Nothings in New York were often subsequently called "Hindoos" by outsiders. See also Anbinder, *Nativism & Slavery*, pp. 81–82.

108. L. L. Pratt to Daniel Ullmann, October 19, 1854, J. P. Faurot to Ullmann, October 20, 1854, Ullmann MSS.

109. Alex Mann to Ullmann, October 9, 1854, L. L. Pratt to Ullmann, October 19, 1854, Ullmann MSS; Fillmore to John P. Kennedy, November 1, 1854, Kennedy MSS; Fillmore to Alexander H. H. Stuart, January 15, 1855, Stuart MSS (University of Virginia). It is clear from Fillmore's letter to Stuart that he greatly accelerated his efforts to get Silver Grays to join Know Nothing lodges after the November returns came in.

110. Alonzo Johnson to Thurlow Weed, October 14, 1854, Rufus J. Baldwin to Alonzo Johnson, October 13, 1854, Weed MSS (RU).

111. J. T. Henry to Daniel Ullmann, October 10, 1854, S. W. Button to Stephen Sammons, October 30, 1854, Ullmann MSS.

112. Non-Know Nothing Democrats carried two districts. In one, where the Whigs had won only 28 percent of the vote in 1852, a Whig regular and a Know Nothing Whig challenger split 29 percent of the 1854 vote. In the upstate seventeenth district, Francis Spinner, an anti-Nebraska Democrat, won in a three-way race that did *not* include a Know Nothing. There the share of the Whig vote dropped from only 38 percent in 1852 to 33 percent in 1854.

113. See Tables 5.6, 5.7, 5.8, and 5.9 in Gienapp, *Origins*, pp. 506–07. Gienapp estimates that Presbyterians favored Ullmann over Clark by an almost five-to-one margin and Lutherans did so by almost forty-to-one. In contrast, Baptists, Methodists, and Congregationalists greatly preferred Clark to Ullmann.

114. George E. Baker to William H. Seward, November 10, 1854, Seward MSS (RU); John O. Charles to Millard Fillmore, November 25, 1854, MFP-O; John P. Kennedy to J. N. Reynolds, November 18, 1854, copy, Kennedy MSS; Robert Kelley to Horatio Seymour, November 15, 1854, Horatio Seymour MSS.

115. James Pollock to John M. Clayton, October 30, 1854, Clayton MSS; Edward Everett to Mrs. Charles Eames, November 13, 1854, Everett MSS; Everett to Millard Fillmore, November 10, 1854, William A. Graham to Fillmore, December 3, 1854, MFP-O.

116. George E. Baker to William H. Seward, November 15, 1854, Charles E. Clarke to Sew-

ard, November 20, 1854, Thomas Chittenden to Seward, November 21, 1854, Seward MSS (RU); John P. Kennedy to J. N. Reynolds, November 18, 1854, Kennedy MSS.

CHAPTER 25

1. George S. Bryan to John P. Kennedy, August 23, 1854, Kennedy MSS.

2. John P. Kennedy to J. N. Reynolds, November 18, 1854, copy, Kennedy MSS.

3. James W. Taylor to Hamilton Fish, November 11, 1854, Fish MSS; George Cook to Thurlow Weed, January 18, 1855, Weed MSS (RU); George E. Baker to William H. Seward, November 15, 1854, Seward MSS (RU).

4. Orsamus B. Matteson to William Schouler, December 14, 1854, Schouler MSS.

5. Charles A. Dana to James S. Pike, November 22, 1854, James S. Pike MSS.

6. Daniel D. Barnard to Hamilton Fish, December 21, 1854, Fish MSS.

7. John T. Bush to Millard Fillmore, November 15, 1854, S. H. Hammond to Fillmore, November 19, 1854, MFP-O; Alex Mann to Daniel Ullmann, November 16, 1854, Ullmann MSS.

8. Millard Fillmore to John P. Kennedy, November 1, 1854, Kennedy MSS; Fillmore to Alexander H. H. Stuart, January 15, 1855, Stuart MSS (University of Virginia).

9. Charles Conrad to Millard Fillmore, December 24, 1854, MFP-O; Fillmore to Edward Everett, December 13, 1854, Everett MSS.

10. Fillmore to Everett, December 13, 1854, Everett MSS; Fillmore to Stuart, January 15, 1855, Stuart MSS.

11. Alex Mann to Daniel Ullmann, November 16, 1854, Ullmann MSS; Solomon G. Haven to Millard Fillmore, December 9, 1854, MFP-O; Fillmore to Stuart, January 15, 1855, Stuart MSS.

12. Ibid.

13. Fillmore to Stuart, January 15, 1855, Stuart MSS; Kennedy to Winthrop, December 25, 1854, copy, Kennedy MSS.

14. Albany *State Register*, January 15, 1855 [misdated 1854], clipping, Stuart MSS (University of Virginia). There is no evidence that Fillmore prompted Hammond, who had apparently become a Know Nothing even before the 1854 election, to write this editorial, but during November and December Fillmore encouraged negotiations by which Know Nothings purchased an interest in the paper to make it an American organ. See John T. Bush to Fillmore, November 15, 16, 23, 25, 1854, S. H. Hammond to Fillmore, November 19, 1854, E. R. Jewett to Fillmore, December 28, 1854, and Solomon G. Haven to Fillmore, December 20, 22, 1854, January 10, 1855, MFP-O.

15. After the Massachusetts election, Rhode Island's conservative Whig John O. Charles made this remark about Winthrop: he "is sadly disconcerted at events [in Massachusetts] & is I think unwisely vehement in denunciation." John O. Charles to Millard Fillmore, November 25, 1854, MFP-O.

16. Millard Fillmore to Isaac Newton, January 3, 1855, in Severance, "Millard Fillmore Papers, Vol. 2," pp. 347–49.

17. Solomon G. Haven to Millard Fillmore, December 9, 20, 1854, January 10, 29 (quotation), 1855, N. K. Hall to Fillmore, December 14, 1854, Isaac Newton to Fillmore, January 18, 1855, MFP-O; Elbridge G. Spaulding to William H. Seward, August 2, 1856, Seward MSS (RU); Gienapp, *Origins*, p. 260.

18. Haven to Fillmore, December 9, 1854, Alex Mann to Fillmore, December 13, 1854, Isaac Newton to Fillmore, January 18, 1855, MFP-O. For New York Know Nothings' insistence that secrecy be maintained, see Darius Perrin to Daniel Ullmann, November 13, 1854, and E. M. Holbrook to Ullmann, December 21, 1854, Ullmann MSS. On March 14, 1855, Robert J. Arundel, a Philadelphia Know Nothing and a long-time fan of McLean, urged McLean to join the Know Nothings, as Fillmore had (Arundel to McLean, March 14, 1855, McLean MSS, LC). This letter indicates not only that, as Haven had predicted, news of Fillmore's membership spread rapidly among Know Nothings once he joined the order, but also that Arundel knew that Fillmore, as an insider, had a decisive advantage in seeking the Know Nothing nomination over McLean if the latter remained an outsider.

19. John McLean to Hector Orr, November 25, 1854, McLean to John J. Prettyman, November 25, 1854, McLean to Robert A. Parrish, March 3, 1855, Ross Wilkins to McLean, January 11, 1855, M. Simpson to McLean, January 13, 1855, Donald McLeod to McLean, March 1, 1855, R. J. Arundel to McLean, March 14, 1855, McLean MSS (LC).

20. For Houston's membership in the order and his popularity with Democratic Know Nothings and non-Know Nothing anti-Nebraska northern Democrats, see Solomon G. Haven to Millard Fillmore, January 10, 1855, MFP-O; John S. Williams to Gideon Welles, November 25, 1854, Welles to Williams, December 9, 1854, draft, Williams to Welles, January 14, 1855, Welles MSS (LC).

21. Alexander H. H. Stuart to Millard Fillmore, November 11, 1854, January 1, 1855, Solomon G. Haven to Fillmore, December 9, 20, 1854, January 10, 17, 1855, MFP-O; Fillmore to Stuart, January 15, 1855, Stuart MSS.

22. John T. Bush to Millard Fillmore, November 25, 1854, MFP-O; John P. Kennedy to John N. Reynolds, February 27, 1855, copy, Kennedy MSS. In the quotation from Bush's letter I have changed his "excluding" to "exclude."

23. Godlove Orth to Will Cumback, April 14, 1855, Schuyler Colfax to Cumback, April 16, 1855, Cumback MSS; Orth to Colfax, November 1854, December 1, 1854, February 5, June 23, 1855, in Schauinger "Orth Letters," 40, pp. 56–58, 60–66.

24. Lewis Campbell to William Schouler, January 1, 1855, Schouler MSS.

25. Haven to Fillmore, December 22, 1854, MFP-O.

26. Cooper in fact gave a speech in the Senate defending the Know Nothings in January 1855, precisely at the time the Pennsylvania legislature took up the election of his successor. Solomon G. Haven to Millard Fillmore, January 29, 1855, MFP-O.

27. On the Pennsylvania senatorial election, see Isaac Newton to Millard Fillmore, January 18, 1855, MFP-O; and especially Anbinder, *Nativism & Slavery*, pp. 150–54. Anbinder estimates, note 67, p. 153, that in the crucial Know Nothing caucus vote on Cameron's nomination, ex-Whigs split almost evenly, twenty-six for and twenty-seven against, whereas ex-Democrats were solidly for him. Free Soil/Know Nothings solidly opposed Cameron.

28. Edward Everett to Millard Fillmore, December 16, 1854, MFP-O; Everett to Mrs. Charles Eames, February 18, 1855, Everett MSS; Robert C. Winthrop to John O. Sargent, February 20, 1855, Sargent MSS; Anbinder, *Nativism & Slavery*, pp. 146–47, 154–56.

29. Rayner is quoted in Anbinder, *Nativism & Slavery*, p. 148.

30. Solomon G. Haven to Millard Fillmore, December 20, 22, 1854, January 10, 1855, John T. Bush to Fillmore, November 15, 16, 1854, MFP-O. The precise partisan composition of the New York legislature is difficult to determine. The figures gathered by Walter Dean Burnham for the Inter-University Consortium list eighty-two Whigs, sixteen Democrats, three Free Soilers, and twenty-six "Others" in the assembly and twenty-two Whigs, seven Democrats, and three "Others" in the state senate. Burnham's "Other" category may refer to Know Nothings, but it is more likely that it included Hardshell or Softshell Democrats since the rival Democratic factions ran separate candidates for the legislature as they had for Congress. S. H. Hammond, the *Albany State Register*'s editor, wrote Fillmore on January 12, 1855, for example, that in both houses combined there were 48 Democrats and 30 Whigs who would vote against Seward. In contrast, Anbinder, *Nativism & Slavery*, pp. 147–49, states that Whigs lacked a majority in the legislature, and he counts thirty-six Whig and twelve Democratic Know Nothings. If he is accurate in denying that Whig/Know Nothings deserved to be counted as Whigs, non-Know Nothing Whigs therefore held 68 of the combined 160 house and senate seats. But Stephen Sammons, the Know Nothing leader, estimated in December that only sixty-six Whigs in the legislature—whether he meant only the assembly or the entire legislature is unclear—were not Silver Grays and that of those sixty-six, twenty were Know Nothings (S. Sammons to Daniel Ullmann, December 15, 1854, Ullmann MSS). Gienapp, *Origins*, p. 177, finally, counts 11 Know Nothings in the 32-seat senate and 40 in the 128-seat assembly.

31. DeWitt C. Stanford to Thurlow Weed, November 23, 1854, Weed MSS (RU); J. McKeon to Caleb Cushing, November 10, 1854, Cushing MSS; John O. Charles to Millard Fillmore, November 25, 1854, MFP-O; and Edward McPherson to J. B. McPherson, November 8, 1854, McPherson MSS.

32. James Kelly to William H. Seward, January 25, 1855, Seward MSS (RU); Seward to Weed, December 24, 1854, Seward to John L. Schoolcraft, December 29, 1854, Weed MSS (RU).

33. L. S. Parsons to Daniel Ullmann, November 11, 1854, F. S. Edwards to Ullmann, December 6, 1854, Ullmann MSS; E. R. Jewett to Millard Fillmore, December 28, 1854, S. H. Hammond to Fillmore, January 12, 1855, J. W. Ferdon to Fillmore, January 12, 1855, and Solomn G. Haven to Fillmore, January 29, 1855, MFP-O.

34. George P. Avery to Thurlow Weed, November 22, 1854, Charles Cooke to Weed, December 20, 1854, Henry Morgan to Weed, February 8, 1855, Weed MSS (RU); George Geddes to William H. Seward, February 7, 1855, Seward MSS (RU).

35. George W. Patterson to Thurlow Weed, February 17, 1855, Stafford C. Cleveland to Weed, February 24, 1855, William H. Burton to Weed, February 26, 1855, Weed MSS (RU); Daniel D. Barnard to Hamilton Fish, January 30, 1855, Fish MSS; E. R. Jewett to Millard Fillmore, February 4, 1855, MFP-O.

36. Anbinder, *Nativism & Slavery*, pp. 147–50; D. W. C. Clarke to William H. Seward, February 6, 1855, George Geddes to Seward, February 7, 1855, Moses H. Grinnell to Seward, February 7, 1855, Seward MSS (RU). "Sam," like "Hindoo" and "Cayenne," was a popular nickname for the Know Nothings.

37. Myron H. Clark to William H. Seward, February 15, 1855, Seward MSS (RU).

38. My account of Rhode Island rests heavily on Burnet, "Creating the 34th Congress," pp. 922–31.

39. Providence *Daily Journal*, March 22, 23, 28, 29, 1855, quoted in Burnet, "Creating the 34th Congress," pp. 925, 926, 927.

40. Durfee got 72 percent of the vote and Thurston got 88 percent.

41. Boston *Courier*, March 1, 1855, and Concord *New Hampshire Patriot*, December 27, 1854, both quoted in Burnet, "Creating the 34th Congress," p. 899. In addition to Burnet's section on New Hampshire, my main secondary sources for this account are Renda, "The Polity and the Party System," 292–319; Gienapp, *Origins*, pp. 173–74; Anbinder, *Nativism & Slavery*, pp. 127, 150; and Sewell, *Hale*, pp. 154–62.

42. John P. Hale to Thurlow Weed, February 2, 1855, Weed MSS (RU).

43. The Congressional Quarterly's *Guide to U.S. Elections* lists no Free Soil vote for 1855, and I have interpolated it from the figures it does list. The regression estimate of the movement of Free Soil voters between 1854 and 1855 is in Renda, "The Polity and the Party System," Table 3.13, p. 376. In 1854, Free Soilers ran Jared Perkins, an unsuccessful Whig congressional candidate in 1853, for governor in order to attract antislavery Whig voters dissatisfied with James Bell, the Whigs' nominee.

44. For estimates of Whig voter movement between 1854 and 1855, see the same table in Renda cited in the preceding note.

45. Schuyler Colfax to E. W. Jackson, March 15, 1855, Colfax MSS (IU); Joshua Leavitt to Salmon P. Chase, March 13–14, 1855, Chase MSS (HSP). Hale was elected to serve the remaining years of a deceased Democratic United States senator's term. James Bell, the Whig/Know Nothing, was picked to fill a full six-year term.

46. Aaron H. Cragin to Thurlow Weed, June 15, 1855, Seward MSS (RU). Cragin, the lone Whig among the three Know Nothing congressmen-elect, announced in this letter that New Hampshire's Know Nothings were already prepared to abandon the nativist party, now that it had successfully shattered the Democrats, for a Republican organization. Later that year the betrayed and outraged Edmund Burke, who had urged anti-Pierce Democrats to vote Know Nothing, also accused Know Nothing leaders of being closet Republicans. "Position of the Old Guard Democracy," undated draft editorial, 1855 folder, Burke MSS.

47. Edward Prentiss to Francis Gillette, December 25, 1854, copy, Hawley MSS; George Baldwin to Emily Baldwin, March 14, 20, 1855, Emily Baldwin to George Baldwin, March 17, April 3, 1855, BFP; Gideon Welles to ?, April 23, 1855, draft, Welles MSS (Conn.HS). For more thorough analyses of the 1855 elections in Connecticut, see Renda, "The Polity and the Party System," 299–323; and Gienapp, *Origins*, pp. 274–78.

48. Gideon Welles to Preston King, November 25, 1854, copy, Welles MSS (LC); Joshua Leavitt to Salmon P. Chase, March 14, 1855, Chase MSS (HSP); Lew Campbell to William

Schouler, February 15, 1855, Schuyler Colfax to Schuyler, March 2, May 1, 1855, Schouler MSS; Colfax to E. W. Jackson, March 15, 1855, Colfax MSS (IU). For evidence that Chase wanted Ohio's Know Nothings included in, rather than alienated from, a Republican party in Ohio that he hoped would nominate him for governor in July, see Chase to E. S. Hamlin, January 22, February 15, 1855, and Oran Follett to Chase, May 2, 1855, Chase MSS (LC); and Chase to James S. Pike, March 22, 1855, Pike MSS.

49. Samuel W. Parker to Samuel Galloway, May 10, 1855, Galloway MSS; Garrett Davis to Lewis Campbell, June 5, 1855, Lewis Campbell MSS; Anbinder, *Nativism & Slavery*, p. 166. Davis' letter to Campbell applauded a proposed platform to be adopted by the June national council meeting that Campbell had sent him and that deplored sectional parties, called for the judiciary to determine the power of Congress over slavery in the territories, and asserted that most questions pertaining to slavery came exclusively under state jurisdiction (Gienapp, *Origins*, p. 183). The position of Orth and Colfax will be documented below.

50. These various southern Whigs, along with the Texas Democrat Sam Houston, are mentioned as having support for the Know Nothing nomination in the following letters to William Schouler in the Schouler MSS: Lew Campbell, December 24, 1854, Henry Wilson, April 16, 1855, Schuyler Colfax, May 1, 1855, Garrett Davis, May 23, 1855, and Ezra Lincoln, May 24, 1855. Wilson, Colfax, and Campbell all stated that they personally did not believe that any Southerner could carry the North. Colfax, as of May 1, favored Pennsylvania's Governor James Pollock for the nomination, and Wilson, intriguingly, said that ex-Senator Truman Smith was Cullom's biggest booster and, just as intriguingly, that "it is hard telling what Weed and the New York politicians go for."

51. Schuyler Colfax to William Schouler, October 23, 1854, March 2, May 1, 1855, Lewis Campbell to Schouler, December 26, 1854, February 15, 1855, Schouler MSS; Solomon G. Haven to Millard Fillmore, February 25, 1855, MFP-O; Lewis Campbell to Samuel Galloway, May 16, 22, 1855, Samuel W. Parker to Gallloway, May 10, 1855, Galloway MSS; Charles A. Dana to James S. Pike, July 14, 1855, Pike MSS. On Campbell's leadership of the midwestern anti-Nebraska Whig/Know Nothings, see also Salmon P. Chase to E. S. Hamlin, February 9, 1855, Chase MSS (LC).

52. Shortly after Seward's reelection by the New York legislature in February 1855, the New York State Know Nothing council adopted a pro-Union platform plank that was then broadcast to the nation to neutralize suspicions that Sewardites controlled the order there. Fillmore's Baltimore friend John P. Kennedy, an outsider, wrote it and secured its adoption through John N. Reynolds and other New York friends in the order. Yet the subsequent actions of New England's Know Nothings mitigated its impact. On Kennedy's role, see John P. Kennedy to John N. Reynolds, February 27, 1855, and especially Kennedy to S. N. Spencer, November 24, 1855, copies, Kennedy MSS.

53. Lew Campbell to William Schouler, December 26, 1854, Henry Wilson to Schouler, April 18, 1855, Schouler MSS; Campbell to Samuel Galloway, May 16, 22, 1855, Galloway MSS; Charles Dana to James S. Pike, July 14, 1855, Pike MSS.

54. Godlove Orth to Will Cumback, April 14, 1855, Schuyler Colfax to Cumback, April 16, 1855, Cumback MSS; Colfax to E. W. Jackson, March 15, 1855, Colfax MSS (IU); Colfax to William Schouler, May 1, 1855, Schouler MSS.

55. Garrett Davis to Lew Campbell, June 5, 1855, Campbell MSS; Davis to Schouler, May 23, 1855, Schouler MSS. For Campbell's hope of southern backing in the impending election for speaker of the House, see Campbell to Galloway, May 16, 22, 1855, Galloway MSS; and Campbell to Schouler, June 26, 1855, Schouler MSS.

56. Kenneth Rayner to Daniel Ullmann, May 4, 1855, Ullmann MSS; for the content of the Union membership oath, see Anbinder, *Nativism & Slavery*, pp. 162–63.

57. Ezra Lincoln to Schouler, May 24, 1855, Schouler MSS.

58. Gienapp, *Origins*, pp. 169–70; Garrett Davis to William Schouler, May 23, 1855, Schouler MSS; Schuyler Colfax to Will Cumback, April 16, 1855, Cumback MSS; Godlove Orth to Schuyler Colfax, June 23, 1855, in Schauinger, "Orth Letters," 40, 65. The quotation about slavery not spreading to Nebraska comes from Conrad to Fillmore, December 24, 1854, MFP-O, but

many southern Whig papers and politicians had publicly declared the same thing since the spring of 1854.

59. Charlotte *North Carolina Whig*, July 6, 1854, and Nashville *Republican Banner*, July 24, 1854, cited in Burnet, "Creating the 34th Congress," pp. 1034, 1095.

60. C. M. Conrad to Fillmore, December 24, 1854, MFP-O.

61. Edward L. Winslow to William H. Seward, July 5, 1855, Seward MSS (RU).

62. Bardstown *Herald*, February 22, 1855; Memphis *Daily Appeal*, June 14, 1855, quoting Walter Coleman; and Fayette *Observer*, May 29, 1855, quoting Kerr's public letter announcing his candidacy, all cited in Burnet, "Creating the 34th Congress," pp. 1149, 1067, 1112. Like Kerr, Coleman attempted to run for Congress as an independent Whig in 1855, and like him, he was crushed by a Know Nothing opponent. The extent and futility of Whig resistance to Know Nothingism in the South will be examined at greater length below.

63. Seth Hawley to Seward, March 30, 1855, Seward MSS (RU); John C. Breckinridge to Joseph A. Wright, April 1, 1855, Wright MSS; William B. Campbell to David Campbell, January 4, February 24, 1855, CFP; *Brownlow's Knoxville Whig*, April 10, 1855, Greensboro *Patriot*, May 5, 1855, and New Orleans *Daily Picayune*, July 27, 1855, all quoted in a preliminary but unpaginated draft of Burnet's "Creating the 34th Congress"; William L. Sharkey to Fontaine, May 3, 1855, Fontaine MSS; public letter of Senator Clement C. Clay, in Huntsville, *Southern Advocate*, July 25, 1855, quoted in Burnet, "Creating the 34th Congress," p. 1186.

64. Alexander H. H. Stuart to Millard Fillmore, November 11, 1854, Solomon G. Haven to Fillmore, January 10, 1855, MFP-O.

65. Ibid.; Alexander H. H. Stuart to Millard Fillmore, January 1, 1855, MFP-O; J. H. Shirrard to William C. Rives, January 16, 1855, Rives MSS; for Wise's nomination and campaign, see the superb biography by Simpson, *Wise*, pp. 106–15. For evidence of Democratic antipathy to Wise in southwestern Virginia, see H. C. Gibbons to Angus R. Blakey, February 5, 1855, Blakey MSS.

66. Botts communicated with the Newark dinner by a letter that was printed in the *New York Times*, November 21, 1854, and is quoted in Burnet, "Creating the 34th Congress," p. 936.

67. J. H. Shirrard to William C. Rives, January 29, 1855, Rives to William M. Burwell, March 19, 1855, Rives MSS; Alexander H. H. Stuart to Millard Fillmore, January 1, 1855, Solomon G. Haven to Fillmore, January 10, 1855, MFP-O.

68. Stuart to Fillmore, November 11, 1854, January 1, 1855, Haven to Fillmore, January 10, 17, 1855, MFP-O; Fillmore to Stuart, January 15, 1855, Stuart MSS.

69. Know Nothings implicitly endorsed anti-Wise Democratic incumbents Thomas Bayly and "Extra-Billy" Smith in the first and seventh districts after both men praised the Know Nothings' call for banning the foreign-born from public office, even while denying membership in the order and denouncing its secrecy. In the tenth district, Whig/Know Nothing John Imboden initially opposed the incumbent Democrat and future governor, John Letcher, but Imboden apparently dropped out of the race before the May balloting. Two of the remaining Whig/Know Nothing candidates, Connally Trigg in the thirteenth district and the venerable Littleton Tazewell in the fourth (Richmond) district, ran against Democratic incumbents who had been unopposed in 1853, and each attracted less than 40 percent of the vote. The other three, however, attracted vote shares ranging between 47 and 49 percent, and all ran more strongly than their Whig predecessors in 1853. The talented Alex Boteler, indeed, lost the eighth (Winchester) district to incumbent Democrat Charles J. Faulkner, himself an apostate Whig, by only 200 votes. In addition to the results listed in the Congressional Quarterly's *Guide to U.S. Elections*, this analysis relies on Burnet, "Creating the 34th Congress," pp. 933–89.

70. Richmond *Enquirer*, May 13, 1855, quoted in Burnet, "Creating the 34th Congress," p. 959; for more on Wise's campaign rhetoric, see Simpson, *Wise*, pp. 106–15. As Simpson points out, Flournoy was vulnerable because he had once argued that the presence of slavery inhibited Virginia's economic development. James M. H. Beale, the Know Nothings' candidate for lieutenant governor and a two-term congressman, had voted in 1850 for the bill abolishing slave pens in the District of Columbia.

71. Rives to William M. Burwell, March 19, 1855, Rives MSS.

72. Kenneth Rayner to Daniel Ullmann, May 8, 1855, Vesparian Ellis to Ullmann, May 29, 1855, J. Timberlake to Ullmann, May 30, 1855, Ullmann MSS; David Campbell to William B. Campbell, June 6, 1855, CFP; William L. Hodge to Fillmore, June 25, 1855, MFP-O Montgomery *Daily Mail*, May 29, 1855, quoted in Burnet, "Creating the 34th Congress," p. 974. For an example of another Know Nothing who blamed "the increased foreign vote" for Flournoy's defeat, see Nathan Sargent to Richard Yates, May 31, 1855, Yates MSS.

73. I have found no such evidence, but some may exist.

74. On Barker, see Gienapp, *Origins*, p. 185.

75. Kennedy was immensely proud of his success in getting his contacts among New York Know Nothings to adopt his platform, which, he told Robert Winthrop, demonstrated that Know Nothings were a "genuine Union party." See John P. Kennedy to J. N. Reynolds, February 27, 1855, Kennedy to Winthrop, April 22, 1855, and Kennedy to S. N. Spencer, November 24, 1855, copies, Kennedy MSS.

76. *New York Tribune*, May 8, 1855; N. Darling to Thurlow Weed, May 30, 1855, Weed MSS (RU); Henry Wilson to William Schouler, April 16, 1855, Schouler MSS; Wilson's later statement is quoted in Gienapp, *Origins*, p. 183.

77. Albert T. Burnley to John J. Crittenden, June 12, 1855, Crittenden MSS (LC); Kenneth Rayner to Daniel Ullmann, June 2, 1856, Ullmann MSS. Superbly detailed, if slightly different accounts of this meeting, can be found in Gienapp, *Origins*, pp. 182–86; and Anbinder, *Nativism & Slavery*, pp. 167–72.

78. A delegation from Louisiana containing Catholics was denied admission, and Section Eight of the platform pledged "Resistance to the aggressive policy and corrupting tendencies of the Roman Catholic Church, in our country" and "jealous resistance of all attempts by any sect, denomination or church to obtain an ascendancy over any other in the State, by means of any special privileges or exemption, by any political combination of its members, or by a division of their civil allegiance with any foreign power, potentate or ecclesiastic." Section Fourteen read: "The National Council declares that all the principles of the order shall be henceforward everywhere openly avowed; and that each member shall be at liberty to make known the existence of the order, and the fact that he himself is a member; and it recommends that there be no concealment of the places of meeting of subordinate councils." The platform is printed in the appendix of Holt, "The Antimasonic and Know Nothing Parties," pp. 701–05.

79. Five men signed both the main and Pennsylvania protests, which thus garnered fifteen signatures. This account is based on the passages in Anbinder and Gienapp cited above.

80. Anbinder, *Nativism & Slavery*, pp. 172–74; Gienapp, *Origins*, pp. 186–87. The all-important New York state council did not explicitly repudiate Section Twelve or insist on restoration of the Missouri Compromise. But it did condemn that repeal and insist that slavery "should derive no extension from such repeal." Anbinder, *Nativism & Slavery*, p. 183.

81. "I shall never cease to thank you for your aid at Philadelphia," Wilson wrote Bowles a week after the council meeting. "To your efforts are we indebted in a great degree for the results." Henry Wilson to Samuel Bowles, June 23, 1855, Bowles MSS.

82. Gienapp, *Origins*, pp. 186–87, quotation from Bowles, p. 186.

83. George E. Baker to Seward, June 19, 1855, Seward MSS (RU); Dana is quoted by Anbinder, *Nativism & Slavery*, p. 172.

84. John P. Kennedy to Robert C. Winthrop, June 18, 1855, copy, Kennedy MSS.

85. Kennedy to Winthrop, June 18, 1855, Kennedy MSS; New Orleans *Bee*, June 18, 1855, and Charlotte *North Carolina Whig*, June 12, 1855, quoted in Burnet, "Creating the 34th Congress," pp. 1002, 1102.

86. Jesse M. Jones to Alexander H. Stephens, July 9, 1855 (quotation), Stephens MSS (LC).

87. For examples of Johnson's attacks, see his speeches of May 11 and June 5, printed in *Johnson Papers*, pp. 301–06, 308–15. For evidence of Whig discontentment with Gentry, see Andrew Johnson to David T. Patterson, February 17, 1855, ibid., pp. 258–59; William B. Campbell to David Campbell, August 4, 1855, CFP; and William Cullom to William Schouler, September 16, 1855, Schouler MSS. Two votes in particular left Gentry vulnerable to demagoguery on the slavery issue. At the end of the second session of the Thirtieth Congress in March 1849, he had

supported a resolution by Indiana's Richard W. Thompson asserting that Mexico's abolition statutes still retained legal force in the Mexican Cession. And in September 1850, he voted for the bill banning slave pens from the District of Columbia. Johnson defeated Henry in 1853, 63,413 (50.9 percent) to 61,163 (49.1 percent); in 1855, he defeated Gentry, 67,499 (50.8 percent) to 65,332 (49.2 percent).

88. Cullom to Schouler, September 16, 1855, Schouler MSS.

89. The quoted remarks come from a speech by Preston printed in the Tuscumbia, Alabama, *Enquirer*, July 20, 1855, which is quoted in Burnet, "Creating the 34th Congress," p. 1152. I have relied on Burnet for the details of all southern congressional elections. Running in Kentucky's seventh (Louisville) district, Preston had amassed 6,609 votes (57.7 percent) in 1853 compared to the Democrats' 4,847 (42.3 percent). In 1855, Preston garnered only 4,378 votes (38.7 percent) to Marshall's 6,932 (61.3 percent). The stunning change in his electoral fortunes testifies to the futility of Whig resistance to the Know Nothing juggernaut in nativist strongholds.

90. Fayetteville *Observer*, May 29, 1855, quoted by Burnet, "Creating the 34th Congress," p. 1112. In 1853, the popular Kerr swamped his Democratic opponent with 6,037 votes, 86.2 percent of the total. In 1855, his total plummeted to 3,756, 34.7 percent of the total.

91. I have counted Alexander Stephens as a Whig in both totals, even though he thought of himself as seceding from the party as early as 1850.

92. Montgomery *Daily Mail*, July 14, 1855, cited by Burnet, "Creating the 34th Congress," p. 1187.

93. New Orleans *Bee*, August 4, 1855, quoted in Burnet, "Creating the 34th Congress," p. 1293; for evidence that French Catholic Whigs refused to vote Know Nothing in 1855, see J. Livingston to Daniel Ullmann, July 31, 1856, Ullmann MSS.

94. Burnet, "Creating the 34th Congress," pp. 1102, 1116; Kruman, *Parties and Politics*, pp. 169–71. Kruman calculated a statistical correlation of .92 between the 1855 Know Nothing vote and that for the Whigs in 1853, but he omitted Kerr's district because of incomplete returns. The figure, which suggests strong Whig support for Know Nothing candidates, would have undoubtedly been lower had that district been included.

95. Burnet, "Creating the 34th Congress," pp. 1356–57, quotes a copy of Johnson's public letter of September 11, 1855, that he found in the New Orleans *Louisiana Courier*, September 28, 1855. Burnet, pp. 1355–56, also quotes Pratt's statement from the Baltimore *American*, September 17, 1855.

96. James A. Pearce to John M. Clayton, September 15, 1855, Clayton MSS.

97. Evitts, *Matter of Allegiances*, pp. 80–91. The St. Mary's and Frederick meetings are quoted in Burnet, "Creating the 34th Congress," p. 1354.

98. John P. Kennedy to B. E. Gautt, November 16, 1855, to S. N. Spencer, November 24, 1855, and to R. C. Winthrop, February 21, 1856, copies, Kennedy MSS. The term of Pratt, an open foe of Know Nothings, was due to run through the Thirty-Fourth Congress until March 1857. But seizing their chance, Know Nothings in the Maryland legislature elected his successor in early 1856. On election day violence in Baltimore in 1855 and subsequent elections, see Evitts, *Matter of Allegiances*, pp. 89–117.

99. Quoted in Volz, "Party, State, and Nation," p. 177. Volz has written by far the best study of Kentucky politics in the 1850s, and my analysis of Kentucky is based heavily on pp. 161–230 of his Ph.D. dissertation.

100. Danville *Kentucky Tribune*, March 16, 1855, and Louisville *Journal*, March 20, 1855, cited in ibid., pp. 188–89.

101. Quoted in ibid., p. 193.

102. That Virginia's Flournoy and Tennessee's Gentry were also strong proponents of Taylor's nomination in 1848 is hardly coincidental. Recall that Taylor had been pushed originally as a No Party man in order to attract Democrats to an ostensibly nonpartisan, indeed antiparty, movement. Know Nothingism presented itself in the same way.

103. Cullom to Schouler, September 16, 1855, Schouler MSS.

104. Dated July 8, Jones' letter is quoted in Burnet, "Creating the 34th Congress," p. 1078.

105. Ibid., p. 1077.

106. Ibid., pp. 1064–67. The Whig/Know Nothing candidate, Thomas Rivers, won the election after Whigs in the Know Nothing order forced Coleman to withdraw.

107. My account of this district is based on ibid., pp. 1045–52. Most Whigs apparently stayed with Taylor, but as the Know Nothing candidate, he also garnered some Democratic votes. In 1853, when Watkins refused to step aside for Taylor and they divided the Whig vote, a Democrat won with 5,525 votes (37.1 percent), Taylor ran second with 5,387 (36.2 percent), and Watkins trailed with 3,988 (26.7 percent). In 1855, Watkins got 7,781 votes (50.9 percent) to Taylor's 7,511 (49.1 percent).

Whig divisions in the newly drawn second district also allowed a Democrat to win in 1853, and in 1855, contenders for the Whig nomination from each rival faction both joined the Know Nothings to get their endorsement. When influential Know Nothing editor Parson Brownlow annointed William Sneed, who originally identified himself as "a party man, a Whig all over, of the old guard," as the better champion of Americanism, Sneed won in consecutive order: the Whig nomination from a Know Nothing-dominated Whig convention, a separate American nomination, and the election. Ibid., pp. 1052–58, quotation, p. 1055.

108. Schott, *Stephens*, pp. 158–59.

109. H. R. Casey to Alexander H. Stephens, May 29, 1855, Stephens MSS (LC).

110. W. W. Paine to Alexander H. Stephens, February 23, 1855, Alfred Iverson to Stephens, June 25, 1855, ? Thwartt to Stephens, June 30, 1855, Stephens MSS (LC).

111. Jesse M. Jones to Alexander Stephens, July 9, 1855, James Mercer Green to Stephens, August 9, 1855, Stephens MSS (LC). Green, for example, identified himself as a member of the "Central Executive Committee of the Democratic Anti K. N. Party of Bible" County.

112. Schott, *Stephens*, pp. 184–87; William Reese to Linton Stephens, August 9, 1855, R. G. Harper to Linton Stephens, August 27, 1855, Alexander Stephens MSS (LC).

113. Thwartt to Alexander H. Stephens, June 30, 1855, John W. Duncan to Stephens, July 13, 1855, J. Lomax to Stephens, August 4, 1855, and H. Walker to Stephens, October 10, 1855 (quotations), Stephens MSS (LC).

114. A third-party Temperance candidate got 6,333 votes (6.1 percent) in the gubernatorial race. For evidence of Democratic converts to Know Nothingism, Andrews' blunders on the campaign trail, and Whig aversion to him, see the following letters, all to Alexander H. Stephens unless specified otherwise, in the Stephens MSS (LC): W. W. Paine, February 23, 1855, Alfred Iverson, June 25, 1855, James Mercer Green to Stephens, August 9, 1855, William Reese to Linton Stephens, August 9, 1855, and H. Walker, October 10, 1855.

115. Savannah *Daily Georgian*, June 19, 1855, quoted in Burnet, "Creating the 34th Congress," p. 1240.

116. John P. Kennedy to Robert C. Winthrop, June 18, 1855, Winthrop to Kennedy, June 20, 1855, Kennedy MSS.

117. Edward Everett to Mrs. Charles Eames, June 18, August 11, 1855, Everett MSS.

118. Washington Hunt to Thurlow Weed, August 10, 1855, Weed MSS; Robert C. Winthrop to John P. Kennedy, August 23, 1855, Kennedy MSS; for Fish, see Gienapp, *Origins*, p. 226.

119. Nathan K. Hall to Millard Fillmore, December 5, 1854, MFP-O; Solomon Foot to Justin Morrill, November 1, 1855, Morrill MSS.

120. Gienapp, *Origins*, pp. 203–08, quotation p. 206.

121. Ibid. and Tables 7.7 and 7.8, p. 512; Edward Kent to William Pitt Fessenden, May 21, June 6, 1855, Noah Smith, Jr., to Fessenden, June 8, 1855, and George W. Ingersoll to Noah Smith, Jr., Fessenden MSS (WRHS).

122. Edward Kent to William H. Seward, October 20, 1855, Seward MSS (RU).

123. Developments in Massachusetts receive excellent, though differing, analyses in Gienapp, *Origins*, pp. 214–223, and Anbinder, *Nativism & Slavery*, pp. 187–92. See also, however, Henry Wilson to Samuel Bowles, June 23, 1855 (quotation), Robert C. Winthrop to Bowles, June 21, 1855, refusing to join a fusion movement, and the many letters from Gardner to Bowles over the summer and fall, Bowles MSS; Edward Everett to Mrs. Charles Eames, September 25, November 7, 1855, Everett MSS; Julius Rockwell to Israel Washburn, Jr., October 13, 1855, Washburn MSS (LC); and the previously cited letters from Winthrop and Everett.

124. Gienapp, *Origins*, Tables 7.12 and 7.13, pp. 514–15. Washburn got 27,279 votes (20.9 percent) in 1854; Walley's share was 9.7 percent. Since Know Nothings retained control of the legislature, Gardner was elected by that body.

125. Edward Everett to Mrs. Charles Eames, November 7, 1855, Everett MSS; Edward L. Pierce to Salmon P. Chase, November 9, 1855, Chase MSS (LC); Henry Wilson to Salmon P. Chase, November 17, 1855, Chase MSS (HSP).

126. For the antislavery thrust of Gardner's campaign, see Anbinder, *Nativism & Slavery*, p. 190.

127. On this gathering, see Anbinder, *Nativism & Slavery*, p. 196; and the reports in the Cincinnati *Gazette*, November 21–24, 1855.

128. James Elliott to Thurlow Weed, November 27, 1855, Weed MSS (RU); Cincinnati *Gazette*, November 24, 1855.

129. John P. Kennedy to John N. Reynolds, November 18, 1855, Kennedy MSS; Haven to Fillmore, December 6, 1855, MFP-O.

130. Gienapp, *Origins*, pp. 208–13, quotation from McClure, p. 209; Holt, *Forging a Majority*, pp. 151–74; George Sanderson to James Buchanan, May 2, 1855, Buchanan MSS (HSP).

131. Since Whigs and Know Nothings both backed James Pollock for governor in 1854, my phrase "Whig holdouts" refers to those men who voted Whig in the race for state supreme court justice when Know Nothings were backing the Native American candidate.

132. H. L. Dieffenbach to William L. Bigler, October 3, 1855, Bigler MSS; George Sanderson to James Buchanan, October 11, 1855, Buchanan MSS (HSP); Gienapp, *Origins*, Table 7.11, p. 514. I have used the returns listed in ibid., p. 274, n. 74. Ballots were also distributed for the original Know Nothing candidate whom Nicholson replaced, and he got 678 votes (0.2 percent).

133. Joshua R. Giddings to George W. Julian, May 30, 1855, Giddings-Julian MSS; Lewis Campbell to Salmon P. Chase, May 28, 1855, Chase MSS (LC). The Chase collections at the Library of Congress and the Historical Society of Pennsylvania are filled with letters relating to this struggle. In addition, the secondary literature on the Ohio race is excellent. See Gienapp, *Origins*, pp. 192–203; Anbinder, *Nativism & Slavery*, pp. 174–80; and Maizlish, *Triumph of Sectionalism*, pp. 206–224.

134. Ben Wade to William Schouler, May 3, 1855, Lewis Campbell to Schouler, May 22, 1855, Schouler MSS. For old line, largely conservative, Whig opposition to Chase, see M. H. Nichols to Salmon P. Chase, April 14, 1855, Chase MSS (LC); and Thomas Corwine to Thomas B. Stevenson, June 17, 1855, Schouler MSS.

135. For one Whig/Know Nothing's anger at Spooner's action in destroying separate Know Nothing nominations in June, see William H. Gibson to Samuel Galloway, April 23, 1855, Galloway MSS.

136. Gienapp, *Origins*, pp. 200–01, 509–11. In a postelection letter, Ben Wade sneered that "our Silver Grays" joined with dissident Know Nothings to run the Trimble ticket. Wade to Israel Washburn, Jr., October 13, 1855, Washburn MSS (LC).

137. Gienapp, *Origins*, pp. 229–30; Anbinder, *Nativism & Slavery*, pp. 183–84. The Know Nothing candidate won a four-way race for secretary of state with 34.1 percent of the vote. For the optimistic reactions of Haven and Kennedy, see John P. Kennedy to Millard Fillmore and to J. N. Reynolds, both dated November 18, 1855, Kennedy MSS; and Solomon G. Haven to Fillmore, December 6, 1855, MFP-O. For examples of Silver Gray/Know Nothings' hostile reactions to Section Twelve, see the following letters to Daniel Ullmann, all in the Ullmann MSS: Killian Miller, June 24, 1855, Congressman-elect F. S. Edwards, June 23, 1855, and James R. Thompson, June 26, 1855.

138. William H. Seward to Lucian Barbour et al., July 2, 1855, Weed to Seward, July 23, 1855, Seward MSS (RU).

139. James C. Hopkins to Thurlow Weed, July 17, 1855, Weed MSS (RU).

140. Horatio Seymour to William L. Marcy, July 31, 1855, Marcy MSS (LC); Solomon G. Haven to Millard Fillmore, June 29, August 15, 1855, Nathan K. Hall to Fillmore, August 18, 1855, MFP-O; Washington Hunt to Thurlow Weed, August 10, 1855, Weed MSS (RU).

141. DeWitt C. Stanford to Myron H. Clark, August 2, 1855, Clark MSS; Alonzo Johnson

to Thurlow Weed, August 17, 1855, Weed MSS (RU); Weed to Seward, July 23, 1855, Seward to E. A. Stansbury, September 14, 1855, Seward MSS (RU). On Seward's continued hesitancy about abandoning the Whig party in New York in 1855, see Gienapp, *Origins*, pp. 224–25.

142. Seymour to Marcy, July 31, 1855, Marcy MSS (LC).

143. Haven to Fillmore, August 15, 1855, Hall to Fillmore, August 18, 1855, MFP-O; James R. Thompson to Daniel Ullmann, September 1, 1855, Ullmann MSS. For a Whig's appalled reaction to the corruption of the canal board in 1855 by the "central clique" of Weed's allies, see W. H. Adams to Fillmore, March 15, 1855, MFP-O.

144. S. B. Jewett to Samuel J. Tilden, October 6, 1855, Tilden MSS; Henry E. Davies to Millard Fillmore, October 1, 1855, MFP-O; Washington Hunt to Hamilton Fish, October 7, 1855, Fish MSS; DeWitt Clinton to Thurlow Weed, October 15, 1855, Weed MSS (RU).

145. George E. Baker to William H. Seward, October 5, 8, 1855, Seward MSS (RU); Berger, *Revolution*, pp. 84–85.

146. *Seward at Washington*, pp. 253–54; Gienapp, *Origins*, pp. 226–27. I rely heavily on Gienapp's superb account of the two conventions.

147. Fillmore's friend Kennedy spotted and rejoiced in this omission. By his logic, Republicans' silence on the matter meant that anti-Nebraska Whig/Know Nothings could also drop it and thus back Fillmore in 1856 without an explicitly anti-Nebraska platform. John P. Kennedy to J. N. Reynolds, November 18, 1855, Kennedy MSS.

148. Nathan K. Hall to Millard Fillmore, November 16, 1855, MFP-O; George E. Baker to William H. Seward, October 13, 1855, Seward MSS (RU); Oliver B. Pierce to Thurlow Weed, November 26, 1855, Weed MSS (RU).

149. Horatio Seymour to William L. Marcy, November 9, 1855, A. J. Parker to Marcy, November 10, 1855 (quotation), Marcy MSS (LC).

150. J. J. Chambers to Myron H. Clark, September 25, 1855, Clark MSS; Gienapp, *Origins*, p. 232; John M. Bradford to Hamilton Fish, November 8, 1855, Fish MSS.

151. Gienapp, *Origins*, Tables 7.14–7.17, pp. 515–17.

152. Washington Hunt to Hamilton Fish, October 7, December 20, 1855, Fish MSS; Seward to Lucian Barbour et al., July 2, 1855, Seward MSS (RU).

153. Speech on the steps of the New York state capitol, Albany, October 12, 1855, in *Seward at Washington*, p. 256.

154. N. K. Hall to Millard Fillmore, November 16, 1855, Solomon G. Haven to Fillmore, December 6, 1855, MFP-O; John P. Kennedy to B. E. Gautt, November 16, 1855, Kennedy to Millard Fillmore, November 18, 1855, Kennedy to J. N. Reynolds, November 18, 1855, Kennedy to S. N. Spencer, November 24, 1855, Kennedy MSS.

155. William H. Seward to Fredrick Seward, November 8, 18, 1855, Seward to George E. Baker, November 1856, in *Seward at Washington*, pp. 258–59.

156. Hunt to Fish, December 20, 1855, Fish MSS.

CHAPTER 26

1. Jackson *Pilot*, July 30, 1870.

2. Samuel Eliot to John O. Sargent, November 10, 1851, Sargent MSS.

3. Granger to Millard Fillmore, June 30, 1852, MFP-BHS.

4. Washington Hunt to Hamilton Fish, December 20, 1855, Fish MSS.

5. Belleville *Advocate*, January 10, 1855, quoted in Burnet, "Creating the 34th Congress," p. 727; Hunt to Fish, December 20, 1855 (quotation), February 17, 1856, Fish MSS.

6. John P. Kennedy to Nathan Sargent, July 19, 1855, copy, Kennedy to J. N. Reynolds, November 18, 1855, copy, Kennedy to S. N. Spencer, November 24, 1855, Kennedy MSS.

7. Andrew Tracy to Justin Morrill, December 10, 1855, Phlinzy H. White to Morrill, December 29, 1855, Sam S. Billings to Morrill, January 20, 1856, Morrill MSS.

8. George Ashmun to Nathaniel P. Banks, October 11, 1856, Banks MSS (Ill.SHL).

9. Daniel D. Barnard to James A. Hamilton, November 23, 28, 1855, copies, Barnard MSS; Robert C. Winthrop to Edward Everett, December 3, 1855, Everett MSS; John P. Kennedy to Robert C. Winthrop, December 23, 1855, copy, Kennedy to James A. Hamilton, December 31, 1855, copy, Kennedy MSS; Robert A. West to Hamilton Fish, January 9, 13 (quotation), 1856,

Washington Hunt to Fish, January 16, 1856, Fish MSS. Kennedy could not attend the meeting, but in his letter to Hamilton of December 31, Kennedy strongly urged the Whigs *not* to nominate Fillmore and to allow the Americans to do so, lest a prior Whig nomination turn Democratic Know Nothings against Fillmore.

10. West to Fish, January 13, 1856, Fish MSS.

11. Gienapp, *Origins*, pp. 239–448, provides by far the fullest and best analysis of the election from the Republicans' perspective. The Democratic campaign is assessed in Nichols, *Disruption of American Democracy*, pp. 17–62. Anbinder, *Nativism & Slavery*, pp. 194–245, also covers the American and Republican campaigns in the North, but some of his interpretations merit skepticism. I have assessed the strategy behind the Fillmore campaign and the reasons that strategy unraveled in "Another Look at the Election of 1856."

12. Anbinder, *Nativism & Slavery*, p. 197, n. 8, suggests that as many as 124 House members were, or had once been, affiliated with the Know Nothings, making them the largest group among the opposition. But he himself admits that his estimate is shaky.

13. An excellent account of the speakership election can be found in Gienapp, *Origins*, pp. 240–48; the classic traditional account is Harrington, "First Northern Victory." Burnet, after examining the congressional elections in all 234 districts, counts 106 verifiable Know Nothings, while Anbinder gives an upper estimate of 124. Thus I have split the difference with 115. Gienapp, p. 240, counts 118 Anti-Nebraska men.

14. Joshua R. Giddings to Gamaliel Bailey, November 11, 1855, Giddings-Julian MSS; Samuel Whitcomb to Justin Morrill, November 22, 1855, Morrill MSS; Schuyler Colfax to Charles Heaton, December 3, 1855, Colfax MSS (NIHS); Preston King to Francis P. Blair, January 3, 1856, Blair-Lee MSS; M. H. Nichols to Salmon P. Chase, December 11, 1855, Gamaliel Bailey to Chase, February 21, 1856, Chase MSS (LC).

15. Schuyler Colfax to Charles Heaton, December 16, 1855, Colfax MSS (NIHS).

16. Solomon G. Haven to Millard Fillmore, December 6, 13, 1855, January 20, 1856, MFP-O; Schuyler Colfax to Charles Heaton, December 3, 11, 16, 1855, Colfax MSS (NIHS); ? Greene to William Schouler, September 1, 1855, J. H. Clay Mudd to Schouler, September 15, 1855, R. W. Corwine to Schouler, December 8, 1855, William Schouler MSS; Albert Gallatin Brown to John F. H. Claiborne, February 4, 1856, Claiborne MSS; M. H. Nichols to Salmon P. Chase, December 11, 1855, Chase MSS (LC); Israel Washburn, Jr., to J. L. Stevens, December 25, 1855, Washburn MSS (LC).

What particularly embittered Campbell was that Cincinnati editor William Schouler, who helped persuade Campbell to withdraw and who, Campbell believed, had come to Washington to lobby congressmen for him, instead betrayed him. Schouler wanted the House printing contracts more than Campbell's election. Once he discovered Democratic/Know Nothings' antipathy to Campbell, he knew that ex-Whigs from Ohio could never win both the speakership and the printer's post. Thus Schouler urged anti-Nebraska men to dump Campbell for Banks, but he still lost the printing contracts. See Lew Campbell to Schouler, February 16, March 10, 24, 30, 1856, and Schouler to George Harrington, April 10, 1856, Schouler MSS.

17. Edward Kent to Israel Washburn, Jr., December 15, 1855, February 9, 1856 (quotation), Washburn MSS (Norlands); G. D. Long to William H. Seward, February 6, 1856 (quotation), Seward MSS (RU); Phlinzy H. White to Justin Morrill, December 29, 1855 (quotation), Sam S. Billings to Morrill, January 20, 1856 (quotation), Morrill MSS; Israel Washburn, Jr., to J. L. Stevens, February 12, 1856, Washburn MSS (LC).

18. Most southern Know Nothings voted for Aiken on the crucial final ballots because Aiken, unlike other Democratic candidates, had not attended the original Democratic caucus that denounced Know Nothingism. If all southern Americans had backed him on the final ballot, he, not Banks, would have won the plurality decision. See Albert Gallatin Brown to John F. H. Claiborne, February 4, 1856, Claiborne MSS.

19. John H. Houston to Nathaniel P. Banks, September 3, 1855, Banks MSS (LC); G. C. to N. P. Banks, November 21, 1855, Banks MSS (Duke); Solomon G. Haven to Millard Fillmore, December 13, 1855, January 20, 1856, MFP-O; Thomas L. Harris to Lanphier and Walker, February 6, 1856, Lanphier MSS; Gamaliel Bailey to Salmon P. Chase, February 21, 1856, Chase MSS (LC).

20. New York's Fillmorites also worried that the wealthy Law, who had already purchased the Albany *State Register* to turn it against Fillmore and had bribed many New York delegates to the American convention, would lavish enough "cigars Brandy & money" on other delegates at Philadelphia to buy the nomination. Fillmore's lieutenants badly needed additional time to organize delegates against Law's juggernaut.

For the desire of Know Nothings from Delaware, the District of Columbia, Maryland, and Kentucky to postpone the convention to avert the "same devil of [sectional] discord" that had plagued the 1855 Know Nothing convention, see John P. Kennedy to Nathan Sargent, July 19, 1855 (above quotation), Kennedy to Solomon G. Haven, January 29, 1856, Kennedy to Rolfe S. Saunders, February 2, 1856, Kennedy MSS; Thomas L. Harris to Lanphier and Walker, February 6, 1856 (reporting on fears of Kentucky Know Nothing Congressman Humphrey Marshall), Lanphier MSS; Vesparian Ellis to Daniel Ullmann, November 14, 1855, Ullmann MSS; Robert P. Letcher to John J. Crittenden, December 13, 1855 ("fatal"), Crittenden MSS (LC); George Pepper Norris to John M. Clayton, February 23, 1856, Clayton MSS.

For New Yorkers' concerns, see L. S. Parsons to Daniel Ullmann, November 17, 1855 ("cigars Brandy & money"), Stephen Sammons to Ullmann, November 26, 1855, James R. Thompson to Ullmann, January 26, 1856, Ullmann MSS; Solomon G. Haven to Millard Fillmore, December 6, 1855, January 20, 1856, Nathan K. Hall to Fillmore, February 4, 7, 1856, MFP-O.

21. Vesparian Ellis to Daniel Ullmann, February 17, 1856, Ullmann MSS; Solomon G. Haven to Millard Fillmore, February 29 (quotation), March 2, 1856, MFP-O.

22. For the Philadelphia meeting of the American national council and nominating convention, I have relied on the reports in the *New York Times*, February 20–26, 1856. Long excerpts from those accounts are reprinted in the appendix to my "The Antimasonic and Know Nothing Parties," pp. 709–32.

23. Ibid., p. 717; John P. Kennedy to Millard Fillmore, March 18, 1856, copy, Kennedy MSS.

24. Fillmore won on the second official ballot with 179 of 241 votes cast, but the *New York Times* provides no sectional breakdown of the vote. On an unofficial straw ballot, when many delegates abstained, however, Fillmore led various competitors by only seventy-one to seventy. And on the first official ballot, from which Maine, Connecticut, New Hampshire, and Iowa delegates totally abstained, as did majorities from Indiana and Illinois, Fillmore got only forty-eight northern votes, compared to seventy-two from the South, while sixty-six Northerners voted for Law, John McLean, Kentucky's Garrett Davis, North Carolina's Kenneth Rayner, New Jersey's Robert Stockton, or Texas' Sam Houston. On that ballot, in fact, Fillmore received no votes at all from nine of sixteen free states.

25. *New York Times*, February 26, 1856; Gienapp, *Origins*, pp. 259–63.

26. Ibid.; John Paul to Salmon P. Chase, February 24, 1856, Chase MSS (HSP); R. W. Corwine to William Schouler, February 24, 28, 1856, Schouler MSS; Thomas J. Marsh to Nathaniel P. Banks, March 19, 1856 (quotation), Isaac Sherman to Banks, April 4, 1856, Banks MSS (LC); Andrew Tracy to Justin Morrill, March 16, 1856, Morrill MSS.

27. Solomon G. Haven to Millard Fillmore, March 2, 1856, MFP-O; John P. Kennedy to Fillmore, March 18, 1856, copy, Kennedy MSS; Daniel D. Barnard to Hamilton Fish, February 29, 1856, Fish MSS.

28. *New York Times*, February 26, 1856; Solomon G. Haven to Millard Fillmore, March 2, 28, April 24, May 11, 1856, N. K. Hall to Fillmore, March 23, 1856, John P. Kennedy to Fillmore, March 18, 28, 1856, Henry E. Davies to Fillmore, March 31, 1856, MFP-O; Robert M. Bird to John M. Clayton, March 2, 1856, Clayton MSS; Haven to Daniel Ullmann, May 11, 1856, Ullmann MSS; William G. Brownlow to Andrew Jackson Donelson, May 24, 1856, Donelson MSS.

29. John P. Kennedy to Joseph F. Randolph, December 1, 1855 (quotation), Kennedy to James A. Hamilton, December 31, 1855, copies, Kennedy MSS.

30. John P. Kennedy to Millard Fillmore, March 18, 1856, copy, Kennedy MSS; Solomon G. Haven to Fillmore, March 28, 1856, Henry E. Davies to Fillmore, March 31, 1856, MFP-O.

31. On these two developments and their impact on northern public opinion, see Gienapp, *Origins*, pp. 297–303; id., "Crime Against Sumner"; and Holt, *Political Crisis*, pp. 192–96.

32. Everett to Fillmore, July 9, 1856, MFP-O; T. M. Monroe to Daniel Ullmann, June 13, 1856, Ullmann MSS; E. P. Walton to Justin Morrill, May 28, 1856, Morrill MSS.

33. The rigging of the North American nomination is analyzed in the books by Gienapp, Anbinder, and Holt cited above, and it can be followed in numerous letters in the Nathaniel P. Banks Papers at the Library of Congress and the Illinois State Historical Library. On Frémont's ultimate nomination by the North Americans, for example, see S. M. Allen to Banks, June 21, 1856, Banks MSS. Not all North Americans could be hoodwinked into supporting Frémont after Banks declined. A few delegates, primarily from New Jersey, defiantly nominated a ticket of Robert Stockton for president and North Carolina's Kenneth Rayner for vice president.

There was also a divisive controversy, lasting until late August, about Frémont's running mate. Along with Banks, the North Americans had originally nominated Pennsylvania's ex-Governor William F. Johnston for vice president, and they expected the Republicans to run Johnston with Frémont. But the Republicans refused and instead nominated William L. Dayton of New Jersey. Only a direct promise from Frémont himself to North American delegates in New York that Dayton would withdraw in favor of Johnston finally persuaded them to endorse Frémont, but Dayton indignantly refused. Some North American state councils, especially in Connecticut and Massachusetts, but, interestingly, not Pennsylvania, therefore insisted on running Frémont-Johnston, not Frémont-Dayton electoral tickets. Johnston was finally induced to withdraw on August 29, apparently by the promise of a cabinet post in Frémont's cabinet and a cash payoff. Gienapp, *Origins*, pp. 343–46, 382–86, traces the flap over the vice presidency with his customary expertise, but it can also be followed in letters to Edwin D. Morgan, chairman of the Republicans' national campaign committee, in the Morgan MSS.

34. Fillmore's letter was addressed to Virginia's Alexander H. H. Stuart, chairman of the American committee that officially notified him of the nomination, and it can be found in the Stuart MSS (University of Virginia). For evidence of its circulation at the North American convention, see Horace H. Day to Nathaniel P. Banks, June 13, 1856, Banks MSS (LC).

35. I provide more detail on these efforts, as well as supporting documentation, in "Another Look at the Election of 1856."

36. William L. Hodge to Millard Fillmore, June 21, 1856 (quotations), MFP-O; Washington *National Intelligencer*, editorial and report of Augusta County, Virginia, Whig meeting, April 7, 1856. "Though shorn of our former strength," vowed the Virginians, "we believe the old line Whigs hold the balance of power in the State, if not the Union, and that we can control the result of the next Presidential election in Virginia."

37. R. W. Corwine to William Schouler, February 28, 1856, Schouler MSS; David T. Disney to Stephen A. Douglas, February 26, 28, 1856, Douglas MSS.

38. Alexander H. H. Stuart to John P. Kennedy, March 16, 1856, Kennedy MSS; George E. Badger to Jeremiah Clemens, July 30, 1856, copy, Badger MSS (SHC, UNC); Richard K. Call to Andrew Jackson Donelson, April 23, 1856, Donelson MSS.

39. James A. Hamilton to Hamilton Fish, March 7, 1856; Daniel D. Barnard to Fish, February 29, April 28 (quotation), 1856, and Washington Hunt to Fish, April 2, 1856, Fish MSS; excerpt from New York *Commercial Advertiser*, quoted in Washington *National Intelligencer*, April 7, 1856.

40. Vesparian Ellis to Daniel Ullmann, March 2, 1856, Ullmann MSS. Anti-Know Nothing Whig Robert C. Winthrop also advised against early Whig endorsements for fear of alienating Democratic Know Nothings. See Winthrop to Hamilton Fish, March 13, 26, 1856, Fish MSS.

41. Edward Everett to William Trescot, January 20, 1856, copy, Everett MSS; A. B. Ely to Millard Fillmore, August 28, September 20 (quotation), 1856, MFP-O; Robert C. Winthrop to Hamilton Fish, March 28, 1856, Fish MSS.

42. John T. Henry to David Davis, March 7, 1856, David Davis MSS; Alexander H. H. Stuart to J. P. Kennedy, March 16, 1856, Kennedy MSS; R. A. West to Hamilton Fish, March 22, 1856 (quotation), Fish MSS; Badger to Jeremiah Clemens, July 30, 1856, Badger MSS.

43. C. G. Baylor to William L. Marcy, March 28, 1856, Marcy MSS (LC); Charles M. Conrad to Fillmore, April 11, 1856, MFP-O; George S. Bryan to J. P. Kennedy, April 4, May 26, 1856, Kennedy MSS; George Badger to John J. Crittenden, August 9, 1856, Crittenden MSS (LC).

44. James E. Harvey to William L. Marcy, March 9, 1856, Marcy MSS (LC); Edward P. Kelly to Nathaniel P. Banks, March 21, 1856, Banks MSS (LC); William D. Lewis to John M. Clayton, July 28, 1856, Clayton MSS.

45. Edwin D. Morgan to Myron H. Clark, April 3, 1856 (quotation), Morgan to John Bigelow, June 2, 1856 (first quotation), copies, Morgan MSS; ? Wales to Nathan P. Banks, July 26, 1856 (quotation), Banks MSS (LC); George T. Curtis to John J. Crittenden, July 10, 1856, Crittenden MSS (LC); D. Worth to George W. Julian, May 13, 1856 (quotation about Indiana), Giddings-Julian MSS.

46. John Law to William L. Marcy, October 10, 1855, Marcy MSS (LC); Thomas Hendricks to Allen Hamilton, March 31, 1856, Hamilton MSS; Rufus Brown to James Buchanan, February 18, 1856, Reverdy Johnson to Buchanan, July 8, 17, 1856, Richard Grayson to Buchanan, August 1, 1856, Buchanan MSS (HSP); George Badger to Jeremiah Clemens, July 30, 1856, copy, Badger MSS; Nevins, *Ordeal: House*, p. 492. Literally scores of additional letters could be cited to document Whig defection to the Democrats. Henry Clay's other living son, Thomas, unlike his brother, James, supported Fillmore and the Americans.

47. John C. Breckinridge to Daniel M. Barringer, October 8, 1856, Barringer MSS; William G. Brownlow to Millard Fillmore, October 6, 1856, MFP-O; George S. Bryan to John P. Kennedy, October 23, 1856, Kennedy MSS.

48. Richard W. Thompson to T. N. Parmalee, September 10, 1856, Thompson MSS (IU); J. O. Jones to Henry S. Lane, June 25, 1856 (quotation), Henry S. Lane MSS.

49. Charles Levi Woodbury to James Buchanan, July 10, 1856, Buchanan MSS (HSP), referring to an address from a Boston meeting of the Massachusetts Whig state committee. The reports from the South come from a meeting of Whigs in Washington, the Norfolk, Virginia, *Herald*, and the Fayetteville, North Carolina, *Observer*, all quoted in the Washington *National Intelligencer*, June 24, 1856. The *Intelligencer* contains the fullest record of these meetings and editorials, and I have relied on its issues for March 8, 27, April 7, May 25, and June 21, 23, 24, 26, 1856, for reports of them and the quotations I use below.

50. All taken from the issues of the *National Intelligencer* cited above, these quotations come, respectively, from a June editorial of the Richmond *Whig*, the Augusta County, Virginia, Whig meeting in April; James Jones' speech to the Washington, D.C., Whig meeting on June 21; the resolutions of that meeting; undated April and June editorials from the New York *Commercial Advertiser*; and an undated excerpt from the Baltimore *Patriot* in June. At least three of these sources explicitly used the phrase "balance of power" to refer to the Whigs' potential role in 1856.

51. Resolutions of Augusta County, Virginia, Whig meeting and editorial of the New York *Commercial Advertiser*, quoted in the Washington *National Intelligencer*, April 7, June 24, 1856.

52. Baltimore *Patriot*, quoted in the *National Intelligencer*, June 24, 1856.

53. H. E. Dummer to Richard Yates, July 9, 1856, Yates MSS; William L. Hodge to Fillmore, June 21, 1856, MFP-O; *National Intelligencer*, June 23, 24, 1856. Dummer, Hodge, and an editorial of the *National Intelligencer* cited July 30 as the date. But the Whig meeting in Washington and the New York *Evening Mirror*, according to reports in that paper, specified July 4.

54. Solomon G. Haven to Alexander H. H. Stuart, June 29, 1856, Stuart MSS (UVa.). For other enthusiastic responses to Fillmore's speeches, see George Robertson to Fillmore, July 3, 1856, Haven to Fillmore, July 4, 1856, and Stuart to Fillmore, July 9, 1856, MFP-O.

55. Fillmore privately explained his preferred Kansas policy to Anna Ella Carroll while simultaneously arguing that he dare not let Southerners see his views. An attempt to reimpose the Missouri Compromise line, as northern Whig/Know Nothings insisted, he argued, would prolong the sectional crisis by infuriating Southerners, but immediate statehood for Kansas would end it. "I would therefore repeal its obnoxious [proslavery] laws, provide for a fair representation of the people in a new legislature, secure to the people free and safe ingress and egress to the territory, and protect them when there from all external violence or intrusion, until the population of the territory entitled them to be admitted as a state; then I would let them, that is, the *resident citizens*, form their own constitution, with or without slavery, and admit them into the Union and thus put an end to this unfortunate controversy." Ostensibly neutral, this policy would almost surely have produced a free state. That is why Fillmore feared letting Southerners

see it. But it was so eminently sensible and fair that his refusal to publish it was one of Fillmore's two biggest mistakes in the campaign. The other was the speeches in New York and Newburgh to be described below. See Fillmore to Anna Ella Carroll, September 8, 1856, microfilm edition of Fillmore Papers (original in Anna Ella Carroll MSS, Maryland Historical Society).

56. For Fillmore's Albany address, see *National Intelligencer*, July 1, 1856. For his speech at Rochester on June 27, see Severance, "Millard Fillmore Papers, Volume 2," pp. 23–26.

57. Washington *National Intelligencer*, June 27, 1856. I have quoted the newspaper version. The later printed edition of the speech worded the matter differently but was no less emphatic about the final death of the Whig party. In it, Fillmore called Clay's defeat in 1844 "the wound inflicted that began the destruction of the Whig party. There was the canker worm that gnawed it to the heart, and subsequently carried it to the grave. These are painful reminiscences all— and let them pass." See Severance, "Millard Fillmore Papers, Volume 2," pp. 9–10.

58. Washington *National Intelligencer*, July 1, 1856.

59. The platform is enclosed with Wyndham Robertson to Fillmore, July 23, 1856, MFP-O.

60. William C. Rives to Millard Fillmore, July 16, 1856, John S. Carlisle to Fillmore, July 18, 1856, Haven to Fillmore, July 18, 1856, MFP-O; Fillmore to Rives, July 23, 1856, Rives MSS.

61. See the letters from William A. Graham, John Kerr, George Robertson, E. C. Cabell, James M. Townshend, Joseph Randolph, George Lunt, and other old line Whigs to Fillmore during July in the MFP-O.

62. Daniel M. Barringer to W. A. Houck, August 6, 1856, Barringer MSS.

63. James McCallum to John Bell, June 1856, John Bell MSS; Henry A. Wise to Edward Everett, August 12, 17, 23, 1856, Everett MSS; William L. Hodge to Millard Fillmore, September 20, 1856 (quotation), MFP-O. Wise and Hodge suggested that the hope of winning printing contracts from the Democrat-controlled Senate also explained their refusal to endorse Fillmore.

64. Everett to Fillmore, July 16, 1856 (quotation), MFP-O; Baltimore *Patriot*, quoted in *National Intelligencer*, June 24, 1856; Thomas Ewing to Thomas Ewing, Jr., July 5, 1856, EFP.

65. Fillmore to Everett, July 9, 1856, Everett MSS; Everett to Fillmore, July 16, 1856, MFP-O; Fillmore to Robert C. Winthrop, August 29, 1856, Winthrop MSS. For the Everett and Winthrop endorsements of Fillmore, see Everett to William Trescot, September 12, 1856, and Winthrop to Everett, October 17, 1856, Everett MSS.

66. Haven to Fillmore, July 20, 1856, MFP-O.

67. A. B. Ely to Fillmore, September 6, 20, 1856, MFP-O.

68. Hamilton Fish to Thurlow Weed, November 22, 1855, Weed MSS (RU); Haven to Millard Fillmore, July 28 (quotation), August 19, 1856, Francis Granger to Fillmore, August 9, 11, 1856, C. D. Bingham to Fillmore, August 9, 1856, William L. Hodge to Fillmore, September 30, 1856, MFP-O; Fish to Edward Everett, September 15, 1856, Everett MSS; Daniel D. Barnard to Fish, September 23, 1856, Fish MSS.

69. Corwin to Fillmore, July 22, 1856, MFP-O.

70. Duncan C. Niven to Fillmore, August 13, 1856, Anna Ella Carroll to Fillmore, August 18, 23, September 6, 11, 23, 1856, Horace H. Day to Fillmore, September 10, 1856, Fillmore to William L. Hodge, September 27, 1856, Corwin to Fillmore, October 5, 1856, MFP-O; Fillmore to Anna Ella Carroll, September 8, 1856, Carroll MSS (microfilm edition of Fillmore MSS).

71. Literally scores of letters to Fillmore conveyed these warnings from the South. For New Jersey and Vermont, see Joseph Randolph to Fillmore, September 1, 1856, and Harry Bradley to Fillmore, July 7 (quotation), August 8, 1856, MFP-O. For the quotation about Gales and Seaton of the *Intelligencer* and Fish's announcement, see Henry A. Wise to Edward Everett, August 17, 1856, and Fish to Everett, September 15, 1856, Everett MSS.

72. I rely on the list of delegates printed in the Richmond *Whig*, September 20, 1856, and reproduced in the appendix of DeScherer, "The Whig National Convention of 1856." Many of these men corresponded with Fillmore in 1856.

73. See accounts, as well, in the Washington *National Intellgencer*, September 18–20, 1856.

74. New York *Herald*, September 18, 1856, quoted in DeScherer, "The Whig National Convention of 1856," p. 3.

75. William L. Hodge to Fillmore, September 20, 1856, William A. Bradley to Fillmore, September 26, 1856, MFP-O.

76. Hodge to Fillmore, September 20, 30, 1856; Levin to Fillmore, September 26, 1856, Fillmore to Hodge, September 27, 1856, MFP-O.

77. Fillmore to William A. Graham, August 9, 1856, microfilm edition of Fillmore MSS.

78. Nathan Sargent to Fillmore, November 7, 1856, MFP-O. I have used the estimates of southern voter movement in Alexander, "Voter Partisan Constancy," pp. 98–99.

79. On Kentucky, see Volz, "Party, State, and Nation," p. 262. Volz regresses the 1856 results against the larger Whig vote of 1848 rather than against Scott's vote in 1852. For Tennessee, see Bergeron, *Antebellum Politics in Tennessee*, p. 118. For North Carolina, I have relied on the correlation analysis in Kruman, *Parties and Politics*, p. 178; and the regression analysis in McFaden, "Sections, Slaveholders, and Safe Concessions," p. 23.

80. "Victorious Defeat" is the title of Gienapp's last chapter in his *Origins*.

81. Ibid., pp. 527–30.

82. William R. Wilson to Fillmore, October 14, 1856, Charles D. Dreschler to Fillmore, October 24, 27, 1856, Andrew Jackson Donelson to Fillmore, October 25, 1856, Andrew Stewart to Fillmore, October 25, 1856, Joseph F. Randolph to Fillmore, October 29, 1856, Benjamin G. Ferris to Fillmore, November 13, 1856, E. B. Bartlett to Fillmore, November 12, 1856, Fillmore to Kenneth Rayner, November 14, 1856 (quotation), and Rayner to Fillmore, November 27, 28, 1856, MFP-O. In his letter to Rayner, Fillmore called for strengthening the American organization. Replying to a letter Fillmore sent him dated November 6, E. B. Bartlett, national president of the American council, told Fillmore on November 12: "You are right in saying that the American party ought, at once, to be re-organized, and new Councils organized where none now exist."

Fillmore's friends hoped to throw the election into the House by depriving Buchanan of Pennsylvania and New Jersey since half of the electors in both states were expected to go for Fillmore. The required majority was at least 149 electoral votes. Had the 34 electoral votes from those two states been shifted from Buchanan and split evenly between Fillmore and Frémont, the totals would have been: Buchanan, 140; Frémont, 132; and Fillmore, 25. But, if all were thrown to Frémont, he would have had exactly 149. Fillmore may have realized that the pressure to do so would have been irresistible, but he had also been warned that 30,000 to 50,000 Americans in Pennsylvania would abstain or go Democratic if the deal was consummated.

83. For the movement of former Fillmore voters into the Republican column by 1860, see Gienapp, "Who Voted for Lincoln?" id., "Nativism and the Creation of a Republican Majority."

84. Gienapp, *Origins*; id., "Nativism and the Creation of a Republican Majority in the North"; Silbey, *Partisan Imperative*, pp. 127–65; and Holt, *Political Crisis*, pp. 175–81.

85. Harry Bradley to Fillmore, July 7, 1856, John Wheeler to Fillmore, October 24, 1856, MFP-O.

86. James Kendall to John Fox Potter, July 8, 1856, Potter MSS; W. B. Thrall to Benjamin Wade, August 5, 1856, Wade MSS; D. F. Williams to Simon Cameron, September 24, 1856, Cameron MSS.

87. Fillmore to Edward Everett, July 12, 1856, Everett MSS.

88. On this point, see especially Freehling, *Road to Disunion*.

89. My reference here is to Freehling's *Road to Disunion*.

90. The literature on southern secession is immense, but for Democratic leadership of the immediatists and Whig opposition to them, see Barney, *Secessionist Impulse*; McCrary et al., "Class and Party in the Secession Crisis"; and especially Crofts, *Reluctant Confederates*.

91. The best analysis of Seward and the Union party movement during the secession crisis is contained in Crofts, *Reluctant Confederates*, but see also my "Abraham Lincoln."

92. Crofts, *Reluctant Confederates*; Holt, "Abraham Lincoln"; Cox, *Politics, Principle, & Prejudice*; and Alexander, "Persistent Whiggery."

93. Perman, *Road to Redemption*.

94. For the reasons for and ramifications of the unique perseverance of North Carolina's Whig party and for Vance's wartime career, see Kruman, *Politics and Parties*.

95. Vance is quoted in Carter, *When the War Was Over*, p. 67.

Abbreviations Used in Notes

ADAH   Alabama Department of Archives and History
BFP   Baldwin Family Papers, Yale University
CFP   Cambell Family Papers, Duke University
CHS   Chicago Historical Society
Conn.HS   Connecticut Historical Society
"Correspondence of Calhoun," J. Franklin Jameson (ed.), "Correspondence of John C. Calhoun,"
            Annual Report of the American Historical Association for 1899, Volume II (Washing-
            ton, 1901).
"Correspondence of Toombs, Stephens, and Cobb," U. B. Phillips (ed.), "Correspondence of Rob-
            ert Toombs, Alexander H. Stephens, and Howell Cobb," *Annual Report of the Amer-
            ican Historical Association for 1911, Volume II* (Washington, 1913).
Duke   Perkins Library, Duke University
EFP   Ewing Family Papers, Library of Congress,
Hayes Diary, Charles R. Williams (ed.), *Diary and Letters of Rutherford Birchard Hayes, Nine-
            teenth President of the United States* (5 volumes; Columbus: Ohio State Archaeological
            and Historical Society, 1922), Volume I.
HSP   Historical Society of Pennsylvania
Ill.SHL   Illinois State Historical Library
Ind.HSL   Indiana Historical Society Library
Ind.SL   Indiana State Library
IU   Lilly Library, Indiana University
LC   Library of Congress
Mangum Papers, Henry T. Shanks (ed.), *The Papers of Willie Person Mangum* (5 volumes;
            Raleigh: North Carolina Department of Archives and History, 1950–56).
Messages and Papers of the Presidents, James D. Richardson (ed.), *Messages and Papers of the
            Presidents, 1789–1897* (10 volumes; Washington: Government Printing Office, 1897).
MFP-BHS   Millard Fillmore Papers, Buffalo and Erie County Historical Society
MFP-O   Millard Fillmore Papers, State University of New York at Oswego
NIHS   Northern Indiana Historical Society, South Bend
Norlands   Washburn Family Library, Norlands, Livermore, Maine
NYPL   New York Public Library, New York City
NYSL   New York State Library, Albany
OHS   Ohio Historical Society, Columbus
RU   Rush Rhees Library, Rochester University
Senate Executive Proceedings, U.S. Congress, *Journal of the Executive Proceedings of the Senate,
            Volume 8, 1848–1852*

SHC, UNC Southern Historical Collection, University of North Carolina

Works of Clay, Calvin Colton (ed.), *The Works of Henry Clay, Comprising His Life, Correspondence, and Speeches* (10 volumes; New York: G. P. Putnam's Sons, 1904).

WRHS   Western Reserve Historical Society

ZT:SWH   Holman Hamilton, *Zachary Taylor: Soldier in the White House,* (reprint edition; Hamden, Conn.: Archon Books, 1966).

Bibliography

Manuscript Collections

Adams Family Papers. Massachusetts Historical Society. Microfilm edition.
James Lusk Alcorn Papers. Mississippi Department of Archives and History.
William Allen Papers. Library of Congress.
Nathan Appleton Papers. Massachusetts Historical Society.
George E. Badger Papers. Southern Historical Collection. University of North Carolina.
George E. Badger Papers. Perkins Library. Duke University.
Baldwin Family Papers. Sterling Library. Yale University.
Nathaniel P. Banks Papers. Perkins Library. Duke University.
Nathaniel P. Banks Papers. Illinois State Historical Library.
Nathaniel P. Banks Papers. Library of Congress.
Daniel D. Barnard Papers. New York State Library.
Daniel M. Barringer Papers. Southern Historical Collection. University of North Carolina.
Battle Family Papers. Southern Historical Collection. University of North Carolina.
Bedinger-Dandridge Family Papers. Perkins Library. Duke University.
James Martin Bell Papers. Perkins Library. Duke University.
John Bell Papers. Library of Congress. Microfilm edition.
John M. Berrien Papers. Southern Historical Collection. University of North Carolina.
William Bigler Papers. Historical Society of Pennsylvania.
William H. Bissell Papers. Chicago Historical Society.
William H. Bissell Papers. Illinois State Historical Library.
Jeremiah Sullivan Black Papers. Library of Congress. Microfilm edition.
Blair Family Papers. Library of Congress.
Blair-Lee Papers. Princeton University.
Angus R. Blakey Papers. Perkins Library. Duke University.
Matthew P. Blue Papers. Alabama Department of Archives and History.
Alexander Boteler Scrapbooks. Perkins Library. Duke University.
Samuel Bowles II Papers. Sterling Library. Yale University.
John Bragg Papers. Southern Historical Collection. University of North Carolina.
Branch Family Papers. Southern Historical Collection. University of North Carolina.
George N. Briggs Papers. American Antiquarian Society.
Albert Gallatin Brown Papers. Mississippi Department of Archives and History.
Austin H. Brown Papers. Indiana State Library.
William P. Browne Papers. Alabama Department of Archives and History.
James Buchanan Papers. Historical Society of Pennsylvania.
James Buchanan Papers. Library of Congress. Microfilm edition.

Buchanan-McClellan Family Papers. Southern Historical Collection. University of North Carolina.

Edmund Burke Papers. Library of Congress.

Benjamin F. Butler Papers. Library of Congress.

Benjamin F. Butler Papers. New York State Library.

David F. Caldwell Papers. Southern Historical Collection. University of North Carolina.

John C. Calhoun Papers. Perkins Library. Duke University.

Samuel Calvin Papers. Perkins Library. Duke University.

Simon Cameron Papers. Dauphin County Historical Society. Microfilm edition.

Campbell Family Papers. Perkins Library. Duke University.

Lewis D. Campbell Papers. Ohio Historical Society.

Robert Caruthers Papers. Southern Historical Collection. University of North Carolina.

Zachariah Chandler Papers. Library of Congress.

Salmon P. Chase Papers. Historical Society of Pennsylvania.

Salmon P. Chase Papers. Library of Congress.

John F. H. Claiborne Papers. Mississippi Department of Archives and History.

Myron H. Clark Papers. New York State Library.

Clement C. Clay Family Papers. Perkins Library. Duke University.

Henry Clay Papers. Perkins Library. Duke University.

Henry Clay Papers. Library of Congress. Microfilm edition.

Henry Clay Papers. Lilly Library. Indiana University.

Thomas J. Clay Papers. Library of Congress. Microfilm edition.

Clingman-Puryear Papers. Southern Historical Collection. University of North Carolina.

Walter Coles Papers. Perkins Library. Duke University.

Schuyler Colfax Papers. Chicago Historical Society.

Schuyler Colfax Papers. Indiana State Library.

Schuyler Colfax Papers. Lilly Library. Indiana University.

Schuyler Colfax Papers. Northern Indiana Historical Society.

Thomas Corwin Papers. Library of Congress.

Thomas Corwin Papers. Ohio Historical Society.

John J. Crittenden Papers. Perkins Library. Duke University.

John J. Crittenden Papers. Library of Congress. Microfilm edition.

William Cumback Papers. Lilly Library. Indiana University.

Caleb Cushing Papers. Library of Congress.

David Davis Papers. Chicago Historical Society.

John Davis Papers. American Antiquarian Society.

John G. Davis Papers. Indiana Historical Society Library.

Moses M. Davis Papers. State Historical Society of Wisconsin.

Henry L. Dawes Papers. Library of Congress.

Andre De Coppet Collection. Princeton University.

Andrew Jackson Donelson Papers. Library of Congress.

James R. Doolittle Papers. New York Public Library.

James R. Doolittle Papers. State Historical Society of Wisconsin.

James D. Doty Papers. State Historical Society of Wisconsin.

Stephen A. Douglas Papers. University of Chicago Library.

George Dunn Papers. Lilly Library. Indiana University.

William H. English Papers. Indiana Historical Society Library.

Edward Everett Papers. Massachusetts Historical Society. Microfilm edition.

Ewing Family Papers. Library of Congress.

Thomas Ewing Papers. Ohio Historical Society.

Erastus Fairbanks Papers. Alabama Department of Archives and History.

Fairchild Collection of Horatio Seymour Manuscripts. New York Historical Society.

John Fairfield Papers. Library of Congress.

William Pitt Fessenden Papers. Library of Congress.

William Pitt Fessenden Papers. Western Reserve Historical Society.

Millard Fillmore Papers. Buffalo and Erie County Historical Society. Microfilm edition.
Millard Fillmore Papers. Library of Congress.
Millard Fillmore Papers. State University of New York at Oswego. Microfilm edition.
Hamilton Fish Papers. Library of Congress.
M. B. Fleming Papers. Perkins Library. Duke University.
Charles Fontaine Papers. Mississippi Department of Archives and History.
Seabury Ford Papers. Ohio Historical Society.
J. Alexander Fulton Papers. Pennsylvania Department of Archives and Manuscripts.
Samuel Galloway Papers. Ohio Historical Society.
Joshua R. Giddings Papers. Ohio Historical Society. Microfilm edition.
Giddings-Julian Papers. Library of Congress.
Joseph Gillespie Papers. Illinois State Historical Library.
Governors' Records. Alabama Department of Archives and History.
Governors' Records. Mississippi Department of Archives and History.
William A. Graham Papers. Southern Historical Collection. University of North Carolina.
Francis Granger Papers. Library of Congress.
Horace Greeley Papers. New York Public Library.
Greeley-Colfax Papers. New York Public Library.
Bolling Hall Papers. Alabama Department of Archives and History.
Allen Hamilton Papers. Indiana State Library.
Joseph R. Hawley Papers. Library of Congress.
Gustavus A. Henry Papers. Southern Historical Collection. University of North Carolina.
Henry W. Hilliard Papers. Alabama Department of Archives and History.
George S. Houston Papers. Perkins Library. Duke University.
Mark Howard Papers. Connecticut Historical Society.
Timothy O. Howe Papers. State Historical Society of Wisconsin.
Jefferson Franklin Jackson Papers. Alabama Department of Archives and History.
Spencer Jarnagin Papers. Southern Historical Collection. University of North Carolina.
Thomas A. Jenckes Papers. Library of Congress.
Herschel V. Johnson Papers. Perkins Library. Duke University.
George W. Jones Papers. Southern Historical Collection. University of North Carolina.
George W. Julian Papers. Indiana State Library.
John Pendleton Kennedy Papers. Enoch Pratt Free Library. Baltimore. Microfilm edition.
Thomas Butler King Papers. Southern Historical Collection. University of North Carolina.
Knollenberg Collection. Sterling Library. Yale University.
Henry S. Lane Papers. Indiana Historical Society Library.
Henry S. Lane Papers. Lilly Library. Indiana University.
Joseph Lane Papers. Lilly Library. Indiana University.
Charles H. Lanphier Papers. Illinois State Historical Library.
Abbott Lawrence Papers. Houghton Library. Harvard University.
Amos A. Lawrence Papers. Massachusetts Historical Society.
Abraham Lincoln Papers. Lilly Library. Indiana University.
Willie P. Mangum Papers. Perkins Library. Duke University.
Willie P. Mangum Papers. Library of Congress.
Willie P. Mangum Papers. Southern Historical Collection. University of North Carolina.
William L. Marcy Papers. Library of Congress.
William L. Marcy Papers. New York State Library.
James McDowell Papers. Southern Historical Collection. University of North Carolina.
Duncan McLaurin Papers. Perkins Library. Duke University.
John McLean Papers. Library of Congress.
John McLean Papers. Ohio Historical Society.
Edward McPherson Papers. Library of Congress.
Samuel Medary Papers. Ohio Historical Society.
William M. Meredith Papers. Historical Society of Pennsylvania.
Edwin D. Morgan Papers. New York State Library.

Justin Smith Morrill Papers. Library of Congress.
Murdock-Wright Family Papers. Southern Historical Collection. University of North Carolina.
Nathaniel Niles Papers. Perkins Library. Duke University.
Godlove S. Orth Papers. Indiana State Library.
David Outlaw Papers. Southern Historical Collection. University of North Carolina.
Robert T. Paine Papers. Southern Historical Collection. University of North Carolina.
Samuel F. Patterson Papers. Perkins Library. Duke University.
Franklin Pierce Papers. Library of Congress. Microfilm edition.
James S. Pike Papers. University of Maine. Microfiche edition.
Polk-Yeatman Papers. Southern Historical Collection. University of North Carolina.
John Fox Potter Papers. State Historical Society of Wisconsin.
William Ballard Preston Papers. Virginia Historical Society.
John A. Quitman Papers. Mississippi Department of Archives and History.
Henry J. Raymond Papers. New York Public Library.
Albert G. Riddle Papers. Western Reserve Historical Society.
William C. Rives Papers. Library of Congress.
William Rockhill Papers. Indiana Historical Society Library.
John O. Sargent Papers. Massachusetts Historical Society.
William Schouler Papers. Massachusetts Historical Society.
Langhorne Scruggs Papers. Perkins Library. Duke University.
Thomas Settle Papers. Southern Historical Collection. University of North Carolina.
William H. Seward Papers. Library of Congress.
William H. Seward Papers. Rush Rhees Library. Rochester University. Microfilm edition.
Horatio Seymour Papers. New York State Library.
Thomas H. Seymour Papers. Connecticut Historical Society.
Caleb B. Smith Papers. Library of Congress.
Alexander H. Stephens Papers. Perkins Library. Duke University.
Alexander H. Stephens Papers. Library of Congress. Microfilm edition.
Thaddeus Stevens Papers. Library of Congress.
Stevenson Family Papers. Library of Congress.
Thomas B. Stevenson Papers. William Henry Smith Collection. Indiana Historical Society Library.
Alexander H. H. Stuart Papers. Library of Congress.
Alexander H. H. Stuart Papers. Alderman Library. University of Virginia.
Milton Sutliffe Papers. Western Reserve Historical Society.
Lyndon Swaim Papers. Perkins Library. Duke University.
Nathaniel P. Tallmadge Papers. State Historical Society of Wisconsin.
Zachary Taylor Papers. Library of Congress. Microfilm edition.
Richard W. Thompson Papers. Indiana State Library.
Richard W. Thompson Papers. Lilly Library. Indiana University.
Richard W. Thompson Papers. Lincoln National Life Foundation. Ft. Wayne.
Waddy Thompson Papers. South Carolinian Library. University of South Carolina.
Samuel J. Tilden Papers. New York Public Library.
Jesse Turner Papers. Perkins Library. Duke University.
Lyman Trumbull Family Papers. Illinois State Historical Library.
Daniel Ullmann Papers. New York Historical Society.
Benjamin F. Wade Papers. Library of Congress. Microfilm edition.
Algernon Sydney Washburn Papers. Perkins Library. Duke University.
Israel Washburn, Jr. Papers. Library of Congress.
Israel Washburn, Jr. Papers. Washburn Family Library. Norlands. Livermore, Maine.
Elihu B. Washburne Papers. Library of Congress.
Elihu B. Washburne Papers. Washburn Family Library. Norlands. Livermore, Maine.
James Watson Webb Papers. Sterling Library. Yale University.
Daniel Webster Papers. Dartmouth College. Microfilm edition.
Thurlow Weed Papers. Library of Congress.

Thurlow Weed Papers. Rush Rhees Library. Rochester University.

Gideon Welles Papers. Connecticut Historical Society.

Gideon Welles Papers. Library of Congress.

Gideon Welles Papers. New York Public Library.

Henry Wilson Papers. Library of Congress.

John Wilson Papers. Bancroft Library. University of California at Berkeley.

Robert C. Winthrop Papers. Massachusetts Historical Society. Microfilm edition.

Joseph A. Wright Papers. Indiana State Library.

Richard Yates Papers. Illinois State Historical Library.

Government Documents

U.S. Bureau of the Census. *Historical Statistics of the United States: Colonial Times to 1970.* Washington, D.C.: Government Printing Office, 1975.

U.S. Congress. *Congressional Globe.* 27th–33rd Congress.

U.S. Congress. *House Executive Documents.* 31st Congress, 1st Session, Volume 2. Documents 4 and 82.

U.S. Congress. *House Journal.* 31st Congress, 1st Session.

U.S. Congress. *House Miscellaneous Documents.* 30th Congress, 2nd Session, Document 6.

U.S. Congress. *Journal of the Executive Proceedings of the Senate, Volume 8, 1848–1852.*

U.S. Congress. *Senate Committee Reports.* 31st Congress, 1st Session. Report 123.

U.S. Congress. *Senate Documents.* 28th Congress, 2nd Session, Volume II. Documents 59 and 173.

U.S. Congress. *Senate Journal.* 31st Congress, 1st Session.

U.S. *Statutes at Large.* Volumes 5 and 9.

Newspapers and Contemporary Periodicals

Albany Evening Journal

American (Whig) Review

Boston *Daily Advertiser*

Harrisburg *Telegraph*

Nashville *Republican Banner*

New Orleans *Bee*

New York *Herald*

New York Times

New York Tribune

Niles Register

Philadelphia *North American and United States Gazette*

Philadelphia *Public Ledger*

Pittsburgh *Commercial Journal*

Pittsburgh *Daily Gazette*

Pittsburgh *Morning Post*

Raleigh *Register*

Richmond *Enquirer*

Richmond *Whig*

Tribune Almanac

Washington *National Intelligencer*

Washington *Union*

Published Correspondence, Diaries, Memoirs, and Public Papers

Basler, Roy P., ed. *The Collected Works of Abraham Lincoln.* 9 volumes. New Brunswick: Rutgers University Press, 1953–55.

Coleman, Mrs. Chapman. *The Life of John J. Crittenden.* 2 volumes. Philadelphia: J. B. Lippincott & Co., 1871.

Colton, Calvin, ed. *The Works of Henry Clay, Comprising His Life, Correspondence, and Speeches.* 10 volumes. New York: G. P. Putnam's Sons, 1904.

Dyer, Oliver. *Great Senators of the United States Forty Years Ago.* New York, 1889.

Flippin, Percy Scott, ed. "Herchel V. Johnson Correspondence," *North Carolina Historical Review,* 4 (January 1927), 182–201.

Graf, Leroy P., and Ralph W. Haskins, eds. *The Papers of Andrew Johnson, Volume 2, 1852–57.* Knoxville: University of Tennessee Press, 1970.

Hamilton, J. G. de Roulhac, and Max R. Williams, eds. *The Papers of William Alexander Graham.* 6 volumes to date. Raleigh: State Department of Archives and History, 1957–.

Hamlin, L. Belle, ed. "Selections from the Letters of Oran Follett," *Quarterly Publications of the Historical and Philosophical Society of Ohio,* Vol. 9 (1914), 71–100; Vol. 10 (1915), 4–33; Vol. 11 (1916), 5–35; and Vol. 13 (1918), 42–78.

Hamlin, L. Belle, ed. "Selections from the William Greene Papers," *Quarterly Publications of the Historical and Philosophical Society of Ohio,* 13 (1918), 4–38.

Jameson, J. Franklin, ed. "Correspondence of John C. Calhoun," *Annual Report of the American Historical Association for 1899, Volume II.* Washington, D.C.: Government Printing Office, 1900.

McClure, Alexander K. *Recollections of Half a Century.* Salem: The Salem Press Company, 1902.

McCormack, Thomas J. *Memoirs of Gustave Koerner, 1809–1896.* Two volumes. Cedar Rapids: The Torch Press, 1909.

McIntosh, James T., et al., eds. *The Papers of Jefferson Davis: Volume 3, July 1846–December 1848.* Baton Rouge: Louisiana State University Press, 1981.

Nevins, Allan, and Milton H. Thomas, eds. *The Diary of George Templeton Strong.* 4 volumes. New York: The Macmillan Company, 1952.

Parks, Joseph H., ed. "Letters from Aaron V. Brown to Alfred O. P. Nicholson, 1844–1850," *Tennessee Historical Quarterly,* 3 (1944), 170–79.

Pease, Theodore Calvin, and Randall, James G., eds. *The Diary of Orville Hickman Browning; Volume I, 1850–1864.* Collections of the Illinois State Historical Library. Volume 20. 1925.

Phillips, Ulrich Bonnell, ed. "The Correspondence of Robert Toombs, Alexander H. Stephens, and Howell Cobb," *Annual Report of the American Historical Association for 1911, Volume II.* Washington: Government Printing Office, 1913.

Richardson, James D., ed. *A Compilation of the Messages and Papers of the Presidents, 1789–1897.* 10 volumes. Washington: Government Printing Office, 1896–99.

Samson, William H., ed. *Letters of Zachary Taylor from the Battlefields of the Mexican War.* Rochester, 1908.

Schauinger, J. Herman, ed. "The Letters of Godlove S. Orth: Hoosier Whig," *Indiana Magazine of History,* 39 (1943), 365–400; 40 (1944), 51–66.

Severance, Frank H., ed. "The Millard Fillmore Papers," *Publications of the Buffalo and Erie County Historical Society,* 10–11, (1907).

Seward, Frederick W., *Seward at Washington as Senator and Secretary of State,* Volume II. New York: Derby and Miller, 1891.

Shanks, Henry T., ed. *The Papers of Willie Person Mangum.* 6 volumes. Raleigh: North Carolina State Department of Archives and History, 1950–56.

Tyler, Lyon G. *The Letters and Times of the Tylers.* 2 volumes. Richmond: Whitter & Shepperson, 1884.

Williams, Charles R., ed. *Diary and Letters of Rutherford Birchard Hayes, Nineteenth President of the United States,* Volume I. Columbus: The Ohio Archaeological and History Society, 1922.

Books and Articles

Adams, William H. *The Whig Party of Louisiana.* Lafayette: University of Southwestern Louisiana, 1973.

Alexander, Thomas B. "Persistent Whiggery in the Confederate South, 1860–1877." *Journal of Southern History,* 27 (1961), 305–29.

Alexander, Thomas B. *Sectional Stress and Party Strength: A Computer Analysis of Roll-Call*

Voting in the United States House of Representatives, 1836–1860. Nashville: Vanderbilt University Press, 1967.

Alexander, Thomas B. "Dimensions of Voter Partisan Constancy in Presidential Elections from 1840 to 1860." *Essays on American Antebellum Politics 1840–1860.* Ed. Stephen E. Maizlish and John J. Kushma. College Station: Texas A & M University Press, 1982.

Alexander, Thomas B. "Harbinger of the Collapse of the Second Two-Party System: The Free Soil Party in 1848." *A Crisis of Republicanism: American Politics during the Civil War Era.* Ed. Lloyd Ambrosius. Lincoln: University of Nebraska Press, 1990.

Anbinder, Tyler. *Nativism & Slavery: The Northern Know Nothings and the Politics of the 1850s.* New York: Oxford University Press, 1992.

Appleby, Joyce. "The Social Origins of American Revolutionary Ideology." *Journal of American History,* 64 (1978), 935–58.

Appleby, Joyce. *Capitalism and the New Social Order: The Republican Vision of the 1790s.* New York: New York University Press, 1984.

Appleby, Joyce. *Liberalism and Republicanism in the Historical Imagination.* Cambridge: Harvard University Press, 1992.

Argersinger, Peter H. "A Place on the Ballot: Fusion Politics and Antifusion Laws." *American Historical Review,* 85 (1980), 287–306.

Ayers, Edward L. *Vengeance and Justice: Crime and Punishment in the Nineteenth-Century American South.* New York: Oxford University Press, 1984.

Baack, Bennett D., and Edward J. Ray. "Tariff Policy and Income Distribution: The Case of the United States, 1830–1860." *Explorations in Economic History,* 11 (1973), 103–21.

Bailyn, Bernard. *The Ideological Origins of the American Revolution.* Cambridge: Harvard University Press, 1967.

Bain, Richard C., and Judith H. Parrish. *Convention Decisions and Voting Records.* Washington: The Brookings Institution, 1973.

Banning, Lance. *The Jeffersonian Persuasion: Evolution of a Party Ideology.* Ithaca: Cornell University Press, 1978.

Barnes, Gilbert Hobbs. *The Anti-Slavery Impulse, 1830–1844.* Reprint edition. New York: Harcourt, Brace, 1964.

Barney, William L. *The Secessionist Impulse: Alabama and Mississippi in 1860.* Princeton: Princeton University Press, 1974.

Barnwell, John. *Love of Order: South Carolina's First Secession Crisis.* Baton Rouge: Louisiana State University Press, 1982.

Bauer, K. Jack. *Zachary Taylor: Soldier, Planter, Statesman of the Old Southwest.* Baton Rouge: Louisiana State University Press, 1985.

Baum, Dale. *The Civil War Party System: The Case of Massachusetts, 1848–1876.* Chapel Hill: University of North Carolina Press, 1984.

Baum, Dale, and Dale T. Knobel. "Anatomy of a Realignment: New York Presidential Politics, 1848–1860." *New York History,* 65 (1984), 61–81.

Benson, Lee. *The Concept of Jacksonian Democracy: New York as a Test Case.* Princeton: Princeton University Press, 1961.

Benson, Lee. "The Mistransference Fallacy in Explanations of Human Behavior." *Historical Methods,* 17 (1984), 118–31.

Benson, Lee, Joel H. Silbey, and Phyllis Field. "Toward a Theory of Stability and Change in American Voting Patterns: New York State, 1792–1970." *The History of American Electoral Behavior.* Ed. Joel H. Silbey, Allan G. Bogue, and William H. Flanigan. Princeton: Princeton University Press, 1978.

Berger, Mark L. *The Revolution in the New York Party Systems, 1840–1860.* Port Washington, N.Y.: Kennikat Press, 1973.

Bergeron, Paul H. *Antebellum Politics in Tennessee.* Lexington: The University Press of Kentucky, 1982.

Billington, Ray Allen. *The Protestant Crusade 1800–1860: A Study of the Origins of American Nativism.* Chicago: Quadrangle Books, 1964.

Binkley, Wilfred E. *American Political Parties: Their National History*. New York: Alfred A. Knopf, 1942.

Birkner, Michael. *Samuel L. Southard: Jeffersonian Whig*. Rutherford, N.J.: Farleigh Dickinson University Press, 1984.

Bloom, Howard S., and Douglas Price. "Voter Response to Short-Run Economic Conditions: The Asymmetric Effect of Prosperity and Recession." *American Political Science Review*, 69 (1975), 1240–54.

Blue, Frederick J. "The Ohio Free Soilers and the Problems of Factionalism." *Ohio History*, 76 (1967), 17–32.

Blue, Frederick J. *The Free Soilers: Third Party Politics, 1848–1854*. Urbana: University of Illinois Press, 1973.

Bolchin, Hal W. "Caleb B. Smith's Opposition to the Mexican War." *Indiana Magazine of History*, 69 (1973), 95–114.

Booraem, Hendrik V. *The Formation of the Republican Party in New York: Politics and Conscience in the Antebellum North*. New York: New York University Press, 1983.

Boritt, Gabor. "Lincoln's Opposition to the Mexican War." *Journal of the Illinois State Historical Society*, 67 (1974), 79–100.

Boritt, Gabor. *Lincoln and the Economics of the American Dream*. Memphis: Memphis State University Press, 1977.

Bowers, Douglas. "Ideology and Political Parties in Maryland, 1851–1856." *Maryland Historical Magazine*, 64 (1969), 197–217.

Brand, Carl F. "The History of the Know Nothing Party in Indiana." *Indiana Magazine of History*, 18 (1922), 47–81.

Brauer, Kinley J. *Cotton versus Conscience: Massachusetts Whig Politics and Southwestern Expansion*. Lexington: University Press of Kentucky, 1967.

Brock, William R. *Parties and Political Conscience: American Dilemmas, 1840–1850*. Millwood, N.Y.: KTO Press, 1979.

Brown, Norman D. *Daniel Webster and the Politics of Availability*. Athens: University of Georgia Press, 1969.

Brown, Richard H. "The Missouri Crisis, Slavery, and the Politics of Jacksonianism." *South Atlantic Quarterly*, 65 (1966), 52–72.

Buel, Richard, Jr. *Securing the Revolution: Ideology in American Politics, 1789–1815*. Ithaca: Cornell University Press, 1972.

Burnham, Walter D. *Presidential Ballots 1836–1892*. Baltimore: The Johns Hopkins University Press, 1955.

Campbell, Stanley W. *The Slave Catchers: Enforcement of the Fugitive Slave Law, 1850–1860*. Chapel Hill: University of North Carolina Press, 1968.

Carman, Harry J., and Reinhard H. Luthin. "The Seward-Fillmore Feud and the Crisis of 1850." *New York History*, 24 (1943), 163–84.

Carman, Harry J., and Reinhard H. Luthin. "The Seward-Fillmore Feud and the Disruption of the Whig Party." *New York History*, 24 (1943), 335–57.

Carroll, E. Malcolm. *The Origins of the Whig Party*. Reprint edition. Gloucester: Peter Smith, 1964.

Carter, Dan T. *When the War Was Over: The Failure of Self-Reconstruction in the South, 1865–1867*. Baton Rouge: Louisiana State University Press, 1985.

Carwardine, Richard. "Evangelicals, Whigs, and the Election of William Henry Harrison." *Journal of American Studies*, 17 (1983), 47–75.

Carwardine, Richard. *Evangelicals and Politics in Antebellum America*. New Haven: Yale University Press, 1993.

Chaffin, Tom. *Fatal Glory: Narcisco López and the First Clandestine U.S. War against Cuba*. Charlottesville: University Press of Virginia, 1996.

Chambers, William N. "The Election of 1840." *History of American Presidential Elections*, Volume I. Ed. Arthur M. Schlesinger, Jr., and Fred Israel. New York: Chelsea House, 1971.

Chitwood, Oliver Perry. *John Tyler: Champion of the Old South*. New York: D. Appleton-Century Company, 1939.

Clubb, Jerome M., William H. Flanigan, and Nancy H. Zingale. *Partisan Realignment: Voters, Parties, and Government in American History*. Beverly Hills: Sage Publications, 1980.

Cohen, Henry. *Business and Politics in America from the Age of Jackson to the Civil War: The Career Biography of W. W. Corcoran*. Westport: Greenwood Press, 1971.

Cole, Arthur C. *The Whig Party in the South*. Reprint edition. Gloucester: Peter Smith, 1962.

Cole, Donald B. *Jacksonian Democracy in New Hampshire*. Cambridge: Harvard University Press, 1970.

Congressional Quarterly. *Guide to U.S. Elections*. Washington: Congressional Quarterly, Inc., 1975.

Cooper, William J., Jr. *The South and the Politics of Slavery, 1828–1856*. Baton Rouge: Louisiana State University Press, 1978.

Cooper, William J., Jr. " 'The Only Door': The Territorial Issue, the Preston Bill, and the Southern Whigs." *A Master's Due: Essays in Honor of David Herbert Donald*. Ed. Michael F. Holt, William J. Cooper, Jr., and John McCardell. Baton Rouge: Louisiana State University Press, 1985.

Cox, Lawanda, and John H. *Politics, Principle, & Prejudice, 1865–1866: Dilemma of Reconstruction America*. Glencoe: The Free Press, 1961.

Crofts, Daniel. *Reluctant Confederates: Upper South Unionists in the Secession Crisis*. Chapel Hill: University of North Carolina Press, 1989.

Current, Richard. *The History of Wisconsin: Volume II, The Civil War Era, 1848–1873*. Madison: State Historical Society of Wisconsin, 1976.

Curtis, James C. *The Fox at Bay: Martin Van Buren and the Presidency*. Lexington: University Press of Kentucky, 1970.

Dalzell, Robert F., Jr. *Daniel Webster and the Trial of American Nationalism, 1843–1852*. Boston: Houghton Mifflin Company, 1973.

Dalzell, Robert F., Jr. *Enterprising Elite: The Boston Associates and the World They Made*. Cambridge: Harvard University Press, 1987.

Danenbaum, Jed. *Drink and Disorder: Temperance Reform in Cincinnati from the Washingtonian Revival to the WCTU*. Urbana: University of Illinois Press, 1984.

Darling, Arthur B. *Political Changes in Massachusetts 1824–1848: A Study of Liberal Movements in Politics*. New Haven: Yale University Press, 1925.

Doherty, Herbert J., Jr. *The Whigs of Florida, 1845–1854*. Gainesville: University of Florida Press, 1959.

Donald, David. *Charles Sumner and the Coming of the Civil War*. New York: Alfred A. Knopf, 1960.

Donald, David. *Lincoln Reconsidered: Essays on the Civil War Era*. New York: Vintage Books, 1961.

Dykstra, Robert R. *Bright Radical Star: Black Freedom and White Supremacy on the Hawkeye Frontier*. Cambridge: Harvard University Press, 1993.

Eiselen, Malcolm Rogers. *The Rise of Pennsylvania Protectionism*. Philadelphia: University of Pennsylvania Press, 1932.

Elkins, Stanley, and Eric McKitrick. *The Age of Federalism: The Early American Republic, 1788–1800*. New York: Oxford University Press, 1993.

Elliot, Charles Winslow. *Winfield Scott: The Soldier and the Man*. New York: The Macmillan Company, 1937.

Ellis, David M. *Landlords and Farmers in the Hudson-Mohawk Region, 1780–1850*. Ithaca: Cornell University Press, 1946.

Ellis, Richard E. *The Jeffersonian Crisis: Courts and Politics in the Young Republic*. New York: W. W. Norton and Company, 1971.

Ellis, Richard E. *The Union at Risk: Jacksonian Democracy, States' Rights and the Nullification Crisis*. New York: Oxford University Press, 1987.

Erickson, Leonard. "Politics and the Repeal of Ohio's Black Laws, 1837–1849." *Ohio History*, 82 (1973), 154–75.

Ershkowitz, Herbert, and William G. Shade, "Consensus or Conflict? Political Behavior in the

State Legislatures during the Jacksonian Era." *Journal of American History*, 58 (1971), 591–622.

Evitts, William J. *A Matter of Allegiances: Maryland from 1850 to 1861*. Baltimore: The Johns Hopkins University Press, 1974.

Feldberg, Michael. *The Philadelphia Riots of 1844: A Study of Ethnic Conflict*. Westport: Greenwood Press, 1975.

Finkelman, Paul. *An Imperfect Union: Slavery, Federalism, and Comity*. Chapel Hill: University of North Carolina Press, 1981.

Fiorina, Morris P. *Retrospective Voting in American National Elections*. New Haven: Yale University Press, 1981.

Flinn, Thomas A. "Continuity and Change in Ohio Politics." *The Journal of Politics*, 24 (1962), 524–37.

Fogel, Robert W. *Without Consent or Contract: The Rise and Fall of American Slavery*. New York: W. W. Norton and Company, 1989.

Fogel, Robert W. "Modeling Complex Dynamic Interactions: The Role of Intergenerational, Cohort, and Period Processes and Conditional Events in the Political Realignment of the 1850s." *Working Paper Series on Historical Factors in Long Run Growth*. National Bureau of Economic Research. Working Paper No. 12. March 1990.

Folsom, Burton, II. "Party Formation and Development in Jacksonian America: The Old South." *Journal of American Studies*, 7 (1973), 217–29.

Folsom, Burton, II. "The Politics of Elites: Prominence and Party in Davidson County, Tennessee, 1835–1861." *Journal of Southern History*, 39 (1973), 359–78.

Foner, Eric. "The Wilmot Proviso Revisited." *Journal of American History*, 56 (1969), 262–79.

Foner, Eric. *Free Soil, Free Labor, Free Men: The Ideology of the Republican Party before the Civil War*. New York: Oxford University Press, 1970.

Foner, Eric. "Politics, Ideology, and the Origins of the American Civil War." *A Nation Divided: Problems and Issues of the Civil War and Reconstruction*. Ed. George Fredrickson. Minneapolis: Burgess Publishing Company, 1975.

Foner, Philip S. *Business & Slavery: The New York Merchants & The Irrepressible Conflict*. Chapel Hill: University of North Carolina Press, 1941.

Forgie, George. *Patricide in the House Divided: A Psychological Interpretation of Lincoln and His Age*. New York: W. W. Norton and Company, 1979.

Formisano, Ronald P. "Political Character, Antipartyism, and the Second Party System." *American Quarterly*, 21 (1969), 683–709.

Formisano, Ronald P. *The Birth of Mass Political Parties: Michigan, 1827–1861*. Princeton: Princeton University Press, 1971.

Formisano, Ronald P. "Deferential-Participant Politics: The Early Republic's Political Culture, 1789–1840." *American Political Science Review*, 68 (1974), 473–87.

Formisano, Ronald P. "Toward a Reorientation of Jacksonian Politics: A Review of the Literature, 1959–1975." *Journal of American History*, 63 (1976), 42–65.

Formisano, Ronald P. "Federalists and Republicans: Parties, Yes—System, No." *The Evolution of American Electoral Systems*. Ed. Paul Kleppner. Westport: Greenwood Press, 1981.

Formisano, Ronald P. *The Transformation of Political Culture: Massachusetts Parties, 1790s–1840s*. New York: Oxford University Press, 1983.

Formisano, Ronald P. "The New Political History and the Election of 1840." *Journal of Interdisciplinary History*, 23 (1993), 661–82.

Fox, Stephen C. "Politicians, Issues and Voter Preference in Jacksonian Ohio: A Critique of an Interpretation." *Ohio History*, 86 (1977), 155–70.

Fox, Stephen C. "The Bank Wars, the Idea of 'Party,' and the Division of the Electorate in Jacksonian Ohio." *Ohio History*, 88 (1979), 253–76.

Freehling, William W. *Prelude to Civil War: The Nullification Controversy in South Carolina, 1816–1836*. New York: Harper & Row, 1966.

Freehling, William W. *The Road to Disunion, Volume I, Secessionists at Bay, 1776–1854*. New York: Oxford University Press, 1990.

Friedman, Jean E. *The Revolt of the Conservative Democrats: An Essay on American Political Culture and Political Development, 1837–1844.* Ann Arbor: UMI Research Press, 1979.

Gatell, Frank Otto. " 'Conscience and Judgment': The Bolt of the Massachusetts Conscience Whigs." *The Historian,* 20 (1959), 18–49.

Gatell, Frank Otto. "Spoils of the Bank War: Political Bias in the Selection of Pet Banks." *American Historical Review,* 70 (1964), 35–58.

Gatell, Frank Otto. "Money and Party in Jacksonian America: A Quantitative Look at New York City's Men of Quality." *Political Science Quarterly,* 82 (1967), 235–52.

Gerrity, Frank. "The Disruption of the Philadelphia Whigocracy: Joseph R. Chandler, Anti-Catholicism, and the Congressional Election of 1854." *Pennsylvania Magazine of History and Biography,* 111 (1987), 161–94.

Gibson, George H. "Opinion in North Carolina Regarding the Annexation of Texas and Cuba, 1835–1855." *North Carolina Historical Review,* 37 (1960), 1–21.

Gienapp, William E. "The Crime Against Sumner: The Caning of Charles Sumner and the Rise of the Republican Party." *Civil War History,* 25 (1979), 218–45.

Gienapp, William E. " 'Politics Seems to Enter Into Everything:' Political Culture in the North, 1840–1860." *Essays on American Antebellum Politics 1840–1860.* Ed. Stephen E. Maizlish and John Kushma. College Station: Texas A & M University Press, 1982.

Gienapp, William E. "The Whig Party, The Compromise of 1850, and the Nomination of Winfield Scott." *Presidential Studies Quarterly,* 14 (1984), 399–415.

Gienapp, William E. "Nativism and the Creation of a Republican Majority in the North before the Civil War." *Journal of American History,* 72 (1985), 529–59.

Gienapp, William E. "Nebraska, Nativism, and Rum: The Failure of Fusion in Pennsylvania, 1854." *Pennsylvania Magazine of History and Biography,* 109 (1986), 425–71.

Gienapp, William E. "Who Voted for Lincoln?" *Abraham Lincoln and the American Political Tradition.* Ed. John L. Thomas. Amherst: University of Massachusetts Press, 1986.

Gienapp, William E. *The Origins of the Republican Party, 1852–1856.* New York: Oxford University Press, 1987.

Gilley, B. H. "Polk's War and the Louisiana Press." *Louisiana History,* 20 (1979), 5–23.

Gilley, B. H. "Tennessee Whigs and the Mexican War." *Tennessee Historical Quarterly,* 40 (1981), 46–67.

Goodman, Paul. *Toward a Christian Republic: Antimasonry and the Great Transition in New England, 1826–1836.* New York: Oxford University Press, 1988.

Goodrich, Carter G., ed. *Canals and American Economic Development.* New York: Columbia University Press, 1961.

Graebner, Norman A. "Thomas Corwin and the Election of 1848: A Study in Conservative Politics." *Journal of Southern History,* 17 (1951), 162–79.

Graebner, Norman A. "Party Politics and the Trist Mission." *Journal of Southern History,* 19 (1953), 137–56.

Gunderson, Robert Gray. *The Log-Cabin Campaign.* Lexington: University of Kentucky Press, 1957.

Hall, Kermit L. *The Politics of Justice: Lower Federal Judicial Selection and the Second Party System.* Lincoln: University of Nebraska Press, 1979.

Hamilton, Holman. *Prologue to Conflict: The Crisis and Compromise of 1850.* New York: W. W. Norton and Company, 1964.

Hamilton, Holman. *Zachary Taylor: Soldier in the White House.* Reprint edition. Hamden, Conn.: Archon Books, 1966.

Hamilton, Holman. *Zachary Taylor: Soldier of the Republic.* Reprint edition. Hamden, Conn.: Archon Books, 1966.

Handlin, Oscar. *Boston's Immigrants: A Study of Acculturation.* New York: Atheneum Press, 1968.

Hargreaves, Mary. *The Presidency of John Quincy Adams.* Lawrence: University of Kansas Press, 1985.

Harrington, Fred Harvey. "The First Northern Victory." *Journal of Southern History,* 5 (1939), 186–205.

Harris, William C. *William Woods Holden: Firebrand of North Carolina Politics*. Baton Rouge: Louisiana State University Press, 1987.

Hays, Samuel P. "Politics and Society: Beyond the Political Party." *The Evolution of American Electoral Systems*. Ed. Paul Kleppner. Westport: Greenwood Press, 1981.

Hibbing, John R., and Alford, John R. "The Electoral Impact of Economic Conditions: Who Is Held Responsible?" *American Journal of Political Science*, 25 (1981), 423–39.

Hofstadter, Richard. *The Idea of a Party System: The Rise of Legitimate Opposition in the United States, 1780–1840*. Berkeley: University of California Press, 1970.

Holt, Edgar A. "Party Politics in Ohio, 1840–1850." *Ohio Archaeological and Historical Publications*, 38 (1929), 47–402.

Holt, Michael F. *Forging a Majority: The Formation of the Republican Party in Pittsburgh, 1848–1860*. New Haven: Yale University Press, 1969.

Holt, Michael F. "The Antimasonic and Know Nothing Parties." *History of U.S. Political Parties*. Volume I. Ed. Arthur M. Schlesinger, Jr. New York: Chelsea House and R. W. Bowker, 1973.

Holt, Michael F. "The Democratic Party, 1828–1860." *History of U.S. Political Parties*. Volume I. Ed. Arthur M. Schlesinger, Jr. New York: Chelsea House and R. W. Bowker, 1973.

Holt, Michael F. "The Politics of Impatience: The Origins of Know Nothingism." *Journal of American History*, 60 (1973), 309–31.

Holt, Michael F. *The Political Crisis of the 1850s*. New York: John Wiley and Sons, 1978.

Holt, Michael F. "Winding Roads to Recovery: The Whig Party from 1844 to 1848." *Essays on American Antebellum Politics, 1840–1860*. Eds. Stephen E. Maizlish and John J. Kushma, College Station: Texas A & M University Press, 1982.

Holt, Michael F. "Abraham Lincoln and the Politics of Union." *Abraham Lincoln and the American Political Tradition*. Ed. John L. Thomas. Amherst: University of Massachusetts Press, 1986.

Holt, Michael F. *Political Parties and American Political Development from the Age of Jackson to the Age of Lincoln*. Baton Rouge: Louisiana State University Press, 1992.

Holt, Michael F. "Rethinking Nineteenth-Century American Political History." *Congress & the Presidency: A Journal of Capital Studies*, 19 (1992), 97–111.

Holt, Michael F. "Another Look at the Election of 1856." *James Buchanan and the Political Crisis of the 1850s*. Ed. Michael J. Birkner. Selingsgrove, Pa.: Susquehanna University Press, 1996.

Howe, Daniel W. *The Political Culture of the American Whigs*. Chicago: University of Chicago Press, 1979.

Howe, Daniel W. "Virtue and Commerce in Jeffersonian America." *Reviews in American History*, 9 (1981), 347–53.

Howe, Daniel W. "The Evangelical Movement and Political Culture in the North during the Second Party System." *Journal of American History*, 77 (1991), 1216–39.

Hummel, Jeffrey R. *Emancipating Slaves, Enslaving Free Men: A History of the American Civil War*. Chicago: Open Court Press, 1996.

Hunt, H. Draper. *Hannibal Hamlin of Maine: Lincoln's First Vice-President*. Syracuse: Syracuse University Press, 1969.

Innes, Stephen. *Creating the Commonwealth: The Economic Culture of Puritan New England*. New York: W. W. Norton and Company, 1995.

Inscoe, John C. "Thomas Clingman, Mountain Whiggery, and the Southern Cause." *Civil War History*, 33 (1987), 42–62.

Jeffrey, Thomas E. "Internal Improvements and Political Parties in Antebellum North Carolina, 1836–1860." *North Carolina Historical Review*, 55 (1978), 111–56.

Jeffrey, Thomas E. " 'Thunder from the Mountains': Thomas Lanier Clingman and the End of Whig Supremacy in North Carolina." *North Carolina Historical Review*, 56 (1979), 366–95.

Johannsen, Robert W. *Stephen A. Douglas*. New York: Oxford University Press, 1973.

Johannsen, Robert W. *To the Halls of the Montezumas: The Mexican War in the American Imagination*. New York: Oxford University Press, 1985.

Johnson, Donald B., ed. *National Party Platforms: Volume I, 1840–1956*. Revised edition. Urbana: University of Illinois Press, 1978.

Johnson, Paul E. *A Shopkeepers' Millennium: Society and Revivals in Rochester, New York, 1815–1837.* New York: Hill & Wang, 1978.

Kallenbach, Joseph E., and Kallenbach, Jessamine S., eds. *American State Governors 1776–1976: Volume I (Electoral and Personal Data).* Dobbs Ferry: Oceana Publications, Inc., 1977.

Kelley, Robert. *The Cultural Pattern in American History: The First Century.* New York: Oxford University Press, 1979.

Kernell, Samuel. "Presidential Popularity and Negative Voting: An Alternative Explanation of the Midterm Congressional Decline of the President's Party." *American Political Science Review,* 71 (1977), 44–66.

Kirwan, Albert D. *John J. Crittenden: The Struggle for the Union.* Lexington: University of Kentucky Press, 1962.

Kleppner, Paul. *The Third Electoral System, 1853–1892: Parties, Voters, and Political Cultures.* Chapel Hill: University of North Carolina Press, 1979.

Kraditor, Aileen. "The Liberty and Free Soil Parties." *History of U.S. Political Parties.* Vol. I. Ed. Arthur M. Schlesinger, Jr. New York: Chelsea House and R. W. Bowker, 1973.

Kruman, Marc W. *Parties and Politics in North Carolina, 1836–1865.* Baton Rouge: Louisiana State University Press, 1983.

Kruman, Marc W. "Thomas L. Clingman and the Whig Party: A Reconsideration." *North Carolina Historical Review,* 64 (1987), 1–18.

Kruman, Marc W. "The Second American Party System and the Transformation of Revolutionary Republicanism." *Journal of the Early Republic,* 12 (1992), 509–38.

Kutolowski, Kathleen. "Antimasonry Reexamined: Social Basis of the Grass-Roots Party." *Journal of American History,* 71 (1984), 269–93.

Lander, Ernest M., Jr. *Reluctant Imperialists: Calhoun, the South Carolinians, and the Mexican War.* Baton Rouge: Louisiana State University Press, 1980.

Larson, John L. "Jefferson's Union and the Problem of Internal Improvements." *Jeffersonian Legacies.* Ed. Peter S. Onuf. Charlottesville: University Press of Virginia, 1993.

Latner, Richard B. "A New Look at Jacksonian Politics." *Journal of American History,* 61 (1975), 943–69.

Leonard, Ira M. "The Rise and Fall of the American Republican Party in New York City, 1843–1845." *New York Historical Society Quarterly,* 50 (1966), 151–92.

Levine, Bruce. *The Spirit of 1848: German Immigrants, Labor Conflict, and the Coming of the Civil War.* Urbana: University of Illinois Press, 1992.

Levine, Peter D. *The Behavior of State Legislative Parties in the Jacksonian Era: New Jersey, 1829–1844.* Rutherford, N.J.: Farleigh Dickinson University Press, 1977.

Livermore, Shaw. *The Twilight of Federalism: The Disintegration of the Federalist Party, 1815–1830.* Princeton: Princeton University Press, 1962.

London, Lawrence F. "George Edmund Badger in the United States Senate, 1846–1849." *North Carolina Historical Review,* 15 (1938), 1–22.

London, Lawrence F. "George Edmund Badger: His Last Years in the Senate, 1851–1855." *North Carolina Historical Review,* 15 (1938), 231–50.

Maizlish, Stephen E. *The Triumph of Sectionalism: The Transformation of Ohio Politics, 1844–1856.* Kent, Ohio: Kent State University Press, 1983.

Marshall, Lynn L. "The Genesis of Grass-Roots Democracy in Kentucky." *Mid-America,* 47 (1965), 269–88.

Marshall, Lynn L. "The Strange Still-Birth of the Whig Party." *American Historical Review,* 72 (1967), 445–68.

May, Robert E. *John A. Quitman: Old South Crusader.* Baton Rouge: Louisiana State University Press, 1985.

Mayfield, John R. *Rehearsal for Republicanism: Free Soil and the Politics of Antislavery.* Port Washington, N.Y.: Kennikat Press, 1980.

McCormick, Richard L. *From Realignment to Reform: Political Change in New York State, 1893–1910.* Ithaca: Cornell University Press, 1981.

McCormick, Richard P. "New Perspectives on Jacksonian Politics." *American Historical Review,* 65 (1960), 288–301.

McCormick, Richard P. *The Second American Party System: Party Formation in the Jacksonian Era.* Chapel Hill: University of North Carolina Press, 1966.

McCormick, Richard P. "Political Development and the Second Party System." *The American Party Systems: Stages of Political Development.* Ed. William N. Chambers and Walter Dean Burnham. New York: Oxford University Press, 1967.

McCormick, Richard P. "Was There a 'Whig Strategy' in 1836?" *Journal of the Early Republic,* 4 (1984), 47–70.

McCoy, Drew R. *The Elusive Republic: Political Economy in Jeffersonian America.* Chapel Hill: University of North Carolina Press, 1980.

McCoy, Drew R. *The Last of the Fathers: James Madison & the Republican Legacy.* New York: Cambridge University Press, 1989.

McCrary, Peyton. *Abraham Lincoln and Reconstruction: The Louisiana Experiment.* Princeton: Princeton University Press, 1978.

McCrary, Peyton, Clark Miller, and Dale Baum. "Class and Party in the Secession Crisis: Voting Behavior in the Deep South, 1856–1861." *Journal of Interdisciplinary History,* 8 (1978), 429–57.

McCrary, Royce C. "Henry W. Hilliard and the Southern Caucus of 1848–49: A Letter to John MacPherson Berrien." *Alabama Historical Quarterly,* 37 (1975), 151–53.

McFaul, John M. *The Politics of Jacksonian Finance.* Ithaca: Cornell University Press, 1972.

Mering, John Vollmer. *The Whig Party in Missouri.* Columbia: University of Missouri Press, 1967.

Merk, Frederick. *Manifest Destiny and Mission in American History.* New York: Vintage Books, 1963.

Merk, Frederick. *Slavery and the Annexation of Texas.* New York: Alfred A. Knopf, 1972.

Meyers, Marvin. *The Jacksonian Persuasion.* Stanford: Stanford University Press, 1957.

Montgomery, Horace. *Cracker Parties.* Baton Rouge: Louisiana State University Press, 1950.

Morgan, Robert J. *A Whig Embattled: The Presidency under John Tyler.* Lincoln: University of Nebraska Press, 1954.

Morrill, James R. "The Presidential Election of 1852: Death Knell of the Whig Party of North Carolina," *North Carolina Historical Review,* 44 (1967), 342–59.

Morrison, Chaplain W. *Democratic Politics and Sectionalism: The Wilmot Proviso Controversy.* Chapel Hill: University of North Carolina Press, 1967.

Morrison, Michael A. *Slavery and the American West: The Eclipse of Manifest Destiny and the Coming of the Civil War.* Chapel Hill: University of North Carolina Press, 1997.

Morse, Jarvis M. *A Neglected Period of Connecticut's History, 1815–1850.* New Haven: Yale University Press, 1925.

Mueller, Henry R. *The Whig Party in Pennsylvania.* New York: Columbia University Press, 1922.

Mulkern, John R. *The Know Nothing Party in Massachusetts: The Rise and Fall of a People's Movement.* Boston: Northeastern University Press, 1990.

Murray, Paul. *The Whig Party in Georgia, 1825–1853.* Chapel Hill: University of North Carolina Press, 1948.

Nathans, Sydney. *Daniel Webster and Jacksonian Democracy.* Baltimore: The Johns Hopkins University Press, 1973.

Nevins, Allan. *Ordeal of the Union: Volume I. Fruits of Manifest Destiny, 1847–1852* and *Volume II. A House Dividing, 1852–1857.* New York: Charles Scribner's Sons, 1947.

Nichols, Roy F. *Franklin Pierce: Young Hickory of the Granite Hills.* Philadelphia: University of Pennsylvania Press, 1931.

Nichols, Roy F. *The Disruption of American Democracy.* New York: Collier Books, 1962.

Nichols, Roy F. "The Kansas-Nebraska Act: A Century of Historiography," *Mississippi Valley Historical Review,* 43 (1956), 187–212.

Nichols, Roy F. *Blueprints for Leviathan: American Style.* New York: Harper & Row, 1966.

Nichols, Roy F., and Nichols, Jeannette. "The Election of 1852." *History of American Presidential Elections.* Volume I. Ed. Arthur M. Schlesinger, Jr., and Fred Israel. New York: Chelsea House, 1971.

Niven, John. *Gideon Welles: Lincoln's Secretary of the Navy*. New York: Oxford University Press, 1973.

Niven, John. *Martin Van Buren: The Romantic Age of American Politics*. New York: Oxford University Press, 1983.

Oakes, James. *The Ruling Race: A History of American Slaveholders*. New York: Alfred A. Knopf, 1982.

Oakes, James. *Slavery and Freedom: An Interpretation of the Old South*. New York: Alfred A. Knopf, 1990.

Parks, Joseph H. "John Bell and the Compromise of 1850." *Journal of Southern History*, 9 (1943), 328–56.

Parks, Joseph H. *John Bell of Tennesssee*. Baton Rouge: Louisiana State University Press, 1950.

Paul, James C. N. *Rift in the Democracy*. New York: A. S. Barnes and Company, 1961.

Penny, Sherry. "Dissension in the Whig Ranks: Daniel Dewey Barnard versus Thurlow Weed." *New York Historical Society Quarterly*, 59 (1975), 71–92.

Perman, Michael. *The Road to Redemption: Southern Politics, 1869–1879*. Chapel Hill: University of North Carolina Press, 1984.

Pershing, B. H. "Membership in the General Assembly of Ohio." *Ohio Archaeological and Historical Quarterly*, 40 (1931), 222–83.

Pessen, Edward. *Jacksonian America: Society, Personality, and Politics*. Homewood, Ill.: The Dorsey Press, 1978.

Peterson, Merrill D. *Olive Branch and Sword: The Compromise of 1833*. Baton Rouge: Louisiana State University Press, 1982.

Peterson, Merrill D. *The Great Triumvirate: Webster, Clay, and Calhoun*. New York: Oxford University Press, 1987.

Phillips, Kim T. "Democrats of the Old School in the Era of Good Feelings." *Pennsylvania Magazine of History and Biography*, 95 (1971), 363–82.

Phillips, Kim T. "The Pennsylvania Origins of the Jackson Movement." *Political Science Quarterly*, 91 (1976), 489–508.

Pletcher, David M. *The Diplomacy of Annexation: Texas, Oregon, and the Mexican War*. Columbia: University of Missouri Press, 1973.

Poage, George Rawlings. *Henry Clay and the Whig Party*. Reprint edition. Gloucester: Peter Smith, 1965.

Potter, David M. *The Impending Crisis, 1848–1861*. Edited and completed by Don E. Fehrenbacher. New York: Harper & Row, 1976.

Ratcliffe, Donald J. "The Role of Voters and Issues in Party Formation: Ohio, 1824." *Journal of American History*, 49 (1973), 847–70.

Ratcliffe, Donald J. "Politics in Jacksonian Ohio: Reflections on the Ethnocultural Interpretation." *Ohio History*, 88 (1979), 5–36.

Rayback, Joseph A. *Free Soil: The Election of 1848*. Lexington: University Press of Kentucky, 1970.

Rayback, Robert J. "The Silver Grey Revolt." *New York History*, 47 (1949), 151–61.

Rayback, Robert J. *Millard Fillmore: Biography of a President*. Buffalo: Henry Stewart, 1959.

Redard, Thomas E. "The Election of 1844 in Louisiana: A New look at the Ethnocultural Approach." *Louisiana History*, 22 (1981), 419–33.

Remini, Robert V. *The Election of Andrew Jackson*. Philadelphia: J. B. Lippincott, 1963.

Remini, Robert V. *Andrew Jackson*. New York: Twayne Publishers, 1966.

Remini, Robert V. *Andrew Jackson and the Bank War*. New York: W. W. Norton and Company, 1967.

Remini, Robert V. "The Election of 1832." *History of American Presidential Elections*, Volume I. Ed. Arthur M. Schlesinger, Jr., and Fred Israel. New York: Chelsea House, 1971.

Remini, Robert V. *Andrew Jackson and the Course of American Freedom*. New York: Harper & Row, 1981.

Remini, Robert V. *Henry Clay: Statesman for the Union*. New York: W. W. Norton and Company, 1991.

Renda, Lex. "Retrospective Voting and the Presidential Election of 1844: The Texas Issue Revisited." *Presidential Studies Quarterly*, 24 (1994), 837–54.

Reynolds, John F., and McCormick, Richard L. "Outlawing 'Treachery': Split Tickets and Ballot Laws in New York and New Jersey, 1880–1910," *Journal of American History*, 72 (1986), 835–68.

Rich, Robert. " 'A Wilderness of Whigs': The Wealthy Men of Boston." *Journal of Social History*, 4 (1971), 263–76.

Risjord, Norman K. *The Old Republicans: Southern Conservatism in the Age of Jefferson*. New York: Columbia University Press, 1965.

Robbins, Roy M. *Our Landed Heritage: The Public Domain, 1776–1970*. Second edition revised. Lincoln: University of Nebraska Press, 1976.

Roll, Charles. *Colonel Dick Thompson: The Persistent Whig*. Indianapolis: Indiana Historical Bureau, 1948.

Rosenberg, Morton M. *Iowa on the Eve of the Civil War: A Decade of Frontier Politics*. Norman: University of Oklahoma Press, 1972.

Ross, Stephen J. "The Transformation of Republican Ideology." *Journal of the Early Republic*, 10 (1990), 323–30.

Russo, David J. "The Major Political Issues of the Jacksonian Period and the Development of Party Loyalty in Congress, 1830–1840." *Transactions of the American Philosophical Society*, 62 (1972), 3–49.

Sartori, Giovanni. *Parties and Party Systems: A Framework of Analysis, Volume I*. Cambridge: Cambridge University Press, 1976.

Schlesinger, Arthur M., Jr. *The Age of Jackson*. Boston: Little, Brown and Company, 1945.

Schott, Thomas E. *Alexander H. Stephens of Georgia: A Biography*. Baton Rouge: Louisiana State University Press, 1988.

Schroeder, John H. *Mr. Polk's War: American Opposition and Dissent, 1846–1848*. Madison: University of Wisconsin Press, 1973.

Seager, Robert, II. *And Tyler Too: A Biography of John and Julia Gardiner Tyler*. New York: McGraw-Hill, 1963.

Sellers, Charles G., Jr. "Banking and Politics in Jackson's Tennessee, 1817–1827." *Mississippi Valley Historical Review*, 41 (1954), 61–84.

Sellers, Charles G., Jr. *James K. Polk: Jacksonian, 1795–1843*. Princeton: Princeton University Press, 1957.

Sellers, Charles G., Jr. *James K. Polk: Continentalist, 1843–1846*. Princeton: Princeton University Press, 1966.

Sellers, Charles G., Jr. "The Election of 1844." *History of American Presidential Elections*, Volume I. Ed. Arthur M. Schlesinger, Jr., and Fred Israel. New York: Chelsea House, 1971.

Sellers, Charles G., Jr. *The Market Revolution: Jacksonian America, 1815–1846*. New York: Oxford University Press, 1991.

Sewell, Richard H. *John P. Hale and the Politics of Abolition*. Cambridge: Harvard University Press, 1965.

Sewell, Richard H. *Ballots for Freedom: Antislavery Politics in the United States, 1837–1860*. New York: Oxford University Press, 1976.

Shade, William G. "Pennsylvania Politics in the Jacksonian Period: A Case Study, Northampton County, 1824–1844." *Pennsylvania History*, 38 (1971), 313–33.

Shade, William G. *Banks or No Banks: The Money Issue in Western Politics, 1832–1865*. Detroit: Wayne State University Press, 1972.

Shade, William G. "Political Pluralism and Party Development: The Creation of a Modern Party System, 1815–1852." *The Evolution of American Electoral Systems*. Ed. Paul Kleppner. Westport: Greenwood Press, 1981.

Shade, William G. *Democratizing the Old Dominion: Virginia and the Second American Party System, 1824–1861*. Charlotteville: University Press of Virginia, 1996.

Shalhope, Robert E. "Toward a Republican Synthesis: The Emergence of an Understanding of Republicanism in American Historiography." *William & Mary Quarterly*, 29 (1972), 49–80.

Sharp, James Roger. *The Jacksonians versus the Banks: Politics in the States after the Panic of 1837*. New York: Columbia University Press, 1970.

Shaw, Robert E. *Erie Water West*. Lexington: University Press of Kentucky, 1966.

Shenton, James P. *Robert John Walker: A Politician from Jackson to Lincoln*. New York: Columbia University Press, 1961.

Shryock, Richard H. *Georgia and the Union in 1850*. Durham: Duke University Press, 1926.

Silbey, Joel H. *The Shrine of Party: Congressional Voting Behavior, 1841–1852*. Pittsburgh: University of Pittsburgh Press, 1967.

Silbey, Joel H. *The Transformation of American Politics, 1840–1860*. Englewood Cliffs: Prentice-Hall, 1967.

Silbey, Joel H. "The Election of 1836." *History of American Presidential Elections*. Volume I. Ed. Arthur M. Schlesinger, Jr., and Fred Israel. New York: Chelsea House, 1971.

Silbey, Joel H. *The Partisan Imperative: The Dynamics of American Politics before the Civil War*. New York: Oxford University Press, 1985.

Simms, H. H. *The Rise of the Whigs in Virginia, 1824–1840*. Richmond: William Byrd Press, 1929.

Simpson, Craig M. *A Good Southerner: The Life of Henry A. Wise of Virginia*. Chapel Hill: University of North Carolina Press, 1985.

Skowronek, Stephen. *The Politics Presidents Make: Leadership from John Adams to George Bush*. Cambridge: Harvard University Press, 1993.

Slaughter, Thomas P. *Bloody Dawn: The Christiana Riot and Racial Violence in the Antebellum North*. New York: Oxford University Press, 1991.

Smith, Elbert B. *The Presidencies of Zachary Taylor and Millard Fillmore*. Lawrence: University Press of Kansas, 1988.

Smith, Willard H. "Schuyler Colfax: Whig Editor, 1845–1855." *Indiana Magazine of History*, 34 (1938), 262–82.

Snyder, Charles M. *The Jacksonian Heritage: Pennsylvania Politics 1833–1848*. Harrisburg: Pennsylvania Historical and Museum Commission, 1958.

Spencer, Donald S. *Louis Kossuth and Young America: A Study of Sectionalism and Foreign Policy*. Columbia: University of Missouri Press, 1977.

Stanley, John L. "Majority Tyranny in Tocqueville's America: The Failure of Negro Suffrage in 1846." *Political Science Quarterly*, 84 (1969), 412–35.

Stegmaier, Mark J. "Zachary Taylor versus the South." *Civil War History*, 36 (1987), 219–41.

Stegmaier, Mark J. *Texas, New Mexico, and the Compromise of 1850: Boundary Dispute & Sectional Crisis*. Kent, Ohio: Kent State University Press, 1996.

Stephenson, George M. *The Political History of the Public Lands from 1840 to 1862*. Boston: Richard G. Badger, 1917.

Stewart, James Brewer. *Joshua R. Giddings and the Tactics of Radical Politics*. Cleveland: Press of Case Western Reserve University, 1970.

Stewart, James Brewer. *Holy Warriors: The Abolitionists and American Slavery*. New York: Hill & Wang, 1976.

Stewart, James Brewer. "Abolitionists, Insurgents, and Third Parties: Sectionalism and Partisan Politics in Northern Whiggery, 1836–1844." *Crusaders and Compromisers: Essays on the Relationship of the Antislavery Struggle to the Antebellum Party System*. Ed. Alan M. Kraut. Westport: Greenwood Press, 1983.

Streeter, Floyd B. *Political Parties in Michigan, 1837–1860*. Lansing: Michigan Historical Commission, 1919.

Summers, Mark W. *The Plundering Generation: Corruption and the Crisis of the Union, 1849–1861*. New York: Oxford University Press, 1987.

Sundquist, James L. *Dynamics of the Party System: Alignment and Realignment of Political Parties in the United States*. Washington: The Brookings Institution, 1973.

Sweeney, Kevin. "Rum, Romanism, Representation, and Reform: Coalition Politics in Massachusetts, 1847–1853." *Civil War History*, 22 (1976), 116–37.

Temin, Peter. *The Jacksonian Economy*. New York: W. W. Norton and Company, 1969.

Thornton, J. Mills, III. *Politics and Power in a Slave Society: Alabama 1800–1860*. Baton Rouge: Louisiana State University Press, 1978.

Timberlake, Richard. "The Specie Circular and Distribution of the Surplus." *Journal of Political Economy*, 68 (1960), 109–17.

Timberlake, Richard. "The Specie Circular and Sales of Public Lands: A Comment." *Journal of Economic History*, 25 (1965), 414–16.

Tomlins, Christopher L. *Law, Labor, and Ideology in the Early American Republic*. New York: Cambridge University Press, 1993.

Trefousse, Hans L. *Benjamin Franklin Wade: Radical Republican from Ohio*. New York: Twayne Publishers, 1963.

Trefousse, Hans L. "The Republican Party, 1854–1864." *History of U.S. Political Parties*. Volume II. Ed. Arthur M. Schlesinger, Jr. New York: Chelsea House and R. W. Bowker, 1973.

Trester, Delmer J. "David Tod and the Gubernatorial Campaign of 1844." *Ohio State Archaeological and Historical Quarterly*, 62 (1953), 162–78.

Tutorow, Norman E. *Texas Annexation and the Mexican War: A Political Study of the Northwest*. Palo Alto: Chadwick House Publishers, 1978.

Tyrell, Ian R. *Sobering Up: From Temperance to Prohibition in Antebellum America, 1800–1860*. Westport: Greenwood Press, 1979.

Van Bolt, Roger H. "Sectional Aspects of Expansion, 1844–1848." *Indiana Magazine of History*, 48 (1952), 119–40.

Van Bolt, Roger H. "The Hoosiers and the 'Eternal Agitation,' 1848–1850." *Indiana Magazine of History*, 48 (1952), 331–68.

Van Bolt, Roger H. "Fusion Out of Confusion." *Indiana Magazine of History*, 49 (1953), 353–90.

Van Bolt, Roger H. "Indiana in Political Transition, 1851–1853." *Indiana Magazine of History*, 49 (1953), 131–60.

Van Deusen, Glyndon G. *The Life of Henry Clay*. Boston: Little, Brown and Company, 1937.

Van Deusen, Glyndon G. *Thurlow Weed: Wizard of the Lobby*. Boston: Little, Brown and Company, 1947.

Van Deusen, Glyndon G. *Horace Greeley: Nineteenth Century Crusader*. New York: Hill & Wang, 1964.

Van Deusen, Glyndon G. *William Henry Seward*. New York: Oxford University Press, 1967.

Van Deusen, Glyndon G. "The Whig Party." *History of U.S. Political Parties*. Volume I. Ed. Arthur M. Schlesinger, Jr. New York: Chelsea House and R. W. Bowker, 1973.

Varon, Elizabeth R. "Tippecanoe and the Ladies, Too: White Women and Party Politics in Antebellum Virginia." *Journal of American History*, 82 (1995), 494–521.

Volpe, Vernon L. "The Anti-Abolitionist Campaign of 1840." *Civil War History*, 32 (1986), 325–39.

Wallace, Michael. "Changing Concepts of Party in the United States, 1815–1828." *American Historical Review*, 74 (1968), 453–91.

Walton, Brian G. "The Elections to the Thirtieth Congress and the Presidential Candidacy of Zachary Taylor." *Journal of Southern History*, 35 (1969), 186–202.

Walton, Brian G. "The Second Party System in Arkansas, 1836–1848." *Arkansas Historical Quarterly*, 28 (1969), 120–55.

Walton, Brian G. "The Second Party System in Tennessee." *East Tennessee Historical Society Publications*, 43 (1971), 18–33.

Walton, Brian G. "A Matter of Timing: Elections to the United States Senate in Tennessee before the Civil War." *Tennessee Historical Quarterly*, 31 (1972), 129–48.

Walton, Brian G. "Elections to the United States Senate in North Carolina, 1835–1861." *North Carolina Historical Review*, 53 (1976), 168–92.

Walton, Brian G. "Georgia's Biennial Legislatures, 1840–1860, and Their Elections to the U.S. Senate." *Georgia Historical Quarterly*, 61 (1977), 140–55.

Watson, Harry L. *Jacksonian Politics and Community Conflict: The Emergence of the Second American Party System in Cumberland County, North Carolina*. Baton Rouge: Louisiana State University Press, 1981.

Watson, Harry L. "Conflict and Collaboration: Yeomen, Slaveholders, and Politics in the Antebellum South." *Journal of Social History*, 10 (1985), 273–98.

Watson, Harry L. *Liberty and Power: The Politics of Jacksonian America*. New York: Hill & Wang, 1990.

Wellington, Raynor G. *The Political and Sectional Influence of the Public Lands, 1828–1842.* Boston: The Riverside Press, 1914.

Welter, Rush. *The Mind of America, 1820–1860.* New York: Columbia University Press, 1975.

Wilburn, Jean. *Biddle's Bank: The Crucial Years.* New York: Columbia University Press, 1967.

Wilentz, Sean. *Chants Democratic: New York City and the Rise of the American Working Class, 1788–1850.* New York: Oxford University Press, 1984.

Williams, Max R. "William A. Graham and the Election of 1844: A Study of North Carolina Politics." *North Carolina Historical Review,* 45 (1968), 23–46.

Williams, Max R. "The Foundations of the Whig Party in North Carolina: A Synthesis and a Modest Proposal." *North Carolina Historical Review,* 47 (1970), 115–29.

Wilson, Major L. "The Concept of Time and the Political Dialogue in the United States, 1828–1848." *American Quarterly,* 19 (1967), 619–44.

Wolff, Gerald. "Party and Section: The Senate and the Kansas-Nebraska Bill." *Civil War History,* 18 (1972), 293–331.

Wolff, Gerald. *The Kansas-Nebraska Bill: Party, Section, and the Coming of the Civil War.* New York, 1977.

Wood, Gordon. *The Creation of the American Republic, 1776–1787.* Chapel Hill: University of North Carolina Press, 1969.

Wood, Gordon. *The Radicalism of the American Revolution.* New York: Alfred A. Knopf, 1992.

Woodward, C. Vann, ed. *Responses of the Presidents to Charges of Misconduct.* New York: Dell Books, 1974.

Wooster, Ralph A. *Politicians, Planters, and Plain Folk: Courthouse and Statehouse in the Upper South, 1850–1860.* Knoxville: University of Tennessee Press, 1975.

Wyatt-Brown, Bertram. "The Antimission Movement in the Jacksonian South: A Study in Regional Folk Culture." *Journal of Southern History,* 36 (1970), 501–29.

Wyatt-Brown, Bertram. *Southern Honor: Ethics and Behavior in the Old South.* New York: Oxford University Press, 1982.

Unpublished Dissertations, Papers, and Theses

Ames, Tim. "Conflict and Consensus: The Wisconsin General Assembly, 1848–1854." Seminar Paper. University of Virginia. 1978.

Anderson, Chace. "The Compromise of 1850 and the Texas Boundary Dispute in the Senate." Seminar Paper. University of Virginia. 1988.

Atkins, Jonathan Moore. " 'A Combat for Liberty': Politics and Parties in Jackson's Tennessee, 1832–1851." Ph.D. Dissertation. University of Michigan. 1991.

Bearss, Sara Beth. " 'How All Occasions Do Inform': Henry Clay's Open Break with Zachary Taylor over the Compromise of 1850." Master's Thesis. University of Virginia. 1984.

Birkner, Michael J. "Politics, Law and Enterprise in Jacksonian America: The Career of Samuel L. Southard." Ph.D. Dissertation. University of Virginia. 1981.

Bobo, Frank R. "Revelry, Reorganization, and Ruin: The Fate of the Whig Party in Georgia from 1848 to 1853." Seminar Paper. University of Virginia. 1992.

Bruser, Lawrence. "Political Antislavery in Connecticut, 1844–1858." Ph.D. Dissertation. Columbia University. 1974.

Burnet, Robert Scott. "Creating the 34th Congress: House and Senate Elections, 1854–1855." Ph.D. Dissertation. University of Virginia. 1997.

Calabro, David J. "The Collapse of the Two-Party System in Florida: 1845–1858." Seminar Paper. University of Virginia. 1978.

Campbell, Ballard C. "Party, Policy, and Political Leadership in Congress during the Nineteenth Century." Paper delivered at the Project '87 Conference on Congress. February 1981.

DeScherer, Chris. "The Whig National Convention of 1856." Seminar Paper. University of Virginia. 1992.

Green, Stephen. "The Collapse of the Whig Party in Maryland." Seminar Paper. Yale College. 1973.

Hampel, Robert M. "The Ohio Whig Party, 1848–1854." Senior Thesis. Yale College. 1972.

Hampel, Robert M. "Constitution-Making at Mid-Century: Indiana, 1850–1852." Seminar Paper. Cornell University. 1973.

Hampel, Robert M. "The Origins of the 1850 Indiana Constitutional Convention." Seminar Paper. Cornell University. 1973.

Harp, Gillis. "The Character of Party Dialogue: Democrats and Whigs in New York State, 1844–1852." Seminar Paper. University of Virginia. 1980.

Hoerl, Hank G. "Land, Rails, and Gresham's Law: The Politics of the Delta, 1842–1854." No place or date. In my possession.

Hoisington, Daniel J. "From Whig to Union: The Whig Party in Georgia, 1849–1853." Master's Thesis. University of Virginia. 1976.

Hunter, Thomas. "A Delegation Divided: North Carolina Politics and the Compromise of 1850." Seminar Paper. University of Virginia. 1989.

Jeffrey, Thomas E. "Party Alignment and Realignment in North Carolina, 1836–1850." Paper presented to the Annual Meeting of the Southern Historical Association. 1979.

Kierner, Cynthia. " 'The Motley Party:' The Know Nothing Interlude and New Jersey's Anti-Democratic Opposition." Seminar Paper. University of Virginia. 1983.

Kirn, John R. "The Third Party System in New York State: Patterns of Electoral Behavior, 1848–1876." Seminar Paper. University of Virginia. 1985.

Kirn, John R. "Elections, Roll Calls, and the Decline of the Second Party System in New York State, 1846–1853." Paper delivered at the Social Science History Annual Meeting. 1995.

Leibiger, Stuart. "Georgia and the Compromise of 1850." Seminar Paper. University of Virginia. 1987.

Lemley, Jane. "The Passage of the Fugitive Slave Act of 1850." Seminar Paper. University of Virginia. 1989.

Lucas, Melvin Philip. "The Second Party System in Mississippi, 1836–1844." Seminar Paper. University of Virginia. 1975.

Lucas, Melvin Philip. "The Period of Political Alchemy: Party in the Mississippi Legislature, 1835–1846." Master's Thesis. Cornell University. 1981.

Maizlish, Stephen. "The Triumph of Sectionalism: The Transformation of Politics in the Antebellum North, Ohio 1844–1860." Ph.D. Dissertation. University of California at Berkeley, 1978.

McDonald, Justin Toby. "The Politics of Compromise: The Compromise of 1850, The Texas Boundary Settlement, and the House of Representatives." Seminar Paper. University of Virginia. 1989.

McFaden, Carlton D. "Sections, Slaveholders, and Safe Concessions: The Demise of the Whig Party in North Carolina from 1848 to 1856." Seminar Paper. University of Virginia. 1992.

Merkel, Philip. "Party and Constitution Making: An Examination of Selected Roll-Calls from the New York Constitutional Convention of 1846." Seminar Paper. University of Virginia. 1983.

Miller, Thomas W. "A New Perspective on Southern Whig Decline: A Comparison of the Mississippi and North Carolina Whig Parties, 1848–1856." Master's Thesis. University of Texas at Austin. 1992.

Mittendorf, Brad. "Mississippi Politics, 1848–1852: The Decline of Partisan Politics." Seminar Paper. University of Virginia. 1990.

Morrison, Christopher. "For Buncombe or Principle: Georgia's Congressional Party Politics in the Crisis and Compromise of 1850." Seminar Paper. University of Virginia. 1990.

Olberg, Peter. "Coalition Politics: Party Formation in Vermont, 1848–1855." Seminar Paper. Yale College. 1972.

Pilkington, Kirk. "Interparty Conflict in the Louisiana House of Representatives, 1848–1854." Seminar Paper. University of Virginia. 1978.

Reed, J. Eric. "The Politics of Internal Improvements: New York's Canals and the Second Party System, 1834–1854." Senior Thesis. University of Virginia. 1987.

Renda, Lex. "Railroads, Revenue, and Reform: Decline of the New Jersey Whigs." Master's Thesis. University of Virginia. 1984.

Renda, Lex. "The Polity and the Party System: Connecticut and New Hampshire, 1840–1876." Ph.D. Dissertation. University of Virginia. 1991.

Shadle, Kurt P. "Consensus and the Decline of the Second Party System: Ohio, 1848–1854." Seminar Paper. University of Virginia. 1978.

Thornton, J. Mills, III. "The Ethic of Subsistence and the Origins of Secession." Public Lecture. University of Florida. November 1987.

Tutorow, Norman E. "Whigs in the Old Northwest and the Mexican War." Ph.D. Dissertation. Stanford University. 1967.

Volz, Harry A., III. "Party, State, and Nation: Kentucky and the Coming of the Civil War." Ph.D. Dissertation. University of Virginia. 1982.

White, Stephen. "The Partisan Political Elements in the Virginia Constitutional Convention of 1850–51." Seminar Paper. University of Virginia. 1980.

Index

California *(continued)*
and Clay Plan, 479, 481–83, 486; constitution of, 437–39, 461, 463, 472, 474, 483–84, 781; Douglas' proposal about, 385–86, 388–89; Fillmore's support for, 617; gold strikes in, 412, 435, 673, 685–87, 776, 790, 804, 955; House debate and vote about, 484, 538; and House speakership, 467–70; immigrants/ Catholics in, 858; and Kansas-Nebraska Act, 857; King's journey to, 443–44, 449–51; Know Nothings in, 858; and little omnibus bill, 539; and Mexican Cession, 385–86, 388–89, 439, 464–65; and Mexican War, 233, 248–50, 252, 310; and northern Democrats, 475, 485, 501, 535, 538; and northern Whigs, 483–84, 487, 489, 533, 536; and omnibus bill, 481, 487, 494–97, 499–501, 503, 506–7, 517, 523, 526–27, 531; patronage in, 547, 660; and Polk administration, 233, 248–50, 252; as pro-northern, 535; reform themes in, 857; Republican party in, 980; and secession threat, 463–64, 484–85, 503, 601, 610, 612; Senate votes about, 537, 542; and Seward's Higher Law speech, 490–91; and slavery, 335–37, 385–86, 388–89, 412, 439, 459, 461–62, 464–65; and southern Democrats, 463–64, 474, 484–85, 494–97, 501, 517, 531; and Southern Rights, 484, 611; and southern Whigs, 464, 476, 482, 484–85, 495, 503, 517, 531, 542; and Taylor administration, 385, 386, 388–89, 412, 437, 438–39, 443–44, 449–51, 459, 461, 463, 472–76, 479, 482–84, 487, 489, 491, 496–98, 501–2; and Texas boundary dispute, 531, 533–36; and Utah, 437–39; and Webster's 7th of March speech, 488–89; and Wilmot Proviso, 385, 436, 459, 463. *See also* California—and election; *specific person or state*
California—and election: of **1849**, 449–51; of **1850**, 565, 569–70, 576, 581, 588; of **1851**, 627, 629, 660; of **1852**, 708, 713, 715, 719–20, 723, 738, 754, 756, 780–81; of **1853**, 780–81, 799, 957; of **1854**, 857–58; of **1856**, 979–80
Call, Richard K., 854
Calvin, Samuel, 340, 578–79
Camden and Amboy Railroad, 53–54, 455, 573–74, 791
Cameron, Simon, 512, 886, 889, 917
Campbell, David, 181, 200, 250, 928
Campbell, James, 670–71, 696–97, 744, 745, 845, 880, 881
Campbell, Lewis D.: and anti-Nebraska coalitions, 859, 863, 866; and Fillmore's presidential ambitions, 916; and Free Soilers, 340; and future of Whig party, 763, 827, 829–30; and House speakership, 923–24, 962–63; and Kansas-Nebraska Act, 811, 827; and Know Nothings, 866, 916, 922, 929, 944; and Kossuth, 696; and southern Whigs, 962; and temperance, 782–83. *See also* Campbell, Lewis D.—and election
Campbell, Lewis D.—and election: of **1848**, 296–97, 316, 322, 327–28, 340; of **1850**, 571; of **1852**, 696, 698, 701–3, 706, 709, 728, 737, 740, 752, 755, 763; of **1853**, 782–83; of **1854–55**, 829–30, 866, 944

Campbell, Robert, 590–91, 701
Campbell, William B.: and California statehood, 464; and Clay's senate return, 397; and Compromise of 1850, 630; and Henrymandering, 795; and Know Nothings, 856, 901; and Mexican War, 253; and New Mexico statehood, 464; retirement of, 770; and slavery, 464. *See also* Campbell, William B.—and election
Campbell, William B.—and election: of **1848**, 355–56; of **1851**, 628–30; of **1852**, 679–80, 699, 728, 735, 754; of **1853–54**, 794, 901
Canada, 97, 101, 604, 700, 739, 750
Canadian Americans, 185, 188, 204
canals, 76, 77, 80–81; and election of **1851**, 647, 650–55; and election of **1853**, 788–90, 799. *See also specific state*
Canandaigua Circular (New York, 1854), 901, 904–5
Cannon, Newton D., 43, 56
Carey, Henry C., 738
Carlisle, John S., 974
Caroline (ship) incident, 97
Carroll, William, 43, 56
Carruthers, Samuel, 821, 850, 851
Casey, Joseph, 504
Cass, Lewis: and Clay, 543; and Committee of Thirteen, 495; and confirmation of Taylor's appointments, 506, 510–12; and Democratic-Whig alliance, 515–17, 543, 548; Democrats refuse to support, 609; and elections, 172; and expansionism, 350; and Fillmore, 515–17; and Free Soilers, 339–40, 342–44; and fugitive slaves, 496; and Kossuth, 693, 695; and Mexican War, 350; and New York politics, 515–17; and omnibus bill, 495–96, 506, 509, 511–13, 516; and patronage, 510–12, 515–17; and popular sovereignty, 475, 513; and slavery, 333–34, 338–44, 350–52, 356–60, 363; and southern Democrats, 495; and Taylor Plan, 485; and Texas annexation, 172; and Wilmot Proviso, 357–60, 485. *See also* election of 1848
Castle Garden (New York): Clay demonstration at, 301; Union party meeting at, 591–92, 606, 617–18, 637, 762
Catholics: and constituencies of political parties, 117–18; and demise of Whig party, 956–58; education of, 155, 779, 842, 845; evangelical Protestants antipathy to, 30; and expansion of Democratic party, 83; and Fillmore's presidential ambitions, 911; and future of Whig party, 775, 837; and Know Nothings, 845–50, 856; and Kossuth, 695–97; as more feared than slavery, 909; and nativism, 187–88, 190, 205; and northern Whigs, 837; and reassessment of Whig party, 206–7; and Republican party, 946, 948; and southern Whigs, 792; and temperance, 691, 696, 742; and Whig morality image, 188. *See also* Catholics—and election; Know Nothings; nativism
Catholics—and election: of **1844**, 190, 192, 203–7, 275; of **1848**, 276, 328; of **1849**, 436; of **1851**, 670–71; of **1852**, 691, 695–97, 730, 741–48, 752–53, 756, 761, 775, 956, 958; of **1853**, 779–80, 786–87, 792, 800, 803; of **1854**, 837, 858, 880–84, 887–91,